THE WORLD FACTBOOK

2000
(CIA's 1999 Edtion)

Prepared by the Central Intelligence Agency

Brassey's
Washington, D.C.

Brassey's Edition 2000 (CIA's 1999 Edition)

The World Factbook is prepared by the Central Intelligence Agency for the use of US Government officials, and the style, format, coverage, and content are designed to meet their specific requirements. Information is provided by the Bureau of Labor Statistics (Department of Labor), Bureau of the Census (Department of Commerce), Central Intelligence Agency, Council of Managers of National Antarctic Programs, Defense Intelligence Agency (Department of Defense), Department of State, Fish and Wildlife Service (Department of the Interior), Maritime Administration (Department of Transportation), National Imagery and Mapping Agency (Department of Defense), Antarctic Information Program (National Science Foundation), Naval Facilities Engineering Command (Department of Defense), Office of Naval Intelligence (Department of Defense), US Board on Geographic Names (Department of Interior), US Coast Guard (Department of Transportation), and other public and private sources.

Brassey's has published a commercial version of *The World Factbook* for eight years in order to extend the limited audience reached by the CIA's publication. This annual is a valuable primary source of information, and Brassey's seeks to make it more readily available to bookstores and libraries so that the taxpayers who fund the US Government can directly benefit from this excellent effort. Brassey's makes no claim to copyright to this publication. Brassey's editions differ in two minor aspects from the CIA publications. This current Brassey's edition is identified by the year 2000, following the pattern Brassey's uses in other annual publications. The CIA completes its volume late each year, and Brassey's republishes it the following year. Also, as a commercial publisher, Brassey's does not include the very simple but expensive four-color maps contained in the CIA publication. The cost to the consumer would be prohibitive, and these maps are not unique and are readily available elsewhere.

ISSN 0277-1527

ISBN 1-57488-266-x

Printed in the United States of America

Contents

		Page
	Notes and Definitions	vii
	Guide to Country Profiles	xxvii
A	Afghanistan	1
	Albania	3
	Algeria	5
	American Samoa	8
	Andorra	9
	Angola	11
	Anguilla	13
	Antarctica	15
	Antigua and Barbuda	17
	Arctic Ocean	19
	Argentina	20
	Armenia	22
	Aruba	25
	Ashmore and Cartier Islands	26
	Atlantic Ocean	27
	Australia	28
	Austria	30
	Azerbaijan	33
B	Bahamas, The	35
	Bahrain	37
	Baker Island	39
	Bangladesh	40
	Barbados	42
	Bassas da India	44
	Belarus	45
	Belgium	48
	Belize	50
	Benin	52
	Bermuda	54
	Bhutan	56
	Bolivia	58
	Bosnia and Herzegovina	61
	Botswana	64
	Bouvet Island	66
	Brazil	66
	British Indian Ocean Territory	69
	British Virgin Islands	70
	Brunei	72
	Bulgaria	74
	Burkina Faso	76
	Burma	78
	Burundi	80
C	Cambodia	82
	Cameroon	85
	Canada	87
	Cape Verde	89
	Cayman Islands	91
	Central African Republic	93

		Page
	Chad	95
	Chile	97
	China (also see separate Hong Kong and Taiwan entries)	100
	Christmas Island	103
	Clipperton Island	104
	Cocos (Keeling) Islands	105
	Colombia	106
	Comoros	109
	Congo, Democratic Republic of the	111
	Congo, Republic of the	113
	Cook Islands	115
	Coral Sea Islands	117
	Costa Rica	118
	Cote d'Ivoire	120
	Croatia	122
	Cuba	125
	Cyprus	128
	Czech Republic	131
D	Denmark	133
	Djibouti	136
	Dominica	138
	Dominican Republic	139
E	Ecuador	142
	Egypt	144
	El Salvador	147
	Equatorial Guinea	149
	Eritrea	151
	Estonia	153
	Ethiopia	156
	Europa Island	158
F	Falkland Islands (Islas Malvinas)	159
	Faroe Islands	160
	Fiji	162
	Finland	164
	France	167
	French Guiana	170
	French Polynesia	172
	French Southern and Antarctic Lands	174
G	Gabon	175
	Gambia, The	177
	Gaza Strip	179
	Georgia	181
	Germany	183
	Ghana	186
	Gibraltar	188
	Glorioso Islands	190
	Greece	191
	Greenland	193
	Grenada	195

		Page
	Guadeloupe	197
	Guam	199
	Guatemala	200
	Guernsey	203
	Guinea	204
	Guinea-Bissau	206
	Guyana	208
H	Haiti	210
	Heard Island and McDonald Islands	212
	Holy See (Vatican City)	213
	Honduras	214
	Hong Kong	217
	Howland Island	219
	Hungary	220
I	Iceland	222
	India	225
	Indian Ocean	227
	Indonesia	228
	Iran	231
	Iraq	233
	Ireland	236
	Israel (also see separate Gaza Strip and West Bank entries)	238
	Italy	241
J	Jamaica	244
	Jan Mayen	246
	Japan	247
	Jarvis Island	249
	Jersey	250
	Johnston Atoll	251
	Jordan	252
	Juan de Nova Island	255
K	Kazakhstan	256
	Kenya	258
	Kingman Reef	261
	Kiribati	261
	Korea, North	263
	Korea, South	266
	Kuwait	268
	Kyrgyzstan	270
L	Laos	273
	Latvia	275
	Lebanon	277
	Lesotho	280
	Liberia	282
	Libya	284
	Liechtenstein	286
	Lithuania	288
	Luxembourg	290
M	Macau	292

		Page
	Macedonia, The Former Yugoslav Republic of	294
	Madagascar	297
	Malawi	299
	Malaysia	301
	Maldives	304
	Mali	305
	Malta	307
	Man, Isle of	309
	Marshall Islands	311
	Martinique	313
	Mauritania	315
	Mauritius	317
	Mayotte	319
	Mexico	321
	Micronesia, Federated States of	323
	Midway Islands	325
	Moldova	326
	Monaco	329
	Mongolia	331
	Montserrat	333
	Morocco	335
	Mozambique	337
N	Namibia	339
	Nauru	341
	Navassa Island	343
	Nepal	344
	Netherlands	346
	Netherlands Antilles	348
	New Caledonia	350
	New Zealand	352
	Nicaragua	355
	Niger	357
	Nigeria	359
	Niue	361
	Norfolk Island	363
	Northern Mariana Islands	364
	Norway	366
O	Oman	368
P	Pacific Ocean	370
	Pakistan	371
	Palau	374
	Palmyra Atoll	376
	Panama	377
	Papua New Guinea	379
	Paracel Islands	381
	Paraguay	382
	Peru	384
	Philippines	386
	Pitcairn Islands	389

		Page
	Poland	390
	Portugal	393
	Puerto Rico	395
Q	Qatar	397
R	Reunion	399
	Romania	401
	Russia	403
	Rwanda	407
S	Saint Helena	409
	Saint Kitts and Nevis	411
	Saint Lucia	412
	Saint Pierre and Miquelon	414
	Saint Vincent and the Grenadines	416
	Samoa	418
	San Marino	420
	Sao Tome and Principe	421
	Saudi Arabia	423
	Senegal	425
	Serbia and Montenegro	427
	Seychelles	430
	Sierra Leone	432
	Singapore	434
	Slovakia	437
	Slovenia	439
	Solomon Islands	441
	Somalia	443
	South Africa	445
	South Georgia and the South Sandwich Islands	448
	Spain	449
	Spratly Islands	452
	Sri Lanka	452
	Sudan	455
	Suriname	457
	Svalbard	459
	Swaziland	461
	Sweden	463
	Switzerland	465
	Syria	468
T	Taiwan entry follows Zimbabwe	
	Tajikistan	471
	Tanzania	473
	Thailand	475
	Togo	478
	Tokelau	480
	Tonga	482
	Trinidad and Tobago	483
	Tromelin Island	485
	Tunisia	486
	Turkey	489

		Page
	Turkmenistan	492
	Turks and Caicos Islands	494
	Tuvalu	496
U	Uganda	497
	Ukraine	500
	United Arab Emirates	503
	United Kingdom	505
	United States	508
	Uruguay	511
	Uzbekistan	514
V	Vanuatu	516
	Venezuela	518
	Vietnam	520
	Virgin Islands	523
W	Wake Atoll	525
	Wallis and Futuna	525
	West Bank	527
	Western Sahara	529
	World	530
Y	Yemen	532
Z	Zambia	534
	Zimbabwe	536
	Taiwan	538

		Page
Appendixes	A: Abbreviations	541
	B: United Nations System	549
	C: International Organizations and Groups	550
	D: Selected International Environmental Agreements	602
	E: Weights and Measures	609
	F: Cross-Reference List of Country Data Codes	622
	G: Cross-Reference List of Hydrographic Data Codes	630
	H: Cross-Reference List of Geographic Names	635

A Brief History of Basic Intelligence and *The World Factbook*

The Intelligence Cycle is the process by which information is acquired, converted into intelligence, and made available to policymakers. **Information** *is raw data from any source, data that may be fragmentary, contradictory, unreliable, ambiguous, deceptive, or wrong.* **Intelligence** *is information that has been collected, integrated, evaluated, analyzed, and interpreted.* **Finished intelligence** *is the final product of the Intelligence Cycle ready to be delivered to the policymaker.*

The three types of finished intelligence are: basic, current, and estimative. Basic intelligence provides the fundamental and factual reference material on a country or issue. Current intelligence reports on new developments. Estimative intelligence judges probable outcomes. The three are mutually supportive: basic intelligence is the foundation on which the other two are constructed; current intelligence continually updates the inventory of knowledge; and estimative intelligence revises overall interpretations of country and issue prospects for guidance of basic and current intelligence. *The World Factbook*, *The President's Daily Brief*, and the *National Intelligence Estimates* are examples of the three types of finished intelligence.

The United States has carried on foreign intelligence activities since the days of George Washington, but only since World War II have they been coordinated on a governmentwide basis. Three programs have highlighted the development of coordinated basic intelligence since that time: (1) the *Joint Army Navy Intelligence Studies* (JANIS), (2) the *National Intelligence Survey* (NIS), and (3) *The World Factbook*.

During World War II, intelligence consumers realized that the production of basic intelligence by different components of the US Government resulted in a great duplication of effort and conflicting information. The Japanese attack on Pearl Harbor in 1941 brought home to leaders in Congress and the executive branch the need for integrating departmental reports to national policymakers. Detailed coordinated information was needed not only on such major powers as Germany and Japan, but also on places of little previous interest. In the Pacific Theater, for example, the Navy and Marines had to launch amphibious operations against many islands about which information was unconfirmed or nonexistent. Intelligence authorities resolved that the United States should never again be caught unprepared.

In 1943, Gen. George B. Strong (G-2), Adm. H. C. Train (Office of Naval Intelligence—ONI), and Gen. William J. Donovan (Director of the Office of Strategic Services—OSS) decided that a joint effort should be initiated. A steering committee was appointed on 27 April 1943 that recommended the formation of a Joint Intelligence Study Publishing Board to assemble, edit, coordinate, and publish the *Joint Army Navy Intelligence Studies* (JANIS). JANIS was the first interdepartmental basic intelligence program to fulfill the needs of the US Government for an authoritative and coordinated appraisal of strategic basic intelligence. Between April 1943 and July 1947, the board published 34 JANIS studies. JANIS performed well in the war effort, and numerous letters of commendation were received, including a statement from Adm. Forrest Sherman, Chief of Staff, Pacific Ocean Areas, which said, "JANIS has become the indispensable reference work for the shore-based planners."

The need for more comprehensive basic intelligence in the postwar world was well expressed in 1946 by George S. Pettee, a noted author on national security. He wrote in *The Future of American Secret Intelligence* (Infantry Journal Press, 1946, page 46) that world leadership in peace requires even more elaborate intelligence than war. "The conduct of peace involves all countries, all human activities—not just the enemy and his war production."

The Central Intelligence Agency was established on 26 July 1947 and officially began operating on 18 September 1947. Effective 1 October 1947, the Director of Central Intelligence assumed operational responsibility for JANIS. On 13 January 1948, the National Security Council issued Intelligence Directive (NSCID) No. 3, which authorized the *National Intelligence Survey* (NIS) program as a peacetime replacement for the wartime JANIS program. Before adequate NIS country sections could be produced, government agencies had to develop more comprehensive gazetteers and better maps. The US Board on Geographic Names (BGN) compiled the names; the Department of the Interior produced the gazetteers; and CIA produced the maps.

The Hoover Commission's Clark Committee, set up in 1954 to study the structure and administration of the CIA, reported to Congress in 1955 that: "The National Intelligence Survey is an invaluable publication which provides the essential elements of basic intelligence on all areas of the world. . . . There will always be a continuing requirement for keeping the Survey up-to-date." The *Factbook* was created as an annual summary and update to the encyclopedic NIS studies. The first classified *Factbook* was published in August 1962, and the first unclassified version was published in June 1971. The NIS program was terminated in 1973 except for the *Factbook*, map, and gazetteer components. The 1975 *Factbook* was the first to be made available to the public with sales through the US Government Printing Office (GPO). The 1996 edition was printed by GPO and the 1997 edition was reprinted by GPO. The year 1999 marks the 52nd anniversary of the establishment of the Central Intelligence Agency and the 56th year of continuous basic intelligence support to the US Government by *The World Factbook* and its two predecessor programs.

Notes and Definitions

In addition to the updating of information, the following changes have been made in this edition of *The World Factbook*. The name Wake Island has been officially changed to Wake Atoll. The **Historical perspective** and **Current issues** entries in the **Introduction** category have been combined into a new **Background** entry. It appears in only a few country profiles at this time. There are new entries on **Population below poverty line**, **Household income or consumption by percentage share**, **Electricity—production by source** (fossil fuel, hydro, nuclear, other), **Electricity—exports**, and **Electricity—imports.** A new reference map of Kosovo has been included and terrain has been added to most of the reference maps. A new physical map of the world has also been added.

Abbreviations: This information is included in **Appendix A: Abbreviations**, which includes all abbreviations and acronyms used in the *Factbook,* with their expansions.

Administrative divisions: This entry generally gives the numbers, designatory terms, and first-order administrative divisions as approved by the US Board on Geographic Names (BGN). Changes that have been reported but not yet acted on by BGN are noted.

Age structure: This entry provides the distribution of the population according to age. Information is included by sex and age group (0-14 years, 15-64 years, 65 years and over). The age structure of a population affects a nation's key socioeconomic issues. Countries with young populations (high percentage under age 15) need to invest more in schools, while countries with older populations (high percentage ages 65 and over) need to invest more in the health sector. The age structure can also be used to help predict potential political issues. For example, the rapid growth of a young adult population unable to find employment can lead to unrest.

Agriculture—products: This entry is a rank ordering of major crops and products starting with the most important.

Airports: This entry gives the total number of airports. The runway(s) may be paved (concrete or asphalt surfaces) or unpaved (grass, dirt, sand, or gravel surfaces), but must be usable. Not all airports have facilities for refueling, maintenance, or air traffic control.

Airports—with paved runways: This entry gives the total number of airports with paved runways (concrete or asphalt surfaces). For airports with more than one runway, only the longest runway is included according to the following five groups —(1) over 3,047 m, (2) 2,438 to 3,047 m, (3) 1,524 to 2,437 m, (4) 914 to 1,523 m, and (5) under 914 m. Only airports with usable runways are included in this listing. Not all airports have facilities for refueling, maintenance, or air traffic control.

Airports—with unpaved runways: This entry gives the total number of airports with unpaved runways (grass, dirt, sand, or gravel surfaces). For airports with more than one runway, only the longest runway is included according to the following five groups—(1) over 3,047 m, (2) 2,438 to 3,047 m, (3) 1,524 to 2,437 m, (4) 914 to 1,523 m, and (5) under 914 m. Only airports with usable runways are included in this listing. Not all airports have facilities for refueling, maintenance, or air traffic control.

Appendixes: This section includes *Factbook*-related material by topic.

Area: This entry includes three subfields. *Total area* is the sum of all land and water areas delimited by international boundaries and/or coastlines. *Land area* is the aggregate of all surfaces delimited by international boundaries and/or coastlines, excluding inland water bodies (lakes, reservoirs, rivers). *Water area* is the sum of all water surfaces delimited by international boundaries and/or coastlines, including inland water bodies (lakes, reservoirs, rivers).

Area—comparative: This entry provides an area comparison based on total area equivalents. Most entities are compared with the entire US or one of the 50 states based on area measurements (1990 revised) provided by the US Bureau of the Census. The smaller entities are compared with Washington, DC (178 sq km, 69 sq mi) or The Mall in Washington, DC (0.59 sq km, 0.23 sq mi, 146 acres).

Background: This entry usually highlights major historic events, current issues, and may include a statement about one or two key future trends. This entry appears for only a few countries at the present time, but will be added to all countries in the future.

Birth rate: This entry gives the average annual number of births during a year per 1,000 persons in the population at midyear; also known as crude birth rate. The birth rate is usually the dominant factor in determining the rate of population growth. It depends on both the level of fertility and the age structure of the population.

Budget: This entry includes revenues, total expenditures, and capital expenditures. These figures are calculated on an exchange rate basis, i.e., not in purchasing power parity (PPP) terms.

Capital: This entry gives the location of the seat of government.

Climate: This entry includes a brief description of typical weather regimes throughout the year.

Coastline: This entry gives the total length of the boundary between the land area (including islands) and the sea.

Communications: This category deals with the means of exchanging information and includes the telephone, radio, and television entries.

Communications—note: This entry includes miscellaneous communications information of significance not included elsewhere.

Constitution: This entry includes the dates of adoption, revisions, and major amendments.

Country map: Most versions of the *Factbook* provide a country map in color. The maps were produced from the best information available at the time of preparation. Names and/or boundaries may have changed subsequently.

Country name: This entry includes all forms of the country's name approved by the US Board on Geographic Names (Italy is used as an example): *conventional long form* (Italian Republic), *conventional short form* (Italy), *local long form* (Repubblica Italiana), *local short form* (Italia), *former* (Kingdom of Italy), as well as the *abbreviation*. Also see the **Terminology** note.

Notes and Definitions *(continued)*

Currency: This entry identifies the national medium of exchange and its basic subunit.

Data code: This entry gives the official US Government digraph that precisely identifies every land entity without overlap, duplication, or omission. AF, for example, is the data code for Afghanistan. This two-letter country code is a standardized geopolitical data element promulgated in the *Federal Information Processing Standards Publication (FIPS) 10-4* by the National Institute of Standards and Technology at the US Department of Commerce and maintained by the Office of the Geographer and Global Issues at the US Department of State. The data code is used to eliminate confusion and incompatibility in the collection, processing, and dissemination of area-specific data and is particularly useful for interchanging data between databases. **Appendix F** cross-references various country data codes and **Appendix G** does the same thing for hydrographic data codes.

Data codes—country: This information is presented in **Appendix F: Cross-Reference List of Country Data Codes** which includes the US Government approved Federal Information Processing Standards (FIPS) codes, the International Organization for Standardization (ISO) codes, and Internet codes for land entities.

Data codes—hydrographic: This information is presented in **Appendix G: Cross-Reference List of Hydrographic Data Codes** which includes the International Hydrographic Organization (IHO) codes, Aeronautical Chart and Information Center (ACIC; now National Imagery and Mapping Agency or NIMA) codes, and Defense Intelligence Agency (DIA) codes for hydrographic entities. The US Government has not yet approved a standard for hydrographic data codes similar to the FIPS 10-4 standard for country data codes.

Date of information: In general, information available as of 1 January 1999, was used in the preparation of this edition.

Death rate: This entry gives the average annual number of deaths during a year per 1,000 population at midyear; also known as crude death rate. The death rate, while only a rough indicator of the mortality situation in a country, accurately indicates the current mortality impact on population growth. This indicator is significantly affected by age distribution, and most countries will eventually show a rise in the overall death rate, in spite of continued decline in mortality at all ages, as declining fertility results in an aging population.

Debt—external: This entry gives the total amount of public foreign financial obligations.

Dependency status: This entry describes the formal relationship between a particular nonindependent entity and an independent state.

Dependent areas: This entry contains an alphabetical listing of all nonindependent entities associated in some way with a particular independent state.

Diplomatic representation: The US Government has diplomatic relations with 184 independent states, including 178 of the 185 UN members (excluded UN members are Bhutan, Cuba, Iran, Iraq, North Korea, former Yugoslavia, and the US itself). In addition, the US has diplomatic relations with 6 independent states that are not in the UN—Holy See, Kiribati, Nauru, Switzerland, Tonga, and Tuvalu.

Notes and Definitions *(continued)*

Diplomatic representation from the US: This entry includes the *chief of mission*, *embassy* address, *mailing address*, *telephone* number, *FAX* number, *branch office* locations, *consulate general* locations, and *consulate* locations.

Diplomatic representation in the US: This entry includes the *chief of* the foreign *mission*, *chancery* address, *telephone* number, *FAX* number, *consulate general* locations, *consulate* locations, *honorary consulate general* locations, and *honorary consulate* locations.

Disputes—international: This entry includes a wide variety of situations that range from traditional bilateral boundary disputes to unilateral claims of one sort or another. Information regarding disputes over international terrestrial and maritime boundaries has been reviewed by the US Department of State. References to other situations involving borders or frontiers may also be included, such as resource disputes, geopolitical questions, or irredentist issues; however, inclusion does not necessarily constitute official acceptance or recognition by the US Government.

Economic aid—donor: This entry refers to net official development assistance (ODA) from OECD nations to developing countries and multilateral organizations. ODA is defined as financial assistance that is concessional in character, has the main objective to promote economic development and welfare of LDCs, and contains a grant element of at least 25%. The entry does not cover other official flows (OOF) or private flows.

Economic aid—recipient: This entry, which is subject to major problems of definition and statistical coverage, refers to the net inflow of Official Development Finance (ODF) to recipient countries. The figure includes assistance from the World Bank, the IMF, and other international organizations and from individual nation donors. Formal commitments of aid are included in the data. Omitted from the data are grants by private organizations. Aid comes in various forms including outright grants and loans. The entry thus is the difference between new inflows and repayments.

Economy: This category includes the entries dealing with the size, development, and management of productive resources, i.e., land, labor, and capital.

Economy—overview: This entry briefly describes the type of economy, including the degree of market orientation, the level of economic development, the most important natural resources, and the unique areas of specialization. It also characterizes major economic events and policy changes in the most recent 12 months and may include a statement about one or two key future macroeconomic trends.

Electricity—consumption: This entry consists of total electricity generated annually plus imports and minus exports, expressed in kilowatt hours.

Electricity—exports: This entry is the total exported electricity in kilowatt hours.

Electricity—imports: This entry is the total imported electricity in kilowatt hours.

Electricity—production: This entry is the annual electricity generated expressed in kilowatt hours.

Electricity—production by source: This entry indicates the percentage share of annual electricity production of each energy source. These are fossil fuel, hydro, nuclear, and other (solar, geothermal, and wind).

Elevation extremes: This entry includes both the *highest point* and the *lowest point.*

Entities: Some of the independent states, dependencies, areas of special sovereignty, and governments included in this publication are not independent, and others are not officially recognized by the US Government. "Independent state" refers to a people politically organized into a sovereign state with a definite territory. "Dependencies" and "areas of special sovereignty" refer to a broad category of political entities that are associated in some way with an independent state. "Country" names used in the table of contents or for page headings are usually the short-form names as approved by the US Board on Geographic Names and may include independent states, dependencies, and areas of special sovereignty, or other geographic entities. There are a total of 266 separate geographic entities in *The World Factbook* that may be categorized as follows:

INDEPENDENT STATES

191 Afghanistan, Albania, Algeria, Andorra, Angola, Antigua and Barbuda, Argentina, Armenia, Australia, Austria, Azerbaijan, The Bahamas, Bahrain, Bangladesh, Barbados, Belarus, Belgium, Belize, Benin, Bhutan, Bolivia, Bosnia and Herzegovina, Botswana, Brazil, Brunei, Bulgaria, Burkina Faso, Burma, Burundi, Cambodia, Cameroon, Canada, Cape Verde, Central African Republic, Chad, Chile, China, Colombia, Comoros, Democratic Republic of the Congo, Republic of the Congo, Costa Rica, Cote d'Ivoire, Croatia, Cuba, Cyprus, Czech Republic, Denmark, Djibouti, Dominica, Dominican Republic, Ecuador, Egypt, El Salvador, Equatorial Guinea, Eritrea, Estonia, Ethiopia, Fiji, Finland, France, Gabon, The Gambia, Georgia, Germany, Ghana, Greece, Grenada, Guatemala, Guinea, Guinea-Bissau, Guyana, Haiti, Holy See, Honduras, Hungary, Iceland, India, Indonesia, Iran, Iraq, Ireland, Israel, Italy, Jamaica, Japan, Jordan, Kazakhstan, Kenya, Kiribati, North Korea, South Korea, Kuwait, Kyrgyzstan, Laos, Latvia, Lebanon, Lesotho, Liberia, Libya, Liechtenstein, Lithuania, Luxembourg, The Former Yugoslav Republic of Macedonia, Madagascar, Malawi, Malaysia, Maldives, Mali, Malta, Marshall Islands, Mauritania, Mauritius, Mexico, Federated States of Micronesia, Moldova, Monaco, Mongolia, Morocco, Mozambique, Namibia, Nauru, Nepal, Netherlands, NZ, Nicaragua, Niger, Nigeria, Norway, Oman, Pakistan, Palau, Panama, Papua New Guinea, Paraguay, Peru, Philippines, Poland, Portugal, Qatar, Romania, Russia, Rwanda, Saint Kitts and Nevis, Saint Lucia, Saint Vincent and the Grenadines, Samoa, San Marino, Sao Tome and Principe, Saudi Arabia, Senegal, Serbia and Montenegro, Seychelles, Sierra Leone, Singapore, Slovakia, Slovenia, Solomon Islands, Somalia, South Africa, Spain, Sri Lanka, Sudan, Suriname, Swaziland, Sweden, Switzerland, Syria, Tajikistan, Tanzania, Thailand, Togo, Tonga, Trinidad and Tobago, Tunisia, Turkey, Turkmenistan, Tuvalu, Uganda, Ukraine, UAE, UK, US, Uruguay, Uzbekistan, Vanuatu, Venezuela, Vietnam, Yemen, Zambia, Zimbabwe

OTHER
   1 Taiwan

DEPENDENCIES AND AREAS OF SPECIAL SOVEREIGNTY
   6 Australia—Ashmore and Cartier Islands, Christmas Island, Cocos
      (Keeling) Islands, Coral Sea Islands, Heard Island and McDonald Islands,
      Norfolk Island
   1 China—Hong Kong
   2 Denmark—Faroe Islands, Greenland
  16 France—Bassas da India, Clipperton Island, Europa Island, French
      Guiana, French Polynesia, French Southern and Antarctic Lands, Glorioso
      Islands, Guadeloupe, Juan de Nova Island, Martinique, Mayotte, New
      Caledonia, Reunion, Saint Pierre and Miquelon, Tromelin Island, Wallis
      and Futuna
   2 Netherlands—Aruba, Netherlands Antilles
   3 New Zealand—Cook Islands, Niue, Tokelau
   3 Norway—Bouvet Island, Jan Mayen, Svalbard
   1 Portugal—Macau
  15 UK—Anguilla, Bermuda, British Indian Ocean Territory, British Virgin
      Islands, Cayman Islands, Falkland Islands, Gibraltar, Guernsey, Jersey,
      Isle of Man, Montserrat, Pitcairn Islands, Saint Helena, South Georgia and
      the South Sandwich Islands, Turks and Caicos Islands
  14 US—American Samoa, Baker Island, Guam, Howland Island, Jarvis
      Island, Johnston Atoll, Kingman Reef, Midway Islands, Navassa Island,
      Northern Mariana Islands, Palmyra Atoll, Puerto Rico, Virgin Islands,
      Wake Atoll

MISCELLANEOUS
   6 Antarctica, Gaza Strip, Paracel Islands, Spratly Islands, West Bank,
      Western Sahara

OTHER ENTITIES
   4 oceans—Arctic Ocean, Atlantic Ocean, Indian Ocean, Pacific Ocean
   1 World
266 Total

Environment—current issues: This entry lists the most pressing and important environmental problems.

Environment—international agreements: This entry separates country participation in international environmental agreements into two levels—*party to* and *signed but not ratified*. Agreements are listed in alphabetical order by the abbreviated form of the full name.

Environmental agreements: This information is presented in **Appendix D: Selected International Environmental Agreements**, which includes the name, abbreviation, date opened for signature, date entered into force, objective, and parties by category.

Ethnic groups: This entry provides a rank ordering of ethnic groups starting with the largest and normally includes the percent of total population.

Exchange rates: This entry provides the official value of a country's monetary unit at a given date or over a given period of time, as expressed in units of local currency per US dollar and as determined by international market forces or official fiat.

Executive branch: This entry includes several subfields. *Chief of state* includes the name and title of the titular leader of the country who represents the state at official and ceremonial functions but may not be involved with the day-to-day activities of the government. *Head of government* includes the name and title of the top administrative leader who is designated to manage the day-to-day activities of the government. *Cabinet* includes the official name for this body of high-ranking advisers and the method for selection of members. *Elections* includes the nature of election process or accession to power, date of the last election, and date of the next election. *Election results* includes the percent of vote for each candidate in the last election. In the UK, the monarch is the chief of state, and the prime minister is the head of government. In the US, the president is both the chief of state and the head of government.

Exports: This entry provides the total US dollar amount of exports on an f.o.b. (free on board) basis.

Exports—commodities: This entry provides a rank ordering of exported products starting with the most important; it sometimes includes the percent of total dollar value.

Exports—partners: This entry provides a rank ordering of trading partners starting with the most important; it sometimes includes the percent of total dollar value.

Fiscal year: This entry identifies the beginning and ending months for a country's accounting period of 12 months, which often is the calendar year but which may begin in any month. FY93/94 refers to the fiscal year that began in calendar year 1993 and ended in calendar year 1994. All yearly references are for the calendar year (CY) unless indicated as a noncalendar fiscal year (FY).

Flag description: This entry provides a written flag description produced from actual flags or the best information available at the time the entry was written. The flags of independent states are used by their dependencies unless there is an officially recognized local flag. Some disputed and other areas do not have flags.

Flag graphic: Most versions of the *Factbook* include a color flag at the beginning of the country profile. The flag graphics were produced from actual flags or the best information available at the time of preparation. The flags of independent states are used by their dependencies unless there is an officially recognized local flag. Some disputed and other areas do not have flags.

GDP: This entry gives the gross domestic product (GDP) or value of all final goods and services produced within a nation in a given year. GDP dollar estimates in the *Factbook* are derived from purchasing power parity (PPP) calculations. See the note on **GDP methodology** for more information.

GDP methodology: In the **Economy** section, GDP dollar estimates for all countries are derived from purchasing power parity (PPP) calculations rather than from conversions at official currency exchange rates. The PPP method involves the use of standardized international dollar price weights, which are applied to the quantities of final goods and services produced in a given economy. The data derived from the PPP method provide the best available starting point for comparisons of economic strength and well-being between countries. The division of a GDP estimate in domestic currency by the corresponding PPP estimate in dollars gives the PPP conversion rate. Whereas PPP estimates for OECD countries are quite reliable, PPP estimates for developing countries are often rough approximations. Most of the GDP estimates are based on extrapolation of PPP numbers published by the UN International Comparison Program (UNICP) and by Professors Robert Summers and Alan Heston of the University of Pennsylvania and their colleagues. In contrast, currency exchange rates depend on a variety of international and domestic financial forces that often have little relation to domestic output. In developing countries with weak currencies the exchange rate estimate of GDP in dollars is typically one-fourth to one-half the PPP estimate. Furthermore, exchange rates may suddenly go up or down by 10% or more because of market forces or official fiat whereas real output has remained unchanged. On 12 January 1994, for example, the 14 countries of the African Financial Community (whose currencies are tied to the French franc) devalued their currencies by 50%. This move, of course, did not cut the real output of these countries by half. One important caution: the proportion of, say, defense expenditures as a percentage of GDP in local currency accounts may differ substantially from the proportion when GDP accounts are expressed in PPP terms, as, for example, when an observer tries to estimate the dollar level of Russian or Japanese military expenditures. Note: the numbers for GDP and other economic data can *not* be chained together from successive volumes of the *Factbook* because of changes in the US dollar measuring rod, revisions of data by statistical agencies, use of new or different sources of information, and changes in national statistical methods and practices. For statistical series on GDP and other economic variables, see the *Handbook of International Economic Statistics* available from the same sources as *The World Factbook.*

GDP—composition by sector: This entry gives the percentage contribution of *agriculture, industry,* and *services* to total GDP.

GDP—per capita: This entry shows GDP on a purchasing power parity basis divided by population as of 1 July for the same year.

GDP—real growth rate: This entry gives GDP growth on an annual basis adjusted for inflation and expressed as a percent.

Geographic coordinates: This entry includes rounded latitude and longitude figures for the purpose of finding the approximate geographic center of an entity and is based on the *Gazetteer of Conventional Names*, Third Edition, August 1988, US Board on Geographic Names and on other sources.

Geographic names: This information is presented in **Appendix H: Cross-Reference List of Geographic Names** which indicates where various geographic names—including alternate names, former names, political or geographical portions of larger entities, and the location of all US Foreign Service posts—can be found in *The World Factbook.* Spellings are normally, but not always, those approved by the US Board on Geographic Names (BGN). Alternate names are included in parentheses, while additional information is included in brackets.

Geography: This category includes the entries dealing with the natural environment and the effects of human activity.

Notes and Definitions *(continued)*

Geography—note: This entry includes miscellaneous geographic information of significance not included elsewhere.

GNP: Gross national product (GNP) is the value of all final goods and services produced within a nation in a given year, plus income earned by its citizens abroad, minus income earned by foreigners from domestic production. The *Factbook*, following current practice, uses GDP rather than GNP to measure national production. However, the user must realize that in certain countries net remittances from citizens working abroad may be important to national well-being.

Government: This category includes the entries dealing with the system for the adoption and administration of public policy.

Government type: This entry gives the basic form of government (e.g., republic, constitutional monarchy, federal republic, parliamentary democracy, military dictatorship).

Government—note: This entry includes miscellaneous government information of significance not included elsewhere.

Gross domestic product: see **GDP**

Gross national product: see **GNP**

Gross world product: see **GWP**

GWP: This entry gives the gross world product (GWP) or aggregate value of all final goods and services produced worldwide in a given year.

Heliports: This entry gives the total number of established helicopter takeoff and landing sites (which may or may not have fuel or other services).

Highways: This entry includes the *total* length of the highway system as well as the length of the *paved* and *unpaved* components.

Household income or consumption by percentage share: Data on household income or consumption come from household surveys, the results adjusted for household size. Nations use different standards and procedures in collecting and adjusting the data. Surveys based on income will normally show a more unequal distribution than surveys based on consumption. The quality of surveys is improving with time, yet caution is still necessary in making inter-country comparisons.

Illicit drugs: This entry gives information on the five categories of illicit drugs—narcotics, stimulants, depressants (sedatives), hallucinogens, and cannabis. These categories include many drugs legally produced and prescribed by doctors as well as those illegally produced and sold outside of medical channels.

Cannabis (Cannabis sativa) is the common hemp plant, which provides hallucinogens with some sedative properties, and includes marijuana (pot, Acapulco gold, grass, reefer), tetrahydrocannabinol (THC, Marinol), hashish (hash), and hashish oil (hash oil).

Coca (mostly Erythroxylum coca) is a bush with leaves that contain the stimulant used to make cocaine. Coca is not to be confused with cocoa, which comes from cacao seeds and is used in making chocolate, cocoa, and cocoa butter.

Cocaine is a stimulant derived from the leaves of the coca bush.

Depressants (sedatives) are drugs that reduce tension and anxiety and include chloral hydrate, barbiturates (Amytal, Nembutal, Seconal, phenobarbital), benzodiazepines (Librium, Valium), methaqualone (Quaalude), glutethimide (Doriden), and others (Equanil, Placidyl, Valmid).

Drugs are any chemical substances that effect a physical, mental, emotional, or behavioral change in an individual.

Drug abuse is the use of any licit or illicit chemical substance that results in physical, mental, emotional, or behavioral impairment in an individual.

Hallucinogens are drugs that affect sensation, thinking, self-awareness, and emotion. Hallucinogens include LSD (acid, microdot), mescaline and peyote (mexc, buttons, cactus), amphetamine variants (PMA, STP, DOB), phencyclidine (PCP, angel dust, hog), phencyclidine analogues (PCE, PCPy, TCP), and others (psilocybin, psilocyn).

Hashish is the resinous exudate of the cannabis or hemp plant (Cannabis sativa).

Heroin is a semisynthetic derivative of morphine.

Mandrax is a trade name for methaqualone, a pharmaceutical depressant.

Marijuana is the dried leaves of the cannabis or hemp plant (Cannabis sativa).

Methaqualone is a pharmaceutical depressant, referred to as mandrax in Southwest Asia.

Narcotics are drugs that relieve pain, often induce sleep, and refer to opium, opium derivatives, and synthetic substitutes. Natural narcotics include opium (paregoric, parepectolin), morphine (MS-Contin, Roxanol), codeine (Tylenol with codeine, Empirin with codeine, Robitussan AC), and thebaine. Semisynthetic narcotics include heroin (horse, smack), and hydromorphone (Dilaudid). Synthetic narcotics include meperidine or Pethidine (Demerol, Mepergan), methadone (Dolophine, Methadose), and others (Darvon, Lomotil).

Opium is the brown, gummy exudate of the incised, unripe seedpod of the opium poppy.

Opium poppy (Papaver somniferum) is the source for the natural and semisynthetic narcotics.

Poppy straw concentrate is the alkaloid derived from the mature, dried opium poppy.

Qat (kat, khat) is a stimulant from the buds or leaves of Catha edulis that is chewed or drunk as tea.

Quaaludes is the North American slang term for methaqualone, a pharmaceutical depressant.

Stimulants are drugs that relieve mild depression, increase energy and activity, and include cocaine (coke, snow, crack), amphetamines (Desoxyn, Dexedrine), phenmetrazine (Preludin), methylphenidate (Ritalin), and others (Cylert, Sanorex, Tenuate).

Imports: This entry provides the total US dollar amount of imports on a c.i.f. (cost, insurance, and freight)or f.o.b. (free on board) basis.

Imports—commodities: This entry provides a rank ordering of imported products starting with the most important; it sometimes includes the percent of total dollar value.

Imports—partners: This entry provides a rank ordering of trading partners starting with the most important; it sometimes includes the percent of total dollar value.

Independence: For most countries, this entry gives the date that sovereignty was achieved, and from which nation, empire, or trusteeship. For the other countries, the date given may not represent "independence" in the strict sense, but rather some significant nationhood event such as traditional founding date, date of unification, federation, confederation, establishment, fundamental change in the form of government, or state succession. Dependent areas include the notation "none" followed by the nature of their dependency status. Also see the **Terminology** note.

Industrial production growth rate: This entry gives the annual percentage increase in industrial production (includes manufacturing, mining, and construction).

Industries: This entry provides a rank ordering of industries starting with the largest by value of annual output.

Infant mortality rate: This entry gives the number of deaths of infants under one year old in a given year per 1,000 live births in the same year. This rate is often used an indicator of the level of health in a country.

Inflation rate (consumer prices): This entry furnishes the annual percent change in consumer prices compared with the previous year's consumer prices.

International disputes: see **Disputes—international**

International organization participation: This entry lists in alphabetical order by abbreviation those international organizations in which the subject country is a member or participates in some other way.

International organizations: This information is presented in **Appendix C: International Organizations and Groups** which includes the name, abbreviation, address, telephone, FAX, date established, aim, and members by category.

Introduction: This category includes one entry, **Background**. At present it appears in only a few country profiles, but will be added to others in the future.

Irrigated land: This entry gives the number of square kilometers of land area that is artificially supplied with water.

Judicial branch: This entry contains the name(s) of the highest court(s) and a brief description of the selection process for members.

Labor force: This entry contains the total labor force figure.

Labor force—by occupation: This entry contains a rank ordering of component parts of the labor force by occupation.

Land boundaries: This entry contains the total length of all land boundaries and the individual lengths for each of the contiguous border countries.

Land use: This entry contains the percentage shares of total land area for five different types of land use. *Arable land*—land cultivated for crops that are replanted after each harvest like wheat, maize, and rice. *Permanent crops*—land cultivated for crops that are not replanted after each harvest like citrus, coffee, and rubber. *Permanent pastures*—land permanently used for herbaceous forage crops. *Forests and woodland*—land under dense or open stands of trees. *Other*—any land type not specifically mentioned above, such as urban areas, roads, desert, etc.

Notes and Definitions *(continued)*

Languages: This entry provides a rank ordering of languages starting with the largest and sometimes includes the percent of total population speaking that language.

Legal system: This entry contains a brief description of the legal system's historical roots, role in government, and acceptance of International Court of Justice (ICJ) jurisdiction.

Legislative branch: This entry contains information on the structure (unicameral, bicameral, tricameral), formal name, number of seats, and term of office. *Elections* includes the nature of election process or accession to power, date of the last election, and date of the next election. *Election results* includes the percent of vote and/or number of seats held by each party in the last election.

Life expectancy at birth: This entry contains the average number of years to be lived by a group of people born in the same year, if mortality at each age remains constant in the future. The entry includes total population as well as the male and female components. Life expectancy at birth is also a measure of overall quality of life in a country and summarizes the mortality at all ages. It can also be thought of as indicating the potential return on investment in human capital and is necessary for the calculation of various actuarial measures.

Literacy: This entry includes a definition of literacy and Census Bureau percentages for the total population, males, and females. There are no universal definitions and standards of literacy. Unless otherwise specified, all rates are based on the most common definition—the ability to read and write at a specified age. Detailing the standards that individual countries use to assess the ability to read and write is beyond the scope of the *Factbook*. Information on literacy, while not a perfect measure of educational results, is probably the most easily available and valid for international comparisons. Low levels of literacy, and education in general, can impede the economic development of a country in the current rapidly changing, technology-driven world.

Location: This entry identifies the country's regional location, neighboring countries, and adjacent bodies of water.

Map references: This entry includes the name of the *Factbook* reference map on which a country may be found. The entry on **Geographic coordinates** may be helpful in finding some smaller countries.

Maritime claims: This entry includes the following claims: contiguous zone, continental shelf, exclusive economic zone, exclusive fishing zone, extended fishing zone, none (usually for a landlocked country), other (unique maritime claims like Libya's Gulf of Sidra Closing Line or North Korea's Military Boundary Line), and territorial sea. The proximity of neighboring states may prevent some national claims from being extended the full distance.

Merchant marine: Merchant marine may be defined as all ships engaged in the carriage of goods; all commercial vessels (as opposed to all nonmilitary ships), which excludes tugs, fishing vessels, offshore oil rigs, etc.; or a grouping of merchant ships by nationality or register. This entry contains information in two subfields—*total* and *ships by type*. *Total* includes the total number of ships (1,000 GRT or over), total DWT for those ships, and total GRT for those ships. *Ships by type* includes a listing of barge carriers, bulk cargo ships, cargo ships, combination bulk carriers, combination ore/oil carriers, container ships, intermodal ships, liquefied gas tankers, livestock carriers, multifunction large-load carriers, oil tankers, passenger ships, passenger-cargo ships, railcar carriers, refrigerated cargo ships, roll-on/roll-off cargo ships, short-sea passenger ships, specialized tankers, tanker tug-barges, and vehicle carriers.

A captive register is a register of ships maintained by a territory, possession, or colony primarily or exclusively for the use of ships owned in the parent country; it is also referred to as an offshore register, the offshore equivalent of an internal register. Ships on a captive register will fly the same flag as the parent country, or a local variant of it, but will be subject to the maritime laws and taxation rules of the offshore territory. Although the nature of a captive register makes it especially desirable for ships owned in the parent country, just as in the internal register, the ships may also be owned abroad. The captive register then acts as a flag of convenience register, except that it is not the register of an independent state.

A flag of convenience register is a national register offering registration to a merchant ship not owned in the flag state. The major flags of convenience (FOC) attract ships to their registers by virtue of low fees, low or nonexistent taxation of profits, and liberal manning requirements. True FOC registers are characterized by having relatively few of the registered ships actually owned in the flag state. Thus, while virtually any flag can be used for ships under a given set of circumstances, an FOC register is one where the majority of the merchant fleet is owned abroad. It is also referred to as an open register.

A flag state is the nation in which a ship is registered and which holds legal jurisdiction over operation of the ship, whether at home or abroad. Maritime legislation of the flag state determines how a ship is crewed and taxed and whether a foreign-owned ship may be placed on the register.

An internal register is a register of ships maintained as a subset of a national register. Ships on the internal register fly the national flag and have that nationality but are subject to a separate set of maritime rules from those on the main national register. These differences usually include lower taxation of profits, use of foreign nationals as crew members, and, usually, ownership outside the flag state (when it functions as an FOC register). The Norwegian International Ship Register and Danish International Ship Register are the most notable examples of an internal register. Both have been instrumental in stemming flight from the national flag to flags of convenience and in attracting foreign-owned ships to the Norwegian and Danish flags.

A merchant ship is a vessel that carries goods against payment of freight; it is commonly used to denote any nonmilitary ship but accurately restricted to commercial vessels only.

A register is the record of a ship's ownership and nationality as listed with the maritime authorities of a country; also, it is the compendium of such individual ships' registrations. Registration of a ship provides it with a nationality and makes it subject to the laws of the country in which registered (the flag state) regardless of the nationality of the ship's ultimate owner.

Military: This category includes the entries dealing with a country's military structure, manpower, and expenditures.

Military branches: This entry lists the names of the ground, naval, air, marine, and other defense or security forces.

Military expenditures—dollar figure: This entry gives current military expenditures in US dollars; the figure is calculated by multiplying the estimated defense spending in percentage terms by the gross domestic product (GDP) calculated on an exchange rate basis *not* purchasing power parity (PPP) terms.

The figure should be treated with caution because of different price patterns and accounting methods among nations, as well as wide variations in the strength of their currencies.

Military expenditures—percent of GDP: This entry gives current military expenditures as an estimated percent of gross domestic product (GDP).

Military manpower—availability: This entry gives the total numbers of males and females age 15-49 and assumes that every individual is fit to serve.

Military manpower—fit for military service: This entry gives the number of males and females age 15-49 fit for military service. This is a more refined measure of potential military manpower availability which tries to correct for the health situation in the country and reduces the maximum potential number to a more realistic estimate of the actual number fit to serve.

Military manpower—military age: This entry gives the minimum age at which an individual may volunteer for military service or be subject to conscription.

Military manpower—reaching military age annually: This entry gives the number of draft-age males and females entering the military manpower pool in any given year and is a measure of the availability of draft-age young adults.

Military—note: This entry includes miscellaneous military information of significance not included elsewhere.

Money figures: All money figures are expressed in contemporaneous US dollars unless otherwise indicated.

National holiday: This entry gives the primary national day of celebration - usually independence day.

Nationality: This entry provides the identifying terms for citizens - *noun* and *adjective*.

Natural hazards: This entry lists potential natural disasters.

Natural resources: This entry lists a country's mineral, petroleum, hydropower, and other resources of commercial importance.

Net migration rate: This entry includes the figure for the difference between the number of persons entering and leaving a country during the year per 1,000 persons (based on midyear population). An excess of persons entering the country is referred to as net immigration (e.g., 3.56 migrants/1,000 population); an excess of persons leaving the country as net emigration (e.g., -9.26 migrants/1,000 population). The net migration rate indicates the contribution of migration to the overall level of population change. High levels of migration can cause problems such as increasing unemployment and potential ethnic strife (if people are coming in) or a reduction in the labor force, perhaps in certain key sectors (if people are leaving).

People: This category includes the entries dealing with the characteristics of the people and their society.

People—note: This entry includes miscellaneous demographic information of significance not included elsewhere.

Notes and Definitions *(continued)*

Personal Names—Capitalization: The *Factbook* capitalizes the surname or family name of individuals for the convenience of our users who are faced with a world of different cultures and naming conventions. An example would be President SADDAM Husayn of Iraq. Saddam is <u>his</u> name and Husayn is his father's name. He may be referred to as President SADDAM Husayn or President SADDAM, but **not** President Husayn. The need for capitalization, bold type, underlining, italics, or some other indicator of the individual's surname is apparent in the following examples: MAO Zedong, Fidel CASTRO Ruz, William Jefferson CLINTON, and TUNKU SALAHUDDIN Abdul Aziz Shah ibni Al-Marhum Sultan Hisammuddin Alam Shah. By knowing the surname, a short form without all capital letters can be used with confidence as in President Saddam, President Castro, Chairman Mao, President Clinton, or Sultan Tunku Salahuddin. The same system of capitalization is extended to the names of leaders with surnames that are not commonly used such as Queen ELIZABETH II.

Personal Names—Spelling: The romanization of personal names in the *Factbook* normally follows the same transliteration system used by the US Board on Geographic Names for spelling place names. At times, however, a foreign leader expressly indicates a preference for, or the media or official documents regularly use, a romanized spelling that differs from the transliteration derived from the US Government standard. In such cases, the *Factbook* uses the alternative spelling.

Personal Names—Titles: The *Factbook* capitalizes any valid title (or short form of it) immediately preceding a person's name. A title standing alone is lowercased. Examples: President YEL'TSIN and President CLINTON are chiefs of state. In Russia, the president is chief of state and the premier is the head of the government, while in the US, the president is both chief of state and head of government.

Pipelines: This entry gives the lengths and types of pipelines for transporting products like natural gas, crude oil, or petroleum products.

Political parties and leaders: This entry includes a listing of significant political organizations and their leaders.

Political pressure groups and leaders: This entry includes a listing of organizations with leaders involved in politics, but not standing for legislative election.

Population: This entry gives an estimate from the US Bureau of the Census based on statistics from population censuses, vital statistics registration systems, or sample surveys pertaining to the recent past and on assumptions about future trends. The total population presents one overall measure of the potential impact of the country on the world and within its region. Note: starting with the 1993 *Factbook*, demographic estimates for some countries (mostly African) have taken into account the effects of the growing incidence of AIDS infections. These countries are Botswana, Brazil, Burkina Faso, Burma, Burundi, Cambodia, Cameroon, Central African Republic, Democratic Republic of the Congo, Republic of the Congo, Cote d'Ivoire, Ethiopia, Guyana, Haiti, Honduras, Kenya, Lesotho, Malawi, Namibia, Nigeria, Rwanda, South Africa, Swaziland, Tanzania, Thailand, Uganda, Zambia, and Zimbabwe.

Notes and Definitions *(continued)*

Population below poverty line: National estimates of the percentage of the population lying below the poverty line are based on surveys of sub-groups, with the results weighted by the number of people in each group. Definitions of poverty vary considerably among nations. For example, rich nations generally employ more generous standards of poverty than poor nations.

Population growth rate: The average annual percent change in the population, resulting from a surplus (or deficit) of births over deaths and the balance of migrants entering and leaving a country. The rate may be positive or negative. The growth rate is a factor in determining how great a burden would be imposed on a country by the changing needs of its people for infrastructure (e.g., schools, hospitals, housing, roads), resources (e.g., food, water, electricity), and jobs. Rapid population growth can be seen as threatening by neighboring countries.

Ports and harbors: This entry lists the major ports and harbors selected on the basis of overall importance to each country. This is determined by evaluating a number of factors (e.g., dollar value of goods handled, gross tonnage, facilities, military significance).

Radio broadcast stations: This entry includes the total number of AM, FM, and shortwave broadcast stations.

Radios: This entry gives the total number of radio receivers.

Railways: This entry includes the *total* length of the railway network and component parts by gauge: *broad*, *dual*, *narrow*, *standard*, and *other*.

Reference maps: This section includes world, regional, and special or current interest maps.

Religions: This entry includes a rank ordering of religions starting with the largest and sometimes includes the percent of total population.

Sex ratio: This entry includes the number of males for each female in five age groups—*at birth*, *under 15 years*, *15-64 years*, *65 years and over*, and for the *total population*. Sex ratio at birth has recently emerged as an indicator of certain kinds of sex discrimination in some countries. For instance, high sex ratios at birth in some Asian countries are now attributed to sex-selective abortion and infanticide due to a strong preference for sons. This will affect future marriage patterns and fertility patterns. Eventually it could cause unrest among young adult males who are unable to find partners. The sex ratio at birth for the World is 1.06 (1999 est.).

Suffrage: This entry gives the age at enfranchisement and whether the right to vote is universal or restricted.

Telephone numbers: All telephone numbers in the *Factbook* consist of the country code in brackets, the city or area code (where required) in parentheses, and the local number. The one component that is not presented is the international access code, which varies from country to country. For example, an international direct dial telephone call placed from the US to Madrid, Spain, would be as follows:

011 [34] (1) 577-xxxx, where
011 is the international access code for station-to-station calls
(01 is for calls other than station-to-station calls),
[34] is the country code for Spain,
(1) is the city code for Madrid,
577 is the local exchange, and
xxxx is the local telephone number.

An international direct dial telephone call placed from another country to the US would be as follows:

international access code + [1] (202) 939-xxxx, where
[1] is the country code for the US,
(202) is the area code for Washington, DC,
939 is the local exchange, and
xxxx is the local telephone number.

Telephone system: This entry includes a brief characterization of the system with details on the *domestic* and *international* components. The following terms and abbreviations are used throughout the entry:

Arabsat—Arab Satellite Communications Organization (Riyadh, Saudi Arabia).

Autodin—Automatic Digital Network (US Department of Defense).

CB—citizen's band mobile radio communications.

cellular telephone system—the telephones in this system are radio transceivers, with each instrument having its own private radio frequency and sufficient radiated power to reach the booster station in its area (cell), from which the telephone signal is fed to a regular telephone exchange.

Central American Microwave System—a trunk microwave radio relay system that links the countries of Central America and Mexico with each other.

coaxial cable—a multichannel communication cable consisting of a central conducting wire, surrounded by and insulated from a cylindrical conducting shell; a large number of telephone channels can be made available within the insulated space by the use of a large number of carrier frequencies.

Comsat—Communications Satellite Corporation (US).

DSN—Defense Switched Network (formerly Automatic Voice Network or Autovon); basic general-purpose, switched voice network of the Defense Communications System (US Department of Defense).

Eutelsat—European Telecommunications Satellite Organization (Paris).

fiber-optic cable—a multichannel communications cable using a thread of optical glass fibers as a transmission medium in which the signal (voice, video, etc.) is in the form of a coded pulse of light.

HF— high-frequency; any radio frequency in the 3,000- to 30,000-kHz range.

Inmarsat—International Mobile Satellite Organization (London); provider of global mobile satellite communications for commercial, distress, and safety applications at sea, in the air, and on land.

Intelsat—International Telecommunications Satellite Organization (Washington, DC).

Intersputnik—International Organization of Space Communications (Moscow); first established in the former Soviet Union and the East European countries, it is now marketing its services worldwide with earth stations in North America, Africa, and East Asia.

landline—communication wire or cable of any sort that is installed on poles or buried in the ground.

Marecs—Maritime European Communications Satellite used in the Inmarsat system on lease from the European Space Agency.

Marisat—satellites of the Comsat Corporation that participate in the Inmarsat system.

Medarabtel—the Middle East Telecommunications Project of the International Telecommunications Union (ITU) providing a modern telecommunications network, primarily by microwave radio relay, linking Algeria, Djibouti, Egypt, Jordan, Libya, Morocco, Saudi Arabia, Somalia, Sudan, Syria, Tunisia, and

Yemen; it was initially started in Morocco in 1970 by the Arab Telecommunications Union (ATU) and was known at that time as the Middle East Mediterranean Telecommunications Network.

microwave radio relay—transmission of long distance telephone calls and television programs by highly directional radio microwaves that are received and sent on from one booster station to another on an optical path.

NMT—Nordic Mobile Telephone; an analog cellular telephone system that was developed jointly by the national telecommunications authorities of the Nordic countries (Denmark, Finland, Iceland, Norway, and Sweden).

Orbita—a Russian television service; also the trade name of a packet-switched digital telephone network.

radiotelephone communications—the two-way transmission and reception of sounds by broadcast radio on authorized frequencies using telephone handsets.

satellite communication system—a communication system consisting of two or more earth stations and at least one satellite that provides long distance transmission of voice, data, and television; the system usually serves as a trunk connection between telephone exchanges; if the earth stations are in the same country, it is a domestic system.

satellite earth station—a communications facility with a microwave radio transmitting and receiving antenna and required receiving and transmitting equipment for communicating with satellites.

satellite link—a radio connection between a satellite and an earth station permitting communication between them, either one-way (down link from satellite to earth station—television receive-only transmission) or two-way (telephone channels).

SHF—super-high-frequency; any radio frequency in the 3,000- to 30,000-MHz range.

shortwave—radio frequencies (from 1.605 to 30 MHz) that fall above the commercial broadcast band and are used for communication over long distances.

Solidaridad—geosynchronous satellites in Mexico's system of international telecommunications in the Western Hemisphere.

Statsionar—Russia's geostationary system for satellite telecommunications.

submarine cable—a cable designed for service under water.

TAT—Trans-Atlantic Telephone; any of a number of high-capacity submarine coaxial telephone cables linking Europe with North America.

telefax—facsimile service between subscriber stations via the public switched telephone network or the international Datel network.

telegraph—a telecommunications system designed for unmodulated electric impulse transmission.

telex—a communication service involving teletypewriters connected by wire through automatic exchanges.

tropospheric scatter—a form of microwave radio transmission in which the troposphere is used to scatter and reflect a fraction of the incident radio waves back to earth; powerful, highly directional antennas are used to transmit and receive the microwave signals; reliable over-the-horizon communications are realized for distances up to 600 miles in a single hop; additional hops can extend the range of this system for very long distances.

trunk network—a network of switching centers, connected by multichannel trunk lines.

UHF— ultra-high-frequency; any radio frequency in the 300- to 3,000-MHz range.

VHF—very-high-frequency; any radio frequency in the 30- to 300-MHz range.

Telephones: This entry gives the total number of subscribers.

Notes and Definitions *(continued)*

Television—broadcast stations: This entry gives the total number of separate broadcast stations plus any repeater stations.

Televisions: This entry gives the total number of television sets.

Terminology: Due to the highly structured nature of the *Factbook* database, some collective generic terms have to be used. For example, the word **Country** in the **Country name** entry refers to a wide variety of dependencies, areas of special sovereignty, uninhabited islands, and other entities in addition to the traditional countries or independent states. **Military** is also used as an umbrella term for various civil defense, security, and defense activities in many entries. The **Independence** entry includes the usual colonial independence dates and former ruling states as well as other significant nationhood dates such as the traditional founding date or the date of unification, federation, confederation, establishment, or state succession that are not strictly independence dates. Dependent areas have the nature of their dependency status noted in this same entry.

Terrain: This entry contains a brief description of the topography.

Total fertility rate: This entry gives a figure for the average number of children that would be born per woman if all women lived to the end of their childbearing years and bore children according to a given fertility rate at each age. The total fertility rate is a more direct measure of the level of fertility than the crude birth rate, since it refers to births per woman. This indicator shows the potential for population growth in the country. High rates will also place some limits on the labor force participation rates for women. Large numbers of children born to women indicate large family sizes that might limit the ability of the families to feed and educate their children.

Transnational Issues: This category includes only two entries at the present time —**Disputes—international** and **Illicit drugs**—that deal with current issues going beyond national boundaries.

Transportation: This category includes the entries dealing with the means for movement of people and goods.

Transportation—note: This entry includes miscellaneous transportation information of significance not included elsewhere.

Unemployment rate: This entry contains the percent of the labor force that is without jobs. Substantial underemployment might be noted.

United Nations System: This information is presented in **Appendix B: United Nations System** as a chart, table, or text (depending on the version of the *Factbook*) that shows the organization of the UN in detail.

Waterways: This entry gives the total length and individual names of navigable rivers, canals, and other inland bodies of water.

Weights and measures: This information is presented in **Appendix E: Weights and Measures** and includes mathematical notations (mathematical powers and names), metric interrelationships (prefix; symbol; length, weight, or capacity; area; volume), and standard conversion factors.

Notes and Definitions *(continued)*

Years: All year references are for the calendar year (CY) unless indicated as fiscal year (FY). The calendar year is an accounting period of 12 months from 1 January to 31 December. The fiscal year is an accounting period of 12 months other than 1 January to 31 December. FY93/94 refers to the fiscal year that began in calendar year 1993 and ended in calendar year 1994.

Note: Information for the US and US dependencies was compiled from material in the public domain and does not represent Intelligence Community estimates.

Guide to Country Profiles *(Categories, Fields, and Subfields)*

Introduction

Background

Geography

Location
Geographic coordinates
Map references
Area
  total
  land
  water
Area—comparative
Land boundaries
  total
  border countries
Coastline
Maritime claims
  contiguous zone
  continental shelf
  exclusive economic zone
  exclusive fishing zone
  extended fishing zone
  territorial sea
Climate
Terrain
Elevation extremes
  lowest point
  highest point
Natural resources
Land use
  arable land
  permanent crops
  permanent pastures
  forests and woodland
  other
Irrigated land
Natural hazards
Environment—current issues
Environment—international agreements
  party to
  signed, but not ratified
Geography—note

People

Population
Age structure
  0-14 years
  15-64 years
  65 years and over
Population growth rate
Birth rate
Death rate
Net migration rate
Sex ratio
  at birth
  under 15 years
  15-64 years
  65 years and over
  total population
Infant mortality rate
Life expectancy at birth
  total population
  male
  female
Total fertility rate
Nationality
  noun
  adjective

Ethnic groups
Religions
Languages
Literacy
  definition
  total population
  male
  female
People - note

Government

Country name
  conventional long form
  conventional short form
  local long form
  local short form
  former
  abbreviation
Data code
Dependency status
Government type
Capital
Administrative divisions
Dependent areas
Independence
National holiday
Constitution
Legal system
Suffrage
Executive branch
  chief of state
  head of government
  cabinet
  elections
  election results
Legislative branch
  elections
  election results
Judicial branch
Political parties and leaders
Political pressure groups and leaders
International organization participation
Diplomatic representation in the US
  chief of mission
  chancery
  telephone
  FAX
  consulate(s) general
  consulate(s)
  honorary consulate(s)
  honorary consulates(s) general
Diplomatic representation from the US
  chief of mission
  embassy
  branch office
  mailing address
  telephone
  FAX
  consulate(s) general
  consulate(s)
Flag description
Government—note

Economy

Economy—overview
GDP
GDP—real growth rate
GDP—per capita
GDP—composition by sector
  agriculture
  industry
  services
Population below poverty line
Household income or consumption by percentage share
Inflation rate (consumer prices)
Labor force
Labor force—by occupation
Unemployment rate
Budget
  revenues
  expenditures
Industries
Industrial production growth rate
Electricity—production
Electricity—production by source
  fossil fuel
  hydro
  nuclear
  other
Electricity—consumption
Electricity—exports
Electricity—imports
Agriculture—products
Exports
Exports—commodities
Exports—partners
Imports
Imports—commodities
Imports—partners
Debt—external
Economic aid—donor
Economic aid—recipient
Currency
Exchange rates
Fiscal year

Communications

Telephones
Telephone system
  domestic
  international
Radio broadcast stations
Radios
Television broadcast stations
Televisions
Communications - note

Transportation

Railways
  total
  broad gauge
  dual gauge
  narrow gauge
  standard gauge
  other gauges
Highways
  total
  paved
  unpaved

Waterways
Pipelines
Ports and harbors
Merchant marine
  total
  ships by type
Airports
Airports—with paved runways
  total
  over 3,047 m
  2,438 to 3,047 m
  1,524 to 2,437 m
  914 to 1,523 m
  under 914 m
Airports—with unpaved runways
  total
  over 3,047 m
  2,438 to 3,047 m
  1,524 to 2,437 m
  914 to 1,523 m
  under 914 m
Heliports
Transportation—note

Military

Military branches
Military manpower—military age
Military manpower—availability
  males age 15-49
  females age 15-49
Military manpower—fit for military service
  males age 15-49
  females age 15-49
Military manpower—reaching military age annually
  males
  females
Military expenditures—dollar figure
Military expenditures—percent of GDP
Military—note

Transnational Issues

Disputes—international
Illicit drugs

Afghanistan

Geography

Location: Southern Asia, north and west of Pakistan, east of Iran
Geographic coordinates: 33 00 N, 65 00 E
Map references: Asia
Area:
total: 647,500 sq km
land: 647,500 sq km
water: 0 sq km
Area - comparative: slightly smaller than Texas
Land boundaries:
total: 5,529 km
border countries: China 76 km, Iran 936 km, Pakistan 2,430 km, Tajikistan 1,206 km, Turkmenistan 744 km, Uzbekistan 137 km
Coastline: 0 km (landlocked)
Maritime claims: none (landlocked)
Climate: arid to semiarid; cold winters and hot summers
Terrain: mostly rugged mountains; plains in north and southwest
Elevation extremes:
lowest point: Amu Darya 258 m
highest point: Nowshak 7,485 m
Natural resources: natural gas, petroleum, coal, copper, talc, barites, sulfur, lead, zinc, iron ore, salt, precious and semiprecious stones
Land use:
arable land: 12%
permanent crops: 0%
permanent pastures: 46%
forests and woodland: 3%
other: 39% (1993 est.)
Irrigated land: 30,000 sq km (1993 est.)
Natural hazards: damaging earthquakes occur in Hindu Kush mountains; flooding
Environment - current issues: soil degradation; overgrazing; deforestation (much of the remaining forests are being cut down for fuel and building materials); desertification

Environment - international agreements:
party to: Desertification, Endangered Species, Environmental Modification, Marine Dumping, Nuclear Test Ban
signed, but not ratified: Biodiversity, Climate Change, Hazardous Wastes, Law of the Sea, Marine Life Conservation
Geography - note: landlocked

People

Population: 25,824,882 (July 1999 est.)
Age structure:
0-14 years: 43% (male 5,640,841; female 5,422,460)
15-64 years: 54% (male 7,273,681; female 6,776,750)
65 years and over: 3% (male 374,666; female 336,484) (1999 est.)
Population growth rate: 3.95% (1999 est.)
note: this rate reflects the continued return of refugees
Birth rate: 41.93 births/1,000 population (1999 est.)
Death rate: 17.02 deaths/1,000 population (1999 est.)
Net migration rate: 14.62 migrant(s)/1,000 population (1999 est.)
Sex ratio:
at birth: 1.05 male(s)/female
under 15 years: 1.04 male(s)/female
15-64 years: 1.07 male(s)/female
65 years and over: 1.11 male(s)/female
total population: 1.06 male(s)/female (1999 est.)
Infant mortality rate: 140.55 deaths/1,000 live births (1999 est.)
Life expectancy at birth:
total population: 47.33 years
male: 47.82 years
female: 46.82 years (1999 est.)
Total fertility rate: 5.94 children born/woman (1999 est.)
Nationality:
noun: Afghan(s)
adjective: Afghan
Ethnic groups: Pashtun 38%, Tajik 25%, Uzbek 6%, Hazara 19%, minor ethnic groups (Aimaks, Turkmen, Baloch, and others)
Religions: Sunni Muslim 84%, Shi'a Muslim 15%, other 1%
Languages: Pashtu 35%, Afghan Persian (Dari) 50%, Turkic languages (primarily Uzbek and Turkmen) 11%, 30 minor languages (primarily Balochi and Pashai) 4%, much bilingualism
Literacy:
definition: age 15 and over can read and write
total population: 31.5%
male: 47.2%
female: 15% (1995 est.)

Government

Country name:
conventional long form: Islamic State of Afghanistan; note - the self-proclaimed Taliban government refers to the country as Islamic Emirate of Afghanistan

conventional short form: Afghanistan
local long form: Dowlat-e Eslami-ye Afghanestan
local short form: Afghanestan
former: Republic of Afghanistan
Data code: AF
Government type: transitional government
Capital: Kabul
Administrative divisions: 30 provinces (velayat, singular - velayat); Badakhshan, Badghis, Baghlan, Balkh, Bamian, Farah, Faryab, Ghazni, Ghowr, Helmand, Herat, Jowzjan, Kabol, Kandahar, Kapisa, Konar, Kondoz, Laghman, Lowgar, Nangarhar, Nimruz, Oruzgan, Paktia, Paktika, Parvan, Samangan, Sar-e Pol, Takhar, Vardak, Zabol
note: there may be two new provinces of Nurestan (Nuristan) and Khowst
Independence: 19 August 1919 (from UK control over Afghan foreign affairs)
National holiday: Victory of the Muslim Nation, 28 April; Remembrance Day for Martyrs and Disabled, 4 May; Independence Day, 19 August
Constitution: none
Legal system: a new legal system has not been adopted but all factions tacitly agree they will follow Shari'a (Islamic law)
Suffrage: undetermined; previously males 15-50 years of age
Executive branch: on 27 September 1996, the ruling members of the Afghan Government were displaced by members of the Islamic Taliban movement; the Islamic State of Afghanistan has no functioning government at this time, and the country remains divided among fighting factions
note: the Taliban have declared themselves the legitimate government of Afghanistan; the UN has deferred a decision on credentials and the Organization of the Islamic Conference has left the Afghan seat vacant until the question of legitimacy can be resolved through negotiations among the warring factions; the country is essentially divided along ethnic lines; the Taliban controls the capital of Kabul and approximately two-thirds of the country including the predominately ethnic Pashtun areas in southern Afghanistan; opposing factions have their stronghold in the ethnically diverse north
Legislative branch: non-functioning as of June 1993
Judicial branch: non-functioning as of March 1995, although there are local Shari'a (Islamic law) courts throughout the country
Political parties and leaders: Taliban (Religious Students Movement) [Mohammad OMAR]; United Islamic Front for the Salvation of Afghanistan comprised of Jumbesh-i-Melli Islami (National Islamic Movement) [Abdul Rashid DOSTAM]; Jamiat-i-Islami (Islamic Society) [Burhanuddin RABBANI and Ahmad Shah MASOOD]; and Hizbi Wahdat-Khalili faction (Islamic Unity Party) [Abdul Karim KHALILI]; other smaller parties are Hizbi Islami-Gulbuddin (Islamic Party) [Gulbuddin HIKMATYAR faction]; Hizbi Islami-Khalis (Islamic Party) [Yunis KHALIS faction]; Ittihad-i-Islami Barai Azadi Afghanistan (Islamic Union

Afghanistan *(continued)*

for the Liberation of Afghanistan) [Abdul Rasul SAYYAF]; Harakat-Inqilab-i-Islami (Islamic Revolutionary Movement) [Mohammad Nabi MOHAMMADI]; Jabha-i-Najat-i-Milli Afghanistan (Afghanistan National Liberation Front) [Sibghatullah MOJADDEDI]; Mahaz-i-Milli-Islami (National Islamic Front) [Sayed Ahamad GAILANI]; Hizbi Wahdat-Akbari faction (Islamic Unity Party) [Mohammad Akbar AKBARI]; Harakat-i-Islami (Islamic Movement) [Mohammed Asif MOHSENI]

Political pressure groups and leaders: tribal elders represent traditional Pashtun leadership; Afghan refugees in Pakistan, Australia, US, and elsewhere have organized politically; Peshawar, Pakistan-based groups such as the Coordination Council for National Unity and Understanding in Afghanistan or CUNUA [Ishaq GAILANI]; Writers Union of Free Afghanistan or WUFA [A. Rasul AMIN]; Mellat (Social Democratic Party) [leader NA]

International organization participation: AsDB, CP, ECO, ESCAP, FAO, G-77, IAEA, IBRD, ICAO, ICRM, IDA, IDB, IFAD, IFC, IFRCS, ILO, IMF, Intelsat, IOC, IOM (observer), ITU, NAM, OIC, OPCW, UN, UNCTAD, UNESCO, UNIDO, UPU, WFTU, WHO, WMO, WToO

Diplomatic representation in the US:
note: embassy operations suspended 21 August 1997
chief of mission: Ambassador (vacant)
chancery: 2341 Wyoming Avenue NW, Washington, DC 20008
telephone: [1] (202) 234-3770
FAX: [1] (202) 328-3516
consulate(s) general: New York

Diplomatic representation from the US: the US embassy in Kabul has been closed since January 1989 due to security concerns

Flag description: three equal horizontal bands of green (top), white, and black with a gold emblem centered on the three bands; the emblem features a temple-like structure with Islamic inscriptions above and below, encircled by a wreath on the left and right and by a bolder Islamic inscription above, all of which are encircled by two crossed scimitars
note: the Taliban uses a plain white flag

Economy

Economy - overview: Afghanistan is an extremely poor, landlocked country, highly dependent on farming and livestock raising (sheep and goats). Economic considerations have played second fiddle to political and military upheavals during two decades of war, including the nearly 10-year Soviet military occupation (which ended 15 February 1989). During that conflict one-third of the population fled the country, with Pakistan and Iran sheltering a combined peak of more than 6 million refugees. Now, only 750,000 registered Afghan refugees remain in Pakistan and about 1.2 million in Iran. Another 1 million have probably moved into and around urban areas within Afghanistan. Gross domestic product has fallen substantially over the past 20 years because of the loss of labor and capital and the disruption of trade

and transport. Much of the population continues to suffer from insufficient food, clothing, housing, and medical care. Inflation remains a serious problem throughout the country, with one estimate putting the rate at 240% in Kabul in 1996. International aid can deal with only a fraction of the humanitarian problem, let alone promote economic development. Government efforts to encourage foreign investment have not worked. The economic situation did not improve in 1998. Numerical data are likely to be either unavailable or unreliable.

GDP: purchasing power parity - $20 billion (1998 est.)
GDP - real growth rate: NA%
GDP - per capita: purchasing power parity - $800 (1998 est.)
GDP - composition by sector:
agriculture: 53%
industry: 28.5%
services: 18.5% (1990)
Population below poverty line: NA%
Household income or consumption by percentage share:
lowest 10%: NA%
highest 10%: NA%
Inflation rate (consumer prices): 240% (1996 est.)
Labor force: 7.1 million
Labor force - by occupation: agriculture and animal husbandry 67.8%, industry 10.2%, construction 6.3%, commerce 5%, services and other 10.7% (1980 est.)
Unemployment rate: 8% (1995 est.)
Budget:
revenues: $NA
expenditures: $NA, including capital expenditures of $NA
Industries: small-scale production of textiles, soap, furniture, shoes, fertilizer, and cement; handwoven carpets; natural gas, oil, coal, copper
Electricity - production: 540 million kWh (1996)
Electricity - production by source:
fossil fuel: 35.19%
hydro: 64.81%
nuclear: 0%
other: 0% (1996)
Electricity - consumption: 660 million kWh (1996)
Electricity - exports: 0 kWh (1996) (1996)
Electricity - imports: 120 million kWh (1996)
Agriculture - products: wheat, fruits, nuts, karakul pelts; wool, mutton
Exports: $80 million (1996 est.)
Exports - commodities: fruits and nuts, handwoven carpets, wool, cotton, hides and pelts, precious and semi-precious gems
Exports - partners: FSU, Pakistan, Iran, Germany, India, UK, Belgium, Luxembourg, Czech Republic
Imports: $150 million (1996 est.)
Imports - commodities: food and petroleum products; most consumer goods
Imports - partners: FSU, Pakistan, Iran, Japan, Singapore, India, South Korea, Germany
Debt - external: $2.3 billion (March 1991 est.)

Economic aid - recipient: $214.6 million (1995); note - US provided $450 million in bilateral assistance (1985-93); US continues to contribute to multilateral assistance through the UN programs of food aid, immunization, land mine removal, and a wide range of aid to refugees and displaced persons
Currency: 1 afghani (AF) = 100 puls
Exchange rates: afghanis (Af) per US$1 - 4,750 (February 1999), 17,000 (December 1996), 7,000 (January 1995), 1,900 (January 1994), 1,019 (March 1993), 850 (1991); note - these rates reflect the free market exchange rates rather than the official exchange rate, which was fixed at 50.600 afghanis to the dollar until 1996, when it rose to 2,262.65 per dollar, and finally became fixed again at 3,000.00 per dollar on April 1996
Fiscal year: 21 March - 20 March

Communications

Telephones: 31,200 (1983 est.)
Telephone system:
domestic: very limited telephone and telegraph service; in 1997, telecommunications links were established between Mazar-e Sharif, Herat, Kandahar, Jalalabad, and Kabul through satellite and microwave systems
international: satellite earth stations - 1 Intelsat (Indian Ocean) linked only to Iran and 1 Intersputnik (Atlantic Ocean region); commercial satellite telephone center in Ghazni
Radio broadcast stations: AM 6 (5 are inactive), FM 1, shortwave 3 (1998)
Radios: 1.67 million (1998 est.)
Television broadcast stations: NA
note: in 1997, there was a station in Mazar-e Sharif reaching four northern Afghanistan provinces; also, the government ran a central television station in Kabul and regional stations in nine of the 30 provinces; it is unknown if any of these stations currently operate
Televisions: 100,000 (1998 est.)

Transportation

Railways:
total: 24.6 km
broad gauge: 9.6 km 1.524-m gauge from Gushgy (Turkmenistan) to Towraghondi; 15 km 1.524-m gauge from Termiz (Uzbekistan) to Kheyrabad transshipment point on south bank of Amu Darya
Highways:
total: 21,000 km
paved: 2,793 km
unpaved: 18,207 km (1996 est.)
Waterways: 1,200 km; chiefly Amu Darya, which handles vessels up to about 500 DWT
Pipelines: petroleum products - Uzbekistan to Bagram and Turkmenistan to Shindand; natural gas 180 km
Ports and harbors: Kheyrabad, Shir Khan
Merchant marine:
total: 1 container ship (1,000 GRT or over) totaling

11,982 GRT/14,101 DWT (1998 est.)
Airports: 44 (1998 est.)
Airports - with paved runways:
total: 11
over 3,047 m: 3
2,438 to 3,047 m: 4
1,524 to 2,437 m: 2
under 914 m: 2 (1998 est.)
Airports - with unpaved runways:
total: 33
2,438 to 3,047 m: 5
1,524 to 2,437 m: 14
914 to 1,523 m: 4
under 914 m: 10 (1998 est.)
Heliports: 3 (1998 est.)

Military

Military branches: NA; note - the military does not exist on a national basis; some elements of the former Army, Air and Air Defense Forces, National Guard, Border Guard Forces, National Police Force (Sarandoi), and tribal militias still exist but are factionalized among the various groups
Military manpower - military age: 22 years of age
Military manpower - availability:
males age 15-49: 6,326,135 (1999 est.)
Military manpower - fit for military service:
males age 15-49: 3,392,336 (1999 est.)
Military manpower - reaching military age annually:
males: 248,320 (1999 est.)
Military expenditures - dollar figure: $NA
Military expenditures - percent of GDP: NA%

Transnational Issues

Disputes - international: support to Islamic militants worldwide by some factions; question over which group should hold Afghanistan's seat at the UN
Illicit drugs: world's second-largest illicit opium producer after Burma (cultivation in 1998 - 41,720 hectares, a 7% increase over 1997; potential production in 1998 - 1,350 metric tons) and a major source of hashish; increasing number of heroin-processing laboratories being set up in the country; major political factions in the country profit from drug trade

Albania

Geography

Location: Southeastern Europe, bordering the Adriatic Sea and Ionian Sea, between Greece and Serbia and Montenegro
Geographic coordinates: 41 00 N, 20 00 E
Map references: Europe
Area:
total: 28,750 sq km
land: 27,400 sq km
water: 1,350 sq km
Area - comparative: slightly smaller than Maryland
Land boundaries:
total: 720 km
border countries: Greece 282 km, The Former Yugoslav Republic of Macedonia 151 km, Serbia and Montenegro 287 km (114 km with Serbia, 173 km with Montenegro)
Coastline: 362 km
Maritime claims:
continental shelf: 200-m depth or to the depth of exploitation
territorial sea: 12 nm
Climate: mild temperate; cool, cloudy, wet winters; hot, clear, dry summers; interior is cooler and wetter
Terrain: mostly mountains and hills; small plains along coast
Elevation extremes:
lowest point: Adriatic Sea 0 m
highest point: Maja e Korabit (Golem Korab) 2,753 m
Natural resources: petroleum, natural gas, coal, chromium, copper, timber, nickel
Land use:
arable land: 21%
permanent crops: 5%
permanent pastures: 15%
forests and woodland: 38%
other: 21% (1993 est.)
Irrigated land: 3,410 sq km (1993 est.)
Natural hazards: destructive earthquakes; tsunamis occur along southwestern coast

Environment - current issues: deforestation; soil erosion; water pollution from industrial and domestic effluents
Environment - international agreements:
party to: Biodiversity, Climate Change, Wetlands
signed, but not ratified: none of the selected agreements
Geography - note: strategic location along Strait of Otranto (links Adriatic Sea to Ionian Sea and Mediterranean Sea)

People

Population: 3,364,571 (July 1999 est.)
Age structure:
0-14 years: 33% (male 568,642; female 530,088)
15-64 years: 61% (male 957,561; female 1,105,870)
65 years and over: 6% (male 84,280; female 118,130) (1999 est.)
Population growth rate: 1.05% (1999 est.)
Birth rate: 20.74 births/1,000 population (1999 est.)
Death rate: 7.35 deaths/1,000 population (1999 est.)
Net migration rate: -2.93 migrant(s)/1,000 population (1999 est.)
Sex ratio:
at birth: 1.08 male(s)/female
under 15 years: 1.07 male(s)/female
15-64 years: 0.87 male(s)/female
65 years and over: 0.71 male(s)/female
total population: 0.92 male(s)/female (1999 est.)
Infant mortality rate: 42.9 deaths/1,000 live births (1999 est.)
Life expectancy at birth:
total population: 69 years
male: 65.92 years
female: 72.33 years (1999 est.)
Total fertility rate: 2.5 children born/woman (1999 est.)
Nationality:
noun: Albanian(s)
adjective: Albanian
Ethnic groups: Albanian 95%, Greeks 3%, other 2% (Vlachs, Gypsies, Serbs, and Bulgarians) (1989 est.)
note: in 1989, other estimates of the Greek population ranged from 1% (official Albanian statistics) to 12% (from a Greek organization)
Religions: Muslim 70%, Albanian Orthodox 20%, Roman Catholic 10%
note: all mosques and churches were closed in 1967 and religious observances prohibited; in November 1990, Albania began allowing private religious practice
Languages: Albanian (Tosk is the official dialect), Greek
Literacy:
definition: age 9 and over can read and write
total population: 93%
male: NA%
female: NA% (1997 est.)

Albania (continued)

Government

Country name:
conventional long form: Republic of Albania
conventional short form: Albania
local long form: Republika e Shqiperise
local short form: Shqiperia
former: People's Socialist Republic of Albania
Data code: AL
Government type: emerging democracy
Capital: Tirana
Administrative divisions: 36 districts (rrethe, singular - rreth) and 1 municipality* (bashki); Berat, Bulqize, Delvine, Devoll (Bilisht), Diber (Peshkopi), Durres, Elbasan, Fier, Gjirokaster, Gramsh, Has (Krume), Kavaje, Kolonje (Erseke), Korce, Kruje, Kucove, Kukes, Lac, Lezhe, Librazhd, Lushnje, Malesi e Madhe (Koplik), Mallakaster (Ballsh), Mat (Burrel), Mirdite (Rreshen), Peqin, Permet, Pogradec, Puke, Sarande, Shkoder, Skrapar (Corovode), Tepelene, Tirane (Tirana), Tirane* (Tirana), Tropoje (Bajram Curri), Vlore
note: administrative divisions have the same names as their administrative centers (exceptions have the administrative center name following in parentheses)
Independence: 28 November 1912 (from Ottoman Empire)
National holiday: Independence Day, 28 November (1912)
Constitution: a new constitution was adopted by popular referendum on 28 November 1998; note - the opposition Democratic Party boycotted the vote
Legal system: has not accepted compulsory ICJ jurisdiction
Suffrage: 18 years of age; universal and compulsory
Executive branch:
chief of state: President of the Republic Rexhep MEIDANI (since 24 July 1997)
head of government: Prime Minister Pandeli MAJKO (since 2 October 1998)
cabinet: Council of Ministers nominated by the prime minister and approved by the president
elections: president elected by the People's Assembly for a five-year term; election last held 24 July 1997 (next to be held NA 2002); prime minister appointed by the president
election results: Rexhep MEIDANI elected president; People's Assembly vote by number - total votes 122, for 110, against 3, abstained 2, invalid 7
Legislative branch: unicameral People's Assembly or Kuvendi Popullor (155 seats; most members are elected by direct popular vote and some by proportional vote for four-year terms)
elections: last held 29 June 1997 (next to be held NA 2001)
election results: percent of vote by party - PS 53.36%, PD 25.33%, PSD 2.5%, PBDNJ 2.78%, PBK 2.36%, PAD 2.85%, PR 2.25%, PLL 3.09%, PDK 1.00%, PBSD 0.84%; seats by party - PS 101, PD 27, PSD 8, PBDNJ 4, PBK 3, PAD 2, PR 2, PLL 2, PDK 1, PBSD 1, PUK 1, independents 3
Judicial branch: Supreme Court, chairman of the Supreme Court is elected by the People's Assembly for a four-year term

Political parties and leaders: Albanian Socialist Party or PS (formerly the Albania Workers Party) [Fatos NANO, chairman]; Democratic Party or PD [Sali BERISHA]; Albanian Republican Party or PR [Fatmir MEHDIU]; Social Democratic Party or PSD [Skender GJINUSHI]; Unity for Human Rights Party or PBDNJ [Vasil MELO, chairman]; National Front (Balli Kombetar) or PBK [Hysen SELFO]; Movement of Legality Party or PLL [Guri DUROLLARI]; Party of National Unity or PUK [Idajet BEQIRI]; Christian Democratic Party or PDK [Zef BUSHATI]; PBSD (expansion unknown) [leader NA]; Democratic Party of the Right or PDD [Petrit KALAKULA]; Democratic Alliance or PAD [Neritan CEKA]; Social Democratic Union Party or USdS [Teodor LACO]; Albanian United Right or DBSH [leader NA]
International organization participation: BSEC, CCC, CE, CEI, EAPC, EBRD, ECE, EU (applicant), FAO, IAEA, IBRD, ICAO, ICRM, IDA, IDB, IFAD, IFC, IFRCS, ILO, IMF, IMO, Intelsat (nonsignatory user), Interpol, IOC, IOM, ISO, ITU, OIC, OPCW, OSCE, PFP, UN, UNCTAD, UNESCO, UNIDO, UNOMIG, UPU, WFTU, WHO, WIPO, WMO, WToO, WTrO (applicant)
Diplomatic representation in the US:
chief of mission: Ambassador Petrit BUSHATI
chancery: 2100 S Street NW, Washington, DC 20008
telephone: [1] (202) 223-4942
FAX: [1] (202) 628-7342
Diplomatic representation from the US:
chief of mission: Ambassador Marisa R. LINO
embassy: Rruga Elbasanit 103, Tirana
mailing address: American Embassy, Tirana, Department of State, Washington, DC 20521-9510
telephone: [355] (42) 47285 through 47289
FAX: [355] (42) 32222
Flag description: red with a black two-headed eagle in the center

Economy

Economy - overview: An extremely poor country by European standards, Albania is making the difficult transition to a more open-market economy. The economy rebounded in 1993-95 after a severe depression accompanying the collapse of the previous centrally planned system in 1990 and 1991. However, a weakening of government resolve to maintain stabilization policies in the election year of 1996 contributed to renewal of inflationary pressures, spurred by the budget deficit which exceeded 12%. The collapse of financial pyramid schemes in early 1997 - which had attracted deposits from a substantial portion of Albania's population - triggered severe social unrest which led to more than 1,500 deaths, widespread destruction of property, and an 8% drop in GDP. The new government installed in July 1997 has taken strong measures to restore public order and to revive economic activity and trade. The economy continues to be bolstered by remittances of some 20% of the labor force which works abroad, mostly in

Greece and Italy. These remittances supplement GDP and help offset the large foreign trade deficit. Most agricultural land was privatized in 1992, substantially improving peasant incomes. In 1998, Albania probably recovered most if not all of the 7% drop in GDP of 1997.
GDP: purchasing power parity - $5 billion (1998 est.)
GDP - real growth rate: 7% (1998 est.)
GDP - per capita: purchasing power parity - $1,490 (1998 est.)
GDP - composition by sector:
agriculture: 56%
industry: 21%
services: 23% (1997)
Population below poverty line: 19.6% (1996 est.)
Household income or consumption by percentage share:
lowest 10%: NA%
highest 10%: NA%
Inflation rate (consumer prices): 40% (1997 est.)
Labor force: 1.692 million (1994 est.) (including 352,000 emigrant workers and 261,000 domestically unemployed)
Labor force - by occupation: agriculture (nearly all private; but some state employed) 49.5%, private business sector 22.2%, state business sector 28.3% (including state-owned industry 7.8%); note - includes only those domestically employed
Unemployment rate: 14% (October 1997) officially, but likely to be as high as 28%
Budget:
revenues: $624 million
expenditures: $996 million, including capital expenditures of $NA
Industries: food processing, textiles and clothing; lumber, oil, cement, chemicals, mining, basic metals, hydropower
Industrial production growth rate: 6% (1995 est.)
Electricity - production: 5.12 billion kWh (1996)
Electricity - production by source:
fossil fuel: 4.3%
hydro: 95.7%
nuclear: 0%
other: 0% (1996)
Electricity - consumption: 5.27 billion kWh (1996)
Electricity - exports: 0 kWh (1996) (1996)
Electricity - imports: 150 million kWh (1996)
Agriculture - products: wide range of temperate-zone crops and livestock
Exports: $212 million (f.o.b., 1998 est.)
Exports - commodities: asphalt, metals and metallic ores, electricity, crude oil, vegetables, fruits, tobacco
Exports - partners: Italy, Greece, Germany, Belgium, US
Imports: $791 million (f.o.b., 1998 est.)
Imports - commodities: machinery, consumer goods, grains
Imports - partners: Italy, Greece, Bulgaria, Turkey, The Former Yugoslav Republic of Macedonia
Debt - external: $645 million (1996)
Economic aid - recipient: $630 million (1997

Albania (continued)

pledged)
Currency: 1 lek (L) = 100 qintars
Exchange rates: leke (L) per US$1 - 139.93
(January 1999), 150.63 (1998), 148.93 (1997), 104.50
(1996), 92.70 (1995), 94.62 (1994)
Fiscal year: calendar year

Communications

Telephones: 55,000
Telephone system:
domestic: obsolete wire system; no longer provides a
telephone for every village; in 1992, following the fall
of the communist government, peasants cut the wire
to about 1,000 villages and used it to build fences
international: inadequate; international traffic carried
by microwave radio relay from the Tirana exchange to
Italy and Greece
Radio broadcast stations: AM 16, FM 3, shortwave
4 (1998)
Radios: 577,000 (1991 est.)
Television broadcast stations: 13 (1997)
Televisions: 300,000 (1993 est.)

Transportation

Railways:
total: 447 km (none electrified)
standard gauge: 447 km 1.435-m gauge (1995)
Highways:
total: 18,000 km
paved: 5,400 km
unpaved: 12,600 km (1996 est.)
Waterways: 43 km plus Albanian sections of Lake
Scutari, Lake Ohrid, and Lake Prespa (1990)
Pipelines: crude oil 145 km; petroleum products 55
km; natural gas 64 km (1991)
Ports and harbors: Durres, Sarande, Shengjin,
Vlore
Merchant marine:
total: 8 cargo ships (1,000 GRT or over) totaling
28,394 GRT/41,429 DWT (1998 est.)
Airports: 9 (1998 est.)
Airports - with paved runways:
total: 3
2,438 to 3,047 m: 3 (1998 est.)
Airports - with unpaved runways:
total: 6
over 3,047 m: 1
1,524 to 2,437 m: 1
914 to 1,523 m: 2
under 914 m: 2 (1998 est.)
Heliports: 1 (1998 est.)

Military

Military branches: Army, Navy, Air and Air Defense
Forces, Interior Ministry Troops, Border Guards
Military manpower - military age: 19 years of age
Military manpower - availability:
males age 15-49: 763,949 (1999 est.)
Military manpower - fit for military service:
males age 15-49: 622,013 (1999 est.)

**Military manpower - reaching military age
annually:**
males: 32,954 (1999 est.)
Military expenditures - dollar figure: $60 million
(1998)
Military expenditures - percent of GDP: 2%
(1998)

Transnational Issues

Disputes - international: the Albanian Government
supports protection of the rights of ethnic Albanians
outside of its borders but has downplayed them to
further its primary foreign policy goal of regional
cooperation; Albanian majority in Kosovo seeks
independence from Serbian Republic; Albanians in
The Former Yugoslav Republic of Macedonia claim
discrimination in education, access to public-sector
jobs, and representation in government
Illicit drugs: increasingly active transshipment point
for Southwest Asian opiates, hashish, and cannabis
transiting the Balkan route and - to a far lesser extent
- cocaine from South America destined for Western
Europe; limited opium and cannabis production;
ethnic Albanian narcotrafficking organizations active
and rapidly expanding in Europe

Algeria

Geography

Location: Northern Africa, bordering the
Mediterranean Sea, between Morocco and Tunisia
Geographic coordinates: 28 00 N, 3 00 E
Map references: Africa
Area:
total: 2,381,740 sq km
land: 2,381,740 sq km
water: 0 sq km
Area - comparative: slightly less than 3.5 times the
size of Texas
Land boundaries:
total: 6,343 km
border countries: Libya 982 km, Mali 1,376 km,
Mauritania 463 km, Morocco 1,559 km, Niger 956 km,
Tunisia 965 km, Western Sahara 42 km
Coastline: 998 km
Maritime claims:
exclusive fishing zone: 32-52 nm
territorial sea: 12 nm
Climate: arid to semiarid; mild, wet winters with hot,
dry summers along coast; drier with cold winters and
hot summers on high plateau; sirocco is a hot, dust/
sand-laden wind especially common in summer
Terrain: mostly high plateau and desert; some
mountains; narrow, discontinuous coastal plain
Elevation extremes:
lowest point: Chott Melrhir -40 m
highest point: Tahat 3,003 m
Natural resources: petroleum, natural gas, iron ore,
phosphates, uranium, lead, zinc
Land use:
arable land: 3%
permanent crops: 0%
permanent pastures: 13%
forests and woodland: 2%
other: 82% (1993 est.)
Irrigated land: 5,550 sq km (1993 est.)
Natural hazards: mountainous areas subject to
severe earthquakes; mud slides

Algeria *(continued)*

Environment - current issues: soil erosion from overgrazing and other poor farming practices; desertification; dumping of raw sewage, petroleum refining wastes, and other industrial effluents is leading to the pollution of rivers and coastal waters; Mediterranean Sea, in particular, becoming polluted from oil wastes, soil erosion, and fertilizer runoff; inadequate supplies of potable water

Environment - international agreements:
party to: Biodiversity, Climate Change, Desertification, Endangered Species, Environmental Modification, Law of the Sea, Ozone Layer Protection, Ship Pollution, Wetlands
signed, but not ratified: Nuclear Test Ban

Geography - note: second-largest country in Africa (after Sudan)

People

Population: 31,133,486 (July 1999 est.)
Age structure:
0-14 years: 37% (male 5,911,910; female 5,696,538)
15-64 years: 59% (male 9,255,702; female 9,063,954)
65 years and over: 4% (male 559,570; female 645,812) (1999 est.)
Population growth rate: 2.1% (1999 est.)
Birth rate: 27 births/1,000 population (1999 est.)
Death rate: 5.52 deaths/1,000 population (1999 est.)
Net migration rate: -0.49 migrant(s)/1,000 population (1999 est.)
Sex ratio:
at birth: 1.04 male(s)/female
under 15 years: 1.04 male(s)/female
15-64 years: 1.02 male(s)/female
65 years and over: 0.87 male(s)/female
total population: 1.02 male(s)/female (1999 est.)
Infant mortality rate: 43.82 deaths/1,000 live births (1999 est.)
Life expectancy at birth:
total population: 69.24 years
male: 68.07 years
female: 70.46 years (1999 est.)
Total fertility rate: 3.27 children born/woman (1999 est.)
Nationality:
noun: Algerian(s)
adjective: Algerian
Ethnic groups: Arab-Berber 99%, European less than 1%
Religions: Sunni Muslim (state religion) 99%, Christian and Jewish 1%
Languages: Arabic (official), French, Berber dialects
Literacy:
definition: age 15 and over can read and write
total population: 61.6%
male: 73.9%
female: 49% (1995 est.)

Government

Country name:
conventional long form: Democratic and Popular Republic of Algeria
conventional short form: Algeria
local long form: Al Jumhuriyah al Jaza'iriyah ad Dimuqratiyah ash Shabiyah
local short form: Al Jaza'ir
Data code: AG
Government type: republic
Capital: Algiers
Administrative divisions: 48 provinces (wilayas, singular - wilaya); Adrar, Ain Defla, Ain Temouchent, Alger, Annaba, Batna, Bechar, Bejaia, Biskra, Blida, Bordj Bou Arreridj, Bouira, Boumerdes, Chlef, Constantine, Djelfa, El Bayadh, El Oued, El Tarf, Ghardaia, Guelma, Illizi, Jijel, Khenchela, Laghouat, Mascara, Medea, Mila, Mostaganem, M'Sila, Naama, Oran, Ouargla, Oum el Bouaghi, Relizane, Saida, Setif, Sidi Bel Abbes, Skikda, Souk Ahras, Tamanghasset, Tebessa, Tiaret, Tindouf, Tipaza, Tissemsilt, Tizi Ouzou, Tlemcen
Independence: 5 July 1962 (from France)
National holiday: Anniversary of the Revolution, 1 November (1954)
Constitution: 19 November 1976, effective 22 November 1976; revised 3 November 1988, 23 February 1989, and 28 November 1996; note - referendum approving the revisions of 28 November 1996 was signed into law 7 December 1996
Legal system: socialist, based on French and Islamic law; judicial review of legislative acts in ad hoc Constitutional Council composed of various public officials, including several Supreme Court justices; has not accepted compulsory ICJ jurisdiction
Suffrage: 18 years of age; universal
Executive branch:
chief of state: President Liamine ZEROUAL (appointed president 31 January 1994, elected president 16 November 1995)
head of government: Interim Prime Minister Smail HAMDANI (since 15 December 1998); note - appointed as interim prime minister until April 1999 presidential elections
cabinet: Council of Ministers appointed by the prime minister
elections: president elected by popular vote for a five-year term; election last held 16 November 1995 (next to be held NA April 1999); note - ZEROUAL announced in September 1998 his intention to step down after early presidential elections); prime minister appointed by the president
election results: Liamine ZEROUAL elected president; percent of vote - Liamine ZEROUAL 61.3%
Legislative branch: bicameral Parliament consists of the National People's Assembly or Al-Majlis Ech-Chaabi Al-Watani (380 seats; members elected by popular vote to serve four-year terms) and the Council of Nations (144 seats; one-third of the members appointed by the president, two-thirds elected by indirect vote; members serve six-year terms; created as a result of the constitutional revision of November 1996)
elections: National People's Assembly - last held 5 June 1997 (next to be held NA 2001); elections for two-thirds of the Council of Nations - last held 25 December 1997 (next to be held NA 2003)
election results: National People's Assembly - percent of vote by party - NA%; seats by party - RND 156, MSP 69, FLN 62, Nahda Movement 34, FFS 20, RCD 19, PT 4, Republican Progressive Party 3, Union for Democracy and Freedoms 1, Liberal Social Party 1, independents 11; Council of Nations - percent of vote by party - NA%; seats by party - RND 80, FLN 10, FFS 4, MSP 2 (remaining 48 seats appointed by the president, party breakdown NA)
Judicial branch: Supreme Court (Cour Supreme)
Political parties and leaders: Islamic Salvation Front or FIS (outlawed April 1992) [Ali BELHADJ, Dr. Abassi MADANI, Rabeh KEBIR (self-exile in Germany)]; National Liberation Front or FLN [Boualem BENHAMOUDA, secretary general]; Socialist Forces Front or FFS [Hocine Ait AHMED, secretary general (self-exile in Switzerland)]; Movement of a Peaceful Society or MSP [Mahfoud NAHNAH, chairman]; Rally for Culture and Democracy or RCD [Said SAADI, secretary general]; Algerian Renewal Party or PRA [Noureddine BOUKROUH, chairman]; Nahda Movement or Al Nahda [Abdallah DJABALLAH, president]; Democratic National Rally or RND [Mohamed BENBAIBECHE, chairman]; Movement for Democracy in Algeria or MDA [Ahmed Ben BELLA]; Workers Party or PT [Louisa HANOUN]; Republican Progressive Party [Khadir DRISS]; Union for Democracy and Freedoms [Mouley BOUKHALAFA]; Liberal Social Party [Ahmed KHELIL]
note: the government established a multiparty system in September 1989 and, as of 31 December 1990, over 50 legal parties existed; a new party law was enacted in March 1997
International organization participation: ABEDA, AfDB, AFESD, AL, AMF, AMU, CCC, ECA, FAO, G-15, G-19, G-24, G-77, IAEA, IBRD, ICAO, ICFTU, ICRM, IDA, IDB, IFAD, IFC, IFRCS, IHO, ILO, IMF, IMO, Inmarsat, Intelsat, Interpol, IOC, ISO, ITU, NAM, OAPEC, OAS (observer), OAU, OIC, OPCW, OPEC, OSCE (partner), UN, UNCTAD, UNESCO, UNHCR, UNIDO, UPU, WCL, WHO, WIPO, WMO, WToO, WTrO (applicant)
Diplomatic representation in the US:
chief of mission: Ambassador Ramtane LAMAMRA
chancery: 2118 Kalorama Road NW, Washington, DC 20008
telephone: [1] (202) 265-2800
FAX: [1] (202) 667-2174
Diplomatic representation from the US:
chief of mission: Ambassador Cameron R. HUME
embassy: 4 Chemin Cheikh Bachir El-Ibrahimi, Algiers
mailing address: B. P. Box 549, Alger-Gare, 16000 Algiers
telephone: [213] (2) 69-11-86, 69-12-55, 69-18-54, 69-38-75
FAX: [213] (2) 69-39-79
Flag description: two equal vertical bands of green (hoist side) and white with a red, five-pointed star

within a red crescent; the crescent, star, and color green are traditional symbols of Islam (the state religion)

Economy

Economy - overview: The hydrocarbons sector is the backbone of the economy, accounting for roughly 52% of budget revenues, 25% of GDP, and over 95% of export earnings. Algeria has the fifth-largest reserves of natural gas in the world and is the second largest gas exporter; it ranks fourteenth for oil reserves. Algiers' efforts to reform one of the most centrally planned economies in the Arab world began after the 1986 collapse of world oil prices plunged the country into a severe recession. In 1989, the government launched a comprehensive, IMF-supported program to achieve economic stabilization and to introduce market mechanisms into the economy. Despite substantial progress toward economic adjustment, in 1992 the reform drive stalled as Algiers became embroiled in political turmoil. In September 1993, a new government was formed, and one priority was the resumption and acceleration of the structural adjustment process. Burdened with a heavy foreign debt, Algiers concluded a one-year standby arrangement with the IMF in April 1994 and the following year signed onto a three-year extended fund facility which ended 30 April 1998. Progress on economic reform, a Paris Club debt rescheduling in 1995, and oil and gas sector expansion have contributed to a recovery since 1995. Investments in developing hydrocarbon resources have spurred growth, but the economy remains heavily dependent on volatile oil and gas revenues. The government has continued efforts to diversify the economy by attracting foreign and domestic investment outside the energy sector in order to reduce high unemployment and improve living standards.

GDP: purchasing power parity - $140.2 billion (1998 est.)

GDP - real growth rate: 3.2% (1998 est.)

GDP - per capita: purchasing power parity - $4,600 (1998 est.)

GDP - composition by sector:
agriculture: 12%
industry: 51%
services: 37% (1997 est.)

Population below poverty line: 22.6% (1995 est.)

Household income or consumption by percentage share:
lowest 10%: 2.8%
highest 10%: 26.8% (1995)

Inflation rate (consumer prices): 9% (1998 est.)

Labor force: 7.8 million (1996 est.)

Labor force - by occupation: government 29.5%, agriculture 22%, construction and public works 16.2%, industry 13.6%, commerce and services 13.5%, transportation and communication 5.2% (1989)

Unemployment rate: 30% (1998 est.)

Budget:
revenues: $14.4 billion

expenditures: $15.7 billion, including capital expenditures of $4.4 million (1998 est.)

Industries: petroleum, natural gas, light industries, mining, electrical, petrochemical, food processing

Industrial production growth rate: -4% (1997 est.)

Electricity - production: 18.4 billion kWh (1996)

Electricity - production by source:
fossil fuel: 98.91%
hydro: 1.09%
nuclear: 0%
other: 0% (1996)

Electricity - consumption: 18.13 billion kWh (1996)

Electricity - exports: 490 million kWh (1996)

Electricity - imports: 220 million kWh (1996)

Agriculture - products: wheat, barley, oats, grapes, olives, citrus, fruits; sheep, cattle

Exports: $14 billion (f.o.b., 1997 est.)

Exports - commodities: petroleum and natural gas 97%

Exports - partners: Italy 18.8%, US 14.8%, France 11.8%, Spain 8%, Germany 7.9% (1995 est.)

Imports: $8.5 billion (f.o.b., 1997 est.)

Imports - commodities: capital goods, food and beverages, consumer goods

Imports - partners: France 29%, Spain 10.5%, Italy 8.2%, US 8%, Germany 5.6% (1995 est.)

Debt - external: $31.4 billion (1998 est.)

Economic aid - recipient: $897.5 million (1994)

Currency: 1 Algerian dinar (DA) = 100 centimes

Exchange rates: Algerian dinars (DA) per US$1 - 61.264 (January 1999), 58.739 (1998), 57.707 (1997), 54.749 (1996), 47.663 (1995), 35.059 (1994)

Fiscal year: calendar year

Communications

Telephones: 1,381,342 (5,200 cellular telephone subscribers) (1997)

Telephone system:
domestic: good service in north but sparse in south; domestic satellite system with 12 earth stations (20 additional domestic earth stations are planned)
international: 5 submarine cables; microwave radio relay to Italy, France, Spain, Morocco, and Tunisia; coaxial cable to Morocco and Tunisia; participant in Medarabtel; satellite earth stations - 2 Intelsat (1 Atlantic Ocean and 1 Indian Ocean), 1 Intersputnik, and 1 Arabsat

Radio broadcast stations: AM 23, FM 1, shortwave 8 (1998 est.)

Radios: 3.5 million (1998 est.)

Television broadcast stations: 18 (not including low-power stations) (1997)

Televisions: 2 million (1998 est.)

Transportation

Railways:
total: 4,772 km
standard gauge: 3,616 km 1.435-m gauge (301 km electrified; 215 km double track)
narrow gauge: 1,156 km 1.055-m gauge

Highways:
total: 102,424 km
paved: 70,570 km (including 608 km of expressways)
unpaved: 31,854 km (1995 est.)

Pipelines: crude oil 6,612 km; petroleum products 298 km; natural gas 2,948 km

Ports and harbors: Algiers, Annaba, Arzew, Bejaia, Beni Saf, Dellys, Djendjene, Ghazaouet, Jijel, Mostaganem, Oran, Skikda, Tenes

Merchant marine:
total: 78 ships (1,000 GRT or over) totaling 933,672 GRT/1,094,104 DWT
ships by type: bulk 9, cargo 27, chemical tanker 7, liquefied gas tanker 11, oil tanker 5, roll-on/roll-off cargo 13, short-sea passenger 5, specialized tanker 1 (1998 est.)

Airports: 137 (1998 est.)

Airports - with paved runways:
total: 51
over 3,047 m: 8
2,438 to 3,047 m: 24
1,524 to 2,437 m: 13
914 to 1,523 m: 5
under 914 m: 1 (1998 est.)

Airports - with unpaved runways:
total: 86
2,438 to 3,047 m: 3
1,524 to 2,437 m: 24
914 to 1,523 m: 40
under 914 m: 19 (1998 est.)

Heliports: 1 (1998 est.)

Military

Military branches: National Popular Army, Navy, Air Force, Territorial Air Defense, National Gendarmerie

Military manpower - military age: 19 years of age

Military manpower - availability:
males age 15-49: 8,237,682 (1999 est.)

Military manpower - fit for military service:
males age 15-49: 5,046,931 (1999 est.)

Military manpower - reaching military age annually:
males: 359,592 (1999 est.)

Military expenditures - dollar figure: $1.3 billion (1994)

Military expenditures - percent of GDP: 2.7% (1994)

Transnational Issues

Disputes - international: part of southeastern region claimed by Libya

American Samoa
(territory of the US)

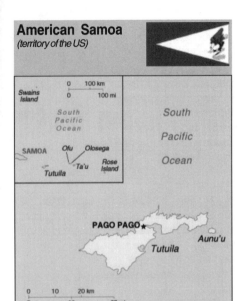

Geography

Location: Oceania, group of islands in the South Pacific Ocean, about one-half of the way from Hawaii to New Zealand

Geographic coordinates: 14 20 S, 170 00 W

Map references: Oceania

Area:
total: 199 sq km
land: 199 sq km
water: 0 sq km
note: includes Rose Island and Swains Island

Area - comparative: slightly larger than Washington, DC

Land boundaries: 0 km

Coastline: 116 km

Maritime claims:
exclusive economic zone: 200 nm
territorial sea: 12 nm

Climate: tropical marine, moderated by southeast trade winds; annual rainfall averages 124 inches; rainy season from November to April, dry season from May to October; little seasonal temperature variation

Terrain: five volcanic islands with rugged peaks and limited coastal plains, two coral atolls (Rose Island, Swains Island)

Elevation extremes:
lowest point: Pacific Ocean 0 m
highest point: Lata 966 m

Natural resources: pumice, pumicite

Land use:
arable land: 5%
permanent crops: 10%
permanent pastures: 0%
forests and woodland: 70%
other: 15% (1993 est.)

Irrigated land: NA sq km

Natural hazards: typhoons common from December to March

Environment - current issues: limited natural fresh water resources; the water division of the government has spent substantial funds in the past few years to improve water catchments and pipelines

Environment - international agreements:
party to: NA
signed, but not ratified: NA

Geography - note: Pago Pago has one of the best natural deepwater harbors in the South Pacific Ocean, sheltered by shape from rough seas and protected by peripheral mountains from high winds; strategic location in the South Pacific Ocean

People

Population: 63,786 (July 1999 est.)

Age structure:
0-14 years: 39% (male 12,840; female 12,074)
15-64 years: 56% (male 17,933; female 18,035)
65 years and over: 5% (male 1,494; female 1,410) (1999 est.)

Population growth rate: 2.64% (1999 est.)

Birth rate: 26.53 births/1,000 population (1999 est.)

Death rate: 4.04 deaths/1,000 population (1999 est.)

Net migration rate: 3.92 migrant(s)/1,000 population (1999 est.)

Sex ratio:
at birth: 1.06 male(s)/female
under 15 years: 1.06 male(s)/female
15-64 years: 0.99 male(s)/female
65 years and over: 1.06 male(s)/female
total population: 1.02 male(s)/female (1999 est.)

Infant mortality rate: 10.19 deaths/1,000 live births (1999 est.)

Life expectancy at birth:
total population: 75.46 years
male: 71.23 years
female: 79.95 years (1999 est.)

Total fertility rate: 3.66 children born/woman (1999 est.)

Nationality:
noun: American Samoan(s)
adjective: American Samoan

Ethnic groups: Samoan (Polynesian) 89%, Caucasian 2%, Tongan 4%, other 5%

Religions: Christian Congregationalist 50%, Roman Catholic 20%, Protestant denominations and other 30%

Languages: Samoan (closely related to Hawaiian and other Polynesian languages), English
note: most people are bilingual

Literacy:
definition: age 15 and over can read and write
total population: 97%
male: 98%
female: 97% (1980 est.)

Government

Country name:
conventional long form: Territory of American Samoa
conventional short form: American Samoa
abbreviation: AS

Data code: AQ

Dependency status: unincorporated and unorganized territory of the US; administered by the Office of Insular Affairs, US Department of the Interior

Government type: NA

Capital: Pago Pago

Administrative divisions: none (territory of the US); there are no first-order administrative divisions as defined by the US Government, but there are three districts and two islands* at the second order; Eastern, Manu'a, Rose Island*, Swains Island*, Western

Independence: none (territory of the US)

National holiday: Territorial Flag Day, 17 April (1900)

Constitution: ratified 1966, in effect 1967

Legal system: NA

Suffrage: 18 years of age; universal

Executive branch:
chief of state: President William Jefferson CLINTON of the US (since 20 January 1993) and Vice President Albert GORE, Jr. (since 20 January 1993)
head of government: Governor Tauese P. SUNIA (since 3 January 1997) and Lieutenant Governor Togiola TULAFONO (since 3 January 1997)
cabinet: NA
elections: US president and vice president elected on the same ticket for four-year terms; governor and lieutenant governor elected on the same ticket by popular vote for four-year terms; election last held 3 November 1996 (next to be held 7 November 2000)
election results: Tauese P. SUNIA elected governor; percent of vote - Tauese P. SUNIA (Democrat) 51%, Peter REID (independent) 49%

Legislative branch: bicameral Fono or Legislative Assembly consists of the House of Representatives (21 seats - 20 of which are elected by popular vote and 1 is an appointed, nonvoting delegate from Swains Island; members serve two-year terms) and the Senate (18 seats; members are elected from local chiefs and serve four-year terms)
elections: House of Representatives - last held NA November 1998 (next to be held NA November 2000); Senate - last held 3 November 1996 (next to be held 7 November 2000)
election results: House of Representatives - percent of vote by party - NA; seats by party - NA; Senate - percent of vote by party - NA; seats by party - NA
note: American Samoa elects one delegate to the US House of Representatives; election last held 3 November 1998 (next to be held 7 November 2000); results - Eni R. F. H. FALEOMAVAEGA (Democrat) reelected as delegate for a sixth term

Judicial branch: High Court (chief justice and associate justices are appointed by the US Secretary of the Interior)

Political parties and leaders: Democratic Party [leader NA]; Republican Party [leader NA]

International organization participation: ESCAP (associate), Interpol (subbureau), IOC, SPC

Diplomatic representation in the US: none (territory of the US)

Diplomatic representation from the US: none (territory of the US)

Flag description: blue, with a white triangle edged

in red that is based on the outer side and extends to the hoist side; a brown and white American bald eagle flying toward the hoist side is carrying two traditional Samoan symbols of authority, a staff and a war club

Economy

Economy - overview: This is a traditional Polynesian economy in which more than 90% of the land is communally owned. Economic activity is strongly linked to the US, with which American Samoa conducts the great bulk of its foreign trade. Tuna fishing and tuna processing plants are the backbone of the private sector, with canned tuna the primary export. Transfers from the US Government add substantially to American Samoa's economic well-being. According to one observer, attempts by the government to develop a larger and broader economy are restrained by Samoa's remote location, its limited transportation, and its devastating hurricanes. Tourism, a developing sector, may be held back by the current financial difficulties in East Asia.

GDP: purchasing power parity - $150 million (1995 est.)

GDP - real growth rate: NA%

GDP - per capita: purchasing power parity - $2,600 (1995 est.)

GDP - composition by sector:
agriculture: NA%
industry: NA%
services: NA%

Population below poverty line: NA%

Household income or consumption by percentage share:
lowest 10%: NA%
highest 10%: NA%

Inflation rate (consumer prices): NA%

Labor force: 13,949 (1996)

Labor force - by occupation: government 33%, tuna canneries 34%, other 33% (1990)

Unemployment rate: 12% (1991)

Budget:
revenues: $121 million (37% in local revenue and 63% in US grants)
expenditures: $127 million, including capital expenditures of $NA (FY96/97)

Industries: tuna canneries (largely dependent on foreign fishing vessels), handicrafts

Industrial production growth rate: NA%

Electricity - production: 105 million kWh (1996)

Electricity - production by source:
fossil fuel: 100%
hydro: 0%
nuclear: 0%
other: 0% (1996)

Electricity - consumption: 105 million kWh (1996)

Electricity - exports: 0 kWh (1996)

Electricity - imports: 0 kWh (1996)

Agriculture - products: bananas, coconuts, vegetables, taro, breadfruit, yams, copra, pineapples, papayas; dairy products, livestock

Exports: $313 million (1996)

Exports - commodities: canned tuna 93%

Exports - partners: US 99.6%

Imports: $471 million (1996)

Imports - commodities: materials for canneries 56%, food 8%, petroleum products 7%, machinery and parts 6%

Imports - partners: US 62%, Japan 9%, NZ 7%, Australia 11%, Fiji 4%, other 7%

Debt - external: $NA

Economic aid - recipient: $NA; note - important financial support from the US

Currency: 1 US dollar (US$) = 100 cents

Exchange rates: US currency is used

Fiscal year: 1 October - 30 September

Communications

Telephones: 9,000 (1994 est.)

Telephone system:
domestic: good telex, telegraph, facsimile and cellular phone services; domestic satellite system with 1 Comsat earth station
international: satellite earth station - 1 Intelsat (Pacific Ocean)

Radio broadcast stations: AM 1, FM 1, shortwave 0 (1998)

Radios: NA

Television broadcast stations: 1 (1997)

Televisions: 12,000 (1994 est.)

Transportation

Railways: 0 km

Highways:
total: 350 km
paved: 150 km
unpaved: 200 km

Ports and harbors: Aunu'u (new construction), Auasi, Faleosao, Ofu, Pago Pago, Ta'u

Merchant marine: none

Airports: 4 (1998 est.)

Airports - with paved runways:
total: 2
2,438 to 3,047 m: 1
under 914 m: 1 (1998 est.)

Airports - with unpaved runways:
total: 2
under 914 m: 2 (1998 est.)

Military

Military - note: defense is the responsibility of the US

Transnational Issues

Disputes - international: none

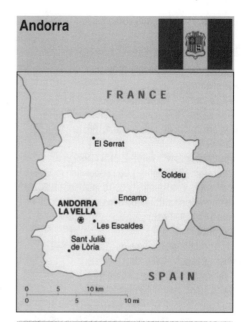

Andorra

Geography

Location: Southwestern Europe, between France and Spain

Geographic coordinates: 42 30 N, 1 30 E

Map references: Europe

Area:
total: 450 sq km
land: 450 sq km
water: 0 sq km

Area - comparative: 2.5 times the size of Washington, DC

Land boundaries:
total: 125 km
border countries: France 60 km, Spain 65 km

Coastline: 0 km (landlocked)

Maritime claims: none (landlocked)

Climate: temperate; snowy, cold winters and warm, dry summers

Terrain: rugged mountains dissected by narrow valleys

Elevation extremes:
lowest point: Riu Valira 840 m
highest point: Coma Pedrosa 2,946 m

Natural resources: hydropower, mineral water, timber, iron ore, lead

Land use:
arable land: 2%
permanent crops: 0%
permanent pastures: 56%
forests and woodland: 22%
other: 20% (1993 est.)

Irrigated land: NA sq km

Natural hazards: snowslides, avalanches

Environment - current issues: deforestation; overgrazing of mountain meadows contributes to soil erosion

Environment - international agreements:
party to: none of the selected agreements
signed, but not ratified: none of the selected agreements

Andorra *(continued)*

Geography - note: landlocked

P e o p l e

Population: 65,939 (July 1999 est.)
Age structure:
0-14 years: 14% (male 4,880; female 4,527)
15-64 years: 73% (male 25,811; female 22,444)
65 years and over: 13% (male 4,196; female 4,081)
(1999 est.)
Population growth rate: 2.24% (1999 est.)
Birth rate: 10.27 births/1,000 population (1999 est.)
Death rate: 5.46 deaths/1,000 population (1999 est.)
Net migration rate: 17.61 migrant(s)/1,000
population (1999 est.)
Sex ratio:
at birth: 1.06 male(s)/female
under 15 years: 1.08 male(s)/female
15-64 years: 1.15 male(s)/female
65 years and over: 1.03 male(s)/female
total population: 1.12 male(s)/female (1999 est.)
Infant mortality rate: 4.08 deaths/1,000 live births
(1999 est.)
Life expectancy at birth:
total population: 83.46 years
male: 80.55 years
female: 86.55 years (1999 est.)
Total fertility rate: 1.25 children born/woman (1999
est.)
Nationality:
noun: Andorran(s)
adjective: Andorran
Ethnic groups: Spanish 61%, Andorran 30%,
French 6%, other 3%
Religions: Roman Catholic (predominant)
Languages: Catalan (official), French, Castilian
Literacy: NA

G o v e r n m e n t

Country name:
conventional long form: Principality of Andorra
conventional short form: Andorra
local long form: Principat d'Andorra
local short form: Andorra
Data code: AN
Government type: parliamentary democracy (since
March 1993) that retains as its heads of state a
coprincipality; the two princes are the president of
France and bishop of Seo de Urgel, Spain, who are
represented locally by officials called veguers
Capital: Andorra la Vella
Administrative divisions: 7 parishes (parroquies,
singular - parroquia); Andorra, Canillo, Encamp, La
Massana, Les Escaldes, Ordino, Sant Julia de Loria
Independence: 1278
National holiday: Mare de Deu de Meritxell, 8
September
Constitution: Andorra's first written constitution was
drafted in 1991; adopted 14 March 1993
Legal system: based on French and Spanish civil
codes; no judicial review of legislative acts; has not
accepted compulsory ICJ jurisdiction

Suffrage: 18 years of age; universal
Executive branch:
chief of state: French Coprince Jacques CHIRAC
(since 17 May 1995) represented by Veguer
Jean-Pierre COURTOIS (since NA); and Spanish
Coprince Episcopal Monseigneur Joan MARTI Alanis
(since 31 January 1971) represented by Veguer
Francesc BADIA Battalla (since NA)
head of government: Executive Council President
Marc FORNE Molne (since 21 December 1994)
cabinet: Executive Council designated by the
Executive Council president
elections: Executive Council president elected by the
General Council and formally appointed by the
coprinces; election last held 16 February 1997 (next to
be held NA 2001)
election results: Marc FORNE Molne elected
executive council president; percent of General
Council vote - NA
Legislative branch: unicameral General Council of
the Valleys or Consell General de las Valls (28 seats;
members are elected by direct popular vote, 14 from
a single national constituency and 14 to represent
each of the 7 parishes; members serve four-year
terms)
elections: last held 16 February 1997 (next to be held
NA February 2001)
election results: percent of vote by party - UL 57%,
AND 21%, IDN 7%, ND 7%, other 8%; seats by party
- UL 16, AND 6, ND 2, IDN 2, UPO 2
Judicial branch: Supreme Court of Andorra at
Perpignan, France, (two civil judges appointed by the
veguers, one appeals judge appointed by the
coprinces alternately); Ecclesiastical Court of the
Bishop of Seo de Urgel (Spain); Tribunal of the Courts
or Tribunal des Cortes, (presided over by the two civil
judges, one appeals judge, the veguers, and two
members of the General Council)
Political parties and leaders: National Democratic
Group or AND [Oscar RIBAS Reig]; Liberal Union or
UL [Francesc CERQUEDA]; New Democracy or ND
[Jaume BARTOMEU Cassany]; Andorran National
Coalition or CNA [Antoni CERQUEDA Gispert];
National Democratic Initiative or IDN [Vincenc
MATEU Zamora]; Liberal Party of Andorra (Partit
Liberal d'Andorra) or PLA [Marc FORNE]; Unio
Parroquial d'Ordino or UDO [leader NA]
note: there are two other small parties
International organization participation: CE,
ECE, ICRM, IFRCS, Interpol, IOC, ITU, OSCE, UN,
UNESCO, WHO, WIPO, WToO
Diplomatic representation in the US:
chief of mission: Ambassador Juli
MINOVES-TRIQUELL (also Permanent
Representative to the UN)
chancery: 2 United Nations Plaza, 25th Floor, New
York, NY 10017
telephone: [1] (212) 750-8064
FAX: [1] (212) 750-6630
Diplomatic representation from the US: the US
does not have an embassy in Andorra; the US
Ambassador to Spain is accredited to Andorra; US

interests in Andorra are represented by the Consulate
General's office in Barcelona (Spain); mailing
address: Paseo Reina Elisenda, 23, 08034
Barcelona, Spain; telephone: (3493) 280-2227; FAX:
(3493) 205-7705; note - Consul General Douglas R.
SMITH makes periodic visits to Andorra
Flag description: three equal vertical bands of blue
(hoist side), yellow, and red with the national coat of
arms centered in the yellow band; the coat of arms
features a quartered shield; similar to the flags of
Chad and Romania that do not have a national coat of
arms in the center

E c o n o m y

Economy - overview: Tourism, the mainstay of
Andorra's tiny, well-to-do economy, accounts for
roughly 80% of GDP. An estimated 10 million tourists
visit annually, attracted by Andorra's duty-free status
and by its summer and winter resorts. Andorra's
comparative advantage has recently eroded as the
economies of neighboring France and Spain have
been opened up, providing broader availability of
goods and lower tariffs. The banking sector, with its
"tax haven" status, also contributes substantially to
the economy. Agricultural production is limited by a
scarcity of arable land, and most food has to be
imported. The principal livestock activity is sheep
raising. Manufacturing consists mainly of cigarettes,
cigars, and furniture. Andorra is a member of the EU
Customs Union and is treated as an EU member for
trade in manufactured goods (no tariffs) and as a
non-EU member for agricultural products.
GDP: purchasing power parity - $1.2 billion (1995
est.)
GDP - real growth rate: NA%
GDP - per capita: purchasing power parity - $18,000
(1995 est.)
GDP - composition by sector:
agriculture: NA%
industry: NA%
services: NA%
Population below poverty line: NA%
**Household income or consumption by percentage
share:**
lowest 10%: NA%
highest 10%: NA%
Inflation rate (consumer prices): NA%
Labor force: NA
Unemployment rate: 0%
Budget:
revenues: $138 million
expenditures: $177 million, including capital
expenditures of $NA (1993)
Industries: tourism (particularly skiing), sheep,
timber, tobacco, banking
Industrial production growth rate: NA%
Electricity - production: 140 million kWh (1992)
Electricity - production by source:
fossil fuel: NA%
hydro: NA%
nuclear: NA%
other: NA%

Andorra *(continued)*

Electricity - consumption: NA kWh
Electricity - exports: NA kWh
Electricity - imports: NA kWh
Agriculture - products: tobacco, rye, wheat, barley, oats, vegetables; sheep
Exports: $47 million (f.o.b., 1995)
Exports - commodities: electricity, tobacco products, furniture
Exports - partners: France 49%, Spain 47%
Imports: $1 billion (1995)
Imports - commodities: consumer goods, food
Imports - partners: France, Spain, US 4.2%
Debt - external: $NA
Economic aid - recipient: none
Currency: 1 French franc (F) = 100 centimes; 1 peseta (Pta) = 100 centimos; the French and Spanish currencies are used
Exchange rates: French francs (F) per US$1 - 5.65 (January 1999), 5.8995 (1998), 5.8367 (1997), 5.1155 (1996), 4.9915 (1995), 5.5520 (1994); Spanish pesetas (Ptas) per US$1 - 143.39 (January 1999), 149.40 (1998), 146.41 (1997), 126.66 (1996), 124.69 (1995), 133.96 (1994)
Fiscal year: calendar year

Communications

Telephones: 21,258 (1983 est.)
Telephone system:
domestic: modern system with microwave radio relay connections between exchanges
international: landline circuits to France and Spain
Radio broadcast stations: AM 0, FM 15, shortwave 0 (1998)
Radios: 10,000 (1993 est.)
Television broadcast stations: 0 (1997)
Televisions: 7,000 (1991 est.)

Transportation

Railways: 0 km
Highways:
total: 269 km
paved: 198 km
unpaved: 71 km (1991 est.)
Ports and harbors: none
Airports: none

Military

Military - note: defense is the responsibility of France and Spain

Transnational Issues

Disputes - international: none

Angola

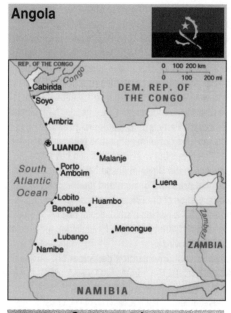

Geography

Location: Southern Africa, bordering the South Atlantic Ocean, between Namibia and Democratic Republic of the Congo
Geographic coordinates: 12 30 S, 18 30 E
Map references: Africa
Area:
total: 1,246,700 sq km
land: 1,246,700 sq km
water: 0 sq km
Area - comparative: slightly less than twice the size of Texas
Land boundaries:
total: 5,198 km
border countries: Democratic Republic of the Congo 2,511 km of which 220 km is the boundary of discontiguous Cabinda Province, Republic of the Congo 201 km, Namibia 1,376 km, Zambia 1,110 km
Coastline: 1,600 km
Maritime claims:
exclusive economic zone: 200 nm
territorial sea: 12 nm
Climate: semiarid in south and along coast to Luanda; north has cool, dry season (May to October) and hot, rainy season (November to April)
Terrain: narrow coastal plain rises abruptly to vast interior plateau
Elevation extremes:
lowest point: Atlantic Ocean 0 m
highest point: Morro de Moco 2,620 m
Natural resources: petroleum, diamonds, iron ore, phosphates, copper, feldspar, gold, bauxite, uranium
Land use:
arable land: 2%
permanent crops: 0%
permanent pastures: 23%
forests and woodland: 43%
other: 32% (1993 est.)
Irrigated land: 750 sq km (1993 est.)

Natural hazards: locally heavy rainfall causes periodic flooding on the plateau
Environment - current issues: the overuse of pastures and subsequent soil erosion attributable to population pressures; desertification; deforestation of tropical rain forest, in response to both international demand for tropical timber and to domestic use as fuel, resulting in loss of biodiversity; soil erosion contributing to water pollution and siltation of rivers and dams; inadequate supplies of potable water
Environment - international agreements:
party to: Biodiversity, Desertification, Law of the Sea
signed, but not ratified: Climate Change
Geography - note: Cabinda is separated from rest of country by the Democratic Republic of the Congo

People

Population: 11,177,537 (July 1999 est.)
Age structure:
0-14 years: 45% (male 2,545,006; female 2,473,732)
15-64 years: 52% (male 2,938,178; female 2,909,844)
65 years and over: 3% (male 143,074; female 167,703) (1999 est.)
Population growth rate: 2.84% (1999 est.)
Birth rate: 43.11 births/1,000 population (1999 est.)
Death rate: 16.35 deaths/1,000 population (1999 est.)
Net migration rate: 1.6 migrant(s)/1,000 population (1999 est.)
Sex ratio:
at birth: 1.05 male(s)/female
under 15 years: 1.03 male(s)/female
15-64 years: 1.01 male(s)/female
65 years and over: 0.85 male(s)/female
total population: 1.01 male(s)/female (1999 est.)
Infant mortality rate: 129.19 deaths/1,000 live births (1999 est.)
Life expectancy at birth:
total population: 48.39 years
male: 46.08 years
female: 50.82 years (1999 est.)
Total fertility rate: 6.12 children born/woman (1999 est.)
Nationality:
noun: Angolan(s)
adjective: Angolan
Ethnic groups: Ovimbundu 37%, Kimbundu 25%, Bakongo 13%, mestico (mixed European and Native African) 2%, European 1%, other 22%
Religions: indigenous beliefs 47%, Roman Catholic 38%, Protestant 15% (1998 est.)
Languages: Portuguese (official), Bantu and other African languages
Literacy:
definition: age 15 and over can read and write
total population: 42%
male: 56%
female: 28% (1998 est.)

Angola (continued)

Government

Country name:
conventional long form: Republic of Angola
conventional short form: Angola
local long form: Republica de Angola
local short form: Angola
former: People's Republic of Angola
Data code: AO
Government type: transitional government, nominally a multiparty democracy with a strong presidential system
Capital: Luanda
Administrative divisions: 18 provinces (provincias, singular - provincia); Bengo, Benguela, Bie, Cabinda, Cuando Cubango, Cuanza Norte, Cuanza Sul, Cunene, Huambo, Huila, Luanda, Lunda Norte, Lunda Sul, Malanje, Moxico, Namibe, Uige, Zaire
Independence: 11 November 1975 (from Portugal)
National holiday: Independence Day, 11 November (1975)
Constitution: 11 November 1975; revised 7 January 1978, 11 August 1980, 6 March 1991, and 26 August 1992
Legal system: based on Portuguese civil law system and customary law; recently modified to accommodate political pluralism and increased use of free markets
Suffrage: 18 years of age; universal
Executive branch:
chief of state: President Jose Eduardo DOS SANTOS (since 21 September 1979); note - the president is both chief of state and head of government
head of government: President Jose Eduardo DOS SANTOS (since January 1999); note - the president is both chief of state and head of government
cabinet: Council of Ministers appointed by the president
elections: President DOS SANTOS originally elected without opposition under a one-party system and stood for reelection in Angola's first multiparty elections in 28-29 September 1992, the last elections to be held (next to be held NA)
election results: DOS SANTOS received 49.6% of the total vote, making a run-off election necessary between him and second-place finisher Jonas SAVIMBI; the run-off was not held and SAVIMBI's National Union for the Total Independence of Angola (UNITA) repudiated the results of the first election; the civil war resumed
Legislative branch: unicameral National Assembly or Assembleia Nacional (220 seats; members elected by proportional vote to serve four-year terms)
elections: last held 29-30 September 1992 (next to be held NA)
election results: percent of vote by party - MPLA 54%, UNITA 34%, others 12%; seats by party - MPLA 129, UNITA 70, PRS 6, FNLA 5, PLD 3, others 7
Judicial branch: Supreme Court or Tribunal da Relacao, judges of the Supreme Court are appointed by the president
Political parties and leaders: Popular Movement for the Liberation of Angola or MPLA [Jose Eduardo DOS SANTOS] ruling party in power since 1975; National Union for the Total Independence of Angola or UNITA [Jonas SAVIMBI], largest opposition party engaged in years of armed resistance before joining the current unity government in April 1997; Social Renewal Party or PRS [leader NA]; National Front for the Liberation of Angola or FNLA [leader NA]; Liberal Democratic Party or PLD [leader NA]
note: about a dozen minor parties participated in the 1992 elections but won few seats and have little influence in the National Assembly
Political pressure groups and leaders: Front for the Liberation of the Enclave of Cabinda or FLEC
note: FLEC is waging a small-scale, highly factionalized, armed struggle for the independence of Cabinda Province
International organization participation: ACP, AfDB, CCC, CEEAC, ECA, FAO, G-77, IBRD, ICAO, ICRM, IDA, IFAD, IFC, IFRCS, ILO, IMF, IMO, Intelsat, Interpol, IOC, IOM, ITU, NAM, OAS (observer), OAU, SADC, UN, UNCTAD, UNESCO, UNIDO, UPU, WCL, WFTU, WHO, WIPO, WMO, WToO, WTrO
Diplomatic representation in the US:
chief of mission: Ambassador Antonio dos Santos FRANCA "N'dalu"
chancery: 1615 M Street, NW, Suite 900, Washington, DC 20036
telephone: [1] (202) 785-1156
FAX: [1] (202) 785-1258
Diplomatic representation from the US:
chief of mission: Ambassador Joseph G. SULLIVAN
embassy: number 32 Rua Houari Boumedienne, Miramar, Luanda
mailing address: international mail: Caixa Postal 6484, Luanda; pouch: American Embassy Luanda, Department of State, Washington, DC 20521-2550
telephone: [244] (2) 345-481, 346-418
FAX: [244] (2) 346-924
Flag description: two equal horizontal bands of red (top) and black with a centered yellow emblem consisting of a five-pointed star within half a cogwheel crossed by a machete (in the style of a hammer and sickle)

Economy

Economy - overview: Angola is an economy in disarray because of more than 20 years of nearly continuous warfare. Despite its abundant natural resources, output per capita is among the world's lowest. Subsistence agriculture provides the main livelihood for 85% of the population. Oil production and the supporting activities are vital to the economy, contributing about 45% to GDP. Notwithstanding the signing of a peace accord in November 1994, sporadic violence continues, millions of land mines remain, and many farmers are reluctant to return to their fields. As a result, much of the country's food must still be imported. To take advantage of its rich resources - gold, diamonds, extensive forests, Atlantic fisheries, arable land, and large oil deposits - Angola will need to implement the peace agreement and reform government policies. The increase in the pace of civil warfare in late 1998 dims economic prospects for 1999 especially if the oil sector were to be damaged.
GDP: purchasing power parity - $11 billion (1998 est.)
GDP - real growth rate: 0.5% (1998 est.)
GDP - per capita: purchasing power parity - $1,000 (1998 est.)
GDP - composition by sector:
agriculture: 13%
industry: 53%
services: 34% (1998 est.)
Population below poverty line: NA%
Household income or consumption by percentage share:
lowest 10%: NA%
highest 10%: NA%
Inflation rate (consumer prices): 90% (1998 est.)
Labor force: 5 million (1997 est.)
Labor force - by occupation: agriculture 85%, industry and services 15% (1997 est.)
Unemployment rate: extensive unemployment and underemployment affecting more than half the population (1997 est.)
Budget:
revenues: $928 million
expenditures: $2.5 billion, including capital expenditures of $963 million (1992 est.)
Industries: petroleum; diamonds, iron ore, phosphates, feldspar, bauxite, uranium, and gold; cement; basic metal products; fish processing; food processing; brewing; tobacco products; sugar; textiles
Industrial production growth rate: NA%
Electricity - production: 1.86 billion kWh (1996)
Electricity - production by source:
fossil fuel: 24.73%
hydro: 75.27%
nuclear: 0%
other: 0% (1996)
Electricity - consumption: 1.86 billion kWh (1996)
Electricity - exports: 0 kWh (1996)
Electricity - imports: 0 kWh (1996)
Agriculture - products: bananas, sugarcane, coffee, sisal, corn, cotton, manioc (tapioca), tobacco, vegetables, plantains; livestock; forest products; fish
Exports: $3.4 billion (f.o.b., 1998 est.)
Exports - commodities: crude oil 90%, diamonds, refined petroleum products, gas, coffee, sisal, fish and fish products, timber, cotton (1998)
Exports - partners: US 65%, EU, China (1997)
Imports: $2.2 billion (f.o.b., 1998 est.)
Imports - commodities: machinery and electrical equipment, vehicles and spare parts; medicines, food, textiles and clothing; substantial military goods
Imports - partners: Portugal 21%, US 15%, France 14%, South Africa (1997)
Debt - external: $13 billion (1998 est.)
Economic aid - recipient: $493.1 million (1995)
Currency: 1 kwanza (NKz) = 100 lwei
Exchange rates: kwanza (NKz) per US$1 - 350,000

Angola (continued)

(February 1999), 392,824 (1998), 229,040 (1997), 128,029 (1996), 2,750 (1995), 59,515 (1994); note - readjusted Kwanzas per US$1,000 through 1994, per US$1 thereafter
Fiscal year: calendar year

Communications

Telephones: 78,000 (1991 est.)
Telephone system: telephone service limited mostly to government and business use; HF radiotelephone used extensively for military links
domestic: limited system of wire, microwave radio relay, and tropospheric scatter
international: satellite earth stations - 2 Intelsat (Atlantic Ocean)
Radio broadcast stations: AM 16, FM 8, shortwave 8 (1998)
Radios: NA
Television broadcast stations: 7 (1997)
Televisions: 50,000 (1993 est.)

Transportation

Railways:
total: 2,952 km (limited trackage in use because of land mines still in place from the civil war) (1997 est.)
narrow gauge: 2,798 km 1.067-m gauge; 154 km 0.600-m gauge
Highways:
total: 76,626 km
paved: 19,156 km
unpaved: 57,470 km (1997 est.)
Waterways: 1,295 km navigable
Pipelines: crude oil 179 km
Ports and harbors: Ambriz, Cabinda, Lobito, Luanda, Malongo, Namibe, Porto Amboim, Soyo
Merchant marine:
total: 10 ships (1,000 GRT or over) totaling 48,384 GRT/78,357 DWT
ships by type: cargo 9, oil tanker 1 (1998 est.)
Airports: 252 (1998 est.)
Airports - with paved runways:
total: 32
over 3,047 m: 4
2,438 to 3,047 m: 9
1,524 to 2,437 m: 12
914 to 1,523 m: 6
under 914 m: 1 (1998 est.)
Airports - with unpaved runways:
total: 220
over 3,047 m: 1
2,438 to 3,047 m: 5
1,524 to 2,437 m: 32
914 to 1,523 m: 100
under 914 m: 82 (1998 est.)

Military

Military branches: Army, Navy, Air and Air Defense Forces, National Police Force
Military manpower - military age: 18 years of age
Military manpower - availability:
males age 15-49: 2,544,203 (1999 est.)

Military manpower - fit for military service:
males age 15-49: 1,280,377 (1999 est.)
Military manpower - reaching military age annually:
males: 111,168 (1999 est.)
Military expenditures - dollar figure: $1 billion (FY97/98)
Military expenditures - percent of GDP: 25% (FY97/98)

Transnational Issues

Disputes - international: none
Illicit drugs: increasingly used as a transshipment point for cocaine and heroin destined for Western Europe and other African states

Anguilla
(overseas territory of the UK)

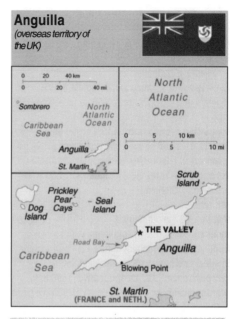

Geography

Location: Caribbean, island in the Caribbean Sea, east of Puerto Rico
Geographic coordinates: 18 15 N, 63 10 W
Map references: Central America and the Caribbean
Area:
total: 91 sq km
land: 91 sq km
water: 0 sq km
Area - comparative: about half the size of Washington, DC
Land boundaries: 0 km
Coastline: 61 km
Maritime claims:
exclusive fishing zone: 200 nm
territorial sea: 3 nm
Climate: tropical; moderated by northeast trade winds
Terrain: flat and low-lying island of coral and limestone
Elevation extremes:
lowest point: Caribbean Sea 0 m
highest point: Crocus Hill 65 m
Natural resources: salt, fish, lobster
Land use:
arable land: 0%
permanent crops: 0%
permanent pastures: 0%
forests and woodland: 0%
other: 100% (mostly rock with sparse scrub oak, few trees, some commercial salt ponds)
Irrigated land: NA sq km
Natural hazards: frequent hurricanes and other tropical storms (July to October)
Environment - current issues: supplies of potable water sometimes cannot meet increasing demand largely because of poor distribution system
Environment - international agreements:
party to: NA
signed, but not ratified: NA

Anguilla (continued)

People

Population: 11,510 (July 1999 est.)
Age structure:
0-14 years: 27% (male 1,581; female 1,529)
15-64 years: 66% (male 3,874; female 3,695)
65 years and over: 7% (male 366; female 465) (1999 est.)
Population growth rate: 3.16% (1999 est.)
Birth rate: 16.68 births/1,000 population (1999 est.)
Death rate: 5.3 deaths/1,000 population (1999 est.)
Net migration rate: 20.24 migrant(s)/1,000 population (1999 est.)
Sex ratio:
at birth: 1.03 male(s)/female
under 15 years: 1.03 male(s)/female
15-64 years: 1.05 male(s)/female
65 years and over: 0.79 male(s)/female
total population: 1.02 male(s)/female (1999 est.)
Infant mortality rate: 18.72 deaths/1,000 live births (1999 est.)
Life expectancy at birth:
total population: 77.71 years
male: 74.72 years
female: 80.78 years (1999 est.)
Total fertility rate: 1.95 children born/woman (1999 est.)
Nationality:
noun: Anguillan(s)
adjective: Anguillan
Ethnic groups: black
Religions: Anglican 40%, Methodist 33%, Seventh-Day Adventist 7%, Baptist 5%, Roman Catholic 3%, other 12%
Languages: English (official)
Literacy:
definition: age 12 and over can read and write
total population: 95%
male: 95%
female: 95% (1984 est.)

Government

Country name:
conventional long form: none
conventional short form: Anguilla
Data code: AV
Dependency status: overseas territory of the UK
Government type: NA
Capital: The Valley
Administrative divisions: none (overseas territory of the UK)
Independence: none (overseas territory of the UK)
National holiday: Anguilla Day, 30 May
Constitution: Anguilla Constitutional Order 1 April 1982; amended 1990
Legal system: based on English common law
Suffrage: 18 years of age; universal
Executive branch:
chief of state: Queen ELIZABETH II (since 6 February 1952); represented by Governor Alan HOOLE (since 1 November 1995)

head of government: Chief Minister Hubert HUGHES (since 16 March 1994)
cabinet: Executive Council appointed by the governor from among the elected members of the House of Assembly
elections: none; the monarch is hereditary; governor appointed by the monarch; chief minister appointed by the governor from among the members of the House of Assembly
Legislative branch: unicameral House of Assembly (11 seats total, 7 elected by direct popular vote; members serve five-year terms)
elections: last held 4 March 1999 (next to be held March 2004)
election results: percent of vote by party - NA; seats by party - ANA 2, AUP 2, ADP 2, independent 1
Judicial branch: High Court (judge provided by Eastern Caribbean Supreme Court)
Political parties and leaders: Anguilla National Alliance or ANA [Osbourne FLEMING]; Anguilla United Party or AUP [Hubert HUGHES]; Anguilla Democratic Party or ADP [Victor BANKS]
International organization participation: Caricom (observer), CDB, Interpol (subbureau), OECS (associate), ECLAC (associate)
Diplomatic representation in the US: none (overseas territory of the UK)
Diplomatic representation from the US: none (overseas territory of the UK)
Flag description: blue, with the flag of the UK in the upper hoist-side quadrant and the Anguillan coat of arms centered in the outer half of the flag; the coat of arms depicts three orange dolphins in an interlocking circular design on a white background with blue wavy water below

Economy

Economy - overview: Anguilla has few natural resources, and the economy depends heavily on luxury tourism, offshore banking, lobster fishing, and remittances from emigrants. The economy, and especially the tourism sector, suffered a setback in late 1995 due to the effects of Hurricane Luis in September but recovered in 1996. Increased activity in the tourism industry, which has spurred the growth of the construction sector, contributed to economic growth in 1997-98. Anguillan officials have put substantial effort into developing the offshore financing sector. A comprehensive package of financial services legislation was enacted in late 1994. In the medium term, prospects for the economy will depend on the tourism sector and, therefore, on continuing income growth in the industrialized nations.
GDP: purchasing power parity - $81 million (1997 est.)
GDP - real growth rate: 6.5% (1997 est.)
GDP - per capita: purchasing power parity - $7,300 (1997 est.)
GDP - composition by sector:
agriculture: 4%
industry: 16%

services: 80% (1996 est.)
Population below poverty line: NA%
Household income or consumption by percentage share:
lowest 10%: NA%
highest 10%: NA%
Inflation rate (consumer prices): 0.6% (1997)
Labor force: 4,400 (1992)
Labor force - by occupation: commerce 36%, services 29%, construction 18%, transportation and utilities 10%, manufacturing 3%, agriculture/fishing/forestry/mining 4%
Unemployment rate: 7% (1992 est.)
Budget:
revenues: $20.4 million
expenditures: $23.3 million, including capital expenditures of $3.8 million (1997 est.)
Industries: tourism, boat building, offshore financial services
Industrial production growth rate: 3.1% (1997 est.)
Electricity - production: NA kWh
Electricity - production by source:
fossil fuel: NA%
hydro: NA%
nuclear: NA%
other: NA%
Electricity - consumption: NA kWh
Electricity - exports: NA kWh
Electricity - imports: NA kWh
Agriculture - products: pigeon peas, corn, sweet potatoes; sheep, goats, pigs, cattle, poultry; fish, lobsters
Exports: $1.6 million (1997)
Exports - commodities: lobster, fish, livestock, salt
Exports - partners: NA
Imports: $54.2 million (1997)
Imports - commodities: NA
Imports - partners: NA
Debt - external: $8.5 million (1996)
Economic aid - recipient: $3.5 million (1995)
Currency: 1 East Caribbean dollar (EC$) = 100 cents
Exchange rates: East Caribbean dollars (EC$) per US$1 - 2.7000 (fixed rate since 1976)
Fiscal year: 1 April - 31 March

Communications

Telephones: 890
Telephone system:
domestic: modern internal telephone system
international: microwave radio relay to island of Saint Martin (Guadeloupe and Netherlands Antilles)
Radio broadcast stations: AM 5, FM 6, shortwave 1 (1998)
Radios: 2,000 (1992 est.)
Television broadcast stations: 1 (1997)
Televisions: NA

Transportation

Railways: 0 km

Anguilla *(continued)*

Highways:
total: 105 km
paved: 65 km
unpaved: 40 km (1992 est.)
Ports and harbors: Blowing Point, Road Bay
Merchant marine: none
Airports: 3 (1998 est.)
Airports - with paved runways:
total: 1
914 to 1,523 m: 1 (1998 est.)
Airports - with unpaved runways:
total: 2
under 914 m: 2 (1998 est.)

Military

Military - note: defense is the responsibility of the UK

Transnational Issues

Disputes - international: none

Antarctica

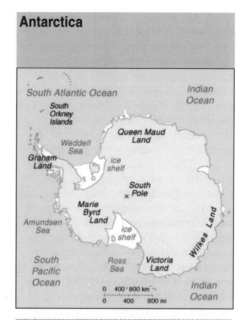

Geography

Location: continent mostly south of the Antarctic Circle
Geographic coordinates: 90 00 S, 0 00 E
Map references: Antarctic Region
Area:
total: 14 million sq km
land: 14 million sq km (280,000 sq km ice-free, 13.72 million sq km ice-covered) (est.)
note: second-smallest continent (after Australia)
Area - comparative: slightly less than 1.5 times the size of the US
Land boundaries: 0 km
note: see entry on International disputes
Coastline: 17,968 km
Maritime claims: none, but see entry on International disputes
Climate: severe low temperatures vary with latitude, elevation, and distance from the ocean; East Antarctica is colder than West Antarctica because of its higher elevation; Antarctic Peninsula has the most moderate climate; higher temperatures occur in January along the coast and average slightly below freezing
Terrain: about 98% thick continental ice sheet and 2% barren rock, with average elevations between 2,000 and 4,000 meters; mountain ranges up to about 5,000 meters; ice-free coastal areas include parts of southern Victoria Land, Wilkes Land, the Antarctic Peninsula area, and parts of Ross Island on McMurdo Sound; glaciers form ice shelves along about half of the coastline, and floating ice shelves constitute 11% of the area of the continent
Elevation extremes:
lowest point: Indian Ocean 0 m
highest point: Vinson Massif 5,140 m
Natural resources: none presently exploited; iron ore, chromium, copper, gold, nickel, platinum and other minerals, and coal and hydrocarbons have been found in small, uncommercial quantities

Land use:
arable land: 0%
permanent crops: 0%
permanent pastures: 0%
forests and woodland: 0%
other: 100% (ice 98%, barren rock 2%)
Irrigated land: 0 sq km (1993)
Natural hazards: katabatic (gravity-driven) winds blow coastward from the high interior; frequent blizzards form near the foot of the plateau; cyclonic storms form over the ocean and move clockwise along the coast; volcanism on Deception Island and isolated areas of West Antarctica; other seismic activity rare and weak
Environment - current issues: in 1998, NASA satellite data showed that the antarctic ozone hole was the largest on record, covering 27 million square kilometers; researchers in 1997 found that increased ultraviolet light coming through the hole damages the DNA of icefish, an antarctic fish lacking hemoglobin; ozone depletion earlier was shown to harm one-celled antarctic marine plants
Environment - international agreements:
party to: none of the selected agreements
signed, but not ratified: none of the selected agreements
Geography - note: the coldest, windiest, highest, and driest continent; during summer, more solar radiation reaches the surface at the South Pole than is received at the Equator in an equivalent period; mostly uninhabitable

People

Population: no indigenous inhabitants, but there are seasonally staffed research stations
note: approximately 29 nations, all signatory to the Antarctic Treaty, send personnel to perform seasonal (summer) and year-round research on the continent and in its surrounding oceans; the population of persons doing and supporting science on the continent and its nearby islands south of 60 degrees south latitude (the region covered by the Antarctic Treaty) varies from approximately 4,000 in summer to 1,000 in winter; in addition, approximately 1,000 personnel including ship's crew and scientists doing onboard research are present in the waters of the treaty region; Summer (January) population - 3,687 total; Argentina 302, Australia 201, Belgium 13, Brazil 80, Bulgaria 16, Chile 352, China 70, Finland 11, France 100, Germany 51, India 60, Italy 106, Japan 136, South Korea 14, Netherlands 10, NZ 60, Norway 40, Peru 28, Poland 70, Russia 254, South Africa 80, Spain 43, Sweden 20, UK 192, US 1,378 (1998-99); Winter (July) population - 964 total; Argentina 165, Australia 75, Brazil 12, Chile 129, China 33, France 33, Germany 9, India 25, Japan 40, South Korea 14, NZ 10, Poland 20, Russia 102, South Africa 10, UK 39, US 248 (1998-99); year-round stations - 42 total; Argentina 6, Australia 4, Brazil 1, Chile 4, China 2, Finland 1, France 1, Germany 1, India 1, Italy 1, Japan 1, South Korea 1, NZ 1, Norway 1, Poland 1, Russia

Antarctica *(continued)*

6, South Africa 1, Spain 1, Ukraine 1, UK 2, US 3, Uruguay 1 (1998-99); Summer-only stations - 32 total; Argentina 3, Australia 4, Bulgaria 1, Chile 7, Germany 1, India 1, Japan 3, NZ 1, Peru 1, Russia 3, Sweden 2, UK 5 (1998-99) in addition, during the austral summer some nations have numerous occupied locations such as tent camps, summer-long temporary facilities, and mobile traverses in support of research

Government

Country name:
conventional long form: none
conventional short form: Antarctica
Data code: AY
Government type: Antarctic Treaty Summary - the Antarctic Treaty, signed on 1 December 1959 and entered into force on 23 June 1961, establishes the legal framework for the management of Antarctica. Administration is carried out through consultative member meetings - the 22nd Antarctic Treaty Consultative Meeting was in Norway in May 1998. At the end of 1998, there were 43 treaty member nations: 27 consultative and 16 acceding. Consultative (voting) members include the seven nations that claim portions of Antarctica as national territory (some claims overlap) and 20 nonclaimant nations. The US and some other nations that have made no claims have reserved the right to do so. The US does not recognize the claims of others. The year in parentheses indicates when an acceding nation was voted to full consultative (voting) status, while no date indicates the country was an original 1959 treaty signatory. Claimant nations are - Argentina, Australia, Chile, France, New Zealand, Norway, and the UK. Nonclaimant consultative nations are - Belgium, Brazil (1983), Bulgaria (1978) China (1985), Ecuador (1990), Finland (1989), Germany (1981), India (1983), Italy (1987), Japan, South Korea (1989), Netherlands (1990), Peru (1989), Poland (1977), Russia, South Africa, Spain (1988), Sweden (1988), Uruguay (1985), and the US. Acceding (nonvoting) members, with year of accession in parentheses, are - Austria (1987), Canada (1988), Colombia (1988), Cuba (1984), Czech Republic (1993), Denmark (1965), Greece (1987), Guatemala (1991), Hungary (1984), North Korea (1987), Papua New Guinea (1981), Romania (1971), Slovakia (1993), Switzerland (1990), Turkey (1995), and Ukraine (1992). Article 1 - area to be used for peaceful purposes only; military activity, such as weapons testing, is prohibited, but military personnel and equipment may be used for scientific research or any other peaceful purpose; Article 2 - freedom of scientific investigation and cooperation shall continue; Article 3 - free exchange of information and personnel in cooperation with the UN and other international agencies; Article 4 - does not recognize, dispute, or establish territorial claims and no new claims shall be asserted while the treaty is in force; Article 5 - prohibits nuclear explosions or disposal of radioactive wastes; Article 6 - includes under the treaty all land and ice shelves south of 60 degrees 00 minutes south; Article 7 - treaty-state observers have free access, including aerial observation, to any area and may inspect all stations, installations, and equipment; advance notice of all activities and of the introduction of military personnel must be given; Article 8 - allows for jurisdiction over observers and scientists by their own states; Article 9 - frequent consultative meetings take place among member nations; Article 10 - treaty states will discourage activities by any country in Antarctica that are contrary to the treaty; Article 11 - disputes to be settled peacefully by the parties concerned or, ultimately, by the ICJ; Articles 12, 13, 14 - deal with upholding, interpreting, and amending the treaty among involved nations. Other agreements - some 200 recommendations adopted at treaty consultative meetings and ratified by governments include - Agreed Measures for the Conservation of Antarctic Fauna and Flora (1964); Convention for the Conservation of Antarctic Seals (1972); Convention on the Conservation of Antarctic Marine Living Resources (1980); a mineral resources agreement was signed in 1988 but was subsequently rejected; the Protocol on Environmental Protection to the Antarctic Treaty was signed 4 October 1991 and entered into force 14 January 1998; this agreement provides for the protection of the Antarctic environment through five specific annexes on marine pollution, fauna, and flora, environmental impact assessments, waste management, and protected areas; it prohibits all activities relating to mineral resources except scientific research.
Legal system: US law, including certain criminal offenses by or against US nationals, such as murder, may apply to areas not under jurisdiction of other countries. Some US laws directly apply to Antarctica. For example, the Antarctic Conservation Act, 16 U.S.C. section 2401 et seq., provides civil and criminal penalties for the following activities, unless authorized by regulation of statute: the taking of native mammals or birds; the introduction of nonindigenous plants and animals; entry into specially protected or scientific areas; the discharge or disposal of pollutants; and the importation into the US of certain items from Antarctica. Violation of the Antarctic Conservation Act carries penalties of up to $10,000 in fines and one year in prison. The Departments of Treasury, Commerce, Transportation, and Interior share enforcement responsibilities. Public Law 95-541, the US Antarctic Conservation Act of 1978, requires expeditions from the US to Antarctica to notify, in advance, the Office of Oceans and Polar Affairs, Room 5801, Department of State, Washington, DC 20520, which reports such plans to other nations as required by the Antarctic Treaty. For more information, contact Permit Office, Office of Polar Programs, National Science Foundation, Arlington, Virginia 22230 (703) 306-1031, or see their website at www.nsf.gov.

Economy

Economy - overview: No economic activity is conducted at present, except for fishing off the coast and small-scale tourism, both based abroad. Antarctic fisheries in 1997-98 reported landing 92,456 metric tons. Unregulated fishing landed five to six times more than the regulated fishery, and allegedly illegal fishing in antarctic waters in 1998 resulted in the seizure (by France and Australia) of at least eight fishing ships. A total of 9,604 tourists visited in the 1997-98 summer, up from the 7,413 who visited the previous year. Nearly all of them were passengers on 13 commercial (nongovernmental) ships that made 92 trips during the summer. Around 200 tourists were on yachts or commercial aircraft. Most tourist trips lasted approximately two weeks.

Communications

Telephones: NA
Telephone system:
domestic: NA
international: NA
Radio broadcast stations: AM NA, FM 2 (American Forces Antarctic Network), shortwave 1 (Argentina Antarctic Base de Egercito Esperanza) (1998)
Radios: NA
Television broadcast stations: 1 (American Forces Antarctic Network-McMurdo) (1997)
Televisions: NA

Transportation

Ports and harbors: none; offshore anchorage
Airports: 17; 27 stations, operated by 16 national governments party to the Antarctic Treaty, have landing facilities for either helicopters and/or fixed-wing aircraft; commercial enterprises operate two additional air facilities; helicopter pads are available at 27 stations; runways at 15 locations are gravel, sea-ice, blue-ice, or compacted snow suitable for landing wheeled, fixed-wing aircraft; of these, 1 is greater than 3 km in length, 6 are between 2 km and 3 km in length, 3 are between 1 km and 2 km in length, 3 are less than 1 km in length, and 2 are of unknown length; snow surface skiways, limited to use by ski-equipped, fixed-wing aircraft, are available at another 15 locations; of these, 4 are greater than 3 km in length, 3 are between 2 km and 3 km in length, 2 are between 1 km and 2 km in length, 2 are less than 1 km in length, and 4 are of unknown length; airports generally subject to severe restrictions and limitations resulting from extreme seasonal and geographic conditions; airports do not meet ICAO standards; advance approval from the respective governmental or nongovernmental operating organization required for landing (1998 est.)
Airports - with unpaved runways:
total: 17
over 3,047 m: 3
2,438 to 3,047 m: 3
1,524 to 2,437 m: 2
914 to 1,523 m: 4
under 914 m: 5 (1998 est.)
Heliports: 1 (1998 est.)

Antarctica *(continued)*

Military

Military - note: the Antarctic Treaty prohibits any measures of a military nature, such as the establishment of military bases and fortifications, the carrying out of military maneuvers, or the testing of any type of weapon; it permits the use of military personnel or equipment for scientific research or for any other peaceful purposes

Transnational Issues

Disputes - international: Antarctic Treaty defers claims (see Antarctic Treaty Summary above); sections (some overlapping) claimed by Argentina, Australia, Chile, France (Adelie Land), New Zealand (Ross Dependency), Norway (Queen Maud Land), and UK; the US and most other nations do not recognize the territorial claims of other nations and have made no claims themselves (the US reserves the right to do so); no formal claims have been made in the sector between 90 degrees west and 150 degrees west

Antigua and Barbuda

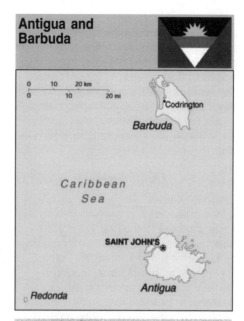

Geography

Location: Caribbean, islands between the Caribbean Sea and the North Atlantic Ocean, east-southeast of Puerto Rico
Geographic coordinates: 17 03 N, 61 48 W
Map references: Central America and the Caribbean
Area:
total: 440 sq km
land: 440 sq km
water: 0 sq km
note: includes Redonda
Area - comparative: 2.5 times the size of Washington, DC
Land boundaries: 0 km
Coastline: 153 km
Maritime claims:
contiguous zone: 24 nm
continental shelf: 200 nm or to the edge of the continental margin
exclusive economic zone: 200 nm
territorial sea: 12 nm
Climate: tropical marine; little seasonal temperature variation
Terrain: mostly low-lying limestone and coral islands, with some higher volcanic areas
Elevation extremes:
lowest point: Caribbean Sea 0 m
highest point: Boggy Peak 402 m
Natural resources: NEGL; pleasant climate fosters tourism
Land use:
arable land: 18%
permanent crops: 0%
permanent pastures: 9%
forests and woodland: 11%
other: 62% (1993 est.)
Irrigated land: NA sq km
Natural hazards: hurricanes and tropical storms (July to October); periodic droughts

Environment - current issues: water management - a major concern because of limited natural fresh water resources - is further hampered by the clearing of trees to increase crop production, causing rainfall to run off quickly
Environment - international agreements:
party to: Biodiversity, Climate Change, Climate Change-Kyoto Protocol, Desertification, Endangered Species, Environmental Modification, Hazardous Wastes, Law of the Sea, Marine Dumping, Nuclear Test Ban, Ozone Layer Protection, Ship Pollution, Whaling
signed, but not ratified: none of the selected agreements

People

Population: 64,246 (July 1999 est.)
Age structure:
0-14 years: 26% (male 8,414; female 8,137)
15-64 years: 69% (male 21,936; female 22,227)
65 years and over: 5% (male 1,504; female 2,028) (1999 est.)
Population growth rate: 0.36% (1999 est.)
Birth rate: 16.22 births/1,000 population (1999 est.)
Death rate: 5.76 deaths/1,000 population (1999 est.)
Net migration rate: -6.9 migrant(s)/1,000 population (1999 est.)
Sex ratio:
at birth: 1.05 male(s)/female
under 15 years: 1.03 male(s)/female
15-64 years: 0.99 male(s)/female
65 years and over: 0.74 male(s)/female
total population: 0.98 male(s)/female (1999 est.)
Infant mortality rate: 20.69 deaths/1,000 live births (1999 est.)
Life expectancy at birth:
total population: 71.46 years
male: 69.06 years
female: 73.98 years (1999 est.)
Total fertility rate: 1.72 children born/woman (1999 est.)
Nationality:
noun: Antiguan(s), Barbudan(s)
adjective: Antiguan, Barbudan
Ethnic groups: black, British, Portuguese, Lebanese, Syrian
Religions: Anglican (predominant), other Protestant sects, some Roman Catholic
Languages: English (official), local dialects
Literacy:
definition: age 15 and over has completed five or more years of schooling
total population: 89%
male: 90%
female: 88% (1960 est.)

Government

Country name:
conventional long form: none
conventional short form: Antigua and Barbuda
Data code: AC

Antigua and Barbuda *(continued)*

Government type: parliamentary democracy
Capital: Saint John's
Administrative divisions: 6 parishes and 2 dependencies*; Barbuda*, Redonda*, Saint George, Saint John, Saint Mary, Saint Paul, Saint Peter, Saint Philip
Independence: 1 November 1981 (from UK)
National holiday: Independence Day, 1 November (1981)
Constitution: 1 November 1981
Legal system: based on English common law
Suffrage: 18 years of age; universal
Executive branch:
chief of state: Queen ELIZABETH II (since 6 February 1952), represented by Governor General James B. CARLISLE (since NA 1993)
head of government: Prime Minister Lester Bryant BIRD (since 8 March 1994)
cabinet: Council of Ministers appointed by the governor general on the advice of the prime minister
elections: none; the monarch is hereditary; governor general chosen by the monarch on the advice of the prime minister; prime minister appointed by the governor general
Legislative branch: bicameral Parliament consists of the Senate (17-member body appointed by the governor general) and the House of Representatives (17 seats; members are elected by proportional representation to serve five-year terms)
elections: House of Representatives - last held 9 March 1999 (next to be held NA March 2004)
election results: percent of vote by party - NA; seats by party - ALP 12, UPP 4, independent 1
Judicial branch: Eastern Caribbean Supreme Court (based in Saint Lucia) (one judge of the Supreme Court is a resident of the islands and presides over the Court of Summary Jurisdiction)
Political parties and leaders: Antigua Labor Party or ALP [Lester Bryant BIRD]; United Progressive Party or UPP [Baldwin SPENCER], a coalition of three opposition political parties - United National Democratic Party or UNDP, Antigua Caribbean Liberation Movement or ACLM, and the Progressive Labor Movement or PLM
Political pressure groups and leaders: Antigua Trades and Labor Union or ATLU [William ROBINSON]; People's Democratic Movement or PDM [Hugh MARSHALL]
International organization participation: ACP, C, Caricom, CDB, ECLAC, FAO, G-77, IBRD, ICAO, ICFTU, ICRM, IFAD, IFC, IFRCS, ILO, IMF, IMO, Intelsat (nonsignatory user), Interpol, IOC, ISO (subscriber), ITU, NAM (observer), OAS, OECS, OPANAL, UN, UNCTAD, UNESCO, UPU, WCL, WFTU, WHO, WMO, WTrO
Diplomatic representation in the US:
chief of mission: Ambassador Lionel Alexander HURST
chancery: 3216 New Mexico Avenue NW, Washington, DC 20016
telephone: [1] (202) 362-5211
FAX: [1] (202) 362-5225

consulate(s) general: Miami
Diplomatic representation from the US: the US does not have an embassy in Antigua and Barbuda (embassy closed 30 June 1994); the US Ambassador to Barbados is accredited to Antigua and Barbuda
Flag description: red, with an inverted isosceles triangle based on the top edge of the flag; the triangle contains three horizontal bands of black (top), light blue, and white, with a yellow rising sun in the black band

Economy

Economy - overview: Tourism continues to be by far the dominant activity in the economy accounting directly or indirectly for more than half of GDP. Increased tourist arrivals have helped spur growth in the construction and transport sectors. The dual island nation's agricultural production is mainly directed to the domestic market; the sector is constrained by the limited water supply and labor shortages that reflect the pull of higher wages in tourism and construction. Manufacturing comprises enclave-type assembly for export with major products being bedding, handicrafts, and electronic components. Prospects for economic growth in the medium term will continue to depend on income growth in the industrialized world, especially in the US, which accounts for about half of all tourist arrivals.
GDP: purchasing power parity - $503 million (1998 est.)
GDP - real growth rate: 6% (1998 est.)
GDP - per capita: purchasing power parity - $7,900 (1998 est.)
GDP - composition by sector:
agriculture: 4%
industry: 12.5%
services: 83.5% (1996 est.)
Population below poverty line: NA%
Household income or consumption by percentage share:
lowest 10%: NA%
highest 10%: NA%
Inflation rate (consumer prices): -1.1% (1997)
Labor force: 30,000
Labor force - by occupation: commerce and services 82%, agriculture 11%, industry 7% (1983)
Unemployment rate: 9% (1997 est.)
Budget:
revenues: $122.6 million
expenditures: $141.2 million, including capital expenditures of $17.3 million (1997 est.)
Industries: tourism, construction, light manufacturing (clothing, alcohol, household appliances)
Industrial production growth rate: 6% (1997 est.)
Electricity - production: 95 million kWh (1996)
Electricity - production by source:
fossil fuel: 100%
hydro: 0%
nuclear: 0%
other: 0% (1996)
Electricity - consumption: 95 million kWh (1996)

Electricity - exports: 0 kWh (1996)
Electricity - imports: 0 kWh (1996)
Agriculture - products: cotton, fruits, vegetables, bananas, coconuts, cucumbers, mangoes, sugarcane; livestock
Exports: $37.8 million (1997)
Exports - commodities: petroleum products 48%, manufactures 23%, food and live animals 4%, machinery and transport equipment 17%
Exports - partners: OECS 26%, Barbados 15%, Guyana 4%, Trinidad and Tobago 2%, US 0.3%
Imports: $325.5 million (1997)
Imports - commodities: food and live animals, machinery and transport equipment, manufactures, chemicals, oil
Imports - partners: US 27%, UK 16%, Canada 4%, OECS 3%, other 50%
Debt - external: $240 million (1997 est.)
Economic aid - recipient: $2.3 million (1995)
Currency: 1 East Caribbean dollar (EC$) = 100 cents
Exchange rates: East Caribbean dollars (EC$) per US$1 - 2.7000 (fixed rate since 1976)
Fiscal year: 1 April - 31 March

Communications

Telephones: 6,700
Telephone system:
domestic: good automatic telephone system
international: 1 coaxial submarine cable; satellite earth station - 1 Intelsat (Atlantic Ocean); tropospheric scatter to Saba (Netherlands Antilles) and Guadeloupe
Radio broadcast stations: AM 4, FM 2, shortwave 0 (repeater transmitters for Deutsche Welle and BBC world broadcasts) (1998)
Radios: NA
Television broadcast stations: 2 (1997)
Televisions: 28,000 (1993 est.)

Transportation

Railways:
total: 77 km
narrow gauge: 64 km 0.760-m gauge; 13 km 0.610-m gauge (used almost exclusively for handling sugarcane)
Highways:
total: 250 km (1996 est.)
paved: NA km
unpaved: NA km
Ports and harbors: Saint John's
Merchant marine:
total: 517 ships (1,000 GRT or over) totaling 2,706,126 GRT/3,542,664 DWT
ships by type: bulk 21, cargo 338, chemical tanker 7, combination bulk 2, container 111, liquefied gas tanker 2, multifunctional large-load carrier 1, oil tanker 4, refrigerated cargo 9, roll-on/roll-off cargo 21, vehicle carrier 1
note: a flag of convenience registry: Germany owns 10 ships, Slovenia 2, and Cyprus 2 (1998 est.)

Airports: 3 (1998 est.)
Airports - with paved runways:
total: 2
2,438 to 3,047 m: 1
under 914 m: 1 (1998 est.)
Airports - with unpaved runways:
total: 1
under 914 m: 1 (1998 est.)

Military

Military branches: Royal Antigua and Barbuda Defense Force, Royal Antigua and Barbuda Police Force (includes Coast Guard)
Military expenditures - dollar figure: $NA
Military expenditures - percent of GDP: NA%

Transnational Issues

Disputes - international: none
Illicit drugs: over the long-term, considered a relatively minor transshipment point for narcotics bound for the US and Europe and recently, a transshipment point for heroin from Europe to the US; potentially more significant as a drug-money-laundering center

Arctic Ocean

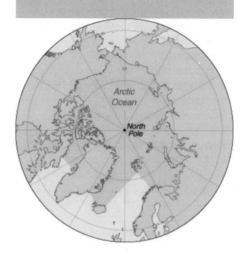

Geography

Location: body of water mostly north of the Arctic Circle
Geographic coordinates: 90 00 N, 0 00 E
Map references: Arctic Region
Area:
total: 14.056 million sq km
note: includes Baffin Bay, Barents Sea, Beaufort Sea, Chukchi Sea, East Siberian Sea, Greenland Sea, Hudson Bay, Hudson Strait, Kara Sea, Laptev Sea, Northwest Passage, and other tributary water bodies
Area - comparative: slightly less than 1.5 times the size of the US; smallest of the world's four oceans (after Pacific Ocean, Atlantic Ocean, and Indian Ocean)
Coastline: 45,389 km
Climate: polar climate characterized by persistent cold and relatively narrow annual temperature ranges; winters characterized by continuous darkness, cold and stable weather conditions, and clear skies; summers characterized by continuous daylight, damp and foggy weather, and weak cyclones with rain or snow
Terrain: central surface covered by a perennial drifting polar icepack that averages about 3 meters in thickness, although pressure ridges may be three times that size; clockwise drift pattern in the Beaufort Gyral Stream, but nearly straight-line movement from the New Siberian Islands (Russia) to Denmark Strait (between Greenland and Iceland); the icepack is surrounded by open seas during the summer, but more than doubles in size during the winter and extends to the encircling landmasses; the ocean floor is about 50% continental shelf (highest percentage of any ocean) with the remainder a central basin interrupted by three submarine ridges (Alpha Cordillera, Nansen Cordillera, and Lomonsov Ridge)
Elevation extremes:
lowest point: Fram Basin -4,665 m
highest point: sea level 0 m

Natural resources: sand and gravel aggregates, placer deposits, polymetallic nodules, oil and gas fields, fish, marine mammals (seals and whales)
Natural hazards: ice islands occasionally break away from northern Ellesmere Island; icebergs calved from glaciers in western Greenland and extreme northeastern Canada; permafrost in islands; virtually icelocked from October to June; ships subject to superstructure icing from October to May
Environment - current issues: endangered marine species include walruses and whales; fragile ecosystem slow to change and slow to recover from disruptions or damage
Environment - international agreements:
party to: none of the selected agreements
signed, but not ratified: none of the selected agreements
Geography - note: major chokepoint is the southern Chukchi Sea (northern access to the Pacific Ocean via the Bering Strait); strategic location between North America and Russia; shortest marine link between the extremes of eastern and western Russia; floating research stations operated by the US and Russia; maximum snow cover in March or April about 20 to 50 centimeters over the frozen ocean; snow cover lasts about 10 months

Government

Data code: none; the US Government has not approved a standard for hydrographic codes - see the Cross-Reference List of Hydrographic Data Codes appendix

Economy

Economy - overview: Economic activity is limited to the exploitation of natural resources, including petroleum, natural gas, fish, and seals.

Communications

Telephone system:
international: no submarine cables

Transportation

Ports and harbors: Churchill (Canada), Murmansk (Russia), Prudhoe Bay (US)
Transportation - note: sparse network of air, ocean, river, and land routes; the Northwest Passage (North America) and Northern Sea Route (Eurasia) are important seasonal waterways

Transnational Issues

Disputes - international: some maritime disputes (see littoral states); Svalbard is the focus of a maritime boundary dispute between Norway and Russia

Argentina

Introduction

Background: A part of the Spanish empire until independence in 1816, Argentina subsequently experienced periods of internal political conflict between conservatives and liberals and between civilian and military factions. Meantime, thanks to rich natural resources and foreign investment, a modern agriculture and a diversified industry were gradually developed. After World War II, a long period of Peronist dictatorship was followed by rule by a military junta. Democratic elections finally came in 1983, but both the political and economic atmosphere remain susceptible to turmoil.

Geography

Location: Southern South America, bordering the South Atlantic Ocean, between Chile and Uruguay
Geographic coordinates: 34 00 S, 64 00 W
Map references: South America
Area:
total: 2,766,890 sq km
land: 2,736,690 sq km
water: 30,200 sq km
Area - comparative: slightly less than three-tenths the size of the US
Land boundaries:
total: 9,665 km
border countries: Bolivia 832 km, Brazil 1,224 km, Chile 5,150 km, Paraguay 1,880 km, Uruguay 579 km
Coastline: 4,989 km
Maritime claims:
contiguous zone: 24 nm
continental shelf: 200 nm or to the edge of the continental margin
exclusive economic zone: 200 nm
territorial sea: 12 nm
Climate: mostly temperate; arid in southeast; subantarctic in southwest
Terrain: rich plains of the Pampas in northern half, flat to rolling plateau of Patagonia in south, rugged Andes along western border
Elevation extremes:
lowest point: Salinas Chicas -40 m (located on Peninsula Valdes)
highest point: Cerro Aconcagua 6,962 m
Natural resources: fertile plains of the pampas, lead, zinc, tin, copper, iron ore, manganese, petroleum, uranium
Land use:
arable land: 9%
permanent crops: 1%
permanent pastures: 52%
forests and woodland: 19%
other: 19% (1993 est.)
Irrigated land: 17,000 sq km (1993 est.)
Natural hazards: San Miguel de Tucuman and Mendoza areas in the Andes subject to earthquakes; pamperos are violent windstorms that can strike the Pampas and northeast; heavy flooding
Environment - current issues: erosion results from inadequate flood controls and improper land use practices; irrigated soil degradation; desertification; air pollution in Buenos Aires and other major cities; water pollution in urban areas; rivers becoming polluted due to increased pesticide and fertilizer use
Environment - international agreements:
party to: Antarctic-Environmental Protocol, Antarctic Treaty, Biodiversity, Climate Change, Desertification, Endangered Species, Environmental Modification, Hazardous Wastes, Law of the Sea, Marine Dumping, Nuclear Test Ban, Ozone Layer Protection, Ship Pollution, Wetlands, Whaling
signed, but not ratified: Climate Change-Kyoto Protocol, Marine Life Conservation
Geography - note: second-largest country in South America (after Brazil); strategic location relative to sea lanes between South Atlantic and South Pacific Oceans (Strait of Magellan, Beagle Channel, Drake Passage)

People

Population: 36,737,664 (July 1999 est.)
Age structure:
0-14 years: 27% (male 5,124,087; female 4,932,060)
15-64 years: 62% (male 11,457,399; female 11,469,346)
65 years and over: 11% (male 1,553,158; female 2,201,614) (1999 est.)
Population growth rate: 1.29% (1999 est.)
Birth rate: 19.91 births/1,000 population (1999 est.)
Death rate: 7.64 deaths/1,000 population (1999 est.)
Net migration rate: 0.65 migrant(s)/1,000 population (1999 est.)
Sex ratio:
at birth: 1.05 male(s)/female
under 15 years: 1.04 male(s)/female
15-64 years: 1 male(s)/female
65 years and over: 0.71 male(s)/female
total population: 0.97 male(s)/female (1999 est.)
Infant mortality rate: 18.41 deaths/1,000 live births (1999 est.)
Life expectancy at birth:
total population: 74.76 years
male: 71.13 years
female: 78.56 years (1999 est.)
Total fertility rate: 2.66 children born/woman (1999 est.)
Nationality:
noun: Argentine(s)
adjective: Argentine
Ethnic groups: white 85%, mestizo, Amerindian, or other nonwhite groups 15%
Religions: nominally Roman Catholic 90% (less than 20% practicing), Protestant 2%, Jewish 2%, other 6%
Languages: Spanish (official), English, Italian, German, French
Literacy:
definition: age 15 and over can read and write
total population: 96.2%
male: 96.2%
female: 96.2% (1995 est.)

Government

Country name:
conventional long form: Argentine Republic
conventional short form: Argentina
local long form: Republica Argentina
local short form: Argentina
Data code: AR
Government type: republic
Capital: Buenos Aires
Administrative divisions: 23 provinces (provincias, singular - provincia), and 1 federal district* (distrito federal); Buenos Aires; Catamarca; Chaco; Chubut; Cordoba; Corrientes; Distrito Federal*; Entre Rios; Formosa; Jujuy; La Pampa; La Rioja; Mendoza; Misiones; Neuquen; Rio Negro; Salta; San Juan; San Luis; Santa Cruz; Santa Fe; Santiago del Estero; Tierra del Fuego, Antartida e Islas del Atlantico Sur; Tucuman
note: the US does not recognize any claims to Antarctica
Independence: 9 July 1816 (from Spain)
National holiday: Revolution Day, 25 May (1810)
Constitution: 1 May 1853; revised August 1994
Legal system: mixture of US and West European legal systems; has not accepted compulsory ICJ jurisdiction

Argentina (continued)

Suffrage: 18 years of age; universal

Executive branch:

chief of state: President Carlos Saul MENEM (since 8 July 1989); Vice President Carlos RUCKAUF (since 8 July 1995); note - the president is both the chief of state and head of government

head of government: President Carlos Saul MENEM (since 8 July 1989); Vice President Carlos RUCKAUF (since 8 July 1995); note - the president is both the chief of state and head of government

cabinet: Cabinet appointed by the president

elections: president and vice president elected on the same ticket by popular vote for four-year terms; election last held 14 May 1995 (next to be held NA October 1999)

election results: Carlos Saul MENEM reelected president; percent of vote - NA

Legislative branch: bicameral National Congress or Congreso Nacional consists of the Senate (72 seats; formerly, three members appointed by each of the provincial legislatures; presently transitioning to one-third of the members being elected every two years to a six-year term) and the Chamber of Deputies (257 seats; one-half of the members elected every two years to four-year terms)

elections: Senate - transition phase will continue through 2001 elections when all seats will be fully contested; winners will randomly draw to determine whether they will serve a two-year, four-year, or full six-year term; Chamber of Deputies - last held 26 October 1997 (next to be held NA October 1999)

election results: Senate - percent of vote by party - NA; seats by party - PJ 39, UCR 1, others 32; Chamber of Deputies - percent of vote by party - NA; seats by party - PJ 119, UCR 69, Frepaso 36, other 33

Judicial branch: Supreme Court (Corte Suprema), the nine Supreme Court judges are appointed by the president with approval of the Senate

Political parties and leaders: Justicialist Party or PJ [Carlos Saul MENEM] (Peronist umbrella political organization); Radical Civic Union or UCR [Fernando DE LA RUA]; Union of the Democratic Center or UCD (conservative party) [leader NA]; Dignity and Independence Political Party or MODIN (right-wing party) [leader NA]; Front for a Country in Solidarity or Frepaso (a four-party coalition) [Carlos ALVAREZ]; Action for the Republic [Domingo CAVALLO]; New Leadership [Gustavo BELIZ]; several provincial parties

Political pressure groups and leaders: Peronist-dominated labor movement; General Confederation of Labor or CGT (Peronist-leaning umbrella labor organization); Argentine Industrial Union (manufacturers' association); Argentine Rural Society (large landowners' association); Argentine Association of Pharmaceutical Labs (CILFA); business organizations; students; the Roman Catholic Church; the Armed Forces

International organization participation: AfDB, Australia Group, BCIE, CCC, ECLAC, FAO, G- 6, G-11, G-15, G-19, G-24, G-77, IADB, IAEA, IBRD, ICAO, ICC, ICFTU, ICRM, IDA, IFAD, IFC, IFRCS, IHO, ILO, IMF, IMO, Inmarsat, Intelsat, Interpol, IOC, IOM, ISO, ITU, LAES, LAIA, Mercosur, MINURSO, MIPONUH, MTCR, NSG, OAS, OPANAL, OPCW, PCA, RG, UN, UNCTAD, UNESCO, UNFICYP, UNHCR, UNIDO, UNIKOM, UNITAR, UNMIBH, UNMOP, UNPREDEP, UNTSO, UNU, UPU, WCL, WFTU, WHO, WIPO, WMO, WToO, WTrO

Diplomatic representation in the US:

chief of mission: Ambassador Diego Ramiro GUELAR

chancery: 1600 New Hampshire Avenue NW, Washington, DC 20009

telephone: [1] (202) 939-6400

FAX: [1] (202) 238-6471

consulate(s) general: Atlanta, Chicago, Houston, Los Angeles, Miami, New York, and San Francisco

Diplomatic representation from the US:

chief of mission: Ambassador (vacant)

embassy: 4300 Colombia, 1425 Buenos Aires

mailing address: international mail: use street address; APO address: Unit 4334, APO AA 34034

telephone: [54] (1) 777-4533, 4534

FAX: [54] (1) 777-0197

Flag description: three equal horizontal bands of light blue (top), white, and light blue; centered in the white band is a radiant yellow sun with a human face known as the Sun of May

Economy

Economy - overview: Argentina benefits from rich natural resources, a highly literate population, an export-oriented agricultural sector, and a diversified industrial base. However, when President Carlos MENEM took office in 1989, the country had piled up huge external debts, inflation had reached 200% per month, and output was plummeting. To combat the economic crisis, the government embarked on a path of trade liberalization, deregulation, and privatization. In 1991, it implemented radical monetary reforms which pegged the peso to the US dollar and limited the growth in the monetary base by law to the growth in reserves. Inflation fell sharply in subsequent years. The Mexican peso crisis produced capital flight, the loss of banking system deposits, and a severe, but short-lived, recession in 1995; a series of reforms to bolster the domestic banking system followed. Real GDP growth recovered strongly, reaching almost 9% in 1997. In 1998, increasing investor anxiety over Brazil, its largest trading partner, produced the highest domestic interest rates in more than three years and slowed growth to 4.3%. Despite the relatively high level of growth in recent years, double-digit unemployment rates have persisted, largely because of rigidities in Argentina's labor laws.

GDP: purchasing power parity - $374 billion (1998 est.)

GDP - real growth rate: 4.3% (1998 est.)

GDP - per capita: purchasing power parity - $10,300 (1998 est.)

GDP - composition by sector:

agriculture: 7%

industry: 37%

services: 56% (1997 est.)

Population below poverty line: 25.5% (1991 est.)

Household income or consumption by percentage share:

lowest 10%: NA%

highest 10%: NA%

Inflation rate (consumer prices): 1% (1998 est.)

Labor force: 14 million (1997)

Labor force - by occupation: agriculture 12%, industry 31%, services 57% (1985 est.)

Unemployment rate: 12% (October 1998)

Budget:

revenues: $56 billion

expenditures: $60 billion, including capital expenditures of $4 billion (1998 est.)

Industries: food processing, motor vehicles, consumer durables, textiles, chemicals and petrochemicals, printing, metallurgy, steel

Industrial production growth rate: 2% (1998)

Electricity - production: 64.669 billion kWh (1996)

Electricity - production by source:

fossil fuel: 45%

hydro: 44.3%

nuclear: 10.7%

other: 0% (1996)

Electricity - consumption: 67.509 billion kWh (1996)

Electricity - exports: 330 million kWh (1996)

Electricity - imports: 3.17 billion kWh (1996)

Agriculture - products: sunflower seeds, lemons, soybeans, grapes, corn, tobacco, peanuts, tea, wheat; livestock

Exports: $26 billion (f.o.b., 1998 est.)

Exports - commodities: cereals, feed, motor vehicles, crude petroleum, steel manufactures

Exports - partners: Brazil 31%, US 8%, Chile 7.0%, China 3%, Uruguay 3% (1997 est.)

Imports: $32 billion (c.i.f., 1998 est.)

Imports - commodities: motor vehicles, motor vehicle parts, organic chemicals, telecommunications equipment, plastics

Imports - partners: Brazil 23%, US 20%, Italy 6%, Germany 5%, France 5% (1997)

Debt - external: $133 billion (1998 est.)

Economic aid - recipient: $2.833 billion (1995)

Currency: 1 peso = 100 centavos

Exchange rates: peso is pegged to the US dollar at an exchange rate of 1 peso = $1

Fiscal year: calendar year

Communications

Telephones: 4.6 million (1990)

Telephone system: 12,000 public telephones; extensive modern system but many families do not have telephones; despite extensive use of microwave radio relay, the telephone system frequently grounds out during rainstorms, even in Buenos Aires

domestic: microwave radio relay and a domestic satellite system with 40 earth stations serve the trunk network

international: satellite earth stations - 2 Intelsat (Atlantic Ocean)

Argentina *(continued)*

Radio broadcast stations: AM 260 (including 10 inactive stations), FM NA (probably more than 1,000, mostly unlicensed), shortwave 6 (1998 est.)
Radios: 22.3 million (1991 est.)
Television broadcast stations: 42 (in addition, there are 444 repeaters) (1997)
Televisions: 7.165 million (1991 est.)

Transportation

Railways:
total: 37,830 km
broad gauge: 23,992 km 1.676-m gauge (167 km electrified)
standard gauge: 2,765 km 1.435-m gauge
narrow gauge: 11,073 km 1.000-m gauge (26 km electrified)
Highways:
total: 208,350 km
paved: 47,550 km (including 567 km of expressways)
unpaved: 160,800 km (1998 est.)
Waterways: 11,000 km navigable
Pipelines: crude oil 4,090 km; petroleum products 2,900 km; natural gas 9,918 km
Ports and harbors: Bahia Blanca, Buenos Aires, Comodoro Rivadavia, Concepcion del Uruguay, La Plata, Mar del Plata, Necochea, Rio Gallegos, Rosario, Santa Fe, Ushuaia
Merchant marine:
total: 29 ships (1,000 GRT or over) totaling 233,856 GRT/363,335 DWT
ships by type: cargo 10, container 1, oil tanker 13, railcar carrier 1, refrigerated cargo 2, roll-on/roll-off cargo 1, short-sea passenger 1 (1998 est.)
Airports: 1,374 (1998 est.)
Airports - with paved runways:
total: 141
over 3,047 m: 5
2,438 to 3,047 m: 26
1,524 to 2,437 m: 58
914 to 1,523 m: 45
under 914 m: 7 (1998 est.)
Airports - with unpaved runways:
total: 1,233
over 3,047 m: 2
2,438 to 3,047 m: 2
1,524 to 2,437 m: 67
914 to 1,523 m: 621
under 914 m: 541 (1998 est.)

Military

Military branches: Argentine Army, Navy of the Argentine Republic (includes Naval Aviation, Marines, and Coast Guard), Argentine Air Force, National Gendarmerie, National Aeronautical Police Force
Military manpower - military age: 20 years of age
Military manpower - availability:
males age 15-49: 9,169,681 (1999 est.)
Military manpower - fit for military service:
males age 15-49: 7,435,551 (1999 est.)

Military manpower - reaching military age annually:
males: 343,038 (1999 est.)
Military expenditures - dollar figure: $4.6 billion (1998)
Military expenditures - percent of GDP: 1.4% (1998)

Transnational Issues

Disputes - international: short section of the southwestern boundary with Chile is indefinite - process to resolve boundary issues is underway; claims UK-administered Falkland Islands (Islas Malvinas); claims UK-administered South Georgia and the South Sandwich Islands; territorial claim in Antarctica
Illicit drugs: increasing use as a transshipment country for cocaine headed for Europe and the US; increasing money-laundering center

Armenia

Introduction

Background: Armenia was one of the 15 successor republics to the USSR in December 1991. Its leaders remain preoccupied by the long conflict with Azerbaijan over the Nagorno-Karabakh enclave. Although a cease-fire has been in effect since May 1994, the sides have not made substantial progress toward a peaceful resolution. In January 1998, differences between President TER-PETROSSIAN and members of his cabinet over the Nagorno-Karabakh peace process came to a head. With the prime minister, defense minister, and security minister arrayed against him, an isolated TER-PETROSSIAN resigned the presidency on 3 February 1998. Prime Minister Robert KOCHARIAN was elected president in March 1998. Concerns about Armenia's economic performance have continued since 1997 with a slowdown in growth and the serious impact of the 1998 financial crisis in Russia.

Geography

Location: Southwestern Asia, east of Turkey
Geographic coordinates: 40 00 N, 45 00 E
Map references: Commonwealth of Independent States
Area:
total: 29,800 sq km
land: 28,400 sq km
water: 1,400 sq km
Area - comparative: slightly smaller than Maryland
Land boundaries:
total: 1,254 km
border countries: Azerbaijan-proper 566 km, Azerbaijan-Naxcivan exclave 221 km, Georgia 164 km, Iran 35 km, Turkey 268 km
Coastline: 0 km (landlocked)
Maritime claims: none (landlocked)
Climate: highland continental, hot summers, cold winters

Armenia (continued)

Terrain: Armenian Highland with mountains; little forest land; fast flowing rivers; good soil in Aras River valley

Elevation extremes:
lowest point: Debed River 400 m
highest point: Aragats Lerr 4,095 m

Natural resources: small deposits of gold, copper, molybdenum, zinc, alumina

Land use:
arable land: 17%
permanent crops: 3%
permanent pastures: 24%
forests and woodland: 15%
other: 41% (1993 est.)

Irrigated land: 2,870 sq km (1993 est.)

Natural hazards: occasionally severe earthquakes; droughts

Environment - current issues: soil pollution from toxic chemicals such as DDT; energy blockade, the result of conflict with Azerbaijan, has led to deforestation when citizens scavenged for firewood; pollution of Hrazdan (Razdan) and Aras Rivers; the draining of Sevana Lich (Lake Sevan), a result of its use as a source for hydropower, threatens drinking water supplies; restart of Metsamor nuclear power plant without adequate (IAEA-recommended) safety and backup systems

Environment - international agreements:
party to: Air Pollution, Biodiversity, Climate Change, Desertification, Nuclear Test Ban, Wetlands
signed, but not ratified: Air Pollution-Persistent Organic Pollutants

Geography - note: landlocked

People

Population: 3,409,234 (July 1999 est.)

Age structure:
0-14 years: 25% (male 442,117; female 425,561)
15-64 years: 66% (male 1,100,334; female 1,148,595)
65 years and over: 9% (male 122,170; female 170,457) (1999 est.)

Population growth rate: -0.38% (1999 est.)

Birth rate: 13.53 births/1,000 population (1999 est.)

Death rate: 9.03 deaths/1,000 population (1999 est.)

Net migration rate: -8.26 migrant(s)/1,000 population (1999 est.)

Sex ratio:
at birth: 1.05 male(s)/female
under 15 years: 1.04 male(s)/female
15-64 years: 0.96 male(s)/female
65 years and over: 0.72 male(s)/female
total population: 0.95 male(s)/female (1999 est.)

Infant mortality rate: 41.12 deaths/1,000 live births (1999 est.)

Life expectancy at birth:
total population: 66.56 years
male: 62.21 years
female: 71.13 years (1999 est.)

Total fertility rate: 1.68 children born/woman (1999 est.)

Nationality:
noun: Armenian(s)
adjective: Armenian

Ethnic groups: Armenian 93%, Azeri 3%, Russian 2%, other (mostly Yezidi Kurds) 2% (1989)
note: as of the end of 1993, virtually all Azeris had emigrated from Armenia

Religions: Armenian Orthodox 94%

Languages: Armenian 96%, Russian 2%, other 2%

Literacy:
definition: age 15 and over can read and write
total population: 99%
male: 99%
female: 98% (1989 est.)

Government

Country name:
conventional long form: Republic of Armenia
conventional short form: Armenia
local long form: Hayastani Hanrapetut'yun
local short form: Hayastan
former: Armenian Soviet Socialist Republic; Armenian Republic

Data code: AM

Government type: republic

Capital: Yerevan

Administrative divisions: 10 provinces (marzer, singular - marz) and 1 city* (k'aghak'ner, singular - k'aghak'); Aragatsotn, Ararat, Armavir, Geghark'unik', Kotayk', Lorri, Shirak, Syunik', Tavush, Vayots' Dzor, Yerevan*

Independence: 28 May 1918-2 December 1920 (First Armenian Republic); 23 September 1991 (from Soviet Union)

National holiday: Referendum Day, 21 September

Constitution: adopted by nationwide referendum 5 July 1995

Legal system: based on civil law system

Suffrage: 18 years of age; universal

Executive branch:
chief of state: President Robert KOCHARIAN (since 30 March 1998)
head of government: Prime Minister Armen DARBINYAN (since 10 April 1998)
cabinet: Council of Ministers appointed by the prime minister
elections: president elected by popular vote for a five-year term; special election last held 30 March 1998 (next election to be held March 2003); prime minister appointed by the president
election results: Robert KOCHARIAN elected president; percent of vote - Robert KOCHARIAN 59%, Karen DEMIRCHYAN 41%

Legislative branch: unicameral National Assembly (Parliament) or Azgayin Zhoghov (190 seats; members serve four-year terms)
elections: last held 5 July 1995 (next to be held in the spring of 1999)
election results: percent of vote by party - NA; seats by party - Republican Bloc 159 (ANM 63, DLP-Hanrapetutyun Bloc 6, Republic Party 4, CDU 3,

Intellectual Armenia 3, Social Democratic Party 2, independents 78), SWM 8, ACP 7, NDU 5, NSDU 3, DLP 1, ARF 1, other 4, vacant 2; note - seats by party change frequently

Judicial branch: Supreme Court; Constitutional Court

Political parties and leaders: Armenian National Movement or ANM [Vano SIRADEGIAN, chairman]; National Democratic Union or NDU [Vazgen MANUKIAN]; Intellectual Armenia [H. TOKMAJIAN]; Social Democratic (Hnchakian) Party [Yeghia NACHARIAN]; Shamiram Women's Movement or SWM [Maria NERSISSIAN]; Armenian Communist Party or ACP [Sergey BADALYAN]; Union of National Self-Determination or NSDU [Paruir HAIRIKIAN, chairman]; Armenian Revolutionary Federation ("Dashnak" Party) or ARF [leader NA]; Christian Democratic Union or CDU [Azat ARSHAKYN, chairman]; Democratic Liberal Party [Orthosis GYONJIAN, chairman]; Republican Party [Andranik MARKARYAN]; People's Party of Armenia [Karen DEMIRCHYAN]; National Democratic 21st Century Party [David SHAKHAZARYAN]; Yerkrapah Parliamentary Group [Smbat AYVAZYAN]

International organization participation: BSEC, CCC, CE (guest), CIS, EAPC, EBRD, ECE, ESCAP, FAO, IAEA, IBRD, ICAO, ICRM, IDA, IFAD, IFC, IFRCS, ILO, IMF, Intelsat, Interpol, IOC, IOM, ISO, ITU, NAM (observer), OPCW, OSCE, PFP, UN, UNCTAD, UNESCO, UNIDO, UPU, WFTU, WHO, WIPO, WMO, WToO, WTrO (applicant)

Diplomatic representation in the US:
chief of mission: Ambassador Rouben R. SHUGARIAN
chancery: 2225 R Street NW, Washington, DC 20008
telephone: [1] (202) 319-1976
FAX: [1] (202) 319-2982
consulate(s) general: Los Angeles

Diplomatic representation from the US:
chief of mission: Ambassador Michael LEMMON
embassy: 18 General Bagramian Avenue, Yerevan
mailing address: American Embassy Yerevan, Department of State, Washington, DC 20521-7020
telephone: [374] (2) 151-551
FAX: [374] (2) 151-550

Flag description: three equal horizontal bands of red (top), blue, and gold

Economy

Economy - overview: Under the old Soviet central planning system, Armenia had developed a modern industrial sector, supplying machine tools, textiles, and other manufactured goods to sister republics in exchange for raw materials and energy. Since the implosion of the USSR in December 1991, Armenia has switched to small-scale agriculture away from the large agroindustrial complexes of the Soviet area. The agricultural sector has long-term needs for more investment and updated technology. The privatization of industry has been at a slower pace, but has been given renewed emphasis by the current

Armenia *(continued)*

administration. Armenia is a food importer, and its mineral deposits (gold, bauxite) are small. The ongoing conflict with Azerbaijan over the ethnic Armenian-dominated region of Nagorno-Karabakh and the breakup of the centrally directed economic system of the former Soviet Union contributed to a severe economic decline in the early 1990s. By 1994, however, the Armenian Government had launched an ambitious IMF-sponsored economic program that has resulted in positive growth rates in 1995-98. Armenia also managed to slash inflation and to privatize most small- and medium-sized enterprises. The chronic energy shortages Armenia suffered in recent years have been largely offset by the energy supplied by one of its nuclear power plants at Metsamor. The Russian financial crisis generated concerns about Armenia's economic performance in 1998. Although inflation dropped to 10% and GDP grew about 6%, the industrial sector remained moribund. Much of Armenia's population remains heavily dependent on remittances from relatives abroad, and remittances from Russia fell off sharply in 1998.

GDP: purchasing power parity - $9.2 billion (1998 est.)

GDP - real growth rate: 6% (1998 est.)

GDP - per capita: purchasing power parity - $2,700 (1998 est.)

GDP - composition by sector:
agriculture: 35%
industry: 30%
services: 35% (1998 est.)

Population below poverty line: 50% (1998 est.)

Household income or consumption by percentage share:
lowest 10%: NA%
highest 10%: NA%

Inflation rate (consumer prices): 10% (1998 est.)

Labor force: 1.6 million (1997)

Labor force - by occupation: manufacturing, mining, and construction 25%, agriculture 38%, services 37%

Unemployment rate: 20% (1998 est.)

Budget:
revenues: $322 million
expenditures: $424 million, including capital expenditures of $80 million (1998 est.)

Industries: much of industry is shut down; metal-cutting machine tools, forging-pressing machines, electric motors, tires, knitted wear, hosiery, shoes, silk fabric, washing machines, chemicals, trucks, watches, instruments, microelectronics

Industrial production growth rate: NA%

Electricity - production: 7.6 billion kWh (1996)

Electricity - production by source:
fossil fuel: 46.05%
hydro: 26.32%
nuclear: 27.63%
other: 0% (1996)

Electricity - consumption: 7.6 billion kWh (1996)

Electricity - exports: 0 kWh (1996)

Electricity - imports: 0 kWh (1996)

Agriculture - products: fruit (especially grapes), vegetables; livestock

Exports: $230 million (f.o.b., 1998 est.)

Exports - commodities: gold and jewelry, aluminum, transport equipment, electrical equipment, scrap metal

Exports - partners: Iran, Russia, Turkmenistan, Georgia

Imports: $840 million (c.i.f., 1998 est.)

Imports - commodities: grain, other foods, fuel, other energy

Imports - partners: Iran, Russia, Turkmenistan, Georgia, US, EU

Debt - external: $820 million (of which $75 million to Russia) (1997 est.)

Economic aid - recipient: $245.5 million (1995)

Currency: 1 dram = 100 luma

Exchange rates: dram per US$1 - 535.62 (January 1999), 504.92 (1998), 490.85 (1997), 414.04 (1996), 405.91 (1995), 288.65 (1994)

Fiscal year: calendar year

Communications

Telephones: 730,000 (1998 est.)

Telephone system: the Ministry of Communications oversees the Ministry of Posts and Telecommunications; the national operator is Armentel; the Greek Telecoms Company owns 90% of Armentel and will provide a $60 million eight-year loan; Armenia has about 4,000 Internet users on one satellite channel
domestic: local - 350,000 telephones are located in Yerevan; a fiber-optic loop provides digital service to 80,000 of Yerevan's customers; GSM cellular is available in Yerevan, as is paging; intercity - the former Soviet system provides service to 380,000 numbers mostly governmental
international: Yerevan is connected to the Trans-Asia-Europe line through Iran; additional international service is available by microwave, land line, and satellite through the Moscow switch; 1 INTELSAT earth station

Radio broadcast stations: AM 9, FM 6, shortwave 1 (1998)

Radios: NA

Television broadcast stations: 3 (in addition, programs are received by relay from Russia; 100% of the population receive Armenian and Russian TV programs) (1997)

Televisions: NA

Transportation

Railways:
total: 825 km in common carrier service; does not include industrial lines
broad gauge: 825 km 1.520-m gauge (1992)

Highways:
total: 8,580 km
paved: 8,580 km
unpaved: 0 km (1996 est.)

Waterways: NA km

Pipelines: natural gas 900 km (1991)

Ports and harbors: none

Airports: 11 (1996 est.)

Airports - with paved runways:
total: 5
over 3,047 m: 2
1,524 to 2,437 m: 1
914 to 1,523 m: 2 (1996 est.)

Airports - with unpaved runways:
total: 6
1,524 to 2,437 m: 2
914 to 1,523 m: 3
under 914 m: 1 (1996 est.)

Military

Military branches: Army, Air Force and Air Defense Aviation, Air Defense Force, Security Forces (internal and border troops)

Military manpower - military age: 18 years of age

Military manpower - availability:
males age 15-49: 922,124 (1999 est.)

Military manpower - fit for military service:
males age 15-49: 732,495 (1999 est.)

Military manpower - reaching military age annually:
males: 32,052 (1999 est.)

Military expenditures - dollar figure: $72.1 million (1999)

Military expenditures - percent of GDP: 4% (1999)

Transnational Issues

Disputes - international: Armenia supports ethnic Armenians in the Nagorno-Karabakh region of Azerbaijan in the longstanding, separatist conflict against the Azerbaijani Government; traditional demands on former Armenian lands in Turkey have subsided

Illicit drugs: illicit cultivator of cannabis mostly for domestic consumption; increasingly used as a transshipment point for illicit drugs - mostly opium and hashish - to Western Europe and the US via Iran, Central Asia, and Russia

Aruba
(part of the Kingdom of the Netherlands)

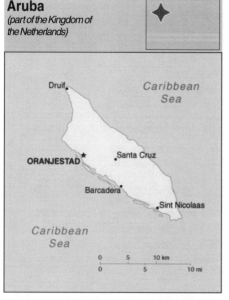

Geography

Location: Caribbean, island in the Caribbean Sea, north of Venezuela

Geographic coordinates: 12 30 N, 69 58 W

Map references: Central America and the Caribbean

Area:
total: 193 sq km
land: 193 sq km
water: 0 sq km

Area - comparative: slightly larger than Washington, DC

Land boundaries: 0 km

Coastline: 68.5 km

Maritime claims:
territorial sea: 12 nm

Climate: tropical marine; little seasonal temperature variation

Terrain: flat with a few hills; scant vegetation

Elevation extremes:
lowest point: Caribbean Sea 0 m
highest point: Mount Jamanota 188 m

Natural resources: NEGL; white sandy beaches

Land use:
arable land: 11%
permanent crops: NA%
permanent pastures: NA%
forests and woodland: NA%
other: 89% (1993 est.)

Irrigated land: NA sq km

Natural hazards: lies outside the Caribbean hurricane belt

Environment - current issues: NA

Environment - international agreements:
party to: NA
signed, but not ratified: NA

People

Population: 68,675 (July 1999 est.)

Age structure:
0-14 years: 22% (male 7,724; female 7,106)
15-64 years: 69% (male 22,723; female 24,747)
65 years and over: 9% (male 2,623; female 3,752) (1999 est.)

Population growth rate: 0.55% (1999 est.)

Birth rate: 13.28 births/1,000 population (1999 est.)

Death rate: 6.48 deaths/1,000 population (1999 est.)

Net migration rate: -1.31 migrant(s)/1,000 population (1999 est.)

Sex ratio:
at birth: 1.05 male(s)/female
under 15 years: 1.09 male(s)/female
15-64 years: 0.92 male(s)/female
65 years and over: 0.7 male(s)/female
total population: 0.93 male(s)/female (1999 est.)

Infant mortality rate: 7.84 deaths/1,000 live births (1999 est.)

Life expectancy at birth:
total population: 77.04 years
male: 73.33 years
female: 80.94 years (1999 est.)

Total fertility rate: 1.8 children born/woman (1999 est.)

Nationality:
noun: Aruban(s)
adjective: Aruban

Ethnic groups: mixed white/Caribbean Amerindian 80%

Religions: Roman Catholic 82%, Protestant 8%, Hindu, Muslim, Confucian, Jewish

Languages: Dutch (official), Papiamento (a Spanish, Portuguese, Dutch, English dialect), English (widely spoken), Spanish

Literacy: NA

Government

Country name:
conventional long form: none
conventional short form: Aruba

Data code: AA

Dependency status: part of the Kingdom of the Netherlands; full autonomy in internal affairs obtained in 1986 upon separation from the Netherlands Antilles

Government type: parliamentary

Capital: Oranjestad

Administrative divisions: none (part of the Kingdom of the Netherlands)

Independence: none (part of the Kingdom of the Netherlands; in 1990, Aruba requested and received from the Netherlands cancellation of the agreement to automatically give independence to the island in 1996)

National holiday: Flag Day, 18 March

Constitution: 1 January 1986

Legal system: based on Dutch civil law system, with some English common law influence

Suffrage: 18 years of age; universal

Executive branch:
chief of state: Queen BEATRIX Wilhelmina Armgard of the Netherlands (since 30 April 1980), represented by Governor General Olindo KOOLMAN (since 1 January 1992)

head of government: Prime Minister Jan (Henny) H. EMAN (since 29 July 1994) and Deputy Prime Minister Glenbert F. CROES

cabinet: Council of Ministers (elected by the Staten)

elections: the monarch is hereditary; governor general appointed for a six-year term by the monarch; prime minister and deputy prime minister elected by the Staten for a four-year term; election last held 12 July 1997 (next to be held by December 2001)

election results: inconclusive; no party won majority in December 1997 parliamentary elections; no new government formed as of May 1998

Legislative branch: unicameral Legislature or Staten (21 seats; members elected by direct popular vote and serve four-year terms)

elections: last held 12 December 1997 (next to be held by NA December 2001)

election results: percent of vote by party - NA; seats by party - AVP 10, MEP 9, OLA 2

Judicial branch: Joint High Court of Justice (judges are appointed by the monarch)

Political parties and leaders: Electoral Movement Party or MEP [Nelson ODUBER]; Aruban People's Party or AVP [Jan (Henny) H. EMAN]; National Democratic Action or ADN [Pedro Charro KELLY]; New Patriotic Party or PPN [Eddy WERLEMEN]; Aruban Patriotic Party or PPA [Benny NISBET]; Aruban Democratic Party or PDA [Leo BERLINSKI]; Democratic Action '86 or AD '86 [Arturo ODUBER]; Aruban Liberal Party or OLA [Glenbert CROES]; Electoral People's Movement or MEP [Betico CROES]; For a Restructured Aruba Now or PARA [Urbana LOPEZ]

International organization participation: Caricom (observer), ECLAC (associate), Interpol, IOC, UNESCO (associate), WCL, WToO (associate)

Diplomatic representation in the US: none (represented by the Kingdom of the Netherlands)

Diplomatic representation from the US:
chief of mission: Consul General James L. WILLIAMS
embassy: J. B. Gorsiraweg #1, Curacao
mailing address: P. O. Box 158, Willemstad, Curacao
telephone: [599] (9) 461-3066
FAX: [599] (9) 461-6489

Flag description: blue, with two narrow, horizontal, yellow stripes across the lower portion and a red, four-pointed star outlined in white in the upper hoist-side corner

Economy

Economy - overview: Tourism is the mainstay of the Aruban economy, although offshore banking and oil refining and storage are also important. The rapid growth of the tourism sector over the last decade has resulted in a substantial expansion of other activities. Construction has boomed, with hotel capacity five times the 1985 level. In addition, the reopening of the country's oil refinery in 1993, a major source of employment and foreign exchange earnings, has

Aruba (continued)

further spurred growth. Aruba's small labor force and less than 1% unemployment rate have led to a large number of unfilled job vacancies, despite sharp rises in wage rates in recent years.

GDP: purchasing power parity - $1.5 billion (1997 est.)

GDP - real growth rate: 6% (1997)

GDP - per capita: purchasing power parity - $22,000 (1997 est.)

GDP - composition by sector:

agriculture: NA%

industry: NA%

services: NA%

Population below poverty line: NA%

Household income or consumption by percentage share:

lowest 10%: NA%

highest 10%: NA%

Inflation rate (consumer prices): 3% (1997)

Labor force: NA

Labor force - by occupation: most employment is in the tourist industry (1996)

Unemployment rate: 0.6% (1996 est.)

Budget:

revenues: $345.3 million

expenditures: $378.5 million, including capital expenditures of $107 million (1997 est.)

Industries: tourism, transshipment facilities, oil refining

Industrial production growth rate: NA%

Electricity - production: 470 million kWh (1996)

Electricity - production by source:

fossil fuel: 100%

hydro: 0%

nuclear: 0%

other: 0% (1996)

Electricity - consumption: 470 million kWh (1996)

Electricity - exports: 0 kWh (1996)

Electricity - imports: 0 kWh (1996)

Agriculture - products: aloes; livestock; fish

Exports: $1.73 billion (including oil reexports)(1997)

Exports - commodities: mostly refined petroleum products

Exports - partners: US 64%, EU

Imports: $2.12 billion (1997)

Imports - commodities: food, consumer goods, manufactures, petroleum products, crude oil for refining and reexport

Imports - partners: US 55.5%, Netherlands 12.3%, Japan 3.5%

Debt - external: $285 million (1996)

Economic aid - recipient: $26 million (1995); note - the Netherlands provided a $127 million aid package to Aruba and Suriname in 1996

Currency: 1 Aruban florin (Af.) = 100 cents

Exchange rates: Aruban florins (Af.) per US$1 - 1.7900 (fixed rate since 1986)

Fiscal year: calendar year

Communications

Telephones: 22,922 (1993 est.)

Telephone system:

domestic: more than adequate

international: 1 submarine cable to Sint Maarten (Netherlands Antilles); extensive interisland microwave radio relay links

Radio broadcast stations: AM 4, FM 6, shortwave 0

Radios: NA

Television broadcast stations: 1 (1997)

Televisions: 19,000 (1993 est.)

Transportation

Railways: 0 km

Highways:

total: 300 km

paved: 130 km

unpaved: 170 km

note: most coastal roads are paved, while unpaved roads serve large tracts of the interior

Ports and harbors: Barcadera, Oranjestad, Sint Nicolaas

Merchant marine:

total: 1 cargo ship (1,000 GRT or over) totaling 1,366 GRT/1,595 DWT (1998 est.)

Airports: 2 (1998 est.)

Airports - with paved runways:

total: 2

2,438 to 3,047 m: 1

914 to 1,523 m: 1 (1998 est.)

Military

Military - note: defense is the responsibility of the Kingdom of the Netherlands

Transnational Issues

Disputes - international: none

Illicit drugs: drug-money-laundering center and transit point for narcotics bound for the US and Europe; added to the US list of major drug producing or drug transit countries in December 1996

Ashmore and Cartier Islands
(territory of Australia)

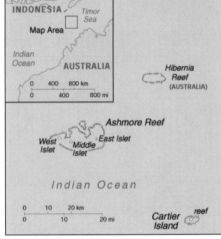

Geography

Location: Southeastern Asia, islands in the Indian Ocean, northwest of Australia

Geographic coordinates: 12 14 S, 123 05 E

Map references: Southeast Asia

Area:

total: 5 sq km

land: 5 sq km

water: 0 sq km

note: includes Ashmore Reef (West, Middle, and East Islets) and Cartier Island

Area - comparative: about eight times the size of The Mall in Washington, DC

Land boundaries: 0 km

Coastline: 74.1 km

Maritime claims:

contiguous zone: 12 nm

continental shelf: 200-m depth or to the depth of exploitation

exclusive fishing zone: 200 nm

territorial sea: 3 nm

Climate: tropical

Terrain: low with sand and coral

Elevation extremes:

lowest point: Indian Ocean 0 m

highest point: unnamed location 3 m

Natural resources: fish

Land use:

arable land: 0%

permanent crops: 0%

permanent pastures: 0%

forests and woodland: 0%

other: 100% (all grass and sand)

Irrigated land: 0 sq km (1993)

Natural hazards: surrounded by shoals and reefs that can pose maritime hazards

Environment - current issues: NA

Environment - international agreements:

party to: NA

signed, but not ratified: NA

Ashmore and Cartier Islands
(continued)

Geography - note: Ashmore Reef National Nature Reserve established in August 1983

Population: no indigenous inhabitants
note: there are only seasonal caretakers

Country name:
conventional long form: Territory of Ashmore and Cartier Islands
conventional short form: Ashmore and Cartier Islands
Data code: AT
Dependency status: territory of Australia; administered from Canberra by the Australian Department of the Environment, Sport, and Territories
Legal system: relevant laws of the Northern Territory of Australia
Diplomatic representation in the US: none (territory of Australia)
Diplomatic representation from the US: none (territory of Australia)
Flag description: the flag of Australia is used

Economy - overview: no economic activity

Ports and harbors: none; offshore anchorage only

Military - note: defense is the responsibility of Australia; periodic visits by the Royal Australian Navy and Royal Australian Air Force

Disputes - international: none

Atlantic Ocean

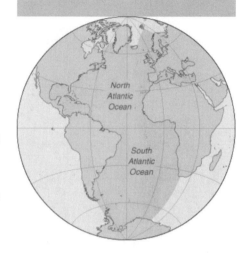

Location: body of water between Africa, Europe, Antarctica, and the Western Hemisphere
Geographic coordinates: 0 00 N, 25 00 W
Map references: World
Area:
total: 82.217 million sq km
note: includes Baltic Sea, Black Sea, Caribbean Sea, Davis Strait, Denmark Strait, Drake Passage, Gulf of Mexico, Mediterranean Sea, North Sea, Norwegian Sea, Scotia Sea, Weddell Sea, and other tributary water bodies
Area - comparative: slightly less than nine times the size of the US; second-largest of the world's four oceans (after the Pacific Ocean, but larger than Indian Ocean or Arctic Ocean)
Coastline: 111,866 km
Climate: tropical cyclones (hurricanes) develop off the coast of Africa near Cape Verde and move westward into the Caribbean Sea; hurricanes can occur from May to December, but are most frequent from August to November
Terrain: surface usually covered with sea ice in Labrador Sea, Denmark Strait, and Baltic Sea from October to June; clockwise warm-water gyre (broad, circular system of currents) in the northern Atlantic, counterclockwise warm-water gyre in the southern Atlantic; the ocean floor is dominated by the Mid-Atlantic Ridge, a rugged north-south centerline for the entire Atlantic basin
Elevation extremes:
lowest point: Milwaukee Deep in the Puerto Rico Trench -8,605 m
highest point: sea level 0 m
Natural resources: oil and gas fields, fish, marine mammals (seals and whales), sand and gravel aggregates, placer deposits, polymetallic nodules, precious stones
Natural hazards: icebergs common in Davis Strait, Denmark Strait, and the northwestern Atlantic Ocean

from February to August and have been spotted as far south as Bermuda and the Madeira Islands; icebergs from Antarctica occur in the extreme southern Atlantic Ocean; ships subject to superstructure icing in extreme northern Atlantic from October to May and extreme southern Atlantic from May to October; persistent fog can be a maritime hazard from May to September
Environment - current issues: endangered marine species include the manatee, seals, sea lions, turtles, and whales; drift net fishing is hastening the decline of fish stocks and contributing to international disputes; municipal sludge pollution off eastern US, southern Brazil, and eastern Argentina; oil pollution in Caribbean Sea, Gulf of Mexico, Lake Maracaibo, Mediterranean Sea, and North Sea; industrial waste and municipal sewage pollution in Baltic Sea, North Sea, and Mediterranean Sea
Environment - international agreements:
party to: none of the selected agreements
signed, but not ratified: none of the selected agreements
Geography - note: major chokepoints include the Dardanelles, Strait of Gibraltar, access to the Panama and Suez Canals; strategic straits include the Strait of Dover, Straits of Florida, Mona Passage, The Sound (Oresund), and Windward Passage; the Equator divides the Atlantic Ocean into the North Atlantic Ocean and South Atlantic Ocean

Data code: none; the US Government has not approved a standard for hydrographic codes - see the Cross-Reference List of Hydrographic Data Codes appendix

Economy - overview: The Atlantic Ocean provides some of the world's most heavily trafficked sea routes, between and within the Eastern and Western Hemispheres. Other economic activity includes the exploitation of natural resources, e.g., fishing, the dredging of aragonite sands (The Bahamas), and production of crude oil and natural gas (Caribbean Sea, Gulf of Mexico, and North Sea).

Telephone system:
international: numerous submarine cables with most between continental Europe and the UK, between North America and the UK, and in the Mediterranean; numerous direct links across Atlantic via satellite networks

Ports and harbors: Alexandria (Egypt), Algiers (Algeria), Antwerp (Belgium), Barcelona (Spain), Buenos Aires (Argentina), Casablanca (Morocco), Colon (Panama), Copenhagen (Denmark), Dakar (Senegal), Gdansk (Poland), Hamburg (Germany),

Atlantic Ocean *(continued)*

Helsinki (Finland), Las Palmas (Canary Islands, Spain), Le Havre (France), Lisbon (Portugal), London (UK), Marseille (France), Montevideo (Uruguay), Montreal (Canada), Naples (Italy), New Orleans (US), New York (US), Oran (Algeria), Oslo (Norway), Peiraiefs or Piraeus (Greece), Rio de Janeiro (Brazil), Rotterdam (Netherlands), Saint Petersburg (Russia), Stockholm (Sweden)
Transportation - note: Kiel Canal and Saint Lawrence Seaway are two important waterways

Transnational Issues

Disputes - international: some maritime disputes (see littoral states)

Australia

Introduction

Background: Australia became a British commonwealth in 1901. Blessed by rich natural resources, the country enjoyed rapid gains in herding, agriculture, and manufacturing and made a major contribution to the British effort in World Wars I and II. Australia subsequently developed its minerals, metals, and fossil fuel markets, all of which have become key Australian exports. Long-term concerns include pollution, particularly depletion of the ozone layer, and management and conservation of coastal areas, especially the Great Barrier Reef. Sydney will host the 2000 summer Olympics.

Geography

Location: Oceania, continent between the Indian Ocean and the South Pacific Ocean
Geographic coordinates: 27 00 S, 133 00 E
Map references: Oceania
Area:
total: 7,686,850 sq km
land: 7,617,930 sq km
water: 68,920 sq km
note: includes Lord Howe Island and Macquarie Island
Area - comparative: slightly smaller than the US
Land boundaries: 0 km
Coastline: 25,760 km
Maritime claims:
contiguous zone: 24 nm
continental shelf: 200 nm or to the edge of the continental margin
exclusive economic zone: 200 nm
territorial sea: 12 nm
Climate: generally arid to semiarid; temperate in south and east; tropical in north
Terrain: mostly low plateau with deserts; fertile plain in southeast
Elevation extremes:
lowest point: Lake Eyre -15 m

highest point: Mount Kosciusko 2,229 m
Natural resources: bauxite, coal, iron ore, copper, tin, silver, uranium, nickel, tungsten, mineral sands, lead, zinc, diamonds, natural gas, petroleum
Land use:
arable land: 6%
permanent crops: 0%
permanent pastures: 54%
forests and woodland: 19%
other: 21% (1993 est.)
Irrigated land: 21,070 sq km (1993 est.)
Natural hazards: cyclones along the coast; severe droughts
Environment - current issues: soil erosion from overgrazing, industrial development, urbanization, and poor farming practices; soil salinity rising due to the use of poor quality water; desertification; clearing for agricultural purposes threatens the natural habitat of many unique animal and plant species; the Great Barrier Reef off the northeast coast, the largest coral reef in the world, is threatened by increased shipping and its popularity as a tourist site; limited natural fresh water resources
Environment - international agreements:
party to: Antarctic-Environmental Protocol, Antarctic Treaty, Biodiversity, Climate Change, Endangered Species, Environmental Modification, Hazardous Wastes, Law of the Sea, Marine Dumping, Marine Life Conservation, Nuclear Test Ban, Ozone Layer Protection, Ship Pollution, Tropical Timber 83, Tropical Timber 94, Wetlands, Whaling
signed, but not ratified: Climate Change-Kyoto Protocol, Desertification
Geography - note: world's smallest continent but sixth-largest country; population concentrated along the eastern and southeastern coasts; regular, tropical, invigorating, sea breeze known as "the Doctor" occurs along the west coast in the summer

People

Population: 18,783,551 (July 1999 est.)
Age structure:
0-14 years: 21% (male 2,023,569; female 1,926,901)
15-64 years: 66% (male 6,317,045; female 6,172,735)
65 years and over: 13% (male 1,022,485; female 1,320,816) (1999 est.)
Population growth rate: 0.9% (1999 est.)
Birth rate: 13.21 births/1,000 population (1999 est.)
Death rate: 6.9 deaths/1,000 population (1999 est.)
Net migration rate: 2.66 migrant(s)/1,000 population (1999 est.)
Sex ratio:
at birth: 1.06 male(s)/female
under 15 years: 1.05 male(s)/female
15-64 years: 1.02 male(s)/female
65 years and over: 0.77 male(s)/female
total population: 0.99 male(s)/female (1999 est.)
Infant mortality rate: 5.11 deaths/1,000 live births (1999 est.)
Life expectancy at birth:
total population: 80.14 years

Australia *(continued)*

male: 77.22 years
female: 83.23 years (1999 est.)
Total fertility rate: 1.81 children born/woman (1999 est.)
Nationality:
noun: Australian(s)
adjective: Australian
Ethnic groups: Caucasian 92%, Asian 7%, aboriginal and other 1%
Religions: Anglican 26.1%, Roman Catholic 26%, other Christian 24.3%, non-Christian 11%
Languages: English, native languages
Literacy:
definition: age 15 and over can read and write
total population: 100%
male: 100%
female: 100% (1980 est.)

Government

Country name:
conventional long form: Commonwealth of Australia
conventional short form: Australia
Data code: AS
Government type: democratic, federal-state system recognizing the British monarch as sovereign
Capital: Canberra
Administrative divisions: 6 states and 2 territories*; Australian Capital Territory*, New South Wales, Northern Territory*, Queensland, South Australia, Tasmania, Victoria, Western Australia
Dependent areas: Ashmore and Cartier Islands, Christmas Island, Cocos (Keeling) Islands, Coral Sea Islands, Heard Island and McDonald Islands, Norfolk Island
Independence: 1 January 1901 (federation of UK colonies)
National holiday: Australia Day, 26 January (1788)
Constitution: 9 July 1900, effective 1 January 1901
Legal system: based on English common law; accepts compulsory ICJ jurisdiction, with reservations
Suffrage: 18 years of age; universal and compulsory
Executive branch:
chief of state: Queen ELIZABETH II (since 6 February 1952), represented by Governor General Sir William DEANE (since 16 February 1996)
head of government: Prime Minister John Winston HOWARD (since 11 March 1996); Deputy Prime Minister Timothy Andrew FISCHER (since 11 March 1996)
cabinet: Cabinet selected from among the members of Federal Parliament by the governor general on the advice of the prime minister
elections: none; the monarch is hereditary; governor general appointed by the monarch; following legislative elections, the leader of the majority party or leader of a majority coalition is usually appointed prime minister by the governor general for a three-year term
Legislative branch: bicameral Federal Parliament consists of the Senate (76 seats - 12 from each of the six states and two from each of the two territories; one-half of the members elected every three years by

popular vote to serve six-year terms) and the House of Representatives (148 seats; members elected by popular vote on the basis of proportional representation to serve three-year terms; no state can have fewer than five representatives)
elections: Senate - last held 3 October 1998 (next to be held by October 2001); House of Representatives - last held 3 October 1998 (next to be held by October 2001)
election results: Senate - percent of vote by party - NA; seats by party - Liberal-National 35, Labor 29, Australian Democrats 9, Greens 1, One Nation 1, independent 1; House of Representatives - percent of vote by party - NA; seats by party - Liberal-National 80, Labor 67, independent 1
Judicial branch: High Court, the Chief Justice and six other justices are appointed by the governor general
Political parties and leaders:
government: coalition of Liberal Party [John Winston HOWARD] and National Party [Timothy Andrew FISCHER]
opposition: Australian Labor Party [Kim BEAZLEY]; Australian Democratic Party [Meg LEES]; Green Party [Bob BROWN]; One Nation Party [Pauline HANSON]
Political pressure groups and leaders: Australian Democratic Labor Party (anti-Communist Labor Party splinter group); Peace and Nuclear Disarmament Action (Nuclear Disarmament Party splinter group)
International organization participation: ANZUS, APEC, AsDB, Australia Group, BIS, C, CCC, CP, EBRD, ESCAP, FAO, IAEA, IBRD, ICAO, ICC, ICFTU, ICRM, IDA, IEA, IFAD, IFC, IFRCS, IHO, ILO, IMF, IMO, Inmarsat, Intelsat, Interpol, IOC, IOM, ISO, ITU, MTCR, NAM (guest), NEA, NSG, OECD, OPCW, PCA, Sparteca, SPC, SPF, UN, UNCTAD, UNESCO, UNFICYP, UNHCR, UNITAR, UNTSO, UNU, UPU, WFTU, WHO, WIPO, WMO, WTrO, ZC
Diplomatic representation in the US:
chief of mission: Ambassador Andrew Sharp PEACOCK
chancery: 1601 Massachusetts Avenue NW, Washington, DC 20036
telephone: [1] (202) 797-3000
FAX: [1] (202) 797-3168
consulate(s) general: Atlanta, Honolulu, Los Angeles, New York, and San Francisco
Diplomatic representation from the US:
chief of mission: Ambassador Genta Hawkins HOLMES
embassy: Moonah Place, Yarralumla, Canberra, Australian Capital Territory 2600
mailing address: APO AP 96549
telephone: [61] (6) 6214-5600
FAX: [61] (6) 6214-5970
consulate(s) general: Melbourne, Perth, and Sydney
Flag description: blue with the flag of the UK in the upper hoist-side quadrant and a large seven-pointed star in the lower hoist-side quadrant; the remaining half is a representation of the Southern Cross constellation in white with one small five-pointed star and four, larger, seven-pointed stars

Economy

Economy - overview: Australia has a prosperous Western-style capitalist economy, with a per capita GDP at the level of the four dominant West European economies. Rich in natural resources, Australia is a major exporter of agricultural products, minerals, metals, and fossil fuels. Commodities account for 57% of the value of total exports, so that a downturn in world commodity prices can have a big impact on the economy. The government is pushing for increased exports of manufactured goods, but competition in international markets continues to be severe. Australia has suffered from the low growth and high unemployment characterizing the OECD countries in the early 1990s, but the economy has expanded at reasonably steady rates in recent years. Canberra's emphasis on reforms is a key factor behind the economy's resilience to the regional crisis and its stronger than expected growth rate that reached 4.5% last year. After a slow start in 1998, exports rebounded in the second half of the year because of a sharp currency depreciation and a redirection of sales to Europe, North America, and Latin America.
GDP: purchasing power parity - $393.9 billion (1998 est.)
GDP - real growth rate: 4.5% (1998 est.)
GDP - per capita: purchasing power parity - $21,200 (1998 est.)
GDP - composition by sector:
agriculture: 4%
industry: 31%
services: 65% (1997 est.)
Population below poverty line: NA%
Household income or consumption by percentage share:
lowest 10%: 2.5%
highest 10%: 24.8% (1989)
Inflation rate (consumer prices): 1% (1998)
Labor force: 9.2 million (December 1997)
Labor force - by occupation: services 73%, industry 22%, agriculture 5% (1997 est.)
Unemployment rate: 8.1% (1998)
Budget:
revenues: $90.73 billion
expenditures: $89.04 billion, including capital expenditures of $NA (FY98/99 est.)
Industries: mining, industrial and transportation equipment, food processing, chemicals, steel
Industrial production growth rate: 1.2% (1995)
Electricity - production: 166.683 billion kWh (1996)
Electricity - production by source:
fossil fuel: 91.14%
hydro: 8.84%
nuclear: 0%
other: 0.02% (1996)
Electricity - consumption: 166.683 billion kWh (1996)
Electricity - exports: 0 kWh (1996)
Electricity - imports: 0 kWh (1996)
Agriculture - products: wheat, barley, sugarcane, fruits; cattle, sheep, poultry

Exports: $56 billion (f.o.b., 1998 est.)
Exports - commodities: coal, gold, meat, wool, alumina, iron ore, wheat, machinery and transport equipment
Exports - partners: Japan 20%, ASEAN 16%, EU 10%, South Korea 9%, US 9%, NZ 8%, Taiwan, Hong Kong, China (1997)
Imports: $61 billion (f.o.b., 1998 est.)
Imports - commodities: machinery and transport equipment, computers and office machines, telecommunication equipment and parts; crude oil and petroleum products
Imports - partners: EU 25%, US 23%, Japan 13%, China, NZ (1997)
Debt - external: $156 billion (June 1997)
Economic aid - donor: ODA, $1.43 billion (FY97/98)
Currency: 1 Australian dollar ($A) = 100 cents
Exchange rates: Australian dollars ($A) per US$1 - 1.56 (February 1999), 1.5888 (1998), 1.3439 (1997), 1.2773 (1996), 1.3486 (1995), 1.3668 (1994)
Fiscal year: 1 July - 30 June

Communications

Telephones: 8.7 million (1987 est.)
Telephone system: excellent domestic and international service
domestic: domestic satellite system
international: submarine cables to New Zealand, Papua New Guinea, and Indonesia; satellite earth stations - 10 Intelsat (4 Indian Ocean and 6 Pacific Ocean), 2 Inmarsat (Indian and Pacific Ocean Regions)
Radio broadcast stations: AM 262, FM 345, shortwave 1 (Australia's only shortwave station, Radio Australia, broadcasts to the world in seven languages, using 23 frequencies) (1998)
Radios: NA
Television broadcast stations: 104 (64 of these stations are government-owned and 40 are commercial) (1997)
Televisions: 9.2 million (1992 est.)

Transportation

Railways:
total: 38,563 km (2,914 km electrified)
broad gauge: 6,083 km 1.600-m gauge
standard gauge: 16,752 km 1.435-m gauge
narrow gauge: 15,728 km 1.067-m gauge
dual gauge: 172 km NA gauges
Highways:
total: 913,000 km
paved: 353,331 km (including 13,630 km of expressways)
unpaved: 559,669 km (1996 est.)
Waterways: 8,368 km; mainly by small, shallow-draft craft
Pipelines: crude oil 2,500 km; petroleum products 500 km; natural gas 5,600 km
Ports and harbors: Adelaide, Brisbane, Cairns, Darwin, Devonport (Tasmania), Fremantle, Geelong,

Hobart (Tasmania), Launceston (Tasmania), Mackay, Melbourne, Sydney, Townsville
Merchant marine:
total: 57 ships (1,000 GRT or over) totaling 1,767,387 GRT/2,426,710 DWT
ships by type: bulk 29, cargo 3, chemical tanker 4, container 4, liquefied gas tanker 4, oil tanker 8, passenger 1, roll-on/roll-off cargo 4 (1998 est.)
Airports: 408 (1998 est.)
Airports - with paved runways:
total: 262
over 3,047 m: 11
2,438 to 3,047 m: 11
1,524 to 2,437 m: 112
914 to 1,523 m: 120
under 914 m: 8 (1998 est.)
Airports - with unpaved runways:
total: 146
1,524 to 2,437 m: 19
914 to 1,523 m: 114
under 914 m: 13 (1998 est.)

Military

Military branches: Australian Army, Royal Australian Navy, Royal Australian Air Force
Military manpower - military age: 17 years of age
Military manpower - availability:
males age 15-49: 4,882,693 (1999 est.)
Military manpower - fit for military service:
males age 15-49: 4,212,272 (1999 est.)
Military manpower - reaching military age annually:
males: 130,570 (1999 est.)
Military expenditures - dollar figure: $6.9 billion (FY97/98)
Military expenditures - percent of GDP: 1.9% (FY97/98)

Transnational Issues

Disputes - international: territorial claim in Antarctica (Australian Antarctic Territory)
Illicit drugs: Tasmania is one of the world's major suppliers of licit opiate products; government maintains strict controls over areas of opium poppy cultivation and output of poppy straw concentrate

Austria

Introduction

Background: Once the center of power for the large Austro-Hungarian empire, Austria was reduced to a small republic after its defeat in World War I. After the annexation to Nazi Germany in 1938 and subsequent occupation by the victorious Allied powers, Austria's 1955 State Treaty declared the country "permanently neutral" as a condition of the Soviet military withdrawal. The Soviet collapse relieved the external pressure to remain unaligned, but neutrality had evolved into a part of Austrian cultural identity, which has led to an ongoing public debate over whether Vienna legitimately can remain outside of European security structures. A wealthy country, Austria joined the European Union in 1995 and, like many EU members, is adjusting to the new European currency and struggling with high unemployment.

Geography

Location: Central Europe, north of Italy and Slovenia
Geographic coordinates: 47 20 N, 13 20 E
Map references: Europe
Area:
total: 83,858 sq km
land: 82,738 sq km
water: 1,120 sq km
Area - comparative: slightly smaller than Maine
Land boundaries:
total: 2,562 km
border countries: Czech Republic 362 km, Germany 784 km, Hungary 366 km, Italy 430 km, Liechtenstein 35 km, Slovakia 91 km, Slovenia 330 km, Switzerland 164 km
Coastline: 0 km (landlocked)
Maritime claims: none (landlocked)
Climate: temperate; continental, cloudy; cold winters with frequent rain in lowlands and snow in mountains; cool summers with occasional showers
Terrain: in the west and south mostly mountains (Alps); along the eastern and northern margins mostly

Austria (continued)

flat or gently sloping
Elevation extremes:
lowest point: Neusiedler See 115 m
highest point: Grossglockner 3,797 m
Natural resources: iron ore, oil, timber, magnesite, lead, coal, lignite, copper, hydropower
Land use:
arable land: 17%
permanent crops: 1%
permanent pastures: 23%
forests and woodland: 39%
other: 20% (1996 est.)
Irrigated land: 40 sq km (1993 est.)
Natural hazards: NA
Environment - current issues: some forest degradation caused by air and soil pollution; soil pollution results from the use of agricultural chemicals; air pollution results from emissions by coal- and oil-fired power stations and industrial plants and from trucks transiting Austria between northern and southern Europe
Environment - international agreements:
party to: Air Pollution, Air Pollution-Nitrogen Oxides, Air Pollution-Sulphur 85, Air Pollution-Sulphur 94, Air Pollution-Volatile Organic Compounds, Antarctic Treaty, Biodiversity, Climate Change, Desertification, Endangered Species, Environmental Modification, Hazardous Wastes, Law of the Sea, Nuclear Test Ban, Ozone Layer Protection, Ship Pollution, Tropical Timber 83, Tropical Timber 94, Wetlands, Whaling
signed, but not ratified: Air Pollution-Persistent Organic Pollutants, Antarctic-Environmental Protocol, Climate Change-Kyoto Protocol
Geography - note: landlocked; strategic location at the crossroads of central Europe with many easily traversable Alpine passes and valleys; major river is the Danube; population is concentrated on eastern lowlands because of steep slopes, poor soils, and low temperatures elsewhere

People

Population: 8,139,299 (July 1999 est.)
Age structure:
0-14 years: 17% (male 702,261; female 666,310)
15-64 years: 68% (male 2,792,484; female 2,713,397)
65 years and over: 15% (male 478,071; female 786,776) (1999 est.)
Population growth rate: 0.09% (1999 est.)
Birth rate: 9.62 births/1,000 population (1999 est.)
Death rate: 10.04 deaths/1,000 population (1999 est.)
Net migration rate: 1.32 migrant(s)/1,000 population (1999 est.)
Sex ratio:
at birth: 1.05 male(s)/female
under 15 years: 1.05 male(s)/female
15-64 years: 1.03 male(s)/female
65 years and over: 0.61 male(s)/female
total population: 0.95 male(s)/female (1999 est.)
Infant mortality rate: 5.1 deaths/1,000 live births (1999 est.)

Life expectancy at birth:
total population: 77.48 years
male: 74.31 years
female: 80.82 years (1999 est.)
Total fertility rate: 1.37 children born/woman (1999 est.)
Nationality:
noun: Austrian(s)
adjective: Austrian
Ethnic groups: German 99.4%, Croatian 0.3%, Slovene 0.2%, other 0.1%
Religions: Roman Catholic 78%, Protestant 5%, other 17%
Languages: German
Literacy:
definition: age 15 and over can read and write
total population: 99% (1974 est.)
male: NA%
female: NA%

Government

Country name:
conventional long form: Republic of Austria
conventional short form: Austria
local long form: Republik Oesterreich
local short form: Oesterreich
Data code: AU
Government type: federal republic
Capital: Vienna
Administrative divisions: 9 states (bundeslaender, singular - bundesland); Burgenland, Kaernten, Niederoesterreich, Oberoesterreich, Salzburg, Steiermark, Tirol, Vorarlberg, Wien
Independence: 1156 (from Bavaria)
National holiday: National Day, 26 October (1955)
Constitution: 1920; revised 1929 (reinstated 1 May 1945)
Legal system: civil law system with Roman law origin; judicial review of legislative acts by the Constitutional Court; separate administrative and civil/penal supreme courts; has not accepted compulsory ICJ jurisdiction
Suffrage: 18 years of age; universal; compulsory for presidential elections
Executive branch:
chief of state: President Thomas KLESTIL (since 8 July 1992)
head of government: Chancellor Viktor KLIMA (since 28 January 1997); Vice Chancellor Wolfgang SCHUESSEL (since 22 April 1995)
cabinet: Council of Ministers chosen by the president on the advice of the chancellor
elections: president elected by popular vote for a six-year term; presidential election last held 19 April 1998 (next to be held in the spring of 2004); chancellor chosen by the president from the majority party in the National Council; vice chancellor chosen by the president on the advice of the chancellor
election results: Thomas KLESTIL reelected president; percent of vote - Thomas KLESTIL 63%, Gertraud KNOLL 14%, Heide SCHMIDT 11%, Richard LUGNER 10%, Karl NOWAK 2%

Legislative branch: bicameral Federal Assembly or Bundesversammlung consists of Federal Council or Bundesrat (64 members; members represent each of the states on the basis of population, but with each state having at least three representatives; members serve a four- or six-year term) and the National Council or Nationalrat (183 seats; members elected by direct popular vote to serve four-year terms)
elections: National Council - last held 17 December 1995 (next to be held in the fall of 1999)
election results: National Council - percent of vote by party - SPOe 38.3%, OeVP 28.3%, FPOe 22.1%, LF 5.3%, Greens 4.6%, other 1.4%; seats by party - SPOe 71, OeVP 53, FPOe 40, LF 10, Greens 9
Judicial branch: Supreme Judicial Court or Oberster Gerichtshof; Administrative Court or Verwaltungsgerichtshof; Constitutional Court or Verfassungsgerichtshof
Political parties and leaders: Social Democratic Party of Austria or SPOe [Viktor KLIMA, chairman]; Austrian People's Party or OeVP [Wolfgang SCHUESSEL, chairman]; Freedom Party of Austria or FPOe [Joerg HAIDER, chairman]; Communist Party or KPOe [Walter BEIER, chairman]; The Greens or GA [Madeleine PETROVIC, parliamentary caucus floor leader and Alexander VAN DER BELLEN, party spokesman]; Liberal Forum or LF [Heide SCHMIDT]
Political pressure groups and leaders: Federal Chamber of Trade and Commerce; Austrian Trade Union Federation (primarily Socialist) or OeGB; three composite leagues of the Austrian People's Party or OeVP representing business, labor, and farmers; OeVP-oriented League of Austrian Industrialists or VOel; Roman Catholic Church, including its chief lay organization, Catholic Action
International organization participation: AfDB, AsDB, Australia Group, BIS, BSEC (observer), CCC, CE, CEI, CERN, EAPC, EBRD, ECE, EIB, EMU, ESA, EU, FAO, G- 9, IADB, IAEA, IBRD, ICAO, ICC, ICFTU, ICRM, IDA, IEA, IFAD, IFC, IFRCS, ILO, IMF, IMO, Intelsat, Interpol, IOC, IOM, ISO, ITU, MINURSO, MTCR, NAM (guest), NEA, NSG, OAS (observer), OECD, OPCW, OSCE, PCA, PFP, UN, UNCTAD, UNDOF, UNESCO, UNFICYP, UNHCR, UNIDO, UNIKOM, UNITAR, UNMIBH, UNMOT, UNOMIG, UNTSO, UNU, UPU, WCL, WEU (observer), WFTU, WHO, WIPO, WMO, WToO, WTrO, ZC
Diplomatic representation in the US:
chief of mission: Ambassador Helmut TUERK
chancery: 3524 International Court NW, Washington, DC 20008-3035
telephone: [1] (202) 895-6700
FAX: [1] (202) 895-6750
consulate(s) general: Chicago, Los Angeles, and New York
Diplomatic representation from the US:
chief of mission: Ambassador Kathryn Walt HALL
embassy: Boltzmanngasse 16, A-1091, Vienna
mailing address: use embassy street address
telephone: [43] (1) 313-39
FAX: [43] (1) 310-0682

Austria *(continued)*

Flag description: three equal horizontal bands of red (top), white, and red

Economy

Economy - overview: Austria has a well-developed market economy with a high standard of living. As a member of the European Monetary Union (EMU), Austria's economy is closely integrated with other EU member countries, especially with Germany. Austria's membership in the EU has drawn an influx of foreign investors attracted by Austria's access to the single European market. Through privatization efforts, the 1996-98 budget consolidation programs, and austerity measures, Austria brought its total public sector deficit down to 2.5% of GDP in 1997 and public debt - at 66% of GDP in 1997 - more or less in line with the 60% of GDP required by the EU's Maastricht criteria. Cuts mainly affect the civil service and Austria's generous social system, the two major causes of the government deficit. To meet increased competition from both EU and Central European countries, Austria will need to emphasize knowledge-based sectors of the economy and deregulate the service sector, particularly telecommunications and energy. The strong GDP growth of 1998 is expected to dwindle back to 2.3% in 1999, and observers caution that this projection may be revised downwards in view of the Asian and Brazilian crises and Germany's lower growth projection.

GDP: purchasing power parity - $184.5 billion (1998 est.)

GDP - real growth rate: 2.9% (1998 est.)

GDP - per capita: purchasing power parity - $22,700 (1998 est.)

GDP - composition by sector:
agriculture: 1.4%
industry: 30.8%
services: 67.8% (1997 est.)

Population below poverty line: NA%

Inflation rate (consumer prices): 0.9% (1998)

Labor force: 3.7 million (1998)

Labor force - by occupation: services 67.7%, industry and crafts 29%, agriculture and forestry 0.7% (salaried employees, 1997 est.)

Unemployment rate: 7% (1999 est.)

Budget:
revenues: $50.4 billion
expenditures: $55.9 billion, including capital expenditures of $NA (1998 est.)

Industries: construction, machinery, vehicles and parts, food, chemicals, lumber and wood processing, paper and paperboard, communications equipment, tourism (1997)

Industrial production growth rate: 4% (1998 est.)

Electricity - production: 52.15 billion kWh (1996)

Electricity - production by source:
fossil fuel: 34.4%
hydro: 65.6%
nuclear: 0%
other: 0% (1997)

Electricity - consumption: 56.1 billion kWh (1997)

Electricity - exports: 9.8 billion kWh (1997)

Electricity - imports: 9 billion kWh (1997)

Agriculture - products: grains, potatoes, sugar beets, wine, fruit; dairy products, cattle, pigs, poultry; lumber

Exports: $62.5 billion (1998)

Exports - commodities: vehicles, machinery and equipment, paper and paperboard, metal goods, iron and steel, telecommunication equipment, textiles, medical and pharmaceutical products (1997)

Exports - partners: EU 62% (Germany 35.1%, Italy 8.3%), Central and Eastern Europe 17.6% (Hungary 4.9%), Japan 1.3%, US 3.7% (1997)

Imports: $65.8 billion (1998)

Imports - commodities: vehicles, machinery and equipment, apparel, metal goods, oil and oil products, office and data-processing machinery, medical and pharmaceutical products, telecommunication equipment, textiles (1997)

Imports - partners: EU 68.9% (Germany 41.7%, Italy 8%), Central and Eastern Europe 11% (Hungary 3.1%), Asia 7.1% (Japan 2.2%), US 5.4% (1997)

Debt - external: $24.33 billion (1997)

Economic aid - donor: ODA, $513 million (1997); of which, bilateral $298 million, multilateral $215 million

Currency: 1 Austrian schilling (AS) = 100 groschen

Exchange rates: Austrian schillings (AS) per US$1 - 11.86 (January 1999), 12.379 (1998), 12.204 (1997), 10.587 (1996), 10.081 (1995), 11.422 (1994)
note: on 9 January 1999, the European Union introduced a common currency that is now being used by financial institutions in some member countries at the rate of 0.8597 euros per US$ and a fixed rate of 13.7603 Austrian shillings per euro; the euro will replace the local currency in consenting countries for all transactions in 2002

Fiscal year: calendar year

Communications

Telephones: 3.47 million (1986 est.)

Telephone system:
domestic: highly developed and efficient
international: satellite earth stations - 2 Intelsat (1 Atlantic Ocean and 1 Indian Ocean) and 2 Eutelsat

Radio broadcast stations: AM 1, FM 61 (several hundred repeaters), shortwave 1 (Austria's single shortwave station, Radio Austria International, transmits its programs to the world in six languages using 12 frequencies and six communication satellite relays) (1998)

Radios: 70% of all households had radios accoding to the 1993 census

Television broadcast stations: 51 (in addition, there are 920 repeaters) (1998)

Televisions: 2,418,584 (1984 est.)

Transportation

Railways:
total: 5,849 km (there is also 594 km of private tracks)
standard gauge: 5,470 km 1.435-m gauge (3,418 km electrified)
narrow gauge: 379 km 1.000-m and 0.760-m gauge

(84 km electrified) (1997)

Highways: 129,061 km
paved: 129,061 km (including 1,613 km of expressways)
unpaved: 0 km (1997 est.)

Waterways: 358 km (1997)

Pipelines: crude oil 777 km; natural gas 840 km (1997)

Ports and harbors: Linz, Vienna, Enns, Krems

Merchant marine:
total: 22 ships (1,000 GRT or over) totaling 67,066 GRT/95,693 DWT
ships by type: bulk 1, cargo 18, combination bulk 2, container 1 (1998 est.)

Airports: 55 (1998 est.)

Airports - with paved runways:
total: 22
over 3,047 m: 1
2,438 to 3,047 m: 5
1,524 to 2,437 m: 1
914 to 1,523 m: 3
under 914 m: 12 (1998 est.)

Airports - with unpaved runways:
total: 33
914 to 1,523 m: 4
under 914 m: 29 (1998 est.)

Heliports: 1 (1998 est.)

Military

Military branches: Army (includes Flying Division)

Military manpower - military age: 19 years of age

Military manpower - availability:
males age 15-49: 2,091,902 (1999 est.)

Military manpower - fit for military service:
males age 15-49: 1,735,469 (1999 est.)

Military manpower - reaching military age annually:
males: 48,872 (1999 est.)

Military expenditures - dollar figure: $1.8 billion (1999 est.)

Military expenditures - percent of GDP: 0.82% (1999 est.)

Transnational Issues

Disputes - international: none

Illicit drugs: transshipment point for Southwest Asian heroin and South American cocaine destined for Western Europe

Azerbaijan

Introduction

Background: In 1806, Azerbaijan, a region of Turkic Muslim people, was conquered by the Russians. In 1918, Azerbaijan declared independence from Russia, but was incorporated into the Soviet Union in 1920. It again declared its independence in 1991, following the collapse of the USSR. The conflict between Azerbaijan and Armenia over the Nagorno-Karabakh region is still unresolved after 10 years and Baku has yet to settle disputes with its neighbors over oil rights in the Caspian Sea. During the war, Karabakh Armenians declared independence and seized almost 20% of the country's territory, creating some 750,000 Azerbaijani refugees in the process. Both sides have generally observed a Russian-mediated cease-fire in place since May 1994.

Geography

Location: Southwestern Asia, bordering the Caspian Sea, between Iran and Russia
Geographic coordinates: 40 30 N, 47 30 E
Map references: Commonwealth of Independent States
Area:
total: 86,600 sq km
land: 86,100 sq km
water: 500 sq km
note: includes the exclave of Naxcivan Autonomous Republic and the Nagorno-Karabakh region; the region's autonomy was abolished by Azerbaijani Supreme Soviet on 26 November 1991
Area - comparative: slightly smaller than Maine
Land boundaries:
total: 2,013 km
border countries: Armenia (with Azerbaijan-proper) 566 km, Armenia (with Azerbaijan-Naxcivan exclave) 221 km, Georgia 322 km, Iran (with Azerbaijan-proper) 432 km, Iran (with Azerbaijan-Naxcivan exclave) 179 km,

Russia 284 km, Turkey 9 km
Coastline: 0 km (landlocked)
note: Azerbaijan borders the Caspian Sea (800 km, est.)
Maritime claims: none (landlocked)
Climate: dry, semiarid steppe
Terrain: large, flat Kur-Araz Ovaligi (Kura-Araks Lowland) (much of it below sea level) with Great Caucasus Mountains to the north, Qarabag Yaylasi (Karabakh Upland) in west; Baku lies on Abseron Yasaqligi (Apsheron Peninsula) that juts into Caspian Sea
Elevation extremes:
lowest point: Caspian Sea -28 m
highest point: Bazarduzu Dagi 4,485 m
Natural resources: petroleum, natural gas, iron ore, nonferrous metals, alumina
Land use:
arable land: 18%
permanent crops: 5%
permanent pastures: 25%
forests and woodland: 11%
other: 41% (1993 est.)
Irrigated land: 10,000 sq km (1993 est.)
Natural hazards: droughts; some lowland areas threatened by rising levels of the Caspian Sea
Environment - current issues: local scientists consider the Abseron Yasaqligi (Apsheron Peninsula) (including Baku and Sumqayit) and the Caspian Sea to be the ecologically most devastated area in the world because of severe air, water, and soil pollution; soil pollution results from the use of DDT as a pesticide and also from toxic defoliants used in the production of cotton
Environment - international agreements:
party to: Climate Change, Desertification, Ozone Layer Protection
signed, but not ratified: Biodiversity
Geography - note: landlocked

People

Population: 7,908,224 (July 1999 est.)
Age structure:
0-14 years: 32% (male 1,292,018; female 1,240,745)
15-64 years: 61% (male 2,361,792; female 2,496,721)
65 years and over: 7% (male 202,755; female 314,193) (1999 est.)
Population growth rate: 0.63% (1999 est.)
Birth rate: 21.58 births/1,000 population (1999 est.)
Death rate: 9.5 deaths/1,000 population (1999 est.)
Net migration rate: -5.76 migrant(s)/1,000 population (1999 est.)
Sex ratio:
at birth: 1.05 male(s)/female
under 15 years: 1.04 male(s)/female
15-64 years: 0.95 male(s)/female
65 years and over: 0.65 male(s)/female
total population: 0.95 male(s)/female (1999 est.)
Infant mortality rate: 82.52 deaths/1,000 live births (1999 est.)

Life expectancy at birth:
total population: 63.08 years
male: 58.76 years
female: 67.63 years (1999 est.)
Total fertility rate: 2.67 children born/woman (1999 est.)
Nationality:
noun: Azerbaijani(s)
adjective: Azerbaijani
Ethnic groups: Azeri 90%, Dagestani Peoples 3.2%, Russian 2.5%, Armenian 2%, other 2.3% (1998 est.)
note: almost all Armenians live in the separatist Nagorno-Karabakh region
Religions: Muslim 93.4%, Russian Orthodox 2.5%, Armenian Orthodox 2.3%, other 1.8% (1995 est.)
note: religious affiliation is still nominal in Azerbaijan; percentages for actual practicing adherents are much lower
Languages: Azeri 89%, Russian 3%, Armenian 2%, other 6% (1995 est.)
Literacy:
definition: age 15 and over can read and write
total population: 97%
male: 99%
female: 96% (1989 est.)

Government

Country name:
conventional long form: Azerbaijani Republic
conventional short form: Azerbaijan
local long form: Azarbaycan Respublikasi
local short form: none
former: Azerbaijan Soviet Socialist Republic
Data code: AJ
Government type: republic
Capital: Baku (Baki)
Administrative divisions: 59 rayons (rayonlar; rayon - singular), 11 cities* (saharlar; sahar - singular), 1 autonomous republic** (muxtar respublika); Abseron Rayonu, Agcabadi Rayonu, Agdam Rayonu, Agdas Rayonu, Agstafa Rayonu, Agsu Rayonu, Ali Bayramli Sahari*, Astara Rayonu, Baki Sahari*, Balakan Rayonu, Barda Rayonu, Beylaqan Rayonu, Bilasuvar Rayonu, Cabrayil Rayonu, Calilabad Rayonu, Daskasan Rayonu, Davaci Rayonu, Fuzuli Rayonu, Gadabay Rayonu, Ganca Sahari*, Goranboy Rayonu, Goycay Rayonu, Haciqabul Rayonu, Imisli Rayonu, Ismayilli Rayonu, Kalbacar Rayonu, Kurdamir Rayonu, Lacin Rayonu, Lankaran Rayonu, Lankaran Sahari*, Lerik Rayonu, Masalli Rayonu, Mingacevir Sahari*, Naftalan Sahari*, Naxcivan Muxtar Respublikasi**, Neftcala Rayonu, Oguz Rayonu, Qabala Rayonu, Qax Rayonu, Qazax Rayonu, Qobustan Rayonu, Quba Rayonu, Qubadli Rayonu, Qusar Rayonu, Saatli Rayonu, Sabirabad Rayonu, Saki Rayonu, Saki Sahari*, Salyan Rayonu, Samaxi Rayonu, Samkir Rayonu, Samux Rayonu, Siyazan Rayonu, Sumqayit Sahari*, Susa Rayonu, Susa Sahari*, Tartar Rayonu, Tovuz Rayonu, Ucar Rayonu, Xacmaz Rayonu, Xankandi Sahari*, Xanlar

Rayonu, Xizi Rayonu, Xocali Rayonu, Xocavand Rayonu, Yardimli Rayonu, Yevlax Rayonu, Yevlax Sahari*, Zangilan Rayonu, Zaqatala Rayonu, Zardab Rayonu

Independence: 30 August 1991 (from Soviet Union)

National holiday: Independence Day, 28 May

Constitution: adopted 12 November 1995

Legal system: based on civil law system

Suffrage: 18 years of age; universal

Executive branch:

chief of state: President Heydar ALIYEV (since 18 June 1993)

head of government: Prime Minister Artur RASIZADE (since 26 November 1996)

cabinet: Council of Ministers appointed by the president and confirmed by the National Assembly

elections: president elected by popular vote to a five-year term; election last held 11 October 1998 (next to be held October 2003); prime minister and first deputy prime ministers appointed by the president and confirmed by the National Assembly

election results: Heydar ALIYEV elected president; percent of vote - Heydar ALIYEV 76%

Legislative branch: unicameral National Assembly or Milli Mejlis (125 seats; members serve five-year terms)

elections: last held 12 and 26 November 1995 (next to be held NA 2000)

election results: percent of vote by party - NA; seats by party - NAP and allies 115, APF 4, PNIA 3, Musavat Party 1, vacant 2

Judicial branch: Supreme Court

Political parties and leaders: New Azerbaijan Party or NAP [Heydar ALIYEV, chairman]; Azerbaijan Popular Front or APF [Abulfaz ELCHIBEY, chairman]; Party for National Independence of Azerbaijan or PNIA [Etibar MAMMADOV, chairman]; Musavat Party [Isa GAMBAR, chairman]; People's Democratic Party of Azerbaijan [Rafig TURABXANLY]; Democratic Party of Independence of Azerbaijan [Vagit KERIMOV]; Communist Party of Azerbaijan (CPA-2) [Firudin HASANOV]; Social Democratic Party of Azerbaijan or SDP [Zardusht ALIZADE, chairman]; Liberal Party of Azerbaijan [Lala HAJIYEVA]; Vahdat Party [Leyla YUNUSOV, Gadzhi ALIZADE]; Azerbaijan Democratic Party or ADP [Ilyas ISMAYLOV]; Civic Solidarity [Sabir RUSTAMXANLI]; Motherland Party [Fazail AGAMALI]

Political pressure groups and leaders: self-proclaimed Armenian Nagorno-Karabakh Republic; Talysh independence movement; Sadval, Lezgin movement

International organization participation: BSEC, CCC, CE (guest), CIS, EAPC, EBRD, ECE, ECO, ESCAP, FAO, IBRD, ICAO, ICRM, IDA, IDB, IFAD, IFC, IFRCS, ILO, IMF, IMO, Intelsat, Interpol, IOC, ITU, NAM (observer), OIC, OPCW, OSCE, PFP, UN, UNCTAD, UNESCO, UNIDO, UPU, WFTU, WHO, WIPO, WMO, WTrO (observer)

Diplomatic representation in the US:

chief of mission: Ambassador Hafiz Mir Jalal PASHAYEV

chancery: (temporary) Suite 700, 927 15th Street NW, Washington, DC 20005 or P. O. Box 28790, Washington, DC 20038-8790

telephone: [1] (202) 842-0001

FAX: [1] (202) 842-0004

Diplomatic representation from the US:

chief of mission: Ambassador Stanley T. ESCUDERO

embassy: Azadliq Prospekt 83, Baku 370007

mailing address: American Embassy Baku, Department of State, Washington, DC 20521-7050

telephone: [9] (9412) 98-03-35, 36, 37

FAX: [9] (9412) 90-66-71

Flag description: three equal horizontal bands of blue (top), red, and green; a crescent and eight-pointed star in white are centered in red band

Economy

Economy - overview: Azerbaijan is less developed industrially than either Armenia or Georgia, the other Caucasian states. It resembles the Central Asian states in its majority Muslim population, high structural unemployment, and low standard of living. The economy's most prominent products are oil, cotton, and natural gas. Production from the Caspian oil field declined through 1997 but registered an increase in 1998. Negotiation of more than a dozen production-sharing arrangements (PSAs) with foreign firms, which have thus far committed $30 billion to oil field development, should generate the funds needed to spur future industrial development. Oil production under the first of these PSAs, with the Azerbaijan International Operating Company, began in November 1997. Azerbaijan shares all the formidable problems of the former Soviet republics in making the transition from a command to a market economy, but its considerable energy resources brighten its long-term prospects. Baku has only recently begun making progress on economic reform, and old economic ties and structures are slowly being replaced. A major short-term obstacle to economic progress, including stepped up foreign investment, is the continuing conflict with Armenia over the Nagorno-Karabakh region. Trade with Russia and the other former Soviet republics is declining in importance while trade is building up with Turkey, Iran, the UAE, and the nations of Europe. A serious long-term challenge is the maintenance of the competitiveness of non-oil exports in world markets.

GDP: purchasing power parity - $12.9 billion (1998 est.)

GDP - real growth rate: 10% (1998 est.)

GDP - per capita: purchasing power parity - $1,640 (1998 est.)

GDP - composition by sector:

agriculture: 22%

industry: 18%

services: 60% (1997 est.)

Population below poverty line: NA%

Household income or consumption by percentage share:

lowest 10%: NA%

highest 10%: NA%

Inflation rate (consumer prices): -7.6% (1998 est.)

Labor force: 2.9 million (1997)

Labor force - by occupation: agriculture and forestry 32%, industry and construction 15%, services 53% (1997)

Unemployment rate: 20% (1996 est.)

Budget:

revenues: $565 million

expenditures: $682 million, including capital expenditures of $NA (1996 est.)

Industries: petroleum and natural gas, petroleum products, oilfield equipment; steel, iron ore, cement; chemicals and petrochemicals; textiles

Industrial production growth rate: NA%

Electricity - production: 16.035 billion kWh (1996)

Electricity - production by source:

fossil fuel: 90.55%

hydro: 9.45%

nuclear: 0%

other: 0% (1996)

Electricity - consumption: 16.8 billion kWh (1997)

Electricity - exports: 600 million kWh (1996)

Electricity - imports: 745 million kWh (1996)

Agriculture - products: cotton, grain, rice, grapes, fruit, vegetables, tea, tobacco; cattle, pigs, sheep, goats

Exports: $781 million (f.o.b., 1997 est.)

Exports - commodities: oil and gas, chemicals, oilfield equipment, textiles, cotton

Exports - partners: CIS, European countries, Turkey

Imports: $794 million (c.i.f., 1997 est.)

Imports - commodities: machinery and parts, consumer durables, foodstuffs, textiles

Imports - partners: CIS, European countries, Turkey

Debt - external: $100 million (of which $75 million to Russia)

Economic aid - recipient: ODA, $113 million (1996)

Currency: manat=100 gopiks

Exchange rates: manats per US$1 - 3,865.00 (November 1998), 3,985.38 (1997), 4,301.26 (1996), 4,413.54 (1995), 1,570.23 (1994)

Fiscal year: calendar year

Communications

Telephones: 1.414 million (1998)

Telephone system: Azerbaijani telecommunications fall under the Ministry of Communications; Azerbaijan's telephone system is a combination of old Soviet era technology used by Azerbaijani citizens and small- to medium-size commercial establishments, and modern cellular phones used by an increasing middle class, large commercial ventures, international companies, and most government officials; the average citizen waits on a 200,000-person list for telephone service; Internet and E-mail service are available in Baku

domestic: local - the majority of telephones are in Baku or other industrial centers; intercity - about 700 villages still do not have public phone service; all long

Azerbaijan (continued)

distance service must use Azertel's (Ministry of Communications) lines; satellite service connects Baku to a modern switch in its separated enclave to Nakhichevan

international: the old Soviet system of cable and microwave is still serviceable; satellite service between Baku and Turkey provides access to 200 countries; additional satellite providers supply services between Baku and specific countries; Azerbaijan is a signator of the Trans-Asia-Europe Fiber-Optic Line (TAE); their lines are not laid but the Turkish satellite and a microwave between Azerbaijan and Iran can provide Azerbaijan worldwide access through this system

Radio broadcast stations: AM 10, FM 17, shortwave 1 (Azerbaijan's single shortwave station transmits its programs to the Middle East in eight languages)

Radios: NA

Television broadcast stations: 2; note - the Ministry of Communications is the monopoly broadcaster and rebroadcaster of television in Azerbaijan; Azerbaijani, Russian, Armenian, Iranian, British broadcasting companies, Voice of America, and other European channels are available via satellite; television is broadcast to Nakhichevan by satellite

Televisions: NA

Transportation

Railways:
total: 2,125 km in common carrier service; does not include industrial lines
broad gauge: 2,125 km 1.520-m gauge (1,278 km electrified) (1993)

Highways:
total: 57,770 km
paved: 54,188 km
unpaved: 3,582 km (1995 est.)

Pipelines: crude oil 1,130 km; petroleum products 630 km; natural gas 1,240 km

Ports and harbors: Baku (Baki)

Merchant marine:
total: 57 ships (1,000 GRT or over) totaling 251,404 GRT/ 306,264 DWT
ships by type: cargo 12, oil tanker 42, roll-on/roll-off cargo 2, short-sea passenger 1 (1998 est.)

Airports: 69 (1996 est.)

Airports - with paved runways:
total: 29
over 3,047 m: 2
2,438 to 3,047 m: 6
1,524 to 2,437 m: 17
914 to 1,523 m: 3
under 914 m: 1 (1996 est.)

Airports - with unpaved runways:
total: 40
914 to 1,523 m: 7
under 914 m: 33 (1996 est.)

Military

Military branches: Army, Navy, Air and Air Defense Forces, Border Guards

Military manpower - military age: 18 years of age

Military manpower - availability:
males age 15-49: 2,041,863 (1999 est.)

Military manpower - fit for military service:
males age 15-49: 1,639,144 (1999 est.)

Military manpower - reaching military age annually:
males: 73,486 (1999 est.)

Military expenditures - dollar figure: $121 million (1999)

Military expenditures - percent of GDP: 2.6% (1999)

Transnational Issues

Disputes - international: Armenia supports ethnic Armenians in the Nagorno-Karabakh region of Azerbaijan in the longstanding, separatist conflict against the Azerbaijani Government; Caspian Sea boundaries are not yet determined among Azerbaijan, Iran, Kazakhstan, Russia, and Turkmenistan

Illicit drugs: limited illicit cultivation of cannabis and opium poppy, mostly for CIS consumption; limited government eradication program; transshipment point for opiates via Iran, Central Asia, and Russia to Western Europe

Bahamas, The

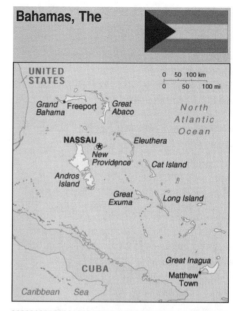

Geography

Location: Caribbean, chain of islands in the North Atlantic Ocean, southeast of Florida

Geographic coordinates: 24 15 N, 76 00 W

Map references: Central America and the Caribbean

Area:
total: 13,940 sq km
land: 10,070 sq km
water: 3,870 sq km

Area - comparative: slightly smaller than Connecticut

Land boundaries: 0 km

Coastline: 3,542 km

Maritime claims:
continental shelf: 200-m depth or to the depth of exploitation
exclusive economic zone: 200 nm
territorial sea: 12 nm

Climate: tropical marine; moderated by warm waters of Gulf Stream

Terrain: long, flat coral formations with some low rounded hills

Elevation extremes:
lowest point: Atlantic Ocean 0 m
highest point: Mount Alvernia, on Cat Island 63 m

Natural resources: salt, aragonite, timber

Land use:
arable land: 1%
permanent crops: 0%
permanent pastures: 0%
forests and woodland: 32%
other: 67% (1993 est.)

Irrigated land: NA sq km

Natural hazards: hurricanes and other tropical storms that cause extensive flood and wind damage

Environment - current issues: coral reef decay; solid waste disposal

Environment - international agreements:
party to: Biodiversity, Climate Change, Endangered

Bahamas, The *(continued)*

Species, Hazardous Wastes, Law of the Sea, Nuclear Test Ban, Ozone Layer Protection, Ship Pollution, Wetlands
signed, but not ratified: none of the selected agreements
Geography - note: strategic location adjacent to US and Cuba; extensive island chain

People

Population: 283,705 (July 1999 est.)
Age structure:
0-14 years: 27% (male 39,271; female 38,740)
15-64 years: 67% (male 92,830; female 96,814)
65 years and over: 6% (male 6,696; female 9,354) (1999 est.)
Population growth rate: 1.36% (1999 est.)
Birth rate: 20.58 births/1,000 population (1999 est.)
Death rate: 5.43 deaths/1,000 population (1999 est.)
Net migration rate: -1.55 migrant(s)/1,000 population (1999 est.)
Sex ratio:
at birth: 1.02 male(s)/female
under 15 years: 1.01 male(s)/female
15-64 years: 0.96 male(s)/female
65 years and over: 0.72 male(s)/female
total population: 0.96 male(s)/female (1999 est.)
Infant mortality rate: 18.38 deaths/1,000 live births (1999 est.)
Life expectancy at birth:
total population: 74.25 years
male: 70.94 years
female: 77.64 years (1999 est.)
Total fertility rate: 2.31 children born/woman (1999 est.)
Nationality:
noun: Bahamian(s)
adjective: Bahamian
Ethnic groups: black 85%, white 15%
Religions: Baptist 32%, Anglican 20%, Roman Catholic 19%, Methodist 6%, Church of God 6%, other Protestant 12%, none or unknown 3%, other 2%
Languages: English, Creole (among Haitian immigrants)
Literacy:
definition: age 15 and over can read and write
total population: 98.2%
male: 98.5%
female: 98% (1995 est.)

Government

Country name:
conventional long form: Commonwealth of The Bahamas
conventional short form: The Bahamas
Data code: BF
Government type: commonwealth
Capital: Nassau
Administrative divisions: 21 districts; Acklins and Crooked Islands, Bimini, Cat Island, Exuma, Freeport, Fresh Creek, Governor's Harbour, Green Turtle Cay, Harbour Island, High Rock, Inagua, Kemps Bay, Long Island, Marsh Harbour, Mayaguana, New Providence, Nicholls Town and Berry Islands, Ragged Island, Rock Sound, Sandy Point, San Salvador and Rum Cay
Independence: 10 July 1973 (from UK)
National holiday: National Day, 10 July (1973)
Constitution: 10 July 1973
Legal system: based on English common law
Suffrage: 18 years of age; universal
Executive branch:
chief of state: Queen ELIZABETH II (since 6 February 1952), represented by Governor General Sir Orville TURNQUEST (since 2 January 1995)
head of government: Prime Minister Hubert Alexander INGRAHAM (since 19 August 1992) and Deputy Prime Minister Frank WATSON (since December 1994)
cabinet: Cabinet appointed by the governor general on the prime minister's recommendation
elections: none; the monarch is hereditary; governor general appointed by the monarch; prime minister and deputy prime minister appointed by the governor general
Legislative branch: bicameral Parliament consists of the Senate (16-member body appointed by the governor general upon the advice of the prime minister and the opposition leader for a five-year term) and the House of Assembly (40 seats; members elected by direct popular vote to serve five-year terms)
elections: last held 14 March 1997 (next to be held by March 2002)
election results: percent of vote by party - NA; seats by party - FNM 35, PLP 5
Judicial branch: Supreme Court
Political parties and leaders: Progressive Liberal Party or PLP [Perry CHRISTIE]; Free National Movement or FNM [Hubert Alexander INGRAHAM]
International organization participation: ACP, C, Caricom, CCC, CDB, ECLAC, FAO, G-77, IADB, IBRD, ICAO, ICFTU, ICRM, IFC, IFRCS, ILO, IMF, IMO, Inmarsat, Intelsat, Interpol, IOC, ITU, NAM, OAS, OPANAL, OPCW, UN, UNCTAD, UNESCO, UNIDO, UPU, WHO, WIPO, WMO, WTrO (applicant)
Diplomatic representation in the US:
chief of mission: Ambassador Arlington Griffith BUTLER
chancery: 2220 Massachusetts Avenue NW, Washington, DC 20008
telephone: [1] (202) 319-2660
FAX: [1] (202) 319-2668
consulate(s) general: Miami and New York
Diplomatic representation from the US:
chief of mission: Ambassador Arthur SCHECHTER
embassy: Queen Street, Nassau
mailing address: local or express mail address: P.O. Box N-8197, Nassau; stateside address: American Embassy Nassau, P.O. Box 599009, Miami, FL 33159-9009; pouch address: Nassau, Department of State, Washington, DC 20521-3370
telephone: [1] (242) 322-1181
FAX: [1] (242) 356-0222
Flag description: three equal horizontal bands of aquamarine (top), gold, and aquamarine, with a black equilateral triangle based on the hoist side

Economy

Economy - overview: The Bahamas is a stable, developing nation with an economy heavily dependent on tourism and offshore banking. Tourism alone accounts for more than 60% of GDP and directly or indirectly employs 40% of the archipelago's labor force. Moderate growth in tourism receipts and a boom in construction of new hotels, resorts, and residences led to an increase of the country's GDP by an estimated 4% in 1998. Manufacturing and agriculture together contribute less than 10% of GDP and show little growth, despite government incentives aimed at those sectors. Overall growth prospects in the short run will depend heavily on the fortunes of the tourism sector and continued income growth in the US, which accounts for the majority of tourist visitors.
GDP: purchasing power parity - $5.63 billion (1998 est.)
GDP - real growth rate: 4% (1998 est.)
GDP - per capita: purchasing power parity - $20,100 (1998 est.)
GDP - composition by sector:
agriculture: 3%
industry: 5%
services: 92% (1997 est.)
Population below poverty line: NA%
Household income or consumption by percentage share:
lowest 10%: NA%
highest 10%: NA%
Inflation rate (consumer prices): 0.4% (1997)
Labor force: 148,000 (1996)
Labor force - by occupation: government 30%, tourism 40%, business services 10%, agriculture 5% (1995 est.)
Unemployment rate: 9% (1998 est.)
Budget:
revenues: $766 million
expenditures: $845 million, including capital expenditures of $97 million (FY97/98)
Industries: tourism, banking, cement, oil refining and transshipment, salt production, rum, aragonite, pharmaceuticals, spiral-welded steel pipe
Industrial production growth rate: NA%
Electricity - production: 1 billion kWh (1996)
Electricity - production by source:
fossil fuel: 100%
hydro: 0%
nuclear: 0%
other: 0% (1996)
Electricity - consumption: 1 billion kWh (1996)
Electricity - exports: 0 kWh (1996)
Electricity - imports: 0 kWh (1996)
Agriculture - products: citrus, vegetables; poultry
Exports: $300 million (1998)
Exports - commodities: pharmaceuticals, cement, rum, crawfish, refined petroleum products
Exports - partners: US 24.5%, EU (excluding UK) 23.9%, UK 12.6%, Singapore 5.6% (1997)

Bahamas, The (continued)

Imports: $1.37 billion (1998)
Imports - commodities: foodstuffs, manufactured goods, crude oil, vehicles, electronics
Imports - partners: US 34.9%, EU 24.3%, Japan 15.5%, Russia 6.3% (1997)
Debt - external: $381.7 million (1997)
Economic aid - recipient: $9.8 million (1995)
Currency: 1 Bahamian dollar (B$) = 100 cents
Exchange rates: Bahamian dollar (B$) per US$1 - 1.000 (fixed rate pegged to the dollar)
Fiscal year: 1 July - 30 June

Communications

Telephones: 200,000 (1997 est.)
Telephone system:
domestic: 91,183 telephone subscribers; totally automatic system; highly developed
international: tropospheric scatter and submarine cable to Florida; 3 coaxial submarine cables; satellite earth station - 1 Intelsat (Atlantic Ocean)
Radio broadcast stations: AM 3, FM 4, shortwave 0 (1998)
Radios: 200,000 (1993 est.)
Television broadcast stations: 1 (1997)
Televisions: 60,000 (1993 est.)

Transportation

Railways: 0 km
Highways:
total: 2,693 km
paved: 1,546 km
unpaved: 1,147 km (1997 est.)
Ports and harbors: Freeport, Matthew Town, Nassau
Merchant marine:
total: 1,079 ships (1,000 GRT or over) totaling 26,631,924 GRT/41,196,326 DWT
ships by type: bulk 209, cargo 241, chemical tanker 43, combination bulk 13, combination ore/oil 22, container 61, liquefied gas tanker 34, livestock carrier 1, oil tanker 170, passenger 62, passenger-cargo 1, railcar carrier 1, refrigerated cargo 140, roll-on/roll-off cargo 48, short-sea passenger 12, specialized tanker 2, vehicle carrier 19
note: a flag of convenience registry; includes ships from 49 countries among which are Norway 177, Greece 141, UK 113, US 61, Denmark 39, Finland 27, Japan 25, Sweden 24, France 22, and Italy 22 (1998 est.)
Airports: 62 (1998 est.)
Airports - with paved runways:
total: 33
over 3,047 m: 2
2,438 to 3,047 m: 1
1,524 to 2,437 m: 15
914 to 1,523 m: 13
under 914 m: 2 (1998 est.)

Airports - with unpaved runways:
total: 29
1,524 to 2,437 m: 1
914 to 1,523 m: 7
under 914 m: 21 (1998 est.)

Military

Military branches: Royal Bahamas Defense Force (Coast Guard only), Royal Bahamas Police Force
Military expenditures - dollar figure: $20 million (FY95/96)
Military expenditures - percent of GDP: NA%

Transnational Issues

Disputes - international: none
Illicit drugs: transshipment point for cocaine and marijuana bound for US and Europe; banking industry vulnerable to money laundering

Bahrain

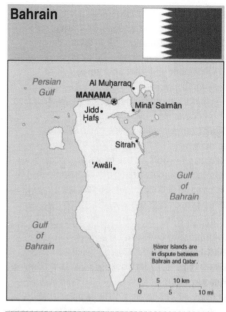

Geography

Location: Middle East, archipelago in the Persian Gulf, east of Saudi Arabia
Geographic coordinates: 26 00 N, 50 33 E
Map references: Middle East
Area:
total: 620 sq km
land: 620 sq km
water: 0 sq km
Area - comparative: 3.5 times the size of Washington, DC
Land boundaries: 0 km
Coastline: 161 km
Maritime claims:
contiguous zone: 24 nm
continental shelf: extending to boundaries to be determined
territorial sea: 12 nm
Climate: arid; mild, pleasant winters; very hot, humid summers
Terrain: mostly low desert plain rising gently to low central escarpment
Elevation extremes:
lowest point: Persian Gulf 0 m
highest point: Jabal ad Dukhan 122 m
Natural resources: oil, associated and nonassociated natural gas, fish
Land use:
arable land: 1%
permanent crops: 1%
permanent pastures: 6%
forests and woodland: 0%
other: 92% (1993 est.)
Irrigated land: 10 sq km (1993 est.)
Natural hazards: periodic droughts; dust storms
Environment - current issues: desertification resulting from the degradation of limited arable land, periods of drought, and dust storms; coastal degradation (damage to coastlines, coral reefs, and sea vegetation) resulting from oil spills and other

Bahrain (continued)

discharges from large tankers, oil refineries, and distribution stations; no natural fresh water resources so that groundwater and sea water are the only sources for all water needs

Environment - international agreements:
party to: Biodiversity, Climate Change, Desertification, Hazardous Wastes, Law of the Sea, Ozone Layer Protection, Wetlands
signed, but not ratified: none of the selected agreements

Geography - note: close to primary Middle Eastern petroleum sources; strategic location in Persian Gulf which much of Western world's petroleum must transit to reach open ocean

People

Population: 629,090 (July 1999 est.)
note: includes 227,801 non-nationals (July 1999 est.)
Age structure:
0-14 years: 31% (male 97,316; female 94,708)
15-64 years: 67% (male 249,594; female 169,337)
65 years and over: 2% (male 9,241; female 8,894) (1999 est.)
Population growth rate: 2% (1999 est.)
Birth rate: 21.86 births/1,000 population (1999 est.)
Death rate: 3.24 deaths/1,000 population (1999 est.)
Net migration rate: 1.42 migrant(s)/1,000 population (1999 est.)
Sex ratio:
at birth: 1.03 male(s)/female
under 15 years: 1.03 male(s)/female
15-64 years: 1.47 male(s)/female
65 years and over: 1.04 male(s)/female
total population: 1.3 male(s)/female (1999 est.)
Infant mortality rate: 14.81 deaths/1,000 live births (1999 est.)
Life expectancy at birth:
total population: 75.32 years
male: 72.75 years
female: 77.96 years (1999 est.)
Total fertility rate: 2.97 children born/woman (1999 est.)
Nationality:
noun: Bahraini(s)
adjective: Bahraini
Ethnic groups: Bahraini 63%, Asian 13%, other Arab 10%, Iranian 8%, other 6%
Religions: Shi'a Muslim 75%, Sunni Muslim 25%
Languages: Arabic, English, Farsi, Urdu
Literacy:
definition: age 15 and over can read and write
total population: 85.2%
male: 89.1%
female: 79.4% (1995 est.)

Government

Country name:
conventional long form: State of Bahrain
conventional short form: Bahrain
local long form: Dawlat al Bahrayn
local short form: Al Bahrayn

Data code: BA
Government type: traditional monarchy
Capital: Manama
Administrative divisions: 12 municipalities (manatiq, singular - mintaqah); Al Hadd, Al Manamah, Al Mintaqah al Gharbiyah, Al Mintaqah al Wusta, Al Mintaqah ash Shamaliyah, Al Muharraq, Ar Rifa' wa al Mintaqah al Janubiyah, Jidd Hafs, Madinat Hamad, Madinat 'Isa, Juzur Hawar, Sitrah
note: all municipalities administered from Manama
Independence: 15 August 1971 (from UK)
National holiday: National Day, 16 December (1971)
Constitution: 26 May 1973, effective 6 December 1973
Legal system: based on Islamic law and English common law
Suffrage: none
Executive branch:
chief of state: Amir HAMAD bin Isa Al Khalifa (since 6 March 1999); Heir Apparent Crown Prince SALMAN bin Hamad (son of the monarch, born NA 1969)
head of government: Prime Minister KHALIFA bin Salman Al Khalifa (since 19 January 1970)
cabinet: Cabinet appointed by the monarch
elections: none; the monarch is hereditary; prime minister appointed by the monarch
Legislative branch: unicameral National Assembly was dissolved 26 August 1975 and legislative powers were assumed by the Cabinet; appointed Advisory Council established 16 December 1992
Judicial branch: High Civil Appeals Court
Political parties and leaders: political parties prohibited
Political pressure groups and leaders: several small, clandestine leftist and Islamic fundamentalist groups are active; following the arrest of a popular Shi'a cleric, Shi'a activists have fomented unrest sporadically since late 1994, demanding the return of an elected National Assembly and an end to unemployment
International organization participation: ABEDA, AFESD, AL, AMF, ESCWA, FAO, G-77, GCC, IBRD, ICAO, ICRM, IDB, IFC, IFRCS, IHO, ILO, IMF, IMO, Inmarsat, Intelsat, Interpol, IOC, ISO (correspondent), ITU, NAM, OAPEC, OIC, OPCW, UN, UN Security Council (temporary), UNCTAD, UNESCO, UNIDO, UPU, WFTU, WHO, WIPO, WMO, WTrO
Diplomatic representation in the US:
chief of mission: Ambassador Dr. Muhammad ABD AL-GHAFFAR Abdallah
chancery: 3502 International Drive NW, Washington, DC 20008
telephone: [1] (202) 342-0741
FAX: [1] (202) 362-2192
consulate(s) general: New York
Diplomatic representation from the US:
chief of mission: Ambassador Johnny YOUNG
embassy: Building No. 979, Road 3119 (next to Al-Ahli Sports Club), Block 3119, Zinj District, Manama
mailing address: American Embassy Manama, PSC

451, FPO AE 09834-5100; International Mail: American Embassy, Box 26431, Manama
telephone: [973] 273-300
FAX: [973] 272-594
Flag description: red with a white serrated band (eight white points) on the hoist side

Economy

Economy - overview: In Bahrain, petroleum production and processing account for about 60% of export receipts, 60% of government revenues, and 30% of GDP. Economic conditions have fluctuated with the changing fortunes of oil since 1985, for example, during and following the Gulf crisis of 1990-91. With its highly developed communication and transport facilities, Bahrain is home to numerous multinational firms with business in the Gulf. A large share of exports consists of petroleum products made from imported crude. Construction proceeds on several major industrial projects. Unemployment, especially among the young, and the depletion of both oil and underground water resources are major long-term economic problems.
GDP: purchasing power parity - $8.2 billion (1998 est.)
GDP - real growth rate: -2% (1998 est.)
GDP - per capita: purchasing power parity - $13,100 (1998 est.)
GDP - composition by sector:
agriculture: 1%
industry: 46%
services: 53% (1996 est.)
Population below poverty line: NA%
Household income or consumption by percentage share:
lowest 10%: NA%
highest 10%: NA%
Inflation rate (consumer prices): -0.2% (1996 est.)
Labor force: 150,000 (1997 est.)
note: 44% of the population in the 15-64 age group is non-national (July 1998 est.)
Labor force - by occupation: industry, commerce, and service 79%, government 20%, agriculture 1% (1997 est.)
Unemployment rate: 15% (1996 est.)
Budget:
revenues: $1.5 billion
expenditures: $1.9 billion, including capital expenditures of $NA (1999 budget)
Industries: petroleum processing and refining, aluminum smelting, offshore banking, ship repairing; tourism
Industrial production growth rate: 3.4% (1995)
Electricity - production: 4.7 billion kWh (1996)
Electricity - production by source:
fossil fuel: 100%
hydro: 0%
nuclear: 0%
other: 0% (1996)
Electricity - consumption: 4.7 billion kWh (1996)
Electricity - exports: 0 kWh (1996)
Electricity - imports: 0 kWh (1996)

Bahrain *(continued)*

Agriculture - products: fruit, vegetables; poultry, dairy products; shrimp, fish
Exports: $4.7 billion (f.o.b., 1997)
Exports - commodities: petroleum and petroleum products 61%, aluminum 7%
Exports - partners: India 18%, Japan 11%, Saudi Arabia 8%, South Korea 7%, UAE 5% (1997)
Imports: $4.4 billion (f.o.b., 1997)
Imports - commodities: nonoil 59%, crude oil 41%
Imports - partners: Saudi Arabia 45%, US 10%, UK 6%, Japan 5%, Germany 4% (1997)
Debt - external: $2 billion (1997)
Economic aid - recipient: $48.4 million (1995)
Currency: 1 Bahraini dinar (BD) = 1,000 fils
Exchange rates: Bahraini dinars (BD) per US$1 - 0.3760 (fixed rate)
Fiscal year: calendar year

Communications

Telephones: 73,552 (1987 est.)
Telephone system: modern system; good domestic services and excellent international connections
domestic: NA
international: tropospheric scatter to Qatar and UAE; microwave radio relay to Saudi Arabia; submarine cable to Qatar, UAE, and Saudi Arabia; satellite earth stations - 2 Intelsat (1 Atlantic Ocean and 1 Indian Ocean) and 1 Arabsat
Radio broadcast stations: AM 2, FM 3, shortwave 0 (1998)
Radios: 320,000 (1993 est.)
Television broadcast stations: 4 (1997)
Televisions: 270,000 (1993 est.)

Transportation

Railways: 0 km
Highways:
total: 3,103 km
paved: 2,374 km
unpaved: 729 km (1997 est.)
Pipelines: crude oil 56 km; petroleum products 16 km; natural gas 32 km
Ports and harbors: Manama, Mina' Salman, Sitrah
Merchant marine:
total: 8 ships (1,000 GRT or over) totaling 228,273 GRT/304,654 DWT
ships by type: bulk 2, cargo 3, container 2, oil tanker 1 (1998 est.)
Airports: 3 (1998 est.)
Airports - with paved runways:
total: 2
over 3,047 m: 2 (1998 est.)
Airports - with unpaved runways:
total: 1
1,524 to 2,437 m: 1 (1998 est.)
Heliports: 1 (1998 est.)

Military

Military branches: Ground Force, Navy, Air Force, Coast Guard, Police Force
Military manpower - military age: 15 years of age

Military manpower - availability:
males age 15-49: 220,670 (1999 est.)
Military manpower - fit for military service:
males age 15-49: 121,451 (1999 est.)
Military manpower - reaching military age annually:
males: NA
Military expenditures - dollar figure: $276.9 million (1994)
Military expenditures - percent of GDP: 4.5% (1998)

Transnational Issues

Disputes - international: territorial dispute with Qatar over the Hawar Islands and maritime boundary dispute with Qatar currently before the International Court of Justice (ICJ)

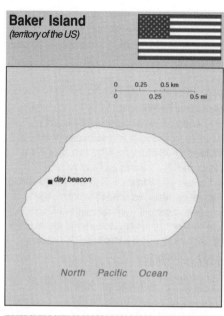

Baker Island
(territory of the US)

Geography

Location: Oceania, atoll in the North Pacific Ocean, about one-half of the way from Hawaii to Australia
Geographic coordinates: 0 13 N, 176 31 W
Map references: Oceania
Area:
total: 1.4 sq km
land: 1.4 sq km
water: 0 sq km
Area - comparative: about 2.5 times the size of The Mall in Washington, DC
Land boundaries: 0 km
Coastline: 4.8 km
Maritime claims:
exclusive economic zone: 200 nm
territorial sea: 12 nm
Climate: equatorial; scant rainfall, constant wind, burning sun
Terrain: low, nearly level coral island surrounded by a narrow fringing reef
Elevation extremes:
lowest point: Pacific Ocean 0 m
highest point: unnamed location 8 m
Natural resources: guano (deposits worked until 1891)
Land use:
arable land: 0%
permanent crops: 0%
permanent pastures: 0%
forests and woodland: 0%
other: 100%
Irrigated land: 0 sq km (1993)
Natural hazards: the narrow fringing reef surrounding the island can be a maritime hazard
Environment - current issues: no natural fresh water resources
Environment - international agreements:
party to: NA
signed, but not ratified: NA
Geography - note: treeless, sparse, and scattered

vegetation consisting of grasses, prostrate vines, and low growing shrubs; primarily a nesting, roosting, and foraging habitat for seabirds, shorebirds, and marine wildlife

People

Population: uninhabited
note: American civilians evacuated in 1942 after Japanese air and naval attacks during World War II; occupied by US military during World War II, but abandoned after the war; public entry is by special-use permit from US Fish and Wildlife Service only and generally restricted to scientists and educators; a cemetery and remnants of structures from early settlement are located near the middle of the west coast; visited annually by US Fish and Wildlife Service

Government

Country name:
conventional long form: none
conventional short form: Baker Island
Data code: FQ
Dependency status: unincorporated territory of the US; administered from Washington, DC by the Fish and Wildlife Service of the US Department of the Interior as part of the National Wildlife Refuge system
Legal system: NA
Flag description: the flag of the US is used

Economy

Economy - overview: no economic activity

Transportation

Ports and harbors: none; offshore anchorage only; note - there is one boat landing area along the middle of the west coast
Airports: 1 abandoned World War II runway of 1,665 m, completely covered with vegetation and unusable
Transportation - note: there is a day beacon near the middle of the west coast

Military

Military - note: defense is the responsibility of the US; visited annually by the US Coast Guard

Transnational Issues

Disputes - international: none

Bangladesh

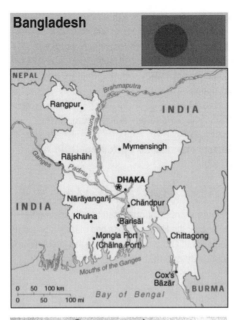

Geography

Location: Southern Asia, bordering the Bay of Bengal, between Burma and India
Geographic coordinates: 24 00 N, 90 00 E
Map references: Asia
Area:
total: 144,000 sq km
land: 133,910 sq km
water: 10,090 sq km
Area - comparative: slightly smaller than Wisconsin
Land boundaries:
total: 4,246 km
border countries: Burma 193 km, India 4,053 km
Coastline: 580 km
Maritime claims:
contiguous zone: 18 nm
continental shelf: up to the outer limits of the continental margin
exclusive economic zone: 200 nm
territorial sea: 12 nm
Climate: tropical; cool, dry winter (October to March); hot, humid summer (March to June); cool, rainy monsoon (June to October)
Terrain: mostly flat alluvial plain; hilly in southeast
Elevation extremes:
lowest point: Indian Ocean 0 m
highest point: Keokradong 1,230 m
Natural resources: natural gas, arable land, timber
Land use:
arable land: 73%
permanent crops: 2%
permanent pastures: 5%
forests and woodland: 15%
other: 5% (1993 est.)
Irrigated land: 31,000 sq km (1993 est.)
Natural hazards: droughts, cyclones; much of the country routinely flooded during the summer monsoon season
Environment - current issues: many people are landless and forced to live on and cultivate flood-prone land; limited access to potable water; water-borne diseases prevalent; water pollution especially of fishing areas results from the use of commercial pesticides; intermittent water shortages because of falling water tables in the northern and central parts of the country; soil degradation; deforestation; severe overpopulation
Environment - international agreements:
party to: Biodiversity, Climate Change, Desertification, Endangered Species, Environmental Modification, Hazardous Wastes, Nuclear Test Ban, Ozone Layer Protection, Wetlands
signed, but not ratified: Law of the Sea

People

Population: 127,117,967 (July 1999 est.)
Age structure:
0-14 years: 38% (male 24,516,722; female 23,346,904)
15-64 years: 59% (male 38,441,064; female 36,586,743)
65 years and over: 3% (male 2,303,613; female 1,922,921) (1999 est.)
Population growth rate: 1.59% (1999 est.)
Birth rate: 25.2 births/1,000 population (1999 est.)
Death rate: 8.5 deaths/1,000 population (1999 est.)
Net migration rate: -0.79 migrant(s)/1,000 population (1999 est.)
Sex ratio:
at birth: 1.06 male(s)/female
under 15 years: 1.05 male(s)/female
15-64 years: 1.05 male(s)/female
65 years and over: 1.2 male(s)/female
total population: 1.06 male(s)/female (1999 est.)
Infant mortality rate: 69.68 deaths/1,000 live births (1999 est.)
Life expectancy at birth:
total population: 60.6 years
male: 60.73 years
female: 60.46 years (1999 est.)
Total fertility rate: 2.86 children born/woman (1999 est.)
Nationality:
noun: Bangladeshi(s)
adjective: Bangladesh
Ethnic groups: Bengali 98%, Biharis 250,000, tribals less than 1 million
Religions: Muslim 88.3%, Hindu 10.5%, other 1.2%
Languages: Bangla (official), English
Literacy:
definition: age 15 and over can read and write
total population: 38.1%
male: 49.4%
female: 26.1% (1995 est.)

Government

Country name:
conventional long form: People's Republic of Bangladesh
conventional short form: Bangladesh
former: East Pakistan

Bangladesh *(continued)*

Data code: BG
Government type: republic
Capital: Dhaka
Administrative divisions: 5 divisions; Barisal, Chittagong, Dhaka, Khulna, Rajshahi
note: there may be one additional division named Sylhet
Independence: 16 December 1971 (from Pakistan)
National holiday: Independence Day, 26 March (1971)
Constitution: 4 November 1972, effective 16 December 1972, suspended following coup of 24 March 1982, restored 10 November 1986, amended many times
Legal system: based on English common law
Suffrage: 18 years of age; universal
Executive branch:
chief of state: President Shahabuddin AHMED (since 9 October 1996); note - the president's duties are normally ceremonial, but with the 13th amendment to the constitution ("Caretaker Government Amendment"), the president's role becomes significant at times when Parliament is dissolved and a caretaker government is installed - at presidential direction - to supervise the elections
head of government: Prime Minister Sheikh HASINA Wajed (since 23 June 1996)
cabinet: Cabinet selected by the prime minister and appointed by the president
elections: president elected by National Parliament for a five-year term; election last held 24 July 1996 (next to be held by NA October 2001); following legislative elections, the leader of the party that wins the most seats is usually appointed prime minister by the president
election results: Shahabuddin AHMED elected president without opposition; percent of National Parliament vote - NA
Legislative branch: unicameral National Parliament or Jatiya Sangsad (330 seats; 300 elected by popular vote from single territorial constituencies, 30 seats reserved for women; members serve five-year terms)
elections: last held 12 June 1996 (next to be held NA 2001)
election results: percent of vote by party - AL 33.87%, BNP 30.87%; seats by party - AL 178, BNP 113, JP 33, JI 3, other 2, election still to be held 1; note - the elections of 12 June 1996 brought to power an Awami League government for the first time in twenty-one years; held under a neutral, caretaker administration, the elections were characterized by a peaceful, orderly process and massive voter turnout, ending a bitter two-year impasse between the former BNP and opposition parties that had paralyzed National Parliament and led to widespread street violence
Judicial branch: Supreme Court, the Chief Justices and other judges are appointed by the president
Political parties and leaders: Bangladesh Nationalist Party or BNP [Khaleda ZIAur Rahman]; Awami League or AL [Sheikh HASINA Wajed]; Jatiyo Party or JP [Hussain Mohammad ERSHAD]; Jamaat-E-Islami or JI [Motiur Rahman NIZAMI];

Bangladesh Communist Party or BCP [Saifuddin Ahmed MANIK]
International organization participation: AsDB, C, CCC, CP, ESCAP, FAO, G-77, IAEA, IBRD, ICAO, ICC, ICFTU, ICRM, IDA, IDB, IFAD, IFC, IFRCS, IHO (pending member), ILO, IMF, IMO, Inmarsat, Intelsat, Interpol, IOC, IOM, ISO, ITU, MINURSO, MONUA, NAM, OIC, OPCW, SAARC, UN, UNCTAD, UNESCO, UNHCR, UNIDO, UNIKOM, UNMIBH, UNMOP, UNMOT, UNOMIG, UNOMIL, UNPREDEP, UNU, UPU, WCL, WFTU, WHO, WIPO, WMO, WToO, WTrO
Diplomatic representation in the US:
chief of mission: Ambassador Khwaja Mohammad SHEHABUDDIN
chancery: 2201 Wisconsin Avenue NW, Washington, DC 20007
telephone: [1] (202) 342-8372
consulate(s) general: Los Angeles and New York
Diplomatic representation from the US:
chief of mission: Ambassador John C. HOLZMAN
embassy: Diplomatic Enclave, Madani Avenue, Baridhara, Dhaka 1212
mailing address: G.P.O. Box 323, Dhaka 1000
telephone: [880] (2) 884700 through 884722
FAX: [880] (2) 883744
Flag description: green with a large red disk slightly to the hoist side of center; the red sun of freedom represents the blood shed to achieve independence; the green field symbolizes the lush countryside, and secondarily, the traditional color of Islam

Economy

Economy - overview: Despite sustained domestic and international efforts to improve economic and demographic prospects, Bangladesh remains one of the world's poorest, most densely populated, and least developed nations. The economy is largely agricultural, with the cultivation of rice the single most important activity in the economy. Major impediments to growth include frequent cyclones and floods, the inefficiency of state-owned enterprises, a rapidly growing labor force that cannot be absorbed by agriculture, delays in exploiting energy resources (natural gas), inadequate power supplies, and slow implementation of economic reforms. Prime Minister Sheikh HASINA Wajed's Awami League government has made some headway improving the climate for foreign investors and liberalizing the capital markets; for example, it has negotiated with foreign firms for oil and gas exploration, better countrywide distribution of cooking gas, and the construction of natural gas pipelines and power plants. Progress on other economic reforms has been halting because of opposition from the bureaucracy, public sector unions, and other vested interest groups. Severe floods, lasting from July to October 1998, endangered the livelihoods of more than 20 million people. Foodgrain production fell by 4 million tons, forcing Dhaka to triple its normal foodgrain imports and placing severe pressure on Bangladesh's balance of payments. The floods increased the country's reliance on large-scale

international aid. So far the East Asian financial crisis has not had major impact on the economy.
GDP: purchasing power parity - $175.5 billion (1998 est.)
GDP - real growth rate: 4% (1998 est.)
GDP - per capita: purchasing power parity - $1,380 (1998 est.)
GDP - composition by sector:
agriculture: 30%
industry: 17%
services: 53% (1997)
Population below poverty line: 35.6% (1995-96 est.)
Household income or consumption by percentage share:
lowest 10%: 4.1%
highest 10%: 23.7% (1992)
Inflation rate (consumer prices): 7% (1998)
Labor force: 56 million
note: extensive export of labor to Saudi Arabia, Kuwait, UAE, and Oman (1996)
Labor force - by occupation: agriculture 65%, services 25%, industry and mining 10% (1996)
Unemployment rate: 35.2% (1996)
Budget:
revenues: $3.8 billion
expenditures: $5.5 billion, including capital expenditures of $NA (1997)
Industries: jute manufacturing, cotton textiles, food processing, steel, fertilizer
Industrial production growth rate: 3.6% (1997)
Electricity - production: 11.5 billion kWh (1997)
Electricity - production by source:
fossil fuel: 97.35%
hydro: 2.65%
nuclear: 0%
other: 0% (1996)
Electricity - consumption: 11.3 billion kWh (1996)
Electricity - exports: 0 kWh (1996)
Electricity - imports: 0 kWh (1996)
Agriculture - products: rice, jute, tea, wheat, sugarcane, potatoes; beef, milk, poultry
Exports: $4.4 billion (1997)
Exports - commodities: garments, jute and jute goods, leather, frozen fish and seafood
Exports - partners: Western Europe 42%, US 30%, Hong Kong 4%, Japan 3% (FY95/96 est.)
Imports: $7.1 billion (1997)
Imports - commodities: capital goods, textiles, food, petroleum products
Imports - partners: India 21%, China 10%, Western Europe 8%, Hong Kong 7%, Singapore 6% (FY95/96 est.)
Debt - external: $16.7 billion (1997)
Economic aid - recipient: $1.475 billion (FY96/97)
Currency: 1 taka (Tk) = 100 poisha
Exchange rates: taka (Tk) per US$1 - 48.500 (January 1999), 46.906 (1998), 43.892 (1997), 41.794 (1996), 40.278 (1995), 40.212 (1994)
Fiscal year: 1 July - 30 June

Bangladesh (continued)

Communications

Telephones: 249,800 (1994 est.)
Telephone system:
domestic: poor domestic telephone service
international: satellite earth stations - 2 Intelsat (Indian Ocean); international radiotelephone communications and landline service to neighboring countries
Radio broadcast stations: AM 12, FM 12, shortwave 2 (one of Bangladesh's two shortwave stations, Bangladesh Betar or Radio Bangladesh, transmits its programs to the world in six languages on four frequencies) (1998)
Radios: NA
Television broadcast stations: 11 (1997)
Televisions: 350,000 (1993 est.)

Transportation

Railways:
total: 2,745 km
broad gauge: 923 km 1.676-m gauge
narrow gauge: 1,822 km 1.000-m gauge (1998 est.)
Highways:
total: 204,022 km
paved: 25,095 km
unpaved: 178,927 km (1996 est.)
Waterways: 5,150-8,046 km navigable waterways (includes 2,575-3,058 km main cargo routes)
Pipelines: natural gas 1,220 km
Ports and harbors: Chittagong, Dhaka, Mongla Port
Merchant marine:
total: 40 ships (1,000 GRT or over) totaling 315,855 GRT/453,002 DWT
ships by type: bulk 2, cargo 33, oil tanker 2, refrigerated cargo 1, roll-on/roll-off cargo 2 (1998 est.)
Airports: 16 (1998 est.)
Airports - with paved runways:
total: 15
over 3,047 m: 1
2,438 to 3,047 m: 2
1,524 to 2,437 m: 4
914 to 1,523 m: 1
under 914 m: 7 (1998 est.)
Airports - with unpaved runways:
total: 1
over 3,047 m: 1 (1998 est.)

Military

Military branches: Army, Navy, Air Force, paramilitary forces (includes Bangladesh Rifles, Bangladesh Ansars, Village Defense Parties, National Cadet Corps)
Military manpower - availability:
males age 15-49: 33,374,195 (1999 est.)
Military manpower - fit for military service:
males age 15-49: 19,772,013 (1999 est.)
Military expenditures - dollar figure: $559 million (FY96/97)
Military expenditures - percent of GDP: 1.8% (FY96/97)

Transnational Issues

Disputes - international: a portion of the boundary with India is indefinite; dispute with India over South Talpatty/New Moore Island
Illicit drugs: transit country for illegal drugs produced in neighboring countries

Barbados

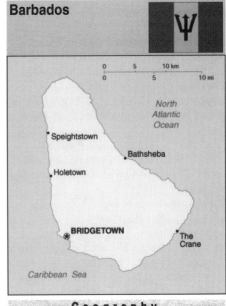

Geography

Location: Caribbean, island between the Caribbean Sea and the North Atlantic Ocean, northeast of Venezuela
Geographic coordinates: 13 10 N, 59 32 W
Map references: Central America and the Caribbean
Area:
total: 430 sq km
land: 430 sq km
water: 0 sq km
Area - comparative: 2.5 times the size of Washington, DC
Land boundaries: 0 km
Coastline: 97 km
Maritime claims:
exclusive economic zone: 200 nm
territorial sea: 12 nm
Climate: tropical; rainy season (June to October)
Terrain: relatively flat; rises gently to central highland region
Elevation extremes:
lowest point: Atlantic Ocean 0 m
highest point: Mount Hillaby 336 m
Natural resources: petroleum, fish, natural gas
Land use:
arable land: 37%
permanent crops: 0%
permanent pastures: 5%
forests and woodland: 12%
other: 46% (1993 est.)
Irrigated land: NA sq km
Natural hazards: infrequent hurricanes; periodic landslides
Environment - current issues: pollution of coastal waters from waste disposal by ships; soil erosion; illegal solid waste disposal threatens contamination of aquifers
Environment - international agreements:
party to: Climate Change, Desertification,

Barbados (continued)

Endangered Species, Hazardous Wastes, Law of the Sea, Marine Dumping, Ozone Layer Protection, Ship Pollution
signed, but not ratified: Biodiversity
Geography - note: easternmost Caribbean island

P e o p l e

Population: 259,191 (July 1999 est.)
Age structure:
0-14 years: 23% (male 30,132; female 29,359)
15-64 years: 67% (male 85,437; female 88,131)
65 years and over: 10% (male 9,862; female 16,270) (1999 est.)
Population growth rate: 0.04% (1999 est.)
Birth rate: 14.46 births/1,000 population (1999 est.)
Death rate: 8.16 deaths/1,000 population (1999 est.)
Net migration rate: -5.86 migrant(s)/1,000 population (1999 est.)
Sex ratio:
at birth: 1.02 male(s)/female
under 15 years: 1.03 male(s)/female
15-64 years: 0.97 male(s)/female
65 years and over: 0.61 male(s)/female
total population: 0.94 male(s)/female (1999 est.)
Infant mortality rate: 16.74 deaths/1,000 live births (1999 est.)
Life expectancy at birth:
total population: 74.98 years
male: 72.22 years
female: 77.81 years (1999 est.)
Total fertility rate: 1.83 children born/woman (1999 est.)
Nationality:
noun: Barbadian(s)
adjective: Barbadian
Ethnic groups: black 80%, white 4%, other 16%
Religions: Protestant 67% (Anglican 40%, Pentecostal 8%, Methodist 7%, other 12%), Roman Catholic 4%, none 17%, other 12%
Languages: English
Literacy:
definition: age 15 and over has ever attended school
total population: 97.4%
male: 98%
female: 96.8% (1995 est.)

G o v e r n m e n t

Country name:
conventional long form: none
conventional short form: Barbados
Data code: BB
Government type: parliamentary democracy
Capital: Bridgetown
Administrative divisions: 11 parishes; Christ Church, Saint Andrew, Saint George, Saint James, Saint John, Saint Joseph, Saint Lucy, Saint Michael, Saint Peter, Saint Philip, Saint Thomas
note: the city of Bridgetown may be given parish status
Independence: 30 November 1966 (from UK)
National holiday: Independence Day, 30 November

(1966)
Constitution: 30 November 1966
Legal system: English common law; no judicial review of legislative acts
Suffrage: 18 years of age; universal
Executive branch:
chief of state: Queen ELIZABETH II (since 6 February 1952), represented by Governor General Sir Clifford Straughn HUSBANDS (since 1 June 1996)
head of government: Prime Minister Owen Seymour ARTHUR (since 6 September 1994); Deputy Prime Minister Billie MILLER (since 6 September 1994)
cabinet: Cabinet appointed by the governor general on the advice of the prime minister
elections: none; the monarch is hereditary monarch; governor general appointed by the monarch; prime minister appointed by the governor general
Legislative branch: bicameral Parliament consists of the Senate (21-member body appointed by the governor general) and the House of Assembly (28 seats; members are elected by direct popular vote to serve five-year terms)
elections: House of Assembly - last held 20 January 1999 (next to be held by January 2004)
election results: House of Assembly - percent of vote by party - NA; seats by party - BLP 26, DLP 2
Judicial branch: Supreme Court of Judicature (judges are appointed by the Service Commissions for the Judicial and Legal Service)
Political parties and leaders: Democratic Labor Party or DLP [David THOMPSON]; Barbados Labor Party or BLP [Owen ARTHUR]; National Democratic Party or NDP [Richard HAYNES]
Political pressure groups and leaders: Barbados Workers Union [Leroy TROTMAN]; People's Progressive Movement [Eric SEALY]; Workers' Party of Barbados [Dr. George BELLE]; Clement Payne Labor Union [David COMMISSIONG]
International organization participation: ACP, C, Caricom, CDB, ECLAC, FAO, G-77, IADB, IBRD, ICAO, ICFTU, ICRM, IFAD, IFC, IFRCS, ILO, IMF, IMO, Intelsat, Interpol, IOC, ISO (correspondent), ITU, LAES, NAM, OAS, OPANAL, UN, UNCTAD, UNESCO, UNIDO, UPU, WFTU, WHO, WIPO, WMO, WTrO
Diplomatic representation in the US:
chief of mission: Ambassador Courtney N. BLACKMAN
chancery: 2144 Wyoming Avenue NW, Washington, DC 20008
telephone: [1] (202) 939-9200
consulate(s) general: Coral Gables (Florida), Miami, and New York
consulate(s): Los Angeles
Diplomatic representation from the US:
chief of mission: Ambassador E. William CROTTY
embassy: Canadian Imperial Bank of Commerce Building, Broad Street, Bridgetown
mailing address: P.O. Box 302, Bridgetown; FPO AA 34055
telephone: [1] (246) 436-4950
FAX: [1] (246) 429-5246

Flag description: three equal vertical bands of blue (hoist side), gold, and blue with the head of a black trident centered on the gold band; the trident head represents independence and a break with the past (the colonial coat of arms contained a complete trident)

E c o n o m y

Economy - overview: Historically, the Barbadian economy had been dependent on sugarcane cultivation and related activities, but production in recent years has diversified into manufacturing and tourism. The start of the Port Charles Marina project in Speightstown helped the tourism industry continue to expand in 1996-98. Offshore finance and informatics are important foreign exchange earners, and there is also a light manufacturing sector. The government continues its efforts to reduce the unacceptably high unemployment rate, encourage direct foreign investment, and privatize remaining state-owned enterprises.
GDP: purchasing power parity - $2.9 billion (1998 est.)
GDP - real growth rate: 3% (1998 est.)
GDP - per capita: purchasing power parity - $11,200 (1998 est.)
GDP - composition by sector:
agriculture: 6%
industry: 15%
services: 79% (1996)
Population below poverty line: NA%
Household income or consumption by percentage share:
lowest 10%: NA%
highest 10%: NA%
Inflation rate (consumer prices): 3.6% (1997)
Labor force: 136,000 (1998 est.)
Labor force - by occupation: services 75%, industry 15%, agriculture 10% (1996 est.)
Unemployment rate: 12% (1998 est.)
Budget:
revenues: $725.5 million
expenditures: $750.6 million, including capital expenditures of $126.3 million (FY97/98 est.)
Industries: tourism, sugar, light manufacturing, component assembly for export
Industrial production growth rate: 0.8% (1996)
Electricity - production: 600 million kWh (1996)
Electricity - production by source:
fossil fuel: 100%
hydro: 0%
nuclear: 0%
other: 0% (1996)
Electricity - consumption: 600 million kWh (1996)
Electricity - exports: 0 kWh (1996)
Electricity - imports: 0 kWh (1996)
Agriculture - products: sugarcane, vegetables, cotton
Exports: $280 million (1997)
Exports - commodities: sugar and molasses, rum, other foods and beverages, chemicals, electrical components, clothing

Barbados (continued)

Exports - partners: Caricom 34.8%, US 18.4%, UK 16.6%, Canada 4.4% (1996)
Imports: $982 million (1997)
Imports - commodities: consumer goods, machinery, foodstuffs, construction materials, chemicals, fuel, electrical components
Imports - partners: US 40.5%, Caricom 14.7%, UK 8.4%, Canada 5% (1996)
Debt - external: $581.4 million (1996)
Economic aid - recipient: $9.1 million (1995)
Currency: 1 Barbadian dollar (Bds$) = 100 cents
Exchange rates: Barbadian dollars (Bds$) per US$1 - 2.0000 (fixed rate pegged to the dollar)
Fiscal year: 1 April - 31 March

Communications

Telephones: 87,343 (1991 est.)
Telephone system:
domestic: island wide automatic telephone system
international: satellite earth station - 1 Intelsat (Atlantic Ocean); tropospheric scatter to Trinidad and Saint Lucia
Radio broadcast stations: AM 2, FM 3, shortwave 0
Radios: NA
Television broadcast stations: 1 (in addition, there are two cable channels) (1997)
Televisions: 69,350 (1993 est.)

Transportation

Railways: 0 km
Highways:
total: 1,650 km
paved: 1,582 km
unpaved: 68 km (1998 est.)
Ports and harbors: Bridgetown, Speightstown (Port Charles Marina)
Merchant marine:
total: 44 ships (1,000 GRT or over) totaling 641,550 GRT/1,087,042 DWT
ships by type: bulk 11, cargo 26, combination bulk 1, oil tanker 4, refrigerated cargo 1, roll-on/roll-off cargo 1
note: a flag of convenience registry; includes ships of 2 countries: Canada owns 2 ships, Hong Kong 1 (1998 est.)
Airports: 1 (1998 est.)
Airports - with paved runways:
total: 1
over 3,047 m: 1 (1998 est.)

Military

Military branches: Royal Barbados Defense Force (includes Ground Forces and Coast Guard), Royal Barbados Police Force
Military manpower - availability:
males age 15-49: 72,111 (1999 est.)
Military manpower - fit for military service:
males age 15-49: 49,600 (1999 est.)
Military expenditures - dollar figure: $NA
Military expenditures - percent of GDP: NA%

Transnational Issues

Disputes - international: none
Illicit drugs: one of many Caribbean transshipment points for narcotics bound for the US and Europe

Bassas da India
(possession of France)

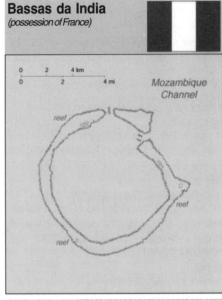

Mozambique Channel

Geography

Location: Southern Africa, islands in the southern Mozambique Channel, about one-half of the way from Madagascar to Mozambique
Geographic coordinates: 21 30 S, 39 50 E
Map references: Africa
Area:
total: 0.2 sq km
land: 0.2 sq km
water: 0 sq km
Area - comparative: about one-third the size of The Mall in Washington, DC
Land boundaries: 0 km
Coastline: 35.2 km
Maritime claims:
exclusive economic zone: 200 nm
territorial sea: 12 nm
Climate: tropical
Terrain: a volcanic rock 2.4 m high
Elevation extremes:
lowest point: Indian Ocean 0 m
highest point: unnamed location 2.4 m
Natural resources: none
Land use:
arable land: 0%
permanent crops: 0%
permanent pastures: 0%
forests and woodland: 0%
other: 100% (all rock)
Irrigated land: 0 sq km (1993)
Natural hazards: maritime hazard since it is usually under water during high tide and surrounded by reefs; subject to periodic cyclones
Environment - current issues: NA
Environment - international agreements:
party to: NA
signed, but not ratified: NA

People

Population: uninhabited

Bassas da India

Government

Country name:
conventional long form: none
conventional short form: Bassas da India
Data code: BS
Dependency status: possession of France; administered by a high commissioner of the Republic, resident in Reunion
Legal system: NA
Diplomatic representation in the US: none (possession of France)
Diplomatic representation from the US: none (possession of France)
Flag description: the flag of France is used

Economy

Economy - overview: no economic activity

Transportation

Ports and harbors: none; offshore anchorage only

Military

Military - note: defense is the responsibility of France

Transnational Issues

Disputes - international: claimed by Madagascar

Belarus

Introduction

Background: For centuries Byelorussia has been fought over, devastated, and partitioned among Russia, Poland, Lithuania, and, in World Wars I and II, Germany. After seven decades as a Soviet republic, the newly named Belarus declared its independence in August 1991. It has retained closer political and economic ties to Russia than any of the other former Soviet republics. On 25 December 1998, Russian President Boris YEL'TSIN and Belarusian President Aleksandr LUKASHENKO signed several agreements intended to provide greater political, economic, and social integration while preserving both states' sovereignty.

Geography

Location: Eastern Europe, east of Poland
Geographic coordinates: 53 00 N, 28 00 E
Map references: Commonwealth of Independent States
Area:
total: 207,600 sq km
land: 207,600 sq km
water: 0 sq km
Area - comparative: slightly smaller than Kansas
Land boundaries:
total: 3,098 km
border countries: Latvia 141 km, Lithuania 502 km, Poland 605 km, Russia 959 km, Ukraine 891 km
Coastline: 0 km (landlocked)
Maritime claims: none (landlocked)
Climate: cold winters, cool and moist summers; transitional between continental and maritime
Terrain: generally flat and contains much marshland
Elevation extremes:
lowest point: Nyoman River 90 m
highest point: Dzyarzhynskaya Hara 346 m
Natural resources: forests, peat deposits, small quantities of oil and natural gas

Land use:
arable land: 29%
permanent crops: 1%
permanent pastures: 15%
forests and woodland: 34%
other: 21% (1993 est.)
Irrigated land: 1,000 sq km (1993 est.)
Natural hazards: NA
Environment - current issues: soil pollution from pesticide use; southern part of the country contaminated with fallout from 1986 nuclear reactor accident at Chornobyl' in northern Ukraine
Environment - international agreements:
party to: Air Pollution, Air Pollution-Nitrogen Oxides, Air Pollution-Sulphur 85, Biodiversity, Environmental Modification, Marine Dumping, Nuclear Test Ban, Ozone Layer Protection
signed, but not ratified: Climate Change, Law of the Sea
Geography - note: landlocked

People

Population: 10,401,784 (July 1999 est.)
Age structure:
0-14 years: 19% (male 1,027,974; female 985,342)
15-64 years: 67% (male 3,390,552; female 3,591,245)
65 years and over: 14% (male 463,369; female 943,302) (1999 est.)
Population growth rate: -0.09% (1999 est.)
Birth rate: 9.7 births/1,000 population (1999 est.)
Death rate: 13.71 deaths/1,000 population (1999 est.)
Net migration rate: 3.13 migrant(s)/1,000 population (1999 est.)
Sex ratio:
at birth: 1.05 male(s)/female
under 15 years: 1.04 male(s)/female
15-64 years: 0.94 male(s)/female
65 years and over: 0.49 male(s)/female
total population: 0.88 male(s)/female (1999 est.)
Infant mortality rate: 14.39 deaths/1,000 live births (1999 est.)
Life expectancy at birth:
total population: 68.13 years
male: 62.04 years
female: 74.52 years (1999 est.)
Total fertility rate: 1.32 children born/woman (1999 est.)
Nationality:
noun: Belarusian(s)
adjective: Belarusian
Ethnic groups: Byelorussian 77.9%, Russian 13.2%, Polish 4.1%, Ukrainian 2.9%, other 1.9%
Religions: Eastern Orthodox 80%, other (including Roman Catholic, Protestant, Jewish, and Muslim) 20% (1997 est.)
Languages: Byelorussian, Russian, other
Literacy:
definition: age 15 and over can read and write
total population: 98%

Belarus (continued)

male: 99%
female: 97% (1989 est.)

Government

Country name:
conventional long form: Republic of Belarus
conventional short form: Belarus
local long form: Respublika Byelarus'
local short form: none
former: Belorussian (Byelorussian) Soviet Socialist Republic
Data code: BO
Government type: republic
Capital: Minsk
Administrative divisions: 6 voblastsi (singular - voblasts') and one municipality* (harady, singular - horad); Brestskaya (Brest), Homyel'skaya (Homyel'), Horad Minsk*, Hrodzyenskaya (Hrodna), Mahilyowskaya (Mahilyow), Minskaya, Vitsyebskaya (Vitsyebsk)
note: administrative divisions have the same names as their administrative centers (exceptions have the administrative center name following in parentheses)
Independence: 25 August 1991 (Belarusian Supreme Soviet declaration of independence from the Soviet Union)
National holiday: Independence Day, 3 July (1944); note - date set by referendum of 24 November 1996; represents Minsk liberation from German occupation
Constitution: 30 March 1994; revised by national referendum of 24 November 1996 giving the presidency greatly expanded powers and became effective 27 November 1996
Legal system: based on civil law system
Suffrage: 18 years of age; universal
Executive branch:
chief of state: President Aleksandr LUKASHENKO (since 20 July 1994)
head of government: Prime Minister Sergey LING (acting since 18 November 1996, confirmed 19 February 1997); First Deputy Prime Ministers Petr PROKOPOVICH (since 23 December 1996) and Vasiliy DOLGOLEV (since 2 December 1998); Deputy Prime Ministers Valeriy KOKOREV (since 23 August 1994), Vladimir ZAMETALIN (since 15 July 1997), Ural LATYPOV (since 30 December 1997), Gennadiy NOVITSKIY (since 11 February 1997), Leonid KOZIK (since 4 February 1997), Aleksandr POPKOV (since 10 November 1998)
cabinet: Council of Ministers
elections: president elected by popular vote for a five-year term; election last held 24 June and 10 July 1994 (next to be held NA; according to the 1994 constitution, the next election should be in 1999, however LUKASHENKO extended his term to 2001 via the November 1996 referendum); prime minister and deputy prime ministers appointed by the president
election results: Aleksandr LUKASHENKO elected president; percent of vote - Aleksandr LUKASHENKO 85%, Vyacheslav KEBICH 15%

note: first presidential elections took place in June-July 1994
Legislative branch: bicameral Parliament or Natsionalnoye Sobranie consists of the Council of the Republic or Soviet Respubliki (64 seats; eight appointed by the president and 56 indirectly elected by deputies of local councils for four-year terms) and the Chamber of Representatives or Palata Pretsaviteley (110 seats; note - present members came from the former Supreme Soviet which LUKASHENKO disbanded in November 1996)
elections: last held May and November-December 1995 (two rounds, each with a run-off; disbanded after the November 1996 referendum; next to be held NA)
election results: after the November 1996 referendum, seats for the Chamber of Representatives were filled by former Supreme Soviet members as follows: PKB 24, Agrarian 14, Party of Peoples Concord 5, LDPB 1, UPNAZ 1, Green World Party 1, Belarusian Social Sports Party 1, Ecological Party 1, Republican Party of Labor and Justice 1, independents 61; 58 of the 64 seats in the Council of the Republic have been appointed/elected
Judicial branch: Supreme Court, judges are appointed by the president; Constitutional Court, half of the judges appointed by the president and half appointed by the Chamber of Representatives
Political parties and leaders: Party of Communists Belarusian or PKB [Sergei KALYAKIN and Vasiliy NOVIKOV, chairmen]; Belarusian Communist Party or KPB [Yetrem SOKOLOV and Viktor CHIKIN, chairmen]; Agrarian Party [Aleksandr PAVLOV, acting chairman]; Belarusian Popular Front or BNF [Levon BARSHEVSKIY, acting chairman]; Civic Accord Bloc (United Civic Party) or CAB [Stanislav BOGDANKEVICH, chairman]; Liberal-Democratic Party or LDPB [Sergei GAYDUKEVICH, chairman]; Belarusian Patriotic Movement (Belarusian Patriotic Party) or BPR [Anatoliy BARANKEVICH, chairman]; Belarusian Labor Party or BPP [Aleksandr BUKHVOSTOV, chairman]; Party of All-Belarusian Unity and Concord or UPNAZ [Dmitriy BULAKOV, chairman]; Belarusian Social-Democrat Hramada or SDBP [Nikolay STATKEVICH, chairman]; Women's Party Nadezhda [Valentina POLEVIKOVA, chairperson]; Green Party of Belarus or BPZ [Nikolay KARTASH, chairman]; Green World Party [Oleg GROMYKO, chairman]; Republican Party of Labor and Justice or RPPS [Anatoliy NETYLKIN, chairman]; Belarus Peasants [Yevgeniy LUGIN, chairman]; Belarusian Social Sports Party or BSSP [Aleksandr ALEKSANDROVICH, chairman]; Ecological Party or BEP [Liudmila YELIZAROVA, chairperson]; Belarusian Socialist Party [Vyacheslav KUZNETSOV]; Savic Assembly Belaya Rus [Nikolai SERGEEV, chairman]; Belarusian Christian-Democratic Unity or BKDZ [Petr SILKO, chairman]; Christian-Democratic Party [Nikolai KRUKOVSKIY, chairman]; Christian-Democratic Choice [Valeriy SOROKA, chairman]; Party of Common Sense [Ivan KARAVAICHIK, chairman];

Belarusian Humanitarian Party [Yevgeniy NOVIKOV, chairman]; Republican Party [Vladimir BELAZOV, chairman]; National Party [Anatoliy ASTAPENKO, chairman]; National Democratic Party [Viktor NAUMENKO, chairman]; People's Party [Viktor TERESCHENKO, chairman]; Belarusian Social-Democratic Party [Stanislav SHUSHKEVICH, chairman]
International organization participation: CCC, CEI, CIS, EAPC, EBRD, ECE, IAEA, IBRD, ICAO, ICRM, IFC, IFRCS, ILO, IMF, Inmarsat, Intelsat (nonsignatory user), Interpol, IOC, IOM (observer), ISO, ITU, OPCW, OSCE, PCA, PFP, UN, UNCTAD, UNESCO, UNIDO, UPU, WFTU, WHO, WIPO, WMO, WTrO (applicant)
Diplomatic representation in the US:
chief of mission: Ambassador (vacant); Charge d'Affaires CHEREPANSKY
chancery: 1619 New Hampshire Avenue NW, Washington, DC 20009
telephone: [1] (202) 986-1604
FAX: [1] (202) 986-1805
consulate(s) general: New York
Diplomatic representation from the US:
chief of mission: Ambassador Daniel V. SPECKHARD (recalled to Washington in June 1998; Charge d'Affaires Randall LE COCQ)
embassy: Starovilenskaya #46-220002, Minsk
mailing address: use embassy street address
telephone: [375] (17) 231-5000
FAX: [375] (17) 234-7853
Flag description: red horizontal band (top) and green horizontal band one-half the width of the red band; a white vertical stripe of white on the hoist side bears the Belarusian national ornament in red

Economy

Economy - overview: Belarus has seen little structural reform since 1995, when President LUKASHENKO launched the country on the path of "market socialism". In keeping with this policy, LUKASHENKO re-imposed administrative controls over prices and currency exchange rates and expanded the state's right to intervene in the management of private enterprise. This produced a climate hostile to private business, inhibiting domestic and foreign investment. The Government of Belarus has artificially revived economic output since mid-1996 by pursuing a policy of rapid credit expansion. In a vain attempt to keep the rapidly rising inflation in check, the government placed strict price controls on food and consumer products, which resulted in food shortages. Long lines for dairy products, chicken, and pork became common in the closing months of 1998. With the goal of slowing down the devaluation of the Belarusian ruble, LUKASHENKO in 1997 introduced a new, complex system of legal buying/selling hard currencies. The new "command" system proved to be totally unworkable and resulted in galloping devaluation. In addition to the burdens imposed on businesses by high inflation and an artificial currency regime, businesses have also been subject to pressure on the part of central and local governments, e.g., arbitrary changes in regulations, numerous rigorous inspections, and retroactive application of new business regulations prohibiting practices that had been legal. A further economic problem is the sizable trade deficit.

GDP: purchasing power parity - $53.7 billion (1998 est.)

GDP - real growth rate: 7% (1998 est.)

GDP - per capita: purchasing power parity - $5,200 (1998 est.)

GDP - composition by sector:
agriculture: 20%
industry: 43%
services: 37% (1997 est.)

Population below poverty line: 77% (1997 est.)

Household income or consumption by percentage share:
lowest 10%: 4.9%
highest 10%: 19.4% (1993)

Inflation rate (consumer prices): 182% (1998)

Labor force: 4.3 million (1998)

Labor force - by occupation: industry and construction 40%, agriculture and forestry 19%, services 41% (1997 est.)

Unemployment rate: 2.3% officially registered unemployed (December 1998); large number of underemployed workers

Budget:
revenues: $4 billion
expenditures: $4.1 billion, including capital expenditures of $180 million (1997 est.)

Industries: tractors, metal-cutting machine tools, off-highway dump trucks up to 110-metric-ton load capacity, wheel-type earth movers for construction and mining, eight-wheel-drive, high-flotation trucks with cargo capacity of 25 metric tons for use in tundra and roadless areas, equipment for animal husbandry and livestock feeding, motorcycles, television sets, chemical fibers, fertilizer, linen fabric, wool fabric, radios, refrigerators, other consumer goods

Industrial production growth rate: 11% (1998 est.)

Electricity - production: 26.1 billion kWh (1998)

Electricity - production by source:
fossil fuel: 99.92%
hydro: 0.08%
nuclear: 0%
other: 0% (1997)

Electricity - consumption: 33.7 billion kWh (1997)

Electricity - exports: 2.7 billion kWh (1997)

Electricity - imports: 10.3 billion kWh (1997)

Agriculture - products: grain, potatoes, vegetables, sugar beets, flax; beef, milk

Exports: $7 billion (f.o.b., 1998)

Exports - commodities: machinery and transport equipment, chemicals, foodstuffs

Exports - partners: Russia, Ukraine, Poland, Germany

Imports: $8.5 billion (c.i.f., 1998)

Imports - commodities: fuel, natural gas, industrial raw materials, textiles, sugar, foodstuffs

Imports - partners: Russia, Ukraine, Poland, Germany

Debt - external: $1.03 billion (1998 est.)

Economic aid - recipient: $194.3 million (1995)

Currency: Belarusian rubel (BR)

Exchange rates: Belarusian rubels per US$1 - 139,000 (25 January 1999 official Belarusian exchange rate), 46,080 (2nd qtr 1998), 25,964 (1997), 15,500 (yearend 1996), 11,500 (yearend 1995), 10,600 (yearend 1994)

Fiscal year: calendar year

Communications

Telephones: 2.55 million (October 1998)

Telephone system: the Ministry of Telecommunications controls all telecommunications through its carrier (a joint stock company) Beltelcom which is a monopoly
domestic: local - Minsk has a digital metropolitan network and a cellular NMT-450 network; waiting lists for telephones are long; local service outside Minsk is neglected and poor; intercity - Belarus has a partly developed fiber-optic backbone system presently serving at least 13 major cities (1998); Belarus's fiber optics form synchronous digital hierarchy rings through other countries' systems; an inadequate analog system remains operational
international: Belarus is a member of the Trans-European Line (TEL), Trans-Asia-Europe Fiber-Optic Line (TAE) and has access to the Trans-Siberia Line (TSL); three fiber-optic segments provide connectivity to Latvia, Poland, Russia, and Ukraine; worldwide service is available to Belarus due to this infrastructure; additional analog lines to Russia; Intelsat, Eutelsat and Intersputnik earth stations

Radio broadcast stations: AM 28, FM 37, shortwave 11

Radios: 3.17 million (1991 est.)

Television broadcast stations: 17 (1997); note - Belarus has a state-run television broadcasting network; independent local television stations exist

Televisions: 9,686,854 (1996)

Transportation

Railways:
total: 5,563 km
broad gauge: 5,563 km 1.520-m gauge (894 km electrified)

Highways:
total: 53,407 km
paved: 52,446 km
unpaved: 961 km (1997 est.)

Waterways: NA km; note - Belarus has extensive and widely used canal and river systems

Pipelines: crude oil 1,470 km; refined products 1,100 km; natural gas 1,980 km (1992)

Ports and harbors: Mazyr

Airports: 118 (1996 est.)

Airports - with paved runways:
total: 36
over 3,047 m: 2
2,438 to 3,047 m: 18
1,524 to 2,437 m: 5
under 914 m: 11 (1996 est.)

Airports - with unpaved runways:
total: 82
over 3,047 m: 1
2,438 to 3,047 m: 6
1,524 to 2,437 m: 4
914 to 1,523 m: 9
under 914 m: 62 (1996 est.)

Military

Military branches: Army, Air Force, Air Defense Force, Interior Ministry Troops, Border Guards

Military manpower - military age: 18 years of age

Military manpower - availability:
males age 15-49: 2,700,034 (1999 est.)

Military manpower - fit for military service:
males age 15-49: 2,115,121 (1999 est.)

Military manpower - reaching military age annually:
males: 79,905 (1999 est.)

Military expenditures - dollar figure: $100 million (1998)

Military expenditures - percent of GDP: 2% (1998)

Transnational Issues

Disputes - international: none

Illicit drugs: limited cultivation of opium poppy and cannabis, mostly for the domestic market; transshipment point for illicit drugs to and via Russia, and to the Baltics and Western Europe

Belgium

Introduction

Background: Belgium became independent from the Netherlands in 1830 and was occupied by Germany during World Wars I and II. In the half century following, it has prospered as a small, modern, technologically advanced European state and member of the European Union. Its unique political circumstance is the long-standing differences between the wealthier Dutch-speaking Flemings of the north and the poorer French-speaking Walloons of the south, differences that are becoming increasingly acute.

Geography

Location: Western Europe, bordering the North Sea, between France and the Netherlands
Geographic coordinates: 50 50 N, 4 00 E
Map references: Europe
Area:
total: 30,510 sq km
land: 30,230 sq km
water: 280 sq km
Area - comparative: about the size of Maryland
Land boundaries:
total: 1,385 km
border countries: France 620 km, Germany 167 km, Luxembourg 148 km, Netherlands 450 km
Coastline: 64 km
Maritime claims:
continental shelf: median line with neighbors
exclusive fishing zone: median line with neighbors (extends about 68 km from coast)
territorial sea: 12 nm
Climate: temperate; mild winters, cool summers; rainy, humid, cloudy
Terrain: flat coastal plains in northwest, central rolling hills, rugged mountains of Ardennes Forest in southeast
Elevation extremes:
lowest point: North Sea 0 m
highest point: Signal de Botrange 694 m
Natural resources: coal, natural gas
Land use:
arable land: 24%
permanent crops: 1%
permanent pastures: 20%
forests and woodland: 21%
other: 34%
Irrigated land: 10 sq km including Luxembourg (1993 est.)
Natural hazards: flooding is a threat in areas of reclaimed coastal land, protected from the sea by concrete dikes
Environment - current issues: the environment is exposed to intense pressures from human activities: urbanization, dense transportation network, industry, intense animal breeding and crop cultivation; air and water pollution also have repercussions for neighboring countries; uncertainties regarding federal and regional responsibilities (now resolved) have impeded progress in tackling environmental challenges
Environment - international agreements:
party to: Air Pollution, Air Pollution-Sulphur 85, Antarctic-Environmental Protocol, Antarctic Treaty, Biodiversity, Climate Change, Desertification, Endangered Species, Environmental Modification, Hazardous Wastes, Law of the Sea, Marine Dumping, Marine Life Conservation, Nuclear Test Ban, Ozone Layer Protection, Ship Pollution, Tropical Timber 83, Tropical Timber 94, Wetlands
signed, but not ratified: Air Pollution-Nitrogen Oxides, Air Pollution-Persistent Organic Pollutants, Air Pollution-Sulphur 94, Air Pollution-Volatile Organic Compounds, Climate Change-Kyoto Protocol
Geography - note: crossroads of Western Europe; majority of West European capitals within 1,000 km of Brussels which is the seat of both the EU and NATO

People

Population: 10,182,034 (July 1999 est.)
Age structure:
0-14 years: 17% (male 895,987; female 853,494)
15-64 years: 66% (male 3,389,572; female 3,318,266)
65 years and over: 17% (male 703,933; female 1,020,782) (1999 est.)
Population growth rate: 0.06% (1999 est.)
Birth rate: 9.98 births/1,000 population (1999 est.)
Death rate: 10.43 deaths/1,000 population (1999 est.)
Net migration rate: 1.01 migrant(s)/1,000 population (1999 est.)
Sex ratio:
at birth: 1.05 male(s)/female
under 15 years: 1.05 male(s)/female
15-64 years: 1.02 male(s)/female
65 years and over: 0.69 male(s)/female
total population: 0.96 male(s)/female (1999 est.)
Infant mortality rate: 6.17 deaths/1,000 live births (1999 est.)
Life expectancy at birth:
total population: 77.53 years
male: 74.31 years
female: 80.9 years (1999 est.)
Total fertility rate: 1.49 children born/woman (1999 est.)
Nationality:
noun: Belgian(s)
adjective: Belgian
Ethnic groups: Fleming 55%, Walloon 33%, mixed or other 12%
Religions: Roman Catholic 75%, Protestant or other 25%
Languages: Flemish 56%, French 32%, German 1%, legally bilingual 11%
Literacy:
definition: age 15 and over can read and write
total population: 99% (1980 est.)
male: NA%
female: NA%

Government

Country name:
conventional long form: Kingdom of Belgium
conventional short form: Belgium
local long form: Royaume de Belgique/Koninkrijk Belgie
local short form: Belgique/Belgie
Data code: BE
Government type: federal parliamentary democracy under a constitutional monarch
Capital: Brussels
Administrative divisions: 10 provinces (French: provinces, singular - province; Flemish: provincien, singular - provincie); Antwerpen, Brabant Wallon, Hainaut, Liege, Limburg, Luxembourg, Namur, Oost-Vlaanderen, Vlaams Brabant, West-Vlaanderen
note: the Brussels Capitol Region is not included within the 10 provinces
Independence: 4 October 1830 (from the Netherlands)
National holiday: National Day, 21 July (ascension of King LEOPOLD I to the throne in 1831)
Constitution: 7 February 1831, last revised 14 July 1993; parliament approved a constitutional package creating a federal state
Legal system: civil law system influenced by English constitutional theory; judicial review of legislative acts; accepts compulsory ICJ jurisdiction, with reservations
Suffrage: 18 years of age; universal and compulsory
Executive branch:
chief of state: King ALBERT II (since 9 August 1993); Heir Apparent Prince PHILIPPE, son of the monarch
head of government: Prime Minister Jean-Luc DEHAENE (since 6 March 1992)
cabinet: Council of Ministers appointed by the monarch and approved by Parliament
elections: none; the monarch is hereditary; prime minister appointed by the monarch and then approved by Parliament
Legislative branch: bicameral Parliament consists

of a Senate or Senaat in Flemish, Senat in French (71 seats; 40 members are directly elected by popular vote, 31 are indirectly elected; members serve four-year terms) and a Chamber of Deputies or Kamer van Volksvertegenwoordigers in Flemish, Chambre des Representants in French (150 seats; members are directly elected by popular vote on the basis of proportional representation to serve four-year terms)

elections: Senate and Chamber of Deputies - last held 21 May 1995 (next to be held in June 1999)

election results: Senate - percent of vote by party - NA; seats by party - CVP 7, SP 6, VLD 6, VU 2, AGALEV 1, VB 3, PS 5, PRL 5, PSC 3, ECOLO 2; note - before the 1995 elections, there were 184 seats; Chamber of Deputies - percent of vote by party - CVP 17.2%, PS 11.9%, SP 12.6%, VLD 13.1%, PRL 10.3%, PSC 7.7%, VB 7.8%, VU 4.7%, ECOLO 4.0%, AGALEV 4.4%, FN 2.3%; seats by party - CVP 29, PS 21, SP 20, VLD 21, PRL 18, PSC 12, VB 11, VU 5, ECOLO 6, AGALEV 5, FN 2; note - before the 1995 elections, there were 212 seats

note: as a result of the 1993 constitutional revision that furthered devolution into a federal state, there are now three levels of government (federal, regional, and linguistic community) with a complex division of responsibilities; this reality leaves six governments each with its own legislative assembly; for other acronyms of the listed parties see Political parties and leaders

Judicial branch: Supreme Court of Justice or Hof van Cassatie in Flemish, Cour de Cassation in French, judges are appointed for life by the Belgian monarch

Political parties and leaders: Flemish Christian Democrats or CVP (Christian People's Party) [Marc VAN PEEL, president]; Francophone Christian Democrats or PSC (Social Christian Party) [Philippe MAYSTADT, president]; Flemish Socialist Party or SP [Fred ERDMAN, president]; Francophone Socialist Party or PS [Philippe BUSQUIN, president]; Flemish Liberal Democrats or VLD [Guy VERHOFSTADT, president]; Francophone Liberal Reformation Party or PRL [Louis MICHEL, president]; Francophone Democratic Front or FDF [Olivier MAINGAIN, president]; Volksunie or VU [Patrik VANKRUNKELSVAN, president]; Vlaams Blok or VB [Frank VANNECKE]; National Front or FN [leader NA]; AGALEV (Flemish Greens) [no president]; ECOLO (Francophone Greens) [no president]; other minor parties

Political pressure groups and leaders: Christian and Socialist Trade Unions; Federation of Belgian Industries; numerous other associations representing bankers, manufacturers, middle-class artisans, and the legal and medical professions; various organizations represent the cultural interests of Flanders and Wallonia; various peace groups such as the Flemish Action Committee Against Nuclear Weapons and Pax Christi

International organization participation: ACCT, AfDB, AsDB, Australia Group, Benelux, BIS, CCC, CE, CERN, EAPC, EBRD, ECE, EIB, EMU, ESA, EU, FAO, G- 9, G-10, IADB, IAEA, IBRD, ICAO, ICC, ICFTU, ICRM, IDA, IEA, IFAD, IFC, IFRCS, IHO, ILO, IMF, IMO, Inmarsat, Intelsat, Interpol, IOC, IOM, ISO, ITU, MTCR, NATO, NEA, NSG, OAS (observer), OECD, OPCW, OSCE, PCA, UN, UNCTAD, UNESCO, UNHCR, UNIDO, UNMOGIP, UNMOP, UNPREDEP, UNRWA, UNTSO, UPU, WCL, WEU, WHO, WIPO, WMO, WTrO, ZC

Diplomatic representation in the US:
chief of mission: Ambassador Alexis REYN
chancery: 3330 Garfield Street NW, Washington, DC 20008
telephone: [1] (202) 333-6900
FAX: [1] (202) 333-3079
consulate(s) general: Atlanta, Chicago, Los Angeles, and New York

Diplomatic representation from the US:
chief of mission: Ambassador Paul CEJAS
embassy: 27 Boulevard du Regent, B-1000 Brussels
mailing address: PSC 82, Box 002, APO AE 09710
telephone: [32] (2) 508-2111
FAX: [32] (2) 511-2725

Flag description: three equal vertical bands of black (hoist side), yellow, and red; the design was based on the flag of France

Economy

Economy - overview: This highly developed private enterprise economy has capitalized on its central geographic location, highly developed transport network, and diversified industrial and commercial base. Industry is concentrated mainly in the populous Flemish area in the north, although the government is encouraging reinvestment in the southern region of Wallonia. With few natural resources, Belgium must import substantial quantities of raw materials and export a large volume of manufactures, making its economy unusually dependent on the state of world markets. Two-thirds of its trade is with other EU countries. Belgium's public debt fell from 127% of GDP in 1996 to 122% of GDP in 1998 and the government is trying to control its expenditures to bring the figure more into line with other industrialized countries. Belgium became a charter member of the European Monetary Union (EMU) in January 1999.

GDP: purchasing power parity - $236 billion (1998 est.)

GDP - real growth rate: 2.8% (1998 est.)

GDP - per capita: purchasing power parity - $23,400 (1998 est.)

GDP - composition by sector:
agriculture: 1.9%
industry: 27.2%
services: 70.9% (1996)

Population below poverty line: NA%

Household income or consumption by percentage share:
lowest 10%: 3.7%
highest 10%: 20.2% (1992)

Inflation rate (consumer prices): 1% (1998 est.)

Labor force: 4.283 million (1997)

Labor force - by occupation: services 69.7%, industry 27.7%, agriculture 2.6% (1992)

Unemployment rate: 12% (1998 est.)

Budget:
revenues: $NA
expenditures: $NA, including capital expenditures of $NA

Industries: engineering and metal products, motor vehicle assembly, processed food and beverages, chemicals, basic metals, textiles, glass, petroleum, coal

Industrial production growth rate: 9.7% (1995)

Electricity - production: 71.066 billion kWh (1996)

Electricity - production by source:
fossil fuel: 41.73%
hydro: 0.33%
nuclear: 57.93%
other: 0.01% (1996)

Electricity - consumption: 75.266 billion kWh (1996)

Electricity - exports: 5.4 billion kWh (1996)

Electricity - imports: 9.6 billion kWh (1996)

Agriculture - products: sugar beets, fresh vegetables, fruits, grain, tobacco; beef, veal, pork, milk

Exports: $145.1 billion (f.o.b., 1998)

Exports - commodities: iron and steel, transportation equipment, tractors, diamonds, petroleum products

Exports - partners: EU 67.2% (Germany 19%), US 5.8% (1994)

Imports: $137.1 billion (f.o.b., 1998)

Imports - commodities: fuels, grains, chemicals, foodstuffs

Imports - partners: EU 75% (Germany 22.1%), US 5% (1997)

Debt - external: $22.3 billion (1998 est.)

Economic aid - donor: ODA, $1 billion (1995)

Currency: 1 Belgian franc (BF) = 100 centimes

Exchange rates: Belgian francs (BF) per US$1 - 34.77 (January 1999), 36.229 (1998), 35.774 (1997), 30.962 (1996), 29.480 (1995), 33.456 (1994)
note: on 1 January 1999, the European Union introduced a common currency that is now being used by financial institutions in some member countries at the rate of 0.8597 euros per US$ and a fixed rate of 40.3399 Belgian francs per euro; the euro will replace the local currency in consenting countries for all transactions in 2002

Fiscal year: calendar year

Communications

Telephones: 5.691 million (1992 est.); 1.7 million cellular telephone subscribers (1998)

Telephone system: highly developed, technologically advanced, and completely automated domestic and international telephone and telegraph facilities
domestic: nationwide cellular telephone system; extensive cable network; limited microwave radio relay network
international: 5 submarine cables; satellite earth

Belgium (continued)

stations - 2 Intelsat (Atlantic Ocean) and 1 Eutelsat
Radio broadcast stations: AM 5, FM 77, shortwave 1 (Belgium's single shortwave station, Radio Vlaanderen Internationaal, transmits its programs internationally in Dutch, English, French, and German, using 21 shortwave frequencies)
Radios: 100,000 (1992 est.)
Television broadcast stations: 24 (in addition, there are Dutch programs on cable, TV-5 Europe by satellite relay, and American Forces Network by relay from Germany) (1997)
Televisions: 3,315,662 (1993 est.)

Transportation

Railways:
total: 3,380 km (2,459 km electrified; 2,563 km double track)
standard gauge: 3,380 km 1.435-m gauge (1996)
Highways:
total: 143,175 km
paved: 143,175 km (including 1,674 km of expressways)
unpaved: 0 km (1996 est.)
Waterways: 2,043 km (1,528 km in regular commercial use)
Pipelines: crude oil 161 km; petroleum products 1,167 km; natural gas 3,300 km
Ports and harbors: Antwerp (one of the world's busiest ports), Brugge, Gent, Hasselt, Liege, Mons, Namur, Oostende, Zeebrugge
Merchant marine:
total: 23 ships (1,000 GRT or over) totaling 35,668 GRT/56,412 DWT
ships by type: bulk 1, cargo 8, chemical tanker 8, oil tanker 6 (1998 est.)
Airports: 42 (1998 est.)
Airports - with paved runways:
total: 24
over 3,047 m: 6
2,438 to 3,047 m: 8
1,524 to 2,437 m: 3
914 to 1,523 m: 1
under 914 m: 6 (1998 est.)
Airports - with unpaved runways:
total: 18
914 to 1,523 m: 2
under 914 m: 16 (1998 est.)
Heliports: 1 (1998 est.)

Military

Military branches: Army, Navy, Air Force, National Gendarmerie
Military manpower - military age: 19 years of age
Military manpower - availability:
males age 15-49: 2,537,544 (1999 est.)
Military manpower - fit for military service:
males age 15-49: 2,098,883 (1999 est.)
Military manpower - reaching military age annually:
males: 64,180 (1999 est.)

Military expenditures - dollar figure: $4.6 billion (1995)
Military expenditures - percent of GDP: 1.7% (1995)

Transnational Issues

Disputes - international: none
Illicit drugs: source of precursor chemicals for South American cocaine processors; transshipment point for cocaine, heroin, hashish, and marijuana entering Western Europe

Belize

Geography

Location: Middle America, bordering the Caribbean Sea, between Guatemala and Mexico
Geographic coordinates: 17 15 N, 88 45 W
Map references: Central America and the Caribbean
Area:
total: 22,960 sq km
land: 22,800 sq km
water: 160 sq km
Area - comparative: slightly smaller than Massachusetts
Land boundaries:
total: 516 km
border countries: Guatemala 266 km, Mexico 250 km
Coastline: 386 km
Maritime claims:
exclusive economic zone: 200 nm
territorial sea: 12 nm in the north, 3 nm in the south; note - from the mouth of the Sarstoon River to Ranguana Cay, Belize's territorial sea is 3 nm; according to Belize's Maritime Areas Act, 1992, the purpose of this limitation is to provide a framework for the negotiation of a definitive agreement on territorial differences with Guatemala
Climate: tropical; very hot and humid; rainy season (May to February)
Terrain: flat, swampy coastal plain; low mountains in south
Elevation extremes:
lowest point: Caribbean Sea 0 m
highest point: Victoria Peak 1,160 m
Natural resources: arable land potential, timber, fish
Land use:
arable land: 2%
permanent crops: 1%
permanent pastures: 2%
forests and woodland: 92%
other: 3% (1993 est.)

Belize (continued)

Irrigated land: 20 sq km (1993 est.)

Natural hazards: frequent, devastating hurricanes (September to December) and coastal flooding (especially in south)

Environment - current issues: deforestation; water pollution from sewage, industrial effluents, agricultural runoff; Hurricane Mitch damage

Environment - international agreements:

party to: Biodiversity, Climate Change, Desertification, Endangered Species, Hazardous Wastes, Law of the Sea, Ozone Layer Protection, Marine Dumping, Ship Pollution, Whaling

signed, but not ratified: none of the selected agreements

Geography - note: national capital moved 80 km inland from Belize City to Belmopan because of hurricanes; only country in Central America without a coastline on the North Pacific Ocean

People

Population: 235,789 (July 1999 est.)

Age structure:

0-14 years: 42% (male 49,991; female 48,074)

15-64 years: 55% (male 65,507; female 63,796)

65 years and over: 3% (male 4,129; female 4,292) (1999 est.)

Population growth rate: 2.42% (1999 est.)

Birth rate: 30.22 births/1,000 population (1999 est.)

Death rate: 5.39 deaths/1,000 population (1999 est.)

Net migration rate: -0.67 migrant(s)/1,000 population (1999 est.)

Sex ratio:

at birth: 1.05 male(s)/female

under 15 years: 1.04 male(s)/female

15-64 years: 1.03 male(s)/female

65 years and over: 0.96 male(s)/female

total population: 1.03 male(s)/female (1999 est.)

Infant mortality rate: 31.57 deaths/1,000 live births (1999 est.)

Life expectancy at birth:

total population: 69.2 years

male: 67.23 years

female: 71.26 years (1999 est.)

Total fertility rate: 3.74 children born/woman (1999 est.)

Nationality:

noun: Belizean(s)

adjective: Belizean

Ethnic groups: mestizo 44%, Creole 30%, Maya 11%, Garifuna 7%, other 8%

Religions: Roman Catholic 62%, Protestant 30% (Anglican 12%, Methodist 6%, Mennonite 4%, Seventh-Day Adventist 3%, Pentecostal 2%, Jehovah's Witnesses 1%, other 2%), none 2%, other 6% (1980)

Languages: English (official), Spanish, Mayan, Garifuna (Carib)

Literacy:

definition: age 14 and over has ever attended school

total population: 70.3%

male: 70.3%

female: 70.3% (1991 est.)

note: other sources list the literacy rate as high as 75%

Government

Country name:

conventional long form: none

conventional short form: Belize

former: British Honduras

Data code: BH

Government type: parliamentary democracy

Capital: Belmopan

Administrative divisions: 6 districts; Belize, Cayo, Corozal, Orange Walk, Stann Creek, Toledo

Independence: 21 September 1981 (from UK)

National holiday: Independence Day, 21 September (1981)

Constitution: 21 September 1981

Legal system: English law

Suffrage: 18 years of age; universal

Executive branch:

chief of state: Queen ELIZABETH II (since 6 February 1952), represented by Governor General Sir Colville YOUNG (since 17 November 1993)

head of government: Prime Minister Said MUSA (since 2 August 1998); Deputy Prime Minister Dean BARROW (since NA July 1993)

cabinet: Cabinet appointed by the governor general on the advice of the prime minister

elections: none; the monarch is hereditary; governor general appointed by the monarch; prime minister appointed by the governor general

Legislative branch: bicameral National Assembly consists of the Senate (eight members; members are appointed for five-year terms, five on the advice of the prime minister, two on the advice of the leader of the opposition, and one after consultation with the Belize Advisory Council - this council serves as an independent body to advise the governor general with respect to difficult decisions such as granting pardons, commutations, stays of execution, the removal of justices of appeal who appear to be incompetent, etc.) and the National Assembly (29 seats; members are elected by direct popular vote to serve five-year terms)

elections: National Assembly - last held 1 August 1998 (next to be held NA August 2003)

election results: percent of vote by party - NA; seats by party - PUP 26, UDP 3

Judicial branch: Supreme Court, the chief justice is appointed by the governor general on advice of the prime minister

Political parties and leaders: People's United Party or PUP [Said MUSA]; United Democratic Party or UDP [Manuel ESQUIVEL, Dean BARROW]; National Alliance for Belizean Rights or NABR [Philip GOLDSON]

Political pressure groups and leaders: Society for the Promotion of Education and Research or SPEAR [Assad SHOMAN]; United Workers Front

International organization participation: ACP, C, Caricom, CDB, ECLAC, FAO, G-77, IADB, IBRD, ICAO, ICFTU, ICRM, IDA, IFAD, IFC, IFRCS, ILO, IMF, IMO, Intelsat (nonsignatory user), Interpol, IOC, IOM (observer), ITU, LAES, NAM, OAS, OPANAL, UN, UNCTAD, UNESCO, UNIDO, UPU, WCL, WHO, WMO, WTrO

Diplomatic representation in the US:

chief of mission: Ambassador James Schofield MURPHY

chancery: 2535 Massachusetts Avenue NW, Washington, DC 20008

telephone: [1] (202) 332-9636

FAX: [1] (202) 332-6888

consulate(s) general: Los Angeles

Diplomatic representation from the US:

chief of mission: Ambassador Carolyn CURIEL

embassy: Gabourel Lane and Hutson Street, Belize City

mailing address: P. O. Box 286, Unit 7401, APO AA 34025

telephone: [501] (2) 77161 through 77163

FAX: [501] (2) 30802

Flag description: blue with a narrow red stripe along the top and the bottom edges; centered is a large white disk bearing the coat of arms; the coat of arms features a shield flanked by two workers in front of a mahogany tree with the related motto SUB UMBRA FLOREO (I Flourish in the Shade) on a scroll at the bottom, all encircled by a green garland

Economy

Economy - overview: The small, essentially private enterprise economy is based primarily on agriculture, agro-based industry, and merchandising, with tourism and construction assuming greater importance. Sugar, the chief crop, accounts for nearly half of exports, while the banana industry is the country's largest employer. The government's tough austerity program in 1997 resulted in an economic slowdown that continued in 1998. The trade deficit has been growing, mostly as a result of low export prices for sugar and bananas. The new government faces important challenges to economic stability. Rapid action to improve tax collection has been promised, but a lack of progress in reigning in spending could bring the exchange rate under pressure.

GDP: purchasing power parity - $700 million (1998 est.)

GDP - real growth rate: 0.5% (1998 est.)

GDP - per capita: purchasing power parity - $3,000 (1998 est.)

GDP - composition by sector:

agriculture: 22%

industry: 22%

services: 56% (1997 est.)

Population below poverty line: NA%

Household income or consumption by percentage share:

lowest 10%: NA%

highest 10%: NA%

Inflation rate (consumer prices): -0.5% (1998 est.)

Labor force: 71,000

note: shortage of skilled labor and all types of technical personnel (1997 est.)

Labor force - by occupation: agriculture 30%,

Belize (continued)

services 16%, government 15.4%, commerce 11.2%, manufacturing 10.3%
Unemployment rate: 13% (1997 est.)
Budget:
revenues: $140 million
expenditures: $142 million, including capital expenditures of $NA (FY97/98 est.)
Industries: garment production, food processing, tourism, construction
Industrial production growth rate: 0.2% (1996 est.)
Electricity - production: 145 million kWh (1996)
Electricity - production by source:
fossil fuel: 100%
hydro: 0%
nuclear: 0%
other: 0% (1996)
Electricity - consumption: 145 million kWh (1996)
Electricity - exports: 0 kWh (1996)
Electricity - imports: 0 kWh (1996)
Agriculture - products: bananas, coca, citrus, sugarcane; lumber; fish, cultured shrimp
Exports: $95.3 million (f.o.b., 1998)
Exports - commodities: sugar 46%, bananas 26%, citrus fruits, clothing, fish products, molasses, wood
Exports - partners: US 45%, UK 30%, Mexico 3%, Canada 3% (1997)
Imports: $149.7 million (c.i.f., 1998)
Imports - commodities: machinery and transportation equipment, manufactured goods, food, fuels, chemicals, pharmaceuticals
Imports - partners: US 52%, Mexico 13%, UK 5% (1997)
Debt - external: $288 million (1996)
Economic aid - recipient: $23.4 million (1995)
Currency: 1 Belizean dollar (Bz$) = 100 cents
Exchange rates: Belizean dollars (Bz$) per US$1 - 2.0000 (fixed rate)
Fiscal year: 1 April - 31 March

Communications

Telephones: 29,000 (1996 est.)
Telephone system: above-average system
domestic: trunk network depends primarily on microwave radio relay
international: satellite earth station - 1 Intelsat (Atlantic Ocean)
Radio broadcast stations: AM 1 (Voice of America relay station), FM 12, shortwave 0 (1998)
Radios: NA
Television broadcast stations: 2 (1997)
Televisions: 27,048 (1993 est.)

Transportation

Railways: 0 km
Highways:
total: 2,248 km
paved: 427 km
unpaved: 1,821 km (1996 est.)
Waterways: 825 km river network used by shallow-draft craft; seasonally navigable

Ports and harbors: Belize City, Big Creek, Corozol, Punta Gorda
Merchant marine:
total: 403 ships (1,000 GRT or over) totaling 1,740,325 GRT/2,511,709 DWT
ships by type: bulk 34, cargo 259, chemical tanker 5, container 9, liquefied gas tanker 1, oil tanker 58, passenger-cargo 2, refrigerated cargo 21, roll-on/roll-off cargo 8, short-sea/passenger 3, specialized tanker 2, vehicle carrier 1
note: a flag of convenience registry; includes ships of 7 countries: Cuba 2, Cyprus 1, Greece 1, Singapore 2, UAE 12, UK 1, and US 1 (1998 est.)
Airports: 44 (1998 est.)
Airports - with paved runways:
total: 3
1,524 to 2,437 m: 1
under 914 m: 2 (1998 est.)
Airports - with unpaved runways:
total: 41
2,438 to 3,047 m: 1
914 to 1,523 m: 10
under 914 m: 30 (1998 est.)

Military

Military branches: Belize Defense Force (includes Ground Forces, Maritime Wing, Air Wing, and Volunteer Guard), Belize National Police
Military manpower - military age: 18 years of age
Military manpower - availability:
males age 15-49: 58,201 (1999 est.)
Military manpower - fit for military service:
males age 15-49: 34,531 (1999 est.)
Military manpower - reaching military age annually:
males: 2,619 (1999 est.)
Military expenditures - dollar figure: $15 million (FY97/98)
Military expenditures - percent of GDP: 2% (FY97/98)

Transnational Issues

Disputes - international: border with Guatemala in dispute
Illicit drugs: transshipment point for cocaine; small-scale illicit producer of cannabis for the international drug trade; minor money-laundering center

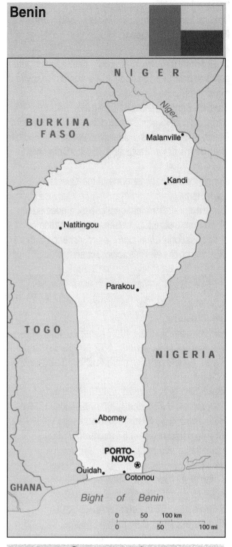

Benin

Geography

Location: Western Africa, bordering the North Atlantic Ocean, between Nigeria and Togo
Geographic coordinates: 9 30 N, 2 15 E
Map references: Africa
Area:
total: 112,620 sq km
land: 110,620 sq km
water: 2,000 sq km
Area - comparative: slightly smaller than Pennsylvania
Land boundaries:
total: 1,989 km
border countries: Burkina Faso 306 km, Niger 266 km, Nigeria 773 km, Togo 644 km
Coastline: 121 km
Maritime claims:
territorial sea: 200 nm
Climate: tropical; hot, humid in south; semiarid in north
Terrain: mostly flat to undulating plain; some hills and low mountains
Elevation extremes:
lowest point: Atlantic Ocean 0 m

highest point: Mont Sokbaro 658 m
Natural resources: small offshore oil deposits, limestone, marble, timber
Land use:
arable land: 13%
permanent crops: 4%
permanent pastures: 4%
forests and woodland: 31%
other: 48% (1993 est.)
Irrigated land: 100 sq km (1993 est.)
Natural hazards: hot, dry, dusty harmattan wind may affect north in winter
Environment - current issues: recent droughts have severely affected marginal agriculture in north; inadequate supplies of potable water; poaching threatens wildlife populations; deforestation; desertification
Environment - international agreements:
party to: Biodiversity, Climate Change, Desertification, Endangered Species, Environmental Modification, Hazardous Wastes, Law of the Sea, Nuclear Test Ban, Ozone Layer Protection
signed, but not ratified: none of the selected agreements
Geography - note: no natural harbors

People

Population: 6,305,567 (July 1999 est.)
Age structure:
0-14 years: 48% (male 1,510,703; female 1,501,437)
15-64 years: 50% (male 1,511,114; female 1,637,155)
65 years and over: 2% (male 62,459; female 82,699) (1999 est.)
Population growth rate: 3.3% (1999 est.)
Birth rate: 45.37 births/1,000 population (1999 est.)
Death rate: 12.4 deaths/1,000 population (1999 est.)
Net migration rate: 0 migrant(s)/1,000 population (1999 est.)
Sex ratio:
at birth: 1.03 male(s)/female
under 15 years: 1.01 male(s)/female
15-64 years: 0.92 male(s)/female
65 years and over: 0.76 male(s)/female
total population: 0.96 male(s)/female (1999 est.)
Infant mortality rate: 97.76 deaths/1,000 live births (1999 est.)
Life expectancy at birth:
total population: 54.08 years
male: 51.98 years
female: 56.24 years (1999 est.)
Total fertility rate: 6.4 children born/woman (1999 est.)
Nationality:
noun: Beninese (singular and plural)
adjective: Beninese
Ethnic groups: African 99% (42 ethnic groups, most important being Fon, Adja, Yoruba, Bariba), Europeans 5,500
Religions: indigenous beliefs 70%, Muslim 15%, Christian 15%

Languages: French (official), Fon and Yoruba (most common vernaculars in south), tribal languages (at least six major ones in north)
Literacy:
definition: age 15 and over can read and write
total population: 37%
male: 48.7%
female: 25.8% (1995 est.)

Government

Country name:
conventional long form: Republic of Benin
conventional short form: Benin
local long form: Republique du Benin
local short form: Benin
former: Dahomey
Data code: BN
Government type: republic under multiparty democratic rule; dropped Marxism-Leninism December 1989; democratic reforms adopted February 1990; transition to multiparty system completed 4 April 1991
Capital: Porto-Novo is the official capital; Cotonou is the seat of government
Administrative divisions: 6 provinces; Atakora, Atlantique, Borgou, Mono, Oueme, Zou
note: six additional provinces have been reported but not confirmed; they are Alibori, Collines, Couffo, Donga, Littoral, and Plateau; moreover, the term "province" may have been changed to "department"
Independence: 1 August 1960 (from France)
National holiday: National Day, 1 August (1990)
Constitution: December 1990
Legal system: based on French civil law and customary law; has not accepted compulsory ICJ jurisdiction
Suffrage: 18 years of age; universal
Executive branch:
chief of state: President Mathieu KEREKOU (since 4 April 1996); note - the president is both the chief of state and head of government
head of government: President Mathieu KEREKOU (since 4 April 1996); note - the president is both the chief of state and head of government
cabinet: Council of Ministers appointed by the president
elections: president elected by popular vote for a five-year term; election last held 18 March 1996 (next to be held NA March 2001)
election results: Mathieu KEREKOU elected president; percent of vote - Mathieu KEREKOU 52.49%, Nicephore SOGLO 47.51%
Legislative branch: unicameral National Assembly or Assemblee Nationale (83 seats; members are elected by direct popular vote to serve four-year terms)
elections: last held 28 March 1995 (next to be held 28 March 1999)
election results: percent of vote by party - NA; seats by party - PRB 20, PRD 19, FARD-ALAFIA 10, PSD 7, NCC 3, RDL-VIVOTEN 3, PCB 2, AC 1, RDP 1, other 17

Judicial branch: Constitutional Court or Cour Constitutionnelle, Supreme Court or Cour Supreme, High Court of Justice
Political parties and leaders: Alliance for Civic Renewal or ARC [leader NA]; Alliance for Democracy and Progress or ADP [Adekpedjou Sylvain AKINDES]; Alliance of the Social Democratic Party or PSD and the National Union for Solidarity and Progress or UNSP [Bruno AMOUSSOU]; Communist Party of Benin or PCB [Pascal FANTONDJI, first secretary]; Democratic Renewal Party or PRD [Adrien HOUNGBEDJI]; Front for Renewal and Development or FARD-ALAFIA [Jerome Sacca KINA]; Liberal Democrats' Rally for National Reconstruction-Vivoten or RDL-Vivoten [Severin ADJOVI]; Parti Ensemble [Albert TEVOEDJRE]
note: as of December 1998, more than 110 political parties were officially recognized; among them are Benin Renaissance Party or PRB, Our Common Cause or NCC, Cameleon Alliance or AC, Rally for Democracy and Pan-Africanism or RDP
International organization participation: ACCT, ACP, AfDB, ECA, ECOWAS, Entente, FAO, FZ, G-77, IBRD, ICAO, ICFTU, ICRM, IDA, IDB, IFAD, IFC, IFRCS, ILO, IMF, IMO, Intelsat, Interpol, IOC, ISO (subscriber), ITU, MINURCA, MIPONUH, NAM, OAU, OIC, OPCW, UN, UNCTAD, UNESCO, UNIDO, UPU, WADB, WAEMU, WCL, WFTU, WHO, WIPO, WMO, WToO, WTrO
Diplomatic representation in the US:
chief of mission: Ambassador Lucien Edgar TONOUKOUIN
chancery: 2737 Cathedral Avenue NW, Washington, DC 20008
telephone: [1] (202) 232-6656
FAX: [1] (202) 265-1996
Diplomatic representation from the US:
chief of mission: Ambassador Robert C. FELDER
embassy: Rue Caporal Bernard Anani, Cotonou
mailing address: B. P. 2012, Cotonou
telephone: [229] 30-06-50, 30-05-13, 30-17-92
FAX: [229] 30-14-39, 30-19-74
Flag description: two equal horizontal bands of yellow (top) and red with a vertical green band on the hoist side

Economy

Economy - overview: The economy of Benin remains underdeveloped and dependent on subsistence agriculture, cotton production, and regional trade. Growth in real output has averaged a sound 4% in 1990-95 and 5% in 1996-98. Rapid population growth has offset much of this growth in output. Inflation has subsided over the past three years. Commercial and transport activities, which make up a large part of GDP, are vulnerable to developments in Nigeria, particularly fuel shortages. Support by the Paris Club and official bilateral creditors has eased the external debt situation in recent years. The government, still burdened with money-losing state enterprises and a bloated civil service, has been gradually implementing a World

Benin (continued)

Bank supported structural adjustment program since 1991.

GDP: purchasing power parity - $7.6 billion (1998 est.)

GDP - real growth rate: 4.4% (1998 est.)

GDP - per capita: purchasing power parity - $1,300 (1998 est.)

GDP - composition by sector:
agriculture: 34%
industry: 14%
services: 52% (1997)

Population below poverty line: 33% (1995 est.)

Household income or consumption by percentage share:
lowest 10%: NA%
highest 10%: NA%

Inflation rate (consumer prices): 5.6% (1998 est.)

Labor force: NA

Unemployment rate: NA%

Budget:
revenues: $299 million
expenditures: $445 million, including capital expenditures of $14 million (1995 est.)

Industries: textiles, cigarettes; beverages, food; construction materials, petroleum

Industrial production growth rate: NA%

Electricity - production: 6 million kWh (1996)

Electricity - production by source:
fossil fuel: 100%
hydro: 0%
nuclear: 0%
other: 0% (1996)

Electricity - consumption: 251 million kWh (1996)

Electricity - exports: 0 kWh (1996)

Electricity - imports: 245 million kWh (1996)

Agriculture - products: corn, sorghum, cassava (tapioca), yams, beans, rice, cotton, palm oil, peanuts; poultry, livestock

Exports: $250 million (f.o.b., 1998)

Exports - commodities: cotton, crude oil, palm products, cocoa

Exports - partners: Brazil 18%, Portugal 11%, Morocco 10%, Libya 6%, France (1997)

Imports: $314 million (f.o.b., 1998)

Imports - commodities: foodstuffs, beverages, tobacco, petroleum products, intermediate goods, capital goods, light consumer goods

Imports - partners: France 21%, UK 9%, Thailand 9%, Hong Kong 8%, China (1997)

Debt - external: $1.6 billion (1996 est.)

Economic aid - recipient: $281.2 million (1995)

Currency: 1 Communaute Financiere Africaine franc (CFAF) = 100 centimes

Exchange rates: CFA francs (CFAF) per US$1 - 566.36 (January 1999), 589.95 (1998), 583.67 (1997), 511.55 (1996), 499.15 (1995), 555.20 (1994)

Fiscal year: calendar year

Communications

Telephones: 38,354 (6,286 cellular telephone subscribers) (1998 est.)

Telephone system:
domestic: fair system of open wire, microwave radio relay, and cellular connections
international: satellite earth station - 1 Intelsat (Atlantic Ocean); submarine cable

Radio broadcast stations: AM 2, FM 9, shortwave 4 (1998 est.)

Radios: 400,000 (1998 est.)

Television broadcast stations: 2 (one privately owned) (1997)

Televisions: 30,000 (1998 est.)

Transportation

Railways:
total: 578 km (single track)
narrow gauge: 578 km 1.000-m gauge (1995 est.)

Highways:
total: 6,787 km
paved: 1,357 km (including 10 km of expressways)
unpaved: 5,430 km (1996 est.)

Waterways: navigable along small sections, important only locally

Ports and harbors: Cotonou, Porto-Novo

Merchant marine: none

Airports: 5 (1998 est.)

Airports - with paved runways:
total: 2
2,438 to 3,047 m: 2 (1998 est.)

Airports - with unpaved runways:
total: 3
1,524 to 2,437 m: 1
914 to 1,523 m: 2 (1998 est.)

Military

Military branches: Armed Forces (includes Army, Navy, Air Force), National Gendarmerie

Military manpower - military age: 18 years of age

Military manpower - availability:
males age 15-49: 1,363,878
females age 15-49: 1,425,987 (1999 est.)
note: both sexes are liable for military service

Military manpower - fit for military service:
males age 15-49: 697,715
females age 15-49: 722,323 (1999 est.)

Military manpower - reaching military age annually:
males: 67,622
females: 67,238 (1999 est.)

Military expenditures - dollar figure: $27 million (1996)

Military expenditures - percent of GDP: 1.2% (1996)

Transnational Issues

Disputes - international: none

Illicit drugs: transshipment point for narcotics associated with Nigerian trafficking organizations and most commonly destined for Western Europe and the US

Bermuda
(overseas territory of the UK)

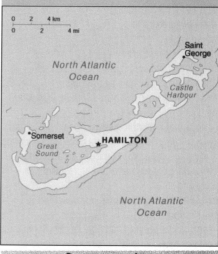

Geography

Location: North America, group of islands in the North Atlantic Ocean, east of North Carolina (US)

Geographic coordinates: 32 20 N, 64 45 W

Map references: North America

Area:
total: 50 sq km
land: 50 sq km
water: 0 sq km

Area - comparative: about 0.3 times the size of Washington, DC

Land boundaries: 0 km

Coastline: 103 km

Maritime claims:
exclusive fishing zone: 200 nm
territorial sea: 12 nm

Climate: subtropical; mild, humid; gales, strong winds common in winter

Terrain: low hills separated by fertile depressions

Elevation extremes:
lowest point: Atlantic Ocean 0 m
highest point: Town Hill 76 m

Natural resources: limestone, pleasant climate fostering tourism

Land use:
arable land: 6%
permanent crops: 0%
permanent pastures: 0%
forests and woodland: 0%
other: 94% (1997 est.)
note: developed (55%) and rural/open space (39%) comprise 94% of Bermudian land area

Irrigated land: NA sq km

Natural hazards: hurricanes (June to November)

Environment - current issues: asbestos disposal; water pollution; preservation of open space

Environment - international agreements:
party to: NA
signed, but not ratified: NA

Geography - note: consists of about 360 small coral

Bermuda *(continued)*

islands with ample rainfall, but no rivers or freshwater lakes; some land, reclaimed and otherwise, was leased by US Government from 1941 to 1995

People

Population: 62,472 (July 1999 est.)
Age structure:
0-14 years: 20% (male 6,174; female 6,023)
15-64 years: 70% (male 21,479; female 22,041)
65 years and over: 10% (male 2,897; female 3,858)
(1999 est.)
Population growth rate: 0.72% (1999 est.)
Birth rate: 11.83 births/1,000 population (1999 est.)
Death rate: 7.27 deaths/1,000 population (1999 est.)
Net migration rate: 2.67 migrant(s)/1,000 population (1999 est.)
Sex ratio:
at birth: 1.05 male(s)/female
under 15 years: 1.03 male(s)/female
15-64 years: 0.97 male(s)/female
65 years and over: 0.75 male(s)/female
total population: 0.96 male(s)/female (1999 est.)
Infant mortality rate: 9.27 deaths/1,000 live births (1999 est.)
Life expectancy at birth:
total population: 76.97 years
male: 75.19 years
female: 78.83 years (1999 est.)
Total fertility rate: 1.71 children born/woman (1999 est.)
Nationality:
noun: Bermudian(s)
adjective: Bermudian
Ethnic groups: black 61%, white and other 39%
Religions: Anglican 28%, Roman Catholic 15%, African Methodist Episcopal (Zion) 12%, Seventh-Day Adventist 6%, Methodist 5%, other 34% (1991)
Languages: English (official), Portuguese
Literacy:
definition: age 15 and over can read and write
total population: 98%
male: 98%
female: 99% (1970 est.)

Government

Country name:
conventional long form: none
conventional short form: Bermuda
Data code: BD
Dependency status: overseas territory of the UK
Government type: NA
Capital: Hamilton
Administrative divisions: 9 parishes and 2 municipalities*; Devonshire, Hamilton, Hamilton*, Paget, Pembroke, Saint George*, Saint Georges, Sandys, Smiths, Southampton, Warwick
Independence: none (overseas territory of the UK)
National holiday: Bermuda Day, 24 May
Constitution: 8 June 1968
Legal system: English law
Suffrage: 18 years of age; universal

Executive branch:
chief of state: Queen ELIZABETH II (since 6 February 1952), represented by Governor Thorold MASEFIELD (since NA June 1997)
head of government: Premier Jennifer SMITH (since 10 November 1998)
cabinet: Cabinet nominated by the premier, appointed by the governor
elections: none; the monarch is hereditary; governor appointed by the monarch; premier appointed by the governor
Legislative branch: bicameral Parliament consists of the Senate (an 11-member body appointed by the governor) and the House of Assembly (40 seats; members are elected by popular vote to serve five-year terms)
elections: last held 9 November 1998 (next to be held NA November 2003)
election results: percent of vote by party - PLP 54%, UBP 44%, NLP 1%, independents 1%; seats by party - PLP 26, UBP 14
Judicial branch: Supreme Court
Political parties and leaders: United Bermuda Party or UBP [Pamela GORDON]; Progressive Labor Party or PLP [Jennifer SMITH]; National Liberal Party or NLP [Charles JEFFERS]
Political pressure groups and leaders: Bermuda Industrial Union or BIU [Derrick BURGESS]; Bermuda Public Services Association or BPSA [Betty CHRISTOPHER]
International organization participation: Caricom (observer), CCC, ICFTU, Interpol (subbureau), IOC
Diplomatic representation in the US: none (overseas territory of the UK)
Diplomatic representation from the US:
chief of mission: Consul General Robert A. FARMER
consulate(s) general: Crown Hill, 16 Middle Road, Devonshire, Hamilton
mailing address: P.O. Box HM325, Hamilton HMBX; American Consulate General Hamilton, Department of State, Washington, DC 20520-5300
telephone: [1] (441) 295-1342
FAX: [1] (441) 295-1592
Flag description: red, with the flag of the UK in the upper hoist-side quadrant and the Bermudian coat of arms (white and blue shield with a red lion holding a scrolled shield showing the sinking of the ship Sea Venture off Bermuda in 1609) centered on the outer half of the flag

Economy

Economy - overview: Bermuda enjoys one of the highest per capita incomes in the world, having successfully exploited its location by providing financial services for international firms and luxury tourist facilities for 360,000 visitors annually. The tourist industry, which accounts for an estimated 28% of GDP, attracts 84% of its business from North America. The industrial sector is small, and agriculture is severely limited by a lack of suitable land. About 80% of food needs are imported. International business contributes over 60% of Bermuda's

economic output; a failed independence vote in late 1995 can be partially attributed to Bermudian fears of scaring away foreign firms.
GDP: purchasing power parity - $1.9 billion (1997 est.)
GDP - real growth rate: 3% (1997 est.)
GDP - per capita: purchasing power parity - $30,000 (1997 est.)
GDP - composition by sector:
agriculture: NA%
industry: NA%
services: NA%
Population below poverty line: NA%
Household income or consumption by percentage share:
lowest 10%: NA%
highest 10%: NA%
Inflation rate (consumer prices): 2.1% (1997)
Labor force: 35,296 (1997)
Labor force - by occupation: clerical 23%, services 22%, laborers 17%, professional and technical 17%, administrative and managerial 12%, sales 7%, agriculture and fishing 2% (1996)
Unemployment rate: NEGL% (1995)
Budget:
revenues: $504.6 million
expenditures: $537 million, including capital expenditures of $75 million (FY97/98)
Industries: tourism, finance, insurance, structural concrete products, paints, perfumes, pharmaceuticals, ship repairing
Industrial production growth rate: NA%
Electricity - production: 480 million kWh (1996)
Electricity - production by source:
fossil fuel: 100%
hydro: 0%
nuclear: 0%
other: 0% (1996)
Electricity - consumption: 480 million kWh (1996)
Electricity - exports: 0 kWh (1996)
Electricity - imports: 0 kWh (1996)
Agriculture - products: bananas, vegetables, citrus, flowers; dairy products
Exports: $57 million (1997)
Exports - commodities: reexports of pharmaceuticals
Exports - partners: Netherlands 50%, Brazil 13%, Canada 6% (1996)
Imports: $617 million (1997)
Imports - commodities: miscellaneous manufactured articles, machinery and transport equipment, food and live animals, chemicals
Imports - partners: US 73%, UK 5%, Canada 4% (1996 est.)
Debt - external: $NA
Economic aid - recipient: $27.9 million (1995)
Currency: 1 Bermudian dollar (Bd$) = 100 cents
Exchange rates: Bermudian dollar (Bd$) per US$1 - 1.0000 (fixed rate)
Fiscal year: 1 April - 31 March

Bermuda (continued)

Communications

Telephones: 54,000 (1991 est.)
Telephone system:
domestic: modern, fully automatic telephone system
international: 3 submarine cables; satellite earth stations - 3 Intelsat (Atlantic Ocean)
Radio broadcast stations: AM 3, FM 3, shortwave 0
Radios: 78,000 (1992 est.)
Television broadcast stations: 3 (1997)
Televisions: 57,000 (1992 est.)

Transportation

Railways: 0 km
Highways:
total: 225 km
paved: 225 km
unpaved: 0 km (1997 est.)
note: in addition, there are 232 km of paved and unpaved roads that are privately owned
Ports and harbors: Hamilton, Saint George
Merchant marine:
total: 97 ships (1,000 GRT or over) totaling 4,647,576 GRT/7,612,686 DWT
ships by type: bulk 18, cargo 3, chemical tanker 1, container 20, liquefied gas tanker 7, oil tanker 27, refrigerated cargo 15, roll-on/roll-off cargo 4, short-sea passenger 2
note: a flag of convenience registry; includes ships from 11 countries among which are UK 24, Canada 12, Hong Kong 11, US 11, Nigeria 4, Sweden 4, Norway 3, and Switzerland 2 (1998 est.)
Airports: 1 (1998 est.)
Airports - with paved runways:
total: 1
2,438 to 3,047 m: 1 (1998 est.)

Military

Military branches: Bermuda Regiment, Bermuda Police Force, Bermuda Reserve Constabulary
Military expenditures - dollar figure: $NA
Military expenditures - percent of GDP: NA%
Military - note: defense is the responsibility of the UK

Transnational Issues

Disputes - international: none

Bhutan

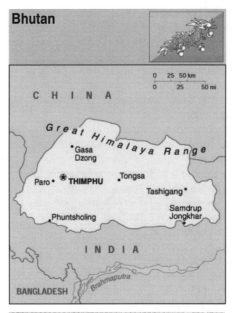

Geography

Location: Southern Asia, between China and India
Geographic coordinates: 27 30 N, 90 30 E
Map references: Asia
Area:
total: 47,000 sq km
land: 47,000 sq km
water: 0 sq km
Area - comparative: about half the size of Indiana
Land boundaries:
total: 1,075 km
border countries: China 470 km, India 605 km
Coastline: 0 km (landlocked)
Maritime claims: none (landlocked)
Climate: varies; tropical in southern plains; cool winters and hot summers in central valleys; severe winters and cool summers in Himalayas
Terrain: mostly mountainous with some fertile valleys and savanna
Elevation extremes:
lowest point: Drangme Chhu 97 m
highest point: Kula Kangri 7,553 m
Natural resources: timber, hydropower, gypsum, calcium carbide
Land use:
arable land: 2%
permanent crops: 0%
permanent pastures: 6%
forests and woodland: 66%
other: 26% (1993 est.)
Irrigated land: 340 sq km (1993 est.)
Natural hazards: violent storms coming down from the Himalayas are the source of the country's name which translates as Land of the Thunder Dragon; frequent landslides during the rainy season
Environment - current issues: soil erosion; limited access to potable water
Environment - international agreements:
party to: Biodiversity, Climate Change, Nuclear Test Ban

signed, but not ratified: Law of the Sea
Geography - note: landlocked; strategic location between China and India; controls several key Himalayan mountain passes

People

Population: 1,951,965 (July 1999 est.)
note: other estimates range as low as 600,000
Age structure:
0-14 years: 40% (male 405,745; female 376,738)
15-64 years: 56% (male 561,754; female 530,420)
65 years and over: 4% (male 39,251; female 38,057) (1999 est.)
Population growth rate: 2.25% (1999 est.)
Birth rate: 36.76 births/1,000 population (1999 est.)
Death rate: 14.26 deaths/1,000 population (1999 est.)
Net migration rate: 0 migrant(s)/1,000 population (1999 est.)
Sex ratio:
at birth: 1.05 male(s)/female
under 15 years: 1.08 male(s)/female
15-64 years: 1.06 male(s)/female
65 years and over: 1.03 male(s)/female
total population: 1.07 male(s)/female (1999 est.)
Infant mortality rate: 109.33 deaths/1,000 live births (1999 est.)
Life expectancy at birth:
total population: 52.75 years
male: 53.19 years
female: 52.29 years (1999 est.)
Total fertility rate: 5.16 children born/woman (1999 est.)
Nationality:
noun: Bhutanese (singular and plural)
adjective: Bhutanese
Ethnic groups: Bhote 50%, ethnic Nepalese 35%, indigenous or migrant tribes 15%
Religions: Lamaistic Buddhism 75%, Indian- and Nepalese-influenced Hinduism 25%
Languages: Dzongkha (official), Bhotes speak various Tibetan dialects, Nepalese speak various Nepalese dialects
Literacy:
definition: age 15 and over can read and write
total population: 42.2%
male: 56.2%
female: 28.1% (1995 est.)
People - note: refugee issue over the presence in Nepal of approximately 91,000 Bhutanese refugees, 90% of whom are in seven United Nations Office of the High Commissioner for Refugees (UNHCR) camps

Government

Country name:
conventional long form: Kingdom of Bhutan
conventional short form: Bhutan
Data code: BT
Government type: monarchy; special treaty relationship with India

Bhutan *(continued)*

Capital: Thimphu

Administrative divisions: 18 districts (dzongkhag, singular and plural); Bumthang, Chhukha, Chirang, Daga, Geylegphug, Ha, Lhuntshi, Mongar, Paro, Pemagatsel, Punakha, Samchi, Samdrup Jongkhar, Shemgang, Tashigang, Thimphu, Tongsa, Wangdi Phodrang

Independence: 8 August 1949 (from India)

National holiday: National Day, 17 December (1907) (Ugyen WANGCHUCK became first hereditary king)

Constitution: no written constitution or bill of rights
note: Bhutan uses 1953 Royal decree for the Constitution of the National Assembly

Legal system: based on Indian law and English common law; has not accepted compulsory ICJ jurisdiction

Suffrage: each family has one vote in village-level elections

Executive branch:
chief of state: King Jigme Singye WANGCHUCK (since 24 July 1972); note - the monarch is both the chief of state and head of government
head of government: King Jigme Singye WANGCHUCK (since 24 July 1972); note - the monarch is both the chief of state and head of government
cabinet: Council of Ministers (Lhengye Shungtsog) appointed by the monarch, approved by the National Assembly
note: there is also a Royal Advisory Council (Lodoi Tsokde), members nominated by the monarch
elections: none; the monarch is hereditary

Legislative branch: unicameral National Assembly or Tshogdu (150 seats; 105 elected from village constituencies, 10 represent religious bodies, and 35 are designated by the monarch to represent government and other secular interests; members serve three-year terms)
elections: last held NA (next to be held NA)
election results: NA

Judicial branch: the Supreme Court of Appeal is the monarch; High Court, judges appointed by the monarch

Political parties and leaders: no legal parties

Political pressure groups and leaders: United Front for Democracy (exiled); Buddhist clergy; Indian merchant community; ethnic Nepalese organizations leading militant antigovernment campaign

International organization participation: AsDB, CP, ESCAP, FAO, G-77, IBRD, ICAO, IDA, IFAD, IMF, Intelsat, IOC, ITU, NAM, OPCW, SAARC, UN, UNCTAD, UNESCO, UNIDO, UPU, WHO, WIPO

Diplomatic representation in the US: none; note - Bhutan has a Permanent Mission to the UN; address: 2 United Nations Plaza, 27th Floor, New York, NY 10017; telephone [1] (212) 826-1919; the Bhutanese mission to the UN has consular jurisdiction in the US
consulate(s) general: New York

Diplomatic representation from the US: the US and Bhutan have no formal diplomatic relations, although informal contact is maintained between the Bhutanese and US Embassy in New Delhi (India)

Flag description: divided diagonally from the lower hoist side corner; the upper triangle is yellow and the lower triangle is orange; centered along the dividing line is a large black and white dragon facing away from the hoist side

Economy

Economy - overview: The economy, one of the world's smallest and least developed, is based on agriculture and forestry, which provide the main livelihood for 90% of the population and account for about 40% of GDP. Agriculture consists largely of subsistence farming and animal husbandry. Rugged mountains dominate the terrain and make the building of roads and other infrastructure difficult and expensive. The economy is closely aligned with India's through strong trade and monetary links. The industrial sector is technologically backward, with most production of the cottage industry type. Most development projects, such as road construction, rely on Indian migrant labor. Bhutan's hydropower potential and its attraction for tourists are key resources. The Bhutanese Government has made some progress in expanding the nation's productive base and improving social welfare. Model education, social, and environment programs in Bhutan are underway with support from multilateral development organizations. Each economic program takes into account the government's desire to protect the country's environment and cultural traditions. Detailed controls and uncertain policies in areas like industrial licensing, trade, labor, and finance continue to hamper foreign investment.

GDP: purchasing power parity - $1.9 billion (1998 est.)

GDP - real growth rate: 6.5% (1998 est.)

GDP - per capita: purchasing power parity - $1,000 (1998 est.)

GDP - composition by sector:
agriculture: 38%
industry: 38%
services: 24% (1997)

Population below poverty line: NA%

Household income or consumption by percentage share:
lowest 10%: NA%
highest 10%: NA%

Inflation rate (consumer prices): 7.4% (1997 est.)

Labor force: NA
note: massive lack of skilled labor

Labor force - by occupation: agriculture 93%, services 5%, industry and commerce 2%

Unemployment rate: NA%

Budget:
revenues: $146 million
expenditures: $152 million, including capital expenditures of $NA (FY95/96 est.)
note: the government of India finances nearly three-fifths of Bhutan's budget expenditures

Industries: cement, wood products, processed fruits, alcoholic beverages, calcium carbide

Industrial production growth rate: 9.3% (1996 est.)

Electricity - production: 1.717 billion kWh (1996)
note: exports electricity to India

Electricity - production by source:
fossil fuel: 0.41%
hydro: 99.59%
nuclear: 0%
other: 0% (1996)

Electricity - consumption: 246 million kWh (1996)

Electricity - exports: 1.475 billion kWh (1996)

Electricity - imports: 4 million kWh (1996)

Agriculture - products: rice, corn, root crops, citrus, foodgrains; dairy products, eggs

Exports: $99 million (f.o.b., 1997 est.)

Exports - commodities: cardamom, gypsum, timber, handicrafts, cement, fruit, electricity (to India), precious stones, spices

Exports - partners: India 94%, Bangladesh

Imports: $131 million (c.i.f., 1997 est.)

Imports - commodities: fuel and lubricants, grain, machinery and parts, vehicles, fabrics, rice

Imports - partners: India 77%, Japan, UK, Germany, US

Debt - external: $87 million (1996)

Economic aid - recipient: $73.8 million (1995)

Currency: 1 ngultrum (Nu) = 100 chetrum; note - Indian currency is also legal tender

Exchange rates: ngultrum (Nu) per US$1 - 42.508 (January 1999), 41.259 (1998), 36.313 (1997), 35.433 (1996), 32.427 (1995), 31.374 (1994); note - the Bhutanese ngultrum is at par with the Indian rupee

Fiscal year: 1 July - 30 June

Communications

Telephones: 4,620 (1991 est.)

Telephone system:
domestic: domestic telephone service is very poor with very few telephones in use
international: international telephone and telegraph service is by landline through India; a satellite earth station was planned (1990)

Radio broadcast stations: AM 0, FM 1, shortwave 1 (1998)

Radios: 23,000 (1989 est.)

Television broadcast stations: 0 (1997)

Televisions: 200 (1985 est.)

Transportation

Railways: 0 km

Highways:
total: 3,285 km
paved: 1,994 km
unpaved: 1,291 km (1996 est.)

Ports and harbors: none

Airports: 2 (1998 est.)

Airports - with paved runways:
total: 1
1,524 to 2,437 m: 1 (1998 est.)

Airports - with unpaved runways:
total: 1
914 to 1,523 m: 1 (1998 est.)

Bhutan (continued)

Military branches: Royal Bhutan Army, Palace Guard, Militia, Royal Police Force
Military manpower - military age: 18 years of age
Military manpower - availability:
males age 15-49: 477,944 (1999 est.)
Military manpower - fit for military service:
males age 15-49: 254,992 (1999 est.)
Military manpower - reaching military age annually:
males: 19,424 (1999 est.)
Military expenditures - dollar figure: $NA
Military expenditures - percent of GDP: NA%

Transnational Issues

Disputes - international: with Nepal over 91,000 Bhutanese refugees in Nepal

Bolivia

Introduction

Background: Bolivia broke away from Spanish rule in 1825. Its subsequent history has been marked by a seemingly endless series of coups, counter-coups, and abrupt changes in leaders and policies. Comparatively democratic civilian rule was established in the 1980s, but the leaders have faced difficult problems of deep-seated poverty, social unrest, strikes, and drug dealing. Current issues include encouraging and negotiating the terms for foreign investment; strengthening the educational system; continuing the privatization program; pursuing judicial reform and an anti-corruption campaign.

Geography

Location: Central South America, southwest of Brazil
Geographic coordinates: 17 00 S, 65 00 W
Map references: South America
Area:
total: 1,098,580 sq km
land: 1,084,390 sq km
water: 14,190 sq km
Area - comparative: slightly less than three times the size of Montana
Land boundaries:
total: 6,743 km
border countries: Argentina 832 km, Brazil 3,400 km, Chile 861 km, Paraguay 750 km, Peru 900 km
Coastline: 0 km (landlocked)
Maritime claims: none (landlocked)
Climate: varies with altitude; humid and tropical to cold and semiarid
Terrain: rugged Andes Mountains with a highland plateau (Altiplano), hills, lowland plains of the Amazon Basin
Elevation extremes:
lowest point: Rio Paraguay 90 m
highest point: Nevado Sajama 6,542 m

Natural resources: tin, natural gas, petroleum, zinc, tungsten, antimony, silver, iron, lead, gold, timber
Land use:
arable land: 2%
permanent crops: 0%
permanent pastures: 24%
forests and woodland: 53%
other: 21% (1993 est.)
Irrigated land: 1,750 sq km (1993 est.)
Natural hazards: cold, thin air of high plateau is obstacle to efficient fuel combustion, as well as to physical activity by those unaccustomed to it from birth; flooding in the northeast (March-April)
Environment - current issues: the clearing of land for agricultural purposes and the international demand for tropical timber are contributing to deforestation; soil erosion from overgrazing and poor cultivation methods (including slash-and-burn agriculture); desertification; loss of biodiversity; industrial pollution of water supplies used for drinking and irrigation
Environment - international agreements:
party to: Biodiversity, Climate Change, Desertification, Endangered Species, Hazardous Wastes, Law of the Sea, Nuclear Test Ban, Tropical Timber 83, Tropical Timber 94
signed, but not ratified: Climate Change-Kyoto Protocol, Environmental Modification, Marine Dumping, Marine Life Conservation, Ozone Layer Protection
Geography - note: landlocked; shares control of Lago Titicaca, world's highest navigable lake (elevation 3,805 m), with Peru

People

Population: 7,982,850 (July 1999 est.)
Age structure:
0-14 years: 39% (male 1,573,391; female 1,540,123)
15-64 years: 56% (male 2,199,077; female 2,307,490)
65 years and over: 5% (male 164,213; female 198,556) (1999 est.)
Population growth rate: 1.96% (1999 est.)
Birth rate: 30.72 births/1,000 population (1999 est.)
Death rate: 9.61 deaths/1,000 population (1999 est.)
Net migration rate: -1.5 migrant(s)/1,000 population (1999 est.)
Sex ratio:
at birth: 1.05 male(s)/female
under 15 years: 1.02 male(s)/female
15-64 years: 0.95 male(s)/female
65 years and over: 0.83 male(s)/female
total population: 0.97 male(s)/female (1999 est.)
Infant mortality rate: 62.02 deaths/1,000 live births (1999 est.)
Life expectancy at birth:
total population: 61.43 years
male: 58.51 years
female: 64.51 years (1999 est.)
Total fertility rate: 3.93 children born/woman (1999 est.)
Nationality:
noun: Bolivian(s)

adjective: Bolivian

Ethnic groups: Quechua 30%, Aymara 25%, mestizo (mixed white and Amerindian ancestry) 30%, white 15%

Religions: Roman Catholic 95%, Protestant (Evangelical Methodist)

Languages: Spanish (official), Quechua (official), Aymara (official)

Literacy:

definition: age 15 and over can read and write

total population: 83.1%

male: 90.5%

female: 76% (1995 est.)

Government

Country name:

conventional long form: Republic of Bolivia

conventional short form: Bolivia

local long form: Republica de Bolivia

local short form: Bolivia

Data code: BL

Government type: republic

Capital: La Paz (seat of government); Sucre (legal capital and seat of judiciary)

Administrative divisions: 9 departments (departamentos, singular - departamento); Chuquisaca, Cochabamba, Beni, La Paz, Oruro, Pando, Potosi, Santa Cruz, Tarija

Independence: 6 August 1825 (from Spain)

National holiday: Independence Day, 6 August (1825)

Constitution: 2 February 1967; revised in August 1994

Legal system: based on Spanish law and Napoleonic Code; has not accepted compulsory ICJ jurisdiction

Suffrage: 18 years of age, universal and compulsory (married); 21 years of age, universal and compulsory (single)

Executive branch:

chief of state: President Hugo BANZER Suarez (since 6 August 1997); Vice President Jorge Fernando QUIROGA Ramirez (since 6 August 1997); note - the president is both the chief of state and head of government

head of government: President Hugo BANZER Suarez (since 6 August 1997); Vice President Jorge Fernando QUIROGA Ramirez (since 6 August 1997); note - the president is both the chief of state and head of government

cabinet: Cabinet appointed by the president from a panel of candidates proposed by the Senate

elections: president and vice president elected on the same ticket by popular vote for five-year terms; election last held 1 June 1997 (next to be held June 2002)

election results: Hugo BANZER Suarez elected president; percent of vote - Hugo BANZER Suarez (ADN) 22%; Jaime PAZ Zamora (MIR) 17%, Juan Carlos DURAN (MNR) 18%, Ivo KULJIS (UCS) 16%, Remedios LOZA (CONDEPA) 17%; no candidate received a majority of the popular vote; Hugo

BANZER Suarez won a congressional runoff election on 5 August 1997 after forming a "megacoalition" with MIR, UCS, CONDEPA, NFR and PDC

Legislative branch: bicameral National Congress or Congreso Nacional consists of Chamber of Senators or Camara de Senadores (27 seats; members are directly elected by popular vote to serve five-year terms) and Chamber of Deputies or Camara de Diputados (130 seats; members are directly elected by popular vote to serve five-year terms)

elections: Chamber of Senators and Chamber of Deputies - last held 1 June 1997 (next to be held June 2002)

election results: Chamber of Senators - percent of vote by party - NA; seats by party - ADN 11, MIR 7, MNR 4, CONDEPA 3, UCS 2; Chamber of Deputies - percent of vote by party - NA; seats by party - ADN 32, MNR 26, MIR 23, UCS 21, CONDEPA 19, MBL 5, IU 4

Judicial branch: Supreme Court (Corte Suprema), judges appointed for a 10-year term by National Congress

Political parties and leaders:

Left Parties: Free Bolivia Movement or MBL [Antonio ARANIBAR]; Patriotic Axis of Convergence or EJE-P [Ramiro BARRANECHEA]; April 9 Revolutionary Vanguard or VR-9 [Carlos SERRATE]; Alternative of Democratic Socialism or ASD [Jerjes JUSTINIANO]; Revolutionary Front of the Left or FRI [Oscar ZAMORA]; Bolivian Communist Party or PCB [Marcos DOMIC]; United Left or IU [Marcos DOMIC]; Front of National Salvation or FSN [Manual MORALES Davila]; Socialist Party One or PS-1 [leader NA]; Bolivian Socialist Falange or FSB [leader NA]; Socialist Unzaguista Movement or MAS [leader NA]

Center-Left Parties: Movement of the Revolutionary Left or MIR [Oscar EID]; Christian Democrat or PDC [Benjamin MIGUEL]; New Youth Force [Alfonso SAAVEDRA Bruno]

Center Party: Nationalist Revolutionary Movement or MNR [Gonzalo SANCHEZ DE LOZADA]

Center-Right Parties: Nationalist Democratic Action or ADN [Enrique TORO]; New Republican Force or NFR [Manfred REYES VILLA]

Populist Parties: Civic Solidarity Union or UCS [Johnny FERNANDEZ]; Conscience of the Fatherland or CONDEPA [Remedios LOZA Alvarado]; Solidarity and Democracy or SYD [leader NA]; Unity and Progress Movement or MUP [Ivo KULJIS]; Popular Patriotic Movement or MPP [Julio MANTILLA]

Evangelical Party: Bolivian Renovating Alliance or ARBOL [Marcelo FERNANDEZ, Hugo VILLEGAS]

Indigenous Parties: Tupac Katari Revolutionary Liberation Movement or MRTK-L [Victor Hugo CARDENAS Conde]; Nationalist Katarista Movement or MKN [Fernando UNTOJA]; Front of Katarista Unity or FULKA [Genaro FLORES]; Katarismo National Unity or KND [Filepe KITTELSON]

International organization participation: CAN, ECLAC, FAO, G-11, G-77, IADB, IAEA, IBRD, ICAO, ICRM, IDA, IFAD, IFC, IFRCS, ILO, IMF, IMO, Intelsat, Interpol, IOC, IOM, ISO (correspondent), ITU, LAES, LAIA, NAM, OAS, OPANAL, OPCW, PCA, RG,

UN, UNCTAD, UNESCO, UNIDO, UPU, WCL, WFTU, WHO, WIPO, WMO, WToO, WTrO

Diplomatic representation in the US:

chief of mission: Ambassador Marcelo PEREZ Monasterios

chancery: 3014 Massachusetts Avenue NW, Washington, DC 20008

telephone: [1] (202) 483-4410

FAX: [1] (202) 328-3712

consulate(s) general: Los Angeles, Miami, New York, and San Francisco

Diplomatic representation from the US:

chief of mission: Ambassador Donna Jean HRINAK

embassy: Avenida Arce 2780, San Jorge, La Paz

mailing address: P. O. Box 425, La Paz; APO AA 34032

telephone: [591] (2) 430251

FAX: [591] (2) 433900

Flag description: three equal horizontal bands of red (top), yellow, and green with the coat of arms centered on the yellow band; similar to the flag of Ghana, which has a large black five-pointed star centered in the yellow band

Economy

Economy - overview: With its long history of semifeudal social controls, dependence on mineral exports, and bouts of hyperinflation, Bolivia has remained one of the poorest and least developed Latin American countries. However, Bolivia has experienced generally improving economic conditions since the PAZ Estenssoro administration (1985-89) introduced market-oriented policies which reduced inflation from 11,700% in 1985 to about 20% in 1988. PAZ Estenssoro was followed as president by Jaime PAZ Zamora (1989-93) who continued the free-market policies of his predecessor, despite opposition from his own party and from Bolivia's once powerful labor movement. President SANCHEZ DE LOZADA (1993-1997) vowed to advance the market-oriented economic reforms he helped launch as PAZ Estenssoro's planning minister. His successes included the signing of a free trade agreement with Mexico and the Southern Cone Common Market (Mercosur) as well as the privatization of the state airline, telephone company, railroad, electric power company, and oil company. Hugo BANZER Suarez has tried to further improve the country's investment climate with an anticorruption campaign. With the scheduled completion of a $2 billion natural gas pipeline to Brazil in 1999, Bolivia hopes to become an energy hub in the region.

GDP: purchasing power parity - $23.4 billion (1998 est.)

GDP - real growth rate: 4.7% (1998 est.)

GDP - per capita: purchasing power parity - $3,000 (1998 est.)

GDP - composition by sector:

agriculture: 17%

industry: 26%

services: 57% (1995 est.)

Population below poverty line: 66%

Bolivia (continued)

Household income or consumption by percentage share:
lowest 10%: 2.3%
highest 10%: 31.7% (1990)
Inflation rate (consumer prices): 4.4% (1998 est.)
Labor force: 2.5 million
Labor force - by occupation: agriculture NA%, services and utilities NA%, manufacturing, mining and construction NA%
Unemployment rate: 11.4% (1997) with widespread underemployment
Budget:
revenues: $2.7 billion
expenditures: $2.7 billion (1998)
Industries: mining, smelting, petroleum, food and beverages, tobacco, handicrafts, clothing
Industrial production growth rate: 4% (1995 est.)
Electricity - production: 2.95 billion kWh (1996)
Electricity - production by source:
fossil fuel: 40.68%
hydro: 59.32%
nuclear: 0%
other: 0% (1996)
Electricity - consumption: 2.948 billion kWh (1996)
Electricity - exports: 2 million kWh (1996)
Electricity - imports: 0 kWh (1996)
Agriculture - products: soybeans, coffee, coca, cotton, corn, sugarcane, rice, potatoes; timber
Exports: $1.1 billion (f.o.b., 1998 est.)
Exports - commodities: metals 34%, natural gas 9.4%, soybeans 8.4%, jewelry 11%, wood 6.9%
Exports - partners: US 22%, UK 9.3%, Colombia 8.7%, Peru 7.4%, Argentina 7.2%
Imports: $1.7 billion (c.i.f. 1998)
Imports - commodities: capital goods 48%, chemicals 11%, petroleum 5%, food 5% (1993 est.)
Imports - partners: US 20%, Japan 13%, Brazil 12, Chile 7.5% (1996)
Debt - external: $4.1 billion (1998)
Economic aid - recipient: $588 million (1997)
Currency: 1 boliviano ($B) = 100 centavos
Exchange rates: bolivianos ($B) per US$1 - 5.6491 (January 1999), 5.5101 (1998), 5.2543 (1997), 5.0746 (1996), 4.8003 (1995), 4.6205 (1994)
Fiscal year: calendar year

Communications

Telephones: 144,300 (1987 est.)
Telephone system: new subscribers face bureaucratic difficulties; most telephones are concentrated in La Paz and other cities
domestic: microwave radio relay system being expanded
international: satellite earth station - 1 Intelsat (Atlantic Ocean)
Radio broadcast stations: AM 177, FM 68, shortwave 112 (1998)
Radios: NA
Television broadcast stations: 48 (1997)
Televisions: 500,000 (1993 est.)

Transportation

Railways:
total: 3,691 km (single track)
narrow gauge: 3,652 km 1.000-m gauge; 39 km 0.760-m gauge (13 km electrified) (1995)
Highways:
total: 52,216 km
paved: 2,872 km (including 27 km of expressways)
unpaved: 49,344 km (1995 est.)
Waterways: 10,000 km of commercially navigable waterways
Pipelines: crude oil 1,800 km; petroleum products 580 km; natural gas 1,495 km
Ports and harbors: none; however, Bolivia has free port privileges in the maritime ports of Argentina, Brazil, Chile, and Paraguay
Merchant marine:
total: 6 ships (1,000 GRT or over) totaling 34,948 GRT/58,472 DWT
ships by type: bulk 1, cargo 5 (1998 est.)
Airports: 1,130 (1998 est.)
Airports - with paved runways:
total: 12
over 3,047 m: 4
2,438 to 3,047 m: 3
1,524 to 2,437 m: 4
914 to 1,523 m: 1 (1998 est.)
Airports - with unpaved runways:
total: 1,118
2,438 to 3,047 m: 3
1,524 to 2,437 m: 70
914 to 1,523 m: 224
under 914 m: 821 (1998 est.)

Military

Military branches: Army (Ejercito Boliviano), Navy (Fuerza Naval Boliviana, includes Marines), Air Force (Fuerza Aerea Boliviana), National Police Force (Policia Nacional de Bolivia)
Military manpower - military age: 19 years of age
Military manpower - availability:
males age 15-49: 1,908,454 (1999 est.)
Military manpower - fit for military service:
males age 15-49: 1,241,311 (1999 est.)
Military manpower - reaching military age annually:
males: 84,481 (1999 est.)
Military expenditures - dollar figure: $154 million (1998)
Military expenditures - percent of GDP: 1.8% (1998)

Transnational Issues

Disputes - international: has wanted a sovereign corridor to the South Pacific Ocean since the Atacama area was lost to Chile in 1884; dispute with Chile over Rio Lauca water rights
Illicit drugs: world's third-largest cultivator of coca (after Peru and Colombia) with an estimated 46,900 hectares under cultivation in 1997, a 2.5% decrease in overall cultivation of coca from 1996 levels; Bolivia, however, is the second-largest producer of coca leaf; even so, farmer abandonment and voluntary and forced eradication programs resulted in leaf production dropping from 75,100 metric tons in 1996 to 73,000 tons in 1997, a 3% decrease from 1996; government considers all but 12,000 hectares illicit; intermediate coca products and cocaine exported to or through Colombia, Brazil, Argentina, and Chile to the US and other international drug markets; alternative crop program aims to reduce illicit coca cultivation

Bosnia and Herzegovina

Introduction

Background: On 21 November 1995, in Dayton, Ohio, the former Yugoslavia's three warring parties signed a peace agreement that brought to a halt over three years of interethnic civil strife in Bosnia and Herzegovina (the final agreement was signed in Paris on 14 December 1995). The Dayton Agreement, signed then by Bosnian President IZETBEGOVIC, Croatian President TUDJMAN, and Serbian President MILOSEVIC, divides Bosnia and Herzegovina roughly equally between the Muslim/Croat Federation and the Republika Srpska while maintaining Bosnia's currently recognized borders. In 1995-96, a NATO-led international peacekeeping force (IFOR) of 60,000 troops served in Bosnia to implement and monitor the military aspects of the agreement. IFOR was succeeded by a smaller, NATO-led Stabilization Force (SFOR) whose mission is to deter renewed hostilities. SFOR remains in place. A High Representative appointed by the UN Security Council is responsible for civilian implementation of the accord, including monitoring implementation, facilitating any difficulties arising in connection with civilian implementation, and coordinating activities of the civilian organizations and agencies in Bosnia. The Bosnian conflict began in the spring of 1992 when the government of Bosnia and Herzegovina held a referendum on independence and the Bosnian Serbs - supported by neighboring Serbia - responded with armed resistance aimed at partitioning the republic along ethnic lines and joining Serb-held areas to form a "greater Serbia." In March 1994, Bosnia's Muslims and Croats reduced the number of warring factions from three to two by signing an agreement in Washington creating their joint Muslim/Croat Federation of Bosnia and Herzegovina. The Federation, formed by the Muslims and Croats in March 1994, is one of two entities (the other being the Bosnian Serb-led Republika Srpska) that comprise Bosnia and Herzegovina.

Geography

Location: Southeastern Europe, bordering the Adriatic Sea and Croatia
Geographic coordinates: 44 00 N, 18 00 E
Map references: Bosnia and Herzegovina, Europe
Area:
total: 51,233 sq km
land: 51,233 sq km
water: 0 sq km
Area - comparative: slightly smaller than West Virginia
Land boundaries:
total: 1,459 km
border countries: Croatia 932 km, Serbia and Montenegro 527 km (312 km with Serbia, 215 km with Montenegro)
Coastline: 20 km
Maritime claims: NA
Climate: hot summers and cold winters; areas of high elevation have short, cool summers and long, severe winters; mild, rainy winters along coast
Terrain: mountains and valleys
Elevation extremes:
lowest point: Adriatic Sea 0 m
highest point: Maglic 2,386 m
Natural resources: coal, iron, bauxite, manganese, forests, copper, chromium, lead, zinc
Land use:
arable land: 14%
permanent crops: 5%
permanent pastures: 20%
forests and woodland: 39%
other: 22% (1993 est.)
Irrigated land: 20 sq km (1993 est.)
Natural hazards: frequent and destructive earthquakes
Environment - current issues: air pollution from metallurgical plants; sites for disposing of urban waste are limited; widespread casualties, water shortages, and destruction of infrastructure because of the 1992-95 civil strife
Environment - international agreements:
party to: Air Pollution, Law of the Sea, Marine Dumping, Marine Life Conservation, Nuclear Test Ban, Ozone Layer Protection
signed, but not ratified: none of the selected agreements
Geography - note: within Bosnia and Herzegovina's recognized borders, the country is divided into a joint Muslim/Croat Federation (about 51% of the territory) and the Bosnian Serb-led Republika Srpska [RS] (about 49% of the territory); the region called Herzegovina is contiguous to Croatia and traditionally has been settled by an ethnic Croat majority

People

Population: 3,482,495 (July 1999 est.)
note: all data dealing with population is subject to considerable error because of the dislocations caused by military action and ethnic cleansing

Age structure:
0-14 years: 17% (male 310,430; female 294,298)
15-64 years: 71% (male 1,221,791; female 1,240,097)
65 years and over: 12% (male 166,876; female 249,003) (1999 est.)
Population growth rate: 3.2% (1999 est.)
Birth rate: 9.36 births/1,000 population (1999 est.)
Death rate: 10.81 deaths/1,000 population (1999 est.)
Net migration rate: 33.42 migrant(s)/1,000 population (1999 est.)
Sex ratio:
at birth: 1.07 male(s)/female
under 15 years: 1.05 male(s)/female
15-64 years: 0.99 male(s)/female
65 years and over: 0.67 male(s)/female
total population: 0.95 male(s)/female (1999 est.)
Infant mortality rate: 24.52 deaths/1,000 live births (1999 est.)
Life expectancy at birth:
total population: 66.98 years
male: 62.55 years
female: 71.71 years (1999 est.)
Total fertility rate: 1.21 children born/woman (1999 est.)
Nationality:
noun: Bosnian(s), Herzegovinian(s)
adjective: Bosnian, Herzegovinian
Ethnic groups: Serb 40%, Muslim 38%, Croat 22% (est.); note - the Croats claim they now make up only 17% of the total population
Religions: Muslim 40%, Orthodox 31%, Catholic 15%, Protestant 4%, other 10%
Languages: Croatian, Serbian, Bosnian
Literacy: NA

Government

Country name:
conventional long form: none
conventional short form: Bosnia and Herzegovina
local long form: none
local short form: Bosna i Hercegovina
Data code: BK
Government type: emerging democracy
Capital: Sarajevo
Administrative divisions: there are two first-order administrative divisions - the Muslim/Croat Federation of Bosnia and Herzegovina (Federacija Bosna i Hercegovina) and the Bosnian Serb-led Republika Srpska; note - the status of Brcko in north eastern Bosnia is to be determined by arbitration
Independence: NA April 1992 (from Yugoslavia)
National holiday: Republika Srpska - "Republic Day," 9 January; Independence Day, 1 March; Federation of Bosnia and Herzegovina - "Republic Day," 25 November
Constitution: the Dayton Agreement, signed 14 December 1995, included a new constitution now in force
Legal system: based on civil law system

Bosnia and Herzegovina (continued)

Suffrage: 16 years of age, if employed; 18 years of age, universal

Executive branch:

chief of state: Chairman of the Presidency Zivko RADISIC (since 13 October 1998 - Serb); other members of the three-member rotating (every 8 months) presidency: Ante JELAVIC (since NA September 1998 - Croat) and Alija IZETBEGOVIC (since 14 March 1996 - Muslim)

head of government: Cochairman of the Council of Ministers Haris SILAJDZIC (since NA January 1997); Cochairman of the Council of Ministers Suetozar MIHAJLOVIC (since 3 February 1999)

cabinet: Council of Ministers nominated by the council chairmen

note: President of the Muslim/Croat Federation of Bosnia and Herzegovina: Ivo ANDRIC-LUZANIC (since 1 January 1999); Vice President is Ejup GANIC; note - president and vice president rotate every 3 months; President of the Republika Srpska: Nikola POPLASEN (since 29 October 1998)

elections: the three-person presidency members (one Muslim, one Croat, one Serb) are elected by popular vote for a four-year term; the president with the most votes becomes the chairman unless he was the incumbent chairman at the time of the election; election last held 12-13 September 1998 (next to be held September 2002); the cochairmen of the Council of Ministers are appointed by the presidency

election results: percent of vote - Zivko RADISIC with 52% of the Serb vote was elected chairman of the collective presidency for the first 8 months; Ante JELAVIC with 52% of the Croat vote will follow RADISIC in the rotation; Alija IZEBEGOVIC with 87% of the Muslim vote won the highest number of votes in the election but was ineligible to serve consecutive terms as chairman

Legislative branch: bicameral Parliamentary Assembly or Skupstina consists of the National House of Representatives or Vijece Opcina (42 seats - 14 Serb, 14 Croat, and 14 Muslim; members elected by popular vote to serve two-year terms) and the House of Peoples or Vijece Gradanstvo (15 seats - 5 Muslim, 5 Croat, 5 Serb; members elected by the Muslim/Croat Federation's House of Representatives and the Republika Srpska's National Assembly to serve two-year terms)

elections: National House of Representatives - elections last held 12-13 September 1998 (next to be held in the fall 2000); House of Peoples - last held NA (next to be held NA)

election results: National House of Representatives - percent of vote by party/coalition - NA; seats by party/ coalition - KCD 17, HDZ-BiH 6, SDP 4, Sloga 4, SDS 4, SDBIH 2, SRS-RS 2, DNZ 1, NHI 1, RSRS 1; House of Peoples - percent of vote by party/coalition - NA; seats by party/coalition - NA

note: the Muslim/Croat Federation has a House of Representatives (140 seats; members elected by popular vote to serve NA year terms); elections last held NA (next to be held NA); percent of vote by party - NA; seats by party/coalition - KCD 68, HDZ-BiH 28,

SDP 19, SDBIH 6, NHI 4, DNZ 3, DSP 2, BPS 2, HSP 2, SPRS 2, BSP 1, KC 1, BOSS 1, HSS 1; the Republika Srpska has a National Assembly (83 seats; members elected by popular vote to serve NA year terms); elections last held NA (next to be held NA); percent of vote by party - NA; seats by party/coalition - SDS 19, KCD 15, SNS 12, SRS-RS 11, SPRS 10, SNSD 6, RSRS 3, SKRS 2, SDP 2, KKO 1, HDZ-BiH 1, NHI 1

Judicial branch: Constitutional Court, consists of nine members: four members are selected by the Muslim/Croat Federation's House of Representatives, two members by the Republika Srpska National Assembly, and three non-Bosnian members by the president of the European Court of Human Rights

Political parties and leaders: Bosnian Party of Rights or BSP [leader NA]; Bosnian Party or BOSS [Mirnes AJANOVIC]; Bosnian Patriotic Party or GPS [Sefer HALILOVIC]; Center Coalition or KC (includes LBO, RS) [leader NA]; Civic Democratic Party or GDS [Ibrahim SPAHIC]; Coalition for King and Fatherland or KKO (Dugravko Prstojevic); Coalition for a United and Democratic BIH or KCD [Alija IZETBEGOVIC; includes SDA, SBH, GDS, LS]; Croatian Democratic Union of BiH or HDZ-BiH [Ante JELAVIC]; Croatian Party of Rights or HSP [Zdravko HRSTIC]; Croatian Peasants Party of BiH or HSS-BiH [Ilija SIMIC]; Democratic Party for Banja Luka and Krajina [Nikola SPIRIC]; Democratic Party of Pensioners or DSP [Alojz KNEZOVIC]; Democratic Peoples Union or DNZ [Fikret ABDIC]; Liberal Bosniak Organization or LBO [Muhamed FILIPOVIC]; Liberal Party or LS [Rasim KADIC, president]; Muslim-Bosnia Organization or MBO [Salih BUREK]; New Croatian Initiative or NHI [Kresimir ZUBAK]; Party for Bosnia and Herzegovina or SBH [Haris SILAJDZIC]; Party for Democratic Action or SDA [Alija IZETBEGOVIC]; Party of Independent Social Democrats or SNSD [Milorad DODIK]; Radical Party Republika Srpska of RSRS [Miroslav RADOVANOVIC]; Republican Party or RS [Sjepan KJLUJIC]; Serb Coalition for Republika Srpska or SKRS [Predrag LAZEREVIC]; Serb Democratic Party or Serb Lands or SDS [Dragan KALINIC]; Serb National Alliance or SNS [Biljana PLAVSIC]; Serb Radical Party-Republika Srpska or SRS-RS [Nikola POPLASEN]; Sloga or Unity [Biljana PLAVSIC; includes SNS, SPRS, SNSD]; Social Democratic Party BIH or SDP (formerly the Democratic Party of Socialists or DSS) [Zlatko LAGUMDZIJA]; Socialist Party of Republika Srpska or SPRS [Zivko RADISIC]

note: SDP and SDBIH announced a merger in 1999

Political pressure groups and leaders: NA

International organization participation: CE (guest), CEI, EBRD, ECE, FAO, G-77, IAEA, IBRD, ICAO, IDA, IFAD, IFC, ILO, IMF, IMO, Intelsat, Interpol, IOC, IOM (observer), ISO, ITU, NAM (guest), OAS (observer), OIC (observer), OPCW, OSCE, UN, UNCTAD, UNESCO, UNIDO, UPU, WHO, WIPO, WMO, WToO

Diplomatic representation in the US:

chief of mission: Ambassador Dragan BOZANIC

chancery: 2109 E Street NW, Washington, DC 20037

telephone: [1] (202) 337-1500

FAX: [1] (202) 337-1502

consulate(s) general: New York

Diplomatic representation from the US:

chief of mission: Ambassador Richard D. KAUZLARICH

embassy: Alipasina 43, 71000 Sarajevo

mailing address: use street address

telephone: [387] (71) 445-700

FAX: [387] (71) 659-722

Flag description: a wide medium blue vertical band on the fly side with a yellow isosceles triangle abutting the band and the top of the flag; the remainder of the flag is medium blue with seven full five-pointed white stars and two half stars top and bottom along the hypotenuse of the triangle

Government - note: Until declaring independence in spring 1992, Bosnia and Herzegovina existed as a republic in the former Yugoslavia. Bosnia was partitioned by fighting during 1992-95 and governed by competing ethnic factions. Bosnia's current governing structures were created by the Dayton Agreement, the 1995 peace agreement which was officially signed in Paris on 14 December 1995 by then Bosnian President IZETBEGOVIC, Croatian President TUDJMAN, and then Serbian President MILOSEVIC. This agreement retained Bosnia's exterior border and created a joint multi-ethnic and democratic government. This national government - based on proportional representation similar to that which existed in the former socialist regime - is charged with conducting foreign, economic, and fiscal policy. The Dayton Agreement also recognized a second tier of government, comprised of two entities - a joint Muslim/Croat Federation and the Bosnian Serb Republika Srpska (RS) - each presiding over roughly one-half the territory. The Federation and RS governments are charged with overseeing internal functions.

Economy

Economy - overview: Bosnia and Herzegovina ranked next to The Former Yugoslav Republic of Macedonia as the poorest republic in the old Yugoslav federation. Although agriculture has been almost all in private hands, farms have been small and inefficient, and the republic traditionally has been a net importer of food. Industry has been greatly overstaffed, one reflection of the rigidities of communist central planning and management. TITO had pushed the development of military industries in the republic with the result that Bosnia hosted a large share of Yugoslavia's defense plants. The bitter interethnic warfare in Bosnia caused production to plummet by 80% from 1990 to 1995, unemployment to soar, and human misery to multiply. With an uneasy peace in place, output has recovered in 1996-98 at high percentage rates on a low base, but remains far below the 1990 level. Key achievements in 1998 included approval of privatization legislation, the introduction of a national currency - the convertible mark, agreement with the Paris Club to reschedule official debt, and the conclusion of a Standby Agreement with the IMF. Economic data are of limited use because, although both entities issue figures, national-level statistics are not available. Moreover, official data do not capture the large share of activity that occurs on the black market. The country receives substantial amounts of reconstruction assistance and humanitarian aid from the international community. Wide regional differences in war damage and access to the outside world have resulted in substantial variations in living conditions among local areas and individual families. In 1999, Bosnia's major goals are to implement privatization and make progress in fiscal reform and management. In addition, Bosnia will have to prepare for an era of declining assistance from the international community.

GDP: purchasing power parity - $5.8 billion (1998 est.)

GDP - real growth rate: 30% (1998 est.)

GDP - per capita: purchasing power parity - $1,720 (1998 est.)

GDP - composition by sector:

agriculture: 19%

industry: 23%

services: 58% (1996 est.)

Population below poverty line: NA%

Household income or consumption by percentage share:

lowest 10%: NA%

highest 10%: NA%

Inflation rate (consumer prices): NA%

Labor force: 1,026,254

Labor force - by occupation: NA%

Unemployment rate: 40%-50% (1996 est.)

Budget:

revenues: $NA

expenditures: $NA, including capital expenditures of $NA

Industries: steel, coal, iron ore, lead, zinc, manganese, bauxite, vehicle assembly, textiles, tobacco products, wooden furniture, tank and aircraft assembly, domestic appliances, oil refining (much of capacity damaged or shut down) (1995)

Industrial production growth rate: 35% (1998 est.)

Electricity - production: 2.3 billion kWh (1996)

Electricity - production by source:

fossil fuel: 34.78%

hydro: 65.22%

nuclear: 0%

other: 0% (1996)

Electricity - consumption: 2.504 billion kWh (1996)

Electricity - exports: 182 million kWh (1996)

Electricity - imports: 386 million kWh (1996)

Agriculture - products: wheat, corn, fruits, vegetables; livestock

Exports: $152 million (1995 est.)

Exports - commodities: NA

Exports - partners: NA

Imports: $1.1 billion (1995 est.)

Imports - commodities: NA

Imports - partners: NA

Debt - external: $3.5 billion (yearend 1995 est.)

Economic aid - recipient: $1.2 billion (1997 pledged)

Currency: 1 convertible marka (KM) = 100 convertible pfenniga

Exchange rates: NA

Fiscal year: calendar year

Communications

Telephones: 727,000

Telephone system: telephone and telegraph network is in need of modernization and expansion; many urban areas are below average when compared with services in other former Yugoslav republics

domestic: NA

international: no satellite earth stations

Radio broadcast stations: AM 8, FM 16, shortwave 1 (1998)

Radios: 840,000

Television broadcast stations: 21 (1997)

Televisions: 1,012,094

Transportation

Railways:

total: 1,021 km (electrified 795 km; operating as diesel or steam until grids are repaired)

standard gauge: 1,021 km 1.435-m gauge (1995); note - some segments still need repair and/or reconstruction

Highways:

total: 21,846 km

paved: 11,425 km

unpaved: 10,421 km (1996 est.)

note: roads need maintenance and repair

Waterways: NA km; large sections of Sava blocked by downed bridges, silt, and debris

Pipelines: crude oil 174 km; natural gas 90 km (1992); note - pipelines now disrupted

Ports and harbors: Bosanska Gradiska, Bosanski Brod, Bosanski Samac, and Brcko (all inland waterway ports on the Sava none of which are fully operational), Orasje

Merchant marine: none

Airports: 25 (1998 est.)

Airports - with paved runways:

total: 9

2,438 to 3,047 m: 4

1,524 to 2,437 m: 2

914 to 1,523 m: 1

under 914 m: 2 (1998 est.)

Airports - with unpaved runways:

total: 16

1,524 to 2,437 m: 1

914 to 1,523 m: 7

under 914 m: 8 (1998 est.)

Heliports: 3 (1998 est.)

Military

Military branches: Federation Army or VF (composed of both Croatian and Bosnian Muslim elements), Army of the Serb Republic (composed of Bosnian Serb elements); note - within both of these forces air and air defense are subordinate commands

Military manpower - military age: 19 years of age

Military manpower - availability:

males age 15-49: 951,541 (1999 est.)

Military manpower - fit for military service:

males age 15-49: 764,992 (1999 est.)

Military manpower - reaching military age annually:

males: 28,438 (1999 est.)

Military expenditures - dollar figure: $NA

Military expenditures - percent of GDP: NA%

Transnational Issues

Disputes - international: disputes with Serbia over Serbian populated areas

Illicit drugs: minor transit point for marijuana and opiate trafficking routes to Western Europe

Botswana

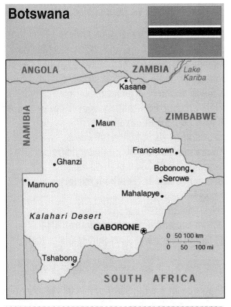

Geography

Location: Southern Africa, north of South Africa
Geographic coordinates: 22 00 S, 24 00 E
Map references: Africa
Area:
total: 600,370 sq km
land: 585,370 sq km
water: 15,000 sq km
Area - comparative: slightly smaller than Texas
Land boundaries:
total: 4,013 km
border countries: Namibia 1,360 km, South Africa 1,840 km, Zimbabwe 813 km
Coastline: 0 km (landlocked)
Maritime claims: none (landlocked)
Climate: semiarid; warm winters and hot summers
Terrain: predominantly flat to gently rolling tableland; Kalahari Desert in southwest
Elevation extremes:
lowest point: junction of the Limpopo and Shashe Rivers 513 m
highest point: Tsodilo Hills 1,489 m
Natural resources: diamonds, copper, nickel, salt, soda ash, potash, coal, iron ore, silver
Land use:
arable land: 1%
permanent crops: 0%
permanent pastures: 46%
forests and woodland: 47%
other: 6% (1993 est.)
Irrigated land: 20 sq km (1993 est.)
Natural hazards: periodic droughts; seasonal August winds blow from the west, carrying sand and dust across the country, which can obscure visibility
Environment - current issues: overgrazing; desertification; limited fresh water resources
Environment - international agreements:
party to: Biodiversity, Climate Change, Desertification, Endangered Species, Hazardous Wastes, Law of the Sea, Nuclear Test Ban, Ozone Layer Protection
signed, but not ratified: none of the selected agreements
Geography - note: landlocked; population concentrated in eastern part of the country

People

Population: 1,464,167 (July 1999 est.)
Age structure:
0-14 years: 42% (male 310,578; female 303,495)
15-64 years: 54% (male 379,836; female 416,073)
65 years and over: 4% (male 20,224; female 33,961) (1999 est.)
Population growth rate: 1.05% (1999 est.)
Birth rate: 31.46 births/1,000 population (1999 est.)
Death rate: 21 deaths/1,000 population (1999 est.)
Net migration rate: 0 migrant(s)/1,000 population (1999 est.)
Sex ratio:
at birth: 1.03 male(s)/female
under 15 years: 1.02 male(s)/female
15-64 years: 0.91 male(s)/female
65 years and over: 0.6 male(s)/female
total population: 0.94 male(s)/female (1999 est.)
Infant mortality rate: 59.08 deaths/1,000 live births (1999 est.)
Life expectancy at birth:
total population: 39.89 years
male: 39.42 years
female: 40.37 years (1999 est.)
Total fertility rate: 3.91 children born/woman (1999 est.)
Nationality:
noun: Motswana (singular), Batswana (plural)
adjective: Motswana (singular), Batswana (plural)
Ethnic groups: Batswana 95%, Kalanga, Basarwa, and Kgalagadi 4%, white 1%
Religions: indigenous beliefs 50%, Christian 50%
Languages: English (official), Setswana
Literacy:
definition: age 15 and over can read and write
total population: 69.8%
male: 80.5%
female: 59.9% (1995 est.)

Government

Country name:
conventional long form: Republic of Botswana
conventional short form: Botswana
former: Bechuanaland
Data code: BC
Government type: parliamentary republic
Capital: Gaborone
Administrative divisions: 10 districts and four town councils*; Central, Chobe, Francistown*, Gaborone*, Ghanzi, Kgalagadi, Kgatleng, Kweneng, Lobatse*, Ngamiland, North-East, Selebi-Pikwe*, South-East, Southern
Independence: 30 September 1966 (from UK)
National holiday: Independence Day, 30 September (1966)
Constitution: March 1965, effective 30 September 1966
Legal system: based on Roman-Dutch law and local customary law; judicial review limited to matters of interpretation; has not accepted compulsory ICJ jurisdiction
Suffrage: 18 years of age; universal
Executive branch:
chief of state: President Festus MOGAE (since 1 April 1998) and Vice President Seretse Ian KHAMA (since NA April 1998); note - the president is both the chief of state and head of government
head of government: President Festus MOGAE (since 1 April 1998) and Vice President Seretse Ian KHAMA (since NA April 1998); note - the president is both the chief of state and head of government
cabinet: Cabinet appointed by the president
elections: president elected by the National Assembly for a five-year term; election last held 15 October 1994 (next to be held NA October 1999); vice president appointed by the president
election results: Sir Ketumile MASIRE elected president; percent of National Assembly vote - NA
note: President MASIRE resigned on 31 March 1998; Vice President MOGAE assumed the presidency pending elections to be held in 1999; on 2 April 1998, Festus MOGAE, then president, designated Seretse Ian KHAMA to be vice president
Legislative branch: bicameral Parliament consists of the House of Chiefs (a largely advisory 15-member body consisting of the chiefs of the eight principal tribes, four elected subchiefs, and three members selected by the other 12) and the National Assembly (44 seats, 40 members are directly elected by popular vote and 4 appointed by the majority party; members serve five-year terms)
elections: National Assembly - elections last held 15 October 1994 (next to be held NA October 1999)
election results: percent of vote by party - NA; seats by party - BDP 27, BNF 13
Judicial branch: High Court; Court of Appeal
Political parties and leaders: Botswana Democratic Party or BDP [Festus MOGAE]; Botswana Freedom Party or BFP [leader NA]; Botswana National Front or BNF [Kenneth KOMA]; Botswana People's Party or BPP [Knight MARIPE]; Independence Freedom Party or IFP [Motsamai MPHO]; Unified Action Party or UAP [Lepetu SETSHWEALD]
International organization participation: ACP, AfDB, C, CCC, ECA, FAO, G-77, IBRD, ICAO, ICFTU, ICRM, IDA, IFAD, IFC, IFRCS, ILO, IMF, Intelsat, Interpol, IOC, ITU, NAM, OAU, SACU, SADC, UN, UNCTAD, UNESCO, UNIDO, UPU, WCL, WFTU, WHO, WIPO, WMO, WToO, WTrO
Diplomatic representation in the US:
chief of mission: Ambassador Archibald Mooketsa MOGWE
chancery: 1531-1533 New Hampshire Avenue NW, Washington, DC 20036
telephone: [1] (202) 244-4990
FAX: [1] (202) 244-4164

Diplomatic representation from the US:
chief of mission: Ambassador Robert C. KRUEGER
embassy: address NA, Gaborone
mailing address: P. O. Box 90, Gaborone
telephone: [267] 353982
FAX: [267] 356947
Flag description: light blue with a horizontal white-edged black stripe in the center

Economy

Economy - overview: Agriculture still provides a livelihood for more than 80% of the population but supplies only about 50% of food needs and accounts for only 4% of GDP. Subsistence farming and cattle raising predominate. Diamond mining and tourism also are important to the economy. The sector is plagued by erratic rainfall and poor soils. Substantial mineral deposits were found in the 1970s and the mining sector grew from 25% of GDP in 1980 to 35% in 1997. Unemployment officially is 21% but unofficial estimates place it closer to 40%.
GDP: purchasing power parity - $5.25 billion (1998 est.)
GDP - real growth rate: 3% (1998 est.)
GDP - per capita: purchasing power parity - $3,600 (1998 est.)
GDP - composition by sector:
agriculture: 4%
industry: 45% (including 35% mining)
services: 51% (1997 est.)
Population below poverty line: NA%
Household income or consumption by percentage share:
lowest 10%: NA%
highest 10%: NA%
Inflation rate (consumer prices): 9% (1997 est.)
Labor force: 235,000 formal sector employees (1995)
Labor force - by occupation: 100,000 public sector; 135,000 private sector, including 14,300 who are employed in various mines in South Africa; most others engaged in cattle raising and subsistence agriculture (1995 est.)
Unemployment rate: 20-40% (1997 est.)
Budget:
revenues: $1.6 billion
expenditures: $1.8 billion, including capital expenditures of $560 million (FY96/97)
Industries: diamonds, copper, nickel, coal, salt, soda ash, potash; livestock processing
Industrial production growth rate: 4.6% (FY92/93)
Electricity - production: 990 million kWh (1996)
Electricity - production by source:
fossil fuel: 100%
hydro: 0%
nuclear: 0%
other: 0% (1996)
Electricity - consumption: 1.675 billion kWh (1996)
Electricity - exports: 0 kWh (1996)
Electricity - imports: 685 million kWh (1996)
Agriculture - products: sorghum, maize, millet, pulses, groundnuts (peanuts), beans, cowpeas, sunflower seed; livestock
Exports: $2.25 billion (f.o.b. 1998 est.)
Exports - commodities: diamonds 76%, copper, nickel 4%, meat (1997)
Exports - partners: EU 74%, Southern African Customs Union (SACU) 21%, Zimbabwe 3% (1996)
Imports: $2.43 billion (f.o.b, 1998 est.)
Imports - commodities: foodstuffs, vehicles and transport equipment, textiles, petroleum products
Imports - partners: Southern African Customs Union (SACU) 78%, Europe 8%, Zimbabwe 6% (1996)
Debt - external: $610 million (1997)
Economic aid - recipient: $73 million (1995)
Currency: 1 pula (P) = 100 thebe
Exchange rates: pulas (P) per US$1 - 4.5725 (January 1999), 4.2258 (1998), 3.6508 (1997), 3.3242 (1996), 2.7722 (1995), 2.6846 (1994)
Fiscal year: 1 April - 31 March

Communications

Telephones: 19,109 (1985 est.)
Telephone system: sparse system
domestic: small system of open-wire lines, microwave radio relay links, and a few radiotelephone communication stations
international: microwave radio relay links to Zambia, Zimbabwe, and South Africa; satellite earth station - 1 Intelsat (Indian Ocean)
Radio broadcast stations: AM 7, FM 15, shortwave 5 (1998)
Radios: NA
Television broadcast stations: 0 (1997)
Televisions: 13,800 (1993 est.)

Transportation

Railways:
total: 971 km
narrow gauge: 971 km 1.067-m gauge (1995)
Highways:
total: 18,482 km
paved: 4,343 km
unpaved: 14,139 km (1996 est.)
Ports and harbors: none
Airports: 92 (1998 est.)
Airports - with paved runways:
total: 12
over 3,047 m: 1
2,438 to 3,047 m: 1
1,524 to 2,437 m: 9
914 to 1,523 m: 1 (1998 est.)
Airports - with unpaved runways:
total: 80
1,524 to 2,437 m: 2
914 to 1,523 m: 57
under 914 m: 21 (1998 est.)

Military

Military branches: Botswana Defense Force (includes Army and Air Wing), Botswana National Police
Military manpower - military age: 18 years of age
Military manpower - availability:
males age 15-49: 344,587 (1999 est.)
Military manpower - fit for military service:
males age 15-49: 182,279 (1999 est.)
Military manpower - reaching military age annually:
males: 18,654 (1999 est.)
Military expenditures - dollar figure: $61 million (FY99/00)
Military expenditures - percent of GDP: 1.2% (FY99/00)

Transnational Issues

Disputes - international: quadripoint with Namibia, Zambia, and Zimbabwe is in disagreement; dispute with Namibia over uninhabited Kasikili (Sidudu) Island in Linyanti (Chobe) River is presently at the ICJ; at least one other island in Linyanti River is contested

Bouvet Island
(territory of Norway)

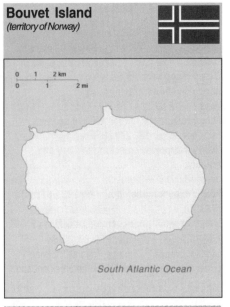

South Atlantic Ocean

Geography

Location: Southern Africa, island in the South Atlantic Ocean, south-southwest of the Cape of Good Hope (South Africa)
Geographic coordinates: 54 26 S, 3 24 E
Map references: Antarctic Region
Area:
total: 58 sq km
land: 58 sq km
water: 0 sq km
Area - comparative: about 0.3 times the size of Washington, DC
Land boundaries: 0 km
Coastline: 29.6 km
Maritime claims:
territorial sea: 4 nm
Climate: antarctic
Terrain: volcanic; maximum elevation about 800 m; coast is mostly inaccessible
Elevation extremes:
lowest point: Atlantic Ocean 0 m
highest point: unnamed location 780 m
Natural resources: none
Land use:
arable land: 0%
permanent crops: 0%
permanent pastures: 0%
forests and woodland: 0%
other: 100% (all ice)
Irrigated land: 0 sq km (1993)
Natural hazards: NA
Environment - current issues: NA
Environment - international agreements:
party to: NA
signed, but not ratified: NA
Geography - note: covered by glacial ice

People

Population: uninhabited

Government

Country name:
conventional long form: none
conventional short form: Bouvet Island
Data code: BV
Dependency status: territory of Norway; administered from Oslo
Legal system: NA
Diplomatic representation in the US: none (territory of Norway)
Diplomatic representation from the US: none (territory of Norway)
Flag description: the flag of Norway is used

Economy

Economy - overview: no economic activity; declared a nature reserve

Communications

Communications - note: automatic meteorological station

Transportation

Ports and harbors: none; offshore anchorage only

Military

Military - note: defense is the responsibility of Norway

Transnational Issues

Disputes - international: none

Brazil

Geography

Location: Eastern South America, bordering the Atlantic Ocean
Geographic coordinates: 10 00 S, 55 00 W
Map references: South America
Area:
total: 8,511,965 sq km
land: 8,456,510 sq km
water: 55,455 sq km
note: includes Arquipelago de Fernando de Noronha, Atol das Rocas, Ilha da Trindade, Ilhas Martin Vaz, and Penedos de Sao Pedro e Sao Paulo
Area - comparative: slightly smaller than the US
Land boundaries:
total: 14,691 km
border countries: Argentina 1,224 km, Bolivia 3,400 km, Colombia 1,643 km, French Guiana 673 km, Guyana 1,119 km, Paraguay 1,290 km, Peru 1,560 km, Suriname 597 km, Uruguay 985 km, Venezuela 2,200 km
Coastline: 7,491 km
Maritime claims:
contiguous zone: 24 nm
continental shelf: 200 nm
exclusive economic zone: 200 nm
territorial sea: 12 nm
Climate: mostly tropical, but temperate in south
Terrain: mostly flat to rolling lowlands in north; some plains, hills, mountains, and narrow coastal belt
Elevation extremes:
lowest point: Atlantic Ocean 0 m
highest point: Pico da Neblina 3,014 m
Natural resources: bauxite, gold, iron ore, manganese, nickel, phosphates, platinum, tin, uranium, petroleum, hydropower, timber
Land use:
arable land: 5%
permanent crops: 1%
permanent pastures: 22%
forests and woodland: 58%
other: 14% (1993 est.)

Brazil (continued)

Irrigated land: 28,000 sq km (1993 est.)
Natural hazards: recurring droughts in northeast; floods and occasional frost in south
Environment - current issues: deforestation in Amazon Basin destroys the habitat and endangers the existence of a multitude of plant and animal species indigenous to the area; air and water pollution in Rio de Janeiro, Sao Paulo, and several other large cities; land degradation and water pollution caused by improper mining activities
Environment - international agreements:
party to: Antarctic-Environmental Protocol, Antarctic Treaty, Biodiversity, Climate Change, Desertification, Endangered Species, Environmental Modification, Hazardous Wastes, Law of the Sea, Marine Dumping, Nuclear Test Ban, Ozone Layer Protection, Ship Pollution, Tropical Timber 83, Tropical Timber 94, Wetlands, Whaling
signed, but not ratified: Climate Change-Kyoto Protocol
Geography - note: largest country in South America; shares common boundaries with every South American country except Chile and Ecuador

People

Population: 171,853,126 (July 1999 est.)
note: Brazil took a census in August 1996 which reported a population of 157,079,573; that figure was about 5% lower than projections by the US Census Bureau, and is close to the implied underenumeration of 4.6% for 1991; the Factbook's demographic statistics for Brazil do not take into consideration the results of the1996 census since the full results have not been released for analysis
Age structure:
0-14 years: 30% (male 26,059,687; female 25,095,236)
15-64 years: 65% (male 55,037,161; female 56,727,196)
65 years and over: 5% (male 3,626,893; female 5,306,953) (1999 est.)
Population growth rate: 1.16% (1999 est.)
Birth rate: 20.42 births/1,000 population (1999 est.)
Death rate: 8.79 deaths/1,000 population (1999 est.)
Net migration rate: -0.03 migrant(s)/1,000 population (1999 est.)
Sex ratio:
at birth: 1.05 male(s)/female
under 15 years: 1.04 male(s)/female
15-64 years: 0.97 male(s)/female
65 years and over: 0.68 male(s)/female
total population: 0.97 male(s)/female (1999 est.)
Infant mortality rate: 35.37 deaths/1,000 live births (1999 est.)
Life expectancy at birth:
total population: 64.06 years
male: 59.35 years
female: 69.01 years (1999 est.)
Total fertility rate: 2.28 children born/woman (1999 est.)
Nationality:
noun: Brazilian(s)

adjective: Brazilian
Ethnic groups: white (includes Portuguese, German, Italian, Spanish, Polish) 55%, mixed white and black 38%, black 6%, other (includes Japanese, Arab, Amerindian) 1%
Religions: Roman Catholic (nominal) 70%
Languages: Portuguese (official), Spanish, English, French
Literacy:
definition: age 15 and over can read and write
total population: 83.3%
male: 83.3%
female: 83.2% (1995 est.)

Government

Country name:
conventional long form: Federative Republic of Brazil
conventional short form: Brazil
local long form: Republica Federativa do Brasil
local short form: Brasil
Data code: BR
Government type: federal republic
Capital: Brasilia
Administrative divisions: 26 states (estados, singular - estado) and 1 federal district* (distrito federal); Acre, Alagoas, Amapa, Amazonas, Bahia, Ceara, Distrito Federal*, Espirito Santo, Goias, Maranhao, Mato Grosso, Mato Grosso do Sul, Minas Gerais, Para, Paraiba, Parana, Pernambuco, Piaui, Rio de Janeiro, Rio Grande do Norte, Rio Grande do Sul, Rondonia, Roraima, Santa Catarina, Sao Paulo, Sergipe, Tocantins
Independence: 7 September 1822 (from Portugal)
National holiday: Independence Day, 7 September (1822)
Constitution: 5 October 1988
Legal system: based on Roman codes; has not accepted compulsory ICJ jurisdiction
Suffrage: voluntary between 16 and 18 years of age and over 70; compulsory over 18 and under 70 years of age
Executive branch:
chief of state: President Fernando Henrique CARDOSO (since 1 January 1995); Vice President Marco MACIEL (since 1 January 1995); note - the president is both the chief of state and head of government
head of government: President Fernando Henrique CARDOSO (since 1 January 1995); Vice President Marco MACIEL (since 1 January 1995); note - the president is both the chief of state and head of government
cabinet: Cabinet appointed by the president
elections: president and vice president elected on the same ticket by popular vote for four-year terms; election last held 4 October 1998 (next to be held NA October 2002)
election results: Fernando Henrique CARDOSO reelected president; percent of vote - 53%
Legislative branch: bicameral National Congress or Congresso Nacional consists of the Federal Senate or Senado Federal (81 seats; three members from each

state or federal district elected according to the principle of majority to serve eight-year terms; one-third elected after a four year period, two-thirds elected after the next four-year period) and the Chamber of Deputies or Camara dos Deputados (513 seats; members are elected by proportional representation to serve four-year terms)
elections: Federal Senate - last held 4 October 1998 for one-third of Senate (next to be held NA October 2002 for two-thirds of the Senate); Chamber of Deputies - last held 4 October 1998 (next to be held NA October 2002)
election results: Federal Senate - percent of vote by party - NA%; seats by party - PMDB 27, PFL 20, PSDB 16, PT 7, PPB 5; Chamber of Deputies - percent of vote by party - NA%; seats by party - PFL 106, PSDB 99, PMDB 82, PPB 60, PT 58
Judicial branch: Supreme Federal Tribunal, 11 judges are appointed for life by the president and confirmed by the Senate
Political parties and leaders: Brazilian Democratic Movement Party or PMDB [Paes DE ANDRADE, president]; Liberal Front Party or PFL [Jose JORGE, president]; Workers' Party or PT [Jose DIRCEU, president]; Brazilian Workers' Party or PTB [Rodrigues PALMA, president]; Democratic Labor Party or PDT [Leonel BRIZOLA, president]; Brazilian Progressive Party or PPB [Espiridiao AMIN, president]; Brazilian Social Democracy Party or PSDB [Artur DA TAVOLA, president]; Popular Socialist Party or PPS [Roberto FREIRE, president]; Communist Party of Brazil or PCdoB [Joao AMAZONAS, chairman]; Liberal Party or PL [Alvaro VALLE, president]
Political pressure groups and leaders: left wing of the Catholic Church, Landless Worker's Movement, and labor unions allied to leftist Workers' Party are critical of government's social and economic policies
International organization participation: AfDB, BIS, CCC, ECLAC, FAO, G-11, G-15, G-19, G-24, G-77, IADB, IAEA, IBRD, ICAO, ICC, ICFTU, ICRM, IDA, IFAD, IFC, IFRCS, IHO, ILO, IMF, IMO, Inmarsat, Intelsat, Interpol, IOC, IOM (observer), ISO, ITU, LAES, LAIA, Mercosur, MONUA, MTCR, NAM (observer), NSG, OAS, OPANAL, OPCW, PCA, RG, UN, UN Security Council (temporary), UNCTAD, UNESCO, UNHCR, UNIDO, UNMOP, UNPREDEP, UNU, UPU, WCL, WFTU, WHO, WIPO, WMO, WToO, WTrO
Diplomatic representation in the US:
chief of mission: Ambassador Rubens Antonio BARBOSA
chancery: 3006 Massachusetts Avenue NW, Washington, DC 20008
telephone: [1] (202) 238-2700
FAX: [1] (202) 238-2827
consulate(s) general: Atlanta, Boston, Chicago, Houston, Los Angeles, Miami, New York, San Juan (Puerto Rico), and San Francisco
Diplomatic representation from the US:
chief of mission: Ambassador-designate J. Brian ATWOOD

Brazil *(continued)*

embassy: Avenida das Nacoes, Quadra 801, Lote 3, Brasilia, Distrito Federal Cep 70403-900 Brazil
mailing address: Unit 3500, APO AA 34030
telephone: [55] (61) 321-7272
FAX: [55] (61) 225-9136
consulate(s) general: Rio de Janeiro, Sao Paulo
consulate(s): Recife

Flag description: green with a large yellow diamond in the center bearing a blue celestial globe with 27 white five-pointed stars (one for each state and the Federal District) arranged in the same pattern as the night sky over Brazil; the globe has a white equatorial band with the motto ORDEM E PROGRESSO (Order and Progress)

Economy

Economy - overview: Possessing large and well-developed agricultural, mining, manufacturing, and service sectors, Brazil's economy outweighs that of all other South American countries and is expanding its presence in world markets. Prior to the institution of a stabilization plan - the Plano Real (Real Plan) in mid-1994, stratospheric inflation rates had disrupted economic activity and discouraged foreign investment. Since then, tight monetary policy has brought inflation under control - consumer prices increased by 2% in 1998 compared to more than 1,000% in 1994. At the same time, GDP growth slowed from 5.7% in 1994 to about 3.0% in 1997 due to tighter credit. The Real Plan faced its strongest challenge in 1998, as the world financial crisis caused investors to more closely examine the country's structural weaknesses. The most severe spillover for Brazil - after Russia's debt default in August 1998 - created unrelenting pressure on the currency which forced the country to hike annual interest rates to 50%. Approximately $30 billion in capital left the country in August and September. After crafting a fiscal adjustment program and pledging progress on structural reform, Brazil received a $41.5 billion IMF-led international support program in November 1998. Capital continued to leach out of the country, and investors, concerned about the rising mountain of debt and currency widely-viewed as overvalued, stayed on the sidelines. In January 1999, Brazil made an abrupt shift of course in exchange rate policy, abandoning the strong currency anti-inflation anchor of the Real Plan. On 13 January 1999, Central Bank officials announced a one-time 8% devaluation of the real, and on 15 January 1999, the currency was declared to be freely floating. President CARDOSO remains committed to limiting inflation and weathering the financial crisis through austerity and sacrifice as the country rides out a deep recession. He hopes the country will resume economic growth in the second half of 1999, so that he can once again focus on his longer-term goal of reducing poverty and income inequality. CARDOSO still hopes to address mandated revenue sharing with the states and cumbersome procedures to amend the constitution before the end of his second term.

GDP: purchasing power parity - $1.0352 trillion (1998 est.)
GDP - real growth rate: 0.5% (1998)
GDP - per capita: purchasing power parity - $6,100 (1998 est.)
GDP - composition by sector:
agriculture: 14%
industry: 36%
services: 50% (1997)
Population below poverty line: 17.4% (1990 est.)
Household income or consumption by percentage share:
lowest 10%: 0.8%
highest 10%: 47.9% (1995)
Inflation rate (consumer prices): 2% (1998)
Labor force: 57 million (1989 est.)
Labor force - by occupation: services 42%, agriculture 31%, industry 27%
Unemployment rate: 8.5% (1998 est.)
Budget:
revenues: $151 billion
expenditures: $149 billion, including capital expenditures of $36 billion (1998)
Industries: textiles, shoes, chemicals, cement, lumber, iron ore, tin, steel, aircraft, motor vehicles and parts, other machinery and equipment
Industrial production growth rate: 4.5% (1997 est.)
Electricity - production: 291.63 billion kWh (1997)
Electricity - production by source:
fossil fuel: 4.38%
hydro: 92.09%
nuclear: 0.8%
other: 2.73% (1996)
Electricity - consumption: 323.215 billion kWh (1996)
Electricity - exports: 8 million kWh (1996)
Electricity - imports: 37.5 billion kWh (1996)
note: imported electricity from Paraguay
Agriculture - products: coffee, soybeans, wheat, rice, corn, sugarcane, cocoa, citrus; beef
Exports: $51 billion (f.o.b., 1998)
Exports - commodities: iron ore, soybean bran, orange juice, footwear, coffee, motor vehicle parts
Exports - partners: EU 28%, Latin America (excluding Argentina) 23%, US 20%, Argentina 12% (1996)
Imports: $57.6 billion (f.o.b., 1998)
Imports - commodities: crude oil, capital goods, chemical products, foodstuffs, coal
Imports - partners: EU 26%, US 22%, Argentina 13%, Japan 5% (1996)
Debt - external: $258.1 billion (December 1998)
Economic aid - recipient: $1.012 billion (1995)
Currency: 1 real (R$) = 100 centavos
Exchange rates: reais (R$) per US$1 - 1.501 (January 1999), 1.161 (1998), 1.078 (1997), 1.005 (1996), 0.918 (1995), 0.639 (1994); CR$ per US$1 - 390.845 (January 1994)
note: the real (R$) was introduced on 1 July 1994, equal to 2,750 cruzeiro reais; from October 1994 through 14 January 1999, the official rate was determined by a managed float; since 15 January 1999, the official rate floats independently with respect to the US$
Fiscal year: calendar year

Communications

Telephones: 14,426,673 (1992 est.)
Telephone system: good working system
domestic: extensive microwave radio relay system and a domestic satellite system with 64 earth stations
international: 3 coaxial submarine cables; satellite earth stations - 3 Intelsat (Atlantic Ocean), 1 Inmarsat (Atlantic Ocean Region East)
Radio broadcast stations: AM 1,627, FM 251, shortwave 114 (of which 91 are associated with AM stations) (1998)
Radios: 60 million (1993 est.)
Television broadcast stations: 138 (1997)
Televisions: 30 million (1993 est.)

Transportation

Railways:
total: 28,862 km (1,187 km electrified)
broad gauge: 4,123 km 1.600-m gauge
narrow gauge: 24,390 km 1.000-m gauge; 13 km 0.760-m gauge
dual gauge: 336 km 1.000-m and 1.600-m gauges (three rails)
Highways:
total: 1.98 million km
paved: 184,140 km
unpaved: 1,795,860 km (1996 est.)
Waterways: 50,000 km navigable
Pipelines: crude oil 2,980 km; petroleum products 4,762 km; natural gas 4,246 km (1998)
Ports and harbors: Belem, Fortaleza, Ilheus, Imbituba, Manaus, Paranagua, Porto Alegre, Recife, Rio de Janeiro, Rio Grande, Salvador, Santos, Vitoria
Merchant marine:
total: 179 ships (1,000 GRT or over) totaling 4,132,037 GRT/6,642,442 DWT
ships by type: bulk 35, cargo 28, chemical tanker 6, combination ore/oil 10, container 10, liquefied gas tanker 10, multifunction large-load carrier 1, oil tanker 61, passenger-cargo 5, refrigerated cargo 1, roll-on/roll-off cargo 11, short-sea passenger 1 (1998 est.)
Airports: 3,265 (1998 est.)
Airports - with paved runways:
total: 514
over 3,047 m: 5
2,438 to 3,047 m: 19
1,524 to 2,437 m: 134
914 to 1,523 m: 325
under 914 m: 31 (1998 est.)
Airports - with unpaved runways:
total: 2,751
1,524 to 2,437 m: 73
914 to 1,523 m: 1,312
under 914 m: 1,366 (1998 est.)

Brazil (continued)

Military

Military branches: Brazilian Army, Brazilian Navy (includes naval air and marines), Brazilian Air Force, Federal Police (paramilitary)
Military manpower - military age: 18 years of age
Military manpower - availability:
males age 15-49: 47,230,426 (1999 est.)
Military manpower - fit for military service:
males age 15-49: 31,723,597 (1999 est.)
Military manpower - reaching military age annually:
males: 1,841,858 (1999 est.)
Military expenditures - dollar figure: $14.7 billion (1998)
Military expenditures - percent of GDP: 1.9% (1998)

Transnational Issues

Disputes - international: two short sections of boundary with Uruguay are in dispute - Arroio Invernada (Arroyo de la Invernada) area of the Rio Quarai (Rio Cuareim) and the islands at the confluence of the Rio Quarai and the Uruguay River
Illicit drugs: limited illicit producer of cannabis, minor coca cultivation in the Amazon region, mostly used for domestic consumption; government has a large-scale eradication program to control cannabis; important transshipment country for Bolivian, Colombian, and Peruvian cocaine headed for the US and Europe; increasingly used by traffickers as a way station for narcotics air transshipments between Peru and Colombia

---

British Indian Ocean Territory
(overseas territory of the UK)

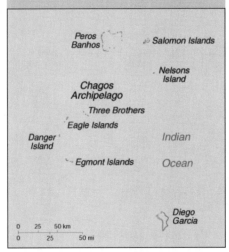

Geography

Location: Southern Asia, archipelago in the Indian Ocean, about one-half the way from Africa to Indonesia
Geographic coordinates: 6 00 S, 71 30 E
Map references: World
Area:
total: 60 sq km
land: 60 sq km
water: 0 sq km
note: includes the entire Chagos Archipelago
Area - comparative: about 0.3 times the size of Washington, DC
Land boundaries: 0 km
Coastline: 698 km
Maritime claims:
exclusive fishing zone: 200 nm
territorial sea: 3 nm
Climate: tropical marine; hot, humid, moderated by trade winds
Terrain: flat and low (up to four meters in elevation)
Elevation extremes:
lowest point: Indian Ocean 0 m
highest point: unnamed location on Diego Garcia 15 m
Natural resources: coconuts, fish
Land use:
arable land: 0%
permanent crops: 0%
permanent pastures: 0%
forests and woodland: NA%
other: NA%
Irrigated land: 0 sq km (1993)
Natural hazards: NA
Environment - current issues: NA
Environment - international agreements:
party to: NA
signed, but not ratified: NA
Geography - note: archipelago of 2,300 islands;

Diego Garcia, largest and southernmost island, occupies strategic location in central Indian Ocean; island is site of joint US-UK military facility

People

Population: no indigenous inhabitants
note: approximately 3,000 native inhabitants, known as the Chagosians or Ilois, were evacuated to Mauritius before construction of UK-US military facilities; now there are UK and US military personnel and civilian contractors living on the island

Government

Country name:
conventional long form: British Indian Ocean Territory
conventional short form: none
abbreviation: BIOT
Data code: IO
Dependency status: overseas territory of the UK; administered by a commissioner, resident in the Foreign and Commonwealth Office in London
Legal system: NA
Executive branch:
chief of state: Queen ELIZABETH II (since 6 February 1952)
head of government: Commissioner David Ross MACLENNAN (since NA 1994); Administrator Don CAIRNS (since NA); note - both reside in the UK
cabinet: NA
elections: none; the monarch is hereditary; commissioner and administrator appointed by the monarch
Diplomatic representation in the US: none (overseas territory of the UK)
Diplomatic representation from the US: none (overseas territory of the UK)
Flag description: white with the flag of the UK in the upper hoist-side quadrant and six blue wavy horizontal stripes bearing a palm tree and yellow crown centered on the outer half of the flag

Economy

Economy - overview: All economic activity is concentrated on the largest island of Diego Garcia, where joint UK-US defense facilities are located. Construction projects and various services needed to support the military installations are done by military and contract employees from the UK, Mauritius, the Philippines, and the US. There are no industrial or agricultural activities on the islands.
Electricity - production: NA kWh
note: electricity supplied by the US military
Electricity - consumption: NA kWh

Communications

Telephones: NA
Telephone system: facilities for military needs only
domestic: NA
international: NA
Radio broadcast stations: AM 1, FM 2, shortwave 0 (1998)

British Indian Ocean Territory
(continued)

Radios: NA
Television broadcast stations: 1 (1997)
Televisions: NA

Highways:
total: NA km
paved: short stretch of paved road of NA km between port and airfield on Diego Garcia
unpaved: NA km
Ports and harbors: Diego Garcia
Airports: 1 (1998 est.)
Airports - with paved runways:
total: 1
over 3,047 m: 1 (1998 est.)

Military

Military - note: defense is the responsibility of the UK; the US lease on Diego Garcia expires in 2016

Transnational Issues

Disputes - international: the Chagos Archipelago is claimed by Mauritius and Seychelles

---

British Virgin Islands
(overseas territory of the UK)

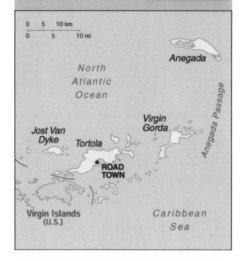

Geography

Location: Caribbean, between the Caribbean Sea and the North Atlantic Ocean, east of Puerto Rico
Geographic coordinates: 18 30 N, 64 30 W
Map references: Central America and the Caribbean
Area:
total: 150 sq km
land: 150 sq km
water: 0 sq km
note: includes the island of Anegada
Area - comparative: about 0.9 times the size of Washington, DC
Land boundaries: 0 km
Coastline: 80 km
Maritime claims:
exclusive fishing zone: 200 nm
territorial sea: 3 nm
Climate: subtropical; humid; temperatures moderated by trade winds
Terrain: coral islands relatively flat; volcanic islands steep, hilly
Elevation extremes:
lowest point: Caribbean Sea 0 m
highest point: Mount Sage 521 m
Natural resources: NEGL
Land use:
arable land: 20%
permanent crops: 7%
permanent pastures: 33%
forests and woodland: 7%
other: 33% (1993 est.)
Irrigated land: NA sq km
Natural hazards: hurricanes and tropical storms (July to October)
Environment - current issues: limited natural fresh water resources (except for a few seasonal streams and springs on Tortola, most of the islands' water supply comes from wells and rainwater catchment)

Environment - international agreements:
party to: NA
signed, but not ratified: NA
Geography - note: strong ties to nearby US Virgin Islands and Puerto Rico

People

Population: 19,156 (July 1999 est.)
Age structure:
0-14 years: 21% (male 2,012; female 1,965)
15-64 years: 74% (male 7,300; female 6,896)
65 years and over: 5% (male 539; female 444) (1999 est.)
Population growth rate: 2.37% (1999 est.)
Birth rate: 15.92 births/1,000 population (1999 est.)
Death rate: 4.65 deaths/1,000 population (1999 est.)
Net migration rate: 12.37 migrant(s)/1,000 population (1999 est.)
Sex ratio:
at birth: 1.05 male(s)/female
under 15 years: 1.02 male(s)/female
15-64 years: 1.06 male(s)/female
65 years and over: 1.21 male(s)/female
total population: 1.06 male(s)/female (1999 est.)
Infant mortality rate: 22.17 deaths/1,000 live births (1999 est.)
Life expectancy at birth:
total population: 75.13 years
male: 74.37 years
female: 75.92 years (1999 est.)
Total fertility rate: 1.71 children born/woman (1999 est.)
Nationality:
noun: British Virgin Islander(s)
adjective: British Virgin Islander
Ethnic groups: black 90%, white, Asian
Religions: Protestant 86% (Methodist 45%, Anglican 21%, Church of God 7%, Seventh-Day Adventist 5%, Baptist 4%, Jehovah's Witnesses 2%, other 2%), Roman Catholic 6%, none 2%, other 6% (1981)
Languages: English (official)
Literacy:
definition: age 15 and over can read and write
total population: 97.8% (1991 est.)
male: NA%
female: NA%

Government

Country name:
conventional long form: none
conventional short form: British Virgin Islands
abbreviation: BVI
Data code: VI
Dependency status: overseas territory of the UK
Government type: NA
Capital: Road Town
Administrative divisions: none (overseas territory of the UK)
Independence: none (overseas territory of the UK)
National holiday: Territory Day, 1 July

British Virgin Islands (continued)

Constitution: 1 June 1977
Legal system: English law
Suffrage: 18 years of age; universal
Executive branch:
chief of state: Queen ELIZABETH II (since 6 February 1952), represented by Governor David MACKILLIGIN (since NA June 1995)
head of government: Chief Minister Ralph T. O'NEAL (since 15 May 1995; appointed after the death of former Chief Minister H. Lavity STOUTT)
cabinet: Executive Council appointed by the governor from members of the Legislative Council
elections: none; the monarch is hereditary; governor appointed by the monarch; chief minister appointed by the governor from among the members of the Legislative Council
Legislative branch: unicameral Legislative Council (13 seats; members are elected by direct popular vote, one member from each of 9 electoral districts, four at-large members; members serve five-year terms)
elections: last held 20 February 1995 (next to be held NA February 2000)
election results: percent of vote by party - NA; seats by party - VIP 6, CCM 2, UP 2, independents 3
Judicial branch: Eastern Caribbean Supreme Court, consisting of the High Court of Justice and the Court of Appeal; (one judge of the Supreme Court is a resident of the islands and presides over the High Court); Magistrate's Court; Juvenile Court; Court of Summary Jurisdiction
Political parties and leaders: United Party or UP [Conrad MADURO]; Virgin Islands Party or VIP [Ralph T. O'NEAL]; Concerned Citizens Movement or CCM [E. Walwyn BREWLEY]; Independent People's Movement or IPM [Omar HODGE and Allen O'NEAL]
International organization participation: Caricom (associate), CDB, ECLAC (associate), Interpol (subbureau), IOC, OECS (associate), UNESCO (associate)
Diplomatic representation in the US: none (overseas territory of the UK)
Diplomatic representation from the US: none (overseas territory of the UK)
Flag description: blue, with the flag of the UK in the upper hoist-side quadrant and the Virgin Islander coat of arms centered in the outer half of the flag; the coat of arms depicts a woman flanked on either side by a vertical column of six oil lamps above a scroll bearing the Latin word VIGILATE (Be Watchful)

Economy

Economy - overview: The economy, one of the most prosperous in the Caribbean, is highly dependent on tourism, which generates an estimated 45% of the national income. In the mid-1980s, the government began offering offshore registration to companies wishing to incorporate in the islands, and incorporation fees now generate substantial revenues. An estimated 250,000 companies were on the offshore registry by yearend 1997. The adoption of a comprehensive insurance law in late 1994, which

provides a blanket of confidentiality with regulated statutory gateways for investigation of criminal offenses, is expected to make the British Virgin Islands even more attractive to international business. Livestock raising is the most important agricultural activity; poor soils limit the islands' ability to meet domestic food requirements. Because of traditionally close links with the US Virgin Islands, the British Virgin Islands has used the dollar as its currency since 1959.
GDP: purchasing power parity - $183 million (1997 est.)
GDP - real growth rate: 4.7% (1997)
GDP - per capita: purchasing power parity - $10,000 (1997 est.)
GDP - composition by sector:
agriculture: 1%
industry: 1.4%
services: 97.6% (1991-95 average)
Population below poverty line: NA%
Household income or consumption by percentage share:
lowest 10%: NA%
highest 10%: NA%
Inflation rate (consumer prices): 6.5% (1997)
Labor force: 4,911 (1980)
Labor force - by occupation: tourism NA%
Unemployment rate: 3% (1995)
Budget:
revenues: $121.5 million
expenditures: $115.5 million, including capital expenditures of $NA (1997)
Industries: tourism, light industry, construction, rum, concrete block, offshore financial center
Industrial production growth rate: 4% (1985)
Electricity - production: 42 million kWh (1996)
Electricity - production by source:
fossil fuel: 100%
hydro: 0%
nuclear: 0%
other: 0% (1996)
Electricity - consumption: 42 million kWh (1996)
Electricity - exports: 0 kWh (1996)
Electricity - imports: 0 kWh (1996)
Agriculture - products: fruits, vegetables; livestock, poultry; fish
Exports: $23.9 million (1996)
Exports - commodities: rum, fresh fish, fruits, animals; gravel, sand
Exports - partners: Virgin Islands (US), Puerto Rico, US
Imports: $121.5 million (1996)
Imports - commodities: building materials, automobiles, foodstuffs, machinery
Imports - partners: Virgin Islands (US), Puerto Rico, US
Debt - external: $34.8 million (1996)
Economic aid - recipient: $2.6 million (1995)
Currency: 1 United States dollar (US$) = 100 cents
Exchange rates: US currency is used
Fiscal year: 1 April - 31 March

Communications

Telephones: 6,291 (1990 est.)
Telephone system: worldwide telephone service
domestic: NA
international: submarine cable to Bermuda
Radio broadcast stations: AM 1, FM 4, shortwave 0 (1998)
Radios: 9,000 (1992 est.)
Television broadcast stations: 1 (in addition, there is one cable company) (1997)
Televisions: 4,000 (1992 est.)

Transportation

Railways: 0 km
Highways:
total: 113 km (1995 est.)
paved: NA km
unpaved: NA km
Ports and harbors: Road Town
Merchant marine: none
Airports: 3 (1998 est.)
Airports - with paved runways:
total: 2
914 to 1,523 m: 1
under 914 m: 1 (1998 est.)
Airports - with unpaved runways:
total: 1
914 to 1,523 m: 1 (1998 est.)

Military

Military - note: defense is the responsibility of the UK

Transnational Issues

Disputes - international: none

Brunei

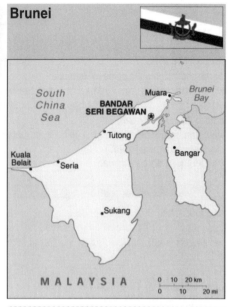

Geography

Location: Southeastern Asia, bordering the South China Sea and Malaysia

Geographic coordinates: 4 30 N, 114 40 E

Map references: Southeast Asia

Area:
total: 5,770 sq km
land: 5,270 sq km
water: 500 sq km

Area - comparative: slightly smaller than Delaware

Land boundaries:
total: 381 km
border countries: Malaysia 381 km

Coastline: 161 km

Maritime claims:
exclusive economic zone: 200 nm or to median line
territorial sea: 12 nm

Climate: tropical; hot, humid, rainy

Terrain: flat coastal plain rises to mountains in east; hilly lowland in west

Elevation extremes:
lowest point: South China Sea 0 m
highest point: Bukit Pagon 1,850 m

Natural resources: petroleum, natural gas, timber

Land use:
arable land: 1%
permanent crops: 1%
permanent pastures: 1%
forests and woodland: 85%
other: 12% (1993 est.)

Irrigated land: 10 sq km (1993 est.)

Natural hazards: typhoons, earthquakes, and severe flooding are very rare

Environment - current issues: seasonal smoke/haze resulting from forest fires in Indonesia

Environment - international agreements:
party to: Endangered Species, Law of the Sea, Ozone Layer Protection, Ship Pollution
signed, but not ratified: none of the selected agreements

Geography - note: close to vital sea lanes through South China Sea linking Indian and Pacific Oceans; two parts physically separated by Malaysia; almost an enclave of Malaysia

People

Population: 322,982 (July 1999 est.)

Age structure:
0-14 years: 33% (male 54,154; female 51,766)
15-64 years: 63% (male 106,492; female 95,921)
65 years and over: 4% (male 7,945; female 6,704) (1999 est.)

Population growth rate: 2.38% (1999 est.)

Birth rate: 24.69 births/1,000 population (1999 est.)

Death rate: 5.21 deaths/1,000 population (1999 est.)

Net migration rate: 4.35 migrant(s)/1,000 population (1999 est.)

Sex ratio:
at birth: 1.06 male(s)/female
under 15 years: 1.05 male(s)/female
15-64 years: 1.11 male(s)/female
65 years and over: 1.19 male(s)/female
total population: 1.09 male(s)/female (1999 est.)

Infant mortality rate: 22.83 deaths/1,000 live births (1999 est.)

Life expectancy at birth:
total population: 71.84 years
male: 70.35 years
female: 73.42 years (1999 est.)

Total fertility rate: 3.33 children born/woman (1999 est.)

Nationality:
noun: Bruneian(s)
adjective: Bruneian

Ethnic groups: Malay 64%, Chinese 20%, other 16%

Religions: Muslim (official) 63%, Buddhism 14%, Christian 8%, indigenous beliefs and other 15% (1981)

Languages: Malay (official), English, Chinese

Literacy:
definition: age 15 and over can read and write
total population: 88.2%
male: 92.6%
female: 83.4% (1995 est.)

Government

Country name:
conventional long form: Negara Brunei Darussalam
conventional short form: Brunei

Data code: BX

Government type: constitutional sultanate

Capital: Bandar Seri Begawan

Administrative divisions: 4 districts (daerah-daerah, singular - daerah); Belait, Brunei and Muara, Temburong, Tutong

Independence: 1 January 1984 (from UK)

National holiday: National Day, 23 February (1984)

Constitution: 29 September 1959 (some provisions suspended under a State of Emergency since December 1962, others since independence on 1 January 1984)

Legal system: based on English common law; for Muslims, Islamic Shari'a law supersedes civil law in a number of areas

Suffrage: none

Executive branch:
chief of state: Sultan and Prime Minister His Majesty Paduka Seri Baginda Sultan Haji HASSANAL Bolkiah Mu'izzaddin Waddaulah (since 5 October 1967); note - the monarch is both the chief of state and head of government
head of government: Sultan and Prime Minister His Majesty Paduka Seri Baginda Sultan Haji HASSANAL Bolkiah Mu'izzaddin Waddaulah (since 5 October 1967); note - the monarch is both the chief of state and head of government
cabinet: Council of Cabinet Ministers appointed and presided over by the monarch; deals with executive matters
note: there is also a Religious Council (members appointed by the monarch) that advises on religious matters, a Privy Council (members appointed by the monarch) that deals with constitutional matters, and the Council of Succession (members appointed by the monarch) that determines the succession to the throne if the need arises
elections: none; the monarch is hereditary

Legislative branch: unicameral Legislative Council or Majlis Masyuarat Megeri (a privy council that serves only in a consultative capacity; NA seats; members appointed by the monarch)
elections: last held in March 1962
note: in 1970 the Council was changed to an appointive body by decree of the monarch; an elected Legislative Council is being considered as part of constitutional reform, but elections are unlikely for several years

Judicial branch: Supreme Court, chief justice and judges are sworn in by the monarch for three-year terms

Political parties and leaders: Brunei Solidarity National Party or PPKB in Malay [Haji Mohd HATTA bin Haji Zainal Abidin, president]; the PPKB is the only legal political party in Brunei; it was registered in 1985, but became largely inactive after 1988; it has less than 200 registered party members; other parties include Brunei People's Party or PRB (banned in 1962) and Brunei National Democratic Party (registered in May 1985, deregistered by the Brunei Government in 1988)

International organization participation: APEC, ASEAN, C, CCC, ESCAP, G-77, IBRD, ICAO, ICRM, IDB, IFRCS, IMF, IMO, Inmarsat, Intelsat, Interpol, IOC, ISO (correspondent), ITU, NAM, OIC, OPCW, UN, UNCTAD, UPU, WHO, WIPO, WMO, WTrO

Diplomatic representation in the US:
chief of mission: Ambassador Pengiran Anak Dato Haji PUTEH Ibni Mohammad Alam
chancery: Watergate, Suite 300, 3rd floor, 2600 Virginia Avenue NW, Washington, DC 20037
telephone: [1] (202) 342-0159
FAX: [1] (202) 342-0158

Brunei *(continued)*

Diplomatic representation from the US:
chief of mission: Ambassador Glen Robert RASE
embassy: Third Floor, Teck Guan Plaza, Jalan Sultan, Bandar Seri Begawan
mailing address: PSC 470 (BSB), FPO AP 96534-0001
telephone: [673] (2) 229670
FAX: [673] (2) 225293
Flag description: yellow with two diagonal bands of white (top, almost double width) and black starting from the upper hoist side; the national emblem in red is superimposed at the center; the emblem includes a swallow-tailed flag on top of a winged column within an upturned crescent above a scroll and flanked by two upraised hands

Economy

Economy - overview: This small, wealthy economy is a mixture of foreign and domestic entrepreneurship, government regulation and welfare measures, and village tradition. It is almost totally supported by exports of crude oil and natural gas, with revenues from the petroleum sector accounting for over half of GDP. Per capita GDP is far above most other Third World countries, and substantial income from overseas investment supplements income from domestic production. The government provides for all medical services and subsidizes food and housing. The government is beginning to show progress on its basic policy of diversifying the economy away from oil and gas. Brunei's leaders are concerned that steadily increased integration in the world economy will undermine internal social cohesion. Because of low world oil prices and the Asian crisis, growth in 1999 is expected to be moderate.
GDP: purchasing power parity - $5.4 billion (1998 est.)
GDP - real growth rate: -1% (1998 est.)
GDP - per capita: purchasing power parity - $17,000 (1998 est.)
GDP - composition by sector:
agriculture: 5%
industry: 46%
services: 49% (1996 est.)
Population below poverty line: NA%
Household income or consumption by percentage share:
lowest 10%: NA%
highest 10%: NA%
Inflation rate (consumer prices): 2% (1997 est.)
Labor force: 144,000 (1995 est.); note - includes foreign workers and military personnel
note: temporary residents make up 41% of labor force (1991)
Labor force - by occupation: government 48%, production of oil, natural gas, services, and construction 42%, agriculture, forestry, and fishing 4%, other 6% (1986 est.)
Unemployment rate: 4.8% (1994 est.)
Budget:
revenues: $2.5 billion
expenditures: $2.6 billion, including capital

expenditures of $768 million (1995 est.)
Industries: petroleum, petroleum refining, liquefied natural gas, construction
Industrial production growth rate: 4% (1997 est.)
Electricity - production: 1.48 billion kWh (1996)
Electricity - production by source:
fossil fuel: 100%
hydro: 0%
nuclear: 0%
other: 0% (1996)
Electricity - consumption: 1.48 billion kWh (1996)
Electricity - exports: 0 kWh (1996)
Electricity - imports: 0 kWh (1996)
Agriculture - products: rice, cassava (tapioca), bananas; water buffalo
Exports: $2.62 billion (f.o.b., 1996 est.)
Exports - commodities: crude oil, liquefied natural gas, petroleum products
Exports - partners: ASEAN 31%, Japan 27%, South Korea 26%, UK, Taiwan (1996 est.)
Imports: $2.65 billion (c.i.f., 1996 est.)
Imports - commodities: machinery and transport equipment, manufactured goods, food, chemicals
Imports - partners: Singapore 29%, UK 19%, US 13%, Malaysia 9%, Japan 5% (1994 est.)
Debt - external: $0
Economic aid - recipient: $4.3 million (1995)
Currency: 1 Bruneian dollar (B$) = 100 cents
Exchange rates: Bruneian dollars (B$) per US$1 - 1.6781 (January 1999), 1.6736 (1998), 1.4848 (1997), 1.4100 (1996), 1.4174 (1995), 1.5274 (1994); note - the Bruneian dollar is at par with the Singapore dollar
Fiscal year: calendar year

Communications

Telephones: 90,000 (1997 est.)
Telephone system: service throughout country is excellent; international service good to Europe, US, and East Asia
domestic: NA
international: satellite earth stations - 2 Intelsat (1 Indian Ocean and 1 Pacific Ocean)
Radio broadcast stations: AM 3, FM 10, shortwave 0 (1998)
Radios: 284,000 (1995 est.)
Television broadcast stations: 2 (1997)
Televisions: 173,000 (1995 est.)

Transportation

Railways:
total: 13 km (private line)
narrow gauge: 13 km 0.610-m gauge
Highways:
total: 1,150 km
paved: 399 km
unpaved: 751 km (1996 est.)
Waterways: 209 km; navigable by craft drawing less than 1.2 m
Pipelines: crude oil 135 km; petroleum products 418 km; natural gas 920 km
Ports and harbors: Bandar Seri Begawan, Kuala

Belait, Muara, Seria, Tutong
Merchant marine:
total: 7 liquefied gas tankers (1,000 GRT or over) totaling 348,476 GRT/340,635 DWT (1998 est.)
Airports: 2 (1998 est.)
Airports - with paved runways:
total: 1
over 3,047 m: 1 (1998 est.)
Airports - with unpaved runways:
total: 1
914 to 1,523 m: 1 (1998 est.)
Heliports: 3 (1998 est.)

Military

Military branches: Land Forces, Navy, Air Force, Royal Brunei Police
Military manpower - military age: 18 years of age
Military manpower - availability:
males age 15-49: 88,628 (1999 est.)
Military manpower - fit for military service:
males age 15-49: 51,270 (1999 est.)
Military manpower - reaching military age annually:
males: 3,078 (1999 est.)
Military expenditures - dollar figure: $343 million (1997)
Military expenditures - percent of GDP: 6% (1997)

Transnational Issues

Disputes - international: possibly involved in a complex dispute over the Spratly Islands with China, Malaysia, Philippines, Taiwan, and Vietnam; in 1984, Brunei established an exclusive fishing zone that encompasses Louisa Reef in the southern Spratly Islands, but has not publicly claimed the island

Bulgaria

Introduction

Background: A Slavic state, Bulgaria achieved independence in 1908 after 500 years of Ottoman rule. Bulgaria fought on the losing side in both World Wars. After World War II it fell within the Soviet sphere of influence. Communist domination ended in 1991 with the dissolution of the USSR, and Bulgaria began the contentious process of moving toward political democracy and a market economy. In addition to the problems of structural economic reform, particularly privatization, Bulgaria faces the serious issues of keeping inflation under control and unemployment, combatting corruption, and curbing black-market and mafia-style crime.

Geography

Location: Southeastern Europe, bordering the Black Sea, between Romania and Turkey
Geographic coordinates: 43 00 N, 25 00 E
Map references: Europe
Area:
total: 110,910 sq km
land: 110,550 sq km
water: 360 sq km
Area - comparative: slightly larger than Tennessee
Land boundaries:
total: 1,808 km
border countries: Greece 494 km, The Former Yugoslav Republic of Macedonia 148 km, Romania 608 km, Serbia and Montenegro 318 km (all with Serbia), Turkey 240 km
Coastline: 354 km
Maritime claims:
contiguous zone: 24 nm
exclusive economic zone: 200 nm
territorial sea: 12 nm
Climate: temperate; cold, damp winters; hot, dry summers
Terrain: mostly mountains with lowlands in north and southeast

Elevation extremes:
lowest point: Black Sea 0 m
highest point: Musala 2,925 m
Natural resources: bauxite, copper, lead, zinc, coal, timber, arable land
Land use:
arable land: 37%
permanent crops: 2%
permanent pastures: 16%
forests and woodland: 35%
other: 10% (1993 est.)
Irrigated land: 12,370 sq km (1993 est.)
Natural hazards: earthquakes, landslides
Environment - current issues: air pollution from industrial emissions; rivers polluted from raw sewage, heavy metals, detergents; deforestation; forest damage from air pollution and resulting acid rain; soil contamination from heavy metals from metallurgical plants and industrial wastes
Environment - international agreements:
party to: Air Pollution, Air Pollution-Nitrogen Oxides, Air Pollution-Sulphur 85, Air Pollution-Volatile Organic Compounds, Antarctic-Environmental Protocol, Antarctic Treaty, Biodiversity, Climate Change, Endangered Species, Environmental Modification, Hazardous Wastes, Law of the Sea, Nuclear Test Ban, Ozone Layer Protection, Ship Pollution, Wetlands
signed, but not ratified: Air Pollution-Persistent Organic Pollutants, Air Pollution-Sulphur 94, Climate Change-Kyoto Protocol
Geography - note: strategic location near Turkish Straits; controls key land routes from Europe to Middle East and Asia

People

Population: 8,194,772 (July 1999 est.)
Age structure:
0-14 years: 16% (male 674,643; female 641,943)
15-64 years: 68% (male 2,744,634; female 2,800,816)
65 years and over: 16% (male 570,766; female 761,970) (1999 est.)
Population growth rate: -0.52% (1999 est.)
Birth rate: 8.71 births/1,000 population (1999 est.)
Death rate: 13.2 deaths/1,000 population (1999 est.)
Net migration rate: -0.66 migrant(s)/1,000 population (1999 est.)
Sex ratio:
at birth: 1.06 male(s)/female
under 15 years: 1.05 male(s)/female
15-64 years: 0.98 male(s)/female
65 years and over: 0.75 male(s)/female
total population: 0.95 male(s)/female (1999 est.)
Infant mortality rate: 12.37 deaths/1,000 live births (1999 est.)
Life expectancy at birth:
total population: 72.27 years
male: 68.72 years
female: 76.03 years (1999 est.)
Total fertility rate: 1.23 children born/woman (1999 est.)

Nationality:
noun: Bulgarian(s)
adjective: Bulgarian
Ethnic groups: Bulgarian 85%, Turk 9%, other 6%
Religions: Bulgarian Orthodox 85%, Muslim 13%, Jewish 0.8%, Roman Catholic 0.5%, Uniate Catholic 0.2%, Protestant, Gregorian-Armenian, and other 0.5%
Languages: Bulgarian, secondary languages closely correspond to ethnic breakdown
Literacy:
definition: age 15 and over can read and write
total population: 98%
male: 99%
female: 97% (1992 est.)

Government

Country name:
conventional long form: Republic of Bulgaria
conventional short form: Bulgaria
Data code: BU
Government type: republic
Capital: Sofia
Administrative divisions: 9 provinces (oblasti, singular - oblast); Burgas, Grad Sofiya, Khaskovo, Lovech, Montana, Plovdiv, Ruse, Sofiya, Varna
Independence: 22 September 1908 (from Ottoman Empire)
National holiday: Independence Day, 3 March (1878)
Constitution: adopted 12 July 1991
Legal system: civil law and criminal law based on Roman law; accepts compulsory ICJ jurisdiction
Suffrage: 18 years of age; universal
Executive branch:
chief of state: President Petar STOYANOV (since 22 January 1997); Vice President Todor KAVALDZHIEV (since 22 January 1997)
head of government: Chairman of the Council of Ministers (Prime Minister) Ivan Kostov (since 19 May 1997); Deputy Prime Ministers Aleksandur BOZHKOV (since 12 February 1997), Evgeniy BAKURDZHIEV (since 21 May 1997), Veselin METODIEV (since 21 May 1997)
cabinet: Council of Ministers elected by the National Assembly
elections: president and vice president elected on the same ticket by popular vote for five-year terms; election last held 27 October and 3 November 1996 (next to be held NA 2001); chairman of the Council of Ministers (prime minister) nominated by the president; deputy prime ministers nominated by the prime minister
election results: Petar STOYANOV elected president; percent of vote - Petar STOYANOV 59.73%
Legislative branch: unicameral National Assembly or Narodno Sobranie (240 seats; members elected by popular vote to serve four-year terms)
elections: last held 19 April 1997 (next to be held NA 2001)
election results: percent of vote by party - UDF 52%, BSP 22%, ANS 7%, Euro-left 5.5%, BBB 4.95%; seats

Bulgaria *(continued)*

by party - UDF 137, BSP 58, ANS 19, Euro-left 14, BBB 12

Judicial branch: Supreme Court, chairman appointed for a seven-year term by the president; Constitutional Court, 12 justices appointed or elected for nine-year terms

Political parties and leaders: Bulgarian Socialist Party or BSP [Georgi PURVANOV, chairman]; Union of Democratic Forces or UDF (an alliance of pro-Democratic parties) [Ivan KOSTOV]; Euro-left [Aleksandur TOMOV]; Alliance for National Salvation or ANS (coalition led mainly by Movement for Rights and Freedoms or DPS [Ahmed DOGAN]); People's Union [Anastasiya MOZER and Stefan SAVOV, cochairmen]

Political pressure groups and leaders: Democratic Alliance for the Republic or DAR; New Union for Democracy or NUD; Podkrepa Labor Confederation; Confederation of Independent Trade Unions of Bulgaria or CITUB; Bulgarian Agrarian National Union - United or BZNS; Bulgarian Democratic Center; "Nikola Petkov" Bulgarian Agrarian National Union; Internal Macedonian Revolutionary Organization or IMRO; agrarian movement; numerous regional, ethnic, and national interest groups with various agendas

International organization participation: ACCT, BIS, BSEC, CCC, CE, CEI, EAPC, EBRD, ECE, EU (applicant), FAO, G- 9, IAEA, IBRD, ICAO, ICFTU, ICRM, IDA, IDB, IFAD, IFC, IFRCS, IHO (pending member), ILO, IMF, IMO, Inmarsat, Intelsat, Interpol, IOC, IOM, ISO, ITU, MONUA, NAM (guest), NSG, OPCW, OSCE, PCA, PFP, UN, UNCTAD, UNESCO, UNIDO, UNMIBH, UNMOP, UPU, WEU (associate partner), WFTU, WHO, WIPO, WMO, WToO, WTrO, ZC

Diplomatic representation in the US:
chief of mission: Ambassador Philip DIMITROV
chancery: 1621 22nd Street NW, Washington, DC 20008
telephone: [1] (202) 387-7969
FAX: [1] (202) 234-7973
consulate(s): New York

Diplomatic representation from the US:
chief of mission: Ambassador Avis T. BOHLEN
embassy: 1 Saborna Street, Sofia
mailing address: American Embassy Sofia, Department of State, Washington, DC 20521-5740
telephone: [359] (2) 980-52-41 through 48
FAX: [359] (2) 981-89-77

Flag description: three equal horizontal bands of white (top), green, and red; the national emblem formerly on the hoist side of the white stripe has been removed - it contained a rampant lion within a wreath of wheat ears below a red five-pointed star and above a ribbon bearing the dates 681 (first Bulgarian state established) and 1944 (liberation from Nazi control)

Economy

Economy - overview: In April 1997, the current ruling Union of Democratic Forces (UDF) government won pre-term parliamentary elections and introduced an IMF currency board system which succeeded in stabilizing the economy. The triple digit inflation of 1996 and 1997 has given way to an official consumer price increase of 1% in 1998. Following declines in GDP in both 1996 and 1997, the economy grew an officially estimated 4% in 1998. In September 1998, the IMF approved a three-year Extended Fund Facility, which provides credits worth approximately $864 million, designed to support Bulgaria's reform efforts. The government's structural reform program includes: (a) privatization and, where appropriate, liquidation of state-owned enterprises (SOEs); (b) liberalization of agricultural policies, including creating conditions for the development of a land market; (c) reform of the country's social insurance programs; and, (d) reforms to strengthen contract enforcement and fight crime and corruption.

GDP: purchasing power parity - $33.6 billion (1998 est.)

GDP - real growth rate: 4% (1998 est.)

GDP - per capita: purchasing power parity - $4,100 (1998 est.)

GDP - composition by sector:
agriculture: 26%
industry: 29%
services: 45% (1997 est.)

Population below poverty line: NA%

Household income or consumption by percentage share:
lowest 10%: 3.3%
highest 10%: 24.7% (1992)

Inflation rate (consumer prices): 1% (1998 est.)

Labor force: 3.57 million (1996 est.)

Labor force - by occupation: NA

Unemployment rate: 12.2% (1998 est.)

Budget:
revenues: $4.1 billion
expenditures: $3.8 billion, including capital expenditures of $NA (1998 est.)

Industries: machine building and metal working, food processing, chemicals, textiles, construction materials, ferrous and nonferrous metals

Industrial production growth rate: NA%

Electricity - production: 41.575 billion kWh (1996)

Electricity - production by source:
fossil fuel: 51.17%
hydro: 6.1%
nuclear: 42.73%
other: 0% (1996)

Electricity - consumption: 41.08 billion kWh (1996)

Electricity - exports: 2.045 billion kWh (1996)

Electricity - imports: 1.55 billion kWh (1996)

Agriculture - products: grain, oilseed, vegetables, fruits, tobacco; livestock

Exports: $4.5 billion (f.o.b., 1998)

Exports - commodities: machinery and equipment; metals, minerals, and fuels; chemicals and plastics; food, textiles (1997)

Exports - partners: Italy 12%, Germany 10%, Turkey, Greece, Russia (1997)

Imports: $4.6 billion (f.o.b., 1998 est.)

Imports - commodities: fuels, minerals, and raw materials; machinery and equipment; metals and ores; chemicals and plastics; food, textiles (1997)

Imports - partners: Russia 28%, Germany 11%, Italy, Greece, US (1997)

Debt - external: $9.3 billion (1998 est.)

Economic aid - recipient: $NA

Currency: 1 lev (Lv) = 100 stotinki

Exchange rates: leva (Lv) per US$1 - 1,685.10 (January 1999), 1,760.36 (1998), 1,681.88 (1997), 177.89 (1996), 67.17 (1995), 54.13 (1994)
note: the official rate is pegged to the euro as of 1 January 1999

Fiscal year: calendar year

Communications

Telephones: 2,773,293 (1993 est.)

Telephone system: almost two-thirds of the lines are residential
domestic: extensive but antiquated transmission system of coaxial cable and microwave radio relay; telephone service is available in most villages
international: direct dialing to 36 countries; satellite earth stations - 1 Intersputnik (Atlantic Ocean region); Intelsat available through a Greek earth station

Radio broadcast stations: AM 24, FM 93, shortwave 2 (1998)

Radios: NA

Television broadcast stations: 33 (in addition, there are two relays of Russian program OK-1 and two relays of TV-5 Europe) (1997)

Televisions: 2.1 million (May 1990 est.)

Transportation

Railways:
total: 4,292 km
standard gauge: 4,047 km 1.435-m gauge (2,650 km electrified; 917 km double track)
narrow gauge: 245 km 0.760-m gauge (1995)

Highways:
total: 36,724 km
paved: 33,786 km (including 314 km of expressways)
unpaved: 2,938 km (1997 est.)

Waterways: 470 km (1987)

Pipelines: crude oil 193 km; petroleum products 525 km; natural gas 1,400 km (1992)

Ports and harbors: Burgas, Lom, Nesebur, Ruse, Varna, Vidin

Merchant marine:
total: 89 ships (1,000 GRT or over) totaling 1,005,092 GRT/1,508,614 DWT
ships by type: bulk 44, cargo 20, chemical tanker 4, container 2, oil tanker 8, passenger-cargo 1, railcar carrier 2, refrigerated cargo 1, roll-on/roll-off cargo 6, short-sea passenger 1 (1998 est.)

Airports: 61 (1998 est.)

Airports - with paved runways:
total: 56
over 3,047 m: 1
2,438 to 3,047 m: 19
1,524 to 2,437 m: 11
under 914 m: 25 (1998 est.)

Bulgaria (continued)

Airports - with unpaved runways:
total: 5
914 to 1,523 m: 1
under 914 m: 4 (1998 est.)

Military

Military branches: Army, Navy, Air and Air Defense Forces, Border Troops, Internal Troops
Military manpower - military age: 19 years of age
Military manpower - availability:
males age 15-49: 2,028,930 (1999 est.)
Military manpower - fit for military service:
males age 15-49: 1,693,597 (1999 est.)
Military manpower - reaching military age annually:
males: 59,887 (1999 est.)
Military expenditures - dollar figure: $226.8 million (1997)
Military expenditures - percent of GDP: 2.2% (1997)

Transnational Issues

Disputes - international: twenty bilateral agreements remain unsigned in a dispute over Bulgarian nonrecognition of Macedonian as a language distinct from Bulgarian
Illicit drugs: major European transshipment point for Southwest Asian heroin and, to a lesser degree, South American cocaine for the European market; limited producer of precursor chemicals; significant producer of amphetamines, much of which are consumed in the Middle East

Burkina Faso

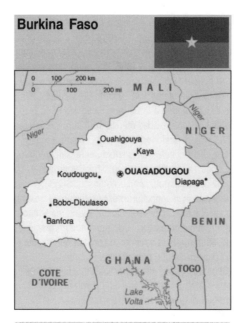

Geography

Location: Western Africa, north of Ghana
Geographic coordinates: 13 00 N, 2 00 W
Map references: Africa
Area:
total: 274,200 sq km
land: 273,800 sq km
water: 400 sq km
Area - comparative: slightly larger than Colorado
Land boundaries:
total: 3,192 km
border countries: Benin 306 km, Ghana 548 km, Cote d'Ivoire 584 km, Mali 1,000 km, Niger 628 km, Togo 126 km
Coastline: 0 km (landlocked)
Maritime claims: none (landlocked)
Climate: tropical; warm, dry winters; hot, wet summers
Terrain: mostly flat to dissected, undulating plains; hills in west and southeast
Elevation extremes:
lowest point: Mouhoun (Black Volta) River 200 m
highest point: Tena Kourou 749 m
Natural resources: manganese, limestone, marble; small deposits of gold, antimony, copper, nickel, bauxite, lead, phosphates, zinc, silver
Land use:
arable land: 13%
permanent crops: 0%
permanent pastures: 22%
forests and woodland: 50%
other: 15% (1993 est.)
Irrigated land: 200 sq km (1993 est.)
Natural hazards: recurring droughts
Environment - current issues: recent droughts and desertification severely affecting agricultural activities, population distribution, and the economy; overgrazing; soil degradation; deforestation
Environment - international agreements:
party to: Biodiversity, Climate Change,

Desertification, Endangered Species, Marine Life Conservation, Ozone Layer Protection, Wetlands
signed, but not ratified: Law of the Sea, Nuclear Test Ban
Geography - note: landlocked

People

Population: 11,575,898 (July 1999 est.)
Age structure:
0-14 years: 48% (male 2,792,895; female 2,759,072)
15-64 years: 49% (male 2,700,253; female 2,978,168)
65 years and over: 3% (male 147,017; female 198,493) (1999 est.)
Population growth rate: 2.7% (1999 est.)
Birth rate: 45.84 births/1,000 population (1999 est.)
Death rate: 17.56 deaths/1,000 population (1999 est.)
Net migration rate: -1.25 migrant(s)/1,000 population (1999 est.)
Sex ratio:
at birth: 1.03 male(s)/female
under 15 years: 1.01 male(s)/female
15-64 years: 0.91 male(s)/female
65 years and over: 0.74 male(s)/female
total population: 0.95 male(s)/female (1999 est.)
Infant mortality rate: 107.19 deaths/1,000 live births (1999 est.)
Life expectancy at birth:
total population: 45.89 years
male: 44.97 years
female: 46.84 years (1999 est.)
Total fertility rate: 6.56 children born/woman (1999 est.)
Nationality:
noun: Burkinabe (singular and plural)
adjective: Burkinabe
Ethnic groups: Mossi about 24%, Gurunsi, Senufo, Lobi, Bobo, Mande, Fulani
Religions: indigenous beliefs 40%, Muslim 50%, Christian (mainly Roman Catholic) 10%
Languages: French (official), tribal languages belonging to Sudanic family, spoken by 90% of the population
Literacy:
definition: age 15 and over can read and write
total population: 19.2%
male: 29.5%
female: 9.2% (1995 est.)

Government

Country name:
conventional long form: none
conventional short form: Burkina Faso
former: Upper Volta
Data code: UV
Government type: parliamentary
Capital: Ouagadougou
Administrative divisions: 30 provinces; Bam, Bazega, Bougouriba, Boulgou, Boulkiemde, Ganzourgou, Gnagna, Gourma, Houe, Kadiogo,

Kenedougou, Komoe, Kossi, Kouritenga, Mouhoun, Namentenga, Naouri, Oubritenga, Oudalan, Passore, Poni, Sanguie, Sanmatenga, Seno, Sissili, Soum, Sourou, Tapoa, Yatenga, Zoundweogo

note: a new electoral code was approved by the National Assembly in January 1997; the number of administrative provinces was increased from 30 to 45 (Bale, Bam, Banwa, Bazega, Bougouriba, Boulgou, Boulkiemde, Comoe, Ganzourgou, Gnagna, Gourma, Houet, Ioba, Kadiogo, Kenedougou, Komandjari, Kompienga, Kossi, Koupelogo, Kouritenga, Kourweogo, Leraba, Loroum, Mouhoun, Nahouri, Namentenga, Nayala, Naumbiel, Oubritenga, Oudalan, Passore, Poni, Samentenga, Sanguie, Seno, Sissili, Soum, Sourou, Tapoa, Tuy, Yagha, Yatenga, Ziro, Zondomo, Zoundweogo)

Independence: 5 August 1960 (from France)

National holiday: Anniversary of the Revolution, 4 August (1983)

Constitution: 2 June 1991

Legal system: based on French civil law system and customary law

Suffrage: universal

Executive branch:

chief of state: President Captain Blaise COMPAORE (since 15 October 1987)

head of government: Prime Minister Kadre Desire OUEDRAOGO (since 6 February 1996)

cabinet: Council of Ministers appointed by the president on the recommendation of the prime minister

elections: president elected by popular vote for a seven-year term; the number of terms which a president may serve is not limited; election last held 15 November 1998 (next to be held NA 2005); prime minister appointed by the president with the consent of the legislature

election results: Blaise COMPAORE reelected president with 88% percent of the vote, with 56% of voter turnout

Legislative branch: bicameral; consists of a National Assembly or Assemblee des Deputes Populaires (ADP) (111 seats; members are elected by popular vote to serve five-year terms) and the purely consultative Chamber of Representations or Chambre des Representants (120 seats; members are appointed to serve three-year terms)

elections: National Assembly election last held 11 May 1997 (next to be held NA 2002)

election results: percent of vote by party - NA; seats by party - CDP 101, PDP 6, RDA 2, ADF 2

Judicial branch: Supreme Court; Appeals Court

Political parties and leaders: Alliance for Democracy and Federation-African Democratic Assembly or ADF-RDA [Herman YAMEOGO]; Burkinabe Bolshevic Party or PBB [leader NA]; Burkinabe Socialist Party or PSB [leader NA]; Burkinabe Socialist Bloc or BSB [Earnest Nongma OUEDRAOGO, president]; Burkinabe Environmentalist Party or UVDB [leader NA]; Congress for Democracy and Progress or CDP [Din Salif SAWADAGO]; Front for Social Forces or FFS

[Fide'le KIENTEGA]; Movement for Social Tolerance and Progress or MTP [leader NA]; New Social Democrats or NSD [leader NA]; Open Revolutionary Party or POR [leader NA]; Party for Democracy and Progress or PDP [Joseph KI-ZERBO]; Party for Progress and Social Development or PPDS [leader NA]; Party for African Independence or PAI [leader NA]; Front de Refus or RDA [Frederic GUIRMA]; Green Party [Ram OUEDRAOGO]; Group for Progressive Democrats or GDP [Issa TIENDREBEOGO]

Political pressure groups and leaders: watchdog/ political action groups throughout the country in both organizations and communities; Burkinabe Movement for Human Rights or HBDHP; Burkinabe General Confederation of Labor or CGTB; National Confederation of Burkinabe Workers or CNTB; National Organization of Free Unions or ONSL; Group of 14 February

International organization participation: ACCT, ACP, AfDB, CCC, ECA, ECOWAS, Entente, FAO, FZ, G-77, IBRD, ICAO, ICC, ICFTU, ICRM, IDA, IDB, IFAD, IFC, IFRCS, ILO, IMF, Intelsat, Interpol, IOC, ITU, MINURCA, NAM, OAU, OIC, OPCW, PCA, UN, UNCTAD, UNESCO, UNIDO, UPU, WADB, WAEMU, WCL, WFTU, WHO, WIPO, WMO, WToO, WTrO

Diplomatic representation in the US:

chief of mission: Ambassador Gaetan Rimwangulya OUEDRAOGO

chancery: 2340 Massachusetts Avenue NW, Washington, DC 20008

telephone: [1] (202) 332-5577

FAX: [1] (202) 667-1882

Diplomatic representation from the US:

chief of mission: Ambassador Sharon P. WILKINSON

embassy: Avenue Raoul Follereau, Ouagadougou

mailing address: 01 B. P. 35, Ouagadougou

telephone: [226] 306723 through 306725

FAX: [226] 303890

Flag description: two equal horizontal bands of red (top) and green with a yellow five-pointed star in the center; uses the popular pan-African colors of Ethiopia

Economy

Economy - overview: One of the poorest countries in the world, landlocked Burkina Faso has a high population density, few natural resources, and a fragile soil. About 85% of the population is engaged in (mainly subsistence) agriculture which is highly vulnerable to variations in rainfall. Industry remains dominated by unprofitable government-controlled corporations. Following the African franc currency devaluation in January 1994 the government updated its development program in conjunction with international agencies, and exports and economic growth have increased. Maintenance of its macroeconomic progress in 1999-2000 depends on continued low inflation, reduction in the trade deficit, and reforms designed to encourage private investment.

GDP: purchasing power parity - $11.6 billion (1998 est.)

GDP - real growth rate: 6% (1998 est.)

GDP - per capita: purchasing power parity - $1,000 (1998 est.)

GDP - composition by sector:

agriculture: 35%

industry: 25%

services: 40% (1997)

Population below poverty line: NA%

Household income or consumption by percentage share:

lowest 10%: NA%

highest 10%: NA%

Inflation rate (consumer prices): 2.5% (1998 est.)

Labor force: 4.679 million (persons 10 years old and over, according to a sample survey taken in 1991)

note: a large part of the male labor force migrates annually to neighboring countries for seasonal employment

Labor force - by occupation: agriculture 85%, industry, commerce, services, government (1998)

Unemployment rate: NA%

Budget:

revenues: $277 million

expenditures: $492 million, including capital expenditures of $233 million (1995 est.)

Industries: cotton lint, beverages, agricultural processing, soap, cigarettes, textiles, gold

Industrial production growth rate: 4.2% (1995)

Electricity - production: 220 million kWh (1996)

Electricity - production by source:

fossil fuel: 63.64%

hydro: 36.36%

nuclear: 0%

other: 0% (1996)

Electricity - consumption: 220 million kWh (1996)

Electricity - exports: 0 kWh (1996)

Electricity - imports: 0 kWh (1996)

Agriculture - products: peanuts, shea nuts, sesame, cotton, sorghum, millet, corn, rice; livestock

Exports: $400 million (f.o.b., 1997 est.)

Exports - commodities: cotton, animal products, gold

Exports - partners: Cote d'Ivoire, France, Italy, Mali

Imports: $700 million (f.o.b., 1997 est.)

Imports - commodities: machinery, food products, petroleum

Imports - partners: Cote d'Ivoire, France, Togo, Nigeria

Debt - external: $715 million (December 1996)

Economic aid - recipient: $484.1 million (1995)

Currency: 1 Communaute Financiere Africaine franc (CFAF) = 100 centimes

Exchange rates: Communaute Financiere Africaine francs (CFAF) per US$1 - 560.01 (December 1998), 589.95 (1998), 583.67 (1997), 511.55 (1996), 499.15 (1995), 555.20 (1994)

Fiscal year: calendar year

Communications

Telephones: 21,000 (1993 est.)
Telephone system: all services only fair
domestic: microwave radio relay, open wire, and radiotelephone communication stations
international: satellite earth station - 1 Intelsat (Atlantic Ocean)
Radio broadcast stations: AM 2, FM 17, shortwave 1 (1998)
Radios: NA
Television broadcast stations: 1 (1997)
Televisions: 49,000 (1991 est.)

Transportation

Railways:
total: 622 km (517 km from Ouagadougou to the Cote d'Ivoire border and 105 km from Ouagadougou to Kaya)
narrow gauge: 622 km 1.000-m gauge (1995 est.)
Highways:
total: 12,506 km
paved: 2,001 km
unpaved: 10,505 km (1995 est.)
Ports and harbors: none
Airports: 33 (1998 est.)
Airports - with paved runways:
total: 2
over 3,047 m: 1
2,438 to 3,047 m: 1 (1998 est.)
Airports - with unpaved runways:
total: 31
2,438 to 3,047 m: 1
1,524 to 2,437 m: 1
914 to 1,523 m: 13
under 914 m: 16 (1998 est.)

Military

Military branches: Army, Air Force, National Gendarmerie, National Police, People's Militia
Military manpower - availability:
males age 15-49: 2,399,724 (1999 est.)
Military manpower - fit for military service:
males age 15-49: 1,230,713 (1999 est.)
Military expenditures - dollar figure: $66 million (1996)
Military expenditures - percent of GDP: 2% (1996)

Transnational Issues

Disputes - international: none

Burma

Geography

Location: Southeastern Asia, bordering the Andaman Sea and the Bay of Bengal, between Bangladesh and Thailand
Geographic coordinates: 22 00 N, 98 00 E
Map references: Southeast Asia
Area:
total: 678,500 sq km
land: 657,740 sq km
water: 20,760 sq km
Area - comparative: slightly smaller than Texas
Land boundaries:
total: 5,876 km
border countries: Bangladesh 193 km, China 2,185 km, India 1,463 km, Laos 235 km, Thailand 1,800 km
Coastline: 1,930 km
Maritime claims:
contiguous zone: 24 nm
continental shelf: 200 nm or to the edge of the continental margin
exclusive economic zone: 200 nm
territorial sea: 12 nm
Climate: tropical monsoon; cloudy, rainy, hot, humid summers (southwest monsoon, June to September);

less cloudy, scant rainfall, mild temperatures, lower humidity during winter (northeast monsoon, December to April)
Terrain: central lowlands ringed by steep, rugged highlands
Elevation extremes:
lowest point: Andaman Sea 0 m
highest point: Hkakabo Razi 5,881 m
Natural resources: petroleum, timber, tin, antimony, zinc, copper, tungsten, lead, coal, some marble, limestone, precious stones, natural gas
Land use:
arable land: 15%
permanent crops: 1%
permanent pastures: 1%
forests and woodland: 49%
other: 34% (1993 est.)
Irrigated land: 10,680 sq km (1993 est.)
Natural hazards: destructive earthquakes and cyclones; flooding and landslides common during rainy season (June to September); periodic droughts
Environment - current issues: deforestation; industrial pollution of air, soil, and water; inadequate sanitation and water treatment contribute to disease
Environment - international agreements:
party to: Biodiversity, Climate Change, Desertification, Law of the Sea, Nuclear Test Ban, Ozone Layer Protection, Ship Pollution, Tropical Timber 83, Tropical Timber 94
signed, but not ratified: none of the selected agreements
Geography - note: strategic location near major Indian Ocean shipping lanes

People

Population: 48,081,302 (July 1999 est.)
Age structure:
0-14 years: 36% (male 8,883,099; female 8,542,087)
15-64 years: 60% (male 14,343,888; female 14,293,233)
65 years and over: 4% (male 906,517; female 1,112,478) (1999 est.)
Population growth rate: 1.61% (1999 est.)
Birth rate: 28.48 births/1,000 population (1999 est.)
Death rate: 12.39 deaths/1,000 population (1999 est.)
Net migration rate: 0 migrant(s)/1,000 population (1999 est.)
Sex ratio:
at birth: 1.06 male(s)/female
under 15 years: 1.04 male(s)/female
15-64 years: 1 male(s)/female
65 years and over: 0.81 male(s)/female
total population: 1.01 male(s)/female (1999 est.)
Infant mortality rate: 76.25 deaths/1,000 live births (1999 est.)
Life expectancy at birth:
total population: 54.74 years
male: 53.24 years
female: 56.32 years (1999 est.)
Total fertility rate: 3.63 children born/woman (1999 est.)

Burma (continued)

Nationality:
noun: Burmese (singular and plural)
adjective: Burmese
Ethnic groups: Burman 68%, Shan 9%, Karen 7%, Rakhine 4%, Chinese 3%, Mon 2%, Indian 2%, other 5%
Religions: Buddhist 89%, Christian 4% (Baptist 3%, Roman Catholic 1%), Muslim 4%, animist beliefs 1%, other 2%
Languages: Burmese, minority ethnic groups have their own languages
Literacy:
definition: age 15 and over can read and write
total population: 83.1%
male: 88.7%
female: 77.7% (1995 est.)

Government

Country name:
conventional long form: Union of Burma
conventional short form: Burma
local long form: Pyidaungzu Myanma Naingngandaw (translated by the US Government as Union of Myanma and by the Burmese as Union of Myanmar)
local short form: Myanma Naingngandaw
former: Socialist Republic of the Union of Burma
Data code: BM
Government type: military regime
Capital: Rangoon (regime refers to the capital as Yangon)
Administrative divisions: 7 divisions* (yin-mya, singular - yin) and 7 states (pyine-mya, singular - pyine); Chin State, Ayeyarwady*, Bago*, Kachin State, Kayin State, Kayah State, Magway*, Mandalay*, Mon State, Rakhine State, Sagaing*, Shan State, Tanintharyi*, Yangon*
Independence: 4 January 1948 (from UK)
National holiday: Independence Day, 4 January (1948)
Constitution: 3 January 1974 (suspended since 18 September 1988); national convention started on 9 January 1993 to draft a new constitution; chapter headings and three of 15 sections have been approved
Legal system: does not accept compulsory ICJ jurisdiction
Suffrage: 18 years of age; universal
Executive branch:
chief of state: Prime Minister and Chairman of the State Peace and Development Council Gen. THAN SHWE (since 23 April 1992); note - the prime minister is both the chief of state and head of government
head of government: Prime Minister and Chairman of the State Peace and Development Council Gen. THAN SHWE (since 23 April 1992); note - the prime minister is both the chief of state and head of government
cabinet: State Peace and Development Council (SPDC); military junta, so named 15 November 1997, which initially assumed power 18 September 1988 under the name State Law and Order Restoration Council; the SPDC oversees the cabinet

elections: none; the prime minister assumed power upon resignation of the former prime minister
Legislative branch: unicameral People's Assembly or Pyithu Hluttaw (485 seats; members elected by popular vote to serve four-year terms)
elections: last held 27 May 1990, but Assembly never convened
election results: percent of vote by party - NA%; seats by party - NLD 396, NUP 10, other 79
Judicial branch: limited; remnants of the British-era legal system in place, but there is no guarantee of a fair public trial; the judiciary is not independent of the executive
Political parties and leaders: National Unity Party or NUP (proregime) [THA KYAW]; National League for Democracy or NLD [AUNG SHWE, chairman, AUNG SAN SUU KYI, general secretary]; Union Solidarity and Development Association or USDA (proregime, a social and political organization) [THAN AUNG, general secretary]; and eight minor legal parties
Political pressure groups and leaders: National Coalition Government of the Union of Burma or NCGUB [Dr. SEIN WIN] consists of individuals legitimately elected to the People's Assembly but not recognized by the military regime; the group fled to a border area and joined with insurgents in December 1990 to form a parallel government; Kachin Independence Army or KIA; United Wa State Army or UWSA; Karen National Union or KNU; several Shan factions; All Burma Student Democratic Front or ABSDF
International organization participation: AsDB, ASEAN, CCC, CP, ESCAP, FAO, G-77, IAEA, IBRD, ICAO, ICRM, IDA, IFAD, IFC, IFRCS, ILO, IMF, IMO, Intelsat (nonsignatory user), Interpol, IOC, ITU, NAM, OPCW, UN, UNCTAD, UNESCO, UNIDO, UPU, WHO, WMO, WToO, WTrO
Diplomatic representation in the US:
chief of mission: Ambassador TIN WINN
chancery: 2300 S Street NW, Washington, DC 20008
telephone: [1] (202) 332-9044
FAX: [1] (202) 332-9046
consulate(s) general: New York
Diplomatic representation from the US:
chief of mission: Ambassador (vacant); Charge d'Affaires Kent M. WIEDEMANN
embassy: 581 Merchant Street, Rangoon (GPO 521)
mailing address: Box B, APO AP 96546
telephone: [95] (1) 282055, 282182 (operator assistance required)
FAX: [95] (1) 280409
Flag description: red with a blue rectangle in the upper hoist-side corner bearing, all in white, 14 five-pointed stars encircling a cogwheel containing a stalk of rice; the 14 stars represent the 14 administrative divisions

Economy

Economy - overview: Burma has a mixed economy with private activity dominant in agriculture, light industry, and transport, and with substantial

state-controlled activity, mainly in energy, heavy industry, and the rice trade. Government policy in the last 10 years, 1989-98, has aimed at revitalizing the economy after three decades of tight central planning. Thus, private activity has markedly increased; foreign investment has been encouraged, so far with moderate success; and efforts continue to increase the efficiency of state enterprises. Published estimates of Burma's foreign trade are greatly understated because of the volume of black-market trade. A major ongoing problem is the failure to achieve monetary and fiscal stability. Although Burma remains a poor Asian country, its rich resources furnish the potential for substantial long-term increases in income, exports, and living standards. The short-term outlook is for continued sluggish growth because of internal unrest, minimal foreign investment, and the large trade deficit.
GDP: purchasing power parity - $56.1 billion (1998 est.)
GDP - real growth rate: 1.1% (1998 est.)
GDP - per capita: purchasing power parity - $1,200 (1998 est.)
GDP - composition by sector:
agriculture: 59%
industry: 11%
services: 30% (1997 est.)
Population below poverty line: NA%
Household income or consumption by percentage share:
lowest 10%: NA%
highest 10%: NA%
Inflation rate (consumer prices): 50% (1998 est.)
Labor force: 18.8 million (FY95/96 est.)
Labor force - by occupation: agriculture 65.2%, industry 14.3%, trade 10.1%, government 6.3%, other 4.1% (FY88/89 est.)
Unemployment rate: NA%
Budget:
revenues: $7.9 billion
expenditures: $12.2 billion, including capital expenditures of $5.7 billion (FY96/97)
Industries: agricultural processing; textiles and footwear; wood and wood products; copper, tin, tungsten, iron; construction materials; pharmaceuticals; fertilizer
Industrial production growth rate: 9.2% (FY95/96 est.)
Electricity - production: 3.75 billion kWh (1996)
Electricity - production by source:
fossil fuel: 61.33%
hydro: 38.67%
nuclear: 0%
other: 0% (1996)
Electricity - consumption: 3.75 billion kWh (1996)
Electricity - exports: 0 kWh (1996)
Electricity - imports: 0 kWh (1996)
Agriculture - products: paddy rice, corn, oilseed, sugarcane, pulses; hardwood
Exports: $940 million (1997)
Exports - commodities: pulses and beans, teak, rice, rubber, hardwood

Burma *(continued)*

Exports - partners: India 17%, Singapore 14%, China 11%, Thailand 9%, Japan 4% (1997)
Imports: $2.2 billion (1997)
Imports - commodities: machinery, transport equipment, construction materials, food products
Imports - partners: Singapore 30%, Japan 17%, China 10%, Thailand 10%, Malaysia 7% (1997)
Debt - external: $4.3 billion (1997 est.)
Economic aid - recipient: $156.9 million (1995)
Currency: 1 kyat (K) = 100 pyas
Exchange rates: kyats (K) per US$1 - 6.1163 (January 1999), 6.3432 (1998), 6.2418 (1997), 5.9176 (1996), 5.6670 (1995), 5.9749 (1994); unofficial - 310-350 (1998)
Fiscal year: 1 April - 31 March

Communications

Telephones: 122,195 (1993 est.)
Telephone system: meets minimum requirements for local and intercity service for business and government; international service is good
domestic: NA
international: satellite earth station - 1 Intelsat (Indian Ocean)
Radio broadcast stations: AM 2, FM 3, shortwave 3 (1998)
Radios: NA
Television broadcast stations: 2 (1998 est.)
Televisions: 88,000 (1992 est.)

Transportation

Railways:
total: 3,740 km
narrow gauge: 3,740 km 1.000-m gauge (1997)
Highways:
total: 28,200 km
paved: 3,440 km
unpaved: 24,760 km (1996 est.)
Waterways: 12,800 km; 3,200 km navigable by large commercial vessels
Pipelines: crude oil 1,343 km; natural gas 330 km
Ports and harbors: Bassein, Bhamo, Chauk, Mandalay, Moulmein, Myitkyina, Rangoon, Akyab (Sittwe), Tavoy
Merchant marine:
total: 41 ships (1,000 GRT or over) totaling 464,478 GRT/695,923 DWT
ships by type: bulk 14, cargo 20, container 2, oil tanker 3, passenger-cargo 2
note: a flag of convenience registry; includes ships of 2 countries: Japan owns 2 ships, US 3 (1998 est.)
Airports: 80 (1998 est.)
Airports - with paved runways:
total: 11
over 3,047 m: 2
2,438 to 3,047 m: 2
1,524 to 2,437 m: 5
914 to 1,523 m: 2 (1998 est.)
Airports - with unpaved runways:
total: 69
over 3,047 m: 2

1,524 to 2,437 m: 12
914 to 1,523 m: 23
under 914 m: 32 (1998 est.)
Heliports: 1 (1998 est.)

Military

Military branches: Army, Navy, Air Force
Military manpower - military age: 18 years of age
Military manpower - availability:
males age 15-49: 12,475,987
females age 15-49: 12,224,947 (1999 est.)
note: both sexes liable for military service
Military manpower - fit for military service:
males age 15-49: 6,660,309
females age 15-49: 6,510,730 (1999 est.)
Military manpower - reaching military age annually:
males: 496,912
females: 477,803 (1999 est.)
Military expenditures - dollar figure: $3.904 billion (FY97/98)
Military expenditures - percent of GDP: 2.1% (FY97/98)

Transnational Issues

Disputes - international: sporadic conflict with Thailand over alignment of border
Illicit drugs: world's largest producer of illicit opium (cultivation in 1998 - 130,300 hectares, a 16% decline from 1997; potential production - 1,750 metric tons, down 26% due to drought and the first eradication effort since the current government took power in 1987) and a minor producer of cannabis for the international drug trade; surrender of drug warlord KHUN SA's Mong Tai Army in January 1996 was hailed by Rangoon as a major counternarcotics success, but lack of serious government commitment and resources continues to hinder the overall antidrug effort; growing role in the production of methamphetamines for regional consumption

Burundi

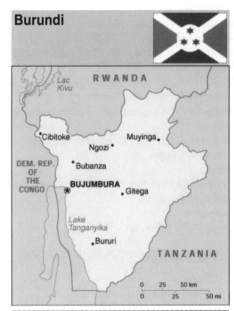

Introduction

Background: Since the end of the Belgian trusteeship in 1962, Burundi has suffered from ethnic uprisings, coups, and other societal dislocations. In a series of waves since October 1993, hundreds of thousands of refugees have fled the ethnic violence between the Hutu and Tutsi factions in Burundi and have crossed into Rwanda, Tanzania, and Zaire (now called the Democratic Republic of the Congo or DROC). Since October 1996, an estimated 120,000 Burundian Hutu refugees from the DROC have been compelled to return to Burundi because of insecurity in the region. Continuing ethnic violence with the Tutsi has caused additional Hutu to flee to Tanzania, thus raising their numbers in the United Nations Office of the High Commissioner for Refugees (UNHCR) camps in that country to about 260,000. Burundian troops have joined armies from Rwanda and Uganda and Congolese Tutsi in trying to overthrow DROC President KABILA and restore security to their borders with the Democratic Republic of the Congo.

Geography

Location: Central Africa, east of Democratic Republic of the Congo
Geographic coordinates: 3 30 S, 30 00 E
Map references: Africa
Area:
total: 27,830 sq km
land: 25,650 sq km
water: 2,180 sq km
Area - comparative: slightly smaller than Maryland
Land boundaries:
total: 974 km
border countries: Democratic Republic of the Congo 233 km, Rwanda 290 km, Tanzania 451 km
Coastline: 0 km (landlocked)
Maritime claims: none (landlocked)
Climate: equatorial; high plateau with considerable altitude variation (772 m to 2,760 m); average annual

temperature varies with altitude from 23 to 17 degrees centigrade but is generally moderate as the average altitude is about 1,700 m; average annual rainfall is about 150 cm; wet seasons from February to May and September to November, and dry seasons from June to August and December to January

Terrain: hilly and mountainous, dropping to a plateau in east, some plains

Elevation extremes:

lowest point: Lake Tanganyika 772 m

highest point: Mount Heha 2,670 m

Natural resources: nickel, uranium, rare earth oxides, peat, cobalt, copper, platinum (not yet exploited), vanadium

Land use:

arable land: 44%

permanent crops: 9%

permanent pastures: 36%

forests and woodland: 3%

other: 8% (1993 est.)

Irrigated land: 140 sq km (1993 est.)

Natural hazards: flooding, landslides

Environment - current issues: soil erosion as a result of overgrazing and the expansion of agriculture into marginal lands; deforestation (little forested land remains because of uncontrolled cutting of trees for fuel); habitat loss threatens wildlife populations

Environment - international agreements:

party to: Biodiversity, Climate Change, Desertification, Endangered Species, Hazardous Wastes, Ozone Layer Protection

signed, but not ratified: Law of the Sea, Nuclear Test Ban

Geography - note: landlocked; straddles crest of the Nile-Congo watershed

People

Population: 5,735,937 (July 1999 est.)

Age structure:

0-14 years: 47% (male 1,349,995; female 1,345,201)

15-64 years: 50% (male 1,392,880; female 1,479,835)

65 years and over: 3% (male 69,748; female 98,278) (1999 est.)

Population growth rate: 3.54% (1999 est.)

Birth rate: 41.27 births/1,000 population (1999 est.)

Death rate: 17.23 deaths/1,000 population (1999 est.)

Net migration rate: 11.33 migrant(s)/1,000 population (1999 est.)

Sex ratio:

at birth: 1.03 male(s)/female

under 15 years: 1 male(s)/female

15-64 years: 0.94 male(s)/female

65 years and over: 0.71 male(s)/female

total population: 0.96 male(s)/female (1999 est.)

Infant mortality rate: 99.36 deaths/1,000 live births (1999 est.)

Life expectancy at birth:

total population: 45.44 years

male: 43.54 years

female: 47.41 years (1999 est.)

Total fertility rate: 6.33 children born/woman (1999 est.)

Nationality:

noun: Burundian(s)

adjective: Burundi

Ethnic groups: Hutu (Bantu) 85%, Tutsi (Hamitic) 14%, Twa (Pygmy) 1%, Europeans 3,000, South Asians 2,000

Religions: Christian 67% (Roman Catholic 62%, Protestant 5%), indigenous beliefs 32%, Muslim 1%

Languages: Kirundi (official), French (official), Swahili (along Lake Tanganyika and in the Bujumbura area)

Literacy:

definition: age 15 and over can read and write

total population: 35.3%

male: 49.3%

female: 22.5% (1995 est.)

Government

Country name:

conventional long form: Republic of Burundi

conventional short form: Burundi

local long form: Republika y'u Burundi

local short form: Burundi

Data code: BY

Government type: republic

Capital: Bujumbura

Administrative divisions: 15 provinces; Bubanza, Bujumbura, Bururi, Cankuzo, Cibitoke, Gitega, Karuzi, Kayanza, Kirundo, Makamba, Muramvya, Muyinga, Ngozi, Rutana, Ruyigi

note: there may be a new province named Mwaro

Independence: 1 July 1962 (from UN trusteeship under Belgian administration)

National holiday: Independence Day, 1 July (1962)

Constitution: 13 March 1992; provided for establishment of a plural political system; supplanted on 6 June 1998 by a Transitional Constitution which enlarged the National Assembly and created two vice presidents

Legal system: based on German and Belgian civil codes and customary law; does not accept compulsory ICJ jurisdiction

Suffrage: NA years of age; universal adult

Executive branch:

chief of state: President Pierre BUYOYA (interim president since 27 September 1996 and officially sworn in on 11 June 1998) is chief of state and head of government and is assisted by First Vice President Frederic BAMVUGINYUMVIRA (since NA) and Second Vice President Mathias SINAMENYA (since NA); note - former President NTIBANTUNGANYA was overthrown in a coup on 25 July 1996

head of government: President Pierre BUYOYA is both chief of state and head of government; assisted by First Vice President Frederic BAMVUGINYUMVIRA (since NA) and Second Vice President Mathias SINAMENYA (since NA)

cabinet: Council of Ministers appointed by president

elections: NA

Legislative branch: unicameral National Assembly

or Assemblee Nationale (81 seats; note - new Transitional Constitution calls for 121 seats; members are elected by popular vote on a proportional basis to serve five-year terms)

elections: last held 29 June 1993 (next was scheduled to be held in 1998, but suspended by presidential decree in 1996)

election results: percent of vote by party - FRODEBU 71%, UPRONA 21.4%; seats by party - FRODEBU 65, UPRONA 16; other parties won too small shares of the vote to win seats in the assembly

Judicial branch: Supreme Court or Cour Supreme

Political parties and leaders: Unity for National Progress or UPRONA [Luc RUKINGAMA, president]; Burundi Democratic Front or FRODEBU [Jean MINANI, president]; Socialist Party of Burundi or PSB [leader NA]; People's Reconciliation Party or PRP [leader NA]

note: opposition parties, legalized in March 1992, include Burundi African Alliance for the Salvation or ABASA; Rally for Democracy and Economic and Social Development or RADDES [Cyrille SIGEJEJE, chairman]; and Party for National Redress or PARENA [Jean-Baptiste BAGAZA]

International organization participation: ACCT, ACP, AfDB, CCC, CEEAC, CEPGL, ECA, FAO, G-77, IBRD, ICAO, ICRM, IDA, IFAD, IFC, IFRCS, ILO, IMF, Intelsat (nonsignatory user), Interpol, IOC, ITU, NAM, OAU, OPCW, UN, UNCTAD, UNESCO, UNIDO, UPU, WHO, WIPO, WMO, WToO, WTrO

Diplomatic representation in the US:

chief of mission: Ambassador Thomas NDIKUMANA

chancery: Suite 212, 2233 Wisconsin Avenue NW, Washington, DC 20007

telephone: [1] (202) 342-2574

FAX: [1] (202) 342-2578

Diplomatic representation from the US:

chief of mission: Ambassador Morris N. HUGHES, Jr.

embassy: Avenue des Etats-Unis, Bujumbura

mailing address: B. P. 1720, Bujumbura

telephone: [257] (2) 223454

FAX: [257] (2) 222926

Flag description: divided by a white diagonal cross into red panels (top and bottom) and green panels (hoist side and outer side) with a white disk superimposed at the center bearing three red six-pointed stars outlined in green arranged in a triangular design (one star above, two stars below)

Economy

Economy - overview: Burundi is a landlocked, resource-poor country with a poorly developed manufacturing sector. The economy is predominately agricultural with roughly 90% of the population dependent on subsistence agriculture. Its economic health depends on the coffee crop, which accounts for 80% of foreign exchange earnings. The ability to pay for imports therefore rests largely on the vagaries of the climate and the international coffee market. Since October 1993 the nation has suffered from massive ethnic-based violence which has resulted in the death of perhaps 250,000 persons and the displacement of

Burundi (continued)

about 800,000 others. Foods, medicines, and electricity remain in short supply.

GDP: purchasing power parity - $4.1 billion (1998 est.)

GDP - real growth rate: 4.5% (1998 est.)

GDP - per capita: purchasing power parity - $740 (1998 est.)

GDP - composition by sector:
agriculture: 58%
industry: 18%
services: 24% (1997 est.)

Population below poverty line: 36.2% (1990 est.)

Household income or consumption by percentage share:
lowest 10%: NA%
highest 10%: NA%

Inflation rate (consumer prices): 17% (1998 est.)

Labor force: 1.9 million

Labor force - by occupation: agriculture 93%, government 4%, industry and commerce 1.5%, services 1.5% (1983 est.)

Unemployment rate: NA%

Budget:
revenues: $NA
expenditures: $165 million, including capital expenditures of $42.6 million (1998 est.)

Industries: light consumer goods such as blankets, shoes, soap; assembly of imported components; public works construction; food processing

Industrial production growth rate: NA%

Electricity - production: 122 million kWh (1996)

Electricity - production by source:
fossil fuel: 1.64%
hydro: 98.36%
nuclear: 0%
other: 0% (1996)

Electricity - consumption: 152 million kWh (1996)

Electricity - exports: 0 kWh (1996)

Electricity - imports: 30 million kWh (1996)

note: imports some electricity from Democratic Republic of the Congo

Agriculture - products: coffee, cotton, tea, corn, sorghum, sweet potatoes, bananas, manioc (tapioca); beef, milk, hides

Exports: $49 million (f.o.b., 1998)

Exports - commodities: coffee, tea, cotton, hides

Exports - partners: UK, Germany, Benelux, Switzerland (1997)

Imports: $102 million f.o.b., 1998)

Imports - commodities: capital goods, petroleum products, foodstuffs, consumer goods

Imports - partners: Benelux, France, Germany, Japan (1997)

Debt - external: $1.1 billion (1995 est.)

Economic aid - recipient: $286.1 million (1995)

Currency: 1 Burundi franc (FBu) = 100 centimes

Exchange rates: Burundi francs (FBu) per US$1 - 508 (January 1999), 477.77 (1998), 352.35 (1997), 302.75 (1996), 249.76 (1995), 252.66 (1994)

Fiscal year: calendar year

Communications

Telephones: 7,200 (1987 est.)

Telephone system: primitive system
domestic: sparse system of open wire, radiotelephone communications, and low-capacity microwave radio relay
international: satellite earth station - 1 Intelsat (Indian Ocean)

Radio broadcast stations: AM 2, FM 2, shortwave 0 (1998)

Radios: NA

Television broadcast stations: 1 (1997)

Televisions: 4,500 (1993 est.)

Transportation

Railways: 0 km

Highways:
total: 14,480 km
paved: 1,028 km
unpaved: 13,452 km (1996 est.)

Waterways: Lake Tanganyika

Ports and harbors: Bujumbura

Airports: 4 (1998 est.)

Airports - with paved runways:
total: 1
over 3,047 m: 1 (1998 est.)

Airports - with unpaved runways:
total: 3
914 to 1,523 m: 2
under 914 m: 1 (1998 est.)

Military

Military branches: Army (includes naval and air units), paramilitary Gendarmerie

Military manpower - military age: 16 years of age

Military manpower - availability:
males age 15-49: 1,260,909 (1999 est.)

Military manpower - fit for military service:
males age 15-49: 658,115 (1999 est.)

Military manpower - reaching military age annually:
males: 73,271 (1999 est.)

Military expenditures - dollar figure: $25 million (1993)

Military expenditures - percent of GDP: 2.6% (1993)

Transnational Issues

Disputes - international: none

Cambodia

Geography

Location: Southeastern Asia, bordering the Gulf of Thailand, between Thailand, Vietnam, and Laos

Geographic coordinates: 13 00 N, 105 00 E

Map references: Southeast Asia

Area:
total: 181,040 sq km
land: 176,520 sq km
water: 4,520 sq km

Area - comparative: slightly smaller than Oklahoma

Land boundaries:
total: 2,572 km
border countries: Laos 541 km, Thailand 803 km, Vietnam 1,228 km

Coastline: 443 km

Maritime claims:
contiguous zone: 24 nm
continental shelf: 200 nm
exclusive economic zone: 200 nm
territorial sea: 12 nm

Climate: tropical; rainy, monsoon season (May to November); dry season (December to April); little seasonal temperature variation

Terrain: mostly low, flat plains; mountains in southwest and north

Elevation extremes:
lowest point: Gulf of Thailand 0 m
highest point: Phnum Aoral 1,810 m

Natural resources: timber, gemstones, some iron ore, manganese, phosphates, hydropower potential

Land use:
arable land: 13%
permanent crops: 0%
permanent pastures: 11%
forests and woodland: 66%
other: 10% (1993 est.)

Irrigated land: 920 sq km (1993 est.)

Natural hazards: monsoonal rains (June to November); flooding; occasional droughts

Environment - current issues: illegal logging

Cambodia (continued)

activities throughout the country and strip mining for gems in the western region along the border with Thailand are resulting in habitat loss and declining biodiversity (in particular, destruction of mangrove swamps threatens natural fisheries); soil erosion; in rural areas, a majority of the population does not have access to potable water; toxic waste delivery from Taiwan sparked unrest in Kampong Saom (Sihanoukville) in December 1998

Environment - international agreements:
party to: Biodiversity, Climate Change, Desertification, Endangered Species, Marine Life Conservation, Ship Pollution, Tropical Timber 94
signed, but not ratified: Law of the Sea, Marine Dumping

Geography - note: a land of paddies and forests dominated by the Mekong River and Tonle Sap

People

Population: 11,626,520 (July 1999 est.)
Age structure:
0-14 years: 45% (male 2,667,768; female 2,587,590)
15-64 years: 52% (male 2,821,772; female 3,197,604)
65 years and over: 3% (male 143,016; female 208,770) (1999 est.)
Population growth rate: 2.49% (1999 est.)
Birth rate: 41.05 births/1,000 population (1999 est.)
Death rate: 16.2 deaths/1,000 population (1999 est.)
Net migration rate: 0 migrant(s)/1,000 population (1999 est.)
Sex ratio:
at birth: 1.05 male(s)/female
under 15 years: 1.03 male(s)/female
15-64 years: 0.88 male(s)/female
65 years and over: 0.69 male(s)/female
total population: 0.94 male(s)/female (1999 est.)
Infant mortality rate: 105.06 deaths/1,000 live births (1999 est.)
Life expectancy at birth:
total population: 48.24 years
male: 46.81 years
female: 49.75 years (1999 est.)
Total fertility rate: 5.81 children born/woman (1999 est.)
Nationality:
noun: Cambodian(s)
adjective: Cambodian
Ethnic groups: Khmer 90%, Vietnamese 5%, Chinese 1%, other 4%
Religions: Theravada Buddhism 95%, other 5%
Languages: Khmer (official), French
Literacy:
definition: age 15 and over can read and write
total population: 35%
male: 48%
female: 22% (1990 est.)

Government

Country name:
conventional long form: Kingdom of Cambodia

conventional short form: Cambodia
local long form: Preahreacheanachakr Kampuchea
local short form: Kampuchea
Data code: CB
Government type: multiparty liberal democracy under a constitutional monarchy established in September 1993
Capital: Phnom Penh
Administrative divisions: 20 provinces (khett, singular and plural) and 3 municipalities* (krong, singular and plural); Banteay Mean Cheay, Batdambang, Kampong Cham, Kampong Chhnang, Kampong Spoe, Kampong Thum, Kampot, Kandal, Kaoh Kong, Keb*, Krachen, Mondol Kiri, Otdar Mean Cheay, Phnum Penh*, Pouthisat, Preah Seihanu* (Sihanoukville), Preah Vihear, Prey Veng, Rotanah Kiri, Siem Reab, Stoeng Treng, Svay Rieng, Takev
note: there may be a new municipality called Pailin
Independence: 9 November 1953 (from France)
National holiday: Independence Day, 9 November (1953)
Constitution: promulgated 21 September 1993
Legal system: primarily a civil law mixture of French-influenced codes from the United Nations Transitional Authority in Cambodia (UNTAC) period, royal decrees, and acts of the legislature, with influences of customary law and remnants of communist legal theory; increasing influence of common law in recent years
Suffrage: 18 years of age; universal
Executive branch:
chief of state: King Norodom SIHANOUK (reinstated 24 September 1993)
head of government: Prime Minister HUN SEN (since 30 November 1998)
cabinet: Council of Ministers appointed by the monarch
elections: none; the monarch is hereditary; prime minister appointed by the monarch after a vote of confidence by the National Assembly
Legislative branch: unicameral National Assembly (122 seats; members elected by popular vote to serve five-year terms)
elections: last held 26 July 1998 (next to be held NA 2003)
election results: percent of vote by party - CPP 41%, FUNCINPEC 32%, SRP 14%, other 13%; seats by party - CPP 64, FUNCINPEC 43, SRP 15
note: pursuant to the coalition agreement signed in November 1998, a Senate is being created and the legislature will thus become bicameral
Judicial branch: Supreme Council of the Magistracy, provided for in the constitution, was formed in December 1997; a Supreme Court and lower courts exercise judicial authority
Political parties and leaders: National United Front for an Independent, Neutral, Peaceful, and Cooperative Cambodia or FUNCINPEC [Prince NORODOM RANARIDDH]; Cambodian Pracheachon Party or Cambodian People's Party or CPP [CHEA SIM]; Sam Rangsi Party or SRP (formerly Khmer Nation Party or KNP) [SAM RANGSI]; Buddhist

Liberal Party or BLP [IENG MOULY]; Populist Party [UNG HUOT]; Khmer Citizen Party or KCP [NGUON SOEUR]
International organization participation: ACCT, AsDB, ASEAN (observer), CP, ESCAP, FAO, G-77, IAEA, IBRD, ICAO, ICRM, IDA, IFAD, IFC, IFRCS, ILO, IMF, IMO, Intelsat (nonsignatory user), Interpol, IOC, ISO (subscriber), ITU, NAM, OPCW, PCA, UN, UNCTAD, UNESCO, UNIDO, UPU, WFTU, WHO, WIPO, WMO, WToO, WTrO (applicant)
Diplomatic representation in the US:
chief of mission: Ambassador VAR HUOTH
chancery: 4500 16th Street NW, Washington, DC 20011
telephone: [1] (202) 726-7742
FAX: [1] (202) 726-8381
Diplomatic representation from the US:
chief of mission: Ambassador Kenneth M. QUINN
embassy: 27 EO Street 240, Phnom Penh
mailing address: Box P, APO AP 96546
telephone: [855] (23) 216-436, 216-438
FAX: [855] (23) 216-811
Flag description: three horizontal bands of blue (top), red (double width), and blue with a white three-towered temple representing Angkor Wat outlined in black in the center of the red band

Economy

Economy - overview: After four years of solid macroeconomic performance, Cambodia's economy slowed dramatically in 1997-98 due to the regional economic crisis, civil violence, and political infighting. Foreign investment fell off, and tourism has declined from 1996 levels. Also, in 1998 the main harvest was hit by drought. The long-term development of the economy after decades of war remains a daunting challenge. Human resource levels in the population are low, particularly in the poverty-ridden countryside. The almost total lack of basic infrastructure in the countryside will continue to hinder development. Recurring political instability and corruption within government discourage foreign investment and delay foreign aid. Even so, growth may resume in 1999 at, say, 2%.
GDP: purchasing power parity - $7.8 billion (1998 est.)
GDP - real growth rate: 0% (1998 est.)
GDP - per capita: purchasing power parity - $700 (1998 est.)
GDP - composition by sector:
agriculture: 51%
industry: 15%
services: 34% (1997 est.)
Population below poverty line: NA%
Household income or consumption by percentage share:
lowest 10%: NA%
highest 10%: NA%
Inflation rate (consumer prices): 15% (1998 est.)
Labor force: 2.5 million to 3 million
Labor force - by occupation: agriculture 80% (1997 est.)

Cambodia *(continued)*

Unemployment rate: NA%
Budget:
revenues: $261 million
expenditures: $496 million, including capital expenditures of $NA (1995 est.)
Industries: rice milling, fishing, wood and wood products, rubber, cement, gem mining, textiles
Industrial production growth rate: 7% (1995 est.)
Electricity - production: 195 million kWh (1996)
Electricity - production by source:
fossil fuel: 61.54%
hydro: 38.46%
nuclear: 0%
other: 0% (1996)
Electricity - consumption: 195 million kWh (1996)
Electricity - exports: 0 kWh (1996)
Electricity - imports: 0 kWh (1996)
Agriculture - products: rice, rubber, corn, vegetables
Exports: $736 million (f.o.b., 1997 est.)
Exports - commodities: timber, garments, rubber, soybeans, sesame
Exports - partners: Singapore, Japan, Thailand, Hong Kong, Indonesia, Malaysia, US
Imports: $1.1 billion (f.o.b., 1997 est.)
Imports - commodities: cigarettes, gold, construction materials, petroleum products, machinery, motor vehicles
Imports - partners: Singapore, Vietnam, Japan, Australia, Hong Kong, Indonesia, Thailand
Debt - external: $2.2 billion (1996 est.)
Economic aid - recipient: $569.8 million (1995)
Currency: 1 new riel (CR) = 100 sen
Exchange rates: riels (CR) per US$1 - 3,772.0 (January 1999), 3,744.4 (1998), 2,946.3 (1997), 2,624.1 (1996), 2,450.8 (1995), 2,545.3 (1994)
Fiscal year: calendar year

Communications

Telephones: 7,000 (1981 est.)
Telephone system: adequate landline and/or cellular service in Phnom Penh and other provincial cities; rural areas have little telephone service
domestic: NA
international: adequate but expensive landline and cellular service available to all countries from Phnom Penh and major provincial cities; satellite earth station - 1 Intersputnik (Indian Ocean Region)
Radio broadcast stations: AM 7, FM 3, shortwave 3 (1998)
Radios: NA
Television broadcast stations: 1 government-operated station and four commercial stations broadcasting to Phnom Penh and major provincial cities via relay (1998)
Televisions: 800,000 (1996 est.)

Transportation

Railways:
total: 603 km
narrow gauge: 603 km 1.000-m gauge

Highways:
total: 35,769 km
paved: 4,165 km
unpaved: 31,604 km (1997 est.)
Waterways: 3,700 km navigable all year to craft drawing 0.6 m; 282 km navigable to craft drawing 1.8 m
Ports and harbors: Kampong Saom (Sihanoukville), Kampot, Krong Kaoh Kong, Phnom Penh
Merchant marine:
total: 141 ships (1,000 GRT or over) totaling 598,867 GRT/841,240 DWT
ships by type: barge carrier 1, bulk 16, cargo 108, container 4, livestock carrier 2, multifunctional large-load carrier 1, oil tankers 1, refrigerated cargo 4, roll-on/roll-off cargo 4
note: a flag of convenience registry; includes ships of 8 countries: Aruba 1, Cyprus 7, Egypt 1, South Korea 1, Malta 1, Panama 1, Russia 5, Singapore 1 (1998 est.)
Airports: 20 (1998 est.)
Airports - with paved runways:
total: 7
2,438 to 3,047 m: 2
1,524 to 2,437 m: 2
914 to 1,523 m: 3 (1998 est.)
Airports - with unpaved runways:
total: 13
1,524 to 2,437 m: 3
914 to 1,523 m: 10 (1998 est.)
Heliports: 3 (1998 est.)

Military

Military branches: Royal Cambodian Armed Forces (RCAF) - created in 1993 by the merger of the Cambodian People's Armed Forces and the two noncommunist resistance armies
note: there are also resistance forces comprised of the Khmer Rouge (also known as the National United Army or NUA) and a separate royalist resistance movement
Military manpower - military age: 18 years of age
Military manpower - availability:
males age 15-49: 2,562,112 (1999 est.)
Military manpower - fit for military service:
males age 15-49: 1,428,523 (1999 est.)
Military manpower - reaching military age annually:
males: 119,839 (1999 est.)
Military expenditures - dollar figure: $85.3 million (1998)
Military expenditures - percent of GDP: 2.4% (1998)

Transnational Issues

Disputes - international: offshore islands and sections of the boundary with Vietnam are in dispute; maritime boundary with Vietnam not defined; parts of border with Thailand are indefinite; maritime boundary with Thailand not clearly defined

Illicit drugs: transshipment site for Golden Triangle heroin; possible money laundering; narcotics-related corruption reportedly involving some in the government, military, and police; possible small-scale opium, heroin, and amphetamine production; large producer of cannabis for the international market

Cameroon

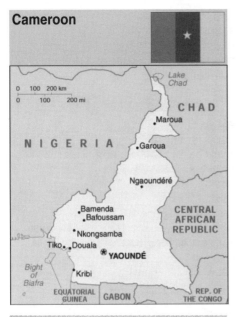

Geography

Location: Western Africa, bordering the Bight of Biafra, between Equatorial Guinea and Nigeria
Geographic coordinates: 6 00 N, 12 00 E
Map references: Africa
Area:
total: 475,440 sq km
land: 469,440 sq km
water: 6,000 sq km
Area - comparative: slightly larger than California
Land boundaries:
total: 4,591 km
border countries: Central African Republic 797 km, Chad 1,094 km, Republic of the Congo 523 km, Equatorial Guinea 189 km, Gabon 298 km, Nigeria 1,690 km
Coastline: 402 km
Maritime claims:
territorial sea: 50 nm
Climate: varies with terrain, from tropical along coast to semiarid and hot in north
Terrain: diverse, with coastal plain in southwest, dissected plateau in center, mountains in west, plains in north
Elevation extremes:
lowest point: Atlantic Ocean 0 m
highest point: Fako 4,095 m
Natural resources: petroleum, bauxite, iron ore, timber, hydropower
Land use:
arable land: 13%
permanent crops: 2%
permanent pastures: 4%
forests and woodland: 78%
other: 3% (1993 est.)
Irrigated land: 210 sq km (1993 est.)
Natural hazards: recent volcanic activity with release of poisonous gases
Environment - current issues: water-borne diseases are prevalent; deforestation; overgrazing; desertification; poaching; overfishing
Environment - international agreements:
party to: Biodiversity, Climate Change, Desertification, Endangered Species, Law of the Sea, Ozone Layer Protection, Tropical Timber 83, Tropical Timber 94
signed, but not ratified: Nuclear Test Ban
Geography - note: sometimes referred to as the hinge of Africa

People

Population: 15,456,092 (July 1999 est.)
Age structure:
0-14 years: 46% (male 3,562,553; female 3,528,778)
15-64 years: 51% (male 3,907,946; female 3,943,035)
65 years and over: 3% (male 231,521; female 282,259) (1999 est.)
Population growth rate: 2.79% (1999 est.)
Birth rate: 41.84 births/1,000 population (1999 est.)
Death rate: 13.95 deaths/1,000 population (1999 est.)
Net migration rate: NA migrant(s)/1,000 population; note - there may be some migration but figures are not available
Sex ratio:
at birth: 1.03 male(s)/female
under 15 years: 1.01 male(s)/female
15-64 years: 0.99 male(s)/female
65 years and over: 0.82 male(s)/female
total population: 0.99 male(s)/female (1999 est.)
Infant mortality rate: 75.69 deaths/1,000 live births (1999 est.)
Life expectancy at birth:
total population: 51.32 years
male: 49.75 years
female: 52.94 years (1999 est.)
Total fertility rate: 5.8 children born/woman (1999 est.)
Nationality:
noun: Cameroonian(s)
adjective: Cameroonian
Ethnic groups: Cameroon Highlanders 31%, Equatorial Bantu 19%, Kirdi 11%, Fulani 10%, Northwestern Bantu 8%, Eastern Nigritic 7%, other African 13%, non-African less than 1%
Religions: indigenous beliefs 51%, Christian 33%, Muslim 16%
Languages: 24 major African language groups, English (official), French (official)
Literacy:
definition: age 15 and over can read and write
total population: 63.4%
male: 75%
female: 52.1% (1995 est.)

Government

Country name:
conventional long form: Republic of Cameroon
conventional short form: Cameroon
former: French Cameroon

Data code: CM
Government type: unitary republic; multiparty presidential regime (opposition parties legalized in 1990)
Capital: Yaounde
Administrative divisions: 10 provinces; Adamaoua, Centre, Est, Extreme-Nord, Littoral, Nord, Nord-Ouest, Ouest, Sud, Sud-Ouest
Independence: 1 January 1960 (from UN trusteeship under French administration)
National holiday: National Day, 20 May (1972)
Constitution: 20 May 1972
Legal system: based on French civil law system, with common law influence; does not accept compulsory ICJ jurisdiction
Suffrage: 21 years of age; universal
Executive branch:
chief of state: President Paul BIYA (since 6 November 1982)
head of government: Prime Minister Peter Mafany MUSONGE (since 19 September 1996)
cabinet: Cabinet appointed by the president
elections: president elected by popular vote for a seven-year term; election last held 12 October 1997 (next to be held NA October 2004); prime minister appointed by the president
election results: President Paul BIYA reelected; percent of vote - Paul BIYA 93%; note - supporters of the opposition candidates boycotted the elections, making a comparison of vote shares relatively meaningless
Legislative branch: unicameral National Assembly or Assemblee Nationale (180 seats; members are elected by direct popular vote to serve five-year terms; note - the president can either lengthen or shorten the term of the legislature)
elections: last held 11 May 1997 (next to be held NA 2002)
election results: percent of vote by party - NA; seats by party - CDPM 109, SDF 43, UNDP 13, UDC 5, UPC-K 1, MDR 1, MLJC 1; note - 7 contested seats will be filled in an election at a time to be set by the Supreme Court
note: the constitution calls for an upper chamber for the legislature, to be called Senate, which the government proposed to establish in 1998
Judicial branch: Supreme Court, judges are appointed by the president
Political parties and leaders: Cameroon People's Democratic Movement or CPDM (government-controlled and the only party until legalization of opposition parties in 1990) [Paul BIYA, president]
major opposition parties: Cameroonian Democratic Union or UDC [Adamou NDAM NJOYA]; Movement for the Defense of the Republic or MDR [Dakole DAISSALA]; Movement for the Youth of Cameroon or MLJC [Marcel YANDO]; National Union for Democracy and Progress or UNDP [Maigari BELLO BOUBA, chairman]; Social Democratic Front or SDF [John FRU NDI]; Union of Cameroonian Populations or UPC [Augustin Frederick KODOG]; Union of

Cameroon (continued)

Cameroonian Democratic Forces or UFOC [Victorin Hameni BIELEU]

Political pressure groups and leaders: Alliance for Change or FAC; Cameroon Anglophone Movement or CAM [Vishe FAI, secretary general]

International organization participation: ACCT, ACP, AfDB, BDEAC, C, CCC, CEEAC, ECA, FAO, FZ, G-19, G-77, IAEA, IBRD, ICAO, ICC, ICFTU, ICRM, IDA, IDB, IFAD, IFC, IFRCS, ILO, IMF, IMO, Inmarsat, Intelsat, Interpol, IOC, ITU, NAM, OAU, OIC, OPCW, PCA, UDEAC, UN, UNCTAD, UNESCO, UNIDO, UNITAR, UPU, WCL, WFTU, WHO, WIPO, WMO, WToO, WTrO

Diplomatic representation in the US:
chief of mission: Ambassador Jerome MENDOUGA
chancery: 2349 Massachusetts Avenue NW, Washington, DC 20008
telephone: [1] (202) 265-8790
FAX: [1] (202) 387-3826

Diplomatic representation from the US:
chief of mission: Ambassador John M. YATES
embassy: Rue Nachtigal, Yaounde
mailing address: B. P. 817, Yaounde; pouch: American Embassy, Department of State, Washington, DC 20521-2520
telephone: [237] 23-45-52
FAX: [237] 23-07-53

Flag description: three equal vertical bands of green (hoist side), red, and yellow with a yellow five-pointed star centered in the red band; uses the popular pan-African colors of Ethiopia

Economy

Economy - overview: Because of its oil resources and favorable agricultural conditions, Cameroon has one of the best-endowed primary commodity economies in sub-Saharan Africa. Still, it faces many of the serious problems facing other underdeveloped countries, such as a top-heavy civil service and a generally unfavorable climate for business enterprise. Since 1990, the government has embarked on various IMF and World Bank programs designed to spur business investment, increase efficiency in agriculture, improve trade, and recapitalize the nation's banks. The government, however, has failed to press forward vigorously with these programs. The latest enhanced structural adjustment agreement was signed in October 1997; the parties hope this will prove more successful, yet government mismanagement and corruption remain problems. Inflation has been brought back under control. Progress toward privatization of remaining state industry may support economic growth in 1999-2000.
GDP: purchasing power parity - $29.6 billion (1998 est.)
GDP - real growth rate: 5% (1998 est.)
GDP - per capita: purchasing power parity - $2,000 (1998 est.)
GDP - composition by sector:
agriculture: 42%
industry: 22%
services: 36% (1997 est.)

Population below poverty line: 40% (1984 est.)
Household income or consumption by percentage share:
lowest 10%: NA%
highest 10%: NA%
Inflation rate (consumer prices): 2.5% (1998 est.)
Labor force: NA
Unemployment rate: 30% (1998 est.)
Budget:
revenues: $2.23 billion
expenditures: $2.23 billion, including capital expenditures of $NA (FY96/97 est.)
Industries: petroleum production and refining, food processing, light consumer goods, textiles, lumber
Industrial production growth rate: NA%
Electricity - production: 2.73 billion kWh (1996)
Electricity - production by source:
fossil fuel: 2.93%
hydro: 97.07%
nuclear: 0%
other: 0% (1996)
Electricity - consumption: 2.73 billion kWh (1996)
Electricity - exports: 0 kWh (1996)
Electricity - imports: 0 kWh (1996)
Agriculture - products: coffee, cocoa, cotton, rubber, bananas, oilseed, grains, root starches; livestock; timber
Exports: $1.6 billion (f.o.b., 1998)
Exports - commodities: crude oil and petroleum products, lumber, cocoa beans, aluminum, coffee, cotton
Exports - partners: Italy 25%, Spain 20%, France 16%, Netherlands 7% (1997 est.)
Imports: $1.3 billion (f.o.b., 1998)
Imports - commodities: machines and electrical equipment, transport equipment, fuel, food
Imports - partners: France 25%, Nigeria 8%, US 8%, Germany 6% (1997 est.)
Debt - external: $8.7 billion (1998 est.)
Economic aid - recipient: $606.1 million (1995); note - France signed two loan agreements totaling $55 million in September 1997, and the Paris Club agreed in October 1997 to reduce the official debt by 50% and to reschedule it on favorable terms with a consolidation of payments due through 2000
Currency: 1 Communaute Financiere Africaine franc (CFAF) = 100 centimes
Exchange rates: Communaute Financiere Africaine francs (CFAF) per US$1 - 575 (January 1999), 589.95 (1998), 583.67 (1997), 511.55 (1996), 499.15 (1995), 555.20 (1994)
Fiscal year: 1 July - 30 June

Communications

Telephones: 36,737 (1991 est.)
Telephone system: available only to business and government
domestic: cable, microwave radio relay, and tropospheric scatter
international: satellite earth stations - 2 Intelsat (Atlantic Ocean)

Radio broadcast stations: AM 11, FM 8, shortwave 3 (1998)
Radios: 6 million (1998 est.)
Television broadcast stations: 1 (1998)
Televisions: 15,000 (1998)

Transportation

Railways:
total: 1,104 km
narrow gauge: 1,104 km 1.000-m gauge (1995 est.)
Highways:
total: 34,300 km
paved: 4,288 km
unpaved: 30,012 km (1995 est.)
Waterways: 2,090 km; of decreasing importance
Ports and harbors: Bonaberi, Douala, Garoua, Kribi, Tiko
Airports: 52 (1998 est.)
Airports - with paved runways:
total: 11
over 3,047 m: 2
2,438 to 3,047 m: 4
1,524 to 2,437 m: 3
914 to 1,523 m: 1
under 914 m: 1 (1998 est.)
Airports - with unpaved runways:
total: 41
1,524 to 2,437 m: 8
914 to 1,523 m: 21
under 914 m: 12 (1998 est.)

Military

Military branches: Army, Navy (includes Naval Infantry), Air Force, National Gendarmerie, Presidential Guard
Military manpower - military age: 18 years of age
Military manpower - availability:
males age 15-49: 3,388,643 (1999 est.)
Military manpower - fit for military service:
males age 15-49: 1,716,285 (1999 est.)
Military manpower - reaching military age annually:
males: 165,670 (1999 est.)
Military expenditures - dollar figure: $155 million (FY98/99)
Military expenditures - percent of GDP: 1.4% (FY98/99)

Transnational Issues

Disputes - international: delimitation of international boundaries in the vicinity of Lake Chad, the lack of which led to border incidents in the past, is completed and awaits ratification by Cameroon, Chad, Niger, and Nigeria; dispute with Nigeria over land and maritime boundaries around the Bakasi Peninsula and Lake Chad is currently before the International Court of Justice

Canada

Introduction

Background: A land of vast distances and rich natural resources, from 1867 on Canada has enjoyed de facto independence while retaining, even to the present day, certain formal ties to the British crown. Economically and technologically the nation has developed in parallel with the US, its neighbor to the south across an unfortified border. Its paramount political problem continues to be the relationship of the province of Quebec, with its French-speaking residents and unique culture, to the remainder of the country.

Geography

Location: Northern North America, bordering the North Atlantic Ocean and North Pacific Ocean, north of the conterminous US
Geographic coordinates: 60 00 N, 95 00 W
Map references: North America
Area:
total: 9,976,140 sq km
land: 9,220,970 sq km
water: 755,170 sq km
Area - comparative: slightly larger than the US
Land boundaries:
total: 8,893 km
border countries: US 8,893 km (includes 2,477 km with Alaska)
Coastline: 243,791 km
Maritime claims:
continental shelf: 200 nm or to the edge of the continental margin
exclusive fishing zone: 200 nm
territorial sea: 12 nm
Climate: varies from temperate in south to subarctic and arctic in north
Terrain: mostly plains with mountains in west and lowlands in southeast
Elevation extremes:
lowest point: Atlantic Ocean 0 m
highest point: Mount Logan 5,950 m

Natural resources: nickel, zinc, copper, gold, lead, molybdenum, potash, silver, fish, timber, wildlife, coal, petroleum, natural gas
Land use:
arable land: 5%
permanent crops: 0%
permanent pastures: 3%
forests and woodland: 54%
other: 38% (1993 est.)
Irrigated land: 7,100 sq km (1993 est.)
Natural hazards: continuous permafrost in north is a serious obstacle to development; cyclonic storms form east of the Rocky Mountains, a result of the mixing of air masses from the Arctic, Pacific, and North American interior, and produce most of the country's rain and snow
Environment - current issues: air pollution and resulting acid rain severely affecting lakes and damaging forests; metal smelting, coal-burning utilities, and vehicle emissions impacting on agricultural and forest productivity; ocean waters becoming contaminated due to agricultural, industrial, mining, and forestry activities
Environment - international agreements:
party to: Air Pollution, Air Pollution-Nitrogen Oxides, Air Pollution-Persistent Organic Pollutants, Air Pollution-Sulphur 85, Air Pollution-Sulphur 94, Antarctic Treaty, Biodiversity, Climate Change, Desertification, Endangered Species, Environmental Modification, Hazardous Wastes, Marine Dumping, Nuclear Test Ban, Ozone Layer Protection, Ship Pollution, Tropical Timber 83, Tropical Timber 94, Wetlands, Whaling
signed, but not ratified: Air Pollution-Volatile Organic Compounds, Antarctic-Environmental Protocol, Climate Change-Kyoto Protocol, Law of the Sea, Marine Life Conservation
Geography - note: second-largest country in world (after Russia); strategic location between Russia and US via north polar route; nearly 90% of the population is concentrated within 160 km of the US/Canada border

Population: 31,006,347 (July 1999 est.)
Age structure:
0-14 years: 20% (male 3,105,944; female 2,960,171)
15-64 years: 68% (male 10,587,553; female 10,461,455)
65 years and over: 12% (male 1,652,044; female 2,239,180) (1999 est.)
Population growth rate: 1.06% (1999 est.)
Birth rate: 11.86 births/1,000 population (1999 est.)
Death rate: 7.26 deaths/1,000 population (1999 est.)
Net migration rate: 5.96 migrant(s)/1,000 population (1999 est.)
Sex ratio:
at birth: 1.05 male(s)/female
under 15 years: 1.05 male(s)/female
15-64 years: 1.01 male(s)/female
65 years and over: 0.74 male(s)/female
total population: 0.98 male(s)/female (1999 est.)
Infant mortality rate: 5.47 deaths/1,000 live births (1999 est.)
Life expectancy at birth:
total population: 79.37 years
male: 76.12 years
female: 82.79 years (1999 est.)
Total fertility rate: 1.65 children born/woman (1999 est.)
Nationality:
noun: Canadian(s)
adjective: Canadian
Ethnic groups: British Isles origin 40%, French origin 27%, other European 20%, Amerindian 1.5%, other, mostly Asian 11.5%
Religions: Roman Catholic 45%, United Church 12%, Anglican 8%, other 35% (1991)
Languages: English (official), French (official)
Literacy:
definition: age 15 and over can read and write
total population: 97% (1986 est.)
male: NA%
female: NA%

Government

Country name:
conventional long form: none
conventional short form: Canada
Data code: CA
Government type: federation with parliamentary democracy
Capital: Ottawa
Administrative divisions: 10 provinces and 3 territories*; Alberta, British Columbia, Manitoba, New Brunswick, Newfoundland, Northwest Territories*, Nova Scotia, Nunavut*, Ontario, Prince Edward Island, Quebec, Saskatchewan, Yukon Territory*
Independence: 1 July 1867 (from UK)
National holiday: Canada Day, 1 July (1867)
Constitution: 17 April 1982 (Constitution Act); originally, the machinery of the government was set up in the British North America Act of 1867; charter of rights and unwritten customs

Canada (continued)

Legal system: based on English common law, except in Quebec, where civil law system based on French law prevails; accepts compulsory ICJ jurisdiction, with reservations
Suffrage: 18 years of age; universal
Executive branch:
chief of state: Queen ELIZABETH II (since 6 February 1952), represented by Governor General Romeo Le BLANC (since 8 February 1995)
head of government: Prime Minister Jean CHRETIEN (since 4 November 1993)
cabinet: Federal Ministry chosen by the prime minister from among the members of his own party sitting in Parliament
elections: none; the monarch is hereditary; governor general appointed by the monarch on the advice of the prime minister for a five-year term; following legislative elections, the leader of the majority party in the House of Commons is automatically designated by the governor general to become prime minister
Legislative branch: bicameral Parliament or Parlement consists of the Senate or Senat (a body whose members are appointed to serve until reaching 75 years of age by the governor general and selected on the advice of the prime minister; its normal limit is 104 senators) and the House of Commons or Chambre des Communes (301 seats; members elected by direct popular vote to serve five-year terms)
elections: House of Commons - last held 2 June 1997 (next to be held by NA June 2002)
election results: percent of vote by party - Liberal Party 38%, Reform Party 19%, Tories 19%, Bloc Quebecois 11%, New Democratic Party 11%, other 2%; seats by party - Liberal Party 155, Reform Party 60, Bloc Quebecois 44, New Democratic Party 21, Progressive Conservative Party 20, independents 1
Judicial branch: Supreme Court, judges are appointed by the prime minister through the governor general
Political parties and leaders: Liberal Party [Jean CHRETIEN]; Bloc Quebecois [Gilles DUCEPPE]; Reform Party [Preston MANNING]; New Democratic Party [Alexa MCDONOUGH]; Progressive Conservative Party [Joe CLARK]
International organization participation: ACCT, AfDB, APEC, AsDB, Australia Group, BIS, C, CCC, CDB (non-regional), CE (observer), CP, EAPC, EBRD, ECE, ECLAC, ESA (cooperating state), FAO, G- 7, G-10, IADB, IAEA, IBRD, ICAO, ICC, ICFTU, ICRM, IDA, IEA, IFAD, IFC, IFRCS, IHO, ILO, IMF, IMO, Inmarsat, Intelsat, Interpol, IOC, IOM, ISO, ITU, MINURCA, MIPONUH, MTCR, NAM (guest), NATO, NEA, NSG, OAS, OECD, OPCW, OSCE, PCA, UN, UNCTAD, UNDOF, UNESCO, UNFICYP, UNHCR, UNIDO, UNIKOM, UNMIBH, UNMOP, UNPREDEP, UNTSO, UNU, UPU, WCL, WFTU, WHO, WIPO, WMO, WTrO, ZC
Diplomatic representation in the US:
chief of mission: Ambassador Raymond A. J. CHRETIEN
chancery: 501 Pennsylvania Avenue NW, Washington, DC 20001

telephone: [1] (202) 682-1740
FAX: [1] (202) 682-7726
consulate(s) general: Atlanta, Boston, Buffalo, Chicago, Dallas, Detroit, Los Angeles, Minneapolis, New York, and Seattle
consulate(s): Miami, Princeton, San Francisco, and San Jose
Diplomatic representation from the US:
chief of mission: Ambassador Gordon D. GIFFIN
embassy: 100 Wellington Street, K1P 5T1, Ottawa
mailing address: P. O. Box 5000, Ogdensburg, NY 13669-0430
telephone: [1] (613) 238-5335, 4470
FAX: [1] (613) 238-5720
consulate(s) general: Calgary, Halifax, Montreal, Quebec, Toronto, and Vancouver
Flag description: three vertical bands of red (hoist side), white (double width, square), and red with a red maple leaf centered in the white band

Economy

Economy - overview: As an affluent, high-tech industrial society, Canada today closely resembles the US in its market-oriented economic system, pattern of production, and high living standards. Since World War II, the impressive growth of the manufacturing, mining, and service sectors has transformed the nation from a largely rural economy into one primarily industrial and urban. Real rates of growth have averaged nearly 3.0% since 1993. Unemployment is falling and government budget surpluses are being partially devoted to reducing the large public sector debt. The 1989 US-Canada Free Trade Agreement (FTA) and 1994 North American Free Trade Agreement (NAFTA) (which included Mexico) have touched off a dramatic increase in trade and economic integration with the US. With its great natural resources, skilled labor force, and modern capital plant Canada can anticipate solid economic prospects in the future. The continuing constitutional impasse between English- and French-speaking areas is raising the possibility of a split in the federation, making foreign investors somewhat edgy.
GDP: purchasing power parity - $688.3 billion (1998 est.)
GDP - real growth rate: 3% (1998 est.)
GDP - per capita: purchasing power parity - $22,400 (1998 est.)
GDP - composition by sector:
agriculture: 3%
industry: 31%
services: 66% (1998)
Population below poverty line: NA%
Household income or consumption by percentage share:
lowest 10%: 2.8%
highest 10%: 23.8% (1994)
Inflation rate (consumer prices): 0.9% (1998)
Labor force: 15.8 million (1998)
Labor force - by occupation: services 75%, manufacturing 16%, construction 5%, agriculture 3%, other 1% (1997)

Unemployment rate: 7.8% (December 1998)
Budget:
revenues: $121.3 billion
expenditures: $112.6 billion, including capital expenditures of $1.7 billion (1998)
Industries: processed and unprocessed minerals, food products, wood and paper products, transportation equipment, chemicals, fish products, petroleum and natural gas
Industrial production growth rate: 0.8% (1998 est.)
Electricity - production: 549.162 billion kWh (1996)
Electricity - production by source:
fossil fuel: 20.34%
hydro: 63.59%
nuclear: 16.05%
other: 0.02% (1996)
Electricity - consumption: 511.586 billion kWh (1996)
Electricity - exports: 45.28 billion kWh (1996)
Electricity - imports: 7.705 billion kWh (1996)
Agriculture - products: wheat, barley, oilseed, tobacco, fruits, vegetables; dairy products; forest products; fish
Exports: $210.7 billion (f.o.b., 1998)
Exports - commodities: motor vehicles and parts, newsprint, wood pulp, timber, crude petroleum, machinery, natural gas, aluminum, telecommunications equipment
Exports - partners: US 81%, Japan 4%, UK, Germany, South Korea, Netherlands, China (1997)
Imports: $202.7 billion (f.o.b., 1998)
Imports - commodities: machinery and equipment, crude oil, chemicals, motor vehicles and parts, durable consumer goods
Imports - partners: US 76%, Japan 3%, UK, Germany, France, Mexico, Taiwan, South Korea (1997)
Debt - external: $253 billion (1996)
Economic aid - donor: ODA, $2.1 billion (1995)
Currency: 1 Canadian dollar (Can$) = 100 cents
Exchange rates: Canadian dollars (Can$) per US$1 - 1.5192 (January 1999), 1.4835 (1998), 1.3846 (1997), 1.3635 (1996), 1.3724 (1995), 1.3656 (1994)
Fiscal year: 1 April - 31 March

Communications

Telephones: 15.3 million (1990)
Telephone system: excellent service provided by modern technology
domestic: domestic satellite system with about 300 earth stations
international: 5 coaxial submarine cables; satellite earth stations - 5 Intelsat (4 Atlantic Ocean and 1 Pacific Ocean) and 2 Intersputnik (Atlantic Ocean region)
Radio broadcast stations: AM 334, FM 35, shortwave 7 (one of the shortwave stations, Radio Canada International, has six transmitters, 48 frequencies, and broadcasts in seven languages; the transmissions are relayed by repeaters in Europe and Asia) (1998)

Canada (continued)

Radios: NA
Television broadcast stations: 80 (in addition, there are many repeaters) (1997)
Televisions: 11.53 million (1983 est.)

Transportation

Railways:
total: 67,773 km; note - there are two major transcontinental freight railway systems: Canadian National (privatized November 1995) and Canadian Pacific Railway; passenger service provided by government-operated firm VIA, which has no trackage of its own
standard gauge: 67,773 km 1.435-m gauge (183 km electrified) (1996)
Highways:
total: 912,200 km
paved: 246,400 km (including 16,600 km of expressways)
unpaved: 665,800 km (1996 est.)
Waterways: 3,000 km, including Saint Lawrence Seaway
Pipelines: crude and refined oil 23,564 km; natural gas 74,980 km
Ports and harbors: Becancour (Quebec), Churchill, Halifax, Hamilton, Montreal, New Westminster, Prince Rupert, Quebec, Saint John (New Brunswick), St. John's (Newfoundland), Sept Isles, Sydney, Trois-Rivieres, Thunder Bay, Toronto, Vancouver, Windsor
Merchant marine:
total: 109 ships (1,000 GRT or over) totaling 1,489,110 GRT/2,205,274 DWT
ships by type: barge carrier 1, bulk 56, cargo 11, chemical tanker 5, combination bulk 2, oil tanker 16, passenger 3, passenger-cargo 1, railcar carrier 2, roll-on/roll-off cargo 7, short-sea passenger 4, specialized tanker 1
note: does not include ships used exclusively in the Great Lakes (1998 est.)
Airports: 1,395 (1998 est.)
Airports - with paved runways:
total: 515
over 3,047 m: 16
2,438 to 3,047 m: 16
1,524 to 2,437 m: 154
914 to 1,523 m: 238
under 914 m: 91 (1998 est.)
Airports - with unpaved runways:
total: 880
1,524 to 2,437 m: 73
914 to 1,523 m: 353
under 914 m: 454 (1998 est.)
Heliports: 16 (1998 est.)

Military

Military branches: Canadian Armed Forces (includes Land Forces Command or LC, Maritime Command or MC, Air Command or AC, Communications Command or CC, Training Command or TC), Royal Canadian Mounted Police (RCMP)
Military manpower - military age: 17 years of age
Military manpower - availability:
males age 15-49: 8,243,859 (1999 est.)
Military manpower - fit for military service:
males age 15-49: 7,061,937 (1999 est.)
Military manpower - reaching military age annually:
males: 210,884 (1999 est.)
Military expenditures - dollar figure: $7.1 billion (FY97/98)
Military expenditures - percent of GDP: 1.2% (FY97/98)

Transnational Issues

Disputes - international: maritime boundary disputes with the US (Dixon Entrance, Beaufort Sea, Strait of Juan de Fuca, Machias Seal Island)
Illicit drugs: illicit producer of cannabis for the domestic drug market; use of hydroponics technology permits growers to plant large quantities of high-quality marijuana indoors; growing role as a transit point for heroin and cocaine entering the US market

Cape Verde

Geography

Location: Western Africa, group of islands in the North Atlantic Ocean, west of Senegal
Geographic coordinates: 16 00 N, 24 00 W
Map references: World
Area:
total: 4,030 sq km
land: 4,030 sq km
water: 0 sq km
Area - comparative: slightly larger than Rhode Island
Land boundaries: 0 km
Coastline: 965 km
Maritime claims: measured from claimed archipelagic baselines
exclusive economic zone: 200 nm
territorial sea: 12 nm
Climate: temperate; warm, dry summer; precipitation meager and very erratic
Terrain: steep, rugged, rocky, volcanic
Elevation extremes:
lowest point: Atlantic Ocean 0 m
highest point: Mt. Fogo 2,829 m (a volcano on Fogo Island)
Natural resources: salt, basalt rock, pozzuolana (a siliceous volcanic ash used to produce hydraulic cement), limestone, kaolin, fish
Land use:
arable land: 11%
permanent crops: 0%
permanent pastures: 6%
forests and woodland: 0%
other: 83% (1993 est.)
Irrigated land: 30 sq km (1993 est.)
Natural hazards: prolonged droughts; harmattan wind can obscure visibility; volcanically and seismically active
Environment - current issues: overgrazing of livestock and improper land use such as the cultivation of crops on steep slopes has led to soil

Cape Verde *(continued)*

erosion; demand for wood used as fuel has resulted in deforestation; desertification; environmental damage has threatened several species of birds and reptiles; overfishing

Environment - international agreements:
party to: Biodiversity, Climate Change, Desertification, Environmental Modification, Law of the Sea, Marine Dumping, Nuclear Test Ban
signed, but not ratified: none of the selected agreements

Geography - note: strategic location 500 km from west coast of Africa near major north-south sea routes; important communications station; important sea and air refueling site

People

Population: 405,748 (July 1999 est.)
Age structure:
0-14 years: 45% (male 92,721; female 91,083)
15-64 years: 49% (male 92,658; female 104,264)
65 years and over: 6% (male 9,936; female 15,086) (1999 est.)
Population growth rate: 1.44% (1999 est.)
Birth rate: 33.49 births/1,000 population (1999 est.)
Death rate: 6.78 deaths/1,000 population (1999 est.)
Net migration rate: -12.35 migrant(s)/1,000 population (1999 est.)
Sex ratio:
at birth: 1.03 male(s)/female
under 15 years: 1.02 male(s)/female
15-64 years: 0.89 male(s)/female
65 years and over: 0.66 male(s)/female
total population: 0.93 male(s)/female (1999 est.)
Infant mortality rate: 45.5 deaths/1,000 live births (1999 est.)
Life expectancy at birth:
total population: 70.96 years
male: 67.66 years
female: 74.36 years (1999 est.)
Total fertility rate: 4.95 children born/woman (1999 est.)
Nationality:
noun: Cape Verdean(s)
adjective: Cape Verdean
Ethnic groups: Creole (mulatto) 71%, African 28%, European 1%
Religions: Roman Catholic (infused with indigenous beliefs); Protestant (mostly Church of the Nazarene)
Languages: Portuguese, Crioulo (a blend of creole Portuguese and West African words)
Literacy:
definition: age 15 and over can read and write
total population: 71.6%
male: 81.4%
female: 63.8% (1995 est.)

Government

Country name:
conventional long form: Republic of Cape Verde
conventional short form: Cape Verde
local long form: Republica de Cabo Verde
local short form: Cabo Verde
Data code: CV
Government type: republic
Capital: Praia
Administrative divisions: 14 districts (concelhos, singular - concelho); Boa Vista, Brava, Fogo, Maio, Paul, Praia, Porto Novo, Ribeira Grande, Sal, Santa Catarina, Santa Cruz, Sao Nicolau, Sao Vicente, Tarrafal
note: there may be a new administrative structure of 16 districts (Boa Vista, Brava, Maio, Mosteiros, Paul, Praia, Porto Novo, Ribeira Grande, Sal, Santa Catarina, Santa Cruz, Sao Domingos, Sao Nicolau, Sao Filipe, Sao Vicente, Tarrafal)
Independence: 5 July 1975 (from Portugal)
National holiday: Independence Day, 5 July (1975)
Constitution: new constitution came into force 25 September 1992
Legal system: derived from the legal system of Portugal
Suffrage: 18 years of age; universal
Executive branch:
chief of state: President Antonio MASCARENHAS Monteiro (since 22 March 1991)
head of government: Prime Minister Carlos Alberto Wahnon de Carvalho VEIGA (since 13 January 1991)
cabinet: Council of Ministers appointed by the president on the recommendation of the prime minister from among the members of the National Assembly
elections: president elected by popular vote for a five-year term; election last held 18 February 1996 (next to be held NA February 2001); prime minister nominated by the National Assembly and appointed by the president
election results: Antonio MASCARENHAS Monteiro elected president; percent of vote - Antonio MASCARENHAS Monteiro (independent) 80.1%
Legislative branch: unicameral National Assembly or Assembleia Nacional (72 seats; members are elected by popular vote to serve five-year terms)
elections: last held 17 December 1995 (next to be held NA 2000)
election results: percent of vote by party - MPD 59%, PAICV 28%, PCD 6%; seats by party - MPD 50, PAICV 21, PCD 1
Judicial branch: Supreme Tribunal of Justice or Supremo Tribunal de Justia
Political parties and leaders: Movement for Democracy or MPD [Prime Minister Carlos VEIGA, founder and president]; African Party for Independence of Cape Verde or PAICV [Pedro Verona Rodrigues PIRES, chairman]; Party for Democratic Convergence or PCD [Dr. Eurico MONTEIRO, president]; Party of Work and Solidarity or PTS [Dr. Oresimo SILVEIRA, president]
International organization participation: ACCT, ACP, AfDB, CCC, ECA, ECOWAS, FAO, G-77, IBRD, ICAO, ICFTU, ICRM, IDA, IFAD, IFC, IFRCS, ILO, IMF, IMO, Intelsat, Interpol, IOC, IOM (observer), ITU, NAM, OAU, OPCW, UN, UNCTAD, UNESCO, UNIDO, UPU, WCL, WHO, WIPO, WMO, WTrO

(applicant)
Diplomatic representation in the US:
chief of mission: Ambassador Ferdinand Amilcar Spencer LOPES
chancery: 3415 Massachusetts Avenue NW, Washington, DC 20007
telephone: [1] (202) 965-6820
FAX: [1] (202) 965-1207
consulate(s) general: Boston
Diplomatic representation from the US:
chief of mission: Ambassador Lawrence Neal BENEDICT
embassy: Rua Abilio Macedo 81, Praia
mailing address: C. P. 201, Praia
telephone: [238] 61 56 16
FAX: [238] 61 13 55
Flag description: three horizontal bands of light blue (top, double width), white (with a horizontal red stripe in the middle third), and light blue; a circle of 10 yellow five-pointed stars is centered on the hoist end of the red stripe and extends into the upper and lower blue bands

Economy

Economy - overview: Cape Verde's low per capita GDP reflects a poor natural resource base, including serious water shortages exacerbated by cycles of long-term drought. The economy is service-oriented, with commerce, transport, and public services accounting for almost 70% of GDP. Although nearly 70% of the population lives in rural areas, the share of agriculture in GDP in 1995 was only 8%, of which fishing accounts for 1.5%. About 90% of food must be imported. The fishing potential, mostly lobster and tuna, is not fully exploited. Cape Verde annually runs a high trade deficit, financed by foreign aid and remittances from emigrants; remittances constitute a supplement to GDP of more than 20%. Economic reforms, launched by the new democratic government in 1991, are aimed at developing the private sector and attracting foreign investment to diversify the economy. Prospects for 1999 depend heavily on the maintenance of aid flows, remittances, and the momentum of the government's development program.
GDP: purchasing power parity - $581 million (1998 est.)
GDP - real growth rate: 7% (1998 est.)
GDP - per capita: purchasing power parity - $1,450 (1998 est.)
GDP - composition by sector:
agriculture: 8%
industry: 18%
services: 74% (1996 est.)
Population below poverty line: NA%
Household income or consumption by percentage share:
lowest 10%: NA%
highest 10%: NA%
Inflation rate (consumer prices): 4.3% (1998)
Labor force: NA
Unemployment rate: NA%

Cape Verde *(continued)*

Budget:
revenues: $188 million
expenditures: $228 million, including capital expenditures of $116 million (1996)
Industries: food and beverages, fish processing, shoes and garments, salt mining, ship repair,
Industrial production growth rate: NA%
Electricity - production: 40 million kWh (1996)
Electricity - production by source:
fossil fuel: 100%
hydro: 0%
nuclear: 0%
other: 0% (1996)
Electricity - consumption: 40 million kWh (1996)
Electricity - exports: 0 kWh (1996)
Electricity - imports: 0 kWh (1996)
Agriculture - products: bananas, corn, beans, sweet potatoes, sugarcane, coffee, peanuts; fish
Exports: $43 million (f.o.b., 1997 est.)
Exports - commodities: shoes, garments, fish, bananas, hides,
Exports - partners: Portugal, Germany, Spain, France, UK, Malaysia
Imports: $215 million (f.o.b., 1997 est.)
Imports - commodities: foodstuffs, consumer goods, industrial products, transport equipment, fuels
Imports - partners: Portugal 25%, Netherlands, France, UK, Spain, US
Debt - external: $220 million (1998)
Economic aid - recipient: $111.3 million (1995)
Currency: 1 Cape Verdean escudo (CVEsc) = 100 centavos
Exchange rates: Cape Verdean escudos (CVEsc) per US$1 - 96.400 (November 1998), 99.41 (1998), 93.177 (1997), 82.591 (1996), 76.853 (1995), 81.891 (1994)
Fiscal year: calendar year

Communications

Telephones: 22,900 (1995 est.)
Telephone system:
domestic: interisland microwave radio relay system with both analog and digital exchanges; work is in progress on a submarine fiber-optic cable system which was scheduled for completion in 1998
international: 2 coaxial submarine cables; HF radiotelephone to Senegal and Guinea-Bissau; satellite earth station - 1 Intelsat (Atlantic Ocean)
Radio broadcast stations: AM 1, FM 6, shortwave 0 (1998)
Radios: NA
Television broadcast stations: 1 (1997 est.)
Televisions: 7,000 (1991 est.)

Transportation

Railways: 0 km
Highways:
total: 1,100 km
paved: 858 km
unpaved: 242 km (1996 est.)
Ports and harbors: Mindelo, Praia, Tarrafal

Merchant marine:
total: 4 ships (1,000 GRT or over) totaling 9,620 GRT/ 13,920 DWT
ships by type: cargo 3, chemical tanker 1 (1998 est.)
Airports: 6 (1998 est.)
Airports - with paved runways:
total: 6
over 3,047 m: 1
914 to 1,523 m: 5 (1998 est.)

Military

Military branches: Armed Forces (AF) (includes all armed force elements, both ground and naval)
Military manpower - availability:
males age 15-49: 84,018 (1999 est.)
Military manpower - fit for military service:
males age 15-49: 47,672 (1999 est.)
Military expenditures - dollar figure: $3.8 million (1996)
Military expenditures - percent of GDP: 1.8% (1996)

Transnational Issues

Disputes - international: none
Illicit drugs: used as a transshipment point for illicit drugs moving from Latin America and Africa destined for Western Europe

Cayman Islands
(overseas territory of the UK)

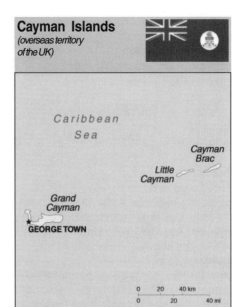

Geography

Location: Caribbean, island group in Caribbean Sea, nearly one-half of the way from Cuba to Honduras
Geographic coordinates: 19 30 N, 80 30 W
Map references: Central America and the Caribbean
Area:
total: 260 sq km
land: 260 sq km
water: 0 sq km
Area - comparative: 1.5 times the size of Washington, DC
Land boundaries: 0 km
Coastline: 160 km
Maritime claims:
exclusive fishing zone: 200 nm
territorial sea: 12 nm
Climate: tropical marine; warm, rainy summers (May to October) and cool, relatively dry winters (November to April)
Terrain: low-lying limestone base surrounded by coral reefs
Elevation extremes:
lowest point: Caribbean Sea 0 m
highest point: The Bluff 43 m
Natural resources: fish, climate and beaches that foster tourism
Land use:
arable land: 0%
permanent crops: 0%
permanent pastures: 8%
forests and woodland: 23%
other: 69% (1993 est.)
Irrigated land: NA sq km
Natural hazards: hurricanes (July to November)
Environment - current issues: no natural fresh water resources; drinking water supplies must be met by rainwater catchment

Cayman Islands *(continued)*

Environment - international agreements:
party to: NA
signed, but not ratified: NA
Geography - note: important location between Cuba and Central America

People

Population: 39,335 (July 1999 est.)
Age structure:
0-14 years: NA
15-64 years: NA
65 years and over: NA
Population growth rate: 4.19% (1999 est.)
Birth rate: 13.66 births/1,000 population (1999 est.)
Death rate: 4.98 deaths/1,000 population (1999 est.)
Net migration rate: 33.2 migrant(s)/1,000 population (1999 est.)
note: major destination for Cubans trying to migrate to the US
Infant mortality rate: 8.4 deaths/1,000 live births (1999 est.)
Life expectancy at birth:
total population: 77.1 years
male: 75.37 years
female: 78.81 years (1999 est.)
Total fertility rate: 1.31 children born/woman (1999 est.)
Nationality:
noun: Caymanian(s)
adjective: Caymanian
Ethnic groups: mixed 40%, white 20%, black 20%, expatriates of various ethnic groups 20%
Religions: United Church (Presbyterian and Congregational), Anglican, Baptist, Roman Catholic, Church of God, other Protestant denominations
Languages: English
Literacy:
definition: age 15 and over has ever attended school
total population: 98%
male: 98%
female: 98% (1970 est.)

Government

Country name:
conventional long form: none
conventional short form: Cayman Islands
Data code: CJ
Dependency status: overseas territory of the UK
Government type: NA
Capital: George Town
Administrative divisions: 8 districts; Creek, Eastern, Midland, South Town, Spot Bay, Stake Bay, West End, Western
Independence: none (overseas territory of the UK)
National holiday: Constitution Day (first Monday in July)
Constitution: 1959, revised 1972 and 1992
Legal system: British common law and local statutes
Suffrage: 18 years of age; universal

Executive branch:
chief of state: Queen ELIZABETH II (since 6 February 1952)
head of government: Governor and President of the Executive Council John Wynne OWEN (since 15 September 1995)
cabinet: Executive Council (three members appointed by the governor, four members elected by the Legislative Assembly)
elections: none; the monarch is hereditary; the governor is appointed by the monarch
Legislative branch: unicameral Legislative Assembly (18 seats, three official members and 15 elected by popular vote; members serve four-year terms)
elections: last held 20 November 1996 (next to be held NA November 2000)
election results: percent of vote - NA; seats - National Team coalition 9, independents 6
Judicial branch: Grand Court; Cayman Islands Court of Appeal
Political parties and leaders: no formal political parties
International organization participation: Caricom (observer), CDB, Interpol (subbureau), IOC
Diplomatic representation in the US: none (overseas territory of the UK)
Diplomatic representation from the US: none (overseas territory of the UK)
Flag description: blue, with the flag of the UK in the upper hoist-side quadrant and the Caymanian coat of arms on a white disk centered on the outer half of the flag; the coat of arms includes a pineapple and turtle above a shield with three stars (representing the three islands) and a scroll at the bottom bearing the motto HE HATH FOUNDED IT UPON THE SEAS

Economy

Economy - overview: With no direct taxation, the islands are a thriving offshore financial center. More than 40,000 companies were registered in the Cayman Islands as of 1997, including almost 600 banks and trust companies; banking assets exceed $500 billion. A stock exchange was opened in 1997. Tourism is also a mainstay, accounting for about 70% of GDP and 75% of foreign currency earnings. The tourist industry is aimed at the luxury market and caters mainly to visitors from North America. Total tourist arrivals exceeded 1.2 million visitors in 1997. About 90% of the islands' food and consumer goods must be imported. The Caymanians enjoy one of the highest outputs per capita and one of the highest standards of living in the world.
GDP: purchasing power parity - $930 million (1997 est.)
GDP - real growth rate: 5.5% (1997 est.)
GDP - per capita: purchasing power parity - $24,500 (1997 est.)
GDP - composition by sector:
agriculture: 1.4%
industry: 3.2%
services: 95.4% (1994 est.)

Population below poverty line: NA%
Household income or consumption by percentage share:
lowest 10%: NA%
highest 10%: NA%
Inflation rate (consumer prices): 2.7% (1997)
Labor force: 19,820 (1995)
Labor force - by occupation: service workers 18.7%, clerical 18.6%, construction 12.5%, finance and investment 6.7%, directors and business managers 5.9% (1979)
Unemployment rate: 5.1% (1996)
Budget:
revenues: $265.2 million
expenditures: $248.9 million, including capital expenditures of $NA (1997)
Industries: tourism, banking, insurance and finance, construction, construction materials, furniture
Industrial production growth rate: NA%
Electricity - production: 290 million kWh (1996)
Electricity - production by source:
fossil fuel: 100%
hydro: 0%
nuclear: 0%
other: 0% (1996)
Electricity - consumption: 290 million kWh (1996)
Electricity - exports: 0 kWh (1996)
Electricity - imports: 0 kWh (1996)
Agriculture - products: vegetables, fruit; livestock, turtle farming
Exports: $2.65 million (1996)
Exports - commodities: turtle products, manufactured consumer goods
Exports - partners: mostly US
Imports: $379.4 million (1996)
Imports - commodities: foodstuffs, manufactured goods
Imports - partners: US, Trinidad and Tobago, UK, Netherlands Antilles, Japan
Debt - external: $70 million (1996)
Economic aid - recipient: $NA
Currency: 1 Caymanian dollar (CI$) = 100 cents
Exchange rates: Caymanian dollars (CI$) per US$1 - 0.83 (3 November 1995), 0.85 (22 November 1993)
Fiscal year: 1 April - 31 March

Communications

Telephones: 21,584 (1993 est.)
Telephone system:
domestic: NA
international: 1 submarine coaxial cable; satellite earth station - 1 Intelsat (Atlantic Ocean)
Radio broadcast stations: AM 1, FM 4 (the four stations have a total of six frequencies), shortwave 0 (1998)
Radios: 28,200 (1992 est.)
Television broadcast stations: NA
Televisions: 6,000 (1992 est.)

Transportation

Railways: 0 km

Cayman Islands *(continued)*

Highways:
total: 406 km
paved: 304 km
unpaved: 102 km
Ports and harbors: Cayman Brac, George Town
Merchant marine:
total: 76 ships (1,000 GRT or over) totaling 1,264,113 GRT/1,970,959 DWT
ships by type: bulk 13, cargo 10, chemical tanker 11, container 4, liquefied gas tanker 1, oil tanker 7, refrigerated cargo 22, roll-on/roll-off cargo 6, specialized tanker 1, vehicle carrier 1
note: a flag of convenience registry; includes ships from 11 countries among which are: Greece 15, US 5, UK 5, Cyprus 2, Denmark 2, Norway 3 (1998 est.)
Airports: 3 (1998 est.)
Airports - with paved runways:
total: 2
1,524 to 2,437 m: 2 (1998 est.)
Airports - with unpaved runways:
total: 1
914 to 1,523 m: 1 (1998 est.)

Military

Military branches: Royal Cayman Islands Police Force (RCIPF)
Military - note: defense is the responsibility of the UK

Transnational Issues

Disputes - international: none
Illicit drugs: vulnerable to drug money laundering and drug transshipment

Central African Republic

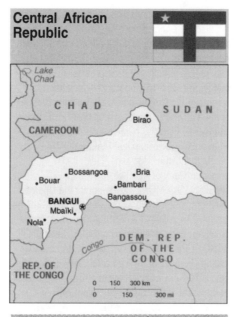

Introduction

Background: In 1996, the country experienced three mutinies by dissident elements of the armed forces, which demanded back pay as well as political and military reforms. Subsequent violence between the government and rebel military groups over pay issues, living conditions, and lack of opposition party representation in the government, destroyed many businesses in the capital, reduced tax revenues, and exacerbated the government's problems in meeting expenses. African peacekeepers restored order in 1997; in April 1998 the United Nations Mission in the Central African Republic (MINURCA) assumed responsibility for peacekeeping operations.

Geography

Location: Central Africa, north of Democratic Republic of the Congo
Geographic coordinates: 7 00 N, 21 00 E
Map references: Africa
Area:
total: 622,980 sq km
land: 622,980 sq km
water: 0 sq km
Area - comparative: slightly smaller than Texas
Land boundaries:
total: 5,203 km
border countries: Cameroon 797 km, Chad 1,197 km, Democratic Republic of the Congo 1,577 km, Republic of the Congo 467 km, Sudan 1,165 km
Coastline: 0 km (landlocked)
Maritime claims: none (landlocked)
Climate: tropical; hot, dry winters; mild to hot, wet summers
Terrain: vast, flat to rolling, monotonous plateau; scattered hills in northeast and southwest
Elevation extremes:
lowest point: Oubangui River 335 m
highest point: Mont Ngaoui 1,420 m
Natural resources: diamonds, uranium, timber,

gold, oil
Land use:
arable land: 3%
permanent crops: 0%
permanent pastures: 5%
forests and woodland: 75%
other: 17% (1993 est.)
Irrigated land: NA sq km
Natural hazards: hot, dry, dusty harmattan winds affect northern areas; floods are common
Environment - current issues: tap water is not potable; poaching has diminished its reputation as one of the last great wildlife refuges; desertification; deforestation
Environment - international agreements:
party to: Biodiversity, Climate Change, Desertification, Endangered Species, Nuclear Test Ban, Ozone Layer Protection, Tropical Timber 94
signed, but not ratified: Law of the Sea
Geography - note: landlocked; almost the precise center of Africa

People

Population: 3,444,951 (July 1999 est.)
Age structure:
0-14 years: 44% (male 757,422; female 749,289)
15-64 years: 53% (male 885,087; female 927,282)
65 years and over: 3% (male 56,309; female 69,562) (1999 est.)
Population growth rate: 2.04% (1999 est.)
Birth rate: 38.28 births/1,000 population (1999 est.)
Death rate: 16.46 deaths/1,000 population (1999 est.)
Net migration rate: -1.45 migrant(s)/1,000 population (1999 est.)
Sex ratio:
at birth: 1.03 male(s)/female
under 15 years: 1.01 male(s)/female
15-64 years: 0.95 male(s)/female
65 years and over: 0.81 male(s)/female
total population: 0.97 male(s)/female (1999 est.)
Infant mortality rate: 103.42 deaths/1,000 live births (1999 est.)
Life expectancy at birth:
total population: 47.19 years
male: 45.35 years
female: 49.09 years (1999 est.)
Total fertility rate: 5.03 children born/woman (1999 est.)
Nationality:
noun: Central African(s)
adjective: Central African
Ethnic groups: Baya 34%, Banda 27%, Sara 10%, Mandjia 21%, Mboum 4%, M'Baka 4%, Europeans 6,500 (including 3,600 French)
Religions: indigenous beliefs 24%, Protestant 25%, Roman Catholic 25%, Muslim 15%, other 11%
note: animistic beliefs and practices strongly influence the Christian majority
Languages: French (official), Sangho (lingua franca and national language), Arabic, Hunsa, Swahili

Central African Republic (continued)

Literacy:
definition: age 15 and over can read and write
total population: 60%
male: 68.5%
female: 52.4% (1995 est.)

Government

Country name:
conventional long form: Central African Republic
conventional short form: none
local long form: Republique Centrafricaine
local short form: none
former: Central African Empire
abbreviation: CAR

Data code: CT

Government type: republic

Capital: Bangui

Administrative divisions: 14 prefectures (prefectures, singular - prefecture), 2 economic prefectures* (prefectures economiques, singular - prefecture economique), and 1 commune**; Bamingui-Bangoran, Bangui**, Basse-Kotto, Gribingui*, Haute-Kotto, Haute-Sangha, Haut-Mbomou, Kemo-Gribingui, Lobaye, Mbomou, Nana-Mambere, Ombella-Mpoko, Ouaka, Ouham, Ouham-Pende, Sangha*, Vakaga

Independence: 13 August 1960 (from France)

National holiday: National Day, 1 December (1958) (proclamation of the republic)

Constitution: passed by referendum 29 December 1994; adopted 7 January 1995

Legal system: based on French law

Suffrage: 21 years of age; universal

Executive branch:
chief of state: President Ange-Felix PATASSE (since 22 October 1993)
head of government: Prime Minister Anicet Georges DOLOGUELE (since January 1999)
cabinet: Council of Ministers
elections: president elected by popular vote for a six-year term; election last held 19 September 1993 (next to be held NA 1999); prime minister appointed by the president
election results: Ange-Felix PATASSE elected president; percent of vote - PATASSE 52.45%, Abel GOUMBA 45.62%

Legislative branch: unicameral National Assembly or Assemblee Nationale (109 seats; members are elected by popular vote to serve five-year terms; note - there were 85 seats in the National Assembly before the 1998 election)
elections: last held 22-23 November and NA December 1998 (next to be held NA 2003)
election results: percent of vote by party - MLPC 43%, RDC 18%, MDD 9%, FPP 6%, PSD 5%, ADP 4%, PUN 3%, FODEM 2%, PLD 2%, UPR 1%, FC 1%, independents 6%; seats by party - MLPC 47, RDC 20, MDD 10, FPP 7, PSD 5, ADP 4, PUN 3, FODEM 2, PLD 2, UPR 1, FC 1, independents 7; note - results of election are being contested
note: the National Assembly is advised by the Economic and Regional Council or Conseil Economique et Regional; when they sit together they are called the Congress or Congres

Judicial branch: Supreme Court or Cour Supreme, judges appointed by the president; Constitutional Court, judges appointed by the president

Political parties and leaders: Alliance for Democracy and Progress or ADP [Tchapka BREDE]; Central African Democratic Assembly or RDC [Andre KOLINGBA]; PUN (full name NA) [leader NA]; Civic Forum or FC [Gen. Timothee MALENDOMA]; FODEM (full name NA) [leader NA]; Liberal Democratic Party or PLD [Nestor KOMBO-NAGUEMON]; Movement for the Liberation of the Central African People or MLPC [the party of the president, Ange-Felix PATASSE]; Movement for Democracy and Development or MDD [David DACKO]; UPR (full name NA) [leader NA]; Patriotic Front for Progress or FPP [Abel GOUMBA]; Social Democratic Party or PSD [leader NA]

International organization participation: ACCT, ACP, AfDB, BDEAC, CCC, CEEAC, ECA, FAO, FZ, G-77, IBRD, ICAO, ICFTU, ICRM, IDA, IFAD, IFC, IFRCS, ILO, IMF, Intelsat, Interpol, IOC, ITU, NAM, OAU, OIC (observer), OPCW, UDEAC, UN, UNCTAD, UNESCO, UNIDO, UPU, WCL, WHO, WIPO, WMO, WToO, WTrO

Diplomatic representation in the US:
chief of mission: Ambassador Henri KOBA
chancery: 1618 22nd Street NW, Washington, DC 20008
telephone: [1] (202) 483-7800
FAX: [1] (202) 332-9893

Diplomatic representation from the US:
chief of mission: Ambassador Robert C. PERRY
embassy: Avenue David Dacko, Bangui
mailing address: B. P. 924, Bangui
telephone: [236] 61 26 21
FAX: [236] 61 44 94

Flag description: four equal horizontal bands of blue (top), white, green, and yellow with a vertical red band in center; there is a yellow five-pointed star on the hoist side of the blue band

Economy

Economy - overview: Subsistence agriculture, together with forestry, remains the backbone of the economy of the Central African Republic (CAR), with more than 70% of the population living in outlying areas. The agricultural sector generates half of GDP. Timber has accounted for about 16% of export earnings and the diamond industry for nearly 54%. Important constraints to economic development include the CAR's landlocked position, a poor transportation system, a largely unskilled work force, and a legacy of misdirected macroeconomic policies. The 50% devaluation of the currencies of 14 Francophone African nations on 12 January 1994 had mixed effects on the CAR's economy. Diamond, timber, coffee, and cotton exports increased, leading an estimated rise of GDP of 7% in 1994 and nearly 5% in 1995. Military rebellions and social unrest in 1996 were accompanied by widespread destruction of property and a drop in GDP of 2%. Ongoing violence between the government and rebel military groups over pay issues, living conditions, and political representation has destroyed many businesses in the capital and reduced tax revenues for the government. The IMF approved an Extended Structure Adjustment Facility in 1998.

GDP: purchasing power parity - $5.5 billion (1998 est.)

GDP - real growth rate: 5.5% (1998 est.)

GDP - per capita: purchasing power parity - $1,640 (1998 est.)

GDP - composition by sector:
agriculture: 53%
industry: 21%
services: 26% (1997 est.)

Population below poverty line: NA%

Household income or consumption by percentage share:
lowest 10%: NA%
highest 10%: NA%

Inflation rate (consumer prices): 2.6% (1998 est.)

Labor force: NA

Unemployment rate: 6% (1993)

Budget:
revenues: $638 million
expenditures: $1.9 billion, including capital expenditures of $888 million (1994 est.)

Industries: diamond mining, sawmills, breweries, textiles, footwear, assembly of bicycles and motorcycles

Industrial production growth rate: NA%

Electricity - production: 100 million kWh (1996)

Electricity - production by source:
fossil fuel: 20%
hydro: 80%
nuclear: 0%
other: 0% (1996)

Electricity - consumption: 100 million kWh (1996)

Electricity - exports: 0 kWh (1996)

Electricity - imports: 0 kWh (1996)

Agriculture - products: cotton, coffee, tobacco, manioc (tapioca), yams, millet, corn, bananas; timber

Exports: $182 million (f.o.b., 1998)

Exports - commodities: diamonds, timber, cotton, coffee, tobacco

Exports - partners: Belgium-Luxembourg 36%, Cote d'Ivoire 5%, Spain 4%, Egypt 3%, France

Imports: $155 million (f.o.b., 1998)

Imports - commodities: food, textiles, petroleum products, machinery, electrical equipment, motor vehicles, chemicals, pharmaceuticals, consumer goods, industrial products

Imports - partners: France 30%, Cote d'Ivoire 18%, Cameroon 11%, Germany 4%, Japan

Debt - external: $930 million (1997 est.)

Economic aid - recipient: $172.2 million (1995); note - traditional budget subsidies from France

Currency: 1 Communaute Financiere Africaine franc (CFAF) = 100 centimes

Exchange rates: Communaute Financiere Africaine francs (CFAF) per US$1 - 560.01 (December 1998),

Central African Republic *(continued)*

589.95 (1998), 583.67 (1997), 511.55 (1996), 499.15 (1995), 555.20 (1994)
Fiscal year: calendar year

Communications

Telephones: 16,867 (1992 est.)
Telephone system: fair system
domestic: network consists principally of microwave radio relay and low-capacity, low-powered radiotelephone communication
international: satellite earth station - 1 Intelsat (Atlantic Ocean)
Radio broadcast stations: AM 1, FM 3 (including Africa No. 1 and R. France Internationale stations located in Bangui), shortwave 1 (1998)
Radios: NA
Television broadcast stations: NA
Televisions: 7,500 (1993 est.)

Transportation

Railways: 0 km
Highways:
total: 23,810 km
paved: 429 km
unpaved: 23,381 km (1995 est.)
Waterways: 800 km; traditional trade carried on by means of shallow-draft dugouts; Oubangui is the most important river
Ports and harbors: Bangui, Nola
Airports: 52 (1998 est.)
Airports - with paved runways:
total: 3
2,438 to 3,047 m: 1
1,524 to 2,437 m: 2 (1998 est.)
Airports - with unpaved runways:
total: 49
2,438 to 3,047 m: 1
1,524 to 2,437 m: 10
914 to 1,523 m: 23
under 914 m: 15 (1998 est.)

Military

Military branches: Central African Armed Forces (includes Republican Guard and Air Force), Presidential Guard, National Gendarmerie, Police Force
Military manpower - availability:
males age 15-49: 782,678 (1999 est.)
Military manpower - fit for military service:
males age 15-49: 409,044 (1999 est.)
Military expenditures - dollar figure: $29 million (1996)
Military expenditures - percent of GDP: 2.2% (1996)

Transnational Issues

Disputes - international: none

Chad

Introduction

Background: In 1960, Chad gained full independence from France. In December 1990, after Chad had endured three decades of ethnic warfare as well as invasions by Libya, former northern guerrilla leader Idriss DEBY seized control of the government. His transitional government eventually suppressed or came to terms with most political-military groups, settled the territorial dispute with Libya on terms favorable to Chad, drafted a democratic constitution which was ratified by popular referendum in 1996, held multiparty national presidential elections in 1996 (DEBY won with 69% of the vote), and held multiparty elections for the National Assembly in 1997 (DEBY's Patriotic Salvation Movement won a majority of the seats). But by the end of 1998, DEBY was beset with numerous problems including heavy casualties in the Democratic Republic of the Congo where Chadian troops had been deployed to support embattled President KABILA, a new rebellion in northern Chad, and further delays in the Doba Basin oil project in the south.

Geography

Location: Central Africa, south of Libya
Geographic coordinates: 15 00 N, 19 00 E
Map references: Africa
Area:
total: 1.284 million sq km
land: 1,259,200 sq km
water: 24,800 sq km
Area - comparative: slightly more than three times the size of California
Land boundaries:
total: 5,968 km
border countries: Cameroon 1,094 km, Central African Republic 1,197 km, Libya 1,055 km, Niger 1,175 km, Nigeria 87 km, Sudan 1,360 km
Coastline: 0 km (landlocked)
Maritime claims: none (landlocked)
Climate: tropical in south, desert in north
Terrain: broad, arid plains in center, desert in north, mountains in northwest, lowlands in south
Elevation extremes:
lowest point: Djourab Depression 160 m
highest point: Emi Koussi 3,415 m
Natural resources: petroleum (unexploited but exploration under way), uranium, natron, kaolin, fish (Lake Chad)
Land use:
arable land: 3%
permanent crops: 0%
permanent pastures: 36%
forests and woodland: 26%
other: 35% (1993 est.)
Irrigated land: 140 sq km (1993 est.)
Natural hazards: hot, dry, dusty harmattan winds occur in north; periodic droughts; locust plagues
Environment - current issues: inadequate supplies of potable water; improper waste disposal in rural areas contributes to soil and water pollution; desertification
Environment - international agreements:
party to: Biodiversity, Climate Change, Desertification, Endangered Species, Nuclear Test Ban, Ozone Layer Protection, Wetlands
signed, but not ratified: Law of the Sea, Marine Dumping
Geography - note: landlocked; Lake Chad is the most significant water body in the Sahel

People

Population: 7,557,436 (July 1999 est.)
Age structure:
0-14 years: 44% (male 1,675,394; female 1,667,717)
15-64 years: 53% (male 1,953,251; female 2,034,883)
65 years and over: 3% (male 99,783; female 126,408) (1999 est.)
Population growth rate: 2.65% (1999 est.)
Birth rate: 43.06 births/1,000 population (1999 est.)
Death rate: 16.57 deaths/1,000 population (1999 est.)

Chad *(continued)*

Net migration rate: 0 migrant(s)/1,000 population (1999 est.)

Sex ratio:

at birth: 1.04 male(s)/female

under 15 years: 1 male(s)/female

15-64 years: 0.96 male(s)/female

65 years and over: 0.79 male(s)/female

total population: 0.97 male(s)/female (1999 est.)

Infant mortality rate: 115.27 deaths/1,000 live births (1999 est.)

Life expectancy at birth:

total population: 48.56 years

male: 46.13 years

female: 51.09 years (1999 est.)

Total fertility rate: 5.69 children born/woman (1999 est.)

Nationality:

noun: Chadian(s)

adjective: Chadian

Ethnic groups: Muslims (Arabs, Toubou, Hadjerai, Fulbe, Kotoko, Kanembou, Baguirmi, Boulala, Zaghawa, and Maba), non-Muslims (Sara, Ngambaye, Mbaye, Goulaye, Moundang, Moussei, Massa), nonindigenous 150,000 (of whom 1,000 are French)

Religions: Muslim 50%, Christian 25%, indigenous beliefs (mostly animism) 25%

Languages: French (official), Arabic (official), Sara and Sango (in south), more than 100 different languages and dialects

Literacy:

definition: age 15 and over can read and write French or Arabic

total population: 48.1%

male: 62.1%

female: 34.7% (1995 est.)

Government

Country name:

conventional long form: Republic of Chad

conventional short form: Chad

local long form: Republique du Tchad

local short form: Tchad

Data code: CD

Government type: republic

Capital: N'Djamena

Administrative divisions: 14 prefectures (prefectures, singular - prefecture); Batha, Biltine, Borkou-Ennedi-Tibesti, Chari-Baguirmi, Guera, Kanem, Lac, Logone Occidental, Logone Oriental, Mayo-Kebbi, Moyen-Chari, Ouaddai, Salamat, Tandjile

Independence: 11 August 1960 (from France)

National holiday: Independence Day, 11 August (1960)

Constitution: 31 March 1995, passed by referendum

Legal system: based on French civil law system and Chadian customary law; does not accept compulsory ICJ jurisdiction

Suffrage: 18 years of age; universal

Executive branch:

chief of state: President Lt. Gen. Idriss DEBY (since 4 December 1990)

head of government: Prime Minister Nassour Guelengdouksia OUAIDOU (since 16 May 1997)

cabinet: Council of State appointed by the president on the recommendation of the prime minister

elections: president elected by popular vote to serve five-year terms; if no candidate receives at least 50% of the total vote, the two candidates receiving the most votes must stand for a second round of voting; last held 2 June and 11 July 1996 (next to be held NA 2001); prime minister appointed by the president

election results: in the first round of voting none of the 15 candidates received the required 50% of the total vote; percent of vote, first round - Lt. Gen. Idress DEBY 47.8%; percent of vote, second round - Lt. Gen. DEBY 69.1%, Wadal Abdelkader KAMOUGUE 30.9%

Legislative branch: unicameral National Assembly (125 seats; members elected by popular vote to serve four-year terms); replaces the Higher Transitional Council or the Conseil Superieur de Transition

elections: National Assembly - last held in two rounds on 5 January and 23 February 1997, (next to be held NA 2001); in the first round of voting some candidates won clear victories by receiving 50% or more of the vote; where that did not happen, the two highest scoring candidates stood for a second round of voting

election results: percent of vote by party - NA; seats by party - MPS 65, URD 29, UNDR 15, RDP 3, others 13

Judicial branch: Supreme Court; Court of Appeal; Criminal Courts; Magistrate Courts

Political parties and leaders: Patriotic Salvation Movement or MPS [Maldom Bada ABBAS, chairman] (originally in opposition but now the party in power and the party of the president); National Union for Development and Renewal or UNDR [Saleh KEBZABO]; Rally for Democracy and Progress or RDP [Lal Mahamat CHOUA]; Union for Renewal and Democracy or URD [Gen. Wadal Abdelkader KAMOUGUE]; note - in mid-1996 Chad had about 60 political parties, of which these are the most prominent in the new National Assembly

International organization participation: ACCT, ACP, AfDB, BDEAC, CEEAC, ECA, FAO, FZ, G-77, IBRD, ICAO, ICFTU, ICRM, IDA, IDB, IFAD, IFC, IFRCS, ILO, IMF, Intelsat, Interpol, IOC, ITU, MINURCA, NAM, OAU, OIC, OPCW, UDEAC, UN, UNCTAD, UNESCO, UNIDO, UPU, WCL, WHO, WIPO, WMO, WToO, WTrO

Diplomatic representation in the US:

chief of mission: Ambassador Hassaballah Abdelhadi Ahmat SOUBIANE

chancery: 2002 R Street NW, Washington, DC 20009

telephone: [1] (202) 462-4009

FAX: [1] (202) 265-1937

Diplomatic representation from the US:

chief of mission: Ambassador David C. HALSTED

embassy: Avenue Felix Eboue, N'Djamena

mailing address: B. P. 413, N'Djamena

telephone: [235] (51) 70-09, (51) 90-52, (51) 92-33

FAX: [235] (51) 56-54

Flag description: three equal vertical bands of blue (hoist side), yellow, and red; similar to the flag of Romania; also similar to the flag of Andorra, which has a national coat of arms featuring a quartered shield centered in the yellow band; design was based on the flag of France

Economy

Economy - overview: Landlocked Chad's economic development suffers from it's geographic remoteness, drought, lack of infrastructure, and political turmoil. About 85% of the population depends on agriculture, including the herding of livestock. Of Africa's Francophone countries, Chad benefited least from the 50% devaluation of their currencies in January 1994. Financial aid from the World Bank, the African Development Fund, and other sources is directed largely at the improvement of agriculture, especially livestock production. Lack of financing and low oil prices, however, are stalling the development of an oil field in the Doba Basin and the construction of a proposed oil pipeline through Cameroon.

GDP: purchasing power parity - $7.5 billion (1998 est.)

GDP - real growth rate: 2.9% (1998 est.)

GDP - per capita: purchasing power parity - $1,000 (1998 est.)

GDP - composition by sector:

agriculture: 39%

industry: 15%

services: 46% (1997)

Population below poverty line: NA%

Household income or consumption by percentage share:

lowest 10%: NA%

highest 10%: NA%

Inflation rate (consumer prices): 15% (1997 est.)

Labor force: NA

Labor force - by occupation: agriculture 85% (subsistence farming, herding, and fishing)

Unemployment rate: NA%

Budget:

revenues: $198 million

expenditures: $218 million, including capital expenditures of $146 million (1998 est.)

Industries: cotton textiles, meat packing, beer brewing, natron (sodium carbonate), soap, cigarettes, construction materials

Industrial production growth rate: 5% (1995)

Electricity - production: 90 million kWh (1996)

Electricity - production by source:

fossil fuel: 100%

hydro: 0%

nuclear: 0%

other: 0% (1996)

Electricity - consumption: 90 million kWh (1996)

Electricity - exports: 0 kWh (1996)

Electricity - imports: 0 kWh (1996)

Agriculture - products: cotton, sorghum, millet, peanuts, rice, potatoes, manioc (tapioca); cattle, sheep, goats, camels

Chad (continued)

Exports: $220 million (f.o.b., 1998 est.)
Exports - commodities: cotton, cattle, textiles
Exports - partners: Portugal 30%, Germany 14%, Thailand, Costa Rica, South Africa, France (1997)
Imports: $252 million (f.o.b., 1998 est.)
Imports - commodities: machinery and transportation equipment, industrial goods, petroleum products, foodstuffs, textiles
Imports - partners: France 41%, Nigeria 10%, Cameroon 7%, India 6% (1997)
Debt - external: $875 million (1995 est.)
Economic aid - recipient: $238.3 million (1995); note - $125 million committed by Taiwan (August 1997); $30 million committed by African Development Bank
Currency: 1 Communaute Financiere Africaine franc (CFAF) = 100 centimes
Exchange rates: Communaute Financiere Africaine Francs (CFAF) per US$1 - 560.01 (December 1998), 589.95 (1998), 583.67 (1997), 511.55 (1996), 499.15 (1995), 555.20 (1994)
Fiscal year: calendar year

Communications

Telephones: 5,000 (1987 est.)
Telephone system: primitive system
domestic: fair system of radiotelephone communication stations
international: satellite earth station - 1 Intelsat (Atlantic Ocean)
Radio broadcast stations: AM 2, FM 3, shortwave 3 (one of the shortwave stations has three frequencies) (1998)
Radios: NA
Television broadcast stations: 1 (broadcasts 1800 to 2100 hours, four days per week) (1997)
Televisions: 7,000 (1991 est.)

Transportation

Railways: 0 km
Highways:
total: 33,400 km
paved: 267 km
unpaved: 33,133 km (1996 est.)
Waterways: 2,000 km navigable
Ports and harbors: none
Airports: 52 (1998 est.)
Airports - with paved runways:
total: 8
over 3,047 m: 1
2,438 to 3,047 m: 2
1,524 to 2,437 m: 2
914 to 1,523 m: 2
under 914 m: 1 (1998 est.)
Airports - with unpaved runways:
total: 44
1,524 to 2,437 m: 12
914 to 1,523 m: 22
under 914 m: 10 (1998 est.)

Military

Military branches: Armed Forces (includes Ground Force, Air Force, and Gendarmerie), Republican Guard, Rapid Intervention Force, Police
Military manpower - military age: 20 years of age
Military manpower - availability:
males age 15-49: 1,689,112 (1999 est.)
Military manpower - fit for military service:
males age 15-49: 875,541 (1999 est.)
Military manpower - reaching military age annually:
males: 70,464 (1999 est.)
Military expenditures - dollar figure: $39 million (1996)
Military expenditures - percent of GDP: 3.5% (1996)

Transnational Issues

Disputes - international: delimitation of international boundaries in the vicinity of Lake Chad, the lack of which led to border incidents in the past, is completed and awaits ratification by Cameroon, Chad, Niger, and Nigeria

Chile

Geography

Location: Southern South America, bordering the South Atlantic Ocean and South Pacific Ocean, between Argentina and Peru
Geographic coordinates: 30 00 S, 71 00 W
Map references: South America
Area:
total: 756,950 sq km
land: 748,800 sq km
water: 8,150 sq km
note: includes Easter Island (Isla de Pascua) and Isla Sala y Gomez
Area - comparative: slightly smaller than twice the size of Montana
Land boundaries:
total: 6,171 km
border countries: Argentina 5,150 km, Bolivia 861 km, Peru 160 km
Coastline: 6,435 km
Maritime claims:
contiguous zone: 24 nm
continental shelf: 200 nm
exclusive economic zone: 200 nm
territorial sea: 12 nm

Chile (continued)

People

Climate: temperate; desert in north; cool and damp in south

Terrain: low coastal mountains; fertile central valley; rugged Andes in east

Elevation extremes:
lowest point: Pacific Ocean 0 m
highest point: Cerro Aconcagua 6,962 m

Natural resources: copper, timber, iron ore, nitrates, precious metals, molybdenum

Land use:
arable land: 5%
permanent crops: 0%
permanent pastures: 18%
forests and woodland: 22%
other: 55% (1993 est.)

Irrigated land: 12,650 sq km (1993 est.)

Natural hazards: severe earthquakes; active volcanism; tsunamis

Environment - current issues: air pollution from industrial and vehicle emissions; water pollution from raw sewage; deforestation contributing to loss of biodiversity; soil erosion; desertification

Environment - international agreements:
party to: Antarctic-Environmental Protocol, Antarctic Treaty, Biodiversity, Climate Change, Desertification, Endangered Species, Environmental Modification, Hazardous Wastes, Law of the Sea, Marine Dumping, Nuclear Test Ban, Ozone Layer Protection, Ship Pollution, Wetlands, Whaling
signed, but not ratified: Climate Change-Kyoto Protocol

Geography - note: strategic location relative to sea lanes between Atlantic and Pacific Oceans (Strait of Magellan, Beagle Channel, Drake Passage); Atacama Desert is one of world's driest regions

People

Population: 14,973,843 (July 1999 est.)

Age structure:
0-14 years: 28% (male 2,137,255; female 2,044,605)
15-64 years: 65% (male 4,845,523; female 4,885,328)
65 years and over: 7% (male 440,010; female 621,122) (1999 est.)

Population growth rate: 1.23% (1999 est.)

Birth rate: 17.81 births/1,000 population (1999 est.)

Death rate: 5.53 deaths/1,000 population (1999 est.)

Net migration rate: 0 migrant(s)/1,000 population (1999 est.)

Sex ratio:
at birth: 1.05 male(s)/female
under 15 years: 1.05 male(s)/female
15-64 years: 0.99 male(s)/female
65 years and over: 0.71 male(s)/female
total population: 0.98 male(s)/female (1999 est.)

Infant mortality rate: 10.02 deaths/1,000 live births (1999 est.)

Life expectancy at birth:
total population: 75.46 years
male: 72.33 years
female: 78.75 years (1999 est.)

Total fertility rate: 2.25 children born/woman (1999 est.)

Nationality:
noun: Chilean(s)
adjective: Chilean

Ethnic groups: white and white-Amerindian 95%, Amerindian 3%, other 2%

Religions: Roman Catholic 89%, Protestant 11%, Jewish less than 1%

Languages: Spanish

Literacy:
definition: age 15 and over can read and write
total population: 95.2%
male: 95.4%
female: 95% (1995 est.)

Government

Country name:
conventional long form: Republic of Chile
conventional short form: Chile
local long form: Republica de Chile
local short form: Chile

Data code: CI

Government type: republic

Capital: Santiago

Administrative divisions: 13 regions (regiones, singular - region); Aisen del General Carlos Ibanez del Campo, Antofagasta, Araucania, Atacama, Bio-Bio, Coquimbo, Libertador General Bernardo O'Higgins, Los Lagos, Magallanes y de la Antartica Chilena, Maule, Region Metropolitana, Tarapaca, Valparaiso
note: the US does not recognize claims to Antarctica

Independence: 18 September 1810 (from Spain)

National holiday: Independence Day, 18 September (1810)

Constitution: 11 September 1980, effective 11 March 1981; amended 30 July 1989

Legal system: based on Code of 1857 derived from Spanish law and subsequent codes influenced by French and Austrian law; judicial review of legislative acts in the Supreme Court; does not accept compulsory ICJ jurisdiction

Suffrage: 18 years of age; universal and compulsory

Executive branch:
chief of state: President Eduardo FREI Ruiz-Tagle (since 11 March 1994); note - the president is both the chief of state and head of government
head of government: President Eduardo FREI Ruiz-Tagle (since 11 March 1994); note - the president is both the chief of state and head of government
cabinet: Cabinet appointed by the president
elections: president elected by popular vote for a six-year term; election last held 11 December 1993 (next to be held NA December 1999)
election results: Eduardo FREI Ruiz-Tagle elected president; percent of vote - Eduardo FREI Ruiz-Tagle (PDC) 58%, Arturo ALESSANDRI 24.4%, other 17.6%

Legislative branch: bicameral National Congress or Congreso Nacional consists of the Senate or Senado (48 seats, 38 elected by popular vote; members serve eight-year terms - one-half elected every four years) and the Chamber of Deputies or Camara de Diputados (120 seats; members are elected by popular vote to serve four-year terms)
elections: Senate - last held 11 December 1997 (next to be held NA December 2001); Chamber of Deputies - last held 11 December 1997 (next to be held NA December 2001)
election results: Senate - percent of vote by party - NA%; seats by party - CPD (PDC 14, PS 4, PPD 2), UPP 17 (RN 7, UDI 10), Chile 2000 (UCCP) 1, independent 10; Chamber of Deputies - percent of vote by party - CPD 50.55% (PDC 22.98%, PS 11.10%, PPD 12.55%, PRSD 3.13%), UPP 36.23% (RN 16.78%, UDI 14.43%); seats by party - CPD 70 (PDC 39, PPD 16, PRSD 4, PS 11), UPP 46 (RN 24, UDI 21, Party of the South 1), right-wing independents 4

Judicial branch: Supreme Court (Corte Suprema), judges are appointed by the president and ratified by the Senate from lists of candidates provided by the court itself; the president of the Supreme Court is elected by the 21-member court

Political parties and leaders: Coalition of Parties for Democracy or CPD consists mainly of: Christian Democratic Party or PDC [Enrique KRAUSS], Socialist Party or PS [Ricardo NUNEZ], Party for Democracy or PPD [Sergio BITAR], Radical Social Democratic Party or PRSD [Anselmo SULE]; Union for the Progress of Chile or UPP consists mainly of two parties: National Renewal or RN [Alberto ESPINA] and Independent Democratic Union or UDI [Pablo LONGUEIRA]; Chile 2000's main party is Progressive Center-Center Union or UCCP [Francisco Javier ERRAZURIZ]

Political pressure groups and leaders: revitalized university student federations at all major universities; United Labor Central or CUT includes trade unionists from the country's five largest labor confederations; Roman Catholic Church

International organization participation: APEC, CCC, ECLAC, FAO, G-11, G-77, IADB, IAEA, IBRD, ICAO, ICC, ICFTU, ICRM, IDA, IFAD, IFC, IFRCS, IHO, ILO, IMF, IMO, Inmarsat, Intelsat, Interpol, IOC, IOM, ISO, ITU, LAES, LAIA, Mercosur (associate), NAM, OAS, OPANAL, OPCW, PCA, RG, UN, UNCTAD, UNESCO, UNIDO, UNITAR, UNMIBH, UNMOGIP, UNTSO, UNU, UPU, WCL, WFTU, WHO, WIPO, WMO, WToO, WTrO

Diplomatic representation in the US:
chief of mission: Ambassador Genaro Luis ARRIAGADA Herrera
chancery: 1732 Massachusetts Avenue NW, Washington, DC 20036
telephone: [1] (202) 785-1746
FAX: [1] (202) 887-5579
consulate(s) general: Chicago, Houston, Los Angeles, Miami, New York, Philadelphia, San Francisco, and San Juan (Puerto Rico)

Diplomatic representation from the US:
chief of mission: Ambassador John O'LEARY
embassy: Avenida Andres Bello 2800, Santiago
mailing address: APO AA 34033

telephone: [56] (2) 232-2600
FAX: [56] (2) 330-3710
Flag description: two equal horizontal bands of white (top) and red; there is a blue square the same height as the white band at the hoist-side end of the white band; the square bears a white five-pointed star in the center; design was based on the US flag

Economy

Economy - overview: Chile has a prosperous, essentially free market economy. Civilian governments - which took over from the military in March 1990 - have continued to reduce the government's role in the economy while shifting the emphasis of public spending toward social programs. Growth in real GDP averaged more than 7.0% in 1991-1997 but fell to about half of that average in 1998 because of spillover from the global financial crisis. Inflation has been on a downward trend and hit a 60-year low in 1998. Chile's currency and foreign reserves also are strong, as sustained foreign capital inflows - including significant direct investment - have more than offset current account deficits and public debt buy-backs. President FREI, who took office in March 1994, has placed improving Chile's education system and developing foreign export markets at the top of his economic agenda. The Chilean economy remains largely dependent on a few sectors - particularly copper mining, fishing, and forestry. Success in meeting the government's goal of sustained annual economic growth of 5% depends largely on world prices for these commodities, continued foreign investor confidence, and the government's ability to maintain a conservative fiscal stance. In 1996, Chile became an associate member of Mercosur and concluded a free trade agreement with Canada.
GDP: purchasing power parity - $184.6 billion (1998 est.)
GDP - real growth rate: 3.5% (1998 est.)
GDP - per capita: purchasing power parity - $12,500 (1998 est.)
GDP - composition by sector:
agriculture: 6%
industry: 33%
services: 61% (1997)
Population below poverty line: 20.5% (1994 est.)
Household income or consumption by percentage share:
lowest 10%: 1.4%
highest 10%: 46.1% (1994)
Inflation rate (consumer prices): 4.7% (1998)
Labor force: 5.8 million (1998 est.)
Labor force - by occupation: services 38.3% (includes government 12%), industry and commerce 33.8%, agriculture, forestry, and fishing 19.2%, mining 2.3%, construction 6.4% (1990)
Unemployment rate: 6.4% (1998)
Budget:
revenues: $17 billion
expenditures: $17 billion, including capital expenditures of $NA (1996 est.)

Industries: copper, other minerals, foodstuffs, fish processing, iron and steel, wood and wood products, transport equipment, cement, textiles
Industrial production growth rate: -1.1% (1998)
Electricity - production: 35.81 billion kWh (1996)
Electricity - production by source:
fossil fuel: 41.89%
hydro: 58.11%
nuclear: 0%
other: 0% (1996)
Electricity - consumption: 35.81 billion kWh (1996)
Electricity - exports: 0 kWh (1996)
Electricity - imports: 0 kWh (1996)
Agriculture - products: wheat, corn, grapes, beans, sugar beets, potatoes, fruit; beef, poultry, wool; timber; fish
Exports: $14.9 billion (f.o.b., 1998)
Exports - commodities: copper 37%, other metals and minerals 8.2%, wood products 7.1%, fish and fishmeal 9.8%, fruits 8.4% (1994)
Exports - partners: EU 25%, US 15%, Asia 34%, Latin America 20% (1995 est.)
Imports: $17.5 billion (f.o.b., 1998)
Imports - commodities: capital goods 25.2%, spare parts 24.8%, raw materials 15.4%, petroleum 10%, foodstuffs 5.7% (1994)
Imports - partners: EU 18%, US 25%, Asia 16%, Latin America 26% (1995 est.)
Debt - external: $31.5 billion (1998)
Economic aid - recipient: ODA, $50.3 million (1996 est.)
Currency: 1 Chilean peso (Ch$) = 100 centavos
Exchange rates: Chilean pesos (Ch$) per US$1 - 475.68 (January 1999), 460.29 (1998), 419.30 (1997), 412.27 (1996), 396.78 (1995), 420.08 (1994)
Fiscal year: calendar year

Communications

Telephones: 1.5 million (1994 est.)
Telephone system: modern system based on extensive microwave radio relay facilities
domestic: extensive microwave radio relay links; domestic satellite system with 3 earth stations
international: satellite earth stations - 2 Intelsat (Atlantic Ocean)
Radio broadcast stations: AM 180 (eight inactive), FM 64, shortwave 17 (one inactive) (1998)
Radios: NA
Television broadcast stations: 63 (in addition, there are 121 repeaters) (1997)
Televisions: 2.85 million (1992 est.)

Transportation

Railways:
total: 6,782 km
broad gauge: 3,743 km 1.676-m gauge (1,653 km electrified)
narrow gauge: 116 km 1.067-m gauge; 2,923 km 1.000-m gauge (40 km electrified) (1995)
Highways:
total: 79,800 km

paved: 11,012 km
unpaved: 68,788 km (1996 est.)
Waterways: 725 km
Pipelines: crude oil 755 km; petroleum products 785 km; natural gas 320 km
Ports and harbors: Antofagasta, Arica, Chanaral, Coquimbo, Iquique, Puerto Montt, Punta Arenas, San Antonio, San Vicente, Talcahuano, Valparaiso
Merchant marine:
total: 42 ships (1,000 GRT or over) totaling 527,201 GRT/787,719 DWT
ships by type: bulk 11, cargo 10, chemical tanker 5, container 2, liquefied gas tanker 1, oil tanker 4, passenger 3, roll-on/roll-off cargo 4, vehicle carrier 2 (1998 est.)
Airports: 378 (1998 est.)
Airports - with paved runways:
total: 58
over 3,047 m: 5
2,438 to 3,047 m: 6
1,524 to 2,437 m: 19
914 to 1,523 m: 19
under 914 m: 9 (1998 est.)
Airports - with unpaved runways:
total: 320
over 3,047 m: 1
2,438 to 3,047 m: 4
1,524 to 2,437 m: 13
914 to 1,523 m: 73
under 914 m: 229 (1998 est.)

Military

Military branches: Army of the Nation, National Navy (includes Naval Air, Coast Guard, and Marines), Air Force of the Nation, Carabineros of Chile (National Police), Investigations Police
Military manpower - military age: 19 years of age
Military manpower - availability:
males age 15-49: 3,968,176 (1999 est.)
Military manpower - fit for military service:
males age 15-49: 2,943,206 (1999 est.)
Military manpower - reaching military age annually:
males: 132,202 (1999 est.)
Military expenditures - dollar figure: $2.12 billion (1998); note - includes earnings from CODELCO Company and costs of pensions; does not include funding for the National Police (Carabineros) and Investigations Police
Military expenditures - percent of GDP: 2.79% (1998)

Transnational Issues

Disputes - international: short section of the southwestern boundary with Argentina is indefinite - process to resolve boundary issues is underway; Bolivia has wanted a sovereign corridor to the South Pacific Ocean since the Atacama area was lost to Chile in 1884; dispute with Bolivia over Rio Lauca water rights; territorial claim in Antarctica (Chilean Antarctic Territory) partially overlaps Argentine and

Chile (continued)

British claims

Illicit drugs: a growing transshipment country for cocaine destined for the US and Europe; economic prosperity has made Chile more attractive to traffickers seeking to launder drug profits; imported precursors pass on to Bolivia

China
(also see separate Hong Kong and Taiwan entries)

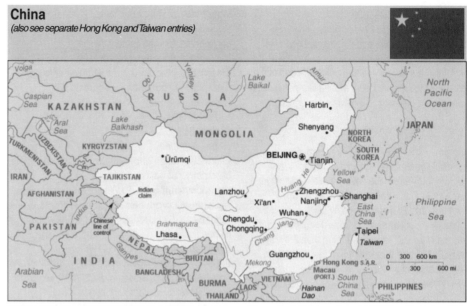

Introduction

Background: For most of its 3,500 years of history, China led the world in agriculture, crafts, and science, then fell behind in the 19th century when the Industrial Revolution gave the West clear superiority in military and economic affairs. In the first half of the 20th century, China continued to suffer from major famines, civil unrest, military defeat, and foreign occupation. After World War II, the Communists under MAO Zedong established a dictatorship that, while ensuring China's autonomy, imposed strict controls over all aspects of life and cost the lives of tens of millions of people. After 1978, his successor DENG Xiaoping decentralized economic decision making; output quadrupled in the next 20 years. Political controls remain tight at the same time economic controls have been weakening. Present issues are: incorporating Hong Kong into the Chinese system; closing down inefficient state-owned enterprises; modernizing the military; fighting corruption; and providing support to tens of millions of displaced workers.

Geography

Location: Eastern Asia, bordering the East China Sea, Korea Bay, Yellow Sea, and South China Sea, between North Korea and Vietnam
Geographic coordinates: 35 00 N, 105 00 E
Map references: Asia
Area:
total: 9,596,960 sq km
land: 9,326,410 sq km
water: 270,550 sq km
Area - comparative: slightly smaller than the US
Land boundaries:
total: 22,143.34 km
border countries: Afghanistan 76 km, Bhutan 470 km, Burma 2,185 km, Hong Kong 30 km, India 3,380 km, Kazakhstan 1,533 km, North Korea 1,416 km, Kyrgyzstan 858 km, Laos 423 km, Macau 0.34 km,

Mongolia 4,673 km, Nepal 1,236 km, Pakistan 523 km, Russia (northeast) 3,605 km, Russia (northwest) 40 km, Tajikistan 414 km, Vietnam 1,281 km
Coastline: 14,500 km
Maritime claims:
contiguous zone: 24 nm
continental shelf: 200 nm or to the edge of the continental margin
territorial sea: 12 nm
Climate: extremely diverse; tropical in south to subarctic in north
Terrain: mostly mountains, high plateaus, deserts in west; plains, deltas, and hills in east
Elevation extremes:
lowest point: Turpan Pendi -154 m
highest point: Mount Everest 8,848 m
Natural resources: coal, iron ore, petroleum, natural gas, mercury, tin, tungsten, antimony, manganese, molybdenum, vanadium, magnetite, aluminum, lead, zinc, uranium, hydropower potential (world's largest)
Land use:
arable land: 10%
permanent crops: 0%
permanent pastures: 43%
forests and woodland: 14%
other: 33% (1993 est.)
Irrigated land: 498,720 sq km (1993 est.)
Natural hazards: frequent typhoons (about five per year along southern and eastern coasts); damaging floods; tsunamis; earthquakes; droughts
Environment - current issues: air pollution (greenhouse gases, sulfur dioxide particulates) from reliance on coal, produces acid rain; water shortages, particularly in the north; water pollution from untreated wastes; deforestation; estimated loss of one-fifth of agricultural land since 1949 to soil erosion and economic development; desertification; trade in endangered species
Environment - international agreements:
party to: Antarctic-Environmental Protocol, Antarctic Treaty, Biodiversity, Climate Change, Desertification,

China (continued)

Endangered Species, Hazardous Wastes, Law of the Sea, Marine Dumping, Ozone Layer Protection, Ship Pollution, Tropical Timber 83, Tropical Timber 94, Wetlands, Whaling

signed, but not ratified: Climate Change-Kyoto Protocol, Nuclear Test Ban

Geography - note: world's fourth-largest country (after Russia, Canada, and US)

People

Population: 1,246,871,951 (July 1999 est.)
Age structure:
0-14 years: 26% (male 169,206,275; female 149,115,216)
15-64 years: 68% (male 435,047,915; female 408,663,265)
65 years and over: 6% (male 39,824,361; female 45,014,919) (1999 est.)
Population growth rate: 0.77% (1999 est.)
Birth rate: 15.1 births/1,000 population (1999 est.)
Death rate: 6.98 deaths/1,000 population (1999 est.)
Net migration rate: -0.41 migrant(s)/1,000 population (1999 est.)
Sex ratio:
at birth: 1.15 male(s)/female
under 15 years: 1.13 male(s)/female
15-64 years: 1.06 male(s)/female
65 years and over: 0.88 male(s)/female
total population: 1.07 male(s)/female (1999 est.)
Infant mortality rate: 43.31 deaths/1,000 live births (1999 est.)
Life expectancy at birth:
total population: 69.92 years
male: 68.57 years
female: 71.48 years (1999 est.)
Total fertility rate: 1.8 children born/woman (1999 est.)
Nationality:
noun: Chinese (singular and plural)
adjective: Chinese
Ethnic groups: Han Chinese 91.9%, Zhuang, Uygur, Hui, Yi, Tibetan, Miao, Manchu, Mongol, Buyi, Korean, and other nationalities 8.1%
Religions: Daoism (Taoism), Buddhism, Muslim 2%-3%, Christian 1% (est.)
note: officially atheist, but traditionally pragmatic and eclectic
Languages: Standard Chinese or Mandarin (Putonghua, based on the Beijing dialect), Yue (Cantonese), Wu (Shanghaiese), Minbei (Fuzhou), Minnan (Hokkien-Taiwanese), Xiang, Gan, Hakka dialects, minority languages (see Ethnic divisions entry)
Literacy:
definition: age 15 and over can read and write
total population: 81.5%
male: 89.9%
female: 72.7% (1995 est.)

Government

Country name:
conventional long form: People's Republic of China
conventional short form: China
local long form: Zhonghua Renmin Gongheguo
local short form: Zhong Guo
abbreviation: PRC
Data code: CH
Government type: Communist state
Capital: Beijing
Administrative divisions: 23 provinces (sheng, singular and plural), 5 autonomous regions* (zizhiqu, singular and plural), and 4 municipalities** (shi, singular and plural); Anhui, Beijing**, Chongqing**, Fujian, Gansu, Guangdong, Guangxi*, Guizhou, Hainan, Hebei, Heilongjiang, Henan, Hubei, Hunan, Jiangsu, Jiangxi, Jilin, Liaoning, Nei Mongol*, Ningxia*, Qinghai, Shaanxi, Shandong, Shanghai**, Shanxi, Sichuan, Tianjin**, Xinjiang*, Xizang* (Tibet), Yunnan, Zhejiang
note: China considers Taiwan its 23rd province; see separate entry for the special administrative region of Hong Kong
Independence: 221 BC (unification under the Qin or Ch'in Dynasty 221 BC; Qing or Ch'ing Dynasty replaced by the Republic on 12 February 1912; People's Republic established 1 October 1949)
National holiday: National Day, 1 October (1949)
Constitution: most recent promulgation 4 December 1982
Legal system: a complex amalgam of custom and statute, largely criminal law; rudimentary civil code in effect since 1 January 1987; new legal codes in effect since 1 January 1980; continuing efforts are being made to improve civil, administrative, criminal, and commercial law
Suffrage: 18 years of age; universal
Executive branch:
chief of state: President JIANG Zemin (since 27 March 1993) and Vice President HU Jintao (since 16 March 1998)
head of government: Premier ZHU Rongji (since 18 March 1998); Vice Premiers QIAN Qichen (since 29 March 1993), LI Lanqing (29 March 1993), WU Bangguo (since 17 March 1995), and WEN Jiabao (since 18 March 1998)
cabinet: State Council appointed by the National People's Congress (NPC)
elections: president and vice president elected by the National People's Congress for five-year terms; elections last held 16-18 March 1998 (next to be held NA March 2003); premier nominated by the president, confirmed by the National People's Congress
election results: JIANG Zemin reelected president by the Ninth National People's Congress with a total of 2,882 votes (36 delegates voted against him, 29 abstained, and 32 did not vote); HU Jintao elected vice president by the Ninth National People's Congress with a total of 2,841 votes (67 delegates voted against him, 39 abstained, and 32 did not vote)
Legislative branch: unicameral National People's Congress or Quanguo Renmin Daibiao Dahui (2,979 seats; members elected by municipal, regional, and provincial people's congresses to serve five-year terms)

elections: last held NA December-NA February 1998 (next to be held late 2002-NA March 2003)
election results: percent of vote - NA; seats - NA
Judicial branch: Supreme People's Court, judges appointed by the National People's Congress
Political parties and leaders: Chinese Communist Party or CCP [JIANG Zemin, General Secretary of the Central Committee]; eight registered small parties controlled by CCP
Political pressure groups and leaders: no meaningful political opposition groups exist
International organization participation: AfDB, APEC, AsDB, BIS, CCC, CDB (non-regional), ESCAP, FAO, G-77, IAEA, IBRD, ICAO, ICC, ICFTU, ICRM, IDA, IFAD, IFC, IFRCS, IHO, ILO, IMF, IMO, Inmarsat, Intelsat, Interpol, IOC, ISO, ITU, LAIA (observer), MINURSO, NAM (observer), OPCW, PCA, UN, UN Security Council, UNCTAD, UNESCO, UNHCR, UNIDO, UNIKOM, UNITAR, UNOMSIL, UNTSO, UNU, UPU, WHO, WIPO, WMO, WToO, WTrO (applicant)
Diplomatic representation in the US:
chief of mission: Ambassador LI Zhaoxing
chancery: 2300 Connecticut Avenue NW, Washington, DC 20008
telephone: [1] (202) 328-2500
consulate(s) general: Chicago, Houston, Los Angeles, New York, and San Francisco
Diplomatic representation from the US:
chief of mission: Ambassador James R. SASSER
embassy: Xiu Shui Bei Jie 3, 100600 Beijing
mailing address: PSC 461, Box 50, FPO AP 96521-0002
telephone: [86] (10) 6532-3831
FAX: [86] (10) 6532-6422
consulate(s) general: Chengdu, Guangzhou, Shanghai, Shenyang
Flag description: red with a large yellow five-pointed star and four smaller yellow five-pointed stars (arranged in a vertical arc toward the middle of the flag) in the upper hoist-side corner

Economy

Economy - overview: Beginning in late 1978 the Chinese leadership has been trying to move the economy from a sluggish Soviet-style centrally planned economy to a more market-oriented economy but still within a rigid political framework of Communist Party control. To this end the authorities switched to a system of household responsibility in agriculture in place of the old collectivization, increased the authority of local officials and plant managers in industry, permitted a wide variety of small-scale enterprise in services and light manufacturing, and opened the economy to increased foreign trade and investment. The result has been a quadrupling of GDP since 1978. Agricultural output doubled in the 1980s, and industry also posted major gains, especially in coastal areas near Hong Kong and opposite Taiwan, where foreign investment helped spur output of both domestic and export goods. On the darker side, the leadership has often experienced in

China (continued)

its hybrid system the worst results of socialism (bureaucracy, lassitude, corruption) and of capitalism (windfall gains and stepped-up inflation). Beijing thus has periodically backtracked, retightening central controls at intervals. In late 1993 China's leadership approved additional long-term reforms aimed at giving still more play to market-oriented institutions and at strengthening the center's control over the financial system; state enterprises would continue to dominate many key industries in what was now termed "a socialist market economy". In 1995-97 inflation dropped sharply, reflecting tighter monetary policies and stronger measures to control food prices. At the same time, the government struggled to (a) collect revenues due from provinces, businesses, and individuals; (b) reduce corruption and other economic crimes; and (c) keep afloat the large state-owned enterprises, most of which had not participated in the vigorous expansion of the economy and many of which had been losing the ability to pay full wages and pensions. From 60 to 100 million surplus rural workers are adrift between the villages and the cities, many subsisting through part-time low-paying jobs. Popular resistance, changes in central policy, and loss of authority by rural cadres have weakened China's population control program, which is essential to maintaining growth in living standards. Another long-term threat to continued rapid economic growth is the deterioration in the environment, notably air pollution, soil erosion, and the steady fall of the water table especially in the north. China continues to lose arable land because of erosion and economic development. The next few years may witness increasing tensions between a highly centralized political system and an increasingly decentralized economic system. Economic growth probably will slow to more moderate levels in 1999-2000.

GDP: purchasing power parity - $4.42 trillion (1998 est.)

GDP - real growth rate: 7.8% (1998 est.) (official figures may substantially overstate growth)

GDP - per capita: purchasing power parity - $3,600 (1998 est.)

GDP - composition by sector:
agriculture: 19%
industry: 49%
services: 32% (1997 est.)

Population below poverty line: NA%

Household income or consumption by percentage share:
lowest 10%: 2.2%
highest 10%: 30.9% (1995)

Inflation rate (consumer prices): -0.8% (1998 est.)

Labor force: 696 million (1997 est.)

Labor force - by occupation: agriculture 50%, industry 24%, services 26% (1997)

Unemployment rate: officially 3% in urban areas; probably 8%-10%; substantial unemployment and underemployment in rural areas (1998 est.)

Budget:
revenues: $NA

expenditures: $NA, including capital expenditures of $NA

Industries: iron and steel, coal, machine building, armaments, textiles and apparel, petroleum, cement, chemical fertilizers, footwear, toys, food processing, autos, consumer electronics, telecommunications

Industrial production growth rate: 8.8% (1998 est.)

Electricity - production: 1.16 trillion kWh (1998)

Electricity - production by source:
fossil fuel: 93%
hydro: 6%
nuclear: 1%
other: 0% (1996 est.)

Electricity - consumption: 994.921 billion kWh (1996)

Electricity - exports: 6.025 billion kWh (1996)

Electricity - imports: 755 million kWh (1996)

Agriculture - products: rice, wheat, potatoes, sorghum, peanuts, tea, millet, barley, cotton, oilseed; pork; fish

Exports: $183.8 billion (f.o.b., 1998)

Exports - commodities: electrical machinery and equipment, machinery and mechanical appliances, woven apparel, knit apparel, footwear, toys and sporting goods (1998)

Exports - partners: Hong Kong 21%, US 21%, Japan 14%, Germany, South Korea, Netherlands, UK, Singapore, Taiwan (1997)

Imports: $140.17 billion (c.i.f., 1998)

Imports - commodities: electrical machinery and equipment, machinery and mechanical appliances, plastics, iron and steel, scientific and photograph equipment, paper and paper board (1998)

Imports - partners: Japan 20%, US 12%, Taiwan 12%, South Korea 11%, Germany, Hong Kong, Singapore, Russia (1997)

Debt - external: $159 billion (1998 est.)

Economic aid - recipient: $6.222 billion (1995)

Currency: 1 yuan (¥) = 10 jiao

Exchange rates: yuan (¥) per US$1 - 8.28 (February 1999), 8.2779 (December 1998), 8.2790 (1998), 8.2898 (1997), 8.3142 (1996), 8.3514 (1995), 8.6187 (1994)

note: beginning 1 January 1994, the People's Bank of China quotes the midpoint rate against the US dollar based on the previous day's prevailing rate in the interbank foreign exchange market

Fiscal year: calendar year

Communications

Telephones: 105 million (1998 est.)

Telephone system: domestic and international services are increasingly available for private use; unevenly distributed domestic system serves principal cities, industrial centers, and all townships
domestic: interprovincial fiber-optic trunk lines and cellular telephone systems have been installed; a domestic satellite system with 55 earth stations is in place
international: satellite earth stations - 5 Intelsat (4 Pacific Ocean and 1 Indian Ocean), 1 Intersputnik

(Indian Ocean Region) and 1 Inmarsat (Pacific and Indian Ocean Regions); several international fiber-optic links to Japan, South Korea, Hong Kong, Russia, and Germany

Radio broadcast stations: AM 569, FM NA, shortwave 173

Radios: 216.5 million (1992 est.)

Television broadcast stations: 209 (China Central Television, government-owned; in addition there are 31 provincial TV stations and nearly 3,000 city TV stations) (1997)

Televisions: 300 million

Transportation

Railways:
total: 64,900 km (including 5,400 km of provincial "local" rails)
standard gauge: 61,300 km 1.435-m gauge (12,000 km electrified; 20,000 km double track)
narrow gauge: 3,600 km 0.750-m gauge local industrial lines (1998 est.)
note: a new total of 68,000 km has been estimated for early 1999

Highways:
total: 1.21 million km
paved: 271,300 km (with at least 24,474 km of motorways)
unpaved: 938,700 km (1998 est.)

Waterways: 109,800 km navigable (1997)

Pipelines: crude oil 9,070 km; petroleum products 560 km; natural gas 9,383 km (1998)

Ports and harbors: Dalian, Fuzhou, Guangzhou, Haikou, Huangpu, Lianyungang, Nanjing, Nantong, Ningbo, Qingdao, Qinhuangdao, Shanghai, Shantou, Tianjin, Xiamen, Xingang, Yantai, Zhanjiang

Merchant marine:
total: 1,759 ships (1,000 GRT or over) totaling 16,828,349 GRT/24,801,291 DWT
ships by type: barge carrier 2, bulk 330, cargo 855, chemical tanker 21, combination bulk 10, combination ore/oil 1, container 121, liquefied gas tanker 20, multifunction large-load carrier 6, oil tanker 245, passenger 8, passenger-cargo 47, refrigerated cargo 25, roll-on/roll-off cargo 24, short-sea passenger 43, vehicle carrier 1 (1998 est.)

Airports: 206 (1996 est.)

Airports - with paved runways:
total: 192
over 3,047 m: 18
2,438 to 3,047 m: 65
1,524 to 2,437 m: 90
914 to 1,523 m: 13
under 914 m: 6 (1996 est.)

Airports - with unpaved runways:
total: 14
1,524 to 2,437 m: 8
914 to 1,523 m: 5
under 914 m: 1 (1996 est.)

China (continued)

Military

Military branches: People's Liberation Army (PLA), which includes the Ground Forces, Navy (includes Marines and Naval Aviation), Air Force, Second Artillery Corps (the strategic missile force), People's Armed Police (internal security troops, nominally subordinate to Ministry of Public Security, but included by the Chinese as part of the "armed forces" and considered to be an adjunct to the PLA in wartime)
Military manpower - military age: 18 years of age
Military manpower - availability:
males age 15-49: 361,267,706 (1999 est.)
Military manpower - fit for military service:
males age 15-49: 198,398,601 (1999 est.)
Military manpower - reaching military age annually:
males: 10,273,696 (1999 est.)
Military expenditures - dollar figure: $12.608 billion (FY99); note-Western analysts believe that China's real defense spending is several times higher than the official figure because several significant items are funded elsewhere
Military expenditures - percent of GDP: NA%

Transnational Issues

Disputes - international: boundary with India in dispute; dispute over at least two small sections of the boundary with Russia remain to be settled, despite 1997 boundary agreement; most of the boundary with Tajikistan in dispute; 33-km section of boundary with North Korea in the Paektu-san (mountain) area is indefinite; involved in a complex dispute over the Spratly Islands with Malaysia, Philippines, Taiwan, Vietnam, and possibly Brunei; maritime boundary dispute with Vietnam in the Gulf of Tonkin; Paracel Islands occupied by China, but claimed by Vietnam and Taiwan; claims Japanese-administered Senkaku-shoto (Senkaku Islands/Diaoyu Tai), as does Taiwan; sections of land border with Vietnam are indefinite
Illicit drugs: major transshipment point for heroin produced in the Golden Triangle; growing domestic drug abuse problem

Christmas Island
(territory of Australia)

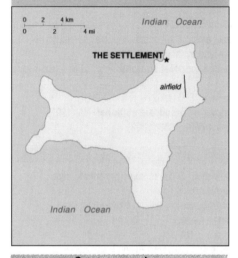

Geography

Location: Southeastern Asia, island in the Indian Ocean, south of Indonesia
Geographic coordinates: 10 30 S, 105 40 E
Map references: Southeast Asia
Area:
total: 135 sq km
land: 135 sq km
water: 0 sq km
Area - comparative: about 0.7 times the size of Washington, DC
Land boundaries: 0 km
Coastline: 138.9 km
Maritime claims:
contiguous zone: 12 nm
exclusive fishing zone: 200 nm
territorial sea: 3 nm
Climate: tropical; heat and humidity moderated by trade winds
Terrain: steep cliffs along coast rise abruptly to central plateau
Elevation extremes:
lowest point: Indian Ocean 0 m
highest point: Murray Hill 361 m
Natural resources: phosphate
Land use:
arable land: NA%
permanent crops: NA%
permanent pastures: NA%
forests and woodland: NA%
other: 100% (1993 est.)
Irrigated land: NA sq km
Natural hazards: the narrow fringing reef surrounding the island can be a maritime hazard
Environment - current issues: NA
Environment - international agreements:
party to: NA
signed, but not ratified: NA
Geography - note: located along major sea lanes of Indian Ocean

People

Population: 2,373 (July 1999 est.)
Age structure:
0-14 years: NA
15-64 years: NA
65 years and over: NA
Population growth rate: 7.77% (1999 est.)
Birth rate: NA births/1,000 population
Death rate: NA deaths/1,000 population
Net migration rate: NA migrant(s)/1,000 population
Infant mortality rate: NA deaths/1,000 live births
Life expectancy at birth:
total population: NA
male: NA
female: NA
Total fertility rate: NA children born/woman
Nationality:
noun: Christmas Islander(s)
adjective: Christmas Island
Ethnic groups: Chinese 61%, Malay 25%, European 11%, other 3%, no indigenous population
Religions: Buddhist 55%, Christian 15%, Muslim 10%, other 20% (1991)
Languages: English

Government

Country name:
conventional long form: Territory of Christmas Island
conventional short form: Christmas Island
Data code: KT
Dependency status: territory of Australia; administered from Canberra by the Australian Department of the Environment, Sport and Territories
Government type: NA
Capital: The Settlement
Administrative divisions: none (territory of Australia)
Independence: none (territory of Australia)
National holiday: NA
Constitution: Christmas Island Act of 1958
Legal system: under the authority of the governor general of Australia and Australian law
Executive branch:
chief of state: Queen ELIZABETH II (since 6 February 1952), represented by the Australian governor general
head of government: Administrator (acting) Graham NICHOLLS (since NA)
elections: none; the monarch is hereditary; administrator appointed by the governor general of Australia and represents the monarch and Australia
Legislative branch: unicameral Christmas Island Shire Council (9 seats; members elected by popular vote to serve one-year terms)
elections: last held NA December 1998 (next to be held NA December 1999)
election results: percent of vote - NA; seats - independents 9
Judicial branch: Supreme Court
Political parties and leaders: none
International organization participation: none

Christmas Island *(continued)*

Diplomatic representation in the US: none
(territory of Australia)
Diplomatic representation from the US: none
(territory of Australia)
Flag description: the flag of Australia is used

Economy

Economy - overview: Phosphate mining had been the only significant economic activity, but in December 1987 the Australian Government closed the mine. In 1990, the mine was reopened by private operators. Australian-based Casinos Austria International Ltd. built a $45 million casino on Christmas Island.
GDP: purchasing power parity - $NA
GDP - real growth rate: NA%
GDP - per capita: purchasing power parity - $NA
GDP - composition by sector:
agriculture: NA%
industry: NA%
services: NA%
Population below poverty line: NA%
Household income or consumption by percentage share:
lowest 10%: NA%
highest 10%: NA%
Inflation rate (consumer prices): NA%
Labor force: NA
Labor force - by occupation: tourism 400 people, mining 100 people
Unemployment rate: NA%
Budget:
revenues: $NA
expenditures: $NA, including capital expenditures of $NA
Industries: tourism, phosphate extraction (near depletion)
Industrial production growth rate: NA%
Electricity - production: NA kWh
Electricity - production by source:
fossil fuel: NA%
hydro: NA%
nuclear: NA%
other: NA%
Electricity - consumption: NA kWh
Electricity - exports: NA kWh
Electricity - imports: NA kWh
Agriculture - products: NA
Exports: $NA
Exports - commodities: phosphate
Exports - partners: Australia, NZ
Imports: $NA
Imports - commodities: consumer goods
Imports - partners: principally Australia
Debt - external: $NA
Economic aid - recipient: $NA
Currency: 1 Australian dollar ($A) = 100 cents
Exchange rates: Australian dollars ($A) per US$1 - 1.5853 (January 1999), 1.5888 (1998), 1.3439 (1997), 1.2773 (1996), 1.3486 (1995), 1.3667 (1994)
Fiscal year: 1 July - 30 June

Communications

Telephones: NA
Telephone system:
domestic: NA
international: NA
note: external telephone and telex services are provided by Intelsat satellite
Radio broadcast stations: AM 1, FM 0, shortwave 0
Radios: 500 (1992)
Television broadcast stations: NA (1997)
Televisions: 350 (1992)

Transportation

Railways: 24 km to serve phosphate mines
Highways:
total: NA km
paved: NA km
unpaved: NA km
Ports and harbors: Flying Fish Cove
Merchant marine: none
Airports: 1 (1998 est.)
Airports - with paved runways:
total: 1
1,524 to 2,437 m: 1 (1998 est.)

Military

Military - note: defense is the responsibility of Australia

Transnational Issues

Disputes - international: none

Clipperton Island
(possession of France)

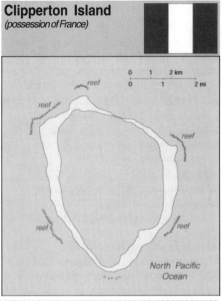

Geography

Location: Middle America, atoll in the North Pacific Ocean, 1,120 km southwest of Mexico
Geographic coordinates: 10 17 N, 109 13 W
Map references: World
Area:
total: 7 sq km
land: 7 sq km
water: 0 sq km
Area - comparative: about 12 times the size of The Mall in Washington, DC
Land boundaries: 0 km
Coastline: 11.1 km
Maritime claims:
territorial sea: 12 nm
Climate: tropical, humid, average temperature 20-32 degrees C, rains May-October
Terrain: coral atoll
Elevation extremes:
lowest point: Pacific Ocean 0 m
highest point: Rocher Clipperton 29 m
Natural resources: none
Land use:
arable land: 0%
permanent crops: 0%
permanent pastures: 0%
forests and woodland: 0%
other: 100% (all coral)
Irrigated land: 0 sq km (1993)
Natural hazards: subject to tornadoes
Environment - current issues: NA
Environment - international agreements:
party to: NA
signed, but not ratified: NA
Geography - note: reef about 8 km in circumference

People

Population: uninhabited

Clipperton Island (continued)

Government

Country name:
conventional long form: none
conventional short form: Clipperton Island
local long form: none
local short form: Ile Clipperton
former: sometimes called Ile de la Passion
Data code: IP
Dependency status: possession of France; administered by France from French Polynesia by a high commissioner of the Republic
Legal system: NA
Diplomatic representation in the US: none (dependent territory of France)
Diplomatic representation from the US: none (dependent territory of France)
Flag description: the flag of France is used

Economy

Economy - overview: Although 115 species of fish have been identified in the territorial waters of Clipperton Island, the only economic activity is a tuna fishing station.

Transportation

Ports and harbors: none; offshore anchorage only

Military

Military - note: defense is the responsibility of France

Transnational Issues

Disputes - international: none

Cocos (Keeling) Islands
(territory of Australia)

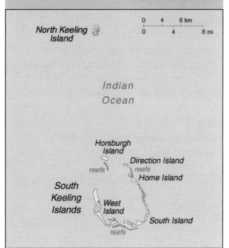

Geography

Location: Southeastern Asia, group of islands in the Indian Ocean, south of Indonesia, about one-half of the way from Australia to Sri Lanka
Geographic coordinates: 12 30 S, 96 50 E
Map references: Southeast Asia
Area:
total: 14 sq km
land: 14 sq km
water: 0 sq km
note: includes the two main islands of West Island and Home Island
Area - comparative: about 24 times the size of The Mall in Washington, DC
Land boundaries: 0 km
Coastline: 2.6 km
Maritime claims:
exclusive fishing zone: 200 nm
territorial sea: 3 nm
Climate: pleasant, modified by the southeast trade wind for about nine months of the year; moderate rainfall
Terrain: flat, low-lying coral atolls
Elevation extremes:
lowest point: Indian Ocean 0 m
highest point: unnamed location 5 m
Natural resources: fish
Land use:
arable land: NA%
permanent crops: NA%
permanent pastures: NA%
forests and woodland: NA%
other: 100% (1993 est.)
Irrigated land: NA sq km
Natural hazards: cyclones may occur in the early months of the year
Environment - current issues: fresh water resources are limited to rainwater accumulations in natural underground reservoirs
Environment - international agreements:

party to: NA
signed, but not ratified: NA
Geography - note: two coral atolls thickly covered with coconut palms and other vegetation

People

Population: 636 (July 1999 est.)
Age structure:
0-14 years: NA
15-64 years: NA
65 years and over: NA (July 1998 est.)
Population growth rate: -0.21% (1999 est.)
Birth rate: NA births/1,000 population
Death rate: NA deaths/1,000 population
Net migration rate: NA migrant(s)/1,000 population
Infant mortality rate: NA deaths/1,000 live births
Life expectancy at birth:
total population: NA
male: NA
female: NA
Total fertility rate: NA children born/woman
Nationality:
noun: Cocos Islander(s)
adjective: Cocos Islander
Ethnic groups: Europeans, Cocos Malays
Religions: Sunni Muslim 57%, Christian 22%, other 21% (1981 est.)
Languages: English, Malay

Government

Country name:
conventional long form: Territory of Cocos (Keeling) Islands
conventional short form: Cocos (Keeling) Islands
Data code: CK
Dependency status: territory of Australia; administered from Canberra by the Australian Department of the Environment, Sport and Territories
Government type: NA
Capital: West Island
Administrative divisions: none (territory of Australia)
Independence: none (territory of Australia)
National holiday: NA
Constitution: Cocos (Keeling) Islands Act of 1955
Legal system: based upon the laws of Australia and local laws
Suffrage: NA
Executive branch:
chief of state: Queen ELIZABETH II (since 6 February 1952), represented by the Australian governor general
head of government: Administrator (acting) Maureen ELLIS (since NA)
cabinet: NA
elections: none; the monarch is hereditary; administrator appointed by the governor general of Australia and represents the monarch and Australia
Legislative branch: unicameral Cocos (Keeling) Islands Shire Council (NA seats)
Judicial branch: Supreme Court

Cocos (Keeling) Islands *(continued)*

Political parties and leaders: none
International organization participation: none
Diplomatic representation in the US: none
(territory of Australia)
Diplomatic representation from the US: none
(territory of Australia)
Flag description: the flag of Australia is used

Economy

Economy - overview: Grown throughout the islands, coconuts are the sole cash crop. Copra and fresh coconuts are the major export earners. Small local gardens and fishing contribute to the food supply, but additional food and most other necessities must be imported from Australia.
GDP: purchasing power parity - $NA
GDP - real growth rate: NA%
GDP - per capita: purchasing power parity - $NA
GDP - composition by sector:
agriculture: NA%
industry: NA%
services: NA%
Population below poverty line: NA%
Household income or consumption by percentage share:
lowest 10%: NA%
highest 10%: NA%
Inflation rate (consumer prices): NA%
Labor force: NA
Labor force - by occupation: the Cocos Islands Cooperative Society Ltd. employs construction workers, stevedores, and lighterage worker operations; tourism employs others
Budget:
revenues: $NA
expenditures: $NA, including capital expenditures of $NA
Industries: copra products and tourism
Industrial production growth rate: NA%
Electricity - production: NA kWh
Electricity - production by source:
fossil fuel: NA%
hydro: NA%
nuclear: NA%
other: NA%
Electricity - consumption: NA kWh
Electricity - exports: NA kWh
Electricity - imports: NA kWh
Agriculture - products: vegetables, bananas, pawpaws, coconuts
Exports: $NA
Exports - commodities: copra
Exports - partners: Australia
Imports: $NA
Imports - commodities: foodstuffs
Imports - partners: Australia
Debt - external: $NA
Economic aid - recipient: $NA
Currency: 1 Australian dollar ($A) = 100 cents
Exchange rates: Australian dollars ($A) per US$1 - 1.5853 (January 1999), 1.5888 (1998), 1.3439 (1997), 1.2773 (1996), 1.3486 (1995), 1.3667 (1994)
Fiscal year: 1 July - 30 June

Communications

Telephones: NA
Telephone system:
domestic: NA
international: telephone, telex, and facsimile communications with Australia and elsewhere via satellite; 1 satellite earth station of NA type
Radio broadcast stations: AM 1, FM 0, shortwave 0
Radios: 300 (1992 est.)
Television broadcast stations: 0 (1997)
Televisions: NA

Transportation

Railways: 0 km
Highways:
total: NA km
paved: NA km
unpaved: NA km
Ports and harbors: none; lagoon anchorage only
Merchant marine: none
Airports: 1 (1998 est.)
Airports - with paved runways:
total: 1
1,524 to 2,437 m: 1 (1998 est.)

Military

Military - note: defense is the responsibility of Australia

Transnational Issues

Disputes - international: none

Colombia

The islands of Malpelo, Providencia, and San Andrés are not shown.

Introduction

Background: Colombia gained its independence from Spain in 1819. Earlier than most countries in the area, it established traditions of civilian government with regular, free elections. In recent years, however, assassinations, widespread guerrilla activities, and drug trafficking have severely disrupted normal public and private activities.

Geography

Location: Northern South America, bordering the Caribbean Sea, between Panama and Venezuela, and bordering the North Pacific Ocean, between Ecuador and Panama
Geographic coordinates: 4 00 N, 72 00 W
Map references: South America, Central America and the Caribbean
Area:
total: 1,138,910 sq km
land: 1,038,700 sq km
water: 100,210 sq km
note: includes Isla de Malpelo, Roncador Cay, Serrana Bank, and Serranilla Bank
Area - comparative: slightly less than three times the size of Montana
Land boundaries:
total: 7,408 km
border countries: Brazil 1,643 km, Ecuador 590 km, Panama 225 km, Peru 2,900 km, Venezuela 2,050 km
Coastline: 3,208 km (Caribbean Sea 1,760 km, North Pacific Ocean 1,448 km)
Maritime claims:
continental shelf: 200-m depth or to the depth of exploitation
exclusive economic zone: 200 nm
territorial sea: 12 nm
Climate: tropical along coast and eastern plains; cooler in highlands
Terrain: flat coastal lowlands, central highlands, high Andes Mountains, eastern lowland plains

---

Colombia *(continued)*

Elevation extremes:
lowest point: Pacific Ocean 0 m
highest point: Nevado del Huila 5,750 m
Natural resources: petroleum, natural gas, coal, iron ore, nickel, gold, copper, emeralds
Land use:
arable land: 4%
permanent crops: 1%
permanent pastures: 39%
forests and woodland: 48%
other: 8% (1993 est.)
Irrigated land: 5,300 sq km (1993 est.)
Natural hazards: highlands subject to volcanic eruptions; occasional earthquakes; periodic droughts
Environment - current issues: deforestation; soil damage from overuse of pesticides; air pollution, especially in Bogota, from vehicle emissions
Environment - international agreements:
party to: Antarctic Treaty, Biodiversity, Climate Change, Endangered Species, Hazardous Wastes, Marine Life Conservation, Nuclear Test Ban, Ozone Layer Protection, Ship Pollution, Tropical Timber 83, Tropical Timber 94
signed, but not ratified: Antarctic-Environmental Protocol, Desertification, Law of the Sea, Marine Dumping
Geography - note: only South American country with coastlines on both North Pacific Ocean and Caribbean Sea

People

Population: 39,309,422 (July 1999 est.)
Age structure:
0-14 years: 33% (male 6,556,566; female 6,402,115)
15-64 years: 62% (male 11,966,306; female 12,593,685)
65 years and over: 5% (male 807,282; female 983,468) (1999 est.)
Population growth rate: 1.85% (1999 est.)
Birth rate: 24.45 births/1,000 population (1999 est.)
Death rate: 5.59 deaths/1,000 population (1999 est.)
Net migration rate: -0.34 migrant(s)/1,000 population (1999 est.)
Sex ratio:
at birth: 1.03 male(s)/female
under 15 years: 1.02 male(s)/female
15-64 years: 0.95 male(s)/female
65 years and over: 0.82 male(s)/female
total population: 0.97 male(s)/female (1999 est.)
Infant mortality rate: 24.3 deaths/1,000 live births (1999 est.)
Life expectancy at birth:
total population: 70.48 years
male: 66.54 years
female: 74.54 years (1999 est.)
Total fertility rate: 2.87 children born/woman (1999 est.)
Nationality:
noun: Colombian(s)
adjective: Colombian
Ethnic groups: mestizo 58%, white 20%, mulatto 14%, black 4%, mixed black-Amerindian 3%, Amerindian 1%
Religions: Roman Catholic 95%
Languages: Spanish
Literacy:
definition: age 15 and over can read and write
total population: 91.3%
male: 91.2%
female: 91.4% (1995 est.)

Government

Country name:
conventional long form: Republic of Colombia
conventional short form: Colombia
local long form: Republica de Colombia
local short form: Colombia
Data code: CO
Government type: republic; executive branch dominates government structure
Capital: Bogota
Administrative divisions: 32 departments (departamentos, singular - departamento) and 1 capital district* (distrito capital); Amazonas, Antioquia, Arauca, Atlantico, Bolivar, Boyaca, Caldas, Caqueta, Casanare, Cauca, Cesar, Choco, Cordoba, Cundinamarca, Guainia, Guaviare, Huila, La Guajira, Magdalena, Meta, Narino, Norte de Santander, Putumayo, Quindio, Risaralda, San Andres y Providencia, Distrito Capital de Santa Fe de Bogota*, Santander, Sucre, Tolima, Valle del Cauca, Vaupes, Vichada
Independence: 20 July 1810 (from Spain)
National holiday: Independence Day, 20 July (1810)
Constitution: 5 July 1991
Legal system: based on Spanish law; a new criminal code modeled after US procedures was enacted in 1992-93; judicial review of executive and legislative acts; accepts compulsory ICJ jurisdiction, with reservations
Suffrage: 18 years of age; universal
Executive branch:
chief of state: President Andres PASTRANA (since 7 August 1998); Vice President Gustavo BELL (since 7 August 1998); note - the president is both the chief of state and head of government
head of government: President Andres PASTRANA (since 7 August 1998); Vice President Gustavo BELL (since 7 August 1998); note - the president is both the chief of state and head of government
cabinet: Cabinet
elections: president elected by popular vote for a four-year term; election last held 31 May 1998 (next to be held NA May 2002); vice president elected by popular vote for a four-year term in a new procedure that replaces the traditional designation of vice presidents by newly elected presidents; election last held 31 May 1998 (next to be held NA May 2002)
election results: no candidate received more than 50% of the total vote, therefore, a run-off election to select a president from the two leading candidates was held 21 June 1998; Andres PASTRANA elected president; percent of vote - NA; Gustavo BELL elected vice president; percent of vote - NA
Legislative branch: bicameral Congress or Congreso consists of the Senate or Senado (102 seats; members are elected by popular vote to serve four-year terms) and the House of Representatives or Camara de Representants (161 seats; members are elected by popular vote to serve four-year terms)
elections: Senate - last held NA March 1998 (next to be held NA March 2002); House of Representatives - last held NA March 1998 (next to be held NA March 2002)
election results: Senate - percent of vote by party - PL 50%, PC 24%, smaller parties (many aligned with conservatives) 26%; seats by party - PL 51, PC 24, smaller parties 27; House of Representatives - percent of vote by party - PL 52%, PC 17%, other 31%; seats by party - NA
Judicial branch: Supreme Court of Justice (Corte Suprema de Justical), highest court of criminal law, judges are selected from the nominees of the Higher Council of Justice for eight-year terms; Council of State, highest court of administrative law, judges are selected from the nominees of the Higher Council of Justice for eight-year terms; Constitutional Court, guards integrity and supremacy of the constitution, rules on constitutionality of laws, amendments to the constitution, and international treaties
Political parties and leaders: Liberal Party or PL [Horaero SERPA]; Conservative Party or PC [Omar YEPES Alzate]; New Democratic Force or NDF [Andres PASTRANA Arango]; Democratic Alliance M-19 or AD/M-19 is a coalition of small leftist parties and dissident liberals and conservatives [leader NA]; Patriotic Union or UP is a legal political party formed by Revolutionary Armed Forces of Colombia or FARC and Colombian Communist Party or PCC [leader NA]
Political pressure groups and leaders: two largest insurgent groups active in Colombia - Revolutionary Armed Forces of Colombia or FARC; and National Liberation Army or ELN
International organization participation: BCIE, CAN, Caricom (observer), CCC, CDB, ECLAC, FAO, G-3, G-11, G-24, G-77, IADB, IAEA, IBRD, ICAO, ICC, ICFTU, ICRM, IDA, IFAD, IFC, IFRCS, IHO (pending member), ILO, IMF, IMO, Inmarsat, Intelsat, Interpol, IOC, IOM, ISO, ITU, LAES, LAIA, NAM, OAS, OPANAL, OPCW, PCA, RG, UN, UNCTAD, UNESCO, UNHCR, UNIDO, UNU, UPU, WCL, WFTU, WHO, WIPO, WMO, WToO, WTrO
Diplomatic representation in the US:
chief of mission: Ambassador Luis Alberto MORENO Mejia
chancery: 2118 Leroy Place NW, Washington, DC 20008
telephone: [1] (202) 387-8338
FAX: [1] (202) 232-8643
consulate(s) general: Boston, Chicago, Houston, Los Angeles, Miami, New Orleans, New York, San Francisco, San Juan (Puerto Rico), and Washington, DC

Colombia (continued)

consulate(s): Atlanta and Tampa

Diplomatic representation from the US:

chief of mission: Ambassador Curtis Warren KAMMAN

embassy: Calle 22D-BIS, numbers 47-51, Apartado Aereo 3831

mailing address: APO AA 34038

telephone: [57] (1) 315-0811

FAX: [57] (1) 315-2197

Flag description: three horizontal bands of yellow (top, double-width), blue, and red; similar to the flag of Ecuador, which is longer and bears the Ecuadorian coat of arms superimposed in the center

Economy

Economy - overview: Colombia ended 1998 in recession with 0.2% GDP growth due to a combination of low world oil prices, reduced export demand, guerrilla violence, and diminished investment flows. The Central Bank resorted to interest rate hikes and tight monetary policy to defend the peso against pressure from Colombia's worsening trade and fiscal deficits. President PASTRANA'S well-respected financial team is working to deal with the myriad economic problems the country faces, including the highest unemployment level in decades and a fiscal deficit of close to 5% of GDP in 1998. The government implemented austerity measures, declared emergency measures to guard against a potential banking crisis resulting from the country's economic slowdown, and is seeking international assistance to fund a peace plan with the guerrillas. Guerrilla violence and low world oil prices will likely continue to undermine the economy in 1999.

GDP: purchasing power parity - $254.7 billion (1998 est.)

GDP - real growth rate: 0.2% (1998)

GDP - per capita: purchasing power parity - $6,600 (1998 est.)

GDP - composition by sector:

agriculture: 19%

industry: 26%

services: 55% (1996)

Population below poverty line: 17.7% (1992 est.)

Household income or consumption by percentage share:

lowest 10%: 1%

highest 10%: 46.9% (1995)

Inflation rate (consumer prices): 16.7% (1998 est.)

Labor force: 16.8 million (1997 est.)

Labor force - by occupation: services 46%, agriculture 30%, industry 24% (1990)

Unemployment rate: 15.7% (1998 est.)

Budget:

revenues: $26 billion (1996 est.)

expenditures: $30 billion, including capital expenditures of $NA (1996 est.)

Industries: textiles, food processing, oil, clothing and footwear, beverages, chemicals, cement; gold, coal, emeralds

Industrial production growth rate: -1.2% (1996)

Electricity - production: 53.725 billion kWh (1996)

Electricity - production by source:

fossil fuel: 19.26%

hydro: 80.74%

nuclear: 0%

other: 0% (1996)

Electricity - consumption: 53.857 billion kWh (1996)

Electricity - exports: 0 kWh (1996)

Electricity - imports: 132 million kWh (1996)

Agriculture - products: coffee, cut flowers, bananas, rice, tobacco, corn, sugarcane, cocoa beans, oilseed, vegetables; forest products; shrimp

Exports: $11.3 billion (f.o.b., 1998 est.)

Exports - commodities: petroleum, coffee, coal, gold, bananas, cut flowers

Exports - partners: US 38%, EU 23%, Andean Community 18%, Japan 3% (1997)

Imports: $14.4 billion (f.o.b., 1998 est.)

Imports - commodities: industrial equipment, transportation equipment, consumer goods, chemicals, paper products, fuels

Imports - partners: US 42%, EU 23%, Andean Community 14%, Japan 4% (1997)

Debt - external: $18 billion (1998 est.)

Economic aid - recipient: $40.7 million (1995)

Currency: 1 Colombian peso (Col$) = 100 centavos

Exchange rates: Colombian pesos (Col$) per US$1 - 1,562.0 (February 1999), 1,426.04 (1998), 1,140.96 (1997), 1,036.69 (1996), 912.83 (1995), 844.84 (1994)

Fiscal year: calendar year

Communications

Telephones: 1.89 million (1986 est.)

Telephone system: modern system in many respects

domestic: nationwide microwave radio relay system; domestic satellite system with 11 earth stations

international: satellite earth stations - 2 Intelsat (Atlantic Ocean)

Radio broadcast stations: AM 463, FM 35, shortwave 45 (1998 est.)

Radios: NA

Television broadcast stations: 60 (includes seven low-power stations) (1997)

Televisions: 5.5 million (1993 est.)

Transportation

Railways:

total: 3,380 km

standard gauge: 150 km 1.435-m gauge (connects Cerrejon coal mines to maritime port at Bahia de Portete)

narrow gauge: 3,230 km 0.914-m gauge (1,830 km in use) (1995)

Highways:

total: 115,564 km

paved: 13,868 km

unpaved: 101,696 km (1997 est.)

Waterways: 14,300 km, navigable by river boats

Pipelines: crude oil 3,585 km; petroleum products

1,350 km; natural gas 830 km; natural gas liquids 125 km

Ports and harbors: Bahia de Portete, Barranquilla, Buenaventura, Cartagena, Leticia, Puerto Bolivar, San Andres, Santa Marta, Tumaco, Turbo

Merchant marine:

total: 14 ships (1,000 GRT or over) totaling 64,7575 GRT/84,518 DWT

ships by type: bulk 4, cargo 5, container 1, multifunction large-load carrier 2, oil tanker 2 (1998 est.)

Airports: 1,120 (1998 est.)

Airports - with paved runways:

total: 89

over 3,047 m: 2

2,438 to 3,047 m: 9

1,524 to 2,437 m: 36

914 to 1,523 m: 35

under 914 m: 7 (1998 est.)

Airports - with unpaved runways:

total: 1,031

2,438 to 3,047 m: 1

1,524 to 2,437 m: 63

914 to 1,523 m: 339

under 914 m: 628 (1998 est.)

Military

Military branches: Army (Ejercito Nacional), Navy (Armada Nacional, includes Marines and Coast Guard), Air Force (Fuerza Aerea Colombiana), National Police (Policia Nacional)

Military manpower - military age: 18 years of age

Military manpower - availability:

males age 15-49: 10,418,211 (1999 est.)

Military manpower - fit for military service:

males age 15-49: 6,980,700 (1999 est.)

Military manpower - reaching military age annually:

males: 360,820 (1999 est.)

Military expenditures - dollar figure: $4 billion (1998)

Military expenditures - percent of GDP: 4.2% (1998)

Transnational Issues

Disputes - international: maritime boundary dispute with Venezuela in the Gulf of Venezuela; territorial disputes with Nicaragua over Archipelago de San Andres y Providencia and Quita Sueno Bank

Illicit drugs: illicit producer of coca, opium poppies, and cannabis; cultivation of coca in 1997 - 79,500 hectares, an 18% increase over 1996; potential production of cocaine in 1997 - 125 metric tons, a 14% increase over 1996; cultivation of opium in 1997 - 6,600 hectares, a 5% increase over 1996; potential production of opium in 1997 - 66 metric tons, a 5% increase over 1996; the world's largest processor of coca derivatives into cocaine; supplier of cocaine to the US and other international drug markets; active aerial eradication program seeks to virtually eliminate coca and opium crops

Comoros

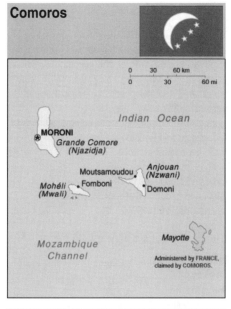

Introduction

Background: Comoros has had difficulty in achieving political stability, having endured 18 coups or attempted coups since receiving independence from France in 1975. Most recently, in August 1997, the islands of Anjouan and Moheli declared their independence from Comoros. An attempt in September 1997 by the government to reestablish control over the rebellious islands by force failed, and presently the Organization of African Unity is brokering negotiations to effect a reconciliation.

Geography

Location: Southern Africa, group of islands in the Mozambique Channel, about two-thirds of the way between northern Madagascar and northern Mozambique
Geographic coordinates: 12 10 S, 44 15 E
Map references: Africa
Area:
total: 2,170 sq km
land: 2,170 sq km
water: 0 sq km
Area - comparative: slightly more than 12 times the size of Washington, DC
Land boundaries: 0 km
Coastline: 340 km
Maritime claims:
exclusive economic zone: 200 nm
territorial sea: 12 nm
Climate: tropical marine; rainy season (November to May)
Terrain: volcanic islands, interiors vary from steep mountains to low hills
Elevation extremes:
lowest point: Indian Ocean 0 m
highest point: Le Kartala 2,360 m
Natural resources: NEGL
Land use:
arable land: 35%

permanent crops: 10%
permanent pastures: 7%
forests and woodland: 18%
other: 30% (1993 est.)
Irrigated land: NA sq km
Natural hazards: cyclones possible during rainy season (December to April); Le Kartala on Grand Comore is an active volcano
Environment - current issues: soil degradation and erosion results from crop cultivation on slopes without proper terracing; deforestation
Environment - international agreements:
party to: Biodiversity, Climate Change, Desertification, Endangered Species, Hazardous Wastes, Law of the Sea, Ozone Layer Protection
signed, but not ratified: none of the selected agreements
Geography - note: important location at northern end of Mozambique Channel

People

Population: 562,723 (July 1999 est.)
Age structure:
0-14 years: 43% (male 120,397; female 119,945)
15-64 years: 54% (male 150,851; female 154,990)
65 years and over: 3% (male 7,878; female 8,662) (1999 est.)
Population growth rate: 3.11% (1999 est.)
Birth rate: 40.29 births/1,000 population (1999 est.)
Death rate: 9.23 deaths/1,000 population (1999 est.)
Net migration rate: 0 migrant(s)/1,000 population (1999 est.)
Sex ratio:
at birth: 1.03 male(s)/female
under 15 years: 1 male(s)/female
15-64 years: 0.97 male(s)/female
65 years and over: 0.91 male(s)/female
total population: 0.98 male(s)/female (1999 est.)
Infant mortality rate: 81.63 deaths/1,000 live births (1999 est.)
Life expectancy at birth:
total population: 60.85 years
male: 58.39 years
female: 63.38 years (1999 est.)
Total fertility rate: 5.43 children born/woman (1999 est.)
Nationality:
noun: Comoran(s)
adjective: Comoran
Ethnic groups: Antalote, Cafre, Makoa, Oimatsaha, Sakalava
Religions: Sunni Muslim 86%, Roman Catholic 14%
Languages: Arabic (official), French (official), Comoran (a blend of Swahili and Arabic)
Literacy:
definition: age 15 and over can read and write
total population: 57.3%
male: 64.2%
female: 50.4% (1995 est.)

Government

Country name:
conventional long form: Federal Islamic Republic of the Comoros
conventional short form: Comoros
local long form: Republique Federale Islamique des Comores
local short form: Comores
Data code: CN
Government type: independent republic
Capital: Moroni
Administrative divisions: three islands; Grande Comore (Njazidja), Anjouan (Nzwani), and Moheli (Mwali)
note: there are also four municipalities named Domoni, Fomboni, Moroni, and Moutsamoudou
Independence: 6 July 1975 (from France)
National holiday: Independence Day, 6 July (1975)
Constitution: 20 October 1996
Legal system: French and Muslim law in a new consolidated code
Suffrage: 18 years of age; universal
Executive branch:
chief of state: Interim President TADJIDDINE Ben Said Massounde (since 6 November 1998); note - President Mohamed TAKI Abdulkarim died in office 6 November 1998 and was succeeded by Interim President MASSOUNDE
head of government: Prime Minister Abbas DJOUSSOUF (since 22 November 1998)
cabinet: Council of Ministers appointed by the president
elections: president elected by popular vote to a five-year term; election last held 16 March 1996 (next to be held NA); prime minister appointed by the president
election results: Mohamed TAKI Abdulkarim elected president; percent of vote - 64%
note: the Comoran constitution stipulates that upon the death of the president, a new president is to be elected within 90 days; however, Interim President TADJIDDINE has stated that a new election cannot be held until Anjouan is reunited with the rest of the country
Legislative branch: bicameral legislature consists of the Senate (15 seats; members selected by regional councils for six-year terms) and a Federal Assembly or Assemblee Federale (43 seats; members elected by popular vote to serve four-year terms)
elections: Federal Assembly - last held 1 and 8 December 1996 (next to be held NA)
election results: Federal Assembly - percent of vote by party - NA; seats by party - RND 39, RND candidate running as independent 1, FNJ 3
Judicial branch: Supreme Court or Cour Supremes, two members are appointed by the president, two members are elected by the Federal Assembly, one by the Council of each island, and former presidents of the republic

Comoros (continued)

Political parties and leaders: Rassemblement National pour le Development or RND, party of the government [leader NA]; Front National pour la Justice or FNJ, Islamic party in opposition [leader NA] *note:* under a new constitution ratified in October 1996, a two-party system was established; former President Mohamed TAKI Abdulkarim called for all parties to dissolve and join him in creating the RND; the constitution stipulates that only parties that win six seats in the Federal Assembly (two from each island) are permitted to be in opposition, but if no party accomplishes that the second most successful party will be in opposition; in the elections of December 1996 the FNJ appeared to qualify as opposition

International organization participation: ACCT, ACP, AfDB, AFESD, AL, CCC, ECA, FAO, FZ, G-77, IBRD, ICAO, IDA, IDB, IFAD, IFC, IFRCS (associate), ILO, IMF, InOC, Intelsat (nonsignatory user), IOC, ITU, NAM, OAU, OIC, OPCW, UN, UNCTAD, UNESCO, UNIDO, UPU, WHO, WMO, WTrO (applicant)

Diplomatic representation in the US:
chief of mission: Ambassador-designate Ahmed DJABIR (ambassador to the US and Canada and permanent representative to the UN)
chancery: (temporary) care of the Permanent Mission of the Federal and Islamic Republic of the Comoros to the United Nations, 336 East 45th Street, 2nd Floor, New York, NY 10017
telephone: [1] (212) 349-2030

Diplomatic representation from the US: the US does not have an embassy in Comoros; the ambassador to Mauritius is accredited to Comoros

Flag description: green with a white crescent in the center of the field, its points facing downward; there are four white five-pointed stars placed in a line between the points of the crescent; the crescent, stars, and color green are traditional symbols of Islam; the four stars represent the four main islands of the archipelago - Mwali, Njazidja, Nzwani, and Mayotte (a territorial collectivity of France, but claimed by Comoros); the design, the most recent of several, is described in the constitution approved by referendum on 7 June 1992

Economy - overview: One of the world's poorest countries, Comoros is made up of three islands that have inadequate transportation links, a young and rapidly increasing population, and few natural resources. The low educational level of the labor force contributes to a subsistence level of economic activity, high unemployment, and a heavy dependence on foreign grants and technical assistance. Agriculture, including fishing, hunting, and forestry, is the leading sector of the economy. It contributes 40% to GDP, employs 80% of the labor force, and provides most of the exports. The country is not self-sufficient in food production; rice, the main staple, accounts for the bulk of imports. The government is struggling to upgrade education and technical training, to privatize commercial and industrial enterprises, to improve

health services, to diversify exports, to promote tourism, and to reduce the high population growth rate. Continued foreign support is essential if the goal of 4% annual GDP growth is to be maintained.

GDP: purchasing power parity - $400 million (1997 est.)

GDP - real growth rate: 3.5% (1997 est.)

GDP - per capita: purchasing power parity - $700 (1997 est.)

GDP - composition by sector:
agriculture: 40%
industry: 14%
services: 46% (1996 est.)

Population below poverty line: NA%

Household income or consumption by percentage share:
lowest 10%: NA%
highest 10%: NA%

Inflation rate (consumer prices): 2.5% (1997)

Labor force: 144,500 (1996 est.)

Labor force - by occupation: agriculture 80%, government 3%

Unemployment rate: 20% (1996 est.)

Budget:
revenues: $48 million
expenditures: $53 million, including capital expenditures of $NA (1997)

Industries: tourism, perfume distillation, textiles, furniture, jewelry, construction materials, soft drinks

Industrial production growth rate: NA%

Electricity - production: 15 million kWh (1996)

Electricity - production by source:
fossil fuel: 86.67%
hydro: 13.33%
nuclear: 0%
other: 0% (1996)

Electricity - consumption: 15 million kWh (1996)

Electricity - exports: 0 kWh (1996)

Electricity - imports: 0 kWh (1996)

Agriculture - products: vanilla, cloves, perfume essences, copra, coconuts, bananas, cassava (tapioca)

Exports: $11.4 million (f.o.b., 1996 est.)

Exports - commodities: vanilla, ylang-ylang, cloves, perfume oil, copra

Exports - partners: France 43%, US 43%, Germany 7% (1996)

Imports: $70 million (f.o.b., 1996 est.)

Imports - commodities: rice and other foodstuffs, consumer goods; petroleum products, cement, transport equipment

Imports - partners: France 59%, South Africa 15%, Kenya 6% (1996)

Debt - external: $219 million (1996 est.)

Economic aid - recipient: $43.3 million (1995)

Currency: 1 Comoran franc (CF) = 100 centimes

Exchange rates: Comoran francs (CF) per US$1 - 420.01 (December 1998), 442.46 (1998), 437.75 (1997), 383.66 (1996), 374.36 (1995), 416.40 (1994)

Fiscal year: calendar year

Telephones: 4,000 (1993 est.)

Telephone system: sparse system of microwave radio relay and HF radiotelephone communication stations
domestic: HF radiotelephone communications and microwave radio relay
international: HF radiotelephone communications to Madagascar and Reunion

Radio broadcast stations: AM 2, FM 1, shortwave 0

Radios: 81,000 (1994)

Television broadcast stations: 0 (1998)

Televisions: 200 (1994

Railways: 0 km

Highways:
total: 880 km
paved: 673 km
unpaved: 207 km (1996 est.)

Ports and harbors: Fomboni, Moroni, Moutsamoudou

Merchant marine: none

Airports: 4 (1998 est.)

Airports - with paved runways:
total: 4
2,438 to 3,047 m: 1
914 to 1,523 m: 3 (1998 est.)

Military branches: Comoran Security Force

Military manpower - availability:
males age 15-49: 132,969 (1999 est.)

Military manpower - fit for military service:
males age 15-49: 79,224 (1999 est.)

Military expenditures - dollar figure: $3 million (1994 est.)

Military expenditures - percent of GDP: NA%

Disputes - international: claims French-administered Mayotte; the islands of Anjouan (Nzwani) and Moheli (Mwali) have moved to secede from Comoros

Congo, Democratic Republic of the

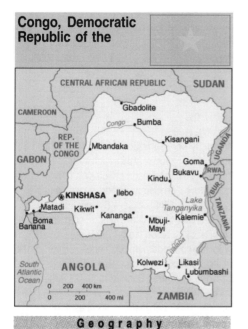

Geography

Location: Central Africa, northeast of Angola
Geographic coordinates: 0 00 N, 25 00 E
Map references: Africa
Area:
total: 2,345,410 sq km
land: 2,267,600 sq km
water: 77,810 sq km
Area - comparative: slightly less than one-fourth the size of the US
Land boundaries:
total: 10,271 km
border countries: Angola 2,511 km, Burundi 233 km, Central African Republic 1,577 km, Republic of the Congo 2,410 km, Rwanda 217 km, Sudan 628 km, Uganda 765 km, Zambia 1,930 km
Coastline: 37 km
Maritime claims:
exclusive economic zone: boundaries with neighbors
territorial sea: 12 nm
Climate: tropical; hot and humid in equatorial river basin; cooler and drier in southern highlands; cooler and wetter in eastern highlands; north of Equator - wet season April to October, dry season December to February; south of Equator - wet season November to March, dry season April to October
Terrain: vast central basin is a low-lying plateau; mountains in east
Elevation extremes:
lowest point: Atlantic Ocean 0 m
highest point: Pic Marguerite on Mont Ngaliema (Mount Stanley) 5,110 m
Natural resources: cobalt, copper, cadmium, petroleum, industrial and gem diamonds, gold, silver, zinc, manganese, tin, germanium, uranium, radium, bauxite, iron ore, coal, hydropower potential, timber
Land use:
arable land: 3%
permanent crops: 0%
permanent pastures: 7%
forests and woodland: 77%

other: 13% (1993 est.)
Irrigated land: 100 sq km (1993 est.)
Natural hazards: periodic droughts in south; volcanic activity
Environment - current issues: poaching threatens wildlife populations; water pollution; deforestation; refugees who arrived in mid-1994 were responsible for significant deforestation, soil erosion, and wildlife poaching in the eastern part of the country (most of those refugees were repatriated in November and December 1996)
Environment - international agreements:
party to: Biodiversity, Climate Change, Desertification, Endangered Species, Hazardous Wastes, Law of the Sea, Marine Dumping, Nuclear Test Ban, Ozone Layer Protection, Tropical Timber 83, Tropical Timber 94, Wetlands
signed, but not ratified: Environmental Modification
Geography - note: straddles Equator; very narrow strip of land that controls the lower Congo river and is only outlet to South Atlantic Ocean; dense tropical rain forest in central river basin and eastern highlands

People

Population: 50,481,305 (July 1999 est.)
Age structure:
0-14 years: 48% (male 12,200,532; female 12,136,372)
15-64 years: 49% (male 12,135,901; female 12,692,057)
65 years and over: 3% (male 564,084; female 752,359) (1999 est.)
Population growth rate: 2.96% (1999 est.)
Birth rate: 46.37 births/1,000 population (1999 est.)
Death rate: 14.99 deaths/1,000 population (1999 est.)
Net migration rate: -1.78 migrant(s)/1,000 population (1999 est.)
note: in 1994, about a million refugees fled into Zaire (now called the Democratic Republic of the Congo or DROC), to escape the fighting between the Hutus and the Tutsis in Rwanda and Burundi; the outbreak of widespread fighting in the DROC between rebels and government forces in October 1996 spurred about 875,000 refugees to return to Rwanda in late 1996 and early 1997; additionally, the DROC is host to 200,000 Angolan, 110,000 Burundi, 100,000 Sudanese, and 15,000 Ugandan refugees; renewed fighting in the DROC in August 1998 resulted in more internal displacement and refugee outflows
Sex ratio:
at birth: 1.03 male(s)/female
under 15 years: 1.01 male(s)/female
15-64 years: 0.96 male(s)/female
65 years and over: 0.75 male(s)/female
total population: 0.97 male(s)/female (1999 est.)
Infant mortality rate: 99.45 deaths/1,000 live births (1999 est.)
Life expectancy at birth:
total population: 49.44 years
male: 47.28 years
female: 51.67 years (1999 est.)

Total fertility rate: 6.45 children born/woman (1999 est.)
Nationality:
noun: Congolese (singular and plural)
adjective: Congolese or Congo
Ethnic groups: over 200 African ethnic groups of which the majority are Bantu; the four largest tribes - Mongo, Luba, Kongo (all Bantu), and the Mangbetu-Azande (Hamitic) make up about 45% of the population
Religions: Roman Catholic 50%, Protestant 20%, Kimbanguist 10%, Muslim 10%, other syncretic sects and traditional beliefs 10%
Languages: French (official), Lingala (a lingua franca trade language), Kingwana (a dialect of Kiswahili or Swahili), Kikongo, Tshiluba
Literacy:
definition: age 15 and over can read and write French, Lingala, Kingwana, or Tshiluba
total population: 77.3%
male: 86.6%
female: 67.7% (1995 est.)

Government

Country name:
conventional long form: Democratic Republic of the Congo
conventional short form: none
local long form: Republique Democratique du Congo
local short form: none
former: Belgian Congo, Congo/Leopoldville, Congo/Kinshasa, Zaire
abbreviation: DROC
Data code: CG
Government type: dictatorship; presumably undergoing a transition to representative government
Capital: Kinshasa
Administrative divisions: 10 provinces (provinces, singular - province) and one city* (ville); Bandundu, Bas-Congo, Equateur, Kasai-Occidental, Kasai-Oriental, Katanga, Kinshasa*, Maniema, Nord-Kivu, Orientale, Sud-Kivu
Independence: 30 June 1960 (from Belgium)
National holiday: anniversary of independence from Belgium, 30 June (1960)
Constitution: 24 June 1967, amended August 1974, revised 15 February 1978, amended April 1990; transitional constitution promulgated in April 1994; following successful rebellion the new government announced on 29 May 1997 a program of constitutional reform and, in November 1998, a draft constitution was approved by President KABILA and awaits ratification by national referendum
Legal system: based on Belgian civil law system and tribal law; has not accepted compulsory ICJ jurisdiction
Suffrage: 18 years of age; universal and compulsory
Executive branch:
chief of state: Laurent Desire KABILA (since 17 May 1997); note - the president is both chief of state and head of government
head of government: Laurent Desire KABILA (since

Congo, Democratic Republic of the *(continued)*

17 May 1997); note - the president is both chief of state and head of government

cabinet: National Executive Council, appointed by the president

elections: before Laurent Desire KABILA seized power, the president was elected by popular vote for a seven-year term; election last held 29 July 1984 (next was to be held in May 1997); formerly, the prime minister was elected by the High Council of the Republic; note - the term of the former government expired in 1991, elections were not held, and former president MOBUTU continued in office until his government was militarily defeated by KABILA on 17 May 1997

election results: MOBUTU Sese Seko Kuku Ngbendu wa Za Banga reelected president in 1984 without opposition

note: Marshal MOBUTU Sese Seko Kuku Ngbendu wa Za Banga was president from 24 November 1965 until forced into exile on 16 May 1997 when his government was overturned militarily by Laurent Desire KABILA, who immediately assumed governing authority; in his 29 May 1997 inaugural address, President KABILA announced a two-year time table for political reform leading to elections by April 1999; subsequently, in December 1998, President KABILA announced that elections would be postponed until all foreign military forces attempting his overthrow had withdrawn from the country

Legislative branch: legislative activity has been suspended pending the establishment of KABILA's promised constitutional reforms and the elections to be held by April 1999 (now postponed indefinitely)

elections: the country's first multi-party presidential and legislative elections had been scheduled for May 1997 but were not held; instead KABILA overthrew the MOBUTU government and seized control of the country

Judicial branch: Supreme Court (Cour Supreme)

Political parties and leaders: sole legal party until January 1991 - Popular Movement of the Revolution or MPR [leader NA]; note - may be replaced by Union for the Republic or UPR [leader NA]; other parties include Union for Democracy and Social Progress or UDPS [Etienne TSHISEKEDI wa Mulumba]; Congolese Rally for Democracy or RCD [Ernest WAMBA dia Wamba]; Democratic Social Christian Party or PDSC [Andre BO-BOLIKO]; Union of Federalists and Independent Republicans or UFERI [Gabriel KYUNGU wa Kumwunzu]; Unified Lumumbast Party or PALU [Antoine GIZENGA]

note: President KABILA, who has banned political party activity indefinitely, currently leads the Alliance of Democratic Forces for the Liberation of Congo-Zaire or AFDL

International organization participation: ACCT, ACP, AfDB, CCC, CEEAC, CEPGL, ECA, FAO, G-19, G-24, G-77, IAEA, IBRD, ICAO, ICFTU, ICRM, IDA, IFAD, IFC, IFRCS, IHO, ILO, IMF, IMO, Intelsat, Interpol, IOC, IOM (observer), ITU, NAM, OAU, OPCW, PCA, SADC, UN, UNCTAD, UNESCO, UNHCR, UNIDO, UPU, WCL, WFTU, WHO, WIPO, WMO, WToO

Diplomatic representation in the US:
chief of mission: Ambassador Faida MITIFU
chancery: 1800 New Hampshire Avenue NW, Washington, DC 20009
telephone: [1] (202) 234-7690, 7691
FAX: [1] (202) 236-0748

Diplomatic representation from the US:
chief of mission: Ambassador William Lacy SWING
embassy: 310 Avenue des Aviateurs, Kinshasa
mailing address: Unit 31550, APO AE 09828
telephone: [243] (12) 21028, 21959
FAX: [243] (88) 43805 43467

Flag description: light blue with a large yellow five-pointed star in the center and a columnar arrangement of six small yellow five-pointed stars along the hoist side

Economy

Economy - overview: The economy of the Democratic Republic of the Congo - a nation endowed with vast potential wealth - has declined significantly since the mid-1980s. The new government instituted a tight fiscal policy that initially curbed inflation and currency depreciation, but these small gains were quickly reversed when the foreign-backed rebellion in the eastern part of the country began in August 1998. The war has dramatically reduced government revenue, and increased external debt. Foreign businesses have curtailed operations due to uncertainty about the outcome of the conflict and because of increased government harassment and restrictions. Poor infrastructure, an uncertain legal framework, corruption, and lack of transparency in government economic policy remain a brake on investment and growth. A number of IMF and World Bank missions have met with the new government to help it develop a coherent economic plan but associated reforms are on hold.

GDP: purchasing power parity - $34.9 billion (1998 est.)

GDP - real growth rate: -3.5% (1998 est.)

GDP - per capita: purchasing power parity - $710 (1998 est.)

GDP - composition by sector:
agriculture: 59%
industry: 15%
services: 26% (1995 est.)

Population below poverty line: NA%

Household income or consumption by percentage share:
lowest 10%: NA%
highest 10%: NA%

Inflation rate (consumer prices): 147% (1998 est.)

Labor force: 14.51 million (1993 est.)

Labor force - by occupation: agriculture 65%, industry 16%, services 19% (1991 est.)

Unemployment rate: NA%

Budget:
revenues: $269 million
expenditures: $244 million, including capital expenditures of $24 million (1996 est.)

Industries: mining, mineral processing, consumer products (including textiles, footwear, cigarettes, processed foods and beverages), cement, diamonds

Industrial production growth rate: NA%

Electricity - production: 6.4 billion kWh (1996)

Electricity - production by source:
fossil fuel: 6.25%
hydro: 93.75%
nuclear: 0%
other: 0% (1996)

Electricity - consumption: 6.265 billion kWh (1996)

Electricity - exports: 195 million kWh (1996)

Electricity - imports: 60 million kWh (1996)

Agriculture - products: coffee, sugar, palm oil, rubber, tea, quinine, cassava (tapioca), palm oil, bananas, root crops, corn, fruits; wood products

Exports: $1.6 billion (f.o.b., 1998 est.)

Exports - commodities: diamonds, copper, coffee, cobalt, crude oil

Exports - partners: Benelux 43%, US 22%, South Africa 8%, France, Germany, Italy, UK, Japan (1997)

Imports: $819 million (f.o.b., 1998 est.)

Imports - commodities: consumer goods, foodstuffs, mining and other machinery, transport equipment, fuels

Imports - partners: South Africa 21%, Benelux 14%, China 8%, Netherlands, US, France, Germany, Italy, Japan, UK (1997)

Debt - external: $15 billion (1997 est.)

Economic aid - recipient: $195.3 million (1995)

Currency: Congolese franc (CF)

Exchange rates: Congolese francs (CF) per US$1 - 2.5 (January 1999); new zaires (Z) per US$1 - 115,000 (January 1998), 83,764 (October 1996), 7,024 (1995), 1,194 (1994)

note: on 30 June 1998 the Congolese franc (CF) was introduced, replacing the new zaire; 1 Congolese franc (CF)=100,000 new zaires

Fiscal year: calendar year

Communications

Telephones: 34,000 (1991 est.)

Telephone system:
domestic: barely adequate wire and microwave radio relay service in and between urban areas; domestic satellite system with 14 earth stations
international: satellite earth station - 1 Intelsat (Atlantic Ocean)

Radio broadcast stations: AM 10, FM 4, shortwave 0

Radios: 3.87 million (1992 est.)

Television broadcast stations: 18 (1997)

Televisions: 55,000 (1992 est.)

Transportation

Railways:
total: 5,138 km (1995); note - severely reduced route-distance in use because of damage to facilities by civil strife
narrow gauge: 3,987 km 1.067-m gauge (858 km electrified); 125 km 1.000-m gauge; 1,026 km 0.600-m gauge

Congo, Democratic Republic of the
(continued)

Highways:
total: 145,000 km
paved: 2,500 km
unpaved: 142,500 km (1993 est.)
Waterways: 15,000 km including the Congo, its tributaries, and unconnected lakes
Pipelines: petroleum products 390 km
Ports and harbors: Banana, Boma, Bukavu, Bumba, Goma, Kalemie, Kindu, Kinshasa, Kisangani, Matadi, Mbandaka
Merchant marine: none
Airports: 233 (1998 est.)
Airports - with paved runways:
total: 23
over 3,047 m: 4
2,438 to 3,047 m: 3
1,524 to 2,437 m: 14
914 to 1,523 m: 2 (1998 est.)
Airports - with unpaved runways:
total: 210
1,524 to 2,437 m: 21
914 to 1,523 m: 95
under 914 m: 94 (1998 est.)

Military

Military branches: Army, Navy, Air Force, Presidential Security Group, Gendarmerie
Military manpower - availability:
males age 15-49: 10,874,744 (1999 est.)
Military manpower - fit for military service:
males age 15-49: 5,536,277 (1999 est.)
Military expenditures - dollar figure: $250 million (1997)
Military expenditures - percent of GDP: 4.6% (1997)

Transnational Issues

Disputes - international: the Democratic Republic of the Congo is in the grip of a civil war that has drawn in military forces from neighboring states, with Uganda and Rwanda supporting the rebel movement which occupies much of the eastern portion of the state; most of the Congo River boundary with the Republic of the Congo is indefinite (no agreement has been reached on the division of the river or its islands, except in the Pool Malebo/Stanley Pool area)
Illicit drugs: illicit producer of cannabis, mostly for domestic consumption

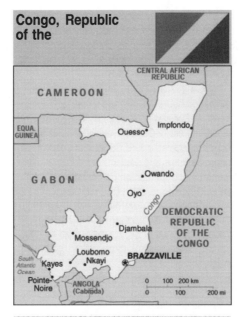

Congo, Republic of the

Geography

Location: Western Africa, bordering the South Atlantic Ocean, between Angola and Gabon
Geographic coordinates: 1 00 S, 15 00 E
Map references: Africa
Area:
total: 342,000 sq km
land: 341,500 sq km
water: 500 sq km
Area - comparative: slightly smaller than Montana
Land boundaries:
total: 5,504 km
border countries: Angola 201 km, Cameroon 523 km, Central African Republic 467 km, Democratic Republic of the Congo 2,410 km, Gabon 1,903 km
Coastline: 169 km
Maritime claims:
territorial sea: 200 nm
Climate: tropical; rainy season (March to June); dry season (June to October); constantly high temperatures and humidity; particularly enervating climate astride the Equator
Terrain: coastal plain, southern basin, central plateau, northern basin
Elevation extremes:
lowest point: Atlantic Ocean 0 m
highest point: Mount Berongou 903 m
Natural resources: petroleum, timber, potash, lead, zinc, uranium, copper, phosphates, natural gas
Land use:
arable land: 0%
permanent crops: 0%
permanent pastures: 29%
forests and woodland: 62%
other: 9% (1993 est.)
Irrigated land: 10 sq km (1993 est.)
Natural hazards: seasonal flooding
Environment - current issues: air pollution from vehicle emissions; water pollution from the dumping of raw sewage; tap water is not potable; deforestation

Environment - international agreements:
party to: Biodiversity, Climate Change, Endangered Species, Ozone Layer Protection, Tropical Timber 83, Tropical Timber 94
signed, but not ratified: Desertification, Law of the Sea
Geography - note: about 70% of the population lives in Brazzaville, Pointe-Noire, or along the railroad between them

People

Population: 2,716,814 (July 1999 est.)
Age structure:
0-14 years: 42% (male 579,940; female 573,847)
15-64 years: 54% (male 718,820; female 751,911)
65 years and over: 4% (male 36,987; female 55,309) (1999 est.)
Population growth rate: 2.16% (1999 est.)
Birth rate: 37.96 births/1,000 population (1999 est.)
Death rate: 16.33 deaths/1,000 population (1999 est.)
Net migration rate: 0 migrant(s)/1,000 population (1999 est.)
Sex ratio:
at birth: 1.03 male(s)/female
under 15 years: 1.01 male(s)/female
15-64 years: 0.96 male(s)/female
65 years and over: 0.67 male(s)/female
total population: 0.97 male(s)/female (1999 est.)
Infant mortality rate: 100.58 deaths/1,000 live births (1999 est.)
Life expectancy at birth:
total population: 47.14 years
male: 45.42 years
female: 48.92 years (1999 est.)
Total fertility rate: 4.89 children born/woman (1999 est.)
Nationality:
noun: Congolese (singular and plural)
adjective: Congolese or Congo
Ethnic groups: Kongo 48%, Sangha 20%, M'Bochi 12%, Teke 17%, Europeans NA%; note - Europeans estimated at 8,500, mostly French, before the 1997 civil war; may be half of that in 1998, following the widespread destruction of foreign businesses in 1997
Religions: Christian 50%, animist 48%, Muslim 2%
Languages: French (official), Lingala and Monokutuba (lingua franca trade languages), many local languages and dialects (of which Kikongo has the most users)
Literacy:
definition: age 15 and over can read and write
total population: 74.9%
male: 83.1%
female: 67.2% (1995 est.)

Government

Country name:
conventional long form: Republic of the Congo
conventional short form: none
local long form: Republique du Congo

Congo, Republic of the (continued)

local short form: none
former: Congo/Brazzaville, Congo
Data code: CF
Government type: republic
Capital: Brazzaville
Administrative divisions: 9 regions (regions, singular - region) and 1 commune*; Bouenza, Brazzaville*, Cuvette, Kouilou, Lekoumou, Likouala, Niari, Plateaux, Pool, Sangha
Independence: 15 August 1960 (from France)
National holiday: Congolese National Day, 15 August (1960)
Constitution: new constitution approved by referendum March 1992 but is now being redrafted by President SASSOU-NGUESSO
Legal system: based on French civil law system and customary law
Suffrage: 18 years of age; universal
Executive branch:
chief of state: President Denis SASSOU-NGUESSO (since 25 October 1997, following the civil war in which he toppled elected president Pascal LISSOUBA); note - the president is both the chief of state and head of government
head of government: normally the prime minister, appointed from the majority party by the president; however, since his inauguration, President Denis SASSOU-NGUESSO has been both chief of state and head of government
cabinet: Council of Ministers appointed by the president
elections: president elected by popular vote for a five-year term; election last held 16 August 1992 (next was to be held 27 July 1997 but will be delayed for several years pending the drafting of a new constitution)
election results: Pascal LISSOUBA elected president in 1992; percent of vote - Pascal LISSOUBA 61%, Bernard KOLELAS 39%; note - LISSOUBA was deposed in 1997, replaced by Denis SASSOU-NGUESSO
Legislative branch: unicameral National Transitional Council (75 seats, members elected by reconciliation forum of 1,420 delegates; note - the National Transitioanl Council replaced the bicameral Paarliament in mid-1997
elections: National Transitional Council - last held NA January 1998 (next to be held NA 2001); note - at that election the National Transitional Council is to be replaced by a bicameral assembly
election results: National Transitional Council - percent of vote by party - NA; seats by party - NA
Judicial branch: Supreme Court (Cour Supreme)
Political parties and leaders: the most important of the many political parties are Congolese Labor Party or PCT [Denis SASSOU-NGUESSO, president]; Association for Democracy and Development or RDD [Joachim YHOMBI-OPANGO, president]; Association for Democracy and Social Progress or RDPS [Jean-Pierre Thystere TCHICAYA, president]; Congolese Movement for Democracy and Integral Development or MCDDI [Michel MAMPOUYA];

Pan-African Union for Social Development or UPADS [Martin MBERI]; Union of Democratic Forces or UFD [Sebastian EBAO]; Union for Democratic Renewal or URD [leader NA]; Union for Development and Social Progress or UDPS [Jean-Michael BOKAMBA-YANGOUMA]
Political pressure groups and leaders: Union of Congolese Socialist Youth or UJSC; Congolese Trade Union Congress or CSC; Revolutionary Union of Congolese Women or URFC; General Union of Congolese Pupils and Students or UGEEC
International organization participation: ACCT, ACP, AfDB, BDEAC, CCC, CEEAC, ECA, FAO, FZ, G-77, IBRD, ICAO, ICFTU, ICRM, IDA, IFAD, IFC, IFRCS, ILO, IMF, IMO, Intelsat, Interpol, IOC, ITU, MONUA, NAM, OAU, OPCW, UDEAC, UN, UNCTAD, UNESCO, UNIDO, UPU, WFTU, WHO, WIPO, WMO, WToO
Diplomatic representation in the US:
chief of mission: (vacant); Charge d'Affaires ad interim Serge MOMBOULI
chancery: 4891 Colorado Avenue NW, Washington, DC 20011
telephone: [1] (202) 726-5500
FAX: [1] (202) 726-1860
Diplomatic representation from the US:
chief of mission: Ambassador J. Aubrey HOOKS
embassy: Avenue Amilcar Cabral, Brazzaville
mailing address: B. P. 1015, Brazzaville
telephone: [242] 83 20 70
FAX: [242] 83 63 38
note: the embassy is temporarily collocated with the US Embassy in the Democratic Republic of the Congo (US Embassy Kinshasa, 310 Avenue des Aviateurs, Kinshasa)
Flag description: divided diagonally from the lower hoist side by a yellow band; the upper triangle (hoist side) is green and the lower triangle is red; uses the popular pan-African colors of Ethiopia

Economy

Economy - overview: The economy is a mixture of village agriculture and handicrafts, an industrial sector based largely on oil, support services, and a government characterized by budget problems and overstaffing. Oil has supplanted forestry as the mainstay of the economy, providing a major share of government revenues and exports. In the early 1980s, rapidly rising oil revenues enabled the government to finance large-scale development projects with GDP growth averaging 5% annually, one of the highest rates in Africa. Subsequently, falling oil prices cut GDP growth by half. Moreover, the government has mortgaged a substantial portion of its oil earnings, contributing to the government's shortage of revenues. The 12 January 1994 devaluation of Franc Zone currencies by 50% resulted in inflation of 61% in 1994 but inflation has subsided since. Economic reform efforts continued with the support of international organizations, notably the World Bank and the IMF. The reform program came to a halt in June 1997 when civil war erupted. Denis

SASSOU-NGUESSO, who returned to power when the war ended in October 1997, publicly expressed interest in moving forward on economic reforms and privatization and in renewing cooperation with international financial institutions. However, economic progress was badly hurt by slumping oil prices in 1998, which worsened the Republic of the Congo's budget deficit. A second blow was the resumption of armed conflict in December 1998.
GDP: purchasing power parity - $3.9 billion (1998 est.)
GDP - real growth rate: 2.5% (1998 est.)
GDP - per capita: purchasing power parity - $1,500 (1998 est.)
GDP - composition by sector:
agriculture: 10%
industry: 59%
services: 31% (1997 est.)
Population below poverty line: NA%
Household income or consumption by percentage share:
lowest 10%: NA%
highest 10%: NA%
Inflation rate (consumer prices): 5% (1997 est.)
Labor force: NA
Unemployment rate: NA%
Budget:
revenues: $870 million
expenditures: $970 million, including capital expenditures of $NA (1997 est.)
Industries: petroleum extraction, cement kilning, lumbering, brewing, sugar milling, palm oil, soap, cigarette making
Industrial production growth rate: NA%
Electricity - production: 438 million kWh (1996)
Electricity - production by source:
fossil fuel: 0.68%
hydro: 99.32%
nuclear: 0%
other: 0% (1996)
Electricity - consumption: 553 million kWh (1996)
Electricity - exports: 0 kWh (1996)
Electricity - imports: 115 million kWh (1996)
Agriculture - products: cassava (tapioca), sugar, rice, corn, peanuts, vegetables, coffee, cocoa; forest products
Exports: $1.7 billion (f.o.b., 1997)
Exports - commodities: petroleum 50%, lumber, plywood, sugar, cocoa, coffee, diamonds
Exports - partners: US 37%, Belgium-Luxembourg 34%, Taiwan, China (1997 est.)
Imports: $803 million (f.o.b. 1997)
Imports - commodities: intermediate manufactures, capital equipment, construction materials, foodstuffs, petroleum products
Imports - partners: France 22%, Italy 16%, US 9%, UK 6% (1997 est.)
Debt - external: $6 billion (1996)
Economic aid - recipient: $159.1 million (1995)
Currency: 1 Communaute Financiere Africaine franc (CFAF) = 100 centimes
Exchange rates: Communaute Financiere Africaine

Congo, Republic of the (continued)

francs (CFAF) per US$1 - 550 (January 1999), 589.95 (1998), 583.67 (1997), 511.55 (1996), 499.15 (1995), 555.20 (1994)
Fiscal year: calendar year

Communications

Telephones: 18,000 (1983 est.)
Telephone system: services barely adequate for government use; key exchanges are in Brazzaville, Pointe-Noire, and Loubomo; inter-city lines frequently out-of-order
domestic: primary network consists of microwave radio relay and coaxial cable
international: satellite earth station - 1 Intelsat (Atlantic Ocean)
Radio broadcast stations: AM 4, FM 1, shortwave 0
Radios: NA
Television broadcast stations: 1 (1997)
Televisions: 8,500 (1993 est.)

Transportation

Railways:
total: 795 km (includes 285 km private track)
narrow gauge: 795 km 1.067-m gauge (1995 est.)
Highways:
total: 12,800 km
paved: 1,242 km
unpaved: 11,558 km (1996 est.)
Waterways: the Congo and Ubangi (Oubangui) Rivers provide 1,120 km of commercially navigable water transport; other rivers are used for local traffic only
Pipelines: crude oil 25 km
Ports and harbors: Brazzaville, Impfondo, Ouesso, Oyo, Pointe-Noire
Airports: 36 (1998 est.)
Airports - with paved runways:
total: 4
over 3,047 m: 1
1,524 to 2,437 m: 3 (1998 est.)
Airports - with unpaved runways:
total: 32
1,524 to 2,437 m: 8
914 to 1,523 m: 14
under 914 m: 10 (1998 est.)

Military

Military branches: NA
Military manpower - military age: 20 years of age
Military manpower - availability:
males age 15-49: 641,543 (1999 est.)
Military manpower - fit for military service:
males age 15-49: 326,834 (1999 est.)
Military manpower - reaching military age annually:
males: 28,976 (1999 est.)
Military expenditures - dollar figure: $110 million (1993)
Military expenditures - percent of GDP: 3.8% (1993)

Transnational Issues

Disputes - international: most of the Congo River boundary with the Democratic Republic of the Congo is indefinite (no agreement has been reached on the division of the river or its islands, except in the Stanley Pool/Pool Malebo area)

Cook Islands
(self-governing in free association with New Zealand)

Introduction

Background: Named after Captain Cook, who sighted them in 1770, the islands became a British protectorate in 1888. By 1900, administrative control was transferred to New Zealand. Residents chose self-government with free association with New Zealand in 1965. The emigration of Cook Islanders to New Zealand in large numbers and resulting loss of skilled labor and government deficits are continuing problems.

Geography

Location: Oceania, group of islands in the South Pacific Ocean, about one-half of the way from Hawaii to New Zealand
Geographic coordinates: 21 14 S, 159 46 W
Map references: Oceania
Area:
total: 240 sq km
land: 240 sq km
water: 0 sq km
Area - comparative: 1.3 times the size of Washington, DC
Land boundaries: 0 km
Coastline: 120 km
Maritime claims:
continental shelf: 200 nm or to the edge of the continental margin
exclusive economic zone: 200 nm
territorial sea: 12 nm
Climate: tropical; moderated by trade winds
Terrain: low coral atolls in north; volcanic, hilly islands in south
Elevation extremes:
lowest point: Pacific Ocean 0 m
highest point: Te Manga 652 m
Natural resources: NEGL
Land use:
arable land: 9%

Cook Islands (continued)

permanent crops: 13%
permanent pastures: NA%
forests and woodland: NA%
other: 78% (1993 est.)
Irrigated land: NA sq km
Natural hazards: typhoons (November to March)
Environment - current issues: NA
Environment - international agreements:
party to: Biodiversity, Climate Change, Desertication,
Law of the Sea
signed, but not ratified: Climate Change-Kyoto
Protocol

People

Population: 20,200 (July 1999 est.)
Age structure:
0-14 years: NA
15-64 years: NA
65 years and over: NA
Population growth rate: 1.04% (1999 est.)
Birth rate: 22.35 births/1,000 population (1999 est.)
Death rate: 5.2 deaths/1,000 population (1999 est.)
Net migration rate: -6.75 migrant(s)/1,000
population (1999 est.)
Infant mortality rate: 24.7 deaths/1,000 live births
(1999 est.)
Life expectancy at birth:
total population: 71.14 years
male: 69.2 years
female: 73.1 years (1999 est.)
Total fertility rate: 3.17 children born/woman (1999
est.)
Nationality:
noun: Cook Islander(s)
adjective: Cook Islander
Ethnic groups: Polynesian (full blood) 81.3%,
Polynesian and European 7.7%, Polynesian and
non-European 7.7%, European 2.4%, other 0.9%
Religions: Christian (majority of populace are
members of the Cook Islands Christian Church)
Languages: English (official), Maori
Literacy: NA

Government

Country name:
conventional long form: none
conventional short form: Cook Islands
Data code: CW
Dependency status: self-governing in free
association with New Zealand; Cook Islands is fully
responsible for internal affairs; New Zealand retains
responsibility for external affairs, in consultation with
the Cook Islands
Government type: self-governing parliamentary
democracy
Capital: Avarua
Administrative divisions: none
Independence: none (became self-governing in free
association with New Zealand on 4 August 1965 and
has the right at any time to move to full independence
by unilateral action)

National holiday: Constitution Day, 4 August
Constitution: 4 August 1965
Legal system: based on New Zealand law and
English common law
Suffrage: NA years of age; universal adult
Executive branch:
chief of state: Queen ELIZABETH II (since 6 February
1952), represented by Apenera SHORT (since NA);
New Zealand High Commissioner Jon JONESSEN
(since NA January 1998), representative of New
Zealand
head of government: Prime Minister Sir Geoffrey A.
HENRY (since 1 February 1989); Deputy Prime
Minister Inatio AKARURU (since 1 February 1989)
cabinet: Cabinet chosen by the prime minister;
collectively responsible to Parliament
elections: none; the monarch is hereditary; the UK
representative is appointed by the monarch; the New
Zealand high commissioner is appointed by the New
Zealand Government; following legislative elections,
the leader of the party that wins the most seats usually
becomes prime minister
Legislative branch: unicameral Parliament (25
seats; members elected by popular vote to serve
five-year terms)
elections: last held 6 March 1994 (next to be held by
June 1999)
election results: percent of vote by party - NA; seats
by party - Cook Islands Party 20, Democratic Party 3,
Democratic Alliance Party 2
note: the House of Arikis (chiefs) advises on
traditional matters, but has no legislative powers
Judicial branch: High Court
Political parties and leaders: Cook Islands Party
[Sir Geoffrey HENRY]; Democratic Party [Sir Thomas
DAVIS]; Democratic Alliance Party [Norman
GEORGE]
International organization participation: AsDB,
ESCAP (associate), FAO, ICAO, ICFTU, IFAD,
Intelsat (nonsignatory user), IOC, OPCW, Sparteca,
SPC, SPF, UNESCO, WHO, WMO
Diplomatic representation in the US: none
(self-governing in free association with New Zealand)
Diplomatic representation from the US: none
(self-governing in free association with New Zealand)
Flag description: blue, with the flag of the UK in the
upper hoist-side quadrant and a large circle of 15
white five-pointed stars (one for every island)
centered in the outer half of the flag

Economy

Economy - overview: Like many other South Pacific
island nations, the Cook Islands' economic
development is hindered by the isolation of the
country from foreign markets, lack of natural
resources, periodic devastation from natural
disasters, and inadequate infrastructure. Agriculture
provides the economic base with major exports made
up of copra and citrus fruit. Manufacturing activities
are limited to fruit-processing, clothing, and
handicrafts. Trade deficits are made up for by
remittances from emigrants and by foreign aid,
overwhelmingly from New Zealand. In 1996, the
government declared bankruptcy, citing a $120 million
public debt. Efforts to exploit tourism potential and
expanding the mining and fishing industries have not
been enough to adequately deal with the financial
crisis. In an effort to stem further erosion of the
economy, the government slashed public service
salaries by 50%, condensed the number of
government ministries from 52 to 22, reduced the
number of civil servants by more than half, began
selling government assets, and closed all overseas
diplomatic posts except for the one in New Zealand.
GDP: purchasing power parity - $79 million
(1994 est.)
GDP - real growth rate: NA%
GDP - per capita: purchasing power parity - $4,000
(1994 est.)
GDP - composition by sector:
agriculture: 17%
industry: 6%
services: 77% (FY90/91)
Population below poverty line: NA%
**Household income or consumption by percentage
share:**
lowest 10%: NA%
highest 10%: NA%
Inflation rate (consumer prices): 2.6% (1994 est.)
Labor force: 6,601 (1993)
Labor force - by occupation: agriculture 29%,
government 27%, services 25%, industry 15%, other
4% (1981)
Unemployment rate: NA%
Budget:
revenues: $NA
expenditures: $NA, including capital expenditures of
$NA
Industries: fruit processing, tourism
Industrial production growth rate: NA%
Electricity - production: 15 million kWh (1996)
Electricity - production by source:
fossil fuel: 100%
hydro: 0%
nuclear: 0%
other: 0% (1996)
Electricity - consumption: 15 million kWh (1996)
Electricity - exports: 0 kWh (1996)
Electricity - imports: 0 kWh (1996)
Agriculture - products: copra, citrus, pineapples,
tomatoes, beans, pawpaws, bananas, yams, taro,
coffee
Exports: $4.2 million (f.o.b., 1994 est.)
Exports - commodities: copra, fresh and canned
citrus fruit, coffee; fish; pearls and pearl shells;
clothing
Exports - partners: NZ 80%, Japan, Hong Kong
(1993)
Imports: $85 million (c.i.f., 1994)
Imports - commodities: foodstuffs, textiles, fuels,
timber, capital goods
Imports - partners: NZ 49%, Italy, Australia (1993)
Debt - external: $160 million (1994)
Economic aid - recipient: $13.1 million (1995);

Cook Islands (continued)

note - New Zealand furnishes the greater part

Currency: 1 New Zealand dollar (NZ$) = 100 cents

Exchange rates: New Zealand dollars (NZ$) per US$1 - 1.8560 (January 1999), 1.8629 (1998), 1.5083 (1997), 1.4543 (1996), 1.5235 (1995), 1.6844 (1994)

Fiscal year: 1 April - 31 March

Communications

Telephones: 4,180 (1994)

Telephone system:

domestic: the individual islands are connected by a combination of satellite earth stations, microwave systems, and VHF and HF radiotelephone; within the islands, service is provided by small exchanges connected to subscribers by open wire, cable, and fiber-optic cable

international: satellite earth station - 1 Intelsat (Pacific Ocean)

Radio broadcast stations: AM 1, FM 1, shortwave 1

Radios: 13,000 (1994 est.)

Television broadcast stations: 2 (in addition, eight low-power repeaters provide good coverage on the island of Rarotonga) (1997)

Televisions: 3,500 (1995 est.)

Transportation

Railways: 0 km

Highways:

total: 187 km

paved: 35 km

unpaved: 152 km (1980 est.)

Ports and harbors: Avarua, Avatiu

Merchant marine:

total: 1 cargo ship (1,000 GRT or over) totaling 2,310 GRT/2,181 DWT (1998 est.)

Airports: 7 (1998 est.)

Airports - with paved runways:

total: 1

1,524 to 2,437 m: 1 (1998 est.)

Airports - with unpaved runways:

total: 6

1,524 to 2,437 m: 3

914 to 1,523 m: 3 (1998 est.)

Military

Military - note: defense is the responsibility of New Zealand, in consultation with the Cook Islands and at its request

Transnational Issues

Disputes - international: none

Coral Sea Islands
(territory of Australia)

Geography

Location: Oceania, islands in the Coral Sea, northeast of Australia

Geographic coordinates: 18 00 S, 152 00 E

Map references: Oceania

Area:

total: less than 3 sq km

land: less than 3 sq km

water: 0 sq km

note: includes numerous small islands and reefs scattered over a sea area of about 1 million sq km, with the Willis Islets the most important

Area - comparative: NA

Land boundaries: 0 km

Coastline: 3,095 km

Maritime claims:

exclusive fishing zone: 200 nm

territorial sea: 3 nm

Climate: tropical

Terrain: sand and coral reefs and islands (or cays)

Elevation extremes:

lowest point: Pacific Ocean 0 m

highest point: unnamed location on Cato Island 6 m

Natural resources: NEGL

Land use:

arable land: 0%

permanent crops: 0%

permanent pastures: 0%

forests and woodland: 0%

other: 100% (mostly grass or scrub cover)

Irrigated land: 0 sq km (1993)

Natural hazards: occasional, tropical cyclones

Environment - current issues: no permanent fresh water resources

Environment - international agreements:

party to: NA

signed, but not ratified: NA

Geography - note: important nesting area for birds and turtles

People

Population: no indigenous inhabitants

note: there is a staff of three to four at the meteorological station

Government

Country name:

conventional long form: Coral Sea Islands Territory

conventional short form: Coral Sea Islands

Data code: CR

Dependency status: territory of Australia; administered from Canberra by the Department of the Environment, Sport and Territories

Legal system: the laws of Australia, where applicable, apply

Executive branch: administered from Canberra by the Department of the Environment, Sport and Territories

Diplomatic representation in the US: none (territory of Australia)

Diplomatic representation from the US: none (territory of Australia)

Flag description: the flag of Australia is used

Economy

Economy - overview: no economic activity

Communications

Communications - note: there are automatic weather relay stations on many of the isles and reefs relaying data to the mainland

Transportation

Ports and harbors: none; offshore anchorage only

Military

Military - note: defense is the responsibility of Australia; visited regularly by the Royal Australian Navy; Australia has control over the activities of visitors

Transnational Issues

Disputes - international: none

Costa Rica

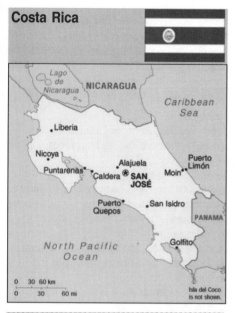

Background: Costa Rica declared its independence from Spain in 1821. After a turbulent beginning it inaugurated an era of peaceful democracy in 1889, subsequently interrupted only twice, by a dictatorial interlude in 1917-19 and an armed uprising in 1948. Increasing the role of the private sector while maintaining the government's social safety net and keeping under control the budget deficit, unemployment, and inflation are key current issues.

Geography

Location: Middle America, bordering both the Caribbean Sea and the North Pacific Ocean, between Nicaragua and Panama
Geographic coordinates: 10 00 N, 84 00 W
Map references: Central America and the Caribbean
Area:
total: 51,100 sq km
land: 50,660 sq km
water: 440 sq km
note: includes Isla del Coco
Area - comparative: slightly smaller than West Virginia
Land boundaries:
total: 639 km
border countries: Nicaragua 309 km, Panama 330 km
Coastline: 1,290 km
Maritime claims:
exclusive economic zone: 200 nm
territorial sea: 12 nm
Climate: tropical; dry season (December to April); rainy season (May to November)
Terrain: coastal plains separated by rugged mountains
Elevation extremes:
lowest point: Pacific Ocean 0 m
highest point: Cerro Chirripo 3,810 m
Natural resources: hydropower

Land use:
arable land: 6%
permanent crops: 5%
permanent pastures: 46%
forests and woodland: 31%
other: 12% (1993 est.)
Irrigated land: 1,200 sq km (1993 est.)
Natural hazards: occasional earthquakes, hurricanes along Atlantic coast; frequent flooding of lowlands at onset of rainy season; active volcanoes
Environment - current issues: deforestation, largely a result of the clearing of land for cattle ranching; soil erosion
Environment - international agreements:
party to: Biodiversity, Climate Change, Desertification, Endangered Species, Environmental Modification, Hazardous Wastes, Law of the Sea, Marine Dumping, Nuclear Test Ban, Ozone Layer Protection, Wetlands, Whaling
signed, but not ratified: Climate Change-Kyoto Protocol, Marine Life Conservation

People

Population: 3,674,490 (July 1999 est.)
Age structure:
0-14 years: 33% (male 622,260; female 593,720)
15-64 years: 62% (male 1,150,900; female 1,121,970)
65 years and over: 5% (male 85,526; female 100,114) (1999 est.)
Population growth rate: 1.89% (1999 est.)
Birth rate: 22.46 births/1,000 population (1999 est.)
Death rate: 4.16 deaths/1,000 population (1999 est.)
Net migration rate: 0.63 migrant(s)/1,000 population (1999 est.)
Sex ratio:
at birth: 1.05 male(s)/female
under 15 years: 1.05 male(s)/female
15-64 years: 1.03 male(s)/female
65 years and over: 0.85 male(s)/female
total population: 1.02 male(s)/female (1999 est.)
Infant mortality rate: 12.89 deaths/1,000 live births (1999 est.)
Life expectancy at birth:
total population: 76.04 years
male: 73.6 years
female: 78.61 years (1999 est.)
Total fertility rate: 2.76 children born/woman (1999 est.)
Nationality:
noun: Costa Rican(s)
adjective: Costa Rican
Ethnic groups: white (including mestizo) 96%, black 2%, Amerindian 1%, Chinese 1%
Religions: Roman Catholic 95%
Languages: Spanish (official), English spoken around Puerto Limon
Literacy:
definition: age 15 and over can read and write
total population: 94.8%
male: 94.7%
female: 95% (1995 est.)

Government

Country name:
conventional long form: Republic of Costa Rica
conventional short form: Costa Rica
local long form: Republica de Costa Rica
local short form: Costa Rica
Data code: CS
Government type: democratic republic
Capital: San Jose
Administrative divisions: 7 provinces (provincias, singular - provincia); Alajuela, Cartago, Guanacaste, Heredia, Limon, Puntarenas, San Jose
Independence: 15 September 1821 (from Spain)
National holiday: Independence Day, 15 September (1821)
Constitution: 9 November 1949
Legal system: based on Spanish civil law system; judicial review of legislative acts in the Supreme Court; has not accepted compulsory ICJ jurisdiction
Suffrage: 18 years of age; universal and compulsory
Executive branch:
chief of state: President Miguel Angel RODRIGUEZ (since 8 May 1998); First Vice President Astrid FISCHEL Volio (since 8 May 1998), Second Vice President Elizabeth ODIO Benito (since 8 May 1998); note - president is both the chief of state and head of government
head of government: President Miguel Angel RODRIGUEZ (since 8 May 1998); First Vice President Astrid FISCHEL Volio (since 8 May 1998), Second Vice President Elizabeth ODIO Benito (since 8 May 1998); note - president is both the chief of state and head of government
cabinet: Cabinet selected by the president
elections: president and vice presidents elected on the same ticket by popular vote for four-year terms; election last held 1 February 1998 (next to be held NA February 2002)
election results: Miguel Angel RODRIGUEZ elected president; percent of vote - Miguel Angel RODRIGUEZ (PUSC) 46.6%, Jose Miguel CORRALES (PLN) 44.6%
Legislative branch: unicameral Legislative Assembly or Asamblea Legislativa (57 seats; members are elected by direct popular vote to serve four-year terms)
elections: last held 1 February 1998 (next to be held NA February 2002)
election results: percent of vote by party - PUSC 41%, PLN 35%, minority parties 24%; seats by party - PUSC 27, PLN 23, minority parties 7
Judicial branch: Supreme Court (Corte Suprema), justices are elected for eight-year terms by the Legislative Assembly
Political parties and leaders: Social Christian Unity Party or PUSC [Miguel Angel RODRIGUEZ Echeverria]; National Liberation Party or PLN [Jose Miguel CORRALES Bolanos]; National Integration Party or PIN [Walter MUNOZ Cespedes]; National Independent Party or PNI [Jorge GONZALEZ Marten]; People United Party or PPU [Norma VARGAS

Costa Rica *(continued)*

Duarte]; National Christian Alliance Party or ANC [Alejandro MADRIGAL Benavides]; Democratic Force Party or PFD [Vladimir DE LA CRUZ de Lemos]; Libertarian Movement Party or PML [Federico MALAVASI Calvo]; Costa Rican Renovation Party or PRC [Sherman Thomas JACKSON]; New Democratic Party or PDN [Rodrigo GUTIERREZ Schwanhauser]; National Rescue Party or PRN [Marina VOLIO Brenes]; Democratic Party or PD [Alvaro GONZALEZ Espinoza]; Independent Party or PI [Yolanda GUTIERREZ Ventura]; Agriculture Labor Action [leader NA]

note: mainly a two-party system - PUSC and PLN; numerous small parties share less than 25% of population's support

Political pressure groups and leaders: Costa Rican Confederation of Democratic Workers or CCTD (Liberation Party affiliate); Confederated Union of Workers or CUT (Communist Party affiliate); Authentic Confederation of Democratic Workers or CATD (Communist Party affiliate); Chamber of Coffee Growers; National Association for Economic Development or ANFE; Free Costa Rica Movement or MCRL (rightwing militants); National Association of Educators or ANDE; Federation of Public Service Workers or FTSP

International organization participation: BCIE, CACM, ECLAC, FAO, G-77, IADB, IAEA, IBRD, ICAO, ICFTU, ICRM, IDA, IFAD, IFC, IFRCS, ILO, IMF, IMO, Inmarsat, Intelsat, Interpol, IOC, IOM, ISO, ITU, LAES, LAIA (observer), NAM (observer), OAS, OPANAL, OPCW, UN, UN Security Council (temporary), UNCTAD, UNESCO, UNIDO, UNU, UPU, WCL, WFTU, WHO, WIPO, WMO, WToO, WTrO

Diplomatic representation in the US:
chief of mission: Ambassador Jaime DAREMBLUM
chancery: 2114 S Street NW, Washington, DC 20008
telephone: [1] (202) 234-2945
FAX: [1] (202) 265-4795
consulate(s) general: Albuquerque, Atlanta, Chicago, Durham, Houston, Los Angeles, Miami, New Orleans, New York, Philadelphia, San Antonio, San Diego, San Francisco, San Juan (Puerto Rico), and Tampa
consulate(s): Austin

Diplomatic representation from the US:
chief of mission: Ambassador Thomas J. DODD
embassy: Pavas Road, San Jose
mailing address: APO AA 34020
telephone: [506] 220-3939
FAX: [506] 220-2305

Flag description: five horizontal bands of blue (top), white, red (double width), white, and blue, with the coat of arms in a white disk on the hoist side of the red band

Economy

Economy - overview: Costa Rica's basically stable economy depends on tourism, agriculture, and electronics exports. Poverty has been substantially reduced over the past 15 years and a strong social safety net has been put into place. Economic growth has rebounded from -0.9% in 1996 to 3% in 1997 and an estimated 5.5% in 1998. Inflation rose to 22.5% in 1995, dropped to 11.1% in 1997, and reached an estimated 12% in 1998. Unemployment appears moderate at 5.6%, but substantial underemployment continues. Furthermore, large government deficits - fueled by interest payments on the massive internal debt - have undermined efforts to maintain the quality of social services. Curbing inflation, reducing the deficit, and improving public sector efficiency remain key challenges to the government. President RODRIGUEZ has called for an increased economic role for the private sector, but political resistance to privatization has stalled much of his economic program.

GDP: purchasing power parity - $24 billion (1998 est.)

GDP - real growth rate: 5.5% (1998 est.)

GDP - per capita: purchasing power parity - $6,700 (1998 est.)

GDP - composition by sector:
agriculture: 15%
industry: 24%
services: 61% (1997)

Population below poverty line: NA%

Household income or consumption by percentage share:
lowest 10%: 1.3%
highest 10%: 34.7% (1996)

Inflation rate (consumer prices): 12% (1998 est.)

Labor force: 868,300

Labor force - by occupation: industry and commerce 23.3%, government and services 55.1%, agriculture 21.6% (1996 est.)

Unemployment rate: 5.6% (1998 est.); much underemployment

Budget:
revenues: $1.1 billion
expenditures: $1.34 billion, including capital expenditures of $110 million (1991 est.)

Industries: food processing, textiles and clothing, construction materials, fertilizer, plastic products

Industrial production growth rate: 10.5% (1992)

Electricity - production: 4.785 billion kWh (1996)

Electricity - production by source:
fossil fuel: 14.11%
hydro: 75.44%
nuclear: 0%
other: 10.45% (1996)

Electricity - consumption: 4.931 billion kWh (1996)

Electricity - exports: 44 million kWh (1996)

Electricity - imports: 190 million kWh (1996)

Agriculture - products: coffee, bananas, sugar, corn, rice, beans, potatoes; beef; timber

Exports: $3.9 billion (f.o.b., 1998)

Exports - commodities: manufactured products, coffee, bananas, textiles, sugar (1997)

Exports - partners: US, Benelux, Germany, Italy, Guatemala, El Salvador, Netherlands, UK, France (1997)

Imports: $4.5 billion (c.i.f., 1998)

Imports - commodities: raw materials, consumer goods, capital equipment, petroleum (1997)

Imports - partners: US, Japan, Mexico, Venezuela, Guatemala, Germany (1997)

Debt - external: $3.2 billion (October 1996 est.)

Economic aid - recipient: $107.1 million (1995)

Currency: 1 Costa Rican colon (C) = 100 centimos

Exchange rates: Costa Rican colones (C) per US$1 - 272.58 (January 1999), 257.23 (1998), 232.60 (1997), 207.69 (1996), 179.73 (1995), 157.07 (1994)

Fiscal year: calendar year

Communications

Telephones: 281,042 (1983 est.)

Telephone system: very good domestic telephone service
domestic: NA
international: connected to Central American Microwave System; satellite earth station - 1 Intelsat (Atlantic Ocean)

Radio broadcast stations: AM 71, FM 0, shortwave 13

Radios: NA

Television broadcast stations: 6 (in addition, there are 11 repeaters) (1997)

Televisions: 340,000 (1993 est.)

Transportation

Railways:
total: 950 km
narrow gauge: 950 km 1.067-m gauge (260 km electrified)

Highways:
total: 35,597 km
paved: 6,051 km
unpaved: 29,546 km (1997 est.)

Waterways: about 730 km, seasonally navigable

Pipelines: petroleum products 176 km

Ports and harbors: Caldera, Golfito, Moin, Puerto Limon, Puerto Quepos, Puntarenas

Merchant marine: none

Airports: 156 (1998 est.)

Airports - with paved runways:
total: 28
2,438 to 3,047 m: 2
1,524 to 2,437 m: 1
914 to 1,523 m: 18
under 914 m: 7 (1998 est.)

Airports - with unpaved runways:
total: 128
914 to 1,523 m: 29
under 914 m: 99 (1998 est.)

Military

Military branches: Coast Guard, Air Section, Ministry of Public Security Force (Fuerza Publica); note - during 1996, the Ministry of Public Security reorganized and eliminated the Civil Guard, Rural Assistance Guard, and Frontier Guards as separate entities; they are now under the Ministry and operate on a geographic command basis performing ground security, law enforcement, counternarcotics, and

Costa Rica *(continued)*

national security (border patrol) functions; the constitution prohibits armed forces
Military manpower - military age: 18 years of age
Military manpower - availability:
males age 15-49: 988,887 (1999 est.)
Military manpower - fit for military service:
males age 15-49: 662,827 (1999 est.)
Military manpower - reaching military age annually:
males: 36,751 (1999 est.)
Military expenditures - dollar figure: $55 million (1995)
Military expenditures - percent of GDP: 2% (1995)

Transnational Issues

Disputes - international: none
Illicit drugs: transshipment country for cocaine and heroin from South America; illicit production of cannabis on small, scattered plots

Cote d'Ivoire

Geography

Location: Western Africa, bordering the North Atlantic Ocean, between Ghana and Liberia
Geographic coordinates: 8 00 N, 5 00 W
Map references: Africa
Area:
total: 322,460 sq km
land: 318,000 sq km
water: 4,460 sq km
Area - comparative: slightly larger than New Mexico
Land boundaries:
total: 3,110 km
border countries: Burkina Faso 584 km, Ghana 668 km, Guinea 610 km, Liberia 716 km, Mali 532 km
Coastline: 515 km
Maritime claims:
continental shelf: 200 nm
exclusive economic zone: 200 nm
territorial sea: 12 nm
Climate: tropical along coast, semiarid in far north; three seasons - warm and dry (November to March), hot and dry (March to May), hot and wet (June to October)
Terrain: mostly flat to undulating plains; mountains in northwest
Elevation extremes:
lowest point: Gulf of Guinea 0 m
highest point: Mont Nimba 1,752 m
Natural resources: petroleum, diamonds, manganese, iron ore, cobalt, bauxite, copper
Land use:
arable land: 8%
permanent crops: 4%
permanent pastures: 41%
forests and woodland: 22%
other: 25% (1993 est.)
Irrigated land: 680 sq km (1993 est.)
Natural hazards: coast has heavy surf and no natural harbors; during the rainy season torrential flooding is possible

Environment - current issues: deforestation (most of the country's forests - once the largest in West Africa - have been cleared by the timber industry); water pollution from sewage and industrial and agricultural effluents
Environment - international agreements:
party to: Biodiversity, Climate Change, Desertification, Endangered Species, Hazardous Wastes, Law of the Sea, Marine Dumping, Nuclear Test Ban, Ozone Layer Protection, Ship Pollution, Tropical Timber 83, Tropical Timber 94, Wetlands
signed, but not ratified: none of the selected agreements

People

Population: 15,818,068 (July 1999 est.)
Age structure:
0-14 years: 47% (male 3,702,051; female 3,664,672)
15-64 years: 51% (male 4,154,440; female 3,952,999)
65 years and over: 2% (male 174,065; female 169,841) (1999 est.)
Population growth rate: 2.35% (1999 est.)
Birth rate: 41.76 births/1,000 population (1999 est.)
Death rate: 16.17 deaths/1,000 population (1999 est.)
Net migration rate: -2.08 migrant(s)/1,000 population (1999 est.)
note: after Liberia's civil war started in 1990, more than 350,000 refugees fled to Cote d'Ivoire and, by September 1998, according to the UNHCR, about 85,000 remain
Sex ratio:
at birth: 1.03 male(s)/female
under 15 years: 1.01 male(s)/female
15-64 years: 1.05 male(s)/female
65 years and over: 1.02 male(s)/female
total population: 1.03 male(s)/female (1999 est.)
Infant mortality rate: 94.17 deaths/1,000 live births (1999 est.)
Life expectancy at birth:
total population: 46.05 years
male: 44.48 years
female: 47.67 years (1999 est.)
Total fertility rate: 5.89 children born/woman (1999 est.)
Nationality:
noun: Ivorian(s)
adjective: Ivorian
Ethnic groups: Baoule 23%, Bete 18%, Senoufou 15%, Malinke 11%, Agni, Africans from other countries (mostly Burkinabe and Malians, about 3 million), non-Africans 130,000 to 330,000 (French 30,000 and Lebanese 100,000 to 300,000)
Religions: Muslim 60%, Christian 22%, indigenous 18% (some of these are also numbered among the Christians and Muslims)
Languages: French (official), 60 native dialects with Dioula the most widely spoken
Literacy:
definition: age 15 and over can read and write
total population: 48.5%

Cote d'Ivoire (continued)

male: 57%
female: 40%

Government

Country name:
conventional long form: Republic of Cote d'Ivoire
conventional short form: Cote d'Ivoire
local long form: Republique de Cote d'Ivoire
local short form: Cote d'Ivoire
former: Ivory Coast
Data code: IV
Government type: republic; multiparty presidential regime established 1960
Capital: Yamoussoukro
note: although Yamoussoukro has been the capital since 1983, Abidjan remains the administrative center; the US, like other countries, maintains its Embassy in Abidjan
Administrative divisions: 50 departments (departements, singular - departement); Abengourou, Abidjan, Aboisso, Adzope, Agboville, Agnibilekrou, Bangolo, Beoumi, Biankouma, Bondoukou, Bongouanou, Bouafle, Bouake, Bouna, Boundiali, Dabakala, Daloa, Danane, Daoukro, Dimbokro, Divo, Duekoue, Ferkessedougou, Gagnoa, Grand-Lahou, Guiglo, Issia, Katiola, Korhogo, Lakota, Man, Mankono, Mbahiakro, Odienne, Oume, Sakassou, San-Pedro, Sassandra, Seguela, Sinfra, Soubre, Tabou, Tanda, Tingrela, Tiassale, Touba, Toumodi, Vavoua, Yamoussoukro, Zuenoula
note: Cote d'Ivoire may have a new administrative structure consisting of 58 departments; the following additional departments have been reported but not yet confirmed by the US Board on Geographic Names (BGN); Adiake', Ale'pe', Dabon, Grand Bassam, Jacqueville, Tiebissou, Toulepleu, Bocanda
Independence: 7 August 1960 (from France)
National holiday: National Day, 7 August
Constitution: 3 November 1960; has been amended numerous times, last time July 1998
Legal system: based on French civil law system and customary law; judicial review in the Constitutional Chamber of the Supreme Court; has not accepted compulsory ICJ jurisdiction
Suffrage: 21 years of age; universal
Executive branch:
chief of state: President Henri Konan BEDIE (since 7 December 1993); note - succeeded to the presidency following the death of President Felix HOUPHOUET-BOIGNY, who had served continuously since November 1960
head of government: Prime Minister Daniel Kablan DUNCAN (since 10 December 1993)
cabinet: Council of Ministers appointed by the president
elections: president elected by popular vote for a five-year term; election last held 22 October 1995 (next to be held October 2000); prime minister appointed by the president
election results: Henri Konan BEDIE elected president; percent of vote - Henri Konan BEDIE 96%
Legislative branch: unicameral National Assembly or Assemblee Nationale (175 seats; members are elected by direct popular vote to serve five-year terms)
elections: elections last held 27 November 1995 (next to be held NA November 2000)
election results: percent of vote by party - NA; seats by party - PDCI 150, RDR 13, FPI 12
note: a Senate will be created in 2000
Judicial branch: Supreme Court (Cour Supreme)
Political parties and leaders: Democratic Party of the Cote d'Ivoire or PDCI [Henri Konan BEDIE]; Rally of the Republicans or RDR [Henriette DAGRI-DIABATE]; Ivorian Popular Front or FPI [Laurent GBAGBO]; Ivorian Worker's Party or PIT [Francis WODIE]; Ivorian Socialist Party or PSI [Morifere BAMBA]; over 20 smaller parties
International organization participation: ACCT, ACP, AfDB, CCC, ECA, ECOWAS, Entente, FAO, FZ, G-24, G-77, IAEA, IBRD, ICAO, ICC, ICFTU, ICRM, IDA, IFAD, IFC, IFRCS, ILO, IMF, IMO, Intelsat, Interpol, IOC, ISO (correspondent), ITU, MINURCA, NAM, OAU, OPCW, UN, UNCTAD, UNESCO, UNIDO, UPU, WADB, WAEMU, WCL, WFTU, WHO, WIPO, WMO, WToO, WTrO
Diplomatic representation in the US:
chief of mission: Ambassador Koffi Moise KOUMOUE-KOFFI
chancery: 2424 Massachusetts Avenue NW, Washington, DC 20008
telephone: [1] (202) 797-0300
Diplomatic representation from the US:
chief of mission: Ambassador George MU
embassy: 5 Rue Jesse Owens, Abidjan
mailing address: 01 B. P. 1712, Abidjan
telephone: [225] 21 09 79, 21 46 72
FAX: [225] 22 32 59
Flag description: three equal vertical bands of orange (hoist side), white, and green; similar to the flag of Ireland, which is longer and has the colors reversed - green (hoist side), white, and orange; also similar to the flag of Italy, which is green (hoist side), white, and red; design was based on the flag of France

Economy

Economy - overview: Cote d'Ivoire is among the world's largest producers and exporters of coffee, cocoa beans, and palm oil. Consequently, the economy is highly sensitive to fluctuations in international prices for these products and to weather conditions. Despite attempts by the government to diversify the economy, it is still largely dependent on agriculture and related activities, which engage roughly 68% of the population. After several years of lagging performance, the Ivorian economy began a comeback in 1994, due to the devaluation of the CFA franc and improved prices for cocoa and coffee, growth in nontraditional primary exports such as pineapples and rubber, limited trade and banking liberalization, offshore oil and gas discoveries, and generous external financing and debt rescheduling by multilateral lenders and France. The 50% devaluation of Franc Zone currencies on 12 January 1994 caused a one-time jump in the inflation rate to 26% in 1994, but the rate fell sharply in 1996-98. Moreover, government adherence to donor-mandated reforms led to a jump in growth to 6% annually in 1996-98. Growth may slow in 1999-2000 because of the difficulty of meeting the conditions of international donors and continued low prices of key exports.
GDP: purchasing power parity - $24.2 billion (1998 est.)
GDP - real growth rate: 6% (1998 est.)
GDP - per capita: purchasing power parity - $1,680 (1998 est.)
GDP - composition by sector:
agriculture: 31%
industry: 20%
services: 49% (1995)
Population below poverty line: NA%
Household income or consumption by percentage share:
lowest 10%: 2.8%
highest 10%: 28.5% (1988)
Inflation rate (consumer prices): 6% (1998 est.)
Labor force: NA
Unemployment rate: NA%
Budget:
revenues: $2.3 billion
expenditures: $2.6 billion, including capital expenditures of $640 million (1997 est.)
Industries: foodstuffs, beverages; wood products, oil refining, automobile assembly, textiles, fertilizer, construction materials, electricity
Industrial production growth rate: 15% (annual rate, first half 1998)
Electricity - production: 1.88 billion kWh (1996)
Electricity - production by source:
fossil fuel: 22%
hydro: 47%
nuclear: 0%
other: 31% (1996)
Electricity - consumption: 1.88 billion kWh (1996)
Electricity - exports: 0 kWh (1996)
Electricity - imports: 0 kWh (1996)
Agriculture - products: coffee, cocoa beans, bananas, palm kernels, corn, rice, manioc (tapioca), sweet potatoes, sugar, cotton, rubber; timber
Exports: $4.3 billion (f.o.b., 1998)
Exports - commodities: cocoa 36%, coffee, tropical woods, petroleum, cotton, bananas, pineapples, palm oil, cotton, fish
Exports - partners: Netherlands 17%, France 15%, Germany 7%, US 6%, Italy 5% (1997)
Imports: $2.5 billion (f.o.b., 1998)
Imports - commodities: food, consumer goods; capital goods, fuel, transport equipment
Imports - partners: France 28%, Nigeria 20%, US 6%, Italy 5%, Germany 4% (1997)
Debt - external: $16.8 billion (1998 est.)
Economic aid - recipient: ODA, $1 billion (1996 est.)
Currency: 1 Communaute Financiere Africaine franc (CFAF) = 100 centimes

Cote d'Ivoire *(continued)*

Exchange rates: CFA francs (CFAF) per US$1 - 560.01 (January 1999), 589.95 (1998), 583.67 (1997), 511.55 (1996), 499.15 (1995), 555.20 (1994)
Fiscal year: calendar year

Communications

Telephones: 200,000 (1988 est.)
Telephone system: well-developed by African standards but operating well below capacity
domestic: open-wire lines and microwave radio relay
international: satellite earth stations - 2 Intelsat (1 Atlantic Ocean and 1 Indian Ocean); 2 coaxial submarine cables
Radio broadcast stations: AM 71, FM 4, shortwave 13
Radios: NA
Television broadcast stations: 14 (1997)
Televisions: 810,000 (1993 est.)

Transportation

Railways:
total: 660 km
narrow gauge: 660 km 1.000-meter gauge; 25 km double track (1995 est.)
Highways:
total: 50,400 km
paved: 4,889 km
unpaved: 45,511 km (1996 est.)
Waterways: 980 km navigable rivers, canals, and numerous coastal lagoons
Ports and harbors: Abidjan, Aboisso, Dabou, San-Pedro
Merchant marine:
total: 1 oil tanker (1,000 GRT or over) totaling 1,200 GRT/1,500 DWT (1998 est.)
Airports: 36 (1998 est.)
Airports - with paved runways:
total: 7
over 3,047 m: 1
2,438 to 3,047 m: 2
1,524 to 2,437 m: 4 (1998 est.)
Airports - with unpaved runways:
total: 29
1,524 to 2,437 m: 8
914 to 1,523 m: 12
under 914 m: 9 (1998 est.)

Military

Military branches: Army, Navy, Air Force, paramilitary Gendarmerie, Republican Guard (includes Presidential Guard), Sapeur-Pompier (Military Fire Group)
Military manpower - military age: 18 years of age
Military manpower - availability:
males age 15-49: 3,677,627 (1999 est.)
Military manpower - fit for military service:
males age 15-49: 1,917,433 (1999 est.)
Military manpower - reaching military age annually:
males: 178,860 (1999 est.)

Military expenditures - dollar figure: $94 million (1998)
Military expenditures - percent of GDP: 0.9% (1996)

Transnational Issues

Disputes - international: none
Illicit drugs: illicit producer of cannabis, mostly for local consumption; minor transshipment point for Southwest and Southeast Asian heroin to Europe and occasionally to the US, and for Latin American cocaine destined for Europe

Croatia

Geography

Location: Southeastern Europe, bordering the Adriatic Sea, between Bosnia and Herzegovina and Slovenia
Geographic coordinates: 45 10 N, 15 30 E
Map references: Europe
Area:
total: 56,538 sq km
land: 56,410 sq km
water: 128 sq km
Area - comparative: slightly smaller than West Virginia
Land boundaries:
total: 2,197 km
border countries: Bosnia and Herzegovina 932 km, Hungary 329 km, Serbia and Montenegro 266 km (241 km with Serbia; 25 km with Montenegro), Slovenia 670 km
Coastline: 5,790 km (mainland 1,778 km, islands 4,012 km)
Maritime claims:
continental shelf: 200-m depth or to the depth of exploitation
territorial sea: 12 nm
Climate: Mediterranean and continental; continental climate predominant with hot summers and cold winters; mild winters, dry summers along coast
Terrain: geographically diverse; flat plains along Hungarian border, low mountains and highlands near Adriatic coast, coastline, and islands
Elevation extremes:
lowest point: Adriatic Sea 0 m
highest point: Dinara 1,830 m
Natural resources: oil, some coal, bauxite, low-grade iron ore, calcium, natural asphalt, silica, mica, clays, salt
Land use:
arable land: 21%
permanent crops: 2%
permanent pastures: 20%

Croatia (continued)

forests and woodland: 38%
other: 19% (1993 est.)
Irrigated land: 30 sq km (1993 est.)
Natural hazards: frequent and destructive earthquakes
Environment - current issues: air pollution (from metallurgical plants) and resulting acid rain is damaging the forests; coastal pollution from industrial and domestic waste; widespread casualties and destruction of infrastructure in border areas affected by civil strife
Environment - international agreements:
party to: Air Pollution, Biodiversity, Climate Change, Hazardous Wastes, Law of the Sea, Nuclear Test Ban, Ozone Layer Protection, Ship Pollution, Wetlands
signed, but not ratified: Air Pollution-Persistent Organic Pollutants, Air Pollution-Sulphur 94, Climate Change-Kyoto Protocol, Desertification
Geography - note: controls most land routes from Western Europe to Aegean Sea and Turkish Straits

People

Population: 4,676,865 (July 1999 est.)
Age structure:
0-14 years: 17% (male 404,761; female 383,088)
15-64 years: 68% (male 1,591,831; female 1,591,106)
65 years and over: 15% (male 272,219; female 433,860) (1999 est.)
Population growth rate: 0.1% (1999 est.)
Birth rate: 10.34 births/1,000 population (1999 est.)
Death rate: 11.14 deaths/1,000 population (1999 est.)
Net migration rate: 1.81 migrant(s)/1,000 population (1999 est.)
Sex ratio:
at birth: 1.07 male(s)/female
under 15 years: 1.06 male(s)/female
15-64 years: 1 male(s)/female
65 years and over: 0.63 male(s)/female
total population: 0.94 male(s)/female (1999 est.)
Infant mortality rate: 7.84 deaths/1,000 live births (1999 est.)
Life expectancy at birth:
total population: 74 years
male: 70.69 years
female: 77.52 years (1999 est.)
Total fertility rate: 1.52 children born/woman (1999 est.)
Nationality:
noun: Croat(s)
adjective: Croatian
Ethnic groups: Croat 78%, Serb 12%, Muslim 0.9%, Hungarian 0.5%, Slovenian 0.5%, others 8.1% (1991)
Religions: Catholic 76.5%, Orthodox 11.1%, Muslim 1.2%, Protestant 0.4%, others and unknown 10.8%
Languages: Serbo-Croatian 96%, other 4% (including Italian, Hungarian, Czech, Slovak, and German)
Literacy:
definition: age 15 and over can read and write

total population: 97%
male: 99%
female: 95% (1991 est.)

Government

Country name:
conventional long form: Republic of Croatia
conventional short form: Croatia
local long form: Republika Hrvatska
local short form: Hrvatska
Data code: HR
Government type: presidential/parliamentary democracy
Capital: Zagreb
Administrative divisions: 21 counties (zupanije, zupanija - singular): Bjelovar-Bilogora, City of Zagreb, Dubrovnik-Neretva, Istra, Karlovac, Koprivnica-Krizevci, Krapina-Zagorje, Lika-Senj, Medimurje, Osijek-Baranja, Pozega-Slavonia, Primorje-Gorski Kotar, Sibenik, Sisak-Moslavina, Slavonski Brod-Posavina, Split-Dalmatia, Varazdin, Virovitica-Podravina, Vukovar-Srijem, Zadar-Knin, Zagreb
note: there are two special self-governing districts (kotari, kotar - singular) under local Serb control: Glina, Knin
Independence: 25 June 1991 (from Yugoslavia)
National holiday: Statehood Day, 30 May (1990)
Constitution: adopted on 22 December 1990
Legal system: based on civil law system
Suffrage: 18 years of age; universal (16 years of age, if employed)
Executive branch:
chief of state: President Franjo TUDJMAN (since 30 May 1990)
head of government: Prime Minister Zlatko MATESA (since 7 November 1995); Deputy Prime Ministers Mate GRANIC (since 8 September 1992), Ivica KOSTOVIC (since 14 October 1993), Jure RADIC (since NA October 1994), Borislav SKEGRO (since 3 April 1993), and Ljerka MINTAS-HODAK (since November 1995)
cabinet: Council of Ministers appointed by the president
elections: president elected by popular vote for a five-year term; election last held 15 June 1997 (next to be held NA 2002); prime minister and deputy prime ministers appointed by the president
election results: President Franjo TUDJMAN reelected; percent of vote - Franjo TUDJMAN 61%, Zdravko TOMAC 21%, Vlado GOTOVAC 18%
Legislative branch: bicameral Assembly or Sabor consists of the House of Counties or Zupanijski Dom (68 seats - 63 directly elected by popular vote, 5 appointed by the president; members serve four-year terms) and House of Representatives or the Zastupnicki Dom (127 seats; members are directly elected by popular vote to serve four-year terms)
elections: House of Counties - last held 13 April 1997 (next to be held NA 2001); House of Representatives - last held 29 October 1995 (next to be held NA 1999)
election results: House of Counties - percent of vote

by party - NA; seats by party - HDZ 42, HDZ/HSS 11, HSS 2, IDS 2, SDP/PGS/HNS 2, SDP/HNS 2, HSLS/HSS/HNS 1, HSLS 1; note - in some districts certain parties ran as coalitions, while in others they ran alone; House of Representatives - percent of vote by party - HDZ 45.23%, HSS/IDS/HNS/HKDU/SBHS 18.26%, HSLS 11.55%, SDP 8.93%, HSP 5.01%; seats by party - HDZ 75, HSLS 12, HSS 10, SDP 10, IDS 4, HSP 4, HNS 2, SNS 2, HND 1, ASH 1, HKDU 1, SBHS 1, independents 4
Judicial branch: Supreme Court, judges appointed for eight-year terms by the Judicial Council of the Republic, which is elected by the House of Representatives; Constitutional Court, judges appointed for eight-year terms by the Judicial Council of the Republic, which is elected by the House of Representatives
Political parties and leaders: Croatian Democratic Union or HDZ [Franjo TUDJMAN, president]; Croatian Democratic Independents or HND [Stjepan MESIC, president]; Croatian Social Liberal Party or HSLS [Drazen BUDISA, president]; Liberal Party or LP [Vlado GOTOVAC, president]; Social Democratic Party of Croatia or SDP [Ivica RACAN]; Croatian Party of Rights or HSP [Anto DJAPIC]; Croatian Party of Rights 1861 or HSP 1861 [Dobroslav PARAGA]; Croatian Peasants' Party or HSS [Zlatko TOMCIC]; Croatian People's Party or HNS [Radimir CACIC, president]; Serbian National Party or SNS [Milan DJUKIC]; Action of the Social Democrats of Croatia or ASH [Silvije DEGEN]; Croatian Christian Democratic Union or HKDU [Marko VESELICA, president]; Istrian Democratic Assembly or IDS [Ivan JAKOVCIC]; Slanvonsko-Baranja Croatian Party or SBHS [Damir JURIC]; Primorje Gorski Kotar Alliance [leader NA]; Independent Democratic Serb Party or SDSS [Vojislav STANIMIROVIC]; Party of Democratic Action or SDA [Semso TANKOVIC]
Political pressure groups and leaders: NA
International organization participation: BIS (pending member), CCC, CE, CEI, EBRD, ECE, FAO, IADB, IAEA, IBRD, ICAO, ICFTU, ICRM, IDA, IFAD, IFC, IFRCS, IHO, ILO, IMF, IMO, Inmarsat, Intelsat, Interpol, IOC, IOM, ISO, ITU, NAM (observer), OAS (observer), OPCW, OSCE, UN, UNCTAD, UNESCO, UNIDO, UPU, WHO, WIPO, WMO, WToO, WTrO (applicant)
Diplomatic representation in the US:
chief of mission: Ambassador Miomir ZUZUL
chancery: 2343 Massachusetts Avenue NW, Washington, DC 20008
telephone: [1] (202) 588-5899
FAX: [1] (202) 588-8936
consulate(s) general: Cleveland, Los Angeles, New York
Diplomatic representation from the US:
chief of mission: Ambassador William D. MONTGOMERY
embassy: Andrije Hebranga 2, Zagreb
mailing address: use street address
telephone: [385] (1) 455-55-00
FAX: [385] (1) 455-85-85

Flag description: red, white, and blue horizontal bands with Croatian coat of arms (red and white checkered)

Economy

Economy - overview: Before the dissolution of Yugoslavia, the Republic of Croatia, after Slovenia, was the most prosperous and industrialized area, with a per capita output perhaps one-third above the Yugoslav average. Croatia faces considerable economic problems stemming from: the legacy of longtime communist mismanagement of the economy; damage during the internecine fighting to bridges, factories, power lines, buildings, and houses; the large refugee and displaced population, both Croatian and Bosnian; and the disruption of economic ties. Western aid and investment, especially in the tourist and oil industries, would help restore the economy. The government has been successful in some reform efforts - partially macroeconomic stabilization policies - and it has normalized relations with its creditors. Yet it still is struggling with privatization of large state enterprises and with bank reform. In 1998, Croatia made progress in reducing its current account deficit to about 8% of GDP from 12% the previous year. Economic growth continues to lag, however, and growing levels of inter-enterprise debt plague the domestic economy. Four commercial banks were put under government control and a major conglomerate is teetering on collapse.

GDP: purchasing power parity - $23.6 billion (1998 est.)

GDP - real growth rate: 3% (1998 est.)

GDP - per capita: purchasing power parity - $5,100 (1998 est.)

GDP - composition by sector:
agriculture: 12%
industry: 24%
services: 64% (1995 est.)

Population below poverty line: NA%

Household income or consumption by percentage share:
lowest 10%: NA%
highest 10%: NA%

Inflation rate (consumer prices): 5.4% (1998)

Labor force: 1.63 million (1998)

Labor force - by occupation: industry and mining 31.1%, agriculture 4.3%, government 19.1% (including education and health), other 45.5% (1993)

Unemployment rate: 18.6% (yearend 1998)

Budget:
revenues: $5.3 billion
expenditures: $6.3 billion, including capital expenditures of $78.5 million (1997 est.)

Industries: chemicals and plastics, machine tools, fabricated metal, electronics, pig iron and rolled steel products, aluminum, paper, wood products, construction materials, textiles, shipbuilding, petroleum and petroleum refining, food and beverages; tourism

Industrial production growth rate: 3.7% (1998 est.)

Electricity - production: 10.682 billion kWh (1996)

Electricity - production by source:
fossil fuel: 29.25%
hydro: 70.75%
nuclear: 0%
other: 0% (1996)

Electricity - consumption: 14.632 billion kWh (1996)

Electricity - exports: 1 billion kWh (1996)

Electricity - imports: 4.95 billion kWh (1996)

Agriculture - products: wheat, corn, sugar beets, sunflower seed, alfalfa, clover, olives, citrus, grapes, vegetables; livestock, dairy products

Exports: $4.5 billion (f.o.b., 1998)

Exports - commodities: machinery and transport equipment 13.6%, miscellaneous manufactures 27.6%, chemicals 14.2%, food and live animals 12.2%, raw materials 6.1%, fuels and lubricants 9.4%, beverages and tobacco 2.7% (1993)

Exports - partners: Germany 22%, Italy 21%, Slovenia 18% (1994)

Imports: $8.4 billion (c.i.f., 1998)

Imports - commodities: machinery and transport equipment 23.1%, fuels and lubricants 8.8%, food and live animals 9.0%, chemicals 14.2%, miscellaneous manufactured articles 16.0%, raw materials 3.5%, beverages and tobacco 1.4% (1993)

Imports - partners: Germany 21%, Italy 19%, Slovenia 10% (1994)

Debt - external: $8 billion (October 1998)

Economic aid - recipient: $NA

Currency: 1 Croatian kuna (HRK) = 100 lipas

Exchange rates: Croatian kuna per US$1 - 6.317 (January 1999), 6.362 (1998), 6.157 (1997), 5.434 (1996), 5.230 (1995), 5.996 (1994)

Fiscal year: calendar year

Communications

Telephones: 1.216 million (1993 est.)

Telephone system:
domestic: NA
international: no satellite earth stations

Radio broadcast stations: AM 14, FM 8, shortwave 0

Radios: 1.1 million

Television broadcast stations: 18 (in addition, there are 145 repeaters) (1997)

Televisions: 1.52 million (1992 est.)

Transportation

Railways:
total: 2,296 km
standard gauge: 2,296 km 1.435-m gauge (796 km electrified)
note: some lines remain inoperative or not in use; disrupted by territorial dispute (1997)

Highways:
total: 27,840 km
paved: 22,690 km (including 330 km of expressways)
unpaved: 5,150 km (1997 est.)

Waterways: 785 km perennially navigable; large sections of Sava blocked by downed bridges, silt, and debris

Pipelines: crude oil 670 km; petroleum products 20 km; natural gas 310 km (1992); note - under repair following territorial dispute

Ports and harbors: Dubrovnik, Dugi Rat, Omisalj, Ploce, Pula, Rijeka, Sibenik, Split, Vukovar (inland waterway port on Danube), Zadar

Merchant marine:
total: 64 ships (1,000 GRT or over) totaling 810,226 GRT/1,227,468 DWT
ships by type: bulk 15, cargo 26, chemical tanker 2, combination bulk 5, container 5, liquefied gas 1, multifunction large-load carrier 3, oil tanker 1, passenger 1, roll-on/roll-off cargo 2, short-sea passenger 3 (1998 est.)

Airports: 72 (1998 est.)

Airports - with paved runways:
total: 21
over 3,047 m: 2
2,438 to 3,047 m: 6
1,524 to 2,437 m: 2
914 to 1,523 m: 4
under 914 m: 7 (1998 est.)

Airports - with unpaved runways:
total: 51
1,524 to 2,437 m: 1
914 to 1,523 m: 8
under 914 m: 42 (1998 est.)

Heliports: 1 (1998 est.)

Military

Military branches: Ground Forces, Naval Forces, Air and Air Defense Forces, Frontier Guard, Home Guard

Military manpower - military age: 19 years of age

Military manpower - availability:
males age 15-49: 1,188,898 (1999 est.)

Military manpower - fit for military service:
males age 15-49: 943,719 (1999 est.)

Military manpower - reaching military age annually:
males: 33,722 (1999 est.)

Military expenditures - dollar figure: $950 million (1999)

Military expenditures - percent of GDP: 5% (1999)

Transnational Issues

Disputes - international: Eastern Slavonia, which was held by ethnic Serbs during the ethnic conflict, was returned to Croatian control by the UN Transitional Administration for Eastern Slavonia on 15 January 1998; Croatia and Italy made progress toward resolving a bilateral issue dating from World War II over property and ethnic minority rights; significant progress has been made with Slovenia toward resolving a maritime border dispute over direct access to the sea in the Adriatic; Serbia and Montenegro is disputing Croatia's claim to the Prevlaka Peninsula in southern Croatia because it controls the entrance to Boka Kotorska in Montenegro; Prevlaka is currently under observation by the UN military observer mission in Prevlaka (UNMOP)

Illicit drugs: transit point along the Balkan route for Southwest Asian heroin to Western Europe; a minor transit point for maritime shipments of South American cocaine bound for Western Europe

Cuba

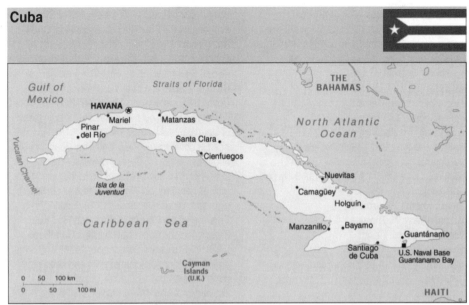

Introduction

Background: Fidel CASTRO led a rebel army to victory in 1959, and his guiding vision has defined Cuba's Communist revolution while his iron will has held the country together for more than four decades. CASTRO brought Cuba onto the world stage by inviting Soviet support in the 1960s, inciting revolutionary movements throughout Latin America and Africa in the 1970s, and sending his army to fight in Angola in the 1980s. At home, Havana provided Cubans with high levels of healthcare, education, and social security while suppressing the Roman Catholic Church and arresting political dissidents. Cuba is slowly recovering from severe economic recession following the withdrawal of former-Soviet subsidies, worth $4billion-$6 billion per year, in 1990.

Geography

Location: Caribbean, island between the Caribbean Sea and the North Atlantic Ocean, south of Florida
Geographic coordinates: 21 30 N, 80 00 W
Map references: Central America and the Caribbean
Area:
total: 110,860 sq km
land: 110,860 sq km
water: 0 sq km
Area - comparative: slightly smaller than Pennsylvania
Land boundaries:
total: 29 km
border countries: US Naval Base at Guantanamo Bay 29 km
note: Guantanamo Naval Base is leased by the US and thus remains part of Cuba
Coastline: 3,735 km
Maritime claims:
exclusive economic zone: 200 nm
territorial sea: 12 nm
Climate: tropical; moderated by trade winds; dry season (November to April); rainy season (May to October)
Terrain: mostly flat to rolling plains, with rugged hills and mountains in the southeast
Elevation extremes:
lowest point: Caribbean Sea 0 m
highest point: Pico Turquino 2,005 m
Natural resources: cobalt, nickel, iron ore, copper, manganese, salt, timber, silica, petroleum
Land use:
arable land: 24%
permanent crops: 7%
permanent pastures: 27%
forests and woodland: 24%
other: 18% (1993 est.)
Irrigated land: 9,100 sq km (1993 est.)
Natural hazards: the east coast is subject to hurricanes from August to October (in general, the country averages about one hurricane every other year); droughts are common
Environment - current issues: pollution of Havana Bay; overhunting threatens wildlife populations; deforestation
Environment - international agreements:
party to: Antarctic Treaty, Biodiversity, Climate Change, Desertification, Endangered Species, Environmental Modification, Hazardous Wastes, Law of the Sea, Marine Dumping, Ozone Layer Protection, Ship Pollution
signed, but not ratified: Antarctic-Environmental Protocol, Marine Life Conservation
Geography - note: largest country in Caribbean

People

Population: 11,096,395 (July 1999 est.)
Age structure:
0-14 years: 22% (male 1,236,899; female 1,172,560)
15-64 years: 69% (male 3,820,255; female 3,801,768)
65 years and over: 9% (male 496,772; female 568,141) (1999 est.)

Cuba *(continued)*

Population growth rate: 0.4% (1999 est.)
Birth rate: 12.9 births/1,000 population (1999 est.)
Death rate: 7.38 deaths/1,000 population (1999 est.)
Net migration rate: -1.52 migrant(s)/1,000 population (1999 est.)
Sex ratio:
at birth: 1.06 male(s)/female
under 15 years: 1.05 male(s)/female
15-64 years: 1 male(s)/female
65 years and over: 0.87 male(s)/female
total population: 1 male(s)/female (1999 est.)
Infant mortality rate: 7.81 deaths/1,000 live births (1999 est.)
Life expectancy at birth:
total population: 75.78 years
male: 73.41 years
female: 78.3 years (1999 est.)
Total fertility rate: 1.58 children born/woman (1999 est.)
Nationality:
noun: Cuban(s)
adjective: Cuban
Ethnic groups: mulatto 51%, white 37%, black 11%, Chinese 1%
Religions: nominally 85% Roman Catholic prior to CASTRO assuming power; Protestants, Jehovah's Witnesses, Jews, and Santeria are also represented
Languages: Spanish
Literacy:
definition: age 15 and over can read and write
total population: 95.7%
male: 96.2%
female: 95.3% (1995 est.)

Government

Country name:
conventional long form: Republic of Cuba
conventional short form: Cuba
local long form: Republica de Cuba
local short form: Cuba
Data code: CU
Government type: Communist state
Capital: Havana
Administrative divisions: 14 provinces (provincias, singular - provincia) and 1 special municipality* (municipio especial); Camaguey, Ciego de Avila, Cienfuegos, Ciudad de La Habana, Granma, Guantanamo, Holguin, Isla de la Juventud*, La Habana, Las Tunas, Matanzas, Pinar del Rio, Sancti Spiritus, Santiago de Cuba, Villa Clara
Independence: 20 May 1902 (from Spain 10 December 1898; administered by the US from 1898 to 1902)
National holiday: Rebellion Day, 26 July (1953); Liberation Day, 1 January (1959)
Constitution: 24 February 1976
Legal system: based on Spanish and American law, with large elements of Communist legal theory; does not accept compulsory ICJ jurisdiction
Suffrage: 16 years of age; universal
Executive branch:

chief of state: President of the Council of State and President of the Council of Ministers Fidel CASTRO Ruz (prime minister from February 1959 until 24 February 1976, when office was abolished; president since 2 December 1976); First Vice President of the Council of State and First Vice President of the Council of Ministers Gen. Raul CASTRO Ruz (since 2 December 1976); note - the president is both the chief of state and head of government
head of government: President of the Council of State and President of the Council of Ministers Fidel CASTRO Ruz (prime minister from February 1959 until 24 February 1976 when office was abolished; president since 2 December 1976); First Vice President of the Council of State and First Vice President of the Council of Ministers Gen. Raul CASTRO Ruz (since 2 December 1976); note - the president is both the chief of state and head of government
cabinet: Council of Ministers proposed by the president of the Council of State, appointed by the National Assembly
note: there is also a Council of State whose members are elected by the National Assembly
elections: president and vice president elected by the National Assembly; election last held 24 February 1998 (next election unscheduled)
election results: Fidel CASTRO Ruz elected president; percent of legislative vote - 100%; Raul CASTRO Ruz elected vice president; percent of legislative vote - 100%
Legislative branch: unicameral National Assembly of People's Power or Asemblea Nacional del Poder Popular (601 seats, elected directly from slates approved by special candidacy commissions; members serve five-year terms)
elections: last held 11 January 1998 (next to be held in 2003)
election results: percent of vote - PCC 94.39%; seats - PCC 601
Judicial branch: People's Supreme Court or Tribunal Supremo Popular (president, vice president, and other judges are elected by the National Assembly)
Political parties and leaders: only party - Cuban Communist Party or PCC [Fidel CASTRO Ruz, first secretary]
International organization participation: CCC, ECLAC, FAO, G-77, IAEA, ICAO, ICRM, IFAD, IFRCS, IHO, ILO, IMO, Inmarsat, Intelsat (nonsignatory user), Interpol, IOC, IOM (observer), ISO, ITU, LAES, LAIA, NAM, OAS (excluded from formal participation since 1962), OPCW, PCA, UN, UNCTAD, UNESCO, UNIDO, UPU, WCL, WFTU, WHO, WIPO, WMO, WToO, WTrO
Diplomatic representation in the US: none; note - Cuba has an Interests Section in the Swiss Embassy, headed by Principal Officer Fernando REMIREZ DE ESTENOZ; address: Cuban Interests Section, Swiss Embassy, 2630 16th Street NW, Washington, DC 20009; telephone: [1] (202) 797-8518
Diplomatic representation from the US: none;

note - the US has an Interests Section in the Swiss Embassy, headed by Principal Officer Michael G. KOZAK; address: USINT, Swiss Embassy, Calzada between L and M Streets, Vedado Seccion, Havana; telephone: 33-3551 through 3559 and 33-3543 through 3547 (operator assistance required); FAX: 33-3700; protecting power in Cuba is Switzerland
Flag description: five equal horizontal bands of blue (top and bottom) alternating with white; a red equilateral triangle based on the hoist side bears a white, five-pointed star in the center

Economy

Economy - overview: The state plays the primary role in the economy and controls practically all foreign trade. The government has undertaken several reforms in recent years to stem excess liquidity, increase labor incentives, and alleviate serious shortages of food, consumer goods, and services. The liberalized agricultural markets introduced in October 1994, at which state and private farmers sell above-quota production at unrestricted prices, have broadened legal consumption alternatives and reduced black market prices. Government efforts to lower subsidies to unprofitable enterprises and to shrink the money supply caused the semi-official exchange rate for the Cuban peso to move from a peak of 120 to the dollar in the summer of 1994 to 21 to the dollar by yearend 1998. New taxes introduced in 1996 helped drive down the number of self-employed workers from 208,000 in January 1996 to 155,000 by July 1998. Havana announced in 1995 that GDP declined by 35% during 1989-93, the result of lost Soviet aid and domestic inefficiencies. The drop in GDP apparently halted in 1994, when Cuba reported 0.7% growth, followed by increases of 2.5% in 1995 and 7.8% in 1996. Growth slowed again in 1997 and 1998 to 2.5% and 1.2% respectively. Export earnings declined 22% in 1998, to $1.4 billion, the result of lower sugar export volume and lower world prices for nickel and sugar. Import expenditures also fell 15% to $3.0 billion, in part due to lower world oil prices. Tourism and remittances play a key role in foreign currency earnings. Living standards for the average Cuban remain at a depressed level compared with 1990.
GDP: purchasing power parity - $17.3 billion (1998 est.)
GDP - real growth rate: 1.2% (1998 est.)
GDP - per capita: purchasing power parity - $1,560 (1998 est.)
GDP - composition by sector:
agriculture: 7.4%
industry: 36.5%
services: 56.1% (1997 est.)
Population below poverty line: NA%
Household income or consumption by percentage share:
lowest 10%: NA%
highest 10%: NA%
Inflation rate (consumer prices): NA%

Cuba (continued)

Labor force: 4.5 million economically active population (1996 est.)
note: state sector 76%, non-state sector 24% (1996 est.)
Labor force - by occupation: services and government 30%, industry 22%, agriculture 20%, commerce 11%, construction 10%, transportation and communications 7% (June 1990)
Unemployment rate: 6.8% (1997 est.)
Budget:
revenues: $12.3 billion
expenditures: $13 billion , including capital expenditures of $NA (1998 est.)
Industries: sugar, petroleum, food, tobacco, textiles, chemicals, paper and wood products, metals (particularly nickel), cement, fertilizers, consumer goods, agricultural machinery
Industrial production growth rate: 6% (1995 est.)
Electricity - production: 14.1 billion kWh (1997)
Electricity - production by source:
fossil fuel: 98.96%
hydro: 1.04%
nuclear: 0%
other: 0% (1996)
Electricity - consumption: 14.1 billion kWh (1997)
Electricity - exports: 0 kWh (1996)
Electricity - imports: 0 kWh (1996)
Agriculture - products: sugarcane, tobacco, citrus, coffee, rice, potatoes, beans; livestock
Exports: $1.4 billion (f.o.b., 1998 est.)
Exports - commodities: sugar, nickel, tobacco, shellfish, medical products, citrus, coffee
Exports - partners: Russia 27%, Canada 18%, Spain 8% (1998 est.)
Imports: $3 billion (c.i.f., 1998 est.)
Imports - commodities: petroleum, food, machinery, chemicals
Imports - partners: Spain 17%, France 9%, Canada 9% (1998 est.)
Debt - external: $10.1 billion (convertible currency, 1997); another $20 billion owed to Russia (1997)
Economic aid - recipient: $46 million (1997 est.)
Currency: 1 Cuban peso (Cu$) = 100 centavos
Exchange rates: Cuban pesos (Cu$) per US$1 - 1.0000 (nonconvertible, official rate, linked to the US dollar)
Fiscal year: calendar year

Communications

Telephones: 229,000
Telephone system: among the world's least developed telephone systems
domestic: NA
international: satellite earth station - 1 Intersputnik (Atlantic Ocean region)
Radio broadcast stations: AM 150, FM 5, shortwave 1
Radios: 2.14 million (1993 est.)
Television broadcast stations: 58 (1997)
Televisions: 2.5 million (1993 est.)

Transportation

Railways:
total: 4,807 km
standard gauge: 4,807 km 1.435-m gauge (147 km electrified)
note: a large amount of track is in private use by sugar plantations
Highways:
total: 60,858 km
paved: 29,820 km (including 638 km of expressway)
unpaved: 31,038 km (1997 est.)
Waterways: 240 km
Ports and harbors: Cienfuegos, Havana, Manzanillo, Mariel, Matanzas, Nuevitas, Santiago de Cuba
Merchant marine:
total: 18 ships (1,000 GRT or over) totaling 89,091 GRT/125,463 DWT
ships by type: bulk 1, cargo 9, liquefied gas tanker 1, oil tanker 2, refrigerated cargo 5 (1998 est.)
Airports: 170 (1998 est.)
Airports - with paved runways:
total: 77
over 3,047 m: 7
2,438 to 3,047 m: 9
1,524 to 2,437 m: 14
914 to 1,523 m: 11
under 914 m: 36 (1998 est.)
Airports - with unpaved runways:
total: 93
914 to 1,523 m: 32
under 914 m: 61 (1998 est.)

Military

Military branches: Revolutionary Armed Forces (FAR) includes ground forces, Revolutionary Navy (MGR), Air and Air Defense Force (DAAFAR), Territorial Troops Militia (MTT), and Youth Labor Army (EJT); the Border Guard (TGF) is controlled by the Interior Ministry
Military manpower - military age: 17 years of age
Military manpower - availability:
males age 15-49: 3,068,140
females age 15-49: 3,014,686 (1999 est.)
Military manpower - fit for military service:
males age 15-49: 1,900,893
females age 15-49: 1,862,411 (1999 est.)
Military manpower - reaching military age annually:
males: 76,328
females: 72,551 (1999 est.)
Military expenditures - dollar figure: $NA
Military expenditures - percent of GDP: roughly 4% (1995 est.)
Military - note: Moscow, for decades the key military supporter and supplier of Cuba, cut off almost all military aid by 1993

Transnational Issues

Disputes - international: US Naval Base at Guantanamo Bay is leased to US and only mutual agreement or US abandonment of the area can terminate the lease
Illicit drugs: territory serves as transshipment zone for cocaine bound for the US and Europe

Cyprus

Geography

Location: Middle East, island in the Mediterranean Sea, south of Turkey

Geographic coordinates: 35 00 N, 33 00 E

Map references: Middle East

Area:
total: 9,250 sq km (note - of which 3,355 sq km are in the Turkish Cypriot area)
land: 9,240 sq km
water: 10 sq km

Area - comparative: about 0.6 times the size of Connecticut

Land boundaries: 0 km

Coastline: 648 km

Maritime claims:
continental shelf: 200-m depth or to the depth of exploitation
territorial sea: 12 nm

Climate: temperate, Mediterranean with hot, dry summers and cool, wet winters

Terrain: central plain with mountains to north and south; scattered but significant plains along southern coast

Elevation extremes:
lowest point: Mediterranean Sea 0 m
highest point: Olympus 1,952 m

Natural resources: copper, pyrites, asbestos, gypsum, timber, salt, marble, clay earth pigment

Land use:
arable land: 12%
permanent crops: 5%
permanent pastures: 0%
forests and woodland: 13%
other: 70% (1993 est.)

Irrigated land: 390 sq km (1993 est.)

Natural hazards: moderate earthquake activity

Environment - current issues: water resource problems (no natural reservoir catchments, seasonal disparity in rainfall; sea water intrusion to island's largest aquifer; increased salination in the north); water pollution from sewage and industrial wastes; coastal degradation; loss of wildlife habitats from urbanization

Environment - international agreements:
party to: Air Pollution, Biodiversity, Climate Change, Endangered Species, Environmental Modification, Hazardous Wastes, Law of the Sea, Marine Dumping, Nuclear Test Ban, Ozone Layer Protection, Ship Pollution
signed, but not ratified: Air Pollution-Persistent Organic Pollutants

People

Population: 754,064 (July 1999 est.)

Age structure:
0-14 years: 24% (male 92,626; female 88,127)
15-64 years: 65% (male 249,083; female 244,750)
65 years and over: 11% (male 34,612; female 44,866) (1999 est.)

Population growth rate: 0.67% (1999 est.)

Birth rate: 13.64 births/1,000 population (1999 est.)

Death rate: 7.42 deaths/1,000 population (1999 est.)

Net migration rate: 0.44 migrant(s)/1,000 population (1999 est.)

Sex ratio:
at birth: 1.05 male(s)/female
under 15 years: 1.05 male(s)/female
15-64 years: 1.02 male(s)/female
65 years and over: 0.77 male(s)/female
total population: 1 male(s)/female (1999 est.)

Infant mortality rate: 7.68 deaths/1,000 live births (1999 est.)

Life expectancy at birth:
total population: 77.1 years
male: 74.91 years
female: 79.39 years (1999 est.)

Total fertility rate: 2 children born/woman (1999 est.)

Nationality:
noun: Cypriot(s)
adjective: Cypriot

Ethnic groups: Greek 78% (99.5% of the Greeks live in the Greek Cypriot area; 0.5% of the Greeks live in the Turkish Cypriot area), Turkish 18% (1.3% of the Turks live in the Greek Cypriot area; 98.7% of the Turks live in the Turkish Cypriot area), other 4% (99.2% of the other ethnic groups live in the Greek Cypriot area; 0.8% of the other ethnic groups live in the Turkish Cypriot area)

Religions: Greek Orthodox 78%, Muslim 18%, Maronite, Armenian Apostolic, and other 4%

Languages: Greek, Turkish, English

Literacy:
definition: age 15 and over can read and write
total population: 94%
male: 98%
female: 91% (1987 est.)

Government

Country name:
conventional long form: Republic of Cyprus
conventional short form: Cyprus
note: the Turkish Cypriot area refers to itself as the "Turkish Republic of Northern Cyprus" (TRNC)

Data code: CY

Government type: republic
note: a disaggregation of the two ethnic communities inhabiting the island began after the outbreak of communal strife in 1963; this separation was further solidified following the Turkish intervention in July 1974 following a Greek junta-based coup attempt, which gave the Turkish Cypriots de facto control in the north; Greek Cypriots control the only internationally recognized government; on 15 November 1983 Turkish Cypriot "President" Rauf DENKTASH declared independence and the formation of a "Turkish Republic of Northern Cyprus" (TRNC), which has been recognized only by Turkey; both sides publicly call for the resolution of intercommunal differences and creation of a new federal system of government

Capital: Nicosia
note: the Turkish Cypriot area's capital is Lefkosa (Nicosia)

Administrative divisions: 6 districts; Famagusta, Kyrenia, Larnaca, Limassol, Nicosia, Paphos; note - Turkish Cypriot area's administrative divisions include Kyrenia, all but a small part of Famagusta, and small parts of Lefkosa (Nicosia) and Larnaca

Independence: 16 August 1960 (from UK)
note: Turkish Cypriot area proclaimed self-rule on 13 February 1975 from Republic of Cyprus

National holiday: Independence Day, 1 October; note - Turkish Cypriot area celebrates 15 November as Independence Day

Constitution: 16 August 1960; negotiations to create the basis for a new or revised constitution to govern the island and to better relations between Greek and Turkish Cypriots have been held intermittently; in 1975 Turkish Cypriots created their own constitution and governing bodies within the "Turkish Federated State of Cyprus," which was renamed the "Turkish Republic of Northern Cyprus" in 1983; a new constitution for the Turkish Cypriot area

Cyprus (continued)

passed by referendum on 5 May 1985

Legal system: based on common law, with civil law modifications

Suffrage: 18 years of age; universal

Executive branch:

chief of state: President Glafcos CLERIDES (since 28 February 1993); note - the president is both the chief of state and head of government; post of vice president is currently vacant; under the 1960 constitution, the post is reserved for a Turkish Cypriot

head of government: President Glafcos CLERIDES (since 28 February 1993); note - the president is both the chief of state and head of government; post of vice president is currently vacant; under the 1960 constitution, the post is reserved for a Turkish Cypriot

cabinet: Council of Ministers appointed jointly by the president and vice president

elections: president elected by popular vote for five-year terms; election last held 15 February 1998 (next to be held NA February 2003)

election results: Glafcos CLERIDES elected president; percent of vote - Glafcos CLERIDES 50.8%, George IAKOVOU 49.2%

note: Rauf R. DENKTASH has been "president" of the Turkish Cypriot area since 13 February 1975 ("president" elected by popular vote for a five-year term); elections last held 15 and 22 April 1995 (next to be held NA April 2000); results - Rauf R. DENKTASH 62.5%, Dervis EROGLU 37.5%; Dervis EROGLU has been "prime minister" of the Turkish Cypriot area since 16 August 1996; there is a Council of Ministers (cabinet) in the Turkish Cypriot area

Legislative branch: unicameral - Greek Cypriot area: House of Representatives or Vouli Antiprosopon (80 seats; 56 assigned to the Greek Cypriots. 24 to Turkish Cypriots; note - only those assigned to Greek Cypriots are filled; members are elected by popular vote to serve five-year terms); Turkish Cypriot area: Assembly of the Republic or Cumhuriyet Meclisi (50 seats; members are elected by popular vote to serve five-year terms)

elections: Greek area: last held 26 May 1996 (next to be held May 2001); Turkish area: last held 6 December 1998 (next to be held December 2003)

election results: Greek area: House of Representatives - percent of vote by party - DISY 34.5%, AKEL (Communist) 33.0%, DIKO 16.4%, EDEK 8.1%, KED 3.7%, others 4.3%; seats by party - DISY 20, AKEL (Communist) 19, DIKO 10, EDEK 5, KED 2; Turkish area: Assembly of the Republic - percent of vote by party - UBP 40.3%, DP 22.6%, TKP 15.4%, CTP 13.4%, UDP 4.6%, YBH 2.5%, BP 1.2%; seats by party - UBP 24, DP 13, TKP 7, CTP 6

Judicial branch: Supreme Court, judges are appointed by the Supreme Council of Judicature

note: there is also a Supreme Court in the Turkish Cypriot area

Political parties and leaders: Greek Cypriot area: Restorative Party of the Working People or AKEL (Communist Party) [Dimitrios CHRISTOFIAS]; Democratic Rally or DISY [Nikos ANASTASIADHIS]; Democratic Party or DIKO [Spyros KYPRIANOU];

United Democratic Union of Cyprus or EDEK [Vassos LYSSARIDIS]; Eurodemocratic Renewal Movement [Alexis GALANOS]; United Democrats Movement or EDI (formerly Free Democrats Movement or KED) [George VASSILIOU]; New Horizons [Nikolaos KOUTSOU, secretary general]; Ecologists [Yeoryios PERDHIKIS]; Turkish Cypriot area: National Unity Party or UBP [Dervis EROGLU]; Communal Liberation Party or TKP [Mustafa AKINCI]; Republican Turkish Party or CTP [Mehmet ALI TALAT]; Unity and Sovereignty Party or BEP [Arif Salih KIRDAG]; Democratic Party or DP [Serdar DENKTASH]; National Birth Party or UDP [Enuer EMIN]; Patriotic Unity Movement or YBH [Alpay DURDURAN]; Our Party or BP [Okyay SADIKOGLU]

Political pressure groups and leaders: Pan-Cyprian Labor Federation or PEO (Communist controlled); Confederation of Cypriot Workers or SEK (pro-West); Federation of Turkish Cypriot Labor Unions or Turk-Sen; Confederation of Revolutionary Labor Unions or Dev-Is

International organization participation: C, CCC, CE, EBRD, ECE, EU (applicant), FAO, G-77, IAEA, IBRD, ICAO, ICC, ICFTU, IDA, IFAD, IFC, IFRCS (associate), IHO, ILO, IMF, IMO, Inmarsat, Intelsat, Interpol, IOC, IOM, ISO, ITU, NAM, OAS (observer), OPCW, OSCE, PCA, UN, UNCTAD, UNESCO, UNIDO, UPU, WCL, WFTU, WHO, WIPO, WMO, WToO, WTrO

Diplomatic representation in the US:

chief of mission: Ambassador Erato KOZAKOU-MARCOULLIS

chancery: 2211 R Street NW, Washington, DC 20008

telephone: [1] (202) 462-5772

FAX: [1] (202) 483-6710

consulate(s) general: New York

note: representative of the Turkish Cypriot area in the US is Ahmet ERDENGIZ; office at 1667 K Street NW, Washington, DC; telephone [1] (202) 887-6198

Diplomatic representation from the US:

chief of mission: Ambassador Kenneth C. BRILL

embassy: corner of Metochiou and Ploutarchou Streets, Engomi, Nicosia

mailing address: P. O. Box 4536, FPO AE 09836

telephone: [357] (2) 776400

FAX: [357] (2) 780944

Flag description: white with a copper-colored silhouette of the island (the name Cyprus is derived from the Greek word for copper) above two green crossed olive branches in the center of the flag; the branches symbolize the hope for peace and reconciliation between the Greek and Turkish communities

note: the Turkish Cypriot flag has a horizontal red stripe at the top and bottom between which is a red crescent and red star on a white field

Economy

Economy - overview: Economic affairs are dominated by the division of the country into the southern (Greek) area controlled by the Cyprus Government and the northern Turkish

Cypriot-administered area. The Greek Cypriot economy is prosperous but highly susceptible to external shocks. Erratic growth rates in the 1990s reflect the economy's vulnerability to swings in tourist arrivals, caused by political instability on the island and fluctuations in economic conditions in Western Europe. Economic policy in the south is focused on meeting the criteria for admission to the EU. As in the Turkish sector, water shortage is a growing problem, and several desalination plants are planned. The Turkish Cypriot economy has about one-fifth the population and one-third the per capita GDP of the south. Because it is recognized only by Turkey, it has had much difficulty arranging foreign financing, and foreign firms have hesitated to invest there. The economy remains heavily dependent on agriculture and government service, which together employ about half of the work force. Moreover, the small, vulnerable economy has suffered because the Turkish lira is legal tender. To compensate for the economy's weakness, Turkey provides direct and indirect aid to nearly every sector, e.g. tourism, education, and industry.

GDP: purchasing power parity - $10 billion (1997 est.)

GDP - real growth rate: 2.3% (1997 est.)

GDP - per capita: purchasing power parity - $13,000 (1997 est.)

GDP - composition by sector: Greek Cypriot area: agriculture 4.4%; industry 22.4%; services 73.2% (1996); Turkish Cypriot area: agriculture 10%; industry 24.6%; services 65.4% (1995)

Population below poverty line: NA%

Household income or consumption by percentage share:

lowest 10%: NA%

highest 10%: NA%

Inflation rate (consumer prices): Greek Cypriot area: 2.3% (1998 est.); Turkish Cypriot area: 87.5% (1997 est.)

Labor force: Greek Cypriot area: 299,700; Turkish Cypriot area: 76,500 (1996)

Labor force - by occupation: Greek Cypriot area: services 62%, industry 25%, agriculture 13% (1995); Turkish Cypriot area: services 66%, industry 11%, agriculture 23% (1995)

Unemployment rate: Greek Cypriot area: 3.3% (1998 est.); Turkish Cypriot area: 6.4% (1996)

Budget:

revenues: Greek Cypriot area - $2.9 billion, Turkish Cypriot area - $171 million

expenditures: Greek Cypriot area - $3.4 billion, including capital expenditures of $345 million, Turkish Cypriot area - $306 million, including capital expenditures of $56.8 million (1997 est.)

Industries: food, beverages, textiles, chemicals, metal products, tourism, wood products

Industrial production growth rate: Greek Cypriot area: -4% (1996); Turkish Cypriot area: 5.1% (1995)

Electricity - production: 2.2 billion kWh (1996)

Electricity - production by source:

fossil fuel: 100%

Cyprus (continued)

hydro: 0%
nuclear: 0%
other: 0% (1996)
Electricity - consumption: 2.2 billion kWh (1996)
Electricity - exports: 0 kWh (1996)
Electricity - imports: 0 kWh (1996)
Agriculture - products: potatoes, citrus, vegetables, barley, grapes, olives, vegetables
Exports: Greek Cypriot area: $1.2 billion (f.o.b., 1998 est.); Turkish Cypriot area: $70.5 million (f.o.b., 1996)
Exports - commodities: Greek Cypriot area: citrus, potatoes, grapes, wine, cement, clothing and shoes (1996); Turkish Cypriot area: citrus, potatoes, textiles (1996)
Exports - partners: Greek Cypriot area: Russia 19.1%, Bulgaria 16.4%, UK 11.3%, Greece 6.3%, Germany 4.8%; Turkish Cypriot area: Turkey 48.2%, UK 21.3%, other EU 13.7% (1997)
Imports: Greek Cypriot area: $3.8 billion (f.o.b., 1998 est.); Turkish Cypriot area: $318.4 million (f.o.b., 1996)
Imports - commodities: Greek Cypriot area: consumer goods, petroleum and lubricants, food and feed grains, machinery (1996); Turkish Cypriot area: food, minerals, chemicals, machinery (1996)
Imports - partners: Greek Cypriot area: US 17.8%, UK 11.9%, Italy 9.7%, Germany 7.5%, Greece 7.6% (1997); Turkish Cypriot area: Turkey 55.3%, UK 13.8%, other EU 11.6% (1997)
Debt - external: Greek Cypriot area: $1.56 billion (1997)
Economic aid - recipient: Greek Cypriot area - $187 million in grants (1990-94); Turkish Cypriot area - $700 million from Turkey in grants and loans (1990-97) that are usually forgiven
Currency: Greek Cypriot area: 1 Cypriot pound (£C) = 100 cents; Turkish Cypriot area: 1 Turkish lira (TL) = 100 kurus
Exchange rates: Cypriot pounds per US1$ - 0.5013 (January 1999), 0.5170 (1998), 0.5135 (1997), 0.4663 (1996), 0.4522 (1995), 0.4915 (1994); Turkish liras (TL) per US$1 - 331,400 (January 1999), 260,724 (1998), 151,865 (1997), 81,405 (1996), 45,845.1 (1995), 29,608.7 (1994)
Fiscal year: calendar year

Communications

Telephones: Greek Cypriot area: 367,000 (1996 est.); Turkish Cypriot area: 80,000 (1996 est.)
Telephone system: excellent in both the Greek Cypriot and Turkish Cypriot areas
domestic: open wire, fiber-optic cable, and microwave radio relay
international: tropospheric scatter; 3 coaxial and 5 fiber-optic submarine cables; satellite earth stations - 3 Intelsat (1 Atlantic Ocean and 2 Indian Ocean), 2 Eutelsat, 2 Intersputnik, and 1 Arabsat
Radio broadcast stations: Greek Cypriot area: AM 4, FM 36, shortwave 1, Turkish Cypriot area: AM 2, FM 6, shortwave 0
Radios: Greek Cypriot area: 500,000 (1996 est.);

Turkish Cypriot area: 130,000 (1996 est.)
Television broadcast stations: Greek Cypriot area: 7 (in addition, there are 35 low-power repeaters) (1997); Turkish Cypriot area: 3 (in addition, there are 4 repeaters) (1997)
Televisions: Greek Cypriot area: 300,000 (1996 est.); Turkish Cypriot area: 90,000 (1996 est.)

Transportation

Railways: 0 km
Highways:
total: Greek Cypriot area: 10,415 km; Turkish Cypriot area: 2,350 km
paved: Greek Cypriot area: 5,947 km; Turkish Cypriot area: 1,370 km
unpaved: Greek Cypriot area: 4,468 km; Turkish Cypriot area: 980 km (1996 est.)
Ports and harbors: Famagusta, Kyrenia, Larnaca, Limassol, Paphos, Vasilikos Bay
Merchant marine:
total: 1,469 ships (1,000 GRT or over) totaling 23,362,067 GRT/36,945,331 DWT
ships by type: barge carrier 2, bulk 430, cargo 530, chemical tanker 23, combination bulk 42, combination ore/oil 11, container 141, liquefied gas tanker 6, oil tanker 152, passenger 7, refrigerated cargo 58, roll-on/roll-off cargo 49, short-sea passenger 14, specialized tanker 3, vehicle carrier 1
note: a flag of convenience registry; includes ships from 37 countries among which are Greece 611, Germany 129, Russia 49, Latvia 278, Netherlands 20, Japan 28, Cuba 16, China 15, Hong Kong 13, and Poland 15 (1998 est.)
Airports: 15 (1998 est.)
Airports - with paved runways:
total: 12
2,438 to 3,047 m: 7
1,524 to 2,437 m: 1
914 to 1,523 m: 3
under 914 m: 1 (1998 est.)
Airports - with unpaved runways:
total: 3
914 to 1,523 m: 1
under 914 m: 2 (1998 est.)
Heliports: 4 (1998 est.)

Military

Military branches: Greek Cypriot area: Greek Cypriot National Guard (GCNG; includes air and naval elements), Hellenic Forces Regiment on Cyprus (ELDYK), Greek Cypriot Police; Turkish Cypriot area: Turkish Cypriot Security Force (TCSF), Turkish Forces Regiment on Cyprus (KTKA), Turkish mainland army units
Military manpower - military age: 18 years of age
Military manpower - availability:
males age 15-49: 194,337 (1999 est.)
Military manpower - fit for military service:
males age 15-49: 133,559 (1999 est.)

Military manpower - reaching military age annually:
males: 6,410 (1999 est.)
Military expenditures - dollar figure: $405 million (1996)
Military expenditures - percent of GDP: 5.4% (1996)

Transnational Issues

Disputes - international: 1974 hostilities divided the island into two de facto autonomous areas, a Greek Cypriot area controlled by the internationally recognized Cypriot Government (59% of the island's land area) and a Turkish-Cypriot area (37% of the island), that are separated by a UN buffer zone (4% of the island); there are two UK sovereign base areas within the Greek Cypriot portion of the island
Illicit drugs: transit point for heroin and hashish via air routes and container traffic to Europe, especially from Lebanon and Turkey; some cocaine transits as well

Czech Republic

Introduction

Background: Once part of the Holy Roman Empire and, later, the Austro-Hungarian monarchy, Czechoslovakia became an independent nation at the end of World War I. Independence ended with the German takeover in 1939. After World War II, Czechoslovakia fell within the Soviet sphere of influence, and in 1968 an invasion by Warsaw Pact troops snuffed out anti-communist demonstrations and riots. With the collapse of Soviet authority in 1991, Czechoslovakia regained its freedom. On 1 January 1993, the country peacefully split into its two ethnic components, the Czech Republic and Slovakia. The Czech Republic, largely by aspiring to become a NATO and EU member, has moved toward integration in world markets, a development that poses both opportunities and risks. But Prague has had a difficult time convincing the public that membership in NATO is crucial to Czech security. At the same time, support for eventual EU membership is waning. Coupled with the country's worsening economic situation, Prague's political scene, troubled for the past three years, will remain so for the foreseeable future.

Geography

Location: Central Europe, southeast of Germany
Geographic coordinates: 49 45 N, 15 30 E
Map references: Europe
Area:
total: 78,703 sq km
land: 78,645 sq km
water: 58 sq km
Area - comparative: slightly smaller than South Carolina
Land boundaries:
total: 1,881 km
border countries: Austria 362 km, Germany 646 km, Poland 658 km, Slovakia 215 km
Coastline: 0 km (landlocked)
Maritime claims: none (landlocked)

Climate: temperate; cool summers; cold, cloudy, humid winters
Terrain: Bohemia in the west consists of rolling plains, hills, and plateaus surrounded by low mountains; Moravia in the east consists of very hilly country
Elevation extremes:
lowest point: Elbe River 115 m
highest point: Snezka 1,602 m
Natural resources: hard coal, soft coal, kaolin, clay, graphite
Land use:
arable land: 41%
permanent crops: 2%
permanent pastures: 11%
forests and woodland: 34%
other: 12% (1993 est.)
Irrigated land: 240 sq km (1993 est.)
Natural hazards: flooding
Environment - current issues: air and water pollution in areas of northwest Bohemia and in northern Moravia around Ostrava present health risks; acid rain damaging forests
Environment - international agreements:
party to: Air Pollution, Air Pollution-Nitrogen Oxides, Air Pollution-Sulphur 85, Air Pollution-Sulphur 94, Air Pollution-Volatile Organic Compounds, Antarctic Treaty, Biodiversity, Climate Change, Endangered Species, Environmental Modification, Hazardous Wastes, Law of the Sea, Nuclear Test Ban, Ozone Layer Protection, Ship Pollution, Wetlands
signed, but not ratified: Air Pollution-Persistent Organic Pollutants, Antarctic-Environmental Protocol, Climate Change-Kyoto Protocol
Geography - note: landlocked; strategically located astride some of oldest and most significant land routes in Europe; Moravian Gate is a traditional military corridor between the North European Plain and the Danube in central Europe

People

Population: 10,280,513 (July 1999 est.)
Age structure:
0-14 years: 17% (male 888,292; female 845,662)
15-64 years: 69% (male 3,569,677; female 3,558,844)
65 years and over: 14% (male 545,305; female 872,733) (1999 est.)
Population growth rate: -0.01% (1999 est.)
Birth rate: 9.84 births/1,000 population (1999 est.)
Death rate: 10.86 deaths/1,000 population (1999 est.)
Net migration rate: 0.91 migrant(s)/1,000 population (1999 est.)
Sex ratio:
at birth: 1.05 male(s)/female
under 15 years: 1.05 male(s)/female
15-64 years: 1 male(s)/female
65 years and over: 0.62 male(s)/female
total population: 0.95 male(s)/female (1999 est.)
Infant mortality rate: 6.67 deaths/1,000 live births (1999 est.)

Life expectancy at birth:
total population: 74.35 years
male: 71.01 years
female: 77.88 years (1999 est.)
Total fertility rate: 1.28 children born/woman (1999 est.)
Nationality:
noun: Czech(s)
adjective: Czech
note: 300,000 Slovaks declared themselves Czech citizens in 1994
Ethnic groups: Czech 94.4%, Slovak 3%, Polish 0.6%, German 0.5%, Gypsy 0.3%, Hungarian 0.2%, other 1%
Religions: atheist 39.8%, Roman Catholic 39.2%, Protestant 4.6%, Orthodox 3%, other 13.4%
Languages: Czech, Slovak
Literacy:
definition: NA
total population: 99% (est.)
male: NA%
female: NA%

Government

Country name:
conventional long form: Czech Republic
conventional short form: Czech Republic
local long form: Ceska Republika
local short form: Ceska Republika
Data code: EZ
Government type: parliamentary democracy
Capital: Prague
Administrative divisions: 73 districts (okresi, singular - okres) and 4 municipalities* (mesta, singular - mesto); Benesov, Beroun, Blansko, Breclav, Brno*, Brno-Venkov, Bruntal, Ceske Budejovice, Ceska Lipa, Cesky Krumlov, Cheb, Chomutov, Chrudim, Decin, Domazlice, Frydek-Mistek, Havlickuv Brod, Hodonin, Hradec Kralove, Jablonec nad Nisou, Jesenik, Jicin, Jihlava, Jindrichuv Hradec, Karlovy Vary, Karvina, Kladno, Klatovy, Kolin, Kromeriz, Kutna Hora, Liberec, Litomerice, Louny, Melnik, Mlada Boleslav, Most, Nachod, Novy Jicin, Nymburk, Olomouc, Opava, Ostrava*, Pardubice, Pelhrimov, Pisek, Plzen*, Plzen-Jih, Plzen-Sever, Prachatice, Praha*, Praha-Vychod, Praha Zapad, Prerov, Pribram, Prostejov, Rakovnik, Rokycany, Rychnov nad Kneznou, Semily, Sokolov, Strakonice, Sumperk, Svitavy, Tabor, Tachov, Teplice, Trebic, Trutnov, Uherske Hradiste, Usti nad Labem, Usti nad Orlici, Vsetin, Vyskov, Zdar nad Sazavou, Zlin, Znojmo
Independence: 1 January 1993 (from Czechoslovakia)
National holiday: National Liberation Day, 8 May; Founding of the Republic, 28 October
Constitution: ratified 16 December 1992; effective 1 January 1993
Legal system: civil law system based on Austro-Hungarian codes; has not accepted compulsory ICJ jurisdiction; legal code modified to bring it in line with Organization on Security and Cooperation in Europe (OSCE) obligations and to

Czech Republic *(continued)*

expunge Marxist-Leninist legal theory
Suffrage: 18 years of age; universal
Executive branch:
chief of state: President Vaclav HAVEL (since 2 February 1993)
head of government: Prime Minister Milos ZEMAN (since 17 July 1998); Deputy Prime Ministers Vladimir SPIDLA (since 17 July 1998), Pavel RYCHETSKY since 17 July 1998), Egon LANSKY (since 17 July 1998), Pavel MERTLIK (since 17 July 1998)
cabinet: Cabinet appointed by the president on the recommendation of the prime minister
elections: president elected by Parliament for a five-year term; election last held 20 January 1998 (next to be held NA January 2003); prime minister appointed by the president
election results: Vaclav HAVEL reelected president; Vaclav HAVEL received 47 of 81 votes in the Senate and 99 out of 200 votes in the Chamber of Deputies (second round of voting)
Legislative branch: bicameral Parliament or Parlament consists of the Senate or Senat (81 seats; members are elected by popular vote to serve staggered two-, four-, and six-year terms) and the Chamber of Deputies or Snemovna Poslancu (200 seats; members are elected by popular vote to serve four-year terms)
elections: Senate - last held 13-14 and 20-21 November 1998 (next to be held NA November 2000 - to replace/reelect 20 senators serving two-year terms); Chamber of Deputies - last held 19-20 June 1998 (early elections to be held NA June 2000)
election results: Senate - percent of vote by party - NA; seats by party - governing coalition (CSSD 23), opposition (ODS 26, KDU-CSL 16, KCSM 4, ODA 7, US 4, DEU 1); Chamber of Deputies - percent of vote by party - NA; seats by party - governing coalition (CSSD 74), opposition (ODS 63, KDU-CSL 20, US 19, KCSM 24)
Judicial branch: Supreme Court, chairman and deputy chairmen are appointed by the president for life; Constitutional Court, chairman and deputy chairmen are appointed by the president for life
Political parties and leaders: Civic Democratic Party or ODS [Vaclav KLAUS, chairman]; Civic Democratic Alliance or ODA [Daniel KROUPA, chairman]; Christian Democratic Union-Czech People's Party or KDU-CSL [Jan KASAL, acting chairman]; Czech Social Democrats or CSSD - left [Milos ZEMAN, chairman]; Communist Party or KSCM - left opposition [Miroslav GREBENICEK, chairman]; Assembly for the Republic or SPR-RSC - extreme right radical [Miroslav SLADEK, chairman]; Democratic Union or DEU [Ratibor MAJZLIK, chairman]; Freedom Union or US [Jan RUML, chairman]
Political pressure groups and leaders: Czech-Moravian Chamber of Trade Unions; Civic Movement
International organization participation: Australia Group, BIS, CCC, CE, CEI, CERN, EAPC, EBRD, ECE, EU (applicant), FAO, IAEA, IBRD, ICAO, ICFTU, ICRM, IDA, IEA (observer), IFC, IFRCS, ILO, IMF, IMO, Inmarsat, Intelsat, Interpol, IOC, IOM, ISO, ITU, NEA, NSG, OAS (observer), OECD, OPCW, OSCE, PCA, PFP, UN, UNCTAD, UNESCO, UNIDO, UNMOP, UNOMIG, UNPREDEP, UPU, WEU (associate partner), WFTU, WHO, WIPO, WMO, WToO, WTrO, ZC
Diplomatic representation in the US:
chief of mission: Ambassador Aleksandr VONDRA
chancery: 3900 Spring of Freedom Street NW, Washington, DC 20008
telephone: [1] (202) 363-6315
FAX: [1] (202) 966-8540
consulate(s) general: Los Angeles and New York
Diplomatic representation from the US:
chief of mission: Ambassador John SHATTUCK
embassy: Trziste 15, 11801 Prague 1
mailing address: use embassy street address
telephone: [420] (2) 5732-0663
FAX: [420] (2) 5732-0583
Flag description: two equal horizontal bands of white (top) and red with a blue isosceles triangle based on the hoist side (almost identical to the flag of the former Czechoslovakia)

Economy

Economy - overview: Political and financial crises in 1997 shattered the Czech Republic's image as one of the most stable and prosperous of post-Communist states. Delays in enterprise restructuring and failure to develop a well-functioning capital market played major roles in Czech economic troubles, which culminated in a currency crisis in May. The currency was forced out of its fluctuation band as investors worried that the current account deficit, which reached nearly 8% of GDP in 1996, would become unsustainable. After expending $3 billion in vain to support the currency, the central bank let it float. The growing current account imbalance reflected a surge in domestic demand and poor export performance, as wage increases outpaced productivity. The government was forced to introduce two austerity packages later in the spring which cut government spending by 2.5% of GDP. A tough 1998 budget continued the painful medicine. These problems were compounded in the summer of 1997 by unprecedented flooding which inundated much of the eastern part of the country. Czech difficulties contrast with earlier achievements of strong GDP growth, a balanced budget, and inflation and unemployment that were among the lowest in the region. The Czech economy's transition problems continue to be too much direct and indirect government influence on the privatized economy, the sometimes ineffective management of privatized firms, and a shortage of experienced financial analysts for the banking system. The country slipped into a mild recession in 1998, but hopes to rebound with 1% growth in 1999.
GDP: purchasing power parity - $116.7 billion (1998 est.)
GDP - real growth rate: -1.5% (1998 est.)
GDP - per capita: purchasing power parity - $11,300 (1998 est.)
GDP - composition by sector:
agriculture: 5%
industry: 33.8%
services: 61.2% (1996)
Population below poverty line: NA%
Household income or consumption by percentage share:
lowest 10%: 4.6%
highest 10%: 23.5% (1993)
Inflation rate (consumer prices): 10.7% (1998)
Labor force: 3.655 million (1998)
Labor force - by occupation: industry 33.1%, agriculture 6.9%, construction 9.1%, transport and communications 7.2%, services 43.7% (1994)
Unemployment rate: 7% (1998 est.)
Budget:
revenues: $16.1 billion
expenditures: $16.6 billion, including capital expenditures of $NA (1997)
Industries: fuels, ferrous metallurgy, machinery and equipment, coal, motor vehicles, glass, armaments
Industrial production growth rate: 6.7% (1998 est.)
Electricity - production: 60.214 billion kWh (1996)
Electricity - production by source:
fossil fuel: 76.69%
hydro: 3.04%
nuclear: 20.27%
other: 0% (1996)
Electricity - consumption: 60.164 billion kWh (1996)
Electricity - exports: 8.8 billion kWh (1996)
Electricity - imports: 8.75 billion kWh (1996)
Agriculture - products: grains, potatoes, sugar beets, hops, fruit; pigs, cattle, poultry; forest products
Exports: $23.8 billion (f.o.b., 1998)
Exports - commodities: manufactured goods 40.5%, machinery and transport equipment 37.7%, chemicals 8.8%, raw materials and fuel 7.8% (1997)
Exports - partners: Germany 35.7%, Slovakia 12.9%, Austria 6.4%, Poland 5.7%, Russia 3.4%, Italy 3.3%, France 2.5% (1997)
Imports: $26.8 billion (f.o.b., 1998)
Imports - commodities: machinery and transport equipment 38.1%, manufactured goods 19.3%, raw materials and fuels 12.4%, chemicals 12.2%, and food 5.2% (1997)
Imports - partners: Germany 26.6%, Slovakia 8.4%, Italy 5.3%, Austria 4.4%, FSU 3.4%, UK 3.4%, Poland 3.2% (1997)
Debt - external: $21.6 billion (1997 est.)
Economic aid - recipient: $351.6 million (1995)
Currency: 1 koruna (Kc) = 100 haleru
Exchange rates: koruny (Kcs) per US$1 - 30.214 (December 1998), 32.294 (1998), 31.698 (1997), 27.145 (1996), 26.541 (1995), 28.785 (1994)
Fiscal year: calendar year

Communications

Telephones: 3,349,539 (1993 est.)

Czech Republic *(continued)*

Telephone system:
domestic: NA
international: satellite earth stations - 2 Intersputnik (Atlantic and Indian Ocean regions)
Radio broadcast stations: AM NA, FM NA, shortwave NA
Radios: NA
Television broadcast stations: 67 (in addition, there are 35 low-power stations and about 51 low-power repeaters) (1997)
Televisions: NA

Transportation

Railways:
total: 9,440 km
standard gauge: 9,344 km 1.435-m standard gauge (2,743 km electrified at three voltages; 1,885 km double track)
narrow gauge: 96 km 0.760-m narrow gauge (1996)
Highways:
total: 55,489 km
paved: 55,489 km (including 423 km of expressways)
unpaved: 0 km (1996 est.)
Waterways: NA km; the Elbe (Labe) is the principal river
Pipelines: natural gas 5,400 km
Ports and harbors: Decin, Prague, Usti nad Labem
Airports: 69 (1998 est.)
Airports - with paved runways:
total: 35
over 3,047 m: 2
2,438 to 3,047 m: 8
1,524 to 2,437 m: 11
914 to 1,523 m: 1
under 914 m: 13 (1998 est.)
Airports - with unpaved runways:
total: 34
914 to 1,523 m: 17
under 914 m: 17 (1998 est.)
Heliports: 1 (1998 est.)

Military

Military branches: Army, Air and Air Defense Forces, Civil Defense, Railroad Units
Military manpower - military age: 18 years of age
Military manpower - availability:
males age 15-49: 2,684,817 (1999 est.)
Military manpower - fit for military service:
males age 15-49: 2,046,079 (1999 est.)
Military manpower - reaching military age annually:
males: 73,072 (1999 est.)
Military expenditures - dollar figure: $1.1 billion (1998)
Military expenditures - percent of GDP: 1.8% (1998)

Transnational Issues

Disputes - international: Liechtenstein claims restitution for 1,600 sq km of property in the Czech Republic confiscated from its royal family in 1918; the Czech Republic insists that restitution does not go back before February 1948, when the communists seized power; individual Sudeten German claims for restitution of property confiscated in connection with their expulsion after World War II; unresolved property issues with Slovakia over redistribution of former Czechoslovak federal property
Illicit drugs: transshipment point for Southwest Asian heroin and hashish and Latin American cocaine to Western Europe; domestic consumption - especially of locally produced synthetic drugs - on the rise

Denmark

Introduction

Background: Once the seat of rapacious Viking raiders and later a major power in northwestern Europe, Denmark has evolved into a modern, prosperous nation that is participating in the political and economic integration of Europe. So far, however, they have opted out of some aspects of the European Union's Maastricht Treaty including the new monetary system launched on 1 January 1999.

Geography

Location: Northern Europe, bordering the Baltic Sea and the North Sea, on a peninsula north of Germany
Geographic coordinates: 56 00 N, 10 00 E
Map references: Europe
Area:
total: 43,094 sq km
land: 42,394 sq km
water: 700 sq km
note: includes the island of Bornholm in the Baltic Sea and the rest of metropolitan Denmark, but excludes the Faroe Islands and Greenland
Area - comparative: slightly less than twice the size of Massachusetts
Land boundaries:
total: 68 km
border countries: Germany 68 km
Coastline: 7,314 km
Maritime claims:
contiguous zone: 4 nm
continental shelf: 200-m depth or to the depth of exploitation
exclusive economic zone: 200 nm
territorial sea: 3 nm
Climate: temperate; humid and overcast; mild, windy winters and cool summers
Terrain: low and flat to gently rolling plains
Elevation extremes:
lowest point: Lammefjord -7 m
highest point: Ejer Bavnehoj 173 m

Denmark *(continued)*

Natural resources: petroleum, natural gas, fish, salt, limestone, stone, gravel and sand

Land use:

arable land: 60%

permanent crops: 0%

permanent pastures: 5%

forests and woodland: 10%

other: 25% (1993 est.)

Irrigated land: 4,350 sq km (1993 est.)

Natural hazards: flooding is a threat in some areas of the country (e.g., parts of Jutland, along the southern coast of the island of Lolland) that are protected from the sea by a system of dikes

Environment - current issues: air pollution, principally from vehicle and power plant emissions; nitrogen and phosphorus pollution of the North Sea; drinking and surface water becoming polluted from animal wastes and pesticides

Environment - international agreements:

party to: Air Pollution, Air Pollution-Nitrogen Oxides, Air Pollution-Sulphur 85, Air Pollution-Sulphur 94, Air Pollution-Volatile Organic Compounds, Antarctic Treaty, Biodiversity, Climate Change, Desertification, Endangered Species, Environmental Modification, Hazardous Wastes, Marine Dumping, Marine Life Conservation, Nuclear Test Ban, Ozone Layer Protection, Ship Pollution, Tropical Timber 83, Tropical Timber 94, Wetlands, Whaling

signed, but not ratified: Air Pollution-Persistent Organic Pollutants, Antarctic-Environmental Protocol, Climate Change-Kyoto Protocol, Law of the Sea

Geography - note: controls Danish Straits (Skagerrak and Kattegat) linking Baltic and North Seas; about one-quarter of the population lives in Copenhagen

People

Population: 5,356,845 (July 1999 est.)

Age structure:

0-14 years: 18% (male 504,182; female 478,547)

15-64 years: 67% (male 1,811,445; female 1,765,038)

65 years and over: 15% (male 331,207; female 466,426) (1999 est.)

Population growth rate: 0.38% (1999 est.)

Birth rate: 11.57 births/1,000 population (1999 est.)

Death rate: 10.97 deaths/1,000 population (1999 est.)

Net migration rate: 3.22 migrant(s)/1,000 population (1999 est.)

Sex ratio:

at birth: 1.05 male(s)/female

under 15 years: 1.05 male(s)/female

15-64 years: 1.03 male(s)/female

65 years and over: 0.71 male(s)/female

total population: 0.98 male(s)/female (1999 est.)

Infant mortality rate: 5.11 deaths/1,000 live births (1999 est.)

Life expectancy at birth:

total population: 76.51 years

male: 73.83 years

female: 79.33 years (1999 est.)

Total fertility rate: 1.62 children born/woman (1999 est.)

Nationality:

noun: Dane(s)

adjective: Danish

Ethnic groups: Scandinavian, Eskimo, Faroese, German

Religions: Evangelical Lutheran 91%, other Protestant and Roman Catholic 2%, other 7% (1988)

Languages: Danish, Faroese, Greenlandic (an Eskimo dialect), German (small minority)

Literacy:

definition: age 15 and over can read and write

total population: 99% (1980 est.)

male: NA%

female: NA%

Government

Country name:

conventional long form: Kingdom of Denmark

conventional short form: Denmark

local long form: Kongeriget Danmark

local short form: Danmark

Data code: DA

Government type: constitutional monarchy

Capital: Copenhagen

Administrative divisions: metropolitan Denmark - 14 counties (amter, singular - amt) and 2 kommunes*; Arhus, Bornholm, Fredericksberg*, Frederiksborg, Fyn, Kobenhavn, Kobenhavns*, Nordjylland, Ribe, Ringkobing, Roskilde, Sonderjylland, Storstrom, Vejle, Vestsjalland, Viborg

note: see separate entries for the Faroe Islands and Greenland, which are part of the Kingdom of Denmark and are self-governing administrative divisions

Independence: first organized as a unified state in 10th century; in 1849 became a constitutional monarchy

National holiday: Birthday of the Queen, 16 April (1940)

Constitution: 1849 was the original constitution; there was a major overhaul 5 June 1953, allowing for a unicameral legislature and a female chief of state

Legal system: civil law system; judicial review of legislative acts; accepts compulsory ICJ jurisdiction, with reservations

Suffrage: 18 years of age; universal

Executive branch:

chief of state: Queen MARGRETHE II (since 14 January 1972); Heir Apparent Crown Prince FREDERIK, elder son of the monarch (born 26 May 1968)

head of government: Prime Minister Poul Nyrup RASMUSSEN (since 25 January 1993)

cabinet: Cabinet appointed by the monarch

elections: none; the monarch is hereditary; prime minister appointed by the monarch

Legislative branch: unicameral Parliament or Folketing (179 seats; members are elected by popular vote on the basis of proportional representation to serve four-year terms)

elections: last held 11 March 1998 (next to be held NA 2002)

election results: percent of vote by party - NA; seats by party - progovernment parties: Social Democrats 65, Socialist People's Party 13, Radical Liberal Party 7, Unity Party 5; opposition: Liberal Party 43, Conservative Party 17, Danish People's Party 13, Center Democrats 8, Christian People's Party 4, Progress Party 4

Judicial branch: Supreme Court, judges are appointed by the monarch for life

Political parties and leaders: Social Democratic Party [Poul Nyrup RASMUSSEN]; Conservative Party [Torben RECHENDORFF]; Liberal Party [Uffe ELLEMANN-JENSEN]; Socialist People's Party [Holger K. NIELSEN]; Progress Party [Kirsten JAKOBSEN]; Center Democratic Party [Mimi JAKOBSEN]; Social Liberal Party [Marianne JELVED]; Unity Party [no leader]; Danish People's Party [Pia KJAERSGAARD]; Radical Liberal Party [Margrethe VESTAGER]; Conservative People's Party [Torben RECHENDORFF]; Christian People's Party [Jann SJURSEN]

International organization participation: AfDB, AsDB, Australia Group, BIS, CBSS, CCC, CE, CERN, EAPC, EBRD, ECE, EIB, ESA, EU, FAO, G- 9, IADB, IAEA, IBRD, ICAO, ICC, ICFTU, ICRM, IDA, IEA, IFAD, IFC, IFRCS, IHO, ILO, IMF, IMO, Inmarsat, Intelsat, Interpol, IOC, IOM, ISO, ITU, MTCR, NATO, NC, NEA, NIB, NSG, OECD, OPCW, OSCE, PCA, UN, UNCTAD, UNESCO, UNHCR, UNIDO, UNIKOM, UNMIBH, UNMOGIP, UNMOP, UNMOT, UNOMIG, UNPREDEP, UNTSO, UPU, WEU (observer), WHO, WIPO, WMO, WTrO, ZC

Diplomatic representation in the US:

chief of mission: Ambassador Knud-Erik TYGESEN

chancery: 3200 Whitehaven Street NW, Washington, DC 20008

telephone: [1] (202) 234-4300

FAX: [1] (202) 328-1470

consulate(s) general: Chicago, Los Angeles, and New York

Diplomatic representation from the US:

chief of mission: Ambassador Edward E. ELSON

embassy: Dag Hammarskjolds Alle 24, 2100 Copenhagen

mailing address: PSC 73, APO AE 09716

telephone: [45] 35 55 31 44

FAX: [45] 35 43 02 23

Flag description: red with a white cross that extends to the edges of the flag; the vertical part of the cross is shifted to the hoist side, and that design element of the Dannebrog (Danish flag) was subsequently adopted by the other Nordic countries of Finland, Iceland, Norway, and Sweden

Economy

Economy - overview: This thoroughly modern market economy features high-tech agriculture, up-to-date small-scale and corporate industry, extensive government welfare measures, comfortable living standards, and high dependence on foreign trade. Denmark is a net exporter of food. The

Denmark (continued)

center-left coalition government will concentrate on reducing the persistently high unemployment rate and the budget deficit as well as following the previous government's policies of maintaining low inflation and a current account surplus. The coalition also vows to maintain a stable currency. The coalition has lowered marginal income taxes while maintaining overall tax revenues; boosted industrial competitiveness through labor market and tax reforms and increased research and development funds; and improved welfare services for the neediest while cutting paperwork and delays. Denmark chose not to join the 11 other EU members who launched the euro on 1 January 1999. Because of the global slowdown, GDP growth may fall to 1% in 1999.

GDP: purchasing power parity - $124.4 billion (1998 est.)

GDP - real growth rate: 2.6% (1998 est.)

GDP - per capita: purchasing power parity - $23,300 (1998 est.)

GDP - composition by sector:
agriculture: 4%
industry: 27%
services: 69% (1997)

Population below poverty line: NA%

Household income or consumption by percentage share:
lowest 10%: 3.6%
highest 10%: 20.5% (1992)

Inflation rate (consumer prices): 1.8% (1998 est.)

Labor force: 2,895,950

Labor force - by occupation: private services 40%, government services 30%, manufacturing and mining 19%, construction 6%, agriculture, forestry, and fishing 5% (1995)

Unemployment rate: 6.5% (1998 est.)

Budget:
revenues: $62.1 billion
expenditures: $66.4 billion, including capital expenditures of $NA (1996 est.)

Industries: food processing, machinery and equipment, textiles and clothing, chemical products, electronics, construction, furniture, and other wood products, shipbuilding

Industrial production growth rate: 1.3% (1996)

Electricity - production: 50.608 billion kWh (1996)

Electricity - production by source:
fossil fuel: 97.6%
hydro: 0.05%
nuclear: 0%
other: 2.35% (1996)

Electricity - consumption: 35.208 billion kWh (1996)

Electricity - exports: 19.2 billion kWh (1996)

Electricity - imports: 3.8 billion kWh (1996)

Agriculture - products: grain, potatoes, rape, sugar beets; beef, dairy products; fish

Exports: $48.8 billion (f.o.b., 1998)

Exports - commodities: machinery and instruments, meat and meat products, fuels, dairy products, ships, fish, chemicals

Exports - partners: Germany 21.4%, Sweden 11.6%, UK 9.6%, Norway 6.2%, France 5.3%, US 4.6%, Netherlands 4.5% (1997)

Imports: $46.1 billion (f.o.b., 1998)

Imports - commodities: machinery and equipment, petroleum, chemicals, grain and foodstuffs, textiles, paper

Imports - partners: Germany 21.7%, Sweden 12.7%, Netherlands 7.8%, UK 7.6%, France 5.6%, Norway 5.2%, US 5.0%, Japan (1997)

Debt - external: $44 billion (1996 est.)

Economic aid - donor: ODA, $1.6 billion (1995)

Currency: 1 Danish krone (DKr) = 100 oere

Exchange rates: Danish kroner (DKr) per US$1 - 6.408 (January 1999), 6.701 (1998), 6.604 (1997), 5.799 (1996), 5.602 (1995), 6.361 (1994)

Fiscal year: calendar year

Communications

Telephones: 3.2 million (1995 est.); 822,000 cellular telephone subscribers

Telephone system: excellent telephone and telegraph services
domestic: buried and submarine cables and microwave radio relay form trunk network, four cellular radio communications systems
international: 18 submarine fiber-optic cables linking Denmark with Norway, Sweden, Russia, Poland, Germany, Netherlands, UK, Faroe Islands, Iceland, and Canada; satellite earth stations - 6 Intelsat, 10 Eutelsat, 1 Orion, 1 Inmarsat (Blaavand-Atlantic-East); note - the Nordic countries (Denmark, Finland, Iceland, Norway, and Sweden) share the Danish earth station and the Eik, Norway, station for world-wide Inmarsat access

Radio broadcast stations: AM 2, FM 3, shortwave 0

Radios: NA

Television broadcast stations: 78 (of which 35 are low-power stations; in addition, there are 51 low-power repeaters) (1997)

Televisions: 3 million (1996 est.)

Transportation

Railways:
total: 3,323 km (458 km privately owned and operated)
standard gauge: 3,323 km 1.435-m gauge (440 km electrified; 760 km double track) (1996)

Highways:
total: 71,600 km
paved: 71,600 km (including 880 km of expressways)
unpaved: 0 km (1996 est.)

Waterways: 417 km

Pipelines: crude oil 110 km; petroleum products 578 km; natural gas 700 km

Ports and harbors: Alborg, Arhus, Copenhagen, Esbjerg, Fredericia, Grena, Koge, Odense, Struer

Merchant marine:
total: 337 ships (1,000 GRT or over) totaling 5,130,643 GRT/6,880,248 DWT
ships by type: bulk 14, cargo 130, chemical tanker 19, container 73, liquefied gas tanker 26, livestock carrier 6, oil tanker 20, railcar carrier 1, refrigerated cargo 15, roll-on/roll-off cargo 21, short-sea passenger 9, specialized tanker 3
note: Denmark has created its own internal register, called the Danish International Ship register (DIS); DIS ships do not have to meet Danish manning regulations, and they amount to a flag of convenience within the Danish register (1998 est.)

Airports: 118 (1998 est.)

Airports - with paved runways:
total: 28
over 3,047 m: 2
2,438 to 3,047 m: 7
1,524 to 2,437 m: 3
914 to 1,523 m: 13
under 914 m: 3 (1998 est.)

Airports - with unpaved runways:
total: 90
1,524 to 2,437 m: 1
914 to 1,523 m: 7
under 914 m: 82 (1998 est.)

Military

Military branches: Royal Danish Army, Royal Danish Navy, Royal Danish Air Force, Home Guard

Military manpower - military age: 20 years of age

Military manpower - availability:
males age 15-49: 1,316,584 (1999 est.)

Military manpower - fit for military service:
males age 15-49: 1,129,870 (1999 est.)

Military manpower - reaching military age annually:
males: 32,130 (1999 est.)

Military expenditures - dollar figure: $2.5 billion (1999)

Military expenditures - percent of GDP: 1.6% (1999)

Transnational Issues

Disputes - international: Rockall continental shelf dispute involving Iceland, Ireland, and the UK (Ireland and the UK have signed a boundary agreement in the Rockall area)

Djibouti

Geography

Location: Eastern Africa, bordering the Gulf of Aden and the Red Sea, between Eritrea and Somalia
Geographic coordinates: 11 30 N, 43 00 E
Map references: Africa
Area:
total: 22,000 sq km
land: 21,980 sq km
water: 20 sq km
Area - comparative: slightly smaller than Massachusetts
Land boundaries:
total: 508 km
border countries: Eritrea 113 km, Ethiopia 337 km, Somalia 58 km
Coastline: 314 km
Maritime claims:
contiguous zone: 24 nm
exclusive economic zone: 200 nm
territorial sea: 12 nm
Climate: desert; torrid, dry
Terrain: coastal plain and plateau separated by central mountains
Elevation extremes:
lowest point: Lac Assal -155 m
highest point: Moussa Ali 2,028 m
Natural resources: geothermal areas
Land use:
arable land: NA%
permanent crops: NA%
permanent pastures: 9%
forests and woodland: 0%
other: 91% (1993 est.)
Irrigated land: NA sq km
Natural hazards: earthquakes; droughts; occasional cyclonic disturbances from the Indian Ocean bring heavy rains and flash floods
Environment - current issues: inadequate supplies of potable water; desertification
Environment - international agreements:

party to: Biodiversity, Climate Change, Desertification, Endangered Species, Law of the Sea, Ship Pollution
signed, but not ratified: none of the selected agreements
Geography - note: strategic location near world's busiest shipping lanes and close to Arabian oilfields; terminus of rail traffic into Ethiopia; mostly wasteland

People

Population: 447,439 (July 1999 est.)
Age structure:
0-14 years: 43% (male 96,222; female 96,023)
15-64 years: 54% (male 128,506; female 114,767)
65 years and over: 3% (male 6,155; female 5,766) (1999 est.)
Population growth rate: 1.51% (1999 est.)
Birth rate: 41.23 births/1,000 population (1999 est.)
Death rate: 14.41 deaths/1,000 population (1999 est.)
Net migration rate: -11.73 migrant(s)/1,000 population (1999 est.)
Sex ratio:
at birth: 1.03 male(s)/female
under 15 years: 1 male(s)/female
15-64 years: 1.12 male(s)/female
65 years and over: 1.07 male(s)/female
total population: 1.07 male(s)/female (1999 est.)
Infant mortality rate: 100.24 deaths/1,000 live births (1999 est.)
Life expectancy at birth:
total population: 51.54 years
male: 49.48 years
female: 53.67 years (1999 est.)
Total fertility rate: 5.87 children born/woman (1999 est.)
Nationality:
noun: Djiboutian(s)
adjective: Djiboutian
Ethnic groups: Somali 60%, Afar 35%, French, Arab, Ethiopian, and Italian 5%
Religions: Muslim 94%, Christian 6%
Languages: French (official), Arabic (official), Somali, Afar
Literacy:
definition: age 15 and over can read and write
total population: 46.2%
male: 60.3%
female: 32.7% (1995 est.)

Government

Country name:
conventional long form: Republic of Djibouti
conventional short form: Djibouti
former: French Territory of the Afars and Issas, French Somaliland
Data code: DJ
Government type: republic
Capital: Djibouti
Administrative divisions: 5 districts (cercles, singular - cercle); 'Ali Sabih, Dikhil, Djibouti, Obock,

Tadjoura
Independence: 27 June 1977 (from France)
National holiday: Independence Day, 27 June (1977)
Constitution: multiparty constitution approved in referendum 4 September 1992
Legal system: based on French civil law system, traditional practices, and Islamic law
Suffrage: NA years of age; universal adult
Executive branch:
chief of state: President HASSAN GOULED Aptidon (since 24 June 1977); note - President HASSAN GOULED announced early in the year that he would resign in April 1999
head of government: Prime Minister BARKAT Gourad Hamadou (since 30 September 1978)
cabinet: Council of Ministers responsible to the president
elections: president elected by popular vote for a six-year term; election last held 7 May 1993 (next to be held 9 April 1999); prime minister appointed by the president
election results: President HASSAN GOULED reelected; percent of vote - NA
Legislative branch: unicameral Chamber of Deputies or Chambre des Deputes (65 seats; members elected by popular vote for five-year terms)
elections: last held 19 December 1997 (next to be held NA 2002)
election results: percent of vote - NA; seats - RPP 65; note - RPP (the ruling party) dominated
Judicial branch: Supreme Court (Cour Supreme)
Political parties and leaders:
ruling party: People's Progress Assembly or RPP [Hassan GOULED Aptidon]
other parties: Democratic Renewal Party or PRD [Mohamed Jama ELABE]; Democratic National Party or PND [ADEN Robleh Awaleh]
Political pressure groups and leaders: Front for the Restoration of Unity and Democracy or FRUD, and affiliates; Movement for Unity and Democracy or MUD
International organization participation: ACCT, ACP, AfDB, AFESD, AL, AMF, ECA, FAO, G-77, IBRD, ICAO, ICFTU, ICRM, IDA, IDB, IFAD, IFC, IFRCS, IGAD, ILO, IMF, IMO, Intelsat (nonsignatory user), Interpol, IOC, ITU, NAM, OAU, OIC, OPCW, UN, UNCTAD, UNESCO, UNIDO, UPU, WFTU, WHO, WMO, WToO, WTrO
Diplomatic representation in the US:
chief of mission: Ambassador ROBLE Olhaye Oudine
chancery: Suite 515, 1156 15th Street NW, Washington, DC 20005
telephone: [1] (202) 331-0270
FAX: [1] (202) 331-0302
Diplomatic representation from the US:
chief of mission: Ambassador Lange SCHERMERHORN
embassy: Plateau du Serpent, Boulevard Marechal Joffre, Djibouti
mailing address: B. P. 185, Djibouti
telephone: [253] 35 39 95

Djibouti *(continued)*

FAX: [253] 35 39 40

Flag description: two equal horizontal bands of light blue (top) and light green with a white isosceles triangle based on the hoist side bearing a red five-pointed star in the center

Economy

Economy - overview: The economy is based on service activities connected with the country's strategic location and status as a free trade zone in northeast Africa. Two-thirds of the inhabitants live in the capital city, the remainder being mostly nomadic herders. Scanty rainfall limits crop production to fruits and vegetables, and most food must be imported. Djibouti provides services as both a transit port for the region and an international transshipment and refueling center. It has few natural resources and little industry. The nation is, therefore, heavily dependent on foreign assistance to help support its balance of payments and to finance development projects. An unemployment rate of 40% to 50% continues to be a major problem. Per capita consumption dropped an estimated 35% over the last seven years because of recession, civil war, and a high population growth rate (including immigrants and refugees). Also, renewed fighting between Ethiopia and Eritrea has disturbed normal external channels of commerce. Faced with a multitude of economic difficulties, the government has fallen in arrears on long-term external debt and has been struggling to meet the stipulations of foreign aid donors.

GDP: purchasing power parity - $530 million (1998 est.)

GDP - real growth rate: 0.6% (1998 est.)

GDP - per capita: purchasing power parity - $1,200 (1998 est.)

GDP - composition by sector:
agriculture: 3%
industry: 20%
services: 77% (1996 est.)

Population below poverty line: NA%

Household income or consumption by percentage share:
lowest 10%: NA%
highest 10%: NA%

Inflation rate (consumer prices): 3% (1997 est.)

Labor force: 282,000

Labor force - by occupation: agriculture 75%, industry 11%, services 14% (1991 est.)

Unemployment rate: 40%-50% (1996 est.)

Budget:
revenues: $156 million
expenditures: $175 million, including capital expenditures of $NA (1997 est.)

Industries: limited to a few small-scale enterprises, such as dairy products and mineral-water bottling

Industrial production growth rate: 3% (1996 est.)

Electricity - production: 175 million kWh (1996)

Electricity - production by source:
fossil fuel: 100%
hydro: 0%
nuclear: 0%

other: 0% (1996)

Electricity - consumption: 175 million kWh (1996)

Electricity - exports: 0 kWh (1996)

Electricity - imports: 0 kWh (1996)

Agriculture - products: fruits, vegetables; goats, sheep, camels

Exports: $39.6 million (f.o.b., 1996 est.)

Exports - commodities: hides and skins, coffee (in transit) (1995)

Exports - partners: Ethiopia 45%, Somalia, Yemen, Saudi Arabia (1996)

Imports: $200.5 million (f.o.b., 1996 est.)

Imports - commodities: foods, beverages, transport equipment, chemicals, petroleum products (1995)

Imports - partners: France, Ethiopia, Italy, Saudi Arabia, Thailand (1996)

Debt - external: $276 million (1996 est.)

Economic aid - recipient: $106.3 million (1995)

Currency: 1 Djiboutian franc (DF) = 100 centimes

Exchange rates: Djiboutian francs (DF) per US$1 - 177.721 (fixed rate since 1973)

Fiscal year: calendar year

Communications

Telephones: 7,200 (1986 est.)

Telephone system: telephone facilities in the city of Djibouti are adequate as are the microwave radio relay connections to outlying areas of the country
domestic: microwave radio relay network
international: submarine cable to Jiddah, Suez, Sicily, Marseilles, Colombo, and Singapore; satellite earth stations - 1 Intelsat (Indian Ocean) and 1 Arabsat; Medarabtel regional microwave radio relay telephone network

Radio broadcast stations: AM 1, FM 2, shortwave 0

Radios: 35,000

Television broadcast stations: 1 (in addition, there are 5 low-power repeaters) (1998)

Televisions: 17,000 (1998)

Transportation

Railways:
total: 97 km (Djibouti segment of the Addis Ababa-Djibouti railroad)
narrow gauge: 97 km 1.000-m gauge
note: in April 1998, Djibouti and Ethiopia announced plans to revitalize the century-old railroad that links their capitals

Highways:
total: 2,890 km
paved: 364 km
unpaved: 2,526 km (1996 est.)

Ports and harbors: Djibouti

Merchant marine:
total: 1 cargo ship (1,000 GRT or over) totaling 1,369 GRT/3,030 DWT (1998 est.)

Airports: 11 (1998 est.)

Airports - with paved runways:
total: 2
over 3,047 m: 1

2,438 to 3,047 m: 1 (1998 est.)

Airports - with unpaved runways:
total: 9
1,524 to 2,437 m: 2
914 to 1,523 m: 5
under 914 m: 2 (1998 est.)

Military

Military branches: Djibouti National Army (includes Navy and Air Force)

Military manpower - availability:
males age 15-49: 105,075 (1999 est.)

Military manpower - fit for military service:
males age 15-49: 61,712 (1999 est.)

Military expenditures - dollar figure: $22.5 million (1997)

Military expenditures - percent of GDP: 4.5% (1997)

Transnational Issues

Disputes - international: none

Dominica

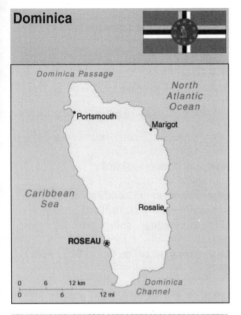

Geography

Location: Caribbean, island between the Caribbean Sea and the North Atlantic Ocean, about one-half of the way from Puerto Rico to Trinidad and Tobago

Geographic coordinates: 15 25 N, 61 20 W

Map references: Central America and the Caribbean

Area:
total: 750 sq km
land: 750 sq km
water: 0 sq km

Area - comparative: slightly more than four times the size of Washington, DC

Land boundaries: 0 km

Coastline: 148 km

Maritime claims:
contiguous zone: 24 nm
exclusive economic zone: 200 nm
territorial sea: 12 nm

Climate: tropical; moderated by northeast trade winds; heavy rainfall

Terrain: rugged mountains of volcanic origin

Elevation extremes:
lowest point: Caribbean Sea 0 m
highest point: Morne Diablatins 1,447 m

Natural resources: timber

Land use:
arable land: 9%
permanent crops: 13%
permanent pastures: 3%
forests and woodland: 67%
other: 8% (1993 est.)

Irrigated land: NA sq km

Natural hazards: flash floods are a constant threat; destructive hurricanes can be expected during the late summer months

Environment - current issues: NA

Environment - international agreements:
party to: Biodiversity, Climate Change, Desertification, Environmental Modification, Hazardous Wastes, Law of the Sea, Ozone Layer Protection, Whaling
signed, but not ratified: none of the selected agreements

People

Population: 64,881 (July 1999 est.)

Age structure:
0-14 years: 27% (male 8,680; female 8,530)
15-64 years: 64% (male 21,090; female 20,294)
65 years and over: 9% (male 2,570; female 3,717) (1999 est.)

Population growth rate: -1.41% (1999 est.)

Birth rate: 16.92 births/1,000 population (1999 est.)

Death rate: 6.35 deaths/1,000 population (1999 est.)

Net migration rate: -24.69 migrant(s)/1,000 population (1999 est.)

Sex ratio:
at birth: 1.05 male(s)/female
under 15 years: 1.02 male(s)/female
15-64 years: 1.04 male(s)/female
65 years and over: 0.69 male(s)/female
total population: 0.99 male(s)/female (1999 est.)

Infant mortality rate: 8.75 deaths/1,000 live births (1999 est.)

Life expectancy at birth:
total population: 78.01 years
male: 75.15 years
female: 81.01 years (1999 est.)

Total fertility rate: 1.89 children born/woman (1999 est.)

Nationality:
noun: Dominican(s)
adjective: Dominican

Ethnic groups: black, Carib Amerindian

Religions: Roman Catholic 77%, Protestant 15% (Methodist 5%, Pentecostal 3%, Seventh-Day Adventist 3%, Baptist 2%, other 2%), none 2%, other 6%

Languages: English (official), French patois

Literacy:
definition: age 15 and over has ever attended school
total population: 94%
male: 94%
female: 94% (1970 est.)

Government

Country name:
conventional long form: Commonwealth of Dominica
conventional short form: Dominica

Data code: DO

Government type: parliamentary democracy

Capital: Roseau

Administrative divisions: 10 parishes; Saint Andrew, Saint David, Saint George, Saint John, Saint Joseph, Saint Luke, Saint Mark, Saint Patrick, Saint Paul, Saint Peter

Independence: 3 November 1978 (from UK)

National holiday: Independence Day, 3 November (1978)

Constitution: 3 November 1978

Legal system: based on English common law

Suffrage: 18 years of age; universal

Executive branch:
chief of state: President Vernon Lorden SHAW (since 7 October 1998)
head of government: Prime Minister Edison C. JAMES (since 12 June 1995)
cabinet: Cabinet appointed by the president on the advice of the prime minister
elections: president elected by the House of Assembly for a five-year term; election last held 7 October 1998 (next to be held NA October 2003); prime minister appointed by the president
election results: Vernon Lorden SHAW elected president; percent of legislative vote - NA

Legislative branch: unicameral House of Assembly (30 seats, 9 appointed senators, 21 elected by popular vote representatives; members serve five-year terms)
elections: last held 12 June 1995 (next to be held by October 2000); byelections held 13 August 1996
election results: percent of vote by party - NA; seats by party - UWP 12, DLP 5, DFP 4

Judicial branch: Eastern Caribbean Supreme Court (located in Saint Lucia), one of the six judges must reside in Dominica and preside over the Court of Summary Jurisdiction

Political parties and leaders: Dominica Freedom Party or DFP [Charles SAVARIN]; Dominica Labor Party or DLP [Rosie DOUGLAS]; United Workers Party or UWP [Edison JAMES]

Political pressure groups and leaders: Dominica Liberation Movement or DLM (a small leftist party)

International organization participation: ACCT, ACP, C, Caricom, CDB, ECLAC, FAO, G-77, IBRD, ICFTU, ICRM, IDA, IFAD, IFC, IFRCS, ILO, IMF, IMO, Interpol, IOC, ITU, NAM (observer), OAS, OECS, OPANAL, OPCW, UN, UNCTAD, UNESCO, UNIDO, UPU, WCL, WHO, WMO, WTrO

Diplomatic representation in the US:
chief of mission: Ambassador Nicholas J. O. LIVERPOOL (resident in Dominica)
chancery: 3216 New Mexico Avenue NW, Washington, DC 20016
telephone: [1] (202) 364-6781
FAX: [1] (202) 364-6791
consulate(s) general: New York

Diplomatic representation from the US: the US does not have an embassy in Dominica; the Ambassador to Dominica resides in Bridgetown (Barbados), but travels frequently to Dominica

Flag description: green, with a centered cross of three equal bands - the vertical part is yellow (hoist side), black, and white and the horizontal part is yellow (top), black, and white; superimposed in the center of the cross is a red disk bearing a sisserou parrot encircled by 10 green, five-pointed stars edged in yellow; the 10 stars represent the 10 administrative divisions (parishes)

Economy

Economy - overview: The economy depends on agriculture and is highly vulnerable to climatic conditions, notably tropical storms. Agriculture, primarily bananas, accounts for 20% of GDP and employs 40% of the labor force. Development of the tourist industry remains difficult because of the rugged coastline, lack of beaches, and the lack of an international airport. Hurricane Luis devastated the country's banana crop in September 1995; tropical storms had wiped out one-quarter of the crop in 1994 as well. The economy began to recover in mid-1998, fueled by increases in construction, soap production, and tourist arrivals. The government is attempting to develop an offshore financial industry in order to diversify the island's production base.

GDP: purchasing power parity - $216 million (1997 est.)

GDP - real growth rate: 1.8% (1997)

GDP - per capita: purchasing power parity - $3,300 (1997 est.)

GDP - composition by sector:
agriculture: 20%
industry: 16%
services: 64% (1996 est.)

Population below poverty line: NA%

Household income or consumption by percentage share:
lowest 10%: NA%
highest 10%: NA%

Inflation rate (consumer prices): 2.2% (1997)

Labor force: 25,000

Labor force - by occupation: agriculture 40%, industry and commerce 32%, services 28%

Unemployment rate: 15% (1992 est.)

Budget:
revenues: $72 million
expenditures: $79.9 million, including capital expenditures of $11.5 million (FY97/98)

Industries: soap, coconut oil, tourism, copra, furniture, cement blocks, shoes

Industrial production growth rate: -10% (1997 est.)

Electricity - production: 40 million kWh (1996)

Electricity - production by source:
fossil fuel: 50%
hydro: 50%
nuclear: 0%
other: 0% (1996)

Electricity - consumption: 40 million kWh (1996)

Electricity - exports: 0 kWh (1996)

Electricity - imports: 0 kWh (1996)

Agriculture - products: bananas, citrus, mangoes, root crops, coconuts; forest and fishery potential not exploited

Exports: $50.4 million (1997)

Exports - commodities: bananas 50%, soap, bay oil, vegetables, grapefruit, oranges

Exports - partners: Caricom countries 47%, UK 36%, US 7% (1996 est.)

Imports: $104.2 million (1997)

Imports - commodities: manufactured goods, machinery and equipment, food, chemicals

Imports - partners: US 41%, Caricom 25%, UK 13%, Netherlands, Canada

Debt - external: $105 million (1997 est.)

Economic aid - recipient: $24.4 million (1995)

Currency: 1 East Caribbean dollar (EC$) = 100 cents

Exchange rates: East Caribbean dollars (EC$) per US$1 - 2.7000 (fixed rate since 1976)

Fiscal year: 1 July - 30 June

Communications

Telephones: 14,613 (1993 est.)

Telephone system:
domestic: fully automatic network
international: microwave radio relay and SHF radiotelephone links to Martinique and Guadeloupe; VHF and UHF radiotelephone links to Saint Lucia

Radio broadcast stations: AM 3, FM 2, shortwave 0

Radios: 45,000 (1993 est.)

Television broadcast stations: 0 (there is one cable television company) (1997)

Televisions: 5,200 (1993 est.)

Transportation

Railways: 0 km

Highways:
total: 780 km
paved: 393 km
unpaved: 387 km (1996 est.)

Ports and harbors: Portsmouth, Roseau

Merchant marine: none

Airports: 2 (1998 est.)

Airports - with paved runways:
total: 2
914 to 1,523 m: 2 (1998 est.)

Military

Military branches: Commonwealth of Dominica Police Force (includes Special Service Unit, Coast Guard)

Military expenditures - dollar figure: $NA

Military expenditures - percent of GDP: NA%

Transnational Issues

Disputes - international: none

Illicit drugs: transshipment point for narcotics bound for the US and Europe; minor cannabis producer; banking industry is vulnerable to money laundering

Dominican Republic

Geography

Location: Caribbean, eastern two-thirds of the island of Hispaniola, between the Caribbean Sea and the North Atlantic Ocean, east of Haiti

Geographic coordinates: 19 00 N, 70 40 W

Map references: Central America and the Caribbean

Area:
total: 48,730 sq km
land: 48,380 sq km
water: 350 sq km

Area - comparative: slightly more than twice the size of New Hampshire

Land boundaries:
total: 275 km
border countries: Haiti 275 km

Coastline: 1,288 km

Maritime claims:
contiguous zone: 24 nm
continental shelf: 200 nm or to the edge of the continental margin
exclusive economic zone: 200 nm
territorial sea: 6 nm

Climate: tropical maritime; little seasonal temperature variation; seasonal variation in rainfall

Terrain: rugged highlands and mountains with fertile valleys interspersed

Elevation extremes:
lowest point: Lago Enriquillo -46 m
highest point: Pico Duarte 3,175 m

Natural resources: nickel, bauxite, gold, silver

Land use:
arable land: 21%
permanent crops: 9%
permanent pastures: 43%
forests and woodland: 12%
other: 15% (1993 est.)

Irrigated land: 2,300 sq km (1993 est.)

Natural hazards: lies in the middle of the hurricane belt and subject to severe storms from June to

Dominican Republic *(continued)*

October; occasional flooding; periodic droughts
Environment - current issues: water shortages; soil eroding into the sea damages coral reefs; deforestation; Hurricane Georges damage
Environment - international agreements:
party to: Biodiversity, Climate Change, Desertification, Endangered Species, Marine Dumping, Marine Life Conservation, Nuclear Test Ban, Ozone Layer Protection
signed, but not ratified: Law of the Sea
Geography - note: shares island of Hispaniola with Haiti (eastern two-thirds is the Dominican Republic, western one-third is Haiti)

People

Population: 8,129,734 (July 1999 est.)
Age structure:
0-14 years: 35% (male 1,447,435; female 1,393,122)
15-64 years: 61% (male 2,501,206; female 2,426,564)
65 years and over: 4% (male 171,049; female 190,358) (1999 est.)
Population growth rate: 1.62% (1999 est.)
Birth rate: 25.97 births/1,000 population (1999 est.)
Death rate: 5.66 deaths/1,000 population (1999 est.)
Net migration rate: -4.14 migrant(s)/1,000 population (1999 est.)
Sex ratio:
at birth: 1.05 male(s)/female
under 15 years: 1.04 male(s)/female
15-64 years: 1.03 male(s)/female
65 years and over: 0.9 male(s)/female
total population: 1.03 male(s)/female (1999 est.)
Infant mortality rate: 42.52 deaths/1,000 live births (1999 est.)
Life expectancy at birth:
total population: 70.07 years
male: 67.86 years
female: 72.4 years (1999 est.)
Total fertility rate: 3.03 children born/woman (1999 est.)
Nationality:
noun: Dominican(s)
adjective: Dominican
Ethnic groups: white 16%, black 11%, mixed 73%
Religions: Roman Catholic 95%
Languages: Spanish
Literacy:
definition: age 15 and over can read and write
total population: 82.1%
male: 82%
female: 82.2% (1995 est.)

Government

Country name:
conventional long form: Dominican Republic
conventional short form: none
local long form: Republica Dominicana
local short form: none
Data code: DR
Government type: republic

Capital: Santo Domingo
Administrative divisions: 29 provinces (provincias, singular - provincia) and 1 district* (distrito); Azua, Baoruco, Barahona, Dajabon, Distrito Nacional*, Duarte, Elias Pina, El Seibo, Espaillat, Hato Mayor, Independencia, La Altagracia, La Romana, La Vega, Maria Trinidad Sanchez, Monsenor Nouel, Monte Cristi, Monte Plata, Pedernales, Peravia, Puerto Plata, Salcedo, Samana, Sanchez Ramirez, San Cristobal, San Juan, San Pedro de Macoris, Santiago, Santiago Rodriguez, Valverde
Independence: 27 February 1844 (from Haiti)
National holiday: Independence Day, 27 February (1844)
Constitution: 28 November 1966
Legal system: based on French civil codes
Suffrage: 18 years of age, universal and compulsory; married persons regardless of age
note: members of the armed forces and police cannot vote
Executive branch:
chief of state: President Leonel FERNANDEZ Reyna (since 16 August 1996); Vice President Jaime David FERNANDEZ Mirabal (since 16 August 1996); note - the president is both the chief of state and head of government
head of government: President Leonel FERNANDEZ Reyna (since 16 August 1996); Vice President Jaime David FERNANDEZ Mirabal (since 16 August 1996); note - the president is both the chief of state and head of government
cabinet: Cabinet nominated by the president
elections: president and vice president elected on the same ticket by popular vote for four-year term; election last held 16 May 1996; runoff election held 30 June 1996 (next to be held 16 May 2000)
election results: Leonel FERNANDEZ Reyna elected president; percent of vote - Leonel FERNANDEZ Reyna (PLD) 51.25%, Jose Francisco PENA Gomez (PRD) 48.75%
Legislative branch: bicameral National Congress or Congreso Nacional consists of the Senate or Senado (30 seats; members are elected by popular vote to serve four-year terms) and the Chamber of Deputies or Camara de Diputados (120 seats; members are elected by popular vote to serve four-year terms)
elections: Senate - last held 16 May 1998 (next to be held NA May 2002); Chamber of Deputies - last held 16 May 1998 (next to be held NA May 2002)
election results: Senate - percent of vote by party - NA; seats by party - PRD 24, PLD 4, PRSC 2; Chamber of Deputies - percent of vote by party - NA; seats by party - PRD 83, PLD 49, PRSC 17
Judicial branch: Supreme Court or Corte Suprema (judges are elected by a Council made up of legislative and executive members with the president presiding)
Political parties and leaders:
major parties: Social Christian Reformist Party or PRSC [Joaquin BALAGUER Ricardo]; Dominican Liberation Party or PLD [Lidio CADET]; Dominican Revolutionary Party or PRD [Enmanuel ESQUEA];

Independent Revolutionary Party or PRI [leader NA]
minor parties: National Veterans and Civilian Party or PNVC [Juan Rene BEAUCHAMPS Javier]; Liberal Party of the Dominican Republic or PLRD [Andres Van Der HORST]; Democratic Quisqueyan Party or PQD [Elias WESSIN Chavez]; National Progressive Force or FNP [Pelegrin CASTILLO]; Popular Christian Party or PPC [Rogelio DELGADO Bogaert]; Dominican Communist Party or PCD [Narciso ISA Conde]; Dominican Workers' Party or PTD [Ivan RODRIGUEZ]; Anti-Imperialist Patriotic Union or UPA [Ignacio RODRIGUEZ Chiappini]; Alliance for Democracy Party or APD [Maximilano Rabelais PUIG Miller, Nelsida MARMOLEJOS, Vicente BENGOA]; Democratic Union or UD [Fernando ALVAREZ Bogaert]
note: in 1983 several leftist parties, including the PCD, joined to form the Dominican Leftist Front or FID; however, they still retain individual party structures
Political pressure groups and leaders: Collective of Popular Organizations or COP
International organization participation: ACP, Caricom (observer), ECLAC, FAO, G-11, G-77, IADB, IAEA, IBRD, ICAO, ICFTU, ICRM, IDA, IFAD, IFC, IFRCS, IHO, ILO, IMF, IMO, Intelsat, Interpol, IOC, IOM, ISO (subscriber), ITU, LAES, LAIA (observer), NAM (guest), OAS, OPANAL, OPCW, PCA, UN, UNCTAD, UNESCO, UNIDO, UPU, WCL, WFTU, WHO, WMO, WToO, WTrO
Diplomatic representation in the US:
chief of mission: Ambassador Bernardo VEGA Boyrie
chancery: 1715 22nd Street NW, Washington, DC 20008
telephone: [1] (202) 332-62801
FAX: [1] (202) 265-8057
consulate(s) general: Boston, Chicago, Los Angeles, Mayaguez (Puerto Rico), Miami, New Orleans, New York, Philadelphia, San Francisco, and San Juan (Puerto Rico)
consulate(s): Charlotte Amalie (Virgin Islands), Detroit, Houston, Jacksonville, Mobile, and Ponce (Puerto Rico)
Diplomatic representation from the US:
chief of mission: Ambassador (vacant)
embassy: corner of Calle Cesar Nicolas Penson and Calle Leopoldo Navarro, Santo Domingo
mailing address: Unit 5500, APO AA 34041-5500
telephone: [1] (809) 221-2171
FAX: [1] (809) 686-7437
Flag description: a centered white cross that extends to the edges divides the flag into four rectangles - the top ones are blue (hoist side) and red, the bottom ones are red (hoist side) and blue; a small coat of arms is at the center of the cross

Economy

Economy - overview: In December 1996, incoming President FERNANDEZ presented a bold reform package for this Caribbean economy - including the devaluation of the peso, income tax cuts, a 50% increase in sales taxes, reduced import tariffs, and increased gasoline prices - in an attempt to create a

Dominican Republic (continued)

market-oriented economy that can compete internationally. Even though most reforms are stalled in the legislature, the economy grew vigorously in 1997-98, with tourism and telecommunications leading the advance. The government is working to increase electric generating capacity, a key to continued economic growth, but the privatization of the state electricity company has met numerous delays. In late September 1998, Hurricane Georges caused approximately $1.3 billion in damages, largely to agriculture and infrastructure.

GDP: purchasing power parity - $39.8 billion (1998 est.)

GDP - real growth rate: 7% (1998 est.)

GDP - per capita: purchasing power parity - $5,000 (1998 est.)

GDP - composition by sector:
agriculture: 19%
industry: 25%
services: 56% (1996 est.)

Population below poverty line: 20.6% (1992 est.)

Household income or consumption by percentage share:
lowest 10%: 1.6%
highest 10%: 39.6% (1989)

Inflation rate (consumer prices): 6% (1998 est.)

Labor force: 2.3 million to 2.6 million

Labor force - by occupation: agriculture 50%, services and government 32%, industry 18% (1991 est.)

Unemployment rate: 16% (1997 est.)

Budget:
revenues: $2.3 billion
expenditures: $2.9 billion, including capital expenditures of $867 million (1999 est.)

Industries: tourism, sugar processing, ferronickel and gold mining, textiles, cement, tobacco

Industrial production growth rate: 6.3% (1995 est.)

Electricity - production: 6.7 billion kWh (1996)

Electricity - production by source:
fossil fuel: 70.15%
hydro: 29.85%
nuclear: 0%
other: 0% (1996)

Electricity - consumption: 6.7 billion kWh (1996)

Electricity - exports: 0 kWh (1996)

Electricity - imports: 0 kWh (1996)

Agriculture - products: sugarcane, coffee, cotton, cocoa, tobacco, rice, beans, potatoes, corn, bananas; cattle, pigs, dairy products, beef, eggs

Exports: $997 million (1997 est.)

Exports - commodities: ferronickel, sugar, gold, coffee, cocoa

Exports - partners: US 45%, EU 19.9%, Canada 3.6%, South Korea 3.3% (1996)

Imports: $3.6 billion (1998)

Imports - commodities: foodstuffs, petroleum, cotton and fabrics, chemicals and pharmaceuticals

Imports - partners: US 44%, EU 16%, Venezuela 11%, Netherlands Antilles, Mexico, Japan (1995)

Debt - external: $3.6 billion (1997)

Economic aid - recipient: $239.6 million (1995)

Currency: 1 Dominican peso (RD$) = 100 centavos

Exchange rates: Dominican pesos (RD$) per US$1 - 15.949 (January 1999), 15.267 (1998), 14.265 (1997), 13.775 (1996), 13.597 (1995), 13.160 (1994)

Fiscal year: calendar year

Communications

Telephones: 190,000 (1987 est.)

Telephone system:
domestic: relatively efficient system based on islandwide microwave radio relay network
international: 1 coaxial submarine cable; satellite earth station - 1 Intelsat (Atlantic Ocean)

Radio broadcast stations: AM 120, FM 0, shortwave 6

Radios: NA

Television broadcast stations: 25 (1997)

Televisions: 728,000 (1993 est.)

Transportation

Railways:
total: 757 km
standard gauge: 375 km 1.435-m gauge (Central Romana Railroad)
narrow gauge: 142 km 0.762-m gauge (Dominica Government Railway); 240 km operated by sugar companies in various gauges (0.558-m, 0.762-m, 1.067-m gauges) (1995)

Highways:
total: 12,600 km
paved: 6,224 km
unpaved: 6,376 km (1996 est.)

Pipelines: crude oil 96 km; petroleum products 8 km

Ports and harbors: Barahona, La Romana, Puerto Plata, San Pedro de Macoris, Santo Domingo

Merchant marine:
total: 1 cargo ship (1,000 GRT or over) totaling 1,587 GRT/1,165 DWT (1998 est.)

Airports: 36 (1998 est.)

Airports - with paved runways:
total: 14
over 3,047 m: 3
2,438 to 3,047 m: 1
1,524 to 2,437 m: 5
914 to 1,523 m: 3
under 914 m: 2 (1998 est.)

Airports - with unpaved runways:
total: 22
1,524 to 2,437 m: 1
914 to 1,523 m: 6
under 914 m: 15 (1998 est.)

Military

Military branches: Army, Navy, Air Force, National Police

Military manpower - military age: 18 years of age

Military manpower - availability:
males age 15-49: 2,156,827 (1999 est.)

Military manpower - fit for military service:
males age 15-49: 1,355,342 (1999 est.)

Military manpower - reaching military age annually:
males: 82,902 (1999 est.)

Military expenditures - dollar figure: $180 million (1998)

Military expenditures - percent of GDP: 1.1% (1998)

Transnational Issues

Disputes - international: none

Illicit drugs: transshipment point for South American drugs destined for the US

Ecuador

Galapagos Islands — Islands not shown in true geographical position.

Geography

Location: Western South America, bordering the Pacific Ocean at the Equator, between Colombia and Peru

Geographic coordinates: 2 00 S, 77 30 W

Map references: South America

Area:
total: 283,560 sq km
land: 276,840 sq km
water: 6,720 sq km
note: includes Galapagos Islands

Area - comparative: slightly smaller than Nevada

Land boundaries:
total: 2,010 km
border countries: Colombia 590 km, Peru 1,420 km

Coastline: 2,237 km

Maritime claims:
continental shelf: claims continental shelf between mainland and Galapagos Islands
territorial sea: 200 nm

Climate: tropical along coast becoming cooler inland

Terrain: coastal plain (costa), inter-Andean central highlands (sierra), and flat to rolling eastern jungle (oriente)

Elevation extremes:
lowest point: Pacific Ocean 0 m
highest point: Chimborazo 6,267 m

Natural resources: petroleum, fish, timber

Land use:
arable land: 6%
permanent crops: 5%
permanent pastures: 18%
forests and woodland: 56%
other: 15% (1993 est.)

Irrigated land: 5,560 sq km (1993 est.)

Natural hazards: frequent earthquakes, landslides, volcanic activity; periodic droughts

Environment - current issues: deforestation; soil erosion; desertification; water pollution; pollution from oil production wastes

Environment - international agreements:
party to: Antarctic-Environmental Protocol, Antarctic Treaty, Biodiversity, Climate Change, Desertification, Endangered Species, Hazardous Wastes, Nuclear Test Ban, Ozone Layer Protection, Ship Pollution, Tropical Timber 83, Tropical Timber 94, Wetlands, Whaling
signed, but not ratified: Climate Change-Kyoto Protocol

Geography - note: Cotopaxi in Andes is highest active volcano in world

People

Population: 12,562,496 (July 1999 est.)

Age structure:
0-14 years: 35% (male 2,250,690; female 2,172,302)
15-64 years: 60% (male 3,745,390; female 3,833,841)
65 years and over: 5% (male 261,090; female 299,183) (1999 est.)

Population growth rate: 1.78% (1999 est.)

Birth rate: 22.26 births/1,000 population (1999 est.)

Death rate: 5.06 deaths/1,000 population (1999 est.)

Net migration rate: 0.55 migrant(s)/1,000 population (1999 est.)

Sex ratio:
at birth: 1.05 male(s)/female
under 15 years: 1.04 male(s)/female
15-64 years: 0.98 male(s)/female
65 years and over: 0.87 male(s)/female
total population: 0.99 male(s)/female (1999 est.)

Infant mortality rate: 30.69 deaths/1,000 live births (1999 est.)

Life expectancy at birth:
total population: 72.16 years
male: 69.54 years
female: 74.9 years (1999 est.)

Total fertility rate: 2.63 children born/woman (1999 est.)

Nationality:
noun: Ecuadorian(s)
adjective: Ecuadorian

Ethnic groups: mestizo (mixed Amerindian and Spanish) 55%, Amerindian 25%, Spanish 10%, black 10%

Religions: Roman Catholic 95%

Languages: Spanish (official), Amerindian languages (especially Quechua)

Literacy:
definition: age 15 and over can read and write
total population: 90.1%
male: 92%
female: 88.2% (1995 est.)

Government

Country name:
conventional long form: Republic of Ecuador
conventional short form: Ecuador
local long form: Republica del Ecuador
local short form: Ecuador
Data code: EC

Government type: republic

Capital: Quito

Administrative divisions: 21 provinces (provincias, singular - provincia); Azuay, Bolivar, Canar, Carchi, Chimborazo, Cotopaxi, El Oro, Esmeraldas, Galapagos, Guayas, Imbabura, Loja, Los Rios, Manabi, Morona-Santiago, Napo, Pastaza, Pichincha, Sucumbios, Tungurahua, Zamora-Chinchipe
note: a new province, Orellana, was reported to have been formed in 1998

Independence: 24 May 1822 (from Spain)

National holiday: Independence Day, 10 August (1809) (independence of Quito)

Constitution: 10 August 1998

Legal system: based on civil law system; has not accepted compulsory ICJ jurisdiction

Suffrage: 18 years of age; universal, compulsory for literate persons ages 18-65, optional for other eligible voters

Executive branch:
chief of state: President Jamil MAHUAD (since 10 August 1998); Vice President Gustavo NOBOA (since 10 August 1998); note - the president is both the chief of state and head of government
head of government: President Jamil MAHUAD (since 10 August 1998); Vice President Gustavo NOBOA (since 10 August 1998); note - the president is both the chief of state and head of government
cabinet: Cabinet appointed by the president
elections: president and vice president elected on the same ticket by popular vote for four-year terms; election last held 31 May 1998; runoff election held 12 July 1998 (next to be held NA 2002)
election results: Jamil MAHUAD elected president; percent of vote - 51%

Legislative branch: unicameral National Congress or Congreso Nacional (121 seats; 79 members are popularly elected at-large nationally to serve four-year terms; 42 members are popularly elected by province - two per province - for four-year terms)
elections: last held 31 May 1998 (next to be held NA May 2002)
election results: percent of vote by party - NA; seats by party - DP 32, PSC 27, PRE 24, ID 18, P-NP 9, FRA 5, PCE 3, MPD 2, CFP 1; note - defections by members of National Congress are commonplace, resulting in frequent changes in the numbers of seats held by the various parties

Judicial branch: Supreme Court (Corte Suprema), new justices are elected by the full Supreme Court

Political parties and leaders:
Center-Right parties: Social Christian Party or PSC [Jaime NEBOT Saadi, president]; Ecuadorian Conservative Party or PCE [Freddy BRAVO]
Center-Left parties: Democratic Left or ID [Rodrigo BORJA Cevallos]; Popular Democracy or DP [Jamil MAHUAD]; Radical Alfarista Front or FRA [Fabian ALARCON, director]
Populist-Left parties: Roldosist Party or PRE [Abdala BUCARAM Ortiz, director]
Populist parties: Concentration of Popular Forces or CFP [Averroes BUCARAM]; Pachakutik-New Country

Ecuador (continued)

or P-NP [Nina PACARI and Freddy EHLERS]
Far-Left parties: Popular Democratic Movement or MPD [Jaime HURTADO Gonzalez]
International organization participation: CAN, ECLAC, FAO, G-11, G-77, IADB, IAEA, IBRD, ICAO, ICC, ICFTU, ICRM, IDA, IFAD, IFC, IFRCS, IHO, ILO, IMF, IMO, Intelsat, Interpol, IOC, IOM, ISO, ITU, LAES, LAIA, NAM, OAS, OPANAL, OPCW, PCA, RG, UN, UNCTAD, UNESCO, UNIDO, UPU, WCL, WFTU, WHO, WIPO, WMO, WToO, WTrO
Diplomatic representation in the US:
chief of mission: Ambassador Ivonne A-BAKI
chancery: 2535 15th Street NW, Washington, DC 20009
telephone: [1] (202) 234-7200
FAX: [1] (202) 667-3482
consulate(s) general: Chicago, Houston, Los Angeles, Miami, New Orleans, New York, Newark, Philadelphia, and San Francisco
Diplomatic representation from the US:
chief of mission: Ambassador Leslie M. ALEXANDER
embassy: Avenida 12 de Octubre y Avenida Patria, Quito
mailing address: APO AA 34039
telephone: [593] (2) 562-890
FAX: [593] (2) 502-052
consulate(s) general: Guayaquil
Flag description: three horizontal bands of yellow (top, double width), blue, and red with the coat of arms superimposed at the center of the flag; similar to the flag of Colombia that is shorter and does not bear a coat of arms

Economy

Economy - overview: Ecuador has substantial oil resources and rich agricultural areas. Because the country exports primary products such as oil, bananas, and shrimp, fluctuations in world market prices can have a substantial domestic impact. Ecuador joined the World Trade Organization in 1996, but has failed to comply with many of its accession commitments. In recent years, growth has been uneven due to ill-conceived fiscal stabilization measures. The populist government of Abdala BUCARAM Ortiz proposed a major currency reform in 1996, but popular discontent with BUCARAM'S austerity measures and rampant official corruption led to his replacement by National Congress with Fabian ALARCON in February 1997. ALARCON adopted a minimalist economic program that put off necessary reforms until August 1998 when President Jamil MAHUAD was elected. MAHAUD inherited an economy in crisis due to mismanagement, El Nino damage to key export sectors such as agriculture, and low world commodity prices in the wake of the Asian financial crisis. MAHAUD announced a fiscal austerity package and expressed interest in an IMF agreement but faces major difficulties in promoting economic growth, including possible political objections to further reform.
GDP: purchasing power parity - $58.7 billion (1998 est.)
GDP - real growth rate: 1% (1998 est.)

GDP - per capita: purchasing power parity - $4,800 (1998 est.)
GDP - composition by sector:
agriculture: 12%
industry: 37%
services: 51% (1996 est.)
Population below poverty line: 35% (1994 est.)
Household income or consumption by percentage share:
lowest 10%: 2.3%
highest 10%: 37.6% (1994)
Inflation rate (consumer prices): 43% (1998 est.)
Labor force: 4.2 million
Labor force - by occupation: agriculture 29%, manufacturing 18%, commerce 15%, services and other activities 38% (1990)
Unemployment rate: 12% with widespread underemployment (November 1998 est.)
Budget:
revenues: planned $5.1 billion not including revenue from potential privatizations
expenditures: $5.1 billion (1999)
Industries: petroleum, food processing, textiles, metal work, paper products, wood products, chemicals, plastics, fishing, lumber
Industrial production growth rate: 2.4% (1997 est.)
Electricity - production: 8.45 billion kWh (1996)
Electricity - production by source:
fossil fuel: 17.16%
hydro: 82.84%
nuclear: 0%
other: 0% (1996)
Electricity - consumption: 8.45 billion kWh (1996)
Electricity - exports: 0 kWh (1996)
Electricity - imports: 0 kWh (1996)
Agriculture - products: bananas, coffee, cocoa, rice, potatoes, manioc (tapioca), plantains, sugarcane; cattle, sheep, pigs, beef, pork, dairy products; balsa wood; fish, shrimp
Exports: $3.4 billion (f.o.b., 1997)
Exports - commodities: petroleum 30%, bananas 26%, shrimp 16%, cut flowers 2%, fish 1.9%
Exports - partners: US 39%, Latin America 25%, EU countries 22%, Asia 12%
Imports: $2.9 billion (c.i.f., 1997)
Imports - commodities: transport equipment, consumer goods, vehicles, machinery, chemicals
Imports - partners: US 32%, EU 19%, Latin America 35%, Asia 11%
Debt - external: $12.5 billion (1997)
Economic aid - recipient: $695.7 million (1995)
Currency: 1 sucre (S/) = 100 centavos
Exchange rates: sucres (S/) per US$1 - 7,133.1 (January 1999), 5,446.6 (1998), 3,988.3 (1997), 3,189.5 (1996), 2,564.5 (1995), 2,196.7 (1994)
Fiscal year: calendar year

Communications

Telephones: 586,300 (1994 est.)
Telephone system:
domestic: facilities generally inadequate and

unreliable
international: satellite earth station - 1 Intelsat (Atlantic Ocean)
Radio broadcast stations: AM 272, FM 0, shortwave 39
Radios: NA
Television broadcast stations: 15 (including one station on the Galapagos Islands) (1997)
Televisions: 940,000 (1992 est.)

Transportation

Railways:
total: 965 km (single track)
narrow gauge: 965 km 1.067-m gauge
Highways:
total: 42,874 km
paved: 5,752 km
unpaved: 37,122 km (1998 est.)
Waterways: 1,500 km
Pipelines: crude oil 800 km; petroleum products 1,358 km
Ports and harbors: Esmeraldas, Guayaquil, La Libertad, Manta, Puerto Bolivar, San Lorenzo
Merchant marine:
total: 23 ships (1,000 GRT or over) totaling 99,078 GRT/162,423 DWT
ships by type: chemical tanker 2, liquefied gas tanker 1, oil tanker 17, passenger 3 (1998 est.)
Airports: 183 (1998 est.)
Airports - with paved runways:
total: 56
over 3,047 m: 2
2,438 to 3,047 m: 6
1,524 to 2,437 m: 15
914 to 1,523 m: 14
under 914 m: 19 (1998 est.)
Airports - with unpaved runways:
total: 127
914 to 1,523 m: 37
under 914 m: 90 (1998 est.)
Heliports: 1 (1998 est.)

Military

Military branches: Army (Ejercito Ecuatoriano), Navy (Armada Ecuatoriana, includes Marines), Air Force (Fuerza Aerea Ecuatoriana), National Police
Military manpower - military age: 20 years of age
Military manpower - availability:
males age 15-49: 3,259,534 (1999 est.)
Military manpower - fit for military service:
males age 15-49: 2,199,704 (1999 est.)
Military manpower - reaching military age annually:
males: 130,208 (1999 est.)
Military expenditures - dollar figure: $720 million (1998)
Military expenditures - percent of GDP: 3.4% (1998)

Transnational Issues

Disputes - international: on 26 October 1998, Peru

Ecuador (continued)

and Ecuador concluded treaties on commerce and navigation and on boundary integration, to complete a package of agreements settling the long-standing boundary dispute between them; demarcation of the agreed-upon boundary was scheduled to begin in mid-January 1999

Illicit drugs: significant transit country for derivatives of coca originating in Colombia, Bolivia, and Peru; importer of precursor chemicals used in production of illicit narcotics; important money-laundering hub

Egypt

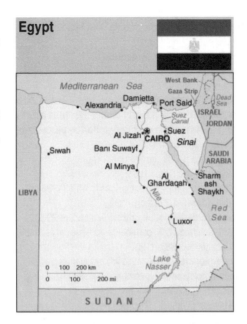

Introduction

Background: One of the four great ancient civilizations, Egypt, ruled by powerful pharaohs, bequeathed to Western civilization numerous advances in technology, science, and the arts. For the last two millennia, however, Egypt has served a series of foreign masters - Persians, Greeks, Romans, Byzantines, Arabs, Turks, and the British. Formal independence came in 1922, and the remnants of British control ended after World War II. The completion of the Aswan High Dam in 1981 altered the time-honored place of the Nile River in the agriculture and ecology of Egypt. A rapidly growing population will stress Egyptian society and resources as it enters the new millenium.

Geography

Location: Northern Africa, bordering the Mediterranean Sea, between Libya and the Gaza Strip
Geographic coordinates: 27 00 N, 30 00 E
Map references: Africa
Area:
total: 1,001,450 sq km
land: 995,450 sq km
water: 6,000 sq km
Area - comparative: slightly more than three times the size of New Mexico
Land boundaries:
total: 2,689 km
border countries: Gaza Strip 11 km, Israel 255 km, Libya 1,150 km, Sudan 1,273 km
Coastline: 2,450 km
Maritime claims:
contiguous zone: 24 nm
continental shelf: 200-m depth or to the depth of exploitation
exclusive economic zone: 200 nm
territorial sea: 12 nm
Climate: desert; hot, dry summers with moderate

winters
Terrain: vast desert plateau interrupted by Nile valley and delta
Elevation extremes:
lowest point: Qattara Depression -133 m
highest point: Mount Catherine 2,629 m
Natural resources: petroleum, natural gas, iron ore, phosphates, manganese, limestone, gypsum, talc, asbestos, lead, zinc
Land use:
arable land: 2%
permanent crops: 0%
permanent pastures: 0%
forests and woodland: 0%
other: 98% (1993 est.)
Irrigated land: 32,460 sq km (1993 est.)
Natural hazards: periodic droughts; frequent earthquakes, flash floods, landslides, volcanic activity; hot, driving windstorm called khamsin occurs in spring; dust storms, sandstorms
Environment - current issues: agricultural land being lost to urbanization and windblown sands; increasing soil salination below Aswan High Dam; desertification; oil pollution threatening coral reefs, beaches, and marine habitats; other water pollution from agricultural pesticides, raw sewage, and industrial effluents; very limited natural fresh water resources away from the Nile which is the only perennial water source; rapid growth in population overstraining natural resources
Environment - international agreements:
party to: Biodiversity, Climate Change, Desertification, Endangered Species, Environmental Modification, Hazardous Wastes, Law of the Sea, Marine Dumping, Nuclear Test Ban, Ozone Layer Protection, Ship Pollution, Tropical Timber 83, Tropical Timber 94, Wetlands, Whaling
signed, but not ratified: none of the selected agreements
Geography - note: controls Sinai Peninsula, only land bridge between Africa and remainder of Eastern Hemisphere; controls Suez Canal, shortest sea link between Indian Ocean and Mediterranean Sea; size, and juxtaposition to Israel, establish its major role in Middle Eastern geopolitics

People

Population: 67,273,906 (July 1999 est.)
Age structure:
0-14 years: 36% (male 12,260,845; female 11,712,752)
15-64 years: 61% (male 20,604,620; female 20,211,012)
65 years and over: 3% (male 1,099,517; female 1,385,160) (1999 est.)
Population growth rate: 1.82% (1999 est.)
Birth rate: 26.8 births/1,000 population (1999 est.)
Death rate: 8.27 deaths/1,000 population (1999 est.)
Net migration rate: -0.35 migrant(s)/1,000 population (1999 est.)
Sex ratio:
at birth: 1.05 male(s)/female

Egypt (continued)

under 15 years: 1.05 male(s)/female
15-64 years: 1.02 male(s)/female
65 years and over: 0.79 male(s)/female
total population: 1.02 male(s)/female (1999 est.)
Infant mortality rate: 67.46 deaths/1,000 live births (1999 est.)
Life expectancy at birth:
total population: 62.39 years
male: 60.39 years
female: 64.49 years (1999 est.)
Total fertility rate: 3.33 children born/woman (1999 est.)
Nationality:
noun: Egyptian(s)
adjective: Egyptian
Ethnic groups: Eastern Hamitic stock (Egyptians, Bedouins, and Berbers) 99%, Greek, Nubian, Armenian, other European (primarily Italian and French) 1%
Religions: Muslim (mostly Sunni) 94% (official estimate), Coptic Christian and other 6% (official estimate)
Languages: Arabic (official), English and French widely understood by educated classes
Literacy:
definition: age 15 and over can read and write
total population: 51.4%
male: 63.6%
female: 38.8% (1995 est.)

Government

Country name:
conventional long form: Arab Republic of Egypt
conventional short form: Egypt
local long form: Jumhuriyat Misr al-Arabiyah
local short form: Misr
former: United Arab Republic (with Syria)
Data code: EG
Government type: republic
Capital: Cairo
Administrative divisions: 26 governorates (muhafazat, singular - muhafazah); Ad Daqahliyah, Al Bahr al Ahmar, Al Buhayrah, Al Fayyum, Al Gharbiyah, Al Iskandariyah, Al Isma'iliyah, Al Jizah, Al Minufiyah, Al Minya, Al Qahirah, Al Qalyubiyah, Al Wadi al Jadid, Ash Sharqiyah, As Suways, Aswan, Asyut, Bani Suwayf, Bur Sa'id, Dumyat, Janub Sina', Kafr ash Shaykh, Matruh, Qina, Shamal Sina', Suhaj
Independence: 28 February 1922 (from UK)
National holiday: Anniversary of the Revolution, 23 July (1952)
Constitution: 11 September 1971
Legal system: based on English common law, Islamic law, and Napoleonic codes; judicial review by Supreme Court and Council of State (oversees validity of administrative decisions); accepts compulsory ICJ jurisdiction, with reservations
Suffrage: 18 years of age; universal and compulsory
Executive branch:
chief of state: President Mohammed Hosni MUBARAK (since 14 October 1981)
head of government: Prime Minister Kamal Ahmed

El-GANZOURI (since 4 January 1996)
cabinet: Cabinet appointed by the president
elections: president nominated by the People's Assembly for a six-year term, the nomination must then be validated by a national, popular referendum; national referendum last held 4 October 1993 (next to be held NA October 1999); prime minister appointed by the president
election results: national referendum validated President MUBARAK's nomination by the People's Assembly to a third term
Legislative branch: bicameral system consists of the People's Assembly or Majlis al-Sha'b (454 seats; 444 elected by popular vote, 10 appointed by the president; members serve five-year terms) and the Advisory Council or Majlis al-Shura - which functions only in a consultative role (264 seats; 176 elected by popular vote, 88 appointed by the president; members serve NA-year terms)
elections: People's Assembly - last held 29 November 1995 (next to be held NA 2000); Advisory Council - last held 7 June 1995 (next to be held NA)
election results: People's Assembly - percent of vote by party - NDP 72%, independents 25%, opposition 3%; seats by party - NDP 317, independents 114, NWP 6, NPUG 5, Nasserist Arab Democratic Party 1, Liberals 1; Advisory Council - percent of vote by party - NDP 99%, independents 1%; seats by party - NA
Judicial branch: Supreme Constitutional Court
Political parties and leaders: National Democratic Party or NDP [President Mohammed Hosni MUBARAK, leader] is the dominant party; legal opposition parties are as follows: New Wafd Party or NWP [Fu'ad SIRAJ AL-DIN]; Socialist Labor Party or SLP [Ibrahim SHUKRI]; National Progressive Unionist Grouping or NPUG [Khalid MUHI AL-DIN]; Socialist Liberal Party [Mustafa Kamal MURAD]; Democratic Unionist Party [Mohammed 'Abd-al-Mun'im TURK]; Umma Party [Ahmad al-SABAHI]; Misr al-Fatah Party (Young Egypt Party) [leader NA]; Nasserist Arab Democratic Party [Dia' al-din DAWUD]; Democratic Peoples' Party [Anwar AFIFI]; The Greens Party [Kamal KIRAH]; Social Justice Party [Muhammad 'ABDAL-'AL]
note: formation of political parties must be approved by government
Political pressure groups and leaders: despite a constitutional ban against religious-based parties, the technically illegal Muslim Brotherhood constitutes MUBARAK's potentially most significant political opposition; MUBARAK tolerated limited political activity by the Brotherhood for his first two terms, but has moved more aggressively in the past two years to block its influence; trade unions and professional associations are officially sanctioned
International organization participation: ABEDA, ACC, ACCT (associate), AfDB, AFESD, AL, AMF, BSEC (observer), CAEU, CCC, EBRD, ECA, ESCWA, FAO, G-15, G-19, G-24, G-77, IAEA, IBRD, ICAO, ICC, ICRM, IDA, IDB, IFAD, IFC, IFRCS, IHO, ILO, IMF, IMO, Inmarsat, Intelsat, Interpol, IOC, IOM, ISO, ITU, MINURCA, MINURSO, MONUA,

NAM, OAPEC, OAS (observer), OAU, OIC, OSCE (partner), PCA, UN, UNCTAD, UNESCO, UNIDO, UNITAR, UNMIBH, UNMOP, UNOMIG, UNOMIL, UNOMSIL, UNPREDEP, UNRWA, UPU, WFTU, WHO, WIPO, WMO, WToO, WTrO
Diplomatic representation in the US:
chief of mission: Ambassador Ahmed MAHER al-Sayed
chancery: 3521 International Court NW, Washington, DC 20008
telephone: [1] (202) 895-5400
FAX: [1] (202) 244-4319, 5131
consulate(s) general: Chicago, Houston, New York, and San Francisco
Diplomatic representation from the US:
chief of mission: Ambassador Daniel C. KURTZER
embassy: (North Gate) 8, Kamel El-Din Salah Street, Garden City, Cairo
mailing address: Unit 64900, APO AE 09839-4900
telephone: [20] (2) 3557371
FAX: [20] (2) 3573200
Flag description: three equal horizontal bands of red (top), white, and black with the national emblem (a shield superimposed on a golden eagle facing the hoist side above a scroll bearing the name of the country in Arabic) centered in the white band; similar to the flag of Yemen, which has a plain white band; also similar to the flag of Syria that has two green stars and to the flag of Iraq, which has three green stars (plus an Arabic inscription) in a horizontal line centered in the white band

Economy

Economy - overview: At the end of the 1980s, Egypt faced problems of low productivity and poor economic management, compounded by the adverse social effects of excessive population growth, high inflation, and massive urban overcrowding. In the face of these pressures, in 1991 Egypt undertook wide-ranging macroeconomic stabilization and structural reform measures. This reform effort has been supported by three IMF arrangements, the last of which expired in September 1998. Egypt's reform efforts - and its participation in the Gulf war coalition - also led to massive debt relief under the Paris Club arrangements. Substantial progress has been made in improving macroeconomic performance. Cairo tamed inflation, slashed budget deficits, and built up foreign reserves to an all-time high. Although the pace of structural reforms - such as privatization and new business legislation - has been slower than envisioned under the IMF program, Egypt's steps toward a more market-oriented economy have prompted increased foreign investment. The November 1997 massacre of foreign tourists in Luxor affected tourism enough to slow the GDP growth rate for 1998 compared to earlier projections. Tourism's slow recovery, coupled with low world oil prices, caused a downturn in foreign exchange earnings in 1998, but external payments are not in crisis.
GDP: purchasing power parity - $188 billion (1998 est.)

Egypt (continued)

GDP - real growth rate: 5% (1998 est.)
GDP - per capita: purchasing power parity - $2,850 (1998 est.)
GDP - composition by sector:
agriculture: 16%
industry: 31%
services: 53% (1997)
Population below poverty line: NA%
Household income or consumption by percentage share:
lowest 10%: 3.9%
highest 10%: 26.7% (1991)
Inflation rate (consumer prices): 3.6% (1998)
Labor force: 17.4 million (1998 est.)
Labor force - by occupation: agriculture 40%, services, including government 38%, industry 22% (1990 est.)
Unemployment rate: 10% (1998 est.)
Budget:
revenues: $20 billion
expenditures: $20.8 billion, including capital expenditures of $4.4 billion (FY97/98)
Industries: textiles, food processing, tourism, chemicals, petroleum, construction, cement, metals
Industrial production growth rate: 9.4% (1997 est.)
Electricity - production: 46 billion kWh (1996)
Electricity - production by source:
fossil fuel: 76.09%
hydro: 23.91%
nuclear: 0%
other: 0% (1996)
Electricity - consumption: 46 billion kWh (1996)
Electricity - exports: 0 kWh (1996)
Electricity - imports: 0 kWh (1996)
Agriculture - products: cotton, rice, corn, wheat, beans, fruits, vegetables; cattle, water buffalo, sheep, goats; fish
Exports: $5.5 billion (f.o.b., FY97/98 est.)
Exports - commodities: crude oil and petroleum products, cotton yarn, raw cotton, textiles, metal products, chemicals
Exports - partners: EU, US, Japan
Imports: $16.7 billion (c.i.f., FY97/98 est.)
Imports - commodities: machinery and equipment, foods, fertilizers, wood products, durable consumer goods, capital goods
Imports - partners: US, EU, Japan
Debt - external: $28 billion (FY97/98 est.)
Economic aid - recipient: ODA, $2.4 billion (1996)
Currency: 1 Egyptian pound (£E) = 100 piasters
Exchange rates: Egyptian pounds (£E) per US$1 - 3.4 (November 1994); market rate - 3.3880 (January 1999), 3.3880 (1998), 3.3880 (1997), 3.3880 (1996), 3.3900 (1995), 3.3910 (1994)
Fiscal year: 1 July - 30 June

Communications

Telephones: 3.168 million (1996); 70,000 digital cellular telephone subscribers (1998); 7,400 analog cellular telephone subscribers (1997)
Telephone system: large system by Third World standards but inadequate for present requirements and undergoing extensive upgrading
domestic: principal centers at Alexandria, Cairo, Al Mansurah, Ismailia, Suez, and Tanta are connected by coaxial cable and microwave radio relay
international: satellite earth stations - 2 Intelsat (Atlantic Ocean and Indian Ocean), 1 Arabsat, and 1 Inmarsat; 5 coaxial submarine cables; tropospheric scatter to Sudan; microwave radio relay to Israel; participant in Medarabtel
Radio broadcast stations: AM 57, FM 14, shortwave 3 (1998 est.)
Radios: 16.45 million (1998 est.)
Television broadcast stations: 42 (in addition, there are nine channels received from Europe by satellite) (1997)
Televisions: 5 million (1998 est.)

Transportation

Railways:
total: 4,751 km
standard gauge: 4,751 km 1,435-m gauge (42 km electrified; 951 km double track)
Highways:
total: 64,000 km
paved: 49,984 km
unpaved: 14,016 km (1996 est.)
Waterways: 3,500 km (including the Nile, Lake Nasser, Alexandria-Cairo Waterway, and numerous smaller canals in the delta); Suez Canal, 193.5 km long (including approaches), used by oceangoing vessels drawing up to 16.1 m of water
Pipelines: crude oil 1,171 km; petroleum products 596 km; natural gas 460 km
Ports and harbors: Alexandria, Al Ghardaqah, Aswan, Asyut, Bur Safajah, Damietta, Marsa Matruh, Port Said, Suez
Merchant marine:
total: 180 ships (1,000 GRT or over) totaling 1,334,406 GRT/2,022,785 DWT
ships by type: bulk 25, cargo 63, container 1, liquefied gas tanker 1, oil tanker 14, passenger 56, refrigerated cargo 1, roll-on/roll-off cargo 16, short-sea passenger 3 (1998 est.)
Airports: 89 (1998 est.)
Airports - with paved runways:
total: 70
over 3,047 m: 10
2,438 to 3,047 m: 37
1,524 to 2,437 m: 16
914 to 1,523 m: 3
under 914 m: 4 (1998 est.)
Airports - with unpaved runways:
total: 19
2,438 to 3,047 m: 2
1,524 to 2,437 m: 2
914 to 1,523 m: 6
under 914 m: 9 (1998 est.)
Heliports: 2 (1998 est.)

Military

Military branches: Army, Navy, Air Force, Air Defense Command
Military manpower - military age: 20 years of age
Military manpower - availability:
males age 15-49: 17,756,706 (1999 est.)
Military manpower - fit for military service:
males age 15-49: 11,507,058 (1999 est.)
Military manpower - reaching military age annually:
males: 694,468 (1999 est.)
Military expenditures - dollar figure: $3.28 billion (FY95/96)
Military expenditures - percent of GDP: 8.2% (FY95/96)

Transnational Issues

Disputes - international: Egypt asserts its claim to the "Hala'ib Triangle," a barren area of 20,580 sq km under partial Sudanese administration that is defined by an administrative boundary which supersedes the treaty boundary of 1899
Illicit drugs: a transit point for Southwest Asian and Southeast Asian heroin and opium moving to Europe and the US; popular transit stop for Nigerian couriers

El Salvador

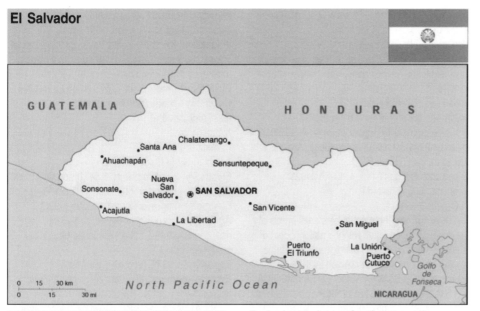

Geography

Location: Middle America, bordering the North Pacific Ocean, between Guatemala and Honduras
Geographic coordinates: 13 50 N, 88 55 W
Map references: Central America and the Caribbean
Area:
total: 21,040 sq km
land: 20,720 sq km
water: 320 sq km
Area - comparative: slightly smaller than Massachusetts
Land boundaries:
total: 545 km
border countries: Guatemala 203 km, Honduras 342 km
Coastline: 307 km
Maritime claims:
territorial sea: 200 nm
Climate: tropical; rainy season (May to October); dry season (November to April)
Terrain: mostly mountains with narrow coastal belt and central plateau
Elevation extremes:
lowest point: Pacific Ocean 0 m
highest point: Cerro El Pital 2,730 m
Natural resources: hydropower, geothermal power, petroleum
Land use:
arable land: 27%
permanent crops: 8%
permanent pastures: 29%
forests and woodland: 5%
other: 31% (1993 est.)
Irrigated land: 1,200 sq km (1993 est.)
Natural hazards: known as the Land of Volcanoes; frequent and sometimes very destructive earthquakes and volcanic activity
Environment - current issues: deforestation; soil erosion; water pollution; contamination of soils from disposal of toxic wastes; Hurricane Mitch damage

Environment - international agreements:
party to: Biodiversity, Climate Change, Climate Change-Kyoto Protocol, Desertification, Hazardous Wastes, Nuclear Test Ban, Ozone Layer Protection
signed, but not ratified: Law of the Sea
Geography - note: smallest Central American country and only one without a coastline on Caribbean Sea

People

Population: 5,839,079 (July 1999 est.)
Age structure:
0-14 years: 37% (male 1,091,500; female 1,044,658)
15-64 years: 58% (male 1,612,847; female 1,786,318)
65 years and over: 5% (male 138,052; female 165,704) (1999 est.)
Population growth rate: 1.53% (1999 est.)
Birth rate: 26.19 births/1,000 population (1999 est.)
Death rate: 6.2 deaths/1,000 population (1999 est.)
Net migration rate: -4.66 migrant(s)/1,000 population (1999 est.)
Sex ratio:
at birth: 1.05 male(s)/female
under 15 years: 1.04 male(s)/female
15-64 years: 0.9 male(s)/female
65 years and over: 0.83 male(s)/female
total population: 0.95 male(s)/female (1999 est.)
Infant mortality rate: 28.38 deaths/1,000 live births (1999 est.)
Life expectancy at birth:
total population: 70.02 years
male: 66.7 years
female: 73.5 years (1999 est.)
Total fertility rate: 2.99 children born/woman (1999 est.)
Nationality:
noun: Salvadoran(s)
adjective: Salvadoran
Ethnic groups: mestizo 94%, Amerindian 5%, white 1%

Religions: Roman Catholic 75%
note: there is extensive activity by Protestant groups throughout the country; by the end of 1992, there were an estimated 1 million Protestant evangelicals in El Salvador
Languages: Spanish, Nahua (among some Amerindians)
Literacy:
definition: age 15 and over can read and write
total population: 71.5%
male: 73.5%
female: 69.8% (1995 est.)

Government

Country name:
conventional long form: Republic of El Salvador
conventional short form: El Salvador
local long form: Republica de El Salvador
local short form: El Salvador
Data code: ES
Government type: republic
Capital: San Salvador
Administrative divisions: 14 departments (departamentos, singular - departamento); Ahuachapan, Cabanas, Chalatenango, Cuscatlan, La Libertad, La Paz, La Union, Morazan, San Miguel, San Salvador, Santa Ana, San Vicente, Sonsonate, Usulutan
Independence: 15 September 1821 (from Spain)
National holiday: Independence Day, 15 September (1821)
Constitution: 20 December 1983
Legal system: based on civil and Roman law, with traces of common law; judicial review of legislative acts in the Supreme Court; accepts compulsory ICJ jurisdiction, with reservations
note: Legislative Assembly passed landmark judicial reforms in 1996
Suffrage: 18 years of age; universal
Executive branch:
chief of state: President Armando CALDERON Sol (since 1 June 1994); Vice President Enrique BORGO Bustamante (since 1 June 1994); note - the president is both the chief of state and head of government
head of government: President Armando CALDERON Sol (since 1 June 1994); Vice President Enrique BORGO Bustamante (since 1 June 1994); note - the president is both the chief of state and head of government
cabinet: Council of Ministers
elections: president and vice president elected on the same ticket by popular vote for five-year terms; election last held 20 March 1994, with a run-off election held 24 April 1994 (next to be held 7 March 1999)
election results: Armando CALDERON Sol elected president; percent of vote - Armando CALDERON Sol (ARENA) 49.03%, Ruben ZAMORA Rivas (CD/FMLN/MNR) 24.09%, Fidel CHAVEZ Mena (PDC) 16.39%, other 10.49%; because no candidate received a majority, a run-off election was held and the results were as follows - Armando CALDERON

Sol (ARENA) 68.35%, Ruben ZAMORA Rivas (CD/FMLN/MNR) 31.65%

note: in the election held 7 March 1999, Francisco FLORES elected president, Carlos QUINTANILLA elected vice president (will take office 1 June 1999); percent of vote - Francisco FLORES (ARENA) 52%, Facundo GUARDADO (FMLN/USC) 29%, Ruben ZAMORA (CD) 8%, other parties 11%

Legislative branch: unicameral Legislative Assembly or Asamblea Legislativa (84 seats; members are elected by direct popular vote to serve three-year terms)

elections: last held 16 March 1997 (next to be held NA March 2000)

election results: percent of vote by party - ARENA 35.4%, FMLN 34.3%, PCN 8.1%, PDC 7.9%, CD 3.8%, PRSC 3.4%, PLD 3.2%, MU 2.1%, PD 1.0%, other 0.8%; seats by party - ARENA 28, FMLN 27, PCN 9, PDC 8, PRSC 3, CD 2, PLD 2, MU 1, PD 1, independent 3

Judicial branch: Supreme Court (Corte Suprema), judges are selected by the Legislative Assembly

Political parties and leaders: National Republican Alliance or ARENA [Alfredo CRISTIANI]; Farabundo Marti National Liberation Front or FMLN [Facundo GUARDADO, general coordinator]; Christian Democratic Party or PDC [Ronal UMANA, secretary general; title in dispute]; National Conciliation Party or PCN [Ciro CRUZ Zepeda, secretary general]; Democratic Convergence or CD [Ruben ZAMORA, secretary general]; Popular Labor Party or PPL [Jose VILANOVA, secretary general]; Liberal Democratic Party or PLD [Kirio Waldo SALGADO, president]; Social Christian Union or USC [Abraham RODRIGUEZ, president]; Democratic Party or PD [Ana Guadeloupe MARTINEZ, president]

note: the Social Christian Union or USC is formed by the union of the Social Christian Renovation Party or PRSC, the Unity Movement or MU, and the MSN

Political pressure groups and leaders:

labor organizations: National Confederation of Salvadoran Workers or CNTS; National Union of Salvadoran Workers or UNTS; Federation of the Construction Industry, Similar Transport and other activities, or FESINCONTRANS; Salvadoran Workers Central or CTS; Port Industry Union of El Salvador or SIPES; Electrical Industry Union of El Salvador or SIES; Workers Union of Electrical Corporation or STCEL

business organizations: Salvadoran Industrial Association or ASI; Salvadoran Assembly Industry Association or ASIC; National Association of Small Enterprise or ANEP

International organization participation: BCIE, CACM, ECLAC, FAO, G-77, IADB, IAEA, IBRD, ICAO, ICFTU, ICRM, IDA, IFAD, IFC, IFRCS, ILO, IMF, IMO, Intelsat, Interpol, IOC, IOM, ISO (correspondent), ITU, LAES, LAIA (observer), MINURSO, NAM (observer), OAS, OPANAL, OPCW, PCA, UN, UNCTAD, UNESCO, UNIDO, UPU, WCL, WFTU, WHO, WIPO, WMO, WToO, WTrO

Diplomatic representation in the US:

chief of mission: Ambassador Rene A. LEON

chancery: 2308 California Street NW, Washington, DC 20008

telephone: [1] (202) 265-9671

consulate(s) general: Chicago, Dallas, Houston, Los Angeles, Miami, New Orleans, New York, and San Francisco

consulate(s): Boston

Diplomatic representation from the US:

chief of mission: Ambassador Anne W. PATTERSON

embassy: Final Boulevard Santa Elena, Antiguo Cuscatlan, San Salvador

mailing address: Unit 3116, APO AA 34023

telephone: [503] 278-4444

FAX: [503] 278-6011

Flag description: three equal horizontal bands of blue (top), white, and blue with the national coat of arms centered in the white band; the coat of arms features a round emblem encircled by the words REPUBLICA DE EL SALVADOR EN LA AMERICA CENTRAL; similar to the flag of Nicaragua, which has a different coat of arms centered in the white band - it features a triangle encircled by the words REPUBLICA DE NICARAGUA on top and AMERICA CENTRAL on the bottom; also similar to the flag of Honduras, which has five blue stars arranged in an X pattern centered in the white band

Economy

Economy - overview: In recent years inflation has fallen to unprecedented levels, and exports have grown substantially. Even so, El Salvador has experienced sizable deficits in both its trade and its fiscal accounts. The trade deficit has been offset by remittances from the large number of Salvadorans living abroad and from external aid. El Salvador sustained damage from Hurricane Mitch, but not as much as other Central American countries. Inflation and the trade deficit are expected to rise somewhat as a result.

GDP: purchasing power parity - $17.5 billion (1998 est.)

GDP - real growth rate: 3.7% (1998 est.)

GDP - per capita: purchasing power parity - $3,000 (1998 est.)

GDP - composition by sector:

agriculture: 15%

industry: 24%

services: 61% (1997 est.)

Population below poverty line: 48.3% (1992 est.)

Household income or consumption by percentage share:

lowest 10%: 1.2%

highest 10%: 38.3% (1995)

Inflation rate (consumer prices): 2.6% (1998)

Labor force: 2.26 million (1997 est.)

Labor force - by occupation: agriculture 40%, commerce 16%, manufacturing 15%, government 13%, financial services 9%, transportation 6%, other 1%

Unemployment rate: 7.7% (1997 est.)

Budget:

revenues: $1.75 billion

expenditures: $1.82 billion, including capital expenditures of $317 million (1997 est.)

Industries: food processing, beverages, petroleum, chemicals, fertilizer, textiles, furniture, light metals

Industrial production growth rate: 7% (1997 est.)

Electricity - production: 3.575 billion kWh (1996)

Electricity - production by source:

fossil fuel: 22.38%

hydro: 61.54%

nuclear: 0%

other: 16.08% (1996)

Electricity - consumption: 3.547 billion kWh (1996)

Electricity - exports: 60 million kWh (1996)

Electricity - imports: 32 million kWh (1996)

Agriculture - products: coffee, sugarcane, corn, rice, beans, oilseed, cotton, sorghum; beef, dairy products; shrimp

Exports: $1.96 billion (f.o.b., 1997 est.)

Exports - commodities: coffee, sugar; shrimp; textiles

Exports - partners: US, Guatemala, Germany, Costa Rica, Honduras

Imports: $3.5 billion (c.i.f., 1997 est.)

Imports - commodities: raw materials, consumer goods, capital goods, fuels

Imports - partners: US, Guatemala, Mexico, Panama, Venezuela, Japan

Debt - external: $2.6 billion (yearend 1997)

Economic aid - recipient: $391.7 million (1995); note - US has committed $280 million in economic assistance to El Salvador for 1995-97 (excludes military aid)

Currency: 1 Salvadoran colon (C) = 100 centavos

Exchange rates: Salvadoran colones (C) per US$1 (end of period) - 8.755 (January 1999-1995), 8.750 (1994)

note: as of 1 June 1990, the rate is based on the average of the buying and selling rates, set on a weekly basis, for official receipts and payments, imports of petroleum, and coffee exports; prior to that date, a system of floating was in effect

Fiscal year: calendar year

Communications

Telephones: 350,000 (1997 est.)

Telephone system:

domestic: nationwide microwave radio relay system

international: satellite earth station - 1 Intelsat (Atlantic Ocean); connected to Central American Microwave System

Radio broadcast stations: AM 18, FM 80, shortwave 2

Radios: 1.5 million (1997 est.)

Television broadcast stations: 5 (1997)

Televisions: 700,000 (1997 est.)

Transportation

Railways:

total: 602 km (single track; note - some sections abandoned, unusable, or operating at reduced capacity)

El Salvador (continued)

narrow gauge: 602 km 0.914-m gauge
Highways:
total: 10,029 km
paved: 1,986 km (including 327 km of expressways)
unpaved: 8,043 km (1997 est.)
Waterways: Rio Lempa partially navigable
Ports and harbors: Acajutla, Puerto Cutuco, La Libertad, La Union, Puerto El Triunfo
Merchant marine: none
Airports: 86 (1998 est.)
Airports - with paved runways:
total: 4
over 3,047 m: 1
1,524 to 2,437 m: 1
914 to 1,523 m: 2 (1998 est.)
Airports - with unpaved runways:
total: 82
914 to 1,523 m: 17
under 914 m: 65 (1998 est.)
Heliports: 1 (1998 est.)

Military

Military branches: Army, Navy, Air Force
Military manpower - military age: 18 years of age
Military manpower - availability:
males age 15-49: 1,393,986 (1999 est.)
Military manpower - fit for military service:
males age 15-49: 884,093 (1999 est.)
Military manpower - reaching military age annually:
males: 65,224 (1999 est.)
Military expenditures - dollar figure: $105 million (1998)
Military expenditures - percent of GDP: 0.9% (1998)

Transnational Issues

Disputes - international: demarcation of boundary with Honduras defined by 1992 International Court of Justice (ICJ) decision has not been completed; small boundary section left unresolved by ICJ decision not yet reported to have been settled; with respect to the maritime boundary in the Golfo de Fonseca, ICJ referred to an earlier agreement in this century and advised that some tripartite resolution among El Salvador, Honduras and Nicaragua likely would be required
Illicit drugs: transshipment point for cocaine; marijuana produced for local consumption

Equatorial Guinea

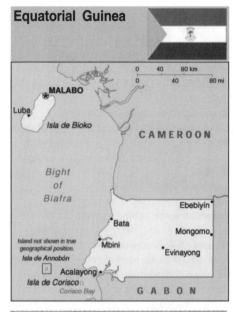

MALABO
Luba
Isla de Bioko
Bight of Biafra
CAMEROON
Ebebiyín
Bata
Mongomo
Mbini
Evinayong
Island not shown in true geographical position.
Isla de Annobón
Acalayong
Isla de Corisco
Corisco Bay
GABON

Geography

Location: Western Africa, bordering the Bight of Biafra, between Cameroon and Gabon
Geographic coordinates: 2 00 N, 10 00 E
Map references: Africa
Area:
total: 28,050 sq km
land: 28,050 sq km
water: 0 sq km
Area - comparative: slightly smaller than Maryland
Land boundaries:
total: 539 km
border countries: Cameroon 189 km, Gabon 350 km
Coastline: 296 km
Maritime claims:
exclusive economic zone: 200 nm
territorial sea: 12 nm
Climate: tropical; always hot, humid
Terrain: coastal plains rise to interior hills; islands are volcanic
Elevation extremes:
lowest point: Atlantic Ocean 0 m
highest point: Pico Basile 3,008 m
Natural resources: petroleum, timber, small unexploited deposits of gold, manganese, uranium
Land use:
arable land: 5%
permanent crops: 4%
permanent pastures: 4%
forests and woodland: 46%
other: 41% (1993 est.)
Irrigated land: NA sq km
Natural hazards: violent windstorms, flash floods
Environment - current issues: tap water is not potable; desertification
Environment - international agreements:
party to: Biodiversity, Desertification, Endangered Species, Law of the Sea, Ship Pollution
signed, but not ratified: none of the selected agreements

Geography - note: insular and continental regions rather widely separated

People

Population: 465,746 (July 1999 est.)
Age structure:
0-14 years: 43% (male 100,334; female 99,826)
15-64 years: 53% (male 118,248; female 129,777)
65 years and over: 4% (male 7,801; female 9,760) (1999 est.)
Population growth rate: 2.55% (1999 est.)
Birth rate: 38.49 births/1,000 population (1999 est.)
Death rate: 12.98 deaths/1,000 population (1999 est.)
Net migration rate: 0 migrant(s)/1,000 population (1999 est.)
note: migration to Spain is a traditional and continuing factor; between 80% and 90% of Equatorial Guinean nationals going to Spain do not return
Sex ratio:
at birth: 1.03 male(s)/female
under 15 years: 1.01 male(s)/female
15-64 years: 0.91 male(s)/female
65 years and over: 0.8 male(s)/female
total population: 0.95 male(s)/female (1999 est.)
Infant mortality rate: 91.18 deaths/1,000 live births (1999 est.)
Life expectancy at birth:
total population: 54.39 years
male: 52.03 years
female: 56.83 years (1999 est.)
Total fertility rate: 5 children born/woman (1999 est.)
Nationality:
noun: Equatorial Guinean(s) or Equatoguinean(s)
adjective: Equatorial Guinean or Equatoguinean
Ethnic groups: Bioko (primarily Bubi, some Fernandinos), Rio Muni (primarily Fang), Europeans less than 1,000, mostly Spanish
Religions: nominally Christian and predominantly Roman Catholic, pagan practices
Languages: Spanish (official), French (official), pidgin English, Fang, Bubi, Ibo
Literacy:
definition: age 15 and over can read and write
total population: 78.5%
male: 89.6%
female: 68.1% (1995 est.)

Government

Country name:
conventional long form: Republic of Equatorial Guinea
conventional short form: Equatorial Guinea
local long form: Republica de Guinea Ecuatorial
local short form: Guinea Ecuatorial
former: Spanish Guinea
Data code: EK
Government type: republic in transition to multiparty democracy (the transition appears to have halted)
Capital: Malabo

Equatorial Guinea (continued)

Administrative divisions: 7 provinces (provincias, singular - provincia); Annobon, Bioko Norte, Bioko Sur, Centro Sur, Kie-Ntem, Litoral, Wele-Nzas
Independence: 12 October 1968 (from Spain)
National holiday: Independence Day, 12 October (1968)
Constitution: approved by national referendum 17 November 1991; amended January 1995
Legal system: partly based on Spanish civil law and tribal custom
Suffrage: 18 years of age; universal adult
Executive branch:
chief of state: President Brig. Gen. (Ret.) Teodoro OBIANG NGUEMA MBASOGO (since 3 August 1979)
head of government: Prime Minister Serafin Seriche DOUGAN (since NA April 1996); First Vice Prime Minister for Foreign Affairs Miguel OYONO NDONG (since NA January 1998); Second Vice Prime Minister for Internal Affairs Demetrio Elo NDONG NGEFUMU (since NA January 1998)
cabinet: Council of Ministers appointed by the president
elections: president elected by popular vote to a seven-year term; election last held 25 February 1996 (next to be held NA February 2003); prime minister and vice prime ministers appointed by the president
election results: President OBIANG NGUEMA MBASOGO reelected with 98% of popular vote in elections marred by widespread fraud
Legislative branch: unicameral House of People's Representatives or Camara de Representantes del Pueblo (80 seats; members directly elected by popular vote to serve five-year terms)
elections: last held 21 November 1993 (next to be held NA 1999)
election results: percent of vote by party - NA; seats by party - PDGE 68, CSDP 6, UDS 5, CLD 1
Judicial branch: Supreme Tribunal
Political parties and leaders:
ruling party: Democratic Party for Equatorial Guinea or PDGE [Augustin Nse NFUMU]
opposition parties: Convergence Party for Social Democracy or CPDS [Placido Miko ABOGO]; Democratic Social Union or UDS [Carmelo MODU, general secretary]; Liberal Democratic Convention or CLD [Alfonso Nsue MOKUY, president]; Liberal Party or PL [Antonio Nkulu Asumu ANGUE]; National Democratic Union or UDENA [Pedro-Cristino Bueriberi BOKESA, president]; Party of the Social Democratic Coalition or PCSD [Buenaventura Monswi M'asumu NSEGUE, general coordinator]; Popular Action of Equatorial Guinea or APGE [Miguel Esono EMAN]; Popular Union or UP [Andres Moises MBA, president]; Party for Progress of Equatorial Guinea or PPGE [Basilio Ava Eworo and Domingo ABUY]; Progressive Democratic Alliance or ADP [Victorino Bolekia BONAY, mayor of Malabo]; Social Democratic and Popular Convergence or CSDP [Secundino Oyono Awong ADA]; Social Democratic Party or PSD [Francisco Mabale NSENG]; Socialist Party of Equatorial Guinea or PSGE [Tomas MECHEBA Fernandez, general secretary]

International organization participation: ACCT, ACP, AfDB, BDEAC, CEEAC, ECA, FAO, FZ, G-77, IBRD, ICAO, ICRM, IDA, IFAD, IFC, IFRCS, ILO, IMF, IMO, Intelsat, Interpol, IOC, ITU, NAM, OAS (observer), OAU, OPCW, UDEAC, UN, UNCTAD, UNESCO, UNIDO, UPU, WHO, WIPO, WToO, WTrO (applicant)
Diplomatic representation in the US:
chief of mission: Ambassador Pastor Micha ONDO BILE
chancery: 1712 I Street NW, Suite 410, Washington, DC 20005
telephone: [1] (202) 393-0525
FAX: [1] (202) 393-0348
Diplomatic representation from the US: the US does not have an embassy in Equatorial Guinea (embassy closed September 1995); US relations with Equatorial Guinea are handled through the US Embassy in Yaounde, Cameroon; the US State Department is considering opening a Consulate Agency in Malabo
Flag description: three equal horizontal bands of green (top), white, and red with a blue isosceles triangle based on the hoist side and the coat of arms centered in the white band; the coat of arms has six yellow six-pointed stars (representing the mainland and five offshore islands) above a gray shield bearing a silk-cotton tree and below which is a scroll with the motto UNIDAD, PAZ, JUSTICIA (Unity, Peace, Justice)

Economy

Economy - overview: The discovery and exploitation of large oil reserves have contributed to dramatic economic growth in recent years. Several large oil companies are expected to bid on oil licenses by May 1999. Forestry, farming, and fishing are also major components of GDP. Subsistence farming predominates. Although pre-independence Equatorial Guinea counted on cocoa production for hard currency earnings, the deterioration of the rural economy under successive brutal regimes has diminished potential for agriculture-led growth. A number of aid programs sponsored by the World Bank and the IMF have been cut off since 1993 because of the government's gross corruption and mismanagement. Businesses, for the most part, are owned by government officials and their family members. Undeveloped natural resources include titanium, iron ore, manganese, uranium, and alluvial gold. The country responded favorably to the devaluation of the CFA franc in January 1994.
GDP: purchasing power parity - $660 million (1997 est.)
GDP - real growth rate: NA%
GDP - per capita: purchasing power parity - $1,500 (1997 est.)
GDP - composition by sector:
agriculture: 46%
industry: 33%
services: 21% (1995 est.)
Population below poverty line: NA%

Household income or consumption by percentage share:
lowest 10%: NA%
highest 10%: NA%
Inflation rate (consumer prices): 6% (1996 est.)
Labor force: NA
Unemployment rate: 30% (1998 est.)
Budget:
revenues: $47 million
expenditures: $43 million, including capital expenditures of $7 million (1996 est.)
Industries: petroleum, fishing, sawmilling, natural gas
Industrial production growth rate: 7.4% (1994 est.)
Electricity - production: 19 million kWh (1996)
Electricity - production by source:
fossil fuel: 89.47%
hydro: 10.53%
nuclear: 0%
other: 0% (1996)
Electricity - consumption: 19 million kWh (1996)
Electricity - exports: 0 kWh (1996)
Electricity - imports: 0 kWh (1996)
Agriculture - products: coffee, cocoa, rice, yams, cassava (tapioca), bananas, palm oil nuts, manioc (tapioca); livestock; timber
Exports: $197 million (f.o.b., 1996 est.)
Exports - commodities: petroleum, timber, cocoa
Exports - partners: US 34%, Japan 17%, Spain 13%, China 13%, Nigeria
Imports: $248 million (c.i.f., 1996 est.)
Imports - commodities: petroleum, food, beverages, clothing, machinery
Imports - partners: Cameroon 40%, Spain 18%, France 14%, US 8%
Debt - external: $254 million (1996 est.)
Economic aid - recipient: $33.8 million (1995)
Currency: Communaute Financiere Africaine franc (CFAF) is used
Exchange rates: Communaute Financiere Africaine francs (CFAF) per US$1 - 560.01 (December 1998), 589.95 (1998), 583.67 (1997), 511.55 (1996), 499.15 (1995), 555.20 (1994)
Fiscal year: 1 April - 31 March

Communications

Telephones: 2,000 (1987 est.)
Telephone system: poor system with adequate government services
domestic: NA
international: international communications from Bata and Malabo to African and European countries; satellite earth station - 1 Intelsat (Indian Ocean)
Radio broadcast stations: AM 2, FM 0, shortwave 0
Radios: NA
Television broadcast stations: 1 (1997)
Televisions: 4,000 (1992 est.)

Equatorial Guinea (continued)

Transportation

Railways:
total: 0 km
Highways:
total: 2,880 km
paved: 0 km
unpaved: 2,880 km (1996 est.)
Ports and harbors: Bata, Luba, Malabo
Merchant marine:
total: 12 ships (1,000 GRT or over) totaling 23,370 GRT/25,194 DWT
ships by type: cargo 9, passenger 2, passenger-cargo 1 (1998 est.)
Airports: 3 (1998 est.)
Airports - with paved runways:
total: 2
2,438 to 3,047 m: 1
1,524 to 2,437 m: 1 (1998 est.)
Airports - with unpaved runways:
total: 1
under 914 m: 1 (1998 est.)

Military

Military branches: Army, Navy, Air Force, Rapid Intervention Force, National Police
Military manpower - availability:
males age 15-49: 102,269 (1999 est.)
Military manpower - fit for military service:
males age 15-49: 51,979 (1999 est.)
Military expenditures - dollar figure: $2.5 million (FY97/98)
Military expenditures - percent of GDP: NA%

Transnational Issues

Disputes - international: maritime boundary dispute with Gabon because of disputed sovereignty over islands in Corisco Bay; maritime boundary dispute with Nigeria because of disputed jurisdiction over oil-rich areas in the Gulf of Guinea

Eritrea

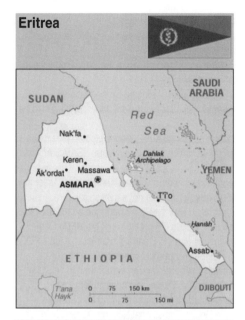

Introduction

Background: On 29 May 1991, ISAIAS Afworki, secretary general of the People's Front for Democracy and Justice (PFDJ), which then served as the country's legislative body, announced the formation of the Provisional Government in Eritrea (PGE) in preparation for the 23-25 April 1993 referendum on independence from Ethiopia. The referendum resulted in a landslide vote for independence, which became effective on 24 May 1993.

Geography

Location: Eastern Africa, bordering the Red Sea, between Djibouti and Sudan
Geographic coordinates: 15 00 N, 39 00 E
Map references: Africa
Area:
total: 121,320 sq km
land: 121,320 sq km
water: 0 sq km
Area - comparative: slightly larger than Pennsylvania
Land boundaries:
total: 1,630 km
border countries: Djibouti 113 km, Ethiopia 912 km, Sudan 605 km
Coastline: 2,234 km total; mainland on Red Sea 1,151 km, islands in Red Sea 1,083 km
Maritime claims: NA
Climate: hot, dry desert strip along Red Sea coast; cooler and wetter in the central highlands (up to 61 cm of rainfall annually); semiarid in western hills and lowlands; rainfall heaviest during June-September except on coastal desert
Terrain: dominated by extension of Ethiopian north-south trending highlands, descending on the east to a coastal desert plain, on the northwest to hilly terrain and on the southwest to flat-to-rolling plains
Elevation extremes:
lowest point: near Kulul within the Denakil depression

-75 m
highest point: Soira 3,018 m
Natural resources: gold, potash, zinc, copper, salt, probably oil and natural gas (currently under exploration), fish
Land use:
arable land: 12%
permanent crops: 1%
permanent pastures: 48%
forests and woodland: 20%
other: 19% (1993 est.)
Irrigated land: 280 sq km (1993 est.)
Natural hazards: frequent droughts
Environment - current issues: deforestation; desertification; soil erosion; overgrazing; loss of infrastructure from civil warfare
Environment - international agreements:
party to: Biodiversity, Climate Change, Desertification, Endangered Species
signed, but not ratified: none of the selected agreements
Geography - note: strategic geopolitical position along world's busiest shipping lanes; Eritrea retained the entire coastline of Ethiopia along the Red Sea upon de jure independence from Ethiopia on 27 April 1993

People

Population: 3,984,723 (July 1999 est.)
Age structure:
0-14 years: 43% (male 859,899; female 852,329)
15-64 years: 54% (male 1,061,921; female 1,078,102)
65 years and over: 3% (male 67,969; female 64,503) (1999 est.)
Population growth rate: 3.88% (1999 est.)
Birth rate: 42.56 births/1,000 population (1999 est.)
Death rate: 12.32 deaths/1,000 population (1999 est.)
Net migration rate: 8.53 migrant(s)/1,000 population (1999 est.)
note: it is estimated that approximately 315,000 Eritrean refugees were still living in Sudan by the end of 1997 according to the UNHCR
Sex ratio:
at birth: 1.03 male(s)/female
under 15 years: 1.01 male(s)/female
15-64 years: 0.98 male(s)/female
65 years and over: 1.05 male(s)/female
total population: 1 male(s)/female (1999 est.)
Infant mortality rate: 76.84 deaths/1,000 live births (1999 est.)
Life expectancy at birth:
total population: 55.74 years
male: 53.61 years
female: 57.95 years (1999 est.)
Total fertility rate: 5.96 children born/woman (1999 est.)
Nationality:
noun: Eritrean(s)
adjective: Eritrean
Ethnic groups: ethnic Tigrinya 50%, Tigre and

Eritrea *(continued)*

Kunama 40%, Afar 4%, Saho (Red Sea coast dwellers) 3%
Religions: Muslim, Coptic Christian, Roman Catholic, Protestant
Languages: Afar, Amharic, Arabic, Tigre and Kunama, Tigrinya, minor ethnic group languages
Literacy: NA

Government

Country name:
conventional long form: State of Eritrea
conventional short form: Eritrea
local long form: Hagere Ertra
local short form: Ertra
former: Eritrea Autonomous Region in Ethiopia
Data code: ER
Government type: transitional government
note: following a successful referendum on independence for the Autonomous Region of Eritrea on 23-25 April 1993, a National Assembly, composed entirely of the People's Front for Democracy and Justice or PFDJ, was established as a transitional legislature; a Constitutional Commission was also established to draft a constitution; ISAIAS Afworki was elected president by the transitional legislature
Capital: Asmara (formerly Asmera)
Administrative divisions: 8 provinces (singular - awraja); Akale Guzay, Barka, Denkel, Hamasen, Sahil, Semhar, Senhit, Seraye
note: in May 1995 the National Assembly adopted a resolution stating that the administrative structure of Eritrea, which had been established by former colonial powers, would consist of only six provinces when the new constitution, then being drafted, became effective in 1997; the new provinces, the names of which had not been recommended by the US Board on Geographic Names for recognition by the US Government, pending acceptable definition of the boundaries, were: Anseba, Debub, Debubawi Keyih Bahri, Gash-Barka, Maakel, and Semanawi Keyih Bahri; more recently, it has been reported that these provinces have been redesignated regions and renamed Southern Red Sea, Northern Red Sea, Anseba, Gash-Barka, Southern, and Central
Independence: 24 May 1993 (from Ethiopia; formerly the Eritrea Autonomous Region)
National holiday: National Day (independence from Ethiopia), 24 May (1993)
Constitution: the transitional constitution, decreed on 19 May 1993, was replaced by a new constitution that was promulgated in May 1997
Legal system: NA
Suffrage: NA; note - it seems likely that the final version of the constitution would follow the example set in the referendum of 1993 and extend suffrage to all persons 18 years of age or older
Executive branch:
chief of state: President ISAIAS Afworki (since 8 June 1993); note - the president is both the chief of state and head of government
head of government: President ISAIAS Afworki (since 8 June 1993); note - the president is both the chief of

state and head of government
cabinet: State Council is the collective executive authority
note: the president is head of the State Council and National Assembly
elections: president elected by the National Assembly; election last held 8 June 1993 (next to be held NA)
election results: ISAIAS Afworki elected president; percent of National Assembly vote - ISAIAS Afworki 95%
Legislative branch: unicameral National Assembly (150 seats; term limits not established)
elections: in May 1997, following the adoption of the new constitution, 75 members of the PFDJ Central Committee (the old Central Committee of the EPLF), 60 members of the 527-member Constituent Assembly which had been established in 1997 to discuss and ratify the new constitution, and 15 representatives of Eritreans living abroad were formed into a Transitional National Assembly to serve as the country's legislative body until country-wide elections to a National Assembly are held; only 75 members will be elected to the National Assembly - the other 75 will be members of the Central Committee of the PFDJ
Judicial branch: the Supreme Court; 10 provincial courts; 29 district courts
Political parties and leaders: People's Front for Democracy and Justice or PFDJ, the only party recognized by the government [ISAIAS Afworki, PETROS Solomon]
Political pressure groups and leaders: Eritrean Islamic Jihad or EIJ; Eritrean Liberation Front or ELF [ABDULLAH Muhammed]; Eritrean Liberation Front-United Organization or ELF-UO [Mohammed Said NAWUD]; Eritrean Liberation Front-Revolutionary Council or ELF-RC [Ahmed NASSER]
International organization participation: ACP, AfDB, CCC, ECA, FAO, G-77, IBRD, ICAO, ICFTU, IDA, IFAD, IFC, IGAD, ILO, IMF, IMO, Intelsat (nonsignatory user), ITU, NAM, OAU, UN, UNCTAD, UNESCO, UNIDO, UPU, WFTU, WHO, WIPO, WMO, WToO
Diplomatic representation in the US:
chief of mission: Ambassador SEMERE Russom
chancery: 1708 New Hampshire Avenue NW, Washington, DC 20009
telephone: [1] (202) 319-1991
FAX: [1] (202) 319-1304
Diplomatic representation from the US:
chief of mission: Ambassador William CLARK
embassy: Franklin D. Roosevelt Street, Asmara
mailing address: P.O. Box 211, Asmara
telephone: [291] (1) 120004
FAX: [291] (1) 127584
Flag description: red isosceles triangle (based on the hoist side) dividing the flag into two right triangles; the upper triangle is green, the lower one is blue; a gold wreath encircling a gold olive branch is centered on the hoist side of the red triangle

Economy

Economy - overview: With independence from Ethiopia on 24 May 1993, Eritrea faced the bitter economic problem of a small, desperately poor African country. The economy is largely based on subsistence agriculture, with over 70% of the population involved in farming and herding. The small industrial sector consists mainly of light industries with outmoded technologies. Domestic output (GDP) is substantially augmented by worker remittances from abroad. Government revenues come from custom duties and taxes on income and sales. Road construction is a top domestic priority. Eritrea has long-term prospects for revenues from the development of offshore oil, offshore fishing, and tourism. Eritrea's economic future depends on its ability to master fundamental social and economic problems, e.g., overcoming illiteracy, promoting job creation, expanding technical training, attracting foreign investment, and streamlining the bureaucracy. The most immediate threat to the economy, however, is the possible expansion of the armed conflict with Ethiopia.
GDP: purchasing power parity - $2.5 billion (1998 est.)
GDP - real growth rate: 5% (1998 est.)
GDP - per capita: purchasing power parity - $660 (1998 est.)
GDP - composition by sector:
agriculture: 18%
industry: 20%
services: 62% (1995 est.)
Population below poverty line: NA%
Household income or consumption by percentage share:
lowest 10%: NA%
highest 10%: NA%
Inflation rate (consumer prices): 8% (1998 est.)
Labor force: NA
Unemployment rate: NA%
Budget:
revenues: $226 million
expenditures: $453 million, including capital expenditures of $88 million (1996 est.)
Industries: food processing, beverages, clothing and textiles
Industrial production growth rate: NA%
Electricity - production: NA kWh
Electricity - production by source:
fossil fuel: NA%
hydro: NA%
nuclear: NA%
other: NA%
Electricity - consumption: NA kWh
Electricity - exports: NA kWh
Electricity - imports: NA kWh
Agriculture - products: sorghum, lentils, vegetables, maize, cotton, tobacco, coffee, sisal; livestock, goats; fish
Exports: $95 million (1996 est.)
Exports - commodities: livestock, sorghum,

Eritrea (continued)

textiles, food, small manufactures
Exports - partners: Ethiopia 67%, Sudan 10%, US 8%, Italy 4%, Saudi Arabia, Yemen (1996)
Imports: $514 million (1996 est.)
Imports - commodities: processed goods, machinery, petroleum products
Imports - partners: Ethiopia, Saudi Arabia, Italy, United Arab Emirates (1996)
Debt - external: $46 million (1996 est.)
Economic aid - recipient: $149.9 million (1995)
Currency: 1 nafka = 100 cents
Exchange rates: nakfa per US$1 = 7.6 (January 1999), 7.2 (March 1998 est.)
note: following independence from Ethiopia, Eritrea continued to use Ethiopian currency until November 1997 when Eritrea issued its own currency, the nakfa, at approximately the same rate as the birr, i.e., 7.2 nakfa per US$1
Fiscal year: calendar year

Telephones: NA
Telephone system:
domestic: very inadequate; about 4 telephones per 100 families, most of which are in Asmara; government is seeking international tenders to improve the system
international: NA
Radio broadcast stations: AM 2, FM 0, shortwave 1
Radios: NA
Television broadcast stations: 1 (government controlled) (1997)
Televisions: NA

Transportation

Railways:
total: 307 km
narrow gauge: 307 km 0.950-m gauge (1995 est.)
note: nonoperational since 1978 except for about a 5 km stretch that was reopened in Massawa in 1994; rehabilitation of the remainder and of the rolling stock is under way; links Ak'ordat and Asmara (formerly Asmera) with the port of Massawa (formerly Mits'iwa)
Highways:
total: 4,010 km
paved: 874 km
unpaved: 3,136 km (1996 est.)
Ports and harbors: Assab (Aseb), Massawa (Mits'iwa)
Merchant marine:
total: 2 ships (1,000 GRT or over) totaling 5,947 GRT/ 5,747 DWT
ships by type: oil tanker 1, roll-on/roll-off cargo 1 (1998 est.)
Airports: 20 (1998 est.)
Airports - with paved runways:
total: 2
over 3,047 m: 1
2,438 to 3,047 m: 1 (1998 est.)
Airports - with unpaved runways:
total: 18

over 3,047 m: 2
2,438 to 3,047 m: 2
1,524 to 2,437 m: 5
914 to 1,523 m: 6
under 914 m: 3 (1998 est.)

Military

Military branches: Army, Navy, Air Force
Military expenditures - dollar figure: $196 million (1997)
Military expenditures - percent of GDP: 28.6% (1997)

Transnational Issues

Disputes - international: dispute over alignment of boundary with Ethiopia led to armed conflict in 1998, which is still unresolved despite arbitration efforts; Hanish Islands dispute with Yemen resolved by arbitral tribunal in October 1998

Estonia

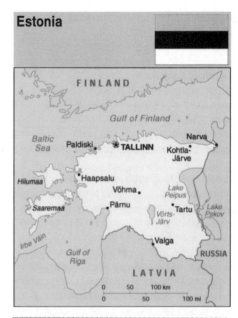

Introduction

Background: In and out of Swedish and Russian control over the centuries, this little Baltic state was re-incorporated into the USSR after German occupation in World War II. Independence came with the collapse of the USSR in 1991; the last Russian troops left in 1994. Estonia thus became free to promote economic and political ties with Western Europe. The position of ethnic Russians (29% of the population) remains an issue of concern to Moscow. European Union (EU) membership negotiations, which began in 1998, remain a domestic issue.

Geography

Location: Eastern Europe, bordering the Baltic Sea and Gulf of Finland, between Latvia and Russia
Geographic coordinates: 59 00 N, 26 00 E
Map references: Europe
Area:
total: 45,226 sq km
land: 43,211 sq km
water: 2,015 sq km
note: includes 1,520 islands in the Baltic Sea
Area - comparative: slightly smaller than New Hampshire and Vermont combined
Land boundaries:
total: 633 km
border countries: Latvia 339 km, Russia 294 km
Coastline: 3,794 km
Maritime claims:
exclusive economic zone: limits fixed in coordination with neighboring states
territorial sea: 12 nm
Climate: maritime, wet, moderate winters, cool summers
Terrain: marshy, lowlands
Elevation extremes:
lowest point: Baltic Sea 0 m
highest point: Suur Munamagi 318 m
Natural resources: shale oil (kukersite), peat,

Estonia *(continued)*

phosphorite, amber, cambrian blue clay, limestone, dolomite

Land use:
arable land: 25%
permanent crops: 0%
permanent pastures: 11%
forests and woodland: 44%
other: 20% (1996 est.)

Irrigated land: 110 sq km (1993 est.)

Natural hazards: flooding occurs frequently in the spring

Environment - current issues: air heavily polluted with sulfur dioxide from oil-shale burning power plants in northeast; contamination of soil and groundwater with petroleum products, chemicals at former Soviet military bases; Estonia has more than 1,400 natural and manmade lakes, the smaller of which in agricultural areas are heavily affected by organic waste; coastal sea water is polluted in many locations

Environment - international agreements:
party to: Biodiversity, Climate Change, Endangered Species, Hazardous Wastes, Ship Pollution, Ozone Layer Protection, Wetlands
signed, but not ratified: Climate Change-Kyoto Protocol

People

Population: 1,408,523 (July 1999 est.)

Age structure:
0-14 years: 18% (male 130,883; female 126,112)
15-64 years: 67% (male 455,112; female 491,819)
65 years and over: 15% (male 66,700; female 137,897) (1999 est.)

Population growth rate: -0.82% (1999 est.)

Birth rate: 9.05 births/1,000 population (1999 est.)

Death rate: 14.21 deaths/1,000 population (1999 est.)

Net migration rate: -3.08 migrant(s)/1,000 population (1999 est.)

Sex ratio:
at birth: 1.05 male(s)/female
under 15 years: 1.04 male(s)/female
15-64 years: 0.93 male(s)/female
65 years and over: 0.48 male(s)/female
total population: 0.86 male(s)/female (1999 est.)

Infant mortality rate: 13.83 deaths/1,000 live births (1999 est.)

Life expectancy at birth:
total population: 68.65 years
male: 62.61 years
female: 75 years (1999 est.)

Total fertility rate: 1.28 children born/woman (1999 est.)

Nationality:
noun: Estonian(s)
adjective: Estonian

Ethnic groups: Estonian 65.1%, Russian 28.1%, Ukrainian 2.5%, Byelorussian 1.5%, Finn 1%, other 1.8% (1998)

Religions: Evangelical Lutheran, Russian Orthodox, Estonian Orthodox, others include Baptist, Methodist, Seventh Day Adventist, Roman Catholic, Pentecostal, Word of Life, Seventh Day Baptist, Judaism

Languages: Estonian (official), Russian, Ukrainian, English, Finnish, other

Literacy:
definition: age 15 and over can read and write
total population: 100%
male: 100%
female: 100% (1998 est.)

Government

Country name:
conventional long form: Republic of Estonia
conventional short form: Estonia
local long form: Eesti Vabariik
local short form: Eesti
former: Estonian Soviet Socialist Republic

Data code: EN

Government type: parliamentary democracy

Capital: Tallinn

Administrative divisions: 15 counties (maakonnad, singular - maakond): Harjumaa (Tallinn), Hiiumaa (Kardla), Ida-Virumaa (Johvi), Jarvamaa (Paide), Jogevamaa (Jogeva), Laanemaa (Haapsalu), Laane-Virumaa (Rakvere), Parnumaa (Parnu), Polvamaa (Polva), Raplamaa (Rapla), Saaremaa (Kuessaare), Tartumaa (Tartu), Valgamaa (Valga), Viljandimaa (Viljandi), Vorumaa (Voru)
note: administrative divisions have the same names as their administrative centers (exceptions have the administrative center name following in parentheses)

Independence: 6 September 1991 (from Soviet Union)

National holiday: Independence Day, 24 February (1918)

Constitution: adopted 28 June 1992

Legal system: based on civil law system; no judicial review of legislative acts

Suffrage: 18 years of age; universal for all Estonian citizens

Executive branch:
chief of state: President Lennart MERI (since 5 October 1992)
head of government: Prime Minister Mart SIIMANN (since 12 March 1997)
cabinet: Council of Ministers appointed by the prime minister, approved by Parliament
elections: president elected by Parliament for a five-year term; if he or she does not secure two-thirds of the votes after three rounds of balloting, then an electoral assembly (made up of Parliament plus members of local governments) elects the president, choosing between the two candidates with the largest percentage of votes; election last held August-September 1996 (next to be held fall 2001); prime minister nominated by the president and approved by Parliament
election results: Lennart MERI elected president by an electoral assembly after Parliament was unable to break a deadlock between MERI and RUUTEL; percent of electoral assembly vote - Lennart MERI 61%, Arnold RUUTEL 39%

Legislative branch: unicameral Parliament or Riigikogu (101 seats; members are elected by popular vote to serve four-year terms)
elections: last held 5 March 1995 (next to be held 7 March 1999)
election results: percent of vote by party - KMU 32.22%, RE 16.18%, K 14.17%, Pro Patria and ERSP 7.85%, M 5.98%, Our Home is Estonia and Right-Wingers 5.0%; seats by party - KMU 41, RE 19, K 16, Pro Patria 8, Our Home is Estonia 6, M 6, Right-Wingers 5

Judicial branch: National Court, chairman appointed by Parliament for life

Political parties and leaders: Coalition Party and Rural Union or KMU [Mart SIIMAN, chairman] made up of four parties: Coalition Party or EK, Country People's Party [Arnold RUUTEL, chairman]/Farmer's Assembly or EME, Rural Union or EM [Arvo SIRENDI, chairman] , and Pensioners' and Families' League or EPPL [Mai TREIAL, chairperson]; Reform Party or RE [Siim KALLAS, chairman]; Center Party or K [Edgar SAVISAAR, chairman]; Union of Pro Patria or Fatherland League (Isamaaliit) [Mart LAAR, chairman]; Our Home is Estonia [Viktor ANDREJEV] made up of two parties: United People's Party and the Russian Party of Estonia; note - Our Home is Estonia split when two Russian Party of Estonia members withdrew; United People's Party [Viktor ANDREJEV, chairman]; Russian Party of Estonia [Nikolai MASPANOV, chairman]; Moderates or M [Andres TARAND] made up of two parties: Social Democratic Party or ESDP and Rural Center Party or EMK; Social Democratic Party [Eiki NESTOR, chairman]; Rural Center Party [Vambo KAAL, chairman]; Development/ Progressive Party [Andra VEIDEMANN, chairwoman] (created by defectors from Center Party in late spring 1996, Development Party faction split and now holds five independent seats); People's Party [Toomas Hendrick KUES]

International organization participation: BIS, CBSS, CCC, CE, EAPC, EBRD, ECE, EU (applicant), FAO, IAEA, IBRD, ICAO, ICFTU, ICRM, IFC, IFRCS, IHO, ILO, IMF, IMO, Interpol, IOC, ISO (correspondent), ITU, OPCW, OSCE, PFP, UN, UNCTAD, UNESCO, UNMIBH, UNTSO, UPU, WEU (associate partner), WHO, WIPO, WMO, WTrO (applicant)

Diplomatic representation in the US:
chief of mission: Ambassador Grigore-Kaleu STOICESCU
chancery: 2131 Massachusetts Avenue NW, Washington, DC 20008
telephone: [1] (202) 588-0101
FAX: [1] (202) 588-0108
consulate(s) general: New York

Diplomatic representation from the US:
chief of mission: Ambassador Melissa WELLS
embassy: Kentmanni 20, Tallinn EE 0001
mailing address: use embassy street address
telephone: [372] (6) 312-021
FAX: [372] (6) 312-025

Flag description: pre-1940 flag restored by Supreme Soviet in May 1990 - three equal horizontal

Estonia (continued)

bands of blue (top), black, and white

Economy

Economy - overview: Estonia's continued adherence to market reforms, disciplined fiscal and monetary policies, and a liberal free trade regime resulted in GDP growth in 1998 of 5.5% and a decrease in inflation to 6.5% from 11.2% in 1997. A high but slightly decreased current account deficit was estimated at 8.6%. The fall in GDP growth is largely due to the impact of Russia's financial crisis and reduced investment in emerging markets in the wake of the Asian financial crisis. Like other small emerging markets, Estonia will face difficulties in 1999 as a result of continuing fallout from Asia. Key events of 1998 were the start of official EU accession talks, banking sector consolidation - nine banks were reduced to five - and the important role that Swedish capital played in the large banks (Swedbank's acquisition of a majority stake in Hansapank has accounted for the large increase in foreign direct investment). The IMF urged Estonia to maintain a stable economy and good reputation in international markets and to avoid populist policies in the run-up to March 1999 parliamentary elections. The government completed restructuring of state-controlled Estonian Telecom, the sale of 49% of which will be the flagship privatization in 1999 and the largest public equity transaction in the Baltics. Estonia expects to join the World Trade Organization in 1999.

GDP: purchasing power parity - $7.8 billion (1998 est.)

GDP - real growth rate: 5.5% (1998 est.)

GDP - per capita: purchasing power parity - $5,500 (1998 est.)

GDP - composition by sector:
agriculture: 6.2%
industry: 24.3%
services: 69.5% (1997 est.)

Population below poverty line: 6.3% (1994 est.)

Household income or consumption by percentage share:
lowest 10%: 3.2%
highest 10%: 28.5% (1996)

Inflation rate (consumer prices): 6.5% (1998 est.)

Labor force: 717,000 (1997 est.)

Labor force - by occupation: industry 42%, agriculture and forestry 11%, services 47% (1996 est.)

Unemployment rate: 9.6% (1998 est.)

Budget:
revenues: $1.37 billion
expenditures: $1.37 billion, including capital expenditures of $NA (1997 est.)

Industries: oil shale, shipbuilding, phosphates, electric motors, excavators, cement, furniture, clothing, textiles, paper, shoes, apparel

Industrial production growth rate: 3% (1996 est.)

Electricity - production: 8.065 billion kWh (1996)

Electricity - production by source:
fossil fuel: 99.96%
hydro: 0.04%

nuclear: 0%
other: 0% (1996)

Electricity - consumption: 5.581 billion kWh (1997)

Electricity - exports: 1.2 billion kWh (1997)

Electricity - imports: 210 million kWh (1997)

Agriculture - products: potatoes, fruits, vegetables; livestock and dairy products; fish

Exports: $2.6 billion (f.o.b., 1998)

Exports - commodities: machinery and equipment 17%, textiles 16%, food products 8%, transport equipment 8%, mineral products 8%, chemical products 8% (1997)

Exports - partners: Finland, Russia, Sweden, Germany, Latvia (1997)

Imports: $3.9 billion (c.i.f., 1998)

Imports - commodities: machinery and equipment 21%, transport equipment 12%, foodstuffs 10%, minerals 9%, textiles 8%, metals 8%, chemical products 8% (1997)

Imports - partners: Finland, Germany, Russia, Sweden, Japan, US (1997)

Debt - external: $270 million (January 1996)

Economic aid - recipient: $137.3 million (1995)

Currency: 1 Estonian kroon (EEK) = 100 cents

Exchange rates: krooni (EEK) per US$1 - 13.473 (January 1999), 14.075 (1998), 13.882 (1997), 12.034 (1996), 11.465 (1995), 12.991 (1994); note - krooni are tied to the German deutsche mark at a fixed rate of 8 to 1

Fiscal year: calendar year

Communications

Telephones: 531,000 (1997)

Telephone system: the Ministry of Transportation and Communications (MOTC) administers Estonia's telephone system; Internet services available throughout most of the country; about 150,000 unfilled subscriber requests
domestic: local - cellular phones services are growing and expanding to develop rural networks under direction of the MOTC; intercity - Estonia has a highly developed fiber-optic backbone (double loop) system presently serving at least 16 major cities (1998)
international: foreign investment in the form of joint business ventures greatly improved Estonia's telephone service; fiber-optic cables to Finland, Sweden, Latvia, and Russia provide worldwide packet switched service

Radio broadcast stations: 27 commercial broadcast stations, 1 government broadcast station (1997); note - by law 51% of shows must be produced within the EU; equal air time must be given to all candidates during elections by public and private stations

Radios: 1.12 million (1997 est.)

Television broadcast stations: 7 (1997); note - Ministry of Culture administers television licensing; mainly Estonian, European, and Russian programming; by law 51% of shows must be produced within the EU; equal air time must be given to all

candidates during elections by public and private stations

Televisions: 1.132 million (1997 est.)

Transportation

Railways:
total: 1,018 km common carrier lines only; does not include dedicated industrial lines
broad gauge: 1,018 km 1.520-m gauge (132 km electrified) (1995)

Highways:
total: 16,437 km
paved: 8,343 km (including 65 km of expressways)
unpaved: 8,094 km (1997 est.)

Waterways: 320 km perennially navigable

Pipelines: natural gas 420 km (1992)

Ports and harbors: Haapsalu, Kunda, Muuga, Paldiski, Parnu, Tallinn

Merchant marine:
total: 52 ships (1,000 GRT or over) totaling 337,163 GRT/348,749 DWT
ships by type: bulk 4, cargo 22, combination bulk 1, container 5, oil tanker 2, roll-on/roll-off cargo 12, short-sea passenger 6 (1998 est.)

Airports: 5 (1997 est.)

Airports - with paved runways:
total: 5
over 3,047 m: 1
2,438 to 3,047 m: 1
914 to 1,523 m: 3 (1997 est.)

Military

Military branches: Ground Forces, Navy/Coast Guard, Air and Air Defense Force (not officially sanctioned), Maritime Border Guard, Volunteer Defense League (Kaitseliit), Security Forces (internal and border troops)

Military manpower - military age: 18 years of age

Military manpower - availability:
males age 15-49: 349,263 (1999 est.)

Military manpower - fit for military service:
males age 15-49: 274,276 (1999 est.)

Military manpower - reaching military age annually:
males: 10,503 (1999 est.)

Military expenditures - dollar figure: $70 million (1999)

Military expenditures - percent of GDP: 1.2% (1999)

Transnational Issues

Disputes - international: Estonian and Russian negotiators reached a technical border agreement in December 1996 which has not been ratified

Illicit drugs: transshipment point for opiates and cannabis from Southwest Asia and the Caucasus via Russia, and cocaine from Latin America to Western Europe and Scandinavia; possible precursor manufacturing and/or trafficking

Ethiopia

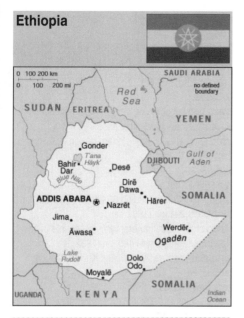

SAUDI ARABIA
no defined
boundary
0 100 200 km
0 100 200 mi
Red Sea
SUDAN ERITREA
YEMEN
Gonder
Tana Hāyk'
Bahir Dar
Desē
Blue Nile
DJIBOUTI
Gulf of Aden
Dirē Dawa
ADDIS ABABA
Nazrēt
Hārer
SOMALIA
Jima
Āwasa
Werdēr
Ogadēn
Lake Rudolf
Dolo Odo
Moyalē
SOMALIA
UGANDA
KENYA
Indian Ocean

Introduction

Background: On 28 May 1991 the Ethiopian People's Revolutionary Democratic Front (EPRDF) toppled the authoritarian government of MENGISTU Haile-Mariam and took control in Addis Ababa. A new constitution was promulgated in December 1994 and national and regional popular elections were held in May and June 1995.

Geography

Location: Eastern Africa, west of Somalia
Geographic coordinates: 8 00 N, 38 00 E
Map references: Africa
Area:
total: 1,127,127 sq km
land: 1,119,683 sq km
water: 7,444 sq km
Area - comparative: slightly less than twice the size of Texas
Land boundaries:
total: 5,311 km
border countries: Djibouti 337 km, Eritrea 912 km, Kenya 830 km, Somalia 1,626 km, Sudan 1,606 km
Coastline: 0 km (landlocked)
Maritime claims: none (landlocked)
Climate: tropical monsoon with wide topographic-induced variation
Terrain: high plateau with central mountain range divided by Great Rift Valley
Elevation extremes:
lowest point: Denakil -125 m
highest point: Ras Dashen Terara 4,620 m
Natural resources: small reserves of gold, platinum, copper, potash, natural gas
Land use:
arable land: 12%
permanent crops: 1%
permanent pastures: 40%
forests and woodland: 25%
other: 22% (1993 est.)

Irrigated land: 1,900 sq km (1993 est.)
Natural hazards: geologically active Great Rift Valley susceptible to earthquakes, volcanic eruptions; frequent droughts
Environment - current issues: deforestation; overgrazing; soil erosion; desertification
Environment - international agreements:
party to: Biodiversity, Climate Change, Desertification, Endangered Species, Ozone Layer Protection
signed, but not ratified: Environmental Modification, Law of the Sea, Nuclear Test Ban
Geography - note: landlocked - entire coastline along the Red Sea was lost with the de jure independence of Eritrea on 24 May 1993

People

Population: 59,680,383 (July 1999 est.)
Age structure:
0-14 years: 46% (male 13,787,810; female 13,703,546)
15-64 years: 51% (male 15,398,123; female 15,141,892)
65 years and over: 3% (male 745,737; female 903,275) (1999 est.)
Population growth rate: 2.16% (1999 est.)
Birth rate: 44.34 births/1,000 population (1999 est.)
Death rate: 21.43 deaths/1,000 population (1999 est.)
Net migration rate: -1.3 migrant(s)/1,000 population (1999 est.)
note: repatriation of Ethiopians who fled to Sudan, Kenya, and Somalia for refuge from war and famine in earlier years, is expected to continue slowly in 1998; small numbers of Sudanese and Somali refugees, who fled to Ethiopia from the fighting in their own countries, began returning to their homes in 1998
Sex ratio:
at birth: 1.03 male(s)/female
under 15 years: 1.01 male(s)/female
15-64 years: 1.02 male(s)/female
65 years and over: 0.83 male(s)/female
total population: 1.01 male(s)/female (1999 est.)
Infant mortality rate: 124.57 deaths/1,000 live births (1999 est.)
Life expectancy at birth:
total population: 40.46 years
male: 39.22 years
female: 41.73 years (1999 est.)
Total fertility rate: 6.81 children born/woman (1999 est.)
Nationality:
noun: Ethiopian(s)
adjective: Ethiopian
Ethnic groups: Oromo 40%, Amhara and Tigrean 32%, Sidamo 9%, Shankella 6%, Somali 6%, Afar 4%, Gurage 2%, other 1%
Religions: Muslim 45%-50%, Ethiopian Orthodox 35%-40%, animist 12%, other 3%-8%
Languages: Amharic, Tigrinya, Orominga, Guaraginga, Somali, Arabic, English (major foreign language taught in schools)

Literacy:
definition: age 15 and over can read and write
total population: 35.5%
male: 45.5%
female: 25.3% (1995 est.)

Government

Country name:
conventional long form: Federal Democratic Republic of Ethiopia
conventional short form: Ethiopia
local long form: Yeltyop'iya Federalawi Demokrasiyawi Ripeblik
local short form: Yeltyop'iya
abbreviation: FDRE
Data code: ET
Government type: federal republic
Capital: Addis Ababa
Administrative divisions: 9 states and 2 chartered cities*: Addis Ababa*; Afar; Amhara; Benshangul/Gumuz (Benishangul-Gumaz); Dire Dawa*; Gambela (Gambella); Harari (Harar); Oromia (Oromiya); Somalia (Somali); Southern Nations, Nationalities, and Peoples (SNNP); Tigray (Tigre)
Independence: oldest independent country in Africa and one of the oldest in the world - at least 2,000 years
National holiday: National Day, 28 May (1991) (defeat of MENGISTU regime)
Constitution: promulgated December 1994
Legal system: currently transitional mix of national and regional courts
Suffrage: 18 years of age; universal
Executive branch:
chief of state: President NEGASSO Gidada (since 22 August 1995)
head of government: Prime Minister MELES Zenawi (since August 1995)
cabinet: Council of Ministers as provided in the December 1994 constitution; ministers are selected by the prime minister and approved by the House of People's Representatives
elections: president elected by the House of People's Representatives for a six-year term; election last held June 1995 (next to be held NA 2001); prime minister designated by the party in power following legislative elections
election results: NEGASSO Gidada elected president; percent of vote by the House of People's Representatives - NA
Legislative branch: bicameral Parliament consists of the House of Federation or upper chamber (117 seats; members are chosen by state assemblies to serve five-year terms) and the House of People's Representatives or lower chamber (548 seats; members are directly elected by popular vote from single-member districts to serve five-year terms)
elections: regional and national popular elections were held in May and June 1995 (next to be held NA 2000)
election results: percent of vote - NA; seats - NA; note - EPRDF won nearly all seats
Judicial branch: Federal Supreme Court; the

Ethiopia (continued)

president and vice president of the Federal Supreme Court are recommended by the prime minister and appointed by the House of People's Representatives; for other federal judges, the prime minister submits candidates selected by the Federal Judicial Administrative Council to the House of People's Representatives for appointment

Political parties and leaders: Ethiopian People's Revolutionary Democratic Front or EPRDF [MELES Zenawi]

Political pressure groups and leaders: Oromo Liberation Front or OLF; All Amhara People's Organization; Southern Ethiopia People's Democratic Coalition; numerous small, ethnically-based groups have formed since former President MENGISTU'S defeat, including several Islamic militant groups

International organization participation: ACP, AfDB, CCC, ECA, FAO, G-24, G-77, IAEA, IBRD, ICAO, ICRM, IDA, IFAD, IFC, IFRCS, IGAD, ILO, IMF, IMO, Intelsat, Interpol, IOC, ISO, ITU, NAM, OAU, OPCW, UN, UNCTAD, UNESCO, UNHCR, UNIDO, UNU, UPU, WFTU, WHO, WIPO, WMO, WToO

Diplomatic representation in the US:
chief of mission: Ambassador BERHANE Gebre-Christos
chancery: 2134 Kalorama Road NW, Washington, DC 20008
telephone: [1] (202) 234-2281
FAX: [1] (202) 328-7950

Diplomatic representation from the US:
chief of mission: Ambassador David H. SHINN
embassy: Entoto Street, Addis Ababa
mailing address: P. O. Box 1014, Addis Ababa
telephone: [251] (1) 550666
FAX: [251] (1) 551328

Flag description: three equal horizontal bands of green (top), yellow, and red with a yellow pentagram and single yellow rays emanating from the angles between the points on a light blue disk centered on the three bands; Ethiopia is the oldest independent country in Africa, and the colors of her flag were so often adopted by other African countries upon independence that they became known as the pan-African colors

Economy

Economy - overview: Ethiopia remains one of the least developed countries in the world. Its economy is based on agriculture, which accounts for more than half of GDP, 90% of exports, and 80% of total employment; coffee generates 60% of export earnings. The agricultural sector suffers from frequent periods of drought, poor cultivation practices, and deterioration of internal security conditions. The manufacturing sector is heavily dependent on inputs from the agricultural sector. Over 90% of large-scale industry, but less than 10% of agriculture, is state-run. The government is considering selling off a portion of state-owned plants and is implementing reform measures that are gradually liberalizing the economy. A major medium-term problem is the improvement of roads, water supply, and other parts of an

infrastructure badly neglected during years of civil strife. Renewed fighting with Eritrea dims economic prospects for 1999.

GDP: purchasing power parity - $32.9 billion (1998 est.)

GDP - real growth rate: 6% (1998 est.)

GDP - per capita: purchasing power parity - $560 (1998 est.)

GDP - composition by sector:
agriculture: 55%
industry: 12%
services: 33% (1995 est.)

Population below poverty line: NA%

Household income or consumption by percentage share:
lowest 10%: NA%
highest 10%: NA%

Inflation rate (consumer prices): 3.9% (1998 est.)

Labor force: NA

Labor force - by occupation: agriculture and animal husbandry 80%, government and services 12%, industry and construction 8% (1985)

Unemployment rate: NA%

Budget:
revenues: $1 billion
expenditures: $1.48 billion, including capital expenditures of $415 million (FY96/97)

Industries: food processing, beverages, textiles, chemicals, metals processing, cement

Industrial production growth rate: NA%

Electricity - production: 1.32 billion kWh (1996)

Electricity - production by source:
fossil fuel: 7.58%
hydro: 87.12%
nuclear: 0%
other: 5.3% (1996)

Electricity - consumption: 1.32 billion kWh (1996)

Electricity - exports: 0 kWh (1996)

Electricity - imports: 0 kWh (1996)

Agriculture - products: cereals, pulses, coffee, oilseed, sugarcane, potatoes; hides, cattle, sheep, goats

Exports: $550 million (f.o.b., 1998)

Exports - commodities: coffee, leather products, gold, oilseeds (1995)

Exports - partners: Germany 26%, Japan 11%, Italy 10%, UK 8%, Djibouti, Saudi Arabia (1996 est.)

Imports: $1.3 billion (f.o.b., 1998 est.)

Imports - commodities: food and live animals, petroleum and petroleum products, chemicals, machinery, motor vehicles and aircraft (1994)

Imports - partners: Italy 11%, US 11%, Germany 7%, Saudi Arabia 4% (1996 est.)

Debt - external: $10 billion (1996)

Economic aid - recipient: $367 million (FY95/96)

Currency: 1 birr (Br) = 100 cents

Exchange rates: birr (Br) per US$1 (end of period) - 7.58 (January 1999), 6.8640 (1997), 6.4260 (1996), 6.3200 (1995), 5.9500 (1994)
note: since May 1993, the birr market rate has been determined in an interbank market supported by weekly wholesale auction; prior to that date, the

official rate was pegged to US$1 = 5.000 birr

Fiscal year: 8 July - 7 July

Communications

Telephones: 100,000 (1983 est.)

Telephone system: open wire and microwave radio relay system adequate for government use
domestic: open wire and microwave radio relay
international: open wire to Sudan and Djibouti; microwave radio relay to Kenya and Djibouti; satellite earth stations - 3 Intelsat (1 Atlantic Ocean and 2 Pacific Ocean)

Radio broadcast stations: AM 5, FM 0, shortwave 1

Radios: 9 million (1998 est.)

Television broadcast stations: 25 (1998)

Televisions: 150,000 (1998 est.)

Transportation

Railways:
total: 681 km (Ethiopian segment of the Addis Ababa-Djibouti railroad)
narrow gauge: 681 km 1.000-m gauge
note: in April 1998, Djibouti and Ethiopia announced plans to revitalize the century-old railroad that links their capitals

Highways:
total: 28,500 km
paved: 4,275 km
unpaved: 24,225 km (1996 est.)

Ports and harbors: none; Ethiopia is landlocked and was by agreement with Eritrea using the ports of Assab and Massawa, but since the border dispute with Eritrea flared, Ethiopia has used the port of Djibouti

Merchant marine:
total: 11 ships (1,000 GRT or over) totaling 71,264 GRT/94,489 DWT
ships by type: cargo 7, oil tanker 1, roll-on/roll-off cargo 3 (1998 est.)

Airports: 84 (1998 est.)

Airports - with paved runways:
total: 11
over 3,047 m: 3
2,438 to 3,047 m: 5
1,524 to 2,437 m: 2
914 to 1,523 m: 1 (1998 est.)

Airports - with unpaved runways:
total: 73
over 3,047 m: 2
2,438 to 3,047 m: 8
1,524 to 2,437 m: 9
914 to 1,523 m: 36
under 914 m: 18 (1998 est.)

Military

Military branches: Ground Forces, Air Force, Police
note: Ethiopia is landlocked and has no navy; following the de jure independence of Eritrea, Ethiopian naval facilities remained in Eritrean possession and ships which belonged to the former

Ethiopia (continued)

Ethiopian Navy and based at Djibouti have been sold

Military manpower - military age: 18 years of age

Military manpower - availability:
males age 15-49: 13,520,302 (1999 est.)

Military manpower - fit for military service:
males age 15-49: 7,052,710 (1999 est.)

Military manpower - reaching military age annually:
males: 655,290 (1999 est.)

Military expenditures - dollar figure: $138 million (FY98/99)

Military expenditures - percent of GDP: 2.5% (FY98/99)

Transnational Issues

Disputes - international: most of the southern half of the boundary with Somalia is a Provisional Administrative Line; territorial dispute with Somalia over the Ogaden; dispute over alignment of boundary with Eritrea led to armed conflict in 1998, which is still unresolved despite arbitration efforts

Illicit drugs: transit hub for heroin originating in Southwest and Southeast Asia and destined for Europe and North America as well as cocaine destined for markets in southern Africa; cultivates qat (chat) for local use and regional export

Europa Island
(possession of France)

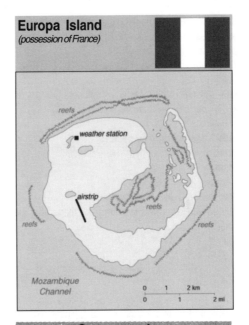

Geography

Location: Southern Africa, island in the Mozambique Channel, about one-half of the way from southern Madagascar to southern Mozambique

Geographic coordinates: 22 20 S, 40 22 E

Map references: Africa

Area:
total: 28 sq km
land: 28 sq km
water: 0 sq km

Area - comparative: about 0.16 times the size of Washington, DC

Land boundaries: 0 km

Coastline: 22.2 km

Maritime claims:
exclusive economic zone: 200 nm
territorial sea: 12 nm

Climate: tropical

Terrain: NA

Elevation extremes:
lowest point: Indian Ocean 0 m
highest point: unnamed location 24 m

Natural resources: negligible

Land use:
arable land: NA%
permanent crops: NA%
permanent pastures: NA%
forests and woodland: NA%
other: NA%

Irrigated land: 0 sq km (1993)

Natural hazards: NA

Environment - current issues: NA

Environment - international agreements:
party to: NA
signed, but not ratified: NA

Geography - note: wildlife sanctuary

People

Population: no indigenous inhabitants
note: there is a small French military garrison

Government

Country name:
conventional long form: none
conventional short form: Europa Island
local long form: none
local short form: Ile Europa

Data code: EU

Dependency status: possession of France; administered by a high commissioner of the Republic, resident in Reunion

Independence: none (possession of France)

Legal system: NA

Diplomatic representation in the US: none (possession of France)

Diplomatic representation from the US: none (possession of France)

Flag description: the flag of France is used

Economy

Economy - overview: no economic activity

Communications

Communications - note: 1 meteorological station

Transportation

Ports and harbors: none; offshore anchorage only

Airports: 1 (1998 est.)

Airports - with unpaved runways:
total: 1
914 to 1,523 m: 1 (1998 est.)

Military

Military - note: defense is the responsibility of France

Transnational Issues

Disputes - international: claimed by Madagascar

Falkland Islands (Islas Malvinas)
(overseas territory of the UK; also claimed by Argentina)

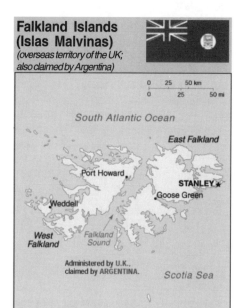

Geography

Location: Southern South America, islands in the South Atlantic Ocean, east of southern Argentina
Geographic coordinates: 51 45 S, 59 00 W
Map references: South America
Area:
total: 12,173 sq km
land: 12,173 sq km
water: 0 sq km
note: includes the two main islands of East and West Falkland and about 200 small islands
Area - comparative: slightly smaller than Connecticut
Land boundaries: 0 km
Coastline: 1,288 km
Maritime claims:
continental shelf: 200 nm
exclusive fishing zone: 200 nm
territorial sea: 12 nm
Climate: cold marine; strong westerly winds, cloudy, humid; rain occurs on more than half of days in year; occasional snow all year, except in January and February, but does not accumulate
Terrain: rocky, hilly, mountainous with some boggy, undulating plains
Elevation extremes:
lowest point: Atlantic Ocean 0 m
highest point: Mount Usborne 705 m
Natural resources: fish, wildlife
Land use:
arable land: 0%
permanent crops: 0%
permanent pastures: 99%
forests and woodland: 0%
other: 1% (1993 est.)
Irrigated land: NA sq km
Natural hazards: strong winds persist throughout the year
Environment - current issues: NA

Environment - international agreements:
party to: NA
signed, but not ratified: NA
Geography - note: deeply indented coast provides good natural harbors; short growing season

People

Population: 2,758 (July 1999 est.)
Age structure:
0-14 years: NA
15-64 years: NA
65 years and over: NA
Population growth rate: 2.43% (1999 est.)
Birth rate: NA births/1,000 population
Death rate: NA deaths/1,000 population
Net migration rate: NA migrant(s)/1,000 population
Infant mortality rate: NA deaths/1,000 live births
Life expectancy at birth:
total population: NA years
male: NA years
female: NA years
Total fertility rate: NA children born/woman
Nationality:
noun: Falkland Islander(s)
adjective: Falkland Island
Ethnic groups: British
Religions: primarily Anglican, Roman Catholic, United Free Church, Evangelist Church, Jehovah's Witnesses, Lutheran, Seventh-Day Adventist
Languages: English

Government

Country name:
conventional long form: Colony of the Falkland Islands
conventional short form: Falkland Islands (Islas Malvinas)
Data code: FA
Dependency status: overseas territory of the UK, also claimed by Argentina
Government type: NA
Capital: Stanley
Administrative divisions: none (overseas territory of the UK; also claimed by Argentina)
Independence: none (overseas territory of the UK; also claimed by Argentina)
National holiday: Liberation Day, 14 June (1982)
Constitution: 3 October 1985; amended 1997
Legal system: English common law
Suffrage: 18 years of age; universal
Executive branch:
chief of state: Queen ELIZABETH II (since 6 February 1952)
head of government: Governor Richard RALPH (since 29 January 1996; to be replaced in May 1999 by Donald LAMONT); Chief Executive A. M. GURR (since NA); Financial Secretary D. F. HOWATT (since NA)
cabinet: Executive Council; three members elected by the Legislative Council, two ex officio members (chief executive and the financial secretary), and the governor

elections: none; the monarch is hereditary; governor appointed by the monarch
Legislative branch: unicameral Legislative Council (10 seats - 8 elected, 2 ex officio; members are elected by popular vote to serve five-year terms)
elections: last held 9 October 1997 (next to be held NA October 2001)
election results: percent of vote - NA; seats - independents 8
Judicial branch: Supreme Court, chief justice is a nonresident
Political parties and leaders: none; all independents
International organization participation: ICFTU
Diplomatic representation in the US: none (overseas territory of the UK; also claimed by Argentina)
Diplomatic representation from the US: none (overseas territory of the UK; also claimed by Argentina)
Flag description: blue with the flag of the UK in the upper hoist-side quadrant and the Falkland Island coat of arms in a white disk centered on the outer half of the flag; the coat of arms contains a white ram (sheep raising is the major economic activity) above the sailing ship Desire (whose crew discovered the islands) with a scroll at the bottom bearing the motto DESIRE THE RIGHT

Economy

Economy - overview: The economy was formerly based on agriculture, mainly sheep farming, but today fishing contributes the bulk of economic activity. In 1987 the government began selling fishing licenses to foreign trawlers operating within the Falklands exclusive fishing zone. These license fees total more than $40 million per year, which goes to support the island's health, education, and welfare system. Squid accounts for 75% of the fish taken. Dairy farming supports domestic consumption; crops furnish winter fodder. Exports feature shipments of high-grade wool to the UK and the sale of postage stamps and coins. To encourage tourism, the Falkland Islands Development Corporation has built three lodges for visitors attracted by the abundant wildlife and trout fishing. The islands are now self-financing except for defense. The British Geological Survey announced a 200-mile oil exploration zone around the islands in 1993, and early seismic surveys suggest substantial reserves capable of producing 500,000 barrels per day; to date no exploitable site has been identified. An agreement between Argentina and the UK in 1995 seeks to defuse licensing and sovereignty conflicts that would dampen foreign interest in exploiting potential oil reserves.
GDP: purchasing power parity - $NA
GDP - real growth rate: NA%
GDP - per capita: purchasing power parity - $NA
GDP - composition by sector:
agriculture: NA%
industry: NA%
services: NA%

Falkland Islands (Islas Malvinas) *(continued)*

Population below poverty line: NA%
Household income or consumption by percentage share:
lowest 10%: NA%
highest 10%: NA%
Inflation rate (consumer prices): NA%
Labor force: 1,100 (est.)
Labor force - by occupation: agriculture 95% (mostly sheepherding and fishing)
Unemployment rate: full employment; labor shortage
Budget:
revenues: $66.1 million
expenditures: $66.8 million, including capital expenditures of $NA (FY97/98 est.)
Industries: wool and fish processing; sale of stamps and coins
Industrial production growth rate: NA%
Electricity - production: 10 million kWh (1996)
Electricity - production by source:
fossil fuel: 100%
hydro: 0%
nuclear: 0%
other: 0% (1996)
Electricity - consumption: 10 million kWh (1996)
Electricity - exports: 0 kWh (1996)
Electricity - imports: 0 kWh (1996)
Agriculture - products: fodder and vegetable crops; sheep, dairy products
Exports: $7.6 million (1995)
Exports - commodities: wool, hides, meat
Exports - partners: UK, Netherlands, Japan (1992)
Imports: $24.7 million (1995)
Imports - commodities: fuel, food and drink, building materials, clothing
Imports - partners: UK, Netherlands Antilles, Japan (1992)
Debt - external: $NA
Economic aid - recipient: $1.7 million (1995)
Currency: 1 Falkland pound (£F) = 100 pence
Exchange rates: Falkland pound (£F) per US$1 - 0.6057 (January 1999), 0.5037 (1998), 0.6106 (1997), 0.6403 (1996), 0.6335 (1995), 0.6529 (1994); note - the Falkland pound is at par with the British pound
Fiscal year: 1 April - 31 March

Communications

Telephones: 1,180 (1991 est.)
Telephone system:
domestic: government-operated radiotelephone and private VHF/CB radiotelephone networks provide effective service to almost all points on both islands
international: satellite earth station - 1 Intelsat (Atlantic Ocean) with links through London to other countries
Radio broadcast stations: 1 (government operated)
Radios: 1,000 (1992 est.)
Television broadcast stations: 2 (operated by the British Forces Broadcasting Service) (1997)
Televisions: NA

Transportation

Railways: 0 km
Highways:
total: 348 km
paved: 83 km
unpaved: 265 km
Ports and harbors: Stanley
Merchant marine: none
Airports: 5 (1998 est.)
Airports - with paved runways:
total: 2
2,438 to 3,047 m: 1
under 914 m: 1 (1998 est.)
Airports - with unpaved runways:
total: 3
under 914 m: 3 (1998 est.)

Military

Military branches: British Forces Falkland Islands (includes Army, Royal Air Force, Royal Navy, and Royal Marines), Police Force
Military expenditures - dollar figure: $NA
Military expenditures - percent of GDP: NA%
Military - note: defense is the responsibility of the UK

Transnational Issues

Disputes - international: claimed by Argentina

Faroe Islands
(part of the Kingdom of Denmark)

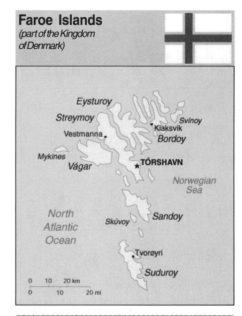

Geography

Location: Northern Europe, island group between the Norwegian Sea and the north Atlantic Ocean, about one-half of the way from Iceland to Norway
Geographic coordinates: 62 00 N, 7 00 W
Map references: Europe
Area:
total: 1,399 sq km
land: 1,399 sq km
water: 0 sq km (some lakes and streams)
Area - comparative: eight times the size of Washington, DC
Land boundaries: 0 km
Coastline: 1,117 km
Maritime claims:
exclusive fishing zone: 200 nm
territorial sea: 3 nm
Climate: mild winters, cool summers; usually overcast; foggy, windy
Terrain: rugged, rocky, some low peaks; cliffs along most of coast
Elevation extremes:
lowest point: Atlantic Ocean 0 m
highest point: Slaettaratindur 882 m
Natural resources: fish, whales
Land use:
arable land: 6%
permanent crops: 0%
permanent pastures: 0%
forests and woodland: 0%
other: 94% (1996)
Irrigated land: 0 sq km
Natural hazards: NA
Environment - current issues: NA
Environment - international agreements:
party to: NA
signed, but not ratified: NA
Geography - note: archipelago of 17 inhabited islands and one uninhabited island, and a few uninhabited islets; strategically located along

Faroe Islands (continued)

important sea lanes in northeastern Atlantic; precipitous terrain limits habitation to small coastal lowlands

People

Population: 41,059 (July 1999 est.)
Age structure:
0-14 years: 23% (male 4,819; female 4,629)
15-64 years: 62% (male 13,600; female 11,811)
65 years and over: 15% (male 2,786; female 3,414) (1999 est.)
Population growth rate: -2.03% (1999 est.)
Birth rate: 12.54 births/1,000 population (1999 est.)
Death rate: 9.08 deaths/1,000 population (1999 est.)
Net migration rate: -23.72 migrant(s)/1,000 population (1999 est.)
Sex ratio:
at birth: 1.04 male(s)/female
under 15 years: 1.04 male(s)/female
15-64 years: 1.15 male(s)/female
65 years and over: 0.82 male(s)/female
total population: 1.07 male(s)/female (1999 est.)
Infant mortality rate: 10.26 deaths/1,000 live births (1999 est.)
Life expectancy at birth:
total population: 78.56 years
male: 75.66 years
female: 81.58 years (1999 est.)
Total fertility rate: 2.36 children born/woman (1999 est.)
Nationality:
noun: Faroese (singular and plural)
adjective: Faroese
Ethnic groups: Scandinavian
Religions: Evangelical Lutheran
Languages: Faroese (derived from Old Norse), Danish
Literacy: NA
note: similar to Denmark proper

Government

Country name:
conventional long form: none
conventional short form: Faroe Islands
local long form: none
local short form: Foroyar
Data code: FO
Dependency status: part of the Kingdom of Denmark; self-governing overseas administrative division of Denmark since 1948
Government type: NA
Capital: Torshavn
Administrative divisions: none (part of the Kingdom of Denmark; self-governing overseas administrative division of Denmark)
Independence: none (part of the Kingdom of Denmark; self-governing overseas administrative division of Denmark)
National holiday: Birthday of the Queen, 16 April (1940)
Constitution: 5 June 1953 (Danish constitution)

Legal system: Danish
Suffrage: 18 years of age; universal
Executive branch:
chief of state: Queen MARGRETHE II of Denmark (since 14 January 1972), represented by High Commissioner Bente KLINTE, chief administrative officer (since NA)
head of government: Prime Minister Anfinn KALLSBERG (since 9 May 1998)
cabinet: Landsstyri elected by the Faroese Parliament
elections: the monarch is hereditary; high commissioner appointed by the monarch; following legislative elections, the leader of the party that wins the most seats is usually elected prime minister by the Faroese Parliament; election last held 30 April 1998 (next to be held NA 2002)
election results: Anfinn KALLSBERG elected prime minister; percent of parliamentary vote - NA
Legislative branch: unicameral Faroese Parliament or Logting (32 seats; members are elected by popular vote on a proportional basis from the seven constituencies to serve four-year terms)
elections: last held 30 April 1998 (next to be held by NA July 2002)
election results: percent of vote by party - Republicans 23.8%, People's Party 21.3%, Social Democrats 21.9%, Coalition Party (Union Party, Labor Front, Home Rule Party) 15%; seats by party - Republicans 8, People's Party 8, Social Democrats 7, Coalition Party 6, other parties 3
note: election of 2 seats to the Danish Parliament was last held on 11 March 1998 (next to be held by NA 2002); results - percent of vote by party - NA; seats by party - Social Democrats 1, Conservatives 1
Judicial branch: none
Political parties and leaders: Social Democratic Party [Joannes EIDESGAARD]; Workers' Party [Alis JACOBSEN]; Home Rule Party [Helena Dam A. NEYSTABO]; Unionist Party [Edmund JOENSEN]; Republican Party [Heini O. HEINESEN]; Center Party [Tordur NICLASEN]; Christian People's Party [Niels Pauli DANIELSEN]; People's Party [Arnfinn KALLSBERG]
International organization participation: NC, NIB
Diplomatic representation in the US: none (self-governing overseas administrative division of Denmark)
Diplomatic representation from the US: none (self-governing overseas administrative division of Denmark)
Flag description: white with a red cross outlined in blue that extends to the edges of the flag; the vertical part of the cross is shifted to the hoist side in the style of the Dannebrog (Danish flag)

Economy

Economy - overview: After the severe economic troubles of the early 1990s, brought on by a drop in the vital fish catch, the Faroe Islands have come back in the last few years, with unemployment down to 5% in mid-1998. Nevertheless the total dependence on fishing means the economy remains extremely

vulnerable. The Faroese hope to broaden their economic base by building new fish-processing plants. Oil finds close to the Faroese area give hope for deposits in the immediate Faroese area, which may lay the basis for sustained economic prosperity. The Faroese are supported by a substantial annual subsidy from Denmark.
GDP: purchasing power parity - $700 million (1996 est.)
GDP - real growth rate: 6% (1996 est.)
GDP - per capita: purchasing power parity - $16,000 (1996 est.)
GDP - composition by sector:
agriculture: 20%
industry: 16%
services: 64% (1996 est.)
Population below poverty line: NA%
Household income or consumption by percentage share:
lowest 10%: NA%
highest 10%: NA%
Inflation rate (consumer prices): 2.8% (1996 est.)
Labor force: 20,345 (1995 est.)
Labor force - by occupation: largely engaged in fishing, manufacturing, transportation, and commerce
Unemployment rate: 5% (1998 est.)
Budget:
revenues: $467 million
expenditures: $468 million, including capital expenditures of $11 million (1996 est.)
Industries: fishing, shipbuilding, construction, handicrafts
Industrial production growth rate: NA%
Electricity - production: 170 million kWh (1996)
Electricity - production by source:
fossil fuel: 52.94%
hydro: 47.06%
nuclear: 0%
other: 0% (1996)
Electricity - consumption: 170 million kWh (1996)
Electricity - exports: 0 kWh (1996)
Electricity - imports: 0 kWh (1996)
Agriculture - products: milk, potatoes, vegetables; sheep; salmon, other fish
Exports: $362 million (f.o.b., 1995)
Exports - commodities: fish and fish products 92%, animal feedstuffs, transport equipment (ships)
Exports - partners: Denmark 22.2%, UK 25.8%, Germany 9.7%, France 8.3%, Norway 6.2%, US 2.0%
Imports: $315.6 (c.i.f., 1995)
Imports - commodities: machinery and transport equipment 17.0%, consumer goods 33%, raw materials and semi-manufactures 26.9%, fuels 11.4%, fish and salt 6.7%
Imports - partners: Denmark 34.5%, Norway 15.9%, UK 8.4% Germany 7.8%, Sweden 5.8%, US 1.5%
Debt - external: $767 million (1995 est.)
Economic aid - recipient: $150 million (annual subsidy from Denmark) (1995)
Currency: 1 Danish krone (DKr) = 100 oere

Faroe Islands (continued)

Exchange rates: Danish kroner (DKr) per US$1 - 6.408 (January 1999), 6.701 (1998), 6.604 (1997), 5.799 (1966), 5.602 (1995), 6.361 (1994)
Fiscal year: calendar year

Communications

Telephones: 22,500 (3,500 cellular telephone subscribers) (1996)
Telephone system: good international communications; good domestic facilities
domestic: digitalization was to hve been completed in 1998
international: satellite earth stations - 1 Orion; 1 fiber-optic submarine cable linking the Faroe Islands with Denmark and Iceland
Radio broadcast stations: AM 1, FM 1 (repeaters 13), shortwave 0
Radios: 11,800 (1996 est.)
Television broadcast stations: 3 (in addition, there are 29 low-power repeaters; satellite relays of MTV Europe, BBC World, and Scansat TV3 Eurosport are also available) (1997)
Televisions: 11,600 (1996 est.)

Transportation

Railways: 0 km
Highways:
total: 458 km
paved: 450 km
unpaved: 8 km (1995 est.)
Ports and harbors: Torshavn, Klaksvik, Tvoroyri, Runavik, Fuglafjorour
Merchant marine:
total: 6 ships (1,000 GRT or over) totaling 22,853 GRT/13,481 DWT
ships by type: cargo 2, oil tanker 1, refrigerated cargo 1, roll-on/roll-off cargo 1, short-sea passenger 1 (1998 est.)
Airports: 1 (1998 est.)
Airports - with paved runways:
total: 1
914 to 1,523 m: 1 (1998 est.)

Military

Military branches: no organized native military forces; only a small Police Force and Coast Guard are maintained
Military expenditures - dollar figure: $NA
Military expenditures - percent of GDP: NA%
Military - note: defense is the responsibility of Denmark

Transnational Issues

Disputes - international: none

Figi

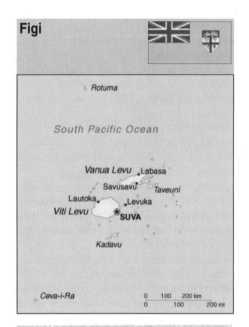

Geography

Location: Oceania, island group in the South Pacific Ocean, about two-thirds of the way from Hawaii to New Zealand
Geographic coordinates: 18 00 S, 175 00 E
Map references: Oceania
Area:
total: 18,270 sq km
land: 18,270 sq km
water: 0 sq km
Area - comparative: slightly smaller than New Jersey
Land boundaries: 0 km
Coastline: 1,129 km
Maritime claims: measured from claimed archipelagic baselines
continental shelf: 200-m depth or to the depth of exploitation; rectilinear shelf claim added
exclusive economic zone: 200 nm
territorial sea: 12 nm
Climate: tropical marine; only slight seasonal temperature variation
Terrain: mostly mountains of volcanic origin
Elevation extremes:
lowest point: Pacific Ocean 0 m
highest point: Tomanivi 1,324 m
Natural resources: timber, fish, gold, copper, offshore oil potential
Land use:
arable land: 10%
permanent crops: 4%
permanent pastures: 10%
forests and woodland: 65%
other: 11% (1993 est.)
Irrigated land: 10 sq km (1993 est.)
Natural hazards: cyclonic storms can occur from November to January
Environment - current issues: deforestation; soil erosion
Environment - international agreements:
party to: Biodiversity, Climate Change, Climate Change-Kyoto Protocol, Desertification, Endangered Species, Law of the Sea, Marine Life Conservation, Nuclear Test Ban, Ozone Layer Protection, Tropical Timber 83, Tropical Timber 94
signed, but not ratified: none of the selected agreements
Geography - note: includes 332 islands of which approximately 110 are inhabited

People

Population: 812,918 (July 1999 est.)
Age structure:
0-14 years: 33% (male 138,796; female 133,428)
15-64 years: 63% (male 257,130; female 256,834)
65 years and over: 4% (male 12,527; female 14,203) (1999 est.)
Population growth rate: 1.28% (1999 est.)
Birth rate: 22.76 births/1,000 population (1999 est.)
Death rate: 6.21 deaths/1,000 population (1999 est.)
Net migration rate: -3.78 migrant(s)/1,000 population (1999 est.)
Sex ratio:
at birth: 1.05 male(s)/female
under 15 years: 1.04 male(s)/female
15-64 years: 1 male(s)/female
65 years and over: 0.88 male(s)/female
total population: 1.01 male(s)/female (1999 est.)
Infant mortality rate: 16.3 deaths/1,000 live births (1999 est.)
Life expectancy at birth:
total population: 66.59 years
male: 64.19 years
female: 69.11 years (1999 est.)
Total fertility rate: 2.7 children born/woman (1999 est.)
Nationality:
noun: Fijian(s)
adjective: Fijian
Ethnic groups: Fijian 51%, Indian 44%, European, other Pacific Islanders, overseas Chinese, and other 5% (1998 est.)
Religions: Christian 52% (Methodist 37%, Roman Catholic 9%), Hindu 38%, Muslim 8%, other 2%
note: Fijians are mainly Christian, Indians are Hindu, and there is a Muslim minority (1986)
Languages: English (official), Fijian, Hindustani
Literacy:
definition: age 15 and over can read and write
total population: 91.6%
male: 93.8%
female: 89.3% (1995 est.)

Government

Country name:
conventional long form: Republic of the Fiji Islands
conventional short form: Fiji
Data code: FJ
Government type: republic
note: military coup leader Maj. Gen. Sitiveni RABUKA formally declared Fiji a republic on 6 October 1987
Capital: Suva

Fiji (continued)

Administrative divisions: 4 divisions and 1 dependency*; Central, Eastern, Northern, Rotuma*, Western

Independence: 10 October 1970 (from UK)

National holiday: Independence Day, 10 October (1970)

Constitution: 10 October 1970 (suspended 1 October 1987); a new constitution was proposed on 23 September 1988 and promulgated on 25 July 1990; amended 25 July 1997 to allow non-ethnic Fijians greater say in government and to make multi-party government mandatory; entered into force 28 July 1998; note - the May 1999 election will be the first test of the amended constitution and will introduce open voting - not racially prescribed - for the first time at the national level

Legal system: based on British system

Suffrage: 21 years of age; universal

Executive branch:

chief of state: President Ratu Sir Kamisese MARA (acting president since 15 December 1993, president since 12 January 1994); Vice President Ratu Josefa Iloilo ULUIVUDA (since 18 January 1999)

head of government: Prime Minister Sitiveni RABUKA (since 2 June 1992); Deputy Prime Minister Taufa VAKATALE (since 7 August 1997)

cabinet: Cabinet appointed by the prime minister from among the members of Parliament and is responsible to Parliament

note: there is also a Presidential Council that advises the president on matters of national importance and a Great Council of Chiefs which consists of the highest ranking members of the traditional chiefly system

elections: president elected by the Great Council of Chiefs for a five-year term; prime minister appointed by the president

election results: Ratu Sir Kamisese MARA elected president; percent of Great Council of Chiefs vote - NA

Legislative branch: bicameral Parliament consists of the Senate (34 seats; 24 reserved for ethnic Fijians, 9 for Indians and others, and 1 for the island of Rotuma; members appointed by the president to serve five-year terms) and the House of Representatives (70 seats; 37 reserved for ethnic Fijians, 27 reserved for ethnic Indians, and 6 for independents and others; members elected by popular vote on a communal basis to serve five-year terms)

elections: House of Representatives - last held 18-25 February 1994 (next to be held 11 May 1999)

election results: House of Representatives - percent of vote by party - NA; seats by party - SVT 31, NFP 20, FLP 7, FAP 5, GVP 4, independents 2, ANC 1; note - results are for the last election before the new constitution came into force

note: when the new constitution is applied to the upcoming May elections, the composition of the legislative branch will change to the following: Senate - 32 seats (14 appointed by the Great Council of Chiefs, nine appointed by the prime minister, eight appointed by the leader of the opposition, and one

appointed by the council of Rotuma) and House of Representatives - 71 seats (23 reserved for ethnic Fijians, 19 reserved for ethnic Indians, three reserved for other ethnic groups, one reserved for the Rotuman constituency encompassing the whole of Fiji, and 25 open seats)

Judicial branch: Supreme Court, judges are appointed by the president

Political parties and leaders: Fijian Political Party or SVT (primarily Fijian) [leader Maj. Gen. Sitivini RABUKA]; National Federation Party or NFP (primarily Indian) [Jai Ram REDDY]; Fijian Nationalist Party or FNP [Sakeasi BUTADROKA]; Fiji Labor Party or FLP [Mahendra CHAUDHRY]; General Voters Party or GVP [Leo SMITH]; Fiji Conservative Party or FCP [leader NA]; Conservative Party of Fiji or CPF [leader NA]; Fiji Indian Liberal Party [leader NA]; Fiji Indian Congress Party [leader NA]; Fiji Independent Labor (Muslim) [leader NA]; Four Corners Party [leader NA]; Fijian Association Party or FAP [Adi Kuini SPEED]; General Electors' Association [David PICKERING]; National Unity Party [Apisai TORA]; Veitokani ni Lewenivanua Vakarisito Party or VLV or Christian Fellowship Party (primarily Methodist Fijian) [leader NA]

note: in early 1995, ethnic Fijian members of the All National Congress or ANC merged with the Fijian Association or FA; the remaining members of the ANC have renamed their party the General Electors' Association

International organization participation: ACP, AsDB, C, CP, ESCAP, FAO, G-77, IBRD, ICAO, ICFTU, ICRM, IDA, IFAD, IFC, IFRCS, IHO, ILO, IMF, IMO, Intelsat, Interpol, IOC, ISO (subscriber), ITU, OPCW, PCA, Sparteca, SPC, SPF, UN, UNCTAD, UNESCO, UNIDO, UNIFIL, UNIKOM, UPU, WFTU, WHO, WIPO, WMO, WToO, WTrO

Diplomatic representation in the US:

chief of mission: Ambassador "Ratu" Napolioni MASIREWA

chancery: Suite 240, 2233 Wisconsin Avenue NW, Washington, DC 20007

telephone: [1] (202) 337-8320

FAX: [1] (202) 337-1996

consulate(s): New York

Diplomatic representation from the US:

chief of mission: Ambassador (vacant); Charge d'Affaires Larry M. DINGER

embassy: 31 Loftus Street, Suva

mailing address: P. O. Box 218, Suva

telephone: [679] 314466

FAX: [679] 300081

Flag description: light blue with the flag of the UK in the upper hoist-side quadrant and the Fijian shield centered on the outer half of the flag; the shield depicts a yellow lion above a white field quartered by the cross of Saint George featuring stalks of sugarcane, a palm tree, bananas, and a white dove

Economy

Economy - overview: Fiji, endowed with forest, mineral, and fish resources, is one of the most

developed of the Pacific island economies, though still with a large subsistence sector. Sugar exports and a growing tourist industry are the major sources of foreign exchange. Sugar processing makes up one-third of industrial activity. Roughly 250,000 tourists visit each year. Political uncertainty and drought, however, contribute to substantial fluctuations in earnings from tourism and sugar and to the emigration of skilled workers. Fiji's growth slowed in 1997 because the sugar industry suffered from low world prices and rent disputes between farmers and landowners. Drought in 1998 further damaged the sugar industry. Overall growth in 1991-98 has averaged less than 2% per year, with long-term problems of low investment and uncertain property rights. The central bank predicts growth of 2% to 3% in 1999.

GDP: purchasing power parity - $5.4 billion (1998 est.)

GDP - real growth rate: 2.4% (1998 est.)

GDP - per capita: purchasing power parity - $6,700 (1998 est.)

GDP - composition by sector:

agriculture: 19%

industry: 22%

services: 59% (1996 est.)

Population below poverty line: NA%

Household income or consumption by percentage share:

lowest 10%: NA%

highest 10%: NA%

Inflation rate (consumer prices): 3% (1997 est.)

Labor force: 235,000

Labor force - by occupation: subsistence agriculture 67%, wage earners 18%, salary earners 15% (1987)

Unemployment rate: 6% (1997 est.)

Budget:

revenues: $540.65 million

expenditures: $742.65 million, including capital expenditures of $NA (1997 est.)

Industries: sugar, tourism, copra, gold, silver, clothing, lumber, small cottage industries

Industrial production growth rate: 2.9% (1995)

Electricity - production: 545 million kWh (1996)

Electricity - production by source:

fossil fuel: 21.1%

hydro: 78.9%

nuclear: 0%

other: 0% (1996)

Electricity - consumption: 545 million kWh (1996)

Electricity - exports: 0 kWh (1996)

Electricity - imports: 0 kWh (1996)

Agriculture - products: sugarcane, coconuts, cassava (tapioca), rice, sweet potatoes, bananas; cattle, pigs, horses, goats; fish

Exports: $655 million (f.o.b., 1996)

Exports - commodities: sugar 32%, clothing, gold, processed fish, lumber

Exports - partners: Australia 27%, UK 14%, NZ 12%, US 8%, Japan (1996)

Imports: $838 million (f.o.b., 1996)

Fiji (continued)

Imports - commodities: machinery and transport equipment, petroleum products, food, chemicals
Imports - partners: Australia 44%, NZ 15%, US 9%, Japan 5%, Singapore 5% (1996)
Debt - external: $217 million (1996 est.)
Economic aid - recipient: $40.3 million (1995)
Currency: 1 Fijian dollar (F$) = 100 cents
Exchange rates: Fijian dollars (F$) per US$1 - 1.9556 (January 1999), 1.9868 (1998), 1.4437 (1997), 1.4033 (1996), 1.4063 (1995), 1.4641 (1994)
Fiscal year: calendar year

Communications

Telephones: 60,017 (1987 est.)
Telephone system: modern local, interisland, and international (wire/radio integrated) public and special-purpose telephone, telegraph, and teleprinter facilities; regional radio communications center
domestic: NA
international: access to important cable link between US and Canada and NZ and Australia; satellite earth station - 1 Intelsat (Pacific Ocean)
Radio broadcast stations: AM 7, FM 1, shortwave 0
Radios: NA
Television broadcast stations: 0
Televisions: 12,000 (1992 est.)

Transportation

Railways:
total: 597 km; note - belongs to the government-owned Fiji Sugar Corporation
narrow gauge: 597 km 0.610-m gauge (1995)
Highways:
total: 3,440 km
paved: 1,692 km
unpaved: 1,748 km (1996 est.)
Waterways: 203 km; 122 km navigable by motorized craft and 200-metric-ton barges
Ports and harbors: Labasa, Lautoka, Levuka, Savusavu, Suva
Merchant marine:
total: 5 ships (1,000 GRT or over) totaling 10,721 GRT/13,145 DWT
ships by type: chemical tanker 2, passenger 1, roll-on/roll-off cargo 1, specialized tanker 1 (1998 est.)
Airports: 24 (1998 est.)
Airports - with paved runways:
total: 3
over 3,047 m: 1
1,524 to 2,437 m: 1
914 to 1,523 m: 1 (1998 est.)
Airports - with unpaved runways:
total: 21
914 to 1,523 m: 4
under 914 m: 17 (1998 est.)

Military

Military branches: Republic of Fiji Military Forces (RFMF; includes ground and naval forces)

Military manpower - military age: 18 years of age
Military manpower - availability:
males age 15-49: 218,853 (1999 est.)
Military manpower - fit for military service:
males age 15-49: 120,555 (1999 est.)
Military manpower - reaching military age annually:
males: 9,326 (1999 est.)
Military expenditures - dollar figure: $34 million (1997)
Military expenditures - percent of GDP: 1.6% (1997)

Transnational Issues

Disputes - international: none

Finland

Introduction

Background: Long ruled by foreign powers, including Sweden and the pre-revolutionary Russian Empire, Finland finally declared independence in 1917. During World War II, Finland fought the USSR twice and then the Germans toward the end of the war. In the following half-century, the Finns made a remarkable transformation from a farm/forest economy to a diversified modern industrial economy. Per capita income has risen to the West European level; Finland is a member of the European Union and is the only Nordic state to join the euro system at its initiation in January 1999.

Geography

Location: Northern Europe, bordering the Baltic Sea, Gulf of Bothnia, and Gulf of Finland, between Sweden and Russia
Geographic coordinates: 64 00 N, 26 00 E
Map references: Europe
Area:
total: 337,030 sq km
land: 305,470 sq km
water: 31,560 sq km

Finland *(continued)*

Area - comparative: slightly smaller than Montana
Land boundaries:
total: 2,628 km
border countries: Norway 729 km, Sweden 586 km, Russia 1,313 km
Coastline: 1,126 km (excludes islands and coastal indentations)
Maritime claims:
contiguous zone: 6 nm
continental shelf: 200-m depth or to the depth of exploitation
exclusive fishing zone: 12 nm
territorial sea: 12 nm (in the Gulf of Finland - 3 nm)
Climate: cold temperate; potentially subarctic, but comparatively mild because of moderating influence of the North Atlantic Current, Baltic Sea, and more than 60,000 lakes
Terrain: mostly low, flat to rolling plains interspersed with lakes and low hills
Elevation extremes:
lowest point: Baltic Sea 0 m
highest point: Haltiatunturi 1,328 m
Natural resources: timber, copper, zinc, iron ore, silver
Land use:
arable land: 8%
permanent crops: NA%
permanent pastures: NA%
forests and woodland: 76%
other: 16% (1993 est.)
Irrigated land: 640 sq km (1993 est.)
Natural hazards: NA
Environment - current issues: air pollution from manufacturing and power plants contributing to acid rain; water pollution from industrial wastes, agricultural chemicals; habitat loss threatens wildlife populations
Environment - international agreements:
party to: Air Pollution, Air Pollution-Nitrogen Oxides, Air Pollution-Sulphur 85, Air Pollution-Sulphur 94, Air Pollution-Volatile Organic Compounds, Antarctic-Environmental Protocol, Antarctic Treaty, Biodiversity, Climate Change, Desertification, Endangered Species, Environmental Modification, Hazardous Wastes, Law of the Sea, Marine Dumping, Marine Life Conservation, Nuclear Test Ban, Ozone Layer Protection, Ship Pollution, Tropical Timber 83, Tropical Timber 94, Wetlands, Whaling
signed, but not ratified: Air Pollution-Persistent Organic Pollutants, Climate Change-Kyoto Protocol
Geography - note: long boundary with Russia; Helsinki is northernmost national capital on European continent; population concentrated on small southwestern coastal plain

People

Population: 5,158,372 (July 1999 est.)
Age structure:
0-14 years: 18% (male 483,700; female 464,431)
15-64 years: 67% (male 1,743,340; female 1,706,873)
65 years and over: 15% (male 289,405; female 470,623) (1999 est.)
Population growth rate: 0.15% (1999 est.)
Birth rate: 10.77 births/1,000 population (1999 est.)
Death rate: 9.67 deaths/1,000 population (1999 est.)
Net migration rate: 0.4 migrant(s)/1,000 population (1999 est.)
Sex ratio:
at birth: 1.04 male(s)/female
under 15 years: 1.04 male(s)/female
15-64 years: 1.02 male(s)/female
65 years and over: 0.61 male(s)/female
total population: 0.95 male(s)/female (1999 est.)
Infant mortality rate: 3.8 deaths/1,000 live births (1999 est.)
Life expectancy at birth:
total population: 77.32 years
male: 73.81 years
female: 80.98 years (1999 est.)
Total fertility rate: 1.68 children born/woman (1999 est.)
Nationality:
noun: Finn(s)
adjective: Finnish
Ethnic groups: Finn 93%, Swede 6%, Lapp 0.11%, Gypsy 0.12%, Tatar 0.02%
Religions: Evangelical Lutheran 89%, Greek Orthodox 1%, none 9%, other 1%
Languages: Finnish 93.5% (official), Swedish 6.3% (official), small Lapp- and Russian-speaking minorities
Literacy:
definition: age 15 and over can read and write
total population: 100% (1980 est.)
male: NA%
female: NA%

Government

Country name:
conventional long form: Republic of Finland
conventional short form: Finland
local long form: Suomen Tasavalta
local short form: Suomi
Data code: FI
Government type: republic
Capital: Helsinki
Administrative divisions: 6 provinces (laanit, singular - laani); Aland, Etela-Suomen Laani, Ita-Suomen Lanni, Lansi-Suomen Laani, Lappi, Oulun Laani
Independence: 6 December 1917 (from Russia)
National holiday: Independence Day, 6 December (1917)
Constitution: 17 July 1919
Legal system: civil law system based on Swedish law; Supreme Court may request legislation interpreting or modifying laws; accepts compulsory ICJ jurisdiction, with reservations
Suffrage: 18 years of age; universal
Executive branch:
chief of state: President Martti AHTISAARI (since 1 March 1994)
head of government: Prime Minister Paavo LIPPONEN (since 13 April 1995) and Deputy Prime Minister Sauli NIINISTO (since 13 April 1995)
cabinet: Council of State or Valtioneuvosto appointed by the president, responsible to Parliament
elections: president elected by popular vote for a six-year term; election last held 31 January-6 February 1994 (next to be held NA January 2000); prime minister and deputy prime minister appointed from the majority party by the president after parliamentary elections
election results: Martti AHTISAARI elected president; percent of vote - Martti AHTISAARI 54%, Elisabeth REHN 46%
Legislative branch: unicameral Parliament or Eduskunta (200 seats; members are elected by popular vote on a proportional basis to serve four-year terms)
elections: last held 21 March 1999 (next to be held NA March 2003)
election results: percent of vote by party - Social Democratic Party 22.9%, Center Party 22.5%, National Coalition (Conservative) Party 21.0%, Leftist Alliance (Communist) 10.9%, Swedish People's Party 5.1%, Green Union 7.2%, Finnish Christian League 4.2%; seats by party - Social Democratic Party 51, Center Party 48, National Coalition (Conservative) Party 46, Leftist Alliance (Communist) 20, Swedish People's Party 11, Green Union 11, Finnish Christian League 10, other 3
Judicial branch: Supreme Court or Korkein Oikeus, judges appointed by the president
Political parties and leaders:
government coalition: Social Democratic Party [Paavo LIPPONEN]; National Coalition (conservative) Party [Sauli NIINISTO]; Leftist Alliance (Communist) composed of People's Democratic League and Democratic Alternative [Claes ANDERSSON]; Swedish People's Party [(Johan) Ole NORRBACK]; Green League [Pekka HAAVISTO]
other: Center Party [Esko AHO]; Finnish Christian League [C. P. Bjarne KALLIS]; Rural Party [Raimo VISTBACKA]; Liberal People's Party [Pekka RYTILA]; Greens Ecological Party or EPV [Eugen PARKATTI]; Young Finns [Risto PENTTILA]
Political pressure groups and leaders: Finnish Communist Party-Unity [Yrjo HAKANEN]; Constitutional Rightist Party; Finnish Pensioners Party; Communist Workers Party [Timo LAHDENMAKI]
International organization participation: AfDB, AsDB, Australia Group, BIS, CBSS, CCC, CE, CERN, EAPC, EBRD, ECE, EIB, EMU, ESA, EU, FAO, G- 9, IADB, IAEA, IBRD, ICAO, ICC, ICFTU, ICRM, IDA, IEA, IFAD, IFC, IFRCS, IHO, ILO, IMF, IMO, Inmarsat, Intelsat, Interpol, IOC, IOM, ISO, ITU, MTCR, NAM (guest), NC, NEA, NIB, NSG, OAS (observer), OECD, OPCW, OSCE, PCA, PFP, UN, UNCTAD, UNESCO, UNFICYP, UNHCR, UNIDO, UNIFIL, UNIKOM, UNMIBH, UNMOGIP, UNMOP, UNPREDEP, UNTSO, UPU, WEU (observer), WFTU, WHO, WIPO, WMO, WToO, WTrO, ZC
Diplomatic representation in the US:
chief of mission: Ambassador Jaakko Tapani LAAJAVA

Finland (continued)

chancery: 3301 Massachusetts Avenue NW,
Washington, DC 20008
telephone: [1] (202) 298-5800
FAX: [1] (202) 298-6030
consulate(s) general: Los Angeles and New York
Diplomatic representation from the US:
chief of mission: Ambassador Eric EDELMAN
embassy: Itainen Puistotie 14A, FIN-00140, Helsinki
mailing address: APO AE 09723
telephone: [358] (9) 171931
FAX: [358] (9) 174681
Flag description: white with a blue cross that extends to the edges of the flag; the vertical part of the cross is shifted to the hoist side in the style of the Dannebrog (Danish flag)

Economy

Economy - overview: Finland has a highly industrialized, largely free-market economy, with per capita output roughly that of the UK, France, Germany, and Italy. Its key economic sector is manufacturing - principally the wood, metals, engineering, telecommunications, and electronics industries. Trade is important, with the export of goods representing about 30% of GDP. Except for timber and several minerals, Finland depends on imports of raw materials, energy, and some components for manufactured goods. Because of the climate, agricultural development is limited to maintaining self-sufficiency in basic products. Forestry, an important export earner, provides a secondary occupation for the rural population. The economy has come back from the recession of 1990-92, which had been caused by economic overheating, depressed foreign markets, and the dismantling of the barter system between Finland and the former Soviet Union. Rapidly increasing integration with Western Europe - Finland was one of the 11 countries joining the euro monetary system (EMU) on 1 January 1999 - will dominate the economic picture over the next several years. Growth in 1999 probably will slow, perhaps to 3%, a barrier to any substantial drop in unemployment.
GDP: purchasing power parity - $103.6 billion (1998 est.)
GDP - real growth rate: 5.1% (1998 est.)
GDP - per capita: purchasing power parity - $20,100 (1998 est.)
GDP - composition by sector:
agriculture: 5%
industry: 32%
services: 63% (1997)
Population below poverty line: NA%
Household income or consumption by percentage share:
lowest 10%: 4.2%
highest 10%: 21.6% (1991)
Inflation rate (consumer prices): 1.5% (1998 est.)
Labor force: 2.533 million
Labor force - by occupation: public services 30.4%, industry 20.9%, commerce 15%, finance, insurance, and business services 10.2%, agriculture and forestry 8.6%, transport and communications 7.7%, construction 7.2%
Unemployment rate: 12% (1998 est.)
Budget:
revenues: $33 billion
expenditures: $40 billion, including capital expenditures of $NA (1996 est.)
Industries: metal products, shipbuilding, pulp and paper, copper refining, foodstuffs, chemicals, textiles, clothing
Industrial production growth rate: 7.4% (1995)
Electricity - production: 67.469 billion kWh (1996)
Electricity - production by source:
fossil fuel: 54.73%
hydro: 17.35%
nuclear: 27.9%
other: 0.02% (1996)
Electricity - consumption: 71.169 billion kWh (1996)
Electricity - exports: 1.7 billion kWh (1996)
Electricity - imports: 5.4 billion kWh (1996)
Agriculture - products: cereals, sugar beets, potatoes; dairy cattle; fish
Exports: $43 billion (f.o.b., 1998)
Exports - commodities: machinery and equipment, chemicals, metals; timber, paper, and pulp
Exports - partners: Germany 11%, UK 10%, Sweden 10%, US 7%, Russia 7%, France 4%, Japan (1997)
Imports: $30.7 billion (f.o.b., 1998)
Imports - commodities: foodstuffs, petroleum and petroleum products, chemicals, transport equipment, iron and steel, machinery, textile yarn and fabrics, fodder grains
Imports - partners: Germany 15%, Sweden 12%, UK 8%, Russia 8%, US 7%, Japan 5% (1997)
Debt - external: $30 billion (December 1993)
Economic aid - donor: ODA, $388 million (1995)
Currency: 1 markka (FMk) or Finmark = 100 pennia
Exchange rates: markkaa (FMk) per US$1 - 5.12 (January 1999), 5.3441 (1998), 5.1914 (1997), 4.5936 (1996), 4.3667 (1995), 5.2235 (1994);
note: on 1 January 1999, the European Union introduced a common currency that is now being used by financial institutions in some member countries at the rate of 0.8597 euros per US$ and a fixed rate of 5.93472 Markkaa per euro; the euro will replace the local currency in consenting countries for all transactions in 2002
Fiscal year: calendar year

Communications

Telephones: 2.5 million (1995 est.)
Telephone system: modern system with excellent service
domestic: cable, microwave radio relay, and an extensive cellular net care for domestic needs
international: 1 submarine cable; satellite earth stations - access to Intelsat transmission service via a Swedish satellite earth station, 1 Inmarsat (Atlantic and Indian Ocean regions); note - Finland shares the Inmarsat earth station with the other Nordic countries (Denmark, Iceland, Norway, and Sweden)

Radio broadcast stations: AM 6, FM 105, shortwave 0
Radios: 4.98 million (1991 est.)
Television broadcast stations: 120 (in addition, there are 431 low-power repeaters) (1997)
Televisions: 1.92 million (1995 est.)

Transportation

Railways:
total: 5,859 km
broad gauge: 5,859 km 1.524-m gauge (2,073 km electrified; 480 km double- or more-track) (1996)
Highways:
total: 77,796 km
paved: 49,789 km (including 444 km of expressways)
unpaved: 28,007 km (1997 est.)
Waterways: 6,675 km total (including Saimaa Canal); 3,700 km suitable for steamers
Pipelines: natural gas 580 km
Ports and harbors: Hamina, Helsinki, Kokkola, Kotka, Loviisa, Oulu, Pori, Rauma, Turku, Uusikaupunki, Varkaus
Merchant marine:
total: 101 ships (1,000 GRT or over) totaling 1,192,559 GRT/1,161,594 DWT
ships by type: bulk 9, cargo 23, chemical tanker 6, oil tanker 11, passenger 1, railcar carrier 1, roll-on/roll-off cargo 38, short-sea passenger 12 (1998 est.)
Airports: 157 (1998 est.)
Airports - with paved runways:
total: 68
over 3,047 m: 3
2,438 to 3,047 m: 26
1,524 to 2,437 m: 10
914 to 1,523 m: 20
under 914 m: 9 (1998 est.)
Airports - with unpaved runways:
total: 89
914 to 1,523 m: 6
under 914 m: 83 (1998 est.)

Military

Military branches: Army, Navy, Air Force, Frontier Guard (includes Sea Guard)
Military manpower - military age: 17 years of age
Military manpower - availability:
males age 15-49: 1,274,654 (1999 est.)
Military manpower - fit for military service:
males age 15-49: 1,050,944 (1999 est.)
Military manpower - reaching military age annually:
males: 34,336 (1999 est.)
Military expenditures - dollar figure: $1.8 billion (1999)
Military expenditures - percent of GDP: 2% (1999)

Transnational Issues

Disputes - international: none
Illicit drugs: minor transshipment point for Latin American cocaine for the West European market

France

Introduction

Background: Although ultimately a victor in World Wars I and II, France lost many men, much wealth, its extensive empire, and its rank as a dominant nation-state. France has struggled since 1958 - arguably with success - to construct a presidential democracy resistant to the severe instabilities inherent in the parliamentary democracy of early 20th century France. In recent years, its reconciliation and cooperation with Germany have proved central to the economic integration of Europe, including the advent of the euro in January 1999.

Geography

Location: Western Europe, bordering the Bay of Biscay and English Channel, between Belgium and Spain southeast of the UK; bordering the Mediterranean Sea, between Italy and Spain
Geographic coordinates: 46 00 N, 2 00 E
Map references: Europe
Area:
total: 547,030 sq km
land: 545,630 sq km
water: 1,400 sq km
note: includes only metropolitan France, but excludes the overseas administrative divisions
Area - comparative: slightly less than twice the size of Colorado
Land boundaries:
total: 2,892.4 km
border countries: Andorra 60 km, Belgium 620 km, Germany 451 km, Italy 488 km, Luxembourg 73 km, Monaco 4.4 km, Spain 623 km, Switzerland 573 km
Coastline: 3,427 km
Maritime claims:
contiguous zone: 24 nm
continental shelf: 200-m depth or to the depth of exploitation
exclusive economic zone: 200 nm (does not apply to the Mediterranean)
territorial sea: 12 nm

Climate: generally cool winters and mild summers, but mild winters and hot summers along the Mediterranean
Terrain: mostly flat plains or gently rolling hills in north and west; remainder is mountainous, especially Pyrenees in south, Alps in east
Elevation extremes:
lowest point: Rhone River delta -2 m
highest point: Mont Blanc 4,807 m
Natural resources: coal, iron ore, bauxite, fish, timber, zinc, potash
Land use:
arable land: 33%
permanent crops: 2%
permanent pastures: 20%
forests and woodland: 27%
other: 18% (1993 est.)
Irrigated land: 16,300 sq km (1995 est.)
Natural hazards: flooding; avalanches
Environment - current issues: some forest damage from acid rain; air pollution from industrial and vehicle emissions; water pollution from urban wastes, agricultural runoff
Environment - international agreements:
party to: Air Pollution, Air Pollution-Nitrogen Oxides, Air Pollution-Sulphur 85, Air Pollution-Sulphur 94, Air Pollution-Volatile Organic Compounds, Antarctic-Environmental Protocol, Antarctic Treaty, Biodiversity, Climate Change, Desertification, Endangered Species, Hazardous Wastes, Law of the Sea, Marine Dumping, Marine Life Conservation, Ozone Layer Protection, Ship Pollution, Tropical Timber 83, Tropical Timber 94, Wetlands, Whaling
signed, but not ratified: Air Pollution-Persistent Organic Pollutants, Climate Change-Kyoto Protocol
Geography - note: largest West European nation; occasional strong, cold, dry, north-to-northwesterly wind known as mistral

People

Population: 58,978,172 (July 1999 est.)
Age structure:
0-14 years: 19% (male 5,638,462; female 5,375,911)
15-64 years: 65% (male 19,302,121; female 19,235,235)
65 years and over: 16% (male 3,825,232; female 5,601,211) (1999 est.)
Population growth rate: 0.27% (1999 est.)
Birth rate: 11.38 births/1,000 population (1999 est.)
Death rate: 9.17 deaths/1,000 population (1999 est.)
Net migration rate: 0.53 migrant(s)/1,000 population (1999 est.)
Sex ratio:
at birth: 1.05 male(s)/female
under 15 years: 1.05 male(s)/female
15-64 years: 1 male(s)/female
65 years and over: 0.68 male(s)/female
total population: 0.95 male(s)/female (1999 est.)
Infant mortality rate: 5.62 deaths/1,000 live births (1999 est.)
Life expectancy at birth:
total population: 78.63 years

male: 74.76 years
female: 82.71 years (1999 est.)
Total fertility rate: 1.61 children born/woman (1999 est.)
Nationality:
noun: Frenchman(men), Frenchwoman(women)
adjective: French
Ethnic groups: Celtic and Latin with Teutonic, Slavic, North African, Indochinese, Basque minorities
Religions: Roman Catholic 90%, Protestant 2%, Jewish 1%, Muslim (North African workers) 1%, unaffiliated 6%
Languages: French 100%, rapidly declining regional dialects and languages (Provencal, Breton, Alsatian, Corsican, Catalan, Basque, Flemish)
Literacy:
definition: age 15 and over can read and write
total population: 99%
male: 99%
female: 99% (1980 est.)

Government

Country name:
conventional long form: French Republic
conventional short form: France
local long form: Republique Francaise
local short form: France
Data code: FR
Government type: republic
Capital: Paris
Administrative divisions: 22 regions (regions, singular - region); Alsace, Aquitaine, Auvergne, Basse-Normandie, Bourgogne, Bretagne, Centre, Champagne-Ardenne, Corse, Franche-Comte, Haute-Normandie, Ile-de-France, Languedoc-Roussillon, Limousin, Lorraine, Midi-Pyrenees, Nord-Pas-de-Calais, Pays de la Loire, Picardie, Poitou-Charentes, Provence-Alpes-Cote d'Azur, Rhone-Alpes
note: metropolitan France is divided into 22 regions (including the "territorial collectivity" of Corse or Corsica) and is subdivided into 96 departments; see separate entries for the overseas departments (French Guiana, Guadeloupe, Martinique, Reunion) and the overseas territorial collectivities (Mayotte, Saint Pierre and Miquelon)
Dependent areas: Bassas da India, Clipperton Island, Europa Island, French Polynesia, French Southern and Antarctic Lands, Glorioso Islands, Juan de Nova Island, New Caledonia, Tromelin Island, Wallis and Futuna
note: the US does not recognize claims to Antarctica
Independence: 486 (unified by Clovis)
National holiday: National Day, Taking of the Bastille, 14 July (1789)
Constitution: 28 September 1958, amended concerning election of president in 1962, amended to comply with provisions of EC Maastricht Treaty in 1992; amended to tighten immigration laws 1993
Legal system: civil law system with indigenous concepts; review of administrative but not legislative acts

France (continued)

Suffrage: 18 years of age; universal

Executive branch:

chief of state: President Jacques CHIRAC (since 17 May 1995)

head of government: Prime Minister Lionel JOSPIN (since 3 June 1997)

cabinet: Council of Ministers appointed by the president on the suggestion of the prime minister

elections: president elected by popular vote for a seven-year term; election last held 23 April and 7 May 1995 (next to be held by May 2002); prime minister nominated by the National Assembly majority and appointed by the president

election results: Jacques CHIRAC elected president; percent of vote, second ballot - Jacques CHIRAC 52.64%, Lionel JOSPIN 47.36%

Legislative branch: bicameral Parliament or Parlement consists of the Senate or Senat (321 seats - 296 for metropolitan France, 13 for overseas departments and territories, and 12 for French nationals abroad; members are indirectly elected by an electoral college to serve nine-year terms; elected by thirds every three years) and the National Assembly or Assemblee Nationale (577 seats; members are elected by popular vote under a single-member majoritarian system to serve five-year terms)

elections: Senate - last held 27 September 1998 (next to be held September 2001); National Assembly - last held 25 May-1 June 1997 (next to be held NA May 2002)

election results: Senate - percent of vote by party - NA; seats by party - RPR 99, Centrist Union 52, Republicans and independents 47, PS 78, PCF 16, other 29; National Assembly - percent of vote by party - NA; seats by party - PS 245, RPR 140, UDF 109, PCF 37, PRS 13, Ecologists 8, MDC 7, LDI-MPF 1, FN 1, various left 9, various right 7

Judicial branch: Supreme Court of Appeals or Cour de Cassation, judges are appointed by the president from nominations of the High Council of the Judiciary; Constitutional Council or Conseil Constitutionnel, three members appointed by the president, three members appointed by the president of the National Assembly, and three appointed by the president of the Senate; Council of State or Conseil d'Etat

Political parties and leaders: Rally for the Republic or RPR [Philippe SEGUIN]; Union for French Democracy or UDF (coalition of PR, FD, RAD, PPDF) [Francois BAYROU]; Parti Republican or PR [Alain MADELIN]; Democratic Force or FD [leader NA]; Socialist Party or PS [Francois HOLLANDE]; Communist Party or PCF [Robert HUE]; National Front or FN [Jean-Marie LE PEN]; The Greens [Jean-Luc BENNAHMIAS]; Generation Ecology or GE [Brice LALONDE]; Citizens Movement or MDC [Jean Pierre CHEVENEMENT]; National Center of Independents and Peasants or CNIP [Oliver d'ORMESSON]; Radical Socialist Party or PRS (previously the Left Radical Movement or MRG) [Jean-Michel BAYLET]; Movement for France or LDI-MPF [Philippe DEVILLIERS]; Mouvement des Reformateurs [Jean-Pierre SOISSON]; Mouvement Ecologiste Independant [Jenevieve ANDUEZA]; Parti Populaire Pour la Democratie Francaise or PPDF [Herve de CHARETTE]; Parti Radical [Thierry CORNILLET]; Adherents Directs [Pierre-Andre WILTZER]; Centrist Union [leader NA]; Republican Party [leader NA]; La Droite [Charles MILLON]; National Front-National Movement [Bruno MEGRET]

Political pressure groups and leaders: Communist-controlled labor union (Confederation Generale du Travail) or CGT, nearly 2.4 million members (claimed); Socialist-leaning labor union (Confederation Francaise Democratique du Travail) or CFDT, about 800,000 members (est.); independent labor union or Force Ouvriere, 1 million members (est.); independent white-collar union or Confederation Generale des Cadres, 340,000 members (claimed); National Council of French Employers (Conseil National du Patronat Francais) or CNPF or Patronat

International organization participation: ACCT, AfDB, AsDB, Australia Group, BDEAC, BIS, CCC, CDB (non-regional), CE, CERN, EAPC, EBRD, ECA (associate), ECE, ECLAC, EIB, EMU, ESA, ESCAP, EU, FAO, FZ, G-5, G-7, G-10, IADB, IAEA, IBRD, ICAO, ICC, ICFTU, ICRM, IDA, IEA, IFAD, IFC, IFRCS, IHO, ILO, IMF, IMO, Inmarsat, InOC, Intelsat, Interpol, IOC, IOM, ISO, ITU, MINURCA, MINURSO, MIPONUH, MONUA, MTCR, NATO, NEA, NSG, OAS (observer), OECD, OPCW, OSCE, PCA, SPC, UN, UN Security Council, UNCTAD, UNESCO, UNHCR, UNIDO, UNIFIL, UNIKOM, UNITAR, UNMIBH, UNOMIG, UNRWA, UNTSO, UNU, UPU, WCL, WEU, WFTU, WHO, WIPO, WMO, WToO, WTrO, ZC

Diplomatic representation in the US:

chief of mission: Ambassador Francois V. BUJON DE L'ESTANG

chancery: 4101 Reservoir Road NW, Washington, DC 20007

telephone: [1] (202) 944-6000

FAX: [1] (202) 944-6166

consulate(s) general: Atlanta, Boston, Chicago, Houston, Los Angeles, Miami, New Orleans, New York, and San Francisco

Diplomatic representation from the US:

chief of mission: Ambassador Felix G. ROHATYN

embassy: 2 Avenue Gabriel, 75382 Paris Cedex 08

mailing address: PSC 116, APO AE 09777

telephone: [33] (1) 43-12-22-22

FAX: [33] (1) 42 66 97 83

consulate(s) general: Marseille, Strasbourg

Flag description: three equal vertical bands of blue (hoist side), white, and red; known as the French Tricouleur (Tricolor); the design and colors are similar to a number of other flags, including those of Belgium, Chad, Ireland, Cote d'Ivoire, and Luxembourg; the official flag for all French dependent areas

---

Economy

Economy - overview: One of the four West European trillion-dollar economies, France matches a growing services sector with a diversified industrial base and substantial agricultural resources. Industry generates one-quarter of GDP and more than 80% of export earnings. The government retains considerable influence over key segments of each sector, with majority ownership of railway, electricity, aircraft, and telecommunication firms. It has been gradually relaxing its control over these sectors since the early 1990s. The government is slowly selling off its holdings in France Telecom, in Air France, and in the insurance, banking, and defense industries. Meanwhile, large tracts of fertile land, the application of modern technology, and subsidies have combined to make France the leading agricultural producer in Western Europe. A major exporter of wheat and dairy products, France is practically self-sufficient in agriculture. The economy expanded by 3% in 1998, following a 2.3% gain in 1997. Persistently high unemployment still poses a major problem for the government. France has shied away from cutting exceptionally generous social welfare benefits or the enormous state bureaucracy, preferring to pare defense spending and raise taxes to keep the deficit down. The JOSPIN administration has pledged both to lower unemployment and trim spending, pinning its hopes for new jobs on economic growth and on legislation to gradually reduce the workweek from 39 to 35 hours by 2002. France joined 10 other EU members to launch the euro on 1 January 1999.

GDP: purchasing power parity - $1.32 trillion (1998 est.)

GDP - real growth rate: 3% (1998 est.)

GDP - per capita: purchasing power parity - $22,600 (1998 est.)

GDP - composition by sector:

agriculture: 2.4%

industry: 28.4%

services: 69.2% (1997)

Population below poverty line: NA%

Household income or consumption by percentage share:

lowest 10%: 2.5%

highest 10%: 24.9% (1989)

Inflation rate (consumer prices): 0.7% (1998)

Labor force: 25.4 million

Labor force - by occupation: services 69%, industry 26%, agriculture 5% (1995)

Unemployment rate: 11.5% (1998)

Budget:

revenues: $222 billion

expenditures: $265 billion, including capital expenditures of $NA (1998 est.)

Industries: steel, machinery, chemicals, automobiles, metallurgy, aircraft, electronics, mining, textiles, food processing, tourism

Industrial production growth rate: 3.9% (1998)

Electricity - production: 480.783 billion kWh (1996)

Electricity - production by source:

fossil fuel: 8.72%

hydro: 12.92%

nuclear: 78.25%

other: 0.11% (1996)

France *(continued)*

Electricity - consumption: 411.743 billion kWh (1996)
Electricity - exports: 72.64 billion kWh (1996)
Electricity - imports: 3.6 billion kWh (1996)
Agriculture - products: wheat, cereals, sugar beets, potatoes, wine grapes; beef, dairy products; fish
Exports: $289 billion (f.o.b., 1998)
Exports - commodities: machinery and transportation equipment, chemicals, foodstuffs, agricultural products, iron and steel products, textiles and clothing
Exports - partners: Germany 16%, UK 10%, Italy 9%, Spain 8%, Belgium-Luxembourg 8%, US 6.5%, Netherlands 4.5%, Japan 2%, Russia 0.9% (1997)
Imports: $255 billion (f.o.b., 1998)
Imports - commodities: crude oil, machinery and equipment, agricultural products, chemicals, iron and steel products
Imports - partners: Germany 17%, Italy 10%, US 9%, Belgium-Luxembourg 8%, UK 8%, Spain 7%, Netherlands 5%, Japan 3%, China 2.5% (1997)
Debt - external: $117.6 billion (1996 est.)
Economic aid - donor: ODA, $8.4 billion (1995)
Currency: 1 French franc (F) = 100 centimes
Exchange rates: French francs (F) per US$1 - 5.65 (January 1999), 5.8995 (1998), 5.8367 (1997), 5.1155 (1996), 4.9915 (1995), 5.5520 (1994)
note: on 1 January 1999, the European Union introduced a common currency that is now being used by financial institutions in some member countries at the rate of 0.8597 euros per US$ and a fixed rate of 6.55957 French francs per euro; the euro will replace the local currency in consenting countries for all transactions in 2002
Fiscal year: calendar year

Telephones: 35 million (1987 est.)
Telephone system: highly developed
domestic: extensive cable and microwave radio relay; extensive introduction of fiber-optic cable; domestic satellite system
international: satellite earth stations - 2 Intelsat (with total of 5 antennas - 2 for Indian Ocean and 3 for Atlantic Ocean), NA Eutelsat, 1 Inmarsat (Atlantic Ocean region); HF radiotelephone communications with more than 20 countries
Radio broadcast stations: AM 41, FM 800 (mostly repeaters), shortwave 0
Radios: 49 million (1993 est.)
Television broadcast stations: 310 (in addition, there are about 1,400 repeaters) (1997)
Televisions: 29.3 million (1993 est.)

Transportation

Railways:
total: 32,027 km (31,940 km are operated by French National Railways (SNCF); 13,803 km of SNCF routes are electrified and 12,132 km are double- or multiple-tracked)
standard gauge: 31,928 km 1.435-m gauge

narrow gauge: 99 km 1.000-m gauge
note: does not include 33 tourist railroads, totaling 469 km, many being of very narrow gauge (1996)
Highways:
total: 892,900 km
paved: 892,900 km (including 9,900 km of expressways)
unpaved: 0 km (1997 est.)
Waterways: 14,932 km; 6,969 km heavily traveled
Pipelines: crude oil 3,059 km; petroleum products 4,487 km; natural gas 24,746 km
Ports and harbors: Bordeaux, Boulogne, Cherbourg, Dijon, Dunkerque, La Pallice, Le Havre, Lyon, Marseille, Mullhouse, Nantes, Paris, Rouen, Saint Nazaire, Saint Malo, Strasbourg
Merchant marine:
total: 64 ships (1,000 GRT or over) totaling 1,826,364 GRT/2,962,338 DWT
ships by type: bulk 5, cargo 5, chemical tanker 6, combination bulk 1, container 6, liquefied gas tanker 4, multifunction large-load carrier 2, oil tanker 20, passenger 3, roll-on/roll-off cargo 5, short-sea passenger 6, specialized tanker 1
note: France also maintains a captive register for French-owned ships in Iles Kerguelen (French Southern and Antarctic Lands) (1998 est.)
Airports: 474 (1998 est.)
Airports - with paved runways:
total: 267
over 3,047 m: 13
2,438 to 3,047 m: 31
1,524 to 2,437 m: 94
914 to 1,523 m: 73
under 914 m: 56 (1998 est.)
Airports - with unpaved runways:
total: 207
1,524 to 2,437 m: 3
914 to 1,523 m: 75
under 914 m: 129 (1998 est.)
Heliports: 3 (1998 est.)

Military

Military branches: Army (includes Marines), Navy (includes Naval Air), Air Force (includes Air Defense, National Gendarmerie
Military manpower - military age: 18 years of age
Military manpower - availability:
males age 15-49: 14,666,286 (1999 est.)
Military manpower - fit for military service:
males age 15-49: 12,203,675 (1999 est.)
Military manpower - reaching military age annually:
males: 411,911 (1999 est.)
Military expenditures - dollar figure: $39.831 billion (1997)
Military expenditures - percent of GDP: 2.5% (1995)

Transnational Issues

Disputes - international: Madagascar claims Bassas da India, Europa Island, Glorioso Islands,

Juan de Nova Island, and Tromelin Island; Comoros claims Mayotte; Mauritius claims Tromelin Island; territorial dispute between Suriname and French Guiana; territorial claim in Antarctica (Adelie Land); Matthew and Hunter Islands east of New Caledonia claimed by France and Vanuatu
Illicit drugs: transshipment point for and consumer of South American cocaine and Southwest Asian heroin

French Guiana
(overseas department of France)

Geography

Location: Northern South America, bordering the North Atlantic Ocean, between Brazil and Suriname
Geographic coordinates: 4 00 N, 53 00 W
Map references: South America
Area:
total: 91,000 sq km
land: 89,150 sq km
water: 1,850 sq km
Area - comparative: slightly smaller than Indiana
Land boundaries:
total: 1,183 km
border countries: Brazil 673 km, Suriname 510 km
Coastline: 378 km
Maritime claims:
exclusive economic zone: 200 nm
territorial sea: 12 nm
Climate: tropical; hot, humid; little seasonal temperature variation
Terrain: low-lying coastal plains rising to hills and small mountains
Elevation extremes:
lowest point: Atlantic Ocean 0 m
highest point: Bellevue de l'Inini 851 m
Natural resources: bauxite, timber, gold (widely scattered), cinnabar, kaolin, fish
Land use:
arable land: 0%
permanent crops: 0%
permanent pastures: 0%
forests and woodland: 83%
other: 17% (1993 est.)
Irrigated land: 20 sq km (1993 est.)
Natural hazards: high frequency of heavy showers and severe thunderstorms; flooding
Environment - current issues: NA
Environment - international agreements:
party to: NA
signed, but not ratified: NA
Geography - note: mostly an unsettled wilderness

People

Population: 167,982 (July 1999 est.)
Age structure:
0-14 years: 31% (male 26,713; female 25,514)
15-64 years: 64% (male 57,935; female 48,959)
65 years and over: 5% (male 4,479; female 4,382)
(1999 est.)
Population growth rate: 3.19% (1999 est.)
Birth rate: 23.27 births/1,000 population (1999 est.)
Death rate: 4.52 deaths/1,000 population (1999 est.)
Net migration rate: 13.1 migrant(s)/1,000 population (1999 est.)
Sex ratio:
at birth: 1.05 male(s)/female
under 15 years: 1.05 male(s)/female
15-64 years: 1.18 male(s)/female
65 years and over: 1.02 male(s)/female
total population: 1.13 male(s)/female (1999 est.)
Infant mortality rate: 12.93 deaths/1,000 live births (1999 est.)
Life expectancy at birth:
total population: 76.61 years
male: 73.41 years
female: 79.97 years (1999 est.)
Total fertility rate: 3.31 children born/woman (1999 est.)
Nationality:
noun: French Guianese (singular and plural)
adjective: French Guianese
Ethnic groups: black or mulatto 66%, white 12%, East Indian, Chinese, Amerindian 12%, other 10%
Religions: Roman Catholic
Languages: French
Literacy:
definition: age 15 and over can read and write
total population: 83%
male: 84%
female: 82% (1982 est.)

Government

Country name:
conventional long form: Department of Guiana
conventional short form: French Guiana
local long form: none
local short form: Guyane
Data code: FG
Dependency status: overseas department of France
Government type: NA
Capital: Cayenne
Administrative divisions: none (overseas department of France)
Independence: none (overseas department of France)
National holiday: National Day, Taking of the Bastille, 14 July (1789)
Constitution: 28 September 1958 (French Constitution)
Legal system: French legal system
Suffrage: 18 years of age; universal
Executive branch:
chief of state: President Jacques CHIRAC of France

(since 17 May 1995), represented by Prefect Dominique VIAN (since NA January 1997)
head of government: President of the General Council Stephan PHINERA (since NA March 1994); President of the Regional Council Antoine KARAM (since NA March 1992)
cabinet: NA
elections: French president elected by popular vote for a seven-year term; prefect appointed by the French president on the advice of the French Ministry of Interior; presidents of the General and Regional Councils are appointed by the members of those councils
Legislative branch: unicameral General Council or Conseil General (19 seats; members are elected by popular vote to serve six-year terms) and a unicameral Regional Council or Conseil Regional (31 seats; members are elected by popular vote to serve six-year terms)
elections: General Council - last held 20-27 March 1994 (next to be held NA 2000); Regional Council - last held 15 March 1998 (next to be held NA 2004)
election results: General Council - percent of vote by party - NA; seats by party - PSG 8, FDG 4, RPR 1, other left 2, other right 2, other 2; Regional Council - percent of vote by party - PS 28.28%, various left parties 22.56%, RPR 15.91%, independents 8.6%, Walwari 6%; seats by party - PS 11, various left parties 9, RPR 6, independents 3, Walwari 2
note: one seat was elected to the French Senate on 27 September 1998 (next to be held NA September 2007); results - percent of vote by party - NA; seats by party - NA; 2 seats were elected to the French National Assembly on 25 May - 1 June 1997 (next to be held NA 2002); results - percent of vote by party - NA; seats by party - RPR 1, PSG 1
Judicial branch: Court of Appeals or Cour d'Appel (highest local court based in Martinique with jurisdiction over Martinique, Guadeloupe, and French Guiana)
Political parties and leaders: Guianese Socialist Party or PSG [Marie-Claude VERDAN]; Socialist Party or PS [Jean BART] (may be a subset of PSG); Nationalist Popular Party of Guyana (Parti Nationaliste Populaire Guiana) or PNPG [Jose DORCY]; Union of Social Democrats (Union des Socialistes Democates) or USD [Leon BERTRAND] (umbrella group of RPR and UDF); Rally for the Republic or RPR [Leon BERTRAND]; Union for French Democracy or UDF [R. CHOW-CHINE]; Guyana Democratic Forces or FDG [Georges OTHILY]; Walwari Committee [Christine TAUBIRA-DELANON]; Action Democrate Guiana or ADG [Andre LECANTE]; Democratic and European Rally of the Senate or RDSE [leader NA]
International organization participation: FZ, WCL, WFTU
Diplomatic representation in the US: none (overseas department of France)
Diplomatic representation from the US: none (overseas department of France)
Flag description: the flag of France is used

French Guiana (continued)

Economy

Economy - overview: The economy is tied closely to that of France through subsidies and imports. Besides the French space center at Kourou, fishing and forestry are the most important economic activities, with exports of fish and fish products (mostly shrimp) accounting for more than 60% of total revenue in 1992. The large reserves of tropical hardwoods, not fully exploited, support an expanding sawmill industry which provides sawn logs for export. Cultivation of crops is limited to the coastal area, where the population is largely concentrated; sugar cane is the major cash crop. French Guiana is heavily dependent on imports of food and energy. Unemployment is a serious problem, particularly among younger workers.

GDP: purchasing power parity - $1 billion (1998 est.)

GDP - real growth rate: NA%

GDP - per capita: purchasing power parity - $6,000 (1998 est.)

GDP - composition by sector:
agriculture: NA%
industry: NA%
services: NA%

Population below poverty line: NA%

Household income or consumption by percentage share:
lowest 10%: NA%
highest 10%: NA%

Inflation rate (consumer prices): 2.5% (1992)

Labor force: 58,800 (1997)

Labor force - by occupation: services, government, and commerce 60.6%, industry 21.2%, agriculture 18.2% (1980)

Unemployment rate: 25.7% (1997 est.)

Budget:
revenues: $191 million
expenditures: $332 million, including capital expenditures of $88 million (1996)

Industries: construction, shrimp processing, forestry products, rum, gold mining

Industrial production growth rate: NA%

Electricity - production: 425 million kWh (1996)

Electricity - production by source:
fossil fuel: 100%
hydro: 0%
nuclear: 0%
other: 0% (1996)

Electricity - consumption: 425 million kWh (1996)

Electricity - exports: 0 kWh (1996)

Electricity - imports: 0 kWh (1996)

Agriculture - products: sugar, rice, corn, manioc (tapioca), cocoa, vegetables, bananas; cattle, pigs, poultry

Exports: $148 million (f.o.b., 1997)

Exports - commodities: shrimp, timber, gold, rum, rosewood essence, clothing

Exports - partners: France 60%, EU 7% (1994)

Imports: $600 million (c.i.f., 1997)

Imports - commodities: food (grains, processed meat), machinery and transport equipment, fuels and chemicals

Imports - partners: France 62%, Germany 4%, Belgium-Luxembourg 4%, US 2% (1994)

Debt - external: $1.2 billion (1988)

Economic aid - recipient: $NA

Currency: 1 French franc (F) = 100 centimes

Exchange rates: French francs (F) per US$1 - 5.65 (January 1999), 5.8995 (1998), 5.8367 (1997), 5.1155 (1996), 4.9915 (1995), 5.5520 (1994)

Fiscal year: calendar year

Communications

Telephones: 31,000 (1990 est.)

Telephone system:
domestic: fair open wire and microwave radio relay system
international: satellite earth station - 1 Intelsat (Atlantic Ocean)

Radio broadcast stations: AM 5, FM 7, shortwave 0

Radios: 79,000 (1992 est.)

Television broadcast stations: 3 (in addition, there are eight low-power repeaters) (1997)

Televisions: 22,000 (1992 est.)

Transportation

Railways: 0 km (1995)

Highways:
total: 1,817 km (national 432 km, departmental 385 km, community 1,000 km)
paved: 727 km
unpaved: 1,090 km (1995 est.)

Waterways: 460 km, navigable by small oceangoing vessels and river and coastal steamers; 3,300 km navigable by native craft

Ports and harbors: Cayenne, Degrad des Cannes, Saint-Laurent du Maroni

Merchant marine: none

Airports: 11 (1998 est.)

Airports - with paved runways:
total: 4
over 3,047 m: 1
914 to 1,523 m: 2
under 914 m: 1 (1998 est.)

Airports - with unpaved runways:
total: 7
914 to 1,523 m: 2
under 914 m: 5 (1998 est.)

Military

Military branches: French Forces, Gendarmerie

Military manpower - availability:
males age 15-49: 47,354 (1999 est.)

Military manpower - fit for military service:
males age 15-49: 30,656 (1999 est.)

Military expenditures - dollar figure: $NA

Military expenditures - percent of GDP: NA%

Military - note: defense is the responsibility of France

Transnational Issues

Disputes - international: Suriname claims area between Riviere Litani and Riviere Marouini (both headwaters of the Lawa)

Illicit drugs: small amount of marijuana grown for local consumption; minor transshipment point to Europe

French Polynesia
(overseas territory of France)

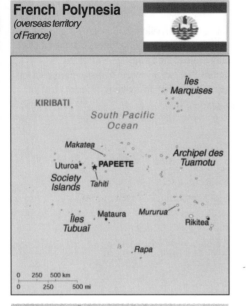

Geography

Location: Oceania, archipelago in the South Pacific Ocean, about one-half of the way from South America to Australia

Geographic coordinates: 15 00 S, 140 00 W

Map references: Oceania

Area:
total: 4,167 sq km (118 islands and atolls)
land: 3,660 sq km
water: 507 sq km

Area - comparative: slightly less than one-third the size of Connecticut

Land boundaries: 0 km

Coastline: 2,525 km

Maritime claims:
exclusive economic zone: 200 nm
territorial sea: 12 nm

Climate: tropical, but moderate

Terrain: mixture of rugged high islands and low islands with reefs

Elevation extremes:
lowest point: Pacific Ocean 0 m
highest point: Mont Orohena 2,241 m

Natural resources: timber, fish, cobalt

Land use:
arable land: 1%
permanent crops: 6%
permanent pastures: 5%
forests and woodland: 31%
other: 57% (1993 est.)

Irrigated land: NA sq km

Natural hazards: occasional cyclonic storms in January

Environment - current issues: NA

Environment - international agreements:
party to: NA
signed, but not ratified: NA

Geography - note: includes five archipelagoes; Makatea in French Polynesia is one of the three great phosphate rock islands in the Pacific Ocean - the others are Banaba (Ocean Island) in Kiribati and Nauru

People

Population: 242,073 (July 1999 est.)

Age structure:
0-14 years: 33% (male 40,422; female 38,913)
15-64 years: 63% (male 78,637; female 72,832)
65 years and over: 4% (male 5,642; female 5,627) (1999 est.)

Population growth rate: 1.72% (1999 est.)

Birth rate: 22.08 births/1,000 population (1999 est.)

Death rate: 5.06 deaths/1,000 population (1999 est.)

Net migration rate: 0.19 migrant(s)/1,000 population (1999 est.)

Sex ratio:
at birth: 1.05 male(s)/female
under 15 years: 1.04 male(s)/female
15-64 years: 1.08 male(s)/female
65 years and over: 1 male(s)/female
total population: 1.06 male(s)/female (1999 est.)

Infant mortality rate: 13.59 deaths/1,000 live births (1999 est.)

Life expectancy at birth:
total population: 72.33 years
male: 69.93 years
female: 74.85 years (1999 est.)

Total fertility rate: 2.64 children born/woman (1999 est.)

Nationality:
noun: French Polynesian(s)
adjective: French Polynesian

Ethnic groups: Polynesian 78%, Chinese 12%, local French 6%, metropolitan French 4%

Religions: Protestant 54%, Roman Catholic 30%, other 16%

Languages: French (official), Tahitian (official)

Literacy:
definition: age 14 and over can read and write
total population: 98%
male: 98%
female: 98% (1977 est.)

Government

Country name:
conventional long form: Territory of French Polynesia
conventional short form: French Polynesia
local long form: Territoire de la Polynesie Francaise
local short form: Polynesie Francaise

Data code: FP

Dependency status: overseas territory of France since 1946

Government type: NA

Capital: Papeete

Administrative divisions: none (overseas territory of France); there are no first-order administrative divisions as defined by the US Government, but there are 5 archipelagic divisions named Archipel des Marquises, Archipel des Tuamotu, Archipel des Tubuai, Iles du Vent, and Iles Sous-le-Vent
note: Clipperton Island is administered by France from French Polynesia

Independence: none (overseas territory of France)

National holiday: National Day, Taking of the Bastille, 14 July (1789)

Constitution: 28 September 1958 (French Constitution)

Legal system: based on French system

Suffrage: 18 years of age; universal

Executive branch:
chief of state: President Jacques CHIRAC of France (since 17 May 1995), represented by High Commissioner of the Republic Paul RONCIERE (since NA 1994)
head of government: President of the Territorial Government of French Polynesia Gaston FLOSSE (since 4 April 1991); President of the Territorial Assembly Justin ARAPARI (since 13 May 1996)
cabinet: Council of Ministers; president submits a list of members of the Territorial Assembly for approval by them to serve as ministers
elections: French president elected by popular vote for a seven-year term; high commissioner appointed by the French president on the advice of the French Ministry of Interior; president of the Territorial Government and the president of the Territorial Assembly are elected by the members of the assembly

Legislative branch: unicameral Territorial Assembly or Assemblee Territoriale (41 seats; members are elected by popular vote to serve five-year terms)
elections: last held 12 May 1996 (next to be held NA 2001)
election results: percent of vote by party - NA; seats by party - People's Rally for the Republic (Gaullist) 22, Polynesian Liberation Front 10, New Fatherland Party 5, other 4
note: one seat was elected to the French Senate on 24 September 1989 (next to be held NA September 1998); results - percent of vote by party - NA; seats by party - UC 1; two seats were elected to the French National Assembly on 25 May - 1 June 1997 (next to be held NA 2002); results - percent of vote by party - NA; seats by party - People's Rally for the Republic (Gaullist) 2

Judicial branch: Court of Appeal or Cour d'Appel; Court of the First Instance or Tribunal de Premiere Instance; Court of Administrative Law or Tribunal Administratif

Political parties and leaders: People's Rally for the Republic (Tahoeraa Huiraatira) [Gaston FLOSSE]; Polynesian Union Party (includes Te Tiarama and Pupu Here Ai'a Party) [Jean JUVENTIN]; Independent Front for the Liberation of Polynesia (Tavini Huiraatira) [Oscar TEMARU]; New Fatherland Party (Ai'a Api) [Emile VERNAUDON]; Independent Party (Ia Mana Te Nunaa) [Jacques DROLLET]; Te Aratia Ote Nunaa (Tinomana Ebb); Haere i Mua [Alexandre LEONTIEFF]; Te e'a No Maohi Nui [Jean-Marius RAAPOTO]; Pupu Taina [Michel LAW]; Entente Polynesian [Arthur CHUNG]; Centrist Union or UC [leader NA]

International organization participation: ESCAP (associate), FZ, ICFTU, SPC, WMO

Diplomatic representation in the US: none

French Polynesia (continued)

(overseas territory of France)
Diplomatic representation from the US: none
(overseas territory of France)
Flag description: two narrow red horizontal bands encase a wide white band; centered on the white band is a disk with blue and white wave pattern on the lower half and gold and white ray pattern on the upper half; a stylized red, blue and white ship rides on the wave pattern; the French flag is used for official occasions

Economy

Economy - overview: Since 1962, when France stationed military personnel in the region, French Polynesia has changed from a subsistence economy to one in which a high proportion of the work force is either employed by the military or supports the tourist industry. Tourism accounts for about 20% of GDP and is a primary source of hard currency earnings. The small manufacturing sector primarily processes agricultural products. The territory benefited from a five-year (1994-98) development agreement with France aimed principally at creating new jobs.
GDP: purchasing power parity - $2.6 billion (1997 est.)
GDP - real growth rate: NA%
GDP - per capita: purchasing power parity - $10,800 (1997 est.)
GDP - composition by sector:
agriculture: 4%
industry: 18%
services: 78% (1997)
Population below poverty line: NA%
Household income or consumption by percentage share:
lowest 10%: NA%
highest 10%: NA%
Inflation rate (consumer prices): 1.5% (1994)
Labor force: 118,744 (of which 70,044 are employed) (1988)
Labor force - by occupation: agriculture 13%, industry 19%, services 68% (1997)
Unemployment rate: 15% (1992 est.)
Budget:
revenues: $652 million
expenditures: $613 million, including capital expenditures of $155 million (1996)
Industries: tourism, pearls, agricultural processing, handicrafts
Industrial production growth rate: NA%
Electricity - production: 350 million kWh (1996)
Electricity - production by source:
fossil fuel: 57.14%
hydro: 42.86%
nuclear: 0%
other: 0% (1996)
Electricity - consumption: 350 million kWh (1996)
Electricity - exports: 0 kWh (1996)
Electricity - imports: 0 kWh (1996)
Agriculture - products: coconuts, vanilla, vegetables, fruits; poultry, beef, dairy products
Exports: $212 million (f.o.b., 1996)
Exports - commodities: cultured pearls 53.8%,
coconut products, mother-of-pearl, vanilla, shark meat (1992)
Exports - partners: France 33%, US 8.5% (1994)
Imports: $860 million (c.i.f., 1996)
Imports - commodities: fuels, foodstuffs, equipment
Imports - partners: France 44.7%, US 13.9% (1994)
Debt - external: $NA
Economic aid - recipient: $450.4 million (1995)
Currency: 1 Comptoirs Francais du Pacifique franc (CFPF) = 100 centimes
Exchange rates: Comptoirs Francais du Pacifique francs (CFPF) per US$1 - 102.72 (January 1999), 107.25 (1998), 106.11 (1997), 93.00 (1996), 90.75 (1995), 100.94 (1994); note - linked at the rate of 18.18 to the French franc
Fiscal year: calendar year

Communications

Telephones: 33,200 (1983 est.)
Telephone system:
domestic: NA
international: satellite earth station - 1 Intelsat (Pacific Ocean)
Radio broadcast stations: AM 5, FM 2, shortwave 0
Radios: 116,000 (1992 est.)
Television broadcast stations: 7 (in addition, there are 17 low-power repeaters) (1997)
Televisions: 35,000 (1992 est.)

Transportation

Railways: 0 km
Highways:
total: 792 km
paved: 792 km (1995 est.)
Ports and harbors: Mataura, Papeete, Rikitea, Uturoa
Merchant marine:
total: 4 ships (1,000 GRT or over) totaling 5,240 GRT/ 7,765 DWT
ships by type: cargo 1, passenger-cargo 2, refrigerated cargo 1 (1998 est.)
Airports: 45 (1998 est.)
Airports - with paved runways:
total: 29
over 3,047 m: 2
1,524 to 2,437 m: 5
914 to 1,523 m: 17
under 914 m: 5 (1998 est.)
Airports - with unpaved runways:
total: 16
914 to 1,523 m: 5
under 914 m: 11 (1998 est.)

Military

Military branches: French Forces (includes Army, Navy, Air Force), Gendarmerie
Military - note: defense is the responsibility of France

Transnational Issues

Disputes - international: none

French Southern and Antarctic Lands
(overseas territory of France)

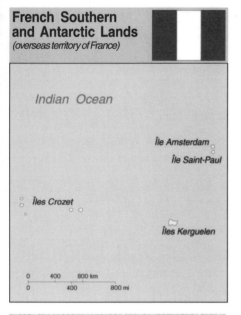

Geography

Location: south of Africa, islands in the southern Indian Ocean, about equidistant between Africa, Antarctica, and Australia; note - French Southern and Antarctic Lands includes Ile Amsterdam, Ile Saint-Paul, Iles Crozet, and Iles Kerguelen in the southern Indian Ocean, along with the French-claimed sector of Antarctica, "Adelie Land"; the US does not recognize the French claim to "Adelie Land"

Geographic coordinates: 43 00 S, 67 00 E

Map references: Antarctic Region

Area:
total: 7,781 sq km
land: 7,781 sq km
water: 0 sq km
note: includes Ile Amsterdam, Ile Saint-Paul, Iles Crozet and Iles Kerguelen; excludes "Adelie Land" claim of about 500,000 sq km in Antarctica that is not recognized by the US

Area - comparative: slightly less than 1.3 times the size of Delaware

Land boundaries: 0 km

Coastline: 1,232 km

Maritime claims:
exclusive economic zone: 200 nm from Iles Kerguelen only
territorial sea: 12 nm

Climate: antarctic

Terrain: volcanic

Elevation extremes:
lowest point: Indian Ocean 0 m
highest point: Mont Ross on Ile Kerguelen 1,850 m

Natural resources: fish, crayfish

Land use:
arable land: 0%
permanent crops: 0%
permanent pastures: 0%
forests and woodland: 0%
other: 100%

Irrigated land: 0 sq km (1993)

Natural hazards: Ile Amsterdam and Ile Saint-Paul are extinct volcanoes

Environment - current issues: NA

Environment - international agreements:
party to: NA
signed, but not ratified: NA

Geography - note: remote location in the southern Indian Ocean

People

Population: no indigenous inhabitants
note: in 1997 there were about 100 researchers whose numbers vary from winter (July) to summer (January)

Government

Country name:
conventional long form: Territory of the French Southern and Antarctic Lands
conventional short form: French Southern and Antarctic Lands
local long form: Territoire des Terres Australes et Antarctiques Francaises
local short form: Terres Australes et Antarctiques Francaises

Data code: FS

Dependency status: overseas territory of France since 1955; administered from Paris by a high commissioner of the Republic

Administrative divisions: none (overseas territory of France); there are no first-order administrative divisions as defined by the US Government, but there are 3 districts named Ile Crozet, Iles Kerguelen, and Iles Saint-Paul et Amsterdam; excludes "Adelie Land" claim in Antarctica that is not recognized by the US

Legal system: NA

Diplomatic representation in the US: none (overseas territory of France)

Diplomatic representation from the US: none (overseas territory of France)

Flag description: the flag of France is used

Economy

Economy - overview: Economic activity is limited to servicing meteorological and geophysical research stations and French and other fishing fleets. The fish catches landed on Iles Kerguelen by foreign ships are exported to France and Reunion.

Budget:
revenues: $19 million
expenditures: $NA, including capital expenditures of $NA (1997)

Transportation

Ports and harbors: none; offshore anchorage only

Merchant marine:
total: 66 ships (1,000 GRT or over) totaling 2,201,120 GRT/3,832,935 DWT
ships by type: bulk 3, cargo 7, chemical tanker 10, container 9, liquefied gas tanker 6, oil tanker 19, refrigerated cargo 2, roll-on/roll-off cargo 10 (1998 est.)

Airports: none

Military

Military - note: defense is the responsibility of France

Transnational Issues

Disputes - international: "Adelie Land" claim in Antarctica is not recognized by the US

Gabon

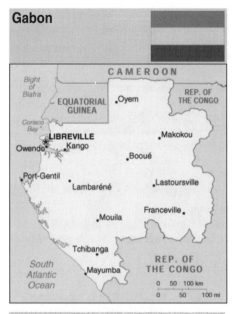

Geography

Location: Western Africa, bordering the Atlantic Ocean at the Equator, between Republic of the Congo and Equatorial Guinea
Geographic coordinates: 1 00 S, 11 45 E
Map references: Africa
Area:
total: 267,670 sq km
land: 257,670 sq km
water: 10,000 sq km
Area - comparative: slightly smaller than Colorado
Land boundaries:
total: 2,551 km
border countries: Cameroon 298 km, Republic of the Congo 1,903 km, Equatorial Guinea 350 km
Coastline: 885 km
Maritime claims:
contiguous zone: 24 nm
exclusive economic zone: 200 nm
territorial sea: 12 nm
Climate: tropical; always hot, humid
Terrain: narrow coastal plain; hilly interior; savanna in east and south
Elevation extremes:
lowest point: Atlantic Ocean 0 m
highest point: Mont Iboundji 1,575 m
Natural resources: petroleum, manganese, uranium, gold, timber, iron ore
Land use:
arable land: 1%
permanent crops: 1%
permanent pastures: 18%
forests and woodland: 77%
other: 3% (1993 est.)
Irrigated land: 40 sq km (1993 est.)
Natural hazards: NA
Environment - current issues: deforestation; poaching
Environment - international agreements:
party to: Biodiversity, Climate Change, Desertification, Endangered Species, Law of the Sea, Marine Dumping, Nuclear Test Ban, Ozone Layer Protection, Ship Pollution, Tropical Timber 83, Tropical Timber 94, Wetlands
signed, but not ratified: none of the selected agreements

People

Population: 1,225,853 (July 1999 est.)
Age structure:
0-14 years: 33% (male 205,076; female 205,198)
15-64 years: 61% (male 376,181; female 370,479)
65 years and over: 6% (male 34,078; female 34,841) (1999 est.)
Population growth rate: 1.48% (1999 est.)
Birth rate: 27.89 births/1,000 population (1999 est.)
Death rate: 13.07 deaths/1,000 population (1999 est.)
Net migration rate: 0 migrant(s)/1,000 population (1999 est.)
Sex ratio:
at birth: 1.03 male(s)/female
under 15 years: 1 male(s)/female
15-64 years: 1.02 male(s)/female
65 years and over: 0.98 male(s)/female
total population: 1.01 male(s)/female (1999 est.)
Infant mortality rate: 83.1 deaths/1,000 live births (1999 est.)
Life expectancy at birth:
total population: 56.98 years
male: 53.98 years
female: 60.08 years (1999 est.)
Total fertility rate: 3.77 children born/woman (1999 est.)
Nationality:
noun: Gabonese (singular and plural)
adjective: Gabonese
Ethnic groups: Bantu tribes including four major tribal groupings (Fang, Eshira, Bapounou, Bateke), other Africans and Europeans 154,000, including 6,000 French and 11,000 persons of dual nationality
Religions: Christian 55%-75%, Muslim less than 1%, animist
Languages: French (official), Fang, Myene, Bateke, Bapounou/Eschira, Bandjabi
Literacy:
definition: age 15 and over can read and write
total population: 63.2%
male: 73.7%
female: 53.3% (1995 est.)

Government

Country name:
conventional long form: Gabonese Republic
conventional short form: Gabon
local long form: Republique Gabonaise
local short form: Gabon
Data code: GB
Government type: republic; multiparty presidential regime (opposition parties legalized 1990)
Capital: Libreville

Administrative divisions: 9 provinces; Estuaire, Haut-Ogooue, Moyen-Ogooue, Ngounie, Nyanga, Ogooue-Ivindo, Ogooue-Lolo, Ogooue-Maritime, Woleu-Ntem
Independence: 17 August 1960 (from France)
National holiday: Independence Day, 17 August (1960) (Gabon granted full independence from France)
Constitution: adopted 14 March 1991
Legal system: based on French civil law system and customary law; judicial review of legislative acts in Constitutional Chamber of the Supreme Court; compulsory ICJ jurisdiction not accepted
Suffrage: 21 years of age; universal
Executive branch:
chief of state: President El Hadj Omar BONGO (since 2 December 1967)
head of government: Prime Minister Jean-Francois NTOUTOUME-EMANE (since 23 January 1999)
cabinet: Council of Ministers appointed by the prime minister in consultation with the president
elections: president elected by popular vote for a seven-year term; election last held 6 December 1998 (next to be held NA 2005); prime minister appointed by the president
election results: President El Hadj Omar BONGO reelected; percent of vote - El Hadj Omar BONGO 66%, Pierre MAMBOUNDOU 17%, Fr. Paul M'BA-ABESSOLE 13%
Legislative branch: bicameral legislature consists of the Senate (91 seats) and the National Assembly or Assemblee Nationale (120 seats); members are elected by direct popular vote to serve five-year terms
elections: National Assembly - last held in December 1996 (next to be held NA December 2001); Senate - last held 12 January 1997 (next to be held in January 2002)
election results: National Assembly - percent of vote by party - NA; seats by party - PDG 100, Morena-Bucherons/RNB 8, PUP 3, CLR 3, FAR 1, UPG 1, USG 2, PGP 2; Senate - percent of vote by party - NA; seats by party - PDG 51, RNB 17, PGP 4, ADERE 3, RDP 1, others 15
Judicial branch: Supreme Court or Cour Supreme consisting of three chambers - Judicial, Administrative, and Accounts; Constitutional Court; Courts of Appeal; Court of State Security; County Courts
Political parties and leaders: African Forum for Reconstruction or FAR [Leon MBOYEBI, secretary general]; Circle of Liberal Reformers or CLR [General Jean Boniface ASSELE]; Gabonese Democratic Party or PDG, former sole party [Jacques ADIAHENOT, secretary general]; Gabonese Party for Progress or PGP [Pierre-Louis AGONDJO-OKAWE, president]; Gabonese People's Union or UPG [Pierre MAMBOUNDOU]; Gabonese Socialist Union or USG [Dr. Serge Mba BEKALE]; National Rally of Woodcutters or Bucherons-RNB [Fr. Paul M'BA-ABESSOLE]; People's Unity Party or PUP [Louis Gaston MAYILA]; Democratic and Republican Alliance or ADERE [Divungui-di-Ndinge DIDJOB];

Gabon *(continued)*

Social Democratic Party or PSD [Pierre Claver MAGANGA-MOUSSAVOU]; Rally for Democracy and Progress or RDP [leader NA]

International organization participation: ACCT, ACP, AfDB, BDEAC, CCC, CEEAC, ECA, FAO, FZ, G-24, G-77, IAEA, IBRD, ICAO, ICFTU, IDA, IDB, IFAD, IFC, IFRCS (associate), ILO, IMF, IMO, Inmarsat, Intelsat, Interpol, IOC, ITU, MINURCA, NAM, OAU, OIC, OPCW, UDEAC, UN, UN Security Council (temporary), UNCTAD, UNESCO, UNIDO, UPU, WCL, WHO, WIPO, WMO, WToO, WTrO

Diplomatic representation in the US:
chief of mission: Ambassador Paul BOUNDOUKOU-LATHA
chancery: Suite 200, 2034 20th Street NW, Washington, DC 20009
telephone: [1] (202) 797-1000
FAX: [1] (202) 332-0668
consulate(s): New York

Diplomatic representation from the US:
chief of mission: Ambassador James V. LEDESMA
embassy: Boulevard de la Mer, Libreville
mailing address: B. P. 4000, Libreville
telephone: [241] 76 20 03 through 76 20 04, 74 34 92
FAX: [241] 74 55 07

Flag description: three equal horizontal bands of green (top), yellow, and blue

Economy

Economy - overview: Gabon enjoys a per capita income four times that of most nations of sub-Saharan Africa. This has supported a sharp decline in extreme poverty; yet because of high income inequality a large proportion of the population remains poor. Gabon depended on timber and manganese until oil was discovered offshore in the early 1970s. The oil sector now accounts for 50% of GDP. Gabon continues to face fluctuating prices for its oil, timber, manganese, and uranium exports. Despite the abundance of natural wealth, the economy is hobbled by poor fiscal management. In 1992, the fiscal deficit widened to 2.4% of GDP, and Gabon failed to settle arrears on its bilateral debt, leading to a cancellation of rescheduling agreements with official and private creditors. Devaluation of its Francophone currency by 50% on 12 January 1994 sparked a one-time inflationary surge, to 35%; the rate dropped to 6% in 1996. The IMF provided a one-year standby arrangement in 1994-95 and a three-year Enhanced Financing Facility (EFF) at near commercial rates beginning in late 1995. Those agreements mandate progress in privatization and fiscal discipline. France provided additional financial support in January 1997 after Gabon had met IMF targets for mid-1996. In 1997, an IMF mission to Gabon criticized the government for overspending on off-budget items, overborrowing from the central bank, and slipping on its schedule for privatization and administrative reform. Growth in 1999 will depend mainly on how world oil prices move.
GDP: purchasing power parity - $7.7 billion (1998 est.)

GDP - real growth rate: 1.7% (1998 est.)
GDP - per capita: purchasing power parity - $6,400 (1998 est.)
GDP - composition by sector:
agriculture: 8%
industry: 67%
services: 25% (1997 est.)
Population below poverty line: NA%
Household income or consumption by percentage share:
lowest 10%: NA%
highest 10%: NA%
Inflation rate (consumer prices): 1% (1998 est.)
Labor force: NA
Labor force - by occupation: agriculture 65%, industry and commerce, services
Unemployment rate: 21% (1997 est.)
Budget:
revenues: $1.5 billion
expenditures: $1.3 billion, including capital expenditures of $302 million (1996 est.)
Industries: food and beverage; textile; lumbering and plywood; cement; petroleum extraction and refining; manganese, uranium, and gold mining; chemicals; ship repair
Industrial production growth rate: 2.3% (1995)
Electricity - production: 930 million kWh (1996)
Electricity - production by source:
fossil fuel: 22.04%
hydro: 77.96%
nuclear: 0%
other: 0% (1996)
Electricity - consumption: 930 million kWh (1996)
Electricity - exports: 0 kWh (1996)
Electricity - imports: 0 kWh (1996)
Agriculture - products: cocoa, coffee, sugar, palm oil, rubber; cattle; okoume (a tropical softwood); fish
Exports: $2.1 billion (f.o.b., 1998 est.)
Exports - commodities: crude oil 81%, timber 12%, manganese 5%, uranium (1996)
Exports - partners: US 67%, China 9%, France 8%, Japan 3% (1997)
Imports: $890 million (f.o.b., 1998 est.)
Imports - commodities: machinery and equipment, foodstuffs, chemicals, petroleum products, construction materials
Imports - partners: France 38%, US 8%, Cameroon 5%, Netherlands 4%, Cote d'Ivoire, Japan (1997)
Debt - external: $4.1 billion (1997)
Economic aid - recipient: $331 million (1995)
Currency: 1 Communaute Financiere Africaine franc (CFAF) = 100 centimes
Exchange rates: Communaute Financiere Africaine francs (CFAF) per US$1 - 577.61 (January 1999), 589.95 (1998), 583.67 (1997), 511.55 (1996), 499.15 (1995), 555.20 (1994)
Fiscal year: calendar year

Communications

Telephones: 22,000 (1991 est.)
Telephone system:
domestic: adequate system of cable, microwave radio

relay, tropospheric scatter, radiotelephone communication stations, and a domestic satellite system with 12 earth stations
international: satellite earth stations - 3 Intelsat (Atlantic Ocean)
Radio broadcast stations: AM 6, FM 6, shortwave 0
Radios: 250,000 (1993 est.)
Television broadcast stations: 4 (in addition, there are five low-power repeaters) (1997)
Televisions: 40,000 (1993 est.)

Transportation

Railways:
total: 649 km Gabon State Railways (OCTRA)
standard gauge: 649 km 1.435-m gauge; single track (1994)
Highways:
total: 7,670 km
paved: 629 km (including 30 km of expressways)
unpaved: 7,041 km (1996 est.)
Waterways: 1,600 km perennially navigable
Pipelines: crude oil 270 km; petroleum products 14 km
Ports and harbors: Cap Lopez, Kango, Lambarene, Libreville, Mayumba, Owendo, Port-Gentil
Merchant marine:
total: 2 ships (1,000 GRT or over) totaling 13,613 GRT/22,599 DWT (1998 est.)
ships by type: bulk 1, cargo 1 (1998 est.)
Airports: 62 (1998 est.)
Airports - with paved runways:
total: 10
over 3,047 m: 1
2,438 to 3,047 m: 1
1,524 to 2,437 m: 7
914 to 1,523 m: 1 (1998 est.)
Airports - with unpaved runways:
total: 52
1,524 to 2,437 m: 10
914 to 1,523 m: 16
under 914 m: 26 (1998 est.)

Military

Military branches: Army, Navy, Air Force, Republican Guard (charged with protecting the president and other senior officials), National Gendarmerie, National Police
Military manpower - military age: 20 years of age
Military manpower - availability:
males age 15-49: 280,719 (1999 est.)
Military manpower - fit for military service:
males age 15-49: 144,133 (1999 est.)
Military manpower - reaching military age annually:
males: 11,392 (1999 est.)
Military expenditures - dollar figure: $91 million (1996)
Military expenditures - percent of GDP: 1.6% (1996)

Gabon (continued)

Transnational Issues

Disputes - international: maritime boundary dispute with Equatorial Guinea because of disputed sovereignty over islands in Corisco Bay

Gambia, The

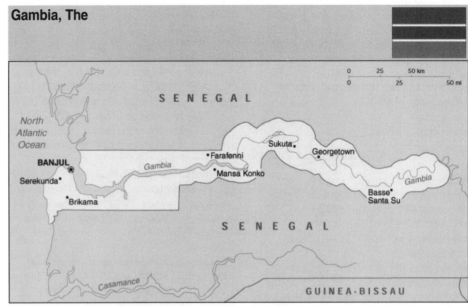

Geography

Location: Western Africa, bordering the North Atlantic Ocean and Senegal
Geographic coordinates: 13 28 N, 16 34 W
Map references: Africa
Area:
total: 11,300 sq km
land: 10,000 sq km
water: 1,300 sq km
Area - comparative: slightly less than twice the size of Delaware
Land boundaries:
total: 740 km
border countries: Senegal 740 km
Coastline: 80 km
Maritime claims:
contiguous zone: 18 nm
continental shelf: not specified
exclusive fishing zone: 200 nm
territorial sea: 12 nm
Climate: tropical; hot, rainy season (June to November); cooler, dry season (November to May)
Terrain: flood plain of the Gambia River flanked by some low hills
Elevation extremes:
lowest point: Atlantic Ocean 0 m
highest point: unnamed location 53 m
Natural resources: fish
Land use:
arable land: 18%
permanent crops: 0%
permanent pastures: 9%
forests and woodland: 28%
other: 45% (1993 est.)
Irrigated land: 150 sq km (1993 est.)
Natural hazards: rainfall has dropped by 30% in the last 30 years
Environment - current issues: deforestation; desertification; water-borne diseases prevalent
Environment - international agreements:
party to: Biodiversity, Climate Change, Desertification, Endangered Species, Hazardous Wastes, Law of the Sea, Nuclear Test Ban, Ozone Layer Protection, Ship Pollution, Wetlands
signed, but not ratified: none of the selected agreements
Geography - note: almost an enclave of Senegal; smallest country on the continent of Africa

People

Population: 1,336,320 (July 1999 est.)
Age structure:
0-14 years: 46% (male 305,839; female 304,905)
15-64 years: 52% (male 341,947; female 348,163)
65 years and over: 2% (male 18,706; female 16,760) (1999 est.)
Population growth rate: 3.35% (1999 est.)
Birth rate: 42.76 births/1,000 population (1999 est.)
Death rate: 12.57 deaths/1,000 population (1999 est.)
Net migration rate: 3.34 migrant(s)/1,000 population (1999 est.)
Sex ratio:
at birth: 1.03 male(s)/female
under 15 years: 1 male(s)/female
15-64 years: 0.98 male(s)/female
65 years and over: 1.12 male(s)/female
total population: 1 male(s)/female (1999 est.)
Infant mortality rate: 75.33 deaths/1,000 live births (1999 est.)
Life expectancy at birth:
total population: 54.39 years
male: 52.02 years
female: 56.83 years (1999 est.)
Total fertility rate: 5.83 children born/woman (1999 est.)
Nationality:
noun: Gambian(s)
adjective: Gambian
Ethnic groups: African 99% (Mandinka 42%, Fula 18%, Wolof 16%, Jola 10%, Serahuli 9%, other 4%), non-African 1%

Religions: Muslim 90%, Christian 9%, indigenous beliefs 1%

Languages: English (official), Mandinka, Wolof, Fula, other indigenous vernaculars

Literacy:
definition: age 15 and over can read and write
total population: 38.6%
male: 52.8%
female: 24.9% (1995 est.)

Government

Country name:
conventional long form: Republic of The Gambia
conventional short form: The Gambia

Data code: GA

Government type: republic under multiparty democratic rule

Capital: Banjul

Administrative divisions: 5 divisions and 1 city*; Banjul*, Lower River, MacCarthy Island, North Bank, Upper River, Western
note: it has been reported but not verified that the name of the MacCarthy Island division has been changed to Central River

Independence: 18 February 1965 (from UK); note - The Gambia and Senegal signed an agreement on 12 December 1981 that called for the creation of a loose confederation to be known as Senegambia, but the agreement was dissolved on 30 September 1989

National holiday: Independence Day, 18 February (1965)

Constitution: 24 April 1970; suspended July 1994; rewritten and approved by national referendum 8 August 1996; reestablished in January 1997

Legal system: based on a composite of English common law, Koranic law, and customary law; accepts compulsory ICJ jurisdiction, with reservations

Suffrage: 18 years of age; universal

Executive branch:
chief of state: President Yahya A. J. J. JAMMEH (since 12 October 1996); Vice President Isatou Njie SAIDY (since 20 March 1997); note - the president is both the chief of state and head of government
head of government: President Yahya A. J. J. JAMMEH (since 18 October 1996); Vice President Isatou Njie SAIDY (since 20 March 1997); note - the president is both the chief of state and head of government
cabinet: Cabinet is appointed by the president
elections: the president is elected by popular vote to a five-year term; the number of terms is not restricted; election last held 26 September 1996 (next to be held NA 2001)
election results: Yahya A. J. J. JAMMEH elected president; percent of vote - Yahya A. J. J. JAMMEH 55.5%, Ousainou DARBOE 35.8%

Legislative branch: unicameral National Assembly; 49 seats (45 elected by popular vote, 4 appointed by the president; all for five-year terms)
elections: last popular election held 2 January 1997 (next to be held NA 2002)
election results: percent of vote by party - NA; seats by party - APRC 33, UDP 7, NRP 2, PDOIS 1, independents 2

Judicial branch: Supreme Court

Political parties and leaders: Alliance for Patriotic Reorientation and Construction or APRC [Yahya A. J. J. JAMMEH]; National Reconciliation Party or NRP [Hamat N. K. BAH]; People's Democratic Organization for Independence and Socialism or PDOIS [Sidia JATTA]; United Democratic Party or UDP [Ousainou DARBOE]; note - in August 1996 the government banned the following from participation in the elections of 1996: People's Progressive Party or PPP [former President Dawda K. JAWARA (in exile)], and two opposition parties - the National Convention Party or NCP [former Vice President Sheriff DIBBA] and the Gambian People's Party or GPP [Hassan Musa CAMARA]

International organization participation: ACP, AfDB, C, CCC, ECA, ECOWAS, FAO, G-77, IBRD, ICAO, ICFTU, ICRM, IDA, IDB, IFAD, IFC, IFRCS, ILO, IMF, IMO, Intelsat (nonsignatory user), Interpol, IOC, ITU, NAM, OAU, OIC, OPCW, UN, UN Security Council (temporary), UNCTAD, UNESCO, UNIDO, UPU, WCL, WFTU, WHO, WIPO, WMO, WToO, WTrO

Diplomatic representation in the US:
chief of mission: Ambassador Crispin GREY-JOHNSON
chancery: Suite 1000, 1155 15th Street NW, Washington, DC 20005
telephone: [1] (202) 785-1399
FAX: [1] (202) 785-1430

Diplomatic representation from the US:
chief of mission: Ambassador George W. HALEY
embassy: Fajara, Kairaba Avenue, Banjul
mailing address: P. M. B. No. 19, Banjul
telephone: [220] 392856, 392858, 391970, 391971
FAX: [220] 392475

Flag description: three equal horizontal bands of red (top), blue with white edges, and green

Economy

Economy - overview: The Gambia has no important mineral or other natural resources and has a limited agricultural base. About 75% of the population depends on crops and livestock for its livelihood. Small-scale manufacturing activity features the processing of peanuts, fish, and hides. Reexport trade normally constitutes a major segment of economic activity, but the 50% devaluation of the CFA franc in January 1994 made Senegalese goods more competitive and hurt the reexport trade. The Gambia has benefited from a rebound in tourism after its decline in response to the military's takeover in July 1994. Short-run economic progress remains highly dependent on sustained bilateral and multilateral aid and on responsible government economic management as forwarded by IMF technical help and advice.

GDP: purchasing power parity - $1.3 billion (1998 est.)

GDP - real growth rate: 3.8% (1998 est.)

GDP - per capita: purchasing power parity - $1,000 (1998 est.)

GDP - composition by sector:
agriculture: 23%
industry: 13%
services: 64% (1997 est.)

Population below poverty line: NA%

Household income or consumption by percentage share:
lowest 10%: NA%
highest 10%: NA%

Inflation rate (consumer prices): 3% (1998 est.)

Labor force: NA

Labor force - by occupation: agriculture 75%, industry, commerce, and services 19%, government 6%

Unemployment rate: NA%

Budget:
revenues: $88.6 million
expenditures: $98.2 million, including capital expenditures of $NA (FY96/97 est.)

Industries: processing peanuts, fish, and hides; tourism; beverages; agricultural machinery assembly, woodworking, metalworking; clothing

Industrial production growth rate: NA%

Electricity - production: 70 million kWh (1996)

Electricity - production by source:
fossil fuel: 100%
hydro: 0%
nuclear: 0%
other: 0% (1996)

Electricity - consumption: 70 million kWh (1996)

Electricity - exports: 0 kWh (1996)

Electricity - imports: 0 kWh (1996)

Agriculture - products: peanuts, millet, sorghum, rice, corn, cassava (tapioca), palm kernels; cattle, sheep, goats; forest and fishery resources not fully exploited

Exports: $120 million (f.o.b., 1997)

Exports - commodities: peanuts and peanut products, fish, cotton lint, palm kernels

Exports - partners: Belgium, Japan, Senegal, Hong Kong, France, Switzerland, UK, US, Indonesia (1997)

Imports: $207 million (f.o.b., 1997)

Imports - commodities: foodstuffs, manufactures, raw materials, fuel, machinery and transport equipment

Imports - partners: Cote d'Ivoire, Hong Kong, UK, Germany, Netherlands, France, Belgium (1997)

Debt - external: $426 million (1995 est.)

Economic aid - recipient: $45.4 million (1995)

Currency: 1 dalasi (D) = 100 butut

Exchange rates: dalasi (D) per US$1 - 10.947 (December 1998), 10.643 (1998), 10.200 (1997), 9.789 (1996), 9.546 (1995), 9.576 (1994)

Fiscal year: 1 July - 30 June

Communications

Telephones: 11,000 (1991 est.)

Telephone system:
domestic: adequate network of microwave radio relay and open wire

international: microwave radio relay links to Senegal and Guinea-Bissau; satellite earth station - 1 Intelsat (Atlantic Ocean)
Radio broadcast stations: AM 2, FM 5, shortwave 0
Radios: 180,000 (1993 est.)
Television broadcast stations: 1 (government owned) (1997)
Televisions: NA

Transportation

Railways: 0 km
Highways:
total: 2,700 km
paved: 956 km
unpaved: 1,744 km (1996 est.)
Waterways: 400 km
Ports and harbors: Banjul
Merchant marine: none
Airports: 1 (1998 est.)
Airports - with paved runways:
total: 1
over 3,047 m: 1 (1998 est.)

Military

Military branches: Army (includes marine unit), National Police, National Guard
Military manpower - availability:
males age 15-49: 296,976 (1999 est.)
Military manpower - fit for military service:
males age 15-49: 149,670 (1999 est.)
Military expenditures - dollar figure: $1.2 million (FY96/97)
Military expenditures - percent of GDP: 2% (FY96/97)

Transnational Issues

Disputes - international: short section of boundary with Senegal is indefinite

Gaza Strip

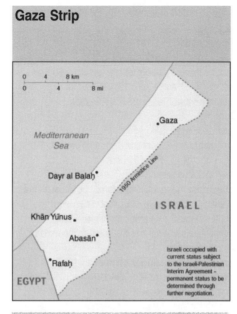

Introduction

Background: The Israel-PLO Declaration of Principles on Interim Self-Government Arrangements ("the DOP"), signed in Washington on 13 September 1993, provides for a transitional period not exceeding five years of Palestinian interim self-government in the Gaza Strip and the West Bank. Permanent status negotiations began on 5 May 1996, but have not resumed since the initial meeting. Under the DOP, Israel agreed to transfer certain powers and responsibilities to the Palestinian Authority, which includes a Palestinian Legislative Council elected in January 1996, as part of interim self-governing arrangements in the West Bank and Gaza Strip. A transfer of powers and responsibilities for the Gaza Strip and Jericho took place pursuant to the Israel-PLO 4 May 1994 Cairo Agreement on the Gaza Strip and the Jericho Area and in additional areas of the West Bank pursuant to the Israel-PLO 28 September 1995 Interim Agreement, the Israel-PLO 15 January 1997 Protocol Concerning Redeployment in Hebron, and the Israel-PLO 23 October, 1998 Wye River Memorandum. The DOP provides that Israel will retain responsibility during the transitional period for external security and for internal security and public order of settlements and Israelis. Permanent status is to be determined through direct negotiations.

Geography

Location: Middle East, bordering the Mediterranean Sea, between Egypt and Israel
Geographic coordinates: 31 25 N, 34 20 E
Map references: Middle East
Area:
total: 360 sq km
land: 360 sq km
water: 0 sq km
Area - comparative: slightly more than twice the size of Washington, DC

Land boundaries:
total: 62 km
border countries: Egypt 11 km, Israel 51 km
Coastline: 40 km
Maritime claims: Israeli-occupied with current status subject to the Israeli-Palestinian Interim Agreement - permanent status to be determined through further negotiation
Climate: temperate, mild winters, dry and warm to hot summers
Terrain: flat to rolling, sand- and dune-covered coastal plain
Elevation extremes:
lowest point: Mediterranean Sea 0 m
highest point: Abu 'Awdah (Joz Abu 'Auda) 105 m
Natural resources: NEGL
Land use:
arable land: 24%
permanent crops: 39%
permanent pastures: 0%
forests and woodland: 11%
other: 26% (1993 est.)
Irrigated land: 120 sq km (1993 est.)
Natural hazards: NA
Environment - current issues: desertification; salination of fresh water; sewage treatment
Environment - international agreements:
party to: none of the selected agreements
signed, but not ratified: none of the selected agreements
Geography - note: there are 24 Israeli settlements and civilian land use sites in the Gaza Strip (August 1998 est.)

People

Population: 1,112,654 (July 1999 est.)
note: in addition, there are some 6,000 Israeli settlers in the Gaza Strip (August 1998 est.)
Age structure:
0-14 years: 52% (male 294,196; female 280,017)
15-64 years: 46% (male 255,209; female 251,317)
65 years and over: 2% (male 13,475; female 18,440) (1999 est.)
Population growth rate: 4.44% (1999 est.)
Birth rate: 48.24 births/1,000 population (1999 est.)
Death rate: 3.8 deaths/1,000 population (1999 est.)
Net migration rate: 0 migrant(s)/1,000 population (1999 est.)
Sex ratio:
at birth: 1.05 male(s)/female
under 15 years: 1.05 male(s)/female
15-64 years: 1.02 male(s)/female
65 years and over: 0.73 male(s)/female
total population: 1.02 male(s)/female (1999 est.)
Infant mortality rate: 22.92 deaths/1,000 live births (1999 est.)
Life expectancy at birth:
total population: 73.44 years
male: 72.01 years
female: 74.95 years (1999 est.)
Total fertility rate: 7.46 children born/woman (1999 est.)

Gaza Strip *(continued)*

Nationality:
noun: NA
adjective: NA
Ethnic groups: Palestinian Arab and other 99.4%, Jewish 0.6%
Religions: Muslim (predominantly Sunni) 98.7%, Christian 0.7%, Jewish 0.6%
Languages: Arabic, Hebrew (spoken by Israeli settlers and many Palestinians), English (widely understood)
Literacy: NA

Government

Country name:
conventional long form: none
conventional short form: Gaza Strip
local long form: none
local short form: Qita Ghazzah
Data code: GZ

Economy

Economy - overview: Economic conditions in the Gaza Strip - under the responsibility of the Palestinian Authority since the Cairo Agreement of May 1994 - have deteriorated since the early 1990s. Real per capita GDP for the West Bank and Gaza Strip (WBGS) declined 36% between 1992 and 1996 owing to the combined effect of falling aggregate incomes and robust population growth. The downturn in economic activity was largely the result of Israeli closure policies - the imposition of generalized border closures in response to security incidents in Israel - which disrupted previously established labor and commodity market relationships between Israel and the WBGS. The most serious negative social effect of this downturn has been the emergence of chronic unemployment; average unemployment rates in the WBGS during the 1980s were generally under 5%, by the mid-1990s this level had risen to over 20%. Since 1997 Israel's use of comprehensive closures has decreased and, in 1998, Israel implemented new policies to reduce the impact of closures and other security procedures on the movement of Palestinian goods and labor. These positive changes to the conduct of economic activity, combined with international donor pledges of over $3 billion made to the Palestinian Authority in November, may fuel a moderate economic recovery in 1999.
GDP: purchasing power parity - $1.1 billion (1998 est.)
GDP - real growth rate: 2.2% (1998 est.)
GDP - per capita: purchasing power parity - $1,000 (1998 est.)
GDP - composition by sector:
agriculture: 33%
industry: 25%
services: 42% (1995 est., includes West Bank)
Population below poverty line: NA%
Household income or consumption by percentage share:
lowest 10%: NA%
highest 10%: NA%

Inflation rate (consumer prices): 8.8% (1997 est.)
Labor force: NA
note: excluding Israeli settlers
Labor force - by occupation: services 66%, industry 21%, agriculture 13% (1996)
Unemployment rate: 26.8% (1997 est.)
Budget:
revenues: $816 million
expenditures: $866 million, including capital expenditures of $NA (1997 est.)
note: includes West Bank
Industries: generally small family businesses that produce textiles, soap, olive-wood carvings, and mother-of-pearl souvenirs; the Israelis have established some small-scale modern industries in an industrial center
Industrial production growth rate: NA%
Electricity - production: NA kWh
note: electricity supplied by Israel
Electricity - production by source:
fossil fuel: NA%
hydro: NA%
nuclear: NA%
other: NA%
Electricity - consumption: NA kWh
Electricity - exports: NA kWh
Electricity - imports: NA kWh
Agriculture - products: olives, citrus, vegetables; beef, dairy products
Exports: $781 million (f.o.b., 1997 est.) (includes West Bank)
Exports - commodities: citrus
Exports - partners: Israel, Egypt, West Bank
Imports: $2.1 billion (c.i.f., 1997 est.) (includes West Bank)
Imports - commodities: food, consumer goods, construction materials
Imports - partners: Israel, Egypt, West Bank
Debt - external: $108 million (1997 est.)
Economic aid - recipient: $NA
Currency: 1 new Israeli shekel (NIS) = 100 new agorot
Exchange rates: new Israeli shekels (NIS) per US$1 - 4.2260 (November 1998), 3.4494 (1997), 3.1917 (1996), 3.0113 (1995), 3.0111 (1994)
Fiscal year: calendar year (since 1 January 1992)

Communications

Telephones: NA; 3.1% of Palestinian households have telephones
Telephone system:
domestic: NA
international: NA
Radio broadcast stations: AM 0, FM 0, shortwave 0
Radios: NA; note - 95% of Palestinian households have radios (1992 est.)
Television broadcast stations: 2 (operated by the Palestinian Broadcasting Corp.) (1997)
Televisions: NA; note - 59% of Palestinian households have televisions (1992 est.)

Transportation

Railways:
total: NA km; note - one line, abandoned and in disrepair, little trackage remains
Highways:
total: NA km
paved: NA km
unpaved: NA km
note: small, poorly developed road network
Ports and harbors: Gaza
Airports: 2 (1998 est.)
note: includes Gaza International Airport that opened on 24 November 1998 as part of agreements stipulated in the 23 October 1998 Wye River Memorandum
Airports - with paved runways:
total: 1
over 3,047 m: 1 (1998 est.)
Airports - with unpaved runways:
total: 1
under 914 m: 1 (1998 est.)

Military

Military branches: NA
Military expenditures - dollar figure: $NA
Military expenditures - percent of GDP: NA%

Transnational Issues

Disputes - international: West Bank and Gaza Strip are Israeli-occupied with current status subject to the Israeli-Palestinian Interim Agreement - permanent status to be determined through further negotiation

Georgia

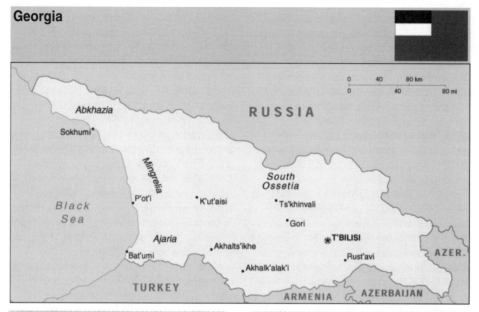

Introduction

Background: Beset by ethnic and civil strife since independence from the Soviet Union in December 1991, Georgia began to stabilize in 1994. Political settlements for separatist conflicts in South Ossetia and Abkhazia remain elusive. The conflict in South Ossetia has been dormant since spring 1994, but sporadic violence continues between Abkhaz forces and Georgian partisans in western Georgia. Russian peacekeepers are deployed in both regions and a UN Observer Mission is operating in Abkhazia. As a result of these conflicts, Georgia still has about 250,000 internally displaced people. In 1995, Georgia adopted a new constitution and conducted generally free and fair nationwide presidential and parliamentary elections. In 1996, the government focused its attention on implementing an ambitious economic reform program and professionalizing its parliament. Violence and organized crime were sharply curtailed in 1995 and 1996, but corruption remains rife. Georgia has taken some steps to reduce its dependence on Russia, acquiring coastal patrol boats in 1997 to replace Russian border units along the Black Sea coast. In 1998, Georgia assumed control of its Black Sea coast and about half of its land border with Turkey in line with a June 1998 agreement with Russia. Since 1997, Georgia's parliament has sharpened its rhetoric against Russia's continued military presence on Georgian territory. In February 1998 an assassination attempt was made against President SHEVARDNADZE by supporters of the late former president Zviad GAMSAKHURDIA. In October 1998, a disaffected military officer led a failed mutiny in western Georgia; the armed forces continue to feel the ripple effect of the uprising. Georgia faces parliamentary elections this fall, and presidential elections next spring. After two years of robust growth, the economy, hurt by the financial crisis in Russia, slowed in 1998.

Geography

Location: Southwestern Asia, bordering the Black Sea, between Turkey and Russia
Geographic coordinates: 42 00 N, 43 30 E
Map references: Commonwealth of Independent States
Area:
total: 69,700 sq km
land: 69,700 sq km
water: 0 sq km
Area - comparative: slightly smaller than South Carolina
Land boundaries:
total: 1,461 km
border countries: Armenia 164 km, Azerbaijan 322 km, Russia 723 km, Turkey 252 km
Coastline: 310 km
Maritime claims: NA
Climate: warm and pleasant; Mediterranean-like on Black Sea coast
Terrain: largely mountainous with Great Caucasus Mountains in the north and Lesser Caucasus Mountains in the south; Kolkhet'is Dablobi (Kolkhida Lowland) opens to the Black Sea in the west; Mtkvari River Basin in the east; good soils in river valley flood plains, foothills of Kolkhida Lowland
Elevation extremes:
lowest point: Black Sea 0 m
highest point: Mt'a Mqinvartsveri (Gora Kazbek) 5,048 m
Natural resources: forests, hydropower, manganese deposits, iron ore, copper, minor coal and oil deposits; coastal climate and soils allow for important tea and citrus growth
Land use:
arable land: 9%
permanent crops: 4%
permanent pastures: 25%
forests and woodland: 34%
other: 28% (1993 est.)
Irrigated land: 4,000 sq km (1993 est.)

Natural hazards: earthquakes
Environment - current issues: air pollution, particularly in Rust'avi; heavy pollution of Mtkvari River and the Black Sea; inadequate supplies of potable water; soil pollution from toxic chemicals
Environment - international agreements:
party to: Air Pollution, Biodiversity, Climate Change, Law of the Sea, Ozone Layer Protection, Ship Pollution, Wetlands
signed, but not ratified: Desertification

People

Population: 5,066,499 (July 1999 est.)
Age structure:
0-14 years: 21% (male 544,055; female 522,491)
15-64 years: 67% (male 1,628,993; female 1,753,527)
65 years and over: 12% (male 236,124; female 381,309) (1999 est.)
Population growth rate: -0.74% (1999 est.)
Birth rate: 11.64 births/1,000 population (1999 est.)
Death rate: 14.3 deaths/1,000 population (1999 est.)
Net migration rate: -4.69 migrant(s)/1,000 population (1999 est.)
Sex ratio:
at birth: 1.05 male(s)/female
under 15 years: 1.04 male(s)/female
15-64 years: 0.93 male(s)/female
65 years and over: 0.62 male(s)/female
total population: 0.91 male(s)/female (1999 est.)
Infant mortality rate: 52.01 deaths/1,000 live births (1999 est.)
Life expectancy at birth:
total population: 64.63 years
male: 61.13 years
female: 68.32 years (1999 est.)
Total fertility rate: 1.53 children born/woman (1999 est.)
Nationality:
noun: Georgian(s)
adjective: Georgian
Ethnic groups: Georgian 70.1%, Armenian 8.1%, Russian 6.3%, Azeri 5.7%, Ossetian 3%, Abkhaz 1.8%, other 5%
Religions: Christian Orthodox 75% (Georgian Orthodox 65%, Russian Orthodox 10%), Muslim 11%, Armenian Apostolic 8%, unknown 6%
Languages: Georgian 71% (official), Russian 9%, Armenian 7%, Azeri 6%, other 7%
note: Abkhaz (official in Abkhazia)
Literacy:
definition: age 15 and over can read and write
total population: 99%
male: 100%
female: 98% (1989 est.)

Government

Country name:
conventional long form: none
conventional short form: Georgia
local long form: none

Georgia (continued)

local short form: Sak'art'velo
former: Georgian Soviet Socialist Republic
Data code: GG
Government type: republic
Capital: T'bilisi
Administrative divisions: 53 rayons (raionebi, singular - raioni), 9 cities* (k'alak'ebi, singular - k'alak'i), and 2 autonomous republics** (avtomnoy respubliki, singular - avtom respublika); Abashis, Abkhazia or Ap'khazet'is Avtonomiuri Respublika** (Sokhumi), Adigenis, Ajaria or Acharis Avtonomiuri Respublika** (Bat'umi), Akhalgoris, Akhalk'alak'is, Akhalts'ikhis, Akhmetis, Ambrolauris, Aspindzis, Baghdat'is, Bolnisis, Borjomis, Chiat'ura*, Ch'khorotsqus, Ch'okhatauris, Dedop'listsqaros, Dmanisis, Dushet'is, Gardabanis, Gori*, Goris, Gurjaanis, Javis, K'arelis, Kaspis, Kharagaulis, Khashuris, Khobis, Khonis, K'ut'aisi*, Lagodekhis, Lanch'khut'is, Lentekhis, Marneulis, Martvilis, Mestiis, Mts'khet'is, Ninotsmindis, Onis, Ozurget'is, P'ot'i*, Qazbegis, Qvarlis, Rust'avi*, Sach'kheris, Sagarejos, Samtrediis, Senakis, Sighnaghis, T'bilisi*, T'elavis, T'erjolis, T'et'ritsqaros, T'ianet'is, Tqibuli*, Ts'ageris, Tsalenjikhis, Tsalkis, Tsqaltubo*, Vanis, Zestap'onis, Zugdidi*, Zugdidis
note: administrative divisions have the same names as their administrative centers (exceptions have the administrative center name following in parentheses)
Independence: 9 April 1991 (from Soviet Union)
National holiday: Independence Day, 26 May (1991)
Constitution: adopted 17 October 1995
Legal system: based on civil law system
Suffrage: 18 years of age; universal
Executive branch:
chief of state: President Eduard Amvrosiyevich SHEVARDNADZE (previously elected chairman of the Government Council 10 March 1992, Council has since been disbanded; previously elected chairman of Parliament 11 October 1992; president since 26 November 1995; note - the president is both the chief of state and head of government
head of government: President Eduard Amvrosiyevich SHEVARDNADZE (previously elected chairman of the Government Council 10 March 1992, Council has since been disbanded; previously elected chairman of Parliament 11 October 1992; president since 26 November 1995; note - the president is both the chief of state and head of government
cabinet: Cabinet of Ministers
elections: president elected by popular vote for a five-year term; election last held 5 November 1995 (next to be held NA 2000)
election results: Eduard SHEVARDNADZE elected president; percent of vote - Eduard SHEVARDNADZE 74%
Legislative branch: unicameral Supreme Council (commonly referred to as Parliament) or Umaghiesi Sabcho (235 seats; members are elected by popular vote to serve four-year terms)
elections: last held 5 November 1995 (next to be held NA 1999)

election results: percent of vote by party - CUG 24%, NDP 8%, AGUR 7%, all other parties received less than 5% each; seats by party - CUG 107, NDP 34, AGUR 32, Progress Bloc 4, SPG 4, others 9, Abkazian deputies 12, independents 29, not filled 4
Judicial branch: Supreme Court, judges elected by the Supreme Council on the president's recommendation; Constitutional Court
Political parties and leaders: Citizen's Union of Georgia or CUG [Eduard SHEVARDNADZE]; People's Party [Mamuka GIORGADZE]; National Democratic Party or NDP [Irina SARISHVILI-CHANTURIA]; Union for "Revival" Party or AGUR [Alsan ABASHIDZE]; Union of Traditionalists or UGT [Akaki ASATIANI]; Socialist Party or SPG [Vakhtang RCHEULISHVILI]; Georgian United Communist Party or UCPG [Panteleimon GIORGADZE, chairman]; Greens Party [Giorgi GACHECHILADZE]; United Republican Party or URP [Nodar NATADZE, chairman]; National Independent Party or NIP [Irakli TSERETELI, chairman]; Labor Party [Shalva NATELASHVILI]; Progressive Bloc (includes the following groups: Democratic Union of Georgia or DUG, Political Association "Georgian Proprietors" - Electoral Association "T'bilisi", Political Union of Young Democrats "Our Choice", Political Union Tanadgoma) [leader NA]
Political pressure groups and leaders: supporters of the late ousted President Zviad GAMSAKHURDYA remain a source of opposition; separatist elements in the breakaway region of Abkhazia; Georgian refugees from Abkhazia (Abkhaz faction in Georgian Parliament)
International organization participation: BSEC, CCC, CE (guest), CIS, EAPC, EBRD, ECE, FAO, IAEA, IBRD, ICAO, IDA, IFAD, IFC, IFRCS, ILO, IMF, IMO, Inmarsat, Interpol, IOC, IOM (observer), ISO (correspondent), ITU, OPCW, OSCE, PFP, UN, UNCTAD, UNESCO, UNIDO, UPU, WHO, WIPO, WMO, WToO, WTrO (applicant)
Diplomatic representation in the US:
chief of mission: Ambassador Tedo JAPARIDZE
chancery: Suite 300, 1615 New Hampshire Avenue NW, Washington, DC 20009
telephone: [1] (202) 393-5959
FAX: [1] (202) 393-4537
Diplomatic representation from the US:
chief of mission: Ambassador Kenneth S. YALOWITZ
embassy: #25 Antoneli Street, T'bilisi 380026
mailing address: use embassy street address
telephone: [995] (32) 989-967
FAX: [995] (32) 933-759
Flag description: maroon field with small rectangle in upper hoist side corner; rectangle divided horizontally with black on top, white below

Economy

Economy - overview: Georgia's economy has traditionally revolved around Black Sea tourism; cultivation of citrus fruits, tea, and grapes; mining of manganese and copper; and output of a small industrial sector producing wine, metals, machinery,

chemicals, and textiles. The country imports the bulk of its energy needs, including natural gas and oil products. Its only sizable internal energy resource is hydropower. Despite the severe damage the economy has suffered due to civil strife, Georgia, with the help of the IMF and World Bank, made substantial economic gains since 1995, increasing GDP growth and slashing inflation. The Georgian economy suffered some setbacks in late 1998, including a large budget deficit due to a failure to collect tax revenue and to the impact of the Russian economic crisis. Georgia also still suffers from energy shortages; it privatized the distribution network in 1998, and deliveries are steadily improving. Georgia is pinning its hopes for long-term recovery on the development of an international transportation corridor through the key Black Sea ports of P'ot'i and Bat'umi. The construction of a Caspian oil pipeline through Georgia - scheduled to open in early 1999 - should spur greater Western investment in the economy. The global economic slowdown, a growing trade deficit, continuing problems with corruption, and political uncertainties cloud the short-term economic picture.
GDP: purchasing power parity - $11.2 billion (1998 est.)
GDP - real growth rate: 4% (1998 est.)
GDP - per capita: purchasing power parity - $2,200 (1998 est.)
GDP - composition by sector:
agriculture: 29%
industry: 16%
services: 55% (1997 est.)
Population below poverty line: NA%
Household income or consumption by percentage share:
lowest 10%: NA%
highest 10%: NA%
Inflation rate (consumer prices): 10.5% (1998 est.)
Labor force: 3.08 million (1997)
Labor force - by occupation: industry and construction 31%, agriculture and forestry 25%, other 44% (1990)
Unemployment rate: 16% (1996 est.)
Budget:
revenues: $364 million
expenditures: $568 million, including capital expenditures of $NA (1998)
Industries: steel, aircraft, machine tools, foundry equipment, electric locomotives, tower cranes, electric welding equipment, machinery for food preparation and meat packing, electric motors, process control equipment, trucks, tractors, textiles, shoes, chemicals, wood products, wine
Industrial production growth rate: -0.3% (1998 est.)
Electricity - production: 6.845 billion kWh (1996)
Electricity - production by source:
fossil fuel: 29.88%
hydro: 70.12%
nuclear: 0%
other: 0% (1996)

Georgia (continued)

Electricity - consumption: 6.949 billion kWh (1996)
Electricity - exports: 300 million kWh (1996)
Electricity - imports: 404 million kWh (1996)
Agriculture - products: citrus, grapes, tea, vegetables, potatoes; livestock
Exports: $230 million (f.o.b., 1997 est.)
Exports - commodities: citrus fruits, tea, wine, other agricultural products; diverse types of machinery; ferrous and nonferrous metals; textiles; chemicals; fuel reexports
Exports - partners: Russia, Turkey, Azerbaijan, Ukraine, Armenia, Bulgaria, Turkey, US, UK, Italy, Germany, Romania (1997)
Imports: $931 million (c.i.f., 1997 est.)
Imports - commodities: fuel, grain and other foods, machinery and parts, transport equipment
Imports - partners: Russia, Turkey, Azerbaijan (1996); note - EU and US send humanitarian food shipments
Debt - external: $1.3 billion (1996 est.)
Economic aid - recipient: $212.7 million (1995)
Currency: lari introduced September 1995 replacing the coupon
Exchange rates: lari per US$1 (end of period) - 1.82 (December 1998), 1.32 (December 1997), 1.28 (December 1996), 1.24 (December 1995)
Fiscal year: calendar year

Communications

Telephones: 760,000 (1996 est.)
Telephone system:
domestic: local - T'bilisi and K'ut'aisi have cellular telephone networks with about 10,000 customers total; urban areas 20 telephones/100 people; rural areas 4 phones/100 people; intercity - a fiber-optic line connects T'bilisi to K'ut'aisi (Georgia's second largest city); nationwide pager service
international: Georgia and Russia are working on a fiber-optic line between P'ot'i and Sochi (Russia); present international service is available by microwave, land line, and satellite through the Moscow switch; international electronic mail and telex service available
Radio broadcast stations: AM NA, FM NA, shortwave NA; note 2 national broadcast stations, 3 regional broadcast stations
Radios: NA
Television broadcast stations: 3
Televisions: NA

Transportation

Railways:
total: 1,583 km in common carrier service; does not include industrial lines
broad gauge: 1,583 km 1.520-m gauge (1993)
Highways:
total: 20,700 km
paved: 19,354 km
unpaved: 1,346 km (1996 est.)
Pipelines: crude oil 370 km; refined products 300 km; natural gas 440 km (1992)

Ports and harbors: Bat'umi, P'ot'i, Sokhumi
Merchant marine:
total: 8 ships (1,000 GRT or over) totaling 86,667 GRT/121,679 DWT
ships by type: cargo 2, oil tanker 5, short-sea passenger 1 (1998 est.)
Airports: 28 (1994 est.)
Airports - with paved runways:
total: 14
over 3,047 m: 1
2,438 to 3,047 m: 7
1,524 to 2,437 m: 4
914 to 1,523 m: 1
under 914 m: 1 (1994 est.)
Airports - with unpaved runways:
total: 14
over 3,047 m: 1
2,438 to 3,047 m: 1
1,524 to 2,437 m: 1
914 to 1,523 m: 5
under 914 m: 6 (1994 est.)
Transportation - note: transportation network is in poor condition and disrupted by ethnic conflict, criminal activities, and fuel shortages; network lacks maintenance and repair

Military

Military branches: Ground Forces, Navy, Air Force, Air Defense Forces, National Guard, Republic Security Forces (internal and border troops)
Military manpower - military age: 18 years of age
Military manpower - availability:
males age 15-49: 1,287,225 (1999 est.)
Military manpower - fit for military service:
males age 15-49: 1,018,309 (1999 est.)
Military manpower - reaching military age annually:
males: 40,604 (1999 est.)
Military expenditures - dollar figure: $57 million (1998)
Military expenditures - percent of GDP: 1% (1998)
Military - note: a CIS peacekeeping force consisting of Russian troops is deployed in the Abkhazia region of Georgia together with a UN military observer group; a Russian peacekeeping battalion is deployed in South Ossetia

Transnational Issues

Disputes - international: none
Illicit drugs: limited cultivation of cannabis and opium poppy, mostly for domestic consumption; used as transshipment point for opiates via Central Asia to Western Europe

Germany

Introduction

Background: Germany - first united in 1871 - suffered defeats in successive world wars and was occupied by the victorious Allied powers of the US, UK, France, and the Soviet Union in 1945. With the beginning of the Cold War and increasing tension between the US and Soviet Union, two German states were formed in 1949: the western Federal Republic of Germany (FRG) and the eastern German Democratic Republic (GDR). The newly democratic FRG embedded itself in key Western economic and security organizations, the EU and NATO, while the Communist GDR was on the front line of the Soviet-led Warsaw Pact. The decline of the Soviet Union and end of the Cold War cleared the path for the fall of the Berlin Wall in 1989 and German re-unification in 1990. Germany has expended considerable funds - roughly $100 billion a year - in subsequent years working to bring eastern productivity and wages up to western standards, with mixed results. Unemployment - which in the east is nearly double that in the west - has grown over the last several years, primarily as a result of structural problems like an inflexible labor market. In January 1999, Germany and 10 other members of the EU formed a common European currency, the euro, and the German government is now looking toward reform of the EU budget and enlargement of the Union into Central Europe.

Geography

Location: Central Europe, bordering the Baltic Sea and the North Sea, between the Netherlands and Poland, south of Denmark
Geographic coordinates: 51 00 N, 9 00 E
Map references: Europe
Area:
total: 356,910 sq km
land: 349,520 sq km
water: 7,390 sq km

Germany (continued)

note: includes the formerly separate Federal Republic of Germany, the German Democratic Republic, and Berlin, following formal unification on 3 October 1990

Area - comparative: slightly smaller than Montana

Land boundaries:

total: 3,621 km

border countries: Austria 784 km, Belgium 167 km, Czech Republic 646 km, Denmark 68 km, France 451 km, Luxembourg 138 km, Netherlands 577 km, Poland 456 km, Switzerland 334 km

Coastline: 2,389 km

Maritime claims:

continental shelf: 200-m depth or to the depth of exploitation

exclusive economic zone: 200 nm

territorial sea: 12 nm

Climate: temperate and marine; cool, cloudy, wet winters and summers; occasional warm, tropical foehn wind; high relative humidity

Terrain: lowlands in north, uplands in center, Bavarian Alps in south

Elevation extremes:

lowest point: Freepsum Lake -2 m

highest point: Zugspitze 2,962 m

Natural resources: iron ore, coal, potash, timber, lignite, uranium, copper, natural gas, salt, nickel

Land use:

arable land: 33%

permanent crops: 1%

permanent pastures: 15%

forests and woodland: 31%

other: 20% (1993 est.)

Irrigated land: 4,750 sq km (1993 est.)

Natural hazards: flooding

Environment - current issues: emissions from coal-burning utilities and industries and lead emissions from vehicle exhausts (the result of continued use of leaded fuels) contribute to air pollution; acid rain, resulting from sulfur dioxide emissions, is damaging forests; pollution in the Baltic Sea from raw sewage and industrial effluents from rivers in eastern Germany; hazardous waste disposal

Environment - international agreements:

party to: Air Pollution, Air Pollution-Nitrogen Oxides, Air Pollution-Sulphur 85, Air Pollution-Sulphur 94, Air Pollution-Volatile Organic Compounds, Antarctic-Environmental Protocol, Antarctic Treaty, Biodiversity, Climate Change, Desertification, Endangered Species, Environmental Modification, Hazardous Wastes, Law of the Sea, Marine Dumping, Nuclear Test Ban, Ozone Layer Protection, Ship Pollution, Tropical Timber 83, Tropical Timber 94, Wetlands, Whaling

signed, but not ratified: Air Pollution-Persistent Organic Pollutants, Climate Change-Kyoto Protocol

Geography - note: strategic location on North European Plain and along the entrance to the Baltic Sea

People

Population: 82,087,361 (July 1999 est.)

Age structure:

0-14 years: 15% (male 6,495,882; female 6,172,359)

15-64 years: 69% (male 28,687,267; female 27,526,698)

65 years and over: 16% (male 4,990,090; female 8,215,065) (1999 est.)

Population growth rate: 0.01% (1999 est.)

Birth rate: 8.68 births/1,000 population (1999 est.)

Death rate: 10.76 deaths/1,000 population (1999 est.)

Net migration rate: 2.12 migrant(s)/1,000 population (1999 est.)

Sex ratio:

at birth: 1.06 male(s)/female

under 15 years: 1.05 male(s)/female

15-64 years: 1.04 male(s)/female

65 years and over: 0.61 male(s)/female

total population: 0.96 male(s)/female (1999 est.)

Infant mortality rate: 5.14 deaths/1,000 live births (1999 est.)

Life expectancy at birth:

total population: 77.17 years

male: 74.01 years

female: 80.5 years (1999 est.)

Total fertility rate: 1.26 children born/woman (1999 est.)

Nationality:

noun: German(s)

adjective: German

Ethnic groups: German 91.5%, Turkish 2.4%, Italians 0.7%, Greeks 0.4%, Poles 0.4%, other 4.6% (made up largely of people fleeing the war in the former Yugoslavia)

Religions: Protestant 38%, Roman Catholic 34%, Muslim 1.7%, unaffiliated or other 26.3%

Languages: German

Literacy:

definition: age 15 and over can read and write

total population: 99% (1977 est.)

male: NA%

female: NA%

Government

Country name:

conventional long form: Federal Republic of Germany

conventional short form: Germany

local long form: Bundesrepublik Deutschland

local short form: Deutschland

Data code: GM

Government type: federal republic

Capital: Berlin

note: the shift from Bonn to Berlin will take place over a period of years, with Bonn retaining many administrative functions and several ministries even after parliament moves in 1999

Administrative divisions: 16 states (Laender, singular - Land); Baden-Wuerttemberg, Bayern, Berlin, Brandenburg, Bremen, Hamburg, Hessen, Mecklenburg-Vorpommern, Niedersachsen, Nordrhein-Westfalen, Rheinland-Pfalz, Saarland, Sachsen, Sachsen-Anhalt, Schleswig-Holstein, Thueringen

Independence: 18 January 1871 (German Empire unification); divided into four zones of occupation (UK, US, USSR, and later, France) in 1945 following World War II; Federal Republic of Germany (FRG or West Germany) proclaimed 23 May 1949 and included the former UK, US, and French zones; German Democratic Republic (GDR or East Germany) proclaimed 7 October 1949 and included the former USSR zone; unification of West Germany and East Germany took place 3 October 1990; all four powers formally relinquished rights 15 March 1991

National holiday: German Unity Day (Day of Unity), 3 October (1990)

Constitution: 23 May 1949, known as Basic Law; became constitution of the united German people 3 October 1990

Legal system: civil law system with indigenous concepts; judicial review of legislative acts in the Federal Constitutional Court; has not accepted compulsory ICJ jurisdiction

Suffrage: 18 years of age; universal

Executive branch:

chief of state: President Roman HERZOG (since 1 July 1994)

head of government: Chancellor Gerhard SCHROEDER (since 27 October 1998)

cabinet: Cabinet appointed by the president upon the proposal of the chancellor

elections: president elected for a five-year term by a Federal Convention including all members of the Federal Assembly and an equal number of delegates elected by the Land Parliaments; election last held 23 May 1994 (next to be held 23 May 1999); chancellor elected by an absolute majority of the Federal Assembly for a four-year term; election last held 27 September 1998 (next to be held in the fall of 2002)

election results: Roman HERZOG elected president; percent of Federal Convention vote - 52.6%; Gerhard SCHROEDER elected chancellor; percent of Federal Assembly - 52.8%

Legislative branch: bicameral chamber (no official name for the two chambers as a whole) consists of the Federal Assembly or Bundestag (656 seats usually, but 669 for the 1998 term; elected by popular vote under a system combining direct and proportional representation; a party must win 5% of the national vote or three direct mandates to gain representation; members serve four-year terms) and the Federal Council or Bundesrat (69 votes; state governments are directly represented by votes; each has 3 to 6 votes depending on population and are required to vote as a block)

elections: Federal Assembly - last held 27 September 1998 (next to be held by the fall of 2002); note - there are no elections for the Bundesrat; composition is determined by the composition of the state-level governments; the composition of the Bundesrat has the potential to change any time one of the 16 states holds an election

election results: Federal Assembly - percent of vote by party - SPD 40.9%, Alliance 90/Greens 6.7%, CDU/CSU 35.1%, FDP 6.2%, PDS 5.1%; seats by

Germany (continued)

party - SPD 298, Alliance 90/Greens 47, CDU/CSU 245, FDP 43, PDS 36; Federal Council - current composition - votes by party - SPD-led states 45, CDU-led states 24

Judicial branch: Federal Constitutional Court or Bundesverfassungsgericht, half the judges are elected by the Bundestag and half by the Bundesrat

Political parties and leaders: Christian Democratic Union or CDU [Wolfgang SCHAEUBLE, chairman]; Christian Social Union or CSU [Edmund STOIBER, chairman]; Free Democratic Party or FDP [Wolfgang GERHARDT, chairman]; Social Democratic Party or SPD [Oskar LAFONTAINE, chairman]; Alliance '90/Greens [Gunda ROESTEL and Antje RADCKE]; Party of Democratic Socialism or PDS [Lothar BISKY, chairman]; German People's Union or DVU [Gerhard FREY, chairman]

Political pressure groups and leaders: employers' organizations, expellee, refugee, trade unions, and veterans groups

International organization participation: AfDB, AsDB, Australia Group, BDEAC, BIS, CBSS, CCC, CDB (non-regional), CE, CERN, EAPC, EBRD, ECE, EIB, EMU, ESA, EU, FAO, G- 5, G- 7, G-10, IADB, IAEA, IBRD, ICAO, ICC, ICFTU, ICRM, IDA, IEA, IFAD, IFC, IFRCS, IHO, ILO, IMF, IMO, Inmarsat, Intelsat, Interpol, IOC, IOM, ISO, ITU, MTCR, NAM (guest), NATO, NEA, NSG, OAS (observer), OECD, OPCW, OSCE, PCA, UN, UNCTAD, UNESCO, UNHCR, UNIDO, UNIKOM, UNMIBH, UNOMIG, UPU, WEU, WHO, WIPO, WMO, WToO, WTrO, ZC

Diplomatic representation in the US:
chief of mission: Ambassador Juergen CHROBOG
chancery: 4645 Reservoir Road NW, Washington, DC 20007
telephone: [1] (202) 298-4000
FAX: [1] (202) 298-4249
consulate(s) general: Atlanta, Boston, Chicago, Detroit, Houston, Los Angeles, Miami, New York, San Francisco, Seattle

Diplomatic representation from the US:
chief of mission: Ambassador John C. KORNBLUM
embassy: Deichmanns Aue 29, 53170 Bonn
mailing address: PSC 117, APO AE 09080
telephone: [49] (228) 3391
FAX: [49] (228) 339-2663
branch office: Berlin; mailing address: Neustaedtische Kirchstrasse 4-5, 10117 Berlin, PSC 120, Box 1000, APO AE 09265; telephone: [49] (30) 238-5174; FAX [49] (30) 238-6290
consulate(s) general: Dusseldorf, Frankfurt am Main, Hamburg, Leipzig, Munich

Flag description: three equal horizontal bands of black (top), red, and gold

Economy

Economy - overview: Germany possesses the world's third most powerful economy, with its capitalist market system tempered by generous welfare benefits. On 1 January 1999, Germany and 10 other European Union countries launched the European Monetary Union (EMU) by permanently fixing their bilateral exchange rates and giving the new European Central Bank control over the zone's monetary policy. Germans expect to have the new European currency, the euro, in pocket by 2002. Domestic demand contributed to a moderate economic upswing in early 1998, although unemployment remains high. Job-creation measures have helped superficially, but structural rigidities - like high wages and costly benefits - make unemployment a long-term, not just a cyclical, problem. Although minimally affected by the Asian crisis in 1998, Germany revised its 1999 forecast downward at the beginning of the year to reflect anticipated effects from the global economic slowdown. Over the long term, Germany faces budgetary problems - lower tax revenues and higher pension outlays - as its population ages. Meanwhile, the German nation continues to wrestle with the integration of eastern Germany, whose adjustment may take decades to complete despite annual transfers from the west of roughly $100 billion a year.

GDP: purchasing power parity - $1.813 trillion (1998 est.)

GDP - real growth rate: 2.7% (1998 est.)

GDP - per capita: purchasing power parity - $22,100 (1998 est.)

GDP - composition by sector:
agriculture: 1.1%
industry: 33.1%
services: 65.8% (1998)

Population below poverty line: NA%

Inflation rate (consumer prices): 0.9% (1998 est.)

Labor force: 38.2 million (1998)

Labor force - by occupation: industry 33.7%, agriculture 2.7%, services 63.6% (1998)

Unemployment rate: 10.6% (1998 est.)

Budget:
revenues: $977 billion
expenditures: $1.024 trillion, including capital expenditures of $NA (1998 est.)

Industries: western: among world's largest and technologically advanced producers of iron, steel, coal, cement, chemicals, machinery, vehicles, machine tools, electronics, food and beverages; eastern: metal fabrication, chemicals, brown coal, shipbuilding, machine building, food and beverages, textiles, petroleum refining

Industrial production growth rate: 5% (1998)

Electricity - production: 515.058 billion kWh (1996)

Electricity - production by source:
fossil fuel: 66.23%
hydro: 3.5%
nuclear: 29.81%
other: 0.46% (1996)

Electricity - consumption: 509.458 billion kWh (1996)

Electricity - exports: 42.5 billion kWh (1996)

Electricity - imports: 36.9 billion kWh (1996)

Agriculture - products: western - potatoes, wheat, barley, sugar beets, fruit, cabbages; cattle, pigs, poultry; eastern - wheat, rye, barley, potatoes, sugar beets, fruit; pork, beef, chickens, milk, hides

Exports: $510 billion (f.o.b., 1998 est.)

Exports - commodities: machinery 31%, vehicles 17%, chemicals 13%, metals and manufactures, foodstuffs, textiles (1997)

Exports - partners: EU 55.5% (France 10.7%, UK 8.5%, Italy 7.4%, Netherlands 7.0%, Belgium-Luxembourg 5.8%), US 8.6%, Japan 2.3% (1997 est.)

Imports: $426 billion (f.o.b., 1998 est.)

Imports - commodities: machinery 22%, vehicles 10%, chemicals 9%, foodstuffs 8%, textiles, metals (1997)

Imports - partners: EU 54.3% (France 10.5%, Netherlands 8.5%, Italy 7.8%, UK 7.0%, Belgium-Luxembourg 6.2%), US 7.7%, Japan 4.9% (1997)

Debt - external: $NA

Economic aid - donor: ODA, $7.5 billion (1995)

Currency: 1 deutsche mark (DM) = 100 pfennige

Exchange rates: deutsche marks (DM) per US$1 - 1.69 (January 1999), 1.7597 (1998), 1.7341 (1997), 1.5048 (1996), 1.4331 (1995), 1.6228 (1994)
note: on 1 January 1999, the European Union introduced a common currency that is now being used by financial institutions in some member countries at the rate of 0.8597 euros per US$ and a fixed rate of 1.95583 deutsche marks per euro; the euro will replace the local currency in consenting countries for all transactions in 2002

Fiscal year: calendar year

Communications

Telephones: 44 million

Telephone system: Germany has one of the world's most technologically advanced telecommunications systems; as a result of intensive capital expenditures since reunification, the formerly backward system of the eastern part of the country has been modernized and integrated with that of the western part
domestic: the region which was formerly West Germany is served by an extensive system of automatic telephone exchanges connected by modern networks of fiber-optic cable, coaxial cable, microwave radio relay, and a domestic satellite system; cellular telephone service is widely available and includes roaming service to many foreign countries; since the reunification of Germany, the telephone system of the eastern region has been upgraded and enjoys all of the advantages of the national system
international: satellite earth stations - 14 Intelsat (12 Atlantic Ocean and 2 Indian Ocean), 1 Eutelsat, 1 Inmarsat (Atlantic Ocean region), 2 Intersputnik (1 Atlantic Ocean region and 1 Indian Ocean region); 7 submarine cable connections; 2 HF radiotelephone communication centers; tropospheric scatter links

Radio broadcast stations: AM 77, FM 1,621, shortwave 37, digital audio broadcasting 130

Radios: 47.1 million (1998 est.)

Television broadcast stations: 9,513 (including repeaters)

Televisions: 51.4 million (1998 est.)

Germany (continued)

Transportation

Railways:

total: 46,300 km including 18,866 km electrified and 14,768 km double- or multiple-tracked (1996)

note: since privatization in 1994, Deutsche Bahn AG (DBAG) no longer publishes details of the tracks it owns; in addition to the DBAG system there are 102 privately owned railway companies which own an approximate 3,000 km to 4,000 km of the total tracks

Highways:

total: 656,074 km

paved: 650,169 km (including 11,309 km of expressways)

unpaved: 5,905 km all-weather (1997 est.)

Waterways: 7,467 km (1997); major rivers include the Rhine and Elbe; Kiel Canal is an important connection between the Baltic Sea and North Sea

Pipelines: crude oil 2,460 km (1997)

Ports and harbors: Berlin, Bonn, Brake, Bremen, Bremerhaven, Cologne, Dresden, Duisburg, Emden, Hamburg, Karlsruhe, Kiel, Lubeck, Magdeburg, Mannheim, Rostock, Stuttgart

Merchant marine:

total: 594 ships (1,000 GRT or over) totaling 7,699,596 GRT/9,629,163 DWT

ships by type: cargo 227, chemical tanker 15, combination bulk 1, container 306, liquefied gas tanker 5, multifunction large-load carrier 5, oil tanker 7, passenger 3, railcar carrier 2, refrigerated cargo 2, roll-on/roll-off cargo 14, short-sea passenger 7 (1998 est.)

Airports: 618 (1998 est.)

Airports - with paved runways:

total: 319

over 3,047 m: 14

2,438 to 3,047 m: 62

1,524 to 2,437 m: 68

914 to 1,523 m: 54

under 914 m: 121 (1998 est.)

Airports - with unpaved runways:

total: 299

over 3,047 m: 2

2,438 to 3,047 m: 6

1,524 to 2,437 m: 6

914 to 1,523 m: 58

under 914 m: 227 (1998 est.)

Heliports: 61 (1998 est.)

Military

Military branches: Army, Navy (includes Naval Air Arm), Air Force, Medical Corps, Border Police, Coast Guard

Military manpower - military age: 18 years of age

Military manpower - availability:

males age 15-49: 20,860,710 (1999 est.)

Military manpower - fit for military service:

males age 15-49: 17,799,070 (1999 est.)

Military manpower - reaching military age annually:

males: 472,708 (1999 est.)

Military expenditures - dollar figure: $32.8 billion (1998)

Military expenditures - percent of GDP: 1.5% (1998)

Transnational Issues

Disputes - international: individual Sudeten German claims for restitution of property confiscated in connection with their expulsion after World War II

Illicit drugs: source of precursor chemicals for South American cocaine processors; transshipment point for and consumer of Southwest Asian heroin and hashish, Latin American cocaine, and European-produced synthetic drugs

Ghana

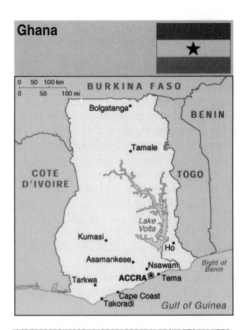

Geography

Location: Western Africa, bordering the Gulf of Guinea, between Cote d'Ivoire and Togo

Geographic coordinates: 8 00 N, 2 00 W

Map references: Africa

Area:

total: 238,540 sq km

land: 230,020 sq km

water: 8,520 sq km

Area - comparative: slightly smaller than Oregon

Land boundaries:

total: 2,093 km

border countries: Burkina Faso 548 km, Cote d'Ivoire 668 km, Togo 877 km

Coastline: 539 km

Maritime claims:

contiguous zone: 24 nm

continental shelf: 200 nm

exclusive economic zone: 200 nm

territorial sea: 12 nm

Climate: tropical; warm and comparatively dry along southeast coast; hot and humid in southwest; hot and dry in north

Terrain: mostly low plains with dissected plateau in south-central area

Elevation extremes:

lowest point: Atlantic Ocean 0 m

highest point: Mount Afadjato 880 m

Natural resources: gold, timber, industrial diamonds, bauxite, manganese, fish, rubber

Land use:

arable land: 12%

permanent crops: 7%

permanent pastures: 22%

forests and woodland: 35%

other: 24% (1993 est.)

Irrigated land: 60 sq km (1993 est.)

Natural hazards: dry, dusty, harmattan winds occur from January to March; droughts

Environment - current issues: recent drought in

Ghana *(continued)*

north severely affecting agricultural activities; deforestation; overgrazing; soil erosion; poaching and habitat destruction threatens wildlife populations; water pollution; inadequate supplies of potable water

Environment - international agreements:
party to: Biodiversity, Climate Change, Desertification, Endangered Species, Environmental Modification, Law of the Sea, Nuclear Test Ban, Ozone Layer Protection, Ship Pollution, Tropical Timber 83, Tropical Timber 94
signed, but not ratified: Marine Life Conservation

Geography - note: Lake Volta is the world's largest artificial lake; northeasterly harmattan wind (January to March)

People

Population: 18,887,626 (July 1999 est.)
Age structure:
0-14 years: 42% (male 4,020,493; female 3,982,816)
15-64 years: 54% (male 5,050,736; female 5,231,951)
65 years and over: 4% (male 284,423; female 317,207) (1999 est.)
Population growth rate: 2.05% (1999 est.)
Birth rate: 31.79 births/1,000 population (1999 est.)
Death rate: 10.4 deaths/1,000 population (1999 est.)
Net migration rate: -0.88 migrant(s)/1,000 population (1999 est.)
Sex ratio:
at birth: 1.03 male(s)/female
under 15 years: 1.01 male(s)/female
15-64 years: 0.97 male(s)/female
65 years and over: 0.9 male(s)/female
total population: 0.98 male(s)/female (1999 est.)
Infant mortality rate: 76.15 deaths/1,000 live births (1999 est.)
Life expectancy at birth:
total population: 57.14 years
male: 55.08 years
female: 59.27 years (1999 est.)
Total fertility rate: 4.11 children born/woman (1999 est.)
Nationality:
noun: Ghanaian(s)
adjective: Ghanaian
Ethnic groups: black African 99.8% (major tribes - Akan 44%, Moshi-Dagomba 16%, Ewe 13%, Ga 8%), European and other 0.2%
Religions: indigenous beliefs 38%, Muslim 30%, Christian 24%, other 8%
Languages: English (official), African languages (including Akan, Moshi-Dagomba, Ewe, and Ga)
Literacy:
definition: age 15 and over can read and write
total population: 64.5%
male: 75.9%
female: 53.5% (1995 est.)

Government

Country name:
conventional long form: Republic of Ghana

conventional short form: Ghana
former: Gold Coast
Data code: GH
Government type: constitutional democracy
Capital: Accra
Administrative divisions: 10 regions; Ashanti, Brong-Ahafo, Central, Eastern, Greater Accra, Northern, Upper East, Upper West, Volta, Western
Independence: 6 March 1957 (from UK)
National holiday: Independence Day, 6 March (1957)
Constitution: new constitution approved 28 April 1992
Legal system: based on English common law and customary law; has not accepted compulsory ICJ jurisdiction
Suffrage: 18 years of age; universal
Executive branch:
chief of state: President Jerry John RAWLINGS (since 7 January 1993); Vice President John Evans Atta MILLS (since 7 January 1993); note - the president is both the chief of state and head of government
head of government: President Jerry John RAWLINGS (since 7 January 1993); Vice President John Evans Atta MILLS (since 7 January 1993); note - the president is both the chief of state and head of government
cabinet: Council of Ministers; president nominates members subject to approval by the Parliament
elections: president and vice president elected on the same ticket by popular vote for four-year terms; election last held 7 December 1996 (next to be held NA 2000)
election results: Jerry John RAWLINGS reelected president; percent of vote - RAWLINGS 57%
Legislative branch: unicameral Parliament (200 seats; members are elected by direct popular vote to serve four-year terms)
elections: last held 7 December 1996 (next to be held NA December 2000)
election results: percent of vote by party - NA; seats by party - NDC 133, NPP 61, PCP 5, PNC 1
Judicial branch: Supreme Court
Political parties and leaders: National Democratic Congress or NDC [Dr. Huudu YAHAYA, general secretary]; New Patriotic Party or NPP [Peter Ala ADJETY]; People's Heritage Party or PHP [Emmanuel Alexander ERSKINE]; National Convention Party or NCP [Sarpong KUMA-KUMA]; Every Ghanian Living Everywhere or EGLE [Owuraku AMOFA, chairman]; People's Convention Party or PCP [P. K. DONKOH-AYIFI, acting chairman]; People's National Convention or PNC [Edward MAHAMA]
International organization participation: ACP, AfDB, C, CCC, ECA, ECOWAS, FAO, G-24, G-77, IAEA, IBRD, ICAO, ICFTU, ICRM, IDA, IFAD, IFC, IFRCS, ILO, IMF, IMO, Inmarsat, Intelsat, Interpol, IOC, IOM (observer), ISO, ITU, MINURSO, NAM, OAU, OPCW, UN, UNCTAD, UNESCO, UNIDO, UNIFIL, UNIKOM, UNMIBH, UNMOP, UNMOT, UNPREDEP, UNU, UPU, WCL, WFTU, WHO, WIPO,

WMO, WToO, WTrO
Diplomatic representation in the US:
chief of mission: Ambassador Kobena KOOMSON
chancery: 3512 International Drive NW, Washington, DC 20008
telephone: [1] (202) 686-4520
FAX: [1] (202) 686-4527
consulate(s) general: New York
Diplomatic representation from the US:
chief of mission: Ambassador Kathryn Dee ROBINSON
embassy: Ring Road East, East of Danquah Circle, Accra
mailing address: P. O. Box 194, Accra
telephone: [233] (21) 775348
FAX: [233] (21) 776008
Flag description: three equal horizontal bands of red (top), yellow, and green with a large black five-pointed star centered in the yellow band; uses the popular pan-African colors of Ethiopia; similar to the flag of Bolivia, which has a coat of arms centered in the yellow band

Economy

Economy - overview: Well endowed with natural resources, Ghana has twice the per capita output of the poorer countries in West Africa. Even so, Ghana remains heavily dependent on international financial and technical assistance. Gold, timber, and cocoa production are major sources of foreign exchange. The domestic economy continues to revolve around subsistence agriculture, which accounts for 41% of GDP and employs 60% of the work force, mainly small landholders. In 1995-97, Ghana made mixed progress under a three-year structural adjustment program in cooperation with the IMF. On the minus side, public sector wage increases and regional peacekeeping commitments have led to continued inflationary deficit financing, depreciation of the cedi, and rising public discontent with Ghana's austerity measures. Power shortages also helped slow growth in 1998.
GDP: purchasing power parity - $33.6 billion (1998 est.)
GDP - real growth rate: 3% (1998 est.)
GDP - per capita: purchasing power parity - $1,800 (1998 est.)
GDP - composition by sector:
agriculture: 41%
industry: 14%
services: 45% (1996 est.)
Population below poverty line: 31.4% (1992 est.)
Household income or consumption by percentage share:
lowest 10%: 3.4%
highest 10%: 27.3% (1992)
Inflation rate (consumer prices): 27.7% (1997 est.)
Labor force: NA
Labor force - by occupation: agriculture and fishing 61%, industry 10%, services 29% (1996 est.)
Unemployment rate: 20% (1997 est.)
Budget:

Ghana (continued)

revenues: $1.39 billion
expenditures: $1.47 billion, including capital expenditures of $370 million (1996 est.)
Industries: mining, lumbering, light manufacturing, aluminum smelting, food processing
Industrial production growth rate: 4.2% (1996 est.)
Electricity - production: 6.1 billion kWh (1996)
Electricity - production by source:
fossil fuel: 0.66%
hydro: 99.34%
nuclear: 0%
other: 0% (1996)
Electricity - consumption: 5.88 billion kWh (1996)
Electricity - exports: 225 million kWh (1996)
Electricity - imports: 5 million kWh (1996)
Agriculture - products: cocoa, rice, coffee, cassava (tapioca), peanuts, corn, shea nuts, bananas; timber
Exports: $1.5 billion (f.o.b., 1997)
Exports - commodities: gold 39%, cocoa 35%, timber 9.4%, tuna, bauxite, aluminum, manganese ore, and diamonds (1996 est.)
Exports - partners: UK, Germany, US, Netherlands, Japan, Nigeria
Imports: $2.1 billion (f.o.b., 1997)
Imports - commodities: capital equipment, petroleum, consumer goods, foods, intermediate goods
Imports - partners: UK, Nigeria, US, Germany, Japan, Netherlands
Debt - external: $5.2 billion (1996 est.)
Economic aid - recipient: $477.3 million (1995)
Currency: 1 new cedi (C) = 100 pesewas
Exchange rates: new cedis per US$1 - 2,324.70 (September 1998), 2,050.17 (1997), 1,637.23 (1996), 1,200.43 (1995), 956.71 (1994)
Fiscal year: calendar year

Communications

Telephones: 100,000 (1997 est.)
Telephone system: poor to fair system
domestic: primarily microwave radio relay
international: satellite earth station - 1 Intelsat (Atlantic Ocean)
Radio broadcast stations: AM 4, FM 23, shortwave 0 (1997)
Radios: 12.5 million (1997 est.)
Television broadcast stations: 7 (in addition, there are eight repeaters) (1997)
Televisions: 1.9 million (1997 est.)

Transportation

Railways:
total: 953 km (undergoing major rehabilitation)
narrow gauge: 953 km 1.067-m gauge (32 km double track) (1997 est.)
Highways:
total: 39,409 km
paved: 11,653 km (including 30 km of expressways)
unpaved: 27,756 km (1997 est.)
Waterways: Volta, Ankobra, and Tano Rivers

provide 168 km of perennial navigation for launches and lighters; Lake Volta provides 1,125 km of arterial and feeder waterways
Pipelines: 0 km
Ports and harbors: Takoradi, Tema
Merchant marine:
total: 5 ships (1,000 GRT or over) totaling 10,552 GRT/14,839 DWT
ships by type: oil tanker 2, refrigerated cargo 3 (1998 est.)
Airports: 12 (1998 est.)
Airports - with paved runways:
total: 6
2,438 to 3,047 m: 1
1,524 to 2,437 m: 3
914 to 1,523 m: 2 (1998 est.)
Airports - with unpaved runways:
total: 6
1,524 to 2,437 m: 1
914 to 1,523 m: 3
under 914 m: 2 (1998 est.)

Military

Military branches: Army, Navy, Air Force, National Police Force, Palace Guard, Civil Defense
Military manpower - military age: 18 years of age
Military manpower - availability:
males age 15-49: 4,520,125 (1999 est.)
Military manpower - fit for military service:
males age 15-49: 2,507,954 (1999 est.)
Military manpower - reaching military age annually:
males: 184,360 (1999 est.)
Military expenditures - dollar figure: $53 million (1999)
Military expenditures - percent of GDP: 0.7% (1999)

Transnational Issues

Disputes - international: none
Illicit drugs: illicit producer of cannabis for the international drug trade; transit hub for Southwest and Southeast Asian heroin and South American cocaine destined for Europe and the US

Gibraltar
(overseas territory of the UK)

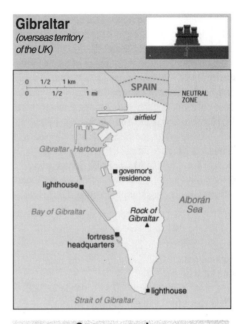

Geography

Location: Southwestern Europe, bordering the Strait of Gibraltar, which links the Mediterranean Sea and the North Atlantic Ocean, on the southern coast of Spain
Geographic coordinates: 36 11 N, 5 22 W
Map references: Europe
Area:
total: 6.5 sq km
land: 6.5 sq km
water: 0 sq km
Area - comparative: about 11 times the size of The Mall in Washington, DC
Land boundaries:
total: 1.2 km
border countries: Spain 1.2 km
Coastline: 12 km
Maritime claims:
territorial sea: 3 nm
Climate: Mediterranean with mild winters and warm summers
Terrain: a narrow coastal lowland borders the Rock of Gibraltar
Elevation extremes:
lowest point: Mediterranean Sea 0 m
highest point: Rock of Gibraltar 426 m
Natural resources: NEGL
Land use:
arable land: NA%
permanent crops: NA%
permanent pastures: NA%
forests and woodland: NA%
other: 100% (1993 est.)
Irrigated land: NA sq km
Natural hazards: NA
Environment - current issues: limited natural freshwater resources; large concrete or natural rock water catchments collect rain water
Environment - international agreements:
party to: NA

signed, but not ratified: NA
Geography - note: strategic location on Strait of Gibraltar that links the North Atlantic Ocean and Mediterranean Sea

People

Population: 29,165 (July 1999 est.)
Age structure:
0-14 years: 20% (male 3,129; female 2,749)
15-64 years: 66% (male 10,888; female 8,247)
65 years and over: 14% (male 1,729; female 2,423) (1999 est.)
Population growth rate: 0.39% (1999 est.)
Birth rate: 12.65 births/1,000 population (1999 est.)
Death rate: 8.81 deaths/1,000 population (1999 est.)
Net migration rate: 0.03 migrant(s)/1,000 population (1999 est.)
Sex ratio:
at birth: 1.05 male(s)/female
under 15 years: 1.14 male(s)/female
15-64 years: 1.32 male(s)/female
65 years and over: 0.71 male(s)/female
total population: 1.17 male(s)/female (1999 est.)
Infant mortality rate: 6.47 deaths/1,000 live births (1999 est.)
Life expectancy at birth:
total population: 78.37 years
male: 75.1 years
female: 81.81 years (1999 est.)
Total fertility rate: 2.16 children born/woman (1999 est.)
Nationality:
noun: Gibraltarian(s)
adjective: Gibraltar
Ethnic groups: Italian, English, Maltese, Portuguese, Spanish
Religions: Roman Catholic 74%, Protestant 11% (Church of England 8%, other 3%), Muslim 8%, Jewish 2%, none or other 5% (1981)
Languages: English (used in schools and for official purposes), Spanish, Italian, Portuguese, Russian
Literacy:
definition: NA
total population: above 95%
male: NA%
female: NA%

Government

Country name:
conventional long form: none
conventional short form: Gibraltar
Data code: GI
Dependency status: overseas territory of the UK
Government type: NA
Capital: Gibraltar
Administrative divisions: none (overseas territory of the UK)
Independence: none (overseas territory of the UK)
National holiday: Commonwealth Day (second Monday of March)
Constitution: 30 May 1969

Legal system: English law
Suffrage: 18 years of age; universal, plus other UK subjects who have been residents six months or more
Executive branch:
chief of state: Queen ELIZABETH II (since 6 February 1952), represented by Governor and Commander-in-Chief, the Right Honorable Sir Richard LUCE (since 24 February 1997)
head of government: Chief Minister Peter CARUANA (since 17 May 1996)
cabinet: Council of Ministers appointed from among the elected members of the House of Assembly by the governor in consultation with the chief minister
note: there is also a Gibraltar Council that advises the governor
elections: none; the monarch is hereditary; governor appointed by the monarch; chief minister appointed by the governor
Legislative branch: unicameral House of Assembly (18 seats - 15 elected, on for the Speaker, and two ex officio; members are elected by popular vote to serve four-year terms)
elections: last held 16 May 1996 (next to be held NA May 2000)
election results: percent of vote by party - SD 53%, SL 42%, NP 3%; seats by party - SD 8, SL 7
Judicial branch: Supreme Court; Court of Appeal
Political parties and leaders: Gibraltar Socialist Labor Party or SL [Joe BOSSANO]; Gibraltar Labor Party/Association for the Advancement of Civil Rights or GCL/AACR [Adolfo CANEPA]; Gibraltar Social Democrats or SD [Peter CARUANA]; Gibraltar National Party or NP [Joe GARCIA]
Political pressure groups and leaders: Housewives Association; Chamber of Commerce; Gibraltar Representatives Organization
International organization participation: Interpol (subbureau)
Diplomatic representation in the US: none (overseas territory of the UK)
Diplomatic representation from the US: none (overseas territory of the UK)
Flag description: two horizontal bands of white (top, double width) and red with a three-towered red castle in the center of the white band; hanging from the castle gate is a gold key centered in the red band

Economy

Economy - overview: Gibraltar benefits from an extensive shipping trade, offshore banking, and its position as an international conference center. The British military presence has been sharply reduced and now contributes about 11% to the local economy. The financial sector accounts for 15% of GDP; tourism (more than 5 million visitors in 1995), shipping services fees, and duties on consumer goods also generate revenue. Because more than 70% of the economy is in the public sector, changes in government spending have a major impact on the level of employment.
GDP: purchasing power parity - $500 million (1997 est.)

GDP - real growth rate: NA%
GDP - per capita: purchasing power parity - $17,500 (1997 est.)
GDP - composition by sector:
agriculture: NA%
industry: NA%
services: NA%
Population below poverty line: NA%
Household income or consumption by percentage share:
lowest 10%: NA%
highest 10%: NA%
Inflation rate (consumer prices): 2.1% (1996)
Labor force: 14,800 (including non-Gibraltar laborers)
Labor force - by occupation: services 60%, industry 40%, agriculture NEGL%
Unemployment rate: 13.5% (1996)
Budget:
revenues: $111.6 million
expenditures: $115.6 million, including capital expenditures of $NA (FY95/96)
Industries: tourism, banking and finance, ship-building and repairing; support to large UK naval and air bases; tobacco, mineral water, beer, canned fish
Industrial production growth rate: NA%
Electricity - production: 85 million kWh (1996)
Electricity - production by source:
fossil fuel: 100%
hydro: 0%
nuclear: 0%
other: 0% (1996)
Electricity - consumption: 85 million kWh (1996)
Electricity - exports: 0 kWh (1996)
Electricity - imports: 0 kWh (1996)
Agriculture - products: none
Exports: $83.7 million (f.o.b., 1995)
Exports - commodities: (principally reexports) petroleum 51%, manufactured goods 41%, other 8%
Exports - partners: UK, Morocco, Portugal, Netherlands, Spain, US, FRG
Imports: $778 million (c.i.f., 1995)
Imports - commodities: fuels, manufactured goods, and foodstuffs
Imports - partners: UK, Spain, Japan, Netherlands
Debt - external: $NA
Economic aid - recipient: $NA
Currency: 1 Gibraltar pound (£G) = 100 pence
Exchange rates: Gibraltar pounds (£G) per US$1 - 0.6057 (January 1999), 0.6037 (1998), 0.6106 (1997), 0.6403 (1996), 0.6335 (1995), 0.6529 (1994); note - the Gibraltar pound is at par with the British pound
Fiscal year: 1 July - 30 June

Communications

Telephones: 19,356 (1994)
Telephone system: adequate, automatic domestic system and adequate international facilities
domestic: automatic exchange facilities
international: radiotelephone; microwave radio relay; satellite earth station - 1 Intelsat (Atlantic Ocean)

Gibraltar *(continued)*

Radio broadcast stations: AM 1, FM 6, shortwave 0

Radios: NA

Television broadcast stations: 1 (in addition, there are 3 low-power repeaters) (1997)

Televisions: NA

Transportation

Railways:

total: NA km; 1.000-m gauge system in dockyard area only

Highways:

total: 49.9 km

paved: 49.9 km

unpaved: 0 km

Pipelines: 0 km

Ports and harbors: Gibraltar

Merchant marine:

total: 18 ships (1,000 GRT or over) totaling 346m951 GRT/588,765 DWT

ships by type: chemical tanker 2, container 4, oil tanker 11, roll-on/roll-off cargo 1 (1998 est.)

Airports: 1 (1998 est.)

Airports - with paved runways:

total: 1

1,524 to 2,437 m: 1 (1998 est.)

Military

Military branches: British Army, Royal Navy, Royal Air Force

Military - note: defense is the responsibility of the UK

Transnational Issues

Disputes - international: source of friction between Spain and the UK

Glorioso Islands
(possession of France)

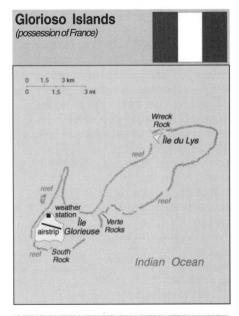

Geography

Location: Southern Africa, group of islands in the Indian Ocean, northwest of Madagascar

Geographic coordinates: 11 30 S, 47 20 E

Map references: Africa

Area:

total: 5 sq km

land: 5 sq km

water: 0 sq km

note: includes Ile Glorieuse, Ile du Lys, Verte Rocks, Wreck Rock, and South Rock

Area - comparative: about eight times the size of The Mall in Washington, DC

Land boundaries: 0 km

Coastline: 35.2 km

Maritime claims:

exclusive economic zone: 200 nm

territorial sea: 12 nm

Climate: tropical

Terrain: NA

Elevation extremes:

lowest point: Indian Ocean 0 m

highest point: unnamed location 12 m

Natural resources: guano, coconuts

Land use:

arable land: NA%

permanent crops: NA%

permanent pastures: NA%

forests and woodland: NA%

other: 100% (all lush vegetation and coconut palms)

Irrigated land: 0 sq km (1993)

Natural hazards: periodic cyclones

Environment - current issues: NA

People

Population: uninhabited

Government

Country name:

conventional long form: none

conventional short form: Glorioso Islands

local long form: none

local short form: Iles Glorieuses

Data code: GO

Dependency status: possession of France; administered by a high commissioner of the Republic, resident in Reunion

Legal system: NA

Diplomatic representation in the US: none (possession of France)

Diplomatic representation from the US: none (possession of France)

Flag description: the flag of France is used

Economy

Economy - overview: no economic activity

Transportation

Ports and harbors: none; offshore anchorage only

Airports: 1 (1998 est.)

Airports - with unpaved runways:

total: 1

914 to 1,523 m: 1 (1998 est.)

Military

Military - note: defense is the responsibility of France

Transnational Issues

Disputes - international: claimed by Madagascar

Greece

Geography

Location: Southern Europe, bordering the Aegean Sea, Ionian Sea, and the Mediterranean Sea, between Albania and Turkey
Geographic coordinates: 39 00 N, 22 00 E
Map references: Europe
Area:
total: 131,940 sq km
land: 130,800 sq km
water: 1,140 sq km
Area - comparative: slightly smaller than Alabama
Land boundaries:
total: 1,210 km
border countries: Albania 282 km, Bulgaria 494 km, Turkey 206 km, The Former Yugoslav Republic of Macedonia 228 km
Coastline: 13,676 km
Maritime claims:
continental shelf: 200-m depth or to the depth of exploitation
territorial sea: 6 nm
Climate: temperate; mild, wet winters; hot, dry summers
Terrain: mostly mountains with ranges extending into sea as peninsulas or chains of islands
Elevation extremes:
lowest point: Mediterranean Sea 0 m
highest point: Mount Olympus 2,917 m
Natural resources: bauxite, lignite, magnesite, petroleum, marble
Land use:
arable land: 19%
permanent crops: 8%
permanent pastures: 41%
forests and woodland: 20%
other: 12% (1993 est.)
Irrigated land: 13,140 sq km (1993 est.)
Natural hazards: severe earthquakes
Environment - current issues: air pollution; water pollution

Environment - international agreements:
party to: Air Pollution, Air Pollution-Nitrogen Oxides, Air Pollution-Sulphur 94, Antarctic-Environmental Protocol, Antarctic Treaty, Biodiversity, Climate Change, Desertification, Endangered Species, Environmental Modification, Hazardous Wastes, Law of the Sea, Marine Dumping, Nuclear Test Ban, Ozone Layer Protection, Ship Pollution, Tropical Timber 83, Tropical Timber 94, Wetlands
signed, but not ratified: Air Pollution-Persistent Organic Pollutants, Air Pollution-Volatile Organic Compounds, Climate Change-Kyoto Protocol
Geography - note: strategic location dominating the Aegean Sea and southern approach to Turkish Straits; a peninsular country, possessing an archipelago of about 2,000 islands

People

Population: 10,707,135 (July 1999 est.)
Age structure:
0-14 years: 16% (male 878,349; female 818,311)
15-64 years: 67% (male 3,619,982; female 3,587,591)
65 years and over: 17% (male 799,053; female 1,003,849) (1999 est.)
Population growth rate: 0.41% (1999 est.)
Birth rate: 9.54 births/1,000 population (1999 est.)
Death rate: 9.44 deaths/1,000 population (1999 est.)
Net migration rate: 4.04 migrant(s)/1,000 population (1999 est.)
Sex ratio:
at birth: 1.07 male(s)/female
under 15 years: 1.07 male(s)/female
15-64 years: 1.01 male(s)/female
65 years and over: 0.8 male(s)/female
total population: 0.98 male(s)/female (1999 est.)
Infant mortality rate: 7.13 deaths/1,000 live births (1999 est.)
Life expectancy at birth:
total population: 78.43 years
male: 75.87 years
female: 81.18 years (1999 est.)
Total fertility rate: 1.3 children born/woman (1999 est.)
Nationality:
noun: Greek(s)
adjective: Greek
Ethnic groups: Greek 98%, other 2%
note: the Greek Government states there are no ethnic divisions in Greece
Religions: Greek Orthodox 98%, Muslim 1.3%, other 0.7%
Languages: Greek (official), English, French
Literacy:
definition: age 15 and over can read and write
total population: 95%
male: 98%
female: 93% (1991 est.)

Government

Country name:
conventional long form: Hellenic Republic

conventional short form: Greece
local long form: Elliniki Dhimokratia
local short form: Ellas or Ellada
former: Kingdom of Greece
Data code: GR
Government type: parliamentary republic; monarchy rejected by referendum 8 December 1974
Capital: Athens
Administrative divisions: 51 prefectures (nomoi, singular - nomos)and 1 autonomous region*; Ayion Oros* (Mt. Athos), Aitolia kai Akarnania, Akhaia, Argolis, Arkadhia, Arta, Attiki, Dhodhekanisos, Drama, Evritania, Evros, Evvoia, Florina, Fokis, Fthiotis, Grevena, Ilia, Imathia, Ioannina, Irakleion, Kardhitsa, Kastoria, Kavala, Kefallinia, Kerkyra, Khalkidhiki, Khania, Khios, Kikladhes, Kilkis, Korinthia, Kozani, Lakonia, Larisa, Lasithi, Lesvos, Levkas, Magnisia, Messinia, Pella, Pieria, Preveza, Rethimni, Rodhopi, Samos, Serrai, Thesprotia, Thessaloniki, Trikala, Voiotia, Xanthi, Zakinthos
Independence: 1829 (from the Ottoman Empire)
National holiday: Independence Day, 25 March (1821) (proclamation of the war of independence)
Constitution: 11 June 1975
Legal system: based on codified Roman law; judiciary divided into civil, criminal, and administrative courts
Suffrage: 18 years of age; universal and compulsory
Executive branch:
chief of state: President Konstandinos (Kostis) STEPHANOPOULOS (since 10 March 1995)
head of government: Prime Minister Konstandinos SIMITIS (since 19 January 1996)
cabinet: Cabinet appointed by the president on the recommendation of the prime minister
elections: president elected by Parliament for a five-year term; election last held 10 March 1995 (next to be held by NA March 2000); prime minister appointed by the president
election results: Konstandinos STEPHANOPOULOS elected president; percent of Parliament vote - NA
Legislative branch: unicameral Parliament or Vouli ton Ellinon (300 seats; members are elected by direct popular vote to serve four-year terms)
elections: elections last held 22 September 1996 (next to be held by NA September 2000)
election results: percent of vote by party - PASOK 41.5%, ND 38.1%, KKE 5.6%, Coalition of the Left and Progress 5.1%, DIKKI 4.4%, Political Spring 2.9%; seats by party - PASOK 162, ND 108, KKE 11, Coalition of the Left and Progress 10, DIKKI 9; note - seating has subsequently changed as a result of disciplinary actions by PASOK, ND, and DIKKI; 1998 seating is PASOK 162, ND 105, KKE 11, Coalition of the Left and Progress 10, DIKKI 8, independents 4
Judicial branch: Supreme Judicial Court, judges appointed for life by the president after consultation with a judicial council; Special Supreme Tribunal, judges appointed for life by the president after consultation with a judicial council
Political parties and leaders: New Democracy or ND (conservative) [Konstandinos KARAMANLIS];

Greece (continued)

Panhellenic Socialist Movement or PASOK [Konstandinos SIMITIS]; Communist Party of Greece or KKE [Aleka PAPARIGA]; Political Spring [Andonis SAMARAS]; Coalition of the Left and Progress (Synaspismos) [Nikolaos KONSTANDOPOULOS]; Democratic Social Movement or DIKKI [Dhimitrios TSOVOLAS]; Rainbow Coalition [Pavlos VOSKOPOULOS]

International organization participation: Australia Group, BIS, BSEC, CCC, CE, CERN, EAPC, EBRD, ECE, EIB, EU, FAO, G- 6, IAEA, IBRD, ICAO, ICC, ICFTU, ICRM, IDA, IEA, IFAD, IFC, IFRCS, IHO, ILO, IMF, IMO, Inmarsat, Intelsat, Interpol, IOC, IOM, ISO, ITU, MINURSO, MTCR, NAM (guest), NATO, NEA, NSG, OAS (observer), OECD, OPCW, OSCE, PCA, UN, UNCTAD, UNESCO, UNHCR, UNIDO, UNIKOM, UNMIBH, UNOMIG, UPU, WEU, WFTU, WHO, WIPO, WMO, WToO, WTrO, ZC

Diplomatic representation in the US:
chief of mission: Ambassador Alexandre PHILON
chancery: 2221 Massachusetts Avenue NW, Washington, DC 20008
telephone: [1] (202) 939-5800
FAX: [1] (202) 939-5824
consulate(s) general: Boston, Chicago, Los Angeles, New York, and San Francisco
consulate(s): Atlanta, Houston, and New Orleans

Diplomatic representation from the US:
chief of mission: Ambassador R. Nicholas BURNS
embassy: 91 Vasilissis Sophias Boulevard, 10160 Athens
mailing address: PSC 108, APO AE 09842-0108
telephone: [30] (1) 721-2951
FAX: [30] (1) 645-6282
consulate(s) general: Thessaloniki

Flag description: nine equal horizontal stripes of blue alternating with white; there is a blue square in the upper hoist-side corner bearing a white cross; the cross symbolizes Greek Orthodoxy, the established religion of the country

Economy

Economy - overview: Greece has a mixed capitalist economy with the public sector accounting for about half of GDP, although the government plans to privatize some leading state enterprises. Tourism is a key industry, providing a large portion of GDP and foreign exchange earnings. Greece is a major beneficiary of EU aid, equal to about 4% of GDP. The economy has improved steadily over the last few years, as the government has tightened policy with the goal of qualifying Greece to join the EU's single currency (the euro) in 2001. In particular, Greece has cut its budget deficit to just over 2% of GDP and tightened monetary policy, with the result that inflation fell below 4% by the end of 1998 - the lowest rate in 26 years. The outlook for 1999 is good with the budget deficit and inflation both expected to decline further, while GDP growth stays near 3% and the current account deficit remains below 2% of GDP.

GDP: purchasing power parity - $143 billion (1998 est.)

GDP - real growth rate: 3% (1998 est.)
GDP - per capita: purchasing power parity - $13,400 (1998 est.)
GDP - composition by sector:
agriculture: 8.5%
industry: 23.5%
services: 68% (1996)
Population below poverty line: NA%
Household income or consumption by percentage share:
lowest 10%: NA%
highest 10%: NA%
Inflation rate (consumer prices): 3.9% (1998 est.)
Labor force: 4.28 million (1998)
Labor force - by occupation: services 59.2%, agriculture 19.8%, industry 21% (1998)
Unemployment rate: 10% (1998 est.)
Budget:
revenues: $45 billion
expenditures: $47.6 billion, including capital expenditures of $NA (1998 est.)
Industries: tourism; food and tobacco processing, textiles; chemicals, metal products; mining, petroleum
Industrial production growth rate: 7.3% (1998 est.)
Electricity - production: 40.028 billion kWh (1996)
Electricity - production by source:
fossil fuel: 89.16%
hydro: 10.75%
nuclear: 0%
other: 0.09% (1996)
Electricity - consumption: 41.388 billion kWh (1996)
Electricity - exports: 1.3 billion kWh (1996)
Electricity - imports: 2.66 billion kWh (1996)
Agriculture - products: wheat, corn, barley, sugar beets, olives, tomatoes, wine, tobacco, potatoes; beef, dairy products
Exports: $12.4 billion (f.o.b., 1998)
Exports - commodities: manufactured goods, foodstuffs, fuels (1998)
Exports - partners: EU 56% (Germany 25%, Italy 11%, UK 8%, France 6%), US 16% (1997)
Imports: $27.7 billion (c.i.f., 1998)
Imports - commodities: manufactured goods, foodstuffs, fuels, chemicals (1998)
Imports - partners: EU 61% (Italy 16%, Germany 16%, France 8%, UK 7%, Netherlands 5%) US 11% (1997)
Debt - external: $40.8 billion (1997)
Economic aid - recipient: $5.4 billion from EU (1997 est.)
Currency: 1 drachma (Dr) = 100 lepta
Exchange rates: drachmae (Dr) per US$1 - 278.78 (January 1999), 295.53 (1998), 273.06 (1997), 240.71 (1996), 231.66 (1995), 242.60 (1994)
Fiscal year: calendar year

Communications

Telephones: 5,571,293 (1993 est.)
Telephone system: adequate, modern networks reach all areas; microwave radio relay carries most traffic; extensive open-wire network; submarine cables to off-shore islands
domestic: microwave radio relay, open wire, and submarine cable
international: tropospheric scatter; 8 submarine cables; satellite earth stations - 2 Intelsat (1 Atlantic Ocean and 1 Indian Ocean), 1 Eutelsat, and 1 Inmarsat (Indian Ocean region)
Radio broadcast stations: AM 29, FM 17 (repeaters 20), shortwave 0
Radios: NA
Television broadcast stations: 64 (in addition, there are about 1,000 low-power repeaters and two stations in the US armed forces network) (1997)
Televisions: 2.3 million (1993 est.)

Transportation

Railways:
total: 2,548 km
standard gauge: 1,565 km 1.435-m gauge (36 km electrified; 23 km double track)
narrow gauge: 961 km 1.000-m gauge; 22 km 0.750-m gauge (a rack type railway for steep grades)
Highways:
total: 117,000 km
paved: 107,406 km (including 470 km of expressways)
unpaved: 9,594 km (1996 est.)
Waterways: 80 km; system consists of three coastal canals; including the Corinth Canal (6 km) which crosses the Isthmus of Corinth connecting the Gulf of Corinth with the Saronic Gulf and shortens the sea voyage from the Adriatic to Peiraiefs (Piraeus) by 325 km; and three unconnected rivers
Pipelines: crude oil 26 km; petroleum products 547 km
Ports and harbors: Alexandroupolis, Elefsis, Irakleion (Crete), Kavala, Kerkyra, Chalkis, Igoumenitsa, Lavrion, Patrai, Peiraiefs (Piraeus), Thessaloniki, Volos
Merchant marine:
total: 810 ships (1,000 GRT or over) totaling 24,798,431 GRT/44,056,618 DWT
ships by type: bulk 307, cargo 66, chemical tanker 19, combination bulk 9, combination ore/oil 12, container 45, liquefied gas tanker 5, multifunction large-load carrier 1, oil tanker 229, passenger 15, passenger-cargo 2, refrigerated cargo 4, roll-on/ roll-off cargo 17, short-sea passenger 76, specialized tanker 3 (1998 est.)
Airports: 78 (1998 est.)
Airports - with paved runways:
total: 63
over 3,047 m: 5
2,438 to 3,047 m: 15
1,524 to 2,437 m: 18
914 to 1,523 m: 16
under 914 m: 9 (1998 est.)
Airports - with unpaved runways:
total: 15
1,524 to 2,437 m: 1
914 to 1,523 m: 3

Greece (continued)

under 914 m: 11 (1998 est.)
Heliports: 2 (1998 est.)

Military

Military branches: Hellenic Army, Hellenic Navy, Hellenic Air Force, National Guard, Police
Military manpower - military age: 21 years of age
Military manpower - availability:
males age 15-49: 2,707,628 (1999 est.)
Military manpower - fit for military service:
males age 15-49: 2,071,670 (1999 est.)
Military manpower - reaching military age annually:
males: 79,376 (1999 est.)
Military expenditures - dollar figure: $4.04 billion (1998 est.)
Military expenditures - percent of GDP: NA%

Transnational Issues

Disputes - international: complex maritime, air, and territorial disputes with Turkey in Aegean Sea; Cyprus question with Turkey; dispute with The Former Yugoslav Republic of Macedonia over name; in September 1995, Skopje and Athens signed an interim accord resolving their dispute over symbols and certain constitutional provisions; Athens also lifted its economic embargo on The Former Yugoslav Republic of Macedonia
Illicit drugs: a gateway to Europe for traffickers smuggling cannabis and heroin from the Middle East and Southwest Asia to the West and precursor chemicals to the East; some South American cocaine transits or is consumed in Greece

Greenland
(part of the Kingdom of Denmark)

Geography

Location: Northern North America, island between the Arctic Ocean and the North Atlantic Ocean, northeast of Canada
Geographic coordinates: 72 00 N, 40 00 W
Map references: Arctic Region
Area:
total: 2,175,600 sq km
land: 2,175,600 sq km (341,600 sq km ice-free, 1,834,000 sq km ice-covered) (est.)
Area - comparative: slightly more than three times the size of Texas
Land boundaries: 0 km
Coastline: 44,087 km
Maritime claims:
exclusive fishing zone: 200 nm
territorial sea: 3 nm
Climate: arctic to subarctic; cool summers, cold winters
Terrain: flat to gradually sloping icecap covers all but a narrow, mountainous, barren, rocky coast
Elevation extremes:
lowest point: Atlantic Ocean 0 m
highest point: Gunnbjorn 3,700 m

Natural resources: zinc, lead, iron ore, coal, molybdenum, gold, platinum, uranium, fish, seals, whales
Land use:
arable land: 0%
permanent crops: 0%
permanent pastures: 1%
forests and woodland: 0%
other: 99% (1993 est.)
Irrigated land: NA sq km
Natural hazards: continuous permafrost over northern two-thirds of the island
Environment - current issues: protection of the arctic environment; preservation of their traditional way of life, including whaling; note - Greenland participates actively in Inuit Circumpolar Conference (ICC)
Environment - international agreements:
party to: NA
signed, but not ratified: NA
Geography - note: dominates North Atlantic Ocean between North America and Europe; sparse population confined to small settlements along coast

People

Population: 59,827 (July 1999 est.)
Age structure:
0-14 years: 26% (male 7,789; female 7,728)
15-64 years: 68% (male 22,248; female 18,678)
65 years and over: 6% (male 1,562; female 1,822) (1999 est.)
Population growth rate: 0.84% (1999 est.)
Birth rate: 15.23 births/1,000 population (1999 est.)
Death rate: 6.79 deaths/1,000 population (1999 est.)
Net migration rate: 0 migrant(s)/1,000 population (1999 est.)
Sex ratio:
at birth: 1 male(s)/female
under 15 years: 1.01 male(s)/female
15-64 years: 1.19 male(s)/female
65 years and over: 0.86 male(s)/female
total population: 1.12 male(s)/female (1999 est.)
Infant mortality rate: 20.06 deaths/1,000 live births (1999 est.)
Life expectancy at birth:
total population: 70.1 years
male: 65.98 years
female: 74.24 years (1999 est.)
Total fertility rate: 2.14 children born/woman (1999 est.)
Nationality:
noun: Greenlander(s)
adjective: Greenlandic
Ethnic groups: Greenlander 87% (Eskimos and Greenland-born whites), Danish and others 13%
Religions: Evangelical Lutheran
Languages: Eskimo dialects, Danish, Greenlandic (an Inuit dialect)
Literacy: NA
note: similar to Denmark proper

Greenland (continued)

Government

Country name:
conventional long form: none
conventional short form: Greenland
local long form: none
local short form: Kalaallit Nunaat
Data code: GL
Dependency status: part of the Kingdom of Denmark; self-governing overseas administrative division of Denmark since 1979
Government type: NA
Capital: Nuuk (Godthab)
Administrative divisions: 3 districts (landsdele); Avannaa (Nordgronland), Tunu (Ostgronland), Kitaa (Vestgronland)
Independence: none (part of the Kingdom of Denmark; self-governing overseas administrative division of Denmark since 1979)
National holiday: Birthday of the Queen, 16 April (1940)
Constitution: 5 June 1953 (Danish constitution)
Legal system: Danish
Suffrage: 18 years of age; universal
Executive branch:
chief of state: Queen MARGRETHE II of Denmark (since 14 January 1972), represented by High Commissioner Gunnar MARTENS (since NA 1995)
head of government: Prime Minister Jonathan MOTZFELDT (since NA September 1997)
cabinet: Landsstyre is formed from the Parliament on the basis of the strength of parties
elections: the monarch is hereditary; high commissioner appointed by the monarch; prime minister is elected by the Parliament (usually the leader of the majority party); election last held 11 March 1999 (next to be held NA 2003)
election results: Jonathan MOTZFELDT reelected prime minister; percent of parliamentary vote - 23 out of 31 votes
Legislative branch: unicameral Parliament or Landsting (31 seats; members are elected by popular vote on the basis of proportional representation to serve four-year terms)
elections: last held on 17 February 1999 (next to be held by NA 2003)
election results: percent of vote by party - Siumut 35.2%, Inuit Ataqatigiit 22%, Atassut Party 25.2%, Candidates' League 12.3%; seats by party - Siumut 11, Atassut Party 8, Inuit Ataqatigiit 7, Candidates' League 4, independent 1
note: 2 representatives were elected to the Danish Parliament or Folketing on NA March 1998 (next to be held by NA 2002); percent of vote by party - Siumut 35.6%, Atassut 35.2%; seats by party - Siumut 1, Atassut 1; Greenlandic representatives are affiliated with Danish political parties
Judicial branch: High Court or Landsret
Political parties and leaders: two-party ruling coalition; Siumut (Forward Party, a moderate socialist party that advocates more distinct Greenlandic identity and greater autonomy from Denmark) [Lars Emil JOHANSEN, chairman]; Inuit Ataqatigiit or IA (Eskimo Brotherhood, a Marxist-Leninist party that favors complete independence from Denmark rather than home rule) [Josef MOTZFELDT]; Atassut Party (Solidarity, a more conservative party that favors continuing close relations with Denmark) [Daniel SKIFTE]; Akulliit Party [Bjarne KREUTZMANN]; Issituup (Polar Party) [Nicolai HEINRICH]; Candidates' League [leader NA]
International organization participation: NC, NIB
Diplomatic representation in the US: none (self-governing overseas administrative division of Denmark)
Diplomatic representation from the US: none (self-governing overseas administrative division of Denmark)
Flag description: two equal horizontal bands of white (top) and red with a large disk slightly to the hoist side of center - the top half of the disk is red, the bottom half is white

Economy

Economy - overview: Greenland suffered negative economic growth in the early 1990s, but since 1993 the economy has improved. The Greenland Home Rule Government (GHRG) has pursued a light fiscal policy since the late 1980s which has helped create surpluses in the public budget and low inflation. Since 1990, Greenland has registered a foreign trade deficit following the closure of the last remaining lead and zinc mine in 1989. Greenland today is critically dependent on fishing and fish exports; the shrimp fishery is by far the largest income earner. Despite resumption of several interesting hydrocarbon and minerals exploration activities, it will take several years before production can materialize. Tourism is the only sector offering any near-term potential and even this is limited due to a short season and high costs. The public sector, including publicly owned enterprises and the municipalities, plays the dominant role in Greenland's economy. About half the government revenues come from grants from the Danish Government, an important supplement of GDP.
GDP: purchasing power parity - $945 million (1997 est.)
GDP - real growth rate: 0.6% (1997 est.)
GDP - per capita: purchasing power parity - $16,100 (1997 est.)
GDP - composition by sector:
agriculture: NA%
industry: NA%
services: NA%
Population below poverty line: NA%
Household income or consumption by percentage share:
lowest 10%: NA%
highest 10%: NA%
Inflation rate (consumer prices): 0.6% (1997 est.)
Labor force: 24,500 (1995 est.)
Unemployment rate: 10.5% (1995 est.)

Budget:
revenues: $706 million
expenditures: $697 million, including capital expenditures of $NA (1995)
Industries: fish processing (mainly shrimp), handicrafts, furs, small shipyards
Industrial production growth rate: NA%
Electricity - production: 245 million kWh (1996)
Electricity - production by source:
fossil fuel: 100%
hydro: 0%
nuclear: 0%
other: 0% (1996)
Electricity - consumption: 245 million kWh (1996)
Electricity - exports: 0 kWh (1996)
Electricity - imports: 0 kWh (1996)
Agriculture - products: forage crops, garden vegetables; sheep; fish
Exports: $363.4 million (f.o.b., 1995)
Exports - commodities: fish and fish products 95%
Exports - partners: Denmark 89%, Japan 5%, UK 5%
Imports: $421 million (c.i.f., 1995)
Imports - commodities: machinery and transport equipment 25%, manufactured goods 18%, food and live animals 11%, petroleum products 6%
Imports - partners: Denmark 7.5%, Iceland 3.8%, Japan 3.3%, Norway 3.1%, US 2.4%, Germany 2.4%, Sweden 1.8%
Debt - external: $243 million (1995)
Economic aid - recipient: $427 million (annual subsidy from Denmark) (1995)
Currency: 1 Danish krone (DKr) = 100 oere
Exchange rates: Danish kroner (DKr) per US$1 - 6.401 (January 1999), 6.701 (1998), 6.604 (1997), 5.799 (1996), 5.602 (1995), 6.361 (1994)
Fiscal year: calendar year

Communications

Telephones: 19,600 (1995 est.)
Telephone system: adequate domestic and international service provided by cables and microwave radio relay; totally digitalized in 1995
domestic: microwave radio relay
international: 2 coaxial submarine cables; satellite earth station - 1 Intelsat (Atlantic Ocean)
Radio broadcast stations: 1 publicly-owned station and some local radio and TV stations
Radios: 23,000 (1991 est.)
Television broadcast stations: 1 publicly-owned station and some local low-power stations; in addition, there are three AFRTS (US Air Force) stations which broadcast in the NTSC system (1997)
Televisions: 12,000 (1991 est.)

Transportation

Railways: 0 km
Highways:
total: 150 km
paved: 60 km
unpaved: 90 km

Greenland *(continued)*

Ports and harbors: Kangerluarsoruseq, Kangerlussuaq, Nanortalik, Narsarsuaq, Nuuk (Godthab), Sisimiut
Merchant marine:
total: 1 passenger (1,000 GRT or over) totaling 1,211 GRT/162 DWT (1998 est.)
Airports: 13 (1998 est.)
Airports - with paved runways:
total: 9
over 3,047 m: 1
2,438 to 3,047 m: 1
1,524 to 2,437 m: 1
914 to 1,523 m: 2
under 914 m: 4 (1998 est.)
Airports - with unpaved runways:
total: 4
1,524 to 2,437 m: 1
914 to 1,523 m: 2
under 914 m: 1 (1998 est.)

Military

Military - note: defense is the responsibility of Denmark

Transnational Issues

Disputes - international: none

Grenada

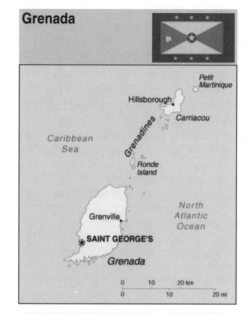

Geography

Location: Caribbean, island between the Caribbean Sea and Atlantic Ocean, north of Trinidad and Tobago
Geographic coordinates: 12 07 N, 61 40 W
Map references: Central America and the Caribbean
Area:
total: 340 sq km
land: 340 sq km
water: 0 sq km
Area - comparative: twice the size of Washington, DC
Land boundaries: 0 km
Coastline: 121 km
Maritime claims:
exclusive economic zone: 200 nm
territorial sea: 12 nm
Climate: tropical; tempered by northeast trade winds
Terrain: volcanic in origin with central mountains
Elevation extremes:
lowest point: Caribbean Sea 0 m
highest point: Mount Saint Catherine 840 m
Natural resources: timber, tropical fruit, deepwater harbors
Land use:
arable land: 15%
permanent crops: 18%
permanent pastures: 3%
forests and woodland: 9%
other: 55% (1993 est.)
Irrigated land: NA sq km
Natural hazards: lies on edge of hurricane belt; hurricane season lasts from June to November
Environment - current issues: NA
Environment - international agreements:
party to: Biodiversity, Climate Change, Desertification, Law of the Sea, Ozone Layer Protection, Whaling
signed, but not ratified: none of the selected agreements

Geography - note: the administration of the islands of the Grenadines group is divided between Saint Vincent and the Grenadines and Grenada

People

Population: 97,008 (July 1999 est.)
Age structure:
0-14 years: 43% (male 21,055; female 20,365)
15-64 years: 53% (male 27,524; female 23,766)
65 years and over: 4% (male 2,034; female 2,264) (1999 est.)
Population growth rate: 0.87% (1999 est.)
Birth rate: 27.62 births/1,000 population (1999 est.)
Death rate: 5.15 deaths/1,000 population (1999 est.)
Net migration rate: -13.74 migrant(s)/1,000 population (1999 est.)
Sex ratio:
at birth: 1.02 male(s)/female
under 15 years: 1.03 male(s)/female
15-64 years: 1.16 male(s)/female
65 years and over: 0.9 male(s)/female
total population: 1.09 male(s)/female (1999 est.)
Infant mortality rate: 11.13 deaths/1,000 live births (1999 est.)
Life expectancy at birth:
total population: 71.6 years
male: 68.97 years
female: 74.29 years (1999 est.)
Total fertility rate: 3.57 children born/woman (1999 est.)
Nationality:
noun: Grenadian(s)
adjective: Grenadian
Ethnic groups: black
Religions: Roman Catholic 53%, Anglican 13.8%, other Protestant sects 33.2%
Languages: English (official), French patois
Literacy:
definition: age 15 and over can read and write
total population: 98%
male: 98%
female: 98% (1970 est.)

Government

Country name:
conventional long form: none
conventional short form: Grenada
Data code: GJ
Government type: parliamentary democracy
Capital: Saint George's
Administrative divisions: 6 parishes and 1 dependency*; Carriacou and Petit Martinique*, Saint Andrew, Saint David, Saint George, Saint John, Saint Mark, Saint Patrick
Independence: 7 February 1974 (from UK)
National holiday: Independence Day, 7 February (1974)
Constitution: 19 December 1973
Legal system: based on English common law
Suffrage: 18 years of age; universal

Grenada (continued)

Executive branch:
chief of state: Queen ELIZABETH II (since 6 February 1952), represented by Governor General Daniel WILLIAMS (since 9 August 1996)
head of government: Prime Minister Keith MITCHELL (since 22 June 1995)
cabinet: Cabinet appointed by the governor general on the advice of the prime minister
elections: none; the monarch is hereditary; governor general appointed by the monarch; prime minister appointed by the governor general from among the members of the House of Assembly
Legislative branch: bicameral Parliament consists of the Senate (a 13-member body, 10 appointed by the government and three by the leader of the opposition) and the House of Representatives (15 seats; members are elected by popular vote to serve five-year terms)
elections: last held on 18 January 1999 (next to be held by NA October 2004)
election results: House of Representatives - percent of vote by party - NA; seats by party - NNP 15
Judicial branch: West Indies Associate States Supreme Court (an associate judge resides in Grenada)
Political parties and leaders: National Democratic Congress or NDC [George BRIZAN]; Grenada United Labor Party or GULP [Herbert PREUDHOMME]; The National Party or TNP [Ben JONES]; New National Party or NNP [Keith MITCHELL]; Maurice Bishop Patriotic Movement or MBPM [Terrence MARRYSHOW]; The Democratic Labor Party or DLP [Francis ALEXIS]
International organization participation: ACP, C, Caricom, CDB, ECLAC, FAO, G-77, IBRD, ICAO, ICFTU, ICRM, IDA, IFAD, IFC, IFRCS, ILO, IMF, Interpol, IOC, ISO (subscriber), ITU, LAES, NAM, OAS, OECS, OPANAL, OPCW, UN, UNCTAD, UNESCO, UNIDO, UPU, WCL, WHO, WToO, WTrO
Diplomatic representation in the US:
chief of mission: Ambassador Denis G. ANTOINE
chancery: 1701 New Hampshire Avenue NW, Washington, DC 20009
telephone: [1] (202) 265-2561
consulate(s): New York
Diplomatic representation from the US:
chief of mission: the ambassador to Barbados is accredited to Grenada
embassy: Point Salines, Saint George's
mailing address: P. O. Box 54, Saint George's, Grenada, West Indies
telephone: [1] (473) 444-1173 through 1176
FAX: [1] (473) 444-4820
Flag description: a rectangle divided diagonally into yellow triangles (top and bottom) and green triangles (hoist side and outer side), with a red border around the flag; there are seven yellow, five-pointed stars with three centered in the top red border, three centered in the bottom red border, and one on a red disk superimposed at the center of the flag; there is also a symbolic nutmeg pod on the hoist-side triangle (Grenada is the world's second-largest producer of nutmeg, after Indonesia); the seven stars represent the seven administrative divisions

Economy

Economy - overview: In this island economy progress in fiscal reforms and prudent macroeconomic management have boosted annual growth to nearly 5% in 1997-98. The increase in economic activity has been led by construction and trade. Tourist facilities are being expanded; tourism is the leading foreign exchange earner. Major short-term concerns are the rising fiscal deficit and the deterioration in the external account balance. Grenada shares a common central bank and a common currency with seven other members of the Organization of Eastern Caribbean States (OECS).
GDP: purchasing power parity - $340 million (1998 est.)
GDP - real growth rate: 5% (1998 est.)
GDP - per capita: purchasing power parity - $3,500 (1998 est.)
GDP - composition by sector:
agriculture: 9.7%
industry: 15%
services: 75.3% (1996 est.)
Population below poverty line: NA%
Household income or consumption by percentage share:
lowest 10%: NA%
highest 10%: NA%
Inflation rate (consumer prices): 1.4% (1998)
Labor force: 36,000
Labor force - by occupation: services 31%, agriculture 24%, construction 8%, manufacturing 5%, other 32% (1985)
Unemployment rate: 20% (1 October 1996)
Budget:
revenues: $85.8 million
expenditures: $102.1 million, including capital expenditures of $28 million (1997)
Industries: food and beverages, textiles, light assembly operations, tourism, construction
Industrial production growth rate: 0.7% (1997 est.)
Electricity - production: 70 million kWh (1996)
Electricity - production by source:
fossil fuel: 100%
hydro: 0%
nuclear: 0%
other: 0% (1996)
Electricity - consumption: 70 million kWh (1996)
Electricity - exports: 0 kWh (1996)
Electricity - imports: 0 kWh (1996)
Agriculture - products: bananas, cocoa, nutmeg, mace, citrus, avocados, root crops, sugarcane, corn, vegetables
Exports: $22 million (1997)
Exports - commodities: bananas, cocoa, nutmeg, fruit and vegetables, clothing, mace
Exports - partners: Caricom 32.3%, UK 20%, US 13%, Netherlands 8.8% (1991)
Imports: $166.5 million (1997)

Imports - commodities: food 25%, manufactured goods 22%, machinery 20%, chemicals 10%, fuel 6% (1989)
Imports - partners: US 31.2%, Caricom 23.6%, UK 13.8%, Japan 7.1% (1991)
Debt - external: $74 million (1997 est.)
Economic aid - recipient: $8.3 million (1995)
Currency: 1 East Caribbean dollar (EC$) = 100 cents
Exchange rates: East Caribbean dollars (EC$) per US$1 - 2.7000 (fixed rate since 1976)
Fiscal year: calendar year

Communications

Telephones: 5,650 (1988 est.)
Telephone system: automatic, islandwide telephone system
domestic: interisland VHF and UHF radiotelephone links
international: new SHF radiotelephone links to Trinidad and Tobago and Saint Vincent; VHF and UHF radio links to Trinidad
Radio broadcast stations: AM 1, FM 0, shortwave 0
Radios: 80,000 (1993 est.)
Television broadcast stations: 2 (1997)
Televisions: 30,000 (1993 est.)

Transportation

Railways: 0 km
Highways:
total: 1,040 km
paved: 638 km
unpaved: 402 km (1996 est.)
Ports and harbors: Grenville, Saint George's
Merchant marine: none
Airports: 3 (1998 est.)
Airports - with paved runways:
total: 2
2,438 to 3,047 m: 1
914 to 1,523 m: 1 (1998 est.)
Airports - with unpaved runways:
total: 1
under 914 m: 1 (1998 est.)

Military

Military branches: Royal Grenada Police Force (includes Special Service Unit), Coast Guard
Military expenditures - dollar figure: $NA
Military expenditures - percent of GDP: NA%

Transnational Issues

Disputes - international: none
Illicit drugs: small-scale cannabis cultivation; lesser transshipment point for marijuana and cocaine to US

Guadeloupe
(overseas department of France)

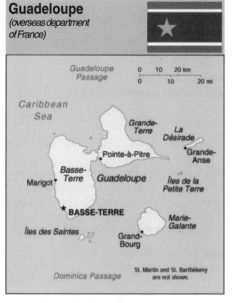

Geography

Location: Caribbean, islands in the eastern Caribbean Sea, southeast of Puerto Rico
Geographic coordinates: 16 15 N, 61 35 W
Map references: Central America and the Caribbean
Area:
total: 1,780 sq km
land: 1,706 sq km
water: 74 sq km
note: Guadeloupe is an archipelago of nine inhabited islands, including Basse-Terre, Grande-Terre, Marie-Galante, La Desirade, Iles des Saintes, Saint Barthelemy, and part of Saint Martin
Area - comparative: 10 times the size of Washington, DC
Land boundaries:
total: 10.2 km
border countries: Netherlands Antilles (Sint Maarten) 10.2 km
Coastline: 306 km
Maritime claims:
exclusive economic zone: 200 nm
territorial sea: 12 nm
Climate: subtropical tempered by trade winds; moderately high humidity
Terrain: Basse-Terre is volcanic in origin with interior mountains; Grande-Terre is low limestone formation; most of the seven other islands are volcanic in origin
Elevation extremes:
lowest point: Caribbean Sea 0 m
highest point: Soufriere 1,467 m
Natural resources: cultivable land, beaches and climate that foster tourism
Land use:
arable land: 14%
permanent crops: 4%
permanent pastures: 14%
forests and woodland: 39%
other: 29% (1993 est.)

Irrigated land: 30 sq km (1993 est.)
Natural hazards: hurricanes (June to October); Soufriere is an active volcano
Environment - current issues: NA
Environment - international agreements:
party to: NA
signed, but not ratified: NA

People

Population: 420,943 (July 1999 est.)
Age structure:
0-14 years: 25% (male 53,427; female 51,234)
15-64 years: 66% (male 138,215; female 141,243)
65 years and over: 9% (male 15,536; female 21,288) (1999 est.)
Population growth rate: 1.06% (1999 est.)
Birth rate: 16.33 births/1,000 population (1999 est.)
Death rate: 5.62 deaths/1,000 population (1999 est.)
Net migration rate: -0.16 migrant(s)/1,000 population (1999 est.)
Sex ratio:
at birth: 1.05 male(s)/female
under 15 years: 1.04 male(s)/female
15-64 years: 0.98 male(s)/female
65 years and over: 0.73 male(s)/female
total population: 0.97 male(s)/female (1999 est.)
Infant mortality rate: 8.54 deaths/1,000 live births (1999 est.)
Life expectancy at birth:
total population: 78.01 years
male: 74.98 years
female: 81.18 years (1999 est.)
Total fertility rate: 1.82 children born/woman (1999 est.)
Nationality:
noun: Guadeloupian(s)
adjective: Guadeloupe
Ethnic groups: black or mulatto 90%, white 5%, East Indian, Lebanese, Chinese less than 5%
Religions: Roman Catholic 95%, Hindu and pagan African 4%, Protestant sects 1%
Languages: French (official) 99%, Creole patois
Literacy:
definition: age 15 and over can read and write
total population: 90%
male: 90%
female: 90% (1982 est.)

Government

Country name:
conventional long form: Department of Guadeloupe
conventional short form: Guadeloupe
local long form: Departement de la Guadeloupe
local short form: Guadeloupe
Data code: GP
Dependency status: overseas department of France
Government type: NA
Capital: Basse-Terre
Administrative divisions: none (overseas department of France)

Independence: none (overseas department of France)
National holiday: National Day, Taking of the Bastille, 14 July (1789)
Constitution: 28 September 1958 (French Constitution)
Legal system: French legal system
Suffrage: 18 years of age; universal
Executive branch:
chief of state: President Jacques CHIRAC of France (since 17 May 1995), represented by Prefect Jean FEDINI (since NA 1996)
head of government: President of the General Council Marcellin LUBETH (since NA 1998); President of the Regional Council Lucette MICHAUX-CHEVRY (since 22 March 1992)
cabinet: NA
elections: French president elected by popular vote for a seven-year term; prefect appointed by the French president on the advice of the French Ministry of Interior; the presidents of the General and Regional Councils are elected by the members of those councils
election results: NA
Legislative branch: unicameral General Council or Conseil General (42 seats; members are elected by popular vote to serve six-year terms) and the unicameral Regional Council or Conseil Regional (41 seats; members are elected by popular vote to serve six-year terms)
elections: General Council - last held 22 March 1998 (next to be held by NA 2002); Regional Council - last held 15 March 1998 (next to be held NA 2004)
election results: General Council - percent of vote by party - NA; seats by party - various left parties 11, PS 8, RPR 8, PPDG 6, various right parties 5, PCC 3, UDF 1; Regional Council - percent of vote by party - RPR 48.03%, PS/PPDG/DVG 24.49%, PCG 5.29%, DVD 5.73%; seats by party - RPR 25, PS/PPDG/DVG 12, PCG 2, DVD 2
note: Guadeloupe elects two representatives to the French Senate; elections last held NA September 1995 (next to be held NA September 2004); percent of vote by party - NA; seats by party - RPR 1, FGPS 1; Guadeloupe elects four representatives to the French National Assembly; elections last held 25 May - 1 June 1997 (next to be held NA 2002); percent of vote by party - NA; seats by party - FGPS 2, RPR 1, PPDG 1
Judicial branch: Court of Appeal or Cour d'Appel with jurisdiction over Guadeloupe, French Guiana, and Martinique
Political parties and leaders: Rally for the Republic or RPR [Lucette MICHAUX-CHEVRY]; Communist Party of Guadeloupe or PCG [Mona CADOCE]; Socialist Party or PS [Georges LOUISOR]; Popular Union for the Liberation of Guadeloupe or UPLG [Claude MAKOUKE]; FGPS Dissidents or FRUI.G [Dominique LARIFLA]; Union for French Democracy or UDF [Marcel ESDRAS]; Progressive Democratic Party or PPDG [Henri BANGOU]; Movement for an Independent Guadeloupe or MPGI [Luc REIETTE];

Guadeloupe *(continued)*

Christian Movement for the Liberation of Guadeloupe or KLPG; DVG (full name NA) [Jacques GILLOT]; DVD (full name NA) [Simon IBO]

Political pressure groups and leaders: Movement for Independent Guadeloupe or MPGI; General Union of Guadeloupe Workers or UGTG; General Federation of Guadeloupe Workers or CGT-G; Christian Movement for the Liberation of Guadeloupe or KLPG

International organization participation: FZ, WCL, WFTU

Diplomatic representation in the US: none (overseas department of France)

Diplomatic representation from the US: none (overseas department of France)

Flag description: three horizontal bands, a narrow green band (top), a wide red band, and a narrow green band; the green bands are separated from the red band by two narrow white stripes; a five-pointed gold star is centered in the red band toward the hoist side; the flag of France is used for official occasions

Economy

Economy - overview: The economy depends on agriculture, tourism, light industry, and services. It also depends on France for large subsidies and imports. Tourism is a key industry, with most tourists from the US; an increasingly large number of cruise ships visit the islands. The traditional sugarcane crop is slowly being replaced by other crops, such as bananas (which now supply about 50% of export earnings), eggplant, and flowers. Other vegetables and root crops are cultivated for local consumption, although Guadeloupe is still dependent on imported food, mainly from France. Light industry features sugar and rum production. Most manufactured goods and fuel are imported. Unemployment is especially high among the young.

GDP: purchasing power parity - $3.7 billion (1996 est.)

GDP - real growth rate: NA%

GDP - per capita: purchasing power parity - $9,000 (1996 est.)

GDP - composition by sector:
agriculture: 6%
industry: 9%
services: 85% (1993 est.)

Population below poverty line: NA%

Household income or consumption by percentage share:
lowest 10%: NA%
highest 10%: NA%

Inflation rate (consumer prices): 3.7% (1990)

Labor force: 128,000

Labor force - by occupation: agriculture 15%, industry 20%, services 65% (1993)

Unemployment rate: 29.5% (1997)

Budget:
revenues: $200 million
expenditures: $350 million, including capital

expenditures of $NA (1997)

Industries: construction, cement, rum, sugar, tourism

Industrial production growth rate: NA%

Electricity - production: 960 million kWh (1996)

Electricity - production by source:
fossil fuel: 100%
hydro: 0%
nuclear: 0%
other: 0% (1996)

Electricity - consumption: 960 million kWh (1996)

Electricity - exports: 0 kWh (1996)

Electricity - imports: 0 kWh (1996)

Agriculture - products: bananas, sugarcane, tropical fruits and vegetables; cattle, pigs, goats

Exports: $133 million (f.o.b., 1997)

Exports - commodities: bananas, sugar, rum

Exports - partners: France 75%, Martinique 13% (1994)

Imports: $1.7 billion (c.i.f., 1997)

Imports - commodities: foodstuffs, fuels, vehicles, clothing and other consumer goods, construction materials

Imports - partners: France 64%, EU 13%, Martinique 4%, US, Japan (1994)

Debt - external: $NA

Economic aid - recipient: $NA; note - substantial annual French subsidies

Currency: 1 French franc (F) = 100 centimes

Exchange rates: French francs (F) per US$1 - 5.65 (January 1999), 5.8995 (1998), 5.8367 (1997), 5.1155(1996), 4.9915 (1995), 5.5520 (1994)

Fiscal year: calendar year

Communications

Telephones: 64,916 (1984 est.)

Telephone system: domestic facilities inadequate
domestic: NA
international: satellite earth station - 1 Intelsat (Atlantic Ocean); microwave radio relay to Antigua and Barbuda, Dominica, and Martinique

Radio broadcast stations: AM 2, FM 8 (private stations licensed to broadcast FM 30), shortwave 0

Radios: 100,000 (1993 est.)

Television broadcast stations: 5 (in addition, there are several low-power repeaters) (1997)

Televisions: 150,000 (1993 est.)

Transportation

Railways:
total: NA km; privately owned, narrow-gauge plantation lines

Highways:
total: 2,082 km
paved: 1,742 km
unpaved: 340 km (1985 est.)
note: in 1996 there were a total of 3,200 km of roads

Ports and harbors: Basse-Terre, Gustavia (on Saint Barthelemy), Marigot, Pointe-a-Pitre

Merchant marine: none

Airports: 9 (1998 est.)

Airports - with paved runways:
total: 8
over 3,047 m: 1
914 to 1,523 m: 2
under 914 m: 5 (1998 est.)

Airports - with unpaved runways:
total: 1
under 914 m: 1 (1998 est.)

Military

Military branches: French Forces, Gendarmerie

Military - note: defense is the responsibility of France

Transnational Issues

Disputes - international: none

Guam
(territory of the US)

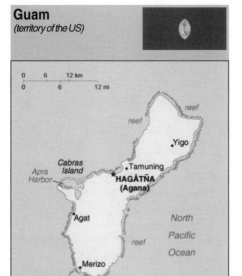

Geography

Location: Oceania, island in the North Pacific Ocean, about three-quarters of the way from Hawaii to the Philippines

Geographic coordinates: 13 28 N, 144 47 E

Map references: Oceania

Area:
total: 541.3 sq km
land: 541.3 sq km
water: 0 sq km

Area - comparative: three times the size of Washington, DC

Land boundaries: 0 km

Coastline: 125.5 km

Maritime claims:
exclusive economic zone: 200 nm
territorial sea: 12 nm

Climate: tropical marine; generally warm and humid, moderated by northeast trade winds; dry season from January to June, rainy season from July to December; little seasonal temperature variation

Terrain: volcanic origin, surrounded by coral reefs; relatively flat coralline limestone plateau (source of most fresh water), with steep coastal cliffs and narrow coastal plains in north, low-rising hills in center, mountains in south

Elevation extremes:
lowest point: Pacific Ocean 0 m
highest point: Mount Lamlam 406 m

Natural resources: fishing (largely undeveloped), tourism (especially from Japan)

Land use:
arable land: 11%
permanent crops: 11%
permanent pastures: 15%
forests and woodland: 18%
other: 45% (1993 est.)

Irrigated land: NA sq km

Natural hazards: frequent squalls during rainy season; relatively rare, but potentially very destructive typhoons (especially in August)

Environment - current issues: extirpation of native bird population by the rapid proliferation of the brown tree snake, an exotic species

Environment - international agreements:
party to: NA
signed, but not ratified: NA

Geography - note: largest and southernmost island in the Mariana Islands archipelago; strategic location in western North Pacific Ocean

People

Population: 151,716 (July 1999 est.)

Age structure:
0-14 years: 35% (male 27,301; female 25,106)
15-64 years: 60% (male 47,691; female 42,714)
65 years and over: 5% (male 4,486; female 4,418) (1999 est.)

Population growth rate: 1.67% (1999 est.)

Birth rate: 26.52 births/1,000 population (1999 est.)

Death rate: 4.35 deaths/1,000 population (1999 est.)

Net migration rate: -5.45 migrant(s)/1,000 population (1999 est.)

Sex ratio:
at birth: 1.11 male(s)/female
under 15 years: 1.09 male(s)/female
15-64 years: 1.12 male(s)/female
65 years and over: 1.02 male(s)/female
total population: 1.1 male(s)/female (1999 est.)

Infant mortality rate: 7.81 deaths/1,000 live births (1999 est.)

Life expectancy at birth:
total population: 77.78 years
male: 74.6 years
female: 81.31 years (1999 est.)

Total fertility rate: 3.92 children born/woman (1999 est.)

Nationality:
noun: Guamanian(s)
adjective: Guamanian

Ethnic groups: Chamorro 47%, Filipino 25%, white 10%, Chinese, Japanese, Korean, and other 18%

Religions: Roman Catholic 98%, other 2%

Languages: English, Chamorro, Japanese

Literacy:
definition: age 15 and over can read and write
total population: 99%
male: 99%
female: 99% (1990 est.)

Government

Country name:
conventional long form: Territory of Guam
conventional short form: Guam

Data code: GQ

Dependency status: organized, unincorporated territory of the US with policy relations between Guam and the US under the jurisdiction of the Office of Insular Affairs, US Department of the Interior

Government type: NA

Capital: Hagatna (Agana)

Administrative divisions: none (territory of the US)

Independence: none (territory of the US)

National holiday: Guam Discovery Day (first Monday in March) (1521); Liberation Day, 21 July (1944)

Constitution: Organic Act of 1 August 1950

Legal system: modeled on US; US federal laws apply

Suffrage: 18 years of age; universal; US citizens, but do not vote in US presidential elections

Executive branch:
chief of state: President William Jefferson CLINTON of the US (since 20 January 1993); Vice President Albert GORE, Jr. (since 20 January 1993)
head of government: Governor Carl GUTIERREZ (since 8 November 1994) and Lieutenant Governor Madeleine BORDALLO (since 8 November 1994)
cabinet: executive departments; heads appointed by the governor with the consent of the Guam legislature
elections: US president and vice president elected on the same ticket for a four-year term; governor and lieutenant governor elected on the same ticket by popular vote for four-year terms; election last held 3 November 1998 (next to be held NA November 2002)
election results: Carl GUTIERREZ reelected governor; percent of vote - Carl GUTIERREZ (Democrat) 53.2%, Joseph ADA (Republican) 46.8%

Legislative branch: unicameral Legislature (15 seats; members are elected by popular vote to serve two-year terms)
elections: last held 3 November 1998 (next to be held NA November 2000)
election results: percent of vote by party - NA; seats by party - Republican 12, Democratic 3
note: Guam elects one delegate to the US House of Representatives; election last held 3 November 1998 (next to be held NA November 2000); results - Robert UNDERWOOD was reelected as delegate; percent of vote by party - NA; seats by party - Democratic 1

Judicial branch: Federal District Court (judge is appointed by the president); Territorial Superior Court (judges appointed for eight-year terms by the governor)

Political parties and leaders: Republican Party (controls the legislature) [leader NA]; Democratic Party (party of the Governor) [leader NA]

International organization participation: ESCAP (associate), Interpol (subbureau), IOC, SPC

Diplomatic representation in the US: none (territory of the US)

Diplomatic representation from the US: none (territory of the US)

Flag description: territorial flag is dark blue with a narrow red border on all four sides; centered is a red-bordered, pointed, vertical ellipse containing a beach scene, outrigger canoe with sail, and a palm tree with the word GUAM superimposed in bold red letters; US flag is the national flag

Economy

Economy - overview: The economy depends mainly on US military spending and on tourist

Guam (continued)

revenue. Over the past 20 years, the tourist industry has grown rapidly, creating a construction boom for new hotels and the expansion of older ones. More than 1 million tourists visit Guam each year. The industry suffered a setback in 1998 because of the continuing Japanese recession; the Japanese normally make up almost 90% of the tourists. Most food and industrial goods are imported. Guam faces the problem of building up the civilian economic sector to offset the impact of military downsizing.

GDP: purchasing power parity - $3 billion (1996 est.)
GDP - real growth rate: NA%
GDP - per capita: purchasing power parity - $19,000 (1996 est.)
GDP - composition by sector:
agriculture: NA%
industry: NA%
services: NA%
Population below poverty line: NA%
Household income or consumption by percentage share:
lowest 10%: NA%
highest 10%: NA%
Inflation rate (consumer prices): 4% (1992 est.)
Labor force: 65,660 (1995)
Labor force - by occupation: federal and territorial government 31%, private 69% (trade 21%, services 33%, construction 12%, other 3%) (1995)
Unemployment rate: 2% (1992 est.)
Budget:
revenues: $524.3 million
expenditures: $361.4 million, including capital expenditures of $NA (1995)
Industries: US military, tourism, construction, transshipment services, concrete products, printing and publishing, food processing, textiles
Industrial production growth rate: NA%
Electricity - production: 800 million kWh (1996)
Electricity - production by source:
fossil fuel: 100%
hydro: 0%
nuclear: 0%
other: 0% (1996)
Electricity - consumption: 800 million kWh (1996)
Electricity - exports: 0 kWh (1996)
Electricity - imports: 0 kWh (1996)
Agriculture - products: fruits, copra, vegetables; eggs, pork, poultry, beef
Exports: $86.1 million (f.o.b., 1992)
Exports - commodities: mostly transshipments of refined petroleum products, construction materials, fish, food and beverage products
Exports - partners: US 25%
Imports: $202.4 million (c.i.f., 1992)
Imports - commodities: petroleum and petroleum products, food, manufactured goods
Imports - partners: US 23%, Japan 19%, other 58%
Debt - external: $NA
Economic aid - recipient: $NA; note - although Guam receives no foreign aid, it does receive large transfer payments from the general revenues of the US Federal Treasury into which Guamanians pay no

income or excise taxes; under the provisions of a special law of Congress, the Guam Treasury, rather than the US Treasury, receives federal income taxes paid by military and civilian Federal employees stationed in Guam
Currency: 1 United States dollar (US$) = 100 cents
Exchange rates: US currency is used
Fiscal year: 1 October - 30 September

Communications

Telephones: 74,317 (March 1997)
Telephone system:
domestic: NA
international: satellite earth stations - 2 Intelsat (Pacific Ocean); submarine cables to US and Japan
Radio broadcast stations: AM 3, FM 3, shortwave 0
Radios: 206,000 (1994)
Television broadcast stations: 5 (1997)
Televisions: 97,000 (1994 est.)

Transportation

Railways: 0 km
Highways:
total: 885 km
paved: 675 km
unpaved: 210 km
note: there is another 685 km of roads classified non-public, including roads located on federal government installations
Ports and harbors: Apra Harbor
Merchant marine: none
Airports: 5 (1998 est.)
Airports - with paved runways:
total: 4
over 3,047 m: 2
2,438 to 3,047 m: 1
914 to 1,523 m: 1 (1998 est.)
Airports - with unpaved runways:
total: 1
under 914 m: 1 (1998 est.)

Military

Military - note: defense is the responsibility of the US

Transnational Issues

Disputes - international: none

Guatemala

Geography

Location: Middle America, bordering the Caribbean Sea, between Honduras and Belize and bordering the North Pacific Ocean, between El Salvador and Mexico
Geographic coordinates: 15 30 N, 90 15 W
Map references: Central America and the Caribbean
Area:
total: 108,890 sq km
land: 108,430 sq km
water: 460 sq km
Area - comparative: slightly smaller than Tennessee
Land boundaries:
total: 1,687 km
border countries: Belize 266 km, El Salvador 203 km, Honduras 256 km, Mexico 962 km
Coastline: 400 km
Maritime claims:
continental shelf: 200-m depth or to the depth of exploitation
exclusive economic zone: 200 nm
territorial sea: 12 nm
Climate: tropical; hot, humid in lowlands; cooler in highlands
Terrain: mostly mountains with narrow coastal plains and rolling limestone plateau (Peten)
Elevation extremes:
lowest point: Pacific Ocean 0 m
highest point: Volcan Tajumulco 4,211 m
Natural resources: petroleum, nickel, rare woods, fish, chicle
Land use:
arable land: 12%
permanent crops: 5%
permanent pastures: 24%
forests and woodland: 54%
other: 5% (1993 est.)
Irrigated land: 1,250 sq km (1993 est.)
Natural hazards: numerous volcanoes in

mountains, with occasional violent earthquakes; Caribbean coast subject to hurricanes and other tropical storms

Environment - current issues: deforestation; soil erosion; water pollution; Hurricane Mitch damage

Environment - international agreements:
party to: Antarctic Treaty, Biodiversity, Climate Change, Desertification, Endangered Species, Environmental Modification, Hazardous Wastes, Law of the Sea, Marine Dumping, Nuclear Test Ban, Ozone Layer Protection, Ship Pollution, Wetlands
signed, but not ratified: Antarctic-Environmental Protocol, Climate Change-Kyoto Protocol

Geography - note: no natural harbors on west coast

People

Population: 12,335,580 (July 1999 est.)

Age structure:
0-14 years: 43% (male 2,688,402; female 2,578,934)
15-64 years: 54% (male 3,312,360; female 3,314,102)
65 years and over: 3% (male 207,014; female 234,768) (1999 est.)

Population growth rate: 2.68% (1999 est.)

Birth rate: 35.57 births/1,000 population (1999 est.)

Death rate: 6.8 deaths/1,000 population (1999 est.)

Net migration rate: -1.93 migrant(s)/1,000 population (1999 est.)

Sex ratio:
at birth: 1.05 male(s)/female
under 15 years: 1.04 male(s)/female
15-64 years: 1 male(s)/female
65 years and over: 0.88 male(s)/female
total population: 1.01 male(s)/female (1999 est.)

Infant mortality rate: 46.15 deaths/1,000 live births (1999 est.)

Life expectancy at birth:
total population: 66.45 years
male: 63.78 years
female: 69.24 years (1999 est.)

Total fertility rate: 4.74 children born/woman (1999 est.)

Nationality:
noun: Guatemalan(s)
adjective: Guatemalan

Ethnic groups: Mestizo (mixed Amerindian-Spanish - in local Spanish called Ladino) 56%, Amerindian or predominantly Amerindian 44%

Religions: Roman Catholic, Protestant, traditional Mayan

Languages: Spanish 60%, Amerindian languages 40% (23 Amerindian languages, including Quiche, Cakchiquel, Kekchi)

Literacy:
definition: age 15 and over can read and write
total population: 55.6%
male: 62.5%
female: 48.6% (1995 est.)

Government

Country name:
conventional long form: Republic of Guatemala
conventional short form: Guatemala
local long form: Republica de Guatemala
local short form: Guatemala

Data code: GT

Government type: republic

Capital: Guatemala

Administrative divisions: 22 departments (departamentos, singular - departamento); Alta Verapaz, Baja Verapaz, Chimaltenango, Chiquimula, El Progreso, Escuintla, Guatemala, Huehuetenango, Izabal, Jalapa, Jutiapa, Peten, Quetzaltenango, Quiche, Retalhuleu, Sacatepequez, San Marcos, Santa Rosa, Solola, Suchitepequez, Totonicapan, Zacapa

Independence: 15 September 1821 (from Spain)

National holiday: Independence Day, 15 September (1821)

Constitution: 31 May 1985, effective 14 January 1986
note: suspended 25 May 1993 by President SERRANO; reinstated 5 June 1993 following ouster of president

Legal system: civil law system; judicial review of legislative acts; has not accepted compulsory ICJ jurisdiction

Suffrage: 18 years of age; universal

Executive branch:
chief of state: President Alvaro Enrique ARZU Irigoyen (since 14 January 1996); Vice President Luis Alberto FLORES Asturias (since 14 January 1996); note - the president is both the chief of state and head of government
head of government: President Alvaro Enrique ARZU Irigoyen (since 14 January 1996); Vice President Luis Alberto FLORES Asturias (since 14 January 1996); note - the president is both the chief of state and head of government
cabinet: Council of Ministers named by the president
elections: president elected by popular vote for a four-year term; election last held 12 November 1995; runoff held 7 January 1996 (next to be held NA November 1999)
election results: Alvaro Enrique ARZU Irigoyen elected president; percent of vote - Alvaro Enrique ARZU Irigoyen (PAN) 51.2%, Jorge PORTILLO Cabrera (FRG) 48.8%

Legislative branch: unicameral Congress of the Republic or Congreso de la Republica (80 seats; members are elected by popular vote to serve four-year terms)
elections: last held on 12 November 1995 (next to be held in November 1999)
election results: percent of vote by party - NA; seats by party - PAN 43, FRG 21, FDNG 6, DCG 4, UCN 3, UD 2, MLN 1
note: on 11 November 1993 the congress approved a procedure that reduced its number from 116 seats to 80; the procedure provided for a special election in mid-1994 to elect an interim congress of 80 members to serve until replaced in the November 1995 general election; the plan was approved in a general referendum in January 1994 and the special election was held on 14 August 1994

Judicial branch: Supreme Court of Justice (Corte Suprema de Justicia); additionally the Court of Constitutionality is presided over by the president of the Supreme Court, judges are elected for a five-year term by Congress

Political parties and leaders: National Centrist Union or UCN [Juan AYERDI Aguilar]; Christian Democratic Party or DCG [Alfonso CABRERA Hidalgo]; National Advancement Party or PAN [Raphael BARRIOS Flores]; National Liberation Movement or MLN [Mario SANDOVAL Alarcon]; Social Democratic Party or PSD [Sergio FLORES Cruz]; Revolutionary Party or PR [Carlos CHAVARRIA Perez]; Guatemalan Republican Front or FRG [Efrain RIOS Montt]; Democratic Union or UD [Jose CHEA Urruela]; New Guatemalan Democratic Front or FDNG [Rafael ARRIAGA Martinez]; Guatemalan National Revolutionary Union or URNG [Jorge SOTO]

Political pressure groups and leaders: Coordinating Committee of Agricultural, Commercial, Industrial, and Financial Associations or CACIF; Mutual Support Group or GAM; Agrarian Owners Group or UNAGRO; Committee for Campesino Unity or CUC; Alliance Against Impunity or AAI

International organization participation: BCIE, CACM, CCC, ECLAC, FAO, G-24, G-77, IADB, IAEA, IBRD, ICAO, ICFTU, ICRM, IDA, IFAD, IFC, IFRCS, IHO, ILO, IMF, IMO, Intelsat, Interpol, IOC, IOM, ISO (correspondent), ITU, LAES, LAIA (observer), NAM, OAS, OPANAL, OPCW, PCA, UN, UNCTAD, UNESCO, UNIDO, UNU, UPU, WCL, WFTU, WHO, WIPO, WMO, WToO, WTrO

Diplomatic representation in the US:
chief of mission: Ambassador William STIXRUD
chancery: 2220 R Street NW, Washington, DC 20008
telephone: [1] (202) 745-4952
FAX: [1] (202) 745-1908
consulate(s) general: Chicago, Houston, Los Angeles, Miami, New York, and San Francisco

Diplomatic representation from the US:
chief of mission: Ambassador Donald J. PLANTY
embassy: 7-01 Avenida de la Reforma, Zone 10, Guatemala City
mailing address: APO AA 34024
telephone: [502] (2) 31-15-41
FAX: [502] (2) 33-48-77

Flag description: three equal vertical bands of light blue (hoist side), white, and light blue with the coat of arms centered in the white band; the coat of arms includes a green and red quetzal (the national bird) and a scroll bearing the inscription LIBERTAD 15 DE SEPTIEMBRE DE 1821 (the original date of independence from Spain) all superimposed on a pair of crossed rifles and a pair of crossed swords and framed by a wreath

Economy

Economy - overview: The agricultural sector accounts for one-fourth of GDP and two-thirds of exports and employs more than half of the labor force. Coffee, sugar, and bananas are the main products.

Guatemala (continued)

Manufacturing and construction account for one-fifth of GDP. Since assuming office in January 1996, President ARZU has worked to implement a program of economic liberalization and political modernization. The signing of the peace accords in December 1996, which ended 36 years of civil war, removed a major obstacle to foreign investment. In 1998, Hurricane Mitch caused relatively little damage to Guatemala compared to its neighbors. Nevertheless, growth will be somewhat smaller due to the storm. Remaining challenges include increasing government revenues, and negotiating a program with the IMF.

GDP: purchasing power parity - $45.7 billion (1998 est.)

GDP - real growth rate: 5% (1998 est.)

GDP - per capita: purchasing power parity - $3,800 (1998 est.)

GDP - composition by sector:
agriculture: 24%
industry: 21%
services: 55% (1997 est.)

Population below poverty line: NA%

Household income or consumption by percentage share:
lowest 10%: 0.6%
highest 10%: 46.6% (1989)

Inflation rate (consumer prices): 6.4% (1998)

Labor force: 3.32 million (1997 est.)

Labor force - by occupation: agriculture 58%, services 14%, manufacturing 14%, commerce 7%, construction 4%, transport 2.6%, utilities 0.3%, mining 0.1% (1995)

Unemployment rate: 5.2% (1997 est.)

Budget:
revenues: $NA
expenditures: $NA

Industries: sugar, textiles and clothing, furniture, chemicals, petroleum, metals, rubber, tourism

Industrial production growth rate: 1.9% (1996)

Electricity - production: 3.1 billion kWh (1996)

Electricity - production by source:
fossil fuel: 29.03%
hydro: 70.97%
nuclear: 0%
other: 0% (1996)

Electricity - consumption: 3.1 billion kWh (1996)

Electricity - exports: 0 kWh (1996)

Electricity - imports: 0 kWh (1996)

Agriculture - products: sugarcane, corn, bananas, coffee, beans, cardamom; cattle, sheep, pigs, chickens

Exports: $2.9 billion (f.o.b., 1997 est.)

Exports - commodities: coffee, sugar, bananas, cardamom, petroleum

Exports - partners: US 37%, El Salvador 13%, Honduras 7%, Costa Rica 5%, Germany 5%

Imports: $3.3 billion (c.i.f., 1997 est.)

Imports - commodities: fuel and petroleum products, machinery, grain, fertilizers, motor vehicles

Imports - partners: US 44%, Mexico 10%, Venezuela 4.6%, Japan, Germany

Debt - external: $3.38 billion (1996 est.)

Economic aid - recipient: $211.9 million (1995)

Currency: 1 quetzal (Q) = 100 centavos

Exchange rates: quetzales (Q) per US$1 - 6.7284 (January 1999), 6.3947 (1998), 6.0653 (1997), 6.0495 (1996), 5.8103 (1995), 5.7512 (1994)

Fiscal year: calendar year

Communications

Telephones: 210,000 (1993 est.)

Telephone system: fairly modern network centered in the city of Guatemala
domestic: NA
international: connected to Central American Microwave System; satellite earth station - 1 Intelsat (Atlantic Ocean)

Radio broadcast stations: AM 91, FM 0, shortwave 15

Radios: 400,000 (1993 est.)

Television broadcast stations: 6 (in addition, there are 17 repeaters) (1997)

Televisions: 475,000 (1993 est.)

Transportation

Railways:
total: 884 km (102 km privately owned)
narrow gauge: 884 km 0.914-m gauge (single track)

Highways:
total: 13,100 km
paved: 3,616 km (including 140 km of expressways)
unpaved: 9,484 km (1996 est.)

Waterways: 260 km navigable year round; additional 730 km navigable during high-water season

Pipelines: crude oil 275 km

Ports and harbors: Champerico, Puerto Barrios, Puerto Quetzal, San Jose, Santo Tomas de Castilla

Merchant marine: none

Airports: 478 (1998 est.)

Airports - with paved runways:
total: 12
2,438 to 3,047 m: 2
1,524 to 2,437 m: 2
914 to 1,523 m: 6
under 914 m: 2 (1998 est.)

Airports - with unpaved runways:
total: 466
2,438 to 3,047 m: 1
1,524 to 2,437 m: 9
914 to 1,523 m: 124
under 914 m: 332 (1998 est.)

Military

Military branches: Army, Navy, Air Force

Military manpower - military age: 18 years of age

Military manpower - availability:
males age 15-49: 2,915,169 (1999 est.)

Military manpower - fit for military service:
males age 15-49: 1,903,382 (1999 est.)

Military manpower - reaching military age annually:
males: 134,964 (1999 est.)

Military expenditures - dollar figure: $124 million (1998)

Military expenditures - percent of GDP: 0.7% (1998)

Transnational Issues

Disputes - international: border with Belize in dispute

Illicit drugs: transit country for cocaine shipments; minor producer of illicit opium poppy and cannabis for the international drug trade; active eradication program of cannabis crop effectively eliminated in 1996

Guernsey
(British crown dependency)

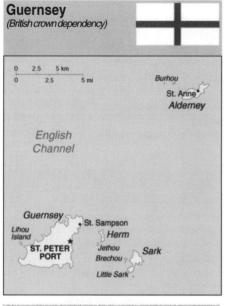

Geography

Location: Western Europe, islands in the English Channel, northwest of France
Geographic coordinates: 49 28 N, 2 35 W
Map references: Europe
Area:
total: 194 sq km
land: 194 sq km
water: 0 sq km
note: includes Alderney, Guernsey, Herm, Sark, and some other smaller islands
Area - comparative: slightly larger than Washington, DC
Land boundaries: 0 km
Coastline: 50 km
Maritime claims:
exclusive fishing zone: 12 nm
territorial sea: 3 nm
Climate: temperate with mild winters and cool summers; about 50% of days are overcast
Terrain: mostly level with low hills in southwest
Elevation extremes:
lowest point: Atlantic Ocean 0 m
highest point: unnamed location on Sark 114 m
Natural resources: cropland
Land use:
arable land: NA%
permanent crops: NA%
permanent pastures: NA%
forests and woodland: NA%
other: NA%
Irrigated land: NA sq km
Natural hazards: NA
Environment - current issues: NA
Environment - international agreements:
party to: NA
signed, but not ratified: NA
Geography - note: large, deepwater harbor at Saint Peter Port

People

Population: 65,386 (July 1999 est.)
Age structure:
0-14 years: 18% (male 6,012; female 5,875)
15-64 years: 66% (male 21,287; female 22,165)
65 years and over: 16% (male 4,069; female 5,978) (1999 est.)
Population growth rate: 1.27% (1999 est.)
Birth rate: 14.16 births/1,000 population (1999 est.)
Death rate: 9.44 deaths/1,000 population (1999 est.)
Net migration rate: 8.01 migrant(s)/1,000 population (1999 est.)
Sex ratio:
at birth: 1.04 male(s)/female
under 15 years: 1.02 male(s)/female
15-64 years: 0.96 male(s)/female
65 years and over: 0.68 male(s)/female
total population: 0.92 male(s)/female (1999 est.)
Infant mortality rate: 8.42 deaths/1,000 live births (1999 est.)
Life expectancy at birth:
total population: 78.72 years
male: 75.78 years
female: 81.77 years (1999 est.)
Total fertility rate: 1.74 children born/woman (1999 est.)
Nationality:
noun: Channel Islander(s)
adjective: Channel Islander
Ethnic groups: UK and Norman-French descent
Religions: Anglican, Roman Catholic, Presbyterian, Baptist, Congregational, Methodist
Languages: English, French, Norman-French dialect spoken in country districts
Literacy: NA

Government

Country name:
conventional long form: Bailiwick of Guernsey
conventional short form: Guernsey
Data code: GK
Dependency status: British crown dependency
Government type: NA
Capital: Saint Peter Port
Administrative divisions: none (British crown dependency)
Independence: none (British crown dependency)
National holiday: Liberation Day, 9 May (1945)
Constitution: unwritten; partly statutes, partly common law and practice
Legal system: English law and local statute; justice is administered by the Royal Court
Suffrage: 18 years of age; universal
Executive branch:
chief of state: Queen ELIZABETH II (since 6 February 1952)
head of government: Lieutenant Governor Sir John COWARD (since NA 1994) and Bailiff Sir Graham Martyn DOREY (since NA February 1992)
cabinet: Advisory and Finance Committee appointed by the Assembly of the States

elections: none; the monarch is hereditary; lieutenant governor appointed by the monarch; bailiff appointed by the monarch
Legislative branch: unicameral Assembly of the States (60 seats - 33 elected by popular vote; members serve six-year terms)
elections: last held 20 April 1994 (next to be held NA 2000)
election results: percent of vote - NA; seats - all independents
Judicial branch: Royal Court
Political parties and leaders: none; all independents
International organization participation: none
Diplomatic representation in the US: none (British crown dependency)
Diplomatic representation from the US: none (British crown dependency)
Flag description: white with the red cross of Saint George (patron saint of England) extending to the edges of the flag

Economy

Economy - overview: Financial services - banking, fund management, insurance, etc. - account for about 55% of total income in this tiny Channel Island economy. Tourism, manufacturing, and horticulture, mainly tomatoes and cut flowers, have been declining. Light tax and death duties make Guernsey a popular tax haven. The evolving economic integration of the EU nations is changing the rules of the game under which Guernsey operates.
GDP: $NA
GDP - real growth rate: NA%
GDP - per capita: $NA
GDP - composition by sector:
agriculture: NA%
industry: NA%
services: NA%
Population below poverty line: NA%
Household income or consumption by percentage share:
lowest 10%: NA%
highest 10%: NA%
Inflation rate (consumer prices): 7% (1988)
Labor force: NA
Unemployment rate: 3%-4% (1994 est.)
Budget:
revenues: $277.9 million
expenditures: $248.8 million, including capital expenditures of $NA (1995 est.)
Industries: tourism, banking
Industrial production growth rate: NA%
Electricity - production: NA kWh
Electricity - production by source:
fossil fuel: NA%
hydro: NA%
nuclear: NA%
other: NA%
Electricity - consumption: NA kWh
Electricity - exports: NA kWh
Electricity - imports: NA kWh

Guernsey *(continued)*

Agriculture - products: tomatoes, greenhouse flowers, sweet peppers, eggplant, fruit; Guernsey cattle
Exports: $NA
Exports - commodities: tomatoes, flowers and ferns, sweet peppers, eggplant, other vegetables
Exports - partners: UK (regarded as internal trade)
Imports: $NA
Imports - commodities: coal, gasoline, oil, machinery and equipment
Imports - partners: UK (regarded as internal trade)
Debt - external: $NA
Economic aid - recipient: $NA
Currency: 1 Guernsey (£G) pound = 100 pence
Exchange rates: Guernsey pounds (£G) per US$1 - 0.6057 (January 1999), 0.6037 (1998), 0.6106 (1997), 0.6403 (1996), 0.6335 (1995), 0.6529 (1994); note - the Guernsey pound is at par with the British pound
Fiscal year: calendar year

Communications

Telephones: 41,850 (1983 est.)
Telephone system:
domestic: NA
international: 1 submarine cable
Radio broadcast stations: AM 1, FM 1, shortwave 0
Radios: NA
Television broadcast stations: 1 (1997)
Televisions: NA

Transportation

Railways: 0 km
Highways:
total: NA km
paved: NA km
unpaved: NA km
Ports and harbors: Saint Peter Port, Saint Sampson
Merchant marine: none
Airports: 2 (1998 est.)
Airports - with paved runways:
total: 2
914 to 1,523 m: 1
under 914 m: 1 (1998 est.)

Military

Military - note: defense is the responsibility of the UK

Transnational Issues

Disputes - international: none

Guinea

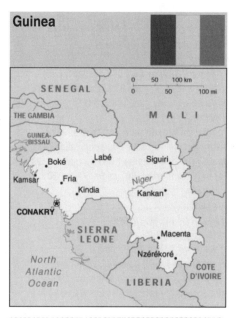

Geography

Location: Western Africa, bordering the North Atlantic Ocean, between Guinea-Bissau and Sierra Leone
Geographic coordinates: 11 00 N, 10 00 W
Map references: Africa
Area:
total: 245,860 sq km
land: 245,860 sq km
water: 0 sq km
Area - comparative: slightly smaller than Oregon
Land boundaries:
total: 3,399 km
border countries: Guinea-Bissau 386 km, Cote d'Ivoire 610 km, Liberia 563 km, Mali 858 km, Senegal 330 km, Sierra Leone 652 km
Coastline: 320 km
Maritime claims:
exclusive economic zone: 200 nm
territorial sea: 12 nm
Climate: generally hot and humid; monsoonal-type rainy season (June to November) with southwesterly winds; dry season (December to May) with northeasterly harmattan winds
Terrain: generally flat coastal plain, hilly to mountainous interior
Elevation extremes:
lowest point: Atlantic Ocean 0 m
highest point: Mont Nimba 1,752 m
Natural resources: bauxite, iron ore, diamonds, gold, uranium, hydropower, fish
Land use:
arable land: 2%
permanent crops: 0%
permanent pastures: 22%
forests and woodland: 59%
other: 17% (1993 est.)
Irrigated land: 930 sq km (1993 est.)
Natural hazards: hot, dry, dusty harmattan haze may reduce visibility during dry season

---

Environment - current issues: deforestation; inadequate supplies of potable water; desertification; soil contamination and erosion; overfishing, overpopulation in forest region
Environment - international agreements:
party to: Biodiversity, Climate Change, Desertification, Endangered Species, Hazardous Wastes, Law of the Sea, Ozone Layer Protection, Wetlands
signed, but not ratified: none of the selected agreements

People

Population: 7,538,953 (July 1999 est.)
Age structure:
0-14 years: 44% (male 1,640,158; female 1,653,184)
15-64 years: 54% (male 1,974,849; female 2,068,221)
65 years and over: 2% (male 83,859; female 118,682) (1999 est.)
Population growth rate: 0.82% (1999 est.)
Birth rate: 40.62 births/1,000 population (1999 est.)
Death rate: 17.3 deaths/1,000 population (1999 est.)
Net migration rate: -15.12 migrant(s)/1,000 population (1999 est.)
note: over the years Guinea has received up to several hundred thousand refugees from the civil wars in Liberia and Sierra Leone, some of whom are now returning to their own countries
Sex ratio:
at birth: 1.03 male(s)/female
under 15 years: 0.99 male(s)/female
15-64 years: 0.95 male(s)/female
65 years and over: 0.71 male(s)/female
total population: 0.96 male(s)/female (1999 est.)
Infant mortality rate: 126.32 deaths/1,000 live births (1999 est.)
Life expectancy at birth:
total population: 46.5 years
male: 44.02 years
female: 49.06 years (1999 est.)
Total fertility rate: 5.53 children born/woman (1999 est.)
Nationality:
noun: Guinean(s)
adjective: Guinean
Ethnic groups: Peuhl 40%, Malinke 30%, Soussou 20%, smaller tribes 10%
Religions: Muslim 85%, Christian 8%, indigenous beliefs 7%
Languages: French (official), each tribe has its own language
Literacy:
definition: age 15 and over can read and write
total population: 35.9%
male: 49.9%
female: 21.9% (1995 est.)

Government

Country name:
conventional long form: Republic of Guinea

Guinea *(continued)*

conventional short form: Guinea
local long form: Republique de Guinee
local short form: Guinee
former: French Guinea
Data code: GV
Government type: republic
Capital: Conakry
Administrative divisions: 4 administrative regions (regions administrative, singular - region administrative) and 1 special zone (zone speciale)*; Conakry*, Guinee, Guinee-Forestiere, Haute-Guinee, Moyen-Guinee
Independence: 2 October 1958 (from France)
National holiday: Anniversary of the Second Republic, 3 April (1984)
Constitution: 23 December 1990 (Loi Fundamentale)
Legal system: based on French civil law system, customary law, and decree; legal codes currently being revised; has not accepted compulsory ICJ jurisdiction
Suffrage: 18 years of age; universal
Executive branch:
chief of state: President Lansana CONTE (head of military government since 5 April 1984, elected president 19 December 1993)
head of government: Prime Minister Lamine SIDIME (since 8 March 1999)
cabinet: Council of Ministers appointed by the president
elections: president elected by popular vote for a five-year term; candidate must receive a majority of the votes cast to be elected president; election last held 14 December 1998 (next to be held NA December 2003); the prime minister appointed by the president
election results: Lansana CONTE reelected president; percent of vote - Lansana CONTE (PUP) 56%, Alpha CONDE (RPG) 16%, Mamadou Boye BA (UNR-PRP) 24%
Legislative branch: unicameral People's National Assembly or Assemblee Nationale Populaire (114 seats; members are elected by direct popular vote to serve five-year terms)
elections: last held 11 June 1995 (next to be held NA 2000)
election results: percent of vote by party - NA; seats by party - PUP 71, RPG 19, PRP 9, UNR 9, UPG 2, PDG 1, UNP 1, PDG-RDA 1, other 1
Judicial branch: Court of Appeal or Cour d'Appel
Political parties and leaders: political parties were legalized on 1 April 1992; of the more than 40 with legal status, the following won seats in the legislature in the 11 June 1995 elections
pro-government: Party for Unity and Progress or PUP [Lansana CONTE]
other: Democratic Party of Guinea-African Democratic Rally or PDG-RDA [El Hadj Ismael Mohamed Gassim GUSHEIN]; Democratic Party of Guinea or PDG-AST [Marcel CROS]; National Union for the Prosperity of Guinea or UNPG [Lt. Col. Facine TOURE]; Party for Renewal and Progress or PRP

[Siradiou DIALLO]; Rally for the Guinean People or RPG [Alpha CONDE]; Union for Progress of Guinea or UPG [Jean-Marie DORE, secretary-general]; Union for a New Republic or UNR [Mamadou Boye BA]; Union for the New Republic or UNR [leader NA]; National Union for Prosperity or UNP [leader NA]
International organization participation: ACCT, ACP, AfDB, CCC, ECA, ECOWAS, FAO, G-77, IBRD, ICAO, ICFTU, ICRM, IDA, IDB, IFAD, IFC, IFRCS, ILO, IMF, IMO, Intelsat, Interpol, IOC, IOM (observer), ISO (correspondent), ITU, MINURSO, NAM, OAU, OIC, OPCW, UN, UNCTAD, UNESCO, UNIDO, UPU, WCL, WFTU, WHO, WIPO, WMO, WToO, WTrO
Diplomatic representation in the US:
chief of mission: Ambassador Mohamed Aly THIAM
chancery: 2112 Leroy Place NW, Washington, DC 20008
telephone: [1] (202) 483-9420
FAX: [1] (202) 483-8688
Diplomatic representation from the US:
chief of mission: Ambassador Tibor P. NAGY, Jr.
embassy: Rue Ka 038, Conakry
mailing address: B. P. 603, Conakry
telephone: [224] 41 15 20, 41 15 21, 41 15 23
FAX: [224] 41 15 22
Flag description: three equal vertical bands of red (hoist side), yellow, and green; uses the popular pan-African colors of Ethiopia; similar to the flag of Rwanda, which has a large black letter R centered in the yellow band

Economy

Economy - overview: Guinea possesses major mineral, hydropower, and agricultural resources, yet remains a poor underdeveloped nation. The agricultural sector employs 80% of the work force. Guinea possesses over 25% of the world's bauxite reserves and is the second largest bauxite producer. The mining sector accounted for about 75% of exports in 1998. Long-run improvements in government fiscal arrangements, literacy, and the legal framework are needed if the country is to move out of poverty. The government made encouraging progress in budget management in 1997-98. Except in the mining industry, foreign investment remains minimal but is expected to pick up in 1999.
GDP: purchasing power parity - $8.8 billion (1998 est.)
GDP - real growth rate: 4.9% (1998 est.)
GDP - per capita: purchasing power parity - $1,180 (1998 est.)
GDP - composition by sector:
agriculture: 24%
industry: 31%
services: 45% (1996 est.)
Population below poverty line: NA%
Household income or consumption by percentage share:
lowest 10%: 0.9%
highest 10%: 31.7% (1991)
Inflation rate (consumer prices): 3.5% (1998 est.)
Labor force: 2.4 million (1983)

Labor force - by occupation: agriculture 80%, industry and commerce 11%, services 5.4%, civil service 3.6%
Unemployment rate: NA%
Budget:
revenues: $553 million
expenditures: $652 million, including capital expenditures of $317 million (1995 est.)
Industries: bauxite, gold, diamonds; alumina refining; light manufacturing and agricultural processing industries
Industrial production growth rate: 3.2% (1994)
Electricity - production: 525 million kWh (1996)
Electricity - production by source:
fossil fuel: 63.81%
hydro: 36.19%
nuclear: 0%
other: 0% (1996)
Electricity - consumption: 525 million kWh (1996)
Electricity - exports: 0 kWh (1996)
Electricity - imports: 0 kWh (1996)
Agriculture - products: rice, coffee, pineapples, palm kernels, cassava (tapioca), bananas, sweet potatoes; cattle, sheep, goats; timber
Exports: $695 million (f.o.b., 1998 est.)
Exports - commodities: bauxite, alumina, diamonds, gold, coffee, fish, agricultural products
Exports - partners: Russia, US, Belgium, Ukraine, Ireland, Spain (1997)
Imports: $560 million (f.o.b., 1998 est.)
Imports - commodities: petroleum products, metals, machinery, transport equipment, textiles, grain and other foodstuffs (1997)
Imports - partners: France, Cote d'Ivoire, US, Belgium, Hong Kong (1997)
Debt - external: $3.15 billion (1998 est.)
Economic aid - recipient: $433.6 million (1995)
Currency: 1 Guinean franc (FG) = 100 centimes
Exchange rates: Guinean francs (FG) per US$1 - 1,292.5 (January 1999), 1,095.3 (1997), 1,004.0 (1996), 991.4 (1995), 976.6 (1994)
note: the official exchange rate of the Guinean franc was set and quoted weekly against the US dollar until the end of October 1993; since 1 November 1994, the exchange rate is determined in the interbank market for foreign exchange
Fiscal year: calendar year

Communications

Telephones: 18,000 (1994 est.)
Telephone system: poor to fair system of open-wire lines, small radiotelephone communication stations, and new microwave radio relay system
domestic: microwave radio relay and radiotelephone communication
international: satellite earth station - 1 Intelsat (Atlantic Ocean)
Radio broadcast stations: AM 3, FM 1, shortwave 0
Radios: 257,000 (1992 est.)
Television broadcast stations: 6 (1997)
Televisions: 65,000 (1993 est.)

Guinea (continued)

Transportation

Railways:
total: 1,086 km
standard gauge: 279 km 1.435-m gauge
narrow gauge: 807 km 1.000-m gauge (includes 662 km in common carrier service from Kankan to Conakry)
Highways:
total: 30,500 km
paved: 5,033 km
unpaved: 25,467 km (1996 est.)
Waterways: 1,295 km navigable by shallow-draft native craft
Ports and harbors: Boke, Conakry, Kamsar
Merchant marine: none
Airports: 15 (1998 est.)
Airports - with paved runways:
total: 5
over 3,047 m: 1
2,438 to 3,047 m: 1
1,524 to 2,437 m: 3 (1998 est.)
Airports - with unpaved runways:
total: 10
1,524 to 2,437 m: 5
914 to 1,523 m: 4
under 914 m: 1 (1998 est.)

Military

Military branches: Army, Navy, Air Force, Republican Guard, Presidential Guard, paramilitary National Gendarmerie, National Police Force (Surete National)
Military manpower - availability:
males age 15-49: 1,726,933 (1999 est.)
Military manpower - fit for military service:
males age 15-49: 871,615 (1999 est.)
Military expenditures - dollar figure: $56 million (1996)
Military expenditures - percent of GDP: 1.4% (1996)

Transnational Issues

Disputes - international: none

Guinea-Bissau

Geography

Location: Western Africa, bordering the North Atlantic Ocean, between Guinea and Senegal
Geographic coordinates: 12 00 N, 15 00 W
Map references: Africa
Area:
total: 36,120 sq km
land: 28,000 sq km
water: 8,120 sq km
Area - comparative: slightly less than three times the size of Connecticut
Land boundaries:
total: 724 km
border countries: Guinea 386 km, Senegal 338 km
Coastline: 350 km
Maritime claims:
exclusive economic zone: 200 nm
territorial sea: 12 nm
Climate: tropical; generally hot and humid; monsoonal-type rainy season (June to November) with southwesterly winds; dry season (December to May) with northeasterly harmattan winds
Terrain: mostly low coastal plain rising to savanna in east
Elevation extremes:
lowest point: Atlantic Ocean 0 m
highest point: unnamed location in the northeast corner of the country 300 m
Natural resources: fish, timber, phosphates, bauxite, unexploited deposits of petroleum
Land use:
arable land: 11%
permanent crops: 1%
permanent pastures: 38%
forests and woodland: 38%
other: 12% (1993 est.)
Irrigated land: 17 sq km (1993 est.)
Natural hazards: hot, dry, dusty harmattan haze may reduce visibility during dry season; brush fires
Environment - current issues: deforestation; soil erosion; overgrazing; overfishing
Environment - international agreements:
party to: Biodiversity, Climate Change, Desertification, Endangered Species, Law of the Sea, Wetlands
signed, but not ratified: none of the selected agreements

People

Population: 1,234,555 (July 1999 est.)
Age structure:
0-14 years: 42% (male 260,821; female 259,520)
15-64 years: 55% (male 322,607; female 356,513)
65 years and over: 3% (male 16,233; female 18,861) (1999 est.)
Population growth rate: 2.31% (1999 est.)
Birth rate: 38.23 births/1,000 population (1999 est.)
Death rate: 15.13 deaths/1,000 population (1999 est.)
Net migration rate: 0 migrant(s)/1,000 population (1999 est.)
Sex ratio:
at birth: 1.03 male(s)/female
under 15 years: 1.01 male(s)/female
15-64 years: 0.9 male(s)/female
65 years and over: 0.86 male(s)/female
total population: 0.94 male(s)/female (1999 est.)
Infant mortality rate: 109.5 deaths/1,000 live births (1999 est.)
Life expectancy at birth:
total population: 49.57 years
male: 47.91 years
female: 51.28 years (1999 est.)
Total fertility rate: 5.09 children born/woman (1999 est.)
Nationality:
noun: Guinean (s)
adjective: Guinean
Ethnic groups: African 99% (Balanta 30%, Fula 20%, Manjaca 14%, Mandinga 13%, Papel 7%), European and mulatto less than 1%
Religions: indigenous beliefs 50%, Muslim 45%, Christian 5%
Languages: Portuguese (official), Crioulo, African languages
Literacy:
definition: age 15 and over can read and write
total population: 53.9%
male: 67.1%
female: 40.7% (1997 est.)

Government

Country name:
conventional long form: Republic of Guinea-Bissau
conventional short form: Guinea-Bissau
local long form: Republica da Guine-Bissau
local short form: Guine-Bissau
former: Portuguese Guinea
Data code: PU
Government type: republic, multiparty since mid-1991

Guinea-Bissau *(continued)*

Capital: Bissau

Administrative divisions: 9 regions (regioes, singular - regiao); Bafata, Biombo, Bissau, Bolama, Cacheu, Gabu, Oio, Quinara, Tombali

note: Bolama may have been renamed Bolama/Bijagos

Independence: 24 September 1973 (unilaterally declared by Guinea-Bissau); 10 September 1974 (recognized by Portugal)

National holiday: Independence Day, 24 September (1973)

Constitution: 16 May 1984, amended 4 May 1991, 4 December 1991, 26 February 1993, 9 June 1993, and 1996

Legal system: NA

Suffrage: 18 years of age; universal

Executive branch:

chief of state: President Joao Bernardo VIEIRA (initially assumed power 14 November 1980 in a coup d'etat)

head of government: Prime Minister Francisco FADUL (since NA November 1998); note - named in an agreement between President VIEIRA and a military-led junta which rebelled against the President FADUL's administration in June 1998

cabinet: none; an interim National Unity Government was provided for in the agreement between President VIEIRA and the military junta and was scheduled be inaugurated in February 1999

elections: president elected by popular vote for a five-year term; election last held 3 July and 7 August 1994 (next to be held NA July 1999); prime minister appointed by the president after consultation with party leaders in the legislature

election results: Joao Bernardo VIEIRA elected president; percent of vote - Joao Bernardo VIEIRA 52%, Koumba YALLA 48%

Legislative branch: unicameral National People's Assembly or Assembleia Nacional Popular (100 seats; members are elected by popular vote to serve a maximum of four years)

elections: last held 3 July and 7 August 1994 (next to be held by NA)

election results: percent of vote by party - PAIGC 46.0%, RGB-MB 19.2%, PRS 10.3%, UM 12.8%, FLING 2.5%, PCD 5.3%, PUSD 2.9%, FCG 0.2%, others 0.8%; seats by party - PAIGC 62, RGB 19, PRS 12, UM 6, FLING 1

Judicial branch: Supreme Court or Supremo Tribunal da Justica, consists of 9 justices who are appointed by the president and serve at his pleasure, final court of appeals in criminal and civil cases; Regional Courts, one in each of nine regions, first court of appeals for sectoral court decisions, hear all felony cases and civil cases valued at over $1,000; 24 Sectoral Courts, judges are not necessarily trained lawyers, hear civil cases under $1,000 and misdemeanor criminal cases

Political parties and leaders: African Party for the Independence of Guinea-Bissau and Cape Verde or PAIGC [Manuel Saturnino da COSTA, secretary general]; Front for the Liberation and Independence of Guinea or FLING [Jose Katengul M. ENDES]; Guinea-Bissau Resistance-Ba Fata Movement or RGB-MB [Domingos FERNANDES Gomes]; Guinean Civic Forum or FCG [Antonieta Rosa GOMES]; International League for Ecological Protection or LIPE [Alhaje Bubacar DJALO, president]; National Union for Democracy and Progress or UNDP [Abubacer BALDE, secretary general]; Party for Democratic Convergence or PCD [Victor MANDINGA]; Social Renovation Party or PRS [Koumba YALLA, leader]; Union for Change or UM [Jorge MANDINGA, president, Dr. Anne SAAD, secretary general]; United Social Democratic Party or PUSD [Victor Sau'de MARIA]

International organization participation: ACCT (associate), ACP, AfDB, ECA, ECOWAS, FAO, FZ, G-77, IBRD, ICAO, ICFTU, ICRM, IDA, IDB, IFAD, IFC, IFRCS, ILO, IMF, IMO, Intelsat (nonsignatory user), Interpol, IOC, IOM (observer), ITU, MONUA, NAM, OAU, OIC, OPCW, UN, UNCTAD, UNESCO, UNIDO, UPU, WAEMU, WFTU, WHO, WIPO, WMO, WToO, WTrO

Diplomatic representation in the US:

chief of mission: Ambassador (vacant); Charge d'Affaires Henrique Adriano DA SILVA

chancery: Suite 519, 1511 K Street, NW, Washington, DC 20005

telephone: [1] (202) 347-3950

FAX: [1] (202) 347-3954

Diplomatic representation from the US: the US Embassy suspended operations on 14 June 1998 in the midst of violent conflict between forces loyal to President VIEIRA and military-led junta

Flag description: two equal horizontal bands of yellow (top) and green with a vertical red band on the hoist side; there is a black five-pointed star centered in the red band; uses the popular pan-African colors of Ethiopia

Economy

Economy - overview: One of the 20 poorest countries in the world, Guinea-Bissau depends mainly on farming and fishing. Cashew crops have increased remarkably in recent years, and the country now ranks sixth in cashew production. Guinea-Bissau exports fish and seafood along with small amounts of peanuts, palm kernels, and timber. Rice is the major crop and staple food. However, intermittent fighting between Senegalese-backed government troops and a military junta destroyed much of the country's infrastructure and caused widespread damage to the economy in 1998. Before the war, trade reform and price liberalization were the most successful part of the country's structural adjustment program under IMF sponsorship. The tightening of monetary policy and the development of the private sector had also begun to reinvigorate the economy. Inflation dropped sharply in the first quarter of 1997. Membership in the WAMU (West African Monetary Union), begun in May 1997, was expected to support 5% annual growth and contribute to fiscal discipline. Because of high costs, the development of petroleum, phosphate, and other mineral resources was not a near-term prospect.

GDP: purchasing power parity - $1.2 billion (1998 est.)

GDP - real growth rate: 3.5% (1998 est.)

GDP - per capita: purchasing power parity - $1,000 (1998 est.)

GDP - composition by sector:

agriculture: 54%

industry: 11%

services: 35% (1996 est.)

Population below poverty line: 48.8% (1991 est.)

Household income or consumption by percentage share:

lowest 10%: 0.5%

highest 10%: 42.4% (1991)

Inflation rate (consumer prices): 25.6% (1997)

Labor force: 480,000

Unemployment rate: NA%

Budget: $NA

Industries: agricultural products processing, beer, soft drinks

Industrial production growth rate: 2.6% (1997 est.)

Electricity - production: 40 million kWh (1996)

Electricity - production by source:

fossil fuel: 100%

hydro: 0%

nuclear: 0%

other: 0% (1996)

Electricity - consumption: 40 million kWh (1996)

Electricity - exports: 0 kWh (1996)

Electricity - imports: 0 kWh (1996)

Agriculture - products: rice, corn, beans, cassava (tapioca), cashew nuts, peanuts, palm kernels, cotton; timber; fish

Exports: $25.8 million (f.o.b., 1996 est.)

Exports - commodities: cashews 95%, fish, peanuts, palm kernels, sawn lumber (1994)

Exports - partners: Spain 35%, India 30%, Thailand 10%, Italy 10% (1995)

Imports: $63 million (f.o.b., 1996 est.)

Imports - commodities: foodstuffs, transport equipment, petroleum products, machinery and equipment (1994)

Imports - partners: Portugal 29.2%, Thailand 8.4%, Netherlands 8.4%, US 7.5% (1996)

Debt - external: $953 million (1996 est.)

Economic aid - recipient: $115.4 million (1995)

Currency: 1 Communaute Financiere Africaine franc (CFAF) = 100 centimes; note - on 1 May 1997, Guinea-Bissau adopted as its currency the CFA franc following its membership into the BCEAO

Exchange rates: Communaute Financiere Africaine francs (CFAF) per US$1 - 566.65 (January 1999), 589.95 (1998), 583.67 (1997); Guinea-Bissauan pesos (PG) per US$1 - 26,373 (1996), 18,073 (1995), 12,892 (1994)

note: as of 2 May 1997, Guinea-Bissau has adopted the CFA franc as the national currency following its membership in BCEAO

Fiscal year: calendar year

Guinea-Bissau *(continued)*

Communications

Telephones: 13,120 (1997 est.)
Telephone system: small system
domestic: combination of microwave radio relay, open-wire lines, radiotelephone, and cellular communications
international: NA
Radio broadcast stations: AM 2, FM 3, shortwave 0
Radios: 40,000 (1994 est.)
Television broadcast stations: 2 (1997)
Televisions: NA

Transportation

Railways: 0 km
Highways:
total: 4,400 km
paved: 453 km
unpaved: 3,947 km (1996 est.)
Waterways: several rivers are accessible to coastal shipping
Ports and harbors: Bissau, Buba, Cacheu, Farim
Merchant marine: none
Airports: 30 (1998 est.)
Airports - with paved runways:
total: 3
over 3,047 m: 1
1,524 to 2,437 m: 1
914 to 1,523 m: 1 (1998 est.)
Airports - with unpaved runways:
total: 27
1,524 to 2,437 m: 1
914 to 1,523 m: 4
under 914 m: 22 (1998 est.)

Military

Military branches: People's Revolutionary Armed Force (FARP; includes Army, Navy, and Air Force), paramilitary force
Military manpower - availability:
males age 15-49: 284,998 (1999 est.)
Military manpower - fit for military service:
males age 15-49: 162,485 (1999 est.)
Military expenditures - dollar figure: $8 million (1996)
Military expenditures - percent of GDP: 2.8% (1996)

Transnational Issues

Disputes - international: none

Guyana

Geography

Location: Northern South America, bordering the North Atlantic Ocean, between Suriname and Venezuela
Geographic coordinates: 5 00 N, 59 00 W
Map references: South America
Area:
total: 214,970 sq km
land: 196,850 sq km
water: 18,120 sq km
Area - comparative: slightly smaller than Idaho
Land boundaries:
total: 2,462 km
border countries: Brazil 1,119 km, Suriname 600 km, Venezuela 743 km
Coastline: 459 km
Maritime claims:
continental shelf: 200 nm or to the outer edge of the continental margin
exclusive fishing zone: 200 nm
territorial sea: 12 nm
Climate: tropical; hot, humid, moderated by northeast trade winds; two rainy seasons (May to mid-August, mid-November to mid-January)
Terrain: mostly rolling highlands; low coastal plain; savanna in south
Elevation extremes:
lowest point: Atlantic Ocean 0 m
highest point: Mount Roraima 2,835 m
Natural resources: bauxite, gold, diamonds, hardwood timber, shrimp, fish
Land use:
arable land: 2%
permanent crops: 0%
permanent pastures: 6%
forests and woodland: 84%
other: 8% (1993 est.)
Irrigated land: 1,300 sq km (1993 est.)
Natural hazards: flash floods are a constant threat during rainy seasons
Environment - current issues: water pollution from sewage and agricultural and industrial chemicals; deforestation
Environment - international agreements:
party to: Biodiversity, Climate Change, Desertification, Endangered Species, Law of the Sea, Ozone Layer Protection, Tropical Timber 83, Tropical Timber 94
signed, but not ratified: none of the selected agreements

People

Population: 705,156 (July 1999 est.)
Age structure:
0-14 years: 30% (male 109,156; female 105,017)
15-64 years: 65% (male 230,624; female 227,677)
65 years and over: 5% (male 14,684; female 17,998) (1999 est.)
Population growth rate: -0.32% (1999 est.)
Birth rate: 18.23 births/1,000 population (1999 est.)
Death rate: 9.04 deaths/1,000 population (1999 est.)
Net migration rate: -12.43 migrant(s)/1,000 population (1999 est.)
Sex ratio:
at birth: 1.05 male(s)/female
under 15 years: 1.04 male(s)/female
15-64 years: 1.01 male(s)/female
65 years and over: 0.82 male(s)/female
total population: 1.01 male(s)/female (1999 est.)
Infant mortality rate: 48.64 deaths/1,000 live births (1999 est.)
Life expectancy at birth:
total population: 61.82 years
male: 59.15 years
female: 64.61 years (1999 est.)
Total fertility rate: 2.09 children born/woman (1999 est.)
Nationality:
noun: Guyanese (singular and plural)
adjective: Guyanese
Ethnic groups: East Indian 49%, black 32%, mixed 12%, Amerindian 6%, white and Chinese 1%
Religions: Christian 57%, Hindu 33%, Muslim 9%, other 1%
Languages: English, Amerindian dialects
Literacy:
definition: age 15 and over has ever attended school

Guyana (continued)

total population: 98.1%
male: 98.6%
female: 97.5% (1995 est.)

Government

Country name:
conventional long form: Co-operative Republic of Guyana
conventional short form: Guyana
former: British Guiana
Data code: GY
Government type: republic
Capital: Georgetown
Administrative divisions: 10 regions; Barima-Waini, Cuyuni-Mazaruni, Demerara-Mahaica, East Berbice-Corentyne, Essequibo Islands-West Demerara, Mahaica-Berbice, Pomeroon-Supenaam, Potaro-Siparuni, Upper Demerara-Berbice, Upper Takutu-Upper Essequibo
Independence: 26 May 1966 (from UK)
National holiday: Republic Day, 23 February (1970)
Constitution: 6 October 1980
Legal system: based on English common law with certain admixtures of Roman-Dutch law; has not accepted compulsory ICJ jurisdiction
Suffrage: 18 years of age; universal
Executive branch:
chief of state: President Janet JAGAN (since NA December 1997)
head of government: Prime Minister Samuel HINDS (since NA December 1997)
cabinet: Cabinet of Ministers appointed by the president, responsible to the legislature
elections: president elected by the majority party in the National Assembly after legislative elections, which must be held within five years; legislative elections last held 15 December 1997 (next to be held NA 2000; this date was part of a negotiated settlement between the two main political parties following a dispute over the December elections); prime minister appointed by the president
Legislative branch: unicameral National Assembly (65 seats, 53 popularly elected; members serve five-year terms)
elections: last held on 15 December 1997 (next to be held by March 2000; this date was negotiated following a dispute over the December elections)
election results: percent of vote by party - PPP 54%, PNC 41%, AFG 1%, TUF 1%; seats by party - PPP 36, PNC 25, AFG 2, TUF 2
Judicial branch: Supreme Court of Judicature
Political parties and leaders: People's Progressive Party or PPP [leader NA]; People's National Congress or PNC [Hugh Desmond HOYTE]; For a Good and Green Guyana or GGG [Hamilton GREEN]; Alliance for Guyana or AFG [Rupert ROOPNARINE]; Democratic Labor Movement or DLM [Paul TENNASSEE]; People's Democratic Movement or PDM [Llewellyn JOHN]; National Democratic Front or NDF [Joseph BACCHUS]; The United Force or TUF [Manzoor NADIR]; National Republican Party or NRP [Robert GANGADEEN]; Guyana Labor Party or GLP

[leader NA]; Guyana Democratic Party or GDP [Asgar ALLY]; Guyanese Organization for Liberty and Democracy Party or GOLD [Anthony MEKDECI]
Political pressure groups and leaders: Trades Union Congress or TUC; Guyana Council of Indian Organizations or GCIO; Civil Liberties Action Committee or CLAC
note: the latter two organizations are small and active but not well organized
International organization participation: ACP, C, Caricom, CCC, CDB, ECLAC, FAO, G-77, IADB, IBRD, ICAO, ICFTU, ICRM, IDA, IFAD, IFC, IFRCS, ILO, IMF, IMO, Intelsat (nonsignatory user), Interpol, IOC, ISO (subscriber), ITU, LAES, NAM, OAS, OIC (observer), OPANAL, OPCW, UN, UNCTAD, UNESCO, UNIDO, UPU, WCL, WFTU, WHO, WIPO, WMO, WTrO
Diplomatic representation in the US:
chief of mission: Ambassador Dr. Ali Odeen ISHMAEL
chancery: 2490 Tracy Place NW, Washington, DC 20008
telephone: [1] (202) 265-6900
consulate(s) general: New York
Diplomatic representation from the US:
chief of mission: Ambassador James F. MACK
embassy: 99-100 Young and Duke Streets, Kingston, Georgetown
mailing address: P. O. Box 10507, Georgetown
telephone: [592] (2) 54900 through 54909, 57960 through 57969
FAX: [592] (2) 59497
Flag description: green, with a red isosceles triangle (based on the hoist side) superimposed on a long, yellow arrowhead; there is a narrow, black border between the red and yellow, and a narrow, white border between the yellow and the green

Economy

Economy - overview: In 1997, Guyana, one of the poorest countries in the Western Hemisphere, posted its sixth straight year of economic growth of 5% or better, with the advance led by gold and bauxite mining and by sugar growing. Favorable growth factors have included expansion in the key agricultural and mining sectors, a more favorable atmosphere for business initiative, a more realistic exchange rate, a moderate inflation rate, and the continued support of international organizations. However, a severe drought and political turmoil following the 1997 elections contributed to a negative growth rate for 1998. Serious underlying economic problems will continue. Electricity has been in short supply and constitutes a major barrier to future gains in national output. The government must persist in efforts to manage its sizable external debt and extend its privatization program.
GDP: purchasing power parity - $1.8 billion (1998 est.)
GDP - real growth rate: -1.8% (1998 est.)
GDP - per capita: purchasing power parity - $2,500 (1998 est.)

GDP - composition by sector:
agriculture: 37%
industry: 22%
services: 41% (1997 est.)
Population below poverty line: NA%
Household income or consumption by percentage share:
lowest 10%: NA%
highest 10%: NA%
Inflation rate (consumer prices): 4.1% (1998)
Labor force: 245,492 (1992)
Labor force - by occupation: agriculture, hunting and forestry 30.2%, commerce 16%, manufacturing 11% (1992)
Unemployment rate: 12% (1992 est.)
Budget:
revenues: $253.7 million
expenditures: $304.1 million, including capital expenditures of $108.8 million (1997 est.)
Industries: bauxite, sugar, rice milling, timber, fishing (shrimp), textiles, gold mining
Industrial production growth rate: 7.1% (1997 est.)
Electricity - production: 325 million kWh (1996)
Electricity - production by source:
fossil fuel: 98.46%
hydro: 1.54%
nuclear: 0%
other: 0% (1996)
Electricity - consumption: 339 million kWh (1996)
Electricity - exports: 0 kWh (1996)
Electricity - imports: 14 million kWh (1996)
Agriculture - products: sugar, rice, wheat, vegetable oils; beef, pork, poultry, dairy products; forest and fishery potential not exploited
Exports: $593.4 million (1997 est.)
Exports - commodities: sugar, gold, bauxite/alumina, rice, shrimp, molasses
Exports - partners: Canada 25.9%, US 20.4%, UK 22.7%, Netherlands Antilles 8.4%, Germany 4.3% (1996)
Imports: $641.6 million (1997 est.)
Imports - commodities: manufactures, machinery, petroleum, food
Imports - partners: US 27.6%, Trinidad and Tobago 17.7%, Netherlands Antilles 12.1%, UK 10.7%, Japan 4.2% (1996)
Debt - external: $1.5 billion (1997)
Economic aid - recipient: $84 million (1995)
Currency: 1 Guyanese dollar (G$) = 100 cents
Exchange rates: Guyanese dollars (G$) per US$1 - 163.7 (December 1998), 150.5 (1998), 142.4 (1997), 140.4 (1996), 142.0 (1995), 138.3 (1994)
Fiscal year: calendar year

Communications

Telephones: 33,000 (1987 est.)
Telephone system: fair system for long-distance calling
domestic: microwave radio relay network for trunk lines
international: tropospheric scatter to Trinidad; satellite

---

earth station - 1 Intelsat (Atlantic Ocean)
Radio broadcast stations: AM 4, FM 3, shortwave 1
Radios: 398,000 (1992 est.)
Television broadcast stations: 1 public station; two private stations relay US satellite services (1997)
Televisions: 32,000 (1992 est.)

Transportation

Railways:
total: 88 km (all dedicated to ore transport)
standard gauge: 40 km 1.435-m gauge
narrow gauge: 48 km 0.914-m gauge
Highways:
total: 7,970 km
paved: 590 km
unpaved: 7,380 km (1996 est.)
Waterways: 6,000 km total of navigable waterways; Berbice, Demerara, and Essequibo Rivers are navigable by oceangoing vessels for 150 km, 100 km, and 80 km, respectively
Ports and harbors: Bartica, Georgetown, Linden, New Amsterdam, Parika
Merchant marine:
total: 2 cargo ships (1,000 GRT or over) totaling 2,340 GRT/4,530 DWT (1998 est.)
Airports: 48 (1998 est.)
Airports - with paved runways:
total: 4
1,524 to 2,437 m: 2
914 to 1,523 m: 1
under 914 m: 1 (1998 est.)
Airports - with unpaved runways:
total: 44
1,524 to 2,437 m: 2
914 to 1,523 m: 7
under 914 m: 35 (1998 est.)

Military

Military branches: Guyana Defense Force (GDF; includes Ground Forces, Coast Guard, and Air Corps), Guyana People's Militia (GPM), Guyana National Service (GNS), Guyana Police Force
Military manpower - availability:
males age 15-49: 202,509 (1999 est.)
Military manpower - fit for military service:
males age 15-49: 152,839 (1999 est.)
Military expenditures - dollar figure: $7 million (1994)
Military expenditures - percent of GDP: 1.7% (1994)

Transnational Issues

Disputes - international: all of the area west of the Essequibo River claimed by Venezuela; Suriname claims area between New (Upper Courantyne) and Courantyne/Kutari [Koetari] Rivers (all headwaters of the Courantyne)
Illicit drugs: transshipment point for narcotics from South America - primarily Venezuela - to Europe and the US; producer of cannabis

Haiti

Geography

Location: Caribbean, western one-third of the island of Hispaniola, between the Caribbean Sea and the North Atlantic Ocean, west of the Dominican Republic
Geographic coordinates: 19 00 N, 72 25 W
Map references: Central America and the Caribbean
Area:
total: 27,750 sq km
land: 27,560 sq km
water: 190 sq km
Area - comparative: slightly smaller than Maryland
Land boundaries:
total: 275 km
border countries: Dominican Republic 275 km
Coastline: 1,771 km
Maritime claims:
contiguous zone: 24 nm
continental shelf: to depth of exploitation
exclusive economic zone: 200 nm
territorial sea: 12 nm
Climate: tropical; semiarid where mountains in east cut off trade winds
Terrain: mostly rough and mountainous
Elevation extremes:
lowest point: Caribbean Sea 0 m
highest point: Chaine de la Selle 2,680 m
Natural resources: none
Land use:
arable land: 20%
permanent crops: 13%
permanent pastures: 18%
forests and woodland: 5%
other: 44% (1993 est.)
Irrigated land: 750 sq km (1993 est.)
Natural hazards: lies in the middle of the hurricane belt and subject to severe storms from June to October; occasional flooding and earthquakes; periodic droughts
Environment - current issues: extensive

deforestation (much of the remaining forested land is being cleared for agriculture and used as fuel); soil erosion; inadequate supplies of potable water
Environment - international agreements:
party to: Biodiversity, Climate Change, Desertification, Law of the Sea, Marine Dumping, Marine Life Conservation
signed, but not ratified: Hazardous Wastes, Nuclear Test Ban
Geography - note: shares island of Hispaniola with Dominican Republic (western one-third is Haiti, eastern two-thirds is the Dominican Republic)

People

Population: 6,884,264 (July 1999 est.)
Age structure:
0-14 years: 42% (male 1,464,529; female 1,420,772)
15-64 years: 54% (male 1,783,884; female 1,932,240)
65 years and over: 4% (male 140,932; female 141,907) (1999 est.)
Population growth rate: 1.53% (1999 est.)
Birth rate: 32.55 births/1,000 population (1999 est.)
Death rate: 13.97 deaths/1,000 population (1999 est.)
Net migration rate: -3.26 migrant(s)/1,000 population (1999 est.)
Sex ratio:
at birth: 1.05 male(s)/female
under 15 years: 1.03 male(s)/female
15-64 years: 0.92 male(s)/female
65 years and over: 0.99 male(s)/female
total population: 0.97 male(s)/female (1999 est.)
Infant mortality rate: 97.64 deaths/1,000 live births (1999 est.)
Life expectancy at birth:
total population: 51.65 years
male: 49.53 years
female: 53.88 years (1999 est.)
Total fertility rate: 4.59 children born/woman (1999 est.)
Nationality:
noun: Haitian(s)
adjective: Haitian
Ethnic groups: black 95%, mulatto plus white 5%
Religions: Roman Catholic 80%, Protestant 16% (Baptist 10%, Pentecostal 4%, Adventist 1%, other 1%), none 1%, other 3% (1982)
note: roughly one-half of the population also practices Voodoo
Languages: French (official) 20%, Creole
Literacy:
definition: age 15 and over can read and write
total population: 45%
male: 48%
female: 42.2% (1995 est.)

Government

Country name:
conventional long form: Republic of Haiti
conventional short form: Haiti

Haiti (continued)

local long form: Republique d'Haiti
local short form: Haiti
Data code: HA
Government type: republic
Capital: Port-au-Prince
Administrative divisions: 9 departments, (departementes, singular - departement); Artibonite, Centre, Grand'Anse, Nord, Nord-Est, Nord-Ouest, Ouest, Sud, Sud-Est
Independence: 1 January 1804 (from France)
National holiday: Independence Day, 1 January (1804)
Constitution: approved March 1987; suspended June 1988, with most articles reinstated March 1989; in October 1991, government claimed to be observing the constitution; return to constitutional rule, October 1994
Legal system: based on Roman civil law system; accepts compulsory ICJ jurisdiction
Suffrage: 18 years of age; universal
Executive branch:
chief of state: President Rene Garcia PREVAL (since 7 February 1996)
head of government: Prime Minister Rosny SMARTH resigned June 1997; currently no prime minister; ratification of a new prime minister held up in political gridlock stemming from controversy over the 6 April 1997 elections
cabinet: Cabinet; chosen by the prime minister in consultation with the president
elections: president elected by popular vote for a five-year term; election last held 17 December 1995 (next to be held by December 2000); prime minister appointed by the president, ratified by the Congress
election results: Rene Garcia PREVAL elected president; percent of vote - Rene Garcia PREVAL 88%, Leon JEUNE 2.5%, Victor BENOIT 2.3%
Legislative branch: bicameral National Assembly or Assemblee Nationale consists of the Senate (27 seats; members serve six-year terms; one-third elected every two years) and the Chamber of Deputies (83 seats; members are elected by popular vote to serve four-year terms)
elections: Senate - last held 25 June 1995, with reruns on 13 August and runoffs on 17 September (election held for nine seats 6 April 1997; results disputed and runoffs postponed indefinitely); Chamber of Deputies - last held 25 June 1995, with reruns on 13 August and runoffs on 17 September (next Senate and Chamber of Deputies elections due November 1998 but delayed indefinitely)
election results: Senate - percent of vote by party - NA; seats by party - OPL 7, FL-leaning 7, independents 3, vacant 10; Chamber of Deputies - percent of vote by party - NA; seats by party - OPL 32, antineoliberal bloc 24, minor parties and independents 22, vacant 5
Judicial branch: Supreme Court (Cour de Cassation)
Political parties and leaders: Lavalas Family or FL [Jean-Bertrand ARISTIDE]; Struggling People's Organization or OPL [Gerard PIERRE-CHARLES];

National Front for Change and Democracy or FNCD [Evans PAUL and Turneb DELPE]; National Congress of Democratic Movements or KONAKOM [Victor BENOIT]; Movement for the Installation of Democracy in Haiti or MIDH [Marc BAZIN]; National Progressive Revolutionary Party or PANPRA [Serge GILLES]; Movement for National Reconstruction or MRN [Rene THEODORE]; Haitian Christian Democratic Party or PDCH [Fritz PIERRE]; Assembly of Progressive National Democrats or RDNP [Leslie MANIGAT]; Mobilization for National Development or MDN [Hubert DE RONCERAY]; Movement for the Organization of the Country or MOP [Gesner COMEAU and Jean MOLIERE]; Open the Gate Party or PLB [Renaud BERNARDIN]; Union of Patriotic Democrats or UPD [Rockefeller GUERRE]; Generation 2004 [Claude ROUMAIN]; Alliance for the Liberation and Advancement of Haiti or ALAH [Reynold GEORGES]; Haitian Democratic Party or PADEMH [Clark PARENT]; National Alliance for Democracy and Progress [leader NA]; Haiti Can or Ayiti Kapab [Ernst VERDIEU]
Political pressure groups and leaders: Roman Catholic Church; Confederation of Haitian Workers or CTH; Federation of Workers Trade Unions or FOS; Autonomous Haitian Workers or CATH; National Popular Assembly or APN; Papaye Peasants Movement or MPP; Popular Organizations Gathering Power or PROP
International organization participation: ACCT, ACP, Caricom (observer), CCC, ECLAC, FAO, G-77, IADB, IAEA, IBRD, ICAO, ICRM, IDA, IFAD, IFC, IFRCS, ILO, IMF, IMO, Intelsat, Interpol, IOC, IOM, ITU, LAES, OAS, OPANAL, OPCW, PCA, UN, UNCTAD, UNESCO, UNIDO, UPU, WCL, WFTU, WHO, WIPO, WMO, WToO, WTrO
Diplomatic representation in the US:
chief of mission: Ambassador (vacant); Charge d'Affaires Louis Harold JOSEPH
chancery: 2311 Massachusetts Avenue NW, Washington, DC 20008
telephone: [1] (202) 332-4090
FAX: [1] (202) 745-7215
consulate(s) general: Boston, Chicago, Miami, New York, and San Juan (Puerto Rico)
Diplomatic representation from the US:
chief of mission: Ambassador Timothy Michael CARNEY
embassy: 5 Harry Truman Boulevard, Port-au-Prince
mailing address: P. O. Box 1761, Port-au-Prince
telephone: [509] 22-0354, 22-0368, 22-0200, 22-0612
FAX: [509] 23-1641
Flag description: two equal horizontal bands of blue (top) and red with a centered white rectangle bearing the coat of arms, which contains a palm tree flanked by flags and two cannons above a scroll bearing the motto L'UNION FAIT LA FORCE (Union Makes Strength)

Economy

Economy - overview: About 75% of the population lives in abject poverty. Nearly 70% of all Haitians

depend on the agriculture sector, which consists mainly of small-scale subsistence farming and employs about two-thirds of the economically active work force. The country has experienced little job creation since President PREVAL took office in February 1996, although the informal economy is growing. Failure to reach agreements with international sponsors have denied Haiti badly needed budget and development assistance. Meeting aid conditions in 1999 will be especially challenging in the face of mounting popular criticism of reforms.
GDP: purchasing power parity - $8.9 billion (1998 est.)
GDP - real growth rate: 3% (1998 est.)
GDP - per capita: purchasing power parity - $1,300 (1998 est.)
GDP - composition by sector:
agriculture: 42%
industry: 14%
services: 44% (1997 est.)
Population below poverty line: 75% (1998 est.)
Household income or consumption by percentage share:
lowest 10%: NA%
highest 10%: NA%
Inflation rate (consumer prices): 8% (1998 est.)
Labor force: 3.6 million (1995)
note: shortage of skilled labor, unskilled labor abundant (1998)
Labor force - by occupation: agriculture 66%, services 25%, industry 9%
Unemployment rate: 60% (1996 est.)
Budget:
revenues: $323 million
expenditures: $363 million, including capital expenditures of $NA (FY97/98 est.)
Industries: sugar refining, flour milling, textiles, cement, tourism, light assembly industries based on imported parts
Industrial production growth rate: 0.6% (1997 est.)
Electricity - production: 415 million kWh (1996)
Electricity - production by source:
fossil fuel: 60.24%
hydro: 39.76%
nuclear: 0%
other: 0% (1996)
Electricity - consumption: 415 million kWh (1996)
Electricity - exports: 0 kWh (1996)
Electricity - imports: 0 kWh (1996)
Agriculture - products: coffee, mangoes, sugarcane, rice, corn, sorghum; wood
Exports: $110 million (f.o.b., 1997)
Exports - commodities: light manufactures 80.5%, coffee 7.6%, other agriculture 7.2%
Exports - partners: US 76%, EU 19% (1997)
Imports: $486 million (f.o.b., 1997)
Imports - commodities: machines and manufactures 50%, food and beverages 39%, petroleum products 2%, chemicals 5%, fats and oils 4%
Imports - partners: US 60%, EU 12% (1997)

Haiti (continued)

Debt - external: $1 billion (1997 est.)
Economic aid - recipient: $730.6 million (1995)
Currency: 1 gourde (G) = 100 centimes
Exchange rates: gourdes (G) per US$1 - 16.778 (January 1999), 16.205 (1998), 17.311 (1997), 15.093 (1996), 16.160 (1995), 12.947 (1994)
Fiscal year: 1 October - 30 September

Communications

Telephones: 50,000 (1990 est.)
Telephone system: domestic facilities barely adequate; international facilities slightly better
domestic: NA
international: satellite earth station - 1 Intelsat (Atlantic Ocean)
Radio broadcast stations: AM 33, FM 0, shortwave 2
Radios: 320,000 (1992 est.)
Television broadcast stations: 2 (in addition, there is a cable TV station) (1997)
Televisions: 32,000 (1992 est.)

Transportation

Railways:
total: 40 km (single track; privately owned industrial line) - closed in early 1990s
narrow gauge: 40 km 0.760-m gauge
Highways:
total: 4,160 km
paved: 1,011 km
unpaved: 3,149 km (1996 est.)
Waterways: NEGL; less than 100 km navigable
Ports and harbors: Cap-Haitien, Gonaives, Jacmel, Jeremie, Les Cayes, Miragoane, Port-au-Prince, Port-de-Paix, Saint-Marc
Merchant marine: none
Airports: 13 (1998 est.)
Airports - with paved runways:
total: 3
2,438 to 3,047 m: 1
1,524 to 2,437 m: 1
914 to 1,523 m: 1 (1998 est.)
Airports - with unpaved runways:
total: 10
914 to 1,523 m: 5
under 914 m: 5 (1998 est.)

Military

Military branches: Haitian National Police (HNP)
note: the regular Haitian Army, Navy, and Air Force have been demobilized but still exist on paper until/unless constitutionally abolished
Military manpower - military age: 18 years of age
Military manpower - availability:
males age 15-49: 1,541,402 (1999 est.)
Military manpower - fit for military service:
males age 15-49: 835,578 (1999 est.)
Military manpower - reaching military age annually:
males: 80,158 (1999 est.)
Military expenditures - dollar figure: $NA; note - mainly for police and security activities

Military expenditures - percent of GDP: NA%
Military - note: the Haitian Armed Forces have been demobilized and replaced by the Haitian National Police

Transnational Issues

Disputes - international: claims US-administered Navassa Island
Illicit drugs: transshipment point for cocaine and marijuana en route to the US and Europe

Heard Island and McDonald Islands
(territory of Australia)

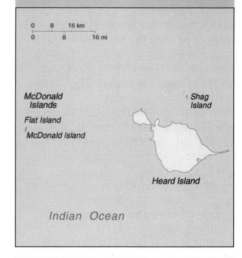

Geography

Location: Southern Africa, islands in the Indian Ocean, about two-thirds of the way from Madagascar to Antarctica
Geographic coordinates: 53 06 S, 72 31 E
Map references: Antarctic Region
Area:
total: 412 sq km
land: 412 sq km
water: 0 sq km
Area - comparative: slightly more than 2 times the size of Washington, DC
Land boundaries: 0 km
Coastline: 101.9 km
Maritime claims:
exclusive fishing zone: 200 nm
territorial sea: 3 nm
Climate: antarctic
Terrain: Heard Island - bleak and mountainous, with a quiescent volcano; McDonald Islands - small and rocky
Elevation extremes:
lowest point: Indian Ocean 0 m
highest point: Big Ben 2,745 m
Natural resources: none
Land use:
arable land: 0%
permanent crops: 0%
permanent pastures: 0%
forests and woodland: 0%
other: 100%
Irrigated land: 0 sq km (1993)
Natural hazards: Heard Island is dominated by a dormant volcano called Big Ben
Environment - current issues: NA
Environment - international agreements:
party to: NA
signed, but not ratified: NA
Geography - note: primarily used for research stations

Heard Island and McDonald Islands
(continued)

People

Population: uninhabited

Government

Country name:
conventional long form: Territory of Heard Island and McDonald Islands
conventional short form: Heard Island and McDonald Islands
Data code: HM
Dependency status: territory of Australia; administered from Canberra by the Department of the Environment, Sport and Territories
Legal system: NA
Diplomatic representation in the US: none (territory of Australia)
Diplomatic representation from the US: none (territory of Australia)
Flag description: the flag of Australia is used

Economy

Economy - overview: no economic activity

Transportation

Ports and harbors: none; offshore anchorage only

Military

Military - note: defense is the responsibility of Australia

Transnational Issues

Disputes - international: none

Holy See (Vatican City)

Introduction

Background: Popes in their secular role ruled much of the Italian peninsula, including Rome, for about a thousand years, until 1870. A dispute between a series of popes and Italy was settled in 1929 by treaties that recognized the Vatican City as an independent sovereignty and gave Roman Catholicism special status in Italy. The US established formal diplomatic relationships with the Vatican in 1984. Present issues in the Vatican concern the ill health of Pope John Paul II, who turns 79 on 20 May 1999, inter-religious dialogue and reconciliation, and the adjustment of church doctrine in an era of rapid change. About 1 billion people worldwide profess the Roman Catholic faith.

Geography

Location: Southern Europe, an enclave of Rome (Italy)
Geographic coordinates: 41 54 N, 12 27 E
Map references: Europe
Area:
total: 0.44 sq km
land: 0.44 sq km
water: 0 sq km
Area - comparative: about 0.7 times the size of The Mall in Washington, DC
Land boundaries:
total: 3.2 km
border countries: Italy 3.2 km
Coastline: 0 km (landlocked)
Maritime claims: none (landlocked)
Climate: temperate; mild, rainy winters (September to mid-May) with hot, dry summers (May to September)
Terrain: low hill
Elevation extremes:
lowest point: unnamed location 19 m
highest point: unnamed location 75 m
Natural resources: none

Land use:
arable land: 0%
permanent crops: 0%
permanent pastures: 0%
forests and woodland: 0%
other: 100% (urban area)
Irrigated land: 0 sq km (1993)
Natural hazards: NA
Environment - current issues: NA
Environment - international agreements:
party to: none of the selected agreements
signed, but not ratified: Air Pollution, Environmental Modification
Geography - note: urban; landlocked; enclave of Rome, Italy; world's smallest state; outside the Vatican City, 13 buildings in Rome and Castel Gandolfo (the pope's summer residence) enjoy extraterritorial rights

People

Population: 870 (July 1999 est.)
Population growth rate: 1.15% (1999 est.)
Nationality:
noun: none
adjective: none
Ethnic groups: Italians, Swiss, other
Religions: Roman Catholic
Languages: Italian, Latin, various other languages

Government

Country name:
conventional long form: The Holy See (State of the Vatican City)
conventional short form: Holy See (Vatican City)
local long form: Santa Sede (Stato della Citta del Vaticano)
local short form: Santa Sede (Citta del Vaticano)
Data code: VT
Government type: monarchical-sacerdotal state
Capital: Vatican City
Independence: 11 February 1929 (from Italy)
National holiday: Installation Day of the Pope (John Paul II), 22 October (1978)
Constitution: Apostolic Constitution of 1967 (effective 1 March 1968)
Legal system: NA
Suffrage: limited to cardinals less than 80 years old
Executive branch:
chief of state: Pope JOHN PAUL II (since 16 October 1978)
head of government: Secretary of State Archbishop Angelo Cardinal SODANO (since 2 December 1990)
cabinet: Pontifical Commission appointed by the pope
elections: pope elected for life by the College of Cardinals; election last held 16 October 1978 (next to be held after the death of the current pope); secretary of state appointed by the pope
election results: Karol WOJTYLA elected pope
Legislative branch: unicameral Pontifical Commission
Judicial branch: none; normally handled by Italy

Holy See (Vatican City) *(continued)*

Political parties and leaders: none
Political pressure groups and leaders: none (exclusive of influence exercised by church officers)
International organization participation: IAEA, ICFTU, Intelsat, IOM (observer), ITU, OAS (observer), OPCW, OSCE, UN (observer), UNCTAD, UNHCR, UPU, WIPO, WToO (observer)
Diplomatic representation in the US:
chief of mission: Apostolic Nuncio Archbishop Gabriel MONTALVO
chancery: 3339 Massachusetts Avenue NW, Washington, DC 20008
telephone: [1] (202) 333-7121
Diplomatic representation from the US:
chief of mission: Ambassador Corrine C. BOGGS
embassy: Villa Domiziana, Via Delle Terme Deciane 26, 00153 Rome
mailing address: PSC 59, Box F, APO AE 09624
telephone: [39] (06) 46741
FAX: [39] (06) 5758346, 57300682
Flag description: two vertical bands of yellow (hoist side) and white with the crossed keys of Saint Peter and the papal miter centered in the white band

Economy

Economy - overview: This unique, noncommercial economy is supported financially by contributions (known as Peter's Pence) from Roman Catholics throughout the world, the sale of postage stamps and tourist mementos, fees for admission to museums, and the sale of publications. The incomes and living standards of lay workers are comparable to, or somewhat better than, those of counterparts who work in the city of Rome.
Population below poverty line: NA%
Household income or consumption by percentage share:
lowest 10%: NA%
highest 10%: NA%
Labor force: NA
Labor force - by occupation: dignitaries, priests, nuns, guards, and 3,000 lay workers who live outside the Vatican
Budget:
revenues: $175.5 million
expenditures: $175 million, including capital expenditures of $NA (1994)
Industries: printing and production of a small amount of mosaics and staff uniforms; worldwide banking and financial activities
Electricity - production: 0 kWh
Electricity - production by source:
fossil fuel: NA%
hydro: NA%
nuclear: NA%
other: NA%
Electricity - consumption: NA kWh
Electricity - exports: NA kWh
Electricity - imports: NA kWh; note - electricity supplied by Italy
Economic aid - recipient: none
Currency: 1 Vatican lira (VLit) = 100 centesimi

Exchange rates: Vatican lire (VLit) per US$1 - 1,688.7 (January 1998), 1,736.2 (1998), 1,703.1 (1997), 1,542.9 (1996), 1,628.9 (1995), 1,612.4 (1994); note - the Vatican lira is at par with the Italian lira which circulates freely
Fiscal year: calendar year

Communications

Telephones: 2,000
Telephone system: automatic exchange
domestic: tied into Italian system
international: uses Italian system
Radio broadcast stations: AM 3, FM 4, shortwave 0
Radios: NA
Television broadcast stations: 1 (1996)
Televisions: NA

Transportation

Railways:
total: 862 m; note - connects to Italy's network at Rome's Saint Peter's station
narrow gauge: 862 m 1.435-m gauge
Highways: none; all city streets
Ports and harbors: none
Airports: none
Heliports: 1 (1998 est.)

Military

Military - note: defense is the responsibility of Italy; Swiss Papal Guards are posted at entrances to the Vatican City

Transnational Issues

Disputes - international: none

Honduras

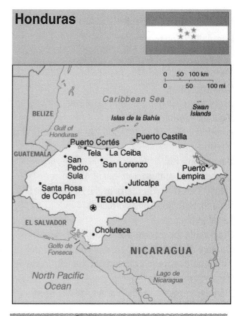

Geography

Location: Middle America, bordering the Caribbean Sea, between Guatemala and Nicaragua and bordering the North Pacific Ocean, between El Salvador and Nicaragua
Geographic coordinates: 15 00 N, 86 30 W
Map references: Central America and the Caribbean
Area:
total: 112,090 sq km
land: 111,890 sq km
water: 200 sq km
Area - comparative: slightly larger than Tennessee
Land boundaries:
total: 1,520 km
border countries: Guatemala 256 km, El Salvador 342 km, Nicaragua 922 km
Coastline: 820 km
Maritime claims:
contiguous zone: 24 nm
continental shelf: natural extension of territory or to 200 nm
exclusive economic zone: 200 nm
territorial sea: 12 nm
Climate: subtropical in lowlands, temperate in mountains
Terrain: mostly mountains in interior, narrow coastal plains
Elevation extremes:
lowest point: Caribbean Sea 0 m
highest point: Cerro Las Minas 2,870 m
Natural resources: timber, gold, silver, copper, lead, zinc, iron ore, antimony, coal, fish
Land use:
arable land: 15%
permanent crops: 3%
permanent pastures: 14%
forests and woodland: 54%
other: 14% (1993 est.)
Irrigated land: 740 sq km (1993 est.)

Honduras *(continued)*

Natural hazards: frequent, but generally mild, earthquakes; damaging hurricanes and floods along Caribbean coast

Environment - current issues: urban population expanding; deforestation results from logging and the clearing of land for agricultural purposes; further land degradation and soil erosion hastened by uncontrolled development and improper land use practices such as farming of marginal lands; mining activities polluting Lago de Yojoa (the country's largest source of fresh water) as well as several rivers and streams with heavy metals; severe Hurricane Mitch damage

Environment - international agreements:
party to: Biodiversity, Climate Change, Desertification, Endangered Species, Hazardous Wastes, Law of the Sea, Marine Dumping, Nuclear Test Ban, Ozone Layer Protection, Tropical Timber 83, Tropical Timber 94, Wetlands
signed, but not ratified: Climate Change-Kyoto Protocol

People

Population: 5,997,327 (July 1999 est.)
Age structure:
0-14 years: 41% (male 1,262,190; female 1,217,752)
15-64 years: 55% (male 1,643,550; female 1,665,666)
65 years and over: 4% (male 98,715; female 109,454) (1999 est.)
Population growth rate: 2.24% (1999 est.)
Birth rate: 30.98 births/1,000 population (1999 est.)
Death rate: 7.14 deaths/1,000 population (1999 est.)
Net migration rate: -1.46 migrant(s)/1,000 population (1999 est.)
Sex ratio:
at birth: 1.05 male(s)/female
under 15 years: 1.04 male(s)/female
15-64 years: 0.99 male(s)/female
65 years and over: 0.9 male(s)/female
total population: 1 male(s)/female (1999 est.)
Infant mortality rate: 40.84 deaths/1,000 live births (1999 est.)
Life expectancy at birth:
total population: 64.68 years
male: 63.16 years
female: 66.27 years (1999 est.)
Total fertility rate: 3.97 children born/woman (1999 est.)
Nationality:
noun: Honduran(s)
adjective: Honduran
Ethnic groups: mestizo (mixed Amerindian and European) 90%, Amerindian 7%, black 2%, white 1%
Religions: Roman Catholic 97%, Protestant minority
Languages: Spanish, Amerindian dialects
Literacy:
definition: age 15 and over can read and write
total population: 72.7%
male: 72.6%
female: 72.7% (1995 est.)

Government

Country name:
conventional long form: Republic of Honduras
conventional short form: Honduras
local long form: Republica de Honduras
local short form: Honduras
Data code: HO
Government type: republic
Capital: Tegucigalpa
Administrative divisions: 18 departments (departamentos, singular - departamento) plus probable Central District (Tegucigalpa); Atlantida, Choluteca, Colon, Comayagua, Copan, Cortes, El Paraiso, Francisco Morazan, Gracias a Dios, Intibuca, Islas de la Bahia, La Paz, Lempira, Ocotepeque, Olancho, Santa Barbara, Valle, Yoro
Independence: 15 September 1821 (from Spain)
National holiday: Independence Day, 15 September (1821)
Constitution: 11 January 1982, effective 20 January 1982
Legal system: rooted in Roman and Spanish civil law; some influence of English common law; accepts ICJ jurisdiction, with reservations
Suffrage: 18 years of age; universal and compulsory
Executive branch:
chief of state: President Carlos Roberto FLORES Facusse (since 27 January 1998); note - the president is both the chief of state and head of government
head of government: President Carlos Roberto FLORES Facusse (since 27 January 1998); note - the president is both the chief of state and head of government
cabinet: Cabinet appointed by president
elections: president elected by popular vote for a four-year term; election last held 30 November 1997 (next to be held NA November 2001)
election results: Carlos Roberto FLORES Facusse elected president; percent of vote - Carlos Roberto FLORES Facusse (PLH) 53%, Nora de MELGAR (PNH) 42%, other 5%
Legislative branch: unicameral National Assembly or Asamblea Nacional (128 seats; members are elected by popular vote to serve four-year terms)
elections: last held on 30 November 1997 (next to be held November 2001)
election results: percent of vote by party - PLH 50%, PNH 42%, PINU-SD 4%, PDCH 2%, other 2%; seats by party - PLH 70, PNH 55, PINU-SD 3
Judicial branch: Supreme Court of Justice (Corte Suprema de Justica), judges are elected for four-year terms by the National Assembly
Political parties and leaders: Liberal Party or PLH [Raphael PINEDA Ponce, president]; National Party of Honduras or PNH [Nora de MELGAR, president]; National Innovation and Unity Party-Social Democratic Party or PINU-SD [Olban VALLADARES, president]; Christian Democratic Party or PDCH [leader NA]
Political pressure groups and leaders: National Association of Honduran Campesinos or ANACH;

Honduran Council of Private Enterprise or COHEP; Confederation of Honduran Workers or CTH; National Union of Campesinos or UNC; General Workers Confederation or CGT; United Federation of Honduran Workers or FUTH; Committee for the Defense of Human Rights in Honduras or CODEH; Coordinating Committee of Popular Organizations or CCOP

International organization participation: BCIE, CACM, ECLAC, FAO, G-77, IADB, IBRD, ICAO, ICFTU, ICRM, IDA, IFAD, IFC, IFRCS, ILO, IMF, IMO, Intelsat, Interpol, IOC, IOM, ITU, LAES, LAIA (observer), MINURSO, NAM, OAS, OPANAL, OPCW, PCA, UN, UNCTAD, UNESCO, UNIDO, UPU, WCL, WFTU, WHO, WIPO, WMO, WTrO
Diplomatic representation in the US:
chief of mission: Ambassador (vacant)
chancery: 3007 Tilden Street NW, Washington, DC 20008
telephone: [1] (202) 966-7702
FAX: [1] (202) 966-9751
consulate(s) general: Chicago, Houston, Los Angeles, Miami, New Orleans, New York, San Francisco, and San Juan (Puerto Rico)
consulate(s): Boston, Detroit, and Jacksonville
Diplomatic representation from the US:
chief of mission: Ambassador James Francis CREAGAN
embassy: Avenida La Paz, Apartado Postal No. 3453, Tegucigalpa
mailing address: American Embassy, APO AA 34022, Tegucigalpa
telephone: [504] 238-5114, 326-9320
FAX: [504] 236-9037
Flag description: three equal horizontal bands of blue (top), white, and blue with five blue five-pointed stars arranged in an X pattern centered in the white band; the stars represent the members of the former Federal Republic of Central America - Costa Rica, El Salvador, Guatemala, Honduras, and Nicaragua; similar to the flag of El Salvador, which features a round emblem encircled by the words REPUBLICA DE EL SALVADOR EN LA AMERICA CENTRAL centered in the white band; also similar to the flag of Nicaragua, which features a triangle encircled by the word REPUBLICA DE NICARAGUA on top and AMERICA CENTRAL on the bottom, centered in the white band

Economy

Economy - overview: Prior to Hurricane Mitch in the fall of 1998, Honduras had been pursuing a moderate economic reform program and had posted strong annual growth numbers. The storm has dramatically changed economic forecasts for Honduras, one of the poorest countries in Central America and the hardest hit by Mitch. Honduras sustained approximately $3 billion in damages and will probably see GDP shrink by 2% in 1999 and unemployment rise. Hardest hit was the all-important agricultural sector, which is responsible for the majority of exports. As a result, the trade deficit is likely to balloon in 1999 to $445 million.

Honduras (continued)

However, significant aid has helped to stabilize the country. In addition, the Paris Club and bilateral creditors have offered substantial debt relief, and Tegucigalpa is currently under consideration for inclusion in the IMF-World Bank Highly Indebted Poor Countries Initiative (HIPC). Additional financing will be needed to restore the economy to its pre-Mitch level.

GDP: purchasing power parity - $14.4 billion (1998 est.)

GDP - real growth rate: 3% (1998 est.)

GDP - per capita: purchasing power parity - $2,400 (1998 est.)

GDP - composition by sector:
agriculture: 20%
industry: 19%
services: 61% (1997)

Population below poverty line: 50% (1992 est.)

Household income or consumption by percentage share:
lowest 10%: 1.2%
highest 10%: 42.1% (1996)

Inflation rate (consumer prices): 14.5% (1998 est.)

Labor force: 1.3 million (1997 est.)

Labor force - by occupation: agriculture 37%, services 39%, industry 24% (1996)

Unemployment rate: 6.3% (1997); underemployed 30% (1997 est.)

Budget:
revenues: $655 million
expenditures: $850 million, including capital expenditures of $150 million (1997 est.)

Industries: sugar, coffee, textiles, clothing, wood products

Industrial production growth rate: 10% (1992 est.)

Electricity - production: 2.73 billion kWh (1996)

Electricity - production by source:
fossil fuel: 12.09%
hydro: 87.91%
nuclear: 0%
other: 0% (1996)

Electricity - consumption: 2.734 billion kWh (1996)

Electricity - exports: 0 kWh (1996)

Electricity - imports: 4 million kWh (1996)

Agriculture - products: bananas, coffee, citrus; beef; timber; shrimp

Exports: $1.3 billion (f.o.b., 1996)

Exports - commodities: bananas, coffee, shrimp, lobster, minerals, meat, lumber

Exports - partners: US 54%, Germany 7%, Belgium 5%, Japan 4%, Spain 3% (1995)

Imports: $1.8 billion (c.i.f. 1996)

Imports - commodities: machinery and transport equipment, industrial raw materials, chemical products, manufactured goods, fuel and oil, foodstuffs

Imports - partners: US 43%, Guatemala 5%, Japan 5%, Germany 4%, Mexico 3%, El Salvador 3% (1995)

Debt - external: $4.1 billion (1995)

Economic aid - recipient: $418.7 million (1995)

Currency: 1 lempira (L) = 100 centavos

Exchange rates: lempiras (L) per US$1 (end of period) - 13.8076 (December 1998), 13.8076 (1998), 13.0942 (1997), 12.8694 (1996), 10.3432 (1995), 9.4001 (1994)

Fiscal year: calendar year

Communications

Telephones: 105,000 (1992 est.)

Telephone system: inadequate system
domestic: NA
international: satellite earth stations - 2 Intelsat (Atlantic Ocean); connected to Central American Microwave System

Radio broadcast stations: AM 176, FM 0, shortwave 7

Radios: 2.115 million (1992 est.)

Television broadcast stations: 11 (in addition, there are 17 repeaters) (1997)

Televisions: 400,000 (1992 est.)

Transportation

Railways:
total: 595 km
narrow gauge: 190 km 1.067-m gauge; 128 km 1.057-m gauge; 277 km 0.914-m gauge

Highways:
total: 14,173 km
paved: 3,126 km
unpaved: 11,047 km (1998 est.)

Waterways: 465 km navigable by small craft

Ports and harbors: La Ceiba, Puerto Castilla, Puerto Cortes, San Lorenzo, Tela, Puerto Lempira

Merchant marine:
total: 247 ships (1,000 GRT or over) totaling 555,534 GRT/730,602 DWT
ships by type: bulk 21, cargo 157, chemical tanker 4, container 7, livestock carrier 1, oil tanker 25, passenger 1, passenger-cargo 4, refrigerated cargo 15, roll-on/roll-off cargo 6, short-sea passenger 5, vehicle carrier 1
note: a flag of convenience registry; Russia owns 6 ships, Vietnam 1, Singapore 3, North Korea 1 (1998 est.)

Airports: 122 (1998 est.)

Airports - with paved runways:
total: 11
2,438 to 3,047 m: 3
1,524 to 2,437 m: 2
914 to 1,523 m: 4
under 914 m: 2 (1998 est.)

Airports - with unpaved runways:
total: 111
2,438 to 3,047 m: 1
1,524 to 2,437 m: 2
914 to 1,523 m: 21
under 914 m: 87 (1998 est.)

Military

Military branches: Army, Navy (includes Marines), Air Force

Military manpower - military age: 18 years of age

Military manpower - availability:
males age 15-49: 1,455,053 (1999 est.)

Military manpower - fit for military service:
males age 15-49: 866,492 (1999 est.)

Military manpower - reaching military age annually:
males: 69,646 (1999 est.)

Military expenditures - dollar figure: $33 million (1998)

Military expenditures - percent of GDP: 0.6% (1998)

Transnational Issues

Disputes - international: demarcation of boundary with El Salvador defined by 1992 International Court of Justice (ICJ) decision has not been completed; small boundary section left unresolved by ICJ decision not yet reported to have been settled; with respect to the maritime boundary in the Golfo de Fonseca, ICJ referred to an earlier agreement in this century and advised that some tripartite resolution among El Salvador, Honduras, and Nicaragua likely would be required; maritime boundary dispute with Nicaragua

Illicit drugs: transshipment point for drugs and narcotics; illicit producer of cannabis, cultivated on small plots and used principally for local consumption

Hong Kong
(special administrative region of China)

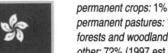

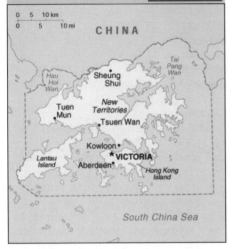

Introduction

Background: Pursuant to the agreement signed by China and the UK on 19 December 1984, Hong Kong became the Hong Kong Special Administrative Region (SAR) of China on 1 July 1997. Under the terms of this agreement, China has promised that under its "one country, two systems" formula its socialist economic system will not be practiced in Hong Kong, and that Hong Kong shall enjoy a high degree of autonomy in all matters except foreign and defense affairs.

Geography

Location: Eastern Asia, bordering the South China Sea and China
Geographic coordinates: 22 15 N, 114 10 E
Map references: Southeast Asia
Area:
total: 1,092 sq km
land: 1,042 sq km
water: 50 sq km
Area - comparative: six times the size of Washington, DC
Land boundaries:
total: 30 km
border countries: China 30 km
Coastline: 733 km
Maritime claims:
territorial sea: 3 nm
Climate: tropical monsoon; cool and humid in winter, hot and rainy from spring through summer, warm and sunny in fall
Terrain: hilly to mountainous with steep slopes; lowlands in north
Elevation extremes:
lowest point: South China Sea 0 m
highest point: Tai Mo Shan 958 m
Natural resources: outstanding deepwater harbor, feldspar
Land use:
arable land: 6%

permanent crops: 1%
permanent pastures: 1%
forests and woodland: 20%
other: 72% (1997 est.)
Irrigated land: 20 sq km (1997 est.)
Natural hazards: occasional typhoons
Environment - current issues: air and water pollution from rapid urbanization
Environment - international agreements:
party to: NA
signed, but not ratified: NA
Geography - note: more than 200 islands

People

Population: 6,847,125 (July 1999 est.)
Age structure:
0-14 years: 18% (male 644,982; female 598,188)
15-64 years: 71% (male 2,397,277; female 2,490,745)
65 years and over: 11% (male 323,949; female 391,984) (1999 est.)
Population growth rate: 1.9% (1999 est.)
Birth rate: 12.9 births/1,000 population (1999 est.)
Death rate: 5.96 deaths/1,000 population (1999 est.)
Net migration rate: 12.07 migrant(s)/1,000 population (1999 est.)
Sex ratio:
at birth: 1.07 male(s)/female
under 15 years: 1.08 male(s)/female
15-64 years: 0.96 male(s)/female
65 years and over: 0.83 male(s)/female
total population: 0.97 male(s)/female (1999 est.)
Infant mortality rate: 5.2 deaths/1,000 live births (1999 est.)
Life expectancy at birth:
total population: 78.91 years
male: 76.15 years
female: 81.85 years (1999 est.)
Total fertility rate: 1.39 children born/woman (1999 est.)
Nationality:
noun: Chinese
adjective: Chinese
Ethnic groups: Chinese 95%, other 5%
Religions: eclectic mixture of local religions 90%, Christian 10%
Languages: Chinese (Cantonese), English
Literacy:
definition: age 15 and over has ever attended school
total population: 92.2%
male: 96%
female: 88.2% (1996 est.)

Government

Country name:
conventional long form: Hong Kong Special Administrative Region
conventional short form: Hong Kong
local long form: Xianggang Tebie Xingzhengqu
local short form: Xianggang
abbreviation: HK

Data code: HK
Dependency status: special administrative region of China
Government type: NA
Capital: Victoria
Administrative divisions: none (special administrative region of China)
Independence: none (special administrative region of China)
National holiday: National Day, 1-2 October; note - 1 July 1997 is celebrated as Hong Kong Special Administrative Region Establishment Day
Constitution: Basic Law approved in March 1990 by China's National People's Congress is Hong Kong's "mini-constitution"
Legal system: based on English common law
Suffrage: direct election 18 years of age; universal for permanent residents living in the territory of Hong Kong for the past seven years; indirect election limited to about 100,000 members of functional constituencies and an 800-member Election Commission drawn from broad regional groupings and other central government bodies
Executive branch:
chief of state: President of China JIANG Zemin (since 27 March 1993)
head of government: Chief Executive TUNG Chee-hwa (since 1 July 1997)
cabinet: Executive Council consists of three ex-officio members and 10 appointed members; ex-officio members are: Chief Secretary Anson CHAN (since 29 November 1993), Financial Secretary Donald TSANG (since 7 March 1995), and Secretary of Justice Elsie LEUNG (since 1 July 1997)
elections: NA
Legislative branch: unicameral Legislative Council or LEGCO (60 seats; 30 indirectly elected by functional constituencies, 20 elected by popular vote, and 10 elected by an 800-member election committee; members serve four-year terms)
elections: last held 25 May 1998 (next to be held NA 2002)
election results: percent of vote by party - NA; seats by party - Democratic Party 13, Liberal Party 9, Democratic Alliance for the Betterment of Hong Kong 9, Hong Kong Progressive Alliance 5, Frontier Party 3, Citizens Party 1, independents 20
Judicial branch: The Court of Final Appeal in the Hong Kong Special Administrative Region
Political parties and leaders: Democratic Party [Martin LEE, chairman]; Liberal Party [leader NA]; Democratic Alliance for the Betterment of Hong Kong [TSANG Yuk-shing, chairman]; Hong Kong Democratic Foundation [Dr. Patrick SHIU Kin-ying, chairman]; Frontier Party [Emily LAN Wai-hang, chairwoman]; Hong Kong Progressive Alliance [leader NA]; Citizens Party [leader NA]
Political pressure groups and leaders: Association for Democracy and People's Livelihood or ADPL [Frederick FUNG Kin Kee, chairman]; Liberal Democratic Federation [HU Fa-kuang, chairman]; Federation of Trade Unions (pro-China) [LEE

Hong Kong (continued)

Chark-tim, president]; Hong Kong and Kowloon Trade Union Council (pro-Taiwan); Confederation of Trade Unions (pro-democracy) [LEE Cheuk-yan, chairman]; Hong Kong General Chamber of Commerce; Chinese General Chamber of Commerce (pro-China); Federation of Hong Kong Industries; Chinese Manufacturers' Association of Hong Kong; Hong Kong Professional Teachers' Union [CHEUNG Man-kwong, president]; Hong Kong Alliance in Support of the Patriotic Democratic Movement in China [Szeto WAH, chairman]

International organization participation: APEC, AsDB, BIS, CCC, ESCAP (associate), ICFTU, IMO (associate), Interpol (subbureau), IOC, ISO (correspondent), WCL, WMO, WTrO

Diplomatic representation in the US: none (special administrative region of China)

Diplomatic representation from the US:

chief of mission: Consul General Richard A. BOUCHER

consulate(s) general: 26 Garden Road, Hong Kong

mailing address: PSC 464, Box 30, FPO AP 96522-0002

telephone: [852] 2523-9011

FAX: [852] 2845-1598

Flag description: red with a stylized, white, five-petal bauhinia flower in the center

Economy

Economy - overview: Hong Kong has a bustling free market economy highly dependent on international trade. Natural resources are limited, and food and raw materials must be imported. Indeed, imports and exports, including reexports, each exceed GDP in dollar value. Even before Hong Kong reverted to Chinese administration on 1 July 1997 it had extensive trade and investment ties with China. Real GDP growth averaged a remarkable 8% in 1987-88 and a still strong 5% in 1989-97. The widespread Asian economic difficulties in 1998 hit this trade-dependent economy quite hard, with GDP down 5%.

GDP: purchasing power parity - $168.1 billion (1998 est.)

GDP - real growth rate: -5% (1998 est.)

GDP - per capita: purchasing power parity - $25,100 (1998 est.)

GDP - composition by sector:

agriculture: 0.1%

industry: 15.9%

services: 84% (1997 est.)

Population below poverty line: NA%

Household income or consumption by percentage share:

lowest 10%: NA%

highest 10%: NA%

Inflation rate (consumer prices): 2.9% (1998 est.)

Labor force: 3.216 million (1998 est.)

Labor force - by occupation: wholesale and retail trade, restaurants, and hotels 31.9%, social services 9.9%, manufacturing 9.2%, financing, insurance, and real estate 13.1%, transport and communications 5.7%, construction 2.6%, other 27.6% (October 1998)

Unemployment rate: 5.5% (1998 est.)

Budget:

revenues: $30.1 billion

expenditures: $26 billion, including capital expenditures of $289 million (FY97/98)

Industries: textiles, clothing, tourism, electronics, plastics, toys, watches, clocks

Industrial production growth rate: -3.7% (1998)

Electricity - production: 27 billion kWh (1996)

Electricity - production by source:

fossil fuel: 100%

hydro: 0%

nuclear: 0%

other: 0% (1996)

Electricity - consumption: 28.598 billion kWh (1997)

Electricity - exports: 1.483 billion kWh (1996)

Electricity - imports: 5.875 billion kWh (1996)

Agriculture - products: fresh vegetables; poultry

Exports: $188.08 billion (including reexports; f.o.b., 1997)

Exports - commodities: clothing, textiles, yarn and fabric, footwear, electrical appliances, watches and clocks, toys

Exports - partners: China 35%, US 22%, Japan 6%, Germany 4%, UK 4% (1997)

Imports: $208.63 billion (c.i.f., 1997)

Imports - commodities: foodstuffs, transport equipment, raw materials, semimanufactures, petroleum; a large share is reexported

Imports - partners: China 38%, Japan 14%, Taiwan 8%, US 8%, Singapore 5% (1997)

Debt - external: none (1996)

Economic aid - recipient: none

Currency: 1 Hong Kong dollar (HK$) = 100 cents

Exchange rates: Hong Kong dollars (HK$) per US$ - 7.74 (1997-99), 7.730 (1996), 7.800 (1995), 7.800 (1994); note - linked to the US dollar at the rate of about 7.8 HK$ per 1 US$

Fiscal year: 1 April - 31 March

Communications

Telephones: 4.47 million (1998)

Telephone system: modern facilities provide excellent domestic and international services

domestic: microwave radio relay links and extensive fiber-optic network

international: satellite earth stations - 3 Intelsat (1 Pacific Ocean and 2 Indian Ocean); coaxial cable to Guangzhou, China; access to 5 international submarine cables providing connections to ASEAN member nations, Japan, Taiwan, Australia, Middle East, and Western Europe

Radio broadcast stations: AM 6, FM 6, shortwave 0

Radios: 3 million (1992 est.)

Television broadcast stations: 4 (in addition, there are two repeaters) (1997)

Televisions: 1.75 million (1992 est.)

Transportation

Railways:

total: 34 km

standard gauge: 34 km 1.435-m gauge (all electrified) (1996 est.)

Highways:

total: 1,831 km

paved: 1,831 km

unpaved: 0 km (1997)

Ports and harbors: Hong Kong

Merchant marine:

total: 195 ships (1,000 GRT or over) totaling 6,075,304 GRT/10,133,186 DWT

ships by type: barge carrier 1, bulk 117, cargo 18, chemical tanker 2, combination bulk 2, container 40, liquefied gas tanker 1, multifunction large-load carrier 2, oil tanker 6, refrigerated cargo 1, roll-on/roll-off cargo 1, short-sea passenger 1, vehicle carrier 3

note: a flag of convenience registry; includes ships from 13 countries among which are UK 16, South Africa 3, China 9, Japan 6, Bermuda 2, Germany 3, Canada 2, Cyprus 1, Belgium 1, and Norway 1 (1998 est.)

Airports: 3 (1998 est.)

Airports - with paved runways:

total: 3

over 3,047 m: 2

1,524 to 2,437 m: 1 (1998 est.)

Heliports: 2 (1998 est.)

Military

Military branches: Hong Kong garrison of the PLA including elements of the PLA Army, the PLA Navy and PLA Air Force; these forces are under the direct leadership of the Central Military Commission in Beijing and under administrative control of the adjacent Guangzhou Military Region

Military manpower - military age: 18 years of age

Military manpower - availability:

males age 15-49: 1,924,304 (1999 est.)

Military manpower - fit for military service:

males age 15-49: 1,452,110 (1999 est.)

Military manpower - reaching military age annually:

males: 45,656 (1999 est.)

Military expenditures - dollar figure: $NA

Military expenditures - percent of GDP: NA%

Military - note: defense is the responsibility of China

Transnational Issues

Disputes - international: none

Illicit drugs: a hub for Southeast Asian heroin trade; transshipment and money-laundering center; increasing indigenous amphetamine abuse

Howland Island
(territory of the US)

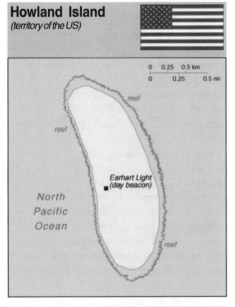

Geography

Location: Oceania, island in the North Pacific Ocean, about one-half of the way from Hawaii to Australia
Geographic coordinates: 0 48 N, 176 38 W
Map references: Oceania
Area:
total: 1.6 sq km
land: 1.6 sq km
water: 0 sq km
Area - comparative: about three times the size of The Mall in Washington, DC
Land boundaries: 0 km
Coastline: 6.4 km
Maritime claims:
exclusive economic zone: 200 nm
territorial sea: 12 nm
Climate: equatorial; scant rainfall, constant wind, burning sun
Terrain: low-lying, nearly level, sandy, coral island surrounded by a narrow fringing reef; depressed central area
Elevation extremes:
lowest point: Pacific Ocean 0 m
highest point: unnamed location 3 m
Natural resources: guano (deposits worked until late 1800s)
Land use:
arable land: 0%
permanent crops: 0%
permanent pastures: 0%
forests and woodland: 5%
other: 95%
Irrigated land: 0 sq km (1998)
Natural hazards: the narrow fringing reef surrounding the island can be a maritime hazard
Environment - current issues: no natural fresh water resources

Environment - international agreements:
party to: NA
signed, but not ratified: NA
Geography - note: almost totally covered with grasses, prostrate vines, and low-growing shrubs; small area of trees in the center; primarily a nesting, roosting, and foraging habitat for seabirds, shorebirds, and marine wildlife

People

Population: uninhabited
note: American civilians evacuated in 1942 after Japanese air and naval attacks during World War II; occupied by US military during World War II, but abandoned after the war; public entry is by special-use permit from US Fish and Wildlife Service only and generally restricted to scientists and educators; visited annually by US Fish and Wildlife Service

Government

Country name:
conventional long form: none
conventional short form: Howland Island
Data code: HQ
Dependency status: unincorporated territory of the US; administered from Washington, DC, by the Fish and Wildlife Service of the US Department of the Interior as part of the National Wildlife Refuge system
Legal system: NA
Flag description: the flag of the US is used

Economy

Economy - overview: no economic activity

Transportation

Ports and harbors: none; offshore anchorage only; note - there is one boat landing area along the middle of the west coast
Airports: airstrip constructed in 1937 for scheduled refueling stop on the round-the-world flight of Amelia Earhart and Fred Noonan - they left Lae, New Guinea, for Howland Island, but were never seen again; the airstrip is no longer serviceable
Transportation - note: Earhart Light is a day beacon near the middle of the west coast that was partially destroyed during World War II, but has since been rebuilt; named in memory of famed aviatrix Amelia Earhart

Military

Military - note: defense is the responsibility of the US; visited annually by the US Coast Guard

Transnational Issues

Disputes - international: none

Hungary

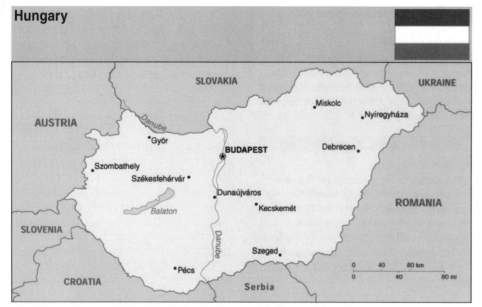

Introduction

Background: After World War II Hungary became part of Soviet-dominated Eastern Europe, and its government and economy were refashioned on the communist model. Increased nationalist opposition, which culminated in the government's announcement of withdrawal from the Warsaw Pact in 1956, led to massive military intervention by Moscow and the swift crushing of the revolt. In the more open GORBACHEV years, Hungary led the movement to dissolve the Warsaw Pact and steadily moved toward multiparty democracy and a market-oriented economy. Following the collapse of the USSR in 1991, Hungary has developed close political and economic relations with western Europe and is now being considered a possible future member of the European Union.

Geography

Location: Central Europe, northwest of Romania
Geographic coordinates: 47 00 N, 20 00 E
Map references: Europe
Area:
total: 93,030 sq km
land: 92,340 sq km
water: 690 sq km
Area - comparative: slightly smaller than Indiana
Land boundaries:
total: 2,009 km
border countries: Austria 366 km, Croatia 329 km, Romania 443 km, Serbia and Montenegro 151 km (all with Serbia), Slovakia 515 km, Slovenia 102 km, Ukraine 103 km
Coastline: 0 km (landlocked)
Maritime claims: none (landlocked)
Climate: temperate; cold, cloudy, humid winters; warm summers
Terrain: mostly flat to rolling plains; hills and low mountains on the Slovakian border
Elevation extremes:
lowest point: Tisza River 78 m

highest point: Kekes 1,014 m
Natural resources: bauxite, coal, natural gas, fertile soils
Land use:
arable land: 51%
permanent crops: 2%
permanent pastures: 13%
forests and woodland: 19%
other: 15% (1993 est.)
Irrigated land: 2,060 sq km (1993 est.)
Environment - current issues: the approximation of Hungary's standards in waste management, energy efficiency, and air, soil, and water pollution with environmental requirements for EU accession will require large investments, estimated by the Government of Hungary at $4 billion over six years; the 1997 budget allocated $9.7 million for this purpose; the 1998 budget allocated $11.3 million; the Central Environmental Fund, which collects monies from product charges, environmental fines, and mining taxes, provided approximately $76.2 million in 1997 and is expected to provide $109.5 million in 1998
Environment - international agreements:
party to: Air Pollution, Air Pollution-Nitrogen Oxides, Air Pollution-Sulphur 85, Air Pollution-Volatile Organic Compounds, Antarctic Treaty, Biodiversity, Climate Change, Endangered Species, Environmental Modification, Hazardous Wastes, Marine Dumping, Nuclear Test Ban, Ozone Layer Protection, Ship Pollution, Wetlands
signed, but not ratified: Air Pollution-Persistent Organic Pollutants, Air Pollution-Sulphur 94, Antarctic-Environmental Protocol, Law of the Sea
Geography - note: landlocked; strategic location astride main land routes between Western Europe and Balkan Peninsula as well as between Ukraine and Mediterranean basin

People

Population: 10,186,372 (July 1999 est.)

Age structure:
0-14 years: 17% (male 908,434; female 865,621)
15-64 years: 68% (male 3,406,512; female 3,524,260)
65 years and over: 15% (male 552,337; female 929,208) (1999 est.)
Population growth rate: -0.2% (1999 est.)
Birth rate: 10.8 births/1,000 population (1999 est.)
Death rate: 13.29 deaths/1,000 population (1999 est.)
Net migration rate: 0.5 migrant(s)/1,000 population (1999 est.)
Sex ratio:
at birth: 1.05 male(s)/female
under 15 years: 1.05 male(s)/female
15-64 years: 0.97 male(s)/female
65 years and over: 0.59 male(s)/female
total population: 0.92 male(s)/female (1999 est.)
Infant mortality rate: 9.46 deaths/1,000 live births (1999 est.)
Life expectancy at birth:
total population: 71.18 years
male: 66.85 years
female: 75.74 years (1999 est.)
Total fertility rate: 1.45 children born/woman (1999 est.)
Nationality:
noun: Hungarian(s)
adjective: Hungarian
Ethnic groups: Hungarian 89.9%, Gypsy 4%, German 2.6%, Serb 2%, Slovak 0.8%, Romanian 0.7%
Religions: Roman Catholic 67.5%, Calvinist 20%, Lutheran 5%, atheist and other 7.5%
Languages: Hungarian 98.2%, other 1.8%
Literacy:
definition: age 15 and over can read and write
total population: 99%
male: 99%
female: 98% (1980 est.)

Government

Country name:
conventional long form: Republic of Hungary
conventional short form: Hungary
local long form: Magyar Koztarsasag
local short form: Magyarorszag
Data code: HU
Government type: republic
Capital: Budapest
Administrative divisions: 19 counties (megyek, singular - megye), 20 urban counties* (singular - megyei varos), and 1 capital city** (fovaros); Bacs-Kiskun, Baranya, Bekes, Bekescsaba*, Borsod-Abauj-Zemplen, Budapest**, Csongrad, Debrecen*, Dunaujvaros*, Eger*, Fejer, Gyor*, Gyor-Moson-Sopron, Hajdu-Bihar, Heves, Hodmezovasarhely*, Jasz-Nagykun-Szolnok, Kaposvar*, Kecskemet*, Komarom-Esztergom, Miskolc*, Nagykanizsa*, Nograd, Nyiregyhaza*, Pecs*, Pest, Somogy, Sopron*, Szabolcs-Szatmar-Bereg, Szeged*, Szekesfehervar*,

Hungary *(continued)*

Szolnok*, Szombathely*, Tatabanya*, Tolna, Vas, Veszprem, Veszprem*, Zala, Zalaegerszeg*

Independence: 1001 (unification by King Stephen I)

National holiday: St. Stephen's Day, 20 August (commemorates the coronation of King Stephen in 1000 AD)

Constitution: 18 August 1949, effective 20 August 1949, revised 19 April 1972; 18 October 1989 revision ensured legal rights for individuals and constitutional checks on the authority of the prime minister and also established the principle of parliamentary oversight; 1997 amendment streamlined the judicial system

Legal system: in process of revision, moving toward rule of law based on Western model

Suffrage: 18 years of age; universal

Executive branch:

chief of state: President Arpad GONCZ (since 3 August 1990; previously interim president since 2 May 1990)

head of government: Prime Minister Viktor ORBAN (since 6 July 1998)

cabinet: Council of Ministers elected by the National Assembly on the recommendation of the president

elections: president elected by the National Assembly for a four-year term; election last held 19 June 1995 (next to be held NA 1999); prime minister elected by the National Assembly on the recommendation of the president

election results: Arpad GONCZ reelected president; a total of 335 votes were cast by the National Assembly, Arpad GONCZ received 259; Viktor ORBAN elected prime minister; percent of legislative vote - NA

Legislative branch: unicameral National Assembly or Orszaggyules (386 seats; members are elected by popular vote under a system of proportional and direct representation to serve four-year terms)

elections: last held on 10 and 24 May 1998 (next to be held May/June 2002)

election results: percent of vote by party (5% or more of the vote required for parliamentary representation in the first round) - MSZP 32.0%, FIDESZ 28.2%, FKGP 13.8%, SZDSZ 7.9%, MIEP 5.5%, MMP 4.1%, MDF 2.8%, KDNP 2.3%, MDNP 1.5%; seats by party - MSZP 134, FIDESZ 148, FKGP 48, SZDSZ 24, MDF 17, MIEP 14, independent 1; note - the MDF won 17 single-member district seats

Judicial branch: Constitutional Court, judges are elected by the National Assembly for a nine-year term

Political parties and leaders: Hungarian Democratic Forum or MDF [Sandor LEZSAK, chairman]; Independent Smallholders or FKGP [Jozsef TORGYAN, president]; Hungarian Socialist Party or MSZP [Laszlo KOVACS, chairman]; Hungarian Civic Party or FIDESZ [Viktor ORBAN, chairman]; Alliance of Free Democrats or SZDSZ [Balint MAGYAR, chairman]; Christian Democratic People's Party or KDNP [Gyorgy GICZY, president]; Hungarian Democratic People's Party or MDNP [Erzebet PUSZTAI, chairman]; Hungarian Justice and Life Party or MIEP [Istvan CSURKA, chairman]; Hungarian Workers' Party or MMP [Gyula THURMER, chairman]

note: the Hungarian Socialist (Communist) Workers' Party or MSZMP renounced communism and became the Hungarian Socialist Party or MSZP in October 1989; the MDNP was formed in March 1996 by breakaway members of the Hungarian Democratic Forum

International organization participation: Australia Group, BIS, CCC, CE, CEI, CERN, EAPC, EBRD, ECE, EU (applicant), FAO, G- 9, IAEA, IBRD, ICAO, ICFTU, ICRM, IDA, IEA, IFC, IFRCS, ILO, IMF, IMO, Inmarsat, Intelsat, Interpol, IOC, IOM, ISO, ITU, MONUA, MTCR, NAM (guest), NEA, NSG, OAS (observer), OECD, OPCW, OSCE, PCA, PFP, UN, UNCTAD, UNESCO, UNFICYP, UNHCR, UNIDO, UNIKOM, UNMIBH, UNOMIG, UNU, UPU, WEU (associate partner), WFTU, WHO, WIPO, WMO, WToO, WTrO, ZC

Diplomatic representation in the US:

chief of mission: Ambassador Geza JESZENSZKY

chancery: 3910 Shoemaker Street NW, Washington, DC 20008

telephone: [1] (202) 966-7726

FAX: [1] (202) 686-6412

consulate(s) general: Los Angeles and New York

Diplomatic representation from the US:

chief of mission: Ambassador Peter F. TUFO

embassy: V. 1054 Szabadsag Ter 12, Budapest

mailing address: pouch: American Embassy Budapest, Department of State, Washington, DC 20521-5270

telephone: [36] (1) 267-4400, 269-9331, 269-9339 (after hours)

FAX: [36] (1) 269-9326

Flag description: three equal horizontal bands of red (top), white, and green

Economy

Economy - overview: Hungary has consolidated its March 1995 stabilization program and undergone enough restructuring to become an established market economy. The country appears to have entered a period of sustainable growth, gradually falling inflation, and stable external balances. The government's main economic priorities are to complete structural reforms, particularly the implementation of the 1997 pension reform act (the first in the region), taxation reform, and planning for comprehensive health care, local government finance reform, and the reform of education at all levels. Foreign investment has totaled more than $17 billion through 1998. In recognition of Hungary's improved macroeconomic situation, all major credit-rating agencies listed the country's foreign currency debt issuances as investment grade in 1996. The current IMF stand-by arrangement expired in February 1998, and Budapest and the IMF agree that there is no need to renew it. The OECD welcomed Hungary as a member in May 1996, and in December 1997 the EU invited Hungary to begin the accession process. Forecasters expect 4%-5% growth in 1999.

GDP: purchasing power parity - $75.4 billion (1998 est.)

GDP - real growth rate: 5% (1998 est.)

GDP - per capita: purchasing power parity - $7,400 (1998 est.)

GDP - composition by sector:

agriculture: 3%

industry: 30.3%

services: 66.7% (1996)

Population below poverty line: 25.3% (1993 est.)

Household income or consumption by percentage share:

lowest 10%: 4.1%

highest 10%: 24% (1993)

Inflation rate (consumer prices): 14% (1998 est.)

Labor force: 4.2 million (1997)

Labor force - by occupation: services 65%, industry 26.7%, agriculture 8.3 (1996)

Unemployment rate: 10.8% (1997)

Budget:

revenues: $11.2 billion

expenditures: $13.2 billion, including capital expenditures of $NA (1998 est.)

Industries: mining, metallurgy, construction materials, processed foods, textiles, chemicals (especially pharmaceuticals), motor vehicles

Industrial production growth rate: 11.1% (1997 est.)

Electricity - production: 33.162 billion kWh (1996)

Electricity - production by source:

fossil fuel: 58.76%

hydro: 0.62%

nuclear: 40.62%

other: 0% (1996)

Electricity - consumption: 35.362 billion kWh (1996)

Electricity - exports: 2.2 billion kWh (1996)

Electricity - imports: 4.4 billion kWh (1996)

Agriculture - products: wheat, corn, sunflower seed, potatoes, sugar beets; pigs, cattle, poultry, dairy products

Exports: $20.7 billion (f.o.b., 1998)

Exports - commodities: machinery and equipment 51.9%, other manufactures 32.7%, agriculture and food products 10.5%, raw materials 2.9%, fuels and electricity 1.9% (1998)

Exports - partners: Germany 37.3%, Austria 11.4%, Italy 6.1%, Russia 5.0% (1997)

Imports: $22.9 billion (f.o.b., 1998)

Imports - commodities: machinery and equipment 46.5%, other manufactures 40.2%, fuels and electricity 6.6%, agricultural and food products 3.7%, raw materials 3.0% (1998)

Imports - partners: Germany 26.7%, Austria 10.5%, Italy 9.5%, Russia 7.4% (1997)

Debt - external: $22.1 billion (1997)

Economic aid - recipient: $122.7 million (1995)

Currency: 1 forint (Ft) = 100 filler

Exchange rates: forints per US$1 - 215.960 (January 1999), 214.402 (1998), 186.789 (1997), 152.647 (1996), 125.681 (1995),105.160 (1994)

Fiscal year: calendar year

Hungary (continued)

Communications

Telephones: 2.16 million (267,000 cellular telephone subscribers) (1996)
Telephone system: 14,213 telex lines; automatic telephone network based on microwave radio relay system; the average waiting time for telephones is expected to drop to one year by the end of 1997 (down from over 10 years in the early 1990s); note - the former state-owned telecommunications firm MATAV - now privatized and managed by a US/German consortium - has ambitious plans to upgrade the inadequate system, including a contract with the German firm Siemens and the Swedish firm Ericsson to provide 600,000 new telephone lines
domestic: microwave radio relay
international: satellite earth stations - 1 Intelsat and 1 Intersputnik (Atlantic Ocean region)
Radio broadcast stations: AM 32, FM 15, shortwave 0
Radios: 6 million (1993 est.)
Television broadcast stations: 39 (in addition, there are low-power stations) (1997)
Televisions: 4.38 million (1993 est.)

Transportation

Railways:
total: 7,606 km
broad gauge: 36 km 1.524-m gauge
standard gauge: 7,394 km 1.435-m gauge (2,207 km electrified; 1,236 km double track)
narrow gauge: 176 km 0.760-m gauge (1996)
note: Hungary and Austria jointly manage the cross-border standard-gauge railway between Gyor, Sopron, Ebenfurt (Gyor-Sopron-Ebenfurti Vasut Rt) a distance of about 101 km in Hungary and 65 km in Austria
Highways:
total: 188,203 km
paved: 81,680 km (including 438 km of expressways)
unpaved: 106,523 km (1997 est.)
Waterways: 1,622 km (1988)
Pipelines: crude oil 1,204 km; natural gas 4,387 km (1991)
Ports and harbors: Budapest, Dunaujvaros
Merchant marine:
total: 3 cargo ships (1,000 GRT or over) totaling 16,210 GRT/19,810 DWT (1998 est.)
Airports: 25 (1998 est.)
Airports - with paved runways:
total: 15
over 3,047 m: 2
2,438 to 3,047 m: 8
1,524 to 2,437 m: 3
914 to 1,523 m: 1
under 914 m: 1 (1998 est.)
Airports - with unpaved runways:
total: 10
2,438 to 3,047 m: 3
1,524 to 2,437 m: 4
914 to 1,523 m: 3 (1998 est.)

Military

Military branches: Ground Forces, Air Force, Border Guard
Military manpower - military age: 18 years of age
Military manpower - availability:
males age 15-49: 2,601,741 (1999 est.)
Military manpower - fit for military service:
males age 15-49: 2,073,419 (1999 est.)
Military manpower - reaching military age annually:
males: 70,393 (1999 est.)
Military expenditures - dollar figure: $645 million (1997)
Military expenditures - percent of GDP: 1.4% (1997)

Transnational Issues

Disputes - international: ongoing Gabcikovo Dam dispute with Slovakia is before the International Court of Justice
Illicit drugs: major transshipment point for Southwest Asian heroin and cannabis and transit point for South American cocaine destined for Western Europe; limited producer of precursor chemicals, particularly for amphetamines and methamphetamines

Iceland

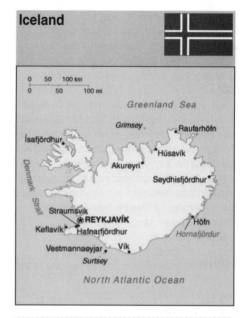

Introduction

Background: Iceland boasts the oldest surviving parliament in the world, the Althing, established in 930. Subsequently this Nordic island, whose small population has largely depended on fishing and sheep-herding for a living, came under the rule of Norway and then Denmark. It gained home rule in 1874 and full independence in 1944. Literacy, longevity, and social cohesion are topnotch by world standards. Tensions continue with Norway, Russia, and other nearby countries over fishing rights in the North Atlantic and adjacent seas.

Geography

Location: Northern Europe, island between the Greenland Sea and the North Atlantic Ocean, northwest of the UK
Geographic coordinates: 65 00 N, 18 00 W
Map references: Arctic Region
Area:
total: 103,000 sq km
land: 100,250 sq km
water: 2,750 sq km
Area - comparative: slightly smaller than Kentucky
Land boundaries: 0 km
Coastline: 4,988 km
Maritime claims:
continental shelf: 200 nm or to the edge of the continental margin
exclusive economic zone: 200 nm
territorial sea: 12 nm
Climate: temperate; moderated by North Atlantic Current; mild, windy winters; damp, cool summers
Terrain: mostly plateau interspersed with mountain peaks, icefields; coast deeply indented by bays and fiords
Elevation extremes:
lowest point: Atlantic Ocean 0 m
highest point: Hvannadalshnukur 2,119 m
Natural resources: fish, hydropower, geothermal power, diatomite

Iceland *(continued)*

Land use:
arable land: 0%
permanent crops: 0%
permanent pastures: 23%
forests and woodland: 1%
other: 76% (1993 est.)
Irrigated land: NA sq km
Natural hazards: earthquakes and volcanic activity
Environment - current issues: water pollution from fertilizer runoff; inadequate wastewater treatment
Environment - international agreements:
party to: Air Pollution, Biodiversity, Climate Change, Desertification, Hazardous Wastes, Law of the Sea, Marine Dumping, Nuclear Test Ban, Ozone Layer Protection, Ship Pollution, Wetlands, Whaling
signed, but not ratified: Air Pollution-Persistent Organic Pollutants, Environmental Modification, Marine Life Conservation
Geography - note: strategic location between Greenland and Europe; westernmost European country; more land covered by glaciers than in all of continental Europe

People

Population: 272,512 (July 1999 est.)
Age structure:
0-14 years: 23% (male 32,608; female 31,061)
15-64 years: 65% (male 89,258; female 87,449)
65 years and over: 12% (male 14,510; female 17,626) (1999 est.)
Population growth rate: 0.57% (1999 est.)
Birth rate: 14.87 births/1,000 population (1999 est.)
Death rate: 7.01 deaths/1,000 population (1999 est.)
Net migration rate: -2.17 migrant(s)/1,000 population (1999 est.)
Sex ratio:
at birth: 1.06 male(s)/female
under 15 years: 1.05 male(s)/female
15-64 years: 1.02 male(s)/female
65 years and over: 0.82 male(s)/female
total population: 1 male(s)/female (1999 est.)
Infant mortality rate: 5.22 deaths/1,000 live births (1999 est.)
Life expectancy at birth:
total population: 78.96 years
male: 76.85 years
female: 81.19 years (1999 est.)
Total fertility rate: 2.03 children born/woman (1999 est.)
Nationality:
noun: Icelander(s)
adjective: Icelandic
Ethnic groups: homogeneous mixture of descendants of Norwegians and Celts
Religions: Evangelical Lutheran 96%, other Protestant and Roman Catholic 3%, none 1% (1988)
Languages: Icelandic
Literacy:
definition: age 15 and over can read and write
total population: 100% (1976 est.)
male: NA%
female: NA%

Government

Country name:
conventional long form: Republic of Iceland
conventional short form: Iceland
local long form: Lyoveldio Island
local short form: Island
Data code: IC
Government type: constitutional republic
Capital: Reykjavik
Administrative divisions: 23 counties (syslar, singular - sysla) and 14 independent towns* (kaupstadhir, singular - kaupstadhur); Akranes*, Akureyri*, Arnessysla, Austur-Bardhastrandarsysla, Austur-Hunavatnssysla, Austur-Skaftafellssysla, Borgarfjardharsysla, Dalasysla, Eyjafjardharsysla, Gullbringusysla, Hafnarfjordhur*, Husavik*, Isafjordhur*, Keflavik*, Kjosarsysla, Kopavogur*, Myrasysla, Neskaupstadhur*, Nordhur-Isafjardharsysla, Nordhur-Mulasys-la, Nordhur-Thingeyjarsysla, Olafsfjordhur*, Rangarvallasysla, Reykjavik*, Saudharkrokur*, Seydhisfjordhur*, Siglufjordhur*, Skagafjardharsysla, Snaefellsnes-og Hnappadalssysla, Strandasysla, Sudhur-Mulasysla, Sudhur-Thingeyjarsysla, Vesttmannaeyjar*, Vestur-Bardhastrandarsysla, Vestur-Hunavatnssysla, Vestur-Isafjardharsysla, Vestur-Skaftafellssysla
Independence: 17 June 1944 (from Denmark)
National holiday: Anniversary of the Establishment of the Republic, 17 June (1944)
Constitution: 16 June 1944, effective 17 June 1944
Legal system: civil law system based on Danish law; does not accept compulsory ICJ jurisdiction
Suffrage: 18 years of age; universal
Executive branch:
chief of state: President Olafur Ragnar GRIMSSON (since 1 August 1996)
head of government: Prime Minister David ODDSSON (since 30 April 1991)
cabinet: Cabinet appointed by the president
elections: president elected by popular vote for a four-year term; election last held 29 June 1996 (next to be held NA June 2000); prime minister appointed by the president
election results: Olafur Ragnar GRIMSSON elected president; percent of vote - 41.4%
Legislative branch: unicameral Parliament or Althing (63 seats; members are elected by popular vote to serve four-year terms)
elections: last held on 8 April 1995 (next to be held by April 1999)
election results: percent of vote by party - Independence Party 37.1%, Progressive Party 23.3%, Social Democratic Party 11.4%, Socialists 14.3%, People's Movement 7.2%, Women's Party 4.9%; seats by party - Independence 25, Progressive 15, Social Democratic 7, Socialists 9, People's Movement 4, Women's Party 3
Judicial branch: Supreme Court or Haestirettur, justices are appointed for life by the president
Political parties and leaders: Independence Party (conservative) or IP [David ODDSSON]; Progressive Party (liberal) or PP [Halldor ASGRIMSSON]; Social Democratic Party or SDP [Sighvatur BJORGVINSSON]; People's Alliance (left socialist) or PA [Margret FRIMANNSDOTTIR]; Women's Party or WL [Kristin ASTGEIRSDOTTIR]; People's Movement (centrist) [leader NA]; National Awakening (People's Revival Party) or PR [Johanna SIGURDARDOTTIR]
International organization participation: Australia Group, BIS, CBSS, CCC, CE, EAPC, EBRD, ECE, EFTA, FAO, IAEA, IBRD, ICAO, ICC, ICFTU, ICRM, IDA, IFC, IFRCS, IHO, ILO, IMF, IMO, Inmarsat, Intelsat, Interpol, IOC, ISO, ITU, MTCR, NATO, NC, NEA, NIB, OECD, OPCW, OSCE, PCA, UN, UNCTAD, UNESCO, UNMIBH, UNU, UPU, WEU (associate), WHO, WIPO, WMO, WTrO
Diplomatic representation in the US:
chief of mission: Ambassador Jon-Baldvin HANNIBALSSON
chancery: Suite 1200, 1156 15th Street NW, Washington, DC 20005
telephone: [1] (202) 265-6653
FAX: [1] (202) 265-6656
consulate(s) general: New York
Diplomatic representation from the US:
chief of mission: Ambassador Day Olin MOUNT
embassy: Laufasvegur 21, Reykjavik
mailing address: US Embassy, PSC 1003, Box 40, FPO AE 09728-0340
telephone: [354] 5629100
FAX: [354] 5629118
Flag description: blue with a red cross outlined in white that extends to the edges of the flag; the vertical part of the cross is shifted to the hoist side in the style of the Dannebrog (Danish flag)

Economy

Economy - overview: Iceland's Scandinavian-type economy is basically capitalistic, yet with an extensive welfare system, low unemployment, and remarkably even distribution of income. The economy depends heavily on the fishing industry, which provides 75% of export earnings and employs 12% of the work force. In the absence of other natural resources - except energy - Iceland's economy is vulnerable to changing world fish prices. The economy remains sensitive to declining fish stocks as well as to drops in world prices for its main exports: fish and fish products, aluminum, and ferrosilicon. The center-right government plans to continue its policies of reducing the budget and current account deficits, limiting foreign borrowing, containing inflation, revising agricultural and fishing policies, diversifying the economy, and privatizing state-owned industries. The government remains opposed to EU membership, primarily because of Icelanders' concern about losing control over their fishing resources. Iceland's economy has been diversifying into manufacturing and service industries in the last decade, and new developments in software production, biotechnology, and financial services are

Iceland *(continued)*

taking place. The tourism sector is also expanding, with the recent trends in ecotourism and whale-watching. Growth is likely to slow in 1999, to a still respectable 4.6%.

GDP: purchasing power parity - $6.06 billion (1998 est.)

GDP - real growth rate: 5.1% (1998 est.)

GDP - per capita: purchasing power parity - $22,400 (1998 est.)

GDP - composition by sector:
agriculture: 13%
industry: 24%
services: 63% (1997 est.)

Population below poverty line: NA%

Household income or consumption by percentage share:
lowest 10%: NA%
highest 10%: NA%

Inflation rate (consumer prices): 1.7% (1998)

Labor force: 130,000 (1998 est.)

Labor force - by occupation: manufacturing 12.9%, fishing and fish processing 11.8%, construction 10.7%, other services 59.5%, agriculture 5.1% (1996 est.)

Unemployment rate: 3% (1998 est.)

Budget:
revenues: $1.9 billion
expenditures: $2.1 billion, including capital expenditures of $146 million (1996 est.)

Industries: fish processing; aluminum smelting, ferrosilicon production, geothermal power; tourism

Industrial production growth rate: NA%

Electricity - production: 5.048 billion kWh (1996)

Electricity - production by source:
fossil fuel: 0.06%
hydro: 93.43%
nuclear: 0%
other: 6.51%

Electricity - consumption: 5.532 billion kWh (1997)

Electricity - exports: 0 kWh (1996)

Electricity - imports: 0 kWh (1996)

Agriculture - products: potatoes, turnips; cattle, sheep; fish

Exports: $1.9 billion (f.o.b., 1998)

Exports - commodities: fish and fish products 70%, animal products, aluminum, diatomite and ferrosilicon

Exports - partners: EU 60% (UK 19%, Germany 13%, France 6%, Denmark 6%), US 14% (1997)

Imports: $2.4 billion (f.o.b., 1998)

Imports - commodities: machinery and equipment, petroleum products, foodstuffs, textiles

Imports - partners: EU 58% (Germany 12%, Norway 12%, UK 10%, Denmark 9%, Sweden 7%), US 9% (1997)

Debt - external: $2.2 billion (1996 est.)

Economic aid - recipient: $NA

Currency: 1 Icelandic krona (IKr) = 100 aurar

Exchange rates: Icelandic kronur (IKr) per US$1 - 69.250 (January 1999), 70.958 (1998), 70.904 (1997), 66.500 (1996), 64.692 (1995), 69.944 (1994)

Fiscal year: calendar year

Communications

Telephones: 143,600 (1993 est.)

Telephone system: adequate domestic service
domestic: the trunk network consists of coaxial and fiber-optic cables and microwave radio relay links
international: satellite earth stations - 2 Intelsat (Atlantic Ocean), 1 Inmarsat (Atlantic and Indian Ocean regions); note - Iceland shares the Inmarsat earth station with the other Nordic countries (Denmark, Finland, Norway, and Sweden)

Radio broadcast stations: AM 5, FM 147 (transmitters and repeaters), shortwave 0

Radios: 91,500 licensed (1993 est.)

Television broadcast stations: 14 (in addition, there are 156 low-power repeaters) (1997)

Televisions: 96,100 (1993 est.)

Transportation

Railways: 0 km

Highways:
total: 12,691 km
paved: 3,262 km
unpaved: 9,429 km (1997 est.)

Ports and harbors: Akureyri, Hornafjordur, Isafjordhur, Keflavik, Raufarhofn, Reykjavik, Seydhisfjordhur, Straumsvik, Vestmannaeyjar

Merchant marine:
total: 3 ships (1,000 GRT or over) totaling 13,085 GRT/16,938 DWT
ships by type: chemical tanker 1, container 1, oil tanker 1 (1998 est.)

Airports: 87 (1998 est.)

Airports - with paved runways:
total: 10
over 3,047 m: 1
1,524 to 2,437 m: 4
914 to 1,523 m: 5 (1998 est.)

Airports - with unpaved runways:
total: 77
1,524 to 2,437 m: 3
914 to 1,523 m: 21
under 914 m: 53 (1998 est.)

Military

Military branches: no regular armed forces; Police, Coast Guard; note - Iceland's defense is provided by the US-manned Icelandic Defense Force (IDF) headquartered at Keflavik

Military manpower - availability:
males age 15-49: 70,958 (1999 est.)

Military manpower - fit for military service:
males age 15-49: 62,570 (1999 est.)

Military expenditures - dollar figure: none

Military - note: Iceland's defense is provided by the US-manned Icelandic Defense Force (IDF) headquartered at Keflavik

Transnational Issues

Disputes - international: Rockall continental shelf dispute involving Denmark, Ireland, and the UK (Ireland and the UK have signed a boundary agreement in the Rockall area)

India

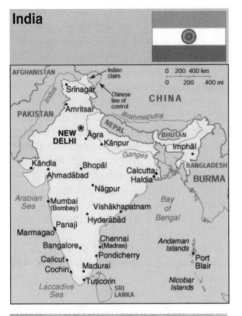

Geography

Location: Southern Asia, bordering the Arabian Sea and the Bay of Bengal, between Burma and Pakistan
Geographic coordinates: 20 00 N, 77 00 E
Map references: Asia
Area:
total: 3,287,590 sq km
land: 2,973,190 sq km
water: 314,400 sq km
Area - comparative: slightly more than one-third the size of the US
Land boundaries:
total: 14,103 km
border countries: Bangladesh 4,053 km, Bhutan 605 km, Burma 1,463 km, China 3,380 km, Nepal 1,690 km, Pakistan 2,912 km
Coastline: 7,000 km
Maritime claims:
contiguous zone: 24 nm
continental shelf: 200 nm or to the edge of the continental margin
exclusive economic zone: 200 nm
territorial sea: 12 nm
Climate: varies from tropical monsoon in south to temperate in north
Terrain: upland plain (Deccan Plateau) in south, flat to rolling plain along the Ganges, deserts in west, Himalayas in north
Elevation extremes:
lowest point: Indian Ocean 0 m
highest point: Kanchenjunga 8,598 m
Natural resources: coal (fourth-largest reserves in the world), iron ore, manganese, mica, bauxite, titanium ore, chromite, natural gas, diamonds, petroleum, limestone
Land use:
arable land: 56%
permanent crops: 1%
permanent pastures: 4%
forests and woodland: 23%
other: 16% (1993 est.)

Irrigated land: 480,000 sq km (1993 est.)
Natural hazards: droughts, flash floods, severe thunderstorms common; earthquakes
Environment - current issues: deforestation; soil erosion; overgrazing; desertification; air pollution from industrial effluents and vehicle emissions; water pollution from raw sewage and runoff of agricultural pesticides; tap water is not potable throughout the country; huge and rapidly growing population is overstraining natural resources
Environment - international agreements:
party to: Antarctic-Environmental Protocol, Antarctic Treaty, Biodiversity, Climate Change, Desertification, Endangered Species, Environmental Modification, Hazardous Wastes, Law of the Sea, Nuclear Test Ban, Ozone Layer Protection, Ship Pollution, Tropical Timber 83, Tropical Timber 94, Wetlands, Whaling
signed, but not ratified: none of the selected agreements
Geography - note: dominates South Asian subcontinent; near important Indian Ocean trade routes

People

Population: 1,000,848,550 (July 1999 est.)
Age structure:
0-14 years: 34% (male 175,463,726; female 165,722,164)
15-64 years: 61% (male 318,004,920; female 295,245,556)
65 years and over: 5% (male 23,571,270; female 22,840,914) (1999 est.)
Population growth rate: 1.68% (1999 est.)
Birth rate: 25.39 births/1,000 population (1999 est.)
Death rate: 8.5 deaths/1,000 population (1999 est.)
Net migration rate: -0.08 migrant(s)/1,000 population (1999 est.)
Sex ratio:
at birth: 1.05 male(s)/female
under 15 years: 1.06 male(s)/female
15-64 years: 1.08 male(s)/female
65 years and over: 1.03 male(s)/female
total population: 1.07 male(s)/female (1999 est.)
Infant mortality rate: 60.81 deaths/1,000 live births (1999 est.)
Life expectancy at birth:
total population: 63.4 years
male: 62.54 years
female: 64.29 years (1999 est.)
Total fertility rate: 3.18 children born/woman (1999 est.)
Nationality:
noun: Indian(s)
adjective: Indian
Ethnic groups: Indo-Aryan 72%, Dravidian 25%, Mongoloid and other 3%
Religions: Hindu 80%, Muslim 14%, Christian 2.4%, Sikh 2%, Buddhist 0.7%, Jains 0.5%, other 0.4%
Languages: English enjoys associate status but is the most important language for national, political, and commercial communication, Hindi the national language and primary tongue of 30% of the people,

Bengali (official), Telugu (official), Marathi (official), Tamil (official), Urdu (official), Gujarati (official), Malayalam (official), Kannada (official), Oriya (official), Punjabi (official), Assamese (official), Kashmiri (official), Sindhi (official), Sanskrit (official), Hindustani (a popular variant of Hindi/Urdu spoken widely throughout northern India)
note: 24 languages each spoken by a million or more persons; numerous other languages and dialects, for the most part mutually unintelligible
Literacy:
definition: age 15 and over can read and write
total population: 52%
male: 65.5%
female: 37.7% (1995 est.)

Government

Country name:
conventional long form: Republic of India
conventional short form: India
Data code: IN
Government type: federal republic
Capital: New Delhi
Administrative divisions: 25 states and 7 union territories*; Andaman and Nicobar Islands*, Andhra Pradesh, Arunachal Pradesh, Assam, Bihar, Chandigarh*, Dadra and Nagar Haveli*, Daman and Diu*, Delhi*, Goa, Gujarat, Haryana, Himachal Pradesh, Jammu and Kashmir, Karnataka, Kerala, Lakshadweep*, Madhya Pradesh, Maharashtra, Manipur, Meghalaya, Mizoram, Nagaland, Orissa, Pondicherry*, Punjab, Rajasthan, Sikkim, Tamil Nadu, Tripura, Uttar Pradesh, West Bengal
Independence: 15 August 1947 (from UK)
National holiday: Anniversary of the Proclamation of the Republic, 26 January (1950)
Constitution: 26 January 1950
Legal system: based on English common law; limited judicial review of legislative acts; accepts compulsory ICJ jurisdiction, with reservations
Suffrage: 18 years of age; universal
Executive branch:
chief of state: President Kicheril Raman NARAYANAN (since 25 July 1997); Vice President Krishnan KANT (since 21 August 1997)
head of government: Prime Minister Atal Behari VAJPAYEE (since 19 March 1998)
cabinet: Council of Ministers appointed by the president on the recommendation of the prime minister
elections: president elected by an electoral college consisting of elected members of both houses of Parliament and the legislatures of the states for a five-year term; election last held 14 July 1997 (next to be held NA July 2002); vice president elected by both houses of Parliament; election last held 16 August 1997 (next to be held NA August 2002); prime minister elected by parliamentary members of the majority party following legislative elections; election last held NA March 1998 (next to be held NA March 2003)
election results: Kicheril Raman NARAYANAN elected president; percent of electoral college vote -

India (continued)

NA; Krishnan KANT elected vice president; percent of Parliament vote - NA; Atal Behari VAJPAYEE elected prime minister; percent of vote - NA

Legislative branch: bicameral Parliament or Sansad consists of the Council of States or Rajya Sabha (a body consisting of not more than 250 members, up to 12 of which are appointed by the president, the remainder are chosen by the elected members of the state and territorial assemblies; members serve six-year terms) and the People's Assembly or Lok Sabha (545 seats; 543 elected by popular vote, 2 appointed by the president; members serve five-year terms)

elections: People's Assembly - last held 16 February through 7 March 1998 (next to be held NA March 2003)

election results: People's Assembly - percent of vote by party - NA; seats by party - BJP 178, Congress (I) Party 141, CPI/M 32, SP 20, ADMK 18, RJD 17, Telugu Desam 12, SAP 12, CPI 9, BJD 9, Akali Dal factions 8, Trinamool Congress 7, SHS 6, DMK 6, Janata Dal Party 6, BSP 5, RSP 5, independents and others 44, vacant 8, appointed by the president 2

Judicial branch: Supreme Court, judges are appointed by the president and remain in office until they reach the age of 65

Political parties and leaders: Bharatiya Janata Party or BJP [Kushabhau THAKRE, president, L. K. ADVANI, A. B. VAJPAYEE]; Congress (I) Party [Sonia GANDHI, president]; Janata Dal Party [Sharad YADAV, president, I. K. GUJRAL]; Janata Dal (Ajit) [Ajit SINGH]; Rashtriya Janata Dal or RJD [Laloo Prasad YADAV]; Communist Party of India/Marxist or CPI/M [Harkishan Singh SURJEET]; Tamil Maanila Congress [G. K. MOOPANAR]; Dravida Munnetra Kazagham or DMK (a regional party in Tamil Nadu) [M. KARUNANIDHI]; Samajwadi Party or SP [Mulayam Singh YADAV (president), Om Prakash CHAUTALA, Devi LAL]; Telugu Desam (a regional party in Andhra Pradesh) [Chandrababu NAIDU]; Communist Party of India or CPI [Indrajit GUPTA]; Revolutionary Socialist Party or RSP [Tridip CHOWDHURY]; Asom Gana Parishad [Prafulla Kumar MAHANTA]; Congress (Tiwari) [Arjun SINGH and N. D. TIWARI]; All India Forward Bloc or AIFB [Prem Dutta PALIWAL (chairman), Chitta BASU (general secretary)]; Muslim League [G. M. BANATWALA]; Madhya Pradesh Vikas Congress [Madhavro SCINDIA]; Karnataka Congress Party [S. BANGARAPPA]; Shiv Sena or SHS [Bal THACKERAY]; Bahujan Samaj Party or BSP [Kanshi RAM]; Communist Party of India/Marxist-Leninist or CPI/ML [Vinod MISHRA]; Akali Dal factions representing Sikh religious community in the Punjab; National Conference or NC (a regional party in Jammu and Kashmir) [Farooq ABDULLAH]; Bihar Peoples Party [Lovely ANAND]; Samata Party or SAP (formerly Janata Dal members) [George FERNANDES]; Indian National League [Suliaman SAIT]; Kerala Congress (Mani faction) [K. M. MANI]; All India Anna Dravida Munnetra Kazhagam or ADMK [leader NA]; Biju Janata Dal or BJD [leader NA];

Trinamool Congress [leader NA]

Political pressure groups and leaders: various separatist groups seeking greater communal and/or regional autonomy; numerous religious or militant/chauvinistic organizations, including Adam Sena, Ananda Marg, Vishwa Hindu Parishad, and Rashtriya Swayamsevak Sangh

International organization participation: AfDB, AsDB, BIS, C, CCC, CP, ESCAP, FAO, G-6, G-15, G-19, G-24, G-77, IAEA, IBRD, ICAO, ICC, ICFTU, ICRM, IDA, IEA (observer), IFAD, IFC, IFRCS, IHO, ILO, IMF, IMO, Inmarsat, Intelsat, Interpol, IOC, IOM (observer), ISO, ITU, MIPONUH, MONUA, NAM, OAS (observer), OPCW, PCA, SAARC, UN, UNCTAD, UNESCO, UNHCR, UNIDO, UNIKOM, UNITAR, UNMIBH, UNOMIL, UNOMSIL, UNU, UPU, WFTU, WHO, WIPO, WMO, WToO, WTrO

Diplomatic representation in the US:
chief of mission: Ambassador Naresh CHANDRA
chancery: 2107 Massachusetts Avenue NW, Washington, DC 20008; note - Embassy located at 2536 Massachusetts Avenue NW, Washington, DC 20008
telephone: [1] (202) 939-7000
FAX: [1] (202) 483-3972
consulate(s) general: Chicago, Houston, New York, and San Francisco

Diplomatic representation from the US:
chief of mission: Ambassador Richard F. CELESTE
embassy: Shanti Path, Chanakyapuri 110021, New Delhi
mailing address: use embassy street address
telephone: [91] (11) 688-9033, 611-3033
FAX: [91] (11) 419-0017
consulate(s) general: Calcutta, Chennai (Madras), Mumbai (Bombay)

Flag description: three equal horizontal bands of orange (top), white, and green with a blue chakra (24-spoked wheel) centered in the white band; similar to the flag of Niger, which has a small orange disk centered in the white band

Economy

Economy - overview: India's economy encompasses traditional village farming, modern agriculture, handicrafts, a wide range of modern industries, and a multitude of support services. 67% of India's labor force work in agriculture, which contributes 25% of the country's GDP. Production, trade, and investment reforms since 1991 have provided new opportunities for Indian businesspersons and an estimated 300 million middle class consumers. New Delhi has avoided debt rescheduling, attracted foreign investment, and revived confidence in India's economic prospects since 1991. Many of the country's fundamentals - including savings rates (26% of GDP) and reserves (now about $30 billion) - are healthy. Even so, the Indian Government needs to restore the early momentum of reform, especially by continuing reductions in the extensive remaining government regulations. India's exports, currency, and foreign

institutional investment were affected by the East Asian crisis in late 1997 and 1998; but capital account controls, a low ratio of short-term debt to reserves, and enhanced supervision of the financial sector helped insulate it from near term balance-of-payments problems. Exports fell 5% in 1998 mainly because of the fall in Asian currencies relative to the rupee. Energy, telecommunications, and transportation bottlenecks continue to constrain growth. A series of weak coalition governments have lacked the political strength to push reforms forward to address these and other problems. Indian think tanks project GDP growth of about 4.5% in 1999. Inflation will remain a worrisome problem.

GDP: purchasing power parity - $1.689 trillion (1998 est.)

GDP - real growth rate: 5.4% (1998 est.)

GDP - per capita: purchasing power parity - $1,720 (1998 est.)

GDP - composition by sector:
agriculture: 25%
industry: 30%
services: 45% (1997)

Population below poverty line: 35% (1994 est.)

Household income or consumption by percentage share:
lowest 10%: 4.1%
highest 10%: 25% (1994)

Inflation rate (consumer prices): 14% (1998 est.)

Labor force: NA

Labor force - by occupation: agriculture 67%, services 18%, industry 15% (1995 est.)

Unemployment rate: NA%

Budget:
revenues: $42.12 billion
expenditures: $63.79 billion, including capital expenditures of $13.8 billion (FY98/99 budget est.)

Industries: textiles, chemicals, food processing, steel, transportation equipment, cement, mining, petroleum, machinery

Industrial production growth rate: 5.5% (1997)

Electricity - production: 404.475 billion kWh (1996)

Electricity - production by source:
fossil fuel: 80.35%
hydro: 17.8%
nuclear: 1.83%
other: 0.02% (1996)

Electricity - consumption: 406.02 billion kWh (1996)

Electricity - exports: 130 million kWh (1996)

Electricity - imports: 1.675 billion kWh (1996)

Agriculture - products: rice, wheat, oilseed, cotton, jute, tea, sugarcane, potatoes; cattle, water buffalo, sheep, goats, poultry; fish

Exports: $32.17 billion (f.o.b., 1998)

Exports - commodities: textile goods, gems and jewelry, engineering goods, chemicals, leather manufactures

Exports - partners: US 19%, Hong Kong 6%, UK 6%, Japan 6%, Germany 5% (1997)

Imports: $41.34 billion (c.i.f., 1998)

Imports - commodities: crude oil and petroleum

products, machinery, gems, fertilizer, chemicals
Imports - partners: US 10%, Belgium 7%, UK 7%, Germany 7%, Saudi Arabia 6%, Japan 6% (1997)
Debt - external: $93 billion (1998)
Economic aid - recipient: $1.604 billion (1995)
Currency: 1 Indian rupee (Re) = 100 paise
Exchange rates: Indian rupees (Rs) per US$1 - 42.508 (January 1999), 41.259 (1998), 36.313 (1997), 35.433 (1996), 32.427 (1995), 31.374 (1994)
Fiscal year: 1 April - 31 March

Telephones: 12 million (1996)
Telephone system: mediocre; local and long distance service provided throughout all regions of the country, with services primarily concentrated in the urban areas; major objective is to continue to expand and modernize long-distance network in order to keep pace with rapidly growing number of local subscriber lines; steady improvement is taking place with the recent admission of private and private-public investors, but demand for communication services is also growing rapidly
domestic: local service is provided by microwave radio relay and coaxial cable, with open wire and obsolete electromechanical and manual switchboard systems still in use in rural areas; starting in the 1980s, a substantial amount of digital switch gear has been introduced for local- and long-distance service; long-distance traffic is carried mostly by coaxial cable and low-capacity microwave radio relay; since 1985, however, significant trunk capacity has been added in the form of fiber-optic cable and a domestic satellite system with 254 earth stations; cellular telephone service in four metropolitan cities
international: satellite earth stations - 8 Intelsat (Indian Ocean) and 1 Inmarsat (Indian Ocean Region); four gateway exchanges operating from Mumbai, New Delhi, Calcutta, and Chennai; submarine cables to Malaysia, UAE, Singapore, and Japan
Radio broadcast stations: AM 153, FM 91, shortwave 62 (1998 est.)
Radios: 111 million (1998 est.)
Television broadcast stations: 562 (82 stations have 1 kW or greater power and 480 stations have less than 1 kW of power) (1997)
Televisions: 50 million (1999 est.)

Railways:
total: 62,915 km (12,307 km electrified; 12,617 km double track)
broad gauge: 40,620 km 1.676-m gauge
narrow gauge: 18,501 km 1.000-m gauge; 3,794 km 0.762-m and 0.610-m gauge (1998 est.)
Highways:
total: 3,319,644 km
paved: 1,517,077 km
unpaved: 1,802,567 km (1996 est.)
Waterways: 16,180 km; 3,631 km navigable by large vessels
Pipelines: crude oil 3,005 km; petroleum products

2,687 km; natural gas 1,700 km (1995)
Ports and harbors: Calcutta, Chennai (Madras), Cochin, Jawaharal Nehru, Kandla, Mumbai (Bombay), Vishakhapatnam
Merchant marine:
total: 311 ships (1,000 GRT or over) totaling 6,627,497 GRT/11,038,723 DWT
ships by type: bulk 126, cargo 63, chemical tanker 11, combination bulk 2, combination ore/oil 3, container 12, liquefied gas tanker 10, oil tanker 76, passenger-cargo 5, short-sea passenger 1, specialized tanker 2 (1998 est.)
Airports: 341 (1998 est.)
Airports - with paved runways:
total: 230
over 3,047 m: 11
2,438 to 3,047 m: 48
1,524 to 2,437 m: 82
914 to 1,523 m: 70
under 914 m: 19 (1998 est.)
Airports - with unpaved runways:
total: 111
2,438 to 3,047 m: 2
1,524 to 2,437 m: 8
914 to 1,523 m: 50
under 914 m: 51 (1998 est.)
Heliports: 17 (1998 est.)

Military branches: Army, Navy (including naval air arm), Air Force, various security or paramilitary forces (includes Border Security Force, Assam Rifles, and Rashtriya Rifles)
Military manpower - military age: 17 years of age
Military manpower - availability:
males age 15-49: 269,339,985 (1999 est.)
Military manpower - fit for military service:
males age 15-49: 158,141,508 (1999 est.)
Military manpower - reaching military age annually:
males: 10,661,786 (1999 est.)
Military expenditures - dollar figure: $10.012 billion (FY98/99)
Military expenditures - percent of GDP: 2.7% (FY98/99)

Disputes - international: boundary with China in dispute; status of Kashmir with Pakistan; water-sharing problems with Pakistan over the Indus River (Wular Barrage); a portion of the boundary with Bangladesh is indefinite; dispute with Bangladesh over New Moore/South Talpatty Island
Illicit drugs: world's largest producer of licit opium for the pharmaceutical trade, but an undetermined quantity of opium is diverted to illicit international drug markets; major transit country for illicit narcotics produced in neighboring countries; illicit producer of hashish and methaqualone; cultivated 2,050 hectares of illicit opium in 1997, a 34% decrease from 1996, with a potential production of 30 metric tons, a 36% decrease from 1996

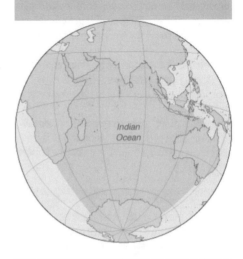

Location: body of water between Africa, Antarctica, Asia, and Australia
Geographic coordinates: 30 00 S, 80 00 E
Map references: World
Area:
total: 73.6 million sq km
note: includes Andaman Sea, Arabian Sea, Bay of Bengal, Great Australian Bight, Gulf of Aden, Gulf of Oman, Mozambique Channel, Persian Gulf, Red Sea, Strait of Malacca, and other tributary water bodies
Area - comparative: slightly less than eight times the size of the US; third-largest ocean (after the Pacific Ocean and Atlantic Ocean, but larger than the Arctic Ocean)
Coastline: 66,526 km
Climate: northeast monsoon (December to April), southwest monsoon (June to October); tropical cyclones occur during May/June and October/November in the northern Indian Ocean and January/February in the southern Indian Ocean
Terrain: surface dominated by counterclockwise gyre (broad, circular system of currents) in the southern Indian Ocean; unique reversal of surface currents in the northern Indian Ocean; low atmospheric pressure over southwest Asia from hot, rising, summer air results in the southwest monsoon and southwest-to-northeast winds and currents, while high pressure over northern Asia from cold, falling, winter air results in the northeast monsoon and northeast-to-southwest winds and currents; ocean floor is dominated by the Mid-Indian Ocean Ridge and subdivided by the Southeast Indian Ocean Ridge, Southwest Indian Ocean Ridge, and Ninetyeast Ridge
Elevation extremes:
lowest point: Java Trench -7,258 m
highest point: sea level 0 m
Natural resources: oil and gas fields, fish, shrimp, sand and gravel aggregates, placer deposits, polymetallic nodules

Indian Ocean *(continued)*

Natural hazards: ships subject to superstructure icing in extreme south near Antarctica from May to October
Environment - current issues: endangered marine species include the dugong, seals, turtles, and whales; oil pollution in the Arabian Sea, Persian Gulf, and Red Sea
Environment - international agreements:
party to: none of the selected agreements
signed, but not ratified: none of the selected agreements
Geography - note: major chokepoints include Bab el Mandeb, Strait of Hormuz, Strait of Malacca, southern access to the Suez Canal, and the Lombok Strait

Government

Data code: none; the US Government has not approved a standard for hydrographic codes - see the Cross-Reference List of Hydrographic Codes appendix

Economy

Economy - overview: The Indian Ocean provides major sea routes connecting the Middle East, Africa, and East Asia with Europe and the Americas. It carries a particularly heavy traffic of petroleum and petroleum products from the oilfields of the Persian Gulf and Indonesia. Its fish are of great and growing importance to the bordering countries for domestic consumption and export. Fishing fleets from Russia, Japan, South Korea, and Taiwan also exploit the Indian Ocean, mainly for shrimp and tuna. Large reserves of hydrocarbons are being tapped in the offshore areas of Saudi Arabia, Iran, India, and western Australia. An estimated 40% of the world's offshore oil production comes from the Indian Ocean. Beach sands rich in heavy minerals and offshore placer deposits are actively exploited by bordering countries, particularly India, South Africa, Indonesia, Sri Lanka, and Thailand.

Communications

Telephone system:
international: submarine cables from India to UAE and Malaysia and from Sri Lanka to Djibouti and Indonesia

Transportation

Ports and harbors: Calcutta (India), Chennai (Madras; India), Colombo (Sri Lanka), Durban (South Africa), Jakarta (Indonesia), Melbourne (Australia), Mumbai (Bombay; India), Richards Bay (South Africa)

Transnational Issues

Disputes - international: some maritime disputes (see littoral states)

Indonesia

Introduction

Background: Indonesia declared its independence in 1945 from the Netherlands, a claim disputed, then recognized by the Dutch in 1949. In 1975 Indonesian troops occupied Portuguese East Timor. Current issues include implementing IMF-mandated reforms (particularly restructuring and recapitalizing the insolvent banking sector), effecting a transition to a popularly elected government, addressing longstanding grievances over the role of the ethnic Chinese business class and charges of cronyism and corruption, alleged human rights violations by the military, the role of the military and religion in politics, and growing pressures for some form of independence or autonomy by Aceh, Irian Jaya, and East Timor.

Geography

Location: Southeastern Asia, archipelago between the Indian Ocean and the Pacific Ocean
Geographic coordinates: 5 00 S, 120 00 E
Map references: Southeast Asia
Area:
total: 1,919,440 sq km
land: 1,826,440 sq km
water: 93,000 sq km
Area - comparative: slightly less than three times the size of Texas
Land boundaries:
total: 2,602 km
border countries: Malaysia 1,782 km, Papua New Guinea 820 km
Coastline: 54,716 km
Maritime claims: measured from claimed archipelagic baselines
exclusive economic zone: 200 nm
territorial sea: 12 nm
Climate: tropical; hot, humid; more moderate in highlands
Terrain: mostly coastal lowlands; larger islands have interior mountains

Elevation extremes:
lowest point: Indian Ocean 0 m
highest point: Puncak Jaya 5,030 m
Natural resources: petroleum, tin, natural gas, nickel, timber, bauxite, copper, fertile soils, coal, gold, silver
Land use:
arable land: 10%
permanent crops: 7%
permanent pastures: 7%
forests and woodland: 62%
other: 14% (1993 est.)
Irrigated land: 45,970 sq km (1993 est.)
Natural hazards: occasional floods, severe droughts, tsunamis, earthquakes, volcanoes
Environment - current issues: deforestation; water pollution from industrial wastes, sewage; air pollution in urban areas; smoke and haze from forest fires
Environment - international agreements:
party to: Biodiversity, Climate Change, Desertification, Endangered Species, Hazardous Wastes, Law of the Sea, Nuclear Test Ban, Ozone Layer Protection, Ship Pollution, Tropical Timber 83, Tropical Timber 94, Wetlands
signed, but not ratified: Climate Change-Kyoto Protocol, Marine Life Conservation
Geography - note: archipelago of 17,000 islands (6,000 inhabited); straddles Equator; strategic location astride or along major sea lanes from Indian Ocean to Pacific Ocean

People

Population: 216,108,345 (July 1999 est.)
Age structure:
0-14 years: 30% (male 33,367,287; female 32,411,786)
15-64 years: 65% (male 70,541,893; female 70,866,972)
65 years and over: 5% (male 3,936,415; female 4,983,992) (1999 est.)

Indonesia (continued)

Population growth rate: 1.46% (1999 est.)
Birth rate: 22.78 births/1,000 population (1999 est.)
Death rate: 8.14 deaths/1,000 population (1999 est.)
Net migration rate: 0 migrant(s)/1,000 population (1999 est.)
Sex ratio:
at birth: 1.05 male(s)/female
under 15 years: 1.03 male(s)/female
15-64 years: 1 male(s)/female
65 years and over: 0.79 male(s)/female
total population: 1 male(s)/female (1999 est.)
Infant mortality rate: 57.3 deaths/1,000 live births (1999 est.)
Life expectancy at birth:
total population: 62.92 years
male: 60.67 years
female: 65.29 years (1999 est.)
Total fertility rate: 2.57 children born/woman (1999 est.)
Nationality:
noun: Indonesian(s)
adjective: Indonesian
Ethnic groups: Javanese 45%, Sundanese 14%, Madurese 7.5%, coastal Malays 7.5%, other 26%
Religions: Muslim 88%, Protestant 5%, Roman Catholic 3%, Hindu 2%, Buddhist 1%, other 1% (1998)
Languages: Bahasa Indonesia (official, modified form of Malay), English, Dutch, local dialects, the most widely spoken of which is Javanese
Literacy:
definition: age 15 and over can read and write
total population: 83.8%
male: 89.6%
female: 78% (1995 est.)

Government

Country name:
conventional long form: Republic of Indonesia
conventional short form: Indonesia
local long form: Republik Indonesia
local short form: Indonesia
former: Netherlands East Indies; Dutch East Indies
Data code: ID
Government type: republic
Capital: Jakarta
Administrative divisions: 24 provinces (propinsi-propinsi, singular - propinsi), 2 special regions* (daerah-daerah istimewa, singular - daerah istimewa), and 1 special capital city district** (daerah khusus ibukota); Aceh*, Bali, Bengkulu, Irian Jaya, Jakarta Raya**, Jambi, Jawa Barat, Jawa Tengah, Jawa Timur, Kalimantan Barat, Kalimantan Selatan, Kalimantan Tengah, Kalimantan Timur, Lampung, Maluku, Nusa Tenggara Barat, Nusa Tenggara Timur, Riau, Sulawesi Selatan, Sulawesi Tengah, Sulawesi Tenggara, Sulawesi Utara, Sumatera Barat, Sumatera Selatan, Sumatera Utara, Timor Timur, Yogyakarta*
Independence: 17 August 1945 (proclaimed independence; on 27 December 1949, Indonesia became legally independent from the Netherlands)
National holiday: Independence Day, 17 August (1945)

Constitution: August 1945, abrogated by Federal Constitution of 1949 and Provisional Constitution of 1950, restored 5 July 1959
Legal system: based on Roman-Dutch law, substantially modified by indigenous concepts and by new criminal procedures code; has not accepted compulsory ICJ jurisdiction
Suffrage: 17 years of age; universal and married persons regardless of age
Executive branch:
note: on 21 May 1998 - less than three months after being selected for a seventh five-year term - President Gen. (Ret.) SOEHARTO resigned from office; immediately following his resignation he announced that Vice President HABIBIE would assume the presidency for the remainder of the term which expires in 2003; on 28 May 1998, HABIBIE and legislative leaders announced an agreement to select a new president in 1999
chief of state: President Bacharuddin J. HABIBIE (since 21 May 1998); note - the president is both the chief of state and head of government
head of government: President Bacharuddin J. HABIBIE (since 21 May 1998); note - the president is both the chief of state and head of government
cabinet: Cabinet
election: president and vice president selected by consensus by the People's Consultative Assembly for five-year terms; selection last held 10 March 1998 (next to be held by 10 November 1999)
election results: Gen. (Ret.) SOEHARTO selected president by consensus by the People's Consultative Assembly; Bacharuddin J. HABIBIE selected vice president by consensus by the People's Consultative Assembly; note - Vice President HABIBIE assumed the presidency after SOEHARTO's resignation
Legislative branch: unicameral House of Representatives or Dewan Perwakilan Rakyat (DPR) (500 seats; 425 elected by popular vote, 75 are appointed military representatives; members serve five-year terms)
elections: last held 29 May 1997 (next to be held 7 June 1999)
election results: percent of vote by party - Golkar 74.5%, PPP 22.43%, PDI 3.07%; seats by party - Golkar 325, PPP 89, PDI 11
note: the People's Consultative Assembly (Majelis Permusyawaratan Rakyat or MPR) includes the DPR plus 200 indirectly selected members; it meets every five years to elect the president and vice president and to approve the broad outlines of national policy
Judicial branch: Supreme Court (Mahkamah Agung), the judges are appointed by the president
Political parties and leaders: Golkar (de facto ruling political party based on functional groups) [Akbar TANSUNG, general chairman]; Indonesia Democracy Party or PDI (federation of former Nationalist and Christian Parties) [Budi HARDJONO, chairman]; Development Unity Party or PPP (federation of former Islamic parties) [Hamzah HAZ, chairman]
International organization participation: APEC,

AsDB, ASEAN, CCC, CP, ESCAP, FAO, G-15, G-19, G-77, IAEA, IBRD, ICAO, ICC, ICFTU, ICRM, IDA, IDB, IFAD, IFC, IFRCS, IHO, ILO, IMF, IMO, Inmarsat, Intelsat, Interpol, IOC, IOM (observer), ISO, ITU, NAM, OIC, OPCW, OPEC, UN, UNCTAD, UNESCO, UNIDO, UNIKOM, UNMIBH, UNMOP, UNMOT, UNOMIG, UNPREDEP, UPU, WCL, WFTU, WHO, WIPO, WMO, WToO, WTrO
Diplomatic representation in the US:
chief of mission: Ambassador DORODJATUN Kuntoro-Jakti
chancery: 2020 Massachusetts Avenue NW, Washington, DC 20036
telephone: [1] (202) 775-5200
FAX: [1] (202) 775-5365
consulate(s) general: Chicago, Houston, Los Angeles, New York, and San Francisco
Diplomatic representation from the US:
chief of mission: Ambassador J. Stapleton ROY
embassy: Medan Merdeka Selatan 5, Jakarta
mailing address: Unit 8129, Box 1, APO AP 96520
telephone: [62] (21) 344-2211
FAX: [62] (21) 386-2259
consulate(s) general: Surabaya
Flag description: two equal horizontal bands of red (top) and white; similar to the flag of Monaco, which is shorter; also similar to the flag of Poland, which is white (top) and red

Economy

Economy - overview: The collapse of the rupiah in late 1997 and early 1998 caused GDP to contract by an estimated 13.7% in 1998 because of Indonesian firms' reliance on short-term dollar-denominated debt and high levels of nonperforming loans in the banking sector. The Indonesian Government initially wavered on meeting the conditions it agreed to in exchange for a $42 billion IMF assistance package, contributing to further loss in investor confidence and outflows of capital. Riots that in many cases targeted ethnic Chinese business owners also set back chances that Indonesia would quickly stabilize its financial crisis and contributed to President SOEHARTO's resignation on 21 May 1998. His successor, B.J. HABIBIE, improved cooperation with the IMF. The money supply - which expanded rapidly early in the year to prop up banks hit by deposit runs - was tightened within a few months, and by October, inflation - which reached a 77% annual rate - was significantly dampened. The government also announced a bank recapitalization program in late 1998, but by early 1999 the plan faced growing challenges over its reliance on public funds. Doubts about whether the program is adequate underlie forecasts of continued - although much less severe - GDP contraction for 1999. Signs of spreading unrest and sectarian violence and concern that social instability will increase as the 7 June 1999 national election approaches also contribute to pessimism about the economy, particularly because foreign investors remain reluctant to begin to increase capital inflows again. The next government will face the challenge of establishing a macroeconomic policy

Indonesia (continued)

framework that addresses longstanding grievances and inequities underlying much of the current unrest without hampering an economic recovery.

GDP: purchasing power parity - $602 billion (1998 est.)

GDP - real growth rate: -13.7% (1998 est.)

GDP - per capita: purchasing power parity - $2,830 (1998 est.)

GDP - composition by sector:
agriculture: 18.8%
industry: 40.3%
services: 40.9% (1998 est.)

Population below poverty line: NA%

Household income or consumption by percentage share:
lowest 10%: 3.6%
highest 10%: 28.3% (1995)

Inflation rate (consumer prices): 77% (1998 est.)

Labor force: 87 million (1997 est.)

Labor force - by occupation: agriculture 41%, trade, restaurant, and hotel 19.8%, manufacturing 14%, construction 4.8%, transport and communications 4.75%, other 15.65% (1997)

Unemployment rate: 15%-20% (1998 est.)

Budget:
revenues: $35 billion (of which $15 billion is from international financial institutions)
expenditures: $35 billion, including capital expenditures of $12 billion (FY98/99 est.)

Industries: petroleum and natural gas; textiles, apparel, and footwear; mining, cement, chemical fertilizers, plywood; rubber; food; tourism

Industrial production growth rate: -13.7% (1998 est.)

Electricity - production: 66.8 billion kWh (1996)

Electricity - production by source:
fossil fuel: 82.34%
hydro: 14.97%
nuclear: 0%
other: 2.69% (1996)

Electricity - consumption: 66.8 billion kWh (1996)

Electricity - exports: 0 kWh (1996)

Electricity - imports: 0 kWh (1996)

Agriculture - products: rice, cassava (tapioca), peanuts, rubber, cocoa, coffee, palm oil, copra; poultry, beef, pork, eggs

Exports: $49 billion (f.o.b., 1998 est.)

Exports - commodities: garments 7.9%, textiles 7.3%, gas 6.4%, electrical appliances 5.9%, pulp and paper 5.3%, oil 4.7%, plywood 4.7%

Exports - partners: Japan 18%, EU 15%, US 14%, Singapore 13%, South Korea 5%, Hong Kong 4%, China 3.9%, Taiwan 3.4% (1998 est.)

Imports: $24 billion (f.o.b., 1998 est.)

Imports - commodities: manufactures 75.3%, raw materials 9.0%, foodstuffs 7.8%, fuels 7.7%

Imports - partners: Japan 20%, US 13%, Germany 9%, Singapore 9%, Australia 6.4%, South Korea 5.4%, Taiwan 3.4%, China 3.1% (1998 est.)

Debt - external: $136 billion (yearend 1997 est.)

Economic aid - recipient: $43 billion from IMF program and other official external financing (1997-2000)

Currency: Indonesian rupiah (Rp)

Exchange rates: Indonesian rupiahs (Rp) per US$1 - 8,714.3 (January 1999), 10,013.6 (1998), 2,909.4 (1997), 2,342.3 (1996), 2,248.6 (1995), 2,160.8 (1994)

Fiscal year: 1 April - 31 March

Communications

Telephones: 1,276,600 (1993 est.)

Telephone system: domestic service fair, international service good
domestic: interisland microwave system and HF radio police net; domestic satellite communications system
international: satellite earth stations - 2 Intelsat (1 Indian Ocean and 1 Pacific Ocean)

Radio broadcast stations: AM 618, FM 38, shortwave 0

Radios: 28.1 million (1992 est.)

Television broadcast stations: 41 (of which 18 are government-owned and 23 are commercial) (1997)

Televisions: 11.5 million (1992 est.)

Transportation

Railways:
total: 6,458 km
narrow gauge: 5,961 km 1.067-m gauge (101 km electrified; 101 km double track); 497 km 0.750-m gauge (1995)

Highways:
total: 342,700 km
paved: 158,670 km
unpaved: 184,030 km (1997 est.)

Waterways: 21,579 km total; Sumatra 5,471 km, Java and Madura 820 km, Kalimantan 10,460 km, Sulawesi (Celebes) 241 km, Irian Jaya 4,587 km

Pipelines: crude oil 2,505 km; petroleum products 456 km; natural gas 1,703 km (1989)

Ports and harbors: Cilacap, Cirebon, Jakarta, Kupang, Palembang, Semarang, Surabaya, Ujungpandang

Merchant marine:
total: 587 ships (1,000 GRT or over) totaling 2,707,004 GRT/3,701,001 DWT
ships by type: bulk 37, cargo 348, chemical tanker 8, container 20, liquefied gas tanker 5, livestock carrier 1, oil tanker 116, passenger 9, passenger-cargo 13, roll-on/roll-off cargo 11, short-sea passenger 7, specialized tanker 7, vehicle carrier 5 (1998 est.)

Airports: 443 (1998 est.)

Airports - with paved runways:
total: 125
over 3,047 m: 4
2,438 to 3,047 m: 11
1,524 to 2,437 m: 41
914 to 1,523 m: 39
under 914 m: 30 (1998 est.)

Airports - with unpaved runways:
total: 318
1,524 to 2,437 m: 5
914 to 1,523 m: 31
under 914 m: 282 (1998 est.)

Heliports: 4 (1998 est.)

Military

Military branches: Army, Navy, Air Force, National Police

Military manpower - military age: 18 years of age

Military manpower - availability:
males age 15-49: 61,087,521 (1999 est.)

Military manpower - fit for military service:
males age 15-49: 35,804,125 (1999 est.)

Military manpower - reaching military age annually:
males: 2,268,638 (1999 est.)

Military expenditures - dollar figure: $959.7 million (FY97/98)

Military expenditures - percent of GDP: 1% (FY97/98)

Transnational Issues

Disputes - international: Indonesian sovereignty over Timor Timur (East Timor Province), which is not recognized by the UN, is the subject of discussions between the UN, Indonesia, and Portugal; two islands in dispute with Malaysia

Illicit drugs: illicit producer of cannabis largely for domestic use; possible growing role as transshipment point for Golden Triangle heroin

Iran

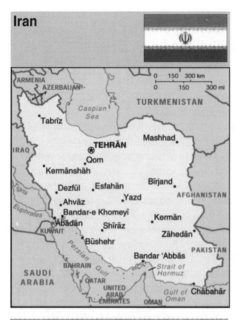

Geography

Location: Middle East, bordering the Gulf of Oman, the Persian Gulf, and the Caspian Sea, between Iraq and Pakistan
Geographic coordinates: 32 00 N, 53 00 E
Map references: Middle East
Area:
total: 1.648 million sq km
land: 1.636 million sq km
water: 12,000 sq km
Area - comparative: slightly larger than Alaska
Land boundaries:
total: 5,440 km
border countries: Afghanistan 936 km, Armenia 35 km, Azerbaijan-proper 432 km, Azerbaijan-Naxcivan exclave 179 km, Iraq 1,458 km, Pakistan 909 km, Turkey 499 km, Turkmenistan 992 km
Coastline: 2,440 km
note: Iran also borders the Caspian Sea (740 km)
Maritime claims:
contiguous zone: 24 nm
continental shelf: natural prolongation
exclusive economic zone: bilateral agreements, or median lines in the Persian Gulf
territorial sea: 12 nm
Climate: mostly arid or semiarid, subtropical along Caspian coast
Terrain: rugged, mountainous rim; high, central basin with deserts, mountains; small, discontinuous plains along both coasts
Elevation extremes:
lowest point: Caspian Sea -28 m
highest point: Qolleh-ye Damavand 5,671 m
Natural resources: petroleum, natural gas, coal, chromium, copper, iron ore, lead, manganese, zinc, sulfur
Land use:
arable land: 10%
permanent crops: 1%
permanent pastures: 27%
forests and woodland: 7%
other: 55% (1993 est.)
Irrigated land: 94,000 sq km (1993 est.)
Natural hazards: periodic droughts, floods; dust storms, sandstorms; earthquakes along western border and in the northeast
Environment - current issues: air pollution, especially in urban areas, from vehicle emissions, refinery operations, and industrial effluents; deforestation; overgrazing; desertification; oil pollution in the Persian Gulf; inadequate supplies of potable water
Environment - international agreements:
party to: Biodiversity, Climate Change, Desertification, Endangered Species, Hazardous Wastes, Marine Dumping, Nuclear Test Ban, Ozone Layer Protection, Wetlands
signed, but not ratified: Environmental Modification, Law of the Sea, Marine Life Conservation

People

Population: 65,179,752 (July 1999 est.)
Age structure:
0-14 years: 36% (male 11,963,438; female 11,447,191)
15-64 years: 60% (male 19,549,935; female 19,276,784)
65 years and over: 4% (male 1,561,877; female 1,380,527) (1999 est.)
Population growth rate: 1.07% (1999 est.)
Birth rate: 20.71 births/1,000 population (1999 est.)
Death rate: 5.39 deaths/1,000 population (1999 est.)
Net migration rate: -4.6 migrant(s)/1,000 population (1999 est.)
Sex ratio:
at birth: 1.05 male(s)/female
under 15 years: 1.05 male(s)/female
15-64 years: 1.01 male(s)/female
65 years and over: 1.13 male(s)/female
total population: 1.03 male(s)/female (1999 est.)
Infant mortality rate: 29.73 deaths/1,000 live births (1999 est.)
Life expectancy at birth:
total population: 69.76 years
male: 68.43 years
female: 71.16 years (1999 est.)
Total fertility rate: 2.45 children born/woman (1999 est.)
Nationality:
noun: Iranian(s)
adjective: Iranian
Ethnic groups: Persian 51%, Azerbaijani 24%, Gilaki and Mazandarani 8%, Kurd 7%, Arab 3%, Lur 2%, Baloch 2%, Turkmen 2%, other 1%
Religions: Shi'a Muslim 89%, Sunni Muslim 10%, Zoroastrian, Jewish, Christian, and Baha'i 1%
Languages: Persian and Persian dialects 58%, Turkic and Turkic dialects 26%, Kurdish 9%, Luri 2%, Balochi 1%, Arabic 1%, Turkish 1%, other 2%
Literacy:
definition: age 15 and over can read and write
total population: 72.1%
male: 78.4%
female: 65.8% (1994 est.)

Government

Country name:
conventional long form: Islamic Republic of Iran
conventional short form: Iran
local long form: Jomhuri-ye Eslami-ye Iran
local short form: Iran
Data code: IR
Government type: theocratic republic
Capital: Tehran
Administrative divisions: 25 provinces (ostanha, singular - ostan); Ardabil, Azarbayjan-e Gharbi, Azarbayjan-e Sharqi, Bushehr, Chahar Mahall va Bakhtiari, Esfahan, Fars, Gilan, Hamadan, Hormozgan, Ilam, Kerman, Kermanshahan, Khorasan, Khuzestan, Kohkiluyeh va Buyer Ahmadi, Kordestan, Lorestan, Markazi, Mazandaran, Semnan, Sistan va Baluchestan, Tehran, Yazd, Zanjan
note: there may be three new provinces named Golestan, Qom, and Qazvin
Independence: 1 April 1979 (Islamic Republic of Iran proclaimed)
National holiday: Islamic Republic Day, 1 April (1979)
Constitution: 2-3 December 1979; revised 1989 to expand powers of the presidency and eliminate the prime ministership
Legal system: the Constitution codifies Islamic principles of government
Suffrage: 15 years of age; universal
Executive branch:
chief of state: Leader of the Islamic Revolution Ayatollah Ali Hoseini-KHAMENEI (since 4 June 1989)
head of government: President (Ali) Mohammad KHATAMI-Ardakani (since 3 August 1997); First Vice President Hasan Ebrahim HABIBI (since NA August 1989)
cabinet: Council of Ministers selected by the president with legislative approval
elections: leader of the Islamic Revolution appointed for life by the Assembly of Experts; president elected by popular vote for a four-year term; election last held 23 May 1997 (next to be held NA May 2001)
election results: (Ali) Mohammad KHATAMI-Ardakani elected president; percent of vote - (Ali) Mohammad KHATAMI-Ardakani 69%
Legislative branch: unicameral Islamic Consultative Assembly or Majles-e-Shura-ye-Eslami (270 seats; members elected by popular vote to serve four-year terms)
elections: last held 8 March and 19 April 1996 (next to be held NA March 2000)
election results: percent of vote - NA; seats - NA
Judicial branch: Supreme Court
Political parties and leaders: since President KHATAMI's election in May 1997, several political parties have been licensed including Executives of Construction, Islamic Iran Solidarity Party, and Islamic Partnership Front; other important political groupings are: Tehran Militant Clergy Association [Secretary

Iran *(continued)*

General Ayatollah Mohammad EMAMI-KASHANI];
Militant Clerics Association [Mehdi
MAHDAVI-KARUBI and Mohammad Asqar
MUSAVI-KHOINIHA]; Islamic Coalition Association
[Habibollah ASQAR-OLADI]
Political pressure groups and leaders: groups
that generally support the Islamic Republic include
Ansar-e Hizballah, Mojahedin of the Islamic
Revolution, Muslim Students Following the Line of the
Imam, and the Islamic Coalition Association;
opposition groups include the Liberation Movement of
Iran and the Nation of Iran party; armed political
groups that have been almost completely repressed
by the government include Mojahedin-e Khalq
Organization (MEK), People's Fedayeen, Democratic
Party of Iranian Kurdistan; the Society for the Defense
of Freedom
International organization participation: CCC,
CP, ECO, ESCAP, FAO, G-19, G-24, G-77, IAEA,
IBRD, ICAO, ICC, ICRM, IDA, IDB, IFAD, IFC, IFRCS,
IHO, ILO, IMF, IMO, Inmarsat, Intelsat, Interpol, IOC,
IOM (observer), ISO, ITU, NAM, OIC, OPCW, OPEC,
PCA, UN, UNCTAD, UNESCO, UNHCR, UNIDO,
UPU, WCL, WFTU, WHO, WMO, WToO
Diplomatic representation in the US: none; note -
Iran has an Interests Section in the Pakistani
Embassy, headed by Fariborz JAHANSUZAN;
address: Iranian Interests Section, Pakistani
Embassy, 2209 Wisconsin Avenue NW, Washington,
DC 20007; telephone: [1] (202) 965-4990
Diplomatic representation from the US: none;
note - protecting power in Iran is Switzerland
Flag description: three equal horizontal bands of
green (top), white, and red; the national emblem (a
stylized representation of the word Allah) in red is
centered in the white band; ALLAH AKBAR (God is
Great) in white Arabic script is repeated 11 times
along the bottom edge of the green band and 11 times
along the top edge of the red band

Economy

Economy - overview: Iran's economy is a mixture of
central planning, state ownership of oil and other large
enterprises, village agriculture, and small-scale private
trading and service ventures. President KHATAMI has
continued to follow the market reform plans of former
President RAFSANJANI and has indicated that he will
pursue diversification of Iran's oil-reliant economy
although he has made little progress toward that goal.
In the early 1990s, Iran experienced a financial crisis
and was forced to reschedule $15 billion in debt. The
strong oil market in 1996 helped ease financial
pressures on Iran and allowed for Tehran's timely debt
service payments. Iran's financial situation tightened in
1997 and deteriorated further in 1998 because of lower
oil prices. As a result Iran has begun to cut imports and
fall into arrears on its debt payments.
GDP: purchasing power parity - $339.7 billion (1998
est.)
GDP - real growth rate: -2.1% (1998 est.)
GDP - per capita: purchasing power parity - $5,000
(1998 est.)

GDP - composition by sector:
agriculture: NA%
industry: NA%
services: NA%
Population below poverty line: 53% (1996 est.)
**Household income or consumption by percentage
share:**
lowest 10%: NA%
highest 10%: NA%
Inflation rate (consumer prices): 24% (1998 est.)
Labor force: 15.4 million
note: shortage of skilled labor
Labor force - by occupation: agriculture 33%,
manufacturing 21% (1988 est.)
Unemployment rate: more than 30% (January 1998
est.)
Budget:
revenues: $34.6 billion
expenditures: $34.9 billion, including capital
expenditures of $11.8 billion (FY96/97)
Industries: petroleum, petrochemicals, textiles,
cement and other construction materials, food
processing (particularly sugar refining and vegetable
oil production), metal fabricating, armaments
Industrial production growth rate: 5.7% (FY95/96
est.)
Electricity - production: 79.5 billion kWh (1996)
Electricity - production by source:
fossil fuel: 90.57%
hydro: 9.43%
nuclear: 0%
other: 0% (1996)
Electricity - consumption: 79.5 billion kWh (1996)
Electricity - exports: 0 kWh (1996)
Electricity - imports: 0 kWh (1996)
Agriculture - products: wheat, rice, other grains,
sugar beets, fruits, nuts, cotton; dairy products, wool;
caviar
Exports: $12.2 billion (f.o.b., 1998 est.)
Exports - commodities: petroleum 80%, carpets,
fruits, nuts, hides, iron, steel
Exports - partners: Japan, Italy, Greece, France,
Spain, South Korea
Imports: $13.8 billion (f.o.b., 1998 est.)
Imports - commodities: machinery, military
supplies, metal works, foodstuffs, pharmaceuticals,
technical services, refined oil products
Imports - partners: Germany, Italy, Japan, UAE,
UK, Belgium
Debt - external: $21.9 billion (1996 est.)
Economic aid - recipient: $116.5 million (1995)
Currency: 10 Iranian rials (IR) = 1 toman; note -
domestic figures are generally referred to in terms of
the toman
Exchange rates: Iranian rials (IR) per US$1 -
1,754.63 (January 1999), 1,751.86 (1998), 1,752.92
(1997), 1,750.76 (1996), 1,747.93 (1995), 1,748.75
(1994); black market rate: 7,000 rials per US$1
(December 1998); note - as of May 1995, the "official
rate" of 1,750 rials per US$1 is used for imports of
essential goods and services and for oil exports,
whereas the "official export rate" of 3,000 rials per

US$1 is used for non-oil exports and imports not
covered by the official rate
Fiscal year: 21 March - 20 March

Communications

Telephones: 8,991,797 (1997 est.)
Telephone system:
domestic: 25 regional telecommunications authorities
created in 1996; these authorities are responsible for
implementing paging services and cellular systems;
microwave radio relay extends throughout the country
with the system centered in Tehran; system is moving
toward digitization and direct-dial capability; 255
long-distance circuits (1999 est.); 366 telephone
exchanges (1995 est.); 204,400 microwave channels
(1996 est.); 230,000 cellular telephone subscribers
(1997 est.); 3,930 pager subscribers (1995 est.)
international: 13,985 international circuits (1999 est.)
with a plan to reach 14,000 by March 1999; satellite
earth stations - 9 Intelsat (with 50 terminals) and 4
Inmarsat; HF radio and microwave radio relay to
Turkey, Azerbaijan, Pakistan, Afghanistan,
Turkmenistan, Syria, Kuwait, Tajikistan, and
Uzbekistan; submarine fiber-optic cable to UAE with
access to Fiber-Optic Link Around the Globe (FLAG);
Trans Asia Europe (TAE) fiber-optic line runs from
Azerbaijan through the northern portion of Iran to
Turkmenistan with expansion to Georgia and
Azerbaijan; four Internet service providers as of 1997
with the number increasing (service limited to
electronic mail to promote Iranian culture)
Radio broadcast stations: AM 72, FM 6, shortwave
5 (1998 est.)
Radios: 13 million (1999 est.)
Television broadcast stations: 28 (in addition,
there are 450 low-power repeaters, all government
controlled) (1997)
Televisions: 7 million (1999 est.)

Transportation

Railways:
total: 7,286 km
broad gauge: 94 km 1.676-m gauge
standard gauge: 7,192 km 1.435-m gauge (146 km
electrified) (1996 est.)
Highways:
total: 162,000 km
paved: 81,000 km (including 470 km of expressways)
unpaved: 81,000 km (1996 est.)
Waterways: 904 km; the Shatt al Arab is usually
navigable by maritime traffic for about 130 km;
channel has been dredged to 3 m and is in use
Pipelines: crude oil 5,900 km; petroleum products
3,900 km; natural gas 4,550 km
Ports and harbors: Abadan (largely destroyed in
fighting during 1980-88 war), Ahvaz, Bandar 'Abbas,
Bandar-e Anzali, Bushehr, Bandar-e Imam Khomeyni,
Bandar-e Lengeh, Bandar-e Mahshahr, Bandar-e
Torkaman, Chabahar (Bandar Beheshti), Jazireh-ye
Khark, Jazireh-ye Lavan, Jazireh-ye Sirri,
Khorramshahr (limited operation since November

Iran (continued)

1992), Now Shahr
Merchant marine:
total: 132 ships (1,000 GRT or over) totaling
3,238,293 GRT/5,658,259 DWT
ships by type: bulk 46, cargo 35, chemical tanker 4,
combination bulk 1, container 5, liquefied gas tanker
1, multifunction large-load carrier 6, oil tanker 21,
refrigerated cargo 2, roll-on/roll-off cargo 10,
short-sea passenger 1 (1998 est.)
Airports: 288 (1998 est.)
Airports - with paved runways:
total: 110
over 3,047 m: 38
2,438 to 3,047 m: 18
1,524 to 2,437 m: 25
914 to 1,523 m: 23
under 914 m: 6 (1998 est.)
Airports - with unpaved runways:
total: 178
over 3,047 m: 1
2,438 to 3,047 m: 5
1,524 to 2,437 m: 14
914 to 1,523 m: 126
under 914 m: 32 (1998 est.)
Heliports: 11 (1998 est.)

Military

Military branches: Islamic Republic of Iran regular
forces (includes Ground Forces, Navy, Air and Air
Defense Forces), Revolutionary Guards (includes
Ground, Air, Navy, Qods, and
Basij-mobilization-forces), Law Enforcement Forces
Military manpower - military age: 21 years of age
Military manpower - availability:
males age 15-49: 17,203,360 (1999 est.)
Military manpower - fit for military service:
males age 15-49: 10,217,269 (1999 est.)
**Military manpower - reaching military age
annually:**
males: 767,152 (1999 est.)
Military expenditures - dollar figure: $5.787 billion
(FY98/99)
Military expenditures - percent of GDP: 2.9%
(FY98/99)

Transnational Issues

Disputes - international: Iran and Iraq restored
diplomatic relations in 1990 but are still trying to work
out written agreements settling outstanding disputes
from their eight-year war concerning border
demarcation, prisoners-of-war, and freedom of
navigation and sovereignty over the Shatt al Arab
waterway; Iran occupies two islands in the Persian
Gulf claimed by the UAE: Lesser Tunb (called Tunb as
Sughra in Arabic by UAE and Jazireh-ye Tonb-e
Kuchek in Persian by Iran) and Greater Tunb (called
Tunb al Kubra in Arabic by UAE and Jazireh-ye
Tonb-e Bozorg in Persian by Iran); it jointly
administers with the UAE an island in the Persian Gulf
claimed by the UAE (called Abu Musa in Arabic by
UAE and Jazireh-ye Abu Musa in Persian by Iran) -

over which Iran has taken steps to exert unilateral
control since 1992, including access restrictions and a
military build-up on the island; the UAE has garnered
significant diplomatic support in the region in
protesting these Iranian actions; Caspian Sea
boundaries are not yet determined among Azerbaijan,
Iran, Kazakhstan, Russia, and Turkmenistan
Illicit drugs: despite substantial interdiction efforts,
Iran remains a key transshipment point for Southwest
Asian heroin to Europe; domestic consumption of
narcotics remains a persistent problem and Iranian
press reports estimate that there are at least 1.2
million drug users in the country

Iraq

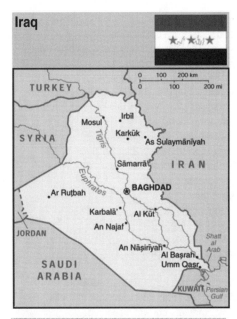

Introduction

Background: Iraq lies in the lower part of the
Tigris-Euphrates valley, the heart of one of the four
great ancient civilizations. The area was overrun by
Arab, Mongol, and Turkish conquerors and became a
British mandate following World War I. Independence
came in 1932. Iraq's pro-Western stance ended in
1958 with the overthrow of the monarchy. Its
subsequent turbulent history has witnessed the
dictatorship of SADDAM Husayn, civil war with the
Kurds, a bloody conflict with neighboring Iran, and, in
1990, an invasion of Kuwait, swiftly turned back by a
Western coalition led by the US. Noncooperation with
UN Security Council resolution obligations and the
UN's inspection of Iraq's nuclear, chemical, biological,
and long-range missile weapons programs remain
major problems.

Geography

Location: Middle East, bordering the Persian Gulf,
between Iran and Kuwait
Geographic coordinates: 33 00 N, 44 00 E
Map references: Middle East
Area:
total: 437,072 sq km
land: 432,162 sq km
water: 4,910 sq km
Area - comparative: slightly more than twice the
size of Idaho
Land boundaries:
total: 3,631 km
border countries: Iran 1,458 km, Jordan 181 km,
Kuwait 242 km, Saudi Arabia 814 km, Syria 605 km,
Turkey 331 km
Coastline: 58 km
Maritime claims:
continental shelf: not specified
territorial sea: 12 nm
Climate: mostly desert; mild to cool winters with dry,
hot, cloudless summers; northern mountainous

Iraq (continued)

regions along Iranian and Turkish borders experience cold winters with occasionally heavy snows that melt in early spring, sometimes causing extensive flooding in central and southern Iraq

Terrain: mostly broad plains; reedy marshes along Iranian border in south with large flooded areas; mountains along borders with Iran and Turkey

Elevation extremes:

lowest point: Persian Gulf 0 m

highest point: Gundah Zhur 3,608 m

Natural resources: petroleum, natural gas, phosphates, sulfur

Land use:

arable land: 12%

permanent crops: 0%

permanent pastures: 9%

forests and woodland: 0%

other: 79% (1993 est.)

Irrigated land: 25,500 sq km (1993 est.)

Natural hazards: dust storms, sandstorms, floods

Environment - current issues: government water control projects have drained most of the inhabited marsh areas east of An Nasiriyah by drying up or diverting the feeder streams and rivers; a once sizable population of Shi'a Muslims, who have inhabited these areas for thousands of years, has been displaced; furthermore, the destruction of the natural habitat poses serious threats to the area's wildlife populations; inadequate supplies of potable water; development of Tigris-Euphrates Rivers system contingent upon agreements with upstream riparian Turkey; air and water pollution; soil degradation (salination) and erosion; desertification

Environment - international agreements:

party to: Law of the Sea, Nuclear Test Ban

signed, but not ratified: Environmental Modification

People

Population: 22,427,150 (July 1999 est.)

Age structure:

0-14 years: 44% (male 4,982,510; female 4,825,129)

15-64 years: 53% (male 6,030,417; female 5,889,543)

65 years and over: 3% (male 326,223; female 373,328) (1999 est.)

Population growth rate: 3.19% (1999 est.)

Birth rate: 38.42 births/1,000 population (1999 est.)

Death rate: 6.56 deaths/1,000 population (1999 est.)

Net migration rate: 0 migrant(s)/1,000 population (1999 est.)

Sex ratio:

at birth: 1.05 male(s)/female

under 15 years: 1.03 male(s)/female

15-64 years: 1.02 male(s)/female

65 years and over: 0.87 male(s)/female

total population: 1.02 male(s)/female (1999 est.)

Infant mortality rate: 62.41 deaths/1,000 live births (1999 est.)

Life expectancy at birth:

total population: 66.52 years

male: 65.54 years

female: 67.56 years (1999 est.)

Total fertility rate: 5.12 children born/woman (1999 est.)

Nationality:

noun: Iraqi(s)

adjective: Iraqi

Ethnic groups: Arab 75%-80%, Kurdish 15%-20%, Turkoman, Assyrian or other 5%

Religions: Muslim 97% (Shi'a 60%-65%, Sunni 32%-37%), Christian or other 3%

Languages: Arabic, Kurdish (official in Kurdish regions), Assyrian, Armenian

Literacy:

definition: age 15 and over can read and write

total population: 58%

male: 70.7%

female: 45% (1995 est.)

Government

Country name:

conventional long form: Republic of Iraq

conventional short form: Iraq

local long form: Al Jumhuriyah al Iraqiyah

local short form: Al Iraq

Data code: IZ

Government type: republic

Capital: Baghdad

Administrative divisions: 18 provinces (muhafazat, singular - muhafazah); Al Anbar, Al Basrah, Al Muthanna, Al Qadisiyah, An Najaf, Arbil, As Sulaymaniyah, At Ta'mim, Babil, Baghdad, Dahuk, Dhi Qar, Diyala, Karbala', Maysan, Ninawa, Salah ad Din, Wasit

Independence: 3 October 1932 (from League of Nations mandate under British administration)

National holiday: Anniversary of the Revolution, 17 July (1968)

Constitution: 22 September 1968, effective 16 July 1970 (provisional Constitution); new constitution drafted in 1990 but not adopted

Legal system: based on Islamic law in special religious courts, civil law system elsewhere; has not accepted compulsory ICJ jurisdiction

Suffrage: 18 years of age; universal

Executive branch:

chief of state: President SADDAM Husayn (since 16 July 1979); Vice President Taha Muhyi al-Din MARUF (since 21 April 1974); Vice President Taha Yasin RAMADAN (since 23 March 1991)

head of government: Prime Minister SADDAM Husayn (since 29 May 1994); Deputy Prime Minister Tariq Mikhail AZIZ (since NA 1979); Deputy Prime Minister Taha Yasin RAMADAN (since NA May 1994); Deputy Prime Minister Muhammad Hamza al-ZUBAYDI (since NA May 1994)

cabinet: Council of Ministers

note: there is also a Revolutionary Command Council; Chairman SADDAM Husayn, Vice Chairman Izzat IBRAHIM al-Duri

elections: president and vice presidents elected by a two-thirds majority of the Revolutionary Command Council; election last held 17 October 1995 (next to be held NA 2002)

election results: SADDAM Husayn reelected president; percent of vote - 99%; Taha Muhyi al-Din MARUF and Taha Yasin RAMADAN elected vice presidents; percent of vote - NA

Legislative branch: unicameral National Assembly or Majlis al-Watani (250 seats; 30 appointed by SADDAM Husayn to represent the three northern provinces of Dahuk, Arbil, and As Sulaymaniyah; 220 elected by popular vote; members serve four-year terms)

elections: last held 24 March 1996 (next to be held NA 2000)

election results: percent of vote by party - NA; seats by party - NA

Judicial branch: Court of Cassation

Political parties and leaders: Ba'th Party [SADDAM Husayn, central party leader]

Political pressure groups and leaders: any formal political activity must be sanctioned by the government; opposition to regime from Kurdish groups and southern Shi'a dissidents

International organization participation: ABEDA, ACC, AFESD, AL, AMF, CAEU, CCC, ESCWA, FAO, G-19, G-77, IAEA, IBRD, ICAO, ICRM, IDA, IDB, IFAD, IFC, IFRCS, ILO, IMF, IMO, Inmarsat, Intelsat, Interpol, IOC, ITU, NAM, OAPEC, OIC, OPEC, PCA, UN, UNCTAD, UNESCO, UNIDO, UPU, WFTU, WHO, WIPO, WMO, WToO

Diplomatic representation in the US: none; note - Iraq has an Interest Section in the Algerian Embassy headed by Dr. Khairi AL ZUBAYDI; address: Iraqi Interests Section, Algerian Embassy, 2118 Kalorama Road NW, Washington, DC 20008; telephone: [1] (202) 265-2800; FAX: [1] (202) 667-2174

Diplomatic representation from the US: none; note - the US has an Interests Section in the Polish Embassy in Baghdad; address: P. O. Box 2051 Hay Babel, Baghdad; telephone: [964] (1) 719-0296; FAX: [964] (1) 718-9297

Flag description: three equal horizontal bands of red (top), white, and black with three green five-pointed stars in a horizontal line centered in the white band; the phrase ALLAHU AKBAR (God is Great) in green Arabic script - Allahu to the right of the middle star and Akbar to the left of the middle star - was added in January 1991 during the Persian Gulf crisis; similar to the flag of Syria that has two stars but no script and the flag of Yemen that has a plain white band; also similar to the flag of Egypt that has a symbolic eagle centered in the white band

Economy

Economy - overview: Iraq's economy has been dominated by the oil sector, which has traditionally provided about 95% of foreign exchange earnings. In the 1980s, financial problems caused by massive expenditures in the eight-year war with Iran and damage to oil export facilities by Iran led the government to implement austerity measures, borrow heavily, and later reschedule foreign debt payments; Iraq suffered economic losses of at least $100 billion from the war. After the end of hostilities in 1988, oil

Iraq *(continued)*

exports gradually increased with the construction of new pipelines and restoration of damaged facilities. Iraq's seizure of Kuwait in August 1990, subsequent international economic embargoes, and military action by an international coalition beginning in January 1991 drastically reduced economic activity and increased prices. The Iraqi Government has been unwilling to abide by UN resolutions so that the economic embargo could be removed. The government's policies of supporting large military and internal security forces and of allocating resources to key supporters of the regime have exacerbated shortages. The implementation of the UN's oil-for-food program in December 1996 has helped improve economic conditions. For the first three six-month phases of the program, Iraq was allowed to export $2 billion worth of oil in exchange for food, medicine, and other humanitarian goods. The UN allowed Iraq to export $5.2 billion of oil beginning with the fourth phase of the program in May 1998. At an average volume of 1.9 million barrels per day during the last half of 1998, oil exports are about three-quarters their prewar level. Per capita food imports have increased significantly, while medical supplies and health care services are steadily improving. Per capita output and living standards are still well below the prewar level, but any estimates have a wide range of error.

GDP: purchasing power parity - $52.3 billion (1998 est.)
GDP - real growth rate: 10% (1998 est.)
GDP - per capita: purchasing power parity - $2,400 (1998 est.)
GDP - composition by sector:
agriculture: NA%
industry: NA%
services: NA%
Population below poverty line: NA%
Household income or consumption by percentage share:
lowest 10%: NA%
highest 10%: NA%
Inflation rate (consumer prices): NA%
Labor force: 4.4 million (1989)
Labor force - by occupation: services 48%, agriculture 30%, industry 22% (1989)
Unemployment rate: NA%
Budget:
revenues: $NA
expenditures: $NA, including capital expenditures of $NA
Industries: petroleum, chemicals, textiles, construction materials, food processing
Industrial production growth rate: NA%
Electricity - production: 27.6 billion kWh (1996)
Electricity - production by source:
fossil fuel: 97.83%
hydro: 2.17%
nuclear: 0%
other: 0% (1996)
Electricity - consumption: 27.6 billion kWh (1996)
Electricity - exports: 0 kWh (1996)

Electricity - imports: 0 kWh (1996)
Agriculture - products: wheat, barley, rice, vegetables, dates, cotton; cattle, sheep
Exports: $5 billion (1998 est.)
Exports - commodities: crude oil
Exports - partners: Russia, France, China, Turkey (1998)
Imports: $3 billion (1998 est.)
Imports - commodities: food, medicine, manufactures
Imports - partners: Russia, France, Jordan, Australia, China (1998)
Debt - external: very heavy relative to GDP but the exact amount is unknown (1998)
Economic aid - recipient: $327.5 million (1995)
Currency: 1 Iraqi dinar (ID) = 1,000 fils
Exchange rates: Iraqi dinars (ID) per US$1 - 0.3109 (fixed official rate since 1982); black market rate - Iraqi dinars (ID) per US$1 - 1,810 (December 1998), 1,530 (December 1997), 3,000 (December 1995); subject to wide fluctuations
Fiscal year: calendar year

Communications

Telephones: 632,000 (1987 est.)
Telephone system: reconstitution of damaged telecommunication facilities began after the Gulf war; most damaged facilities have been rebuilt
domestic: the network consists of coaxial cables and microwave radio relay links
international: satellite earth stations - 2 Intelsat (1 Atlantic Ocean and 1 Indian Ocean), 1 Intersputnik (Atlantic Ocean region) and 1 Arabsat (inoperative); coaxial cable and microwave radio relay to Jordan, Kuwait, Syria, and Turkey; Kuwait line is probably nonoperational
Radio broadcast stations: AM 16, FM 1, shortwave 0
Radios: 3.7 million (1998 est.)
Television broadcast stations: 13 (government controlled) (1997)
Televisions: 1 million (1992 est.)

Transportation

Railways:
total: 2,032 km
standard gauge: 2,032 km 1.435-m gauge
Highways:
total: 47,400 km
paved: 40,764 km
unpaved: 6,636 km (1996 est.)
Waterways: 1,015 km; Shatt al Arab is usually navigable by maritime traffic for about 130 km; channel has been dredged to 3 meters and is in use; Tigris and Euphrates Rivers have navigable sections for shallow-draft watercraft; Shatt al Basrah canal was navigable by shallow-draft craft before closing in 1991 because of the Persian Gulf war
Pipelines: crude oil 4,350 km; petroleum products 725 km; natural gas 1,360 km

Ports and harbors: Umm Qasr, Khawr az Zubayr, and Al Basrah have limited functionality
Merchant marine:
total: 30 ships (1,000 GRT or over) totaling 456,845 GRT/780,318 DWT
ships by type: cargo 14, oil tanker 11, passenger 1, passenger-cargo 1, refrigerated cargo 1, roll-on/roll-off cargo 2 (1998 est.)
Airports: 109 (1998 est.)
Airports - with paved runways:
total: 77
over 3,047 m: 20
2,438 to 3,047 m: 36
1,524 to 2,437 m: 7
914 to 1,523 m: 7
under 914 m: 7 (1998 est.)
Airports - with unpaved runways:
total: 32
over 3,047 m: 3
2,438 to 3,047 m: 5
1,524 to 2,437 m: 3
914 to 1,523 m: 10
under 914 m: 11 (1998 est.)
Heliports: 4 (1998 est.)

Military

Military branches: Army, Republican Guard and Special Republican Guard, Navy, Air Force, Air Defense Force, Border Guard Force, Internal Security Forces
Military manpower - military age: 18 years of age
Military manpower - availability:
males age 15-49: 5,459,998 (1999 est.)
Military manpower - fit for military service:
males age 15-49: 3,058,098 (1999 est.)
Military manpower - reaching military age annually:
males: 259,915 (1999 est.)
Military expenditures - dollar figure: $NA
Military expenditures - percent of GDP: NA%

Transnational Issues

Disputes - international: Iran and Iraq restored diplomatic relations in 1990 but are still trying to work out written agreements settling outstanding disputes from their eight-year war concerning border demarcation, prisoners-of-war, and freedom of navigation and sovereignty over the Shatt al Arab waterway; in November 1994, Iraq formally accepted the UN-demarcated border with Kuwait which had been spelled out in Security Council Resolutions 687 (1991), 773 (1993), and 883 (1993); this formally ends earlier claims to Kuwait and to Bubiyan and Warbah islands although the government continues periodic rhetorical challenges; dispute over water development plans by Turkey for the Tigris and Euphrates Rivers

Ireland

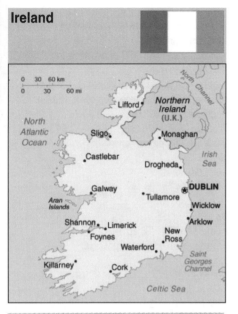

Introduction

Background: Growing Irish nationalism resulted in independence from the United Kingdom in 1921, with six largely Protestant northern counties remaining within the UK. After World War II bloody strife between Catholics and Protestants over the status of Northern Ireland cost thousands of lives. In 1998, substantial steps toward peace were agreed to by the British and Irish governments and the Roman Catholics and Protestants of Northern Ireland.

Geography

Location: Western Europe, occupying five-sixths of the island of Ireland in the North Atlantic Ocean, west of Great Britain
Geographic coordinates: 53 00 N, 8 00 W
Map references: Europe
Area:
total: 70,280 sq km
land: 68,890 sq km
water: 1,390 sq km
Area - comparative: slightly larger than West Virginia
Land boundaries:
total: 360 km
border countries: UK 360 km
Coastline: 1,448 km
Maritime claims:
continental shelf: not specified
exclusive fishing zone: 200 nm
territorial sea: 12 nm
Climate: temperate maritime; modified by North Atlantic Current; mild winters, cool summers; consistently humid; overcast about half the time
Terrain: mostly level to rolling interior plain surrounded by rugged hills and low mountains; sea cliffs on west coast
Elevation extremes:
lowest point: Atlantic Ocean 0 m
highest point: Carrauntoohill 1,041 m

Natural resources: zinc, lead, natural gas, barite, copper, gypsum, limestone, dolomite, peat, silver
Land use:
arable land: 13%
permanent crops: 0%
permanent pastures: 68%
forests and woodland: 5%
other: 14% (1993 est.)
Irrigated land: NA sq km
Natural hazards: NA
Environment - current issues: water pollution, especially of lakes, from agricultural runoff
Environment - international agreements:
party to: Air Pollution, Air Pollution-Nitrogen Oxides, Air Pollution-Sulphur 94, Biodiversity, Climate Change, Desertification, Environmental Modification, Hazardous Wastes, Law of the Sea, Marine Dumping, Nuclear Test Ban, Ozone Layer Protection, Ship Pollution, Tropical Timber 83, Wetlands, Whaling
signed, but not ratified: Air Pollution-Persistent Organic Pollutants, Climate Change-Kyoto Protocol, Endangered Species, Marine Life Conservation, Tropical Timber 94
Geography - note: strategic location on major air and sea routes between North America and northern Europe; over 40% of the population resides within 97 km of Dublin

People

Population: 3,632,944 (July 1999 est.)
Age structure:
0-14 years: 21% (male 399,379; female 377,366)
15-64 years: 67% (male 1,232,072; female 1,213,364)
65 years and over: 12% (male 174,519; female 236,244) (1999 est.)
Population growth rate: 0.38% (1999 est.)
Birth rate: 13.58 births/1,000 population (1999 est.)
Death rate: 8.43 deaths/1,000 population (1999 est.)
Net migration rate: -1.31 migrant(s)/1,000 population (1999 est.)
Sex ratio:
at birth: 1.07 male(s)/female
under 15 years: 1.06 male(s)/female
15-64 years: 1.02 male(s)/female
65 years and over: 0.74 male(s)/female
total population: 0.99 male(s)/female (1999 est.)
Infant mortality rate: 5.94 deaths/1,000 live births (1999 est.)
Life expectancy at birth:
total population: 76.39 years
male: 73.64 years
female: 79.32 years (1999 est.)
Total fertility rate: 1.81 children born/woman (1999 est.)
Nationality:
noun: Irishman(men), Irishwoman(men), Irish (collective plural)
adjective: Irish
Ethnic groups: Celtic, English
Religions: Roman Catholic 92%, Anglican 3%, Islamic 0.11%, Jehovah's Witness 0.1%, Jewish

0.04%, other 4.75% (1991)
Languages: English is the language generally used, Irish (Gaelic) spoken mainly in areas located along the western seaboard
Literacy:
definition: age 15 and over can read and write
total population: 98% (1981 est.)
male: NA%
female: NA%

Government

Country name:
conventional long form: none
conventional short form: Ireland
Data code: EI
Government type: republic
Capital: Dublin
Administrative divisions: 26 counties; Carlow, Cavan, Clare, Cork, Donegal, Dublin, Galway, Kerry, Kildare, Kilkenny, Laois, Leitrim, Limerick, Longford, Louth, Mayo, Meath, Monaghan, Offaly, Roscommon, Sligo, Tipperary, Waterford, Westmeath, Wexford, Wicklow
Independence: 6 December 1921 (from UK)
National holiday: Saint Patrick's Day, 17 March
Constitution: 29 December 1937; adopted 1 July 1937 by plebiscite
Legal system: based on English common law, substantially modified by indigenous concepts; judicial review of legislative acts in Supreme Court; has not accepted compulsory ICJ jurisdiction
Suffrage: 18 years of age; universal
Executive branch:
chief of state: President Mary MCALEESE (since 11 November 1997)
head of government: Prime Minister Bertie AHERN (since 26 June 1997)
cabinet: Cabinet appointed by the president with previous nomination by the prime minister and approval of the House of Representatives
elections: president elected by popular vote for a seven-year term; election last held 31 October 1997 (next to be held NA November 2004); prime minister nominated by the House of Representatives and appointed by the president
election results: Mary MCALEESE elected president; percent of vote - Mary MCALEESE 44.8%, Mary BANOTTI 29.6%
Legislative branch: bicameral Parliament or Oireachtas consists of the Senate or Seanad Eireann (60 seats - 49 elected by the universities and from candidates put forward by five vocational panels, 11 are nominated by the prime minister; members serve five-year terms) and the House of Representatives or Dail Eireann (166 seats; members are elected by popular vote on the basis of proportional representation to serve five-year terms)
elections: Senate - last held NA August 1997 (next to be held NA 2002); House of Representatives - last held 6 June 1997 (next to be held NA 2002)
election results: Senate - percent of vote by party - NA; seats by party - NA; House of Representatives -

Ireland (continued)

percent of vote by party - NA; seats by party - Fianna Fail 76, Fine Gael 53, Labor Party 19, Progressive Democrats 4, Democratic Left 4, Greens 2, Sinn Fein 1, independents 7

Judicial branch: Supreme Court, judges appointed by the president on the advice of the government (prime minister and cabinet)

Political parties and leaders: Fianna Fail [Bertie AHERN]; Labor Party [Ruairi QUINN]; Fine Gael [John BRUTON]; Communist Party of Ireland [Michael O'RIORDAN]; Sinn Fein [Gerry ADAMS]; Progressive Democrats [Mary HARNEY]; The Workers' Party [Marion DONNELLY]; Green Alliance [Patricia HOWARD]

note: Prime Minister AHERN heads a two-party coalition consisting of Fianna Fail and the Progressive Democrats; Democratic Left merged into the Labor Party on 1 February 1999

International organization participation: Australia Group, BIS, CCC, CE, EBRD, ECE, EIB, EMU, ESA, EU, FAO, IAEA, IBRD, ICAO, ICC, ICFTU, ICRM, IDA, IEA, IFAD, IFC, IFRCS, ILO, IMF, IMO, Intelsat, Interpol, IOC, IOM (observer), ISO, ITU, MINURSO, MTCR, NEA, NSG, OECD, OPCW, OSCE, UN, UNCTAD, UNESCO, UNFICYP, UNIDO, UNIFIL, UNIKOM, UNITAR, UNMIBH, UNMOP, UNPREDEP, UNTSO, UPU, WEU (observer), WHO, WIPO, WMO, WTrO, ZC

Diplomatic representation in the US:
chief of mission: Ambassador Sean O'HUIGINN
chancery: 2234 Massachusetts Avenue NW, Washington, DC 20008
telephone: [1] (202) 462-3939
FAX: [1] (202) 232-5993
consulate(s) general: Boston, Chicago, New York, and San Francisco

Diplomatic representation from the US:
chief of mission: Ambassador Michael SULLIVAN
embassy: 42 Elgin Road, Ballsbridge, Dublin
mailing address: use embassy street address
telephone: [353] (1) 6688777
FAX: [353] (1) 6689946

Flag description: three equal vertical bands of green (hoist side), white, and orange; similar to the flag of Cote d'Ivoire, which is shorter and has the colors reversed - orange (hoist side), white, and green; also similar to the flag of Italy, which is shorter and has colors of green (hoist side), white, and red

Economy

Economy - overview: Ireland is a small, modern, trade-dependent economy with growth averaging 9.5% in 1995-98. Agriculture, once the most important sector, is now dwarfed by industry, which accounts for 39% of GDP, about 80% of exports, and employs 28% of the labor force. Although exports remain the primary engine for Ireland's robust growth, the economy is also benefiting from a rise in consumer spending and recovery in both construction and business investment. Over the past decade, the Irish government has implemented a series of national economic programs designed to curb inflation, reduce government spending, and promote foreign investment. Although the unemployment rate has been halved, it remains high, and job creation is a primary concern of government policy. Recent efforts have concentrated on improving workers qualifications and the education system. Ireland joined in launching the euro currency system in January 1999 along with 10 other EU nations.

GDP: purchasing power parity - $67.1 billion (1998 est.)

GDP - real growth rate: 9.5% (1998 est.)

GDP - per capita: purchasing power parity - $18,600 (1998 est.)

GDP - composition by sector:
agriculture: 7%
industry: 39%
services: 54% (1997)

Population below poverty line: NA%

Household income or consumption by percentage share:
lowest 10%: 2.5%
highest 10%: 27.4% (1987)

Inflation rate (consumer prices): 2.4% (1998)

Labor force: 1.52 million (1997 est.)

Labor force - by occupation: services 62.1%, manufacturing and construction 27%, agriculture, forestry, and fishing 10%, utilities 0.9% (1996 est.)

Unemployment rate: 7.7% (1998 est.)

Budget:
revenues: $23.5 billion
expenditures: $20.6 billion, including capital expenditures of $NA (1998)

Industries: food products, brewing, textiles, clothing, chemicals, pharmaceuticals, machinery, transportation equipment, glass and crystal

Industrial production growth rate: 15.8% (1998 est.)

Electricity - production: 17.843 billion kWh (1996)

Electricity - production by source:
fossil fuel: 95.83%
hydro: 3.99%
nuclear: 0%
other: 0.18% (1996)

Electricity - consumption: 17.743 billion kWh (1996)

Electricity - exports: 200 million kWh (1996)

Electricity - imports: 100 million kWh (1996)

Agriculture - products: turnips, barley, potatoes, sugar beets, wheat; beef, dairy products

Exports: $60.9 billion (f.o.b., 1998)

Exports - commodities: chemicals, data processing equipment, industrial machinery, live animals, animal products (1997)

Exports - partners: EU 67% (UK 24%, Germany 12%, France 8%), US 11% (1997)

Imports: $43.7 billion (c.i.f., 1998)

Imports - commodities: food, animal feed, data processing equipment, petroleum and petroleum products, machinery, textiles, clothing (1997)

Imports - partners: EU 55% (UK 34%, Germany 6%, France 6%), US 15% (1997)

Debt - external: $11 billion (1998)

Economic aid - donor: ODA, $153 million (1995)

Currency: 1 Irish pound (£Ir) = 100 pence

Exchange rates: Irish pounds (£Ir) per US$1 - 0.6815 (January 1999), 0.7014 (1998), 0.6588 (1997), 0.6248 (1996), 0.6235 (1995), 0.6676 (1994)

note: on 1 January 1999, the European Union introduced a common currency that is now being used by financial institutions in some member countries at the rate of 0.8597 euros per US$ and a fixed rate of 0.78764 Irish pounds per euro; the euro will replace the local currency in consenting countries for all transactions in 2002

Fiscal year: calendar year

Communications

Telephones: 900,000 (1987 est.)

Telephone system: modern digital system using cable and microwave radio relay
domestic: microwave radio relay
international: satellite earth station - 1 Intelsat (Atlantic Ocean)

Radio broadcast stations: AM 9, FM 45, shortwave 0

Radios: 2.2 million (1991 est.)

Television broadcast stations: 10 (in addition, there are 36 low-power repeaters) (1997)

Televisions: 1.025 million (1990 est.)

Transportation

Railways:
total: 1,947 km
broad gauge: 1,947 km 1.600-m gauge (38 km electrified; 485 km double track) (1996)

Highways:
total: 92,500 km
paved: 87,042 km (including 80 km of expressways)
unpaved: 5,458 km (1996 est.)

Waterways: limited for commercial traffic

Pipelines: natural gas 225 km

Ports and harbors: Arklow, Cork, Drogheda, Dublin, Foynes, Galway, Limerick, New Ross, Waterford

Merchant marine:
total: 31 ships (1,000 GRT or over) totaling 79,284 GRT/117,652 DWT
ships by type: bulk 1, cargo 28, container 2 (1998 est.)

Airports: 44 (1998 est.)

Airports - with paved runways:
total: 16
over 3,047 m: 1
2,438 to 3,047 m: 1
1,524 to 2,437 m: 4
914 to 1,523 m: 3
under 914 m: 7 (1998 est.)

Airports - with unpaved runways:
total: 28
914 to 1,523 m: 3
under 914 m: 25 (1998 est.)

Ireland (continued)

Military

Military branches: Army (includes Naval Service and Air Corps), National Police (Garda Siochana)
Military manpower - military age: 17 years of age
Military manpower - availability:
males age 15-49: 974,226 (1999 est.)
Military manpower - fit for military service:
males age 15-49: 790,155 (1999 est.)
Military manpower - reaching military age annually:
males: 33,810 (1999 est.)
Military expenditures - dollar figure: $771 million (1997)
Military expenditures - percent of GDP: 1% (1997)

Transnational Issues

Disputes - international: Northern Ireland issue with the UK (historic peace agreement signed 10 April 1998); Rockall continental shelf dispute involving Denmark, Iceland, and the UK (Ireland and the UK have signed a boundary agreement in the Rockall area)
Illicit drugs: transshipment point for and consumer of hashish from North Africa to the UK and Netherlands and of European-produced synthetic drugs; transshipment point for heroin and cocaine destined for Western Europe

Israel
(also see separate Gaza Strip and West Bank entries)

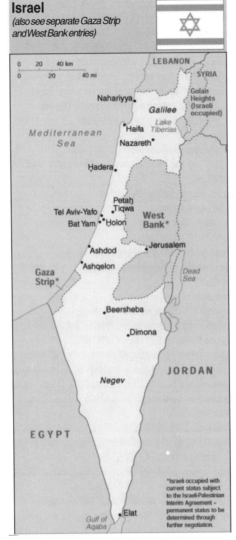

Introduction

Background: The territories occupied by Israel since the 1967 war are not included in the data below, unless otherwise noted. In keeping with the framework established at the Madrid Conference in October 1991, bilateral negotiations are being conducted between Israel and Palestinian representatives, and Israel and Syria, to achieve a permanent settlement between them. On 25 April 1982, Israel withdrew from the Sinai pursuant to the 1979 Israel-Egypt Peace treaty. Outstanding territorial and other disputes with Jordan were resolved in the 26 October 1994 Israel-Jordan Treaty of Peace.

Geography

Location: Middle East, bordering the Mediterranean Sea, between Egypt and Lebanon
Geographic coordinates: 31 30 N, 34 45 E
Map references: Middle East
Area:
total: 20,770 sq km
land: 20,330 sq km
water: 440 sq km
Area - comparative: slightly smaller than New Jersey

Land boundaries:
total: 1,006 km
border countries: Egypt 255 km, Gaza Strip 51 km, Jordan 238 km, Lebanon 79 km, Syria 76 km, West Bank 307 km
Coastline: 273 km
Maritime claims:
continental shelf: to depth of exploitation
territorial sea: 12 nm
Climate: temperate; hot and dry in southern and eastern desert areas
Terrain: Negev desert in the south; low coastal plain; central mountains; Jordan Rift Valley
Elevation extremes:
lowest point: Dead Sea -408 m
highest point: Har Meron 1,208 m
Natural resources: copper, phosphates, bromide, potash, clay, sand, sulfur, asphalt, manganese, small amounts of natural gas and crude oil
Land use:
arable land: 17%
permanent crops: 4%
permanent pastures: 7%
forests and woodland: 6%
other: 66% (1993 est.)
Irrigated land: 1,800 sq km (1993 est.)
Natural hazards: sandstorms may occur during spring and summer
Environment - current issues: limited arable land and natural fresh water resources pose serious constraints; desertification; air pollution from industrial and vehicle emissions; groundwater pollution from industrial and domestic waste, chemical fertilizers, and pesticides
Environment - international agreements:
party to: Biodiversity, Climate Change, Desertification, Endangered Species, Hazardous Wastes, Nuclear Test Ban, Ozone Layer Protection, Ship Pollution, Wetlands
signed, but not ratified: Climate Change-Kyoto Protocol, Marine Life Conservation
Geography - note: there are 216 Israeli settlements and civilian land use sites in the West Bank, 42 in the Israeli-occupied Golan Heights, 24 in the Gaza Strip, and 29 in East Jerusalem (August 1998 est.)

People

Population: 5,749,760 (July 1999 est.)
note: includes about 166,000 Israeli settlers in the West Bank, about 19,000 in the Israeli-occupied Golan Heights, about 6,000 in the Gaza Strip, and about 176,000 in East Jerusalem (August 1998 est.)
Age structure:
0-14 years: 28% (male 822,192; female 783,905)
15-64 years: 62% (male 1,792,062; female 1,783,755)
65 years and over: 10% (male 244,438; female 323,408) (1999 est.)
Population growth rate: 1.81% (1999 est.)
Birth rate: 19.83 births/1,000 population (1999 est.)
Death rate: 6.16 deaths/1,000 population (1999 est.)

Net migration rate: 4.42 migrant(s)/1,000 population (1999 est.)

Sex ratio:

at birth: 1.05 male(s)/female

under 15 years: 1.05 male(s)/female

15-64 years: 1 male(s)/female

65 years and over: 0.76 male(s)/female

total population: 0.99 male(s)/female (1999 est.)

Infant mortality rate: 7.78 deaths/1,000 live births (1999 est.)

Life expectancy at birth:

total population: 78.61 years

male: 76.71 years

female: 80.61 years (1999 est.)

Total fertility rate: 2.68 children born/woman (1999 est.)

Nationality:

noun: Israeli(s)

adjective: Israeli

Ethnic groups: Jewish 80.1% (Europe/America-born 32.1%, Israel-born 20.8%, Africa-born 14.6%, Asia-born 12.6%), non-Jewish 19.9% (mostly Arab) (1996 est.)

Religions: Judaism 80.1%, Islam 14.6% (mostly Sunni Muslim), Christian 2.1%, other 3.2% (1996 est.)

Languages: Hebrew (official), Arabic used officially for Arab minority, English most commonly used foreign language

Literacy:

definition: age 15 and over can read and write

total population: 95%

male: 97%

female: 93% (1992 est.)

Government

Country name:

conventional long form: State of Israel

conventional short form: Israel

local long form: Medinat Yisra'el

local short form: Yisra'el

Data code: IS

Government type: republic

Capital: Jerusalem

note: Israel proclaimed Jerusalem as its capital in 1950, but the US, like nearly all other countries, maintains its Embassy in Tel Aviv

Administrative divisions: 6 districts (mehozot, singular - mehoz); Central, Haifa, Jerusalem, Northern, Southern, Tel Aviv

Independence: 14 May 1948 (from League of Nations mandate under British administration)

National holiday: Independence Day, 14 May 1948; note - Israel declared independence on 14 May 1948, but the Jewish calendar is lunar and the holiday may occur in April or May

Constitution: no formal constitution; some of the functions of a constitution are filled by the Declaration of Establishment (1948), the basic laws of the parliament (Knesset), and the Israeli citizenship law

Legal system: mixture of English common law, British Mandate regulations, and, in personal matters, Jewish, Christian, and Muslim legal systems; in

December 1985, Israel informed the UN Secretariat that it would no longer accept compulsory ICJ jurisdiction

Suffrage: 18 years of age; universal

Executive branch:

chief of state: President Ezer WEIZMAN (since 13 May 1993)

head of government: Prime Minister Binyamin NETANYAHU (since 18 June 1996)

cabinet: Cabinet selected from and approved by the Knesset

elections: president elected by the Knesset for a five-year term; election last held 4 March 1998 (next to be held NA March 2003); prime minister elected by popular vote for a four-year term; election last held 29 May 1996 (early elections are scheduled for 17 May 1999); note - in March 1992, the Knesset approved legislation, effective in 1996, which allowed for the direct election of the prime minister; under the new law, each voter casts two ballots - one for the direct election of the prime minister and one for the party in the Knesset; the candidate that receives the largest percentage of the popular vote then works to form a coalition with other parties to achieve a parliamentary majority of 61 seats; finally, the candidate must submit his or her cabinet to the Knesset for approval and this must be done within 45 days of the election; in contrast to the old system, under the new law, the prime minister's party need not be the single-largest party in the Knesset

election results: Ezer WEIZMAN reelected president by the Knesset with a total of 63 votes, other candidate, Shaul AMOR, received 49 votes (there were seven abstentions and one absence); Binyamin NETANYAHU elected prime minister; percent of vote - Binyamin NETANYAHU 50.4%, Shimon PERES 49.5%

Legislative branch: unicameral Knesset or parliament (120 seats; members elected by popular vote to serve four-year terms)

elections: last held 29 May 1996 (early elections are scheduled for 17 May 1999)

election results: percent of vote by party - NA; seats by party - Labor Party 34, Likud Party 32, SHAS 10, MERETZ 9, National Religious Party 9, Yisra'el Ba'Aliya 7, Hadash-Balad 5, Third Way 4, United Arab List 4, United Jewish Torah 4, Moledet 2; note - Likud, Tzomet, and Gesher candidates ran on a joint list

Judicial branch: Supreme Court, appointed for life by the president

Political parties and leaders:

government coalition: Likud Party [Prime Minister Binyamin NETANYAHU]; Tzomet [Rafael EITAN]; SHAS [Arieh DERI]; National Religious Party [Yitzhak LEVI]; Yisra'el Ba'Aliya [Natan SHARANSKY]; United Jewish Torah [Meir PORUSH]; Third Way [Avigdor KAHALANI]

opposition: Labor Party [Ehud BARAK]; MERETZ [Yossi SARID]; United Arab List [Abd al-Malik DAHAMSHAH]; Hadash-Balad [Hashim MAHAMID]

other: Moledet [Rehavam ZEEVI]; Gesher [David LEVI]

Political pressure groups and leaders: Gush Emunim, Israeli nationalists advocating Jewish settlement on the West Bank and Gaza Strip; Peace Now supports territorial concessions in the West Bank and is critical of government's Lebanon policy

International organization participation: BSEC (observer), CCC, CE (observer), CERN (observer), EBRD, ECE, FAO, IADB, IAEA, IBRD, ICAO, ICC, ICFTU, IDA, IFAD, IFC, ILO, IMF, IMO, Inmarsat, Intelsat, Interpol, IOC, IOM, ISO, ITU, OAS (observer), OPCW, OSCE (partner), PCA, UN, UNCTAD, UNESCO, UNHCR, UNIDO, UPU, WHO, WIPO, WMO, WToO, WTrO

Diplomatic representation in the US:

chief of mission: Ambassador Zalman SHOVAL

chancery: 3514 International Drive NW, Washington, DC 20008

telephone: [1] (202) 364-5500

FAX: [1] (202) 364-5610

consulate(s) general: Atlanta, Boston, Chicago, Houston, Los Angeles, Miami, New York, Philadelphia, and San Francisco

Diplomatic representation from the US:

chief of mission: Ambassador Edward S. WALKER, Jr.

embassy: 71 Hayarkon Street, Tel Aviv

mailing address: PSC 98, Unit 7228, APO AE 09830

telephone: [972] (3) 519-7575

FAX: [972] (3) 517-3227

consulate(s) general: Jerusalem; note - an independent US mission, established in 1928, whose members are not accredited to a foreign government

Flag description: white with a blue hexagram (six-pointed linear star) known as the Magen David (Shield of David) centered between two equal horizontal blue bands near the top and bottom edges of the flag

Economy

Economy - overview: Israel has a technologically advanced market economy with substantial government participation. It depends on imports of crude oil, grains, raw materials, and military equipment. Despite limited natural resources, Israel has intensively developed its agricultural and industrial sectors over the past 20 years. Manufacturing and construction employ about 28% of Israeli workers; agriculture, forestry, and fishing 2.6%; and services the rest. Israel is largely self-sufficient in food production except for grains. Diamonds, high-technology equipment, and agricultural products (fruits and vegetables) are leading exports. Israel usually posts sizable current account deficits, which are covered by large transfer payments from abroad and by foreign loans. Roughly half of the government's external debt is owed to the US, which is its major source of economic and military aid. The influx of Jewish immigrants from the former USSR topped 750,000 during the period 1989-98, bringing the population of Israel from the former Soviet Union to one million, one-sixth of the total population and adding scientific and professional expertise of

Israel *(continued)*

substantial value for the economy's future. The influx, coupled with the opening of new markets at the end of the Cold War, energized Israel's economy, which grew rapidly in the early 1990s. But growth began slowing in 1996 when the government imposed tighter fiscal and monetary policies and the immigration bonus petered out.

GDP: purchasing power parity - $101.9 billion (1998 est.)

GDP - real growth rate: 1.9% (1998 est.)

GDP - per capita: purchasing power parity - $18,100 (1998 est.)

GDP - composition by sector:
agriculture: 2%
industry: 17%
services: 81% (1997 est.)

Population below poverty line: NA%

Household income or consumption by percentage share:
lowest 10%: 2.8%
highest 10%: 26.9% (1992)

Inflation rate (consumer prices): 5.4% (1998 est.)

Labor force: 2.3 million (1997)

Labor force - by occupation: public services 31.2%, manufacturing 20.2%, finance and business 13.1%, commerce 12.8%, construction 7.5%, personal and other services 6.4%, transport, storage, and communications 6.2%, agriculture, forestry, and fishing 2.6% (1996)

Unemployment rate: 8.7% (1998 est.)

Budget:
revenues: $55 billion
expenditures: $58 billion, including capital expenditures of $NA (1998 est.)

Industries: food processing, diamond cutting and polishing, textiles and apparel, chemicals, metal products, military equipment, transport equipment, electrical equipment, potash mining, high-technology electronics, tourism

Industrial production growth rate: 5.4% (1996)

Electricity - production: 28.035 billion kWh (1996)

Electricity - production by source:
fossil fuel: 99.88%
hydro: 0.12%
nuclear: 0%
other: 0% (1996)

Electricity - consumption: 27.725 billion kWh (1996)

Electricity - exports: 310 million kWh (1996)

Electricity - imports: 0 kWh (1996)

Agriculture - products: citrus, vegetables, cotton; beef, poultry, dairy products

Exports: $22.1 billion (f.o.b., 1998)

Exports - commodities: machinery and equipment, cut diamonds, chemicals, textiles and apparel, agricultural products, metals

Exports - partners: US 32%, UK, Hong Kong, Benelux, Japan, Netherlands (1997)

Imports: $26.1 billion (f.o.b., 1998)

Imports - commodities: raw materials, military equipment, investment goods, rough diamonds, oil, consumer goods

Imports - partners: US 19%, Benelux 12%, Germany 9%, UK 8%, Italy 7%, Switzerland 6% (1997)

Debt - external: $18.7 billion (1997)

Economic aid - recipient: $1.241 billion (1994); note - $1.2 billion from the US (1997)

Currency: 1 new Israeli shekel (NIS) = 100 new agorot

Exchange rates: new Israeli shekels (NIS) per US$1 - 4.2269 (November 1998), 3.4494 (1997), 3.1917 (1996), 3.0113 (1995), 3.0111 (1994)

Fiscal year: calendar year (since 1 January 1992)

Communications

Telephones: 2.6 million (1996)

Telephone system: most highly developed system in the Middle East although not the largest
domestic: good system of coaxial cable and microwave radio relay
international: 3 submarine cables; satellite earth stations - 3 Intelsat (2 Atlantic Ocean and 1 Indian Ocean)

Radio broadcast stations: AM 9, FM 45, shortwave 0

Radios: 2.25 million (1993 est.)

Television broadcast stations: 24 (in addition, there are 31 low-power repeaters) (1997)

Televisions: 1.5 million (1993 est.)

Transportation

Railways:
total: 610 km
standard gauge: 610 km 1.435-m gauge (1996)

Highways:
total: 15,464 km
paved: 15,464 km (including 56 km of expressways)
unpaved: 0 km (1997 est.)

Pipelines: crude oil 708 km; petroleum products 290 km; natural gas 89 km

Ports and harbors: Ashdod, Ashqelon, Elat (Eilat), Hadera, Haifa, Tel Aviv-Yafo

Merchant marine:
total: 23 ships (1,000 GRT or over) totaling 736,419 GRT/855,497 DWT
ships by type: cargo 1, container 21, roll-on/roll-off cargo 1 (1998 est.)

Airports: 54 (1998 est.)

Airports - with paved runways:
total: 31
over 3,047 m: 2
2,438 to 3,047 m: 5
1,524 to 2,437 m: 7
914 to 1,523 m: 10
under 914 m: 7 (1998 est.)

Airports - with unpaved runways:
total: 23
2,438 to 3,047 m: 1
1,524 to 2,437 m: 1
914 to 1,523 m: 3
under 914 m: 18 (1998 est.)

Heliports: 2 (1998 est.)

Military

Military branches: Israel Defense Forces (includes ground, naval, and air components), Pioneer Fighting Youth (Nahal), Frontier Guard, Chen (women); note - historically there have been no separate Israeli military services

Military manpower - military age: 18 years of age

Military manpower - availability:
males age 15-49: 1,474,046
females age 15-49: 1,439,569 (1999 est.)

Military manpower - fit for military service:
males age 15-49: 1,206,320
females age 15-49: 1,173,818 (1999 est.)

Military manpower - reaching military age annually:
males: 50,737
females: 48,546 (1999 est.)

Military expenditures - dollar figure: $8.7 billion (1999)

Military expenditures - percent of GDP: 9.5% (1999)

Transnational Issues

Disputes - international: West Bank and Gaza Strip are Israeli-occupied with current status subject to the Israeli-Palestinian Interim Agreement - permanent status to be determined through further negotiation; Golan Heights is Israeli-occupied; Israeli troops in southern Lebanon since June 1982

Illicit drugs: increasingly concerned about cocaine and heroin abuse; drugs primarily arrive in country from Lebanon

Italy

Introduction

Background: Italy failed to secure political unification until the 1860s, thus lacking the military and imperial power of Spain, Britain, and France. The fascist dictatorship of MUSSOLINI after World War I, led to the disastrous alliance with HITLER's Germany and defeat in World War II. Italy was a founding member of the European Economic Community (EEC) and joined in the growing political and economic unification of Western Europe, including the introduction of the euro in January 1999. On-going problems include illegal immigration, the ravages of organized crime, high unemployment, and the low incomes and technical standards of Southern Italy compared with the North.

Geography

Location: Southern Europe, a peninsula extending into the central Mediterranean Sea, northeast of Tunisia

Geographic coordinates: 42 50 N, 12 50 E

Map references: Europe

Area:
total: 301,230 sq km
land: 294,020 sq km
water: 7,210 sq km
note: includes Sardinia and Sicily

Area - comparative: slightly larger than Arizona

Land boundaries:
total: 1,932.2 km
border countries: Austria 430 km, France 488 km, Holy See (Vatican City) 3.2 km, San Marino 39 km, Slovenia 232 km, Switzerland 740 km

Coastline: 7,600 km

Maritime claims:
continental shelf: 200-m depth or to the depth of exploitation
territorial sea: 12 nm

Climate: predominantly Mediterranean; Alpine in far north; hot, dry in south

Terrain: mostly rugged and mountainous; some plains, coastal lowlands

Elevation extremes:
lowest point: Mediterranean Sea 0 m
highest point: Mont Blanc (Monte Bianco) 4,807 m

Natural resources: mercury, potash, marble, sulfur, dwindling natural gas and crude oil reserves, fish, coal

Land use:
arable land: 31%
permanent crops: 10%
permanent pastures: 15%
forests and woodland: 23%
other: 21% (1993 est.)

Irrigated land: 27,100 sq km (1993 est.)

Natural hazards: regional risks include landslides, mudflows, avalanches, earthquakes, volcanic eruptions, flooding; land subsidence in Venice

Environment - current issues: air pollution from industrial emissions such as sulfur dioxide; coastal and inland rivers polluted from industrial and agricultural effluents; acid rain damaging lakes; inadequate industrial waste treatment and disposal facilities

Environment - international agreements:
party to: Air Pollution, Air Pollution-Nitrogen Oxides, Air Pollution-Sulphur 85, Air Pollution-Sulphur 94, Air Pollution-Volatile Organic Compounds, Antarctic-Environmental Protocol, Antarctic Treaty, Biodiversity, Climate Change, Desertification, Endangered Species, Environmental Modification, Hazardous Wastes, Law of the Sea, Marine Dumping, Nuclear Test Ban, Ozone Layer Protection, Ship Pollution, Tropical Timber 83, Tropical Timber 94, Wetlands, Whaling
signed, but not ratified: Air Pollution-Persistent Organic Pollutants, Climate Change-Kyoto Protocol

Geography - note: strategic location dominating central Mediterranean as well as southern sea and air approaches to Western Europe

People

Population: 56,735,130 (July 1999 est.)

Age structure:
0-14 years: 14% (male 4,161,841; female 3,925,413)
15-64 years: 68% (male 19,205,293; female 19,285,848)
65 years and over: 18% (male 4,169,098; female 5,987,637) (1999 est.)

Population growth rate: -0.08% (1999 est.)

Birth rate: 9.27 births/1,000 population (1999 est.)

Death rate: 10.28 deaths/1,000 population (1999 est.)

Net migration rate: 0.17 migrant(s)/1,000 population (1999 est.)

Sex ratio:
at birth: 1.06 male(s)/female
under 15 years: 1.06 male(s)/female
15-64 years: 1 male(s)/female
65 years and over: 0.7 male(s)/female
total population: 0.94 male(s)/female (1999 est.)

Infant mortality rate: 6.3 deaths/1,000 live births (1999 est.)

Life expectancy at birth:
total population: 78.51 years
male: 75.4 years
female: 81.82 years (1999 est.)

Total fertility rate: 1.22 children born/woman (1999 est.)

Nationality:
noun: Italian(s)
adjective: Italian

Ethnic groups: Italian (includes small clusters of German-, French-, and Slovene-Italians in the north and Albanian-Italians and Greek-Italians in the south)

Religions: Roman Catholic 98%, other 2%

Languages: Italian, German (parts of Trentino-Alto Adige region are predominantly German speaking), French (small French-speaking minority in Valle d'Aosta region), Slovene (Slovene-speaking minority in the Trieste-Gorizia area)

Literacy:
definition: age 15 and over can read and write
total population: 97%
male: 98%
female: 96% (1990 est.)

Government

Country name:
conventional long form: Italian Republic
conventional short form: Italy
local long form: Repubblica Italiana
local short form: Italia
former: Kingdom of Italy

Data code: IT

Government type: republic

Capital: Rome

Administrative divisions: 20 regions (regioni, singular - regione); Abruzzi, Basilicata, Calabria, Campania, Emilia-Romagna, Friuli-Venezia Giulia, Lazio, Liguria, Lombardia, Marche, Molise, Piemonte, Puglia, Sardegna, Sicilia, Toscana, Trentino-Alto Adige, Umbria, Valle d'Aosta, Veneto

Independence: 17 March 1861 (Kingdom of Italy proclaimed)

National holiday: Anniversary of the Republic, 2 June (1946)

Constitution: 1 January 1948

Legal system: based on civil law system, with ecclesiastical law influence; appeals treated as trials de novo; judicial review under certain conditions in Constitutional Court; has not accepted compulsory ICJ jurisdiction

Suffrage: 18 years of age; universal (except in senatorial elections, where minimum age is 25)

Executive branch:
chief of state: President Oscar Luigi SCALFARO (since 28 May 1992)
head of government: Prime Minister (referred to in Italy as the president of the Council of Ministers) Massimo D'ALEMA (since 27 October 1998)
cabinet: Council of Ministers nominated by the prime minister and approved by the president
elections: president elected by an electoral college consisting of both houses of Parliament and 58

Italy (continued)

regional representatives for a seven-year term; election last held 25 May 1992 (next to be held NA June 1999); prime minister appointed by the president and confirmed by parliament

election results: Oscar Luigi SCALFARO elected president; percent of electoral college vote - NA

Legislative branch: bicameral Parliament or Parlamento consists of the Senate or Senato della Repubblica (326 seats - 315 elected by popular vote of which 232 are directly elected and 83 are elected by regional proportional representation, 11 are appointed senators-for-life; members serve five-year terms) and the Chamber of Deputies or Camera dei Deputati (630 seats; 475 are directly elected, 155 by regional proportional representation; members serve five-year terms)

elections: Senate - last held 21 April 1996 (next to be held by NA April 2001); Chamber of Deputies - last held 21 April 1996 (next to be held by NA April 2001)

election results: Senate - percent of vote by party - NA; seats by party - Olive Tree 157, Freedom Alliance 116, Northern League 27, Refounded Communists 10, regional lists 3, Social Movement-Tricolor Flames 1, Panella Reformers 1; Chamber of Deputies - percent of vote by party - NA; seats by party - Olive Tree 284, Freedom Alliance 246, Northern League 59, Refounded Communists 35, Southern Tyrol List 3, Autonomous List 2, other 1

Judicial branch: Constitutional Court or Corte Costituzionale, composed of 15 judges (one-third appointed by the president, one-third elected by Parliament, one-third elected by the ordinary and administrative supreme courts)

Political parties and leaders:

Olive Tree (Ulivo): Democrats of the Left or DS [Walter VELTRONI]; Greens (Verdi) [Luigi MANCONI]; Italian Popular Party or PPI [Franco MARINI]

Freedom Pole: Forza Italia or FI [Silvio BERLUSCONI]; National Alliance or AN [Gianfranco FINI]; Christian Democratic Center or CCD [Pierferdinando CASINI]; Democratic Union for the Republic or UDR [Clemente MASTELLA]

other: Northern League or NL [Umberto BOSSI]; Communist Refoundation or RC [Fausto BERTINOTTI]; Italian Social Movement-Tricolor Flame or MSI-Fiamma Tricolore [Pino RAUTI]; Italian Socialists or SI [Enrico BOSSELLI]; Italian Communist Party or PDCI [Armando COSSUTTA]; Autonomous List (a group of minor parties) [leader NA]; Southern Tyrols People's Party or SVP (German speakers) [leader NA]; Italy of Values [Antonio DIPIETRO]

Political pressure groups and leaders: the Roman Catholic Church; three major trade union confederations (Confederazione Generale Italiana del Lavoro or CGIL [Sergio COFFERATI] which is left wing, Confederazione Italiana dei Sindacati Lavoratori or CISL [Sergio D'ANTONI] which is Catholic centrist, and Unione Italiana del Lavoro or UIL [Pietro LARIZZA] which is lay centrist); Italian manufacturers and merchants associations (Confindustria, Confcommercio); organized farm groups (Confcoltivatori, Confagricoltura)

International organization participation: AfDB, AsDB, Australia Group, BIS, BSEC (observer), CCC, CDB (non-regional), CE, CEI, CERN, EAPC, EBRD, ECE, ECLAC, EIB, EMU, ESA, EU, FAO, G- 7, G-10, IADB, IAEA, IBRD, ICAO, ICC, ICFTU, ICRM, IDA, IEA, IFAD, IFC, IFRCS, IHO, ILO, IMF, IMO, Inmarsat, Intelsat, Interpol, IOC, IOM, ISO, ITU, LAIA (observer), MINURSO, MTCR, NAM (guest), NATO, NEA, NSG, OAS (observer), OECD, OPCW, OSCE, PCA, UN, UNCTAD, UNESCO, UNHCR, UNIDO, UNIFIL, UNIKOM, UNITAR, UNMIBH, UNMOGIP, UNTSO, UPU, WCL, WEU, WHO, WIPO, WMO, WToO, WTrO, ZC

Diplomatic representation in the US:

chief of mission: Ambassador Ferdinando SALLEO

chancery: 1601 Fuller Street NW, Washington, DC 20009 and 2700 16th Street NW, Washington, DC 20009

telephone: [1] (202) 328-5500

FAX: [1] (202) 483-2187

consulate(s) general: Boston, Chicago, Houston, Miami, New York, Los Angeles, Philadelphia, and San Francisco

consulate(s): Detroit

Diplomatic representation from the US:

chief of mission: Ambassador Thomas M. FOGLIETTA

embassy: Via Veneto 119/A, 00187-Rome

mailing address: PSC 59, Box 100, APO AE 09624

telephone: [39] (06) 46741

FAX: [39] (06) 488-2672

consulate(s) general: Florence, Milan, Naples

Flag description: three equal vertical bands of green (hoist side), white, and red; similar to the flag of Ireland, which is longer and is green (hoist side), white, and orange; also similar to the flag of the Cote d'Ivoire, which has the colors reversed - orange (hoist side), white, and green

Economy

Economy - overview: Since World War II, the Italian economy has changed from one based on agriculture into a ranking industrial economy, with approximately the same total and per capita output as France and the UK. This basically capitalistic economy is still divided into a developed industrial north, dominated by private companies, and a less developed agricultural south, with large public enterprises and more than 20% unemployment. Most raw materials needed by industry and over 75% of energy requirements must be imported. In the second half of 1992, Rome became unsettled by the prospect of not qualifying to participate in EU plans for economic and monetary union later in the decade; thus, it finally began to address its huge fiscal imbalances. Subsequently, the government has adopted fairly stringent budgets, abandoned its inflationary wage indexation system, and started to scale back its generous social welfare programs, including pension and health care benefits. In December 1998, Italy adopted a budget compliant with the requirements of the European Monetary Union (EMU); representatives of government, labor, and employers agreed to an update of the 1993 "social pact," which has been widely credited with having brought Italy's inflation into conformity with EMU requirements. In 1999, Italy must adjust to the loss of an independent monetary policy, which it has used quite liberally in the past to help cope with external shocks. Italy also must work to stimulate employment, promote wage flexibility, and tackle the informal economy.

GDP: purchasing power parity - $1.181 trillion (1998 est.)

GDP - real growth rate: 1.5% (1998 est.)

GDP - per capita: purchasing power parity - $20,800 (1998 est.)

GDP - composition by sector:

agriculture: 3.3%

industry: 33%

services: 63.7% (1994)

Population below poverty line: NA%

Household income or consumption by percentage share:

lowest 10%: 2.9%

highest 10%: 23.7% (1991)

Inflation rate (consumer prices): 1.8% (1998 est.)

Labor force: 23.193 million

Labor force - by occupation: services 61%, industry 32%, agriculture 7% (1996)

Unemployment rate: 12.5% (1998 est.)

Budget:

revenues: $559 billion

expenditures: $589 billion, including capital expenditures of $NA (1998 est.)

Industries: tourism, machinery, iron and steel, chemicals, food processing, textiles, motor vehicles, clothing, footwear, ceramics

Industrial production growth rate: 0.5% (1996 est.)

Electricity - production: 226.707 billion kWh (1996)

Electricity - production by source:

fossil fuel: 80.02%

hydro: 18.25%

nuclear: 0%

other: 1.73%

Electricity - consumption: 264.007 billion kWh (1996)

Electricity - exports: 800 million kWh (1996)

Electricity - imports: 38.1 billion kWh (1996)

Agriculture - products: fruits, vegetables, grapes, potatoes, sugar beets, soybeans, grain, olives; beef, dairy products; fish

Exports: $243 billion (f.o.b., 1998)

Exports - commodities: engineering products, textiles and clothing, production machinery, motor vehicles, transport equipment, chemicals; food, beverages and tobacco; minerals and nonferrous metals

Exports - partners: Germany 16.4%, France 12.2%, US 7.9%, UK 7.1%, Spain 5.2%, Netherlands 2.8% (1997)

Imports: $202 billion (f.o.b., 1998)

Imports - commodities: engineering products,

chemicals, transport equipment, energy products, minerals and nonferrous metals, textiles and clothing; food, beverages and tobacco

Imports - partners: Germany 18.0%, France 13.2%, UK 6.7%, Netherlands 6.2%, US 5.0%, Belgium-Luxembourg 4.7% (1997)

Debt - external: $45 billion (1996 est.)

Economic aid - donor: ODA, $1.6 billion (1995)

Currency: 1 Italian lira (Lit) = 100 centesimi

Exchange rates: Italian lire (Lit) per US$1 - 1,688.7 (January 1999), 1,736.2 (1998), 1,703.1 (1997), 1,542.9 (1996), 1,628.9 (1995), 1,612.4 (1994) *note:* on 1 January 1999, the European Union introduced a common currency that is now being used by financial institutions in some member countries at the rate of 0.8597 euros per US$ and a fixed rate of 1,936.27 lire per euro; the euro will replace the local currency in consenting countries for all transactions in 2002

Fiscal year: calendar year

Communications

Telephones: 25.6 million (1996 est.)

Telephone system: modern, well-developed, fast; fully automated telephone, telex, and data services *domestic:* high-capacity cable and microwave radio relay trunks *international:* satellite earth stations - 3 Intelsat (with a total of 5 antennas - 3 for Atlantic Ocean and 2 for Indian Ocean), 1 Inmarsat (Atlantic Ocean region), and NA Eutelsat; 21 submarine cables

Radio broadcast stations: AM 135, FM 28 (repeaters 1,840), shortwave 0

Radios: 45.7 million (1996 est.)

Television broadcast stations: 6,317 (consisting of 117 public stations with two kW of power or more, about 5,300 low-power public stations, and about 900 low-power private stations, mostly in local service) (1997)

Televisions: 17 million (1996 est.)

Transportation

Railways:
total: 19,272 km
standard gauge: 17,983 km 1.435-m gauge; Italian Railways (FS) operates 15,942 km of the total standard gauge routes (10,889 km electrified)
narrow gauge: 112 km 1.000-m gauge (112 km electrified); 1,177 km 0.950-m gauge (19 km electrified) (1996)

Highways:
total: 317,000 km
paved: 317,000 km (including 9,500 km of expressways)
unpaved: 0 km (1996 est.)

Waterways: 2,400 km for various types of commercial traffic, although of limited overall value

Pipelines: crude oil 1,703 km; petroleum products 2,148 km; natural gas 19,400 km

Ports and harbors: Augusta (Sicily), Bagnoli, Bari, Brindisi, Gela, Genoa, La Spezia, Livorno, Milazzo, Naples, Porto Foxi, Porto Torres (Sardinia), Salerno, Savona, Taranto, Trieste, Venice

Merchant marine:
total: 393 ships (1,000 GRT or over) totaling 5,982,870 GRT/8,413,850 DWT
ships by type: bulk 38, cargo 46, chemical tanker 60, combination ore/oil 2, container 16, liquefied gas tanker 35, livestock carrier 1, multifunction large-load carrier 1, oil tanker 84, passenger 6, roll-on/roll-off cargo 53, short-sea passenger 28, specialized tanker 12, vehicle carrier 11 (1998 est.)

Airports: 136 (1998 est.)

Airports - with paved runways:
total: 97
over 3,047 m: 5
2,438 to 3,047 m: 33
1,524 to 2,437 m: 17
914 to 1,523 m: 30
under 914 m: 12 (1998 est.)

Airports - with unpaved runways:
total: 39
1,524 to 2,437 m: 2
914 to 1,523 m: 19
under 914 m: 18 (1998 est.)

Heliports: 2 (1998 est.)

Military

Military branches: Army, Navy, Air Force, Carabinieri

Military manpower - military age: 18 years of age

Military manpower - availability:
males age 15-49: 14,142,889 (1999 est.)

Military manpower - fit for military service:
males age 15-49: 12,200,780 (1999 est.)

Military manpower - reaching military age annually:
males: 315,952 (1999 est.)

Military expenditures - dollar figure: $21.095 billion (FY97)

Military expenditures - percent of GDP: 1.9% (1995)

Transnational Issues

Disputes - international: Italy and Slovenia made progress in resolving bilateral issues; Croatia and Italy made progress toward resolving a bilateral issue dating from World War II over property and ethnic minority rights

Illicit drugs: important gateway for and consumer of Latin American cocaine and Southwest Asian heroin entering the European market

Jamaica

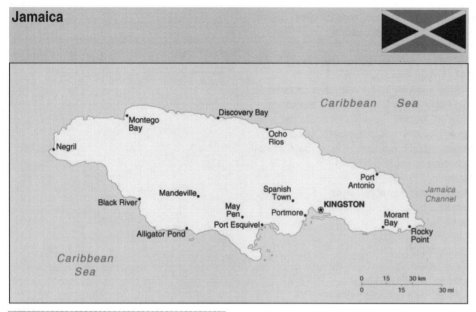

Geography

Location: Caribbean, island in the Caribbean Sea, south of Cuba

Geographic coordinates: 18 15 N, 77 30 W

Map references: Central America and the Caribbean

Area:

total: 10,990 sq km

land: 10,830 sq km

water: 160 sq km

Area - comparative: slightly smaller than Connecticut

Land boundaries: 0 km

Coastline: 1,022 km

Maritime claims: measured from claimed archipelagic baselines

continental shelf: 200-m depth or to the depth of exploitation

exclusive economic zone: 200 nm

territorial sea: 12 nm

Climate: tropical; hot, humid; temperate interior

Terrain: mostly mountains, with narrow, discontinuous coastal plain

Elevation extremes:

lowest point: Caribbean Sea 0 m

highest point: Blue Mountain Peak 2,256 m

Natural resources: bauxite, gypsum, limestone

Land use:

arable land: 14%

permanent crops: 6%

permanent pastures: 24%

forests and woodland: 17%

other: 39% (1993 est.)

Irrigated land: 350 sq km (1993 est.)

Natural hazards: hurricanes (especially July to November)

Environment - current issues: deforestation; coastal waters polluted by industrial waste, sewage, and oil spills; damage to coral reefs; air pollution in Kingston results from vehicle emissions

Environment - international agreements:

party to: Biodiversity, Climate Change, Desertification, Law of the Sea, Marine Dumping, Marine Life Conservation, Nuclear Test Ban, Ozone Layer Protection, Ship Pollution, Wetlands, Whaling

signed, but not ratified: none of the selected agreements

Geography - note: strategic location between Cayman Trench and Jamaica Channel, the main sea lanes for Panama Canal

People

Population: 2,652,443 (July 1999 est.)

Age structure:

0-14 years: 31% (male 421,127; female 402,593)

15-64 years: 62% (male 819,956; female 828,176)

65 years and over: 7% (male 79,747; female 100,844) (1999 est.)

Population growth rate: 0.64% (1999 est.)

Birth rate: 20.22 births/1,000 population (1999 est.)

Death rate: 5.39 deaths/1,000 population (1999 est.)

Net migration rate: -8.39 migrant(s)/1,000 population (1999 est.)

Sex ratio:

at birth: 1.05 male(s)/female

under 15 years: 1.05 male(s)/female

15-64 years: 0.99 male(s)/female

65 years and over: 0.79 male(s)/female

total population: 0.99 male(s)/female (1999 est.)

Infant mortality rate: 13.93 deaths/1,000 live births (1999 est.)

Life expectancy at birth:

total population: 75.62 years

male: 73.22 years

female: 78.13 years (1999 est.)

Total fertility rate: 2.26 children born/woman (1999 est.)

Nationality:

noun: Jamaican(s)

adjective: Jamaican

Ethnic groups: black 90.4%, East Indian 1.3%, white 0.2%, Chinese 0.2%, mixed 7.3%, other 0.6%

Religions: Protestant 61.3% (Church of God 21.2%, Baptist 8.8%, Anglican 5.5%, Seventh-Day Adventist 9%, Pentecostal 7.6%, Methodist 2.7%, United Church 2.7%, Brethren 1.1%, Jehovah's Witness 1.6%, Moravian 1.1%), Roman Catholic 4%, other, including some spiritual cults 34.7%

Languages: English, Creole

Literacy:

definition: age 15 and over has ever attended school

total population: 85%

male: 80.8%

female: 89.1% (1995 est.)

Government

Country name:

conventional long form: none

conventional short form: Jamaica

Data code: JM

Government type: parliamentary democracy

Capital: Kingston

Administrative divisions: 14 parishes; Clarendon, Hanover, Kingston, Manchester, Portland, Saint Andrew, Saint Ann, Saint Catherine, Saint Elizabeth, Saint James, Saint Mary, Saint Thomas, Trelawny, Westmoreland

Independence: 6 August 1962 (from UK)

National holiday: Independence Day (first Monday in August) (1962)

Constitution: 6 August 1962

Legal system: based on English common law; has not accepted compulsory ICJ jurisdiction

Suffrage: 18 years of age; universal

Executive branch:

chief of state: Queen ELIZABETH II (since 6 February 1952), represented by Governor General Sir Howard Felix COOKE (since 1 August 1991)

head of government: Prime Minister Percival James PATTERSON (since 30 March 1992) and Deputy Prime Minister Seymour MULLINGS (since NA 1993)

cabinet: Cabinet appointed by the governor general on the advice of the prime minister

elections: none; the monarch is hereditary; governor general appointed by the monarch on the recommendation of the prime minister; prime minister and deputy prime minister appointed by the governor general

Legislative branch: bicameral Parliament consists of the Senate (a 21-member body appointed by the governor general on the recommendations of the prime minister and the leader of the opposition; ruling party 13 seats, opposition eight seats) and the House of Representatives (60 seats; members are elected by popular vote to serve five-year terms)

elections: last held 18 December 1997 (next to be held by March 2002)

election results: percent of vote by party - NA; seats by party - PNP 50, JLP 10

Judicial branch: Supreme Court (judges appointed by the governor general on the advice of the prime minister)

Jamaica *(continued)*

Political parties and leaders: People's National Party or PNP [P. J. PATTERSON]; Jamaica Labor Party or JLP [Edward SEAGA]; National Democratic Movement or NDM [Bruce GOLDING]
Political pressure groups and leaders: Rastafarians (black religious/racial cultists, pan-Africanists); New Beginnings Movement or NBM
International organization participation: ACP, C, Caricom, CCC, CDB, ECLAC, FAO, G-15, G-19, G-77, IADB, IAEA, IBRD, ICAO, ICFTU, ICRM, IFAD, IFC, IFRCS, IHO (pending member), ILO, IMF, IMO, Intelsat, Interpol, IOC, IOM (observer), ISO, ITU, LAES, NAM, OAS, OPANAL, OPCW, UN, UNCTAD, UNESCO, UNIDO, UPU, WCL, WFTU, WHO, WIPO, WMO, WToO, WTrO
Diplomatic representation in the US:
chief of mission: Ambassador Richard Leighton BERNAL
chancery: 1520 New Hampshire Avenue NW, Washington, DC 20036
telephone: [1] (202) 452-0660
FAX: [1] (202) 452-0081
consulate(s) general: Miami and New York
Diplomatic representation from the US:
chief of mission: Ambassador Stanley Louis MCLELLAND
embassy: Jamaica Mutual Life Center, 2 Oxford Road, 3rd floor, Kingston
mailing address: use embassy street address
telephone: [1] (809) 929-4850 through 4859
FAX: [1] (809) 926-6743
Flag description: diagonal yellow cross divides the flag into four triangles - green (top and bottom) and black (hoist side and outer side)

Economy

Economy - overview: Key sectors in this island economy are bauxite (alumina and bauxite account for more than half of exports) and tourism. Since assuming office in 1992, Prime Minister PATTERSON has eliminated most price controls, streamlined tax schedules, and privatized government enterprises. Continued tight monetary and fiscal policies have helped slow inflation - although inflationary pressures are mounting - and stabilize the exchange rate, but have resulted in the slowdown of economic growth (moving from 1.5% in 1992 to 0.5% in 1995). In 1996, GDP showed negative growth (-1.4%) and remained negative through 1998. Serious problems include: high interest rates; increased foreign competition; the weak financial condition of business in general resulting in receiverships or closures and downsizings of companies; the shift in investment portfolios to non-productive, short-term high yield instruments; a pressured, sometimes sliding, exchange rate; a widening merchandise trade deficit; and a growing internal debt for government bailouts to various ailing sectors of the economy, particularly the financial sector. Jamaica's medium-term prospects will depend upon encouraging investment in the productive sectors, maintaining a competitive exchange rate, stabilizing the labor environment, selling off reacquired firms, and implementing proper fiscal and monetary policies.
GDP: purchasing power parity - $8.8 billion (1998 est.)
GDP - real growth rate: -2% (1998 est.)
GDP - per capita: purchasing power parity - $3,300 (1998 est.)
GDP - composition by sector:
agriculture: 7.4%
industry: 42.1%
services: 50.5% (1997 est.)
Population below poverty line: 34.2% (1992 est.)
Household income or consumption by percentage share:
lowest 10%: 2.4%
highest 10%: 31.9% (1991)
Inflation rate (consumer prices): 9.9% (1998 est.)
Labor force: 1.14 million (1996)
Labor force - by occupation: services 41%, agriculture 22.5%, industry 19% (1989)
Unemployment rate: 16.5% (1997 est.)
Budget:
revenues: $2.27 billion
expenditures: $3.66 billion, including capital expenditures of $1.265 billion (FY98/99 est.)
Industries: tourism, bauxite, textiles, food processing, light manufactures
Industrial production growth rate: NA%
Electricity - production: 6.125 billion kWh (1996)
Electricity - production by source:
fossil fuel: 97.96%
hydro: 2.04%
nuclear: 0%
other: 0% (1996)
Electricity - consumption: 6.125 billion kWh (1996)
Electricity - exports: 0 kWh (1996)
Electricity - imports: 0 kWh (1996)
Agriculture - products: sugarcane, bananas, coffee, citrus, potatoes, vegetables; poultry, goats, milk
Exports: $1.7 billion (1997)
Exports - commodities: alumina, bauxite, sugar, bananas, rum
Exports - partners: US 33.3%, EU (excluding UK and Norway) 17.1%, Canada 14.1%, UK 13.4%, Norway 6.1%, Caricom 3.4%
Imports: $2.8 billion (1997)
Imports - commodities: machinery and transport equipment, construction materials, fuel, food, chemicals
Imports - partners: US 47.7%, EU (excluding UK) 12.8%, Caricom 10.2%, Latin America 6.7%, UK 3.7% (1997)
Debt - external: $4.2 billion (1997 est.)
Economic aid - recipient: $102.7 million (1995)
Currency: 1 Jamaican dollar (J$) = 100 cents
Exchange rates: Jamaican dollars (J$) per US$1 - 35.57 (December 1998), 35.404 (1997), 37.120 (1996), 35.142 (1995), 33.086 (1994)
Fiscal year: 1 April - 31 March

Communications

Telephones: 350,000 (1997 est.)
Telephone system: fully automatic domestic telephone network
domestic: NA
international: satellite earth stations - 2 Intelsat (Atlantic Ocean); 3 coaxial submarine cables
Radio broadcast stations: AM 1, FM 7, shortwave 0 (1997)
Radios: 1.973 million (1997)
Television broadcast stations: 7 (1997)
Televisions: 330,000 (1992 est.)

Transportation

Railways:
total: 370 km
standard gauge: 370 km 1.435-m gauge; note - 207 km belong to the Jamaica Railway Corporation in common carrier service, but are no longer operational; the remaining track is privately owned and used to transport bauxite
Highways:
total: 18,700 km
paved: 13,100 km
unpaved: 5,600 km (1997 est.)
Pipelines: petroleum products 10 km
Ports and harbors: Alligator Pond, Discovery Bay, Kingston, Montego Bay, Ocho Rios, Port Antonio, Rocky Point, Port Esquivel (Longswharf)
Merchant marine:
total: 2 ships (1,000 GRT or over) totaling 3,478 GRT/ 5,878 DWT
ships by type: oil tanker 1, roll-on/roll-off cargo 1 (1998 est.)
Airports: 36 (1998 est.)
Airports - with paved runways:
total: 11
2,438 to 3,047 m: 2
1,524 to 2,437 m: 1
914 to 1,523 m: 3
under 914 m: 5 (1998 est.)
Airports - with unpaved runways:
total: 25
914 to 1,523 m: 2
under 914 m: 23 (1998 est.)

Military

Military branches: Jamaica Defense Force (includes Ground Forces, Coast Guard, and Air Wing), Jamaica Constabulary Force
Military manpower - military age: 18 years of age
Military manpower - availability:
males age 15-49: 715,260 (1999 est.)
Military manpower - fit for military service:
males age 15-49: 503,667 (1999 est.)
Military manpower - reaching military age annually:
males: 26,108 (1999 est.)
Military expenditures - dollar figure: $47.9 million (FY97/98 est.)
Military expenditures - percent of GDP: NA%

Disputes - international: none
Illicit drugs: transshipment point for cocaine from Central and South America to North America and Europe; illicit cultivation of cannabis; government has an active manual cannabis eradication program

Jan Mayen
(territory of Norway)

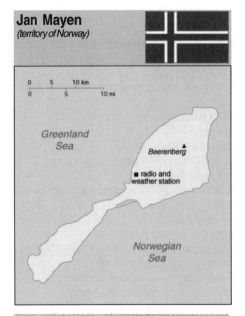

Geography

Location: Northern Europe, island between the Greenland Sea and the Norwegian Sea, northeast of Iceland
Geographic coordinates: 71 00 N, 8 00 W
Map references: Arctic Region
Area:
total: 373 sq km
land: 373 sq km
water: 0 sq km
Area - comparative: slightly more than twice the size of Washington, DC
Land boundaries: 0 km
Coastline: 124.1 km
Maritime claims:
contiguous zone: 10 nm
continental shelf: 200-m depth or to the depth of exploitation
exclusive economic zone: 200 nm
territorial sea: 4 nm
Climate: arctic maritime with frequent storms and persistent fog
Terrain: volcanic island, partly covered by glaciers
Elevation extremes:
lowest point: Norwegian Sea 0 m
highest point: Haakon VII Toppen/Beerenberg 2,277 m
Natural resources: none
Land use:
arable land: 0%
permanent crops: 0%
permanent pastures: 0%
forests and woodland: 0%
other: 100%
Irrigated land: 0 sq km (1993)
Natural hazards: dominated by the volcano Haakon VII Toppen/Beerenberg; volcanic activity resumed in 1970
Environment - current issues: NA

Environment - international agreements:
party to: NA
signed, but not ratified: NA
Geography - note: barren volcanic island with some moss and grass

People

Population: no indigenous inhabitants
note: there are personnel who operate the Long Range Navigation (Loran) C base and the weather and coastal services radio station

Government

Country name:
conventional long form: none
conventional short form: Jan Mayen
Data code: JN
Dependency status: territory of Norway; administered from Oslo through a governor (sysselmann) resident in Longyearbyen (Svalbard); however, authority has been delegated to a station commander of the Norwegian Defense Communication Service
Legal system: NA
Diplomatic representation in the US: none (territory of Norway)
Diplomatic representation from the US: none (territory of Norway)
Flag description: the flag of Norway is used

Economy

Economy - overview: Jan Mayen is a volcanic island with no exploitable natural resources. Economic activity is limited to providing services for employees of Norway's radio and meteorological stations located on the island.

Communications

Radio broadcast stations: AM NA, FM NA, shortwave NA
note: radio and meteorological station

Transportation

Ports and harbors: none; offshore anchorage only
Airports: 1 (1998 est.)
Airports - with unpaved runways:
total: 1
914 to 1,523 m: 1 (1998 est.)

Military

Military - note: defense is the responsibility of Norway

Transnational Issues

Disputes - international: none

Japan

Geography

Location: Eastern Asia, island chain between the North Pacific Ocean and the Sea of Japan, east of the Korean Peninsula

Geographic coordinates: 36 00 N, 138 00 E

Map references: Asia

Area:
total: 377,835 sq km
land: 374,744 sq km
water: 3,091 sq km
note: includes Bonin Islands (Ogasawara-gunto), Daito-shoto, Minami-jima, Okino-tori-shima, Ryukyu Islands (Nansei-shoto), and Volcano Islands (Kazan-retto)

Area - comparative: slightly smaller than California

Land boundaries: 0 km

Coastline: 29,751 km

Maritime claims:
exclusive economic zone: 200 nm
territorial sea: 12 nm; between 3 nm and 12 nm in the international straits - La Perouse or Soya, Tsugaru, Osumi, and Eastern and Western Channels of the Korea or Tsushima Strait

Climate: varies from tropical in south to cool temperate in north

Terrain: mostly rugged and mountainous

Elevation extremes:
lowest point: Hachiro-gata -4 m
highest point: Fujiyama 3,776 m

Natural resources: negligible mineral resources, fish

Land use:
arable land: 11%
permanent crops: 1%
permanent pastures: 2%
forests and woodland: 67%
other: 19% (1993 est.)

Irrigated land: 27,820 sq km (1993 est.)

Natural hazards: many dormant and some active volcanoes; about 1,500 seismic occurrences (mostly tremors) every year; tsunamis

Environment - current issues: air pollution from power plant emissions results in acid rain; acidification of lakes and reservoirs degrading water quality and threatening aquatic life; Japan is one of the largest consumers of fish and tropical timber, contributing to the depletion of these resources in Asia and elsewhere

Environment - international agreements:
party to: Antarctic-Environmental Protocol, Antarctic Treaty, Biodiversity, Climate Change, Desertication, Endangered Species, Environmental Modification, Hazardous Wastes, Law of the Sea, Marine Dumping, Nuclear Test Ban, Ozone Layer Protection, Ship Pollution, Tropical Timber 83, Tropical Timber 94, Wetlands, Whaling
signed, but not ratified: Climate Change-Kyoto Protocol

Geography - note: strategic location in northeast Asia

People

Population: 126,182,077 (July 1999 est.)

Age structure:
0-14 years: 15% (male 9,697,851; female 9,242,027)
15-64 years: 68% (male 43,405,024; female 43,023,885)
65 years and over: 17% (male 8,686,347; female 12,126,943) (1999 est.)

Population growth rate: 0.2% (1999 est.)

Birth rate: 10.48 births/1,000 population (1999 est.)

Death rate: 8.12 deaths/1,000 population (1999 est.)

Net migration rate: -0.34 migrant(s)/1,000 population (1999 est.)

Sex ratio:
at birth: 1.05 male(s)/female
under 15 years: 1.05 male(s)/female
15-64 years: 1.01 male(s)/female
65 years and over: 0.72 male(s)/female
total population: 0.96 male(s)/female (1999 est.)

Infant mortality rate: 4.07 deaths/1,000 live births (1999 est.)

Life expectancy at birth:
total population: 80.11 years
male: 77.02 years
female: 83.35 years (1999 est.)

Total fertility rate: 1.48 children born/woman (1999 est.)

Nationality:
noun: Japanese (singular and plural)
adjective: Japanese

Ethnic groups: Japanese 99.4%, other 0.6% (mostly Korean)

Religions: observe both Shinto and Buddhist 84%, other 16% (including Christian 0.7%)

Languages: Japanese

Literacy:
definition: age 15 and over can read and write
total population: 99% (1970 est.)
male: NA%
female: NA%

Government

Country name:
conventional long form: none
conventional short form: Japan

Data code: JA

Government type: constitutional monarchy

Capital: Tokyo

Administrative divisions: 47 prefectures; Aichi, Akita, Aomori, Chiba, Ehime, Fukui, Fukuoka, Fukushima, Gifu, Gumma, Hiroshima, Hokkaido, Hyogo, Ibaraki, Ishikawa, Iwate, Kagawa, Kagoshima, Kanagawa, Kochi, Kumamoto, Kyoto, Mie, Miyagi, Miyazaki, Nagano, Nagasaki, Nara, Niigata, Oita, Okayama, Okinawa, Osaka, Saga, Saitama, Shiga, Shimane, Shizuoka, Tochigi, Tokushima, Tokyo, Tottori, Toyama, Wakayama, Yamagata, Yamaguchi, Yamanashi

Independence: 660 BC (traditional founding by Emperor Jimmu)

National holiday: Birthday of the Emperor, 23 December (1933)

Constitution: 3 May 1947

Legal system: modeled after European civil law system with English-American influence; judicial review of legislative acts in the Supreme Court; accepts compulsory ICJ jurisdiction, with reservations

Suffrage: 20 years of age; universal

Executive branch:
chief of state: Emperor AKIHITO (since 7 January 1989)
head of government: Prime Minister Keizo OBUCHI (since 30 July 1998)
cabinet: Cabinet appointed by the prime minister
elections: none; the monarch is hereditary; the Diet designates the prime minister; the constitution requires that the prime minister must command a parliamentary majority, therefore, following legislative elections, the leader of the majority party or leader of a majority coalition in the House of Representatives usually becomes prime minister

Legislative branch: bicameral Diet or Kokkai consists of the House of Councillors or Sangi-in (252 seats; one-half of the members elected every three years - 76 seats of which are elected from the 47 multi-seat prefectural districts and 50 of which are elected from a single nationwide list with voters casting ballots by party; members elected by popular vote to serve six-year terms) and the House of Representatives or Shugi-in (500 seats - 200 of which are elected from 11 regional blocks on a proportional representation basis and 300 of which are elected from 300 single-seat districts; members elected by popular vote to serve four-year terms)
elections: House of Councillors - last held 12 July 1998 (next to be held NA July 2001); House of Representatives - last held 20 October 1996 (next to be held by October 2000)
election results: House of Councillors - percent of vote by party - NA; seats by party - LDP 102, DPJ 47, JCP 23, Komeito 22, SDP 13, Liberal Party 12, independents 26, others 7; note - the distribution of

Japan *(continued)*

seats as of January 1999 is as follows - LDP 104, DPJ 56, Komeito 24, JCP 23, SDP 14, Liberal Party 12, independents 5, others 14; House of Representatives - percent of vote by party - NA; seats by party - LDP 240, NFP 142, DPJ 52, JCP 26, SDP 15, Sun Party 10, others 15; note - the distribution of seats as of January 1999 is as follows - LDP 266, DPJ 94, Komeito/Reform Club 52, Liberal Party 39, JCP 26, SDP 14, independents 5, others 4

Judicial branch: Supreme Court, chief justice is appointed by the monarch after designation by the cabinet, all other justices are appointed by the cabinet

Political parties and leaders: Liberal Democratic Party or LDP [Keizo OBUCHI, president, Yoshiro MORI, secretary general]; Democratic Party of Japan or DPJ [Naoto KAN, leader, Tsutomu HATA, secretary general]; Komeito [Takenori KANZAKI, president, Tetsuzo FUYUSHIBA, secretary general]; Liberal Party [Ichiro OZAWA, president, Hirohisa FUJII, secretary general]; Japan Communist Party or JCP [Tetsuzo FUWA, chairman, Kazuo SHII, secretary general]; Social Democratic Party or SDP [Takako DOI, chairperson, Sadao FUCHIGAMI, secretary general]; Reform Club [Tatsuo OZAWA, leader, Katsuyuki ISHIDA, secretary general]

note: subsequent to the last legislative elections, the New Frontier Party or NFP and the Sun Party disbanded; the DPJ was formed by former members of the SDP and Sakigake and, in April 1998, was joined by three additional parties which had formed after the NFP disbanded; New Peace Party and Komei merged to form Komeito in November 1998

International organization participation: AfDB, APEC, AsDB, Australia Group, BIS, CCC, CE (observer), CERN (observer), CP, EBRD, ESCAP, FAO, G-5, G-7, G-10, IADB, IAEA, IBRD, ICAO, ICC, ICFTU, ICRM, IDA, IEA, IFAD, IFC, IFRCS, IHO, ILO, IMF, IMO, Inmarsat, Intelsat, Interpol, IOC, IOM, ISO, ITU, MTCR, NEA, NSG, OAS (observer), OECD, OPCW, OSCE (partner), PCA, UN, UN Security Council (temporary), UNCTAD, UNDOF, UNESCO, UNHCR, UNIDO, UNITAR, UNRWA, UNU, UPU, WFTU, WHO, WIPO, WMO, WToO, WTrO, ZC

Diplomatic representation in the US:
chief of mission: Ambassador Kunihiko SAITO
chancery: 2520 Massachusetts Avenue NW, Washington, DC 20008
telephone: [1] (202) 238-6700
FAX: [1] (202) 328-2187
consulate(s) general: Hagatna (Guam), Anchorage, Atlanta, Boston, Chicago, Detroit, Honolulu, Houston, Kansas City (Missouri), Los Angeles, Miami, New Orleans, New York, Portland (Oregon), San Francisco, and Seattle
consulate(s): Saipan (Northern Mariana Islands)
Diplomatic representation from the US:
chief of mission: Ambassador Thomas S. FOLEY
embassy: 10-5, Akasaka 1-chome, Minato-ku, Tokyo 107-8420
mailing address: Unit 45004, Box 258, APO AP 96337-5004
telephone: [81] (3) 3224-5000

FAX: [81] (3) 3505-1862
consulate(s) general: Naha (Okinawa), Osaka-Kobe, Sapporo
consulate(s): Fukuoka, Nagoya
Flag description: white with a large red disk (representing the sun without rays) in the center

Economy

Economy - overview: Government-industry cooperation, a strong work ethic, mastery of high technology, and a comparatively small defense allocation (1% of GDP) have helped Japan advance with extraordinary rapidity to the rank of second most powerful economy in the world. One notable characteristic of the economy is the working together of manufacturers, suppliers, and distributors in closely knit groups called keiretsu. A second basic feature has been the guarantee of lifetime employment for a substantial portion of the urban labor force; this guarantee is eroding. Industry, the most important sector of the economy, is heavily dependent on imported raw materials and fuels. The much smaller agricultural sector is highly subsidized and protected, with crop yields among the highest in the world. Usually self-sufficient in rice, Japan must import about 50% of its requirements of other grain and fodder crops. Japan maintains one of the world's largest fishing fleets and accounts for nearly 15% of the global catch. For three decades overall real economic growth had been spectacular: a 10% average in the 1960s, a 5% average in the 1970s, and a 4% average in the 1980s. Growth slowed markedly in 1992-95 largely because of the aftereffects of overinvestment during the late 1980s and contractionary domestic policies intended to wring speculative excesses from the stock and real estate markets. Growth picked up to 3.9% in 1996, largely a reflection of stimulative fiscal and monetary policies as well as low rates of inflation. But in 1997-98 Japan experienced a wrenching recession, centered about financial difficulties in the banking system and real estate markets and exacerbated by rigidities in corporate structures and labor markets. In early 1999 output has started to stabilize as emergency government spending begins to take hold. The crowding of habitable land area and the aging of the population are two major long-run problems.

GDP: purchasing power parity - $2.903 trillion (1998 est.)
GDP - real growth rate: -2.6% (1998 est.)
GDP - per capita: purchasing power parity - $23,100 (1998 est.)
GDP - composition by sector:
agriculture: 2%
industry: 38%
services: 60% (1997)
Population below poverty line: NA%
Household income or consumption by percentage share:
lowest 10%: NA%
highest 10%: NA%

Inflation rate (consumer prices): 0.9% (1998 est.)
Labor force: 67.72 million (November 1998)
Labor force - by occupation: trade and services 50%, manufacturing, mining, and construction 33%, utilities and communication 7%, agriculture, forestry, and fishing 6%, government 3% (1994)
Unemployment rate: 4.4% (November 1998)
Budget:
revenues: $407 billion
expenditures: $711 billion, including capital expenditures (public works only) of about $86 billion (FY99/00 est.)
Industries: among world's largest and technologically advanced producers of steel and nonferrous metallurgy, heavy electrical equipment, construction and mining equipment, motor vehicles and parts, electronic and telecommunication equipment, machine tools, automated production systems, locomotives and railroad rolling stock, ships, chemicals; textiles, processed foods
Industrial production growth rate: -6.9% (1998)
Electricity - production: 948.559 billion kWh (1996)
Electricity - production by source:
fossil fuel: 61.47%
hydro: 8.34%
nuclear: 29.83%
other: 0.36% (1996)
Electricity - consumption: 948.559 billion kWh (1996)
Electricity - exports: 0 kWh (1996)
Electricity - imports: 0 kWh (1996)
Agriculture - products: rice, sugar beets, vegetables, fruit; pork, poultry, dairy products, eggs; fish
Exports: $440 billion (f.o.b., 1998)
Exports - commodities: manufactures 96% (including machinery 50%, motor vehicles 19%, consumer electronics 3%)
Exports - partners: US 30%, EU 18%, Southeast Asia 12%, China 5%
Imports: $319 billion (c.i.f., 1998)
Imports - commodities: manufactures 54%, foodstuffs and raw materials 28%, fossil fuels 16%
Imports - partners: US 24%, Southeast Asia 14%, EU 14%, China 13%
Debt - external: $NA
Economic aid - donor: ODA, $9.1 billion (1999)
Currency: yen (¥)
Exchange rates: yen (¥) per US$1 - 113.18 (January 1999), 130.91 (1998), 120.99 (1997), 108.78 (1996), 94.06 (1995), 102.21 (1994)
Fiscal year: 1 April - 31 March

Communications

Telephones: 64 million (1987 est.)
Telephone system: excellent domestic and international service
domestic: NA
international: satellite earth stations - 5 Intelsat (4 Pacific Ocean and 1 Indian Ocean), 1 Intersputnik (Indian Ocean region), and 1 Inmarsat (Pacific and Indian Ocean regions); submarine cables to China,

Japan (continued)

Philippines, Russia, and US (via Guam)
Radio broadcast stations: AM 318, FM 58, shortwave 0
Radios: 97 million (1993 est.)
Television broadcast stations: 7,549 (consisting of 6,995 non-government and non-commercial stations, of which 95 are main stations of 1 kW or greater power and 6,900 are low-power stations, and 554 commercial stations of which 113 are main stations and 441 are repeaters); note - in addition, US Forces are served by 3 TV stations and 2 TV cable stations (1997)
Televisions: 100 million (1993 est.)

Transportation

Railways:
total: 23,670.7 km
standard gauge: 2,893.1 km 1.435-m gauge (entirely electrified)
narrow gauge: 89.8 km 1.372-m gauge (89.8 km electrified); 20,656.8 km 1.067-m gauge (10,383.6 km electrified); 31 km 0.762-m gauge (3.6 km electrified) (1994)
Highways:
total: 1.16 million km
paved: 859,560 km (including 6,070 km of expressways)
unpaved: 300,440 km (1996 est.)
Waterways: about 1,770 km; seagoing craft ply all coastal inland seas
Pipelines: crude oil 84 km; petroleum products 322 km; natural gas 1,800 km
Ports and harbors: Akita, Amagasaki, Chiba, Hachinohe, Hakodate, Higashi-Harima, Himeji, Hiroshima, Kawasaki, Kinuura, Kobe, Kushiro, Mizushima, Moji, Nagoya, Osaka, Sakai, Sakaide, Shimizu, Tokyo, Tomakomai
Merchant marine:
total: 713 ships (1,000 GRT or over) totaling 13,753,027 GRT/19,311,312 DWT
ships by type: bulk 159, cargo 54, chemical tanker 13, combination bulk 16, combination ore/oil 4, container 27, liquefied gas tanker 40, oil tanker 232, passenger 10, passenger-cargo 2, refrigerated cargo 27, roll-on/roll-off cargo 48, short-sea passenger 13, vehicle carrier 68 (1998 est.)
Airports: 170 (1998 est.)
Airports - with paved runways:
total: 140
over 3,047 m: 5
2,438 to 3,047 m: 35
1,524 to 2,437 m: 39
914 to 1,523 m: 30
under 914 m: 31 (1998 est.)
Airports - with unpaved runways:
total: 30
914 to 1,523 m: 2
under 914 m: 28 (1998 est.)
Heliports: 14 (1998 est.)

Military

Military branches: Japan Ground Self-Defense Force (Army), Japan Maritime Self-Defense Force (Navy), Japan Air Self-Defense Force (Air Force)
Military manpower - military age: 18 years of age
Military manpower - availability:
males age 15-49: 30,646,516 (1999 est.)
Military manpower - fit for military service:
males age 15-49: 26,438,961 (1999 est.)
Military manpower - reaching military age annually:
males: 784,658 (1999 est.)
Military expenditures - dollar figure: $42.9 billion (FY98/99)
Military expenditures - percent of GDP: 0.9% (FY98/99)

Transnational Issues

Disputes - international: islands of Etorofu, Kunashiri, Shikotan, and the Habomai group occupied by the Soviet Union in 1945, now administered by Russia, claimed by Japan; Liancourt Rocks (Takeshima/Tokdo) disputed with South Korea; Senkaku-shoto (Senkaku Islands) claimed by China and Taiwan

Jarvis Island
(territory of the US)

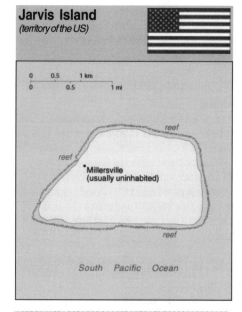

Geography

Location: Oceania, island in the South Pacific Ocean, about one-half of the way from Hawaii to the Cook Islands
Geographic coordinates: 0 22 S, 160 03 W
Map references: Oceania
Area:
total: 4.5 sq km
land: 4.5 sq km
water: 0 sq km
Area - comparative: about eight times the size of The Mall in Washington, DC
Land boundaries: 0 km
Coastline: 8 km
Maritime claims:
exclusive economic zone: 200 nm
territorial sea: 12 nm
Climate: tropical; scant rainfall, constant wind, burning sun
Terrain: sandy, coral island surrounded by a narrow fringing reef
Elevation extremes:
lowest point: Pacific Ocean 0 m
highest point: unnamed location 7 m
Natural resources: guano (deposits worked until late 1800s)
Land use:
arable land: 0%
permanent crops: 0%
permanent pastures: 0%
forests and woodland: 0%
other: 100%
Irrigated land: 0 sq km (1998)
Natural hazards: the narrow fringing reef surrounding the island can be a maritime hazard
Environment - current issues: no natural fresh water resources
Environment - international agreements:
party to: NA
signed, but not ratified: NA

Jarvis Island (continued)

Geography - note: sparse bunch grass, prostrate vines, and low-growing shrubs; primarily a nesting, roosting, and foraging habitat for seabirds, shorebirds, and marine wildlife

People

Population: uninhabited

note: Millersville settlement on western side of island occasionally used as a weather station from 1935 until World War II, when it was abandoned; reoccupied in 1957 during the International Geophysical Year by scientists who left in 1958; public entry is by special-use permit from US Fish and Wildlife Service only and generally restricted to scientists and educators; visited annually by US Fish and Wildlife Service

Government

Country name:
conventional long form: none
conventional short form: Jarvis Island
Data code: DQ
Dependency status: unincorporated territory of the US; administered from Washington, DC by the Fish and Wildlife Service of the US Department of the Interior as part of the National Wildlife Refuge system
Legal system: NA
Flag description: the flag of the US is used

Economy

Economy - overview: no economic activity

Transportation

Ports and harbors: none; offshore anchorage only; note - there is one boat landing area in the middle of the west coast and another near the southwest corner of the island
Transportation - note: there is a day beacon near the middle of the west coast

Military

Military - note: defense is the responsibility of the US; visited annually by the US Coast Guard

Transnational Issues

Disputes - international: none

Jersey
(British crown dependency)

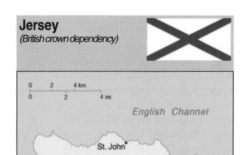

Geography

Location: Western Europe, island in the English Channel, northwest of France
Geographic coordinates: 49 15 N, 2 10 W
Map references: Europe
Area:
total: 116 sq km
land: 116 sq km
water: 0 sq km
Area - comparative: about 0.7 times the size of Washington, DC
Land boundaries: 0 km
Coastline: 70 km
Maritime claims:
exclusive fishing zone: 12 nm
territorial sea: 3 nm
Climate: temperate; mild winters and cool summers
Terrain: gently rolling plain with low, rugged hills along north coast
Elevation extremes:
lowest point: Atlantic Ocean 0 m
highest point: unnamed location 143 m
Natural resources: agricultural land
Land use:
arable land: 66%
permanent crops: NA%
permanent pastures: NA%
forests and woodland: NA%
other: 34%
Irrigated land: NA sq km
Natural hazards: NA
Environment - current issues: NA
Environment - international agreements:
party to: NA
signed, but not ratified: NA
Geography - note: largest and southernmost of Channel Islands; about 30% of population concentrated in Saint Helier

People

Population: 89,721 (July 1999 est.)
Age structure:
0-14 years: 18% (male 8,308; female 7,663)
15-64 years: 68% (male 30,168; female 30,754)
65 years and over: 14% (male 5,348; female 7,480) (1999 est.)
Population growth rate: 0.63% (1999 est.)
Birth rate: 11.85 births/1,000 population (1999 est.)
Death rate: 9.08 deaths/1,000 population (1999 est.)
Net migration rate: 3.49 migrant(s)/1,000 population (1999 est.)
Sex ratio:
at birth: 1.11 male(s)/female
under 15 years: 1.08 male(s)/female
15-64 years: 0.98 male(s)/female
65 years and over: 0.71 male(s)/female
total population: 0.95 male(s)/female (1999 est.)
Infant mortality rate: 2.76 deaths/1,000 live births (1999 est.)
Life expectancy at birth:
total population: 78.83 years
male: 76.08 years
female: 81.87 years (1999 est.)
Total fertility rate: 1.5 children born/woman (1999 est.)
Nationality:
noun: Channel Islander(s)
adjective: Channel Islander
Ethnic groups: UK and Norman-French descent
Religions: Anglican, Roman Catholic, Baptist, Congregational New Church, Methodist, Presbyterian
Languages: English (official), French (official), Norman-French dialect spoken in country districts
Literacy: NA

Government

Country name:
conventional long form: Bailiwick of Jersey
conventional short form: Jersey
Data code: JE
Dependency status: British crown dependency
Government type: NA
Capital: Saint Helier
Administrative divisions: none (British crown dependency)
Independence: none (British crown dependency)
National holiday: Liberation Day, 9 May (1945)
Constitution: unwritten; partly statutes, partly common law and practice
Legal system: English law and local statute
Suffrage: NA years of age; universal adult
Executive branch:
chief of state: Queen ELIZABETH II (since 6 February 1952)
head of government: Lieutenant Governor and Commander in Chief Sir Michael WILKES (since NA 1995) and Bailiff Philip Martin BAILHACHE (since NA 1995)
cabinet: committees appointed by the Assembly of the States

Jersey *(continued)*

elections: none; the monarch is hereditary; lieutenant governor and bailiff appointed by the monarch
Legislative branch: unicameral Assembly of the States (57 seats - 53 elected including 12 senators popularly elected for six-year terms, half retiring every third year, 12 constables popularly elected triennially, and 29 deputies popularly elected triennially)
elections: last held NA (next to be held NA)
election results: percent of vote - NA; seats - independents 52
Judicial branch: Royal Court, judges elected by an electoral college and the bailiff
Political parties and leaders: none; all independents
International organization participation: none
Diplomatic representation in the US: none (British crown dependency)
Diplomatic representation from the US: none (British crown dependency)
Flag description: white with the diagonal red cross of Saint Patrick (patron saint of Ireland) extending to the corners of the flag

Economy

Economy - overview: The economy is based largely on financial services, agriculture, and tourism. Potatoes, cauliflower, tomatoes, and especially flowers are important export crops, shipped mostly to the UK. The Jersey breed of dairy cattle is known worldwide and represents an important export earner. Milk products go to the UK and other EU countries. In 1996 the finance sector accounted for about 60% of the island's output. Tourism, another mainstay of the economy, accounts for 24% of GDP. In recent years, the government has encouraged light industry to locate in Jersey, with the result that an electronics industry has developed alongside the traditional manufacturing of knitwear. All raw material and energy requirements are imported, as well as a large share of Jersey's food needs. Light tax and death duties make the island a popular tax haven.
GDP: purchasing power parity - $NA
GDP - real growth rate: NA%
GDP - per capita: purchasing power parity - $NA
GDP - composition by sector:
agriculture: 5%
industry: 2%
services: 93% (1995)
Population below poverty line: NA%
Household income or consumption by percentage share:
lowest 10%: NA%
highest 10%: NA%
Inflation rate (consumer prices): 3.7% (1996)
Labor force: 57,050 (1996)
Unemployment rate: 0.7% (1996)
Budget:
revenues: $666.9 million
expenditures: $618.5 million, including capital expenditures of $128.4 million (1996 est.)
Industries: tourism, banking and finance, dairy
Industrial production growth rate: NA%

Electricity - production: NA kWh
Electricity - production by source:
fossil fuel: NA%
hydro: NA%
nuclear: NA%
other: NA%
Electricity - consumption: 467 million kWh (1995)
Electricity - exports: 0 kWh
Electricity - imports: NA kWh; note - much electricity supplied by France
Agriculture - products: potatoes, cauliflowers, tomatoes; beef, dairy products
Exports: $NA
Exports - commodities: light industrial and electrical goods, foodstuffs, textiles
Exports - partners: UK
Imports: $NA
Imports - commodities: machinery and transport equipment, manufactured goods, foodstuffs, mineral fuels, chemicals
Imports - partners: UK
Debt - external: none
Economic aid - recipient: none
Currency: 1 Jersey pound (£J) = 100 pence
Exchange rates: Jersey pounds (£J) per US$1 - 0.6057 (January 1999), 0.6037 (1998), 0.6106 (1997), 0.6403 (1996), 0.6335 (1995), 0.6529 (1994); the Jersey pound is at par with the British pound
Fiscal year: 1 April - 31 March

Communications

Telephones: 61,447 (1983 est.)
Telephone system:
domestic: NA
international: 3 submarine cables
Radio broadcast stations: AM 1, FM 1, shortwave 0
Radios: NA
Television broadcast stations: 1 (1997)
Televisions: NA

Transportation

Railways: 0 km
Highways:
total: 577 km (1995)
paved: NA km
unpaved: NA km
Ports and harbors: Gorey, Saint Aubin, Saint Helier
Merchant marine: none
Airports: 1 (1998 est.)
Airports - with paved runways:
total: 1
1,524 to 2,437 m: 1 (1998 est.)

Military

Military - note: defense is the responsibility of the UK

Transnational Issues

Disputes - international: none

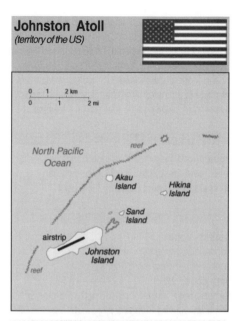

Johnston Atoll
(territory of the US)

Geography

Location: Oceania, atoll in the North Pacific Ocean, about one-third of the way from Hawaii to the Marshall Islands
Geographic coordinates: 16 45 N, 169 30 W
Map references: Oceania
Area:
total: 2.8 sq km
land: 2.8 sq km
water: 0 sq km
Area - comparative: about 4.7 times the size of The Mall in Washington, DC
Land boundaries: 0 km
Coastline: 10 km
Maritime claims:
exclusive economic zone: 200 nm
territorial sea: 12 nm
Climate: tropical, but generally dry; consistent northeast trade winds with little seasonal temperature variation
Terrain: mostly flat
Elevation extremes:
lowest point: Pacific Ocean 0 m
highest point: Summit Peak 5 m
Natural resources: NA; guano deposits worked until depletion about 1890
Land use:
arable land: 0%
permanent crops: 0%
permanent pastures: 0%
forests and woodland: 0%
other: 100%
Irrigated land: 0 sq km (1998)
Natural hazards: NA
Environment - current issues: no natural fresh water resources
Environment - international agreements:
party to: NA
signed, but not ratified: NA
Geography - note: strategic location in the North

Johnston Atoll (continued)

Pacific Ocean; Johnston Island and Sand Island are natural islands, which have been expanded by coral dredging; North Island (Akau) and East Island (Hikina) are manmade islands formed from coral dredging; closed to the public; former US nuclear weapons test site; site of Johnston Atoll Chemical Agent Disposal System (JACADS); some low-growing vegetation

People

Population: no indigenous inhabitants
note: there are 1,200 US military and civilian contractor personnel (January 1999 est.)

Government

Country name:
conventional long form: none
conventional short form: Johnston Atoll
Data code: JQ
Dependency status: unincorporated territory of the US; administered from Washington, DC, by the US Defense Threat Reduction Agency (DTRA) and managed cooperatively by DTRA and the Fish and Wildlife Service of the US Department of the Interior as part of the National Wildlife Refuge system
Legal system: NA
Flag description: the flag of the US is used

Economy

Economy - overview: Economic activity is limited to providing services to US military personnel and contractors located on the island. All food and manufactured goods must be imported.
Electricity - production: NAkWh
note: there are six 25,000 kWh generators supplied by the base operating support contractor
Electricity - consumption: NAkWh

Communications

Telephone system: 13 outgoing and 10 incoming commercial lines; adequate telecommunications
domestic: 60-channel submarine cable, 22 DSN circuits by satellite, Autodin with standard remote terminal, digital telephone switch, Military Affiliated Radio System (MARS station), UHF/VHF air-ground radio, a link to the Pacific Consolidated Telecommunications Network (PCTN) satellite
international: NA
Radio broadcast stations: AM NA, FM 5 channels; also 1 local volunteer FM radio station;, shortwave NA;
Television broadcast stations: commercial satellite television system, with 16 channels (1997)

Transportation

Ports and harbors: Johnston Island
Airports: 1 (1998 est.)
Airports - with paved runways:
total: 1
2,438 to 3,047 m: 1 (1998 est.)

Military

Military - note: defense is the responsibility of the US

Transnational Issues

Disputes - international: none

Jordan

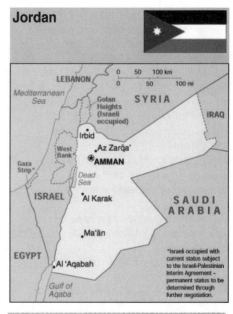

*Israeli occupied with current status subject to the Israeli-Palestinian Interim Agreement – permanent status to be determined through further negotiation.

Geography

Location: Middle East, northwest of Saudi Arabia
Geographic coordinates: 31 00 N, 36 00 E
Map references: Middle East
Area:
total: 89,213 sq km
land: 88,884 sq km
water: 329 sq km
Area - comparative: slightly smaller than Indiana
Land boundaries:
total: 1,619 km
border countries: Iraq 181 km, Israel 238 km, Saudi Arabia 728 km, Syria 375 km, West Bank 97 km
Coastline: 26 km
Maritime claims:
territorial sea: 3 nm
Climate: mostly arid desert; rainy season in west (November to April)
Terrain: mostly desert plateau in east, highland area in west; Great Rift Valley separates East and West Banks of the Jordan River
Elevation extremes:
lowest point: Dead Sea -408 m
highest point: Jabal Ram 1,754 m
Natural resources: phosphates, potash, shale oil
Land use:
arable land: 4%
permanent crops: 1%
permanent pastures: 9%
forests and woodland: 1%
other: 85% (1993 est.)
Irrigated land: 630 sq km (1993 est.)
Natural hazards: NA
Environment - current issues: limited natural fresh water resources; deforestation; overgrazing; soil erosion; desertification
Environment - international agreements:
party to: Biodiversity, Climate Change, Desertification, Endangered Species, Hazardous Wastes, Law of the Sea, Marine Dumping, Nuclear

Jordan (continued)

Test Ban, Ozone Layer Protection, Wetlands
signed, but not ratified: none of the selected agreements

P e o p l e

Population: 4,561,147 (July 1999 est.)
Age structure:
0-14 years: 43% (male 1,005,211; female 954,968)
15-64 years: 54% (male 1,265,116; female 1,200,372)
65 years and over: 3% (male 67,852; female 67,628) (1999 est.)
Population growth rate: 3.05% (1999 est.)
Birth rate: 34.31 births/1,000 population (1999 est.)
Death rate: 3.85 deaths/1,000 population (1999 est.)
Net migration rate: 0 migrant(s)/1,000 population (1999 est.)
Sex ratio:
at birth: 1.06 male(s)/female
under 15 years: 1.05 male(s)/female
15-64 years: 1.05 male(s)/female
65 years and over: 1 male(s)/female
total population: 1.05 male(s)/female (1999 est.)
Infant mortality rate: 32.7 deaths/1,000 live births (1999 est.)
Life expectancy at birth:
total population: 73.06 years
male: 71.15 years
female: 75.08 years (1999 est.)
Total fertility rate: 4.64 children born/woman (1999 est.)
Nationality:
noun: Jordanian(s)
adjective: Jordanian
Ethnic groups: Arab 98%, Circassian 1%, Armenian 1%
Religions: Sunni Muslim 96%, Christian 4% (1997 est.)
Languages: Arabic (official), English widely understood among upper and middle classes
Literacy:
definition: age 15 and over can read and write
total population: 86.6%
male: 93.4%
female: 79.4% (1995 est.)

G o v e r n m e n t

Country name:
conventional long form: Hashemite Kingdom of Jordan
conventional short form: Jordan
local long form: Al Mamlakah al Urduniyah al Hashimiyah
local short form: Al Urdun
former: Transjordan
Data code: JO
Government type: constitutional monarchy
Capital: Amman
Administrative divisions: 12 governorates (muhafazat, singular - muhafazah); Ajlun, Al 'Aqabah, Al Balqa', Al Karak, Al Mafraq, 'Amman, At Tafilah, Az Zarqa', Irbid, Jarash, Ma'an, Madaba
Independence: 25 May 1946 (from League of Nations mandate under British administration)
National holiday: Independence Day, 25 May (1946)
Constitution: 8 January 1952
Legal system: based on Islamic law and French codes; judicial review of legislative acts in a specially provided High Tribunal; has not accepted compulsory ICJ jurisdiction
Suffrage: 20 years of age; universal
Executive branch:
chief of state: King ABDULLAH II (since 7 February 1999)
head of government: Prime Minister Fayez TARAWNEH (since 20 August 1998)
cabinet: Cabinet appointed by the prime minister in consultation with the monarch
elections: none; the monarch is hereditary; prime minister appointed by the monarch
Legislative branch: bicameral National Assembly or Majlis al-'Umma consists of the Senate (a 40-member body appointed by the monarch from designated categories of public figures; members serve four-year terms) and the House of Representatives (80 seats; members elected by popular vote on the basis of proportional representation to serve four-year terms)
elections: House of Representatives - last held 4 November 1997 (next to be held NA November 2001)
election results: House of Representatives - percent of vote by party - NA; seats by party - National Constitutional Party 2, Arab Land Party 1, independents 75, other 2
note: the House of Representatives has been convened and dissolved by the monarch several times since 1974; in November 1989 the first parliamentary elections in 22 years were held
Judicial branch: Court of Cassation
Political parties and leaders: Al-Ahrar (Freedom) Party [Dr. Ahmad ZO'BI, secretary general]; Arab Ba'th Progressive Party [Mahmoud al-MA'AYTAH, secretary general]; Arab Islamic Democratic Party (Doa'a) [Yousif ABU BAKR, secretary general]; Arab Jordanian Ansar Party [Muhammad MAJALI, secretary general]; Arab Land Party [Dr. Muhammad al-'ORAN, secretary general]; Democratic Party of the Left [Musa MA'AITAH, secretary general]; Islamic Action Front [Dr. Ishaq al-FARHAN, secretary general]; Jordanian Arab Constitutional Front Party [Milhem TELL, secretary general]; Jordanian Ba'th Arab Socialist Party [Tayseer al-HOMSI, secretary general]; Jordanian Communist Party [Ya'acoub ZAYADIN, secretary general]; Jordanian Democratic Popular Unity Party [Sa'eed MUSTAPHA, secretary general]; Jordanian Labor Party [Muhammad KHATAYIBAH, secretary general]; Jordanian Peace Party [Dr. Shaher KHREIS, secretary general]; Jordanian People's Democratic Party or HASHD [Salem NAHHAS, secretary general]; Al-Mustaqbal (Future) Party [Suleiman 'ARAR, secretary general]; National Action Party or Haqq [Muhammad ZO'BI, secretary general]; National Constitutional Party [Abdul Hadi MAJALI, secretary general]; National Democratic Public Movement Party [Muhammad al-'AMER, secretary general]; Progressive Party [Na'el BARAKAT, secretary general]; Al-Umma (Nation) Party [Ahmad HNEIDI, secretary general]
International organization participation: ABEDA, ACC, AFESD, AL, AMF, CAEU, CCC, ESCWA, FAO, G-77, IAEA, IBRD, ICAO, ICC, ICFTU, ICRM, IDA, IDB, IFAD, IFC, IFRCS, ILO, IMF, IMO, Intelsat, Interpol, IOC, IOM (observer), ISO (correspondent), ITU, MONUA, NAM, OIC, OPCW, PCA, UN, UNCTAD, UNESCO, UNIDO, UNMIBH, UNMOP, UNMOT, UNOMIG, UNPREDEP, UNRWA, UPU, WFTU, WHO, WIPO, WMO, WToO, WTrO (applicant)
Diplomatic representation in the US:
chief of mission: Ambassador Marwan Jamil MUASHIR
chancery: 3504 International Drive NW, Washington, DC 20008
telephone: [1] (202) 966-2664
FAX: [1] (202) 966-3110
Diplomatic representation from the US:
chief of mission: Ambassador William BURNS
embassy: Jabel Amman, Amman
mailing address: P. O. Box 354, Amman 11118 Jordan; APO AE 09892-0200
telephone: [962] (6) 5920101
FAX: [962] (6) 5927712
Flag description: three equal horizontal bands of black (top), white, and green with a red isosceles triangle based on the hoist side bearing a small white seven-pointed star; the seven points on the star represent the seven fundamental laws of the Koran

E c o n o m y

Economy - overview: Jordan is a small Arab country with inadequate supplies of water and other natural resources such as oil and coal. Jordan benefited from increased Arab aid during the oil boom of the late 1970s and early 1980s, when its annual real GNP growth averaged more than 10%. In the remainder of the 1980s, however, reductions in both Arab aid and worker remittances slowed real economic growth to an average of roughly 2% per year. Imports - mainly oil, capital goods, consumer durables, and food - outstripped exports, with the difference covered by aid, remittances, and borrowing. In mid-1989, the Jordanian Government began debt-rescheduling negotiations and agreed to implement an IMF-supported program designed to gradually reduce the budget deficit and implement badly needed structural reforms. The Persian Gulf crisis that began in August 1990, however, aggravated Jordan's already serious economic problems, forcing the government to shelve the IMF program, stop most debt payments, and suspend rescheduling negotiations. Aid from Gulf Arab states, worker remittances, and trade contracted; and refugees flooded the country, producing serious balance-of-payments problems, stunting GDP growth, and straining government resources. The economy rebounded in 1992, largely due to the influx of capital repatriated by workers returning from the Gulf, but recovery was uneven. A preliminary agreement with the IMF in early 1999 will provide new loans over the next three years. Sluggish growth, along with debt, poverty, and unemployment are fundamental ongoing economic problems.

GDP: purchasing power parity - $15.5 billion (1998 est.)

GDP - real growth rate: 2.2% (1998 est.)

GDP - per capita: purchasing power parity - $3,500 (1998 est.)

GDP - composition by sector:
agriculture: 6%
industry: 30%
services: 64% (1995 est.)

Population below poverty line: 30% (1998 est.)

Household income or consumption by percentage share:
lowest 10%: 2.4%
highest 10%: 34.7% (1991)

Inflation rate (consumer prices): 4% (1998 est.)

Labor force: 1.15 million
note: in addition, there are 300,000 foreign workers (1997 est.)

Labor force - by occupation: industry 11.4%, commerce, restaurants, and hotels 10.5%, construction 10%, transport and communications 8.7%, agriculture 7.4%, other services 52% (1992)

Unemployment rate: 15% official rate; note - actual rate is 25%-30% (1998 est.)

Budget:
revenues: $2.8 billion
expenditures: $3 billion, including capital expenditures of $672 million (1999 est.)

Industries: phosphate mining, petroleum refining, cement, potash, light manufacturing

Industrial production growth rate: -3.4% (1996)

Electricity - production: 5.52 billion kWh (1996)

Electricity - production by source:
fossil fuel: 99.64%
hydro: 0.36%
nuclear: 0%
other: 0% (1996)

Electricity - consumption: 5.52 billion kWh (1996)

Electricity - exports: 0 kWh (1996)

Electricity - imports: 0 kWh (1996)

Agriculture - products: wheat, barley, citrus, tomatoes, melons, olives; sheep, goats, poultry

Exports: $1.5 billion (f.o.b., 1997 est.)

Exports - commodities: phosphates, fertilizers, potash, agricultural products, manufactures

Exports - partners: Iraq, India, Saudi Arabia, EU, Indonesia, UAE, Syria, Ethiopia

Imports: $3.9 billion (c.i.f., 1997 est.)

Imports - commodities: crude oil, machinery, transport equipment, food, live animals, manufactured goods

Imports - partners: EU, Iraq, US, Japan, Turkey, Malaysia, Syria, China

Debt - external: $7.5 billion (1998 est.)

Economic aid - recipient: $1.097 billion (1995); note - received $320 million from ODA in 1998 (est.)

Currency: 1 Jordanian dinar (JD) = 1,000 fils

Exchange rates: Jordanian dinars (JD) per US$1 - 0.7090 (January 1999-1996), 0.7005 (1995), 0.6987 (1994), 0.6928 (1993)
note: since May 1989, the dinar has been pegged to a basket of currencies

Fiscal year: calendar year

Communications

Telephones: 425,000 (1998)

Telephone system:
domestic: microwave radio relay, coaxial and fiber-optic cable, and cellular; Jordan has two cellular telephone providers (with approximately 50,000 subscribers in 1998), ten data service providers, and four Internet service providers (with approximately 8,000 subscribers in 1998)
international: satellite earth stations - 3 Intelsat, 1 Arabsat, and 29 land and maritime Inmarsat terminals (1996); coaxial cable, fiber-optic cable, and microwave radio relay to Iraq, Saudi Arabia, Syria, and Israel; building a Red Sea Fiber-Optic Link Around the Globe (FLAG) fiber-optic submarine cable link and planning to update links with Saudi Arabia and Israel to fiber-optic cable; 4,000 international circuits (1998 est.); participant in Medarabtel

Radio broadcast stations: AM 6, FM 7, shortwave 1 (1998 est.)

Radios: 1.1 million (1992 est.)

Television broadcast stations: 8 (in addition, there are approximately 42 repeaters and 1 TV receive-only satellite link) (1997)

Televisions: 350,000 (1992 est.)

Transportation

Railways:
total: 677 km
narrow gauge: 677 km 1.050-m gauge; note - an additional 110 km stretch of the old Hejaz railroad is out of use (1998 est.)

Highways:
total: 8,000 km
paved: 8,000 km
unpaved: 0 km (1998 est.)

Pipelines: crude oil 209 km

Ports and harbors: Al 'Aqabah

Merchant marine:
total: 7 ships (1,000 GRT or over) totaling 42,746 GRT/59,100 DWT
ships by type: bulk 2, cargo 2, container 1, livestock carrier 1, roll-on/roll-off cargo 1 (1998 est.)

Airports: 17 (1998 est.)

Airports - with paved runways:
total: 14
over 3,047 m: 9
2,438 to 3,047 m: 4
under 914 m: 1 (1998 est.)

Airports - with unpaved runways:
total: 3
914 to 1,523 m: 1
under 914 m: 2 (1998 est.)

Military

Military branches: Jordanian Armed Forces (JAF; includes Royal Jordanian Land Force, Royal Naval Force, and Royal Jordanian Air Force); Badiya (irregular) Border Guards; Ministry of the Interior's Public Security Force (falls under JAF only in wartime or crisis situations)

Military manpower - military age: 18 years of age

Military manpower - availability:
males age 15-49: 1,113,998 (1999 est.)

Military manpower - fit for military service:
males age 15-49: 793,002 (1999 est.)

Military manpower - reaching military age annually:
males: 49,954 (1999 est.)

Military expenditures - dollar figure: $608.9 million (FY 98)

Military expenditures - percent of GDP: 7.8% (1997)

Transnational Issues

Disputes - international: none

Juan de Nova Island
(possession of France)

Geography

Location: Southern Africa, island in the Mozambique Channel, about one-third of the way between Madagascar and Mozambique
Geographic coordinates: 17 03 S, 42 45 E
Map references: Africa
Area:
total: 4.4 sq km
land: 4.4 sq km
water: 0 sq km
Area - comparative: about seven times the size of The Mall in Washington, DC
Land boundaries: 0 km
Coastline: 24.1 km
Maritime claims:
contiguous zone: 12 nm
continental shelf: 200-m depth or to depth the of exploitation
exclusive economic zone: 200 nm
territorial sea: 12 nm
Climate: tropical
Terrain: NA
Elevation extremes:
lowest point: Indian Ocean 0 m
highest point: unnamed location 10 m
Natural resources: guano deposits and other fertilizers
Land use:
arable land: 0%
permanent crops: 0%
permanent pastures: 0%
forests and woodland: 90%
other: 10%
Irrigated land: 0 sq km (1993)
Natural hazards: periodic cyclones
Environment - current issues: NA
Environment - international agreements:
party to: NA
signed, but not ratified: NA
Geography - note: wildlife sanctuary

People

Population: uninhabited

Government

Country name:
conventional long form: none
conventional short form: Juan de Nova Island
local long form: none
local short form: Ile Juan de Nova
Data code: JU
Dependency status: possession of France; administered by a high commissioner of the Republic, resident in Reunion
Legal system: NA
Diplomatic representation in the US: none (possession of France)
Diplomatic representation from the US: none (possession of France)
Flag description: the flag of France is used

Economy

Economy - overview: no economic activity

Transportation

Railways:
total: NA km; short line going to a jetty
Ports and harbors: none; offshore anchorage only
Airports: 1 (1998 est.)
Airports - with unpaved runways:
total: 1
914 to 1,523 m: 1 (1998 est.)

Military

Military - note: defense is the responsibility of France

Transnational Issues

Disputes - international: claimed by Madagascar

Kazakhstan

Introduction

Background: As a republic within the USSR (1920-91), Kazakhstan suffered greatly from Stalinist purges, from environmental damage, and saw the ethnic Russian portion of its population rise to 37% while other non-Kazakhs made up almost 20%. Current issues include the pace of market reform and privatization; fair and free elections and democratic reform; ethnic differences between Russians and Kazakhs; environmental problems; and how to convert the country's abundant energy resources into a better standard of living.

Geography

Location: Central Asia, northwest of China
Geographic coordinates: 48 00 N, 68 00 E
Map references: Commonwealth of Independent States
Area:
total: 2,717,300 sq km
land: 2,669,800 sq km
water: 47,500 sq km
Area - comparative: slightly less than four times the size of Texas
Land boundaries:
total: 12,012 km
border countries: China 1,533 km, Kyrgyzstan 1,051 km, Russia 6,846 km, Turkmenistan 379 km, Uzbekistan 2,203 km
Coastline: 0 km (landlocked)
note: Kazakhstan borders the Aral Sea, now split into two bodies of water (1,070 km), and the Caspian Sea (1,894 km)
Maritime claims: none (landlocked)
Climate: continental, cold winters and hot summers, arid and semiarid
Terrain: extends from the Volga to the Altai Mountains and from the plains in western Siberia to oases and desert in Central Asia
Elevation extremes:
lowest point: Vpadina Kaundy -132 m

highest point: Zhengis Shingy (Pik Khan-Tengri) 6,995 m
Natural resources: major deposits of petroleum, natural gas, coal, iron ore, manganese, chrome ore, nickel, cobalt, copper, molybdenum, lead, zinc, bauxite, gold, uranium
Land use:
arable land: 12%
permanent crops: 11%
permanent pastures: 57%
forests and woodland: 4%
other: 16% (1996 est.)
Irrigated land: 22,000 sq km (1996 est.)
Natural hazards: earthquakes in the south, mudslides around Almaty
Environment - current issues: radioactive or toxic chemical sites associated with its former defense industries and test ranges are found throughout the country and pose health risks for humans and animals; industrial pollution is severe in some cities; because the two main rivers which flowed into the Aral Sea have been diverted for irrigation, it is drying up and leaving behind a harmful layer of chemical pesticides and natural salts; these substances are then picked up by the wind and blown into noxious dust storms; pollution in the Caspian Sea; soil pollution from overuse of agricultural chemicals and salination from faulty irrigation practices
Environment - international agreements:
party to: Biodiversity, Climate Change, Desertification, Ozone Layer Protection, Ship Pollution
signed, but not ratified: none of the selected agreements
Geography - note: landlocked

People

Population: 16,824,825 (July 1999 est.)
Age structure:
0-14 years: 28% (male 2,432,519; female 2,359,375)
15-64 years: 65% (male 5,279,877; female 5,580,271)

65 years and over: 7% (male 392,934; female 779,849) (1999 est.)
Population growth rate: -0.09% (1999 est.)
Birth rate: 17.16 births/1,000 population (1999 est.)
Death rate: 10.34 deaths/1,000 population (1999 est.)
Net migration rate: -7.73 migrant(s)/1,000 population (1999 est.)
Sex ratio:
at birth: 1.05 male(s)/female
under 15 years: 1.03 male(s)/female
15-64 years: 0.95 male(s)/female
65 years and over: 0.5 male(s)/female
total population: 0.93 male(s)/female (1999 est.)
Infant mortality rate: 58.82 deaths/1,000 live births (1999 est.)
Life expectancy at birth:
total population: 63.39 years
male: 57.92 years
female: 69.13 years (1999 est.)
Total fertility rate: 2.09 children born/woman (1999 est.)
Nationality:
noun: Kazakhstani(s)
adjective: Kazakhstani
Ethnic groups: Kazakh (Qazaq) 46%, Russian 34.7%, Ukrainian 4.9%, German 3.1%, Uzbek 2.3%, Tatar 1.9%, other 7.1% (1996)
Religions: Muslim 47%, Russian Orthodox 44%, Protestant 2%, other 7%
Languages: Kazakh (Qazaq) (state language) 40%, Russian (official, used in everyday business) 66%
Literacy:
definition: age 15 and over can read and write
total population: 98%
male: 99%
female: 96% (1989 est.)

Government

Country name:
conventional long form: Republic of Kazakhstan
conventional short form: Kazakhstan
local long form: Qazaqstan Respublikasy
local short form: none
former: Kazakh Soviet Socialist Republic
Data code: KZ
Government type: republic
Capital: Astana
note: the government moved from Almaty to Astana in December 1998
Administrative divisions: 14 oblystar (singular - oblysy) and 3 cities (qala, singular - qalasy)*; Almaty, Almaty*, Aqmola (Astana), Aqtobe, Astana*, Atyrau, Batys Qazaqstan (Oral), Bayqongyr*, Mangghystau (Aqtau; formerly Gur'yev), Ongtustik Qazaqstan (Shymkent), Pavlodar, Qaraghandy, Qostanay, Qyzylorda, Shyghys Qazaqstan (Oskemen; formerly Ust'-Kamenogorsk), Soltustik Qazaqstan (Petropavl), Zhambyl (Taraz; formerly Dzhambul)
note: administrative divisions have the same names as their administrative centers (exceptions have the administrative center name following in parentheses);

Kazakhstan (continued)

in 1995 the Governments of Kazakhstan and Russia entered into an agreement whereby Russia would lease for a period of 20 years an area of 6,000 sq km enclosing the Bayqongyr (Baykonur) space launch facilities and the city of Bayqongyr (formerly Leninsk)

Independence: 16 December 1991 (from the Soviet Union)

National holiday: Day of the Republic, 25 October (1990) (date on which Kazakhstan declared its sovereignty)

Constitution: adopted by national referendum 30 August 1995; first post-independence constitution was adopted 28 January 1993

Legal system: based on civil law system

Suffrage: 18 years of age; universal

Executive branch:

chief of state: President Nursultan A. NAZARBAYEV (chairman of the Supreme Soviet from 22 February 1990-91, president since 1 December 1991)

head of government: Prime Minister Nurlan BALGIMBAYEV (since 10 October 1997) and First Deputy Prime Minister Uraz ZHANDOSOV (since 20 February 1998)

cabinet: Council of Ministers appointed by the president

elections: president elected by popular vote for a seven-year term; election last held 10 January 1999, a year before it was previously scheduled (next to be held NA 2006); note - President NAZARBAYEV's previous term had been extended to 2000 by a nationwide referendum held 30 April 1995; prime minister and first deputy prime minister appointed by the president

election results: Nursultan A. NAZARBAYEV elected president; percent of vote - Nursultan NAZARBAYEV 82%, Serikbolsyn ABDILDIN 12%

note: President NAZARBAYEV expanded his presidential powers by decree: only he can initiate constitutional amendments, appoint and dismiss the government, dissolve Parliament, call referenda at his discretion, and appoint administrative heads of regions and cities

Legislative branch: bicameral Parliament consists of the Senate (47 seats; 7 senators are appointed by the president; other members are popularly elected, two from each oblast and Almaty, to serve four-year terms) and the Majilis (67 seats; members are popularly elected to serve four-year terms); note - with the oblasts being reduced to 14, the Senate will eventually be reduced to 37

elections: Senate - (indirect) last held 5 December 1995 (next to be held NA 1999); Majilis - last held 9 December and 23 December 1995 (next to be held NA 1999)

election results: Senate - percent of vote by party - NA; seats by party - party members 13, no party affiliation 34, of which "independent" state officials 25, nominated by the president 7, elected by popular vote 15; Majilis - percent of vote by party - NA; seats by party - PUP 24, December National Democratic Party 12, Kazakhstan Agrarian Union 5, Confederation of

Kazakh Trade Unions 5, KPK 2, independents and others 19

Judicial branch: Supreme Court (44 members); Constitutional Council (7 members)

Political parties and leaders: People's Unity Party or PUP (was Union of People's Unity) [Akhan BIZHANOV, chairman]; People's Congress of Kazakhstan or NKK [Anuar ISMAILOV, chairman]; AZAMAT Movement [Petr SVOIK, Murat AUEZOV, and Galym ABILSIITOV, cochairmen]; Communist Party or KPK [Serikbolsyn ABDILDIN, first secretary]; December National Democratic Party [Hasen KOZHAKHMETOV, chairman]; Labor and Workers Movement [Madel ISMAILOV, chairman]; Republican People's Slavic Movement-Harmony or Lad [Aleksander SAMARKIN, chairman]; Russian Center or RT [Nina SIDOROVA, chairwoman]; Pensioners Movement or Pokoleniye [Irina SAVOSTINA, chairwoman]; Kazakhstan Agrarian Union [leader NA]; Confederation of Kazakh Trade Unions [leader NA]

Political pressure groups and leaders: Independent Trade Union Center [Leonid SOLOMIN, president]; Kazakhstan International Bureau on Human Rights [Yevgeniy ZHOVTIS, executive director]; Democratic Committee on Human Rights [Baretta YERGALIEVA, chairwoman]; Independent Miners Union [Victor GAIPOV, president]; The Almaty-Helsinki Foundation for Human Rights [Ninel FOKINA, chairwoman]; Legal Development of Kazakhstan [Vitaliy VORONOV, chairman]

International organization participation: AsDB, CCC, CIS, EAPC, EBRD, ECE, ECO, ESCAP, FAO, IAEA, IBRD, ICAO, IDA, IFC, ILO, IMF, IMO, Intelsat, Interpol, IOC, IOM (observer), ITU, OAS (observer), OIC, OPCW, OSCE, PFP, UN, UNCTAD, UNESCO, UPU, WFTU, WHO, WIPO, WMO, WToO, WTrO (applicant)

Diplomatic representation in the US:

chief of mission: Ambassador Bolat K. NURGALIYEV

chancery: 1401 16th Street, NW, Washington, DC 20036

telephone: [1] (202) 232-5488

FAX: [1] (202) 232-5845

consulate(s): New York

Diplomatic representation from the US:

chief of mission: Ambassador Richard H. JONES

embassy: 99/97A Furmanova Street, Almaty, Republic of Kazakhstan 480091

mailing address: American Embassy Almaty, Department of State, Washington, DC 20521-7030

telephone: [7] (3272) 63-39-21, 63-13-75, 50-76-23

FAX: [7] (3272) 63-38-83

Flag description: sky blue background representing the endless sky and a gold sun with 32 rays soaring above a golden steppe eagle in the center; on the hoist side is a "national ornamentation" in yellow

Economy

Economy - overview: Kazakhstan, the second largest of the former Soviet republics in territory, possesses enormous untapped fossil fuel reserves as

well as plentiful supplies of other minerals and metals. It also has considerable agricultural potential with its vast steppe lands accommodating both livestock and grain production. Kazakhstan's industrial sector rests on the extraction and processing of these natural resources and also on a relatively large machine building sector specializing in construction equipment, tractors, agricultural machinery, and some defense items. The breakup of the USSR and the collapse of demand for Kazakhstan's traditional heavy industry products have resulted in a sharp contraction of the economy since 1991, with the steepest annual decline occurring in 1994. In 1995-97 the pace of the government program of economic reform and privatization quickened, resulting in a substantial shifting of assets into the private sector. The December 1996 signing of the Caspian Pipeline Consortium agreement to build a new pipeline from western Kazakhstan's Tengiz oil field to the Black Sea increases prospects for substantially larger oil exports in several years. Kazakhstan's economy turned downward in 1998 with a 2.5% decline in GDP growth due to slumping oil prices and the August financial crisis in Russia. 1999 will also be a difficult year.

GDP: purchasing power parity - $52.9 billion (1998 est.)

GDP - real growth rate: -2.5% (1998 est.)

GDP - per capita: purchasing power parity - $3,100 (1998 est.)

GDP - composition by sector:

agriculture: 11.5%

industry: 32.6%

services: 55.9% (1997 est.)

Population below poverty line: NA%

Household income or consumption by percentage share:

lowest 10%: 3.1%

highest 10%: 24.9% (1993)

Inflation rate (consumer prices): 10% (1998 est.)

Labor force: 8.8 million (1997)

Labor force - by occupation: industry 27%, agriculture and forestry 23%, other 50% (1996)

Unemployment rate: 13.7% (1998 est.)

Budget:

revenues: $2.9 billion

expenditures: $4.2 billion, including capital expenditures of $NA (1998 est.)

Industries: oil, coal, iron ore, manganese, chromite, lead, zinc, copper, titanium, bauxite, gold, silver, phosphates, sulfur, iron and steel, nonferrous metal, tractors and other agricultural machinery, electric motors, construction materials; much of industrial capacity is shut down and/or is in need of repair

Industrial production growth rate: -2.1% (1998 est.)

Electricity - production: 52 billion kWh (1997)

Electricity - production by source:

fossil fuel: 86.3%

hydro: 13.6%

nuclear: 0.1%

other: 0% (1997)

Electricity - consumption: 64.34 billion kWh (1996)

Kazakhstan *(continued)*

Electricity - exports: 1.75 billion kWh (1996)
Electricity - imports: 8.5 billion kWh (1996)
Agriculture - products: grain (mostly spring wheat), cotton; wool, livestock
Exports: $6.3 billion (1998 est.)
Exports - commodities: oil, ferrous and nonferrous metals, chemicals, grain, wool, meat, coal
Exports - partners: Russia, UK, Ukraine, Uzbekistan, Netherlands, China, Italy, Germany (1997)
Imports: $7.4 billion (1998 est.)
Imports - commodities: machinery and parts, industrial materials, oil and gas, consumer goods
Imports - partners: Russia, Ukraine, US, Uzbekistan, Turkey, UK, Germany, South Korea (1997)
Debt - external: $3.1 billion (1998 est.)
Economic aid - recipient: $409.6 million (1995)
Currency: 1 Kazakhstani tenge = 100 tiyn
Exchange rates: tenges per US$1 - 85.2 (February 1999), 78.30 (1998), 75.44 (1997), 67.30 (1996), 60.95 (1995), 35.54 (1994)
Fiscal year: calendar year

Communications

Telephones: 2 million (1997)
Telephone system: service is poor
domestic: landline and microwave radio relay; AMPS standard cellular systems are available in most of Kazakhstan
international: international traffic with other former Soviet republics and China carried by landline and microwave radio relay and with other countries by satellite and through 8 international telecommunications circuits at the Moscow international gateway switch; satellite earth stations - 1 Intelsat and a new digital satellite earth station established at Almaty; a third satellite earth station at Atyrau provides teleconnectivity to the AT&T network via Intelsat; cable connected by the Trans-Asia-Europe Fiber-Optic Line
Radio broadcast stations: AM NA, FM NA, shortwave NA
Radios: 4.088 million (with multiple speakers for program diffusion 6.082 million)
Television broadcast stations: 20 (of which at least eight are government stations and at least 12 are private stations - seven of those are satellite TV relay stations) (1997)
Televisions: 4.75 million

Transportation

Railways:
total: 14,400 km in common carrier service; does not include industrial lines
broad gauge: 14,400 km 1.520-m gauge (3,299 km electrified) (1997)
Highways:
total: 141,000 km
paved: 104,200 km
unpaved: 36,800 km (1997 est.)

Waterways: 3,900 km on the Syrdariya (Syr Darya) and Ertis (Irtysh)
Pipelines: crude oil 2,850 km; refined products 1,500 km; natural gas 3,480 km (1992)
Ports and harbors: Aqtau (Shevchenko), Atyrau (Gur'yev), Oskemen (Ust-Kamenogorsk), Pavlodar, Semey (Semipalatinsk)
Airports: 10 (1997 est.)
Airports - with paved runways:
total: 9
over 3,047 m: 4
2,438 to 3,047 m: 3
1,524 to 2,437 m: 2 (1997 est.)
Airports - with unpaved runways:
total: 1
914 to 1,523 m: 1 (1997 est.)

Military

Military branches: General Purpose Forces (Army), Air Force, Border Guards, Navy, Republican Guard
Military manpower - military age: 18 years of age
Military manpower - availability:
males age 15-49: 4,450,258 (1999 est.)
Military manpower - fit for military service:
males age 15-49: 3,550,645 (1999 est.)
Military manpower - reaching military age annually:
males: 155,767 (1999 est.)
Military expenditures - dollar figure: $232.4 million (1998)
Military expenditures - percent of GDP: 1% (1998)

Transnational Issues

Disputes - international: Caspian Sea boundaries are not yet determined among Azerbaijan, Iran, Kazakhstan, Russia, and Turkmenistan; Russia leases approximately 6,000 sq km of territory enclosing the Baykonur Cosmodrome
Illicit drugs: significant illicit cultivation of cannabis and limited cultivation of opium poppy and ephedra (for the drug ephedrone); limited government eradication program; cannabis consumed largely in the CIS; used as transshipment point for illicit drugs to Russia, North America, and Western Europe from Southwest Asia

Kenya

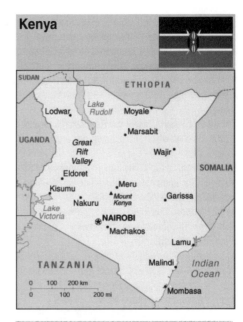

Geography

Location: Eastern Africa, bordering the Indian Ocean, between Somalia and Tanzania
Geographic coordinates: 1 00 N, 38 00 E
Map references: Africa
Area:
total: 582,650 sq km
land: 569,250 sq km
water: 13,400 sq km
Area - comparative: slightly more than twice the size of Nevada
Land boundaries:
total: 3,446 km
border countries: Ethiopia 830 km, Somalia 682 km, Sudan 232 km, Tanzania 769 km, Uganda 933 km
Coastline: 536 km
Maritime claims:
continental shelf: 200-m depth or to the depth of exploitation
exclusive economic zone: 200 nm
territorial sea: 12 nm
Climate: varies from tropical along coast to arid in interior
Terrain: low plains rise to central highlands bisected by Great Rift Valley; fertile plateau in west
Elevation extremes:
lowest point: Indian Ocean 0 m
highest point: Mount Kenya 5,199 m
Natural resources: gold, limestone, soda ash, salt barites, rubies, fluorspar, garnets, wildlife
Land use:
arable land: 7%
permanent crops: 1%
permanent pastures: 37%
forests and woodland: 30%
other: 25% (1993 est.)
Irrigated land: 660 sq km (1993 est.)
Natural hazards: recurring drought in northern and eastern regions; flooding during rainy seasons
Environment - current issues: water pollution from

urban and industrial wastes; degradation of water quality from increased use of pesticides and fertilizers; deforestation; soil erosion; desertification; poaching

Environment - international agreements:
party to: Biodiversity, Climate Change, Desertification, Endangered Species, Law of the Sea, Marine Dumping, Marine Life Conservation, Nuclear Test Ban, Ozone Layer Protection, Ship Pollution, Wetlands, Whaling
signed, but not ratified: none of the selected agreements

Geography - note: the Kenyan Highlands comprise one of the most successful agricultural production regions in Africa; glaciers on Mt. Kenya; unique physiography supports abundant and varied wildlife of scientific and economic value

People

Population: 28,808,658 (July 1999 est.)
Age structure:
0-14 years: 43% (male 6,244,321; female 6,104,181)
15-64 years: 54% (male 7,845,083; female 7,826,442)
65 years and over: 3% (male 343,449; female 445,182) (1999 est.)
Population growth rate: 1.59% (1999 est.)
Birth rate: 30.8 births/1,000 population (1999 est.)
Death rate: 14.58 deaths/1,000 population (1999 est.)
Net migration rate: -0.34 migrant(s)/1,000 population (1999 est.)
Sex ratio:
at birth: 1.03 male(s)/female
under 15 years: 1.02 male(s)/female
15-64 years: 1 male(s)/female
65 years and over: 0.77 male(s)/female
total population: 1 male(s)/female (1999 est.)
Infant mortality rate: 59.07 deaths/1,000 live births (1999 est.)
Life expectancy at birth:
total population: 47.02 years
male: 46.56 years
female: 47.49 years (1999 est.)
Total fertility rate: 3.88 children born/woman (1999 est.)
Nationality:
noun: Kenyan(s)
adjective: Kenyan
Ethnic groups: Kikuyu 22%, Luhya 14%, Luo 13%, Kalenjin 12%, Kamba 11%, Kisii 6%, Meru 6%, other African 15%, non-African (Asian, European, and Arab) 1%
Religions: Protestant 38%, Roman Catholic 28%, indigenous beliefs 26%, Muslim 7%, other 1%
Languages: English (official), Swahili (official), numerous indigenous languages
Literacy:
definition: age 15 and over can read and write
total population: 78.1%
male: 86.3%
female: 70% (1995 est.)

Government

Country name:
conventional long form: Republic of Kenya
conventional short form: Kenya
former: British East Africa
Data code: KE
Government type: republic
Capital: Nairobi
Administrative divisions: 7 provinces and 1 area*; Central, Coast, Eastern, Nairobi Area*, North Eastern, Nyanza, Rift Valley, Western
Independence: 12 December 1963 (from UK)
National holiday: Independence Day, 12 December (1963)
Constitution: 12 December 1963, amended as a republic 1964; reissued with amendments 1979, 1983, 1986, 1988, 1991, 1992, and 1997
Legal system: based on English common law, tribal law, and Islamic law; judicial review in High Court; accepts compulsory ICJ jurisdiction, with reservations; constitutional amendment of 1982 making Kenya a de jure one-party state repealed in 1991
Suffrage: 18 years of age; universal
Executive branch:
chief of state: President Daniel Toroitich arap MOI (since 14 October 1978); note - the president is both the chief of state and head of government
head of government: President Daniel Toroitich arap MOI (since 14 October 1978); note - the president is both the chief of state and head of government
cabinet: Cabinet appointed by the president
elections: president elected by popular vote from among the members of the National Assembly for a five-year term; election last held 29 December 1997 (next to be held by early 2003); vice president appointed by the president
election results: President Daniel T. arap MOI reelected; percent of vote - Daniel T. arap MOI (KANU) 40.12%, Mwai KIBAKI (DP) 31.09%, Raila ODINGA (NDP) 10.2%, Michael WAMALWA (FORD-Kenya) 8.29%, Charity NGILU (SDP) 7.71%
Legislative branch: unicameral National Assembly or Bunge (222 seats, 12 appointed by the president, 210 members elected by popular vote to serve five-year terms)
elections: last held 29 December 1997 (next to be held between 1 December 2002 and 30 April 2003)
election results: percent of vote by party - NA; seats by party - KANU 107, FORD-A 1, FORD-K 17, FORD-People 3, DP 39, NDP 21, SDP 15, SAFINA 5, smaller parties 2; seats appointed by the president - KANU 6, FORD-Kenya 1, DP 2, SDP 1, NDP 1, SAFINA 1
Judicial branch: Court of Appeal, chief justice is appointed by the president; High Court
Political parties and leaders:
ruling party: Kenya African National Union or KANU [President Daniel Toroitich arap MOI]
opposition party: Democratic Party of Kenya or DP [Mwai KIBAKI]; Forum for the Restoration of Democracy-Asili or FORD-A [Martin SHIKUKU, chairman]; Forum for the Restoration of Democracy-Kenya or FORD-K [Michael Kijana WAMALWA]; Forum for the Restoration of Democracy-People or FORD-People [Raymond MATIBA]; National Development Party or NDP [Raila ODINGA, president and Dr. Charles MARANGA, secretary general]; Social Democratic Party or SDP [Anyang N'YANGO, secretary general]; SAFINA [Farah MAALIM, chairman, Mghanga MWANDAWIRO, secretary general]
Political pressure groups and leaders: National Convention Executive Council or NCEC, a proreform coalition of political parties and nongovernment organizations [Kivutha KIBWANA]; Roman Catholic and other Christian churches; human rights groups; labor unions; Muslim organizations; Protestant National Council of Churches of Kenya or NCCK [Mutava MUSYIMI]; Supreme Council of Kenyan Muslims or SUPKEM [Shaykh Abdul Gafur al-BUSAIDY, chairman]
International organization participation: ACP, AfDB, C, CCC, EADB, ECA, FAO, G-77, IAEA, IBRD, ICAO, ICFTU, ICRM, IDA, IFAD, IFC, IFRCS, IGAD, ILO, IMF, IMO, Intelsat, Interpol, IOC, IOM, ISO, ITU, MINURSO, MONUA, NAM, OAU, OPCW, UN, UN Security Council (temporary), UNCTAD, UNESCO, UNIDO, UNIKOM, UNMOP, UNOMIL, UNOMSIL, UNPREDEP, UNU, UPU, WCL, WHO, WIPO, WMO, WToO, WTrO
Diplomatic representation in the US:
chief of mission: Ambassador Samuel K. CHEMAI
chancery: 2249 R Street NW, Washington, DC 20008
telephone: [1] (202) 387-6101
FAX: [1] (202) 462-3829
consulate(s) general: Los Angeles and New York
Diplomatic representation from the US:
chief of mission: Ambassador Prudence B. BUSHNELL
embassy: USAID Building, The Crescent, Parklands, Nairobi (temporary location)
mailing address: P. O. Box 30137, Box 21A, Unit 64100, APO AE 09831
telephone: [254] (2) 751613
FAX: [254] (2) 743204
Flag description: three equal horizontal bands of black (top), red, and green; the red band is edged in white; a large warrior's shield covering crossed spears is superimposed at the center

Economy

Economy - overview: Since 1993, the government of Kenya has implemented a program of economic liberalization and reform. Steps have included the removal of import licensing and price controls, removal of foreign exchange controls, fiscal and monetary restraint, and reduction of the public sector through privatizing publicly owned companies and downsizing the civil service. With the support of the World Bank, IMF, and other donors, these reforms have led to a turnaround in economic performance following a period of negative growth in the early

Kenya (continued)

1990s. Kenya's real GDP grew at 5% in 1995 and 4% in 1996, and inflation remained under control. Growth slowed in 1997-98. Political violence damaged the tourist industry, and the IMF allowed Kenya's Enhanced Structural Adjustment Program to lapse due to the government's failure to enact reform conditions and to adequately address public sector corruption. Moreover, El Nino rains destroyed crops and damaged an already crumbling infrastructure in 1997 and 1998. Long-term barriers to development include electricity shortages, the government's continued and inefficient dominance of key sectors, endemic corruption, and the country's high population growth rate.

GDP: purchasing power parity - $43.9 billion (1998 est.)

GDP - real growth rate: 1.6% (1998 est.)

GDP - per capita: purchasing power parity - $1,550 (1998 est.)

GDP - composition by sector:
agriculture: 29%
industry: 17%
services: 54% (1997)

Population below poverty line: 42% (1992 est.)

Household income or consumption by percentage share:
lowest 10%: 1.2%
highest 10%: 47.7% (1992)

Inflation rate (consumer prices): 2.5% (1998)

Labor force: 9.2 million (1998 est.)

Labor force - by occupation: agriculture 75%-80%, nonagriculture 20%-25%

Unemployment rate: 50% (1998 est.)

Budget:
revenues: $2.6 billion
expenditures: $2.7 billion, including capital expenditures of $NA (1997 est.)

Industries: small-scale consumer goods (plastic, furniture, batteries, textiles, soap, cigarettes, flour), agricultural products processing; oil refining, cement; tourism

Industrial production growth rate: 3.8% (1995)

Electricity - production: 3.81 billion kWh (1996)

Electricity - production by source:
fossil fuel: 10.5%
hydro: 81.63%
nuclear: 0%
other: 7.87% (1996)

Electricity - consumption: 3.985 billion kWh (1996)

Electricity - exports: 0 kWh (1996)

Electricity - imports: 175 million kWh (1996)

Agriculture - products: coffee, tea, corn, wheat, sugarcane, fruit, vegetables; dairy products, beef, pork, poultry, eggs

Exports: $2 billion (f.o.b., 1998)

Exports - commodities: tea 18%, coffee 15%, petroleum products (1995)

Exports - partners: Uganda 16.1%, Tanzania 12.8%, UK 10.4%, Germany 7.5% (1996)

Imports: $3.05 billion (f.o.b., 1998)

Imports - commodities: machinery and transportation equipment 31%, consumer goods 13%, petroleum products 12% (1995)

Imports - partners: UK 13.2%, UAE 8.2%, South Africa 7.6%, Germany 7.4% (1996)

Debt - external: $6.45 billion (1997 est.)

Economic aid - recipient: $642.8 million (1995)

Currency: 1 Kenyan shilling (KSh) = 100 cents

Exchange rates: Kenyan shillings (KSh) per US$1 - 61.802 (January 1999), 60.367 (1998), 58.732 (1997), 57.115 (1996), 51.430 (1995), 56.051 (1994)

Fiscal year: 1 July - 30 June

Communications

Telephones: 383,676 (1997); 3,077 cellular telephone subscribers (1998)

Telephone system:
domestic: primarily microwave radio relay
international: satellite earth stations - 4 Intelsat

Radio broadcast stations: AM 24, FM 7, shortwave 2

Radios: 5 million

Television broadcast stations: 8 (of which six are government-controlled and two are commercial) (1997)

Televisions: 500,000

Transportation

Railways:
total: 2,652 km
narrow gauge: 2,652 km 1.000-m gauge

Highways:
total: 63,800 km
paved: 8,868 km
unpaved: 54,932 km (1996 est.)

Waterways: part of the Lake Victoria system is within the boundaries of Kenya

Pipelines: petroleum products 483 km

Ports and harbors: Kisumu, Lamu, Mombasa

Merchant marine:
total: 2 ships (1,000 GRT or over) totaling 4,883 GRT/6,255 DWT
ships by type: oil tanker 1, roll-on/roll-off cargo 1 (1998 est.)

Airports: 232 (1998 est.)

Airports - with paved runways:
total: 21
over 3,047 m: 4
2,438 to 3,047 m: 1
1,524 to 2,437 m: 2
914 to 1,523 m: 14 (1998 est.)

Airports - with unpaved runways:
total: 211
2,438 to 3,047 m: 1
1,524 to 2,437 m: 14
914 to 1,523 m: 113
under 914 m: 83 (1998 est.)

Military

Military branches: Army, Navy, Air Force, paramilitary General Service Unit of the Police

Military manpower - availability:
males age 15-49: 7,094,151 (1999 est.)

Military manpower - fit for military service:
males age 15-49: 4,397,008 (1999 est.)

Military expenditures - dollar figure: $197 million (FY98/99)

Military expenditures - percent of GDP: 1.9% (FY98/99)

Transnational Issues

Disputes - international: administrative boundary with Sudan does not coincide with international boundary

Illicit drugs: widespread harvesting of small, wild plots of marijuana and qat (chat); transit country for South Asian heroin destined for Europe and, sometimes, North America; Indian methaqualone also transits on way to South Africa

Kingman Reef
(territory of the US)

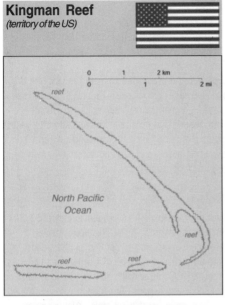

Geography

Location: Oceania, reef in the North Pacific Ocean, about one-half of the way from Hawaii to American Samoa

Geographic coordinates: 6 24 N, 162 24 W

Map references: Oceania

Area:
total: 1 sq km
land: 1 sq km
water: 0 sq km

Area - comparative: about 1.7 times the size of The Mall in Washington, DC

Land boundaries: 0 km

Coastline: 3 km

Maritime claims:
exclusive economic zone: 200 nm
territorial sea: 12 nm

Climate: tropical, but moderated by prevailing winds

Terrain: low and nearly level

Elevation extremes:
lowest point: Pacific Ocean 0 m
highest point: unnamed location 1 m

Natural resources: none

Land use:
arable land: 0%
permanent crops: 0%
permanent pastures: 0%
forests and woodland: 0%
other: 100%

Irrigated land: 0 sq km (1996)

Natural hazards: wet or awash most of the time, maximum elevation of about 1 meter makes Kingman Reef a maritime hazard

Environment - current issues: none

Environment - international agreements:
party to: NA
signed, but not ratified: NA

Geography - note: barren coral atoll with deep interior lagoon; closed to the public

People

Population: uninhabited

Government

Country name:
conventional long form: none
conventional short form: Kingman Reef

Data code: KQ

Dependency status: unincorporated territory of the US; administered from Washington, DC by the US Navy; however, it is awash the majority of the time, so it is not usable and is uninhabited

Capital: none; administered from Washington, DC

Legal system: NA

Flag description: the flag of the US is used

Economy

Economy - overview: no economic activity

Transportation

Ports and harbors: none; offshore anchorage only

Airports: lagoon was used as a halfway station between Hawaii and American Samoa by Pan American Airways for flying boats in 1937 and 1938

Military

Military - note: defense is the responsibility of the US

Transnational Issues

Disputes - international: none

Kiribati

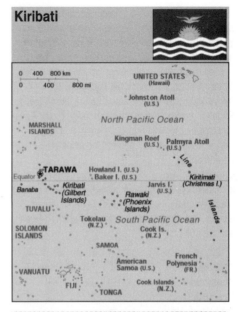

Geography

Location: Oceania, group of islands in the Pacific Ocean, straddling the equator, about one-half of the way from Hawaii to Australia; note - on 1 January 1995, Kiribati unilaterally moved the International Date Line from the middle of the country to include its easternmost islands and make it the same day throughout the country

Geographic coordinates: 1 25 N, 173 00 E

Map references: Oceania

Area:
total: 717 sq km
land: 717 sq km
water: 0 sq km
note: includes three island groups - Gilbert Islands, Line Islands, Phoenix Islands

Area - comparative: four times the size of Washington, DC

Land boundaries: 0 km

Coastline: 1,143 km

Maritime claims:
exclusive economic zone: 200 nm
territorial sea: 12 nm

Climate: tropical; marine, hot and humid, moderated by trade winds

Terrain: mostly low-lying coral atolls surrounded by extensive reefs

Elevation extremes:
lowest point: Pacific Ocean 0 m
highest point: unnamed location on Banaba 81 m

Natural resources: phosphate (production discontinued in 1979)

Land use:
arable land: NA%
permanent crops: 51%
permanent pastures: NA%
forests and woodland: 3%
other: 46% (1993 est.)

Irrigated land: NA sq km

Natural hazards: typhoons can occur any time, but

usually November to March; occasional tornadoes

Environment - current issues: heavy pollution in lagoon of south Tarawa atoll due to heavy migration mixed with traditional practices such as lagoon latrines and open-pit dumping; ground water at risk

Environment - international agreements:

party to: Biodiversity, Climate Change, Desertification, Endangered Species, Marine Dumping, Ozone Layer Protection

signed, but not ratified: none of the selected agreements

Geography - note: 20 of the 33 islands are inhabited; Banaba (Ocean Island) in Kiribati is one of the three great phosphate rock islands in the Pacific Ocean - the others are Makatea in French Polynesia and Nauru

People

Population: 85,501 (July 1999 est.)

Age structure:

0-14 years: NA

15-64 years: NA

65 years and over: NA

Population growth rate: 1.78% (1999 est.)

Birth rate: 26.13 births/1,000 population (1999 est.)

Death rate: 7.53 deaths/1,000 population (1999 est.)

Net migration rate: -0.77 migrant(s)/1,000 population (1999 est.)

Infant mortality rate: 48.22 deaths/1,000 live births (1999 est.)

Life expectancy at birth:

total population: 62.88 years

male: 61.02 years

female: 64.98 years (1999 est.)

Total fertility rate: 3.09 children born/woman (1999 est.)

Nationality:

noun: I-Kiribati (singular and plural)

adjective: I-Kiribati

Ethnic groups: Micronesian

Religions: Roman Catholic 53%, Protestant (Congregational) 41%, Seventh-Day Adventist, Baha'i, Church of God, Mormon 6% (1985 est.)

Languages: English (official), Gilbertese

Literacy: NA

Government

Country name:

conventional long form: Republic of Kiribati

conventional short form: Kiribati

note: pronounced kir-ih-bahss

former: Gilbert Islands

Data code: KR

Government type: republic

Capital: Tarawa

Administrative divisions: 3 units; Gilbert Islands, Line Islands, Phoenix Islands

note: in addition, there are 6 districts (Banaba, Central Gilberts, Line Islands, Northern Gilberts, Southern Gilberts, Tarawa) and 21 island councils - one for each of the inhabited islands (Abaiang, Abemama, Aranuka, Arorae, Banaba, Beru, Butaritari, Kanton, Kiritimati, Kuria, Maiana, Makin, Marakei, Nikunau, Nonouti, Onotoa, Tabiteuea, Tabuaeran, Tamana, Tarawa, Teraina)

Independence: 12 July 1979 (from UK)

National holiday: Independence Day, 12 July (1979)

Constitution: 12 July 1979

Legal system: NA

Suffrage: 18 years of age; universal

Executive branch:

chief of state: President (Beretitenti) Teburoro TITO (since 1 October 1994); Vice President (Kauoman-ni-Beretitenti) Tewareka TENTOA (since 12 October 1994); note - the president is both the chief of state and head of government

head of government: President (Beretitenti) Teburoro TITO (since 1 October 1994); Vice President (Kauoman-ni-Beretitenti) Tewareka TENTOA (since 12 October 1994); note - the president is both the chief of state and head of government

cabinet: Cabinet appointed by the president from among the members of the House of Assembly, includes the president, vice president, attorney general, and up to eight other ministers

elections: president elected by popular vote for a four-year term; note - the House of Assembly chooses the presidential candidates from among their members and then those candidates compete in a general election; election last held 27 November 1998 (next to be held by NA November 2002); vice president appointed by the president

election results: Teburoro TITO reelected president; percent of vote - Teburoro TITO 52.3%, Dr. Harry TONG 45.8%, Amberoti NIKORA 1.9%, Taberannang TIMEON 0%

Legislative branch: unicameral House of Assembly or Maneaba Ni Maungatabu (41 seats; 39 elected by popular vote, one ex officio member, and one nominated to represent Banaba; members serve four-year terms)

elections: last held 23 September 1998 (next to be held by NA September 2002)

election results: percent of vote by party - NA; seats by party - Maneaban Te Mauri Party 14, National Progressive Party 11, independents 14

Judicial branch: Court of Appeal, judges at all levels are appointed by the president; High Court, judges at all levels are appointed by the president; 26 Magistrates' courts, judges at all levels are appointed by the president

Political parties and leaders: National Progressive Party [Teatao TEANNAKI]; New Movement Party [leader NA]; Liberal Party [Tewareka TENTOA]; Maneaban Te Mauri Party [Teburoro TITO]

note: there is no tradition of formally organized political parties in Kiribati; they more closely resemble factions or interest groups because they have no party headquarters, formal platforms, or party structures

International organization participation: ACP, AsDB, C, ESCAP, IBRD, ICAO, ICFTU, ICRM, IDA, IFC, IFRCS, IMF, Intelsat (nonsignatory user), Interpol, ITU, Sparteca, SPC, SPF, UNESCO, UPU, WHO, WTrO (applicant)

Diplomatic representation in the US: Kiribati does not have an embassy in the US; there is an honorary consulate in Honolulu

Diplomatic representation from the US: the US does not have an embassy in Kiribati; the ambassador to the Marshall Islands is accredited to Kiribati

Flag description: the upper half is red with a yellow frigate bird flying over a yellow rising sun, and the lower half is blue with three horizontal wavy white stripes to represent the ocean

Economy

Economy - overview: A remote country of 33 scattered coral atolls, Kiribati has few national resources. Commercially viable phosphate deposits were exhausted at the time of independence from the UK in 1979. Copra and fish now represent the bulk of production and exports. The economy has fluctuated widely in recent years. Economic development is constrained by a shortage of skilled workers, weak infrastructure, and remoteness from international markets. The financial sector is at an early stage of development as is the expansion of private sector initiatives. Foreign financial aid, largely from the UK and Japan, is a critical supplement to GDP, equal to 25%-50% of GDP in recent years. Remittances from workers abroad account for more than $5 million each year.

GDP: purchasing power parity - $62 million (1996 est.)

GDP - real growth rate: 1.9% (1996 est.)

GDP - per capita: purchasing power parity - $800 (1996 est.)

GDP - composition by sector:

agriculture: 14%

industry: 7%

services: 79% (1996 est.)

Population below poverty line: NA%

Household income or consumption by percentage share:

lowest 10%: NA%

highest 10%: NA%

Inflation rate (consumer prices): -0.6% (1996 est.)

Labor force: 7,870 economically active, not including subsistence farmers (1985 est.)

Unemployment rate: 2%; underemployment 70% (1992 est.)

Budget:

revenues: $33.3 million

expenditures: $47.7 million, including capital expenditures of $NA million (1996 est.)

Industries: fishing, handicrafts

Industrial production growth rate: 0.7% (1992 est.)

Electricity - production: 7 million kWh (1996)

Electricity - production by source:

fossil fuel: 100%

hydro: 0%

nuclear: 0%

other: 0% (1996)

Kiribati *(continued)*

Electricity - consumption: 7 million kWh (1996)
Electricity - exports: 0 kWh (1996)
Electricity - imports: 0 kWh (1996)
Agriculture - products: copra, taro, breadfruit, sweet potatoes, vegetables; fish
Exports: $6.7 million (f.o.b., 1996 est.)
Exports - commodities: copra 62%, seaweed, fish
Exports - partners: US, Australia, NZ (1996)
Imports: $37.4 million (c.i.f., 1996 est.)
Imports - commodities: foodstuffs, machinery and equipment, miscellaneous manufactured goods, fuel
Imports - partners: Australia 46%, Fiji, Japan, NZ, US (1996)
Debt - external: $7.2 million (1996 est.)
Economic aid - recipient: $15.5 million (1995)
Currency: 1 Australian dollar ($A) = 100 cents
Exchange rates: Australian dollars ($A) per US$1 - 1.5853 (January 1999), 1.5888 (1998), 1.3439 (1997), 1.2773 (1996), 1.3486 (1995), 1.3667 (1994)
Fiscal year: NA

Communications

Telephones: 1,400 (1984 est.)
Telephone system:
domestic: NA
international: satellite earth station - 1 Intelsat (Pacific Ocean)
note: Kiribati is being linked to the Pacific Ocean Cooperative Telecommunications Network, which should improve telephone service
Radio broadcast stations: AM 1, FM 0, shortwave 0
Radios: 15,000 (1992 est.)
Television broadcast stations: 1 (1997)
Televisions: 0 (1988)

Transportation

Railways: 0 km
Highways:
total: 670 km (1996 est.)
paved: NA km
unpaved: NA km
Waterways: small network of canals, totaling 5 km, in Line Islands
Ports and harbors: Banaba, Betio, English Harbor, Kanton
Merchant marine:
total: 1 passenger-cargo (1,000 GRT or over) totaling 1,291 GRT/1,295 DWT (1998 est.)
Airports: 21 (1998 est.)
Airports - with paved runways:
total: 4
1,524 to 2,437 m: 4 (1998 est.)
Airports - with unpaved runways:
total: 17
914 to 1,523 m: 12
under 914 m: 5 (1998 est.)

Military

Military branches: no regular military forces; Police Force (carries out law enforcement functions and paramilitary duties; small police posts are on all islands)
Military expenditures - dollar figure: $NA
Military expenditures - percent of GDP: NA%
Military - note: Kiribati does not have military forces; defense assistance is provided by Australia and NZ

Transnational Issues

Disputes - international: none

Korea, North

Introduction

Background: At the end of World War II, the US and the Soviet Union agreed that US troops would accept the surrender of Japanese forces south of the 38th parallel and the Soviet Union would do so in the north. In 1948, the UN proposed nationwide elections; after P'yongyang's refusal to allow UN inspectors in the north, elections were held in the south and the Republic of Korea was established. The Democratic People's Republic of Korea was established the following month in the north. Communist North Korean forces invaded South Korea in 1950. US and other UN forces intervened to defend the South and Chinese forces intervened on behalf of the North. After a bitter three-year war, an armistice was signed in 1953, establishing a military demarcation line near the 38th parallel. The North's heavy investment in military forces has produced an army of 1 million troops equipped with thousands of tanks and artillery pieces. Despite growing economic hardships, North Korea continues to devote a significant portion of its scarce resources to the military.

Geography

Location: Eastern Asia, northern half of the Korean Peninsula bordering the Korea Bay and the Sea of Japan, between China and South Korea
Geographic coordinates: 40 00 N, 127 00 E
Map references: Asia
Area:
total: 120,540 sq km
land: 120,410 sq km
water: 130 sq km
Area - comparative: slightly smaller than Mississippi
Land boundaries:
total: 1,673 km
border countries: China 1,416 km, South Korea 238 km, Russia 19 km
Coastline: 2,495 km

Maritime claims:

territorial sea: 12 nm

exclusive economic zone: 200 nm

note: military boundary line 50 nm in the Sea of Japan and the exclusive economic zone limit in the Yellow Sea where all foreign vessels and aircraft without permission are banned

Climate: temperate with rainfall concentrated in summer

Terrain: mostly hills and mountains separated by deep, narrow valleys; coastal plains wide in west, discontinuous in east

Elevation extremes:

lowest point: Sea of Japan 0 m

highest point: Paektu-san 2,744 m

Natural resources: coal, lead, tungsten, zinc, graphite, magnesite, iron ore, copper, gold, pyrites, salt, fluorspar, hydropower

Land use:

arable land: 14%

permanent crops: 2%

permanent pastures: 0%

forests and woodland: 61%

other: 23% (1993 est.)

Irrigated land: 14,600 sq km (1993 est.)

Natural hazards: late spring droughts often followed by severe flooding; occasional typhoons during the early fall

Environment - current issues: localized air pollution attributable to inadequate industrial controls; water pollution; inadequate supplies of potable water

Environment - international agreements:

party to: Antarctic Treaty, Biodiversity, Climate Change, Environmental Modification, Ozone Layer Protection, Ship Pollution

signed, but not ratified: Antarctic-Environmental Protocol, Law of the Sea

Geography - note: strategic location bordering China, South Korea, and Russia; mountainous interior is isolated, nearly inaccessible, and sparsely populated

People

Population: 21,386,109 (July 1999 est.)

Age structure:

0-14 years: 26% (male 2,800,748; female 2,666,207)

15-64 years: 68% (male 7,143,969; female 7,447,147)

65 years and over: 6% (male 412,161; female 915,877) (1999 est.)

Population growth rate: 1.45% (1999 est.)

Birth rate: 21.37 births/1,000 population (1999 est.)

Death rate: 6.92 deaths/1,000 population (1999 est.)

Net migration rate: 0 migrant(s)/1,000 population (1999 est.)

Sex ratio:

at birth: 1.05 male(s)/female

under 15 years: 1.05 male(s)/female

15-64 years: 0.96 male(s)/female

65 years and over: 0.45 male(s)/female

total population: 0.94 male(s)/female (1999 est.)

Infant mortality rate: 25.52 deaths/1,000 live births

(1999 est.)

Life expectancy at birth:

total population: 70.07 years

male: 67.41 years

female: 72.86 years (1999 est.)

Total fertility rate: 2.3 children born/woman (1999 est.)

Nationality:

noun: Korean(s)

adjective: Korean

Ethnic groups: racially homogeneous; there is a small Chinese community and a few ethnic Japanese

Religions: Buddhism and Confucianism, some Christianity and syncretic Chondogyo

note: autonomous religious activities now almost nonexistent; government-sponsored religious groups exist to provide illusion of religious freedom

Languages: Korean

Literacy:

definition: age 15 and over can read and write Korean

total population: 99%

male: 99%

female: 99% (1990 est.)

Government

Country name:

conventional long form: Democratic People's Republic of Korea

conventional short form: North Korea

local long form: Choson-minjujuui-inmin-konghwaguk

local short form: none

note: the North Koreans generally use the term "Choson" to refer to their country

abbreviation: DPRK

Data code: KN

Government type: Communist state; one-man dictatorship

Capital: P'yongyang

Administrative divisions: 9 provinces (do, singular and plural) and 3 special cities* (si, singular and plural); Chagang-do (Chagang Province), Hamgyong-bukto (North Hamgyong Province), Hamgyong-namdo (South Hamgyong Province), Hwanghae-bukto (North Hwanghae Province), Hwanghae-namdo (South Hwanghae Province), Kaesong-si* (Kaesong City), Kangwon-do (Kangwon Province), Namp'o-si* (Namp'o City), P'yongan-bukto (North P'yongan Province), P'yongan-namdo (South P'yongan Province), P'yongyang-si* (P'yongyang City), Yanggang-do (Yanggang Province)

Independence: 9 September 1948, Democratic People's Republic of Korea (DPRK) Foundation Day

note: 15 August 1945, date of independence from the Japanese and celebrated in North Korea as National Liberation Day

National holiday: Foundation Day, 9 September (1948)

Constitution: adopted 1948, completely revised 27 December 1972, revised again in April 1992 and September 1998

Legal system: based on German civil law system with Japanese influences and Communist legal

theory; no judicial review of legislative acts; has not accepted compulsory ICJ jurisdiction

Suffrage: 17 years of age; universal

Executive branch:

chief of state: KIM Chong-il; note - in September 1998, KIM Chong-il was reelected Chairman of the National Defense Commission, a position accorded the nation's "highest administrative authority"; KIM Young-nam was named President of the Supreme People's Assembly Presidium and given the responsibility of representing the state and receiving diplomatic credentials

head of government: Premier HONG Song-nam (since 5 September 1998)

cabinet: renamed DPRK Cabinet (naegak) on 5 September 1998; was previously called the State Administrative Council; Cabinet members, except for the Minister of People's Armed Forces, are appointed by the Supreme People's Assembly

elections: premier elected by the Supreme People's Assembly

election results: NA

Legislative branch: unicameral Supreme People's Assembly or Ch'oego Inmin Hoeui (687 seats; members elected by popular vote to serve five-year terms)

elections: last held 26 July 1998 (next to be held NA)

election results: percent of vote by party - NA; seats by party - the KWP approves a single list of candidates who are elected without opposition; minor parties hold a few seats

Judicial branch: Central Court, judges are elected by the Supreme People's Assembly

Political parties and leaders: major party - Korean Workers' Party or KWP [KIM Chong-il, General Secretary]; Korean Social Democratic Party [KIM Pyong-sik, chairman]; Chondoist Chongu Party [YU Mi-yong, chairwoman]

International organization participation: ESCAP, FAO, ICAO, ICRM, IFAD, IFRCS, IHO, IMO, Intelsat (nonsignatory user), IOC, ISO, ITU, NAM, UN, UNCTAD, UNESCO, UNIDO, UPU, WFTU, WHO, WIPO, WMO, WToO

Diplomatic representation in the US: none; note - North Korea has a Permanent Mission to the UN in New York, headed by YI Hyong-chol

Diplomatic representation from the US: none

Flag description: three horizontal bands of blue (top), red (triple width), and blue; the red band is edged in white; on the hoist side of the red band is a white disk with a red five-pointed star

Economy

Economy - overview: North Korea is the world's most centrally planned economy. Agricultural land is collectivized, state-owned industry produces nearly all manufactured goods, and heavy and military industries have long been developed at the expense of light and consumer industries. Open-air markets since 1995 have gained increasing importance in the distribution of food and consumer goods but private production remains extremely limited. Total economic output has fallen steadily since 1991 - perhaps by as much as one-half - when the country's economic ties to the Soviet Union and Eastern Bloc collapsed. The slide has also been fueled by serious energy shortages, aging industrial facilities, and a lack of maintenance and new investment. The leadership has tried to maintain a high level of military spending but the armed forces have nonetheless been affected by the general economic decline. Although North Korea has long depended on imports to meet food needs, serious fertilizer shortages in recent years have combined with structural constraints - such as a shortage of arable land and a short growing season - to reduce staple grain output to more than 1 million tons below what the country needs to meet even minimal demand. Widespread famine and disease have cost the lives of hundreds of thousands of North Koreans in 1994-98. The US, China, the international community, and nongovernmental organizations have sent aid but the problems remain extremely serious.

GDP: purchasing power parity - $21.8 billion (1998 est.)
GDP - real growth rate: -5% (1998 est.)
GDP - per capita: purchasing power parity - $1,000 (1998 est.)
GDP - composition by sector:
agriculture: 25%
industry: 60%
services: 15% (1995 est.)
Population below poverty line: NA%
Household income or consumption by percentage share:
lowest 10%: NA%
highest 10%: NA%
Inflation rate (consumer prices): NA%
Labor force: 9.615 million
Labor force - by occupation: agricultural 36%, nonagricultural 64%
Unemployment rate: NA%
Budget:
revenues: $19.3 billion
expenditures: $19.3 billion, including capital expenditures of $NA (1992 est.)
Industries: military products; machine building, electric power, chemicals; mining (coal, iron ore, magnesite, graphite, copper, zinc, lead, and precious metals), metallurgy; textiles, food processing
Industrial production growth rate: -7% to -9% (1992 est.)
Electricity - production: 34 billion kWh (1996)
Electricity - production by source:
fossil fuel: 35.29%
hydro: 64.71%
nuclear: 0%
other: 0% (1996)
Electricity - consumption: 34 billion kWh (1996)
Electricity - exports: 0 kWh (1996)
Electricity - imports: 0 kWh (1996)
Agriculture - products: rice, corn, potatoes, soybeans, pulses; cattle, pigs, pork, eggs
Exports: $743 million (f.o.b., 1997 est.)

Exports - commodities: minerals, metallurgical products, agricultural and fishery products, manufactures (including armaments)
Exports - partners: Japan 28%, South Korea 21%, China 5%, Germany 4%, Russia 1% (1995)
Imports: $1.83 billion (c.i.f., 1997 est.)
Imports - commodities: petroleum, grain, coking coal, machinery and equipment, consumer goods
Imports - partners: China 33%, Japan 17%, Russia 5%, South Korea 4%, Germany 3% (1995)
Debt - external: $12 billion (1996 est.)
Economic aid - recipient: $NA; note - an estimated $200 million to $300 million in humanitarian aid from US, South Korea, Japan, and EU in 1997
Currency: 1 North Korean won (Wn) = 100 chon
Exchange rates: official: North Korean won (Wn) per US$1 - 2.15 (May 1994), 2.13 (May 1992), 2.14 (September 1991), 2.1 (January 1990), 2.3 (December 1989); market: North Korean won (Wn) per US$1 - 200
Fiscal year: calendar year

Communications

Telephones: 1.4 million (1998 est.)
Telephone system:
domestic: system is being expanded with installation of fiber-optic cable nationwide; access traditionally reserved for official and business subscribers; public access is expected to increase
international: satellite earth stations - 1 Intelsat (Indian Ocean) and 1 Intersputnik (Indian Ocean Region); other international connections through Moscow and Beijing
Radio broadcast stations: AM 27, FM 14, shortwave 3
Radios: 4.7 million
Television broadcast stations: 38
Televisions: 2 million

Transportation

Railways:
broad gauge: NA km
total: 5,000 km
standard gauge: 4,095 km 1.435-m gauge (3,500 km electrified; 159 km double track)
narrow gauge: 665 km 0.762-m gauge
dual gauge: 240 km 1.435-m and 1.600-m gauges (three rails) (1996 est.)
Highways:
total: 31,200 km
paved: 1,997 km
unpaved: 29,203 km (1996 est.)
Waterways: 2,253 km; mostly navigable by small craft only
Pipelines: crude oil 37 km; petroleum product 180 km
Ports and harbors: Ch'ongjin, Haeju, Hungnam (Hamhung), Kimch'aek, Kosong, Najin, Namp'o, Sinuiju, Songnim, Sonbong (formerly Unggi), Ungsang, Wonsan

Merchant marine:
total: 110 ships (1,000 GRT or over) totaling 691,802 GRT/992,789 DWT
ships by type: bulk 8, cargo 91, combination bulk 1, multifunction large-load carrier 1, oil tanker 4, passenger 2, passenger-cargo 1, short-sea passenger 2 (1998 est.)
Airports: 49 (1994 est.) (1998 est.)
Airports - with paved runways:
total: 22
over 3,047 m: 2
2,438 to 3,047 m: 15
1,524 to 2,437 m: 2
914 to 1,523 m: 1
under 914 m: 2 (1994 est.)
Airports - with unpaved runways:
total: 27
2,438 to 3,047 m: 4
1,524 to 2,437 m: 5
914 to 1,523 m: 12
under 914 m: 6 (1994 est.)

Military

Military branches: Korean People's Army (includes Army, Navy, Air Force), Civil Security Forces
Military manpower - military age: 18 years of age
Military manpower - availability:
males age 15-49: 5,768,038 (1999 est.)
Military manpower - fit for military service:
males age 15-49: 3,483,188 (1999 est.)
Military manpower - reaching military age annually:
males: 177,888 (1999 est.)
Military expenditures - dollar figure: $5 billion to $7 billion (1997 est.)
Military expenditures - percent of GDP: 25% to 33% (1997 est.)

Transnational Issues

Disputes - international: 33-km section of boundary with China in the Paektu-san (mountain) area is indefinite; Demarcation Line with South Korea

Korea, South

Introduction

Background: At the end of World War II, the US and the Soviet Union agreed that US troops would accept the surrender of Japanese forces south of the 38th parallel and the Soviet Union would do so in the north. In 1948, the UN proposed nationwide elections; after P'yongyang's refusal to allow UN inspectors in the north, elections were held in the south and the Republic of Korea was established. The Democratic People's Republic of Korea was established the following month in the north. Communist North Korean forces invaded South Korea in 1950. US and other UN forces intervened to defend the South and Chinese forces intervened on behalf of the North. After a bitter three-year war, an armistice was signed in 1953, establishing a military demarcation line near the 38th parallel. Thereafter, South Korea achieved amazing economic growth, with per capita output rising to 13 times the level in the North. Since late 1997, however, the nation has suffered widespread financial and organizational difficulties. Continuing tensions between North and South have raised concerns of provocative military actions by the North.

Geography

Location: Eastern Asia, southern half of the Korean Peninsula bordering the Sea of Japan and the Yellow Sea
Geographic coordinates: 37 00 N, 127 30 E
Map references: Asia
Area:
total: 98,480 sq km
land: 98,190 sq km
water: 290 sq km
Area - comparative: slightly larger than Indiana
Land boundaries:
total: 238 km
border countries: North Korea 238 km
Coastline: 2,413 km
Maritime claims:
contiguous zone: 24 nm

continental shelf: not specified
exclusive economic zone: 200 nm
territorial sea: 12 nm; between 3 nm and 12 nm in the Korea Strait
Climate: temperate, with rainfall heavier in summer than winter
Terrain: mostly hills and mountains; wide coastal plains in west and south
Elevation extremes:
lowest point: Sea of Japan 0 m
highest point: Halla-san 1,950 m
Natural resources: coal, tungsten, graphite, molybdenum, lead, hydropower
Land use:
arable land: 19%
permanent crops: 2%
permanent pastures: 1%
forests and woodland: 65%
other: 13% (1993 est.)
Irrigated land: 13,350 sq km (1993 est.)
Natural hazards: occasional typhoons bring high winds and floods; low-level seismic activity common in southwest
Environment - current issues: air pollution in large cities; water pollution from the discharge of sewage and industrial effluents; driftnet fishing
Environment - international agreements:
party to: Antarctic-Environmental Protocol, Antarctic Treaty, Biodiversity, Climate Change, Endangered Species, Environmental Modification, Hazardous Wastes, Law of the Sea, Nuclear Test Ban, Ozone Layer Protection, Ship Pollution, Tropical Timber 83, Tropical Timber 94, Wetlands, Whaling
signed, but not ratified: Climate Change-Kyoto Protocol, Desertification

People

Population: 46,884,800 (July 1999 est.)
Age structure:
0-14 years: 22% (male 5,504,333; female 4,874,974)
15-64 years: 71% (male 16,949,807; female 16,432,951)
65 years and over: 7% (male 1,192,688; female 1,930,047) (1999 est.)
Population growth rate: 1% (1999 est.)
Birth rate: 15.95 births/1,000 population (1999 est.)
Death rate: 5.68 deaths/1,000 population (1999 est.)
Net migration rate: -0.3 migrant(s)/1,000 population (1999 est.)
Sex ratio:
at birth: 1.13 male(s)/female
under 15 years: 1.13 male(s)/female
15-64 years: 1.03 male(s)/female
65 years and over: 0.62 male(s)/female
total population: 1.02 male(s)/female (1999 est.)
Infant mortality rate: 7.57 deaths/1,000 live births (1999 est.)
Life expectancy at birth:
total population: 74.3 years
male: 70.75 years
female: 78.32 years (1999 est.)

Total fertility rate: 1.79 children born/woman (1999 est.)
Nationality:
noun: Korean(s)
adjective: Korean
Ethnic groups: homogeneous (except for about 20,000 Chinese)
Religions: Christianity 49%, Buddhism 47%, Confucianism 3%, pervasive folk religion (shamanism), Chondogyo (Religion of the Heavenly Way), and other 1%
Languages: Korean, English widely taught in junior high and high school
Literacy:
definition: age 15 and over can read and write
total population: 98%
male: 99.3%
female: 96.7% (1995 est.)

Government

Country name:
conventional long form: Republic of Korea
conventional short form: South Korea
local long form: Taehan-min'guk
local short form: none
note: the South Koreans generally use the term "Han-guk" to refer to their country
abbreviation: ROK
Data code: KS
Government type: republic
Capital: Seoul
Administrative divisions: 9 provinces (do, singular and plural) and 6 special cities* (gwangyoksi, singular and plural); Cheju-do, Cholla-bukto, Cholla-namdo, Ch'ungch'ong-bukto, Ch'ungch'ong-namdo, Inch'on-gwangyoksi*, Kangwon-do, Kwangju-gwangyoksi*, Kyonggi-do, Kyongsang-bukto, Kyongsang-namdo, Pusan-gwangyoksi*, Soul-t'ukpyolsi*, Taegu-gwangyoksi*, Taejon-gwangyoksi*
Independence: 15 August 1945, date of liberation from Japanese colonial rule
National holiday: Liberation Day, 15 August (1945)
Constitution: 25 February 1988
Legal system: combines elements of continental European civil law systems, Anglo-American law, and Chinese classical thought
Suffrage: 20 years of age; universal
Executive branch:
chief of state: President KIM Dae-jung (since 25 February 1998)
head of government: Prime Minister KIM Chong-p'il (since 3 March 1998)
cabinet: State Council appointed by the president on the prime minister's recommendation
elections: president elected by popular vote for a single five-year term; election last held 18 December 1997 (next to be held by 18 December 2002); prime minister appointed by the president; deputy prime ministers appointed by the president on the prime minister's recommendation
election results: KIM Dae-jung elected president;

Korea, South *(continued)*

percent of vote - KIM Dae-jung (NCNP) 40.3%, YI Hoe-chang (GNP) 38.7%, YI In-che (NPP) 19.2%

Legislative branch: unicameral National Assembly or Kukhoe (299 seats; members elected by popular vote to serve four-year terms)

elections: last held 11 April 1996 (next to be held NA 2000)

election results: percent of vote by party - NA; seats by party - NKP 139, NCNP 79, ULD 50, DP 15, independents 16; note - the distribution of seats as of February 1999 was GNP 137, NCNP 105, ULD 53, independents 4

Judicial branch: Supreme Court, justices are appointed by the president subject to the consent of the National Assembly

Political parties and leaders: Grand National Party or GNP [CHO Sun, president]; National Congress for New Politics or NCNP [KIM Dae-jung, president]; United Liberal Democrats or ULD [PAK Tae-chun, president]

note: subsequent to the legislative election of April 1996 the following parties disbanded - New Korea Party or NKP and Democratic Party or DP; New People's Party or NPP merged with the NCNP in August 1998

Political pressure groups and leaders: Korean National Council of Churches; National Democratic Alliance of Korea; National Federation of Student Associations; National Federation of Farmers' Associations; National Council of Labor Unions; Federation of Korean Trade Unions; Korean Veterans' Association; Federation of Korean Industries; Korean Traders Association; Korean Confederation of Trade Unions

International organization participation: AfDB, APEC, AsDB, BIS, CCC, CP, EBRD, ESCAP, FAO, G-77, IAEA, IBRD, ICAO, ICC, ICFTU, ICRM, IDA, IEA (observer), IFAD, IFC, IFRCS, IHO, ILO, IMF, IMO, Inmarsat, Intelsat, Interpol, IOC, IOM, ISO, ITU, MINURSO, NEA, NSG, OAS (observer), OECD, OPCW, OSCE (partner), UN, UNCTAD, UNESCO, UNIDO, UNMOGIP, UNOMIG, UNU, UPU, WHO, WIPO, WMO, WToO, WTrO

Diplomatic representation in the US:
chief of mission: Ambassador YI Hong-ku
chancery: 2450 Massachusetts Avenue NW, Washington, DC 20008
telephone: [1] (202) 939-5600
FAX: [1] (202) 387-0205
consulate(s) general: Agana (Guam), Anchorage, Atlanta, Boston, Chicago, Honolulu, Houston, Los Angeles, Miami, New York, San Francisco, and Seattle

Diplomatic representation from the US:
chief of mission: Ambassador Stephen W. BOSWORTH
embassy: 82 Sejong-Ro, Chongro-ku, Seoul
mailing address: American Embassy, Unit 15550, APO AP 96205-0001
telephone: [82] (2) 397-4114
FAX: [82] (2) 738-8845

Flag description: white with a red (top) and blue yin-yang symbol in the center; there is a different black trigram from the ancient I Ching (Book of Changes) in each corner of the white field

Economy

Economy - overview: As one of the Four Dragons of East Asia, South Korea has achieved an incredible record of growth. Three decades ago its GDP per capita was comparable with levels in the poorer countries of Africa and Asia. Today its GDP per capita is seven times India's, 13 times North Korea's, and already near the lesser economies of the European Union. This success through the late 1980s was achieved by a system of close government business ties, including directed credit, import restrictions, sponsorship of specific industries, and a strong labor effort. The government promoted the import of raw materials and technology at the expense of consumer goods and encouraged savings and investment over consumption. The Asian financial crisis of 1997-98 exposed certain longstanding weaknesses in South Korea's development model, including high debt/equity ratios, massive foreign borrowing, and an undisciplined financial sector. By the end of 1998 it had recovered financial stability, rebuilding foreign exchange reserves to record levels by running a current account surplus of $40 billion. As of December 1998, the first tentative signs of a rebound in the economy emerged, and most forecasters expect GDP growth to turn positive at least in the second half of 1999. Seoul has also made a positive start on a program to get the country's largest business groups to swap subsidiaries to promote specialization, and the administration has directed many of the mid-sized conglomerates into debt-workout programs with creditor banks. Challenges for the future include cutting redundant staff, which reaches 20%-30% at most firms and maintaining the impetus for structural reform.

GDP: purchasing power parity - $584.7 billion (1998 est.)

GDP - real growth rate: -6.8% (1998 est.)

GDP - per capita: purchasing power parity - $12,600 (1998 est.)

GDP - composition by sector:
agriculture: 6%
industry: 43%
services: 51% (1997 est.)

Population below poverty line: NA%

Household income or consumption by percentage share:
lowest 10%: NA%
highest 10%: NA%

Inflation rate (consumer prices): 7.5% (1998)

Labor force: 20 million

Labor force - by occupation: services and other 52%, mining and manufacturing 27%, agriculture, fishing, forestry 21% (1991)

Unemployment rate: 7.9% (1998)

Budget:
revenues: $100.4 billion
expenditures: $100.5 billion, including capital expenditures of $NA (1997 est.)

Industries: electronics, automobile production, chemicals, shipbuilding, steel, textiles, clothing, footwear, food processing

Industrial production growth rate: 3.1% (1997 est.)

Electricity - production: 194.163 billion kWh (1996)

Electricity - production by source:
fossil fuel: 61.18%
hydro: 2.65%
nuclear: 36.17%
other: 0% (1996)

Electricity - consumption: 194.163 billion kWh (1996)

Electricity - exports: 0 kWh (1996)

Electricity - imports: 0 kWh (1996)

Agriculture - products: rice, root crops, barley, vegetables, fruit; cattle, pigs, chickens, milk, eggs; fish

Exports: $133 billion (f.o.b., 1998)

Exports - commodities: electronic and electrical equipment, machinery, steel, automobiles, ships; textiles, clothing, footwear; fish

Exports - partners: US 17%, EU 13%, Japan 12% (1995)

Imports: $94 billion (c.i.f., 1998)

Imports - commodities: machinery, electronics and electronic equipment, oil, steel, transport equipment, textiles, organic chemicals, grains

Imports - partners: US 22%, Japan 21%, EU 13% (1995)

Debt - external: $154 billion (1998 est.)

Economic aid - recipient: $NA

Currency: 1 South Korean won (W) = 100 chun (theoretical)

Exchange rates: South Korean won (W) per US$1 - 1,174.00 (January 1999), 1,401.44 (1998), 951.29 (1997), 804.45 (1996), 771.27 (1995), 803.45 (1994)

Fiscal year: calendar year

Communications

Telephones: 16.6 million (1993)

Telephone system: excellent domestic and international services
domestic: NA
international: fiber-optic submarine cable to China; satellite earth stations - 3 Intelsat (2 Pacific Ocean and 1 Indian Ocean) and 1 Inmarsat (Pacific Ocean region)

Radio broadcast stations: AM 79, FM 46, shortwave 0

Radios: 42 million (1993 est.)

Television broadcast stations: 121 (in addition, there are 850 relay stations and eight-channel American Forces Korea Network) (1997)

Televisions: 9.3 million (1992 est.)

Transportation

Railways:
total: 6,240 km
standard gauge: 6,240 km 1.435-m gauge (525 km electrified) (1998 est.)

Korea, South *(continued)*

Highways:
total: 63,500 km
paved: 46,800 km (including 1,720 km of expressways)
unpaved: 16,700 km (1998 est.)
Waterways: 1,609 km; use restricted to small native craft
Pipelines: petroleum products 455 km; note - additionally, there is a parallel petroleum, oils, and lubricants (POL) pipeline being completed
Ports and harbors: Chinhae, Inch'on, Kunsan, Masan, Mokp'o, P'ohang, Pusan, Tonghae-hang, Ulsan, Yosu
Merchant marine:
total: 442 ships (1,000 GRT or over) totaling 5,212,089 GRT/8,161,845 DWT
ships by type: bulk 106, cargo 133, chemical tanker 36, combination bulk 5, container 52, liquefied gas tanker 13, multifunction large-load carrier 1, oil tanker 56, passenger 3, refrigerated cargo 22, roll-on/roll-off cargo 2, short-sea passenger 1, specialized tanker 3, vehicle carrier 9 (1998 est.)
Airports: 103 (1998 est.)
Airports - with paved runways:
total: 68
over 3,047 m: 1
2,438 to 3,047 m: 18
1,524 to 2,437 m: 15
914 to 1,523 m: 13
under 914 m: 21 (1998 est.)
Airports - with unpaved runways:
total: 35
914 to 1,523 m: 3
under 914 m: 32 (1998 est.)
Heliports: 200 (1998 est.)

Military

Military branches: Army, Navy, Air Force, Marine Corps, National Maritime Police (Coast Guard)
Military manpower - military age: 18 years of age
Military manpower - availability:
males age 15-49: 13,954,916 (1999 est.)
Military manpower - fit for military service:
males age 15-49: 8,890,144 (1999 est.)
Military manpower - reaching military age annually:
males: 400,468 (1999 est.)
Military expenditures - dollar figure: $9.9 billion (FY98/99)
Military expenditures - percent of GDP: 3.2% (FY98/99)

Transnational Issues

Disputes - international: Demarcation Line with North Korea; Liancourt Rocks (Takeshima/Tokdo) claimed by Japan

Kuwait

Geography

Location: Middle East, bordering the Persian Gulf, between Iraq and Saudi Arabia
Geographic coordinates: 29 30 N, 45 45 E
Map references: Middle East
Area:
total: 17,820 sq km
land: 17,820 sq km
water: 0 sq km
Area - comparative: slightly smaller than New Jersey
Land boundaries:
total: 464 km
border countries: Iraq 242 km, Saudi Arabia 222 km
Coastline: 499 km
Maritime claims:
territorial sea: 12 nm
Climate: dry desert; intensely hot summers; short, cool winters
Terrain: flat to slightly undulating desert plain
Elevation extremes:
lowest point: Persian Gulf 0 m
highest point: unnamed location 306 m
Natural resources: petroleum, fish, shrimp, natural gas
Land use:
arable land: 0%
permanent crops: 0%
permanent pastures: 8%
forests and woodland: 0%
other: 92% (1993 est.)
Irrigated land: 20 sq km (1993 est.)
Natural hazards: sudden cloudbursts are common from October to April; they bring inordinate amounts of rain which can damage roads and houses; sandstorms and dust storms occur throughout the year, but are most common between March and August
Environment - current issues: limited natural fresh water resources; some of world's largest and most

sophisticated desalination facilities provide much of the water; air and water pollution; desertification
Environment - international agreements:
party to: Climate Change, Desertification, Environmental Modification, Hazardous Wastes, Law of the Sea, Nuclear Test Ban, Ozone Layer Protection
signed, but not ratified: Biodiversity, Endangered Species, Marine Dumping
Geography - note: strategic location at head of Persian Gulf

People

Population: 1,991,115 (July 1999 est.)
note: includes 1,220,935 non-nationals (July 1999 est.)
Age structure:
0-14 years: 32% (male 343,461; female 285,129)
15-64 years: 66% (male 850,689; female 468,618)
65 years and over: 2% (male 26,593; female 16,625) (1999 est.)
Population growth rate: 3.88% (1999 est.)
note: this rate reflects the continued post-Gulf crisis return of expatriates
Birth rate: 20.45 births/1,000 population (1999 est.)
Death rate: 2.31 deaths/1,000 population (1999 est.)
Net migration rate: 20.65 migrant(s)/1,000 population (1999 est.)
Sex ratio:
at birth: 1.05 male(s)/female
under 15 years: 1.2 male(s)/female
15-64 years: 1.82 male(s)/female
65 years and over: 1.6 male(s)/female
total population: 1.58 male(s)/female (1999 est.)
Infant mortality rate: 10.26 deaths/1,000 live births (1999 est.)
Life expectancy at birth:
total population: 77.15 years
male: 75.11 years
female: 79.3 years (1999 est.)
Total fertility rate: 3.34 children born/woman (1999 est.)
Nationality:
noun: Kuwaiti(s)
adjective: Kuwaiti
Ethnic groups: Kuwaiti 45%, other Arab 35%, South Asian 9%, Iranian 4%, other 7%
Religions: Muslim 85% (Sunni 45%, Shi'a 40%), Christian, Hindu, Parsi, and other 15%
Languages: Arabic (official), English widely spoken
Literacy:
definition: age 15 and over can read and write
total population: 78.6%
male: 82.2%
female: 74.9% (1995 est.)

Government

Country name:
conventional long form: State of Kuwait
conventional short form: Kuwait
local long form: Dawlat al Kuwayt
local short form: Al Kuwayt

Kuwait (continued)

Data code: KU
Government type: nominal constitutional monarchy
Capital: Kuwait
Administrative divisions: 5 governorates (muhafazat, singular - muhafazah); Al Ahmadi, Al Farwaniyah, Al 'Asimah, Al Jahra', Hawalli
Independence: 19 June 1961 (from UK)
National holiday: National Day, 25 February (1950)
Constitution: approved and promulgated 11 November 1962
Legal system: civil law system with Islamic law significant in personal matters; has not accepted compulsory ICJ jurisdiction
Suffrage: adult males who have been naturalized for 30 years or more or have resided in Kuwait since before 1920 and their male descendants at age 21
note: only 10% of all citizens are eligible to vote; in 1996, naturalized citizens who do not meet the pre-1920 qualification but have been naturalized for 30 years were eligible to vote for the first time
Executive branch:
chief of state: Amir JABIR al-Ahmad al-Jabir Al Sabah (since 31 December 1977)
head of government: Prime Minister and Crown Prince SAAD al-Abdallah al-Salim Al Sabah (since 8 February 1978); First Deputy Prime Minister SABAH al-Ahmad al-Jabir Al Sabah (since 17 October 1992); Second Deputy Prime Minister SALIM al-Sabah al-Salim Al Sabah (since 7 October 1996)
cabinet: Council of Ministers appointed by the prime minister and approved by the monarch
elections: none; the monarch is hereditary; prime minister and deputy prime ministers appointed by the monarch
Legislative branch: unicameral National Assembly or Majlis al-Umma (50 seats; members elected by popular vote to serve four-year terms)
elections: last held 7 October 1996 (next to be held approximately October 2000)
election results: percent of vote - NA; seats - independents 50; note - all cabinet ministers are also ex officio members of the National Assembly
Judicial branch: High Court of Appeal
Political parties and leaders: none
Political pressure groups and leaders: several political groups act as de facto parties: Bedouins, merchants, Sunni and Shi'a activists, and secular leftists and nationalists
International organization participation: ABEDA, AfDB, AFESD, AL, AMF, BDEAC, CAEU, CCC, ESCWA, FAO, G-77, GCC, IAEA, IBRD, ICAO, ICC, ICRM, IDA, IDB, IFAD, IFC, IFRCS, IHO (pending member), ILO, IMF, IMO, Inmarsat, Intelsat, Interpol, IOC, ISO (correspondent), ITU, NAM, OAPEC, OIC, OPCW, OPEC, UN, UNCTAD, UNESCO, UNIDO, UPU, WFTU, WHO, WMO, WToO, WTrO
Diplomatic representation in the US:
chief of mission: Ambassador MUHAMMAD al-Sabah al-Salim Al SABAH
chancery: 2940 Tilden Street NW, Washington, DC 20008
telephone: [1] (202) 966-0702

FAX: [1] (202) 966-0517
Diplomatic representation from the US:
chief of mission: Ambassador James A. LAROCCO
embassy: Bayan, near the Bayan palace, Kuwait City
mailing address: P.O. Box 77 Safat, 13001 Safat, Kuwait; Unit 69000, APO AE 09880-9000
telephone: [965] 539-5307 or 539-5308
FAX: [965] 538-0282
Flag description: three equal horizontal bands of green (top), white, and red with a black trapezoid based on the hoist side

Economy

Economy - overview: Kuwait is a small and relatively open economy with proved crude oil reserves of about 94 billion barrels - 10% of world reserves. Petroleum accounts for nearly half of GDP, 90% of export revenues, and 75% of government income. Kuwait lacks water and has practically no arable land, thus preventing development of agriculture. With the exception of fish, it depends almost wholly on food imports. About 75% of potable water must be distilled or imported. The economy improved moderately in 1994-97, but in 1998 suffered from the large decline in world oil prices. The Kuwaiti cabinet approved a reform package in January 1999, including reducing subsidies and increasing taxes on large consumer goods. Nevertheless, Kuwait anticipates continuing budget deficits for the next few years. Kuwait is attracting foreign oil companies to develop fields in the northern part of the country.
GDP: purchasing power parity - $43.7 billion (1998 est.)
GDP - real growth rate: -5% (1998 est.)
GDP - per capita: purchasing power parity - $22,700 (1998 est.)
GDP - composition by sector:
agriculture: 0%
industry: 55%
services: 45% (1996)
Population below poverty line: NA%
Household income or consumption by percentage share:
lowest 10%: NA%
highest 10%: NA%
Inflation rate (consumer prices): 1% (1997 est.)
Labor force: 1.1 million (1996 est.)
note: 68% of the population in the 15-64 age group is non-national (July 1998 est.)
Labor force - by occupation: government and social services 50%, services 40%, industry and agriculture 10% (1996 est.)
Unemployment rate: 1.8% (official 1996 est.)
Budget:
revenues: $8.1 billion
expenditures: $14.5 billion, including capital expenditures of $NA (FY98/99 budget est.)
Industries: petroleum, petrochemicals, desalination, food processing, construction materials, salt, construction
Industrial production growth rate: 1% (1997 est.)
Electricity - production: 23 billion kWh (1996)

Electricity - production by source:
fossil fuel: 100%
hydro: 0%
nuclear: 0%
other: 0% (1996)
Electricity - consumption: 23 billion kWh (1996)
Electricity - exports: 0 kWh (1996)
Electricity - imports: 0 kWh (1996)
Agriculture - products: practically no crops; fish
Exports: $14.3 billion (f.o.b., 1997)
Exports - commodities: oil and refined products, fertilizers
Exports - partners: Japan 24%, India 16%, US 13%, South Korea 11%, Singapore 8% (1997)
Imports: $7.8 billion (f.o.b., 1996)
Imports - commodities: food, construction materials, vehicles and parts, clothing
Imports - partners: US 22%, Japan 15%, UK 13%, Germany 8%, Italy 6% (1997)
Debt - external: $7.3 billion (1997 est.)
Economic aid - recipient: $27.6 million (1995)
Currency: 1 Kuwaiti dinar (KD) = 1,000 fils
Exchange rates: Kuwaiti dinars (KD) per US$1 - 0.3018 (January 1999), 0.3047 (1998), 0.3033 (1997), 0.2994 (1996), 0.2984 (1995), 0.2976 (1994)
Fiscal year: 1 July - 30 June

Communications

Telephones: 408,000 (1998)
Telephone system: the civil network suffered some damage as a result of the Gulf war, but most of the telephone exchanges were left intact and, by the end of 1994, domestic and international telecommunications had been restored to normal operation; the quality of service is excellent
domestic: new telephone exchanges provide a large capacity for new subscribers; trunk traffic is carried by microwave radio relay, coaxial cable, open wire and fiber-optic cable; a cellular telephone system operates throughout Kuwait (with approximately 150,000 subscribers in 1996) and the country is well supplied with pay telephones; approximately 15,000 Internet subscribers in 1996
international: coaxial cable and microwave radio relay to Saudi Arabia; satellite earth stations - 3 Intelsat (1 Atlantic Ocean, 2 Indian Ocean), 1 Inmarsat (Atlantic Ocean), and 1 Arabsat
Radio broadcast stations: AM 3, FM 0, shortwave 0
Radios: 720,000 (1992 est.)
Television broadcast stations: 13 (in addition, there are several satellite channels) (1997)
Televisions: 800,000 (1993 est.)

Transportation

Railways: 0 km
Highways:
total: 4,450 km
paved: 3,587 km
unpaved: 863 km (1996 est.)

Kuwait (continued)

Pipelines: crude oil 877 km; petroleum products 40 km; natural gas 165 km

Ports and harbors: Ash Shu'aybah, Ash Shuwaykh, Kuwait, Mina' 'Abd Allah, Mina' al Ahmadi, Mina' Su'ud

Merchant marine:

total: 49 ships (1,000 GRT or over) totaling 2,509,061 GRT/4,046,739 DWT

ships by type: bulk 1, cargo 10, container 6, liquefied gas tanker 7, livestock carrier 3, oil tanker 22 (1998 est.)

Airports: 8 (1998 est.)

Airports - with paved runways:

total: 4

over 3,047 m: 2

2,438 to 3,047 m: 2 (1998 est.)

Airports - with unpaved runways:

total: 4

1,524 to 2,437 m: 1

914 to 1,523 m: 1

under 914 m: 2 (1998 est.)

Heliports: 1 (1998 est.)

Military

Military branches: Army, Navy, Air Force, National Police Force, National Guard, Coast Guard

Military manpower - military age: 18 years of age

Military manpower - availability:

males age 15-49: 718,061 (1999 est.)

Military manpower - fit for military service:

males age 15-49: 425,126 (1999 est.)

Military manpower - reaching military age annually:

males: 20,854 (1999 est.)

Military expenditures - dollar figure: $2.7035 billion (FY98/99)

Military expenditures - percent of GDP: 7.9% (FY98/99)

Transnational Issues

Disputes - international: in November 1994, Iraq formally accepted the UN-demarcated border with Kuwait which had been spelled out in Security Council Resolutions 687 (1991), 773 (1993), and 883 (1993); this formally ends earlier claims to Kuwait and to Bubiyan and Warbah islands; ownership of Qaruh and Umm al Maradim islands disputed by Saudi Arabia

Kyrgyzstan

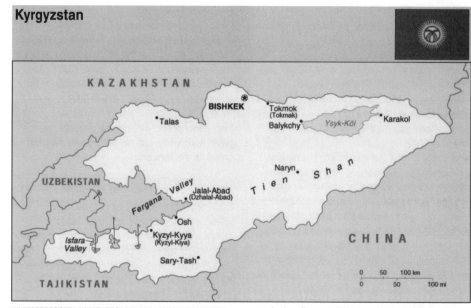

Introduction

Background: A country of incredible natural beauty and proud nomadic traditions, Kyrgyzstan became part of the Russian empire in 1864. In the Czarist and Soviet periods, Russian managers and technicians were sent to Kyrgyzstan and have recently made up more than one-fifth of the population. Many Russians have been returning home since Kyrgyzstan gained its independence in 1991 when the USSR collapsed. Privatization of state-owned enterprises, expansion of democracy and political freedoms, and inter-ethnic relations are current issues.

Geography

Location: Central Asia, west of China

Geographic coordinates: 41 00 N, 75 00 E

Map references: Commonwealth of Independent States

Area:

total: 198,500 sq km

land: 191,300 sq km

water: 7,200 sq km

Area - comparative: slightly smaller than South Dakota

Land boundaries:

total: 3,878 km

border countries: China 858 km, Kazakhstan 1,051 km, Tajikistan 870 km, Uzbekistan 1,099 km

Coastline: 0 km (landlocked)

Maritime claims: none (landlocked)

Climate: dry continental to polar in high Tien Shan; subtropical in southwest (Fergana Valley); temperate in northern foothill zone

Terrain: peaks of Tien Shan and associated valleys and basins encompass entire nation

Elevation extremes:

lowest point: Kara-Darya 132 m

highest point: Jengish Chokusu (Pik Pobedy) 7,439 m

Natural resources: abundant hydroelectric potential; significant deposits of gold and rare earth metals; locally exploitable coal, oil, and natural gas; other deposits of nepheline, mercury, bismuth, lead, and zinc

Land use:

arable land: 7%

permanent crops: 0%

permanent pastures: 44%

forests and woodland: 4%

other: 45% (1993 est.)

note: Kyrgyzstan has the world's largest natural growth walnut forest

Irrigated land: 9,000 sq km (1993 est.)

Natural hazards: NA

Environment - current issues: water pollution; many people get their water directly from contaminated streams and wells; as a result, water-borne diseases are prevalent; increasing soil salinity from faulty irrigation practices

Environment - international agreements:

party to: Biodiversity, Desertification, Hazardous Wastes

signed, but not ratified: none of the selected agreements

Geography - note: landlocked

People

Population: 4,546,055 (July 1999 est.)

Age structure:

0-14 years: 35% (male 804,502; female 788,076)

15-64 years: 59% (male 1,308,145; female 1,362,140)

65 years and over: 6% (male 105,442; female 177,750) (1999 est.)

Population growth rate: 0.68% (1999 est.)

Birth rate: 21.83 births/1,000 population (1999 est.)

Death rate: 8.74 deaths/1,000 population (1999 est.)

Net migration rate: -6.28 migrant(s)/1,000 population (1999 est.)

Sex ratio:

at birth: 1.05 male(s)/female

under 15 years: 1.02 male(s)/female

15-64 years: 0.96 male(s)/female
65 years and over: 0.59 male(s)/female
total population: 0.95 male(s)/female (1999 est.)
Infant mortality rate: 75.92 deaths/1,000 live births (1999 est.)
Life expectancy at birth:
total population: 63.57 years
male: 59.25 years
female: 68.1 years (1999 est.)
Total fertility rate: 2.63 children born/woman (1999 est.)
Nationality:
noun: Kyrgyzstani(s)
adjective: Kyrgyzstani
Ethnic groups: Kirghiz 52.4%, Russian 18%, Uzbek 12.9%, Ukrainian 2.5%, German 2.4%, other 11.8%
Religions: Muslim 75%, Russian Orthodox 20%, other 5%
Languages: Kirghiz (Kyrgyz) - official language, Russian - official language
note: in March 1996, the Kyrgyzstani legislature amended the constitution to make Russian an official language, along with Kirghiz, in territories and work places where Russian-speaking citizens predominate
Literacy:
definition: age 15 and over can read and write
total population: 97%
male: 99%
female: 96% (1989 est.)

Government

Country name:
conventional long form: Kyrgyz Republic
conventional short form: Kyrgyzstan
local long form: Kyrgyz Respublikasy
local short form: none
former: Kirghiz Soviet Socialist Republic
Data code: KG
Government type: republic
Capital: Bishkek
Administrative divisions: 6 oblasttar (singular - oblast) and 1 city* (singular - shaar); Bishkek Shaary*, Chuy Oblasty (Bishkek), Jalal-Abad Oblasty, Naryn Oblasty, Osh Oblasty, Talas Oblasty, Ysyk-Kol Oblasty (Karakol)
note: administrative divisions have the same names as their administrative centers (exceptions have the administrative center name following in parentheses)
Independence: 31 August 1991 (from Soviet Union)
National holiday: National Day, 2 December; Independence Day, 31 August (1991)
Constitution: adopted 5 May 1993
note: amendment proposed by President AKAYEV and passed in a national referendum on 10 February 1996 significantly expands the powers of the president at the expense of the legislature
Legal system: based on civil law system
Suffrage: 18 years of age; universal
Executive branch:
chief of state: President Askar AKAYEV (since 28 October 1990)
head of government: Prime Minister Jumabek

IBRAIMOV (since NA December 1998)
cabinet: Cabinet of Ministers appointed by the president on the recommendation of the prime minister
elections: president elected by popular vote for a five-year term; elections last held 24 December 1995 (next to be held NA 2000); prime minister appointed by the president
election results: Askar AKAYEV reelected president; percent of vote - Askar AKAYEV 75%; note - elections were held early which gave the two opposition candidates little time to campaign; AKAYEV may have orchestrated the "deregistration" of two other candidates, one of whom was a major rival
Legislative branch: bicameral Supreme Council or Zhogorku Kenesh consists of the Assembly of People's Representatives (70 seats; members are elected by popular vote to serve five-year terms) and the Legislative Assembly (35 seats; members are elected by popular vote to serve five-year terms)
elections: Assembly of People's Representatives - last held 5 February 1995 (next to be held NA 2000); Legislative Assembly - last held 5 February 1995 (next to be held NA 2000)
election results: Assembly of People's Representatives - percent of vote by party - NA; seats by party - NA; note - not all of the 70 seats were filled at the 5 February 1995 elections; as a result, run-off elections were held at later dates; the assembly meets twice yearly; Legislative Assembly - percent of vote by party - NA; seats by party - NA; note - not all of the 35 seats were filled at the 5 February 1995 elections; as a result, run-off elections were held at later dates
note: the legislature became bicameral for the 5 February 1995 elections
Judicial branch: Supreme Court, judges are appointed for 10-year terms by the Supreme Council on recommendation of the president; Constitutional Court; Higher Court of Arbitration
Political parties and leaders: Social Democratic Party or PSD [Zh. IBRAMOV]; Democratic Movement of Kyrgyzstan or DDK [Jypar JEKSHEYEV, chairman]; National Unity Democratic Movement or DDNE [Yury RAZGULYAYEV]; Communist Party of Kyrgyzstan or PKK [Absamat MASALIYEV, chairman]; Kyrgyzstan Erkin Party (Democratic Movement of Free Kyrgyzstan) or ErK [Tursunbay Bakir UULU]; Republican Popular Party of Kyrgyzstan [Zh. SHARSHENALIYEV]; Agrarian Party of Kyrgyzstan [A. ALIYEV]; Fatherland or Alta Mekel Party [Omurbek TEKEBAYEV]; Banner National Rivival Party or ASABA [Chaprashty BAZARBAY]; Movement for the People's Salvation [Djumgalbek AMAMBAYEV]; Mutual Help Movement or Ashar [Zhumagazy USUPOV]; Peasant Party [leader NA]; Agrarian Party [leader NA]
Political pressure groups and leaders: National Unity Democratic Movement; Council of Free Trade Unions; Union of Entrepreneurs; Kyrgyz Committee on Human Rights [Ramazan DYRYIDAYEV]
International organization participation: AsDB, CIS, EAPC, EBRD, ECE, ECO, ESCAP, FAO, IBRD,

ICAO, ICRM, IDA, IDB, IFAD, IFC, IFRCS, ILO, IMF, Intelsat, Interpol, IOC, IOM (observer), ISO (correspondent), ITU, OIC, OPCW, OSCE, PCA, PFP, UN, UNCTAD, UNESCO, UNIDO, UNOMSIL, UPU, WFTU, WHO, WIPO, WMO, WToO, WTrO
Diplomatic representation in the US:
chief of mission: Ambassador Bakyt ABDRISAYEV
chancery: 1732 Wisconsin Avenue NW, Washington, DC 20007
telephone: [1] (202) 338-5141
FAX: [1] (202) 338-5139
Diplomatic representation from the US:
chief of mission: Ambassador Anne M. SIGMUND
embassy: 171 Prospect Mira, 720016 Bishkek
mailing address: use embassy street address
telephone: [996] (3312) 22-29-20, 22-27-77
FAX: [996] (3312) 22-35-51
Flag description: red field with a yellow sun in the center having 40 rays representing the 40 Kirghiz tribes; on the obverse side the rays run counterclockwise, on the reverse, clockwise; in the center of the sun is a red ring crossed by two sets of three lines, a stylized representation of the roof of the traditional Kirghiz yurt

Economy

Economy - overview: Kyrgyzstan is a small, poor, mountainous country with a predominantly agricultural economy. Cotton, wool, and meat are the main agricultural products and exports. Industrial exports include gold, mercury, uranium, and hydropower. Kyrgyzstan has been one of the most progressive countries of the former Soviet Union in carrying out market reforms. Following a successful stabilization program, which lowered inflation from 88% in 1994 to 15% for 1997, attention is turning toward stimulating growth. Much of the government's stock in enterprises has been sold. Drops in production have been severe since the breakup of the Soviet Union in December 1991, but by mid-1995 production began to recover and exports began to increase. Pensioners, unemployed workers, and government workers with salary arrears continue to suffer. Foreign assistance played a substantial role in the country's economic turnaround in 1996-97. The government has adopted a series of measures to combat some of the severe economic problems such as excessive debt and inadequate revenue collection, encountered in 1998.
GDP: purchasing power parity - $9.8 billion (1998 est.)
GDP - real growth rate: 1.8% (1998 est.)
GDP - per capita: purchasing power parity - $2,200 (1998 est.)
GDP - composition by sector:
agriculture: 47%
industry: 12%
services: 41% (1996 est.)
Population below poverty line: 40% (1993 est.)
Household income or consumption by percentage share:
lowest 10%: 2.7%
highest 10%: 26.2% (1993)

Kyrgyzstan *(continued)*

Inflation rate (consumer prices): 18.4% (1998 est.)
Labor force: 1.7 million
Labor force - by occupation: agriculture and forestry 40%, industry and construction 19%, other 41% (1995 est.)
Unemployment rate: 6% 1998 est.)
Budget:
revenues: $225 million
expenditures: $308 million, including capital expenditures of $11 million (1996 est.)
Industries: small machinery, textiles, food processing, cement, shoes, sawn logs, refrigerators, furniture, electric motors, gold, rare earth metals
Industrial production growth rate: 14% (1998 est.)
note: the gold industry spurted in 1998 giving industry as a whole a boost on a small base while the rest of the economy, including agriculture, lagged
Electricity - production: 13.49 billion kWh (1996)
Electricity - production by source:
fossil fuel: 9.56%
hydro: 90.44%
nuclear: 0%
other: 0% (1996)
Electricity - consumption: 10.92 billion kWh (1996)
Electricity - exports: 6.32 billion kWh (1996)
Electricity - imports: 3.75 billion kWh (1996)
Agriculture - products: tobacco, cotton, potatoes, vegetables, grapes, fruits and berries; sheep, goats, cattle, wool
Exports: $630 million (1998 est.)
Exports - commodities: cotton, wool, meat, tobacco; gold, mercury, uranium, hydropower; machinery; shoes
Exports - partners: China, UK, FSU
Imports: $670 million (1998 est.)
Imports - commodities: grain, lumber, industrial products, ferrous metals, fuel, machinery, textiles, footwear
Imports - partners: Turkey, Cuba, US, Germany
Debt - external: $935 million (1997 est.)
Economic aid - recipient: $329.4 million (1995)
Currency: 1 Kyrgyzstani som (KGS) = 100 tyiyn
Exchange rates: soms (KGS) per US$1 - 30.25 (February 1999), 20.838 (1998), 17.362 (1997), 12.810 (1996), 10.822 (1995), 10.842 (1994)
Fiscal year: calendar year

Communications

Telephones: 356,000 (1996 est.)
Telephone system: poorly developed; about 100,000 unsatisfied applications for household telephones
domestic: principally microwave radio relay; one cellular provider, probably only limited to Bishkek region
international: connections with other CIS countries by landline or microwave radio relay and with other countries by leased connections with Moscow international gateway switch and by satellite; satellite earth stations - 1 Intersputnik and 1 Intelsat;

connected internationally by the Trans-Asia-Europe Fiber-Optic Line
Radio broadcast stations: AM NA, FM NA, shortwave NA; note - one state-run radio broadcast station
Radios: 825,000 (radio receiver systems with multiple speakers for program diffusion 748,000)
Television broadcast stations: NA (repeater stations throughout the country relay programs from Russia, Uzbekistan, Kazakhstan, and Turkey) (1997)
Televisions: 875,000

Transportation

Railways:
total: 370 km in common carrier service; does not include industrial lines
broad gauge: 370 km 1.520-m gauge (1990)
Highways:
total: 18,500 km
paved: 16,854 km (including 140 km of expressways)
unpaved: 1,646 km (1996 est.)
Waterways: 600 km (1990)
Pipelines: natural gas 200 km
Ports and harbors: Balykchy (Ysyk-Kol or Rybach'ye)
Airports: 54 (1994 est.)
Airports - with paved runways:
total: 14
over 3,047 m: 1
2,438 to 3,047 m: 3
1,524 to 2,437 m: 9
under 914 m: 1 (1994 est.)
Airports - with unpaved runways:
total: 40
1,524 to 2,437 m: 4
914 to 1,523 m: 4
under 914 m: 32 (1994 est.)

Military

Military branches: Army, National Guard, Security Forces (internal and border troops), Civil Defense
note: border troops controlled by Russia
Military manpower - military age: 18 years of age
Military manpower - availability:
males age 15-49: 1,146,595 (1999 est.)
Military manpower - fit for military service:
males age 15-49: 930,017 (1999 est.)
Military manpower - reaching military age annually:
males: 46,561 (1999 est.)
Military expenditures - dollar figure: $10.8 million (1996)
Military expenditures - percent of GDP: 1% (1996)

Transnational Issues

Disputes - international: territorial dispute with Tajikistan on southwestern boundary in Isfara Valley area
Illicit drugs: limited illicit cultivator of cannabis and opium poppy, mostly for CIS consumption; limited

government eradication program; increasingly used as transshipment point for illicit drugs to Russia and Western Europe from Southwest Asia

Laos

Geography

Location: Southeastern Asia, northeast of Thailand, west of Vietnam
Geographic coordinates: 18 00 N, 105 00 E
Map references: Southeast Asia
Area:
total: 236,800 sq km
land: 230,800 sq km
water: 6,000 sq km
Area - comparative: slightly larger than Utah
Land boundaries:
total: 5,083 km
border countries: Burma 235 km, Cambodia 541 km, China 423 km, Thailand 1,754 km, Vietnam 2,130 km
Coastline: 0 km (landlocked)
Maritime claims: none (landlocked)
Climate: tropical monsoon; rainy season (May to November); dry season (December to April)
Terrain: mostly rugged mountains; some plains and plateaus
Elevation extremes:
lowest point: Mekong River 70 m
highest point: Phou Bia 2,817 m
Natural resources: timber, hydropower, gypsum, tin, gold, gemstones
Land use:
arable land: 3%
permanent crops: 0%
permanent pastures: 3%
forests and woodland: 54%
other: 40% (1993 est.)
Irrigated land: 1,250 sq km (1993 est.)
note: rainy season irrigation - 2,169 sq km; dry season irrigation - 750 sq km (1998 est.)
Natural hazards: floods, droughts, and blight
Environment - current issues: unexploded ordnance; deforestation; soil erosion; a majority of the population does not have access to potable water
Environment - international agreements:
party to: Biodiversity, Climate Change,

Desertification, Environmental Modification, Law of the Sea, Nuclear Test Ban, Ozone Layer Protection
signed, but not ratified: none of the selected agreements
Geography - note: landlocked

People

Population: 5,407,453 (July 1999 est.)
Age structure:
0-14 years: 45% (male 1,235,797; female 1,203,520)
15-64 years: 52% (male 1,360,991; female 1,434,378)
65 years and over: 3% (male 78,195; female 94,572) (1999 est.)
Population growth rate: 2.74% (1999 est.)
Birth rate: 39.93 births/1,000 population (1999 est.)
Death rate: 12.56 deaths/1,000 population (1999 est.)
Net migration rate: 0 migrant(s)/1,000 population (1999 est.)
Sex ratio:
at birth: 1.05 male(s)/female
under 15 years: 1.03 male(s)/female
15-64 years: 0.95 male(s)/female
65 years and over: 0.83 male(s)/female
total population: 0.98 male(s)/female (1999 est.)
Infant mortality rate: 89.32 deaths/1,000 live births (1999 est.)
Life expectancy at birth:
total population: 54.21 years
male: 52.63 years
female: 55.87 years (1999 est.)
Total fertility rate: 5.55 children born/woman (1999 est.)
Nationality:
noun: Lao(s) or Laotian(s)
adjective: Lao or Laotian
Ethnic groups: Lao Loum (lowland) 68%, Lao Theung (upland) 22%, Lao Soung (highland) including the Hmong ("Meo") and the Yao (Mien) 9%, ethnic Vietnamese/Chinese 1%
Religions: Buddhist 60%, animist and other 40%
Languages: Lao (official), French, English, and various ethnic languages
Literacy:
definition: age 15 and over can read and write
total population: 60%
male: 70%
female: 48% (1998 est.)

Government

Country name:
conventional long form: Lao People's Democratic Republic
conventional short form: Laos
local long form: Sathalanalat Paxathipatai Paxaxon Lao
local short form: none
Data code: LA
Government type: Communist state
Capital: Vientiane

Administrative divisions: 16 provinces (khoueng, singular and plural), 1 municipality* (kampheng nakhon, singular and plural), and 1 special zone** (khetphiset, singular and plural); Attapu, Bokeo, Bolikhamxai, Champasak, Houaphan, Khammouan, Louangnamtha, Louangphabang, Oudomxai, Phongsali, Salavan, Savannakhet, Viangchan*, Viangchan, Xaignabouli, Xaisomboun**, Xekong, Xiangkhoang
Independence: 19 July 1949 (from France)
National holiday: National Day, 2 December (1975) (proclamation of the Lao People's Democratic Republic)
Constitution: promulgated 14 August 1991
Legal system: based on traditional customs, French legal norms and procedures, and Socialist practice
Suffrage: 18 years of age; universal
Executive branch:
chief of state: President KHAMTAI Siphandon (since 26 February 1998); Vice President OUDOM Khattiya (since 26 February 1998)
head of government: Prime Minister SISAVAT Keobounphan (since 26 February 1998); Senior Deputy Prime Minister BOUNGNANG Volachit (since 20 April 1996); Deputy Prime Ministers KHAMPHOUI Keoboualapha (since 15 August 1991), CHOUMMALI Saignason (since 26 February 1998), SOMSAVAT Lengsavad (since 26 February 1998)
cabinet: Council of Ministers appointed by the president, approved by the National Assembly
elections: president elected by the National Assembly for a five-year term; election last held 21 December 1997 (next to be held NA 2002); prime minister appointed by the president with the approval of the National Assembly for a five-year term
election results: KHAMTAI Siphandon elected president; percent of National Assembly vote - NA
Legislative branch: unicameral National Assembly (99 seats; members elected by popular vote to serve five-year terms; note - by presidential decree, on 27 October 1997, the number of seats increased from 85 to 99)
elections: last held 21 December 1997 (next to be held NA 2002)
election results: percent of vote by party - NA; seats by party - LPRP or LPRP-approved (independent, non-party members) 99
Judicial branch: People's Supreme Court, the president of the People's Supreme Court is elected by the National Assembly on the recommendation of the National Assembly Standing Committee, the vice president of the People's Supreme Court and the judges are appointed by the National Assembly Standing Committee
Political parties and leaders: Lao People's Revolutionary Party or LPRP [KHAMTAI Siphandon, party president]; other parties proscribed
Political pressure groups and leaders: noncommunist political groups proscribed; most opposition leaders fled the country in 1975
International organization participation: ACCT, AsDB, ASEAN, CP, ESCAP, FAO, G-77, IBRD, ICAO,

Laos (continued)

ICRM, IDA, IFAD, IFC, IFRCS, ILO, IMF, Intelsat (nonsignatory user), Interpol, IOC, ITU, NAM, OPCW, PCA, UN, UNCTAD, UNESCO, UNIDO, UPU, WFTU, WHO, WIPO, WMO, WToO, WTrO (observer)

Diplomatic representation in the US:
chief of mission: Ambassador VANG Rattanavong
chancery: 2222 S Street NW, Washington, DC 20008
telephone: [1] (202) 332-6416
FAX: [1] (202) 332-4923

Diplomatic representation from the US:
chief of mission: Ambassador Wendy Jean CHAMBERLIN
embassy: Rue Bartholonie, B.P. 114, Vientiane
mailing address: American Embassy, Box V, APO AP 96546
telephone: [856] (21) 212581, 212582, 212585
FAX: [856] (21) 212584

Flag description: three horizontal bands of red (top), blue (double width), and red with a large white disk centered in the blue band

Economy

Economy - overview: The government of Laos - one of the few remaining official communist states - has been decentralizing control and encouraging private enterprise since 1986. The results, starting from an extremely low base, have been striking - growth averaged 7% in 1988-96. Because Laos depends heavily on its trade with Thailand, it fell victim to the financial crisis in the region beginning in 1997. Laos is a landlocked country with a primitive infrastructure. It has no railroads, a rudimentary road system, and limited external and internal telecommunications. Electricity is available in only a few urban areas. Subsistence agriculture accounts for half of GDP and provides 80% of total employment. The predominant crop is glutinous rice. In non-drought years, Laos is self-sufficient overall in food, but each year flood, pests, and localized drought cause shortages in various parts of the country. For the foreseeable future the economy will continue to depend on aid from the IMF and other international sources; Japan is currently the largest bilateral aid donor; aid from the former USSR/Eastern Europe has been cut sharply. As in many developing countries, deforestation and soil erosion will hamper efforts to regain a high rate of GDP growth.
GDP: purchasing power parity - $6.6 billion (1998 est.)
GDP - real growth rate: 4% (1998 est.)
GDP - per capita: purchasing power parity - $1,260 (1998 est.)
GDP - composition by sector:
agriculture: 51%
industry: 21%
services: 28% (1998 est.)
Population below poverty line: 46.1% (1993 est.)
Household income or consumption by percentage share:
lowest 10%: 4.2%
highest 10%: 26.4% (1992)
Inflation rate (consumer prices): 112% (1998 est.)

Labor force: 1 million-1.5 million
Labor force - by occupation: agriculture 80% (1997 est.)
Unemployment rate: 5.7% (1997 est.)
Budget:
revenues: $230.2 million
expenditures: $365.9 million, including capital expenditures of $317 million (1996)
Industries: tin and gypsum mining, timber, electric power, agricultural processing, construction, garments
Industrial production growth rate: 8.9% (1998 est.)
Electricity - production: 900 million kWh (1996)
Electricity - production by source:
fossil fuel: 0.04%
hydro: 99.96%
nuclear: 0%
other: 0% (1998)
Electricity - consumption: 287 million kWh (1996)
Electricity - exports: 640 million kWh (1996)
Electricity - imports: 27 million kWh (1996)
Agriculture - products: sweet potatoes, vegetables, corn, coffee, sugarcane, tobacco, cotton; water buffalo, pigs, cattle, poultry
Exports: $330 million (f.o.b., 1998)
Exports - commodities: wood products, garments, electricity, coffee, tin
Exports - partners: Vietnam, Thailand, Germany, France
Imports: $630 million (c.i.f., 1998)
Imports - commodities: machinery and equipment, vehicles, fuel
Imports - partners: Thailand, Japan, Vietnam, China, Singapore
Debt - external: $1.2 billion (1996)
Economic aid - recipient: $290 million (1998)
Currency: 1 new kip (NK) = 100 at
Exchange rates: new kips (NK) per US$1 - 4,217 (January 1999), 3,299.21 (1998), 1,256.73 (1997), 921.14 (1996), 804.69 (1995), 717.67 (1994)
note: as of September 1995, a floating exchange rate policy was adopted
Fiscal year: 1 October - 30 September

Communications

Telephones: 28,000 (1998 est.)
Telephone system: service to general public is poor but improving, with over 28,000 telephones currently in service and an additional 48,000 expected by 2001; the government relies on a radiotelephone network to communicate with remote areas
domestic: radiotelephone communications
international: satellite earth station - 1 Intersputnik (Indian Ocean Region)
Radio broadcast stations: AM 9, FM 5, shortwave 4 (1998)
Radios: 580,000 (1995)
Television broadcast stations: 4 (1997)
Televisions: 32,000 (1993 est.)

Transportation

Railways: 0 km
Highways:
total: 21,716 km
paved: 9,673.5 km
unpaved: 12,042.5 km (1998 est.)
Waterways: about 4,587 km, primarily Mekong and tributaries; 2,897 additional kilometers are sectionally navigable by craft drawing less than 0.5 m
Pipelines: petroleum products 136 km
Ports and harbors: none
Merchant marine:
total: 1 cargo ship (1,000 GRT or over) totaling 2,370 GRT/3,000 DWT (1998 est.)
Airports: 52 (1998 est.)
Airports - with paved runways:
total: 9
over 3,047 m: 1
1,524 to 2,437 m: 5
914 to 1,523 m: 3 (1998 est.)
Airports - with unpaved runways:
total: 43
1,524 to 2,437 m: 1
914 to 1,523 m: 17
under 914 m: 25 (1998 est.)

Military

Military branches: Lao People's Army (LPA; includes militia element), Lao People's Navy (LPN; includes riverine element), Air Force, National Police Department
Military manpower - military age: 18 years of age
Military manpower - availability:
males age 15-49: 1,200,664 (1999 est.)
Military manpower - fit for military service:
males age 15-49: 648,087 (1999 est.)
Military manpower - reaching military age annually:
males: 57,047 (1999 est.)
Military expenditures - dollar figure: $77.4 million (FY96/97)
Military expenditures - percent of GDP: 4.2% (FY96/97)

Transnational Issues

Disputes - international: parts of the border with Thailand are indefinite
Illicit drugs: world's third-largest illicit opium producer (estimated cultivation in 1998 - 26,100 hectares, a 7% decrease over 1997; estimated potential production in 1998 - 140 metric tons, a 33% decrease over 1997); potential heroin producer; transshipment point for heroin and methamphetamines produced in Burma; illicit producer of cannabis

Latvia

Introduction

Background: Along with most of the other small nations of Europe, Latvia shares a history of invasion by a succession of expansionist nations, e.g., Sweden, Poland, Germany, and Russia. After a brief period of independence between the two World Wars, Latvia was annexed by the USSR in 1940 under the Molotov-Ribbentrop Pact. The USSR recaptured Latvia from its German occupiers in 1944. Latvia reestablished its independence in August 1991, a few months prior to the collapse of the Soviet Union; the last Russian troops left in 1994. The status of ethnic Russians, who make up 30% of the population, is an issue of concern to Moscow. Unemployment has become a growing problem and Latvia hopes to receive an invitation to begin EU accession talks by the end of 1999.

Geography

Location: Eastern Europe, bordering the Baltic Sea, between Estonia and Lithuania
Geographic coordinates: 57 00 N, 25 00 E
Map references: Europe
Area:
total: 64,589 sq km
land: 64,589 sq km
water: 0 sq km
Area - comparative: slightly larger than West Virginia
Land boundaries:
total: 1,150 km
border countries: Belarus 141 km, Estonia 339 km, Lithuania 453 km, Russia 217 km
Coastline: 531 km
Maritime claims:
continental shelf: 200-m depth or to the depth of exploitation
exclusive economic zone: 200 nm
territorial sea: 12 nm
Climate: maritime; wet, moderate winters

Terrain: low plain
Elevation extremes:
lowest point: Baltic Sea 0 m
highest point: Gaizinkalns 312 m
Natural resources: minimal; amber, peat, limestone, dolomite
Land use:
arable land: 27%
permanent crops: 0%
permanent pastures: 13%
forests and woodland: 46%
other: 14% (1993 est.)
Irrigated land: 160 sq km (1993 est.)
Natural hazards: NA
Environment - current issues: air and water pollution because of a lack of waste conversion equipment; Gulf of Riga and Daugava River heavily polluted; contamination of soil and groundwater with chemicals and petroleum products at military bases
Environment - international agreements:
party to: Air Pollution, Biodiversity, Climate Change, Endangered Species, Hazardous Wastes, Ozone Layer Protection, Ship Pollution, Wetlands
signed, but not ratified: Air Pollution-Persistent Organic Pollutants, Climate Change-Kyoto Protocol

People

Population: 2,353,874 (July 1999 est.)
Age structure:
0-14 years: 18% (male 216,369; female 207,242)
15-64 years: 67% (male 749,396; female 825,988)
65 years and over: 15% (male 114,038; female 240,841) (1999 est.)
Population growth rate: -1.25% (1999 est.)
Birth rate: 8.1 births/1,000 population (1999 est.)
Death rate: 15.82 deaths/1,000 population (1999 est.)
Net migration rate: -4.75 migrant(s)/1,000 population (1999 est.)
Sex ratio:
at birth: 1.05 male(s)/female

under 15 years: 1.04 male(s)/female
15-64 years: 0.91 male(s)/female
65 years and over: 0.47 male(s)/female
total population: 0.85 male(s)/female (1999 est.)
Infant mortality rate: 17.19 deaths/1,000 live births (1999 est.)
Life expectancy at birth:
total population: 67.3 years
male: 61.24 years
female: 73.66 years (1999 est.)
Total fertility rate: 1.18 children born/woman (1999 est.)
Nationality:
noun: Latvian(s)
adjective: Latvian
Ethnic groups: Latvian 56.5%, Russian 30.4%, Byelorussian 4.3%, Ukrainian 2.8%, Polish 2.6%, other 3.4%
Religions: Lutheran, Roman Catholic, Russian Orthodox
Languages: Lettish (official), Lithuanian, Russian, other
Literacy:
definition: age 15 and over can read and write
total population: 100%
male: 100%
female: 99% (1989 est.)

Government

Country name:
conventional long form: Republic of Latvia
conventional short form: Latvia
local long form: Latvijas Republika
local short form: Latvija
former: Latvian Soviet Socialist Republic
Data code: LG
Government type: parliamentary democracy
Capital: Riga
Administrative divisions: 26 counties (singular - rajons) and 7 municipalities*: Aizkraukles Rajons, Aluksnes Rajons, Balvu Rajons, Bauskas Rajons, Cesu Rajons, Daugavpils*, Daugavpils Rajons, Dobeles Rajons, Gulbenes Rajons, Jekabpils Rajons, Jelgava*, Jelgavas Rajons, Jurmala*, Kraslavas Rajons, Kuldigas Rajons, Leipaja*, Liepajas Rajons, Limbazu Rajons, Ludzas Rajons, Madonas Rajons, Ogres Rajons, Preilu Rajons, Rezekne*, Rezeknes Rajons, Riga*, Rigas Rajons, Saldus Rajons, Talsu Rajons, Tukuma Rajons, Valkas Rajons, Valmieras Rajons, Ventspils*, Ventspils Rajons
Independence: 6 September 1991 (from Soviet Union)
National holiday: Independence Day, 18 November (1918)
Constitution: the 1991 Constitutional Law which supplements the 1922 constitution, provides for basic rights and freedoms
Legal system: based on civil law system
Suffrage: 18 years of age; universal for Latvian citizens
Executive branch:
chief of state: President Guntis ULMANIS (since 7

Latvia (continued)

July 1993)

head of government: Prime Minister Vilis KRISTOPANS (since 21 November 1998)

cabinet: Council of Ministers nominated by the prime minister and appointed by the Parliament

elections: president elected by Parliament for a four-year term (amended from a three-year term on 4 December 1997); election last held 18 June 1996 (next to be held by NA June/July 1999); prime minister appointed by the president

election results: Guntis ULMANIS elected president in the first round of balloting; percent of parliamentary vote - Guntis ULMANIS 53%, Ilga KREITUSE 25%

Legislative branch: unicameral Parliament or Saeima (100 seats; members are elected by direct popular vote to serve four-year terms - amended from three-year term on 4 December 1997)

elections: last held 3 October 1998 (next to be held NA October 2002)

election results: percent of vote by party - People's Party 21%, LC 18%, TSP 14%, TVB/LNNK 14%, Social Democrats 13%, New Party 8%; seats by party - People's Party 24, LC 21, TSP 16, TVB/LNNK 17, Social Democrats 14, New Party 8

Judicial branch: Supreme Court, judges' appointments are confirmed by Parliament

Political parties and leaders: New Party [Raimonds PAULS]; People's Party [Andris SKELE]; Democratic Party "Saimnieks" or DPS [Ziedonis CEVERS, chairman]; Latvia's Way or LC [Andrei PANTELEJEVS]; For Fatherland and Freedom or TVB [Maris GRINBLATS], merged with LNNK; Latvian Unity Party or LVP [Alberis KAULS]; Latvian National Conservative Party or LNNK [Andrejs KRASTINS]; Green Party or LZP [Olegs BATAREVSK]; Latvian Farmers Union or LZS [Andris ROZENTALS]; Christian Democrat Union or LKDS [Talavs JUNDZIS]; National Harmony Party or TSP [Janis JURKANS]; Latvian Socialist Party or LSP [Sergejs DIAMANIS]; Latvian Liberal Party or LLP [J. DANOSS]; Political Association of the Underprivileged or MPA [B. PELSE, V. DIMANTS, J. KALNINS]; Latvian Democratic Labor Party or LDDP [J. BOJARS]; Party of Russian Citizens or LKPP [V. SOROCHIN, V. IVANOV]; Christian People's Party or KTP (formerly People's Front of Latvia or LTF) [Uldis AUGSTKALNS]; Political Union of Economists or TPA [Edvins KIDE]; Latvian National Democratic Party or LNDP [A. MALINS]; "Our Land" or MZ [M. DAMBEKALNE]; Anticommunist Union or PA [P. MUCENIEKS]; Latvian Social-Democratic Workers Party or LSDSP [Janis DINEVICS]; Party for the Defense of Latvia's Defrauded People [leader NA]; Latvian Independence Party or LNP [Valdis KONOVALOVS]; Association of Latvian Social Democrats [Juris BOJARS, Janis ADAMSONS]

International organization participation: BIS, CBSS, CCC, CE, EAPC, EBRD, ECE, EU (applicant), FAO, IAEA, IBRD, ICAO, ICFTU, ICRM, IDA, IFC, IFRCS, ILO, IMF, IMO, Intelsat (nonsignatory user), Interpol, IOC, IOM (observer), ISO (correspondent), ITU, OAS (observer), OPCW, OSCE, PFP, UN, UNCTAD, UNESCO, UNIDO, UPU, WEU (associate partner), WHO, WIPO, WMO, WTrO

Diplomatic representation in the US:

chief of mission: Ambassador Ojars Eriks KALNINS

chancery: 4325 17th Street NW, Washington, DC 20011

telephone: [1] (202) 726-8213, 8214

FAX: [1] (202) 726-6785

Diplomatic representation from the US:

chief of mission: Ambassador James H. HOLMES

embassy: Raina Boulevard 7, LV-1510, Riga

mailing address: American Embassy Riga, PSC 78, Box Riga, APO AE 09723

telephone: [371] 721-0005

FAX: [371] 782-0047

Flag description: three horizontal bands of maroon (top), white (half-width), and maroon

Economy

Economy - overview: Developments in 1998 include an invitation to join the World Trade Organization (the first Baltic country invited), GDP growth of 3.6% (down from 6% in 1997), and reduced inflation at 4.7% (from 8.4% in 1997). The drop in GDP growth is largely attributable to the impact of Russia's financial crisis and reduced investment in emerging markets following the Asian financial troubles. Unofficial sanctions that Russia imposed in the spring initially hit Latvia's exporters - Russia is among Latvia's top three trade partners - but also prompted them to seek alternative markets. Latvia continued its strict fiscal and monetary policy, including its second balanced budget and had a 1.8% budget surplus. Its draft 1999 budget is based on conservative projections of 2% to 4% GDP growth and 4.5% inflation. Unemployment climbed to 9.2% in 1998, a considerable increase over the 6.7% rate in 1997. Latvia continued to have a high current account deficit, estimated at about 9%. Privatization of large state utilities - especially the energy sector - was postponed and is unlikely to resume before late 1999. EU accession remains Latvia's top priority, and Latvia expects to be invited to start EU accession talks by the end of 1999. Continued troubles in the Russian and East Asian economies probably will hold growth to around 2.5% in 1999.

GDP: purchasing power parity - $9.7 billion (1998 est.)

GDP - real growth rate: 3.6% (1998 est.)

GDP - per capita: purchasing power parity - $4,100 (1998 est.)

GDP - composition by sector:

agriculture: 7%

industry: 28%

services: 65% (1997)

Population below poverty line: NA%

Household income or consumption by percentage share:

lowest 10%: 4.3%

highest 10%: 22.1% (1993)

Inflation rate (consumer prices): 4.7% (1998 est.)

Labor force: 1.4 million (1997)

Labor force - by occupation: industry 41%, agriculture and forestry 16%, services 43% (1990)

Unemployment rate: 9.2% (1998)

Budget:

revenues: $1.33 billion

expenditures: $1.27 billion, including capital expenditures of $NA (1998 est.)

Industries: buses, vans, street and railroad cars, synthetic fibers, agricultural machinery, fertilizers, washing machines, radios, electronics, pharmaceuticals, processed foods, textiles; dependent on imports for energy, raw materials, and intermediate products

Industrial production growth rate: 3% (1998 est.)

Electricity - production: 3.2 billion kWh (1996)

Electricity - production by source:

fossil fuel: 28.12%

hydro: 71.88%

nuclear: 0%

other: 0% (1996)

Electricity - consumption: 6.18 billion kWh (1996)

Electricity - exports: 300 million kWh (1996)

Electricity - imports: 3.28 billion kWh (1996)

Agriculture - products: grain, sugar beets, potatoes, vegetables; beef, milk, eggs; fish

Exports: $1.9 billion (f.o.b., 1998)

Exports - commodities: wood and wood products, machinery and equipment, textiles, foodstuffs

Exports - partners: Russia 21%, Germany 14%, UK 14%, Sweden 8% (1997)

Imports: $3.1 billion (f.o.b., 1998)

Imports - commodities: fuels, machinery and equipment, chemicals

Imports - partners: Russia 16%, Germany 16%, Finland 10%, Sweden 8% (1997)

Debt - external: $212 million (1998)

Economic aid - recipient: $96.2 million (1995)

Currency: 1 Latvian lat (LVL) = 100 santims

Exchange rates: lats (LVL) per US$1 - 0.570 (January 1999), 0.590 (1998), 0.581 (1997), 0.551 (1996), 0.528 (1995), 0.560 (1994)

Fiscal year: calendar year

Communications

Telephones: 710,848 (1997)

Telephone system: Lattelekom is 51% state owned, plans to privatize in 2000 to satisfy EU concerns; 50,000 people are on the waiting list to receive telephone service; Internet service is available throughout Latvia

domestic: local - two cellular service providers; NMT-450 and GSM standards provide service nationwide; over 75% of population covered; intercity - two synchronous digital hierarchy fiber-optic rings form the national backbone; 11 digital switching centers, 3 service centers

international: Latvia has international fiber-optic connectivity to Belarus, Estonia, Lithuania, and an undersea fiber-optic cable to Sweden

Radio broadcast stations: AM NA, FM NA, shortwave NA; note - there are 25 stations of unknown type; 75% of commercial broadcasts must be in the

Latvia (continued)

Latvian language; remainder mostly in Russian and European languages
Radios: 1.4 million (1993 est.)
Television broadcast stations: 30 (origin of TV broadcasts must be 40% Latvian and 40% other European languages)
Televisions: NA; note - almost 100% of the population have TV access, 16% have VCRs, and 20% have cable or satellite dishes (1995)

Transportation

Railways:
total: 2,412 km
broad gauge: 2,379 km 1.520-m gauge (271 km electrified) (1992)
narrow gauge: 33 km 0.750-m gauge (1994)
Highways:
total: 55,942 km
paved: 21,426 km
unpaved: 34,516 km (1997 est.)
Waterways: 300 km perennially navigable
Pipelines: crude oil 750 km; refined products 780 km; natural gas 560 km (1992)
Ports and harbors: Daugavpils, Liepaja, Riga, Ventspils
Merchant marine:
total: 11 ships (1,000 GRT or over) totaling 42,429 GRT/44,583 DWT
ships by type: cargo 3, oil tanker 4, refrigerated cargo 3, roll-on/roll-off cargo 1 (1998 est.)
Airports: 50 (1994 est.)
Airports - with paved runways:
total: 36
2,438 to 3,047 m: 6
1,524 to 2,437 m: 2
914 to 1,523 m: 1
under 914 m: 27 (1994 est.)
Airports - with unpaved runways:
total: 14
2,438 to 3,047 m: 2
914 to 1,523 m: 2
under 914 m: 10 (1994 est.)

Military

Military branches: Ground Forces, Navy, Air and Air Defense Forces, Security Forces, Border Guard, Home Guard (Zemessardze)
Military manpower - military age: 18 years of age
Military manpower - availability:
males age 15-49: 565,811 (1999 est.)
Military manpower - fit for military service:
males age 15-49: 443,879 (1999 est.)
Military manpower - reaching military age annually:
males: 16,883 (1999 est.)
Military expenditures - dollar figure: $60 million (1999)
Military expenditures - percent of GDP: 0.9% (1999)

Transnational Issues

Disputes - international: draft treaty delimiting the boundary with Russia has not been signed; ongoing talks over maritime boundary dispute with Lithuania (primary concern is oil exploration rights)
Illicit drugs: transshipment point for opiates and cannabis from Central and Southwest Asia to Western Europe and Scandinavia and Latin American cocaine and some synthetics from Western Europe to CIS; limited production of illicit amphetamines, ephedrine, and ecstasy for export

Lebanon

Introduction

Background: Lebanon has made progress toward rebuilding its political institutions and regaining its national sovereignty since the end of the devastating 16-year civil war, which ended in 1991. Under the Ta'if Accord - the blueprint for national reconciliation - the Lebanese have established a more equitable political system, particularly by giving Muslims a greater say in the political process while institutionalizing sectarian divisions in the government. Since the end of the civil war, the Lebanese have formed six cabinets, conducted two legislative elections, and held their first municipal elections in 35 years. Most of the militias have been weakened or disbanded. The Lebanese Armed Forces (LAF) has seized vast quantities of weapons used by the militias during the war and extended central government authority over about one-half of the country. Hizballah, the radical Shi'a party, retains its weapons. Foreign forces still occupy areas of Lebanon. Israel maintains troops in southern Lebanon and continues to support a proxy militia, the Army of South Lebanon (ASL), along a narrow stretch of territory contiguous to its border. The ASL's enclave encompasses this self-declared security zone and about 20 kilometers north to the strategic town of Jazzin. Syria maintains about 25,000 troops in Lebanon based mainly in Beirut, North Lebanon, and the Bekaa Valley. Syria's deployment was legitimized by the Arab League during Lebanon's civil war and in the Ta'if Accord. Citing the continued weakness of the LAF, Beirut's requests, and failure of the Lebanese Government to implement all of the constitutional reforms in the Ta'if Accord, Damascus has so far refused to withdraw its troops from Lebanon.

Geography

Location: Middle East, bordering the Mediterranean Sea, between Israel and Syria
Geographic coordinates: 33 50 N, 35 50 E
Map references: Middle East

Lebanon (continued)

Area:
total: 10,400 sq km
land: 10,230 sq km
water: 170 sq km
Area - comparative: about 0.7 times the size of Connecticut
Land boundaries:
total: 454 km
border countries: Israel 79 km, Syria 375 km
Coastline: 225 km
Maritime claims:
territorial sea: 12 nm
Climate: Mediterranean; mild to cool, wet winters with hot, dry summers; Lebanon mountains experience heavy winter snows
Terrain: narrow coastal plain; Al Biqa' (Bekaa Valley) separates Lebanon and Anti-Lebanon Mountains
Elevation extremes:
lowest point: Mediterranean Sea 0 m
highest point: Jabal al Makmal 3,087 m
Natural resources: limestone, iron ore, salt, water-surplus state in a water-deficit region
Land use:
arable land: 21%
permanent crops: 9%
permanent pastures: 1%
forests and woodland: 8%
other: 61% (1993 est.)
Irrigated land: 860 sq km (1993 est.)
Natural hazards: dust storms, sandstorms
Environment - current issues: deforestation; soil erosion; desertification; air pollution in Beirut from vehicular traffic and the burning of industrial wastes; pollution of coastal waters from raw sewage and oil spills
Environment - international agreements:
party to: Biodiversity, Climate Change, Desertification, Hazardous Wastes, Law of the Sea, Nuclear Test Ban, Ozone Layer Protection, Ship Pollution
signed, but not ratified: Environmental Modification, Marine Dumping, Marine Life Conservation
Geography - note: Nahr al Litani only major river in Near East not crossing an international boundary; rugged terrain historically helped isolate, protect, and develop numerous factional groups based on religion, clan, and ethnicity

People

Population: 3,562,699 (July 1999 est.)
Age structure:
0-14 years: 30% (male 535,596; female 515,776)
15-64 years: 64% (male 1,084,121; female 1,196,678)
65 years and over: 6% (male 105,133; female 125,395) (1999 est.)
Population growth rate: 1.61% (1999 est.)
Birth rate: 22.5 births/1,000 population (1999 est.)
Death rate: 6.45 deaths/1,000 population (1999 est.)
Net migration rate: 0 migrant(s)/1,000 population (1999 est.)

Sex ratio:
at birth: 1.05 male(s)/female
under 15 years: 1.04 male(s)/female
15-64 years: 0.91 male(s)/female
65 years and over: 0.84 male(s)/female
total population: 0.94 male(s)/female (1999 est.)
Infant mortality rate: 30.53 deaths/1,000 live births (1999 est.)
Life expectancy at birth:
total population: 70.93 years
male: 68.34 years
female: 73.66 years (1999 est.)
Total fertility rate: 2.25 children born/woman (1999 est.)
Nationality:
noun: Lebanese (singular and plural)
adjective: Lebanese
Ethnic groups: Arab 95%, Armenian 4%, other 1%
Religions: Islam 70% (5 legally recognized Islamic groups - Alawite or Nusayri, Druze, Isma'ilite, Shi'a, Sunni), Christian 30% (11 legally recognized Christian groups - 4 Orthodox Christian, 6 Catholic, 1 Protestant), Judaism NEGL%
Languages: Arabic (official), French, English, Armenian widely understood
Literacy:
definition: age 15 and over can read and write
total population: 86.4%
male: 90.8%
female: 82.2% (1997 est.)

Government

Country name:
conventional long form: Lebanese Republic
conventional short form: Lebanon
local long form: Al Jumhuriyah al Lubnaniyah
local short form: Lubnan
Data code: LE
Government type: republic
Capital: Beirut
Administrative divisions: 5 governorates (muhafazat, singular - muhafazah); Al Biqa', Al Janub, Ash Shamal, Bayrut, Jabal Lubnan
Independence: 22 November 1943 (from League of Nations mandate under French administration)
National holiday: Independence Day, 22 November (1943)
Constitution: 23 May 1926, amended a number of times
Legal system: mixture of Ottoman law, canon law, Napoleonic code, and civil law; no judicial review of legislative acts; has not accepted compulsory ICJ jurisdiction
Suffrage: 21 years of age; compulsory for all males; authorized for women at age 21 with elementary education
Executive branch:
chief of state: President Emile LAHUD (since 24 November 1998)
head of government: Prime Minister Salim al-HUSS (since 4 December 1998)
cabinet: Cabinet chosen by the prime minister in

consultation with the president and members of the National Assembly; the current Cabinet was formed in 1998
elections: president elected by the National Assembly for a six-year term; election last held 15 October 1998 (next to be held NA 2004); prime minister and deputy prime minister appointed by the president in consultation with the National Assembly; by custom, the president is a Maronite Christian, the prime minister is a Sunni Muslim, and the speaker of the legislature is a Shi'a Muslim
election results: Emile LAHUD elected president; National Assembly vote - 118 votes in favor, 0 against, 10 abstentions
Legislative branch: unicameral National Assembly or Majlis Alnuwab (Arabic) or Assemblee Nationale (French) (128 seats; members elected by popular vote on the basis of sectarian proportional representation to serve four-year terms)
elections: last held in the summer of 1996 (next to be held NA 2000)
election results: percent of vote by party - NA; seats by party - NA (one-half Christian and one-half Muslim)
Judicial branch: four Courts of Cassation (three courts for civil and commercial cases and one court for criminal cases); Constitutional Council (called for in Ta'if Accord) rules on constitutionality of laws; Supreme Council (hears charges against the president and prime minister as needed)
Political parties and leaders: political party activity is organized along largely sectarian lines; numerous political groupings exist, consisting of individual political figures and followers motivated by religious, clan, and economic considerations
International organization participation: ABEDA, ACCT, AFESD, AL, AMF, CCC, ESCWA, FAO, G-24, G-77, IAEA, IBRD, ICAO, ICC, ICFTU, ICRM, IDA, IDB, IFAD, IFC, IFRCS, ILO, IMF, IMO, Inmarsat, Intelsat, Interpol, IOC, ISO (correspondent), ITU, NAM, OAS (observer), OIC, PCA, UN, UNCTAD, UNESCO, UNHCR, UNIDO, UNRWA, UPU, WFTU, WHO, WIPO, WMO, WToO
Diplomatic representation in the US:
chief of mission: Ambassador-designate Farid ABBOUD
chancery: 2560 28th Street NW, Washington, DC 20008
telephone: [1] (202) 939-6300
FAX: [1] (202) 939-6324
consulate(s) general: Detroit, New York, and Los Angeles
Diplomatic representation from the US:
chief of mission: Ambassador David SATTERFIELD
embassy: Antelias, Beirut
mailing address: P. O. Box 70-840, Beirut; PSC 815, Box 2, FPO AE 09836-0002
telephone: [961] (1) 402200, 403300, 426183, 417774, 889926
FAX: [961] (1) 407112
Flag description: three horizontal bands of red (top), white (double width), and red with a green and brown cedar tree centered in the white band

Lebanon (continued)

Economy

Economy - overview: The 1975-91 civil war seriously damaged Lebanon's economic infrastructure, cut national output by half, and all but ended Lebanon's position as a Middle Eastern entrepot and banking hub. Peace has enabled the central government to restore control in Beirut, begin collecting taxes, and regain access to key port and government facilities. Economic recovery has been helped by a financially sound banking system and resilient small- and medium-scale manufacturers, with family remittances, banking services, manufactured and farm exports, and international aid as the main sources of foreign exchange. Lebanon's economy has made impressive gains since the launch of "Horizon 2000," the government's $20 billion reconstruction program in 1993. Real GDP grew 8% in 1994 and 7% in 1995 before Israel's Operation Grapes of Wrath in April 1996 stunted economic activity. During 1992-98, annual inflation fell from more than 100% to 5%, and foreign exchange reserves jumped to more than $6 billion from $1.4 billion. Burgeoning capital inflows have generated foreign payments surpluses, and the Lebanese pound has remained relatively stable. Progress also has been made in rebuilding Lebanon's war-torn physical and financial infrastructure. Solidere, a $2-billion firm, is managing the reconstruction of Beirut's central business district; the stock market reopened in January 1996; and international banks and insurance companies are returning. The government nonetheless faces serious challenges in the economic arena. It has had to fund reconstruction by tapping foreign exchange reserves and boosting borrowing. Reducing the government budget deficit is a major goal of the LAHUD government. The stalled peace process and ongoing violence in southern Lebanon could lead to wider hostilities that would disrupt vital capital inflows. Furthermore, the gap between rich and poor has widened in the 1990's, resulting in grassroots dissatisfaction over the skewed distribution of the reconstruction's benefits and leading the government to shift its focus from rebuilding infrastructure to improving living conditions.

GDP: purchasing power parity - $15.8 billion (1998 est.)

GDP - real growth rate: 3% (1998 est.)

GDP - per capita: purchasing power parity - $4,500 (1998 est.)

GDP - composition by sector:
agriculture: 4%
industry: 23%
services: 73% (1997 est.)

Population below poverty line: NA%

Household income or consumption by percentage share:
lowest 10%: NA%
highest 10%: NA%

Inflation rate (consumer prices): 5% (1998 est.)

Labor force: 1 million

note: in addition, there are as many as 1 million foreign workers (1996 est.)

Labor force - by occupation: services 62%, industry 31%, agriculture 7% (1997 est.)

Unemployment rate: 18% (1997 est.)

Budget:
revenues: $4.9 billion
expenditures: $7.9 billion, including capital expenditures of $NA (1998 est.)

Industries: banking; food processing; jewelry; cement; textiles; mineral and chemical products; wood and furniture products; oil refining; metal fabricating

Industrial production growth rate: 25% (1993 est.)

Electricity - production: 8.4 billion kWh (1997 est.)

Electricity - production by source:
fossil fuel: 87.72%
hydro: 12.28%
nuclear: 0%
other: 0% (1996)

Electricity - consumption: 6.01 billion kWh (1996)

Electricity - exports: 0 kWh (1996)

Electricity - imports: 310 million kWh (1996)

Agriculture - products: citrus, grapes, tomatoes, apples, vegetables, potatoes, olives, tobacco, hemp (hashish); sheep, goats

Exports: $711 million (f.o.b., 1997)

Exports - commodities: foodstuffs and tobacco 20%, textiles 12%, chemicals 11%, metal and metal products 11%, electrical equipment and products 10%, jewelry 10%, paper and paper products 8% (1997)

Exports - partners: Saudi Arabia 14%, UAE 9%, France 7%, Syria 6%, US 6%, Kuwait 4%, Jordan 4%, Turkey 4%

Imports: $7.5 billion (c.i.f., 1997)

Imports - commodities: foodstuffs 29%, machinery and transport equipment 28%, consumer goods 18%, chemicals 9%, textiles 5%, metals 5%, fuels 3%, agricultural foods 3% (1997)

Imports - partners: Italy 13%, US 9%, France 9%, Germany 8%, Switzerland 7%, Japan 4%, UK 4%, Syria 4% (1997)

Debt - external: $3 billion (1998 est.)

Economic aid - recipient: $3.5 billion (pledges 1997-2001)

Currency: 1 Lebanese pound (£L) = 100 piasters

Exchange rates: Lebanese pounds (£L) per US$1 - 1,508.0 (January 1999), 1,516.1 (1998), 1,539.5 (1997), 1,571.4 (1996), 1,621.4 (1995), 1,680.1 (1994)

Fiscal year: calendar year

Communications

Telephones: 150,000 (1990 est.)

Telephone system: telecommunications system severely damaged by civil war; rebuilding well underway
domestic: primarily microwave radio relay and cable
international: satellite earth stations - 2 Intelsat (1 Indian Ocean and 1 Atlantic Ocean) (erratic operations); coaxial cable to Syria; microwave radio relay to Syria but inoperable beyond Syria to Jordan; 3 submarine coaxial cables

Radio broadcast stations: AM 5, FM 3, shortwave 1

note: government is licensing a limited number of the more than 100 AM and FM stations operated sporadically by various factions that sprang up during the civil war

Radios: 2.37 million (1992 est.)

Television broadcast stations: 28 (1997)

Televisions: 1.1 million (1993 est.)

Transportation

Railways:
total: 222 km
standard gauge: 222 km 1.435-m (from Beirut to the Syrian border)

Highways:
total: 6,270 km
paved: 6,270 km
unpaved: 0 km (1998 est.)

Pipelines: crude oil 72 km (none in operation)

Ports and harbors: Al Batrun, Al Mina', An Naqurah, Antilyas, Az Zahrani, Beirut, Jubayl, Juniyah, Shikka, Sidon, Tripoli, Tyre

Merchant marine:
total: 64 ships (1,000 GRT or over) totaling 267,562 GRT/403,252 DWT
ships by type: bulk 6, cargo 41, chemical tanker 1, combination bulk 1, combination ore/oil 1, container 3, livestock carrier 6, roll-on/roll-off cargo 2, vehicle carrier 3 (1998 est.)

Airports: 9 (1998 est.)

Airports - with paved runways:
total: 7
over 3,047 m: 1
2,438 to 3,047 m: 2
1,524 to 2,437 m: 2
914 to 1,523 m: 1
under 914 m: 1 (1998 est.)

Airports - with unpaved runways:
total: 2
914 to 1,523 m: 1
under 914 m: 1 (1998 est.)

Military

Military branches: Lebanese Armed Forces (LAF; includes Army, Navy, and Air Force)

Military manpower - availability:
males age 15-49: 925,834 (1999 est.)

Military manpower - fit for military service:
males age 15-49: 573,093 (1999 est.)

Military expenditures - dollar figure: $445 million (1997)

Military expenditures - percent of GDP: 5% (1997)

Transnational Issues

Disputes - international: Israeli troops in southern Lebanon since June 1982; Syrian troops in northern, central, and eastern Lebanon since October 1976

Lebanon (continued)

Illicit drugs: inconsequential producer of hashish and heroin; some heroine and cocaine processing mostly in the Bekaa valley; a Lebanese/Syrian eradication campaign started in the early 1990s has practically eliminated the opium and cannabis crops

Lesotho

Geography

Location: Southern Africa, an enclave of South Africa
Geographic coordinates: 29 30 S, 28 30 E
Map references: Africa
Area:
total: 30,350 sq km
land: 30,350 sq km
water: 0 sq km
Area - comparative: slightly smaller than Maryland
Land boundaries:
total: 909 km
border countries: South Africa 909 km
Coastline: 0 km (landlocked)
Maritime claims: none (landlocked)
Climate: temperate; cool to cold, dry winters; hot, wet summers
Terrain: mostly highland with plateaus, hills, and mountains
Elevation extremes:
lowest point: junction of the Orange and Makhaleng Rivers 1,400 m
highest point: Thabana Ntlenyana 3,482 m
Natural resources: water, agricultural and grazing land, some diamonds and other minerals
Land use:
arable land: 11%
permanent crops: NA%
permanent pastures: 66%
forests and woodland: NA%
other: 23% (1993 est.)
Irrigated land: 30 sq km (1993 est.)
Natural hazards: periodic droughts
Environment - current issues: population pressure forcing settlement in marginal areas results in overgrazing, severe soil erosion, and soil exhaustion; desertification; Highlands Water Project controls, stores, and redirects water to South Africa
Environment - international agreements:
party to: Biodiversity, Climate Change,

Desertification, Marine Life Conservation, Ozone Layer Protection
signed, but not ratified: Endangered Species, Law of the Sea, Marine Dumping
Geography - note: landlocked; surrounded by South Africa

People

Population: 2,128,950 (July 1999 est.)
Age structure:
0-14 years: 40% (male 424,355; female 422,892)
15-64 years: 56% (male 573,285; female 610,636)
65 years and over: 4% (male 40,604; female 57,178) (1999 est.)
Population growth rate: 1.8% (1999 est.)
Birth rate: 31.26 births/1,000 population (1999 est.)
Death rate: 13.23 deaths/1,000 population (1999 est.)
Net migration rate: 0 migrant(s)/1,000 population (1999 est.)
Sex ratio:
at birth: 1.03 male(s)/female
under 15 years: 1 male(s)/female
15-64 years: 0.94 male(s)/female
65 years and over: 0.71 male(s)/female
total population: 0.95 male(s)/female (1999 est.)
Infant mortality rate: 77.58 deaths/1,000 live births (1999 est.)
Life expectancy at birth:
total population: 52.99 years
male: 51.37 years
female: 54.65 years (1999 est.)
Total fertility rate: 4.03 children born/woman (1999 est.)
Nationality:
noun: Mosotho (singular), Basotho (plural)
adjective: Basotho
Ethnic groups: Sotho 99.7%, Europeans 1,600, Asians 800
Religions: Christian 80%, rest indigenous beliefs
Languages: Sesotho (southern Sotho), English (official), Zulu, Xhosa
Literacy:
definition: age 15 and over can read and write
total population: 71.3%
male: 81.1%
female: 62.3% (1995 est.)

Government

Country name:
conventional long form: Kingdom of Lesotho
conventional short form: Lesotho
former: Basutoland
Data code: LT
Government type: parliamentary constitutional monarchy
Capital: Maseru
Administrative divisions: 10 districts; Berea, Butha-Buthe, Leribe, Mafeteng, Maseru, Mohales Hoek, Mokhotlong, Qacha's Nek, Quthing, Thaba-Tseka

Independence: 4 October 1966 (from UK)
National holiday: Independence Day, 4 October (1966)
Constitution: 2 April 1993
Legal system: based on English common law and Roman-Dutch law; judicial review of legislative acts in High Court and Court of Appeal; has not accepted compulsory ICJ jurisdiction
Suffrage: 18 years of age; universal
Executive branch:
chief of state: King LETSIE III (since 7 February 1996, succeeded to the throne following the death of his father, King MOSHOESHOE II, on 16 January 1996); note - King LETSIE III formerly occupied the throne (November 1990 to February 1995) while his father was in exile
head of government: Prime Minister Pakalitha MOSISILI (since NA May 1998)
cabinet: Cabinet
elections: none; the monarch is hereditary, but, under the terms of the constitution which came into effect after the March 1993 election, the monarch is a "living symbol of national unity" with no executive or legislative powers; under traditional law the college of chiefs has the power to determine who is next in the line of succession, who shall serve as regent in the event that the successor is not of mature age, and may even depose the monarch
Legislative branch: bicameral Parliament consists of the Senate (33 members - 22 principal chiefs and 11 other members appointed by the ruling party) and the Assembly (80 seats; members elected by popular vote for five-year terms); note - number of seats in the Assembly rose from 65 to 80 in the May 1998 election
elections: last held 23 May 1998 (next to be held in late 1999 or early 2000)
election results: percent of vote by party - LCD 61%; seats by party - LCD 79, BCP 1
note: results contested; LCD, with only 61% of the vote, won 79 out of 80 parliamentary seats based on a historical political consensus for a "winner take all" formula
Judicial branch: High Court, chief justice appointed by the monarch; Court of Appeal; Magistrate's Court; customary or traditional court
Political parties and leaders:
ruling party: Lesotho Congress for Democracy or LCD [Dr. Pakalitha MOSISILI, leader; Shakhane MOKHEHLE, secretary general]
opposition party: Basotho National Party or BNP [leader NA]; Basotholand Congress Party or BCP [Molapo QHOBELA]; Lesotho Labor Party/United Democratic Party Alliance or LLP/UDP [Charles MOFELI and Mamolefi RANTHIMO]; Maremátlou Freedom Party or MFP [Vincent MALEBO]; National Progressive Party or NPP [Chief Peete Nkoebe PEETE]; Sefate Democratic Union or SDU [Bofihla NKUEBE]; Lesotho Congress for Democracy or LCD [leader NA]
International organization participation: ACP, AfDB, C, CCC, ECA, FAO, G-77, IBRD, ICAO, ICFTU, ICRM, IDA, IFAD, IFC, IFRCS, ILO, IMF, Intelsat (nonsignatory user), Interpol, IOC, ITU, NAM, OAU, OPCW, SACU, SADC, UN, UNCTAD, UNESCO, UNHCR, UNIDO, UPU, WCL, WFTU, WHO, WIPO, WMO, WToO, WTrO
Diplomatic representation in the US:
chief of mission: Ambassador Dr. Eunice M. BULANE
chancery: 2511 Massachusetts Avenue NW, Washington, DC 20008
telephone: [1] (202) 797-5533 through 5536
FAX: [1] (202) 234-6815
Diplomatic representation from the US:
chief of mission: Ambassador Katherine H. PETERSON
embassy: 254 Kingsway, Maseru West (Consular Section)
mailing address: P. O. Box 333, Maseru 100, Lesotho
telephone: [266] 312666
FAX: [266] 310116
Flag description: divided diagonally from the lower hoist side corner; the upper half is white, bearing the brown silhouette of a large shield with crossed spear and club; the lower half is a diagonal blue band with a green triangle in the corner

Economy

Economy - overview: Small, landlocked, and mountainous, Lesotho's only important natural resource is water. Its economy is based on subsistence agriculture, livestock, and remittances from miners employed in South Africa. The number of such mine workers has declined steadily over the past several years. In 1996 their remittances added about 33% to GDP compared with the addition of roughly 67% in 1990. A small manufacturing base depends largely on farm products which support the milling, canning, leather, and jute industries. Agricultural products are exported primarily to South Africa. Proceeds from membership in a common customs union with South Africa form the majority of government revenue. Although drought has decreased agricultural activity over the past few years, completion of a major hydropower facility in January 1998 now permits the sale of water to South Africa, generating royalties that will be an important source of income for Lesotho. The pace of parastatal privatization has increased in recent years. Civil disorder in September 1998 destroyed 80% of the commercial infrastructure in Maseru and two other major towns. Most firms were not covered by insurance, and the rebuilding of small and medium business will be a significant challenge in terms of both economic growth and employment levels.
GDP: purchasing power parity - $5.1 billion (1997 est.)
GDP - real growth rate: 10% (1997 est.)
GDP - per capita: purchasing power parity - $2,400 (1997 est.)
GDP - composition by sector:
agriculture: 14%
industry: 42%
services: 44% (1996 est.)
Population below poverty line: 49.2% (1993 est.)
Household income or consumption by percentage share:
lowest 10%: 0.9%
highest 10%: 43.4% (1986-87)
Inflation rate (consumer prices): 8% (1997 est.)
Labor force: 689,000 economically active
Labor force - by occupation: 86% of resident population engaged in subsistence agriculture; roughly 35% of the active male wage earners work in South Africa
Unemployment rate: substantial unemployment and underemployment effecting more than half of the labor force (1996 est.)
Budget:
revenues: $507 million
expenditures: $487 million, including capital expenditures of $170 million (FY96/97 est.)
Industries: food, beverages, textiles, handicrafts; construction; tourism
Industrial production growth rate: 19.7% (1995)
Electricity - production: 0 kWh (1995)
note: electricity supplied by South Africa
Electricity - production by source:
fossil fuel: NA%
hydro: NA%
nuclear: NA%
other: NA%
Electricity - consumption: 335 million kWh (1996)
Electricity - exports: 0 kWh (1996)
Electricity - imports: 335 million kWh (1996)
Agriculture - products: corn, wheat, pulses, sorghum, barley; livestock
Exports: $200 million (f.o.b., 1997 est.)
Exports - commodities: manufactures 65% (clothing, footwear, road vehicles), wool and mohair 7%, food and live animals 7% (1996)
Exports - partners: South African Customs Union 66%, North America 26%, EU 4% (1996)
Imports: $880 million (f.o.b., 1997 est.)
Imports - commodities: food; building materials, vehicles, machinery, medicines, petroleum products (1995)
Imports - partners: South African Customs Union 90%, Asia 6%, EU 2% (1995)
Debt - external: $660 million (1997 est.)
Economic aid - recipient: $123.7 million (1995)
Currency: 1 loti (L) = 100 lisente
note: maloti (M) is the plural form of loti
Exchange rates: maloti (M) per US$1 - 5.98380 (January 1999), 5.52828 (1998), 4.60796 (1997), 4.29935 (1996), 3.62709 (1995), 3.55080 (1994); note - the Basotho loti is at par with the South African rand
Fiscal year: 1 April - 31 March

Communications

Telephones: 12,000 (1991 est.)
Telephone system: rudimentary system
domestic: consists of a few landlines, a small microwave radio relay system, and a minor radiotelephone communication system
international: satellite earth station - 1 Intelsat (Atlantic Ocean)

Lesotho (continued)

Radio broadcast stations: AM 3, FM 4, shortwave 0
Radios: 66,000
Television broadcast stations: NA
Televisions: 11,000 (1992 est.)

Transportation

Railways:
total: 2.6 km; note - owned by, operated by, and included in the statistics of South Africa
narrow gauge: 2.6 km 1.067-m gauge (1995)
Highways:
total: 4,955 km
paved: 887 km
unpaved: 4,068 km (1996 est.)
Ports and harbors: none
Airports: 29 (1998 est.)
Airports - with paved runways:
total: 4
over 3,047 m: 1
914 to 1,523 m: 1
under 914 m: 2 (1998 est.)
Airports - with unpaved runways:
total: 25
914 to 1,523 m: 4
under 914 m: 21 (1998 est.)

Military

Military branches: Lesotho Defense Force (LDF; includes Army and Air Wing), Royal Lesotho Mounted Police (RLMP)
Military manpower - availability:
males age 15-49: 504,442 (1999 est.)
Military manpower - fit for military service:
males age 15-49: 271,925 (1999 est.)
Military expenditures - dollar figure: $NA
Military expenditures - percent of GDP: NA%

Transnational Issues

Disputes - international: none

Liberia

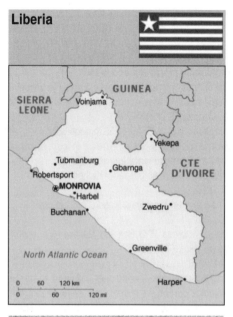

Introduction

Background: The 1995 Abuja Peace Accords ended seven years of civil warfare in Liberia. More than 20,000 of the estimated 33,000 factional fighters gave up their arms to the Cease-Fire Monitoring Group of the Economic Community of West African States (ECOMOG). Free and open presidential and legislative elections were held 19 July 1997; former faction leader, Charles TAYLOR, and his National Patriotic Party won overwhelming victories. The years of civil strife coupled with the flight of most business people disrupted formal economic activity. A short-lived armed clash in September 1998 between government forces and supporters of factional leader Roosevelt JOHNSON and continuing uncertainty about the security situation have slowed the process of rebuilding the social and economic structure of the war-torn country. For two centuries the US has had uniquely close ties to Liberia and today is a major aid donor.

Geography

Location: Western Africa, bordering the North Atlantic Ocean, between Cote d'Ivoire and Sierra Leone
Geographic coordinates: 6 30 N, 9 30 W
Map references: Africa
Area:
total: 111,370 sq km
land: 96,320 sq km
water: 15,050 sq km
Area - comparative: slightly larger than Tennessee
Land boundaries:
total: 1,585 km
border countries: Guinea 563 km, Cote d'Ivoire 716 km, Sierra Leone 306 km
Coastline: 579 km
Maritime claims:
territorial sea: 200 nm
Climate: tropical; hot, humid; dry winters with hot

days and cool to cold nights; wet, cloudy summers with frequent heavy showers
Terrain: mostly flat to rolling coastal plains rising to rolling plateau and low mountains in northeast
Elevation extremes:
lowest point: Atlantic Ocean 0 m
highest point: Mount Wuteve 1,380 m
Natural resources: iron ore, timber, diamonds, gold
Land use:
arable land: 1%
permanent crops: 3%
permanent pastures: 59%
forests and woodland: 18%
other: 19% (1993 est.)
Irrigated land: 20 sq km (1993 est.)
Natural hazards: dust-laden harmattan winds blow from the Sahara (December to March)
Environment - current issues: tropical rain forest subject to deforestation; soil erosion; loss of biodiversity; pollution of coastal waters from oil residue and raw sewage
Environment - international agreements:
party to: Desertification, Endangered Species, Nuclear Test Ban, Ozone Layer Protection, Ship Pollution, Tropical Timber 83, Tropical Timber 94
signed, but not ratified: Biodiversity, Climate Change, Environmental Modification, Law of the Sea, Marine Dumping, Marine Life Conservation

People

Population: 2,923,725 (July 1999 est.)
Age structure:
0-14 years: 45% (male 656,101; female 649,389)
15-64 years: 52% (male 775,429; female 738,904)
65 years and over: 3% (male 50,126; female 53,776) (1999 est.)
Population growth rate: 4.92% (1999 est.)
Birth rate: 41.49 births/1,000 population (1999 est.)
Death rate: 11.03 deaths/1,000 population (1999 est.)
Net migration rate: 18.77 migrant(s)/1,000 population (1999 est.)
note: evidence from UNHCR indicates Liberians are being repatriated
Sex ratio:
at birth: 1.03 male(s)/female
under 15 years: 1.01 male(s)/female
15-64 years: 1.05 male(s)/female
65 years and over: 0.93 male(s)/female
total population: 1.03 male(s)/female (1999 est.)
Infant mortality rate: 100.63 deaths/1,000 live births (1999 est.)
Life expectancy at birth:
total population: 59.88 years
male: 57.2 years
female: 62.64 years (1999 est.)
Total fertility rate: 6.02 children born/woman (1999 est.)
Nationality:
noun: Liberian(s)
adjective: Liberian
Ethnic groups: indigenous African tribes 95%

Liberia *(continued)*

(including Kpelle, Bassa, Gio, Kru, Grebo, Mano, Krahn, Gola, Gbandi, Loma, Kissi, Vai, and Bella), Americo-Liberians 2.5% (descendants of immigrants from the US who had been slaves)

Religions: traditional 70%, Muslim 20%, Christian 10%

Languages: English 20% (official), about 20 tribal languages, of which a few can be written and are used in correspondence

Literacy:

definition: age 15 and over can read and write

total population: 38.3%

male: 53.9%

female: 22.4% (1995 est.)

note: these figures are increasing because of the improving school system

Government

Country name:

conventional long form: Republic of Liberia

conventional short form: Liberia

Data code: LI

Government type: republic

Capital: Monrovia

Administrative divisions: 13 counties; Bomi, Bong, Grand Bassa, Grand Cape Mount, Grand Gedeh, Grand Kru, Lofa, Margibi, Maryland, Montserrado, Nimba, River Cess, Sinoe

Independence: 26 July 1847

National holiday: Independence Day, 26 July (1847)

Constitution: 6 January 1986

Legal system: dual system of statutory law based on Anglo-American common law for the modern sector and customary law based on unwritten tribal practices for indigenous sector

Suffrage: 18 years of age; universal

Executive branch:

chief of state: President Charles Ghankay TAYLOR (since 2 August 1997); note - the president is both the chief of state and head of government

head of government: President Charles Ghankay TAYLOR (since 2 August 1997); note - the president is both the chief of state and head of government

cabinet: Cabinet appointed by the president

elections: president elected by popular vote for a four-year term (renewable); election last held 19 July 1997 (next to be held NA July 2001)

election results: Charles Ghankay TAYLOR elected president; percent of vote - Charles Ghankay TAYLOR (NPP) 75.3%, Ellen Johnson SIRLEAF (UP) 9.6%, Alhaji KROMAH (ALCOP) 4%, other 11.1%

Legislative branch: bicameral National Assembly consists of the Senate (26 seats; members elected by popular vote to serve four-year terms) and the House of Representatives (64 seats; members elected by popular vote to serve four-year terms)

elections: Senate - last held 19 July 1997 (next to be held in NA 2001); House of Representatives - last held 19 July 1997 (next to be held in NA 2001)

election results: Senate - percent of vote by party - NA; seats by party - NPP 21, UP 3, ALCOP 2; House

of Representatives - percent of vote by party - NA; seats by party - NPP 49, UP 7, ALCOP 3, Alliance of Political Parties 2, UPP 2, LPP 1; note - the Alliance of Political Parties was a coalition of the LAP and the LUP

Judicial branch: Supreme Court

Political parties and leaders:

ruling party: National Patriotic Party or NPP [Charles Ghankay TAYLOR]

opposition party: All Liberia Coalition Party or ALCOP [Alhaji KROMAH, chairman]; Free Democratic Party or FDP [George T. WASHINGTON, chairman]; Liberian Action Party or LAP [Cletus WOTORSON]; Liberian National Union or LINU [Henry MONIBA, chairman]; Liberian People's Party or LPP [Togba-Nah TIPOTEH, chairman]; Liberian Unification Party or LUP [Laveli SUPUWOOD]; National Democratic Party of Liberia or NDPL [Dr. George E. Saigbe BOLEY, chairman]; National Reformation Party or NRP [Martin SHERIF, chairman]; People's Democratic Party of Liberia or PDPL [Fiyah GBULIE, chairman]; People's Progressive Party or PPP [Chea CHEAPOO, chairman]; Reformation Alliance Party or RAP [Henry Boimah FAHNBULLEH, chairman]; True Whig Party or TWP [Rudolph SHERMAN, chairman]; Unity Party or UP [Ellen JOHNSON-SIRLEAF, chairman]; United People's Party or UPP [Gabriel Baccus MATTHEWS, chairman]

International organization participation: ACP, AfDB, CCC, ECA, ECOWAS, FAO, G-77, IAEA, IBRD, ICAO, ICFTU, ICRM, IDA, IFAD, IFC, IFRCS, ILO, IMF, IMO, Inmarsat, Intelsat (nonsignatory user), Interpol, IOC, IOM, ITU, NAM, OAU, OPCW, UN, UNCTAD, UNESCO, UNIDO, UPU, WCL, WFTU, WHO, WIPO, WMO

Diplomatic representation in the US:

chief of mission: Ambassador Rachel DIGGS

chancery: 5201 16th Street NW, Washington, DC 20011

telephone: [1] (202) 723-0437

FAX: [1] (202) 723-0436

consulate(s) general: New York

Diplomatic representation from the US:

chief of mission: Ambassador (vacant); Charge d'Affaires Donald PETTERSON

embassy: 111 United Nations Drive, Mamba Point, Monrovia

mailing address: use embassy street address

telephone: [231] 226-370 through 226-382

FAX: [231] 226-148, 226-147

Flag description: 11 equal horizontal stripes of red (top and bottom) alternating with white; there is a white five-pointed star on a blue square in the upper hoist-side corner; the design was based on the US flag

Economy

Economy - overview: A civil war in 1989-97 has destroyed much of Liberia's economy, especially the infrastructure in and around Monrovia. Many businessmen have fled the country, taking capital and

expertise with them. Some returned during 1997. Many will not return. Richly endowed with water, mineral resources, forests, and a climate favorable to agriculture, Liberia had been a producer and exporter of basic products, while local manufacturing, mainly foreign owned, had been small in scope. The democratically elected government, installed in August 1997, inherited massive international debts and currently relies on revenues from its maritime registry to provide the bulk of its foreign exchange earnings. The restoration of the infrastructure and the raising of incomes in this ravaged economy depends on the implementation of sound macro- and micro-economic policies of the new government, including the encouragement of foreign investment.

GDP: purchasing power parity - $2.8 billion (1998 est.)

GDP - real growth rate: NA%

GDP - per capita: purchasing power parity - $1,000 (1998 est.)

GDP - composition by sector:

agriculture: 30%

industry: 36%

services: 34%

Population below poverty line: 80%

Household income or consumption by percentage share:

lowest 10%: NA%

highest 10%: NA%

Inflation rate (consumer prices): NA%

Labor force - by occupation: agriculture 70%

Unemployment rate: 70%

Budget:

revenues: $NA

expenditures: $NA

Industries: rubber processing, palm oil processing, diamonds

Industrial production growth rate: 0%

Electricity - production: 480 million kWh (1996)

Electricity - production by source:

fossil fuel: 100%

hydro: 0%

nuclear: 0%

other: 0% (1996)

Electricity - consumption: 480 million kWh (1996)

Electricity - exports: 0 kWh (1996)

Electricity - imports: 0 kWh (1996)

Agriculture - products: rubber, coffee, cocoa, rice, cassava (tapioca), palm oil, sugarcane, bananas; sheep, goats; timber

Exports: $1.1 billion (f.o.b., 1998 est.)

Exports - commodities: diamonds, iron ore, rubber, timber, coffee

Exports - partners: Belgium, Norway, Ukraine, Singapore (1997)

Imports: $3.65 billion (f.o.b., 1998 est.)

Imports - commodities: fuels, chemicals, machinery, transportation equipment, manufactured goods; rice and other foodstuffs

Imports - partners: South Korea, Japan, Italy, Singapore (1997)

Debt - external: $2 billion (1997 est.)

Liberia *(continued)*

Economic aid - recipient: $122.8 million (1995)
Currency: 1 Liberian dollar (L$) = 100 cents
Exchange rates: Liberian dollars (L$) per US$1 -
1.0000 (officially fixed rate since 1940); market
exchange rate: Liberian dollars (L$) per US$1 - 40
(December 1998), 50 (October 1995), 7 (January
1992); market rate floats against the US dollar
Fiscal year: calendar year

Communications

Telephones: fewer than 25,000 (1998 est.)
Telephone system: telephone and telegraph
service via microwave radio relay network; main
center is Monrovia
domestic: NA
international: satellite earth station - 1 Intelsat
(Atlantic Ocean)
Radio broadcast stations: AM 3, FM 10, shortwave
0
note: two of the FM radio stations are limited to a small
area
Radios: 675,000 (1995 est.); note - 10,000 windup
radios were distributed in the country prior to the 1997
election
Television broadcast stations: 1 (in addition, there
are four low-power repeaters; the station is located in
Monrovia) (1997)
Televisions: 56,000 (1995 est.)

Transportation

Railways:
total: 480 km (328 km single track); note - three rail
systems owned and operated by foreign steel and
financial interests in conjunction with the Liberian
Government; one of these, the Lamco Railroad,
closed in 1989 after iron ore production ceased; the
other two were shut down by the civil war; large
sections of the rail lines have been dismantled;
approximately 60 km of railroad track was exported for
scrap
standard gauge: NA km 1.435-m gauge
narrow gauge: NA km 1.067-m gauge
Highways:
total: 10,037 km (there is major deterioration on all
highways due to lack of maintenance since the civil
war began)
paved: 603 km
unpaved: 9,434 km (1996 est.)
Ports and harbors: Buchanan, Greenville, Harper,
Monrovia
Merchant marine:
total: 1,651 ships (1,000 GRT or over) totaling
59,804,012 GRT/96,650,752 DWT
ships by type: barge carrier 4, bulk 408, cargo 106,
chemical tanker 176, combination bulk 25,
combination ore/oil 50, container 193, liquefied gas
tanker 89, multifunction large-load carrier 2, oil tanker
413, passenger 37, refrigerated cargo 69, roll-on/
roll-off cargo 19, short-sea passenger 3, specialized
tanker 12, vehicle carrier 45
note: a flag of convenience registry; includes ships

from 54 countries among which are Germany 186, US
161, Norway 142, Greece 144, Japan 124, Hong Kong
100, China 53, UK 32, Singapore 39, and Monaco 38
(1998 est.)
Airports: 45 (1998 est.)
Airports - with paved runways:
total: 2
over 3,047 m: 1
1,524 to 2,437 m: 1 (1998 est.)
Airports - with unpaved runways:
total: 43
1,524 to 2,437 m: 3
914 to 1,523 m: 5
under 914 m: 35 (1998 est.)

Military

Military branches: Army, Air Force, Navy
Military manpower - availability:
males age 15-49: 667,032 (1999 est.)
Military manpower - fit for military service:
males age 15-49: 356,825 (1999 est.)
Military expenditures - dollar figure: $1.4 million
(1998)
Military expenditures - percent of GDP: 2%
(1998)

Transnational Issues

Disputes - international: none
Illicit drugs: increasingly a transshipment point for
Southeast and Southwest Asian heroin and South
American cocaine for the European and US markets

Libya

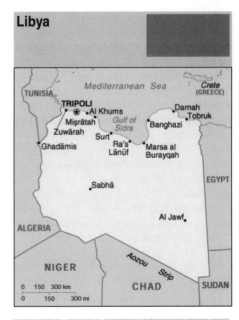

Geography

Location: Northern Africa, bordering the
Mediterranean Sea, between Egypt and Tunisia
Geographic coordinates: 25 00 N, 17 00 E
Map references: Africa
Area:
total: 1,759,540 sq km
land: 1,759,540 sq km
water: 0 sq km
Area - comparative: slightly larger than Alaska
Land boundaries:
total: 4,383 km
border countries: Algeria 982 km, Chad 1,055 km,
Egypt 1,150 km, Niger 354 km, Sudan 383 km,
Tunisia 459 km
Coastline: 1,770 km
Maritime claims:
territorial sea: 12 nm
note: Gulf of Sidra closing line - 32 degrees 30
minutes north
Climate: Mediterranean along coast; dry, extreme
desert interior
Terrain: mostly barren, flat to undulating plains,
plateaus, depressions
Elevation extremes:
lowest point: Sabkhat Ghuzayyil -47 m
highest point: Bikku Bitti 2,267 m
Natural resources: petroleum, natural gas, gypsum
Land use:
arable land: 1%
permanent crops: 0%
permanent pastures: 8%
forests and woodland: 0%
other: 91% (1993 est.)
Irrigated land: 4,700 sq km (1993 est.)
Natural hazards: hot, dry, dust-laden ghibli is a
southern wind lasting one to four days in spring and
fall; dust storms, sandstorms
Environment - current issues: desertification; very
limited natural fresh water resources; the Great

Libya *(continued)*

Manmade River Project, the largest water development scheme in the world, is being built to bring water from large aquifers under the Sahara to coastal cities

Environment - international agreements:
party to: Desertification, Marine Dumping, Nuclear Test Ban, Ozone Layer Protection
signed, but not ratified: Biodiversity, Climate Change, Law of the Sea

People

Population: 4,992,838 (July 1999 est.)
note: includes 161,251 non-nationals (July 1999 est.)
Age structure:
0-14 years: 36% (male 930,661; female 891,046)
15-64 years: 60% (male 1,545,958; female 1,437,120)
65 years and over: 4% (male 93,726; female 94,327) (1999 est.)
Population growth rate: 2.4% (1999 est.)
Birth rate: 27.33 births/1,000 population (1999 est.)
Death rate: 3.35 deaths/1,000 population (1999 est.)
Net migration rate: 0 migrant(s)/1,000 population (1999 est.)
Sex ratio:
at birth: 1.05 male(s)/female
under 15 years: 1.04 male(s)/female
15-64 years: 1.08 male(s)/female
65 years and over: 0.99 male(s)/female
total population: 1.06 male(s)/female (1999 est.)
Infant mortality rate: 28.15 deaths/1,000 live births (1999 est.)
Life expectancy at birth:
total population: 75.73 years
male: 73.81 years
female: 77.74 years (1999 est.)
Total fertility rate: 3.79 children born/woman (1999 est.)
Nationality:
noun: Libyan(s)
adjective: Libyan
Ethnic groups: Berber and Arab 97%, Greeks, Maltese, Italians, Egyptians, Pakistanis, Turks, Indians, Tunisians
Religions: Sunni Muslim 97%
Languages: Arabic, Italian, English, all are widely understood in the major cities
Literacy:
definition: age 15 and over can read and write
total population: 76.2%
male: 87.9%
female: 63% (1995 est.)

Government

Country name:
conventional long form: Socialist People's Libyan Arab Jamahiriya
conventional short form: Libya
local long form: Al Jumahiriyah al Arabiyah al Libiyah ash Shabiyah al Ishtirakiyah
local short form: none

Data code: LY
Government type: Jamahiriya (a state of the masses) in theory, governed by the populace through local councils; in fact, a military dictatorship
Capital: Tripoli
Administrative divisions: 25 municipalities (baladiyat, singular - baladiyah); Ajdabiya, Al 'Aziziyah, Al Fatih, Al Jabal al Akhdar, Al Jufrah, Al Khums, Al Kufrah, An Nuqat al Khams, Ash Shati', Awbari, Az Zawiyah, Banghazi, Darnah, Ghadamis, Gharyan, Misratah, Murzuq, Sabha, Sawfajjin, Surt, Tarabulus, Tarhunah, Tubruq, Yafran, Zlitan
note: the 25 municipalities may have been replaced by 13 regions
Independence: 24 December 1951 (from Italy)
National holiday: Revolution Day, 1 September (1969)
Constitution: 11 December 1969, amended 2 March 1977
Legal system: based on Italian civil law system and Islamic law; separate religious courts; no constitutional provision for judicial review of legislative acts; has not accepted compulsory ICJ jurisdiction
Suffrage: 18 years of age; universal and compulsory
Executive branch:
chief of state: Revolutionary Leader Col. Muammar Abu Minyar al-QADHAFI (since 1 September 1969); note - holds no official title, but is de facto chief of state
head of government: Secretary of the General People's Committee (Premier) Muhammad Ahmad al-MANQUSH (since NA January 1998)
cabinet: General People's Committee established by the General People's Congress
elections: national elections are indirect through a hierarchy of peoples' committees; head of government elected by the General People's Congress; election last held NA (next to be held NA)
election results: Muhammad Ahmad al-MANQUSH elected head of government; percent of General People's Congress vote - NA
Legislative branch: unicameral General People's Congress (NA seats; members elected indirectly through a hierarchy of peoples' committees)
Judicial branch: Supreme Court
Political parties and leaders: none
Political pressure groups and leaders: various Arab nationalist movements with almost negligible memberships may be functioning clandestinely, as well as some Islamic elements
International organization participation: ABEDA, AfDB, AFESD, AL, AMF, AMU, CAEU, CCC, ECA, FAO, G-77, IAEA, IBRD, ICAO, ICRM, IDA, IDB, IFAD, IFC, IFRCS, ILO, IMF, IMO, Intelsat, Interpol, IOC, ISO, ITU, NAM, OAPEC, OAU, OIC, OPEC, PCA, UN, UNCTAD, UNESCO, UNIDO, UNITAR, UPU, WFTU, WHO, WIPO, WMO, WToO
Diplomatic representation in the US: Libya does not have an embassy in the US
Diplomatic representation from the US: the US suspended all embassy activities in Tripoli on 2 May 1980
Flag description: plain green; green is the

traditional color of Islam (the state religion)

Economy

Economy - overview: The socialist-oriented economy depends primarily upon revenues from the oil sector, which contributes practically all export earnings and about one-third of GDP. These oil revenues and a small population give Libya one of the highest per capita GDPs in Africa, but little of this income flows down to the lower orders of society. Low oil prices in 1998 cut back revenue sharply, and GDP growth fell by 1%. In this statist society, import restrictions and inefficient resource allocations have led to periodic shortages of basic goods and foodstuffs. The nonoil manufacturing and construction sectors, which account for about 20% of GDP, have expanded from processing mostly agricultural products to include the production of petrochemicals, iron, steel, and aluminum. Agriculture accounts for only 5% of GDP; it employs 18% of the labor force. Climatic conditions and poor soils severely limit farm output, and Libya imports about 75% of its food requirements. The UN sanctions imposed in April 1992 do not have a major impact on the economy although they have increased transaction and transportation costs.
GDP: purchasing power parity - $38 billion (1998 est.)
GDP - real growth rate: -1% (1998 est.)
GDP - per capita: purchasing power parity - $6,700 (1998 est.)
GDP - composition by sector:
agriculture: 5%
industry: 55%
services: 40% (1996 est.)
Population below poverty line: NA%
Household income or consumption by percentage share:
lowest 10%: NA%
highest 10%: NA%
Inflation rate (consumer prices): 24.2% (1998 est.)
Labor force: 1 million
Labor force - by occupation: industry 31%, services 27%, government 24%, agriculture 18%
Unemployment rate: 30% (1998 est.)
Budget:
revenues: $3.6 billion
expenditures: $5.1 billion, including capital expenditures of $NA (1998 est.)
Industries: petroleum, food processing, textiles, handicrafts, cement
Industrial production growth rate: NA%
Electricity - production: 17 billion kWh (1996)
Electricity - production by source:
fossil fuel: 100%
hydro: 0%
nuclear: 0%
other: 0% (1996)
Electricity - consumption: 17 billion kWh (1996)
Electricity - exports: 0 kWh (1996)
Electricity - imports: 0 kWh (1996)

Libya (continued)

Agriculture - products: wheat, barley, olives, dates, citrus, vegetables, peanuts; beef, eggs
Exports: $6.8 billion (f.o.b., 1998 est.)
Exports - commodities: crude oil, refined petroleum products, natural gas
Exports - partners: Italy, Germany, Spain, France, Turkey, Greece, Egypt
Imports: $6.9 billion (c.i.f., 1998 est.)
Imports - commodities: machinery, transport equipment, food, manufactured goods
Imports - partners: Italy, Germany, UK, France, Spain, Turkey, Tunisia, Eastern Europe
Debt - external: $4 billion (1998 est.)
Economic aid - recipient: $8.4 million (1995)
Currency: 1 Libyan dinar (LD) = 1,000 dirhams
Exchange rates: Libyan dinars (LD) per US$1 -
0.3799 (November 1998), 0.3891 (1997), 0.3651
(1996), 0.3532 (1995), 0.3596 (1994); official rate:
0.45 (December 1998)
Fiscal year: calendar year

Communications

Telephones: 411,000 (1999 est.)
Telephone system: telecommunications system is being modernized; cellular telephone system became operational in 1996
domestic: microwave radio relay, coaxial cable, cellular, tropospheric scatter, and a domestic satellite system with 14 earth stations
international: satellite earth stations - 4 Intelsat, NA Arabsat, and NA Intersputnik; submarine cables to France and Italy; microwave radio relay to Tunisia and Egypt; tropospheric scatter to Greece; participant in Medarabtel
Radio broadcast stations: AM 17, FM 3, shortwave 3 (1998 est.)
Radios: 1 million (1998 est.)
Television broadcast stations: 12 (in addition, there is one low-power repeater) (1997)
Televisions: 550,000 (1998 est.)

Transportation

Railways:
note: Libya has had no railroad in operation since 1965, all previous systems having been dismantled; current plans are to construct a 1.435-m standard gauge line from the Tunisian frontier to Tripoli and Misratah, then inland to Sabha, center of a mineral-rich area, but there has been no progress; other plans made jointly with Egypt would establish a rail line from As Sallum, Egypt, to Tobruk with completion set for mid-1994; no progress has been reported
Highways:
total: 83,200 km
paved: 47,590 km
unpaved: 35,610 km (1996 est.)
Waterways: none
Pipelines: crude oil 4,383 km; petroleum products 443 km (includes liquefied petroleum gas or LPG 256 km); natural gas 1,947 km

Ports and harbors: Al Khums, Banghazi, Darnah, Marsa al Burayqah, Misratah, Ra's Lanuf, Tobruk, Tripoli, Zuwarah
Merchant marine:
total: 30 ships (1,000 GRT or over) totaling 588,928 GRT/989,662 DWT
ships by type: cargo 9, chemical tanker 1, liquefied gas tanker 3, oil tanker 9, roll-on/roll-off cargo 4, short-sea passenger 4 (1998 est.)
Airports: 143 (1998 est.)
Airports - with paved runways:
total: 60
over 3,047 m: 24
2,438 to 3,047 m: 6
1,524 to 2,437 m: 22
914 to 1,523 m: 5
under 914 m: 3 (1998 est.)
Airports - with unpaved runways:
total: 83
over 3,047 m: 5
2,438 to 3,047 m: 2
1,524 to 2,437 m: 15
914 to 1,523 m: 42
under 914 m: 19 (1998 est.)

Military

Military branches: Army, Navy, Air and Air Defense Command
Military manpower - military age: 17 years of age
Military manpower - availability:
males age 15-49: 1,372,261 (1999 est.)
Military manpower - fit for military service:
males age 15-49: 816,186 (1999 est.)
Military manpower - reaching military age annually:
males: 62,098 (1999 est.)
Military expenditures - dollar figure: $NA
Military expenditures - percent of GDP: NA%

Transnational Issues

Disputes - international: maritime boundary dispute with Tunisia; Libya claims about 19,400 sq km in northern Niger and part of southeastern Algeria

Liechtenstein

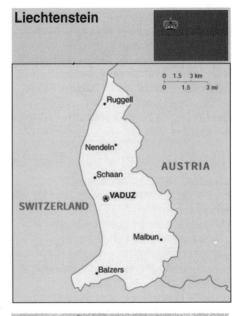

Geography

Location: Central Europe, between Austria and Switzerland
Geographic coordinates: 47 10 N, 9 32 E
Map references: Europe
Area:
total: 160 sq km
land: 160 sq km
water: 0 sq km
Area - comparative: about 0.9 times the size of Washington, DC
Land boundaries:
total: 76 km
border countries: Austria 35 km, Switzerland 41 km
Coastline: 0 km (landlocked)
Maritime claims: none (landlocked)
Climate: continental; cold, cloudy winters with frequent snow or rain; cool to moderately warm, cloudy, humid summers
Terrain: mostly mountainous (Alps) with Rhine Valley in western third
Elevation extremes:
lowest point: Ruggeller Riet 430 m
highest point: Grauspitz 2,599 m
Natural resources: hydroelectric potential
Land use:
arable land: 24%
permanent crops: 0%
permanent pastures: 16%
forests and woodland: 35%
other: 25% (1993 est.)
Irrigated land: NA sq km
Natural hazards: NA
Environment - current issues: NA
Environment - international agreements:
party to: Air Pollution, Air Pollution-Nitrogen Oxides, Air Pollution-Sulphur 85, Air Pollution-Sulphur 94, Air Pollution-Volatile Organic Compounds, Biodiversity, Climate Change, Endangered Species, Hazardous Wastes, Ozone Layer Protection, Wetlands

Liechtenstein (continued)

signed, but not ratified: Air Pollution-Persistent Organic Pollutants, Climate Change-Kyoto Protocol, Law of the Sea

Geography - note: along with Uzbekistan, one of only two doubly landlocked countries in the world; variety of microclimatic variations based on elevation

People

Population: 32,057 (July 1999 est.)
Age structure:
0-14 years: 19% (male 3,076; female 2,949)
15-64 years: 70% (male 11,209; female 11,247)
65 years and over: 11% (male 1,484; female 2,092) (1999 est.)
Population growth rate: 1.08% (1999 est.)
Birth rate: 12.23 births/1,000 population (1999 est.)
Death rate: 7.33 deaths/1,000 population (1999 est.)
Net migration rate: 5.9 migrant(s)/1,000 population (1999 est.)
Sex ratio:
at birth: 1.04 male(s)/female
under 15 years: 1.04 male(s)/female
15-64 years: 1 male(s)/female
65 years and over: 0.71 male(s)/female
total population: 0.97 male(s)/female (1999 est.)
Infant mortality rate: 5.23 deaths/1,000 live births (1999 est.)
Life expectancy at birth:
total population: 78.11 years
male: 75.64 years
female: 80.69 years (1999 est.)
Total fertility rate: 1.6 children born/woman (1999 est.)
Nationality:
noun: Liechtensteiner(s)
adjective: Liechtenstein
Ethnic groups: Alemannic 87.5%, Italian, Turkish, and other 12.5%
Religions: Roman Catholic 80%, Protestant 7.4%, unknown 7.7%, other 4.9% (1996)
Languages: German (official), Alemannic dialect
Literacy:
definition: age 10 and over can read and write
total population: 100%
male: 100%
female: 100% (1981 est.)

Government

Country name:
conventional long form: Principality of Liechtenstein
conventional short form: Liechtenstein
local long form: Fuerstentum Liechtenstein
local short form: Liechtenstein
Data code: LS
Government type: hereditary constitutional monarchy
Capital: Vaduz
Administrative divisions: 11 communes (Gemeinden, singular - Gemeinde); Balzers, Eschen, Gamprin, Mauren, Planken, Ruggell, Schaan, Schellenberg, Triesen, Triesenberg, Vaduz

Independence: 23 January 1719 (Imperial Principality of Liechtenstein established)
National holiday: Assumption Day, 15 August
Constitution: 5 October 1921
Legal system: local civil and penal codes; accepts compulsory ICJ jurisdiction, with reservations
Suffrage: 20 years of age; universal
Executive branch:
chief of state: Prince Hans ADAM II (since 13 November 1989, assumed executive powers 26 August 1984); Heir Apparent Prince ALOIS von und zu Liechtenstein, son of the monarch (born 11 June 1968)
head of government: Head of Government Mario FRICK (since 15 December 1993) and Deputy Head of Government Michael RITTER (since 2 February 1997)
cabinet: Cabinet elected by the Diet; confirmed by the monarch
elections: none; the monarch is hereditary; following legislative elections, the leader of the majority party in the Diet is usually appointed the head of government by the monarch and the leader of the largest minority party in the Diet is usually appointed the deputy head of government by the monarch
Legislative branch: unicameral Diet or Landtag (25 seats; members are elected by direct popular vote under proportional representation to serve four-year terms)
elections: last held on 2 February 1997 (next to be held by NA 2001)
election results: percent of vote by party - VU 50.1%, FBPL 41.3%, FL 8.5%; seats by party - VU 13, FBPL 10, FL 2
Judicial branch: Supreme Court or Oberster Gerichtshof; Superior Court or Obergericht
Political parties and leaders: Fatherland Union or VU [Dr. Oswald KRANZ]; Progressive Citizens' Party or FBPL [Norbert SEEGER]; The Free List or FL [Paul VOGT]
International organization participation: CE, EBRD, ECE, EFTA, IAEA, ICRM, IFRCS, Intelsat, Interpol, IOC, ITU, OPCW, OSCE, PCA, UN, UNCTAD, UPU, WCL, WIPO, WTrO
Diplomatic representation in the US: Liechtenstein does not have an embassy in the US, but is represented by the Swiss embassy in routine diplomatic matters
Diplomatic representation from the US: the US does not have an embassy in Liechtenstein, but the US Ambassador to Switzerland is also accredited to Liechtenstein
Flag description: two equal horizontal bands of blue (top) and red with a gold crown on the hoist side of the blue band

Economy

Economy - overview: Despite its small size and limited natural resources, Liechtenstein has developed into a prosperous, highly industrialized, free-enterprise economy with a vital financial service sector and living standards on a par with the urban areas of its large European neighbors. Low business taxes - the maximum tax rate is 18% - and easy incorporation rules have induced about 73,700 holding or so-called letter box companies to establish nominal offices in Liechtenstein, providing 30% of state revenues. The country participates in a customs union with Switzerland and uses the Swiss franc as its national currency. It imports more than 90% of its energy requirements. Liechtenstein is a member of the European Economic Area (an organization serving as a bridge between European Free Trade Association (EFTA) and EU) since May 1995. The government is working to harmonize its economic policies with those of an integrated Europe.
GDP: purchasing power parity - $730 million (1998 est.)
GDP - real growth rate: NA%
GDP - per capita: purchasing power parity - $23,000 (1998 est.)
GDP - composition by sector:
agriculture: NA%
industry: NA%
services: NA%
Population below poverty line: NA%
Household income or consumption by percentage share:
lowest 10%: NA%
highest 10%: NA%
Inflation rate (consumer prices): 0.5% (1997 est.)
Labor force: 22,891 of which 13,847 are foreigners; 8,231 commute from Austria and Switzerland to work each day
Labor force - by occupation: industry, trade, and building 45%, services 53%, agriculture, fishing, forestry, and horticulture 2% (1997 est.)
Unemployment rate: 1.6% (1997)
Budget:
revenues: $455 million
expenditures: $435 million, including capital expenditures of $NA (1996 est.)
Industries: electronics, metal manufacturing, textiles, ceramics, pharmaceuticals, food products, precision instruments, tourism
Industrial production growth rate: NA%
Electricity - production: 150 million kWh (1995)
Electricity - production by source:
fossil fuel: NA%
hydro: NA%
nuclear: NA%
other: NA%
Electricity - consumption: NA kWh
Electricity - exports: NA kWh
Electricity - imports: NA kWh
Agriculture - products: wheat, barley, maize, potatoes; livestock, dairy products
Exports: $2.47 billion (1996)
Exports - commodities: small specialty machinery, dental products, stamps, hardware, pottery
Exports - partners: EU and EFTA countries 60.57% (Switzerland 15.7%) (1995)
Imports: $917.3 million (1996)
Imports - commodities: machinery, metal goods,

Liechtenstein (continued)

textiles, foodstuffs, motor vehicles
Imports - partners: EU countries, Switzerland (1996)
Debt - external: $0 (1996)
Economic aid - recipient: none
Currency: 1 Swiss franc, franken, or franco (SwF) = 100 centimes, rappen, or centesimi
Exchange rates: Swiss francs, franken, or franchi (SwF) per US$1 - 1.3837 (January 1999), 1.4498 (1998), 1.4513 (1997), 1.2360 (1996), 1.1825 (1995), 1.3677 (1994)
Fiscal year: calendar year

Communications

Telephones: 22,857 (1996 est.)
Telephone system: automatic telephone system
domestic: NA
international: linked to Swiss networks by cable and microwave radio relay
Radio broadcast stations: 1 broadcast station in Triesen
note: linked to Swiss networks
Radios: 12,134 (1996)
Television broadcast stations: NA (linked to Swiss networks) (1997)
Televisions: 11,785 (1996)

Transportation

Railways:
total: 18.5 km; note - owned, operated, and included in statistics of Austrian Federal Railways
standard gauge: 18.5 km 1.435-m gauge (electrified)
Highways:
total: 250 km
paved: 250 km
unpaved: 0 km
Ports and harbors: none
Airports: none

Military

Military - note: defense is the responsibility of Switzerland

Transnational Issues

Disputes - international: claims 1,600 sq km of property in the Czech Republic confiscated from its royal family in 1918; the Czech Republic insists that restitution does not go back before February 1948, when the communists seized power

Lithuania

Geography

Location: Eastern Europe, bordering the Baltic Sea, between Latvia and Russia
Geographic coordinates: 56 00 N, 24 00 E
Map references: Europe
Area:
total: 65,200 sq km
land: 65,200 sq km
water: 0 sq km
Area - comparative: slightly larger than West Virginia
Land boundaries:
total: 1,273 km
border countries: Belarus 502 km, Latvia 453 km, Poland 91 km, Russia (Kaliningrad) 227 km
Coastline: 99 km
Maritime claims:
territorial sea: 12 nm
Climate: transitional, between maritime and continental; wet, moderate winters and summers
Terrain: lowland, many scattered small lakes, fertile soil
Elevation extremes:
lowest point: Baltic Sea 0 m
highest point: Juozapines/Kalnas 292 m
Natural resources: peat
Land use:
arable land: 35%
permanent crops: 12%
permanent pastures: 7%
forests and woodland: 31%
other: 15% (1993 est.)
Irrigated land: 430 sq km (1993 est.)
Natural hazards: NA
Environment - current issues: contamination of soil and groundwater with petroleum products and chemicals at military bases
Environment - international agreements:
party to: Biodiversity, Climate Change, Ozone Layer Protection, Ship Pollution, Wetlands

signed, but not ratified: Air Pollution-Persistent Organic Pollutants, Climate Change-Kyoto Protocol

People

Population: 3,584,966 (July 1999 est.)
Age structure:
0-14 years: 20% (male 365,149; female 350,070)
15-64 years: 67% (male 1,156,161; female 1,239,145)
65 years and over: 13% (male 160,963; female 313,478) (1999 est.)
Population growth rate: -0.4% (1999 est.)
Birth rate: 10.52 births/1,000 population (1999 est.)
Death rate: 12.93 deaths/1,000 population (1999 est.)
Net migration rate: -1.58 migrant(s)/1,000 population (1999 est.)
Sex ratio:
at birth: 1.05 male(s)/female
under 15 years: 1.04 male(s)/female
15-64 years: 0.93 male(s)/female
65 years and over: 0.51 male(s)/female
total population: 0.88 male(s)/female (1999 est.)
Infant mortality rate: 14.71 deaths/1,000 live births (1999 est.)
Life expectancy at birth:
total population: 68.96 years
male: 62.91 years
female: 75.31 years (1999 est.)
Total fertility rate: 1.45 children born/woman (1999 est.)
Nationality:
noun: Lithuanian(s)
adjective: Lithuanian
Ethnic groups: Lithuanian 80.6%, Russian 8.7%, Polish 7%, Byelorussian 1.6%, other 2.1%
Religions: primarily Roman Catholic, others include Lutheran, Russian Orthodox, Protestant, evangelical Christian Baptist, Islam, Judaism
Languages: Lithuanian (official), Polish, Russian
Literacy:
definition: age 15 and over can read and write
total population: 98%
male: 99%
female: 98% (1989 est.)

Government

Country name:
conventional long form: Republic of Lithuania
conventional short form: Lithuania
local long form: Lietuvos Respublika
local short form: Lietuva
former: Lithuanian Soviet Socialist Republic
Data code: LH
Government type: parliamentary democracy
Capital: Vilnius
Administrative divisions: 44 regions (rajonai, singular - rajonas) and 11 municipalities*: Akmenes Rajonas, Alytaus Rajonas, Alytus*, Anyksciu Rajonas, Birstonas*, Birzu Rajonas, Druskininkai*, Ignalinos Rajonas, Jonavos Rajonas, Joniskio Rajonas,

Jurbarko Rajonas, Kaisiadoriu Rajonas, Kaunas*, Kauno Rajonas, Kedainiu Rajonas, Kelmes Rajonas, Klaipeda*, Klaipedos Rajonas, Kretingos Rajonas, Kupiskio Rajonas, Lazdiju Rajonas, Marijampole*, Marijampoles Rajonas, Mazeikiu Rajonas, Moletu Rajonas, Neringa* Pakruojo Rajonas, Palanga*, Panevezio Rajonas, Panevezys*, Pasvalio Rajonas, Plunges Rajonas, Prienu Rajonas, Radviliskio Rajonas, Raseiniu Rajonas, Rokiskio Rajonas, Sakiu Rajonas, Salcininku Rajonas, Siauliai*, Siauliu Rajonas, Silales Rajonas, Silutes Rajonas, Sirvintu Rajonas, Skuodo Rajonas, Svencioniu Rajonas, Taurages Rajonas, Telsiu Rajonas, Traku Rajonas, Ukmerges Rajonas, Utenos Rajonas, Varenos Rajonas, Vilkaviskio Rajonas, Vilniaus Rajonas, Vilnius*, Zarasu Rajonas

Independence: 6 September 1991 (from Soviet Union)

National holiday: Statehood Day, 16 February (1918)

Constitution: adopted 25 October 1992

Legal system: based on civil law system; no judicial review of legislative acts

Suffrage: 18 years of age; universal

Executive branch:

chief of state: President Valdas ADAMKUS (since 26 February 1998)

head of government: Premier Gediminas VAGNORIUS (since 28 November 1996)

cabinet: Council of Ministers appointed by the president on the nomination of the premier

elections: president elected by popular vote for a five-year term; election last held 21 December 1997 and 5 January 1998 (next to be held NA 2003); premier appointed by the president on the approval of the Parliament

election results: Valdas ADAMKUS elected president; percent of vote - Valdas ADAMKUS 50.37%, Arturas PAULAUSKAS 49.7%

Legislative branch: unicameral Parliament or Seimas (141 seats, 71 members are directly elected by popular vote, 70 are elected by proportional representation; members serve four-year terms)

elections: last held 20 October and 10 November 1996 (next to be held NA October 2000)

election results: percent of vote by party - NA; seats by party - TS 69, LKDP 15, LCS 15, LDDP 12, LSDP 10, DP 2, independents 12, others 6

Judicial branch: Supreme Court, judges appointed by the Parliament; Court of Appeal, judges appointed by the Parliament

Political parties and leaders: Christian Democratic Party or LKDP [Algirdas SAUDARGAS, chairman]; Democratic Labor Party of Lithuania or LDDP [Ceslovas JURSENAS, chairman]; Lithuanian Nationalist Union or LTS [Rimantas SMETONA, chairman]; Lithuanian Social Democratic Party or LSDP [Aloyzas SAKALAS, chairman]; Lithuanian Farmer's Party or LUP (previously Farmers' Union) [Albinas VAIZMUZIS, chairman]; Lithuanian Center Union or LCS [Romualdas OZOLAS, chairman]; Homeland Union/Conservative Party or TS [Vytautas

LANDSBERGIS, chairman]; Lithuanian Polish Union or LLS [Rsztardas MACIEKIANIEC, chairman]; Democratic Party or DP [Lydie WURTH-POLFER, president]

Political pressure groups and leaders: Lithuanian Future Forum

International organization participation: BIS, CBSS, CCC, CE, EAPC, EBRD, ECE, EU (applicant), FAO, IAEA, IBRD, ICAO, ICC, ICFTU, ICRM, IFC, IFRCS, ILO, IMF, IMO, Intelsat (nonsignatory user), Interpol, IOC, IOM (observer), ISO (correspondent), ITU, OPCW, OSCE, PFP, UN, UNCTAD, UNESCO, UPU, WEU (associate partner), WHO, WIPO, WMO, WTrO (applicant)

Diplomatic representation in the US:

chief of mission: Ambassador Stasys SAKALAUSKAS

chancery: 2622 16th Street NW, Washington, DC 20009

telephone: [1] (202) 234-5860

FAX: [1] (202) 328-0466

consulate(s) general: Chicago and New York

Diplomatic representation from the US:

chief of mission: Ambassador Keith C. SMITH

embassy: Akmenu 6, 2600 Vilnius

mailing address: American Embassy, Vilnius, PSC 78, Box V, APO AE 09723

telephone: [370] (2) 223-031

FAX: [370] (6) 706-084

Flag description: three equal horizontal bands of yellow (top), green, and red

Economy

Economy - overview: Lithuania has benefited from its disciplined approach to market reform and its adherence to strict fiscal and monetary policies imposed by the IMF, measures that have helped constrain the growth of the money supply, reduce inflation to 5.1%, and support GDP growth of 6% in 1997 and 4.5% in 1998. Foreign direct investment and the privatization program maintained their momentum in 1998. However, the current account deficit has hovered around 8% to 10% of GDP annually since 1995 - the result of greater demand for consumer goods and falling growth in exports. Reducing this deficit is the immediate economic challenge for 1999.

GDP: purchasing power parity - $17.6 billion (1998 est.)

GDP - real growth rate: 4.5% (1998 est.)

GDP - per capita: purchasing power parity - $4,900 (1998 est.)

GDP - composition by sector:

agriculture: 13%

industry: 32%

services: 55% (1997 est.)

Population below poverty line: NA%

Household income or consumption by percentage share:

lowest 10%: 3.4%

highest 10%: 28% (1993)

Inflation rate (consumer prices): 5.1% (1998 est.)

Labor force: 1.8 million

Labor force - by occupation: industry and construction 42%, agriculture and forestry 20%, other 38% (1997)

Unemployment rate: 6.7% (January 1998)

Budget:

revenues: $1.5 billion

expenditures: $1.7 billion, including capital expenditures of $NA (1997 est.)

Industries: metal-cutting machine tools, electric motors, television sets, refrigerators and freezers, petroleum refining, shipbuilding (small ships), furniture making, textiles, food processing, fertilizers, agricultural machinery, optical equipment, electronic components, computers, amber

Industrial production growth rate: 4.7% (1998 est.)

Electricity - production: 14.51 billion kWh (1996)

Electricity - production by source:

fossil fuel: 9.65%

hydro: 3.03%

nuclear: 87.32%

other: 0% (1996)

Electricity - consumption: 9.58 billion kWh (1996)

Electricity - exports: 5.23 billion kWh (1996)

Electricity - imports: 300 million kWh (1996)

Agriculture - products: grain, potatoes, sugar beets, flax, vegetables; beef, milk, eggs; fish

Exports: $4.2 billion (f.o.b., 1998)

Exports - commodities: machinery and equipment 19%, mineral products 16%, textiles 15%, chemicals 8%, foodstuffs 8% (1997)

Exports - partners: Russia 24%, Germany 11%, Belarus 10%, Latvia 9%, Ukraine 9% (1997)

Imports: $5.9 billion (f.o.b., 1998)

Imports - commodities: machinery and equipment 30%, mineral products 18%, chemicals 9%, textiles 8%, foodstuffs (1997)

Imports - partners: Russia 24%, Germany 19%, Poland, Denmark, Finland (1997)

Debt - external: $NA

Economic aid - recipient: $228.5 million (1995)

Currency: 1 Lithuanian litas = 100 centas

Exchange rates: litai per US$1 - 4.000 (fixed rate since 1 May 1994), 3.978 (1994), 4.344 (1993), 1.773 (1992)

Fiscal year: calendar year

Communications

Telephones: 1.08 million (1998)

Telephone system: the Ministry of Communications and Informatics, Ministry of Defense, and Ministry of Internal Affairs oversee Lithuania's telecommunications; the national operator is Lietuvos Telomas; Internet is available

domestic: local - three cellular service providers; NMT-450 and GSM standards provide services nationwide; 80% of customers are on the two GSM networks; 157,000 cellular customers; intercity - Lithuania is close to completing its fiber-optic backbone consisting of two small rings inside a larger ring

international: Lithuania has international fiber-optic

Lithuania *(continued)*

connectivity to Latvia, Poland, and an undersea fiber-optic cable to Sweden
Radio broadcast stations: AM 13, FM 26, shortwave 1
Radios: 1.42 million (1993 est.)
Television broadcast stations: 3
Televisions: NA; note - 93% of the population have TV, 30% have cable or satellite dish, and 16% own VCRs (1996)

Transportation

Railways:
total: 2,002 km
broad gauge: 2,002 km 1.524-m gauge (122 km electrified) (1994)
Highways:
total: 68,161 km
paved: 60,527 km (including 410 km of expressways)
unpaved: 7,634 km (1997 est.)
Waterways: 600 km perennially navigable
Pipelines: crude oil, 105 km; natural gas 760 km (1992)
Ports and harbors: Kaunas, Klaipeda
Merchant marine:
total: 54 ships (1,000 GRT or over) totaling 316,616 GRT/353,683 DWT
ships by type: cargo 26, combination bulk 11, oil tanker 2, railcar carrier 1, refrigerated cargo 10, roll-on/roll-off cargo 1, short-sea passenger 3 (1998 est.)
Airports: 96 (1994 est.)
Airports - with paved runways:
total: 25
over 3,047 m: 3
2,438 to 3,047 m: 2
1,524 to 2,437 m: 4
914 to 1,523 m: 2
under 914 m: 14 (1994 est.)
Airports - with unpaved runways:
total: 71
2,438 to 3,047 m: 1
1,524 to 2,437 m: 1
914 to 1,523 m: 6
under 914 m: 63 (1994 est.)

Military

Military branches: Ground Forces, Navy, Air and Air Defense Force, Security Forces (internal and border troops), National Guard (Skat)
Military manpower - military age: 18 years of age
Military manpower - availability:
males age 15-49: 906,687 (1999 est.)
Military manpower - fit for military service:
males age 15-49: 713,436 (1999 est.)
Military manpower - reaching military age annually:
males: 26,168 (1999 est.)
Military expenditures - dollar figure: $181 million (1999)
Military expenditures - percent of GDP: 1.5% (1999)

Transnational Issues

Disputes - international: ongoing talks over maritime boundary dispute with Latvia (primary concern is oil exploration rights); 1997 border agreement with Russia not yet ratified
Illicit drugs: transshipment point for opiates and other illicit drugs from Southwest Asia, Latin America, and Western Europe to Western Europe and Scandinavia

Luxembourg

Geography

Location: Western Europe, between France and Germany
Geographic coordinates: 49 45 N, 6 10 E
Map references: Europe
Area:
total: 2,586 sq km
land: 2,586 sq km
water: 0 sq km
Area - comparative: slightly smaller than Rhode Island
Land boundaries:
total: 359 km
border countries: Belgium 148 km, France 73 km, Germany 138 km
Coastline: 0 km (landlocked)
Maritime claims: none (landlocked)
Climate: modified continental with mild winters, cool summers
Terrain: mostly gently rolling uplands with broad, shallow valleys; uplands to slightly mountainous in the north; steep slope down to Moselle floodplain in the southeast
Elevation extremes:
lowest point: Moselle River 133 m
highest point: Burgplatz 559 m
Natural resources: iron ore (no longer exploited)
Land use:
arable land: 24%
permanent crops: 1%
permanent pastures: 20%
forests and woodland: 21%
other: 34%
Irrigated land: 10 sq km (including Belgium (1993 est.)
Natural hazards: NA
Environment - current issues: air and water pollution in urban areas
Environment - international agreements:
party to: Air Pollution, Air Pollution-Nitrogen Oxides, Air Pollution-Sulphur 85, Air Pollution-Sulphur 94, Air

Luxembourg *(continued)*

Pollution-Volatile Organic Compounds, Biodiversity, Climate Change, Desertification, Endangered Species, Hazardous Wastes, Marine Dumping, Nuclear Test Ban, Ozone Layer Protection, Ship Pollution, Tropical Timber 83, Tropical Timber 94 *signed, but not ratified:* Air Pollution-Persistent Organic Pollutants, Climate Change-Kyoto Protocol, Environmental Modification, Law of the Sea
Geography - note: landlocked

People

Population: 429,080 (July 1999 est.)
Age structure:
0-14 years: 18% (male 39,701; female 37,998)
15-64 years: 67% (male 146,336; female 140,717)
65 years and over: 15% (male 26,201; female 38,127) (1999 est.)
Population growth rate: 0.88% (1999 est.)
Birth rate: 10.35 births/1,000 population (1999 est.)
Death rate: 9.32 deaths/1,000 population (1999 est.)
Net migration rate: 7.78 migrant(s)/1,000 population (1999 est.)
Sex ratio:
at birth: 1.03 male(s)/female
under 15 years: 1.04 male(s)/female
15-64 years: 1.04 male(s)/female
65 years and over: 0.69 male(s)/female
total population: 0.98 male(s)/female (1999 est.)
Infant mortality rate: 4.99 deaths/1,000 live births (1999 est.)
Life expectancy at birth:
total population: 77.65 years
male: 74.58 years
female: 80.83 years (1999 est.)
Total fertility rate: 1.57 children born/woman (1999 est.)
Nationality:
noun: Luxembourger(s)
adjective: Luxembourg
Ethnic groups: Celtic base (with French and German blend), Portuguese, Italian, and European (guest and worker residents)
Religions: Roman Catholic 97%, Protestant and Jewish 3%
Languages: Luxembourgian, German, French, English
Literacy:
definition: age 15 and over can read and write
total population: 100%
male: 100%
female: 100% (1980 est.)

Government

Country name:
conventional long form: Grand Duchy of Luxembourg
conventional short form: Luxembourg
local long form: Grand-Duche de Luxembourg
local short form: Luxembourg
Data code: LU
Government type: constitutional monarchy
Capital: Luxembourg

Administrative divisions: 3 districts; Diekirch, Grevenmacher, Luxembourg
Independence: 1839 (from the Netherlands)
National holiday: National Day, 23 June (1921) (public celebration of the Grand Duke's birthday)
Constitution: 17 October 1868, occasional revisions
Legal system: based on civil law system; accepts compulsory ICJ jurisdiction
Suffrage: 18 years of age; universal and compulsory
Executive branch:
chief of state: Grand Duke JEAN (since 12 November 1964); Heir Apparent Prince HENRI (son of the monarch, born 16 April 1955)
head of government: Prime Minister Jean-Claude JUNCKER (since 1 January 1995) and Vice Prime Minister Jacques F. POOS (since 21 July 1984)
cabinet: Council of Ministers appointed by the monarch, responsible to the Chamber of Deputies
elections: none; the monarch is hereditary; prime minister and vice prime minister appointed by the monarch but are responsible to the Chamber of Deputies
Legislative branch: unicameral Chamber of Deputies or Chambre des Deputes (60 seats; members are elected by direct popular vote to serve five-year terms)
elections: last held 12 June 1994 (next to be held by 13 June 1999)
election results: percent of vote by party - NA; seats by party - CSV 21, LSAP 17, DP 12, Action Committee for Democracy and Pension Rights 5, Greens 5
note: the Council of State or Conseil d'Etat, which has 21 members who are appointed for life, is an advisory body whose views are considered by the Chamber of Deputies
Judicial branch: Superior Court of Justice or Cour Superieure de Justice, judges are appointed for life by the monarch; Administrative Court or Tribunale Administratin, judges are appointed for life by the monarch
Political parties and leaders: Christian Social People's Party or CSV [Erna HENNICOT-SCHOEPGES]; Luxembourg Socialist Workers' Party or LSAP [Ben FAYOT]; Democratic Party or DP [Lydie Wurth POLFER]; Action Committee for Democracy and Pension Rights [Roby MEHLEN]; the Green Alternative [Abbes JACOBY]; other minor parties
Political pressure groups and leaders: group of steel companies representing iron and steel industry; Centrale Paysanne representing agricultural producers; Christian and Socialist labor unions; Federation of Industrialists; Artisans and Shopkeepers Federation
International organization participation: ACCT, Australia Group, Benelux, CCC, CE, EAPC, EBRD, ECE, EIB, EMU, EU, FAO, IAEA, IBRD, ICAO, ICC, ICFTU, ICRM, IDA, IEA, IFAD, IFC, IFRCS, ILO, IMF, IMO, Intelsat, Interpol, IOC, IOM, ITU, MTCR, NATO, NEA, NSG, OECD, OPCW, OSCE, PCA, UN, UNCTAD, UNESCO, UNIDO, UPU, WCL, WEU, WHO, WIPO, WMO, WTrO, ZC

Diplomatic representation in the US:
chief of mission: Ambassador Arlette CONZEMIUS
chancery: 2200 Massachusetts Avenue NW, Washington, DC 20008
telephone: [1] (202) 265-4171
FAX: [1] (202) 328-8270
consulate(s) general: New York and San Francisco
Diplomatic representation from the US:
chief of mission: Ambassador (vacant); Charge d'Affaires Marie MURRAY
embassy: 22 Boulevard Emmanuel-Servais, 2535 Luxembourg City
mailing address: American Embassy Luxembourg, Unit 1410, APO AE 09126-1410 (official mail); American Embassy Luxembourg, PSC 9, Box 9500, APO AE 09123 (personal mail)
telephone: [352] 46 01 23
FAX: [352] 46 14 01
Flag description: three equal horizontal bands of red (top), white, and light blue; similar to the flag of the Netherlands, which uses a darker blue and is shorter; design was based on the flag of France

Economy

Economy - overview: The stable, prosperous economy features moderate growth, low inflation, and low unemployment. The industrial sector, until recently dominated by steel, has become increasingly more diversified. During the past decades, growth in the financial sector has more than compensated for the decline in steel. Services, especially banking, account for a growing proportion of the economy. Agriculture is based on small family-owned farms. Luxembourg has especially close trade and financial ties to Belgium and the Netherlands, and as a member of the EU, enjoys the advantages of the open European market. It joined with 10 other EU members to launch the euro on 1 January 1999.
GDP: purchasing power parity - $13.9 billion (1998 est.)
GDP - real growth rate: 2.9% (1998 est.)
GDP - per capita: purchasing power parity - $32,700 (1998 est.)
GDP - composition by sector:
agriculture: 1%
industry: 22%
services: 77% (1998 est.)
Population below poverty line: NA%
Household income or consumption by percentage share:
lowest 10%: NA%
highest 10%: NA%
Inflation rate (consumer prices): 1.4% (1998)
Labor force: 226,500 (one-third of labor force is foreign workers, mostly from Portugal, Italy, France, Belgium, and Germany) (1998 est.)
Labor force - by occupation: services 83.2%, industry 14.3%, agriculture 2.5% (1998 est.)
Unemployment rate: 3% (1998 est.)
Budget:
revenues: $5.46 billion
expenditures: $5.44 billion, including capital

Luxembourg (continued)

expenditures of $NA (1997 est.)

Industries: banking, iron and steel, food processing, chemicals, metal products, engineering, tires, glass, aluminum

Industrial production growth rate: 3.3% (1995 est.)

Electricity - production: 1.158 billion kWh (1997)

Electricity - production by source:

fossil fuel: 90.12%

hydro: 9.88%

nuclear: 0%

other: 0% (1996)

Electricity - consumption: 5.381 billion kWh (1996)

Electricity - exports: 800 million kWh (1996)

Electricity - imports: 5.8 billion kWh (1996)

Agriculture - products: barley, oats, potatoes, wheat, fruits, wine grapes; livestock products

Exports: $7.1 billion (f.o.b., 1996)

Exports - commodities: finished steel products, chemicals, rubber products, glass, aluminum, other industrial products

Exports - partners: Germany 28%, France 18%, Belgium 15%, UK 7%, Netherlands 5%

Imports: $9.4 billion (c.i.f., 1996)

Imports - commodities: minerals, metals, foodstuffs, quality consumer goods

Imports - partners: Belgium 38%, Germany 25%, France 11%, Netherlands 4%

Debt - external: $NA

Economic aid - donor: ODA, $65 million (1995)

Currency: 1 Luxembourg franc (LuxF) = 100 centimes; note - centimes no longer in use

Exchange rates: Luxembourg francs (LuxF) per US$1 - 34.77 (January 1999), 36.299 (1998), 35.774 (1997), 30.962 (1996), 29.480 (1995), 33.456 (1994); note - the Luxembourg franc is at par with the Belgian franc, which circulates freely in Luxembourg

note: on 1 January 1999, the European Union introduced a common currency that is now being used by financial institutions in some member countries at the rate of 0.8597 euros per US$ and a fixed rate of 40.3399 francs per euro; the euro will replace the local currency in consenting countries for all transactions in 2002

Fiscal year: calendar year

Communications

Telephones: 279,736 (1997)

Telephone system: highly developed, completely automated and efficient system, mainly buried cables

domestic: nationwide cellular telephone system; buried cable

international: 3 channels leased on TAT-6 coaxial submarine cable (Europe to North America)

Radio broadcast stations: AM 0, FM 6, shortwave 0

Radios: 230,000 (1993 est.)

Television broadcast stations: 5 (1997)

Televisions: 100,500 (1993 est.)

Transportation

Railways:

total: 275 km

standard gauge: 275 km 1.435-m gauge (262 km electrified; 178 km double track) (1995)

Highways:

total: 5,137 km

paved: 5,086 km (including 123 km of expressways)

unpaved: 51 km (1996 est.)

note: one source lists roads 2,863 km; expressways 115 km

Waterways: 37 km; Moselle

Pipelines: petroleum products 48 km

Ports and harbors: Mertert

Merchant marine:

total: 37 ships (1,000 GRT or over) totaling 1,033,045 GRT/1,480,023 DWT

ships by type: bulk 1, chemical tanker 6, liquefied gas tanker 13, oil tanker 6, passenger 4, roll-on/roll-off cargo 6, vehicle carrier 1 (1998 est.)

Airports: 2 (1998 est.)

Airports - with paved runways:

total: 1

over 3,047 m: 1 (1998 est.)

Airports - with unpaved runways:

total: 1

under 914 m: 1 (1998 est.)

Military

Military branches: Army, National Gendarmerie

Military manpower - military age: 19 years of age

Military manpower - availability:

males age 15-49: 108,285 (1999 est.)

Military manpower - fit for military service:

males age 15-49: 88,813 (1999 est.)

Military manpower - reaching military age annually:

males: 2,452 (1999 est.)

Military expenditures - dollar figure: $124 million (FY97)

Military expenditures - percent of GDP: 0.8% (1995)

Transnational Issues

Disputes - international: none

Macau
(Chinese territory under Portuguese administration)

Geography

Location: Eastern Asia, bordering the South China Sea and China

Geographic coordinates: 22 10 N, 113 33 E

Map references: Southeast Asia

Area:

total: 21 sq km

land: 21 sq km

water: 0 sq km

Area - comparative: about 0.1 times the size of Washington, DC

Land boundaries:

total: 0.34 km

border countries: China 0.34 km

Coastline: 40 km

Maritime claims: not specified

Climate: subtropical; marine with cool winters, warm summers

Terrain: generally flat

Elevation extremes:

lowest point: South China Sea 0 m

highest point: Coloane Alto 174 m

Natural resources: NEGL

Macau (continued)

Land use:

arable land: 0%

permanent crops: 2%

permanent pastures: 0%

forests and woodland: 0%

other: 98% (1998 est.)

Irrigated land: NA sq km

Natural hazards: NA

Environment - current issues: NA

Environment - international agreements:

party to: Ozone Layer Protection (extended from Portugal)

signed, but not ratified: NA

Geography - note: essentially urban; one causeway and two bridges connect the two islands of Coloane and Taipa to the peninsula on mainland

Population: 437,312 (July 1999 est.)

Age structure:

0-14 years: 24% (male 54,456; female 50,912)

15-64 years: 69% (male 142,575; female 158,132)

65 years and over: 7% (male 12,547; female 18,690) (1999 est.)

Population growth rate: 1.86% (1999 est.)

Birth rate: 12.5 births/1,000 population (1999 est.)

Death rate: 3.48 deaths/1,000 population (1999 est.)

Net migration rate: 9.59 migrant(s)/1,000 population (1999 est.)

Sex ratio:

at birth: 1.05 male(s)/female

under 15 years: 1.07 male(s)/female

15-64 years: 0.9 male(s)/female

65 years and over: 0.67 male(s)/female

total population: 0.92 male(s)/female (1999 est.)

Infant mortality rate: 4.23 deaths/1,000 live births (1999 est.)

Life expectancy at birth:

total population: 81.88 years

male: 78.79 years

female: 85.13 years (1999 est.)

Total fertility rate: 1.27 children born/woman (1999 est.)

Nationality:

noun: Macanese (singular and plural)

adjective: Macau

Ethnic groups: Chinese 95%, Portuguese 3%, other 2%

Religions: Buddhist 50%, Roman Catholic 15%, none and other 35% (1997 est.)

Languages: Portuguese, Chinese (Cantonese)

Literacy:

definition: age 15 and over can read and write

total population: 90%

male: 93%

female: 86% (1981 est.)

Country name:

conventional long form: none

conventional short form: Macau

local long form: none

local short form: Ilha de Macau

Data code: MC

Dependency status: Chinese territory under Portuguese administration; note - scheduled to revert to China on 20 December 1999

Government type: NA

Capital: Macau

Administrative divisions: 2 districts (concelhos, singular - concelho); Ilhas, Macau

Independence: none (Chinese territory under Portuguese administration; Portugal signed an agreement with China on 13 April 1987 to return Macau to Chinese administration on 20 December 1999; in the joint declaration, China promises to respect Macau's existing social and economic systems and lifestyle for 50 years after transition)

National holiday: Day of Portugal, 10 June (1580)

Constitution: 17 February 1976, Organic Law of Macau; Macau's future constitution, the "Basic Law", promulgated by China's National People's Congress on 31 March 1993, will go into effect 20 December 1999

Legal system: Portuguese civil law system

Suffrage: 18 years of age; universal

Executive branch:

chief of state: President Jorge SAMPAIO of Portugal (since 9 March 1996)

head of government: Governor General Vasco Joaquim Rocha VIEIRA (since 20 March 1991)

cabinet: Consultative Council consists of a total of 15 members - five appointed by the governor, two nominated by the governor, five elected for a four-year term (two represent administrative bodies, one represents moral, cultural, and welfare interests, and two represent economic interests), and three statutory members

elections: Portuguese president elected by popular vote for a five-year term; governor general appointed by the Portuguese president after consultation with the Legislative Assembly

Legislative branch: unicameral Legislative Assembly (23 seats; 8 elected by popular vote, 8 by indirect vote, and 7 appointed by the governor; members serve four-year terms)

elections: last held 22 September 1996 (next to be held NA 2000)

election results: percent of vote by party - NA; seats by party - APPEM 2, CODEM 1, UDM 1, UNIPRO 2, UPD 1, ANMD 1

Judicial branch: Supreme Court, consisting of five magistrates including the president; lower court judges appointed for three-year terms by the governor

Political parties and leaders: Uniao Promotora para o Progresso or UNIPRO [leader NA]; Associacao Promotora para a Economia de Macau or APPEM [leader NA]; Uniao para o Desenvolvimento or UPD [leader NA]; Associacao de Novo Macau Democratico or ANMD [leader NA]; Convergencia para o Desenvolvimento or CODEM [leader NA]; Uniao para o Desenvolvimento or UDM [leader NA]; Uniao Geral para o Desenvolvimento de Macau or UDM [leader NA]; Associacao de Amizade or AMI [leader NA]; Alianca para o Desenvolvimento da Economia or ADE [leader NA]; Associacao dos Empregados e Assalariados or AEA [leader NA]; Associacao pela Democracia e BemEstar Social de Macau or ADBSM [leader NA]

note: there are no formal political parties, but civic associations are used instead

Political pressure groups and leaders: wealthy Macanese and Chinese representing local interests, wealthy procommunist merchants representing China's interests; in January 1967 the Macau Government acceded to Chinese demands that gave China veto power over administration

International organization participation: CCC, ESCAP (associate), IMO (associate), Interpol (subbureau), UNESCO (associate), WMO, WToO (associate), WTrO

Diplomatic representation in the US: none (Chinese territory under Portuguese administration)

Diplomatic representation from the US: the US has no offices in Macau, and US interests are monitored by the US Consulate General in Hong Kong

Flag description: the flag of Portugal is used

Economy - overview: The economy is based largely on tourism (including gambling) and textile and fireworks manufacturing. Efforts to diversify have spawned other small industries - toys, artificial flowers, and electronics. The tourist sector has accounted for roughly 25% of GDP, and the clothing industry has provided about two-thirds of export earnings; the gambling industry probably represents over 40% of GDP. Macau depends on China for most of its food, fresh water, and energy imports. Japan and Hong Kong are the main suppliers of raw materials and capital goods. Macau is scheduled to revert to Chinese administration on 20 December 1999.

GDP: purchasing power parity - $6.9 billion (1998 est.)

GDP - real growth rate: -0.1% (1998 est.)

GDP - per capita: purchasing power parity - $16,000 (1998 est.)

GDP - composition by sector:

agriculture: 1%

industry: 40%

services: 59% (1997)

Population below poverty line: NA%

Household income or consumption by percentage share:

lowest 10%: NA%

highest 10%: NA%

Inflation rate (consumer prices): 3.5% (1997)

Labor force: 277,676 (1997)

Labor force - by occupation: industry 28%, restaurants and hotels 28%, other services 44%

Unemployment rate: 3.8% (1998 est.)

Budget:

revenues: $1.3 billion

expenditures: $1.07 billion, including capital expenditures of $NA (1995 est.)

Industries: clothing, textiles, toys, electronics,

footwear, tourism
Industrial production growth rate: NA%
Electricity - production: 1.125 billion kWh (1996)
Electricity - production by source:
fossil fuel: 100%
hydro: 0%
nuclear: 0%
other: 0% (1996)
Electricity - consumption: 1.522 billion kWh (1996)
Electricity - exports: 3 million kWh (1996)
Electricity - imports: 400 million kWh (1996)
Agriculture - products: rice, vegetables
Exports: $2.14 billion (f.o.b., 1997)
Exports - commodities: textiles, clothing, toys, electronics, cement, footwear, machinery
Exports - partners: US 45%, EU 24%, Hong Kong 8%, China 6% (1997)
Imports: $2.075 billion (c.i.f., 1997)
Imports - commodities: raw materials, foodstuffs, capital goods, fuels, lubricants
Imports - partners: China 29%, Hong Kong 25%, EU 12.4%, Japan 9% (1997)
Debt - external: $0 (1996)
Economic aid - recipient: $NA
Currency: 1 pataca (P) = 100 avos
Exchange rates: patacas (P) per US$1 - 7.74 (1998), 7.99 (1997), 7.962 (1996), 8.034 (1993-95), 7.973 (1992); note - linked to the Hong Kong dollar at the rate of 1.03 patacas per Hong Kong dollar
Fiscal year: calendar year

Telephones: 200,000 (1997 est.)
Telephone system: fairly modern communication facilities maintained for domestic and international services
domestic: NA
international: HF radiotelephone communication facility; access to international communications carriers provided via Hong Kong and China; satellite earth station - 1 Intelsat (Indian Ocean)
Radio broadcast stations: AM 4, FM 3, shortwave 0
Radios: 135,000 (1992 est.)
Television broadcast stations: 0 (receives Hong Kong broadcasts) (1997)
Televisions: 34,000 (1992 est.)

Railways: 0 km
Highways:
total: 50 km
paved: 50 km
unpaved: 0 km (1996 est.)
Ports and harbors: Macau
Merchant marine: none
Airports: 1 (1998 est.)
Airports - with paved runways:
total: 1
over 3,047 m: 1 (1998 est.)

Military branches: no regular military forces, Police Force
Military manpower - availability:
males age 15-49: 121,355 (1999 est.)
Military manpower - fit for military service:
males age 15-49: 66,744 (1999 est.)
Military - note: defense is currently the responsibility of Portugal, but will become the responsibility of China on 20 December 1999

Disputes - international: none

Macedonia, The Former Yugoslav Republic of

Location: Southeastern Europe, north of Greece
Geographic coordinates: 41 50 N, 22 00 E
Map references: Europe
Area:
total: 25,333 sq km
land: 24,856 sq km
water: 477 sq km
Area - comparative: slightly larger than Vermont
Land boundaries:
total: 748 km
border countries: Albania 151 km, Bulgaria 148 km, Greece 228 km, Serbia and Montenegro 221 km (all with Serbia)
Coastline: 0 km (landlocked)
Maritime claims: none (landlocked)
Climate: warm, dry summers and autumns and relatively cold winters with heavy snowfall
Terrain: mountainous territory covered with deep basins and valleys; three large lakes, each divided by a frontier line; country bisected by the Vardar River
Elevation extremes:
lowest point: Vardar River 50 m
highest point: Golem Korab (Majae Korabit) 2,753 m
Natural resources: chromium, lead, zinc, manganese, tungsten, nickel, low-grade iron ore, asbestos, sulfur, timber
Land use:
arable land: 24%
permanent crops: 2%
permanent pastures: 25%
forests and woodland: 39%
other: 10% (1993 est.)
Irrigated land: 830 sq km (1993 est.)
Natural hazards: high seismic risks
Environment - current issues: air pollution from metallurgical plants
Environment - international agreements:
party to: Air Pollution, Biodiversity, Climate Change,

Macedonia, The Former Yugoslav Republic of *(continued)*

Hazardous Wastes, Law of the Sea, Ozone Layer Protection

signed, but not ratified: none of the selected agreements

Geography - note: landlocked; major transportation corridor from Western and Central Europe to Aegean Sea and Southern Europe to Western Europe

People

Population: 2,022,604 (July 1999 est.)

note: the Macedonian Government census of July 1994 put the population at 1.94 million, but ethnic allocations were likely undercounted

Age structure:

0-14 years: 23% (male 243,190; female 228,491)

15-64 years: 67% (male 680,692; female 673,923)

65 years and over: 10% (male 88,116; female 108,192) (1999 est.)

Population growth rate: 0.64% (1999 est.)

Birth rate: 15.21 births/1,000 population (1999 est.)

Death rate: 8.03 deaths/1,000 population (1999 est.)

Net migration rate: -0.83 migrant(s)/1,000 population (1999 est.)

Sex ratio:

at birth: 1.08 male(s)/female

under 15 years: 1.06 male(s)/female

15-64 years: 1.01 male(s)/female

65 years and over: 0.81 male(s)/female

total population: 1 male(s)/female (1999 est.)

Infant mortality rate: 18.68 deaths/1,000 live births (1999 est.)

Life expectancy at birth:

total population: 73.05 years

male: 70.93 years

female: 75.34 years (1999 est.)

Total fertility rate: 2 children born/woman (1999 est.)

Nationality:

noun: Macedonian(s)

adjective: Macedonian

Ethnic groups: Macedonian 66%, Albanian 23%, Turkish 4%, Serb 2%, Gypsies 3%, other 2%

Religions: Eastern Orthodox 67%, Muslim 30%, other 3%

Languages: Macedonian 70%, Albanian 21%, Turkish 3%, Serbo-Croatian 3%, other 3%

Literacy: NA

Government

Country name:

conventional long form: The Former Yugoslav Republic of Macedonia

conventional short form: none

local long form: Republika Makedonija

local short form: Makedonija

abbreviation: FYROM

Data code: MK

Government type: emerging democracy

Capital: Skopje

Administrative divisions: 34 counties (opstinas, singular - opstina) Berovo, Bitola, Brod, Debar, Delcevo, Gevgelija, Gostivar, Kavadarci, Kicevo, Kocani, Kratovo, Kriva Palanka, Krusevo, Kumanovo, Murgasevo, Negotino, Ohrid, Prilep, Probistip, Radovis, Resen, Skopje-Centar, Skopje-Cair, Skopje-Karpos, Skopje-Kisela Voda, Skopje-Gazi Baba, Stip, Struga, Strumica, Sveti Nikole, Tetovo, Titov Veles, Valandovo, Vinica

note: in September 1996, the Macedonian Assembly passed legislation changing the territorial division of the country; names of the 123 new municipalities are not yet available

Independence: 17 September 1991 (from Yugoslavia)

National holiday: 8 September

Constitution: adopted 17 November 1991, effective 20 November 1991

Legal system: based on civil law system; judicial review of legislative acts

Suffrage: 18 years of age; universal

Executive branch:

chief of state: President Kiro GLIGOROV (since 27 January 1991)

head of government: Prime Minister Ljubco GEORGIEVSKI (since 30 November 1998)

cabinet: Council of Ministers elected by the majority vote of all the deputies in the Assembly; note - cabinet formed by the government coalition parties VMRO-DPMNE, DA, and DPA

elections: president elected by popular vote for a five-year term; election last held 16 October 1994 (next to be held NA October 1999)

election results: Kiro GLIGOROV elected president; percent of vote - Kiro GLIGOROV 78.4%

Legislative branch: unicameral Assembly or Sobranje (120 seats - 85 members are elected by popular vote; 35 members come from lists of candidates submitted by parties based on the percentage that parties gain from the overall vote; all serve four-year terms)

elections: last held 18 October and 1 November 1998 (next to be held NA 2002)

election results: percent of vote by party - NA; seats by party - VMRO 49, SDSM 27, PDP 14, DA 13, DPA 11, LDP 4, Socialists 1, Roma Party 1

Judicial branch: Constitutional Court, judges are elected by the Judicial Council; Judicial Court of the Republic, judges are elected by the Judicial Council

Political parties and leaders: Social-Democratic Alliance of Macedonia or SDSM (former Communist Party) [Branko CRVENKOVSKI, president]; Party for Democratic Prosperity or PDP [Abdurahman ALITI, president]; Liberal Democratic Party or LDP [Petar GOSEV]; Socialist Party of Macedonia or SP [Ljubislav IVANOV-ZINGO, president]; Internal Macedonian Revolutionary Organization - Democratic Party for Macedonian National Unity or VMRO-DPMNE [Ljubcho GEORGIEVSKI, president]; Democratic Party for Albanians or DPA [Arben XHAFERI, president]; Democratic Alternative or DA [Vasil TUPURKOVSKI, president]; Movement for All Macedonian Action or MAAK [Straso ANGELOVSKI]; Democratic Party of Serbs or DPSM [leader NA]; Democratic Party of Turks [leader NA]; Party for Democratic Action [Slavic MUSLIM]; Party for the Complete Emancipation of Romas or PCER [Bajram BORNT]; Democratic Party of Macedonia or DPM [Tomislav STOJANOVSKI]; Democratic Progressive Party of Romas [leader NA]; Civic Liberal Party [leader NA]; Worker Party [leader NA]; Movement for Renewal in Macedonia or VMRO [leader NA]; Alliance of Communists [leader NA]; Communist Party [leader NA]; Alliance of Romas [leader NA]; Republican Party for National Unity [leader NA]; Party for Democratic Action-True Path [leader NA]; Social Democratic Party of Macedonia or SDPM [leader NA]; League of Democracy [leader NA]; Social Christian Party of Macedonia [leader NA]; Party of Pensioners of Macedonia [leader NA]

International organization participation: BIS (pending member), CCC, CE, CEI, EAPC, EBRD, ECE, FAO, IAEA, IBRD, ICAO, ICRM, IDA, IFAD, IFC, IFRCS, ILO, IMF, IMO, Intelsat (nonsignatory user), Interpol, IOC, ISO, ITU, OSCE, PFP, UN, UNCTAD, UNESCO, UNIDO, UPU, WHO, WIPO, WMO, WToO, WTrO (applicant)

Diplomatic representation in the US:

chief of mission: Ambassador Ljubica Z. ACEVSKA

chancery: 3050 K Street, NW, Suite 210, Washington, DC 20007

telephone: [1] (202) 337 3063

FAX: [1] (202) 337-3093

consulate(s) general: New York

Diplomatic representation from the US:

chief of mission: Ambassador Christopher Robert HILL

embassy: Bul. Ilindenska bb, 91000 Skopje

mailing address: American Embassy Skopje, Department of State, Washington, DC 20521-7120 (pouch)

telephone: [389] (91) 116-180

FAX: [389] (91) 117-103

Flag description: a rising yellow sun with eight rays extending to the edges of the red field

Economy

Economy - overview: The breakup of Yugoslavia in 1991 deprived Macedonia, its poorest republic, of key protected markets and large transfer payments from the center. Worker remittances and foreign aid have softened the subsequent volatile recovery period. Continued recovery depends on Macedonia's ability to attract investment, to redevelop trade ties with Greece and Serbia and Montenegro, and to maintain its commitment to economic liberalization. The economy can meet its basic food needs but depends on outside sources for all of its oil and gas and most of its modern machinery and parts.

GDP: purchasing power parity - $2.1 billion (1998 est.)

GDP - real growth rate: 4.5% (1998 est.)

GDP - per capita: purchasing power parity - $1,050 (1998 est.)

GDP - composition by sector:

agriculture: 20.4%

Macedonia, The Former Yugoslav Republic of (continued)

industry: 38.6%

services: 41% (1995 est.)

Population below poverty line: NA%

Household income or consumption by percentage share:

lowest 10%: NA%

highest 10%: NA%

Inflation rate (consumer prices): 3% (1998 est.)

Labor force: 591,773 (June 1994)

Labor force - by occupation: manufacturing and mining 40% (1992)

Unemployment rate: 30% (1998 est.); note - many employed workers are, in fact, furloughees

Budget:

revenues: $1.06 billion

expenditures: $1 billion, including capital expenditures of $107 million (1996 est.)

Industries: coal, metallic chromium, lead, zinc, ferronickel, textiles, wood products, tobacco

Industrial production growth rate: 3.4% (1997 est.)

Electricity - production: 6.06 billion kWh (1996)

Electricity - production by source:

fossil fuel: 80.2%

hydro: 19.8%

nuclear: 0%

other: 0% (1996)

Electricity - consumption: 6.06 billion kWh (1996)

Electricity - exports: 0 kWh (1996)

Electricity - imports: 0 kWh (1996)

Agriculture - products: rice, tobacco, wheat, corn, millet, cotton, sesame, mulberry leaves, citrus, vegetables; beef, pork, poultry, mutton

Exports: $1.2 billion (f.o.b., 1997)

Exports - commodities: food, beverages, tobacco 17.0%, machinery and transport equipment 13.3%, other manufactured goods 58%

Exports - partners: Bulgaria, other former Yugoslav republics, Germany, Italy

Imports: $1.6 billion (c.i.f., 1997)

Imports - commodities: machinery and equipment 19%, chemicals 14%, fuels 12%

Imports - partners: other former Yugoslav republics, Germany, Bulgaria, Italy, Austria

Debt - external: $1.06 billion (June 1997)

Economic aid - recipient: ODA, $100 million (1996 est.)

Currency: 1 Macedonian denar (MKD) = 100 deni

Exchange rates: denars per US$1 - 52.156 (January 1999), 54.462 (1998), 50.004 (1997), 39.981 (1996), 37.882 (1995), 43.263 (1994)

Fiscal year: calendar year

Communications

Telephones: 125,000

Telephone system:

domestic: NA

international: NA

Radio broadcast stations: AM 6, FM 2, shortwave 0

Radios: 350,000 (1992 est.)

Television broadcast stations: 136 (of which 22 are main stations and 114 are low-power stations) (1997)

Televisions: 327,011 (1992 est.)

Transportation

Railways:

total: 922 km

standard gauge: 922 km 1.435-m gauge (232 km electrified) (1997)

Highways:

total: 10,591 km

paved: 5,500 km (including 133 km of expressways)

unpaved: 5,091 km (1997 est.)

Waterways: none, lake transport only

Pipelines: 0 km

Ports and harbors: none

Airports: 16 (1998 est.)

Airports - with paved runways:

total: 10

2,438 to 3,047 m: 2

under 914 m: 8 (1998 est.)

Airports - with unpaved runways:

total: 6

914 to 1,523 m: 2

under 914 m: 4 (1998 est.)

Military

Military branches: Army, Navy, Air and Air Defense Forces, Police Force

Military manpower - military age: 19 years of age

Military manpower - availability:

males age 15-49: 539,329 (1999 est.)

Military manpower - fit for military service:

males age 15-49: 434,468 (1999 est.)

Military manpower - reaching military age annually:

males: 17,291 (1999 est.)

Military expenditures - dollar figure: $71 million (1998)

Military expenditures - percent of GDP: 2.2% (1998)

Transnational Issues

Disputes - international: dispute with Greece over name; in September 1995, Skopje and Athens signed an interim accord resolving their dispute over symbols and certain constitutional provisions; Athens also lifted its economic embargo on The Former Yugoslav Republic of Macedonia; the border commission formed by The Former Yugoslav Republic of Macedonia and Serbia and Montenegro in April 1996 to resolve differences in delineation of their mutual border has made no progress so far; Albanians in Macedonia claim discrimination in education, access to public-sector jobs and representation in government; Party for Democratic Action (DPA), which is now a member party of the government, calls for a rewrite of the constitution to declare ethnic Albanians a national group and allow for regional autonomy

Illicit drugs: increasing transshipment point for Southwest Asian heroin and hashish; minor transit point for South American cocaine destined for Europe

Madagascar

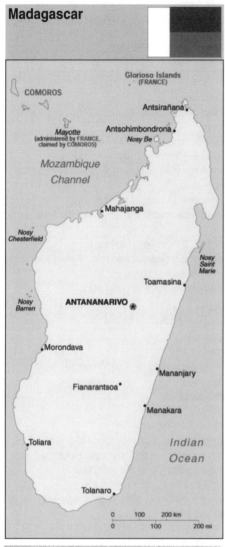

Geography

Location: Southern Africa, island in the Indian Ocean, east of Mozambique
Geographic coordinates: 20 00 S, 47 00 E
Map references: Africa
Area:
total: 587,040 sq km
land: 581,540 sq km
water: 5,500 sq km
Area - comparative: slightly less than twice the size of Arizona
Land boundaries: 0 km
Coastline: 4,828 km
Maritime claims:
contiguous zone: 24 nm
continental shelf: 200 nm or 100 nm from the 2,500-m deep isobath
exclusive economic zone: 200 nm
territorial sea: 12 nm
Climate: tropical along coast, temperate inland, arid in south
Terrain: narrow coastal plain, high plateau and mountains in center
Elevation extremes:
lowest point: Indian Ocean 0 m

highest point: Maromokotro 2,876 m
Natural resources: graphite, chromite, coal, bauxite, salt, quartz, tar sands, semiprecious stones, mica, fish
Land use:
arable land: 4%
permanent crops: 1%
permanent pastures: 41%
forests and woodland: 40%
other: 14% (1993 est.)
Irrigated land: 10,870 sq km (1993 est.)
Natural hazards: periodic cyclones
Environment - current issues: soil erosion results from deforestation and overgrazing; desertification; surface water contaminated with raw sewage and other organic wastes; several species of flora and fauna unique to the island are endangered
Environment - international agreements:
party to: Biodiversity, Desertification, Endangered Species, Marine Life Conservation, Nuclear Test Ban, Ozone Layer Protection
signed, but not ratified: Climate Change, Law of the Sea
Geography - note: world's fourth-largest island; strategic location along Mozambique Channel

People

Population: 14,873,387 (July 1999 est.)
Age structure:
0-14 years: 45% (male 3,356,104; female 3,279,056)
15-64 years: 52% (male 3,841,248; female 3,908,209)
65 years and over: 3% (male 234,549; female 254,221) (1999 est.)
Population growth rate: 2.8% (1999 est.)
Birth rate: 41.52 births/1,000 population (1999 est.)
Death rate: 13.56 deaths/1,000 population (1999 est.)
Net migration rate: 0 migrant(s)/1,000 population (1999 est.)
Sex ratio:
at birth: 1.03 male(s)/female
under 15 years: 1.02 male(s)/female
15-64 years: 0.98 male(s)/female
65 years and over: 0.92 male(s)/female
total population: 1 male(s)/female (1999 est.)
Infant mortality rate: 89.1 deaths/1,000 live births (1999 est.)
Life expectancy at birth:
total population: 53.24 years
male: 52.01 years
female: 54.51 years (1999 est.)
Total fertility rate: 5.7 children born/woman (1999 est.)
Nationality:
noun: Malagasy (singular and plural)
adjective: Malagasy
Ethnic groups: Malayo-Indonesian (Merina and related Betsileo), Cotiers (mixed African, Malayo-Indonesian, and Arab ancestry - Betsimisaraka, Tsimihety, Antaisaka, Sakalava), French, Indian, Creole, Comoran

Religions: indigenous beliefs 52%, Christian 41%, Muslim 7%
Languages: French (official), Malagasy (official)
Literacy:
definition: age 15 and over can read and write
total population: 80%
male: 88%
female: 73% (1990 est.)

Government

Country name:
conventional long form: Republic of Madagascar
conventional short form: Madagascar
local long form: Republique de Madagascar
local short form: Madagascar
former: Malagasy Republic
Data code: MA
Government type: republic
Capital: Antananarivo
Administrative divisions: 6 provinces (faritany); Antananarivo, Antsiranana, Fianarantsoa, Mahajanga, Toamasina, Toliara
Independence: 26 June 1960 (from France)
National holiday: Independence Day, 26 June (1960)
Constitution: 19 August 1992 by national referendum
Legal system: based on French civil law system and traditional Malagasy law; has not accepted compulsory ICJ jurisdiction
Suffrage: 18 years of age; universal
Executive branch:
chief of state: President Didier RATSIRAKA (since 10 February 1997)
head of government: Prime Minister Tantely Rene Gabriot ANDRIANARIVO (since NA 1998)
cabinet: Council of Ministers appointed by the prime minister
elections: president elected by popular vote for a five-year term; election last held 29 December 1996 (next to be held NA 2002); prime minister appointed by the president from a list of candidates nominated by the National Assembly
election results: Didier RATSIRAKA elected president; percent of vote - Didier RATSIRAKA (AREMA) 50.7%, Albert ZAFY (AFFA) 49.3%
Legislative branch: unicameral National Assembly or Assemblee Nationale (150 seats; members are directly elected by popular vote to serve four-year terms); note - the legislature is scheduled to become a bicameral Paliament with the establishment of a Senate; two-thirds of the seats of this Senate will be filled by regional assemblies whose members will be elected by popular vote; the remaining one-third of the seats will be appointed by the president; the total number of seats will be determined by the National Assembly; all members will serve four-year terms
elections: National Assembly - last held 17 May 1998 (next to be held NA 2002)
election results: National Assembly - percent of vote by party - NA; seats by party - AREMA 62, LEADER/ Fanilo 15, AVI 14, RPSD 11, AFFA 6, MFM 3, AKFM/

Madagascar *(continued)*

Fanavaozana 3, GRAD/Iloafo 1, Fihaonana 1, independents 34

Judicial branch: Supreme Court (Cour Supreme); High Constitutional Court (Haute Cour Constitutionnelle)

Political parties and leaders: Association for the Rebirth of Madagascar or AREMA [Pierrot RAJAONARIVELO]; Economic Liberalism and Democratic Action for National Recovery or LEADER/Fanilo [Herizo RAZAFIMAHALEO]; Judged by Your Work or AVI [Norbert RATSIRAHONANA]; Renewal of the Social Democratic Party or RPSD [Evariste MARSON]; Action, Truth, Development, and Harmony or AFFA [Professor Albert ZAFY]; Movement for the Progress of Madagascar or MFM [Manandafy RAKOTONIRINA]; Congress Party for Malagasy Independence or AKFM/Fanavaozana [Pastor Richard ANDRIAMANJATO]; Group of Reflection and Action for the Development of Madagascar or GRAD/Iloafo [Tovonanahary RABETSITONTA]; Fihaonana Rally or Fihaonana [Guy RAZANAMASY]

Political pressure groups and leaders: National Council of Christian Churches or FFKM; Federalist Movement

International organization participation: ACCT, ACP, AfDB, CCC, ECA, FAO, G-77, IAEA, IBRD, ICAO, ICC, ICFTU, ICRM, IDA, IFAD, IFC, IFRCS, ILO, IMF, IMO, InOC, Intelsat, Interpol, IOC, IOM (observer), ITU, NAM, OAU, OPCW, UN, UNCTAD, UNESCO, UNHCR, UNIDO, UPU, WCL, WFTU, WHO, WIPO, WMO, WToO, WTrO

Diplomatic representation in the US:
chief of mission: Ambassador (vacant); Charge d'Affaires Biclair Henri ANDRIANANTOANDRO
chancery: 2374 Massachusetts Avenue NW, Washington, DC 20008
telephone: [1] (202) 265-5525, 5526
consulate(s) general: New York

Diplomatic representation from the US:
chief of mission: Ambassador (vacant); Charge d'Affaires Howard T. PERLOW
embassy: 14-16 Rue Rainitovo, Antsahavola, Antananarivo
mailing address: B. P. 620, Antananarivo
telephone: [261] (2) 212-57, 200-89, 207-18
FAX: [261] (2) 345-39

Flag description: two equal horizontal bands of red (top) and green with a vertical white band of the same width on hoist side

Economy

Economy - overview: Madagascar suffers from chronic malnutrition, underfunded health and education facilities, a roughly 3% annual population growth rate, and severe loss of forest cover, accompanied by erosion. Agriculture, including fishing and forestry, is the mainstay of the economy, accounting for 32% of GDP and contributing more than 70% to export earnings. Industry features textile manufacturing and the processing of agricultural products. Growth in output in 1992-97 averaged less than the growth rate of the population. Growth has

been held back by antigovernment strikes and demonstrations, a decline in world coffee demand, and the erratic commitment of the government to economic reform. Formidable obstacles stand in the way of Madagascar's realizing its considerable growth potential; the extent of government reforms, outside financial aid, and foreign investment will be key determinants.

GDP: purchasing power parity - $10.3 billion (1997 est.)

GDP - real growth rate: 3% (1997 est.)

GDP - per capita: purchasing power parity - $730 (1997 est.)

GDP - composition by sector:
agriculture: 32%
industry: 13%
services: 55% (1997 est.)

Population below poverty line: NA%

Household income or consumption by percentage share:
lowest 10%: 2.3%
highest 10%: 34.9% (1993)

Inflation rate (consumer prices): 4.5% (1997)

Labor force: 7 million (1995)

Unemployment rate: NA%

Budget:
revenues: $477 million
expenditures: $706 million, including capital expenditures of $264 million (1996 est.)

Industries: meat processing, soap, breweries, tanneries, sugar, textiles, glassware, cement, automobile assembly plant, paper, petroleum, tourism

Industrial production growth rate: 3.8% (1993 est.)

Electricity - production: 595 million kWh (1996)

Electricity - production by source:
fossil fuel: 41.18%
hydro: 58.82%
nuclear: 0%
other: 0% (1996)

Electricity - consumption: 595 million kWh (1996)

Electricity - exports: 0 kWh (1996)

Electricity - imports: 0 kWh (1996)

Agriculture - products: coffee, vanilla, sugarcane, cloves, cocoa, rice, cassava (tapioca), beans, bananas, peanuts; livestock products

Exports: $170 million (f.o.b., 1997)

Exports - commodities: coffee 45%, vanilla 20%, cloves, shellfish, sugar, petroleum products (1995 est.)

Exports - partners: France 31.7%, Japan 15.8%, Germany 6.4%, Reunion 5.7% (1996)

Imports: $477 million (f.o.b., 1997)

Imports - commodities: intermediate manufactures 30%, capital goods 28%, petroleum 15%, consumer goods 14%, food 13% (1995 est.)

Imports - partners: France 31.0%, Iran 9.1%, South Africa 8.2%, Japan 5.8%, US 5.0% (1996)

Debt - external: $4.4 billion (1996 est.)

Economic aid - recipient: $298.5 million (1995)

Currency: 1 Malagasy franc (FMG) = 100 centimes

Exchange rates: Malagasy francs (FMG) per US$1 -

5,468.5 (January 1999), 5,441.4 (1998), 5,090.9 (1997), 4,061.3 (1996), 4,265.6 (1995), 3,067.3 (1994)

Fiscal year: calendar year

Communications

Telephones: 34,000 (1994)

Telephone system: system is above average for Africa
domestic: open-wire lines, coaxial cables, microwave radio relay, and tropospheric scatter links
international: submarine cable to Bahrain; satellite earth stations - 1 Intelsat (Indian Ocean) and 1 Intersputnik (Atlantic Ocean region)

Radio broadcast stations: AM 17, FM 3, shortwave 0

Radios: 2.74 million (1994 est.)

Television broadcast stations: 1 (in addition, there are 36 repeaters) (1997)

Televisions: 280,000 (1994 est.)

Transportation

Railways:
total: 883 km
narrow gauge: 883 km 1.000-m gauge (1994)

Highways:
total: 49,837 km
paved: 5,781 km
unpaved: 44,056 km (1996 est.)

Waterways: of local importance only; isolated streams and small portions of Lakandranon' Ampangalana (Canal des Pangalanes)

Ports and harbors: Antsiranana, Antsohimbondrona, Mahajanga, Toamasina, Toliara

Merchant marine:
total: 12 ships (1,000 GRT or over) totaling 23,311 GRT/31,533 DWT
ships by type: cargo 6, chemical tanker 1, liquefied gas tanker 1, oil tanker 2, roll-on/roll-off cargo 2 (1998 est.)

Airports: 133 (1998 est.)

Airports - with paved runways:
total: 29
over 3,047 m: 1
2,438 to 3,047 m: 2
1,524 to 2,437 m: 4
914 to 1,523 m: 20
under 914 m: 2 (1998 est.)

Airports - with unpaved runways:
total: 104
1,524 to 2,437 m: 3
914 to 1,523 m: 59
under 914 m: 42 (1998 est.)

Military

Military branches: Popular Armed Forces (includes Intervention Forces, Development Forces, Aeronaval Forces - includes Navy and Air Force), Gendarmerie, Presidential Security Regiment

Military manpower - military age: 20 years of age

Madagascar *(continued)*

Military manpower - availability:
males age 15-49: 3,415,726 (1999 est.)
Military manpower - fit for military service:
males age 15-49: 2,027,757 (1999 est.)
Military manpower - reaching military age annually:
males: 144,779 (1999 est.)
Military expenditures - dollar figure: $29 million (1994)
Military expenditures - percent of GDP: 1% (1994)

Transnational Issues

Disputes - international: claims Bassas da India, Europa Island, Glorioso Islands, Juan de Nova Island, and Tromelin Island (all administered by France)
Illicit drugs: illicit producer of cannabis (cultivated and wild varieties) used mostly for domestic consumption; transshipment point for heroin

Malawi

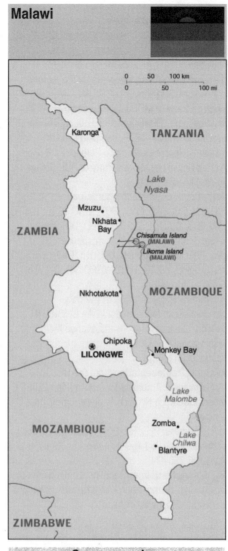

Geography

Location: Southern Africa, east of Zambia
Geographic coordinates: 13 30 S, 34 00 E
Map references: Africa
Area:
total: 118,480 sq km
land: 94,080 sq km
water: 24,400 sq km
Area - comparative: slightly smaller than Pennsylvania
Land boundaries:
total: 2,881 km
border countries: Mozambique 1,569 km, Tanzania 475 km, Zambia 837 km
Coastline: 0 km (landlocked)
Maritime claims: none (landlocked)
Climate: tropical; rainy season (November to May); dry season (May to November)
Terrain: narrow elongated plateau with rolling plains, rounded hills, some mountains
Elevation extremes:
lowest point: junction of the Shire River and international boundary with Mozambique 37 m
highest point: Sapitwa 3,002 m

Natural resources: limestone, unexploited deposits of uranium, coal, and bauxite
Land use:
arable land: 18%
permanent crops: 0%
permanent pastures: 20%
forests and woodland: 39%
other: 23% (1993 est.)
Irrigated land: 280 sq km (1993 est.)
Natural hazards: NA
Environment - current issues: deforestation; land degradation; water pollution from agricultural runoff, sewage, industrial wastes; siltation of spawning grounds endangers fish populations
Environment - international agreements:
party to: Biodiversity, Climate Change, Desertification, Endangered Species, Environmental Modification, Hazardous Wastes, Marine Life Conservation, Nuclear Test Ban, Ozone Layer Protection, Wetlands
signed, but not ratified: Law of the Sea
Geography - note: landlocked

People

Population: 10,000,416 (July 1999 est.)
Age structure:
0-14 years: 45% (male 2,265,526; female 2,246,135)
15-64 years: 52% (male 2,580,125; female 2,637,464)
65 years and over: 3% (male 112,813; female 158,353) (1999 est.)
Population growth rate: 1.57% (1999 est.)
Birth rate: 39.54 births/1,000 population (1999 est.)
Death rate: 23.84 deaths/1,000 population (1999 est.)
Net migration rate: 0 migrant(s)/1,000 population (1999 est.)
Sex ratio:
at birth: 1.03 male(s)/female
under 15 years: 1.01 male(s)/female
15-64 years: 0.98 male(s)/female
65 years and over: 0.71 male(s)/female
total population: 0.98 male(s)/female (1999 est.)
Infant mortality rate: 132.14 deaths/1,000 live births (1999 est.)
Life expectancy at birth:
total population: 36.3 years
male: 36.49 years
female: 36.11 years (1999 est.)
Total fertility rate: 5.48 children born/woman (1999 est.)
Nationality:
noun: Malawian(s)
adjective: Malawian
Ethnic groups: Chewa, Nyanja, Tumbuko, Yao, Lomwe, Sena, Tonga, Ngoni, Ngonde, Asian, European
Religions: Protestant 55%, Roman Catholic 20%, Muslim 20%, traditional indigenous beliefs
Languages: English (official), Chichewa (official), other languages important regionally

Malawi (continued)

Literacy:
definition: age 15 and over can read and write
total population: 56.4%
male: 71.9%
female: 41.8% (1995 est.)

Government

Country name:
conventional long form: Republic of Malawi
conventional short form: Malawi
former: Nyasaland
Data code: MI
Government type: multiparty democracy
Capital: Lilongwe
Administrative divisions: 24 districts; Blantyre, Chikwawa, Chiradzulu, Chitipa, Dedza, Dowa, Karonga, Kasungu, Lilongwe, Machinga (Kasupe), Mangochi, Mchinji, Mulanje, Mwanza, Mzimba, Ntcheu, Nkhata Bay, Nkhotakota, Nsanje, Ntchisi, Rumphi, Salima, Thyolo, Zomba
Independence: 6 July 1964 (from UK)
National holiday: Independence Day 6 July (1964); Republic Day 6 July (1966)
Constitution: 18 May 1995
Legal system: based on English common law and customary law; judicial review of legislative acts in the Supreme Court of Appeal; has not accepted compulsory ICJ jurisdiction
Suffrage: 18 years of age; universal
Executive branch:
chief of state: President Bakili MULUZI (since 21 May 1994); note - the president is both the chief of state and head of government
head of government: President Bakili MULUZI (since 21 May 1994); note - the president is both the chief of state and head of government
cabinet: Cabinet named by the president
elections: president elected by popular vote for a five-year term; election last held 17 May 1994 (next to be held by May 1999)
election results: Bakili MULUZI elected president; percent of vote - NA
Legislative branch: unicameral National Assembly (177 seats; members are elected by popular vote to serve five-year terms)
elections: last held 17 May 1994 (next to be held by May 1999)
election results: percent of vote by party - NA; seats by party - UDF 84, AFORD 33, MCP 55, others 5; note - because of defections and byelections, the distribution of seats in the National Assembly had changed at the end of the 1996 as follows: UDF 84, MCP 47, AFORD 34, independents 8, and vacant 4
note: the constitution of 18 May 1995, in addition to reducing the age at which universal suffrage is conferred from 21 to 18 years, provided for a bicameral legislature; by 1999, in addition to the existing National Assembly, a Senate of 80 seats is to be elected
Judicial branch: Supreme Court of Appeal; High Court (chief justice appointed by the president, puisne judges appointed on the advice of the Judicial Service Commission); magistrate's courts
Political parties and leaders:
ruling party: United Democratic Front or UDF [Bakili MULUZI]
opposition groups: Alliance for Democracy or AFORD [Chakufwa CHIHANA]; Congress for the Second Republic or CSR [Kanyama CHIUME]; Malawi Congress Party or MCP [Gwanda CHAKUAMBA, president, John TEMBO, vice president]; Malawi Democratic Party or MDP [Kampelo KALUA, president]; People Democratic Party or PDP [Rolf PATEL]; Social Democratic Party or SDP [Eston KAKHOME, president]
International organization participation: ACP, AfDB, C, CCC, ECA, FAO, G-77, IBRD, ICAO, ICFTU, ICRM, IDA, IFAD, IFC, IFRCS, ILO, IMF, IMO, Intelsat, Interpol, IOC, ISO (correspondent), ITU, NAM, OAU, OPCW, SADC, UN, UNCTAD, UNESCO, UNIDO, UPU, WFTU, WHO, WIPO, WMO, WToO, WTrO
Diplomatic representation in the US:
chief of mission: Ambassador Willie CHOKANI
chancery: 2408 Massachusetts Avenue NW, Washington, DC 20008
telephone: [1] (202) 797-1007
Diplomatic representation from the US:
chief of mission: Ambassador Amelia Ellen SHIPPY
embassy: address NA, in new development area in Lilongwe
mailing address: P. O. Box 30016, Lilongwe 3, Malawi
telephone: [265] 783 166
FAX: [265] 780 471
Flag description: three equal horizontal bands of black (top), red, and green with a radiant, rising, red sun centered in the black band

Economy

Economy - overview: Landlocked Malawi ranks among the world's least developed countries. The economy is predominately agricultural, with about 90% of the population living in rural areas. Agriculture accounts for 45% of GDP and 90% of export revenues. The economy depends on substantial inflows of economic assistance from the IMF, the World Bank, and individual donor nations. The new government faces strong challenges, e.g., to spur exports, to improve educational and health facilities, and to deal with environmental problems of deforestation and erosion.
GDP: purchasing power parity - $8.9 billion (1998 est.)
GDP - real growth rate: 3.2% (1998 est.)
GDP - per capita: purchasing power parity - $940 (1998 est.)
GDP - composition by sector:
agriculture: 45%
industry: 30%
services: 25% (1995 est.)
Population below poverty line: 54% (1990-91 est.)
Household income or consumption by percentage share:
lowest 10%: NA%
highest 10%: NA%
Inflation rate (consumer prices): 83.4% (1995)
Labor force: 3.5 million
Labor force - by occupation: agriculture 86%, wage earners 14% (1990 est.)
Unemployment rate: NA%
Budget:
revenues: $530 million
expenditures: $674 million, including capital expenditures of $129 million (1993)
Industries: tea, tobacco, sugar, sawmill products, cement, consumer goods
Industrial production growth rate: 0.9% (1995)
Electricity - production: 800 million kWh (1996)
Electricity - production by source:
fossil fuel: 2.5%
hydro: 97.5%
nuclear: 0%
other: 0% (1996)
Electricity - consumption: 800 million kWh (1996)
Electricity - exports: 0 kWh (1996)
Electricity - imports: 0 kWh (1996)
Agriculture - products: tobacco, sugarcane, cotton, tea, corn, potatoes, cassava (tapioca), sorghum, pulses; cattle, goats
Exports: $405 million (f.o.b., 1995)
Exports - commodities: tobacco, tea, sugar, coffee, peanuts, wood products
Exports - partners: US, South Africa, Germany, Japan
Imports: $475 million (f.o.b., 1995)
Imports - commodities: food, petroleum products, semimanufactures, consumer goods, transportation equipment
Imports - partners: South Africa, Zimbabwe, Japan, US, UK, Germany
Debt - external: $2.3 billion (1996 est.)
Economic aid - recipient: $416.5 million (1995)
Currency: 1 Malawian kwacha (MK) = 100 tambala
Exchange rates: Malawian kwachas (MK) per US$1 - 43.5426 (January 1999), 31.0727 (1998), 16.4442 (1997), 15.3085 (1996), 15.2837 (1995), 8.7364 (1994)
Fiscal year: 1 April - 31 March

Communications

Telephones: 43,000 (1985 est.)
Telephone system:
domestic: fair system of open-wire lines, microwave radio relay links, and radiotelephone communications stations
international: satellite earth stations - 2 Intelsat (1 Indian Ocean and 1 Atlantic Ocean)
Radio broadcast stations: AM 10, FM 17, shortwave 0
Radios: 1.011 million (1995)
Television broadcast stations: 0 (1997 est.)
Televisions: NA

Malawi (continued)

Transportation

Railways:
total: 789 km
narrow gauge: 789 km 1.067-m gauge
Highways:
total: 28,400 km
paved: 5,254 km
unpaved: 23,146 km (1996 est.)
Waterways: Lake Nyasa (Lake Malawi); Shire River, 144 km
Ports and harbors: Chipoka, Monkey Bay, Nkhata Bay, Nkhotakota
Airports: 45 (1998 est.)
Airports - with paved runways:
total: 5
over 3,047 m: 1
1,524 to 2,437 m: 1
914 to 1,523 m: 3 (1998 est.)
Airports - with unpaved runways:
total: 40
1,524 to 2,437 m: 1
914 to 1,523 m: 16
under 914 m: 23 (1998 est.)

Military

Military branches: Army (includes Air Wing and Naval Detachment), Police (includes paramilitary Mobile Force Unit)
Military manpower - availability:
males age 15-49: 2,314,509 (1999 est.)
Military manpower - fit for military service:
males age 15-49: 1,186,341 (1999 est.)
Military expenditures - dollar figure: $17 million (FY96/97)
Military expenditures - percent of GDP: 0.8% (FY96/97)

Transnational Issues

Disputes - international: dispute with Tanzania over the boundary in Lake Nyasa (Lake Malawi)

Malaysia

Geography

Location: Southeastern Asia, peninsula and northern one-third of the island of Borneo, bordering Indonesia and the South China Sea, south of Vietnam
Geographic coordinates: 2 30 N, 112 30 E
Map references: Southeast Asia
Area:
total: 329,750 sq km
land: 328,550 sq km
water: 1,200 sq km
Area - comparative: slightly larger than New Mexico
Land boundaries:
total: 2,669 km
border countries: Brunei 381 km, Indonesia 1,782 km, Thailand 506 km
Coastline: 4,675 km (Peninsular Malaysia 2,068 km, East Malaysia 2,607 km)
Maritime claims:
continental shelf: 200-m depth or to the depth of exploitation; specified boundary in the South China Sea
exclusive economic zone: 200 nm
territorial sea: 12 nm
Climate: tropical; annual southwest (April to October) and northeast (October to February) monsoons
Terrain: coastal plains rising to hills and mountains
Elevation extremes:
lowest point: Indian Ocean 0 m
highest point: Gunung Kinabalu 4,100 m
Natural resources: tin, petroleum, timber, copper, iron ore, natural gas, bauxite
Land use:
arable land: 3%
permanent crops: 12%
permanent pastures: 0%
forests and woodland: 68%
other: 17% (1993 est.)
Irrigated land: 2,941 sq km (1998 est.)
Natural hazards: flooding, landslides
Environment - current issues: air pollution from industrial and vehicular emissions; water pollution from raw sewage; deforestation; smoke/haze from Indonesian forest fires
Environment - international agreements:
party to: Biodiversity, Climate Change, Desertification, Endangered Species, Hazardous Wastes, Law of the Sea, Marine Life Conservation, Nuclear Test Ban, Ozone Layer Protection, Ship Pollution, Tropical Timber 83, Tropical Timber 94
signed, but not ratified: none of the selected agreements
Geography - note: strategic location along Strait of Malacca and southern South China Sea

People

Population: 21,376,066 (July 1999 est.)
Age structure:
0-14 years: 35% (male 3,879,012; female 3,680,895)
15-64 years: 61% (male 6,478,910; female 6,482,909)
65 years and over: 4% (male 369,639; female 484,701) (1999 est.)
Population growth rate: 2.08% (1999 est.)
Birth rate: 26.05 births/1,000 population (1999 est.)
Death rate: 5.29 deaths/1,000 population (1999 est.)
Net migration rate: 0 migrant(s)/1,000 population (1999 est.)
note: does not include illegal immigrants - large numbers from Indonesia and smaller numbers from the Philippines, Bangladesh, Burma, China, and India
Sex ratio:
at birth: 1.06 male(s)/female
under 15 years: 1.05 male(s)/female
15-64 years: 1 male(s)/female
65 years and over: 0.76 male(s)/female
total population: 1.01 male(s)/female (1999 est.)
Infant mortality rate: 21.68 deaths/1,000 live births (1999 est.)
Life expectancy at birth:
total population: 70.67 years
male: 67.62 years

Malaysia (continued)

female: 73.9 years (1999 est.)
Total fertility rate: 3.35 children born/woman (1999 est.)
Nationality:
noun: Malaysian(s)
adjective: Malaysian
Ethnic groups: Malay and other indigenous 58%, Chinese 26%, Indian 7%, others 9%
Religions: Islam, Buddhism, Daoism, Hinduism, Christianity, Sikhism; note - in addition, Shamanism is practiced on East Malaysia
Languages: Bahasa Melayu (official), English, Chinese dialects (Cantonese, Mandarin, Hokkien, Hakka, Hainan, Foochow), Tamil, Telugu, Malalalam, Panjabi, Thai; note - in addition, in East Malaysia several indigenous languages are spoken, the largest of which are Iban and Kadazan
Literacy:
definition: age 15 and over can read and write
total population: 83.5%
male: 89.1%
female: 78.1% (1995 est.)

Government

Country name:
conventional long form: none
conventional short form: Malaysia
former: Malayan Union
Data code: MY
Government type: constitutional monarchy
note: Malaya (what is now Peninsular Malaysia) formed 31 August 1957; Federation of Malaysia (Malaya, Sabah, Sarawak, and Singapore) formed 9 July 1963 (Singapore left the federation on 9 August 1965); nominally headed by the paramount ruler (king) and a bicameral Parliament consisting of a nonelected upper house and an elected lower house; Peninsular Malaysian states - hereditary rulers in all but Melaka, Penang, Sabah, and Sarawak, where governors are appointed by the Malaysian Government; powers of state governments are limited by the federal constitution; under terms of the federation, Sabah and Sarawak retain certain constitutional prerogatives (e.g., the right to maintain their own immigration controls); Sabah - holds 20 seats in House of Representatives, with foreign affairs, defense, internal security, and other powers delegated to federal government; Sarawak - holds 27 seats in House of Representatives, with foreign affairs, defense, internal security, and other powers delegated to federal government
Capital: Kuala Lumpur
Administrative divisions: 13 states (negeri-negeri, singular - negeri) and 2 federal territories* (wilayah-wilayah persekutuan, singular - wilayah persekutuan); Johor, Kedah, Kelantan, Labuan*, Melaka, Negeri Sembilan, Pahang, Perak, Perlis, Pulau Pinang, Sabah, Sarawak, Selangor, Terengganu, Wilayah Persekutuan*
note: the city of Kuala Lumpur is located within the federal territory of Wilayah Persekutuan; the terms therefore are not interchangeable

Independence: 31 August 1957 (from UK)
National holiday: National Day, 31 August (1957)
Constitution: 31 August 1957, amended 16 September 1963
Legal system: based on English common law; judicial review of legislative acts in the Supreme Court at request of supreme head of the federation; has not accepted compulsory ICJ jurisdiction
Suffrage: 21 years of age; universal
Executive branch:
chief of state: Paramount Ruler TUANKU JA'AFAR ibni Al-Marhum Tuanku Abdul Rahman (since 26 April 1994) and Deputy Paramount Ruler Sultan TUNKU SALAHUDDIN Abdul Aziz Shah ibni Al-Marhum Sultan Hisammuddin Alam Shah (since 26 April 1994)
head of government: Prime Minister Dr. MAHATHIR bin Mohamad (since 16 July 1981); Deputy Prime Minister ABDULLAH bin Ahmad Badawi (since 8 January 1999)
cabinet: Cabinet appointed by the prime minister from among the members of Parliament with consent of the paramount ruler
elections: paramount ruler and deputy paramount ruler elected by and from the hereditary rulers of nine of the states for five-year terms; election last held 4 February 1994 (next to be held NA 1999); prime minister designated from among the members of the House of Representatives; following legislative elections, the leader of the party that wins a plurality of seats in the House of Representatives becomes prime minister
election results: TUANKU JA'AFAR ibni Al-Marhum Tuanku Abdul Rahman elected paramount ruler; Sultan TUNKU SALAHUDDIN Abdul Aziz Shah ibni Al-Marhum Sultan Hisammuddin Alam Shah elected deputy paramount ruler
Legislative branch: bicameral Parliament or Parlimen consists of nonelected Senate or Dewan Negara (69 seats; 43 appointed by the paramount ruler, 26 appointed by the state legislatures) and the House of Representatives or Dewan Rakyat (192 seats; members elected by popular vote directly weighted toward the rural Malay population to serve five-year terms)
elections: House of Representatives - last held 24-25 April 1995 (next to be held by April 2000)
election results: House of Representatives - percent of vote by party - National Front 63%, other 37%; seats by party - National Front 162, DAP 9, PBS 8, PAS 7, Spirit of '46 6; note - subsequent to the election there was a change in the distribution of seats, the current distribution is - National Front 168, DAP 8, PAS 8, PBS 5, independents 3
Judicial branch: Supreme Court, judges appointed by the paramount ruler on the advice of the prime minister
Political parties and leaders:
Peninsular Malaysia: National Front (a confederation of 13 political parties dominated by United Malays National Organization or UMNO [MAHATHIR bin Mohamad]); Malaysian Chinese Association or MCA [LING Liong Sik]; Gerakan Rakyat Malaysia [LIM

Keng Yaik]; Malaysian Indian Congress or MIC [S. Samy VELLU]; major opposition parties are Parti Islam SeMalaysia or PAS [Ustaz Fadzil Mohamed NOOR] and the Democratic Action Party or DAP [LIM Kit Siang]
Sabah: National Front, dominated by the UMNO [leader NA]; Sabah Progressive Party or SAPP [Datuk YONG Teck Lee]; Parti Democratic Sabah or PDS [Bernard DOMPOK]; Parti Bersatu Rakyat Sabah or PBRS [Datuk Joseph KURUP]; Parti Akar [Datuk PANDIKAR Amin Mulia]
Sarawak: National Front, composed of the Party Pesaka Bumiputra Bersatu or PBB [Datuk Patinggi Haji Abdul TAIB Mahmud]; Sarawak United People's Party or SUPP [Datuk Dr. George CHAN Hong Nam]; Sarawak National Party or SNAP [Datuk Amar James WONG]; Parti Bansa Dayak Sarawak or PBDS [Datuk Leo MOGGIE]; major opposition party is Democratic Action Party or DAP [LIM Kit Siang]
note: subsequent to the election, the following parties were dissolved - Spirit of '46 or Semangat '46 [Tengku Tan Sri RAZALEIGH, president] and Sabah United Party (Parti Bersatu Sabah) or PBS [Datuk Seri Joseph PAIRIN Kitingan]
International organization participation: APEC, AsDB, ASEAN, C, CCC, CP, ESCAP, FAO, G-15, G-77, IAEA, IBRD, ICAO, ICFTU, ICRM, IDA, IDB, IFAD, IFC, IFRCS, IHO, ILO, IMF, IMO, Inmarsat, Intelsat, Interpol, IOC, ISO, ITU, MINURSO, MONUA, NAM, OIC, OPCW, UN, UNCTAD, UNESCO, UNIDO, UNIKOM, UNMIBH, UNOMIL, UPU, WCL, WFTU, WHO, WIPO, WMO, WToO, WTrO
Diplomatic representation in the US:
chief of mission: Ambassador Dato' GHAZZALI Sheikh Abdul Khalid
chancery: 2401 Massachusetts Avenue NW, Washington, DC 20008
telephone: [1] (202) 328-2700
FAX: [1] (202) 483-7661
consulate(s) general: Los Angeles and New York
Diplomatic representation from the US:
chief of mission: Ambassador B. Lynn PASCOE
embassy: 376 Jalan Tun Razak, 50400 Kuala Lumpur
mailing address: P. O. Box No. 10035, 50700 Kuala Lumpur; American Embassy Kuala Lumpur, APO AP 96535-8152
telephone: [60] (3) 248-9011
FAX: [60] (3) 242-2207
Flag description: 14 equal horizontal stripes of red (top) alternating with white (bottom); there is a blue rectangle in the upper hoist-side corner bearing a yellow crescent and a yellow fourteen-pointed star; the crescent and the star are traditional symbols of Islam; the design was based on the flag of the US

Economy

Economy - overview: After a decade of 8% average GDP growth, the Malaysian economy - severely hit by the regional financial crisis - declined 7% in 1998. Malaysia will likely remain in recession for the first half of 1999; official statistics continue to show anemic exports, and some private financial analysts forecast

Malaysia *(continued)*

a further drop in GDP of 1% in 1999. Prime Minister MAHATHIR has imposed capital controls to protect the local currency while cutting interest rates to stimulate the economy. Kuala Lumpur also announced an expansionary budget for 1999 to combat rising unemployment. Malaysia continues to seek funding from domestic and international sources to help finance its budget deficit and recapitalize its weakened banking sector.

GDP: purchasing power parity - $215.4 billion (1998 est.)

GDP - real growth rate: -7% (1998 est.)

GDP - per capita: purchasing power parity - $10,300 (1998 est.)

GDP - composition by sector:
agriculture: 13%
industry: 46%
services: 41% (1997 est.)

Population below poverty line: 15.5% (1989 est.)

Household income or consumption by percentage share:
lowest 10%: 1.9%
highest 10%: 37.9% (1989)

Inflation rate (consumer prices): 5.3% (1998)

Labor force: 8.398 million (1996 est.)

Labor force - by occupation: manufacturing 25%, agriculture, forestry, and fisheries 21%, local trade and tourism 17%, services 12%, government 11%, construction 8% (1996)

Unemployment rate: 2.6% (1996 est.)

Budget:
revenues: $22.6 billion
expenditures: $22 billion, including capital expenditures of $5.3 billion (1996 est.)

Industries: Peninsular Malaysia - rubber and oil palm processing and manufacturing, light manufacturing industry, electronics, tin mining and smelting, logging and processing timber; Sabah - logging, petroleum production; Sarawak - agriculture processing, petroleum production and refining, logging

Industrial production growth rate: 14.4% (1995)

Electricity - production: 48 billion kWh (1996)

Electricity - production by source:
fossil fuel: 83.33%
hydro: 16.67%
nuclear: 0%
other: 0% (1996)

Electricity - consumption: 47.977 billion kWh (1996)

Electricity - exports: 174 million kWh (1996)

Electricity - imports: 151 million kWh (1996)

Agriculture - products: Peninsular Malaysia - rubber, palm oil, rice; Sabah - subsistence crops, rubber, timber, coconuts, rice; Sarawak - rubber, pepper; timber

Exports: $74.3 billion (f.o.b., 1998)

Exports - commodities: electronic equipment, petroleum and petroleum products, palm oil, wood and wood products, rubber, textiles

Exports - partners: US 21%, Singapore 20%, Japan 12%, Hong Kong 5%, UK 4%, Thailand 4%,
Germany 3% (1995)

Imports: $59.3 billion (f.o.b., 1998)

Imports - commodities: machinery and equipment, chemicals, food

Imports - partners: Japan 27%, US 16%, Singapore 12%, Taiwan 5%, Germany 4%, South Korea 4% (1995)

Debt - external: $39.8 billion (1998)

Economic aid - recipient: $125 million (1995)

Currency: 1 ringgit (M$) = 100 sen

Exchange rates: ringgits (M$) per US$1 - 3.8000 (January 1999), 3.9244 (1998), 2.8133 (1997), 2.5159 (1996), 2.5044 (1995), 2.6243 (1994)

Fiscal year: calendar year

Communications

Telephones: 2,550,957 (1992 est.)

Telephone system: international service good
domestic: good intercity service provided on Peninsular Malaysia mainly by microwave radio relay; adequate intercity microwave radio relay network between Sabah and Sarawak via Brunei; domestic satellite system with 2 earth stations
international: submarine cables to India, Hong Kong and Singapore; satellite earth stations - 2 Intelsat (1 Indian Ocean and 1 Pacific Ocean)

Radio broadcast stations: AM 28, FM 3, shortwave 0

Radios: 8.08 million (1992 est.)

Television broadcast stations: 27 (of which 26 are government-owned and one is independent and has 15 high-power repeater stations to relay its programs) (1997)

Televisions: 2 million (1993 est.)

Transportation

Railways:
total: 1,798 km
narrow gauge: 1,798 km 1.000-m gauge (148 km electrified) (1998 est.)

Highways:
total: 94,500 km
paved: 70,970 km (including 580 km of expressways)
unpaved: 23,530 km (1996 est.)

Waterways: 7,296 km (Peninsular Malaysia 3,209 km, Sabah 1,569 km, Sarawak 2,518 km)

Pipelines: crude oil 1,307 km; natural gas 379 km

Ports and harbors: Bintulu, Kota Kinabalu, Kuantan, Kuching, Kudat, Labuan, Lahad Datu, Lumut, Miri, Pasir Gudang, Penang, Port Dickson, Port Kelang, Sandakan, Sibu, Tanjung Berhala, Tanjung Kidurong, Tawau

Merchant marine:
total: 378 ships (1,000 GRT or over) totaling 5,059,272 GRT/7,428,623 DWT
ships by type: bulk 62, cargo 128, chemical tanker 30, container 58, liquefied gas tanker 19, livestock carrier 1, oil tanker 61, passenger 2, refrigerated cargo 2, roll-on/roll-off cargo 6, specialized tanker 2, vehicle carrier 7 (1998 est.)

Airports: 115 (1998 est.)

Airports - with paved runways:
total: 32
over 3,047 m: 5
2,438 to 3,047 m: 4
1,524 to 2,437 m: 11
914 to 1,523 m: 6
under 914 m: 6 (1998 est.)

Airports - with unpaved runways:
total: 83
1,524 to 2,437 m: 1
914 to 1,523 m: 8
under 914 m: 74 (1998 est.)

Heliports: 1 (1998 est.)

Military

Military branches: Malaysian Army, Royal Malaysian Navy, Royal Malaysian Air Force, Royal Malaysian Police Force, Marine Police, Sarawak Border Scouts

Military manpower - military age: 21 years of age

Military manpower - availability:
males age 15-49: 5,526,555 (1999 est.)

Military manpower - fit for military service:
males age 15-49: 3,349,066 (1999 est.)

Military manpower - reaching military age annually:
males: 183,928 (1999 est.)

Military expenditures - dollar figure: $2.1 billion (1998)

Military expenditures - percent of GDP: 2.1% (1998)

Transnational Issues

Disputes - international: involved in a complex dispute over the Spratly Islands with China, Philippines, Taiwan, Vietnam, and possibly Brunei; Philippines have not fully revoked claim to Sabah State; two islands in dispute with Singapore; two islands in dispute with Indonesia

Illicit drugs: transit point for some illicit drugs going to Western markets; drug trafficking prosecuted vigorously and carries severe penalties

Maldives

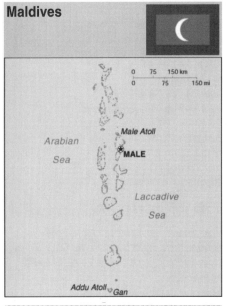

Geography

Location: Southern Asia, group of atolls in the Indian Ocean, south-southwest of India

Geographic coordinates: 3 15 N, 73 00 E

Map references: Asia

Area:
total: 300 sq km
land: 300 sq km
water: 0 sq km

Area - comparative: about 1.7 times the size of Washington, DC

Land boundaries: 0 km

Coastline: 644 km

Maritime claims: measured from claimed archipelagic baselines
contiguous zone: 24 nm
exclusive economic zone: 200 nm
territorial sea: 12 nm

Climate: tropical; hot, humid; dry, northeast monsoon (November to March); rainy, southwest monsoon (June to August)

Terrain: flat, with white sandy beaches

Elevation extremes:
lowest point: Indian Ocean 0 m
highest point: unnamed location on Wilingili island in the Addu Atoll 2.4 m

Natural resources: fish

Land use:
arable land: 10%
permanent crops: 0%
permanent pastures: 3%
forests and woodland: 3%
other: 84% (1993 est.)

Irrigated land: NA sq km

Natural hazards: low level of islands makes them very sensitive to sea level rise

Environment - current issues: depletion of freshwater aquifers threatens water supplies

Environment - international agreements:
party to: Biodiversity, Climate Change, Climate

Change-Kyoto Protocol, Hazardous Wastes, Ozone Layer Protection
signed, but not ratified: Law of the Sea

Geography - note: 1,190 coral islands grouped into 26 atolls; archipelago of strategic location astride and along major sea lanes in Indian Ocean

People

Population: 300,220 (July 1999 est.)

Age structure:
0-14 years: 47% (male 72,414; female 68,764)
15-64 years: 50% (male 76,446; female 73,275)
65 years and over: 3% (male 4,944; female 4,377) (1999 est.)

Population growth rate: 3.37% (1999 est.)

Birth rate: 39.3 births/1,000 population (1999 est.)

Death rate: 5.63 deaths/1,000 population (1999 est.)

Net migration rate: 0 migrant(s)/1,000 population (1999 est.)

Sex ratio:
at birth: 1.05 male(s)/female
under 15 years: 1.05 male(s)/female
15-64 years: 1.04 male(s)/female
65 years and over: 1.13 male(s)/female
total population: 1.05 male(s)/female (1999 est.)

Infant mortality rate: 38.14 deaths/1,000 live births (1999 est.)

Life expectancy at birth:
total population: 68.29 years
male: 66.53 years
female: 70.15 years (1999 est.)

Total fertility rate: 5.73 children born/woman (1999 est.)

Nationality:
noun: Maldivian(s)
adjective: Maldivian

Ethnic groups: Sinhalese, Dravidian, Arab, African

Religions: Sunni Muslim

Languages: Maldivian Divehi (dialect of Sinhala, script derived from Arabic), English spoken by most government officials

Literacy:
definition: age 15 and over can read and write
total population: 93.2%
male: 93.3%
female: 93% (1995 est.)

Government

Country name:
conventional long form: Republic of Maldives
conventional short form: Maldives
local long form: Dhivehi Raajjeyge Jumhooriyyaa
local short form: Dhivehi Raajje

Data code: MV

Government type: republic

Capital: Male

Administrative divisions: 19 atolls (atholhu, singular and plural) and 1 other first-order administrative division*; Alifu, Baa, Dhaalu, Faafu, Gaafu Alifu, Gaafu Dhaalu, Gnaviyani, Haa Alifu, Haa Dhaalu, Kaafu, Laamu, Lhaviyani, Maale*, Meemu,

Noonu, Raa, Seenu, Shaviyani, Thaa, Vaavu

Independence: 26 July 1965 (from UK)

National holiday: Independence Day, 26 July (1965)

Constitution: 4 June 1968

Legal system: based on Islamic law with admixtures of English common law primarily in commercial matters; has not accepted compulsory ICJ jurisdiction

Suffrage: 21 years of age; universal

Executive branch:
chief of state: President Maumoon Abdul GAYOOM (since 11 November 1978); note - the president is both the chief of state and head of government
head of government: President Maumoon Abdul GAYOOM (since 11 November 1978); note - the president is both the chief of state and head of government
cabinet: Ministry of Atolls appointed by the president; note - need not be members of Majlis
elections: president elected by secret ballot of the Majlis for a five-year term; election last held 1 October 1993 (next to be held NA October 1998)
election results: President Maumoon Abdul GAYOOM reelected; percent of Majlis vote - Maumoon Abdul GAYOOM 92.76%

Legislative branch: unicameral Citizens' Council or Majlis (48 seats; 40 elected by popular vote, 8 appointed by the president; members serve five-year terms)
elections: last held 2 December 1994 (next to be held NA December 1999)
election results: percent of vote - NA; seats - independents 40

Judicial branch: High Court

Political parties and leaders: although political parties are not banned, none exist

International organization participation: AsDB, C, CCC, CP, ESCAP, FAO, G-77, IBRD, ICAO, IDA, IDB, IFAD, IFC, IMF, IMO, Intelsat (nonsignatory user), Interpol, IOC, ITU, NAM, OIC, OPCW, SAARC, UN, UNCTAD, UNESCO, UNIDO, UPU, WHO, WMO, WToO, WTrO

Diplomatic representation in the US: Maldives does not have an embassy in the US, but does have a Permanent Mission to the UN in New York

Diplomatic representation from the US: the US does not have an embassy in Maldives; the US Ambassador to Sri Lanka is accredited to Maldives and makes periodic visits there

Flag description: red with a large green rectangle in the center bearing a vertical white crescent; the closed side of the crescent is on the hoist side of the flag

Economy

Economy - overview: Tourism, Maldives largest industry, accounts for about 18% of GDP and more than 60% of the Maldives' foreign exchange receipts. Over 90% of government tax revenue comes from import duties and tourism-related taxes. About 350,000 tourists visited the islands in 1997. Fishing is a second leading growth sector. The Maldivian Government began an economic reform program in

1989 initially by lifting import quotas and opening some exports to the private sector. Subsequently, it has liberalized regulations to allow more foreign investment. Agriculture and manufacturing continue to play a minor role in the economy, constrained by the limited availability of cultivable land and the shortage of domestic labor. Most staple foods must be imported. Industry, which consists mainly of garment production, boat building, and handicrafts, accounts for about 15% of GDP. Maldivian authorities worry about the impact of erosion and possible global warming on their low-lying country; 80% of the area is one meter or less above sea level.

GDP: purchasing power parity - $500 million (1998 est.)

GDP - real growth rate: 5.8% (1998 est.)

GDP - per capita: purchasing power parity - $1,840 (1998 est.)

GDP - composition by sector:
agriculture: 22%
industry: 15%
services: 63% (1994 est.)

Population below poverty line: NA%

Household income or consumption by percentage share:
lowest 10%: NA%
highest 10%: NA%

Inflation rate (consumer prices): 6.3% (1996)

Labor force: 56,435 (1990 est.)

Labor force - by occupation: fishing industry and agriculture 25%, services 21%, manufacturing and construction 21%, trade, restaurants, and hotels 16%, transportation and communication 10%, other 7%

Unemployment rate: NEGL%

Budget:
revenues: $88 million (excluding foreign grants)
expenditures: $141 million, including capital expenditures of $NA (1995 est.)

Industries: fish processing, tourism, shipping, boat building, coconut processing, garments, woven mats, rope, handicrafts, coral and sand mining

Industrial production growth rate: 6.3% (1994 est.)

Electricity - production: 60 million kWh (1996)

Electricity - production by source:
fossil fuel: 100%
hydro: 0%
nuclear: 0%
other: 0% (1996)

Electricity - consumption: 60 million kWh (1996)

Electricity - exports: 0 kWh (1996)

Electricity - imports: 0 kWh (1996)

Agriculture - products: coconuts, corn, sweet potatoes; fish

Exports: $59 million (f.o.b., 1996)

Exports - commodities: fish, clothing

Exports - partners: Sri Lanka, US, Germany, Singapore, UK

Imports: $302 million (f.o.b., 1996)

Imports - commodities: consumer goods, intermediate and capital goods, petroleum products

Imports - partners: Singapore, India, Sri Lanka, Hong Kong, Japan, Thailand

Debt - external: $179 million (1996 est.)

Economic aid - recipient: $NA

Currency: 1 rufiyaa (Rf) = 100 laari

Exchange rates: rufiyaa (Rf) per US$1 - 11.770 (1995-January 1999), 11.586 (1994), 10.957 (1993)

Fiscal year: calendar year

Communications

Telephones: 8,523 (1992 est.)

Telephone system: minimal domestic and international facilities
domestic: inter-atoll communication primarily through HF transceivers and VHF/UHF telephones
international: satellite earth station - 1 Intelsat (Indian Ocean)

Radio broadcast stations: AM 2, FM 1, shortwave 0

Radios: 28,284 (1992 est.)

Television broadcast stations: 1 (1997)

Televisions: 7,309 (1992 est.)

Transportation

Railways: 0 km

Highways:
total: NA km
paved: NA km
unpaved: NA km; note - Male has 9.6 km of coral highways within the city (1988 est.)

Ports and harbors: Gan, Male

Merchant marine:
total: 21 ships (1,000 GRT or over) totaling 75,585 GRT/115,590 DWT
ships by type: cargo 18, container 1, oil tanker 1, short-sea passenger 1 (1998 est.)

Airports: 5 (1998 est.)

Airports - with paved runways:
total: 2
over 3,047 m: 1
2,438 to 3,047 m: 1 (1998 est.)

Airports - with unpaved runways:
total: 3
914 to 1,523 m: 3 (1998 est.)

Military

Military branches: National Security Service (paramilitary police force)

Military manpower - availability:
males age 15-49: 66,554 (1999 est.)

Military manpower - fit for military service:
males age 15-49: 37,086 (1999 est.)

Military expenditures - dollar figure: $NA

Military expenditures - percent of GDP: NA%

Transnational Issues

Disputes - international: none

Mali

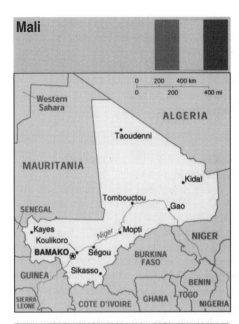

Geography

Location: Western Africa, southwest of Algeria

Geographic coordinates: 17 00 N, 4 00 W

Map references: Africa

Area:
total: 1.24 million sq km
land: 1.22 million sq km
water: 20,000 sq km

Area - comparative: slightly less than twice the size of Texas

Land boundaries:
total: 7,243 km
border countries: Algeria 1,376 km, Burkina Faso 1,000 km, Guinea 858 km, Cote d'Ivoire 532 km, Mauritania 2,237 km, Niger 821 km, Senegal 419 km

Coastline: 0 km (landlocked)

Maritime claims: none (landlocked)

Climate: subtropical to arid; hot and dry February to June; rainy, humid, and mild June to November; cool and dry November to February

Terrain: mostly flat to rolling northern plains covered by sand; savanna in south, rugged hills in northeast

Elevation extremes:
lowest point: Senegal River 23 m
highest point: Hombori Tondo 1,155 m

Natural resources: gold, phosphates, kaolin, salt, limestone, uranium, bauxite, iron ore, manganese, tin, and copper deposits are known but not exploited

Land use:
arable land: 2%
permanent crops: 0%
permanent pastures: 25%
forests and woodland: 6%
other: 67% (1993 est.)

Irrigated land: 780 sq km (1993 est.)

Natural hazards: hot, dust-laden harmattan haze common during dry seasons; recurring droughts

Environment - current issues: deforestation; soil erosion; desertification; inadequate supplies of potable water; poaching

Mali (continued)

Environment - international agreements:
party to: Biodiversity, Climate Change, Desertification, Endangered Species, Law of the Sea, Ozone Layer Protection, Wetlands
signed, but not ratified: Climate Change-Kyoto Protocol, Nuclear Test Ban
Geography - note: landlocked

People

Population: 10,429,124 (July 1999 est.)
Age structure:
0-14 years: 47% (male 2,482,301; female 2,460,894)
15-64 years: 49% (male 2,447,712; female 2,708,978)
65 years and over: 4% (male 155,178; female 174,061) (1999 est.)
Population growth rate: 3.01% (1999 est.)
Birth rate: 49.5 births/1,000 population (1999 est.)
Death rate: 18.56 deaths/1,000 population (1999 est.)
Net migration rate: -0.87 migrant(s)/1,000 population (1999 est.)
Sex ratio:
at birth: 1.03 male(s)/female
under 15 years: 1.01 male(s)/female
15-64 years: 0.9 male(s)/female
65 years and over: 0.89 male(s)/female
total population: 0.95 male(s)/female (1999 est.)
Infant mortality rate: 119.44 deaths/1,000 live births (1999 est.)
Life expectancy at birth:
total population: 47.5 years
male: 46.09 years
female: 48.96 years (1999 est.)
Total fertility rate: 6.96 children born/woman (1999 est.)
Nationality:
noun: Malian(s)
adjective: Malian
Ethnic groups: Mande 50% (Bambara, Malinke, Sarakole), Peul 17%, Voltaic 12%, Songhai 6%, Tuareg and Moor 10%, other 5%
Religions: Muslim 90%, indigenous beliefs 9%, Christian 1%
Languages: French (official), Bambara 80%, numerous African languages
Literacy:
definition: age 15 and over can read and write
total population: 31%
male: 39.4%
female: 23.1% (1995 est.)

Government

Country name:
conventional long form: Republic of Mali
conventional short form: Mali
local long form: Republique de Mali
local short form: Mali
former: French Sudan
Data code: ML
Government type: republic

Capital: Bamako
Administrative divisions: 8 regions (regions, singular - region); Gao, Kayes, Kidal, Koulikoro, Mopti, Segou, Sikasso, Tombouctou
Independence: 22 September 1960 (from France)
National holiday: Anniversary of the Proclamation of the Republic, 22 September (1960)
Constitution: adopted 12 January 1992
Legal system: based on French civil law system and customary law; judicial review of legislative acts in Constitutional Court (which was formally established on 9 March 1994); has not accepted compulsory ICJ jurisdiction
Suffrage: 21 years of age; universal
Executive branch:
chief of state: President Alpha Oumar KONARE (since 8 June 1992)
head of government: Prime Minister Ibrahim Boubacar KEITA (since March 1994)
cabinet: Council of Ministers appointed by the prime minister
elections: president elected by popular vote for a five-year term; election last held 11 May 1997 (next to be held May 2002); prime minister appointed by the president
election results: Alpha Oumar KONARE reelected president; percent of vote - Alpha Oumar KONARE 85.15%, Mamadou DIABY 4.09%, other 10.76%
Legislative branch: unicameral National Assembly or Assemblee Nationale (147 seats; members are elected by popular vote to serve five-year terms)
elections: last held 20 July and 3 August 1997 (next to be held in two rounds in 2002); note - much of the opposition boycotted the election
election results: percent of vote by party - NA; seats by party - ADEMA 130, PARENA 8, CDS 4, UDD 3, PDP 2
Judicial branch: Supreme Court (Cour Supreme)
Political parties and leaders: Alliance for Democracy or ADEMA [Ibrahim N'DIAYE, secretary general]; Party for National Renewal or PARENA [Yoro DIAKITE, chairman; Tiebile DRAME, secretary general]; Democratic and Social Convention or CDS [Mamadou Bakary SANGARE, chairman]; Union for Democracy and Development or UDD [Moussa Balla COULIBALY]; Party for Democracy and Progress or PDP [Me Idrissa TRAORE]; National Congress for Democratic Initiative or CNID [Mountaga TALL, chairman]; Sudanese Union/African Democratic Rally or US/RDA [Mamadou Bamou TOURE, secretary general]; Rally for Democracy and Progress or RDP [Almamy SYLLA, chairman]; Rally for Democracy and Labor or RDT [Ali GNANGADO]; Union of Democratic Forces for Progress or UFDP [Youssouf TOURE, secretary general]; Movement for the Independence, Renaissance and Integration of Africa or MIRIA [Mohamed Lamine TRAORE, Mouhamedou DICKO]
Political pressure groups and leaders: United Movement and Fronts of Azawad or MFUA; Patriotic Movement of the Ghanda Koye or MPGK
International organization participation: ACCT, ACP, AfDB, CCC, ECA, ECOWAS, FAO, FZ, G-77,

IAEA, IBRD, ICAO, ICFTU, ICRM, IDA, IDB, IFAD, IFC, IFRCS, ILO, IMF, Intelsat, Interpol, IOC, ITU, MINURCA, MIPONUH, MONUA, NAM, OAU, OIC, OPCW, UN, UNCTAD, UNESCO, UNIDO, UNOMSIL, UPU, WADB, WAEMU, WCL, WFTU, WHO, WIPO, WMO, WToO, WTrO
Diplomatic representation in the US:
chief of mission: Ambassador Cheick Oumar DIARRAH
chancery: 2130 R Street NW, Washington, DC 20008
telephone: [1] (202) 332-2249, 939-8950
FAX: [1] (202) 332-6603
Diplomatic representation from the US:
chief of mission: Ambassador David P. RAWSON
embassy: Rue Rochester NY and Rue Mohamed V, Bamako
mailing address: B. P. 34, Bamako
telephone: [223] 22 54 70
FAX: [223] 22 37 12
Flag description: three equal vertical bands of green (hoist side), yellow, and red; uses the popular pan-African colors of Ethiopia

Economy

Economy - overview: Mali is among the poorest countries in the world, with 65% of its land area desert or semidesert. Economic activity is largely confined to the riverine area irrigated by the Niger. About 10% of the population is nomadic and some 80% of the labor force is engaged in farming and fishing. Industrial activity is concentrated on processing farm commodities. Mali is heavily dependent on foreign aid and vulnerable to fluctuations in world prices for cotton, its main export. In 1997, the government continued its successful implementation of an IMF-recommended structural adjustment program that is helping the economy grow, diversify, and attract foreign investment. Mali's adherence to economic reform, and the 50% devaluation of the African franc in January 1994, has pushed up economic growth. Several multinational corporations increased gold mining operations in 1996-98, and the government anticipates that Mali will become a major Sub-Saharan gold exporter in the next few years. Annual growth thus may fall in the 5% range in 1999-2000, and inflation held to 5% or less.
GDP: purchasing power parity - $8 billion (1998 est.)
GDP - real growth rate: 4.6% (1998 est.)
GDP - per capita: purchasing power parity - $790 (1998 est.)
GDP - composition by sector:
agriculture: 49%
industry: 17%
services: 34% (1995)
Population below poverty line: NA%
Household income or consumption by percentage share:
lowest 10%: NA%
highest 10%: NA%
Inflation rate (consumer prices): 5% (1998 est.)
Labor force: NA

Labor force - by occupation: agriculture and fishing 80% (1998 est.)

Unemployment rate: NA%

Budget:

revenues: $730 million

expenditures: $770 million, including capital expenditures of $320 million (1997 est.)

Industries: minor local consumer goods production and food processing; construction; phosphate and gold mining

Industrial production growth rate: 0.6% (1995 est.)

Electricity - production: 288 million kWh (1996)

Electricity - production by source:

fossil fuel: 21.88%

hydro: 78.12%

nuclear: 0%

other: 0% (1996)

Electricity - consumption: 288 million kWh (1996)

Electricity - exports: 0 kWh (1996)

Electricity - imports: 0 kWh (1996)

Agriculture - products: cotton, millet, rice, corn, vegetables, peanuts; cattle, sheep, goats

Exports: $590 million (f.o.b., 1998 est.)

Exports - commodities: cotton 50%, gold, livestock (1998 est.)

Exports - partners: Thailand 20%, Italy 20%, China 9%, Brazil, franc zone (1997)

Imports: $600 million (f.o.b., 1998 est.)

Imports - commodities: machinery and equipment, construction materials, petroleum, foodstuffs, textiles

Imports - partners: Cote d'Ivoire 19%, France 17%, other franc zone and EU countries (1997)

Debt - external: $3.1 billion (1998)

Economic aid - recipient: $596.4 million (1995)

Currency: 1 Communaute Financiere Africaine franc (CFAF) = 100 centimes

Exchange rates: Communaute Financiere Africaine francs (CFAF) per US$1 - 567.81 (January 1999), 589.95 (1998), 583.67 (1997), 511.55 (1996), 499.15 (1995), 555.20 (1994)

Fiscal year: calendar year

Communications

Telephones: 11,000 (1982 est.)

Telephone system: domestic system poor but improving; provides only minimal service

domestic: network consists of microwave radio relay, open wire, and radiotelephone communications stations; expansion of microwave radio relay in progress

international: satellite earth stations - 2 Intelsat (1 Atlantic Ocean and 1 Indian Ocean)

Radio broadcast stations: AM 2, FM 2, shortwave 1

Radios: 430,000 (1992 est.)

Television broadcast stations: 1 (in addition, there are two repeaters) (1997)

Televisions: 11,000 (1992 est.)

Transportation

Railways:

total: 641 km; (linked to Senegal's rail system through Kayes)

narrow gauge: 641 km 1.000-m gauge (1995)

Highways:

total: 15,100 km

paved: 1,827 km

unpaved: 13,273 km (1996 est.)

Waterways: 1,815 km navigable

Ports and harbors: Koulikoro

Airports: 28 (1998 est.)

Airports - with paved runways:

total: 6

2,438 to 3,047 m: 4

914 to 1,523 m: 2 (1998 est.)

Airports - with unpaved runways:

total: 22

2,438 to 3,047 m: 1

1,524 to 2,437 m: 3

914 to 1,523 m: 8

under 914 m: 10 (1998 est.)

Military

Military branches: Army, Air Force, Gendarmerie, Republican Guard, National Guard, National Police (Surete Nationale)

Military manpower - availability:

males age 15-49: 2,128,375 (1999 est.)

Military manpower - fit for military service:

males age 15-49: 1,218,732 (1999 est.)

Military expenditures - dollar figure: $49 million (1996)

Military expenditures - percent of GDP: 2% (1996)

Transnational Issues

Disputes - international: none

Malta

Geography

Location: Southern Europe, islands in the Mediterranean Sea, south of Sicily (Italy)

Geographic coordinates: 35 50 N, 14 35 E

Map references: Europe

Area:

total: 320 sq km

land: 320 sq km

water: 0 sq km

Area - comparative: slightly less than twice the size of Washington, DC

Land boundaries: 0 km

Coastline: 140 km

Maritime claims:

contiguous zone: 24 nm

continental shelf: 200-m depth or to the depth of exploitation

exclusive fishing zone: 25 nm

territorial sea: 12 nm

Climate: Mediterranean with mild, rainy winters and hot, dry summers

Terrain: mostly low, rocky, flat to dissected plains; many coastal cliffs

Elevation extremes:

lowest point: Mediterranean Sea 0 m

highest point: Ta'Dmejrek 253 m (near Dingli)

Natural resources: limestone, salt

Land use:

arable land: 38%

permanent crops: 3%

permanent pastures: NA%

forests and woodland: NA%

other: 59% (1993 est.)

Irrigated land: 10 sq km (1993 est.)

Natural hazards: NA

Environment - current issues: very limited natural fresh water resources; increasing reliance on desalination

Environment - international agreements:

party to: Air Pollution, Climate Change,

Malta (continued)

Desertification, Endangered Species, Law of the Sea, Marine Dumping, Nuclear Test Ban, Ozone Layer Protection, Ship Pollution, Wetlands
signed, but not ratified: Biodiversity, Climate Change-Kyoto Protocol
Geography - note: the country comprises an archipelago, with only the three largest islands (Malta, Ghawdex or Gozo, and Kemmuna or Comino) being inhabited; numerous bays provide good harbors

People

Population: 381,603 (July 1999 est.)
Age structure:
0-14 years: 20% (male 40,058; female 37,810)
15-64 years: 68% (male 130,282; female 128,390)
65 years and over: 12% (male 18,996; female 26,067) (1999 est.)
Population growth rate: 0.49% (1999 est.)
Birth rate: 11.02 births/1,000 population (1999 est.)
Death rate: 7.37 deaths/1,000 population (1999 est.)
Net migration rate: 1.24 migrant(s)/1,000 population (1999 est.)
Sex ratio:
at birth: 1.06 male(s)/female
under 15 years: 1.06 male(s)/female
15-64 years: 1.01 male(s)/female
65 years and over: 0.73 male(s)/female
total population: 0.98 male(s)/female (1999 est.)
Infant mortality rate: 7.42 deaths/1,000 live births (1999 est.)
Life expectancy at birth:
total population: 77.76 years
male: 75.43 years
female: 80.23 years (1999 est.)
Total fertility rate: 1.63 children born/woman (1999 est.)
Nationality:
noun: Maltese (singular and plural)
adjective: Maltese
Ethnic groups: Maltese (descendants of ancient Carthaginians and Phoenicians, with strong elements of Italian and other Mediterranean stock)
Religions: Roman Catholic 98%
Languages: Maltese (official), English (official)
Literacy:
definition: age 10 and over can read and write
total population: 88%
male: 88%
female: 88% (1985)

Government

Country name:
conventional long form: Republic of Malta
conventional short form: Malta
local long form: Repubblika ta' Malta
local short form: Malta
Data code: MT
Government type: parliamentary democracy
Capital: Valletta
Administrative divisions: none (administered directly from Valletta)

Independence: 21 September 1964 (from UK)
National holiday: Independence Day, 21 September (1964)
Constitution: 1964 constitution substantially amended on 13 December 1974
Legal system: based on English common law and Roman civil law; has accepted compulsory ICJ jurisdiction, with reservations
Suffrage: 18 years of age; universal
Executive branch:
chief of state: President Ugo MIFSUD BONNICI (since 4 April 1994)
head of government: Prime Minister Eddie Fenech ADAMI (since 6 September 1998); Deputy Prime Minister Guido de MARCO (since 8 September 1998)
cabinet: Cabinet appointed by the president on the advice of the prime minister
elections: president elected by the House of Representatives for a five-year term; election last held NA April 1994 (next to be held by NA April 1999); following House of Representatives elections, the leader of the majority party or leader of a majority coalition is usually appointed prime minister by the president for a five-year term; the deputy prime minister is appointed by the president on the advice of the prime minister
election results: Ugo MIFSUD BONNICI elected president; percent of House of Representatives vote - NA
Legislative branch: unicameral House of Representatives (usually 65 seats; note - additional seats are given to the party with the largest popular vote to ensure a legislative majority; current total: 69 seats; members are elected by popular vote on the basis of proportional representation to serve five-year terms)
elections: last held 5 September 1998 (next to be held by September 2003)
election results: percent of vote by party - PN 51.8%, MLP 46.9%, AD 1.2%; seats by party - PN 35, MLP 30
Judicial branch: Constitutional Court, judges are appointed by the president on the advice of the prime minister; Court of Appeal, judges are appointed by the president on the advice of the prime minister
Political parties and leaders: Nationalist Party or PN [Edward FENECH ADAMI]; Malta Labor Party or MLP [Alfred SANT]; Alternativa Demokratika/Alliance for Social Justice or AD [Wenzu MINTOFF]
International organization participation: C, CCC, CE, EBRD, ECE, EU (applicant), FAO, G-77, IAEA, IBRD, ICAO, ICFTU, ICRM, IFAD, IFRCS, ILO, IMF, IMO, Inmarsat, Intelsat, Interpol, IOC, IOM (observer), ISO (correspondent), ITU, NAM, OPCW, OSCE, PCA, UN, UNCTAD, UNESCO, UNIDO, UPU, WCL, WHO, WIPO, WMO, WToO, WTrO
Diplomatic representation in the US:
chief of mission: Ambassador (vacant); Charge d'Affaires Anthony DARMANIN
chancery: 2017 Connecticut Avenue NW, Washington, DC 20008
telephone: [1] (202) 462-3611, 3612
FAX: [1] (202) 387-5470

consulate(s): New York
Diplomatic representation from the US:
chief of mission: Ambassador Kathryn Haycock PROFFITT
embassy: 2nd Floor, Development House, Saint Anne Street, Floriana, Malta
mailing address: P. O. Box 535, Valletta
telephone: [356] 235960
FAX: [356] 223322
Flag description: two equal vertical bands of white (hoist side) and red; in the upper hoist-side corner is a representation of the George Cross, edged in red

Economy

Economy - overview: Significant resources are limestone, a favorable geographic location, and a productive labor force. Malta produces only about 20% of its food needs, has limited freshwater supplies, and has no domestic energy sources. The economy is dependent on foreign trade, manufacturing (especially electronics and textiles), and tourism; the state-owned Malta drydocks employs about 3,800 people. In 1998, almost 1 million tourists visited the island. Per capita GDP of roughly $13,000 places Malta in the ranks of the less affluent EU countries. The island is divided politically over the question of joining the EU. The sizable budget deficit remains a key concern.
GDP: purchasing power parity - $5 billion (1998 est.)
GDP - real growth rate: 4% (1998 est.)
GDP - per capita: purchasing power parity - $13,000 (1998 est.)
GDP - composition by sector:
agriculture: 3%
industry: 26%
services: 71% (1997 est.)
Population below poverty line: NA%
Household income or consumption by percentage share:
lowest 10%: NA%
highest 10%: NA%
Inflation rate (consumer prices): 2.8% (1997 est.)
Labor force: 148,085 (September 1996)
Labor force - by occupation: public services 34%, other services 32%, manufacturing and construction 22%, agriculture 2% (1996)
Unemployment rate: 5% (1997)
Budget:
revenues: $1.32 billion
expenditures: $1.76 billion, including capital expenditures of $NA (1998 est.)
Industries: tourism; electronics, ship building and repair, construction; food and beverages, textiles, footwear, clothing, tobacco
Industrial production growth rate: NA%
Electricity - production: 1.425 billion kWh (1996)
Electricity - production by source:
fossil fuel: 100%
hydro: 0%
nuclear: 0%
other: 0% (1996)
Electricity - consumption: 1.425 billion kWh (1996)
Electricity - exports: 0 kWh (1996)

Malta *(continued)*

Electricity - imports: 0 kWh (1996)
Agriculture - products: potatoes, cauliflowers, grapes, wheat, barley, tomatoes, citrus, cut flowers, green peppers; pork, milk, poultry, eggs
Exports: $1.7 billion (f.o.b., 1997)
Exports - commodities: machinery and transport equipment, manufactures (1996)
Exports - partners: France 18%, US 15%, Germany 15%, UK 8%, Italy 6% (1997)
Imports: $2.3 billion (f.o.b., 1997)
Imports - commodities: machinery and transport equipment, manufactured goods; food, drink, and tobacco
Imports - partners: Italy 20%, France 16%, UK 15%, Germany 10%, US 8% (1997)
Debt - external: $130 million (1997)
Economic aid - recipient: $NA
Currency: 1 Maltese lira (LM) = 100 cents
Exchange rates: Maltese liri (LM) per US$1 - 0.3797 (January 1999), 0.3884 (1998), 0.3857 (1997), 0.3604 (1996), 0.3529 (1995), 0.3776 (1994)
Fiscal year: 1 April - 31 March

Communications

Telephones: 191,876 (1992 est.)
Telephone system: automatic system satisfies normal requirements
domestic: submarine cable and microwave radio relay between islands
international: 2 submarine cables; satellite earth station - 1 Intelsat (Atlantic Ocean)
Radio broadcast stations: AM 8, FM 4, shortwave 0
Radios: 189,000 (1992 est.)
Television broadcast stations: 2 (1997)
Televisions: 300,000 (1996 est.)

Transportation

Railways: 0 km
Highways:
total: 1,582 km
paved: 1,471 km
unpaved: 111 km (1993 est.)
Ports and harbors: Marsaxlokk, Valletta
Merchant marine:
total: 1,361 ships (1,000 GRT or over) totaling 24,436,956 GRT/40,706,665 DWT
ships by type: bulk 370, cargo 400, chemical tanker 49, combination bulk 18, combination ore/oil 17, container 56, liquefied gas tanker 2, livestock carrier 3, multifunction large-load carrier 3, oil tanker 302, passenger 7, refrigerated cargo 46, roll-on/roll-off cargo 47, short-sea passenger 19, specialized tanker 4, vehicle carrier 18
note: a flag of convenience registry; includes ships from 49 countries among which includes Greece 445, Russia 51, Switzerland 45, Italy 44, Norway 40, Croatia 26, Turkey 35, Germany 32, Georgia 23, and Monaco 24 (1998 est.)
Airports: 1 (1998 est.)

Airports - with paved runways:
total: 1
over 3,047 m: 1 (1998 est.)

Military

Military branches: Armed Forces (including an air squadron, a maritime squadron, and the Revenue Security Corps), Maltese Police Force
Military manpower - availability:
males age 15-49: 99,067 (1999 est.)
Military manpower - fit for military service:
males age 15-49: 78,855 (1999 est.)
Military expenditures - dollar figure: $65.5 million (FY96/97)
Military expenditures - percent of GDP: 2.7% (FY96/97)

Transnational Issues

Disputes - international: Malta and Tunisia are discussing the commercial exploitation of the continental shelf between their countries, particularly for oil exploration
Illicit drugs: minor transshipment point for hashish from North Africa to Western Europe

Man, Isle of
(British crown dependency)

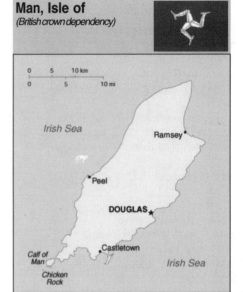

Geography

Location: Western Europe, island in the Irish Sea, between Great Britain and Ireland
Geographic coordinates: 54 15 N, 4 30 W
Map references: Europe
Area:
total: 588 sq km
land: 588 sq km
water: 0 sq km
Area - comparative: slightly more than three times the size of Washington, DC
Land boundaries: 0 km
Coastline: 113 km
Maritime claims:
exclusive fishing zone: 12 nm
territorial sea: 12 nm
Climate: cool summers and mild winters; humid; overcast about half the time
Terrain: hills in north and south bisected by central valley
Elevation extremes:
lowest point: Irish Sea 0 m
highest point: Snaefell 620 m
Natural resources: lead, iron ore
Land use:
arable land: 12%
permanent crops: 0%
permanent pastures: 56%
forests and woodland: 32%
other: 0%
Irrigated land: NA sq km
Natural hazards: NA
Environment - current issues: NA
Environment - international agreements:
party to: NA
signed, but not ratified: NA
Geography - note: one small islet, the Calf of Man, lies to the southwest, and is a bird sanctuary

Man, Isle of *(continued)*

People

Population: 75,686 (July 1999 est.)
Age structure:
0-14 years: 18% (male 6,906; female 6,597)
15-64 years: 65% (male 24,655; female 24,604)
65 years and over: 17% (male 5,156; female 7,768)
(1999 est.)
Population growth rate: 0.71% (1999 est.)
Birth rate: 12.43 births/1,000 population (1999 est.)
Death rate: 11.52 deaths/1,000 population (1999 est.)
Net migration rate: 6.17 migrant(s)/1,000 population (1999 est.)
Sex ratio:
at birth: 1.05 male(s)/female
under 15 years: 1.05 male(s)/female
15-64 years: 1 male(s)/female
65 years and over: 0.66 male(s)/female
total population: 0.94 male(s)/female (1999 est.)
Infant mortality rate: 2.45 deaths/1,000 live births (1999 est.)
Life expectancy at birth:
total population: 77.79 years
male: 74.28 years
female: 81.47 years (1999 est.)
Total fertility rate: 1.67 children born/woman (1999 est.)
Nationality:
noun: Manxman, Manxwoman
adjective: Manx
Ethnic groups: Manx (Norse-Celtic descent), Briton
Religions: Anglican, Roman Catholic, Methodist, Baptist, Presbyterian, Society of Friends
Languages: English, Manx Gaelic
Literacy: NA

Government

Country name:
conventional long form: none
conventional short form: Isle of Man
Data code: IM
Dependency status: British crown dependency
Government type: NA
Capital: Douglas
Administrative divisions: none (British crown dependency)
Independence: none (British crown dependency)
National holiday: Tynwald Day, 5 July
Constitution: 1961, Isle of Man Constitution Act
Legal system: English law and local statute
Suffrage: 21 years of age; universal
Executive branch:
chief of state: Lord of Mann Queen ELIZABETH II (since 6 February 1952), represented by Lieutenant Governor His Excellency Sir Timothy DAUNT (since NA 1995)
head of government: President of the Tynwald and the Legislative Council Sir Charles KERRUISH (since NA 1990)
cabinet: Council of Ministers
elections: the monarch is hereditary; lieutenant governor appointed by the monarch for a five-year term; president of theTwnwald and the Legislative Council elected by the Tynwald for a five-year term; election last held NA (next to be held NA)
election results: Sir Charles KERRUISH elected president of the Legislative Council; percent of legislative vote - NA
Legislative branch: bicameral Tynwald consists of the Legislative Council (a 10-member body composed of the Lord Bishop of Sodor and Man, a nonvoting attorney general, and 8 others named by the House of Keys) and the House of Keys (24 seats; members are elected by popular vote to serve five-year terms)
elections: House of Keys - last held 21 November 1996 (next to be held NA 2001)
election results: House of Keys - percent of vote by party - NA; seats by party - independents 24
Judicial branch: High Court of Justice, justices are appointed by the Lord Chancellor of England on the nomination of the lieutenant governor
Political parties and leaders: there is no party system; members sit as independents
International organization participation: none
Diplomatic representation in the US: none (British crown dependency)
Diplomatic representation from the US: none (British crown dependency)
Flag description: red with the Three Legs of Man emblem (Trinacria), in the center; the three legs are joined at the thigh and bent at the knee; in order to have the toes pointing clockwise on both sides of the flag, a two-sided emblem is used

Economy

Economy - overview: Offshore banking, manufacturing, and tourism are key sectors of the economy. The government's policy of offering incentives to high-technology companies and financial institutions to locate on the island has paid off in expanding employment opportunities in high-income industries. As a result, agriculture and fishing, once the mainstays of the economy, have declined in their shares of GDP. Banking and other services now contribute more than four fifths of GDP. Trade is mostly with the UK. The Isle of Man enjoys free access to EU markets.
GDP: purchasing power parity - $985 million (1998 est.)
GDP - real growth rate: NA%
GDP - per capita: purchasing power parity - $13,100 (1998 est.)
GDP - composition by sector:
agriculture: 2%
industry: 16%
services: 82% (1998 est.)
Population below poverty line: NA%
Household income or consumption by percentage share:
lowest 10%: NA%
highest 10%: NA%
Inflation rate (consumer prices): 2.9% (1998 est.)
Labor force: 33,577 (1996)
Labor force - by occupation: manufacturing 11%, construction 10%, transport and communication 8%, retail distribution 9%, professional and scientific services 18%, public administration 6%, banking and finance 18%
Unemployment rate: 1% (1998 est.)
Budget:
revenues: $437.7 million
expenditures: $432.5 million, including capital expenditures of $102.2 million (FY98/99 est.)
Industries: financial services, light manufacturing, tourism
Industrial production growth rate: NA%
Electricity - production: NA kWh
Electricity - production by source:
fossil fuel: 100%
hydro: 0%
nuclear: 0%
other: 0%
Electricity - consumption: NA kWh
Electricity - exports: NA kWh
Electricity - imports: NA kWh
Agriculture - products: cereals, vegetables; cattle, sheep, pigs, poultry
Exports: $NA
Exports - commodities: tweeds, herring, processed shellfish, beef, lamb
Exports - partners: UK
Imports: $NA
Imports - commodities: timber, fertilizers, fish
Imports - partners: UK
Debt - external: $NA
Economic aid - recipient: $NA
Currency: 1 Manx pound (£M) = 100 pence
Exchange rates: Manx pounds (£M) per US$1 - 0.6057 (January 1999), 0.6037 (1998), 0.6106 (1997), 0.6403 (1996), 0.6335 (1995), 0.6529 (1994)); the Manx pound is at par with the British pound
Fiscal year: 1 April - 31 March

Communications

Telephones: 46,000 (1996)
Telephone system:
domestic: NA
international: NA
Radio broadcast stations: AM 1, FM 4, shortwave 0
Radios: NA
Television broadcast stations: 0 (receives broadcasts from the UK) (1997)
Televisions: 24,450 (1996)

Transportation

Railways:
total: 52 km (27 km electrified)
Highways:
total: 640 km
paved: 320 km
unpaved: 320 km
Ports and harbors: Castletown, Douglas, Peel, Ramsey

Man, Isle of (continued)

Merchant marine:
total: 148 ships (1,000 GRT or over) totaling 4,161,154 GRT/6,880,170 DWT
ships by type: bulk 28, cargo 7, chemical tanker 14, combination bulk 3, container 20, liquefied gas tanker 14, oil tanker 43, refrigerated cargo 3, roll-on/roll-off cargo 14, vehicle carrier 2
note: a flag of convenience registry; UK owns 8 ships, Denmark 1, Sweden 1, Belgium 1, and Netherlands 1 (1998 est.)
Airports: 1 (1998 est.)
Airports - with paved runways:
total: 1
1,524 to 2,437 m: 1 (1998 est.)

Military

Military - note: defense is the responsibility of the UK

Transnational Issues

Disputes - international: none

Marshall Islands

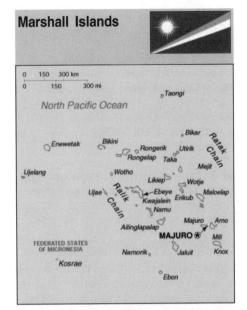

Geography

Location: Oceania, group of atolls and reefs in the North Pacific Ocean, about one-half of the way from Hawaii to Papua New Guinea
Geographic coordinates: 9 00 N, 168 00 E
Map references: Oceania
Area:
total: 181.3 sq km
land: 181.3 sq km
water: 0 sq km
note: includes the atolls of Bikini, Enewetak, and Kwajalein
Area - comparative: about the size of Washington, DC
Land boundaries: 0 km
Coastline: 370.4 km
Maritime claims:
contiguous zone: 24 nm
exclusive economic zone: 200 nm
territorial sea: 12 nm
Climate: wet season from May to November; hot and humid; islands border typhoon belt
Terrain: low coral limestone and sand islands
Elevation extremes:
lowest point: Pacific Ocean 0 m
highest point: unnamed location on Likiep 10 m
Natural resources: phosphate deposits, marine products, deep seabed minerals
Land use:
arable land: NA%
permanent crops: 60%
permanent pastures: NA%
forests and woodland: NA%
other: 40%
Irrigated land: NA sq km
Natural hazards: occasional typhoons
Environment - current issues: inadequate supplies of potable water
Environment - international agreements:
party to: Biodiversity, Climate Change, Desertification,

Law of the Sea, Ozone Layer Protection, Ship Pollution
signed, but not ratified: Climate Change-Kyoto Protocol
Geography - note: two archipelagic island chains of 30 atolls and 1,152 islands; Bikini and Enewetak are former US nuclear test sites; Kwajalein, the famous World War II battleground, is now used as a US missile test range

People

Population: 65,507 (July 1999 est.)
Age structure:
0-14 years: 50% (male 16,622; female 15,957)
15-64 years: 48% (male 16,106; female 15,386)
65 years and over: 2% (male 677; female 759) (1999 est.)
Population growth rate: 3.86% (1999 est.)
Birth rate: 45.31 births/1,000 population (1999 est.)
Death rate: 6.73 deaths/1,000 population (1999 est.)
Net migration rate: 0 migrant(s)/1,000 population (1999 est.)
Sex ratio:
at birth: 1.05 male(s)/female
under 15 years: 1.04 male(s)/female
15-64 years: 1.05 male(s)/female
65 years and over: 0.89 male(s)/female
total population: 1.04 male(s)/female (1999 est.)
Infant mortality rate: 43.38 deaths/1,000 live births (1999 est.)
Life expectancy at birth:
total population: 64.81 years
male: 63.21 years
female: 66.5 years (1999 est.)
Total fertility rate: 6.67 children born/woman (1999 est.)
Nationality:
noun: Marshallese (singular and plural)
adjective: Marshallese
Ethnic groups: Micronesian
Religions: Christian (mostly Protestant)
Languages: English (universally spoken and is the official language), two major Marshallese dialects from the Malayo-Polynesian family, Japanese
Literacy:
definition: age 15 and over can read and write
total population: 93%
male: 100%
female: 88% (1980 est.)

Government

Country name:
conventional long form: Republic of the Marshall Islands
conventional short form: Marshall Islands
former: Marshall Islands District (Trust Territory of the Pacific Islands)
Data code: RM
Government type: constitutional government in free association with the US; the Compact of Free Association entered into force 21 October 1986

Marshall Islands (continued)

Capital: Majuro

Administrative divisions: 33 municipalities; Ailinginae, Ailinglaplap, Ailuk, Arno, Aur, Bikar, Bikini, Bokak, Ebon, Enewetak, Erikub, Jabat, Jaluit, Jemo, Kili, Kwajalein, Lae, Lib, Likiep, Majuro, Maloelap, Mejit, Mili, Namorik, Namu, Rongelap, Rongrik, Toke, Ujae, Ujelang, Utirik, Wotho, Wotje

Independence: 21 October 1986 (from the US-administered UN trusteeship)

National holiday: Proclamation of the Republic of the Marshall Islands, 1 May (1979)

Constitution: 1 May 1979

Legal system: based on adapted Trust Territory laws, acts of the legislature, municipal, common, and customary laws

Suffrage: 18 years of age; universal

Executive branch:

chief of state: President Imata KABUA (since 14 January 1997); note - the president is both the chief of state and head of government

head of government: President Imata KABUA (since 14 January 1997); note - the president is both the chief of state and head of government

cabinet: Cabinet selected by the president from among the members of Parliament

elections: president elected by Parliament from among its own members for a four-year term; election last held 14 January 1997 (next to be held NA November 1999); note - Imata KABUA elected to succeed and complete the term of the late President Amata KABUA

election results: Imata KABUA elected president; percent of Parliament vote - 63%

Legislative branch: unicameral Parliament or Nitijela (33 seats; members elected by popular vote to serve four-year terms)

elections: last held 20 November 1995 (next to be held NA November 1999)

election results: percent of vote by party - NA; seats by party - NA

note: the Council of Chiefs is a 12-member body that advises on matters affecting customary law and practice

Judicial branch: Supreme Court; High Court

Political parties and leaders: traditionally there have been no formally organized political parties; what has existed more closely resembles factions or interest groups because they do not have party headquarters, formal platforms, or party structures; the following two "groupings" have competed in legislative balloting in recent years - Our Islands Party [leader NA] and Ralik/Ratak Democratic Party or RRDP [Ramsey REIMERS]

International organization participation: AsDB, ESCAP, G-77, IAEA, IBRD, ICAO, IDA, IFC, IMF, Inmarsat, Intelsat (nonsignatory user), Interpol, ITU, OPCW, Sparteca, SPC, SPF, UN, UNCTAD, UNESCO, WHO

Diplomatic representation in the US:

chief of mission: Ambassador Banny DE BRUM

chancery: 2433 Massachusetts Avenue NW, Washington, DC 20008

telephone: [1] (202) 234-5414

FAX: [1] (202) 232-3236

consulate(s) general: Honolulu

Diplomatic representation from the US:

chief of mission: Ambassador Joan M. PLAISTED

embassy: Oceanside, Mejen Weto, Long Island, Majuro

mailing address: P. O. Box 1379, Majuro, Republic of the Marshall Islands 96960-1379

telephone: [692] 247-4011

FAX: [692] 247-4012

Flag description: blue with two stripes radiating from the lower hoist-side corner - orange (top) and white; there is a white star with four large rays and 20 small rays on the hoist side above the two stripes

Economy

Economy - overview: US Government assistance is the mainstay of this tiny island economy. Agricultural production is concentrated on small farms, and the most important commercial crops are coconuts, tomatoes, melons, and breadfruit. Small-scale industry is limited to handicrafts, fish processing, and copra. The tourist industry, now a small source of foreign exchange employing less than 10% of the labor force, remains the best hope for future added income. The islands have few natural resources, and imports far exceed exports. Under the terms of the Compact of Free Association, the US provides roughly $65 million in annual aid, equal to about 70% of GDP. Negotiations will get underway in 1999 for an extended agreement. Government downsizing, drought, a drop in construction, and the decline in tourism and foreign investment due to the Asian financial difficulties have caused GDP to fall in 1996-98.

GDP: purchasing power parity - $91 million (1998 est.)

GDP - real growth rate: -5% (1998 est.)

GDP - per capita: purchasing power parity - $1,450 (1998 est.)

GDP - composition by sector:

agriculture: 15%

industry: 13%

services: 72% (1995)

Population below poverty line: NA%

Household income or consumption by percentage share:

lowest 10%: NA%

highest 10%: NA%

Inflation rate (consumer prices): 5% (1997)

Labor force: NA

Labor force - by occupation: NA

Unemployment rate: 16% (1991 est.)

Budget:

revenues: $80.1 million

expenditures: $77.4 million, including capital expenditures of $19.5 million (FY95/96 est.)

Industries: copra, fish, tourism, craft items from shell, wood, and pearls, offshore banking (embryonic)

Industrial production growth rate: NA%

Electricity - production: 57 million kWh (1994)

Electricity - production by source:

fossil fuel: NA%

hydro: NA%

nuclear: NA%

other: NA%

Electricity - consumption: 57 million kWh (1994)

Electricity - exports: 0 kWh (1994)

Electricity - imports: 0 kWh (1994)

Agriculture - products: coconuts, cacao, taro, breadfruit, fruits; pigs, chickens

Exports: $17.5 million (f.o.b., 1996 est.)

Exports - commodities: fish, coconut oil, fish, trochus shells

Exports - partners: US, Japan, Australia

Imports: $71.8 million (c.i.f., 1996 est.)

Imports - commodities: foodstuffs, machinery and equipment, fuels, beverages and tobacco

Imports - partners: US, Japan, Australia, NZ

Debt - external: $125 million (FY96/97 est.)

Economic aid - recipient: $NA; note - approximately $65 million annually from the US

Currency: 1 United States dollar (US$) = 100 cents

Exchange rates: US currency is used

Fiscal year: 1 October - 30 September

Communications

Telephones: 2,000 (1997 est.)

Telephone system: telex services

domestic: Majuro Atoll and Ebeye and Kwajalein islands have regular, seven-digit, direct-dial telephones; other islands interconnected by shortwave radiotelephone (used mostly for government purposes)

international: satellite earth stations - 2 Intelsat (Pacific Ocean); US Government satellite communications system on Kwajalein

Radio broadcast stations: AM 1, FM 2, shortwave 1

Radios: NA

Television broadcast stations: 3 (of which one is an independent station and two are US military stations) (1997)

Televisions: NA

Transportation

Railways: 0 km

Highways:

total: NA km

paved: NA km

unpaved: NA km

note: paved roads on major islands (Majuro, Kwajalein), otherwise stone-, coral-, or laterite-surfaced roads and tracks

Ports and harbors: Majuro

Merchant marine:

total: 131 ships (1,000 GRT or over) totaling 6,572,915 GRT/11,208,214 DWT

ships by type: bulk 56, cargo 5, chemical tanker 3, container 20, liquefied gas tanker 2, oil tanker 42, roll-on/roll-off cargo 2, vehicle carrier 1

note: a flag of convenience registry; includes the ships

of Canada 1, China 1, Germany 1, Japan 1, and US 7 (1998 est.)
Airports: 16 (1998 est.)
Airports - with paved runways:
total: 4
1,524 to 2,437 m: 3
914 to 1,523 m: 1 (1998 est.)
Airports - with unpaved runways:
total: 12
914 to 1,523 m: 7
under 914 m: 5 (1998 est.)

Military

Military branches: no regular military forces (a coast guard may be established); Police Force
Military - note: defense is the responsibility of the US

Transnational Issues

Disputes - international: claims US territory of Wake Atoll

Martinique
(overseas department of France)

Geography

Location: Caribbean, island in the Caribbean Sea, north of Trinidad and Tobago
Geographic coordinates: 14 40 N, 61 00 W
Map references: Central America and the Caribbean
Area:
total: 1,100 sq km
land: 1,060 sq km
water: 40 sq km
Area - comparative: slightly more than six times the size of Washington, DC
Land boundaries: 0 km
Coastline: 350 km
Maritime claims:
exclusive economic zone: 200 nm
territorial sea: 12 nm
Climate: tropical; moderated by trade winds; rainy season (June to October); vulnerable to devastating cyclones (hurricanes) every eight years on average; average temperature 17.3 degrees C; humid
Terrain: mountainous with indented coastline; dormant volcano
Elevation extremes:
lowest point: Caribbean Sea 0 m
highest point: Montagne Pelee 1,397 m
Natural resources: coastal scenery and beaches, cultivable land
Land use:
arable land: 8%
permanent crops: 8%
permanent pastures: 17%
forests and woodland: 44%
other: 23% (1993 est.)
Irrigated land: 40 sq km (1993 est.)
Natural hazards: hurricanes, flooding, and volcanic activity (an average of one major natural disaster every five years)
Environment - current issues: NA
Environment - international agreements:
party to: NA

signed, but not ratified: NA

People

Population: 411,539 (July 1999 est.)
Age structure:
0-14 years: 23% (male 47,933; female 46,957)
15-64 years: 67% (male 136,058; female 138,935)
65 years and over: 10% (male 17,530; female 24,126) (1999 est.)
Population growth rate: 1.03% (1999 est.)
Birth rate: 16.3 births/1,000 population (1999 est.)
Death rate: 5.94 deaths/1,000 population (1999 est.)
Net migration rate: -0.09 migrant(s)/1,000 population (1999 est.)
Sex ratio:
at birth: 1.02 male(s)/female
under 15 years: 1.02 male(s)/female
15-64 years: 0.98 male(s)/female
65 years and over: 0.73 male(s)/female
total population: 0.96 male(s)/female (1999 est.)
Infant mortality rate: 6.76 deaths/1,000 live births (1999 est.)
Life expectancy at birth:
total population: 79.27 years
male: 76.47 years
female: 82.13 years (1999 est.)
Total fertility rate: 1.8 children born/woman (1999 est.)
Nationality:
noun: Martiniquais (singular and plural)
adjective: Martiniquais
Ethnic groups: African and African-white-Indian mixture 90%, white 5%, East Indian, Lebanese, Chinese less than 5%
Religions: Roman Catholic 95%, Hindu and pagan African 5%
Languages: French, Creole patois
Literacy:
definition: age 15 and over can read and write
total population: 93%
male: 92%
female: 93% (1982 est.)

Government

Country name:
conventional long form: Department of Martinique
conventional short form: Martinique
local long form: Departement de la Martinique
local short form: Martinique
Data code: MB
Dependency status: overseas department of France
Government type: NA
Capital: Fort-de-France
Administrative divisions: none (overseas department of France)
Independence: none (overseas department of France)
National holiday: National Day, Taking of the Bastille, 14 July (1789)
Constitution: 28 September 1958 (French Constitution)

Martinique *(continued)*

Legal system: French legal system
Suffrage: 18 years of age; universal
Executive branch:
chief of state: President Jacques CHIRAC of France (since 17 May 1995); Prefect Dominique BELLION (since NA October 1998)
head of government: President of the General Council Claude LISE (since 22 March 1992); President of the Regional Council Alfred MARIE-JEANNE (since NA March 1998)
cabinet: NA
elections: French president elected by popular vote for a seven-year term; prefect appointed by the French president on the advice of the French Ministry of Interior; the presidents of the General and Regional Councils are elected by the members of those councils
Legislative branch: unicameral General Council or Conseil General (45 seats; members are elected by popular vote to serve six-year terms) and a unicameral Regional Assembly or Conseil Regional (41 seats; members are elected by popular vote to serve six-year terms)
elections: General Council - last held NA March 1994 (next to be held NA 2000); Regional Assembly - last held on NA March 1998 (next to be held by March 2004)
election results: General Council - percent of vote by party - NA; seats by party - NA; note - the PPM won a plurality; Regional Assembly - percent of vote by party - NA; seats by party - NA
note: Martinique elects 2 seats to the French Senate; elections last held 24 September 1995 (next to be held September 1998); results - percent of vote by party - NA; seats by party - PS 2; Martinique also elects 4 seats to the French National Assembly; elections last held 1 June 1997 (next to be held NA 2002); results - percent of vote by party - NA; seats by party - RPR 2, PS 1, independent 1
Judicial branch: Court of Appeal or Cour d'Appel
Political parties and leaders: Rally for the Republic or RPR [Andre LESUEUR]; Martinique Forces [Maurice LAOUCHEZ]; Martinique Socialist Party or PPM [Ernest WAN-AJOUHU]; Socialist Federation of Martinique or FSM [Jean CRUSOL]; Martinique Communist Party or PCM [George ERICHOT]; Martinique Patriots or PM [leader NA]; Union for French Democracy or UDF [Miguel LAVENTURE]; Martinique Independence Movement or MIM [Alfred MARIE-JEANNE]; Republican Party or PR [Jean BAILLY]; National Council of Popular Committees [Robert SAE]; Rally for Democratic Martinique [Felix HILAIRE-FORTUNE]; Movement for a Liberated Martinique [Philippe PETIT]; Union for the Renewal of Ste. Marie [Guy LORDINOT]; Combat Worker [Gerard BEAUJOUR]
Political pressure groups and leaders: Proletarian Action Group or GAP; Socialist Revolution Group or GRS [Philippe PIERRE-CHARLES]; Caribbean Revolutionary Alliance or ARC; Central Union for Martinique Workers or CSTM [Marc PULVAR]; Frantz Fanon Circle; League of Workers

and Peasants; Association for the Protection of Martinique's Heritage (ecologist) [Garcin MALSA]
International organization participation: FZ, WCL, WFTU
Diplomatic representation in the US: none (overseas department of France)
Diplomatic representation from the US: none (overseas department of France)
Flag description: a light blue background is divided into four quadrants by a white cross; in the center of each rectangle is a white snake; the flag of France is used for official occasions

Economy

Economy - overview: The economy is based on sugarcane, bananas, tourism, and light industry. Agriculture accounts for about 6% of GDP and the small industrial sector for 11%. Sugar production has declined, with most of the sugarcane now used for the production of rum. Banana exports are increasing, going mostly to France. The bulk of meat, vegetable, and grain requirements must be imported, contributing to a chronic trade deficit that requires large annual transfers of aid from France. Tourism has become more important than agricultural exports as a source of foreign exchange. The majority of the work force is employed in the service sector and in administration.
GDP: purchasing power parity - $4.24 billion (1996 est.)
GDP - real growth rate: NA%
GDP - per capita: purchasing power parity - $10,700 (1996 est.)
GDP - composition by sector:
agriculture: 6%
industry: 11%
services: 83% (1997 est.)
Population below poverty line: NA%
Household income or consumption by percentage share:
lowest 10%: NA%
highest 10%: NA%
Inflation rate (consumer prices): 3.9% (1990)
Labor force: 160,000
Labor force - by occupation: agriculture 10%, industry 17%, services 73% (1997)
Unemployment rate: 24% (1997)
Budget:
revenues: $775 million
expenditures: $2.15 billion, including capital expenditures of $118 million (1996)
Industries: construction, rum, cement, oil refining, sugar, tourism
Industrial production growth rate: NA%
Electricity - production: 855 million kWh (1996)
Electricity - production by source:
fossil fuel: 100%
hydro: 0%
nuclear: 0%
other: 0% (1996)
Electricity - consumption: 855 million kWh (1996)
Electricity - exports: 0 kWh (1996)

Electricity - imports: 0 kWh (1996)
Agriculture - products: pineapples, avocados, bananas, flowers, vegetables, sugarcane
Exports: $200 million (f.o.b., 1997)
Exports - commodities: refined petroleum products, bananas, rum, pineapples
Exports - partners: France 57%, Guadeloupe 31%, French Guiana (1991)
Imports: $1.6 billion (c.i.f., 1997)
Imports - commodities: petroleum products, crude oil, foodstuffs, construction materials, vehicles, clothing and other consumer goods
Imports - partners: France 62%, UK, Italy, Germany, Japan, US (1991)
Debt - external: $180 million (1994)
Economic aid - recipient: $NA; note - substantial annual aid from France
Currency: 1 French franc (F) = 100 centimes
Exchange rates: French francs (F) per US$1 - 5.65 (January 1999), 5.8995 (1998), 5.8367 (1997), 5.1155 (1996), 4.9915 (1995), 5.5520 (1994)
Fiscal year: calendar year

Communications

Telephones: 209,672 (1994 est.)
Telephone system: domestic facilities are adequate
domestic: NA
international: microwave radio relay to Guadeloupe, Dominica, and Saint Lucia; satellite earth stations - 2 Intelsat (Atlantic Ocean)
Radio broadcast stations: AM 1, FM 6, shortwave 0
Radios: 74,000 (1992 est.)
Television broadcast stations: 11 (in addition, there are nine repeaters) (1997)
Televisions: 65,000 (1993 est.)

Transportation

Railways: 0 km
Highways:
total: 2,724 km
paved: NA km
unpaved: NA km (1994)
Ports and harbors: Fort-de-France, La Trinite
Merchant marine: none
Airports: 2 (1998 est.)
Airports - with paved runways:
total: 1
over 3,047 m: 1 (1998 est.)
Airports - with unpaved runways:
total: 1
914 to 1,523 m: 1 (1998 est.)

Military

Military branches: French forces (Army, Navy, Air Force), Gendarmerie
Military - note: defense is the responsibility of France

Martinique (continued)

Transnational Issues

Disputes - international: none
Illicit drugs: transshipment point for cocaine and marijuana bound for the US and Europe

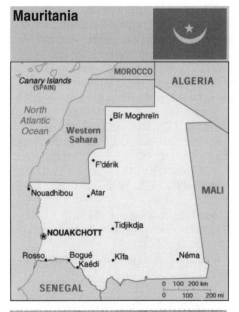

Mauritania

Geography

Location: Northern Africa, bordering the North Atlantic Ocean, between Senegal and Western Sahara
Geographic coordinates: 20 00 N, 12 00 W
Map references: Africa
Area:
total: 1,030,700 sq km
land: 1,030,400 sq km
water: 300 sq km
Area - comparative: slightly larger than three times the size of New Mexico
Land boundaries:
total: 5,074 km
border countries: Algeria 463 km, Mali 2,237 km, Senegal 813 km, Western Sahara 1,561 km
Coastline: 754 km
Maritime claims:
contiguous zone: 24 nm
continental shelf: 200 nm or to the edge of the continental margin
exclusive economic zone: 200 nm
territorial sea: 12 nm
Climate: desert; constantly hot, dry, dusty
Terrain: mostly barren, flat plains of the Sahara; some central hills
Elevation extremes:
lowest point: Sebkha de Ndrhamcha -3 m
highest point: Kediet Ijill 910 m
Natural resources: iron ore, gypsum, fish, copper, phosphate
Land use:
arable land: 0%
permanent crops: 0%
permanent pastures: 38%
forests and woodland: 4%
other: 58% (1993 est.)
Irrigated land: 490 sq km (1993 est.)
Natural hazards: hot, dry, dust/sand-laden sirocco wind blows primarily in March and April; periodic droughts

Environment - current issues: overgrazing, deforestation, and soil erosion aggravated by drought are contributing to desertification; very limited natural fresh water resources away from the Senegal which is the only perennial river
Environment - international agreements:
party to: Biodiversity, Climate Change, Desertification, Hazardous Wastes, Law of the Sea, Nuclear Test Ban, Ozone Layer Protection, Ship Pollution, Wetlands
signed, but not ratified: none of the selected agreements
Geography - note: most of the population concentrated in the cities of Nouakchott and Nouadhibou and along the Senegal River in the southern part of the country

People

Population: 2,581,738 (July 1999 est.)
Age structure:
0-14 years: 47% (male 600,901; female 600,225)
15-64 years: 51% (male 641,481; female 678,951)
65 years and over: 2% (male 25,156; female 35,024) (1999 est.)
Population growth rate: 2.99% (1999 est.)
Birth rate: 44.1 births/1,000 population (1999 est.)
Death rate: 14.2 deaths/1,000 population (1999 est.)
Net migration rate: 0 migrant(s)/1,000 population (1999 est.)
Sex ratio:
at birth: 1.03 male(s)/female
under 15 years: 1 male(s)/female
15-64 years: 0.94 male(s)/female
65 years and over: 0.72 male(s)/female
total population: 0.96 male(s)/female (1999 est.)
Infant mortality rate: 76.46 deaths/1,000 live births (1999 est.)
Life expectancy at birth:
total population: 50.48 years
male: 47.39 years
female: 53.65 years (1999 est.)
Total fertility rate: 6.35 children born/woman (1999 est.)
Nationality:
noun: Mauritanian(s)
adjective: Mauritanian
Ethnic groups: mixed Maur/black 40%, Maur 30%, black 30%
Religions: Muslim 100%
Languages: Hasaniya Arabic (official), Pular, Soninke, Wolof (official), French
Literacy:
definition: age 15 and over can read and write
total population: 37.7%
male: 49.6%
female: 26.3% (1995 est.)

Government

Country name:
conventional long form: Islamic Republic of

Mauritania *(continued)*

Mauritania
conventional short form: Mauritania
local long form: Al Jumhuriyah al Islamiyah al Muritaniyah
local short form: Muritaniyah
Data code: MR
Government type: republic
Capital: Nouakchott
Administrative divisions: 12 regions (regions, singular - region) and 1 capital district; Adrar, Assaba, Brakna, Dakhlet Nouadhibou, Gorgol, Guidimaka, Hodh Ech Chargui, Hodh El Gharbi, Inchiri, Nouakchott*, Tagant, Tiris Zemmour, Trarza
Independence: 28 November 1960 (from France)
National holiday: Independence Day, 28 November (1960)
Constitution: 12 July 1991
Legal system: a combination of Shari'a (Islamic law) and modern law
Suffrage: 18 years of age; universal
Executive branch:
chief of state: President Col. Maaouya Ould Sid Ahmed TAYA (since 12 December 1984)
head of government: Prime Minister Cheikel Afia Ould Mohamed KHOUNA (since 16 November 1998)
cabinet: Council of Ministers
elections: president elected by popular vote for a six-year term; election last held 12 December 1997 (next to be held NA December 2003); prime minister appointed by the president
election results: President Col. Maaouya Ould Sid Ahmed TAYA reelected with 90% of the vote
Legislative branch: bicameral legislature consists of the Senate or Majlis al-Shuyukh (56 seats; 17 up for election every two years; members elected by municipal leaders to serve six-year terms) and the National Assembly or Majlis al-Watani (79 seats; members elected by popular vote to serve five-year terms)
elections: Senate - last held 17 April 1998 (next to be held NA 2000); National Assembly - last held 11 and 18 October 1996 (next to be held NA 2001)
election results: Senate - percent of vote by party - NA; seats by party - NA; National Assembly - percent of vote by party - NA; seats by party - PRDS 71, AC 1, independents and other 7
Judicial branch: three-tier system: lower, appeals, and Supreme Court (Cour Supreme)
Political parties and leaders: legalized by constitution passed 12 July 1991, however, politics continue to be tribally based; emerging parties include Democratic and Social Republican Party or PRDS [led by President Col. Maaouya Ould Sid'Ahmed TAYA]; Union of Democratic Forces-New Era or UFD/NE [headed by Ahmed Ould DADDAH]; Assembly for Democracy and Unity or RDU [Ahmed Ould SIDI BABA]; Popular Social and Democratic Union or UPSD [Mohamed Mahmoud Ould MAH]; Mauritanian Party for Renewal or PMR [Hameida BOUCHRAYA]; National Avant-Garde Party or PAN [Khattry Ould JIDDOU]; Mauritanian Party of the Democratic Center or PCDM [Bamba Ould SIDI BADI]; Action for Change

or AC [Messoud Ould BOULKHEIR]
Political pressure groups and leaders: Mauritanian Workers Union or UTM [Mohamed Ely Ould BRAHIM, secretary general]; General Confederation of Mauritanian Workers or CGTM [Abdallahi Ould MOHAMED, secretary general]
International organization participation: ABEDA, ACCT (associate), ACP, AfDB, AFESD, AL, AMF, AMU, CAEU, CCC, ECA, ECOWAS, FAO, G-77, IBRD, ICAO, ICRM, IDA, IDB, IFAD, IFC, IFRCS, IHO (pending member), ILO, IMF, IMO, Intelsat, Interpol, IOC, ITU, NAM, OAU, OIC, OPCW, UN, UNCTAD, UNESCO, UNIDO, UPU, WHO, WIPO, WMO, WToO, WTrO
Diplomatic representation in the US:
chief of mission: Ambassador-designate Ahmed Ould Khalifa OULD JIDDOU
chancery: 2129 Leroy Place NW, Washington, DC 20008
telephone: [1] (202) 232-5700
FAX: [1] (202) 319-2623
Diplomatic representation from the US:
chief of mission: Ambassador Timberlake FOSTER
embassy: Rue Abdallahi Ould Oubeid, Nouakchott
mailing address: B. P. 222, Nouakchott
telephone: [222] (2) 526-60, 526-63
FAX: [222] (2) 515-92
Flag description: green with a yellow five-pointed star above a yellow, horizontal crescent; the closed side of the crescent is down; the crescent, star, and color green are traditional symbols of Islam

Economy

Economy - overview: A majority of the population still depends on agriculture and livestock for a livelihood, even though most of the nomads and many subsistence farmers were forced into the cities by recurrent droughts in the 1970s and 1980s. Mauritania has extensive deposits of iron ore, which account for almost 50% of total exports. The decline in world demand for this ore, however, has led to cutbacks in production. The nation's coastal waters are among the richest fishing areas in the world, but overexploitation by foreigners threatens this key source of revenue. The country's first deepwater port opened near Nouakchott in 1986. In recent years, drought and economic mismanagement have resulted in a substantial buildup of foreign debt. The government has begun the second stage of an economic reform program in consultation with the World Bank, the IMF, and major donor countries. Short-term growth prospects are uncertain because of the heavy debt service burden, rapid population growth, and vulnerability to climatic conditions.
GDP: purchasing power parity - $4.7 billion (1998 est.)
GDP - real growth rate: 4.2% (1998 est.)
GDP - per capita: purchasing power parity - $1,890 (1998 est.)
GDP - composition by sector:
agriculture: 26%
industry: 31%

services: 43% (1996)
Population below poverty line: 57% (1990 est.)
Household income or consumption by percentage share:
lowest 10%: 0.7%
highest 10%: 30.4% (1988)
Inflation rate (consumer prices): 4.7% (1996)
Labor force: 465,000 (1981 est.); 45,000 wage earners (1980)
Labor force - by occupation: agriculture 47%, services 29%, industry and commerce 14%, government 10%
Unemployment rate: 23% (1995 est.)
Budget:
revenues: $329 million
expenditures: $265 million, including capital expenditures of $75 million (1996 est.)
Industries: fish processing, mining of iron ore and gypsum
Industrial production growth rate: 7.2% (1994)
Electricity - production: 150 million kWh (1996)
Electricity - production by source:
fossil fuel: 80%
hydro: 20%
nuclear: 0%
other: 0% (1996)
Electricity - consumption: 150 million kWh (1996)
Electricity - exports: 0 kWh (1996)
Electricity - imports: 0 kWh (1996)
Agriculture - products: dates, millet, sorghum, root crops; cattle, sheep; fish products
Exports: $562 million (f.o.b., 1997)
Exports - commodities: fish and fish products, iron ore, gold
Exports - partners: Japan 22%, Italy 16%, France 14%
Imports: $552 million (f.o.b., 1997)
Imports - commodities: foodstuffs, consumer goods, petroleum products, capital goods
Imports - partners: France 30%, Algeria 10%, Spain 7%, China 6%, US 3%
Debt - external: $2.5 billion (1995)
Economic aid - recipient: $227.9 million (1995)
Currency: 1 ouguiya (UM) = 5 khoums
Exchange rates: ouguiyas (UM) per US$1 - 204.600 (January 1999), 151.853 (1997), 137.222 (1996), 129.768 (1995), 123.575 (1994)
Fiscal year: calendar year

Communications

Telephones: 17,000 (1991 est.)
Telephone system: poor system of cable and open-wire lines, minor microwave radio relay links, and radiotelephone communications stations (improvements being made)
domestic: mostly cable and open-wire lines; a recently completed domestic satellite telecommunications system links Nouakchott with regional capitals
international: satellite earth stations - 1 Intelsat (Atlantic Ocean) and 2 Arabsat
Radio broadcast stations: AM 1, FM 2, shortwave 1 (1998 est.)

Mauritania (continued)

Radios: 1 million (1998 est.)
Television broadcast stations: 1 (1997)
Televisions: 50,000 (1995 est.)

Transportation

Railways:
total: 704 km (single track); note - owned and operated by government mining company
standard gauge: 704 km 1.435-m gauge (1995)
Highways:
total: 7,660 km
paved: 866 km
unpaved: 6,794 km (1996 est.)
Waterways: mostly ferry traffic on the Senegal River
Ports and harbors: Bogue, Kaedi, Nouadhibou, Nouakchott, Rosso
Merchant marine: none
Airports: 26 (1998 est.)
Airports - with paved runways:
total: 8
2,438 to 3,047 m: 3
1,524 to 2,437 m: 4
914 to 1,523 m: 1 (1998 est.)
Airports - with unpaved runways:
total: 18
2,438 to 3,047 m: 2
1,524 to 2,437 m: 5
914 to 1,523 m: 9
under 914 m: 2 (1998 est.)

Military

Military branches: Army, Navy, Air Force, National Gendarmerie, National Guard, National Police, Presidential Guard
Military manpower - availability:
males age 15-49: 571,521 (1999 est.)
Military manpower - fit for military service:
males age 15-49: 277,620 (1999 est.)
Military expenditures - dollar figure: $30 million (1996)
Military expenditures - percent of GDP: 2.5% (1996)

Transnational Issues

Disputes - international: none

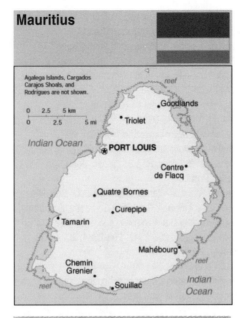

Mauritius

Agalega Islands, Cargados Carajos Shoals, and Rodrigues are not shown.

Geography

Location: Southern Africa, island in the Indian Ocean, east of Madagascar
Geographic coordinates: 20 17 S, 57 33 E
Map references: World
Area:
total: 1,860 sq km
land: 1,850 sq km
water: 10 sq km
note: includes Agalega Islands, Cargados Carajos Shoals (Saint Brandon), and Rodrigues
Area - comparative: almost 11 times the size of Washington, DC
Land boundaries: 0 km
Coastline: 177 km
Maritime claims:
continental shelf: 200 nm or to the edge of the continental margin
exclusive economic zone: 200 nm
territorial sea: 12 nm
Climate: tropical, modified by southeast trade winds; warm, dry winter (May to November); hot, wet, humid summer (November to May)
Terrain: small coastal plain rising to discontinuous mountains encircling central plateau
Elevation extremes:
lowest point: Indian Ocean 0 m
highest point: Mont Piton 828 m
Natural resources: arable land, fish
Land use:
arable land: 49%
permanent crops: 3%
permanent pastures: 3%
forests and woodland: 22%
other: 23% (1993 est.)
Irrigated land: 170 sq km (1993 est.)
Natural hazards: cyclones (November to April); almost completely surrounded by reefs that may pose maritime hazards
Environment - current issues: water pollution

Environment - international agreements:
party to: Biodiversity, Climate Change, Desertification, Endangered Species, Environmental Modification, Hazardous Wastes, Law of the Sea, Marine Life Conservation, Nuclear Test Ban, Ozone Layer Protection, Ship Pollution, Whaling
signed, but not ratified: none of the selected agreements

People

Population: 1,182,212 (July 1999 est.)
Age structure:
0-14 years: 26% (male 156,616; female 153,698)
15-64 years: 68% (male 398,557; female 402,674)
65 years and over: 6% (male 28,586; female 42,081) (1999 est.)
Population growth rate: 1.18% (1999 est.)
Birth rate: 18.49 births/1,000 population (1999 est.)
Death rate: 6.69 deaths/1,000 population (1999 est.)
Net migration rate: 0 migrant(s)/1,000 population (1999 est.)
Sex ratio:
at birth: 1 male(s)/female
under 15 years: 1.02 male(s)/female
15-64 years: 0.99 male(s)/female
65 years and over: 0.68 male(s)/female
total population: 0.98 male(s)/female (1999 est.)
Infant mortality rate: 16.2 deaths/1,000 live births (1999 est.)
Life expectancy at birth:
total population: 71.09 years
male: 67.21 years
female: 74.96 years (1999 est.)
Total fertility rate: 2.21 children born/woman (1999 est.)
Nationality:
noun: Mauritian(s)
adjective: Mauritian
Ethnic groups: Indo-Mauritian 68%, Creole 27%, Sino-Mauritian 3%, Franco-Mauritian 2%
Religions: Hindu 52%, Christian 28.3% (Roman Catholic 26%, Protestant 2.3%), Muslim 16.6%, other 3.1%
Languages: English (official), Creole, French, Hindi, Urdu, Hakka, Bojpoori
Literacy:
definition: age 15 and over can read and write
total population: 82.9%
male: 87.1%
female: 78.8% (1995 est.)

Government

Country name:
conventional long form: Republic of Mauritius
conventional short form: Mauritius
Data code: MP
Government type: parliamentary democracy
Capital: Port Louis
Administrative divisions: 9 districts and 3 dependencies*; Agalega Islands*, Black River, Cargados Carajos Shoals*, Flacq, Grand Port, Moka,

Pamplemousses, Plaines Wilhems, Port Louis, Riviere du Rempart, Rodrigues*, Savanne
Independence: 12 March 1968 (from UK)
National holiday: Independence Day, 12 March (1968)
Constitution: 12 March 1968; amended 12 March 1992
Legal system: based on French civil law system with elements of English common law in certain areas
Suffrage: 18 years of age; universal
Executive branch:
chief of state: President Cassam UTEEM (since 1 July 1992) and Vice President Angidi Verriah CHETTIAR (since 28 June 1997)
head of government: Prime Minister Navinchandra RAMGOOLAM (since 27 December 1995)
cabinet: Council of Ministers appointed by the president on the recommendation of the prime minister
elections: president and vice president elected by the National Assembly for five-year terms; election last held 28 June 1997 (next to be held NA 2002); prime minister and deputy prime minister appointed by the president and are responsible to the National Assembly
election results: Cassam UTEEM reelected president and Angidi Verriah CHETTIAR elected vice president; percent of vote by the National Assembly - NA
Legislative branch: unicameral National Assembly (66 seats - 62 elected by popular vote, 4 appointed by the election commission from the losing political parties to give representation to various ethnic minorities; members serve five-year terms)
elections: last held on 20 December 1995 (next to be held by December 2000)
election results: percent of vote by party - MLP/MMM 65%, MSM/MMR 20%, other 15%; seats by party - MLP 35, MMM 25, allies of MLP and MMM on Rodrigues Island 2; appointed were Rodrigues Movement 2, PMSD 1, Hizbullah 1
Judicial branch: Supreme Court
Political parties and leaders:
government party: Mauritian Labor Party or MLP [Navinchandra RAMGOOLAM]
opposition parties: Hizbullah [Imam Mustapha BEEHARRY]; MSM/MMR alliance consisting of the Militant Socialist Movement or MSM [Sir Anerood JUGNAUTH] and the Mauritian Militant Renaissance or MMR [Dr. Paramhansa NABABSING]; Mauritian Social Democrat Party or PMSD [Xavier-Luc DUVAL]; Mauritian Militant Movement or MMM [Paul BERENGER]; Organization of the People of Rodrigues or OPR [Louis Serge CLAIR]; Rodrigues Movement [Nicholas Von MALLY]
Political pressure groups and leaders: various labor unions
International organization participation: ACCT, ACP, AfDB, C, CCC, ECA, FAO, G-77, IAEA, IBRD, ICAO, ICFTU, ICRM, IDA, IFAD, IFC, IFRCS, ILO, IMF, IMO, Inmarsat, InOC, Intelsat, Interpol, IOC, ISO, ITU, NAM, OAU, OPCW, PCA, SADC, UN, UNCTAD, UNESCO, UNIDO, UPU, WCL, WFTU,

WHO, WIPO, WMO, WToO, WTrO
Diplomatic representation in the US:
chief of mission: Ambassador Chitmansing JESSERAMSING
chancery: Suite 441, 4301 Connecticut Avenue NW, Washington, DC 20008
telephone: [1] (202) 244-1491, 1492
FAX: [1] (202) 966-0983
Diplomatic representation from the US:
chief of mission: Ambassador Harold Walter GEISEL
embassy: 4th Floor, Rogers House, John Kennedy Street, Port Louis
mailing address: international mail: P.O. Box 544, Port Louis; US mail: American Embassy, Port Louis, Department of State, Washington, DC 20521-2450
telephone: [230] 208-2347, 208-2354, 208-9763 through 9767
FAX: [230] 208-9534
Flag description: four equal horizontal bands of red (top), blue, yellow, and green

Economy

Economy - overview: Since independence in 1968, Mauritius has developed from a low income, agriculturally based economy to a middle income diversified economy with growing industrial, financial services, and tourist sectors. For most of the period, annual growth has been of the order of 5% to 6%. This remarkable achievement has been reflected in increased life expectancy, lowered infant mortality, and a much improved infrastructure. Sugarcane is grown on about 90% of the cultivated land area and accounts for 25% of export earnings. The government's development strategy centers on industrialization (with a view to modernization and to exports), agricultural diversification, and tourism. Economic performance in 1991-98 continued strong with solid growth and low unemployment.
GDP: purchasing power parity - $11.7 billion (1998 est.)
GDP - real growth rate: 5% (1998 est.)
GDP - per capita: purchasing power parity - $10,000 (1998 est.)
GDP - composition by sector:
agriculture: 8%
industry: 29%
services: 63% (1996)
Population below poverty line: 10.6% (1992 est.)
Household income or consumption by percentage share:
lowest 10%: NA%
highest 10%: NA%
Inflation rate (consumer prices): 6.8% (1997)
Labor force: 514,000 (1995)
Labor force - by occupation: construction and industry 36%, services 24%, agriculture and fishing 14%, trade, restaurants, hotels 16%, transportation and communication 7%, finance 3% (1995)
Unemployment rate: 2% (1996 est.)
Budget:
revenues: $824 million (FY94/95)
expenditures: $1 billion, including capital

expenditures of $198 million (FY95/96 est.)
Industries: food processing (largely sugar milling), textiles, clothing; chemicals, metal products, transport equipment, nonelectrical machinery; tourism
Industrial production growth rate: 5.8% (1992)
Electricity - production: 1.125 billion kWh (1996)
Electricity - production by source:
fossil fuel: 86.67%
hydro: 13.33%
nuclear: 0%
other: 0% (1996)
Electricity - consumption: 1.125 billion kWh (1996)
Electricity - exports: 0 kWh (1996)
Electricity - imports: 0 kWh (1996)
Agriculture - products: sugarcane, tea, corn, potatoes, bananas, pulses; cattle, goats; fish
Exports: $1.6 billion (f.o.b., 1997)
Exports - commodities: clothing and textiles 55%, sugar 24% (1995)
Exports - partners: UK 34.4%, France 19.5%, US 13.0%, Germany 5.6%, Italy 4.0% (1996)
Imports: $2.3 billion (c.i.f., 1997)
Imports - commodities: manufactured goods 37%, capital equipment 19%, foodstuffs 13%, petroleum products 8%, chemicals 7% (1995)
Imports - partners: South Africa 12.0%, France 11.1%, India 8.9%, UK 6.5%, Germany 4.7%, (1996)
Debt - external: $1.2 billion (1996 est.)
Economic aid - recipient: $5.2 million (1995)
Currency: 1 Mauritian rupee (MauR) = 100 cents
Exchange rates: Mauritian rupees (MauRs) per US$1 - 24.099 (January 1999), 22.803 (1998), 20.561 (1997), 17.948 (1996), 17.386 (1995), 17.960 (1994)
Fiscal year: 1 July - 30 June

Communications

Telephones: 107,000 (1993)
Telephone system: small system with good service
domestic: primarily microwave radio relay
international: satellite earth station - 1 Intelsat (Indian Ocean); new microwave link to Reunion; HF radiotelephone links to several countries
Radio broadcast stations: AM 2, FM 0, shortwave 0
Radios: 399,000 (1993 est.)
Television broadcast stations: 2 (in addition, there are 11 repeaters) (1997)
Televisions: 242,000 (1993 est.)

Transportation

Railways: 0 km
Highways:
total: 1,860 km
paved: 1,732 km (including 30 km of expressways)
unpaved: 128 km (1996 est.)
Ports and harbors: Port Louis
Merchant marine:
total: 17 ships (1,000 GRT or over) totaling 178,846 GRT/236,308 DWT
ships by type: cargo 6, combination bulk 2, container 6, liquefied gas tanker 1, refrigerated cargo 2

Mauritius *(continued)*

note: a flag of convenience registry; India owns 1 ship (1998 est.)
Airports: 5 (1998 est.)
Airports - with paved runways:
total: 2
2,438 to 3,047 m: 1
914 to 1,523 m: 1 (1998 est.)
Airports - with unpaved runways:
total: 3
914 to 1,523 m: 1
under 914 m: 2 (1998 est.)

Military

Military branches: National Police Force (includes the paramilitary Special Mobile Force or SMF, Special Support Units or SSU, and National Coast Guard)
Military manpower - availability:
males age 15-49: 339,218 (1999 est.)
Military manpower - fit for military service:
males age 15-49: 171,705 (1999 est.)
Military expenditures - dollar figure: $11.2 million (FY97/98)
Military expenditures - percent of GDP: 0.4% (FY97/98)

Transnational Issues

Disputes - international: claims the Chagos Archipelago in UK-administered British Indian Ocean Territory; claims French-administered Tromelin Island
Illicit drugs: illicit producer of cannabis for the international drug trade; heroin consumption and transshipment are growing problems

Mayotte
(territorial collectivity of France)

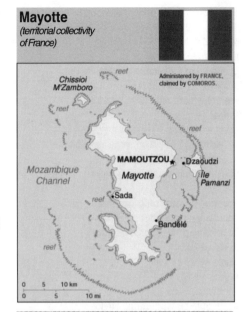

Administered by FRANCE, claimed by COMOROS.

Geography

Location: Southern Africa, island in the Mozambique Channel, about one-half of the way from northern Madagascar to northern Mozambique
Geographic coordinates: 12 50 S, 45 10 E
Map references: Africa
Area:
total: 375 sq km
land: 375 sq km
water: 0 sq km
Area - comparative: slightly more than twice the size of Washington, DC
Land boundaries: 0 km
Coastline: 185.2 km
Maritime claims:
exclusive economic zone: 200 nm
territorial sea: 12 nm
Climate: tropical; marine; hot, humid, rainy season during northeastern monsoon (November to May); dry season is cooler (May to November)
Terrain: generally undulating, with deep ravines and ancient volcanic peaks
Elevation extremes:
lowest point: Indian Ocean 0 m
highest point: Benara 660 m
Natural resources: NEGL
Land use:
arable land: NA%
permanent crops: NA%
permanent pastures: NA%
forests and woodland: NA%
other: NA%
Irrigated land: NA sq km
Natural hazards: cyclones during rainy season
Environment - current issues: NA
Environment - international agreements:
party to: NA
signed, but not ratified: NA
Geography - note: part of Comoro Archipelago

People

Population: 149,336 (July 1999 est.)
Age structure:
0-14 years: 47% (male 34,838; female 34,798)
15-64 years: 52% (male 42,073; female 35,068)
65 years and over: 1% (male 1,257; female 1,302) (1999 est.)
Population growth rate: 5% (1999 est.)
Birth rate: 46.12 births/1,000 population (1999 est.)
Death rate: 8.9 deaths/1,000 population (1999 est.)
Net migration rate: 12.73 migrant(s)/1,000 population (1999 est.)
Sex ratio:
at birth: 1.03 male(s)/female
under 15 years: 1 male(s)/female
15-64 years: 1.2 male(s)/female
65 years and over: 0.97 male(s)/female
total population: 1.1 male(s)/female (1999 est.)
Infant mortality rate: 69.06 deaths/1,000 live births (1999 est.)
Life expectancy at birth:
total population: 60.02 years
male: 57.61 years
female: 62.51 years (1999 est.)
Total fertility rate: 6.41 children born/woman (1999 est.)
Nationality:
noun: Mahorais (singular and plural)
adjective: Mahoran
Ethnic groups: NA
Religions: Muslim 99%, Christian (mostly Roman Catholic)
Languages: Mahorian (a Swahili dialect), French
Literacy: NA

Government

Country name:
conventional long form: Territorial Collectivity of Mayotte
conventional short form: Mayotte
Data code: MF
Dependency status: territorial collectivity of France
Government type: NA
Capital: Mamoutzou
Administrative divisions: none (territorial collectivity of France)
Independence: none (territorial collectivity of France)
National holiday: National Day, Taking of the Bastille, 14 July (1789)
Constitution: 28 September 1958 (French Constitution)
Legal system: French law
Suffrage: 18 years of age; universal
Executive branch:
chief of state: President Jacques CHIRAC of France (since 17 May 1995), represented by Prefect Philippe BOISADAM (since NA)
head of government: President of the General Council Younoussa BAMANA (since NA 1977)
cabinet: NA

Mayotte *(continued)*

elections: French president elected by popular vote for a seven-year term; prefect appointed by the French president on the advice of the French Ministry of the Interior; president of the General Council elected by the members of the General Council for a six-year term

Legislative branch: unicameral General Council or Conseil General (19 seats; members are elected by popular vote to serve three-year terms)

elections: last held 23 March 1997 (next to be held NA March 2000)

election results: percent of vote by party - NA; note - only nine of the 19 seats were subjected to voting in March 1997; after the election, seats by party were as follows: MPM 8, RPR 5, independents 5, PS 1

note: Mayotte elects one member of the French Senate; elections last held 24 September 1995 (next to be held 24 September 2001); results - percent of vote by party - NA; seats by party - MPM 1; Mayotte also elects one member to the French National Assembly; elections last held 25 May and 1 June 1997 (next to be held as a special election on NA May 2002); results - percent of vote by party - UDF/FD 51.7%, RPR 48.3%; seats by party - UDF/FD 1

Judicial branch: Supreme Court (Tribunal Superieur d'Appel)

Political parties and leaders: Mahoran Popular Movement or MPM [Younoussa BAMANA]; Mahoran Rally for the Republic or RPR [Mansour KAMARDINE]; Democratic Front or FD [Youssouf MOUSSA]; Association for French Mayotte or Association Pour Mayotte Francaise [Didier BEOUTIS]; Socialist Party or PS (local branch of French Parti Socialiste) [leader NA]; Union for French Democracy or UDF [Henri JEAN-BAPTISTE]

International organization participation: FZ

Diplomatic representation in the US: none (territorial collectivity of France)

Diplomatic representation from the US: none (territorial collectivity of France)

Flag description: the flag of France is used

Economy

Economy - overview: Economic activity is based primarily on the agricultural sector, including fishing and livestock raising. Mayotte is not self-sufficient and must import a large portion of its food requirements, mainly from France. The economy and future development of the island are heavily dependent on French financial assistance, an important supplement to GDP. Mayotte's remote location is an obstacle to the development of tourism.

GDP: purchasing power parity - $85 million (1998 est.)

GDP - real growth rate: NA%

GDP - per capita: purchasing power parity - $600 (1998 est.)

GDP - composition by sector:
agriculture: NA%
industry: NA%
services: NA%

Population below poverty line: NA%

Household income or consumption by percentage share:
lowest 10%: NA%
highest 10%: NA%

Inflation rate (consumer prices): NA%

Labor force: NA

Unemployment rate: 38% (1991 est.)

Budget:
revenues: $NA
expenditures: $73 million, including capital expenditures of $NA (1991 est.)

Industries: newly created lobster and shrimp industry

Industrial production growth rate: NA%

Electricity - production: NA kWh

Electricity - production by source:
fossil fuel: NA%
hydro: NA%
nuclear: NA%
other: NA%

Electricity - consumption: NA kWh

Electricity - exports: NA kWh

Electricity - imports: NA kWh

Agriculture - products: vanilla, ylang-ylang (perfume essence), coffee, copra

Exports: $3.64 million (f.o.b., 1996)

Exports - commodities: ylang-ylang (perfume essence), vanilla, copra

Exports - partners: France 80%, Comoros 15%, Reunion

Imports: $131.5 million (f.o.b., 1996)

Imports - commodities: building materials, machinery and transportation equipment, metals, chemicals, rice, clothing, flour

Imports - partners: France 66%, Africa 14%, Southeast Asia 20%

Debt - external: $NA

Economic aid - recipient: $107.7 million (1995); note - extensive French financial assistance

Currency: 1 French franc (F) = 100 centimes

Exchange rates: French francs (F) per US$1 - 5.65 (January 1999), 5.8995 (1998), 5.8367 (1997), 5.1155 (1996), 4.9915 (1995), 5.5520 (1994)

Fiscal year: calendar year

Communications

Telephones: 450

Telephone system: small system administered by French Department of Posts and Telecommunications
domestic: NA
international: microwave radio relay and HF radiotelephone communications to Comoros and other international connections

Radio broadcast stations: AM 1, FM 0, shortwave 0

Radios: 30,000 (1994 est.)

Television broadcast stations: 3 (1997)

Televisions: 3,500 (1994 est.)

Transportation

Railways: 0 km

Highways:
total: 93 km
paved: 72 km
unpaved: 21 km

Ports and harbors: Dzaoudzi

Merchant marine: none

Airports: 1 (1998 est.)

Airports - with paved runways:
total: 1
914 to 1,523 m: 1 (1998 est.)

Military

Military - note: defense is the responsibility of France; small contingent of French forces stationed on the island

Transnational Issues

Disputes - international: claimed by Comoros

Mexico

Geography

Location: Middle America, bordering the Caribbean Sea and the Gulf of Mexico, between Belize and the US and bordering the North Pacific Ocean, between Guatemala and the US

Geographic coordinates: 23 00 N, 102 00 W

Map references: North America

Area:
total: 1,972,550 sq km
land: 1,923,040 sq km
water: 49,510 sq km

Area - comparative: slightly less than three times the size of Texas

Land boundaries:
total: 4,538 km
border countries: Belize 250 km, Guatemala 962 km, US 3,326 km

Coastline: 9,330 km

Maritime claims:
contiguous zone: 24 nm
continental shelf: 200 nm or to the edge of the continental margin
exclusive economic zone: 200 nm
territorial sea: 12 nm

Climate: varies from tropical to desert

Terrain: high, rugged mountains; low coastal plains; high plateaus; desert

Elevation extremes:
lowest point: Laguna Salada -10 m
highest point: Volcan Pico de Orizaba 5,700 m

Natural resources: petroleum, silver, copper, gold, lead, zinc, natural gas, timber

Land use:
arable land: 12%
permanent crops: 1%
permanent pastures: 39%
forests and woodland: 26%
other: 22% (1993 est.)

Irrigated land: 61,000 sq km (1993 est.)

Natural hazards: tsunamis along the Pacific coast, volcanoes and destructive earthquakes in the center and south, and hurricanes on the Gulf of Mexico and Caribbean coasts

Environment - current issues: natural fresh water resources scarce and polluted in north, inaccessible and poor quality in center and extreme southeast; raw sewage and industrial effluents polluting rivers in urban areas; deforestation; widespread erosion; desertification; serious air pollution in the national capital and urban centers along US-Mexico border

Environment - international agreements:
party to: Biodiversity, Climate Change, Desertification, Endangered Species, Hazardous Wastes, Law of the Sea, Marine Dumping, Marine Life Conservation, Nuclear Test Ban, Ozone Layer Protection, Ship Pollution, Wetlands, Whaling
signed, but not ratified: Climate Change-Kyoto Protocol

Geography - note: strategic location on southern border of US

People

Population: 100,294,036 (July 1999 est.)

Age structure:
0-14 years: 35% (male 17,987,500; female 17,289,875)
15-64 years: 61% (male 29,610,813; female 31,216,342)
65 years and over: 4% (male 1,873,986; female 2,315,520) (1999 est.)

Population growth rate: 1.73% (1999 est.)

Birth rate: 24.99 births/1,000 population (1999 est.)

Death rate: 4.83 deaths/1,000 population (1999 est.)

Net migration rate: -2.84 migrant(s)/1,000 population (1999 est.)

Sex ratio:
at birth: 1.05 male(s)/female
under 15 years: 1.04 male(s)/female
15-64 years: 0.95 male(s)/female
65 years and over: 0.81 male(s)/female
total population: 0.97 male(s)/female (1999 est.)

Infant mortality rate: 24.62 deaths/1,000 live births (1999 est.)

Life expectancy at birth:
total population: 72 years
male: 68.98 years
female: 75.17 years (1999 est.)

Total fertility rate: 2.85 children born/woman (1999 est.)

Nationality:
noun: Mexican(s)
adjective: Mexican

Ethnic groups: mestizo (Amerindian-Spanish) 60%, Amerindian or predominantly Amerindian 30%, white 9%, other 1%

Religions: nominally Roman Catholic 89%, Protestant 6%

Languages: Spanish, various Mayan, Nahuatl, and other regional indigenous languages

Literacy:
definition: age 15 and over can read and write
total population: 89.6%
male: 91.8%
female: 87.4% (1995 est.)

Government

Country name:
conventional long form: United Mexican States
conventional short form: Mexico
local long form: Estados Unidos Mexicanos
local short form: Mexico

Data code: MX

Government type: federal republic operating under a centralized government

Capital: Mexico

Administrative divisions: 31 states (estados, singular - estado) and 1 federal district* (distrito federal); Aguascalientes, Baja California, Baja California Sur, Campeche, Chiapas, Chihuahua, Coahuila de Zaragoza, Colima, Distrito Federal*, Durango, Guanajuato, Guerrero, Hidalgo, Jalisco, Mexico, Michoacan de Ocampo, Morelos, Nayarit, Nuevo Leon, Oaxaca, Puebla, Queretaro de Arteaga, Quintana Roo, San Luis Potosi, Sinaloa, Sonora, Tabasco, Tamaulipas, Tlaxcala, Veracruz-Llave, Yucatan, Zacatecas

Independence: 16 September 1810 (from Spain)

National holiday: Independence Day, 16 September (1810)

Constitution: 5 February 1917

Legal system: mixture of US constitutional theory and civil law system; judicial review of legislative acts; accepts compulsory ICJ jurisdiction, with reservations

Suffrage: 18 years of age; universal and compulsory (but not enforced)

Executive branch:
chief of state: President Ernesto ZEDILLO Ponce de Leon (since 1 December 1994); note - the president is both the chief of state and head of government
head of government: President Ernesto ZEDILLO Ponce de Leon (since 1 December 1994); note - the president is both the chief of state and head of government
cabinet: Cabinet appointed by the president with consent of the Senate

Mexico (continued)

elections: president elected by popular vote for a six-year term; election last held 21 August 1994 (next to be held in July or August 2000)

election results: Ernesto ZEDILLO Ponce de Leon elected president; percent of vote - Ernesto ZEDILLO Ponce de Leon (PRI) 50.18%, Cuauhtemoc CARDENAS Solorzano (PRD) 17.08%, Diego FERNANDEZ DE CEVALLOS (PAN) 26.69%, other 6.05%

Legislative branch: bicameral National Congress or Congreso de la Union consists of the Senate or Camara de Senadores (128 seats; half are elected by popular vote to serve six-year terms, and half are allocated on the basis of each party's popular vote) and the Chamber of Deputies or Camara de Diputados (500 seats; 300 members are directly elected by popular vote to serve three-year terms; remaining 200 members are allocated on the basis of each party's popular vote, also for three-year terms)

elections: Senate - last held 6 July 1997 for one-quarter of the seats; Chamber of Deputies - last held 6 July 1997 (the next legislative elections will coincide with the presidential election in July or August 2000)

election results: Senate - percent of vote by party - NA; seats by party - PRI 77, PAN 33, PRD 16, PVEM 1, PT 1; note - the distribution of seats as of May 1998 is as follows - PRI 77, PAN 31, PRD 15, PT 1, independents 4; Chamber of Deputies - percent of vote by party - PRI 39%, PAN 27%, PRD 26%; seats by party - PRI 239, PRD 125, PAN 121, PVEM 8, PT 7; note - the distribution of seats as of May 1998 is as follows - PRI 237, PRD 127, PAN 120, PT 7, PVEM 6, independents 3

Judicial branch: Supreme Court of Justice or Corte Suprema de Justicia (judges are appointed by the president with consent of the Senate)

Political parties and leaders: recognized parties - Institutional Revolutionary Party or PRI [Mariano PALACIOS Alocer]; National Action Party or PAN [Felipe CALDERON Hinojosa]; Party of the Democratic Revolution or PRD [Andres Manuel LOPEZ Obrador]; Mexican Green Ecologist Party or PVEM [Jorge GONZALEZ Torres]; Workers Party or PT [Alberto ANAYA Gutierrez]

Political pressure groups and leaders: Roman Catholic Church; Confederation of Mexican Workers or CTM; Confederation of Industrial Chambers or CONCAMIN; Confederation of National Chambers of Commerce or CONCANACO; National Peasant Confederation or CNC; Revolutionary Workers Party or PRT; Revolutionary Confederation of Workers and Peasants or CROC; Regional Confederation of Mexican Workers or CROM; Confederation of Employers of the Mexican Republic or COPARMEX; National Chamber of Transformation Industries or CANACINTRA; Coordinator for Foreign Trade Business Organizations or COECE; Federation of Unions Providing Goods and Services or FESEBES; National Union of Workers or UNT

International organization participation: APEC, BCIE, BIS, Caricom (observer), CCC, CDB, EBRD, ECLAC, FAO, G-3, G-6, G-11, G-15, G-19, G-24, IADB, IAEA, IBRD, ICAO, ICC, ICFTU, ICRM, IDA, IEA (observer), IFAD, IFC, IFRCS, ILO, IMF, IMO, Inmarsat, Intelsat, Interpol, IOC, IOM (observer), ISO, ITU, LAES, LAIA, NAM (observer), NEA, OAS, OECD, OPANAL, OPCW, PCA, RG, UN, UNCTAD, UNESCO, UNIDO, UNU, UPU, WCL, WFTU, WHO, WIPO, WMO, WToO, WTrO

Diplomatic representation in the US:

chief of mission: Ambassador Jesus REYES HEROLES Gonzalez Garza

chancery: 1911 Pennsylvania Avenue NW, Washington, DC 20006

telephone: [1] (202) 728-1600

FAX: [1] (202) 728-1698

consulate(s) general: Atlanta, Austin, Boston, Chicago, Dallas, Denver, El Paso, Houston, Laredo (Texas), Los Angeles, Miami, New Orleans, New York, Nogales (Arizona), Phoenix, Sacramento, San Antonio, San Diego, San Francisco, San Juan (Puerto Rico)

consulate(s): Albuquerque, Brownsville (Texas), Calexico (California), Corpus Christi, Del Rio (Texas), Detroit, Douglas (Arizona), Eagle Pass (Texas), Fresno (California), McAllen (Texas), Midland (Texas), Orlando, Oxnard (California), Philadelphia, Portland (Oregon), St. Louis, Salt Lake City, San Bernardino, San Jose, Santa Ana (California), Seattle, Tucson

Diplomatic representation from the US:

chief of mission: Ambassador Jeffery DAVIDOW

embassy: Paseo de la Reforma 305, Colonia Cuauhtemoc, 06500 Mexico, Distrito Federal

mailing address: P. O. Box 3087, Laredo, TX 78044-3087

telephone: [52] (5) 209-9100

FAX: [52] (5) 208-3373, 511-9980

consulate(s) general: Ciudad Juarez, Guadalajara, Monterrey, Tijuana

consulate(s): Hermosillo, Matamoros, Merida, Nuevo Laredo, Nogales

Flag description: three equal vertical bands of green (hoist side), white, and red; the coat of arms (an eagle perched on a cactus with a snake in its beak) is centered in the white band

Economy

Economy - overview: Mexico has a free market economy with a mixture of modern and outmoded industry and agriculture, increasingly dominated by the private sector. The number of state-owned enterprises in Mexico has fallen from more than 1,000 in 1982 to fewer than 200 in 1998. The ZEDILLO administration is privatizing and expanding competition in sea ports, railroads, telecommunications, electricity, natural gas distribution, and airports. A strong export sector helped to cushion the economy's decline in 1995 and led the recovery in 1996 and 1997. In 1998, private consumption became the leading driver of growth, which was accompanied by increased employment and higher wages. The government expects the economy to slow in 1999 because of low commodity prices, tighter international liquidity, and slacker demand for exports. Mexico still needs to overcome many structural problems as it strives to modernize its economy and raise living standards. Income distribution is very unequal, with the top 20% of income earners accounting for 55% of income. Trade with the US and Canada has nearly doubled since NAFTA was implemented in 1994. Mexico is pursuing additional trade agreements with most countries in Latin America and with the EU to lessen its dependence on the US.

GDP: purchasing power parity - $815.3 billion (1998 est.)

GDP - real growth rate: 4.8% (1998 est.)

GDP - per capita: purchasing power parity - $8,300 (1998 est.)

GDP - composition by sector:

agriculture: 6%

industry: 26%

services: 68% (1997)

Population below poverty line: 27% (1998 est.)

Household income or consumption by percentage share:

lowest 10%: 1.8%

highest 10%: 36.6% 1996)

Inflation rate (consumer prices): 18.6% (1998)

Labor force: 37.5 million (1998)

Labor force - by occupation: services 28.8%, agriculture, forestry, hunting, and fishing 21.8%, commerce 17.1%, manufacturing 16.1%, construction 5.2%, public administration and national defense 4.4%, transportation and communications 4.1%

Unemployment rate: 2.6% (1998) urban; plus considerable underemployment

Budget:

revenues: $117 billion

expenditures: $123 billion, including capital expenditures of $NA (1998 est.)

Industries: food and beverages, tobacco, chemicals, iron and steel, petroleum, mining, textiles, clothing, motor vehicles, consumer durables, tourism

Industrial production growth rate: 6% (1998 est.)

Electricity - production: 154.395 billion kWh (1996)

Electricity - production by source:

fossil fuel: 71.46%

hydro: 20.16%

nuclear: 4.85%

other: 3.53% (1996)

Electricity - consumption: 154.448 billion kWh (1996)

Electricity - exports: 1.263 billion kWh (1996)

Electricity - imports: 1.316 billion kWh (1996)

Agriculture - products: corn, wheat, soybeans, rice, beans, cotton, coffee, fruit, tomatoes; beef, poultry, dairy products; wood products

Exports: $117.5 billion (f.o.b., 1998), includes in-bond industries (assembly plant operations with links to US companies)

Exports - commodities: crude oil, oil products, coffee, silver, engines, motor vehicles, cotton, consumer electronics

Mexico *(continued)*

Exports - partners: US 87.5%, Canada 1.3%, Japan 0.8%, Spain 0.6%, Chile 0.6%, Brazil 0.5% (1998 est.)
Imports: $111.5 billion (f.o.b., 1998), includes in-bond industries (assembly plant operations with links to US companies)
Imports - commodities: metal-working machines, steel mill products, agricultural machinery, electrical equipment, car parts for assembly, repair parts for motor vehicles, aircraft, and aircraft parts
Imports - partners: US 74.2%, Japan 3.7%, Germany 3.7%, Canada 1.8%, South Korea 1.5%, Italy 1.3%, France 1.2% (1998 est.)
Debt - external: $154 billion (1997)
Economic aid - recipient: $1.166 billion (1995)
Currency: 1 New Mexican peso (Mex$) = 100 centavos
Exchange rates: Mexican pesos (Mex$) per US$1 - 10.1104 (January 1999), 9.1360 (1998), 7.9141 (1997), 7.5994(1996), 6.4194 (1995), 3.3751 (1994)
Fiscal year: calendar year

Communications

Telephones: 11,890,868 (1993 est.)
Telephone system: highly developed system with extensive microwave radio relay links; privatized in December 1990; opened to competition January 1997
domestic: adequate telephone service for business and government, but the population is poorly served; domestic satellite system with 120 earth stations; extensive microwave radio relay network
international: satellite earth stations - 5 Intelsat (4 Atlantic Ocean and 1 Pacific Ocean); launched Solidaridad I satellite in November 1993 and Solidaridad II in October 1994, giving Mexico improved access to South America, Central America and much of the US as well as enhancing domestic communications; linked to Central American Microwave System of trunk connections
Radio broadcast stations: AM 824 (1999 est.), FM 500 (1998 est.), shortwave 19 (1999 est.)
Radios: 22.5 million (1992 est.)
Television broadcast stations: 236 (not including repeaters) (1997)
Televisions: 13.1 million (1992 est.)

Transportation

Railways:
total: 31,048 km
standard gauge: 30,958 km 1.435-m gauge (246 km electrified)
narrow gauge: 90 km 0.914-m gauge (1998 est.)
Highways:
total: 252,000 km
paved: 94,248 km (including 6,740 km of expressways)
unpaved: 157,752 km (1996 est.)
Waterways: 2,900 km navigable rivers and coastal canals
Pipelines: crude oil 28,200 km; petroleum products

10,150 km; natural gas 13,254 km; petrochemical 1,400 km
Ports and harbors: Acapulco, Altamira, Coatzacoalcos, Ensenada, Guaymas, La Paz, Lazaro Cardenas, Manzanillo, Mazatlan, Progreso, Salina Cruz, Tampico, Topolobampo, Tuxpan, Veracruz
Merchant marine:
total: 52 ships (1,000 GRT or over) totaling 852,004 GRT/1,236,475 DWT
ships by type: bulk 2, cargo 1, chemical tanker 4, container 4, liquefied gas tanker 7, oil tanker 28, roll-on/roll-off cargo 3, short-sea passenger 3 (1998 est.)
Airports: 1,805 (1998 est.)
Airports - with paved runways:
total: 232
over 3,047 m: 10
2,438 to 3,047 m: 27
1,524 to 2,437 m: 91
914 to 1,523 m: 78
under 914 m: 26 (1998 est.)
Airports - with unpaved runways:
total: 1,573
over 3,047 m: 1
2,438 to 3,047 m: 1
1,524 to 2,437 m: 63
914 to 1,523 m: 468
under 914 m: 1,040 (1998 est.)
Heliports: 1 (1998 est.)

Military

Military branches: National Defense Secretariat (includes Army and Air Force), Navy Secretariat (includes Naval Air and Marines)
Military manpower - military age: 18 years of age
Military manpower - availability:
males age 15-49: 25,675,266 (1999 est.)
Military manpower - fit for military service:
males age 15-49: 18,675,524 (1999 est.)
Military manpower - reaching military age annually:
males: 1,085,042 (1999 est.)
Military expenditures - dollar figure: $6 billion (1998)
Military expenditures - percent of GDP: 1.3% (1998)

Transnational Issues

Disputes - international: none
Illicit drugs: illicit cultivation of opium poppy (cultivation in 1998 - 5,500 hectares; potential production - 60 metric tons) and cannabis cultivation in 1998 - 4,600 hectares; government eradication efforts have been key in keeping illicit crop levels low; major supplier of heroin and marijuana to the US market; continues as the primary transshipment country for US-bound cocaine from South America; involved in the production and distribution of methamphetamines

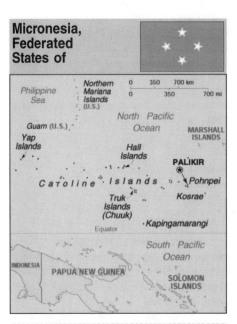

Micronesia, Federated States of

Geography

Location: Oceania, island group in the North Pacific Ocean, about three-quarters of the way from Hawaii to Indonesia
Geographic coordinates: 6 55 N, 158 15 E
Map references: Oceania
Area:
total: 702 sq km
land: 702 sq km
water: 0 sq km
note: includes Pohnpei (Ponape), Truk (Chuuk) Islands, Yap Islands, and Kosrae
Area - comparative: four times the size of Washington, DC
Land boundaries: 0 km
Coastline: 6,112 km
Maritime claims:
exclusive economic zone: 200 nm
territorial sea: 12 nm
Climate: tropical; heavy year-round rainfall, especially in the eastern islands; located on southern edge of the typhoon belt with occasionally severe damage
Terrain: islands vary geologically from high mountainous islands to low, coral atolls; volcanic outcroppings on Pohnpei, Kosrae, and Truk
Elevation extremes:
lowest point: Pacific Ocean 0 m
highest point: Totolom 791 m
Natural resources: forests, marine products, deep-seabed minerals
Land use:
arable land: NA%
permanent crops: NA%
permanent pastures: NA%
forests and woodland: NA%
other: NA%
Irrigated land: NA sq km
Natural hazards: typhoons (June to December)

Micronesia, Federated States of (continued)

Environment - current issues: NA
Environment - international agreements:
party to: Biodiversity, Climate Change, Desertification, Hazardous Wastes, Law of the Sea, Ozone Layer Protection
signed, but not ratified: Climate Change-Kyoto Protocol
Geography - note: four major island groups totaling 607 islands

People

Population: 131,500 (July 1999 est.)
Age structure:
0-14 years: NA
15-64 years: NA
65 years and over: NA
Population growth rate: 3.3% (1999 est.)
Birth rate: 27.32 births/1,000 population (1999 est.)
Death rate: 6.01 deaths/1,000 population (1999 est.)
Net migration rate: 11.65 migrant(s)/1,000 population (1999 est.)
Infant mortality rate: 33.99 deaths/1,000 live births (1999 est.)
Life expectancy at birth:
total population: 68.48 years
male: 66.52 years
female: 70.48 years (1999 est.)
Total fertility rate: 3.87 children born/woman (1999 est.)
Nationality:
noun: Micronesian(s)
adjective: Micronesian; Kosrae(s), Pohnpeian(s), Trukese, Yapese
Ethnic groups: nine ethnic Micronesian and Polynesian groups
Religions: Roman Catholic 50%, Protestant 47%, other and none 3%
Languages: English (official and common language), Trukese, Pohnpeian, Yapese, Kosrean
Literacy:
definition: age 15 and over can read and write
total population: 89%
male: 91%
female: 88% (1980 est.)

Government

Country name:
conventional long form: Federated States of Micronesia
conventional short form: none
former: Kosrae, Ponape, Truk, and Yap Districts (Trust Territory of the Pacific Islands)
abbreviation: FSM
Data code: FM
Government type: constitutional government in free association with the US; the Compact of Free Association entered into force 3 November 1986
Capital: Palikir
Administrative divisions: 4 states; Chuuk (Truk), Kosrae, Pohnpei, Yap
Independence: 3 November 1986 (from the US-administered UN Trusteeship)

National holiday: Proclamation of the Federated States of Micronesia, 10 May (1979)
Constitution: 10 May 1979
Legal system: based on adapted Trust Territory laws, acts of the legislature, municipal, common, and customary laws
Suffrage: 18 years of age; universal
Executive branch:
chief of state: President Jacob NENA (acting president since NA July 1996, president since 9 May 1997); Vice President Leo A. FALCAM (since 9 May 1997); note - the president is both the chief of state and head of government; Vice President Jacob NENA became acting president in July 1996 after President Bailey OLTER suffered a stroke; OLTER was declared incapacitated in November 1996; as provided for by the constitution, 180 days later, with OLTER still unable to resume his duties, NENA was sworn in as the new president; he will serve for the remaining two years of OLTER's term
head of government: President Jacob NENA (acting president since NA July 1996, president since 9 May 1997); Vice President Leo A. FALCAM (since 9 May 1997); note - the president is both the chief of state and head of government; Vice President Jacob NENA became acting president in July 1996 after President Bailey OLTER suffered a stroke; OLTER was declared incapacitated in November 1996; as provided for by the constitution, 180 days later, with OLTER still unable to resume his duties, NENA was sworn in as the new president; he will serve for the remaining two years of OLTER's term
cabinet: Cabinet
elections: president and vice president elected by Congress from among the four senators-at-large for four-year terms; election last held 11 May 1995 (next to be held NA May 1999); note - because of the vacancy to the post of vice president created after NENA left to become acting president, a new election to fill the position of vice president for the remaining two years of the term was held on 9 May 1997 (next to be held NA May 1999)
election results: Bailey OLTER reelected president; percent of Congress vote - NA; Leo A. FALCAM elected vice president; percent of Congress vote - NA
Legislative branch: unicameral Congress (14 seats; members elected by popular vote; four - one elected from each of state - to serve four-year terms and 10 - elected from single-member districts delineated by population - to serve two-year terms)
elections: elections for four-year term seats last held 7 March 1995 (next to be held 2 March 1999); elections for two-year term seats last held 3 March 1997 (next to be held NA March 1999)
election results: percent of vote - NA; seats - independents 14
Judicial branch: Supreme Court
Political parties and leaders: no formal parties
International organization participation: AsDB, ESCAP, G-77, IBRD, ICAO, IDA, IFC, IMF, Intelsat, ITU, OPCW, Sparteca, SPC, SPF, UN, UNCTAD, WHO, WMO
Diplomatic representation in the US:
chief of mission: Ambassador Jesse Bibiano MAREHALAU
chancery: 1725 N Street NW, Washington, DC 20036
telephone: [1] (202) 223-4383
FAX: [1] (202) 223-4391
consulate(s) general: Honolulu and Tamuning (Guam)
Diplomatic representation from the US:
chief of mission: Ambassador (vacant); Charge d'Affaires Ann WRIGHT
embassy: address NA, Kolonia
mailing address: P. O. Box 1286, Pohnpei, Federated States of Micronesia 96941
telephone: [691] 320-2187
FAX: [691] 320-2186
Flag description: light blue with four white five-pointed stars centered; the stars are arranged in a diamond pattern

Economy

Economy - overview: Economic activity consists primarily of subsistence farming and fishing. The islands have few mineral deposits worth exploiting, except for high-grade phosphate. The potential for a tourist industry exists, but the remoteness of the location and a lack of adequate facilities hinder development. Financial assistance from the US is the primary source of revenue, with the US pledged to spend $1 billion in the islands in the 1990s. Geographical isolation and a poorly developed infrastructure are major impediments to long-term growth.
GDP: purchasing power parity - $220 million (1996 est.)
note: GDP is supplemented by grant aid, averaging perhaps $100 million annually
GDP - real growth rate: 1% (1996 est.)
GDP - per capita: purchasing power parity - $1,760 (1996 est.)
GDP - composition by sector:
agriculture: NA%
industry: NA%
services: NA%
Population below poverty line: NA%
Household income or consumption by percentage share:
lowest 10%: NA%
highest 10%: NA%
Inflation rate (consumer prices): 4% (1996 est.)
Labor force: NA
Labor force - by occupation: two-thirds are government employees
Unemployment rate: 27% (1989)
Budget:
revenues: $58 million
expenditures: $52 million, including capital expenditures of $4.7 million (FY95/96 est.)
Industries: tourism, construction, fish processing, craft items from shell, wood, and pearls
Industrial production growth rate: NA%

Micronesia, Federated States of (continued)

Electricity - production: NA kWh
Electricity - production by source:
fossil fuel: NA%
hydro: NA%
nuclear: NA%
other: NA%
Electricity - consumption: NA kWh
Electricity - exports: NA kWh
Electricity - imports: NA kWh
Agriculture - products: black pepper, tropical fruits and vegetables, coconuts, cassava (tapioca), sweet potatoes; pigs, chickens
Exports: $73 million (f.o.b., 1996 est.)
Exports - commodities: fish, garments, bananas, black pepper
Exports - partners: Japan, US, Guam
Imports: $168 million (c.i.f., 1996 est.)
Imports - commodities: food, manufactured goods, machinery and equipment, beverages
Imports - partners: US, Japan, Australia
Debt - external: $129 million
Economic aid - recipient: $77.4 million (1995); note - under terms of the Compact of Free Association, the US will provide $1.3 billion in grant aid during the period 1986-2001
Currency: 1 United States dollar (US$) = 100 cents
Exchange rates: US currency is used
Fiscal year: 1 October - 30 September

Telephones: 960
Telephone system:
domestic: islands interconnected by shortwave radiotelephone (used mostly for government purposes)
international: satellite earth stations - 4 Intelsat (Pacific Ocean)
Radio broadcast stations: AM 5, FM 1, shortwave 1
Radios: 17,000 (1993 est.)
Television broadcast stations: 2 (1997)
Televisions: 1,290 (1993 est.)

Transportation

Railways: 0 km
Highways:
total: 240 km
paved: 42 km
unpaved: 198 km (1996 est.)
Ports and harbors: Colonia (Yap), Kolonia (Pohnpei), Lele, Moen
Merchant marine: none
Airports: 6 (1998 est.)
Airports - with paved runways:
total: 5
1,524 to 2,437 m: 4
914 to 1,523 m: 1 (1998 est.)
Airports - with unpaved runways:
total: 1
914 to 1,523 m: 1 (1998 est.)

Military

Military - note: Federated States of Micronesia (FSM) is a sovereign, self-governing state in free association with the US; FSM is totally dependent on the US for its defense

Transnational Issues

Disputes - international: none

Midway Islands
(territory of the US)

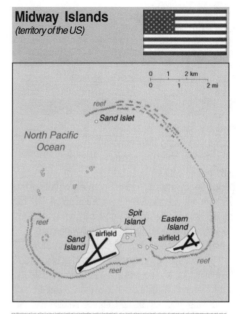

Geography

Location: Oceania, atoll in the North Pacific Ocean, about one-third of the way from Honolulu to Tokyo
Geographic coordinates: 28 13 N, 177 22 W
Map references: Oceania
Area:
total: 6.2 sq km
land: 6.2 sq km
water: 0 sq km
note: includes Eastern Island, Sand Island, and Spit Island
Area - comparative: about nine times the size of The Mall in Washington, DC
Land boundaries: 0 km
Coastline: 15 km
Maritime claims:
exclusive economic zone: 200 nm
territorial sea: 12 nm
Climate: subtropical, but moderated by prevailing easterly winds
Terrain: low, nearly level
Elevation extremes:
lowest point: Pacific Ocean 0 m
highest point: unnamed location 4 m
Natural resources: wildlife, terrestrial and aquatic
Land use:
arable land: 0%
permanent crops: 0%
permanent pastures: 0%
forests and woodland: 0%
other: 100%
Irrigated land: 0 sq km (1998)
Natural hazards: NA
Environment - current issues: NA
Environment - international agreements:
party to: NA
signed, but not ratified: NA
Geography - note: a coral atoll managed as a national wildlife refuge and open to the public for wildlife-related recreation in the form of wildlife

Midway Islands *(continued)*

observation and photography, sport fishing, snorkeling, and scuba diving

Population: no indigenous inhabitants

Government

Country name:
conventional long form: none
conventional short form: Midway Islands
Data code: MQ
Dependency status: unincorporated territory of the US; formerly administered from Washington, DC, by the US Navy, under Naval Facilities Engineering Command, Pacific Division; this facility has been operationally closed since 10 September 1993; on 31 October 1996, through a presidential executive order, the jurisdiction and control of the atoll was transferred to the Fish and Wildlife Service of the US Department of the Interior as part of the National Wildlife Refuge system
Capital: none; administered from Washington, DC
Legal system: NA
Flag description: the flag of the US is used

Economy

Economy - overview: The economy is based on providing support services for the national wildlife refuge activities located on the islands. All food and manufactured goods must be imported.

Transportation

Highways:
total: 32 km
paved: NA km
unpaved: NA km
Pipelines: 7.8 km
Ports and harbors: Sand Island
Airports: 3 (1998 est.)
Airports - with paved runways:
total: 2
1,524 to 2,437 m: 2 (1998 est.)
Airports - with unpaved runways:
total: 1
914 to 1,523 m: 1 (1998 est.)

Military

Military - note: defense is the responsibility of the US

Transnational Issues

Disputes - international: none

Moldova

Geography

Location: Eastern Europe, northeast of Romania
Geographic coordinates: 47 00 N, 29 00 E
Map references: Commonwealth of Independent States
Area:
total: 33,843 sq km
land: 33,371 sq km
water: 472 sq km
Area - comparative: slightly larger than Maryland
Land boundaries:
total: 1,389 km
border countries: Romania 450 km, Ukraine 939 km
Coastline: 0 km (landlocked)
Maritime claims: none (landlocked)
Climate: moderate winters, warm summers
Terrain: rolling steppe, gradual slope south to Black Sea
Elevation extremes:
lowest point: Nistru River 2 m
highest point: Mount Balaneshty 430 m
Natural resources: lignite, phosphorites, gypsum
Land use:
arable land: 53%
permanent crops: 14%

permanent pastures: 13%
forests and woodland: 13%
other: 7% (1993 est.)
Irrigated land: 3,110 sq km (1993 est.)
Natural hazards: landslides (57 cases in 1998)
Environment - current issues: heavy use of agricultural chemicals, including banned pesticides such as DDT, has contaminated soil and groundwater; extensive soil erosion from poor farming methods
Environment - international agreements:
party to: Air Pollution, Biodiversity, Climate Change, Desertification, Hazardous Wastes, Ozone Layer Protection
signed, but not ratified: Air Pollution-Persistent Organic Pollutants
Geography - note: landlocked

People

Population: 4,460,838 (July 1999 est.)
Age structure:
0-14 years: 24% (male 555,096; female 535,625)
15-64 years: 66% (male 1,408,334; female 1,529,542)
65 years and over: 10% (male 160,317; female 271,924) (1999 est.)
Population growth rate: 0.1% (1999 est.)
Birth rate: 14.43 births/1,000 population (1999 est.)
Death rate: 12.5 deaths/1,000 population (1999 est.)
Net migration rate: -0.92 migrant(s)/1,000 population (1999 est.)
Sex ratio:
at birth: 1.05 male(s)/female
under 15 years: 1.04 male(s)/female
15-64 years: 0.92 male(s)/female
65 years and over: 0.59 male(s)/female
total population: 0.91 male(s)/female (1999 est.)
Infant mortality rate: 43.52 deaths/1,000 live births (1999 est.)
Life expectancy at birth:
total population: 64.39 years
male: 59.76 years
female: 69.24 years (1999 est.)
Total fertility rate: 1.86 children born/woman (1999 est.)
Nationality:
noun: Moldovan(s)
adjective: Moldovan
Ethnic groups: Moldavian/Romanian 64.5%, Ukrainian 13.8%, Russian 13%, Gagauz 3.5%, Jewish 1.5%, Bulgarian 2%, other 1.7% (1989 est.)
note: internal disputes with ethnic Russians in the Transdniester region
Religions: Eastern Orthodox 98.5%, Jewish 1.5%, Baptist (only about 1,000 members) (1991)
note: the large majority of churchgoers are ethnic Moldovans
Languages: Moldovan (official, virtually the same as the Romanian language), Russian, Gagauz (a Turkish dialect)
Literacy:
definition: age 15 and over can read and write

Moldova (continued)

total population: 96%
male: 99%
female: 94% (1989 est.)

Country name:
conventional long form: Republic of Moldova
conventional short form: Moldova
local long form: Republica Moldova
local short form: none
former: Soviet Socialist Republic of Moldova; Moldavia
Data code: MD
Government type: republic
Capital: Chisinau
Administrative divisions: 40 raions (singular - raion) and 4 municipalities*; Anenii Noi, Balti*, Basarabeasca, Bender*, Briceni, Cahul, Cainari, Calarasi, Camenca, Cantemir, Causeni, Ceadir-Lunga, Chisinau*, Cimislia, Comrat, Criuleni, Donduseni, Drochia, Dubasari, Edinet, Falesti, Floresti, Glodeni, Grigoriopol, Hincesti, Ialoveni, Leova, Nisporeni, Ocnita, Orhei, Rezina, Ribnita, Riscani, Singerei, Slobozia, Soldanesti, Soroca, Stefan-Voda, Straseni, Taraclia, Telenesti, Tiraspol*, Ungheni, Vulcanesti
note: in accordance with the Law on Territorial Administrative Reform, the 40 raions have been reorganized into 9 counties (judets), one municipality*, and 2 territorial units**: Baltsi, Cahul, Chisinau, Chisinau*, Dubossary district (Transnistria)**, Edinets, Gagauzia**, Lapushna, Orhei, Soroca, Tighina, Ungheni; the status of the Dubossary district is still under negotiation
Independence: 27 August 1991 (from Soviet Union)
National holiday: Independence Day, 27 August 1991
Constitution: new constitution adopted 28 July 1994; replaces old Soviet constitution of 1979
Legal system: based on civil law system; Constitutional Court reviews legality of legislative acts and governmental decisions of resolution; it is unclear if Moldova accepts compulsory ICJ jurisdiction but accepts many UN and Organization for Security and Cooperation in Europe (OSCE) documents
Suffrage: 18 years of age; universal
Executive branch:
chief of state: President Petru LUCINSCHI (since 15 January 1997)
head of government: Prime Minister Ion CIUBUC (since 15 January 1997) and four deputy prime ministers
cabinet: Council of Ministers appointed by the president on the recommendation of the prime minister
elections: president elected by popular vote for a four-year term; election last held 17 November 1996; runoff election 1 December 1996 (next to be held NA November 2000); following legislative elections, the leader of the majority party or leader of the majority coalition is usually elected prime minister by Parliament; names of deputy prime ministers are

submitted by the prime minister for acceptance by the president
election results: Petru LUCINSCHI ran against Mircea SNEGUR and was elected president; percent of vote - LUCINSCHI 54%, SNEGUR 46%; Prime Minister Ion CIUBUC was appointed by the president 15 January 1997 and was elected by a parliamentary vote of 75-15 on 24 January 1997
Legislative branch: unicameral Parliament or Parlamentul (101 seats; members are directly elected by popular vote to serve four-year terms)
elections: last held 22 March 1998 (next to be held spring 2002)
election results: percent of vote by party - PCM 30%, CDM 19%, PMDP 18%, PFD 9%; seats by party - PCM 40, CDM 26, PMDP 24, PFD 11
note: the comparative breakdown of seats by faction is approximate
Judicial branch: Supreme Court
Political parties and leaders: Communist Party or PCM [Vladimir VORONIN, first chairman]; The Democratic Convention or CDM (includes the Christian Democratic Popular Front or FPCD and the Party of Rivival and Conciliation or PRC) [Mircea SNEGUR and Iurie ROSCA, chairmen]; Party of Democratic Forces or PFD [Valeriu MATEI, chairman]; Bloc for a Democratic and Prosperous Moldova or PMDP [Dumitru DIACOV]; Socialist Unity Faction or US of the Socialist Party of Moldova or PSM [leader NA]; Social Democratic Party of Moldova or PSDM [Oazu NANTOI, chairman]; Agrarian Democratic Party of Moldova or PDAM [Dumitru MOTPAN, chairman]; Peasants and Intellectuals Bloc [Lidia ISTRATI, chairwoman]; Liberal Party of Moldova or PLM [Mircea RUSU, chairman]; Socialist Party of Moldova or PSM [Valeriu SENIC and Victor MOREV, cochairmen]; Party for Social Progress or PPSM [Eugen SOBOR, chairman]; Civic Unity [Vladimir SOLONARI]; Moldovan National Peasant Party or PNTM [Simeon CERTAN]; Party of People's Social Justice [Maricica LITVITCHI]
Political pressure groups and leaders: The Ecology Movement of Moldova or EMM [Alecu RENITSA, chairman]; The Christian Democratic League of Women of Moldova or CDLWM [Lidia ISTRATI, chairwoman]; National Christian Party of Moldova or NCPM [V. NIKU, leader]; The Peoples Movement Gagauz Khalky or GKh [S. GULGAR, leader]; The Democratic Party of Gagauzia or DPG [G. SAVOSTIN, chairman]; The Alliance of Working People of Moldova or AWPM [G. POLOGOV, president]; Liberal Convention of Moldova (now the Liberal Party); Association of Victims of Repression [Alexander USATIUC]; Christian Democratic Youth Organization [Valeriu BARBA]; National Youth League [Valeriu STRELETS]; Union of Youth of Moldova [Petru GAVTON]
International organization participation: ACCT, BIS, BSEC, CCC, CE, CEI, CIS, EAPC, EBRD, ECE, FAO, IAEA, IBRD, ICAO, ICFTU, IDA, IFAD, IFC, ILO, IMF, Intelsat (nonsignatory user), Interpol, IOC, IOM (observer), ISO (correspondent), ITU, OPCW, OSCE,

PFP, UN, UNCTAD, UNESCO, UNIDO, UPU, WHO, WIPO, WMO, WToO, WTrO (applicant)
Diplomatic representation in the US:
chief of mission: Ambassador Ceslav CIOBANU
chancery: 2101 S Street NW, Washington, DC 20008
telephone: [1] (202) 667-1130
FAX: [1] (202) 667-1204
Diplomatic representation from the US:
chief of mission: Ambassador Rudolf Villem PERINA
embassy: Strada Alexei Mateevicie, #103, Chisinau 2009
mailing address: use embassy street address; pouch address - American Embassy Chisinau, Department of State, Washington, DC 20521-7080
telephone: [373] (2) 23-37-72
FAX: [373] (2) 23-30-44
Flag description: same color scheme as Romania - three equal vertical bands of blue (hoist side), yellow, and red; emblem in center of flag is of a Roman eagle of gold outlined in black with a red beak and talons carrying a yellow cross in its beak and a green olive branch in its right talons and a yellow scepter in its left talons; on its breast is a shield divided horizontally red over blue with a stylized ox head, star, rose, and crescent all in black-outlined yellow

Economy - overview: Moldova enjoys a favorable climate and good farmland but has no major mineral deposits. As a result, the economy depends heavily on agriculture, featuring fruits, vegetables, wine, and tobacco. Moldova must import all of its supplies of oil, coal, and natural gas, largely from Russia. Energy shortages contributed to sharp production declines after the breakup of the Soviet Union in 1991. The Moldovan Government has recently been making progress on an ambitious economic reform agenda. As part of its reform efforts, Moldova introduced a stable convertible currency, freed all prices, stopped issuing preferential credits to state enterprises and backed steady land privatization, removed export controls, and freed interest rates. In 1998, the economic troubles of Russia, with whom Moldova conducts 55% of its trade, was a major cause of the 8.6% drop in GDP. In 1999, the IMF resumed payment on Moldova's Extended Fund Facility, which had been suspended since 1997. The IMF intends to grant $135 million in 1999.
GDP: purchasing power parity - $10 billion (1998 est.)
GDP - real growth rate: -8.6% (1998 est.)
GDP - per capita: purchasing power parity - $2,200 (1998 est.)
GDP - composition by sector:
agriculture: 30%
industry: 29%
services: 41% (1997)
Population below poverty line: NA%
Household income or consumption by percentage share:
lowest 10%: 2.7%
highest 10%: 25.8% (1992)

Moldova *(continued)*

Inflation rate (consumer prices): 18.3% (1998 est.)
Labor force: 1.7 million (1998)
Labor force - by occupation: agriculture 40.2%, industry 14.3%, other 45.5% (1998)
Unemployment rate: 2% (includes only officially registered unemployed; large numbers of underemployed workers) (September 1998)
Budget:
revenues: $536 million
expenditures: $594 million, including capital expenditures of $NA (1998 est.)
Industries: food processing, agricultural machinery, foundry equipment, refrigerators and freezers, washing machines, hosiery, sugar, vegetable oil, shoes, textiles
Industrial production growth rate: -5% (1998 est.)
Electricity - production: 8.325 billion kWh (1996)
Electricity - production by source:
fossil fuel: 96.1%
hydro: 3.9%
nuclear: 0%
other: 0% (1996)
Electricity - consumption: 6.825 billion kWh (1996)
Electricity - exports: 3.1 billion kWh (1996)
Electricity - imports: 1.6 billion kWh (1996)
Agriculture - products: vegetables, fruits, wine, grain, sugar beets, sunflower seed, tobacco; beef, milk
Exports: $633 million (f.o.b., 1998)
Exports - commodities: foodstuffs, wine, tobacco, textiles and footwear, machinery
Exports - partners: Russia 58%, Kazakhstan, Ukraine, Belarus, Romania, US, Germany, Italy (1997)
Imports: $1.02 billion (f.o.b., 1998)
Imports - commodities: oil, gas, coal, steel, machinery, chemical products, metals, metal products, foodstuffs, automobiles, other consumer durables
Imports - partners: Russia 26%, Ukraine 20%, Belarus, Romania, Germany, Italy (1997)
Debt - external: more than $1.2 billion (February 1999)
Economic aid - recipient: $100.8 million (1995); note - $547 million from the IMF and World Bank (1992-99)
Currency: the Moldovan leu (MLD) (plural lei) was introduced in late 1993
Exchange rates: lei (MLD) per US$1 (end of period) - 8.3226 (December 1998), 8.3395 (1998), 4.6605 (1997), 4.6500 (1996), 4.4990 (1995), 4.2700 (1994); period average - 4.6758 (January 1998), 4.6236 (1997), 4.6045 (1996), 4.4958 (1995)
Fiscal year: calendar year

Communications

Telephones: 600,000 (1998 est.)
Telephone system: the Ministry of Information, Computers, and Telecommunications controls telecommunications; the carrier is Modtelecom
domestic: local - Chisinau has a fiber-optic loop and one cellular GSM provider; the waiting list for telephones is long; local service outside Chisinau is poor; intercity - Moldova's two fiber-optic segments form a synchronous digital hierarchy ring through Romania's system; an analog backbone system runs from south to north in Moldova
international: two fiber-optic segments provide connectivity to Romania; worldwide service can be available to Moldova through this infrastructure; additional analog lines are to Russia; Intelsat, Eutelsat, and Intersputnik earth stations
Radio broadcast stations: AM 4, FM 8, shortwave NA (1999)
Radios: NA
Television broadcast stations: 1 national station, 3 private stations, 15 small local stations outside Chisinau (1998)
Televisions: 93 televisions/100 people (1996)

Transportation

Railways:
total: 1,328 km
broad gauge: 1,328 km 1.520-m gauge (1992)
Highways:
total: 12,300 km
paved: 10,738 km
unpaved: 1,562 km (1996 est.)
Waterways: 424 km (1994)
Pipelines: natural gas 310 km (1992)
Ports and harbors: none
Airports: 26 (1994 est.)
Airports - with paved runways:
total: 8
over 3,047 m: 1
2,438 to 3,047 m: 2
1,524 to 2,437 m: 2
under 914 m: 3 (1994 est.)
Airports - with unpaved runways:
total: 18
2,438 to 3,047 m: 3
1,524 to 2,437 m: 2
914 to 1,523 m: 5
under 914 m: 8 (1994 est.)

Military

Military branches: Ground Forces, Air and Air Defense Forces, Republic Security Forces (internal and border troops)
Military manpower - military age: 18 years of age
Military manpower - availability:
males age 15-49: 1,151,674 (1999 est.)
Military manpower - fit for military service:
males age 15-49: 908,347 (1999 est.)
Military manpower - reaching military age annually:
males: 38,666 (1999 est.)
Military expenditures - dollar figure: $6.3 million (FY99)
Military expenditures - percent of GDP: 1% (1999)

Transnational Issues

Disputes - international: separatist Transdniester region, comprising the area between the Nistru (Dniester) River and Ukraine, has its own de facto government, dominated by Moldovan Slavs
Illicit drugs: limited cultivation of opium poppy and cannabis, mostly for CIS consumption; transshipment point for illicit drugs from Southwest Asia via Central Asia to Russia, Western Europe and possibly the United States

Monaco

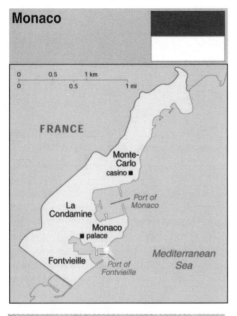

Geography

Location: Western Europe, bordering the Mediterranean Sea, on the southern coast of France, near the border with Italy
Geographic coordinates: 43 44 N, 7 24 E
Map references: Europe
Area:
total: 1.95 sq km
land: 1.95 sq km
water: 0 sq km
Area - comparative: about three times the size of The Mall in Washington, DC
Land boundaries:
total: 4.4 km
border countries: France 4.4 km
Coastline: 4.1 km
Maritime claims:
territorial sea: 12 nm
Climate: Mediterranean with mild, wet winters and hot, dry summers
Terrain: hilly, rugged, rocky
Elevation extremes:
lowest point: Mediterranean Sea 0 m
highest point: Mont Agel 140 m
Natural resources: none
Land use:
arable land: 0%
permanent crops: 0%
permanent pastures: 0%
forests and woodland: 0%
other: 100% (urban area)
Irrigated land: NA sq km
Natural hazards: NA
Environment - current issues: NA
Environment - international agreements:
party to: Biodiversity, Climate Change, Desertification, Endangered Species, Hazardous Wastes, Law of the Sea, Marine Dumping, Ozone Layer Protection, Ship Pollution, Wetlands, Whaling
signed, but not ratified: Climate Change-Kyoto Protocol

Geography - note: second smallest independent state in world (after Holy See); almost entirely urban

People

Population: 32,149 (July 1999 est.)
Age structure:
0-14 years: 17% (male 2,723; female 2,645)
15-64 years: 64% (male 10,014; female 10,530)
65 years and over: 19% (male 2,302; female 3,935) (1999 est.)
Population growth rate: 0.31% (1999 est.)
Birth rate: 10.7 births/1,000 population (1999 est.)
Death rate: 11.79 deaths/1,000 population (1999 est.)
Net migration rate: 4.17 migrant(s)/1,000 population (1999 est.)
Sex ratio:
at birth: 1.05 male(s)/female
under 15 years: 1.03 male(s)/female
15-64 years: 0.95 male(s)/female
65 years and over: 0.59 male(s)/female
total population: 0.88 male(s)/female (1999 est.)
Infant mortality rate: 6.47 deaths/1,000 live births (1999 est.)
Life expectancy at birth:
total population: 78.58 years
male: 75 years
female: 82.35 years (1999 est.)
Total fertility rate: 1.7 children born/woman (1999 est.)
Nationality:
noun: Monegasque(s) or Monacan(s)
adjective: Monegasque or Monacan
Ethnic groups: French 47%, Monegasque 16%, Italian 16%, other 21%
Religions: Roman Catholic 95%
Languages: French (official), English, Italian, Monegasque
Literacy: NA

Government

Country name:
conventional long form: Principality of Monaco
conventional short form: Monaco
local long form: Principaute de Monaco
local short form: Monaco
Data code: MN
Government type: constitutional monarchy
Capital: Monaco
Administrative divisions: none; there are no first-order administrative divisions as defined by the US Government, but there are four quarters (quartiers, singular - quartier); Fontvieille, La Condamine, Monaco-Ville, Monte-Carlo
Independence: 1419 (beginning of the rule by the House of Grimaldi)
National holiday: National Day, 19 November
Constitution: 17 December 1962
Legal system: based on French law; has not accepted compulsory ICJ jurisdiction
Suffrage: 21 years of age; universal

Executive branch:
chief of state: Prince RAINIER III (since 9 May 1949); Heir Apparent Prince ALBERT Alexandre Louis Pierre, son of the monarch (born 14 March 1958)
head of government: Minister of State Michel LEVEQUE (since 3 February 1997)
cabinet: Council of Government is under the authority of the monarch
elections: none; the monarch is hereditary; minister of state appointed by the monarch from a list of three French national candidates presented by the French Government
Legislative branch: unicameral National Council or Conseil National (18 seats; members are elected by popular vote to serve five-year terms)
elections: last held 1 and 8 February 1998 (next to be held NA January 2003)
election results: percent of vote by party - NA; seats by party - National and Democratic Union 18
Judicial branch: Supreme Court or Tribunal Supreme, judges named by the monarch on the basis of nominations by the National Council
Political parties and leaders: National and Democratic Union or UND [Jean-Louis CAMPORA]
International organization participation: ACCT, ECE, IAEA, ICAO, ICRM, IFRCS, IHO, IMO, Inmarsat, Intelsat, Interpol, IOC, ITU, OPCW, OSCE, UN, UNCTAD, UNESCO, UPU, WHO, WIPO, WMO
Diplomatic representation in the US: Monaco does not have an embassy in the US
consulate(s): New York
Diplomatic representation from the US: the US does not have an embassy in Monaco; the US Consul General in Marseille (France) is accredited to Monaco
Flag description: two equal horizontal bands of red (top) and white; similar to the flag of Indonesia which is longer and the flag of Poland which is white (top) and red

Economy

Economy - overview: Monaco, situated on the French Mediterranean coast, is a popular resort, attracting tourists to its casino and pleasant climate. The Principality has successfully sought to diversify into services and small, high-value-added, nonpolluting industries. The state has no income tax and low business taxes and thrives as a tax haven both for individuals who have established residence and for foreign companies that have set up businesses and offices. The state retains monopolies in a number of sectors, including tobacco, the telephone network, and the postal service. About 55% of Monaco's annual revenue comes from value-added taxes on hotels, banks, and the industrial sector. Living standards are high, roughly comparable to those in prosperous French metropolitan areas.
GDP: purchasing power parity - $800 million (1996 est.)
GDP - real growth rate: NA%
GDP - per capita: purchasing power parity - $25,000 (1996 est.)

Monaco (continued)

GDP - composition by sector:
agriculture: NA%
industry: NA%
services: NA%
Population below poverty line: NA%
Household income or consumption by percentage share:
lowest 10%: NA%
highest 10%: NA%
Inflation rate (consumer prices): NA%
Labor force: 30,540 (January 1994)
Unemployment rate: 3.1% (1994)
Budget:
revenues: $518 million
expenditures: $531 million, including capital expenditures of $NA (1995)
Industrial production growth rate: NA%
Electricity - production: NA kWh
Electricity - production by source:
fossil fuel: NA%
hydro: NA%
nuclear: NA%
other: NA%
Electricity - consumption: NA kWh
Electricity - exports: NA kWh
Electricity - imports: NA kWh
Agriculture - products: none
Exports: $NA; full customs integration with France, which collects and rebates Monegasque trade duties; also participates in EU market system through customs union with France
Imports: $NA; full customs integration with France, which collects and rebates Monegasque trade duties; also participates in EU market system through customs union with France
Debt - external: $NA
Economic aid - recipient: $NA
Currency: 1 French franc (F) = 100 centimes
Exchange rates: French francs (F) per US$1 - 5.65 (January 1999), 5.8995 (1998), 5.8367 (1997), 5.1155 (1996), 4.9915 (1995), 5.5520 (1994)
Fiscal year: calendar year

Communications

Telephones: 53,180 (1994 est.)
Telephone system: automatic telephone system
domestic: NA
international: no satellite earth stations; connected by cable into the French communications system
Radio broadcast stations: AM 3, FM 4, shortwave 0
Radios: 33,000 (1994 est.)
Television broadcast stations: 5 (1997)
Televisions: 24,000 (1994 est.)

Transportation

Railways:
total: 1.7 km
standard gauge: 1.7 km 1.435-m gauge

Highways:
total: 50 km
paved: 50 km
unpaved: 0 km (1996 est.)
Ports and harbors: Monaco
Merchant marine: none
Airports: linked to airport in Nice, France, by helicopter service

Military

Military - note: defense is the responsibility of France

Transnational Issues

Disputes - international: none

Mongolia

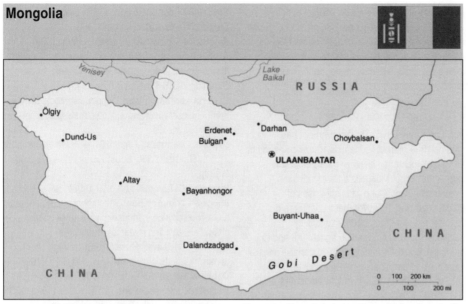

Geography

Location: Northern Asia, between China and Russia
Geographic coordinates: 46 00 N, 105 00 E
Map references: Asia
Area:
total: 1.565 million sq km
land: 1.565 million sq km
water: 0 sq km
Area - comparative: slightly smaller than Alaska
Land boundaries:
total: 8,114 km
border countries: China 4,673 km, Russia 3,441 km
Coastline: 0 km (landlocked)
Maritime claims: none (landlocked)
Climate: desert; continental (large daily and seasonal temperature ranges)
Terrain: vast semidesert and desert plains; mountains in west and southwest; Gobi Desert in southeast
Elevation extremes:
lowest point: Hoh Nuur 518 m
highest point: Tavan Bogd Uul 4,374 m
Natural resources: oil, coal, copper, molybdenum, tungsten, phosphates, tin, nickel, zinc, wolfram, fluorspar, gold
Land use:
arable land: 1%
permanent crops: 0%
permanent pastures: 80%
forests and woodland: 9%
other: 10% (1993 est.)
Irrigated land: 800 sq km (1993 est.)
Natural hazards: dust storms can occur in the spring; grassland fires
Environment - current issues: limited natural fresh water resources; policies of the former communist regime promoting rapid urbanization and industrial growth have raised concerns about their negative effects on the environment; the burning of soft coal and the concentration of factories in Ulaanbaatar have severely polluted the air; deforestation, overgrazing, the converting of virgin land to agricultural production have increased soil erosion from wind and rain; desertification; mining activities have also had a deleterious effect on the environment
Environment - international agreements:
party to: Biodiversity, Climate Change, Desertification, Endangered Species, Environmental Modification, Hazardous Wastes, Law of the Sea, Nuclear Test Ban, Ozone Layer Protection, Wetlands
signed, but not ratified: none of the selected agreements
Geography - note: landlocked; strategic location between China and Russia

People

Population: 2,617,379 (July 1999 est.)
Age structure:
0-14 years: 36% (male 480,087; female 464,609)
15-64 years: 60% (male 787,222; female 787,405)
65 years and over: 4% (male 42,219; female 55,837) (1999 est.)
Population growth rate: 1.45% (1999 est.)
Birth rate: 22.51 births/1,000 population (1999 est.)
Death rate: 7.97 deaths/1,000 population (1999 est.)
Net migration rate: 0 migrant(s)/1,000 population (1999 est.)
Sex ratio:
at birth: 1.05 male(s)/female
under 15 years: 1.03 male(s)/female
15-64 years: 1 male(s)/female
65 years and over: 0.76 male(s)/female
total population: 1 male(s)/female (1999 est.)
Infant mortality rate: 64.63 deaths/1,000 live births (1999 est.)
Life expectancy at birth:
total population: 61.81 years
male: 59.71 years
female: 64.02 years (1999 est.)
Total fertility rate: 2.6 children born/woman (1999 est.)
Nationality:
noun: Mongolian(s)
adjective: Mongolian
Ethnic groups: Mongol 90%, Kazakh 4%, Chinese 2%, Russian 2%, other 2%
Religions: predominantly Tibetan Buddhist, Muslim 4%
note: previously limited religious activity because of communist regime
Languages: Khalkha Mongol 90%, Turkic, Russian, Chinese
Literacy:
definition: age 15 and over can read and write
total population: 82.9%
male: 88.6%
female: 77.2% (1988 est.)

Government

Country name:
conventional long form: none
conventional short form: Mongolia
local long form: none
local short form: Mongol Uls
former: Outer Mongolia
Data code: MG
Government type: republic
Capital: Ulaanbaatar
Administrative divisions: 18 provinces (aymguud, singular - aymag) and 3 municipalities* (hotuud, singular - hot); Arhangay, Bayanhongor, Bayan-Olgiy, Bulgan, Darhan*, Dornod, Dornogovi, Dundgovi, Dzavhan, Erdenet*, Govi-Altay, Hentiy, Hovd, Hovsgol, Omnogovi, Ovorhangay, Selenge, Suhbaatar, Tov, Ulaanbaatar*, Uvs
Independence: 13 March 1921 (from China)
National holiday: National Day, 11 July (1921)
Constitution: 12 February 1992
Legal system: blend of Russian, Chinese, and Turkish systems of law; no constitutional provision for judicial review of legislative acts; has not accepted compulsory ICJ jurisdiction
Suffrage: 18 years of age; universal
Executive branch:
chief of state: President Natsagiyn BAGABANDI (since 20 June 1997)
head of government: Prime Minister Janlavyn NARANTSATSRALT (since 9 December 1998)
cabinet: Cabinet appointed by the State Great Hural in consultation with the president
elections: president nominated by parties in the State Great Hural and elected by popular vote for a four-year term; election last held 18 May 1997 (next to be held summer 2001); following legislative elections, the leader of the majority party or majority coalition is usually elected prime minister by the State Great Hural
election results: Natsagiyn BAGABANDI elected president; percent of vote - Natsagiyn BAGABANDI (MPRP) 60.8%, Punsalmaagiyn OCHIRBAT (MNDP and MSDP) 29.8%, Jambyn GOMBOJAV (MUTP) 6.6%; following five months of political deadlock which left Mongolia without a working government, Janlavyn NARANTSATSRALT was elected prime minister on 9 December 1998 by a vote in the State Great Hural of

36 to 21, with nine abstentions and 10 absentees

Legislative branch: unicameral State Great Hural (76 seats; members elected by popular vote to serve four-year terms)

elections: last held 30 June 1996 (next to be held NA June 2000)

election results: percent of vote by party - DUC 66%, MPRP 33%, MCP 1%; seats by party - DUC 50 (MNDP 34, MSDP 13, independents 3), MPRP 25, MCP 1

Judicial branch: Supreme Court, serves as appeals court for people's and provincial courts, but to date rarely overturns verdicts of lower courts, judges are nominated by the General Council of Courts for approval by the State Great Hural

Political parties and leaders: Mongolian People's Revolutionary Party or MPRP [N. ENKHBAYAR, general secretary]; Democratic Union Coalition or DUC [Mendsaihan ENHSAIHAN, general secretary] (includes Mongolian National Democratic Party or MNDP [T. ELBEGDORJ, chairman], Mongolian Social Democratic Party or MSDP [Radnaasumbereliyn GONCHIGDORJ, chairman], Green Party [NYAM]; and Mongolian Democratic Party of Believers or MDPB [leader NA]); Mongolian Conservative Party or MCP [JARGALSAIHAN]; Democratic Power Coalition [D. BYAMBASUREN, chairman] (includes Mongolian Democratic Renaissance Party or MDRP [BYAMBASUREN, chairman] and Mongolian People's Party or MPP [leader NA]); Mongolian National Solidarity Party or MNSP [leader NA]; Bourgeois Party/Capitalist Party [VARGALSAIHAN, chairman]; United Heritage Party or UHP [B. JAMTSAI] (includes United Party of Herdsman and Farmers [leader NA], Independence Party [leader NA], Traditional United Conservative Party [leader NA], and Mongolian United Private Property Owners Party [leader NA]); Workers' Party [leader NA]

International organization participation: AsDB, ASEAN (observer), CCC, ESCAP, FAO, G-77, IAEA, IBRD, ICAO, ICFTU, ICRM, IDA, IFAD, IFC, IFRCS, ILO, IMF, IMO, Intelsat, Interpol, IOC, ISO, ITU, OPCW, UN, UNCTAD, UNESCO, UNIDO, UPU, WHO, WIPO, WMO, WToO, WTrO

Diplomatic representation in the US:

chief of mission: Ambassador Jalbuugiyn CHOINHOR

chancery: 2833 M Street NW, Washington, DC 20007

telephone: [1] (202) 333-7117

FAX: [1] (202) 298-9227

consulate(s) general: New York

Diplomatic representation from the US:

chief of mission: Ambassador Alphonse F. LA PORTA

embassy: inner north side of the Big Ring, just west of the Selbe Gol, Ulaanbaatar

mailing address: c/o American Embassy Beijing, Micro Region 11, Big Ring Road, C.P.O. 1021, Ulaanbaatar 13; PSC 461, Box 300, FPO AP 96521-0002

telephone: [976] (1) 329095

FAX: [976] (1) 320776

Flag description: three equal, vertical bands of red (hoist side), blue, and red; centered on the hoist-side red band in yellow is the national emblem ("soyombo" - a columnar arrangement of abstract and geometric representation for fire, sun, moon, earth, water, and the yin-yang symbol)

Economy

Economy - overview: The government has embraced free-market economics, freezing spending, easing price controls, liberalizing domestic and international trade. Mongolia's severe climate, scattered population, and wide expanses of unproductive land, however, have constrained economic development. Economic activity traditionally has been based on agriculture and the breeding of livestock. In past years, extensive mineral resources had been developed with Soviet support; total Soviet assistance at its height amounted to 30% of GDP, but disappeared almost overnight in 1990-91. The mining and processing of coal, copper, molybdenum, tin, tungsten, and gold account for a large part of industrial production. The Mongolian leadership has been soliciting support from foreign donors and economic growth picked up in 1997 and 1998 after stalling in 1996 due to a series of natural disasters and declines in world prices of copper and cashmere. Mongolia joined the World Trade Organization in 1997.

GDP: purchasing power parity - $5.8 billion (1998 est.)

GDP - real growth rate: 3.5% (1998 est.)

GDP - per capita: purchasing power parity - $2,250 (1998 est.)

GDP - composition by sector:

agriculture: 31%

industry: 35%

services: 34% (1997 est.)

Population below poverty line: 36.3% (1995 est.)

Household income or consumption by percentage share:

lowest 10%: 2.9%

highest 10%: 24.5% (1995)

Inflation rate (consumer prices): 6% (1998)

Labor force: 1.115 million (mid-1993 est.)

Labor force - by occupation: primarily herding/agricultural

Unemployment rate: 4.5% (1998)

Budget:

revenues: $260 million (1998)

expenditures: $330 million (1998)

Industries: copper, construction materials, mining (particularly coal); food and beverage, processing of animal products

Industrial production growth rate: 4.5% (1997 est.)

Electricity - production: 2.3 billion kWh (1996)

Electricity - production by source:

fossil fuel: 100%

hydro: 0%

nuclear: 0%

other: 0% (1996)

Electricity - consumption: 2.681 billion kWh (1996)

Electricity - exports: 0 kWh (1996)

Electricity - imports: 381 million kWh (1996)

Agriculture - products: wheat, barley, potatoes, forage crops; sheep, goats, cattle, camels, horses

Exports: $316.8 million (f.o.b., 1998)

Exports - commodities: copper, livestock, animal products, cashmere, wool, hides, fluorspar, other nonferrous metals

Exports - partners: China 30.1%, Switzerland 21.5%, Russia 12.1%, South Korea 9.7%, US 8.1% (1998)

Imports: $472.4 million (f.o.b., 1998)

Imports - commodities: machinery and equipment, fuels, food products, industrial consumer goods, chemicals, building materials, sugar, tea

Imports - partners: Russia 30.6%, China 13.3%, Japan 11.7%, South Korea 7.5%, US 6.9% (1998)

Debt - external: $500 million (1996 est.)

Economic aid - recipient: $250 million (1998 est.)

Currency: 1 tughrik (Tug) = 100 mongos

Exchange rates: tughriks (Tug) per US$1 - 902 (January 1999), 840.83 (1998), 789.99 (1997), 548.40 (1996), 449.61 (1995), 412.72 (1994)

Fiscal year: calendar year

Communications

Telephones: 93,600 (1998)

Telephone system:

domestic: NA

international: satellite earth station - 1 Intersputnik (Indian Ocean Region)

Radio broadcast stations: AM 12, FM 1, shortwave 0

Radios: 220,000

Television broadcast stations: 1 (in addition, there are 18 provincial repeaters) (1997)

Televisions: 120,000 (1993 est.)

Transportation

Railways:

total: 1,928 km

broad gauge: 1,928 km 1.524-m gauge (1994)

Highways:

total: 46,470 km

paved: 3,730 km

unpaved: 42,740 km (1997 est.)

note: much of the unpaved rural road system consists of rough cross-country tracks

Waterways: 397 km of principal routes (1988)

Ports and harbors: none

Airports: 34 (1994 est.)

Airports - with paved runways:

total: 8

2,438 to 3,047 m: 7

under 914 m: 1 (1994 est.)

Airports - with unpaved runways:

total: 26

over 3,047 m: 3

2,438 to 3,047 m: 5

1,524 to 2,437 m: 10

Mongolia (continued)

914 to 1,523 m: 3
under 914 m: 5 (1994 est.)

Military

Military branches: Mongolian People's Army (includes Internal Security Forces and Frontier Guards), Air Force
Military manpower - military age: 18 years of age
Military manpower - availability:
males age 15-49: 702,141 (1999 est.)
Military manpower - fit for military service:
males age 15-49: 457,270 (1999 est.)
Military manpower - reaching military age annually:
males: 28,613 (1999 est.)
Military expenditures - dollar figure: $20.3 million (1997)
Military expenditures - percent of GDP: 2% (1997)

Transnational Issues

Disputes - international: none

Montserrat
(overseas territory of the UK)

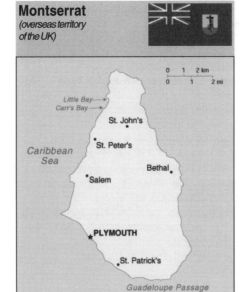

Geography

Location: Caribbean, island in the Caribbean Sea, southeast of Puerto Rico
Geographic coordinates: 16 45 N, 62 12 W
Map references: Central America and the Caribbean
Area:
total: 100 sq km
land: 100 sq km
water: 0 sq km
Area - comparative: about 0.6 times the size of Washington, DC
Land boundaries: 0 km
Coastline: 40 km
Maritime claims:
exclusive fishing zone: 200 nm
territorial sea: 3 nm
Climate: tropical; little daily or seasonal temperature variation
Terrain: volcanic islands, mostly mountainous, with small coastal lowland
Elevation extremes:
lowest point: Caribbean Sea 0 m
highest point: Chances Peak 914 m
Natural resources: NEGL
Land use:
arable land: 20%
permanent crops: 0%
permanent pastures: 10%
forests and woodland: 40%
other: 30% (1993 est.)
Irrigated land: NA sq km
Natural hazards: severe hurricanes (June to November); volcanic eruptions (full-scale eruptions of the Soufriere Hills volcano occurred during 1996-97)
Environment - current issues: land erosion occurs on slopes that have been cleared for cultivation
Environment - international agreements:
party to: NA
signed, but not ratified: NA

People

Population: 12,853 (July 1999 est.)
note: demographic figures include an estimated 8,000 refugees who left the island following the resumption of volcanic activity in July 1995
Age structure:
0-14 years: NA
15-64 years: NA
65 years and over: NA
Population growth rate: 0.21% (1999 est.)
Birth rate: 13.87 births/1,000 population (1999 est.)
Death rate: 9.88 deaths/1,000 population (1999 est.)
Net migration rate: -1.94 migrant(s)/1,000 population (1999 est.)
Infant mortality rate: 12 deaths/1,000 live births (1999 est.)
Life expectancy at birth:
total population: 75.56 years
male: 73.79 years
female: 77.37 years (1999 est.)
Total fertility rate: 1.78 children born/woman (1999 est.)
Nationality:
noun: Montserratian(s)
adjective: Montserratian
Ethnic groups: black, white
Religions: Anglican, Methodist, Roman Catholic, Pentecostal, Seventh-Day Adventist, other Christian denominations
Languages: English
Literacy:
definition: age 15 and over has ever attended school
total population: 97%
male: 97%
female: 97% (1970 est.)

Government

Country name:
conventional long form: none
conventional short form: Montserrat
Data code: MH
Dependency status: overseas territory of the UK
Government type: NA
Capital: Plymouth (abandoned in 1997 due to volcanic activity; interim government buildings have been built at Brades, in the Carr's Bay/Little Bay vicinity at the northwest end of Montserrat)
Administrative divisions: 3 parishes; Saint Anthony, Saint Georges, Saint Peter's
Independence: none (overseas territory of the UK)
National holiday: Celebration of the Birthday of the Queen (second Saturday of June)
Constitution: present constitution came into force 19 December 1989
Legal system: English common law and statutory law
Suffrage: 18 years of age; universal
Executive branch:
chief of state: Queen ELIZABETH II (since 6 February 1952), represented by Governor Anthony John ABBOTT (since NA September 1997)

Montserrat (continued)

head of government: Chief Minister David BRANDT (since 22 August 1997)
cabinet: Executive Council consists of the governor, the chief minister, three other ministers, the attorney general, and the finance secretary
elections: the monarch is hereditary; governor appointed by the monarch; following legislative elections, the leader of the majority party usually becomes chief minister; note - as a result of the last election, a coalition party was formed between NPP, NDP, and one of the independent candidates
Legislative branch: unicameral Legislative Council (11 seats, 7 popularly elected; members serve five-year terms)
elections: last held 11 November 1996 (next to be held by NA 2001)
election results: percent of vote by party - NA; seats by party - PPA 2, MNR 2, NPP 1, independent 2
Judicial branch: Eastern Caribbean Supreme Court (based in Saint Lucia) (one judge of the Supreme Court is a resident of the islands and presides over the High Court)
Political parties and leaders: National Progressive Party or NPP [Reuben T. MEADE]; Movement for National Reconstruction or MNR [Percival Austin BRAMBLE]; People's Progressive Alliance or PPA [Bertrand OSBORNE]; National Development Party or NDP [leader NA]
International organization participation: Caricom, CDB, ECLAC (associate), ICFTU, Interpol (subbureau), OECS, WCL
Diplomatic representation in the US: none (overseas territory of the UK)
Diplomatic representation from the US: none (overseas territory of the UK)
Flag description: blue, with the flag of the UK in the upper hoist-side quadrant and the Montserratian coat of arms centered in the outer half of the flag; the coat of arms features a woman standing beside a yellow harp with her arm around a black cross

Economy

Economy - overview: Severe volcanic activity, which began in July 1995, put a damper on this small, open economy throughout 1996-98. A catastrophic eruption in June 1997 closed the air and sea ports, causing further economic and social dislocation. Two-thirds of the 12,000 inhabitants fled the island. Some began to return in 1998, but lack of housing limited the number. The agriculture sector continued to be affected by the lack of suitable land for farming and the destruction of crops. Construction was the dominant activity in 1997 and 1998. GDP probably declined again in 1998. Prospects for the economy depend largely on developments in relation to the volcano and on public sector construction activity. The UK has committed about $100 million in 1996-98 to help reconstruct the economy.
GDP: purchasing power parity - $36 million (1997 est.)
GDP - real growth rate: -18.5% (1997 est.)
GDP - per capita: purchasing power parity - $NA

GDP - composition by sector:
agriculture: 5.4%
industry: 13.6%
services: 81% (1996 est.)
Population below poverty line: NA%
Household income or consumption by percentage share:
lowest 10%: NA%
highest 10%: NA%
Inflation rate (consumer prices): 5% (1997)
Labor force: 4,521 (1992); note - later substantially lowered by flight of people from volcanic activity
Labor force - by occupation: community, social, and personal services 40.5%, construction 13.5%, trade, restaurants, and hotels 12.3%, manufacturing 10.5%, agriculture, forestry, and fishing 8.8%, other 14.4% (1983 est.)
Unemployment rate: 20% (1996 est.)
Budget:
revenues: $31.4 million
expenditures: $31.6 million, including capital expenditures of $8.4 million (1997 est.)
Industries: tourism, rum, textiles, electronic appliances
Industrial production growth rate: NA%
Electricity - production: 15 million kWh (1996)
Electricity - production by source:
fossil fuel: 100%
hydro: 0%
nuclear: 0%
other: 0% (1996)
Electricity - consumption: 15 million kWh (1996)
Electricity - exports: 0 kWh (1996)
Electricity - imports: 0 kWh (1996)
Agriculture - products: cabbages, carrots, cucumbers, tomatoes, onions, peppers; livestock products
Exports: $8.2 million (1997)
Exports - commodities: electronic components, plastic bags, apparel, hot peppers, live plants, cattle
Exports - partners: US, Ireland
Imports: $26.1 million (1997)
Imports - commodities: machinery and transportation equipment, foodstuffs, manufactured goods, fuels, lubricants, and related materials
Imports - partners: NA
Debt - external: $8.9 million (1997)
Economic aid - recipient: $9.8 million (1995); note - about $100 million (1996-98) in reconstruction aid from the UK
Currency: 1 East Caribbean dollar (EC$) = 100 cents
Exchange rates: East Caribbean dollars (EC$) per US$1 - 2.7000 (fixed rate since 1976)
Fiscal year: 1 April - 31 March

Communications

Telephones: 3,000
Telephone system:
domestic: NA
international: NA
Radio broadcast stations: AM 8, FM 4, shortwave 0

Radios: 6,000 (1992 est.)
Television broadcast stations: 1 (1997)
Televisions: 2,000 (1992 est.)

Transportation

Railways: 0 km
Highways:
total: 269 km
paved: 203 km
unpaved: 66 km (1995)
Ports and harbors: Plymouth (abandoned), Little Bay (anchorages and ferry landing), Carr's Bay
Merchant marine: none
Airports: 1 (1998 est.)
Airports - with paved runways:
total: 1
914 to 1,523 m: 1 (1998 est.)

Military

Military branches: Police Force
Military - note: defense is the responsibility of the UK

Transnational Issues

Disputes - international: none

Morocco

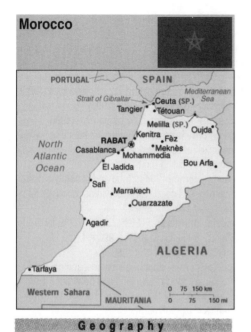

Geography

Location: Northern Africa, bordering the North Atlantic Ocean and the Mediterranean Sea, between Algeria and Western Sahara
Geographic coordinates: 32 00 N, 5 00 W
Map references: Africa
Area:
total: 446,550 sq km
land: 446,300 sq km
water: 250 sq km
Area - comparative: slightly larger than California
Land boundaries:
total: 2,017.9 km
border countries: Algeria 1,559 km, Western Sahara 443 km, Spain (Ceuta) 6.3 km, Spain (Melilla) 9.6 km
Coastline: 1,835 km
Maritime claims:
contiguous zone: 24 nm
continental shelf: 200-m depth or to the depth of exploitation
exclusive economic zone: 200 nm
territorial sea: 12 nm
Climate: Mediterranean, becoming more extreme in the interior
Terrain: northern coast and interior are mountainous with large areas of bordering plateaus, intermontane valleys, and rich coastal plains
Elevation extremes:
lowest point: Sebkha Tah -55 m
highest point: Jebel Toubkal 4,165 m
Natural resources: phosphates, iron ore, manganese, lead, zinc, fish, salt
Land use:
arable land: 21%
permanent crops: 1%
permanent pastures: 47%
forests and woodland: 20%
other: 11% (1993 est.)
Irrigated land: 12,580 sq km (1993 est.)
Natural hazards: northern mountains geologically

unstable and subject to earthquakes; periodic droughts
Environment - current issues: land degradation/desertification (soil erosion resulting from farming of marginal areas, overgrazing, destruction of vegetation); water supplies contaminated by raw sewage; siltation of reservoirs; oil pollution of coastal waters
Environment - international agreements:
party to: Biodiversity, Climate Change, Desertification, Endangered Species, Hazardous Wastes, Marine Dumping, Nuclear Test Ban, Ozone Layer Protection, Ship Pollution, Wetlands
signed, but not ratified: Environmental Modification, Law of the Sea
Geography - note: strategic location along Strait of Gibraltar

People

Population: 29,661,636 (July 1999 est.)
Age structure:
0-14 years: 36% (male 5,409,322; female 5,208,742)
15-64 years: 60% (male 8,773,625; female 8,922,976)
65 years and over: 4% (male 619,164; female 727,807) (1999 est.)
Population growth rate: 1.84% (1999 est.)
Birth rate: 25.78 births/1,000 population (1999 est.)
Death rate: 6.12 deaths/1,000 population (1999 est.)
Net migration rate: -1.27 migrant(s)/1,000 population (1999 est.)
Sex ratio:
at birth: 1.05 male(s)/female
under 15 years: 1.04 male(s)/female
15-64 years: 0.98 male(s)/female
65 years and over: 0.85 male(s)/female
total population: 1 male(s)/female (1999 est.)
Infant mortality rate: 50.96 deaths/1,000 live births (1999 est.)
Life expectancy at birth:
total population: 68.87 years
male: 66.85 years
female: 70.99 years (1999 est.)
Total fertility rate: 3.24 children born/woman (1999 est.)
Nationality:
noun: Moroccan(s)
adjective: Moroccan
Ethnic groups: Arab-Berber 99.1%, other 0.7%, Jewish 0.2%
Religions: Muslim 98.7%, Christian 1.1%, Jewish 0.2%
Languages: Arabic (official), Berber dialects, French often the language of business, government, and diplomacy
Literacy:
definition: age 15 and over can read and write
total population: 43.7%
male: 56.6%
female: 31% (1995 est.)

Government

Country name:
conventional long form: Kingdom of Morocco
conventional short form: Morocco
local long form: Al Mamlakah al Maghribiyah
local short form: Al Maghrib
Data code: MO
Government type: constitutional monarchy
Capital: Rabat
Administrative divisions: 37 provinces and 2 wilayas*; Agadir, Al Hoceima, Azilal, Beni Mellal, Ben Slimane, Boulemane, Casablanca*, Chaouen, El Jadida, El Kelaa des Srarhna, Er Rachidia, Essaouira, Fes, Figuig, Guelmim, Ifrane, Kenitra, Khemisset, Khenifra, Khouribga, Laayoune, Larache, Marrakech, Meknes, Nador, Ouarzazate, Oujda, Rabat-Sale*, Safi, Settat, Sidi Kacem, Tanger, Tan-Tan, Taounate, Taroudannt, Tata, Taza, Tetouan, Tiznit
note: three additional provinces of Ad Dakhla (Oued Eddahab), Boujdour, and Es Smara as well as parts of Tan-Tan and Laayoune fall within Moroccan-claimed Western Sahara; decentralization/regionalization law passed by the legislature in March 1997 creating many new provinces/regions; specific details and scope of the reorganization not yet available
Independence: 2 March 1956 (from France)
National holiday: National Day, 3 March (1961) (anniversary of King HASSAN II's accession to the throne)
Constitution: 10 March 1972, revised 4 September 1992, amended (to create bicameral legislature) September 1996
Legal system: based on Islamic law and French and Spanish civil law system; judicial review of legislative acts in Constitutional Chamber of Supreme Court
Suffrage: 21 years of age; universal
Executive branch:
chief of state: King HASSAN II (since 3 March 1961)
head of government: Prime Minister Abderrahmane YOUSSOUFI (since 14 March 1998)
cabinet: Council of Ministers appointed by the monarch
elections: none; the monarch is hereditary; prime minister appointed by the monarch following legislative elections
Legislative branch: bicameral Parliament consists of an upper house or Chamber of Counselors (270 seats; members elected indirectly by local councils, professional organizations, and labor syndicates for nine-year terms; one-third of the members are renewed every three years) and a lower house or Chamber of Representatives (325 seats; members elected by popular vote for five-year terms)
elections: Chamber of Counselors - last held 5 December 1997 (next to be held NA December 2000); Chamber of Representatives - last held 14 November 1997 (next to be held NA November 2002)
election results: Chamber of Counselors - percent of vote by party - NA; seats by party - RNI 42, MDS 33, UC 28, MP 27, PND 21, IP 21, USFP 16, MNP 15, UT 13, FFD 12, CDT 11, UTM 8, PPS 7, PSD 4, PDI 4,

Morocco *(continued)*

UGTM 3, UNMT 2, other 3; Chamber of Representatives - percent of vote by party - NA; seats by party - USFP 57, UC 50, RNI 46, MP 40, MDS 32, IP 32, MNP 19, PND 10, MPCD 9, PPS 9, FFD 9, PSD 5, OADP 4, PA 2, PDI 1

Judicial branch: Supreme Court, judges are appointed on the recommendation of the Supreme Council of the Judiciary, presided over by the monarch

Political parties and leaders:

opposition: Socialist Union of Popular Forces or USFP [Abderrahmane YOUSSOUFI]; Istiqlal Party or IP [Abbas EL-FASSI]; Party of Progress and Socialism or PPS [Moulay Ismail al ALAOUI]; Organization of Democratic and Popular Action or OADP [Mohamed BENSAID]; Democratic Socialist Party or PSD [Issa al-OUARDIGHI]; Democratic Forces Front or FFD [Thami KHIARI]; Popular Constitutional and Democratic Movement or MPCD [Dr. Abdelkarim al-KHATIB]

pro-government: Constitutional Union or UC [Abdellatif SEMLALI]; Popular Movement or MP [Mohamed LAENSER]; National Democratic Party or PND [Mohamed Arsalane EL-JADIDI]; National Popular Movement or MNP [Mahjoubi AHARDANE]; Social Democratic Movement or MDS [Mahmoud ARCHANE]

independents: National Rally of Independents or RNI [Ahmed OSMAN]; Democracy and Istiqlal Party or PDI [Abdelwahed MACHE]; Action Party or PA [Ahmed ABAKIL]; Labor Party or UT [leader NA]

labor unions and community organizations (indirect elections only): Democratic Confederation of Labor or CDT [Noubir AMAOUI]; General Union of Moroccan Workers or UGTM [Abderrazzak AFILAL]; Moroccan Union of Workers or UTM [Mahjoub BENSEDIQ]; Party of Shura and Istiqla [Abdelwaheb MAASH]; Labor Union Commissions or CS [leader NA]; Democratic Trade Union or SD [leader NA]; Association of Popular Trade Unions or ADP [leader NA]; Democratic National Trade Union or USND [leader NA]; Moroccan National Workers Union or UNMT [leader NA]

International organization participation: ABEDA, ACCT (associate), AfDB, AFESD, AL, AMF, AMU, CCC, EBRD, ECA, FAO, G-77, IAEA, IBRD, ICAO, ICC, ICFTU, ICRM, IDA, IDB, IFAD, IFC, IFRCS, IHO (pending member), ILO, IMF, IMO, Intelsat, Interpol, IOC, IOM (observer), ISO, ITU, NAM, OAS (observer), OIC, OPCW, OSCE (partner), UN, UNCTAD, UNESCO, UNHCR, UNIDO, UPU, WHO, WIPO, WMO, WToO, WTrO

Diplomatic representation in the US:

chief of mission: Ambassador Mohamed BENAISSA

chancery: 1601 21st Street NW, Washington, DC 20009

telephone: [1] (202) 462-7979 through 7982

FAX: [1] (202) 265-0161

consulate(s) general: New York

Diplomatic representation from the US:

chief of mission: Ambassador Edward M. GABRIEL

embassy: 2 Avenue de Marrakech, Rabat

mailing address: PSC 74, Box 3, APO AE 09718

telephone: [212] (7) 76 22 65

FAX: [212] (7) 76 56 61

consulate(s) general: Casablanca

Flag description: red with a green pentacle (five-pointed, linear star) known as Solomon's seal in the center of the flag; green is the traditional color of Islam

Economy

Economy - overview: Morocco faces the problems typical of developing countries - restraining government spending, reducing constraints on private activity and foreign trade, and keeping inflation within manageable bounds. Since the early 1980s the government has pursued an economic program toward these objectives with the support of the IMF, the World Bank, and the Paris Club of creditors. The dirham is now fully convertible for current account transactions; reforms of the financial sector have been implemented; and state enterprises are slowly being privatized. Drought conditions in 1997 depressed activity in the key agricultural sector, holding down exports and contributing to a 2.2% contraction in real GDP. Favorable rainfalls in the fall of 1997 have led to 6.8% real GDP growth in 1998. Growth is forecast to be about 4.0% in 1999. Formidable long-term challenges include: servicing the external debt; preparing the economy for freer trade with the EU; and improving education and attracting foreign investment to improve living standards and job propects for Morocco's youthful population.

GDP: purchasing power parity - $92.9 billion (1998 est.)

GDP - real growth rate: 6.8% (1998 est.)

GDP - per capita: purchasing power parity - $3,200 (1998 est.)

GDP - composition by sector:

agriculture: 14%

industry: 33%

services: 53% (1997)

Population below poverty line: 13.1% (1990-91 est.)

Household income or consumption by percentage share:

lowest 10%: 2.8%

highest 10%: 30.5% (1990-91)

Inflation rate (consumer prices): 2%-3% (1998 est.)

Labor force: 11 million (1997 est.)

Labor force - by occupation: agriculture 50%, services 26%, industry 15%, other 9% (1985)

Unemployment rate: 19% (1998 est.)

Budget:

revenues: $8.4 billion

expenditures: $10 billion, including capital expenditures of $1.8 billion (FY97/98 est.)

Industries: phosphate rock mining and processing, food processing, leather goods, textiles, construction, tourism

Industrial production growth rate: 4.1% (1997 est.)

Electricity - production: 11.5 billion kWh (1996)

Electricity - production by source:

fossil fuel: 95.65%

hydro: 4.35%

nuclear: 0%

other: 0% (1996)

Electricity - consumption: 12.52 billion kWh (1996)

Electricity - exports: 0 kWh (1996)

Electricity - imports: 1.02 billion kWh (1996)

Agriculture - products: barley, wheat, citrus, wine, vegetables, olives; livestock

Exports: $7 billion (f.o.b., 1997)

Exports - commodities: food and beverages 30%, semiprocessed goods 23%, consumer goods 21%, phosphates 17% (1995 est.)

Exports - partners: EU 63%, Japan 7.7%, India 6.6%, US 3.4%, Libya 3.4% (1996 est.)

Imports: $10 billion (c.i.f., 1997)

Imports - commodities: semiprocessed goods 26%, capital goods 25%, food and beverages 18%, fuel and lubricants 15%, consumer goods 12%, raw materials 4% (1995 est.)

Imports - partners: EU 57%, US 6.6%, Saudi Arabia 5.3%, Brazil 2.8% (1996 est.)

Debt - external: $20.9 billion (1998 est.)

Economic aid - recipient: $565.6 million (1995)

Currency: 1 Moroccan dirham (DH) = 100 centimes

Exchange rates: Moroccan dirhams (DH) per US$1 - 9.320 (January 1999), 9.604 (1998), 9.527 (1997), 8.716 (1996), 8.540 (1995), 9.203 (1994)

Fiscal year: July 1-June 30

Communications

Telephones: 1,312,596 (1999 est.)

Telephone system:

domestic: good system composed of open-wire lines, cables, and microwave radio relay links; principal centers are Casablanca and Rabat; secondary centers are Fes, Marrakech, Oujda, Tangier, and Tetouan

international: 5 submarine cables; satellite earth stations - 2 Intelsat (Atlantic Ocean) and 1 Arabsat; microwave radio relay to Gibraltar, Spain, and Western Sahara; coaxial cable and microwave radio relay to Algeria; participant in Medarabtel

Radio broadcast stations: AM 22, FM 7, shortwave 5 (1998 est.)

Radios: 5.1 million (1998 est.)

Television broadcast stations: 26 (in addition, there are 35 repeaters) (1997)

Televisions: 1.21 million (1998 est.)

Transportation

Railways:

total: 1,907 km

standard gauge: 1,907 km 1.435-m gauge (1,003 km electrified; 246 km double track) (1994)

Highways:

total: 60,626 km

paved: 30,556 km (including 219 km of expressways)

unpaved: 30,070 km (1996 est.)

Pipelines: crude oil 362 km; petroleum products 491

Morocco (continued)

km (abandoned); natural gas 241 km

Ports and harbors: Agadir, El Jadida, Casablanca, El Jorf Lasfar, Kenitra, Mohammedia, Nador, Rabat, Safi, Tangier; also Spanish-controlled Ceuta and Melilla

Merchant marine:

total: 40 ships (1,000 GRT or over) totaling 217,869 GRT/263,033 DWT

ships by type: cargo 8, chemical tanker 6, container 3, oil tanker 3, passenger 1, refrigerated cargo 10, roll-on/roll-off cargo 8, short-sea passenger 1 (1998 est.)

Airports: 69 (1998 est.)

Airports - with paved runways:

total: 26

over 3,047 m: 11

2,438 to 3,047 m: 4

1,524 to 2,437 m: 8

914 to 1,523 m: 2

under 914 m: 1 (1998 est.)

Airports - with unpaved runways:

total: 43

2,438 to 3,047 m: 1

1,524 to 2,437 m: 10

914 to 1,523 m: 21

under 914 m: 11 (1998 est.)

Heliports: 1 (1998 est.)

Military

Military branches: Royal Armed Forces (includes Army, Navy, Air Force), Gendarmerie, Auxiliary Forces

Military manpower - military age: 18 years of age

Military manpower - availability:

males age 15-49: 7,735,597 (1999 est.)

Military manpower - fit for military service:

males age 15-49: 4,888,595 (1999 est.)

Military manpower - reaching military age annually:

males: 320,040 (1999 est.)

Military expenditures - dollar figure: $1.3611 billion (FY97/98)

Military expenditures - percent of GDP: 3.8% (FY97/98)

Transnational Issues

Disputes - international: claims and administers Western Sahara, but sovereignty is unresolved and the UN is attempting to hold a referendum on the issue; the UN-administered cease-fire has been in effect since September 1991; Spain controls five places of sovereignty (plazas de soberania) on and off the coast of Morocco - the coastal enclaves of Ceuta and Melilla which Morocco contests, as well as the islands of Penon de Alhucemas, Penon de Velez de la Gomera, and Islas Chafarinas

Illicit drugs: illicit producer of hashish; trafficking on the increase for both domestic and international drug markets; shipments of hashish mostly directed to Western Europe; transit point for cocaine from South America destined for Western Europe

Mozambique

Geography

Location: Southern Africa, bordering the Mozambique Channel, between South Africa and Tanzania

Geographic coordinates: 18 15 S, 35 00 E

Map references: Africa

Area:

total: 801,590 sq km

land: 784,090 sq km

water: 17,500 sq km

Area - comparative: slightly less than twice the size of California

Land boundaries:

total: 4,571 km

border countries: Malawi 1,569 km, South Africa 491 km, Swaziland 105 km, Tanzania 756 km, Zambia 419 km, Zimbabwe 1,231 km

Coastline: 2,470 km

Maritime claims:

exclusive economic zone: 200 nm

territorial sea: 12 nm

Climate: tropical to subtropical

Terrain: mostly coastal lowlands, uplands in center, high plateaus in northwest, mountains in west

Elevation extremes:

lowest point: Indian Ocean 0 m

highest point: Monte Binga 2,436 m

Natural resources: coal, titanium, natural gas

Land use:

arable land: 4%

permanent crops: 0%

permanent pastures: 56%

forests and woodland: 18%

other: 22% (1993 est.)

Irrigated land: 1,180 sq km (1993 est.)

Natural hazards: severe droughts and floods occur in central and southern provinces; devastating cyclones

Environment - current issues: a long civil war and recurrent drought in the hinterlands have resulted in increased migration of the population to urban and coastal areas with adverse environmental consequences; desertification; pollution of surface and coastal waters

Environment - international agreements:

party to: Biodiversity, Climate Change, Desertification, Endangered Species, Hazardous Wastes, Law of the Sea, Ozone Layer Protection

signed, but not ratified: none of the selected agreements

People

Population: 19,124,335 (July 1999 est.)

note: the 1997 Mozambican census reported a population of 16,542,800; other estimates range as low as 16.9 million

Age structure:

0-14 years: 45% (male 4,236,545; female 4,325,586)

15-64 years: 53% (male 4,941,048; female 5,181,282)

65 years and over: 2% (male 182,857; female 257,017) (1999 est.)

Population growth rate: 2.54% (1999 est.)

Birth rate: 42.75 births/1,000 population (1999 est.)

Death rate: 17.31 deaths/1,000 population (1999 est.)

Net migration rate: 0 migrant(s)/1,000 population (1999 est.)

Sex ratio:

at birth: 1.03 male(s)/female

under 15 years: 0.98 male(s)/female

15-64 years: 0.95 male(s)/female

65 years and over: 0.71 male(s)/female

total population: 0.96 male(s)/female (1999 est.)

Infant mortality rate: 117.56 deaths/1,000 live births (1999 est.)

Life expectancy at birth:

total population: 45.89 years

male: 44.73 years

female: 47.09 years (1999 est.)

Total fertility rate: 5.88 children born/woman (1999 est.)

Nationality:

noun: Mozambican(s)

adjective: Mozambican

Ethnic groups: indigenous tribal groups 99.66%

Mozambique (continued)

(Shangaan, Chokwe, Manyika, Sena, Makua, and others), Europeans 0.06%, Euro-Africans 0.2%, Indians 0.08%

Religions: indigenous beliefs 50%, Christian 30%, Muslim 20%

Languages: Portuguese (official), indigenous dialects

Literacy:
definition: age 15 and over can read and write
total population: 40.1%
male: 57.7%
female: 23.3% (1995 est.)

Government

Country name:
conventional long form: Republic of Mozambique
conventional short form: Mozambique
local long form: Republica de Mocambique
local short form: Mocambique

Data code: MZ

Government type: republic

Capital: Maputo

Administrative divisions: 10 provinces (provincias, singular - provincia); Cabo Delgado, Gaza, Inhambane, Manica, Maputo, Nampula, Niassa, Sofala, Tete, Zambezia

Independence: 25 June 1975 (from Portugal)

National holiday: Independence Day, 25 June (1975)

Constitution: 30 November 1990

Legal system: based on Portuguese civil law system and customary law

Suffrage: 18 years of age; universal

Executive branch:
chief of state: President Joaquim Alberto CHISSANO (since 6 November 1986); note - before being popularly elected, CHISSANO was elected president by Frelimo's Central Committee 4 November 1986 (reelected by the Committee 30 July 1989)
head of government: Prime Minister Pascoal MOCUMBI (since NA December 1994)
cabinet: Cabinet
elections: president elected by popular vote for a five-year term; election last held 27 October 1994 (next to be held NA October 1999); prime minister appointed by the president
election results: Joaquim Alberto CHISSANO elected president; percent of vote - Joaquim CHISSANO 53.3%, Afonso DHLAKAMA 33.3%

Legislative branch: unicameral Assembly of the Republic or Assembleia da Republica (250 seats; members are directly elected by popular vote on a secret ballot to serve five-year terms)
elections: last held 27-29 October 1994 (next to be held NA October 1999)
election results: percent of vote by party - Frelimo 44.33%, Renamo 33.78%, DU 5.15%, other 16.74%; seats by party - Frelimo 129, Renamo 112, DU 9

Judicial branch: Supreme Court, judges appointed by the president and judges elected by the Assembly

Political parties and leaders: Front for the Liberation of Mozambique (Frente de Liberatacao de Mocambique) or Frelimo [Joaquim Alberto CHISSANO, chairman]; Mozambique National Resistance (Resistencia Nacional Mocambicana) or Renamo [Afonso DHLAKAMA, president]; Democratic Union or DU [Antonio PALANGE, general secretary]; note - the DU may have broken up into the three parties that composed it - Liberal and Democratic Party of Mozambique, National Democratic Party, and National Party of Mozambique

International organization participation: ACP, AfDB, C, CCC, ECA, FAO, G-77, IBRD, ICAO, ICFTU, ICRM, IDA, IDB, IFAD, IFC, IFRCS, IHO (pending member), ILO, IMF, IMO, Inmarsat, Intelsat, Interpol, IOC, IOM (observer), ISO (correspondent), ITU, NAM, OAU, OIC, SADC, UN, UNCTAD, UNESCO, UNIDO, UPU, WFTU, WHO, WIPO, WMO, WToO, WTrO

Diplomatic representation in the US:
chief of mission: Ambassador Marcos Geraldo NAMASHULUA
chancery: Suite 570, 1990 M Street NW, Washington, DC 20036
telephone: [1] (202) 293-7146
FAX: [1] (202) 835-0245

Diplomatic representation from the US:
chief of mission: Ambassador Bryan Dean CURRAN
embassy: Avenida Kenneth Kuanda 193, Maputo
mailing address: P. O. Box 783, Maputo
telephone: [258] (1) 492797
FAX: [258] (1) 490114

Flag description: three equal horizontal bands of green (top), black, and yellow with a red isosceles triangle based on the hoist side; the black band is edged in white; centered in the triangle is a yellow five-pointed star bearing a crossed rifle and hoe in black superimposed on an open white book

Economy

Economy - overview: Before the peace accord of October 1992, Mozambique's economy was devastated by a protracted civil war and socialist mismanagement. In 1994, it ranked as one of the poorest countries in the world. Since then, Mozambique has undertaken a series of economic reforms. Almost all aspects of the economy have been liberalized to some extent. More than 900 state enterprises have been privatized. Pending are tax and much needed commercial code reform, as well as greater private sector involvement in the transportation, telecommunications, and energy sectors. Since 1996, inflation has been low and foreign exchange rates stable. Albeit from a small base, Mozambique achieved one of the highest growth rates in the world in 1997-98. Still, the country depends on foreign assistance to balance the budget and to pay for a trade imbalance in which imports outnumber exports by three to one. The medium-term outlook for the country looks bright, as trade and transportation links to South Africa and the rest of the region are expected to improve and sizable foreign investments materialize. Among these investments are metal production (aluminum, steel), natural gas, power generation, agriculture (cotton, sugar), fishing, timber, and transportation services. Additional exports in these areas should bring in needed foreign exchange.

GDP: purchasing power parity - $16.8 billion (1998 est.)

GDP - real growth rate: 11% (1998 est.)

GDP - per capita: purchasing power parity - $900 (1998 est.)

GDP - composition by sector:
agriculture: 35%
industry: 13%
services: 52% (1996 est.)

Population below poverty line: NA%

Household income or consumption by percentage share:
lowest 10%: NA%
highest 10%: NA%

Inflation rate (consumer prices): -1.3% (1998 est.)

Labor force: NA

Labor force - by occupation: agriculture 80%, industry 9.5%, services 5.5%, wage earners working abroad 5% (1993 est)

Unemployment rate: NA

Budget:
revenues: $402 million
expenditures: $799 million, including capital expenditures of $NA (1997 est.)

Industries: food, beverages, chemicals (fertilizer, soap, paints), petroleum products, textiles, cement, glass, asbestos, tobacco

Industrial production growth rate: 39% (1997)

Electricity - production: 426 million kWh (1997)

Electricity - production by source: NA%

Electricity - consumption: 1.11 billion kWh (1997)

Electricity - exports: 0 kWh (1996)

Electricity - imports: 685.6 million kWh (1997)

Agriculture - products: cotton, cashew nuts, sugarcane, tea, cassava (tapioca), corn, rice, tropical fruits; beef, poultry

Exports: $295 million (f.o.b., 1998 est.)

Exports - commodities: shrimp 40%, cashews, cotton, sugar, copra, citrus (1997)

Exports - partners: Spain 17%, South Africa 16%, Portugal 12%, US 10%, Japan, Malawi, India, Zimbabwe (1996 est.)

Imports: $965 million (c.i.f., 1998 est.)

Imports - commodities: food, clothing, farm equipment, petroleum (1997)

Imports - partners: South Africa 55%, Zimbabwe 7%, Saudi Arabia 5%, Portugal 4%, US, Japan, India (1996 est.)

Debt - external: $5.7 billion (December 1997)

Economic aid - recipient: $1.115 billion (1995)

Currency: 1 metical (Mt) = 100 centavos

Exchange rates: meticais (Mt) per US$1 - 12,394.0 (January 1999), 11,874.6 (1998), 11.543.6 (1997), 11,293.8 (1996), 9,024.3 (1995), 6,038.6 (1994)

Fiscal year: calendar year

Communications

Telephones: 70,000 (1998 est.)

Telephone system: fair system of tropospheric scatter, open-wire lines, and microwave radio relay

---

domestic: microwave radio relay and tropospheric scatter

international: satellite earth stations - 5 Intelsat (2 Atlantic Ocean and 3 Indian Ocean)
Radio broadcast stations: AM 29, FM 4, shortwave 0
Radios: 700,000 (1992 est.)
Television broadcast stations: 1 (1997)
Televisions: 44,000 (1992 est.)

Transportation

Railways:
total: 3,131 km
narrow gauge: 2,988 km 1.067-m gauge; 143 km 0.762-m gauge (1994)
Highways:
total: 30,400 km
paved: 5,685 km
unpaved: 24,715 km (1996 est.)
Waterways: about 3,750 km of navigable routes
Pipelines: crude oil 306 km; petroleum products 289 km
note: not operating
Ports and harbors: Beira, Inhambane, Maputo, Nacala, Pemba, Quelimane
Merchant marine:
total: 3 cargo ships (1,000 GRT or over) totaling 4,125 GRT/7,024 DWT (1998 est.)
Airports: 174 (1998 est.)
Airports - with paved runways:
total: 22
over 3,047 m: 1
2,438 to 3,047 m: 3
1,524 to 2,437 m: 10
914 to 1,523 m: 4
under 914 m: 4 (1998 est.)
Airports - with unpaved runways:
total: 152
2,438 to 3,047 m: 1
1,524 to 2,437 m: 16
914 to 1,523 m: 39
under 914 m: 96 (1998 est.)

Military

Military branches: Army, Naval Command, Air and Air Defense Forces, Militia
Military manpower - availability:
males age 15-49: 4,385,483 (1999 est.)
Military manpower - fit for military service:
males age 15-49: 2,526,447 (1999 est.)
Military expenditures - dollar figure: $72 million (FY97)
Military expenditures - percent of GDP: 4.7% (1997)

Transnational Issues

Disputes - international: none
Illicit drugs: Southern African transit hub for South American cocaine probably destined for the European and US markets; producer of hashish and methaqualone

Namibia

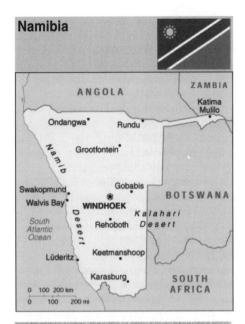

Geography

Location: Southern Africa, bordering the South Atlantic Ocean, between Angola and South Africa
Geographic coordinates: 22 00 S, 17 00 E
Map references: Africa
Area:
total: 825,418 sq km
land: 825,418 sq km
water: 0 sq km
Area - comparative: slightly more than half the size of Alaska
Land boundaries:
total: 3,824 km
border countries: Angola 1,376 km, Botswana 1,360 km, South Africa 855 km, Zambia 233 km
Coastline: 1,572 km
Maritime claims:
contiguous zone: 24 nm
exclusive economic zone: 200 nm
territorial sea: 12 nm
Climate: desert; hot, dry; rainfall sparse and erratic
Terrain: mostly high plateau; Namib Desert along coast; Kalahari Desert in east
Elevation extremes:
lowest point: Atlantic Ocean 0 m
highest point: Konigstein 2,606 m
Natural resources: diamonds, copper, uranium, gold, lead, tin, lithium, cadmium, zinc, salt, vanadium, natural gas, fish; suspected deposits of oil, natural gas, coal, iron ore
Land use:
arable land: 1%
permanent crops: 0%
permanent pastures: 46%
forests and woodland: 22%
other: 31% (1993 est.)
Irrigated land: 60 sq km (1993 est.)
Natural hazards: prolonged periods of drought
Environment - current issues: very limited natural fresh water resources; desertification

Environment - international agreements:
party to: Biodiversity, Climate Change, Desertification, Endangered Species, Hazardous Wastes, Law of the Sea, Ozone Layer Protection, Wetlands
signed, but not ratified: none of the selected agreements

People

Population: 1,648,270 (July 1999 est.)
Age structure:
0-14 years: 44% (male 366,030; female 358,105)
15-64 years: 52% (male 424,879; female 435,116)
65 years and over: 4% (male 26,787; female 37,353) (1999 est.)
Population growth rate: 1.57% (1999 est.)
Birth rate: 35.63 births/1,000 population (1999 est.)
Death rate: 19.92 deaths/1,000 population (1999 est.)
Net migration rate: 0 migrant(s)/1,000 population (1999 est.)
Sex ratio:
at birth: 1.03 male(s)/female
under 15 years: 1.02 male(s)/female
15-64 years: 0.98 male(s)/female
65 years and over: 0.72 male(s)/female
total population: 0.98 male(s)/female (1999 est.)
Infant mortality rate: 65.94 deaths/1,000 live births (1999 est.)
Life expectancy at birth:
total population: 41.26 years
male: 41.64 years
female: 40.87 years (1999 est.)
Total fertility rate: 4.94 children born/woman (1999 est.)
Nationality:
noun: Namibian(s)
adjective: Namibian
Ethnic groups: black 86%, white 6.6%, mixed 7.4%
note: about 50% of the population belong to the Ovambo tribe and 9% to the Kavangos tribe; other ethnic groups are: Herero 7%, Damara 7%, Nama 5%, Caprivian 4%, Bushmen 3%, Baster 2%, Tswana 0.5%
Religions: Christian 80% to 90% (Lutheran 50% at least, other Christian denominations 30%), native religions 10% to 20%
Languages: English 7% (official), Afrikaans common language of most of the population and about 60% of the white population, German 32%, indigenous languages: Oshivambo, Herero, Nama
Literacy:
definition: age 15 and over can read and write
total population: 38%
male: 45%
female: 31% (1960 est.)

Government

Country name:
conventional long form: Republic of Namibia
conventional short form: Namibia

Namibia (continued)

Data code: WA
Government type: republic
Capital: Windhoek
Administrative divisions: 13 regions; Caprivi, Erongo, Hardap, Karas, Khomas, Kunene, Ohangwena, Okavango, Omaheke, Omusati, Oshana, Oshikoto, Otjozondjupa
Independence: 21 March 1990 (from South African mandate)
National holiday: Independence Day, 21 March (1990)
Constitution: ratified 9 February 1990; effective 12 March 1990
Legal system: based on Roman-Dutch law and 1990 constitution
Suffrage: 18 years of age; universal
Executive branch:
chief of state: President Sam NUJOMA (since 21 March 1990); note - the president is both the chief of state and head of government
head of government: President Sam NUJOMA (since 21 March 1990); note - the president is both the chief of state and head of government
cabinet: Cabinet appointed by the president from among the members of the National Assembly
elections: president elected by popular vote for a five-year term; election last held 7-8 December 1994 (next to be held NA December 1999)
election results: Sam NUJOMA elected president; percent of vote - 76%
Legislative branch: bicameral legislature consists of the National Council (26 seats; two members are chosen from each regional council to serve six-year terms) and the National Assembly (72 seats; members are elected by popular vote to serve five-year terms)
elections: National Council - last held 30 November-1 December 1998 (next to be held by December 2004); National Assembly - last held 7-8 December 1994 (next to be held NA December 1999)
election results: National Council - percent of vote by party - NA; seats by party - NA; National Assembly - percent of vote by party - SWAPO 73.89%, DTA 20.78%, UDF 2.72%, DCN 0.83%, MAG 0.82%; seats by party - SWAPO 53, DTA 15, UDF 2, MAG 1, DCN 1
note: the National Council is a purely advisory body
Judicial branch: Supreme Court, judges appointed by the president
Political parties and leaders: South West Africa People's Organization or SWAPO [Sam NUJOMA]; National Democratic Party for Justice or NDPFJ [Nbhwete NDJOBA]; Democratic Turnhalle Alliance of Namibia or DTA [Katuutire KAURA, president]; United Democratic Front or UDF [Justus GAROEB]; Monitor Action Group or MAG [Kosie PRETORIUS]; Democratic Coalition of Namibia or DCN [Moses K. KATJIUONGUA]
Political pressure groups and leaders: NA
International organization participation: ACP, AfDB, C, CCC, ECA, FAO, G-77, IAEA, IBRD, ICAO, ICRM, IFAD, IFC, IFRCS, ILO, IMF, IMO, Intelsat, Interpol, IOC, IOM (observer), ISO (subscriber), ITU, MONUA, NAM, OAU, OPCW, SACU, SADC, UN, UNCTAD, UNESCO, UNHCR, UNIDO, UPU, WCL, WHO, WIPO, WMO, WToO, WTrO

Diplomatic representation in the US:
chief of mission: Ambassador (vacant); Charge d'Affaires Usko SHIVUTE
chancery: 1605 New Hampshire Avenue NW, Washington, DC 20009
telephone: [1] (202) 986-0540
FAX: [1] (202) 986-0443
Diplomatic representation from the US:
chief of mission: Ambassador George F. WARD, Jr.
embassy: Ausplan Building, 14 Lossen St., Private Bag 12029 Ausspannplatz, Windhoek
mailing address: use embassy street address
telephone: [264] (61) 221601
FAX: [264] (61) 229792
Flag description: a large blue triangle with a yellow sunburst fills the upper left section and an equal green triangle (solid) fills the lower right section; the triangles are separated by a red stripe that is contrasted by two narrow white-edge borders

Economy

Economy - overview: The economy is heavily dependent on the extraction and processing of minerals for export. Mining accounts for 20% of GDP. Namibia is the fourth-largest exporter of nonfuel minerals in Africa and the world's fifth-largest producer of uranium. Rich alluvial diamond deposits make Namibia a primary source for gem-quality diamonds. Namibia also produces large quantities of lead, zinc, tin, silver, and tungsten. Half of the population depends on agriculture (largely subsistence agriculture) for its livelihood. Namibia must import some of its food. Although per capita GDP is three times the per capita GDP of Africa's poorer countries, the majority of Namibia's people live in pronounced poverty because of the great inequality of income distribution and the large amounts going to foreigners. The Namibian economy has close links to South Africa.
GDP: purchasing power parity - $6.6 billion (1998 est.)
GDP - real growth rate: 2% (1998 est.)
GDP - per capita: purchasing power parity - $4,100 (1998 est.)
GDP - composition by sector:
agriculture: 11%
industry: 34%
services: 55% (1997 est.)
Population below poverty line: NA%
Household income or consumption by percentage share:
lowest 10%: NA%
highest 10%: NA%
Inflation rate (consumer prices): 7% (1996 est.)
Labor force: 500,000
Labor force - by occupation: agriculture 49%, industry and commerce 25%, services 5%, government 18%, mining 3% (1994 est.)
Unemployment rate: 30% to 40%, including underemployment (1997 est.)

Budget:
revenues: $1.1 billion
expenditures: $1.2 billion, including capital expenditures of $193 million (FY96/97 est.)
Industries: meat packing, fish processing, dairy products; mining (diamond, lead, zinc, tin, silver, tungsten, uranium, copper)
Industrial production growth rate: 10% (1994)
Electricity - production: 0 kWh (1996)
Electricity - production by source:
fossil fuel: NA%
hydro: NA%
nuclear: NA%
other: NA%
Electricity - consumption: 1.11 billion kWh (1996)
Electricity - exports: 0 kWh (1996)
Electricity - imports: 1.11 billion kWh (1996)
note: imports electricity from South Africa
Agriculture - products: millet, sorghum, peanuts; livestock; fish
Exports: $1.44 billion (f.o.b., 1998 est.)
Exports - commodities: diamonds, copper, gold, zinc, lead, uranium; cattle, processed fish, karakul skins
Exports - partners: UK 38%, South Africa 24%, Spain 12%, Japan 7% (1996 est.)
Imports: $1.48 billion (f.o.b., 1998 est.)
Imports - commodities: foodstuffs; petroleum products and fuel, machinery and equipment, chemicals
Imports - partners: South Africa 87%, Germany, US, Japan (1995 est.)
Debt - external: $315 million (1996 est.)
Economic aid - recipient: $127 million (1998)
Currency: 1 Namibian dollar (N$) = 100 cents
Exchange rates: Namibian dollars (N$) per US$1 - 5.98380 (January 1999), 5.52828 (1998), 4.60796 (1997), 4.29935 (1996), 3.62709 (1995), 3.55080 (1994)
Fiscal year: 1 April - 31 March

Communications

Telephones: 89,722 (1992 est.)
Telephone system:
domestic: good urban services; fair rural service; microwave radio relay links major towns; connections to other populated places are by open wire
international: NA
note: a fully automated digital network is being implemented
Radio broadcast stations: AM 4, FM 40, shortwave 0
Radios: 195,000 (1992 est.)
Television broadcast stations: 8 (of which five are main stations and three are low-power stations; there are also about 20 low-power repeaters) (1997)
Televisions: 27,000 (1993 est.)

Transportation

Railways:
total: 2,382 km

Namibia (continued)

narrow gauge: 2,382 km 1.067-m gauge; single track (1995)
Highways:
total: 64,799 km
paved: 7,841 km
unpaved: 56,958 km (1996 est.)
Ports and harbors: Luderitz, Walvis Bay
Merchant marine: none
Airports: 135 (1998 est.)
Airports - with paved runways:
total: 22
over 3,047 m: 2
2,438 to 3,047 m: 2
1,524 to 2,437 m: 15
914 to 1,523 m: 3 (1998 est.)
Airports - with unpaved runways:
total: 113
2,438 to 3,047 m: 2
1,524 to 2,437 m: 20
914 to 1,523 m: 70
under 914 m: 21 (1998 est.)

Military

Military branches: National Defense Force (Army), Police
Military manpower - availability:
males age 15-49: 380,528 (1999 est.)
Military manpower - fit for military service:
males age 15-49: 228,225 (1999 est.)
Military expenditures - dollar figure: $90 million (FY97/98)
Military expenditures - percent of GDP: 2.6% (FY97/98)

Transnational Issues

Disputes - international: quadripoint with Botswana, Zambia, and Zimbabwe is in disagreement; dispute with Botswana over uninhabited Kasikili (Sidudu) Island in Linyanti (Chobe) River is presently at the ICJ; at least one other island in Linyanti River is contested

Nauru

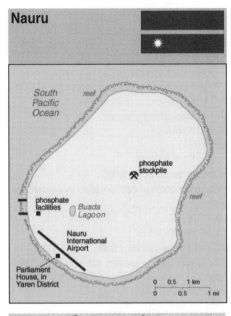

Geography

Location: Oceania, island in the South Pacific Ocean, south of the Marshall Islands
Geographic coordinates: 0 32 S, 166 55 E
Map references: Oceania
Area:
total: 21 sq km
land: 21 sq km
water: 0 sq km
Area - comparative: about 0.1 times the size of Washington, DC
Land boundaries: 0 km
Coastline: 30 km
Maritime claims:
exclusive fishing zone: 200 nm
territorial sea: 12 nm
Climate: tropical; monsoonal; rainy season (November to February)
Terrain: sandy beach rises to fertile ring around raised coral reefs with phosphate plateau in center
Elevation extremes:
lowest point: Pacific Ocean 0 m
highest point: unnamed location along plateau rim 61 m
Natural resources: phosphates
Land use:
arable land: NA%
permanent crops: NA%
permanent pastures: NA%
forests and woodland: NA%
other: 100% (1993 est.)
Irrigated land: NA sq km
Natural hazards: periodic droughts
Environment - current issues: limited natural fresh water resources, roof storage tanks collect rainwater; intensive phosphate mining during the past 90 years - mainly by a UK, Australia, and New Zealand consortium - has left the central 90% of Nauru a wasteland and threatens limited remaining land resources

Environment - international agreements:
party to: Biodiversity, Climate Change, Desertification, Law of the Sea, Marine Dumping
signed, but not ratified: none of the selected agreements
Geography - note: Nauru is one of the three great phosphate rock islands in the Pacific Ocean - the others are Banaba (Ocean Island) in Kiribati and Makatea in French Polynesia; only 53 km south of Equator

People

Population: 10,605 (July 1999 est.)
Age structure:
0-14 years: NA
15-64 years: NA
65 years and over: NA
Population growth rate: 0% (1999 est.)
Birth rate: NA
Death rate: 0 deaths/1,000 population (1999 est.)
Net migration rate: 0 migrant(s)/1,000 population (1999 est.)
Infant mortality rate: NA deaths/1,000 live births
Life expectancy at birth:
total population: NA
male: NA
female: NA
Total fertility rate: NA children born/woman
Nationality:
noun: Nauruan(s)
adjective: Nauruan
Ethnic groups: Nauruan 58%, other Pacific Islander 26%, Chinese 8%, European 8%
Religions: Christian (two-thirds Protestant, one-third Roman Catholic)
Languages: Nauruan (official, a distinct Pacific Island language), English widely understood, spoken, and used for most government and commercial purposes
Literacy: NA

Government

Country name:
conventional long form: Republic of Nauru
conventional short form: Nauru
former: Pleasant Island
Data code: NR
Government type: republic
Capital: no official capital; government offices in Yaren District
Administrative divisions: 14 districts; Aiwo, Anabar, Anetan, Anibare, Baiti, Boe, Buada, Denigomodu, Ewa, Ijuw, Meneng, Nibok, Uaboe, Yaren
Independence: 31 January 1968 (from the Australia-, New Zealand-, and UK-administered UN trusteeship)
National holiday: Independence Day, 31 January (1968)
Constitution: 29 January 1968
Legal system: acts of the Nauru Parliament and

Nauru (continued)

British common law

Suffrage: 20 years of age; universal and compulsory

Executive branch:

chief of state: President Bernard DOWIYOGO (since 17 June 1998); note - the president is both the chief of state and head of government

head of government: President Bernard DOWIYOGO (since 17 June 1998); note - the president is both the chief of state and head of government

cabinet: Cabinet appointed by the president from among the members of Parliament

elections: president elected by Parliament for a three-year term; election last held 17 June 1998 (next to be held NA 2001)

election results: Bernard DOWIYOGO elected president; percent of Parliament vote - NA

note: former President Kinza CLODUMAR was deposed in a no-confidence vote

Legislative branch: unicameral Parliament (18 seats; members elected by popular vote to serve three-year terms)

elections: last held 8 February 1997 (next to be held NA February 2000)

election results: percent of vote - NA; seats - independents 18

Judicial branch: Supreme Court

Political parties and leaders: loose multi-party system; Nauru Party (informal) [Bernard DOWIYOGO]; Democratic Party [Kennan ADEANG]

International organization participation: AsDB, C (special), ESCAP, ICAO, Intelsat (nonsignatory user), Interpol, IOC, ITU, OPCW, Sparteca, SPC, SPF, UNESCO, UPU, WHO

Diplomatic representation in the US: Nauru does not have an embassy in the US

consulate(s): Hagatna (Guam)

Diplomatic representation from the US: the US does not have an embassy in Nauru; the US Ambassador to Fiji is accredited to Nauru

Flag description: blue with a narrow, horizontal, yellow stripe across the center and a large white 12-pointed star below the stripe on the hoist side; the star indicates the country's location in relation to the Equator (the yellow stripe) and the 12 points symbolize the 12 original tribes of Nauru

Economy

Economy - overview: Revenues come from exports of phosphates, but reserves are expected to be exhausted by the year 2000. Phosphates have given Nauruans one of the highest per capita incomes in the Third World. Few other resources exist, thus most necessities must be imported, including fresh water from Australia. The rehabilitation of mined land and the replacement of income from phosphates are serious long-term problems. Substantial amounts of phosphate income are invested in trust funds to help cushion the transition. The government also has been borrowing heavily from the trusts to finance fiscal deficits. To cut costs the government has called a freezing of wages, a reduction of over-staffed public service departments, privatization of numerous

government agencies, and closure of some overseas consulates.

GDP: purchasing power parity - $100 million (1993 est.)

GDP - real growth rate: NA%

GDP - per capita: purchasing power parity - $10,000 (1993 est.)

GDP - composition by sector:

agriculture: NA%

industry: NA%

services: NA%

Population below poverty line: NA%

Household income or consumption by percentage share:

lowest 10%: NA%

highest 10%: NA%

Inflation rate (consumer prices): -3.6% (1993)

Labor force - by occupation: employed in mining phosphates, public administration, education, and transportation

Unemployment rate: 0%

Budget:

revenues: $23.4 million

expenditures: $64.8 million, including capital expenditures of $NA (FY95/96)

Industries: phosphate mining, financial services, coconut products

Industrial production growth rate: NA%

Electricity - production: 32 million kWh (1996)

Electricity - production by source:

fossil fuel: 100%

hydro: 0%

nuclear: 0%

other: 0% (1996)

Electricity - consumption: 32 million kWh (1996)

Electricity - exports: 0 kWh (1996)

Electricity - imports: 0 kWh (1996)

Agriculture - products: coconuts

Exports: $25.3 million (f.o.b., 1991)

Exports - commodities: phosphates

Exports - partners: Australia, NZ

Imports: $21.1 million (c.i.f., 1991)

Imports - commodities: food, fuel, manufactures, building materials, machinery

Imports - partners: Australia, UK, NZ, Japan

Debt - external: $33.3 million

Economic aid - recipient: $2.5 million (1995); note - $2.25 million from Australia (FY96/97 est.)

Currency: 1 Australian dollar ($A) = 100 cents

Exchange rates: Australian dollars ($A) per US$1 - 1.5853 (January 1999), 1.5888 (1998), 1.3439 (1997), 1.2773 (1996), 1.3486 (1995), 1.3667 (1994)

Fiscal year: 1 July - 30 June

Communications

Telephones: 2,000 (1989 est.)

Telephone system: adequate local and international radiotelephone communications provided via Australian facilities

domestic: NA

international: satellite earth station - 1 Intelsat (Pacific Ocean)

Radio broadcast stations: AM 1, FM 0, shortwave 0

Radios: 4,000 (1993 est.)

Television broadcast stations: 1 (1997)

Televisions: NA

Transportation

Railways:

total: 3.9 km; note - used to haul phosphates from the center of the island to processing facilities on the southwest coast

Highways:

total: 30 km

paved: 24 km

unpaved: 6 km (1996 est.)

Ports and harbors: Nauru

Merchant marine: none

Airports: 1 (1998 est.)

Airports - with paved runways:

total: 1

1,524 to 2,437 m: 1 (1998 est.)

Military

Military branches: no regular armed forces; Directorate of the Nauru Police Force

Military expenditures - dollar figure: $NA

Military expenditures - percent of GDP: NA%

Military - note: Nauru maintains no defense forces; under an informal agreement, Australia is responsible for defense of the island

Transnational Issues

Disputes - international: none

Navassa Island
(territory of the US)

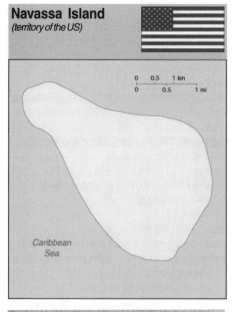

Caribbean
Sea

Geography

Location: Caribbean, island in the Caribbean Sea, about one-fourth of the way from Haiti to Jamaica
Geographic coordinates: 18 25 N, 75 02 W
Map references: Central America and the Caribbean
Area:
total: 5.2 sq km
land: 5.2 sq km
water: 0 sq km
Area - comparative: about nine times the size of The Mall in Washington, DC
Land boundaries: 0 km
Coastline: 8 km
Maritime claims:
exclusive economic zone: 200 nm
territorial sea: 12 nm
Climate: marine, tropical
Terrain: raised coral and limestone plateau, flat to undulating; ringed by vertical white cliffs (9 to 15 meters high)
Elevation extremes:
lowest point: Caribbean Sea 0 m
highest point: unnamed location on southwest side 77 m
Natural resources: guano
Land use:
arable land: 0%
permanent crops: 0%
permanent pastures: 10%
forests and woodland: 0%
other: 90%
Irrigated land: 0 sq km (1998)
Natural hazards: NA
Environment - current issues: NA
Environment - international agreements:
party to: NA
signed, but not ratified: NA
Geography - note: strategic location 160 km south of the US Naval Base at Guantanamo Bay, Cuba;

mostly exposed rock, but enough grassland to support goat herds; dense stands of fig-like trees, scattered cactus

People

Population: uninhabited
note: transient Haitian fishermen and others camp on the island

Government

Country name:
conventional long form: none
conventional short form: Navassa Island
Data code: BQ
Dependency status: unincorporated territory of the US; administered from Washington, DC, by the Office of Insular Affairs, US Department of the Interior; in September 1996, the Coast Guard ceased operations and maintenance of Navassa Island Light, a 46-meter-tall lighthouse located on the southern side of the island; there has also been a private claim advanced against the island
Capital: none; administered from Washington, DC
Legal system: NA
Flag description: the flag of the US is used

Economy

Economy - overview: no economic activity

Transportation

Ports and harbors: none; offshore anchorage only

Military

Military - note: defense is the responsibility of the US

Transnational Issues

Disputes - international: claimed by Haiti

Nepal

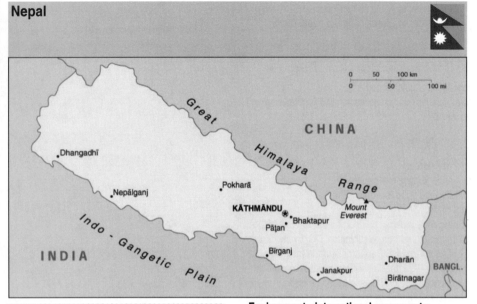

Geography

Location: Southern Asia, between China and India
Geographic coordinates: 28 00 N, 84 00 E
Map references: Asia
Area:
total: 140,800 sq km
land: 136,800 sq km
water: 4,000 sq km
Area - comparative: slightly larger than Arkansas
Land boundaries:
total: 2,926 km
border countries: China 1,236 km, India 1,690 km
Coastline: 0 km (landlocked)
Maritime claims: none (landlocked)
Climate: varies from cool summers and severe winters in north to subtropical summers and mild winters in south
Terrain: Terai or flat river plain of the Ganges in south, central hill region, rugged Himalayas in north
Elevation extremes:
lowest point: Kanchan Kalan 70 m
highest point: Mount Everest 8,848 m
Natural resources: quartz, water, timber, hydropower potential, scenic beauty, small deposits of lignite, copper, cobalt, iron ore
Land use:
arable land: 17%
permanent crops: 0%
permanent pastures: 15%
forests and woodland: 42%
other: 26% (1993 est.)
Irrigated land: 8,500 sq km (1993 est.)
Natural hazards: severe thunderstorms, flooding, landslides, drought, and famine depending on the timing, intensity, and duration of the summer monsoons
Environment - current issues: the almost total dependence on wood for fuel and cutting down trees to expand agricultural land without replanting has resulted in widespread deforestation; soil erosion; water pollution (use of contaminated water presents human health risks)

Environment - international agreements:
party to: Biodiversity, Climate Change, Desertification, Endangered Species, Hazardous Wastes, Law of the Sea, Nuclear Test Ban, Ozone Layer Protection, Tropical Timber 83, Tropical Timber 94, Wetlands
signed, but not ratified: Marine Dumping, Marine Life Conservation
Geography - note: landlocked; strategic location between China and India; contains eight of world's 10 highest peaks

People

Population: 24,302,653 (July 1999 est.)
Age structure:
0-14 years: 41% (male 5,182,829; female 4,869,895)
15-64 years: 55% (male 6,856,905; female 6,571,916)
65 years and over: 4% (male 407,797; female 413,311) (1999 est.)
Population growth rate: 2.51% (1999 est.)
Birth rate: 35.32 births/1,000 population (1999 est.)
Death rate: 10.18 deaths/1,000 population (1999 est.)
Net migration rate: 0 migrant(s)/1,000 population (1999 est.)
Sex ratio:
at birth: 1.05 male(s)/female
under 15 years: 1.06 male(s)/female
15-64 years: 1.04 male(s)/female
65 years and over: 0.99 male(s)/female
total population: 1.05 male(s)/female (1999 est.)
Infant mortality rate: 73.58 deaths/1,000 live births (1999 est.)
Life expectancy at birth:
total population: 58.42 years
male: 58.47 years
female: 58.36 years (1999 est.)
Total fertility rate: 4.78 children born/woman (1999 est.)
Nationality:
noun: Nepalese (singular and plural)

adjective: Nepalese
Ethnic groups: Newars, Indians, Tibetans, Gurungs, Magars, Tamangs, Bhotias, Rais, Limbus, Sherpas
Religions: Hindu 90%, Buddhist 5%, Muslim 3%, other 2% (1981)
note: only official Hindu state in the world, although no sharp distinction between many Hindu and Buddhist groups
Languages: Nepali (official), 20 other languages divided into numerous dialects
Literacy:
definition: age 15 and over can read and write
total population: 27.5%
male: 40.9%
female: 14% (1995 est.)
People - note: refugee issue over the presence in Nepal of approximately 91,000 Bhutanese refugees, 90% of whom are in seven United Nations Office of the High Commissioner for Refugees (UNHCR) camps

Government

Country name:
conventional long form: Kingdom of Nepal
conventional short form: Nepal
Data code: NP
Government type: parliamentary democracy as of 12 May 1991
Capital: Kathmandu
Administrative divisions: 14 zones (anchal, singular and plural); Bagmati, Bheri, Dhawalagiri, Gandaki, Janakpur, Karnali, Kosi, Lumbini, Mahakali, Mechi, Narayani, Rapti, Sagarmatha, Seti
Independence: 1768 (unified by Prithvi Narayan Shah)
National holiday: Birthday of His Majesty the King, 28 December (1945)
Constitution: 9 November 1990
Legal system: based on Hindu legal concepts and English common law; has not accepted compulsory ICJ jurisdiction
Suffrage: 18 years of age; universal
Executive branch:
chief of state: King BIRENDRA Bir Bikram Shah Dev (succeeded to the throne 31 January 1972 following the death of his father King MAHENDRA Bir Bikram Shah Dev, crowned king 24 February 1975); Heir Apparent Crown Prince DIPENDRA Bir Bikram
head of government: Prime Minister Girija Prasad KOIRALA (since 15 April 1998)
cabinet: Cabinet appointed by the monarch on the recommendation of the prime minister
elections: none; the monarch is hereditary; following legislative elections, the leader of the majority party or leader of a majority coalition is usually appointed prime minister by the monarch
Legislative branch: bicameral Parliament consists of the National Council (60 seats; 35 appointed by the House of Representatives, 10 by the king, and 15 elected by an electoral college; one-third of the members elected every two years to serve six-year

Nepal *(continued)*

terms) and the House of Representatives (205 seats; members elected by popular vote to serve five-year terms)

elections: House of Representatives - last held 15 November 1994 (next to be held 3 May 1999)

election results: House of Representatives - percent of vote by party - NCP 33%, CPN/UML 31%, NDP 18%, Nepal Sadbhavana (Goodwill) Party 3%, NWPP 1%; seats by party - CPN/UML 88, NCP 83, NDP 20, NWPP 4, Nepal Sadbhavana (Goodwill) Party 3, independents 7

Judicial branch: Supreme Court (Sarbochha Adalat), chief justice is appointed by the monarch on recommendation of the Constitutional Council, the other judges are appointed by the monarch on the recommendation of the Judicial Council

Political parties and leaders: Communist Party of Nepal/United Marxist-Leninist or CPN/UML [Man Mohan ADHIKARI, party president, Madhar KUMAR, general secretary]; Nepali Congress Party or NCP [Girija Prasad KOIRALA, party president, Daranath Rana DHATT, general secretary]; National Democratic Party or NDP (also called Rastriya Prajantra Party or RPP) [Surya Bahadur THAPA]; Nepal Sadbhavana (Goodwill) Party [Gajendra Narayan SINGH, president]; Nepal Workers and Peasants Party or NWPP [Narayan Man BIJUKCHHE, party chair]

Political pressure groups and leaders: numerous small, left-leaning student groups in the capital; several small, radical Nepalese antimonarchist groups

International organization participation: AsDB, CCC, CP, ESCAP, FAO, G-77, IBRD, ICAO, ICFTU, ICRM, IDA, IFAD, IFC, IFRCS, ILO, IMF, IMO, Intelsat, Interpol, IOC, ISO (correspondent), ITU, NAM, OPCW, SAARC, UN, UNCTAD, UNESCO, UNIDO, UNIFIL, UNMIBH, UNMOP, UNPREDEP, UPU, WFTU, WHO, WIPO, WMO, WToO, WTrO (applicant)

Diplomatic representation in the US:

chief of mission: Ambassador THAPA Bekh Bahadur

chancery: 2131 Leroy Place NW, Washington, DC 20008

telephone: [1] (202) 667-4550

FAX: [1] (202) 667-5534

consulate(s) general: New York

Diplomatic representation from the US:

chief of mission: Ambassador Ralph FRANK

embassy: Pani Pokhari, Kathmandu

mailing address: use embassy street address

telephone: [977] (1) 411179

FAX: [977] (1) 419963

Flag description: red with a blue border around the unique shape of two overlapping right triangles; the smaller, upper triangle bears a white stylized moon and the larger, lower triangle bears a white 12-pointed sun

Economy

Economy - overview: Nepal is among the poorest and least developed countries in the world with nearly half of its population living below the poverty line. Agriculture is the mainstay of the economy, providing a livelihood for over 80% of the population and accounting for 41% of GDP. Industrial activity mainly involves the processing of agricultural produce including jute, sugarcane, tobacco, and grain. Production of textiles and carpets has expanded recently and accounted for about 80% of foreign exchange earnings in the past three years. Apart from agricultural land and forests, exploitable natural resources are mica, hydropower, and tourism. Agricultural production is growing by about 5% on average as compared with annual population growth of 2.5%. Since May 1991, the government has been moving forward with economic reforms particularly those that encourage trade and foreign investment, e.g., by eliminating business licenses and registration requirements in order to simplify investment procedures. The government has also been cutting expenditures by reducing subsidies, privatizing state industries, and laying off civil servants. More recently, however, political instability - five different governments over the past few years - has hampered Kathmandu's ability to forge consensus to implement key economic reforms. Nepal has considerable scope for accelerating economic growth by exploiting its potential in hydropower and tourism, areas of recent foreign investment interest. Prospects for foreign trade or investment in other sectors will remain poor, however, because of the small size of the economy, its technological backwardness, its remoteness, its landlocked geographic location, and its susceptibility to natural disaster. The international community's role of funding more than 60% of Nepal's development budget and more than 28% of total budgetary expenditures will likely continue as a major ingredient of growth.

GDP: purchasing power parity - $26.2 billion (1998 est.)

GDP - real growth rate: 4.9% (1998 est.)

GDP - per capita: purchasing power parity - $1,100 (1998 est.)

GDP - composition by sector:

agriculture: 41%

industry: 22%

services: 37% (1997)

Population below poverty line: 42% (1995-96 est.)

Household income or consumption by percentage share:

lowest 10%: 3.2%

highest 10%: 29.8% (1995-96)

Inflation rate (consumer prices): 7.8% (1998 est.)

Labor force: 10 million (1996 est.)

note: severe lack of skilled labor

Labor force - by occupation: agriculture 81%, services 16%, industry 3%

Unemployment rate: NA%; substantial underemployment (1996)

Budget:

revenues: $536 million

expenditures: $818 million, including capital expenditures of $NA (FY96/97 est.)

Industries: tourism, carpet, textile; small rice, jute, sugar, and oilseed mills; cigarette; cement and brick production

Industrial production growth rate: 14.7% (FY94/95 est.)

Electricity - production: 1.032 billion kWh (1996)

Electricity - production by source:

fossil fuel: 3.1%

hydro: 96.9%

nuclear: 0%

other: 0% (1996)

Electricity - consumption: 1.013 billion kWh (1996)

Electricity - exports: 89 million kWh (1996)

Electricity - imports: 70 million kWh (1996)

Agriculture - products: rice, corn, wheat, sugarcane, root crops; milk, water buffalo meat

Exports: $394 million (f.o.b., 1997), but does not include unrecorded border trade with India

Exports - commodities: carpets, clothing, leather goods, jute goods, grain

Exports - partners: India, US, Germany, UK

Imports: $1.7 billion (c.i.f., 1997)

Imports - commodities: petroleum products 20%, fertilizer 11%, machinery 10%

Imports - partners: India, Singapore, Japan, Germany

Debt - external: $2.4 billion (1997)

Economic aid - recipient: $411 million (FY97/98)

Currency: 1 Nepalese rupee (NR) = 100 paisa

Exchange rates: Nepalese rupees (NRs) per US$1 - 67.675 (January 1999), 65.976 (1998), 58.010 (1997), 56.692 (1996), 51.890 (1995), 49.398 (1994)

Fiscal year: 16 July - 15 July

Communications

Telephones: 115,911 (1996 est.)

Telephone system: poor telephone and telegraph service; fair radiotelephone communication service

domestic: NA

international: radiotelephone communications; satellite earth station - 1 Intelsat (Indian Ocean)

Radio broadcast stations: AM 88, FM 1, shortwave 0

Radios: 690,000 (1992 est.)

Television broadcast stations: 6 (1998 est.)

Televisions: 45,000 (1992 est.)

Transportation

Railways:

total: 101 km; note - all in Kosi close to Indian border

narrow gauge: 101 km 0.762-m gauge

Highways:

total: 7,700 km

paved: 3,196 km

unpaved: 4,504 km (1996 est.)

Ports and harbors: none

Airports: 45 (1998 est.)

Airports - with paved runways:

total: 5

over 3,047 m: 1

1,524 to 2,437 m: 3

Nepal (continued)

914 to 1,523 m: 1 (1998 est.)
Airports - with unpaved runways:
total: 40
1,524 to 2,437 m: 2
914 to 1,523 m: 9
under 914 m: 29 (1998 est.)

Military

Military branches: Royal Nepalese Army, Royal
Nepalese Army Air Service, Nepalese Police Force
Military manpower - military age: 17 years of age
Military manpower - availability:
males age 15-49: 5,924,732 (1999 est.)
Military manpower - fit for military service:
males age 15-49: 3,079,569 (1999 est.)
**Military manpower - reaching military age
annually:**
males: 281,658 (1999 est.)
Military expenditures - dollar figure: $44 million
(FY96/97)
Military expenditures - percent of GDP: 0.9%
(FY96/97)

Transnational Issues

Disputes - international: with Bhutan over 91,000
Bhutanese refugees in Nepal
Illicit drugs: illicit producer of cannabis for the
domestic and international drug markets; transit point
for opiates from Southeast Asia to the West

Netherlands

Geography

Location: Western Europe, bordering the North Sea,
between Belgium and Germany
Geographic coordinates: 52 30 N, 5 45 E
Map references: Europe
Area:
total: 41,532 sq km
land: 33,889 sq km
water: 7,643 sq km
Area - comparative: slightly less than twice the size
of New Jersey
Land boundaries:
total: 1,027 km
border countries: Belgium 450 km, Germany 577 km
Coastline: 451 km
Maritime claims:
exclusive fishing zone: 200 nm
territorial sea: 12 nm
Climate: temperate; marine; cool summers and mild
winters
Terrain: mostly coastal lowland and reclaimed land
(polders); some hills in southeast
Elevation extremes:
lowest point: Prins Alexanderpolder -7 m
highest point: Vaalserberg 321 m
Natural resources: natural gas, petroleum, fertile
soil
Land use:
arable land: 25%
permanent crops: 3%
permanent pastures: 25%
forests and woodland: 8%
other: 39% (1996 est.)
Irrigated land: 6,000 sq km (1996 est.)
Natural hazards: the extensive system of dikes and
dams protects nearly one-half of the total area from
being flooded
Environment - current issues: water pollution in
the form of heavy metals, organic compounds, and
nutrients such as nitrates and phosphates; air
pollution from vehicles and refining activities; acid rain

Environment - international agreements:
party to: Air Pollution, Air Pollution-Nitrogen Oxides,
Air Pollution-Sulphur 85, Air Pollution-Sulphur 94, Air
Pollution-Volatile Organic Compounds,
Antarctic-Environmental Protocol, Antarctic Treaty,
Biodiversity, Climate Change, Desertification,
Endangered Species, Environmental Modification,
Hazardous Wastes, Law of the Sea, Marine Dumping,
Marine Life Conservation, Nuclear Test Ban, Ozone
Layer Protection, Ship Pollution, Tropical Timber 83,
Tropical Timber 94, Wetlands, Whaling
signed, but not ratified: Air Pollution-Persistent
Organic Pollutants, Biodiversity, Climate
Change-Kyoto Protocol
Geography - note: located at mouths of three major
European rivers (Rhine, Maas or Meuse, and
Schelde)

People

Population: 15,807,641 (July 1999 est.)
Age structure:
0-14 years: 18% (male 1,475,606; female 1,410,088)
15-64 years: 68% (male 5,482,193; female
5,288,948)
65 years and over: 14% (male 875,847; female
1,274,959) (1999 est.)
Population growth rate: 0.47% (1999 est.)
Birth rate: 11.36 births/1,000 population (1999 est.)
Death rate: 8.69 deaths/1,000 population (1999 est.)
Net migration rate: 1.99 migrant(s)/1,000
population (1999 est.)
Sex ratio:
at birth: 1.05 male(s)/female
under 15 years: 1.05 male(s)/female
15-64 years: 1.04 male(s)/female
65 years and over: 0.69 male(s)/female
total population: 0.98 male(s)/female (1999 est.)
Infant mortality rate: 5.11 deaths/1,000 live births
(1999 est.)
Life expectancy at birth:
total population: 78.15 years
male: 75.28 years
female: 81.17 years (1999 est.)
Total fertility rate: 1.49 children born/woman (1999
est.)
Nationality:
noun: Dutchman(men), Dutchwoman(women)
adjective: Dutch
Ethnic groups: Dutch 94%, Moroccans, Turks, and
other 6% (1988)
Religions: Roman Catholic 34%, Protestant 25%,
Muslim 3%, other 2%, unaffiliated 36% (1991)
Languages: Dutch
Literacy:
definition: age 15 and over can read and write
total population: 99% (1979 est.)
male: NA%
female: NA%

Government

Country name:
conventional long form: Kingdom of the Netherlands

conventional short form: Netherlands
local long form: Koninkrijk der Nederlanden
local short form: Nederland
Data code: NL
Government type: constitutional monarchy
Capital: Amsterdam; The Hague is the seat of government
Administrative divisions: 12 provinces (provincien, singular - provincie); Drenthe, Flevoland, Friesland, Gelderland, Groningen, Limburg, Noord-Brabant, Noord-Holland, Overijssel, Utrecht, Zeeland, Zuid-Holland
Dependent areas: Aruba, Netherlands Antilles
Independence: 1579 (from Spain)
National holiday: Queen's Day, 30 April
Constitution: adopted 1814; amended many times, last time 17 February 1983
Legal system: civil law system incorporating French penal theory; constitution does not permit judicial review of acts of the States General; accepts compulsory ICJ jurisdiction, with reservations
Suffrage: 18 years of age; universal
Executive branch:
chief of state: Queen BEATRIX Wilhelmina Armgard (since 30 April 1980); Heir Apparent WILLEM-ALEXANDER (born 27 April 1967), Prince of Orange, son of the monarch
head of government: Prime Minister Wim KOK (since 22 August 1994) and Vice Prime Ministers Annemarie JORRITSMA (since 3 August 1998) and Els BORST-EILERS (since 3 August 1998)
cabinet: Cabinet appointed by the monarch
elections: none; the monarch is hereditary; following Second Chamber elections, the leader of the majority party or leader of a majority coalition is usually appointed prime minister by the monarch; vice prime ministers appointed by the monarch
note: there is a Council of State composed of the monarch, heir apparent, and councillors consulted by the executive on legislative and administrative policy
Legislative branch: bicameral States General or Staten Generaal consists of the First Chamber or Eerste Kamer (75 seats; members indirectly elected by the country's 12 provincial councils for four-year terms) and the Second Chamber or Tweede Kamer (150 seats; members directly elected by popular vote to serve four-year terms)
elections: First Chamber - last held 9 June 1995 (next to be held 25 May 1999); Second Chamber - last held 6 May 1998 (next to be held May 2002)
election results: First Chamber - percent of vote by party - NA; seats by party - VVD 23, CDA 19, PvdA 14, D'66 7, other 12; Second Chamber - percent of vote by party - PvdA 30.0%, VVD 25.3%, CDA 19.3%, D'66 9.3%, other 16.1%; seats by party - PvdA 45, VVD 38, CDA 29, D'66 14, other 24
Judicial branch: Supreme Court or Hoge Raad, justices are nominated for life by the monarch
Political parties and leaders: Christian Democratic Appeal or CDA [Jaap DE HOOP SCHEFFER]; Labor Party or PvdA [Wim KOK]; People's Party for Freedom and Democracy (Liberal) or VVD [Hans F. DIJKSTAL];

Democrats '66 or D'66 [Thom DE GRAAF]; a host of minor parties
Political pressure groups and leaders: large multinational firms; Federation of Netherlands Trade Union Movement (comprising Socialist and Catholic trade unions) and a Protestant trade union; Federation of Catholic and Protestant Employers Associations; the nondenominational Federation of Netherlands Enterprises; and Interchurch Peace Council or IKV
International organization participation: AfDB, AsDB, Australia Group, Benelux, BIS, CCC, CE, CERN, EAPC, EBRD, ECE, ECLAC, EIB, EMU, ESA, ESCAP, EU, FAO, G-10, IADB, IAEA, IBRD, ICAO, ICC, ICFTU, ICRM, IDA, IEA, IFAD, IFC, IFRCS, IHO, ILO, IMF, IMO, Inmarsat, Intelsat, Interpol, IOC, IOM, ISO, ITU, MTCR, NAM (guest), NATO, NEA, NSG, OAS (observer), OECD, OPCW, OSCE, PCA, UN, UNCTAD, UNESCO, UNHCR, UNIDO, UNMIBH, UNTSO, UNU, UPU, WCL, WEU, WHO, WIPO, WMO, WToO, WTrO, ZC
Diplomatic representation in the US:
chief of mission: Ambassador Joris M. VOS
chancery: 4200 Linnean Avenue NW, Washington, DC 20008
telephone: [1] (202) 244-5300
FAX: [1] (202) 362-3430
consulate(s) general: Chicago, Houston, Los Angeles, New York
Diplomatic representation from the US:
chief of mission: Ambassador Cynthia P. SCHNEIDER
embassy: Lange Voorhout 102, 2514 EJ, The Hague
mailing address: PSC 71, Box 1000, APO AE 09715
telephone: [31] (70) 310-9209
FAX: [31] (70) 361-4688
consulate(s) general: Amsterdam
Flag description: three equal horizontal bands of red (top), white, and blue; similar to the flag of Luxembourg, which uses a lighter blue and is longer

Economy

Economy - overview: This prosperous and open economy is based on private enterprise with the government's presence felt in many aspects of the economy. Industrial activity features food processing, petroleum refining, and metalworking. The highly mechanized agricultural sector employs only 4% of the labor force, but provides large surpluses for export and the domestic food-processing industry. As a result, the Netherlands ranks third worldwide in value of agricultural exports, behind the US and France. Sharp cuts in subsidy and social security spending since the 1980s helped the Dutch achieve sustained economic growth combined with falling unemployment and moderate inflation. The economy achieved a strong 3.7% growth in 1998; a dip in the business cycle probably will cause the economy to decelerate to slightly over 2% growth in 1999. Unemployment in 1999 is expected to be less than 5% of the labor force, and inflation probably will decline. The Dutch joined the first wave of 11 EU countries

launching the euro system on 1 January 1999.
GDP: purchasing power parity - $348.6 billion (1998 est.)
GDP - real growth rate: 3.7% (1998 est.)
GDP - per capita: purchasing power parity - $22,200 (1998 est.)
GDP - composition by sector:
agriculture: 3.2%
industry: 27.5%
services: 69.3% (1998 est.)
Population below poverty line: NA%
Household income or consumption by percentage share:
lowest 10%: 2.9%
highest 10%: 24.7% (1991)
Inflation rate (consumer prices): 2% (1998)
Labor force: 7 million (1998 est.)
Labor force - by occupation: services 73%, manufacturing and construction 23%, agriculture 4% (1998 est.)
Unemployment rate: 4.1% (1998 est.)
Budget:
revenues: $163 billion
expenditures: $170 billion, including capital expenditures of $NA (1999 est.)
Industries: agroindustries, metal and engineering products, electrical machinery and equipment, chemicals, petroleum, construction, microelectronics, fishing
Industrial production growth rate: 2.4% (1998)
Electricity - production: 83.3 billion kWh (1997)
Electricity - production by source:
fossil fuel: 94.51%
hydro: 0.1%
nuclear: 4.95%
other: 0.44% (1996)
Electricity - consumption: 90.366 billion kWh (1996)
Electricity - exports: 700 million kWh (1996)
Electricity - imports: 11.3 billion kWh (1996)
Agriculture - products: grains, potatoes, sugar beets, fruits, vegetables; livestock
Exports: $160 billion (f.o.b., 1998)
Exports - commodities: machinery and equipment, chemicals, fuels, food and tobacco
Exports - partners: EU 78% (Germany 27%, Belgium-Luxembourg 13%, France 11%, UK 10%, Italy 6%), Central and Eastern Europe, US (1997)
Imports: $142 billion (f.o.b., 1998)
Imports - commodities: machinery and transport equipment, chemicals, foodstuffs, fuels, consumer goods
Imports - partners: EU 61% (Germany 21%, Belgium-Luxembourg 11%, UK 10%), US 9%, Central and Eastern Europe (1997)
Debt - external: $0
Economic aid - donor: ODA, $2.9 billion (1997)
Currency: 1 Netherlands guilder, gulden, or florin (f.) = 100 cents; note - on 1 January 2002 to be replaced by the euro
Exchange rates: Netherlands guilders, gulden, or florins (f.) per US$1 - 1.8904 (January 1999), 1.9837

(1998), 1.9513 (1997), 1.6859 (1996), 1.6057 (1995), 1.8200 (1994)

note: on 1 January 1999, the European Union introduced a common currency that is now being used by financial institutions in some member countries at the rate of 0.8597 euros per US$ and a fixed rate of 2.20371 guilders per euro; the euro will replace the local currency in consenting countries for all transactions in 2002

Fiscal year: calendar year

Communications

Telephones: 8.431 million (1998 est.); 3.4 million cellular telephone subscribers (1998 est.)

Telephone system: highly developed and well maintained; system of multi-conductor cables gradually being supplemented/replaced by a glass-fiber based telecommunication infrastructure; Mobile GSM-based mobile telephony density rapidly growing; third generation Universal Mobile Telecommunications System expected for introduction by the year 2001

domestic: nationwide cellular telephone system; microwave radio relay

international: 5 submarine cables; satellite earth stations - 3 Intelsat (1 Indian Ocean and 2 Atlantic Ocean), 1 Eutelsat, and 1 Inmarsat (Atlantic and Indian Ocean Regions)

Radio broadcast stations: AM 3 (relays 3), FM 12 (repeaters 39), shortwave 0

Radios: 14 million (1994 est.)

Television broadcast stations: 15 (in addition, there are five low-power repeaters) (1997)

Televisions: 7.6 million (1994 est.)

Transportation

Railways:
total: 2,813 km
standard gauge: 2,813 km 1.435-m gauge; (1,991 km electrified) (1996)

Highways:
total: 127,000 km
paved: 114,427 km (including 2,360 km of expressways)
unpaved: 12,573 km (1996 est.)

Waterways: 5,046 km, of which 47% is usable by craft of 1,000 metric ton capacity or larger

Pipelines: crude oil 418 km; petroleum products 965 km; natural gas 10,230 km

Ports and harbors: Amsterdam, Delfzijl, Dordrecht, Eemshaven, Groningen, Haarlem, Ijmuiden, Maastricht, Rotterdam, Terneuzen, Utrecht

Merchant marine:
total: 510 ships (1,000 GRT or over) totaling 3,632,477 GRT/4,097,328 DWT
ships by type: bulk 4, cargo 303, chemical tanker 42, combination bulk 1, container 52, liquefied gas tanker 17, livestock carrier 1, multifunction large-load carrier 9, oil tanker 24, passenger 8, refrigerated cargo 30, roll-on/roll-off cargo 12, short-sea passenger 3, specialized tanker 4

note: many Dutch-owned ships are also operating under the registry of Netherlands Antilles (1998 est.)

Airports: 28 (1998 est.)

Airports - with paved runways:
total: 19
over 3,047 m: 2
2,438 to 3,047 m: 7
1,524 to 2,437 m: 6
914 to 1,523 m: 3
under 914 m: 1 (1998 est.)

Airports - with unpaved runways:
total: 9
914 to 1,523 m: 3
under 914 m: 6 (1998 est.)

Heliports: 1 (1998 est.)

Military

Military branches: Royal Netherlands Army, Royal Netherlands Navy (includes Naval Air Service and Marine Corps), Royal Netherlands Air Force, Royal Constabulary

Military manpower - military age: 20 years of age

Military manpower - availability:
males age 15-49: 4,117,376 (1999 est.)

Military manpower - fit for military service:
males age 15-49: 3,595,693 (1999 est.)

Military manpower - reaching military age annually:
males: 95,368 (1999 est.)

Military expenditures - dollar figure: $6.604 billion (FY97)

Military expenditures - percent of GDP: 2.1% (1995)

Transnational Issues

Disputes - international: none

Illicit drugs: important gateway for cocaine, heroin, and hashish entering Europe; major European producer of illicit amphetamines and other synthetic drugs

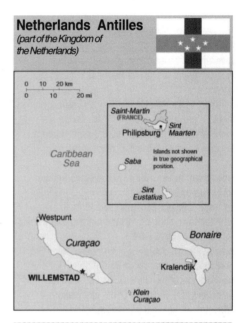

Netherlands Antilles
(part of the Kingdom of the Netherlands)

Geography

Location: Caribbean, two island groups in the Caribbean Sea - one includes Curacao and Bonaire north of Venezuela and the other is east of the Virgin Islands

Geographic coordinates: 12 15 N, 68 45 W

Map references: Central America and the Caribbean

Area:
total: 960 sq km
land: 960 sq km
water: 0 sq km
note: includes Bonaire, Curacao, Saba, Sint Eustatius, and Sint Maarten (Dutch part of the island of Saint Martin)

Area - comparative: more than five times the size of Washington, DC

Land boundaries:
total: 10.2 km
border countries: Guadeloupe (Saint Martin) 10.2 km

Coastline: 364 km

Maritime claims:
exclusive fishing zone: 12 nm
territorial sea: 12 nm

Climate: tropical; ameliorated by northeast trade winds

Terrain: generally hilly, volcanic interiors

Elevation extremes:
lowest point: Caribbean Sea 0 m
highest point: Mount Scenery 862 m

Natural resources: phosphates (Curacao only), salt (Bonaire only)

Land use:
arable land: 10%
permanent crops: 0%
permanent pastures: 0%
forests and woodland: 0%
other: 90% (1993 est.)

Irrigated land: NA sq km

Netherlands Antilles (continued)

Natural hazards: Curacao and Bonaire are south of Caribbean hurricane belt and are rarely threatened; Sint Maarten, Saba, and Sint Eustatius are subject to hurricanes from July to October
Environment - current issues: NA
Environment - international agreements:
party to: NA
signed, but not ratified: NA

People

Population: 207,827 (July 1999 est.)
Age structure:
0-14 years: 26% (male 27,160; female 26,149)
15-64 years: 67% (male 65,781; female 73,054)
65 years and over: 7% (male 6,538; female 9,145) (1999 est.)
Population growth rate: 1.01% (1999 est.)
Birth rate: 17.11 births/1,000 population (1999 est.)
Death rate: 6.58 deaths/1,000 population (1999 est.)
Net migration rate: -0.43 migrant(s)/1,000 population (1999 est.)
Sex ratio:
at birth: 1.05 male(s)/female
under 15 years: 1.04 male(s)/female
15-64 years: 0.9 male(s)/female
65 years and over: 0.72 male(s)/female
total population: 0.92 male(s)/female (1999 est.)
Infant mortality rate: 12.59 deaths/1,000 live births (1999 est.)
Life expectancy at birth:
total population: 74.25 years
male: 72.19 years
female: 76.41 years (1999 est.)
Total fertility rate: 2.09 children born/woman (1999 est.)
Nationality:
noun: Netherlands Antillean(s)
adjective: Netherlands Antillean
Ethnic groups: mixed black 85%, Carib Amerindian, white, East Asian
Religions: Roman Catholic, Protestant, Jewish, Seventh-Day Adventist
Languages: Dutch (official), Papiamento (a Spanish-Portuguese-Dutch-English dialect) predominates, English widely spoken, Spanish
Literacy:
definition: age 15 and over can read and write
total population: 98%
male: 98%
female: 99% (1981 est.)

Government

Country name:
conventional long form: none
conventional short form: Netherlands Antilles
local long form: none
local short form: Nederlandse Antillen
Data code: NT
Dependency status: part of the Kingdom of the Netherlands; full autonomy in internal affairs granted in 1954

Government type: parliamentary
Capital: Willemstad
Administrative divisions: none (part of the Kingdom of the Netherlands)
note: each island has its own government
Independence: none (part of the Kingdom of the Netherlands)
National holiday: Queen's Day, 30 April (1938)
Constitution: 29 December 1954, Statute of the Realm of the Netherlands, as amended
Legal system: based on Dutch civil law system, with some English common law influence
Suffrage: 18 years of age; universal
Executive branch:
chief of state: Queen BEATRIX Wilhelmina Armgard of the Netherlands (since 30 April 1980), represented by Governor General Jaime SALEH (since NA October 1989)
head of government: Prime Minister Miguel POURIER (since 25 February 1994)
cabinet: Council of Ministers elected by the Staten
elections: the monarch is hereditary; governor general appointed by the monarch for a six-year term; following legislative elections, the leader of the majority party is usually elected prime minister by the Staten; election last held 30 January 1998 (next to be held by NA 2002)
election results: Miguel POURIER elected prime minister; percent of legislative vote - NA
Legislative branch: unicameral States or Staten (22 seats; members are elected by popular vote to serve four-year terms)
elections: last held 30 January 1998 (next to be held by NA 2002)
election results: percent of vote by party - NA; seats by party - PAR 4, PNP 3, SPA 1, PDB 2, UPB 1, MAN 2, PLKP 3, WIPM 1, SEA 1, DP-St.M 2, FOL 2; no party won enough seats to form a government
note: the government of Prime Minister Miguel POURIER is a coalition of several parties
Judicial branch: Joint High Court of Justice (judges appointed by the monarch)
Political parties and leaders:
Bonaire: Democratic Party of Bonaire or PDB [Jopi ABRAHAM]; Patriotic Union of Bonaire or UPB [Rudy ELLIS]
Curacao: Antillean Restructuring Party or PAR [Miguel POURIER]; National People's Party or PNP [Suzy ROMER]; New Antilles Movement or MAN [Domenico Felip Don MARTINA]; Workers' Liberation Front or FOL [Wilson GODETT, Jr.]; Socialist Independent or SI [George HUECK]; Democratic Party of Curacao or DP [Ephraim JONCKHEER]; Nos Patria [Chin BEHILIA]; Social Action Cause or KAS [Benny DEMEI]; Labor Party People's Crusade or PLKP [Errol COVA]; Foundation Energetic Management Anti-Narcotics or FAME [Eric LODEWIJKS]; Pro Curacao Party or PPK [Winston LOURENS]; C 93 [Stanley BROWN]; People's Party or PAPU [Richard HODI]
Saba: Windward Islands People's Movement or WIPM Saba [Ray HASSELL]; Saba Democratic Labor

Movement [Steve HASSELL]; Saba Unity Party [Carmen SIMMONDS]
Sint Eustatius: Democratic Party of Sint Eustatius or DP-St. E [Julian WOODLEY]; Windward Islands People's Movement or WIPM [leader NA]; St. Eustatius Alliance or SEA [Ingrid WHITFIELD]
Sint Maarten: Democratic Party of Sint Maarten or DP-St. M [Sarah WESTCOTT-WILLIAMS]; Patriotic Movement of Sint Maarten or SPA [William MARLIN]; Serious Alternative People's Party or SAPP [Julian ROLLOCKS]
note: political parties are indigenous to each island
International organization participation: Caricom (observer), ECLAC (associate), Interpol, IOC, UNESCO (associate), UPU, WMO, WToO (associate)
Diplomatic representation in the US: none (represented by the Kingdom of the Netherlands)
Diplomatic representation from the US:
chief of mission: Consul General James L. WILLIAMS
consulate(s) general: J.B. Gorsiraweg #1, Curacao
mailing address: P. O. Box 158, Willemstad, Curacao
telephone: [599] (9) 4613066
FAX: [599] (9) 4616489
Flag description: white, with a horizontal blue stripe in the center superimposed on a vertical red band, also centered; five white, five-pointed stars are arranged in an oval pattern in the center of the blue band; the five stars represent the five main islands of Bonaire, Curacao, Saba, Sint Eustatius, and Sint Maarten

Economy

Economy - overview: Tourism, petroleum transshipment, and offshore finance are the mainstays of this small economy, which is closely tied to the outside world. The islands enjoy a high per capita income and a well-developed infrastructure as compared with other countries in the region. Almost all consumer and capital goods are imported, with Venezuela, the US, and Mexico being the major suppliers. Poor soils and inadequate water supplies hamper the development of agriculture.
GDP: purchasing power parity - $2.4 billion (1997 est.)
GDP - real growth rate: -1.8% (1997)
GDP - per capita: purchasing power parity - $11,500 (1997 est.)
GDP - composition by sector:
agriculture: 1%
industry: 15%
services: 84% (1996 est.)
Population below poverty line: NA%
Household income or consumption by percentage share:
lowest 10%: NA%
highest 10%: NA%
Inflation rate (consumer prices): 3.3% (1997)
Labor force: 89,000
Labor force - by occupation: government 65%, industry and commerce 28% (1983)
Unemployment rate: 14.9% (1998 est.)

Netherlands Antilles *(continued)*

Budget:
revenues: $710.8 million
expenditures: $741.6 million, including capital expenditures of $NA (1997 est.)
Industries: tourism (Curacao, Sint Maarten, and Bonaire), petroleum refining (Curacao), petroleum transshipment facilities (Curacao and Bonaire), light manufacturing (Curacao)
Industrial production growth rate: NA%
Electricity - production: 1.4 billion kWh (1996)
Electricity - production by source:
fossil fuel: 100%
hydro: 0%
nuclear: 0%
other: 0% (1996)
Electricity - consumption: 1.4 billion kWh (1996)
Electricity - exports: 0 kWh (1996)
Electricity - imports: 0 kWh (1996)
Agriculture - products: aloes, sorghum, peanuts, vegetables, tropical fruit
Exports: $268.2 million (f.o.b., 1997)
Exports - commodities: petroleum products 98% (1993)
Exports - partners: US 28.6%, Honduras 6.4%, Belgium-Luxembourg 6%, Italy 4.9%, Guatemala 4.5%, Costa Rica 4% (1996)
Imports: $1.4 billion (c.i.f., 1997)
Imports - commodities: crude petroleum 64%, food, manufactures (1993)
Imports - partners: Venezuela 34%, US 16.4%, Mexico 15.5%, Netherlands 5%, Italy 3.5%, Brazil 2.8% (1996)
Debt - external: $1.35 billion (1996)
Economic aid - recipient: $NA; note - the Netherlands provided a $97 million aid package in 1996
Currency: 1 Netherlands Antillean guilder, gulden, or florin (NAf.) = 100 cents
Exchange rates: Netherlands Antillean guilders, gulden, or florins (NAf.) per US$1 - 1.790 (fixed rate since 1989)
Fiscal year: calendar year

Communications

Telephones: NA
Telephone system: generally adequate facilities
domestic: extensive interisland microwave radio relay links
international: 2 submarine cables; satellite earth stations - 2 Intelsat (Atlantic Ocean)
Radio broadcast stations: AM 9, FM 4, shortwave 0
Radios: 205,000 (1992 est.)
Television broadcast stations: 3 (in addition, there is a cable service which supplies programs received from various US satellite networks) (1997)
Televisions: 64,000 (1992 est.)

Transportation

Railways: 0 km
Highways:
total: 600 km

paved: 300 km
unpaved: 300 km (1992 est.)
Ports and harbors: Kralendijk, Philipsburg, Willemstad
Merchant marine:
total: 95 ships (1,000 GRT or over) totaling 811,782 GRT/1,045,989 DWT
ships by type: bulk 2, cargo 26, chemical tanker 2, combination ore/oil 3, container 10, liquefied gas tanker 4, multifunction large-load carrier 19, oil tanker 4, passenger 1, refrigerated cargo 18, roll-on/roll-off cargo 6
note: a flag of convenience registry; includes ships of 2 countries: Belgium owns 9 ships, Germany 1 (1998 est.)
Airports: 5 (1998 est.)
Airports - with paved runways:
total: 5
over 3,047 m: 1
1,524 to 2,437 m: 2
914 to 1,523 m: 1
under 914 m: 1 (1998 est.)

Military

Military branches: Royal Netherlands Navy, Marine Corps, Royal Netherlands Air Force, National Guard, Police Force
Military manpower - military age: 20 years of age
Military manpower - availability:
males age 15-47: 53,285 (1999 est.)
Military manpower - fit for military service:
males age 15-49: 29,888 (1999 est.)
Military manpower - reaching military age annually:
males: 1,457 (1999 est.)
Military - note: defense is the responsibility of the Kingdom of the Netherlands

Transnational Issues

Disputes - international: none
Illicit drugs: money-laundering center; transshipment point for South American drugs bound for the US and Europe

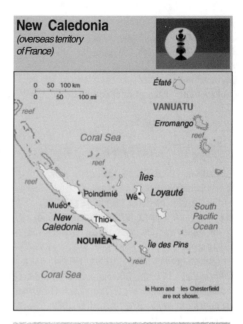

New Caledonia
(overseas territory of France)

Geography

Location: Oceania, islands in the South Pacific Ocean, east of Australia
Geographic coordinates: 21 30 S, 165 30 E
Map references: Oceania
Area:
total: 19,060 sq km
land: 18,575 sq km
water: 485 sq km
Area - comparative: slightly smaller than New Jersey
Land boundaries: 0 km
Coastline: 2,254 km
Maritime claims:
exclusive economic zone: 200 nm
territorial sea: 12 nm
Climate: tropical; modified by southeast trade winds; hot, humid
Terrain: coastal plains with interior mountains
Elevation extremes:
lowest point: Pacific Ocean 0 m
highest point: Mont Panie 1,628 m
Natural resources: nickel, chrome, iron, cobalt, manganese, silver, gold, lead, copper
Land use:
arable land: 0%
permanent crops: 0%
permanent pastures: 12%
forests and woodland: 39%
other: 49% (1993 est.)
Irrigated land: NA sq km
Natural hazards: typhoons most frequent from November to March
Environment - current issues: NA
Environment - international agreements:
party to: NA
signed, but not ratified: NA

People

Population: 197,361 (July 1999 est.)

New Caledonia (continued)

Age structure:
0-14 years: 29% (male 29,610; female 28,485)
15-64 years: 65% (male 64,552; female 63,229)
65 years and over: 6% (male 5,443; female 6,042)
(1999 est.)
Population growth rate: 1.59% (1999 est.)
Birth rate: 20.68 births/1,000 population (1999 est.)
Death rate: 4.82 deaths/1,000 population (1999 est.)
Net migration rate: 0.08 migrant(s)/1,000
population (1999 est.)
Sex ratio:
at birth: 1.05 male(s)/female
under 15 years: 1.04 male(s)/female
15-64 years: 1.02 male(s)/female
65 years and over: 0.9 male(s)/female
total population: 1.02 male(s)/female (1999 est.)
Infant mortality rate: 12.15 deaths/1,000 live births
(1999 est.)
Life expectancy at birth:
total population: 75.35 years
male: 72.1 years
female: 78.77 years (1999 est.)
Total fertility rate: 2.43 children born/woman (1999
est.)
Nationality:
noun: New Caledonian(s)
adjective: New Caledonian
Ethnic groups: Melanesian 42.5%, European
37.1%, Wallisian 8.4%, Polynesian 3.8%, Indonesian
3.6%, Vietnamese 1.6%, other 3%
Religions: Roman Catholic 60%, Protestant 30%,
other 10%
Languages: French, 28 Melanesian-Polynesian
dialects
Literacy:
definition: age 15 and over can read and write
total population: 91%
male: 92%
female: 90% (1976 est.)

Government

Country name:
conventional long form: Territory of New Caledonia
and Dependencies
conventional short form: New Caledonia
local long form: Territoire des Nouvelle-Caledonie et
Dependances
local short form: Nouvelle-Caledonie
Data code: NC
Dependency status: overseas territory of France
since 1956
Government type: NA
Capital: Noumea
Administrative divisions: none (overseas territory
of France); there are no first-order administrative
divisions as defined by the US Government, but there
are 3 provinces named Iles Loyaute, Nord, and Sud
Independence: none (overseas territory of France);
note - a referendum on independence was held in
1998 but did not pass
National holiday: National Day, Taking of the
Bastille, 14 July (1789)

Constitution: 28 September 1958 (French
Constitution)
Legal system: the 1988 Matignon Accords grant
substantial autonomy to the islands; formerly under
French law
Suffrage: 18 years of age; universal
Executive branch:
chief of state: President Jacques CHIRAC of France
(since 17 May 1995), represented by High
Commissioner and President of the Council of
Government Dominque BUR (since NA August 1995)
head of government: President of the Territorial
Congress Simon LOUECKHOTE (since NA 1998)
cabinet: Consultative Committee
elections: French president elected by popular vote
for a seven-year term; high commissioner appointed
by the French president on the advice of the French
Ministry of Interior; president of the Territorial
Congress elected by the members of the congress
Legislative branch: unicameral Territorial Congress
or Congres Territorial (54 seats; members are
members of the three Provincial Assemblies or
Assemblees Provinciales elected by popular vote to
serve six-year terms)
elections: last held 9 July 1995 (next to be held NA
July 2001)
election results: percent of vote by party - NA; seats
by party - RPR 22, FLNKS 12, UNCT 9, UNI 5,
DEPCA 2, FN 2, RCF 2, and other 2
note: New Caledonia elects 1 seat to the French
Senate; elections last held 27 September 1992 (next
to be held NA September 2001); results - percent of
vote by party - NA; seats by party - RPR 1; New
Caledonia also elects 2 seats to the French National
Assembly; elections last held 25 May-1 June 1997
(next to be held NA 2002); results - percent of vote by
party - NA; seats by party - RPR 2
Judicial branch: Court of Appeal or Cour d'Appel
Political parties and leaders: Progressive
Melanesian Union or UPM [Edmond NEKIRIAI];
Melanesian proindependence Kanaka Socialist
National Liberation Front or FLNKS [Rock
WAMYTAN]; Melanesian moderate Kanak Socialist
Liberation or LKS [Nidoish NAISSELINE]; National
Front or FN (extreme right) [Guy GEORGE]; Socialist
Party of Kanaky or PSK [Jacques VIOLETTE]; Union
Oceanienne or UO (conservative) [Michel HEMA];
Front de Developpement des Iles Loyautes or FDIL
[Cono HAMU]; Union Caledonian or UC [Bernard
LEPEU, president]; A New Caledonia for All or UNCT
[Didier LEROUX]; Kanaque Liberation Party or
PALIKA [Paul NEAOUTYINE and Elie POIGOUNE];
New Caledonia National Party [Georges CHATENEY];
Oceanic Democratic Rally or RDO [Alois SAKO];
Kanaque Federal Party of OPAO [Gabrielle PAITA and
Auguste SIAPO]; Caledonian Generation
[Jean-Raymond POSTIC]; Union des Synicates de
Travailleurs Kanaks Exploites or USTKE [Louis Kotra
UREGEY]; Federation for a New Caledonian Society
or FNSC [Jean-Pierre AIFA]; Union to Construct
Independence [Frances POADOUY]; Movement for
France or MPF [Claude SARAAN]; Rally for Caledonia

in the Republic or RPCR is a coalition of 5 parties:
Union for the Rebirth of Caledonia [Jean-Louis MIR];
Christian Social Democrats - All Ethnic Group Accord
[Raymond MURA]; Rally for Caledonia [Jacques
LAFLEUR]; Rally of the Republic [Dick UKEIWE];
Liberal Caledonian Movement [Jean LEQUES]; Union
Nationale pour l'Independance or UNI [leader NA];
Developper Ensemble pour Construire l'Avenir or
DEPCA [leader NA]; Rassemblement pour une
Caledonie dans la France or RCF [leader NA]
International organization participation: ESCAP
(associate), FZ, ICFTU, SPC, WFTU, WMO
Diplomatic representation in the US: none
(overseas territory of France)
Diplomatic representation from the US: none
(overseas territory of France)
Flag description: three horizontal bands, blue (top),
red, and green, with a yellow disk enclosing a black
symbol centered to the hoist side; the flag of France is
used for official occasions

Economy

Economy - overview: New Caledonia has more
than 20% of the world's known nickel resources. In
recent years, the economy has suffered because of
depressed international demand for nickel, the
principal source of export earnings. Only a negligible
amount of the land is suitable for cultivation, and food
accounts for about 25% of imports. In addition to
nickel, financial support from France and tourism are
key to the health of the economy. Performance in
1998 was hampered by the spillover of financial
problems in East Asia and by lower expected prices
for nickel.
GDP: purchasing power parity - $2.1 billion (1996
est.)
GDP - real growth rate: NA%
GDP - per capita: purchasing power parity - $11,400
(1996 est.)
GDP - composition by sector:
agriculture: 3%
industry: 25%
services: 72% (1996)
Population below poverty line: NA%
**Household income or consumption by percentage
share:**
lowest 10%: NA%
highest 10%: NA%
Inflation rate (consumer prices): 1.7% (1996 est.)
Labor force: 70,044 (1988)
Labor force - by occupation: agriculture 20%,
industry 16%, services 60%, mining 4% (1996)
Unemployment rate: 15% (1994)
Budget:
revenues: $755.6 million
expenditures: $755.6 million, including capital
expenditures of $NA (1995 est.)
Industries: nickel mining and smelting
Industrial production growth rate: NA%
Electricity - production: 1.145 billion kWh (1996)
Electricity - production by source:
fossil fuel: 69.87%

New Caledonia (continued)

hydro: 30.13%
nuclear: 0%
other: 0% (1996)
Electricity - consumption: 1.145 billion kWh (1996)
Electricity - exports: 0 kWh (1996)
Electricity - imports: 0 kWh (1996)
Agriculture - products: vegetables; beef, other livestock products
Exports: $500 million (f.o.b., 1996)
Exports - commodities: ferronickels, nickel ore
Exports - partners: Japan 31%, France 29%, US 12%, Australia 7%, Taiwan 6% (1996 est.)
Imports: $845 million (c.i.f., 1996)
Imports - commodities: foods, transport equipment, machinery and electrical equipment, fuels, minerals
Imports - partners: France 45%, Australia 18%, Singapore 7%, New Zealand 6%, Japan 4% (1996 est.)
Debt - external: $NA
Economic aid - recipient: $446.3 million (1995); note - about $50 million yearly support from France for government operations
Currency: 1 Comptoirs Francais du Pacifique franc (CFPF) = 100 centimes
Exchange rates: Comptoirs Francais du Pacifique francs (CFPF) per US$1 - 102.72 (January 1999), 107.25 (1998), 106.11 (1997), 93.00 (1996), 90.75 (1995), 100.93 (1994); note - linked at the rate of 18.18 to the French franc
Fiscal year: calendar year

Communications

Telephones: 38,748 (1993 est.)
Telephone system:
domestic: NA
international: satellite earth station - 1 Intelsat (Pacific Ocean)
Radio broadcast stations: AM 5, FM 3, shortwave 0
Radios: 97,000 (1992 est.)
Television broadcast stations: 6 (in addition, there are 25 low-power repeaters) (1997)
Televisions: 47,000 (1992 est.)

Transportation

Railways: 0 km
Highways:
total: 5,562 km
paved: 975 km
unpaved: 4,587 km (1993)
Ports and harbors: Mueo, Noumea, Thio
Merchant marine: none
Airports: 27 (1998 est.)
Airports - with paved runways:
total: 5
over 3,047 m: 1
914 to 1,523 m: 3
under 914 m: 1 (1998 est.)
Airports - with unpaved runways:
total: 22

914 to 1,523 m: 11
under 914 m: 11 (1998 est.)
Heliports: 7 (1998 est.)

Military

Military branches: French Armed Forces (Army, Navy, Air Force, Gendarmerie); Police Force
Military expenditures - dollar figure: $NA
Military expenditures - percent of GDP: NA%
Military - note: defense is the responsibility of France

Transnational Issues

Disputes - international: Matthew and Hunter Islands claimed by France and Vanuatu

New Zealand

Antipodes Islands, Auckland Islands, Bounty Islands, Campbell Island, Chatham Islands, and Kermadec Islands are not shown.

Geography

Location: Oceania, islands in the South Pacific Ocean, southeast of Australia
Geographic coordinates: 41 00 S, 174 00 E
Map references: Oceania
Area:
total: 268,680 sq km
land: 268,670 sq km
water: 10 sq km
note: includes Antipodes Islands, Auckland Islands, Bounty Islands, Campbell Island, Chatham Islands, and Kermadec Islands
Area - comparative: about the size of Colorado
Land boundaries: 0 km
Coastline: 15,134 km
Maritime claims:
continental shelf: 200 nm or to the edge of the continental margin
exclusive economic zone: 200 nm
territorial sea: 12 nm
Climate: temperate with sharp regional contrasts
Terrain: predominately mountainous with some large coastal plains
Elevation extremes:
lowest point: Pacific Ocean 0 m

New Zealand (continued)

highest point: Mount Cook 3,764 m
Natural resources: natural gas, iron ore, sand, coal, timber, hydropower, gold, limestone
Land use:
arable land: 9%
permanent crops: 5%
permanent pastures: 50%
forests and woodland: 28%
other: 8% (1993 est.)
Irrigated land: 2,850 sq km (1993 est.)
Natural hazards: earthquakes are common, though usually not severe; volcanic activity
Environment - current issues: deforestation; soil erosion; native flora and fauna hard-hit by species introduced from outside
Environment - international agreements:
party to: Antarctic-Environmental Protocol, Antarctic Treaty, Biodiversity, Climate Change, Endangered Species, Environmental Modification, Hazardous Wastes, Law of the Sea, Marine Dumping, Nuclear Test Ban, Ozone Layer Protection, Tropical Timber 83, Tropical Timber 94, Wetlands, Whaling
signed, but not ratified: Climate Change-Kyoto Protocol, Marine Life Conservation
Geography - note: about 80% of the population lives in cities

People

Population: 3,662,265 (July 1999 est.)
Age structure:
0-14 years: 23% (male 430,105; female 409,302)
15-64 years: 65% (male 1,202,762; female 1,195,006)
65 years and over: 12% (male 184,048; female 241,042) (1999 est.)
Population growth rate: 0.99% (1999 est.)
Birth rate: 14.42 births/1,000 population (1999 est.)
Death rate: 7.53 deaths/1,000 population (1999 est.)
Net migration rate: 3.01 migrant(s)/1,000 population (1999 est.)
Sex ratio:
at birth: 1.05 male(s)/female
under 15 years: 1.05 male(s)/female
15-64 years: 1.01 male(s)/female
65 years and over: 0.76 male(s)/female
total population: 0.98 male(s)/female (1999 est.)
Infant mortality rate: 6.22 deaths/1,000 live births (1999 est.)
Life expectancy at birth:
total population: 77.82 years
male: 74.55 years
female: 81.27 years (1999 est.)
Total fertility rate: 1.85 children born/woman (1999 est.)
Nationality:
noun: New Zealander(s)
adjective: New Zealand
Ethnic groups: New Zealand European 74.5%, Maori 9.7%, other European 4.6%, Pacific Islander 3.8%, Asian and others 7.4%
Religions: Anglican 24%, Presbyterian 18%, Roman Catholic 15%, Methodist 5%, Baptist 2%, other

Protestant 3%, unspecified or none 33% (1986)
Languages: English (official), Maori
Literacy:
definition: age 15 and over can read and write
total population: 99% (1980 est.)
male: NA%
female: NA%

Government

Country name:
conventional long form: none
conventional short form: New Zealand
abbreviation: NZ
Data code: NZ
Government type: parliamentary democracy
Capital: Wellington
Administrative divisions: 93 counties, 9 districts*, and 3 town districts**; Akaroa, Amuri, Ashburton, Bay of Islands, Bruce, Buller, Chatham Islands, Cheviot, Clifton, Clutha, Cook, Dannevirke, Egmont, Eketahuna, Ellesmere, Eltham, Eyre, Featherston, Franklin, Golden Bay, Great Barrier Island, Grey, Hauraki Plains, Hawera*, Hawke's Bay, Heathcote, Hikurangi**, Hobson, Hokianga, Horowhenua, Hurunui, Hutt, Inangahua, Inglewood, Kaikoura, Kairanga, Kiwitea, Lake, Mackenzie, Malvern, Manaia**, Manawatu, Mangonui, Maniototo, Marlborough, Masterton, Matamata, Mount Herbert, Ohinemuri, Opotiki, Oroua, Otamatea, Otorohanga*, Oxford, Pahiatua, Paparua, Patea, Piako, Pohangina, Raglan, Rangiora*, Rangitikei, Rodney, Rotorua*, Runanga, Saint Kilda, Silverpeaks, Southland, Stewart Island, Stratford, Strathallan, Taranaki, Taumarunui, Taupo, Tauranga, Thames-Coromandel*, Tuapeka, Vincent, Waiapu, Waiheke, Waihemo, Waikato, Waikohu, Waimairi, Waimarino, Waimate, Waimate West, Waimea, Waipa, Waipawa*, Waipukurau*, Wairarapa South, Wairewa, Wairoa, Waitaki, Waitomo*, Waitotara, Wallace, Wanganui, Waverley**, Westland, Whakatane*, Whangarei, Whangaroa, Woodville
note: there may be a new administrative structure of 16 regions (Auckland, Bay of Plenty, Canterbury, Gisborne, Hawke's Bay, Marlborough, Nelson, Northland, Otago, Southland, Taranaki, Tasman, Waikato, Wanganui-Manawatu, Wellington, West Coast) that are subdivided into 57 districts and 16 cities* (Ashburton, Auckland*, Banks Peninsula, Buller, Carterton, Central Hawke's Bay, Central Otago, Christchurch*, Clutha, Dunedin*, Far North, Franklin, Gisborne, Gore, Grey, Hamilton*, Hastings, Hauraki, Horowhenua, Hurunui, Hutt*, Invercargill*, Kaikoura, Kaipara, Kapiti Coast, Kawerau, Mackenzie, Manawatu, Manukau*, Marlborough, Masterton, Matamata Piako, Napier*, Nelson*, New Plymouth, North Shore*, Opotiki, Otorohanga, Palmerston North*, Papakura*, Porirua*, Queenstown Lakes, Rangitikei, Rodney, Rotorua, Ruapehu, Selwyn, Southland, South Taranaki, South Waikato, South Wairarapa, Stratford, Tararua, Tasman, Taupo, Tauranga, Thames Coromandel, Timaru, Upper Hutt*, Waikato, Waimakariri, Waimate, Waipa, Wairoa,

Waitakere*, Waitaki, Waitomo, Wanganui, Wellington*, Western Bay of Plenty, Westland, Whakatane, Whangarei)
Dependent areas: Cook Islands, Niue, Tokelau
Independence: 26 September 1907 (from UK)
National holiday: Waitangi Day, 6 February (1840) (Treaty of Waitangi established British sovereignty)
Constitution: no formal, written constitution; consists of various documents, including certain acts of the UK and New Zealand Parliaments; Constitution Act 1986 was to have come into force 1 January 1987, but has not been enacted
Legal system: based on English law, with special legislation and land courts for Maoris; accepts compulsory ICJ jurisdiction, with reservations
Suffrage: 18 years of age; universal
Executive branch:
chief of state: Queen ELIZABETH II (since 6 February 1952), represented by Governor General Sir Michael HARDIE BOYS (since 21 March 1996)
head of government: Prime Minister Jenny SHIPLEY (since 8 December 1997) and Deputy Prime Minister Wyatt CREECH (since NA August 1998); note - the coalition government of the National Party and the New Zealand First Party was dissolved on 18 August 1998
cabinet: Executive Council appointed by the governor general on the recommendation of the prime minister
elections: none; the monarch is hereditary; governor general appointed by the monarch; following legislative elections, the leader of the majority party or the leader of a majority coalition is usually appointed prime minister by the governor general for a three-year term; deputy prime minister appointed by the governor general
Legislative branch: unicameral House of Representatives - commonly called Parliament (120 seats; members elected by popular vote in single-member constituencies to serve three-year terms)
elections: last held 12 October 1996 (next must be called by October 1999)
election results: percent of vote by party - NP 34.1%, NZLP 28.3%, NZFP 13.1%, Alliance 10.1%, ACT 6.17%, UNZ 0.91%; seats by party - NP 44, NZLP 37, NZFP 17, Alliance 13, ACT 8, UNZ 1
Judicial branch: High Court; Court of Appeal
Political parties and leaders: National Party or NP [Jenny SHIPLEY]; New Zealand First Party or NZFP [Winston PETERS]; New Zealand Labor Party or NZLP (opposition) [Helen CLARK]; Alliance (a coalition of five small parties - New Labor Party [Jim ANDERTON], Democratic Party [John WRIGHT], New Zealand Liberal Party [Frank GROVER], Green Party [coleaders Jeanette FITZSIMONS and Rod DONALD], and Mana Motuhake [Sandra LEE]); United New Zealand or UNZ [Peter DUNNE]; Conservative Party (formerly Right of Centre Party) [Trevor ROGERS]; ACT, New Zealand [Richard PREBBLE]; Christian Coalition (a coalition of the Christian Democrats and Christian Heritage Party) [Rev. Graham CAPILL]; Mauri Pacific Party

(composed of members who broke away from the NZFP) [Tau HENARE]

International organization participation: ANZUS (US suspended security obligations to NZ on 11 August 1986), APEC, AsDB, Australia Group, C, CCC, CP, EBRD, ESCAP, FAO, IAEA, IBRD, ICAO, ICFTU, ICRM, IDA, IEA, IFAD, IFC, IFRCS, IHO, ILO, IMF, IMO, Inmarsat, Intelsat, Interpol, IOC, IOM (observer), ISO, ITU, MONUA, MTCR, NAM (guest), NSG, OECD, OPCW, PCA, Sparteca, SPC, SPF, UN, UNCTAD, UNESCO, UNIDO, UNMOP, UNOMSIL, UNPREDEP, UNTSO, UPU, WFTU, WHO, WIPO, WMO, WTrO

Diplomatic representation in the US:
chief of mission: Ambassador James Brendan BOLGER
chancery: 37 Observatory Circle NW, Washington, DC 20008
telephone: [1] (202) 328-4800
consulate(s) general: Los Angeles, New York

Diplomatic representation from the US:
chief of mission: Ambassador Josiah Horton BEEMAN
embassy: 29 Fitzherbert Terrace, Thorndon, Wellington
mailing address: P. O. Box 1190, Wellington; PSC 467, Box 1, FPO AP 96531-1001
telephone: [64] (4) 472-2068
FAX: [64] (4) 471-2380
consulate(s) general: Auckland

Flag description: blue with the flag of the UK in the upper hoist-side quadrant with four red five-pointed stars edged in white centered in the outer half of the flag; the stars represent the Southern Cross constellation

Economy

Economy - overview: Since 1984 the government has accomplished major economic restructuring, moving an agrarian economy dependent on a concessionary British market access toward a more industrialized, free market economy that can compete globally. This dynamic growth has boosted real incomes, broadened and deepened the technological capabilities of the industrial sector, and contained inflationary pressures. Inflation remains among the lowest in the industrial world. Per capita GDP has been moving up toward the levels of the big West European economies. New Zealand's heavy dependence on trade leaves its growth prospects vulnerable to economic performance in Asia, Europe, and the US. The slump in demand in Asian markets largely explains the slight drop in GDP in 1998.
GDP: purchasing power parity - $61.1 billion (1998 est.)
GDP - real growth rate: -0.2% (1998)
GDP - per capita: purchasing power parity - $17,000 (1998 est.)
GDP - composition by sector:
agriculture: 9%
industry: 25%
services: 66% (1997)

Population below poverty line: NA%
Household income or consumption by percentage share:
lowest 10%: NA%
highest 10%: NA%
Inflation rate (consumer prices): 1.1% (1998)
Labor force: 1.86 million (1998)
Labor force - by occupation: services 65.1%, industry 25.1%, agriculture 9.8% (1995)
Unemployment rate: 7.6% (1998)
Budget:
revenues: $24.9 billion
expenditures: $23.7 billion, including capital expenditures of $NA (FY97/98 est.)
Industries: food processing, wood and paper products, textiles, machinery, transportation equipment, banking and insurance, tourism, mining
Industrial production growth rate: NA%
Electricity - production: 35.534 billion kWh (1996)
Electricity - production by source:
fossil fuel: 18.72%
hydro: 75.67%
nuclear: 0%
other: 5.61% (1996)
Electricity - consumption: 35.534 billion kWh (1996)
Electricity - exports: 0 kWh (1996)
Electricity - imports: 0 kWh (1996)
Agriculture - products: wheat, barley, potatoes, pulses, fruits, vegetables; wool, beef, dairy products; fish
Exports: $12.9 billion (1998 est.)
Exports - commodities: wool, lamb, mutton, beef, fish, cheese, chemicals, forestry products, fruits and vegetables, manufactures, dairy products, wood
Exports - partners: Australia 20%, Japan 15%, US 10%, UK 6% (1997)
Imports: $13 billion (1998 est.)
Imports - commodities: machinery and equipment, vehicles and aircraft, petroleum, consumer goods, plastics
Imports - partners: Australia 27%, US 19%, Japan 12%, UK 6% (1997)
Debt - external: $53.2 billion (March 1998)
Economic aid - donor: ODA, $123 million (1995)
Currency: 1 New Zealand dollar (NZ$) = 100 cents
Exchange rates: New Zealand dollars (NZ$) per US$1 - 1.85 (February 1999), 1.8629 (1998), 1.5083 (1997), 1.4543 (1996), 1.5235 (1995), 1.6844 (1994)
Fiscal year: 1 July - 30 June

Communications

Telephones: 1.7 million (1986 est.)
Telephone system: excellent international and domestic systems
domestic: NA
international: submarine cables to Australia and Fiji; satellite earth stations - 2 Intelsat (Pacific Ocean)
Radio broadcast stations: AM 64, FM 2, shortwave 0
Radios: 3.215 million (1992 est.)
Television broadcast stations: 41 (in addition,

there are 52 medium-power repeaters and over 650 low-power repeaters) (1997)
Televisions: 1.53 million (1992 est.)

Transportation

Railways:
total: 3,973 km
narrow gauge: 3,973 km 1.067-m gauge (519 km electrified)
Highways:
total: 92,200 km
paved: 53,568 km (including at least 144 km of expressways)
unpaved: 38,632 km (1996 est.)
Waterways: 1,609 km; of little importance to transportation
Pipelines: petroleum products 160 km; natural gas 1,000 km; liquefied petroleum gas or LPG 150 km
Ports and harbors: Auckland, Christchurch, Dunedin, Tauranga, Wellington
Merchant marine:
total: 14 ships (1,000 GRT or over) totaling 138,687 GRT/183,372 DWT
ships by type: bulk 4, cargo 1, liquefied gas tanker 1, oil tanker 3, railcar carrier 1, roll-on/roll-off cargo 4 (1998 est.)
Airports: 111 (1998 est.)
Airports - with paved runways:
total: 44
over 3,047 m: 2
1,524 to 2,437 m: 10
914 to 1,523 m: 29
under 914 m: 3 (1998 est.)
Airports - with unpaved runways:
total: 67
1,524 to 2,437 m: 1
914 to 1,523 m: 23
under 914 m: 43 (1998 est.)

Military

Military branches: New Zealand Army, Royal New Zealand Navy, Royal New Zealand Air Force
Military manpower - military age: 20 years of age
Military manpower - availability:
males age 15-49: 943,624 (1999 est.)
Military manpower - fit for military service:
males age 15-49: 793,814 (1999 est.)
Military manpower - reaching military age annually:
males: 26,046 (1999 est.)
Military expenditures - dollar figure: $562 million (FY97/98)
Military expenditures - percent of GDP: 1.05% (FY97/98)

Transnational Issues

Disputes - international: territorial claim in Antarctica (Ross Dependency)

Nicaragua

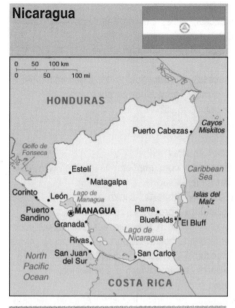

Geography

Location: Middle America, bordering both the Caribbean Sea and the North Pacific Ocean, between Costa Rica and Honduras

Geographic coordinates: 13 00 N, 85 00 W

Map references: Central America and the Caribbean

Area:
total: 129,494 sq km
land: 120,254 sq km
water: 9,240 sq km

Area - comparative: slightly smaller than the state of New York

Land boundaries:
total: 1,231 km
border countries: Costa Rica 309 km, Honduras 922 km

Coastline: 910 km

Maritime claims:
contiguous zone: 25-nm security zone
continental shelf: natural prolongation
territorial sea: 200 nm

Climate: tropical in lowlands, cooler in highlands

Terrain: extensive Atlantic coastal plains rising to central interior mountains; narrow Pacific coastal plain interrupted by volcanoes

Elevation extremes:
lowest point: Pacific Ocean 0 m
highest point: Mogoton 2,438 m

Natural resources: gold, silver, copper, tungsten, lead, zinc, timber, fish

Land use:
arable land: 9%
permanent crops: 1%
permanent pastures: 46%
forests and woodland: 27%
other: 17% (1993 est.)

Irrigated land: 880 sq km (1993 est.)

Natural hazards: destructive earthquakes, volcanoes, landslides, and occasionally severe hurricanes

Environment - current issues: deforestation; soil erosion; water pollution; Hurricane Mitch damage

Environment - international agreements:
party to: Biodiversity, Climate Change, Desertification, Endangered Species, Hazardous Wastes, Nuclear Test Ban, Ozone Layer Protection, Wetlands
signed, but not ratified: Climate Change-Kyoto Protocol, Environmental Modification, Law of the Sea

People

Population: 4,717,132 (July 1999 est.)

Age structure:
0-14 years: 44% (male 1,037,269; female 1,018,909)
15-64 years: 54% (male 1,236,326; female 1,297,356)
65 years and over: 2% (male 54,706; female 72,566) (1999 est.)

Population growth rate: 2.84% (1999 est.)

Birth rate: 35.04 births/1,000 population (1999 est.)

Death rate: 5.6 deaths/1,000 population (1999 est.)

Net migration rate: -1.06 migrant(s)/1,000 population (1999 est.)

Sex ratio:
at birth: 1.04 male(s)/female
under 15 years: 1.02 male(s)/female
15-64 years: 0.95 male(s)/female
65 years and over: 0.75 male(s)/female
total population: 0.97 male(s)/female (1999 est.)

Infant mortality rate: 40.47 deaths/1,000 live births (1999 est.)

Life expectancy at birth:
total population: 67.08 years
male: 64.7 years
female: 69.56 years (1999 est.)

Total fertility rate: 4.14 children born/woman (1999 est.)

Nationality:
noun: Nicaraguan(s)
adjective: Nicaraguan

Ethnic groups: mestizo (mixed Amerindian and white) 69%, white 17%, black 9%, Amerindian 5%

Religions: Roman Catholic 95%, Protestant 5%

Languages: Spanish (official)
note: English- and Amerindian-speaking minorities on Atlantic coast

Literacy:
definition: age 15 and over can read and write
total population: 65.7%
male: 64.6%
female: 66.6% (1995 est.)

Government

Country name:
conventional long form: Republic of Nicaragua
conventional short form: Nicaragua
local long form: Republica de Nicaragua
local short form: Nicaragua

Data code: NU

Government type: republic

Capital: Managua

Administrative divisions: 15 departments (departamentos, singular - departamento), 2 autonomous regions* (regiones autonomistas, singular - region autonomista); Boaco, Carazo, Chinandega, Chontales, Esteli, Granada, Jinotega, Leon, Madriz, Managua, Masaya, Matagalpa, Nueva Segovia, Rio San Juan, Rivas, Atlantico Norte*, Atlantico Sur*

Independence: 15 September 1821 (from Spain)

National holiday: Independence Day, 15 September (1821)

Constitution: 9 January 1987

Legal system: civil law system; Supreme Court may review administrative acts

Suffrage: 16 years of age; universal

Executive branch:
chief of state: President Arnoldo ALEMAN Lacayo (10 January 1997); Vice President Enrique BOLANOS Geyer (10 January 1997); note - the president is both chief of state and head of government
head of government: President Arnoldo ALEMAN Lacayo (10 January 1997); Vice President Enrique BOLANOS Geyer (10 January 1997); note - the president is both chief of state and head of government
cabinet: Cabinet
elections: president and vice president elected on the same ticket by popular vote for a five-year term; election last held 20 October 1996 (next to be held NA 2001); note - in July 1995 the term of the office of the president was amended to five years
election results: Arnoldo ALEMAN Lacayo (Liberal Alliance [ruling party] - includes PLC, PALI, PLIUN, and PUCA) 51.03%, Daniel ORTEGA Saavedra (FSLN) 37.75%, Guillermo OSORNO (PCCN) 4.10%, Noel VIDAURRE (PCN) 2.26%, Benjamin LANZAS (PRONAL) 0.53%, other (18 other candidates) remaining 4.33%

Legislative branch: unicameral National Assembly or Asamblea Nacional (93 seats; members are elected by proportional representation to serve five-year terms)
elections: last held 20 October 1996 (next to be held NA 2001)
election results: percent of vote by party - Liberal Alliance (ruling party - includes PLC, PALI, PLIUN, and PUCA) 46.03%, FSLN 36.55%, PCCN 3.73%, PCN 2.12%, MRS 1.33%; seats by party - Liberal Alliance 42, FSLN 36, PCCN 4, PCN 3, PRONAL 2, MRS 1, PRN 1, PNC 1, PLI 1, AU 1, UNO-96 Alliance 1

Judicial branch: Supreme Court (Corte Suprema), 12 judges elected for seven-year terms by the National Assembly

Political parties and leaders:
right: Nicaraguan Party of the Christian Road or PCCN [Guillermo OSORNO, Roberto RODRIGUEZ]; Liberal Constitutionalist Party or PLC [Jose RIZO Castellon]; Independent Liberal Party for National Unity or PLIUN [Carlos GUERRA Gallardo]; Conservative National Party or PNC [Adolfo

Nicaragua *(continued)*

CALERO, Noel VIDAURRE]; Nationalist Liberal Party or PLN [Enrique SANCHEZ Herdocia]
center right: Neoliberal Party or PALI [Adolfo GARCIA Esquivel]; Nicaraguan Resistance Party or PRN [Fabio GADEA]; Independent Liberal Party or PLI [Virgilio GODOY]; National Project or PRONAL [Antonio LACAYO Oyanguren]; Conservative Action Movement or MAC [Hernaldo ZUNIGA]
center left: Sandinista Renovation Movement or MRS [Sergio RAMIREZ]; Social Democratic Party or PSD [Adolfo JARQUIN]; Social Christian Party or PSC [Erick RAMIREZ]; Movement for Revolutionary Unity or MUR [leader NA]; Central American Integrationist Party or PIAC [leader NA]; Unity Alliance or AU [Alejandro SERRANO]; Conservative Party of Nicaragua or PCN [Dr. Fernando AGUERO Rocha]; National Democratic Party or PND [Alfredo CESAR Aguirre]; Central American Unionist Party or PUCA [Blanca ROJAS Echaverry]; UNO-96 Alliance [Alfredo CESAR Aguirre]; Nicaraguan Democratic Movement or MDN [Alfredo GUZMAN]
left: Sandinista National Liberation Front or FSLN [Daniel ORTEGA Saavedra]
Political pressure groups and leaders: National Workers Front or FNT is a Sandinista umbrella group of eight labor unions: Sandinista Workers Central or CST; Farm Workers Association or ATC; Health Workers Federation or FETASALUD; National Union of Employees or UNE; National Association of Educators of Nicaragua or ANDEN; Union of Journalists of Nicaragua or UPN; Heroes and Martyrs Confederation of Professional Associations or CONAPRO; and the National Union of Farmers and Ranchers or UNAG; Permanent Congress of Workers or CPT is an umbrella group of four non-Sandinista labor unions: Confederation of Labor Unification or CUS; Autonomous Nicaraguan Workers Central or CTN-A; Independent General Confederation of Labor or CGT-I; and Labor Action and Unity Central or CAUS; Nicaraguan Workers' Central or CTN is an independent labor union; Superior Council of Private Enterprise or COSEP is a confederation of business groups
International organization participation: BCIE, CACM, ECLAC, FAO, G-77, IADB, IAEA, IBRD, ICAO, ICFTU, ICRM, IDA, IFAD, IFC, IFRCS, ILO, IMF, IMO, Intelsat, Interpol, IOC, IOM, ITU, LAES, LAIA (observer), NAM, OAS, OPANAL, OPCW, PCA, UN, UNCTAD, UNESCO, UNHCR, UNIDO, UPU, WCL, WHO, WIPO, WMO, WToO, WTrO
Diplomatic representation in the US:
chief of mission: Ambassador Francisco AGUIRRE Sacasa
chancery: 1627 New Hampshire Avenue NW, Washington, DC 20009
telephone: [1] (202) 939-6570
consulate(s) general: Houston, Los Angeles, Miami, New Orleans, New York
Diplomatic representation from the US:
chief of mission: Ambassador Lino GUTIERREZ
embassy: Kilometer 4.5 Carretera Sur, Managua
mailing address: APO AA 34021

telephone: [505] (2) 662298, 666010, 666012, 666013, 666015, 666018, 666026, 666027, 666032, 666033
FAX: [505] (2) 669074
Flag description: three equal horizontal bands of blue (top), white, and blue with the national coat of arms centered in the white band; the coat of arms features a triangle encircled by the words REPUBLICA DE NICARAGUA on the top and AMERICA CENTRAL on the bottom; similar to the flag of El Salvador, which features a round emblem encircled by the words REPUBLICA DE EL SALVADOR EN LA AMERICA CENTRAL centered in the white band; also similar to the flag of Honduras, which has five blue stars arranged in an X pattern centered in the white band

Economy

Economy - overview: Prior to Hurricane Mitch in the fall of 1998, Nicaragua had been pursuing a number of impressive economic reforms and had begun to shed the legacy of a decade of civil war and economic mismanagement by posting strong annual growth numbers. The storm has put the reform effort on hold and has changed economic forecasts for the foreseeable future - Nicaragua, the poorest country in Central America was one of the hardest hit by the hurricane. Nicaragua sustained approximately $1 billion in damages and will probably see GDP growth slow by at least one percentage point in 1999. Hardest hit was the all-important agriculture sector, which is responsible for the majority of exports. As a result, the trade deficit is likely to balloon in 1999 to roughly $900 million. Significant aid and relief have helped to stabilize the country. In addition, the Paris Club and other creditors have offered substantial debt relief. Nevertheless, additional financing will be needed to restore the economy to its pre-Mitch condition.
GDP: purchasing power parity - $11.6 billion (1998 est.)
GDP - real growth rate: 4% (1998 est.)
GDP - per capita: purchasing power parity - $2,500 (1998 est.)
GDP - composition by sector:
agriculture: 32%
industry: 24%
services: 44% (1997)
Population below poverty line: 50.3% (1993 est.)
Household income or consumption by percentage share:
lowest 10%: 1.6%
highest 10%: 39.8% (1993)
Inflation rate (consumer prices): 16% (1998 est.)
Labor force: 1.5 million
Labor force - by occupation: services 54%, agriculture 31%, industry 15% (1995 est.)
Unemployment rate: 14%; underemployment 36% (1997 est.)
Budget:
revenues: $389 million
expenditures: $551 million, including capital expenditures of $NA (1996 est.)

Industries: food processing, chemicals, metal products, textiles, clothing, petroleum refining and distribution, beverages, footwear
Industrial production growth rate: 1.4% (1994 est.)
Electricity - production: 1.665 billion kWh (1996)
Electricity - production by source:
fossil fuel: 48.95%
hydro: 21.02%
nuclear: 0%
other: 30.03% (1996)
Electricity - consumption: 1.665 billion kWh (1996)
Electricity - exports: 0 kWh (1996)
Electricity - imports: 0 kWh (1996)
Agriculture - products: coffee, bananas, sugarcane, cotton, rice, corn, cassava (tapioca), citrus, beans; beef, veal, pork, poultry, dairy products
Exports: $704 million (f.o.b., 1997)
Exports - commodities: coffee, seafood, meat, sugar, gold, bananas
Exports - partners: US, Central America, Germany, Canada
Imports: $1.45 billion (c.i.f., 1997)
Imports - commodities: consumer goods, machinery and equipment, petroleum products
Imports - partners: Central America, US, Venezuela, Japan
Debt - external: $6 billion (1996 est.)
Economic aid - recipient: $839.9 million (1995)
Currency: 1 gold cordoba (C$) = 100 centavos
Exchange rates: gold cordobas (C$) per US$1 - 11.14 (December 1998), 10.58 (1998), 9.45 (1997), 8.44 (1996), 7.55 (1995), 6.72 (1994)
Fiscal year: calendar year

Communications

Telephones: 66,810 (1993 est.)
Telephone system: low-capacity microwave radio relay and wire system being expanded; connected to Central American Microwave System
domestic: wire and microwave radio relay
international: satellite earth stations - 1 Intersputnik (Atlantic Ocean region) and 1 Intelsat (Atlantic Ocean)
Radio broadcast stations: AM 45, FM 0, shortwave 3
Radios: 1.037 million (1992 est.)
Television broadcast stations: 3 (in addition, there are seven low-power repeaters) (1997)
Televisions: 260,000 (1992 est.)

Transportation

Highways:
total: 16,382 km
paved: 1,818 km
unpaved: 14,564 km (1998 est.)
Waterways: 2,220 km, including 2 large lakes
Pipelines: crude oil 56 km
Ports and harbors: Bluefields, Corinto, El Bluff, Puerto Cabezas, Puerto Sandino, Rama, San Juan del Sur
Merchant marine: none

Nicaragua (continued)

Airports: 184 (1998 est.)
Airports - with paved runways:
total: 13
over 3,047 m: 1
2,438 to 3,047 m: 1
1,524 to 2,437 m: 3
914 to 1,523 m: 3
under 914 m: 5 (1998 est.)
Airports - with unpaved runways:
total: 171
1,524 to 2,437 m: 1
914 to 1,523 m: 27
under 914 m: 143 (1998 est.)

Military

Military branches: Ground Forces, Navy, Air Force
Military manpower - military age: 18 years of age
Military manpower - availability:
males age 15-49: 1,108,146 (1999 est.)
Military manpower - fit for military service:
males age 15-49: 681,495 (1999 est.)
Military manpower - reaching military age annually:
males: 53,508 (1999 est.)
Military expenditures - dollar figure: $26 million (1998)
Military expenditures - percent of GDP: 1.2% (1998)

Transnational Issues

Disputes - international: territorial disputes with Colombia over the Archipelago de San Andres y Providencia and Quita Sueno Bank; with respect to the maritime boundary question in the Golfo de Fonseca, the International Court of Justice (ICJ) referred the disputants to an earlier agreement in this century and advised that some tripartite resolution among El Salvador, Honduras, and Nicaragua likely would be required; maritime boundary dispute with Honduras
Illicit drugs: transshipment point for cocaine destined for the US

Niger

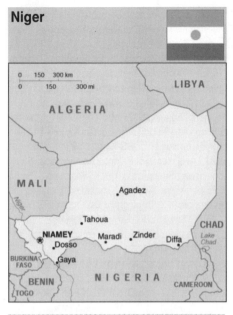

Geography

Location: Western Africa, southeast of Algeria
Geographic coordinates: 16 00 N, 8 00 E
Map references: Africa
Area:
total: 1.267 million sq km
land: 1,266,700 sq km
water: 300 sq km
Area - comparative: slightly less than twice the size of Texas
Land boundaries:
total: 5,697 km
border countries: Algeria 956 km, Benin 266 km, Burkina Faso 628 km, Chad 1,175 km, Libya 354 km, Mali 821 km, Nigeria 1,497 km
Coastline: 0 km (landlocked)
Maritime claims: none (landlocked)
Climate: desert; mostly hot, dry, dusty; tropical in extreme south
Terrain: predominately desert plains and sand dunes; flat to rolling plains in south; hills in north
Elevation extremes:
lowest point: Niger River 200 m
highest point: Mont Greboun 1,944 m
Natural resources: uranium, coal, iron ore, tin, phosphates, gold, petroleum
Land use:
arable land: 3%
permanent crops: 0%
permanent pastures: 7%
forests and woodland: 2%
other: 88% (1993 est.)
Irrigated land: 660 sq km (1993 est.)
Natural hazards: recurring droughts
Environment - current issues: overgrazing; soil erosion; deforestation; desertification; wildlife populations (such as elephant, hippopotamus, giraffe, and lion) threatened because of poaching and habitat destruction
Environment - international agreements:
party to: Biodiversity, Climate Change, Desertification, Endangered Species, Environmental Modification, Hazardous Wastes, Nuclear Test Ban, Ozone Layer Protection, Wetlands
signed, but not ratified: Climate Change-Kyoto Protocol, Law of the Sea
Geography - note: landlocked

People

Population: 9,962,242 (July 1999 est.)
Age structure:
0-14 years: 48% (male 2,445,536; female 2,346,844)
15-64 years: 50% (male 2,421,971; female 2,518,248)
65 years and over: 2% (male 121,253; female 108,390) (1999 est.)
Population growth rate: 2.95% (1999 est.)
Birth rate: 52.31 births/1,000 population (1999 est.)
Death rate: 22.78 deaths/1,000 population (1999 est.)
Net migration rate: 0 migrant(s)/1,000 population (1999 est.)
Sex ratio:
at birth: 1.03 male(s)/female
under 15 years: 1.04 male(s)/female
15-64 years: 0.96 male(s)/female
65 years and over: 1.12 male(s)/female
total population: 1 male(s)/female (1999 est.)
Infant mortality rate: 112.79 deaths/1,000 live births (1999 est.)
Life expectancy at birth:
total population: 41.96 years
male: 42.22 years
female: 41.7 years (1999 est.)
Total fertility rate: 7.24 children born/woman (1999 est.)
Nationality:
noun: Nigerien(s)
adjective: Nigerien
Ethnic groups: Hausa 56%, Djerma 22%, Fula 8.5%, Tuareg 8%, Beri Beri (Kanouri) 4.3%, Arab, Toubou, and Gourmantche 1.2%, about 1,200 French expatriates
Religions: Muslim 80%, remainder indigenous beliefs and Christians
Languages: French (official), Hausa, Djerma
Literacy:
definition: age 15 and over can read and write
total population: 13.6%
male: 20.9%
female: 6.6% (1995 est.)

Government

Country name:
conventional long form: Republic of Niger
conventional short form: Niger
local long form: Republique du Niger
local short form: Niger
Data code: NG
Government type: republic
Capital: Niamey
Administrative divisions: 7 departments (departements, singular - departement), and 1 capital

district* (capitale district); Agadez, Diffa, Dosso, Maradi, Niamey*, Tahoua, Tillaberi, Zinder

Independence: 3 August 1960 (from France)

National holiday: Republic Day, 18 December (1958)

Constitution: the constitution of January 1993 was revised by national referendum on 12 May 1996

Legal system: based on French civil law system and customary law; has not accepted compulsory ICJ jurisdiction

Suffrage: 18 years of age; universal

Executive branch:

chief of state: President Ibrahim BARE Mainassara (since 28 January 1996); note - the president is both chief of state and head of government

head of government: President Ibrahim BARE Mainassara (since 28 January 1996); note - Ibrahim MAYAKI (since 27 November 1997) was appointed prime minister by the president but does not exercise any executive authority and is only the implementor of the president's programs; the president is both chief of state and head of government

note: President Ibrahim BARE was assasinated on the 9 April 1999

cabinet: Council of Ministers appointed by the president

elections: president elected by popular vote for a five-year term; last held 7-8 July 1996 (next to be held NA 2001); note - Ibrahim BARE Mainassara initially became president when he ousted President Mahamane OUSMANE in a coup on 27 January 1996 and subsequently defeated him in the flawed election of July 1996

election results: percent of vote - Ibrahim BARE Mainassara 52.22%, Mahamane OUSMANE 19.75%, Tandja MAMADOU 15.65%, Mahamadou ISSOUFOU 7.60%, Moumouni AMADOU Djermakoye 4.77%

Legislative branch: two-chamber National Assembly; one chamber with 83 seats (members elected by popular vote for five-year terms); selection process for second chamber not established

elections: last held 23 November 1996 (next to be held NA 2001)

election results: percent of vote by party - NA; seats by party - UNIRD 59, ANDPS-Zaman Lahiya 8, UDPS-Amana 3, coalition of independents 3, MDP-Alkwali 1, UPDP-Shamuwa 4, DARAJA 3, PMT-Albarka 2

Judicial branch: State Court or Cour d'Etat; Court of Appeal or Cour d'Appel

Political parties and leaders: Alliance for Democracy and Progress or ADP-AUMUNCI [Issoufou BACHARD, chairman]; DARAJA [Ali TALBA, chairman]; Democratic and Social Convention-Rahama or CDS-Rahama [Mahamane OUSMANE]; Movement for Development and Pan-Africanism or MDP-Alkwali [Mai Manga BOUCAR, chairman]; National Movement of the Development Society-Nassara or MNSD-Nassara [Tandja MAMADOU, chairman]; National Union of Independents for Democratic Revival or UNIRD [President Ibrahim BARE Mainassara]; Niger

Progressive Party-African Democratic Rally or PPN-RDA [Dandiko KOULODO]; Niger Social Democrat Party or PADN [Malam Adji WAZIRI]; Nigerien Party for Democracy and Socialism-Tarayya or PNDS-Tarayya [Mahamadou ISSOUFOU]; Nigerien Alliance for Democracy and Social Progress-Zaman Lahia or ANDPS-Zaman Lahia [Moumouni Adamou DJERMAKOYE]; PMT-Albarka [Idi Ango OMAR]; Union for Democracy and Social Progress-Amana or UDPS-Amana [Mohamed ABDULLAHI]; Union of Patriots, Democrats, and Progressives-Shamuwa or UPDP-Shamuwa [Professor Andre' SALIFOU, chairman]; Union of Popular Forces for Democracy and Progress-Sawaba or UFPDP-Sawaba [Issoufou ASSOUMANE, secretary general]; Rally for Democracy and Progress or RDP [leader NA]

International organization participation: ACCT, ACP, AfDB, CCC, ECA, ECOWAS, Entente, FAO, FZ, G-77, IAEA, IBRD, ICAO, ICFTU, ICRM, IDA, IDB, IFAD, IFC, IFRCS, ILO, IMF, Intelsat, Interpol, IOC, ITU, MIPONUH, NAM, OAU, OIC, OPCW, UN, UNCTAD, UNESCO, UNIDO, UPU, WADB, WAEMU, WCL, WFTU, WHO, WIPO, WMO, WToO, WTrO

Diplomatic representation in the US:

chief of mission: Ambassador Joseph DIATTA

chancery: 2204 R Street NW, Washington, DC 20008

telephone: [1] (202) 483-4224 through 4227

Diplomatic representation from the US:

chief of mission: Ambassador Charles O. CECIL

embassy: Rue Des Ambassades, Niamey

mailing address: B. P. 11201, Niamey

telephone: [227] 72 26 61 through 72 26 64

FAX: [227] 73 31 67

Flag description: three equal horizontal bands of orange (top), white, and green with a small orange disk (representing the sun) centered in the white band; similar to the flag of India, which has a blue spoked wheel centered in the white band

Economy

Economy - overview: Niger is a poor, landlocked Sub-Saharan nation, whose economy centers on subsistence agriculture, animal husbandry, reexport trade, and increasingly less on uranium, its major export since the 1970s. The 50% devaluation of the West African franc in January 1994 boosted exports of livestock, cowpeas, onions, and the products of Niger's small cotton industry. The government relies on bilateral and multilateral aid for operating expenses and public investment and is strongly induced to adhere to structural adjustment programs designed by the IMF and the World Bank. Short-term prospects depend largely on upcoming negotiations on debt relief and extended aid.

GDP: purchasing power parity - $9.4 billion (1998 est.)

GDP - real growth rate: 4.5% (1998 est.)

GDP - per capita: purchasing power parity - $970 (1998 est.)

GDP - composition by sector:

agriculture: 40%

industry: 18%

services: 42% (1997)

Population below poverty line: NA%

Household income or consumption by percentage share:

lowest 10%: 3%

highest 10%: 29.3% (1992)

Inflation rate (consumer prices): 4.8% (1998)

Labor force: 70,000 receive regular wages or salaries

Labor force - by occupation: agriculture 90%, industry and commerce 6%, government 4%

Unemployment rate: NA%

Budget:

revenues: $370 million (including $160 million from foreign sources)

expenditures: $370 million, including capital expenditures of $186 million (1998 est.)

Industries: cement, brick, textiles, food processing, chemicals, slaughterhouses, and a few other small light industries; uranium mining

Industrial production growth rate: NA%

Electricity - production: 170 million kWh (1996)

Electricity - production by source:

fossil fuel: 100%

hydro: 0%

nuclear: 0%

other: 0% (1996)

Electricity - consumption: 365 million kWh (1996)

Electricity - exports: 0 kWh (1996)

Electricity - imports: 195 million kWh (1996)

note: imports electricity from Nigeria

Agriculture - products: cowpeas, cotton, peanuts, millet, sorghum, cassava (tapioca), rice; cattle, sheep, goats, camels, donkeys, horses, poultry

Exports: $269 million (f.o.b., 1997)

Exports - commodities: uranium ore 50%, livestock products 20%, cowpeas, onions (1996 est.)

Exports - partners: Greece 21%, Canada 18%, France 12%, Nigeria 7% (1996 est.)

Imports: $295 million (c.i.f., 1997)

Imports - commodities: consumer goods, primary materials, machinery, vehicles and parts, petroleum, cereals

Imports - partners: France 17%, Cote d'Ivoire 7%, US 5%, Belgium-Luxembourg 4%, Nigeria (1996 est.)

Debt - external: $1.2 billion (1998 est.)

Economic aid - recipient: $222 million (1995)

Currency: 1 Communaute Financiere Africaine franc (CFAF) = 100 centimes

Exchange rates: Communaute Financiere Africaine francs (CFAF) per US$1 - 560.01 (January 1999), 589.95 (1998), 583.67 (1997), 511.55 (1996), 499.15 (1995), 555.20 (1994)

Fiscal year: calendar year

Communications

Telephones: 14,000 (1995 est.)

Telephone system: small system of wire, radiotelephone communications, and microwave radio relay links concentrated in southwestern area

domestic: wire, radiotelephone communications, and

Niger *(continued)*

microwave radio relay; domestic satellite system with 3 earth stations and 1 planned
international: satellite earth stations - 2 Intelsat (1 Atlantic Ocean and 1 Indian Ocean)
Radio broadcast stations: AM 15, FM 6, shortwave 0
Radios: 620,000 (1995 est.)
Television broadcast stations: 10 (in addition, there are seven low-power repeaters) (1997)
Televisions: 105,000 (1995 est.)

Transportation

Railways: 0 km
Highways:
total: 10,100 km
paved: 798 km
unpaved: 9,302 km (1996 est.)
Waterways: Niger river is navigable 300 km from Niamey to Gaya on the Benin frontier from mid-December through March
Ports and harbors: none
Airports: 27 (1998 est.)
Airports - with paved runways:
total: 9
2,438 to 3,047 m: 2
1,524 to 2,437 m: 6
914 to 1,523 m: 1 (1998 est.)
Airports - with unpaved runways:
total: 18
1,524 to 2,437 m: 1
914 to 1,523 m: 15
under 914 m: 2 (1998 est.)

Military

Military branches: Army, Air Force, National Gendarmerie, Republican Guard, National Police
Military manpower - military age: 18 years of age
Military manpower - availability:
males age 15-49: 2,117,868 (1999 est.)
Military manpower - fit for military service:
males age 15-49: 1,143,355 (1999 est.)
Military manpower - reaching military age annually:
males: 102,762 (1999 est.)
Military expenditures - dollar figure: $20 million (FY96/97)
Military expenditures - percent of GDP: 1.1% (FY96/97)

Transnational Issues

Disputes - international: Libya claims about 19,400 sq km in northern Niger; delimitation of international boundaries in the vicinity of Lake Chad, the lack of which led to border incidents in the past, is completed and awaits ratification by Cameroon, Chad, Niger, and Nigeria

Nigeria

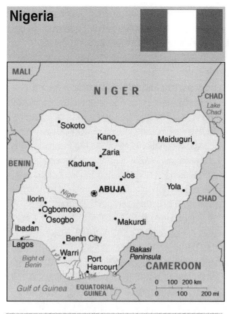

Geography

Location: Western Africa, bordering the Gulf of Guinea, between Benin and Cameroon
Geographic coordinates: 10 00 N, 8 00 E
Map references: Africa
Area:
total: 923,770 sq km
land: 910,770 sq km
water: 13,000 sq km
Area - comparative: slightly more than twice the size of California
Land boundaries:
total: 4,047 km
border countries: Benin 773 km, Cameroon 1,690 km, Chad 87 km, Niger 1,497 km
Coastline: 853 km
Maritime claims:
continental shelf: 200-m depth or to the depth of exploitation
exclusive economic zone: 200 nm
territorial sea: 30 nm
Climate: varies; equatorial in south, tropical in center, arid in north
Terrain: southern lowlands merge into central hills and plateaus; mountains in southeast, plains in north
Elevation extremes:
lowest point: Atlantic Ocean 0 m
highest point: Chappal Waddi 2,419 m
Natural resources: petroleum, tin, columbite, iron ore, coal, limestone, lead, zinc, natural gas
Land use:
arable land: 33%
permanent crops: 3%
permanent pastures: 44%
forests and woodland: 12%
other: 8% (1993 est.)
Irrigated land: 9,570 sq km (1993 est.)
Natural hazards: periodic droughts
Environment - current issues: soil degradation; rapid deforestation; desertification; recent droughts in north severely affecting marginal agricultural activities

Environment - international agreements:
party to: Biodiversity, Climate Change, Desertification, Endangered Species, Hazardous Wastes, Law of the Sea, Marine Dumping, Marine Life Conservation, Nuclear Test Ban, Ozone Layer Protection
signed, but not ratified: none of the selected agreements

People

Population: 113,828,587 (July 1999 est.)
Age structure:
0-14 years: 45% (male 25,613,974; female 25,397,166)
15-64 years: 52% (male 30,272,539; female 29,197,611)
65 years and over: 3% (male 1,678,732; female 1,668,565) (1999 est.)
Population growth rate: 2.92% (1999 est.)
Birth rate: 41.84 births/1,000 population (1999 est.)
Death rate: 12.98 deaths/1,000 population (1999 est.)
Net migration rate: 0.31 migrant(s)/1,000 population (1999 est.)
Sex ratio:
at birth: 1.03 male(s)/female
under 15 years: 1.01 male(s)/female
15-64 years: 1.04 male(s)/female
65 years and over: 1.01 male(s)/female
total population: 1.02 male(s)/female (1999 est.)
Infant mortality rate: 69.46 deaths/1,000 live births (1999 est.)
Life expectancy at birth:
total population: 53.3 years
male: 52.55 years
female: 54.06 years (1999 est.)
Total fertility rate: 6.02 children born/woman (1999 est.)
Nationality:
noun: Nigerian(s)
adjective: Nigerian
Ethnic groups: Hausa, Fulani, Yoruba, Ibo, Ijaw, Kanuri, Ibibio, Tiv
Religions: Muslim 50%, Christian 40%, indigenous beliefs 10%
Languages: English (official), Hausa, Yoruba, Ibo, Fulani
Literacy:
definition: age 15 and over can read and write
total population: 57.1%
male: 67.3%
female: 47.3% (1995 est.)

Government

Country name:
conventional long form: Federal Republic of Nigeria
conventional short form: Nigeria
Data code: NI
Government type: republic transitioning from military to civilian rule
Capital: Abuja

Nigeria (continued)

note: on 12 December 1991 the capital was officially moved from Lagos to Abuja; many government offices remain in Lagos pending completion of facilities in Abuja

Administrative divisions: 30 states and 1 territory*; Abia, Abuja Federal Capital Territory*, Adamawa, Akwa Ibom, Anambra, Bauchi, Benue, Borno, Cross River, Delta, Edo, Enugu, Imo, Jigawa, Kaduna, Kano, Katsina, Kebbi, Kogi, Kwara, Lagos, Niger, Ogun, Ondo, Osun, Oyo, Plateau, Rivers, Sokoto, Taraba, Yobe

note: the government has announced the creation of six additional states named Bayelsa, Ebonyi, Ekiti, Gombe, Nassarawa, and Zamfara as part of the process of transition to a civilian government

Independence: 1 October 1960 (from UK)

National holiday: Independence Day, 1 October (1960)

Constitution: 1979 constitution still partially in force

Legal system: based on English common law, Islamic law, and tribal law

Suffrage: 18 years of age; universal

Executive branch:

chief of state: Chairman of the Provisional Ruling Council and Commander in Chief of Armed Forces Gen. Abdulsalami ABUBAKAR (since 9 June 1998) will remain chief of state and head of government until 29 May 1999 when President-elect Olusegun OBASANJO will be inaugurated

head of government: Chairman of the Provisional Ruling Council and Commander in Chief of Armed Forces Gen. Abdulsalami ABUBAKAR (since 9 June 1998) will remain chief of state and head of government until 29 May 1999 when President-elect Olusegun OBASANJO will be inaugurated

cabinet: Federal Executive Council

elections: the president is elected by popular vote for no more than two four-year terms; election last held 27 February 1999 (next election to be held NA 2003)

election results: Olusegun OBASANJO (PDP) won the election with NA% of the vote, Olu FALAE (APP-AD) NA%

Legislative branch: bicameral National Assembly consists of Senate (109 seats, three from each state and one from the Federal Capital Territory; members elected by popular vote to serve seven-year terms) and House of Representatives (360 seats, members elected by popular vote to serve seven-year terms)

elections: Senate - last held 20-24 February 1999 (next to be held NA 2006); House of Representatives - last held 20-24 February 1999 (next to be held NA 2006)

election results: Senate - percent of vote by party - NA; seats by party - PDP 61, APP 24, AD 20, other 4; House of Representatives - percent of vote by party - NA; seats by party - PDP 206, APP 74, AD 68, others 12

note: the National Assembly was suspended by the military government following the military takeover on 17 November 1993; the new civilian government which was elected on 20 February 1999 is expected to be inaugurated on 29 May 1999

Judicial branch: Supreme Court, judges appointed by the Provisional Ruling Council; Federal Court of Appeal, judges are appointed by the federal government on the advice of the Advisory Judicial Committee

Political parties and leaders: political parties, suppressed by the military government, were allowed to form in July 1998; three parties were registered by the Provisional Ruling Council for participation in local, state and national elections; All People's Party or APP [Mahmud WAZIRI]; People's Democratic Party or PDP [Soloman LAR]; Alliance for Democracy or AD [Ayo ADEBANJO]

International organization participation: ACP, AfDB, C (suspended), CCC, ECA, ECOWAS, FAO, G-15, G-19, G-24, G-77, IAEA, IBRD, ICAO, ICC, ICRM, IDA, IFAD, IFC, IFRCS, IHO, ILO, IMF, IMO, Inmarsat, Intelsat, Interpol, IOC, ISO, ITU, MINURSO, MONUA, NAM, OAU, OIC, OPCW, OPEC, PCA, UN, UNCTAD, UNESCO, UNHCR, UNIDO, UNIKOM, UNITAR, UNMIBH, UNMOP, UNMOT, UNPREDEP, UNU, UPU, WCL, WFTU, WHO, WIPO, WMO, WToO, WTrO

Diplomatic representation in the US:

chief of mission: Ambassador Wakili Hassan ADAMU

chancery: 1333 16th Street NW, Washington, DC 20036

telephone: [1] (202) 986-8400

FAX: [1] (202) 775-1385

consulate(s) general: New York

Diplomatic representation from the US:

chief of mission: Ambassador William H. TWADDELL

embassy: 2 Eleke Crescent, Lagos

mailing address: P. O. Box 554, Lagos

telephone: [234] (1) 261-0097

FAX: [234] (1) 261-0257

Flag description: three equal vertical bands of green (hoist side), white, and green

Economy

Economy - overview: The oil-rich Nigerian economy continues to be hobbled by political instability, corruption, and poor macroeconomic management. Nigeria's unpopular military rulers have failed to make significant progress in diversifying the economy away from overdependence on the capital intensive oil sector which provides 30% of GDP, 95% of foreign exchange earnings, and about 80% of budgetary revenues. The government's resistance to initiating greater transparency and accountability in managing the country's multibillion dollar oil earnings continues to limit economic growth and prevent an agreement with the IMF and bilateral creditors on a staff-monitored program and debt relief. The largely subsistence agricultural sector has failed to keep up with rapid population growth, and Nigeria, once a large net exporter of food, now must import food. Growth in 1999 may become negative because of continued low oil prices and persistent inefficiencies in the system.

GDP: purchasing power parity - $106.2 billion (1998 est.)

GDP - real growth rate: i._% (1998 est.)

GDP - per capita: purchasing power parity - $960 (1998 est.)

GDP - composition by sector:

agriculture: 33%

industry: 42%

services: 25% (1997 est.)

Population below poverty line: 34.1% (1992-93 est.)

Household income or consumption by percentage share:

lowest 10%: 1.3%

highest 10%: 31.4% (1992-93)

Inflation rate (consumer prices): 15% (1998 est.)

Labor force: 42.844 million

Labor force - by occupation: agriculture 54%, industry, commerce, and services 19%, government 15%

Unemployment rate: 28% (1992 est.)

Budget:

revenues: $13.9 billion (1998 est.)

expenditures: $13.9 billion, including capital expenditures of $NA billion (1998 est.)

Industries: crude oil, coal, tin, columbite, palm oil, peanuts, cotton, rubber, wood, hides and skins, textiles, cement and other construction materials, food products, footwear, chemicals, fertilizer, printing, ceramics, steel

Industrial production growth rate: 4.1% (1996)

Electricity - production: 13.78 billion kWh (1996)

Electricity - production by source:

fossil fuel: 60.94%

hydro: 39.06%

nuclear: 0%

other: 0% (1996)

Electricity - consumption: 13.74 billion kWh (1996)

Electricity - exports: 50 million kWh (1996)

Electricity - imports: 0 kWh (1996)

Agriculture - products: cocoa, peanuts, palm oil, corn, rice, sorghum, millet, cassava (tapioca), yams, rubber; cattle, sheep, goats, pigs; timber; fish

Exports: $9.7 billion (f.o.b., 1998)

Exports - commodities: petroleum and petroleum products 95%, cocoa, rubber

Exports - partners: US 35%, Spain 11%, Italy 6%, France 6% (1997 est.)

Imports: $9.8 billion (f.o.b., 1998)

Imports - commodities: machinery, chemicals, transportation equipment, manufactured goods, food and animals

Imports - partners: US 14%, UK 11%, Germany 10%, France 8%, Netherlands 5% (1997 est.)

Debt - external: $32 billion (1998 est.)

Economic aid - recipient: $39.2 million (1995)

Currency: 1 naira (N) = 100 kobo

Exchange rates: nairas (N) per US$1 - 21.886 (December 1998), 21.886 (1998), 21.886 (1997), 21.895 (1995), 21.996 (1994)

Fiscal year: calendar year

Communications

Telephones: 405,100 (1995 est.)

Telephone system: average system limited by poor

Nigeria *(continued)*

maintenance; major expansion in progress
domestic: intercity traffic is carried by coaxial cable, microwave radio relay, cellular network, and a domestic communications satellite system with 20 earth stations
international: satellite earth stations - 3 Intelsat (2 Atlantic Ocean and 1 Indian Ocean); 1 coaxial submarine cable
Radio broadcast stations: AM 82, FM 32, shortwave 10 (1998 est.)
Radios: 17.2 million (1998 est.)
Television broadcast stations: 1 (government-controlled)
Televisions: 6.1 million (1998 est.)

Transportation

Railways:
total: 3,557 km
narrow gauge: 3,505 km 1.067-m gauge
standard gauge: 52 km 1.435-m gauge (1995)
note: years of neglect of both the rolling stock and the right-of-way have seriously reduced the capacity and utility of the system; a project to restore Nigeria's railways is now underway
Highways:
total: 51,000 km
paved: 26,000 km (including 2,044 km of expressways)
unpaved: 25,000 km (1998 est.)
note: many of the roads reported as paved may be graveled; because of poor maintenance and years of heavy freight traffic (in part the result of the failure of the railroad system), much of the road system is barely useable
Waterways: 8,575 km consisting of the Niger and Benue rivers and smaller rivers and creeks
Pipelines: crude oil 2,042 km; petroleum products 3,000 km; natural gas 500 km
Ports and harbors: Calabar, Lagos, Onne, Port Harcourt, Sapele, Warri
Merchant marine:
total: 38 ships (1,000 GRT or over) totaling 371,499 GRT/631,425 DWT
ships by type: bulk 1, cargo 13, chemical tanker 3, oil tanker 20, roll-on/roll-off cargo 1 (1998 est.)
Airports: 72 (1998 est.)
Airports - with paved runways:
total: 36
over 3,047 m: 6
2,438 to 3,047 m: 10
1,524 to 2,437 m: 10
914 to 1,523 m: 8
under 914 m: 2 (1998 est.)
Airports - with unpaved runways:
total: 36
over 3,047 m: 1
1,524 to 2,437 m: 1
914 to 1,523 m: 16
under 914 m: 18 (1998 est.)
Heliports: 1 (1998 est.)

Military

Military branches: Army, Navy, Air Force, Police Force
Military manpower - military age: 18 years of age
Military manpower - availability:
males age 15-49: 25,967,281 (1999 est.)
Military manpower - fit for military service:
males age 15-49: 14,890,337 (1999 est.)
Military manpower - reaching military age annually:
males: 1,201,738 (1999 est.)
Military expenditures - dollar figure: $236 million (1999)
Military expenditures - percent of GDP: 0.7% (1999)

Transnational Issues

Disputes - international: delimitation of international boundaries in the vicinity of Lake Chad, the lack of which led to border incidents in the past, is completed and awaits ratification by Cameroon, Chad, Niger, and Nigeria; dispute with Cameroon over land and maritime boundaries around the Bakasi Peninsula is currently before the International Court of Justice; maritime boundary dispute with Equatorial Guinea because of disputed jurisdiction over oil-rich areas in the Gulf of Guinea
Illicit drugs: facilitates movement of heroin en route from Southeast and Southwest Asia to Western Europe and North America; increasingly a transit route for cocaine from South America intended for European, East Asian, and North American markets

Niue
(self-governing in free association with New Zealand)

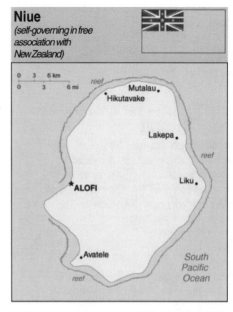

Geography

Location: Oceania, island in the South Pacific Ocean, east of Tonga
Geographic coordinates: 19 02 S, 169 52 W
Map references: Oceania
Area:
total: 260 sq km
land: 260 sq km
water: 0 sq km
Area - comparative: 1.5 times the size of Washington, DC
Land boundaries: 0 km
Coastline: 64 km
Maritime claims:
exclusive economic zone: 200 nm
territorial sea: 12 nm
Climate: tropical; modified by southeast trade winds
Terrain: steep limestone cliffs along coast, central plateau
Elevation extremes:
lowest point: Pacific Ocean 0 m
highest point: unnamed location near Mutalau settlement 68 m
Natural resources: fish, arable land
Land use:
arable land: 19%
permanent crops: 8%
permanent pastures: 4%
forests and woodland: 19%
other: 50% (1993 est.)
Irrigated land: NA sq km
Natural hazards: typhoons
Environment - current issues: traditional methods of burning brush and trees to clear land for agriculture have threatened soil supplies which are not naturally very abundant
Environment - international agreements:
party to: Biodiversity, Climate Change, Desertification
signed, but not ratified: Climate Change-Kyoto

Niue *(continued)*

Protocol, Law of the Sea
Geography - note: one of world's largest coral islands

Population: 2,103 (July 1999 est.)
Age structure:
0-14 years: NA
15-64 years: NA
65 years and over: NA
Population growth rate: 0.5% (1999 est.)
Birth rate: NA births/1,000 population
Death rate: NA deaths/1,000 population
Net migration rate: NA migrant(s)/1,000 population
Infant mortality rate: NA deaths/1,000 live births
Life expectancy at birth:
total population: NA
male: NA
female: NA
Total fertility rate: NA children born/woman
Nationality:
noun: Niuean(s)
adjective: Niuean
Ethnic groups: Polynesian (with some 200 Europeans, Samoans, and Tongans)
Religions: Ekalesia Niue (Niuean Church) 75% - a Protestant church closely related to the London Missionary Society, Latter-Day Saints 10%, other 15% (mostly Roman Catholic, Jehovah's Witnesses, Seventh-Day Adventist)
Languages: Polynesian closely related to Tongan and Samoan, English
Literacy:
definition: NA
total population: 95%
male: NA%
female: NA%

Country name:
conventional long form: none
conventional short form: Niue
Data code: NE
Dependency status: self-governing in free association with New Zealand; Niue fully responsible for internal affairs; New Zealand retains responsibility for external affairs
Government type: self-governing parliamentary democracy
Capital: Alofi
Administrative divisions: none; note - there are no first-order administrative divisions as defined by the US Government, but there are 14 villages each with its own village council whose members are elected and serve three-year terms
Independence: on 19 October 1974, Niue became a self-governing parliamentary government in free association with New Zealand
National holiday: Waitangi Day, 6 February (1840) (Treaty of Waitangi established British sovereignty)
Constitution: 19 October 1974 (Niue Constitution Act)

Legal system: English common law
Suffrage: 18 years of age; universal
Executive branch:
chief of state: Queen ELIZABETH II (since 6 February 1952); the UK and New Zealand are represented by New Zealand High Commissioner Warren SEARELL (since NA August 1993)
head of government: Premier Frank Fakaotimanava LUI (since 12 March 1993)
cabinet: Cabinet consists of the premier and three ministers
elections: the monarch is hereditary; premier elected by the Legislative Assembly for a three-year term; election last held 23 February 1996 (next to be held NA March 1999)
election results: Frank Fakaotimanava LUI elected premier; percent of Legislative Assembly vote - NA
Legislative branch: unicameral Legislative Assembly (20 seats; members elected by popular vote to serve three-year terms; six elected from a common roll and 14 are village representatives)
elections: last held 23 February 1996 (next to be held NA March 1999)
election results: percent of vote by party - NA; seats by party - NPP 9, independents 11
Judicial branch: Supreme Court of New Zealand; High Court of Niue
Political parties and leaders: Niue People's Action Party or NPP [Young VIVIAN]
International organization participation: ESCAP (associate), Intelsat (nonsignatory user), Sparteca, SPC, SPF, UNESCO, WHO, WMO
Diplomatic representation in the US: none (self-governing territory in free association with New Zealand)
Diplomatic representation from the US: none (self-governing territory in free association with New Zealand)
Flag description: yellow with the flag of the UK in the upper hoist-side quadrant; the flag of the UK bears five yellow five-pointed stars - a large one on a blue disk in the center and a smaller one on each arm of the bold red cross

Economy - overview: The economy is heavily dependent on aid and remittances from New Zealand as Niue has no indigenous export products. Government expenditures regularly exceed revenues, and the shortfall is made up by grants from New Zealand which are used to pay wages to public employees. Niue has cut government expenditures by reducing the public service by almost half. The agricultural sector consists mainly of subsistence gardening, although some cash crops are grown for export. Industry consists primarily of small factories to process passion fruit, lime oil, honey, and coconut cream. The sale of postage stamps to foreign collectors is an important source of revenue. The island in recent years has suffered a serious loss of population because of migration of Niueans to New Zealand.

GDP: purchasing power parity - $2.4 million (1993 est.)
GDP - real growth rate: NA%
GDP - per capita: purchasing power parity - $1,200 (1993 est.)
GDP - composition by sector:
agriculture: NA%
industry: NA%
services: NA%
Population below poverty line: NA%
Household income or consumption by percentage share:
lowest 10%: NA%
highest 10%: NA%
Inflation rate (consumer prices): 5% (1992)
Labor force: 450 (1992 est.)
Labor force - by occupation: most work on family plantations; paid work exists only in government service, small industry, and the Niue Development Board
Unemployment rate: NA%
Budget:
revenues: $5.5 million
expenditures: $6.3 million, including capital expenditures of $NA (1985 est.)
Industries: tourism, handicrafts, food processing
Industrial production growth rate: NA%
Electricity - production: 3 million kWh (1996)
Electricity - production by source:
fossil fuel: 100%
hydro: 0%
nuclear: 0%
other: 0% (1996)
Electricity - consumption: 3 million kWh (1996)
Electricity - exports: 0 kWh (1996)
Electricity - imports: 0 kWh (1996)
Agriculture - products: coconuts, passion fruit, honey, limes, taro, yams, cassava (tapioca), sweet potatoes; pigs, poultry, beef cattle
Exports: $117,500 (f.o.b., 1989)
Exports - commodities: canned coconut cream, copra, honey, passion fruit products, pawpaw, root crops, limes, footballs, stamps, handicrafts
Exports - partners: NZ 89%, Fiji, Cook Islands, Australia
Imports: $4.1 million (c.i.f., 1989)
Imports - commodities: food, live animals, manufactured goods, machinery, fuels, lubricants, chemicals, drugs
Imports - partners: NZ 59%, Fiji 20%, Japan 13%, Samoa, Australia, US
Debt - external: $NA
Economic aid - recipient: $8.3 million (1995)
Currency: 1 New Zealand dollar (NZ$) = 100 cents
Exchange rates: New Zealand dollars (NZ$) per US$1 - 1.8560 (January 1999), 1.8629 (1998), 1.5082 (1997), 1.4543 (1996), 1.5235 (1995), 1.6844 (1994)
Fiscal year: 1 April - 31 March

Niue (continued)

Communications

Telephones: 276 (1992 est.)
Telephone system:
domestic: single-line telephone system connects all villages on island
international: NA
Radio broadcast stations: AM 1, FM 1, shortwave 0 (1987 est.)
Radios: 1,000
Television broadcast stations: 1 (1997)
Televisions: 312 (1991 est.)

Transportation

Railways: 0 km
Highways:
total: 234 km
paved: 0 km
unpaved: 234 km
Ports and harbors: none; offshore anchorage only
Merchant marine: none
Airports: 1 (1998 est.)
Airports - with paved runways:
total: 1
1,524 to 2,437 m: 1 (1998 est.)

Military

Military branches: Police Force
Military - note: defense is the responsibility of New Zealand

Transnational Issues

Disputes - international: none

Norfolk Island
(territory of Australia)

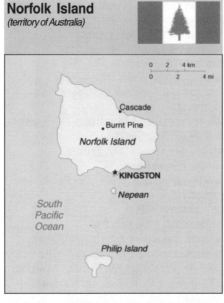

Geography

Location: Oceania, island in the South Pacific Ocean, east of Australia
Geographic coordinates: 29 02 S, 167 57 E
Map references: Oceania
Area:
total: 34.6 sq km
land: 34.6 sq km
water: 0 sq km
Area - comparative: about 0.2 times the size of Washington, DC
Land boundaries: 0 km
Coastline: 32 km
Maritime claims:
exclusive fishing zone: 200 nm
territorial sea: 3 nm
Climate: subtropical, mild, little seasonal temperature variation
Terrain: volcanic formation with mostly rolling plains
Elevation extremes:
lowest point: Pacific Ocean 0 m
highest point: Mount Bates 319 m
Natural resources: fish
Land use:
arable land: NA%
permanent crops: NA%
permanent pastures: 25%
forests and woodland: NA%
other: 75% (1993 est.)
Irrigated land: NA sq km
Natural hazards: typhoons (especially May to July)
Environment - current issues: NA
Environment - international agreements:
party to: NA
signed, but not ratified: NA

People

Population: 1,905 (July 1999 est.)
Age structure:
0-14 years: NA

15-64 years: NA
65 years and over: NA
Population growth rate: -0.71% (1999 est.)
Birth rate: NA births/1,000 population
Death rate: NA deaths/1,000 population
Net migration rate: NA migrant(s)/1,000 population
Infant mortality rate: NA deaths/1,000 live births
Life expectancy at birth:
total population: NA
male: NA
female: NA
Total fertility rate: NA children born/woman
Nationality:
noun: Norfolk Islander(s)
adjective: Norfolk Islander(s)
Ethnic groups: descendants of the Bounty mutineers, Australian, New Zealander, Polynesians
Religions: Anglican 39%, Roman Catholic 11.7%, Uniting Church in Australia 16.4%, Seventh-Day Adventist 4.4%, none 9.2%, unknown 16.9%, other 2.4% (1986)
Languages: English (official), Norfolk a mixture of 18th century English and ancient Tahitian

Government

Country name:
conventional long form: Territory of Norfolk Island
conventional short form: Norfolk Island
Data code: NF
Dependency status: territory of Australia; Canberra administers Commonwealth responsibilities on Norfolk Island through the Department of Environment, Sport and Territories
Government type: NA
Capital: Kingston
Administrative divisions: none (territory of Australia)
Independence: none (territory of Australia)
National holiday: Pitcairners Arrival Day Anniversary, 8 June (1856)
Constitution: Norfolk Island Act of 1979
Legal system: based on the laws of Australia, local ordinances and acts; English common law applies in matters not covered by either Australian or Norfolk Island law
Suffrage: 18 years of age; universal
Executive branch:
chief of state: Queen ELIZABETH II (since 6 February 1952); the UK and Australia are represented by Administrator A. J. MESSNER (since 4 August 1997)
head of government: Assembly President and Chief Minister George Charles Smith (since 30 April 1997)
cabinet: Executive Council is made up of four of the nine members of the Legislative Assembly; the council devises government policy and acts as an advisor to the Administrator
elections: the monarch is hereditary; administrator appointed by the governor general of Australia; chief minister elected by the Legislative Assembly for a term of not more than three years; election last held 30 April 1997 (next to be held by May 2000)
election results: George Charles Smith elected chief

Norfolk Island (continued)

minister; percent of Legislative Assembly vote - NA

Legislative branch: unicameral Legislative Assembly (9 seats; members elected by electors who have nine equal votes each but only four votes can be given to any one candidate; members serve three-year terms)

elections: last held 30 April 1997 (next to be held by May 2000)

election results: percent of vote - NA; seats - independents 9

Judicial branch: Supreme Court; Court of Petty Sessions

Political parties and leaders: none

International organization participation: none

Diplomatic representation in the US: none (territory of Australia)

Diplomatic representation from the US: none (territory of Australia)

Flag description: three vertical bands of green (hoist side), white, and green with a large green Norfolk Island pine tree centered in the slightly wider white band

Economy

Economy - overview: Tourism, the primary economic activity, has steadily increased over the years and has brought a level of prosperity unusual among inhabitants of the Pacific islands. Revenues from tourism have helped the agricultural sector to become self-sufficient in the production of beef, poultry, and eggs.

GDP: purchasing power parity - $NA

GDP - real growth rate: NA%

GDP - per capita: purchasing power parity - $NA

GDP - composition by sector:

agriculture: NA%

industry: NA%

services: NA%

Population below poverty line: NA%

Household income or consumption by percentage share:

lowest 10%: NA%

highest 10%: NA%

Inflation rate (consumer prices): NA%

Labor force: 1,395 (1991 est.)

Labor force - by occupation: tourism NA%, subsistence agriculture NA%

Unemployment rate: NA%

Budget:

revenues: $4.6 million

expenditures: $4.8 million, including capital expenditures of $NA (FY92/93)

Industries: tourism

Industrial production growth rate: NA%

Electricity - production: NA kWh

Electricity - production by source:

fossil fuel: NA%

hydro: NA%

nuclear: NA%

other: NA%

Electricity - consumption: NA kWh

Electricity - exports: NA kWh

Electricity - imports: NA kWh

Agriculture - products: Norfolk Island pine seed, Kentia palm seed, cereals, vegetables, fruit; cattle, poultry

Exports: $1.5 million (f.o.b., FY91/92)

Exports - commodities: postage stamps, seeds of the Norfolk Island pine and Kentia palm, small quantities of avocados

Exports - partners: Australia, other Pacific island countries, NZ, Asia, Europe

Imports: $17.9 million (c.i.f., FY91/92)

Imports - commodities: NA

Imports - partners: Australia, other Pacific island countries, NZ, Asia, Europe

Debt - external: $NA

Economic aid - recipient: $NA

Currency: 1 Australian dollar ($A) = 100 cents

Exchange rates: Australian dollars ($A) per US$1 - 1.5853 (January 1999), 1.5888 (1998), 1.3439 (1997), 1.2773 (1996), 1.3486 (1995), 1.3667 (1994)

Fiscal year: 1 July - 30 June

Communications

Telephones: 1,087 (1983 est.)

Telephone system:

domestic: NA

international: radiotelephone service with Sydney (Australia)

Radio broadcast stations: AM 1, FM 0, shortwave 0

Radios: 2,000 (1993 est.)

Television broadcast stations: 1 (local programming station; in addition, there are two repeaters that bring in Australian programs by satellite) (1998)

Televisions: 1,500 (1995 est.)

Transportation

Railways: 0 km

Highways:

total: 80 km

paved: 53 km

unpaved: 27 km

Ports and harbors: none; loading jetties at Kingston and Cascade

Merchant marine: none

Airports: 1 (1998 est.)

Airports - with paved runways:

total: 1

1,524 to 2,437 m: 1 (1998 est.)

Military

Military - note: defense is the responsibility of Australia

Transnational Issues

Disputes - international: none

Nothern Mariana Islands
(commonwealth in political union with the US)

Geography

Location: Oceania, islands in the North Pacific Ocean, about three-quarters of the way from Hawaii to the Philippines

Geographic coordinates: 15 12 N, 145 45 E

Map references: Oceania

Area:

total: 477 sq km

land: 477 sq km

water: 0 sq km

note: includes 14 islands including Saipan, Rota, and Tinian

Area - comparative: 2.5 times the size of Washington, DC

Land boundaries: 0 km

Coastline: 1,482 km

Maritime claims:

exclusive economic zone: 200 nm

territorial sea: 12 nm

Climate: tropical marine; moderated by northeast trade winds, little seasonal temperature variation; dry season December to June, rainy season July to October

Terrain: southern islands are limestone with level terraces and fringing coral reefs; northern islands are volcanic

Elevation extremes:

lowest point: Pacific Ocean 0 m

highest point: unnamed location on Agrihan 965 m

Natural resources: arable land, fish

Land use:

arable land: 21%

permanent crops: 0%

permanent pastures: 19%

forests and woodland: 0%

other: 60%

Irrigated land: NA sq km

Natural hazards: active volcanoes on Pagan and Agrihan; typhoons (especially August to November)

Environment - current issues: contamination of groundwater on Saipan may contribute to disease; clean-up of landfill; protection of endangered species conflicts with development

Environment - international agreements:
party to: NA
signed, but not ratified: NA

Geography - note: strategic location in the North Pacific Ocean

Population: 69,398 (July 1999 est.)

Age structure:
0-14 years: 24% (male 8,459; female 8,197)
15-64 years: 74% (male 24,651; female 26,949)
65 years and over: 2% (male 550; female 592) (1999 est.)

Population growth rate: 3.99% (1999 est.)

Birth rate: 22.19 births/1,000 population (1999 est.)

Death rate: 2.42 deaths/1,000 population (1999 est.)

Net migration rate: 20.14 migrant(s)/1,000 population (1999 est.)

Sex ratio:
at birth: 1.06 male(s)/female
under 15 years: 1.03 male(s)/female
15-64 years: 0.91 male(s)/female
65 years and over: 0.93 male(s)/female
total population: 0.94 male(s)/female (1999 est.)

Infant mortality rate: 6.8 deaths/1,000 live births (1999 est.)

Life expectancy at birth:
total population: 75.36 years
male: 72.19 years
female: 78.72 years (1999 est.)

Total fertility rate: 1.86 children born/woman (1999 est.)

Nationality:
noun: NA
adjective: NA

Ethnic groups: Chamorro, Carolinians and other Micronesians, Caucasian, Japanese, Chinese, Korean

Religions: Christian (Roman Catholic majority, although traditional beliefs and taboos may still be found)

Languages: English, Chamorro, Carolinian
note: 86% of population speaks a language other than English at home

Literacy:
definition: age 15 and over can read and write
total population: 97%
male: 97%
female: 96% (1980 est.)

Country name:
conventional long form: Commonwealth of the Northern Mariana Islands
conventional short form: Northern Mariana Islands

Data code: CQ

Dependency status: commonwealth in political union with the US; federal funds to the Commonwealth administered by the US Department of the Interior, Office of Insular Affairs

Government type: commonwealth; self-governing with locally elected governor, lieutenant governor, and legislature

Capital: Saipan

Administrative divisions: none (commonwealth in political union with the US); there are no first-order administrative divisions as defined by the US Government, but there are four municipalities at the second order; Northern Islands, Rota, Saipan, Tinian

Independence: none (commonwealth in political union with the US)

National holiday: Commonwealth Day, 8 January (1978)

Constitution: Covenant Agreement effective 4 November 1986 and the Constitution of the Commonwealth of the Northern Mariana Islands effective 1 January 1978

Legal system: based on US system, except for customs, wages, immigration laws, and taxation

Suffrage: 18 years of age; universal; indigenous inhabitants are US citizens but do not vote in US presidential elections

Executive branch:
chief of state: President William Jefferson CLINTON of the US (since 20 January 1993); Vice President Albert GORE, Jr. (since 20 January 1993)
head of government: Governor Pedro P. TENORIO (since NA January 1998) and Lieutenant Governor Jesus R. SABLAN (since NA January 1998)
cabinet: NA
elections: US president and vice president elected on the same ticket for four-year terms; governor and lieutenant governor elected on the same ticket by popular vote for four-year terms; election last held in NA November 1997 (next to be held NA November 2001)
election results: Pedro P. TENORIO elected governor in a three-way race; percent of vote - Pedro P. TENORIO (Republican) 47%

Legislative branch: bicameral Legislature consists of the Senate (9 seats; members are elected by popular vote to serve four-year staggered terms) and the House of Representatives (18 seats; members are elected by popular vote to serve two-year terms)
elections: Senate - last held NA November 1997 (next to be held NA November 1999); House of Representatives - last held NA November 1997 (next to be held NA November 1999)
election results: Senate - percent of vote by party - NA; seats by party - Republicans 8, Democrats 1; House of Representatives - percent of vote by party - NA; seats by party - Republicans 13, Democrats 5
note: the Commonwealth does not have a nonvoting delegate in Congress; instead, it has an elected official or "resident representative" located in Washington, DC; seats by party - Republican 1 (Juan N. BABAUTA)

Judicial branch: Commonwealth Supreme Court; Superior Court; Federal District Court

Political parties and leaders: Republican Party [Benigno R. FITIAL]; Democratic Party [chairman (currently vacant)]

International organization participation: ESCAP (associate), Interpol (subbureau), SPC

Flag description: blue, with a white, five-pointed star superimposed on the gray silhouette of a latte stone (a traditional foundation stone used in building) in the center, surrounded by a wreath

Economy - overview: The economy benefits substantially from financial assistance from the US. The rate of funding has declined as locally generated government revenues have grown. An agreement for the years 1986 to 1992 entitled the islands to $228 million for capital development, government operations, and special programs. Since 1992, funding has been extended one year at a time. The commonwealth received $27.7 million from FY93/94 through FY95/96. For FY96/97 through FY02/03, funding of $11 million will be provided for infrastructure, with an equal local match. A rapidly growing chief source of income is the tourist industry, which now employs about 50% of the work force. Japanese tourists predominate. The agricultural sector is of minor importance and is made up of cattle ranches and small farms producing coconuts, breadfruit, tomatoes, and melons. Garment production is the fastest growing industry with employment of 12,000 mostly Chinese workers and shipments of $1 billion to the US in 1998 under duty and quota exemptions.

GDP: purchasing power parity - $524 million (1996 est.)
note: GDP numbers reflect US spending

GDP - real growth rate: NA%

GDP - per capita: purchasing power parity - $9,300 (1996 est.)

GDP - composition by sector:
agriculture: NA%
industry: NA%
services: NA%

Population below poverty line: NA%

Household income or consumption by percentage share:
lowest 10%: NA%
highest 10%: NA%

Inflation rate (consumer prices): 6.5% (1994 est.)

Labor force: 6,006 total indigenous labor force; 2,699 unemployed; 28,717 foreign workers (1995)

Labor force - by occupation: managerial 20.5%, technical, sales 16.4%, services 19.3%, farming 3.1%, precision production 13.8%, operators, fabricators 26.9%

Unemployment rate: 14% (residents)

Budget:
revenues: $221 million
expenditures: $213 million, including capital expenditures of $17.7 million (1996)

Industries: tourism, construction, garments, handicrafts

Industrial production growth rate: NA%

Electricity - production: NA kWh

Electricity - production by source:
fossil fuel: 100%

Northern Mariana Islands (continued)

hydro: NA%
nuclear: NA%
other: NA%
Electricity - consumption: NA kWh
Electricity - exports: NA kWh
Electricity - imports: NA kWh
Agriculture - products: coconuts, fruits, vegetables; cattle
Exports: $1 billion (1998)
Exports - commodities: garments
Exports - partners: US
Imports: $NA
Imports - commodities: food, construction equipment and materials, petroleum products
Imports - partners: US, Japan
Debt - external: $NA
Economic aid - recipient: $21.1 million (1995)
Currency: 1 United States dollar (US$) = 100 cents
Exchange rates: US currency is used
Fiscal year: 1 October - 30 September

Communications

Telephones: 13,618 (1993 est.)
Telephone system:
domestic: NA
international: satellite earth stations - 2 Intelsat (Pacific Ocean)
Radio broadcast stations: AM 2, FM 3
Radios: 15,460 (1995 est.)
Television broadcast stations: 1 (on Saipan and one station planned for Rota; in addition, two cable stations on Saipan provide varied programming from satellite networks) (1997)
Televisions: 15,460 (1995 est.)

Transportation

Railways: 0 km
Highways:
total: 362 km (1991 est.)
paved: NA km
unpaved: NA km
Waterways: none
Ports and harbors: Saipan, Tinian
Merchant marine: none
Airports: 5 (1998 est.)
Airports - with paved runways:
total: 3
2,438 to 3,047 m: 1
1,524 to 2,437 m: 2 (1998 est.)
Airports - with unpaved runways:
total: 2
2,438 to 3,047 m: 1
under 914 m: 1 (1998 est.)
Heliports: 1 (1998 est.)

Military

Military - note: defense is the responsibility of the US

Transnational Issues

Disputes - international: none

Norway

Introduction

Background: Norway gained its independence from Sweden in 1905. As a separate realm, Norway stayed free of World War I but suffered German occupation in World War II. Discovery of oil and gas in adjacent waters in the late 1960s gave a strong boost to Norway's economic fortunes. Norway is planning for the time when its oil and gas reserves are depleted and is focusing on containing spending on its extensive welfare system. It has decided at this time not to join the European Union and the new euro currency regime.

Geography

Location: Northern Europe, bordering the North Sea and the North Atlantic Ocean, west of Sweden
Geographic coordinates: 62 00 N, 10 00 E
Map references: Europe
Area:
total: 324,220 sq km
land: 307,860 sq km
water: 16,360 sq km
Area - comparative: slightly larger than New Mexico
Land boundaries:
total: 2,515 km
border countries: Finland 729 km, Sweden 1,619 km, Russia 167 km
Coastline: 21,925 km (includes mainland 3,419 km, large islands 2,413 km, long fjords, numerous small islands, and minor indentations 16,093 km)
Maritime claims:
contiguous zone: 10 nm
continental shelf: 200 nm
exclusive economic zone: 200 nm
territorial sea: 4 nm
Climate: temperate along coast, modified by North Atlantic Current; colder interior; rainy year-round on west coast
Terrain: glaciated; mostly high plateaus and rugged mountains broken by fertile valleys; small, scattered plains; coastline deeply indented by fjords; arctic tundra in north

Elevation extremes:
lowest point: Norwegian Sea 0 m
highest point: Glittertinden 2,472 m
Natural resources: petroleum, copper, natural gas, pyrites, nickel, iron ore, zinc, lead, fish, timber, hydropower
Land use:
arable land: 3%
permanent crops: NA%
permanent pastures: 0%
forests and woodland: 27%
other: 70% (1993 est.)
Irrigated land: 970 sq km (1993 est.)
Natural hazards: NA
Environment - current issues: water pollution; acid rain damaging forests and adversely affecting lakes, threatening fish stocks; air pollution from vehicle emissions
Environment - international agreements:
party to: Air Pollution, Air Pollution-Nitrogen Oxides, Air Pollution-Sulphur 85, Air Pollution-Sulphur 94, Air Pollution-Volatile Organic Compounds, Antarctic-Environmental Protocol, Antarctic Treaty, Biodiversity, Climate Change, Desertification, Endangered Species, Environmental Modification, Hazardous Wastes, Law of the Sea, Marine Dumping, Nuclear Test Ban, Ozone Layer Protection, Ship Pollution, Tropical Timber 83, Tropical Timber 94, Wetlands, Whaling
signed, but not ratified: Air Pollution-Persistent Organic Pollutants, Climate Change-Kyoto Protocol
Geography - note: about two-thirds mountains; some 50,000 islands off its much indented coastline; strategic location adjacent to sea lanes and air routes in North Atlantic; one of most rugged and longest coastlines in world; Norway is the only NATO member having a land boundary with Russia

People

Population: 4,438,547 (July 1999 est.)
Age structure:
0-14 years: 20% (male 447,607; female 423,844)
15-64 years: 65% (male 1,462,906; female 1,415,992)
65 years and over: 15% (male 286,339; female 401,859) (1999 est.)
Population growth rate: 0.4% (1999 est.)
Birth rate: 12.54 births/1,000 population (1999 est.)
Death rate: 10.12 deaths/1,000 population (1999 est.)
Net migration rate: 1.62 migrant(s)/1,000 population (1999 est.)
Sex ratio:
at birth: 1.06 male(s)/female
under 15 years: 1.06 male(s)/female
15-64 years: 1.03 male(s)/female
65 years and over: 0.71 male(s)/female
total population: 0.98 male(s)/female (1999 est.)
Infant mortality rate: 4.96 deaths/1,000 live births (1999 est.)

Life expectancy at birth:
total population: 78.36 years
male: 75.55 years
female: 81.35 years (1999 est.)
Total fertility rate: 1.77 children born/woman (1999 est.)
Nationality:
noun: Norwegian(s)
adjective: Norwegian
Ethnic groups: Germanic (Nordic, Alpine, Baltic), Lapps (Sami) 20,000
Religions: Evangelical Lutheran 87.8% (state church), other Protestant and Roman Catholic 3.8%, none 3.2%, unknown 5.2% (1980)
Languages: Norwegian (official)
note: small Lapp- and Finnish-speaking minorities
Literacy:
definition: age 15 and over can read and write
total population: 99% (1976 est.)
male: NA%
female: NA%

Government

Country name:
conventional long form: Kingdom of Norway
conventional short form: Norway
local long form: Kongeriket Norge
local short form: Norge
Data code: NO
Government type: constitutional monarchy
Capital: Oslo
Administrative divisions: 19 provinces (fylker, singular - fylke); Akershus, Aust-Agder, Buskerud, Finnmark, Hedmark, Hordaland, More og Romsdal, Nordland, Nord-Trondelag, Oppland, Oslo, Ostfold, Rogaland, Sogn og Fjordane, Sor-Trondelag, Telemark, Troms, Vest-Agder, Vestfold
Dependent areas: Bouvet Island, Jan Mayen, Svalbard
Independence: 26 October 1905 (from Sweden)
National holiday: Constitution Day, 17 May (1814)
Constitution: 17 May 1814, modified in 1884
Legal system: mixture of customary law, civil law system, and common law traditions; Supreme Court renders advisory opinions to legislature when asked; accepts compulsory ICJ jurisdiction, with reservations
Suffrage: 18 years of age; universal
Executive branch:
chief of state: King HARALD V (since 17 January 1991); Heir Apparent Crown Prince HAAKON MAGNUS, son of the monarch (born 20 July 1973)
head of government: Prime Minister Kjell Magne BONDEVIK (since 15 October 1997)
cabinet: State Council appointed by the monarch with the approval of the Parliament
elections: none; the monarch is hereditary; following parliamentary elections, the leader of the majority party or leader of a majority coalition is usually appointed prime minister by the monarch with the approval of the Parliament
Legislative branch: modified unicameral Parliament or Storting which, for certain purposes, divides itself into two chambers (165 seats; members are elected by popular vote by proportional representation to serve four-year terms)
elections: last held 15 September 1997 (next to be held NA September 2001)
election results: percent of vote by party - Labor 35%, Center Party 7.9%, Conservatives 14.3%, Christian People's 13.7%, Socialist Left 6%, Progress 15.3%, Liberal Party 4.4%, other parties 1.6%; seats by party - Labor 65, Center Party 11, Conservatives 23, Christian People's 25, Socialist Left 9, Progress 25, Liberal Party 6, other parties 1
note: for certain purposes, the Parliament divides itself into two chambers and elects one-fourth of its membership to an upper house or Lagting
Judicial branch: Supreme Court or Hoyesterett, justices appointed by the monarch
Political parties and leaders: Labor Party [Thorbjorn JAGLAND]; Conservative Party [Jan PETERSEN]; Center Party [Anne ENGER LAHNSTEIN]; Christian People's Party [Valgerd HAUGLAND]; Socialist Left Party [Kristin HALVORSEN]; Norwegian Communist Party [Kare Andre NILSEN]; Progress Party [Carl I. HAGEN]; Liberal Party [Lars SPONHEIM]; Red Electoral Alliance [Aslak Sira MYHRE]
International organization participation: AfDB, AsDB, Australia Group, BIS, CBSS, CCC, CE, CERN, EAPC, EBRD, ECE, EFTA, ESA, FAO, IADB, IAEA, IBRD, ICAO, ICC, ICFTU, ICRM, IDA, IEA, IFAD, IFC, IFRCS, IHO, ILO, IMF, IMO, Inmarsat, Intelsat, Interpol, IOC, IOM, ISO, ITU, MONUA, MTCR, NAM (guest), NATO, NC, NEA, NIB, NSG, OPCW, OSCE, PCA, UN, UNCTAD, UNESCO, UNHCR, UNIDO, UNMIBH, UNMOP, UNPREDEP, UPU, WEU (associate), WHO, WIPO, WMO, WTrO, ZC
Diplomatic representation in the US:
chief of mission: Ambassador Tom Erik VRAALSON
chancery: 2720 34th Street NW, Washington, DC 20008
telephone: [1] (202) 333-6000
FAX: [1] (202) 337-0870
consulate(s) general: Houston, Miami, Minneapolis, New York, and San Francisco
Diplomatic representation from the US:
chief of mission: Ambassador David B. HERMELIN
embassy: Drammensveien 18, 0244 Oslo
mailing address: PSC 69, Box 1000, APO AE 09707
telephone: [47] (22) 44 85 50
FAX: [47] (22) 44 33 63
Flag description: red with a blue cross outlined in white that extends to the edges of the flag; the vertical part of the cross is shifted to the hoist side in the style of the Dannebrog (Danish flag)

Economy

Economy - overview: Norway is a prosperous bastion of welfare capitalism. The economy consists of a combination of free market activity and government intervention. The government controls key areas, such as the vital petroleum sector (through large-scale state enterprises), and extensively subsidizes agriculture, fishing, and areas with sparse resources. Norway maintains an extensive welfare system that helps propel public sector expenditures to more than 50% of GDP and results in one of the highest average tax levels in the world. A major shipping nation, with a high dependence on international trade, Norway is basically an exporter of raw materials and semiprocessed goods. The country is richly endowed with natural resources - petroleum, hydropower, fish, forests, and minerals - and is highly dependent on its oil production and international oil prices. Only Saudi Arabia exports more oil than Norway. Norway imports more than half its food needs. Oslo opted to stay out of the EU during a referendum in November 1994. Economic growth in 1999 should drop to about 1%. Despite their high per capita income and generous welfare benefits, Norwegians worry about that time in the 21st century when the oil and gas run out.
GDP: purchasing power parity - $109 billion (1998 est.)
GDP - real growth rate: 2.4% (1998 est.)
GDP - per capita: purchasing power parity - $24,700 (1998 est.)
GDP - composition by sector:
agriculture: 2%
industry: 30%
services: 68% (1997)
Population below poverty line: NA%
Household income or consumption by percentage share:
lowest 10%: 4.1%
highest 10%: 21.2% (1991)
Inflation rate (consumer prices): 2.3% (1998 est.)
Labor force: 2.3 million (1998 est.)
Labor force - by occupation: services 71%, industry 23%, agriculture, forestry, and fishing 6% (1993)
Unemployment rate: 2.6% (yearend 1997)
Budget:
revenues: $48.6 billion
expenditures: $53 billion, including capital expenditures of $NA (1994 est.)
Industries: petroleum and gas, food processing, shipbuilding, pulp and paper products, metals, chemicals, timber, mining, textiles, fishing
Industrial production growth rate: 2.7% (1998 est.)
Electricity - production: 103.374 billion kWh (1996)
Electricity - production by source:
fossil fuel: 0.76%
hydro: 99.23%
nuclear: 0%
other: 0.01% (1996)
Electricity - consumption: 112.374 billion kWh (1996)
Electricity - exports: 4.2 billion kWh (1996)
Electricity - imports: 13.2 billion kWh (1996)
Agriculture - products: oats, other grains; beef, milk; fish
Exports: $39.8 billion (f.o.b., 1998)
Exports - commodities: petroleum and petroleum

Norway *(continued)*

products 55%, machinery and equipment, metals, chemicals, ships, fish (1997)
Exports - partners: EU 76% (UK 19%, Germany 10%, Netherlands 11%, Sweden 9%, France 8%), US 6% (1997)
Imports: $37.1 billion (f.o.b., 1998)
Imports - commodities: machinery and equipment, chemicals, metals, foodstuffs
Imports - partners: EU 68% (Sweden 16%, Germany 14%, UK 9%, Denmark 7%, Netherlands 4%), US 6%, Japan 4%(1997)
Debt - external: none - Norway is a net external creditor
Economic aid - donor: ODA, $1.4 billion (1998)
Currency: 1 Norwegian krone (NKr) = 100 oere
Exchange rates: Norwegian kroner (NKr) per US$1 - 7.4524 (January 1999), 7.5451 (1998), 7.0734 (1997), 6.4498 (1996), 6.3352 (1995), 7.0576 (1994)
Fiscal year: calendar year

Communications

Telephones: 2.39 million (1994 est.); 470,000 cellular telephone subscribers (1994)
Telephone system: high-quality domestic and international telephone, telegraph, and telex services
domestic: NA domestic satellite earth stations
international: 2 buried coaxial cable systems; 4 coaxial submarine cables; satellite earth stations - NA Eutelsat, NA Intelsat (Atlantic Ocean), and 1 Inmarsat (Atlantic and Indian Ocean regions); note - Norway shares the Inmarsat earth station with the other Nordic countries (Denmark, Finland, Iceland, and Sweden)
Radio broadcast stations: AM 46, FM 493 (350 private and 143 government), shortwave 0
Radios: 3.3 million (1993 est.)
Television broadcast stations: 209 (1997)
Televisions: 1.5 million (1993 est.)

Transportation

Railways:
total: 4,012 km
standard gauge: 4,012 km 1.435-m gauge (2,422 km electrified; 96 km double track) (1996)
Highways:
total: 91,180 km
paved: 67,473 km (including 109 km of expressways)
unpaved: 23,707 km (1997 est.)
Waterways: 1,577 km along west coast; navigable by 2.4 m draft vessels maximum
Pipelines: refined petroleum products 53 km
Ports and harbors: Bergen, Drammen, Floro, Hammerfest, Harstad, Haugesund, Kristiansand, Larvik, Narvik, Oslo, Porsgrunn, Stavanger, Tromso, Trondheim
Merchant marine:
total: 788 ships (1,000 GRT or over) totaling 21,200,416 GRT/33,642,888 DWT
ships by type: bulk 106, cargo 150, chemical tanker 99, combination bulk 8, combination ore/oil 39, container 19, liquefied gas tanker 86, multifunction large-load carrier 1, oil tanker 143, passenger 12, refrigerated cargo 15, roll-on/roll-off cargo 52,

short-sea passenger 22, vehicle carrier 36
note: the government has created an internal register, the Norwegian International Ship register (NIS), as a subset of the Norwegian register; ships on the NIS enjoy many benefits of flags of convenience and do not have to be crewed by Norwegians (1998 est.)
Airports: 103 (1998 est.)
Airports - with paved runways:
total: 66
over 3,047 m: 1
2,438 to 3,047 m: 11
1,524 to 2,437 m: 14
914 to 1,523 m: 11
under 914 m: 29 (1998 est.)
Airports - with unpaved runways:
total: 37
914 to 1,523 m: 5
under 914 m: 32 (1998 est.)
Heliports: 1 (1998 est.)

Military

Military branches: Norwegian Army, Royal Norwegian Navy (includes Coast Artillery and Coast Guard), Royal Norwegian Air Force, Home Guard
Military manpower - military age: 20 years of age
Military manpower - availability:
males age 15-49: 1,103,738 (1999 est.)
Military manpower - fit for military service:
males age 15-49: 917,244 (1999 est.)
Military manpower - reaching military age annually:
males: 27,448 (1999 est.)
Military expenditures - dollar figure: NA
Military expenditures - percent of GDP: 2.2% (1998)

Transnational Issues

Disputes - international: territorial claim in Antarctica (Queen Maud Land); Svalbard is the focus of a maritime boundary dispute in the Barents Sea between Norway and Russia
Illicit drugs: minor transshipment point for drugs shipped via the CIS and Baltic states for the European market; increasing domestic consumption of cannabis and amphetamines

Oman

Geography

Location: Middle East, bordering the Arabian Sea, Gulf of Oman, and Persian Gulf, between Yemen and UAE
Geographic coordinates: 21 00 N, 57 00 E
Map references: Middle East
Area:
total: 212,460 sq km
land: 212,460 sq km
water: 0 sq km
Area - comparative: slightly smaller than Kansas
Land boundaries:
total: 1,374 km
border countries: Saudi Arabia 676 km, UAE 410 km, Yemen 288 km
Coastline: 2,092 km
Maritime claims:
contiguous zone: 24 nm
exclusive economic zone: 200 nm
territorial sea: 12 nm
Climate: dry desert; hot, humid along coast; hot, dry interior; strong southwest summer monsoon (May to September) in far south
Terrain: vast central desert plain, rugged mountains in north and south
Elevation extremes:
lowest point: Arabian Sea 0 m
highest point: Jabal Shams 2,980 m
Natural resources: petroleum, copper, asbestos, some marble, limestone, chromium, gypsum, natural gas
Land use:
arable land: 0%
permanent crops: 0%
permanent pastures: 5%
forests and woodland: NA%
other: 95% (1993 est.)
Irrigated land: 580 sq km (1993 est.)
Natural hazards: summer winds often raise large sandstorms and dust storms in interior; periodic droughts

Oman (continued)

People and Government column

Environment - current issues: rising soil salinity; beach pollution from oil spills; very limited natural fresh water resources

Environment - international agreements:
party to: Biodiversity, Climate Change, Desertification, Hazardous Wastes, Law of the Sea, Marine Dumping, Ship Pollution, Whaling
signed, but not ratified: none of the selected agreements

Geography - note: strategic location with small foothold on Musandam Peninsula adjacent to Strait of Hormuz, a vital transit point for world crude oil

Population: 2,446,645 (July 1999 est.)
Age structure:
0-14 years: 41% (male 508,681; female 489,453)
15-64 years: 57% (male 856,062; female 535,123)
65 years and over: 2% (male 30,083; female 27,243) (1999 est.)
Population growth rate: 3.45% (1999 est.)
Birth rate: 37.98 births/1,000 population (1999 est.)
Death rate: 4.29 deaths/1,000 population (1999 est.)
Net migration rate: 0.84 migrant(s)/1,000 population (1999 est.)
Sex ratio:
at birth: 1.05 male(s)/female
under 15 years: 1.04 male(s)/female
15-64 years: 1.6 male(s)/female
65 years and over: 1.1 male(s)/female
total population: 1.33 male(s)/female (1999 est.)
Infant mortality rate: 24.71 deaths/1,000 live births (1999 est.)
Life expectancy at birth:
total population: 71.3 years
male: 69.31 years
female: 73.39 years (1999 est.)
Total fertility rate: 6.11 children born/woman (1999 est.)
Nationality:
noun: Omani(s)
adjective: Omani
Ethnic groups: Arab, Baluchi, South Asian (Indian, Pakistani, Sri Lankan, Bangladeshi), African
Religions: Ibadhi Muslim 75%, Sunni Muslim, Shi'a Muslim, Hindu
Languages: Arabic (official), English, Baluchi, Urdu, Indian dialects
Literacy:
definition: NA
total population: approaching 80%
male: NA%
female: NA%

Country name:
conventional long form: Sultanate of Oman
conventional short form: Oman
local long form: Saltanat Uman
local short form: Uman
Data code: MU

Government type: monarchy
Capital: Muscat
Administrative divisions: 6 regions (mintaqat, singular - mintaqah) and 2 governorates* (muhafazat, singular - muhafazah) Ad Dakhiliyah, Al Batinah, Al Wusta, Ash Sharqiyah, Az Zahirah, Masqat, Musandam*, Zufar*
Independence: 1650 (expulsion of the Portuguese)
National holiday: National Day, 18 November (1940)
Constitution: none; note - on 6 November 1996, Sultan QABOOS issued a royal decree promulgating a new basic law which, among other things, clarifies the royal succession, provides for a prime minister, bars ministers from holding interests in companies doing business with the government, establishes a bicameral Omani council, and guarantees basic civil liberties for Omani citizens
Legal system: based on English common law and Islamic law; ultimate appeal to the monarch; has not accepted compulsory ICJ jurisdiction
Suffrage: limited to approximately 50,000 Omanis chosen by the government to vote in elections for the Majlis ash-Shura
Executive branch:
chief of state: Sultan and Prime Minister QABOOS bin Said Al Said (since 23 July 1970); note - the monarch is both the chief of state and head of government
head of government: Sultan and Prime Minister QABOOS bin Said Al Said (since 23 July 1970); note - the monarch is both the chief of state and head of government
cabinet: Cabinet appointed by the monarch
elections: none; the monarch is hereditary
Legislative branch: bicameral Majlis Oman consists of an upper chamber or Majlis ad-Dawla (41 seats; members appointed by the monarch; has advisory powers only) and a lower chamber or Majlis ash-Shura (82 seats; members elected by limited suffrage, however, the monarch makes final selections and can negate election results; body has some limited power to propose legislation, but otherwise has only advisory powers)
elections: last held NA October 1997 (next to be held NA 2000)
election results: NA
Judicial branch: none; traditional Islamic judges and a nascent civil court system, administered by region
Political parties and leaders: none
Political pressure groups and leaders: NA
International organization participation: ABEDA, AFESD, AL, AMF, ESCWA, FAO, G-77, GCC, IBRD, ICAO, IDA, IDB, IFAD, IFC, IHO, ILO, IMF, IMO, Inmarsat, Intelsat, Interpol, IOC, ISO (correspondent), ITU, NAM, OIC, OPCW, UN, UNCTAD, UNESCO, UNIDO, UPU, WFTU, WHO, WIPO, WMO, WTrO (applicant)
Diplomatic representation in the US:
chief of mission: Ambassador Abdallah bin Muhammad bin Aqil al-DHAHAB
chancery: 2535 Belmont Road, NW, Washington, DC 20008

telephone: [1] (202) 387-1980 through 1981, 1988
FAX: [1] (202) 745-4933
Diplomatic representation from the US:
chief of mission: Ambassador John D. CRAIG
embassy: Jameat A'Duwal Al Arabiya Street, Al Khuwair area, Muscat
mailing address: international: P. O. Box 202, Code No. 115, Medinat Qaboos, Muscat
telephone: [968] 698989
FAX: [968] 699779
Flag description: three horizontal bands of white, red, and green of equal width with a broad, vertical, red band on the hoist side; the national emblem (a khanjar dagger in its sheath superimposed on two crossed swords in scabbards) in white is centered at the top of the vertical band

Economy - overview: Economic performance is closely tied to the fortunes of the oil industry. Petroleum accounts for 75% of export earnings and government revenues and for roughly 40% of GDP. Oman has proved oil reserves of 4 billion barrels, equivalent to about 20 years' production at the current rate of extraction. Agriculture is carried on at a subsistence level and the general population depends on imported food. The government is encouraging private investment, both domestic and foreign, as a prime force for further economic development. In 1998-99 the economy is suffering from weak world oil prices.
GDP: purchasing power parity - $18.6 billion (1998 est.)
GDP - real growth rate: -8.5% (1998 est.)
GDP - per capita: purchasing power parity - $7,900 (1998 est.)
GDP - composition by sector:
agriculture: 2%
industry: 50%
services: 48% (1997 est.)
Population below poverty line: NA%
Household income or consumption by percentage share:
lowest 10%: NA%
highest 10%: NA%
Inflation rate (consumer prices): -0.2% (1997 est.)
Labor force: 850,000 (1997 est.)
Labor force - by occupation: NA
Unemployment rate: NA%
Budget:
revenues: $4 billion
expenditures: $5.6 billion, including capital expenditures of $NA (1999 budget est.)
Industries: crude oil production and refining, natural gas production, construction, cement, copper
Industrial production growth rate: 2% (1997 est.)
Electricity - production: 8 billion kWh (1996)
Electricity - production by source:
fossil fuel: 100%
hydro: 0%
nuclear: 0%
other: 0% (1996)

Oman (continued)

Electricity - consumption: 8 billion kWh (1996)
Electricity - exports: 0 kWh (1996)
Electricity - imports: 0 kWh (1996)
Agriculture - products: dates, limes, bananas, alfalfa, vegetables; camels, cattle; fish
Exports: $7.6 billion (f.o.b., 1997)
Exports - commodities: petroleum, reexports, fish, metals, textiles
Exports - partners: Japan 26%, China 19%, Thailand 19%, South Korea 14%, US 4% (1997)
Imports: $4 billion (f.o.b., 1997)
Imports - commodities: machinery, transportation equipment, manufactured goods, food, livestock, lubricants
Imports - partners: UAE 23% (largely reexports), Japan 16%, UK 14%, US 8%, Germany 5% (1997)
Debt - external: $3 billion (1997 est.)
Economic aid - recipient: $76.4 million (1995)
Currency: 1 Omani rial (RO) = 1,000 baiza
Exchange rates: Omani rials (RO) per US$1 - 0.3845 (fixed rate since 1986)
Fiscal year: calendar year

Communications

Telephones: 150,000 (1994 est.)
Telephone system: modern system consisting of open wire, microwave, and radiotelephone communication stations; limited coaxial cable
domestic: open wire, microwave, radiotelephone communications, and a domestic satellite system with 8 earth stations
international: satellite earth stations - 2 Intelsat (Indian Ocean) and 1 Arabsat
Radio broadcast stations: AM 2, FM 4, shortwave 1
Radios: 1.043 million (1992 est.)
Television broadcast stations: 13 (in addition, there are 25 low-power repeaters) (1997)
Televisions: 1.195 million (1992 est.)

Transportation

Railways: 0 km
Highways:
total: 32,800 km
paved: 9,840 km (including 550 km of expressways)
unpaved: 22,960 km (1996 est.)
Pipelines: crude oil 1,300 km; natural gas 1,030 km
Ports and harbors: Matrah, Mina' al Fahl, Mina' Raysut
Merchant marine:
total: 3 ships (1,000 GRT or over) totaling 16,306 GRT/8,210 DWT
ships by type: cargo 1, passenger 1, passenger-cargo 1 (1998 est.)
Airports: 143 (1998 est.)
Airports - with paved runways:
total: 6
over 3,047 m: 4
2,438 to 3,047 m: 1
914 to 1,523 m: 1 (1998 est.)
Airports - with unpaved runways:
total: 137

over 3,047 m: 2
2,438 to 3,047 m: 6
1,524 to 2,437 m: 58
914 to 1,523 m: 36
under 914 m: 35 (1998 est.)
Heliports: 1 (1998 est.)

Military

Military branches: Army, Navy, Air Force, paramilitary (includes Royal Oman Police)
Military manpower - military age: 14 years of age
Military manpower - availability:
males age 15-49: 752,637 (1999 est.)
Military manpower - fit for military service:
males age 15-49: 420,361 (1999 est.)
Military manpower - reaching military age annually:
males: NA
Military expenditures - dollar figure: $1.672 billion (1998)
Military expenditures - percent of GDP: 11.1% (1998)

Transnational Issues

Disputes - international: southern boundary with the United Arab Emirates has not been bilaterally defined; northern section in the Musandam Peninsula is an administrative boundary

Pacific Ocean

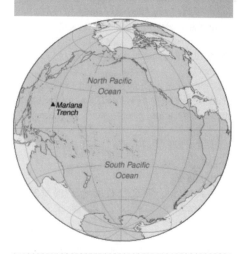

Geography

Location: body of water between Antarctica, Asia, Australia, and the Western Hemisphere
Geographic coordinates: 0 00 N, 160 00 W
Map references: World
Area:
total: 165.384 million sq km
note: includes Bali Sea, Bellingshausen Sea, Bering Sea, Bering Strait, Coral Sea, East China Sea, Flores Sea, Gulf of Alaska, Gulf of Tonkin, Java Sea, Philippine Sea, Ross Sea, Savu Sea, Sea of Japan, Sea of Okhotsk, South China Sea, Tasman Sea, Timor Sea, and other tributary water bodies
Area - comparative: about 18 times the size of the US; the largest ocean (followed by the Atlantic Ocean, the Indian Ocean, and the Arctic Ocean); covers about one-third of the global surface; larger than the total land area of the world
Coastline: 135,663 km
Climate: planetary air pressure systems and resultant wind patterns exhibit remarkable uniformity in the south and east; trade winds and westerly winds are well-developed patterns, modified by seasonal fluctuations; tropical cyclones (hurricanes) may form south of Mexico from June to October and affect Mexico and Central America; continental influences cause climatic uniformity to be much less pronounced in the eastern and western regions at the same latitude in the North Pacific Ocean; the western Pacific is monsoonal - a rainy season occurs during the summer months, when moisture-laden winds blow from the ocean over the land, and a dry season during the winter months, when dry winds blow from the Asian landmass back to the ocean; tropical cyclones (typhoons) may strike southeast and east Asia from May to December
Terrain: surface currents in the northern Pacific are dominated by a clockwise, warm-water gyre (broad circular system of currents) and in the southern Pacific by a counterclockwise, cool-water gyre; in the

Pacific Ocean *(continued)*

northern Pacific, sea ice forms in the Bering Sea and Sea of Okhotsk in winter; in the southern Pacific, sea ice from Antarctica reaches its northernmost extent in October; the ocean floor in the eastern Pacific is dominated by the East Pacific Rise, while the western Pacific is dissected by deep trenches, including the Mariana Trench, which is the world's deepest

Elevation extremes:

lowest point: Challenger Deep in the Mariana Trench -10,924 m

highest point: sea level 0 m

Natural resources: oil and gas fields, polymetallic nodules, sand and gravel aggregates, placer deposits, fish

Natural hazards: surrounded by a zone of violent volcanic and earthquake activity sometimes referred to as the "Pacific Ring of Fire"; subject to tropical cyclones (typhoons) in southeast and east Asia from May to December (most frequent from July to October); tropical cyclones (hurricanes) may form south of Mexico and strike Central America and Mexico from June to October (most common in August and September); southern shipping lanes subject to icebergs from Antarctica; cyclical El Nino phenomenon occurs off the coast of Peru, when the trade winds slacken and the warm Equatorial countercurrent moves south, killing the plankton that is the primary food source for anchovies; consequently, the anchovies move to better feeding grounds, causing resident marine birds to starve by the thousands because of the loss of their food source; ships subject to superstructure icing in extreme north from October to May and in extreme south from May to October; persistent fog in the northern Pacific can be a maritime hazard from June to December

Environment - current issues: endangered marine species include the dugong, sea lion, sea otter, seals, turtles, and whales; oil pollution in Philippine Sea and South China Sea

Environment - international agreements:

party to: none of the selected agreements

signed, but not ratified: none of the selected agreements

Geography - note: the major chokepoints are the Bering Strait, Panama Canal, Luzon Strait, and the Singapore Strait; the Equator divides the Pacific Ocean into the North Pacific Ocean and the South Pacific Ocean; dotted with low coral islands and rugged volcanic islands in the southwestern Pacific Ocean

Government

Data code: none; the US Government has not approved a standard for hydrographic codes - see the Cross-Reference List of Hydrographic Codes appendix

Economy

Economy - overview: The Pacific Ocean is a major contributor to the world economy and particularly to those nations its waters directly touch. It provides low-cost sea transportation between East and West, extensive fishing grounds, offshore oil and gas fields, minerals, and sand and gravel for the construction industry. In 1996, over 60% of the world's fish catch came from the Pacific Ocean. Exploitation of offshore oil and gas reserves is playing an ever-increasing role in the energy supplies of Australia, NZ, China, US, and Peru. The high cost of recovering offshore oil and gas, combined with the wide swings in world prices for oil since 1985, has slowed but not stopped new drillings.

Communications

Telephone system:

international: several submarine cables with network nodal points on Guam and Hawaii

Transportation

Ports and harbors: Bangkok (Thailand), Hong Kong, Kao-hsiung (Taiwan), Los Angeles (US), Manila (Philippines), Pusan (South Korea), San Francisco (US), Seattle (US), Shanghai (China), Singapore, Sydney (Australia), Vladivostok (Russia), Wellington (NZ), Yokohama (Japan)

Transnational Issues

Disputes - international: some maritime disputes (see littoral states)

Pakistan

Geography

Location: Southern Asia, bordering the Arabian Sea, between India on the east and Iran and Afghanistan on the west and China in the north

Geographic coordinates: 30 00 N, 70 00 E

Map references: Asia

Area:

total: 803,940 sq km

land: 778,720 sq km

water: 25,220 sq km

Area - comparative: slightly less than twice the size of California

Land boundaries:

total: 6,774 km

border countries: Afghanistan 2,430 km, China 523 km, India 2,912 km, Iran 909 km

Coastline: 1,046 km

Maritime claims:

contiguous zone: 24 nm

continental shelf: 200 nm or to the edge of the continental margin

exclusive economic zone: 200 nm

territorial sea: 12 nm

Climate: mostly hot, dry desert; temperate in northwest; arctic in north

Terrain: flat Indus plain in east; mountains in north and northwest; Balochistan plateau in west

Elevation extremes:

lowest point: Indian Ocean 0 m

highest point: K2 (Mt. Godwin-Austen) 8,611 m

Natural resources: land, extensive natural gas reserves, limited petroleum, poor quality coal, iron ore, copper, salt, limestone

Land use:

arable land: 27%

permanent crops: 1%

permanent pastures: 6%

forests and woodland: 5%

other: 61% (1993 est.)

Irrigated land: 171,100 sq km (1993 est.)

Pakistan (continued)

Natural hazards: frequent earthquakes, occasionally severe especially in north and west; flooding along the Indus after heavy rains (July and August)

Environment - current issues: water pollution from raw sewage, industrial wastes, and agricultural runoff; limited natural fresh water resources; a majority of the population does not have access to potable water; deforestation; soil erosion; desertification

Environment - international agreements:
party to: Biodiversity, Climate Change, Desertification, Endangered Species, Environmental Modification, Hazardous Wastes, Law of the Sea, Nuclear Test Ban, Ozone Layer Protection, Ship Pollution, Wetlands
signed, but not ratified: Marine Life Conservation

Geography - note: controls Khyber Pass and Bolan Pass, traditional invasion routes between Central Asia and the Indian Subcontinent

People

Population: 138,123,359 (July 1999 est.)
Age structure:
0-14 years: 41% (male 29,423,876; female 27,763,774)
15-64 years: 55% (male 38,533,918; female 36,804,592)
65 years and over: 4% (male 2,768,942; female 2,828,257) (1999 est.)
Population growth rate: 2.18% (1999 est.)
Birth rate: 33.51 births/1,000 population (1999 est.)
Death rate: 10.45 deaths/1,000 population (1999 est.)
Net migration rate: -1.3 migrant(s)/1,000 population (1999 est.)
Sex ratio:
at birth: 1.05 male(s)/female
under 15 years: 1.06 male(s)/female
15-64 years: 1.05 male(s)/female
65 years and over: 0.98 male(s)/female
total population: 1.05 male(s)/female (1999 est.)
Infant mortality rate: 91.86 deaths/1,000 live births (1999 est.)
Life expectancy at birth:
total population: 59.38 years
male: 58.49 years
female: 60.3 years (1999 est.)
Total fertility rate: 4.73 children born/woman (1999 est.)
Nationality:
noun: Pakistani(s)
adjective: Pakistani
Ethnic groups: Punjabi, Sindhi, Pashtun (Pathan), Baloch, Muhajir (immigrants from India and their descendants)
Religions: Muslim 97% (Sunni 77%, Shi'a 20%), Christian, Hindu, and other 3%
Languages: Punjabi 48%, Sindhi 12%, Siraiki (a Punjabi variant) 10%, Pashtu 8%, Urdu (official) 8%, Balochi 3%, Hindko 2%, Brahui 1%, English (official and lingua franca of Pakistani elite and most government ministries), Burushaski, and other 8%

Literacy:
definition: age 15 and over can read and write
total population: 37.8%
male: 50%
female: 24.4% (1995 est.)

Government

Country name:
conventional long form: Islamic Republic of Pakistan
conventional short form: Pakistan
former: West Pakistan
Data code: PK
Government type: federal republic
Capital: Islamabad
Administrative divisions: 4 provinces, 1 territory*, and 1 capital territory**; Balochistan, Federally Administered Tribal Areas*, Islamabad Capital Territory**, North-West Frontier, Punjab, Sindh
note: the Pakistani-administered portion of the disputed Jammu and Kashmir region includes Azad Kashmir and the Northern Areas
Independence: 14 August 1947 (from UK)
National holiday: Pakistan Day, 23 March (1956) (proclamation of the republic)
Constitution: 10 April 1973, suspended 5 July 1977, restored with amendments 30 December 1985
Legal system: based on English common law with provisions to accommodate Pakistan's status as an Islamic state; accepts compulsory ICJ jurisdiction, with reservations
Suffrage: 21 years of age; universal; separate electorates and reserved parliamentary seats for non-Muslims
Executive branch:
chief of state: President Mohammad Rafiq TARAR (since 31 December 1997)
head of government: Prime Minister Mohammad Nawaz SHARIF (since 17 February 1997)
cabinet: Cabinet appointed by the prime minister
elections: president elected by Parliament for a five-year term; election last held 31 December 1997 (next to be held no later than 1 January 2003); following legislative elections, the leader of the majority party or leader of a majority coalition is usually elected prime minister by the National Assembly; election last held 3 February 1997 (next to be held NA February 2002)
election results: Mohammad Rafiq TARAR elected president; percent of Parliament and provincial vote - NA; Mohammad Nawaz SHARIF elected prime minister; percent of National Assembly vote - NA
Legislative branch: bicameral Parliament or Majlis-e-Shoora consists of the Senate (87 seats; members indirectly elected by provincial assemblies to serve six-year terms; one-third of the members up for election every two years) and the National Assembly (217 seats - 10 represent non-Muslims; members elected by popular vote to serve five-year terms)
elections: Senate - last held 12 March 1997 (next to be held NA March 1999); National Assembly - last held 3 February 1997 (next to be held NA February 2002)

election results: Senate - percent of vote by party - NA; seats by party - PML/N 30, PPP 17, ANP 7, MQM/A 6, JWP 5, BNP 4, JUI/F 2, PML/J 2, BNM/M 1, PKMAP 1, TJP 1, independents 6, vacant 5; National Assembly - percent of vote by party - NA; seats by party - PML/N 137, PPP 18, MQM/A 12, ANP 10, BNP 3, JWP 2, JUI/F 2, PPP/SB 1, NPP 1, independents 21, minorities 10
Judicial branch: Supreme Court, judicial chiefs are appointed by the president; Federal Islamic (Shari'a) Court
Political parties and leaders:
government: Pakistan Muslim League, Nawaz Sharif faction or PML/N [Nawaz SHARIF]; Balochistan National Movement/Mengal Group or BNM/M [Sardar Akhtar MENGAL]; Jamiat-al-Hadith or JAH [leader NA]; Jamhoori Watan Party or JWP [Akbar Khan BUGTI]; Pakistan People's Party/Shaheed Bhutto or PPP/SB [Ghinva BHUTTO]; Baluch National Party or BNP [leader NA]
opposition: Pakistan People's Party or PPP [Benazir BHUTTO]; Pakistan Muslim League, Junejo faction or PML/J [Hamid Nasir CHATTHA]; National People's Party or NPP [Ghulam Mustapha JATOI]; Pakhtun Khwa Milli Awami Party or PKMAP [Mahmood Khan ACHAKZAI]; Balochistan National Movement/Hayee Group or BNM/H [Dr. HAYEE Baluch]; Pakhtun Quami Party or PKQP [Mohammed AFZAL Khan]; Awami National Party or ANP [Wali KHAN]; Mutahida Qaumi Movement, Altaf faction or MQM/A [Altaf HUSSAIN]
frequently shifting: Jamiat Ulema-i-Pakistan, Niazi faction or JUP/NI [leader NA]; Pakistan Muslim League, Functional Group or PML/F [Pir PAGARO]; Pakistan National Party or PNP [leader NA]; Milli Yakjheti Council or MYC is an umbrella organization which includes Jamaat-i-Islami or JI [Qazi Hussain AHMED], Jamiat Ulema-i-Islam, Sami-ul-Haq faction or JUI/S, Tehrik-I-Jafria Pakistan or TJP [Allama Sajid NAQVI], and Jamiat Ulema-i-Pakistan, Noorani faction or JUP/NO
note: political alliances in Pakistan can shift frequently; subsequent to the election Jamiat Ulema-i-Islami, Fazlur Rehman group or JUI/F was disbanded
Political pressure groups and leaders: military remains important political force; ulema (clergy), landowners, industrialists, and small merchants also influential
International organization participation: AsDB, C, CCC, CP, ECO, ESCAP, FAO, G-19, G-24, G-77, IAEA, IBRD, ICAO, ICC, ICFTU, ICRM, IDA, IDB, IFAD, IFC, IFRCS, IHO, ILO, IMF, IMO, Inmarsat, Intelsat, Interpol, IOC, IOM, ISO, ITU, MINURSO, MONUA, NAM, OAS (observer), OIC, OPCW, PCA, SAARC, UN, UNCTAD, UNESCO, UNHCR, UNIDO, UNIKOM, UNITAR, UNMIBH, UNMOP, UNOMIG, UNOMIL, UNOMSIL, UNPREDEP, UPU, WCL, WFTU, WHO, WIPO, WMO, WToO, WTrO
Diplomatic representation in the US:
chief of mission: Ambassador Riaz Hussain KHOKHAR

Pakistan *(continued)*

chancery: 2315 Massachusetts Avenue NW, Washington, DC 20008
telephone: [1] (202) 939-6205
FAX: [1] (202) 387-0484
consulate(s) general: Los Angeles and New York
Diplomatic representation from the US:
chief of mission: Ambassador William MILAM
embassy: Diplomatic Enclave, Ramna 5, Islamabad
mailing address: P. O. Box 1048, Unit 62200, APO AE 09812-2200
telephone: [92] (51) 826161 through 826179
FAX: [92] (51) 276427
consulate(s) general: Karachi
consulate(s): Lahore, Peshawar
Flag description: green with a vertical white band (symbolizing the role of religious minorities) on the hoist side; a large white crescent and star are centered in the green field; the crescent, star, and color green are traditional symbols of Islam

Economy

Economy - overview: Pakistan continues to suffer through a damaging foreign exchange crisis - stemming from years of loose fiscal policies that have exacerbated inflation and allowed public debt to explode. After accruing more than $1.5 billion in debt arrears in the first six months of FY98/99, Pakistani officials approached multilateral creditors requesting balance-of-payments relief and structural support. In January 1999, Islamabad received more than $1 billion in loans along with $3 billion in debt relief following the Finance Minister DAR's pledge to implement an economic reform program to reduce the budget deficit, deepen the financial sector, and broaden the industrial base. Although the economy has shown signs of improvement following implementation of some corrective measures, Prime Minister SHARIF - historically - has failed to implement the tough structural reforms necessary for sustained, longer-term growth. The government must also cope with long-standing economic vulnerabilities - inadequate infrastructure and low levels of literacy.
GDP: purchasing power parity - $270 billion (1998 est.)
GDP - real growth rate: 5% (1998 est.)
GDP - per capita: purchasing power parity - $2,000 (1998 est.)
GDP - composition by sector:
agriculture: 24.2%
industry: 26.4%
services: 49.4% (1997)
Population below poverty line: 34% (1991 est.)
Household income or consumption by percentage share:
lowest 10%: 3.4%
highest 10%: 25.2% (1991)
Inflation rate (consumer prices): 7.8% (FY97/98)
Labor force: 37.8 million (1998)
note: extensive export of labor, mostly to the Middle East, and use of child labor
Labor force - by occupation: agriculture 47%, mining and manufacturing 17%, services 17%, other 19%

Unemployment rate: NA%
Budget:
revenues: $10.8 billion
expenditures: $12 billion, including capital expenditures of $NA (FY96/97)
Industries: textiles, food processing, beverages, construction materials, clothing, paper products, shrimp
Industrial production growth rate: 2% (FY97/98)
Electricity - production: 59.336 billion kWh (1996)
Electricity - production by source:
fossil fuel: 57.3%
hydro: 42.13%
nuclear: 0.57%
other: 0% (1997)
Electricity - consumption: 59.336 billion kWh (1996)
Electricity - exports: 0 kWh (1996)
Electricity - imports: 0 kWh (1996)
Agriculture - products: cotton, wheat, rice, sugarcane, fruits, vegetables; milk, beef, mutton, eggs
Exports: $8.5 billion (FY97/98)
Exports - commodities: cotton, textiles, clothing, rice, leather, carpets
Exports - partners: EU, US, Hong Kong, Japan
Imports: $10.1 billion (FY97/98)
Imports - commodities: petroleum, petroleum products, machinery, transportation equipment, vegetable oils, animal fats, chemicals
Imports - partners: EU, Japan, US, China
Debt - external: $34 billion (1998 est.)
Economic aid - recipient: $2 billion (FY97/98)
Currency: 1 Pakistani rupee (PRe) = 100 paisa
Exchange rates: Pakistani rupees (PRs) per US$1 - 46.000 (January 1999), 45.033 (1998), 41.086 (1997), 36.056 (1996), 31.623 (1995), 30.548 (1994); note - annual average of official rate; parallel market rate is higher
Fiscal year: 1 July - 30 June

Communications

Telephones: 2.828 million (1998)
Telephone system: the domestic system is mediocre, but improving; service is adequate for government and business use, in part because major businesses have established their own private systems; since 1988, the government has promoted investment in the national telecommunications system on a priority basis, significantly increasing network capacity; despite major improvements in trunk and urban systems, telecommunication services are still not readily available to the majority of the rural population
domestic: microwave radio relay, coaxial cable, fiber-optic cable, cellular, and satellite
international: satellite earth stations - 3 Intelsat (1 Atlantic Ocean and 2 Indian Ocean); 3 operational international gateway exchanges (1 at Karachi and 2 at Islamabad); microwave radio relay to neighboring countries
Radio broadcast stations: AM 26, FM 3, shortwave 18 (1998 est.)

Radios: 10.2 million (1998 est.)
Television broadcast stations: 22 (in addition, there are seven low-power repeaters) (1997)
Televisions: 2.08 million (1998 est.)

Transportation

Railways:
total: 8,163 km
broad gauge: 7,718 km 1.676-m gauge (293 km electrified; 1,037 km double track)
narrow gauge: 445 km 1.000-m gauge (1996 est.)
Highways:
total: 224,774 km
paved: 128,121 km
unpaved: 96,653 km (1996 est.)
Pipelines: crude oil 250 km; petroleum products 885 km; natural gas 4,044 km (1987)
Ports and harbors: Karachi, Port Muhammad bin Qasim
Merchant marine:
total: 23 ships (1,000 GRT or over) totaling 384,304 GRT/619,668 DWT
ships by type: bulk 4, cargo 15, container 3, oil tanker 1 (1998 est.)
Airports: 116 (1998 est.)
Airports - with paved runways:
total: 80
over 3,047 m: 11
2,438 to 3,047 m: 20
1,524 to 2,437 m: 31
914 to 1,523 m: 15
under 914 m: 3 (1998 est.)
Airports - with unpaved runways:
total: 36
over 3,047 m: 1
1,524 to 2,437 m: 8
914 to 1,523 m: 9
under 914 m: 18 (1998 est.)
Heliports: 7 (1998 est.)

Military

Military branches: Army, Navy, Air Force, Civil Armed Forces, National Guard
Military manpower - military age: 17 years of age
Military manpower - availability:
males age 15-49: 33,496,712 (1999 est.)
Military manpower - fit for military service:
males age 15-49: 20,519,762 (1999 est.)
Military manpower - reaching military age annually:
males: 1,553,310 (1999 est.)
Military expenditures - dollar figure: $2.48 billion (FY98/99)
Military expenditures - percent of GDP: 4.4% (FY98/99)

Transnational Issues

Disputes - international: status of Kashmir with India; water-sharing problems with India over the Indus River (Wular Barrage)
Illicit drugs: producer of illicit opium and hashish for

the international drug trade (poppy cultivation in 1998 - 3,030 hectares, a 26% drop from 1997 because of eradication and alternative development); limited center for processing Afghan heroin; key transit area for Southwest Asian heroin moving to Western markets; narcotics still move from Afghanistan into Baluchistan Province

Palau

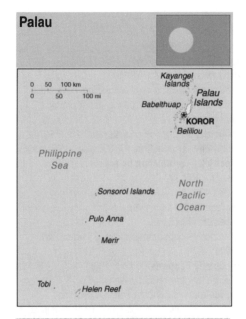

Geography

Location: Oceania, group of islands in the North Pacific Ocean, southeast of the Philippines
Geographic coordinates: 7 30 N, 134 30 E
Map references: Oceania
Area:
total: 458 sq km
land: 458 sq km
water: 0 sq km
Area - comparative: slightly more than 2.5 times the size of Washington, DC
Land boundaries: 0 km
Coastline: 1,519 km
Maritime claims:
continental shelf: 200-m depth or to the depth of exploitation
exclusive fishing zone: 12 nm
extended fishing zone: 200 nm
territorial sea: 3 nm
Climate: wet season May to November; hot and humid
Terrain: varying geologically from the high, mountainous main island of Babelthuap to low, coral islands usually fringed by large barrier reefs
Elevation extremes:
lowest point: Pacific Ocean 0 m
highest point: Mount Ngerchelchauus 242 m
Natural resources: forests, minerals (especially gold), marine products, deep-seabed minerals
Land use:
arable land: NA%
permanent crops: NA%
permanent pastures: NA%
forests and woodland: NA%
other: NA%
Irrigated land: NA sq km
Natural hazards: typhoons (June to December)
Environment - current issues: inadequate facilities for disposal of solid waste; threats to the marine ecosystem from sand and coral dredging, illegal fishing practices, and overfishing

Environment - international agreements:
party to: Biodiversity, Law of the Sea
signed, but not ratified: none of the selected agreements
Geography - note: includes World War II battleground of Beliliou (Peleliu) and world-famous rock islands; archipelago of six island groups totaling over 200 islands in the Caroline chain

People

Population: 18,467 (July 1999 est.)
Age structure:
0-14 years: 27% (male 2,595; female 2,446)
15-64 years: 68% (male 6,867; female 5,675)
65 years and over: 5% (male 416; female 468) (1999 est.)
Population growth rate: 1.94% (1999 est.)
Birth rate: 21.55 births/1,000 population (1999 est.)
Death rate: 7.74 deaths/1,000 population (1999 est.)
Net migration rate: 5.63 migrant(s)/1,000 population (1999 est.)
Sex ratio:
at birth: 1.06 male(s)/female
under 15 years: 1.06 male(s)/female
15-64 years: 1.21 male(s)/female
65 years and over: 0.89 male(s)/female
total population: 1.15 male(s)/female (1999 est.)
Infant mortality rate: 18.5 deaths/1,000 live births (1999 est.)
Life expectancy at birth:
total population: 67.75 years
male: 64.69 years
female: 70.98 years (1999 est.)
Total fertility rate: 2.66 children born/woman (1999 est.)
Nationality:
noun: Palauan(s)
adjective: Palauan
Ethnic groups: Palauans are a composite of Polynesian, Malayan, and Melanesian races
Religions: Christian (Catholics, Seventh-Day Adventists, Jehovah's Witnesses, the Assembly of God, the Liebenzell Mission, and Latter-Day Saints), Modekngei religion (one-third of the population observes this religion which is indigenous to Palau)
Languages: English (official in all of Palau's 16 states), Sonsorolese (official in the state of Sonsoral), Angaur and Japanese (in the state of Anguar), Tobi (in the state of Tobi), Palauan (in the other 13 states)
Literacy:
definition: age 15 and over can read and write
total population: 92%
male: 93%
female: 90% (1980 est.)

Government

Country name:
conventional long form: Republic of Palau
conventional short form: Palau
local long form: Beluu er a Belau
local short form: Belau
former: Trust Territory of the Pacific Islands

Data code: PS
Government type: constitutional government in free association with the US; the Compact of Free Association entered into force 1 October 1994
Capital: Koror
note: a new capital is being built about 20 km northeast of Koror
Administrative divisions: 18 states; Aimeliik, Airai, Angaur, Hatobohei, Kayangel, Koror, Melekeok, Ngaraard, Ngarchelong, Ngardmau, Ngatpang, Ngchesar, Ngeremlengui, Ngiwal, Palau Island, Peleliu, Sonsoral, Tobi
Independence: 1 October 1994 (from the US-administered UN Trusteeship)
National holiday: Constitution Day, 9 July (1979)
Constitution: 1 January 1981
Legal system: based on Trust Territory laws, acts of the legislature, municipal, common, and customary laws
Suffrage: 18 years of age; universal
Executive branch:
chief of state: President Kuniwo NAKAMURA (since 1 January 1993) and Vice President Tommy E. REMENGESAU Jr. (since 1 January 1993); note - the president is both the chief of state and head of government
head of government: President Kuniwo NAKAMURA (since 1 January 1993) and Vice President Tommy E. REMENGESAU Jr. (since 1 January 1993); note - the president is both the chief of state and head of government
cabinet: Cabinet
elections: president and vice president elected on separate tickets by popular vote for four-year terms; election last held 11 November 1996 (next to be held NA November 2000)
election results: Kuniwo NAKAMURA reelected president; percent of vote - Kuniwo NAKAMURA 64%, Chief Ibedul Yutaka GIBBONS 36%; Tommy E. REMENGESAU Jr. reelected vice president; percent of vote - Tommy E. REMENGESAU Jr. 69%, Kione ISECHAL 31%
Legislative branch: bicameral Parliament or Olbiil Era Kelulau (OEK) consists of the Senate (14 seats; members elected by popular vote on a population basis to serve four-year terms) and the House of Delegates (16 seats - one from each state; members elected by popular vote to serve four-year terms)
elections: Senate - last held 11 November 1996 (next to be held NA November 2000); House of Delegates - last held 11 November 1996 (next to be held NA November 2000)
election results: Senate - percent of vote by party - NA; seats by party - NA; House of Delegates - percent of vote by party - NA; seats by party - NA
Judicial branch: Supreme Court; National Court; Court of Common Pleas
Political parties and leaders: Palau Nationalist Party [Polycarp BASILIUS]
International organization participation: ESCAP, IBRD, ICAO, ICRM, IDA, IFC, IFRCS, IMF, Sparteca, SPC, SPF, UN, UNCTAD, WHO

Diplomatic representation in the US:
chief of mission: Ambassador Hersey KYOTA
chancery: 1150 18th Street NW, Suite 750, Washington, DC 20036
telephone: [1] (202) 452-6814
FAX: [1] (202) 452-6281
Diplomatic representation from the US:
chief of mission: Ambassador Thomas C. HUBBARD (resident in Manila); Charge d'Affaires Allen E. NUGENT
embassy: address NA, Koror
mailing address: P.O. Box 6028, Republic of Palau 96940
telephone: [680] 488-2920, 2990
FAX: [680] 488-2911
Flag description: light blue with a large yellow disk (representing the moon) shifted slightly to the hoist side

Economy

Economy - overview: The economy consists primarily of subsistence agriculture and fishing. The government is the major employer of the work force, relying heavily on financial assistance from the US. The population enjoys a per capita income of more than twice that of the Philippines and much of Micronesia. Long-run prospects for the tourist sector have been greatly bolstered by the expansion of air travel in the Pacific and the rising prosperity of leading East Asian countries.
GDP: purchasing power parity - $160 million (1997 est.)
note: GDP numbers reflect US spending
GDP - real growth rate: 10% (1997 est.)
GDP - per capita: purchasing power parity - $8,800 (1997 est.)
GDP - composition by sector:
agriculture: NA%
industry: NA%
services: NA%
Population below poverty line: NA%
Household income or consumption by percentage share:
lowest 10%: NA%
highest 10%: NA%
Inflation rate (consumer prices): NA%
Labor force: NA
Labor force - by occupation: NA
Unemployment rate: 7%
Budget:
revenues: $52.9 million
expenditures: $59.9 million, including capital expenditures of $NA (1997 est.)
Industries: tourism, craft items (from shell, wood, pearls), some commercial fishing and agriculture
Industrial production growth rate: NA%
Electricity - production: 200 million kWh (1996)
Electricity - production by source:
fossil fuel: 85%
hydro: 15%
nuclear: 0%
other: 0% (1996)

Electricity - consumption: 200 million kWh (1996)
Electricity - exports: 0 kWh (1996)
Electricity - imports: 0 kWh (1996)
Agriculture - products: coconuts, copra, cassava (tapioca), sweet potatoes
Exports: $14.3 million (f.o.b., 1996)
Exports - commodities: trochus (type of shellfish), tuna, copra, handicrafts
Exports - partners: US, Japan
Imports: $72.4 million (f.o.b., 1996)
Imports - commodities: NA
Imports - partners: US
Debt - external: about $100 million (1989)
Economic aid - recipient: $155.8 million (1995); note - the Compact of Free Association with the US, entered into after the end of the UN trusteeship on 1 October 1994, will provide Palau with up to $700 million in US aid over 15 years in return for furnishing military facilities
Currency: 1 United States dollar (US$) = 100 cents
Exchange rates: US currency is used
Fiscal year: 1 October - 30 September

Communications

Telephones: 1,500 (1988 est.)
Telephone system:
domestic: NA
international: satellite earth station - 1 Intelsat (Pacific Ocean)
Radio broadcast stations: AM 1, FM 1, shortwave 0
Radios: 9,000 (1993 est.)
Television broadcast stations: 1 (1997)
Televisions: 1,600 (1993 est.)

Transportation

Railways: 0 km
Highways:
total: 61 km
paved: 36 km
unpaved: 25 km
Ports and harbors: Koror
Merchant marine: none
Airports: 3 (1998 est.)
Airports - with paved runways:
total: 1
1,524 to 2,437 m: 1 (1998 est.)
Airports - with unpaved runways:
total: 2
1,524 to 2,437 m: 2 (1998 est.)

Military

Military branches: NA
Military expenditures - dollar figure: $NA
Military expenditures - percent of GDP: NA%
Military - note: defense is the responsibility of the US; under a Compact of Free Association between Palau and the US, the US military is granted access to the islands for 50 years

Palau (continued)

Transnational Issues

Disputes - international: none

Palmyra Atoll
(territory of the US)

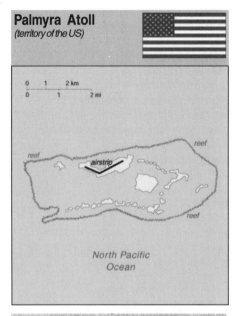

Geography

Location: Oceania, atoll in the North Pacific Ocean, about one-half of the way from Hawaii to American Samoa

Geographic coordinates: 5 52 N, 162 06 W

Map references: Oceania

Area:

total: 11.9 sq km

land: 11.9 sq km

water: 0 sq km

Area - comparative: about 20 times the size of The Mall in Washington, DC

Land boundaries: 0 km

Coastline: 14.5 km

Maritime claims:

exclusive economic zone: 200 nm

territorial sea: 12 nm

Climate: equatorial, hot, and very rainy

Terrain: very low

Elevation extremes:

lowest point: Pacific Ocean 0 m

highest point: unnamed location 2 m

Natural resources: none

Land use:

arable land: 0%

permanent crops: 0%

permanent pastures: 0%

forests and woodland: 100%

other: 0%

Irrigated land: 0 sq km (1993)

Natural hazards: NA

Environment - current issues: NA

Environment - international agreements:

party to: NA

signed, but not ratified: NA

Geography - note: about 50 islets covered with dense vegetation, coconut trees, and balsa-like trees up to 30 meters tall

People

Population: uninhabited

Government

Country name:

conventional long form: none

conventional short form: Palmyra Atoll

Data code: LQ

Dependency status: incorporated territory of the US; privately owned, but administered from Washington, DC by the Office of Insular Affairs, US Department of the Interior

Legal system: NA

Flag description: the flag of the US is used

Economy

Economy - overview: no economic activity

Transportation

Highways: much of the road and many causeways built during World War II are unserviceable and overgrown

Ports and harbors: West Lagoon

Airports: 1 (1998 est.)

note: some overgrowth of vegetation on runway but still serviceable

Airports - with unpaved runways:

total: 1

1,524 to 2,437 m: 1 (1998 est.)

Military

Military - note: defense is the responsibility of the US

Transnational Issues

Disputes - international: none

Panama

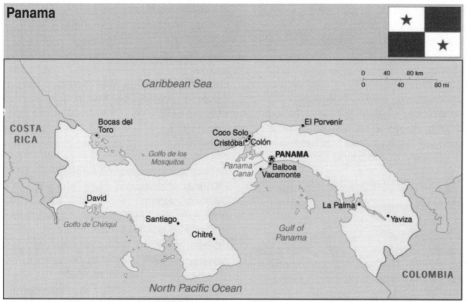

Geography

Location: Middle America, bordering both the Caribbean Sea and the North Pacific Ocean, between Colombia and Costa Rica
Geographic coordinates: 9 00 N, 80 00 W
Map references: Central America and the Caribbean
Area:
total: 78,200 sq km
land: 75,990 sq km
water: 2,210 sq km
Area - comparative: slightly smaller than South Carolina
Land boundaries:
total: 555 km
border countries: Colombia 225 km, Costa Rica 330 km
Coastline: 2,490 km
Maritime claims:
territorial sea: 200 nm
Climate: tropical; hot, humid, cloudy; prolonged rainy season (May to January), short dry season (January to May)
Terrain: interior mostly steep, rugged mountains and dissected, upland plains; coastal areas largely plains and rolling hills
Elevation extremes:
lowest point: Pacific Ocean 0 m
highest point: Volcan de Chiriqui 3,475 m
Natural resources: copper, mahogany forests, shrimp
Land use:
arable land: 7%
permanent crops: 2%
permanent pastures: 20%
forests and woodland: 44%
other: 27% (1993 est.)
Irrigated land: 320 sq km (1993 est.)
Natural hazards: NA
Environment - current issues: water pollution from agricultural runoff threatens fishery resources; deforestation of tropical rain forest; land degradation
Environment - international agreements:
party to: Biodiversity, Climate Change, Climate Change-Kyoto Protocol, Desertification, Endangered Species, Hazardous Wastes, Law of the Sea, Marine Dumping, Nuclear Test Ban, Ozone Layer Protection, Ship Pollution, Tropical Timber 83, Tropical Timber 94, Wetlands, Whaling
signed, but not ratified: Marine Life Conservation
Geography - note: strategic location on eastern end of isthmus forming land bridge connecting North and South America; controls Panama Canal that links North Atlantic Ocean via Caribbean Sea with North Pacific Ocean

People

Population: 2,778,526 (July 1999 est.)
Age structure:
0-14 years: 32% (male 446,792; female 429,811)
15-64 years: 63% (male 882,541; female 859,455)
65 years and over: 5% (male 76,648; female 83,279) (1999 est.)
Population growth rate: 1.53% (1999 est.)
Birth rate: 21.69 births/1,000 population (1999 est.)
Death rate: 5.14 deaths/1,000 population (1999 est.)
Net migration rate: -1.22 migrant(s)/1,000 population (1999 est.)
Sex ratio:
at birth: 1.04 male(s)/female
under 15 years: 1.04 male(s)/female
15-64 years: 1.03 male(s)/female
65 years and over: 0.92 male(s)/female
total population: 1.02 male(s)/female (1999 est.)
Infant mortality rate: 23.35 deaths/1,000 live births (1999 est.)
Life expectancy at birth:
total population: 74.66 years
male: 71.91 years
female: 77.51 years (1999 est.)
Total fertility rate: 2.54 children born/woman (1999 est.)

Nationality:
noun: Panamanian(s)
adjective: Panamanian
Ethnic groups: mestizo (mixed Amerindian and white) 70%, Amerindian and mixed (West Indian) 14%, white 10%, Amerindian 6%
Religions: Roman Catholic 85%, Protestant 15%
Languages: Spanish (official), English 14%
note: many Panamanians bilingual
Literacy:
definition: age 15 and over can read and write
total population: 90.8%
male: 91.4%
female: 90.2% (1995 est.)

Government

Country name:
conventional long form: Republic of Panama
conventional short form: Panama
local long form: Republica de Panama
local short form: Panama
Data code: PM
Government type: constitutional republic
Capital: Panama
Administrative divisions: 9 provinces (provincias, singular - provincia) and 2 territories* (comarca); Bocas del Toro, Chiriqui, Cocle, Colon, Darien, Herrera, Los Santos, Panama, San Blas*, Veraguas, and a new, as yet unnamed territory* or comarca created 7 March 1997 when President PEREZ BALLADARES signed a bill designating a reserve stretched across three provinces
Independence: 3 November 1903 (from Colombia; became independent from Spain 28 November 1821)
National holiday: Independence Day, 3 November (1903)
Constitution: 11 October 1972; major reforms adopted April 1983
Legal system: based on civil law system; judicial review of legislative acts in the Supreme Court of Justice; accepts compulsory ICJ jurisdiction, with reservations
Suffrage: 18 years of age; universal and compulsory
Executive branch:
chief of state: President Ernesto PEREZ BALLADARES (since 1 September 1994); First Vice President Tomas ALTAMIRANO Duque (since 1 September 1994); Second Vice President Felipe VIRZI (since 1 September 1994); note - the president is both the chief of state and head of government
head of government: President Ernesto PEREZ BALLADARES (since 1 September 1994); First Vice President Tomas ALTAMIRANO Duque (since 1 September 1994); Second Vice President Felipe VIRZI (since 1 September 1994); note - the president is both the chief of state and head of government
cabinet: Cabinet appointed by the president
elections: president and vice presidents elected on the same ticket by popular vote for five-year terms; election last held 8 May 1994 (next to be held 2 May 1999)
election results: Ernesto PEREZ BALLADARES

---

elected president; percent of vote - Ernesto PEREZ BALLADARES (PRD) 33%, Mireya MOSCOSO DE GRUBER (PA) 29%, Ruben BLADES (MPE) 17%, Ruben Dario CARLES (MOLIRENA) 16%

Legislative branch: unicameral Legislative Assembly or Asamblea Legislativa (72 seats; members are elected by popular vote to serve five-year terms)

elections: last held 8 May 1994 (next to be held 2 May 1999)

election results: percent of vote by party - NA; seats by party - PRD 32, PS 4, PALA 1, PA 14, MPE 6, MOLIRENA 4, PLA 3, PRC 3, PLN 2, PDC 1, UDI 1, MORENA 1

note: legislators from outlying rural districts are chosen on a plurality basis while districts located in more populous towns and cities elect multiple legislators by means of a proportion-based formula

Judicial branch: Supreme Court of Justice (Corte Suprema de Justicia), nine judges appointed for 10-year terms; five superior courts; three courts of appeal

Political parties and leaders:

governing coalition: Democratic Revolutionary Party or PRD [Gerardo GONZALEZ]; National Liberal Party or PLN [Raul ARANGO, founder]; Popular Nationalist Party [Jorge FLORES]

other parties: Solidarity Party or PS [Carlos CLEMENT]; Nationalist Republican Liberal Movement or MOLIRENA [Guillermo FORD]; Arnulfista Party or PA [Mireya MOSCOSO DE GRUBER]; Christian Democratic Party or PDC [Ruben AROSEMENA]; Papa Egoro Movement or MPE [Ruben BLADES]; Civic Renewal Party or PRC [Sandra ESCORCIA]; National Renovation Movement or MORENA [Pedro VALLARINO]; Authentic Liberal Party or PLA [leader NA]; Labor Party or PALA [leader NA]; Independent Democratic Union or UDI [leader NA]

Political pressure groups and leaders: National Council of Organized Workers or CONATO; National Council of Private Enterprise or CONEP; Panamanian Association of Business Executives or APEDE; National Civic Crusade; Chamber of Commerce; Panamanian Industrialists Society or SIP; Workers Confederation of the Republic of Panama or CTRP

International organization participation: CAN (associate), CCC, ECLAC, FAO, G-77, IADB, IAEA, IBRD, ICAO, ICFTU, ICRM, IDA, IFAD, IFC, IFRCS, ILO, IMF, IMO, Inmarsat, Intelsat, Interpol, IOC, IOM, ISO, ITU, LAES, LAIA (observer), NAM, OAS, OPANAL, OPCW, PCA, RG, UN, UNCTAD, UNESCO, UNIDO, UPU, WCL, WFTU, WHO, WIPO, WMO, WToO, WTrO

Diplomatic representation in the US:

chief of mission: Ambassador Eloy ALFARO de Alba

chancery: 2862 McGill Terrace NW, Washington, DC 20008

telephone: [1] (202) 483-1407

consulate(s) general: Atlanta, Houston, Miami, New Orleans, New York, Philadelphia, San Francisco, San Juan (Puerto Rico), Tampa

Diplomatic representation from the US:

chief of mission: Ambassador Simon FERRO

embassy: Avenida Balboa and Calle 38, Apartado 6959, Panama City 5

mailing address: American Embassy Panama, Unit 0945, APO AA 34002

telephone: [507] 227-1377

FAX: [507] 227-1964

Flag description: divided into four, equal rectangles; the top quadrants are white (hoist side) with a blue five-pointed star in the center and plain red, the bottom quadrants are plain blue (hoist side) and white with a red five-pointed star in the center

Economy

Economy - overview: Because of its key geographic location, Panama's economy is service-based, heavily weighted toward banking, commerce, and tourism. Since taking office in 1994, President PEREZ BALLADARES has advanced an economic reform program designed to liberalize the trade regime, attract foreign investment, privatize state-owned enterprises, institute fiscal reform, and encourage job creation through labor code reform. The government privatized its two remaining ports along the Panama Canal in 1997 and approved the sale of the railroad in early 1998. It also plans to sell other assets, including the electric company. Panama joined the World Trade Organization (WTrO) and approved a tariff reduction that will give the country the lowest average tariff rates in Latin America. A banking reform law was approved by the legislature in early 1998. The most important sectors driving growth have been the Panama Canal and other shipping and port activities.

GDP: purchasing power parity - $19.9 billion (1998 est.)

GDP - real growth rate: 2.7% (1998 est.)

GDP - per capita: purchasing power parity - $7,300 (1998 est.)

GDP - composition by sector:

agriculture: 8%

industry: 18%

services: 74% (1997 est.)

Population below poverty line: NA%

Household income or consumption by percentage share:

lowest 10%: 0.5%

highest 10%: 42.5% (1991)

Inflation rate (consumer prices): 1.4% (1998)

Labor force: 1.044 million (1997 est.)

note: shortage of skilled labor, but an oversupply of unskilled labor

Labor force - by occupation: government and community services 31.8%, agriculture, hunting, and fishing 26.8%, commerce, restaurants, and hotels 16.4%, manufacturing and mining 9.4%, construction 3.2%, transportation and communications 6.2%, finance, insurance, and real estate 4.3%

Unemployment rate: 13.1% (1997 est.)

Budget:

revenues: $2.4 billion

expenditures: $2.4 billion, including capital expenditures of $341 million (1997 est.)

Industries: construction, petroleum refining, brewing, cement and other construction materials, sugar milling

Industrial production growth rate: 0.4% (1995 est.)

Electricity - production: 3.55 billion kWh (1996)

Electricity - production by source:

fossil fuel: 29.58%

hydro: 70.42%

nuclear: 0%

other: 0% (1996)

Electricity - consumption: 3.488 billion kWh (1996)

Electricity - exports: 157 million kWh (1996)

Electricity - imports: 95 million kWh (1996)

Agriculture - products: bananas, rice, corn, coffee, sugarcane, vegetables; livestock; shrimp

Exports: $6.68 billion (f.o.b., 1997)

Exports - commodities: bananas 43%, shrimp 11%, sugar 4%, clothing 5%, coffee 2%

Exports - partners: US 37%, EU, Central America and Caribbean

Imports: $7.38 billion (f.o.b., 1997)

Imports - commodities: capital goods 21%, crude oil 11%, foodstuffs 9%, consumer goods, chemicals

Imports - partners: US 48%, EU, Central America and Caribbean, Japan

Debt - external: $7.26 billion (1996 est.)

Economic aid - recipient: $197.1 million (1995)

Currency: 1 balboa (B) = 100 centesimos

Exchange rates: balboas (B) per US$1 - 1.000 (fixed rate)

Fiscal year: calendar year

Communications

Telephones: 273,000 (1991 est.)

Telephone system: domestic and international facilities well developed

domestic: NA

international: 1 coaxial submarine cable; satellite earth stations - 2 Intelsat (Atlantic Ocean); connected to the Central American Microwave System

Radio broadcast stations: AM 91, FM 0, shortwave 0

Radios: 564,000 (1992 est.)

Television broadcast stations: 9 (in addition, there are 17 repeaters) (1997)

Televisions: 420,000 (1992 est.)

Transportation

Railways:

total: 355 km

broad gauge: 76 km 1.524-m gauge

narrow gauge: 279 km 0.914-m gauge

Highways:

total: 11,100 km

paved: 3,730 km (including 30 km of expressways)

unpaved: 7,370 km (1996 est.)

Waterways: 800 km navigable by shallow draft vessels; 82 km Panama Canal

Pipelines: crude oil 130 km

Ports and harbors: Balboa, Cristobal, Coco Solo,

Panama (continued)

Manzanillo (part of Colon area), Vacamonte
Merchant marine:
total: 4,632 ships (1,000 GRT or over) totaling
98,433,972 GRT/149,800,820 DWT
ships by type: bulk 1,335, cargo 1,028, chemical
tanker 288, combination bulk 68, combination ore/oil
15, container 507, liquefied gas tanker 176, livestock
carrier 9, multifunction large-load carrier 6, oil tanker
498, passenger 41, passenger-cargo 5, railcar carrier
2, refrigerated cargo 312, roll-on/roll-off cargo 102,
short-sea passenger 40, specialized tanker 23,
vehicle carrier 177
note: a flag of convenience registry; includes ships
from 71 countries among which are Japan 1,262,
Greece 378, Hong Kong 244, South Korea 259,
Taiwan 229, China 193, Singapore 103, US 116,
Switzerland 78, and Indonesia 53 (1998 est.)
Airports: 110 (1998 est.)
Airports - with paved runways:
total: 43
over 3,047 m: 1
2,438 to 3,047 m: 1
1,524 to 2,437 m: 5
914 to 1,523 m: 14
under 914 m: 22 (1998 est.)
Airports - with unpaved runways:
total: 67
914 to 1,523 m: 17
under 914 m: 50 (1998 est.)

Military

Military branches: an amendment to the
Constitution abolished the armed forces, but there are
security forces (Panamanian Public Forces or PPF
includes the National Police, National Maritime
Service, and National Air Service)
Military manpower - availability:
males age 15-49: 746,910 (1999 est.)
Military manpower - fit for military service:
males age 15-49: 511,866 (1999 est.)
Military expenditures - dollar figure: $132 million
(1997)
Military expenditures - percent of GDP: 1.6%
(1997)
Military - note: in October 1994, a month after
President PEREZ BALLADARES assumed office,
Panama's Legislative Assembly approved a
constitutional amendment prohibiting the creation of a
standing military force, but allowing the temporary
establishment of a "special police force" to counter
acts of "external aggression"

Transnational Issues

Disputes - international: none
Illicit drugs: major cocaine transshipment point and
major drug-money-laundering center; no recent signs
of coca cultivation; monitoring of financial transactions
is improving

Papua New Guinea

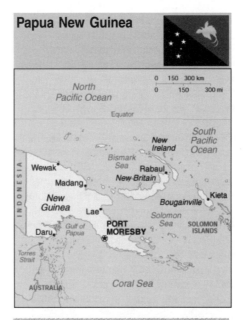

Geography

Location: Southeastern Asia, group of islands
including the eastern half of the island of New Guinea
between the Coral Sea and the South Pacific Ocean,
east of Indonesia
Geographic coordinates: 6 00 S, 147 00 E
Map references: Oceania
Area:
total: 462,840 sq km
land: 452,860 sq km
water: 9,980 sq km
Area - comparative: slightly larger than California
Land boundaries:
total: 820 km
border countries: Indonesia 820 km
Coastline: 5,152 km
Maritime claims: measured from claimed
archipelagic baselines
continental shelf: 200-m depth or to the depth of
exploitation
exclusive fishing zone: 200 nm
territorial sea: 12 nm
Climate: tropical; northwest monsoon (December to
March), southeast monsoon (May to October); slight
seasonal temperature variation
Terrain: mostly mountains with coastal lowlands and
rolling foothills
Elevation extremes:
lowest point: Pacific Ocean 0 m
highest point: Mount Wilhelm 4,509 m
Natural resources: gold, copper, silver, natural gas,
timber, oil, fisheries
Land use:
arable land: 0.1%
permanent crops: 1%
permanent pastures: 0%
forests and woodland: 92.9%
other: 6% (1993 est.)
Irrigated land: NA sq km
Natural hazards: active volcanism; situated along
the Pacific "Rim of Fire"; the country is subject to

frequent and sometimes severe earthquakes; mud
slides
Environment - current issues: rain forest subject to
deforestation as a result of growing commercial
demand for tropical timber; pollution from mining
projects; severe drought
Environment - international agreements:
party to: Antarctic Treaty, Biodiversity, Climate
Change, Endangered Species, Environmental
Modification, Hazardous Wastes, Law of the Sea,
Marine Dumping, Nuclear Test Ban, Ozone Layer
Protection, Ship Pollution, Tropical Timber 83,
Tropical Timber 94, Wetlands
signed, but not ratified: Antarctic-Environmental
Protocol, Climate Change-Kyoto Protocol
Geography - note: shares island of New Guinea
with Indonesia; one of world's largest swamps along
southwest coast

People

Population: 4,705,126 (July 1999 est.)
Age structure:
0-14 years: 39% (male 951,532; female 902,841)
15-64 years: 58% (male 1,411,053; female
1,298,937)
65 years and over: 3% (male 64,101; female 76,662)
(1999 est.)
Population growth rate: 2.26% (1999 est.)
Birth rate: 32.04 births/1,000 population (1999 est.)
Death rate: 9.47 deaths/1,000 population (1999 est.)
Net migration rate: 0 migrant(s)/1,000 population
(1999 est.)
Sex ratio:
at birth: 1.05 male(s)/female
under 15 years: 1.05 male(s)/female
15-64 years: 1.09 male(s)/female
65 years and over: 0.84 male(s)/female
total population: 1.07 male(s)/female (1999 est.)
Infant mortality rate: 55.58 deaths/1,000 live births
(1999 est.)
Life expectancy at birth:
total population: 58.47 years
male: 57.58 years
female: 59.4 years (1999 est.)
Total fertility rate: 4.17 children born/woman (1999
est.)
Nationality:
noun: Papua New Guinean(s)
adjective: Papua New Guinean
Ethnic groups: Melanesian, Papuan, Negrito,
Micronesian, Polynesian
Religions: Roman Catholic 22%, Lutheran 16%,
Presbyterian/Methodist/London Missionary Society
8%, Anglican 5%, Evangelical Alliance 4%,
Seventh-Day Adventist 1%, other Protestant sects
10%, indigenous beliefs 34%
Languages: English spoken by 1%-2%, pidgin
English widespread, Motu spoken in Papua region
note: 715 indigenous languages
Literacy:
definition: age 15 and over can read and write
total population: 72.2%

Papua New Guinea (continued)

male: 81%
female: 62.7% (1995 est.)

Government

Country name:
conventional long form: Independent State of Papua New Guinea
conventional short form: Papua New Guinea
abbreviation: PNG
Data code: PP
Government type: parliamentary democracy
Capital: Port Moresby
Administrative divisions: 20 provinces; Bougainville, Central, Chimbu, Eastern Highlands, East New Britain, East Sepik, Enga, Gulf, Madang, Manus, Milne Bay, Morobe, National Capital, New Ireland, Northern, Sandaun, Southern Highlands, Western, Western Highlands, West New Britain
Independence: 16 September 1975 (from the Australian-administered UN trusteeship)
National holiday: Independence Day, 16 September (1975)
Constitution: 16 September 1975
Legal system: based on English common law
Suffrage: 18 years of age; universal
Executive branch:
chief of state: Queen ELIZABETH II (since 6 February 1952), represented by Governor General Silas ATOPARE (since 13 November 1997)
head of government: Prime Minister Bill SKATE (since 22 July 1997); Deputy Prime Minister Iairo LASARO (since 20 October 1998)
cabinet: National Executive Council appointed by the governor general on the recommendation of the prime minister
elections: none; the monarch is hereditary; governor general appointed by the National Executive Council; prime minister and deputy prime minister appointed by the governor general for up to five years on the basis of majority support in National Parliament
Legislative branch: unicameral National Parliament - sometimes referred to as the House of Assembly (109 seats - 89 elected from open electorates and 20 from provincial electorates; members elected by popular vote to serve five-year terms)
elections: last held 14-28 June 1997 (next to be held NA June 2002)
election results: percent of vote by party - PPP 15%, Pangu Pati 14%, NA 14%, PDM 8%, PNC 6%, PAP 5%, UP 3%, NP 1%, PUP 1%, independents 33%; seats by party - PPP 16, Pangu Pati 15, NA 15, PDM 9, PNC 7, PAP 5, UP 3, NP 1, PUP 1, independents 37; note - association with political parties is very fluid
Judicial branch: Supreme Court, the chief justice is appointed by the governor general on the proposal of the National Executive Council after consultation with the minister responsible for justice, other judges are appointed by the Judicial and Legal Services Commission
Political parties and leaders: Bougainville Unity Alliance or BUA [Samuel AKOITAI]; People's Progress Party or PPP [Michael NALI]; Papua New Guinea United Party or Pangu Pati [Chris HAIVETA]; National Alliance or NA [Michael SOMARE]; People's Democratic Movement or PDM [Iario LASARO]; People's Action Party or PAP [Ted DIRO]; United Party or UP [Rimbiuk PATO]; National Party or NP [Paul PORA]; People's Unity Party or PUP [Alfred KAIABE]; Melanesian Alliance or MA [Fr. John MOMIS]; Movement for Greater Autonomy [Stephen POKAWIN]; Christian Democratic Party [Dilu GOMA]; Papua New Guinea First Party (includes People's National Congress or PNC [Bill SKATE] and Christian Country Party [Avusi TANO]); People's Resources Awareness Party [leader NA]; Liberal Party [Rabbie SAMAI]; People's Solidarity Party [Kala SWOKIM]; Melanesian Labour Party [Paul MONDIA]; Black Action Party [Paul WANJIK]; League for National Advancement or LNA [leader NA]; United Resource Party [Masket IANGALIO]; Hausman Party [Waim TOKAM]; Milne Bay Party [Simon MUMURIK]
International organization participation: ACP, APEC, AsDB, ASEAN (observer), C, CP, ESCAP, FAO, G-77, IBRD, ICAO, ICFTU, ICRM, IDA, IFAD, IFC, IFRCS, IHO, ILO, IMF, IMO, Intelsat, Interpol, IOC, ISO (correspondent), ITU, NAM, OPCW, Sparteca, SPC, SPF, UN, UNCTAD, UNESCO, UNIDO, UPU, WFTU, WHO, WIPO, WMO, WTrO
Diplomatic representation in the US:
chief of mission: Ambassador Nagora Y. BOGAN
chancery: 1779 Massachusetts Avenue NW, Washington, DC 20036
telephone: [1] (202) 745-3680
FAX: [1] (202) 745-3679
Diplomatic representation from the US:
chief of mission: Ambassador Arma Jane KARAER
embassy: Douglas Street, Port Moresby
mailing address: P. O. Box 1492, Port Moresby
telephone: [675] 321-1455
FAX: [675] 321-3423
Flag description: divided diagonally from upper hoist-side corner; the upper triangle is red with a soaring yellow bird of paradise centered; the lower triangle is black with five white five-pointed stars of the Southern Cross constellation centered

Economy

Economy - overview: Papua New Guinea is richly endowed with natural resources, but exploitation has been hampered by the rugged terrain and the high cost of developing infrastructure. Agriculture provides a subsistence livelihood for the bulk of the population. Mineral deposits, including oil, copper, and gold, account for 72% of export earnings. Budgetary support from Australia and development aid under World Bank auspices have helped sustain the economy. In 1995, Port Moresby reached agreement with the IMF and World Bank on a structural adjustment program, of which the first phase was successfully completed in 1996. In 1997, droughts caused by the El Nino weather pattern wreaked havoc on Papua New Guinea's coffee, cocoa, and coconut production, the mainstays of the agricultural-based economy and major sources of export earnings. The coffee crop was slashed by up to 50% in 1997. Despite problems with drought, the year 1998 saw a small recovery in GDP.
GDP: purchasing power parity - $11.1 billion (1998 est.)
GDP - real growth rate: 1.6% (1998 est.)
GDP - per capita: purchasing power parity - $2,400 (1998 est.)
GDP - composition by sector:
agriculture: 28.2%
industry: 34.5%
services: 37.3% (1997 est.)
Population below poverty line: NA%
Household income or consumption by percentage share:
lowest 10%: 1.7%
highest 10%: 40.5% (1996)
Inflation rate (consumer prices): 12% (FY97/98 est.)
Labor force: 1.941 million
Labor force - by occupation: agriculture 64% (1993 est.)
Unemployment rate: NA%
Budget:
revenues: $1.5 billion
expenditures: $1.35 billion, including capital expenditures of $NA (1997 est.)
Industries: copra crushing, palm oil processing, plywood production, wood chip production; mining of gold, silver, and copper; crude oil production; construction, tourism
Industrial production growth rate: NA%
Electricity - production: 1.7 billion kWh (1996)
Electricity - production by source:
fossil fuel: 70.59%
hydro: 29.41%
nuclear: 0%
other: 0% (1996)
Electricity - consumption: 1.7 billion kWh (1996)
Electricity - exports: 0 kWh (1996)
Electricity - imports: 0 kWh (1996)
Agriculture - products: coffee, cocoa, coconuts, palm kernels, tea, rubber, sweet potatoes, fruit, vegetables; poultry, pork
Exports: $2.2 billion (f.o.b., 1997)
Exports - commodities: gold, copper ore, oil, logs, palm oil, coffee, cocoa, crayfish and prawns
Exports - partners: Australia, Japan, Germany, UK, South Korea, China
Imports: $1.5 billion (c.i.f., 1997)
Imports - commodities: machinery and transport equipment, manufactured goods, food, fuels, chemicals
Imports - partners: Australia, Singapore, Japan, US, New Zealand, Malaysia
Debt - external: $3.2 billion (1995)
Economic aid - recipient: $376.3 million (1995)
Currency: 1 kina (K) = 100 toea
Exchange rates: kina (K) per US$1 - 0.47 (December 1998), 0.6975 (1997), 0.7588 (1996), 0.7835 (1995), 0.9950 (1994); note - the government floated the kina on 10 October 1994
Fiscal year: calendar year

Papua New Guinea (continued)

Communications

Telephones: 63,212 (1986 est.)
Telephone system: services are adequate and being improved; facilities provide radiotelephone and telegraph, coastal radio, aeronautical radio, and international radio communication services
domestic: mostly radiotelephone
international: submarine cables to Australia and Guam; satellite earth station - 1 Intelsat (Pacific Ocean); international radio communication service
Radio broadcast stations: AM 31, FM 2, shortwave 0
Radios: 298,000 (1992 est.)
Television broadcast stations: 3 (1997)
Televisions: 10,000 (1992 est.)

Transportation

Railways: 0 km
Highways:
total: 19,600 km
paved: 686 km
unpaved: 18,914 km (1996 est.)
Waterways: 10,940 km
Ports and harbors: Kieta, Lae, Madang, Port Moresby, Rabaul
Merchant marine:
total: 20 ships (1,000 GRT or over) totaling 35,400 GRT/50,869 DWT
ships by type: bulk 2, cargo 6, chemical tanker 1, combination ore/oil 5, container 1, oil tanker 2, roll-on/roll-off 3 (1998 est.)
Airports: 492 (1998 est.)
Airports - with paved runways:
total: 19
2,438 to 3,047 m: 1
1,524 to 2,437 m: 14
914 to 1,523 m: 3
under 914 m: 1 (1998 est.)
Airports - with unpaved runways:
total: 473
1,524 to 2,437 m: 13
914 to 1,523 m: 60
under 914 m: 400 (1998 est.)
Heliports: 2 (1998 est.)

Military

Military branches: Papua New Guinea Defense Force (includes Ground, Naval, and Air Forces, and Special Forces Unit)
Military manpower - availability:
males age 15-49: 1,238,683 (1999 est.)
Military manpower - fit for military service:
males age 15-49: 687,978 (1999 est.)
Military expenditures - dollar figure: $41.5 million (1998)
Military expenditures - percent of GDP: 1% (1998)

Transnational Issues

Disputes - international: none

Paracel Islands

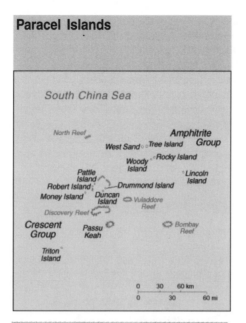

Geography

Location: Southeastern Asia, group of small islands and reefs in the South China Sea, about one-third of the way from central Vietnam to the northern Philippines
Geographic coordinates: 16 30 N, 112 00 E
Map references: Southeast Asia
Area:
total: NA sq km
land: NA sq km
water: 0 sq km
Area - comparative: NA
Land boundaries: 0 km
Coastline: 518 km
Maritime claims: NA
Climate: tropical
Terrain: NA
Elevation extremes:
lowest point: South China Sea 0 m
highest point: unnamed location on Rocky Island 14 m
Natural resources: none
Land use:
arable land: 0%
permanent crops: 0%
permanent pastures: 0%
forests and woodland: 0%
other: 100%
Irrigated land: 0 sq km (1993)
Natural hazards: typhoons
Environment - current issues: NA
Environment - international agreements:
party to: none of the selected agreements
signed, but not ratified: none of the selected agreements

People

Population: no indigenous inhabitants
note: there are scattered Chinese garrisons

Government

Country name:
conventional long form: none
conventional short form: Paracel Islands
Data code: PF

Economy

Economy - overview: China announced plans in 1997 to open the islands for tourism.

Transportation

Ports and harbors: small Chinese port facilities on Woody Island and Duncan Island being expanded
Airports: 1 (1998 est.)
Airports - with paved runways:
total: 1
1,524 to 2,437 m: 1 (1998 est.)

Military

Military - note: occupied by China

Transnational Issues

Disputes - international: occupied by China, but claimed by Taiwan and Vietnam

Paraguay

Geography

Location: Central South America, northeast of Argentina
Geographic coordinates: 23 00 S, 58 00 W
Map references: South America
Area:
total: 406,750 sq km
land: 397,300 sq km
water: 9,450 sq km
Area - comparative: slightly smaller than California
Land boundaries:
total: 3,920 km
border countries: Argentina 1,880 km, Bolivia 750 km, Brazil 1,290 km
Coastline: 0 km (landlocked)
Maritime claims: none (landlocked)
Climate: subtropical; substantial rainfall in the eastern portions, becoming semiarid in the far west
Terrain: grassy plains and wooded hills east of Rio Paraguay; Gran Chaco region west of Rio Paraguay mostly low, marshy plain near the river, and dry forest and thorny scrub elsewhere
Elevation extremes:
lowest point: junction of Rio Paraguay and Rio Parana 46 m
highest point: Cerro San Rafael 850 m
Natural resources: hydropower, timber, iron ore, manganese, limestone
Land use:
arable land: 6%
permanent crops: 0%
permanent pastures: 55%
forests and woodland: 32%
other: 7% (1993 est.)
Irrigated land: 670 sq km (1993 est.)
Natural hazards: local flooding in southeast (early September to June); poorly drained plains may become boggy (early October to June)
Environment - current issues: deforestation (an estimated 2 million hectares of forest land have been lost from 1958-85); water pollution; inadequate means for waste disposal present health risks for many urban residents
Environment - international agreements:
party to: Biodiversity, Climate Change, Desertification, Endangered Species, Hazardous Wastes, Law of the Sea, Ozone Layer Protection, Wetlands
signed, but not ratified: Climate Change-Kyoto Protocol, Nuclear Test Ban
Geography - note: landlocked; lies between Argentina, Bolivia, and Brazil

People

Population: 5,434,095 (July 1999 est.)
Age structure:
0-14 years: 39% (male 1,086,107; female 1,049,833)
15-64 years: 56% (male 1,528,127; female 1,517,213)
65 years and over: 5% (male 116,761; female 136,054) (1999 est.)
Population growth rate: 2.65% (1999 est.)
Birth rate: 31.87 births/1,000 population (1999 est.)
Death rate: 5.23 deaths/1,000 population (1999 est.)
Net migration rate: -0.09 migrant(s)/1,000 population (1999 est.)
Sex ratio:
at birth: 1.05 male(s)/female
under 15 years: 1.03 male(s)/female
15-64 years: 1.01 male(s)/female
65 years and over: 0.86 male(s)/female
total population: 1.01 male(s)/female (1999 est.)
Infant mortality rate: 36.35 deaths/1,000 live births (1999 est.)
Life expectancy at birth:
total population: 72.43 years
male: 70.47 years
female: 74.49 years (1999 est.)
Total fertility rate: 4.22 children born/woman (1999 est.)
Nationality:
noun: Paraguayan(s)
adjective: Paraguayan
Ethnic groups: mestizo (mixed Spanish and Amerindian) 95%, white plus Amerindian 5%
Religions: Roman Catholic 90%, Mennonite and other Protestant denominations
Languages: Spanish (official), Guarani
Literacy:
definition: age 15 and over can read and write
total population: 92.1%
male: 93.5%
female: 90.6% (1995 est.)

Government

Country name:
conventional long form: Republic of Paraguay
conventional short form: Paraguay
local long form: Republica del Paraguay
local short form: Paraguay
Data code: PA

Government type: republic
Capital: Asuncion
Administrative divisions: 18 departments (departamentos, singular - departamento); Alto Paraguay, Alto Parana, Amambay, Asuncion, Boqueron, Caaguazu, Caazapa, Canindeyu, Central, Concepcion, Cordillera, Guaira, Itapua, Misiones, Neembucu, Paraguari, Presidente Hayes, San Pedro
Independence: 14 May 1811 (from Spain)
National holiday: Independence Days, 14-15 May (1811)
Constitution: promulgated 20 June 1992
Legal system: based on Argentine codes, Roman law, and French codes; judicial review of legislative acts in Supreme Court of Justice; does not accept compulsory ICJ jurisdiction
Suffrage: 18 years of age; universal and compulsory up to age 60
Executive branch:
chief of state: President Luis GONZALEZ Macchi (since 28 March 1999); note - the president is both the chief of state and head of government
head of government: President Luis GONZALEZ Macchi (since 28 March 1999); note - the president is both the chief of state and head of government
cabinet: Council of Ministers nominated by the president
elections: president and vice president elected on the same ticket by popular vote for five-year terms; election last held 10 May 1998 (next to be held NA May 2003)
election results: Raul CUBAS Grau elected president; percent of vote - 55.3%; resigned 28 March 1999
note: President Luis GONZALEZ Macchi, formerly president of the Chamber of Senators, constitutionally succeeded President Raul CUBAS Grau, who resigned following the assassination of Vice President Luis Maria ARGANA; the successor to ARGANA will be decided in an election to be held in late 1999
Legislative branch: bicameral Congress or Congreso consists of the Chamber of Senators or Camara de Senadores (45 seats; members are elected by popular vote to serve five-year terms) and the Chamber of Deputies or Camara de Diputados (80 seats; members are elected by popular vote to serve five-year terms)
elections: Chamber of Senators - last held 10 May 1998 (next to be held NA May 2003); Chamber of Deputies - last held 10 May 1998 (next to be held NA May 2003)
election results: Chamber of Senators - percent of vote by party - NA; seats by party - Colorado Party 24, PLRA/PEN 20, other 1; Chamber of Deputies - percent of vote by party - NA; seats by party - Colorado Party 45, PLRA/PEN 35
Judicial branch: Supreme Court of Justice (Corte Suprema de Justicia), judges appointed on the proposal of the Counsel of Magistrates (Consejo de la Magistratura)
Political parties and leaders: National Republican Association - Colorado Party [acting president Bader RACHID LICHI]; Authentic Radical Liberal Party or

Paraguay (continued)

PLRA [Domingo LAINO]; National Encounter or PEN [Carlos FILIZZOLA]; Christian Democratic Party or PDC [Miguel MONTANER]; Febrerista Revolutionary Party or PRF [Carlos Maria LJUBETIC]

Political pressure groups and leaders: Unitary Workers Central or CUT; Roman Catholic Church; National Workers Central or CNT; Paraguayan Workers Confederation or CPT

International organization participation: CCC, ECLAC, FAO, G-77, IADB, IAEA, IBRD, ICAO, ICFTU, ICRM, IDA, IFAD, IFC, IFRCS, ILO, IMF, IMO, Intelsat, Interpol, IOC, IOM, ISO (correspondent), ITU, LAES, LAIA, Mercosur, OAS, OPANAL, OPCW, PCA, RG, UN, UNCTAD, UNESCO, UNIDO, UPU, WCL, WHO, WIPO, WMO, WToO, WTrO

Diplomatic representation in the US:
chief of mission: Ambassador (vacant)
chancery: 2400 Massachusetts Avenue NW, Washington, DC 20008
telephone: [1] (202) 483-6960 through 6962
FAX: [1] (202) 234-4508
consulate(s) general: Los Angeles, Miami, New Orleans, New York

Diplomatic representation from the US:
chief of mission: Ambassador Maura A. HARTY
embassy: 1776 Avenida Mariscal Lopez, Casilla Postal 402, Asuncion
mailing address: Unit 4711, APO AA 34036-0001
telephone: [595] (21) 213-715
FAX: [595] (21) 213-728

Flag description: three equal, horizontal bands of red (top), white, and blue with an emblem centered in the white band; unusual flag in that the emblem is different on each side; the obverse (hoist side at the left) bears the national coat of arms (a yellow five-pointed star within a green wreath capped by the words REPUBLICA DEL PARAGUAY, all within two circles); the reverse (hoist side at the right) bears the seal of the treasury (a yellow lion below a red Cap of Liberty and the words Paz y Justicia (Peace and Justice) capped by the words REPUBLICA DEL PARAGUAY, all within two circles)

Economy

Economy - overview: Paraguay has a market economy marked by a large informal sector. The informal sector features both reexport of imported consumer goods (electronics, whiskeys, perfumes, cigarettes, and office equipment) to neighboring countries as well as the activities of thousands of microenterprises and urban street vendors. The formal sector is largely oriented toward services. A large percentage of the population derive their living from agricultural activity, often on a subsistence basis. The formal economy has grown an average of about 3% over the past six years, but GDP declined in 1998. However, population has increased at about the same rate over the same period, leaving per capita income nearly stagnant. The new government of Raul CUBAS Grau was pursuing an economic reform agenda, albeit with limited success because of in-fighting in the ruling party and resistance from the opposition.

GDP: purchasing power parity - $19.8 billion (1998 est.)
GDP - real growth rate: -0.5% (1998 est.)
GDP - per capita: purchasing power parity - $3,700 (1998 est.)
GDP - composition by sector:
agriculture: 27%
industry: 30%
services: 43% (1997)
Population below poverty line: 21.8% (1991 est.)
Household income or consumption by percentage share:
lowest 10%: 0.7%
highest 10%: 46.6% (1995)
Inflation rate (consumer prices): 14.6% (1998)
Labor force: 1.8 million (1995 est.)
Labor force - by occupation: agriculture 45%
Unemployment rate: 8.2% (urban) (1996 est.)
Budget:
revenues: $1.25 billion
expenditures: $1.66 billion, including capital expenditures of $357 million (1995 est.)
Industries: meat packing, oilseed crushing, milling, brewing, textiles, other light consumer goods, cement, construction
Industrial production growth rate: 5.1% (1995)
Electricity - production: 45.03 billion kWh (1996)
Electricity - production by source:
fossil fuel: 0.07%
hydro: 99.93%
nuclear: 0%
other: 0% (1996)
Electricity - consumption: 4.768 billion kWh (1996)
Electricity - exports: 40.262 billion kWh (1996)
Electricity - imports: 0 kWh (1996)
Agriculture - products: cotton, sugarcane, soybeans, corn, wheat, tobacco, cassava (tapioca), fruits, vegetables; beef, pork, eggs, milk; timber
Exports: $1.1 billion (f.o.b., 1997 est.)
Exports - commodities: cotton, soybeans, timber, vegetable oils, meat products, coffee, tung oil
Exports - partners: Brazil 48%, Netherlands 22%, Argentina 9%, US 4%, Uruguay 3%, Chile 2% (1997)
Imports: $2.5 billion (c.i.f., 1996 est.)
Imports - commodities: capital goods, consumer goods, foodstuffs, raw materials, fuels
Imports - partners: Brazil 29%, US 22%, Argentina 14%, Hong Kong 9% (1995)
Debt - external: $1.3 billion (1996)
Economic aid - recipient: $180.4 million (1995)
Currency: 1 guarani (G) = 100 centimos
Exchange rates: guaranies (G) per US$ - 2,866.3 (January 1999), 2,755.7 (1998), 2,191.0 (1997), 2,062.8 (1996), 1,970.4 (1995), 1,911.5 (1994)
Fiscal year: calendar year

Communications

Telephones: 88,730 (1985 est.)
Telephone system: meager telephone service; principal switching center is Asuncion
domestic: fair microwave radio relay network

international: satellite earth station - 1 Intelsat (Atlantic Ocean)
Radio broadcast stations: AM 40, FM 0, shortwave 7
Radios: 775,000 (1992 est.)
Television broadcast stations: 10 (1997)
Televisions: 370,000 (1992 est.)

Transportation

Railways:
total: 971 km
standard gauge: 441 km 1.435-m gauge
narrow gauge: 60 km 1.000-m gauge
note: there are 470 km of various gauges that are privately owned
Highways:
total: 29,500 km
paved: 2,803 km
unpaved: 26,697 km (1996 est.)
Waterways: 3,100 km
Ports and harbors: Asuncion, Villeta, San Antonio, Encarnacion
Merchant marine:
total: 21 ships (1,000 GRT or over) totaling 30,287 GRT/32,510 DWT
ships by type: cargo 15, chemical tanker 1, oil tanker 4, roll-on/roll-off 1 (1998 est.)
Airports: 941 (1998 est.)
Airports - with paved runways:
total: 10
over 3,047 m: 3
1,524 to 2,437 m: 3
914 to 1,523 m: 4 (1998 est.)
Airports - with unpaved runways:
total: 931
over 3,047 m: 1
1,524 to 2,437 m: 29
914 to 1,523 m: 349
under 914 m: 552 (1998 est.)

Military

Military branches: Army, Navy (includes Naval Air and Marines), Air Force
Military manpower - military age: 17 years of age
Military manpower - availability:
males age 15-49: 1,311,382 (1999 est.)
Military manpower - fit for military service:
males age 15-49: 947,347 (1999 est.)
Military manpower - reaching military age annually:
males: 55,065 (1999 est.)
Military expenditures - dollar figure: $125 million (1998)
Military expenditures - percent of GDP: 1.4% (1998)

Transnational Issues

Illicit drugs: illicit producer of cannabis for the international drug trade; transshipment country for Bolivian cocaine headed for Europe and the US

Peru

Geography

Location: Western South America, bordering the South Pacific Ocean, between Chile and Ecuador
Geographic coordinates: 10 00 S, 76 00 W
Map references: South America
Area:
total: 1,285,220 sq km
land: 1.28 million sq km
water: 5,220 sq km
Area - comparative: slightly smaller than Alaska
Land boundaries:
total: 6,940 km
border countries: Bolivia 900 km, Brazil 1,560 km, Chile 160 km, Colombia 2,900 km, Ecuador 1,420 km
Coastline: 2,414 km
Maritime claims:
continental shelf: 200 nm
territorial sea: 200 nm
Climate: varies from tropical in east to dry desert in west
Terrain: western coastal plain (costa), high and rugged Andes in center (sierra), eastern lowland jungle of Amazon Basin (selva)
Elevation extremes:
lowest point: Pacific Ocean 0 m
highest point: Nevado Huascaran 6,768 m
Natural resources: copper, silver, gold, petroleum, timber, fish, iron ore, coal, phosphate, potash
Land use:
arable land: 3%
permanent crops: 0%
permanent pastures: 21%
forests and woodland: 66%
other: 10% (1993 est.)
Irrigated land: 12,800 sq km (1993 est.)
Natural hazards: earthquakes, tsunamis, flooding, landslides, mild volcanic activity
Environment - current issues: deforestation; overgrazing of the slopes of the costa and sierra leading to soil erosion; desertification; air pollution in Lima; pollution of rivers and coastal waters from municipal and mining wastes
Environment - international agreements:
party to: Antarctic-Environmental Protocol, Antarctic Treaty, Biodiversity, Climate Change, Desertification, Endangered Species, Hazardous Wastes, Nuclear Test Ban, Ozone Layer Protection, Ship Pollution, Tropical Timber 83, Tropical Timber 94, Wetlands, Whaling
signed, but not ratified: Climate Change-Kyoto Protocol
Geography - note: shares control of Lago Titicaca, world's highest navigable lake, with Bolivia

People

Population: 26,624,582 (July 1999 est.)
Age structure:
0-14 years: 35% (male 4,786,048; female 4,637,280)
15-64 years: 60% (male 8,045,747; female 7,939,760)
65 years and over: 5% (male 557,252; female 658,495) (1999 est.)
Population growth rate: 1.93% (1999 est.)
Birth rate: 26.09 births/1,000 population (1999 est.)
Death rate: 5.7 deaths/1,000 population (1999 est.)
Net migration rate: -1.13 migrant(s)/1,000 population (1999 est.)
Sex ratio:
at birth: 1.05 male(s)/female
under 15 years: 1.03 male(s)/female
15-64 years: 1.01 male(s)/female
65 years and over: 0.85 male(s)/female
total population: 1.01 male(s)/female (1999 est.)
Infant mortality rate: 38.97 deaths/1,000 live births (1999 est.)
Life expectancy at birth:
total population: 70.38 years
male: 68.08 years
female: 72.78 years (1999 est.)
Total fertility rate: 3.23 children born/woman (1999 est.)
Nationality:
noun: Peruvian(s)
adjective: Peruvian
Ethnic groups: Amerindian 45%, mestizo (mixed Amerindian and white) 37%, white 15%, black, Japanese, Chinese, and other 3%
Religions: Roman Catholic
Languages: Spanish (official), Quechua (official), Aymara
Literacy:
definition: age 15 and over can read and write
total population: 88.7%
male: 94.5%
female: 83% (1995 est.)

Government

Country name:
conventional long form: Republic of Peru
conventional short form: Peru
local long form: Republica del Peru
local short form: Peru
Data code: PE
Government type: republic
Capital: Lima
Administrative divisions: 24 departments (departamentos, singular - departamento) and 1 constitutional province* (provincia constitucional); Amazonas, Ancash, Apurimac, Arequipa, Ayacucho, Cajamarca, Callao*, Cusco, Huancavelica, Huanuco, Ica, Junin, La Libertad, Lambayeque, Lima, Loreto, Madre de Dios, Moquegua, Pasco, Piura, Puno, San Martin, Tacna, Tumbes, Ucayali
note: the 1979 constitution mandated the creation of regions (regiones, singular - region) to function eventually as autonomous economic and administrative entities; so far, 12 regions have been constituted from 23 of the 24 departments - Amazonas (from Loreto), Andres Avelino Caceres (from Huanuco, Pasco, Junin), Arequipa (from Arequipa), Chavin (from Ancash), Grau (from Tumbes, Piura), Inca (from Cusco, Madre de Dios, Apurimac), La Libertad (from La Libertad), Los Libertadores-Huari (from Ica, Ayacucho, Huancavelica), Mariategui (from Moquegua, Tacna, Puno), Nor Oriental del Maranon (from Lambayeque, Cajamarca, Amazonas), San Martin (from San Martin), Ucayali (from Ucayali); formation of another region has been delayed by the reluctance of the constitutional province of Callao to merge with the department of Lima; because of inadequate funding from the central government and organizational and political difficulties, the regions have yet to assume major responsibilities; the 1993 constitution retains the regions but limits their authority; the 1993 constitution also reaffirms the roles of departmental and municipal governments
Independence: 28 July 1821 (from Spain)
National holiday: Independence Day, 28 July (1821)
Constitution: 31 December 1993
Legal system: based on civil law system; has not accepted compulsory ICJ jurisdiction
Suffrage: 18 years of age; universal
Executive branch:
chief of state: President Alberto Kenyo FUJIMORI Fujimori (since 28 July 1990); note - the president is both the chief of state and head of government
head of government: President Alberto Kenyo FUJIMORI Fujimori (since 28 July 1990); note - the president is both the chief of state and head of government
note: Prime Minister Victor JOYWAY (since 4 January 1999) does not exercise executive power; this power is in the hands of the president
cabinet: Council of Ministers appointed by the president
elections: president elected by popular vote for a five-year term; election last held 9 April 1995 (next to be held NA 2000)
election results: President FUJIMORI reelected; percent of vote - Alberto FUJIMORI 64.42%, Javier PEREZ de CUELLAR 21.80%, Mercedes CABANILLAS 4.11%, other 9.67%

Legislative branch: unicameral Democratic Constituent Congress or Congresso Constituyente Democratico (120 seats; members are elected by popular vote to serve five-year terms)
elections: last held 9 April 1995 (next to be held NA April 2000)
election results: percent of vote by party - C90/NM 52.1%, UPP 14%, other parties 33.9%; seats by party - C90/NM 67, UPP 17, APRA 8, FIM 6, CODE-Pais Posible 5, AP 4, PPC 3, Renovation 3, IU 2, OBRAS 2, other parties 3
Judicial branch: Supreme Court of Justice (Corte Suprema de Justicia), judges are appointed by the National Council of the Judiciary
Political parties and leaders: Change 90-New Majority or C90/NM [Alberto FUJIMORI]; Union for Peru or UPP [Javier PEREZ de CUELLAR]; American Popular Revolutionary Alliance or APRA [Luis ALVA Castro]; Independent Moralizing Front or FIM [Fernando OLIVERA Vega]; Democratic Coordinator or CODE-Pais Posible [Jose BARBA Caballero and Alejandro TOLEDO]; Popular Action Party or AP [Juan DIAZ Leon]; Popular Christian Party or PPC [Luis BEDOYA Reyes]; Renovation Party [Rafael REY Rey]; Civic Works Movement or OBRAS [Ricardo BELMONT]; United Left or IU [leader NA]; Independent Agrarian Movement or MIA [leader NA]
Political pressure groups and leaders: leftist guerrilla groups include Shining Path [Abimael GUZMAN Reynoso (imprisoned), Oscar RAMIREZ Durand (top leader at-large)]; Tupac Amaru Revolutionary Movement or MRTA [Victor POLAY (imprisoned), Hugo AVALLENEDA Valdez (top leader at-large)]
International organization participation: APEC, CAN, CCC, ECLAC, FAO, G-11, G-15, G-19, G-24, G-77, IADB, IAEA, IBRD, ICAO, ICC, ICFTU, ICRM, IDA, IFAD, IFC, IFRCS, IHO, ILO, IMF, IMO, Inmarsat, Intelsat, Interpol, IOC, IOM, ISO (correspondent), ITU, LAES, LAIA, NAM, OAS, OPANAL, OPCW, PCA, RG, UN, UNCTAD, UNESCO, UNIDO, UPU, WCL, WFTU, WHO, WIPO, WMO, WToO, WTrO
Diplomatic representation in the US:
chief of mission: Ambassador Ricardo V. LUNA MENDOZA
chancery: 1700 Massachusetts Avenue NW, Washington, DC 20036
telephone: [1] (202) 833-9860 through 9869
FAX: [1] (202) 659-8124
consulate(s) general: Chicago, Houston, Los Angeles, Miami, New York, Paterson (New Jersey), San Francisco
Diplomatic representation from the US:
chief of mission: Ambassador Dennis C. JETT
embassy: Avenida Encalada, Cuadra 17, Monterrico, Lima
mailing address: P. O. Box 1995, Lima 1; American Embassy (Lima), APO AA 34031-5000
telephone: [51] (1) 434-3000
FAX: [51] (1) 434-3037
Flag description: three equal, vertical bands of red

(hoist side), white, and red with the coat of arms centered in the white band; the coat of arms features a shield bearing a llama, cinchona tree (the source of quinine), and a yellow cornucopia spilling out gold coins, all framed by a green wreath

Economy

Economy - overview: The Peruvian economy has become increasingly market-oriented, with major privatizations completed since 1990 in the mining, electricity, and telecommunications industries. An austerity program implemented shortly after the FUJIMORI government took office in July 1990 contributed to a short-lived contraction of economic activity, but the slide came to a halt late that year, and in 1991 output rose 2.4%. By working with the IMF and World Bank on new financial conditions and arrangements, the government succeeded in ending its arrears by March 1993. In 1992, GDP fell by 2.8%, in part because a warmer-than-usual El Nino current resulted in a 30% drop in the fish catch, but the economy rebounded as strong foreign investment helped push growth to 7% in 1993, about 13% in 1994, and 6.8% in 1995. Growth slowed to 2.8% in 1996 as the government adopted tight fiscal and monetary policy to reduce the current account deficit and meet its IMF targets. Growth then rebounded to 7.3% in 1997 even as inflation fell to its lowest level in 23 years. Capital inflows surged to record levels in early 1997 and have remained strong. In 1998, El Nino's impact on agriculture, the financial crisis in Asia, and instability in Brazilian markets undercut growth. While Lima publicly projects a rebound to 5% in 1999, private sector analysts believe this figure is overly optimistic.
GDP: purchasing power parity - $111.8 billion (1998 est.)
GDP - real growth rate: 1.8% (1998 est.)
GDP - per capita: purchasing power parity - $4,300 (1998 est.)
GDP - composition by sector:
agriculture: 7%
industry: 37%
services: 56% (1997)
Population below poverty line: 54% (1991 est.)
Household income or consumption by percentage share:
lowest 10%: 1.9%
highest 10%: 34.3% (1994)
Inflation rate (consumer prices): 6.7% (1997 est.)
Labor force: 7.6 million (1996 est.)
Labor force - by occupation: agriculture, mining and quarrying, manufacturing, construction, transport, services
Unemployment rate: 8.2%; extensive underemployment (1996)
Budget:
revenues: $8.5 billion
expenditures: $9.3 billion, including capital expenditures of $2 billion (1996 est.)
Industries: mining of metals, petroleum, fishing, textiles, clothing, food processing, cement, auto assembly, steel, shipbuilding, metal fabrication

Industrial production growth rate: 1.2% (1996)
Electricity - production: 16.211 billion kWh (1996)
Electricity - production by source:
fossil fuel: 19.25%
hydro: 80.75%
nuclear: 0%
other: 0% (1996)
Electricity - consumption: 16.211 billion kWh (1996)
Electricity - exports: 0 kWh (1996)
Electricity - imports: 0 kWh (1996)
Agriculture - products: coffee, cotton, sugarcane, rice, wheat, potatoes, plantains, coca; poultry, beef, dairy products, wool; fish
Exports: $6.8 billion (f.o.b., 1997)
Exports - commodities: copper, zinc, fishmeal, crude petroleum and byproducts, lead, refined silver, coffee, cotton
Exports - partners: US 20%, Japan 7%, UK 7%, China 7%, Germany 5% (1996)
Imports: $10.3 billion (c.i.f., 1997)
Imports - commodities: machinery, transport equipment, foodstuffs, petroleum, iron and steel, chemicals, pharmaceuticals
Imports - partners: US 31%, Colombia 7%, Chile 6%, Venezuela 6%, UK 6% (1996)
Debt - external: $25.7 billion (1996 est.)
Economic aid - recipient: $895.1 million (1995)
Currency: 1 nuevo sol (S/.) = 100 centimos
Exchange rates: nuevo sol (S/.) per US$1 - 3.250 (January 1999), 2.930 (1998), 2.664 (1997), 2.453 (1996), 2.253 (1995), 2.195 (1994)
Fiscal year: calendar year

Communications

Telephones: 779,306 (1990 est.)
Telephone system: adequate for most requirements
domestic: nationwide microwave radio relay system and a domestic satellite system with 12 earth stations
international: satellite earth stations - 2 Intelsat (Atlantic Ocean)
Radio broadcast stations: AM 273, FM 0, shortwave 144
Radios: 5.7 million (1992 est.)
Television broadcast stations: 13 (in addition, there are 112 repeaters) (1997)
Televisions: 2 million (1993 est.)

Transportation

Railways:
total: 2,041 km
standard gauge: 1,726 km 1.435-m gauge
narrow gauge: 315 km 0.914-m gauge (1997)
Highways:
total: 72,146 km
paved: 7,353 km
unpaved: 64,793 km (1998 est.)
Waterways: 8,600 km of navigable tributaries of Amazon system and 208 km of Lago Titicaca
Pipelines: crude oil 800 km; natural gas and natural gas liquids 64 km

Peru *(continued)*

Ports and harbors: Callao, Chimbote, Ilo, Matarani, Paita, Puerto Maldonado, Salaverry, San Martin, Talara, Iquitos, Pucallpa, Yurimaguas
note: Iquitos, Pucallpa, and Yurimaguas are all on the upper reaches of the Amazon and its tributaries
Merchant marine:
total: 7 ships (1,000 GRT or over) totaling 51,518 GRT/75,018 DWT
ships by type: cargo 6, oil tanker 1 (1998 est.)
Airports: 244 (1998 est.)
Airports - with paved runways:
total: 44
over 3,047 m: 7
2,438 to 3,047 m: 15
1,524 to 2,437 m: 12
914 to 1,523 m: 8
under 914 m: 2 (1998 est.)
Airports - with unpaved runways:
total: 200
over 3,047 m: 1
2,438 to 3,047 m: 3
1,524 to 2,437 m: 24
914 to 1,523 m: 73
under 914 m: 99 (1998 est.)

Military

Military branches: Army (Ejercito Peruano), Navy (Marina de Guerra del Peru; includes Naval Air, Marines, and Coast Guard), Air Force (Fuerza Aerea del Peru), National Police
Military manpower - military age: 20 years of age
Military manpower - availability:
males age 15-49: 6,913,471 (1999 est.)
Military manpower - fit for military service:
males age 15-49: 4,657,649 (1999 est.)
Military manpower - reaching military age annually:
males: 268,624 (1999 est.)
Military expenditures - dollar figure: $913 million (1998); note - may not include off-budget purchases related to military modernization program
Military expenditures - percent of GDP: 1.4% (1998)

Transnational Issues

Disputes - international: on 26 October 1998, Peru and Ecuador concluded treaties on commerce and navigation and on boundary integration, to complete a package of agreements settling the long-standing boundary dispute between them; demarcation of the agreed-upon boundary was scheduled to begin in mid-January 1999
Illicit drugs: until recently the world's largest coca leaf producer, Peru has reduced the area of coca under cultivation by 26%, from 68,800 hectares in 1997 to 51,000 hectares at the end of 1998; most of cocaine base is shipped to neighboring Colombia and Brazil for processing into cocaine for the international drug market, but exports of finished cocaine are increasing

Philippines

Geography

Location: Southeastern Asia, archipelago between the Philippine Sea and the South China Sea, east of Vietnam
Geographic coordinates: 13 00 N, 122 00 E
Map references: Southeast Asia
Area:
total: 300,000 sq km
land: 298,170 sq km
water: 1,830 sq km
Area - comparative: slightly larger than Arizona
Land boundaries: 0 km
Coastline: 36,289 km
Maritime claims: measured from claimed archipelagic baselines
continental shelf: to depth of exploitation
exclusive economic zone: 200 nm
territorial sea: irregular polygon extending up to 100 nm from coastline as defined by 1898 treaty; since late 1970s has also claimed polygonal-shaped area in South China Sea up to 285 nm in breadth
Climate: tropical marine; northeast monsoon (November to April); southwest monsoon (May to October)

Terrain: mostly mountains with narrow to extensive coastal lowlands
Elevation extremes:
lowest point: Philippine Sea 0 m
highest point: Mount Apo 2,954 m
Natural resources: timber, petroleum, nickel, cobalt, silver, gold, salt, copper
Land use:
arable land: 19%
permanent crops: 12%
permanent pastures: 4%
forests and woodland: 46%
other: 19% (1993 est.)
Irrigated land: 15,800 sq km (1993 est.)
Natural hazards: astride typhoon belt, usually affected by 15 and struck by five to six cyclonic storms per year; landslides; active volcanoes; destructive earthquakes; tsunamis
Environment - current issues: uncontrolled deforestation in watershed areas; soil erosion; air and water pollution in Manila; increasing pollution of coastal mangrove swamps which are important fish breeding grounds
Environment - international agreements:
party to: Biodiversity, Climate Change, Endangered Species, Hazardous Wastes, Law of the Sea, Marine Dumping, Nuclear Test Ban, Ozone Layer Protection, Tropical Timber 83, Tropical Timber 94, Wetlands, Whaling
signed, but not ratified: Climate Change-Kyoto Protocol, Desertification

People

Population: 79,345,812 (July 1999 est.)
Age structure:
0-14 years: 37% (male 15,057,698; female 14,555,430)
15-64 years: 59% (male 23,168,043; female 23,715,877)
65 years and over: 4% (male 1,269,522; female 1,579,242) (1999 est.)
Population growth rate: 2.04% (1999 est.)
Birth rate: 27.88 births/1,000 population (1999 est.)
Death rate: 6.45 deaths/1,000 population (1999 est.)
Net migration rate: -1.03 migrant(s)/1,000 population (1999 est.)
Sex ratio:
at birth: 1.05 male(s)/female
under 15 years: 1.03 male(s)/female
15-64 years: 0.98 male(s)/female
65 years and over: 0.8 male(s)/female
total population: 0.99 male(s)/female (1999 est.)
Infant mortality rate: 33.89 deaths/1,000 live births (1999 est.)
Life expectancy at birth:
total population: 66.58 years
male: 63.79 years
female: 69.5 years (1999 est.)
Total fertility rate: 3.46 children born/woman (1999 est.)
Nationality:
noun: Filipino(s)

Philippines *(continued)*

adjective: Philippine

Ethnic groups: Christian Malay 91.5%, Muslim Malay 4%, Chinese 1.5%, other 3%

Religions: Roman Catholic 83%, Protestant 9%, Muslim 5%, Buddhist and other 3%

Languages: Pilipino (official, based on Tagalog), English (official)

Literacy:

definition: age 15 and over can read and write

total population: 94.6%

male: 95%

female: 94.3% (1995 est.)

Government

Country name:

conventional long form: Republic of the Philippines

conventional short form: Philippines

local long form: Republika ng Pilipinas

local short form: Pilipinas

Data code: RP

Government type: republic

Capital: Manila

Administrative divisions: 72 provinces and 61 chartered cities*; Abra, Agusan del Norte, Agusan del Sur, Aklan, Albay, Angeles*, Antique, Aurora, Bacolod*, Bago*, Baguio*, Bais*, Basilan, Basilan City*, Bataan, Batanes, Batangas, Batangas City*, Benguet, Bohol, Bukidnon, Bulacan, Butuan*, Cabanatuan*, Cadiz*, Cagayan, Cagayan de Oro*, Calbayog*, Caloocan*, Camarines Norte, Camarines Sur, Camiguin, Canlaon*, Capiz, Catanduanes, Cavite, Cavite City*, Cebu, Cebu City*, Cotabato*, Dagupan*, Danao*, Dapitan*, Davao City* Davao, Davao del Sur, Davao Oriental, Dipolog*, Dumaguete*, Eastern Samar, General Santos*, Gingoog*, Ifugao, Iligan*, Ilocos Norte, Ilocos Sur, Iloilo, Iloilo City*, Iriga*, Isabela, Kalinga-Apayao, La Carlota*, Laguna, Lanao del Norte, Lanao del Sur, Laoag*, Lapu-Lapu*, La Union, Legaspi*, Leyte, Lipa*, Lucena*, Maguindanao, Mandaue*, Manila*, Marawi*, Marinduque, Masbate, Mindoro Occidental, Mindoro Oriental, Misamis Occidental, Misamis Oriental, Mountain, Naga*, Negros Occidental, Negros Oriental, North Cotabato, Northern Samar, Nueva Ecija, Nueva Vizcaya, Olongapo*, Ormoc*, Oroquieta*, Ozamis*, Pagadian*, Palawan, Palayan*, Pampanga, Pangasinan, Pasay*, Puerto Princesa*, Quezon, Quezon City*, Quirino, Rizal, Romblon, Roxas*, Samar, San Carlos* (in Negros Occidental), San Carlos* (in Pangasinan), San Jose*, San Pablo*, Silay*, Siquijor, Sorsogon, South Cotabato, Southern Leyte, Sultan Kudarat, Sulu, Surigao*, Surigao del Norte, Surigao del Sur, Tacloban*, Tagaytay*, Tagbilaran*, Tangub*, Tarlac, Tawitawi, Toledo*, Trece Martires*, Zambales, Zamboanga*, Zamboanga del Norte, Zamboanga del Sur

Independence: 4 July 1946 (from US)

National holiday: Independence Day, 12 June (1898) (from Spain)

Constitution: 2 February 1987, effective 11 February 1987

Legal system: based on Spanish and Anglo-American law; accepts compulsory ICJ jurisdiction, with reservations

Suffrage: 18 years of age; universal

Executive branch:

chief of state: President Joseph Ejercito ESTRADA (since 30 June 1998) and Vice President Gloria MACAPAGAL-ARROYO (since 30 June 1998); note - the president is both the chief of state and head of government

head of government: President Joseph Ejercito ESTRADA (since 30 June 1998) and Vice President Gloria MACAPAGAL-ARROYO (since 30 June 1998); note - the president is both the chief of state and head of government

cabinet: Cabinet appointed by the president with the consent of the Commission of Appointments

elections: president and vice president elected on separate tickets by popular vote for six-year terms; election last held 11 May 1998 (next to be held 11 May 2004)

election results: Joseph Ejercito ESTRADA elected president; percent of vote - NA%; Gloria MACAPAGAL-ARROYO elected vice president; percent of vote - NA%

Legislative branch: bicameral Congress or Kongreso consists of the Senate or Senado (24 seats - one-half elected every three years; members elected by popular vote to serve six-year terms) and the House of Representatives or Kapulungan Ng Mga Kinatawan (221 seats; members elected by popular vote to serve three-year terms; note - an additional 50 members may be appointed by the president)

elections: Senate - last held 11 May 1998 (next to be held 11 May 2001); House of Representatives - elections last held 11 May 1998 (next to be held 11 May 2001)

election results: Senate - percent of vote by party - NA; seats by party - LAMP 12, Lakas 5, PRP 2, LP 1, other 3; note - the Senate now has only 23 members with one seat vacated when Gloria MACAPAGAL-ARROYO became vice president; the seat can only be filled by election and is likely to remain open until the next regular election in 2001; House of Representatives - percent of vote by party - NA; seats by party - LAMP 135, Lakas 37, LP 13, Aksyon Demokratiko 1, other 35

Judicial branch: Supreme Court, justices are appointed for four-year terms by the president on the recommendation of the Judicial and Bar Council

Political parties and leaders: Laban Ng Masang Pilipino or LAMP (Struggle of the Filipino Masses) [Joseph ESTRADA, titular head; Eduardo "Danding" COJUANGO, chairman, Edgardo ANGARA, party president]; Lakas [Raul MANGLAPUS, chairman, Gloria MACAPAGAL-ARROYO, secretary general, Jose DE VENECIA, party president]; Liberal Party or LP [Raul DAZA, president, Jovito SALONGA, chairman, Florencio ABAD, secretary general]; People's Reform Party or PRP [Miriam DEFENSOR-SANTIAGO]; Aksyon Demokratiko or Democratic Action [Raul ROCO]

International organization participation: APEC, AsDB, ASEAN, CCC, CP, ESCAP, FAO, G-24, G-77, IAEA, IBRD, ICAO, ICFTU, ICRM, IDA, IFAD, IFC, IFRCS, IHO, ILO, IMF, IMO, Inmarsat, Intelsat, Interpol, IOC, IOM, ISO, ITU, NAM, OPCW, UN, UNCTAD, UNESCO, UNHCR, UNIDO, UNU, UPU, WCL, WFTU, WHO, WIPO, WMO, WToO, WTrO

Diplomatic representation in the US:

chief of mission: Ambassador Raul Chaves RABE

chancery: 1600 Massachusetts Avenue NW, Washington, DC 20036

telephone: [1] (202) 467-9300

FAX: [1] (202) 328-7614

consulate(s) general: Chicago, Honolulu, Los Angeles, New York, San Francisco, and Tamuning (Guam)

consulate(s): San Diego and Susupe (Saipan)

Diplomatic representation from the US:

chief of mission: Ambassador Thomas C. HUBBARD

embassy: 1201 Roxas Boulevard, Ermita Manila 1000

mailing address: FPO 96515

telephone: [63] (2) 523-1001

FAX: [63] (2) 522-4361

Flag description: two equal horizontal bands of blue (top) and red with a white equilateral triangle based on the hoist side; in the center of the triangle is a yellow sun with eight primary rays (each containing three individual rays) and in each corner of the triangle is a small yellow five-pointed star

Economy

Economy - overview: In 1998 the Philippine economy - a mixture of agriculture, light industry, and supporting services - deteriorated as a result of spillover from the Asian financial crisis and poor weather conditions. Growth fell to about -0.5% in 1998 from 5% in 1997, but is expected to recover to more than 2% in 1999. The government has promised to continue its economic reforms to help the Philippines match the pace of development in the newly industrialized countries of East Asia. The strategy includes improving infrastructure, overhauling the tax system to bolster government revenues, and moving toward further deregulation and privatization of the economy.

GDP: purchasing power parity - $270.5 billion (1998 est.)

GDP - real growth rate: -0.5% (1998 est.)

GDP - per capita: purchasing power parity - $3,500 (1998 est.)

GDP - composition by sector:

agriculture: 20%

industry: 32%

services: 48% (1997 est.)

Population below poverty line: 32% (1997 est.)

Household income or consumption by percentage share:

lowest 10%: 2.4%

highest 10%: 33.5% (1994)

Inflation rate (consumer prices): 9.7% (1998)

Labor force: 31.3 million (1998 est.)

Labor force - by occupation: agriculture 39.8%, government and social services 19.4%, services

Philippines *(continued)*

17.7%, manufacturing 9.8%, construction 5.8%, other 7.5% (1998 est.)

Unemployment rate: 9.6% (October 1998)

Budget:

revenues: $14.5 billion

expenditures: $12.6 billion (1998 est.)

Industries: textiles, pharmaceuticals, chemicals, wood products, food processing, electronics assembly, petroleum refining, fishing

Industrial production growth rate: -1.7% (1998 est.)

Electricity - production: 32.2 billion kWh (1996)

Electricity - production by source:

fossil fuel: 62.11%

hydro: 20.19%

nuclear: 0%

other: 17.7% (1996)

Electricity - consumption: 32.2 billion kWh (1996)

Electricity - exports: 0 kWh (1996)

Electricity - imports: 0 kWh (1996)

Agriculture - products: rice, coconuts, corn, sugarcane, bananas, pineapples, mangoes; pork, eggs, beef; fish

Exports: $25 billion (f.o.b., 1998 est.)

Exports - commodities: electronics and telecommunications 51%, machinery and transport 10%, garments 9%, other 30%

Exports - partners: US 34%, Japan 17%, EU 17%, ASEAN 14%, Hong Kong 4%, Taiwan 4% (1997 est.)

Imports: $29 billion (f.o.b., 1998 est.)

Imports - commodities: raw materials and intermediate goods 43%, capital goods 36%, consumer goods 9%, fuels 9%

Imports - partners: Japan 21%, US 20%, ASEAN 12%, EU 10%, Taiwan 5%, Hong Kong 4%, Saudi Arabia 4% (1997 est.)

Debt - external: $46.4 billion (September 1998)

Economic aid - recipient: ODA, $1.1 billion (1998)

Currency: 1 Philippine peso (P) = 100 centavos

Exchange rates: Philippine pesos (P) per US$1 - 38.404 (January 1999), 40.893 (1998), 29.471 (1997), 26.216 (1996), 25.714 (1995), 26.417 (1994)

Fiscal year: calendar year

Telephones: 1.9 million (1997)

Telephone system: good international radiotelephone and submarine cable services; domestic and interisland service adequate

domestic: domestic satellite system with 11 earth stations

international: submarine cables to Hong Kong, Guam, Singapore, Taiwan, and Japan; satellite earth stations - 3 Intelsat (1 Indian Ocean and 2 Pacific Ocean)

Radio broadcast stations: AM 261, FM 55, shortwave 0

Radios: 9.03 million (1992 est.)

Television broadcast stations: 37 (includes six stations of the US Armed Forces Radio and TV Service) (1997)

Televisions: 9.2 million (1998)

Transportation

Railways:

total: 897 km of which 492 km in operation

narrow gauge: 492 km 1.067-m gauge (1996)

Highways:

total: 161,313 km

paved: 290 km

unpaved: 161,023 km (1997)

Waterways: 3,219 km; limited to shallow-draft (less than 1.5 m) vessels

Pipelines: petroleum products 357 km

Ports and harbors: Batangas, Cagayan de Oro, Cebu, Davao, Guimaras Island, Iligan, Iloilo, Jolo, Legaspi, Manila, Masao, Puerto Princesa, San Fernando, Subic Bay, Zamboanga

Merchant marine:

total: 513 ships (1,000 GRT or over) totaling 6,544,029 GRT/10,052,418 DWT

ships by type: bulk 179, cargo 131, chemical tanker 6, combination bulk 13, container 9, liquefied gas tanker 12, livestock carrier 10, oil tanker 48, passenger 4, passenger-cargo 13, refrigerated cargo 19, roll-on/roll-off cargo 17, short-sea passenger 31, specialized tanker 1, vehicle carrier 20

note: a flag of convenience registry; Japan owns 19 ships, Hong Kong 5, Cyprus 1, Denmark 1, Greece 1, Netherlands 1, Singapore 1, and UK 1 (1998 est.)

Airports: 260 (1998 est.)

Airports - with paved runways:

total: 75

over 3,047 m: 4

2,438 to 3,047 m: 5

1,524 to 2,437 m: 26

914 to 1,523 m: 30

under 914 m: 10 (1998 est.)

Airports - with unpaved runways:

total: 185

1,524 to 2,437 m: 3

914 to 1,523 m: 61

under 914 m: 121 (1998 est.)

Heliports: 1 (1998 est.)

Military

Military branches: Army, Navy (includes Coast Guard and Marine Corps), Air Force

Military manpower - military age: 20 years of age

Military manpower - availability:

males age 15-49: 20,228,797 (1999 est.)

Military manpower - fit for military service:

males age 15-49: 14,261,514 (1999 est.)

Military manpower - reaching military age annually:

males: 818,006 (1999 est.)

Military expenditures - dollar figure: $995 million (1998)

Military expenditures - percent of GDP: 1.5% (1998)

Transnational Issues

Disputes - international: involved in a complex dispute over the Spratly Islands with China, Malaysia, Taiwan, Vietnam, and possibly Brunei; claim to Malaysia's Sabah State has not been fully revoked

Illicit drugs: exports locally produced marijuana and hashish to East Asia, the US, and other Western markets; serves as a transit point for heroin and crystal methamphetamine

Pitcairn Islands
(overseas territory of the UK)

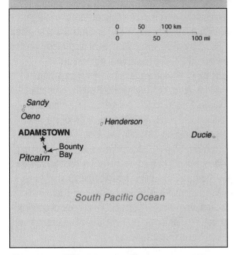

Geography

Location: Oceania, islands in the South Pacific Ocean, about one-half of the way from Peru to New Zealand
Geographic coordinates: 25 04 S, 130 06 W
Map references: Oceania
Area:
total: 47 sq km
land: 47 sq km
water: 0 sq km
Area - comparative: about 0.3 times the size of Washington, DC
Land boundaries: 0 km
Coastline: 51 km
Maritime claims:
exclusive economic zone: 200 nm
territorial sea: 3 nm
Climate: tropical, hot, humid; modified by southeast trade winds; rainy season (November to March)
Terrain: rugged volcanic formation; rocky coastline with cliffs
Elevation extremes:
lowest point: Pacific Ocean 0 m
highest point: Pawala Valley Ridge 347 m
Natural resources: miro trees (used for handicrafts), fish
note: manganese, iron, copper, gold, silver, and zinc have been discovered offshore
Land use:
arable land: NA%
permanent crops: NA%
permanent pastures: NA%
forests and woodland: NA%
other: NA%
Irrigated land: NA sq km
Natural hazards: typhoons (especially November to March)
Environment - current issues: deforestation (only a small portion of the original forest remains because of burning and clearing for settlement)

Environment - international agreements:
party to: NA
signed, but not ratified: NA

People

Population: 49 (July 1999 est.)
Age structure:
0-14 years: NA
15-64 years: NA
65 years and over: NA
Population growth rate: -2.04% (1999 est.)
Birth rate: NA births/1,000 population
Death rate: NA deaths/1,000 population
Net migration rate: NA migrant(s)/1,000 population
Infant mortality rate: NA deaths/1,000 live births
Life expectancy at birth:
total population: NA years
male: NA years
female: NA years
Total fertility rate: NA children born/woman
Nationality:
noun: Pitcairn Islander(s)
adjective: Pitcairn Islander
Ethnic groups: descendants of the Bounty mutineers and their Tahitian wives
Religions: Seventh-Day Adventist 100%
Languages: English (official), Pitcairnese, Tahitian, 18th century English dialect

Government

Country name:
conventional long form: Pitcairn, Henderson, Ducie, and Oeno Islands
conventional short form: Pitcairn Islands
Data code: PC
Dependency status: overseas territory of the UK
Government type: NA
Capital: Adamstown
Administrative divisions: none (overseas territory of the UK)
Independence: none (overseas territory of the UK)
National holiday: Celebration of the Birthday of the Queen (second Saturday in June)
Constitution: Local Government Ordinance of 1964
Legal system: local island by-laws
Suffrage: 18 years of age; universal with three years residency
Executive branch:
chief of state: Queen ELIZABETH II (since 6 February 1952), represented by UK High Commissioner to New Zealand and Governor (nonresident) of the Pitcairn Islands Robert John ALSTON (since NA August 1994); Commissioner (nonresident) G. D. HARRAWAY (since NA; is the liaison person between the governor and the Island Council)
head of government: Island Magistrate and Chairman of the Island Council Jay WARREN (since NA)
cabinet: NA
elections: the monarch is hereditary; high commissioner and commissioner appointed by the monarch; island magistrate elected by popular vote

for a three-year term; last known election held NA December 1993 (next to be held NA December 1996)
election results: Jay WARREN reelected island magistrate; percent of vote - NA
Legislative branch: unicameral Island Council (10 seats - 6 elected by popular vote, 1 appointed by the 6 elected members, 2 appointed by the governor, and 1 seat for the Island Secretary; members serve one-year terms)
elections: take place each December; last held NA December 1998 (next to be held NA December 1999)
election results: percent of vote - NA; seats - all independents
Judicial branch: Island Court, island magistrate presides over the court and is elected every three years
Political parties and leaders: none
Political pressure groups and leaders: NA
International organization participation: SPC
Diplomatic representation in the US: none (overseas territory of the UK)
Diplomatic representation from the US: none (overseas territory of the UK)
Flag description: blue with the flag of the UK in the upper hoist-side quadrant and the Pitcairn Islander coat of arms centered on the outer half of the flag; the coat of arms is yellow, green, and light blue with a shield featuring a yellow anchor

Economy

Economy - overview: The inhabitants exist on fishing and subsistence farming. The fertile soil of the valleys produces a wide variety of fruits and vegetables, including citrus, sugarcane, watermelons, bananas, yams, and beans. Bartering is an important part of the economy. The major sources of revenue are the sale of postage stamps to collectors and the sale of handicrafts to passing ships.
GDP: purchasing power parity - $NA
GDP - real growth rate: NA%
GDP - per capita: purchasing power parity - $NA
GDP - composition by sector:
agriculture: NA%
industry: NA%
services: NA%
Population below poverty line: NA%
Household income or consumption by percentage share:
lowest 10%: NA%
highest 10%: NA%
Inflation rate (consumer prices): NA%
Labor force: 14 able-bodied men (1993)
Labor force - by occupation: no business community in the usual sense; some public works; subsistence farming and fishing
Unemployment rate: NA%
Budget:
revenues: $729,884
expenditures: $878,119, including capital expenditures of $NA (FY94/95 est.)
Industries: postage stamps, handicrafts
Industrial production growth rate: NA%

Pitcairn Islands *(continued)*

Electricity - production: NA kWh
Electricity - production by source:
fossil fuel: NA%
hydro: NA%
nuclear: NA%
other: NA%
Electricity - consumption: NA kWh
Electricity - exports: NA kWh
Electricity - imports: NA kWh
Agriculture - products: wide variety of fruits and vegetables
Exports: $NA
Exports - commodities: fruits, vegetables, curios
Exports - partners: NA
Imports: $NA
Imports - commodities: fuel oil, machinery, building materials, flour, sugar, other foodstuffs
Imports - partners: NA
Debt - external: $NA
Economic aid - recipient: $NA
Currency: 1 New Zealand dollar (NZ$) = 100 cents
Exchange rates: New Zealand dollars (NZ$) per US$1 - 1.8560 (January 1999), 1.8629 (1998), 1.5083 (1997), 1.4543 (1996), 1.5235 (1995), 1.6844 (1994)
Fiscal year: 1 April - 31 March

Telephones: 24
Telephone system: party line telephone service on the island
domestic: NA
international: radiotelephone
Radio broadcast stations: AM 1, FM 0, shortwave 0
Radios: NA
Television broadcast stations: 0 (1997)
Televisions: NA

Transportation

Railways: 0 km
Highways:
total: 6.4 km
paved: 0 km
unpaved: 6.4 km
Ports and harbors: Bounty Bay
Merchant marine: none
Airports: none

Military

Military - note: defense is the responsibility of the UK

Transnational Issues

Disputes - international: none

Poland

Geography

Location: Central Europe, east of Germany
Geographic coordinates: 52 00 N, 20 00 E
Map references: Europe
Area:
total: 312,683 sq km
land: 304,510 sq km
water: 8,173 sq km
Area - comparative: slightly smaller than New Mexico
Land boundaries:
total: 2,888 km
border countries: Belarus 605 km, Czech Republic 658 km, Germany 456 km, Lithuania 91 km, Russia (Kaliningrad Oblast) 206 km, Slovakia 444 km, Ukraine 428 km
Coastline: 491 km
Maritime claims:
exclusive economic zone: defined by international treaties
territorial sea: 12 nm
Climate: temperate with cold, cloudy, moderately severe winters with frequent precipitation; mild summers with frequent showers and thundershowers
Terrain: mostly flat plain; mountains along southern border
Elevation extremes:
lowest point: Raczki Elblaskie -2 m
highest point: Rysy 2,499 m
Natural resources: coal, sulfur, copper, natural gas, silver, lead, salt
Land use:
arable land: 47%
permanent crops: 1%
permanent pastures: 13%
forests and woodland: 29%
other: 10% (1993 est.)
Irrigated land: 1,000 sq km (1993 est.)
Natural hazards: NA
Environment - current issues: situation has improved since 1989 due to decline in heavy industry

and increased environmental concern by postcommunist governments; air pollution nonetheless remains serious because of sulfur dioxide emissions from coal-fired power plants, and the resulting acid rain has caused forest damage; water pollution from industrial and municipal sources is also a problem, as is disposal of hazardous wastes
Environment - international agreements:
party to: Air Pollution, Antarctic-Environmental Protocol, Antarctic Treaty, Biodiversity, Climate Change, Endangered Species, Environmental Modification, Hazardous Wastes, Law of the Sea, Marine Dumping, Nuclear Test Ban, Ozone Layer Protection, Ship Pollution, Wetlands
signed, but not ratified: Air Pollution-Nitrogen Oxides, Air Pollution-Persistent Organic Pollutants, Air Pollution-Sulphur 94, Climate Change-Kyoto Protocol
Geography - note: historically, an area of conflict because of flat terrain and the lack of natural barriers on the North European Plain

People

Population: 38,608,929 (July 1999 est.)
Age structure:
0-14 years: 20% (male 3,921,093; female 3,734,223)
15-64 years: 68% (male 13,076,231; female 13,243,716)
65 years and over: 12% (male 1,762,135; female 2,871,531) (1999 est.)
Population growth rate: 0.05% (1999 est.)
Birth rate: 10.61 births/1,000 population (1999 est.)
Death rate: 9.72 deaths/1,000 population (1999 est.)
Net migration rate: -0.4 migrant(s)/1,000 population (1999 est.)
Sex ratio:
at birth: 1.06 male(s)/female
under 15 years: 1.05 male(s)/female
15-64 years: 0.99 male(s)/female
65 years and over: 0.61 male(s)/female
total population: 0.95 male(s)/female (1999 est.)
Infant mortality rate: 12.76 deaths/1,000 live births (1999 est.)
Life expectancy at birth:
total population: 73.06 years
male: 68.93 years
female: 77.41 years (1999 est.)
Total fertility rate: 1.45 children born/woman (1999 est.)
Nationality:
noun: Pole(s)
adjective: Polish
Ethnic groups: Polish 97.6%, German 1.3%, Ukrainian 0.6%, Byelorussian 0.5% (1990 est.)
Religions: Roman Catholic 95% (about 75% practicing), Eastern Orthodox, Protestant, and other 5%
Languages: Polish
Literacy:
definition: age 15 and over can read and write
total population: 99%
male: 99%
female: 98% (1978 est.)

Poland (continued)

Government

Country name:
conventional long form: Republic of Poland
conventional short form: Poland
local long form: Rzeczpospolita Polska
local short form: Polska
Data code: PL
Government type: democratic state
Capital: Warsaw
Administrative divisions: 16 provinces
(wojewodztwa, singular - wojewodztwo);
Dolnoslaskie, Kujawsko-Pomorskie, Lodzkie,
Lubelskie, Lubuskie, Malopolskie, Mazowieckie,
Opolskie, Podkarpackie, Podlaskie, Pomorskie,
Slaskie, Swietokrzyskie, Warminsko-Mazurskie,
Wielkopolskie, Zachodniopomorskie
Independence: 11 November 1918 (independent
republic proclaimed)
National holiday: Constitution Day, 3 May (1791);
Independence Day, November 11 (1918)
Constitution: 16 October 1997; adopted by the
National Assembly on 2 April 1997; passed by
national referendum 23 May 1997
Legal system: mixture of Continental (Napoleonic)
civil law and holdover communist legal theory;
changes being gradually introduced as part of broader
democratization process; limited judicial review of
legislative acts although under the new constitution,
the Constitutional Tribunal ruling will become final as
of October 1999; court decisions can be appealed to
the European Court of Justice in Strasbourg
Suffrage: 18 years of age; universal
Executive branch:
chief of state: President Aleksander KWASNIEWSKI
(since 23 December 1995)
head of government: Prime Minister Jerzy BUZEK
(since NA October 1997), Deputy Prime Ministers
Leszek BALCEROWICZ (since 31 October 1997),
Janusz TOMASZEWSKI (since 31 October 1997)
cabinet: Council of Ministers responsible to the prime
minister and the Sejm; the prime minister proposes,
the president appoints, and the Sejm approves the
Council of Ministers
elections: president elected by popular vote for a
five-year term; election first round held 5 November
1995, second round held 19 November 1995 (next to
be held NA November 2000); prime minister and
deputy prime ministers appointed by the president
and confirmed by the Sejm
election results: Aleksander KWASNIEWSKI elected
president in 1995; percent of popular vote, second
round - Aleksander KWASNIEWSKI 51.7%, Lech
WALESA 48.3%; Jerzy BUZEK selected prime
minister in 1997
Legislative branch: bicameral National Assembly or
Zgromadzenie Narodowe consists of the Sejm (460
seats; members are elected under a complex system
of proportional representation to serve four-year
terms) and the Senate or Senat (100 seats; members
are elected by a majority vote on a provincial basis to
serve four-year terms)
elections: Sejm elections last held 21 September

1997 (next to be held by NA September 2001); Senate
- last held 21 September 1997 (next to be held by NA
September 2001)
election results: Sejm - percent of vote by party - AWS
33.8%, SLD 27.1%, UW 13.4%, PSL 7.3%, ROP
5.6%, MN 0.4%, other 12.4%; seats by party - AWS
201, SLD 164, UW 60, PSL 27, ROP 6, MN 2; Senate
- percent of vote by party - NA; seats by party - AWS
51, SLD 28, UW 8, ROP 5, PSL 3, independents 5;
note - seats by party in the Sejm as of December
1997: AWS 200, SLD 164, UW 60, PSL 26, ROP 4,
MN 2, other 4
note: four seats are constitutionally assigned to ethnic
German parties
Judicial branch: Supreme Court, judges are
appointed by the president on the recommendation of
the National Council of the Judiciary for an indefinite
period; Constitutional Tribunal, judges are chosen by
the Sejm for nine-year terms
Political parties and leaders:
post-Communist: Democratic Left Alliance or SLD
(Social Democracy of Poland) [Leszek MILLER];
Polish Peasant Party or PSL [Jaroslaw KALINOWSKI]
post-Solidarity parties: Freedom Union or UW; note -
Democratic Union and Liberal Democratic Congress
merged to form Freedom Union [Leszek
BALCEROWICZ]; Christian-National Union or ZCHN
[Marian PILKA]; Center Alliance Party or PC [Jaroslaw
KACZYNSKI]; Peasant Alliance or PL [Gabriel
JANOWSKI]; Solidarity Electoral Action Social
Movement or RS AWS [Jerzy BUZEK]; Union of Labor
or UP [Aleksander MALACHOWSKI]; Conservative
Party or PK [Aleksander HALL]
non-Communist, non-Solidarity: Movement for the
Reconstruction of Poland or ROP [Jan OLSZEWSKI];
Confederation for an Independent Poland or KPN
[Adam SLOMKA]; German Minority or MN [Henryk
KROLL]; Union of Real Politics or UPR [Stanislaw
MICHALKIEWICZ]
Political pressure groups and leaders: powerful
Roman Catholic Church; Solidarity (trade union); All
Poland Trade Union Alliance or OPZZ (trade union)
International organization participation: Australia
Group, BIS, BSEC (observer), CBSS, CCC, CE, CEI,
CERN, EAPC, EBRD, ECE, EU (applicant), FAO,
IAEA, IBRD, ICAO, ICFTU, ICRM, IDA, IEA
(observer), IFC, IFRCS, IHO, ILO, IMF, IMO,
Inmarsat, Intelsat, Interpol, IOC, IOM, ISO, ITU,
MINURSO, MONUA, NAM (guest), NSG, OAS
(observer), OECD, OPCW, OSCE, PCA, PFP, UN,
UNCTAD, UNDOF, UNESCO, UNHCR, UNIDO,
UNIFIL, UNIKOM, UNMIBH, UNMOP, UNMOT,
UNOMIG, UNPREDEP, UPU, WCL, WEU (associate
partner), WFTU, WHO, WIPO, WMO, WToO, WTrO,
ZC
Diplomatic representation in the US:
chief of mission: Ambassador Jerzy KOZMINSKI
chancery: 2640 16th Street NW, Washington, DC
20009
telephone: [1] (202) 234-3800 through 3802
FAX: [1] (202) 328-6271
consulate(s) general: Chicago, Los Angeles, and New
York

Diplomatic representation from the US:
chief of mission: Ambassador Daniel FRIED
embassy: Aleje Ujazdowskie 29/31 00-054, Warsaw
P1
mailing address: American Embassy Warsaw, US
Department of State, Washington, DC 20521-5010
(pouch)
telephone: [48] (22) 628-30-41
FAX: [48] (22) 625-67-31
consulate(s) general: Krakow
Flag description: two equal horizontal bands of
white (top) and red; similar to the flags of Indonesia
and Monaco which are red (top) and white

Economy

Economy - overview: Poland today stands out as
one of the most successful and open transition
economies. The privatization of small and medium
state-owned companies and a liberal law on
establishing new firms marked the rapid development
of a private sector now responsible for 70% of
economic activity. In contrast to the vibrant expansion
of private non-farm activity, the large agriculture
component remains handicapped by structural
problems, surplus labor, inefficient small farms, and
lack of investment. The government's determination to
enter the EU as soon as possible affects all aspects of
its economic policies. Improving Poland's worsening
current account deficit also is a priority. To date, the
government has resisted pressure for protectionist
solutions and continues to support regional free trade
initiatives. The government export strategy
emphasizes a more aggressive export assistance
program. Warsaw continues to hold the budget deficit
to less than 2% of GDP. Further progress on public
finance depends mainly on comprehensive reform of
the social welfare system and privatization of Poland's
remaining state sector. Restructuring and privatization
of "sensitive sectors" (e.g., coal, steel, and
telecommunications) has begun. Long-awaited
privatizations in aviation and energy are scheduled for
1999.
GDP: purchasing power parity - $263 billion (1998
est.)
GDP - real growth rate: 5.6% (1998 est.)
GDP - per capita: purchasing power parity - $6,800
(1998 est.)
GDP - composition by sector:
agriculture: 5.1%
industry: 26.6%
services: 68.3% (1997)
Population below poverty line: 23.8% (1993 est.)
**Household income or consumption by percentage
share:**
lowest 10%: 4%
highest 10%: 22.1% (1992)
Inflation rate (consumer prices): 11% (1998 est.)
Labor force: 17.4 million (1998 est.)
Labor force - by occupation: industry and
construction 29.9%, agriculture 26%, services 44.1%
(1996)
Unemployment rate: 10% (1998)

Poland (continued)

Budget:
revenues: $36.5 billion
expenditures: $38.3 billion, including capital
expenditures of $NA (1997 est.)
Industries: machine building, iron and steel, coal
mining, chemicals, shipbuilding, food processing,
glass, beverages, textiles
Industrial production growth rate: 7.9% (1998
est.)
Electricity - production: 134.731 billion kWh (1996)
Electricity - production by source:
fossil fuel: 97.09%
hydro: 2.91%
nuclear: 0%
other: 0% (1996)
Electricity - consumption: 132.291 billion kWh
(1996)
Electricity - exports: 7.925 billion kWh (1996)
Electricity - imports: 5.485 billion kWh (1996)
Agriculture - products: potatoes, fruits, vegetables,
wheat; poultry, eggs, pork, beef, milk, cheese
Exports: $27.2 billion (f.o.b., 1997)
Exports - commodities: manufactured goods,
chemicals 57%, machinery and equipment 21%, food
and live animals 12%, mineral fuels 7%, other 3%
Exports - partners: Germany 32.9%, Russia 8.4%,
Italy 5.9%, Ukraine 4.7%, Netherlands 4.7%, France
4.4%
Imports: $38.5 billion (f.o.b., 1997)
Imports - commodities: manufactured goods,
chemical 43%, machinery and equipment 36%,
mineral fuels 9%, food and live animals 8%, other 4%
Imports - partners: Germany 24.1%, Italy 9.9%,
Russia 6.3%, UK 5.5%, US 4.5%, France 5.9%
Debt - external: $42 billion (1997)
Economic aid - recipient: $4.312 billion (1995)
Currency: 1 zloty (Zl) = 100 groszy
Exchange rates: zlotych (Zl) per US$1 - 3.5409
(January 1999), 3.4754 (1998), 3.2793 (1997), 2.6961
(1996), 2.4250 (1995); note - a currency reform on 1
January 1995 replaced 10,000 old zlotys with 1 new
zloty; 22,723 (1994)
Fiscal year: calendar year

Communications

Telephones: 8.2 million (1996)
Telephone system: underdeveloped and outmoded
system; government aims to have 10 million
telephones in service by 2000; the process of partial
privatization of the state-owned telephone monopoly
has begun
domestic: cable, open wire, and microwave radio
relay; 3 cellular networks
international: satellite earth stations - 2 Intelsat, NA
Eutelsat, 2 Inmarsat (Atlantic and Indian Ocean
regions), and 1 Intersputnik (Atlantic Ocean region)
Radio broadcast stations: AM 27, FM 75,
shortwave 1 (1994 est.)
Radios: 9.9 million registered (1996)
Television broadcast stations: 150 (1997)
Televisions: 9.4 million registered (1996)

Transportation

Railways:
total: 24,313 km
broad gauge: 652 km 1.520-m gauge
standard gauge: 22,243 km 1.435-m gauge (11,648
km electrified; 8,978 km double track)
narrow gauge: 1,418 km various gauges including
1.000-m, 0.785-m, 0.750-m, and 0.600-m (1996)
Highways:
total: 377,048 km
paved: 247,721 km (including 264 km of
expressways)
unpaved: 129,327 km (1997 est.)
Waterways: 3,812 km navigable rivers and canals
(1996)
Pipelines: crude oil and petroleum products 2,280
km; natural gas 17,000 km (1996)
Ports and harbors: Gdansk, Gdynia, Gliwice,
Kolobrzeg, Szczecin, Swinoujscie, Ustka, Warsaw,
Wrocaw
Merchant marine:
total: 61 ships (1,000 GRT or over) totaling 1,162,954
GRT/1,866,462 DWT
ships by type: bulk 53, cargo 3, chemical tanker 2,
roll-on/roll-off cargo 1, short-sea passenger 2 (1998
est.)
Airports: 92 (1998 est.)
Airports - with paved runways:
total: 74
over 3,047 m: 2
2,438 to 3,047 m: 25
1,524 to 2,437 m: 38
914 to 1,523 m: 6
under 914 m: 3 (1998 est.)
Airports - with unpaved runways:
total: 18
2,438 to 3,047 m: 1
1,524 to 2,437 m: 1
914 to 1,523 m: 9
under 914 m: 7 (1998 est.)
Heliports: 3 (1998 est.)

Military

Military branches: Army, Navy, Air and Air Defense
Force
Military manpower - military age: 19 years of age
Military manpower - availability:
males age 15-49: 10,417,314 (1999 est.)
Military manpower - fit for military service:
males age 15-49: 8,104,484 (1999 est.)
**Military manpower - reaching military age
annually:**
males: 334,420 (1999 est.)
Military expenditures - dollar figure: $3.3 billion
(1998)
Military expenditures - percent of GDP: 2.2%
(1998)

Transnational Issues

Disputes - international: none
Illicit drugs: major illicit producer of amphetamines
for the international market; transshipment point for
Asian and Latin American illicit drugs to Western
Europe

Portugal

Geography

Location: Southwestern Europe, bordering the North Atlantic Ocean, west of Spain
Geographic coordinates: 39 30 N, 8 00 W
Map references: Europe
Area:
total: 92,391 sq km
land: 91,951 sq km
water: 440 sq km
note: includes Azores and Madeira Islands
Area - comparative: slightly smaller than Indiana
Land boundaries:
total: 1,214 km
border countries: Spain 1,214 km
Coastline: 1,793 km
Maritime claims:
continental shelf: 200-m depth or to the depth of exploitation
exclusive economic zone: 200 nm
territorial sea: 12 nm
Climate: maritime temperate; cool and rainy in north, warmer and drier in south
Terrain: mountainous north of the Tagus River, rolling plains in south

Elevation extremes:
lowest point: Atlantic Ocean 0 m
highest point: Ponta do Pico (Pico or Pico Alto) on Ilha do Pico in the Azores 2,351 m
Natural resources: fish, forests (cork), tungsten, iron ore, uranium ore, marble
Land use:
arable land: 26%
permanent crops: 9%
permanent pastures: 9%
forests and woodland: 36%
other: 20% (1993 est.)
Irrigated land: 6,300 sq km (1993 est.)
Natural hazards: Azores subject to severe earthquakes
Environment - current issues: soil erosion; air pollution caused by industrial and vehicle emissions; water pollution, especially in coastal areas
Environment - international agreements:
party to: Air Pollution, Biodiversity, Climate Change, Desertification, Endangered Species, Hazardous Wastes, Law of the Sea, Marine Dumping, Marine Life Conservation, Ozone Layer Protection, Ship Pollution, Tropical Timber 83, Wetlands
signed, but not ratified: Air Pollution-Persistent Organic Pollutants, Air Pollution-Volatile Organic Compounds, Climate Change-Kyoto Protocol, Environmental Modification, Nuclear Test Ban, Tropical Timber 94
Geography - note: Azores and Madeira Islands occupy strategic locations along western sea approaches to Strait of Gibraltar

People

Population: 9,918,040 (July 1999 est.)
Age structure:
0-14 years: 17% (male 866,115; female 820,438)
15-64 years: 68% (male 3,283,345; female 3,428,427)
65 years and over: 15% (male 619,086; female 900,629) (1999 est.)
Population growth rate: -0.13% (1999 est.)
Birth rate: 10.49 births/1,000 population (1999 est.)
Death rate: 10.25 deaths/1,000 population (1999 est.)
Net migration rate: -1.51 migrant(s)/1,000 population (1999 est.)
Sex ratio:
at birth: 1.06 male(s)/female
under 15 years: 1.06 male(s)/female
15-64 years: 0.96 male(s)/female
65 years and over: 0.69 male(s)/female
total population: 0.93 male(s)/female (1999 est.)
Infant mortality rate: 6.73 deaths/1,000 live births (1999 est.)
Life expectancy at birth:
total population: 75.88 years
male: 72.51 years
female: 79.46 years (1999 est.)
Total fertility rate: 1.34 children born/woman (1999 est.)

Nationality:
noun: Portuguese (singular and plural)
adjective: Portuguese
Ethnic groups: homogeneous Mediterranean stock; citizens of black African descent who immigrated to mainland during decolonization number less than 100,000
Religions: Roman Catholic 97%, Protestant denominations 1%, other 2%
Languages: Portuguese
Literacy:
definition: age 15 and over can read and write
total population: 85%
male: 89%
female: 82% (1990 est.)

Government

Country name:
conventional long form: Portuguese Republic
conventional short form: Portugal
local long form: Republica Portuguesa
local short form: Portugal
Data code: PO
Government type: parliamentary democracy
Capital: Lisbon
Administrative divisions: 18 districts (distritos, singular - distrito) and 2 autonomous regions* (regioes autonomas, singular - regiao autonoma); Aveiro, Acores (Azores)*, Beja, Braga, Braganca, Castelo Branco, Coimbra, Evora, Faro, Guarda, Leiria, Lisboa, Madeira*, Portalegre, Porto, Santarem, Setubal, Viana do Castelo, Vila Real, Viseu
Dependent areas: Macau (scheduled to revert to China on 20 December 1999)
Independence: 1140 (independent republic proclaimed 5 October 1910)
National holiday: Day of Portugal, 10 June (1580)
Constitution: 25 April 1976, revised 30 October 1982, 1 June 1989, 5 November 1992, and 3 September 1997
Legal system: civil law system; the Constitutional Tribunal reviews the constitutionality of legislation; accepts compulsory ICJ jurisdiction, with reservations
Suffrage: 18 years of age; universal
Executive branch:
chief of state: President Jorge SAMPAIO (since 9 March 1996)
head of government: Prime Minister Antonio Manuel de Oliviera GUTERRES (since 28 October 1995)
cabinet: Council of Ministers appointed by the president on the recommendation of the prime minister
note: there is also a Council of State that acts as a consultative body to the president
elections: president elected by popular vote for a five-year term; election last held 14 January 1996 (next to be held NA January 2001); following legislative elections, the leader of the majority party or leader of a majority coalition is usually appointed prime minister by the president
election results: Jorge SAMPAIO elected president; percent of vote - Jorge SAMPAIO (Socialist) 53.8%,

Portugal (continued)

Anibal CAVACO SILVA (Social Democrat) 46.2%
Legislative branch: unicameral Assembly of the Republic or Assembleia da Republica (230 seats; members are elected by popular vote to serve four-year terms)

elections: last held 1 October 1995 (next to be held by 1 October 1999)

election results: percent of vote by party - PSD 34.0%, PS 43.8%, CDU 8.6%, CDS/PP 9.1%; seats by party - PSD 88, PS 112, CDU 15, CDS/PP 15

Judicial branch: Supreme Court or Supremo Tribunal de Justica, judges appointed for life by the Conselho Superior da Magistratura

Political parties and leaders: Social Democratic Party or PSD [Marcelo Rebelo DE SOUSA]; Portuguese Socialist Party or PS [Antonio GUTERRES]; Portuguese Communist Party or PCP [Carlos CARVALHAS]; Popular Party or PP (formerly known as Center Democratic Party or CDS) [Rebelo DE SOUSA]; National Solidarity Party or PSN [Manuel SERGIO]; United Democratic Coalition or CDU (communists; includes the PCP and a number of small leftist groups) [leader NA]

International organization participation: AfDB, Australia Group, BIS, CCC, CE, CERN, EAPC, EBRD, ECE, ECLAC, EIB, EMU, EU, FAO, IADB, IAEA, IBRD, ICAO, ICC, ICFTU, ICRM, IDA, IEA, IFAD, IFC, IFRCS, IHO, ILO, IMF, IMO, Inmarsat, Intelsat, Interpol, IOC, IOM, ISO, ITU, LAIA (observer), MINURCA, MINURSO, MONUA, MTCR, NAM (guest), NATO, NEA, NSG, OAS (observer), OECD, OPCW, OSCE, PCA, UN, UN Security Council (temporary), UNCTAD, UNESCO, UNIDO, UNMIBH, UNMOP, UNPREDEP, UPU, WCL, WEU, WFTU, WHO, WIPO, WMO, WToO, WTrO, ZC

Diplomatic representation in the US:
chief of mission: Ambassador Fernando Antonio de Lacerda ANDRESEN GUIMARAES
chancery: 2125 Kalorama Road NW, Washington, DC 20008
telephone: [1] (202) 328-8610
FAX: [1] (202) 462-3726
consulate(s) general: Boston, New York, Newark (New Jersey), New Bedford (Massachusetts), Providence (Rhode Island), and San Francisco
consulate(s): Los Angeles

Diplomatic representation from the US:
chief of mission: Ambassador Gerald S. MCGOWAN
embassy: Avenida das Forcas Armadas, 1600 Lisbon
mailing address: PSC 83, APO AE 09726
telephone: [351] (1) 727-3300
FAX: [351] (1) 726-9109
consulate(s): Ponta Delgada (Azores)

Flag description: two vertical bands of green (hoist side, two-fifths) and red (three-fifths) with the Portuguese coat of arms centered on the dividing line

Economy

Economy - overview: Portugal, in 1998, continued to see strong economic growth, falling interest rates, and low unemployment. The country qualified for the European Monetary Union (EMU) in 1998 and joined with 10 other European countries in launching the euro on 1 January 1999. Portugal's inflation rate for 1998, 2.8%, was low but higher than most of its European partners. The country continues to run a trade deficit and a balance of payments deficit. The government is working to modernize capital plant and increase the country's competitiveness in the increasingly integrated world markets. Growth is expected to slow to 3% in 1999 because of a slowdown in public investment and sluggish demand for exports.

GDP: purchasing power parity - $144.8 billion (1998 est.)

GDP - real growth rate: 4.2% (1998 est.)

GDP - per capita: purchasing power parity - $14,600 (1998 est.)

GDP - composition by sector:
agriculture: 4%
industry: 36%
services: 60% (1998 est.)

Population below poverty line: NA%

Household income or consumption by percentage share:
lowest 10%: NA%
highest 10%: NA%

Inflation rate (consumer prices): 2.8% (1998 est.)

Labor force: 4.75 million (1998 est.)

Labor force - by occupation: services 56%, manufacturing 22%, agriculture, forestry, fisheries 12%, construction 9%, mining 1% (1998 est.)

Unemployment rate: 5% (August 1998)

Budget:
revenues: $48 billion
expenditures: $52 billion, including capital expenditures of $7.4 billion (1996 est.)

Industries: textiles and footwear; wood pulp, paper, and cork; metalworking; oil refining; chemicals; fish canning; wine; tourism

Industrial production growth rate: 4.1% (1998 est.)

Electricity - production: 32.839 billion kWh (1996)

Electricity - production by source:
fossil fuel: 55%
hydro: 45%
nuclear: 0%
other: 0% (1998 est.)

Electricity - consumption: 31.92 billion kWh (1997)

Electricity - exports: 3 billion kWh (1996)

Electricity - imports: 4.2 billion kWh (1996)

Agriculture - products: grain, potatoes, olives, grapes; sheep, cattle, goats, poultry, beef, dairy products

Exports: $25 billion (f.o.b., 1998)

Exports - commodities: clothing and footwear, machinery, chemicals, cork and paper products, hides

Exports - partners: EU 81% (Germany 20%, Spain 15%, France 14%, UK 12% Netherlands 5%, Benelux 5%, Italy 4%), US 5% (1997)

Imports: $34.9 billion (f.o.b., 1998)

Imports - commodities: machinery and transport equipment, chemicals, petroleum, textiles, agricultural products

Imports - partners: EU 76% (Spain 24%, Germany 15%, France 11%, Italy 8%, UK 7%, Netherlands 5%), US 3%, Japan 2% (1997)

Debt - external: $13.1 billion (1997 est.)

Economic aid - donor: ODA, $271 million (1995)

Currency: 1 Portuguese escudo (Esc) = 100 centavos

Exchange rates: Portuguese escudos (Esc) per US$1 - 172.78 (January 1999), 180.10 (1998), 175.31 (1997), 154.24 (1996), 151.11 (1995), 165.99 (1994)
note: on 1 January 1999, the European Union introduced a common currency that is now being used by financial institutions in some member countries at the rate of 0.8597 euros per US$ and a fixed rate of 200.482 escudos per euro; the euro will replace the local currency in consenting countries for all transactions in 2002

Fiscal year: calendar year

Communications

Telephones: 3.7 million (1996 est.)

Telephone system:
domestic: generally adequate integrated network of coaxial cables, open wire, microwave radio relay, and domestic satellite earth stations
international: 6 submarine cables; satellite earth stations - 3 Intelsat (2 Atlantic Ocean and 1 Indian Ocean), NA Eutelsat; tropospheric scatter to Azores; note - an earth station for Inmarsat (Atlantic Ocean region) is planned

Radio broadcast stations: AM 57, FM 66 (repeaters 22), shortwave 0

Radios: 2.2 million (1993 est.)

Television broadcast stations: 36 (in addition, there are 62 repeaters) (1997)

Televisions: 2,970,892 (1993 est.)

Transportation

Railways:
total: 3,072 km
broad gauge: 2,769 km 1.668-m gauge (528 km electrified; 426 km double track)
narrow gauge: 303 km 1.000-m gauge (1996)

Highways:
total: 68,732 km
paved: 59,110 km (including 687 km of expressways)
unpaved: 9,622 km (1995 est.)

Waterways: 820 km navigable; relatively unimportant to national economy, used by shallow-draft craft limited to 300 metric-ton cargo capacity

Pipelines: crude oil 22 km; petroleum products 58 km; natural gas 700 km
note: the secondary lines for the natural gas pipeline that will be 300 km long have not yet been built

Ports and harbors: Aveiro, Funchal (Madeira Islands), Horta (Azores), Leixoes, Lisbon, Porto, Ponta Delgada (Azores), Praia da Vitoria (Azores), Setubal, Viana do Castelo

Portugal (continued)

Merchant marine:

total: 132 ships (1,000 GRT or over) totaling 894,640 GRT/1,366,955 DWT

ships by type: bulk 13, cargo 72, chemical tanker 14, container 7, liquefied gas tanker 7, oil tanker 9, refrigerated cargo 1, roll-on/roll-off cargo 3, short-sea passenger 4, vehicle carrier 2

note: Portugal has created a captive register on Madeira for Portuguese-owned ships; ships on the Madeira Register (MAR) will have taxation and crewing benefits of a flag of convenience (1998 est.)

Airports: 66 (1998 est.)

Airports - with paved runways:

total: 40

over 3,047 m: 5

2,438 to 3,047 m: 7

1,524 to 2,437 m: 5

914 to 1,523 m: 18

under 914 m: 5 (1998 est.)

Airports - with unpaved runways:

total: 26

914 to 1,523 m: 1

under 914 m: 25 (1998 est.)

Military

Military branches: Army, Navy (includes Marines), Air Force, National Republican Guard

Military manpower - military age: 20 years of age

Military manpower - availability:

males age 15-49: 2,542,188 (1999 est.)

Military manpower - fit for military service:

males age 15-49: 2,042,730 (1999 est.)

Military manpower - reaching military age annually:

males: 73,405 (1999 est.)

Military expenditures - dollar figure: $2.458 billion (1997)

Military expenditures - percent of GDP: 2.6% (1997)

Transnational Issues

Disputes - international: as former colonial power, Portugal plays a key role in the issue of Indonesia's sovereignty over Timor Timur (East Timor Province), which has not been recognized by the UN

Illicit drugs: important gateway country for Latin American cocaine entering the European market; transshipment point for hashish from North Africa to Europe; consumer of Southwest Asian heroin

Puerto Rico
(commonwealth associated with the US)

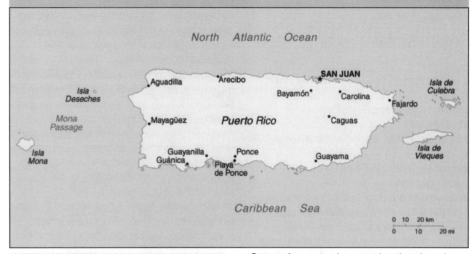

Geography

Location: Caribbean, island between the Caribbean Sea and the North Atlantic Ocean, east of the Dominican Republic

Geographic coordinates: 18 15 N, 66 30 W

Map references: Central America and the Caribbean

Area:

total: 9,104 sq km

land: 8,959 sq km

water: 145 sq km

Area - comparative: slightly less than three times the size of Rhode Island

Land boundaries: 0 km

Coastline: 501 km

Maritime claims:

exclusive economic zone: 200 nm

territorial sea: 12 nm

Climate: tropical marine, mild; little seasonal temperature variation

Terrain: mostly mountains, with coastal plain belt in north; mountains precipitous to sea on west coast; sandy beaches along most coastal areas

Elevation extremes:

lowest point: Caribbean Sea 0 m

highest point: Cerro de Punta 1,338 m

Natural resources: some copper and nickel; potential for onshore and offshore oil

Land use:

arable land: 4%

permanent crops: 5%

permanent pastures: 26%

forests and woodland: 16%

other: 49% (1993 est.)

Irrigated land: 390 sq km (1993 est.)

Natural hazards: periodic droughts; hurricanes

Environment - current issues: erosion; occasional drought causing water shortages

Environment - international agreements:

party to: NA

signed, but not ratified: NA

Geography - note: important location along the Mona Passage - a key shipping lane to the Panama Canal; San Juan is one of the biggest and best natural harbors in the Caribbean; many small rivers and high central mountains ensure land is well watered; south coast relatively dry; fertile coastal plain belt in north

People

Population: 3,887,652 (July 1999 est.)

Age structure:

0-14 years: 24% (male 482,111; female 459,940)

15-64 years: 65% (male 1,220,682; female 1,323,787)

65 years and over: 11% (male 173,133; female 227,999) (1999 est.)

Population growth rate: 0.59% (1999 est.)

Birth rate: 15.9 births/1,000 population (1999 est.)

Death rate: 7.87 deaths/1,000 population (1999 est.)

Net migration rate: -2.15 migrant(s)/1,000 population (1999 est.)

Sex ratio:

at birth: 1.06 male(s)/female

under 15 years: 1.05 male(s)/female

15-64 years: 0.92 male(s)/female

65 years and over: 0.76 male(s)/female

total population: 0.93 male(s)/female (1999 est.)

Infant mortality rate: 10.79 deaths/1,000 live births (1999 est.)

Life expectancy at birth:

total population: 75.06 years

male: 70.95 years

female: 79.41 years (1999 est.)

Total fertility rate: 1.94 children born/woman (1999 est.)

Nationality:

noun: Puerto Rican(s) (US citizens)

adjective: Puerto Rican

Ethnic groups: Hispanic

Religions: Roman Catholic 85%, Protestant denominations and other 15%

Languages: Spanish, English

Puerto Rico (continued)

Literacy:
definition: age 15 and over can read and write
total population: 89%
male: 90%
female: 88% (1980 est.)

Government

Country name:
conventional long form: Commonwealth of Puerto Rico
conventional short form: Puerto Rico
Data code: RQ
Dependency status: commonwealth associated with the US
Government type: commonwealth
Capital: San Juan
Administrative divisions: none (commonwealth associated with the US); there are no first-order administrative divisions as defined by the US Government, but there are 78 municipalities (municipios, singular - municipio) at the second order; Adjuntas, Aguada, Aguadilla, Aguas Buenas, Aibonito, Anasco, Arecibo, Arroyo, Barceloneta, Barranquitas, Bayamon, Cabo Rojo, Caguas, Camuy, Canovanas, Carolina, Catano, Cayey, Ceiba, Ciales, Cidra, Coamo, Comerio, Corozal, Culebra, Dorado, Fajardo, Florida, Guanica, Guayama, Guayanilla, Guaynabo, Gurabo, Hatillo, Hormigueros, Humacao, Isabela, Jayuya, Juana Diaz, Juncos, Lajas, Lares, Las Marias, Las Piedras, Loiza, Luquillo, Manati, Maricao, Maunabo, Mayaguez, Moca, Morovis, Naguabo, Naranjito, Orocovis, Patillas, Penuelas, Ponce, Quebradillas, Rincon, Rio Grande, Sabana Grande, Salinas, San German, San Juan, San Lorenzo, San Sebastian, Santa Isabel, Toa Alta, Toa Baja, Trujillo Alto, Utuado, Vega Alta, Vega Baja, Vieques, Villalba, Yabucoa, Yauco
Independence: none (commonwealth associated with the US)
National holiday: US Independence Day, 4 July (1776)
Constitution: ratified 3 March 1952; approved by US Congress 3 July 1952; effective 25 July 1952
Legal system: based on Spanish civil code
Suffrage: 18 years of age; universal; indigenous inhabitants are US citizens but do not vote in US presidential elections
Executive branch:
chief of state: President William Jefferson CLINTON of the US (since 20 January 1993); Vice President Albert GORE, Jr. (since 20 January 1993)
head of government: Governor Pedro ROSSELLO (since 2 January 1993)
cabinet: NA
elections: US president and vice president elected on the same ticket for four-year terms; governor elected by popular vote for a four-year term; election last held 5 November 1996 (next to be held 7 November 2000)
election results: Pedro ROSSELLO reelected governor; percent of vote - 51.1%
Legislative branch: bicameral Legislative Assembly consists of the Senate (28 seats; members are directly elected by popular vote to serve four-year terms) and the House of Representatives (54 seats; members are directly elected by popular vote to serve four-year terms)
elections: Senate - last held 5 November 1996 (next to be held 7 November 2000); House of Representatives - last held 5 November 1996 (next to be held 7 November 2000)
election results: Senate - percent of vote by party - NA; seats by party - PNP 19, PPD 8, PIP 1; House of Representatives - percent of vote by party - NA; seats by party - PNP 37, PPD 16, PIP 1
note: Puerto Rico elects one nonvoting representative to the US House of Representatives; elections last held 5 November 1996 (next to be held 7 November 2000); results - percent of vote by party - NA; seats by party - PNP 1 (Carlos Romero BARCELO)
Judicial branch: Supreme Court (justices appointed by the governor with the consent of the Senate); Superior Courts (justices appointed by the governor with the consent of the Senate); Municipal Courts (justices appointed by the governor with the consent of the Senate)
Political parties and leaders: National Republican Party of Puerto Rico [Luis FERRE]; Popular Democratic Party or PPD [Anibal ACEVIDA Vila]; New Progressive Party or PNP [Pedro ROSSELLO]; Puerto Rican Independence Party or PIP [Ruben BERRIOS Martinez]; National Democratic Party [William MIRANDA]
Political pressure groups and leaders: Armed Forces for National Liberation or FALN; Volunteers of the Puerto Rican Revolution; Boricua Popular Army (also known as the Macheteros); Armed Forces of Popular Resistance
International organization participation: Caricom (observer), ECLAC (associate), FAO (associate), ICFTU, Interpol (subbureau), IOC, WCL, WFTU, WHO (associate)
Diplomatic representation in the US: none (commonwealth associated with the US)
Diplomatic representation from the US: none (commonwealth associated with the US)
Flag description: five equal horizontal bands of red (top and bottom) alternating with white; a blue isosceles triangle based on the hoist side bears a large, white, five-pointed star in the center; design based on the US flag

Economy

Economy - overview: Puerto Rico has one of the most dynamic economies in the Caribbean region. A diverse industrial sector has surpassed agriculture as the primary locus of economic activity and income. Encouraged by duty-free access to the US and by tax incentives, US firms have invested heavily in Puerto Rico since the 1950s. US minimum wage laws apply. Sugar production has lost out to dairy production and other livestock products as the main source of income in the agricultural sector. Tourism has traditionally been an important source of income for the island, with estimated arrivals of nearly 4 million tourists in 1993. Construction and tourism were the leading sectors in economic growth in 1998.
GDP: purchasing power parity - $34.7 billion (1998 est.)
GDP - real growth rate: 3.1% (1998 est.)
GDP - per capita: purchasing power parity - $9,000 (1998 est.)
GDP - composition by sector:
agriculture: NA%
industry: NA%
services: NA%
Population below poverty line: NA%
Household income or consumption by percentage share:
lowest 10%: NA%
highest 10%: NA%
Inflation rate (consumer prices): 5.7% (1998 est.)
Labor force: 1.3 million (1996)
Labor force - by occupation: government 19%, manufacturing 13%, trade 17%, construction 5%, other 32%, unemployed 14% (1996)
Unemployment rate: 13% (FY96/97 est.)
Budget:
revenues: $6.7 billion
expenditures: $9.6 billion (FY 1999/2000
Industries: pharmaceuticals, electronics, apparel, food products; tourism
Industrial production growth rate: 5% (1994 est.)
Electricity - production: 18.3 billion kWh (1996)
Electricity - production by source:
fossil fuel: 98.36%
hydro: 1.64%
nuclear: 0%
other: 0% (1996)
Electricity - consumption: 18.3 billion kWh (1996)
Electricity - exports: 0 kWh (1996)
Electricity - imports: 0 kWh (1996)
Agriculture - products: sugarcane, coffee, pineapples, plantains, bananas; livestock products, chickens
Exports: $30.3 billion (f.o.b. 1998)
Exports - commodities: pharmaceuticals, electronics, apparel, canned tuna, rum, beverage concentrates, medical equipment
Exports - partners: US 88% (1997 est.)
Imports: $21.8 billion (c.i.f. 1996)
Imports - commodities: chemicals, machinery and equipment, clothing, food, fish, petroleum products
Imports - partners: US 62% (1997 est.)
Debt - external: $NA
Economic aid - recipient: $NA
Currency: 1 US dollar (US$) = 100 cents
Exchange rates: US currency is used
Fiscal year: 1 July - 30 June

Communications

Telephones: 1.389 million (1996 est.)
Telephone system: modern system, integrated with that of the US by high-capacity submarine cable and Intelsat with high-speed data capability
domestic: digital telephone system with about 1 million lines (1990 est.); cellular telephone service

international: satellite earth station - 1 Intelsat; submarine cable to US
Radio broadcast stations: AM 50, FM 63, shortwave 0
note: there were 118 radio stations in 1995
Radios: 2.6 million (1994 est.)
Television broadcast stations: 18 (in addition, there are three stations of the US Armed Forces Radio and Television Service) (1997)
Televisions: 973,000 (1994 est.)

Transportation

Railways:
total: 96 km
narrow gauge: 96 km 1.000-m gauge, rural, narrow-gauge system for hauling sugarcane; no passenger service
Highways:
total: 14,400 km
paved: 14,400 km
unpaved: 0 km (1996 est.)
Ports and harbors: Guanica, Guayanilla, Guayama, Playa de Ponce, San Juan
Merchant marine: none
Airports: 30 (1998 est.)
Airports - with paved runways:
total: 21
over 3,047 m: 3
1,524 to 2,437 m: 3
914 to 1,523 m: 9
under 914 m: 6 (1998 est.)
Airports - with unpaved runways:
total: 9
914 to 1,523 m: 2
under 914 m: 7 (1998 est.)

Military

Military branches: paramilitary National Guard, Police Force
Military - note: defense is the responsibility of the US

Transnational Issues

Disputes - international: none

Qatar

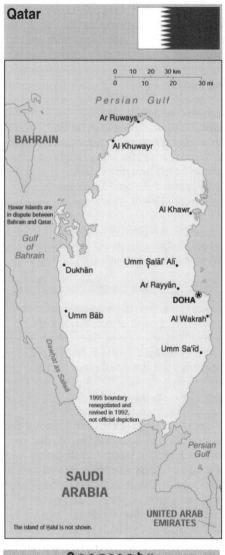

Geography

Location: Middle East, peninsula bordering the Persian Gulf and Saudi Arabia
Geographic coordinates: 25 30 N, 51 15 E
Map references: Middle East
Area:
total: 11,437 sq km
land: 11,437 sq km
water: 0 sq km
Area - comparative: slightly smaller than Connecticut
Land boundaries:
total: 60 km
border countries: Saudi Arabia 60 km
Coastline: 563 km
Maritime claims:
contiguous zone: 24 nm
exclusive economic zone: 200 nm
territorial sea: 12 nm
Climate: desert; hot, dry; humid and sultry in summer
Terrain: mostly flat and barren desert covered with loose sand and gravel
Elevation extremes:
lowest point: Persian Gulf 0 m

highest point: Qurayn Abu al Bawl 103 m
Natural resources: petroleum, natural gas, fish
Land use:
arable land: 1%
permanent crops: NA%
permanent pastures: 5%
forests and woodland: NA%
other: 94% (1993 est.)
Irrigated land: 80 sq km (1993 est.)
Natural hazards: haze, dust storms, sandstorms common
Environment - current issues: limited natural fresh water resources are increasing dependence on large-scale desalination facilities
Environment - international agreements:
party to: Biodiversity, Climate Change, Hazardous Wastes, Ozone Layer Protection
signed, but not ratified: Law of the Sea
Geography - note: strategic location in central Persian Gulf near major petroleum deposits

People

Population: 723,542 (July 1999 est.)
Age structure:
0-14 years: 27% (male 99,232; female 95,421)
15-64 years: 71% (male 367,213; female 145,925)
65 years and over: 2% (male 11,047; female 4,704) (1999 est.)
Population growth rate: 3.62% (1999 est.)
Birth rate: 16.75 births/1,000 population (1999 est.)
Death rate: 3.57 deaths/1,000 population (1999 est.)
Net migration rate: 23.03 migrant(s)/1,000 population (1999 est.)
Sex ratio:
at birth: 1.05 male(s)/female
under 15 years: 1.04 male(s)/female
15-64 years: 2.52 male(s)/female
65 years and over: 2.35 male(s)/female
total population: 1.94 male(s)/female (1999 est.)
Infant mortality rate: 17.25 deaths/1,000 live births (1999 est.)
Life expectancy at birth:
total population: 74.23 years
male: 71.7 years
female: 76.89 years (1999 est.)
Total fertility rate: 3.42 children born/woman (1999 est.)
Nationality:
noun: Qatari(s)
adjective: Qatari
Ethnic groups: Arab 40%, Pakistani 18%, Indian 18%, Iranian 10%, other 14%
Religions: Muslim 95%
Languages: Arabic (official), English commonly used as a second language
Literacy:
definition: age 15 and over can read and write
total population: 79.4%
male: 79.2%
female: 79.9% (1995 est.)

Qatar *(continued)*

Government

Country name:
conventional long form: State of Qatar
conventional short form: Qatar
local long form: Dawlat Qatar
local short form: Qatar
note: closest approximation of the native pronunciation falls between cutter and gutter, but not like guitar
Data code: QA
Government type: traditional monarchy
Capital: Doha
Administrative divisions: 9 municipalities (baladiyat, singular - baladiyah); Ad Dawhah, Al Ghuwayriyah, Al Jumayliyah, Al Khawr, Al Wakrah, Ar Rayyan, Jarayan al Batinah, Madinat ash Shamal, Umm Salal
Independence: 3 September 1971 (from UK)
National holiday: Independence Day, 3 September (1971)
Constitution: provisional constitution enacted 19 April 1972
Legal system: discretionary system of law controlled by the amir, although civil codes are being implemented; Islamic law is significant in personal matters
Suffrage: none
Executive branch:
chief of state: Amir HAMAD bin Khalifa Al Thani (since 27 June 1995 when, as crown prince, he ousted his father, Amir KHALIFA bin Hamad Al Thani, in a bloodless coup); Crown Prince JASSIM bin Hamad bin Khalifa Al Thani, third son of the monarch (selected crown prince by the monarch 22 October 1996); note - Amir HAMAD also holds the positions of minister of defense and commander-in-chief of the armed forces
head of government: Prime Minister ABDALLAH bin Khalifa Al Thani, brother of the monarch (since 30 October 1996); Deputy Prime Minister MUHAMMAD bin Khalifa Al Thani, brother of the monarch (since 20 January 1998)
cabinet: Council of Ministers appointed by the monarch
elections: none; the monarch is hereditary
Legislative branch: unicameral Advisory Council or Majlis al-Shura (35 seats; members appointed by the monarch)
note: the constitution calls for elections for part of this consultative body, but no elections have been held since 1970, when there were partial elections to the body; Council members have had their terms extended every four years since
Judicial branch: Court of Appeal
Political parties and leaders: none
International organization participation: ABEDA, AFESD, AL, AMF, CCC, ESCWA, FAO, G-77, GCC, IAEA, IBRD, ICAO, ICRM, IDB, IFAD, IFRCS, IHO (pending member), ILO, IMF, IMO, Inmarsat, Intelsat, Interpol, IOC, ISO (correspondent), ITU, NAM, OAPEC, OIC, OPCW, OPEC, UN, UNCTAD,

UNESCO, UNIDO, UPU, WHO, WIPO, WMO, WTrO
Diplomatic representation in the US:
chief of mission: Ambassador Saad Muhammad al-KUBAYSI
chancery: Suite 200, 4200 Wisconsin Avenue NW, Washington, DC 20016
telephone: [1] (202) 274-1600
consulate(s) general: Houston
Diplomatic representation from the US:
chief of mission: Ambassador Elizabeth MCKUNE
embassy: 149 Ahmed Bin Ali St., Fariq Bin Omran (opposite the television station), Doha
mailing address: P. O. Box 2399, Doha
telephone: [974] 864701 through 864703
FAX: [974] 861669
note: work week is Saturday-Wednesday
Flag description: maroon with a broad white serrated band (nine white points) on the hoist side

Economy

Economy - overview: Oil is the backbone of the economy and accounts for more than 30% of GDP, roughly 70% of export earnings, and 66% of government revenues. Proved oil reserves of 3.7 billion barrels should ensure continued output at current levels for 23 years. Oil has given Qatar a per capita GDP comparable to the leading West European industrial countries. Qatar's proved reserves of natural gas exceed 7 trillion cubic meters, more than 5% of the world total, third largest in the world. Production and export of natural gas are becoming increasingly important. Long-term goals feature the development of off-shore petroleum and the diversification of the economy. Lower world oil prices brought GDP down in 1998.
GDP: purchasing power parity - $12 billion (1998 est.)
GDP - real growth rate: -3% (1998 est.)
GDP - per capita: purchasing power parity - $17,100 (1998 est.)
GDP - composition by sector:
agriculture: 1%
industry: 49%
services: 50% (1996 est.)
Population below poverty line: NA%
Household income or consumption by percentage share:
lowest 10%: NA%
highest 10%: NA%
Inflation rate (consumer prices): 7.4% (1996)
Labor force: 233,000 (1993 est.)
Unemployment rate: NA%
Budget:
revenues: $3.4 billion
expenditures: $4.3 billion, including capital expenditures of $700 million (FY98/99 budget est.)
Industries: crude oil production and refining, fertilizers, petrochemicals, steel reinforcing bars, cement
Industrial production growth rate: -4% (1995)
Electricity - production: 5.2 billion kWh (1996)

Electricity - production by source:
fossil fuel: 100%
hydro: 0%
nuclear: 0%
other: 0% (1996)
Electricity - consumption: 5.2 billion kWh (1996)
Electricity - exports: 0 kWh (1996)
Electricity - imports: 0 kWh (1996)
Agriculture - products: fruits, vegetables; poultry, dairy products, beef; fish
Exports: $5.6 billion (f.o.b., 1997 est.)
Exports - commodities: petroleum products 80%, fertilizers, steel
Exports - partners: Japan 49%, Singapore 12%, South Korea 12%, Thailand 4%, US 3% (1997)
Imports: $4.4 billion (f.o.b., 1997 est.)
Imports - commodities: machinery and equipment, consumer goods, food, chemicals
Imports - partners: UK 25%, France 13%, Japan 10%, US 9%, Italy 6% (1997)
Debt - external: $11 billion (1997 est.)
Economic aid - recipient: $NA
Currency: 1 Qatari riyal (QR) = 100 dirhams
Exchange rates: Qatari riyals (QR) per US$1 - 3.6400 riyals (fixed rate)
Fiscal year: 1 April - 31 March

Communications

Telephones: 160,717 (1992 est.)
Telephone system: modern system centered in Doha
domestic: NA
international: tropospheric scatter to Bahrain; microwave radio relay to Saudi Arabia and UAE; submarine cable to Bahrain and UAE; satellite earth stations - 2 Intelsat (1 Atlantic Ocean and 1 Indian Ocean) and 1 Arabsat
Radio broadcast stations: AM 2, FM 3, shortwave 0
Radios: 201,000 (1992 est.)
Television broadcast stations: 2 (in addition, there are three repeaters) (1997)
Televisions: 205,000 (1992 est.)

Transportation

Railways: 0 km
Highways:
total: 1,230 km
paved: 1,107 km
unpaved: 123 km (1996 est.)
Pipelines: crude oil 235 km; natural gas 400 km
Ports and harbors: Doha, Halul Island, Umm Sa'id
Merchant marine:
total: 22 ships (1,000 GRT or over) totaling 713,014 GRT/1,112,829 DWT
ships by type: cargo 10, combination ore/oil 2, container 5, oil tanker 5 (1998 est.)
Airports: 4 (1998 est.)
Airports - with paved runways:
total: 2
over 3,047 m: 2 (1998 est.)

Airports - with unpaved runways:
total: 2
914 to 1,523 m: 1
under 914 m: 1 (1998 est.)
Heliports: 1 (1998 est.)

Military

Military branches: Army, Navy, Air Force, Public Security
Military manpower - military age: 18 years of age
Military manpower - availability:
males age 15-49: 301,451 (1999 est.)
note: includes non-nationals
Military manpower - fit for military service:
males age 15-49: 158,114 (1999 est.)
Military manpower - reaching military age annually:
males: 6,125 (1999 est.)
Military expenditures - dollar figure: $940 million (FY98/99)
Military expenditures - percent of GDP: 9.6% (FY98/99)

Transnational Issues

Disputes - international: territorial dispute with Bahrain over the Hawar Islands and maritime boundary dispute with Bahrain currently before the International Court of Justice (ICJ); in 1996, agreed with Saudi Arabia to demarcate border per 1992 accord; that process is ongoing

---

Reunion
(overseas department of France)

Geography

Location: Southern Africa, island in the Indian Ocean, east of Madagascar
Geographic coordinates: 21 06 S, 55 36 E
Map references: World
Area:
total: 2,510 sq km
land: 2,500 sq km
water: 10 sq km
Area - comparative: slightly smaller than Rhode Island
Land boundaries: 0 km
Coastline: 201 km
Maritime claims:
exclusive economic zone: 200 nm
territorial sea: 12 nm
Climate: tropical, but temperature moderates with elevation; cool and dry from May to November, hot and rainy from November to April
Terrain: mostly rugged and mountainous; fertile lowlands along coast
Elevation extremes:
lowest point: Indian Ocean 0 m
highest point: Piton des Neiges 3,069 m
Natural resources: fish, arable land
Land use:
arable land: 17%
permanent crops: 2%
permanent pastures: 5%
forests and woodland: 35%
other: 41% (1993 est.)
Irrigated land: 60 sq km (1993 est.)
Natural hazards: periodic, devastating cyclones (December to April); Piton de la Fournaise on the southeastern coast is an active volcano
Environment - current issues: NA
Environment - international agreements:
party to: NA
signed, but not ratified: NA

People

Population: 717,723 (July 1999 est.)
Age structure:
0-14 years: 32% (male 118,401; female 112,878)
15-64 years: 62% (male 218,952; female 225,292)
65 years and over: 6% (male 17,506; female 24,694) (1999 est.)
Population growth rate: 1.75% (1999 est.)
Birth rate: 22.16 births/1,000 population (1999 est.)
Death rate: 4.64 deaths/1,000 population (1999 est.)
Net migration rate: 0 migrant(s)/1,000 population (1999 est.)
Sex ratio:
at birth: 1.05 male(s)/female
under 15 years: 1.05 male(s)/female
15-64 years: 0.97 male(s)/female
65 years and over: 0.71 male(s)/female
total population: 0.98 male(s)/female (1999 est.)
Infant mortality rate: 6.9 deaths/1,000 live births (1999 est.)
Life expectancy at birth:
total population: 75.73 years
male: 72.69 years
female: 78.93 years (1999 est.)
Total fertility rate: 2.64 children born/woman (1999 est.)
Nationality:
noun: Reunionese (singular and plural)
adjective: Reunionese
Ethnic groups: French, African, Malagasy, Chinese, Pakistani, Indian
Religions: Roman Catholic 86%, Hindu, Islam, Buddhist (1995)
Languages: French (official), Creole widely used
Literacy:
definition: age 15 and over can read and write
total population: 79%
male: 76%
female: 80% (1982 est.)

Government

Country name:
conventional long form: Department of Reunion
conventional short form: Reunion
local long form: none
local short form: Ile de la Reunion
Data code: RE
Dependency status: overseas department of France
Government type: NA
Capital: Saint-Denis
Administrative divisions: none (overseas department of France); there are no first-order administrative divisions as defined by the US Government, but there are four arrondissements, 24 communes, and 47 cantons
Independence: none (overseas department of France)
National holiday: National Day, Taking of the Bastille, 14 July (1789)

Reunion *(continued)*

Constitution: 28 September 1958 (French Constitution)
Legal system: French law
Suffrage: 18 years of age; universal
Executive branch:
chief of state: President Jacques CHIRAC of France (since 17 May 1995), represented by Prefect Robert POMMIES (since NA 1996)
head of government: President of the General Council Christophe PAYET (since 4 April 1994) and President of the Regional Council Margarite SUDRE (since 25 June 1993)
cabinet: NA
elections: French president elected by popular vote for a seven-year term; prefect appointed by the French president on the advice of the French Ministry of the Interior; the presidents of the General and Regional Councils are elected by the members of those councils
Legislative branch: unicameral General Council (47 seats; members are elected by direct popular vote to serve six-year terms) and unicameral Regional Council (45 seats; members are elected by direct popular vote to serve six-year terms)
elections: General Council - last held NA March 1994 (next to be held NA 2000); Regional Council - last held 25 June 1993 (next to be held NA 1999)
election results: General Council - percent of vote by party - NA; seats by party - PCR 12, PS 12, UDF 11, RPR 5, others 7; Regional Council - percent of vote by party - NA; seats by party - UPF 17, Free-Dom Movement 13, PCR 9, PS 6
note: Reunion elects three representatives to the French Senate; elections last held 14 April 1996 (next to be held NA); results - percent of vote by party - NA; seats by party - RPR 1, PCR 2; Reunion also elects five deputies to the French National Assembly; elections last held 25 May and 1 June 1997 (next to be held NA2002); results - percent of vote by party - NA; seats by party - PCR 3, PS 1, and RPR-UDF 1
Judicial branch: Court of Appeals or Cour d'Appel
Political parties and leaders: Rally for the Republic or RPR [Andre Maurice PIHOUEE]; Union for French Democracy or UDF [Ibrahim DINDAN]; Communist Party of Reunion or PCR [Paul VERGES]; France-Reunion Future or FRA [Andre THIEN AH KOON]; Socialist Party or PS [Jean-Claude FRUTEAU]; Center of Social Democrats or CDS [leader NA]; Union for France or UPF (includes RPR and UDF) [leader NA]; Free-DOM Movement [Marguerite SUDRE]; National Front or FN [Alix MOREL]
International organization participation: FZ, InOC, WFTU
Diplomatic representation in the US: none (overseas department of France)
Diplomatic representation from the US: none (overseas department of France)
Flag description: the flag of France is used

Economy

Economy - overview: The economy has traditionally been based on agriculture. Sugarcane has been the primary crop for more than a century, and in some years it accounts for 85% of exports. The government has been pushing the development of a tourist industry to relieve high unemployment, which recently amounted to one-third of the labor force. The gap in Reunion between the well-off and the poor is extraordinary and accounts for the persistent social tensions. The white and Indian communities are substantially better off than other segments of the population, often approaching European standards, whereas indigenous groups suffer the poverty and unemployment typical of the poorer nations of the African continent. The outbreak of severe rioting in February 1991 illustrates the seriousness of socioeconomic tensions. The economic well-being of Reunion depends heavily on continued financial assistance from France.
GDP: purchasing power parity - $3.4 billion (1998 est.)
GDP - real growth rate: 3.8% (1998 est.)
GDP - per capita: purchasing power parity - $4,800 (1998 est.)
GDP - composition by sector:
agriculture: NA%
industry: NA%
services: NA%
Population below poverty line: NA%
Household income or consumption by percentage share:
lowest 10%: NA%
highest 10%: NA%
Inflation rate (consumer prices): NA%
Labor force: 261,000 (1995)
Labor force - by occupation: agriculture 8%, industry 19%, services 73% (1990)
Unemployment rate: 35% (1994)
Budget:
revenues: $856.7 million
expenditures: $2.2437 billion, including capital expenditures of $NA (1993)
Industries: sugar, rum, cigarettes, handicraft items, flower oil extraction
Industrial production growth rate: NA%
Electricity - production: 1.1 billion kWh (1996)
Electricity - production by source:
fossil fuel: 54.55%
hydro: 45.45%
nuclear: 0%
other: 0% (1996)
Electricity - consumption: 1.1 billion kWh (1996)
Electricity - exports: 0 kWh (1996)
Electricity - imports: 0 kWh (1996)
Agriculture - products: sugarcane, vanilla, tobacco, tropical fruits, vegetables, corn
Exports: $171.78 million (f.o.b., 1994)
Exports - commodities: sugar 63%, rum and molasses 4%, perfume essences 2%, lobster 3%, (1993)
Exports - partners: France 74%, Japan 6%, Comoros 4% (1994)
Imports: $2.35 billion (c.i.f., 1994)
Imports - commodities: manufactured goods, food, beverages, tobacco, machinery and transportation equipment, raw materials, and petroleum products

Imports - partners: France 67%, Bahrain 4%, Italy 3% (1994)
Debt - external: $NA
Economic aid - recipient: $NA; note - substantial annual subsidies from France
Currency: 1 French franc (F) = 100 centimes
Exchange rates: French francs (F) per US$1 - 5.65 (January 1999), 5.8995 (1998), 5.8367 (1997), 5.1155 (1996), 4.9915 (1995), 5.5520 (1994)
Fiscal year: calendar year

Communications

Telephones: 219,000 (1995)
Telephone system: adequate system; principal center is Saint-Denis
domestic: modern open wire and microwave radio relay network
international: radiotelephone communication to Comoros, France, Madagascar; new microwave route to Mauritius; satellite earth station - 1 Intelsat (Indian Ocean)
Radio broadcast stations: AM 3, FM 13, shortwave 0
Radios: 158,000 (1994)
Television broadcast stations: 22 (in addition, there are 18 low-power repeaters) (1997)
Televisions: 116,181 (1992 est.)

Transportation

Railways: 0 km
Highways:
total: 2,784 km
paved: 2,187 km
unpaved: 597 km (1987 est.)
Ports and harbors: Le Port, Pointe des Galets
Merchant marine:
total: 1 chemical tanker (1,000 GRT or over) totaling 28,264 GRT/44,885 DWT (1998 est.)
Airports: 2 (1998 est.)
Airports - with paved runways:
total: 2
2,438 to 3,047 m: 1
914 to 1,523 m: 1 (1998 est.)

Military

Military branches: French forces (Army, Navy, Air Force, and Gendarmerie)
Military manpower - military age: 18 years of age
Military manpower - availability:
males age 15-49: 185,800 (1999 est.)
Military manpower - fit for military service:
males age 15-49: 95,068 (1999 est.)
Military manpower - reaching military age annually:
males: 5,902 (1999 est.)
Military - note: defense is the responsibility of France

Transnational Issues

Disputes - international: none

Romania

Geography

Location: Southeastern Europe, bordering the Black Sea, between Bulgaria and Ukraine
Geographic coordinates: 46 00 N, 25 00 E
Map references: Europe
Area:
total: 237,500 sq km
land: 230,340 sq km
water: 7,160 sq km
Area - comparative: slightly smaller than Oregon
Land boundaries:
total: 2,508 km
border countries: Bulgaria 608 km, Hungary 443 km, Moldova 450 km, Serbia and Montenegro 476 km (all with Serbia), Ukraine (north) 362 km, Ukraine (east) 169 km
Coastline: 225 km
Maritime claims:
contiguous zone: 24 nm
continental shelf: 200-m depth or to the depth of exploitation
exclusive economic zone: 200 nm
territorial sea: 12 nm
Climate: temperate; cold, cloudy winters with frequent snow and fog; sunny summers with frequent showers and thunderstorms
Terrain: central Transylvanian Basin is separated from the Plain of Moldavia on the east by the Carpathian Mountains and separated from the Walachian Plain on the south by the Transylvanian Alps
Elevation extremes:
lowest point: Black Sea 0 m
highest point: Moldoveanu 2,544 m
Natural resources: petroleum (reserves declining), timber, natural gas, coal, iron ore, salt
Land use:
arable land: 41%
permanent crops: 3%
permanent pastures: 21%
forests and woodland: 29%

other: 6% (1993 est.)
Irrigated land: 31,020 sq km (1993 est.)
Natural hazards: earthquakes most severe in south and southwest; geologic structure and climate promote landslides
Environment - current issues: soil erosion and degradation; water pollution; air pollution in south from industrial effluents; contamination of Danube delta wetlands
Environment - international agreements:
party to: Air Pollution, Antarctic Treaty, Biodiversity, Climate Change, Desertification, Endangered Species, Environmental Modification, Hazardous Wastes, Law of the Sea, Nuclear Test Ban, Ozone Layer Protection, Ship Pollution, Wetlands
signed, but not ratified: Air Pollution-Persistent Organic Pollutants, Antarctic-Environmental Protocol, Climate Change-Kyoto Protocol
Geography - note: controls most easily traversable land route between the Balkans, Moldova, and Ukraine

People

Population: 22,334,312 (July 1999 est.)
Age structure:
0-14 years: 19% (male 2,117,289; female 2,027,940)
15-64 years: 68% (male 7,563,695; female 7,663,491)
65 years and over: 13% (male 1,234,760; female 1,727,137) (1999 est.)
Population growth rate: -0.23% (1999 est.)
Birth rate: 10.09 births/1,000 population (1999 est.)
Death rate: 11.55 deaths/1,000 population (1999 est.)
Net migration rate: -0.87 migrant(s)/1,000 population (1999 est.)
Sex ratio:
at birth: 1.05 male(s)/female
under 15 years: 1.04 male(s)/female
15-64 years: 0.99 male(s)/female
65 years and over: 0.71 male(s)/female
total population: 0.96 male(s)/female (1999 est.)
Infant mortality rate: 18.12 deaths/1,000 live births (1999 est.)
Life expectancy at birth:
total population: 70.83 years
male: 67.05 years
female: 74.81 years (1999 est.)
Total fertility rate: 1.27 children born/woman (1999 est.)
Nationality:
noun: Romanian(s)
adjective: Romanian
Ethnic groups: Romanian 89.1%, Hungarian 8.9%, German 0.4%, Ukrainian, Serb, Croat, Russian, Turk, and Gypsy 1.6%
Religions: Romanian Orthodox 70%, Roman Catholic 6% (of which 3% are Uniate), Protestant 6%, unaffiliated 18%
Languages: Romanian, Hungarian, German
Literacy:
definition: age 15 and over can read and write

total population: 97%
male: 98%
female: 95% (1992 est.)

Government

Country name:
conventional long form: none
conventional short form: Romania
local long form: none
local short form: Romania
Data code: RO
Government type: republic
Capital: Bucharest
Administrative divisions: 40 counties (judete, singular - judet) and 1 municipality* (municipiu); Alba, Arad, Arges, Bacau, Bihor, Bistrita-Nasaud, Botosani, Braila, Brasov, Bucuresti*, Buzau, Calarasi, Caras-Severin, Cluj, Constanta, Covasna, Dimbovita, Dolj, Galati, Gorj, Giurgiu, Harghita, Hunedoara, Ialomita, Iasi, Maramures, Mehedinti, Mures, Neamt, Olt, Prahova, Salaj, Satu Mare, Sibiu, Suceava, Teleorman, Timis, Tulcea, Vaslui, Vilcea, Vrancea
Independence: 1881 (from Turkey; republic proclaimed 30 December 1947)
National holiday: National Day of Romania, 1 December (1990)
Constitution: 8 December 1991
Legal system: former mixture of civil law system and communist legal theory; is now based on the constitution of France's Fifth Republic
Suffrage: 18 years of age; universal
Executive branch:
chief of state: President Emil CONSTANTINESCU (since 29 November 1996)
head of government: Prime Minister Radu VASILE (since 17 April 1998)
cabinet: Council of Ministers appointed by the prime minister
elections: president elected by popular vote for a four-year term; election last held 3 November 1996, with runoff between the top two candidates held 17 November 1996 (next to be held NA November/ December 2000); prime minister appointed by the president
election results: percent of vote - Emil CONSTANTINESCU 54.4%, Ion ILIESCU 45.6%
Legislative branch: bicameral Parliament or Parlament consists of the Senate or Senat (143 seats; members are elected by direct popular vote on a proportional representation basis to serve four-year terms) and the Chamber of Deputies or Adunarea Deputatilor (343 seats; members are elected by direct popular vote on a proportional representation basis to serve four-year terms)
elections: Senate - last held 3 November 1996 (next to be held NA 2000); Chamber of Deputies - last held 3 November 1996 (next to be held NA 2000)
election results: Senate - percent of vote by party - CDR 30.7%, PDSR 23.1%, USD 13.2%, UDMR 6.8%, PRM 4.5%, PUNR 4.2%, others 17.5%; seats by party - CDR 53, PDSR 41, USD 23, UDMR 11, PRM 8, PUNR 7; Chamber of Deputies - percent of vote by

Romania (continued)

party - CDR 30.2%, PDSR 21.5%, USD 12.9%, UDMR 6.6% PRM 4.5% PUNR 4.4%, others 19.9%; seats by party - CDR 122, PDSR 91, USD 53, UDMR 25, PRM 19, PUNR 18, ethnic minorities 15

Judicial branch: Supreme Court of Justice, judges are appointed by the president on the recommendation of the Superior Council of Magistrates

Political parties and leaders: Democratic Party or PD [Petre ROMAN]; Romanian Social Democratic Party or PSDR [Sergiu CUNESCU]; Party of Social Democracy in Romania or PDSR [Ion ILIESCU]; Democratic Union of Hungarians in Romania or UDMR [Bela MARKO]; National Liberal Party or PNL [Mircea IONESCU-QUINTUS]; National Peasants' Christian and Democratic Party or PNTCD [Ion DIACONESCU]; Romanian National Unity Party or PUNR [Valeriu TABARA]; Socialist Labor Party or PSM [Ilie VERDET]; Agrarian Democratic Party of Romania or PDAR [Mihai BERCA]; The Democratic Convention or CDR [Ion DIACONESCU]; Romania Mare Party (Greater Romanian Party) or PRM [Corneliu Vadim TUDOR]; Civic Alliance Party or PAC [Nicolae MANOLESCU, chairman]; Liberal Party '93 or PL-93 [Dinu PATRICIU]; National Liberal Party-Democratic Convention or PNL-CD [Nicolae CERVENI]; Socialist Party or PS [Tudor MOHORA]
note: to increase their voting strength several of the above-mentioned parties united under umbrella organizations: PNTCD, PNL, and PNL-CD form the bulk of the Democratic Convention or CDR [Ion DIACONESCU]; PD and PSDR form the Union of Social Democrats or USD [Petre ROMAN]; and PAC and PL-93 form the National Liberal Alliance or ANL [Nicolae MANOLESCU]; PSM, PS, ANL, and numerous other small parties failed to gain representation in the most recent election

Political pressure groups and leaders: various human rights and professional associations

International organization participation: ACCT, BIS, BSEC, CCC, CE, CEI, EAPC, EBRD, ECE, EU (applicant), FAO, G-9, G-77, IAEA, IBRD, ICAO, ICFTU, ICRM, IFAD, IFC, IFRCS, ILO, IMF, IMO, Inmarsat, Intelsat, Interpol, IOC, IOM (observer), ISO, ITU, LAIA (observer), MONUA, NAM (guest), NSG, OAS (observer), OPCW, OSCE, PCA, PFP, UN, UNCTAD, UNESCO, UNIDO, UNIKOM, UPU, WCL, WEU (associate partner), WFTU, WHO, WIPO, WMO, WToO, WTrO, ZC

Diplomatic representation in the US:
chief of mission: Ambassador Mircea Dan GEOANA
chancery: 1607 23rd Street NW, Washington, DC 20008
telephone: [1] (202) 332-4846, 4848, 4851
FAX: [1] (202) 232-4748
consulate(s) general: Los Angeles and New York

Diplomatic representation from the US:
chief of mission: Ambassador James C. ROSAPEPE
embassy: Strada Tudor Arghezi 7-9, Bucharest
mailing address: American Embassy Bucharest, Department of State, Washington, DC 20521-5260 (pouch)

telephone: [40] (1) 210 01 49, 210 40 42
FAX: [40] (1) 210 03 95
branch office: Cluj-Napoca

Flag description: three equal vertical bands of blue (hoist side), yellow, and red; the national coat of arms that used to be centered in the yellow band has been removed; now similar to the flags of Andorra and Chad

Economy

Economy - overview: After the collapse of the Soviet Bloc in 1989-91, Romania was left with an obsolete industrial base and a pattern of industrial capacity wholly unsuited to its needs. In February 1997, Romania embarked on a comprehensive macroeconomic stabilization and structural reform program, but reform subsequently has been a stop-and-go process. Restructuring programs include liquidating large energy-intensive industries and major agricultural and financial sector reforms. Today, Romania is continuing its difficult transition to a market-based economy. GDP contracted by an estimated 7.3% in 1998 after a 6.6% decline in 1997. Tight monetary policy and slower exchange rate depreciation earlier in 1998 helped lower inflation to an estimated 41% from 152% in 1997. The large current account deficit and concerns about meeting debt payments in 1999 contributed to increased pressure on the exchange rate towards the end of 1998. Replacing the IMF standby agreement (suspended because of lack of progress on structural reforms), servicing large debt payments, and bringing the budget under control are key priorities for 1999.

GDP: purchasing power parity - $90.6 billion (1998 est.)
GDP - real growth rate: -7.3% (1998 est.)
GDP - per capita: purchasing power parity - $4,050 (1998 est.)
GDP - composition by sector:
agriculture: 19%
industry: 41%
services: 40% (1997)
Population below poverty line: 21.5% (1994 est.)
Household income or consumption by percentage share:
lowest 10%: 3.8%
highest 10%: 20.2% (1992)
Inflation rate (consumer prices): 41% (1998 est.)
Labor force: 10.1 million (1996 est.)
Labor force - by occupation: NA%
Unemployment rate: 9% (1998 est.)
Budget:
revenues: $10 billion
expenditures: $11.7 billion, including capital expenditures of $1.3 billion (1997 est.)
Industries: mining, timber, construction materials, metallurgy, chemicals, machine building, food processing, petroleum production and refining
Industrial production growth rate: -17% (1998 est.)
Electricity - production: 59.245 billion kWh (1996)
Electricity - production by source:
fossil fuel: 72.11%

hydro: 26.35%
nuclear: 1.54%
other: 0% (1996)
Electricity - consumption: 60.045 billion kWh (1996)
Electricity - exports: 0 kWh (1996)
Electricity - imports: 800 million kWh (1996)
Agriculture - products: wheat, corn, sugar beets, sunflower seed, potatoes, grapes; milk, eggs, beef
Exports: $8.2 billion (f.o.b., 1998 est.)
Exports - commodities: textiles and footwear 23%, metals and metal products 18%, machinery and equipment 9%, chemicals 7% (1997)
Exports - partners: Italy 20%, Germany 17%, France 6%, Turkey 4% (1997)
Imports: $10.8 billion (f.o.b., 1998 est.)
Imports - commodities: machinery and equipment 23%, fuels and minerals 19%, chemicals 8%, foodstuffs (1997)
Imports - partners: Germany 16%, Italy 16%, Russia 12%, France 6% (1997)
Debt - external: $10 billion (1998 est.)
Economic aid - recipient: $510.1 million (1995)
Currency: 1 leu (L) = 100 bani
Exchange rates: lei (L) per US$1 - 11,353.6 (January 1999), 8,875.6 (1998), 7,167.9 (1997), 3,084.2 (1996), 2,033.3 (1995), 1,655.1 (1994)
Fiscal year: calendar year

Communications

Telephones: 2.6 million (1993 est.)
Telephone system:
domestic: poor service; 89% of telephone network is automatic; trunk network is microwave radio relay; roughly 3,300 villages with no service (February 1990 est.)
international: satellite earth station - 1 Intelsat; new digital international direct-dial exchanges are in Bucharest (1993 est.)
Radio broadcast stations: AM 12, FM 5, shortwave 0
note: in 1995, 135 local radio stations were registered
Radios: 4.64 million (1992 est.)
Television broadcast stations: 130 (in addition, there are about 400 low-power repeaters) (1997)
Televisions: 4.58 million (1992 est.)

Transportation

Railways:
total: 11,376 km
broad gauge: 60 km 1.524-m gauge
standard gauge: 10,889 km 1.435-m gauge (3,723 km electrified; 3,060 km double track)
narrow gauge: 427 km 0.760-m gauge (1994)
Highways:
total: 153,358 km
paved: 78,213 km (including 113 km of expressways)
unpaved: 75,145 km (1996 est.)
Waterways: 1,724 km (1984)
Pipelines: crude oil 2,800 km; petroleum products 1,429 km; natural gas 6,400 km (1992)

Romania (continued)

Ports and harbors: Braila, Constanta, Galati, Mangalia, Sulina, Tulcea

Merchant marine:

total: 199 ships (1,000 GRT or over) totaling 1,996,157 GRT/2,917,895 DWT

ships by type: bulk 35, cargo 141, container 2, oil tanker 7, passenger 1, passenger-cargo 1, railcar carrier 2, roll-on/roll-off cargo 9, specialized tanker 1 (1998 est.)

Airports: 27 (1998 est.)

Airports - with paved runways:

total: 21

over 3,047 m: 4

2,438 to 3,047 m: 6

1,524 to 2,437 m: 11 (1998 est.)

Airports - with unpaved runways:

total: 6

1,524 to 2,437 m: 1

914 to 1,523 m: 3

under 914 m: 2 (1998 est.)

Heliports: 2 (1998 est.)

Military

Military branches: Army, Navy, Air and Air Defense Forces, Paramilitary Forces, Civil Defense

Military manpower - military age: 20 years of age

Military manpower - availability:

males age 15-49: 5,876,912 (1999 est.)

Military manpower - fit for military service:

males age 15-49: 4,938,953 (1999 est.)

Military manpower - reaching military age annually:

males: 193,264 (1999 est.)

Military expenditures - dollar figure: $650 million (1996)

Military expenditures - percent of GDP: 2.5% (1996)

Transnational Issues

Disputes - international: dispute with Ukraine over continental shelf of the Black Sea under which significant gas and oil deposits may exist; agreed in 1997 to two-year negotiating period, after which either party can refer dispute to the International Court of Justice

Illicit drugs: important transshipment point for Southwest Asian heroin transiting the Balkan route and small amounts of Latin American cocaine bound for Western Europe

Russia

Introduction

Background: Russia, a vast Eurasian expanse of field, forest, desert, and tundra, has endured many "times of trouble" - the Mongol rule of the 13th to 15th century; czarist reigns of terror; massive invasions by Swedes, French, and Germans; and the deadly communist period (1917-91) in which Russia dominated an immense Soviet Union. General Secretary Mikhail GORBACHEV, in charge during 1985-91, introduced glasnost (openness) and perestroika (restructuring) in an attempt to modernize communism, but also inadvertently released forces that shattered the USSR into 15 independent republics in December 1991. Russia has struggled in its efforts to build a democratic political system and market economy to replace the strict social, political, and economic controls of the communist period. These reform efforts have resulted in contradictory and confusing economic and political regulations and practices. Industry, agriculture, the military, the central government, and the ruble have suffered, but Russia has successfully held one presidential, two legislative, and numerous regional elections since 1991. The severe illnesses of President Boris YEL'TSIN have contributed to a lack of policy focus at the center.

Geography

Location: Northern Asia (that part west of the Urals is sometimes included with Europe), bordering the Arctic Ocean, between Europe and the North Pacific Ocean

Geographic coordinates: 60 00 N, 100 00 E

Map references: Asia

Area:

total: 17,075,200 sq km

land: 16,995,800 sq km

water: 79,400 sq km

Area - comparative: slightly less than 1.8 times the size of the US

Land boundaries:

total: 19,917 km

border countries: Azerbaijan 284 km, Belarus 959 km, China (southeast) 3,605 km, China (south) 40 km, Estonia 294 km, Finland 1,313 km, Georgia 723 km, Kazakhstan 6,846 km, North Korea 19 km, Latvia 217 km, Lithuania (Kaliningrad Oblast) 227 km, Mongolia 3,441 km, Norway 167 km, Poland (Kaliningrad Oblast) 206 km, Ukraine 1,576 km

Coastline: 37,653 km

Maritime claims:

continental shelf: 200-m depth or to the depth of exploitation

exclusive economic zone: 200 nm

territorial sea: 12 nm

Climate: ranges from steppes in the south through humid continental in much of European Russia; subarctic in Siberia to tundra climate in the polar north; winters vary from cool along Black Sea coast to frigid in Siberia; summers vary from warm in the steppes to cool along Arctic coast

Terrain: broad plain with low hills west of Urals; vast coniferous forest and tundra in Siberia; uplands and mountains along southern border regions

Elevation extremes:

lowest point: Caspian Sea -28 m

highest point: Mount El'brus 5,633 m

Natural resources: wide natural resource base including major deposits of oil, natural gas, coal, and many strategic minerals, timber

note: formidable obstacles of climate, terrain, and distance hinder exploitation of natural resources

Land use:

arable land: 8%

permanent crops: 0%

permanent pastures: 4%

forests and woodland: 46%

other: 42% (1993 est.)

Irrigated land: 40,000 sq km (1993 est.)

Natural hazards: permafrost over much of Siberia is a major impediment to development; volcanic activity in the Kuril Islands; volcanoes and earthquakes on the Kamchatka Peninsula

Russia (continued)

Environment - current issues: air pollution from heavy industry, emissions of coal-fired electric plants, and transportation in major cities; industrial, municipal, and agricultural pollution of inland waterways and sea coasts; deforestation; soil erosion; soil contamination from improper application of agricultural chemicals; scattered areas of sometimes intense radioactive contamination

Environment - international agreements:
party to: Air Pollution, Air Pollution-Nitrogen Oxides, Air Pollution-Sulphur 85, Antarctic-Environmental Protocol, Antarctic Treaty, Biodiversity, Climate Change, Endangered Species, Environmental Modification, Hazardous Wastes, Law of the Sea, Marine Dumping, Nuclear Test Ban, Ozone Layer Protection, Ship Pollution, Tropical Timber 83, Wetlands, Whaling
signed, but not ratified: Air Pollution-Sulphur 94, Climate Change-Kyoto Protocol

Geography - note: largest country in the world in terms of area but unfavorably located in relation to major sea lanes of the world; despite its size, much of the country lacks proper soils and climates (either too cold or too dry) for agriculture

People

Population: 146,393,569 (July 1999 est.)
Age structure:
0-14 years: 19% (male 14,224,033; female 13,666,440)
15-64 years: 68% (male 48,407,409; female 51,768,664)
65 years and over: 13% (male 5,698,356; female 12,628,667) (1999 est.)
Population growth rate: -0.33% (1999 est.)
Birth rate: 9.64 births/1,000 population (1999 est.)
Death rate: 14.96 deaths/1,000 population (1999 est.)
Net migration rate: 2.05 migrant(s)/1,000 population (1999 est.)
Sex ratio:
at birth: 1.05 male(s)/female
under 15 years: 1.04 male(s)/female
15-64 years: 0.94 male(s)/female
65 years and over: 0.45 male(s)/female
total population: 0.88 male(s)/female (1999 est.)
Infant mortality rate: 23 deaths/1,000 live births (1999 est.)
Life expectancy at birth:
total population: 65.12 years
male: 58.83 years
female: 71.72 years (1999 est.)
Total fertility rate: 1.34 children born/woman (1999 est.)
Nationality:
noun: Russian(s)
adjective: Russian
Ethnic groups: Russian 81.5%, Tatar 3.8%, Ukrainian 3%, Chuvash 1.2%, Bashkir 0.9%, Byelorussian 0.8%, Moldavian 0.7%, other 8.1%
Religions: Russian Orthodox, Muslim, other
Languages: Russian, other

Literacy:
definition: age 15 and over can read and write
total population: 98%
male: 100%
female: 97% (1989 est.)

Government

Country name:
conventional long form: Russian Federation
conventional short form: Russia
local long form: Rossiyskaya Federatsiya
local short form: Rossiya
former: Russian Soviet Federative Socialist Republic
Data code: RS
Government type: federation
Capital: Moscow
Administrative divisions: oblasts (oblastey, singular - oblast'), 21 autonomous republics* (avtonomnyk respublik, singular - avtonomnaya respublika), 10 autonomous okrugs**(avtonomnykh okrugov, singular - avtonomnyy okrug), 6 krays*** (krayev, singular - kray), 2 federal cities (singular - gorod)****, and 1 autonomous oblast*****(avtonomnaya oblast'); Adygeya (Maykop)*, Aginskiy Buryatskiy (Aginskoye)**, Altay (Gorno-Altaysk)*, Altayskiy (Barnaul)***, Amurskaya (Blagoveshchensk), Arkhangel'skaya, Astrakhanskaya, Bashkortostan (Ufa)*, Belgorodskaya, Bryanskaya, Buryatiya (Ulan-Ude)*, Chechnya (Groznyy)*, Chelyabinskaya, Chitinskaya, Chukotskiy (Anadyr')**, Chuvashiya (Cheboksary)*, Dagestan (Makhachkala)*, Evenkiyskiy (Tura)**, Ingushetiya (Nazran')*, Irkutskaya, Ivanovskaya, Kabardino-Balkariya (Nal'chik)*, Kaliningradskaya, Kalmykiya (Elista)*, Kaluzkskaya, Kamchatskaya (Petropavlovsk-Kamchatskiy), Karachayevo-Cherkesiya (Cherkessk)*, Kareliya (Petrozavodsk)*, Kemerovskaya, Khabarovskiy***, Khakasiya (Abakan)*, Khanty-Mansiyskiy (Khanty-Mansiysk)**, Kirovskaya, Komi (Syktyvkar)*, Koryakskiy (Palana)**, Kostromskaya, Krasnodarskiy***, Krasnoyarskiy***, Kurganskaya, Kurskaya, Leningradskaya, Lipetskaya, Magadanskaya, Mariy-El (Yoshkar-Ola)*, Mordoviya (Saransk)*, Moskovskaya, Moskva (Moscow)****, Murmanskaya, Nenetskiy (Nar'yan-Mar)**, Nizhegorodskaya, Novgorodskaya, Novosibirskaya, Omskaya, Orenburgskaya, Orlovskaya (Orel), Penzenskaya, Permskaya, Komi-Permyatskiy (Kudymkar)**, Primorskiy (Vladivostok)***, Pskovskaya, Rostovskaya, Ryazanskaya, Sakha (Yakutsk)*, Sakhalinskaya (Yuzhno-Sakhalinsk), Samarskaya, Sankt-Peterburg (Saint Petersburg)****, Saratovskaya, Severnaya Osetiya-Alaniya (Vladikavkaz)*, Smolenskaya, Stavropol'skiy***, Sverdlovskaya (Yekaterinburg), Tambovskaya, Tatarstan (Kazan')*, Taymryskiy (Dudinka)**, Tomskaya, Tul'skaya, Tverskaya, Tyumenskaya, Tyva (Kyzyl)*, Udmurtiya (Izhevsk)*, Ul'yanovskaya, Ust'-Ordynskiy Buryatskiy (Ust'-Ordynskiy)**, Vladimirskaya, Volgogradskaya, Vologodskaya, Voronezhskaya, Yamalo-Nenetskiy (Salekhard)**,

Yaroslavskaya, Yevreyskaya*****; note - when using a place name with an adjectival ending 'skaya' or 'skiy,' the word Oblast' or Avonomnyy Okrug or Kray should be added to the place name
note: the autonomous republics of Chechnya and Ingushetiya were formerly the autonomous republic of Checheno-Ingushetia (the boundary between Chechnya and Ingushetia has yet to be determined); administrative divisions have the same names as their administrative centers (exceptions have the administrative center name following in parentheses)
Independence: 24 August 1991 (from Soviet Union)
National holiday: Independence Day, June 12 (1990)
Constitution: adopted 12 December 1993
Legal system: based on civil law system; judicial review of legislative acts
Suffrage: 18 years of age; universal
Executive branch:
chief of state: President Boris Nikolayevich YEL'TSIN (since 12 June 1991)
head of government: Premier Yevgeniy Maksimovich PRIMAKOV (since 11 September 1998), First Deputy Premiers Yuriy Dmitriyevich MASLYUKOV (since 11 September 1998) and Vadim Anatol'yevich GUSTOV (since 11 September 1998); Deputy Premiers Vladimir Broisovich BULGAK (since 11 September 1998), Gennadiy Vasil'yevich KULIK (since 11 September 1998), and Valentin Ivanovna MATVIYENKO (since 11 September 1998)
cabinet: Ministries of the Government or "Government" composed of the premier and his deputies, ministers, and other agency heads; all are appointed by the president
note: there is also a Presidential Administration (PA) that provides staff and policy support to the president, drafts presidential decrees, and coordinates policy among government agencies; a Security Council also reports directly to the president
elections: president elected by popular vote for a four-year term; election last held 16 June 1996 with runoff election on 3 July 1996 (next to be held NA June 2000); note - no vice president; if the president dies in office, cannot exercise his powers because of ill health, is impeached, or resigns, the premier succeeds him; the premier serves as acting president until a new presidential election is held, which must be within three months; premier and deputy premiers appointed by the president with the approval of the Duma
election results: Boris Nikolayevich YEL'TSIN elected president; percent of vote in runoff - YEL'TSIN 54%, Gennadiy Andreyevich ZYUGANOV 40%
Legislative branch: bicameral Federal Assembly or Federal'noye Sobraniye consists of the Federation Council or Sovet Federatsii (178 seats, filled ex-officio by the top executive and legislative officials in each of the 89 federal administrative units - oblasts, krays, republics, autonomous okrugs and oblasts, and the federal cities of Moscow and St. Petersburg; members serve four-year terms) and the State Duma or Gosudarstvennaya Duma (450 seats, half elected in

single-member districts and half elected from national party lists; members are elected by direct popular vote to serve four-year terms)

elections: State Duma - last held 17 December 1995 (next to be held NA December 1999)

election results: State Duma - percent of vote received by parties clearing the 5% threshold entitling them to a proportional share of the 225 party list seats - Communist Party of the Russian Federation 22.3%, Liberal Democratic Party of Russia 11.2%, Our Home Is Russia 10.1%, Yabloko Bloc 6.9%; seats by party - Communist Party of the Russian Federation 157, independents 78, Our Home Is Russia 55, Liberal Democratic Party of Russia 51, Yabloko Bloc 45, Agrarian Party of Russia 20, Russia's Democratic Choice 9, Power To the People 9, Congress of Russian Communities 5, Forward, Russia! 3, Women of Russia 3, other parties 15

Judicial branch: Constitutional Court, judges are appointed for life by the Federation Council on the recommendation of the president; Supreme Court, judges are appointed for life by the Federation Council on the recommendation of the president; Superior Court of Arbitration, judges are appointed for life by the Federation Council on the recommendation of the president

Political parties and leaders:

pro-market democrats: Yabloko Bloc [Grigoriy Alekseyevich YAVLINSKIY]; Pravoye Delo (Just Cause), a coalition of reformist, western-oriented movements [Yegor Timurovich GAYDAR, Anatoliy Borisovich CHUBAYS, Boris Yefimovich NEMTSOV, Sergey Vladlenovich KIRIYENKO]

centrists/special interest parties: Fatherland [Yuriy Mikhailovich LUZHKOV]; Russian People's Republican Party [Aleksandr Ivanovich LEBED]; Our Home Is Russia [Viktor Stepanovich CHERNOMYRDIN]

anti-market and/or ultranationalist: Communist Party of the Russian Federation [Gennadiy Andreyevich ZYUGANOV]; Liberal Democratic Party of Russia [Vladimir Vol'fovich ZHIRINOVSKIY]; Agrarian Party [Mikhail Ivanovich LAPSHIN]; Working Russia [Viktor Ivanovich ANPILOV and Stanislav TEREKHOV]; Russian National Unity [Aleksandr BARKASHOV]

note: some 150 political parties, blocs, and movements registered with the Justice Ministry as of the 19 December 1998 deadline to be eligible to participate in the scheduled December 1999 Duma elections; in 1995, 43 political organizations qualified to run slates of candidates on the Duma party list ballot; among the parties not listed above but holding seats in the Duma were Russia's Democratic Choice, Power To the People, Congress of Russian Communities, Forward, Russia!, and Women of Russia

Political pressure groups and leaders: NA

International organization participation: APEC, BIS, BSEC, CBSS, CCC, CE, CERN (observer), CIS, EAPC, EBRD, ECE, ESCAP, IAEA, IBRD, ICAO, ICRM, IDA, IFC, IFRCS, IHO, ILO, IMF, IMO, Inmarsat, Intelsat, Interpol, IOC, IOM (observer), ISO, ITU, LAIA (observer), MINURSO, MONUA, MTCR, NSG, OAS (observer), OPCW, OSCE, PCA, PFP, UN, UN Security Council, UNCTAD, UNESCO, UNHCR, UNIDO, UNIKOM, UNITAR, UNMIBH, UNMOP, UNOMIG, UNOMSIL, UNPREDEP, UNTSO, UPU, WFTU, WHO, WIPO, WMO, WToO, WTrO (applicant), ZC

Diplomatic representation in the US:

chief of mission: Ambassador Yuliy Mikhaylovich VORONTSOV

chancery: 2650 Wisconsin Avenue NW, Washington, DC 20007

telephone: [1] (202) 298-5700 through 5704

FAX: [1] (202) 298-5735

consulate(s) general: New York, San Francisco, and Seattle

Diplomatic representation from the US:

chief of mission: Ambassador James F. COLLINS

embassy: Novinskiy Bul'var 19/23, Moscow

mailing address: APO AE 09721

telephone: [7] (095) 252-24-51 through 59

FAX: [7] (095) 956-42-61

consulate(s) general: St. Petersburg, Vladivostok, Yekaterinburg

Flag description: three equal horizontal bands of white (top), blue, and red

Economy

Economy - overview: Seven years after the collapse of the USSR, Russia is still struggling to establish a modern market economy and achieve strong economic growth. Russian GDP has contracted an estimated 43% since 1991, including a 5% drop in 1998, despite the country's wealth of natural resources, its well-educated population, and its diverse - although increasingly dilapidated - industrial base. By the end of 1997, Russia had achieved some progress. Inflation had been brought under control, the ruble was stabilized, and an ambitious privatization program had transferred thousands of enterprises to private ownership. Some important market-oriented laws were also passed, including a commercial code governing business relations and an arbitration court for resolving economic disputes. But in 1998, the Asian financial crisis swept through the country, contributing to a sharp decline in russia's earnings from oil exports and resulting in an exodus of foreign investors. Matters came to a head in August 1998 when the government allowed the ruble to fall precipitously and stopped payment on $40 billion in ruble bonds. Ongoing problems include an undeveloped legal and financial system, poor progress on restructuring the military-industrial complex, and persistently large budget deficits, largely reflecting the inability of successive governments to collect sufficient taxes. Russia's transition to a market economy has also been slowed by the growing prevalence of payment arrears and barter and by widespread corruption. The severity of Russia's economic problems is dramatized by the large annual decline in population, estimated by some observers at 800,000 people, caused by environmental hazards, the decline in health care, and the unwillingness of people to have children.

GDP: purchasing power parity - $593.4 billion (1998 est.)

GDP - real growth rate: -5% (1998 est.)

GDP - per capita: purchasing power parity - $4,000 (1998 est.)

GDP - composition by sector:

agriculture: 7%

industry: 39%

services: 54% (1997)

Population below poverty line: 28.6% (1998 est.)

Household income or consumption by percentage share:

lowest 10%: 3%

highest 10%: 22.2% (1993)

Inflation rate (consumer prices): 84% (1998 est.)

Labor force: 66 million (1997)

Labor force - by occupation: NA

Unemployment rate: 11.5% (1998 est.) with considerable additional underemployment

Budget:

revenues: $40 billion

expenditures: $63 billion, including capital expenditures of $NA (1998 est.)

Industries: complete range of mining and extractive industries producing coal, oil, gas, chemicals, and metals; all forms of machine building from rolling mills to high-performance aircraft and space vehicles; shipbuilding; road and rail transportation equipment; communications equipment; agricultural machinery, tractors, and construction equipment; electric power generating and transmitting equipment; medical and scientific instruments; consumer durables, textiles, foodstuffs, handicrafts

Industrial production growth rate: -5.5% (1998 est.)

Electricity - production: 834 billion kWh (1997)

Electricity - production by source:

fossil fuel: 68.14%

hydro: 19%

nuclear: 12.82%

other: 0.04% (1997)

Electricity - consumption: 788.036 billion kWh (1996)

Electricity - exports: 24.2 billion kWh (1996)

Electricity - imports: 6.6 billion kWh (1996)

Agriculture - products: grain, sugar beets, sunflower seed, vegetables, fruits; beef, milk

Exports: $71.8 billion (1998 est.)

Exports - commodities: petroleum and petroleum products, natural gas, wood and wood products, metals, chemicals, and a wide variety of civilian and military manufactures

Exports - partners: Ukraine, Germany, US, Belarus, other Western and less developed countries

Imports: $58.5 billion (1998 est.)

Imports - commodities: machinery and equipment, consumer goods, medicines, meat, grain, sugar, semifinished metal products

Imports - partners: Europe, North America, Japan, and less developed countries

Russia (continued)

Debt - external: $164 billion (yearend 1998)
Economic aid - recipient: $8.523 billion (1995)
Currency: 1 ruble (R) = 100 kopeks
Exchange rates: rubles per US$1 - 22.2876 (January 1999), 9.7051 (1998), 5,785 (1997), 5,121 (1996), 4,559 (1995), 2,191 (1994)
note: the post-1 January 1998 ruble is equal to 1,000 of the pre-1 January 1998 rubles
Fiscal year: calendar year

Communications

Telephones: 23.8 million (1997 est.)
Telephone system: the telephone system has undergone significant changes in the 1990's; there are more than 1,000 companies licensed to offer communication services; access to digital lines has improved, particularly in urban centers; Internet and e-mail services are improving; Russia has made progress toward building the telecommunications infrastructure necessary for a market economy
domestic: cross country digital trunk lines run from St. Petersburg to Khabarovsk, and from Moscow to Novorossiysk; the telephone systems in 60 regional capitals have modern digital infrastructures; cellular services, both analog and digital, are available in many areas; in rural areas, the telephone services are still outdated, inadequate, and low density
international: Russia is connected internationally by three undersea fiber-optic cables; digital switches in several cities provide more than 50,000 lines for international calls; satellite earth stations provide access to Intelsat, Intersputnik, Eutelsat, Inmarsat, and Orbita
Radio broadcast stations: AM NA, FM NA, shortwave NA; note - there are about 1,050 (including AM, FM, and shortwave) radio broadcast stations throughout the country
Radios: 50 million (1993 est.) (74.3 million radio receivers with multiple speaker systems for program diffusion)
Television broadcast stations: 11,000 (1996 est.)
Televisions: 54.85 million (1992 est.)

Transportation

Railways:
total: 150,000 km; note - 87,000 km in common carrier service; 63,000 km serve specific industries and are not available for common carrier use
broad gauge: 150,000 km 1.520-m gauge (January 1997 est.)
Highways:
total: 948,000 km (including 416,000 km which serve specific industries or farms and are not maintained by governmental highway maintenance departments)
paved: 336,000 km
unpaved: 612,000 km (including 411,000 km of graveled or some other form of surfacing and 201,000 km of unstabilized earth) (1995 est.)
Waterways: total navigable routes in general use 101,000 km; routes with navigation guides serving the Russian River Fleet 95,900 km; routes with night navigational aids 60,400 km; man-made navigable routes 16,900 km (January 1994 est.)
Pipelines: crude oil 48,000 km; petroleum products 15,000 km; natural gas 140,000 km (June 1993 est.)
Ports and harbors: Arkhangel'sk, Astrakhan', Kaliningrad, Kazan', Khabarovsk, Kholmsk, Krasnoyarsk, Moscow, Murmansk, Nakhodka, Nevel'sk, Novorossiysk, Petropavlovsk-Kamchatskiy, St. Petersburg, Rostov, Sochi, Tuapse, Vladivostok, Volgograd, Vostochnyy, Vyborg
Merchant marine:
total: 617 ships (1,000 GRT or over) totaling 4,146,329 GRT/5,278,909 DWT
ships by type: barge carrier 1, bulk 19, cargo 309, combination bulk 21, combination ore/oil 6, container 25, multifunction large-load carrier 1, oil tanker 149, passenger 35, passenger-cargo 3, refrigerated cargo 16, roll-on/roll-off cargo 25, short-sea passenger 7 (1998 est.)
Airports: 2,517 (1994 est.)
Airports - with paved runways:
total: 630
over 3,047 m: 54
2,438 to 3,047 m: 202
1,524 to 2,437 m: 108
914 to 1,523 m: 115
under 914 m: 151 (1994 est.)
Airports - with unpaved runways:
total: 1,887
over 3,047 m: 25
2,438 to 3,047 m: 45
1,524 to 2,437 m: 134
914 to 1,523 m: 291
under 914 m: 1,392 (1994 est.)

Military

Military branches: Ground Forces, Navy, Air Forces, Strategic Rocket Forces
note: the Air Defense Force merged into the Air Force in March 1998
Military manpower - military age: 18 years of age
Military manpower - availability:
males age 15-49: 38,665,138 (1999 est.)
Military manpower - fit for military service:
males age 15-49: 30,173,495 (1999 est.)
Military manpower - reaching military age annually:
males: 1,149,536 (1999 est.)
Military expenditures - dollar figure: $NA
note: the Intelligence Community estimates that defense spending in Russia fell by about 10% in real terms in 1996, reducing Russian defense outlays to about one-sixth of peak Soviet levels in the late 1980s (1997 est.)
Military expenditures - percent of GDP: NA%

Transnational Issues

Disputes - international: dispute over at least two small sections of the boundary with China remain to be settled, despite 1997 boundary agreement; islands of Etorofu, Kunashiri, and Shikotan and the Habomai group occupied by the Soviet Union in 1945, now administered by Russia, claimed by Japan; Caspian Sea boundaries are not yet determined among Azerbaijan, Iran, Kazakhstan, Russia, and Turkmenistan; Estonian and Russian negotiators reached a technical border agreement in December 1996 which has not been ratified; draft treaty delimiting the boundary with Latvia has not been signed; has made no territorial claim in Antarctica (but has reserved the right to do so) and does not recognize the claims of any other nation; 1997 border agreement with Lithuania not yet ratified; Svalbard is the focus of a maritime boundary dispute in the Barents Sea between Norway and Russia
Illicit drugs: limited cultivation of illicit cannabis and opium poppy and producer of amphetamines, mostly for domestic consumption; government has active eradication program; increasingly used as transshipment point for Southwest and Southeast Asian opiates and cannabis and Latin American cocaine to Western Europe, possibly to the US, and growing domestic market

Rwanda

Introduction

Background: Throughout their colonial rule, first Germany and then Belgium favored Rwanda's minority Tutsi ethnic group in education and employment. In 1959, the majority ethnic group, the Hutus, overthrew the ruling Tutsi monarch. The Hutus killed hundreds of Tutsis and drove tens of thousands into exile in neighboring countries. The children of these exiles later formed a rebel group, the Rwandan Patriotic Front (RPF), and began a civil war in October 1990. The war, along with several political and economic upheavals, exasperated ethnic tensions culminating in April 1994 in a genocide in which roughly 800,000 Tutsis and moderate Hutus were killed. The Tutsi rebels defeated the Hutu regime and ended the genocide in July 1994, but approximately 2 million Hutu refugees - many fearing Tutsi retribution - fled to neighboring Burundi, Tanzania, Uganda, and Zaire, now called the Democratic Republic of the Congo (DROC). According to the UN Office of the High Commissioner for Refugees, in 1996 and early 1997 nearly 1.3 million Hutus returned to Rwanda. Even with substantial international aid, these civil dislocations have hindered efforts to foster reconciliation and to boost investment and agricultural output. Although much of the country is now at peace, members of the former regime continue to destabilize the northwest area of the country through a low-intensity insurgency. Rwandan troops are currently involved in a crisis engulfing neighboring DROC.

Geography

Location: Central Africa, east of Democratic Republic of the Congo
Geographic coordinates: 2 00 S, 30 00 E
Map references: Africa
Area:
total: 26,340 sq km
land: 24,950 sq km

water: 1,390 sq km
Area - comparative: slightly smaller than Maryland
Land boundaries:
total: 893 km
border countries: Burundi 290 km, Democratic Republic of the Congo 217 km, Tanzania 217 km, Uganda 169 km
Coastline: 0 km (landlocked)
Maritime claims: none (landlocked)
Climate: temperate; two rainy seasons (February to April, November to January); mild in mountains with frost and snow possible
Terrain: mostly grassy uplands and hills; relief is mountainous with altitude declining from west to east
Elevation extremes:
lowest point: Rusizi River 950 m
highest point: Volcan Karisimbi 4,519 m
Natural resources: gold, cassiterite (tin ore), wolframite (tungsten ore), methane, hydropower
Land use:
arable land: 35%
permanent crops: 13%
permanent pastures: 18%
forests and woodland: 22%
other: 12% (1993 est.)
Irrigated land: 40 sq km (1993 est.)
Natural hazards: periodic droughts; the volcanic Birunga mountains are in the northwest along the border with Democratic Republic of the Congo
Environment - current issues: deforestation results from uncontrolled cutting of trees for fuel; overgrazing; soil exhaustion; soil erosion; widespread poaching
Environment - international agreements:
party to: Biodiversity, Climate Change, Desertification, Endangered Species, Nuclear Test Ban
signed, but not ratified: Law of the Sea
Geography - note: landlocked; predominantly rural population

People

Population: 8,154,933 (July 1999 est.)
Age structure:
0-14 years: 44% (male 1,807,695; female 1,793,590)
15-64 years: 53% (male 2,148,477; female 2,179,119)
65 years and over: 3% (male 92,490; female 133,562) (1999 est.)
Population growth rate: 2.43% (1999 est.)
Birth rate: 38.97 births/1,000 population (1999 est.)
Death rate: 19.53 deaths/1,000 population (1999 est.)
Net migration rate: 4.91 migrant(s)/1,000 population (1999 est.)
note: following the outbreak of genocidal strife in Rwanda in April 1994 between Tutsi and Hutu factions, more than 2 million refugees fled to neighboring Burundi, Tanzania, Uganda, and Democratic Republic of the Congo (formerly Zaire); according to the UN High Commission on Refugees, in 1996 and early 1997 nearly 1.3 million Hutus

returned to Rwanda - of these 720,000 returned from Democratic Republic of the Congo, 480,000 from Tanzania, 88,000 from Burundi, and 10,000 from Uganda; probably fewer than 100,000 Rwandans remained outside of Rwanda by the end of 1997
Sex ratio:
at birth: 1.03 male(s)/female
under 15 years: 1.01 male(s)/female
15-64 years: 0.99 male(s)/female
65 years and over: 0.69 male(s)/female
total population: 0.99 male(s)/female (1999 est.)
Infant mortality rate: 112.86 deaths/1,000 live births (1999 est.)
Life expectancy at birth:
total population: 41.31 years
male: 40.84 years
female: 41.8 years (1999 est.)
Total fertility rate: 5.8 children born/woman (1999 est.)
Nationality:
noun: Rwandan(s)
adjective: Rwandan
Ethnic groups: Hutu 80%, Tutsi 19%, Twa (Pygmoid) 1%
Religions: Roman Catholic 65%, Protestant 9%, Muslim 1%, indigenous beliefs and other 25%
Languages: Kinyarwanda (official) universal Bantu vernacular, French (official), English (official), Kiswahili (Swahili) used in commercial centers
Literacy:
definition: age 15 and over can read and write
total population: 60.5%
male: 69.8%
female: 51.6% (1995 est.)

Government

Country name:
conventional long form: Rwandese Republic
conventional short form: Rwanda
local long form: Republika y'u Rwanda
local short form: Rwanda
Data code: RW
Government type: republic; presidential, multiparty system
Capital: Kigali
Administrative divisions: 12 prefectures (in French - prefectures, singular - prefecture; in Kinyarwanda - plural - NA, singular - prefegitura); Butare, Byumba, Cyangugu, Gikongoro, Gisenyi, Gitarama, Kibungo, Kibuye, Kigali, Kigaliville, Umutara, Ruhengeri
Independence: 1 July 1962 (from Belgium-administered UN trusteeship)
National holiday: Independence Day, 1 July (1962)
Constitution: on 5 May 1995, the Transitional National Assembly adopted a new constitution which included elements of the constitution of 18 June 1991 as well as provisions of the 1993 Arusha peace accord and the November 1994 multi-party protocol of understanding
Legal system: based on German and Belgian civil law systems and customary law; judicial review of legislative acts in the Supreme Court; has not

accepted compulsory ICJ jurisdiction
Suffrage: NA years of age; universal adult
Executive branch:
chief of state: President Pasteur BIZIMUNGU (since 19 July 1994); Vice President Maj. Gen. Paul KAGAME (since 19 July 1994)
head of government: Prime Minister Celestin RWIGEMA (since 1 September 1995)
cabinet: Council of Ministers appointed by the president
elections: normally the president is elected by popular vote for a five-year term; election last held in December 1988 (next to be held NA); prime minister is appointed by the president
election results: Juvenal HABYARIMANA elected president; percent of vote - 99.98% (HABYARIMANA was the sole candidate)
note: President HABYARIMANA was killed in a plane crash on 6 April 1994 which ignited the genocide and was replaced by President BIZIMUNGU who was installed by the military forces of the ruling Rwandan Patriotic Front on 19 July 1994
Legislative branch: unicameral Transitional National Assembly or Assemblee Nationale de Transition (a power-sharing body with 70 seats established on 12 December 1994 following a multi-party protocol understanding; members were predetermined by the Arusha peace accord)
elections: the last national legislative elections were held 16 December 1988 for the National Development Council (the legislature prior to the advent of the Transitional National Assembly); no elections have been held for the Transitional National Assembly as the distribution of seats was predetermined by the Arusha peace accord
election results: percent of vote by party - NA; seats by party - RPF 19, MDR 13, PSD 13, PL 13, PDC 6, PSR 2, PDI 2, other 2; note - the distribution of seats was predetermined
Judicial branch: Constitutional Court, consists of the Court of Cassation and the Council of State in joint session
Political parties and leaders: significant parties include: Rwandan Patriotic Front or RPF [Charles MULIGANDE, secretary general]; Democratic Republican Movement or MDR [leader NA]; Liberal Party or PL [leader NA]; Democratic and Socialist Party or PSD [leader NA]; Christian Democratic Party or PDC [leader NA]; Islamic Democratic Party or PDI [leader NA]; Rwandan Socialist Party or PSR [leader NA]; National Movement for Democracy and Development or MRND (former ruling party) [leader NA]
Political pressure groups and leaders: Rwanda Patriotic Army or RPA [Maj. Gen. Paul KAGAME, commander]; Rally for the Democracy and Return (RDR)
International organization participation: ACCT, ACP, AfDB, CCC, CEEAC, CEPGL, ECA, FAO, G-77, IBRD, ICAO, ICFTU, ICRM, IDA, IFAD, IFC, IFRCS, ILO, IMF, Intelsat, Interpol, IOC, IOM (observer), ITU, NAM, OAU, OPCW, UN, UNCTAD, UNESCO,

UNIDO, UPU, WCL, WHO, WIPO, WMO, WToO, WTrO
Diplomatic representation in the US:
chief of mission: Ambassador Theogene N. RUDASINGWA
chancery: 1714 New Hampshire Ave. NW, Washington, DC 20009
telephone: [1] (202) 232-2882
FAX: [1] (202) 232-4544
Diplomatic representation from the US:
chief of mission: Ambassador George M. STAPLES
embassy: Boulevard de la Revolution, Kigali
mailing address: B. P. 28, Kigali
telephone: [250] 756 01 through 03, 721 26, 771 47
FAX: [250] 721 28
Flag description: three equal vertical bands of red (hoist side), yellow, and green with a large black letter R centered in the yellow band; uses the popular pan-African colors of Ethiopia; similar to the flag of Guinea, which has a plain yellow band

Economy

Economy - overview: Rwanda is a rural country with about 90% of the population engaged in (mainly subsistence) agriculture. It is the most densely populated country in Africa; is landlocked, and has few natural resources and minimal industry. Primary exports are coffee and tea. The 1994 genocide decimated Rwanda's fragile economic base, severely impoverished the population, particularly women, and eroded the country's ability to attract private and external investment. However, Rwanda has made significant progress in stabilizing and rehabilitating its economy. GDP has rebounded, and inflation has been curbed. In June 1998, Rwanda signed an Enhanced Structural Adjustment Facility (ESAF) with the IMF. Rwanda has also embarked upon an ambitious privatization program with the World Bank.
GDP: purchasing power parity - $5.5 billion (1998 est.)
GDP - real growth rate: 10.5% (1998 est.)
GDP - per capita: purchasing power parity - $690 (1998 est.)
GDP - composition by sector:
agriculture: 36%
industry: 24%
services: 40% (1997 est.)
Population below poverty line: 51.2% (1993 est.)
Household income or consumption by percentage share:
lowest 10%: 4.2%
highest 10%: 24.2% (1983-85)
Inflation rate (consumer prices): 10% (1998)
Labor force: 3.6 million
Labor force - by occupation: agriculture 90%, government and services, industry and commerce
Unemployment rate: NA%
Budget:
revenues: $231 million
expenditures: $319 million, including capital expenditures of $13 million (1996 est.)
Industries: production of cement, processing of

agricultural products, small-scale beverage production, manufacture of soap, furniture, shoes, plastic goods, textiles, cigarettes
Industrial production growth rate: 4.9% (1995 est.)
Electricity - production: 164 million kWh (1996)
Electricity - production by source:
fossil fuel: 2.44%
hydro: 97.56%
nuclear: 0%
other: 0% (1996)
Electricity - consumption: 177 million kWh (1996)
Electricity - exports: 2 million kWh (1996)
Electricity - imports: 15 million kWh (1996)
Agriculture - products: coffee, tea, pyrethrum (insecticide made from chrysanthemums), bananas, beans, sorghum, potatoes; livestock
Exports: $82.1 million (f.o.b., 1998 est.)
Exports - commodities: coffee 55%, tea 21%, hides, tin ore (1997)
Exports - partners: Brazil 49%, Germany 16%, US, Netherlands, UK (1996)
Imports: $326 million (f.o.b., 1998 est.)
Imports - commodities: foodstuffs, machinery and equipment, steel, petroleum products, cement and construction material (1997)
Imports - partners: Italy, Kenya, Tanzania, US, Belgium-Luxembourg (1997)
Debt - external: $1.2 billion (1998)
Economic aid - recipient: $711.2 million (1995); note - since 1994, World Bank financing to Rwanda has totaled more than $120 million; in June 1998, Rwanda signed an Enhanced Structural Adjustment Facility (ESAF) with the IMF; in summer 1998, Rwanda presented its policy objectives and development priorities to donor governments resulting in multi-year pledges in the amount of $250 million
Currency: 1 Rwandan franc (RF) = 100 centimes
Exchange rates: Rwandan francs (RF) per US$1 - 320.63 (February 1999), 312.31 (1998), 301.53 (1997), 306.82 (1996), 262.20 (1995)
Fiscal year: calendar year

Communications

Telephones: 6,400 (1983 est.)
Telephone system: telephone system primarily serves business and government
domestic: the capital, Kigali, is connected to the centers of the prefectures by microwave radio relay; the remainder of the network depends on wire and HF radiotelephone
international: international connections employ microwave radio relay to neighboring countries and satellite communications to more distant countries; satellite earth stations - 1 Intelsat (Indian Ocean) in Kigali (includes telex and telefax service)
Radio broadcast stations: AM 1, FM 1, shortwave 0
Radios: 630,000 (1993 est.)
Television broadcast stations: 2 (1997)
Televisions: NA

Transportation

Railways: 0 km
Highways:
total: 12,000 km
paved: 1,000 km
unpaved: 11,000 km (1997 est.)
Waterways: Lac Kivu navigable by shallow-draft barges and native craft
Ports and harbors: Cyangugu, Gisenyi, Kibuye
Airports: 7 (1998 est.)
Airports - with paved runways:
total: 4
over 3,047 m: 1
914 to 1,523 m: 2
under 914 m: 1 (1998 est.)
Airports - with unpaved runways:
total: 3
914 to 1,523 m: 1
under 914 m: 2 (1998 est.)

Military

Military branches: Army, Gendarmerie
Military manpower - availability:
males age 15-49: 1,964,118 (1999 est.)
Military manpower - fit for military service:
males age 15-49: 1,000,204 (1999 est.)
Military expenditures - dollar figure: $92 million (1999)
Military expenditures - percent of GDP: 3.8% (1999)

Transnational Issues

Disputes - international: Rwandan military forces are supporting the rebel forces in the civil war in the Democratic Republic of the Congo

Saint Helena
(overseas territory of the UK)

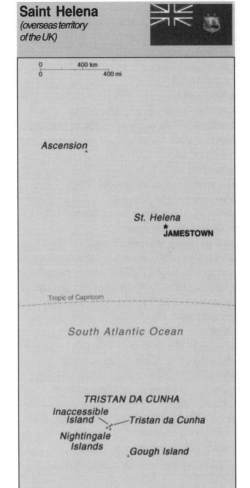

Geography

Location: islands in the South Atlantic Ocean, about mid-way between South America and Africa
Geographic coordinates: 15 56 S, 5 42 W
Map references: Africa
Area:
total: 410 sq km
land: 410 sq km
water: 0 sq km
note: includes Ascension, Gough Island, Inaccessible Island, Nightingale Islands, and Tristan da Cunha Island
Area - comparative: slightly more than two times the size of Washington, DC
Land boundaries: 0 km
Coastline: 60 km
Maritime claims:
exclusive fishing zone: 200 nm
territorial sea: 12 nm
Climate: Saint Helena - tropical; marine; mild, tempered by trade winds; Tristan da Cunha - temperate; marine, mild, tempered by trade winds (tends to be cooler than Saint Helena)
Terrain: Saint Helena - rugged, volcanic; small scattered plateaus and plains

note: the other islands of the group have a volcanic origin
Elevation extremes:
lowest point: Atlantic Ocean 0 m
highest point: Queen Mary's Peak on Tristan da Cunha 2,060 m
Natural resources: fish
Land use:
arable land: 6%
permanent crops: NA%
permanent pastures: 6%
forests and woodland: 6%
other: 82% (1993 est.)
Irrigated land: NA sq km
Natural hazards: active volcanism on Tristan da Cunha
Environment - current issues: NA
Environment - international agreements:
party to: NA
signed, but not ratified: NA
Geography - note: Napoleon Bonaparte's place of exile and burial (his remains were taken to Paris in 1840); harbors at least 40 species of plants unknown anywhere else in the world; Ascension is a breeding ground for sea turtles and sooty terns

People

Population: 7,145 (July 1999 est.)
Age structure:
0-14 years: 20% (male 713; female 690)
15-64 years: 72% (male 2,664; female 2,449)
65 years and over: 8% (male 259; female 370) (1999 est.)
Population growth rate: 0.74% (1999 est.)
Birth rate: 13.86 births/1,000 population (1999 est.)
Death rate: 6.44 deaths/1,000 population (1999 est.)
Net migration rate: 0 migrant(s)/1,000 population (1999 est.)
Sex ratio:
at birth: 1.04 male(s)/female
under 15 years: 1.03 male(s)/female
15-64 years: 1.09 male(s)/female
65 years and over: 0.7 male(s)/female
total population: 1.04 male(s)/female (1999 est.)
Infant mortality rate: 27.98 deaths/1,000 live births (1999 est.)
Life expectancy at birth:
total population: 75.88 years
male: 72.78 years
female: 79.13 years (1999 est.)
Total fertility rate: 1.5 children born/woman (1999 est.)
Nationality:
noun: Saint Helenian(s)
adjective: Saint Helenian
Ethnic groups: African descent, white
Religions: Anglican (majority), Baptist, Seventh-Day Adventist, Roman Catholic
Languages: English
Literacy:
definition: age 20 and over can read and write
total population: 97%

Saint Helena (continued)

male: 97%
female: 98% (1987 est.)

Country name:
conventional long form: none
conventional short form: Saint Helena
Data code: SH
Dependency status: overseas territory of the UK
Government type: NA
Capital: Jamestown
Administrative divisions: 1 administrative area and 2 dependencies*; Ascension*, Saint Helena, Tristan da Cunha*
Independence: none (overseas territory of the UK)
National holiday: Celebration of the Birthday of the Queen (second Saturday in June)
Constitution: 1 January 1989
Legal system: NA
Suffrage: NA years of age
Executive branch:
chief of state: Queen ELIZABETH II (since 6 February 1952)
head of government: Governor and Commander in Chief David Leslie SMALLMAN (since NA 1995)
cabinet: Executive Council consists of the governor, two ex officio officers, and six elected members of the Legislative Council
elections: none; the monarch is hereditary; governor is appointed by the monarch
Legislative branch: unicameral Legislative Council (15 seats, including the governor, 2 ex officio and 12 elected members; members are elected by popular vote to serve four-year terms)
elections: last held 9 July 1997 (next to be held NA July 2001)
election results: percent of vote - NA; seats - independents 15
Judicial branch: Supreme Court
Political parties and leaders: none
International organization participation: ICFTU
Diplomatic representation in the US: none (overseas territory of the UK)
Diplomatic representation from the US: none (overseas territory of the UK)
Flag description: blue with the flag of the UK in the upper hoist-side quadrant and the Saint Helenian shield centered on the outer half of the flag; the shield features a rocky coastline and three-masted sailing ship

Economy - overview: The economy depends largely on financial assistance from the UK, which amounted to about $5 million in 1998. The local population earns income from fishing, the raising of livestock, and sales of handicrafts. Because there are few jobs, a large proportion of the work force has left to seek employment overseas.
GDP: purchasing power parity - $13.9 million (FY94/95 est.)

GDP - real growth rate: NA%
GDP - per capita: purchasing power parity - $2,000 (FY94/95 est.)
GDP - composition by sector:
agriculture: NA%
industry: NA%
services: NA%
Population below poverty line: NA%
Household income or consumption by percentage share:
lowest 10%: NA%
highest 10%: NA%
Inflation rate (consumer prices): NA%
Labor force: 2,416 (1991 est.)
note: a large proportion of the work force has left to seek employment overseas
Labor force - by occupation: professional, technical, and related workers 8.7%, managerial, administrative, and clerical 12.8%, sales people 8.1%, farmers, fishermen 5.4%, craftspersons, production process workers 14.7%, others 50.3% (1987)
Unemployment rate: NA%
Budget:
revenues: $11.2 million
expenditures: $11 million, including capital expenditures of $NA (FY92/93)
Industries: crafts (furniture, lacework, fancy woodwork), fishing
Industrial production growth rate: NA%
Electricity - production: 6 million kWh (1996)
Electricity - production by source:
fossil fuel: 100%
hydro: 0%
nuclear: 0%
other: 0% (1996)
Electricity - consumption: 6 million kWh (1996)
Electricity - exports: 0 kWh (1996)
Electricity - imports: 0 kWh (1996)
Agriculture - products: maize, potatoes, vegetables; timber; fish, crawfish (on Tristan da Cunha)
Exports: $704,000 (f.o.b., 1995)
Exports - commodities: fish (frozen, canned, and salt-dried skipjack, tuna), coffee, handicrafts
Exports - partners: South Africa, UK
Imports: $14.434 million (c.i.f., 1995)
Imports - commodities: food, beverages, tobacco, fuel oils, animal feed, building materials, motor vehicles and parts, machinery and parts
Imports - partners: UK, South Africa
Debt - external: $NA
Economic aid - recipient: $12.6 million (1995); note - $5.3 million from UK (1997)
Currency: 1 Saint Helenian pound (£S) = 100 pence
Exchange rates: Saint Helenian pounds (£S) per US$1 - 0.6057 (January 1999), 0.6037 (1998), 0.6047 (1997), 0.6403 (1996), 0.6335 (1995), 0.6529 (1994); note - the Saint Helenian pound is at par with the British pound
Fiscal year: 1 April - 31 March

Telephones: 550
Telephone system:
domestic: automatic network; HF radiotelephone from Saint Helena to Ascension, then into worldwide submarine cable and satellite networks
international: major coaxial submarine cable relay point between South Africa, Portugal, and UK at Ascension; satellite earth stations - 2 Intelsat (Atlantic Ocean)
Radio broadcast stations: AM 1, FM 0, shortwave 0
Radios: 2,500 (1993 est.)
Television broadcast stations: 0 (1997)
Televisions: NA
Communications - note: Gough Island has a meteorological station

Railways: 0 km
Highways:
total: NA km (Saint Helena 118 km, Ascension NA km, Tristan da Cunha NA km)
paved: 180.7 km (Saint Helena 98 km, Ascension 80 km, Tristan da Cunha 2.70 km)
unpaved: NA km (Saint Helena 20 km, Ascension NA km, Tristan da Cunha NA km)
Ports and harbors: Georgetown (on Ascension), Jamestown
Merchant marine: none
Airports: 1 (1998 est.)
Airports - with paved runways:
total: 1
over 3,047 m: 1 (1998 est.)

Military - note: defense is the responsibility of the UK

Disputes - international: none

Saint Kitts and Nevis

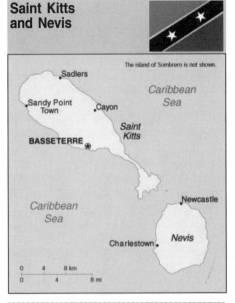

The island of Sombrero is not shown.

Map labels: Sadlers, Sandy Point Town, Cayon, BASSETERRE, Saint Kitts, Caribbean Sea, Newcastle, Charlestown, Nevis, Caribbean Sea

0 4 8 km
0 4 8 mi

Geography

Location: Caribbean, islands in the Caribbean Sea, about one-third of the way from Puerto Rico to Trinidad and Tobago

Geographic coordinates: 17 20 N, 62 45 W

Map references: Central America and the Caribbean

Area:
total: 269 sq km
land: 269 sq km
water: 0 sq km

Area - comparative: 1.5 times the size of Washington, DC

Land boundaries: 0 km

Coastline: 135 km

Maritime claims:
continental shelf: 200 nm or to the edge of the continental margin
territorial sea: 12 nm
contiguous zone: 24 nm
exclusive economic zone: 200 nm

Climate: subtropical tempered by constant sea breezes; little seasonal temperature variation; rainy season (May to November)

Terrain: volcanic with mountainous interiors

Elevation extremes:
lowest point: Caribbean Sea 0 m
highest point: Mount Liamuiga 1,156 m

Natural resources: NEGL

Land use:
arable land: 22%
permanent crops: 17%
permanent pastures: 3%
forests and woodland: 17%
other: 41% (1993 est.)

Irrigated land: NA sq km

Natural hazards: hurricanes (July to October)

Environment - current issues: NA

Environment - international agreements:
party to: Biodiversity, Climate Change, Desertification, Endangered Species, Hazardous Wastes, Law of the Sea, Ozone Layer Protection, Whaling
signed, but not ratified: none of the selected agreements

People

Population: 42,838 (July 1999 est.)

Age structure:
0-14 years: 33% (male 7,178; female 6,826)
15-64 years: 61% (male 13,226; female 13,083)
65 years and over: 6% (male 1,020; female 1,505) (1999 est.)

Population growth rate: 1.34% (1999 est.)

Birth rate: 22.6 births/1,000 population (1999 est.)

Death rate: 8.15 deaths/1,000 population (1999 est.)

Net migration rate: -1.05 migrant(s)/1,000 population (1999 est.)

Sex ratio:
at birth: 1.06 male(s)/female
under 15 years: 1.05 male(s)/female
15-64 years: 1.01 male(s)/female
65 years and over: 0.68 male(s)/female
total population: 1 male(s)/female (1999 est.)

Infant mortality rate: 17.39 deaths/1,000 live births (1999 est.)

Life expectancy at birth:
total population: 67.94 years
male: 64.87 years
female: 71.21 years (1999 est.)

Total fertility rate: 2.42 children born/woman (1999 est.)

Nationality:
noun: Kittitian(s), Nevisian(s)
adjective: Kittitian, Nevisian

Ethnic groups: black

Religions: Anglican, other Protestant sects, Roman Catholic

Languages: English

Literacy:
definition: age 15 and over has ever attended school
total population: 97%
male: 97%
female: 98% (1980 est.)

Government

Country name:
conventional long form: Federation of Saint Kitts and Nevis
conventional short form: Saint Kitts and Nevis
former: Federation of Saint Christopher and Nevis

Data code: SC

Government type: constitutional monarchy

Capital: Basseterre

Administrative divisions: 14 parishes; Christ Church Nichola Town, Saint Anne Sandy Point, Saint George Basseterre, Saint George Gingerland, Saint James Windward, Saint John Capisterre, Saint John Figtree, Saint Mary Cayon, Saint Paul Capisterre, Saint Paul Charlestown, Saint Peter Basseterre, Saint Thomas Lowland, Saint Thomas Middle Island, Trinity Palmetto Point

Independence: 19 September 1983 (from UK)

National holiday: Independence Day, 19 September (1983)

Constitution: 19 September 1983

Legal system: based on English common law

Suffrage: 18 years of age; universal

Executive branch:
chief of state: Queen ELIZABETH II (since 6 February 1952), represented by Governor General Dr. Cuthbert Montraville SEBASTIAN (since 1 January 1996)
head of government: Prime Minister Dr. Denzil DOUGLAS (since 6 July 1995) and Deputy Prime Minister Sam CONDOR (since 6 July 1995)
cabinet: Cabinet appointed by the governor general in consultation with the prime minister
elections: none; the monarch is hereditary; the governor general is appointed by the monarch; following legislative elections, the leader of the majority party or leader of a majority coalition is usually appointed prime minister by the governor general; deputy prime minister appointed by the governor general

Legislative branch: unicameral House of Assembly (14 seats, 11 popularly elected from single-member constituencies; members serve five-year terms)
elections: last held 3 July 1995 (next to be held by July 2000)
election results: percent of vote by party - SKLNP 58%, PAM 41%; seats by party - SKNLP 7, PAM 1, NRP 1, CCM 2

Judicial branch: Eastern Caribbean Supreme Court (based on Saint Lucia) (one judge of the Supreme Court resides in Saint Kitts)

Political parties and leaders: People's Action Movement or PAM [Dr. Kennedy SIMMONDS]; Saint Kitts and Nevis Labor Party or SKNLP [Dr. Denzil DOUGLAS]; Nevis Reformation Party or NRP [Joseph PARRY]; Concerned Citizens Movement or CCM [Vance AMORY]

International organization participation: ACP, C, Caricom, CDB, ECLAC, FAO, G-77, IBRD, ICFTU, ICRM, IDA, IFAD, IFC, IFRCS, ILO, IMF, Interpol, IOC, OAS, OECS, OPANAL, OPCW, UN, UNCTAD, UNESCO, UNIDO, UPU, WCL, WHO, WIPO, WTrO

Diplomatic representation in the US:
chief of mission: Ambassador Edwards ERSTEIN
chancery: 3216 New Mexico Avenue NW, Washington, DC 20016
telephone: [1] (202) 686-2636
FAX: [1] (202) 686-5740

Diplomatic representation from the US: the US does not have an embassy in Saint Kitts and Nevis; US interests are monitored by the embassy in Bridgetown (Barbados)

Flag description: divided diagonally from the lower hoist side by a broad black band bearing two white, five-pointed stars; the black band is edged in yellow; the upper triangle is green, the lower triangle is red

Saint Kitts and Nevis *(continued)*

Economy

Economy - overview: The economy has traditionally depended on the growing and processing of sugarcane; decreasing world prices have hurt the industry in recent years. Tourism, export-oriented manufacturing, and offshore banking activity have assumed larger roles. Most food is imported. The government has undertaken a program designed to revitalize the faltering sugar sector. It is also working to improve revenue collection in order to better fund social programs. In 1997 some leaders in Nevis were urging separation from Saint Kitts on the basis that Nevis was paying far more in taxes than it was receiving in government services, but the vote on cessation failed in August 1998. In late September 1998, Hurricane Georges caused approximately $445 million in damages.

GDP: purchasing power parity - $235 million (1997 est.)

GDP - real growth rate: 6.3% (1997 est.)

GDP - per capita: purchasing power parity - $6,000 (1997 est.)

GDP - composition by sector:
agriculture: 5.5%
industry: 22.5%
services: 72% (1996)

Population below poverty line: NA%

Household income or consumption by percentage share:
lowest 10%: NA%
highest 10%: NA%

Inflation rate (consumer prices): 11.3% (1997)

Labor force: 18,172 (June 1995)

Labor force - by occupation: services 69%, manufacturing 31%

Unemployment rate: 4% (1997 est.)

Budget:
revenues: $64.1 million
expenditures: $73.3 million, including capital expenditures of $10.4 million (1997 est.)

Industries: sugar processing, tourism, cotton, salt, copra, clothing, footwear, beverages

Industrial production growth rate: NA%

Electricity - production: 81 million kWh (1996)

Electricity - production by source:
fossil fuel: 100%
hydro: 0%
nuclear: 0%
other: 0% (1996)

Electricity - consumption: 81 million kWh (1996)

Electricity - exports: 0 kWh (1996)

Electricity - imports: 0 kWh (1996)

Agriculture - products: sugarcane, rice, yams, vegetables, bananas; fish

Exports: $43.7 million (1997)

Exports - commodities: machinery, food, electronics, beverages and tobacco

Exports - partners: US 68.5%, UK 22.3%, Caricom nations 5.5% (1995 est.)

Imports: $129.6 million (1997)

Imports - commodities: machinery, manufactures, food, fuels

Imports - partners: US 42.4%, Caricom nations 17.2%, UK 11.3% (1995 est.)

Debt - external: $56 million (1995 est.)

Economic aid - recipient: $5.5 million (1995)

Currency: 1 East Caribbean dollar (EC$) = 100 cents

Exchange rates: East Caribbean dollars (EC$) per US$1 - 2.7000 (fixed rate since 1976)

Fiscal year: calendar year

Communications

Telephones: 3,800 (1986 est.)

Telephone system: good interisland VHF/UHF/SHF radiotelephone connections and international link via Antigua and Barbuda and Saint Martin (Guadeloupe and Netherlands Antilles)
domestic: interisland links are handled by VHF/UHF/SHF radiotelephone
international: international calls are carried by radiotelephone to Antigua and Barbuda and from there switched to submarine cable or to Intelsat, or carried to Saint Martin (Guadeloupe and Netherlands Antilles) by radiotelephone and switched to Intelsat

Radio broadcast stations: AM 2, FM 0, shortwave 0

Radios: 25,000 (1993 est.)

Television broadcast stations: 1 (in addition, there are three repeaters) (1997)

Televisions: 9,500 (1993 est.)

Transportation

Railways:
total: 58 km
narrow gauge: 58 km 0.762-m gauge on Saint Kitts to serve sugarcane plantations (1995)

Highways:
total: 320 km
paved: 136 km
unpaved: 184 km (1996 est.)

Ports and harbors: Basseterre, Charlestown

Merchant marine: none

Airports: 2 (1998 est.)

Airports - with paved runways:
total: 2
1,524 to 2,437 m: 1
914 to 1,523 m: 1 (1998 est.)

Military

Military branches: Royal Saint Kitts and Nevis Defense Force, Royal Saint Kitts and Nevis Police Force, Coast Guard

Military expenditures - dollar figure: $NA

Military expenditures - percent of GDP: NA%

Transnational Issues

Disputes - international: none

Illicit drugs: transshipment points for South American drugs destined for the US

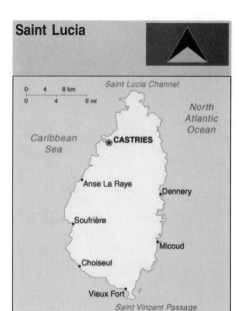

Saint Lucia

Geography

Location: Caribbean, island between the Caribbean Sea and North Atlantic Ocean, north of Trinidad and Tobago

Geographic coordinates: 13 53 N, 60 68 W

Map references: Central America and the Caribbean

Area:
total: 620 sq km
land: 610 sq km
water: 10 sq km

Area - comparative: 3.5 times the size of Washington, DC

Land boundaries: 0 km

Coastline: 158 km

Maritime claims: 200 nm
contiguous zone: 24 nm
exclusive economic zone: 200 nm
territorial sea: 12 nm

Climate: tropical, moderated by northeast trade winds; dry season from January to April, rainy season from May to August

Terrain: volcanic and mountainous with some broad, fertile valleys

Elevation extremes:
lowest point: Caribbean Sea 0 m
highest point: Mount Gimie 950 m

Natural resources: forests, sandy beaches, minerals (pumice), mineral springs, geothermal potential

Land use:
arable land: 8%
permanent crops: 21%
permanent pastures: 5%
forests and woodland: 13%
other: 53% (1993 est.)

Irrigated land: 10 sq km (1993 est.)

Natural hazards: hurricanes and volcanic activity

Environment - current issues: deforestation; soil erosion, particularly in the northern region

Saint Lucia (continued)

Environment - international agreements:
party to: Biodiversity, Climate Change, Desertification, Endangered Species, Environmental Modification, Hazardous Wastes, Law of the Sea, Marine Dumping, Ozone Layer Protection, Whaling *signed, but not ratified:* Climate Change-Kyoto Protocol

People

Population: 154,020 (July 1999 est.)
Age structure:
0-14 years: 33% (male 26,068; female 25,359)
15-64 years: 61% (male 46,265; female 48,100)
65 years and over: 6% (male 3,097; female 5,131) (1999 est.)
Population growth rate: 1.09% (1999 est.)
Birth rate: 21.63 births/1,000 population (1999 est.)
Death rate: 5.58 deaths/1,000 population (1999 est.)
Net migration rate: -5.19 migrant(s)/1,000 population (1999 est.)
Sex ratio:
at birth: 1.07 male(s)/female
under 15 years: 1.03 male(s)/female
15-64 years: 0.96 male(s)/female
65 years and over: 0.6 male(s)/female
total population: 0.96 male(s)/female (1999 est.)
Infant mortality rate: 16.55 deaths/1,000 live births (1999 est.)
Life expectancy at birth:
total population: 71.81 years
male: 68.14 years
female: 75.74 years (1999 est.)
Total fertility rate: 2.27 children born/woman (1999 est.)
Nationality:
noun: Saint Lucian(s)
adjective: Saint Lucian
Ethnic groups: black 90%, mixed 6%, East Indian 3%, white 1%
Religions: Roman Catholic 90%, Protestant 7%, Anglican 3%
Languages: English (official), French patois
Literacy:
definition: age 15 and over has ever attended school
total population: 67%
male: 65%
female: 69% (1980 est.)

Government

Country name:
conventional long form: none
conventional short form: Saint Lucia
Data code: ST
Government type: constitutional monarchy
Capital: Castries
Administrative divisions: 11 quarters; Anse-la-Raye, Castries, Choiseul, Dauphin, Dennery, Gros Islet, Laborie, Micoud, Praslin, Soufriere, Vieux Fort
Independence: 22 February 1979 (from UK)
National holiday: Independence Day, 22 February (1979)

Constitution: 22 February 1979
Legal system: based on English common law
Suffrage: 18 years of age; universal
Executive branch:
chief of state: Queen ELIZABETH II (since 6 February 1952), represented by Governor General Dr. Perlette LOUISY (since September 1997)
head of government: Prime Minister Kenny ANTHONY (since 24 May 1997) and Deputy Prime Minister Mario MICHEL (since 24 May 1997)
cabinet: Cabinet appointed by the governor general on the advice of the prime minister
elections: none; the monarch is hereditary; the governor general is appointed by the monarch; following legislative elections, the leader of the majority party or leader of a majority coalition is usually appointed prime minister by the governor general
Legislative branch: bicameral Parliament consists of the Senate (an 11-member body, six appointed on the advice of the prime minister, three on the advice of the leader of the opposition, and two after consultation with religious, economic, and social groups) and the House of Assembly (17 seats; members are elected by popular vote from single-member constituencies to serve five-year terms)
elections: House of Assembly - last held 23 May 1997 (next to be held NA 2002)
election results: House of Assembly - percent of vote by party - NA; seats by party - SLP 16, UWP 1
Judicial branch: Eastern Caribbean Supreme Court (jurisdiction extends to Anguilla, Antigua and Barbuda, the British Virgin Islands, Dominica, Grenada, Montserrat, Saint Kitts and Nevis, Saint Lucia, and Saint Vincent and the Grenadines)
Political parties and leaders: United Workers Party or UWP [leader NA]; Saint Lucia Labor Party or SLP [Kenneth ANTHONY]; National Freedom Party or NFP [Martinus FRANCOIS]
International organization participation: ACCT (associate), ACP, C, Caricom, CDB, ECLAC, FAO, G-77, IBRD, ICAO, ICFTU, ICRM, IDA, IFAD, IFC, IFRCS, ILO, IMF, IMO, Intelsat (nonsignatory user), Interpol, IOC, ISO (subscriber), ITU, NAM, OAS, OECS, OPANAL, OPCW, UN, UNCTAD, UNESCO, UNIDO, UPU, WCL, WFTU, WHO, WIPO, WMO, WTrO
Diplomatic representation in the US:
chief of mission: Ambassador (vacant); Charge d'Affaires Juliet Elaine MALLET PHILLIP
chancery: 3216 New Mexico Avenue NW, Washington, DC 20016
telephone: [1] (202) 364-6792 through 6795
FAX: [1] (202) 364-6728
consulate(s) general: New York
Diplomatic representation from the US: the US does not have an embassy in Saint Lucia; the Ambassador to Saint Lucia resides in Bridgetown (Barbados)
Flag description: blue, with a gold isosceles triangle below a black arrowhead; the upper edges of the arrowhead have a white border

Economy

Economy - overview: The economy remains vulnerable due to its heavy dependence on banana production, which is subject to periodic droughts and tropical storms. Increased competition from Latin American bananas will probably further reduce market prices, exacerbating Saint Lucia's need to diversify its economy in coming years, e.g., by further expanding tourism, manufacturing, and construction. In 1997, strong activity in tourism and other service sectors offset the contraction in agriculture, manufacturing, and construction sectors. Improvement in the construction sector and growth of the tourism industry was expected to expand GDP in 1998. The agriculture sector registered its fifth year of decline in 1997 primarily because of a severe decline in banana production.
GDP: purchasing power parity - $625 million (1997 est.)
GDP - real growth rate: 2.2% (1997)
GDP - per capita: purchasing power parity - $4,100 (1997 est.)
GDP - composition by sector:
agriculture: 10.7%
industry: 32.3%
services: 57% (1996 est.)
Population below poverty line: NA%
Household income or consumption by percentage share:
lowest 10%: NA%
highest 10%: NA%
Inflation rate (consumer prices): 1.9% (1997)
Labor force: 43,800
Labor force - by occupation: agriculture 43.4%, services 38.9%, industry and commerce 17.7% (1983 est.)
Unemployment rate: 15% (1996 est.)
Budget:
revenues: $141.2 million
expenditures: $146.7 million, including capital expenditures of $25.1 million (FY97/98 est.)
Industries: clothing, assembly of electronic components, beverages, corrugated cardboard boxes, tourism, lime processing, coconut processing
Industrial production growth rate: -8.9% (1997 est.)
Electricity - production: 110 million kWh (1996)
Electricity - production by source:
fossil fuel: 100%
hydro: 0%
nuclear: 0%
other: 0% (1996)
Electricity - consumption: 110 million kWh (1996)
Electricity - exports: 0 kWh (1996)
Electricity - imports: 0 kWh (1996)
Agriculture - products: bananas, coconuts, vegetables, citrus, root crops, cocoa
Exports: $70.1 million (1997)
Exports - commodities: bananas 41%, clothing, cocoa, vegetables, fruits, coconut oil

Saint Lucia (continued)

Exports - partners: UK 50%, US 24%, Caricom countries 16% (1995)
Imports: $292.4 million (1997)
Imports - commodities: food 23%, manufactured goods 21%, machinery and transportation equipment 19%, chemicals, fuels
Imports - partners: US 36%, Caricom countries 22%, UK 11%, Japan 5%, Canada 4% (1995)
Debt - external: $159 million (1997)
Economic aid - recipient: $51.8 million (1995)
Currency: 1 East Caribbean dollar (EC$) = 100 cents
Exchange rates: East Caribbean dollars (EC$) per US$1 - 2.7000 (fixed rate since 1976)
Fiscal year: 1 April - 31 March

Communications

Telephones: 26,000 (1992 est.)
Telephone system:
domestic: system is automatically switched
international: direct microwave radio relay link with Martinique and Saint Vincent and the Grenadines; tropospheric scatter to Barbados; international calls beyond these countries are carried by Intelsat from Martinique
Radio broadcast stations: AM 4, FM 1, shortwave 0
Radios: 104,000 (1992 est.)
Television broadcast stations: 3 (of which two are commercial stations and one is a community antenna television [CATV] channel) (1997)
Televisions: 26,000 (1992 est.)

Transportation

Railways: 0 km
Highways:
total: 1,210 km
paved: 63 km
unpaved: 1,147 km (1996 est.)
Ports and harbors: Castries, Vieux Fort
Merchant marine: none
Airports: 2 (1998 est.)
Airports - with paved runways:
total: 2
2,438 to 3,047 m: 1
1,524 to 2,437 m: 1 (1998 est.)

Military

Military branches: Royal Saint Lucia Police Force (includes Special Service Unit), Coast Guard
Military expenditures - dollar figure: $5 million (1991); note - for police force
Military expenditures - percent of GDP: 2% (1991)

Transnational Issues

Disputes - international: none
Illicit drugs: transit point for South American drugs destined for the US and Europe

---

Saint Pierre and Miquelon
(territorial collectivity of France)

Geography

Location: Northern North America, islands in the North Atlantic Ocean, south of Newfoundland (Canada)
Geographic coordinates: 46 50 N, 56 20 W
Map references: North America
Area:
total: 242 sq km
land: 242 sq km
water: 0 sq km
note: includes eight small islands in the Saint Pierre and the Miquelon groups
Area - comparative: 1.5 times the size of Washington, DC
Land boundaries: 0 km
Coastline: 120 km
Maritime claims:
exclusive economic zone: 200 nm
territorial sea: 12 nm
Climate: cold and wet, with much mist and fog; spring and autumn are windy
Terrain: mostly barren rock
Elevation extremes:
lowest point: Atlantic Ocean 0 m
highest point: Morne de la Grande Montagne 240 m
Natural resources: fish, deepwater ports
Land use:
arable land: 13%
permanent crops: NA%
permanent pastures: NA%
forests and woodland: 4%
other: 83% (1993 est.)
Irrigated land: NA sq km
Natural hazards: persistent fog throughout the year can be a maritime hazard
Environment - current issues: NA
Environment - international agreements:
party to: NA
signed, but not ratified: NA

Geography - note: vegetation scanty

People

Population: 6,966 (July 1999 est.)
Age structure:
0-14 years: NA
15-64 years: NA
65 years and over: NA
Population growth rate: 0.75% (1999 est.)
Birth rate: 12.27 births/1,000 population (1999 est.)
Death rate: 5.41 deaths/1,000 population (1999 est.)
Net migration rate: 0.59 migrant(s)/1,000 population (1999 est.)
Infant mortality rate: 8.12 deaths/1,000 live births (1999 est.)
Life expectancy at birth:
total population: 77.13 years
male: 75.58 years
female: 79 years (1999 est.)
Total fertility rate: 1.58 children born/woman (1999 est.)
Nationality:
noun: Frenchman(men), Frenchwoman(women)
adjective: French
Ethnic groups: Basques and Bretons (French fishermen)
Religions: Roman Catholic 99%
Languages: French
Literacy:
definition: age 15 and over can read and write
total population: 99%
male: 99%
female: 99% (1982 est.)

Government

Country name:
conventional long form: Territorial Collectivity of Saint Pierre and Miquelon
conventional short form: Saint Pierre and Miquelon
local long form: Departement de Saint-Pierre et Miquelon
local short form: Saint-Pierre et Miquelon
Data code: SB
Dependency status: self-governing territorial collectivity of France
Government type: NA
Capital: Saint-Pierre
Administrative divisions: none (territorial collectivity of France)
note: there are no first-order administrative divisions approved by the US Government, but there are two communes - Saint Pierre, Miquelon
Independence: none (territorial collectivity of France; has been under French control since 1763)
National holiday: National Day, Taking of the Bastille, 14 July (1789)
Constitution: 28 September 1958 (French Constitution)
Legal system: French law with special adaptations for local conditions, such as housing and taxation
Suffrage: 18 years of age; universal

Saint Pierre and Miquelon *(continued)*

Executive branch:

chief of state: President Jacques CHIRAC of France (since 17 May 1995), represented by Prefect Remi THUAU (since NA)

head of government: President of the General Council Bernard LE SOAVEC (since NA 1996)

cabinet: NA

elections: French president elected by popular vote for a seven-year term; prefect appointed by the French president on the advice of the French Ministry of Interior; president of the General Council is elected by the members of the council

Legislative branch: unicameral General Council or Conseil General (19 seats - 15 from Saint Pierre and 4 from Miquelon; members are elected by popular vote to serve six-year terms)

elections: elections last held 20 March 1994 (next to be held NA April 2000)

election results: percent of vote by party - NA; seats by party - RPR 15, other 4

note: Saint Pierre and Miquelon elect 1 seat to the French Senate; elections last held NA September 1995 (next to be held NA September 2004); results - percent of vote by party - NA; seats by party - RPR 1; Saint Pierre and Miquelon also elects 1 seat to the French National Assembly; elections last held 25 May-1 June 1997 (next to be held NA 2002); results - percent of vote by party - NA; seats by party - UDF 1

Judicial branch: Superior Tribunal of Appeals or Tribunal Superieur d'Appel

Political parties and leaders: Socialist Party or PS [leader NA]; Rassemblement pour la Republique or RPR [leader NA]; Union pour la Democratie Francaise or UDF [leader NA]

International organization participation: FZ, WFTU

Diplomatic representation in the US: none (territorial collectivity of France)

Diplomatic representation from the US: none (territorial collectivity of France)

Flag description: a yellow sailing ship rides on a dark blue background with a black wave line under the ship; on the hoist side, a vertical band is divided into three parts: the top part is red with a green diagonal cross extending to the corners overlaid by a white cross dividing the square into four sections; the middle part has a white background with an ermine pattern; the third part has a red background with two stylized yellow lions outlined in black, one on top of the other; the flag of France is used for official occasions

Economy

Economy - overview: The inhabitants have traditionally earned their livelihood by fishing and by servicing fishing fleets operating off the coast of Newfoundland. The economy has been declining, however, because the number of ships stopping at Saint Pierre has dropped steadily over the years. In 1992, an arbitration panel awarded the islands an exclusive economic zone of 12,348 sq km to settle a longstanding territorial dispute with Canada, although it represents only 25% of what France had sought.

The islands are heavily subsidized by France. Imports come primarily from Canada and France.

GDP: purchasing power parity - $74 million (1996 est.)

GDP - real growth rate: NA%

GDP - per capita: purchasing power parity - $11,000 (1996 est.)

GDP - composition by sector:

agriculture: NA%

industry: NA%

services: NA%

Population below poverty line: NA%

Household income or consumption by percentage share:

lowest 10%: NA%

highest 10%: NA%

Inflation rate (consumer prices): NA%

Labor force: 3,000 (1996)

Labor force - by occupation: NA

Unemployment rate: 9.8% (1997)

Budget:

revenues: $70 million

expenditures: $60 million, including capital expenditures of $24 million (1996 est.)

Industries: fish processing and supply base for fishing fleets; tourism

Industrial production growth rate: NA%

Electricity - production: 39 million kWh (1996)

Electricity - production by source:

fossil fuel: 100%

hydro: 0%

nuclear: 0%

other: 0% (1996)

Electricity - consumption: 39 million kWh (1996)

Electricity - exports: 0 kWh (1996)

Electricity - imports: 0 kWh (1996)

Agriculture - products: vegetables; cattle, sheep, pigs; fish

Exports: $1.2 million (f.o.b., 1996)

Exports - commodities: fish and fish products, fox and mink pelts

Exports - partners: US 58%, France 17%, UK 11%, Canada, Portugal (1990)

Imports: $60.5 million (c.i.f., 1996)

Imports - commodities: meat, clothing, fuel, electrical equipment, machinery, building materials

Imports - partners: Canada, France, US, Netherlands, UK

Debt - external: $NA

Economic aid - recipient: $NA

Currency: 1 French franc (F) = 100 centimes

Exchange rates: French francs (F) per US$1 - 5.65 (January 1999), 5.8995 (1998), 5.8367 (1997), 5.1155 (1996), 4.9915 (1995), 5.5520 (1994)

Fiscal year: calendar year

Communications

Telephones: 3,650 (1994 est.)

Telephone system:

domestic: NA

international: radiotelephone communication with most countries in the world; 1 earth station in French domestic satellite system

Radio broadcast stations: AM 1, FM 3, shortwave 0

Radios: 3,000 (1992 est.)

Television broadcast stations: 0 (there are, however, two repeaters which rebroadcast programs from France, Canada, and the US) (1997)

Televisions: 2,000 (1992 est.)

Transportation

Railways: 0 km

Highways:

total: 114 km

paved: 69 km

unpaved: 45 km (1994 est.)

Ports and harbors: Saint Pierre

Merchant marine: none

Airports: 2 (1998 est.)

Airports - with paved runways:

total: 2

914 to 1,523 m: 2 (1998 est.)

Military

Military - note: defense is the responsibility of France

Transnational Issues

Disputes - international: none

Saint Vincent and the Grenadines

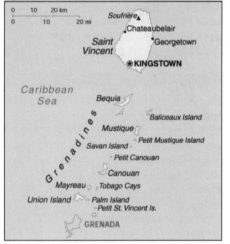

Geography

Location: Caribbean, islands in the Caribbean Sea, north of Trinidad and Tobago
Geographic coordinates: 13 15 N, 61 12 W
Map references: Central America and the Caribbean
Area:
total: 340 sq km
land: 340 sq km
water: 0 sq km
Area - comparative: twice the size of Washington, DC
Land boundaries: 0 km
Coastline: 84 km
Maritime claims:
contiguous zone: 24 nm
continental shelf: 200 nm
exclusive economic zone: 200 nm
territorial sea: 12 nm
Climate: tropical; little seasonal temperature variation; rainy season (May to November)
Terrain: volcanic, mountainous
Elevation extremes:
lowest point: Caribbean Sea 0 m
highest point: Soufriere 1,234 m
Natural resources: NEGL
Land use:
arable land: 10%
permanent crops: 18%
permanent pastures: 5%
forests and woodland: 36%
other: 31% (1993 est.)
Irrigated land: 10 sq km (1993 est.)
Natural hazards: hurricanes; Soufriere volcano on the island of Saint Vincent is a constant threat
Environment - current issues: pollution of coastal waters and shorelines from discharges by pleasure yachts and other effluents; in some areas, pollution is severe enough to make swimming prohibitive
Environment - international agreements:
party to: Biodiversity, Climate Change, Desertification, Endangered Species, Hazardous Wastes, Law of the Sea, Ozone Layer Protection, Ship Pollution, Whaling
signed, but not ratified: Climate Change-Kyoto Protocol
Geography - note: the administration of the islands of the Grenadines group is divided between Saint Vincent and the Grenadines and Grenada

People

Population: 120,519 (July 1999 est.)
Age structure:
0-14 years: 30% (male 18,160; female 17,524)
15-64 years: 65% (male 39,448; female 38,672)
65 years and over: 5% (male 2,762; female 3,953) (1999 est.)
Population growth rate: 0.57% (1999 est.)
Birth rate: 18.34 births/1,000 population (1999 est.)
Death rate: 5.23 deaths/1,000 population (1999 est.)
Net migration rate: -7.43 migrant(s)/1,000 population (1999 est.)
Sex ratio:
at birth: 1.03 male(s)/female
under 15 years: 1.04 male(s)/female
15-64 years: 1.02 male(s)/female
65 years and over: 0.7 male(s)/female
total population: 1 male(s)/female (1999 est.)
Infant mortality rate: 15.16 deaths/1,000 live births (1999 est.)
Life expectancy at birth:
total population: 73.8 years
male: 72.29 years
female: 75.36 years (1999 est.)
Total fertility rate: 1.94 children born/woman (1999 est.)
Nationality:
noun: Saint Vincentian(s) or Vincentian(s)
adjective: Saint Vincentian or Vincentian
Ethnic groups: black, white, East Indian, Carib Amerindian
Religions: Anglican, Methodist, Roman Catholic, Seventh-Day Adventist
Languages: English, French patois
Literacy:
definition: age 15 and over has ever attended school
total population: 96%
male: 96%
female: 96% (1970 est.)

Government

Country name:
conventional long form: none
conventional short form: Saint Vincent and the Grenadines
Data code: VC
Government type: constitutional monarchy
Capital: Kingstown
Administrative divisions: 6 parishes; Charlotte, Grenadines, Saint Andrew, Saint David, Saint George, Saint Patrick

Independence: 27 October 1979 (from UK)
National holiday: Independence Day, 27 October (1979)
Constitution: 27 October 1979
Legal system: based on English common law
Suffrage: 18 years of age; universal
Executive branch:
chief of state: Queen ELIZABETH II (since 6 February 1952), represented by Governor General David JACK (since NA)
head of government: Prime Minister James F. MITCHELL (since 30 July 1984)
cabinet: Cabinet appointed by the governor general on the advice of the prime minister
elections: none; the monarch is hereditary; the governor general is appointed by the monarch; following legislative elections, the leader of the majority party is usually appointed prime minister by the governor general; deputy prime minister appointed by the governor general on the advice of the prime minister
Legislative branch: unicameral House of Assembly (21 seats, 15 elected representatives and 6 appointed senators; representatives are elected by popular vote from single-member constituencies to serve five-year terms)
elections: last held 15 June 1998 (next to be held by NA May 2003)
election results: percent of vote by party - NA; seats by party - NDP 8, ULP 7
Judicial branch: Eastern Caribbean Supreme Court (based on Saint Lucia); one judge of the Supreme Court resides in Saint Vincent
Political parties and leaders: New Democratic Party or NDP [James F. MITCHELL]; United People's Movement or UPM [Adrian SAUNDERS]; National Reform Party or NRP [Joel MIGUEL]; Unity Labor Party or ULP [Ralph GONSALVES] (formed by the coalition of Saint Vincent Labor Party or SVLP and the Movement for National Unity or MNU)
International organization participation: ACP, C, Caricom, CDB, ECLAC, FAO, G-77, IBRD, ICAO, ICFTU, ICRM, IDA, IFAD, IFRCS, ILO, IMF, IMO, Intelsat (nonsignatory user), Interpol, IOC, ITU, OAS, OECS, OPANAL, OPCW, UN, UNCTAD, UNESCO, UNIDO, UPU, WCL, WFTU, WHO, WIPO, WTrO
Diplomatic representation in the US:
chief of mission: Ambassador Kingsley C. A. LAYNE
chancery: 3216 New Mexico Avenue NW, Washington, DC 20016
telephone: [1] (202) 364-6730
FAX: [1] (202) 364-6736
Diplomatic representation from the US: the US does not have an embassy in Saint Vincent and the Grenadines; the Ambassador to Saint Vincent and the Grenadines resides in Bridgetown (Barbados)
Flag description: three vertical bands of blue (hoist side), gold (double width), and green; the gold band bears three green diamonds arranged in a V pattern

Saint Vincent and the Grenadines (continued)

Economy

Economy - overview: Agriculture, dominated by banana production, is the most important sector of this lower-middle-income economy. The services sector, based mostly on a growing tourist industry, is also important. The government has been relatively unsuccessful at introducing new industries, and high unemployment rates of 35%-40% continue. The continuing dependence on a single crop represents the biggest obstacle to the islands' development; tropical storms wiped out substantial portions of crops in both 1994 and 1995. The tourism sector has considerable potential for development over the next decade. Recent growth has been stimulated by strong activity in the construction sector and an improvement in tourism.

GDP: purchasing power parity - $289 million (1998 est.)

GDP - real growth rate: 4% (1998 est.)

GDP - per capita: purchasing power parity - $2,400 (1998 est.)

GDP - composition by sector:
agriculture: 10.6%
industry: 17.5%
services: 71.9% (1996 est.)

Population below poverty line: NA%

Household income or consumption by percentage share:
lowest 10%: NA%
highest 10%: NA%

Inflation rate (consumer prices): 3.6% (1996)

Labor force: 67,000 (1984 est.)

Labor force - by occupation: agriculture 26%, industry 17%, services 57% (1980 est.)

Unemployment rate: 35%-40% (1994 est.)

Budget:
revenues: $85.7 million
expenditures: $98.6 million, including capital expenditures of $25.7 million (1997 est.)

Industries: food processing, cement, furniture, clothing, starch

Industrial production growth rate: -0.9% (1997 est.)

Electricity - production: 62 million kWh (1996)

Electricity - production by source:
fossil fuel: 67.74%
hydro: 32.26%
nuclear: 0%
other: 0% (1996)

Electricity - consumption: 62 million kWh (1996)

Electricity - exports: 0 kWh (1996)

Electricity - imports: 0 kWh (1996)

Agriculture - products: bananas, coconuts, sweet potatoes, spices; small numbers of cattle, sheep, pigs, goats; fish

Exports: $47.3 million (1997)

Exports - commodities: bananas 39%, eddoes and dasheen (taro), arrowroot starch, tennis racquets

Exports - partners: Caricom countries 49%, UK 16%, US 10% (1995)

Imports: $158.8 million (1997)

Imports - commodities: foodstuffs, machinery and equipment, chemicals and fertilizers, minerals and fuels

Imports - partners: US 36%, Caricom countries 28%, UK 13% (1995)

Debt - external: $83.6 million (1997)

Economic aid - recipient: $47.5 million (1995); note - Stabex (EU) $34.5 million (1998)

Currency: 1 East Caribbean dollar (EC$) = 100 cents

Exchange rates: East Caribbean dollars (EC$) per US$1 - 2.7000 (fixed rate since 1976)

Fiscal year: calendar year

Communications

Telephones: 6,189 (1983 est.)

Telephone system:
domestic: islandwide, fully automatic telephone system; VHF/UHF radiotelephone from Saint Vincent to the other islands of the Grenadines
international: VHF/UHF radiotelephone from Saint Vincent to Barbados; new SHF radiotelephone to Grenada and to Saint Lucia; access to Intelsat earth station in Martinique through Saint Lucia

Radio broadcast stations: AM 2, FM 0, shortwave 0

Radios: 76,000 (1992 est.)

Television broadcast stations: 1 (in addition, there are three repeaters) (1997)

Televisions: 20,600 (1992 est.)

Transportation

Railways: 0 km

Highways:
total: 1,040 km
paved: 320 km
unpaved: 720 km (1996 est.)

Ports and harbors: Kingstown

Merchant marine:
total: 814 ships (1,000 GRT or over) totaling 7,726,930 GRT/11,835,144 DWT
ships by type: barge carrier 1, bulk 138, cargo 402, chemical tanker 26, combination bulk 11, combination ore/oil 7, container 47, liquefied gas tanker 3, livestock carrier 4, multifunction large-load carrier 2, oil tanker 64, passenger 2, refrigerated cargo 40, roll-on/roll-off cargo 51, short-sea passenger 10, specialized tanker 5, vehicle carrier 1
note: a flag of convenience registry; includes ships from 20 countries among which are Croatia 17, Slovenia 7, China 5, Greece 5, UAE 3, Norway 2, Japan 2, and Ukraine 2 (1998 est.)

Airports: 6 (1998 est.)

Airports - with paved runways:
total: 5
914 to 1,523 m: 2
under 914 m: 3 (1998 est.)

Airports - with unpaved runways:
total: 1
under 914 m: 1 (1998 est.)

Military

Military branches: Royal Saint Vincent and the Grenadines Police Force (includes Special Service Unit), Coast Guard

Military expenditures - dollar figure: $NA

Military expenditures - percent of GDP: NA%

Transnational Issues

Disputes - international: none

Illicit drugs: transshipment point for South American drugs destined for the US and Europe

Samoa

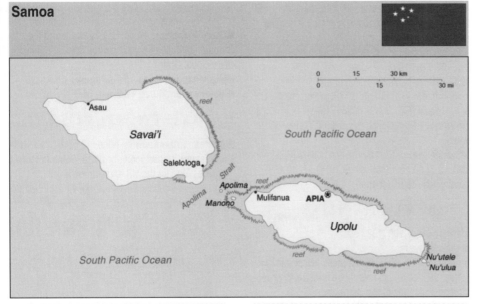

Geography

Location: Oceania, group of islands in the South Pacific Ocean, about one-half of the way from Hawaii to New Zealand

Geographic coordinates: 13 35 S, 172 20 W

Map references: Oceania

Area:
total: 2,860 sq km
land: 2,850 sq km
water: 10 sq km

Area - comparative: slightly smaller than Rhode Island

Land boundaries: 0 km

Coastline: 403 km

Maritime claims:
exclusive economic zone: 200 nm
territorial sea: 12 nm

Climate: tropical; rainy season (October to March), dry season (May to October)

Terrain: narrow coastal plain with volcanic, rocky, rugged mountains in interior

Elevation extremes:
lowest point: Pacific Ocean 0 m
highest point: Mauga Silisili 1,857 m

Natural resources: hardwood forests, fish

Land use:
arable land: 19%
permanent crops: 24%
permanent pastures: 0%
forests and woodland: 47%
other: 10%

Irrigated land: NA sq km

Natural hazards: occasional typhoons; active volcanism

Environment - current issues: soil erosion

Environment - international agreements:
party to: Biodiversity, Climate Change, Desertification, Law of the Sea, Nuclear Test Ban, Ozone Layer Protection
signed, but not ratified: Climate Change-Kyoto Protocol

People

Population: 229,979 (July 1999 est.)
note: other estimates range as low as 162,000

Age structure:
0-14 years: 39% (male 45,647; female 44,141)
15-64 years: 57% (male 68,054; female 62,612)
65 years and over: 4% (male 4,477; female 5,048) (1999 est.)

Population growth rate: 2.3% (1999 est.)

Birth rate: 28.81 births/1,000 population (1999 est.)

Death rate: 5.4 deaths/1,000 population (1999 est.)

Net migration rate: -0.39 migrant(s)/1,000 population (1999 est.)

Sex ratio:
at birth: 1.05 male(s)/female
under 15 years: 1.03 male(s)/female
15-64 years: 1.09 male(s)/female
65 years and over: 0.89 male(s)/female
total population: 1.06 male(s)/female (1999 est.)

Infant mortality rate: 30.5 deaths/1,000 live births (1999 est.)

Life expectancy at birth:
total population: 69.82 years
male: 67.43 years
female: 72.33 years (1999 est.)

Total fertility rate: 3.61 children born/woman (1999 est.)

Nationality:
noun: Samoan(s)
adjective: Samoan

Ethnic groups: Samoan 92.6%, Euronesians 7% (persons of European and Polynesian blood), Europeans 0.4%

Religions: Christian 99.7% (about one-half of population associated with the London Missionary Society; includes Congregational, Roman Catholic, Methodist, Latter-Day Saints, Seventh-Day Adventist)

Languages: Samoan (Polynesian), English

Literacy:
definition: age 15 and over can read and write
total population: 97%

Government

Country name:
conventional long form: Independent State of Samoa
conventional short form: Samoa
former: Western Samoa

Data code: WS

Government type: constitutional monarchy under native chief

Capital: Apia

Administrative divisions: 11 districts; A'ana, Aiga-i-le-Tai, Atua, Fa'asaleleaga, Gaga'emauga, Gagaifomauga, Palauli, Satupa'itea, Tuamasaga, Va'a-o-Fonoti, Vaisigano

Independence: 1 January 1962 (from New Zealand-administered UN trusteeship)

National holiday: National Day, 1 June (1962)

Constitution: 1 January 1962

Legal system: based on English common law and local customs; judicial review of legislative acts with respect to fundamental rights of the citizen; has not accepted compulsory ICJ jurisdiction

Suffrage: 21 years of age; universal

Executive branch:
chief of state: Chief Susuga MALIETOA Tanumafili II (cochief of state from 1 January 1962 until becoming sole chief of state 5 April 1963)
head of government: Prime Minister TUILA'EPA Sailele Malielegaoi (since 24 November 1998); note - TUILA'EPA served as deputy prime minister since 1992; he assumed the prime ministership in November 1998 when former Prime Minister TOFILAU Eti Alesana resigned in poor health; the post of deputy prime minister is currently vacant
cabinet: Cabinet consists of 12 members, appointed by the chief of state with the prime minister's advice
elections: upon the death of Chief Susuga MALIETOA Tanumafili II, a new chief of state will be elected by the Legislative Assembly to serve a five-year term; prime minister appointed by the chief of state with the approval of the Legislative Assembly

Legislative branch: unicameral Legislative Assembly or Fono (49 seats - 47 elected by Samoans, 2 elected by non-Samoans; only chiefs (matai) may stand for election to the Fono; members serve five-year terms)
elections: last held 26 April 1996 (next to be held by NA April 2001)
election results: percent of vote by party - HRPP 45.17%, SNDP 27.1%, independents 23.7%; seats by party - HRPP 25, SNDP 13, independents 11

Judicial branch: Supreme Court; Court of Appeal

Political parties and leaders: Human Rights Protection Party or HRPP [TUILA'EPA Sailele Malielegaoi, chairman]; Samoan National Development Party or SNDP [TAPUA Tamasese Efi, chairman] (opposition); Samoan Progressive Conservative Party [LEOTA Ituau Ale]; Samoa All People's Party or SAPP [Matatumua MAIMOAGA]

International organization participation: ACP,

Samoa (continued)

AsDB, C, ESCAP, FAO, G-77, IBRD, ICAO, ICFTU, ICRM, IDA, IFAD, IFC, IFRCS, IMF, IMO, Intelsat (nonsignatory user), IOC, ITU, OPCW, Sparteca, SPC, SPF, UN, UNCTAD, UNESCO, UPU, WHO, WIPO, WMO

Diplomatic representation in the US:
chief of mission: Ambassador Tuiloma Neroni SLADE
chancery: 820 Second Avenue, Suite 800D, New York, NY 10017
telephone: [1] (212) 599-6196, 6197
FAX: [1] (212) 599-0797

Diplomatic representation from the US:
chief of mission: Ambassador Josiah Horton BEEMAN (Ambassador to New Zealand and Samoa, resides in Wellington, New Zealand)
embassy: 5th floor, Beach Road, Apia
mailing address: P.O. Box 3430, Apia
telephone: [685] 21631
FAX: [685] 22030

Flag description: red with a blue rectangle in the upper hoist-side quadrant bearing five white five-pointed stars representing the Southern Cross constellation

Economy

Economy - overview: The economy of Samoa has traditionally been dependent on development aid, private family remittances from overseas, and agricultural exports. The country is vulnerable to devastating storms. Agriculture employs two-thirds of the labor force, and furnishes 90% of exports, featuring coconut cream, coconut oil, and copra. Outside of a large automotive wire harness factory, the manufacturing sector mainly processes agricultural products. Tourism is an expanding sector; more than 70,0000 tourists visited the islands in 1996. The Samoan Government has called for deregulation of the financial sector, encouragement of investment, and continued fiscal discipline. Observers point to the flexibility of the labor market as a basic strength for future economic advances.

GDP: purchasing power parity - $470 million (1997 est.)
GDP - real growth rate: 3.4% (1997 est.)
GDP - per capita: purchasing power parity - $2,100 (1997 est.)
GDP - composition by sector:
agriculture: 40%
industry: 25%
services: 35% (1996 est.)
Population below poverty line: NA%
Household income or consumption by percentage share:
lowest 10%: NA%
highest 10%: NA%
Inflation rate (consumer prices): 2.2% (1998 est.)
Labor force: 82,500 (1991 est.)
Labor force - by occupation: agriculture 65%, services 30%, industry 5% (1995 est.)
Unemployment rate: NA%
Budget:
revenues: $52 million

expenditures: $99 million, including capital expenditures of $37 million (FY96/97 est.)
Industries: timber, tourism, food processing, fishing
Industrial production growth rate: 14% (1996 est.)
Electricity - production: 65 million kWh (1996)
Electricity - production by source:
fossil fuel: 61.54%
hydro: 38.46%
nuclear: 0%
other: 0% (1996)
Electricity - consumption: 65 million kWh (1996)
Electricity - exports: 0 kWh (1996)
Electricity - imports: 0 kWh (1996)
Agriculture - products: coconuts, bananas, taro, yams
Exports: $14.6 million (f.o.b., 1997)
Exports - commodities: coconut oil and cream, copra, fish, beer
Exports - partners: Australia 82%, New Zealand 6%, Slovakia, Germany, American Samoa (1996)
Imports: $99.7 million (f.o.b., 1997)
Imports - commodities: intermediate goods, food, capital goods
Imports - partners: Australia 33%, New Zealand 25%, Japan 15%, Fiji 8%, US 8% (1996)
Debt - external: $167 million (1996 est.)
Economic aid - recipient: $42.9 million (1995)
Currency: 1 tala (WS$) = 100 sene
Exchange rates: tala (WS$) per US$1 - 2.9011 (January 1999), 2.9429 (1998), 2.5562 (1997), 2.4618 (1996), 2.4722 (1995), 2.5349 (1994)
Fiscal year: calendar year

Communications

Telephones: 7,500 (1988 est.)
Telephone system:
domestic: NA
international: satellite earth station - 1 Intelsat (Pacific Ocean)
Radio broadcast stations: AM 1, FM 0, shortwave 0
Radios: 76,000 (1992 est.)
Television broadcast stations: 6 (1997)
Televisions: 6,000 (1992 est.)

Transportation

Railways: 0 km
Highways:
total: 790 km
paved: 332 km
unpaved: 458 km (1996 est.)
Ports and harbors: Apia, Asau, Mulifanua, Salelologa
Airports: 3 (1998 est.)
Airports - with paved runways:
total: 1
2,438 to 3,047 m: 1 (1998 est.)
Airports - with unpaved runways:
total: 2
under 914 m: 2 (1998 est.)

Military

Military branches: no regular armed services; Samoa Police Force
Military expenditures - dollar figure: $NA
Military expenditures - percent of GDP: NA%
Military - note: Samoa has no formal defense structure or regular armed forces; informal defense ties exist with NZ, which is required to consider any Samoan request for assistance under the 1962 Treaty of Friendship

Transnational Issues

Disputes - international: none

San Marino

ITALY

La Dogana
Serravalle
Domagnano
Acquaviva
Borgo Maggiore
⊛ SAN MARINO
Faetano
Chiesanuova
Fiorentino
ITALY

Geography

Location: Southern Europe, an enclave in central Italy
Geographic coordinates: 43 46 N, 12 25 E
Map references: Europe
Area:
total: 60 sq km
land: 60 sq km
water: 0 sq km
Area - comparative: about 0.3 times the size of Washington, DC
Land boundaries:
total: 39 km
border countries: Italy 39 km
Coastline: 0 km (landlocked)
Maritime claims: none (landlocked)
Climate: Mediterranean; mild to cool winters; warm, sunny summers
Terrain: rugged mountains
Elevation extremes:
lowest point: Torrente Ausa 55 m
highest point: Monte Titano 749 m
Natural resources: building stone
Land use:
arable land: 17%
permanent crops: NA%
permanent pastures: NA%
forests and woodland: NA%
other: 83% (1993 est.)
Irrigated land: NA sq km
Natural hazards: NA
Environment - current issues: NA
Environment - international agreements:
party to: Biodiversity, Climate Change, Nuclear Test Ban
signed, but not ratified: Air Pollution
Geography - note: landlocked; smallest independent state in Europe after the Holy See and Monaco; dominated by the Apennines

People

Population: 25,061 (July 1999 est.)
Age structure:
0-14 years: 16% (male 2,008; female 2,036)
15-64 years: 67% (male 8,501; female 8,294)
65 years and over: 17% (male 1,774; female 2,448) (1999 est.)
Population growth rate: 0.64% (1999 est.)
Birth rate: 10.41 births/1,000 population (1999 est.)
Death rate: 8.22 deaths/1,000 population (1999 est.)
Net migration rate: 4.23 migrant(s)/1,000 population (1999 est.)
Sex ratio:
at birth: 1 male(s)/female
under 15 years: 0.99 male(s)/female
15-64 years: 1.02 male(s)/female
65 years and over: 0.72 male(s)/female
total population: 0.96 male(s)/female (1999 est.)
Infant mortality rate: 5.39 deaths/1,000 live births (1999 est.)
Life expectancy at birth:
total population: 81.47 years
male: 77.59 years
female: 85.35 years (1999 est.)
Total fertility rate: 1.51 children born/woman (1999 est.)
Nationality:
noun: Sammarinese (singular and plural)
adjective: Sammarinese
Ethnic groups: Sammarinese, Italian
Religions: Roman Catholic
Languages: Italian
Literacy:
definition: age 10 and over can read and write
total population: 96%
male: 97%
female: 95% (1976 est.)

Government

Country name:
conventional long form: Republic of San Marino
conventional short form: San Marino
local long form: Repubblica di San Marino
local short form: San Marino
Data code: SM
Government type: republic
Capital: San Marino
Administrative divisions: 9 municipalities (castelli, singular - castello); Acquaviva, Borgo Maggiore, Chiesanuova, Domagnano, Faetano, Fiorentino, Monte Giardino, San Marino, Serravalle
Independence: 301 (by tradition)
National holiday: Anniversary of the Foundation of the Republic, 3 September
Constitution: 8 October 1600; electoral law of 1926 serves some of the functions of a constitution
Legal system: based on civil law system with Italian law influences; has not accepted compulsory ICJ jurisdiction
Suffrage: 18 years of age; universal

Executive branch:
chief of state: cochiefs of state Captain Regent Pietro BERTI and Captain Regent Paolo BOLLINI (for the period 1 October 1998-31 March 1999)
head of government: Secretary of State for Foreign and Political Affairs Gabriele GATTI (since NA July 1986)
cabinet: Congress of State elected by the Great and General Council for a five-year term
elections: cochiefs of state (captain regents) elected by the Great and General Council for a six-month term; election last held NA September 1998 (next to be held NA March 1999); secretary of state for foreign and political affairs elected by the Great and General Council for a five-year term; election last held NA June 1998 (next to be held NA June 2003)
election results: Pietro BERTI and Paolo BOLLINI elected captain regents; percent of legislative vote - NA; Gabriele GATTI reelected secretary of state for foreign and political affairs; percent of legislative vote - NA
note: the popularly elected parliament (Great and General Council) selects two of its members to serve as the Captains Regent (cochiefs of state) for a six-month period; they preside over meetings of the Great and General Council and its cabinet (Congress of State) which has ten other members, all selected by the Great and General Council; assisting the captains regent are three secretaries of state - Foreign Affairs, Internal Affairs, and Finance - and several additional secretaries; the secretary of state for Foreign Affairs has assumed many of the prerogatives of a prime minister
Legislative branch: unicameral Great and General Council or Consiglio Grande e Generale (60 seats; members are elected by direct popular vote to serve five-year terms)
elections: last held 31 May 1998 (next to be held by NA May 2003)
election results: percent of vote by party - PDCS 40.8%, PSS 23.3%, PPDS 18.6%, AP 9.8%, RC 3.3%, Reformist Socialists 4.2%; seats by party - PDCS 25, PSS 14, PPDS 11, AP 6, RC 2, RS 2
Judicial branch: Council of Twelve or Consiglio dei XII
Political parties and leaders: Christian Democratic Party or PDCS [Piermarino MENICUCCI, secretary general]; Democratic Progressive Party or PPDS (formerly San Marino Communist Party or PSS) [Stefano MACINA, secretary general]; Reformist Socialists or RS (formerly San Marino Socialist Party or PSS) [Maurizio RATTINI, secretary general]; Democratic Movement or MD [Emilio DELLA BALDA]; Popular Alliance or AP [Antonella MULARONI]; Communist Renewal or RC [Giuseppe AMICHI]; Reformist Movement [leader NA]
International organization participation: CE, ECE, ICAO, ICFTU, ICRM, IFRCS, ILO, IMF, IOC, IOM (observer), ITU, NAM (guest), OPCW, OSCE, UN, UNCTAD, UNESCO, UPU, WHO, WIPO, WToO

San Marino (continued)

Diplomatic representation in the US: San Marino does not have an embassy in the US
honorary consulate(s) general: Washington, DC, and New York
honorary consulate(s): Detroit
Diplomatic representation from the US: the US does not have an embassy in San Marino; the US Consul General in Florence (Italy) is accredited to San Marino
Flag description: two equal horizontal bands of white (top) and light blue with the national coat of arms superimposed in the center; the coat of arms has a shield (featuring three towers on three peaks) flanked by a wreath, below a crown and above a scroll bearing the word LIBERTAS (Liberty)

Economy

Economy - overview: The tourist sector contributes over 50% of GDP. In 1995 more than 3.3 million tourists visited San Marino. The key industries are banking, wearing apparel, electronics, and ceramics. Main agricultural products are wine and cheeses. The per capita level of output and standard of living are comparable to those of Italy, which supplies much of its food.
GDP: purchasing power parity - $500 million (1997 est.)
GDP - real growth rate: NA%
GDP - per capita: purchasing power parity - $20,000 (1997 est.)
GDP - composition by sector:
agriculture: NA%
industry: NA%
services: NA%
Population below poverty line: NA%
Household income or consumption by percentage share:
lowest 10%: NA%
highest 10%: NA%
Inflation rate (consumer prices): 5.3% (1995)
Labor force: 15,600 (1995)
Labor force - by occupation: services 55%, industry 43%, agriculture 2% (1995)
Unemployment rate: 3.6% (April 1996)
Budget:
revenues: $320 million
expenditures: $320 million, including capital expenditures of $26 million (1995 est.)
Industries: tourism, textiles, electronics, ceramics, cement, wine
Industrial production growth rate: NA%
Electricity - production: NA kWh
Electricity - production by source:
fossil fuel: NA%
hydro: NA%
nuclear: NA%
other: NA%
Electricity - consumption: NA kWh
Electricity - exports: NA kWh
Electricity - imports: NA kWh
note: electricity supplied by Italy
Agriculture - products: wheat, grapes, maize, olives; cattle, pigs, horses, beef, cheese, hides
Exports: trade data are included with the statistics for Italy
Exports - commodities: building stone, lime, wood, chestnuts, wheat, wine, baked goods, hides, and ceramics
Imports: trade data are included with the statistics for Italy
Imports - commodities: wide variety of consumer manufactures, food
Debt - external: $NA
Economic aid - recipient: $NA
Currency: 1 Italian lira (Lit) = 100 centesimi; note - also mints its own coins
Exchange rates: Italian lire (Lit) per US$1 - 1,668.7 (January 1998),1,736.2 (1998), 1,703.1 (1997), 1,542.9 (1996), 1,628.9 (1995), 1,612.4 (1994)
Fiscal year: calendar year

Communications

Telephones: 15,000 (1995 est.)
Telephone system:
domestic: automatic telephone system completely integrated into Italian system
international: microwave radio relay and cable connections to Italian network; no satellite earth stations
Radio broadcast stations: AM 0, FM 0, shortwave 0
Radios: 15,000 (1994 est.)
Television broadcast stations: 1 (San Marino residents also receive broadcasts from Italy) (1997)
Televisions: 9,000 (1994 est.)

Transportation

Railways: 0 km; note - there is a 1.5 km cable railway connecting the city of San Marino to Borgo Maggiore
Highways:
total: 220 km
paved: NA km
unpaved: NA km
Ports and harbors: none
Airports: none

Military

Military branches: Voluntary Military Force, Police Force
Military expenditures - dollar figure: $3.7 million (1995)
Military expenditures - percent of GDP: 1% (1995)

Transnational Issues

Disputes - international: none

Sao Tome and Principe

Geography

Location: Western Africa, islands in the Gulf of Guinea, straddling the Equator, west of Gabon
Geographic coordinates: 1 00 N, 7 00 E
Map references: Africa
Area:
total: 1,000 sq km
land: 1,000 sq km
water: 0 sq km
Area - comparative: more than five times the size of Washington, DC
Land boundaries: 0 km
Coastline: 209 km
Maritime claims: measured from claimed archipelagic baselines
exclusive economic zone: 200 nm
territorial sea: 12 nm
Climate: tropical; hot, humid; one rainy season (October to May)
Terrain: volcanic, mountainous
Elevation extremes:
lowest point: Atlantic Ocean 0 m
highest point: Pico de Sao Tome 2,024 m
Natural resources: fish
Land use:
arable land: 2%
permanent crops: 36%
permanent pastures: 1%
forests and woodland: NA%
other: 61% (1993 est.)
Irrigated land: 100 sq km (1993 est.)
Natural hazards: NA
Environment - current issues: deforestation; soil erosion and exhaustion
Environment - international agreements:
party to: Desertification, Environmental Modification, Law of the Sea
signed, but not ratified: Biodiversity, Climate Change

People

Population: 154,878 (July 1999 est.)

Sao Tome and Principe *(continued)*

Age structure:
0-14 years: 48% (male 37,322; female 36,423)
15-64 years: 48% (male 36,067; female 38,730)
65 years and over: 4% (male 2,876; female 3,460)
(1999 est.)
Population growth rate: 3.14% (1999 est.)
Birth rate: 43.31 births/1,000 population (1999 est.)
Death rate: 8.08 deaths/1,000 population (1999 est.)
Net migration rate: -3.88 migrant(s)/1,000
population (1999 est.)
Sex ratio:
at birth: 1.03 male(s)/female
under 15 years: 1.02 male(s)/female
15-64 years: 0.93 male(s)/female
65 years and over: 0.83 male(s)/female
total population: 0.97 male(s)/female (1999 est.)
Infant mortality rate: 52.93 deaths/1,000 live births
(1999 est.)
Life expectancy at birth:
total population: 64.71 years
male: 63.18 years
female: 66.28 years (1999 est.)
Total fertility rate: 6.14 children born/woman (1999
est.)
Nationality:
noun: Sao Tomean(s)
adjective: Sao Tomean
Ethnic groups: mestico, angolares (descendants of
Angolan slaves), forros (descendants of freed slaves),
servicais (contract laborers from Angola,
Mozambique, and Cape Verde), tongas (children of
servicais born on the islands), Europeans (primarily
Portuguese)
Religions: Roman Catholic, Evangelical Protestant,
Seventh-Day Adventist
Languages: Portuguese (official)
Literacy:
definition: age 15 and over can read and write
total population: 73%
male: 85%
female: 62% (1991 est.)

Government

Country name:
conventional long form: Democratic Republic of Sao
Tome and Principe
conventional short form: Sao Tome and Principe
local long form: Republica Democratica de Sao Tome
e Principe
local short form: Sao Tome e Principe
Data code: TP
Government type: republic
Capital: Sao Tome
Administrative divisions: 2 provinces; Principe,
Sao Tome
note: Principe has had self-government since 29 April
1995
Independence: 12 July 1975 (from Portugal)
National holiday: Independence Day, 12 July
(1975)
Constitution: approved March 1990; effective 10
September 1990

Legal system: based on Portuguese legal system
and customary law; has not accepted compulsory ICJ
jurisdiction
Suffrage: 18 years of age; universal
Executive branch:
chief of state: President Miguel TROVOADA (since 4
April 1991)
head of government: Prime Minister Guilherma
Posser da COSTA (since 30 December 1998)
cabinet: Council of Ministers appointed by the
president on the proposal of the prime minister
elections: president elected by popular vote for a
five-year term; election last held 30 June and 15 July
1996 (next to be held in 2001); prime minister chosen by
the National Assembly and approved by the president
election results: Miguel TROVOADA reelected
president in Sao Tome's second multiparty
presidential election; percent of vote - Miguel
TROVOADA 52.74%, Manuel Pinto da COSTA
47.26%
Legislative branch: unicameral National Assembly
or Assembleia Nacional (55 seats; members are
elected by direct popular vote to serve five-year terms)
elections: last held 8 November 1998 (next to be held
NA 2003)
election results: percent of vote by party -
MLSTP-PSD 56%, PCD 14.5%%, ADI 29%; seats by
party - MLSTP-PSD 31, ADI 16, PCD 8
Judicial branch: Supreme Court, judges are
appointed by the National Assembly
Political parties and leaders: Party for Democratic
Convergence or PCD [Armindo AGUIAR, secretary
general]; Movement for the Liberation of Sao Tome
and Principe-Social Democratic Party or MLSTP-PSD
[Manuel Pinto Da COSTA]; Christian Democratic
Front or FDC [Alphonse Dos SANTOS]; Democratic
Opposition Coalition or CODO [leader NA];
Independent Democratic Action or ADI [Carlos
NEVES]; other small parties
International organization participation: ACCT,
ACP, AfDB, CCC, CEEAC, ECA, FAO, G-77, IBRD,
ICAO, ICRM, IDA, IFAD, IFRCS, ILO, IMF, IMO,
Intelsat (nonsignatory user), Interpol, IOC, IOM
(observer), ITU, NAM, OAU, UN, UNCTAD,
UNESCO, UNIDO, UPU, WHO, WIPO, WMO, WToO,
WTrO (applicant)
Diplomatic representation in the US: Sao Tome
and Principe does not have an embassy in the US, but
does have a Permanent Mission to the UN, headed by
First Secretary Domingos AUGUSTO Ferreira,
located at 122 East 42nd Street, Suite 1604, New
York, NY 10168, telephone [1] (212) 697-4211
Diplomatic representation from the US: the US
does not have an embassy in Sao Tome and Principe;
the Ambassador to Gabon is accredited to Sao Tome
and Principe on a nonresident basis and makes
periodic visits to the islands
Flag description: three horizontal bands of green
(top), yellow (double width), and green with two black
five-pointed stars placed side by side in the center of
the yellow band and a red isosceles triangle based on
the hoist side; uses the popular pan-African colors of
Ethiopia

Economy

Economy - overview: This small poor island
economy has become increasingly dependent on
cocoa since independence over 20 years ago.
However, cocoa production has substantially declined
because of drought and mismanagement. The
resulting shortage of cocoa for export has created a
persistent balance-of-payments problem. Sao Tome
has to import all fuels, most manufactured goods,
consumer goods, and a significant amount of food.
Over the years, it has been unable to service its
external debt and has had to depend on concessional
aid and debt rescheduling. Considerable potential
exists for development of a tourist industry, and the
government has taken steps to expand facilities in
recent years. The government also has attempted to
reduce price controls and subsidies, but economic
growth has remained sluggish. Sao Tome is also
optimistic that significant petroleum discoveries are
forthcoming in its territorial waters in the oil-rich waters
of the Gulf of Guinea. Corruption scandals continue to
weaken the economy.
GDP: purchasing power parity - $164 million (1998
est.)
GDP - real growth rate: 2.5% (1998 est.)
GDP - per capita: purchasing power parity - $1,100
(1998 est.)
GDP - composition by sector:
agriculture: 23%
industry: 19%
services: 58% (1997 est.)
Population below poverty line: NA%
**Household income or consumption by percentage
share:**
lowest 10%: NA%
highest 10%: NA%
Inflation rate (consumer prices): 21% (1998 est.)
Labor force: NA
Labor force - by occupation: population mainly
engaged in subsistence agriculture and fishing
note: there are shortages of skilled workers
Unemployment rate: 50% in the formal business
sector (1998 est.)
Budget:
revenues: $58 million
expenditures: $114 million, including capital
expenditures of $54 million (1993 est.)
Industries: light construction, textiles, soap, beer;
fish processing; timber
Industrial production growth rate: NA%
Electricity - production: 15 million kWh (1996)
Electricity - production by source:
fossil fuel: 46.67%
hydro: 53.33%
nuclear: 0%
other: 0% (1996)
Electricity - consumption: 15 million kWh (1996)
Electricity - exports: 0 kWh (1996)
Electricity - imports: 0 kWh (1996)
Agriculture - products: cocoa, coconuts, palm
kernels, copra, cinnamon, pepper, coffee, bananas,

Sao Tome and Principe *(continued)*

papayas, beans; poultry; fish
Exports: $5.3 million (f.o.b., 1997 est.)
Exports - commodities: cocoa 90%, copra, coffee, palm oil (1997)
Exports - partners: Netherlands 51%, Germany 6%, Portugal 6% (1997)
Imports: $19.2 million (f.o.b., 1997 est.)
Imports - commodities: machinery and electrical equipment, food products, petroleum products
Imports - partners: Portugal 26%, France 18%, Angola, Belgium, Japan (1997)
Debt - external: $267 million (1997)
Economic aid - recipient: $57.3 million (1995)
Currency: 1 dobra (Db) = 100 centimos
Exchange rates: dobras (Db) per US$1 - 6,873.5 (October 1998), 4,552.5 (1997), 2,203.2 (1996), 1,420.3 (1995), 732.6 (1994)
Fiscal year: calendar year

Communications

Telephones: 2,200 (1986 est.)
Telephone system:
domestic: minimal system
international: satellite earth station - 1 Intelsat (Atlantic Ocean)
Radio broadcast stations: AM 1, FM 2, shortwave 0
Radios: 33,000 (1992 est.)
Television broadcast stations: 2 (1997)
Televisions: NA

Transportation

Railways: 0 km
Highways:
total: 320 km
paved: 218 km
unpaved: 102 km (1996 est.)
Ports and harbors: Santo Antonio, Sao Tome
Merchant marine:
total: 3 cargo ships (1,000 GRT or over) totaling 7,610 GRT/9,446 DWT (1998 est.)
Airports: 2 (1998 est.)
Airports - with paved runways:
total: 2
1,524 to 2,437 m: 1
914 to 1,523 m: 1 (1998 est.)

Military

Military branches: Army, Navy, Security Police
Military manpower - availability:
males age 15-49: 31,724 (1999 est.)
Military manpower - fit for military service:
males age 15-49: 16,766 (1999 est.)
Military expenditures - dollar figure: $500,000 (1994)
Military expenditures - percent of GDP: 1.5% (1994)

Transnational Issues

Disputes - international: none

Saudi Arabia

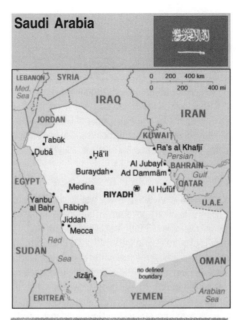

Geography

Location: Middle East, bordering the Persian Gulf and the Red Sea, north of Yemen
Geographic coordinates: 25 00 N, 45 00 E
Map references: Middle East
Area:
total: 1,960,582 sq km
land: 1,960,582 sq km
water: 0 sq km
Area - comparative: slightly more than one-fifth the size of the US
Land boundaries:
total: 4,415 km
border countries: Iraq 814 km, Jordan 728 km, Kuwait 222 km, Oman 676 km, Qatar 60 km, UAE 457 km, Yemen 1,458 km
Coastline: 2,640 km
Maritime claims:
contiguous zone: 18 nm
continental shelf: not specified
territorial sea: 12 nm
Climate: harsh, dry desert with great extremes of temperature
Terrain: mostly uninhabited, sandy desert
Elevation extremes:
lowest point: Persian Gulf 0 m
highest point: Jabal Sawda' 3,133 m
Natural resources: petroleum, natural gas, iron ore, gold, copper
Land use:
arable land: 2%
permanent crops: 0%
permanent pastures: 56%
forests and woodland: 1%
other: 41% (1993 est.)
Irrigated land: 4,350 sq km (1993 est.)
Natural hazards: frequent sand and dust storms
Environment - current issues: desertification; depletion of underground water resources; the lack of perennial rivers or permanent water bodies has

---

prompted the development of extensive seawater desalination facilities; coastal pollution from oil spills
Environment - international agreements:
party to: Climate Change, Desertification, Endangered Species, Hazardous Wastes, Law of the Sea, Ozone Layer Protection
signed, but not ratified: none of the selected agreements
Geography - note: extensive coastlines on Persian Gulf and Red Sea provide great leverage on shipping (especially crude oil) through Persian Gulf and Suez Canal

People

Population: 21,504,613 (July 1999 est.)
note: includes 5,321,938 non-nationals (July 1999 est.)
Age structure:
0-14 years: 43% (male 4,705,724; female 4,543,918)
15-64 years: 54% (male 6,925,020; female 4,783,570)
65 years and over: 3% (male 291,449; female 254,932) (1999 est.)
Population growth rate: 3.39% (1999 est.)
Birth rate: 37.38 births/1,000 population (1999 est.)
Death rate: 4.86 deaths/1,000 population (1999 est.)
Net migration rate: 1.4 migrant(s)/1,000 population (1999 est.)
Sex ratio:
at birth: 1.05 male(s)/female
under 15 years: 1.04 male(s)/female
15-64 years: 1.45 male(s)/female
65 years and over: 1.14 male(s)/female
total population: 1.24 male(s)/female (1999 est.)
Infant mortality rate: 38.8 deaths/1,000 live births (1999 est.)
Life expectancy at birth:
total population: 70.55 years
male: 68.67 years
female: 72.53 years (1999 est.)
Total fertility rate: 6.34 children born/woman (1999 est.)
Nationality:
noun: Saudi(s)
adjective: Saudi or Saudi Arabian
Ethnic groups: Arab 90%, Afro-Asian 10%
Religions: Muslim 100%
Languages: Arabic
Literacy:
definition: age 15 and over can read and write
total population: 62.8%
male: 71.5%
female: 50.2% (1995 est.)

Government

Country name:
conventional long form: Kingdom of Saudi Arabia
conventional short form: Saudi Arabia
local long form: Al Mamlakah al Arabiyah as Suudiyah
local short form: Al Arabiyah as Suudiyah
Data code: SA

Saudi Arabia (continued)

Government type: monarchy
Capital: Riyadh
Administrative divisions: 13 provinces (mintaqat, singular - mintaqah); Al Bahah, Al Hudud ash Shamaliyah, Al Jawf, Al Madinah, Al Qasim, Ar Riyad, Ash Sharqiyah (Eastern Province), 'Asir, Ha'il, Jizan, Makkah, Najran, Tabuk
Independence: 23 September 1932 (unification)
National holiday: Unification of the Kingdom, 23 September (1932)
Constitution: governed according to Shari'a (Islamic law); the Basic Law that articulates the government's rights and responsibilities was introduced in 1993
Legal system: based on Islamic law, several secular codes have been introduced; commercial disputes handled by special committees; has not accepted compulsory ICJ jurisdiction
Suffrage: none
Executive branch:
chief of state: King and Prime Minister FAHD bin Abd al-Aziz Al Saud (since 13 June 1982); Crown Prince and First Deputy Prime Minister ABDALLAH bin Abd al-Aziz Al Saud (half-brother to the monarch, heir to the throne since 13 June 1982, regent from 1 January to 22 February 1996); note - the monarch is both the chief of state and head of government
head of government: King and Prime Minister FAHD bin Abd al-Aziz Al Saud (since 13 June 1982); Crown Prince and First Deputy Prime Minister ABDALLAH bin Abd al-Aziz Al Saud (half-brother to the monarch, heir to the throne since 13 June 1982, regent from 1 January to 22 February 1996); note - the monarch is both the chief of state and head of government
cabinet: Council of Ministers is appointed by the monarch and includes many royal family members
elections: none; the monarch is hereditary
Legislative branch: a consultative council (90 members and a chairman appointed by the monarch for four-year terms)
Judicial branch: Supreme Council of Justice
Political parties and leaders: none allowed
International organization participation: ABEDA, AfDB, AFESD, AL, AMF, BIS, CCC, ESCWA, FAO, G-19, G-77, GCC, IAEA, IBRD, ICAO, ICC, ICRM, IDA, IDB, IFAD, IFC, IFRCS, ILO, IMF, IMO, Inmarsat, Intelsat, Interpol, IOC, ISO, ITU, NAM, OAPEC, OAS (observer), OIC, OPCW, OPEC, UN, UNCTAD, UNESCO, UNIDO, UPU, WFTU, WHO, WIPO, WMO, WTrO (applicant)
Diplomatic representation in the US:
chief of mission: Ambassador BANDAR bin Sultan bin Abd al-Aziz Al Saud
chancery: 601 New Hampshire Avenue NW, Washington, DC 20037
telephone: [1] (202) 342-3800
consulate(s) general: Houston, Los Angeles, and New York
Diplomatic representation from the US:
chief of mission: Ambassador Wyche FOWLER, Jr.
embassy: Collector Road M, Diplomatic Quarter, Riyadh
mailing address: American Embassy Riyadh, Unit

61307, APO AE 09803-1307; International Mail: P. O. Box 94309, Riyadh 11693
telephone: [966] (1) 488-3800
FAX: [966] (1) 488-7360
consulate(s) general: Dhahran, Jiddah (Jeddah)
Flag description: green with large white Arabic script (that may be translated as There is no God but God; Muhammad is the Messenger of God) above a white horizontal saber (the tip points to the hoist side); green is the traditional color of Islam

Economy

Economy - overview: This is a well-to-do oil-based economy with strong government controls over major economic activities. Saudi Arabia has the largest reserves of petroleum in the world (26% of the proved total), ranks as the largest exporter of petroleum, and plays a leading role in OPEC. The petroleum sector accounts for roughly 75% of budget revenues, 40% of GDP, and 90% of export earnings. About 35% of GDP comes from the private sector. Roughly 4 million foreign workers play an important role in the Saudi economy, for example, in the oil and service sectors. The Saudi economy was severely hit by the large decline in world oil prices in 1998. GDP fell by nearly 11%; the budget deficit rose to $12.3 billion; and the current account recorded a $13 billion deficit - the first in three years. The government announced plans to implement large spending cuts in 1999 because of weak oil prices and will continue to call on greater private sector involvement in the economy. Shortages of water and rapid population growth will constrain government efforts to increase self-sufficiency in agricultural products.
GDP: purchasing power parity - $186 billion (1998 est.)
GDP - real growth rate: -10.8% (1998 est.)
GDP - per capita: purchasing power parity - $9,000 (1998 est.)
GDP - composition by sector:
agriculture: 6%
industry: 53%
services: 41% (1996)
Population below poverty line: NA%
Household income or consumption by percentage share:
lowest 10%: NA%
highest 10%: NA%
Inflation rate (consumer prices): -0.2% (1998 est.)
Labor force: 7 million
note: 35% of the population in the 15-64 age group is non-national (July 1998 est.)
Labor force - by occupation: government 40%, industry, construction, and oil 25%, services 30%, agriculture 5%
Unemployment rate: NA%
Budget:
revenues: $32.3 billion
expenditures: $44 billion, including capital expenditures of $NA (1999 budget est.)
Industries: crude oil production, petroleum refining, basic petrochemicals, cement, two small steel-rolling

mills, construction, fertilizer, plastics
Industrial production growth rate: 1% (1997 est.)
Electricity - production: 95 billion kWh (1996)
Electricity - production by source:
fossil fuel: 100%
hydro: 0%
nuclear: 0%
other: 0% (1996)
Electricity - consumption: 95 billion kWh (1996)
Electricity - exports: 0 kWh (1996)
Electricity - imports: 0 kWh (1996)
Agriculture - products: wheat, barley, tomatoes, melons, dates, citrus; mutton, chickens, eggs, milk
Exports: $59.7 billion (f.o.b., 1997)
Exports - commodities: petroleum and petroleum products 90%
Exports - partners: Japan 18%, US 15%, South Korea 11%, Singapore 8%, India 4% (1997 est.)
Imports: $26.2 billion (f.o.b., 1997)
Imports - commodities: machinery and equipment, foodstuffs, chemicals, motor vehicles, textiles
Imports - partners: US 23%, UK 17%, Japan 8%, Germany 8%, Italy 5% (1997 est.)
Debt - external: $NA
Economic aid - donor: pledged $100 million in 1993 to fund reconstruction of Lebanon; since 1993, Saudi Arabia has committed $208 million for assistance to the Palestinians
Currency: 1 Saudi riyal (SR) = 100 halalah
Exchange rates: Saudi riyals (SR) per US$1 - 3.7450 (fixed rate since June 1986)
Fiscal year: calendar year

Communications

Telephones: 1.46 million (1993)
Telephone system: modern system
domestic: extensive microwave radio relay and coaxial and fiber-optic cable systems
international: microwave radio relay to Bahrain, Jordan, Kuwait, Qatar, UAE, Yemen, and Sudan; coaxial cable to Kuwait and Jordan; submarine cable to Djibouti, Egypt and Bahrain; satellite earth stations - 5 Intelsat (3 Atlantic Ocean and 2 Indian Ocean), 1 Arabsat, and 1 Inmarsat (Indian Ocean region)
Radio broadcast stations: AM 43, FM 13, shortwave 0
Radios: 5 million (1993 est.)
Television broadcast stations: 117 (1997)
Televisions: 4.5 million (1993 est.)

Transportation

Railways:
total: 1,390 km
standard gauge: 1,390 km 1.435-m gauge (448 km double track) (1992)
Highways:
total: 162,000 km
paved: 69,174 km
unpaved: 92,826 km (1996 est.)
Pipelines: crude oil 6,400 km; petroleum products 150 km; natural gas 2,200 km (includes natural gas liquids 1,600 km)

Ports and harbors: Ad Dammam, Al Jubayl, Duba, Jiddah, Jizan, Rabigh, Ra's al Khafji, Mishab, Ras Tanura, Yanbu' al Bahr, Madinat Yanbu' al Sinaiyah

Merchant marine:

total: 73 ships (1,000 GRT or over) totaling 1,124,110 GRT/1,467,121 DWT

ships by type: bulk 1, cargo 13, chemical tanker 7, container 5, liquefied gas tanker 1, livestock carrier 4, oil tanker 17, passenger 1, refrigerated cargo 4, roll-on/roll-off cargo 12, short-sea passenger 8 (1998 est.)

Airports: 205 (1998 est.)

Airports - with paved runways:

total: 70

over 3,047 m: 30

2,438 to 3,047 m: 12

1,524 to 2,437 m: 23

914 to 1,523 m: 3

under 914 m: 2 (1998 est.)

Airports - with unpaved runways:

total: 135

over 3,047 m: 1

2,438 to 3,047 m: 5

1,524 to 2,437 m: 78

914 to 1,523 m: 38

under 914 m: 13 (1998 est.)

Heliports: 4 (1998 est.)

Military

Military branches: Land Force (Army), Navy, Air Force, Air Defense Force, National Guard, Ministry of Interior Forces

Military manpower - military age: 18 years of age

Military manpower - availability:

males age 15-49: 5,696,772 (1999 est.)

Military manpower - fit for military service:

males age 15-49: 3,171,860 (1999 est.)

Military manpower - reaching military age annually:

males: 197,386 (1999 est.)

Military expenditures - dollar figure: $18.1 billion (1997 est.)

Military expenditures - percent of GDP: 12% (1997 est.)

Transnational Issues

Disputes - international: large section of boundary with Yemen not defined; location and status of boundary with UAE is not final, de facto boundary reflects 1974 agreement; Kuwaiti ownership of Qaruh and Umm al Maradim islands is disputed by Saudi Arabia; in 1996, agreed with Qatar to demarcate border per 1992 accord; that process is ongoing

Illicit drugs: death penalty for traffickers; increasing consumption of heroin and cocaine

Senegal

Geography

Location: Western Africa, bordering the North Atlantic Ocean, between Guinea-Bissau and Mauritania

Geographic coordinates: 14 00 N, 14 00 W

Map references: Africa

Area:

total: 196,190 sq km

land: 192,000 sq km

water: 4,190 sq km

Area - comparative: slightly smaller than South Dakota

Land boundaries:

total: 2,640 km

border countries: The Gambia 740 km, Guinea 330 km, Guinea-Bissau 338 km, Mali 419 km, Mauritania 813 km

Coastline: 531 km

Maritime claims:

contiguous zone: 24 nm

continental shelf: 200 nm or to the edge of the continental margin

exclusive economic zone: 200 nm

territorial sea: 12 nm

Climate: tropical; hot, humid; rainy season (May to November) has strong southeast winds; dry season (December to April) dominated by hot, dry, harmattan wind

Terrain: generally low, rolling, plains rising to foothills in southeast

Elevation extremes:

lowest point: Atlantic Ocean 0 m

highest point: unnamed feature near Nepen Diakha 581 m

Natural resources: fish, phosphates, iron ore

Land use:

arable land: 12%

permanent crops: 0%

permanent pastures: 16%

forests and woodland: 54%

other: 18% (1993 est.)

Irrigated land: 710 sq km (1993 est.)

Natural hazards: lowlands seasonally flooded; periodic droughts

Environment - current issues: wildlife populations threatened by poaching; deforestation; overgrazing; soil erosion; desertification; overfishing

Environment - international agreements:

party to: Biodiversity, Climate Change, Desertification, Endangered Species, Hazardous Wastes, Law of the Sea, Marine Life Conservation, Nuclear Test Ban, Ozone Layer Protection, Ship Pollution, Wetlands, Whaling

signed, but not ratified: Marine Dumping

Geography - note: The Gambia is almost an enclave of Senegal

People

Population: 10,051,930 (July 1999 est.)

Age structure:

0-14 years: 48% (male 2,403,384; female 2,416,791)

15-64 years: 49% (male 2,360,113; female 2,594,278)

65 years and over: 3% (male 134,765; female 142,599) (1999 est.)

Population growth rate: 3.32% (1999 est.)

Birth rate: 43.88 births/1,000 population (1999 est.)

Death rate: 10.71 deaths/1,000 population (1999 est.)

Net migration rate: 0 migrant(s)/1,000 population (1999 est.)

Sex ratio:

at birth: 1.03 male(s)/female

under 15 years: 0.99 male(s)/female

15-64 years: 0.91 male(s)/female

65 years and over: 0.95 male(s)/female

total population: 0.95 male(s)/female (1999 est.)

Infant mortality rate: 59.81 deaths/1,000 live births (1999 est.)

Life expectancy at birth:

total population: 57.83 years

male: 54.95 years

female: 60.78 years (1999 est.)

Total fertility rate: 6.11 children born/woman (1999 est.)

Nationality:

noun: Senegalese (singular and plural)

adjective: Senegalese

Ethnic groups: Wolof 43.3%, Pular 23.8%, Serer 14.7%, Diola 3.7%, Mandink 3%, Soninke 1.1%, European and Lebanese 1%, other 9.4%

Religions: Muslim 92%, indigenous beliefs 6%, Christian 2% (mostly Roman Catholic)

Languages: French (official), Wolof, Pulaar, Diola, Mandingo

Literacy:

definition: age 15 and over can read and write

total population: 33.1%

male: 43%

female: 23.2% (1995 est.)

Senegal (continued)

Government

Country name:
conventional long form: Republic of Senegal
conventional short form: Senegal
local long form: Republique du Senegal
local short form: Senegal
Data code: SG
Government type: republic under multiparty democratic rule
Capital: Dakar
Administrative divisions: 10 regions (regions, singular - region); Dakar, Diourbel, Fatick, Kaolack, Kolda, Louga, Saint-Louis, Tambacounda, Thies, Ziguinchor
Independence: 4 April 1960 from France; complete independence was achieved upon dissolution of federation with Mali on 20 August 1960 (The Gambia and Senegal signed an agreement on 12 December 1981 that called for the creation of a loose confederation to be known as Senegambia, but the agreement was dissolved on 30 September 1989)
National holiday: Independence Day, 4 April (1960)
Constitution: 3 March 1963, revised 1991
Legal system: based on French civil law system; judicial review of legislative acts in Constitutional Court; the Council of State audits the government's accounting office; Senegal has not accepted compulsory ICJ jurisdiction
Suffrage: 18 years of age; universal
Executive branch:
chief of state: President Abdou DIOUF (since 1 January 1981)
head of government: Prime Minister Mamadou Lamine LOUM (since 4 July 1998)
cabinet: Council of Ministers appointed by the prime minister in consultation with the president
elections: president elected by popular vote for a seven-year term; election last held 21 February 1993 (next to be held NA February 2000); prime minister appointed by the president
election results: Abdou DIOUF reelected president; percent of vote - Abdou DIOUF (PS) 58.4%, Abdoulaye WADE (PDS) 32.03%, other 9.57%
Legislative branch: unicameral National Assembly or Assemblee Nationale (140 seats; members are elected by direct popular vote to serve five-year terms)
elections: last held 24 May 1998 (next to be held NA May 2003)
election results: percent of vote by party - PS 50.19%, PDS 19%, UDS-R 13%, And/Jef-PADS 5%, LD/MPT 4%, CDP/Garab-Gi 2%, FSD 1%, PDS-R 1%, RND 1%, BCG 1%, PIT 1% ; seats by party - PS 93, PDS 23, UDS-R 11, And-Jef/PADS 4, LD-MPT 3, CDP/Garab-Gi 1, FSD 1, PDS-R 1, RND 1, BCG 1, PIT 1
Judicial branch: under the terms of a reform of the judicial system implemented in 1992, the principal organs of the judiciary are as follows; Constitutional Court; Council of State; Court of Final Appeals or Cour de Cassation; Court of Appeals
Political parties and leaders: African Party for Democracy and Socialism or And-Jef/PADS (also known as PADS/AJ) [Landing SAVANE, secretary general]; Democratic League-Labor Party Movement or LD-MPT [Dr. Abdoulaye BATHILY]; Democratic and Patriotic Convention or CDP Garab-Gi [Dr. Iba Der THIAM]; Independent Labor Party or PIT [Amath DANSOKHO]; National Democratic Rally or RND [Madier DIOUF]; Senegalese Democratic Party or PDS [Abdoulaye WADE]; Senegalese Democratic Party-Renewal or PDS-R [Serigne Lamine DIOP, secretary general]; Senegalese Democratic Union-Renewal or UDS-R [Mamadou Puritain FALL]; Socialist Party or PS [President Abdou DIOUF]; African Party of Independence [Majhemout DIOP]; Front pour le socialisme et la democratie or FSD [leader NA]; Bloc des centristes Gainde or BCG [leader NA]; other small parties
Political pressure groups and leaders: students; teachers; labor; Muslim brotherhoods
International organization participation: ACCT, ACP, AfDB, CCC, ECA, ECOWAS, FAO, FZ, G-15, G-77, IAEA, IBRD, ICAO, ICC, ICFTU, ICRM, IDA, IDB, IFAD, IFC, IFRCS, ILO, IMF, IMO, Inmarsat, Intelsat, Interpol, IOC, IOM, ITU, MINURCA, MIPONUH, MONUA, NAM, OAU, OIC, OPCW, PCA, UN, UNAVEM III, UNCTAD, UNESCO, UNIDO, UNIKOM, UNMIBH, UPU, WADB, WAEMU, WCL, WFTU, WHO, WIPO, WMO, WToO, WTrO
Diplomatic representation in the US:
chief of mission: Ambassador Mamadou Mansour SECK
chancery: 2112 Wyoming Avenue NW, Washington, DC 20008
telephone: [1] (202) 234-0540
Diplomatic representation from the US:
chief of mission: Ambassador Dane Farnsworth SMITH, Jr.
embassy: Avenue Jean XXIII at the corner of Avenue Kleber, Dakar
mailing address: B. P. 49, Dakar
telephone: [221] 823-4296, 823-7384
FAX: [221] 822-2991
Flag description: three equal vertical bands of green (hoist side), yellow, and red with a small green five-pointed star centered in the yellow band; uses the popular pan-African colors of Ethiopia

Economy

Economy - overview: In January 1994, Senegal undertook a bold and ambitious economic reform program with the support of the international donor community. This reform began with a 50% devaluation of Senegal's currency, the CFA franc, which is linked at a fixed rate to the French franc. Government price controls and subsidies have been steadily dismantled. After seeing its economy contract by 2.1% in 1993, Senegal made an important turnaround, thanks to the reform program, with real growth in GDP averaging 5% annually in 1995-98. Annual inflation has been pushed below 2%, and the fiscal deficit has been cut to less than 1.5% of GDP. Investment rose steadily from 13.8% of GDP in 1993 to 16.5% in 1997. As a member of the West African Economic and Monetary Union (UEMOA), Senegal is working toward greater regional integration with a unified external tariff. Senegal also realized full Internet connectivity in 1996, creating a miniboom in information technology-based services. Private activity now accounts for 82% of GDP. On the negative side, Senegal faces deep-seated urban problems of chronic unemployment, juvenile delinquency, and drug addiction. Forecasters predict growth will continue in the 5% range in 1999-2000.
GDP: purchasing power parity - $15.6 billion (1998 est.)
GDP - real growth rate: 5.7% (1998 est.)
GDP - per capita: purchasing power parity - $1,600 (1998 est.)
GDP - composition by sector:
agriculture: 19%
industry: 17%
services: 64% (1996 est.)
Population below poverty line: NA%
Household income or consumption by percentage share:
lowest 10%: 1.4%
highest 10%: 42.8% (1991)
Inflation rate (consumer prices): 1.8% (1998 est.)
Labor force: NA
Labor force - by occupation: agriculture 60%
Unemployment rate: NA%; urban youth 40%
Budget:
revenues: $885 million
expenditures: $885 million, including capital expenditures of $125 million (1996 est.)
Industries: agricultural and fish processing, phosphate mining, fertilizer production, petroleum refining, construction materials
Industrial production growth rate: 7% (1998 est.)
Electricity - production: 1.027 billion kWh (1997 est.)
Electricity - production by source:
fossil fuel: 100%
hydro: 0%
nuclear: 0%
other: 0% (1996)
Electricity - consumption: 730 million kWh (1996)
Electricity - exports: 0 kWh (1997)
Electricity - imports: 0 kWh (1997)
Agriculture - products: peanuts, millet, corn, sorghum, rice, cotton, tomatoes, green vegetables; cattle, poultry, pigs; fish
Exports: $925 million (f.o.b., 1998)
Exports - commodities: fish, ground nuts (peanuts), petroleum products, phosphates, cotton
Exports - partners: France 20%, other EU countries, India, Cote d'Ivoire, Mali (1996)
Imports: $1.2 billion (f.o.b., 1998)
Imports - commodities: foods and beverages, consumer goods, capital goods, petroleum products
Imports - partners: France 36%, other EU countries, Nigeria, Cameroon, Cote d'Ivoire, Algeria, US, China, Japan (1996)
Debt - external: $3.8 billion (1997)
Economic aid - recipient: $647.5 million (1995)

Senegal (continued)

Currency: 1 Communaute Financiere Africaine franc (CFAF) = 100 centimes
Exchange rates: Communaute Financiere Africaine francs (CFAF) per US$1 - 560.01 (December 1998), 589.95 (1998), 583.67 (1997), 511.55 (1966), 499.15 (1995), 555.20 (1994)
Fiscal year: calendar year

Communications

Telephones: 81,988 (1995 est.)
Telephone system:
domestic: above-average urban system; microwave radio relay, coaxial cable and fiber-optic cable in trunk system
international: 4 submarine cables; satellite earth station - 1 Intelsat (Atlantic Ocean)
Radio broadcast stations: AM 8, FM 6, shortwave 1
Radios: 850,000 (1993 est.)
Television broadcast stations: 1 (1997)
Televisions: 61,000 (1993 est.)

Transportation

Railways:
total: 904 km
narrow gauge: 904 km 1.000-meter gauge (70 km double track) (1995)
Highways:
total: 14,576 km
paved: 4,271 km
unpaved: 10,305 km (1996 est.)
Waterways: 897 km total; 785 km on the Senegal river, and 112 km on the Saloum river
Ports and harbors: Dakar, Kaolack, Matam, Podor, Richard-Toll, Saint-Louis, Ziguinchor
Merchant marine:
total: 1 bulk ship (1,000 GRT or over) totaling 1,995 GRT/3,775 DWT (1998 est.)
Airports: 20 (1998 est.)
Airports - with paved runways:
total: 10
over 3,047 m: 1
1,524 to 2,437 m: 7
914 to 1,523 m: 2 (1998 est.)
Airports - with unpaved runways:
total: 10
1,524 to 2,437 m: 5
914 to 1,523 m: 4
under 914 m: 1 (1998 est.)

Military

Military branches: Army, Navy, Air Force, National Gendarmerie, National Police (Surete Nationale)
Military manpower - military age: 18 years of age
Military manpower - availability:
males age 15-49: 2,096,438 (1999 est.)
Military manpower - fit for military service:
males age 15-49: 1,095,047 (1999 est.)
Military manpower - reaching military age annually:
males: 103,348 (1999 est.)

Military expenditures - dollar figure: $68 million (1997)
Military expenditures - percent of GDP: 1.4% (1997)

Transnational Issues

Disputes - international: short section of boundary with The Gambia is indefinite
Illicit drugs: transshipment point for Southwest and Southeast Asian heroin moving to Europe and North America; illicit cultivator of cannabis

Serbia and Montenegro

Serbia and Montenegro have asserted the formation of a joint independent state, but this entity has not been formally recognized as a state by the United States.

Introduction

Background: Serbia and Montenegro have asserted the formation of a joint independent state, but this entity has not been formally recognized as a state by the US. The US view is that the Socialist Federal Republic of Yugoslavia (SFRY) has dissolved and that none of the successor republics represents its continuation.

Geography

Location: Southeastern Europe, bordering the Adriatic Sea, between Albania and Bosnia and Herzegovina
Geographic coordinates: 44 00 N, 21 00 E
Map references: Europe
Area:
total: 102,350 sq km (Serbia 88,412 sq km; Montenegro 13,938 sq km)
land: 102,136 sq km (Serbia 88,412 sq km; Montenegro 13,724 sq km)
water: 214 sq km (Serbia 0 sq km; Montenegro 214 sq km)
Area - comparative: slightly smaller than Kentucky (Serbia is slightly larger than Maine; Montenegro is slightly smaller than Connecticut)
Land boundaries:
total: 2,246 km
border countries: Albania 287 km (114 km with Serbia, 173 km with Montenegro), Bosnia and Herzegovina 527 km (312 km with Serbia, 215 km with Montenegro), Bulgaria 318 km (with Serbia), Croatia (north) 241 km (with Serbia), Croatia (south) 25 km (with Montenegro), Hungary 151 km (with Serbia), The Former Yugoslav Republic of Macedonia 221 km (with Serbia), Romania 476 km (with Serbia)
note: the internal boundary between Montenegro and Serbia is 211 km
Coastline: 199 km (Montenegro 199 km, Serbia 0 km)
Maritime claims: NA

Serbia and Montenegro *(continued)*

Climate: in the north, continental climate (cold winter and hot, humid summers with well distributed rainfall); central portion, continental and Mediterranean climate; to the south, Adriatic climate along the coast, hot, dry summers and autumns and relatively cold winters with heavy snowfall inland

Terrain: extremely varied; to the north, rich fertile plains; to the east, limestone ranges and basins; to the southeast, ancient mountains and hills; to the southwest, extremely high shoreline with no islands off the coast

Elevation extremes:

lowest point: Adriatic Sea 0 m

highest point: Daravica 2,656 m

Natural resources: oil, gas, coal, antimony, copper, lead, zinc, nickel, gold, pyrite, chrome

Land use:

arable land: NA%

permanent crops: NA%

permanent pastures: NA%

forests and woodland: NA%

other: NA%

Irrigated land: NA sq km

Natural hazards: destructive earthquakes

Environment - current issues: pollution of coastal waters from sewage outlets, especially in tourist-related areas such as Kotor; air pollution around Belgrade and other industrial cities; water pollution from industrial wastes dumped into the Sava which flows into the Danube

Environment - international agreements:

party to: none of the selected agreements

signed, but not ratified: none of the selected agreements

Geography - note: controls one of the major land routes from Western Europe to Turkey and the Near East; strategic location along the Adriatic coast

People

Population: 11,206,847 (Serbia - 10,526,478; Montenegro - 680,369) (July 1999 est.)

note: all data dealing with population is subject to considerable error because of the dislocations caused by military action and ethnic cleansing

Age structure:

0-14 years: Serbia - 20% (male 1,102,109; female 1,025,069); Montenegro - 21% (male 75,633; female 70,464)

15-64 years: Serbia - 67% (male 3,538,689; female 3,483,192); Montenegro - 68% (male 232,223; female 227,371)

65 years and over: Serbia - 13% (male 595,200; female 782,219); Montenegro - 11% (male 30,829; female 43,849) (July 1999 est.)

Population growth rate: Serbia - 0.02%; Montenegro - 0.07% (1999 est.)

Birth rate: Serbia - 12.54 births/1,000 population; Montenegro - 13.19 births/1,000 population (1999 est.)

Death rate: Serbia - 9.68 deaths/1,000 population; Montenegro - 7.44 deaths/1,000 population (1999 est.)

Net migration rate: Serbia - -2.65 migrants/1,000 population; Montenegro - -5.09 migrants/1,000 population (1999 est.)

Sex ratio:

at birth: Serbia - 1.08 male(s)/female; Montenegro - 1.08 male(s)/female

under 15 years: Serbia - 1.08 male(s)/female; Montenegro - 1.07 male(s)/female

15-64 years: Serbia - 1.02 male(s)/female; Montenegro - 1.02 male(s)/female

65 years and over: Serbia - 0.76 male(s)/female; Montenegro - 0.70 male(s)/female

total population: Serbia - 0.99 male(s)/female; Montenegro - 0.99 male(s)/female (1999 est.)

Infant mortality rate: Serbia - 16.49 deaths/1,000 live births; Montenegro - 10.99 deaths/1,000 live births (1999 est.)

Life expectancy at birth:

total population: Serbia - 73.45 years; Montenegro - 76.32 years

male: Serbia - 71.03 years; Montenegro - 72.87 years

female: Serbia - 76.05 years; Montenegro - 80.07 years (1999 est.)

Total fertility rate: Serbia - 1.74 children born/woman; Montenegro - 1.76 children born/woman (1999 est.)

Nationality:

noun: Serb(s); Montenegrin(s)

adjective: Serbian; Montenegrin

Ethnic groups: Serbs 63%, Albanians 14%, Montenegrins 6%, Hungarians 4%, other 13%

Religions: Orthodox 65%, Muslim 19%, Roman Catholic 4%, Protestant 1%, other 11%

Languages: Serbo-Croatian 95%, Albanian 5%

Literacy: NA

Government

Country name:

conventional long form: none

conventional short form: Serbia and Montenegro

local long form: none

local short form: Srbija-Crna Gora

note: Serbia and Montenegro has self-proclaimed itself the "Federal Republic of Yugoslavia" (FRY) but the US view is that the Socialist Federal Republic of Yugoslavia (SFRY) has dissolved and that none of the successor republics represents its continuation

Data code: Serbia - SR; Montenegro - MW

Government type: republic

Capital: Belgrade (Serbia), Podgorica (Montenegro)

Administrative divisions: 2 republics (republike, singular - republika); and 2 nominally autonomous provinces* (autonomn pokrajine, singular - autonomna pokrajina); Kosovo*, Montenegro, Serbia, Vojvodina*

Independence: 11 April 1992 (Federal Republic of Yugoslavia or FRY formed as self-proclaimed successor to the Socialist Federal Republic of Yugoslavia or SFRY)

National holiday: St. Vitus Day, 28 June

Constitution: 27 April 1992

Legal system: based on civil law system

Suffrage: 16 years of age, if employed; 18 years of age, universal

Executive branch:

chief of state: President Slobodan MILOSEVIC (since 23 July 1997); note - Milan MILUTINOVIC is president of Serbia (since 21 December 1997); Milo DJUKANOVIC is president of Montenegro (since 21 December 1997)

head of government: Prime Minister Momir BULATOVIC (since 20 May 1998); Deputy Prime Ministers Nikola SAINOVIC (since 15 September 1995), Vuk DRASKOVIC (since 1 February 1999), Jovan ZEBIC (since 9 April 1998), and Vladan KUTLESIC (since 20 March 1997), Zoran LILIC (since 20 May 1998), Danilo VUKSANOVIC (since 20 May 1998)

cabinet: Federal Executive Council

elections: president elected by the Federal Assembly for a four-year term; election last held 23 July 1997 (next to be held NA 2001); prime minister appointed by the president

election results: Slobodan MILOSEVIC elected president; percent of legislative vote - Slobodan MILOSEVIC 90%

Legislative branch: bicameral Federal Assembly or Savezna Skupstina consists of the Chamber of Republics or Vece Republika (40 seats - 20 Serbian, 20 Montenegrin; members distributed on the basis of party representation in the republican assemblies to serve four-year terms) and the Chamber of Citizens or Vece Gradjana (138 seats -, 108 Serbian with half elected by constituency majorities and half by proportional representation, 30 Montenegrin with six elected by constituency and 24 proportionally; members serve four-year terms)

elections: Chamber of Republics - last held 24 December 1996 (next to be held NA 2000); Chamber of Citizens - last held 3 November 1996 (next to be held NA 2000)

election results: Chamber of Republics - percent of vote by party - NA; seats by party - NA; note - seats are filled on a proportional basis to reflect the composition of the legislatures of the republics of Montenegro and Serbia; Chamber of Citizens - percent of vote by party - NA; seats by party - SPS/JUL/ND 64, Zajedno 22, DPSCG 20, SRS 16, NS 8, SVM 3, other 5; note - Zajedno coalition includes SPO, DS, GSS

Judicial branch: Federal Court or Savezni Sud, judges are elected by the Federal Assembly for nine-year terms; Constitutional Court, judges are elected by the Federal Assembly for nine-year terms

Political parties and leaders: Serbian Socialist Party or SPS (former Communist Party) [Slobodan MILOSEVIC]; Serbian Radical Party or SRS [Vojislav SESELJ]; Serbian Renewal Movement or SPO [Vuk DRASKOVIC, president]; Democratic Party or DS [Zoran DJINDJIC]; Democratic Party of Serbia or DSS [Vojislav KOSTUNICA]; Democratic Party of Socialists of Montenegro or DPSCG [Milo DJUKANOVIC]; People's Party of Montenegro or NS [Novak KILIBARDA]; Socialist People's Party of

Montenegro or SNP [Momir BULATOVIC]; Social Democratic Party of Montenegro or SDP [Zarko RAKCEVIC]; Liberal Alliance of Montenegro [Slavko PEROVIC]; Democratic Community of Vojvodina Hungarians or DZVM [Sandor PALL]; League of Social Democrats of Vojvodina or LSV [Nenad CANAK]; Reformist Democratic Party of Vojvodina or RDSV [Aleksandar POPOV]; Democratic Alliance of Vojvodina Croats or DSHV [Bela TONKOVIC]; League of Communists-Movement for Yugoslavia or SK-PJ [Dragomir DRASKOVIC]; Democratic Alliance of Kosovo or LDK [Dr. Ibrahim RUGOVA, president]; Democratic League of Albanians [Rexhep QOSJA]; Parliamentary Party of Kosovo or PPK [Bajram KOSUMI]; Party of Democratic Action or SDA [Dr. Sulejman UGLJANIN]; Civic Alliance of Serbia or GSS [Vesna PESIC, chairman]; Yugoslav United Left or JUL [Mirjana MARKOVIC (MILOSEVIC's wife)]; New Democracy or ND [Dusan MIHAJLOVIC]; Alliance of Vojvodina Hungarians or SVM [Jozsef KASZA]; Together or Zajedno [leader NA]

Political pressure groups and leaders: NA

International organization participation: ICFTU, IOC, OPCW

Diplomatic representation in the US: the US and Serbia and Montenegro do not maintain full diplomatic relations; the Embassy of the former Socialist Federal Republic of Yugoslavia continues to function in the US

chief of mission: Ambassador (vacant); Counselor, Charge d'Affaires ad interim Nebojsa VUJOVIC

chancery: 2410 California St. NW, Washington, DC 20008

telephone: [1] (202) 462-6566

Diplomatic representation from the US: the US and Serbia and Montenegro do not maintain full diplomatic relations

chief of mission: Ambassador (vacant); Chief of Mission Richard M. MILES

embassy: Kneza Milosa 50, 11000 Belgrade

mailing address: American Embassy, Belgrade, United States Department of State, Washington, DC 20521-5070 (pouch)

telephone: [381] (11) 645655

FAX: [381] (11) 645221

Economy

Economy - overview: The swift collapse of the Yugoslav federation in 1991 has been followed by highly destructive warfare, the destabilization of republic boundaries, and the breakup of important interrepublic trade flows. Output in Serbia and Montenegro dropped by half in 1992-93. Like the other former Yugoslav republics, it had depended on its sister republics for large amounts of energy and manufactures. Wide differences in climate, mineral resources, and levels of technology among the republics accentuated this interdependence, as did the communist practice of concentrating much industrial output in a small number of giant plants. The breakup of many of the trade links, the sharp drop in output as industrial plants lost suppliers and markets, and the destruction of physical assets in the fighting all

have contributed to the economic difficulties of the republics. One singular factor in the economic situation of Serbia is the continuation in office of a government that is primarily interested in political and military mastery, not economic reform. Hyperinflation ended with the establishment of a new currency unit in June 1993; prices were relatively stable from 1995 through 1997, but inflationary pressures resurged in 1998. Reliable statistics continue to be hard to come by, and the GDP estimate is extremely rough. The economic boom anticipated by the government after the suspension of UN sanctions in December 1995 has failed to materialize. Government mismanagement of the economy is largely to blame. Also, the Outer Wall sanctions that exclude Belgrade from international financial institutions and an investment ban and asset freeze imposed in 1998 because of Belgrade's repressive actions in Kosovo have added to economic difficulties.

GDP: purchasing power parity - $25.4 billion (1998 est.)

GDP - real growth rate: 3.5% (1998 est.)

GDP - per capita: purchasing power parity - $2,300 (1998 est.)

GDP - composition by sector:

agriculture: 25%

industry: 50%

services: 25% (1994 est.)

Population below poverty line: NA%

Household income or consumption by percentage share:

lowest 10%: NA%

highest 10%: NA%

Inflation rate (consumer prices): 48% (1998 est.)

Labor force: NA

Labor force - by occupation: industry 41%, services 35%, trade and tourism 12%, transportation and communication 7%, agriculture 5% (1994)

Unemployment rate: more than 35% (1995 est.)

Budget:

revenues: $NA

expenditures: $NA, including capital expenditures of $NA

Industries: machine building (aircraft, trucks, and automobiles; tanks and weapons; electrical equipment; agricultural machinery); metallurgy (steel, aluminum, copper, lead, zinc, chromium, antimony, bismuth, cadmium); mining (coal, bauxite, nonferrous ore, iron ore, limestone); consumer goods (textiles, footwear, foodstuffs, appliances); electronics, petroleum products, chemicals, and pharmaceuticals

Industrial production growth rate: 8% (1997 est.)

Electricity - production: 36.155 billion kWh (1996)

Electricity - production by source:

fossil fuel: 63.44%

hydro: 36.56%

nuclear: 0%

other: 0% (1996)

Electricity - consumption: 35.999 billion kWh (1996)

Electricity - exports: 156 million kWh (1996)

Electricity - imports: 0 kWh (1996)

Agriculture - products: cereals, fruits, vegetables, tobacco, olives; cattle, sheep, goats

Exports: $2.3 billion (1998 est.)

Exports - commodities: manufactured goods, food and live animals, raw materials

Exports - partners: Bosnia and Herzegovina, Italy, The Former Yugoslav Republic of Macedonia

Imports: $3.9 billion (1998 est.)

Imports - commodities: machinery and transport equipment, fuels and lubricants, manufactured goods, chemicals, food and live animals, raw materials

Imports - partners: Germany, Italy, Russia

Debt - external: $11.2 billion (1995 est.)

Economic aid - recipient: $NA

Currency: 1 Yugoslav New Dinar (YD) = 100 paras

Exchange rates: Yugoslav New Dinars (YD) per US $1 - official rate: 10.0 (December 1998), 5.85 (December 1997), 5.02 (September 1996), 1.5 (early 1995); black market rate: 14.5 (December 1998), 8.9 (December 1997), 2 to 3 (early 1995)

Fiscal year: calendar year

Communications

Telephones: 700,000

Telephone system:

domestic: NA

international: satellite earth station - 1 Intelsat (Atlantic Ocean)

Radio broadcast stations: 27 (public or state-owned 1, private 26)

Radios: 2.015 million

Television broadcast stations: more than 771 (consisting of 86 strong stations, 685 low-power stations, and 20 repeaters in the principal networks; there are also numerous local or private stations in Serbia and Vojvodina) (1997)

Televisions: 1 million

Transportation

Railways:

total: 3,987 km

standard gauge: 3,987 km 1.435-m gauge (1,377 km partially electrified since 1992) (1998)

Highways:

total: 50,414 km

paved: 45,020 km (including 545 km of expressways)

unpaved: 5,394 km (1997 est.)

Waterways: NA km

Pipelines: crude oil 415 km; petroleum products 130 km; natural gas 2,110 km

Ports and harbors: Bar, Belgrade, Kotor, Novi Sad, Pancevo, Tivat, Zelenika

Merchant marine:

total: 1 short-sea passenger (1,000 GRT or over) totaling 2,437 GRT/400 DWT (owned by Montenegro) (1998 est.)

Airports: 48 (Serbia 43, Montenegro 5) (1998 est.)

Airports - with paved runways:

total: 18

over 3,047 m: 2 (Serbia 2, Montenegro 0)

2,438 to 3,047 m: 5 (Serbia 3, Montenegro 2)

1,524 to 2,437 m: 5 (Serbia 4, Montenegro 1)
914 to 1,523 m: 2 (Serbia 2, Montenegro 0)
under 914 m: 4 (Serbia 4, Montenegro 0) (1998 est.)
Airports - with unpaved runways:
total: 30
1,524 to 2,437 m: 2 (Serbia 2, Montenegro 0)
914 to 1,523 m: 14 (Serbia 13, Montenegro 1)
under 914 m: 14 (Serbia 13, Montenegro 1) (1998 est.)

Military

Military branches: Army (including ground forces with border troops, naval forces, air and air defense forces)
Military manpower - military age: Serbia - NA years of age; Montenegro - 19 years of age
Military manpower - availability:
males age 15-49: Serbia - 2,727,292; Montenegro - 187,198 (1999 est.)
Military manpower - fit for military service:
males age 15-49: Serbia - 2,183,534; Montenegro - 150,415 (1999 est.)
Military manpower - reaching military age annually:
males: Serbia - NA; Montenegro - 5,671 (1999 est.)
Military expenditures - dollar figure: $911 million (1999)
Military expenditures - percent of GDP: 6.5% (1999)

Transnational Issues

Disputes - international: disputes with Bosnia and Herzegovina over Serbian populated areas; Albanian majority in Kosovo seeks independence from Serbian republic; Serbia and Montenegro is disputing Croatia's claim to the Prevlaka Peninsula in southern Croatia because it controls the entrance to Boka Kotorska in Montenegro; Prevlaka is currently under observation by the UN military observer mission in Prevlaka (UNMOP); the border commission formed by The Former Yugoslav Republic of Macedonia and Serbia and Montenegro in April 1996 to resolve differences in delineation of their mutual border has made no progress so far
Illicit drugs: major transshipment point for Southwest Asian heroin moving to Western Europe on the Balkan route

Seychelles

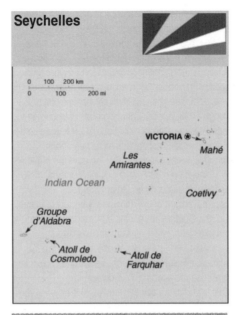

Geography

Location: Eastern Africa, group of islands in the Indian Ocean, northeast of Madagascar
Geographic coordinates: 4 35 S, 55 40 E
Map references: Africa
Area:
total: 455 sq km
land: 455 sq km
water: 0 sq km
Area - comparative: 2.5 times the size of Washington, DC
Land boundaries: 0 km
Coastline: 491 km
Maritime claims:
continental shelf: 200 nm or to the edge of the continental margin
exclusive economic zone: 200 nm
territorial sea: 12 nm
Climate: tropical marine; humid; cooler season during southeast monsoon (late May to September); warmer season during northwest monsoon (March to May)
Terrain: Mahe Group is granitic, narrow coastal strip, rocky, hilly; others are coral, flat, elevated reefs
Elevation extremes:
lowest point: Indian Ocean 0 m
highest point: Morne Seychellois 905 m
Natural resources: fish, copra, cinnamon trees
Land use:
arable land: 2%
permanent crops: 13%
permanent pastures: NA%
forests and woodland: 11%
other: 74% (1993 est.)
Irrigated land: NA sq km
Natural hazards: lies outside the cyclone belt, so severe storms are rare; short droughts possible
Environment - current issues: water supply depends on catchments to collect rain water

Environment - international agreements:
party to: Biodiversity, Climate Change, Desertification, Endangered Species, Hazardous Wastes, Law of the Sea, Marine Dumping, Nuclear Test Ban, Ozone Layer Protection, Ship Pollution, Whaling
signed, but not ratified: Climate Change-Kyoto Protocol
Geography - note: 40 granitic and about 50 coralline islands

People

Population: 79,164 (July 1999 est.)
Age structure:
0-14 years: 29% (male 11,712; female 11,569)
15-64 years: 64% (male 24,879; female 26,038)
65 years and over: 7% (male 1,709; female 3,257) (1999 est.)
Population growth rate: 0.65% (1999 est.)
Birth rate: 19.39 births/1,000 population (1999 est.)
Death rate: 6.56 deaths/1,000 population (1999 est.)
Net migration rate: -6.32 migrant(s)/1,000 population (1999 est.)
Sex ratio:
at birth: 1.03 male(s)/female
under 15 years: 1.01 male(s)/female
15-64 years: 0.96 male(s)/female
65 years and over: 0.52 male(s)/female
total population: 0.94 male(s)/female (1999 est.)
Infant mortality rate: 16.65 deaths/1,000 live births (1999 est.)
Life expectancy at birth:
total population: 70.95 years
male: 66.61 years
female: 75.42 years (1999 est.)
Total fertility rate: 1.97 children born/woman (1999 est.)
Nationality:
noun: Seychellois (singular and plural)
adjective: Seychelles
Ethnic groups: Seychellois (mixture of Asians, Africans, Europeans)
Religions: Roman Catholic 90%, Anglican 8%, other 2%
Languages: English (official), French (official), Creole
Literacy:
definition: age 15 and over can read and write
total population: 58%
male: 56%
female: 60% (1971 est.)

Government

Country name:
conventional long form: Republic of Seychelles
conventional short form: Seychelles
Data code: SE
Government type: republic
Capital: Victoria
Administrative divisions: 23 administrative districts; Anse aux Pins, Anse Boileau, Anse Etoile,

Seychelles (continued)

Anse Louis, Anse Royale, Baie Lazare, Baie Sainte Anne, Beau Vallon, Bel Air, Bel Ombre, Cascade, Glacis, Grand' Anse (on Mahe), Grand' Anse (on Praslin), La Digue, La Riviere Anglaise, Mont Buxton, Mont Fleuri, Plaisance, Pointe La Rue, Port Glaud, Saint Louis, Takamaka

Independence: 29 June 1976 (from UK)

National holiday: National Day, 18 June (1993) (adoption of the constitution)

Constitution: 18 June 1993

Legal system: based on English common law, French civil law, and customary law

Suffrage: 17 years of age; universal

Executive branch:

chief of state: President France Albert RENE (since 5 June 1977); note - the president is both the chief of state and head of government

head of government: President France Albert RENE (since 5 June 1977); note - the president is both the chief of state and head of government

cabinet: Council of Ministers appointed by the president

elections: president elected by popular vote for a five-year term; election last held 20-22 March 1998 (next to be held by NA 2003)

election results: President France Albert RENE reelected; percent of vote - France Albert RENE (SPPF) 61%, Wavel RAMKALAWAN (UO) 27%, Sir James MANCHAM (DP) 12%

Legislative branch: unicameral National Assembly or Assemblee Nationale (35 seats - 25 elected by popular vote, 10 allocated on a proportional basis to parties winning at least nine percent of the vote; members serve five-year terms)

elections: last held 20-22 March 1998 (next to be held by NA 2003)

election results: percent of vote by party - NA; seats by party (elected) - SPPF 24, DP 1; seats by party (awarded) - SPPF 6, DP 1, UO 3

note: the 10 awarded seats are apportioned according to the share of each party in the total vote

Judicial branch: Court of Appeal, judges are appointed by the president; Supreme Court, judges are appointed by the president

Political parties and leaders: ruling party - Seychelles People's Progressive Front or SPPF [France Albert RENE]; Democratic Party or DP [leader NA]; United Opposition or UO [Wavel RAMKALAWAN] - a coalition of the following parties: Seychelles Party or PS [Wavel RAMKALAWAN], Seychelles Democratic Movement or MSPD [Jacques HONDOUL], and Seychelles Liberal Party or SLP [Ogilvie BERLOUIS]; New Democratic Party [Christopher GILL (former member of DP)]

Political pressure groups and leaders: trade unions; Roman Catholic Church

International organization participation: ACCT, ACP, AfDB, C, ECA, FAO, G-77, IBRD, ICAO, ICFTU, ICRM, IFAD, IFC, IFRCS, ILO, IMF, IMO, InOC, Intelsat (nonsignatory user), Interpol, IOC, NAM, OAU, OPCW, SADC, UN, UNCTAD, UNESCO, UNIDO, UPU, WCL, WHO, WMO, WToO, WTrO (applicant)

Diplomatic representation in the US:

chief of mission: Ambassador Claude MOREL

chancery: 800 Second Avenue, Suite 400C, New York, NY 10017

telephone: [1] (212) 972-1785

FAX: [1] (212) 972-1786

Diplomatic representation from the US: the US does not have an embassy in Seychelles; the ambassador to Mauritius is accredited to Seychelles

Flag description: five oblique bands of blue (hoist side), yellow, red, white, and green (bottom) radiating from the bottom of the hoist side

Economy

Economy - overview: Since independence in 1976, per capita output in this Indian Ocean archipelago has expanded to roughly seven times the old near-subsistence level. Growth has been led by the tourist sector, which employs about 30% of the labor force and provides more than 70% of hard currency earnings, and by tuna fishing, which accounted for 70% of GDP in 1996-97. In recent years the government has encouraged foreign investment in order to upgrade hotels and other services. At the same time, the government has moved to reduce the dependence on tourism by promoting the development of farming, fishing, and small-scale manufacturing. The vulnerability of the tourist sector was illustrated by the sharp drop in 1991-92 due largely to the Gulf war. Although the industry has rebounded, the government recognizes the continuing need for upgrading the sector in the face of stiff international competition. Other issues facing the government are the curbing of the budget deficit and further privatization of public enterprises.

GDP: purchasing power parity - $550 million (1997 est.)

GDP - real growth rate: 4.3% (1997 est.)

GDP - per capita: purchasing power parity - $7,000 (1997 est.)

GDP - composition by sector:

agriculture: 4%

industry: 15%

services: 81% (1994)

Population below poverty line: NA%

Household income or consumption by percentage share:

lowest 10%: NA%

highest 10%: NA%

Inflation rate (consumer prices): 0.6% (1997)

Labor force: 26,000 (1996)

Labor force - by occupation: industry 19%, services 57%, government 14%, fishing, agriculture, and forestry 10% (1989)

Unemployment rate: NA%

Budget:

revenues: $220 million

expenditures: $241 million, including capital expenditures of $36 million (1994 est.)

Industries: fishing; tourism; processing of coconuts and vanilla, coir (coconut fiber) rope, boat building, printing, furniture; beverages

Industrial production growth rate: 4% (1992)

Electricity - production: 125 million kWh (1996)

Electricity - production by source:

fossil fuel: 100%

hydro: 0%

nuclear: 0%

other: 0% (1996)

Electricity - consumption: 125 million kWh (1996)

Electricity - exports: 0 kWh (1996)

Electricity - imports: 0 kWh (1996)

Agriculture - products: coconuts, cinnamon, vanilla, sweet potatoes, cassava (tapioca), bananas; broiler chickens; tuna fish

Exports: $53 million (f.o.b., 1995)

Exports - commodities: fish, cinnamon bark, copra, petroleum products (reexports)

Exports - partners: France, UK, China, Germany, Japan (1993)

Imports: $340 million (c.i.f., 1997)

Imports - commodities: manufactured goods, food, petroleum products, tobacco, beverages, machinery and transportation equipment

Imports - partners: China, Singapore, South Africa, UK (1993)

Debt - external: $170 million (1994 est.)

Economic aid - recipient: $16.4 million (1995)

Currency: 1 Seychelles rupee (SRe) = 100 cents

Exchange rates: Seychelles rupees (SRe) per US$1 - 5.4540 (January 1999), 5.2622 (1998), 5.0263 (1997), 4.9700 (1996), 4.7620 (1995), 5.0559 (1994)

Fiscal year: calendar year

Communications

Telephones: 13,000 (1995 est.)

Telephone system:

domestic: radiotelephone communications between islands in the archipelago

international: direct radiotelephone communications with adjacent island countries and African coastal countries; satellite earth station - 1 Intelsat (Indian Ocean)

Radio broadcast stations: AM 3, FM 0, shortwave 0

Radios: 50,000 (1996 est.)

Television broadcast stations: 2 (in addition, there are 9 repeaters) (1997)

Televisions: 12,000 (1996 est.)

Transportation

Railways: 0 km

Highways:

total: 280 km

paved: 176 km

unpaved: 104 km (1996 est.)

Ports and harbors: Victoria

Merchant marine: none

Airports: 14 (1998 est.)

Airports - with paved runways:

total: 6

2,438 to 3,047 m: 1

914 to 1,523 m: 3

under 914 m: 2 (1998 est.)

Seychelles *(continued)*

Airports - with unpaved runways:
total: 8
914 to 1,523 m: 4
under 914 m: 4 (1998 est.)

Military

Military branches: Army, Coast Guard, Marines, air wing, National Guard, Presidential Protection Unit, Police Force
Military manpower - availability:
males age 15-49: 22,420 (1999 est.)
Military manpower - fit for military service:
males age 15-49: 11,242 (1999 est.)
Military expenditures - dollar figure: $13.7 million (1995)
Military expenditures - percent of GDP: NA%

Transnational Issues

Disputes - international: claims Chagos Archipelago in British Indian Ocean Territory

Sierra Leone

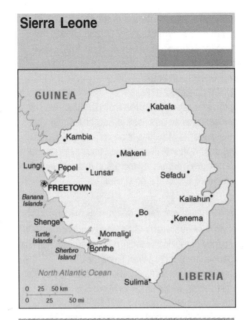

Introduction

Background: On 25 May 1997, the democratically-elected government of President Ahmad Tejan KABBAH was overthrown by a disgruntled coalition of army personnel from the Armed Forces Revolutionary Council (AFRC) and the Revolutionary United Front (RUF) under the command of Major Johnny Paul KOROMA; President KABBAH fled to exile in Guinea. The Economic Community of West African States Cease-Fire Monitoring Group (ECOMOG) forces, led by a strong Nigerian contingent, undertook the suppression of the rebellion. They were initially unsuccessful, but, by October 1997, they forced the rebels to agree to a cease-fire and to a plan to return the government to democratic control. President KABBAH returned to office on 10 March 1998 to face the task of restoring order to a demoralized population and a disorganized and severely damaged economy. Many of the leaders of the coup were tried and executed in October 1998. In January 1999, the situation had deteriorated even further, with commerce at a standstill, hundreds of thousands of people driven from their homes, and bitter fighting between the AFRC/RUF and ECOMOG troops intensifying by large-scale import of arms.

Geography

Location: Western Africa, bordering the North Atlantic Ocean, between Guinea and Liberia
Geographic coordinates: 8 30 N, 11 30 W
Map references: Africa
Area:
total: 71,740 sq km
land: 71,620 sq km
water: 120 sq km
Area - comparative: slightly smaller than South Carolina
Land boundaries:
total: 958 km
border countries: Guinea 652 km, Liberia 306 km

Coastline: 402 km
Maritime claims:
territorial sea: 200 nm
continental shelf: 200-m depth or to the depth of exploitation
Climate: tropical; hot, humid; summer rainy season (May to December); winter dry season (December to April)
Terrain: coastal belt of mangrove swamps, wooded hill country, upland plateau, mountains in east
Elevation extremes:
lowest point: Atlantic Ocean 0 m
highest point: Loma Mansa (Bintimani) 1,948 m
Natural resources: diamonds, titanium ore, bauxite, iron ore, gold, chromite
Land use:
arable land: 7%
permanent crops: 1%
permanent pastures: 31%
forests and woodland: 28%
other: 33% (1993 est.)
Irrigated land: 290 sq km (1993 est.)
Natural hazards: dry, sand-laden harmattan winds blow from the Sahara (November to May); sandstorms, dust storms
Environment - current issues: rapid population growth pressuring the environment; overharvesting of timber, expansion of cattle grazing, and slash-and-burn agriculture have resulted in deforestation and soil exhaustion; civil war depleting natural resources; overfishing
Environment - international agreements:
party to: Biodiversity, Climate Change, Desertification, Endangered Species, Law of the Sea, Marine Life Conservation, Nuclear Test Ban
signed, but not ratified: Environmental Modification

People

Population: 5,296,651 (July 1999 est.)
Age structure:
0-14 years: 45% (male 1,182,181; female 1,219,956)
15-64 years: 52% (male 1,307,475; female 1,423,046)
65 years and over: 3% (male 82,374; female 81,619) (1999 est.)
Population growth rate: 4.34% (1999 est.)
Birth rate: 45.62 births/1,000 population (1999 est.)
Death rate: 16.77 deaths/1,000 population (1999 est.)
Net migration rate: 14.5 migrant(s)/1,000 population (1999 est.)
Sex ratio:
at birth: 1.03 male(s)/female
under 15 years: 0.97 male(s)/female
15-64 years: 0.92 male(s)/female
65 years and over: 1.01 male(s)/female
total population: 0.94 male(s)/female (1999 est.)
Infant mortality rate: 126.23 deaths/1,000 live births (1999 est.)
Life expectancy at birth:
total population: 49.13 years
male: 46.07 years

Sierra Leone (continued)

female: 52.27 years (1999 est.)
Total fertility rate: 6.16 children born/woman (1999 est.)
Nationality:
noun: Sierra Leonean(s)
adjective: Sierra Leonean
Ethnic groups: 20 native African tribes 90% (Temne 30%, Mende 30%, other 30%), Creole 10% (descendents of freed Jamaican slaves who were settled in the Freetown area in the late-eighteenth century), refugees from Liberia's recent civil war, small numbers of Europeans, Lebanese, Pakistanis, and Indians
Religions: Muslim 60%, indigenous beliefs 30%, Christian 10%
Languages: English (official, regular use limited to literate minority), Mende (principal vernacular in the south), Temne (principal vernacular in the north), Krio (English-based Creole, spoken by the descendents of freed Jamaican slaves who were settled in the Freetown area, a lingua franca and a first language for 10% of the population but understood by 95%)
Literacy:
definition: age 15 and over can read and write English, Mende, Temne, or Arabic
total population: 31.4%
male: 45.4%
female: 18.2% (1995 est.)

Government

Country name:
conventional long form: Republic of Sierra Leone
conventional short form: Sierra Leone
Data code: SL
Government type: constitutional democracy
Capital: Freetown
Administrative divisions: 3 provinces and 1 area*; Eastern, Northern, Southern, Western*
Independence: 27 April 1961 (from UK)
National holiday: Republic Day, 27 April (1961)
Constitution: 1 October 1991; subsequently amended several times
Legal system: based on English law and customary laws indigenous to local tribes; has not accepted compulsory ICJ jurisdiction
Suffrage: 18 years of age; universal
Executive branch:
chief of state: President Ahmad Tejan KABBAH (since 29 March 1996, reinstated 10 March 1998); note - the president is both the chief of state and head of government
head of government: President Ahmad Tejan KABBAH (since 29 March 1996, reinstated 10 March 1998); note - the president is both the chief of state and head of government
cabinet: Ministers of State appointed by the president with the approval of the House of Representatives; the cabinet is responsible to the president
elections: president elected by popular vote for a five-year term; election held 26-27 February 1996 (next to be held NA 2001); note - president's tenure of office is limited to two five-year terms

election results: Ahmad Tejan KABBAH elected president; percent of vote - first round - KABBAH 36.0%, second round - KABBAH 59.5%
Legislative branch: unicameral House of Representatives (80 seats - 68 elected by popular vote, 12 filled by paramount chiefs elected in separate elections; members serve five-year terms)
elections: last held 26-27 February 1996 (next to be held 2001)
election results: percent of vote by party - NA; seats by party - SLPP 27, UNPP 17, PDP 12, APC 5, NUP 4, DCP 3; note - first elections since the former House of Representatives was shut down by the military coup of 29 April 1992
Judicial branch: Supreme Court
Political parties and leaders: 15 parties registered for the February 1996 elections; National People's Party or NPP [Andrew TURAY]; Democratic Center Party or DCP [Abu KOROMA]; People's Progressive Party or PPP [Abass Chernok BUNDU, chairman]; Coalition for Progress Party or CPP [Geredine WILLIAMS-SARHO]; National Unity Movement or NUM [John Desmond Fashole LUKE]; United National People's Party or UNPP [John KARIFA-SMART]; People's Democratic Party or PDP [Thaimu BANGURA, chairman]; All People's Congress or APC [Edward Mohammed TURAY, chairman]; National Republican Party or NRP [Sahr Stephen MAMBU]; Social Democratic Party or SDP [Andrew Victor LUNGAY]; People's National Convention or PNC [Edward John KARGBO, chairman]; National Unity Party or NUP [Dr. John KARIMU, chairman]; Sierra Leone People's Party or SLPP [President Ahmad Tejan KABBAH, chairman]; National Democratic Alliance or NDA [Amadu M. B. JALLOH]; National Alliance for Democracy Party or NADP [Mohamed Yahya SILLAH]
International organization participation: ACP, AfDB, C, CCC, ECA, ECOWAS, FAO, G-77, IAEA, IBRD, ICAO, ICFTU, ICRM, IDA, IDB, IFAD, IFC, IFRCS, ILO, IMF, IMO, Intelsat (nonsignatory user), Interpol, IOC, ITU, NAM, OAU, OIC, OPCW, UN, UNCTAD, UNESCO, UNIDO, UPU, WCL, WFTU, WHO, WIPO, WMO, WToO, WTrO
Diplomatic representation in the US:
chief of mission: Ambassador John Ernest LEIGH
chancery: 1701 19th Street NW, Washington, DC 20009
telephone: [1] (202) 939-9261 through 9263
FAX: [1] (202) 483-1793
Diplomatic representation from the US:
chief of mission: Ambassador Joseph MELROSE; note - embassy closed in late December 1998
embassy: Corner of Walpole and Siaka Stevens Streets, Freetown
mailing address: use embassy street address
telephone: [232] (22) 226481 through 226485
FAX: [232] (22) 225471
Flag description: three equal horizontal bands of light green (top), white, and light blue

Economy

Economy - overview: Sierra Leone has substantial mineral, agricultural, and fishery resources. However, the economic and social infrastructure is not well developed, and serious social disorders continue to hamper economic development. The period of AFRC/RUF junta rule (May 1997-February 1998) led to UN sanctions and 20% drop in GDP in 1997. The continued fighting at yearend 1997 set back what small progress had been made by the KABBAH government in recovering from the junta period and reestablishing a viable economy. About two-thirds of the working-age population engages in subsistence agriculture. Manufacturing consists mainly of the processing of raw materials and of light manufacturing for the domestic market. Bauxite and rutile mines have been shut down by civil strife. The major source of hard currency is found in the mining of diamonds, the large majority of which are smuggled out of the country. The fate of the economy in 1999 depends on the outcome of negotiations to end the civil strife.
GDP: purchasing power parity - $2.7 billion (1998 est.)
GDP - real growth rate: 0.7% (1998 est.)
GDP - per capita: purchasing power parity - $530 (1998 est.)
GDP - composition by sector:
agriculture: 52%
industry: 16%
services: 32% (1996)
Population below poverty line: 68% (1989 est.)
Household income or consumption by percentage share:
lowest 10%: 0.5%
highest 10%: 43.6% (1989)
Inflation rate (consumer prices): 37.4% (1998 est.)
Labor force: 1.369 million (1981 est.)
note: only about 65,000 wage earners (1985)
Labor force - by occupation: agriculture 65%, industry 19%, services 16% (1981 est.)
Unemployment rate: NA%
Budget:
revenues: $96 million
expenditures: $150 million, including capital expenditures of $NA (1996 est.)
Industries: mining (diamonds); small-scale manufacturing (beverages, textiles, cigarettes, footwear); petroleum refining
Industrial production growth rate: NA%
Electricity - production: 230 million kWh (1996)
Electricity - production by source:
fossil fuel: 100%
hydro: 0%
nuclear: 0%
other: 0% (1996)
Electricity - consumption: 230 million kWh (1996)
Electricity - exports: 0 kWh (1996)
Electricity - imports: 0 kWh (1996)
Agriculture - products: rice, coffee, cocoa, palm

Sierra Leone *(continued)*

kernels, palm oil, peanuts; poultry, cattle, sheep, pigs; fish
Exports: $41 million (f.o.b., 1998)
Exports - commodities: diamonds, rutile, cocoa, coffee, fish
Exports - partners: Belgium 49%, Spain 10%, US 8%, UK 3% (1997)
Imports: $166 million (f.o.b., 1998)
Imports - commodities: foodstuffs, machinery and equipment, fuels and lubricants
Imports - partners: UK 16%, US 9%, Cote d'Ivoire 8%, Belgium-Luxembourg 3% (1997)
Debt - external: $1.15 billion (1998)
Economic aid - recipient: $203.7 million (1995)
Currency: 1 leone (Le) = 100 cents
Exchange rates: leones (Le) per US$1 - 1,630.5 (January 1999), 1,597.2 (1998), 981.48 (1997), 920.73 (1996), 755.22 (1995), 586.74 (1994)
Fiscal year: 1 July - 30 June

Communications

Telephones: 17,526 (1991 est.)
Telephone system: marginal telephone and telegraph service
domestic: national microwave radio relay system made unserviceable by military activities
international: satellite earth station - 1 Intelsat (Atlantic Ocean)
Radio broadcast stations: AM 1, FM 1, shortwave NA
Radios: 980,000 (1992 est.)
Television broadcast stations: 2 (1997)
Televisions: 45,000 (1992 est.)

Transportation

Railways:
total: 84 km used on a limited basis because the mine at Marampa is closed
narrow gauge: 84 km 1.067-m gauge
Highways:
total: 11,700 km
paved: 1,287 km
unpaved: 10,413 km (1996 est.)
Waterways: 800 km; 600 km navigable year round
Ports and harbors: Bonthe, Freetown, Pepel
Merchant marine: none
Airports: 10 (1998 est.)
Airports - with paved runways:
total: 2
over 3,047 m: 1
914 to 1,523 m: 1 (1998 est.)
Airports - with unpaved runways:
total: 8
914 to 1,523 m: 5
under 914 m: 3 (1998 est.)
Heliports: 1 (1998 est.)

Military

Military branches: Army
Military manpower - availability:
males age 15-49: 1,119,239 (1999 est.)

Military manpower - fit for military service:
males age 15-49: 543,210 (1999 est.)
Military expenditures - dollar figure: $46 million (FY96/97)
Military expenditures - percent of GDP: 2% (FY96/97)

Transnational Issues

Disputes - international: none

Singapore

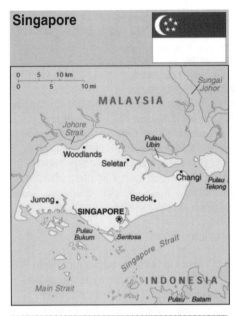

Geography

Location: Southeastern Asia, islands between Malaysia and Indonesia
Geographic coordinates: 1 22 N, 103 48 E
Map references: Southeast Asia
Area:
total: 647.5 sq km
land: 637.5 sq km
water: 10 sq km
Area - comparative: slightly more than 3.5 times the size of Washington, DC
Land boundaries: 0 km
Coastline: 193 km
Maritime claims:
exclusive fishing zone: within and beyond territorial sea, as defined in treaties and practice
territorial sea: 3 nm
Climate: tropical; hot, humid, rainy; no pronounced rainy or dry seasons; thunderstorms occur on 40% of all days (67% of days in April)
Terrain: lowland; gently undulating central plateau contains water catchment area and nature preserve
Elevation extremes:
lowest point: Singapore Strait 0 m
highest point: Bukit Timah 166 m
Natural resources: fish, deepwater ports
Land use:
arable land: 2%
permanent crops: 6%
permanent pastures: NA%
forests and woodland: 5%
other: 87% (1993 est.)
Irrigated land: NA sq km
Natural hazards: NA
Environment - current issues: industrial pollution; limited natural fresh water resources; limited land availability presents waste disposal problems; seasonal smoke/haze resulting from forest fires in Indonesia

Singapore (continued)

Environment - international agreements:
party to: Biodiversity, Climate Change, Endangered Species, Hazardous Wastes, Law of the Sea, Nuclear Test Ban, Ozone Layer Protection, Ship Pollution
signed, but not ratified: none of the selected agreements
Geography - note: focal point for Southeast Asian sea routes

People

Population: 3,531,600 (July 1999 est.)
Age structure:
0-14 years: 21% (male 387,786; female 364,018)
15-64 years: 72% (male 1,265,291; female 1,268,458)
65 years and over: 7% (male 109,418; female 136,629) (1999 est.)
Population growth rate: 1.15% (1999 est.)
Birth rate: 13.38 births/1,000 population (1999 est.)
Death rate: 4.69 deaths/1,000 population (1999 est.)
Net migration rate: 2.83 migrant(s)/1,000 population (1999 est.)
Sex ratio:
at birth: 1.08 male(s)/female
under 15 years: 1.07 male(s)/female
15-64 years: 1 male(s)/female
65 years and over: 0.8 male(s)/female
total population: 1 male(s)/female (1999 est.)
Infant mortality rate: 3.84 deaths/1,000 live births (1999 est.)
Life expectancy at birth:
total population: 78.84 years
male: 75.79 years
female: 82.14 years (1999 est.)
Total fertility rate: 1.47 children born/woman (1999 est.)
Nationality:
noun: Singaporean(s)
adjective: Singapore
Ethnic groups: Chinese 76.4%, Malay 14.9%, Indian 6.4%, other 2.3%
Religions: Buddhist (Chinese), Muslim (Malays), Christian, Hindu, Sikh, Taoist, Confucianist
Languages: Chinese (official), Malay (official and national), Tamil (official), English (official)
Literacy:
definition: age 15 and over can read and write
total population: 91.1%
male: 95.9%
female: 86.3% (1995 est.)

Government

Country name:
conventional long form: Republic of Singapore
conventional short form: Singapore
Data code: SN
Government type: republic within Commonwealth
Capital: Singapore
Administrative divisions: none
Independence: 9 August 1965 (from Malaysia)
National holiday: National Day, 9 August (1965)

Constitution: 3 June 1959, amended 1965 (based on preindependence State of Singapore Constitution)
Legal system: based on English common law; has not accepted compulsory ICJ jurisdiction
Suffrage: 20 years of age; universal and compulsory
Executive branch:
chief of state: President ONG Teng Cheong (since 1 September 1993)
head of government: Prime Minister GOH Chok Tong (since 28 November 1990) and Deputy Prime Ministers LEE Hsien Loong (since 28 November 1990) and Tony TAN Keng Yam (since 1 August 1995)
cabinet: Cabinet appointed by the president, responsible to Parliament
elections: president elected by popular vote for a six-year term; election last held 28 August 1993 (next to be held NA August 1999); following legislative elections, the leader of the majority party or the leader of a majority coalition is usually appointed prime minister by the president; deputy prime ministers appointed by the president
election results: ONG Teng Cheong elected president in the country's first popular election for president; percent of vote - ONG Teng Cheong 59%, CHUA Kim Yeow 41%
Legislative branch: unicameral Parliament (83 seats; members elected by popular vote to serve five-year terms)
elections: last held 2 January 1997 (next to be held by 2002)
election results: percent of vote by party - PAP 65% (in contested constituencies), other 35%; seats by party - PAP 81, WP 1, SPP 1
Judicial branch: Supreme Court, chief justice is appointed by the president with the advice of the prime minister, other judges are appointed by the president with the advice of the chief justice; Court of Appeals
Political parties and leaders:
government: People's Action Party or PAP [GOH Chok Tong, secretary general]
opposition: Singapore Democratic Party or SDP [CHEE Soon Juan]; Workers' Party or WP [J. B. JEYARETNAM]; National Solidarity Party or NSP [C. K. TAN]; Singapore People's Party or SPP [CHIAM See Tong]; Democratic Action Party [LIM Kit Siang, secretary general]
International organization participation: APEC, AsDB, ASEAN, Australia Group (observer), BIS, C, CCC, CP, ESCAP, G-77, IAEA, IBRD, ICAO, ICC, ICFTU, ICRM, IFC, IFRCS, IHO, ILO, IMF, IMO, Inmarsat, Intelsat, Interpol, IOC, ISO, ITU, NAM, OPCW, PCA, UN, UNCTAD, UNIKOM, UPU, WHO, WIPO, WMO, WTrO
Diplomatic representation in the US:
chief of mission: Ambassador CHAN Heng Chee
chancery: 3501 International Place NW, Washington, DC 20008
telephone: [1] (202) 537-3100
FAX: [1] (202) 537-0876
consulate(s): New York

Diplomatic representation from the US:
chief of mission: Ambassador Steven J. GREEN
embassy: 27 Napier Street, Singapore 258508
mailing address: FPO AP 96534-0001
telephone: [65] 476-9100
FAX: [65] 476-9340
Flag description: two equal horizontal bands of red (top) and white; near the hoist side of the red band, there is a vertical, white crescent (closed portion is toward the hoist side) partially enclosing five white five-pointed stars arranged in a circle

Economy

Economy - overview: Singapore has an open economy with strong service and manufacturing sectors and excellent international trading links derived from its entrepot history. Extraordinarily strong fundamentals allowed Singapore to weather the effects of the Asian financial crisis better than its neighbors, but the crisis did pull GDP growth down to 1.3% in 1998 from 6% in 1997. Projections for 1999 GDP growth are in the -1% to 1% range. Rising labor costs and appreciation of the Singapore dollar against its neighbors' currencies continue to be a threat to Singapore's competitiveness. The government's strategy to address this problem includes cutting costs, increasing productivity, improving infrastructure, and encouraging higher value-added industries. In applied technology, per capita output, investment, and labor discipline, Singapore has key attributes of a developed country.
GDP: purchasing power parity - $91.7 billion (1998 est.)
GDP - real growth rate: 1.3% (1998 est.)
GDP - per capita: purchasing power parity - $26,300 (1998 est.)
GDP - composition by sector:
agriculture: NEGL%
industry: 28%
services: 72%
Population below poverty line: NA%
Household income or consumption by percentage share:
lowest 10%: NA%
highest 10%: NA%
Inflation rate (consumer prices): -0.5% (1998 est.)
Labor force: 1.856 million (1997 est.)
Labor force - by occupation: financial, business, and other services 33.5%, manufacturing 25.6%, commerce 22.9%, construction 6.6%, other 11.4% (1994)
Unemployment rate: 5% (1999 est.)
Budget:
revenues: $16.3 billion
expenditures: $13.6 billion, including capital expenditures of $NA (FY97/98 est.)
Industries: electronics, financial services, oil drilling equipment, petroleum refining, rubber processing and rubber products, processed food and beverages, ship repair, entrepot trade, biotechnology
Industrial production growth rate: 3% (1998 est.)
Electricity - production: 28 billion kWh (1998)

Singapore *(continued)*

Electricity - production by source:
fossil fuel: 100%
hydro: 0%
nuclear: 0%
other: 0% (1996)
Electricity - consumption: 28 billion kWh (1998)
Electricity - exports: 0 kWh (1998)
Electricity - imports: 0 kWh (1998)
Agriculture - products: rubber, copra, fruit, vegetables; poultry
Exports: $128 billion (1998 est.)
Exports - commodities: computer equipment, rubber and rubber products, petroleum products, telecommunications equipment
Exports - partners: Malaysia 19%, US 18%, Hong Kong 9%, Japan 8%, Thailand 6% (1995)
Imports: $133.9 billion (1997 est.)
Imports - commodities: aircraft, petroleum, chemicals, foodstuffs
Imports - partners: Japan 21%, Malaysia 15%, US 15%, Thailand 5%, Taiwan 4%, South Korea 4% (1995)
Debt - external: $NA
Economic aid - recipient: $NA
Currency: 1 Singapore dollar (S$) = 100 cents
Exchange rates: Singapore dollars (S$) per US$1 - 1.6781 (January 1999), 1.6736 (1998), 1.4848 (1997), 1.4100 (1996), 1.4174 (1995), 1.5274 (1994)
Fiscal year: 1 April - 31 March

Communications

Telephones: 1.4 million (1997 est.)
Telephone system: good domestic facilities; good international service
domestic: NA
international: submarine cables to Malaysia (Sabah and Peninsular Malaysia), Indonesia, and the Philippines; satellite earth stations - 2 Intelsat (1 Indian Ocean and 1 Pacific Ocean), and 1 Inmarsat (Pacific Ocean region)
Radio broadcast stations: AM 13, FM 4, shortwave 0
Radios: NA
Television broadcast stations: 4 (1997)
Televisions: 1.05 million (1992 est.)

Transportation

Railways:
total: 38.6 km
narrow gauge: 38.6 km 1.000-m gauge
note: there is a 67 km mass transit system with 42 stations
Highways:
total: 3,017 km
paved: 2,936 km (including 148 km of expressways)
unpaved: 81 km (1997 est.)
Ports and harbors: Singapore
Merchant marine:
total: 875 ships (1,000 GRT or over) totaling 19,734,146 GRT/31,442,482 DWT
ships by type: bulk 142, cargo 132, chemical tanker 51, combination bulk 6, combination ore/oil 6, container 154, liquefied gas tanker 27, livestock carrier 1, multifunction large-load carrier 6, oil tanker 291, refrigerated cargo 8, roll-on/roll-off cargo 11, short-sea passenger 1, specialized tanker 9, vehicle carrier 30
note: a flag of convenience registry; includes ships from 22 countries among which are Japan 41, Denmark 35, Sweden 28, Thailand 28, Hong Kong 26, Germany 19, Taiwan 19, and Indonesia 11 (1998 est.)
Airports: 9 (1998 est.)
Airports - with paved runways:
total: 9
over 3,047 m: 2
2,438 to 3,047 m: 1
1,524 to 2,437 m: 4
914 to 1,523 m: 1
under 914 m: 1 (1998 est.)
Heliports: 1 (1998 est.)

Military

Military branches: Army, Navy, Air Force, People's Defense Force, Police Force
Military manpower - availability:
males age 15-49: 1,042,587 (1999 est.)
Military manpower - fit for military service:
males age 15-49: 757,940 (1999 est.)
Military expenditures - dollar figure: $4.244 billion (FY98/99)
Military expenditures - percent of GDP: 5.1% (FY98/99)

Transnational Issues

Disputes - international: two islands in dispute with Malaysia
Illicit drugs: transit point for Golden Triangle heroin going to the US, Western Europe, and the Third World; also a money-laundering center

Slovakia

Infant mortality rate: 9.48 deaths/1,000 live births (1999 est.)
Life expectancy at birth:
total population: 73.46 years
male: 69.71 years
female: 77.4 years (1999 est.)
Total fertility rate: 1.2 children born/woman (1999 est.)
Nationality:
noun: Slovak(s)
adjective: Slovak
Ethnic groups: Slovak 85.7%, Hungarian 10.7%, Gypsy 1.5% (the 1992 census figures underreport the Gypsy/Romany community, which is about 500,000), Czech 1%, Ruthenian 0.3%, Ukrainian 0.3%, German 0.1%, Polish 0.1%, other 0.3%
Religions: Roman Catholic 60.3%, atheist 9.7%, Protestant 8.4%, Orthodox 4.1%, other 17.5%
Languages: Slovak (official), Hungarian
Literacy: NA

Introduction

Background: After centuries under foreign rule, mainly by Hungary, the Slovaks joined with their neighbors to form the new nation of Czechoslovakia in 1918. Following the chaos of World War II, Czechoslovakia became a communist nation within Soviet-ruled Eastern Europe. Soviet influence collapsed in 1989, and Czechoslovakia once more was an independent country turning toward the West. The Slovaks and the Czechs agreed to separate peacefully on 1 January 1993. Slovakia has experienced more difficulty than the Czech Republic in developing a modern market economy.

Geography

Location: Central Europe, south of Poland
Geographic coordinates: 48 40 N, 19 30 E
Map references: Europe
Area:
total: 48,845 sq km
land: 48,800 sq km
water: 45 sq km
Area - comparative: about twice the size of New Hampshire
Land boundaries:
total: 1,355 km
border countries: Austria 91 km, Czech Republic 215 km, Hungary 515 km, Poland 444 km, Ukraine 90 km
Coastline: 0 km (landlocked)
Maritime claims: none (landlocked)
Climate: temperate; cool summers; cold, cloudy, humid winters
Terrain: rugged mountains in the central and northern part and lowlands in the south
Elevation extremes:
lowest point: Bodrok River 94 m
highest point: Gerlachovka 2,655 m
Natural resources: brown coal and lignite; small amounts of iron ore, copper and manganese ore; salt
Land use:
arable land: 31%

permanent crops: 3%
permanent pastures: 17%
forests and woodland: 41%
other: 8% (1993 est.)
Irrigated land: 800 sq km (1993 est.)
Natural hazards: NA
Environment - current issues: air pollution from metallurgical plants presents human health risks; acid rain damaging forests
Environment - international agreements:
party to: Air Pollution, Air Pollution-Nitrogen Oxides, Air Pollution-Sulphur 85, Air Pollution-Sulphur 94, Antarctic Treaty, Biodiversity, Climate Change, Endangered Species, Environmental Modification, Hazardous Wastes, Law of the Sea, Nuclear Test Ban, Ozone Layer Protection, Ship Pollution, Wetlands
signed, but not ratified: Air Pollution-Persistent Organic Pollutants, Antarctic-Environmental Protocol, Climate Change-Kyoto Protocol
Geography - note: landlocked

People

Population: 5,396,193 (July 1999 est.)
Age structure:
0-14 years: 20% (male 551,847; female 528,236)
15-64 years: 69% (male 1,837,788; female 1,861,305)
65 years and over: 11% (male 237,710; female 379,307) (1999 est.)
Population growth rate: 0.04% (1999 est.)
Birth rate: 9.52 births/1,000 population (1999 est.)
Death rate: 9.43 deaths/1,000 population (1999 est.)
Net migration rate: 0.29 migrant(s)/1,000 population (1999 est.)
Sex ratio:
at birth: 1.05 male(s)/female
under 15 years: 1.04 male(s)/female
15-64 years: 0.99 male(s)/female
65 years and over: 0.63 male(s)/female
total population: 0.95 male(s)/female (1999 est.)

Government

Country name:
conventional long form: Slovak Republic
conventional short form: Slovakia
local long form: Slovenska Republika
local short form: Slovensko
Data code: LO
Government type: parliamentary democracy
Capital: Bratislava
Administrative divisions: 8 departments (kraje, singular - kraj); Banskobystricky, Bratislavsky, Kosicky, Nitriansky, Presovsky, Trenciansky, Trnavsky, Zilinsky
Independence: 1 January 1993 (from Czechoslovakia)
National holiday: Slovak Constitution Day, 1 September (1992); Anniversary of Slovak National Uprising, 29 August (1944)
Constitution: ratified 1 September 1992, fully effective 1 January 1993
Legal system: civil law system based on Austro-Hungarian codes; has not accepted compulsory ICJ jurisdiction; legal code modified to comply with the obligations of Organization on Security and Cooperation in Europe (OSCE) and to expunge Marxist-Leninist legal theory
Suffrage: 18 years of age; universal
Executive branch:
chief of state: President (vacant); note - President NOVAC retired at the end of his term; the government has announced its intention to hold direct presidential election in early 1999; in the meantime the prime minister takes over the president's duties
head of government: Prime Minister Mikulas DZURINDA (since 30 October 1998)
cabinet: Cabinet appointed by the president on the recommendation of the prime minister
elections: president elected by National Council secret ballot that must yield a three-fifths majority for a five-year term; election last held NA March 1998 but no candidate was able to win a three-fifths majority

Slovakia (continued)

required by law (next to be held NA 1999); following National Council elections, the leader of the majority party or the leader of a majority coalition is usually appointed prime minister by the president
election results: presidency vacant
Legislative branch: unicameral National Council of the Slovak Republic or Narodna Rada Slovensky Repubiky (150 seats; members are elected by popular vote to serve four-year terms)
elections: last held 25-26 September 1998 (next to be held NA September 2003)
election results: percent of vote by party - HZDS 27%, SDK 16.3%, SDL 14.7%, SMK 9.1%, SNS 9.1%, SOP 8%; seats by party - governing coalition 93 (SDK 42, SDL 23, SMK 15, SOP 13), opposition 57 (HZDS 43, SNS 14)
Judicial branch: Supreme Court, judges are elected by the National Council; Constitutional Court
Political parties and leaders: Movement for a Democratic Slovakia or HZDS [Vladimir MECIAR, chairman]; Slovak Democratic Coalition or SDK (includes KDH, DS, DU, SSDS, SZS) [Mikulas DZURINDA]; Party of the Democratic Left or SDL [Jozef MIGAS, chairman]; Party of the Hungarian Coalition or SMK (includes MKDH, MOS, and Coexistence) [Bela BUGAR]; Slovak National Party or SNS [Jan SLOTA, chairman]; Party of Civic Understanding or SOP [Rudolf SCHUSTER, chairman]; Hungarian Christian Democratic Movement or MKDH [Bela BUGAR]; Hungarian Civic Party or MOS [Laszlo A. NAGY, president]; Coexistence [Miklos DURAY, chairman]; Christian Democratic Movement or KDH [Jan CARNOGURSKY, chairman]; Democratic Union or DU [Jozef MORAVCIK, chairman]; Association of Slovak Workers or ZRS [Jan LUPTAK, chairman]; Social Democratic Party of Slovakia or SSDS [Jaroslav VOLF, chairman]; Party of Greens in Slovakia or SZS [Zdenka TOTHOVA, chairman]; Democratic Party or DS [Jan LANGOS, chairman]
Political pressure groups and leaders: Party of Entrepreneurs and Businessmen of Slovakia; Christian Social Union; Confederation of Trade Unions or KOZ; Metal Workers Unions or KOVO and METALURG; Association of Employers of Slovakia; Association of Towns and Villages or ZMOS
International organization participation: Australia Group, BIS, BSEC (observer), CCC, CE, CEI, CERN, EAPC, EBRD, ECE, EU (applicant), FAO, IAEA, IBRD, ICAO, ICFTU, ICRM, IDA, IFC, IFRCS, ILO, IMF, IMO, Inmarsat, Intelsat (nonsignatory user), Interpol, IOC, IOM, ISO, ITU, MONUA, NSG, OPCW, OSCE, PCA, PFP, UN, UNCTAD, UNESCO, UNIDO, UPU, WEU (associate partner), WFTU, WHO, WIPO, WMO, WToO, WTrO, ZC
Diplomatic representation in the US:
chief of mission: Ambassador-designate Martin BUTORA
chancery: (temporary) Suite 250, 2201 Wisconsin Avenue NW, Washington, DC 20007
telephone: [1] (202) 965-5161
FAX: [1] (202) 965-5166

Diplomatic representation from the US:
chief of mission: Ambassador Ralph R. JOHNSON
embassy: Hviezdoslavovo Namestie 4, 81102 Bratislava
mailing address: use embassy street address
telephone: [42] (7) 5443-0861, 5443-3338
FAX: [42] (7) 5443-5439

Flag description: three equal horizontal bands of white (top), blue, and red superimposed with the Slovak cross in a shield centered on the hoist side; the cross is white centered on a background of red and blue

Economy

Economy - overview: Slovakia, continuing the difficult transition from a centrally controlled economy to a modern market-oriented economy, begins 1999 with clouds on the horizon: GDP growth is slowing sharply; budget and current account deficits are too large; external debt is growing uncomfortably fast; unemployment is high and rising; corrupt insider deals persist; and demand is weakening for Slovakia's key primary goods exports, especially as Russia and Ukraine slump and as EU growth slows. International credit rating agencies have downgraded Slovak debt to below investment grade. The new government intends to address the economy's ills by giving priority to joining the OECD and EU, cutting government wage and infrastructure spending, boosting some taxes and regulated prices, expanding privatization to companies formerly considered strategic, restructuring the financial section, encouraging foreign investment, and reenergizing the social partnership with labor and employers. Government officials believe as long as two years may be needed before its structural reforms improve economic performance. In 1999, the government expects GDP growth to slow from 5% in 1998 to 2%, inflation to rise from 6% to 10%, and unemployment to rise from less than 14% to 15% or 16%, but hopes to bring the budget deficit down to no more than 2% of GDP and the current account deficit down to 5% to 6% of GDP.
GDP: purchasing power parity - $44.5 billion (1998 est.)
GDP - real growth rate: 5% (1998 est.)
GDP - per capita: purchasing power parity - $8,300 (1998 est.)
GDP - composition by sector:
agriculture: 4.8%
industry: 33.4%
services: 61.8% (1997)
Population below poverty line: NA%
Household income or consumption by percentage share:
lowest 10%: 5.1%
highest 10%: 18.2% (1992)
Inflation rate (consumer prices): 7.4% (1998)
Labor force: 3.32 million (1997)
Labor force - by occupation: industry 29.3%, agriculture 8.9%, construction 8%, transport and communication 8.2%, services 45.6% (1994)
Unemployment rate: 14% (1998 est.)

Budget:
revenues: $5.4 billion
expenditures: $6.5 billion, including capital expenditures of $NA (1997)
Industries: metal and metal products; food and beverages; electricity, gas, coke, oil, and nuclear fuel; chemicals and manmade fibers; machinery; paper and printing; earthenware and ceramics; transport vehicles; textiles; electrical and optical apparatus; rubber products
Industrial production growth rate: 2.7% (1997)
Electricity - production: 25.81 billion kWh (1996)
Electricity - production by source:
fossil fuel: 35.57%
hydro: 20.81%
nuclear: 43.62%
other: 0% (1996)
Electricity - consumption: 26.353 billion kWh (1996)
Electricity - exports: 2.607 billion kWh (1996)
Electricity - imports: 3.15 billion kWh (1996)
Agriculture - products: grains, potatoes, sugar beets, hops, fruit; pigs, cattle, poultry; forest products
Exports: $10.7 billion (f.o.b., 1998)
Exports - commodities: machinery and transport equipment 37%; intermediate manufactured goods 30%, miscellaneous manufactured goods 13%; chemicals 9%; raw materials 4% (1998)
Exports - partners: EU 56% (Germany 29%), Czech Republic 20%, Austria 7%, Poland 7% (1998)
Imports: $12.9 billion (f.o.b., 1998)
Imports - commodities: machinery and transport equipment 40%; intermediate manufactured goods 18%; fuels 11%; chemicals 11%; miscellaneous manufactured goods 10% (1998)
Imports - partners: EU 50% (Germany 26%), Czech Republic 18%, Russia 10%, Italy 6% (1998)
Debt - external: $10.7 billion (1997)
Economic aid - recipient: $421.9 million (1995)
Currency: 1 koruna (Sk) = 100 halierov
Exchange rates: koruny (Sk) per US$1 - 36.207 (January 1999), 35.233 (1998). 33.616 (1997), 30.654 (1996), 29.713 (1995), 32.045 (1994)
Fiscal year: calendar year

Communications

Telephones: 1,362,178 (1992 est.)
Telephone system:
domestic: NA
international: NA
Radio broadcast stations: AM NA, FM NA, shortwave NA; note - there are 22 private broadcast stations and two public (state) broadcast stations
Radios: 915,000 (1995 est.)
Television broadcast stations: 41 (1997)
Televisions: 1.2 million (1995 est.)

Transportation

Railways:
total: 3,660 km
broad gauge: 102 km 1.520-m gauge

standard gauge: 3,507 km 1.435-m gauge (1424 km electrified)

narrow gauge: 51 km (46 km 1,000-m gauge; 5 km 0.750-m gauge) (1996)

Highways:

total: 38,000 km

paved: 37,500 km (including 280 km of expressways)

unpaved: 500 km (1998 est.)

Waterways: 172 km on the Danube

Pipelines: petroleum products NA km; natural gas 2,700 km

Ports and harbors: Bratislava, Komarno

Merchant marine:

total: 3 cargo ships (1,000 GRT or over) totaling 15,041 GRT/19,517 DWT (1998 est.)

Airports: 15 (1998 est.)

Airports - with paved runways:

total: 10

over 3,047 m: 2

2,438 to 3,047 m: 2

1,524 to 2,437 m: 3

914 to 1,523 m: 1

under 914 m: 2 (1998 est.)

Airports - with unpaved runways:

total: 5

914 to 1,523 m: 2

under 914 m: 3 (1998 est.)

Military

Military branches: Army, Air and Air Defense Forces, Reserve Force (Home Guards), Civil Defense Force

Military manpower - military age: 18 years of age

Military manpower - availability:

males age 15-49: 1,478,729 (1999 est.)

Military manpower - fit for military service:

males age 15-49: 1,130,482 (1999 est.)

Military manpower - reaching military age annually:

males: 45,919 (1999 est.)

Military expenditures - dollar figure: $436 million (1998)

Military expenditures - percent of GDP: 2.1% (1998)

Transnational Issues

Disputes - international: ongoing Gabcikovo Dam dispute with Hungary is before the International Court of Justice; unresolved property issues with Czech Republic over redistribution of former Czechoslovak federal property

Illicit drugs: minor, but increasing, transshipment point for Southwest Asian heroin and hashish bound for Western Europe

Slovenia

Geography

Location: Southeastern Europe, eastern Alps bordering the Adriatic Sea, between Austria and Croatia

Geographic coordinates: 46 00 N, 15 00 E

Map references: Europe

Area:

total: 20,256 sq km

land: 20,256 sq km

water: 0 sq km

Area - comparative: slightly smaller than New Jersey

Land boundaries:

total: 1,334 km

border countries: Austria 330 km, Croatia 670 km, Italy 232 km, Hungary 102 km

Coastline: 46.6 km

Maritime claims: NA

Climate: Mediterranean climate on the coast, continental climate with mild to hot summers and cold winters in the plateaus and valleys to the east

Terrain: a short coastal strip on the Adriatic, an alpine mountain region adjacent to Italy and Austria, mixed mountain and valleys with numerous rivers to the east

Elevation extremes:

lowest point: Adriatic Sea 0 m

highest point: Triglav 2,864 m

Natural resources: lignite coal, lead, zinc, mercury, uranium, silver

Land use:

arable land: 12%

permanent crops: 3%

permanent pastures: 24%

forests and woodland: 54%

other: 7% (1996 est.)

Irrigated land: 20 sq km (1993 est.)

Natural hazards: flooding and earthquakes

Environment - current issues: Sava River polluted with domestic and industrial waste; pollution of coastal waters with heavy metals and toxic chemicals; forest damage near Koper from air pollution (originating at metallurgical and chemical plants) and resulting acid rain

Environment - international agreements:

party to: Air Pollution, Air Pollution-Sulphur 94, Biodiversity, Climate Change, Hazardous Wastes, Law of the Sea, Marine Dumping, Nuclear Test Ban, Ozone Layer Protection, Ship Pollution, Wetlands

signed, but not ratified: Air Pollution-Persistent Organic Pollutants, Climate Change-Kyoto Protocol

People

Population: 1,970,570 (July 1999 est.)

Age structure:

0-14 years: 16% (male 163,816; female 155,509)

15-64 years: 70% (male 693,382; female 687,060)

65 years and over: 14% (male 99,121; female 171,682) (1999 est.)

Population growth rate: -0.04% (1999 est.)

Birth rate: 8.97 births/1,000 population (1999 est.)

Death rate: 9.62 deaths/1,000 population (1999 est.)

Net migration rate: 0.23 migrant(s)/1,000 population (1999 est.)

Sex ratio:

at birth: 1.06 male(s)/female

under 15 years: 1.05 male(s)/female

15-64 years: 1.01 male(s)/female

65 years and over: 0.58 male(s)/female

total population: 0.94 male(s)/female (1999 est.)

Infant mortality rate: 5.28 deaths/1,000 live births (1999 est.)

Life expectancy at birth:

total population: 75.36 years

male: 71.71 years

female: 79.21 years (1999 est.)

Total fertility rate: 1.23 children born/woman (1999 est.)

Nationality:

noun: Slovene(s)

adjective: Slovenian

Ethnic groups: Slovene 91%, Croat 3%, Serb 2%,

Slovenia (continued)

Muslim 1%, other 3%

Religions: Roman Catholic 70.8% (including 2% Uniate), Lutheran 1%, Muslim 1%, atheist 4.3%, other 22.9%

Languages: Slovenian 91%, Serbo-Croatian 6%, other 3%

Literacy:
definition: NA
total population: 99%
male: NA%
female: NA%

Government

Country name:
conventional long form: Republic of Slovenia
conventional short form: Slovenia
local long form: Republika Slovenije
local short form: Slovenija

Data code: SI

Government type: parliamentary democratic republic

Capital: Ljubljana

Administrative divisions: 136 municipalities (obcine, singular - obcina) and 11 urban municipalities* (obcine mestne, singular - obcina mestna) Ajdovscina, Beltinci, Bled, Bohinj, Borovnica, Bovec, Brda, Brezice, Brezovica, Cankova-Tisina, Celje*, Cerklje na Gorenjskem, Cerknica, Cerkno, Crensovci, Crna na Koroskem, Crnomelj, Destrnik-Trnovska Vas, Divaca, Dobrepolje, Dobrova-Horjul-Polhov Gradec, Dol pri Ljubljani, Domzale, Dornava, Dravograd, Duplek, Gorenja Vas-Poljane, Gorisnica, Gornja Radgona, Gornji Grad, Gornji Petrovci, Grosuplje, Hodos Salovci, Hrastnik, Hrpelje-Kozina, Idrija, Ig, Ilirska Bistrica, Ivancna Gorica, Izola, Jesenice, Jursinci, Kamnik, Kanal, Kidricevo, Kobarid, Kobilje, Kocevje, Komen, Koper*, Kozje, Kranj*, Kranjska Gora, Krsko, Kungota, Kuzma, Lasko, Lenart, Lendava, Litija, Ljubljana*, Ljubno, Ljutomer, Logatec, Loska Dolina, Loski Potok, Luce, Lukovica, Majsperk, Maribor*, Medvode, Menges, Metlika, Mezica, Miren-Kostanjevica, Mislinja, Moravce, Moravske Toplice, Mozirje, Murska Sobota*, Muta, Naklo, Nazarje, Nova Gorica*, Novo Mesto*, Odranci, Ormoz, Osilnica, Pesnica, Piran, Pivka, Podcetrtek, Podvelka-Ribnica, Postojna, Preddvor, Ptuj*, Puconci, Race-Fram, Radece, Radenci, Radlje ob Dravi, Radovljica, Ravne-Prevalje, Ribnica, Rogasevci, Rogaska Slatina, Rogatec, Ruse, Semic, Sencur, Sentilj, Sentjernej, Sentjur pri Celju, Sevnica, Sezana, Skocjan, Skofja Loka, Skofljica, Slovenj Gradec*, Slovenska Bistrica, Slovenske Konjice, Smarje pri Jelsah, Smartno ob Paki, Sostanj, Starse, Store, Sveti Jurij, Tolmin, Trbovlje, Trebnje, Trzic, Turnisce, Velenje*, Velike Lasce, Videm, Vipava, Vitanje, Vodice, Vojnik, Vrhnika, Vuzenica, Zagorje ob Savi, Zalec, Zavrc, Zelezniki, Ziri, Zrece

Independence: 25 June 1991 (from Yugoslavia)

National holiday: National Statehood Day, 25 June (1991)

Constitution: adopted 23 December 1991, effective 23 December 1991

Legal system: based on civil law system

Suffrage: 18 years of age; universal (16 years of age, if employed)

Executive branch:
chief of state: President Milan KUCAN (since 22 April 1990)
head of government: Prime Minister Janez DRNOVSEK (since 14 May 1992)
cabinet: Council of Ministers nominated by the prime minister and elected by the National Assembly
elections: president elected by popular vote for a five-year term; election last held 24 November 1997 (next to be held NA 2002); following National Assembly elections, the leader of the majority party or the leader of a majority coalition is usually nominated to become prime minister by the president and elected by the National Assembly; election last held 10 November 1996 (next to be held NA November 2000)
election results: Milan KUCAN elected president; percent of vote - Milan KUCAN 56.3%, Janez PODOBNIK 18%; Janez DRNOVSEK elected prime minister; percent of National Assembly vote - 51%

Legislative branch: unicameral National Assembly or Drzavni Zbor (90 seats, 40 are directly elected and 50 are selected on a proportional basis; note - the numbers of directly elected and proportionally elected seats varies with each election; members are elected by popular vote to serve four-year terms)
elections: National Assembly - last held 10 November 1996 (next to be held Fall 2000)
election results: percent of vote by party - LDS 27.01%, SLS 19.38%, SDS 16.13%, SKD 9.62%, ZLDS 9.03%, DeSUS 4.32%, SNS 3.22%; seats by party - LDS 25, SLS 19, SDS 16, SKD 10, ZLSD 9, DeSUS 5, SNS 4, Hungarian minority 1, Italian minority 1; note - seating as of January 1997 is as follows: LDS 25, SLS 19, SDS 16, SKD 9, ZLSD 9, DeSUS 5, SNS 4, Hungarian minority 1, Italian minority 1, independents 1
note: the National Council or Drzavni Svet is an advisory body with limited legislative powers; it may propose laws and ask to review any National Assembly decisions; in the election of NA November 1997, 40 members were elected to represent local, professional, and socioeconomic interests (next election to be held in the fall of 2002)

Judicial branch: Supreme Court, judges are elected by the National Assembly on the recommendation of the Judicial Council; Constitutional Court, judges elected for nine-year terms by the National Assembly and nominated by the president

Political parties and leaders: Liberal Democratic or LDS [Janez DRNOVSEK, chairman]; Slovene Christian Democrats or SKD [Lozje PETERLE, chairman]; Social Democratic Party of Slovenia or SDS [Janez JANSA, chairman]; Slovene People's Party or SLS [Marjan PODOBNIK, chairman]; United List (former Communists and allies) or ZLSD [Borut PAHOR, chairman]; Slovene National Party or SNS [Zmago JELINCIC, chairman]; Democratic Party of Retired (Persons) of Slovenia or DeSUS [Joze GLOBACNIK]

Political pressure groups and leaders: none

International organization participation: CCC, CE, CEI, EAPC, EBRD, ECE, FAO, IADB, IAEA, IBRD, ICAO, ICRM, IDA, IFC, IFRCS, ILO, IMF, IMO, Intelsat (nonsignatory user), Interpol, IOC, IOM (observer), ISO, ITU, NAM (guest), OPCW, OSCE, PCA, PFP, UN, UN Security Council (temporary), UNCTAD, UNESCO, UNFICYP, UNIDO, UPU, WEU (associate partner), WHO, WIPO, WMO, WToO, WTrO

Diplomatic representation in the US:
chief of mission: Ambassador Dimitrij RUPEL
chancery: 1525 New Hampshire Avenue NW, Washington, DC 20036
telephone: [1] (202) 667-5363
FAX: [1] (202) 667-4563
consulate(s) general: New York

Diplomatic representation from the US:
chief of mission: Ambassador (vacant); Charge d'Affaires J. Paul REID
embassy: address NA, Ljubljana
mailing address: P.O. Box 254, Prazakova 4, 1000 Ljubljana; American Embassy Ljubljana, Department of State, Washington, DC 20521-7140
telephone: [386] (61) 301-427, 472, 485
FAX: [386] (61) 301-401

Flag description: three equal horizontal bands of white (top), blue, and red with the Slovenian seal (a shield with the image of Triglav, Slovenia's highest peak, in white against a blue background at the center, beneath it are two wavy blue lines depicting seas and rivers, and above it, there are three six-sided stars arranged in an inverted triangle which are taken from the coat of arms of the Counts of Celje, the great Slovene dynastic house of the late 14th and early 15th centuries); the seal is located in the upper hoist side of the flag centered in the white and blue bands

Economy

Economy - overview: Today, Slovenia exhibits one of the highest per capita GDPs of the transition economies of the region, fairly moderate inflation, and a comfortable level of international reserves. Slovenia received an invitation in 1997 to begin accession negotiations with the EU - a reflection of its sound economic footing. Slovenia must press on with privatization, enterprise restructuring, institution reform, and liberalization of financial markets, thereby creating conditions conducive to foreign investment and the maintenance of a stable tolar. Critical to the future success of the economy is the development of export sales in increasingly competitive international markets.

GDP: purchasing power parity - $20.4 billion (1998 est.)

GDP - real growth rate: 3.6% (1998 est.)

GDP - per capita: purchasing power parity - $10,300 (1998 est.)

GDP - composition by sector:
agriculture: 5%
industry: 35%

Slovenia (continued)

services: 60% (1997 est.)
Population below poverty line: NA%
Household income or consumption by percentage share:
lowest 10%: 4%
highest 10%: 24.5% (1993)
Inflation rate (consumer prices): 8% (1998 est.)
Labor force: 857,400
Labor force - by occupation: NA
Unemployment rate: 7.1% (1997 est.)
Budget:
revenues: $8.48 billion
expenditures: $8.53 billion, including capital expenditures of $455 million (1996 est.)
Industries: ferrous metallurgy and rolling mill products, aluminum reduction and rolled products, lead and zinc smelting, electronics (including military electronics), trucks, electric power equipment, wood products, textiles, chemicals, machine tools
Industrial production growth rate: 0.8% (1996)
Electricity - production: 12.075 billion kWh (1996)
Electricity - production by source:
fossil fuel: 34.58%
hydro: 29.31%
nuclear: 36.11%
other: 0% (1996)
Electricity - consumption: 11.295 billion kWh (1996)
Electricity - exports: 2.03 billion kWh (1996)
Electricity - imports: 1.25 billion kWh (1996)
Agriculture - products: potatoes, hops, wheat, sugar beets, corn, grapes; cattle, sheep, poultry
Exports: $9.2 billion (f.o.b., 1998)
Exports - commodities: manufactured goods 45%, machinery and transport equipment 30%, chemicals 10%, food 3% (1997)
Exports - partners: Germany 29%, Italy 15%, Croatia 10%, France, Austria, US (1997)
Imports: $9.9 billion (f.o.b., 1998)
Imports - commodities: machinery and transport equipment 31%, manufactured goods 31%, chemicals 11%, fuels and lubricants, food (1997)
Imports - partners: Germany 21%, Italy 17%, France 10%, Austria 8%, Croatia 5%, Hungary, US (1997)
Debt - external: $4.4 billion (1998 est.)
Economic aid - recipient: ODA, $5 million (1993)
Currency: 1 tolar (SIT) = 100 stotins
Exchange rates: tolars (SIT) per US$1 - 162.50 (January 1999), 166.13 (1998), 159.69 (1997), 135.36 (1996), 118.52 (1995), 128.81 (1994)
Fiscal year: calendar year

Communications

Telephones: 691,240 (1997 est.)
Telephone system:
domestic: 70% digital; full digitalization scheduled by 2000
international: NA
Radio broadcast stations: AM 6, FM 5, shortwave 0
note: there are more than 20 regional and local radio broadcast stations

Radios: 596,100 (1993 est.)
Television broadcast stations: 23 (consisting of 20 network stations and three private stations; there are also about 400 low-power repeaters) (1997)
Televisions: 454,400 (1993 est.)

Transportation

Railways:
total: 1,201 km
standard gauge: 1,201 km 1.435-m gauge (electrified 489 km) (1998)
Highways:
total: 14,830 km
paved: 12,309 km (including 251 km of expressways)
unpaved: 2,521 km (1997 est.)
Waterways: NA
Pipelines: crude oil 290 km; natural gas 305 km
Ports and harbors: Izola, Koper, Piran
Airports: 14 (1998 est.)
Airports - with paved runways:
total: 6
over 3,047 m: 1
2,438 to 3,047 m: 1
1,524 to 2,437 m: 1
914 to 1,523 m: 2
under 914 m: 1 (1998 est.)
Airports - with unpaved runways:
total: 8
1,524 to 2,437 m: 2
914 to 1,523 m: 2
under 914 m: 4 (1998 est.)

Military

Military branches: Slovenian Army (includes Air and Naval Forces)
Military manpower - military age: 19 years of age
Military manpower - availability:
males age 15-49: 530,182 (1999 est.)
Military manpower - fit for military service:
males age 15-49: 421,864 (1999 est.)
Military manpower - reaching military age annually:
males: 15,294 (1999 est.)
Military expenditures - dollar figure: $272 million (1998)
Military expenditures - percent of GDP: 1.8% (1998)

Transnational Issues

Disputes - international: significant progress has been made with Croatia resolving a maritime border dispute over direct access to the sea in the Adriatic; Italy and Slovenia made progress in resolving bilateral issues
Illicit drugs: transit point for Southwest Asian heroin bound for Western Europe and for precursor chemicals

Solomon Islands

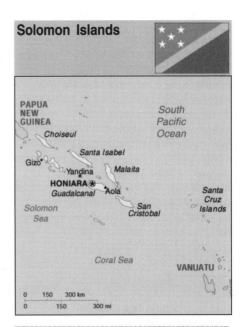

Introduction

Background: In 1893, Britain made the southern Solomon Islands a protectorate. Other islands were added to the group, including some ceded to Britain by Germany. The Solomon Islands were occupied by the Japanese during World War II. Following the war, internal self-government was established in 1976, and independence from the UK came two years later. Current issues include government deficits, deforestation, and malaria control.

Geography

Location: Oceania, group of islands in the South Pacific Ocean, east of Papua New Guinea
Geographic coordinates: 8 00 S, 159 00 E
Map references: Oceania
Area:
total: 28,450 sq km
land: 27,540 sq km
water: 910 sq km
Area - comparative: slightly smaller than Maryland
Land boundaries: 0 km
Coastline: 5,313 km
Maritime claims: measured from claimed archipelagic baselines
continental shelf: 200 nm
exclusive economic zone: 200 nm
territorial sea: 12 nm
Climate: tropical monsoon; few extremes of temperature and weather
Terrain: mostly rugged mountains with some low coral atolls
Elevation extremes:
lowest point: Pacific Ocean 0 m
highest point: Mount Makarakomburu 2,447 m
Natural resources: fish, forests, gold, bauxite, phosphates, lead, zinc, nickel
Land use:
arable land: 1%
permanent crops: 1%

Solomon Islands (continued)

permanent pastures: 1%

forests and woodland: 88%

other: 9% (1993 est.)

Irrigated land: NA sq km

Natural hazards: typhoons, but they are rarely destructive; geologically active region with frequent earth tremors; volcanic activity

Environment - current issues: deforestation; soil erosion; much of the surrounding coral reefs are dead or dying

Environment - international agreements:

party to: Biodiversity, Climate Change, Environmental Modification, Law of the Sea, Marine Dumping, Marine Life Conservation, Ozone Layer Protection, Whaling

signed, but not ratified: Climate Change-Kyoto Protocol

People

Population: 455,429 (July 1999 est.)

Age structure:

0-14 years: 45% (male 103,844; female 99,972)

15-64 years: 52% (male 120,518; female 117,298)

65 years and over: 3% (male 6,808; female 6,989) (1999 est.)

Population growth rate: 3.18% (1999 est.)

Birth rate: 35.92 births/1,000 population (1999 est.)

Death rate: 4.11 deaths/1,000 population (1999 est.)

Net migration rate: 0 migrant(s)/1,000 population (1999 est.)

Sex ratio:

at birth: 1.05 male(s)/female

under 15 years: 1.04 male(s)/female

15-64 years: 1.03 male(s)/female

65 years and over: 0.97 male(s)/female

total population: 1.03 male(s)/female (1999 est.)

Infant mortality rate: 23 deaths/1,000 live births (1999 est.)

Life expectancy at birth:

total population: 72.09 years

male: 69.55 years

female: 74.75 years (1999 est.)

Total fertility rate: 4.96 children born/woman (1999 est.)

Nationality:

noun: Solomon Islander(s)

adjective: Solomon Islander

Ethnic groups: Melanesian 93%, Polynesian 4%, Micronesian 1.5%, European 0.8%, Chinese 0.3%, other 0.4%

Religions: Anglican 34%, Roman Catholic 19%, Baptist 17%, United (Methodist/Presbyterian) 11%, Seventh-Day Adventist 10%, other Protestant 5%, traditional beliefs 4%

Languages: Melanesian pidgin in much of the country is lingua franca, English spoken by 1%-2% of population

note: 120 indigenous languages

Literacy: NA

Government

Country name:

conventional long form: none

conventional short form: Solomon Islands

former: British Solomon Islands

Data code: BP

Government type: parliamentary democracy

Capital: Honiara

Administrative divisions: 7 provinces and 1 town*; Central, Guadalcanal, Honiara*, Isabel, Makira, Malaita, Temotu, Western

note: there may be two new provinces of Choiseul (Lauru) and Rennell/Bellona and the administrative unit of Honiara may have been abolished

Independence: 7 July 1978 (from UK)

National holiday: Independence Day, 7 July (1978)

Constitution: 7 July 1978

Legal system: English common law

Suffrage: 21 years of age; universal

Executive branch:

chief of state: Queen ELIZABETH II (since 6 February 1952), represented by Governor General Moses PITAKAKA (since 10 June 1994)

head of government: Prime Minister Bartholomew ULUFA'ALU (since 27 August 1997); Deputy Prime Minister Sir Baddeley DEVESI (since 27 August 1997)

cabinet: Cabinet appointed by the governor general on the advice of the prime minister from among the members of Parliament

elections: none; the monarch is hereditary; governor general appointed by the monarch on the advice of Parliament for up to five years; following legislative elections, the leader of the majority party or the leader of a majority coalition is usually elected prime minister by Parliament; deputy prime minister appointed by the governor general on the advice of the prime minister from among the members of Parliament

Legislative branch: unicameral National Parliament (50 seats; members elected from single member constituencies by popular vote to serve four-year terms)

elections: last held 6 August 1997 (next to be held by August 2001)

election results: percent of vote by party - NA; seats by party - GNUR 21, PAP 7, NAPSI 5, SILP 4, UP 4, independents 6, other 3

Judicial branch: Court of Appeal

Political parties and leaders: characterized by fluid coalitions; Liberal Party [Bartholomew ULUFA'ALU]; Solomon Islands National Unity, Reconciliation, and Progressive Party or SINURP [Job Duddley TAUSINGA] (leader of opposition); People's Alliance Party or PAP [leader NA]; Group for National Unity and Reconciliation or GNUR [leader NA]; National Action Party of Solomon Islands or NAPSI [leader NA]; Solomon Islands Labor Party or SILP [leader NA]; United Party or UP [leader NA]; Nationalist Front for Progress or NFP [Andrew NORI]; Labor Party or LP [Joses TUHANUKU]; Christian Fellowship [leader NA]; National Party [leader NA]

International organization participation: ACP, AsDB, C, ESCAP, FAO, G-77, IBRD, ICAO, ICRM, IDA, IFAD, IFC, IFRCS, ILO, IMF, IMO, Intelsat (nonsignatory user), IOC, ITU, Sparteca, SPC, SPF, UN, UNCTAD, UNESCO, UPU, WFTU, WHO, WMO, WTrO

Diplomatic representation in the US:

chief of mission: Ambassador Stephen Rex HOROI (represents the country as both the Permanent Representative to the UN and the ambassador to the US)

chancery: 800 Second Avenue, Suite 400L, New York, NY 10017

telephone: [1] (212) 599-6192, 6193

FAX: [1] (212) 661-8925

Diplomatic representation from the US: the US does not have an embassy in Solomon Islands (embassy closed July 1993); the ambassador to Papua New Guinea is accredited to the Solomon Islands

Flag description: divided diagonally by a thin yellow stripe from the lower hoist-side corner; the upper triangle (hoist side) is blue with five white five-pointed stars arranged in an X pattern; the lower triangle is green

Economy

Economy - overview: The bulk of the population depend on agriculture, fishing, and forestry for at least part of their livelihood. Most manufactured goods and petroleum products must be imported. The islands are rich in undeveloped mineral resources such as lead, zinc, nickel, and gold. Economic troubles in Southeast Asia led to a steep downturn in the timber industry, and economic output declined by about 10% in 1998. The government instituted public service pay cuts and other retrenchments.

GDP: purchasing power parity - $1.15 billion (1998 est.)

GDP - real growth rate: -10% (1998 est.)

GDP - per capita: purchasing power parity - $2,600 (1998 est.)

GDP - composition by sector:

agriculture: NA%

industry: NA%

services: NA%

Population below poverty line: NA%

Household income or consumption by percentage share:

lowest 10%: NA%

highest 10%: NA%

Inflation rate (consumer prices): 11.8% (1996)

Labor force: 26,842

Labor force - by occupation: services 41.5%, agriculture, forestry, and fishing 23.7%, commerce, transport, and finance 21.7%, construction, manufacturing, and mining 13.1% (1992 est.)

Unemployment rate: NA%

Budget:

revenues: $147 million

expenditures: $168 million, including capital

Solomon Islands (continued)

expenditures of $NA (1997 est.)
Industries: copra, fish (tuna)
Industrial production growth rate: NA%
Electricity - production: 30 million kWh (1996)
Electricity - production by source:
fossil fuel: 100%
hydro: 0%
nuclear: 0%
other: 0% (1996)
Electricity - consumption: 30 million kWh (1996)
Electricity - exports: 0 kWh (1996)
Electricity - imports: 0 kWh (1996)
Agriculture - products: cocoa, beans, coconuts, palm kernels, rice, potatoes, vegetables, fruit; cattle, pigs; timber; fish
Exports: $184 million (f.o.b., 1996)
Exports - commodities: timber, fish, palm oil, cocoa, copra
Exports - partners: Japan 50%, Spain 16%, UK, Thailand 5% (1996)
Imports: $151 million (c.i.f., 1996 est.)
Imports - commodities: plant and equipment, manufactured goods, food and live animals, fuel
Imports - partners: Australia 42%, Japan 10%, Singapore 9%, NZ 8%, US 5% (1996)
Debt - external: $145 million (1996 est.)
Economic aid - recipient: $46.4 million (1995)
Currency: 1 Solomon Islands dollar (SI$) = 100 cents
Exchange rates: Solomon Islands dollars (SI$) per US$1 - 4.9334 (January 1999), 4.8156 (1998), 3.5664 (1997), 3.4059 (1995), 3.2914 (1994)
Fiscal year: calendar year

Communications

Telephones: 5,000 (1991 est.)
Telephone system:
domestic: NA
international: satellite earth station - 1 Intelsat (Pacific Ocean)
Radio broadcast stations: AM 4, FM 0, shortwave 0
Radios: 38,000 (1993 est.)
Television broadcast stations: 0 (1997)
Televisions: 2,000 (1992 est.)

Transportation

Railways: 0 km
Highways:
total: 1,360 km
paved: 34 km
unpaved: 1,326 km (includes about 800 km of private plantation roads) (1996 est.)
Ports and harbors: Aola Bay, Honiara, Lofung, Noro, Viru Harbor, Yandina
Merchant marine: none
Airports: 33 (1998 est.)
Airports - with paved runways:
total: 2
1,524 to 2,437 m: 1
914 to 1,523 m: 1 (1998 est.)

Airports - with unpaved runways:
total: 31
1,524 to 2,437 m: 1
914 to 1,523 m: 9
under 914 m: 21 (1998 est.)

Military

Military branches: no regular military forces; Solomon Islands National Reconnaissance and Surveillance Force; Royal Solomon Islands Police (RSIP)
Military expenditures - dollar figure: $NA
Military expenditures - percent of GDP: NA%

Transnational Issues

Disputes - international: none

Somalia

Geography

Location: Eastern Africa, bordering the Gulf of Aden and the Indian Ocean, east of Ethiopia
Geographic coordinates: 10 00 N, 49 00 E
Map references: Africa
Area:
total: 637,660 sq km
land: 627,340 sq km
water: 10,320 sq km
Area - comparative: slightly smaller than Texas
Land boundaries:
total: 2,366 km
border countries: Djibouti 58 km, Ethiopia 1,626 km, Kenya 682 km
Coastline: 3,025 km
Maritime claims:
territorial sea: 200 nm
Climate: principally desert; December to February - northeast monsoon, moderate temperatures in north and very hot in south; May to October - southwest monsoon, torrid in the north and hot in the south, irregular rainfall, hot and humid periods (tangambili) between monsoons
Terrain: mostly flat to undulating plateau rising to hills in north
Elevation extremes:
lowest point: Indian Ocean 0 m
highest point: Shimbiris 2,416 m
Natural resources: uranium and largely unexploited reserves of iron ore, tin, gypsum, bauxite, copper, salt
Land use:
arable land: 2%
permanent crops: 0%
permanent pastures: 69%
forests and woodland: 26%
other: 3% (1993 est.)
Irrigated land: 1,800 sq km (1993 est.)
Natural hazards: recurring droughts; frequent dust storms over eastern plains in summer
Environment - current issues: famine; use of contaminated water contributes to human health

Somalia (continued)

problems; deforestation; overgrazing; soil erosion; desertification

Environment - international agreements:
party to: Endangered Species, Law of the Sea
signed, but not ratified: Marine Dumping, Nuclear Test Ban

Geography - note: strategic location on Horn of Africa along southern approaches to Bab el Mandeb and route through Red Sea and Suez Canal

People

Population: 7,140,643 (July 1999 est.)
note: this estimate was derived from an official census taken in 1987 by the Somali Government with the cooperation of the UN and the US Bureau of the Census; population estimates are updated between censuses by factoring in growth rates and by taking account of refugee movements and losses due to famine; lower estimates of Somalia's population in mid-1996 (on the order of 6.0 million to 6.5 million) have been made by aid and relief agencies, based on the number of persons being fed; population counting in Somalia is complicated by the large numbers of nomads and by refugee movements in response to famine and clan warfare

Age structure:
0-14 years: 44% (male 1,588,025; female 1,584,770)
15-64 years: 53% (male 1,898,794; female 1,865,487)
65 years and over: 3% (male 92,419; female 111,148) (1999 est.)

Population growth rate: 4.13% (1999 est.)
Birth rate: 47.98 births/1,000 population (1999 est.)
Death rate: 18.62 deaths/1,000 population (1999 est.)
Net migration rate: 11.9 migrant(s)/1,000 population (1999 est.)

Sex ratio:
at birth: 1.03 male(s)/female
under 15 years: 1 male(s)/female
15-64 years: 1.02 male(s)/female
65 years and over: 0.83 male(s)/female
total population: 1.01 male(s)/female (1999 est.)

Infant mortality rate: 125.77 deaths/1,000 live births (1999 est.)

Life expectancy at birth:
total population: 46.23 years
male: 44.66 years
female: 47.85 years (1999 est.)

Total fertility rate: 7.25 children born/woman (1999 est.)

Nationality:
noun: Somali(s)
adjective: Somali

Ethnic groups: Somali 85%, Bantu, Arabs 30,000
Religions: Sunni Muslim
Languages: Somali (official), Arabic, Italian, English

Literacy:
definition: age 15 and over can read and write
total population: 24%
male: 36%
female: 14% (1990 est.)

Government

Country name:
conventional long form: none
conventional short form: Somalia
former: Somali Republic, Somali Democratic Republic
Data code: SO
Government type: none
Capital: Mogadishu
Administrative divisions: 18 regions (plural - NA, singular - gobolka); Awdal, Bakool, Banaadir, Bari, Bay, Galguduud, Gedo, Hiiraan, Jubbada Dhexe, Jubbada Hoose, Mudug, Nugaal, Sanaag, Shabeellaha Dhexe, Shabeellaha Hoose, Sool, Togdheer, Woqooyi Galbeed

Independence: 1 July 1960 (from a merger of British Somaliland, which became independent from the UK on 26 June 1960, and Italian Somaliland, which became independent from the Italian-administered UN trusteeship on 1 July 1960, to form the Somali Republic)

National holiday: NA
Constitution: 25 August 1979, presidential approval 23 September 1979
Legal system: NA
Suffrage: 18 years of age; universal
Executive branch: Somalia has no functioning government; the United Somali Congress (USC) ousted the regime of Major General Mohamed SIAD Barre on 27 January 1991; the present political situation is one of anarchy, marked by interclan fighting and random banditry

Legislative branch: unicameral People's Assembly or Golaha Shacbiga
note: not functioning

Judicial branch: (not functioning); note - following the breakdown of national government, most regions have reverted to Islamic law with a provision for appeal of all sentences

Political parties and leaders: none
Political pressure groups and leaders: numerous clan and subclan factions are currently vying for power

International organization participation: ACP, AfDB, AFESD, AL, AMF, CAEU, ECA, FAO, G-77, IBRD, ICAO, ICRM, IDA, IDB, IFAD, IFC, IFRCS, IGAD, ILO, IMF, IMO, Intelsat, Interpol, IOC, IOM (observer), ITU, NAM, OAU, OIC, UN, UNCTAD, UNESCO, UNHCR, UNIDO, UPU, WFTU, WHO, WIPO, WMO, WTrO (observer)

Diplomatic representation in the US: Somalia does not have an embassy in the US (ceased operations on 8 May 1991)

Diplomatic representation from the US: the US does not have an embassy in Somalia; US interests are represented by the US Embassy in Nairobi at Moi Avenue and Haile Selassie Avenue; mail address: P. O. Box 30137, Unit 64100, Nairobi; APO AE 09831; telephone: [254] (2) 334141; FAX [254] (2) 340838

Flag description: light blue with a large white five-pointed star in the center; design based on the flag of the UN (Italian Somaliland was a UN trust territory)

Government - note: While chaos and clan fighting continue in most of Somalia, some orderly government has been established in the northern part. In May 1991, the elders of clans in former British Somaliland established the independent Republic of Somaliland, which, although not recognized by any government, maintains a stable existence, aided by the overwhelming dominance of the ruling clan and the economic infrastructure left behind by British, Russian and American military assistance programs. The economy has been growing and in February 1996 the EU agreed to finance the reconstruction of the port of Berbera; since then, other aid projects have been assumed by the EU and by a non-governmental Italian organization.

Economy

Economy - overview: One of the world's poorest and least developed countries, Somalia has few resources. Moreover, much of the economy has been devastated by the civil war. Agriculture is the most important sector, with livestock accounting for about 40% of GDP and about 65% of export earnings. Nomads and semi-nomads, who are dependent upon livestock for their livelihood, make up a large portion of the population. After livestock, bananas are the principal export; sugar, sorghum, corn, and fish are products for the domestic market. The small industrial sector, based on the processing of agricultural products, accounts for 10% of GDP; most facilities have been shut down because of the civil strife. Moreover, as of early 1999, ongoing civil disturbances in Mogadishu and outlying areas are interfering with any substantial economic advance.

GDP: purchasing power parity - $4 billion (1998 est.)
GDP - real growth rate: NA%
GDP - per capita: purchasing power parity - $600 (1998 est.)
GDP - composition by sector:
agriculture: 59%
industry: 10%
services: 31% (1995 est.)

Population below poverty line: NA%
Household income or consumption by percentage share:
lowest 10%: NA%
highest 10%: NA%
Inflation rate (consumer prices): NA%
Labor force: 3.7 million (very few are skilled laborers)(1993 est.)
Labor force - by occupation: agriculture (mostly pastoral nomadism) 71%, industry and services 29%
Unemployment rate: NA%
Budget:
revenues: $NA
expenditures: $NA, including capital expenditures of $NA

Industries: a few small industries, including sugar refining, textiles, petroleum refining (mostly shut down)
Industrial production growth rate: NA%
Electricity - production: 258 million kWh (1996)

Somalia *(continued)*

Electricity - production by source:
fossil fuel: 100%
hydro: 0%
nuclear: 0%
other: 0% (1996)
Electricity - consumption: 258 million kWh (1996)
Electricity - exports: 0 kWh (1996)
Electricity - imports: 0 kWh (1996)
Agriculture - products: bananas, sorghum, corn, sugarcane, mangoes, sesame seeds, beans; cattle, sheep, goats; fish
Exports: $123 million (f.o.b., 1995 est.)
Exports - commodities: livestock, bananas, hides, fish (1997)
Exports - partners: Saudi Arabia 55%, Yemen 19%, Italy 11%, UAE, US (1996 est.)
Imports: $60 million (f.o.b., 1995 est.)
Imports - commodities: manufactures, petroleum products, foodstuffs, construction materials (1995)
Imports - partners: Kenya 28%, Djibouti 21%, Brazil 6%, Pakistan (1996 est.)
Debt - external: $2.6 billion (1996 est.)
Economic aid - recipient: $191.5 million (1995)
Currency: 1 Somali shilling (So. Sh.) = 100 cents
Exchange rates: Somali shillings (So. Sh.) per US$1 - 2,620 (January 1999), 7,500 (November 1997 est.), 7,000 (January 1996 est.), 5,000 (1 January 1995), 2,616 (1 July 1993), 4,200 (December 1992)
note: the Republic of Somaliland, a self-declared independent country not recognized by any government, issues its own currency, the Somaliland shilling (So. Sh.)
Fiscal year: NA

Communications

Telephones: 9,000 (1991 est.)
Telephone system: the public telecommunications system was completely destroyed or dismantled by the civil war factions; all relief organizations depend on their own private systems
domestic: recently, local cellular telephone systems have been established in Mogadishu and in several other population centers
international: international connections are available from Mogadishu by satellite
Radio broadcast stations: AM NA, FM NA, shortwave 5
Radios: 300,000
Television broadcast stations: 1 (1997)
Televisions: 118,000 (1993 est.)

Transportation

Railways: 0 km
Highways:
total: 22,100 km
paved: 2,608 km
unpaved: 19,492 km (1996 est.)
Pipelines: crude oil 15 km
Ports and harbors: Bender Cassim (Boosaaso), Berbera, Chisimayu (Kismaayo), Merca, Mogadishu
Merchant marine: none

Airports: 61 (1998 est.)
Airports - with paved runways:
total: 7
over 3,047 m: 4
2,438 to 3,047 m: 1
1,524 to 2,437 m: 1
914 to 1,523 m: 1 (1998 est.)
Airports - with unpaved runways:
total: 54
2,438 to 3,047 m: 3
1,524 to 2,437 m: 13
914 to 1,523 m: 28
under 914 m: 10 (1998 est.)

Military

Military branches: NA; note - no functioning central government military forces; clan militias continue to battle for control of key economic or political prizes
Military manpower - availability:
males age 15-49: 1,730,450 (1999 est.)
Military manpower - fit for military service:
males age 15-49: 962,545 (1999 est.)
Military expenditures - dollar figure: $NA
Military expenditures - percent of GDP: NA%

Transnational Issues

Disputes - international: most of the southern half of the boundary with Ethiopia is a Provisional Administrative Line; territorial dispute with Ethiopia over the Ogaden

South Africa

Geography

Location: Southern Africa, at the southern tip of the continent of Africa
Geographic coordinates: 29 00 S, 24 00 E
Map references: Africa
Area:
total: 1,219,912 sq km
land: 1,219,912 sq km
water: 0 sq km
note: includes Prince Edward Islands (Marion Island and Prince Edward Island)
Area - comparative: slightly less than twice the size of Texas
Land boundaries:
total: 4,750 km
border countries: Botswana 1,840 km, Lesotho 909 km, Mozambique 491 km, Namibia 855 km, Swaziland 430 km, Zimbabwe 225 km
Coastline: 2,798 km
Maritime claims:
continental shelf: 200-m depth or to the depth of exploitation
exclusive economic zone: 200 nm
territorial sea: 12 nm
Climate: mostly semiarid; subtropical along east coast; sunny days, cool nights
Terrain: vast interior plateau rimmed by rugged hills and narrow coastal plain
Elevation extremes:
lowest point: Atlantic Ocean 0 m
highest point: Njesuthi 3,408 m
Natural resources: gold, chromium, antimony, coal, iron ore, manganese, nickel, phosphates, tin, uranium, gem diamonds, platinum, copper, vanadium, salt, natural gas
Land use:
arable land: 10%
permanent crops: 1%
permanent pastures: 67%
forests and woodland: 7%

South Africa (continued)

other: 15% (1993 est.)
Irrigated land: 12,700 sq km (1993 est.)
Natural hazards: prolonged droughts
Environment - current issues: lack of important arterial rivers or lakes requires extensive water conservation and control measures; growth in water usage threatens to outpace supply; pollution of rivers from agricultural runoff and urban discharge; air pollution resulting in acid rain; soil erosion; desertification
Environment - international agreements:
party to: Antarctic-Environmental Protocol, Antarctic Treaty, Biodiversity, Climate Change, Desertification, Endangered Species, Hazardous Wastes, Law of the Sea, Marine Dumping, Marine Life Conservation, Nuclear Test Ban, Ozone Layer Protection, Ship Pollution, Wetlands, Whaling
signed, but not ratified: none of the selected agreements
Geography - note: South Africa completely surrounds Lesotho and almost completely surrounds Swaziland

People

Population: 43,426,386 (July 1999 est.)
note: South Africa took a census 10 October 1996 which showed a population of 37,859,000 (after a 6.8% adjustment for underenumeration based on a post-enumeration survey); this figure is still about 10% below projections from earlier censuses; since the full results of that census have not been released for analysis, the numbers shown for South Africa do not take into consideration the results of this 1996 census
Age structure:
0-14 years: 34% (male 7,541,840; female 7,403,235)
15-64 years: 61% (male 13,180,925; female 13,312,917)
65 years and over: 5% (male 798,825; female 1,188,644) (1999 est.)
Population growth rate: 1.32% (1999 est.)
Birth rate: 25.94 births/1,000 population (1999 est.)
Death rate: 12.81 deaths/1,000 population (1999 est.)
Net migration rate: 0.08 migrant(s)/1,000 population (1999 est.)
Sex ratio:
at birth: 1.03 male(s)/female
under 15 years: 1.02 male(s)/female
15-64 years: 0.99 male(s)/female
65 years and over: 0.67 male(s)/female
total population: 0.98 male(s)/female (1999 est.)
Infant mortality rate: 51.99 deaths/1,000 live births (1999 est.)
Life expectancy at birth:
total population: 54.76 years
male: 52.68 years
female: 56.9 years (1999 est.)
Total fertility rate: 3.09 children born/woman (1999 est.)
Nationality:
noun: South African(s)
adjective: South African

Ethnic groups: black 75.2%, white 13.6%, Colored 8.6%, Indian 2.6%
Religions: Christian 68% (includes most whites and Coloreds, about 60% of blacks and about 40% of Indians), Muslim 2%, Hindu 1.5% (60% of Indians), traditional and animistic 28.5%
Languages: 11 official languages, including Afrikaans, English, Ndebele, Pedi, Sotho, Swazi, Tsonga, Tswana, Venda, Xhosa, Zulu
Literacy:
definition: age 15 and over can read and write
total population: 81.8%
male: 81.9%
female: 81.7% (1995 est.)

Government

Country name:
conventional long form: Republic of South Africa
conventional short form: South Africa
abbreviation: RSA
Data code: SF
Government type: republic
Capital: Pretoria (administrative); Cape Town (legislative); Bloemfontein (judicial)
Administrative divisions: 9 provinces; Eastern Cape, Free State, Gauteng, KwaZulu-Natal, Mpumalanga, North-West, Northern Cape, Northern Province, Western Cape
Independence: 31 May 1910 (from UK)
National holiday: Freedom Day, 27 April (1994)
Constitution: 10 December 1996; this new constitution was certified by the Constitutional Court on 4 December 1996, was signed by President MANDELA on 10 December 1996, and entered into effect on 3 February 1997; it is being implemented in phases
Legal system: based on Roman-Dutch law and English common law; accepts compulsory ICJ jurisdiction, with reservations
Suffrage: 18 years of age; universal
Executive branch:
chief of state: President Nelson MANDELA (since 10 May 1994); Executive Deputy President Thabo MBEKI (since 10 May 1994); note - the president is both the chief of state and head of government
head of government: President Nelson MANDELA (since 10 May 1994); Executive Deputy President Thabo MBEKI (since 10 May 1994); note - the president is both the chief of state and head of government
cabinet: Cabinet appointed by the president
elections: president and executive deputy presidents elected by the National Assembly for five-year terms; election last held 9 May 1994 (next scheduled for sometime between May and July 1999)
election results: Nelson MANDELA elected president; percent of National Assembly vote - 100% (by acclamation); Thabo MBEKI and Frederik W. DE KLERK elected executive deputy presidents; percent of National Assembly vote - 100% (by acclamation)
note: the initial governing coalition, made up of the ANC, the IFP, and the NP, which constituted a

Government of National Unity or GNU, no longer includes the NP which was withdrawn by DE KLERK on 30 June 1996 when he voluntarily gave up his position as executive deputy president and distanced himself from the programs of the ANC
Legislative branch: bicameral parliament consisting of the National Assembly (400 seats; members are elected by popular vote under a system of proportional representation to serve five-year terms) and the National Council of Provinces (90 seats, 10 members elected by each of the nine provincial legislatures for five-year terms; has special powers to protect regional interests, including the safeguarding of cultural and linguistic traditions among ethnic minorities); note - following the implementation of the new constitution on 3 February 1997 the former Senate was disbanded and replaced by the National Council of Provinces with essentially no change in membership and party affiliations, although the new institution's responsibilities have been changed somewhat by the new constitution
elections: National Assembly and Senate - last held 26-29 April 1994 (next to be held 2 June 1999); note - the Senate was disbanded and replaced by the National Council of Provinces on 6 February 1997
election results: National Assembly - percent of vote by party - ANC 62.6%, NP 20.4%, IFP 10.5%, FF 2.2%, DP 1.7%, PAC 1.2%, ACDP 0.5%, other 0.9%; seats by party - ANC 252, NP 82, IFP 43, FF 9, DP 7, PAC 5, ACDP 2; Senate - percent of vote by party - NA; seats by party - ANC 61, NP 17, FF 4, IFP 5, DP 3
Judicial branch: Constitutional Court; Supreme Court of Appeals; High Courts; Magistrate Courts
Political parties and leaders: African Christian Democratic Party or ACDP [Kenneth MESHOE, president]; African National Congress or ANC [Thabo MBEKI, president]; Democratic Party or DP [Tony LEON, president]; Freedom Front or FF [Constand VILJOEN, president]; Inkatha Freedom Party or IFP [Mangosuthu BUTHELEZI, president]; National Party (now the New National Party) or NP [Marthinus VAN SCHALKWYK, executive director]; Pan-Africanist Congress or PAC [Stanley MOGOBA, president]; United Democratic Movement or UDM [Roelf MEYER, Bantu HOLOMISA]
note: 11 other parties won votes in the April 1994 elections but not enough to gain seats in the National Assembly
Political pressure groups and leaders: Congress of South African Trade Unions or COSATU [Sam SHILOWA, general secretary]; South African Communist Party or SACP [Charles NQAKULA, general secretary]; South African National Civics Organization or SANCO [Mlungisi HLONGWANE, national president]; note - COSATU and SACP are in a formal alliance with the ANC
International organization participation: AfDB, BIS, C, CCC, ECA, FAO, G-77, IAEA, IBRD, ICAO, ICC, ICFTU, ICRM, IDA, IFAD, IFC, IFRCS, IHO, ILO, IMF, IMO, Inmarsat, Intelsat, Interpol, IOC, IOM, ISO, ITU, MTCR, NAM, NSG, OAU, OPCW, SACU, SADC, UN, UNCTAD, UNESCO, UNHCR, UPU, WFTU,

South Africa *(continued)*

WHO, WIPO, WMO, WToO, WTrO, ZC
Diplomatic representation in the US:
chief of mission: Ambassador (vacant)
chancery: 3051 Massachusetts Avenue NW, Washington, DC 20008
telephone: [1] (202) 232-4400
FAX: [1] (202) 265-1607
consulate(s) general: Beverly Hills (California), Chicago, and New York
Diplomatic representation from the US:
chief of mission: Ambassador James A. JOSEPH
embassy: 877 Pretorius St., Arcadia 0083
mailing address: P.O. Box 9536, Pretoria 0001
telephone: [27] (12) 342-1048
FAX: [27] (12) 342-2244
consulate(s) general: Cape Town, Durban, Johannesburg
Flag description: two equal width horizontal bands of red (top) and blue separated by a central green band which splits into a horizontal Y, the arms of which end at the corners of the hoist side, embracing a black isosceles triangle from which the arms are separated by narrow yellow bands; the red and blue bands are separated from the green band and its arms by narrow white stripes
note: prior to 26 April 1994, the flag was actually four flags in one - three miniature flags reproduced in the center of the white band of the former flag of the Netherlands, which has three equal horizontal bands of orange (top), white, and blue; the miniature flags are a vertically hanging flag of the old Orange Free State with a horizontal flag of the UK adjoining on the hoist side and a horizontal flag of the old Transvaal Republic adjoining on the other side

Economy

Economy - overview: South Africa is a middle-income, developing country with an abundant supply of resources, well-developed financial, legal, communications, energy, and transport sectors, a stock exchange that ranks among the 10 largest in the world, and a modern infrastructure supporting an efficient distribution of goods to major urban centers throughout the region. However, growth has not been strong enough to cut into the 30% unemployment, and daunting economic problems remain from the apartheid era, especially the problems of poverty and lack of economic empowerment among the disadvantaged groups. Other problems are crime and corruption. The new government demonstrated its commitment to open markets, privatization, and a favorable investment climate with the release of its macroeconomic strategy in June 1996. Called "Growth, Employment and Redistribution," this policy framework includes the introduction of tax incentives to stimulate new investment in labor-intensive projects, expansion of basic infrastructure services, the restructuring and partial privatization of state assets, continued reduction of tariffs, subsidies to promote economic efficiency, improved services to the disadvantaged, and integration into the global economy. Serious structural rigidities remain, including a complicated and relatively protectionist trade regime, and concentration of wealth and economic control.

GDP: purchasing power parity - $290.6 billion (1998 est.)
GDP - real growth rate: 0.3% (1998 est.)
GDP - per capita: purchasing power parity - $6,800 (1998 est.)
GDP - composition by sector:
agriculture: 5%
industry: 39%
services: 56% (1996 est.)
Population below poverty line: NA%
Household income or consumption by percentage share:
lowest 10%: 1.4%
highest 10%: 47.3% (1993)
Inflation rate (consumer prices): 9% (1998 est.)
Labor force: 15 million economically active (1997)
Labor force - by occupation: services 35%, agriculture 30%, industry 20%, mining 9%, other 6%
Unemployment rate: 30% (1998 est.)
Budget:
revenues: $30.5 billion
expenditures: $38 billion, including capital expenditures of $2.6 billion (FY94/95 est.)
Industries: mining (world's largest producer of platinum, gold, chromium), automobile assembly, metalworking, machinery, textile, iron and steel, chemical, fertilizer, foodstuffs
Industrial production growth rate: -1% (1998 est.)
Electricity - production: 186.949 billion kWh (1996)
Electricity - production by source:
fossil fuel: 93%
hydro: 0.7%
nuclear: 6.3%
other: NA% (1996)
Electricity - consumption: 181.404 billion kWh (1996)
Electricity - exports: 5.575 billion kWh (1996)
Electricity - imports: 30 million kWh (1996)
Agriculture - products: corn, wheat, sugarcane, fruits, vegetables; beef, poultry, mutton, wool, dairy products
Exports: $28.7 billion (f.o.b., 1998)
Exports - commodities: gold 20%, other minerals and metals 20%-25%, food 5%, chemicals 3% (1997)
Exports - partners: UK, Italy, Japan, US, Germany (1997)
Imports: $27.2 billion (f.o.b., 1998)
Imports - commodities: machinery, transport equipment, chemicals, petroleum products, textiles, scientific instruments (1997)
Imports - partners: Germany, US, UK, Japan (1997)
Debt - external: $23.5 billion (1997 est.)
Economic aid - recipient: $676.3 million
Currency: 1 rand (R) = 100 cents
Exchange rates: rand (R) per US$1 - 5.98380 (January 1999), 5.52828 (1998), 4.60796 (1997), 4.29935 (1996), 3.62709 (1995), 3.55080 (1994)
Fiscal year: 1 April - 31 March

Communications

Telephones: 4.2 million (1997)
Telephone system: the system is the best developed, most modern, and has the highest capacity in Africa
domestic: consists of carrier-equipped open-wire lines, coaxial cables, microwave radio relay links, fiber-optic cable, and radiotelephone communication stations; key centers are Bloemfontein, Cape Town, Durban, Johannesburg, Port Elizabeth, and Pretoria
international: 1 submarine cable; satellite earth stations - 3 Intelsat (1 Indian Ocean and 2 Atlantic Ocean)
Radio broadcast stations: AM 15, FM 164, shortwave 1
Radios: 7.5 million (1999 est.)
Television broadcast stations: 556 (includes 156 network stations and 400 privately-owned low-power stations; in addition, there are 144 network repeaters) (1997)
Televisions: 7.5 million

Transportation

Railways:
total: 21,431 km
narrow gauge: 20,995 km 1.067-m gauge (9,087 km electrified); 436 km 0.610-m gauge (1995)
Highways:
total: 331,265 km
paved: 137,475 km (including 1,142 km of expressways)
unpaved: 193,790 km (1995 est.)
Pipelines: crude oil 931 km; petroleum products 1,748 km; natural gas 322 km
Ports and harbors: Cape Town, Durban, East London, Mosselbaai, Port Elizabeth, Richards Bay, Saldanha
Merchant marine:
total: 9 ships (1,000 GRT or over) totaling 274,797 GRT/270,837 DWT
ships by type: container 6, oil tanker 2, roll-on/roll-off cargo 1 (1998 est.)
Airports: 749 (1998 est.)
Airports - with paved runways:
total: 144
over 3,047 m: 10
2,438 to 3,047 m: 4
1,524 to 2,437 m: 45
914 to 1,523 m: 75
under 914 m: 10 (1998 est.)
Airports - with unpaved runways:
total: 605
1,524 to 2,437 m: 35
914 to 1,523 m: 304
under 914 m: 266 (1998 est.)

Military

Military branches: South African National Defense Force or SANDF (includes Army, Navy, Air Force, and Medical Services), South African Police Service or SAPS

South Africa (continued)

Military manpower - military age: 18 years of age
Military manpower - availability:
males age 15-49: 11,330,692 (1999 est.)
Military manpower - fit for military service:
males age 15-49: 6,889,631 (1999 est.)
Military manpower - reaching military age annually:
males: 453,610 (1999 est.)
Military expenditures - dollar figure: $2 billion (FY99/00)
Military expenditures - percent of GDP: 2.2% (FY95/96)
Military - note: the National Defense Force continues to integrate former military, black homelands forces, and ex-opposition forces

Transnational Issues

Disputes - international: Swaziland has asked South Africa to open negotiations on reincorporating some nearby South African territories that are populated by ethnic Swazis or that were long ago part of the Swazi Kingdom
Illicit drugs: transshipment center for heroin and cocaine; cocaine consumption on the rise; world's largest market for illicit methaqualone, usually imported illegally from India through various east African countries; illicit cultivation of marijuana

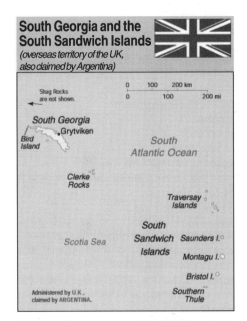

South Georgia and the South Sandwich Islands
(overseas territory of the UK, also claimed by Argentina)

Geography

Location: Southern South America, islands in the South Atlantic Ocean, east of the tip of South America
Geographic coordinates: 54 30 S, 37 00 W
Map references: Antarctic Region
Area:
total: 4,066 sq km
land: 4,066 sq km
water: 0 sq km
note: includes Shag Rocks, Clerke Rocks, Bird Island
Area - comparative: slightly larger than Rhode Island
Land boundaries: 0 km
Coastline: NA km
Maritime claims:
exclusive fishing zone: 200 nm
territorial sea: 12 nm
Climate: variable, with mostly westerly winds throughout the year interspersed with periods of calm; nearly all precipitation falls as snow
Terrain: most of the islands, rising steeply from the sea, are rugged and mountainous; South Georgia is largely barren and has steep, glacier-covered mountains; the South Sandwich Islands are of volcanic origin with some active volcanoes
Elevation extremes:
lowest point: Atlantic Ocean 0 m
highest point: Mount Paget 2,915 m
Natural resources: fish
Land use:
arable land: 0%
permanent crops: 0%
permanent pastures: 0%
forests and woodland: 0%
other: 100% (largely covered by permanent ice and snow with some sparse vegetation consisting of grass, moss, and lichen)
Irrigated land: 0 sq km (1993)

Natural hazards: the South Sandwich Islands have prevailing weather conditions that generally make them difficult to approach by ship; they are also subject to active volcanism
Environment - current issues: NA
Environment - international agreements:
party to: NA
signed, but not ratified: NA
Geography - note: the north coast of South Georgia has several large bays, which provide good anchorage; reindeer, introduced early in this century, live on South Georgia

People

Population: no indigenous inhabitants
note: there is a small military garrison on South Georgia, and the British Antarctic Survey has a biological station on Bird Island; the South Sandwich Islands are uninhabited

Government

Country name:
conventional long form: South Georgia and the South Sandwich Islands
conventional short form: none
Data code: SX
Dependency status: overseas territory of the UK, also claimed by Argentina; administered from the Falkland Island by a UK civil commissioner; Grytviken on South Georgia is the garrison town
Capital: none; Grytviken on South Georgia is the garrison town
Legal system: NA
Diplomatic representation in the US: none (overseas territory of the UK, also claimed by Argentina)
Diplomatic representation from the US: none (overseas territory of the UK, also claimed by Argentina)
Flag description: the flag of the UK is used

Economy

Economy - overview: Some fishing takes place in adjacent waters. There is a potential source of income from harvesting fin fish and krill. The islands receive income from postage stamps produced in the UK.
Budget:
revenues: $291,777
expenditures: $451,000, including capital expenditures of $NA (1988 est.)

Communications

Telephone system:
domestic: NA
international: coastal radiotelephone station at Grytviken

Transportation

Ports and harbors: Grytviken
Airports: none

South Georgia and the South Sandwich Islands (continued)

Military

Military - note: defense is the responsibility of the UK

Transnational Issues

Disputes - international: claimed by Argentina

Spain

Canary Islands are not shown.

Introduction

Background: A powerful world empire in the 16th and 17th centuries, Spain ultimately yielded command of the seas to England, beginning with the defeat of the Armada in 1588. Spain subsequently failed to embrace the mercantile and industrial revolutions and fell behind Britain, France, and Germany in economic and political power. Spain remained neutral in World Wars I and II. In the second half of the 20th century Spain played a catch-up role in the western international community. Continuing problems are large-scale unemployment and the Basque separatist movement.

Geography

Location: Southwestern Europe, bordering the Bay of Biscay, Mediterranean Sea, North Atlantic Ocean, and Pyrenees Mountains, southwest of France
Geographic coordinates: 40 00 N, 4 00 W
Map references: Europe
Area:
total: 504,750 sq km
land: 499,400 sq km
water: 5,350 sq km
note: includes Balearic Islands, Canary Islands, and five places of sovereignty (plazas de soberania) on and off the coast of Morocco - Ceuta, Melilla, Islas Chafarinas, Penon de Alhucemas, and Penon de Velez de la Gomera
Area - comparative: slightly more than twice the size of Oregon
Land boundaries:
total: 1,919.1 km
border countries: Andorra 65 km, France 623 km, Gibraltar 1.2 km, Portugal 1,214 km, Morocco (Ceuta) 6.3 km, Morocco (Melilla) 9.6 km
Coastline: 4,964 km
Maritime claims:
exclusive economic zone: 200 nm (applies only to the Atlantic Ocean)
territorial sea: 12 nm

Climate: temperate; clear, hot summers in interior, more moderate and cloudy along coast; cloudy, cold winters in interior, partly cloudy and cool along coast
Terrain: large, flat to dissected plateau surrounded by rugged hills; Pyrenees in north
Elevation extremes:
lowest point: Atlantic Ocean 0 m
highest point: Pico de Teide (Tenerife) on Canary Islands 3,718 m
Natural resources: coal, lignite, iron ore, uranium, mercury, pyrites, fluorspar, gypsum, zinc, lead, tungsten, copper, kaolin, potash, hydropower
Land use:
arable land: 30%
permanent crops: 9%
permanent pastures: 21%
forests and woodland: 32%
other: 8% (1993 est.)
Irrigated land: 34,530 sq km (1993 est.)
Natural hazards: periodic droughts
Environment - current issues: pollution of the Mediterranean Sea from raw sewage and effluents from the offshore production of oil and gas; water quality and quantity nationwide; air pollution; deforestation; desertification
Environment - international agreements:
party to: Air Pollution, Air Pollution-Nitrogen Oxides, Air Pollution-Sulphur 94, Air Pollution-Volatile Organic Compounds, Antarctic-Environmental Protocol, Antarctic Treaty, Biodiversity, Climate Change, Endangered Species, Environmental Modification, Hazardous Wastes, Law of the Sea, Marine Dumping, Marine Life Conservation, Nuclear Test Ban, Ozone Layer Protection, Ship Pollution, Tropical Timber 83, Tropical Timber 94, Wetlands, Whaling
signed, but not ratified: Air Pollution-Persistent Organic Pollutants, Climate Change-Kyoto Protocol, Desertification
Geography - note: strategic location along approaches to Strait of Gibraltar

People

Population: 39,167,744 (July 1999 est.)
Age structure:
0-14 years: 15% (male 3,012,907; female 2,835,455)
15-64 years: 68% (male 13,411,046; female 13,406,214)
65 years and over: 17% (male 2,702,654; female 3,799,468) (1999 est.)
Population growth rate: 0.1% (1999 est.)
Birth rate: 9.99 births/1,000 population (1999 est.)
Death rate: 9.69 deaths/1,000 population (1999 est.)
Net migration rate: 0.66 migrant(s)/1,000 population (1999 est.)
Sex ratio:
at birth: 1.07 male(s)/female
under 15 years: 1.06 male(s)/female
15-64 years: 1 male(s)/female
65 years and over: 0.71 male(s)/female
total population: 0.95 male(s)/female (1999 est.)
Infant mortality rate: 6.41 deaths/1,000 live births (1999 est.)

Spain (continued)

Life expectancy at birth:
total population: 77.71 years
male: 73.97 years
female: 81.71 years (1999 est.)
Total fertility rate: 1.24 children born/woman (1999 est.)
Nationality:
noun: Spaniard(s)
adjective: Spanish
Ethnic groups: composite of Mediterranean and Nordic types
Religions: Roman Catholic 99%, other 1%
Languages: Castilian Spanish 74%, Catalan 17%, Galician 7%, Basque 2%
Literacy:
definition: age 15 and over can read and write
total population: 96%
male: 98%
female: 94% (1986 est.)

Government

Country name:
conventional long form: Kingdom of Spain
conventional short form: Spain
local short form: Espana
Data code: SP
Government type: parliamentary monarchy
Capital: Madrid
Administrative divisions: 17 autonomous communities (comunidades autonomas, singular - comunidad autonoma); Andalucia, Aragon, Asturias, Baleares (Balearic Islands), Canarias (Canary Islands), Cantabria, Castilla-La Mancha, Castilla y Leon, Cataluna, Communidad Valencian, Extremadura, Galicia, La Rioja, Madrid, Murcia, Navarra, Pais Vasco (Basque Country)
note: there are five places of sovereignty on and off the coast of Morocco: Ceuta and Melilla are administered as autonomous communities; Islas Chafarinas, Penon de Alhucemas, and Penon de Velez de la Gomera are under direct Spanish administration
Independence: 1492 (expulsion of the Moors and unification)
National holiday: National Day, 12 October
Constitution: 6 December 1978, effective 29 December 1978
Legal system: civil law system, with regional applications; does not accept compulsory ICJ jurisdiction
Suffrage: 18 years of age; universal
Executive branch:
chief of state: King JUAN CARLOS I (since 22 November 1975); Heir Apparent Prince FELIPE, son of the monarch, born 30 January 1968
head of government: President of the Government Jose Maria AZNAR Lopez (since 5 May 1996); First Vice President Francisco ALVAREZ CASCOS Fernandez (since 5 May 1996) and Second Vice President (and Minister of Economy and Finance) Rodrigo RATO Figaredo (since 5 May 1996)
cabinet: Council of Ministers designated by the president
note: there is also a Council of State that is the supreme consultative organ of the government
elections: the monarch is hereditary; president proposed by the monarch and elected by the National Assembly following legislative elections; election last held 3 March 1996 (next to be held by NA April 2000); vice presidents appointed by the monarch on proposal of the president
election results: Jose Maria AZNAR elected president; percent of National Assembly vote - NA
Legislative branch: bicameral; the General Courts or National Assembly or Las Cortes Generales consists of the Senate or Senado (256 seats - 208 members directly elected by popular vote and the other 48 appointed by the regional legislatures to serve four-year terms) and the Congress of Deputies or Congreso de los Diputados (350 seats; members are elected by popular vote on block lists by proportional representation to serve four-year terms)
elections: Senate - last held 3 March 1996 (next to be held by April 2000); Congress of Deputies - last held 3 March 1996 (next to be held by April 2000)
election results: Senate - percent of vote by party - NA; seats by party - PP 132, PSOE 96, CiU 11, PNV 6, IU 2, others 9; Congress of Deputies - percent of vote by party - PP 38.9%, PSOE 37.5%, IU 10.7%, CiU 4.6%; seats by party - PP 156, PSOE 141, IU 21, CiU 16, other 16
Judicial branch: Supreme Court or Tribunal Supremo
Political parties and leaders:
principal national parties, from right to left: Popular Party or PP [Jose Maria AZNAR Lopez]; Spanish Socialist Workers Party or PSOE [Joaquin ALMUNIA Amann, secretary general]; Spanish Communist Party or PCE [Julio ANGUITA Gonzalez]; United Left or IU (a coalition of parties including the PCE and other small parties) [Julio ANGUITA Gonzalez]
chief regional parties: Convergence and Union or CiU [Jordi PUJOL i Soley, secretary general] (a coalition of the Democratic Convergence of Catalonia or CDC [Jordi PUJOL i Soley] and the Democratic Union of Catalonia or UDC [Josep Antoni DURAN y LLEIDA]); Basque Nationalist Party or PNV [Xabier ARZALLUS Antia]; Canarian Coalition or CC (a coalition of five parties) [Lorenzo OLLARTE Cullen]
Political pressure groups and leaders: on the extreme left, the Basque Fatherland and Liberty or ETA and the First of October Antifascist Resistance Group or GRAPO use terrorism to oppose the government; Euskal Herritarok or EH [Herri BATASUNA]; free labor unions (authorized in April 1977); Workers Confederation or CC.OO; the Socialist General Union of Workers or UGT and the smaller independent Workers Syndical Union or USO; business and landowning interests; the Catholic Church; Opus Dei; university students
International organization participation: AfDB, AsDB, Australia Group, BIS, CCC, CE, CERN, EAPC, EBRD, ECE, ECLAC, EIB, EMU, ESA, EU, FAO, IADB, IAEA, IBRD, ICAO, ICC, ICFTU, ICRM, IDA, IEA, IFAD, IFC, IFRCS, IHO, ILO, IMF, IMO, Inmarsat, Intelsat, Interpol, IOC, IOM (observer), ISO, ITU, LAIA (observer), MTCR, NAM (guest), NATO, NEA, NSG, OAS (observer), OECD, OPCW, OSCE, PCA, UN, UNCTAD, UNESCO, UNHCR, UNIDO, UNMIBH, UNU, UPU, WCL, WEU, WHO, WIPO, WMO, WToO, WTrO, ZC
Diplomatic representation in the US:
chief of mission: Ambassador Antonio OYARZABAL MARCHESI
chancery: 2375 Pennsylvania Avenue NW, Washington, DC 20037
telephone: [1] (202) 452-0100, 728-2340
FAX: [1] (202) 833-5670
consulate(s) general: Boston, Chicago, Houston, Los Angeles, Miami, New Orleans, New York, San Francisco, and San Juan (Puerto Rico)
Diplomatic representation from the US:
chief of mission: Ambassador Edward L. ROMERO
embassy: Serrano 75, 28006 Madrid
mailing address: APO AE 09642
telephone: [34] (91) 587-2200
FAX: [34] (91) 587-2303
consulate(s) general: Barcelona
Flag description: three horizontal bands of red (top), yellow (double width), and red with the national coat of arms on the hoist side of the yellow band; the coat of arms includes the royal seal framed by the Pillars of Hercules, which are the two promontories (Gibraltar and Ceuta) on either side of the eastern end of the Strait of Gibraltar

Economy

Economy - overview: Spain's mixed capitalist economy supports a GDP that on a per capita basis is three-fourths that of the four leading West European economies. Its center-right government successfully worked to gain admission to the first group of countries launching the European single currency on 1 January 1999. The deficit-to-GDP ratio is 2.1%, the debt-to-GDP ratio is around 68%, and inflation is approximately 2%. Moreover, the AZNAR administration has continued to advocate liberalization, privatization, and deregulation of the economy and has introduced some tax reforms to that end. Unemployment, nonetheless, remains the highest in the EU at 20%. The government, for political reasons, has made only limited progress in changing labor laws or reforming pension schemes, which are key to the sustainability of both Spain's internal economic advances and its competitiveness in a single currency area. Adjustment to the monetary and other economic policies of an integrated Europe will pose difficult challenges to Spain in the next few years.
GDP: purchasing power parity - $645.6 billion (1998 est.)
GDP - real growth rate: 3.5% (1998 est.)
GDP - per capita: purchasing power parity - $16,500 (1998 est.)
GDP - composition by sector:
agriculture: 3.4%

Spain *(continued)*

industry: 33.3%
services: 63.3% (1997 est.)
Population below poverty line: NA%
Household income or consumption by percentage share:
lowest 10%: 2.8%
highest 10%: 25.2% (1990)
Inflation rate (consumer prices): 2% (1998 est.)
Labor force: 16.2 million
Labor force - by occupation: services 64%, manufacturing, mining, and construction 28%, agriculture 8% (1997 est.)
Unemployment rate: 20% (1998 est.)
Budget:
revenues: $113 billion
expenditures: $139 billion, including capital expenditures of $15 billion (1995)
Industries: textiles and apparel (including footwear), food and beverages, metals and metal manufactures, chemicals, shipbuilding, automobiles, machine tools, tourism
Industrial production growth rate: 5.8% (1998)
Electricity - production: 163.468 billion kWh (1996)
Electricity - production by source:
fossil fuel: 43.17%
hydro: 23.92%
nuclear: 32.74%
other: 0.17% (1996)
Electricity - consumption: 164.568 billion kWh (1996)
Electricity - exports: 5.7 billion kWh (1996)
Electricity - imports: 6.8 billion kWh (1996)
Agriculture - products: grain, vegetables, olives, wine grapes, sugar beets, citrus; beef, pork, poultry, dairy products; fish
Exports: $111.1 billion (f.o.b., 1998 est.)
Exports - commodities: cars and trucks, other machinery and manufactured goods, foodstuffs, and other consumer goods
Exports - partners: EU 70% (France 20%, Germany 18%, Italy 10%, Portugal 9%, UK 8%), US 4.4% (1997)
Imports: $132.3 billion (f.o.b., 1998 est.)
Imports - commodities: machinery, transport equipment, fuels, semifinished goods, foodstuffs, consumer goods, chemicals (1997)
Imports - partners: EU 65% (France 17%, Germany 15%, Italy 9%, UK 8%, Benelux 7%), US 6%, Japan 3% (1997)
Debt - external: $90 billion (1993 est.)
Economic aid - donor: ODA, $1.3 billion (1995)
Currency: 1 peseta (Pta) = 100 centimos
Exchange rates: pesetas (Ptas) per US$1 - 143.39 (January 1999), 149.40 (1998), 146.41 (1997), 126.66 (1996), 124.69 (1995), 133.96 (1994)
note: on 1 January 1999, the European Union introduced a common currency that is now being used by financial institutions in some member countries at the rate of 0.8597 euros per US$ and a fixed rate of 166.386 pesetas per euro; the euro will replace the local currency in consenting countries for all transactions in 2002
Fiscal year: calendar year

Communications

Telephones: 12.6 million (1990 est.)
Telephone system: generally adequate, modern facilities
domestic: NA
international: 22 coaxial submarine cables; satellite earth stations - 2 Intelsat (1 Atlantic Ocean and 1 Indian Ocean), NA Eutelsat, NA Inmarsat, and NA Marecs; tropospheric scatter to adjacent countries
Radio broadcast stations: AM 190, FM 406 (repeaters 134), shortwave 0
Radios: 12 million (1992 est.)
Television broadcast stations: 542 (382 network stations, 160 low-power stations, and one US Air Force Europe station) (1997)
Televisions: 15.7 million (1992 est.)

Transportation

Railways:
total: 15,079 km
broad gauge: 12,781 km 1.668-m gauge (6,355 km electrified; 2,295 km double track)
standard gauge: 525 km 1.435-m gauge (480 km electrified)
narrow gauge: 1,773 km 1.000-m gauge (594 km electrified) (1996)
Highways:
total: 346,858 km
paved: 343,389 km (including 9,063 km of expressways)
unpaved: 3,469 km (1997 est.)
Waterways: 1,045 km, but of minor economic importance
Pipelines: crude oil 265 km; petroleum products 1,794 km; natural gas 1,666 km
Ports and harbors: Aviles, Barcelona, Bilbao, Cadiz, Cartagena, Castellon de la Plana, Ceuta, Huelva, La Coruna, Las Palmas (Canary Islands), Malaga, Melilla, Pasajes, Gijon, Santa Cruz de Tenerife (Canary Islands), Santander, Tarragona, Valencia, Vigo
Merchant marine:
total: 137 ships (1,000 GRT or over) totaling 1,094,408 GRT/1,695,708 DWT
ships by type: bulk 11, cargo 29, chemical tanker 10, container 10, liquefied gas tanker 3, oil tanker 25, passenger 1, refrigerated cargo 6, roll-on/roll-off cargo 35, short-sea passenger 6, specialized tanker 1 (1998 est.)
Airports: 99 (1998 est.)
Airports - with paved runways:
total: 66
over 3,047 m: 15
2,438 to 3,047 m: 11
1,524 to 2,437 m: 16
914 to 1,523 m: 15
under 914 m: 9 (1998 est.)
Airports - with unpaved runways:
total: 33
1,524 to 2,437 m: 1
914 to 1,523 m: 11

under 914 m: 21 (1998 est.)
Heliports: 2 (1998 est.)

Military

Military branches: Army, Navy, Air Force, Marines, Civil Guard, National Police, Coastal Civil Guard
Military manpower - military age: 20 years of age
Military manpower - availability:
males age 15-49: 10,374,314 (1999 est.)
Military manpower - fit for military service:
males age 15-49: 8,346,155 (1999 est.)
Military manpower - reaching military age annually:
males: 311,350 (1999 est.)
Military expenditures - dollar figure: $6.3 billion (1995)
Military expenditures - percent of GDP: 1.4% (1995)

Transnational Issues

Disputes - international: Gibraltar issue with UK; Spain controls five places of sovereignty (plazas de soberania) on and off the coast of Morocco - the coastal enclaves of Ceuta and Melilla, which Morocco contests, as well as the islands of Penon de Alhucemas, Penon de Velez de la Gomera, and Islas Chafarinas
Illicit drugs: key European gateway country for Latin American cocaine and North African hashish entering the European market; transshipment point for and consumer of Southwest Asian heroin

Spratly Islands

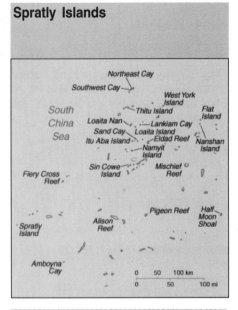

Geography

Location: Southeastern Asia, group of reefs and islands in the South China Sea, about two-thirds of the way from southern Vietnam to the southern Philippines
Geographic coordinates: 8 38 N, 111 55 E
Map references: Southeast Asia
Area:
total: less than 5 sq km
land: less than 5 sq km
water: 0 sq km
note: includes 100 or so islets, coral reefs, and sea mounts scattered over an area of nearly 410,000 sq km of the central South China Sea
Area - comparative: NA
Land boundaries: 0 km
Coastline: 926 km
Maritime claims: NA
Climate: tropical
Terrain: flat
Elevation extremes:
lowest point: South China Sea 0 m
highest point: unnamed location on Southwest Cay 4 m
Natural resources: fish, guano, undetermined oil and natural gas potential
Land use:
arable land: 0%
permanent crops: 0%
permanent pastures: 0%
forests and woodland: 0%
other: 100%
Irrigated land: 0 sq km (1993)
Natural hazards: typhoons; serious maritime hazard because of numerous reefs and shoals
Environment - current issues: NA
Environment - international agreements:
party to: none of the selected agreements
signed, but not ratified: none of the selected agreements

Geography - note: strategically located near several primary shipping lanes in the central South China Sea; includes numerous small islands, atolls, shoals, and coral reefs

People

Population: no indigenous inhabitants
note: there are scattered garrisons occupied by personnel of several claimant states

Government

Country name:
conventional long form: none
conventional short form: Spratly Islands
Data code: PG

Economy

Economy - overview: Economic activity is limited to commercial fishing. The proximity to nearby oil- and gas-producing sedimentary basins suggests the potential for oil and gas deposits, but the region is largely unexplored, and there are no reliable estimates of potential reserves; commercial exploitation has yet to be developed.

Transportation

Ports and harbors: none
Airports: 4 (1998 est.)
Airports - with paved runways:
total: 1
914 to 1,523 m: 1 (1998 est.)
Airports - with unpaved runways:
total: 3
914 to 1,523 m: 1
under 914 m: 2 (1998 est.)

Military

Military - note: Spratly Islands consist of more than 100 small islands or reefs, of which about 45 are claimed and occupied by China, Malaysia, the Philippines, Taiwan, and Vietnam

Transnational Issues

Disputes - international: all of the Spratly Islands are claimed by China, Taiwan, and Vietnam; parts of them are claimed by Malaysia and the Philippines; in 1984, Brunei established an exclusive fishing zone, which encompasses Louisa Reef in the southern Spratly Islands, but has not publicly claimed the island

Sri Lanka

Geography

Location: Southern Asia, island in the Indian Ocean, south of India
Geographic coordinates: 7 00 N, 81 00 E
Map references: Asia
Area:
total: 65,610 sq km
land: 64,740 sq km
water: 870 sq km
Area - comparative: slightly larger than West Virginia
Land boundaries: 0 km
Coastline: 1,340 km
Maritime claims:
contiguous zone: 24 nm
continental shelf: 200 nm or to the edge of the continental margin
exclusive economic zone: 200 nm
territorial sea: 12 nm
Climate: tropical monsoon; northeast monsoon (December to March); southwest monsoon (June to October)
Terrain: mostly low, flat to rolling plain; mountains in south-central interior
Elevation extremes:
lowest point: Indian Ocean 0 m
highest point: Pidurutalagala 2,524 m
Natural resources: limestone, graphite, mineral sands, gems, phosphates, clay
Land use:
arable land: 14%
permanent crops: 15%
permanent pastures: 7%
forests and woodland: 32%
other: 32% (1993 est.)
Irrigated land: 5,500 sq km (1993 est.)
Natural hazards: occasional cyclones and tornadoes
Environment - current issues: deforestation; soil erosion; wildlife populations threatened by poaching; coastal degradation from mining activities and

Sri Lanka (continued)

increased pollution; freshwater resources being polluted by industrial wastes and sewage runoff

Environment - international agreements:
party to: Biodiversity, Climate Change, Desertification, Endangered Species, Environmental Modification, Hazardous Wastes, Law of the Sea, Nuclear Test Ban, Ozone Layer Protection, Wetlands
signed, but not ratified: Marine Life Conservation

Geography - note: strategic location near major Indian Ocean sea lanes

People

Population: 19,144,875 (July 1999 est.)
note: since the outbreak of hostilities between the government and armed Tamil separatists in the mid-1980s, several hundred thousand Tamil civilians have fled the island; as of late 1996, 63,068 were housed in refugee camps in south India, another 30,000-40,000 lived outside the Indian camps, and more than 200,000 Tamils have sought political asylum in the West

Age structure:
0-14 years: 27% (male 2,650,135; female 2,535,092)
15-64 years: 67% (male 6,231,987; female 6,500,782)
65 years and over: 6% (male 592,539; female 634,340) (1999 est.)

Population growth rate: 1.1% (1999 est.)

Birth rate: 18.16 births/1,000 population (1999 est.)

Death rate: 6.02 deaths/1,000 population (1999 est.)

Net migration rate: -1.13 migrant(s)/1,000 population (1999 est.)

Sex ratio:
at birth: 1.05 male(s)/female
under 15 years: 1.05 male(s)/female
15-64 years: 0.96 male(s)/female
65 years and over: 0.93 male(s)/female
total population: 0.98 male(s)/female (1999 est.)

Infant mortality rate: 16.12 deaths/1,000 live births (1999 est.)

Life expectancy at birth:
total population: 72.67 years
male: 69.89 years
female: 75.59 years (1999 est.)

Total fertility rate: 2.1 children born/woman (1999 est.)

Nationality:
noun: Sri Lankan(s)
adjective: Sri Lankan

Ethnic groups: Sinhalese 74%, Tamil 18%, Moor 7%, Burgher, Malay, and Vedda 1%

Religions: Buddhist 69%, Hindu 15%, Christian 8%, Muslim 8%

Languages: Sinhala (official and national language) 74%, Tamil (national language) 18%
note: English is commonly used in government and is spoken by about 10% of the population

Literacy:
definition: age 15 and over can read and write
total population: 90.2%
male: 93.4%
female: 87.2% (1995 est.)

Government

Country name:
conventional long form: Democratic Socialist Republic of Sri Lanka
conventional short form: Sri Lanka
former: Ceylon

Data code: CE

Government type: republic

Capital: Colombo

Administrative divisions: 8 provinces; Central, North Central, North Eastern, North Western, Sabaragamuwa, Southern, Uva, Western

Independence: 4 February 1948 (from UK)

National holiday: Independence and National Day, 4 February (1948)

Constitution: adopted 16 August 1978

Legal system: a highly complex mixture of English common law, Roman-Dutch, Muslim, Sinhalese, and customary law; has not accepted compulsory ICJ jurisdiction

Suffrage: 18 years of age; universal

Executive branch:
chief of state: President Chandrika Bandaranaike KUMARATUNGA (since 12 November 1994); note - Sirimavo BANDARANAIKE is the prime minister; in Sri Lanka the president is considered to be both the chief of state and the head of the government, this is in contrast to the more common practice of dividing the roles between the president and the prime minister when both offices exist
head of government: President Chandrika Bandaranaike KUMARATUNGA (since 12 November 1994); note - Sirimavo BANDARANAIKE is the prime minister; in Sri Lanka the president is considered to be both the chief of state and the head of the government, this is in contrast to the more common practice of dividing the roles between the president and the prime minister when both offices exist
cabinet: Cabinet appointed by the president in consultation with the prime minister
elections: president elected by popular vote for a six-year term; election last held 9 November 1994 (next to be held NA November 2000)
election results: Chandrika Bandaranaike KUMARATUNGA elected president; percent of vote - Chandrika Bandaranaike KUMARATUNGA (People's Alliance) 62%, Srima DISSANAYAKE (United National Party) 37%, other 1%

Legislative branch: unicameral Parliament (225 seats; members elected by popular vote on the basis of a modified proportional representation system to serve six-year terms)
elections: last held 16 August 1994 (next to be held by August 2000)
election results: percent of vote by party - PA 49.0%, UNP 44.0%, SLMC 1.8%, TULF 1.7%, SLPF 1.1%, EPDP 0.3%, UPF 0.3%, PLOTE 0.1%, other 1.7%; seats by party - PA 105, UNP 94, EPDP 9, SLMC 7, TULF 5, PLOTE 3, SLPF 1, UPF 1

Judicial branch: Supreme Court, judges are appointed by the Judicial Service Commission; Court of Appeals

Political parties and leaders: All Ceylon Tamil Congress or ACTC [C. G. Kumar PONNAMBALAM]; Ceylon Workers Congress or CLDC [S. THONDAMAN]; Communist Party [K. P. SILVA]; Communist Party/Beijing or CP/B [N. SHANMUGATHASAN]; Democratic People's Liberation Front or DPLF [leader NA]; Democratic United National (Lalith) Front or DUNLF [Srimani ATHULATHMUDALI]; Eelam People's Democratic Party or EPDP [Douglas DEVANANDA]; Eelam People's Revolutionary Liberation Front or EPRL [Suresh PREMACHANDRAN]; Eelam Revolutionary Organization of Students or EROS [Shankar RAJI]; Janatha Vimukthi Peramuna or JVP [Somawansa AMERASINGHE]; Lanka Socialist Party/Trotskyite or LSSP (Lanka Sama Samaja Party) [Batty WEERAKOON]; Liberal Party or LP [Rajira WIJESINGHE]; New Socialist Party or NSSP (Nava Sama Samaja Party) [Vasudeva NANAYAKKARA]; People's Alliance or PA [Chandrika Bandaranaike KUMARATUNGA]; People's Liberation Organization of Tamil Eelam or PLOTE [Uma MAHESWARAN]; People's United Front or MEP (Mahajana Eksath Peramuna) [Dinesh GUNAWARDENE]; Sri Lanka Freedom Party or SLFP [Chandrika Bandaranaike KUMARATUNGA]; Sri Lanka Muslim Congress or SLMC [M. H. M. ASHRAFF]; Sri Lanka People's Party or SLMP (Sri Lanka Mahajana Party) [Y. P. DE SILVA]; Sri Lanka Progressive Front or SLPF [Ariya BULEGODA]; Tamil Eelam Liberation Organization or TELO [M. K. SIVAJILINGHAM]; Tamil United Liberation Front or TULF [M. SIVASITHAMBARAM]; United National Party or UNP [Ranil WICHREMESINGHE]; Upcountry People's Front or UPF [Periyasamy CHANDRASEKARAN]; Desha Vimukthi Janatha Party or DVJP [P.M. Podi APPUHAMY]; several ethnic Tamil and Muslim parties, represented in either parliament or provincial councils

Political pressure groups and leaders: Liberation Tigers of Tamil Eelam or LTTE; other radical chauvinist Sinhalese groups; Buddhist clergy; Sinhalese Buddhist lay groups; labor unions

International organization participation: AsDB, C, CCC, CP, ESCAP, FAO, G-24, G-77, IAEA, IBRD, ICAO, ICC, ICFTU, ICRM, IDA, IFAD, IFC, IFRCS, IHO, ILO, IMF, IMO, Inmarsat, Intelsat, Interpol, IOC, IOM, ISO, ITU, NAM, OAS (observer), OPCW, PCA, SAARC, UN, UNCTAD, UNESCO, UNIDO, UNU, UPU, WCL, WFTU, WHO, WIPO, WMO, WToO, WTrO

Diplomatic representation in the US:
chief of mission: Ambassador Warnasena RASAPUTRAM
chancery: 2148 Wyoming Avenue NW, Washington, DC 20008
telephone: [1] (202) 483-4025 through 4028
FAX: [1] (202) 232-7181
consulate(s): New York

Diplomatic representation from the US:
chief of mission: Ambassador Shaun E. DONNELLY
embassy: 210 Galle Road, Colombo 3

Sri Lanka (continued)

mailing address: P. O. Box 106, Colombo
telephone: [94] (1) 448007
FAX: [94] (1) 437345, 446013
Flag description: yellow with two panels; the smaller hoist-side panel has two equal vertical bands of green (hoist side) and orange; the other panel is a large dark red rectangle with a yellow lion holding a sword, and there is a yellow bo leaf in each corner; the yellow field appears as a border that goes around the entire flag and extends between the two panels

Economy

Economy - overview: In 1977, Colombo abandoned statist economic policies and its import substitution trade policy for market-oriented policies and export-oriented trade. Sri Lanka's most dynamic industries now are food processing, textiles and apparel, food and beverages, telecommunications, and insurance and banking. By 1996 plantation crops made up only 20% of exports (compared with 93% in 1970), while textiles and garments accounted for 63%. GDP grew at an annual average rate of 5.5% throughout the 1990s until a drought and a deteriorating security situation lowered growth to 3.8% in 1996. The economy rebounded in 1997-98 with growth of 6.4% and 4.7%. For the next round of reforms, the central bank of Sri Lanka recommends that Colombo expand market mechanisms in nonplantation agriculture, dismantle the government's monopoly on wheat imports, and promote more competition in the financial sector. A continuing cloud over the economy is the fighting between the Sinhalese and the minority Tamils, which has cost 50,000 lives in the past 15 years. The global slowdown will temper growth in 1999.
GDP: purchasing power parity - $48.1 billion (1998 est.)
GDP - real growth rate: 4.7% (1998 est.)
GDP - per capita: purchasing power parity - $2,500 (1998 est.)
GDP - composition by sector:
agriculture: 18%
industry: 31%
services: 51% (1997)
Population below poverty line: 35.3% (1990-91 est.)
Household income or consumption by percentage share:
lowest 10%: 3.8%
highest 10%: 25.2% (1990)
Inflation rate (consumer prices): 9.3% (1998)
Labor force: 6.2 million (1997)
Labor force - by occupation: services 46%, agriculture 37%, industry 17% (1997 est.)
Unemployment rate: 11% (1997 est.)
Budget:
revenues: $3 billion
expenditures: $4.2 billion, including capital expenditures of $1 billion (1997 est.)
Industries: processing of rubber, tea, coconuts, and other agricultural commodities; clothing, cement, petroleum refining, textiles, tobacco

Industrial production growth rate: 6.5% (1996 est.)
Electricity - production: 5.05 billion kWh (1996)
Electricity - production by source:
fossil fuel: 4.95%
hydro: 95.05%
nuclear: 0%
other: 0% (1996)
Electricity - consumption: 5.05 billion kWh (1996)
Electricity - exports: 0 kWh (1996)
Electricity - imports: 0 kWh (1996)
Agriculture - products: rice, sugarcane, grains, pulses, oilseed, spices, tea, rubber, coconuts; milk, eggs, hides, beef
Exports: $4.5 billion (f.o.b., 1998)
Exports - commodities: textiles and apparel, tea, diamonds and other gems, coconut products, rubber products, petroleum products (1997)
Exports - partners: US 36%, UK 11%, Japan 6%, Germany 5%, Belgium-Luxembourg 4% (1997)
Imports: $5.3 billion (f.o.b., 1998)
Imports - commodities: machinery and equipment, textiles, petroleum, building materials, sugar (1997)
Imports - partners: India 10%, Japan 9%, South Korea 8%, Hong Kong 7%, Taiwan 7% (1997)
Debt - external: $8.8 billion (1998)
Economic aid - recipient: $559.3 million (1995)
Currency: 1 Sri Lankan rupee (SLRe) = 100 cents
Exchange rates: Sri Lankan rupees (SLRes) per US$1 - 67.948 (January 1999), 64.593 (1998), 58.995 (1997), 55.271 (1996), 51.252 (1995), 49.415 (1994)
Fiscal year: calendar year

Communications

Telephones: 352,681 (1997 est.); 114,888 cellular telephone subscribers (1997 est.)
Telephone system: very inadequate domestic service, but expanding with the entry of two wireless loop operators and privatization of national telephone company; good international service
domestic: NA
international: submarine cables to Indonesia and Djibouti; satellite earth stations - 2 Intelsat (Indian Ocean)
Radio broadcast stations: AM 12, FM 5, shortwave 0
Radios: 3.6 million (1996 est.)
Television broadcast stations: 21 (19 network stations, two low-power stations) (1997)
Televisions: 1.6 million (1996 est.)

Transportation

Railways:
total: 1,501 km
broad gauge: 1,442 km 1.676-m gauge
narrow gauge: 59 km 0.762-m gauge (1995)
Highways:
total: 99,200 km
paved: 39,680 km
unpaved: 59,520 km (1996 est.)
Waterways: 430 km; navigable by shallow-draft craft

Pipelines: crude oil and petroleum products 62 km (1987)
Ports and harbors: Colombo, Galle, Jaffna, Trincomalee
Merchant marine:
total: 22 ships (1,000 GRT or over) totaling 178,867 GRT/276,363 DWT
ships by type: bulk 1, cargo 14, container 1, oil tanker 1, refrigerated cargo 5 (1998 est.)
Airports: 13 (1998 est.)
Airports - with paved runways:
total: 12
over 3,047 m: 1
1,524 to 2,437 m: 5
914 to 1,523 m: 6 (1998 est.)
Airports - with unpaved runways:
total: 1
1,524 to 2,437 m: 1 (1998 est.)

Military

Military branches: Army, Navy, Air Force, Police Force
Military manpower - military age: 18 years of age
Military manpower - availability:
males age 15-49: 5,223,590 (1999 est.)
Military manpower - fit for military service:
males age 15-49: 4,062,758 (1999 est.)
Military manpower - reaching military age annually:
males: 199,196 (1999 est.)
Military expenditures - dollar figure: $719 million (1998)
Military expenditures - percent of GDP: 4.2% (1998)

Transnational Issues

Disputes - international: none

Sudan

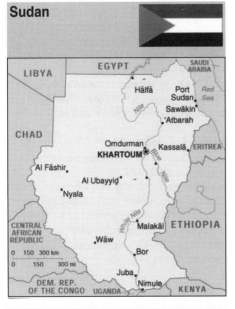

Location: Northern Africa, bordering the Red Sea, between Egypt and Eritrea
Geographic coordinates: 15 00 N, 30 00 E
Map references: Africa
Area:
total: 2,505,810 sq km
land: 2.376 million sq km
water: 129,810 sq km
Area - comparative: slightly more than one-quarter the size of the US
Land boundaries:
total: 7,687 km
border countries: Central African Republic 1,165 km, Chad 1,360 km, Democratic Republic of the Congo 628 km, Egypt 1,273 km, Eritrea 605 km, Ethiopia 1,606 km, Kenya 232 km, Libya 383 km, Uganda 435 km
Coastline: 853 km
Maritime claims:
contiguous zone: 18 nm
continental shelf: 200-m depth or to the depth of exploitation
territorial sea: 12 nm
Climate: tropical in south; arid desert in north; rainy season (April to October)
Terrain: generally flat, featureless plain; mountains in east and west
Elevation extremes:
lowest point: Red Sea 0 m
highest point: Kinyeti 3,187 m
Natural resources: petroleum; small reserves of iron ore, copper, chromium ore, zinc, tungsten, mica, silver, gold
Land use:
arable land: 5%
permanent crops: 0%
permanent pastures: 46%
forests and woodland: 19%
other: 30% (1993 est.)
Irrigated land: 19,460 sq km (1993 est.)

Natural hazards: dust storms
Environment - current issues: inadequate supplies of potable water; wildlife populations threatened by excessive hunting; soil erosion; desertification
Environment - international agreements:
party to: Biodiversity, Climate Change, Desertification, Endangered Species, Law of the Sea, Nuclear Test Ban, Ozone Layer Protection
signed, but not ratified: none of the selected agreements
Geography - note: largest country in Africa; dominated by the Nile and its tributaries

Population: 34,475,690 (July 1999 est.)
Age structure:
0-14 years: 45% (male 7,941,909; female 7,614,225)
15-64 years: 53% (male 9,094,712; female 9,061,194)
65 years and over: 2% (male 423,389; female 340,261) (1999 est.)
Population growth rate: 2.71% (1999 est.)
Birth rate: 39.34 births/1,000 population (1999 est.)
Death rate: 10.6 deaths/1,000 population (1999 est.)
Net migration rate: -1.68 migrant(s)/1,000 population (1999 est.)
Sex ratio:
at birth: 1.05 male(s)/female
under 15 years: 1.04 male(s)/female
15-64 years: 1 male(s)/female
65 years and over: 1.24 male(s)/female
total population: 1.03 male(s)/female (1999 est.)
Infant mortality rate: 70.94 deaths/1,000 live births (1999 est.)
Life expectancy at birth:
total population: 56.4 years
male: 55.41 years
female: 57.44 years (1999 est.)
Total fertility rate: 5.58 children born/woman (1999 est.)
Nationality:
noun: Sudanese (singular and plural)
adjective: Sudanese
Ethnic groups: black 52%, Arab 39%, Beja 6%, foreigners 2%, other 1%
Religions: Sunni Muslim 70% (in north), indigenous beliefs 25%, Christian 5% (mostly in south and Khartoum)
Languages: Arabic (official), Nubian, Ta Bedawie, diverse dialects of Nilotic, Nilo-Hamitic, Sudanic languages, English
note: program of Arabization in process
Literacy:
definition: age 15 and over can read and write
total population: 46.1%
male: 57.7%
female: 34.6% (1995 est.)

Country name:
conventional long form: Republic of the Sudan

conventional short form: Sudan
local long form: Jumhuriyat as-Sudan
local short form: As-Sudan
former: Anglo-Egyptian Sudan
Data code: SU
Government type: transitional - previously ruling military junta; presidential and National Assembly elections held in March 1996; new constitution drafted by Presidential Committee, went into effect on 30 June 1998 after being approved in nationwide referendum
Capital: Khartoum
Administrative divisions: 26 states (wilayat, singular - wilayah); A'ali an Nil, Al Bahr al Ahmar, Al Buhayrat, Al Jazirah, Al Khartum, Al Qadarif, Al Wahdah, An Nil al Abyad, An Nil al Azraq, Ash Shamaliyah, Bahr al Jabal, Gharb al Istiwa'iyah, Gharb Bahr al Ghazal, Gharb Darfur, Gharb Kurdufan, Janub Darfur, Janub Kurdufan, Junqali, Kassala, Nahr an Nil, Shamal Bahr al Ghazal, Shamal Darfur, Shamal Kurdufan, Sharq al Istiwa'iyah, Sinnar, Warab
Independence: 1 January 1956 (from Egypt and UK)
National holiday: Independence Day, 1 January (1956)
Constitution: 12 April 1973, suspended following coup of 6 April 1985; interim constitution of 10 October 1985 suspended following coup of 30 June 1989; new constitution implemented on 30 June 1998
Legal system: based on English common law and Islamic law; as of 20 January 1991, the now defunct Revolutionary Command Council imposed Islamic law in the northern states; Islamic law applies to all residents of the northern states regardless of their religion; some separate religious courts; accepts compulsory ICJ jurisdiction, with reservations
Suffrage: NA years of age; universal, but noncompulsory
Executive branch:
chief of state: President Lt. General Umar Hasan Ahmad al-BASHIR (since 16 October 1993); First Vice President Ali Uthman Muhammad TAHA (since 17 February 1998), Second Vice President (Police) Maj. General George KONGOR AROP (since NA February 1994); note - the president is both the chief of state and head of government
head of government: President Lt. General Umar Hasan Ahmad al-BASHIR (since 16 October 1993); First Vice President Ali Uthman Muhammad TAHA (since 17 February 1998), Second Vice President (Police) Maj. General George KONGOR AROP (since NA February 1994); note - the president is both the chief of state and head of government
cabinet: Cabinet appointed by the president; note - President al-BASHIR's government is dominated by members of Sudan's National Islamic Front (NIF), a fundamentalist political organization formed from the Muslim Brotherhood in 1986; in 1998, the NIF created the National Congress as its legal front; the National Congress/NIF dominates much of Khartoum's overall domestic and foreign policies; President al-BASHIR named a new cabinet on 20 April 1996 which includes members of the National Islamic Front, serving and

retired military officers, and civilian technocrats; on 8 March 1998, he reshuffled the cabinet and brought in several former rebel and opposition members as ministers

elections: president elected by popular vote for a five-year term; election last held 6-17 March 1996 (next to be held NA 2001)

election results: Umar Hasan Ahmad al-BASHIR elected president; percent of vote - Umar Hasan Ahmad al-BASHIR 75.7%; note - about forty other candidates ran for president

note: al-BASHIR, as chairman of the Revolutionary Command Council for National Salvation (RCC), assumed power on 30 June 1989 and served concurrently as chief of state, chairman of the RCC, prime minister, and minister of defense until 16 October 1993 when he was appointed president by the RCC; upon its dissolution on 16 October 1993, the RCC's executive and legislative powers were devolved to the president and the Transitional National Assembly (TNA), Sudan's appointed legislative body, which has since been replaced by the National Assembly which was elected in March 1996

Legislative branch: unicameral National Assembly (400 seats; 275 elected by popular vote, 125 elected by a supraassembly of interest groups known as the National Congress)

elections: last held 6-17 March 1996 (next to be held NA 2001)

election results: NA; the March 1996 elections were held on a nonparty basis; parties are banned in the new National Assembly

Judicial branch: Supreme Court; Special Revolutionary Courts

Political parties and leaders: political parties were banned following 30 June 1989 coup, however, political "associations" are allowed under a new law drafted in 1998 and implemented on 1 January 1999 and include - National Congress [Umar Hasan Ahmad al-BASHIR]

Political pressure groups and leaders: National Islamic Front or NIF [Hasan al-TURABI] (banned, but the National Congress operates as its legal front)

International organization participation: ABEDA, ACP, AfDB, AFESD, AL, AMF, CAEU, CCC, ECA, FAO, G-77, IAEA, IBRD, ICAO, ICRM, IDA, IDB, IFAD, IFC, IFRCS, IGAD, ILO, IMF, IMO, Intelsat, Interpol, IOC, IOM (observer), ITU, NAM, OAU, OIC, PCA, UN, UNCTAD, UNESCO, UNHCR, UNIDO, UNU, UPU, WFTU, WHO, WIPO, WMO, WToO

Diplomatic representation in the US:
chief of mission: Ambassador Mahdi Ibrahim MAHAMMAD (recalled to Khartoum in August 1998)
chancery: 2210 Massachusetts Avenue NW, Washington, DC 20008
telephone: [1] (202) 338-8565
FAX: [1] (202) 667-2406

Diplomatic representation from the US: US officials at the US Embassy in Khartoum were moved for security reasons in February 1996 and have been relocated to the US Embassies in Nairobi, Kenya and Cairo, Egypt; they visit Khartoum monthly, but the Sudanese Government has not allowed such visits since August 1998; the US Embassy in Khartoum (located on Sharia Abdul Latif Avenue; mailing address - P.O. Box 699, Khartoum; APO AE 09829; telephone - [249] (11) 774611 or 774700; FAX - [249] (11) 774137) is kept open by local employees; the US Embassy in Nairobi, Kenya is located temporarily in the USAID Building at The Crescent, Parkland, Nairobi; mailing address - P.O. Box 30137, Box 21A, Unit 64100, APO AE 09831; telephone - [254] (2) 751613; FAX - [254] (2) 743204; the US Embassy in Cairo, Egypt is located at (North Gate) 8, Kamel El-Din Salah Street, Garden City, Cairo; mailing address - Unit 64900, APO AE 09839-4900; telephone - [20] (2) 3557371; FAX - [20] (2) 3573200

Flag description: three equal horizontal bands of red (top), white, and black with a green isosceles triangle based on the hoist side

Economy

Economy - overview: Sudan is buffeted by civil war, chronic political instability, adverse weather, high inflation, a drop in remittances from abroad, and counterproductive economic policies. The private sector's main areas of activity are agriculture and trading, with most private industrial investment predating 1980. Agriculture employs 80% of the work force. Industry mainly processes agricultural items. Sluggish economic performance over the past decade, attributable largely to declining annual rainfall, has kept per capita income at low levels. A large foreign debt and huge arrears continue to cause difficulties. In 1990 the International Monetary Fund took the unusual step of declaring Sudan noncooperative because of its nonpayment of arrears to the Fund. After Sudan backtracked on promised reforms in 1992-93, the IMF threatened to expel Sudan from the Fund. To avoid expulsion, Khartoum agreed to make payments on its arrears to the Fund, liberalize exchange rates, and reduce subsidies, measures it has partially implemented. The government's continued prosecution of the civil war and its growing international isolation continued to inhibit growth in the nonagricultural sectors of the economy during 1998. Hyperinflation has raised consumer prices above the reach of most. In 1998, a top priority was to develop potentially lucrative oilfields in southcentral Sudan; the government is working with foreign partners to exploit the oil sector.

GDP: purchasing power parity - $31.2 billion (1998 est.)

GDP - real growth rate: 6.1% (1998 est.)

GDP - per capita: purchasing power parity - $930 (1998 est.)

GDP - composition by sector:
agriculture: 33%
industry: 17%
services: 50% (1992 est.)

Population below poverty line: NA%

Household income or consumption by percentage share:
lowest 10%: NA%
highest 10%: NA%

Inflation rate (consumer prices): 27% (mid-1997 est.)

Labor force: 11 million (1996 est.)
note: labor shortages for almost all categories of skilled employment (1983 est.)

Labor force - by occupation: agriculture 80%, industry and commerce 10%, government 6%

Unemployment rate: 30% (FY92/93 est.)

Budget:
revenues: $482 million
expenditures: $1.5 billion, including capital expenditures of $30 million (1996)

Industries: cotton ginning, textiles, cement, edible oils, sugar, soap distilling, shoes, petroleum refining

Industrial production growth rate: 5% (1996 est.)

Electricity - production: 1.315 billion kWh (1996)

Electricity - production by source:
fossil fuel: 27.76%
hydro: 72.24%
nuclear: 0%
other: 0% (1996)

Electricity - consumption: 1.315 billion kWh (1996)

Electricity - exports: 0 kWh (1996)

Electricity - imports: 0 kWh (1996)

Agriculture - products: cotton, groundnuts (peanuts), sorghum, millet, wheat, gum arabic, sesame; sheep

Exports: $594 million (f.o.b., 1997)

Exports - commodities: cotton 23%, sesame 22%, livestock/meat 13%, gum arabic 5% (1996)

Exports - partners: Saudi Arabia 20%, UK 14%, China 11%, Italy 8% (1996)

Imports: $1.42 billion (f.o.b., 1997)

Imports - commodities: foodstuffs, petroleum products, manufactured goods, machinery and equipment, medicines and chemicals, textiles (1996)

Imports - partners: Saudi Arabia 10%, South Korea 7%, Germany 6%, Egypt 6% (1996)

Debt - external: $20.3 billion (1996 est.)

Economic aid - recipient: $254.4 million (1995)

Currency: 1 Sudanese pound (£Sd) = 100 piastres

Exchange rates: Sudanese pounds (£Sd) per US$1 - 1,819.70 (April 1998), 1,873.53 (2d Qtr 1998), 1,575.74 (1997), 1,250.79 (1996), 580.87 (1995), 289.61 (1994), 159.31 (1993)

Fiscal year: calendar year
note: prior to July 1995, Sudan had a fiscal year that began on 1 July and ended on 30 June; as a transition to their new fiscal year, a six-month budget was implemented for 1 July-31 December 1995; the new calendar year (1 January-31 December) fiscal year became effective 1 January 1996

Communications

Telephones: 77,215 (1983 est.)

Telephone system: large, well-equipped system by African standards, but barely adequate and poorly maintained by modern standards
domestic: consists of microwave radio relay, cable, radiotelephone communications, tropospheric scatter, and a domestic satellite system with 14 earth stations
international: satellite earth stations - 1 Intelsat

Sudan *(continued)*

(Atlantic Ocean) and 1 Arabsat
Radio broadcast stations: AM 11, FM 1, shortwave 1 (1998 est.)
Radios: 5.75 million (1998 est.)
Television broadcast stations: 3 (1997)
Televisions: 250,000 (1998 est.)

Transportation

Railways:
total: 5,516 km
narrow gauge: 4,800 km 1.067-m gauge; 716 km 1.6096-m gauge plantation line
Highways:
total: 11,900 km
paved: 4,320 km
unpaved: 7,580 km (1996 est.)
Waterways: 5,310 km navigable
Pipelines: refined products 815 km
Ports and harbors: Juba, Khartoum, Kusti, Malakal, Nimule, Port Sudan, Sawakin
Merchant marine:
total: 4 ships (1,000 GRT or over) totaling 38,093 GRT/49,727 DWT
ships by type: cargo 2, roll-on/roll-off cargo 2 (1998 est.)
Airports: 63 (1998 est.)
Airports - with paved runways:
total: 12
over 3,047 m: 1
2,438 to 3,047 m: 8
1,524 to 2,437 m: 3 (1998 est.)
Airports - with unpaved runways:
total: 51
1,524 to 2,437 m: 14
914 to 1,523 m: 26
under 914 m: 11 (1998 est.)
Heliports: 1 (1998 est.)

Military

Military branches: Army, Navy, Air Force, Popular Defense Force Militia
Military manpower - military age: 18 years of age
Military manpower - availability:
males age 15-49: 7,942,139 (1999 est.)
Military manpower - fit for military service:
males age 15-49: 4,889,557 (1999 est.)
Military manpower - reaching military age annually:
males: 379,174 (1999 est.)
Military expenditures - dollar figure: $550 million (FY98/99)
Military expenditures - percent of GDP: NA%

Transnational Issues

Disputes - international: administrative boundary with Kenya does not coincide with international boundary; Egypt asserts its claim to the "Hala'ib Triangle," a barren area of 20,580 sq km under partial Sudanese administration that is defined by an administrative boundary which supersedes the treaty boundary of 1899

Suriname

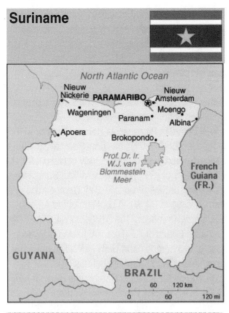

Geography

Location: Northern South America, bordering the North Atlantic Ocean, between French Guiana and Guyana
Geographic coordinates: 4 00 N, 56 00 W
Map references: South America
Area:
total: 163,270 sq km
land: 161,470 sq km
water: 1,800 sq km
Area - comparative: slightly larger than Georgia
Land boundaries:
total: 1,707 km
border countries: Brazil 597 km, French Guiana 510 km, Guyana 600 km
Coastline: 386 km
Maritime claims:
exclusive economic zone: 200 nm
territorial sea: 12 nm
Climate: tropical; moderated by trade winds
Terrain: mostly rolling hills; narrow coastal plain with swamps
Elevation extremes:
lowest point: unnamed location in the coastal plain -2 m
highest point: Wilhelmina Gebergte 1,286 m
Natural resources: timber, hydropower, fish, kaolin, shrimp, bauxite, gold, and small amounts of nickel, copper, platinum, iron ore
Land use:
arable land: NA%
permanent crops: NA%
permanent pastures: 0%
forests and woodland: 96%
other: 4% (1993 est.)
Irrigated land: 600 sq km (1993 est.)
Natural hazards: NA
Environment - current issues: deforestation as timber is cut for export; pollution of inland waterways by small-scale mining activities

Environment - international agreements:
party to: Biodiversity, Climate Change, Endangered Species, Law of the Sea, Marine Dumping, Nuclear Test Ban, Ozone Layer Protection, Ship Pollution, Tropical Timber 94, Wetlands
signed, but not ratified: none of the selected agreements
Geography - note: mostly tropical rain forest; great diversity of flora and fauna that, for the most part, is increasingly threatened by new development; relatively small population, most of which lives along the coast

People

Population: 431,156 (July 1999 est.)
Age structure:
0-14 years: 33% (male 72,673; female 69,212)
15-64 years: 62% (male 135,573; female 130,700)
65 years and over: 5% (male 10,585; female 12,413) (1999 est.)
Population growth rate: 0.71% (1999 est.)
Birth rate: 21.75 births/1,000 population (1999 est.)
Death rate: 5.75 deaths/1,000 population (1999 est.)
Net migration rate: -8.92 migrant(s)/1,000 population (1999 est.)
Sex ratio:
at birth: 1.05 male(s)/female
under 15 years: 1.05 male(s)/female
15-64 years: 1.04 male(s)/female
65 years and over: 0.85 male(s)/female
total population: 1.03 male(s)/female (1999 est.)
Infant mortality rate: 26.52 deaths/1,000 live births (1999 est.)
Life expectancy at birth:
total population: 70.89 years
male: 68.32 years
female: 73.59 years (1999 est.)
Total fertility rate: 2.55 children born/woman (1999 est.)
Nationality:
noun: Surinamer(s)
adjective: Surinamese
Ethnic groups: Hindustani (also known locally as "East Indians"; their ancestors emigrated from northern India in the latter part of the 19th century) 37%, Creole (mixed white and black) 31%, Javanese 15.3%, "Maroons" (their African ancestors were brought to the country in the 17th and 18th centuries as slaves and escaped to the interior) 10.3%, Amerindian 2.6%, Chinese 1.7%, white 1%, other 1.1%
Religions: Hindu 27.4%, Muslim 19.6%, Roman Catholic 22.8%, Protestant 25.2% (predominantly Moravian), indigenous beliefs 5%
Languages: Dutch (official), English (widely spoken), Sranang Tongo (Surinamese, sometimes called Taki-Taki, is native language of Creoles and much of the younger population and is lingua franca among others), Hindustani (a dialect of Hindi), Javanese
Literacy:
definition: age 15 and over can read and write

Suriname (continued)

total population: 93%
male: 95%
female: 91% (1995 est.)

Country name:
conventional long form: Republic of Suriname
conventional short form: Suriname
local long form: Republiek Suriname
local short form: Suriname
former: Netherlands Guiana, Dutch Guiana
Data code: NS
Government type: republic
Capital: Paramaribo
Administrative divisions: 10 districts (distrikten, singular - distrikt); Brokopondo, Commewijne, Coronie, Marowijne, Nickerie, Para, Paramaribo, Saramacca, Sipaliwini, Wanica
Independence: 25 November 1975 (from Netherlands)
National holiday: Independence Day, 25 November (1975)
Constitution: ratified 30 September 1987
Legal system: based on Dutch legal system incorporating French penal theory
Suffrage: 18 years of age; universal
Executive branch:
chief of state: President Jules WIJDENBOSCH (since 14 September 1996); Vice President Pretaapnarian RADHAKISHUN (since 14 September 1996); note - the president is both the chief of state and head of government
head of government: President Jules WIJDENBOSCH (since 14 September 1996); Vice President Pretaapnarian RADHAKISHUN (since 14 September 1996); note - the president is both the chief of state and head of government
cabinet: Cabinet of Ministers appointed by the president from among the members of the National Assembly
note: First Advisor of State maintains significant power
elections: president and vice president elected by the National Assembly or, if no presidential or vice presidential candidate receives a constitutional majority vote in the National Assembly after two votes, by the larger People's Assembly (869 representatives from the national, local, and regional councils), for five-year terms; election last held 23 May 1996; runoff election held 5 September 1996 (next to be held NA May 2001)
election results: Jules WIJDENBOSCH elected president; percent of legislative vote - NA; National Assembly failed to elect president; results reflect votes cast by the People's Assembly - Jules WIJDENBOSCH (NDP) received 438 votes, Ronald VENETIAAN (NF) received 407 votes
Legislative branch: unicameral National Assembly or National Assemblee (51 seats; members are elected by popular vote to serve five-year terms)
elections: last held 23 May 1996 (next to be held NA May 2001)

election results: percent of vote by party - NA; seats by party - NDP 16, NF 14, BVD 5, KTPI 5, Pertjaja Luhur 4, The Progressive Development Alliance 3, DA '91 2, OPDA 2
Judicial branch: Supreme Court (justices nominated for life)
Political parties and leaders: The New Front or NF (a coalition of three parties NPS, VHP, SPA) [Ronald R. VENETIAAN]; Progressive Reform Party or VHP [Jaggernath LACHMON]; National Party of Suriname or NPS [Ronald VENETIAAN]; Party of National Unity and Solidarity or KTPI [Willy SOEMITA]; Suriname Labor Party or SPA [Fred DERBY]; Democratic Alternative '91 or DA '91 (a coalition of the AF and BEP, formed in January 1991) [Winston JESSURUN]; Alternative Forum or AF [Rick VAN RAVENSWAY]; Party for Brotherhood and Unity in Politics or BEP [Caprino ALLENDY]; Pertjaja Luhur [Paul SOMOHARDJO]; National Democratic Party or NDP [Desire BOUTERSE]; Progressive Workers' and Farm Laborers' Union or PALU [Ir Iwan KROLIS]; The Progressive Development Alliance (a combination of two parties, HPP and PVF) [Harry KISOENSINGH]; Democratic Party or DP [Frank PLAYFAIR]; Reformed Progressive Party or HPP [Harry KISOENSINGH]; Party of the Federation of Land Workers or PVF [Jwan SITAL]; Party for Renewal and Democracy or BVD [Atta MUNGRA]; Independent Progressive Democratic Alternative or OPDA [Joginder RAMKHILAWAN]
Political pressure groups and leaders: Union for Liberation and Democracy [Kofi AFONGPONG]; Mandela Bushnegro Liberation Movement [Leendert ADAMS]; Tucayana Amazonica [Alex JUBITANA, Thomas SABAJO]; General Liberation and Development Party or ABOP [Ronnie BRUNSWIJK]
International organization participation: ACP, Caricom, ECLAC, FAO, G-77, IADB, IBRD, ICAO, ICFTU, ICRM, IFAD, IHO, ILO, IMF, IMO, Intelsat (nonsignatory user), Interpol, IOC, ISO (correspondent), ITU, LAES, NAM, OAS, OIC, OPANAL, OPCW, PCA, UN, UNCTAD, UNESCO, UNIDO, UPU, WCL, WHO, WIPO, WMO, WTrO
Diplomatic representation in the US:
chief of mission: Ambassador Arnold Theodoor HALFHIDE
chancery: Suite 460, 4301 Connecticut Avenue NW, Washington, DC 20008
telephone: [1] (202) 244-7488
FAX: [1] (202) 244-5878
consulate(s) general: Miami
Diplomatic representation from the US:
chief of mission: Ambassador Dennis K. HAYS
embassy: Dr. Sophie Redmondstraat 129, Paramaribo
mailing address: P. O. Box 1821, American Embassy Paramaribo, Department of State, Washington, DC, 20521-3390
telephone: [597] 472900, 477881, 476459
FAX: [597] 420800
Flag description: five horizontal bands of green (top, double width), white, red (quadruple width),

white, and green (double width); there is a large, yellow, five-pointed star centered in the red band

Economy - overview: The economy is dominated by the bauxite industry, which accounts for more than 15% of GDP and 70% of export earnings. After assuming power in the fall of 1996, the WIJDENBOSCH government ended the structural adjustment program of the previous government, claiming it was unfair to the poorer elements of society. Tax revenues fell as old taxes lapsed and the government failed to implement new tax alternatives. By the end of 1997, the allocation of new Dutch development funds was frozen as Surinamese Government relations with the Netherlands deteriorated. Economic growth slowed in 1998, with decline in the mining, construction, and utility sectors. Suriname's economic prospects for the medium term will depend on renewed commitment to responsible monetary and fiscal policies and to the introduction of structural reforms to liberalize markets and promote competition.
GDP: purchasing power parity - $1.48 billion (1998 est.)
GDP - real growth rate: 2% (1998 est.)
GDP - per capita: purchasing power parity - $3,500 (1998 est.)
GDP - composition by sector:
agriculture: 10%
industry: 32%
services: 58% (1996)
Population below poverty line: NA%
Household income or consumption by percentage share:
lowest 10%: NA%
highest 10%: NA%
Inflation rate (consumer prices): 20% (1998 est.)
Labor force: NA
Labor force - by occupation: agriculture NA%, industry NA%, services NA%
Unemployment rate: 20% (1997)
Budget:
revenues: $393 million
expenditures: $403 million, including capital expenditures of $34 million (1997 est.)
Industries: bauxite and gold mining, alumina and aluminum production, lumbering, food processing, fishing
Industrial production growth rate: 6.5% (1994 est.)
Electricity - production: 1.62 billion kWh (1996)
Electricity - production by source:
fossil fuel: 19.75%
hydro: 80.25%
nuclear: 0%
other: 0% (1996)
Electricity - consumption: 1.62 billion kWh (1996)
Electricity - exports: 0 kWh (1996)
Electricity - imports: 0 kWh (1996)
Agriculture - products: paddy rice, bananas, palm kernels, coconuts, plantains, peanuts; beef, chickens;

Suriname (continued)

forest products; shrimp
Exports: $548.84 million (1997)
Exports - commodities: alumina, aluminum, crude oil, lumber, shrimp and fish, rice, bananas
Exports - partners: Norway 24%, Netherlands 22%, US 22%, France 9.5%, Japan 7.6%, UK 6.5% (1997)
Imports: $551.8 million (1997)
Imports - commodities: capital equipment, petroleum, foodstuffs, cotton, consumer goods
Imports - partners: US 48%, Netherlands 21.2%, UK 5.1%, Japan 4% (1997)
Debt - external: $216 million (1996 est.)
Economic aid - recipient: $76.4 million (1995); note - the Netherlands provided a $127 million aid package to Aruba and Suriname in 1996
Currency: 1 Surinamese guilder, gulden, or florin (Sf.) = 100 cents
Exchange rates: Surinamese guilders, gulden, or florins (Sf.) per US$1 - 850 (January 1999); central bank midpoint rate: 401.00 (1998), 401.00 (1997), 401.26 (1996), 442.23 (1995), 134.12 (1994); parallel rate: 800 (December 1998), 412 (December 1995), 510 (December 1994)
note: beginning July 1994, the central bank midpoint exchange rate was unified and became market determined; during 1998, the exchange rate splintered into four distinct rates; in January 1999 the government floated the guilder
Fiscal year: calendar year

Communications

Telephones: 43,522 (1992 est.)
Telephone system: international facilities good
domestic: microwave radio relay network
international: satellite earth stations - 2 Intelsat (Atlantic Ocean)
Radio broadcast stations: AM 5, FM 32, shortwave 1
Radios: 290,256 (1993 est.)
Television broadcast stations: 3 (in addition, there are seven repeaters) (1997)
Televisions: 59,598 (1993 est.)

Transportation

Railways:
total: 166 km (single track)
standard gauge: 80 km 1.435-m gauge
narrow gauge: 86 km 1.000-m gauge
Highways:
total: 4,530 km
paved: 1,178 km
unpaved: 3,352 km (1996 est.)
Waterways: 1,200 km; most important means of transport; oceangoing vessels with drafts ranging up to 7 m can navigate many of the principal waterways
Ports and harbors: Albina, Moengo, New Nickerie, Paramaribo, Paranam, Wageningen
Airports: 46 (1998 est.)
Airports - with paved runways:
total: 5
over 3,047 m: 1

under 914 m: 4 (1998 est.)
Airports - with unpaved runways:
total: 41
914 to 1,523 m: 7
under 914 m: 34 (1998 est.)

Military

Military branches: National Army (includes small Navy and Air Force elements), Civil Police
Military manpower - availability:
males age 15-49: 118,686 (1999 est.)
Military manpower - fit for military service:
males age 15-49: 69,842 (1999 est.)
Military expenditures - dollar figure: $8.5 million (1997 est.)
Military expenditures - percent of GDP: 1.6% (1997 est.)

Transnational Issues

Disputes - international: claims area in French Guiana between Litani Rivier and Riviere Marouini (both headwaters of the Lawa Rivier); claims area in Guyana between New (Upper Courantyne) and Courantyne/Koetari [Kutari] Rivers (all headwaters of the Courantyne)
Illicit drugs: transshipment point for South American drugs destined mostly for Europe

Svalbard
(territory of Norway)

Geography

Location: Northern Europe, islands between the Arctic Ocean, Barents Sea, Greenland Sea, and Norwegian Sea, north of Norway
Geographic coordinates: 78 00 N, 20 00 E
Map references: Arctic Region
Area:
total: 62,049 sq km
land: 62,049 sq km
water: 0 sq km
note: includes Spitsbergen and Bjornoya (Bear Island)
Area - comparative: slightly smaller than West Virginia
Land boundaries: 0 km
Coastline: 3,587 km
Maritime claims:
exclusive fishing zone: 200 nm unilaterally claimed by Norway but not recognized by Russia
territorial sea: 4 nm
Climate: arctic, tempered by warm North Atlantic Current; cool summers, cold winters; North Atlantic Current flows along west and north coasts of Spitsbergen, keeping water open and navigable most of the year
Terrain: wild, rugged mountains; much of high land ice covered; west coast clear of ice about one-half of the year; fjords along west and north coasts
Elevation extremes:
lowest point: Arctic Ocean 0 m
highest point: Newtontoppen 1,717 m
Natural resources: coal, copper, iron ore, phosphate, zinc, wildlife, fish
Land use:
arable land: 0%
permanent crops: 0%
permanent pastures: 0%
forests and woodland: 0%
other: 100% (no trees and the only bushes are crowberry and cloudberry)

Svalbard (continued)

Irrigated land: NA sq km
Natural hazards: ice floes often block up the entrance to Bellsund (a transit point for coal export) on the west coast and occasionally make parts of the northeastern coast inaccessible to maritime traffic
Environment - current issues: NA
Environment - international agreements:
party to: NA
signed, but not ratified: NA
Geography - note: northernmost part of the Kingdom of Norway; consists of nine main islands; glaciers and snowfields cover 60% of the total area

People

Population: 2,503 (July 1999 est.)
Age structure:
0-14 years: NA
15-64 years: NA
65 years and over: NA
Population growth rate: -3.55% (1999 est.)
Birth rate: NA births/1,000 population
Death rate: NA deaths/1,000 population
Net migration rate: NA migrant(s)/1,000 population
Infant mortality rate: NA deaths/1,000 live births
Life expectancy at birth:
total population: NA years
male: NA years
female: NA years
Total fertility rate: NA children born/woman
Ethnic groups: Russian and Ukrainian 62%, Norwegian 38%, other NEGL% (1994)
Languages: Russian, Norwegian

Government

Country name:
conventional long form: none
conventional short form: Svalbard (sometimes referred to as Spitzbergen)
Data code: SV
Dependency status: territory of Norway; administered by the Ministry of Industry, Oslo, through a governor (sysselmann) residing in Longyearbyen, Spitsbergen; by treaty (9 February 1920) sovereignty was given to Norway
Government type: NA
Capital: Longyearbyen
Independence: none (territory of Norway)
National holiday: NA
Legal system: NA
Executive branch:
chief of state: King HARALD V of Norway (since 17 January 1991)
head of government: Governor Ann-Kristin OLSEN (since NA) and Assistant Governor Jan-Atle HANSEN (since NA September 1993)
elections: none; the monarch is hereditary; governor and assistant governor responsible to the Polar Department of the Ministry of Justice
International organization participation: none
Flag description: the flag of Norway is used

Economy

Economy - overview: Coal mining is the major economic activity on Svalbard. The treaty of 9 February 1920 gives the 41 signatories equal rights to exploit mineral deposits, subject to Norwegian regulation. Although US, UK, Dutch, and Swedish coal companies have mined in the past, the only companies still mining are Norwegian and Russian. The settlements on Svalbard are essentially company towns. The Norwegian state-owned coal company employs nearly 60% of the Norwegian population on the island, runs many of the local services, and provides most of the local infrastructure. There is also some trapping of seal, polar bear, fox, and walrus.
GDP: $NA
GDP - real growth rate: NA%
GDP - per capita: $NA
Population below poverty line: NA%
Household income or consumption by percentage share:
lowest 10%: NA%
highest 10%: NA%
Inflation rate (consumer prices): NA%
Labor force: NA
Budget:
revenues: $11.7 million
expenditures: $11.7 million, including capital expenditures of $NA (1997 est.)
Industrial production growth rate: NA%
Electricity - production: NA kWh
Electricity - production by source:
fossil fuel: NA%
hydro: NA%
nuclear: NA%
other: NA%
Electricity - consumption: NA kWh
Electricity - exports: NA kWh
Electricity - imports: NA kWh
Exports: $NA
Imports: $NA
Economic aid - recipient: $8.7 million from Norway (1997)
Currency: 1 Norwegian krone (NKr) = 100 oere
Exchange rates: Norwegian kroner (NKr) per US$1 - 7.4524 (January 1999), 7.5451 (1998), 7.0734 (1997), 6.4498 (1996), 6.3352 (1995), 7.0576 (1994)

Communications

Telephones: NA
Telephone system:
domestic: local telephone service
international: satellite earth station - 1 of NA type (for communication with Norwegian mainland only)
Radio broadcast stations: AM 1, FM 1 (repeaters 2), shortwave 0
note: there are five meteorological/radio stations
Radios: NA
Television broadcast stations: NA
Televisions: NA

Transportation

Railways: 0 km
Highways:
total: NA km
paved: NA km
unpaved: NA km
Ports and harbors: Barentsburg, Longyearbyen, Ny-Alesund, Pyramiden
Merchant marine: none
Airports: 4 (1998 est.)
Airports - with paved runways:
total: 1
1,524 to 2,437 m: 1 (1998 est.)
Airports - with unpaved runways:
total: 3
under 914 m: 3 (1998 est.)

Military

Military - note: demilitarized by treaty (9 February 1920)

Transnational Issues

Disputes - international: Svalbard is the focus of a maritime boundary dispute in the Barents Sea between Norway and Russia

Swaziland

Geography

Location: Southern Africa, between Mozambique and South Africa
Geographic coordinates: 26 30 S, 31 30 E
Map references: Africa
Area:
total: 17,360 sq km
land: 17,200 sq km
water: 160 sq km
Area - comparative: slightly smaller than New Jersey
Land boundaries:
total: 535 km
border countries: Mozambique 105 km, South Africa 430 km
Coastline: 0 km (landlocked)
Maritime claims: none (landlocked)
Climate: varies from tropical to near temperate
Terrain: mostly mountains and hills; some moderately sloping plains
Elevation extremes:
lowest point: Great Usutu River 21 m
highest point: Emlembe 1,862 m
Natural resources: asbestos, coal, clay, cassiterite, hydropower, forests, small gold and diamond deposits, quarry stone, and talc
Land use:
arable land: 11%
permanent crops: 0%
permanent pastures: 62%
forests and woodland: 7%
other: 20% (1993 est.)
Irrigated land: 670 sq km (1993 est.)
Natural hazards: NA
Environment - current issues: limited supplies of potable water; wildlife populations being depleted because of excessive hunting; overgrazing; soil degradation; soil erosion
Environment - international agreements:
party to: Biodiversity, Climate Change, Endangered Species, Nuclear Test Ban, Ozone Layer Protection
signed, but not ratified: Desertification, Law of the Sea
Geography - note: landlocked; almost completely surrounded by South Africa

People

Population: 985,335 (July 1999 est.)
Age structure:
0-14 years: 46% (male 227,675; female 228,733)
15-64 years: 51% (male 243,853; female 259,950)
65 years and over: 3% (male 9,866; female 15,258) (1999 est.)
Population growth rate: 1.91% (1999 est.)
Birth rate: 40.8 births/1,000 population (1999 est.)
Death rate: 21.72 deaths/1,000 population (1999 est.)
Net migration rate: 0 migrant(s)/1,000 population (1999 est.)
Sex ratio:
at birth: 1.03 male(s)/female
under 15 years: 1 male(s)/female
15-64 years: 0.94 male(s)/female
65 years and over: 0.65 male(s)/female
total population: 0.96 male(s)/female (1999 est.)
Infant mortality rate: 101.87 deaths/1,000 live births (1999 est.)
Life expectancy at birth:
total population: 38.11 years
male: 36.86 years
female: 39.4 years (1999 est.)
Total fertility rate: 5.92 children born/woman (1999 est.)
Nationality:
noun: Swazi(s)
adjective: Swazi
Ethnic groups: African 97%, European 3%
Religions: Christian 60%, indigenous beliefs 40%
Languages: English (official, government business conducted in English), siSwati (official)
Literacy:
definition: age 15 and over can read and write
total population: 76.7%
male: 78%
female: 75.6% (1995 est.)

Government

Country name:
conventional long form: Kingdom of Swaziland
conventional short form: Swaziland
Data code: WZ
Government type: monarchy; independent member of Commonwealth
Capital: Mbabane; note - Lobamba is the royal and legislative capital
Administrative divisions: 4 districts; Hhohho, Lubombo, Manzini, Shiselweni
Independence: 6 September 1968 (from UK)
National holiday: Somhlolo (Independence) Day, 6 September (1968)
Constitution: none; constitution of 6 September 1968 was suspended 12 April 1973; a new constitution was promulgated 13 October 1978, but was not formally presented to the people; since then a few more outlines for a constitution have been compiled but so far none have been accepted
Legal system: based on South African Roman-Dutch law in statutory courts and Swazi traditional law and custom in traditional courts; has not accepted compulsory ICJ jurisdiction
Suffrage: NA; note - no suffrage before September 1993; 55 of the 65 seats in the House of Assembly were filled by popular vote in the elections of September and October 1993; of a population of less than 1 million, the electorate numbered 283,693
Executive branch:
chief of state: King MSWATI III (since 25 April 1986)
head of government: Prime Minister Sibusiso Barnabas DLAMINI (since 9 August 1996)
cabinet: Cabinet recommended by the prime minister and confirmed by the monarch
elections: none; the monarch is hereditary; prime minister appointed by the monarch
Legislative branch: bicameral Parliament or Libandla, an advisory body, consists of the Senate (20 seats - 10 appointed by the House of Assembly and 10 appointed by the monarch; members serve five-year terms) and the House of Assembly (65 seats - 10 appointed by the monarch and 55 elected by popular vote; members serve five-year terms)
elections: House of Assembly - last held NA September and NA October 1998 (next to be held NA 2003)
election results: House of Assembly - balloting is done on a nonparty basis; candidates for election are nominated by the local council of each constituency and for each constituency the three candidates with the most votes in the first round of voting are narrowed to a single winner by a second round
Judicial branch: High Court, judges are appointed by the monarch; Court of Appeal, judges are appointed by the monarch
Political parties and leaders:
note: political parties are banned by the constitution promulgated on 13 October 1978; illegal parties are prohibited from holding large public gatherings
illegal parties: People's United Democratic Movement or PUDEMO [Mario MASUKU]; Swaziland Youth Congress or SWAYOCO (included in PUDEMO); Swaziland Communist Party or SWACOPA [Mphandlana SHONGWE]; Swaziland Liberation Front or FROLISA [leader NA]; Convention for Full Democracy in Swaziland or COFUDESWA [Sabelo DLAMINI]; Swaziland National Front or SWANAFRO [leader NA]; Ngwane Socialist Revolutionary Party or NGWASOREP [leader NA]; Swaziland Democratic Alliance (represents key opposition parties) [Jerry NXUMALO]; Swaziland Federation of Trade Unions or SFTU [Jan SITHOLE]
International organization participation: ACP, AfDB, C, CCC, ECA, FAO, G-77, IBRD, ICAO, ICFTU, ICRM, IDA, IFAD, IFC, IFRCS, ILO, IMF, Intelsat, Interpol, IOC, ITU, NAM, OAU, OPCW, PCA, SACU,

Swaziland (continued)

SADC, UN, UNCTAD, UNESCO, UNIDO, UPU, WHO, WIPO, WMO, WTrO
Diplomatic representation in the US:
chief of mission: Ambassador Mary Madzandza KANYA
chancery: Suite 3M, 3400 International Drive NW, Washington, DC 20008
telephone: [1] (202) 362-6683
FAX: [1] (202) 244-8059
Diplomatic representation from the US:
chief of mission: Ambassador Alan R. McKEE
embassy: Central Bank Building, Warner Street, Mbabane
mailing address: P. O. Box 199, Mbabane
telephone: [268] 404-6441 through 404-6445
FAX: [268] 404-5959
Flag description: three horizontal bands of blue (top), red (triple width), and blue; the red band is edged in yellow; centered in the red band is a large black and white shield covering two spears and a staff decorated with feather tassels, all placed horizontally

Economy

Economy - overview: In this small landlocked economy, subsistence agriculture occupies more than 60% of the population. Manufacturing features a number of agroprocessing factories. Mining has declined in importance in recent years; high-grade iron ore deposits were depleted by 1978, and health concerns have cut world demand for asbestos. Exports of soft drink concentrate, sugar and wood pulp are the main earners of hard currency. Surrounded by South Africa, except for a short border with Mozambique, Swaziland is heavily dependent on South Africa from which it receives nearly all of its imports and to which it sends more than half of its exports. Remittances from Swazi workers in South African mines supplement domestically earned income by as much as 20%. The government is trying to improve the atmosphere for foreign investment. Overgrazing, soil depletion, and drought persist as problems for the future.
GDP: purchasing power parity - $4 billion (1998 est.)
GDP - real growth rate: 2.6% (1998 est.)
GDP - per capita: purchasing power parity - $4,200 (1998 est.)
GDP - composition by sector:
agriculture: 10%
industry: 42%
services: 48% (1997 est.)
Population below poverty line: NA%
Household income or consumption by percentage share:
lowest 10%: NA%
highest 10%: NA%
Inflation rate (consumer prices): 8% (1998)
Labor force: NA
Labor force - by occupation: private sector about 70%, public sector about 30%
Unemployment rate: 22% (1995 est.)
Budget:
revenues: $400 million

expenditures: $450 million, including capital expenditures of $115 million (FY96/97)
Industries: mining (coal and asbestos), wood pulp, sugar, soft drink concentrates
Industrial production growth rate: 3.7% (FY95/96)
Electricity - production: 415 million kWh (1996)
Electricity - production by source:
fossil fuel: 49.4%
hydro: 50.6%
nuclear: 0%
other: 0% (1996)
Electricity - consumption: 986 million kWh (1996)
Electricity - exports: 0 kWh (1996)
Electricity - imports: 571 million kWh (1996)
note: imports about 60% of its electricity from South Africa
Agriculture - products: sugarcane, cotton, maize, tobacco, rice, citrus, pineapples, corn, sorghum, peanuts; cattle, goats, sheep
Exports: $972 million (f.o.b., 1998)
Exports - commodities: soft drink concentrates, sugar, wood pulp, cotton yarn, citrus and canned fruit (1996)
Exports - partners: South Africa 58%, EU 17%, Mozambique, North Korea (1995)
Imports: $1.2 billion (f.o.b., 1998)
Imports - commodities: motor vehicles, machinery, transport equipment, foodstuffs, petroleum products, chemicals (1996)
Imports - partners: South Africa 96%, Japan, UK, Singapore (FY95/96)
Debt - external: $175 million (1998)
Economic aid - recipient: $55 million (1995)
Currency: 1 lilangeni (E) = 100 cents
Exchange rates: emalangeni (E) per US$1 - 5.9812 (January 1999), 5.4807 (1998), 4.6032 (1997), 4.2706 (1996), 3.6266 (1995), 3.5490 (1994); note - the Swazi lilangeni is at par with the South African rand
Fiscal year: 1 April - 31 March

Communications

Telephones: NA; 45,000 cellular telephone subscribers (1993 est.)
Telephone system:
domestic: system consists of carrier-equipped, open-wire lines and low-capacity, microwave radio relay
international: satellite earth station - 1 Intelsat (Atlantic Ocean)
Radio broadcast stations: AM 7, FM 6, shortwave 0
Radios: 200,000 (1998 est.)
Television broadcast stations: 2 (in addition, there are seven repeaters) (1997)
Televisions: 20,000 (1998 est.)

Transportation

Railways:
total: 297 km; note - includes 71 km which are not in use

narrow gauge: 297 km 1.067-m gauge
Highways:
total: 3,810 km
paved: NA km
unpaved: NA km (1996 est.)
Ports and harbors: none
Airports: 18 (1998 est.)
Airports - with paved runways:
total: 1
2,438 to 3,047 m: 1 (1998 est.)
Airports - with unpaved runways:
total: 17
914 to 1,523 m: 7
under 914 m: 10 (1998 est.)

Military

Military branches: Umbutfo Swaziland Defense Force (Army), Royal Swaziland Police Force
Military manpower - availability:
males age 15-49: 221,199 (1999 est.)
Military manpower - fit for military service:
males age 15-49: 128,806 (1999 est.)
Military expenditures - dollar figure: $23 million (FY95/96)
Military expenditures - percent of GDP: 1.9% (FY95/96)

Transnational Issues

Disputes - international: Swaziland has asked South Africa to open negotiations on reincorporating some nearby South African territories that are populated by ethnic Swazis or that were long ago part of the Swazi Kingdom

Sweden

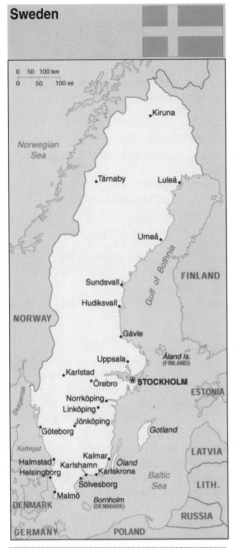

Introduction

Background: Having long lost its military prowess of the 17th century, Sweden has evolved into a prosperous and peaceful constitutional monarchy with a capitalist system interlarded with substantial welfare elements. As the 20th century comes to an end, this long successful formula is being undermined by high unemployment; the rising cost of a "cradle to the grave" welfare state; the decline of Sweden's competitive position in world markets; and indecision over the country's role in the political and economic integration of Europe. A member of the European Union, Sweden chose not to participate in the introduction of the euro on 1 January 1999.

Geography

Location: Northern Europe, bordering the Baltic Sea, Gulf of Bothnia, Kattegat, and Skagerrak, between Finland and Norway

Geographic coordinates: 62 00 N, 15 00 E

Map references: Europe

Area:
total: 449,964 sq km
land: 410,928 sq km

water: 39,036 sq km

Area - comparative: slightly larger than California

Land boundaries:
total: 2,205 km
border countries: Finland 586 km, Norway 1,619 km

Coastline: 3,218 km

Maritime claims:
continental shelf: 200-m depth or to the depth of exploitation
exclusive economic zone: agreed boundaries or midlines
territorial sea: 12 nm (adjustments made to return a portion of straits to high seas)

Climate: temperate in south with cold, cloudy winters and cool, partly cloudy summers; subarctic in north

Terrain: mostly flat or gently rolling lowlands; mountains in west

Elevation extremes:
lowest point: Baltic Sea 0 m
highest point: Kebnekaise 2,111 m

Natural resources: zinc, iron ore, lead, copper, silver, timber, uranium, hydropower

Land use:
arable land: 7%
permanent crops: 0%
permanent pastures: 1%
forests and woodland: 68%
other: 24% (1993 est.)

Irrigated land: 1,150 sq km (1993 est.)

Natural hazards: ice floes in the surrounding waters, especially in the Gulf of Bothnia, can interfere with maritime traffic

Environment - current issues: acid rain damaging soils and lakes; pollution of the North Sea and the Baltic Sea

Environment - international agreements:
party to: Air Pollution, Air Pollution-Nitrogen Oxides, Air Pollution-Sulphur 85, Air Pollution-Sulphur 94, Air Pollution-Volatile Organic Compounds, Antarctic-Environmental Protocol, Antarctic Treaty, Biodiversity, Climate Change, Desertification, Endangered Species, Environmental Modification, Hazardous Wastes, Law of the Sea, Marine Dumping, Nuclear Test Ban, Ozone Layer Protection, Ship Pollution, Tropical Timber 83, Tropical Timber 94, Wetlands, Whaling
signed, but not ratified: Air Pollution-Persistent Organic Pollutants, Climate Change-Kyoto Protocol

Geography - note: strategic location along Danish Straits linking Baltic and North Seas

People

Population: 8,911,296 (July 1999 est.)

Age structure:
0-14 years: 19% (male 856,819; female 812,958)
15-64 years: 64% (male 2,896,383; female 2,802,571)
65 years and over: 17% (male 651,549; female 891,016) (1999 est.)

Population growth rate: 0.29% (1999 est.)

Birth rate: 12 births/1,000 population (1999 est.)

Death rate: 10.77 deaths/1,000 population (1999 est.)

Net migration rate: 1.68 migrant(s)/1,000 population (1999 est.)

Sex ratio:
at birth: 1.05 male(s)/female
under 15 years: 1.05 male(s)/female
15-64 years: 1.03 male(s)/female
65 years and over: 0.73 male(s)/female
total population: 0.98 male(s)/female (1999 est.)

Infant mortality rate: 3.91 deaths/1,000 live births (1999 est.)

Life expectancy at birth:
total population: 79.29 years
male: 76.61 years
female: 82.11 years (1999 est.)

Total fertility rate: 1.83 children born/woman (1999 est.)

Nationality:
noun: Swede(s)
adjective: Swedish

Ethnic groups: white, Lapp (Sami), foreign-born or first-generation immigrants 12% (Finns, Yugoslavs, Danes, Norwegians, Greeks, Turks)

Religions: Evangelical Lutheran 94%, Roman Catholic 1.5%, Pentecostal 1%, other 3.5% (1987)

Languages: Swedish
note: small Lapp- and Finnish-speaking minorities

Literacy:
definition: age 15 and over can read and write
total population: 99% (1979 est.)
male: NA%
female: NA%

Government

Country name:
conventional long form: Kingdom of Sweden
conventional short form: Sweden
local long form: Konungariket Sverige
local short form: Sverige

Data code: SW

Government type: constitutional monarchy

Capital: Stockholm

Administrative divisions: 21 counties (lan, singular and plural); Blekinge, Dalarnas, Gavleborgs, Gotlands, Hallands, Jamtlands, Jonkopings, Kalmar, Kronobergs, Norrbottens, Orebro, Ostergotlands, Skane, Sodermanlands, Stockholms, Uppsala, Varmlands, Vasterbottens, Vasternorrlands, Vastmanlands, Vastra Gotalands

Independence: 6 June 1523 (Gustav VASA elected king); 6 June 1809 (constitutional monarchy was established)

National holiday: Day of the Swedish Flag, 6 June

Constitution: 1 January 1975

Legal system: civil law system influenced by customary law; accepts compulsory ICJ jurisdiction, with reservations

Suffrage: 18 years of age; universal

Executive branch:
chief of state: King CARL XVI GUSTAF (since 19 September 1973); Heir Apparent Princess VICTORIA Ingrid Alice Desiree, daughter of the monarch (born 14 July 1977)

Sweden (continued)

head of government: Prime Minister Goran PERSSON (since 21 March 1996)

cabinet: Cabinet appointed by the prime minister

elections: the monarch is hereditary; prime minister elected by the Parliament; election last held NA September 1998 (next to be held NA 2002)

election results: Goran PERSSON reelected prime minister; percent of parliamentary vote - 131 votes out of 349

Legislative branch: unicameral Parliament or Riksdag (349 seats; members are elected by popular vote on a proportional representation basis to serve four-year terms)

elections: last held 20 September 1998 (next to be held NA September 2002)

election results: percent of vote by party - Social Democrats 36.5%, Moderates 22.7%, Left Party 12%, Christian Democrats 11.8%, Center Party 5.1%, Liberal Party 4.7%, Greens 4.5%; seats by party - Social Democrats 131, Moderates 82, Left Party 43, Christian Democrats 42, Center Party 18, Liberal Party 17, Greens 16

Judicial branch: Supreme Court or Hogsta Domstolen, judges are appointed by the government (prime minister and cabinet)

Political parties and leaders: Social Democratic Party [Goran PERSSON]; Moderate Party (conservative) [Carl BILDT]; Liberal People's Party [Maria LEISSNER]; Center Party [Lennart DALEUS]; Christian Democratic Party [Alf SVENSSON]; New Democracy Party [Vivianne FRANZEN]; Left Party or VP (formerly Communist) [Gudrun SCHYMAN]; Communist Workers' Party [Rolf HAGEL]; Green Party [no formal leader but party spokesperson is Briger SCHLAUG]

International organization participation: ACCT, AfDB, AsDB, Australia Group, BIS, CCC, CE, CERN, EAPC, EBRD, ECE, EFTA, ESA, FAO, G-10, IADB, IAEA, IBRD, ICAO, ICC, ICFTU, ICRM, IDA, IEA, IFAD, IFC, IFRCS, ILO, IMF, IMO, Inmarsat, Intelsat, Interpol, IOC, IOM, ISO, ITU, LAIA (observer), MTCR, NAM (guest), NEA, NSG, OAS (observer), OECD, OPCW, OSCE, PCA, PFP, UN (observer), UNCTAD, UNESCO, UNHCR, UNIDO, UNITAR, UNMIBH, UNMOP, UNMOT, UNOMIG, UNPREDEP, UNTSO, UNU, UPU, WCL, WHO, WIPO, WMO, WToO, WTrO, ZC

Diplomatic representation in the US:

chief of mission: Ambassador Rolf EKEUS

chancery: 1501 M Street NW, Washington, DC 20005-1702

telephone: [1] (202) 467-2600

FAX: [1] (202) 467-2699

consulate(s) general: Los Angeles and New York

Diplomatic representation from the US:

chief of mission: Ambassador Lyndon Lowell OLSON, Jr.

embassy: Strandvagen 101, S-115 89 Stockholm

mailing address: American Embassy Stockholm, Department of State, Washington, DC 20521-5750 (pouch)

telephone: [46] (8) 783 53 00

FAX: [46] (8) 661 19 64

Flag description: blue with a yellow cross that extends to the edges of the flag; the vertical part of the cross is shifted to the hoist side in the style of the Dannebrog (Danish flag)

Economy

Economy - overview: Aided by peace and neutrality for the whole twentieth century, Sweden has achieved an enviable standard of living under a mixed system of high-tech capitalism and extensive welfare benefits. It has a modern distribution system, excellent internal and external communications, and a skilled labor force. Timber, hydropower, and iron ore constitute the resource base of an economy heavily oriented toward foreign trade. Privately owned firms account for about 90% of industrial output, of which the engineering sector accounts for 50% of output and exports. Agriculture accounts for only 2% of GDP and 2% of the jobs. In recent years, however, this extraordinarily favorable picture has been clouded by budgetary difficulties, inflation, high unemployment, and a gradual loss of competitiveness in international markets. Sweden has harmonized its economic policies with those of the EU, which it joined at the start of 1995. Sweden decided not to join the euro system at its outset in January 1999 but plans to hold a referendum in 2000 on whether to join. Annual GDP growth is forecast for 2.2% and 2.6% in 1999 and 2000 respectively. Budgetary problems and shaky business confidence will constrain government plans to reduce unemployment.

GDP: purchasing power parity - $175 billion (1998 est.)

GDP - real growth rate: 2.9% (1998 est.)

GDP - per capita: purchasing power parity - $19,700 (1998 est.)

GDP - composition by sector:

agriculture: 2.2%

industry: 30.5%

services: 67.3% (1997)

Population below poverty line: NA%

Household income or consumption by percentage share:

lowest 10%: 3.7%

highest 10%: 20.1% (1992)

Inflation rate (consumer prices): 2% (1998 est.)

Labor force: 4.552 million (1992)

Labor force - by occupation: community, social and personal services 38.3%, mining and manufacturing 21.2%, commerce, hotels, and restaurants 14.1%, banking, insurance 9%, communications 7.2%, construction 7%, agriculture, fishing, and forestry 3.2% (1991)

Unemployment rate: 6.3% plus about 5% in training programs (1998 est.)

Budget:

revenues: $109.4 billion

expenditures: $146.1 billion, including capital expenditures of $NA (FY95/96)

Industries: iron and steel, precision equipment (bearings, radio and telephone parts, armaments), wood pulp and paper products, processed foods, motor vehicles

Industrial production growth rate: 4.4% (1998)

Electricity - production: 135.192 billion kWh (1996)

Electricity - production by source:

fossil fuel: 9.75%

hydro: 37.52%

nuclear: 52.62%

other: 0.11% (1996)

Electricity - consumption: 141.392 billion kWh (1996)

Electricity - exports: 9.7 billion kWh (1996)

Electricity - imports: 15.9 billion kWh (1996)

Agriculture - products: grains, sugar beets, potatoes; meat, milk

Exports: $85.5 billion (f.o.b., 1998)

Exports - commodities: machinery 35%, motor vehicles, paper products, pulp and wood, iron and steel products, chemicals

Exports - partners: EU 55% (Germany 11%, UK 9%, Denmark 6%, Finland 5%), Norway 8%, US 8% (1994)

Imports: $66.6 billion (f.o.b., 1998)

Imports - commodities: machinery, petroleum and petroleum products, chemicals, motor vehicles, foodstuffs, iron and steel, clothing

Imports - partners: EU 68% (Germany 19%, UK 10%, Denmark 8%, France 6%), Norway 8%, US 6% (1997)

Debt - external: $66.5 billion (1994)

Economic aid - donor: ODA, $1.7 billion (1995)

Currency: 1 Swedish krona (SKr) = 100 oere

Exchange rates: Swedish kronor (SKr) per US$1 - 7.8193 (January 1999), 7.9499 (1998), 7.6349 (1997), 6.7060 (1996), 7.1333 (1995), 7.7160 (1994)

Fiscal year: calendar year

Communications

Telephones: 13 million (1996 est.)

Telephone system: excellent domestic and international facilities; automatic system

domestic: coaxial and multiconductor cable carry most voice traffic; parallel microwave radio relay network carries some additional telephone channels

international: 5 submarine coaxial cables; satellite earth stations - 1 Intelsat (Atlantic Ocean), 1 Eutelsat, and 1 Inmarsat (Atlantic and Indian Ocean regions); note - Sweden shares the Inmarsat earth station with the other Nordic countries (Denmark, Finland, Iceland, and Norway)

Radio broadcast stations: AM 5, FM 360 (mostly repeaters), shortwave 0

Radios: 7.272 million (1993 est.)

Television broadcast stations: 163 (1997)

Televisions: 3.5 million

Transportation

Railways:

total: 13,415 km (includes 3,594 km of privately-owned railways) *standard gauge:* 13,415 km 1.435-m gauge (7,917 km electrified and 1,152 km double track) (1996)

Highways:

total: 138,000 km

paved: 105,018 km (including 1,330 km of expressways)

unpaved: 32,982 km (1996 est.)

Waterways: 2,052 km navigable for small steamers and barges

Pipelines: natural gas 84 km

Ports and harbors: Gavle, Goteborg, Halmstad, Helsingborg, Hudiksvall, Kalmar, Karlshamn, Malmo, Solvesborg, Stockholm, Sundsvall

Merchant marine:

total: 154 ships (1,000 GRT or over) totaling 1,894,783 GRT/1,528,077 DWT

ships by type: bulk 6, cargo 28, chemical tanker 28, combination ore/oil 4, liquefied gas tanker 1, oil tanker 24, railcar carrier 1, refrigerated cargo 1, roll-on/roll-off cargo 39, short-sea passenger 5, specialized tanker 4, vehicle carrier 13 (1998 est.)

Airports: 255 (1998 est.)

Airports - with paved runways:

total: 145

over 3,047 m: 2

2,438 to 3,047 m: 10

1,524 to 2,437 m: 82

914 to 1,523 m: 27

under 914 m: 24 (1998 est.)

Airports - with unpaved runways:

total: 110

914 to 1,523 m: 5

under 914 m: 105 (1998 est.)

Heliports: 1 (1998 est.)

Military

Military branches: Swedish Army, Royal Swedish Navy, Swedish Air Force

Military manpower - military age: 19 years of age

Military manpower - availability:

males age 15-49: 2,076,903 (1999 est.)

Military manpower - fit for military service:

males age 15-49: 1,817,554 (1999 est.)

Military manpower - reaching military age annually:

males: 52,486 (1999 est.)

Military expenditures - dollar figure: $4.9 billion (FY97/98)

Military expenditures - percent of GDP: 2.2% (FY97/98)

Transnational Issues

Disputes - international: none

Illicit drugs: minor transshipment point for and consumer of narcotics shipped via the CIS and Baltic states; increasing consumer of European amphetamines

Switzerland

Introduction

Background: Switzerland's independence and neutrality have long been honored by the major European powers and Switzerland did not participate in either World War I or II. The political and economic integration of Europe since World War II may be rendering obsolete Switzerland's concern for neutrality.

Geography

Location: Central Europe, east of France, north of Italy

Geographic coordinates: 47 00 N, 8 00 E

Map references: Europe

Area:

total: 41,290 sq km

land: 39,770 sq km

water: 1,520 sq km

Area - comparative: slightly less than twice the size of New Jersey

Land boundaries:

total: 1,852 km

border countries: Austria 164 km, France 573 km, Italy 740 km, Liechtenstein 41 km, Germany 334 km

Coastline: 0 km (landlocked)

Maritime claims: none (landlocked)

Climate: temperate, but varies with altitude; cold, cloudy, rainy/snowy winters; cool to warm, cloudy, humid summers with occasional showers

Terrain: mostly mountains (Alps in south, Jura in northwest) with a central plateau of rolling hills, plains, and large lakes

Elevation extremes:

lowest point: Lake Maggiore 195 m

highest point: Dufourspitze 4,634 m

Natural resources: hydropower potential, timber, salt

Land use:

arable land: 10%

permanent crops: 2%

permanent pastures: 28%

forests and woodland: 32%

other: 28% (1993 est.)

Irrigated land: 250 sq km (1993 est.)

Natural hazards: avalanches, landslides, flash floods

Environment - current issues: air pollution from vehicle emissions and open-air burning; acid rain; water pollution from increased use of agricultural fertilizers; loss of biodiversity

Environment - international agreements:

party to: Air Pollution, Air Pollution-Nitrogen Oxides, Air Pollution-Sulphur 85, Air Pollution-Sulphur 94, Air Pollution-Volatile Organic Compounds, Antarctic Treaty, Biodiversity, Climate Change, Desertification, Endangered Species, Environmental Modification, Hazardous Wastes, Marine Dumping, Marine Life Conservation, Nuclear Test Ban, Ozone Layer Protection, Ship Pollution, Tropical Timber 83, Tropical Timber 94, Wetlands, Whaling

signed, but not ratified: Air Pollution-Persistent Organic Pollutants, Antarctic-Environmental Protocol, Climate Change-Kyoto Protocol, Law of the Sea

Geography - note: landlocked; crossroads of northern and southern Europe; along with southeastern France and northern Italy, contains the highest elevations in Europe

People

Population: 7,275,467 (July 1999 est.)

Age structure:

0-14 years: 17% (male 639,970; female 611,876)

15-64 years: 68% (male 2,509,988; female 2,417,580)

65 years and over: 15% (male 444,482; female 651,571) (1999 est.)

Population growth rate: 0.2% (1999 est.)

Birth rate: 10.53 births/1,000 population (1999 est.)

Death rate: 9.06 deaths/1,000 population (1999 est.)

Net migration rate: 0.49 migrant(s)/1,000 population (1999 est.)

Switzerland *(continued)*

Sex ratio:
at birth: 1.05 male(s)/female
under 15 years: 1.05 male(s)/female
15-64 years: 1.04 male(s)/female
65 years and over: 0.68 male(s)/female
total population: 0.98 male(s)/female (1999 est.)
Infant mortality rate: 4.87 deaths/1,000 live births (1999 est.)
Life expectancy at birth:
total population: 78.99 years
male: 75.83 years
female: 82.32 years (1999 est.)
Total fertility rate: 1.46 children born/woman (1999 est.)
Nationality:
noun: Swiss (singular and plural)
adjective: Swiss
Ethnic groups: German 65%, French 18%, Italian 10%, Romansch 1%, other 6%
Religions: Roman Catholic 46.1%, Protestant 40%, other 5%, no religion 8.9% (1990)
Languages: German 63.7%, French 19.2%, Italian 7.6%, Romansch 0.6%, other 8.9%
Literacy:
definition: age 15 and over can read and write
total population: 99% (1980 est.)
male: NA%
female: NA%

Government

Country name:
conventional long form: Swiss Confederation
conventional short form: Switzerland
local long form: Schweizerische Eidgenossenschaft (German), Confederation Suisse (French), Confederazione Svizzera (Italian)
local short form: Schweiz (German), Suisse (French), Svizzera (Italian)
Data code: SZ
Government type: federal republic
Capital: Bern
Administrative divisions: 26 cantons (cantons, singular - canton in French; cantoni, singular - cantone in Italian; kantone, singular - kanton in German); Aargau, Ausser-Rhoden, Basel-Landschaft, Basel-Stadt, Bern, Fribourg, Geneve, Glarus, Graubunden, Inner-Rhoden, Jura, Luzern, Neuchatel, Nidwalden, Obwalden, Sankt Gallen, Schaffhausen, Schwyz, Solothurn, Thurgau, Ticino, Uri, Valais, Vaud, Zug, Zurich
Independence: 1 August 1291
National holiday: Anniversary of the Founding of the Swiss Confederation, 1 August (1291)
Constitution: 29 May 1874
Legal system: civil law system influenced by customary law; judicial review of legislative acts, except with respect to federal decrees of general obligatory character; accepts compulsory ICJ jurisdiction, with reservations
Suffrage: 18 years of age; universal
Executive branch:
chief of state: President Ruth DREIFUSS (since 1

January 1999); Vice President Adolf OGI (since 1 January 1999); note - the president is both the chief of state and head of government
head of government: President Ruth DREIFUSS (since 1 January 1999); Vice President Adolf OGI (since 1 January 1999); note - the president is both the chief of state and head of government
cabinet: Federal Council or Bundesrat (in German), Conseil Federal (in French), Consiglio Federale (in Italian) elected by the Federal Assembly from among its own members for a four-year term
elections: president and vice president elected by the Federal Assembly from among the members of the Federal Council for one-year terms that run concurrently; election last held NA December 1998 (next to be held NA December 1999)
election results: Ruth DREIFUSS elected president; percent of Federal Assembly vote - Ruth DREIFUSS 75%; Adolf OGI elected vice president; percent of legislative vote - NA
Legislative branch: bicameral Federal Assembly or Bundesversammlung (in German), Assemblee Federale (in French), Assemblea Federale (in Italian) consists of the Council of States or Standerat (in German), Conseil des Etats (in French), Consiglio degli Stati (in Italian) (46 seats - members serve four-year terms) and the National Council or Nationalrat (in German), Conseil National (in French), Consiglio Nazionale (in Italian) (200 seats - members are elected by popular vote on a basis of proportional representation to serve four-year terms)
elections: Council of States - last held throughout 1997 (each canton determines when the next election will be held); National Council - last held 20 October 1995 (next to be held probably 24 October 1999)
election results: Council of States - percent of vote by party - NA; seats by party - FDP 17, CVP 16, SVP 5, SPS 5, LPS 2, LdU 1; National Council - percent of vote by party - NA; seats by party - FDP 45, SPS 54, CVP 34, SVP 29, Greens 9, LPS 7, FPS 7, LdU 3, EVP 2, SD 3, PdAdS 3, Ticino League 1, EDU 1, FRAP 1, CSP 1
Judicial branch: Federal Supreme Court, judges elected for six-year terms by the Federal Assembly
Political parties and leaders: Radical Free Democratic Party (Freisinnig-Demokratische Partei der Schweiz or FDP, Parti Radical-Democratique Suisse or PRD, Partitio Liberal-Radicale Svizzero or PLR) [Franz STEINEGGER, president]; Social Democratic Party (Sozialdemokratische Partei der Schweiz or SPS, Parti Socialist Suisse or PSS, Partito Socialista Svizzero or PSS, Partida Socialdemocratica de la Svizra or PSS) [Ursula KOCH, president]; Christian Democratic People's Party (Christichdemokratische Volkspartei der Schweiz or CVP, Parti Democrate-Chretien Suisse or PDC, Partito Democratico-Cristiano Popolare Svizzero or PDC, Partida Cristiandemocratica dalla Svizra or PCD) [Adalbert DURRER, president]; Swiss People's Party (Schweizerische Volkspartei or SVP, Union Democratique du Centre or UDC, Unione Democratica de Centro or UDC, Uniun Democratica

dal Center or UDC) [Ueli MAURER, president]; Green Party (Grune Partei der Schweiz or Grune, Parti Ecologiste Suisse or Les Verts, Partito Ecologista Svizzero or I Verdi, Partida Ecologica Svizra or La Verda) [Ruedi BAUMANN, president]; Freedom Party or FPS [Roland BORER]; Alliance of Independents' Party (Landesring der Unabhaengigen or LdU, Alliance des Independants or AdI) [Anton SCHALLER, president]; Ticino League (Lega dei Ticinesi) [leader NA]; and other minor parties including Swiss Democratic Party (Schweizer Demokraten or SD, Democrates Suisses or DS, Democratici Svizzeri or DS), Liberal Party (Liberale Partei der Schweiz or LPS, Parti Liberal Suisse or PLS, Partito Liberale Svizzero or PLS), Workers' Party (Parti Suisse du Travail or PST, Partei der Arbeit der Schweiz or PdAdS, Partito Svizzero del Lavoro or PSdL), Evangelical People's Party (Evangelische Volkspartei der Schweiz or EVP, Parti Evangelique Suisse or PEV, Partito Evangelico Svizzero or PEV), and the Union of Federal Democrats (Eidgenossisch-Demokratische Union or EDU, Union Democratique Federale or UDF, Unione Democratica Federale or UDF)
International organization participation: ACCT, AfDB, AsDB, Australia Group, BIS, CCC, CE, CERN, EAPC, EBRD, ECE, EFTA, ESA, FAO, G-10, IADB, IAEA, IBRD, ICAO, ICC, ICFTU, ICRM, IDA, IEA, IFAD, IFC, IFRCS, ILO, IMF, IMO, Inmarsat, Intelsat, Interpol, IOC, IOM, ISO, ITU, LAIA (observer), MTCR, NAM (guest), NEA, NSG, OAS (observer), OECD, OSCE, PCA, PFP, UN (observer), UNCTAD, UNESCO, UNHCR, UNIDO, UNITAR, UNMIBH, UNMOP, UNMOT, UNOMIG, UNPREDEP, UNTSO, UNU, UPU, WCL, WHO, WIPO, WMO, WToO, WTrO, ZC
Diplomatic representation in the US:
chief of mission: Ambassador Alfred DEFAGO
chancery: 2900 Cathedral Avenue NW, Washington, DC 20008
telephone: [1] (202) 745-7900
FAX: [1] (202) 387-2564
consulate(s) general: Atlanta, Chicago, Houston, Los Angeles, New York, and San Francisco
Diplomatic representation from the US:
chief of mission: Ambassador Madeleine May KUNIN
embassy: Jubilaeumstrasse 93, 3005 Bern
mailing address: use embassy street address
telephone: [41] (31) 357 70 11
FAX: [41] (31) 357 73 44
Flag description: red square with a bold, equilateral white cross in the center that does not extend to the edges of the flag

Economy

Economy - overview: Switzerland, a fundamentally prosperous and stable modern economy with a per capita GDP 15%-20% above that of the big West European economies, experienced an export-driven upturn in its economy in 1998. The downturn in the global economy, however, will have a cooling effect on the 1998 boom in the Swiss export sector, including

Switzerland (continued)

financial services, biotechnology, pharmaceuticals, and special-purpose machines. A major downturn in the Swiss economy should still be avoided, as consumer and capital spending have picked up and will keep the economy moving in 1999. GDP growth in 1999 is expected to come in around 1.4%. The growing political and economic union of Europe suggests that Switzerland's time-honored neutral separation is becoming increasingly obsolete. Thus, when the surrounding trade partners launched the euro on 1 January 1999, their firms began prodding Swiss exporters and importers to keep their accounts in euros.

GDP: purchasing power parity - $191.8 billion (1998 est.)

GDP - real growth rate: 2% (1998 est.)

GDP - per capita: purchasing power parity - $26,400 (1998 est.)

GDP - composition by sector:
agriculture: 2.8%
industry: 31.1%
services: 66.1% (1995)

Population below poverty line: NA%

Household income or consumption by percentage share:
lowest 10%: 2.9%
highest 10%: 28.6% (1982)

Inflation rate (consumer prices): 0% (1998)

Labor force: 3.8 million (850,000 foreign workers, mostly Italian)

Labor force - by occupation: services 67%, manufacturing and construction 29%, agriculture and forestry 4% (1995)

Unemployment rate: 3.6% (1998 est.)

Budget:
revenues: $32.66 billion
expenditures: $34.89 billion, including capital expenditures of $2.3 billion (1998 est.)

Industries: machinery, chemicals, watches, textiles, precision instruments

Industrial production growth rate: 6% (1998 est.)

Electricity - production: 54.815 billion kWh (1996)

Electricity - production by source:
fossil fuel: 3.99%
hydro: 52.73%
nuclear: 43.27%
other: 0.01% (1996)

Electricity - consumption: 53.765 billion kWh (1996)

Electricity - exports: 24.2 billion kWh (1996)

Electricity - imports: 23.15 billion kWh (1996)

Agriculture - products: grains, fruits, vegetables; meat, eggs

Exports: $94.4 billion (f.o.b., 1998)

Exports - commodities: machinery 29%, chemicals 28%, metals, watches, agricultural products (1997)

Exports - partners: EU 61% (Germany 23%, France 9%, Italy 8%, UK 6%, Austria 3%), US 10%, Japan 4% (1997)

Imports: $95.5 billion (f.o.b., 1998)

Imports - commodities: machinery 22%, chemicals 16%, vehicles, metals, agricultural products, textiles (1997)

Imports - partners: EU 79% (Germany 32%, France 12%, Italy 10%, Netherlands 5%, UK 5%),, US 7%, Japan 3% (1997)

Debt - external: $NA

Economic aid - donor: ODA, $1.1 billion (1995)

Currency: 1 Swiss franc, franken, or franco (SFR) = 100 centimes, rappen, or centesimi

Exchange rates: Swiss francs, franken, or franchi (SFR) per US$1 - 1.3837 (January 1999), 1.4498 (1998), 1.4513 (1997), 1.2360 (1996), 1.1825 (1995), 1.3677 (1994)

Fiscal year: calendar year

Communications

Telephones: 5.24 million (1996 est.); 307,000 cellular telephone subscribers (1994 est.)

Telephone system: excellent domestic and international services
domestic: extensive cable and microwave radio relay networks
international: satellite earth stations - 2 Intelsat (Atlantic Ocean and Indian Ocean)

Radio broadcast stations: AM 7, FM 50, shortwave 1 (1997)

Radios: 2.8 million (1996)

Television broadcast stations: 108 (1997)

Televisions: 2.647 million licenses (1996)

Transportation

Railways:
total: 4,479 km (1,564 km double track)
standard gauge: 3,304 km 1.435-m gauge (3,288 km electrified)
narrow gauge: 1,165 km 1.000-m gauge (1,057 km electrified); 10 km 0.750-m or 0.800-m gauge (1996)

Highways:
total: 71,048 km (including 1,613 km of expressways)
paved: NA km
unpaved: NA km (1997 est.)

Waterways: 65 km; Rhine (Basel to Rheinfelden, Schaffhausen to Bodensee); 12 navigable lakes

Pipelines: crude oil 314 km; natural gas 1,506 km

Ports and harbors: Basel

Merchant marine:
total: 20 ships (1,000 GRT or over) totaling 412,459 GRT/724,995 DWT
ships by type: bulk 13, cargo 1, chemical tanker 5, oil tanker 1 (1998 est.)

Airports: 67 (1998 est.)

Airports - with paved runways:
total: 42
over 3,047 m: 3
2,438 to 3,047 m: 5
1,524 to 2,437 m: 12
914 to 1,523 m: 7
under 914 m: 15 (1998 est.)

Airports - with unpaved runways:
total: 25
under 914 m: 25 (1998 est.)

Military

Military branches: Army, Air Force, Frontier Guards, Fortification Guards

Military manpower - military age: 20 years of age

Military manpower - availability:
males age 15-49: 1,867,290 (1999 est.)

Military manpower - fit for military service:
males age 15-49: 1,592,696 (1999 est.)

Military manpower - reaching military age annually:
males: 41,204 (1999 est.)

Military expenditures - dollar figure: $3.1 billion (1999)

Military expenditures - percent of GDP: 1.2% (1999)

Transnational Issues

Disputes - international: none

Illicit drugs: because of more stringent government regulations, used significantly less as a money-laundering center; transit country for and consumer of South American cocaine and Southwest Asian heroin

Syria

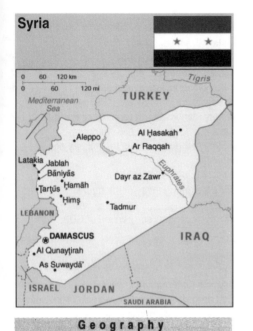

Geography

Location: Middle East, bordering the Mediterranean Sea, between Lebanon and Turkey
Geographic coordinates: 35 00 N, 38 00 E
Map references: Middle East
Area:
total: 185,180 sq km
land: 184,050 sq km
water: 1,130 sq km
note: includes 1,295 sq km of Israeli-occupied territory
Area - comparative: slightly larger than North Dakota
Land boundaries:
total: 2,253 km
border countries: Iraq 605 km, Israel 76 km, Jordan 375 km, Lebanon 375 km, Turkey 822 km
Coastline: 193 km
Maritime claims:
contiguous zone: 41 nm
territorial sea: 35 nm
Climate: mostly desert; hot, dry, sunny summers (June to August) and mild, rainy winters (December to February) along coast; cold weather with snow or sleet periodically hitting Damascus
Terrain: primarily semiarid and desert plateau; narrow coastal plain; mountains in west
Elevation extremes:
lowest point: unnamed location near Lake Tiberias -200 m
highest point: Mount Hermon 2,814 m
Natural resources: petroleum, phosphates, chrome and manganese ores, asphalt, iron ore, rock salt, marble, gypsum
Land use:
arable land: 28%
permanent crops: 4%
permanent pastures: 43%
forests and woodland: 3%
other: 22% (1993 est.)
Irrigated land: 9,060 sq km (1993 est.)

Natural hazards: dust storms, sandstorms
Environment - current issues: deforestation; overgrazing; soil erosion; desertification; water pollution from dumping of raw sewage and wastes from petroleum refining; inadequate supplies of potable water
Environment - international agreements:
party to: Biodiversity, Climate Change, Desertification, Hazardous Wastes, Nuclear Test Ban, Ozone Layer Protection, Ship Pollution
signed, but not ratified: Environmental Modification
Geography - note: there are 42 Israeli settlements and civilian land use sites in the Israeli-occupied Golan Heights (August 1998 est.)

People

Population: 17,213,871 (July 1999 est.)
note: in addition, there are about 37,200 people living in the Israeli-occupied Golan Heights - 18,200 Arabs (16,500 Druze and 1,700 Alawites) and about 19,000 Israeli settlers (August 1998 est.)
Age structure:
0-14 years: 46% (male 4,032,620; female 3,840,431)
15-64 years: 51% (male 4,515,274; female 4,322,415)
65 years and over: 3% (male 246,812; female 256,319) (1999 est.)
Population growth rate: 3.15% (1999 est.)
Birth rate: 36.95 births/1,000 population (1999 est.)
Death rate: 5.4 deaths/1,000 population (1999 est.)
Net migration rate: 0 migrant(s)/1,000 population (1999 est.)
Sex ratio:
at birth: 1.05 male(s)/female
under 15 years: 1.05 male(s)/female
15-64 years: 1.04 male(s)/female
65 years and over: 0.96 male(s)/female
total population: 1.04 male(s)/female (1999 est.)
Infant mortality rate: 36.42 deaths/1,000 live births (1999 est.)
Life expectancy at birth:
total population: 68.09 years
male: 66.75 years
female: 69.48 years (1999 est.)
Total fertility rate: 5.37 children born/woman (1999 est.)
Nationality:
noun: Syrian(s)
adjective: Syrian
Ethnic groups: Arab 90.3%, Kurds, Armenians, and other 9.7%
Religions: Sunni Muslim 74%, Alawite, Druze, and other Muslim sects 16%, Christian (various sects) 10%, Jewish (tiny communities in Damascus, Al Qamishli, and Aleppo)
Languages: Arabic (official); Kurdish, Armenian, Aramaic, Circassian widely understood; French, English somewhat understood
Literacy:
definition: age 15 and over can read and write
total population: 70.8%
male: 85.7%

female: 55.8% (1997 est.)

Government

Country name:
conventional long form: Syrian Arab Republic
conventional short form: Syria
local long form: Al Jumhuriyah al Arabiyah as Suriyah
local short form: Suriyah
former: United Arab Republic (with Egypt)
Data code: SY
Government type: republic under military regime since March 1963
Capital: Damascus
Administrative divisions: 14 provinces (muhafazat, singular - muhafazah); Al Hasakah, Al Ladhiqiyah, Al Qunaytirah, Ar Raqqah, As Suwayda', Dar'a, Dayr az Zawr, Dimashq, Halab, Hamah, Hims, Idlib, Rif Dimashq, Tartus
Independence: 17 April 1946 (from League of Nations mandate under French administration)
National holiday: National Day, 17 April (1946)
Constitution: 13 March 1973
Legal system: based on Islamic law and civil law system; special religious courts; has not accepted compulsory ICJ jurisdiction
Suffrage: 18 years of age; universal
Executive branch:
chief of state: President Hafiz al-ASAD (since 22 February 1971); note - President ASAD seized power in the November 1970 coup, assumed presidential powers 22 February 1971, and was confirmed as president in the 12 March 1971 national elections; Vice Presidents 'Abd al-Halim ibn Said KHADDAM (since 11 March 1984) and Muhammad Zuhayr MASHARIQA (since 11 March 1984)
head of government: Prime Minister Mahmud ZUBI (since 1 November 1987), Deputy Prime Ministers Lt. Gen. Mustafa TALAS (since 11 March 1984), Dr. Salim YASIN (since NA December 1981), and Rashid AKHTARINI (since 4 July 1992)
cabinet: Council of Ministers appointed by the president
elections: president elected by popular vote for a seven-year term; referendum/election last held 8 February 1999 (next to be held NA 2006); vice presidents appointed by the president; prime minister and deputy prime ministers appointed by the president
election results: Hafiz al-ASAD reelected president; percent of vote - Hafiz al-ASAD 99%
Legislative branch: unicameral People's Council or Majlis al-shaab (250 seats; members elected by popular vote to serve four-year terms)
elections: last held 30 November-1 December 1998 (next to be held NA 2002)
election results: percent of vote by party - NPF 67%, non-NPF 33%; seats by party - NPF 167, independents 83; note - the constitution guarantees that the Ba'th Party (part of the NPF alliance) receive one-half of the seats
Judicial branch: Supreme Constitutional Court, justices are appointed for four-year terms by the

Syria *(continued)*

president; High Judicial Council; Court of Cassation; State Security Courts

Political parties and leaders:
National Progressive Front (NPF) includes: the ruling Arab Socialist Renaissance (Ba'th) Party [Hafiz al-ASAD, president of the republic, secretary general of the party, and chairman of the National Progressive Front]; Syrian Arab Socialist Party or ASP [Ghassan 'Abd-al-Aziz UTHMAN]; Arab Socialist Union or ASU [Fayiz ISMAIL]; Syrian Communist Party or SCP [Yusuf FAYSAL]; Arab Socialist Unionist Party [Safwan QUDSI]; Socialist Union Democratic Party [Ahmad al-ASAD]

Political pressure groups and leaders: non-Ba'th parties have little effective political influence; Communist party ineffective; conservative religious leaders; Muslim Brotherhood (operates in exile in Jordan and Yemen)

International organization participation: ABEDA, AFESD, AL, AMF, CAEU, CCC, ESCWA, FAO, G-24, G-77, IAEA, IBRD, ICAO, ICC, ICRM, IDA, IDB, IFAD, IFC, IFRCS, IHO, ILO, IMF, IMO, Intelsat, Interpol, IOC, ISO, ITU, NAM, OAPEC, OIC, UN, UNCTAD, UNESCO, UNIDO, UNRWA, UPU, WFTU, WHO, WMO, WToO

Diplomatic representation in the US:
chief of mission: Ambassador Walid MUALEM
chancery: 2215 Wyoming Avenue NW, Washington, DC 20008
telephone: [1] (202) 232-6313
FAX: [1] (202) 234-9548

Diplomatic representation from the US:
chief of mission: Ambassador Ryan CROCKER
embassy: Abou Roumaneh, Al-Mansur Street, No. 2, Damascus
mailing address: P. O. Box 29, Damascus
telephone: [963] (11) 333-2814, 333-0788, 332-0783
FAX: [963] (11) 224-7938

Flag description: three equal horizontal bands of red (top), white, and black with two small green five-pointed stars in a horizontal line centered in the white band; similar to the flag of Yemen, which has a plain white band and of Iraq, which has three green stars (plus an Arabic inscription) in a horizontal line centered in the white band; also similar to the flag of Egypt, which has a symbolic eagle centered in the white band

Economy

Economy - overview: Syria's predominantly statist economy is on a shaky footing because of Damascus's failure to implement extensive economic reform. The dominant agricultural sector remains underdeveloped, with roughly 80% of agricultural land still dependent on rain-fed sources. Although Syria has sufficient water supplies in the aggregate at normal levels of precipitation, the great distance between major water supplies and population centers poses serious distribution problems. The water problem is exacerbated by rapid population growth, industrial expansion, and increased water pollution. Private investment is critical to the modernization of the agricultural, energy, and export sectors. Oil production is leveling off, and the efforts of the nonoil sector to penetrate international markets have fallen short. Syria's inadequate infrastructure, outmoded technological base, and weak educational system make it vulnerable to future shocks and hamper competition with neighbors such as Jordan and Israel.

GDP: purchasing power parity - $41.7 billion (1998 est.)
GDP - real growth rate: 2% (1998 est.)
GDP - per capita: purchasing power parity - $2,500 (1998 est.)
GDP - composition by sector:
agriculture: 26%
industry: 21%
services: 53% (1997)
Population below poverty line: 15%-25%
Household income or consumption by percentage share:
lowest 10%: NA%
highest 10%: NA%
Inflation rate (consumer prices): 15%-20% (1997 est.)
Labor force: 4.7 million (1998 est.)
Labor force - by occupation: services 40%, agriculture 40%, industry 20% (1996 est.)
Unemployment rate: 12%-15% (1998 est.)
Budget:
revenues: $3.5 billion
expenditures: $4.2 billion, including capital expenditures of $NA (1997 est.)
Industries: petroleum, textiles, food processing, beverages, tobacco, phosphate rock mining
Industrial production growth rate: 0.2% (1996 est.)
Electricity - production: 19.3 billion kWh (1996)
Electricity - production by source:
fossil fuel: 63.73%
hydro: 36.27%
nuclear: 0%
other: 0% (1996)
Electricity - consumption: 19.3 billion kWh (1996)
Electricity - exports: 0 kWh (1996)
Electricity - imports: 0 kWh (1996)
Agriculture - products: wheat, barley, cotton, lentils, chickpeas, olives, sugar beets; beef, mutton, eggs, poultry, milk
Exports: $4.2 billion (f.o.b., 1998 est.)
Exports - commodities: petroleum 65%, textiles 16%, food and live animals 13%, manufactures 6% (1997 est.)
Exports - partners: Italy 18%, Germany 13%, France 12%, Turkey 10%, Lebanon 7%, Spain 6% (1997 est.)
Imports: $5.7 billion (c.i.f., 1997)
Imports - commodities: machinery and equipment 40%, foodstuffs/animals 15%, metal and metal products 15%, textiles 10%, chemicals 10%, consumer goods 5% (1997 est.)
Imports - partners: Ukraine 14%, Italy 7%, Germany 6%, Turkey 5%, France 4%, South Korea 4%, Japan 4%, US 3% (1997 est.)

Debt - external: $22 billion (1998 est.)
Economic aid - recipient: $327.3 million (1995)
Currency: 1 Syrian pound (£S) = 100 piastres
Exchange rates: Syrian pounds (£S) per US$1 - 46 (1998), 41.9 (January 1997); official fixed rate 11.225
Fiscal year: calendar year

Communications

Telephones: 541,465 (1992 est.)
Telephone system: fair system currently undergoing significant improvement and digital upgrades, including fiber-optic technology
domestic: coaxial cable and microwave radio relay network
international: satellite earth stations - 1 Intelsat (Indian Ocean) and 1 Intersputnik (Atlantic Ocean region); 1 submarine cable; coaxial cable and microwave radio relay to Iraq, Jordan, Lebanon, and Turkey; participant in Medarabtel
Radio broadcast stations: AM 9, FM 1, shortwave 0
Radios: 3.392 million (1992 est.)
Television broadcast stations: 54 (of which 36 are low-power stations and repeaters) (1997)
Televisions: 700,000 (1993 est.)

Transportation

Railways:
total: 1,998 km
broad gauge: 1,766 km 1.435-m gauge
narrow gauge: 232 km 1.050-m gauge
Highways:
total: 41,451 km
paved: 9,575 km (including 877 km of expressways)
unpaved: 31,876 km (1997 est.)
Waterways: 870 km; minimal economic importance
Pipelines: crude oil 1,304 km; petroleum products 515 km
Ports and harbors: Baniyas, Jablah, Latakia, Tartus
Merchant marine:
total: 131 ships (1,000 GRT or over) totaling 401,407 GRT/578,081 DWT
ships by type: bulk 11, cargo 115, livestock carrier 4, roll-on/roll-off cargo 1 (1998 est.)
Airports: 104 (1998 est.)
Airports - with paved runways:
total: 24
over 3,047 m: 5
2,438 to 3,047 m: 16
914 to 1,523 m: 1
under 914 m: 2 (1998 est.)
Airports - with unpaved runways:
total: 80
1,524 to 2,437 m: 3
914 to 1,523 m: 14
under 914 m: 63 (1998 est.)
Heliports: 2 (1998 est.)

Syria (continued)

Military branches: Syrian Arab Army, Syrian Arab Navy, Syrian Arab Air Force, Syrian Arab Air Defense Forces, Police and Security Force
Military manpower - military age: 19 years of age
Military manpower - availability:
males age 15-49: 4,060,995 (1999 est.)
Military manpower - fit for military service:
males age 15-49: 2,271,539 (1999 est.)
Military manpower - reaching military age annually:
males: 188,546 (1999 est.)
Military expenditures - dollar figure: $800 million-$1 billion (1997 est.); note - based on official budget data that understate actual spending
Military expenditures - percent of GDP: 8% (1995 est.)

Transnational Issues

Disputes - international: Golan Heights is Israeli occupied; dispute with upstream riparian Turkey over Turkish water development plans for the Tigris and Euphrates Rivers; Syrian troops in northern, central, and eastern Lebanon since October 1976
Illicit drugs: a transit point for opiates and hashish bound for regional and Western markets

Taiwan

Entry

follows

Zimbabwe

Tajikistan

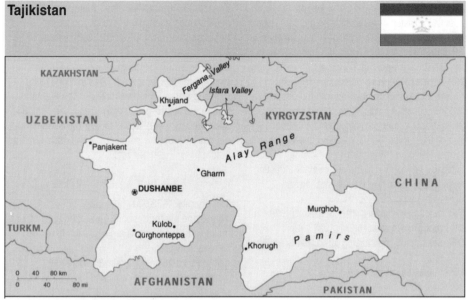

Introduction

Background: Tajikistan has experienced three changes of government and a civil war since it gained independence in September 1991 when the USSR collapsed. A peace agreement was signed in June 1997, but implementation is progressing slowly. Russian-led peacekeeping troops are deployed throughout the country, and Russian-commanded border guards are stationed along the Tajikistani-Afghan border.

Geography

Location: Central Asia, west of China
Geographic coordinates: 39 00 N, 71 00 E
Map references: Commonwealth of Independent States
Area:
total: 143,100 sq km
land: 142,700 sq km
water: 400 sq km
Area - comparative: slightly smaller than Wisconsin
Land boundaries:
total: 3,651 km
border countries: Afghanistan 1,206 km, China 414 km, Kyrgyzstan 870 km, Uzbekistan 1,161 km
Coastline: 0 km (landlocked)
Maritime claims: none (landlocked)
Climate: midlatitude continental, hot summers, mild winters; semiarid to polar in Pamir Mountains
Terrain: Pamir and Alay mountains dominate landscape; western Fergana Valley in north, Kofarnihon and Vakhsh Valleys in southwest
Elevation extremes:
lowest point: Syrdariya 300 m
highest point: Qullai Kommunizm 7,495 m
Natural resources: significant hydropower potential, some petroleum, uranium, mercury, brown coal, lead, zinc, antimony, tungsten
Land use:
arable land: 6%
permanent crops: 0%

permanent pastures: 25%
forests and woodland: 4%
other: 65% (1993 est.)
Irrigated land: 6,390 sq km (1993 est.)
Natural hazards: NA
Environment - current issues: inadequate sanitation facilities; increasing levels of soil salinity; industrial pollution; excessive pesticides; part of the basin of the shrinking Aral Sea suffers from severe overutilization of available water for irrigation and associated pollution
Environment - international agreements:
party to: Biodiversity, Climate Change, Desertification, Ozone Layer Protection
signed, but not ratified: none of the selected agreements
Geography - note: landlocked

People

Population: 6,102,854 (July 1999 est.)
Age structure:
0-14 years: 41% (male 1,250,344; female 1,224,355)
15-64 years: 55% (male 1,661,488; female 1,681,839)
65 years and over: 4% (male 122,065; female 162,763) (1999 est.)
Population growth rate: 1.43% (1999 est.)
Birth rate: 27.46 births/1,000 population (1999 est.)
Death rate: 7.85 deaths/1,000 population (1999 est.)
Net migration rate: -5.34 migrant(s)/1,000 population (1999 est.)
Sex ratio:
at birth: 1.05 male(s)/female
under 15 years: 1.02 male(s)/female
15-64 years: 0.99 male(s)/female
65 years and over: 0.75 male(s)/female
total population: 0.99 male(s)/female (1999 est.)
Infant mortality rate: 114.78 deaths/1,000 live births (1999 est.)
Life expectancy at birth:
total population: 64.28 years

male: 61.15 years
female: 67.57 years (1999 est.)
Total fertility rate: 3.48 children born/woman (1999 est.)
Nationality:
noun: Tajikistani(s)
adjective: Tajikistani
Ethnic groups: Tajik 64.9%, Uzbek 25%, Russian 3.5% (declining because of emigration), other 6.6%
Religions: Sunni Muslim 80%, Shi'a Muslim 5%
Languages: Tajik (official), Russian widely used in government and business
Literacy:
definition: age 15 and over can read and write
total population: 98%
male: 99%
female: 97% (1989 est.)

Government

Country name:
conventional long form: Republic of Tajikistan
conventional short form: Tajikistan
local long form: Jumhurii Tojikiston
local short form: none
former: Tajik Soviet Socialist Republic
Data code: TI
Government type: republic
Capital: Dushanbe
Administrative divisions: 2 oblasts (viloyatho, singular - viloyat) and one autonomous oblast* (viloyati mukhtori); Viloyati Mukhtori Kuhistoni Badakhshoni* (Khorugh - formerly Khorog), Viloyati Khatlon (Qurghonteppa - formerly Kurgan-Tyube), Viloyati Leninobod (Khujand - formerly Leninabad)
note: the administrative center name follows in parentheses
Independence: 9 September 1991 (from Soviet Union)
National holiday: National Day, 9 September (1991)
Constitution: 6 November 1994
Legal system: based on civil law system; no judicial review of legislative acts
Suffrage: 18 years of age; universal
Executive branch:
chief of state: President Emomali RAHMONOV (since 6 November 1994; head of state and Supreme Assembly chairman since 19 November 1992)
head of government: Prime Minister Yahyo AZIMOV (since 8 February 1996)
cabinet: Council of Ministers appointed by the president, approved by the Supreme Assembly for approval
elections: president elected by popular vote for a five-year term; election last held 6 November 1994 (next to be held NA 1999); prime minister appointed by the president
election results: Emomali RAHMONOV elected president; percent of vote - Emomali RAHMONOV 58%, Abdumalik ABDULLOJANOV 40%
Legislative branch: unicameral Supreme Assembly or Majlisi Oli (181 seats; members are elected by popular vote to serve five-year terms)

Tajikistan (continued)

elections: last held 26 February and 12 March 1995 (next to be held NA 1999)

election results: percent of vote by party - NA; estimated seats by party - Communist Party and affiliates 100, People's Party 10, Party of People's Unity 6, Party of Economic and Political Renewal 1, other 64

Judicial branch: Supreme Court, judges are appointed by the president

Political parties and leaders: Tajik Communist Party or CPT [Shodi SHABDOLOV]; People's Democratic Party of Tajikistan or PDPT [Abdulmajid DOSTIEV]; Rastokhez (Rebirth) Movement [Tohiri ABDUJABBOR]; National Unity Party [Abdulmalik ABDULLOJANOV] - evolved from the People's Party and Party of People's Unity; United Tajik Opposition or UTO [Said Abdullo NURI] - an umbrella group including; Islamic Revival Movement of Tajikistan or IMP [Said Abdullo NURI, chairman]; Democratic Party or TDP [Jumaboy NIYOZOV, chairman]; Lali Badakhshan Movement [Atobek AMIRBEKOV]; Party for the Political and Economic Renewal of Tajikistan or PPERT [Valijon BABAYEV]; Citizenship, Patriotism, Unity Party [Bobokhon MAHMADOV]; Adolatho "Justice" Party [Abdurahmon KARIMOV, chairman]; Party of Justice and Development [Rahmutullo ZAINAV]

International organization participation: CCC, CIS, EAPC, EBRD, ECE, ECO, ESCAP, FAO, IBRD, ICAO, ICRM, IDA, IFAD, IFC, IFRCS, ILO, IMF, Intelsat, IOC, IOM, ITU, OIC, OPCW, OSCE, UN, UNCTAD, UNESCO, UNIDO, UPU, WFTU, WHO, WIPO, WMO, WTrO (observer)

Diplomatic representation in the US: Tajikistan does not have an embassy in the US, but has a mission at the UN: address - 136 East 67th Street, New York, NY 10021, telephone - [1] (212) 472-7645, FAX - [1] (212) 628-0252; permanent representative to the UN is Rashid ALIMOV

Diplomatic representation from the US:
chief of mission: Ambassador Robert FINN
embassy: temporarily collocated with the US Embassy in Almaty
mailing address: use embassy street address
telephone: NA
FAX: NA

Flag description: three horizontal stripes of red (top), a wider stripe of white, and green; a gold crown surmounted by seven five-pointed gold stars is located in the center of the white stripe

Economy

Economy - overview: Tajikistan has the lowest per capita GDP among the former Soviet republics. Agriculture dominates the economy, with cotton the most important crop. Mineral resources, varied but limited in amount, include silver, gold, uranium, and tungsten. Industry consists only of a large aluminum plant, hydropower facilities, and small obsolete factories mostly in light industry and food processing. The Tajikistani economy has been gravely weakened by five years of civil conflict and by the loss of subsidies from Moscow and of markets for its products. Tajikistan thus depends on aid from Russia and Uzbekistan and on international humanitarian assistance for much of its basic subsistence needs. Even if the peace agreement of June 1997 is honored, the country faces major problems in integrating refugees and former combatants into the economy. Moreover, constant political turmoil and the continued dominance by former communist officials have impeded the introduction of meaningful economic reforms. Still in a post-conflict status, the future of Tajikistan's economy and the potential for attracting foreign investment depend upon stability and progress in the peace process.

GDP: purchasing power parity - $6 billion (1998 est.)

GDP - real growth rate: 5.3% (1998 est.)

GDP - per capita: purchasing power parity - $990 (1998 est.)

GDP - composition by sector:
agriculture: 25%
industry: 35%
services: 40% (1997)

Population below poverty line: NA%

Household income or consumption by percentage share:
lowest 10%: NA%
highest 10%: NA%

Inflation rate (consumer prices): 46.3% (1998 est.)

Labor force: 1.9 million (1996)

Labor force - by occupation: agriculture and forestry 52%, manufacturing, mining, and construction 17%, services 31% (1995)

Unemployment rate: 5.7% includes only officially registered unemployed; also large numbers of underemployed workers and unregistered unemployed people (December 1998)

Budget:
revenues: $NA
expenditures: $NA, including capital expenditures of $NA

Industries: aluminum, zinc, lead, chemicals and fertilizers, cement, vegetable oil, metal-cutting machine tools, refrigerators and freezers

Industrial production growth rate: 8% (1998 est.)

Electricity - production: 13.555 billion kWh (1996)

Electricity - production by source:
fossil fuel: 4.09%
hydro: 95.91%
nuclear: 0%
other: 0% (1996)

Electricity - consumption: 12.555 billion kWh (1996)

Electricity - exports: 3.8 billion kWh (1996)

Electricity - imports: 2.8 billion kWh (1996)

Agriculture - products: cotton, grain, fruits, grapes, vegetables; cattle, sheep, goats

Exports: $740 million (1998 est.)

Exports - commodities: cotton, aluminum, fruits, vegetable oil, textiles

Exports - partners: FSU 78%, Netherlands (1994)

Imports: $810 million (1998 est.)

Imports - commodities: fuel, chemicals, machinery and transport equipment, textiles, foodstuffs

Imports - partners: FSU 55%, Switzerland, UK (1994)

Debt - external: $1 billion (1997 est.)

Economic aid - recipient: $64.7 million (1995)

Currency: the Tajikistani ruble (TJR) = 100 tanga

Exchange rates: Tajikistani rubles (TJR) per US$1 - 998 (January 1999), 350 (January 1997), 284 (January 1996)

Fiscal year: calendar year

Communications

Telephones: 303,000 (1991 est.)

Telephone system: poorly developed and not well maintained; many towns are not reached by the national network
domestic: cable and microwave radio relay
international: linked by cable and microwave radio relay to other CIS republics, and by leased connections to the Moscow international gateway switch; Dushanbe linked by Intelsat to international gateway switch in Ankara (Turkey); satellite earth stations - 1 Orbita and 2 Intelsat

Radio broadcast stations: 1 state-owned radio broadcast station of NA type

Radios: NA

Television broadcast stations: 0 (there are, however, repeaters that relay programs from Russia, Iran, and Turkey) (1997)

Televisions: NA

Transportation

Railways:
total: 480 km in common carrier service; does not include industrial lines (1990)

Highways:
total: 13,700 km
paved: 11,330 km (note - these roads are said to be hard-surfaced, meaning that some are paved and some are all-weather gravel surfaced)
unpaved: 2,370 km (1996 est.)

Pipelines: natural gas 400 km (1992)

Ports and harbors: none

Airports: 59 (1994 est.)

Airports - with paved runways:
total: 14
over 3,047 m: 1
2,438 to 3,047 m: 5
1,524 to 2,437 m: 7
914 to 1,523 m: 1 (1994 est.)

Airports - with unpaved runways:
total: 45
914 to 1,523 m: 9
under 914 m: 36 (1994 est.)

Military

Military branches: Army, Air Force, Air Defense Forces, Presidential National Guard, Security Forces (internal and border troops)

Military manpower - military age: 18 years of age

Tajikistan *(continued)*

Military manpower - availability:
males age 15-49: 1,478,551 (1999 est.)
Military manpower - fit for military service:
males age 15-49: 1,211,514 (1999 est.)
Military manpower - reaching military age annually:
males: 65,001 (1999 est.)
Military expenditures - dollar figure: $19.3 million (1997)
Military expenditures - percent of GDP: 1.8% (1997)

Transnational Issues

Disputes - international: most of the boundary with China in dispute; territorial dispute with Kyrgyzstan on northern boundary in Isfara Valley area
Illicit drugs: limited illicit cultivation of cannabis, mostly for domestic consumption; opium poppy cultivation negligible in 1998 because of government eradication program; increasingly used as transshipment point for illicit drugs from Southwest Asia to Russia and Western Europe

Tanzania

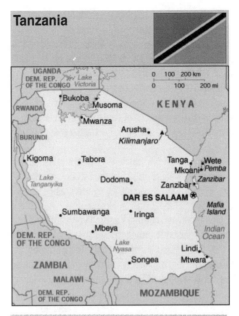

Geography

Location: Eastern Africa, bordering the Indian Ocean, between Kenya and Mozambique
Geographic coordinates: 6 00 S, 35 00 E
Map references: Africa
Area:
total: 945,090 sq km
land: 886,040 sq km
water: 59,050 sq km
note: includes the islands of Mafia, Pemba, and Zanzibar
Area - comparative: slightly larger than twice the size of California
Land boundaries:
total: 3,402 km
border countries: Burundi 451 km, Kenya 769 km, Malawi 475 km, Mozambique 756 km, Rwanda 217 km, Uganda 396 km, Zambia 338 km
Coastline: 1,424 km
Maritime claims:
exclusive economic zone: 200 nm
territorial sea: 12 nm
Climate: varies from tropical along coast to temperate in highlands
Terrain: plains along coast; central plateau; highlands in north, south
Elevation extremes:
lowest point: Indian Ocean 0 m
highest point: Kilimanjaro 5,895 m
Natural resources: hydropower, tin, phosphates, iron ore, coal, diamonds, gemstones, gold, natural gas, nickel
Land use:
arable land: 3%
permanent crops: 1%
permanent pastures: 40%
forests and woodland: 38%
other: 18% (1993 est.)
Irrigated land: 1,500 sq km (1993 est.)
Natural hazards: the tsetse fly; flooding on the central plateau during the rainy season; drought

Environment - current issues: soil degradation; deforestation; desertification; destruction of coral reefs threatens marine habitats; recent droughts affected marginal agriculture
Environment - international agreements:
party to: Biodiversity, Climate Change, Desertification, Endangered Species, Hazardous Wastes, Law of the Sea, Nuclear Test Ban, Ozone Layer Protection
signed, but not ratified: none of the selected agreements
Geography - note: Kilimanjaro is highest point in Africa

People

Population: 31,270,820 (July 1999 est.)
Age structure:
0-14 years: 44% (male 6,926,149; female 6,967,416)
15-64 years: 53% (male 8,030,141; female 8,437,978)
65 years and over: 3% (male 415,074; female 494,062) (1999 est.)
Population growth rate: 2.14% (1999 est.)
Birth rate: 40.37 births/1,000 population (1999 est.)
Death rate: 16.75 deaths/1,000 population (1999 est.)
Net migration rate: -2.24 migrant(s)/1,000 population (1999 est.)
Sex ratio:
at birth: 1.03 male(s)/female
under 15 years: 0.99 male(s)/female
15-64 years: 0.95 male(s)/female
65 years and over: 0.84 male(s)/female
total population: 0.97 male(s)/female (1999 est.)
Infant mortality rate: 95.27 deaths/1,000 live births (1999 est.)
Life expectancy at birth:
total population: 46.17 years
male: 43.85 years
female: 48.57 years (1999 est.)
Total fertility rate: 5.4 children born/woman (1999 est.)
Nationality:
noun: Tanzanian(s)
adjective: Tanzanian
Ethnic groups: mainland - native African 99% (of which 95% are Bantu consisting of more than 130 tribes), other 1% (consisting of Asian, European, and Arab); Zanzibar - Arab, native African, mixed Arab and native African
Religions: mainland - Christian 45%, Muslim 35%, indigenous beliefs 20; Zanzibar - more than 99% Muslim
Languages: Kiswahili or Swahili (official), Kiunguju (name for Swahili in Zanzibar), English (official, primary language of commerce, administration, and higher education), Arabic (widely spoken in Zanzibar), many local languages
note: Kiswahili (Swahili) is the mother tongue of the Bantu people living in Zanzibar and nearby coastal Tanzania; although Kiswahili is Bantu in structure and origin, its vocabulary draws on a variety of sources,

including Arabic and English, and it has become the lingua franca of central and eastern Africa; the first language of most people is one of the local languages

Literacy:
definition: age 15 and over can read and write Kiswahili (Swahili), English, or Arabic
total population: 67.8%
male: 79.4%
female: 56.8% (1995 est.)

Government

Country name:
conventional long form: United Republic of Tanzania
conventional short form: Tanzania
former: United Republic of Tanganyika and Zanzibar
Data code: TZ
Government type: republic
Capital: Dar es Salaam
note: some government offices have been transferred to Dodoma, which is planned as the new national capital; the National Assembly now meets there on regular basis
Administrative divisions: 25 regions; Arusha, Dar es Salaam, Dodoma, Iringa, Kigoma, Kilimanjaro, Lindi, Mara, Mbeya, Morogoro, Mtwara, Mwanza, Pemba North, Pemba South, Pwani, Rukwa, Ruvuma, Shinyanga, Singida, Tabora, Tanga, Zanzibar Central/South, Zanzibar North, Zanzibar Urban/West, Ziwa Magharibi
note: Ziwa Magharibi may have been renamed Kagera
Independence: 26 April 1964; Tanganyika became independent 9 December 1961 (from UK-administered UN trusteeship); Zanzibar became independent 19 December 1963 (from UK); Tanganyika united with Zanzibar 26 April 1964 to form the United Republic of Tanganyika and Zanzibar; renamed United Republic of Tanzania 29 October 1964
National holiday: Union Day, 26 April (1964)
Constitution: 25 April 1977; major revisions October 1984
Legal system: based on English common law; judicial review of legislative acts limited to matters of interpretation; has not accepted compulsory ICJ jurisdiction
Suffrage: 18 years of age; universal
Executive branch:
chief of state: President Benjamin William MKAPA (since 23 November 1995); Vice President Omar Ali JUMA (since 23 November 1995); note the president is both chief of state and head of government
head of government: President Benjamin William MKAPA (since 23 November 1995); Vice President Omar Ali JUMA (since 23 November 1995); note - the president is both chief of state and head of government
note: Zanzibar elects a president who is head of government for matters internal to Zanzibar; Dr. Salmin AMOUR was elected to that office on 22 October 1995 in a popular election
cabinet: Cabinet ministers, including the prime

minister, are appointed by the president from among the members of the National Assembly
elections: president and vice president elected on the same ballot by popular vote for five-year terms; election last held 29 October-19 November 1995 (next to be held NA October 2000); prime minister appointed by the president
election results: percent of vote - Benjamin William MKAPA 62%, MREMA 28%, LIPUMBA 6%, CHEYO 4%
Legislative branch: unicameral National Assembly or Bunge (274 seats - 232 elected by popular vote, 37 allocated to women nominated by the president, five to members of the Zanzibar House of Representatives; members serve five-year terms); note - in addition to enacting laws that apply to the entire United Republic of Tanzania, the Assembly enacts laws that apply only to the mainland; Zanzibar has its own House of Representatives to make laws especially for Zanzibar (the Zanzibar House of Representatives has 50 seats, directly elected by universal suffrage to serve five-year terms)
elections: last held 29 October-19 November 1995 (next to be held NA October 2000)
election results: National Assembly: percent of vote by party - NA; seats by party - CCM 186, CUF 24, NCCR-Mageuzi 16, CHADEMA 3, UDP 3; Zanzibar House of Representatives: percent of vote by party - NA; seats by party - CCM 26, CUF 24
Judicial branch: Court of Appeal; High Court, judges appointed by the president
Political parties and leaders: Chama Cha Mapinduzi or CCM (Revolutionary Party) [Benjamin William MKAPA]; Civic United Front or CUF [Seif Sharif HAMAD]; National Convention for Construction and Reform or NCCR [Lyatonga (Augustine) MREMA]; Union for Multiparty Democracy or UMD [Abdullah FUNDIKIRA]; Chama Cha Demokrasia na Maendeleo or CHADEMA [Edwin I. M. MTEI, chairman]; Democratic Party (unregistered) [Reverend MTIKLA]; United Democratic Party or UDP [John CHEYO]
International organization participation: ACP, AfDB, C, CCC, EADB, ECA, FAO, G- 6, G-77, IAEA, IBRD, ICAO, ICFTU, ICRM, IDA, IFAD, IFC, IFRCS, ILO, IMF, IMO, Intelsat, Interpol, IOC, IOM (observer), ISO, ITU, MONUA, NAM, OAU, OPCW, SADC, UN, UNCTAD, UNESCO, UNHCR, UNIDO, UPU, WCL, WFTU, WHO, WIPO, WMO, WToO, WTrO
Diplomatic representation in the US:
chief of mission: Ambassador Mustafa Salim NYANG'ANYI
chancery: 2139 R Street NW, Washington, DC 20008
telephone: [1] (202) 518-6647
FAX: [1] (202) 797-7408
Diplomatic representation from the US:
chief of mission: Ambassador Charles R. STITH
embassy: 285 Toure Drive, Dar es Salaam (temporary location)
mailing address: P. O. Box 9123, Dar es Salaam
telephone: [255] (51) 666010 through 666015
FAX: [255] (51) 666701

Flag description: divided diagonally by a yellow-edged black band from the lower hoist-side corner; the upper triangle (hoist side) is green and the lower triangle is blue

Economy

Economy - overview: Tanzania is one of the poorest countries in the world. The economy is heavily dependent on agriculture, which accounts for 56% of GDP, provides 85% of exports, and employs 90% of the work force. Topography and climatic conditions, however, limit cultivated crops to only 4% of the land area. Industry accounts for 15% of GDP and is mainly limited to processing agricultural products and light consumer goods. The economic recovery program announced in mid-1986 has generated notable increases in agricultural production and financial support for the program by bilateral donors. The World Bank, the International Monetary Fund, and bilateral donors have provided funds to rehabilitate Tanzania's deteriorated economic infrastructure. Growth in 1991-98 has featured a pickup in industrial production and a substantial increase in output of minerals, led by gold. Natural gas exploration in the Rufiji Delta looks promising and production could start by 2002. Recent banking reforms have helped increase private sector growth and investment. Short-term economic progress also depends on curbing corruption.
GDP: purchasing power parity - $22.1 billion (1998 est.)
GDP - real growth rate: 3.8% (1998 est.)
GDP - per capita: purchasing power parity - $730 (1998 est.)
GDP - composition by sector:
agriculture: 56%
industry: 15%
services: 29% (1996 est.)
Population below poverty line: 51.1% (1991 est.)
Household income or consumption by percentage share:
lowest 10%: 2.9%
highest 10%: 30.2% (1993)
Inflation rate (consumer prices): 13.5% (1998)
Labor force: 13.495 million
Labor force - by occupation: agriculture 90%, industry and commerce 10% (1995 est.)
Unemployment rate: NA%
Budget:
revenues: $700 million
expenditures: $1 billion, including capital expenditures of $NA (FY98/99 est.)
Industries: primarily agricultural processing (sugar, beer, cigarettes, sisal twine), diamond and gold mining, oil refining, shoes, cement, textiles, wood products, fertilizer, salt
Industrial production growth rate: 0.4% (1995 est.)
Electricity - production: 1.82 billion kWh (1996)
Electricity - production by source:
fossil fuel: 12.09%
hydro: 87.91%
nuclear: 0%

Tanzania (continued)

other: 0% (1996)
Electricity - consumption: 1.82 billion kWh (1996)
Electricity - exports: 0 kWh (1996)
Electricity - imports: 0 kWh (1996)
Agriculture - products: coffee, sisal, tea, cotton, pyrethrum (insecticide made from chrysanthemums), cashew nuts, tobacco, cloves (Zanzibar), corn, wheat, cassava (tapioca), bananas, fruits, vegetables; cattle, sheep, goats
Exports: $952 million (f.o.b., 1998 est.)
Exports - commodities: coffee, manufactured goods, cotton, cashew nuts, minerals, tobacco, sisal (1996)
Exports - partners: India 9.8%, Germany 8.9%, Japan 7.8%, Malaysia 6.5%, Rwanda 5.2%, Netherlands 4.7% (1997)
Imports: $1.46 billion (f.o.b., 1998 est.)
Imports - commodities: consumer goods, machinery and transportation equipment, industrial raw materials, crude oil
Imports - partners: South Africa 12.9%, Kenya 9.6%, UK 8.7%, Saudi Arabia 6.6%, Japan 4.9%, China 4.6% (1997)
Debt - external: $8.3 billion (1998 est.)
Economic aid - recipient: $860.9 million (1995)
Currency: 1 Tanzanian shilling (TSh) = 100 cents
Exchange rates: Tanzanian shillings (TSh) per US$1 - 668.3 (February 1999), 664.67 (1998), 612.12 (1997), 579.98 (1996), 574.76 (1995), 509.63 (1994)
Fiscal year: 1 July - 30 June

Communications

Telephones: 88,000 (1994)
Telephone system: fair system operating below capacity
domestic: open wire, microwave radio relay, tropospheric scatter
international: satellite earth stations - 2 Intelsat (1 Indian Ocean and 1 Atlantic Ocean)
Radio broadcast stations: AM 12, FM 4, shortwave 0
Radios: 740,000 (1994 est.)
Television broadcast stations: 4 (1998)
Televisions: 60,000 (1994 est.)

Transportation

Railways:
total: 3,569 km (1995)
narrow gauge: 2,600 km 1.000-m gauge; 969 km 1.067-m gauge
note: the Tanzania-Zambia Railway Authority (TAZARA), which operates 1,860 km of 1.067-m narrow gauge track between Dar es Salaam and Kapiri Mposhi in Zambia (of which 969 km are in Tanzania and 891 km are in Zambia) is not a part of Tanzania Railways Corporation; because of the difference in gauge, this system does not connect to Tanzania Railways
Highways:
total: 88,200 km
paved: 3,704 km

unpaved: 84,496 km (1996 est.)
Waterways: Lake Tanganyika, Lake Victoria, Lake Nyasa
Pipelines: crude oil 982 km
Ports and harbors: Bukoba, Dar es Salaam, Kigoma, Kilwa Masoko, Lindi, Mtwara, Mwanza, Pangani, Tanga, Wete, Zanzibar
Merchant marine:
total: 7 ships (1,000 GRT or over) totaling 20,618 GRT/26,321 DWT
ships by type: cargo 2, oil tanker 2, passenger-cargo 2, roll-on/roll-off cargo 1 (1998 est.)
Airports: 129 (1998 est.)
Airports - with paved runways:
total: 10
over 3,047 m: 1
2,438 to 3,047 m: 2
1,524 to 2,437 m: 5
914 to 1,523 m: 1
under 914 m: 1 (1998 est.)
Airports - with unpaved runways:
total: 119
over 3,047 m: 1
1,524 to 2,437 m: 18
914 to 1,523 m: 65
under 914 m: 35 (1998 est.)

Military

Military branches: Tanzanian People's Defense Force or TPDF (includes Army, Navy, and Air Force), paramilitary Police Field Force Unit, Militia
Military manpower - availability:
males age 15-49: 7,119,106 (1999 est.)
Military manpower - fit for military service:
males age 15-49: 4,120,617 (1999 est.)
Military expenditures - dollar figure: $21 million (FY98/99)
Military expenditures - percent of GDP: 0.2% (FY98/99)

Transnational Issues

Disputes - international: dispute with Malawi over the boundary in Lake Nyasa (Lake Malawi)
Illicit drugs: growing role in transshipment of Southwest and Southeast Asian heroin and South American cocaine destined for European and US markets and of South Asian methaqualone bound for Southern Africa

Thailand

Geography

Location: Southeastern Asia, bordering the Andaman Sea and the Gulf of Thailand, southeast of Burma
Geographic coordinates: 15 00 N, 100 00 E
Map references: Southeast Asia
Area:
total: 514,000 sq km
land: 511,770 sq km
water: 2,230 sq km
Area - comparative: slightly more than twice the size of Wyoming
Land boundaries:
total: 4,863 km
border countries: Burma 1,800 km, Cambodia 803 km, Laos 1,754 km, Malaysia 506 km
Coastline: 3,219 km
Maritime claims:
continental shelf: 200-m depth or to the depth of exploitation
exclusive economic zone: 200 nm
territorial sea: 12 nm
Climate: tropical; rainy, warm, cloudy southwest monsoon (mid-May to September); dry, cool northeast

Thailand (continued)

monsoon (November to mid-March); southern isthmus always hot and humid

Terrain: central plain; Khorat Plateau in the east; mountains elsewhere

Elevation extremes:
lowest point: Gulf of Thailand 0 m
highest point: Doi Inthanon 2,576 m

Natural resources: tin, rubber, natural gas, tungsten, tantalum, timber, lead, fish, gypsum, lignite, fluorite

Land use:
arable land: 34%
permanent crops: 6%
permanent pastures: 2%
forests and woodland: 26%
other: 32% (1993 est.)

Irrigated land: 44,000 sq km (1993 est.)

Natural hazards: land subsidence in Bangkok area resulting from the depletion of the water table; droughts

Environment - current issues: air pollution from vehicle emissions; water pollution from organic and factory wastes; deforestation; soil erosion; wildlife populations threatened by illegal hunting

Environment - international agreements:
party to: Climate Change, Endangered Species, Hazardous Wastes, Marine Life Conservation, Nuclear Test Ban, Ozone Layer Protection, Tropical Timber 83, Tropical Timber 94
signed, but not ratified: Biodiversity, Climate Change-Kyoto Protocol, Law of the Sea

Geography - note: controls only land route from Asia to Malaysia and Singapore

People

Population: 60,609,046 (July 1999 est.)

Age structure:
0-14 years: 24% (male 7,364,411; female 7,095,428)
15-64 years: 70% (male 20,878,602; female 21,493,735)
65 years and over: 6% (male 1,664,113; female 2,112,757) (1999 est.)

Population growth rate: 0.93% (1999 est.)

Birth rate: 16.46 births/1,000 population (1999 est.)

Death rate: 7.16 deaths/1,000 population (1999 est.)

Net migration rate: 0 migrant(s)/1,000 population (1999 est.)

Sex ratio:
at birth: 1.05 male(s)/female
under 15 years: 1.04 male(s)/female
15-64 years: 0.97 male(s)/female
65 years and over: 0.79 male(s)/female
total population: 0.97 male(s)/female (1999 est.)

Infant mortality rate: 29.54 deaths/1,000 live births (1999 est.)

Life expectancy at birth:
total population: 69.21 years
male: 65.58 years
female: 73.01 years (1999 est.)

Total fertility rate: 1.82 children born/woman (1999 est.)

Nationality:
noun: Thai (singular and plural)
adjective: Thai

Ethnic groups: Thai 75%, Chinese 14%, other 11%

Religions: Buddhism 95%, Muslim 3.8%, Christianity 0.5%, Hinduism 0.1%, other 0.6% (1991)

Languages: Thai, English (secondary language of the elite), ethnic and regional dialects

Literacy:
definition: age 15 and over can read and write
total population: 93.8%
male: 96%
female: 91.6% (1995 est.)

Government

Country name:
conventional long form: Kingdom of Thailand
conventional short form: Thailand

Data code: TH

Government type: constitutional monarchy

Capital: Bangkok

Administrative divisions: 76 provinces (changwat, singular and plural); Amnat Charoen, Ang Thong, Buriram, Chachoengsao, Chai Nat, Chaiyaphum, Chanthaburi, Chiang Mai, Chiang Rai, Chon Buri, Chumphon, Kalasin, Kamphaeng Phet, Kanchanaburi, Khon Kaen, Krabi, Krung Thep Mahanakhon (Bangkok), Lampang, Lamphun, Loei, Lop Buri, Mae Hong Son, Maha Sarakham, Mukdahan, Nakhon Nayok, Nakhon Pathom, Nakhon Phanom, Nakhon Ratchasima, Nakhon Sawan, Nakhon Si Thammarat, Nan, Narathiwat, Nong Bua Lamphu, Nong Khai, Nonthaburi, Pathum Thani, Pattani, Phangnga, Phatthalung, Phayao, Phetchabun, Phetchaburi, Phichit, Phitsanulok, Phra Nakhon Si Ayutthaya, Phrae, Phuket, Prachin Buri, Prachuap Khiri Khan, Ranong, Ratchaburi, Rayong, Roi Et, Sa Kaeo, Sakon Nakhon, Samut Prakan, Samut Sakhon, Samut Songkhram, Sara Buri, Satun, Sing Buri, Sisaket, Songkhla, Sukhothai, Suphan Buri, Surat Thani, Surin, Tak, Trang, Trat, Ubon Ratchathani, Udon Thani, Uthai Thani, Uttaradit, Yala, Yasothon

Independence: 1238 (traditional founding date; never colonized)

National holiday: Birthday of His Majesty the King, 5 December (1927)

Constitution: new constitution signed by King PHUMIPHON on 11 October 1997

Legal system: based on civil law system, with influences of common law; has not accepted compulsory ICJ jurisdiction

Suffrage: 18 years of age; universal and compulsory

Executive branch:
chief of state: King PHUMIPHON Adunyadet (since 9 June 1946)
head of government: Prime Minister CHUAN Likphai (since 15 November 1997)
cabinet: Council of Ministers
note: there is also a Privy Council
elections: none; the monarch is hereditary; prime minister designated from among the members of the

House of Representatives; following a national election for the House of Representatives, the leader of the party that can organize a majority coalition usually becomes prime minister

Legislative branch: bicameral National Assembly or Rathasapha consists of the Senate or Wuthisapha (a 253-member appointed body which will be phased into a 200-member elected body starting in March 2000; members serve six-year terms) and the House of Representatives or Sapha Phuthaen Ratsadon (currently has 391 members, but will become a 500-member body after the next election; members elected by popular vote to serve four-year terms)
elections: House of Representatives - last held 17 November 1996 (next scheduled to be held by 17 November 2000, but may be held earlier)
election results: House of Representatives - percent of vote by party - NA; seats by party - NAP 125, DP 123, NDP 52, TNP 39, SAP 20, TCP 18, SP 8, LDP 4, MP 2

Judicial branch: Supreme Court (Sandika), judges appointed by the monarch

Political parties and leaders: Thai Nation Party or TNP (Chat Thai Party) [BANHAN Sinlapa-acha]; Democratic Party or DP (Prachathipat Party) [CHUAN Likphai]; New Aspiration Party or NAP (Khwamwang Mai) [Gen. CHAWALIT Yongchaiyut]; National Development Party or NDP (Chat Phattana) [KON Thappharangsi]; Phalang Dharma Party or PDP (Phalang Tham) [CHAIWAT Sinsuwong]; Social Action Party or SAP (Kitsangkhom Party) [BUNPHAN Khaewatthana]; Thai Citizen's Party or TCP (Prachakon Thai) [SAMAK Sunthonwet]; Liberal Democratic Party or LDP (Seri Tham) [PHINIT Charusombat]; Solidarity Party or SP (Ekkaphap Party) [CHAIYOT Sasomsap]; Thai Love Thai Party or TRTP (Thai Rak Thai Party) [THAKSIN Chinnawat]; Mass Party or MP [CHALERM Yoobamrung, SOPHON Petchsavang]

International organization participation: APEC, AsDB, ASEAN, CCC, CP, ESCAP, FAO, G-77, IAEA, IBRD, ICAO, ICFTU, ICRM, IDA, IFAD, IFC, IFRCS, IHO, ILO, IMF, IMO, Inmarsat, Intelsat, Interpol, IOC, IOM, ISO, ITU, NAM, OPCW, PCA, UN, UNCTAD, UNESCO, UNHCR, UNIDO, UNIKOM, UNMIBH, UNU, UPU, WCL, WFTU, WHO, WIPO, WMO, WToO, WTrO

Diplomatic representation in the US:
chief of mission: Ambassador NIT Phibunsongkhram
chancery: 1024 Wisconsin Avenue NW, Washington, DC 20007
telephone: [1] (202) 944-3600
FAX: [1] (202) 944-3611
consulate(s) general: Chicago, Los Angeles, and New York

Diplomatic representation from the US:
chief of mission: Ambassador Richard HECKLINGER
embassy: 120 Wireless Road, Bangkok
mailing address: APO AP 96546
telephone: [66] (2) 205-4000
FAX: [66] (2) 254-2990
consulate(s) general: Chiang Mai

Thailand (continued)

Flag description: five horizontal bands of red (top), white, blue (double width), white, and red

Economy - overview: After months of speculative pressure on the Thai baht, the government decided to float the currency in July 1997, the symbolic beginning of the country's current economic crisis. The crisis - which began in the country's financial sector - has spread throughout the economy. After years of rapid economic growth averaging 9% earlier this decade, the Thai economy contracted 0.4% in 1997 and shrunk another 8.5% in 1998. In the years before the crisis, Thailand ran persistent current account deficits. With the depreciation of the Thai baht and the collapse of domestic demand, however, imports have fallen off sharply - by more than 33% - and Thailand posted a trade surplus of approximately $12 billion in 1998. Foreign investment for new projects, the long-time catalyst of Thailand's economic growth, has also slowed. The CHUAN government has closely adhered to the economic recovery program prescribed by the IMF. The cooperation afforded Thailand stability in the value of its currency in the second half of 1998 and helped replenish foreign reserves. Tough measures - including passage of adequate bankruptcy and foreclosure legislation as well as privatization of state-owned companies and recapitalization of the financial sector - remain undone. Bangkok is also trying to establish a social safety net for those displaced by the current economic crisis and is working to increase the quality of Thailand's labor force.
GDP: purchasing power parity - $369 billion (1998 est.)
GDP - real growth rate: -8.5% (1998 est.)
GDP - per capita: purchasing power parity - $6,100 (1998 est.)
GDP - composition by sector:
agriculture: 12%
industry: 39%
services: 49% (1997 est.)
Population below poverty line: 13.1% (1992 est.)
Household income or consumption by percentage share:
lowest 10%: 2.5%
highest 10%: 37.1% (1992)
Inflation rate (consumer prices): 4.3% (1998 est.)
Labor force: 32.6 million (1997 est.)
Labor force - by occupation: agriculture 54%, industry 15%, services (including government) 31% (1996 est.)
Unemployment rate: 4.5% (1998 est.)
Budget:
revenues: $24 billion
expenditures: $25 billion, including capital expenditures of $8 billion (FY96/97)
Industries: tourism; textiles and garments, agricultural processing, beverages, tobacco, cement, light manufacturing, such as jewelry; electric appliances and components, computers and parts, integrated circuits, furniture, plastics; world's

second-largest tungsten producer and third-largest tin producer
Industrial production growth rate: -10% (1998)
Electricity - production: 82 billion kWh (1996)
Electricity - production by source:
fossil fuel: 91.46%
hydro: 8.54%
nuclear: 0%
other: 0% (1996)
Electricity - consumption: 82.561 billion kWh (1996)
Electricity - exports: 79 million kWh (1996)
Electricity - imports: 640 million kWh (1996)
Agriculture - products: rice, cassava (tapioca), rubber, corn, sugarcane, coconuts, soybeans
Exports: $51.6 billion (f.o.b., 1997)
Exports - commodities: manufactures 82% (computers and parts 16%), agricultural products and fisheries 14% (1997)
Exports - partners: US 19.6%, Japan 14.9%, Singapore 11%, Hong Kong 5.7%, Malaysia 4.3%, UK 3.7% (1997)
Imports: $73.5 billion (c.i.f., 1996)
Imports - commodities: capital goods 50%, intermediate goods and raw materials 22%, consumer goods 10.2%, fuels 8.7% (1997)
Imports - partners: Japan 25.6%, US 13.9%, Singapore 5%, Taiwan 4.6%, Germany 4.5%, Malaysia 4.1% (1997)
Debt - external: $90 billion (1997)
Economic aid - recipient: $1.732 billion (1995)
Currency: 1 baht (B) = 100 satang
Exchange rates: baht (B) per US$1 - 36.624 (January 1999), 41.359 (1998), 31.364 (1997), 25.343 (1996), 24.915 (1995), 25.150 (1994)
Fiscal year: 1 October - 30 September

Telephones: 1,553,200 (1994 est.)
Telephone system: service to general public adequate, but investments in technological upgrades reduced by recession; bulk of service to government activities provided by multichannel cable and microwave radio relay network
domestic: microwave radio relay and multichannel cable; domestic satellite system being developed
international: satellite earth stations - 2 Intelsat (1 Indian Ocean and 1 Pacific Ocean)
Radio broadcast stations: AM 200 (in government-controlled network), FM 100 (in government-controlled network), shortwave 0
Radios: 10.75 million (1992 est.)
Television broadcast stations: 5 (all in Bangkok; in addition, there are 131 repeaters) (1997)
Televisions: 3.3 million (1993 est.)

Railways:
total: 4,623 km
narrow gauge: 4,623 km 1.000-m gauge (99 km double track)

Highways:
total: 64,600 km
paved: 62,985 km
unpaved: 1,615 km (1996 est.)
Waterways: 3,999 km principal waterways; 3,701 km with navigable depths of 0.9 m or more throughout the year; numerous minor waterways navigable by shallow-draft native craft
Pipelines: petroleum products 67 km; natural gas 350 km
Ports and harbors: Bangkok, Laem Chabang, Pattani, Phuket, Sattahip, Si Racha, Songkhla
Merchant marine:
total: 293 ships (1,000 GRT or over) totaling 1,848,626 GRT/2,989,382 DWT
ships by type: bulk 41, cargo 135, chemical tanker 5, combination bulk 1, container 13, liquefied gas tanker 17, multifunction large-load carrier 3, oil tanker 61, passenger 1, refrigerated cargo 11, roll-on/roll-off cargo 2, short-sea passenger 1, specialized tanker 2 (1998 est.)
Airports: 107 (1998 est.)
Airports - with paved runways:
total: 56
over 3,047 m: 6
2,438 to 3,047 m: 9
1,524 to 2,437 m: 17
914 to 1,523 m: 20
under 914 m: 4 (1998 est.)
Airports - with unpaved runways:
total: 51
1,524 to 2,437 m: 1
914 to 1,523 m: 15
under 914 m: 35 (1998 est.)
Heliports: 3 (1998 est.)

Military branches: Royal Thai Army, Royal Thai Navy (includes Royal Thai Marine Corps), Royal Thai Air Force, Paramilitary Forces
Military manpower - military age: 18 years of age
Military manpower - availability:
males age 15-49: 17,486,014 (1999 est.)
Military manpower - fit for military service:
males age 15-49: 10,536,417 (1999 est.)
Military manpower - reaching military age annually:
males: 585,562 (1999 est.)
Military expenditures - dollar figure: $1.95 billion (FY97/98)
Military expenditures - percent of GDP: 2.5% (FY97/98)

Disputes - international: parts of the border with Laos are indefinite; maritime boundary with Vietnam resolved, August 1997; parts of border with Cambodia are indefinite; maritime boundary with Cambodia not clearly defined; sporadic conflict with Burma over alignment of border
Illicit drugs: a minor producer of opium, heroin, and

Thailand (continued)

marijuana; major illicit transit point for heroin en route to the international drug market from Burma and Laos; eradication efforts have reduced the area of cannabis cultivation and shifted some production to neighboring countries; opium poppy cultivation has been reduced by eradication efforts; also a drug money-laundering center; minor role in amphetamine production for regional consumption; increasing indigenous abuse of methamphetamines and heroin

Togo

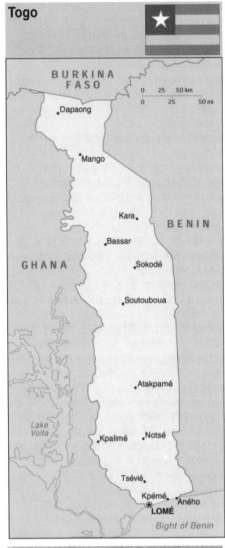

Geography

Location: Western Africa, bordering the Bight of Benin, between Benin and Ghana
Geographic coordinates: 8 00 N, 1 10 E
Map references: Africa
Area:
total: 56,790 sq km
land: 54,390 sq km
water: 2,400 sq km
Area - comparative: slightly smaller than West Virginia
Land boundaries:
total: 1,647 km
border countries: Benin 644 km, Burkina Faso 126 km, Ghana 877 km
Coastline: 56 km
Maritime claims:
exclusive economic zone: 200 nm
territorial sea: 30 nm
Climate: tropical; hot, humid in south; semiarid in north
Terrain: gently rolling savanna in north; central hills; southern plateau; low coastal plain with extensive lagoons and marshes

Elevation extremes:
lowest point: Atlantic Ocean 0 m
highest point: Pic Agou 986 m
Natural resources: phosphates, limestone, marble
Land use:
arable land: 38%
permanent crops: 7%
permanent pastures: 4%
forests and woodland: 17%
other: 34% (1993 est.)
Irrigated land: 70 sq km (1993 est.)
Natural hazards: hot, dry harmattan wind can reduce visibility in north during winter; periodic droughts
Environment - current issues: deforestation attributable to slash-and-burn agriculture and the use of wood for fuel; recent droughts affecting agriculture
Environment - international agreements:
party to: Biodiversity, Climate Change, Desertification, Endangered Species, Law of the Sea, Nuclear Test Ban, Ozone Layer Protection, Ship Pollution, Tropical Timber 83, Tropical Timber 94, Wetlands
signed, but not ratified: none of the selected agreements

People

Population: 5,081,413 (July 1999 est.)
Age structure:
0-14 years: 48% (male 1,229,026; female 1,218,956)
15-64 years: 50% (male 1,223,371; female 1,299,519)
65 years and over: 2% (male 49,890; female 60,651) (1999 est.)
Population growth rate: 3.51% (1999 est.)
Birth rate: 44.78 births/1,000 population (1999 est.)
Death rate: 9.69 deaths/1,000 population (1999 est.)
Net migration rate: 0 migrant(s)/1,000 population (1999 est.)
Sex ratio:
at birth: 1.03 male(s)/female
under 15 years: 1.01 male(s)/female
15-64 years: 0.94 male(s)/female
65 years and over: 0.82 male(s)/female
total population: 0.97 male(s)/female (1999 est.)
Infant mortality rate: 77.55 deaths/1,000 live births (1999 est.)
Life expectancy at birth:
total population: 59.25 years
male: 56.93 years
female: 61.64 years (1999 est.)
Total fertility rate: 6.53 children born/woman (1999 est.)
Nationality:
noun: Togolese (singular and plural)
adjective: Togolese
Ethnic groups: native African (37 tribes; largest and most important are Ewe, Mina, and Kabre) 99%, European and Syrian-Lebanese less than 1%
Religions: indigenous beliefs 70%, Christian 20%, Muslim 10%
Languages: French (official and the language of

Togo *(continued)*

commerce), Ewe and Mina (the two major African languages in the south), Kabye (sometimes spelled Kabiye) and Dagomba (the two major African languages in the north)

Literacy:
definition: age 15 and over can read and write
total population: 51.7%
male: 67%
female: 37% (1995 est.)

Government

Country name:
conventional long form: Togolese Republic
conventional short form: Togo
local long form: Republique Togolaise
local short form: none
former: French Togo
Data code: TO
Government type: republic under transition to multiparty democratic rule
Capital: Lome
Administrative divisions: 5 regions (regions, singular - region); De La Kara, Des Plateaux, Des Savanes, Du Centre, Maritime
Independence: 27 April 1960 (from French-administered UN trusteeship)
National holiday: Independence Day, 27 April (1960)
Constitution: multiparty draft constitution approved by High Council of the Republic 1 July 1992; adopted by public referendum 27 September 1992
Legal system: French-based court system
Suffrage: NA years of age; universal adult
Executive branch:
chief of state: President Gen. Gnassingbe EYADEMA (since 14 April 1967)
head of government: Prime Minister Kwassi KLUTSE (since August 1996)
cabinet: Council of Ministers appointed by the president and the prime minister
elections: president elected by popular vote for a five-year term; election last held 21 June 1998 (next to be held NA 2003); prime minister appointed by the president
election results: Gnassingbe EYADEMA reelected president; percent of vote - Gnassingbe EYADEMA 52.13%
Legislative branch: unicameral National Assembly (81 seats; members are elected by popular vote to serve five-year terms)
elections: last held 6 and 20 February 1994 (next to be held NA February 1999)
election results: percent of vote by party - NA; seats by party - CAR 36, RPT 35, UTD 7, UJD 2, CFN 1
note: as a result of defections from the CAR to the RPT and the merging of the UJD with the RPT, representation in the National Assembly in August 1997 was RPT 42, CAR 32, UTD 5, CFN 1, independent 1
Judicial branch: Court of Appeal or Cour d'Appel; Supreme Court or Cour Supreme
Political parties and leaders: Rally of the Togolese People or RPT [President Gen. Gnassingbe EYADEMA]; Coordination des Forces Nouvelles or CFN [Joseph KOFFIGOH]; Togolese Union for Democracy or UTD [Edem KODJO]; Action Committee for Renewal or CAR [Yao AGBOYIBOR]; Union for Democracy and Solidarity or UDS [Antoine FOLLY]; Pan-African Sociodemocrats Group or GSP, an alliance of three radical parties: CDPA, PDR, and PSP [leader NA]; Democratic Convention of African Peoples or CDPA [Leopold GNININVI]; Party for Democracy and Renewal or PDR [Zarifou AYEVA]; Pan-African Social Party or PSP [Francis AGBAGLI]; Union of Forces for Change or UFC [Gilchrist OLYMPIO (in exile), Jeane-Pierre FABRE, general secretary in Togo]; Union of Justice and Democracy or UJD [Lal TAXPANDJAN]
note: Rally of the Togolese People or RPT, led by President EYADEMA, was the only party until the formation of multiple parties was legalized 12 April 1991
International organization participation: ACCT, ACP, AfDB, CCC, ECA, ECOWAS, Entente, FAO, FZ, G-77, IBRD, ICAO, ICC, ICFTU, ICRM, IDA, IFAD, IFC, IFRCS, ILO, IMF, IMO, Intelsat, Interpol, IOC, ITU, MINURCA, MINURSO, MIPONUH, NAM, OAU, OIC, OPCW, UN, UNCTAD, UNESCO, UNIDO, UPU, WADB, WAEMU, WCL, WFTU, WHO, WIPO, WMO, WToO, WTrO
Diplomatic representation in the US:
chief of mission: Ambassador Akosita FINEANGANOFO
chancery: 2208 Massachusetts Avenue NW, Washington, DC 20008
telephone: [1] (202) 234-4212
FAX: [1] (202) 232-3190
Diplomatic representation from the US:
chief of mission: Ambassador Brenda Brown SCHOONOVER
embassy: Rue Pelletier Caventou and Rue Vauban, Lome
mailing address: B. P. 852, Lome
telephone: [228] 21 77 17, 21 29 91 through 21 29 94
FAX: [228] 21 79 52
Flag description: five equal horizontal bands of green (top and bottom) alternating with yellow; there is a white five-pointed star on a red square in the upper hoist-side corner; uses the popular pan-African colors of Ethiopia

Economy

Economy - overview: This small sub-Saharan economy is heavily dependent on both commercial and subsistence agriculture, which provides employment for 65% of the labor force. Cocoa, coffee, and cotton together generate about 30% of export earnings. Togo is self-sufficient in basic foodstuffs when harvests are normal, with occasional regional supply difficulties. In the industrial sector, phosphate mining is by far the most important activity, although it has suffered from the collapse of world phosphate prices and increased foreign competition. Togo serves as a regional commercial and trade center. The government's decade-long effort, supported by the World Bank and the IMF, to implement economic reform measures, encourage foreign investment, and bring revenues in line with expenditures has stalled. Political unrest, including private and public sector strikes throughout 1992 and 1993, jeopardized the reform program, shrunk the tax base, and disrupted vital economic activity. The 12 January 1994 devaluation of the currency by 50% provided an important impetus to renewed structural adjustment; these efforts were facilitated by the end of strife in 1994 and a return to overt political calm. Progress depends on following through on privatization, increased transparency in government accounting to accommodate increased social service outlays, and possible downsizing of the military, on which the regime has depended to stay in place. However, in late 1998 the EU suspended aid and trade preferences for Togo because of grave doubts over the conduct of the presidential elections. The World Bank also suspended its disbursements at yearend 1998 because Togo was unable to pay its arrears.

GDP: purchasing power parity - $8.2 billion (1998 est.)
GDP - real growth rate: 3.8% (1998 est.)
GDP - per capita: purchasing power parity - $1,670 (1998 est.)
GDP - composition by sector:
agriculture: 32%
industry: 23%
services: 45% (1995)
Population below poverty line: 32.3% (1987-89 est.)
Household income or consumption by percentage share:
lowest 10%: NA%
highest 10%: NA%
Inflation rate (consumer prices): 7.2% (1997)
Labor force: 1.538 million (1993 est.)
Labor force - by occupation: agriculture 65%, industry 5%, services 30% (1998 est.)
Unemployment rate: NA%
Budget:
revenues: $232 million
expenditures: $252 million, including capital expenditures of $NA (1997 est.)
Industries: phosphate mining, agricultural processing, cement; handicrafts, textiles, beverages
Industrial production growth rate: 13.6% (1995)
Electricity - production: 88 million kWh (1996)
Electricity - production by source:
fossil fuel: 93.18%
hydro: 6.82%
nuclear: 0%
other: 0% (1996)
Electricity - consumption: 408 million kWh (1996)
Electricity - exports: 0 kWh (1996)
Electricity - imports: 320 million kWh (1996)
note: imports electricity from Ghana
Agriculture - products: coffee, cocoa, cotton, yams, cassava (tapioca), corn, beans, rice, millet, sorghum; livestock; fish

Togo (continued)

Exports: $345 million (f.o.b., 1997)
Exports - commodities: cotton, phosphates, coffee, cocoa
Exports - partners: Canada 7.6%, Taiwan 7.1%, Nigeria 6.8%, South Africa 5.2% (1996 est.)
Imports: $400 million (f.o.b., 1997)
Imports - commodities: machinery and equipment, consumer goods, petroleum products
Imports - partners: Ghana 19.1%, France 10.8%, China 8.2%, Cameroon 6.8% (1996 est.)
Debt - external: $1.5 billion (1996)
Economic aid - recipient: $201.1 million (1995)
Currency: 1 Communaute Financiere Africaine franc (CFAF) = 100 centimes
Exchange rates: Communaute Financiere Africaine francs (CFAF) per US$1 - 560.01 (December 1998), 589.95 (1998), 583.67 (1997), 511.55 (1996), 499.15 (1995), 555.20 (1994)
Fiscal year: calendar year

Communications

Telephones: 47,000 (10,000 cellular telephone subscribers) (1998 est.)
Telephone system: fair system based on network of microwave radio relay routes supplemented by open-wire lines and cellular system
domestic: microwave radio relay and open-wire lines for conventional system; cellular system has capacity of 10,000 telephones
international: satellite earth stations - 1 Intelsat (Atlantic Ocean) and 1 Symphonie
Radio broadcast stations: AM 2, FM 0, shortwave 0
Radios: 795,000 (1992 est.)
Television broadcast stations: 3 (in addition, there are two repeaters) (1997)
Televisions: 24,000 (1992 est.)

Transportation

Railways:
total: 525 km (1995)
narrow gauge: 525 km 1.000-m gauge
Highways:
total: 7,520 km
paved: 2,376 km
unpaved: 5,144 km (1996 est.)
Waterways: 50 km Mono river
Ports and harbors: Kpeme, Lome
Merchant marine: none
Airports: 9 (1998 est.)
Airports - with paved runways:
total: 2
2,438 to 3,047 m: 2 (1998 est.)
Airports - with unpaved runways:
total: 7
914 to 1,523 m: 5
under 914 m: 2 (1998 est.)

Military

Military branches: Army, Navy, Air Force, Gendarmerie
Military manpower - availability:
males age 15-49: 1,102,453 (1999 est.)
Military manpower - fit for military service:
males age 15-49: 578,109 (1999 est.)
Military expenditures - dollar figure: $27 million (1996)
Military expenditures - percent of GDP: 2% (1996)

Transnational Issues

Disputes - international: none
Illicit drugs: transit hub for Nigerian heroin and cocaine traffickers

Tokelau
(territory of New Zealand)

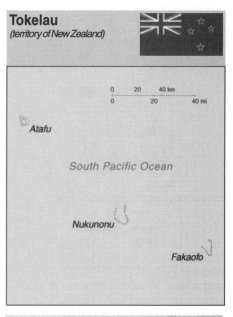

Geography

Location: Oceania, group of three islands in the South Pacific Ocean, about one-half of the way from Hawaii to New Zealand
Geographic coordinates: 9 00 S, 172 00 W
Map references: Oceania
Area:
total: 10 sq km
land: 10 sq km
water: 0 sq km
Area - comparative: about 17 times the size of The Mall in Washington, DC
Land boundaries: 0 km
Coastline: 101 km
Maritime claims:
exclusive economic zone: 200 nm
territorial sea: 12 nm
Climate: tropical; moderated by trade winds (April to November)
Terrain: low-lying coral atolls enclosing large lagoons
Elevation extremes:
lowest point: Pacific Ocean 0 m
highest point: unnamed location 5 m
Natural resources: NEGL
Land use:
arable land: 0% (soil is thin and infertile)
permanent crops: 0%
permanent pastures: 0%
forests and woodland: 0%
other: 100% (1993 est.)
Irrigated land: NA sq km
Natural hazards: lies in Pacific typhoon belt
Environment - current issues: very limited natural resources and overcrowding are contributing to emigration to New Zealand
Environment - international agreements:
party to: NA
signed, but not ratified: NA

Tokelau *(continued)*

People

Population: 1,471 (July 1999 est.)
Age structure:
0-14 years: NA
15-64 years: NA
65 years and over: NA
Population growth rate: -0.92% (1999 est.)
Birth rate: NA births/1,000 population
Death rate: NA deaths/1,000 population
Net migration rate: NA migrant(s)/1,000 population
Infant mortality rate: NA deaths/1,000 live births
Life expectancy at birth:
total population: NA
male: NA
female: NA
Total fertility rate: NA children born/woman
Nationality:
noun: Tokelauan(s)
adjective: Tokelauan
Ethnic groups: Polynesian
Religions: Congregational Christian Church 70%, Roman Catholic 28%, other 2%
note: on Atafu, all Congregational Christian Church of Samoa; on Nukunonu, all Roman Catholic; on Fakaofo, both denominations, with the Congregational Christian Church predominant
Languages: Tokelauan (a Polynesian language), English

Government

Country name:
conventional long form: none
conventional short form: Tokelau
Data code: TL
Dependency status: territory of New Zealand; note - Tokelauans are drafting a constitution, developing institutions and patterns of self-government as Tokelau moves toward free association with Wellington
Government type: NA
Capital: none; each atoll has its own administrative center
Administrative divisions: none (territory of New Zealand)
Independence: none (territory of New Zealand)
National holiday: Waitangi Day, 6 February (1840) (Treaty of Waitangi established British sovereignty over New Zealand)
Constitution: administered under the Tokelau Islands Act of 1948, as amended in 1970
Legal system: British and local statutes
Suffrage: 21 years of age; universal
Executive branch:
chief of state: Queen ELIZABETH II (since 6 February 1952); the UK and New Zealand are represented by Administrator Lindsay WATT (since NA March 1993)
head of government: Aliki Faipule FALIMATEAO (since NA 1997)
cabinet: the Council of Faipule, consisting of three elected leaders, one from each atoll; functions as a cabinet

elections: none; the monarch is hereditary; administrator appointed by the Minister of Foreign Affairs and Trade in New Zealand; the head of government is chosen from the Council of Faipule and serves a one-year term
Legislative branch: unicameral General Fono (45 seats - 15 from each of the three atolls; members chosen by each atoll's Council of Elders or Taupulega to serve three-year terms); note - the Tokelau Amendment Act of 1996 confers legislative power on the General Fono
Judicial branch: Supreme Court in New Zealand exercises civil and criminal jurisdiction
Political parties and leaders: none
International organization participation: SPC, WHO (associate)
Diplomatic representation in the US: none (territory of New Zealand)
Diplomatic representation from the US: none (territory of New Zealand)
Flag description: the flag of New Zealand is used

Economy

Economy - overview: Tokelau's small size (three villages), isolation, and lack of resources greatly restrain economic development and confine agriculture to the subsistence level. The people must rely on aid from New Zealand to maintain public services, annual aid being substantially greater than GDP. The principal sources of revenue come from sales of copra, postage stamps, souvenir coins, and handicrafts. Money is also remitted to families from relatives in New Zealand.
GDP: purchasing power parity - $1.5 million (1993 est.)
GDP - real growth rate: NA%
GDP - per capita: purchasing power parity - $1,000 (1993 est.)
GDP - composition by sector:
agriculture: NA%
industry: NA%
services: NA%
Population below poverty line: NA%
Household income or consumption by percentage share:
lowest 10%: NA%
highest 10%: NA%
Inflation rate (consumer prices): NA%
Labor force: NA
Unemployment rate: NA%
Budget:
revenues: $430,830
expenditures: $2.8 million, including capital expenditures of $37,300 (1987 est.)
Industries: small-scale enterprises for copra production, wood work, plaited craft goods; stamps, coins; fishing
Industrial production growth rate: NA%
Electricity - production: NA kWh
Electricity - production by source:
fossil fuel: NA%
hydro: NA%

nuclear: NA%
other: NA%
Electricity - consumption: NA kWh
Electricity - exports: NA kWh
Electricity - imports: NA kWh
Agriculture - products: coconuts, copra, breadfruit, papayas, bananas; pigs, poultry, goats
Exports: $98,000 (f.o.b., 1983)
Exports - commodities: stamps, copra, handicrafts
Exports - partners: NZ
Imports: $323,400 (c.i.f., 1983)
Imports - commodities: foodstuffs, building materials, fuel
Imports - partners: NZ
Debt - external: $0
Economic aid - recipient: $3.8 million (1995)
Currency: 1 New Zealand dollar (NZ$) = 100 cents
Exchange rates: New Zealand dollars (NZ$) per US$1 - 1.8560 (January 1999), 1.8629 (1998), 1.5083 (1997), 1.4543 (1996), 1.5235 (1995), 1.6844 (1994)
Fiscal year: 1 April - 31 March

Communications

Telephones: NA
Telephone system:
domestic: radiotelephone service between islands
international: radiotelephone service to Western Samoa; government-regulated telephone service (TeleTok), with three satellite earth stations, established in 1997
Radio broadcast stations: AM NA, FM NA, shortwave NA
note: each atoll has a radio broadcast station of NA type that broadcasts shipping and weather reports
Radios: 1,000 (1993 est.)
Television broadcast stations: NA (1997)
Televisions: NA

Transportation

Railways: 0 km
Highways:
total: NA km
paved: NA km
unpaved: NA km
Ports and harbors: none; offshore anchorage only
Merchant marine: none
Airports: none; lagoon landings by amphibious aircraft from Western Samoa

Military

Military - note: defense is the responsibility of New Zealand

Transnational Issues

Disputes - international: none

Tonga

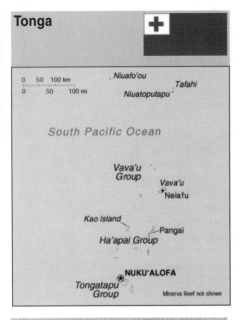

Geography

Location: Oceania, archipelago in the South Pacific Ocean, about two-thirds of the way from Hawaii to New Zealand
Geographic coordinates: 20 00 S, 175 00 W
Map references: Oceania
Area:
total: 748 sq km
land: 718 sq km
water: 30 sq km
Area - comparative: four times the size of Washington, DC
Land boundaries: 0 km
Coastline: 419 km
Maritime claims:
continental shelf: 200-m depth or to the depth of exploitation
exclusive economic zone: 200 nm
territorial sea: 12 nm
Climate: tropical; modified by trade winds; warm season (December to May), cool season (May to December)
Terrain: most islands have limestone base formed from uplifted coral formation; others have limestone overlying volcanic base
Elevation extremes:
lowest point: Pacific Ocean 0 m
highest point: unnamed location on Kao Island 1,033 m
Natural resources: fish, fertile soil
Land use:
arable land: 24%
permanent crops: 43%
permanent pastures: 6%
forests and woodland: 11%
other: 16% (1993 est.)
Irrigated land: NA sq km
Natural hazards: cyclones (October to April); earthquakes and volcanic activity on Fonuafo'ou
Environment - current issues: deforestation

results as more and more land is being cleared for agriculture and settlement; some damage to coral reefs from starfish and indiscriminate coral and shell collectors; overhunting threatens native sea turtle populations
Environment - international agreements:
party to: Biodiversity, Climate Change, Desertification, Law of the Sea, Marine Life Conservation, Nuclear Test Ban, Ozone Layer Protection, Ship Pollution
signed, but not ratified: none of the selected agreements
Geography - note: archipelago of 170 islands (36 inhabited)

People

Population: 109,082 (July 1999 est.)
Age structure:
0-14 years: NA
15-64 years: NA
65 years and over: NA
Population growth rate: 0.8% (1999 est.)
Birth rate: 25.92 births/1,000 population (1999 est.)
Death rate: 6 deaths/1,000 population (1999 est.)
Net migration rate: -1.19 migrant(s)/1,000 population (1999 est.)
Infant mortality rate: 37.93 deaths/1,000 live births (1999 est.)
Life expectancy at birth:
total population: 69.78 years
male: 67.73 years
female: 72.22 years (1999 est.)
Total fertility rate: 3.56 children born/woman (1999 est.)
Nationality:
noun: Tongan(s)
adjective: Tongan
Ethnic groups: Polynesian, Europeans about 300
Religions: Christian (Free Wesleyan Church claims over 30,000 adherents)
Languages: Tongan, English
Literacy:
definition: can read and write Tongan and/or English
total population: 98.5%
male: 98.4%
female: 98.7% (1996 est.)

Government

Country name:
conventional long form: Kingdom of Tonga
conventional short form: Tonga
former: Friendly Islands
Data code: TN
Government type: hereditary constitutional monarchy
Capital: Nuku'alofa
Administrative divisions: three island groups; Ha'apai, Tongatapu, Vava'u
Independence: 4 June 1970 (emancipation from UK protectorate)
National holiday: Emancipation Day, 4 June (1970)

Constitution: 4 November 1875, revised 1 January 1967
Legal system: based on English law
Suffrage: 21 years of age; universal
Executive branch:
chief of state: King Taufa'ahau TUPOU IV (since 16 December 1965)
head of government: Prime Minister Baron VAEA (since 22 August 1991) and Deputy Prime Minister S. Langi KAVALIKU (since 22 August 1991)
cabinet: Cabinet appointed by the monarch
note: there is also a Privy Council that consists of the monarch and the Cabinet
elections: none; the monarch is hereditary; prime minister and deputy prime minister appointed for life by the monarch
Legislative branch: unicameral Legislative Assembly or Fale Alea (30 seats - 12 reserved for cabinet ministers sitting ex officio, nine for nobles selected by the country's 33 nobles, and nine elected by popular vote; members serve three-year terms)
elections: last held 24-25 January 1996 (next to be held NA March 1999)
election results: percent of vote - NA; seats - 7 proreform, 2 traditionalist
Judicial branch: Supreme Court, judges are appointed by the monarch; Privy Council with the addition of the chief justice of the Supreme Court sits as the Court of Appeal
Political parties and leaders: Tonga People's Party [Viliami FUKOFUKA]
International organization participation: ACP, AsDB, C, ESCAP, FAO, G-77, IBRD, ICAO, ICFTU, ICRM, IDA, IFAD, IFC, IFRCS, IHO, IMF, Intelsat (nonsignatory user), Interpol, IOC, ITU, Sparteca, SPC, SPF, UNCTAD, UNESCO, UNIDO, UPU, WHO, WMO, WTrO (applicant)
Diplomatic representation in the US: Tonga does not have an embassy in the US; Ambassador Akosita FINEANGANOFO, resides in London; address: Embassy of the Kingdom of Tonga, c/o Tonga High Commission, 36 Molyneux Street, London W1H 6AB, telephone [44] (171) 724-5828, FAX [44] (171) 723-9074
consulate(s) general: San Francisco
Diplomatic representation from the US: the US does not have an embassy in Tonga; the ambassador to Fiji is accredited to Tonga
Flag description: red with a bold red cross on a white rectangle in the upper hoist-side corner

Economy

Economy - overview: The economy's base is agriculture, which contributes 32% to GDP. Squash, coconuts, bananas, and vanilla beans are the main crops, and agricultural exports make up two-thirds of total exports. The country must import a high proportion of its food, mainly from New Zealand. The industrial sector accounts for only 10% of GDP. Tourism is the primary source of hard currency earnings. The country remains dependent on sizable external aid and remittances to offset its trade deficit.

Tonga (continued)

The government is emphasizing the development of the private sector, especially the encouragement of investment.

GDP: purchasing power parity - $232 million (FY97/98 est.)

GDP - real growth rate: -1.5% (FY97/98 est.)

GDP - per capita: purchasing power parity - $2,100 (FY97/98 est.)

GDP - composition by sector:
agriculture: 32%
industry: 10%
services: 58% (1996)

Population below poverty line: NA%

Household income or consumption by percentage share:
lowest 10%: NA%
highest 10%: NA%

Inflation rate (consumer prices): 2% (1997 est.)

Labor force: 36,665 (1994)

Labor force - by occupation: agriculture 65% (1997 est.)

Unemployment rate: 11.8% (FY93/94)

Budget:
revenues: $49 million
expenditures: $120 million, including capital expenditures of $75 million (FY96/97 est.)

Industries: tourism, fishing

Industrial production growth rate: 1.9% (FY95/96)

Electricity - production: 30 million kWh (1996)

Electricity - production by source:
fossil fuel: 100%
hydro: 0%
nuclear: 0%
other: 0% (1996)

Electricity - consumption: 30 million kWh (1996)

Electricity - exports: 0 kWh (1996)

Electricity - imports: 0 kWh (1996)

Agriculture - products: squash, coconuts, copra, bananas, vanilla beans, cocoa, coffee, ginger, black pepper; fish

Exports: $11.9 million (f.o.b., FY97/98)

Exports - commodities: squash, fish, vanilla, root crops, coconut oil

Exports - partners: Japan 43%, US 19%, Canada 14%, NZ 5%, Australia 5% (1996 est.)

Imports: $78.9 million (f.o.b., FY97/98)

Imports - commodities: food products, live animals, machinery and transport equipment, manufactures, fuels, chemicals

Imports - partners: NZ 34%, Australia 16%, US 10%, UK 8%, Japan 6% (1996 est.)

Debt - external: $62 million (1998)

Economic aid - recipient: $38.8 million (1995)

Currency: 1 pa'anga (T$) = 100 seniti

Exchange rates: pa'anga (T$) per US$1 - 1.6171 (December 1998), 1.4921 (1998), 1.2635 (1997), 1.2323 (1996), 1.2709 (1995), 1.3202 (1994)

Fiscal year: 1 July - 30 June

Communications

Telephones: 6,000 (1994 est.)

Telephone system:
domestic: NA
international: satellite earth station - 1 Intelsat (Pacific Ocean)

Radio broadcast stations: AM 1, FM 0, shortwave 0

Radios: 66,000 (1993 est.)

Television broadcast stations: 1 (1997)

Televisions: 2,000 (1994 est.)

Transportation

Railways: 0 km

Highways:
total: 680 km
paved: 184 km
unpaved: 496 km (1996 est.)

Ports and harbors: Neiafu, Nuku'alofa, Pangai

Merchant marine:
total: 7 ships (1,000 GRT or over) totaling 17,754 GRT/25,969 DWT
ships by type: bulk 1, cargo 2, chemical tanker 1, liquefied gas tanker 2, roll-on/roll-off cargo 1 (1998 est.)

Airports: 6 (1998 est.)

Airports - with paved runways:
total: 1
2,438 to 3,047 m: 1 (1998 est.)

Airports - with unpaved runways:
total: 5
1,524 to 2,437 m: 1
914 to 1,523 m: 2
under 914 m: 2 (1998 est.)

Military

Military branches: Tonga Defense Services (includes, Royal Tongan Marines, Tongan Royal Guards, Maritime Force, Police); note - a new Air Wing which will be subordinate to the Defense Ministry is being developed

Military expenditures - dollar figure: $NA

Military expenditures - percent of GDP: NA%

Transnational Issues

Disputes - international: none

Trinidad and Tobago

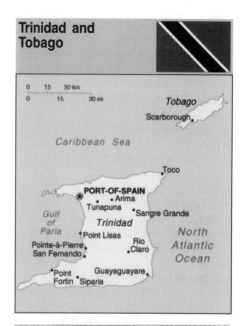

Geography

Location: Caribbean, islands between the Caribbean Sea and the North Atlantic Ocean, northeast of Venezuela

Geographic coordinates: 11 00 N, 61 00 W

Map references: Central America and the Caribbean

Area:
total: 5,130 sq km
land: 5,130 sq km
water: 0 sq km

Area - comparative: slightly smaller than Delaware

Land boundaries: 0 km

Coastline: 362 km

Maritime claims:
contiguous zone: 24 nm
continental shelf: 200 nm or to the outer edge of the continental margin
exclusive economic zone: 200 nm
territorial sea: 12 nm

Climate: tropical; rainy season (June to December)

Terrain: mostly plains with some hills and low mountains

Elevation extremes:
lowest point: Caribbean Sea 0 m
highest point: El Cerro del Aripo 940 m

Natural resources: petroleum, natural gas, asphalt

Land use:
arable land: 15%
permanent crops: 9%
permanent pastures: 2%
forests and woodland: 46%
other: 28% (1993 est.)

Irrigated land: 220 sq km (1993 est.)

Natural hazards: outside usual path of hurricanes and other tropical storms

Environment - current issues: water pollution from agricultural chemicals, industrial wastes, and raw sewage; oil pollution of beaches; deforestation; soil erosion

Trinidad and Tobago (continued)

Environment - international agreements:

party to: Biodiversity, Climate Change, Climate Change-Kyoto Protocol, Endangered Species, Hazardous Wastes, Law of the Sea, Marine Life Conservation, Nuclear Test Ban, Ozone Layer Protection, Tropical Timber 83, Tropical Timber 94, Wetlands

signed, but not ratified: none of the selected agreements

People

Population: 1,102,096 (July 1999 est.)
Age structure:
0-14 years: 27% (male 150,862; female 144,589)
15-64 years: 66% (male 377,894; female 346,375)
65 years and over: 7% (male 37,001; female 45,375) (1999 est.)
Population growth rate: -1.35% (1999 est.)
Birth rate: 14.46 births/1,000 population (1999 est.)
Death rate: 8.14 deaths/1,000 population (1999 est.)
Net migration rate: -19.8 migrant(s)/1,000 population (1999 est.)
Sex ratio:
at birth: 1.03 male(s)/female
under 15 years: 1.04 male(s)/female
15-64 years: 1.09 male(s)/female
65 years and over: 0.82 male(s)/female
total population: 1.05 male(s)/female (1999 est.)
Infant mortality rate: 18.56 deaths/1,000 live births (1999 est.)
Life expectancy at birth:
total population: 70.66 years
male: 68.19 years
female: 73.19 years (1999 est.)
Total fertility rate: 2.06 children born/woman (1999 est.)
Nationality:
noun: Trinidadian(s), Tobagonian(s)
adjective: Trinidadian, Tobagonian
Ethnic groups: black 40%, East Indian (a local term - primarily immigrants from northern India) 40.3%, mixed 14%, white 1%, Chinese 1%, other 3.7%
Religions: Roman Catholic 32.2%, Hindu 24.3%, Anglican 14.4%, other Protestant 14%, Muslim 6%, none or unknown 9.1%
Languages: English (official), Hindi, French, Spanish
Literacy:
definition: age 15 and over can read and write
total population: 97.9%
male: 98.8%
female: 97% (1995 est.)

Government

Country name:
conventional long form: Republic of Trinidad and Tobago
conventional short form: Trinidad and Tobago
Data code: TD
Government type: parliamentary democracy
Capital: Port-of-Spain

Administrative divisions: 8 counties, 3 municipalities*, and 1 ward**; Arima*, Caroni, Mayaro, Nariva, Port-of-Spain*, Saint Andrew, Saint David, Saint George, Saint Patrick, San Fernando*, Tobago**, Victoria
Independence: 31 August 1962 (from UK)
National holiday: Independence Day, 31 August (1962)
Constitution: 1 August 1976
Legal system: based on English common law; judicial review of legislative acts in the Supreme Court; has not accepted compulsory ICJ jurisdiction
Suffrage: 18 years of age; universal
Executive branch:
chief of state: President Arthur Napoleon Raymond ROBINSON (since 19 March 1997)
head of government: Prime Minister Basdeo PANDAY (since 9 November 1995)
cabinet: Cabinet appointed from among the members of Parliament
elections: president elected by an electoral college, which consists of the members of the Senate and House of Representatives, for a five-year term; election last held NA February 1997 (next to be held NA 2002); prime minister appointed from among the members of Parliament; following legislative elections, the leader of the majority party in the House of Representatives is usually appointed prime minister
election results: Arthur Napoleon Raymond ROBINSON elected president; percent of electoral college vote - 69%
Legislative branch: bicameral Parliament consists of the Senate (31 seats; members appointed by the president for a maximum term of five years) and the House of Representatives (36 seats; members are elected by popular vote to serve five-year terms)
elections: House of Representatives - last held 6 November 1995 (next to be held by December 2000)
election results: House of Representatives - percent of vote - PNM 52%, UNC 42.2%, NAR 5.2%; seats by party - PNM 15, UNC 19, NAR 1, independent 1; note - the UNC formed a coalition with the NAR
note: Tobago has a unicameral House of Assembly, with 15 members serving four-year terms
Judicial branch: Court of Appeal (judges are appointed by the president on the advice of the prime minister); Supreme Court (judges are appointed by the president on the advice of the prime minister)
Political parties and leaders: People's National Movement or PNM [Patrick MANNING]; United National Congress or UNC [Basdeo PANDAY]; National Alliance for Reconstruction or NAR [Nizam MOHAMMED]; Movement for Social Transformation or MOTION [David ABDULLAH]; National Joint Action Committee or NJAC [Makandal DAAGA]; National Development Party or NDP [Carson CHARLES]; Movement for Unity and Progress or MUP [Hulsie BHAGGAN]
International organization participation: ACP, C, Caricom, CCC, CDB, ECLAC, FAO, G-24, G-77, IADB, IBRD, ICAO, ICFTU, ICRM, IDA, IFAD, IFC,

IFRCS, IHO, ILO, IMF, IMO, Intelsat, Interpol, IOC, ISO, ITU, LAES, NAM, OAS, OPANAL, OPCW, UN, UNCTAD, UNESCO, UNIDO, UNU, UPU, WFTU, WHO, WIPO, WMO, WTrO
Diplomatic representation in the US:
chief of mission: Ambassador Michael A. ARNEAUD
chancery: 1708 Massachusetts Avenue NW, Washington, DC 20036
telephone: [1] (202) 467-6490
FAX: [1] (202) 785-3130
consulate(s) general: Miami and New York
Diplomatic representation from the US:
chief of mission: Ambassador Edward E. SHUMAKER, III
embassy: 15 Queen's Park West, Port-of-Spain
mailing address: P. O. Box 752, Port-of-Spain
telephone: [1] (809) 622-6372 through 6376, 6176
FAX: [1] (809) 628-5462
Flag description: red with a white-edged black diagonal band from the upper hoist side

Economy

Economy - overview: Trinidad and Tobago has earned a reputation as an excellent investment site for international businesses. Successful economic reforms were implemented in 1995, and foreign investment and trade are flourishing. Unemployment - a main cause of the country's socioeconomic problems - is high, but has decreased to its lowest point in six years. An investment boom in the energy sector led to a surge in imports in 1997. The resulting trade deficit is expected to return to a surplus once construction is completed and the plants come on line. The petrochemical sector has spurred growth in other related sectors, reinforcing the government's commitment to economic diversification. Tourism is a major foreign exchange earner, with 260,000 arrivals in 1995, 80% from Europe.
GDP: purchasing power parity - $8.85 billion (1998 est.)
GDP - real growth rate: 4.3% (1998 est.)
GDP - per capita: purchasing power parity - $8,000 (1998 est.)
GDP - composition by sector:
agriculture: 2.2%
industry: 44%
services: 53.8% (1997 est.)
Population below poverty line: 21% (1992 est.)
Household income or consumption by percentage share:
lowest 10%: NA%
highest 10%: NA%
Inflation rate (consumer prices): 3.7% (1997)
Labor force: 541,000 (1997 est.)
Labor force - by occupation: construction and utilities 12.4%, manufacturing, mining, and quarrying 14%, agriculture 9.5%, services 64.1% (1997 est.)
Unemployment rate: 14% (June 1998)
Budget:
revenues: $1.59 billion
expenditures: $1.54 billion, including capital expenditures of $165.8 million (1997)

Trinidad and Tobago *(continued)*

Industries: petroleum, chemicals, tourism, food processing, cement, beverage, cotton textiles
Industrial production growth rate: 7.5% (1995)
Electricity - production: 4 billion kWh (1996)
Electricity - production by source:
fossil fuel: 100%
hydro: 0%
nuclear: 0%
other: 0% (1996)
Electricity - consumption: 4 billion kWh (1996)
Electricity - exports: 0 kWh (1996)
Electricity - imports: 0 kWh (1996)
Agriculture - products: cocoa, sugarcane, rice, citrus, coffee, vegetables; poultry
Exports: $2.4 billion (f.o.b., 1997)
Exports - commodities: petroleum and petroleum products, chemicals, steel products, fertilizer, sugar, cocoa, coffee, citrus, flowers
Exports - partners: US 39.7%, Caricom countries 24.5%, Latin America 10.3%, EU 8.2% (1997)
Imports: $3.3 billion (c.i.f., 1997)
Imports - commodities: machinery, transportation equipment, manufactured goods, food, live animals
Imports - partners: US 52.2%, Latin America 16.5%, EU 13.8%, Japan 3.6% (1997)
Debt - external: $2.8 billion (1997 est.)
Economic aid - recipient: $121.4 million (1995)
Currency: 1 Trinidad and Tobago dollar (TT$) = 100 cents
Exchange rates: Trinidad and Tobago dollars (TT$) per US$1 - 6.2761 (January 1999), 6.2840 (1998), 6.2517 (1997), 6.0051 (1996), 5.9478 (1995), 5.9249 (1994)
Fiscal year: 1 October-30 September

Communications

Telephones: 170,000 (1992 est.)
Telephone system: excellent international service; good local service
domestic: NA
international: satellite earth station - 1 Intelsat (Atlantic Ocean); tropospheric scatter to Barbados and Guyana
Radio broadcast stations: AM 1, FM 10, shortwave 0
Radios: 700,000 (1993 est.)
Television broadcast stations: 4 (1997)
Televisions: 400,000 (1992 est.)

Transportation

Railways: minimal agricultural railroad system near San Fernando; railway service was discontinued in 1968
Highways:
total: 8,320 km
paved: 4,252 km
unpaved: 4,068 km (1996 est.)
Pipelines: crude oil 1,032 km; petroleum products 19 km; natural gas 904 km
Ports and harbors: Pointe-a-Pierre, Point Fortin, Point Lisas, Port-of-Spain, Scarborough, Tembladora

Merchant marine:
total: 1 cargo ship (1,000 GRT or over) totaling 1,336 GRT/2,567 DWT (1998 est.)
Airports: 6 (1998 est.)
Airports - with paved runways:
total: 3
over 3,047 m: 1
2,438 to 3,047 m: 1
1,524 to 2,437 m: 1 (1998 est.)
Airports - with unpaved runways:
total: 3
914 to 1,523 m: 1
under 914 m: 2 (1998 est.)

Military

Military branches: Trinidad and Tobago Defense Force (includes Ground Forces, Coast Guard, and Air Wing), Trinidad and Tobago Police Service
Military manpower - availability:
males age 15-49: 312,870 (1999 est.)
Military manpower - fit for military service:
males age 15-49: 223,200 (1999 est.)
Military expenditures - dollar figure: $83 million (1994)
Military expenditures - percent of GDP: NA%

Transnational Issues

Disputes - international: none
Illicit drugs: transshipment point for South American drugs destined for the US and Europe; producer of cannabis

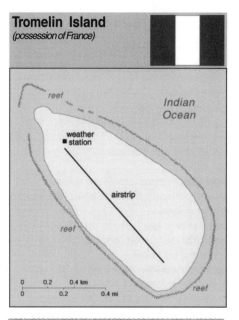

Tromelin Island
(possession of France)

Geography

Location: Southern Africa, island in the Indian Ocean, east of Madagascar
Geographic coordinates: 15 52 S, 54 25 E
Map references: Africa
Area:
total: 1 sq km
land: 1 sq km
water: 0 sq km
Area - comparative: about 1.7 times the size of The Mall in Washington, DC
Land boundaries: 0 km
Coastline: 3.7 km
Maritime claims:
contiguous zone: 12 nm
continental shelf: 200-m depth or to the depth of exploitation
exclusive economic zone: 200 nm
territorial sea: 12 nm
Climate: tropical
Terrain: sandy
Elevation extremes:
lowest point: Indian Ocean 0 m
highest point: unnamed location 7 m
Natural resources: fish
Land use:
arable land: 0%
permanent crops: 0%
permanent pastures: 0%
forests and woodland: 0%
other: 100% (scattered bushes)
Irrigated land: 0 sq km (1993)
Natural hazards: NA
Environment - current issues: NA
Environment - international agreements:
party to: NA
signed, but not ratified: NA
Geography - note: climatologically important location for forecasting cyclones; wildlife sanctuary

Tromelin Island *(continued)*

People

Population: uninhabited

Government

Country name:
conventional long form: none
conventional short form: Tromelin Island
local long form: none
local short form: Ile Tromelin
Data code: TE
Dependency status: possession of France; administered by a high commissioner of the Republic, resident in Reunion
Legal system: NA
Diplomatic representation in the US: none (possession of France)
Diplomatic representation from the US: none (possession of France)
Flag description: the flag of France is used

Economy

Economy - overview: no economic activity

Communications

Communications - note: important meteorological station

Transportation

Ports and harbors: none; offshore anchorage only
Airports: 1 (1998 est.)
Airports - with unpaved runways:
total: 1
under 914 m: 1 (1998 est.)

Military

Military - note: defense is the responsibility of France

Transnational Issues

Disputes - international: claimed by Madagascar and Mauritius

---

Tunisia

Geography

Location: Northern Africa, bordering the Mediterranean Sea, between Algeria and Libya
Geographic coordinates: 34 00 N, 9 00 E
Map references: Africa
Area:
total: 163,610 sq km
land: 155,360 sq km
water: 8,250 sq km
Area - comparative: slightly larger than Georgia
Land boundaries:
total: 1,424 km
border countries: Algeria 965 km, Libya 459 km
Coastline: 1,148 km
Maritime claims:
contiguous zone: 24 nm
territorial sea: 12 nm
Climate: temperate in north with mild, rainy winters and hot, dry summers; desert in south
Terrain: mountains in north; hot, dry central plain; semiarid south merges into the Sahara
Elevation extremes:
lowest point: Shatt al Gharsah -17 m
highest point: Jabal ash Shanabi 1,544 m

Natural resources: petroleum, phosphates, iron ore, lead, zinc, salt
Land use:
arable land: 19%
permanent crops: 13%
permanent pastures: 20%
forests and woodland: 4%
other: 44% (1993 est.)
Irrigated land: 3,850 sq km (1993 est.)
Natural hazards: NA
Environment - current issues: toxic and hazardous waste disposal is ineffective and presents human health risks; water pollution from raw sewage; limited natural fresh water resources; deforestation; overgrazing; soil erosion; desertification
Environment - international agreements:
party to: Biodiversity, Climate Change, Desertification, Endangered Species, Environmental Modification, Hazardous Wastes, Law of the Sea, Marine Dumping, Nuclear Test Ban, Ozone Layer Protection, Ship Pollution, Wetlands
signed, but not ratified: Marine Life Conservation
Geography - note: strategic location in central Mediterranean

People

Population: 9,513,603 (July 1999 est.)
Age structure:
0-14 years: 31% (male 1,513,296; female 1,417,166)
15-64 years: 63% (male 3,006,029; female 3,018,411)
65 years and over: 6% (male 283,026; female 275,675) (1999 est.)
Population growth rate: 1.39% (1999 est.)
Birth rate: 19.72 births/1,000 population (1999 est.)
Death rate: 5.05 deaths/1,000 population (1999 est.)
Net migration rate: -0.74 migrant(s)/1,000 population (1999 est.)
Sex ratio:
at birth: 1.08 male(s)/female
under 15 years: 1.07 male(s)/female
15-64 years: 1 male(s)/female
65 years and over: 1.03 male(s)/female
total population: 1.02 male(s)/female (1999 est.)
Infant mortality rate: 31.38 deaths/1,000 live births (1999 est.)
Life expectancy at birth:
total population: 73.35 years
male: 71.95 years
female: 74.86 years (1999 est.)
Total fertility rate: 2.38 children born/woman (1999 est.)
Nationality:
noun: Tunisian(s)
adjective: Tunisian
Ethnic groups: Arab 98%, European 1%, Jewish and other 1%
Religions: Muslim 98%, Christian 1%, Jewish and other 1%
Languages: Arabic (official and one of the languages of commerce), French (commerce)

Tunisia *(continued)*

Literacy:
definition: age 15 and over can read and write
total population: 66.7%
male: 78.6%
female: 54.6% (1995 est.)

Government

Country name:
conventional long form: Republic of Tunisia
conventional short form: Tunisia
local long form: Al Jumhuriyah at Tunisiyah
local short form: Tunis
Data code: TS
Government type: republic
Capital: Tunis
Administrative divisions: 23 governorates; Al Kaf, Al Mahdiyah, Al Munastir, Al Qasrayn, Al Qayrawan, Aryanah, Bajah, Banzart, Bin 'Arus, Jundubah, Madanin, Nabul, Qabis, Qafsah, Qibili, Safaqis, Sidi Bu Zayd, Silyanah, Susah, Tatawin, Tawzar, Tunis, Zaghwan
Independence: 20 March 1956 (from France)
National holiday: National Day, 20 March (1956)
Constitution: 1 June 1959; amended 12 July 1988
Legal system: based on French civil law system and Islamic law; some judicial review of legislative acts in the Supreme Court in joint session
Suffrage: 20 years of age; universal
Executive branch:
chief of state: President Zine El Abidine BEN ALI (since 7 November 1987)
head of government: Prime Minister Hamed KAROUI (since 26 September 1989)
cabinet: Council of Ministers appointed by the president
elections: president elected by popular vote for a five-year term; election last held 20 March 1994 (next to be held NA 1999); prime minister appointed by the president
election results: President Zine El Abidine BEN ALI reelected without opposition; percent of vote - Zine El Abidine BEN ALI 99%
Legislative branch: unicameral Chamber of Deputies or Majlis al-Nuwaab (163 seats; members elected by popular vote to serve five-year terms)
elections: last held 20 March 1994 (next to be held NA 1999)
election results: percent of vote by party - RCD 97.7%, MDS 1.0%, others 1.3%; seats by party - RCD 144, MDS 10, others 9; note - the government changed the electoral code to guarantee that the opposition won seats
Judicial branch: Court of Cassation (Cour de Cassation)
Political parties and leaders: Constitutional Democratic Rally Party or RCD [President BEN ALI (official ruling party)]; Movement of Democratic Socialists or MDS [leader NA]; five other political parties are legal, including the Communist Party
Political pressure groups and leaders: the Islamic fundamentalist party, Al Nahda (Renaissance), is outlawed

International organization participation: ABEDA, ACCT, AfDB, AFESD, AL, AMF, AMU, BSEC (observer), CCC, ECA, FAO, G-77, IAEA, IBRD, ICAO, ICC, ICFTU, ICRM, IDA, IDB, IFAD, IFC, IFRCS, IHO, ILO, IMF, IMO, Inmarsat, Intelsat, Interpol, IOC, IOM (observer), ISO, ITU, MINURCA, MINURSO, MIPONUH, NAM, OAS (observer), OAU, OIC, OPCW, OSCE (partner), UN, UNCTAD, UNESCO, UNHCR, UNIDO, UNMIBH, UPU, WFTU, WHO, WIPO, WMO, WToO, WTrO
Diplomatic representation in the US:
chief of mission: Ambassador Noureddine MEJDOUB
chancery: 1515 Massachusetts Avenue NW, Washington, DC 20005
telephone: [1] (202) 862-1850
Diplomatic representation from the US:
chief of mission: Ambassador Robin L. RAPHEL
embassy: 144 Avenue de la Liberte, 1002 Tunis-Belvedere
mailing address: use embassy street address
telephone: [216] (1) 782-566
FAX: [216] (1) 789-719
Flag description: red with a white disk in the center bearing a red crescent nearly encircling a red five-pointed star; the crescent and star are traditional symbols of Islam

Economy

Economy - overview: Tunisia has a diverse economy, with important agricultural, mining, energy, tourism, and manufacturing sectors. Governmental control of economic affairs while still heavy has gradually lessened over the past decade with increasing privatization, simplification of the tax structure, and a prudent approach to debt. Real growth averaged 4.0% in 1993-97 and reached 5.0% in 1998. Inflation has been moderate. Growth in tourism and increased trade have been key elements in this steady growth. Tunisia's association agreement with the European Union entered into force on 1 March 1998, the first such accord between the EU and Mediterranean countries to be activated. Under the agreement Tunisia will gradually remove barriers to trade with the EU over the next decade. Broader privatization, further liberalization of the investment code to increase foreign investment, and improvements in government efficiency are among the challenges for the future.
GDP: purchasing power parity - $49 billion (1998 est.)
GDP - real growth rate: 5% (1998 est.)
GDP - per capita: purchasing power parity - $5,200 (1998 est.)
GDP - composition by sector:
agriculture: 14%
industry: 28%
services: 58% (1996 est.)
Population below poverty line: 14.1% (1990 est.)
Household income or consumption by percentage share:
lowest 10%: 2.3%
highest 10%: 30.7% (1990)

Inflation rate (consumer prices): 3.3% (1998 est.)
Labor force: 3.3 million (1995 est.)
note: shortage of skilled labor
Labor force - by occupation: services 55%, industry 23%, agriculture 22% (1995 est.)
Unemployment rate: 15.6% (1998 est.)
Budget:
revenues: $5.8 billion
expenditures: $6.5 billion, including capital expenditures to $1.4 billion (1998 est.)
Industries: petroleum, mining (particularly phosphate and iron ore), tourism, textiles, footwear, food, beverages
Industrial production growth rate: 4.2% (1997 est.)
Electricity - production: 7.535 billion kWh (1996)
Electricity - production by source:
fossil fuel: 99.54%
hydro: 0.46%
nuclear: 0%
other: 0% (1996)
Electricity - consumption: 7.616 billion kWh (1996)
Electricity - exports: 0 kWh (1996)
Electricity - imports: 81 million kWh (1996)
Agriculture - products: olives, dates, oranges, almonds, grain, sugar beets, grapes; poultry, beef, dairy products
Exports: $5.4 billion (f.o.b., 1997 est.)
Exports - commodities: hydrocarbons, textiles, agricultural products, phosphates and chemicals
Exports - partners: EU 80%, North African countries 6%, Asia 4%, US 1% (1996)
Imports: $7.9 billion (c.i.f., 1997 est.)
Imports - commodities: industrial goods and equipment 57%, hydrocarbons 13%, food 12%, consumer goods
Imports - partners: EU countries 80%, North African countries 5.5%, Asia 5.5%, US 5% (1996)
Debt - external: $12.1 billion (1998 est.)
Economic aid - recipient: $933.2 million (1995); note - ODA, $90 million (1998 est.)
Currency: 1 Tunisian dinar (TD) = 1,000 millimes
Exchange rates: Tunisian dinars (TD) per US$1 - 1.1027 (December 1998), 1.1393 (1998), 1.1059 (1997), 0.9734 (1996), 0.9458 (1995), 1.0116 (1994)
Fiscal year: calendar year

Communications

Telephones: 560,000 (1996 est.); 3,185 cellular telephone subscribers (1998 est.)
Telephone system: the system is above the African average and is continuing to be upgraded; key centers are Sfax, Sousse, Bizerte, and Tunis; Internet access is available through two private service providers licensed by the government
domestic: trunk facilities consist of open-wire lines, coaxial cable, and microwave radio relay
international: 5 submarine cables; satellite earth stations - 1 Intelsat (Atlantic Ocean) and 1 Arabsat with back-up control station; coaxial cable and microwave radio relay to Algeria and Libya; participant in Medarabtel

Tunisia (continued)

Radio broadcast stations: AM 7, FM 8, shortwave 1 (1998 est.)
Radios: 1.7 million (1998 est.)
Television broadcast stations: 19 (these are network stations; there are some additional stations of low power) (1997)
Televisions: 650,000 (1998 est.)

Transportation

Railways:
total: 2,260 km
standard gauge: 492 km 1.435-m gauge
narrow gauge: 1,758 km 1.000-m gauge
dual gauge: 10 km 1.000-m and 1.435-m gauges (three rails) (1993 est.)
Highways:
total: 23,100 km
paved: 18,226 km
unpaved: 4,874 km (1996 est.)
Pipelines: crude oil 797 km; petroleum products 86 km; natural gas 742 km
Ports and harbors: Bizerte, Gabes, La Goulette, Sfax, Sousse, Tunis, Zarzis
Merchant marine:
total: 20 ships (1,000 GRT or over) totaling 188,345 GRT/215,749 DWT
ships by type: bulk 4, cargo 5, chemical tanker 3, liquefied gas tanker 1, oil tanker 3, short-sea passenger 3, specialized tanker 1 (1998 est.)
Airports: 32 (1998 est.)
Airports - with paved runways:
total: 14
over 3,047 m: 3
2,438 to 3,047 m: 5
1,524 to 2,437 m: 3
914 to 1,523 m: 3 (1998 est.)
Airports - with unpaved runways:
total: 18
2,438 to 3,047 m: 1
1,524 to 2,437 m: 2
914 to 1,523 m: 8
under 914 m: 7 (1998 est.)

Military

Military branches: Army, Navy, Air Force, paramilitary forces, National Guard
Military manpower - military age: 20 years of age
Military manpower - availability:
males age 15-49: 2,601,928 (1999 est.)
Military manpower - fit for military service:
males age 15-49: 1,486,964 (1999 est.)
Military manpower - reaching military age annually:
males: 99,597 (1999 est.)
Military expenditures - dollar figure: $356 million (1999)
Military expenditures - percent of GDP: 1.5% (1999)

Transnational Issues

Disputes - international: maritime boundary dispute with Libya; Malta and Tunisia are discussing the commercial exploitation of the continental shelf between their countries, particularly for oil exploration

Turkey

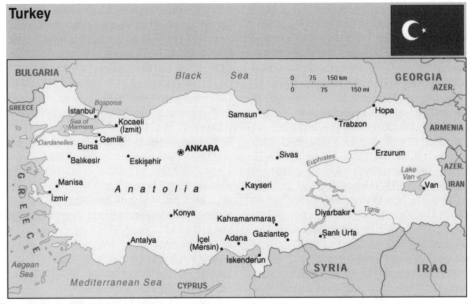

Geography

Location: southwestern Asia (that part west of the Bosporus is sometimes included with Europe), bordering the Black Sea, between Bulgaria and Georgia, and bordering the Aegean Sea and the Mediterranean Sea, between Greece and Syria
Geographic coordinates: 39 00 N, 35 00 E
Map references: Middle East
Area:
total: 780,580 sq km
land: 770,760 sq km
water: 9,820 sq km
Area - comparative: slightly larger than Texas
Land boundaries:
total: 2,627 km
border countries: Armenia 268 km, Azerbaijan 9 km, Bulgaria 240 km, Georgia 252 km, Greece 206 km, Iran 499 km, Iraq 331 km, Syria 822 km
Coastline: 7,200 km
Maritime claims:
exclusive economic zone: in Black Sea only: to the maritime boundary agreed upon with the former USSR
territorial sea: 6 nm in the Aegean Sea; 12 nm in Black Sea and in Mediterranean Sea
Climate: temperate; hot, dry summers with mild, wet winters; harsher in interior
Terrain: mostly mountains; narrow coastal plain; high central plateau (Anatolia)
Elevation extremes:
lowest point: Mediterranean Sea 0 m
highest point: Mount Ararat 5,166 m
Natural resources: antimony, coal, chromium, mercury, copper, borate, sulfur, iron ore
Land use:
arable land: 32%
permanent crops: 4%
permanent pastures: 16%
forests and woodland: 26%
other: 22% (1993 est.)
Irrigated land: 36,740 sq km (1993 est.)

Natural hazards: very severe earthquakes, especially in northern Turkey, along an arc extending from the Sea of Marmara to Lake Van
Environment - current issues: water pollution from dumping of chemicals and detergents; air pollution, particularly in urban areas; deforestation; concern for oil spills from increasing Bosporus ship traffic
Environment - international agreements:
party to: Air Pollution, Antarctic Treaty, Biodiversity, Desertification, Hazardous Wastes, Nuclear Test Ban, Ozone Layer Protection, Ship Pollution, Wetlands
signed, but not ratified: Antarctic-Environmental Protocol, Environmental Modification
Geography - note: strategic location controlling the Turkish Straits (Bosporus, Sea of Marmara, Dardanelles) that link Black and Aegean Seas

People

Population: 65,599,206 (July 1999 est.)
Age structure:
0-14 years: 30% (male 10,148,457; female 9,781,452)
15-64 years: 64% (male 21,255,506; female 20,560,070)
65 years and over: 6% (male 1,775,164; female 2,078,557) (1999 est.)
Population growth rate: 1.57% (1999 est.)
Birth rate: 20.92 births/1,000 population (1999 est.)
Death rate: 5.27 deaths/1,000 population (1999 est.)
Net migration rate: 0 migrant(s)/1,000 population (1999 est.)
Sex ratio:
at birth: 1.05 male(s)/female
under 15 years: 1.04 male(s)/female
15-64 years: 1.03 male(s)/female
65 years and over: 0.85 male(s)/female
total population: 1.02 male(s)/female (1999 est.)
Infant mortality rate: 35.81 deaths/1,000 live births (1999 est.)
Life expectancy at birth:
total population: 73.29 years

male: 70.81 years
female: 75.88 years (1999 est.)
Total fertility rate: 2.41 children born/woman (1999 est.)
Nationality:
noun: Turk(s)
adjective: Turkish
Ethnic groups: Turkish 80%, Kurdish 20%
Religions: Muslim 99.8% (mostly Sunni), other 0.2% (Christian and Jews)
Languages: Turkish (official), Kurdish, Arabic
Literacy:
definition: age 15 and over can read and write
total population: 82.3%
male: 91.7%
female: 72.4% (1995 est.)

Government

Country name:
conventional long form: Republic of Turkey
conventional short form: Turkey
local long form: Turkiye Cumhuriyeti
local short form: Turkiye
Data code: TU
Government type: republican parliamentary democracy
Capital: Ankara
Administrative divisions: 80 provinces (iller, singular - il); Adana, Adiyaman, Afyon, Agri, Aksaray, Amasya, Ankara, Antalya, Ardahan, Artvin, Aydin, Balikesir, Bartin, Batman, Bayburt, Bilecik, Bingol, Bitlis, Bolu, Burdur, Bursa, Canakkale, Cankiri, Corum, Denizli, Diyarbakir, Edirne, Elazig, Erzincan, Erzurum, Eskisehir, Gazi Antep, Giresun, Gumushane, Hakkari, Hatay, Icel, Igdir, Isparta, Istanbul, Izmir, Kahraman Maras, Karabuk, Karaman, Kars, Kastamonu, Kayseri, Kilis, Kirikkale, Kirklareli, Kirsehir, Kocaeli, Konya, Kutahya, Malatya, Manisa, Mardin, Mugla, Mus, Nevsehir, Nigde, Ordu, Osmaniye, Rize, Sakarya, Samsun, Sanli Urfa, Siirt, Sinop, Sirnak, Sivas, Tekirdag, Tokat, Trabzon, Tunceli, Usak, Van, Yalova, Yozgat, Zonguldak
note: Karabuk, Kilis, Osmaniye and Yalova are the four newest provinces; the US Board on Geographic Names is awaiting an official Turkish administrative map for verification of the boundaries
Independence: 29 October 1923 (successor state to the Ottoman Empire)
National holiday: Anniversary of the Declaration of the Republic, 29 October (1923)
Constitution: 7 November 1982
Legal system: derived from various European continental legal systems; accepts compulsory ICJ jurisdiction, with reservations
Suffrage: 18 years of age; universal
Executive branch:
chief of state: President Suleyman DEMIREL (since 16 May 1993)
head of government: Prime Minister Bulent ECEVIT (since 11 January 1999)
cabinet: Council of Ministers appointed by the president on the nomination of the prime minister

Turkey (continued)

note: there is also a National Security Council that serves as an advisory body to the president and the cabinet

elections: president elected by the National Assembly for a seven-year term; election last held 16 May 1993 (next scheduled to be held NA May 2000); prime minister and deputy prime minister appointed by the president

election results: Suleyman DEMIREL elected president; percent of National Assembly vote - 54%

Legislative branch: unicameral Grand National Assembly of Turkey or Turkiye Buyuk Millet Meclisi (550 seats; members are elected by popular vote to serve five-year terms)

elections: last held 24 December 1995 (next to be held 18 April 1999)

election results: percent of vote by party - RP 21.38%, DYP 19.18%, ANAP 19.65%, DSP 14.64%, CHP 10.71%, independent 0.48%; seats by party - RP 158, DYP 135, ANAP 133, DSP 75, CHP 49; note - seats held by various parties are subject to change due to defections, creation of new parties, and ouster or death of sitting deputies; seating by party as of 1 January 1999: FP 144, ANAP 137, DYP 97, DSP 61, CHP 55, DTP 12, BBP 8, MHP 3, DP 1, DEPAR 1, independents 20, vacant 11

Judicial branch: Constitutional Court, judges appointed by the president; Court of Appeals, judges are elected by the Supreme Council of Judges and Prosecutors

Political parties and leaders: Motherland Party or ANAP [Mesut YILMAZ]; Democratic Left Party or DSP [Bulent ECEVIT]; True Path Party or DYP [Tansu CILLER]; Nationalist Action Party or MHP [Devlet BAHCELI]; Republican People's Party or CHP [Deniz BAYKAL]; Workers' Party or IP [Dogu PERINCEK]; Nation Party or MP [Aykut EDIBALI]; Democratic Party or DP [Korkut OZAL]; Grand Unity Party or BBP [Muhsin YAZICIOGLU]; Rebirth Party or YDP [Hasan Celal GUZEL]; People's Democracy Party or HADEP [Murat BOZLAK]; Main Path Party or ANAYOL [Gurcan BASER]; Democratic Target Party or DHP [Abdulkadir Yasar TURK]; Liberal Democratic Party or LDP [Besim TIBUK]; New Democracy Movement or YDH [Huseyin ERGUN]; Labor Party or EP [Ihsan CARALAN]; Democracy and Peace Party or DBP [Refik KARAKOC]; Freedom and Solidarity Party or ODP [Ufuk URAS]; Peace Party or BP [Mehmet ETI]; Democratic Mass Party or DKP [Serafettin ELCI]; Democratic Turkey Party or DTP [Husamettin CINDORUK]; Virtue Party or FP [Recai KUTAN]; Changing Turkey Party or DEPAR [Gokhan CAPOGLU]; Shining Turkey Party or ATP [Tugrul TURKES]; National Unity Party or UBP [Fehmi KURAL]; My Turkey Party or TP [Durmus Ali EKER]; Socialist Power Party or SIP [leader NA]

note: Welfare Party or RP [Necmettin ERBAKAN] was officially outlawed on 22 February 1998

Political pressure groups and leaders: Turkish Confederation of Labor or Turk-Is [Bayram MERAL]; Confederation of Revolutionary Workers Unions or DISK [Ridvan BUDAK]; Moral Rights Workers Union or Hak-Is [Salim USLU]; Turkish Industrialists' and Businessmen's Association or TUSIAD [Muharrem KAYHAN]; Turkish Union of Chambers of Commerce and Commodity Exchanges or TOBB [Fuat MIRAS]; Turkish Confederation of Employers' Unions or TISK [Refik BAYDUR]; Independent Industrialists and Businessmen's Association or MUSIAD [Erol YARAR]

International organization participation: AsDB, BIS, BSEC, CCC, CE, CERN (observer), EAPC, EBRD, ECE, ECO, ESCAP, FAO, IAEA, IBRD, ICAO, ICC, ICFTU, ICRM, IDA, IDB, IEA, IFAD, IFC, IFRCS, IHO, ILO, IMF, IMO, Intelsat, Interpol, IOC, IOM (observer), ISO, ITU, NATO, NEA, OECD, OIC, OPCW, OSCE, PCA, UN, UNCTAD, UNESCO, UNHCR, UNIDO, UNIKOM, UNMIBH, UNOMIG, UNPREDEP, UNRWA, UPU, WEU (associate), WFTU, WHO, WIPO, WMO, WToO, WTrO

Diplomatic representation in the US:
chief of mission: Ambassador Baki ILKIN
chancery: 1714 Massachusetts Avenue NW, Washington, DC 20036
telephone: [1] (202) 659-8200
consulate(s) general: Chicago, Houston, Los Angeles, and New York

Diplomatic representation from the US:
chief of mission: Ambassador Mark R. PARRIS
embassy: 110 Ataturk Boulevard, Ankara
mailing address: PSC 93, Box 5000, APO AE 09823
telephone: [90] (312) 468-6110
FAX: [90] (312) 467-0019
consulate(s) general: Istanbul
consulate(s): Adana

Flag description: red with a vertical white crescent (the closed portion is toward the hoist side) and white five-pointed star centered just outside the crescent opening

Economy

Economy - overview: Turkey has a dynamic economy that is a complex mix of modern industry and commerce along with traditional village agriculture and crafts. It has a strong and rapidly growing private sector, yet the state still plays a major role in basic industry, banking, transport, and communication. Its most important industry - and largest exporter - is textiles and clothing, which is almost entirely in private hands. The economic situation in recent years has been marked by rapid growth coupled with partial success in implementing structural reform measures. Inflation declined to 70% in 1998, down from 99% in 1997, but the public sector fiscal deficit probably remained near 10% of GDP - due in large part to interest payments which accounted for 42% of central government spending in 1998. The government enacted a new tax law and speeded up privatization in 1998 but made no progress on badly needed social security reform. Ankara is trying to increase trade with other countries in the region yet most of Turkey's trade is still with OECD countries. Despite the implementation in January 1996 of a customs union with the EU, foreign direct investment in the country remains low - about $1 billion annually - perhaps because potential investors are concerned about still-high inflation and the unsettled political situation. Economic growth will remain about the same in 1999; inflation should decline further.

GDP: purchasing power parity - $425.4 billion (1998 est.)

GDP - real growth rate: 2.8% (1998 est.)

GDP - per capita: purchasing power parity - $6,600 (1998 est.)

GDP - composition by sector:
agriculture: 14.4%
industry: 28.7%
services: 56.9% (1998)

Population below poverty line: NA%

Household income or consumption by percentage share:
lowest 10%: NA%
highest 10%: NA%

Inflation rate (consumer prices): 70% (1998)

Labor force: 22.7 million (April 1998)

note: about 1.5 million Turks work abroad (1994)

Labor force - by occupation: agriculture 42.5%, services 34.5%, industry 23% (1996)

Unemployment rate: 10% (1998 est.)

Budget:
revenues: $44.4 billion
expenditures: $58.5 billion, including capital expenditures of $3.7 billion (1998)

Industries: textiles, food processing, autos, mining (coal, chromite, copper, boron), steel, petroleum, construction, lumber, paper

Industrial production growth rate: 4.1% (1998 est.)

Electricity - production: 103 billion kWh (1997)

Electricity - production by source:
fossil fuel: 62.4%
hydro: 37.1%
nuclear: 0%
other: 0.5% (1997)

Electricity - consumption: 91.16 billion kWh (1996)

Electricity - exports: 300 million kWh (1996)

Electricity - imports: 265 million kWh (1996)

Agriculture - products: tobacco, cotton, grain, olives, sugar beets, pulse, citrus; livestock

Exports: $31 billion (f.o.b., 1998)

Exports - commodities: textiles and apparel 30%, foodstuffs 15%, iron and steel products 13% (1997)

Exports - partners: Germany 20%, US 9%, Russia 5%, UK 6%, Italy 6% (1998)

Imports: $47 billion (f.o.b., 1998)

Imports - commodities: machinery and equipment 50%, fuels, minerals, foodstuffs (1997)

Imports - partners: Germany 16%, Italy 9%, US 9%, Russia 6%, UK 6%, France 2% (1997)

Debt - external: $93.4 billion (1998)

Economic aid - recipient: ODA, $195 million (1993)

Currency: Turkish lira (TL)

Exchange rates: Turkish liras (TL) per US$1 - 331,400 (January 1999), 260,724 (1998), 151,865 (1997), 81,405 (1996), 45,845.1 (1995), 29,608.7 (1994)

Fiscal year: calendar year

Turkey *(continued)*

Communications

Telephones: 17 million (in addition, there are 1.5 million cellular telephone subscribers) (1997 est.)
Telephone system: fair domestic and international systems; undergoing modernization and refurbishment programs
domestic: cable; AMPS standard cellular system in Ashkhabad with plans for expansion
international: 12 satellite earth stations - Intelsat (Atlantic Ocean), Eutelsat, and Inmarsat (Indian and Atlantic Ocean regions); 3 submarine fiber-optic cables (1996); connected internationally by the Trans-Asia-Europe Fiber-Optic Line that became operational in 1998
Radio broadcast stations: AM NA, FM NA, shortwave NA
note: there are 36 national broadcast stations, 108 regional broadcast stations, and 1,058 local broadcast stations (1996)
Radios: 9.4 million (1992 est.)
Television broadcast stations: 69 (in addition, there are 476 low-power repeaters) (1997)
Televisions: 10.53 million (1993 est.)

Transportation

Railways:
total: 10,386 km
standard gauge: 10,386 km 1.435-m gauge (1,088 km electrified)
Highways:
total: 382,397 km
paved: 95,599 km (including 1,560 km of expressways)
unpaved: 286,798 km (1997 est.)
Waterways: about 1,200 km
Pipelines: crude oil 1,738 km; petroleum products 2,321 km; natural gas 708 km
Ports and harbors: Gemlik, Hopa, Iskenderun, Istanbul, Izmir, Kocaeli (Izmit), Icel (Mersin), Samsun, Trabzon
Merchant marine:
total: 531 ships (1,000 GRT or over) totaling 5,913,171 GRT/9,832,994 DWT
ships by type: bulk 159, cargo 239, chemical tanker 32, combination bulk 5, combination ore/oil 6, container 12, liquefied gas tanker 5, oil tanker 36, passenger-cargo 1, refrigerated cargo 3, roll-on/roll-off cargo 21, short-sea passenger 9, specialized tanker 3 (1998 est.)
Airports: 117 (1998 est.)
Airports - with paved runways:
total: 81
over 3,047 m: 16
2,438 to 3,047 m: 25
1,524 to 2,437 m: 19
914 to 1,523 m: 16
under 914 m: 5 (1998 est.)

Airports - with unpaved runways:
total: 36
1,524 to 2,437 m: 1
914 to 1,523 m: 9
under 914 m: 26 (1998 est.)
Heliports: 2 (1998 est.)

Military

Military branches: Land Forces, Navy (includes Naval Air and Naval Infantry), Air Force, Coast Guard, Gendarmerie
Military manpower - military age: 20 years of age
Military manpower - availability:
males age 15-49: 18,168,658 (1999 est.)
Military manpower - fit for military service:
males age 15-49: 11,024,173 (1999 est.)
Military manpower - reaching military age annually:
males: 659,338 (1999 est.)
Military expenditures - dollar figure: $6.737 billion (1997)
Military expenditures - percent of GDP: 4.3% (1997)

Transnational Issues

Disputes - international: complex maritime, air, and territorial disputes with Greece in Aegean Sea; Cyprus question with Greece; dispute with downstream riparian states (Syria and Iraq) over water development plans for the Tigris and Euphrates Rivers; traditional demands on former Armenian lands in Turkey have subsided
Illicit drugs: major transit route for Southwest Asian heroin and hashish to Western Europe and - to a far lesser extent the US - via air, land, and sea routes; major Turkish, Iranian, and other international trafficking organizations operate out of Istanbul; laboratories to convert imported morphine base into heroin are in remote regions of Turkey as well as near Istanbul; government maintains strict controls over areas of legal opium poppy cultivation and output of poppy straw concentrate

Turkmenistan

Geography

Location: Central Asia, bordering the Caspian Sea, between Iran and Kazakhstan
Geographic coordinates: 40 00 N, 60 00 E
Map references: Commonwealth of Independent States
Area:
total: 488,100 sq km
land: 488,100 sq km
water: 0 sq km
Area - comparative: slightly larger than California
Land boundaries:
total: 3,736 km
border countries: Afghanistan 744 km, Iran 992 km, Kazakhstan 379 km, Uzbekistan 1,621 km
Coastline: 0 km
note: Turkmenistan borders the Caspian Sea (1,768 km)
Maritime claims: none (landlocked)
Climate: subtropical desert
Terrain: flat-to-rolling sandy desert with dunes rising to mountains in the south; low mountains along border with Iran; borders Caspian Sea in west
Elevation extremes:
lowest point: Vpadina Akchanaya -81 m (note - Sarygamysh Koli is a lake in north eastern Turkmenistan whose water levels fluctuate widely; at its shallowest, its level is -110 m; it is presently at -60 m, 20 m above Vpadina Akchanaya)
highest point: Ayrybaba 3,139 m
Natural resources: petroleum, natural gas, coal, sulfur, salt
Land use:
arable land: 3%
permanent crops: 0%
permanent pastures: 63%
forests and woodland: 8%
other: 26% (1993 est.)
Irrigated land: 13,000 sq km (1993 est.)
Natural hazards: NA
Environment - current issues: contamination of soil and groundwater with agricultural chemicals, pesticides; salination, water-logging of soil due to poor irrigation methods; Caspian Sea pollution; diversion of a large share of the flow of the Amu Darya into irrigation contributes to that river's inability to replenish the Aral Sea; desertification
Environment - international agreements:
party to: Biodiversity, Climate Change, Desertification, Hazardous Wastes, Ozone Layer Protection
signed, but not ratified: Climate Change-Kyoto Protocol
Geography - note: landlocked

People

Population: 4,366,383 (July 1999 est.)
Age structure:
0-14 years: 38% (male 845,584; female 813,223)
15-64 years: 58% (male 1,243,031; female 1,283,985)
65 years and over: 4% (male 68,496; female 112,064) (1999 est.)
Population growth rate: 1.58% (1999 est.)
Birth rate: 25.91 births/1,000 population (1999 est.)
Death rate: 8.77 deaths/1,000 population (1999 est.)
Net migration rate: -1.35 migrant(s)/1,000 population (1999 est.)
Sex ratio:
at birth: 1.05 male(s)/female
under 15 years: 1.04 male(s)/female
15-64 years: 0.97 male(s)/female
65 years and over: 0.61 male(s)/female
total population: 0.98 male(s)/female (1999 est.)
Infant mortality rate: 73.1 deaths/1,000 live births (1999 est.)
Life expectancy at birth:
total population: 61.11 years
male: 57.48 years
female: 64.91 years (1999 est.)
Total fertility rate: 3.21 children born/woman (1999 est.)

Nationality:
noun: Turkmen(s)
adjective: Turkmen
Ethnic groups: Turkmen 77%, Uzbek 9.2%, Russian 6.7%, Kazakh 2%, other 5.1% (1995)
Religions: Muslim 89%, Eastern Orthodox 9%, unknown 2%
Languages: Turkmen 72%, Russian 12%, Uzbek 9%, other 7%
Literacy:
definition: age 15 and over can read and write
total population: 98%
male: 99%
female: 97% (1989 est.)

Government

Country name:
conventional long form: none
conventional short form: Turkmenistan
local long form: none
local short form: Turkmenistan
former: Turkmen Soviet Socialist Republic
Data code: TX
Government type: republic
Capital: Ashgabat
Administrative divisions: 5 welayatlar (singular - welayat): Ahal Welayaty (Ashgabat), Balkan Welayaty (Nebitdag), Dashhowuz Welayaty (formerly Tashauz), Lebap Welayaty (Charjew), Mary Welayaty
note: administrative divisions have the same names as their administrative centers (exceptions have the administrative center name following in parentheses)
Independence: 27 October 1991 (from the Soviet Union)
National holiday: Independence Day, 27 October (1991)
Constitution: adopted 18 May 1992
Legal system: based on civil law system
Suffrage: 18 years of age; universal
Executive branch:
chief of state: President and Chairman of the Cabinet of Ministers Saparmurat NIYAZOV (since 27 October 1990, when the first direct presidential election occurred); note - the president is both the chief of state and head of government
head of government: President and Chairman of the Cabinet of Ministers Saparmurat NIYAZOV (since 27 October 1990, when the first direct presidential election occurred); note - the president is both the chief of state and head of government; Deputy Chairmen of the Cabinet of Ministers Mukhamed ABALAKOV (since NA), Orazgeldy AYDOGDIYEV (since NA 1992), Hudaayguly HALYKOV (since NA 1996), Rejep SAPAROV (since NA 1992), Boris SHIKHMURADOV (since NA 1993), Batyr SARJAYEV (since NA 1993), Ilaman SHIKHIYEV (since NA 1995), Yolly GURBANMURADOV (since NA 1997), Saparmurat NURIYEV (since NA 1997)
cabinet: Council of Ministers appointed by the president
note: NIYAZOV has been asked by various local groups, most recently on 21 December 1998 at the

Turkmenistan *(continued)*

Second Congress of the Democratic Party, to be "president for life," but he has declined, saying the status would require an amendment to the constitution
elections: president elected by popular vote for a five-year term; election last held 21 June 1992 (next to be held NA 2002; note - extension of President NIYAZOV's term for an additional five years overwhelmingly approved by national referendum held 15 January 1994); deputy chairmen of the cabinet of ministers are appointed by the president
election results: Saparmurat NIYAZOV elected president without opposition; percent of vote - Saparmurat NIYAZOV 99.5%
Legislative branch: under the 1992 constitution, there are two parliamentary bodies, a unicameral People's Council or Halk Maslahaty (more than 100 seats, some of which are elected by popular vote and some of which are appointed; meets infrequently) and a unicameral Assembly or Majlis (50 seats; members are elected by popular vote to serve five-year terms)
elections: People's Council - NA; Assembly - last held 11 December 1994 (next to be held NA December 1999)
election results: Assembly - percent of vote by party - NA; seats by party - Democratic Party 45, other 5; note - all 50 preapproved by President NIYAZOV
Judicial branch: Supreme Court, judges are appointed by the president
Political parties and leaders: Democratic Party of Turkmenistan or DPT [Saparmurat NIYAZOV]
note: formal opposition parties are outlawed; unofficial, small opposition movements exist underground or in foreign countries
International organization participation: CCC, CIS, EAPC, EBRD, ECE, ECO, ESCAP, FAO, IBRD, ICAO, ICRM, IDB, IFC, IFRCS, ILO, IMF, IMO, Intelsat (nonsignatory user), IOC, IOM (observer), ISO (correspondent), ITU, NAM, OIC, OPCW, OSCE, PFP, UN, UNCTAD, UNESCO, UPU, WFTU, WHO, WIPO, WMO, WToO, WTrO (observer)
Diplomatic representation in the US:
chief of mission: Ambassador Halil UGUR
chancery: 2207 Massachusetts Avenue NW, Washington, DC 20008
telephone: [1] (202) 588-1500
FAX: [1] (202) 588-0697
Diplomatic representation from the US:
chief of mission: Ambassador Steven R. MANN
embassy: 9 Pushkin Street, Ashgabat
mailing address: use embassy street address
telephone: [9] (9312) 35-00-45, 35-00-46, 35-00-42, 51-13-06, Tie Line [8] 962-0000
FAX: [9] (9312) 51-13-05
Flag description: green field with a vertical red stripe near the hoist side, containing five carpet guls (designs used in producing rugs) stacked above two crossed olive branches similar to the olive branches on the UN flag; a white crescent moon and five white stars appear in the upper corner of the field just to the fly side of the red stripe

Economy

Economy - overview: Turkmenistan is largely desert country with nomadic cattle raising, intensive agriculture in irrigated oases, and huge gas and oil resources. One-half of its irrigated land is planted in cotton, making it the world's tenth largest producer. It also possesses the world's fifth largest reserves of natural gas and substantial oil resources. Until the end of 1993, Turkmenistan had experienced less economic disruption than other former Soviet states because its economy received a boost from higher prices for oil and gas and a sharp increase in hard currency earnings. In 1994, Russia's refusal to export Turkmen gas to hard currency markets and mounting debts of its major customers in the former USSR for gas deliveries contributed to a sharp fall in industrial production and caused the budget to shift from a surplus to a slight deficit. The economy bottomed out in 1996, but high inflation continued. Furthermore, with an authoritarian ex-communist regime in power and a tribally based social structure, Turkmenistan has taken a cautious approach to economic reform, hoping to use gas and cotton sales to sustain its inefficient economy. In 1996, the government set in place a stabilization program aimed at a unified and market-based exchange rate, allocation of government credits by auction, and strict limits on budget deficits. Privatization goals remain limited. Turkmenistan is working hard to open new gas export channels through Iran and Turkey to Europe, but these will take many years to realize. In 1998 Turkmenistan faced revenue shortfalls due to the continued lack of adequate export routes for natural gas and obligations on extensive short-term external debt.
GDP: purchasing power parity - $7 billion (1998 est.)
GDP - real growth rate: 5% (1998)
GDP - per capita: purchasing power parity - $1,630 (1998 est.)
GDP - composition by sector:
agriculture: 18%
industry: 50%
services: 32% (1996 est.)
Population below poverty line: NA%
Household income or consumption by percentage share:
lowest 10%: 2.7%
highest 10%: 26.9% (1993)
Inflation rate (consumer prices): 19.8% (1998 est.)
Labor force: 2.34 million (1996)
Labor force - by occupation: agriculture and forestry 44%, industry and construction 19%, other 37% (1996)
Unemployment rate: NA%
Budget:
revenues: $521 million
expenditures: $548 million, including capital expenditures of $83 million (1996 est.)
Industries: natural gas, oil, petroleum products, textiles, food processing

Industrial production growth rate: NA%
Electricity - production: 9.484 billion kWh (1996)
Electricity - production by source:
fossil fuel: 99.96%
hydro: 0.04%
nuclear: 0%
other: 0% (1996)
Electricity - consumption: 7.134 billion kWh (1996)
Electricity - exports: 2.7 billion kWh (1996)
Electricity - imports: 350 million kWh (1996)
Agriculture - products: cotton, grain; livestock
Exports: $689 million (1997 est.)
Exports - commodities: natural gas, cotton, petroleum products, textiles, electricity, carpets
Exports - partners: FSU, Hong Kong, Switzerland, US, Germany, Turkey (1996)
Imports: $1.1 billion (1997 est.)
Imports - commodities: machinery and parts, grain and food, plastics and rubber, consumer durables, textiles
Imports - partners: FSU, US, Turkey, Germany, Cyprus (1996)
Debt - external: $1.7 billion (1998 est.)
Economic aid - recipient: $27.2 million (1995)
Currency: 1 Turkmen manat (TMM) = 100 tenesi
Exchange rates: manats per US$1 - 5,350 (January 1999), 4,070 (January 1997), 2,400 (January 1996)
Fiscal year: calendar year

Communications

Telephones: NA
Telephone system: poorly developed
domestic: NA
international: linked by cable and microwave radio relay to other CIS republics and to other countries by leased connections to the Moscow international gateway switch; a new telephone link from Ashgabat to Iran has been established; a new exchange in Ashgabat switches international traffic through Turkey via Intelsat; satellite earth stations - 1 Orbita and 1 Intelsat
Radio broadcast stations: 1 state-owned radio broadcast station of NA type
Radios: NA
Television broadcast stations: 3 (much programming relayed from Russia and Turkey) (1997)
Televisions: NA

Transportation

Railways:
total: 2,187 km
broad gauge: 2,187 km 1.520-m gauge (1996 est.)
Highways:
total: 24,000 km
paved: 19,488 km (note - these roads are said to be hard-surfaced, meaning that some are paved and some are all-weather gravel surfaced)
unpaved: 4,512 km (1996 est.)
Waterways: the Amu Darya is an important inland waterway
Pipelines: crude oil 250 km; natural gas 4,400 km

Turkmenistan (continued)

Ports and harbors: Turkmenbashy
Merchant marine:
total: 1 oil tanker (1,000 GRT or over) totaling 1,896 GRT/3,389 DWT (1998 est.)
Airports: 64 (1994 est.)
Airports - with paved runways:
total: 22
2,438 to 3,047 m: 13
1,524 to 2,437 m: 8
914 to 1,523 m: 1 (1994 est.)
Airports - with unpaved runways:
total: 42
914 to 1,523 m: 7
under 914 m: 35 (1994 est.)

Military

Military branches: Ministry of Defense (Army, Air and Air Defense, Navy, Border Troops, and Internal Troops), National Guard
Military manpower - military age: 18 years of age
Military manpower - availability:
males age 15-49: 1,110,606 (1999 est.)
Military manpower - fit for military service:
males age 15-49: 901,735 (1999 est.)
Military manpower - reaching military age annually:
males: 45,050 (1999 est.)
Military expenditures - dollar figure: $88 million (1998)
Military expenditures - percent of GDP: 3% (1998)

Transnational Issues

Disputes - international: Caspian Sea boundaries are not yet determined among Azerbaijan, Iran, Kazakhstan, Russia, and Turkmenistan
Illicit drugs: limited illicit cultivator of opium poppy, mostly for domestic consumption; limited government eradication program; increasingly used as transshipment point for illicit drugs from Southwest Asia to Russia and Western Europe; also a transshipment point for acetic anhydride destined for Afghanistan

Turks and Caicos Islands
(overseas territory of the UK)

Geography

Location: Caribbean, two island groups in the North Atlantic Ocean, southeast of The Bahamas
Geographic coordinates: 21 45 N, 71 35 W
Map references: Central America and the Caribbean
Area:
total: 430 sq km
land: 430 sq km
water: 0 sq km
Area - comparative: 2.5 times the size of Washington, DC
Land boundaries: 0 km
Coastline: 389 km
Maritime claims:
exclusive fishing zone: 200 nm
territorial sea: 12 nm
Climate: tropical; marine; moderated by trade winds; sunny and relatively dry
Terrain: low, flat limestone; extensive marshes and mangrove swamps
Elevation extremes:
lowest point: Caribbean Sea 0 m
highest point: Blue Hills 49 m
Natural resources: spiny lobster, conch
Land use:
arable land: 2%
permanent crops: NA%
permanent pastures: NA%
forests and woodland: NA%
other: 98% (1993 est.)
Irrigated land: NA sq km
Natural hazards: frequent hurricanes
Environment - current issues: limited natural fresh water resources, private cisterns collect rainwater
Environment - international agreements:
party to: NA
signed, but not ratified: NA
Geography - note: 30 islands (eight inhabited)

People

Population: 16,863 (July 1999 est.)
Age structure:
0-14 years: 32% (male 2,777; female 2,697)
15-64 years: 63% (male 5,619; female 5,085)
65 years and over: 5% (male 305; female 380) (1999 est.)
Population growth rate: 3.65% (1999 est.)
Birth rate: 26.39 births/1,000 population (1999 est.)
Death rate: 4.86 deaths/1,000 population (1999 est.)
Net migration rate: 15 migrant(s)/1,000 population (1999 est.)
Sex ratio:
at birth: 1.05 male(s)/female
under 15 years: 1.03 male(s)/female
15-64 years: 1.11 male(s)/female
65 years and over: 0.8 male(s)/female
total population: 1.07 male(s)/female (1999 est.)
Infant mortality rate: 21.11 deaths/1,000 live births (1999 est.)
Life expectancy at birth:
total population: 72.35 years
male: 70.4 years
female: 74.4 years (1999 est.)
Total fertility rate: 3.28 children born/woman (1999 est.)
Nationality:
noun: none
adjective: none
Ethnic groups: black
Religions: Baptist 41.2%, Methodist 18.9%, Anglican 18.3%, Seventh-Day Adventist 1.7%, other 19.9% (1980)
Languages: English (official)
Literacy:
definition: age 15 and over has ever attended school
total population: 98%
male: 99%
female: 98% (1970 est.)

Government

Country name:
conventional long form: none
conventional short form: Turks and Caicos Islands
Data code: TK
Dependency status: overseas territory of the UK
Government type: NA
Capital: Grand Turk (Cockburn Town)
Administrative divisions: none (overseas territory of the UK)
Independence: none (overseas territory of the UK)
National holiday: Constitution Day, 30 August (1976)
Constitution: introduced 30 August 1976; suspended in 1986; restored and revised 5 March 1988
Legal system: based on laws of England and Wales, with a small number adopted from Jamaica and The Bahamas
Suffrage: 18 years of age; universal

Turks and Caicos Islands (continued)

Executive branch:

chief of state: Queen ELIZABETH II (since 6 February 1953), represented by Governor John KELLY (since NA September 1996)

head of government: Chief Minister Derek H. TAYLOR (since 31 January 1995)

cabinet: Executive Council consists of three ex officio members and five appointed by the governor from among the members of the Legislative Council

elections: none; the monarch is hereditary; governor appointed by the monarch; chief minister appointed by the governor

Legislative branch: unicameral Legislative Council (19 seats, of which 13 are popularly elected; members serve four-year terms)

elections: last held 31 January 1995 (next to be held by NA December 1999)

election results: percent of vote by party - NA; seats by party - PDM 8, PNP 4, independent (Norman SAUNDERS) 1

Judicial branch: Supreme Court

Political parties and leaders: Progressive National Party or PNP [Washington MISICK]; People's Democratic Movement or PDM [Derek H. TAYLOR]; United Democratic Party or UDP [Wendal SWANN]

International organization participation: Caricom (associate), CDB, Interpol (subbureau)

Diplomatic representation in the US: none (overseas territory of the UK)

Diplomatic representation from the US: none (overseas territory of the UK)

Flag description: blue, with the flag of the UK in the upper hoist-side quadrant and the colonial shield centered on the outer half of the flag; the shield is yellow and contains a conch shell, lobster, and cactus

Economy

Economy - overview: The Turks and Caicos economy is based on tourism, fishing, and offshore financial services. Most capital goods and food for domestic consumption are imported. The US was the leading source of tourists in 1996, accounting for more than half of the 87,000 visitors. Major sources of government revenue include fees from offshore financial activities and customs receipts.

GDP: purchasing power parity - $117 million (1997 est.)

GDP - real growth rate: 4% (1997 est.)

GDP - per capita: purchasing power parity - $7,700 (1997 est.)

GDP - composition by sector:
agriculture: NA%
industry: NA%
services: NA%

Population below poverty line: NA%

Household income or consumption by percentage share:
lowest 10%: NA%
highest 10%: NA%

Inflation rate (consumer prices): 4% (1995)

Labor force: 4,848 (1990 est.)

Labor force - by occupation: about 33% in government and 20% in agriculture and fishing; significant numbers in tourism and financial and other services (1997 est.)

Unemployment rate: 10% (1997 est.)

Budget:
revenues: $47 million
expenditures: $33.6 million, including capital expenditures of $NA (1997/98 est.)

Industries: tourism, offshore financial services

Industrial production growth rate: NA%

Electricity - production: 5 million kWh (1996)

Electricity - production by source:
fossil fuel: 100%
hydro: 0%
nuclear: 0%
other: 0% (1996)

Electricity - consumption: 5 million kWh (1996)

Electricity - exports: 0 kWh (1996)

Electricity - imports: 0 kWh (1996)

Agriculture - products: corn, beans, cassava (tapioca), citrus fruits; fish

Exports: $4.7 million (1993)

Exports - commodities: lobster, dried and fresh conch, conch shells

Exports - partners: US, UK

Imports: $46.6 million (1993)

Imports - commodities: food and beverages, tobacco, clothing, manufactures, construction materials

Imports - partners: US, UK

Debt - external: $NA

Economic aid - recipient: $5.7 million (1995)

Currency: 1 United States dollar (US$) = 100 cents

Exchange rates: US currency is used

Fiscal year: calendar year

Communications

Telephones: 1,359 (1988 est.)

Telephone system: fair cable and radiotelephone services
domestic: NA
international: 2 submarine cables; satellite earth station - 1 Intelsat (Atlantic Ocean)

Radio broadcast stations: AM 3, FM 0, shortwave 0

Radios: 7,000 (1992 est.)

Television broadcast stations: 0 (broadcasts from The Bahamas are received; cable television is established) (1997)

Televisions: NA

Transportation

Railways: 0 km

Highways:
total: 121 km
paved: 24 km
unpaved: 97 km

Ports and harbors: Grand Turk, Providenciales

Merchant marine: none

Airports: 7 (1998 est.)

Airports - with paved runways:
total: 4

1,524 to 2,437 m: 3
914 to 1,523 m: 1 (1998 est.)

Airports - with unpaved runways:
total: 3
914 to 1,523 m: 2
under 914 m: 1 (1998 est.)

Military

Military - note: defense is the responsibility of the UK

Transnational Issues

Disputes - international: none

Illicit drugs: transshipment point for South American narcotics destined for the US

Tuvalu

Geography

Location: Oceania, island group consisting of nine coral atolls in the South Pacific Ocean, about one-half of the way from Hawaii to Australia
Geographic coordinates: 8 00 S, 178 00 E
Map references: Oceania
Area:
total: 26 sq km
land: 26 sq km
water: 0 sq km
Area - comparative: 0.1 times the size of Washington, DC
Land boundaries: 0 km
Coastline: 24 km
Maritime claims:
contiguous zone: 24 nm
exclusive economic zone: 200 nm
territorial sea: 12 nm
Climate: tropical; moderated by easterly trade winds (March to November); westerly gales and heavy rain (November to March)
Terrain: very low-lying and narrow coral atolls
Elevation extremes:
lowest point: Pacific Ocean 0 m
highest point: unnamed location 5 m
Natural resources: fish
Land use:
arable land: 0%
permanent crops: 0%
permanent pastures: 0%
forests and woodland: 0%
other: 100% (1993 est.)
Irrigated land: NA sq km
Natural hazards: severe tropical storms are usually rare, but, in 1997, there were three cyclones
Environment - current issues: since there are no streams or rivers and groundwater is not potable, all water needs must be met by catchment systems with storage facilities; beachhead erosion because of the use of sand for building materials; excessive

clearance of forest undergrowth for use as fuel; damage to coral reefs from the spread of the Crown of Thorns starfish; Tuvalu is very concerned about global increases in greenhouse gas emissions and their effect on rising sea levels, which threaten the country's underground water table
Environment - international agreements:
party to: Climate Change, Climate Change-Kyoto Protocol, Desertification, Endangered Species, Marine Dumping, Ozone Layer Protection, Ship Pollution
signed, but not ratified: Biodiversity, Law of the Sea

People

Population: 10,588 (July 1999 est.)
Age structure:
0-14 years: 35% (male 1,870; female 1,799)
15-64 years: 61% (male 3,062; female 3,360)
65 years and over: 4% (male 225; female 272) (1999 est.)
Population growth rate: 1.34% (1999 est.)
Birth rate: 21.91 births/1,000 population (1999 est.)
Death rate: 8.5 deaths/1,000 population (1999 est.)
Net migration rate: 0 migrant(s)/1,000 population (1999 est.)
Sex ratio:
at birth: 1.05 male(s)/female
under 15 years: 1.04 male(s)/female
15-64 years: 0.91 male(s)/female
65 years and over: 0.83 male(s)/female
total population: 0.95 male(s)/female (1999 est.)
Infant mortality rate: 25.53 deaths/1,000 live births (1999 est.)
Life expectancy at birth:
total population: 64.15 years
male: 63.01 years
female: 65.34 years (1999 est.)
Total fertility rate: 3.11 children born/woman (1999 est.)
Nationality:
noun: Tuvaluan(s)
adjective: Tuvaluan
Ethnic groups: Polynesian 96%
Religions: Church of Tuvalu (Congregationalist) 97%, Seventh-Day Adventist 1.4%, Baha'i 1%, other 0.6%
Languages: Tuvaluan, English
Literacy: NA; note - education is free and compulsory from ages 6 through 13

Government

Country name:
conventional long form: none
conventional short form: Tuvalu
former: Ellice Islands
Data code: TV
Government type: constitutional monarchy with a parliamentary democracy; began debating republic status in 1992
Capital: Funafuti
Administrative divisions: none

Independence: 1 October 1978 (from UK)
National holiday: Independence Day, 1 October (1978)
Constitution: 1 October 1978
Legal system: NA
Suffrage: 18 years of age; universal
Executive branch:
chief of state: Queen ELIZABETH II (since 6 February 1952), represented by Governor General Sir Tomasi PUAPUA, M.D. (since NA June 1998)
head of government: Prime Minister Bikenibeu PAENIU (since 23 December 1996) and Deputy Prime Minister Kokeiya MALUA (since 8 April 1998);
cabinet: Cabinet appointed by the governor general on the recommendation of the prime minister
elections: the monarch is hereditary; governor general appointed by the monarch on the recommendation of the prime minister; prime minister and deputy prime minister elected by and from the members of Parliament; election last held 8 April 1998 (next to be held NA 2002)
election results: Bikenibeu PAENIU reelected prime minister by a vote in Parliament of 10 to 2; Kokeiya MALUA elected deputy prime minister; percent of Parliament vote - NA
Legislative branch: unicameral Parliament or Fale I Fono, also called House of Assembly (12 seats - two from each island with more than 1,000 inhabitants, one from all the other inhabited islands; members elected by popular vote to serve four-year terms)
elections: last held 26-27 March 1998 (next to be held by NA 2002)
election results: percent of vote - NA; seats - independents 12
Judicial branch: eight Island Courts; High Court; note - a chief justice visits twice a year to preside over sessions of the High Court
Political parties and leaders: there are no political parties but members of Parliament usually align themselves in informal groupings
International organization participation: ACP, AsDB, C (special), ESCAP, IFRCS (associate), Intelsat (nonsignatory user), ITU, Sparteca, SPC, SPF, UNESCO, UPU, WHO, WTrO (applicant)
Diplomatic representation in the US: Tuvalu does not have an embassy in the US
Diplomatic representation from the US: the US does not have an embassy in Tuvalu; the US ambassador to Fiji is accredited to Tuvalu
Flag description: light blue with the flag of the UK in the upper hoist-side quadrant; the outer half of the flag represents a map of the country with nine yellow five-pointed stars symbolizing the nine islands

Economy

Economy - overview: Tuvalu consists of a densely populated, scattered group of nine coral atolls with poor soil. The country has no known mineral resources and few exports. Subsistence farming and fishing are the primary economic activities. Government revenues largely come from the sale of stamps and coins and worker remittances. About

Tuvalu *(continued)*

1,000 Tuvaluans work in Nauru in the phosphate mining industry. Nauru has begun repatriating Tuvaluans, however, as phosphate resources decline. Substantial income is received annually from an international trust fund established in 1987 by Australia, NZ, and the UK and supported also by Japan and South Korea. In an effort to reduce its dependence on foreign aid, the government is pursuing public sector reforms, including privatization of some government functions and personnel cuts of up to 7%. In 1998, Tuvalu began selling internet addresses in its TV domain and reportedly has derived revenue from use of its area code for "900" lines. Low-lying Tuvalu is particularly vulnerable to any future global warming.

GDP: purchasing power parity - $7.8 million (1995 est.)

GDP - real growth rate: 8.7% (1995)

GDP - per capita: purchasing power parity - $800 (1995 est.)

GDP - composition by sector:
agriculture: NA%
industry: NA%
services: NA%

Population below poverty line: NA%

Household income or consumption by percentage share:
lowest 10%: NA%
highest 10%: NA%

Inflation rate (consumer prices): 3.9% (average 1985-93)

Labor force: NA

Labor force - by occupation: people make a living mainly through exploitation of the sea, reefs, and atolls and from wages sent home by those working abroad (mostly workers in the phosphate industry and sailors)

Unemployment rate: NA%

Budget:
revenues: $4.3 million
expenditures: $4.3 million, including capital expenditures of $NA (1989 est.)

Industries: fishing, tourism, copra

Industrial production growth rate: NA%

Electricity - production: 3 million kWh (1995)

Electricity - production by source:
fossil fuel: NA%
hydro: NA%
nuclear: NA%
other: NA%

Electricity - consumption: 3 million kWh (1995)

Electricity - exports: 0 kWh (1995)

Electricity - imports: 0 kWh (1995)

Agriculture - products: coconuts; fish

Exports: $165,000 (f.o.b., 1989)

Exports - commodities: copra

Exports - partners: Fiji, Australia, NZ

Imports: $4.4 million (c.i.f., 1989)

Imports - commodities: food, animals, mineral fuels, machinery, manufactured goods

Imports - partners: Fiji, Australia, NZ

Debt - external: $NA

Economic aid - recipient: $7.9 million (1995); note - substantial annual support from an international trust fund

Currency: 1 Tuvaluan dollar ($T) or 1 Australian dollar ($A) = 100 cents

Exchange rates: Tuvaluan dollars ($T) or Australian dollars ($A) per US$1 - 1.5853 (January 1999), 1.5888 (1998), 1.3439 (1997), 1.2773 (1996), 1.3486 (1995), 1.3667 (1994)

Fiscal year: calendar year

Communications

Telephones: 130 (1983 est.)

Telephone system:
domestic: radiotelephone communications between islands
international: NA

Radio broadcast stations: AM 1, FM 0, shortwave 0

Radios: 4,000 (1993 est.)

Television broadcast stations: 0 (1997)

Televisions: NA

Transportation

Railways: 0 km

Highways:
total: 8 km (1996 est.)
paved: NA km
unpaved: NA km

Ports and harbors: Funafuti, Nukufetau

Merchant marine:
total: 10 ships (1,000 GRT or over) totaling 44,371 GRT/70,137 DWT
ships by type: cargo 6, chemical tanker 2, oil tanker 1, passenger-cargo 1 (1998 est.)

Airports: 1 (1998 est.)

Airports - with unpaved runways:
total: 1
1,524 to 2,437 m: 1 (1998 est.)

Military

Military branches: no regular military forces; Police Force (consists of 56 full- and part-time personnel), Police Force (includes Maritime Surveillance Unit for search and rescue missions and surveillance operations)

Military expenditures - dollar figure: $NA

Military expenditures - percent of GDP: NA%

Transnational Issues

Disputes - international: none

Uganda

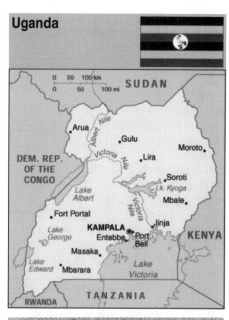

Geography

Location: Eastern Africa, west of Kenya

Geographic coordinates: 1 00 N, 32 00 E

Map references: Africa

Area:
total: 236,040 sq km
land: 199,710 sq km
water: 36,330 sq km

Area - comparative: slightly smaller than Oregon

Land boundaries:
total: 2,698 km
border countries: Democratic Republic of the Congo 765 km, Kenya 933 km, Rwanda 169 km, Sudan 435 km, Tanzania 396 km

Coastline: 0 km (landlocked)

Maritime claims: none (landlocked)

Climate: tropical; generally rainy with two dry seasons (December to February, June to August); semiarid in northeast

Terrain: mostly plateau with rim of mountains

Elevation extremes:
lowest point: Lake Albert 621 m
highest point: Margherita Peak on Mount Stanley 5,110 m

Natural resources: copper, cobalt, limestone, salt

Land use:
arable land: 25%
permanent crops: 9%
permanent pastures: 9%
forests and woodland: 28%
other: 29% (1993 est.)

Irrigated land: 90 sq km (1993 est.)

Natural hazards: NA

Environment - current issues: draining of wetlands for agricultural use; deforestation; overgrazing; soil erosion; poaching is widespread

Environment - international agreements:
party to: Biodiversity, Climate Change, Desertification, Endangered Species, Hazardous Wastes, Law of the Sea, Marine Life Conservation,

Uganda (continued)

Nuclear Test Ban, Ozone Layer Protection
signed, but not ratified: Environmental Modification
Geography - note: landlocked

People

Population: 22,804,973 (July 1999 est.)
Age structure:
0-14 years: 51% (male 5,857,254; female 5,820,526)
15-64 years: 47% (male 5,301,208; female 5,330,005)
65 years and over: 2% (male 239,434; female 256,546) (1999 est.)
Population growth rate: 2.83% (1999 est.)
Birth rate: 48.54 births/1,000 population (1999 est.)
Death rate: 18.43 deaths/1,000 population (1999 est.)
Net migration rate: -1.84 migrant(s)/1,000 population (1999 est.)
note: according to the UNHCR, by the end of 1997, Uganda was host to refugees from a number of neighboring countries, including: Sudan 160,000, Democratic Republic of the Congo 14,000, and Rwanda 12,000
Sex ratio:
at birth: 1.03 male(s)/female
under 15 years: 1.01 male(s)/female
15-64 years: 0.99 male(s)/female
65 years and over: 0.93 male(s)/female
total population: 1 male(s)/female (1999 est.)
Infant mortality rate: 90.68 deaths/1,000 live births (1999 est.)
Life expectancy at birth:
total population: 43.06 years
male: 42.2 years
female: 43.94 years (1999 est.)
Total fertility rate: 7.03 children born/woman (1999 est.)
Nationality:
noun: Ugandan(s)
adjective: Ugandan
Ethnic groups: Baganda 17%, Karamojong 12%, Basogo 8%, Iteso 8%, Langi 6%, Rwanda 6%, Bagisu 5%, Acholi 4%, Lugbara 4%, Bunyoro 3%, Batobo 3%, non-African (European, Asian, Arab) 1%, other 23%
Religions: Roman Catholic 33%, Protestant 33%, Muslim 16%, indigenous beliefs 18%
Languages: English (official national language, taught in grade schools, used in courts of law and by most newspapers and some radio broadcasts), Ganda or Luganda (most widely used of the Niger-Congo languages, preferred for native language publications and may be taught in school), other Niger-Congo languages, Nilo-Saharan languages, Swahili, Arabic
Literacy:
definition: age 15 and over can read and write
total population: 61.8%
male: 73.7%
female: 50.2% (1995 est.)

Government

Country name:
conventional long form: Republic of Uganda
conventional short form: Uganda
Data code: UG
Government type: republic
Capital: Kampala
Administrative divisions: 39 districts; Apac, Arua, Bundibugyo, Bushenyi, Gulu, Hoima, Iganga, Jinja, Kabale, Kabarole, Kalangala, Kampala, Kamuli, Kapchorwa, Kasese, Kibale, Kiboga, Kisoro, Kitgum, Kotido, Kumi, Lira, Luwero, Masaka, Masindi, Mbale, Mbarara, Moroto, Moyo, Mpigi, Mubende, Mukono, Nebbi, Ntungamo, Pallisa, Rakai, Rukungiri, Soroti, Tororo
Independence: 9 October 1962 (from UK)
National holiday: Independence Day, 9 October (1962)
Constitution: 8 October 1995; adopted by the interim, 284-member Constituent Assembly, charged with debating the draft constitution that had been proposed in May 1993; the Constituent Assembly was dissolved upon the promulgation of the constitution in October 1995
Legal system: in 1995, the government restored the legal system to one based on English common law and customary law; accepts compulsory ICJ jurisdiction, with reservations
Suffrage: 18 years of age; universal
Executive branch:
chief of state: President Lt. Gen. Yoweri Kaguta MUSEVENI (since seizing power 29 January 1986); note - the president is both chief of state and head of government
head of government: President Lt. Gen. Yoweri Kaguta MUSEVENI (since seizing power 29 January 1986); Prime Minister Kintu MUSOKE (since 18 November 1994); note - the president is both chief of state and head of government; the prime minister assists the president in the supervision of the cabinet
cabinet: Cabinet appointed by the president from among elected legislators
elections: president elected by popular vote for a NA-year term; election last held 9 May 1996 (next to be held by 31 May 2001); note - first popular election for president since independence in 1962 was held in 1996; prime minister appointed by the president
election results: Lt. Gen. Yoweri Kaguta MUSEVENI elected president; percent of vote - Lt. Gen. Yoweri Kaguta MUSEVENI 74%, Paul Kawanga SSEMOGERERE 24%, Muhammad MAYANJA 2%
Legislative branch: unicameral National Assembly (276 members - 214 directly elected by popular vote, 62 nominated by legally established special interest groups and approved by the president - women 39, army 10, disabled 5, youth 5, labor 3; members serve five-year terms)
elections: last held 27 June 1996 (next to be held NA 2001);
election results: NA; note - election campaigning by party was not permitted

Judicial branch: Court of Appeal, judges are appointed by the president; High Court, judges are appointed by the president
Political parties and leaders: only one political organization, the National Resistance Movement or NRM [Dr. Samson KISEKKA, chairman] is recognized; note - this is the party of President MUSEVENI; the president maintains that the NRM is not a political party, but a movement which claims the loyalty of all Ugandans
note: of the political parties that exist but are prohibited from sponsoring candidates, the most important are the Ugandan People's Congress or UPC [Milton OBOTE]; Democratic Party or DP [Paul SSEMOGERERE]; and Conservative Party or CP [Joshua S. MAYANJA-NKANGI]; the new constitution requires the suspension of political party activity until a referendum is held on the matter in 2000
International organization participation: ACP, AfDB, C, CCC, EADB, ECA, FAO, G-77, IAEA, IBRD, ICAO, ICFTU, ICRM, IDA, IDB, IFAD, IFC, IFRCS, IGAD, ILO, IMF, Intelsat, Interpol, IOC, IOM, ISO (correspondent), ITU, NAM, OAU, OIC, OPCW, PCA, UN, UNCTAD, UNESCO, UNHCR, UNIDO, UPU, WFTU, WHO, WIPO, WMO, WToO, WTrO
Diplomatic representation in the US:
chief of mission: Ambassador Edith Grace SSEMPALA
chancery: 5911 16th Street NW, Washington, DC 20011
telephone: [1] (202) 726-7100 through 7102, 0416
FAX: [1] (202) 726-1727
Diplomatic representation from the US:
chief of mission: Ambassador Nancy J. POWELL
embassy: Parliament Avenue, Kampala
mailing address: P. O. Box 7007, Kampala
telephone: [256] (41) 259792, 259793, 259795
FAX: [256] (41) 259794
Flag description: six equal horizontal bands of black (top), yellow, red, black, yellow, and red; a white disk is superimposed at the center and depicts a red-crested crane (the national symbol) facing the hoist side

Economy

Economy - overview: Uganda has substantial natural resources, including fertile soils, regular rainfall, and sizable mineral deposits of copper and cobalt. Agriculture is the most important sector of the economy, employing over 80% of the work force. Coffee is the major export crop and accounts for the bulk of export revenues. Since 1986, the government - with the support of foreign countries and international agencies - has acted to rehabilitate and stabilize the economy by undertaking currency reform, raising producer prices on export crops, increasing prices of petroleum products, and improving civil service wages. The policy changes are especially aimed at dampening inflation and boosting production and export earnings. In 1990-98, the economy turned in a solid performance based on continued investment in the rehabilitation of infrastructure, improved

Uganda (continued)

incentives for production and exports, reduced inflation, gradually improved domestic security, and the return of exiled Indian-Ugandan entrepreneurs. Continuation of this performance, while possible, appears difficult because of Ugandan involvement in the war in the Democratic Republic of the Congo, growing corruption within the government, and slippage in the government's determination to press reforms.

GDP: purchasing power parity - $22.7 billion (1998 est.)

GDP - real growth rate: 5.5% (1998 est.)

GDP - per capita: purchasing power parity - $1,020 (1998 est.)

GDP - composition by sector:
agriculture: 44%
industry: 17%
services: 39% (1997 est.)

Population below poverty line: 55% (1993 est.)

Household income or consumption by percentage share:
lowest 10%: 3%
highest 10%: 33.4% (1992)

Inflation rate (consumer prices): 2.6% (1998)

Labor force: 8.361 million (1993 est.)

Labor force - by occupation: agriculture 86%, industry 4%, services 10% (1980 est.)

Unemployment rate: NA%

Budget:
revenues: $869 million
expenditures: $985 million, including capital expenditures of $69 million (FY95/96)

Industries: sugar, brewing, tobacco, cotton textiles, cement

Industrial production growth rate: 19.7% (FY95/96)

Electricity - production: 787 million kWh (1996)

Electricity - production by source:
fossil fuel: 0.89%
hydro: 99.11%
nuclear: 0%
other: 0% (1996)

Electricity - consumption: 677 million kWh (1996)

Electricity - exports: 110 million kWh (1996)

Electricity - imports: 0 kWh (1996)

Agriculture - products: coffee, tea, cotton, tobacco, cassava (tapioca), potatoes, corn, millet, pulses; beef, goat meat, milk, poultry

Exports: $476 million (f.o.b., 1998)

Exports - commodities: coffee 54%, gold, fish and fish products, cotton, tea, corn (1997)

Exports - partners: Spain 14%, Germany 14%, Netherlands 10%, France 8%, Italy (1997)

Imports: $1.4 billion (c.i.f., 1998)

Imports - commodities: transportation equipment, petroleum, medical supplies, iron and steel (1996)

Imports - partners: Kenya 31%, UK 12%, Japan 6%, India 6%, South Africa 5% (1997)

Debt - external: $2.9 billion (1998 est.)

Economic aid - recipient: $827.3 million (1993)

Currency: 1 Ugandan shilling (USh) = 100 cents

Exchange rates: Ugandan shillings (USh) per US$1 - 1,368.4 (December 1998), 1,240.2 (1998), 1,083.0 (1997), 1,046.1 (1996), 968.9 (1995), 979.4 (1994)

Fiscal year: 1 July - 30 June

Communications

Telephones: 61,600 (1990 est.)

Telephone system: fair system but in serious need of expansion and better maintenance; a cellular system has been introduced as a stopgap but the communications problems will not be solved without substantial investment in the conventional telephone infrastructure; e-mail and Internet services are available
domestic: intercity traffic by wire, microwave radio relay, and radiotelephone communications stations, cellular system for short range traffic
international: satellite earth station - 1 Intelsat (Atlantic Ocean)

Radio broadcast stations: AM 10, FM 0, shortwave 0

Radios: 2.13 million (1993 est.)

Television broadcast stations: 8 (in addition, there is one low-power repeater) (1997)

Televisions: 220,000 (1993 est.)

Transportation

Railways:
total: 1,241 km
narrow gauge: 1,241 km 1.000-m gauge
note: a program to rehabilitate the railroad is underway (1995)

Highways:
total: 27,000 km
paved: 1,800 km
unpaved: 25,200 km (of which about 4,800 km are all-weather roads) (1990 est.)

Waterways: Lake Victoria, Lake Albert, Lake Kyoga, Lake George, Lake Edward, Victoria Nile, Albert Nile

Ports and harbors: Entebbe, Jinja, Port Bell

Merchant marine:
total: 3 roll-on/roll-off cargo ships (1,000 GRT or over) totaling 5,091 GRT/8,229 DWT (1998 est.)

Airports: 27 (1998 est.)

Airports - with paved runways:
total: 4
over 3,047 m: 3
1,524 to 2,437 m: 1 (1998 est.)

Airports - with unpaved runways:
total: 23
2,438 to 3,047 m: 1
1,524 to 2,437 m: 6
914 to 1,523 m: 9
under 914 m: 7 (1998 est.)

Military

Military branches: Army, Navy, Air Wing

Military manpower - availability:
males age 15-49: 4,812,363 (1999 est.)

Military manpower - fit for military service:
males age 15-49: 2,611,096 (1999 est.)

Military expenditures - dollar figure: $95 million (FY98/99)

Military expenditures - percent of GDP: 1.9% (FY98/99)

Transnational Issues

Disputes - international: Ugandan military forces are supporting the rebel forces in the civil war in the Democratic Republic of the Congo

Ukraine

Geography

Location: Eastern Europe, bordering the Black Sea, between Poland and Russia
Geographic coordinates: 49 00 N, 32 00 E
Map references: Commonwealth of Independent States
Area:
total: 603,700 sq km
land: 603,700 sq km
water: 0 sq km
Area - comparative: slightly smaller than Texas
Land boundaries:
total: 4,558 km
border countries: Belarus 891 km, Hungary 103 km, Moldova 939 km, Poland 428 km, Romania (south) 169 km, Romania (west) 362 km, Russia 1,576 km, Slovakia 90 km
Coastline: 2,782 km
Maritime claims:
continental shelf: 200-m or to the depth of exploitation
exclusive economic zone: 200 nm
territorial sea: 12 nm
Climate: temperate continental; Mediterranean only on the southern Crimean coast; precipitation disproportionately distributed, highest in west and north, lesser in east and southeast; winters vary from cool along the Black Sea to cold farther inland; summers are warm across the greater part of the country, hot in the south
Terrain: most of Ukraine consists of fertile plains (steppes) and plateaus, mountains being found only in the west (the Carpathians), and in the Crimean Peninsula in the extreme south
Elevation extremes:
lowest point: Black Sea 0 m
highest point: Hora Hoverla 2,061 m
Natural resources: iron ore, coal, manganese, natural gas, oil, salt, sulfur, graphite, titanium, magnesium, kaolin, nickel, mercury, timber
Land use:
arable land: 58%

permanent crops: 2%
permanent pastures: 13%
forests and woodland: 18%
other: 9% (1993 est.)
Irrigated land: 26,050 sq km (1993 est.)
Natural hazards: NA
Environment - current issues: inadequate supplies of potable water; air and water pollution; deforestation; radiation contamination in the northeast from 1986 accident at Chornobyl' Nuclear Power Plant
Environment - international agreements:
party to: Air Pollution, Air Pollution-Nitrogen Oxides, Air Pollution-Sulphur 85, Antarctic Treaty, Biodiversity, Climate Change, Environmental Modification, Marine Dumping, Nuclear Test Ban, Ozone Layer Protection, Ship Pollution
signed, but not ratified: Air Pollution-Persistent Organic Pollutants, Air Pollution-Sulphur 94, Air Pollution-Volatile Organic Compounds, Antarctic-Environmental Protocol, Law of the Sea
Geography - note: strategic position at the crossroads between Europe and Asia; second-largest country in Europe

People

Population: 49,811,174 (July 1999 est.)
Age structure:
0-14 years: 18% (male 4,690,318; female 4,498,239)
15-64 years: 68% (male 16,136,296; female 17,572,011)
65 years and over: 14% (male 2,251,664; female 4,662,646) (1999 est.)
Population growth rate: -0.62% (1999 est.)
Birth rate: 9.54 births/1,000 population (1999 est.)
Death rate: 16.38 deaths/1,000 population (1999 est.)
Net migration rate: 0.63 migrant(s)/1,000 population (1999 est.)
Sex ratio:
at birth: 1.05 male(s)/female
under 15 years: 1.04 male(s)/female

15-64 years: 0.92 male(s)/female
65 years and over: 0.48 male(s)/female
total population: 0.86 male(s)/female (1999 est.)
Infant mortality rate: 21.73 deaths/1,000 live births (1999 est.)
Life expectancy at birth:
total population: 65.91 years
male: 60.23 years
female: 71.87 years (1999 est.)
Total fertility rate: 1.34 children born/woman (1999 est.)
Nationality:
noun: Ukrainian(s)
adjective: Ukrainian
Ethnic groups: Ukrainian 73%, Russian 22%, Jewish 1%, other 4%
Religions: Ukrainian Orthodox - Moscow Patriarchate, Ukrainian Orthodox - Kiev Patriarchate, Ukrainian Autocephalous Orthodox, Ukrainian Catholic (Uniate), Protestant, Jewish
Languages: Ukrainian, Russian, Romanian, Polish, Hungarian
Literacy:
definition: age 15 and over can read and write
total population: 98%
male: 100%
female: 97% (1989 est.)

Government

Country name:
conventional long form: none
conventional short form: Ukraine
local long form: none
local short form: Ukrayina
former: Ukrainian Soviet Socialist Republic
Data code: UP
Government type: republic
Capital: Kiev (Kyyiv)
Administrative divisions: 24 oblasti (singular - oblast'), 1 autonomous republic* (avtomnaya respublika), and 2 municipalities (mista, singular - misto) with oblast status**; Cherkas'ka (Cherkasy), Chernihivs'ka (Chernihiv), Chernivets'ka (Chernivtsi), Dnipropetrovs'ka (Dnipropetrovs'k), Donets'ka (Donets'k), Ivano-Frankivs'ka (Ivano-Frankivs'k), Kharkivs'ka (Kharkiv), Khersons'ka (Kherson), Khmel'nyts'ka (Khmel'nyts'kyy), Kirovohrads'ka (Kirovohrad), Kyyiv**, Kyyivs'ka (Kiev), Luhans'ka (Luhans'k), L'vivs'ka (L'viv), Mykolayivs'ka (Mykolayiv), Odes'ka (Odesa), Poltavs'ka (Poltava), Avtonomna Respublika Krym* (Simferopol'), Rivnens'ka (Rivne), Sevastopol'** (Sums'ka (Sumy), Ternopil's'ka (Ternopil'), Vinnyts'ka (Vinnytsya), Volyns'ka (Luts'k), Zakarpats'ka (Uzhhorod), Zaporiz'ka (Zaporizhzhya), Zhytomyrs'ka (Zhytomyr)
note: oblasts have the administrative center name following in parentheses
Independence: 1 December 1991 (from Soviet Union)
National holiday: Independence Day, 24 August (1991)
Constitution: adopted 28 June 1996

Ukraine *(continued)*

Legal system: based on civil law system; judicial review of legislative acts

Suffrage: 18 years of age; universal

Executive branch:

chief of state: President Leonid D. KUCHMA (since 19 July 1994)

head of government: Prime Minister Valeriy PUSTOVOYTENKO (since 16 July 1997), First Deputy Prime Minister Volodymyr KURATCHENKO (since 14 January 1999), and three deputy prime ministers

cabinet: Cabinet of Ministers appointed by the president and approved by the Supreme Council

note: there is also a National Security and Defense Council or NSDC originally created in 1992 as the National Security Council, but significantly revamped and strengthened under President KUCHMA; the NSDC staff is tasked with developing national security policy on domestic and international matters and advising the president; a Presidential Administration that helps draft presidential edicts and provides policy support to the president; and a Council of Regions that serves as an advisory body created by President KUCHMA in September 1994 that includes chairmen of the Kyyiv (Kiev) and Sevastopol' municipalities and chairmen of the Oblasti

elections: president elected by popular vote for a five-year term; election last held 26 June and 10 July 1994 (next to be held NA October 1999); prime minister and deputy prime ministers appointed by the president and approved by the People's Council

election results: Leonid D. KUCHMA elected president; percent of vote - Leonid KUCHMA 52.15%, Leonid KRAVCHUK 45.06%

Legislative branch: unicameral Supreme Council or Verkhovna Rada (450 seats; under Ukraine's new election law, half of the Rada's seats are allocated on a proportional basis to those parties that gain 4% of the national electoral vote; the other 225 members are elected by popular vote in single-mandate constituencies; all serve four-year terms)

elections: last held 29 March 1998 (next to be held NA 2002); note - repeat elections continuing to fill vacant seats

election results: percent of vote by party (for parties clearing 4% hurdle on 29 March 1998) - Communist 24.7%, Rukh 9.4%, Socialist/Peasant 8.6%, Green 5.3%, People's Democratic Party 5.0%, Hromada 4.7%, Progressive Socialist 4.0%, United Social Democratic Party 4.0%; seats by party (as of 8 July 1998) - Communist 120, People's Democratic Party 88, Rukh 47, Hromada 45, Socialist/Peasant 33, United Social Democratic 25, Green 24, Progressive Socialist 14, independents 26, vacant 28

Judicial branch: Supreme Court; Constitutional Court

Political parties and leaders: Communist Party of Ukraine [Petro SYMONENKO]; Hromad [Pavlo LAZARENKO]; Ukrainian Popular Movement or Rukh [Vyacheslav CHORNOVIL, chairman]; Socialist Party of Ukraine or SPU [Oleksandr MOROZ, chairman]; Peasant Party of Ukraine or SelPU [Serhiy DOVAN];

People's Democratic Party or NDPU [Anatoliy MATVIYENKO, chairman]; Reforms and Order Party [Viktor PYNZENYK]; United Social Democratic Party of Ukraine [Vasyl ONOPENKO]; Agrarian Party of Ukraine or APU [Kateryna VASHCHUK]; Liberal Party of Ukraine or LPU [Volodymyr SHCHERBAN]; Green Party of Ukraine or PZU [Vitaliy KONONOV, leader]; Progressive Socialist Party [Natalya VITRENKO]

note: and numerous smaller parties

Political pressure groups and leaders: New Ukraine (Nova Ukrayina); Congress of National Democratic Forces

International organization participation: BSEC, CCC, CE, CEI, CIS, EAPC, EBRD, ECE, IAEA, IBRD, ICAO, ICRM, IFC, IFRCS, IHO (pending member), ILO, IMF, IMO, Inmarsat, Intelsat (nonsignatory user), Interpol, IOC, IOM (observer), ISO, ITU, MONUA, NSG, OAS (observer), OPCW, OSCE, PCA, PFP, UN, UNCTAD, UNESCO, UNIDO, UNMIBH, UNMOP, UNMOT, UNPREDEP, UPU, WFTU, WHO, WIPO, WMO, WToO, WTrO (applicant)

Diplomatic representation in the US:

chief of mission: Ambassador Anton Denysovych BUTEYKO

chancery: 3350 M Street NW, Washington, DC 20007

telephone: [1] (202) 333-0606

FAX: [1] (202) 333-0817

consulate(s) general: Chicago and New York

Diplomatic representation from the US:

chief of mission: Ambassador Steven Karl PIFER

embassy: 10 Yuria Kotsyubynskoho, 254053 Kiev 53

mailing address: use embassy street address

telephone: [380] (44) 246-9750

FAX: [380] (44) 244-7350

Flag description: two equal horizontal bands of azure (top) and golden yellow represent grainfields under a blue sky

---

Economy

Economy - overview: After Russia, the Ukrainian republic was far and away the most important economic component of the former Soviet Union, producing about four times the output of the next-ranking republic. Its fertile black soil generated more than one-fourth of Soviet agricultural output, and its farms provided substantial quantities of meat, milk, grain, and vegetables to other republics. Likewise, its diversified heavy industry supplied equipment and raw materials to industrial and mining sites in other regions of the former USSR. Ukraine depends on imports of energy, especially natural gas. Shortly after the implosion of the USSR in December 1991, the Ukrainian Government liberalized most prices and erected a legal framework for privatization, but widespread resistance to reform within the government and the legislature soon stalled reform efforts and led to some backtracking. Output in 1992-98 fell to less than half the 1991 level. Loose monetary policies pushed inflation to hyperinflationary levels in late 1993. Since his election in July 1994, President KUCHMA has pushed economic reforms, maintained financial discipline, and tried to remove

almost all remaining controls over prices and foreign trade. The onset of the financial crisis in Russia dashed Ukraine's hopes for its first year of economic growth in 1998 due to a sharp fall in export revenue and reduced domestic demand. Although administrative currency controls will be lifted in early 1999, they are likely to be reimposed when the hryvnia next comes under pressure. The currency is only likely to collapse further if Ukraine abandons tight monetary policies or threatens default. Despite increasing pressure from the IMF to accelerate reform, significant economic restructuring remains unlikely in 1999.

GDP: purchasing power parity - $108.5 billion (1998 est.)

GDP - real growth rate: -1.7% (1998 est.)

GDP - per capita: purchasing power parity - $2,200 (1998 est.)

GDP - composition by sector:

agriculture: 14%

industry: 30%

services: 56% (1997 est.)

Population below poverty line: 50% (1997 est.)

Household income or consumption by percentage share:

lowest 10%: 4.1%

highest 10%: 20.8% (1992)

Inflation rate (consumer prices): 20% (yearend 1998 est.)

Labor force: 22.8 million (yearend 1997)

Labor force - by occupation: industry and construction 32%, agriculture and forestry 24%, health, education, and culture 17%, trade and distribution 8%, transport and communication 7%, other 12% (1996)

Unemployment rate: 3.7% officially registered; large number of unregistered or underemployed workers (December 1998)

Budget:

revenues: $18 billion

expenditures: $21 billion, including capital expenditures of $NA (1997 est.)

Industries: coal, electric power, ferrous and nonferrous metals, machinery and transport equipment, chemicals, food-processing (especially sugar)

Industrial production growth rate: -1.5% (1998 est.)

Electricity - production: 171.8 billion kWh (1998)

Electricity - production by source:

fossil fuel: 47%

hydro: 9.2%

nuclear: 43.8%

other: 0% (1998)

Electricity - consumption: 174 billion kWh (1998)

Electricity - exports: 5 billion kWh (1998)

Electricity - imports: 7 billion kWh (1998)

Agriculture - products: grain, sugar beets, sunflower seeds, vegetables; beef, milk

Exports: $11.3 billion (1998 est.)

Exports - commodities: ferrous and nonferrous metals, chemicals, machinery and transport equipment, food products

Ukraine *(continued)*

Exports - partners: Russia, China,, Turkey, Germany, Belarus (1998)
Imports: $13.1 billion (1998 est.)
Imports - commodities: energy, machinery and parts, transportation equipment, chemicals, plastics and rubber
Imports - partners: Russia, Germany, US, Poland, Italy (1998)
Debt - external: $10.9 billion (October 1998)
Economic aid - recipient: $637.7 million (1995); IMF Extended Funds Facility $2.2 billion (1998)
Currency: 1 hryvna=100 kopiykas
Exchange rates: hryvnia per US$1 - 3.4270 (February 1999), 2.4495 (1998), 1.8617 (1997), 1.8295 (1996), 1.4731 (1995), 0.3275 (1994)
note: in August 1998, Ukraine introduced currency controls in an attempt to fend off the impact of the Russian financial crisis; it created an exchange rate corridor for the hryvnia of 2.5-3.5 hryvnia per US$1
Fiscal year: calendar year

Communications

Telephones: 12,531,277 (1998)
Telephone system: Ukraine's phone systems are administered through the State Committee for Communications; Ukraine has a telecommunication development plan through 2005; Internet service is available in large cities
domestic: local - Kiev has a digital loop connected to the national digital backbone; Kiev has several cellular phone companies providing service in the different standards; some companies offer intercity roaming and even limited international roaming; cellular phone service is offered in at least 100 cities nationwide
international: foreign investment in the form of joint business ventures greatly improved the Ukrainian telephone system; Ukraine's two main fiber-optic lines are part of the Trans-Asia-Europe Fiber-Optic Line (TAE); these lines connect Ukraine to worldwide service through Belarus, Hungary, and Poland; Odesa is a landing point for the Italy-Turkey-Ukraine-Russia Undersea Fiber-Optic Cable (ITUR) giving Ukraine an additional fiber-optic link to worldwide service; Ukraine has Intelsat, Inmarsat, and Intersputnik earth stations
Radio broadcast stations: AM NA, FM NA, shortwave NA; note - at least 25 local broadcast stations of NA type (1998)
Radios: 15 million (1990)
Television broadcast stations: at least 33 (in addition 21 repeater stations that relay ORT broadcasts from Russia) (1997)
Televisions: 17.3 million (1992)

Transportation

Railways:
total: 23,350 km
broad gauge: 23,350 km 1.524-m gauge (8,600 km electrified)
Highways:
total: 172,565 km
paved: 163,937 km (including 1,875 km of expressways); note - these roads are said to be hard-surfaced, meaning that some are paved and some are all-weather gravel surfaced
unpaved: 8,628 km (1996 est.)
Waterways: 4,400 km navigable waterways, of which 1,672 km were on the Pryp"yat' and Dnistr (1990)
Pipelines: crude oil 4,000 km (1995); petroleum products 4,500 km (1995); natural gas 34,400 km (1998)
Ports and harbors: Berdyans'k, Illichivs'k, Izmayil, Kerch, Kherson, Kiev (Kyyiv), Mariupol', Mykolayiv, Odesa, Reni
Merchant marine:
total: 181 ships (1,000 GRT or over) totaling 1,022,047 GRT/1,101,278 DWT
ships by type: bulk 9, cargo 117, liquefied gas tanker 1, container 4, multifunction large-load carrier 2, oil tanker 16, passenger 12, passenger-cargo 3, railcar carrier 2, refrigerated cargo 2, roll-on/roll-off cargo 10, short-sea passenger 3 (1998 est.)
Airports: 706 (1994 est.)
Airports - with paved runways:
total: 163
over 3,047 m: 14
2,438 to 3,047 m: 55
1,524 to 2,437 m: 34
914 to 1,523 m: 3
under 914 m: 57 (1994 est.)
Airports - with unpaved runways:
total: 543
over 3,047 m: 7
2,438 to 3,047 m: 7
1,524 to 2,437 m: 16
914 to 1,523 m: 37
under 914 m: 476 (1994 est.)

Military

Military branches: Army, Navy, Air Force, Air Defense Force, Internal Troops, National Guard, Border Troops
Military manpower - military age: 18 years of age
Military manpower - availability:
males age 15-49: 12,434,486 (1999 est.)
Military manpower - fit for military service:
males age 15-49: 9,740,684 (1999 est.)
Military manpower - reaching military age annually:
males: 365,762 (1999 est.)
Military expenditures - dollar figure: $414 million (1999)
Military expenditures - percent of GDP: 1.4% (1999)

Transnational Issues

Disputes - international: dispute with Romania over continental shelf of the Black Sea under which significant gas and oil deposits may exist; agreed in 1997 to two-year negotiating period, after which either party can refer dispute to the International Court of Justice (ICJ); has made no territorial claim in Antarctica (but has reserved the right to do so) and does not recognize the claims of any other nation
Illicit drugs: limited cultivation of cannabis and opium poppy, mostly for CIS consumption; some synthetic drug production for export to West; limited government eradication program; used as transshipment point for opiates and other illicit drugs from Africa, Latin America, and Turkey, and to Europe and Russia; drug-related money laundering a minor, but growing, problem

United Arab Emirates

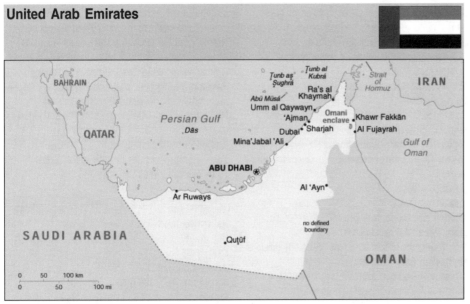

23%, South Asian 50%, other expatriates (includes Westerners and East Asians) 8% (1982)
note: less than 20% are UAE citizens (1982)
Religions: Muslim 96% (Shi'a 16%), Christian, Hindu, and other 4%
Languages: Arabic (official), Persian, English, Hindi, Urdu
Literacy:
definition: age 15 and over can read and write
total population: 79.2%
male: 78.9%
female: 79.8% (1995 est.)

Government

Country name:
conventional long form: United Arab Emirates
conventional short form: none
local long form: Al Imarat al Arabiyah al Muttahidah
local short form: none
former: Trucial States
abbreviation: UAE
Data code: TC
Government type: federation with specified powers delegated to the UAE federal government and other powers reserved to member emirates
Capital: Abu Dhabi
Administrative divisions: 7 emirates (imarat, singular - imarah); Abu Zaby (Abu Dhabi), 'Ajman, Al Fujayrah, Ash Shariqah (Sharjah), Dubayy (Dubai), Ra's al Khaymah, Umm al Qaywayn
Independence: 2 December 1971 (from UK)
National holiday: National Day, 2 December (1971)
Constitution: 2 December 1971 (made permanent in 1996)
Legal system: federal court system introduced in 1971; all emirates except Dubayy (Dubai) and Ra's al Khaymah have joined the federal system; all emirates have secular and Islamic law for civil, criminal, and high courts
Suffrage: none
Executive branch:
chief of state: President ZAYID bin Sultan Al Nuhayyan (since 2 December 1971), ruler of Abu Zaby (Abu Dhabi) (since 6 August 1966) and Vice President MAKTUM bin Rashid al-Maktum (since 8 October 1990), ruler of Dubayy (Dubai)
head of government: Prime Minister MAKTUM bin Rashid al-Maktum (since 8 October 1990), ruler of Dubayy (Dubai); Deputy Prime Minister SULTAN bin Zayid Al Nuhayyan (since 20 November 1990)
cabinet: Council of Ministers appointed by the president
note: there is also a Federal Supreme Council (FSC) which is composed of the seven emirate rulers; the council is the highest constitutional authority in the UAE; establishes general policies and sanctions federal legislation, Abu Zaby (Abu Dhabi) and Dubayy (Dubai) rulers have effective veto power; meets four times a year
elections: president and vice president elected by the FSC (a group of seven electors) for five-year terms; election last held NA October 1996 (next to be held

Geography

Location: Middle East, bordering the Gulf of Oman and the Persian Gulf, between Oman and Saudi Arabia
Geographic coordinates: 24 00 N, 54 00 E
Map references: Middle East
Area:
total: 82,880 sq km
land: 82,880 sq km
water: 0 sq km
Area - comparative: slightly smaller than Maine
Land boundaries:
total: 867 km
border countries: Oman 410 km, Saudi Arabia 457 km
Coastline: 1,318 km
Maritime claims:
contiguous zone: 24 nm
continental shelf: 200 nm or to the edge of the continental margin
exclusive economic zone: 200 nm
territorial sea: 12 nm
Climate: desert; cooler in eastern mountains
Terrain: flat, barren coastal plain merging into rolling sand dunes of vast desert wasteland; mountains in east
Elevation extremes:
lowest point: Persian Gulf 0 m
highest point: Jabal Yibir 1,527 m
Natural resources: petroleum, natural gas
Land use:
arable land: 0%
permanent crops: 0%
permanent pastures: 2%
forests and woodland: 0%
other: 98% (1993 est.)
Irrigated land: 50 sq km (1993 est.)
Natural hazards: frequent sand and dust storms
Environment - current issues: lack of natural freshwater resources being overcome by desalination plants; desertification; beach pollution from oil spills

Environment - international agreements:
party to: Climate Change, Desertification, Endangered Species, Hazardous Wastes, Marine Dumping, Ozone Layer Protection
signed, but not ratified: Biodiversity, Law of the Sea
Geography - note: strategic location along southern approaches to Strait of Hormuz, a vital transit point for world crude oil

People

Population: 2,344,402 (July 1999 est.)
note: includes 1,576,589 non-nationals (July 1999 est.)
Age structure:
0-14 years: 31% (male 368,844; female 353,183)
15-64 years: 67% (male 1,015,690; female 558,902)
65 years and over: 2% (male 32,935; female 14,848) (1999 est.)
Population growth rate: 1.78% (1999 est.)
Birth rate: 18.86 births/1,000 population (1999 est.)
Death rate: 3.13 deaths/1,000 population (1999 est.)
Net migration rate: 2.03 migrant(s)/1,000 population (1999 est.)
Sex ratio:
at birth: 1.05 male(s)/female
under 15 years: 1.04 male(s)/female
15-64 years: 1.82 male(s)/female
65 years and over: 2.22 male(s)/female
total population: 1.53 male(s)/female (1999 est.)
Infant mortality rate: 14.1 deaths/1,000 live births (1999 est.)
Life expectancy at birth:
total population: 75.24 years
male: 73.83 years
female: 76.72 years (1999 est.)
Total fertility rate: 3.5 children born/woman (1999 est.)
Nationality:
noun: Emirian(s)
adjective: Emirian
Ethnic groups: Emiri 19%, other Arab and Iranian

NA 2001); prime minister and deputy prime minister appointed by the president

election results: ZAYID bin Sultan Al Nuhayyan reelected president; percent of FSC vote - NA, but believed to be unanimous; MAKTUM bin Rashid al-Maktum elected vice president; percent of FSC vote - NA, but believed to be unanimous

Legislative branch: unicameral Federal National Council or Majlis al-Ittihad al-Watani (40 seats; members appointed by the rulers of the constituent states to serve two-year terms)

elections: none

note: reviews legislation, but cannot change or veto

Judicial branch: Union Supreme Court, judges appointed by the president

Political parties and leaders: none

Political pressure groups and leaders: NA

International organization participation: ABEDA, AfDB, AFESD, AL, AMF, CAEU, CCC, ESCWA, FAO, G-77, GCC, IAEA, IBRD, ICAO, ICRM, IDA, IDB, IFAD, IFC, IFRCS, IHO, ILO, IMF, IMO, Inmarsat, Intelsat, Interpol, IOC, ISO (correspondent), ITU, NAM, OAPEC, OIC, OPCW, OPEC, UN, UNCTAD, UNESCO, UNIDO, UPU, WHO, WIPO, WMO, WTrO

Diplomatic representation in the US:

chief of mission: Ambassador Muhammad bin Husayn al-SHAALI

chancery: Suite 700, 1255 22nd Street NW, Washington, DC 20037

telephone: [1] (202) 955-7999

Diplomatic representation from the US:

chief of mission: Ambassador Theodore H. KATTOUF

embassy: Al-Sudan Street, Abu Dhabi

mailing address: P. O. Box 4009, Abu Dhabi; American Embassy Abu Dhabi, Department of State, Washington, DC 20521-6010 (pouch); note - work week is Saturday through Wednesday

telephone: [971] (2) 436691, 436692

FAX: [971] (2) 434771

consulate(s) general: Dubai

Flag description: three equal horizontal bands of green (top), white, and black with a thicker vertical red band on the hoist side

Economy

Economy - overview: The UAE has an open economy with one of the world's highest per capita incomes and with a sizable annual trade surplus. Its wealth is based on oil and gas output (about 33% of GDP), and the fortunes of the economy fluctuate with the prices of those commodities. Since 1973, the UAE has undergone a profound transformation from an impoverished region of small desert principalities to a modern state with a high standard of living. At present levels of production, oil and gas reserves should last for over 100 years. The UAE Government is encouraging increased privatization within the economy. Industrial development has picked up in 1997-98, but lower world oil prices caused GDP to drop 5% in 1998.

GDP: purchasing power parity - $40 billion (1998 est.)

GDP - real growth rate: -5% (1998 est.)

GDP - per capita: purchasing power parity - $17,400 (1998 est.)

GDP - composition by sector:

agriculture: 3%

industry: 52%

services: 45% (1996 est.)

Population below poverty line: NA%

Household income or consumption by percentage share:

lowest 10%: NA%

highest 10%: NA%

Inflation rate (consumer prices): 5% (1997 est.)

Labor force: 1.3 million (1997 est.)

note: 75% of the population in the 15-64 age group is non-national (July 1998 est.)

Labor force - by occupation: services 60%, industry 32%, agriculture 8% (1996 est.)

Unemployment rate: NA%

Budget:

revenues: $5.4 billion

expenditures: $5.8 billion, including capital expenditures of $350 million (1998 budget est.)

Industries: petroleum, fishing, petrochemicals, construction materials, some boat building, handicrafts, pearling

Industrial production growth rate: 0% (1997 est.)

Electricity - production: 18 billion kWh (1996)

Electricity - production by source:

fossil fuel: 100%

hydro: 0%

nuclear: 0%

other: 0% (1996)

Electricity - consumption: 18 billion kWh (1996)

Electricity - exports: 0 kWh (1996)

Electricity - imports: 0 kWh (1996)

Agriculture - products: dates, vegetables, watermelons; poultry, eggs, dairy products; fish

Exports: $38 billion (f.o.b., 1997 est.)

Exports - commodities: crude oil 45%, natural gas, reexports, dried fish, dates

Exports - partners: Japan 36%, South Korea 9%, Singapore 5%, India 5%, Oman 3% (1997)

Imports: $29.7 billion (f.o.b., 1997 est.)

Imports - commodities: manufactured goods, machinery and transport equipment, chemicals, food

Imports - partners: US 9%, Japan 9%, UK 9%, Germany 6%, India 6% (1997)

Debt - external: $14 billion (1996 est.)

Economic aid - recipient: $NA

Currency: 1 Emirian dirham (Dh) = 100 fils

Exchange rates: Emirian dirhams (Dh) per US$1 - central bank mid-point rate: 3.6725 (January 1999), 3.6725 (1998); fixed rate: 3.6710 (1994-1997)

Fiscal year: calendar year

Communications

Telephones: 677,793 (1993 est.)

Telephone system: modern system consisting of microwave radio relay and coaxial cable; key centers are Abu Dhabi and Dubai

domestic: microwave radio relay and coaxial cable

international: satellite earth stations - 3 Intelsat (1 Atlantic Ocean and 2 Indian Ocean) and 1 Arabsat; submarine cables to Qatar, Bahrain, India, and Pakistan; tropospheric scatter to Bahrain; microwave radio relay to Saudi Arabia

Radio broadcast stations: AM 8, FM 3, shortwave 0

Radios: 545,000 (1992 est.)

Television broadcast stations: 15 (1997)

Televisions: 170,000 (1993 est.)

Transportation

Railways: 0 km

Highways:

total: 4,835 km

paved: 4,835 km

unpaved: 0 km (1996 est.)

Pipelines: crude oil 830 km; natural gas, including natural gas liquids, 870 km

Ports and harbors: 'Ajman, Al Fujayrah, Das Island, Khawr Fakkan, Mina' Jabal 'Ali, Mina' Khalid, Mina' Rashid, Mina' Saqr, Mina' Zayid, Umm al Qaywayn

Merchant marine:

total: 74 ships (1,000 GRT or over) totaling 1,093,795 GRT/1,757,189 DWT

ships by type: bulk 4, cargo 20, chemical tanker 4, container 8, liquefied gas tanker 1, livestock carrier 1, oil tanker 28, refrigerated cargo 1, roll-on/roll-off cargo 7 (1998 est.)

Airports: 41 (1998 est.)

Airports - with paved runways:

total: 21

over 3,047 m: 8

2,438 to 3,047 m: 3

1,524 to 2,437 m: 3

914 to 1,523 m: 3

under 914 m: 4 (1998 est.)

Airports - with unpaved runways:

total: 20

over 3,047 m: 1

2,438 to 3,047 m: 1

1,524 to 2,437 m: 4

914 to 1,523 m: 9

under 914 m: 5 (1998 est.)

Heliports: 2 (1998 est.)

Military

Military branches: Army, Navy, Air Force, Air Defense, paramilitary (includes Federal Police Force)

Military manpower - military age: 18 years of age

Military manpower - availability:

males age 15-49: 791,097 (1999 est.)

note: includes non-nationals

Military manpower - fit for military service:

males age 15-49: 425,248 (1999 est.)

Military manpower - reaching military age annually:

males: 23,358 (1999 est.)

Military expenditures - dollar figure: $2.118 billion (1999)

United Arab Emirates (continued)

Military expenditures - percent of GDP: 5% (1999)

Transnational Issues

Disputes - international: location and status of boundary with Saudi Arabia is not final, de facto boundary reflects 1974 agreement; no defined boundary with most of Oman, but Administrative Line in far north; claims two islands in the Persian Gulf occupied by Iran: Lesser Tunb (called Tunb as Sughra in Arabic by UAE and Jazireh-ye Tonb-e Kuchek in Persian by Iran) and Greater Tunb (called Tunb al Kubra in Arabic by UAE and Jazireh-ye Tonb-e Bozorg in Persian by Iran); claims island in the Persian Gulf jointly administered with Iran (called Abu Musa in Arabic by UAE and Jazireh-ye Abu Musa in Persian by Iran) - over which Iran has taken steps to exert unilateral control since 1992, including access restrictions and a military build-up on the island; the UAE has garnered significant diplomatic support in the region in protesting these Iranian actions

Illicit drugs: growing role as heroin transshipment and money-laundering center due to its proximity to southwest Asian producing countries and the bustling free trade zone in Dubai

United Kingdom

Introduction

Background: Britain, the dominant industrial and maritime power of the nineteenth century, played a leading role in developing parliamentary democracy and in advancing literature and science. The British Empire covered approximately one-fourth of the earth's surface at its zenith. In the first half of the twentieth century its strength was seriously depleted by two world wars. Since the end of World War II, the British Empire has been dismantled, and Britain has rebuilt itself into a prosperous, modern European nation with significant international political, cultural, and economic influence. As the twentieth century draws to a close, Britain is debating the degree of its integration with continental Europe. While a member of the EU, for the time being it is staying out of the euro system introduced in January 1999. Constitutional reform, including the House of Lords and the devolution of power to Scotland, Wales, and Northern Ireland, is an ongoing issue in Great Britain.

Geography

Location: Western Europe, islands including the northern one-sixth of the island of Ireland between the North Atlantic Ocean and the North Sea, northwest of France

Geographic coordinates: 54 00 N, 2 00 W

Map references: Europe

Area:
total: 244,820 sq km
land: 241,590 sq km
water: 3,230 sq km
note: includes Rockall and Shetland Islands

Area - comparative: slightly smaller than Oregon

Land boundaries:
total: 360 km
border countries: Ireland 360 km

Coastline: 12,429 km

Maritime claims:
continental shelf: as defined in continental shelf orders or in accordance with agreed upon boundaries
exclusive fishing zone: 200 nm
territorial sea: 12 nm

Climate: temperate; moderated by prevailing southwest winds over the North Atlantic Current; more than one-half of the days are overcast

Terrain: mostly rugged hills and low mountains; level to rolling plains in east and southeast

Elevation extremes:
lowest point: Fenland -4 m
highest point: Ben Nevis 1,343 m

Natural resources: coal, petroleum, natural gas, tin, limestone, iron ore, salt, clay, chalk, gypsum, lead, silica

Land use:
arable land: 25%
permanent crops: 0%
permanent pastures: 46%
forests and woodland: 10%
other: 19% (1993 est.)

Irrigated land: 1,080 sq km (1993 est.)

Natural hazards: NA

Environment - current issues: sulfur dioxide emissions from power plants contribute to air pollution; some rivers polluted by agricultural wastes; and coastal waters polluted because of large-scale disposal of sewage at sea

Environment - international agreements:
party to: Air Pollution, Air Pollution-Nitrogen Oxides, Air Pollution-Sulphur 94, Air Pollution-Volatile Organic Compounds, Antarctic-Environmental Protocol, Antarctic Treaty, Biodiversity, Climate Change, Desertification, Endangered Species, Environmental Modification, Hazardous Wastes, Law of the Sea, Marine Dumping, Marine Life Conservation, Nuclear Test Ban, Ozone Layer Protection, Ship Pollution, Tropical Timber 83, Tropical Timber 94, Wetlands, Whaling
signed, but not ratified: Air Pollution-Persistent Organic Pollutants, Climate Change-Kyoto Protocol

Geography - note: lies near vital North Atlantic sea lanes; only 35 km from France and now linked by tunnel under the English Channel; because of heavily indented coastline, no location is more than 125 km from tidal waters

United Kingdom (continued)

Population: 59,113,439 (July 1999 est.)
Age structure:
0-14 years: 19% (male 5,822,901; female 5,522,122)
15-64 years: 65% (male 19,393,706; female 19,103,882)
65 years and over: 16% (male 3,821,181; female 5,449,647) (1999 est.)
Population growth rate: 0.24% (1999 est.)
Birth rate: 11.9 births/1,000 population (1999 est.)
Death rate: 10.64 deaths/1,000 population (1999 est.)
Net migration rate: 1.11 migrant(s)/1,000 population (1999 est.)
Sex ratio:
at birth: 1.05 male(s)/female
under 15 years: 1.05 male(s)/female
15-64 years: 1.02 male(s)/female
65 years and over: 0.7 male(s)/female
total population: 0.97 male(s)/female (1999 est.)
Infant mortality rate: 5.78 deaths/1,000 live births (1999 est.)
Life expectancy at birth:
total population: 77.37 years
male: 74.73 years
female: 80.15 years (1999 est.)
Total fertility rate: 1.71 children born/woman (1999 est.)
Nationality:
noun: Briton(s), British (collective plural)
adjective: British
Ethnic groups: English 81.5%, Scottish 9.6%, Irish 2.4%, Welsh 1.9%, Ulster 1.8%, West Indian, Indian, Pakistani, and other 2.8%
Religions: Anglican 27 million, Roman Catholic 9 million, Muslim 1 million, Presbyterian 800,000, Methodist 760,000, Sikh 400,000, Hindu 350,000, Jewish 300,000 (1991 est.)
Languages: English, Welsh (about 26% of the population of Wales), Scottish form of Gaelic (about 60,000 in Scotland)
Literacy:
definition: age 15 and over has completed five or more years of schooling
total population: 99% (1978 est.)
male: NA%
female: NA%

Country name:
conventional long form: United Kingdom of Great Britain and Northern Ireland
conventional short form: United Kingdom
abbreviation: UK
Data code: UK
Government type: constitutional monarchy
Capital: London
Administrative divisions: 47 counties, 7 metropolitan counties, 26 districts, 9 regions, and 3 islands areas; England - 39 counties, 7 metropolitan counties*; Avon, Bedford, Berkshire, Buckingham,
Cambridge, Cheshire, Cleveland, Cornwall, Cumbria, Derby, Devon, Dorset, Durham, East Sussex, Essex, Gloucester, Greater London*, Greater Manchester*, Hampshire, Hereford and Worcester, Hertford, Humberside, Isle of Wight, Kent, Lancashire, Leicester, Lincoln, Merseyside*, Norfolk, Northampton, Northumberland, North Yorkshire, Nottingham, Oxford, Shropshire, Somerset, South Yorkshire*, Stafford, Suffolk, Surrey, Tyne and Wear*, Warwick, West Midlands*, West Sussex, West Yorkshire*, Wiltshire; Northern Ireland - 26 districts; Antrim, Ards, Armagh, Ballymena, Ballymoney, Banbridge, Belfast, Carrickfergus, Castlereagh, Coleraine, Cookstown, Craigavon, Down, Dungannon, Fermanagh, Larne, Limavady, Lisburn, Londonderry, Magherafelt, Moyle, Newry and Mourne, Newtownabbey, North Down, Omagh, Strabane; Scotland - 9 regions, 3 islands areas*; Borders, Central, Dumfries and Galloway, Fife, Grampian, Highland, Lothian, Orkney*, Shetland*, Strathclyde, Tayside, Western Isles*; Wales - 8 counties; Clwyd, Dyfed, Gwent, Gwynedd, Mid Glamorgan, Powys, South Glamorgan, West Glamorgan
note: England may now have 35 counties and Wales 9 counties
Dependent areas: Anguilla, Bermuda, British Indian Ocean Territory, British Virgin Islands, Cayman Islands, Falkland Islands, Gibraltar, Guernsey, Jersey, Isle of Man, Montserrat, Pitcairn Islands, Saint Helena, South Georgia and the South Sandwich Islands, Turks and Caicos Islands
Independence: England has existed as a unified entity since the 10th century; the union between England and Wales was enacted under the Statute of Rhuddlan in 1284; in the Act of Union of 1707, England and Scotland agreed to permanent union as Great Britain; the legislative union of Great Britain and Ireland was implemented in 1801, with the adoption of the name the United Kingdom of Great Britain and Ireland; the Anglo-Irish treaty of 1921 formalized a partition of Ireland; six northern Irish counties remained part of the United Kingdom as Northern Ireland and the current name of the country, the United Kingdom of Great Britain and Northern Ireland, was adopted in 1927
National holiday: Celebration of the Birthday of the Queen (second Saturday in June)
Constitution: unwritten; partly statutes, partly common law and practice
Legal system: common law tradition with early Roman and modern continental influences; no judicial review of Acts of Parliament; accepts compulsory ICJ jurisdiction, with reservations; British courts and legislation are increasingly subject to review by European Union courts
Suffrage: 18 years of age; universal
Executive branch:
chief of state: Queen ELIZABETH II (since 6 February 1952); Heir Apparent Prince CHARLES (son of the queen, born 14 November 1948)
head of government: Prime Minister Anthony C. L.
(Tony) BLAIR (since 2 May 1997)
cabinet: Cabinet of Ministers appointed by the prime minister
elections: none; the monarch is hereditary; the prime minister is the leader of the majority party in the House of Commons (assuming there is no majority party, a prime minister would have a majority coalition or at least a coalition that was not rejected by the majority)
Legislative branch: bicameral Parliament consists of House of Lords (1,200 seats; four-fifths of the members are hereditary peers, two archbishops, 24 other senior bishops, serving and retired Lords of Appeal in Ordinary, other life peers, Scottish peers) and House of Commons (659 seats; members are elected by popular vote to serve five-year terms unless the House is dissolved earlier)
elections: House of Lords - no elections; House of Commons - last held 1 May 1997 (next to be held by NA May 2002); note - in 1998 elections were held for a Northern Ireland Parliament; in 1999 there will be elections for a new Scottish parliament and a new Welsh Assembly
election results: House of Commons - percent of vote by party - Labor 44.5%, Conservative 31%, Liberal Democratic 17%, other 7.5%; seats by party - Labor 418, Conservative 165, Liberal Democrat 46, other 30
Judicial branch: House of Lords, several Lords of Appeal in Ordinary are appointed by the monarch for life
Political parties and leaders: Conservative and Unionist Party [William HAGUE]; Labor Party [Anthony (Tony) Blair]; Liberal Democrats [Jeremy (Paddy) ASHDOWN]; Scottish National Party [Alex SALMOND]; Welsh National Party (Plaid Cymru) [Dafydd Iwan WIGLEY]; Ulster Unionist Party (Northern Ireland) [David TRIMBLE]; Democratic Unionist Party (Northern Ireland) [Rev. Ian PAISLEY]; Social Democratic and Labor Party or SDLP (Northern Ireland) [John HUME]; Sinn Fein (Northern Ireland) [Gerry ADAMS]; Alliance Party (Northern Ireland) [Seamus CLOSE]
Political pressure groups and leaders: Trades Union Congress; Confederation of British Industry; National Farmers' Union; Campaign for Nuclear Disarmament
International organization participation: AfDB, AsDB, Australia Group, BIS, C, CCC, CDB (non-regional), CE, CERN, CP, EAPC, EBRD, ECA (associate), ECE, ECLAC, EIB, ESA, ESCAP, EU, FAO, G-5, G-7, G-10, IADB, IAEA, IBRD, ICAO, ICC, ICFTU, ICRM, IDA, IEA, IFAD, IFC, IFRCS, IHO, ILO, IMF, IMO, Inmarsat, Intelsat, Interpol, IOC, IOM (observer), ISO, ITU, MTCR, NATO, NEA, NSG, OAS (observer), OECD, OPCW, OSCE, PCA, UN, UN Security Council, UNCTAD, UNESCO, UNFICYP, UNHCR, UNIDO, UNIKOM, UNMIBH, UNOMIG, UNOMSIL, UNRWA, UNU, UPU, WCL, WEU, WHO, WIPO, WMO, WTrO, ZC
Diplomatic representation in the US:
chief of mission: Ambassador Sir Christopher J. R. MEYER
chancery: 3100 Massachusetts Avenue NW,

United Kingdom *(continued)*

Washington, DC 20008
telephone: [1] (202) 588-6500
FAX: [1] (202) 588-7870
consulate(s) general: Atlanta, Boston, Chicago, Cleveland, Houston, Los Angeles, New York, and San Francisco
consulate(s): Dallas, Miami, and Seattle
Diplomatic representation from the US:
chief of mission: Ambassador Philip LADER
embassy: 24/31 Grosvenor Square, London, W. 1A1AE
mailing address: PSC 801, Box 40, FPO AE 09498-4040
telephone: [44] (171) 499-9000
FAX: [44] (171) 409-1637
consulate(s) general: Belfast, Edinburgh
Flag description: blue with the red cross of Saint George (patron saint of England) edged in white superimposed on the diagonal red cross of Saint Patrick (patron saint of Ireland) which is superimposed on the diagonal white cross of Saint Andrew (patron saint of Scotland); known as the Union Flag or Union Jack; the design and colors (especially the Blue Ensign) have been the basis for a number of other flags including other Commonwealth countries and their constituent states or provinces, as well as British overseas territories

Economy

Economy - overview: The UK is one of the world's great trading powers and financial centers, and its essentially capitalistic economy ranks among the four largest in Western Europe. Over the past two decades the government has greatly reduced public ownership and contained the growth of social welfare programs. Agriculture is intensive, highly mechanized, and efficient by European standards, producing about 60% of food needs with only 1% of the labor force. The UK has large coal, natural gas, and oil reserves; primary energy production accounts for 10% of GDP, one of the highest shares of any industrial nation. Services, particularly banking, insurance, and business services, account by far for the largest proportion of GDP while industry continues to decline in importance, now employing only 18% of the work force. Economic growth is slowing, and Britain may experience a short recession in 1999. As a result, unemployment probably will begin to rise again. The BLAIR government has put off the question of participation in the euro system until after the next election, not expected until 2001, but Chancellor of the Exchequer BROWN is committed to preparing the British economy for eventual membership.
GDP: purchasing power parity - $1.252 trillion (1998 est.)
GDP - real growth rate: 2.6% (1998 est.)
GDP - per capita: purchasing power parity - $21,200 (1998 est.)
GDP - composition by sector:
agriculture: 1.5%
industry: 31.5%
services: 67% (1997)

Population below poverty line: 17%
Household income or consumption by percentage share:
lowest 10%: 2.4%
highest 10%: 24.7% (1986)
Inflation rate (consumer prices): 2.7% (1998)
Labor force: 28.8 million (1998)
Labor force - by occupation: services 68.9%, manufacturing and construction 17.5%, government 11.3%, energy 1.2%, agriculture 1.1% (1996)
Unemployment rate: 7.5% (1998 est.)
Budget:
revenues: $487.7 billion
expenditures: $492.6 billion, including capital expenditures of $23.1 billion (1997 est.)
Industries: production machinery including machine tools, electric power equipment, automation equipment, railroad equipment, shipbuilding, aircraft, motor vehicles and parts, electronics and communications equipment, metals, chemicals, coal, petroleum, paper and paper products, food processing, textiles, clothing, and other consumer goods
Industrial production growth rate: 0.5% (1998 est.)
Electricity - production: 309.672 billion kWh (1996)
Electricity - production by source:
fossil fuel: 72.28%
hydro: 1.28%
nuclear: 26.33%
other: 0.11% (1996)
Electricity - consumption: 326.322 billion kWh (1996)
Electricity - exports: 0 kWh (1996)
Electricity - imports: 16.65 billion kWh (1996)
Agriculture - products: cereals, oilseed, potatoes, vegetables; cattle, sheep, poultry; fish
Exports: $271 billion (f.o.b., 1998)
Exports - commodities: manufactured goods, fuels, chemicals; food, beverages, tobacco
Exports - partners: EU countries 56% (Germany 12%, France 10%, Netherlands 8%), US 12% (1997)
Imports: $304 billion (f.o.b., 1998)
Imports - commodities: manufactured goods, machinery, fuels, foodstuffs
Imports - partners: EU countries 53% (Germany 14%, France 10%, Netherlands 7%, Ireland 5%), US 13% (1997)
Debt - external: $NA
Economic aid - donor: ODA, $3.4 billion (1996)
Currency: 1 British pound (£) = 100 pence
Exchange rates: British pounds (£) per US$1 - 0.6057 (January 1999), 0.6037 (1998), 0.6106 (1997), 0.6403 (1996), 0.6335 (1995), 0.6529 (1994)
Fiscal year: 1 April - 31 March

Communications

Telephones: 29.5 million (1987 est.)
Telephone system: technologically advanced domestic and international system
domestic: equal mix of buried cables, microwave radio relay, and fiber-optic systems

international: 40 coaxial submarine cables; satellite earth stations - 10 Intelsat (7 Atlantic Ocean and 3 Indian Ocean), 1 Inmarsat (Atlantic Ocean region), and 1 Eutelsat; at least 8 large international switching centers
Radio broadcast stations: AM 225, FM 525 (mostly repeaters), shortwave 0
Radios: 70 million
Television broadcast stations: 78 (in addition, there are 869 repeaters) (1997)
Televisions: 20 million

Transportation

Railways:
total: 16,878 km
broad gauge: 342 km 1.600-m gauge (190 km double track); note - all 1.600-m gauge track, of which 342 km is in common carrier use, is in Northern Ireland
standard gauge: 16,536 km 1.435-m gauge (4,928 km electrified; 12,591 km double or multiple track) (1996)
Highways:
total: 372,000 km
paved: 372,000 km (including 3,270 km of expressways)
unpaved: 0 km (1996 est.)
Waterways: 3,200 km
Pipelines: crude oil (almost all insignificant) 933 km; petroleum products 2,993 km; natural gas 12,800 km
Ports and harbors: Aberdeen, Belfast, Bristol, Cardiff, Dover, Falmouth, Felixstowe, Glasgow, Grangemouth, Hull, Leith, Liverpool, London, Manchester, Peterhead, Plymouth, Scapa Flow, Sullom Voe, Tees, Tyne
Merchant marine:
total: 155 ships (1,000 GRT or over) totaling 2,460,361 GRT/2,517,875 DWT
ships by type: bulk 3, cargo 29, chemical tanker 6, combination ore/oil 1, container 25, liquefied gas tanker 1, oil tanker 51, passenger 8, passenger-cargo 1, roll-on/roll-off cargo 17, short-sea passenger 12, specialized tanker 1 (1998 est.)
Airports: 497 (1998 est.)
Airports - with paved runways:
total: 356
over 3,047 m: 10
2,438 to 3,047 m: 32
1,524 to 2,437 m: 169
914 to 1,523 m: 91
under 914 m: 54 (1998 est.)
Airports - with unpaved runways:
total: 141
1,524 to 2,437 m: 1
914 to 1,523 m: 23
under 914 m: 117 (1998 est.)
Heliports: 12 (1998 est.)

Military

Military branches: Army, Royal Navy (includes Royal Marines), Royal Air Force
Military manpower - availability:
males age 15-49: 14,458,646 (1999 est.)

United Kingdom *(continued)*

Military manpower - fit for military service:
males age 15-49: 12,053,320 (1999 est.)
Military expenditures - dollar figure: $36.7 billion
(FY98/99)
Military expenditures - percent of GDP: 2.6%
(FY98/99)

Transnational Issues

Disputes - international: Northern Ireland issue
with Ireland (historic peace agreement signed 10 April
1998); Gibraltar issue with Spain; Argentina claims
Falkland Islands (Islas Malvinas); Argentina claims
South Georgia and the South Sandwich Islands;
Mauritius claims island of Diego Garcia in British
Indian Ocean Territory; Rockall continental shelf
dispute involving Denmark, Iceland, and Ireland
(Ireland and the UK have signed a boundary
agreement in the Rockall area); territorial claim in
Antarctica (British Antarctic Territory); Seychelles
claims Chagos Archipelago in British Indian Ocean
Territory
Illicit drugs: gateway country for Latin American
cocaine entering the European market; producer and
major consumer of synthetic drugs, synthetic
precursor chemicals; transshipment point for
Southwest Asian heroin; money-laundering center

United States

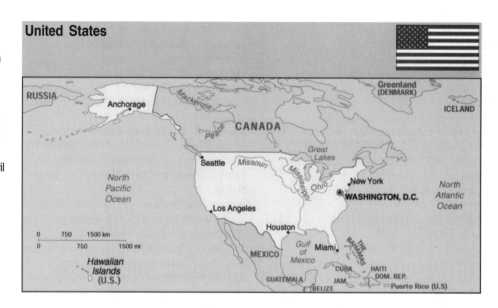

Introduction

Background: Buoyed by victories in World Wars I
and II and the end of the Cold War in 1991, the US
remains the world's most powerful nation-state. The
economy is marked by steady growth, low
unemployment, low inflation, and rapid advances in
technology. The biggest cloud over this affluent
society is the distribution of gains - since 1975 most of
the increase in national income has gone to the 20%
of people at the top of the income ladder.

Geography

Location: North America, bordering both the North
Atlantic Ocean and the North Pacific Ocean, between
Canada and Mexico
Geographic coordinates: 38 00 N, 97 00 W
Map references: North America
Area:
total: 9,629,091 sq km
land: 9,158,960 sq km
water: 470,131 sq km
note: includes only the 50 states and District of
Columbia
Area - comparative: about one-half the size of
Russia; about three-tenths the size of Africa; about
one-half the size of South America (or slightly larger
than Brazil); slightly larger than China; about two and
one-half times the size of Western Europe
Land boundaries:
total: 12,248 km
border countries: Canada 8,893 km (including 2,477
km with Alaska), Cuba 29 km (US Naval Base at
Guantanamo Bay), Mexico 3,326 km
note: Guantanamo Naval Base is leased by the US
and thus remains part of Cuba
Coastline: 19,924 km
Maritime claims:
contiguous zone: 12 nm
continental shelf: not specified
exclusive economic zone: 200 nm
territorial sea: 12 nm

Climate: mostly temperate, but tropical in Hawaii and
Florida, arctic in Alaska, semiarid in the great plains
west of the Mississippi River, and arid in the Great
Basin of the southwest; low winter temperatures in the
northwest are ameliorated occasionally in January
and February by warm chinook winds from the eastern
slopes of the Rocky Mountains
Terrain: vast central plain, mountains in west, hills
and low mountains in east; rugged mountains and
broad river valleys in Alaska; rugged, volcanic
topography in Hawaii
Elevation extremes:
lowest point: Death Valley -86 m
highest point: Mount McKinley 6,194 m
Natural resources: coal, copper, lead,
molybdenum, phosphates, uranium, bauxite, gold,
iron, mercury, nickel, potash, silver, tungsten, zinc,
petroleum, natural gas, timber
Land use:
arable land: 19%
permanent crops: 0%
permanent pastures: 25%
forests and woodland: 30%
other: 26% (1993 est.)
Irrigated land: 207,000 sq km (1993 est.)
Natural hazards: tsunamis, volcanoes, and
earthquake activity around Pacific Basin; hurricanes
along the Atlantic and Gulf of Mexico coasts;
tornadoes in the midwest and southeast; mud slides in
California; forest fires in the west; flooding; permafrost
in northern Alaska, a major impediment to
development
Environment - current issues: air pollution
resulting in acid rain in both the US and Canada; the
US is the largest single emitter of carbon dioxide from
the burning of fossil fuels; water pollution from runoff
of pesticides and fertilizers; very limited natural fresh
water resources in much of the western part of the
country require careful management; desertification
Environment - international agreements:
party to: Air Pollution, Air Pollution-Nitrogen Oxides,

United States (continued)

Antarctic-Environmental Protocol, Antarctic Treaty, Climate Change, Endangered Species, Environmental Modification, Marine Dumping, Marine Life Conservation, Nuclear Test Ban, Ozone Layer Protection, Ship Pollution, Tropical Timber 83, Tropical Timber 94, Wetlands, Whaling
signed, but not ratified: Air Pollution-Persistent Organic Pollutants, Air Pollution-Volatile Organic Compounds, Biodiversity, Climate Change-Kyoto Protocol, Desertification, Hazardous Wastes
Geography - note: world's third-largest country (after Russia and Canada)

People

Population: 272,639,608 (July 1999 est.)
Age structure:
0-14 years: 22% (male 30,097,125; female 28,699,568)
15-64 years: 66% (male 89,024,052; female 90,379,328)
65 years and over: 12% (male 14,189,132; female 20,250,403) (1999 est.)
Population growth rate: 0.85% (1999 est.)
Birth rate: 14.3 births/1,000 population (1999 est.)
Death rate: 8.8 deaths/1,000 population (1999 est.)
Net migration rate: 3 migrant(s)/1,000 population (1999 est.)
Sex ratio:
at birth: 1.05 male(s)/female
under 15 years: 1.05 male(s)/female
15-64 years: 0.99 male(s)/female
65 years and over: 0.7 male(s)/female
total population: 0.96 male(s)/female (1999 est.)
Infant mortality rate: 6.33 deaths/1,000 live births (1999 est.)
Life expectancy at birth:
total population: 76.23 years
male: 72.95 years
female: 79.67 years (1999 est.)
Total fertility rate: 2.07 children born/woman (1999 est.)
Nationality:
noun: American(s)
adjective: American
Ethnic groups: white 83.5%, black 12.4%, Asian 3.3%, Amerindian 0.8% (1992)
Religions: Protestant 56%, Roman Catholic 28%, Jewish 2%, other 4%, none 10% (1989)
Languages: English, Spanish (spoken by a sizable minority)
Literacy:
definition: age 15 and over can read and write
total population: 97%
male: 97%
female: 97% (1979 est.)

Government

Country name:
conventional long form: United States of America
conventional short form: United States
abbreviation: US or USA

Data code: US
Government type: federal republic; strong democratic tradition
Capital: Washington, DC
Administrative divisions: 50 states and 1 district*; Alabama, Alaska, Arizona, Arkansas, California, Colorado, Connecticut, Delaware, District of Columbia*, Florida, Georgia, Hawaii, Idaho, Illinois, Indiana, Iowa, Kansas, Kentucky, Louisiana, Maine, Maryland, Massachusetts, Michigan, Minnesota, Mississippi, Missouri, Montana, Nebraska, Nevada, New Hampshire, New Jersey, New Mexico, New York, North Carolina, North Dakota, Ohio, Oklahoma, Oregon, Pennsylvania, Rhode Island, South Carolina, South Dakota, Tennessee, Texas, Utah, Vermont, Virginia, Washington, West Virginia, Wisconsin, Wyoming
Dependent areas: American Samoa, Baker Island, Guam, Howland Island, Jarvis Island, Johnston Atoll, Kingman Reef, Midway Islands, Navassa Island, Northern Mariana Islands, Palmyra Atoll, Puerto Rico, Virgin Islands, Wake Atoll
note: from 18 July 1947 until 1 October 1994, the US administered the Trust Territory of the Pacific Islands, but recently entered into a new political relationship with all four political units: the Northern Mariana Islands is a commonwealth in political union with the US (effective 3 November 1986); Palau concluded a Compact of Free Association with the US (effective 1 October 1994); the Federated States of Micronesia signed a Compact of Free Association with the US (effective 3 November 1986); the Republic of the Marshall Islands signed a Compact of Free Association with the US (effective 21 October 1986)
Independence: 4 July 1776 (from England)
National holiday: Independence Day, 4 July (1776)
Constitution: 17 September 1787, effective 4 March 1789
Legal system: based on English common law; judicial review of legislative acts; accepts compulsory ICJ jurisdiction, with reservations
Suffrage: 18 years of age; universal
Executive branch:
chief of state: President William Jefferson CLINTON (since 20 January 1993) and Vice President Albert GORE, Jr. (since 20 January 1993); note - the president is both the chief of state and head of government
head of government: President William Jefferson CLINTON (since 20 January 1993) and Vice President Albert GORE, Jr. (since 20 January 1993); note - the president is both the chief of state and head of government
cabinet: Cabinet appointed by the president with Senate approval
elections: president and vice president elected on the same ticket by a college of representatives who are elected directly from each state; president and vice president serve four-year terms; election last held 5 November 1996 (next to be held 7 November 2000)
election results: William Jefferson CLINTON reelected president; percent of popular vote - William

Jefferson CLINTON (Democratic Party) 49.2%, Robert DOLE (Republican Party) 40.7%, Ross PEROT (Reform Party) 8.4%, other 1.7%
Legislative branch: bicameral Congress consists of Senate (100 seats, one-third are renewed every two years; two members are elected from each state by popular vote to serve six-year terms) and House of Representatives (435 seats; members are directly elected by popular vote to serve two-year terms)
elections: Senate - last held 2 November 1998 (next to be held 7 November 2000); House of Representatives - last held 2 November 1998 (next to be held 7 November 2000)
election results: Senate - percent of vote by party - NA; seats by party - Republican Party 55, Democratic Party 45; House of Representatives - percent of vote by party - NA; seats by party - Republican Party 223, Democratic Party 211, independent 1
Judicial branch: Supreme Court (the nine justices are appointed for life by the president with confirmation by the Senate)
Political parties and leaders: Republican Party [Jim NICHOLSON, national committee chairman]; Democratic Party [Steve GROSSMAN, national committee chairman]; several other groups or parties of minor political significance
International organization participation: AfDB, ANZUS, APEC, AsDB, Australia Group, BIS, CCC, CE (observer), CERN (observer), CP, EAPC, EBRD, ECE, ECLAC, ESCAP, FAO, G-5, G-7, G-10, IADB, IAEA, IBRD, ICAO, ICC, ICFTU, ICRM, IDA, IEA, IFAD, IFC, IFRCS, IHO, ILO, IMF, IMO, Inmarsat, Intelsat, Interpol, IOC, IOM, ISO, ITU, MINURSO, MIPONUH, MTCR, NATO, NEA, NSG, OAS, OECD, OPCW, OSCE, PCA, SPC, UN, UN Security Council, UNCTAD, UNHCR, UNIDO, UNIKOM, UNMIBH, UNOMIG, UNPREDEP, UNRWA, UNTSO, UNU, UPU, WCL, WHO, WIPO, WMO, WTrO, ZC
Flag description: thirteen equal horizontal stripes of red (top and bottom) alternating with white; there is a blue rectangle in the upper hoist-side corner bearing 50 small, white, five-pointed stars arranged in nine offset horizontal rows of six stars (top and bottom) alternating with rows of five stars; the 50 stars represent the 50 states, the 13 stripes represent the 13 original colonies; known as Old Glory; the design and colors have been the basis for a number of other flags, including Chile, Liberia, Malaysia, and Puerto Rico

Economy

Economy - overview: The US has the most powerful, diverse, and technologically advanced economy in the world, with a per capita GDP of $31,500, the largest among major industrial nations. In this market-oriented economy, private individuals and business firms make most of the decisions, and government buys needed goods and services predominantly in the private marketplace. US business firms enjoy considerably greater flexibility than their counterparts in Western Europe and Japan in decisions to expand capital plant, lay off surplus workers, and develop new products. At the same time, they face higher barriers to entry in their rivals' home markets than the barriers to entry of foreign firms in US markets. US firms are at or near the forefront in technological advances, especially in computers and in medical, aerospace, and military equipment, although their advantage has narrowed since the end of World War II. The onrush of technology largely explains the gradual development of a "two-tier labor market" in which those at the bottom lack the education and the professional/technical skills of those at the top and, more and more, fail to get pay raises, health insurance coverage, and other benefits. Since 1975, practically all the gains in household income have gone to the top 20% of households. The years 1994-98 witnessed solid increases in real output, low inflation rates, and a drop in unemployment to below 5%. Long-term problems include inadequate investment in economic infrastructure, rapidly rising medical costs of an aging population, sizable trade deficits, and stagnation of family income in the lower economic groups. The outlook for 1999 is for GDP growth somewhat below 1998's, continued low inflation, and about the same level of unemployment. Two shadows for 1999 are the severe financial crises in East Asia and Russia and the exuberant level of stock prices in relation to corporate earnings.

GDP: purchasing power parity - $8.511 trillion (1998 est.)

GDP - real growth rate: 3.9% (1998 est.)

GDP - per capita: purchasing power parity - $31,500 (1998 est.)

GDP - composition by sector:
agriculture: 2%
industry: 23%
services: 75% (1998 est.)

Population below poverty line: 13% (1997 est.)

Household income or consumption by percentage share:
lowest 10%: 1.5%
highest 10%: 28.5% (1994)

Inflation rate (consumer prices): 1.6% (1998)

Labor force: 137.7 million (includes unemployed) (1998)

Labor force - by occupation: managerial and professional 29.6%, technical, sales and administrative support 29.3%, services 13.6%, manufacturing, mining, transportation, and crafts 24.8%, farming, forestry, and fishing 2.7% (1998)
note: figures exclude the unemployed

Unemployment rate: 4.5% (1998)

Budget:
revenues: $1.722 trillion
expenditures: $1.653 trillion, including capital expenditures of $NA (1998)

Industries: leading industrial power in the world, highly diversified and technologically advanced; petroleum, steel, motor vehicles, aerospace, telecommunications, chemicals, electronics, food processing, consumer goods, lumber, mining

Industrial production growth rate: 3.6% (1998)

Electricity - production: 3.629 trillion kWh (1996)

Electricity - production by source:
fossil fuel: 65.1%
hydro: 9.6%
nuclear: 18.59%
other: 6.71% (1996)

Electricity - consumption: 3.666 trillion kWh (1996)

Electricity - exports: 9.02 billion kWh (1996)

Electricity - imports: 46.543 billion kWh (1996)

Agriculture - products: wheat, other grains, corn, fruits, vegetables, cotton; beef, pork, poultry, dairy products; forest products; fish

Exports: $663 billion (f.o.b., 1998 est.)

Exports - commodities: capital goods, automobiles, industrial supplies and raw materials, consumer goods, agricultural products

Exports - partners: Canada 22%, Western Europe 21%, Japan 10%, Mexico 10% (1997)

Imports: $912 billion (c.i.f., 1998 est.)

Imports - commodities: crude oil and refined petroleum products, machinery, automobiles, consumer goods, industrial raw materials, food and beverages

Imports - partners: Canada, 19%, Western Europe 18%, Japan 14%, Mexico 10%, China 7% (1997)

Debt - external: $862 billion (1995 est.)

Economic aid - donor: ODA, $7.4 billion (1995)

Currency: 1 United States dollar (US$) = 100 cents

Exchange rates: British pounds (£) per US$ - 0.6057 (January 1999), 0.6037 (1998), 0.6106 (1997), 0.6403 (1996), 0.6335 (1995), 0.6529 (1994); Canadian dollars (Can$) per US$ - 1.5192 (January 1999), 1.4835 (1998), 1.3846 (1997), 1.3635 (1996), 1.3724 (1995), 1.3656 (1994); French francs (F) per US$ - 5.65 (January 1999), 5.8995 (1998), 5.8367 (1997), 5.1155 (1996), 4.9915 (1995), 5.5520 (1994); Italian lire (Lit) per US$ - 1,668.7 (January 1999), 1,763.2 (1998), 1,703.1 (1997), 1,542.9 (1996), 1,628.9 (1995), 1,612.4 (1994); Japanese yen (¥) per US$ - 113.18 (January 1999), 130.91 (1998), 120.99 (1997), 108.78 (1996), 94.06 (1995), 102.21 (1994); German deutsche marks (DM) per US$ - 1.69 (January 1999), 1.9692 (1998), 1.7341 (1997), 1.5048 (1996), 1.4331 (1995), 1.6228 (1994); Euro per US$ - 0.8597 (January 1999)

Fiscal year: 1 October - 30 September

Communications

Telephones: 182.558 million (1987 est.)

Telephone system:
domestic: a large system of fiber-optic cable, microwave radio relay, coaxial cable, and domestic satellites carries conventional telephone traffic; a rapidly growing cellular system carries mobile telephone traffic throughout country
international: 24 ocean cable systems in use; satellite earth stations - 61 Intelsat (45 Atlantic Ocean and 16 Pacific Ocean), 5 Intersputnik (Atlantic Ocean region), and 4 Inmarsat (Pacific and Atlantic Ocean regions) (1990 est.)

Radio broadcast stations: AM 4,987, FM 4,932, shortwave 0

Radios: 540.5 million (1992 est.)

Television broadcast stations: more than 1,500 (including nearly 1,000 stations affiliated with the five major networks - NBC, ABC, CBS, FOX, and PBS; in addition, there are about 9,000 cable TV systems) (1997)

Televisions: 215 million (1993 est.)

Transportation

Railways:
total: 240,000 km mainline routes (nongovernment owned)
standard gauge: 240,000 km 1.435-m gauge (1989)

Highways:
total: 6.42 million km
paved: 3,903,360 km (including 88,400 km of expressways)
unpaved: 2,516,640 km (1996 est.)

Waterways: 41,009 km of navigable inland channels, exclusive of the Great Lakes

Pipelines: petroleum products 276,000 km; natural gas 331,000 km (1991)

Ports and harbors: Anchorage, Baltimore, Boston, Charleston, Chicago, Duluth, Hampton Roads, Honolulu, Houston, Jacksonville, Los Angeles, New Orleans, New York, Philadelphia, Port Canaveral, Portland (Oregon), Prudhoe Bay, San Francisco, Savannah, Seattle, Tampa, Toledo

Merchant marine:
total: 385 ships (1,000 GRT or over) totaling 11,123,848 GRT/15,255,996 DWT
ships by type: barge carrier 10, bulk 61, cargo 28, chemical tanker 13, combination bulk 2, container 83, liquefied gas tanker 9, multifunctional large-load carrier 3, oil tanker 114, passenger 7, passenger-cargo 1, roll-on/roll-off cargo 43, short-sea passenger 3, specialized tanker 1, vehicle carrier 7 (1998 est.)

Airports: 14,459 (1998 est.)

Airports - with paved runways:
total: 5,167
over 3,047 m: 180
2,438 to 3,047 m: 219
1,524 to 2,437 m: 1,294
914 to 1,523 m: 2,447
under 914 m: 1,027 (1998 est.)

Airports - with unpaved runways:
total: 9,292
over 3,047 m: 1
2,438 to 3,047 m: 6
1,524 to 2,437 m: 156
914 to 1,523 m: 1,647
under 914 m: 7,482 (1998 est.)

Heliports: 122 (1998 est.)

Military

Military branches: Department of the Army, Department of the Navy (includes Marine Corps), Department of the Air Force
note: the Coast Guard falls under the Department of Transportation, but in wartime reports to the

United States (continued)

Department of the Navy
Military manpower - military age: 18 years of age
Military manpower - fit for military service:
males age 15-49: NA
Military expenditures - dollar figure: $267.2 billion (1997 est.)
Military expenditures - percent of GDP: 3.4% (1997 est.)

Transnational Issues

Disputes - international: maritime boundary disputes with Canada (Dixon Entrance, Beaufort Sea, Strait of Juan de Fuca, Machias Seal Island); US Naval Base at Guantanamo Bay is leased from Cuba and only mutual agreement or US abandonment of the area can terminate the lease; Haiti claims Navassa Island; US has made no territorial claim in Antarctica (but has reserved the right to do so) and does not recognize the claims of any other nation; Marshall Islands claims Wake Atoll
Illicit drugs: consumer of cocaine shipped from Colombia through Mexico and the Caribbean; consumer of heroin, marijuana, and increasingly methamphetamines from Mexico; consumer of high-quality Southeast Asian heroin; illicit producer of cannabis, marijuana, depressants, stimulants, hallucinogens, and methamphetamines; drug-money-laundering center

Uruguay

Geography

Location: Southern South America, bordering the South Atlantic Ocean, between Argentina and Brazil
Geographic coordinates: 33 00 S, 56 00 W
Map references: South America
Area:
total: 176,220 sq km
land: 173,620 sq km
water: 2,600 sq km
Area - comparative: slightly smaller than the state of Washington
Land boundaries:
total: 1,564 km
border countries: Argentina 579 km, Brazil 985 km
Coastline: 660 km
Maritime claims:
continental shelf: 200-m depth or to the depth of exploitation
territorial sea: 200 nm; overflight and navigation guaranteed beyond 12 nm
Climate: warm temperate; freezing temperatures almost unknown
Terrain: mostly rolling plains and low hills; fertile coastal lowland
Elevation extremes:
lowest point: Atlantic Ocean 0 m
highest point: Cerro Catedral 514 m
Natural resources: fertile soil, hydropower, minor minerals, fisheries
Land use:
arable land: 7%
permanent crops: 0%
permanent pastures: 77%
forests and woodland: 6%
other: 10% (1997 est.)
Irrigated land: 7,700 sq km (1997 est.)
Natural hazards: seasonally high winds (the pampero is a chilly and occasional violent wind which blows north from the Argentine pampas), droughts, floods; because of the absence of mountains, which

act as weather barriers, all locations are particularly vulnerable to rapid changes in weather fronts
Environment - current issues: Working with Brazil to monitor and minimize transboundary pollution caused by Brazilian power plant near border; water pollution from meat packing/tannery industry; inadequate solid/hazardous waste disposal
Environment - international agreements:
party to: Antarctic-Environmental Protocol, Antarctic Treaty, Biodiversity, Climate Change, Desertification, Endangered Species, Environmental Modification, Hazardous Wastes, Law of the Sea, Nuclear Test Ban, Ozone Layer Protection, Ship Pollution, Wetlands, Whaling
signed, but not ratified: Climate Change-Kyoto Protocol, Marine Dumping, Marine Life Conservation

People

Population: 3,308,523 (July 1999 est.)
Age structure:
0-14 years: 24% (male 407,990; female 388,293)
15-64 years: 63% (male 1,026,554; female 1,054,513)
65 years and over: 13% (male 179,331; female 251,842) (1999 est.)
Population growth rate: 0.73% (1999 est.)
Birth rate: 16.84 births/1,000 population (1999 est.)
Death rate: 8.81 deaths/1,000 population (1999 est.)
Net migration rate: -0.78 migrant(s)/1,000 population (1999 est.)
Sex ratio:
at birth: 1.06 male(s)/female
under 15 years: 1.05 male(s)/female
15-64 years: 0.97 male(s)/female
65 years and over: 0.71 male(s)/female
total population: 0.95 male(s)/female (1999 est.)
Infant mortality rate: 13.49 deaths/1,000 live births (1999 est.)
Life expectancy at birth:
total population: 75.83 years
male: 72.69 years
female: 79.15 years (1999 est.)
Total fertility rate: 2.27 children born/woman (1999 est.)
Nationality:
noun: Uruguayan(s)
adjective: Uruguayan
Ethnic groups: white 88%, mestizo 8%, black 4%, Amerindian, practically nonexistent
Religions: Roman Catholic 66% (less than one-half of the adult population attends church regularly), Protestant 2%, Jewish 2%, nonprofessing or other 30%
Languages: Spanish, Portunol, or Brazilero (Portuguese-Spanish mix on the Brazilian frontier)
Literacy:
definition: age 15 and over can read and write
total population: 97.3%
male: 96.9%
female: 97.7% (1995 est.)

Uruguay (continued)

Uruguay (continued)

Government

Country name:
conventional long form: Oriental Republic of Uruguay
conventional short form: Uruguay
local long form: Republica Oriental del Uruguay
local short form: Uruguay
Data code: UY
Government type: republic
Capital: Montevideo
Administrative divisions: 19 departments (departamentos, singular - departamento); Artigas, Canelones, Cerro Largo, Colonia, Durazno, Flores, Florida, Lavalleja, Maldonado, Montevideo, Paysandu, Rio Negro, Rivera, Rocha, Salto, San Jose, Soriano, Tacuarembo, Treinta y Tres
Independence: 25 August 1825 (from Brazil)
National holiday: Independence Day, 25 August (1825)
Constitution: 27 November 1966, effective February 1967, suspended 27 June 1973, new constitution rejected by referendum 30 November 1980; two constitutional reforms approved by plebiscite 26 November 1989 and 7 January 1997
Legal system: based on Spanish civil law system; accepts compulsory ICJ jurisdiction
Suffrage: 18 years of age; universal and compulsory
Executive branch:
chief of state: President Julio Maria SANGUINETTI (since 1 March 1995) and Vice President Hugo FERNANDEZ Faingold (since 5 October 1998); note - the president is both the chief of state and head of government
head of government: President Julio Maria SANGUINETTI (since 1 March 1995) and Vice President Hugo FERNANDEZ Faingold (since 5 October 1998); note - the president is both the chief of state and head of government
cabinet: Council of Ministers appointed by the president with parliamentary approval
elections: president and vice president elected on the same ticket by popular vote for five-year terms; election last held 27 November 1994 (next to be held 31 October 1999 with run-off election if necessary on 28 November 1999)
election results: Julio Maria SANGUINETTI elected president; percent of vote - 23%
Legislative branch: bicameral General Assembly or Asamblea General consists of Chamber of Senators or Camara de Senadores (30 seats; members are elected by popular vote to serve five-year terms) and Chamber of Representatives or Camara de Representantes (99 seats; members are elected by popular vote to serve five-year terms)
elections: Chamber of Senators - last held 27 November 1994 (next to be held 31 October 1999); Chamber of Representatives - last held 27 November 1994 (next to be held 31 October 1999)
election results: Chamber of Senators - percent of vote by party - Colorado 36%, Blanco 34%, Encuentro Progresista 27%, New Sector/Space 3%; seats by party - Colorado 11, Blanco 10, Encuentro Progresista

8, New Sector/Space 1; Chamber of Representatives - percent of vote by party - Colorado 32%, Blanco 31%, Encuentro Progresista 31%, New Sector/Space 5%; seats by party - Colorado 32, Blanco 31, Encuentro Progresista 31, New Sector/Space 5
Judicial branch: Supreme Court, judges are nominated by the president and elected for 10-year terms by the General Assembly
Political parties and leaders: National Party or Blanco [Walter SANTORO]; Herrerista faction of the National Party [Luis LACALLE]; Herrero Wilsonista faction of the National Party [Alaberto VOLONTE]; Colorado Party [Julio M. SANGUINETTI]; Battleist faction of the Colorado Party [Luis LACALLE]; Broad Front Coalition [historical leader - Gen. Liber SEREGNI]; Progressive Encounter in the Broad Front or Encuentro Progresista [Tabare VAZQUEZ]; New Sector/Space Coalition or Nuevo Espacio [Rafael MICHELINI]
International organization participation: CCC, ECLAC, FAO, G-11, G-77, IADB, IAEA, IBRD, ICAO, ICC, ICRM, IFAD, IFC, IFRCS, IHO, ILO, IMF, IMO, Intelsat, Interpol, IOC, IOM, ISO, ITU, LAES, LAIA, Mercosur, MINURSO, MONUA, NAM (observer), OAS, OPANAL, OPCW, PCA, RG, UN, UNCTAD, UNESCO, UNIDO, UNIKOM, UNMOGIP, UNMOT, UNOMIG, UPU, WCL, WFTU, WHO, WIPO, WMO, WToO, WTrO
Diplomatic representation in the US:
chief of mission: Ambassador Alvaro DIEZ DE MEDINA SUAREZ
chancery: 2715 M Street, NW, Washington, DC 20007
telephone: [1] (202) 331-1313 through 1316
FAX: [1] (202) 331-8142
consulate(s) general: Los Angeles, Miami, and New York
Diplomatic representation from the US:
chief of mission: Ambassador Christopher C. ASHBY
embassy: Lauro Muller 1776, Montevideo
mailing address: APO AA 34035
telephone: [598] (2) 23 60 61, 48 77 77
FAX: [598] (2) 48 86 11
Flag description: nine equal horizontal stripes of white (top and bottom) alternating with blue; there is a white square in the upper hoist-side corner with a yellow sun bearing a human face known as the Sun of May and 16 rays alternately triangular and wavy

Economy

Economy - overview: Uruguay's small economy benefits from a favorable climate for agriculture and substantial hydropower production. The SANGUINETTI government's conservative monetary and fiscal policies are aimed at reducing inflation; other priorities include moving toward a more market-oriented economy, completing reform of the social security system, and increasing investment in education. Economic performance remains sensitive to conditions in Argentina and Brazil, largely because more than half of Uruguay's trade is conducted with its

partners in Mercosur (the Southern Cone Common Market).
GDP: purchasing power parity - $28.4 billion (1998 est.)
GDP - real growth rate: 3% (1998 est.)
GDP - per capita: purchasing power parity - $8,600 (1998 est.)
GDP - composition by sector:
agriculture: 8%
industry: 26%
services: 66% (1997)
Population below poverty line: NA%
Household income or consumption by percentage share:
lowest 10%: NA%
highest 10%: NA%
Inflation rate (consumer prices): 8.6% (1998)
Labor force: 1.38 million (1997 est.)
Labor force - by occupation: government 25%, manufacturing 19%, agriculture 11%, commerce 12%, utilities, construction, transport, and communications 12%, other services 21% (1988 est.)
Unemployment rate: 10.5% (November 1998)
Budget:
revenues: $4 billion
expenditures: $4.3 billion, with capital expenditures of $385 million (1997 est.)
Industries: meat processing, wool and hides, sugar, textiles, footwear, leather apparel, tires, cement, petroleum refining, wine
Industrial production growth rate: 5.6% (1997)
Electricity - production: 8.35 billion kWh (1996)
Electricity - production by source:
fossil fuel: 10.18%
hydro: 89.82%
nuclear: 0%
other: 0% (1996)
Electricity - consumption: 8.223 billion kWh (1996)
Electricity - exports: 437 million kWh (1996)
Electricity - imports: 310 million kWh (1996)
Agriculture - products: wheat, rice, corn, sorghum; livestock; fish
Exports: $2.7 billion (f.o.b., 1997)
Exports - commodities: wool and textile manufactures, beef and other animal products, rice, fish and shellfish, chemicals
Exports - partners: Brazil, Argentina, US, Germany, Italy, UK
Imports: $3.7 billion (c.i.f., 1997)
Imports - commodities: machinery and equipment, vehicles, chemicals, minerals, plastics, oil
Imports - partners: Brazil, Argentina, US, Italy, Germany, France, Spain
Debt - external: $4.6 billion (1996 est.)
Economic aid - recipient: $79.7 million (1995)
Currency: 1 Uruguayan peso ($Ur) = 100 centesimos
Exchange rates: Uruguayan pesos ($Ur) per US$1 - 11.08 (January 1999), 9.98 (January 1998), 9.4418 (1997), 7.9718 (1996), 6.3491 (1995), 5.0529 (1994)
Fiscal year: calendar year

Uruguay *(continued)*

Communications

Telephones: 767,333 (1997)
Telephone system: some modern facilities
domestic: most modern facilities concentrated in Montevideo; new nationwide microwave radio relay network
international: satellite earth stations - 2 Intelsat (Atlantic Ocean)
Radio broadcast stations: AM 72, FM 0, shortwave 28
Radios: 1.89 million (1992 est.)
Television broadcast stations: 26 (in addition, there are ten low-power repeaters for the Montevideo station) (1997)
Televisions: 1,131,065 (1996)

Transportation

Railways:
total: 2,994 km
standard gauge: 2,073 km 1.435-m gauge (921 km closed) (1997)
Highways:
total: 8,420 km
paved: 7,578 km
unpaved: 842 km (1996 est.)
Waterways: 1,600 km; used by coastal and shallow-draft river craft
Ports and harbors: Fray Bentos, Montevideo, Nueva Palmira, Paysandu, Punta del Este, Colonia, Piriapolis
Merchant marine:
total: 2 oil tankers (1,000 GRT or over) totaling 44,042 GRT/83,684 DWT (1998 est.)
Airports: 65 (1998 est.)
Airports - with paved runways:
total: 15
2,438 to 3,047 m: 1
1,524 to 2,437 m: 5
914 to 1,523 m: 8
under 914 m: 1 (1998 est.)
Airports - with unpaved runways:
total: 50
1,524 to 2,437 m: 2
914 to 1,523 m: 15
under 914 m: 33 (1998 est.)

Military

Military branches: Army, Navy (includes Naval Air Arm, Coast Guard, Marines), Air Force, Police (Coracero Guard, Grenadier Guard)
Military manpower - availability:
males age 15-49: 806,451 (1999 est.)
Military manpower - fit for military service:
males age 15-49: 653,796 (1999 est.)
Military expenditures - dollar figure: $172 million (1998)
Military expenditures - percent of GDP: 0.9% (1998)

Transnational Issues

Disputes - international: two short sections of the boundary with Brazil are in dispute - Arroyo de la Invernada (Arroio Invernada) area of the Rio Cuareim (Rio Quarai) and the islands at the confluence of the Rio Cuareim (Rio Quarai) and the Uruguay River

Uzbekistan

Geography

Location: Central Asia, north of Afghanistan
Geographic coordinates: 41 00 N, 64 00 E
Map references: Commonwealth of Independent States
Area:
total: 447,400 sq km
land: 425,400 sq km
water: 22,000 sq km
Area - comparative: slightly larger than California
Land boundaries:
total: 6,221 km
border countries: Afghanistan 137 km, Kazakhstan 2,203 km, Kyrgyzstan 1,099 km, Tajikistan 1,161 km, Turkmenistan 1,621 km
Coastline: 0 km
note: Uzbekistan includes the southern portion of the Aral Sea with a 420 km shoreline
Maritime claims: none (doubly landlocked)
Climate: mostly midlatitude desert, long, hot summers, mild winters; semiarid grassland in east
Terrain: mostly flat-to-rolling sandy desert with dunes; broad, flat intensely irrigated river valleys along course of Amu Darya, Sirdaryo (Syr Darya), and Zarafshon; Fergana Valley in east surrounded by mountainous Tajikistan and Kyrgyzstan; shrinking Aral Sea in west
Elevation extremes:
lowest point: Sariqarnish Kuli -12 m
highest point: Adelunga Toghi 4,301 m
Natural resources: natural gas, petroleum, coal, gold, uranium, silver, copper, lead and zinc, tungsten, molybdenum
Land use:
arable land: 9%
permanent crops: 1%
permanent pastures: 46%
forests and woodland: 3%
other: 41% (1993 est.)
Irrigated land: 40,000 sq km (1993 est.)
Natural hazards: NA

Environment - current issues: drying up of the Aral Sea is resulting in growing concentrations of chemical pesticides and natural salts; these substances are then blown from the increasingly exposed lake bed and contribute to desertification; water pollution from industrial wastes and the heavy use of fertilizers and pesticides is the cause of many human health disorders; increasing soil salination; soil contamination from agricultural chemicals, including DDT
Environment - international agreements:
party to: Biodiversity, Climate Change, Desertification, Endangered Species, Environmental Modification, Hazardous Wastes, Ozone Layer Protection
signed, but not ratified: Climate Change-Kyoto Protocol
Geography - note: along with Liechtenstein, one of the only two doubly landlocked countries in the world

People

Population: 24,102,473 (July 1999 est.)
Age structure:
0-14 years: 37% (male 4,556,973; female 4,413,617)
15-64 years: 58% (male 6,938,090; female 7,068,839)
65 years and over: 5% (male 443,604; female 681,350) (1999 est.)
Population growth rate: 1.32% (1999 est.)
Birth rate: 23.43 births/1,000 population (1999 est.)
Death rate: 7.75 deaths/1,000 population (1999 est.)
Net migration rate: -2.44 migrant(s)/1,000 population (1999 est.)
Sex ratio:
at birth: 1.05 male(s)/female
under 15 years: 1.03 male(s)/female
15-64 years: 0.98 male(s)/female
65 years and over: 0.65 male(s)/female
total population: 0.98 male(s)/female (1999 est.)
Infant mortality rate: 71.58 deaths/1,000 live births (1999 est.)

Life expectancy at birth:
total population: 63.91 years
male: 60.29 years
female: 67.71 years (1999 est.)
Total fertility rate: 2.82 children born/woman (1999 est.)
Nationality:
noun: Uzbekistani(s)
adjective: Uzbekistani
Ethnic groups: Uzbek 80%, Russian 5.5%, Tajik 5%, Kazakh 3%, Karakalpak 2.5%, Tatar 1.5%, other 2.5% (1996 est.)
Religions: Muslim 88% (mostly Sunnis), Eastern Orthodox 9%, other 3%
Languages: Uzbek 74.3%, Russian 14.2%, Tajik 4.4%, other 7.1%
Literacy:
definition: age 15 and over can read and write
total population: 99%
male: 99%
female: 99% (yearend 1996)

Government

Country name:
conventional long form: Republic of Uzbekistan
conventional short form: Uzbekistan
local long form: Uzbekiston Respublikasi
local short form: none
former: Uzbek Soviet Socialist Republic
Data code: UZ
Government type: republic; effectively authoritarian presidential rule, with little power outside the executive branch; executive power concentrated in the presidency
Capital: Tashkent (Toshkent)
Administrative divisions: 12 wiloyatlar (singular - wiloyat), 1 autonomous republic* (respublikasi), and 1 city** (shahri); Andijon Wiloyati, Bukhoro Wiloyati, Farghona Wiloyati, Jizzakh Wiloyati, Khorazm Wiloyati (Urganch), Namangan Wiloyati, Nawoiy Wiloyati, Qashqadaryo Wiloyati (Qarshi), Qoraqalpoghiston* (Nukus), Samarqand Wiloyati, Sirdaryo Wiloyati (Guliston), Surkhondaryo Wiloyati (Termiz), Toshkent Shahri**, Toshkent Wiloyati
note: administrative divisions have the same names as their administrative centers (exceptions have the administrative center name following in parentheses)
Independence: 31 August 1991 (from Soviet Union)
National holiday: Independence Day, 1 September (1991)
Constitution: new constitution adopted 8 December 1992
Legal system: evolution of Soviet civil law; still lacks independent judicial system
Suffrage: 18 years of age; universal
Executive branch:
chief of state: President Islom KARIMOV (since 24 March 1990, when he was elected president by the then Supreme Soviet)
head of government: Prime Minister Otkir SULTONOV (since 21 December 1995) and 10 deputy prime ministers

Uzbekistan (continued)

cabinet: Cabinet of Ministers appointed by the president with approval of the Supreme Assembly
elections: president elected by popular vote for a five-year term; election last held 29 December 1991 (next to be held NA January 2000; note - extension of President KARIMOV's term for an additional four years overwhelmingly approved - 99.6% of total vote in favor - by national referendum held 26 March 1995); prime minister and all other ministers appointed by the president
election results: Islom KARIMOV elected president; percent of vote - Islom KARIMOV 86%, Muhammed SOLIH 12%, other 2%
Legislative branch: unicameral Supreme Assembly or Oliy Majlis (250 seats; members elected by popular vote to serve five-year terms)
elections: last held 25 December 1994 (next to be held NA December 1999)
election results: percent of vote by party - NA; seats by party - People's Democratic Party 207, Fatherland Progress Party 12, other 31; note - seating following the final runoff elections were held 22 January 1995: People's Democratic Party 69, Fatherland Progress Party 14, Social Democratic Party 47, local government 120
note: all parties in parliament support President KARIMOV
Judicial branch: Supreme Court, judges are nominated by the president and confirmed by the Supreme Assembly
Political parties and leaders: People's Democratic Party or NDP (formerly Communist Party) [Abdulkhafiz JALOLOV, first secretary]; Fatherland Progress Party (Vatan Tarakiyoti) or VTP [Anvar YULDASHEV, chairman]; Adolat (Justice) Social Democratic Party [Turgunpulat DAMINOV, first secretary]; Democratic National Rebirth Party (Milly Tiklanish) or MTP [Ibrahim GAFUROV, chairman]; Self-Sacrificers Party or Fidoskorlar [Erkin NORBOTAEV, general secretary]
Political pressure groups and leaders: Birlik (Unity) Movement [Abdurakhim PULATOV, chairman]; Erk (Freedom) Democratic Party [Muhamd SOLIH, chairman] was banned 9 December 1992; Human Rights Society of Uzbekistan [Abdumanob PULATOV, chairman]; Independent Human Rights Society of Uzbekistan [Mikhail AROZINOV, chairman]
International organization participation: AsDB, CCC, CIS, EAPC, EBRD, ECE, ECO, ESCAP, IAEA, IBRD, ICAO, ICRM, IDA, IFC, IFRCS, ILO, IMF, Intelsat, Interpol, IOC, ISO, ITU, NAM, OIC, OPCW, OSCE, PFP, UN, UNCTAD, UNESCO, UNIDO, UPU, WFTU, WHO, WIPO, WMO, WToO, WTrO (applicant)
Diplomatic representation in the US:
chief of mission: Ambassador Sadyk SAFAYEV
chancery: 1746 Massachusetts Avenue NW, Washington, DC 20036
telephone: [1] (202) 887-5300
FAX: [1] (202) 293-6804
consulate(s) general: New York

Diplomatic representation from the US:
chief of mission: Ambassador Joseph A. PRESEL
embassy: 82 Chilanzarskaya, Tashkent 700115
mailing address: use embassy street address; US Embassy Tashkent, Department of State, Washington, DC 20521-7110
telephone: [998] (71) 120-5450
FAX: [998] (71) 120-6335
Flag description: three equal horizontal bands of blue (top), white, and green separated by red fimbriations with a white crescent moon and 12 white stars in the upper hoist-side quadrant

Economy

Economy - overview: Uzbekistan is a dry, landlocked country of which 10% consists of intensely cultivated, irrigated river valleys. It was one of the poorest areas of the former Soviet Union with more than 60% of its population living in densely populated rural communities. Uzbekistan is now the world's third largest cotton exporter, a major producer of gold and natural gas, and a regionally significant producer of chemicals and machinery. Following independence in December 1991, the government sought to prop up its Soviet-style command economy with subsidies and tight controls on production and prices. Faced with high rates of inflation, however, the government began to reform in mid-1994, by introducing tighter monetary policies, expanding privatization, slightly reducing the role of the state in the economy, and improving the environment for foreign investors. Nevertheless, the state continues to be a dominating influence in the economy, and reforms have so far failed to bring about much-needed structural changes. The IMF suspended Uzbekistan's $185 million standby arrangement in late 1996 because of governmental steps that made impossible fulfillment of Fund conditions. Uzbekistan has responded to the negative external conditions generated by the Asian and Russian financial crises by tightening export and currency controls within its already largely closed economy.
GDP: purchasing power parity - $59.2 billion (1998 est.)
GDP - real growth rate: 1% (1998 est.)
GDP - per capita: purchasing power parity - $2,500 (1998 est.)
GDP - composition by sector:
agriculture: 26%
industry: 27%
services: 47% (1996 est.)
Population below poverty line: NA%
Household income or consumption by percentage share:
lowest 10%: NA%
highest 10%: NA%
Inflation rate (consumer prices): 40% (1998 est.)
Labor force: 11.9 million (1998 est.)
Labor force - by occupation: agriculture and forestry 44%, industry 20%, services 36% (1995)

Unemployment rate: 5% plus another 10% underemployed (December 1996 est.)
Budget:
revenues: $4.4 billion
expenditures: $4.7 billion, including capital expenditures of $1.1 billion (1997 est.)
Industries: textiles, food processing, machine building, metallurgy, natural gas
Industrial production growth rate: 5% (1998)
Electricity - production: 47.9 billion kWh (1998)
Electricity - production by source:
fossil fuel: 84.18%
hydro: 15.82%
nuclear: 0%
other: 0% (1996)
Electricity - consumption: 43.885 billion kWh (1996)
Electricity - exports: 5.6 billion kWh (1996)
Electricity - imports: 6.5 billion kWh (1996)
Agriculture - products: cotton, vegetables, fruits, grain; livestock
Exports: $3.8 billion (1998)
Exports - commodities: cotton, gold, natural gas, mineral fertilizers, ferrous metals, textiles, food products, autos
Exports - partners: Russia, Ukraine, Eastern Europe, Western Europe
Imports: $4.1 billion (1998)
Imports - commodities: grain, machinery and parts, consumer durables, other foods
Imports - partners: principally other FSU, Czech Republic, Western Europe
Debt - external: $2.6 billion (1997 est.)
Economic aid - recipient: $276.6 million (1995)
Currency: Uzbekistani som (UKS)
Exchange rates: Uzbekistani soms (UKS) per US$1 - 111.9 (February 1999), 110.95 (December 1998), 75.8 (September 1997), 41.1 (1996), 30.2 (1995), 11.4 (1994), 1.0 (1993)
Fiscal year: calendar year

Communications

Telephones: 1.475 million (1998 est.)
Telephone system: poorly developed; ambitiously engaged in telecommunications modernization
domestic: in 1998 there were six cellular networks operating in Uzbekistan; 4 GSM, 1 D-AMPS, 1 AMPS standard
international: linked by landline or microwave radio relay with CIS member states and to other countries by leased connection via the Moscow international gateway switch; new Intelsat links to Tokyo (Japan) and Ankara (Turkey) give Uzbekistan international access independent of Russian facilities; satellite earth stations - NA Orbita and NA Intelsat; Trans-Asia-Europe Fiber-Optic Line
Radio broadcast stations: AM NA, FM NA, shortwave NA; note - there are 12 radio broadcast stations including one state-owned broadcast station of NA type and four independent stations

Radios: 29,016,870
Television broadcast stations: 4 (in addition, there are two repeater stations that relay Russian ORT programs and Kazakh, Kyrgyz, and Tadzhik programs) (1997)
Televisions: 24,497,850

Transportation

Railways:
total: 3,380 km in common carrier service; does not include industrial lines
broad gauge: 3,380 km 1.520-m gauge (300 km electrified) (1993)
Highways:
total: 81,600 km
paved: 71,237 km (note - these roads are said to be hard surfaced, meaning that some are paved and some are all-weather gravel surfaced)
unpaved: 10,363 km dirt (1996 est.)
Waterways: 1,100 (1990)
Pipelines: crude oil 250 km; petroleum products 40 km; natural gas 810 km (1992)
Ports and harbors: Termiz (Amu Darya river)
Airports: 3 (1997 est.)
Airports - with paved runways:
total: 3
over 3,047 m: 2
2,438 to 3,047 m: 1 (1997 est.)

Military

Military branches: Army, Air and Air Defense Forces, Security Forces (internal and border troops), National Guard
Military manpower - military age: 18 years of age
Military manpower - availability:
males age 15-49: 6,172,436 (1999 est.)
Military manpower - fit for military service:
males age 15-49: 5,012,944 (1999 est.)
Military manpower - reaching military age annually:
males: 254,114 (1999 est.)
Military expenditures - dollar figure: $200 million (1997)
Military expenditures - percent of GDP: 1.4% (1997)

Transnational Issues

Disputes - international: none
Illicit drugs: limited illicit cultivation of cannabis and very small amounts of opium poppy, mostly for domestic consumption, almost entirely eradicated by an effective government eradication program; increasingly used as transshipment point for illicit drugs from Afghanistan to Russia and Western Europe and for acetic anhydride destined for Afghanistan

Vanatu

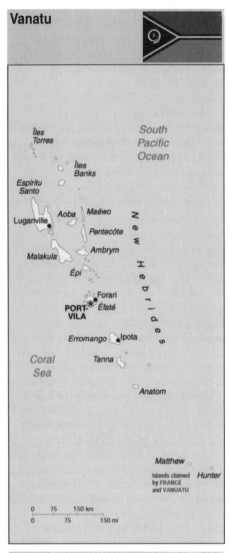

Geography

Location: Oceania, group of islands in the South Pacific Ocean, about three-quarters of the way from Hawaii to Australia
Geographic coordinates: 16 00 S, 167 00 E
Map references: Oceania
Area:
total: 14,760 sq km
land: 14,760 sq km
water: 0 sq km
note: includes more than 80 islands
Area - comparative: slightly larger than Connecticut
Land boundaries: 0 km
Coastline: 2,528 km
Maritime claims: measured from claimed archipelagic baselines
contiguous zone: 24 nm
continental shelf: 200 nm or to the edge of the continental margin
exclusive economic zone: 200 nm
territorial sea: 12 nm
Climate: tropical; moderated by southeast trade winds
Terrain: mostly mountains of volcanic origin; narrow

coastal plains
Elevation extremes:
lowest point: Pacific Ocean 0 m
highest point: Tabwemasana 1,877 m
Natural resources: manganese, hardwood forests, fish
Land use:
arable land: 2%
permanent crops: 10%
permanent pastures: 2%
forests and woodland: 75%
other: 11% (1993 est.)
Irrigated land: NA sq km
Natural hazards: tropical cyclones or typhoons (January to April); volcanism causes minor earthquakes
Environment - current issues: a majority of the population does not have access to a potable and reliable supply of water; deforestation
Environment - international agreements:
party to: Biodiversity, Climate Change, Endangered Species, Ozone Layer Protection, Ship Pollution
signed, but not ratified: Desertification, Law of the Sea

People

Population: 189,036 (July 1999 est.)
Age structure:
0-14 years: 39% (male 37,040; female 35,760)
15-64 years: 58% (male 56,649; female 53,799)
65 years and over: 3% (male 3,125; female 2,663) (1999 est.)
Population growth rate: 2.02% (1999 est.)
Birth rate: 28.49 births/1,000 population (1999 est.)
Death rate: 8.26 deaths/1,000 population (1999 est.)
Net migration rate: 0 migrant(s)/1,000 population (1999 est.)
Sex ratio:
at birth: 1.05 male(s)/female
under 15 years: 1.04 male(s)/female
15-64 years: 1.05 male(s)/female
65 years and over: 1.17 male(s)/female
total population: 1.05 male(s)/female (1999 est.)
Infant mortality rate: 59.58 deaths/1,000 live births (1999 est.)
Life expectancy at birth:
total population: 61.44 years
male: 59.41 years
female: 63.57 years (1999 est.)
Total fertility rate: 3.61 children born/woman (1999 est.)
Nationality:
noun: Ni-Vanuatu (singular and plural)
adjective: Ni-Vanuatu
Ethnic groups: indigenous Melanesian 94%, French 4%, Vietnamese, Chinese, Pacific Islanders
Religions: Presbyterian 36.7%, Anglican 15%, Catholic 15%, indigenous beliefs 7.6%, Seventh-Day Adventist 6.2%, Church of Christ 3.8%, other 15.7%
Languages: English (official), French (official), pidgin (known as Bislama or Bichelama)

Vanuatu (continued)

Literacy:
definition: age 15 and over can read and write
total population: 53%
male: 57%
female: 48% (1979 est.)

Government

Country name:
conventional long form: Republic of Vanuatu
conventional short form: Vanuatu
former: New Hebrides
Data code: NH
Government type: republic
Capital: Port-Vila
Administrative divisions: 6 provinces; Malampa, Penama, Sanma, Shefa, Tafea, Torba
Independence: 30 July 1980 (from France and UK)
National holiday: Independence Day, 30 July (1980)
Constitution: 30 July 1980
Legal system: unified system being created from former dual French and British systems
Suffrage: 18 years of age; universal
Executive branch:
chief of state: President Jean Marie LEYE (since 2 March 1994)
head of government: Prime Minister Donald KALPOKAS (since 30 March 1998); Deputy Prime Minister Willie JIMMY (since 19 October 1998)
cabinet: Council of Ministers appointed by the prime minister, responsible to Parliament
elections: president elected by an electoral college consisting of Parliament and the presidents of the regional councils for a five-year term; election for president last held 2 March 1994 (next to be held NA 1999); following legislative elections, the leader of the majority party or majority coalition is usually elected prime minister by Parliament from among its members; election for prime minister last held 6 March 1998 (next to be held NA 2002)
election results: Jean Marie LEYE elected president; percent of electoral college vote - NA; Donald KALPOKAS elected prime minister by Parliament with a total of 35 votes; other candidate, Rialuth Serge VOHOR, received 17 votes
note: the general legislative elections in November 1995 did not give a majority to any of the political parties; since the election, there have been four changes of government - all of which have been coalitions formed by Parliamentary vote; Rialuth Serge VOHOR was prime minister from November 1995 until he resigned 7 February 1996 when faced with a no-confidence vote in Parliament; Maxime Carlot KORMAN was then elected prime minister and served until he was ousted in a no-confidence motion on 30 September 1996; VOHOR was then elected prime minister for a second time; as a result of legislative elections in March 1998, KALPOKAS was elected prime minister and formed a coalition government with Father LINI's National United Party (NUP)
Legislative branch: unicameral Parliament (52 seats; members elected by popular vote to serve four-year terms)
elections: last held 6 March 1998 (next to be held NA 2002)
election results: percent of vote by party - NA; seats by party - VP 18, UMP 12, NUP 11, other and independent 11; note - political party associations are fluid; there have been four changes of government since the November 1995 elections
note: the National Council of Chiefs advises on matters of custom and land
Judicial branch: Supreme Court, chief justice is appointed by the president after consultation with the prime minister and the leader of the opposition, three other justices are appointed by the president on the advice of the Judicial Service Commission
Political parties and leaders: Union of Moderate Parties or UMP [Serge VOHOR]; National United Party or NUP [leader NA]; Vanuatu Party or VP [Donald KALPOKAS]; Melanesian Progressive Party or MPP [Barak SOPE]; Tan Union or TU [Vincent BOULEKONE]; Na-Griamel Movement [Frankie STEVENS]; Friend Melanesian Party [Albert RAVUTIA]; John Frum Movement [leader NA]; Vanuatu Republican Party [Maxime Carlot KORMAN]
International organization participation: ACCT, ACP, AsDB, C, ESCAP, FAO, G-77, IBRD, ICAO, ICFTU, ICRM, IDA, IFC, IFRCS, IMF, IMO, Intelsat (nonsignatory user), IOC, ITU, NAM, Sparteca, SPC, SPF, UN, UNCTAD, UNESCO, UNIDO, UPU, WFTU, WHO, WMO, WTrO (applicant)
Diplomatic representation in the US: Vanuatu does not have an embassy in the US, it does, however, have a Permanent Mission to the UN
Diplomatic representation from the US: the US does not have an embassy in Vanuatu; the ambassador to Papua New Guinea is accredited to Vanuatu
Flag description: two equal horizontal bands of red (top) and green with a black isosceles triangle (based on the hoist side) all separated by a black-edged yellow stripe in the shape of a horizontal Y (the two points of the Y face the hoist side and enclose the triangle); centered in the triangle is a boar's tusk encircling two crossed namele leaves, all in yellow

Economy

Economy - overview: The economy is based primarily on subsistence or small-scale agriculture which provides a living for 65% of the population. Fishing, offshore financial services, and tourism, with about 50,000 visitors in 1997, are other mainstays of the economy. Mineral deposits are negligible; the country has no known petroleum deposits. A small light industry sector caters to the local market. Tax revenues come mainly from import duties. Economic development is hindered by dependence on relatively few commodity exports, vulnerability to natural disasters, and long distances from main markets and between constituent islands.
GDP: purchasing power parity - $240 million (1997 est.)
GDP - real growth rate: NA%
GDP - per capita: purchasing power parity - $1,300 (1997 est.)
GDP - composition by sector:
agriculture: 23%
industry: 13%
services: 64% (1996)
Population below poverty line: NA%
Household income or consumption by percentage share:
lowest 10%: NA%
highest 10%: NA%
Inflation rate (consumer prices): 2.2% (1997 est.)
Labor force: NA
Labor force - by occupation: agriculture 65%, services 32%, industry 3% (1995 est.)
Unemployment rate: NA%
Budget:
revenues: $94.4 million
expenditures: $99.8 million, including capital expenditures of $30.4 million (1996 est.)
Industries: food and fish freezing, wood processing, meat canning
Industrial production growth rate: 6.4% (1996 est.)
Electricity - production: 30 million kWh (1996)
Electricity - production by source:
fossil fuel: 100%
hydro: 0%
nuclear: 0%
other: 0% (1996)
Electricity - consumption: 30 million kWh (1996)
Electricity - exports: 0 kWh (1996)
Electricity - imports: 0 kWh (1996)
Agriculture - products: copra, coconuts, cocoa, coffee, taro, yams, coconuts, fruits, vegetables; fish, beef
Exports: $30 million (f.o.b., 1996)
Exports - commodities: copra, beef, cocoa, timber, coffee
Exports - partners: Japan 28%, Spain 21%, Germany 14%, UK 7%, Cote d'Ivoire 7%, Australia, New Caledonia (1996 est.)
Imports: $97 million (f.o.b., 1996)
Imports - commodities: machines and vehicles, food and beverages, basic manufactures, raw materials and fuels, chemicals
Imports - partners: Japan 47%, Australia 23%, Singapore 8%, New Zealand 6%, France 3%, Fiji (1996 est.)
Debt - external: $63 million (1996 est.)
Economic aid - recipient: $45.8 million (1995)
Currency: 1 vatu (VT) = 100 centimes
Exchange rates: vatu (VT) per US$1 - 129.66 (January 1999), 127.52 (1998), 115.87 (1997), 111.72 (1996), 112.11 (1995), 116.41 (1994)
Fiscal year: calendar year

Communications

Telephones: 4,000 (1994 est.)
Telephone system:
domestic: NA

Vanuatu *(continued)*

international: satellite earth station - 1 Intelsat (Pacific Ocean)

Radio broadcast stations: AM 2, FM 0, shortwave 0

Radios: 49,000 (1994 est.)

Television broadcast stations: 1 (1997)

Televisions: 2,000 (1994 est.)

Transportation

Railways: 0 km

Highways:

total: 1,070 km

paved: 256 km

unpaved: 814 km (1996 est.)

Ports and harbors: Forari, Port-Vila, Santo (Espiritu Santo)

Merchant marine:

total: 82 ships (1,000 GRT or over) totaling 1,327,078 GRT/1,764,558 DWT

ships by type: bulk 31, cargo 24, chemical tanker 3, combination bulk 1, liquefied gas tanker 4, oil tanker 2, refrigerated cargo 11, vehicle carrier 6

note: a flag of convenience registry; includes ships from 15 countries among which are ships of Japan 28, India 10, US 10, Greece 3, Hong Kong 3, Australia 2, Canada 1, China 1, and France 1 (1998 est.)

Airports: 32 (1998 est.)

Airports - with paved runways:

total: 3

2,438 to 3,047 m: 1

1,524 to 2,437 m: 1

914 to 1,523 m: 1 (1998 est.)

Airports - with unpaved runways:

total: 29

1,524 to 2,437 m: 1

914 to 1,523 m: 11

under 914 m: 17 (1998 est.)

Military

Military branches: no regular military forces; Vanuatu Police Force (VPF; includes the paramilitary Vanuatu Mobile Force or VMF)

Military expenditures - dollar figure: $NA

Military expenditures - percent of GDP: NA%

Transnational Issues

Disputes - international: claims Matthew and Hunter Islands east of New Caledonia

Venezuela

Geography

Location: Northern South America, bordering the Caribbean Sea and the North Atlantic Ocean, between Colombia and Guyana

Geographic coordinates: 8 00 N, 66 00 W

Map references: South America, Central America and the Caribbean

Area:

total: 912,050 sq km

land: 882,050 sq km

water: 30,000 sq km

Area - comparative: slightly more than twice the size of California

Land boundaries:

total: 4,993 km

border countries: Brazil 2,200 km, Colombia 2,050 km, Guyana 743 km

Coastline: 2,800 km

Maritime claims:

contiguous zone: 15 nm

continental shelf: 200-m depth or to the depth of exploitation

exclusive economic zone: 200 nm

territorial sea: 12 nm

Climate: tropical; hot, humid; more moderate in highlands

Terrain: Andes Mountains and Maracaibo Lowlands in northwest; central plains (llanos); Guiana Highlands in southeast

Elevation extremes:

lowest point: Caribbean Sea 0 m

highest point: Pico Bolivar (La Columna) 5,007 m

Natural resources: petroleum, natural gas, iron ore, gold, bauxite, other minerals, hydropower, diamonds

Land use:

arable land: 4%

permanent crops: 1%

permanent pastures: 20%

forests and woodland: 34%

other: 41% (1993 est.)

Irrigated land: 1,900 sq km (1993 est.)

Natural hazards: subject to floods, rockslides, mud slides; periodic droughts

Environment - current issues: sewage pollution of Lago de Valencia; oil and urban pollution of Lago de Maracaibo; deforestation; soil degradation; urban and industrial pollution, especially along the Caribbean coast

Environment - international agreements:

party to: Biodiversity, Climate Change, Desertification, Endangered Species, Hazardous Wastes, Marine Life Conservation, Nuclear Test Ban, Ozone Layer Protection, Ship Pollution, Tropical Timber 83, Tropical Timber 94, Wetlands, Whaling

signed, but not ratified: Marine Dumping

Geography - note: on major sea and air routes linking North and South America

People

Population: 23,203,466 (July 1999 est.)

Age structure:

0-14 years: 33% (male 3,988,499; female 3,741,568)

15-64 years: 62% (male 7,231,546; female 7,184,769)

65 years and over: 5% (male 484,071; female 573,013) (1999 est.)

Population growth rate: 1.71% (1999 est.)

Birth rate: 22.25 births/1,000 population (1999 est.)

Death rate: 4.93 deaths/1,000 population (1999 est.)

Net migration rate: -0.23 migrant(s)/1,000 population (1999 est.)

Sex ratio:

at birth: 1.08 male(s)/female

under 15 years: 1.07 male(s)/female

15-64 years: 1.01 male(s)/female

65 years and over: 0.84 male(s)/female

total population: 1.02 male(s)/female (1999 est.)

Infant mortality rate: 26.51 deaths/1,000 live births (1999 est.)

Life expectancy at birth:

total population: 72.95 years

male: 69.97 years

female: 76.16 years (1999 est.)

Total fertility rate: 2.61 children born/woman (1999 est.)

Nationality:

noun: Venezuelan(s)

adjective: Venezuelan

Ethnic groups: Spanish, Italian, Portuguese, Arab, German, African, indigenous people

Religions: nominally Roman Catholic 96%, Protestant 2%

Languages: Spanish (official), numerous indigenous dialects

Literacy:

definition: age 15 and over can read and write

total population: 91.1%

male: 91.8%

female: 90.3% (1995 est.)

Venezuela (continued)

Government

Country name:
conventional long form: Republic of Venezuela
conventional short form: Venezuela
local long form: Republica de Venezuela
local short form: Venezuela
Data code: VE
Government type: republic
Capital: Caracas
Administrative divisions: 22 states (estados, singular - estado),1 federal district* (distrito federal), and 1 federal dependency** (dependencia federal); Amazonas, Anzoategui, Apure, Aragua, Barinas, Bolivar, Carabobo, Cojedes, Delta Amacuro, Dependencias Federales**, Distrito Federal*, Falcon, Guarico, Lara, Merida, Miranda, Monagas, Nueva Esparta, Portuguesa, Sucre, Tachira, Trujillo, Yaracuy, Zulia
note: the federal dependency consists of 11 federally controlled island groups with a total of 72 individual islands
Independence: 5 July 1811 (from Spain)
National holiday: Independence Day, 5 July (1811)
Constitution: 23 January 1961
Legal system: based on Napoleonic code; judicial review of legislative acts in Cassation Court only; has not accepted compulsory ICJ jurisdiction
Suffrage: 18 years of age; universal
Executive branch:
chief of state: President Hugo CHAVEZ Frias (since 3 February 1999); note - the president is both the chief of state and head of government
head of government: President Hugo CHAVEZ Frias (since 3 February 1999); note - the president is both the chief of state and head of government
cabinet: Council of Ministers appointed by the president
elections: president elected by popular vote for a five-year term; election last held 6 December 1998 (next to be held NA December 2003)
election results: Hugo CHAVEZ Frias elected president; percent of vote - NA%
Legislative branch: bicameral Congress of the Republic or Congreso de la Republica consists of the Senate or Senado (52 seats, two from each state and the federal district (46), one for each of the retired presidents, and others representing minorities (6); members are elected by popular vote to serve five-year terms) and Chamber of Deputies or Camara de Diputados (207 seats; members are elected by popular vote to serve five-year terms)
elections: Senate - last held 6 December 1998 (next to be held NA December 2003); Chamber of Deputies - last held 6 December 1998 (next to be held NA December 2003)
election results: Senate - percent of vote by party - NA; seats by party - AD 16, COPEI 14, Causa R 9, National Convergence 5, MAS 3, independents 5; note - two former presidents (1 from AD, 1 from COPEI) hold lifetime Senate seats; Chamber of Deputies - percent of vote by party - AD 25.6%,

COPEI 24.6%, MAS 10.6%, National Convergence 8.7%, Causa R 19.3%; seats by party - AD 53, COPEI 51, Causa R 40, MAS 22, National Convergence 18, other 23
Judicial branch: Supreme Court of Justice (Corte Suprema de Justicia), magistrates are elected by both chambers in joint session for a nine-year term, one-third are reelected every three years
Political parties and leaders: National Convergence or Convergencia [Jose Miguel UZCATEGUI, president, Juan Jose CALDERA, national coordinator]; Social Christian Party or COPEI [Luis HERRERA Campins, president, and Donald RAMIREZ, secretary general]; Democratic Action or AD [David MORALES Bello, president, and Luis ALFARO Ucero, secretary general]; Movement Toward Socialism or MAS [Felipe MUJICA, president, and Leopoldo PUCHI, secretary general]; Radical Cause or La Causa R [Lucas MATHEUS, secretary general]; Homeland for All or PPT [Alexis ROSAS, director]
Political pressure groups and leaders: FEDECAMARAS, a conservative business group; Venezuelan Confederation of Workers or CTV (labor organization dominated by the Democratic Action); VECINOS groups
International organization participation: CAN, Caricom (observer), CCC, CDB, ECLAC, FAO, G-3, G-11, G-15, G-19, G-24, G-77, IADB, IAEA, IBRD, ICAO, ICC, ICFTU, ICRM, IFAD, IFC, IFRCS, IHO, ILO, IMF, IMO, Intelsat, Interpol, IOC, IOM, ISO, ITU, LAES, LAIA, MINURSO, NAM, OAS, OPANAL, OPCW, OPEC, PCA, RG, UN, UNCTAD, UNESCO, UNHCR, UNIDO, UNIKOM, UNU, UPU, WCL, WFTU, WHO, WIPO, WMO, WToO, WTrO
Diplomatic representation in the US:
chief of mission: Ambassador (vacant)
chancery: 1099 30th Street NW, Washington, DC 20007
telephone: [1] (202) 342-2214
FAX: [1] (202) 342-6820
consulate(s) general: Boston, Chicago, Houston, Miami, New Orleans, New York, San Francisco, and San Juan (Puerto Rico)
Diplomatic representation from the US:
chief of mission: Ambassador John Francis MAISTO
embassy: Calle F con Calle Suapure, Colinas de Valle Arriba, Caracas 1060
mailing address: P. O. Box 62291, Caracas 1060-A; APO AA 34037
telephone: [58] (2) 977-2011
FAX: [58] (2) 977-0843
Flag description: three equal horizontal bands of yellow (top), blue, and red with the coat of arms on the hoist side of the yellow band and an arc of seven white five-pointed stars centered in the blue band

Economy

Economy - overview: The petroleum sector dominates the economy, accounting for roughly a third of GDP, around 80% of export earnings, and more than half of government operating revenues. As

a result, the steep downturn in international oil prices has had a severe impact on the economy; fiscal cuts spurred by the loss of revenues, high interest rates, and the sharp downturn in export earnings drove the economy into recession in 1998. The recession continued into 1999 with oil prices forecast to stay relatively low, but rising. Although the government has pursued moderate austerity measures to address the downturn in revenues, Venezuela's ongoing reform program has largely stalled. Pressure on the bolivar - overvalued by as much as 40% - was also significant through much of 1998, increasing the probability of an adjustment of the currency in 1999. Newly elected President Hugo CHAVEZ will be hard pressed to address Venezuela's many economic ills. He has promised to strike a balance between reforms designed to address the structural deformities of the economy and addressing declining living standards. CHAVEZ has sought to play down the populism that marked his political campaign for the presidency in an effort to allay investor concerns. The wide range of viewpoints represented on CHAVEZ's economic team is likely to make rapid implementation of a coherent policy difficult.
GDP: purchasing power parity - $194.5 billion (1998 est.)
GDP - real growth rate: -0.9% (1998 est.)
GDP - per capita: purchasing power parity - $8,500 (1998 est.)
GDP - composition by sector:
agriculture: 4%
industry: 63%
services: 33% (1997 est.)
Population below poverty line: 31.3% (1989 est.)
Household income or consumption by percentage share:
lowest 10%: 1.5%
highest 10%: 35.6% (1995)
Inflation rate (consumer prices): 29.9% (1998)
Labor force: 9.2 million
Labor force - by occupation: services 64%, industry 23%, agriculture 13% (1997 est.)
Unemployment rate: 11.5% (1997 est.)
Budget:
revenues: $11.99 billion
expenditures: $11.48 billion, including capital expenditures of $3 billion (1996 est.)
Industries: petroleum, iron ore mining, construction materials, food processing, textiles, steel, aluminum, motor vehicle assembly
Industrial production growth rate: 0.5% (1995 est.)
Electricity - production: 73 billion kWh (1996)
Electricity - production by source:
fossil fuel: 20.55%
hydro: 79.45%
nuclear: 0%
other: 0% (1996)
Electricity - consumption: 72.85 billion kWh (1996)
Electricity - exports: 150 million kWh (1996)
Electricity - imports: 0 kWh (1996)
Agriculture - products: corn, sorghum, sugarcane,

Venezuela *(continued)*

rice, bananas, vegetables, coffee; beef, pork, milk, eggs; fish

Exports: $16.9 billion (f.o.b., 1998)

Exports - commodities: petroleum, bauxite and aluminum, steel, chemicals, agricultural products, basic manufactures (1998)

Exports - partners: US and Puerto Rico 57%, Colombia, Brazil (1997)

Imports: $12.4 billion (f.o.b., 1998)

Imports - commodities: raw materials, machinery and equipment, transport equipment, construction materials (1998)

Imports - partners: US 53%, Japan, Colombia, Italy, Germany (1997)

Debt - external: $26.5 billion (1996)

Economic aid - recipient: $50.8 million (1995)

Currency: 1 bolivar (Bs) = 100 centimos

Exchange rates: bolivares (Bs) per US$1 - 570.267 (January 1999), 547.556 (1998), 488.635 (1997), 417.333 (1996), 176.843 (1995), 148.503 (1994)

Fiscal year: calendar year

Communications

Telephones: 1.44 million (1987 est.)

Telephone system: modern and expanding

domestic: domestic satellite system with 3 earth stations

international: 3 submarine coaxial cables; satellite earth station - 1 Intelsat (Atlantic Ocean)

Radio broadcast stations: AM 181, FM 0, shortwave 26

Radios: 9.04 million (1992 est.)

Television broadcast stations: 66 (in addition, there are 45 repeaters) (1997)

Televisions: 3.3 million (1992 est.)

Transportation

Railways:

total: 584 km (248 km privately owned)

standard gauge: 584 km 1.435-m gauge

Highways:

total: 84,300 km

paved: 33,214 km

unpaved: 51,086 km (1996 est.)

Waterways: 7,100 km; Rio Orinoco and Lago de Maracaibo accept oceangoing vessels

Pipelines: crude oil 6,370 km; petroleum products 480 km; natural gas 4,010 km

Ports and harbors: Amuay, Bajo Grande, El Tablazo, La Guaira, La Salina, Maracaibo, Matanzas, Palua, Puerto Cabello, Puerto la Cruz, Puerto Ordaz, Puerto Sucre, Punta Cardon

Merchant marine:

total: 32 ships (1,000 GRT or over) totaling 535,882 GRT/937,461 DWT

ships by type: bulk 5, cargo 9, combination bulk 1, liquefied gas tanker 2, oil tanker 8, passenger-cargo 1, roll-on/roll-off cargo 5, short-sea passenger 1 (1998 est.)

Airports: 371 (1998 est.)

Airports - with paved runways:

total: 122

over 3,047 m: 5

2,438 to 3,047 m: 10

1,524 to 2,437 m: 32

914 to 1,523 m: 59

under 914 m: 16 (1998 est.)

Airports - with unpaved runways:

total: 249

1,524 to 2,437 m: 10

914 to 1,523 m: 94

under 914 m: 145 (1998 est.)

Heliports: 1 (1998 est.)

Military

Military branches: National Armed Forces (Fuerzas Armadas Nacionales or FAN) includes Ground Forces or Army (Fuerzas Terrestres or Ejercito), Naval Forces (Fuerzas Navales or Armada), Air Force (Fuerzas Aereas or Aviacion), Armed Forces of Cooperation or National Guard (Fuerzas Armadas de Cooperacion or Guardia Nacional)

Military manpower - military age: 18 years of age

Military manpower - availability:

males age 15-49: 6,268,982 (1999 est.)

Military manpower - fit for military service:

males age 15-49: 4,522,757 (1999 est.)

Military manpower - reaching military age annually:

males: 242,362 (1999 est.)

Military expenditures - dollar figure: $1.1 billion (1998)

Military expenditures - percent of GDP: 1% (1998)

Transnational Issues

Disputes - international: claims all of Guyana west of the Essequibo River; maritime boundary dispute with Colombia in the Gulf of Venezuela

Illicit drugs: illicit producer of cannabis, opium, and coca leaf for the international drug trade on a small scale; however, large quantities of cocaine and heroin transit the country from Colombia bound for US and Europe; important money-laundering hub; active eradication program primarily targeting opium

Vietnam

Geography

Location: Southeastern Asia, bordering the Gulf of Thailand, Gulf of Tonkin, and South China Sea, alongside China, Laos, and Cambodia

Geographic coordinates: 16 00 N, 106 00 E

Map references: Southeast Asia

Area:

total: 329,560 sq km

land: 325,360 sq km

water: 4,200 sq km

Area - comparative: slightly larger than New Mexico

Land boundaries:

total: 4,639 km

border countries: Cambodia 1,228 km, China 1,281 km, Laos 2,130 km

Coastline: 3,444 km (excludes islands)

Maritime claims:

contiguous zone: 24 nm

continental shelf: 200 nm or to the edge of the continental margin

exclusive economic zone: 200 nm

territorial sea: 12 nm

Climate: tropical in south; monsoonal in north with hot, rainy season (mid-May to mid-September) and

Vietnam (continued)

warm, dry season (mid-October to mid-March)
Terrain: low, flat delta in south and north; central highlands; hilly, mountainous in far north and northwest
Elevation extremes:
lowest point: South China Sea 0 m
highest point: Ngoc Linh 3,143 m
Natural resources: phosphates, coal, manganese, bauxite, chromate, offshore oil and gas deposits, forests
Land use:
arable land: 17%
permanent crops: 4%
permanent pastures: 1%
forests and woodland: 30%
other: 48% (1993 est.)
Irrigated land: 18,600 sq km (1993 est.)
Natural hazards: occasional typhoons (May to January) with extensive flooding
Environment - current issues: logging and slash-and-burn agricultural practices contribute to deforestation and soil degradation; water pollution and overfishing threaten marine life populations; groundwater contamination limits potable water supply; growing urban industrialization and population migration are rapidly degrading environment in Hanoi and Ho Chi Minh City
Environment - international agreements:
party to: Biodiversity, Climate Change, Desertification, Endangered Species, Environmental Modification, Hazardous Wastes, Law of the Sea, Ozone Layer Protection, Ship Pollution, Wetlands
signed, but not ratified: Climate Change-Kyoto Protocol, Nuclear Test Ban

People

Population: 77,311,210 (July 1999 est.)
Age structure:
0-14 years: 34% (male 13,377,315; female 12,603,906)
15-64 years: 61% (male 22,934,553; female 24,277,488)
65 years and over: 5% (male 1,645,288; female 2,472,660) (1999 est.)
Population growth rate: 1.37% (1999 est.)
Birth rate: 20.78 births/1,000 population (1999 est.)
Death rate: 6.56 deaths/1,000 population (1999 est.)
Net migration rate: -0.53 migrant(s)/1,000 population (1999 est.)
Sex ratio:
at birth: 1.06 male(s)/female
under 15 years: 1.06 male(s)/female
15-64 years: 0.94 male(s)/female
65 years and over: 0.67 male(s)/female
total population: 0.96 male(s)/female (1999 est.)
Infant mortality rate: 34.84 deaths/1,000 live births (1999 est.)
Life expectancy at birth:
total population: 68.1 years
male: 65.71 years

female: 70.64 years (1999 est.)
Total fertility rate: 2.41 children born/woman (1999 est.)
Nationality:
noun: Vietnamese (singular and plural)
adjective: Vietnamese
Ethnic groups: Vietnamese 85%-90%, Chinese 3%, Muong, Tai, Meo, Khmer, Man, Cham
Religions: Buddhist, Taoist, Roman Catholic, indigenous beliefs, Islam, Protestant, Cao Dai, Hoa Hao
Languages: Vietnamese (official), Chinese, English, French, Khmer, tribal languages (Mon-Khmer and Malayo-Polynesian)
Literacy:
definition: age 15 and over can read and write
total population: 93.7%
male: 96.5%
female: 91.2% (1995 est.)

Government

Country name:
conventional long form: Socialist Republic of Vietnam
conventional short form: Vietnam
local long form: Cong Hoa Chu Nghia Viet Nam
local short form: Viet Nam
abbreviation: SRV
Data code: VM
Government type: Communist state
Capital: Hanoi
Administrative divisions: 58 provinces (tinh, singular and plural), 3 municipalities* (thu do, singular and plural); An Giang, Bac Giang, Bac Kan, Bac Lieu, Bac Ninh, Ba Ria-Vung Tau, Ben Tre, Binh Dinh, Binh Duong, Binh Phuoc, Binh Thuan, Ca Mau, Can Tho, Cao Bang, Dac Lac, Da Nang, Dong Nai, Dong Thap, Gia Lai, Ha Giang, Hai Duong, Hai Phong*, Ha Nam, Ha Noi*, Ha Tay, Ha Tinh, Hoa Binh, Ho Chi Minh*, Hung Yen, Khanh Hoa, Kien Giang, Kon Tum, Lai Chau, Lam Dong, Lang Son, Lao Cai, Long An, Nam Dinh, Nghe An, Ninh Binh, Ninh Thuan, Phu Tho, Phu Yen, Quang Binh, Quang Nam, Quang Ngai, Quang Ninh, Quang Tri, Soc Trang, Son La, Tay Ninh, Thai Binh, Thai Nguyen, Thanh Hoa, Thua Thien-Hue, Tien Giang, Tra Vinh, Tuyen Quang, Vinh Long, Vinh Phuc, Yen Bai
Independence: 2 September 1945 (from France)
National holiday: Independence Day, 2 September (1945)
Constitution: 15 April 1992
Legal system: based on communist legal theory and French civil law system
Suffrage: 18 years of age; universal
Executive branch:
chief of state: President Tran Duc LUONG (since 24 September 1997) and Vice President Nguyen Thi BINH (since NA October 1992)
head of government: Prime Minister Phan Van KHAI (since 25 September 1997); First Deputy Prime Minister Nguyen Tan DUNG (since 29 September 1997); Deputy Prime Ministers Nguyen Cong TAN (since 29 September 1997), Ngo Xuan LOC (since 29

September 1997), Nguyen Manh CAM (since 29 September 1997), and Pham Gia KHIEM (since 29 September 1997)
cabinet: Cabinet appointed by the president on the proposal of the prime minister and ratification of the National Assembly
elections: president elected by the National Assembly from among its members for a five-year term; election last held 25 September 1997 (next to be held when National Assembly meets following legislative elections in NA 2002); prime minister appointed by the president from among the members of the National Assembly; deputy prime ministers appointed by the prime minister
election results: Tran Duc LUONG elected president; percent of National Assembly vote - NA
Legislative branch: unicameral National Assembly or Quoc-Hoi (450 seats; members elected by popular vote to serve five-year terms)
elections: last held 20 July 1997 (next to be held NA 2002)
election results: percent of vote by party - CPV 92%, other 8% (the 8% are not CPV members but are approved by the CPV to stand for election); seats by party - CPV or CPV-approved 450
Judicial branch: Supreme People's Court, chief justice is elected for a five-year term by the National Assembly on the recommendation of the president
Political parties and leaders: only party - Communist Party of Vietnam or CPV [Le Kha PHIEU, general secretary]
International organization participation: ACCT, APEC, AsDB, ASEAN, CCC, ESCAP, FAO, G-77, IAEA, IBRD, ICAO, ICRM, IDA, IFAD, IFC, IFRCS, ILO, IMF, IMO, Intelsat, Interpol, IOC, IOM (observer), ISO, ITU, NAM, OPCW, UN, UNCTAD, UNESCO, UNIDO, UPU, WCL, WFTU, WHO, WIPO, WMO, WToO, WTrO (applicant)
Diplomatic representation in the US:
chief of mission: Ambassador LE VAN BANG
chancery: 1233 20th Street NW, Washington, DC 20036, Suite 400
telephone: [1] (202) 861-0737
FAX: [1] (202) 861-0917
consulate(s) general: San Francisco
Diplomatic representation from the US:
chief of mission: Ambassador Douglas B. "Pete" Peterson
embassy: 7 Lang Ha Road, Ba Dinh District, Hanoi
mailing address: PSC 461, Box 400, FPO AP 96521-0002
telephone: [84] (4) 8431500
FAX: [84] (4) 8350484
consulate(s) general: Ho Chi Minh City
Flag description: red with a large yellow five-pointed star in the center

Economy

Economy - overview: Vietnam is a poor, densely populated country that has had to recover from the ravages of war, the loss of financial support from the old Soviet Bloc, and the rigidities of a centrally

Vietnam *(continued)*

planned economy. Substantial progress has been achieved over the past 10 years in moving forward from an extremely low starting point, though the regional downturn is now limiting that progress. GDP growth of 8.5% in 1997 fell to 4% in 1998. These numbers masked some major difficulties that are emerging in economic performance. Many domestic industries, including coal, cement, steel, and paper, have reported large stockpiles of inventory and tough competition from more efficient foreign producers, giving Vietnam a trade deficit of $3.3 billion in 1997. While disbursements of aid and foreign direct investment have risen, they are not large enough to finance the rapid increase in imports; and it is widely believed that Vietnam may be using short-term trade credits to bridge the gap - a risky strategy that could result in a foreign exchange crunch. Meanwhile, Vietnamese authorities continue to move slowly toward implementing the structural reforms needed to revitalize the economy and produce more competitive, export-driven industries. Privatization of state enterprises remains bogged down in political controversy, while the country's dynamic private sector is denied both financing and access to markets. Reform of the banking sector is proceeding slowly, raising concerns that the country will be unable to tap sufficient domestic savings to maintain current high levels of growth. Administrative and legal barriers are also causing costly delays for foreign investors and are raising similar doubts about Vietnam's ability to maintain the inflow of foreign capital. Ideological bias in favor of state intervention and control of the economy is slowing progress toward a more liberalized investment environment.

GDP: purchasing power parity - $134.8 billion (1998 est.)
GDP - real growth rate: 4% (1998 est.)
GDP - per capita: purchasing power parity - $1,770 (1998 est.)
GDP - composition by sector:
agriculture: 28%
industry: 30%
services: 42% (1996 est.)
Population below poverty line: 50.9% (1993 est.)
Household income or consumption by percentage share:
lowest 10%: 3.5%
highest 10%: 29% (1993)
Inflation rate (consumer prices): 9% (1998)
Labor force: 32.7 million
Labor force - by occupation: agriculture 65%, industry and services 35% (1990 est.)
Unemployment rate: 25% (1995 est.)
Budget:
revenues: $5.6 billion
expenditures: $6 billion, including capital expenditures of $1.7 billion (1996 est.)
Industries: food processing, garments, shoes, machine building, mining, cement, chemical fertilizer, glass, tires, oil, coal, steel, paper
Industrial production growth rate: 12% (1998 est.)

Electricity - production: 14.88 billion kWh (1996)
Electricity - production by source:
fossil fuel: 12.1%
hydro: 84%
nuclear: 0%
other: 3.9% (1996)
Electricity - consumption: 14.88 billion kWh (1996)
Electricity - exports: 0 kWh (1996)
Electricity - imports: 0 kWh (1996)
Agriculture - products: paddy rice, corn, potatoes, rubber, soybeans, coffee, tea, bananas; poultry, pigs; fish
Exports: $9.4 billion (f.o.b., 1998 est.)
Exports - commodities: crude oil, marine products, rice, coffee, rubber, tea, garments, shoes
Exports - partners: Japan, Germany, Singapore, Taiwan, Hong Kong, France, South Korea
Imports: $11.4 billion (f.o.b., 1998 est.)
Imports - commodities: machinery and equipment, petroleum products, fertilizer, steel products, raw cotton, grain, cement, motorcycles
Imports - partners: Singapore, South Korea, Japan, France, Hong Kong, Taiwan
Debt - external: $7.3 billion Western countries; $4.5 billion CEMA debts primarily to Russia; $9 billion to $18 billion nonconvertible debt (former CEMA, Iraq, Iran)
Economic aid - recipient: $2.2 billion in credits and grants pledged by international donors for 1999
Currency: 1 new dong (D) = 100 xu
Exchange rates: new dong (D) per US$1 - 13,900 (December 1998), 11,100 (December 1996), 11,193 (1995 average), 11,000 (October 1994), 10,800 (November 1993), 8,100 (July 1991)
Fiscal year: calendar year

Communications

Telephones: 800,000 (1995 est.)
Telephone system: while Vietnam's telecommunication sector lags far behind other countries in Southeast Asia, Hanoi has made considerable progress since 1991 in upgrading the system; Vietnam has digitized all provincial switch boards, while fiber-optic and microwave transmission systems have been extended from Hanoi, Da Nang, and Ho Chi Minh City to all provinces; the density of telephone receivers nationwide doubled from 1993 to 1995, but is still far behind other countries in the region; Vietnam's telecommunications strategy aims to increase telephone density to 30 per 1,000 inhabitants by the year 2000 and authorities estimate that approximately $2.7 billion will be spent on telecommunications upgrades through the end of the decade
domestic: NA
international: satellite earth stations - 2 Intersputnik (Indian Ocean region)
Radio broadcast stations: AM NA, FM 228, shortwave 0
Radios: 7.215 million (1992 est.)
Television broadcast stations: NA
Televisions: 2.9 million (1992 est.)

Transportation

Railways:
total: 2,835 km (in addition, there are 224 km not restored to service after war damage)
standard gauge: 151 km 1.435-m gauge
narrow gauge: 2,454 km 1.000-m gauge
dual gauge: 230 km NA-m gauges (three rails)
Highways:
total: 93,300 km
paved: 23,418 km
unpaved: 69,882 km (1996 est.)
Waterways: 17,702 km navigable; more than 5,149 km navigable at all times by vessels up to 1.8 m draft
Pipelines: petroleum products 150 km
Ports and harbors: Cam Ranh, Da Nang, Haiphong, Ho Chi Minh City, Hong Gai, Qui Nhon, Nha Trang
Merchant marine:
total: 123 ships (1,000 GRT or over) totaling 527,920 GRT/820,515 DWT
ships by type: bulk 7, cargo 98, chemical tanker 1, combination bulk 1, oil tanker 12, refrigerated cargo 4 (1998 est.)
Airports: 48 (1994 est.)
Airports - with paved runways:
total: 36
over 3,047 m: 8
2,438 to 3,047 m: 3
1,524 to 2,437 m: 5
914 to 1,523 m: 13
under 914 m: 7 (1994 est.)
Airports - with unpaved runways:
total: 12
1,524 to 2,437 m: 2
914 to 1,523 m: 5
under 914 m: 5 (1994 est.)

Military

Military branches: People's Army of Vietnam (PAVN) (includes Ground Forces, Navy, and Air Force), Coast Guard
Military manpower - military age: 17 years of age
Military manpower - availability:
males age 15-49: 20,492,806 (1999 est.)
Military manpower - fit for military service:
males age 15-49: 12,933,945 (1999 est.)
Military manpower - reaching military age annually:
males: 877,714 (1999 est.)
Military expenditures - dollar figure: $650 million (1997)
Military expenditures - percent of GDP: 9.3% (1997)

Transnational Issues

Disputes - international: maritime boundary with Cambodia not defined; involved in a complex dispute over the Spratly Islands with China, Malaysia, Philippines, Taiwan, and possibly Brunei; maritime boundary with Thailand resolved, August 1997;

Vietnam *(continued)*

maritime boundary dispute with China in the Gulf of Tonkin; Paracel Islands occupied by China but claimed by Vietnam and Taiwan; offshore islands and sections of boundary with Cambodia are in dispute; sections of land border with China are indefinite

Illicit drugs: minor producer of opium poppy with 3,000 hectares cultivated in 1998, capable of producing 20 metric tons of opium; probably minor transit point for Southeast Asian heroin destined for the US and Europe; growing opium/heroin addiction; possible small-scale heroin production

Virgin Islands
(territory of the US)

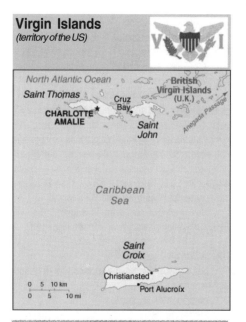

Geography

Location: Caribbean, islands between the Caribbean Sea and the North Atlantic Ocean, east of Puerto Rico

Geographic coordinates: 18 20 N, 64 50 W

Map references: Central America and the Caribbean

Area:
total: 352 sq km
land: 349 sq km
water: 3 sq km

Area - comparative: twice the size of Washington, DC

Land boundaries: 0 km

Coastline: 188 km

Maritime claims:
exclusive economic zone: 200 nm
territorial sea: 12 nm

Climate: subtropical, tempered by easterly trade winds, relatively low humidity, little seasonal temperature variation; rainy season May to November

Terrain: mostly hilly to rugged and mountainous with little level land

Elevation extremes:
lowest point: Caribbean Sea 0 m
highest point: Crown Mountain 474 m

Natural resources: sun, sand, sea, surf

Land use:
arable land: 15%
permanent crops: 6%
permanent pastures: 26%
forests and woodland: 6%
other: 47% (1993 est.)

Irrigated land: NA sq km

Natural hazards: several hurricanes in recent years; frequent and severe droughts and floods; occasional earthquakes

Environment - current issues: lack of natural freshwater resources

Environment - international agreements:
party to: NA

signed, but not ratified: NA

Geography - note: important location along the Anegada Passage - a key shipping lane for the Panama Canal; Saint Thomas has one of the best natural, deepwater harbors in the Caribbean

People

Population: 119,827 (July 1999 est.)
note: West Indian (45% born in the Virgin Islands and 29% born elsewhere in the West Indies) 74%, US mainland 13%, Puerto Rican 5%, other 8%

Age structure:
0-14 years: 28% (male 17,454; female 16,585)
15-64 years: 63% (male 34,712; female 41,325)
65 years and over: 9% (male 4,237; female 5,514) (1999 est.)

Population growth rate: 1.19% (1999 est.)

Birth rate: 17.08 births/1,000 population (1999 est.)

Death rate: 5.34 deaths/1,000 population (1999 est.)

Net migration rate: 0.13 migrant(s)/1,000 population (1999 est.)

Sex ratio:
at birth: 1.06 male(s)/female
under 15 years: 1.05 male(s)/female
15-64 years: 0.84 male(s)/female
65 years and over: 0.77 male(s)/female
total population: 0.89 male(s)/female (1999 est.)

Infant mortality rate: 10.07 deaths/1,000 live births (1999 est.)

Life expectancy at birth:
total population: 77.74 years
male: 74.04 years
female: 81.67 years (1999 est.)

Total fertility rate: 2.42 children born/woman (1999 est.)

Nationality:
noun: Virgin Islander(s)
adjective: Virgin Islander

Ethnic groups: black 80%, white 15%, other 5%

Religions: Baptist 42%, Roman Catholic 34%, Episcopalian 17%, other 7%

Languages: English (official), Spanish, Creole

Literacy: NA

Government

Country name:
conventional long form: Virgin Islands of the United States
conventional short form: Virgin Islands
former: Danish West Indies

Data code: VQ

Dependency status: organized, unincorporated territory of the US; administered by the Office of Insular Affairs, US Department of the Interior

Government type: NA

Capital: Charlotte Amalie

Administrative divisions: none (territory of the US); there are no first-order administrative divisions as defined by the US Government, but there are three islands at the second order; Saint Croix, Saint John, Saint Thomas

Virgin Islands *(continued)*

National holiday: Transfer Day, 31 March (1917) (from Denmark to US)
Constitution: Revised Organic Act of 22 July 1954
Legal system: based on US laws
Suffrage: 18 years of age; universal; note - indigenous inhabitants are US citizens but do not vote in US presidential elections
Executive branch:
chief of state: President William Jefferson CLINTON of the US (since 20 January 1993); Vice President Albert GORE, Jr. (since 20 January 1993)
head of government: Governor Dr. Charles Wesley TURNBULL (since 5 January 1999) and Lieutenant Governor Gerald LUZ James II (since 5 January 1999)
cabinet: NA
elections: US president and vice president elected on the same ticket for four-year terms; governor and lieutenant governor elected by popular vote for four-year terms; election last held 3 November 1998 (next to be held NA November 2002)
election results: Dr. Charles Wesley TURNBULL elected governor; percent of vote - Dr. Charles W. TURNBULL (Democrat) 58.9%, former Governor Roy L. SCHNEIDER (ICM) 41.1%
Legislative branch: unicameral Senate (15 seats; members are elected by popular vote to serve two-year terms)
elections: last held 3 November 1998 (next to be held NA November 2000)
election results: percent of vote by party - NA; seats by party - Democratic Party 6, independents 5, Republican Party 2, Independent Citizens Movement 2
note: the Virgin Islands elect one representative to the US House of Representatives; election last held 3 November 1998 (next to be held NA November 2000); results - Dr. Donna GREEN (Democrat) 80%, Victor O. FRAZER (ICM) 20%
Judicial branch: US District Court (judges are appointed by the president); Territorial Court (judges appointed by the governor)
Political parties and leaders: Democratic Party [James O'BRYON Jr.]; Independent Citizens' Movement or ICM [Virdin C. BROWN]; Republican Party [Charlotte-Poole DAVIS]
International organization participation: ECLAC (associate), Interpol (subbureau), IOC
Diplomatic representation in the US: none (territory of the US)
Diplomatic representation from the US: none (territory of the US)
Flag description: white, with a modified US coat of arms in the center between the large blue initials V and I; the coat of arms shows a yellow eagle holding an olive branch in one talon and three arrows in the other with a superimposed shield of vertical red and white stripes below a blue panel

Economy

Economy - overview: Tourism is the primary economic activity, accounting for more than 70% of GDP and 70% of employment. The islands normally host 2 million visitors a year. The number of US tourists in the first five months of 1996 was down by 55% from the same period in 1995, the lingering result of the fierce hurricanes of 1995. Unemployment rose sharply in 1996. The manufacturing sector consists of textile, electronics, pharmaceutical, and watch assembly plants. The agricultural sector is small, with most food being imported. International business and financial services are a small but growing component of the economy. One of the world's largest petroleum refineries is at Saint Croix. A major economic problem at the beginning of 1997 was the more than $1 billion in governmental arrears, income tax refunds, payments to vendors, and overdue wages.
GDP: purchasing power parity - $1.2 billion (1987 est.)
GDP - real growth rate: NA%
GDP - per capita: purchasing power parity - $12,500 (1987 est.)
GDP - composition by sector:
agriculture: NA%
industry: NA%
services: NA%
Population below poverty line: NA%
Household income or consumption by percentage share:
lowest 10%: NA%
highest 10%: NA%
Inflation rate (consumer prices): NA%
Labor force: 47,443 (1990 est.)
Labor force - by occupation: agriculture 1%, industry 20%, services 62%, other 17% (1990)
Unemployment rate: 6.2% (March 1994)
Budget:
revenues: $364.4 million
expenditures: $364.4 million, including capital expenditures of $NA (1990 est.)
Industries: tourism, petroleum refining, watch assembly, rum distilling, construction, pharmaceuticals, textiles, electronics
Industrial production growth rate: NA%
Electricity - production: 1.02 billion kWh (1996)
Electricity - production by source:
fossil fuel: 100%
hydro: 0%
nuclear: 0%
other: 0% (1996)
Electricity - consumption: 1.02 billion kWh (1996)
Electricity - exports: 0 kWh (1996)
Electricity - imports: 0 kWh (1996)
Agriculture - products: truck garden products, fruit, vegetables, sorghum; Senepol cattle
Exports: $1.8 billion (f.o.b., 1992)
Exports - commodities: refined petroleum products
Exports - partners: US, Puerto Rico
Imports: $2.2 billion (c.i.f., 1992)
Imports - commodities: crude oil, foodstuffs, consumer goods, building materials
Imports - partners: US, Puerto Rico
Debt - external: $NA
Economic aid - recipient: $NA
Currency: 1 United States dollar (US$) = 100 cents
Exchange rates: US currency is used
Fiscal year: 1 October - 30 September

Communications

Telephones: 60,000 (1990 est.)
Telephone system:
domestic: modern, uses fiber-optic cable and microwave radio relay
international: submarine cable and satellite communications; satellite earth stations - NA
Radio broadcast stations: AM 4, FM 8, shortwave 0 (1988)
Radios: 105,000 (1994 est.)
Television broadcast stations: 2 (1997)
Televisions: 66,000 (1994 est.)

Transportation

Railways: 0 km
Highways:
total: 856 km
paved: NA km
unpaved: NA km
Ports and harbors: Charlotte Amalie, Christiansted, Cruz Bay, Port Alucroix
Merchant marine: none
Airports: 2
note: international airports on Saint Thomas and Saint Croix; there is an airfield on St. John (1998 est.)
Airports - with paved runways:
total: 2
1,524 to 2,437 m: 2 (1998 est.)

Military

Military - note: defense is the responsibility of the US

Transnational Issues

Disputes - international: none

Wake Atoll
(territory of the US)

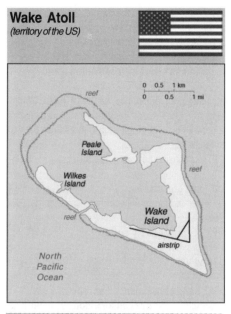

Geography

Location: Oceania, atoll in the North Pacific Ocean, about two-thirds of the way from Hawaii to the Northern Mariana Islands
Geographic coordinates: 19 17 N, 166 36 E
Map references: Oceania
Area:
total: 6.5 sq km
land: 6.5 sq km
water: 0 sq km
Area - comparative: about 11 times the size of The Mall in Washington, DC
Land boundaries: 0 km
Coastline: 19.3 km
Maritime claims:
exclusive economic zone: 200 nm
territorial sea: 12 nm
Climate: tropical
Terrain: atoll of three coral islands built up on an underwater volcano; central lagoon is former crater, islands are part of the rim
Elevation extremes:
lowest point: Pacific Ocean 0 m
highest point: unnamed location 6 m
Natural resources: none
Land use:
arable land: 0%
permanent crops: 0%
permanent pastures: 0%
forests and woodland: 0%
other: 100%
Irrigated land: 0 sq km (1998)
Natural hazards: occasional typhoons
Environment - current issues: NA
Environment - international agreements:
party to: NA
signed, but not ratified: NA
Geography - note: strategic location in the North Pacific Ocean; emergency landing location for transpacific flights

People

Population: no indigenous inhabitants
note: US military personnel have left the island, but some civilian personnel remain (1999 est.)

Government

Country name:
conventional long form: none
conventional short form: Wake Atoll
Data code: WQ
Dependency status: unincorporated territory of the US; administered from Washington, DC by the Department of the Interior; occasional activities on the island are managed by the US Army under a US Air Force contract
Legal system: NA
Flag description: the flag of the US is used

Economy

Economy - overview: Economic activity is limited to providing services to contractors located on the island. All food and manufactured goods must be imported.
Electricity - production: NA kWh
note: electricity supplied by the US military
Electricity - consumption: NA kWh

Communications

Telephone system: satellite communications; 1 DSN circuit off the Overseas Telephone System (OTS)
domestic: NA
international: NA
Radio broadcast stations: AM 0, FM NA, shortwave NA
note: Armed Forces Radio/Television Service (AFRTS) radio service provided by satellite
Television broadcast stations: 0 (1997)

Transportation

Ports and harbors: none; two offshore anchorages for large ships
Airports: 1 (1998 est.)
Airports - with paved runways:
total: 1
2,438 to 3,047 m: 1 (1998 est.)
Transportation - note: formerly an important commercial aviation base, now occasionally used by US military, some commercial cargo planes, and for emergency landings

Military

Military - note: defense is the responsibility of the US

Transnational Issues

Disputes - international: claimed by Marshall Islands

Wallis and Futuna
(overseas territory of France)

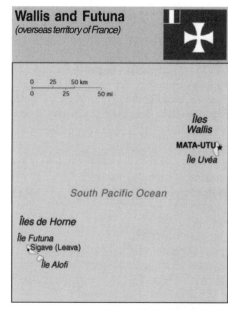

Geography

Location: Oceania, islands in the South Pacific Ocean, about two-thirds of the way from Hawaii to New Zealand
Geographic coordinates: 13 18 S, 176 12 W
Map references: Oceania
Area:
total: 274 sq km
land: 274 sq km
water: 0 sq km
note: includes Ile Uvea (Wallis Island), Ile Futuna (Futuna Island), Ile Alofi, and 20 islets
Area - comparative: 1.5 times the size of Washington, DC
Land boundaries: 0 km
Coastline: 129 km
Maritime claims:
exclusive economic zone: 200 nm
territorial sea: 12 nm
Climate: tropical; hot, rainy season (November to April); cool, dry season (May to October); rains 2,500-3,000 mm per year (80% humidity); average temperature 26.6 degrees C
Terrain: volcanic origin; low hills
Elevation extremes:
lowest point: Pacific Ocean 0 m
highest point: Mont Singavi 765 m
Natural resources: NEGL
Land use:
arable land: 5%
permanent crops: 20%
permanent pastures: NA%
forests and woodland: NA%
other: 75% (1993 est.)
Irrigated land: NA sq km
Natural hazards: NA
Environment - current issues: deforestation (only small portions of the original forests remain) largely as a result of the continued use of wood as the main fuel source; as a consequence of cutting down the forests,

the mountainous terrain of Futuna is particularly prone to erosion; there are no permanent settlements on Alofi because of the lack of natural fresh water resources

Environment - international agreements:

party to: NA

signed, but not ratified: NA

Geography - note: both island groups have fringing reefs

People

Population: 15,129 (July 1999 est.)

Age structure:

0-14 years: NA%

15-64 years: NA%

65 years and over: NA%

Population growth rate: 1.04% (1999 est.)

Birth rate: 22.34 births/1,000 population (1999 est.)

Death rate: 4.66 deaths/1,000 population (1999 est.)

Net migration rate: -7.26 migrant(s)/1,000 population (1999 est.)

Infant mortality rate: NA deaths/1,000 live births

Life expectancy at birth:

total population: NA years

male: NA years

female: NA years

Total fertility rate: NA children born/woman

Nationality:

noun: Wallisian(s), Futunan(s), or Wallis and Futuna Islanders

adjective: Wallisian, Futunan, or Wallis and Futuna Islander

Ethnic groups: Polynesian

Religions: Roman Catholic 100%

Languages: French, Wallisian (indigenous Polynesian language)

Literacy:

definition: age 15 and over can read and write

total population: 50%

male: 50%

female: 50% (1969 est.)

Government

Country name:

conventional long form: Territory of the Wallis and Futuna Islands

conventional short form: Wallis and Futuna

local long form: Territoire des Iles Wallis et Futuna

local short form: Wallis et Futuna

Data code: WF

Dependency status: overseas territory of France

Government type: NA

Capital: Mata-Utu (on Ile Uvea)

Administrative divisions: none (overseas territory of France); there are no first-order administrative divisions as defined by the US Government, but there are three kingdoms named Wallis, Sigave, Alo

Independence: none (overseas territory of France)

Constitution: 28 September 1958 (French Constitution)

Legal system: French legal system

Suffrage: 18 years of age; universal

Executive branch:

chief of state: President Jacques CHIRAC of France (since 17 May 1995), represented by High Administrator Claude PIERRET (since NA)

head of government: President of the Territorial Assembly Victor BRIAL (since 1 June 1997)

cabinet: Council of the Territory consists of three kings and three members appointed by the high administrator on the advice of the Territorial Assembly

note: there are three traditional kings with limited powers

elections: French president elected by popular vote for a seven-year term; high administrator appointed by the French president on the advice of the French Ministry of the Interior; the presidents of the Territorial Government and the Territorial Assembly are elected by the members of the assembly

Legislative branch: unicameral Territorial Assembly or Assemblee Territoriale (20 seats; members are elected by popular vote to serve five-year terms)

elections: last held 16 March 1997 (next to be held NA March 2002)

election results: percent of vote by party - NA; seats by party - NA

note: Wallis and Futuna elects one senator to the French Senate and one deputy to the French National Assembly; French Senate - elections last held 27 September 1998 (next to be held by NA September 2007); results - percent of vote by party - NA; seats - RPR 1; French National Assembly - elections last held 25 May-1 June 1997 (next to be held by NA March 2002); results - percent of vote by party - NA; seats - RPR 1

Judicial branch: none; justice generally administered under French law by the high administrator, but the three traditional kings administer customary law and there is a magistrate in Mata-Utu

Political parties and leaders: Rally for the Republic or RPR [leader NA]; Union Populaire Locale or UPL [leader NA]; Union Pour la Democratie Francaise or UDF [leader NA]; Lua kae tahi (Giscardians) [leader NA]; Mouvement des Radicaux de Gauche or MRG [leader NA]; Taumu'a Lelei [leader NA]

International organization participation: FZ, SPC

Diplomatic representation in the US: none (overseas territory of France)

Diplomatic representation from the US: none (overseas territory of France)

Flag description: a large white modified Maltese cross centered on a red background; the flag of France outlined in white on two sides is in the upper hoist quadrant; the flag of France is used for official occasions

Economy

Economy - overview: The economy is limited to traditional subsistence agriculture, with about 80% of the labor force earning its livelihood from agriculture (coconuts and vegetables), livestock (mostly pigs),

and fishing. About 4% of the population is employed in government. Revenues come from French Government subsidies, licensing of fishing rights to Japan and South Korea, import taxes, and remittances from expatriate workers in New Caledonia. Wallis and Futuna imports food - particularly flour, sugar, rice, and beef - fuel, clothing, machinery, and transport equipment, but its exports are negligible, consisting mostly of breadfruit, yams, and taro root.

GDP: purchasing power parity - $28.7 million (1995 est.)

GDP - real growth rate: NA%

GDP - per capita: purchasing power parity - $2,000 (1995 est.)

GDP - composition by sector:

agriculture: NA%

industry: NA%

services: NA%

Population below poverty line: NA%

Household income or consumption by percentage share:

lowest 10%: NA%

highest 10%: NA%

Inflation rate (consumer prices): NA%

Labor force: NA

Labor force - by occupation: agriculture, livestock, and fishing 80%, government 4% (est.)

Unemployment rate: NA%

Budget:

revenues: $20 million

expenditures: $20 million, including capital expenditures of $NA (1997 est.)

Industries: copra, handicrafts, fishing, lumber

Industrial production growth rate: NA%

Electricity - production: NA kWh

Electricity - production by source:

fossil fuel: NA%

hydro: NA%

nuclear: NA%

other: NA%

Electricity - consumption: NA kWh

Electricity - exports: NA kWh

Electricity - imports: NA kWh

Agriculture - products: breadfruit, yams, taro, bananas; pigs, goats

Exports: $370,000 (f.o.b., 1995 est.)

Exports - commodities: copra, handicrafts

Exports - partners: NA

Imports: $13.5 million (c.i.f., 1995 est.)

Imports - commodities: foodstuffs, manufactured goods, transportation equipment, fuel, clothing

Imports - partners: France, Australia, New Zealand

Debt - external: $NA

Economic aid - recipient: $1 million (1995)

Currency: 1 Comptoirs Francais du Pacifique franc (CFPF) = 100 centimes

Exchange rates: Comptoirs Francais du Pacifique francs (CFPF) per US$1 - 102.72 (January 1999), 107.25 (1998), 106.11 (1997), 93.00 (1996), 90.75 (1995), 100.94 (1994); note - linked at the rate of 18.18 to the French franc

Wallis and Futuna *(continued)*

Fiscal year: calendar year

Telephones: 340 (1985 est.)
Telephone system:
domestic: NA
international: NA
Radio broadcast stations: AM 1, FM 0, shortwave 0
Radios: NA
Television broadcast stations: 2 (1997)
Televisions: NA

Transportation

Railways: 0 km
Highways:
total: 120 km (Ile Uvea 100 km, Ile Futuna 20 km)
paved: 16 km (all on Ile Uvea)
unpaved: 104 km (Ile Uvea 84 km, Ile Futuna 20 km)
Waterways: none
Ports and harbors: Leava, Mata-Utu
Merchant marine:
total: 2 ships (1,000 GRT or over) totaling 44,160 GRT/41,656 DWT
ships by type: oil tanker 1, passenger 1 (1998 est.)
Airports: 2 (1998 est.)
Airports - with paved runways:
total: 1
1,524 to 2,437 m: 1 (1998 est.)
Airports - with unpaved runways:
total: 1
914 to 1,523 m: 1 (1998 est.)

Military

Military - note: defense is the responsibility of France

Transnational Issues

Disputes - international: none

West Bank

West Bank is Israeli occupied with current status subject to the Israeli-Palestinian Interim Agreement - permanent status to be determined through further negotiation.

Introduction

Background: The Israel-PLO Declaration of Principles on Interim Self-Government Arrangements ("the DOP"), signed in Washington on 13 September 1993, provides for a transitional period not exceeding five years of Palestinian interim self-government in the Gaza Strip and the West Bank. Permanent status negotiations began on 5 May 1996, but have not resumed since the initial meeting. Under the DOP, Israel agreed to transfer certain powers and responsibilities to the Palestinian Authority, which includes a Palestinian Legislative Council elected in January 1996, as part of interim self-governing arrangements in the West Bank and Gaza Strip. A transfer of powers and responsibilities for the Gaza Strip and Jericho took place pursuant to the Israel-PLO 4 May 1994 Cairo Agreement on the Gaza Strip and the Jericho Area and in additional areas of the West Bank pursuant to the Israel-PLO 28 September 1995 Interim Agreement, the Israel-PLO 15 January 1997 Protocol Concerning Redeployment in Hebron, and the Israel-PLO 23 October 1998 Wye River Memorandum. The DOP provides that Israel will retain responsibility during the transitional period for external security and for internal security and public order of settlements and Israelis. Permanent status is to be determined through direct negotiations.

Geography

Location: Middle East, west of Jordan
Geographic coordinates: 32 00 N, 35 15 E
Map references: Middle East
Area:
total: 5,860 sq km
land: 5,640 sq km
water: 220 sq km
note: includes West Bank, Latrun Salient, and the northwest quarter of the Dead Sea, but excludes Mt. Scopus; East Jerusalem and Jerusalem No Man's Land are also included only as a means of depicting the entire area occupied by Israel in 1967
Area - comparative: slightly smaller than Delaware
Land boundaries:
total: 404 km
border countries: Israel 307 km, Jordan 97 km
Coastline: 0 km (landlocked)
Maritime claims: none (landlocked)
Climate: temperate, temperature and precipitation vary with altitude, warm to hot summers, cool to mild winters
Terrain: mostly rugged dissected upland, some vegetation in west, but barren in east
Elevation extremes:
lowest point: Dead Sea -408 m
highest point: Tall Asur 1,022 m
Natural resources: NEGL
Land use:
arable land: 27%
permanent crops: 0%
permanent pastures: 32%
forests and woodland: 1%
other: 40%
Irrigated land: NA sq km
Natural hazards: NA
Environment - current issues: adequacy of fresh water supply; sewage treatment
Environment - international agreements:
party to: none of the selected agreements
signed, but not ratified: none of the selected agreements
Geography - note: landlocked; highlands are main recharge area for Israel's coastal aquifers; there are 216 Israeli settlements and civilian land use sites in the West Bank and 29 in East Jerusalem (August 1998 est.)

People

Population: 1,611,109 (July 1999 est.)
note: in addition, there are some 166,000 Israeli settlers in the West Bank and about 176,000 in East Jerusalem (August 1998 est.)
Age structure:
0-14 years: 45% (male 370,770; female 352,803)
15-64 years: 52% (male 422,209; female 411,597)
65 years and over: 3% (male 22,376; female 31,354)

West Bank *(continued)*

(1999 est.)

Population growth rate: 3.14% (1999 est.)

Birth rate: 35.59 births/1,000 population (1999 est.)

Death rate: 4.2 deaths/1,000 population (1999 est.)

Net migration rate: 0 migrant(s)/1,000 population (1999 est.)

Sex ratio:

at birth: 1.05 male(s)/female

under 15 years: 1.05 male(s)/female

15-64 years: 1.03 male(s)/female

65 years and over: 0.71 male(s)/female

total population: 1.02 male(s)/female (1999 est.)

Infant mortality rate: 25.22 deaths/1,000 live births (1999 est.)

Life expectancy at birth:

total population: 72.83 years

male: 70.96 years

female: 74.79 years (1999 est.)

Total fertility rate: 4.78 children born/woman (1999 est.)

Nationality:

noun: NA

adjective: NA

Ethnic groups: Palestinian Arab and other 83%, Jewish 17%

Religions: Muslim 75% (predominantly Sunni), Jewish 17%, Christian and other 8%

Languages: Arabic, Hebrew (spoken by Israeli settlers and many Palestinians), English (widely understood)

Literacy: NA

Government

Country name:

conventional long form: none

conventional short form: West Bank

Data code: WE

Economy

Economy - overview: Economic conditions in the West Bank - where economic activity is governed by the Paris Economic Protocol of April 1994 between Israel and the Palestinian Authority - have deteriorated since the early 1990s. Real per capita GDP for the West Bank and Gaza Strip (WBGS) declined 36.1% between 1992 and 1996 owing to the combined effect of falling aggregate incomes and robust population growth. The downturn in economic activity was largely the result of Israeli closure policies - the imposition of generalized border closures in response to security incidents in Israel - which disrupted previously established labor and commodity market relationships between Israel and the WBGS. The most serious negative social effect of this downturn has been the emergence of chronic unemployment; average unemployment rates in the WBGS during the 1980s were generally under 5%, by the mid-1990s this level had risen to over 20%. Since 1997 Israel's use of comprehensive closures has decreased and, in 1998, Israel implemented new policies to reduce the impact of closures and other security procedures on the movement of Palestinian goods and labor. These positive changes to the conduct of economic activity, combined with international donor pledges of over $3 billion made to the Palestinian Authority in November, may fuel a moderate economic recovery in 1999.

GDP: purchasing power parity - $3.1 billion (1998 est.)

GDP - real growth rate: 2.2% (1998 est.)

GDP - per capita: purchasing power parity - $2,000 (1998 est.)

GDP - composition by sector:

agriculture: 33%

industry: 25%

services: 42% (1995 est., includes Gaza Strip)

Population below poverty line: NA%

Household income or consumption by percentage share:

lowest 10%: NA%

highest 10%: NA%

Inflation rate (consumer prices): 7.6% (1997 est.)

Labor force: NA

note: excluding Israeli settlers

Labor force - by occupation: agriculture 13%, industry 13%, commerce, restaurants, and hotels 12%, construction 8%, other services 54% (1996)

Unemployment rate: 17.3% (1997 est.)

Budget:

revenues: $816 million

expenditures: $866 million, including capital expenditures of $NA (1997 est.)

note: includes Gaza Strip

Industries: generally small family businesses that produce cement, textiles, soap, olive-wood carvings, and mother-of-pearl souvenirs; the Israelis have established some small-scale, modern industries in the settlements and industrial centers

Industrial production growth rate: NA%

Electricity - production: NA kWh

note: most electricity imported from Israel; East Jerusalem Electric Company buys and distributes electricity to Palestinians in East Jerusalem and its concession in the West Bank; the Israel Electric Company directly supplies electricity to most Jewish residents and military facilities; at the same time, some Palestinian municipalities, such as Nabulus and Janin, generate their own electricity from small power plants

Electricity - production by source:

fossil fuel: NA%

hydro: NA%

nuclear: NA%

other: NA%

Electricity - consumption: NA kWh

Electricity - exports: NA kWh

Electricity - imports: NA kWh

Agriculture - products: olives, citrus, vegetables; beef, dairy products

Exports: $781 million (f.o.b., 1997 est.) (includes Gaza Strip)

Exports - commodities: olives, fruit, vegetables, limestone

Exports - partners: Israel, Jordan

Imports: $2.1 billion (c.i.f., 1997 est.) (includes Gaza Strip)

Imports - commodities: food, consumer goods, construction materials

Imports - partners: Israel, Jordan

Debt - external: $108 million (1997 est.)

Economic aid - recipient: $NA

Currency: 1 new Israeli shekel (NIS) = 100 new agorot; 1 Jordanian dinar (JD) = 1,000 fils

Exchange rates: new Israeli shekels (NIS) per US$1 - 4.2260 (November 1998), 3.4494 (1997), 3.1917 (1996), 3.0113 (1995), 3.0111 (1994); Jordanian dinars (JD) per US$1 - 0.7090 (January 1999), 0.7090 (1998), 0.7090 (1997), 0.7090 (1996), 0.7005 (1995), 0.6987 (1994)

Fiscal year: calendar year (since 1 January 1992)

Communications

Telephones: NA; 3.1% of Palestinian households have telephones

Telephone system:

domestic: NA

international: NA

note: Israeli company BEZEK and the Palestinian company PALTEL are responsible for communication services in the West Bank

Radio broadcast stations: AM 1, FM 0, shortwave 0

Radios: NA; note - 82% of Palestinian households have radios (1992 est.)

Television broadcast stations: NA

Televisions: NA; note - 54% of Palestinian households have televisions (1992 est.)

Transportation

Railways: 0 km

Highways:

total: 4,500 km

paved: 2,700 km

unpaved: 1,800 km (1997 est.)

note: Israelis have developed many highways to service Jewish settlements

Ports and harbors: none

Airports: 2 (1998 est.)

Airports - with paved runways:

total: 2

1,524 to 2,437 m: 1

under 914 m: 1 (1998 est.)

Military

Military branches: NA

Military expenditures - dollar figure: $NA

Military expenditures - percent of GDP: NA%

Transnational Issues

Disputes - international: West Bank and Gaza Strip are Israeli-occupied with current status subject to the Israeli-Palestinian Interim Agreement - permanent status to be determined through further negotiation

Western Sahara

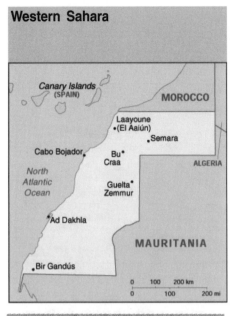

Geography

Location: Northern Africa, bordering the North Atlantic Ocean, between Mauritania and Morocco
Geographic coordinates: 24 30 N, 13 00 W
Map references: Africa
Area:
total: 266,000 sq km
land: 266,000 sq km
water: 0 sq km
Area - comparative: about the size of Colorado
Land boundaries:
total: 2,046 km
border countries: Algeria 42 km, Mauritania 1,561 km, Morocco 443 km
Coastline: 1,110 km
Maritime claims: contingent upon resolution of sovereignty issue
Climate: hot, dry desert; rain is rare; cold offshore air currents produce fog and heavy dew
Terrain: mostly low, flat desert with large areas of rocky or sandy surfaces rising to small mountains in south and northeast
Elevation extremes:
lowest point: Sebjet Tah -55 m
highest point: unnamed location 463 m
Natural resources: phosphates, iron ore
Land use:
arable land: 0%
permanent crops: 0%
permanent pastures: 19%
forests and woodland: 0%
other: 81%
Irrigated land: NA sq km
Natural hazards: hot, dry, dust/sand-laden sirocco wind can occur during winter and spring; widespread harmattan haze exists 60% of time, often severely restricting visibility
Environment - current issues: sparse water and arable land

Environment - international agreements:
party to: none of the selected agreements
signed, but not ratified: none of the selected agreements

People

Population: 239,333 (July 1999 est.)
Age structure:
0-14 years: NA
15-64 years: NA
65 years and over: NA
Population growth rate: 2.34% (1999 est.)
Birth rate: 45.42 births/1,000 population (1999 est.)
Death rate: 16.58 deaths/1,000 population (1999 est.)
Net migration rate: -5.41 migrant(s)/1,000 population (1999 est.)
Infant mortality rate: 136.67 deaths/1,000 live births (1999 est.)
Life expectancy at birth:
total population: 49.1 years
male: 47.98 years
female: 50.57 years (1999 est.)
Total fertility rate: 6.7 children born/woman (1999 est.)
Nationality:
noun: Sahrawi(s), Sahraoui(s)
adjective: Sahrawian, Sahraouian
Ethnic groups: Arab, Berber
Religions: Muslim
Languages: Hassaniya Arabic, Moroccan Arabic
Literacy: NA

Government

Country name:
conventional long form: none
conventional short form: Western Sahara
Data code: WI
Government type: legal status of territory and question of sovereignty unresolved; territory contested by Morocco and Polisario Front (Popular Front for the Liberation of the Saguia el Hamra and Rio de Oro), which in February 1976 formally proclaimed a government-in-exile of the Sahrawi Arab Democratic Republic (SADR); territory partitioned between Morocco and Mauritania in April 1976, with Morocco acquiring northern two-thirds; Mauritania, under pressure from Polisario guerrillas, abandoned all claims to its portion in August 1979; Morocco moved to occupy that sector shortly thereafter and has since asserted administrative control; the Polisario's government-in-exile was seated as an OAU member in 1984; guerrilla activities continued sporadically, until a UN-monitored cease-fire was implemented 6 September 1991
Capital: none
Administrative divisions: none (under de facto control of Morocco)
Suffrage: none; a UN sponsored voter identification campaign has yet to be completed

Executive branch: none
International organization participation: none
Diplomatic representation in the US: none
Diplomatic representation from the US: none

Economy

Economy - overview: Western Sahara, a territory poor in natural resources and lacking sufficient rainfall, depends on pastoral nomadism, fishing, and phosphate mining as the principal sources of income for the population. Most of the food for the urban population must be imported. All trade and other economic activities are controlled by the Moroccan Government. Incomes and standards of living are substantially below the Moroccan level.
GDP: purchasing power parity - $NA
GDP - real growth rate: NA%
GDP - per capita: purchasing power parity - $NA
GDP - composition by sector:
agriculture: NA%
industry: NA%
services: 40%-45% (1996 est.)
Population below poverty line: NA%
Household income or consumption by percentage share:
lowest 10%: NA%
highest 10%: NA%
Inflation rate (consumer prices): NA%
Labor force: 12,000
Labor force - by occupation: animal husbandry and subsistence farming 50%
Unemployment rate: NA%
Budget:
revenues: $NA
expenditures: $NA, including capital expenditures of $NA
Industries: phosphate mining, handicrafts
Industrial production growth rate: NA%
Electricity - production: 85 million kWh (1996)
Electricity - production by source:
fossil fuel: 100%
hydro: 0%
nuclear: 0%
other: 0% (1996)
Electricity - consumption: 85 million kWh (1996)
Electricity - exports: 0 kWh (1996)
Electricity - imports: 0 kWh (1996)
Agriculture - products: fruits and vegetables (grown in the few oases); camels, sheep, goats (kept by nomads)
Exports: $NA
Exports - commodities: phosphates 62%
Exports - partners: Morocco claims and administers Western Sahara, so trade partners are included in overall Moroccan accounts
Imports: $NA
Imports - commodities: fuel for fishing fleet, foodstuffs
Imports - partners: Morocco claims and administers Western Sahara, so trade partners are included in overall Moroccan accounts

Western Sahara (continued)

Debt - external: $NA
Economic aid - recipient: $NA
Currency: 1 Moroccan dirham (DH) = 100 centimes
Exchange rates: Moroccan dirhams (DH) per US$1
- 9.320 (January 1999), 9.604 (1998), 9.527 (1997),
8.716 (1996), 8.540 (1995), 9.203 (1994)
Fiscal year: calendar year

Communications

Telephones: 2,000
Telephone system: sparse and limited system
domestic: NA
international: tied into Morocco's system by
microwave radio relay, tropospheric scatter, and
satellite; satellite earth stations - 2 Intelsat (Atlantic
Ocean) linked to Rabat, Morocco
Radio broadcast stations: AM 2, FM 0, shortwave
0
Radios: NA
Television broadcast stations: NA
Televisions: NA

Transportation

Railways: 0 km
Highways:
total: 6,200 km
paved: 1,350 km
unpaved: 4,850 km (1991 est.)
Ports and harbors: Ad Dakhla, Cabo Bojador,
Laayoune (El Aaiun)
Airports: 12 (1998 est.)
Airports - with paved runways:
total: 3
2,438 to 3,047 m: 3 (1998 est.)
Airports - with unpaved runways:
total: 9
1,524 to 2,437 m: 1
914 to 1,523 m: 5
under 914 m: 3 (1998 est.)
Heliports: 1 (1998 est.)

Military

Military branches: NA
Military expenditures - dollar figure: $NA
Military expenditures - percent of GDP: NA%

Transnational Issues

Disputes - international: claimed and administered
by Morocco, but sovereignty is unresolved and the UN
is attempting to hold a referendum on the issue; the
UN-administered cease-fire has been in effect since
September 1991

World

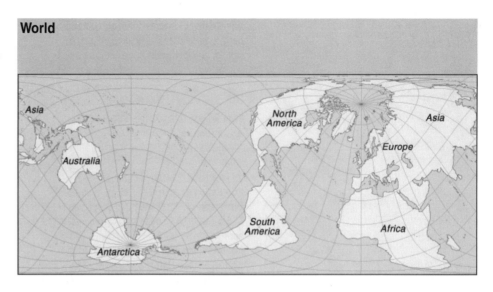

Geography

Map references: World, Time Zones
Area:
total: 510.072 million sq km
land: 148.94 million sq km
water: 361.132 million sq km
note: 70.8% of the world's surface is water, 29.2% is
land
Area - comparative: land area about 15 times the
size of the US
Land boundaries: the land boundaries in the world
total 251,480.24 km (not counting shared boundaries
twice)
Coastline: 356,000 km
Maritime claims:
contiguous zone: 24 nm claimed by most, but can
vary
continental shelf: 200-m depth claimed by most or to
depth of exploitation; others claim 200 nm or to the
edge of the continental margin
exclusive fishing zone: 200 nm claimed by most, but
can vary
exclusive economic zone: 200 nm claimed by most,
but can vary
territorial sea: 12 nm claimed by most, but can vary
note: boundary situations with neighboring states
prevent many countries from extending their fishing or
economic zones to a full 200 nm; 43 nations and other
areas that are landlocked include Afghanistan, Andorra,
Armenia, Austria, Azerbaijan, Belarus, Bhutan, Bolivia,
Botswana, Burkina Faso, Burundi, Central African
Republic, Chad, Czech Republic, Ethiopia, Holy See
(Vatican City), Hungary, Kazakhstan, Kyrgyzstan,
Laos, Lesotho, Liechtenstein, Luxembourg, Malawi,
Mali, Moldova, Mongolia, Nepal, Niger, Paraguay,
Rwanda, San Marino, Slovakia, Swaziland,
Switzerland, Tajikistan, The Former Yugoslav Republic
of Macedonia, Turkmenistan, Uganda, Uzbekistan,
West Bank, Zambia, Zimbabwe
Climate: two large areas of polar climates separated
by two rather narrow temperate zones from a wide
equatorial band of tropical to subtropical climates
Terrain: the greatest ocean depth is the Mariana
Trench at 10,924 m in the Pacific Ocean
Elevation extremes:
lowest point: Dead Sea -408 m
highest point: Mount Everest 8,848 m
Natural resources: the rapid using up of
nonrenewable mineral resources, the depletion of
forest areas and wetlands, the extinction of animal
and plant species, and the deterioration in air and
water quality (especially in Eastern Europe, the former
USSR, and China) pose serious long-term problems
that governments and peoples are only beginning to
address
Land use:
arable land: 10%
permanent crops: 1%
permanent pastures: 26%
forests and woodland: 32%
other: 31% (1993 est.)
Irrigated land: 2,481,250 sq km (1993 est.)
Natural hazards: large areas subject to severe
weather (tropical cyclones), natural disasters
(earthquakes, landslides, tsunamis, volcanic
eruptions)
Environment - current issues: large areas subject
to overpopulation, industrial disasters, pollution (air,
water, acid rain, toxic substances), loss of vegetation
(overgrazing, deforestation, desertification), loss of
wildlife, soil degradation, soil depletion, erosion
Environment - international agreements: selected
international environmental agreements are included
under the Environment - international agreements
entry for each country and in the Selected
International Environmental Agreements appendix

People

Population: 5,995,544,836 (July 1999 est.)
Age structure:
0-14 years: 30% (male 934,816,288; female
884,097,095)

15-64 years: 63% (male 1,905,701,066; female 1,861,265,079)

65 years and over: 7% (male 179,094,601; female 230,570,707) (1999 est.)

Population growth rate: 1.3% (1999 est.)

Birth rate: 22 births/1,000 population (1999 est.)

Death rate: 9 deaths/1,000 population (1999 est.)

Sex ratio:

at birth: 1.06 male(s)/female

under 15 years: 1.06 male(s)/female

15-64: 1.02 male(s)/female

65 years and over: 0.78 male(s)/female

total population: 1.02 male(s)/female (1999 est.)

Infant mortality rate: 56 deaths/1,000 live births (1999 est.)

Life expectancy at birth:

total population: 63 years

male: 61 years

female: 65 years (1999 est.)

Total fertility rate: 2.8 children born/woman (1999 est.)

Government

Data code: none; there is no FIPS 10-4 country code for the World, so the Factbook uses the "W" data code from DIAM 65-18 "Geopolitical Data Elements and Related Features," Data Standard No. 3, March 1984, published by the Defense Intelligence Agency; see the Cross-Reference List of Country Data Codes appendix

Administrative divisions: 266 nations, dependent areas, other, and miscellaneous entries

Legal system: all members of the UN (excluding Yugoslavia) plus Nauru and Switzerland are parties to the statute that established the International Court of Justice (ICJ) or World Court

Economy

Economy - overview: Growth in global output (gross world product, GWP) dropped to 2% in 1998 from 4% in 1997 because of continued recession in Japan, severe financial difficulties in other East Asian countries, and widespread dislocations in the Russian economy. The US economy continued its remarkable sustained prosperity, growing at 3.9% in 1998, and accounted for 22% of GWP. Western Europe's economies grew at roughly 2.5%, not enough to cut deeply into the region's high unemployment; these economies produced 21% of GWP. China, the second largest economy in the world, continued its rapid growth and accounted for 11% of GWP. Japan posted a decline of 2.6% in 1998 and its share in GWP dropped to 7.4%. As usual, the 15 successor nations of the USSR and the other old Warsaw Pact nations experienced widely different rates of growth. Russia's national product dropped by 5% whereas the nations of central and eastern Europe grew by 3.4% on average. The developing nations varied widely in their growth results, with many countries facing population increases that eat up gains in output. Externally, the nation-state, as a bedrock economic-political

institution, is steadily losing control over international flows of people, goods, funds, and technology. Internally, the central government finds its control over resources slipping as separatist regional movements - typically based on ethnicity - gain momentum, e.g., in the successor states of the former Soviet Union, in the former Yugoslavia, in India, and in Canada. In Western Europe, governments face the difficult political problem of channeling resources away from welfare programs in order to increase investment and strengthen incentives to seek employment. The addition of more than 80 million people each year to an already overcrowded globe is exacerbating the problems of pollution, desertification, underemployment, epidemics, and famine. Because of their own internal problems, the industrialized countries have inadequate resources to deal effectively with the poorer areas of the world, which, at least from the economic point of view, are becoming further marginalized. In 1998, serious financial difficulties in several high-growth East Asia countries cast a shadow over short-term global economic prospects. The introduction of the euro as the common currency of much of Western Europe in January 1999 poses serious economic risks because of varying levels of income and cultural and political differences among the participating nations. (For specific economic developments in each country of the world in 1998, see the individual country entries.)

GDP: GWP (gross world product) - purchasing power parity - $39 trillion (1998 est.)

GDP - real growth rate: 2% (1998 est.)

GDP - per capita: purchasing power parity - $6,600 (1998 est.)

GDP - composition by sector:

agriculture: NA%

industry: NA%

services: NA%

Household income or consumption by percentage share:

lowest 10%: NA%

highest 10%: NA%

Inflation rate (consumer prices): all countries 25%; developed countries 2% to 4% typically; developing countries 10% to 60% typically (1998 est.)

note: national inflation rates vary widely in individual cases, from stable prices in Japan to hyperinflation in a number of Third World countries

Labor force: NA

Labor force - by occupation: NA

Unemployment rate: 30% combined unemployment and underemployment in many non-industrialized countries; developed countries typically 5%-12% unemployment (1998 est.)

Industries: dominated by the onrush of technology, especially in computers, robotics, telecommunications, and medicines and medical equipment; most of these advances take place in OECD nations; only a small portion of non-OECD countries have succeeded in rapidly adjusting to these technological forces; the accelerated development of new industrial (and agricultural) technology is

complicating already grim environmental problems

Industrial production growth rate: 5% (1997 est.)

Electricity - production: 12.3427 trillion kWh (1994)

Electricity - production by source:

fossil fuel: NA%

hydro: NA%

nuclear: NA%

other: NA%

Electricity - consumption: 12.3427 trillion kWh (1994)

Exports: $5 trillion (f.o.b., 1998 est.)

Exports - commodities: the whole range of industrial and agricultural goods and services

Exports - partners: in value, about 75% of exports from the developed countries

Imports: $5 trillion (f.o.b., 1998 est.)

Imports - commodities: the whole range of industrial and agricultural goods and services

Imports - partners: in value, about 75% of imports by the developed countries

Debt - external: $2 trillion for less developed countries (1998 est.)

Economic aid - recipient: traditional worldwide foreign aid $50 billion (1995 est.)

Communications

Telephones: NA

Telephone system:

domestic: NA

international: NA

Radio broadcast stations: AM NA, FM NA, shortwave NA

Radios: NA

Television broadcast stations: NA

Televisions: NA

Transportation

Railways:

total: 1,201,337 km includes about 190,000 to 195,000 km of electrified routes of which 147,760 km are in Europe, 24,509 km in the Far East, 11,050 km in Africa, 4,223 km in South America, and 4,160 km in North America; note - fastest speed in daily service is 300 km/hr attained by France's Societe Nationale des Chemins-de-Fer Francais (SNCF) Le Train a Grande Vitesse (TGV) - Atlantique line

broad gauge: 251,153 km

standard gauge: 710,754 km

narrow gauge: 239,430 km

Highways:

total: NA km

paved: NA km

unpaved: NA km

Ports and harbors: Chiba, Houston, Kawasaki, Kobe, Marseille, Mina' al Ahmadi (Kuwait), New Orleans, New York, Rotterdam, Yokohama

Merchant marine:

total: 28,310 ships (1,000 GRT or over) totaling 495,299,489 GRT/764,129,056 DWT

ships by type: barge carrier 23, bulk 5,745, cargo 8,766, chemical tanker 1,326, combination bulk 319,

World *(continued)*

combination ore/oil 227, container 2,615, liquefied gas tanker 802, livestock carrier 60, multifunction large-load carrier 90, oil tanker 4,521, passenger 392, passenger-cargo 126, railcar carrier 19, refrigerated cargo 1,067, roll-on/roll-off cargo 1,117, short-sea passenger 484, specialized tanker 118, vehicle carrier 493 (1998 est.)

Military

Military branches: ground, maritime, and air forces at all levels of technology
Military expenditures - dollar figure: aggregate real expenditure on arms worldwide in 1998 remained at approximately the 1997 level, about three-quarters of a trillion dollars (1998 est.)
Military expenditures - percent of GDP: roughly 2% of gross world product (1998 est.)

Yemen

Geography

Location: Middle East, bordering the Arabian Sea, Gulf of Aden, and Red Sea, between Oman and Saudi Arabia
Geographic coordinates: 15 00 N, 48 00 E
Map references: Middle East
Area:
total: 527,970 sq km
land: 527,970 sq km
water: 0 sq km
note: includes Perim, Socotra, the former Yemen Arab Republic (YAR or North Yemen), and the former People's Democratic Republic of Yemen (PDRY or South Yemen)
Area - comparative: slightly larger than twice the size of Wyoming
Land boundaries:
total: 1,746 km
border countries: Oman 288 km, Saudi Arabia 1,458 km
Coastline: 1,906 km
Maritime claims:
contiguous zone: 18 nm in the North; 24 nm in the South
continental shelf: 200 nm or to the edge of the continental margin
exclusive economic zone: 200 nm
territorial sea: 12 nm
Climate: mostly desert; hot and humid along west coast; temperate in western mountains affected by seasonal monsoon; extraordinarily hot, dry, harsh desert in east
Terrain: narrow coastal plain backed by flat-topped hills and rugged mountains; dissected upland desert plains in center slope into the desert interior of the Arabian Peninsula
Elevation extremes:
lowest point: Arabian Sea 0 m
highest point: Jabal an Nabi Shu'ayb 3,760 m
Natural resources: petroleum, fish, rock salt,

marble, small deposits of coal, gold, lead, nickel, and copper, fertile soil in west
Land use:
arable land: 3%
permanent crops: 0%
permanent pastures: 30%
forests and woodland: 4%
other: 63% (1993 est.)
Irrigated land: 3,600 sq km (1993 est.)
Natural hazards: sandstorms and dust storms in summer
Environment - current issues: very limited natural fresh water resources; inadequate supplies of potable water; overgrazing; soil erosion; desertification
Environment - international agreements:
party to: Biodiversity, Climate Change, Desertification, Environmental Modification, Hazardous Wastes, Law of the Sea, Nuclear Test Ban, Ozone Layer Protection
signed, but not ratified: none of the selected agreements
Geography - note: strategic location on Bab el Mandeb, the strait linking the Red Sea and the Gulf of Aden, one of world's most active shipping lanes

People

Population: 16,942,230 (July 1999 est.)
Age structure:
0-14 years: 48% (male 4,118,292; female 3,971,886)
15-64 years: 49% (male 4,243,809; female 4,065,429)
65 years and over: 3% (male 278,133; female 264,681) (1999 est.)
Population growth rate: 3.34% (1999 est.)
Birth rate: 43.31 births/1,000 population (1999 est.)
Death rate: 9.88 deaths/1,000 population (1999 est.)
Net migration rate: 0 migrant(s)/1,000 population (1999 est.)
Sex ratio:
at birth: 1.05 male(s)/female
under 15 years: 1.04 male(s)/female
15-64 years: 1.04 male(s)/female
65 years and over: 1.05 male(s)/female
total population: 1.04 male(s)/female (1999 est.)
Infant mortality rate: 69.82 deaths/1,000 live births (1999 est.)
Life expectancy at birth:
total population: 59.98 years
male: 58.17 years
female: 61.88 years (1999 est.)
Total fertility rate: 7.06 children born/woman (1999 est.)
Nationality:
noun: Yemeni(s)
adjective: Yemeni
Ethnic groups: predominantly Arab; Afro-Arab concentrations in western coastal locations; South Asians in southern regions; small European communities in major metropolitan areas
Religions: Muslim including Shaf'i (Sunni) and Zaydi (Shi'a), small numbers of Jewish, Christian, and Hindu
Languages: Arabic

Yemen (continued)

Literacy:
definition: age 15 and over can read and write
total population: 38%
male: 53%
female: 26% (1990 est.)

Government

Country name:
conventional long form: Republic of Yemen
conventional short form: Yemen
local long form: Al Jumhuriyah al Yamaniyah
local short form: Al Yaman
Data code: YM
Government type: republic
Capital: Sanaa
Administrative divisions: 17 governorates (muhafazat, singular - muhafazah); Abyan, 'Adan, Al Bayda', Al Hudaydah, Al Jawf, Al Mahrah, Al Mahwit, 'Ataq, Dhamar, Hadhramawt, Hajjah, Ibb, Lahij, Ma'rib, Sa'dah, San'a', Ta'izz
note: there may be a new governorate for the capital city of Sanaa
Independence: 22 May 1990 Republic of Yemen was established with the merger of the Yemen Arab Republic [Yemen (Sanaa) or North Yemen] and the Marxist-dominated People's Democratic Republic of Yemen [Yemen (Aden) or South Yemen]; previously North Yemen had become independent on NA November 1918 (from the Ottoman Empire) and South Yemen had become independent on 30 November 1967 (from the UK)
National holiday: Proclamation of the Republic, 22 May (1990)
Constitution: 16 May 1991; amended 29 September 1994
Legal system: based on Islamic law, Turkish law, English common law, and local tribal customary law; does not accept compulsory ICJ jurisdiction
Suffrage: 18 years of age; universal
Executive branch:
chief of state: President Lt. Gen. Ali Abdallah SALIH (since 22 May 1990, the former president of North Yemen, assumed office upon the merger of North and South Yemen); Vice President Maj. Gen. Abd al-Rab Mansur al-HADI (since NA October 1994)
head of government: Prime Minister Dr. Abd al-Karim Ali al-IRYANI (since NA April 1998)
cabinet: Council of Ministers appointed by the president on the advice of the prime minister
elections: President SALIH was elected by the House of Representatives for a five-year term, however, future presidents will be elected by direct, popular vote for five-year terms; election last held 1 October 1994 (next to be held NA 1999); vice president appointed by the president; prime minister and deputy prime ministers appointed by the president
election results: Ali Abdallah SALIH elected president; percent of House of Representatives vote - NA
Legislative branch: unicameral House of Representatives (301 seats; members elected by popular vote to serve four-year terms)
elections: last held 27 April 1997 (next to be held NA April 2001)
election results: percent of vote by party - NA; seats by party - GPC 189, Islah 52, Nasserite Unionist Party 3, National Arab Socialist Baath Party 2, independents 54, election pending 1
note: in May 1997, the president created a consultative council, sometimes referred to as the upper house of Parliament; its 59 members are all appointed by the president
Judicial branch: Supreme Court
Political parties and leaders: there are over 12 political parties active in Yemen, some of the more prominent are: General People's Congress or GPC [President Ali Abdallah SALIH]; Islamic Reform Grouping or Islah [Shaykh Abdallah bin Husayn al-AHMAR]; Yemeni Socialist Party or YSP [Ali Salih UBAYD]; Nasserite Unionist Party [leader NA]; National Arab Socialist Baath Party [Dr. Qassim SALAAM]
note: President SALIH's General People's Congress or GPC won a landslide victory in the April 1997 legislative election and no longer governs in coalition with Shaykh Abdallah bin Husayn al-AHMAR's Islamic Reform Grouping or Islaah - the two parties had been in coalition since the end of the civil war in 1994; the YSP, a loyal opposition party, boycotted the April 1997 legislative election
Political pressure groups and leaders: NA
International organization participation: ACC, AFESD, AL, AMF, CAEU, CCC, ESCWA, FAO, G-77, IAEA, IBRD, ICAO, ICRM, IDA, IDB, IFAD, IFC, IFRCS, ILO, IMF, IMO, Intelsat, Interpol, IOC, ITU, NAM, OIC, OPCW, UN, UNCTAD, UNESCO, UNIDO, UPU, WFTU, WHO, WIPO, WMO, WToO, WTrO (applicant)
Diplomatic representation in the US:
chief of mission: Ambassador Abd al-Wahhab Abdallah al-HAJRI
chancery: Suite 705, 2600 Virginia Avenue NW, Washington, DC 20037
telephone: [1] (202) 965-4760
FAX: [1] (202) 337-2017
Diplomatic representation from the US:
chief of mission: Ambassador Barbara K. BODINE
embassy: Dhahr Himyar Zone, Sheraton Hotel District, Sanaa
mailing address: P. O. Box 22347, Sanaa
telephone: [967] (1) 238843 through 238852
FAX: [967] (1) 251563
Flag description: three equal horizontal bands of red (top), white, and black; similar to the flag of Syria which has two green stars and of Iraq which has three green stars (plus an Arabic inscription) in a horizontal line centered in the white band; also similar to the flag of Egypt which has a symbolic eagle centered in the white band

Economy

Economy - overview: Yemen, one of the poorest countries in the Arab world, reported strong growth in the mid-1990s with the onset of oil production, but was harmed by low oil prices in 1998. Yemen has embarked on an IMF-supported structural adjustment program designed to modernize and streamline the economy, which has led to foreign debt relief and restructuring. Yemen will work in 1999 to maintain tight control over spending and implement additional components of the IMF program. The high population growth rate of 3.3%, internal political dissension, and continued low prices make the government's task especially difficult.
GDP: purchasing power parity - $12.1 billion (1998 est.)
GDP - real growth rate: 1.8% (1998 est.)
GDP - per capita: purchasing power parity - $740 (1998 est.)
GDP - composition by sector:
agriculture: 16%
industry: 46%
services: 38% (1996)
Population below poverty line: NA%
Household income or consumption by percentage share:
lowest 10%: 2.3%
highest 10%: 30.8% (1992)
Inflation rate (consumer prices): 11% (1998 est.)
Labor force: NA
Labor force - by occupation: most people are employed in agriculture and herding or as expatriate laborers; services, construction, industry, and commerce account for less than one-half of the labor force
Unemployment rate: 30% (1995 est.)
Budget:
revenues: $2.3 billion
expenditures: $2.6 billion, including capital expenditures of $NA (1998 budget est.)
Industries: crude oil production and petroleum refining; small-scale production of cotton textiles and leather goods; food processing; handicrafts; small aluminum products factory; cement
Industrial production growth rate: NA%
Electricity - production: 1.9 billion kWh (1996)
Electricity - production by source:
fossil fuel: 100%
hydro: 0%
nuclear: 0%
other: 0% (1996)
Electricity - consumption: 1.9 billion kWh (1996)
Electricity - exports: 0 kWh (1996)
Electricity - imports: 0 kWh (1996)
Agriculture - products: grain, fruits, vegetables, qat (mildly narcotic shrub), coffee, cotton; dairy products, poultry, beef; fish
Exports: $1.6 billion (f.o.b., 1998 est.)
Exports - commodities: crude oil, cotton, coffee, dried and salted fish
Exports - partners: China 31%, South Korea 19%, Thailand 17%, Thailand 5%, Brazil 5%, Japan 5% (1997)
Imports: $2.8 billion (c.i.f., 1998 est.)
Imports - commodities: food and live animals, machinery and equipment, manufactured goods
Imports - partners: UAE 9%, Saudi Arabia 8%, US

Yemen *(continued)*

7%, France 6%, Brazil 5% (1997)
Debt - external: $4.9 billion (1998)
Economic aid - recipient: $176.1 million (1995)
Currency: Yemeni rial (YRI) (new currency)
Exchange rates: Yemeni rials (YRI) per US$1 -
140.940 (October 1998), 129.286 (1997), 94.157
(1996), 40.839 (1995), 12.010 (official fixed rate
1991-94)
Fiscal year: calendar year

Communications

Telephones: 131,655 (1992 est.)
Telephone system: since unification in 1990, efforts
have been made to create a national
telecommunications network
domestic: the network consists of microwave radio
relay, cable, and tropospheric scatter
international: satellite earth stations - 3 Intelsat (2
Indian Ocean and 1 Atlantic Ocean), 1 Intersputnik
(Atlantic Ocean region), and 2 Arabsat; microwave
radio relay to Saudi Arabia and Djibouti
Radio broadcast stations: AM 4, FM 1, shortwave
0
Radios: 325,000 (1993 est.)
Television broadcast stations: 7 (in addition, there
are several low-power repeaters) (1997)
Televisions: 100,000 (1993 est.)

Transportation

Railways: 0 km
Highways:
total: 64,725 km
paved: 5,243 km
unpaved: 59,482 km (1996 est.)
Pipelines: crude oil 644 km; petroleum products 32
km
Ports and harbors: Aden, Al Hudaydah, Al Mukalla,
As Salif, Mocha, Nishtun
Merchant marine:
total: 3 ships (1,000 GRT or over) totaling 12,059
GRT/18,563 DWT
ships by type: cargo 1, oil tanker 2 (1998 est.)
Airports: 48 (1998 est.)
Airports - with paved runways:
total: 12
over 3,047 m: 2
2,438 to 3,047 m: 7
1,524 to 2,437 m: 1
914 to 1,523 m: 1
under 914 m: 1 (1998 est.)
Airports - with unpaved runways:
total: 36
over 3,047 m: 2
2,438 to 3,047 m: 9
1,524 to 2,437 m: 10
914 to 1,523 m: 12
under 914 m: 3 (1998 est.)

Military

Military branches: Army, Navy, Air Force, Air
Defense Forces, paramilitary (includes Police)

Military manpower - military age: 18 years of age
Military manpower - availability:
males age 15-49: 3,776,075 (1999 est.)
Military manpower - fit for military service:
males age 15-49: 2,119,308 (1999 est.)
**Military manpower - reaching military age
annually:**
males: 212,005 (1999 est.)
Military expenditures - dollar figure: $413.6
million (1999)
Military expenditures - percent of GDP: 7.6%
(1999)

Transnational Issues

Disputes - international: a large section of
boundary with Saudi Arabia is not defined; Hanish
Islands dispute with Eritrea resolved by arbitral
tribunal in October 1998

Zambia

Geography

Location: Southern Africa, east of Angola
Geographic coordinates: 15 00 S, 30 00 E
Map references: Africa
Area:
total: 752,610 sq km
land: 740,720 sq km
water: 11,890 sq km
Area - comparative: slightly larger than Texas
Land boundaries:
total: 5,664 km
border countries: Angola 1,110 km, Democratic
Republic of the Congo 1,930 km, Malawi 837 km,
Mozambique 419 km, Namibia 233 km, Tanzania 338
km, Zimbabwe 797 km
Coastline: 0 km (landlocked)
Maritime claims: none (landlocked)
Climate: tropical; modified by altitude; rainy season
(October to April)
Terrain: mostly high plateau with some hills and
mountains
Elevation extremes:
lowest point: Zambezi river 329 m
highest point: unnamed location in Mafinga Hills
2,301 m
Natural resources: copper, cobalt, zinc, lead, coal,
emeralds, gold, silver, uranium, hydropower
Land use:
arable land: 7%
permanent crops: 0%
permanent pastures: 40%
forests and woodland: 39%
other: 14% (1993 est.)
Irrigated land: 460 sq km (1993 est.)
Natural hazards: tropical storms (November to
April)
Environment - current issues: air pollution and
resulting acid rain in the mineral extraction and
refining region; poaching seriously threatens
rhinoceros and elephant populations; deforestation;

Zambia (continued)

soil erosion; desertification; lack of adequate water treatment presents human health risks

Environment - international agreements:
party to: Biodiversity, Climate Change, Desertification, Endangered Species, Hazardous Wastes, Law of the Sea, Nuclear Test Ban, Ozone Layer Protection, Wetlands
signed, but not ratified: Climate Change-Kyoto Protocol

Geography - note: landlocked

People

Population: 9,663,535 (July 1999 est.)
Age structure:
0-14 years: 49% (male 2,381,937; female 2,355,807)
15-64 years: 49% (male 2,308,715; female 2,379,994)
65 years and over: 2% (male 107,427; female 129,655) (1999 est.)
Population growth rate: 2.12% (1999 est.)
Birth rate: 44.51 births/1,000 population (1999 est.)
Death rate: 22.56 deaths/1,000 population (1999 est.)
Net migration rate: -0.78 migrant(s)/1,000 population (1999 est.)
Sex ratio:
at birth: 1.03 male(s)/female
under 15 years: 1.01 male(s)/female
15-64 years: 0.97 male(s)/female
65 years and over: 0.83 male(s)/female
total population: 0.99 male(s)/female (1999 est.)
Infant mortality rate: 91.85 deaths/1,000 live births (1999 est.)
Life expectancy at birth:
total population: 36.96 years
male: 36.72 years
female: 37.21 years (1999 est.)
Total fertility rate: 6.35 children born/woman (1999 est.)
Nationality:
noun: Zambian(s)
adjective: Zambian
Ethnic groups: African 98.7%, European 1.1%, other 0.2%
Religions: Christian 50%-75%, Muslim and Hindu 24%-49%, indigenous beliefs 1%
Languages: English (official), major vernaculars - Bemba, Kaonda, Lozi, Lunda, Luvale, Nyanja, Tonga, and about 70 other indigenous languages
Literacy:
definition: age 15 and over can read and write English
total population: 78.2%
male: 85.6%
female: 71.3% (1995 est.)

Government

Country name:
conventional long form: Republic of Zambia
conventional short form: Zambia
former: Northern Rhodesia
Data code: ZA

Government type: republic
Capital: Lusaka
Administrative divisions: 9 provinces; Central, Copperbelt, Eastern, Luapula, Lusaka, Northern, North-Western, Southern, Western
Independence: 24 October 1964 (from UK)
National holiday: Independence Day, 24 October (1964)
Constitution: 2 August 1991
Legal system: based on English common law and customary law; judicial review of legislative acts in an ad hoc constitutional council; has not accepted compulsory ICJ jurisdiction
Suffrage: 18 years of age; universal
Executive branch:
chief of state: President Frederick CHILUBA (since 31 October 1991); Vice President Christon TEMBO (since NA December 1997); note - the president is both the chief of state and head of government
head of government: President Frederick CHILUBA (since 31 October 1991); Vice President Christon TEMBO (since NA December 1997); note - the president is both the chief of state and head of government
cabinet: Cabinet appointed by the president from among the members of the National Assembly
elections: president elected by popular vote for a five-year term; election last held 18 November 1996 (next to be held NA October 2001); vice president appointed by the president
election results: Frederick CHILUBA reelected president; percent of vote - Frederick CHILUBA 70%, Dean MUNGO'MBA 12%, Humphrey MULEMBA 6%, Akashambatwa LEWANIKA 4%, Chama CHAKOMBOKA 3%, others 5%
Legislative branch: unicameral National Assembly (150 seats; members are elected by popular vote to serve five-year terms)
elections: last held 18 November 1996 (next to be held NA October 2001)
election results: percent of vote by party - NA; seats by party - MMD 130, NP 5, ZADECO 2, AZ 2, independents 11
Judicial branch: Supreme Court, justices are appointed by the president
Political parties and leaders: Agenda for Zambia or AZ [Akashambatwa LEWANIKA]; Labor Party or LP [Chibiza MFUNI]; Liberal Progressive Front or LPF [Roger CHONGWE, president]; Movement for Democratic Process or MDP [Chama CHAKOM BOKA]; Movement for Multiparty Democracy or MMD [Frederick CHILUBA]; National Lima Party or NLP [Guy SCOTT and Ben KAPITA]; National Party or NP [Daniel LISULO]; United National Independence Party or UNIP [Kenneth KAUNDA]; Zambia Democratic Congress or ZADECO [Dean MUNG'OMBA]
International organization participation: ACP, AfDB, C, CCC, ECA, FAO, G-19, G-77, IAEA, IBRD, ICAO, ICFTU, ICRM, IDA, IFAD, IFC, IFRCS, ILO, IMF, Intelsat, Interpol, IOC, IOM, ITU, MONUA, NAM, OAU, OPCW, SADC, UN, UNCTAD, UNESCO, UNIDO, UNOMSIL, UPU, WCL, WHO, WIPO, WMO,

WToO, WTrO
Diplomatic representation in the US:
chief of mission: Ambassador Dunstan Weston KAMANA
chancery: 2419 Massachusetts Avenue NW, Washington, DC 20008
telephone: [1] (202) 265-9717 through 9719
FAX: [1] (202) 332-0826
Diplomatic representation from the US:
chief of mission: Ambassador Arlene RENDER
embassy: corner of Independence and United Nations Avenues
mailing address: P. O. Box 31617, Lusaka
telephone: [260] (1) 250-955, 252-230
FAX: [260] (1) 252-225
Flag description: green with a panel of three vertical bands of red (hoist side), black, and orange below a soaring orange eagle, on the outer edge of the flag

Economy

Economy - overview: Despite progress in privatization and budgetary reform, Zambia's economy has a long way to go. Inflation, while slowing somewhat, continues to be a major concern to the CHILUBA government. Zambia's copper mining sector, which accounts for over 80% of the nation's foreign currency intake, is struggling. Production rates are down as are world copper prices. Aid cuts by Zambia's donors, arising out of concern for the November 1996 flawed election, also have damaged Zambia's economic prospects. Urged by the World Bank, Zambia has embarked on a privatization program which is to include the all-important copper industry. Until a deal on the copper sector is concluded, perhaps by mid-1999, economic prospects will remain clouded.
GDP: purchasing power parity - $8.3 billion (1998 est.)
GDP - real growth rate: -2% (1998 est.)
GDP - per capita: purchasing power parity - $880 (1998 est.)
GDP - composition by sector:
agriculture: 23%
industry: 40%
services: 37% (1997 est.)
Population below poverty line: 86% (1993 est.)
Household income or consumption by percentage share:
lowest 10%: 1.5%
highest 10%: 31.3% (1993)
Inflation rate (consumer prices): 43.9% (1996)
Labor force: 3.4 million
Labor force - by occupation: agriculture 85%, mining, manufacturing, and construction 6%, transport and services 9%
Unemployment rate: 22% (1991)
Budget:
revenues: $888 million
expenditures: $835 million, including capital expenditures of $110 million (1995 est.)
Industries: copper mining and processing, construction, foodstuffs, beverages, chemicals,

Zambia (continued)

textiles, fertilizer
Industrial production growth rate: 3.5% (1996)
Electricity - production: 7.84 billion kWh (1996)
Electricity - production by source:
fossil fuel: 0.51%
hydro: 99.49%
nuclear: 0%
other: 0% (1996)
Electricity - consumption: 6.393 billion kWh (1996)
Electricity - exports: 1.47 billion kWh (1996)
Electricity - imports: 23 million kWh (1996)
Agriculture - products: corn, sorghum, rice, peanuts, sunflower seed, tobacco, cotton, sugarcane, cassava (tapioca); cattle, goats, pigs, poultry, beef, pork, poultry meat, milk, eggs, hides
Exports: $905 million (f.o.b., 1998 est.)
Exports - commodities: copper, cobalt, zinc, lead, tobacco
Exports - partners: Japan, South Africa, US, Saudi Arabia, India, Thailand, Malaysia (1997)
Imports: $1.1 billion (f.o.b., 1998 est.)
Imports - commodities: machinery, transportation equipment, foodstuffs, fuels, petroleum products, electricity, fertilizer
Imports - partners: South Africa 48%, Saudi Arabia, UK, Zimbabwe (1997)
Debt - external: $7.1 billion (1997 est.)
Economic aid - recipient: $1.991 billion (1995)
Currency: 1 Zambian kwacha (ZK) = 100 ngwee
Exchange rates: Zambian kwacha (ZK) per US$1 - 1,428 (October 1998), 1,333.81 (1997), 1,203.71 (1996), 857.23 (1995), 669.37 (1994)
Fiscal year: calendar year

Communications

Telephones: 80,900 (1987 est.)
Telephone system: facilities are among the best in Sub-Saharan Africa
domestic: high-capacity microwave radio relay connects most larger towns and cities
international: satellite earth stations - 2 Intelsat (1 Indian Ocean and 1 Atlantic Ocean)
Radio broadcast stations: AM 11, FM 5, shortwave 0
Radios: 1,889,140
Television broadcast stations: 9 (1997)
Televisions: 215,000 (1995 est.)

Transportation

Railways:
total: 2,164 km (1995)
narrow gauge: 2,164 km 1.067-m gauge (13 km double track)
note: the total includes 891 km of the Tanzania-Zambia Railway Authority (TAZARA), which operates 1,860 km of 1.067-m narrow gauge track between Dar es Salaam and Kapiri Mposhi where it connects to the Zambia Railways system; TAZARA is not a part of Zambia Railways
Highways:
total: 39,700 km

paved: 7,265 km (including 60 km of expressways)
unpaved: 32,435 km (1996 est.)
Waterways: 2,250 km, including Zambezi and Luapula rivers, Lake Tanganyika
Pipelines: crude oil 1,724 km
Ports and harbors: Mpulungu
Airports: 112 (1998 est.)
Airports - with paved runways:
total: 12
over 3,047 m: 1
2,438 to 3,047 m: 3
1,524 to 2,437 m: 5
914 to 1,523 m: 2
under 914 m: 1 (1998 est.)
Airports - with unpaved runways:
total: 100
2,438 to 3,047 m: 1
1,524 to 2,437 m: 2
914 to 1,523 m: 66
under 914 m: 31 (1998 est.)

Military

Military branches: Army, Air Force, paramilitary forces, Police
Military manpower - availability:
males age 15-49: 2,102,167 (1999 est.)
Military manpower - fit for military service:
males age 15-49: 1,113,174 (1999 est.)
Military expenditures - dollar figure: $76 million (1997)
Military expenditures - percent of GDP: 1.8% (1997)

Transnational Issues

Disputes - international: quadripoint with Botswana, Namibia, and Zimbabwe is in disagreement
Illicit drugs: transshipment point for methaqualone, heroin, and cocaine bound for Southern Africa and Europe; regional money-laundering center

Zimbabwe

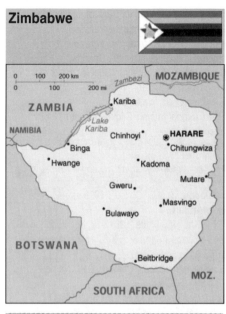

Geography

Location: Southern Africa, northeast of Botswana
Geographic coordinates: 20 00 S, 30 00 E
Map references: Africa
Area:
total: 390,580 sq km
land: 386,670 sq km
water: 3,910 sq km
Area - comparative: slightly larger than Montana
Land boundaries:
total: 3,066 km
border countries: Botswana 813 km, Mozambique 1,231 km, South Africa 225 km, Zambia 797 km
Coastline: 0 km (landlocked)
Maritime claims: none (landlocked)
Climate: tropical; moderated by altitude; rainy season (November to March)
Terrain: mostly high plateau with higher central plateau (high veld); mountains in east
Elevation extremes:
lowest point: junction of the Runde and Save rivers 162 m
highest point: Inyangani 2,592 m
Natural resources: coal, chromium ore, asbestos, gold, nickel, copper, iron ore, vanadium, lithium, tin, platinum group metals
Land use:
arable land: 7%
permanent crops: 0%
permanent pastures: 13%
forests and woodland: 23%
other: 57% (1993 est.)
Irrigated land: 1,930 sq km (1993 est.)
Natural hazards: recurring droughts; floods and severe storms are rare
Environment - current issues: deforestation; soil erosion; land degradation; air and water pollution; the black rhinoceros herd - once the largest concentration of the species in the world - has been significantly reduced by poaching

Zimbabwe *(continued)*

Environment - international agreements:
party to: Biodiversity, Climate Change, Desertification, Endangered Species, Law of the Sea, Ozone Layer Protection
signed, but not ratified: none of the selected agreements
Geography - note: landlocked

People

Population: 11,163,160 (July 1999 est.)
Age structure:
0-14 years: 43% (male 2,432,785; female 2,389,029)
15-64 years: 54% (male 2,986,531; female 3,059,186)
65 years and over: 3% (male 132,532; female 163,097) (1999 est.)
Population growth rate: 1.02% (1999 est.)
Birth rate: 30.64 births/1,000 population (1999 est.)
Death rate: 20.43 deaths/1,000 population (1999 est.)
Net migration rate: NA migrant(s)/1,000 population
note: there is a small but steady flow of Zimbabweans into South Africa in search of better paid employment
Sex ratio:
at birth: 1.03 male(s)/female
under 15 years: 1.02 male(s)/female
15-64 years: 0.98 male(s)/female
65 years and over: 0.81 male(s)/female
total population: 0.99 male(s)/female (1999 est.)
Infant mortality rate: 61.21 deaths/1,000 live births (1999 est.)
Life expectancy at birth:
total population: 38.86 years
male: 38.77 years
female: 38.94 years (1999 est.)
Total fertility rate: 3.71 children born/woman (1999 est.)
Nationality:
noun: Zimbabwean(s)
adjective: Zimbabwean
Ethnic groups: African 98% (Shona 71%, Ndebele 16%, other 11%), white 1%, mixed and Asian 1%
Religions: syncretic (part Christian, part indigenous beliefs) 50%, Christian 25%, indigenous beliefs 24%, Muslim and other 1%
Languages: English (official), Shona, Sindebele (the language of the Ndebele, sometimes called Ndebele), numerous but minor tribal dialects
Literacy:
definition: age 15 and over can read and write English
total population: 85%
male: 90%
female: 80% (1995 est.)

Government

Country name:
conventional long form: Republic of Zimbabwe
conventional short form: Zimbabwe
former: Southern Rhodesia
Data code: ZI
Government type: parliamentary democracy

Capital: Harare
Administrative divisions: 8 provinces and 2 cities* with provincial status; Bulawayo*, Harare*, Manicaland, Mashonaland Central, Mashonaland East, Mashonaland West, Masvingo, Matabeleland North, Matabeleland South, Midlands
Independence: 18 April 1980 (from UK)
National holiday: Independence Day, 18 April (1980)
Constitution: 21 December 1979
Legal system: mixture of Roman-Dutch and English common law
Suffrage: 18 years of age; universal
Executive branch:
chief of state: Executive President Robert Gabriel MUGABE (since 31 December 1987); Co-Vice Presidents Simon Vengai MUZENDA (since 31 December 1987) and Joshua M. NKOMO (since 6 August 1990); note - the president is both the chief of state and head of government
head of government: Executive President Robert Gabriel MUGABE (since 31 December 1987); Co-Vice Presidents Simon Vengai MUZENDA (since 31 December 1987) and Joshua M. NKOMO (since 6 August 1990); note - the president is both the chief of state and head of government
cabinet: Cabinet appointed by the president; responsible to the House of Assembly
elections: president nominated by the House of Assembly for a six-year term (if more than one nomination, an electoral college consisting of members of the House of Assembly elects the president); election last held 26-27 March 1996 (next to be held NA March 2002); co-vice presidents appointed by the president
election results: Robert Gabriel MUGABE reelected president; percent of electoral college vote - Robert Gabriel MUGABE 92.7%, Abel MUZOREWA 4.8%; Ndabaningi SITHOLE 2.4%
Legislative branch: unicameral parliament, called House of Assembly (150 seats - 120 elected by popular vote for six-year terms, 12 nominated by the president, 10 occupied by traditional chiefs chosen by their peers, and 8 occupied by provincial governors)
elections: last held 8-9 April 1995 (next to be held NA April 2001)
election results: percent of vote by party - NA; seats by party - ZANU-PF 117, ZANU-Ndonga 2, independent 1
Judicial branch: Supreme Court
Political parties and leaders: Zimbabwe African National Union-Patriotic Front or ZANU-PF [Robert MUGABE]; Zimbabwe African National Union-NDONGA or ZANU-NDONGA [Ndabaningi SITHOLE]; Zimbabwe Unity Movement or ZUM [Edgar TEKERE]; Democratic Party or DP [Emmanuel MAGOCHE]; Forum Party of Zimbabwe [Enock DUMBUTSHENA]; United Parties [Abel MUZOREWA]
International organization participation: ACP, AfDB, C, CCC, ECA, FAO, G-15, G-77, IAEA, IBRD, ICAO, ICFTU, ICRM, IDA, IFAD, IFC, IFRCS, ILO,

IMF, Intelsat, Interpol, IOC, IOM (observer), ISO, ITU, MONUA, NAM, OAU, OPCW, PCA, SADC, UN, UNCTAD, UNESCO, UNIDO, UPU, WCL, WFTU, WHO, WIPO, WMO, WToO, WTrO
Diplomatic representation in the US:
chief of mission: Ambassador Amos Bernard Muvengwa MIDZI
chancery: 1608 New Hampshire Avenue NW, Washington, DC 20009
telephone: [1] (202) 332-7100
FAX: [1] (202) 483-9326
Diplomatic representation from the US:
chief of mission: Ambassador Thomas McDONALD
embassy: 172 Herbert Chitepo Avenue, Harare
mailing address: P. O. Box 3340, Harare
telephone: [263] (4) 794521
FAX: [263] (4) 796488
Flag description: seven equal horizontal bands of green, yellow, red, black, red, yellow, and green with a white equilateral triangle edged in black based on the hoist side; a yellow Zimbabwe bird is superimposed on a red five-pointed star in the center of the triangle

Economy

Economy - overview: The government of Zimbabwe faces a wide variety of difficult economic problems as it struggles to consolidate earlier progress in developing a market-oriented economy. Its involvement in the war in the Democratic Republic of the Congo, for example, has already drained hundreds of millions of dollars from the economy. Badly needed support from the IMF suffers delays in part because of the country's failure to meet budgetary goals. Inflation rose from an annual rate of 25% in January 1998 to 47% in December and will almost certainly continue to increase in 1999. The economy is being steadily weakened by AIDS; Zimbabwe has one of the highest rates of infection in the world. Per capita GDP, which is twice the average of the poorer sub-Saharan nations, will increase little if any in the near-term, and Zimbabwe will suffer continued frustrations in developing its agricultural and mineral resources.
GDP: purchasing power parity - $26.2 billion (1998 est.)
GDP - real growth rate: 1.5% (1998 est.)
GDP - per capita: purchasing power parity - $2,400 (1998 est.)
GDP - composition by sector:
agriculture: 28%
industry: 32%
services: 40% (1997 est.)
Population below poverty line: 25.5% (1990-91 est.)
Household income or consumption by percentage share:
lowest 10%: 1.8%
highest 10%: 46.9% (1990)
Inflation rate (consumer prices): 32% (1998 est.)
Labor force: 5 million (1997 est.)
Labor force - by occupation: NA

Zimbabwe *(continued)*

Unemployment rate: at least 45% (1994 est.)
Budget:
revenues: $2.5 billion
expenditures: $2.9 billion, including capital expenditures of $279 million (FY96/97 est.)
Industries: mining (coal, clay, numerous metallic and nonmetallic ores), copper, steel, nickel, tin, wood products, cement, chemicals, fertilizer, clothing and footwear, foodstuffs, beverages
Industrial production growth rate: 10% (1994)
Electricity - production: 8.5 billion kWh (1996)
Electricity - production by source:
fossil fuel: 71.76%
hydro: 28.24%
nuclear: 0%
other: 0% (1996)
Electricity - consumption: 10.769 billion kWh (1996)
Electricity - exports: 1 million kWh (1996)
Electricity - imports: 2.27 billion kWh (1996)
Agriculture - products: corn, cotton, tobacco, wheat, coffee, sugarcane, peanuts; cattle, sheep, goats, pigs
Exports: $1.7 billion (f.o.b., 1998 est.)
Exports - commodities: tobacco, gold, ferroalloys, cotton (1997)
Exports - partners: South Africa 12%, UK 11%, Germany 8%, Japan 6%, US 6% (1997 est.)
Imports: $2 billion (f.o.b., 1998 est.)
Imports - commodities: machinery and transport equipment 39%, other manufactures 18%, chemicals 15%, fuels 10% (1997 est.)
Imports - partners: South Africa 37%, UK 7%, US 6%, Japan 6% (1997 est.)
Debt - external: $5 billion (1998)
Economic aid - recipient: $437.6 million (1995)
Currency: 1 Zimbabwean dollar (Z$) = 100 cents
Exchange rates: Zimbabwean dollars (Z$) per US$1 - 39.3701 (January 1999), 21.4133 (1998), 11.8906 (1997), 9.9206 (1996), 8.6580 (1995), 8.1500 (1994)
Fiscal year: 1 July - 30 June

Telephones: 301,000 (1990 est.)
Telephone system: system was once one of the best in Africa, but now suffers from poor maintenance
domestic: consists of microwave radio relay links, open-wire lines, and radiotelephone communication stations
international: satellite earth station - 1 Intelsat (Atlantic Ocean)
Radio broadcast stations: AM 8, FM 18, shortwave 0
Radios: 890,000 (1992 est.)
Television broadcast stations: 16 (1997)
Televisions: 280,000 (1992 est.)

Transportation

Railways:
total: 2,759 km (1995)

narrow gauge: 2,759 km 1.067-m gauge (313 km electrified; 42 km double track) (1995 est.)
Highways:
total: 18,338 km
paved: 8,692 km
unpaved: 9,646 km (1996 est.)
Waterways: the Mazoe and Zambezi rivers are used for transporting chrome ore from Harare to Mozambique
Pipelines: petroleum products 212 km
Ports and harbors: Binga, Kariba
Airports: 467 (1998 est.)
Airports - with paved runways:
total: 18
over 3,047 m: 3
2,438 to 3,047 m: 2
1,524 to 2,437 m: 4
914 to 1,523 m: 9 (1998 est.)
Airports - with unpaved runways:
total: 449
1,524 to 2,437 m: 4
914 to 1,523 m: 220
under 914 m: 225 (1998 est.)

Military

Military branches: Zimbabwe National Army, Air Force of Zimbabwe, Zimbabwe Republic Police (includes Police Support Unit, Paramilitary Police)
Military manpower - availability:
males age 15-49: 2,738,963 (1999 est.)
Military manpower - fit for military service:
males age 15-49: 1,707,348 (1999 est.)
Military expenditures - dollar figure: $427 million (FY97/98)
Military expenditures - percent of GDP: 4.6% (FY97/98)

Transnational Issues

Disputes - international: quadripoint with Botswana, Namibia, and Zambia is in disagreement
Illicit drugs: significant transit point for African cannabis and South Asian heroin, mandrax, and methamphetamines destined for the South African and European markets

Taiwan

Introduction

Background: In 1895, military defeat forced China to cede Taiwan to Japan, however it reverted to Chinese control after World War II. Following the Communist victory on the mainland in 1949, 2 million Nationalists fled to Taiwan and established a government that over five decades has gradually democratized and incorporated native Taiwanese within its structure. Throughout this period, the island has prospered as one of East Asia's economic tigers. The dominant political issue continues to be the relationship between Taiwan and Mainland China and the question of eventual reunification.

Geography

Location: Eastern Asia, islands bordering the East China Sea, Philippine Sea, South China Sea, and Taiwan Strait, north of the Philippines, off the southeastern coast of China
Geographic coordinates: 23 30 N, 121 00 E
Map references: Southeast Asia
Area:
total: 35,980 sq km
land: 32,260 sq km
water: 3,720 sq km
note: includes the Pescadores, Matsu, and Quemoy
Area - comparative: slightly smaller than Maryland and Delaware combined
Land boundaries: 0 km
Coastline: 1,448 km
Maritime claims:
exclusive economic zone: 200 nm
territorial sea: 12 nm
Climate: tropical; marine; rainy season during southwest monsoon (June to August); cloudiness is persistent and extensive all year
Terrain: eastern two-thirds mostly rugged mountains; flat to gently rolling plains in west
Elevation extremes:
lowest point: South China Sea 0 m

Taiwan (continued)

highest point: Yu Shan 3,997 m
Natural resources: small deposits of coal, natural gas, limestone, marble, and asbestos
Land use:
arable land: 24%
permanent crops: 1%
permanent pastures: 5%
forests and woodland: 55%
other: 15%
Irrigated land: NA sq km
Natural hazards: earthquakes and typhoons
Environment - current issues: air pollution; water pollution from industrial emissions, raw sewage; contamination of drinking water supplies; trade in endangered species; low-level radioactive waste disposal
Environment - international agreements:
party to: none of the selected agreements
signed, but not ratified: none of the selected agreements

People

Population: 22,113,250 (July 1999 est.)
Age structure:
0-14 years: 22% (male 2,515,398; female 2,338,506)
15-64 years: 70% (male 7,825,953; female 7,574,836)
65 years and over: 8% (male 989,040; female 869,517) (1999 est.)
Population growth rate: 0.93% (1999 est.)
Birth rate: 14.63 births/1,000 population (1999 est.)
Death rate: 5.32 deaths/1,000 population (1999 est.)
Net migration rate: -0.02 migrant(s)/1,000 population (1999 est.)
Sex ratio:
at birth: 1.08 male(s)/female
under 15 years: 1.08 male(s)/female
15-64 years: 1.03 male(s)/female
65 years and over: 1.14 male(s)/female
total population: 1.05 male(s)/female (1999 est.)
Infant mortality rate: 6.01 deaths/1,000 live births (1999 est.)
Life expectancy at birth:
total population: 77.49 years
male: 74.38 years
female: 80.85 years (1999 est.)
Total fertility rate: 1.77 children born/woman (1999 est.)
Nationality:
noun: Chinese (singular and plural)
adjective: Chinese
Ethnic groups: Taiwanese (including Hakka) 84%, mainland Chinese 14%, aborigine 2%
Religions: mixture of Buddhist, Confucian, and Taoist 93%, Christian 4.5%, other 2.5%
Languages: Mandarin Chinese (official), Taiwanese (Min), Hakka dialects
Literacy:
definition: age 15 and over can read and write
total population: 94% (1998 est.)
male: 93% (1980 est.)
female: 79% (1980 est.)

Government

Country name:
conventional long form: none
conventional short form: Taiwan
local long form: none
local short form: T'ai-wan
Data code: TW
Government type: multiparty democratic regime headed by popularly elected president
Capital: Taipei
Administrative divisions: since in the past the authorities claimed to be the government of all China, the central administrative divisions include the provinces of Fu-chien (some 20 offshore islands of Fujian Province including Quemoy and Matsu) and Taiwan (the island of Taiwan and the Pescadores islands); note - the more commonly referenced administrative divisions are those of Taiwan Province - 16 counties (hsien, singular and plural), 5 municipalities* (shih, singular and plural), and 2 special municipalities** (chuan-shih, singular and plural); Chang-hua, Chia-i, Chia-i*, Chi-lung*, Hsin-chu, Hsin-chu*, Hua-lien, I-lan, Kao-hsiung, Kao-hsiung**, Miao-li, Nan-t'ou, P'eng-hu, P'ing-tung, T'ai-chung, T'ai-chung*, T'ai-nan, T'ai-nan*, T'ai-pei, T'ai-pei**, T'ai-tung, T'ao-yuan, and Yun-lin; the provincial capital is at Chung-hsing-hsin-ts'un
note: Taiwan uses the Wade-Giles system for romanization
National holiday: National Day, 10 October (1911) (Anniversary of the Chinese Revolution)
Constitution: 1 January 1947, amended in 1992, 1994, and 1997
Legal system: based on civil law system; accepts compulsory ICJ jurisdiction, with reservations
Suffrage: 20 years of age; universal
Executive branch:
chief of state: President LEE Teng-hui (succeeded to the presidency following the death of President CHIANG Ching-kuo 13 January 1988, elected by the National Assembly 21 March 1990, elected by popular vote in the first-ever direct elections for president 23 March 1996); Vice President LIEN Chan (since 20 May 1996)
head of government: Premier (President of the Executive Yuan) Vincent SIEW (since 1 September 1997) and Vice Premier (Vice President of the Executive Yuan) LIU Chao-shiuan (since 10 December 1997)
cabinet: Executive Yuan appointed by the president
elections: president and vice president elected on the same ticket by popular vote for four-year terms; election last held 23 March 1996 (next to be held NA 2000); premier appointed by the president; vice premiers appointed by the president on the recommendation of the premier
election results: LEE Teng-hui elected president; percent of vote - LEE Teng-hui 54%, PENG Ming-min 21%, LIN Yang-kang 15%, and CHEN Li-an 10%
Legislative branch: unicameral Legislative Yuan (225 seats - 168 elected by popular vote, 41 elected on the basis of the proportion of nationwide votes received by participating political parties, eight elected from overseas Chinese constituencies on the basis of the proportion of nationwide votes received by participating political parties, eight elected by popular vote among the aboriginal populations; members serve three-year terms) and unicameral National Assembly (334 seats; members elected by popular vote to serve four-year terms)
elections: Legislative Yuan - last held 5 December 1998 (next to be held NA December 2001); National Assembly - last held 23 March 1996 (next to be held NA 2000)
election results: Legislative Yuan - percent of vote by party - KMT 46%, DPP 29%, CNP 7%, independents 10%, other parties 8%; seats by party - KMT 123, DPP 70, CNP 11, independents 15, other parties 6; National Assembly - percent of vote by party - KMT 55%, DPP 30%, CNP 14%, other 1%; seats by party - KMT 183, DPP 99, CNP 46, other 6
Judicial branch: Judicial Yuan, justices appointed by the president with the consent of the National Assembly
Political parties and leaders: Kuomintang or KMT (Nationalist Party) [LEE Teng-hui, chairman]; Democratic Progressive Party or DPP [LIN Yi-Hsiung, chairman]; Chinese New Party or CNP [leader NA]; Taiwan Independence Party or TAIP [HSU Shih-Kai]; other various parties
Political pressure groups and leaders: Taiwan independence movement, various business and environmental groups
note: debate on Taiwan independence has become acceptable within the mainstream of domestic politics on Taiwan; political liberalization and the increased representation of opposition parties in Taiwan's legislature have opened public debate on the island's national identity; advocates of Taiwan independence oppose the ruling party's traditional stand that the island will eventually reunify with mainland China; goals of the Taiwan independence movement include establishing a sovereign nation on Taiwan and entering the UN; other organizations supporting Taiwan independence include the World United Formosans for Independence and the Organization for Taiwan Nation Building
International organization participation: APEC, AsDB, BCIE, ICC, IOC, WCL, WTrO (applicant)
Diplomatic representation in the US: none; unofficial commercial and cultural relations with the people of the US are maintained through a private instrumentality, the Taipei Economic and Cultural Representative Office (TECRO) with headquarters in Taipei and field offices in Washington and 12 other US cities
Diplomatic representation from the US: none; unofficial commercial and cultural relations with the people on Taiwan are maintained through a private institution, the American Institute in Taiwan (AIT), which has its headquarters in Rosslyn, Virginia (telephone: [1] (703) 525-8474 and FAX: [1] (703) 841-1385) and offices in Taipei at #7 Lane 134, Hsin

Taiwan *(continued)*

Yi Road, Section 3, telephone [886] (2) 2709-2000, FAX [886] (2) 2702-7675, and in Kao-hsiung at #2 Chung Cheng 3d Road, telephone [886] (7) 224-0154 through 0157, FAX [886] (7) 223-8237, and the American Trade Center at Room 3207 International Trade Building, Taipei World Trade Center, 333 Keelung Road Section 1, Taipei 10548, telephone [886] (2) 2720-1550, FAX [886] (2) 2757-7162
Flag description: red with a dark blue rectangle in the upper hoist-side corner bearing a white sun with 12 triangular rays

Economy

Economy - overview: Taiwan has a dynamic capitalist economy with gradually decreasing guidance of investment and foreign trade by government authorities and partial government ownership of some large banks and industrial firms. Real growth in GDP has averaged about 8.5% a year during the past three decades. Export growth has been even faster and has provided the impetus for industrialization. Inflation and unemployment are low, and foreign reserves are the world's third largest. Agriculture contributes less than 3% to GDP, down from 35% in 1952. Traditional labor-intensive industries are steadily being moved off-shore and replaced with more capital- and technology-intensive industries. Taiwan has become a major investor in China, Thailand, Indonesia, the Philippines, Malaysia, and Vietnam. The tightening of labor markets has led to an influx of foreign workers, both legal and illegal. Because of its conservative financial approach and its entrepreneurial strengths, Taiwan suffered little compared with many of its neighbors from "the Asian flu" in 1998.
GDP: purchasing power parity - $362 billion (1998 est.)
GDP - real growth rate: 4.8% (1998 est.)
GDP - per capita: purchasing power parity - $16,500 (1998 est.)
GDP - composition by sector:
agriculture: 2.7%
industry: 35.3%
services: 62% (1997)
Population below poverty line: NA%
Household income or consumption by percentage share:
lowest 10%: NA%
highest 10%: NA%
Inflation rate (consumer prices): 2.1% (1998)
Labor force: 9.4 million (1997)
Labor force - by occupation: services 52%, industry 38%, agriculture 10% (1996)
Unemployment rate: 2.7% (1998)
Budget:
revenues: $40 billion
expenditures: $55 billion, including capital expenditures of $NA (1998 est.)
Industries: electronics, textiles, chemicals, clothing, food processing, plywood, sugar milling, cement, shipbuilding, petroleum refining
Industrial production growth rate: 7% (1997)

Electricity - production: 134.906 billion kWh (1996)
Electricity - production by source:
fossil fuel: 63.2%
hydro: 7.1%
nuclear: 29.7%
other: 0% (1997)
Electricity - consumption: 134.906 billion kWh (1996)
Electricity - exports: 0 kWh (1996)
Electricity - imports: 0 kWh (1996)
Agriculture - products: rice, wheat, corn, soybeans, vegetables, fruit, tea; pigs, poultry, beef, milk; fish
Exports: $122.1 billion (f.o.b., 1997)
Exports - commodities: machinery and electrical equipment 21.7%, electronic products 14.8%, information/communications 11.8%, textile products 11.6% (1997)
Exports - partners: US 24.2%, Hong Kong 23.5%, Europe 15.1%, Japan 9.6% (1997)
Imports: $114.4 billion (c.i.f., 1997)
Imports - commodities: machinery and electrical equipment 16.5%, electronic products 16.3%, chemicals 10.0%, precision instrument 5.6% (1997)
Imports - partners: Japan 25.4%, US 20.3%, Europe 18.9%, Hong Kong 1.7% (1997)
Debt - external: $80 million (1997 est.)
Economic aid - recipient: $NA
Currency: 1 New Taiwan dollar (NT$) = 100 cents
Exchange rates: New Taiwan dollars per US$1 - 32.45 (yearend 1997), 27.5 (1996), 27.4 (1995), 26.2 (1994)
Fiscal year: 1 July - 30 June

Communications

Telephones: 11.526 million (1998 est.)
Telephone system:
domestic: extensive microwave radio relay trunk system on east and west coasts
international: satellite earth stations - 2 Intelsat (1 Pacific Ocean and 1 Indian Ocean); submarine cables to Japan (Okinawa), Philippines, Guam, Singapore, Hong Kong, Indonesia, Australia, Middle East, and Western Europe
Radio broadcast stations: AM 158, FM 48, shortwave 21
Radios: 8.62 million
Television broadcast stations: 29 (in addition, there are two repeaters) (1997)
Televisions: 10.8 million (1996 est.)

Transportation

Railways:
total: 4,600 km (519 km electrified); note - 1,108 km belongs to the Taiwan Railway Administration and the remaining 3,492 km is dedicated to industrial use
narrow gauge: 4,600 km 1.067-m
Highways:
total: 19,634 km
paved: 17,171 km (including 548 km of expressways)
unpaved: 2,463 km (1997)

Pipelines: petroleum products 615 km; natural gas 97 km
Ports and harbors: Chi-lung (Keelung), Hua-lien, Kao-hsiung, Su-ao, T'ai-chung
Merchant marine:
total: 180 ships (1,000 GRT or over) totaling 5,106,573 GRT/7,963,834 DWT
ships by type: bulk 47, cargo 30, combination bulk 3, container 72, oil tanker 17, refrigerated cargo 9, roll-on/roll-off cargo 2 (1998 est.)
Airports: 39 (1998 est.)
Airports - with paved runways:
total: 36
over 3,047 m: 8
2,438 to 3,047 m: 12
1,524 to 2,437 m: 6
914 to 1,523 m: 6
under 914 m: 4 (1998 est.)
Airports - with unpaved runways:
total: 3
1,524 to 2,437 m: 1
under 914 m: 2 (1998 est.)
Heliports: 2 (1998 est.)

Military

Military branches: Army, Navy (includes Marines), Air Force, Coastal Patrol and Defense Command, Armed Forces Reserve Command, Combined Service Forces
Military manpower - military age: 19 years of age
Military manpower - availability:
males age 15-49: 6,544,602 (1999 est.)
Military manpower - fit for military service:
males age 15-49: 5,019,737 (1999 est.)
Military manpower - reaching military age annually:
males: 204,711 (1999 est.)
Military expenditures - dollar figure: $7.446 billion (FY98/99)
Military expenditures - percent of GDP: 2.8% (FY98/99)

Transnational Issues

Disputes - international: involved in complex dispute over the Spratly Islands with China, Malaysia, Philippines, Vietnam, and possibly Brunei; Paracel Islands occupied by China, but claimed by Vietnam and Taiwan; claims Japanese-administered Senkaku-shoto (Senkaku Islands/Diaoyu Tai), as does China
Illicit drugs: considered an important heroin transit point; major problem with domestic consumption of methamphetamines and heroin

Appendix A:

Abbreviations

A	ABEDA	Arab Bank for Economic Development in Africa
	ACC	Arab Cooperation Council
	ACCT	Agence de Cooperation Culturelle et Technique; see Agency for Cultural and Technical Cooperation; changed name in 1996 to Agence de la francophonie or Agency for the French-Speaking Community
	ACP Group	African, Caribbean, and Pacific Group of States
	AfDB	African Development Bank
	AFESD	Arab Fund for Economic and Social Development
	AG	Andean Group; see Andean Community of Nations (CAN)
	Air Pollution	Convention on Long-Range Transboundary Air Pollution
	Air Pollution-Nitrogen Oxides	Protocol to the 1979 Convention on Long-Range Transboundary Air Pollution Concerning the Control of Emissions of Nitrogen Oxides or Their Transboundary Fluxes
	Air Pollution-Persistent Organic Pollutants	Protocol to the 1979 Convention on Long-Range Transboundary Air Pollution on Persistent·Organic Pollutants
	Air Pollution-Sulphur 85	Protocol to the 1979 Convention on Long-Range Transboundary Air Pollution on the Reduction of Sulphur Emissions or Their Transboundary Fluxes by at Least 30%
	Air Pollution-Sulphur 94	Protocol to the 1979 Convention on Long-Range Transboundary Air Pollution on Further Reduction of Sulphur Emissions
	Air Pollution-Volatile Organic Compounds	Protocol to the 1979 Convention on Long-Range Transboundary Air Pollution Concerning the Control of Emissions of Volatile Organic Compounds or Their Transboundary Fluxes
	AL	Arab League
	ALADI	Asociacion Latinoamericana de Integracion; see Latin American Integration Association (LAIA)
	AMF	Arab Monetary Fund
	AMU	Arab Maghreb Union
	Ancom	Andean Common Market; see Andean Community ofNations (CAN)
	Antarctic-Environmental Protocol	Protocol on Environmental Protection to the Antarctic Treaty
	ANZUS	Australia-New Zealand-United States Security Treaty
	APEC	Asia Pacific Economic Cooperation
	Arabsat	Arab Satellite Communications Organization
	AsDB	Asian Development Bank
	ASEAN	Association of Southeast Asian Nations
	Autodin	Automatic Digital Network
B	BAD	Banque africaine de developpement; see African Development Bank (AfDB)
	BADEA	Banque Arabe de Developpement Economique en Afrique; see Arab Bank for Economic Development in Africa (ABEDA)
	BCIE	Banco Centroamericano de Integracion Economico; see Central American Bank for Economic Integration (BCIE)
	BDEAC	Banque de Developpment des Etats de l'Afrique Centrale; see Central African States Development Bank (BDEAC)
	Benelux	Benelux Economic Union

Appendix A: Abbreviations (continued)

	BID	Banco Interamericano de Desarrollo; see Inter-American Development Bank (IADB) Biodiversity Convention on Biological Diversity
	BIS	Bank for International Settlements
	BOAD	Banque Ouest-Africaine de Developpement; see West African Development Bank (WADB)
	BSEC	Black Sea Economic Cooperation Zone
C	C	Commonwealth
	CACM	Central American Common Market
	CAEU	Council of Arab Economic Unity
	CAN	Andean Community of Nations
	Caricom	Caribbean Community and Common Market
	CB	citizen's band mobile radio communications
	CBSS	Council of the Baltic Sea States
	CCC	Customs Cooperation Council
	CDB	Caribbean Development Bank
	CE	Council of Europe
	CEAO	Communaute Economique de l'Afrique de l'Ouest; see West African Economic Community (CEAO)
	CEEAC	Communaute Economique des Etats de l'Afrique Centrale; see Economic Community of Central African States (CEEAC)
	CEI	Central European Initiative
	CEMA	Council for Mutual Economic Assistance; also known as CMEA or Comecon
	CEPGL	Communaute Economique des Pays des Grands Lacs; see Economic Community of the Great Lakes Countries (CEPGL)
	CERN	Conseil Europeen pour la Recherche Nucleaire; see European Organization for Nuclear Research (CERN)
	CG	Contadora Group
	c.i.f.	cost, insurance, and freight
	CIS	Commonwealth of Independent States
	CITES	see Endangered Species
	Climate Change	United Nations Framework Convention on Climate Change
	Climate Change-Kyoto Protocol	Kyoto Protocol to the United Nations Framework Convention on Climate Change
	CMEA	Council for Mutual Economic Assistance (CEMA); also known as Comecon
	COCOM	Coordinating Committee on Export Controls
	Comecon	Council for Mutual Economic Assistance (CEMA); also known as CMEA
	Comsat	Communications Satellite Corporation
	CP	Colombo Plan
	CSCE	Conference on Security and Cooperation in Europe; see Organization on Security and Cooperation in Europe (OSCE)
	CY	calendar year
D	DC	developed country
	Desertification	United Nations Convention to Combat Desertification in Those Countries Experiencing Serious Drought and/or Desertification, Particularly in Africa
	DSN	Defense Switched Network
	DWT	deadweight ton

Appendix A: Abbreviations (continued)

E	EADB	East African Development Bank
	EAPC	Euro-Atlantic Partnership Council
	EBRD	European Bank for Reconstruction and Development
	EC	European Community; see European Union (EU)
	ECA	Economic Commission for Africa
	ECAFE	Economic Commission for Asia and the Far East; see Economic and Social Commission for Asia and the Pacific (ESCAP)
	ECE	Economic Commission for Europe
	ECLA	Economic Commission for Latin America; see Economic Commission for Latin America and the Caribbean (ECLAC)
	ECLAC	Economic Commission for Latin America and the Caribbean
	ECO	Economic Cooperation Organization
	ECOSOC	Economic and Social Council
	ECOWAS	Economic Community of West African States
	ECSC	European Coal and Steel Community; see European Union (EU)
	ECWA	Economic Commission for Western Asia; see Economic and Social Commission for Western Asia (ESCWA)
	EEC	European Economic Community; see European Union (EU)
	EFTA	European Free Trade Association
	EIB	European Investment Bank
	EMU	European Monetary Union
	Endangered Species	Convention on the International Trade in Endangered Species of Wild Flora and Fauna (CITES)
	Entente	Council of the Entente
	Environmental Modification	Convention on the Prohibition of Military or Any Other Hostile Use of Environmental Modification Techniques
	ESA	European Space Agency
	ESCAP	Economic and Social Commission for Asia and the Pacific
	ESCWA	Economic and Social Commission for Western Asia
	est.	estimate
	EU	European Union
	Euratom	European Atomic Energy Community; see European Community (EC)
	Eutelsat	European Telecommunications Satellite Organization
	Ex-Im	Export-Import Bank of the United States
F	FAO	Food and Agriculture Organization
	FAX	facsimile
	f.o.b.	free on board
	FLS	Front Line States
	FRG	Federal Republic of Germany (West Germany); used for information dated before 3 October 1990 or CY91
	FSU	former Soviet Union
	FY	fiscal year (FY93/94, for example, began in calendar year 1993 and ended in calendar year 1994)
	FYROM	The Former Yugoslav Republic of Macedonia
	FZ	Franc Zone

543

Appendix A: Abbreviations (continued)

G	G-2	Group of 2
	G-3	Group of 3
	G-5	Group of 5
	G-6	Group of 6 (not to be confused with the Big Six)
	G-7	Group of 7
	G-8	Group of 8
	G-9	Group of 9
	G-10	Group of 10
	G-11	Group of 11
	G-15	Group of 15
	G-19	Group of 19
	G-24	Group of 24
	G-30	Group of 30
	G-33	Group of 33
	G-77	Group of 77
	GATT	General Agreement on Tariffs and Trade; subsumed by the World Trade Organization (WTrO) on 1 January 1995
	GCC	Gulf Cooperation Council
	GDP	gross domestic product
	GDR	German Democratic Republic (East Germany); used for information dated before 3 October 1990 or CY91
	GNP	gross national product
	GRT	gross register ton
	GWP	gross world product
H	Hazardous Wastes	Basel Convention on the Control of Transboundary Movements of Hazardous Wastes and Their Disposal
	HF	high-frequency
I	IADB	Inter-American Development Bank
	IAEA	International Atomic Energy Agency
	IBEC	International Bank for Economic Cooperation
	IBRD	International Bank for Reconstruction and Development (World Bank)
	ICAO	International Civil Aviation Organization
	ICC	International Chamber of Commerce
	ICEM	Intergovernmental Committee for European Migration; see International Organization for Migration (IOM)
	ICFTU	International Confederation of Free Trade Unions; see World Confederation of Labor (WCL)
	ICJ	International Court of Justice
	ICM	Intergovernmental Committee for Migration; see International Organization for Migration (IOM)
	ICRC	International Committee of the Red Cross
	ICRM	International Red Cross and Red Crescent Movement
	IDA	International Development Association
	IDB	Islamic Development Bank
	IEA	International Energy Agency
	IFAD	International Fund for Agricultural Development

Appendix A: Abbreviations (continued)

IFC	International Finance Corporation
IFCTU	International Federation of Christian Trade Unions
IFRCS	International Federation of Red Cross and Red Crescent Societies
IGAD	Inter-Governmental Authority on Development
IGADD	Inter-Governmental Authority on Drought and Development
IHO	International Hydrographic Organization
IIB	International Investment Bank
ILO	International Labor Organization
IMCO	Intergovernmental Maritime Consultative Organization; see International Maritime Organization (IMO)
IMF	International Monetary Fund
IMO	International Maritime Organization
Inmarsat	International Mobile Satellite Organization
InOC	Indian Ocean Commission
Intelsat	International Telecommunications Satellite Organization
Interpol	International Criminal Police Organization
Intersputnik	International Organization of Space Communications
IOC	International Olympic Committee
IOM	International Organization for Migration
ISO	International Organization for Standardization
ITU	International Telecommunication Union

K

kHz	kilohertz
km	kilometer
kW	kilowatt
kWh	kilowatt hour

L

LAES	Latin American Economic System
LAIA	Latin American Integration Association
LAS	League of Arab States; see Arab League (AL)
Law of the Sea	United Nations Convention on the Law of the Sea (LOS)
LDC	less developed country
LLDC	least developed country
London Convention	see Marine Dumping
LORCS	League of Red Cross and Red Crescent Societies; see International Federation of Red Cross and Red Crescent Societies (IFRCS)
LOS	see Law of the Sea

M

m	meter
Marecs	Maritime European Communications Satellite
Marine Dumping	Convention on the Prevention of Marine Pollution by Dumping Wastes and Other Matter
Marine Life Conservation	Convention on Fishing and Conservation of Living Resources of the High Seas
MARPOL	see Ship Pollution
Medarabtel	Middle East Telecommunications Project of the International Telecommunications Union
Mercosur	Mercado Comun del Cono Sur; see Southern Cone Common Market
MHz	megahertz
MINURSO	United Nations Mission for the Referendum in Western Sahara

Appendix A: Abbreviations (continued)

MINUGUA	United Nations Verification Mission in Guatemala
MIPONUH	United Nations Civilian Police Mission in Haiti
MONUA	United Nations Observer Mission in Angola
MTCR	Missile Technology Control Regime

N

NA	not available
NACC	North Atlantic Cooperation Council; see Euro-Atlantic Partnership Council (EAPC)
NAM	Nonaligned Movement
NATO	North Atlantic Treaty Organization
NC	Nordic Council
NEA	Nuclear Energy Agency
NEGL	negligible
NIB	Nordic Investment Bank
NIC	newly industrializing country; see newly industrializing economy (NIE)
NIE	newly industrializing economy
nm	nautical mile
NMT	Nordic Mobile Telephone
NSG	Nuclear Suppliers Group
Nuclear Test Ban	Treaty Banning Nuclear Weapons Tests in the Atmosphere, in Outer Space, and Under Water
NZ	New Zealand

O

OAPEC	Organization of Arab Petroleum Exporting Countries
OAS	Organization of American States
OAU	Organization of African Unity
ODA	official development assistance
OECD	Organization for Economic Cooperation and Development
OECS	Organization of Eastern Caribbean States
OIC	Organization of the Islamic Conference
ONUMOZ	see United Nations Operation in Mozambique (UNOMOZ)
ONUSAL	United Nations Observer Mission in El Salvador
OOF	other official flows
OPANAL	Organismo para la Proscripcion de las Armas Nucleares en la America Latina y el Caribe; see Agency for the Prohibition of Nuclear Weapons in Latin America and the Caribbean
OPCW	Organization for the Prohibition of Chemical Weapons
OPEC	Organization of Petroleum Exporting Countries
OSCE	Organization on Security and Cooperation in Europe Ozone Layer Protection Montreal Protocol on Substances That Deplete the Ozone Layer

P

PCA	Permanent Court of Arbitration
PDRY	People's Democratic Republic of Yemen [Yemen (Aden) or South Yemen]; used for information dated before 22 May 1990 or CY91
PFP	Partnership for Peace

R

Ramsar	see Wetlands
RG	Rio Group

S

SAARC	South Asian Association for Regional Cooperation
SACU	Southern African Customs Union
SADC	Southern African Development Community

	SADCC	Southern African Development Coordination Conference; see Southern African Development Community (SADC)
	SELA	Sistema Economico Latinoamericana; see Latin American Economic System (LAES)
	SFRY	Socialist Federal Republic of Yugoslavia; dissolved 5 December 1991
	SHF	super-high-frequency
	Ship Pollution	Protocol of 1978 Relating to the International Convention for the Prevention of Pollution From Ships, 1973 (MARPOL)
	Sparteca	South Pacific Regional Trade and Economic Cooperation Agreement
	SPC	South Pacific Commission
	SPF	South Pacific Forum
	sq km	square kilometer
	sq mi	square mile
T	TAT	Trans-Atlantic Telephone
	Tropical Timber 83	International Tropical Timber Agreement, 1983
	Tropical Timber 94	International Tropical Timber Agreement, 1994
U	UAE	United Arab Emirates
	UDEAC	Union Douaniere et Economique de l'Afrique Centrale; see Central African Customs and Economic Union (UDEAC)
	UEMOA	Union economique et monetaire Ouest africaine; see West African Economic and Monetary Union (WAEMU)
	UHF	ultra-high-frequency
	UK	United Kingdom
	UN	United Nations
	UNAMIR	United Nations Assistance Mission for Rwanda
	UNAVEM III	United Nations Angola Verification Mission III
	UNCRO	United Nations Confidence Restoration Operation in Croatia
	UNCTAD	United Nations Conference on Trade and Development
	UNDOF	United Nations Disengagement Observer Force
	UNDP	United Nations Development Program
	UNEP	United Nations Environment Program
	UNESCO	United Nations Educational, Scientific, and Cultural Organization
	UNFICYP	United Nations Peace-keeping Force in Cyprus
	UNFPA	United Nations Fund for Population Activities; see UN Population Fund (UNFPA)
	UNHCR	United Nations High Commissioner for Refugees
	UNICEF	United Nations Children's Fund
	UNIDO	United Nations Industrial Development Organization
	UNIFIL	United Nations Interim Force in Lebanon
	UNIKOM	United Nations Iraq-Kuwait Observation Mission
	UNITAR	United Nations Institute for Training and Research
	UNMIH	United Nations Mission in Haiti
	UNMIBH	United Nations Mission in Bosnia and Herzegovina
	UNMOGIP	United Nations Military Observer Group in India and Pakistan
	UNMOP	United Nations Mission of Observers in Prevlaka
	UNMOT	United Nations Mission of Observers in Tajikistan
	UNOMIG	United Nations Observer Mission in Georgia

Appendix A: Abbreviations (continued)

	UNOMIL	United Nations Observer Mission in Liberia
	UNOMOZ	United Nations Operation in Mozambique
	UNOMSIL	United Nations Mission of Observers in Sierra Leone
	UNOMUR	United Nations Observer Mission Uganda-Rwanda
	UNOSOM II	United Nations Operation in Somalia II
	UNPREDEP	United Nations Preventive Deployment Force
	UNPROFOR	United Nations Protection Force
	UNRISD	United Nations Research Institute for Social Development
	UNRWA	United Nations Relief and Works Agency for Palestine Refugees in the Near East
	UNSMIH	United Nations Support Mission in Haiti
	UNTAC	United Nations Transitional Authority in Cambodia
	UNTAES	United Nations Transitional Administration in Eastern Slavonia, Baranja, and Western Sirmium
	UNTSO	United Nations Truce Supervision Organization
	UNU	United Nations University
	UPU	Universal Postal Union
	US	United States
	USSR	Union of Soviet Socialist Republics (Soviet Union); used for information dated before 25 December 1991
	USSR/EE	Union of Soviet Socialist Republics/Eastern Europe
V	VHF	very-high-frequency
W	WADB	West African Development Bank
	WAEMU	West African Economic and Monetary Union
	WCL	World Confederation of Labor
	WCO	World Customs Organization; see Customs Cooperation Council
	Wetlands	Convention on Wetlands of International Importance Especially As Waterfowl Habitat
	WEU	Western European Union
	WFC	World Food Council
	WFP	World Food Program
	WFTU	World Federation of Trade Unions
	Whaling	International Convention for the Regulation of Whaling
	WHO	World Health Organization
	WIPO	World Intellectual Property Organization
	WMO	World Meteorological Organization
	WP	Warsaw Pact
	WTO	see WToO for World Tourism Organization or WTrO for World Trade Organization
	WToO	World Tourism Organization
	WTrO	World Trade Organization
Y	YAR	Yemen Arab Republic [Yemen (Sanaa) or North Yemen]; used for information dated before 22 May 1990 or CY91
Z	ZC	Zangger Committee

Appendix B:

United Nations System

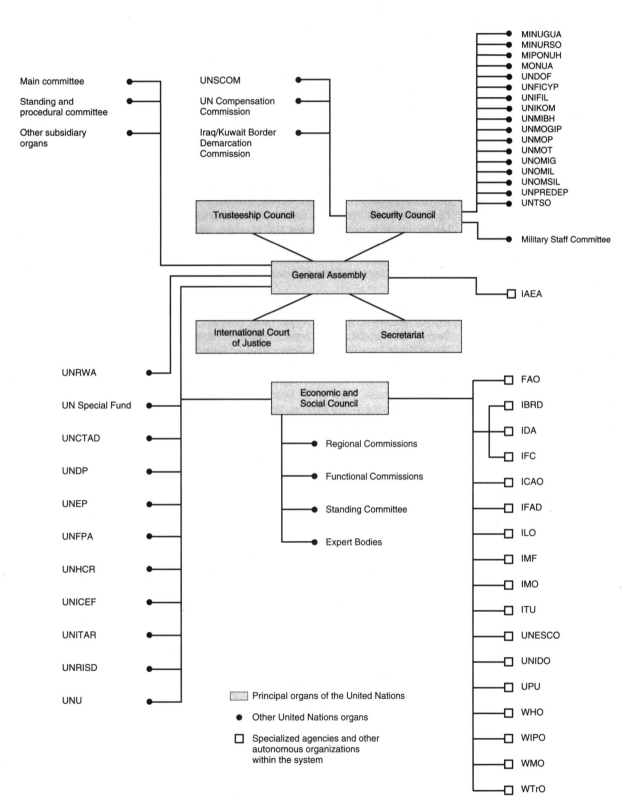

Based on chart from the *UN Chronicle*

Appendix C:

International Organizations and Groups

advanced developing countries	another term for those less developed countries (LDCs) with particularly rapid industrial development; see newly industrializing economies (NIEs)
advanced economies	a new term used by the International Monetary FUND (IMF) for the top group in its hierarchy of advanced economies, countries in transition, and developing countries; recently published IMF statistics include the following 28 advanced economies: Australia, Austria, Belgium, Canada, Denmark, Finland, France, Germany, Greece, Hong Kong, Iceland, Ireland, Israel, Italy, Japan, South Korea, Luxembourg, Netherlands, NZ, Norway, Portugal, Singapore, Spain, Sweden, Switzerland, Taiwan, UK, US; *note*—this group would presumably also cover the following seven smaller countries of Andorra, Bermuda, Faroe Islands, Holy See, Liechtenstein, Monaco, and San Marino which are included in the more comprehensive group of developed countries"
African, Caribbean, and Pacific Group of States (ACP Group) *address*—Avenue Georges Henri 451, B-1200 Brussels, Belgium *telephone*—[32] (2) 743 06 00 *FAX*—[32] (2) 735 55 73 *established*—1 April 1976 *aim*—to manage their preferential economic and aid relationship with the EU	*members*—(70) Angola, Antigua and Barbuda, The Bahamas, Barbados, Belize, Benin, Botswana, Burkina Faso, Burundi, Cameroon, Cape Verde, Central African Republic, Chad, Comoros, Democratic Republic of the Congo, Republic of the Congo, Cote d'Ivoire, Djibouti, Dominica, Dominican Republic, Equatorial Guinea, Eritrea, Ethiopia, Fiji, Gabon, The Gambia, Ghana, Grenada, Guinea, Guinea-Bissau, Guyana, Haiti, Jamaica, Kenya, Kiribati, Lesotho, Liberia, Madagascar, Malawi, Mali, Mauritania, Mauritius, Mozambique, Namibia, Niger, Nigeria, Papua New Guinea, Rwanda, Saint Kitts and Nevis, Saint Lucia, Saint Vincent and the Grenadines, Samoa, Sao Tome and Principe, Senegal, Seychelles, Sierra Leone, Solomon Islands, Somalia, Sudan, Suriname, Swaziland, Tanzania, Togo, Tonga, Trinidad and Tobago, Tuvalu, Uganda, Vanuatu, Zambia, Zimbabwe
African Development Bank (AfDB) *note*—also known as Banque Africaine de Developpement (BAD) *address*—01 BP 1387, Abidjan 01, Cote d'Ivoire *telephone*—[225] 20 44 44 *FAX*—[225] 21 77 53 *established*—4 August 1963 *aim*—to promote economic and social development	*regional members*—(53) Algeria, Angola, Benin, Botswana, Burkina Faso, Burundi, Cameroon, Cape Verde, Central African Republic, Chad, Comoros, Democratic Republic of the Congo, Republic of the Congo, Cote d'Ivoire, Djibouti, Egypt, Equatorial Guinea, Eritrea, Ethiopia, Gabon, The Gambia, Ghana, Guinea, Guinea-Bissau, Kenya, Lesotho, Liberia, Libya, Madagascar, Malawi, Mali, Mauritania, Mauritius, Morocco, Mozambique, Namibia, Niger, Nigeria, Rwanda, Sao Tome and Principe, Senegal, Seychelles, Sierra Leone, Somalia, South Africa, Sudan, Swaziland, Tanzania, Togo, Tunisia, Uganda, Zambia, Zimbabwe *nonregional members*—(25) Argentina, Austria, Belgium, Brazil, Canada, China, Denmark, Finland, France, Germany, India, Italy, Japan, South Korea, Kuwait, Netherlands, Norway, Portugal, Saudi Arabia, Spain, Sweden, Switzerland, UAE, UK, US
Agence de Cooperation Culturelle et Technique (ACCT)	see Agency for the French-speaking Community (ACCT)
Agence de la francophonie (ACCT)	see Agency for the French-speaking Community (ACCT)
Agency for Cultural and Technical Cooperation (ACCT)	see Agency for the French-speaking Community (ACCT); acronym from Agence de Cooperation Culturelle et Technique

Note: The Socialist Federal Republic of Yugoslavia (SFRY) ceases to exist. None of the successor states of the former Yugoslavia, including Serbia and Montenegro, have been permitted to participate solely on the basis of the membership of the former Yugoslavia in the United Nations General Assembly and Economic and Social Council and their subsidiary bodies and in various United Nations specialized agencies. The United Nations, however, permits the seat and nameplate of the SFRY to remain, permits the SFRY mission to continue to function, and continues to fly the flag of the former Yugoslavia. For a variety of reasons, a number of other organizations have not yet taken action with regard to the membership of the former Yugoslavia. *The World Factbook* therefore continues to list Yugoslavia under international organizations where the SFRY seat remains or where no action has yet been taken.

550

Appendix C: International Organizations and Groups (continued)

Agency for the French-Speaking Community (ACCT)

note—formerly Agency for Cultural and Technical Cooperation
address—13 Quai Andre-Citroen, F-75015 Paris, France
telephone—[33] (1) 44 37 33 00
FAX—[33] (1) 45 79 14 98
established—21 March 1970
name changed—1996
aim—to promote cultural and technical cooperation among French-speaking countries

members—(41) Belgium, Benin, Bulgaria, Burkina Faso, Burundi, Cambodia, Cameroon, Canada, Cape Verde, Central African Republic, Chad, Comoros, Democratic Republic of the Congo (may have dropped out), Republic of the Congo, Cote d'Ivoire, Djibouti, Dominica, Equatorial Guinea, France, Gabon, Guinea, Haiti, Laos, Lebanon, Luxembourg, Madagascar, Mali, Mauritius, Moldova, Monaco, Niger, Romania, Rwanda, Sao Tome and Principe, Senegal, Seychelles, Switzerland, Togo, Tunisia, Vanuatu, Vietnam
associate members—(5) Egypt, Guinea-Bissau, Mauritania, Morocco, Saint Lucia
participating governments—(2) New Brunswick (Canada), Quebec (Canada)

Agency for the Prohibition of Nuclear Weapons in Latin America and the Caribbean (OPANAL)

note—acronym from Organismo para la Proscripcion de las Armas Nucleares en la America Latina y el Caribe (OPANAL)
address—Temistocles 78, Col Polanco, CP 011560, Mexico City 5 DF, Mexico
telephone—[52] (5) 280 4923, 280 5064, 280 2715
FAX—[52] (5) 280 2965
established—14 February 1967
aim—to encourage the peaceful uses of atomic energy and prohibit nuclear weapons

members—(32) Antigua and Barbuda, Argentina, The Bahamas, Barbados, Belize, Bolivia, Brazil, Chile, Colombia, Costa Rica, Dominica, Dominican Republic, Ecuador, El Salvador, Grenada, Guatemala, Guyana, Haiti, Honduras, Jamaica, Mexico, Nicaragua, Panama, Paraguay, Peru, Saint Kitts and Nevis, Saint Lucia, Saint Vincent and the Grenadines, Suriname, Trinidad and Tobago, Uruguay, Venezuela

Andean Community of Nations (CAN)

aim—formerly known as the Andean Group (AG), the Andean Parliament, and the Andean Common Market (Ancom)
address—c/o JUNAC, Pasco de la Republica 3895, Casilla 18-1177, Lima 18, Peru
telephone—[51] (1) 221 2222
FAX—[51] (1) 221 3329
established—26 May 1969
effective—16 October 1969
aim—to promote harmonious development through economic integration

members—(5) Bolivia, Colombia, Ecuador, Peru, Venezuela
associate members—(1) Panama

Andean Group (AG)

see Andean Community of Nations (CAN)

Arab Bank for Economic Development in Africa (ABEDA)

note—also known as Banque Arabe de Developpement Economique en Afrique (BADEA)
address—Abdel Rahman El Mahdi Avenue, P.O. Box 2640, Khartoum, Sudan
telephone—[249] (11) 770498, 773646, 773709
FAX—[249] (11) 770600
established—18 February 1974
effective—16 September 1974
aim—to promote economic development

members—(17 plus the Palestine Liberation Organization) Algeria, Bahrain, Egypt, Iraq, Jordan, Kuwait, Lebanon, Libya, Mauritania, Morocco, Oman, Qatar, Saudi Arabia, Sudan, Syria, Tunisia, UAE, Palestine Liberation Organization; *note*—these are all the members of the Arab League excluding Comoros, Djibouti, Somalia, Yemen

Appendix C: International Organizations and Groups (continued)

Arab Cooperation Council (ACC)

established—16 February 1989
aim—to promote economic cooperation and integration, possibly leading to an Arab Common Market

members—(4) Egypt, Iraq, Jordan, Yemen

Arab Fund for Economic and Social Development (AFESD)

address—P.O. Box 21923, Safat 13080, Kuwait
telephone—[965] 4844500
FAX—[965] 4815750, 4815760, 4815770
established—16 May 1968
aim—to promote economic and social development

members—(21 plus the Palestine Liberation Organization) Algeria, Bahrain, Comoros, Djibouti, Egypt (suspended from 1979 to 1988), Iraq (suspended 1993), Jordan, Kuwait, Lebanon, Libya, Mauritania, Morocco, Oman, Qatar, Saudi Arabia, Somalia (suspended 1993), Sudan (suspended 1993), Syria, Tunisia, UAE, Yemen, Palestine Liberation Organization

---

Arab League (AL)

note—also known as League of Arab States (LAS)
address—Midan Attahrir, Tahrir Square, P.O. Box 11642, Cairo, Egypt
telephone—[20] (2) 750 511
FAX—[20] (2) 740 331
established—22 March 1945
aim—to promote economic, social, political, and military cooperation

members—(21 plus the Palestine Liberation Organization) Algeria, Bahrain, Comoros, Djibouti, Egypt, Iraq, Jordan, Kuwait, Lebanon, Libya, Mauritania, Morocco, Oman, Qatar, Saudi Arabia, Somalia, Sudan, Syria, Tunisia, UAE, Yemen, Palestine Liberation Organization

---

Arab Maghreb Union (AMU)

address—27 Avenue Okba Agdal, Rabat, Morocco
telephone—[212] (7) 77 26 82, 77 26 76, 77 26 68
FAX—[212] (7) 77 26 93
established—17 February 1989
aim—to promote cooperation and integration among the Arab states of northern Africa

members—(5) Algeria, Libya, Mauritania, Morocco, Tunisia

Arab Monetary Fund (AMF)

address—P.O. Box 2818, Abu Dhabi, United Arab Emirates
telephone—[971] (2) 215000, 328500
FAX—[971] (2) 326454
established—27 April 1976
effective—2 February 1977
aim—to promote Arab cooperation, development, and integration in monetary and economic affairs

members—(20 plus the Palestine Liberation Organization) Algeria, Bahrain, Djibouti, Egypt, Iraq, Jordan, Kuwait, Lebanon, Libya, Mauritania, Morocco, Oman, Qatar, Saudi Arabia, Somalia, Sudan, Syria, Tunisia, UAE, Yemen, Palestine Liberation Organization

Appendix C: International Organizations and Groups (continued)

Asia-Pacific Economic Cooperation (APEC)

address—438 Alexandra Road, Alexandra Point Building, 14th Floor 01/04, Singapore 119958, Singapore
telephone—[65] 276 1880
FAX—[65] 276 1775
established—7 November 1989
aim—to promote trade and investment in the Pacific basin

members—(21) Australia, Brunei, Canada, Chile, China, Hong Kong, Indonesia, Japan, South Korea, Malaysia, Mexico, NZ, Papua New Guinea, Peru, Philippines, Russia, Singapore, Taiwan, Thailand, US, Vietnam
observers—(3) Association of Southeast Asian Nations, Pacific Economic Cooperation Conference, South Pacific Forum

Asian Development Bank (AsDB)

address—6 ADB Avenue, Mandaluyong, 0401 METRO Manila, Philippines
telephone—[63] (2) 711 3851
FAX—[63] (2) 741 7961, 631 6816
established—19 December 1966
aim—to promote regional economic cooperation

regional members—(40) Afghanistan, Australia, Bangladesh, Bhutan, Burma, Cambodia, China, Cook Islands, Fiji, Hong Kong, India, Indonesia, Japan, Kazakhstan, Kiribati, South Korea, Kyrgyzstan, Laos, Malaysia, Maldives, Marshall Islands, Federated States of Micronesia, Mongolia, Nauru, Nepal, NZ, Pakistan, Papua New Guinea, Philippines, Samoa, Singapore, Solomon Islands, Sri Lanka, Taiwan, Thailand, Tonga, Tuvalu, Uzbekistan, Vanuatu, Vietnam
nonregional members—(16) Austria, Belgium, Canada, Denmark, Finland, France, Germany, Italy, Netherlands, Norway, Spain, Sweden, Switzerland, Turkey, UK, US

Asociacion Latinoamericana de Integracion (ALADI)

see Latin American Integration Association (LAIA)

Association of Southeast Asian Nations (ASEAN)

note—the ASEAN Regional Forum (ARF) consists of the 9 ASEAN members, 2 observers, 2 consultative partners, and 8 dialogue partners: Australia, Canada, EU, India, Japan, South Korea, New Zealand, US
address—70 A Jalan Sisingamangaraja, Kebayoran Baru, P.O. Box 2072, Jakarta 12110, Indonesia
telephone—[62] (21) 7262410, 7262991, 7262272, 7251988
FAX—[62] (21) 7398234, 7243348
established—9 August 1967
aim—to encourage regional economic, social, and cultural cooperation among the non-Communist countries of Southeast Asia

members—(9) Brunei, Burma, Indonesia, Laos, Malaysia, Philippines, Singapore, Thailand, Vietnam
observers—(2) Cambodia, Papua New Guinea; *note*—Cambodia has been accepted as a member of ASEAN but must go through the entry ceremony
associate partners—(2) China, Russia

Australia Group

established—1984
aim—to consult on and coordinate export controls related to chemical and biological weapons

members—(28) Argentina, Australia, Austria, Belgium, Canada, Czech Republic, Denmark, Finland, France, Germany, Greece, Hungary, Iceland, Ireland, Italy, Japan, Luxembourg, Netherlands, NZ, Norway, Poland, Portugal, Slovakia, Spain, Sweden, Switzerland, UK, US; *note*—may now include only 23 countries
observer—(1) Singapore

Appendix C: International Organizations and Groups (continued)

Australia-New Zealand-United States Security Treaty (ANZUS) *address*—c/o Department of Foreign Affairs and Trade, Bag 8, Queen Victoria Terrace, Canberra ACT 2600, Australia *telephone*—[61] (6) 261 91 11 *FAX*—[61] (6) 261 21 51 *established*—1 September 1951 *effective*—29 April 1952 *aim*—to implement a trilateral mutual security agreement, although the US suspended security obligations to NZ on 11 August 1986; Australia and the US continue to hold annual meetings	*members*—(3) Australia, NZ, US
Banco Centroamericano de Integracion Economico (BCIE)	see Central American Bank for Economic Integration (BCIE)
Banco Interamericano de Desarrollo (BID)	see Inter-American Development Bank (IADB)
Bank for International Settlements (BIS) *address*—Centralbahnplatz 2, CH-4002 Basel, Switzerland *telephone*—[41] (61) 280 80 80 *FAX*—[41] (61) 280 91 00, 280 81 00 *established*—20 January 1930 *effective*—17 March 1930 *aim*—to promote cooperation among central banks in international financial settlements	*members*—(42) Australia, Austria, Belgium, Brazil, Bulgaria, Canada, China, Czech Republic, Denmark, Estonia, Finland, France, Germany, Greece, Hong Kong, Hungary, Iceland, India, Ireland, Italy, Japan, South Korea, Latvia, Lithuania, Mexico, Netherlands, Norway, Poland, Portugal, Romania, Russia, Saudi Arabia, Singapore, Slovakia, South Africa, Spain, Sweden, Switzerland, Turkey, UK, US, Yugoslavia (suspended) *pending members*—(2) Croatia, Macedonia
Banque Africaine de Developpement (BAD)	see African Development Bank (AfDB)
Banque Arabe de Developpement Economique en Afrique (BADEA)	see Arab Bank for Economic Development in Africa (ABEDA)
Banque de Developpement des Etats de l'Afrique Centrale (BDEAC)	see Central African States Development Bank (BDEAC)
Banque Ouest-Africaine de Developpement (BOAD)	see West African Development Bank (WADB)
Benelux Economic Union (Benelux) *note*—acronym from Belgium, Netherlands, and Luxembourg *address*—Rue de la Regence 39, B-1000 Brussels, Belgium *telephone*—[32] (2) 519 38 11 *FAX*—[32] (2) 513 42 06 *established*—3 February 1958 *effective*—1 November 1960 *aim*—to develop closer economic cooperation and integration	*members*—(3) Belgium, Luxembourg, Netherlands

Appendix C: International Organizations and Groups (continued)

Big Seven

note—membership is the same as the Group of 7
established—NA 1975
aim—to discuss and coordinate major economic policies

members—(7) Big Six (Canada, France, Germany, Italy, Japan, UK) plus the US

Big Six

note—not to be confused with the Group of 6
established—NA 1967
aim—to foster economic cooperation

members—(6) Canada, France, Germany, Italy, Japan, UK

Black Sea Economic Cooperation Zone (BSEC)

address—Istinye Cad Musir Fuad Pasa Yalisi Eski Tersame, Istinye 80860, Istanbul, Turkey
telephone—[90] (212) 229 6330
FAX—[90] (212) 229 6336
established—25 June 1992
aim—to enhance regional stability through economic cooperation

members—(11) Albania, Armenia, Azerbaijan, Bulgaria, Georgia, Greece, Moldova, Romania, Russia, Turkey, Ukraine
observers—(7) Austria, Egypt, Israel, Italy, Poland, Slovakia, Tunisia

---

Caribbean Community and Common Market (Caricom)

address—Caricom, P.O. Box 10827, Bank of Guyana Building, 3rd floor, Avenue of the Republic, Georgetown, Guyana
telephone—[592] (2) 69281 through 69289
FAX—[592] (2) 66091, 67816, 57341
established—4 July 1973
effective—1 August 1973
aim—to promote economic integration and development, especially among the less developed countries

members—(14) Antigua and Barbuda, The Bahamas, Barbados, Belize, Dominica, Grenada, Guyana, Jamaica, Montserrat, Saint Kitts and Nevis, Saint Lucia, Saint Vincent and the Grenadines, Suriname, Trinidad and Tobago
associate members—(2) British Virgin Islands, Turks and Caicos Islands
observers—(11) Anguilla, Aruba, Bermuda, Cayman Islands, Colombia, Dominican Republic, Haiti, Mexico, Netherlands Antilles, Puerto Rico, Venezuela

---

Caribbean Development Bank (CDB)

address—P.O. Box 408, Wildey, St. Michael, Barbados
telephone—[1] (246) 431 1600
FAX—[1] (246) 426 7269
established—18 October 1969
effective—26 January 1970
aim—to promote economic development and cooperation

regional members—(20) Anguilla, Antigua and Barbuda, The Bahamas, Barbados, Belize, British Virgin Islands, Cayman Islands, Colombia, Dominica, Grenada, Guyana, Jamaica, Mexico, Montserrat, Saint Kitts and Nevis, Saint Lucia, Saint Vincent and the Grenadines, Trinidad and Tobago, Turks and Caicos Islands, Venezuela
nonregional members—(6) Canada, China, France, Germany, Italy, UK

Cartagena Group

see Group of 11

Appendix C: International Organizations and Groups (continued)

Central African Customs and Economic Union (UDEAC)

note—acronym from Union Douaniere et Economique de l'Afrique Centrale
address—BP 969, Bangui, Central African Republic
telephone—[236] 61 09 22, 61 45 77
FAX—[236] 61 21 35
established—8 December 1964
effective—1 January 1966
aim—to promote the establishment of a Central African Common Market

members—(6) Cameroon, Central African Republic, Chad, Republic of the Congo, Equatorial Guinea, Gabon

---

Central African States Development Bank (BDEAC)

note—acronym from Banque de Developpement des Etats de l'Afrique Centrale
address—BDEAC, Place du Gouvernement, BP 1177, Brazzaville, Republic of the Congo
telephone—[242] 83 01 26, 83 01 49, 81 02 12, 81 02 21
FAX—[242] 83 02 66
established—3 December 1975
aim—to provide loans for economic development

members—(9) Cameroon, Central African Republic, Chad, Republic of the Congo, Equatorial Guinea, France, Gabon, Germany, Kuwait

---

Central American Bank for Economic Integration (BCIE)

note—acronym from Banco Centroamericano de Integracion Economico
address—Apartado Postal 772, Tegucigalpa DC, Honduras
telephone—[504] 372230 through 372239, 371184 through 371188
FAX—[504] 370793, 373904
established—13 December 1960
aim—to promote economic integration and development

members—(5) Costa Rica, El Salvador, Guatemala, Honduras, Nicaragua
nonregional members—(4) Argentina, Colombia, Mexico, Taiwan

Central American Common Market (CACM)

address—c/o SIECA, Apart Postal 1237, 4a Avenida 10-25, Zona 14, Guatemala 01901, Guatemala
telephone—[502] (2) 682151, 682152, 682153, 682154
FAX—[502] (2) 681071
established—13 December 1960
effective—3 June 1961
aim—to promote establishment of a Central American Common Market

members—(5) Costa Rica, El Salvador, Guatemala, Honduras, Nicaragua; *note*—Panama pursues full regional cooperation

---

Appendix C: International Organizations and Groups (continued)

Central European Initiative (CEI)

note—evolved from the Hexagonal Group
address—European Bank for Reconstruction and Development, One Exchange Square, London EC2A 2EH, UK
telephone—[44] (171) 338 6152
FAX—[44] (171) 338 7472
established—27 July 1991
aim—to form an economic and political cooperation group for the region between the Adriatic and the Baltic Seas

members—(16) Albania, Austria, Belarus, Bosnia and Herzegovina, Bulgaria, Croatia, Czech Republic, Hungary, Italy, The Former Yugoslav Republic of Macedonia, Moldova, Poland, Romania, Slovakia, Slovenia, Ukraine

---

centrally planned economies

a term applied mainly to the traditionally communist states that looked to the former USSR for leadership; most are now evolving toward more democratic and market-oriented systems; also known formerly as the Second World or as the communist countries; through the 1980s, this group included Albania, Bulgaria, Cambodia, China, Cuba, Czechoslovakia, GDR, Hungary, North Korea, Laos, Mongolia, Poland, Romania, USSR, Vietnam, Yugoslavia

---

Colombo Plan (CP)

address—Colombo Plan Bureau, P.O. Box 596, 12 Melbourne Avenue, Colombo 4, Sri Lanka
telephone—[94] (1) 581813, 581853, 581754
FAX—[94] (1) 581754
established—1 July 1951
aim—to promote economic and social development in Asia and the Pacific

members—(26) Afghanistan, Australia, Bangladesh, Bhutan, Burma, Cambodia, Canada, Fiji, India, Indonesia, Iran, Japan, South Korea, Laos, Malaysia, Maldives, Nepal, NZ, Pakistan, Papua New Guinea, Philippines, Singapore, Sri Lanka, Thailand, UK, US

Commission for Social Development

note—formerly Social Commission
address—Division Policy Coordination ECOSOC Affairs, Department Policy Coordination and Sustainable Development, United Nations, Room S-29631, New York, NY 10017, US
telephone—[1] (212) 963 1234
FAX—[1] (212) 963 5935
established—21 June 1946 as the Social Commission, renamed 29 July 1966
aim—to deal, as part of the Economic and Social Council, with social development programs of UN

members—(46) selected on a rotating basis from all regions

Commission on Crime Prevention and Criminal Justice

address—Crime Prevention and Criminal Justice Division, Vienna International Center, P.O. Box 500, A-1400 Vienna, Austria
telephone—[43] (1) 21345, extension 4272
FAX—[43] (1) 21345 5898
established—6 February 1992
aim—to provide guidance, as part of the Economic and Social Council, on crime prevention and criminal justice

members—(40) selected on a rotating basis from all regions

Appendix C: International Organizations and Groups (continued)

Commission on Human Rights

address—c/o Secretariat, United Nations Office of the High Commissioner of Human Rights, Palais des Nations, CH-1211 Geneva 10, Switzerland
telephone—[41] (22) 917 12 34, 907 12 34
FAX—[41] (22) 733 32 46
established—18 February 1946
aim—to assist, as part of the Economic and Social Council, with human rights programs of UN

members—(53) selected on a rotating basis from all regions

Commission on Narcotic Drugs

address—c/o United Nations Drug Control Programme, Treaty Implementation and Legal Affairs Branch, P.O. Box 500, A-1400 Vienna, Austria
telephone—[43] (1) 213450
FAX—[43] (1) 21345-5885
established—16 February 1946
aim—Economic and Social Council organization dealing with illicit drugs programs of UN

members—(53) selected on a rotating basis from all regions with emphasis on producing and processing countries

---

Commission on Population and Development

address—Division for Policy and Coordination and ECOSOC Affairs, Department for Policy Coordination and Sustainable Development, United Nations, Room 2963, New York, NY 10017, US
telephone—[1] (212) 963 1234
FAX—[1] (212) 963 5935
established—3 October 1946
aim—to deal with population matters of importance to the UN, as part of Economic and Social Council

members—(47) selected on a rotating basis from all regions

Commission on Science and Technology for Development

address—United Nations, New York, NY 10017, US
telephone—[1] (212) 963 1234
FAX—[1] (212) 758 2718
established—30 April 1992
aim—to promote international cooperation, as part of the Economic and Social Council, in the field of science and technology

members—(53) selected on a rotating basis from all regions

Appendix C: International Organizations and Groups (continued)

Commission on the Status of Women

address—Division for the Advancement of Women, Department for Ecumenical and Social Affairs, United Nations, Room DC2-1200, New York, NY 10017, US
telephone—[1] (212) 963 4666
FAX—[1] (212) 963 3463
established—21 June 1946
aim—to deal, as part of the Economic and Social Council, with women's rights goals of UN

members—(45) selected on a rotating basis from all regions

Commission on Sustainable Development

address—Division for Sustainable Development, UN DPCSD, Room DC2-2274, New York, NY 10017, US
telephone—[1] (212) 963 0902
FAX—[1] (212) 963 4260
established—12 February 1993
aim—to monitor, as part of the Economic and Social Council, implementation of agreements reached at the UN Conference on Environment and Development

members—(53) selected on a rotating basis from all regions

Commonwealth (C)

note—also known as Commonwealth of Nations
address—c/o Commonwealth Secretariat, Marlborough House, Pall Mall, London SW1Y 5HX, UK
telephone—[44] (171) 839 3411
FAX—[44] (171) 930 0827
established—31 December 1931
aim—to foster multinational cooperation and assistance, as a voluntary association that evolved from the British Empire

members—(52) Antigua and Barbuda, Australia, The Bahamas, Bangladesh, Barbados, Belize, Botswana, Brunei, Cameroon, Canada, Cyprus, Dominica, Fiji, The Gambia, Ghana, Grenada, Guyana, India, Jamaica, Kenya, Kiribati, Lesotho, Malawi, Malaysia, Maldives, Malta, Mauritius, Mozambique, Namibia, NZ, Nigeria (suspended), Pakistan, Papua New Guinea, Saint Kitts and Nevis, Saint Lucia, Saint Vincent and the Grenadines, Samoa, Seychelles, Sierra Leone, Singapore, Solomon Islands, South Africa, Sri Lanka, Swaziland, Tanzania, Tonga, Trinidad and Tobago, Uganda, UK, Vanuatu, Zambia, Zimbabwe
special members—(2) Nauru (soon to become full member), Tuvalu

---

Commonwealth of Independent States (CIS)

address—Kirov Street 17, 220000 Minsk, Belarus
telephone—[375] 293434, 293517
FAX—[375] 261894, 261944
established—8 December 1991
effective—21 December 1991
aim—to coordinate intercommonwealth relations and to provide a mechanism for the orderly dissolution of the USSR

members—(12) Armenia, Azerbaijan, Belarus, Georgia, Kazakhstan, Kyrgyzstan, Moldova, Russia, Tajikistan, Turkmenistan, Ukraine, Uzbekistan

---

Commonwealth of Nations

see Commonwealth (C)

Communaute Economique de l'Afrique de l'Ouest (CEAO)

see West African Economic Community (CEAO)

Communaute Economique des Etats de l'Afrique Centrale (CEEAC)

see Economic Community of Central African States (CEEAC)

Communaute Economique des Pays des Grands Lacs (CEPGL)

see Economic Community of the Great Lakes Countries (CEPGL)

Appendix C: International Organizations and Groups (continued)

communist countries	traditionally the Marxist-Leninist states with authoritarian governments and command economies based on the Soviet model; most of the original and the successor states are no longer communist; see centrally planned economies
Conference on Security and Cooperation in Europe (CSCE)	see Organization for Security and Cooperation in Europe (OSCE)
Conseil Europeen pour la Recherche Nucleaire (CERN)	see European Organization for Nuclear Research (CERN)
Contadora Group (CG)	established 5 January 1983 (on the Panamanian island of Contadora) to reduce tensions and conflicts in Central America; has evolved into the Rio Group (RG); members included Colombia, Mexico, Panama, Venezuela
Cooperation Council for the Arab States of the Gulf	see Gulf Cooperation Council (GCC)
Coordinating Committee on Export Controls (COCOM)	established in 1949 to control the export of strategic products and technical data from member countries to proscribed destinations; members were Australia, Belgium, Canada, Denmark, France, Germany, Greece, Italy, Japan, Luxembourg, Netherlands, Norway, Portugal, Spain, Turkey, UK, US; abolished 31 March 1994; COCOM members are working on a new organization with expanded membership which focuses on nonproliferation export controls as opposed to East-West control of advanced technology
Council for Mutual Economic Assistance (CEMA) *note*—also known as CMEA or Comecon	established 25 January 1949 to promote the development of socialist economies and abolished 1 January 1991; members included Afghanistan (observer), Albania (had not participated since 1961 break with USSR), Angola (observer), Bulgaria, Cuba, Czechoslovakia, Ethiopia (observer), GDR, Hungary, Laos (observer), Mongolia, Mozambique (observer), Nicaragua (observer), Poland, Romania, USSR, Vietnam, Yemen (observer), Yugoslavia (associate)
Council of Arab Economic Unity (CAEU) *address*—International Trade Centre Building, 12th Floor, 1191 Cornish El Nile, P.O. Box 1, Mohamad Fareed, Cairo, Egypt *telephone*—[20] (2) 754252, 755321 *FAX*—[20] (2) 754090 *established*—3 June 1957 *effective*—30 May 1964 *aim*—to promote economic integration among Arab nations	*members*—(11 plus the Palestine Liberation Organization) Egypt, Iraq, Jordan, Kuwait, Libya, Mauritania, Somalia, Sudan, Syria, UAE, Yemen, Palestine Liberation Organization
Council of Europe (CE) *address*—Palais de l'Europe, F-67075 Strasbourg CEDEX, France *telephone*—[33] (3) 88 41 20 00 *FAX*—[33] (3) 88 41 27 81, 88 41 27 82 *established*—5 May 1949 *effective*—3 August 1949 *aim*—to promote increased unity and quality of life in Europe	*members*—(40) Albania, Andorra, Austria, Belgium, Bulgaria, Croatia, Cyprus, Czech Republic, Denmark, Estonia, Finland, France, Germany, Greece, Hungary, Iceland, Ireland, Italy, Latvia, Liechtenstein, Lithuania, Luxembourg, The Former Yugoslav Republic of Macedonia, Malta, Moldova, Netherlands, Norway, Poland, Portugal, Romania, Russia, San Marino, Slovakia, Slovenia, Spain, Sweden, Switzerland, Turkey, Ukraine, UK *guests*—(4) Armenia, Azerbaijan, Bosnia and Herzegovina, Georgia *observers*—(5) Canada, Israel, Italy, Japan, US
Council of the Baltic Sea States (CBSS) *address*—Ministry for Foreign Affairs, Box 16121, S-10323 Stockholm, Sweden *telephone*—[46] (8) 405 1000 *FAX*—[46] (8) 723 1176 *established*—5 March 1992 *aim*—to promote cooperation among the Baltic Sea states in the areas of aid to new democratic institutions, economic development, humanitarian aid, energy and the environment, cultural programs and education, and transportation and communication	*members*—(12) Denmark, Estonia, EU, Finland, Germany, Iceland, Latvia, Lithuania, Norway, Poland, Russia, Sweden

Appendix C: International Organizations and Groups (continued)

Council of the Entente (Entente)

address—01 BP 3734, Angle Avenue
Verdier-Rue de Tessieres, Abidjan 01,
Cote d'Ivoire
telephone—[225] 33 10 01, 33 28 35, 32 10 74
FAX—[225] 33 11 49
established—29 May 1959
aim—to promote economic, social, and political
coordination

members—(5) Benin, Burkina Faso, Cote d'Ivoire, Niger, Togo

---

countries in transition

a new term used by the International Monetary FUND (IMF) for the middle group in its hierarchy of advanced economies, countries in transition, and developing countries; recently published IMF statistics include the following 28 countries in transition: Albania, Armenia, Azerbaijan, Belarus, Bosnia and Herzegovina, Bulgaria, Croatia, Czech Republic, Estonia, Georgia, Hungary, Kazakhstan, Kyrgyzstan, Latvia, Lithuania, The Former Yugoslav Republic of Macedonia, Moldova, Mongolia, Poland, Romania, Russia, Serbia and Montenegro, Slovakia, Slovenia, Tajikistan, Turkmenistan, Ukraine, Uzbekistan; *note*—this group is identical to the group traditionally referred to as the "former USSR/Eastern Europe" except for the addition of Mongolia

---

Customs Cooperation Council (CCC)

note—also known as World Customs
Organization (WCO)
address—Rue de l'Industrie 26-38, B-1040
Brussels, Belgium
telephone—[32] (2) 508 42 11
FAX—[32] (2) 508 42 40
established—15 December 1950
aim—to promote international cooperation in
customs matters

members—(144) Albania, Algeria, Angola, Argentina, Armenia, Australia, Austria, Azerbaijan, The Bahamas, Bangladesh, Belarus, Belgium, Bermuda, Botswana, Brazil, Brunei, Bulgaria, Burkina Faso, Burma, Burundi, Cameroon, Canada, Cape Verde, Central African Republic, Chile, China, Colombia, Comoros, Democratic Republic of the Congo, Republic of the Congo, Cote d'Ivoire, Croatia, Cuba, Cyprus, Czech Republic, Denmark, Egypt, Eritrea, Estonia, Ethiopia, Finland, France, Gabon, The Gambia, Georgia, Germany, Ghana, Greece, Guatemala, Guinea, Guyana, Haiti, Hong Kong, Hungary, Iceland, India, Indonesia, Iran, Iraq, Ireland, Israel, Italy, Jamaica, Japan, Jordan, Kazakhstan, Kenya, South Korea, Kuwait, Latvia, Lebanon, Lesotho, Liberia, Libya, Lithuania, Luxembourg, Macau, The Former Yugoslav Republic of Macedonia, Madagascar, Malawi, Malaysia, Maldives, Mali, Malta, Mauritania, Mauritius, Mexico, Moldova, Mongolia, Morocco, Mozambique, Namibia, Nepal, Netherlands, NZ, Niger, Nigeria, Norway, Pakistan, Panama, Paraguay, Peru, Philippines, Poland, Portugal, Qatar, Romania, Russia, Rwanda, Sao Tome and Principe, Saudi Arabia, Senegal, Sierra Leone, Singapore, Slovakia, Slovenia, South Africa, Spain, Sri Lanka, Sudan, Swaziland, Sweden, Switzerland, Syria, Tajikistan, Tanzania, Thailand, Togo, Trinidad and Tobago, Tunisia, Turkey, Turkmenistan, Uganda, Ukraine, UAE, UK, US, Uruguay, Uzbekistan, Venezuela, Vietnam, Yemen, Zambia, Zimbabwe

---

developed countries (DCs)

the top group in the hierarchy of developed countries (DCs), former USSR/Eastern Europe (former USSR/EE), and less developed countries (LDCs); includes the market-oriented economies of the mainly democratic nations in the Organization for Economic Cooperation and Development (OECD), Bermuda, Israel, South Africa, and the European ministates; also known as the First World, high-income countries, the North, industrial countries; generally have a per capita GDP in excess of $10,000 although four OECD countries and South Africa have figures well under $10,000 and two of the excluded OPEC countries have figures of more than $10,000; the 35 DCs are: Andorra, Australia, Austria, Belgium, Bermuda, Canada, Denmark, Faroe Islands, Finland, France, Germany, Greece, Holy See, Iceland, Ireland, Israel, Italy, Japan, Liechtenstein, Luxembourg, Malta, Mexico, Monaco, Netherlands, NZ, Norway, Portugal, San Marino, South Africa, Spain, Sweden, Switzerland, Turkey, UK, US; *note*—similar to the new International Monetary Fund (IMF) term "advanced economies" which adds Hong Kong, South Korea, Singapore, and Taiwan but drops Malta, Mexico, South Africa, and Turkey

Appendix C: International Organizations and Groups (continued)

developing countries

a new term used by the International Monetary FUND (IMF) for the bottom group in its hierarchy of advanced economies, countries in transition, and developing countries; recently published IMF statistics include the following 126 developing countries: Afghanistan, Algeria, Angola, Antigua and Barbuda, Argentina, Aruba, The Bahamas, Bahrain, Bangladesh, Barbados, Belize, Benin, Bhutan, Bolivia, Botswana, Brazil, Burkina Faso, Burma, Burundi, Cambodia, Cameroon, Cape Verde, Central African Republic, Chad, Chile, China, Colombia, Comoros, Democratic Republic of the Congo, Republic of the Congo, Costa Rica, Cote d'Ivoire, Cyprus, Djibouti, Dominica, Dominican Republic, Ecuador, Egypt, El Salvador, Equatorial Guinea, Ethiopia, Fiji, Gabon, The Gambia, Ghana, Grenada, Guatemala, Guinea, Guinea-Bissau, Guyana, Haiti, Honduras, India, Indonesia, Iran, Iraq, Jamaica, Jordan, Kenya, Kiribati, Kuwait, Laos, Lebanon, Lesotho, Liberia, Libya, Madagascar, Malawi, Malaysia, Maldives, Mali, Malta, Marshall Islands, Mauritania, Mauritius, Mexico, Federated States of Micronesia, Morocco, Mozambique, Namibia, Nepal, Netherlands Antilles, Nicaragua, Niger, Nigeria, Oman, Pakistan, Panama, Papua New Guinea, Paraguay, Peru, Philippines, Qatar, Rwanda, Saint Kitts and Nevis, Saint Lucia, Saint Vincent and the Grenadines, Samoa, Sao Tome and Principe, Saudi Arabia, Senegal, Seychelles, Sierra Leone, Solomon Islands, Somalia, South Africa, Sri Lanka, Sudan, Suriname, Swaziland, Syria, Tanzania, Thailand, Togo, Trinidad and Tobago, Tunisia, Turkey, UAE, Uganda, Uruguay, Vanuatu, Venezuela, Vietnam, Yemen, Zambia, Zimbabwe; *note*—this category would presumably also cover the following 46 other countries that are traditionally included in the more comprehensive group of "less developed countries": American Samoa, Anguilla, British Virgin Islands, Brunei, Cayman Islands, Christmas Island, Cocos Islands, Cook Islands, Cuba, Eritrea, Falkland Islands, French Guiana, French Polynesia, Gaza Strip, Gibraltar, Greenland, Grenada, Guadeloupe, Guam, Guernsey, Jersey, North Korea, Macau, Isle of Man, Martinique, Mayotte, Montserrat, Nauru, New Caledonia, Niue, Norfolk Island, Northern Mariana Islands, Palau, Pitcairn Islands, Puerto Rico, Reunion, Saint Helena, Saint Pierre and Miquelon, Tokelau, Tonga, Turks and Caicos Islands, Tuvalu, Virgin Islands, Wallis and Futuna, West Bank, Western Sahara

East African Development Bank (EADB)

address—4 Nile Avenue, P.O. Box 7128, Kampala, Uganda
telephone—[256] (41) 230021, 230825
FAX—[256] (41) 259763
established—6 June 1967
effective—1 December 1967
aim—to promote economic development

members—(3) Kenya, Tanzania, Uganda

Economic and Social Commission for Asia and the Pacific (ESCAP)

address—United Nations Building, Rajadamnern Avenue, Bangkok 10200, Thailand
telephone—[66] (2) 2881234
FAX—[66] (2) 2881000
established—28 March 1947 as Economic Commission for Asia and the Far East (ECAFE)
aim—to carry out the commitment of the Economic and Social Council of the UN to promote economic development

members—(51) Afghanistan, Armenia, Australia, Azerbaijan, Bangladesh, Bhutan, Brunei, Burma, Cambodia, China, Fiji, France, India, Indonesia, Iran, Japan, Kazakhstan, Kiribati, North Korea, South Korea, Kyrgyzstan, Laos, Malaysia, Maldives, Marshall Islands, Federated States of Micronesia, Mongolia, Nauru, Nepal, Netherlands, NZ, Pakistan, Palau, Papua New Guinea, Philippines, Russia, Samoa, Singapore, Solomon Islands, Sri Lanka, Tajikistan, Thailand, Tonga, Turkey, Turkmenistan, Tuvalu, UK, US, Uzbekistan, Vanuatu, Vietnam
associate members—(9) American Samoa, Cook Islands, French Polynesia, Guam, Hong Kong, Macau, New Caledonia, Niue, Northern Mariana Islands

Economic and Social Commission for Western Asia (ESCWA)

address—P.O. Box 11-8575, Riad El-Sohl Square, Beirut, Lebanon
telephone—[961] (10) 981301
FAX—[961] (10) 981510
established—9 August 1973 as Economic Commission for Western Asia (ECWA)
aim—to promote economic development as a regional commission for the UN's Economic and Social Council

members—(12 plus the Palestine Liberation Organization) Bahrain, Egypt, Iraq, Jordan, Kuwait, Lebanon, Oman, Qatar, Saudi Arabia, Syria, UAE, Yemen, Palestine Liberation Organization

Appendix C: International Organizations and Groups (continued)

Economic and Social Council (ECOSOC)

address—United Nations, New York, NY 10017, US
telephone—[1] (212) 963 1234
FAX—[1] (212) 758 2718
established—26 June 1945
effective—24 October 1945
aim—to coordinate the economic and social work of the UN; includes five regional commissions (see Economic Commission for Africa, Economic Commission for Europe, Economic Commission for Latin America and the Caribbean, Economic and Social Commission for Asia and the Pacific, Economic and Social Commission for Western Asia) and 10 functional commissions (see Commission for Social Development, Commission on Human Rights, Commission on Narcotic Drugs, Commission on the Status of Women, Commission on Population and Development, Statistical Commission, Commission on Science and Technology for Development, Commission on Sustainable Development, and Commission on Crime Prevention and Criminal Justice)

members—(54) selected on a rotating basis from all regions

Economic Commission for Africa (ECA)

address—P.O. Box 3001-3005, Addis Ababa, Ethiopia
telephone—[251] (1) 51 72 00
FAX—[251] (1) 51 44 16
established—29 April 1958
aim—to promote economic development as a regional commission of the UN's Economic and Social Council

members—(53) Algeria, Angola, Benin, Botswana, Burkina Faso, Burundi, Cameroon, Cape Verde, Central African Republic, Chad, Comoros, Democratic Republic of the Congo, Republic of the Congo, Cote d'Ivoire, Djibouti, Egypt, Equatorial Guinea, Eritrea, Ethiopia, Gabon, The Gambia, Ghana, Guinea, Guinea-Bissau, Kenya, Lesotho, Liberia, Libya, Madagascar, Malawi, Mali, Mauritania, Mauritius, Morocco, Mozambique, Namibia, Niger, Nigeria, Rwanda, Sao Tome and Principe, Senegal, Seychelles, Sierra Leone, Somalia, South Africa, Sudan, Swaziland, Tanzania, Togo, Tunisia, Uganda, Zambia, Zimbabwe
associate members—(2) France, UK

Economic Commission for Asia and the Far East (ECAFE)

see Economic and Social Commission for Asia and the Pacific (ESCAP)

Economic Commission for Europe (ECE)

address—Palais des Nations, CH-1211 Geneva 10, Switzerland
telephone—[41] (22) 917 2727, 917 4444
FAX—[41] (22) 917 0505
established—28 March 1947
aim—to promote economic development as a regional commission of the UN's Economic and Social Council

members—(55) Albania, Andorra, Armenia, Austria, Azerbaijan, Belarus, Belgium, Bosnia and Herzegovina, Bulgaria, Canada, Croatia, Cyprus, Czech Republic, Denmark, Estonia, Finland, France, Georgia, Germany, Greece, Hungary, Iceland, Ireland, Israel, Italy, Kazakhstan, Kyrgyzstan, Latvia, Liechtenstein, Lithuania, Luxembourg, The Former Yugoslav Republic of Macedonia, Malta, Moldova, Monaco, Netherlands, Norway, Poland, Portugal, Romania, Russia, San Marino, Slovakia, Slovenia, Spain, Sweden, Switzerland, Tajikistan, Turkey, Turkmenistan, Ukraine, UK, US, Uzbekistan, Yugoslavia

Economic Commission for Latin America (ECLA)	see Economic Commission for Latin America and the Caribbean (ECLAC)
Economic Commission for Latin America and the Caribbean (ECLAC) *address*—Edificio Naciones Unidas, Avenida Dag Hammarskjold, Casilla 179 D, Santiago, Chile *telephone*—[56] (2) 2102000 *FAX*—[56] (2) 2080252, 2081946 *established*—25 February 1948 as Economic Commission for Latin America (ECLA) *aim*—to promote economic development as a regional commission of the UN's Economic and Social Council	*members*—(41) Antigua and Barbuda, Argentina, The Bahamas, Barbados, Belize, Bolivia, Brazil, Canada, Chile, Colombia, Costa Rica, Cuba, Dominica, Dominican Republic, Ecuador, El Salvador, France, Grenada, Guatemala, Guyana, Haiti, Honduras, Italy, Jamaica, Mexico, Netherlands, Nicaragua, Panama, Paraguay, Peru, Portugal, Saint Kitts and Nevis, Saint Lucia, Saint Vincent and the Grenadines, Spain, Suriname, Trinidad and Tobago, UK, US, Uruguay, Venezuela *associate members*—(7) Anguilla, Aruba, British Virgin Islands, Montserrat, Netherlands Antilles, Puerto Rico, Virgin Islands
Economic Commission for Western Asia (ECWA)	see Economic and Social Commission for Western Asia (ESCWA)
Economic Community of Central African States (CEEAC) *note*—acronym from Communaute Economique des Etats de l'Afrique Centrale *address*—CEEAC, BP 2112, Libreville, Gabon *telephone*—[241] 73 35 47, 73 35 48, 73 36 77 *established*—18 October 1983 *aim*—to promote regional economic cooperation and establish a Central African Common Market	*members*—(11) Angola, Burundi, Cameroon, Central African Republic, Chad, Democratic Republic of the Congo, Republic of the Congo, Equatorial Guinea, Gabon, Rwanda, Sao Tome and Principe
Economic Community of the Great Lakes Countries (CEPGL) *note*—acronym from Communaute Economique des Pays des Grands Lacs *address*—IRAZ-CEPGL, BP 91, Gitega, Burundi *established*—26 September 1976 *aim*—to promote regional economic cooperation and integration	*members*—(3) Burundi, Democratic Republic of the Congo, Rwanda
Economic Community of West African States (ECOWAS) *address*—6 King George V Road, PMB 12745, Lagos, Nigeria *telephone*—[234] (1) 636839, 636841, 636064, 630398 *FAX*—[234] (1) 636822 *established*—28 May 1975 *aim*—to promote regional economic cooperation	*members*—(16) Benin, Burkina Faso, Cape Verde, Cote d'Ivoire, The Gambia, Ghana, Guinea, Guinea-Bissau, Liberia, Mali, Mauritania, Niger, Nigeria, Senegal, Sierra Leone, Togo

Appendix C: International Organizations and Groups (continued)

Economic Cooperation Organization (ECO)

address—No. 1 Goulbou Alley, Kamraniyeh, P.O. Box 14155-6176, Teheran, Iran Islamic Republic
telephone—[98] (21) 2831731, 2831733
FAX—[98] (21) 2831732
established—NA 1985
aim—to promote regional cooperation in trade, transportation, communications, tourism, cultural affairs, and economic development

members—(10) Afghanistan, Azerbaijan, Iran, Kazakhstan, Kyrgyzstan, Pakistan, Tajikistan, Turkey, Turkmenistan, Uzbekistan
associate members—(1) "Turkish Republic of Northern Cyprus"

Euro-Atlantic Partnership Council (EAPC)

note—began as the North Atlantic Cooperation Council (NACC); an extension of NATO
address—c/o NATO, B-1110 Brussels, Belgium
telephone—[32] (2) 728 41 11
FAX—[32] (2) 728 45 79
established—8 November 1991
effective—20 December 1991
aim—to discuss cooperation on mutual political and security issues

members—(44) Albania, Armenia, Austria, Azerbaijan, Belarus, Belgium, Bulgaria, Canada, Czech Republic, Denmark, Estonia, Finland, France, Georgia, Germany, Greece, Hungary, Iceland, Italy, Kazakhstan, Kyrgyzstan, Latvia, Lithuania, Luxembourg, The Former Yugoslav Republic of Macedonia, Moldova, Netherlands, Norway, Poland, Portugal, Romania, Russia, Slovakia, Slovenia, Spain, Sweden, Switzerland, Tajikistan, Turkey, Turkmenistan, Ukraine, UK, US, Uzbekistan

European Bank for Reconstruction and Development (EBRD)

address—EBRD Headquarters, One Exchange Square, London EC2A 2EH, UK
telephone—[44] (171) 338 6000
FAX—[44] (171) 338 6100
established—15 April 1991
aim—to facilitate the transition of seven centrally planned economies in Europe (Bulgaria, former Czechoslovakia, Hungary, Poland, Romania, former USSR, and former Yugoslavia) to market economies by committing 60% of its loans to privatization

members—(60) Albania, Armenia, Australia, Austria, Azerbaijan, Belarus, Belgium, Bosnia and Herzegovina, Bulgaria, Canada, Croatia, Cyprus, Czech Republic, Denmark, Egypt, EU, European Investment Bank (EIB), Estonia, Finland, France, Georgia, Germany, Greece, Hungary, Iceland, Ireland, Israel, Italy, Japan, Kazakhstan, South Korea, Kyrgyzstan, Latvia, Liechtenstein, Lithuania, Luxembourg, The Former Yugoslav Republic of Macedonia, Malta, Mexico, Moldova, Morocco, Netherlands, NZ, Norway, Poland, Portugal, Romania, Russia, Slovakia, Slovenia, Spain, Sweden, Switzerland, Tajikistan, Turkey, Turkmenistan, Ukraine, UK, US, Uzbekistan;
note—includes all 25 members of the OECD; also includes the EU as a single entity

European Community (or European Communities, EC)

was established 8 April 1965 to integrate the European Atomic Energy Community (Euratom), the European Coal and Steel Community (ESC), the European Economic Community (EEC or Common Market), and to establish a completely integrated common market and an eventual federation of Europe; merged into the European Union (EU) on 7 February 1992; member states at the time of merger were Belgium, Denmark, France, Germany, Greece, Ireland, Italy, Luxembourg, Netherlands, Portugal, Spain, UK

European Free Trade Association (EFTA)

address—9-11 Rue de Varembe, CH-1202 Geneva 20, Switzerland
telephone—[41] (22) 749 13 35
FAX—[41] (22) 733 92 91
established—4 January 1960
effective—3 May 1960
aim—to promote expansion of free trade

members—(4) Iceland, Liechtenstein, Norway, Switzerland

Appendix C: International Organizations and Groups (continued)

European Investment Bank (EIB)

address—Bd Konrad Adenauer 100, L-2950
Luxembourg, Luxembourg
telephone—[352] 43791
FAX—[352] 437704
established—25 March 1957
effective—1 January 1958
aim—to promote economic development of the
EU and its predecessors, the EEC and the EC

members—(15) Austria, Belgium, Denmark, Finland, France, Germany, Greece, Ireland, Italy, Luxembourg, Netherlands, Portugal, Spain, Sweden, UK

European Monetary Union (EMU)

note—an integral part of the European Union
address—c/o European Commission, Rue de la
Loi 200, B-1049 Bruxelles, Belgium
telephone—[32] (2) 299 11 11
proposed—7 February 1992
aim—to promote a single market by creating a
single currency, the euro; time table—2 May
1998: European exchange rates fixed for 1
January 1999; 1 January 1999: all banks and
stock exchanges begin using euros; 1 January
2002: the euro goes into circulation; 1 July 2002
local currencies no longer accepted

members—(11) Austria, Belgium, Finland, France, Germany, Ireland, Italy, Luxembourg, Netherlands, Portugal, Spain; note—Denmark, Sweden, and UK decided not to join, and Greece did not meet all the criteria to take part

European Organization for Nuclear Research (CERN)

note—acronym retained from the predecessor
organization Conseil Europeen pour la
Recherche Nucleaire
address—CH-1211 Geneva 23, Switzerland
telephone—[41] (22) 767 61 11
FAX—[41] (22) 767 65 55
established—1 July 1953
effective—29 September 1954
aim—to foster nuclear research for peaceful
purposes only

members—(19) Austria, Belgium, Czech Republic, Denmark, Finland, France, Germany, Greece, Hungary, Italy, Netherlands, Norway, Poland, Portugal, Slovakia, Spain, Sweden, Switzerland, UK
observers—(8) EU, Israel, Japan, Russia, Turkey, United Nations Educational, Scientific, and Cultural Organization (UNESCO), US, Yugoslavia (suspended)

European Space Agency (ESA)

address—ESA Headquarters, 8-10 Rue Mario
Nikis, F-75738 Paris CEDEX 15, France
telephone—[33] (1) 53 69 76 54
FAX—[33] (1) 53 69 75 60
established—31 July 1973
effective—1 May 1975
aim—to promote peaceful cooperation in space
research and technology

members—(14) Austria, Belgium, Denmark, Finland, France, Germany, Ireland, Italy, Netherlands, Norway, Spain, Sweden, Switzerland, UK
cooperating state—(1) Canada

Appendix C: International Organizations and Groups (continued)

European Union (EU)

note—evolved from the European Community (EC)
address—c/o European Commission, Rue de la Loi 200, B-1049 Brussels, Belgium
telephone—[32] (2) 299 11 11
FAX—[32] (2) 295 01 38 through 295 01 40
established—7 February 1992
effective—1 November 1993
aim—to coordinate policy among the 15 members in three fields: economics, building on the European Economic Community's (EEC) efforts to establish a common market and eventually a common currency to be called the 'euro', which will supercede the EU's accounting unit, the ECU; defense, within the concept of a Common Foreign and Security Policy (CFSP); and justice and home affairs, including immigration, drugs, terrorism, and improved living and working conditions

members—(15) Austria, Belgium, Denmark, Finland, France, Germany, Greece, Ireland, Italy, Luxembourg, Netherlands, Portugal, Spain, Sweden, UK
members—(12) Albania, Bulgaria, Cyprus, Czech Republic, Estonia, Hungary, Latvia, Lithuania, Malta, Poland, Romania, Slovakia

First World

another term for countries with advanced, industrialized economies; this term is fading from use; see developed countries (DCs)

Food and Agriculture Organization (FAO)

address—Viale delle Terme di Caracalla, I-00100 Rome, Italy
telephone—[39] (6) 57051
FAX—[39] (6) 5705 3152
established—16 October 1945
aim—to raise living standards and increase availability of agricultural products, as a UN specialized agency

members—(176) Afghanistan, Albania, Algeria, Angola, Antigua and Barbuda, Argentina, Armenia, Australia, Austria, Azerbaijan, The Bahamas, Bahrain, Bangladesh, Barbados, Belgium, Belize, Benin, Bhutan, Bolivia, Bosnia and Herzegovina, Botswana, Brazil, Bulgaria, Burkina Faso, Burma, Burundi, Cambodia, Cameroon, Canada, Cape Verde, Central African Republic, Chad, Chile, China, Colombia, Comoros, Democratic Republic of the Congo, Republic of the Congo, Cook Islands, Costa Rica, Cote d'Ivoire, Croatia, Cuba, Cyprus, Czech Republic, Denmark, Djibouti, Dominica, Dominican Republic, Ecuador, Egypt, El Salvador, Equatorial Guinea, Eritrea, Estonia, Ethiopia, EU, Fiji, Finland, France, Gabon, The Gambia, Georgia, Germany, Ghana, Greece, Grenada, Guatemala, Guinea, Guinea-Bissau, Guyana, Haiti, Honduras, Hungary, Iceland, India, Indonesia, Iran, Iraq, Ireland, Israel, Italy, Jamaica, Japan, Jordan, Kazakhstan, Kenya, North Korea, South Korea, Kuwait, Kyrgyzstan, Laos, Latvia, Lebanon, Lesotho, Liberia, Libya, Lithuania, Luxembourg, The Former Yugoslav Republic of Macedonia, Madagascar, Malawi, Malaysia, Maldives, Mali, Malta, Mauritania, Mauritius, Mexico, Moldova, Mongolia, Morocco, Mozambique, Namibia, Nepal, Netherlands, NZ, Nicaragua, Niger, Nigeria, Norway, Oman, Pakistan, Panama, Papua New Guinea, Paraguay, Peru, Philippines, Poland, Portugal, Qatar, Romania, Rwanda, Saint Kitts and Nevis, Saint Lucia, Saint Vincent and the Grenadines, Samoa, Sao Tome and Principe, Saudi Arabia, Senegal, Seychelles, Sierra Leone, Slovakia, Slovenia, Solomon Islands, Somalia, South Africa, Spain, Sri Lanka, Sudan, Suriname, Swaziland, Sweden, Switzerland, Syria, Tajikistan, Tanzania, Thailand, Togo, Tonga, Trinidad and Tobago, Tunisia, Turkey, Turkmenistan, Uganda, UAE, UK, US, Uruguay, Vanuatu, Venezuela, Vietnam, Yemen, Yugoslavia (suspended), Zambia, Zimbabwe
associate member—(1) Puerto Rico

former Soviet Union (FSU)

a collective term often used to identify as a group the successor nations to the Soviet Union or USSR; this group of 15 countries consists of Armenia, Azerbaijan, Belarus, Estonia, Georgia, Kazakhstan, Kyrgyzstan, Latvia, Lithuania, Moldova, Russia, Tajikistan, Turkmenistan, Ukraine, Uzbekistan

former USSR/Eastern Europe (former USSR/EE)

the middle group in the hierarchy of developed countries (DCs), former USSR/Eastern Europe (former USSR/EE), and less developed countries (LDCs); these countries are in political and economic transition and may well be grouped differently in the near future; this group of 27 countries consists of Albania, Armenia, Azerbaijan, Belarus, Bosnia and Herzegovina, Bulgaria, Croatia, Czech Republic, Estonia, Georgia, Hungary, Kazakhstan, Kyrgyzstan, Latvia, Lithuania, The Former Yugoslav Republic of Macedonia, Moldova, Poland, Romania, Russia, Serbia and Montenegro, Slovakia, Slovenia, Tajikistan, Turkmenistan, Ukraine, Uzbekistan; this group is identical to the IMF group "countries in transition" except for the IMF's inclusion of Mongolia

Appendix C: International Organizations and Groups (continued)

Four Dragons	the four small Asian less developed countries (LDCs) that have experienced unusually rapid economic growth; also known as the Four Tigers; this group consists of Hong Kong, South Korea, Singapore, Taiwan; these countries are included in the IMF's "advanced economies" group
Four Tigers	another term for the Four Dragons; see Four Dragons
Franc Zone (FZ) *note*—also known as Conference des Ministres des Finances des Pays de la Zone Franc *address*—c/o Banque de France, Service de la Zone Franc, 39 Rue des Croix des Petits Champs, F-75001 Paris, France *telephone*—[33] (1) 42 92 42 92 *FAX*—[33] (1) 42 96 04 23 *established*—20 December 1945 *aim*—to form a monetary union among countries whose currencies are linked to the French franc	*members*—(16) Benin, Burkina Faso, Cameroon, Central African Republic, Chad, Comoros, Republic of the Congo, Cote d'Ivoire, Equatorial Guinea, France, Gabon, Guinea-Bissau, Mali, Niger, Senegal, Togo; *note*—France includes metropolitan France, the four overseas departments of France (French Guiana, Guadeloupe, Martinique, Reunion), the two territorial collectivities of France (Mayotte, Saint Pierre and Miquelon), and the three overseas territories of France (French Polynesia, New Caledonia, Wallis and Futuna)
Front Line States (FLS)	established to achieve black majority rule in South Africa; has since gone out of existence; members included Angola, Botswana, Mozambique, Namibia, Tanzania, Zambia, Zimbabwe
General Agreement on Tariffs and Trade (GATT)	was established 30 October 1947 to promote the expansion of international trade on a nondiscriminatory basis; subsumed by the World Trade Organization (WTrO) on 1 January 1995; members at the time were Angola, Antigua and Barbuda, Argentina, Australia, Austria, Bahrain, Bangladesh, Barbados, Belgium, Belize, Benin, Bolivia, Botswana, Brazil, Brunei, Burkina Faso, Burma, Burundi, Cameroon, Canada, Central African Republic, Chad, Chile, Colombia, Democratic Republic of the Congo, Republic of the Congo, Costa Rica, Cote d'Ivoire, Cuba, Cyprus, Czech Republic, Denmark, Dominica, Dominican Republic, Egypt, El Salvador, Fiji, Finland, France, Gabon, The Gambia, Germany, Ghana, Greece, Grenada, Guatemala, Guinea-Bissau, Guyana, Haiti, Honduras, Hong Kong, Hungary, Iceland, India, Indonesia, Ireland, Israel, Italy, Jamaica, Japan, Kenya, South Korea, Kuwait, Lesotho, Liechtenstein, Luxembourg, Macau, Madagascar, Malawi, Malaysia, Maldives, Mali, Malta, Mauritania, Mauritius, Mexico, Morocco, Mozambique, Namibia, Netherlands, NZ, Nicaragua, Niger, Nigeria, Norway, Pakistan, Paraguay, Peru, Philippines, Poland, Portugal, Qatar, Romania, Rwanda, Saint Kitts and Nevis, Saint Lucia, Saint Vincent and the Grenadines, Senegal, Sierra Leone, Singapore, Slovakia, South Africa, Spain, Sri Lanka, Suriname, Swaziland, Sweden, Switzerland, Tanzania, Thailand, Togo, Trinidad and Tobago, Tunisia, Turkey, Uganda, UAE, UK, US, Uruguay, Venezuela, Yugoslavia (suspended), Zambia, Zimbabwe
Group of 2 (G-2)	informal term that came into use about 1986; to facilitate bilateral economic cooperation between the two most powerful economic giants Japan, US
Group of 3 (G-3) *address*—c/o Ministry of Foreign Affairs, Grupo de los tres, Caracas, Venezuela *established*—NA October 1990 *aim*—mechanism for policy coordination	*members*—(3) Colombia, Mexico, Venezuela
Group of 5 (G-5) *established*—22 September 1985 *aim*—to coordinate the economic policies of five major noncommunist economic powers	*members*—(5) France, Germany, Japan, UK, US
Group of 6 (G-6) *note*—also known as Groupe des Six Sur le Desarmement; not to be confused with the Big Six *established*—22 May 1984 *aim*—to achieve nuclear disarmament	*members*—(6) Argentina, Greece, India, Mexico, Sweden, Tanzania

Appendix C: International Organizations and Groups (continued)

Group of 7 (G-7)

note—membership is the same as the Big Seven
established—22 September 1985
aim—to facilitate economic cooperation among the seven major noncommunist economic powers

members—(7) Group of 5 (France, Germany, Japan, UK, US) plus Canada and Italy

Group of 8 (G-8)

established NA October 1975 to facilitate economic cooperation among the developed countries (DCs) that participated in the Conference on International Economic Cooperation (CIEC), held in several sessions between NA December 1975 and 3 June 1977; members were Australia, Canada, EU (as one member), Japan, Spain, Sweden, Switzerland, US

Group of 9 (G-9)

established—NA
aim—to discuss matters of mutual interest on an informal basis

members—(9) Austria, Belgium, Bulgaria, Denmark, Finland, Hungary, Romania, Sweden, Yugoslavia

Group of 10 (G-10)

note—also known as the Paris Club; includes the wealthiest members of the IMF who provide most of the money to be loaned and act as the informal steering committee; name persists in spite of the addition of Switzerland on NA April 1984
address—c/o IMF Office in Europe, 64-66 Avenue d'Iena, F-75116 Paris, France
telephone—[33] (1) 40 69 30 80
FAX—[33] (1) 47 23 40 89
established—NA October 1962
aim—to coordinate credit policy

members— (11) Belgium, Canada, France, Germany, Italy, Japan, Netherlands, Sweden, Switzerland, UK, US
nonstate participants—(4) BIS, EU, IMF, OECD

Group of 11 (G-11)

note—also known as the Cartagena Group
established—22 June 1984, in Cartagena, Colombia
aim—to provide a forum for largest debtor nations in Latin America

members—(11) Argentina, Bolivia, Brazil, Chile, Colombia, Dominican Republic, Ecuador, Mexico, Peru, Uruguay, Venezuela

Group of 15 (G-15)

note—byproduct of the Nonaligned Movement
address—Technical Support Facility, Ch du Champ d'Ancier 17, Case Postale 326, CH-1211 Geneva 19, Switzerland
telephone—[41] (22) 798 42 10
FAX—[41] (22) 798 38 49
established—September 1989
aim—to promote economic cooperation among developing nations; to act as the main political organ for the Nonaligned Movement

members—(15) Algeria, Argentina, Brazil, Egypt, India, Indonesia, Jamaica, Malaysia, Mexico, Nigeria, Peru, Senegal, Venezuela, former Yugoslavia, Zimbabwe

Appendix C: International Organizations and Groups (continued)

Group of 19 (G-19)

established—NA October 1975
aim—to represent the interests of the less developed countries (LDCs) that participated in the Conference on International Economic Cooperation (CIEC) held in several sessions between NA December 1975 and 3 June 1977

members—(19) Algeria, Argentina, Brazil, Cameroon, Democratic Republic of the Congo, Egypt, India, Indonesia, Iran, Iraq, Jamaica, Mexico, Nigeria, Pakistan, Peru, Saudi Arabia, Venezuela, Yugoslavia, Zambia

Group of 24 (G-24)

address—c/o European Commission, DGIA - G-24 Coordination Unit, Rue de la Loi 200, B-1049 Brussels, Belgium
telephone—[32] (2) 299 22 44
FAX—[32] (2) 299 06 02
established—NA January 1972
aim—to promote the interests of developing countries in Africa, Asia, and Latin America within the IMF

members—(24) Algeria, Argentina, Brazil, Colombia, Democratic Republic of the Congo, Cote d'Ivoire, Egypt, Ethiopia, Gabon, Ghana, Guatemala, India, Iran, Lebanon, Mexico, Nigeria, Pakistan, Peru, Philippines, Sri Lanka, Syria, Trinidad and Tobago, Venezuela, Yugoslavia

Group of 30 (G-30)

address—1990 M Street NW, Suite 450, Washington, DC 20036, US
telephone—[1] (202) 331 2472
FAX—[1] (202) 785 9423
established—NA 1979
aim—to discuss and propose solutions to the world's economic problems

members—(30) informal group of 30 leading international bankers, economists, financial experts, and business leaders organized by Johannes Witteveen (former managing director of the IMF)

Group of 33 (G-33)

established—NA 1987
aim—to promote solutions to international economic problems

members—(33) leading economists from 13 countries

Group of 77 (G-77)

address—Office of the Chairman, United Nations, Room S-3959, P.O. Box 20, New York, NY 10017, US
telephone—[1] (212) 963 3816, 963 0192, 963 4777
FAX—[1] (212) 963 3515, 963 1753
established—NA October 1967
aim—to promote economic cooperation among developing countries; name persists in spite of increased membership

members—(131 plus the Palestine Liberation Organization) Afghanistan, Algeria, Angola, Antigua and Barbuda, Argentina, The Bahamas, Bahrain, Bangladesh, Barbados, Belize, Benin, Bhutan, Bolivia, Bosnia and Herzegovina, Botswana, Brazil, Brunei, Burkina Faso, Burma, Burundi, Cambodia, Cameroon, Cape Verde, Central African Republic, Chad, Chile, China, Colombia, Comoros, Democratic Republic of the Congo, Republic of the Congo, Costa Rica, Cote d'Ivoire, Cuba, Cyprus, Djibouti, Dominica, Dominican Republic, Ecuador, Egypt, El Salvador, Equatorial Guinea, Eritrea, Ethiopia, Fiji, Gabon, The Gambia, Ghana, Grenada, Guatemala, Guinea, Guinea-Bissau, Guyana, Haiti, Honduras, India, Indonesia, Iran, Iraq, Jamaica, Jordan, Kenya, South Korea, Kuwait, Laos, Lebanon, Lesotho, Liberia, Libya, Madagascar, Malawi, Malaysia, Maldives, Mali, Malta, Marshall Islands, Mauritania, Mauritius, Federated States of Micronesia, Mongolia, Morocco, Mozambique, Namibia, Nepal, Nicaragua, Niger, Nigeria, Oman, Pakistan, Panama, Papua New Guinea, Paraguay, Peru, Philippines, Qatar, Romania, Rwanda, Saint Kitts and Nevis, Saint Lucia, Saint Vincent and the Grenadines, Samoa, Sao Tome and Principe, Saudi Arabia, Senegal, Seychelles, Sierra Leone, Singapore, Solomon Islands, Somalia, South Africa, Sri Lanka, Sudan, Suriname, Swaziland, Syria, Tanzania, Thailand, Togo, Tonga, Trinidad and Tobago, Tunisia, Uganda, UAE, Uruguay, Vanuatu, Venezuela, Vietnam, Yemen, Yugoslavia, Zambia, Zimbabwe, Palestine Liberation Organization

Appendix C: International Organizations and Groups (continued)

Gulf Cooperation Council (GCC)	*members*—(6) Bahrain, Kuwait, Oman, Qatar, Saudi Arabia, UAE
note—also known as the Cooperation Council for the Arab States of the Gulf *address*—P.O. Box 7153, Riyadh 11462, Saudi Arabia *telephone*—[966] (1) 482 7777, extension 1238 *FAX*—[966] (1) 482 9109 *established*—25 May 1981 *aim*—to promote regional cooperation in economic, social, political, and military affairs	
Hexagonal Group	see Central European Initiative (CEI)
high-income countries	another term for the industrialized countries with high per capita GDPs; see developed countries (DCs)
Indian Ocean Commission (InOC)	*members*—(5) Comoros, France (for Reunion), Madagascar, Mauritius, Seychelles
address—Q4 Avenue Sir Guy Forget, BP7, Quatre Bornes, Mauritius *telephone*—[230] 425 9564, 425 1652 *FAX*—[230] 425 1209 *established*—17 July 1982 *aim*—to organize and promote regional cooperation in all sectors, especially economic	
industrial countries	another term for the developed countries; see developed countries (DCs)
Inter-American Development Bank (IADB)	*members*—(46) Argentina, Austria, The Bahamas, Barbados, Belgium, Belize, Bolivia, Brazil, Canada, Chile, Colombia, Costa Rica, Croatia, Denmark, Dominican Republic, Ecuador, El Salvador, Finland, France, Germany, Guatemala, Guyana, Haiti, Honduras, Israel, Italy, Jamaica, Japan, Mexico, Netherlands, Nicaragua, Norway, Panama, Paraguay, Peru, Portugal, Slovenia, Spain, Suriname, Sweden, Switzerland, Trinidad and Tobago, UK, US, Uruguay, Venezuela
note—also known as Banco Interamericano de Desarrollo (BID) *address*—1300 New York Avenue NW, Washington, DC 20577, US *telephone*—[1] (202) 623 1000 *FAX*—[1] (202) 623 3096 *established*—8 April 1959 *effective*—30 December 1959 *aim*—to promote economic and social development in Latin America	
Inter-Governmental Authority on Drought and Development (IGADD)	see Inter-Governmental Authority on Development (IGAD)
Inter-Governmental Authority on Development (IGAD)	*members*—(7) Djibouti, Eritrea, Ethiopia, Kenya, Somalia, Sudan, Uganda
note—formerly known as Inter-Governmental Authority on Drought and Development (IGADD) *address*—P. O. Box 2653, Djibouti, Djibouti *telephone*—[253] 354050 *FAX*—[253] 356994, 356284 *established*—15-16 January 1986 as the Inter-Governmental Authority on Drought and Development *revitalized*—21 March 1996 as the Inter-Governmental Authority on Development *aim*—to promote a social, economic, and scientific community among its members	

Appendix C: International Organizations and Groups (continued)

International Atomic Energy Agency (IAEA) *address*—Wagramerstrasse 5, P.O. Box 100, A-1400 Vienna, Austria *telephone*—[43] (1) 20600 *FAX*—[43] (1) 20607 *established*—26 October 1956 *effective*—29 July 1957 *aim*—to promote peaceful uses of atomic energy	*members*—(127) Afghanistan, Albania, Algeria, Argentina, Armenia, Australia, Austria, Bangladesh, Belarus, Belgium, Bolivia, Bosnia and Herzegovina, Brazil, Bulgaria, Burma, Cambodia, Cameroon, Canada, Chile, China, Colombia, Democratic Republic of the Congo, Costa Rica, Cote d'Ivoire, Croatia, Cuba, Cyprus, Czech Republic, Denmark, Dominican Republic, Ecuador, Egypt, El Salvador, Estonia, Ethiopia, Finland, France, Gabon, Georgia, Germany, Ghana, Greece, Guatemala, Haiti, Holy See, Hungary, Iceland, India, Indonesia, Iran, Iraq, Ireland, Israel, Italy, Jamaica, Japan, Jordan, Kazakhstan, Kenya, South Korea, Kuwait, Latvia, Lebanon, Liberia, Libya, Liechtenstein, Lithuania, Luxembourg, The Former Yugoslav Republic of Macedonia, Madagascar, Malaysia, Mali, Malta, Marshall Islands, Mauritius, Mexico, Moldova, Monaco, Mongolia, Morocco, Namibia, Netherlands, NZ, Nicaragua, Niger, Nigeria, Norway, Pakistan, Panama, Paraguay, Peru, Philippines, Poland, Portugal, Qatar, Romania, Russia, Saudi Arabia, Senegal, Sierra Leone, Singapore, Slovakia, Slovenia, South Africa, Spain, Sri Lanka, Sudan, Sweden, Switzerland, Syria, Tanzania, Thailand, Tunisia, Turkey, Uganda, Ukraine, UAE, UK, US, Uruguay, Uzbekistan, Venezuela, Vietnam, Yemen, Yugoslavia (suspended), Zambia, Zimbabwe
International Bank for Economic Cooperation (IBEC)	was established on 22 October 1963 to promote economic cooperation and development; members were Bulgaria, Cuba, Czechoslovakia, GDR, Hungary, Mongolia, Poland, Romania, USSR, Vietnam; now it is a Russian bank with a new charter
International Bank for Reconstruction and Development (IBRD) *note*—also known as the World Bank *address*—1818 H Street NW, Washington, DC 20433, US *telephone*—[1] (202) 477 1234 *FAX*—[1] (202) 477 6391 *established*—22 July 1944 *effective*—27 December 1945 *aim*—to provide economic development loans; a UN specialized agency	*members*—(181) Afghanistan, Albania, Algeria, Angola, Antigua and Barbuda, Argentina, Armenia, Australia, Austria, Azerbaijan, The Bahamas, Bahrain, Bangladesh, Barbados, Belarus, Belgium, Belize, Benin, Bhutan, Bolivia, Bosnia and Herzegovina, Botswana, Brazil, Brunei, Bulgaria, Burkina Faso, Burma, Burundi, Cambodia, Cameroon, Canada, Cape Verde, Central African Republic, Chad, Chile, China, Colombia, Comoros, Democratic Republic of the Congo, Republic of the Congo, Costa Rica, Cote d'Ivoire, Croatia, Cyprus, Czech Republic, Denmark, Djibouti, Dominica, Dominican Republic, Ecuador, Egypt, El Salvador, Equatorial Guinea, Eritrea, Estonia, Ethiopia, Fiji, Finland, France, Gabon, The Gambia, Georgia, Germany, Ghana, Greece, Grenada, Guatemala, Guinea, Guinea-Bissau, Guyana, Haiti, Honduras, Hungary, Iceland, India, Indonesia, Iran, Iraq, Ireland, Israel, Italy, Jamaica, Japan, Jordan, Kazakhstan, Kenya, Kiribati, South Korea, Kuwait, Kyrgyzstan, Laos, Latvia, Lebanon, Lesotho, Liberia, Libya, Lithuania, Luxembourg, The Former Yugoslav Republic of Macedonia, Madagascar, Malawi, Malaysia, Maldives, Mali, Malta, Marshall Islands, Mauritania, Mauritius, Mexico, Federated States of Micronesia, Moldova, Mongolia, Morocco, Mozambique, Namibia, Nepal, Netherlands, NZ, Nicaragua, Niger, Nigeria, Norway, Oman, Pakistan, Palau, Panama, Papua New Guinea, Paraguay, Peru, Philippines, Poland, Portugal, Qatar, Romania, Russia, Rwanda, Saint Kitts and Nevis, Saint Lucia, Saint Vincent and the Grenadines, Samoa, Sao Tome and Principe, Saudi Arabia, Senegal, Seychelles, Sierra Leone, Singapore, Slovakia, Slovenia, Solomon Islands, Somalia, South Africa, Spain, Sri Lanka, Sudan, Suriname, Swaziland, Sweden, Switzerland, Syria, Tajikistan, Tanzania, Thailand, Togo, Tonga, Trinidad and Tobago, Tunisia, Turkey, Turkmenistan, Uganda, Ukraine, UAE, UK, US, Uruguay, Uzbekistan, Vanuatu, Venezuela, Vietnam, Yemen, Zambia, Zimbabwe
International Chamber of Commerce (ICC) *address*—38 Cours Albert 1st, F-75008 Paris, France *telephone*—[33] (1) 49 53 28 28 *FAX*—[33] (1) 49 53 29 42 *established*—NA 1919 *aim*—to promote free trade and private enterprise and to represent business interests at national and international levels	*members*—(62 national councils) Argentina, Australia, Austria, Bangladesh, Belgium, Brazil, Burkina Faso, Cameroon, Canada, Chile, China, Colombia, Cote d'Ivoire, Cyprus, Denmark, Ecuador, Egypt, Finland, France, Germany, Greece, Iceland, India, Indonesia, Iran, Ireland, Israel, Italy, Japan, Jordan, South Korea, Kuwait, Lebanon, Lithuania, Luxembourg, Madagascar, Mexico, Morocco, Netherlands, Nigeria, Norway, Pakistan, Peru, Portugal, Saudi Arabia, Senegal, Singapore, South Africa, Spain, Sri Lanka, Sweden, Switzerland, Syria, Taiwan, Togo, Tunisia, Turkey, UK, US, Uruguay, Venezuela, Yugoslavia

Appendix C: International Organizations and Groups (continued)

International Civil Aviation Organization (ICAO)

address—ICAO, 999 University Street, Montreal H3C 5H7, Canada
telephone—[1] (514) 954 8219
FAX—[1] (514) 954 6077
established—7 December 1944
effective—4 April 1947
aim—to promote international cooperation in civil aviation; a UN specialized agency

members—(185) Afghanistan, Albania, Algeria, Angola, Antigua and Barbuda, Argentina, Armenia, Australia, Austria, Azerbaijan, The Bahamas, Bahrain, Bangladesh, Barbados, Belarus, Belgium, Belize, Benin, Bhutan, Bolivia, Bosnia and Herzegovina, Botswana, Brazil, Brunei, Bulgaria, Burkina Faso, Burma, Burundi, Cambodia, Cameroon, Canada, Cape Verde, Central African Republic, Chad, Chile, China, Colombia, Comoros, Democratic Republic of the Congo, Republic of the Congo, Cook Islands, Costa Rica, Cote d'Ivoire, Croatia, Cuba, Cyprus, Czech Republic, Denmark, Djibouti, Dominican Republic, Ecuador, Egypt, El Salvador, Equatorial Guinea, Eritrea, Estonia, Ethiopia, Fiji, Finland, France, Gabon, The Gambia, Georgia, Germany, Ghana, Greece, Grenada, Guatemala, Guinea, Guinea-Bissau, Guyana, Haiti, Honduras, Hungary, Iceland, India, Indonesia, Iran, Iraq, Ireland, Israel, Italy, Jamaica, Japan, Jordan, Kazakhstan, Kenya, Kiribati, North Korea, South Korea, Kuwait, Kyrgyzstan, Laos, Latvia, Lebanon, Lesotho, Liberia, Libya, Lithuania, Luxembourg, The Former Yugoslav Republic of Macedonia, Madagascar, Malawi, Malaysia, Maldives, Mali, Malta, Marshall Islands, Mauritania, Mauritius, Mexico, Federated States of Micronesia, Moldova, Monaco, Mongolia, Morocco, Mozambique, Namibia, Nauru, Nepal, Netherlands, NZ, Nicaragua, Niger, Nigeria, Norway, Oman, Palau, Pakistan, Panama, Papua New Guinea, Paraguay, Peru, Philippines, Poland, Portugal, Qatar, Romania, Russia, Rwanda, Saint Lucia, Saint Vincent and the Grenadines, Samoa, San Marino, Sao Tome and Principe, Saudi Arabia, Senegal, Seychelles, Sierra Leone, Singapore, Slovakia, Slovenia, Solomon Islands, Somalia, South Africa, Spain, Sri Lanka, Sudan, Suriname, Swaziland, Sweden, Switzerland, Syria, Tajikistan, Tanzania, Thailand, Togo, Tonga, Trinidad and Tobago, Tunisia, Turkey, Turkmenistan, Uganda, Ukraine, UAE, UK, US, Uruguay, Uzbekistan, Vanuatu, Venezuela, Vietnam, Yemen, Zambia, Zimbabwe

International Committee of the Red Cross (ICRC)

address—ICRC, 19 Avenue de la Paix, CH-1202 Geneva, Switzerland
telephone—[41] (22) 734 60 01
FAX—[41] (22) 733 20 57
established—NA 1863
aim—to provide humanitarian aid in wartime

members—(25 individuals) all Swiss nationals

International Confederation of Free Trade Unions (ICFTU)

address—International Trade Union House, Boulevard Emile Jacqmain 155, B-1210 Brussels, Belgium
telephone—[32] (2) 224 02 11
FAX—[32] (2) 201 58 15, 203 07 56
established—NA December 1949
aim—to promote the trade union movement

members—(206 affiliated organizations in the following 141 countries) Algeria, Antigua and Barbuda, Argentina, Australia, Austria, The Bahamas, Bangladesh, Barbados, Basque Country, Belgium, Belize, Benin, Bermuda, Botswana, Brazil, Bulgaria, Burkina Faso, Cameroon, Canada, Cape Verde, Central African Republic, Chad, Chile, China, Colombia, Democratic Republic of the Congo, Republic of the Congo, Cook Islands, Costa Rica, Cote d'Ivoire, Croatia, Curacao, Cyprus, Czech Republic, Denmark, Djibouti, Dominica, Dominican Republic, Ecuador, El Salvador, Eritrea, Estonia, Falkland Islands, Fiji, Finland, France, French Polynesia, Gabon, The Gambia, Germany, Ghana, Greece, Grenada, Guatemala, Guinea, Guinea-Bissau, Guyana, Holy See, Honduras, Hong Kong, Hungary, Iceland, India, Indonesia, Ireland, Israel, Italy, Jamaica, Japan, Jordan, Kenya, Kiribati, South Korea, Latvia, Lebanon, Liberia, Lithuania, Luxembourg, Madagascar, Malawi, Malaysia, Mali, Malta, Mauritius, Mexico, Moldova, Mongolia, Montserrat, Morocco, Mozambique, Nepal, Netherlands, New Caledonia, NZ, Nicaragua, Niger, Norway, Pakistan, Panama, Papua New Guinea, Paraguay, Peru, Philippines, Poland, Portugal, Puerto Rico, Romania, Rwanda, Saint Helena, Saint Kitts and Nevis, Saint Lucia, Saint Vincent and the Grenadines, Samoa, San Marino, Senegal, Serbia and Montenegro, Seychelles, Sierra Leone, Singapore, Slovakia, South Africa, Spain, Sri Lanka, Suriname, Swaziland, Sweden, Switzerland, Tanzania, Thailand, Togo, Tonga, Trinidad and Tobago, Tunisia, Turkey, Uganda, UK, US, Vanuatu, Venezuela, Zambia, Zimbabwe

International Court of Justice (ICJ)

note—also known as the World Court
address—Peace Palace, NL-2517 KJ The Hague, Netherlands
telephone—[31] (70) 302 23 23
FAX—[31] (70) 364 99 28
established—26 June 1945
effective—24 October 1945
aim—primary judicial organ of the UN

members—(15 judges) elected by the UN General Assembly and Security Council to represent all principal legal systems

Appendix C: International Organizations and Groups (continued)

International Criminal Police Organization (Interpol)

address—BP 6041, F-69411 Lyon CEDEX 06, France
telephone—[33] (4) 72 44 70 00
FAX—[33] (4) 72 44 71 63
established—13 June 1956
aim—to promote international cooperation among police authorities in fighting crime

members—(177) Albania, Algeria, Andorra, Angola, Antigua and Barbuda, Argentina, Armenia, Aruba, Australia, Austria, Azerbaijan, The Bahamas, Bahrain, Bangladesh, Barbados, Belarus, Belgium, Belize, Benin, Bolivia, Bosnia and Herzegovina, Botswana, Brazil, Brunei, Bulgaria, Burkina Faso, Burma, Burundi, Cambodia, Cameroon, Canada, Cape Verde, Central African Republic, Chad, Chile, China, Colombia, Democratic Republic of the Congo, Republic of the Congo, Costa Rica, Cote d'Ivoire, Croatia, Cuba, Cyprus, Czech Republic, Denmark, Djibouti, Dominica, Dominican Republic, Ecuador, Egypt, El Salvador, Equatorial Guinea, Estonia, Ethiopia, Fiji, Finland, France, Gabon, The Gambia, Georgia, Germany, Ghana, Greece, Grenada, Guatemala, Guinea, Guinea-Bissau, Guyana, Haiti, Honduras, Hungary, Iceland, India, Indonesia, Iran, Iraq, Ireland, Israel, Italy, Jamaica, Japan, Jordan, Kazakhstan, Kenya, Kiribati, South Korea, Kuwait, Kyrgyzstan, Laos, Latvia, Lebanon, Lesotho, Liberia, Libya, Liechtenstein, Lithuania, Luxembourg, The Former Yugoslav Republic of Macedonia, Madagascar, Malawi, Malaysia, Maldives, Mali, Malta, Marshall Islands, Mauritania, Mauritius, Mexico, Moldova, Monaco, Mongolia, Morocco, Mozambique, Namibia, Nauru, Nepal, Netherlands, Netherlands Antilles, NZ, Nicaragua, Niger, Nigeria, Norway, Oman, Pakistan, Panama, Papua New Guinea, Paraguay, Peru, Philippines, Poland, Portugal, Qatar, Romania, Russia, Rwanda, Saint Kitts and Nevis, Saint Lucia, Saint Vincent and the Grenadines, Sao Tome and Principe, Saudi Arabia, Senegal, Seychelles, Sierra Leone, Singapore, Slovakia, Slovenia, Somalia, South Africa, Spain, Sri Lanka, Sudan, Suriname, Swaziland, Sweden, Switzerland, Syria, Tanzania, Thailand, Togo, Tonga, Trinidad and Tobago, Tunisia, Turkey, Uganda, Ukraine, UAE, UK, US, Uruguay, Uzbekistan, Venezuela, Vietnam, Yemen, Zambia, Zimbabwe

subbureaus—(14) American Samoa, Anguilla, Bermuda, British Virgin Islands, Cayman Islands, Gibraltar, Guam, Hong Kong, Macau, Montserrat, Northern Mariana Islands, Puerto Rico, Turks and Caicos Islands, Virgin Islands

International Development Association (IDA)

address—1818 H Street NW, Washington, DC 20433, US
telephone—[1] (202) 477 1234
FAX—[1] (202) 477 6391
established—26 January 1960
effective—24 September 1960
aim—UN specialized agency and IBRD affiliate that provides economic loans for low income countries

members—(160)
Part I—(26 developed countries) Australia, Austria, Belgium, Canada, Denmark, Finland, France, Germany, Iceland, Ireland, Italy, Japan, Kuwait, Luxembourg, Netherlands, NZ, Norway, Portugal, Russia, South Africa, Spain, Sweden, Switzerland, UAE, UK, US
Part II—(134 less developed countries) Afghanistan, Albania, Algeria, Angola, Argentina, Armenia, Azerbaijan, Bangladesh, Belize, Benin, Bhutan, Bolivia, Bosnia and Herzegovina, Botswana, Brazil, Burkina Faso, Burma, Burundi, Cambodia, Cameroon, Cape Verde, Central African Republic, Chad, Chile, China, Colombia, Comoros, Democratic Republic of the Congo, Republic of the Congo, Costa Rica, Cote d'Ivoire, Croatia, Cyprus, Czech Republic, Djibouti, Dominica, Dominican Republic, Ecuador, Egypt, El Salvador, Equatorial Guinea, Eritrea, Ethiopia, Fiji, Gabon, The Gambia, Georgia, Ghana, Greece, Grenada, Guatemala, Guinea, Guinea-Bissau, Guyana, Haiti, Honduras, Hungary, India, Indonesia, Iran, Iraq, Israel, Jordan, Kazakhstan, Kenya, Kiribati, South Korea, Kyrgyzstan, Laos, Latvia, Lebanon, Lesotho, Liberia, Libya, The Former Yugoslav Republic of Macedonia, Madagascar, Malawi, Malaysia, Maldives, Mali, Marshall Islands, Mauritania, Mauritius, Mexico, Federated States of Micronesia, Moldova, Mongolia, Morocco, Mozambique, Nepal, Nicaragua, Niger, Nigeria, Oman, Pakistan, Palau, Panama, Papua New Guinea, Paraguay, Peru, Philippines, Poland, Rwanda, Saint Kitts and Nevis, Saint Lucia, Saint Vincent and the Grenadines, Samoa, Sao Tome and Principe, Saudi Arabia, Senegal, Sierra Leone, Slovakia, Slovenia, Solomon Islands, Somalia, Sri Lanka, Sudan, Swaziland, Syria, Tajikistan, Tanzania, Thailand, Togo, Tonga, Trinidad and Tobago, Tunisia, Turkey, Uganda, Uzbekistan, Vanuatu, Vietnam, Yemen, Zambia, Zimbabwe

International Energy Agency (IEA)

address—2 Rue Andre Pascal, F-75775 Paris CEDEX 16, France
telephone—[33] (1) 45 24 82 00
FAX—[33] (1) 45 24 99 88
established—15 November 1974
aim—to promote cooperation on energy matters, especially emergency oil sharing and relations between oil consumers and oil producers; established by the OECD

members—(24) Australia, Austria, Belgium, Canada, Denmark, Finland, France, Germany, Greece, Hungary, Ireland, Italy, Japan, Luxembourg, Netherlands, NZ, Norway, Portugal, Spain, Sweden, Switzerland, Turkey, UK, US
observers—(16) Commission of the European Communities, Czech Republic, Iceland, South Korea, Mexico, Poland

Appendix C: International Organizations and Groups (continued)

International Federation of Red Cross and Red Crescent Societies (IFRCS)

note—formerly known as League of Red Cross and Red Crescent Societies (LORCS)
address—Chemin des Crets 17, CP 372, Petit-Saconnex, CH-1211 Geneva 19, Switzerland
telephone—[41] (22) 730 4222
FAX—[41] (22) 733 0395
established—5 May 1919
aim—to organize, coordinate, and direct international relief actions; to promote humanitarian activities; to represent and encourage the development of National Societies; to bring help to victims of armed conflicts, refugees, and displaced people; to reduce the vulnerability of people through development programs

members—(175) Afghanistan, Albania, Algeria, Andorra, Angola, Antigua and Barbuda, Argentina, Armenia, Australia, Austria, Azerbaijan, The Bahamas, Bahrain, Bangladesh, Barbados, Belarus, Belgium, Belize, Benin, Bolivia, Botswana, Brazil, Brunei, Bulgaria, Burkina Faso, Burma, Burundi, Cambodia, Cameroon, Canada, Cape Verde, Central African Republic, Chad, Chile, China, Colombia, Democratic Republic of the Congo, Republic of the Congo, Costa Rica, Cote d'Ivoire, Croatia, Cuba, Czech Republic, Denmark, Djibouti, Dominica, Dominican Republic, Ecuador, Egypt, El Salvador, Equatorial Guinea, Estonia, Ethiopia, Fiji, Finland, France, The Gambia, Georgia, Germany, Ghana, Greece, Grenada, Guatemala, Guinea, Guinea-Bissau, Guyana, Haiti, Honduras, Hungary, Iceland, India, Indonesia, Iran, Iraq, Ireland, Italy, Jamaica, Japan, Jordan, Kenya, Kiribati, North Korea, South Korea, Kuwait, Kyrgyzstan, Laos, Latvia, Lebanon, Lesotho, Liberia, Libya, Liechtenstein, Lithuania, Luxembourg, The Former Yugoslav Republic of Macedonia, Madagascar, Malawi, Malaysia, Mali, Malta, Mauritania, Mauritius, Mexico, Monaco, Mongolia, Morocco, Mozambique, Namibia, Nepal, Netherlands, NZ, Nicaragua, Niger, Nigeria, Norway, Pakistan, Palau, Panama, Papua New Guinea, Paraguay, Peru, Philippines, Poland, Portugal, Qatar, Romania, Russia, Rwanda, Saint Kitts and Nevis, Saint Lucia, Saint Vincent and the Grenadines, Samoa, San Marino, Sao Tome and Principe, Saudi Arabia, Senegal, Seychelles, Sierra Leone, Singapore, Slovakia, Slovenia, Solomon Islands, Somalia, South Africa, Spain, Sri Lanka, Sudan, Suriname, Swaziland, Sweden, Switzerland, Syria, Tajikistan, Tanzania, Thailand, Togo, Tonga, Trinidad and Tobago, Tunisia, Turkey, Turkmenistan, Uganda, Ukraine, UAE, UK, US, Uruguay, Uzbekistan, Vanuatu, Venezuela, Vietnam, Yemen, Yugoslavia, Zambia, Zimbabwe
associate members—(4) Comoros, Cyprus, Gabon, Tuvalu

International Finance Corporation (IFC)

address—2121 Pennsylvania Avenue NW, Washington, DC 20433, US
telephone—[1] (202) 473 0631, 477 1234
FAX—[1] (202) 974 4384, 477 6391
established—25 May 1955
effective—20 July 1956
aim—to support private enterprise in international economic development; a UN specialized agency and IBRD affiliate

members—(174) Afghanistan, Albania, Algeria, Angola, Antigua and Barbuda, Argentina, Armenia, Australia, Austria, Azerbaijan, The Bahamas, Bahrain, Bangladesh, Barbados, Belarus, Belgium, Belize, Benin, Bolivia, Bosnia and Herzegovina, Botswana, Brazil, Bulgaria, Burkina Faso, Burma, Burundi, Cambodia, Cameroon, Canada, Cape Verde, Central African Republic, Chad, Chile, China, Colombia, Comoros, Democratic Republic of the Congo, Republic of the Congo, Costa Rica, Cote d'Ivoire, Croatia, Cyprus, Czech Republic, Denmark, Djibouti, Dominica, Dominican Republic, Ecuador, Egypt, El Salvador, Equatorial Guinea, Eritrea, Estonia, Ethiopia, Fiji, Finland, France, Gabon, The Gambia, Georgia, Germany, Ghana, Greece, Grenada, Guatemala, Guinea, Guinea-Bissau, Guyana, Haiti, Honduras, Hungary, Iceland, India, Indonesia, Iran, Iraq, Ireland, Israel, Italy, Jamaica, Japan, Jordan, Kazakhstan, Kenya, Kiribati, South Korea, Kuwait, Kyrgyzstan, Laos, Latvia, Lebanon, Lesotho, Liberia, Libya, Lithuania, Luxembourg, The Former Yugoslav Republic of Macedonia, Madagascar, Malawi, Malaysia, Maldives, Mali, Marshall Islands, Mauritania, Mauritius, Mexico, Federated States of Micronesia, Moldova, Mongolia, Morocco, Mozambique, Namibia, Nepal, Netherlands, NZ, Nicaragua, Niger, Nigeria, Norway, Oman, Pakistan, Palau, Panama, Papua New Guinea, Paraguay, Peru, Philippines, Poland, Portugal, Romania, Russia, Rwanda, Saint Kitts and Nevis, Saint Lucia, Samoa, Saudi Arabia, Senegal, Seychelles, Sierra Leone, Singapore, Slovakia, Slovenia, Solomon Islands, Somalia, South Africa, Spain, Sri Lanka, Sudan, Swaziland, Sweden, Switzerland, Syria, Tajikistan, Tanzania, Thailand, Togo, Tonga, Trinidad and Tobago, Tunisia, Turkey, Turkmenistan, Uganda, Ukraine, UAE, UK, US, Uruguay, Uzbekistan, Vanuatu, Venezuela, Vietnam, Yemen, Zambia, Zimbabwe

International Fund for Agricultural Development (IFAD)

address—Via del Serafico 107, I-00142 Rome, Italy
telephone—[39] (6) 54591
FAX—[39] (6) 5043463
established—NA November 1974
aim—to promote agricultural development; a UN specialized agency

members—(160)
Category I—(22 industrialized aid contributors) Australia, Austria, Belgium, Canada, Denmark, Finland, France, Germany, Greece, Ireland, Italy, Japan, Luxembourg, Netherlands, NZ, Norway, Portugal, Spain, Sweden, Switzerland, UK, US
Category II—(12 petroleum-exporting aid contributors) Algeria, Gabon, Indonesia, Iran, Iraq, Kuwait, Libya, Nigeria, Qatar, Saudi Arabia, UAE, Venezuela
Category III—(126 aid recipients) Afghanistan, Albania, Angola, Antigua and Barbuda, Argentina, Armenia, Azerbaijan, Bangladesh, Barbados, Belize, Benin, Bhutan, Bolivia, Bosnia and Herzegovina, Botswana, Brazil, Burkina Faso, Burma, Burundi, Cambodia, Cameroon, Cape Verde, Central African Republic, Chad, Chile, China, Colombia, Comoros, Democratic Republic of the Congo, Republic of the Congo, Cook Islands, Costa Rica, Cote d'Ivoire, Croatia, Cuba, Cyprus, Djibouti, Dominica, Dominican Republic, Ecuador, Egypt, El Salvador, Equatorial Guinea, Eritrea, Ethiopia, Fiji, The Gambia, Georgia, Ghana, Grenada, Guatemala, Guinea, Guinea-Bissau, Guyana, Haiti, Honduras, India, Israel, Jamaica, Jordan, Kenya, North Korea, South Korea, Kyrgyzstan, Laos, Lebanon, Lesotho, Liberia, The Former Yugoslav Republic of Macedonia, Madagascar, Malawi, Malaysia, Maldives, Mali, Malta, Mauritania, Mauritius, Mexico, Moldova, Mongolia, Morocco, Mozambique, Namibia, Nepal, Nicaragua, Niger, Oman, Pakistan, Panama, Papua New Guinea, Paraguay, Peru, Philippines, Romania, Rwanda, Saint Kitts and Nevis, Saint Lucia, Saint Vincent and the Grenadines, Samoa, Sao Tome and Principe, Senegal, Seychelles, Sierra Leone, Solomon Islands, Somalia, South Africa, Sri Lanka, Sudan, Suriname, Swaziland, Syria, Tajikistan, Tanzania, Thailand, Togo, Tonga, Trinidad and Tobago, Tunisia, Turkey, Uganda, Uruguay, Vietnam, Yemen, Yugoslavia (suspended), Zambia, Zimbabwe

International Hydrographic Organization (IHO)

note—name changed from International Hydrographic Bureau on 22 September 1970
address—BP 445, 4 Quai Antoine 1st, Monaco MC 98011, CEDEX, Monaco
telephone—[33] (93) 01 81 00
FAX—[33] (93) 10 81 40
established—NA June 1919
effective—NA June 1921
aim—to train hydrographic surveyors and nautical cartographers to achieve standardization in nautical charts and electronic chart displays; to provide advice on nautical cartography and hydrography; to develop the sciences in the field of hydrography and techniques used for descriptive oceanography

members—(64) Algeria, Argentina, Australia, Bahrain, Belgium, Brazil, Canada, Chile, China, Democratic Republic of the Congo, Croatia, Cuba, Cyprus, Denmark, Dominican Republic, Ecuador, Egypt, Estonia, Fiji, Finland, France, Germany, Greece, Guatemala, Iceland, India, Indonesia, Iran, Italy, Japan, North Korea, South Korea, Malaysia, Monaco, Netherlands, NZ, Nigeria, Norway, Oman, Pakistan, Papua New Guinea, Peru, Philippines, Poland, Portugal, Russia, Singapore, South Africa, Spain, Sri Lanka, Suriname, Sweden, Syria, Thailand, Tonga, Trinidad and Tobago, Tunisia, Turkey, UAE, UK, US, Uruguay, Venezuela, Yugoslavia
membership pending—(10) Bangladesh, Bulgaria, Colombia, Jamaica, Kuwait, Mauritania, Morocco, Mozambique, Qatar, Ukraine

International Investment Bank (IIB)

established on 7 July 1970; to promote economic development; members were Bulgaria, Cuba, Czechoslovakia, East Germany, Hungary, Mongolia, Poland, Romania, USSR, Vietnam; now it is a Russian bank with a new charter

International Labor Organization (ILO)

address—International Labor Office, 4 route des Morillons, CH-1211 Geneva 22, Switzerland
telephone—[41] (22) 799 61 11
FAX—[41] (22) 798 86 85
established—11 April 1919 (affiliated with the UN 14 December 1946)
aim—to deal with world labor issues; a UN specialized agency

members—(174) Afghanistan, Albania, Algeria, Angola, Antigua and Barbuda, Argentina, Armenia, Australia, Austria, Azerbaijan, The Bahamas, Bahrain, Bangladesh, Barbados, Belarus, Belgium, Belize, Benin, Bolivia, Bosnia and Herzegovina, Botswana, Brazil, Bulgaria, Burkina Faso, Burma, Burundi, Cambodia, Cameroon, Canada, Cape Verde, Central African Republic, Chad, Chile, China, Colombia, Comoros, Democratic Republic of the Congo, Republic of the Congo, Costa Rica, Cote d'Ivoire, Croatia, Cuba, Cyprus, Czech Republic, Denmark, Djibouti, Dominica, Dominican Republic, Ecuador, Egypt, El Salvador, Equatorial Guinea, Eritrea, Estonia, Ethiopia, Fiji, Finland, France, Gabon, The Gambia, Georgia, Germany, Ghana, Greece, Grenada, Guatemala, Guinea, Guinea-Bissau, Guyana, Haiti, Honduras, Hungary, Iceland, India, Indonesia, Iran, Iraq, Ireland, Israel, Italy, Jamaica, Japan, Jordan, Kazakhstan, Kenya, South Korea, Kuwait, Kyrgyzstan, Laos, Latvia, Lebanon, Lesotho, Liberia, Libya, Lithuania, Luxembourg, The Former Yugoslav Republic of Macedonia, Madagascar, Malawi, Malaysia, Mali, Malta, Mauritania, Mauritius, Mexico, Moldova, Mongolia, Morocco, Mozambique, Namibia, Nepal, Netherlands, NZ, Nicaragua, Niger, Nigeria, Norway, Oman, Pakistan, Panama, Papua New Guinea, Paraguay, Peru, Philippines, Poland, Portugal, Qatar, Romania, Russia, Rwanda, Saint Kitts and Nevis, Saint Lucia, Saint Vincent and the Grenadines, San Marino, Sao Tome and Principe, Saudi Arabia, Senegal, Seychelles, Sierra Leone, Singapore, Slovakia, Slovenia, Solomon Islands, Somalia, South Africa, Spain, Sri Lanka, Sudan, Suriname, Swaziland, Sweden, Switzerland, Syria, Tajikistan, Tanzania, Thailand, Togo, Trinidad and Tobago, Tunisia, Turkey, Turkmenistan, Uganda, Ukraine, UAE, UK, US, Uruguay, Uzbekistan, Venezuela, Vietnam, Yemen, Yugoslavia (suspended), Zambia, Zimbabwe

International Maritime Organization (IMO)

note—name changed from Intergovernmental Maritime Consultative Organization (IMCO) on 22 May 1982
address—4 Albert Embankment, London SE1 7SR, UK
telephone—[44] (171) 735 7611
FAX—[44] (171) 587 3210
established—17 March 1958
aim—to deal with international maritime affairs; a UN specialized agency

members—(155) Albania, Algeria, Angola, Antigua and Barbuda, Argentina, Australia, Austria, Azerbaijan, The Bahamas, Bahrain, Bangladesh, Barbados, Belgium, Belize, Benin, Bolivia, Bosnia and Herzegovina, Brazil, Brunei, Bulgaria, Burma, Cambodia, Cameroon, Canada, Cape Verde, Chile, China, Colombia, Democratic Republic of the Congo, Republic of the Congo, Costa Rica, Cote d'Ivoire, Croatia, Cuba, Cyprus, Czech Republic, Denmark, Djibouti, Dominica, Dominican Republic, Ecuador, Egypt, El Salvador, Equatorial Guinea, Eritrea, Estonia, Ethiopia, Fiji, Finland, France, Gabon, The Gambia, Georgia, Germany, Ghana, Greece, Guatemala, Guinea, Guinea-Bissau, Guyana, Haiti, Honduras, Hungary, Iceland, India, Indonesia, Iran, Iraq, Ireland, Israel, Italy, Jamaica, Japan, Jordan, Kazakhstan, Kenya, North Korea, South Korea, Kuwait, Latvia, Lebanon, Liberia, Libya, Lithuania, Luxembourg, The Former Yugoslav Republic of Macedonia, Madagascar, Malawi, Malaysia, Maldives, Malta, Mauritania, Mauritius, Mexico, Monaco, Mongolia, Morocco, Mozambique, Namibia, Nepal, Netherlands, NZ, Nicaragua, Nigeria, Norway, Oman, Pakistan, Panama, Papua New Guinea, Paraguay, Peru, Philippines, Poland, Portugal, Qatar, Romania, Russia, Saint Lucia, Saint Vincent and the Grenadines, Samoa, Sao Tome and Principe, Saudi Arabia, Senegal, Seychelles, Sierra Leone, Singapore, Slovakia, Slovenia, Solomon Islands, Somalia, South Africa, Spain, Sri Lanka, Sudan, Suriname, Sweden, Switzerland, Syria, Tanzania, Thailand, Togo, Trinidad and Tobago, Tunisia, Turkey, Turkmenistan, Ukraine, UAE, UK, US, Uruguay, Vanuatu, Venezuela, Vietnam, Yemen, Yugoslavia (suspended)
associate members—(2) Hong Kong, Macau

International Maritime Satellite Organization (Inmarsat)

see International Mobile Satellite Organization (Inmarsat)

Appendix C: International Organizations and Groups (continued)

International Mobile Satellite Organization (Inmarsat)

note—formerly International Maritime Satellite Organization
address—99 City Road, London EC1Y 1AX, UK
telephone—[44] (171) 728 1212
FAX—[44] (171) 728 1602
established—3 September 1976
effective—26 July 1979
aim—to provide worldwide communications for commercial, distress, and safety applications, at sea, in the air, and on land

members—(81) Algeria, Argentina, Australia, The Bahamas, Bahrain, Bangladesh, Belarus, Belgium, Brazil, Brunei, Bulgaria, Cameroon, Canada, Chile, China, Colombia, Costa Rica, Croatia, Cuba, Cyprus, Czech Republic, Denmark, Egypt, Finland, France, Gabon, Georgia, Germany, Ghana, Greece, Hungary, Iceland, India, Indonesia, Iran, Iraq, Israel, Italy, Japan, South Korea, Kuwait, Lebanon, Liberia, Malaysia, Malta, Marshall Islands, Mauritius, Mexico, Monaco, Mozambique, Netherlands, NZ, Nigeria, Norway, Oman, Pakistan, Panama, Peru, Philippines, Poland, Portugal, Qatar, Romania, Russia, Saudi Arabia, Senegal, Singapore, Slovakia, South Africa, Spain, Sri Lanka, Sweden, Switzerland, Thailand, Tunisia, Turkey, Ukraine, UAE, UK, US, Yugoslavia

International Monetary Fund (IMF)

address—700 19th Street NW, Washington, DC 20431, US
telephone—[1] (202) 623 7000
FAX—[1] (202) 623 4661, 623 7491, 623 4662
established—22 July 1944
effective—27 December 1945
aim—to promote world monetary stability and economic development; a UN specialized agency

members—(182) Afghanistan, Albania, Algeria, Angola, Antigua and Barbuda, Argentina, Armenia, Australia, Austria, Azerbaijan, The Bahamas, Bahrain, Bangladesh, Barbados, Belarus, Belgium, Belize, Benin, Bhutan, Bolivia, Bosnia and Herzegovina, Botswana, Brazil, Brunei, Bulgaria, Burkina Faso, Burma, Burundi, Cambodia, Cameroon, Canada, Cape Verde, Central African Republic, Chad, Chile, China, Colombia, Comoros, Democratic Republic of the Congo, Republic of the Congo, Costa Rica, Cote d'Ivoire, Croatia, Cyprus, Czech Republic, Denmark, Djibouti, Dominica, Dominican Republic, Ecuador, Egypt, El Salvador, Equatorial Guinea, Eritrea, Estonia, Ethiopia, Fiji, Finland, France, Gabon, The Gambia, Georgia, Germany, Ghana, Greece, Grenada, Guatemala, Guinea, Guinea-Bissau, Guyana, Haiti, Honduras, Hungary, Iceland, India, Indonesia, Iran, Iraq, Ireland, Israel, Italy, Jamaica, Japan, Jordan, Kazakhstan, Kenya, Kiribati, South Korea, Kuwait, Kyrgyzstan, Laos, Latvia, Lebanon, Lesotho, Liberia, Libya, Lithuania, Luxembourg, The Former Yugoslav Republic of Macedonia, Madagascar, Malawi, Malaysia, Maldives, Mali, Malta, Marshall Islands, Mauritania, Mauritius, Mexico, Federated States of Micronesia, Moldova, Mongolia, Morocco, Mozambique, Namibia, Nepal, Netherlands, NZ, Nicaragua, Niger, Nigeria, Norway, Oman, Pakistan, Palua, Panama, Papua New Guinea, Paraguay, Peru, Philippines, Poland, Portugal, Qatar, Romania, Russia, Rwanda, Saint Kitts and Nevis, Saint Lucia, Saint Vincent and the Grenadines, Samoa, San Marino, Sao Tome and Principe, Saudi Arabia, Senegal, Seychelles, Sierra Leone, Singapore, Slovakia, Slovenia, Solomon Islands, Somalia, South Africa, Spain, Sri Lanka, Sudan, Suriname, Swaziland, Sweden, Switzerland, Syria, Tajikistan, Tanzania, Thailand, Togo, Tonga, Trinidad and Tobago, Tunisia, Turkey, Turkmenistan, Uganda, Ukraine, UAE, UK, US, Uruguay, Uzbekistan, Vanuatu, Venezuela, Vietnam, Yemen, Zambia, Zimbabwe

International Olympic Committee (IOC)

note—there are 194 National Olympic Committees of which 185 are recognized by the International Olympic Committee
address—Chateau de Vidy, CH-1007 Lausanne, Switzerland
telephone—[41] (21) 621 61 11
FAX—[41] (21) 621 62 16
established—23 June 1894
aim—to promote the Olympic ideals and administer the Olympic games: 2000 Summer Olympics in Sydney, Australia; 2002 Winter Olympics in Salt Lake City, United States; 2004 Summer Olympics in Athens, Greece

National Olympic Committees—(196 and the Palestine Liberation Organization) Afghanistan, Albania, Algeria, American Samoa, Andorra, Angola, Antigua and Barbuda, Argentina, Armenia, Aruba, Australia, Austria, Azerbaijan, The Bahamas, Bahrain, Bangladesh, Barbados, Belarus, Belgium, Belize, Benin, Bermuda, Bhutan, Bolivia, Bosnia and Herzegovina, Botswana, Brazil, British Virgin Islands, Brunei, Bulgaria, Burkina Faso, Burma, Burundi, Cambodia, Cameroon, Canada, Cape Verde, Cayman Islands, Central African Republic, Chad, Chile, China, Colombia, Comoros, Democratic Republic of the Congo, Republic of the Congo, Cook Islands, Costa Rica, Cote d'Ivoire, Croatia, Cuba, Cyprus, Czech Republic, Denmark, Djibouti, Dominica, Dominican Republic, Ecuador, Egypt, El Salvador, Equatorial Guinea, Estonia, Ethiopia, Fiji, Finland, France, Gabon, The Gambia, Georgia, Germany, Ghana, Greece, Grenada, Guam, Guatemala, Guinea, Guinea-Bissau, Guyana, Haiti, Honduras, Hong Kong, Hungary, Iceland, India, Indonesia, Iran, Iraq, Ireland, Israel, Italy, Jamaica, Japan, Jordan, Kazakhstan, Kenya, North Korea, South Korea, Kuwait, Kyrgyzstan, Laos, Latvia, Lebanon, Lesotho, Liberia, Libya, Liechtenstein, Lithuania, Luxembourg, The Former Yugoslav Republic of Macedonia, Madagascar, Malawi, Malaysia, Maldives, Mali, Malta, Mauritania, Mauritius, Mexico, Moldova, Monaco, Mongolia, Morocco, Mozambique, Namibia, Nauru, Nepal, Netherlands, Netherlands Antilles, NZ, Nicaragua, Niger, Nigeria, Norway, Oman, Pakistan, Panama, Papua New Guinea, Paraguay, Peru, Philippines, Poland, Portugal, Puerto Rico, Qatar, Romania, Russia, Rwanda, Saint Kitts and Nevis, Saint Lucia, Saint Vincent and the Grenadines, Samoa, San Marino, Sao Tome and Principe, Saudi Arabia, Senegal, Seychelles, Sierra Leone, Singapore, Slovakia, Slovenia, Solomon Islands, Somalia, South Africa, Spain, Sri Lanka, Sudan, Suriname, Swaziland, Sweden, Switzerland, Syria, Taiwan, Tajikistan, Tanzania, Thailand, Togo, Tonga, Trinidad and Tobago, Tunisia, Turkey, Turkmenistan, Uganda, Ukraine, UAE, UK, US, Uruguay, Uzbekistan, Vanuatu, Venezuela, Vietnam, Virgin Islands, Yemen, Yugoslavia (Serbia and Montenegro), Zambia, Zimbabwe, Palestine Liberation Organization

Appendix C: International Organizations and Groups (continued)

International Organization for Migration (IOM)

note—established as Provisional Intergovernmental Committee for the Movement of Migrants from Europe; renamed Intergovernmental Committee for European Migration (ICEM) on 15 November 1952; renamed Intergovernmental Committee for Migration (ICM) in November 1980; current name adopted 14 November 1989
address—17 route des Morillons, CP 71, CH-1211 Geneva 19, Switzerland
telephone—[41] (22) 717 91 11
FAX—[41] (22) 798 61 50
established—5 December 1951
aim—to facilitate orderly international emigration and immigration

members—(60) Albania, Angola, Argentina, Armenia, Australia, Austria, Bangladesh, Belgium, Bolivia, Bulgaria, Canada, Chile, Colombia, Costa Rica, Croatia, Cyprus, Czech Republic, Denmark, Dominican Republic, Ecuador, Egypt, El Salvador, Finland, France, Germany, Greece, Guatemala, Haiti, Honduras, Hungary, Israel, Italy, Japan, Kenya, South Korea, Liberia, Luxembourg, Netherlands, Nicaragua, Norway, Pakistan, Panama, Paraguay, Peru, Philippines, Poland, Portugal, Senegal, Slovakia, South Africa, Sri Lanka, Sweden, Switzerland, Tajikistan, Thailand, Uganda, US, Uruguay, Venezuela, Zambia
observers—(49) Afghanistan, Belarus, Belize, Bosnia and Herzegovina, Brazil, Cape Verde, Democratic Republic of the Congo, Cuba, Georgia, Ghana, Guinea, Guinea-Bissau, Holy See, India, Indonesia, Iran, Ireland, Jamaica, Jordan, Kazakhstan, Kyrgyzstan, Latvia, Lithuania, Madagascar, Malta, Mexico, Moldova, Morocco, Mozambique, Namibia, NZ, Romania, Russia, Rwanda, San Marino, Sao Tome and Principe, Slovenia, Somalia, Spain, Sudan, Tanzania, Tunisia, Turkey, Turkmenistan, Ukraine, UK, Vietnam, Yugoslavia, Zimbabwe

International Organization for Standardization (ISO)

address—CP 56, 1 Rue de Varembe, CH-1211 Geneva 20, Switzerland
telephone—[41] (22) 749 01 11
FAX—[41] (22) 733 34 30
established—NA February 1947
aim—to promote the development of international standards with a view to facilitating international exchange of goods and services and to developing cooperation in the sphere of intellectual, scientific, technological and economic activity

members—(85 national standards organizations) Albania, Algeria, Argentina, Armenia, Australia, Austria, Bangladesh, Belarus, Belgium, Bosnia and Herzegovina, Brazil, Bulgaria, Canada, Chile, China, Colombia, Costa Rica, Croatia, Cuba, Cyprus, Czech Republic, Denmark, Ecuador, Egypt, Ethiopia, Finland, France, Germany, Ghana, Greece, Hungary, Iceland, India, Indonesia, Iran, Ireland, Israel, Italy, Jamaica, Japan, Kenya, North Korea, South Korea, Libya, The Former Yugoslav Republic of Macedonia, Malaysia, Mauritius, Mexico, Mongolia, Morocco, Netherlands, NZ, Nigeria, Norway, Pakistan, Panama, Philippines, Poland, Portugal, Romania, Russia, Saudi Arabia, Singapore, Slovakia, Slovenia, South Africa, Spain, Sri Lanka, Sweden, Switzerland, Syria, Tanzania, Thailand, Trinidad and Tobago, Tunisia, Turkey, Ukraine, UK, US, Uruguay, Uzbekistan, Venezuela, Vietnam, Yugoslavia, Zimbabwe
correspondent members—(32) Bahrain, Barbados, Bolivia, Botswana, Brunei, Cote d'Ivoire, El Salvador, Estonia, Georgia, Guatemala, Guinea, Hong Kong, Jordan, Kuwait, Kyrgyzstan, Latvia, Lebanon, Lithuania, Malawi, Malta, Moldova, Mozambique, Nepal, Oman, Papua New Guinea, Paraguay, Peru, Qatar, Sudan, Turkmenistan, Uganda, UAE
subscriber members—(10) Antigua and Barbuda, Benin, Bolivia, Cambodia, Dominican Republic, Fiji, Grenada, Guyana, Namibia, Saint Lucia

International Red Cross and Red Crescent Movement (ICRM)

address—CICR, 19 Avenue de la Paix, CH-1202 Geneva, Switzerland
telephone—[41] (22) 734 60 01
FAX—[41] (22) 733 20 57
established—NA 1928
aim—to promote worldwide humanitarian aid through the International Committee of the Red Cross (ICRC) in wartime, and International Federation of Red Cross and Red Crescent Societies (IFRCS; formerly League of Red Cross and Red Crescent Societies or LORCS) in peacetime

National Societies—(175 countries) Afghanistan, Albania, Algeria, Andorra, Angola, Antigua and Barbuda, Argentina, Armenia Australia, Austria, Azerbaijan, The Bahamas, Bahrain, Bangladesh, Barbados, Belarus, Belgium, Belize, Benin, Bolivia, Botswana, Brazil, Brunei, Bulgaria, Burkina Faso, Burma, Burundi, Cambodia, Cameroon, Canada, Cape Verde, Central African Republic, Chad, Chile, China, Colombia, Democratic Republic of the Congo, Republic of the Congo, Costa Rica, Cote d'Ivoire, Croatia, Cuba, Czech Republic, Denmark, Djibouti, Dominica, Dominican Republic, Ecuador, Egypt, El Salvador, Equatorial Guinea, Estonia, Ethiopia, Fiji, Finland, France, The Gambia, Germany, Ghana, Greece, Grenada, Guatemala, Guinea, Guinea-Bissau, Guyana, Haiti, Honduras, Hungary, Iceland, India, Indonesia, Iran, Iraq, Ireland, Italy, Jamaica, Japan, Jordan, Kenya, Kiribati, North Korea, South Korea, Kuwait, Kyrgyzstan, Laos, Latvia, Lebanon, Lesotho, Liberia, Libya, Liechtenstein, Lithuania, Luxembourg, The Former Yugoslav Republic of Macedonia, Madagascar, Malawi, Malaysia, Mali, Malta, Mauritania, Mauritius, Mexico, Monaco, Mongolia, Morocco, Mozambique, Namibia, Nepal, Netherlands, NZ, Nicaragua, Niger, Nigeria, Norway, Pakistan, Palau, Panama, Papua New Guinea, Paraguay, Peru, Philippines, Poland, Portugal, Qatar, Romania, Russia, Rwanda, Saint Kitts and Nevis, Saint Lucia, Saint Vincent and the Grenadines, Samoa, San Marino, Sao Tome and Principe, Saudi Arabia, Senegal, Seychelles, Sierra Leone, Singapore, Slovakia, Slovenia, Solomon Islands, Somalia, South Africa, Spain, Sri Lanka, Sudan, Suriname, Swaziland, Sweden, Switzerland, Syria, Tajikistan, Tanzania, Thailand, Togo, Tonga, Trinidad and Tobago, Tunisia, Turkey, Turkmenistan, Uganda, Ukraine, UAE, UK, US, Uruguay, Uzbekistan, Vanuatu, Venezuela, Vietnam, Yemen, Yugoslavia, Zambia, Zimbabwe

Appendix C: International Organizations and Groups (continued)

International Telecommunication Union (ITU)

address—Place des Nations, CH-1211 Geneva 20, Switzerland
telephone—[41] (22) 730 6184
FAX—[41] (22) 733 7256, 730 6614
established—9 December 1932
effective—1 January 1934
affiliated with the UN—15 November 1947
aim—to deal with world telecommunications issues; a UN specialized agency

members—(188) Afghanistan, Albania, Algeria, Andorra, Angola, Antigua and Barbuda, Argentina, Armenia, Australia, Austria, Azerbaijan, The Bahamas, Bahrain, Bangladesh, Barbados, Belarus, Belgium, Belize, Benin, Bhutan, Bolivia, Bosnia and Herzegovina, Botswana, Brazil, Brunei, Bulgaria, Burkina Faso, Burma, Burundi, Cambodia, Cameroon, Canada, Cape Verde, Central African Republic, Chad, Chile, China, Colombia, Comoros, Democratic Republic of the Congo, Republic of the Congo, Costa Rica, Cote d'Ivoire, Croatia, Cuba, Cyprus, Czech Republic, Denmark, Djibouti, Dominica, Dominican Republic, Ecuador, Egypt, El Salvador, Equatorial Guinea, Eritrea, Estonia, Ethiopia, Fiji, Finland, France, Gabon, The Gambia, Georgia, Germany, Ghana, Greece, Grenada, Guatemala, Guinea, Guinea-Bissau, Guyana, Haiti, Holy See, Honduras, Hungary, Iceland, India, Indonesia, Iran, Iraq, Ireland, Israel, Italy, Jamaica, Japan, Jordan, Kazakhstan, Kenya, Kiribati, North Korea, South Korea, Kuwait, Kyrgyzstan, Laos, Latvia, Lebanon, Lesotho, Liberia, Libya, Liechtenstein, Lithuania, Luxembourg, The Former Yugoslav Republic of Macedonia, Madagascar, Malawi, Malaysia, Maldives, Mali, Malta, Marshall Islands, Mauritania, Mauritius, Mexico, Federated States of Micronesia, Moldova, Monaco, Mongolia, Morocco, Mozambique, Namibia, Nauru, Nepal, Netherlands, NZ, Nicaragua, Niger, Nigeria, Norway, Oman, Pakistan, Panama, Papua New Guinea, Paraguay, Peru, Philippines, Poland, Portugal, Qatar, Romania, Russia, Rwanda, Saint Lucia, Saint Vincent and the Grenadines, Samoa, San Marino, Sao Tome and Principe, Saudi Arabia, Senegal, Sierra Leone, Singapore, Slovakia, Slovenia, Solomon Islands, Somalia, South Africa, Spain, Sri Lanka, Sudan, Suriname, Swaziland, Sweden, Switzerland, Syria, Tajikistan, Tanzania, Thailand, Togo, Tonga, Trinidad and Tobago, Tunisia, Turkey, Turkmenistan, Tuvalu, Uganda, Ukraine, UAE, UK, US, Uruguay, Uzbekistan, Vanuatu, Venezuela, Vietnam, Yemen, Yugoslavia (suspended), Zambia, Zimbabwe

International Telecommunications Satellite Organization (Intelsat)

address—Intelsat, 3400 International Drive NW, Washington, DC 20008-3098, US
telephone—[1] (202) 944 7500
FAX—[1] (202) 944 7890
established—20 August 1971
effective—12 February 1973
aim—to develop and operate a global commercial telecommunications satellite system

members—(142) Afghanistan, Algeria, Angola, Argentina, Armenia, Australia, Austria, Azerbaijan, The Bahamas, Bahrain, Bangladesh, Barbados, Belgium, Benin, Bhutan, Bolivia, Bosnia and Herzegovina, Botswana, Brazil, Brunei, Bulgaria, Burkina Faso, Cameroon, Canada, Cape Verde, Central African Republic, Chad, Chile, China, Colombia, Democratic Republic of the Congo, Republic of the Congo, Costa Rica, Cote d'Ivoire, Croatia, Cyprus, Czech Republic, Denmark, Dominican Republic, Ecuador, Egypt, El Salvador, Equatorial Guinea, Ethiopia, Fiji, Finland, France, Gabon, Germany, Ghana, Greece, Guatemala, Guinea, Haiti, Holy See, Honduras, Hungary, Iceland, India, Indonesia, Iran, Iraq, Ireland, Israel, Italy, Jamaica, Japan, Jordan, Kazakhstan, Kenya, South Korea, Kuwait, Kyrgyzstan, Lebanon, Libya, Liechtenstein, Luxembourg, Madagascar, Malawi, Malaysia, Mali, Malta, Mauritania, Mauritius, Mexico, Federated States of Micronesia, Monaco, Mongolia, Morocco, Mozambique, Namibia, Nepal, Netherlands, NZ, Nicaragua, Niger, Nigeria, Norway, Oman, Pakistan, Panama, Papua New Guinea, Paraguay, Peru, Philippines, Poland, Portugal, Qatar, Romania, Russia, Rwanda, Saudi Arabia, Senegal, Singapore, Somalia, South Africa, Spain, Sri Lanka, Sudan, Swaziland, Sweden, Switzerland, Syria, Tajikistan, Tanzania, Thailand, Togo, Trinidad and Tobago, Tunisia, Turkey, Uganda, UAE, UK, US, Uruguay, Uzbekistan, Venezuela, Vietnam, Yemen, Yugoslavia, Zambia, Zimbabwe
nonsignatory users—(43) Albania, Antigua and Barbuda, Belarus, Belize, Burma, Burundi, Cambodia, Comoros, Cook Islands, Cuba, Djibouti, Eritrea, The Gambia, Guinea-Bissau, Guyana, Kiribati, North Korea, Laos, Latvia, Lesotho, Liberia, Lithuania, The Former Yugoslav Republic of Macedonia, Maldives, Marshall Islands, Moldova, Nauru, Niue, Saint Lucia, Saint Vincent and the Grenadines, Samoa, Sao Tome and Principe, Seychelles, Sierra Leone, Slovakia, Slovenia, Solomon Islands, Suriname, Tonga, Turkmenistan, Tuvalu, Ukraine, Vanuatu

Islamic Development Bank (IDB)

address—P.O. Box 5925, Jeddah 21432, Saudi Arabia
telephone—[966] (2) 6361400
FAX—[966] (2) 6366871
established—15 December 1973
aim—to promote Islamic economic aid and social development

members—(48 plus the Palestine Liberation Organization) Afghanistan, Albania, Algeria, Azerbaijan, Bahrain, Bangladesh, Benin, Brunei, Burkina Faso, Cameroon, Chad, Comoros, Djibouti, Egypt, Gabon, The Gambia, Guinea, Guinea-Bissau, Indonesia, Iran, Iraq, Jordan, Kuwait, Kyrgyzstan, Lebanon, Libya, Malaysia, Maldives, Mali, Mauritania, Morocco, Mozambique, Niger, Oman, Pakistan, Qatar, Saudi Arabia, Senegal, Sierra Leone, Somalia, Sudan, Syria, Tunisia, Turkey, Turkmenistan, Uganda, UAE, Yemen, Palestine Liberation Organization

Latin American Economic System (LAES)

note—also known as Sistema Economico Latinoamericana (SELA)
address—SELA, Avda Francisco de Miranda, Torre Europa, Piso 4, Chacaito, Apartado de Correos 17035, Caracas 1010-A, Venezuela
telephone—[58] (2) 905 5111
FAX—[58] (2) 951 6953, 951 7246
established—17 October 1975
aim—to promote economic and social development through regional cooperation

members—(27) Argentina, Barbados, Belize, Bolivia, Brazil, Chile, Colombia, Costa Rica, Cuba, Dominican Republic, Ecuador, El Salvador, Grenada, Guatemala, Guyana, Haiti, Honduras, Jamaica, Mexico, Nicaragua, Panama, Paraguay, Peru, Suriname, Trinidad and Tobago, Uruguay, Venezuela

Latin American Integration Association (LAIA)

note—also known as Asociacion Latinoamericana de Integracion (ALADI)
address—Calle Cebollati 1461, Casilla de Correo 577, 11000 Montevideo, Uruguay
telephone—[598] (2) 400 11 21, 409 59 15
FAX—[598] (2) 409 06 49
established—12 August 1980
effective—18 March 1981
aim—to promote freer regional trade

members—(11) Argentina, Bolivia, Brazil, Chile, Colombia, Cuba, Ecuador, Mexico, Paraguay, Peru, Uruguay, Venezuela
observers—(20) China, Commission of the European Communities, Costa Rica, Dominican Republic, El Salvador, Guatemala, Honduras, Inter-American Development Bank, Italy, Nicaragua, Organization of American States, Panama, Portugal, Romania, Russia, Spain, Switzerland, United Nations Development Program, United Nations Economic Commission for Latin America and the Caribbean

League of Arab States (LAS)

see Arab League (AL)

League of Red Cross and Red Crescent Societies (LORCS)

see International Federation of Red Cross and Red Crescent Societies (IFRCS)

least developed countries (LLDCs)

that subgroup of the less developed countries (LDCs) initially identified by the UN General Assembly in 1971 as having no significant economic growth, per capita GDPs normally less than $1,000, and low literacy rates; also known as the undeveloped countries; the 42 LLDCs are: Afghanistan, Bangladesh, Benin, Bhutan, Botswana, Burkina Faso, Burma, Burundi, Cape Verde, Central African Republic, Chad, Comoros, Djibouti, Equatorial Guinea, Eritrea, Ethiopia, The Gambia, Guinea, Guinea-Bissau, Haiti, Kiribati, Laos, Lesotho, Malawi, Maldives, Mali, Mauritania, Mozambique, Nepal, Niger, Rwanda, Samoa, Sao Tome and Principe, Sierra Leone, Somalia, Sudan, Tanzania, Togo, Tuvalu, Uganda, Vanuatu, Yemen

less developed countries (LDCs)	the bottom group in the hierarchy of developed countries (DCs), former USSR/Eastern Europe (former USSR/EE), and less developed countries (LDCs); mainly countries and dependent areas with low levels of output, living standards, and technology; per capita GDPs are generally below $5,000 and often less than $1,500; however, the group also includes a number of countries with high per capita incomes, areas of advanced technology, and rapid rates of growth; includes the advanced developing countries, developing countries, Four Dragons (Four Tigers), least developed countries (LLDCs), low-income countries, middle-income countries, newly industrializing economies (NIEs), the South, Third World, underdeveloped countries, undeveloped countries; the 172 LDCs are: Afghanistan, Algeria, American Samoa, Angola, Anguilla, Antigua and Barbuda, Argentina, Aruba, The Bahamas, Bahrain, Bangladesh, Barbados, Belize, Benin, Bhutan, Bolivia, Botswana, Brazil, British Virgin Islands, Brunei, Burkina Faso, Burma, Burundi, Cambodia, Cameroon, Cape Verde, Cayman Islands, Central African Republic, Chad, Chile, China, Christmas Island, Cocos Islands, Colombia, Comoros, Democratic Republic of the Congo, Republic of the Congo, Cook Islands, Costa Rica, Cote d'Ivoire, Cuba, Cyprus, Djibouti, Dominica, Dominican Republic, Ecuador, Egypt, El Salvador, Equatorial Guinea, Eritrea, Ethiopia, Falkland Islands, Fiji, French Guiana, French Polynesia, Gabon, The Gambia, Gaza Strip, Ghana, Gibraltar, Greenland, Grenada, Guadeloupe, Guam, Guatemala, Guernsey, Guinea, Guinea-Bissau, Guyana, Haiti, Honduras, Hong Kong, India, Indonesia, Iran, Iraq, Jamaica, Jersey, Jordan, Kenya, Kiribati, North Korea, South Korea, Kuwait, Laos, Lebanon, Lesotho, Liberia, Libya, Macau, Madagascar, Malawi, Malaysia, Maldives, Mali, Isle of Man, Marshall Islands, Martinique, Mauritania, Mauritius, Mayotte, Federated States of Micronesia, Mongolia, Montserrat, Morocco, Mozambique, Namibia, Nauru, Nepal, Netherlands Antilles, New Caledonia, Nicaragua, Niger, Nigeria, Niue, Norfolk Island, Northern Mariana Islands, Oman, Palau, Pakistan, Panama, Papua New Guinea, Paraguay, Peru, Philippines, Pitcairn Islands, Puerto Rico, Qatar, Reunion, Rwanda, Saint Helena, Saint Kitts and Nevis, Saint Lucia, Saint Pierre and Miquelon, Saint Vincent and the Grenadines, Samoa, Sao Tome and Principe, Saudi Arabia, Senegal, Seychelles, Sierra Leone, Singapore, Solomon Islands, Somalia, Sri Lanka, Sudan, Suriname, Swaziland, Syria, Taiwan, Tanzania, Thailand, Togo, Tokelau, Tonga, Trinidad and Tobago, Tunisia, Turks and Caicos Islands, Tuvalu, UAE, Uganda, Uruguay, Vanuatu, Venezuela, Vietnam, Virgin Islands, Wallis and Futuna, West Bank, Western Sahara, Yemen, Zambia, Zimbabwe; *note*—similar to the new International Monetary Fund (IMF) term "developing countries" which adds Malta, Mexico, South Africa, and Turkey but omits in its recently published statistics American Samoa, Anguilla, British Virgin Islands, Brunei, Cayman Islands, Christmas Island, Cocos Islands, Cook Islands, Cuba, Eritrea, Falkland Islands, French Guiana, French Polynesia, Gaza Strip, Gibraltar, Greenland, Grenada, Guadeloupe, Guam, Guernsey, Jersey, North Korea, Macau, Isle of Man, Martinique, Mayotte, Montserrat, Nauru, New Caledonia, Niue, Norfolk Island, Northern Mariana Islands, Palau, Pitcairn Islands, Puerto Rico, Reunion, Saint Helena, Saint Pierre and Miquelon, Tokelau, Tonga, Turks and Caicos Islands, Tuvalu, Virgin Islands, Wallis and Futuna, West Bank, Western Sahara
low-income countries	another term for those less developed countries with below-average per capita GDPs; see less developed countries (LDCs)
London Suppliers Group	see Nuclear Suppliers Group (NSG)
Mercado Comun del Cono Sur (Mercosur)	see Southern Cone Common Market
middle-income countries	another term for those less developed countries with above-average per capita GDPs; see less developed countries (LDCs)
Missile Technology Control Regime (MTCR) *established*—16 April 1987 *aim*—to arrest the proliferation of missiles (unmanned delivery vehicles of mass destruction) by controlling the export of key missile technologies and equipment	*members*—(28) Argentina, Australia, Austria, Belgium, Brazil, Canada, Denmark, Finland, France, Germany, Greece, Hungary, Iceland, Ireland, Italy, Japan, Luxembourg, Netherlands, NZ, Norway, Portugal, Russia, South Africa, Spain, Sweden, Switzerland, UK, US
Near Abroad	Russian term for the 14 non-Russian successor states of the USSR, in which 25 million ethnic Russians live and in which Moscow has expressed a strong national security interest; the 14 countries are Armenia, Azerbaijan, Belarus, Estonia, Georgia, Kazakhstan, Kyrgyzstan, Latvia, Lithuania, Moldova, Tajikistan, Turkmenistan, Ukraine, Uzbekistan

Appendix C: International Organizations and Groups (continued)

newly industrializing countries (NICs)	former term for the newly industrializing economies; see newly industrializing economies (NIEs)
newly industrializing economies (NIEs)	that subgroup of the less developed countries (LDCs) that has experienced particularly rapid industrialization of their economies; formerly known as the newly industrializing countries (NICs); also known as advanced developing countries; usually includes the Four Dragons (Hong Kong, South Korea, Singapore, Taiwan), and Brazil
Nonaligned Movement (NAM) *address*—Permanent Representative of Colombia to the United Nations, 140 East 57th Street, New York, NY 10022, US *telephone*—[1] (212) 355 7776 *FAX*—[1] (212) 371 2813 *established*—1-6 September 1961 *aim*—to establish political and military cooperation apart from the traditional East or West blocs	*members*—(112 plus the Palestine Liberation Organization) Afghanistan, Algeria, Angola, The Bahamas, Bahrain, Bangladesh, Barbados, Belize, Benin, Bhutan, Bolivia, Botswana, Brunei, Burkina Faso, Burma, Burundi, Cambodia, Cameroon, Cape Verde, Central African Republic, Chad, Chile, Colombia, Comoros, Democratic Republic of the Congo, Republic of the Congo, Cote d'Ivoire, Cuba, Cyprus, Djibouti, Ecuador, Egypt, Equatorial Guinea, Eritrea, Ethiopia, Gabon, The Gambia, Ghana, Grenada, Guatemala, Guinea, Guinea-Bissau, Guyana, Honduras, India, Indonesia, Iran, Iraq, Jamaica, Jordan, Kenya, North Korea, Kuwait, Laos, Lebanon, Lesotho, Liberia, Libya, Madagascar, Malawi, Malaysia, Maldives, Mali, Malta, Mauritania, Mauritius, Mongolia, Morocco, Mozambique, Namibia, Nepal, Nicaragua, Niger, Nigeria, Oman, Pakistan, Panama, Papua New Guinea, Peru, Philippines, Qatar, Rwanda, Saint Lucia, Sao Tome and Principe, Saudi Arabia, Senegal, Seychelles, Sierra Leone, Singapore, Somalia, South Africa, Sri Lanka, Sudan, Suriname, Swaziland, Syria, Tanzania, Thailand, Togo, Trinidad and Tobago, Tunisia, Turkmenistan, Uganda, UAE, Uzbekistan, Vanuatu, Venezuela, Vietnam, Yemen, Yugoslavia, Zambia, Zimbabwe, Palestine Liberation Organization *observers*—(18) Afro-Asian Solidarity Organization, Antigua and Barbuda, Arab League, Armenia, Azerbaijan, Brazil, China, Costa Rica, Croatia, Dominica, El Salvador, Kanaka Socialist National Liberation Front (New Caledonia), Mexico, Organization of African Unity, Organization of the Islamic Conference, Socialist Party of Puerto Rico, UN, Uruguay *guests*—(22) Australia, Austria, Bosnia and Herzegovina, Bulgaria, Canada, Dominican Republic, Finland, Germany, Greece, Hungary, Italy, Netherlands, NZ, Norway, Poland, Portugal, Romania, San Marino, Slovenia, Spain, Sweden, Switzerland
Nordic Council (NC) *address*—Store Strandstraede 18, PB 3043, DK-1021 Kobenhavn K, Denmark *telephone*—[45] 33 96 04 00 *FAX*—[45] 33 11 18 70 *established*—16 March 1952 *effective*—12 February 1953 *aim*—to promote regional economic, cultural, and environmental cooperation	*members*—(5) Denmark (including Faroe Islands and Greenland), Finland (including Aland Islands), Iceland, Norway, Sweden *observers*—(3) the Sami (Lapp) local parliaments of Finland, Norway, and Sweden
Nordic Investment Bank (NIB) *address*—Fabianinkatu 34, P.O. Box 249, FIN-00171 Helsinki, Finland *telephone*—[358] (0) 18001 *FAX*—[358] (0) 1800210 *established*—4 December 1975 *effective*—1 June 1976 *aim*—to promote economic cooperation and development	*members*—(5) Denmark (including Faroe Islands and Greenland), Finland (including Aland Islands), Iceland, Norway, Sweden
North	a popular term for the rich industrialized countries generally located in the northern portion of the Northern Hemisphere; the counterpart of the South; see developed countries (DCs)
North Atlantic Cooperation Council (NACC)	see Euro-Atlantic Partnership Council (EAPC)
North Atlantic Treaty Organization (NATO) *address*—B-1110 Brussels, Belgium *telephone*—[32] (2) 707 4111 *FAX*—[32] (2) 707 4579 *established*—17 September 1949 *aim*—to promote mutual defense and cooperation	*members*—(16) Belgium, Canada, Denmark, France, Germany, Greece, Iceland, Italy, Luxembourg, Netherlands, Norway, Portugal, Spain, Turkey, UK, US; *note*—Czech Republic, Hungary, and Poland to join in April 1999

Appendix C: International Organizations and Groups (continued)

Nuclear Energy Agency (NEA)

address—AEN/NEA, Le Seine St. Germain, 12 Boulevard des Iles, F-92130 Issy-les-Moulineaux, France
telephone—[33] (1) 45 24 10 10
FAX—[33] (1) 45 24 11 10
established—NA 1958
aim—to promote the peaceful uses of nuclear energy; associated with OECD

members—(27) Australia, Austria, Belgium, Canada, Czech Republic, Denmark, Finland, France, Germany, Greece, Hungary, Iceland, Ireland, Italy, Japan, South Korea, Luxembourg, Mexico, Netherlands, Norway, Portugal, Spain, Sweden, Switzerland, Turkey, UK, US

Nuclear Suppliers Group (NSG)

note—also known as the London Suppliers Group or the London Group
address—c/o Permanent Mission of Japan in Vienna, Prinz-Eugen Strasse 8-10, A-1040 Vienna, Austria
telephone—[43] (1) 505 5467
FAX—[43] (1) 505 6167
established—NA 1974
effective—NA 1975
aim—to establish guidelines for exports of nuclear materials, processing equipment for uranium enrichment, and technical information to countries of proliferation concern and regions of conflict and instability

members—(34) Argentina, Australia, Austria, Belgium, Brazil, Bulgaria, Canada, Czech Republic, Denmark, Finland, France, Germany, Greece, Hungary, Ireland, Italy, Japan, South Korea, Luxembourg, Netherlands, NZ, Norway, Poland, Portugal, Romania, Russia, Slovakia, South Africa, Spain, Sweden, Switzerland, Ukraine, UK, US
observer—(1) European Commission (a policy-planning body for the EU)

Organismo para la Proscripcion de las Armas Nucleares en la America Latina y el Caribe (OPANAL)

see Agency for the Prohibition of Nuclear Weapons in Latin America and the Caribbean (OPANAL)

Organization for Economic Cooperation and Development (OECD)

address—2 Rue Andre Pascal, F-75775 Paris CEDEX 16, France
telephone—[33] (1) 45 24 82 00
FAX—[33] (1) 45 24 85 00, 45 24 81 76
established—14 December 1960
effective—30 September 1961
aim—to promote economic cooperation and development

members—(29) Australia, Austria, Belgium, Canada, Czech Republic, Denmark, Finland, France, Germany, Greece, Hungary, Iceland, Ireland, Italy, Japan, South Korea, Luxembourg, Mexico, Netherlands, NZ, Norway, Poland, Portugal, Spain, Sweden, Switzerland, Turkey, UK, US
special member—(1) EU

Organization for Security and Cooperation in Europe (OSCE)

note—formerly the Conference on Security and Cooperation in Europe (CSCE)
address—Karntner Ring 5-7, A-1010 Vienna, Austria
telephone—[43] (1) 514 36-190
FAX—[43] (1) 514 36-96
established—1 January 1995
aim—to foster the implementation of human rights, fundamental freedoms, democracy, and the rule of law; to act as an instrument of early warning, conflict prevention and crisis management; and to serve as a framework for conventional arms control and confidence building measures

members—(55) Albania, Andorra, Armenia, Austria, Azerbaijan, Belarus, Belgium, Bosnia and Herzegovina, Bulgaria, Canada, Croatia, Cyprus, Czech Republic, Denmark, Estonia, Finland, France, Georgia, Germany, Greece, Holy See, Hungary, Iceland, Ireland, Italy, Kazakhstan, Kyrgyzstan, Latvia, Liechtenstein, Lithuania, Luxembourg, The Former Yugoslav Republic of Macedonia, Malta, Moldova, Monaco, Netherlands, Norway, Poland, Portugal, Romania, Russia, San Marino, Slovakia, Slovenia, Spain, Sweden, Switzerland, Tajikistan, Turkey, Turkmenistan, Ukraine, UK, US, Uzbekistan, Yugoslavia (suspended)
partners for cooperation—(7) Algeria, Egypt, Israel, Japan, South Korea, Morocco, Tunisia

Organization for the Prohibition of Chemical Weapons (OPCW)

address—Johan de Wittlaan 32, NL-2517 JR The Hague, Netherlands
telephone—[31] (70) 376 17 00
FAX—[31] (70) 360 09 44
established—29 April 1997
aim—to enforce the Convention on the Prohibition of the Development, Production, Stockpiling and Use of Chemical Weapons and on Their Destruction; to provide a forum for consultation and cooperation among the signatories of the Convention

members—(168) Afghanistan, Albania, Algeria, Argentina, Armenia, Australia, Austria, Azerbaijan, The Bahamas, Bahrain, Bangladesh, Belarus, Belgium, Benin, Bhutan, Bolivia, Bosnia and Herzegovina, Brazil, Brunei, Bulgaria, Burkina Faso, Burma, Burundi, Cambodia, Cameroon, Canada, Cape Verde, Central African Republic, Chad, Chile, China, Colombia, Comoros, Democratic Republic of the Congo, Republic of the Congo, Cook Islands, Costa Rica, Cote d'Ivoire, Croatia, Cuba, Cyprus, Czech Republic, Denmark, Djibouti, Dominica, Dominican Republic, Ecuador, El Salvador, Equatorial Guinea, Estonia, Ethiopia, Fiji, Finland, France, Gabon, The Gambia, Georgia, Germany, Ghana, Greece, Grenada, Guatemala, Guinea, Guinea-Bissau, Guyana, Haiti, Holy See, Honduras, Hungary, Iceland, India, Indonesia, Iran, Ireland, Israel, Italy, Jamaica, Japan, Jordan, Kazakhstan, Kenya, South Korea, Kuwait, Kyrgyzstan, Laos, Latvia, Lesotho, Liberia, Liechtenstein, Lithuania, Luxembourg, Madagascar, Malawi, Malaysia, Maldives, Mali, Malta, Marshall Islands, Mauritania, Mauritius, Mexico, Federated States of Micronesia, Moldova, Monaco, Mongolia, Morocco, Namibia, Nauru, Nepal, Netherlands, NZ, Nicaragua, Niger, Nigeria, Norway, Oman, Pakistan, Panama, Papua New Guinea, Paraguay, Peru, Philippines, Poland, Portugal, Qatar, Romania, Russia, Rwanda, Saint Kitts and Nevis, Saint Lucia, Saint Vincent and the Grenadines, Samoa, San Marino, Saudi Arabia, Senegal, Serbia and Montenegro, Seychelles, Sierra Leone, Singapore, Slovakia, Slovenia, South Africa, Spain, Sri Lanka, Suriname, Swaziland, Sweden, Switzerland, Tajikistan, Tanzania, Thailand, Togo, Trinidad and Tobago, Tunisia, Turkey, Turkmenistan, Uganda, Ukraine, UAE, UK, US, Uruguay, Uzbekistan, Venezuela, Vietnam, Yemen, Zambia, Zimbabwe

Organization of African Unity (OAU)

address—P. O. Box 3243, Addis Ababa, Ethiopia
telephone—[251] (1) 517700
FAX—[251] (1) 512622, 517844
established—25 May 1963
aim—to promote unity and cooperation among African states

members—(53) Algeria, Angola, Benin, Botswana, Burkina Faso, Burundi, Cameroon, Cape Verde, Central African Republic, Chad, Comoros, Democratic Republic of the Congo, Republic of the Congo, Cote d'Ivoire, Djibouti, Egypt, Equatorial Guinea, Eritrea, Ethiopia, Gabon, The Gambia, Ghana, Guinea, Guinea-Bissau, Kenya, Lesotho, Liberia, Libya, Madagascar, Malawi, Mali, Mauritania, Mauritius, Mozambique, Namibia, Niger, Nigeria, Rwanda, Sahrawi Arab Democratic Republic, Sao Tome and Principe, Senegal, Seychelles, Sierra Leone, Somalia, South Africa, Sudan, Swaziland, Tanzania, Togo, Tunisia, Uganda, Zambia, Zimbabwe

Organization of American States (OAS)

address—corner of 17th Street and Constitution Avenue NW, Washington, DC 20006, US
telephone—[1] (202) 458 3000
FAX—[1] (202) 458 3967
established—30 April 1948
effective—13 December 1951
aim—to promote regional peace and security as well as economic and social development

members—(35) Antigua and Barbuda, Argentina, The Bahamas, Barbados, Belize, Bolivia, Brazil, Canada, Chile, Colombia, Costa Rica, Cuba (excluded from formal participation since 1962), Dominica, Dominican Republic, Ecuador, El Salvador, Grenada, Guatemala, Guyana, Haiti, Honduras, Jamaica, Mexico, Nicaragua, Panama, Paraguay, Peru, Saint Kitts and Nevis, Saint Lucia, Saint Vincent and the Grenadines, Suriname, Trinidad and Tobago, US, Uruguay, Venezuela
observers—(40) Algeria, Angola, Austria, Belgium, Bosnia and Herzegovina, Croatia, Cyprus, Czech Republic, Egypt, Equatorial Guinea, EU, Finland, France, Germany, Greece, Holy See, Hungary, India, Israel, Italy, Japan, Kazakhstan, South Korea, Latvia, Lebanon, Morocco, Netherlands, Pakistan, Poland, Portugal, Romania, Russia, Saudi Arabia, Spain, Sri Lanka, Sweden, Switzerland, Tunisia, Ukraine, UK

Appendix C: International Organizations and Groups (continued)

Organization of Arab Petroleum Exporting Countries (OAPEC)

address—P.O. Box 20501, Safat 13066, Kuwait
telephone—[965] 4844500
FAX—[965] 4815747
established—9 January 1968
aim—to promote cooperation in the petroleum industry

members—(10) Algeria, Bahrain, Egypt, Iraq, Kuwait, Libya, Qatar, Saudi Arabia, Syria, UAE

Organization of Eastern Caribbean States (OECS)

address—OECS, P.O. Box 179, Morne Fortune, Castries, Saint Lucia
telephone—[1] (758) 45 22537, 45 22538
FAX—[1] (758) 45 31628
established—18 June 1981
effective—4 July 1981
aim—to promote political, economic, and defense cooperation

members—(7) Antigua and Barbuda, Dominica, Grenada, Montserrat, Saint Kitts and Nevis, Saint Lucia, Saint Vincent and the Grenadines
associate members—(2) Anguilla, British Virgin Islands

Organization of Petroleum Exporting Countries (OPEC)

address—Obere Donaustrasse 93, A-1020 Vienna, Austria
telephone—[43] (1) 21 11 20
FAX—[43] (1) 216 43 20
established—14 September 1960
aim—to coordinate petroleum policies

members—(11) Algeria, Indonesia, Iran, Iraq, Kuwait, Libya, Nigeria, Qatar, Saudi Arabia, UAE, Venezuela

---

Organization of the Islamic Conference (OIC)

address—6 km Makkah Al-Mukarramah Road, P.O. Box 178, Jeddah 21411, Saudi Arabia
telephone—[966] (2) 680-0800
FAX—[966] (2) 687-6568
established—22-25 September 1969
aim—to promote Islamic solidarity in economic, social, cultural, and political affairs

members—(54 plus the Palestine Liberation Organization) Afghanistan, Albania, Algeria, Azerbaijan, Bahrain, Bangladesh, Benin, Brunei, Burkina Faso, Cameroon, Chad, Comoros, Djibouti, Egypt, Gabon, The Gambia, Guinea, Guinea-Bissau, Indonesia, Iran, Iraq, Jordan, Kazakhstan, Kuwait, Kyrgyzstan, Lebanon, Libya, Malaysia, Maldives, Mali, Mauritania, Morocco, Mozambique, Niger, Nigeria, Oman, Pakistan, Qatar, Saudi Arabia, Senegal, Sierra Leone, Somalia, Sudan, Suriname, Syria, Tajikistan, Togo, Tunisia, Turkey, Turkmenistan, Uganda, UAE, Uzbekistan, Yemen, Palestine Liberation Organization
observers—(4) Bosnia and Herzegovina, Central African Republic, Guyana, "Turkish Republic of Northern Cyprus"

Paris Club

see Group of 10

Partnership for Peace (PFP)

address—NATO Office of Information and Press, B-1110 Brussels, Belgium
telephone—[32] (2) 728 44 15
FAX—[32] (2) 728 45 79
established—10-11 January 1994
aim—to expand and intensify political and military cooperation throughout Europe, increase stability, diminish threats to peace, and build relationships by promoting the spirit of practical cooperation and commitment to democratic principles that underpin NATO; program under the auspices of NATO

members—(27) Albania, Armenia, Austria, Azerbaijan, Belarus, Bulgaria, Czech Republic, Estonia, Finland, Georgia, Hungary, Kazakhstan, Kyrgyzstan, Latvia, Lithuania, The Former Yugoslav Republic of Macedonia, Moldova, Poland, Romania, Russia, Slovakia, Slovenia, Sweden, Switzerland, Turkmenistan, Ukraine, Uzbekistan

---

Appendix C: International Organizations and Groups (continued)

Permanent Court of Arbitration (PCA) *address*—Peace Palace, Carnegieplein 2, NL-2517 KJ The Hague, Netherlands *telephone*—[31] (70) 302 42 42 *FAX*—[31] (70) 302 41 67 *established*—29 July 1899 *aim*—to facilitate the settlement of international disputes	*members*—(83) Argentina, Australia, Austria, Belarus, Belgium, Bolivia, Brazil, Bulgaria, Burkina Faso, Cambodia, Cameroon, Canada, Chile, China, Colombia, Democratic Republic of the Congo, Cuba, Cyprus, Czech Republic, Denmark, Dominican Republic, Ecuador, Egypt, El Salvador, Fiji, Finland, France, Germany, Greece, Guatemala, Haiti, Honduras, Hungary, Iceland, India, Iran, Iraq, Israel, Italy, Japan, Jordan, Kyrgyzstan, Laos, Lebanon, Libya, Liechtenstein, Luxembourg, Malta, Mauritius, Mexico, Netherlands, NZ, Nicaragua, Nigeria, Norway, Pakistan, Panama, Paraguay, Peru, Poland, Portugal, Romania, Russia, Senegal, Singapore, Slovakia, Slovenia, Spain, Sri Lanka, Sudan, Suriname, Swaziland, Sweden, Switzerland, Thailand, Turkey, Uganda, Ukraine, UK, US, Uruguay, Venezuela, Zimbabwe
Population Commission	see Commission on Population and Development
Rio Group (RG) *note*—formerly known as Grupo de los Ocho, established in December 1986 *address*—Ministerio de Relaciones Exteriores, Edificio AYFRA, Piso 10, Pdte Franco y Ayolas, Asuncion, Paraguay *telephone*—[595] (21) 448409, 493872 *FAX*—[595] (21) 450911, 493910 *established*—NA 1988 *aim*—to consult on regional Latin American issues	*members*—(12) Argentina, Bolivia, Brazil, Chile, Colombia, Ecuador, Mexico, Panama, Paraguay, Peru, Uruguay, Venezuela
Second World	another term for the traditionally Marxist-Leninist states of the USSR and Eastern Europe, with authoritarian governments and command economies based on the Soviet model; the term is fading from use; see centrally planned economies
Sistema Economico Latinoamericana (SELA)	see Latin American Economic System (LAES)
Social Commission	see Commission for Social Development
socialist countries	in general, countries in which the government owns and plans the use of the major factors of production; *note*—the term is sometimes used incorrectly as a synonym for communist countries
South	a popular term for the poorer, less industrialized countries generally located south of the developed countries; the counterpart of the North; see less developed countries (LDCs)
South Asian Association for Regional Cooperation (SAARC) *address*—P.O. Box 4222, Kathmandu, Nepal *telephone*—[977] (1) 221785, 226350, 221792, 228029 *FAX*—[977] (1) 227033, 223991 *established*—8 December 1985 *aim*—to promote economic, social, and cultural cooperation	*members*—(7) Bangladesh, Bhutan, India, Maldives, Nepal, Pakistan, Sri Lanka
South Pacific Commission (SPC) *address*—BP D5, 98848 Noumea CEDEX, New Caledonia *telephone*—[687] 26 20 00 *FAX*—[687] 26 38 18 *established*—6 February 1947 *effective*—29 July 1948 *aim*—to promote regional cooperation in economic and social matters	*members*—(26) American Samoa, Australia, Cook Islands, Fiji, France, French Polynesia, Guam, Kiribati, Marshall Islands, Federated States of Micronesia, Nauru, New Caledonia, NZ, Niue, Northern Mariana Islands, Palau, Papua New Guinea, Pitcairn Islands, Samoa, Solomon Islands, Tokelau, Tonga, Tuvalu, US, Vanuatu, Wallis and Futuna

Appendix C: International Organizations and Groups (continued)

South Pacific Forum (SPF)	*members*—(16) Australia, Cook Islands, Fiji, Kiribati, Marshall Islands, Federated States of Micronesia, Nauru, NZ, Niue, Palau, Papua New Guinea, Samoa, Solomon Islands, Tonga, Tuvalu, Vanuatu
address—c/o Forum Secretariat, Ratu Sukuna Road, Private Mail Bag, Suva, Fiji *telephone*—[679] 312 600, 303 106 *FAX*—[679] 301 102, 305 573 *established*—5 August 1971 *aim*—to promote regional cooperation in political matters	
South Pacific Regional Trade and Economic Cooperation Agreement (Sparteca)	*members*—(16) Australia, Cook Islands, Fiji, Kiribati, Marshall Islands, Federated States of Micronesia, Nauru, NZ, Niue, Palau, Papua New Guinea, Samoa, Solomon Islands, Tonga, Tuvalu, Vanuatu
address—c/o forum Secretariat, Ratu Sukuna Road GPO Box 856, Suva, Fiji *telephone*—[679] 312 600, 303 106 *FAX*—[679] 302 204 *established*—NA 1981 *aim*—to redress unequal trade relationships of Australia and New Zealand with small island economies in the Pacific region	
Southern African Customs Union (SACU)	*members*—(5) Botswana, Lesotho, Namibia, South Africa, Swaziland
address—Director of Customs and Excise, Ministry of Finance, Private Bag 13295, Windhoek, Namibia *established*—11 December 1969 *aim*—to promote free trade and cooperation in customs matters	
Southern African Development Community (SADC)	*members*—(14) Angola, Botswana, Democratic Republic of the Congo, Lesotho, Malawi, Mauritius, Mozambique, Namibia, Seychelles, South Africa, Swaziland, Tanzania, Zambia, Zimbabwe
note—evolved from the Southern African Development Coordination Conference (SADCC) *address*—Private Bag 0095, Gaborone, Botswana *telephone*—[267] (31) 351863, 351864, 351865 *FAX*—[267] (31) 372848 *established*—17 August 1992 *aim*—to promote regional economic development and integration	
Southern Cone Common Market (Mercosur)	*members*—(4) Argentina, Brazil, Paraguay, Uruguay *associate member*—(1) Chile
note—also known as Mercado Comun del Cono Sur (Mercosur) *address*—Rincon 575 Piso 12, 11000 Montevideo, Uruguay *telephone*—[598] (2) 9164590 *FAX*—[598] (2) 9164591 *established*—26 March 1991 *aim*—to increase regional economic cooperation	

Appendix C: International Organizations and Groups (continued)

Statistical Commission *address*—Division for Policy and Coordination and ECOSOC Affairs, Department for Policy Coordination and Sustainable Development, United Nations, Room 2963, New York, NY 10017, US *telephone*—[1] (212) 963 1234 *FAX*—[1] (212) 963 5935 *established*—21 June 1946 *aim*—to deal with development and standardization of national statistics of interest to the UN, as part of the Economic and Social Council organization	*members*—(24) selected on a rotating basis from all regions
Third World	another term for the less developed countries; the term is obsolescent; see less developed countries (LDCs)
underdeveloped countries	refers to those less developed countries with the potential for above-average economic growth; see less developed countries (LDCs)
undeveloped countries	refers to those extremely poor less developed countries (LDCs) with little prospect for economic growth; see least developed countries (LLDCs)
Union Douaniere et Economique de l'Afrique Centrale (UDEAC)	see Central African Customs and Economic Union (UDEAC)
United Nations (UN) *address*—United Nations, New York, NY 10017, US *telephone*—[1] (212) 963 1234 *FAX*—[1] (212) 963 4879 *established*—26 June 1945 *effective*—24 October 1945 *aim*—to maintain international peace and security and to promote cooperation involving economic, social, cultural, and humanitarian problems	*members*—(184 excluding Yugoslavia) Afghanistan, Albania, Algeria, Andorra, Angola, Antigua and Barbuda, Argentina, Armenia, Australia, Austria, Azerbaijan, The Bahamas, Bahrain, Bangladesh, Barbados, Belarus, Belgium, Belize, Benin, Bhutan, Bolivia, Bosnia and Herzegovina, Botswana, Brazil, Brunei, Bulgaria, Burkina Faso, Burma, Burundi, Cambodia, Cameroon, Canada, Cape Verde, Central African Republic, Chad, Chile, China, Colombia, Comoros, Democratic Republic of the Congo, Republic of the Congo, Costa Rica, Cote d'Ivoire, Croatia, Cuba, Cyprus, Czech Republic, Denmark, Djibouti, Dominica, Dominican Republic, Ecuador, Egypt, El Salvador, Equatorial Guinea, Eritrea, Estonia, Ethiopia, Fiji, Finland, France, Gabon, The Gambia, Georgia, Germany, Ghana, Greece, Grenada, Guatemala, Guinea, Guinea-Bissau, Guyana, Haiti, Honduras, Hungary, Iceland, India, Indonesia, Iran, Iraq, Ireland, Israel, Italy, Jamaica, Japan, Jordan, Kazakhstan, Kenya, North Korea, South Korea, Kuwait, Kyrgyzstan, Laos, Latvia, Lebanon, Lesotho, Liberia, Libya, Liechtenstein, Lithuania, Luxembourg, The Former Yugoslav Republic of Macedonia, Madagascar, Malawi, Malaysia, Maldives, Mali, Malta, Marshall Islands, Mauritania, Mauritius, Mexico, Federated States of Micronesia, Moldova, Monaco, Mongolia, Morocco, Mozambique, Namibia, Nepal, Netherlands, NZ, Nicaragua, Niger, Nigeria, Norway, Oman, Pakistan, Palau, Panama, Papua New Guinea, Paraguay, Peru, Philippines, Poland, Portugal, Qatar, Romania, Russia, Rwanda, Saint Kitts and Nevis, Saint Lucia, Saint Vincent and the Grenadines, Samoa, San Marino, Sao Tome and Principe, Saudi Arabia, Senegal, Seychelles, Sierra Leone, Singapore, Slovakia, Slovenia, Solomon Islands, Somalia, South Africa, Spain, Sri Lanka, Sudan, Suriname, Swaziland, Sweden, Syria, Tajikistan, Tanzania, Thailand, Togo, Trinidad and Tobago, Tunisia, Turkey, Turkmenistan, Uganda, Ukraine, UAE, UK, US, Uruguay, Uzbekistan, Vanuatu, Venezuela, Vietnam, Yemen, Yugoslavia (suspended), Zambia, Zimbabwe; note - all UN members are represented in the General Assembly *observers*—(2 plus the Palestine Liberation Organization) Holy See, Switzerland, Palestine Liberation Organization
United Nations Angola Verification Mission (UNAVEM III)	successor to original UNAVEM and UNAVEM II; established 20 December 1988; renewed for third time 8 February 1995; aim was to assist the parties in restoring peace and achieving national reconciliation in Angola on the basis of the Peace Accords, the Lusaka Protocol, and relevant Security Council resolutions; established by the UN Security Council; members Bangladesh, Brazil, Bulgaria, Egypt, Fiji, Guinea-Bissau, Hungary, India, Jordan, Mongolia, Mali, Morocco, Netherlands, Nigeria, Portugal, Sweden, Tanzania, Uruguay, Zambia, Zimbabwe; disbanded 30 June 1997
United Nations Assistance Mission for Rwanda (UNAMIR)	established 5 October 1993 to support and provide safe conditions for displaced persons and human rights monitors, and to assist in training a new national police force; established by the UN Security Council; members were Argentina, Australia, Austria, Bangladesh, Canada, Chad, Republic of the Congo, Djibouti, Fiji, Germany, Ghana, Guinea, Guinea-Bissau, India, Jordan, Malawi, Mali, Niger, Nigeria, Pakistan, Russia, Senegal, Switzerland, Tunisia, Uruguay, Zambia, Zimbabwe; terminated 8 March 1996

Appendix C: International Organizations and Groups (continued)

United Nations Children's Fund (UNICEF)

note—acronym retained from the predecessor organization UN International Children's Emergency Fund
address—UNICEF House, Three United Nations Plaza, New York, NY 10017, US
telephone—[1] (212) 326 7000
FAX—[1] (212) 888 7465, 888 7454
established—11 December 1946
aim—to help establish child health and welfare services

members—(36) selected on a rotating basis from all regions

United Nations Civilian Police Mission in Haiti (MIPONUH)

address—c/o Department of Peace-keeping Operations, Room S-3260E, United Nations, New York, NY 10017, US
telephone—[1] (212) 963 1234
FAX—[1] (212) 963 4879
established—1 December 1997
aim—to support the professionalization of the Haitian National Police; established by UN Security Council; completion was expected by 30 November 1998

members—(11) Argentina, Benin, Canada, France, India, Mali, Niger, Senegal, Togo, Tunisia, US

United Nations Civilian Police Support Group in Croatia

established—19 December 1997
aim—to monitor the Croatian police with respect to the return of displaced persons

members—(20) Argentina, Austria, Denmark, Egypt, Fiji, Finland, Indonesia, Ireland, Jordan, Kenya, Lithuania, Nepal, Nigeria, Norway, Poland, Russia, Sweden, Tunisia, Ukraine, US

United Nations Conference on Trade and Development (UNCTAD)

address—UNCTAD, Palais des Nations, CH-1211 Geneva 10, Switzerland
telephone—[41] (22) 917 12 34, 907 12 34
FAX—[41] (22) 907 00 57
established—30 December 1964
aim—to promote international trade

members—(188) all UN members plus Holy See, Switzerland, Tonga

United Nations Confidence Restoration Operation in Croatia (UNCRO)

established 31 March 1995 to separate Croatian and Krajina Serb forces; to monitor demilitarization of the Prevlaka Peninsula; to maintain a presence on Croatia's international borders; to monitor and report the crossing of military personnel, equipment, supplies and weapons; to facilitate delivery of humanitarian assistance; to aid refugees and displaced persons; to protect ethnic minorities; and to clear mines; established by the UN Security Council; members were Argentina, Bangladesh, Belgium, Brazil, Canada, Czech Republic, Denmark, Egypt, Estonia, Finland, France, Germany, Ghana, Indonesia, Ireland, Jordan, Kenya, Lithuania, Malaysia, Nepal, Netherlands, Nigeria, Norway, Pakistan, Poland, Portugal, Russia, Senegal, Slovakia, Spain, Sweden, Tunisia, Turkey, Ukraine, UK, US; disbanded January 1996

Appendix C: International Organizations and Groups (continued)

United Nations Development Program (UNDP)

address—One United National Plaza, New York, NY 10017, US
telephone—[1] (212) 906 5788, 906 5000
FAX—[1] (212) 906 5365
established—22 November 1965
aim—to provide technical assistance to stimulate economic and social development

members—(36) selected on a rotating basis from all regions

United Nations Disengagement Observer Force (UNDOF)

address—c/o Department of Peace-keeping Operations, United Nations, Room S-3260E, New York, NY 10017, US
telephone—[1] (212) 963 1234
FAX—[1] (212) 963 4879
established—31 May 1974
aim—to observe the 1973 Arab-Israeli cease-fire; established by the UN Security Council

members—(4) Austria, Canada, Japan, Poland

United Nations Educational, Scientific, and Cultural Organization (UNESCO)

address—7 place de Fontenoy, F-75352 Paris 07SP, France
telephone—[33] (1) 45 68 10 00
FAX—[33] (1) 45 67 16 90
established—16 November 1945
effective—4 November 1946
aim—to promote cooperation in education, science, and culture

members—(186) Afghanistan, Albania, Algeria, Andorra, Angola, Antigua and Barbuda, Argentina, Armenia, Australia, Austria, Azerbaijan, The Bahamas, Bahrain, Bangladesh, Barbados, Belarus, Belgium, Belize, Benin, Bhutan, Bolivia, Bosnia and Herzegovina, Botswana, Brazil, Bulgaria, Burkina Faso, Burma, Burundi, Cambodia, Cameroon, Canada, Cape Verde, Central African Republic, Chad, Chile, China, Colombia, Comoros, Democratic Republic of the Congo, Republic of the Congo, Cook Islands, Costa Rica, Cote d'Ivoire, Croatia, Cuba, Cyprus, Czech Republic, Denmark, Djibouti, Dominica, Dominican Republic, Ecuador, Egypt, El Salvador, Equatorial Guinea, Eritrea, Estonia, Ethiopia, Fiji, Finland, France, Gabon, The Gambia, Georgia, Germany, Ghana, Greece, Grenada, Guatemala, Guinea, Guinea-Bissau, Guyana, Haiti, Honduras, Hungary, Iceland, India, Indonesia, Iran, Iraq, Ireland, Israel, Italy, Jamaica, Japan, Jordan, Kazakhstan, Kenya, Kiribati, North Korea, South Korea, Kuwait, Kyrgyzstan, Laos, Latvia, Lebanon, Lesotho, Liberia, Libya, Lithuania, Luxembourg, The Former Yugoslav Republic of Macedonia, Madagascar, Malawi, Malaysia, Maldives, Mali, Malta, Marshall Islands, Mauritania, Mauritius, Mexico, Moldova, Monaco, Mongolia, Morocco, Mozambique, Namibia, Nauru, Nepal, Netherlands, NZ, Nicaragua, Niger, Nigeria, Niue, Norway, Oman, Pakistan, Panama, Papua New Guinea, Paraguay, Peru, Philippines, Poland, Portugal, Qatar, Romania, Russia, Rwanda, Saint Kitts and Nevis, Saint Lucia, Saint Vincent and the Grenadines, Samoa, San Marino, Sao Tome and Principe, Saudi Arabia, Senegal, Seychelles, Sierra Leone, Slovakia, Slovenia, Solomon Islands, Somalia, South Africa, Spain, Sri Lanka, Sudan, Suriname, Swaziland, Sweden, Switzerland, Syria, Tajikistan, Tanzania, Thailand, Togo, Tonga, Trinidad and Tobago, Tunisia, Turkey, Turkmenistan, Tuvalu, Uganda, Ukraine, UAE, UK, Uruguay, Uzbekistan, Vanuatu, Venezuela, Vietnam, Yemen, Yugoslavia (suspended), Zambia, Zimbabwe
associate members—(4) Aruba, British Virgin Islands, Macau, Netherlands Antilles

---

United Nations Environment Program (UNEP)

address—P.O. Box 30552, Nairobi, Kenya
telephone—[254] (2) 230800, 520600, 621234
FAX—[254] (2) 226890, 623927
established—15 December 1972
aim—to promote international cooperation on all environmental matters

members—(58) selected on a rotating basis from all regions

Appendix C: International Organizations and Groups (continued)

United Nations General Assembly *address*—see United Nations *established*—26 June 1945 *effective*—24 October 1945 *aim*—to function as the primary deliberative organ of the UN	*members*—(185) all UN members are represented in the General Assembly
United Nations High Commissioner for Refugees (UNHCR) *address*—Case Postale 2500, Depot, CH-1211 Geneva 2, Switzerland *telephone*—[41] (22) 739 81 11 *FAX*—[41] (22) 731 95 46 *established*—3 December 1949 *effective*—1 January 1951 *aim*—to ensure the humanitarian treatment of refugees and find permanent solutions to refugee problems	*members*—(52) Algeria, Argentina, Australia, Austria, Bangladesh, Belgium, Brazil, Canada, China, Colombia, Democratic Republic of the Congo, Denmark, Ethiopia, Finland, France, Germany, Greece, Holy See, Hungary, India, Iran, Israel, Italy, Japan, Lebanon, Lesotho, Madagascar, Morocco, Namibia, Netherlands, Nicaragua, Nigeria, Norway, Pakistan, Philippines, Poland, Russia, Somalia, South Africa, Spain, Sudan, Sweden, Switzerland, Tanzania, Thailand, Tunisia, Turkey, Uganda, UK, US, Venezuela, Yugoslavia
United Nations Industrial Development Organization (UNIDO) *address*—Vienna International Center, P.O. Box 300, A-1400 Vienna, Austria *telephone*—[43] (1) 211 310 *FAX*—[43] (1) 23 21 56 *established*—17 November 1966 *effective*—1 January 1967 *aim*—UN specialized agency that promotes industrial development especially among the members	*members*—(168) Afghanistan, Albania, Algeria, Angola, Argentina, Armenia, Austria, Azerbaijan, The Bahamas, Bahrain, Bangladesh, Barbados, Belarus, Belgium, Belize, Benin, Bhutan, Bolivia, Bosnia and Herzegovina, Botswana, Brazil, Bulgaria, Burkina Faso, Burma, Burundi, Cambodia, Cameroon, Canada, Cape Verde, Central African Republic, Chad, Chile, China, Colombia, Comoros, Democratic Republic of the Congo, Republic of the Congo, Costa Rica, Cote d'Ivoire, Croatia, Cuba, Cyprus, Czech Republic, Denmark, Djibouti, Dominica, Dominican Republic, Ecuador, Egypt, El Salvador, Equatorial Guinea, Eritrea, Ethiopia, Fiji, Finland, France, Gabon, The Gambia, Georgia, Germany, Ghana, Greece, Grenada, Guatemala, Guinea, Guinea-Bissau, Guyana, Haiti, Honduras, Hungary, India, Indonesia, Iran, Iraq, Ireland, Israel, Italy, Jamaica, Japan, Jordan, Kenya, North Korea, South Korea, Kuwait, Kyrgyzstan, Laos, Latvia, Lebanon, Lesotho, Liberia, Libya, Luxembourg, The Former Yugoslav Republic of Macedonia, Madagascar, Malawi, Malaysia, Maldives, Mali, Malta, Mauritania, Mauritius, Mexico, Moldova, Mongolia, Morocco, Mozambique, Namibia, Nepal, Netherlands, NZ, Nicaragua, Niger, Nigeria, Norway, Oman, Pakistan, Panama, Papua New Guinea, Paraguay, Peru, Philippines, Poland, Portugal, Qatar, Romania, Russia, Rwanda, Saint Kitts and Nevis, Saint Lucia, Saint Vincent and the Grenadines, Sao Tome and Principe, Saudi Arabia, Senegal, Seychelles, Sierra Leone, Slovakia, Slovenia, Somalia, Spain, Sri Lanka, Sudan, Suriname, Swaziland, Sweden, Switzerland, Syria, Tajikistan, Tanzania, Thailand, Togo, Tonga, Trinidad and Tobago, Tunisia, Turkey, Uganda, Ukraine, UAE, UK, US, Uruguay, Uzbekistan, Vanuatu, Venezuela, Vietnam, Yemen, Yugoslavia (suspended), Zambia, Zimbabwe
United Nations Institute for Training and Research (UNITAR) *address*—Palais des Nations, Bureau 1070, CH-1211, Geneva 10, Switzerland *telephone*—[41] (22) 798-58-50, 798-84-00 *FAX*—[41] (22) 733-13-83 *established*—11 December 1963 *aim*—to help the UN become more effective through training and research	*members (Board of Trustees)*—(17) Argentina, Australia, Austria, Cameroon, Chile, China, Egypt, France, India, Ireland, Italy, Japan, Libya, Nigeria, Pakistan, Russia, Switzerland; *note*—the UN Secretary General can appoint up to 30 members

Appendix C: International Organizations and Groups (continued)

United Nations Interim Force in Lebanon (UNIFIL) *address*—c/o Department of Peace-keeping Operations, Room S-3260E, United Nations, New York, NY 10017, US *telephone*—[1] (212) 963 1234 *FAX*—[1] (212) 963 4879 *established*—19 March 1978 *aim*—to confirm the withdrawal of Israeli forces, and assist in reestablishing Lebanese authority in southern Lebanon; established by the UN Security Council	*members*—(9) Fiji, Finland, France, Ghana, Ireland, Italy, Nepal, Norway, Poland
United Nations Iraq-Kuwait Observation Mission (UNIKOM) *address*—c/o Department of Peace-keeping Operations, Room S-3260E, United Nations, New York, NY 10017, USA *telephone*—[1] (212) 963 1234 *FAX*—[1] (212) 963 4879 *established*—9 April 1991 *aim*—to observe and monitor the demilitarized zone established between Iraq and Kuwait; established by the UN Security Council	*members*—(33) Argentina, Austria, Bangladesh, Canada, China, Denmark, Fiji, Finland, France, Germany, Ghana, Greece, Hungary, India, Indonesia, Ireland, Italy, Kenya, Malaysia, Nigeria, Pakistan, Poland, Romania, Russia, Senegal, Singapore, Sweden, Thailand, Turkey, UK, US, Uruguay, Venezuela
United Nations Military Observer Group in India and Pakistan (UNMOGIP) *address*—c/o Department of Peace-keeping Operations, Room 3727, United Nations, New York, NY 10017, US *telephone*—[1] (212) 963 5721 *FAX*—[1] (212) 758 2718 *established*—13 August 1948 *aim*—to observe the 1949 India-Pakistan cease-fire; established by the UN Security Council	*members*—(8) Belgium, Chile, Denmark, Finland, Italy, South Korea, Sweden, Uruguay
United Nations Mission for the Referendum in Western Sahara (MINURSO) *address*—c/o Department of Peace-keeping Operations, Room S-3260E, United Nations, New York, NY 10017, US *telephone*—[1] (212) 963 1234 *FAX*—[1] (212) 963 4879 *established*—29 April 1991 *aim*—to supervise the cease-fire and conduct a referendum in Western Sahara; established by the UN Security Council	*members*—(27) Argentina, Austria, Bangladesh, China, Egypt, El Salvador, France, Ghana, Greece, Guinea, Honduras, Ireland, Italy, Kenya, South Korea, Malaysia, Nigeria, Pakistan, Poland, Portugal, Russia, Sweden, Togo, Tunisia, US, Uruguay, Venezuela

Appendix C: International Organizations and Groups (continued)

United Nations Mission in Bosnia and Herzegovina (UNMIBH)

address—c/o Department of Peace-keeping Operations, Room S-3260E, United Nations, New York, NY 10017, US
telephone—[1] (212) 963 1234
FAX—[1] (212) 758 2718
established—13 December 1995
aim—to establish an International Police Task Force (IPTF) to implement the Dayton Peace Agreement in Bosnia and Herzegovina

members—(40) Argentina, Austria, Bangladesh, Bulgaria, Canada, Chile, Denmark, Egypt, Estonia, Finland, France, Germany, Ghana, Greece, Hungary, Iceland, India, Indonesia, Ireland, Italy, Jordan, Malaysia, Nepal, Netherlands, Nigeria, Norway, Pakistan, Poland, Portugal, Russia, Senegal, Spain, Sweden, Switzerland, Thailand, Tunisia, Turkey, Ukraine, UK, US

United Nations Mission in Haiti (UNMIH)

established 23 September 1993; aim was to assist in implementing the agreement to transfer power back into the civilian government; established by the UN Security Council; became the United Nations Support Mission in Haiti (UNSMIH) 28 June 1996 with the aim to assist in the professionalization of the Haitian National Police; members were Algeria, Canada, France, India, Mali, Pakistan, Togo, US; disbanded 31 July 1997

United Nations Mission in the Central African Republic (MINURCA)

address—c/o Department of Peacekeeping Operations, Room S-3260E, United Nations, New York, NY 10017, US
telephone—[1] (212) 963-1234
FAX—[1] (212) 758-2718
established—17 March 1998
aim—to provide security in the capital as the government undertakes the necessary reforms to provide its own security; to provide training to civilian police

members—(13) Benin, Burkina Faso, Canada, Chad, Cote d'Ivoire, Egypt, France, Gabon, Mali, Portugal, Senegal, Togo, Tunisia

---

United Nations Mission of Observers in Prevlaka (UNMOP)

address—c/o Department of Peace-keeping Operations, Room S-3260E, United Nations, New York, NY 10017, US
telephone—[1] (212) 963 1234
FAX—[1] (212) 758 2718
established—13 December 1992
aim—to monitor the demilitarization of the Prevlaka peninsula

members—(25) Argentina, Bangladesh, Belgium, Brazil, Canada, Czech Republic, Denmark, Egypt, Finland, Ghana, Indonesia, Ireland, Jordan, Kenya, Nepal, NZ, Nigeria, Norway, Pakistan, Poland, Portugal, Russia, Sweden, Switzerland, Ukraine

---

United Nations Mission of Observers in Sierra Leone (UNOMSIL)

address—c/o Department of Peacekeeping Operations, Room S-3260E, United Nations, New York, NY 10017, US
telephone—[1] (212) 963-1234
FAX—[1] (212) 758-2718
established—13 July 1998
aim—to monitor the military and security situation in Sierra Leone; to monitor the disarmament and demobilization of combatants and members of the Civil Defense Forces (CFD); to assist in monitoring respect for international humanitarian law

members—(11) China, Egypt, India, Kenya, Kyrgyzstan, Mali, NZ, Pakistan, Russia, UK, Zambia

Appendix C: International Organizations and Groups (continued)

United Nations Mission of Observers in Tajikistan (UNMOT)	*members*—(12) Austria, Bangladesh, Bulgaria, Denmark, Ghana, Indonesia, Jordan, Nigeria, Poland, Switzerland, Ukraine, Uruguay
address—c/o Department of Peace-keeping Operations, Room S-3260E, United Nations, New York, NY 10017, US *telephone*—[1] (212) 963 1234 *FAX*—[1] (212) 758 2718 *established*—16 December 1994 *aim*—to monitor and investigate violations of the cease-fire of 17 September 1994 between Tajikistan and the Tajik opposition and to assist in the political negotiation process; established by the UN Security Council	
United Nations Observer Mission in Angola (MONUA)	*members*—(30) Bangladesh, Brazil, Bulgaria, Republic of the Congo, Egypt, France, Guinea-Bissau, Hungary, India, Jordan, Kenya, Malaysia, Mali, Namibia, NZ, Nigeria, Norway, Pakistan, Poland, Portugal, Romania, Russia, Senegal, Slovakia, Sweden, Tanzania, Ukraine, Uruguay, Zambia, Zimbabwe
address—c/o Department of Peace-keeping operations, Room S-3260E, United Nations, New York, NY 10017, US *telephone*—[1] (212) 758 2718 *established*—1 July 1997 *aim*—to assist in implementation of peace agreement; oversee normalization of state administration throughout National territory; established by UN Security Council	
United Nations Observer Mission in El Salvador (ONUSAL)	established 20 May 1991 to verify cease-fire arrangements and to monitor the maintenance of public order pending the organization of a new National Civil Police; established by the UN Security Council; members were Argentina, Austria, Brazil, Canada, Chile, Colombia, France, Guyana, Ireland, Italy, Mexico, Spain, Sweden, Venezuela; disbanded April 1995
United Nations Observer Mission in Georgia (UNOMIG)	*members*—(22) Albania, Austria, Bangladesh, Czech Republic, Denmark, Egypt, France, Germany, Greece, Hungary, Indonesia, Jordan, South Korea, Pakistan, Poland, Russia, Sweden, Switzerland, Turkey, UK, US, Uruguay
address—c/o Department of Peace-keeping Operations, Room S-3260E, United Nations, New York, NY 10017, US *telephone*—[1] (212) 963 1234 *FAX*—[1] (212) 963 4879 *established*—August 1993 *aim*—to verify compliance with the cease-fire agreement, to monitor weapons exclusion zone, and to supervise CIS peacekeeping force for Abkhazia; established by the UN Security Council	
United Nations Observer Mission in Liberia (UNOMIL)	*members*—(6) Bangladesh, Egypt, India, Kenya, Malaysia, Pakistan
address—c/o Department of Peace-keeping Operations, Room S-3260E, United Nations, New York, NY 10017, US *telephone*—[1] (212) 963 1234 *FAX*—[1] (212) 963 4879 *established*—22 September 1993 *aim*—to assist in the implementation of the peace agreement; established by the UN Security Council	

Appendix C: International Organizations and Groups (continued)

United Nations Observer Mission Uganda-Rwanda (UNOMUR)	established 1993 for six months to monitor the Uganda/Rwanda border to verify that no military assistance reaches Rwanda across the border; established by the UN Security Council; members were Bangladesh, Botswana, Brazil, Hungary, Netherlands, Senegal, Slovakia, Zimbabwe; subsumed by UNAMIR
United Nations Operation in Mozambique (UNOMOZ)	established 16 December 1992 to supervise the cease-fire; established by the UN Security Council; members were Argentina, Austria, Bangladesh, Botswana, Brazil, Canada, Cape Verde, China, Czech Republic, Egypt, Guinea-Bissau, Hungary, India, Ireland, Italy, Japan, Jordan, Malaysia, Netherlands, Norway, Portugal, Russia, Spain, Sweden, US, Uruguay, Zambia; shut down operations 31 January 1995
United Nations Operation in Somalia (UNOSOM II)	established 24 April 1992 to facilitate an immediate cessation of hostilities, to maintain a cease-fire in order to promote a political settlement, and to provide urgent humanitarian assistance; established by the UN Security Council; members were Australia, Bangladesh, Botswana, Canada, Egypt, India, Ireland, Malaysia, Nepal, NZ, Nigeria, Pakistan, Romania, Zimbabwe; UN peacekeepers left Somalia on 1 March 1995; some UN personnel remain in Somalia engaged in humanitarian work
United Nations Peace-keeping Force in Cyprus (UNFICYP) *address*—Chief of Mission, P.O. Box 1642, Nicosia, Cyprus *telephone*—[357] (2) 359 700 *FAX*—[357] (2) 359 753 *established*—4 March 1964 *aim*—to serve as a peacekeeping force between Greek Cypriots and Turkish Cypriots in Cyprus; established by the UN Security Council	*members*—(9) Argentina, Australia, Austria, Canada, Finland, Hungary Ireland, Slovenia, UK
United Nations Population Fund (UNFPA) *note*—acronym retained from predecessor organization UN Fund for Population Activities *address*—220 East 42nd Street, 19th Floor, Room DN-1901, New York, NY 10017, US *telephone*—[1] (212) 297 5000 *FAX*—[1] (212) 557 6416 *established*—NA July 1967 *aim*—to assist both developed and developing countries to deal with their population problems	*members*—(34) selected on a rotating basis from all regions
United Nations Preventive Deployment Force (UNPREDEP)	established 31 March 1995; to monitor border activity in the Former Yugoslav Republic of Macedonia; members were Argentina, Bangladesh, Belgium, Brazil, Canada, Czech Republic, Denmark, Egypt, Finland, Ghana, Indonesia, Ireland, Jordan, Kenya, Nepal, NZ, Nigeria, Norway, Pakistan, Poland, Portugal, Russia, Sweden, Switzerland, Turkey, Ukraine, US; mandate ended 25 March 1999
United Nations Protection Force (UNPROFOR)	established 28 February 1992; to create conditions for peace and security required for the negotiation of an overall settlement of the "Yugoslav" crisis; established by the UN Security Council; members were Bangladesh, Belgium, Brazil, Canada, Czech Republic, Denmark, Egypt, Finland, France, Germany, Ghana, Indonesia, Ireland, Jordan, Kenya, Malaysia, Nepal, Netherlands, NZ, Nigeria, Norway, Pakistan, Poland, Portugal, Russia, Spain, Sweden, Switzerland, Ukraine, UK, US; disbanded December 1995; replaced by the Implementation Force (IFOR), which has been replaced by the Stabilization Force (SFOR)

Appendix C: International Organizations and Groups (continued)

United Nations Relief and Works Agency for Palestine Refugees in the Near East (UNRWA)

address—P. O. Box 371, Gaza City, Cisjordania-Gaza
telephone—[972] (7) 677 7333, 824 508
FAX—[972] (7) 677 7555
established—8 December 1949
aim—to provide assistance to Palestinian refugees

members—(10) Belgium, Egypt, France, Japan, Jordan, Lebanon, Syria, Turkey, UK, US

United Nations Research Institute for Social Development (UNRISD)

address—Palais des Nations, CH-1211 Geneva 10, Switzerland
telephone—[41] (22) 798 84 00, 798 58 50
FAX—[41] (22) 740 07 91
established—1 July 1964
aim—to conduct research into the problems of economic development during different phases of economic growth

members—no country members, but a Board of Directors consisting of a chairman appointed by the UN secretary general and 10 individual members

---

United Nations Secretariat

address—see United Nations
established—26 June 1945
effective—24 October 1945
aim—to serve as the primary administrative organ of the UN; a Secretary General is appointed for a five-year term by the General Assembly on the recommendation of the Security Council

members—the UN Secretary General and staff

United Nations Security Council

address—c/o United Nations, Room S-3520A, New York, NY 10017, US
telephone—[1] (212) 963 1234
FAX—[1] (212) 758 2718
established—26 June 1945
effective—24 October 1945
aim—to maintain international peace and security

permanent members—(5) China, France, Russia, UK, US
nonpermanent members—(10) elected for two-year terms by the UN General Assembly; Bahrain (1998-99), Brazil (1998-99), Costa Rica (1997-98), Gabon (1998-99), The Gambia (1998-99), Japan (1997-98), Kenya (1997-98), Portugal (1997-98), Slovenia (1998-99), Sweden (1997-98)

United Nations Transitional Administration in Eastern Slavonia, Baranja, and Western Sirmium (UNTAES)

established 12 November 1995; aim to facilitate and supervise the Basic Agreement between the government of the Republic of Croatia and the local Serbian community that will lead to a peaceful integration of that region into the national state of Croatia; members were Argentina, Bangladesh, Belgium, Brazil, Czech Republic, Denmark, Egypt, Fiji, Finland, Ghana, Indonesia, Ireland, Jordan, Kenya, Nepal, NZ, Niger, Norway, Pakistan, Poland, Russian, Slovakia, Sweden, Switzerland, Tunisia, Ukraine, UK, US; disbanded 15 January 1998; a UN Civilian Police Support Group was established in December 1997 as follow-on mission to UNTAES; the support group will continue to monitor the Croatian police in the Danube region, particularly in connection with the return of displaced people

---

United Nations Transitional Authority in Cambodia (UNTAC)

established by the UN Security Council on 28 February 1992 to contribute to the restoration and maintenance of peace and to the holding of free elections; disbanded sometime after the UN-supervised election in May 1993; members were Algeria, Argentina, Australia, Austria, Bangladesh, Belgium, Brunei, Bulgaria, Cameroon, Canada, Chile, China, Colombia, Egypt, Fiji, France, Germany, Ghana, Hungary, India, Indonesia, Ireland, Italy, Japan, Jordan, Kenya, Malaysia, Morocco, Nepal, Netherlands, NZ, Nigeria, Norway, Pakistan, Philippines, Poland, Russia, Senegal, Singapore, Sweden, Thailand, Tunisia, UK, US, Uruguay

Appendix C: International Organizations and Groups (continued)

United Nations Truce Supervision Organization (UNTSO)

address—Government House, P.O. Box 490, Jerusalem 91004, Israel
telephone—[972] (2) 673 4223
FAX—[972] (2) 673 5282, 673 4223 extension 400
established—NA May 1948
aim—to supervise the 1948 Arab-Israeli cease-fire; currently supports timely deployment of reinforcements to other peacekeeping operations in the region as needed; initially established by the UN Security Council

members—(20) Argentina, Australia, Austria, Belgium, Canada, Chile, China, Denmark, Estonia, Finland, France, Ireland, Italy, Netherlands, NZ, Norway, Russia, Sweden, Switzerland, US

United Nations Trusteeship Council

established on 26 June 1945, effective on 24 October 1945, to supervise the administration of the 11 UN trust territories; members were China, France, Russia, UK, US; it formally suspended operations 1 November 1995 after the Trust Territory of the Pacific Islands (Palau) became the Republic of Palau, a constitutional government in free association with the US; the Trusteeship Council was not dissolved

---

United Nations University (UNU)

address—53-70 Jingumae 5-chome, Shibuya-ku, Tokyo 150, Japan
telephone—[81] (3) 3499 2811
FAX—[81] (3) 3499 2828
established—6 December 1973
aim—to conduct research in development, welfare, and human survival and to train scholars

members—(38 associated institutes in 33 countries) Argentina, Australia, Austria, Bangladesh, Brazil, Canada, Chile, China, Colombia, Costa Rica, Ethiopia, France, Ghana, Guatemala, Hungary, Iceland, India, Japan, Kenya, South Korea, Mexico, Netherlands, Nigeria, Philippines, Spain, Sri Lanka, Sudan, Switzerland, Thailand, Trinidad and Tobago, UK, US, Venezuela

---

United National Verification Mission in Guatemala (MINUGUA)

established on 20 January 1997; to verify fulfillment of cease-fire provisions; established by UN Security Council; members were Argentina, Australia, Austria, Brazil, Canada, Columbia, Ecuador, Germany, Italy, Norway, Russia, Singapore, Spain, Sweden, Ukraine, US, Uruguay, Venezuela; mandate terminated in May 1997

Universal Postal Union (UPU)

address—Bureau International de l'UPU, Weltpoststrasse 4, CH-3000 Berne 15, Switzerland
telephone—[41] (31) 350 31 11
FAX—[41] (31) 350 31 10
established—9 October 1874, affiliated with the UN 15 November 1947
effective—1 July 1948
aim—to promote international postal cooperation; a UN specialized agency

members—(189) Afghanistan, Albania, Algeria, Angola, Antigua and Barbuda, Argentina, Armenia, Australia, Austria, Azerbaijan, The Bahamas, Bahrain, Bangladesh, Barbados, Belarus, Belgium, Belize, Benin, Bhutan, Bolivia, Bosnia and Herzegovina, Botswana, Brazil, Brunei, Bulgaria, Burkina Faso, Burma, Burundi, Cambodia, Cameroon, Canada, Cape Verde, Central African Republic, Chad, Chile, China, Colombia, Comoros, Democratic Republic of the Congo, Republic of the Congo, Costa Rica, Cote d'Ivoire, Croatia, Cuba, Cyprus, Czech Republic, Denmark, Djibouti, Dominica, Dominican Republic, Ecuador, Egypt, El Salvador, Equatorial Guinea, Eritrea, Estonia, Ethiopia, Fiji, Finland, France, Gabon, The Gambia, Georgia, Germany, Ghana, Greece, Grenada, Guatemala, Guinea, Guinea-Bissau, Guyana, Haiti, Holy See, Honduras, Hungary, Iceland, India, Indonesia, Iran, Iraq, Ireland, Israel, Italy, Jamaica, Japan, Jordan, Kazakhstan, Kenya, Kiribati, North Korea, South Korea, Kuwait, Kyrgyzstan, Laos, Latvia, Lebanon, Lesotho, Liberia, Libya, Liechtenstein, Lithuania, Luxembourg, The Former Yugoslav Republic of Macedonia, Madagascar, Malawi, Malaysia, Maldives, Mali, Malta, Mauritania, Mauritius, Mexico, Moldova, Monaco, Mongolia, Morocco, Mozambique, Namibia, Nauru, Nepal, Netherlands, Netherlands Antilles, NZ, Nicaragua, Niger, Nigeria, Norway, Oman, Overseas Territories of the UK, Pakistan, Panama, Papua New Guinea, Paraguay, Peru, Philippines, Poland, Portugal, Qatar, Romania, Russia, Rwanda, Saint Kitts and Nevis, Saint Lucia, Saint Vincent and the Grenadines, Samoa, San Marino, Sao Tome and Principe, Saudi Arabia, Senegal, Seychelles, Sierra Leone, Singapore, Slovakia, Slovenia, Solomon Islands, Somalia, South Africa, Spain, Sri Lanka, Sudan, Suriname, Swaziland, Sweden, Switzerland, Syria, Tajikistan, Tanzania, Thailand, Togo, Tonga, Trinidad and Tobago, Tunisia, Turkey, Turkmenistan, Tuvalu, Uganda, Ukraine, UAE, UK, US, Uruguay, Uzbekistan, Vanuatu, Venezuela, Vietnam, Yemen, Yugoslavia (suspended), Zambia, Zimbabwe

---

Warsaw Pact (WP)

established 14 May 1955 to promote mutual defense; members met 1 July 1991 to dissolve the alliance; member states at the time of dissolution were Bulgaria, Czechoslovakia, Hungary, Poland, Romania, and the USSR; earlier members included GDR and Albania

Appendix C: International Organizations and Groups (continued)

West African Development Bank (WADB) *note*—also known as Banque Ouest-Africaine de Developpement (BOAD); is a financial institution of WAEMU *address*—68 Avenue de la Liberation, BP 1172, Lome, Togo *telephone*—[228] 21 59 06, 21 42 44, 21 01 13 *FAX*—[228] 21 52 67, 21 72 69 *established*—14 November 1973 *aim*—to promote regional economic development and integration	*members*—(7) Benin, Burkina Faso, Cote d'Ivoire, Mali, Niger, Senegal, Togo
West African Economic and Monetary Union (WAEMU) *note*—also known as Union Economique et Monetaire Ouest africaine (UEMOA) *address*—Commission de l'UEMOA, 01 BP 543, Ouadgadougou, Burkina Faso *telephone*—[226] (35) 31 88 73 through 76 *FAX*—[226] (35) 31 88 72 *established*—1 August 1994 *aim*—to increase competitiveness of members' economic markets; to create a common market	*members*—(8) Benin, Burkina Faso, Cote d'Ivoire, Guinea-Bissau, Mali, Niger, Senegal, Togo
West African Economic Community (CEAO) *note*—acronym from Communaute Economique de l'Afrique de l'Ouest	established on 3 June 1972 to promote regional economic development; its members were Benin, Burkina Faso, Cote d'Ivoire, Mali, Mauritania, Niger, Senegal; it was disbanded in 1994
Western European Union (WEU) *address*—Rue de la Regence 4, B-1000 Brussels, Belgium *telephone*—[32] (2) 500 44 11 *FAX*—[32] (2) 511 32 70 *established*—23 October 1954 *effective*—6 May 1955 *aim*—to provide mutual defense and to move toward political unification	*members*—(10) Belgium, France, Germany, Greece, Italy, Luxembourg, Netherlands, Portugal, Spain, UK *associate members*—(3) Iceland, Norway, Turkey *associate partners*—(10) Bulgaria, Czech Republic, Estonia, Hungary, Latvia, Lithuania, Poland, Romania, Slovakia, Slovenia *observers*—(5) Austria, Denmark, Finland, Ireland, Sweden
World Bank	see International Bank for Reconstruction and Development (IBRD)
World Bank Group	includes International Bank for Reconstruction and Development (IBRD), International Development Association (IDA), and International Finance Corporation (IFC)
World Confederation of Labor (WCL) *address*—Rue de Treves 33, B-1040 Brussels, Belgium *telephone*—[32] (2) 230 62 95 *FAX*—[32] (2) 230 87 22 *established*—19 June 1920 as the International Federation of Christian Trade Unions (IFCTU), renamed 4 October 1968 *aim*—to promote the trade union movement	*members*—(99 national organizations) Algeria, Angola, Antigua and Barbuda, Argentina, Aruba, Austria, Bangladesh, Belgium, Belize, Benin, Bolivia, Bonaire Island, Botswana, Brazil, Burkina Faso, Cameroon, Canada, Cape Verde, Central African Republic, Chad, Chile, Colombia, Democratic Republic of the Congo, Costa Rica, Cote d'Ivoire, Cuba, Curacao, Cyprus, Dominica, Dominican Republic, Ecuador, El Salvador, France, French Guiana, Gabon, The Gambia, Ghana, Grenada, Guadeloupe, Guatemala, Guinea, Guyana, Haiti, Honduras, Hong Kong, Indonesia, Iran, Italy, Jamaica, Kenya, Lesotho, Liberia, Liechtenstein, Luxembourg, Madagascar, Malaysia, Mali, Malta, Martinique, Mauritius, Mexico, Montserrat, Namibia, Netherlands, Nicaragua, Niger, Nigeria, Pakistan, Panama, Paraguay, Peru, Philippines, Poland, Portugal, Puerto Rico, Romania, Rwanda, Saint Kitts and Nevis, Saint Lucia, Saint Martin, Saint Vincent and the Grenadines, Senegal, Seychelles, Sierra Leone, Spain, Sri Lanka, Suriname, Switzerland, Taiwan, Tanzania, Thailand, Togo, UK, US, Uruguay, Venezuela, Vietnam, Zambia, Zimbabwe
World Court	see International Court of Justice (ICJ)
World Customs Organization (WCO)	see Customs Cooperation Council (CCC)

Appendix C: International Organizations and Groups (continued)

World Federation of Trade Unions (WFTU)

address—Branicka 112, 14000 Prague 4, Czech Republic
telephone—[42] (2) 44 46 21 40, 44 46 20 85, 44 46 29 61
FAX—[42] (2) 44 46 13 78
established—3 October 1945
aim—to promote the trade union movement

members—(125 and the Palestine Liberation Organization) Afghanistan, Albania, Angola, Antigua and Barbuda, Argentina, Armenia, Australia, Austria, Azerbaijan, Bahrain, Bangladesh, Barbados, Belarus, Benin, Bolivia, Botswana, Brazil, Bulgaria, Burkina Faso, Cambodia, Cameroon, Canada, Chile, Colombia, Democratic Republic of the Congo, Republic of the Congo, Costa Rica, Cote d'Ivoire, Cuba, Cyprus, Czech Republic, Djibouti, Dominican Republic, Ecuador, Egypt, El Salvador, Eritrea, Ethiopia, Fiji, Finland, France, French Guiana, The Gambia, Ghana, Greece, Guadeloupe, Guatemala, Guinea, Guinea-Bissau, Guyana, Haiti, Honduras, Hungary, India, Indonesia, Iran, Iraq, Jamaica, Japan, Jordan, Kazakhstan, North Korea, Kuwait, Kyrgyzstan, Laos, Lebanon, Lesotho, Liberia, Libya, Madagascar, Malawi, Malaysia, Mali, Martinique, Mauritius, Mexico, Mozambique, Nepal, New Caledonia, NZ, Niger, Nigeria, Oman, Pakistan, Panama, Papua New Guinea, Peru, Philippines, Poland, Portugal, Puerto Rico, Reunion, Romania, Russia, Saint Lucia, Saint Pierre and Miquelon, Saint Vincent and the Grenadines, Saudi Arabia, Senegal, Sierra Leone, Slovakia, Solomon Islands, Somalia, South Africa, Sri Lanka, Sudan, Sweden, Syria, Tajikistan, Tanzania, Thailand, Togo, Trinidad and Tobago, Tunisia, Turkey, Turkmenistan, Uganda, Ukraine, Uruguay, Uzbekistan, Vanuatu, Venezuela, Vietnam, Yemen, Zimbabwe, Palestine Liberation Organization

World Food Council (WFC)

established 17 December 1974; to study world food problems and to recommend solutions; ECOSOC organization; there were 36 members selected on a rotating basis from all regions; subsumed by the World Food Program and Food and Agriculture Organization

World Food Program (WFP)

address—Via Cesare Giullio Viola, 68/70 Parco de Medici, I-00148 Rome, Italy
telephone—[39] (6) 522821
FAX—[39] (6) 59602348, 52282840
established—24 November 1961
aim—to provide food aid in support of economic development or disaster relief; an ECOSOC organization

members—(36) selected on a rotating basis from all regions

World Health Organization (WHO)

address—CH-1211 Geneva 27, Switzerland
telephone—[41] (22) 791 21 11, 791 32 23
FAX—[41] (22) 791 07 46
established—22 July 1946
effective—7 April 1948
aim—to deal with health matters worldwide; a UN specialized agency

members—(191) Afghanistan, Albania, Algeria, Andorra, Angola, Antigua and Barbuda, Argentina, Armenia, Australia, Austria, Azerbaijan, The Bahamas, Bahrain, Bangladesh, Barbados, Belarus, Belgium, Belize, Benin, Bhutan, Bolivia, Bosnia and Herzegovina, Botswana, Brazil, Brunei, Bulgaria, Burkina Faso, Burma, Burundi, Cambodia, Cameroon, Canada, Cape Verde, Central African Republic, Chad, Chile, China, Colombia, Comoros, Democratic Republic of the Congo, Republic of the Congo, Cook Islands, Costa Rica, Cote d'Ivoire, Croatia, Cuba, Cyprus, Czech Republic, Denmark, Djibouti, Dominica, Dominican Republic, Ecuador, Egypt, El Salvador, Equatorial Guinea, Eritrea, Estonia, Ethiopia, Fiji, Finland, France, Gabon, The Gambia, Georgia, Germany, Ghana, Greece, Grenada, Guatemala, Guinea, Guinea-Bissau, Guyana, Haiti, Honduras, Hungary, Iceland, India, Indonesia, Iran, Iraq, Ireland, Israel, Italy, Jamaica, Japan, Jordan, Kazakhstan, Kenya, Kiribati, North Korea, South Korea, Kuwait, Kyrgyzstan, Laos, Latvia, Lebanon, Lesotho, Liberia, Libya, Lithuania, Luxembourg, The Former Yugoslav Republic of Macedonia, Madagascar, Malawi, Malaysia, Maldives, Mali, Malta, Marshall Islands, Mauritania, Mauritius, Mexico, Federated States of Micronesia, Moldova, Monaco, Mongolia, Morocco, Mozambique, Namibia, Nauru, Nepal, Netherlands, NZ, Nicaragua, Niue, Niger, Nigeria, Norway, Oman, Pakistan, Palau, Panama, Papua New Guinea, Paraguay, Peru, Philippines, Poland, Portugal, Qatar, Romania, Russia, Rwanda, Saint Kitts and Nevis, Saint Lucia, Saint Vincent and the Grenadines, Samoa, San Marino, Sao Tome and Principe, Saudi Arabia, Senegal, Seychelles, Sierra Leone, Singapore, Slovakia, Slovenia, Solomon Islands, Somalia, South Africa, Spain, Sri Lanka, Sudan, Suriname, Swaziland, Sweden, Switzerland, Syria, Tajikistan, Tanzania, Thailand, Togo, Tonga, Trinidad and Tobago, Tunisia, Turkey, Turkmenistan, Tuvalu, Uganda, Ukraine, UAE, UK, US, Uruguay, Uzbekistan, Vanuatu, Venezuela, Vietnam, Yemen, Yugoslavia (suspended), Zambia, Zimbabwe
associate members—(2) Puerto Rico, Tokelau

Appendix C: International Organizations and Groups (continued)

World Intellectual Property Organization (WIPO)

address—34 Chemin des Colombettes, Case Postale 18, CH-1211 Geneva 20, Switzerland
telephone—[41] (22) 730 9111
FAX—[41] (22) 733 5428
established—14 July 1967
effective—26 April 1970
aim—to furnish protection for literary, artistic, and scientific works; a UN specialized agency

members—(168) Albania, Algeria, Andorra, Angola, Argentina, Armenia, Australia, Austria, Azerbaijan, The Bahamas, Bahrain, Bangladesh, Barbados, Belarus, Belgium, Benin, Bhutan, Bolivia, Bosnia and Herzegovina, Botswana, Brazil, Brunei, Bulgaria, Burkina Faso, Burundi, Cambodia, Cameroon, Canada, Cape Verde, Central African Republic, Chad, Chile, China, Colombia, Democratic Republic of the Congo, Republic of the Congo, Costa Rica, Cote d'Ivoire, Croatia, Cuba, Cyprus, Czech Republic, Denmark, Ecuador, Egypt, El Salvador, Equatorial Guinea, Eritrea, Estonia, Ethiopia, Fiji, Finland, France, Gabon, The Gambia, Georgia, Germany, Ghana, Greece, Guatemala, Guinea, Guinea-Bissau, Guyana, Haiti, Holy See, Honduras, Hungary, Iceland, India, Indonesia, Iraq, Ireland, Israel, Italy, Jamaica, Japan, Jordan, Kazakhstan, Kenya, North Korea, South Korea, Kyrgyzstan, Laos, Latvia, Lebanon, Lesotho, Liberia, Libya, Liechtenstein, Lithuania, Luxembourg, The Former Yugoslav Republic of Macedonia, Madagascar, Malawi, Malaysia, Mali, Malta, Mauritania, Mauritius, Mexico, Moldova, Monaco, Mongolia, Morocco, Mozambique, Namibia, Nepal, Netherlands, NZ, Nicaragua, Niger, Nigeria, Norway, Oman, Pakistan, Panama, Papua New Guinea, Paraguay, Peru, Philippines, Poland, Portugal, Qatar, Romania, Russia, Rwanda, Saint Kitts and Nevis, Saint Lucia, Saint Vincent and the Grenadines, Samoa, San Marino, Sao Tome and Principe, Saudi Arabia, Senegal, Sierra Leone, Singapore, Slovakia, Slovenia, Somalia, South Africa, Spain, Sri Lanka, Sudan, Suriname, Swaziland, Sweden, Switzerland, Tajikistan, Tanzania, Thailand, Togo, Trinidad and Tobago, Tunisia, Turkey, Turkmenistan, Uganda, Ukraine, UAE, UK, US, Uruguay, Uzbekistan, Venezuela, Vietnam, Yemen, Yugoslavia (suspended), Zambia, Zimbabwe

World Meteorological Organization (WMO)

address—Case Postale 2300, 41 Avenue Giuseppe-Motta, CH-1211 Geneva 2, Switzerland
telephone—[41] (22) 730 81 11
FAX—[41] (22) 734 23 26
established—11 October 1947
effective—4 April 1951
aim—to sponsor meteorological cooperation; a UN specialized agency

members—(185) Afghanistan, Albania, Algeria, Angola, Antigua and Barbuda, Argentina, Armenia, Australia, Austria, Azerbaijan, The Bahamas, Bahrain, Bangladesh, Barbados, Belarus, Belgium, Belize, Benin, Bolivia, Bosnia and Herzegovina, Botswana, Brazil, British Caribbean Territories, Brunei, Bulgaria, Burkina Faso, Burma, Burundi, Cambodia, Cameroon, Canada, Cape Verde, Central African Republic, Chad, Chile, China, Colombia, Comoros, Democratic Republic of the Congo, Republic of the Congo, Cook Islands, Costa Rica, Cote d'Ivoire, Croatia, Cuba, Cyprus, Czech Republic, Denmark, Djibouti, Dominica, Dominican Republic, Ecuador, Egypt, El Salvador, Eritrea, Estonia, Ethiopia, Fiji, Finland, France, French Polynesia, Gabon, The Gambia, Georgia, Germany, Ghana, Greece, Guatemala, Guinea, Guinea-Bissau, Guyana, Haiti, Honduras, Hong Kong, Hungary, Iceland, India, Indonesia, Iran, Iraq, Ireland, Israel, Italy, Jamaica, Japan, Jordan, Kazakhstan, Kenya, North Korea, South Korea, Kuwait, Kyrgyzstan, Laos, Latvia, Lebanon, Lesotho, Liberia, Libya, Lithuania, Luxembourg, Macau, The Former Yugoslav Republic of Macedonia, Madagascar, Malawi, Malaysia, Maldives, Mali, Malta, Mauritania, Mauritius, Mexico, Federated States of Micronesia, Moldova, Monaco, Mongolia, Morocco, Mozambique, Namibia, Nepal, Netherlands, Netherlands Antilles, New Caledonia, NZ, Nicaragua, Niger, Nigeria, Niue, Norway, Oman, Pakistan, Panama, Papua New Guinea, Paraguay, Peru, Philippines, Poland, Portugal, Qatar, Romania, Russia, Rwanda, Saint Lucia, Samoa, Sao Tome and Principe, Saudi Arabia, Senegal, Seychelles, Sierra Leone, Singapore, Slovakia, Slovenia, Solomon Islands, Somalia, South Africa, Spain, Sri Lanka, Sudan, Suriname, Swaziland, Sweden, Switzerland, Syria, Tajikistan, Tanzania, Thailand, Togo, Tonga, Trinidad and Tobago, Tunisia, Turkey, Turkmenistan, Uganda, Ukraine, UAE, UK, US, Uruguay, Uzbekistan, Vanuatu, Venezuela, Vietnam, Yemen, Yugoslavia (suspended), Zambia, Zimbabwe

World Tourism Organization (WToO)

address—Calle Capitan Haya 42, 28020 Madrid, Spain
telephone—[34] (1) 567 81 00
FAX—[34] (1) 571 37 33
established—2 January 1975
aim—to promote tourism as a means of contributing to economic development, international understanding, and peace

members—(133) Afghanistan, Albania, Algeria, Andorra, Angola, Argentina, Armenia, Austria, Bangladesh, Benin, Bolivia, Bosnia and Herzegovina, Botswana, Brazil, Bulgaria, Burkina Faso, Burma, Burundi, Cambodia, Cameroon, Central African Republic, Chad, Chile, China, Colombia, Democratic Republic of the Congo, Republic of the Congo, Costa Rica, Cote d'Ivoire, Croatia, Cuba, Cyprus, Czech Republic, Djibouti, Dominican Republic, Ecuador, Egypt, El Salvador, Equatorial Guinea, Eritrea, Ethiopia, Fiji, Finland, France, Gabon, The Gambia, Georgia, Germany, Ghana, Greece, Grenada, Guatemala, Guinea, Guinea-Bissau, Haiti, Hungary, India, Indonesia, Iran, Iraq, Israel, Italy, Jamaica, Japan, Jordan, Kazakhstan, Kenya, North Korea, South Korea, Kuwait, Kyrgyzstan, Laos, Lebanon, Lesotho, Libya, The Former Yugoslav Republic of Macedonia, Madagascar, Malawi, Malaysia, Maldives, Mali, Malta, Mauritania, Mauritius, Mexico, Moldova, Mongolia, Morocco, Mozambique, Namibia, Nepal, Netherlands, Nicaragua, Niger, Nigeria, Pakistan, Panama, Paraguay, Peru, Philippines, Poland, Portugal, Romania, Russia, Rwanda, San Marino, Sao Tome and Principe, Senegal, Seychelles, Sierra Leone, Slovakia, Slovenia, South Africa, Spain, Sri Lanka, Sudan, Switzerland, Syria, Tanzania, Thailand, Togo, Tunisia, Turkey, Turkmenistan, Uganda, Ukraine, Uruguay, Uzbekistan, Venezuela, Vietnam, Yemen, Zambia, Zimbabwe
associate members—(4) Aruba, Macau, Madeira Islands, Netherlands Antilles
observer—(1) Holy See

Appendix C: International Organizations and Groups (continued)

World Trade Organization (WTrO)

note—succeeded General Agreement on Tariff and Trade (GATT)
address—Centre William Rappard, 154 Rue de Lausanne, CH-1211 Geneva 21, Switzerland
telephone—[41] (22) 739 51 11
FAX—[41] (22) 739 54 58
established—15 April 1994
effective—1 January 1995
aim—to provide a means to resolve trade conflicts between members and to carry on negotiations with the goal of further lowering and/or eliminating tariffs and other trade barriers

members—(134) Angola, Antigua and Barbuda, Argentina, Australia, Austria, Bahrain, Bangladesh, Barbados, Belgium, Belize, Benin, Bolivia, Botswana, Brazil, Brunei, Bulgaria, Burkina Faso, Burma, Burundi, Cameroon, Canada, Central African Republic, Chad, Chile, Colombia, Democratic Republic of the Congo, Republic of the Congo, Costa Rica, Cote d'Ivoire, Cuba, Cyprus, Czech Republic, Denmark, Djibouti, Dominica, Dominican Republic, Ecuador, Egypt, El Salvador, EU, Fiji, Finland, France, Gabon, The Gambia, Germany, Ghana, Greece, Grenada, Guatemala, Guinea, Guinea-Bissau, Guyana, Haiti, Honduras, Hong Kong, Hungary, Iceland, India, Indonesia, Ireland, Israel, Italy, Jamaica, Japan, Kenya, South Korea, Kuwait, Kyrgyzstan, Latvia, Lesotho, Liechtenstein, Luxembourg, Macau, Madagascar, Malawi, Malaysia, Maldives, Mali, Malta, Mauritania, Mauritius, Mexico, Mongolia, Morocco, Mozambique, Namibia, Netherlands, NZ, Nicaragua, Niger, Nigeria, Norway, Pakistan, Panama, Papua New Guinea, Paraguay, Peru, Philippines, Poland, Portugal, Qatar, Romania, Rwanda, Saint Kitts and Nevis, Saint Lucia, Saint Vincent and the Grenadines, Senegal, Sierra Leone, Singapore, Slovakia, Slovenia, Solomon Islands, South Africa, Spain, Sri Lanka, Suriname, Swaziland, Sweden, Switzerland, Tanzania, Thailand, Togo, Trinidad and Tobago, Tunisia, Turkey, Uganda, UAE, UK, US, Uruguay, Venezuela, Zambia, Zimbabwe
observers—(5) Azerbaijan, Laos, Somalia, Tajikistan, Turkmenistan
applicants—(33) Albania, Algeria, Armenia, The Bahamas, Belarus, Cambodia, Cape Verde, China, Comoros, Croatia, Equatorial Guinea, Estonia, Georgia, Jordan, Kazakhstan, Kiribati, Lithuania, The Former Yugoslav Republic of Macedonia, Moldova, Nepal, Oman, Russia, Sao Tome and Principe, Saudi Arabia, Seychelles, Tonga, Tuvalu, Ukraine, Uzbekistan, Vanuatu, Vietnam, Yemen, Taiwan; *note*—some of these countries applied to GATT and are still under consideration for membership in WTrO; the following member of GATT had not become a member of WTrO as of 1 January 1998: Yugoslavia (suspended)

Zangger Committee (ZC)

established—early 1970s
aim—to establish guidelines for the export control provisions of the Nonproliferation of Nuclear Weapons Treaty (NPT)

members—(29) Australia, Austria, Belgium, Bulgaria, Canada, Czech Republic, Denmark, Finland, France, Germany, Greece, Hungary, Ireland, Italy, Japan, Luxembourg, Netherlands, Norway, Poland, Portugal, Romania, Russia, Slovakia, South Africa, Spain, Sweden, Switzerland, UK, US

Appendix D:

Selected International Environmental Agreements

Air Pollution	see Convention on Long-Range Transboundary Air Pollution
Air Pollution-Nitrogen Oxides	see Protocol to the 1979 Convention on Long-Range Transboundary Air Pollution Concerning the Control of Emissions of Nitrogen Oxides or Their Transboundary Fluxes
Air Pollution-Persistent Organic Pollutants	see Protocol to the 1979 Convention on Long-Range Transboundary Air Pollution on Persistent Organic Pollutants
Air Pollution-Sulphur 85	see Protocol to the 1979 Convention on Long-Range Transboundary Air Pollution on the Reduction of Sulphur Emissions or Their Transboundary Fluxes by at least 30%
Air Pollution-Sulphur 94	see Protocol to the 1979 Convention on Long-Range Transboundary Air Pollution on Further Reduction of Sulphur Emissions
Air Pollution-Volatile Organic Compounds	see Protocol to the 1979 Convention on Long-Range Transboundary Air Pollution Concerning the Control of Emissions of Volatile Organic Compounds or Their Transboundary Fluxes
Antarctic-Environmental Protocol	see Protocol on Environmental Protection to the Antarctic Treaty
Antarctic Treaty *opened for signature*—1 December 1959 *entered into force*—23 June 1961 *objective*—to ensure that Antarctica is used for peaceful purposes, such as, for international cooperation in scientific research, and that it does not become the scene or object of international discord	*parties*—(43) Argentina, Australia, Austria, Belgium, Brazil, Bulgaria, Canada, Chile, China, Colombia, Cuba, Czech Republic, Denmark, Ecuador, Finland, France, Germany, Greece, Guatemala, Hungary, India, Italy, Japan, North Korea, South Korea, Netherlands, NZ, Norway, Papua New Guinea, Peru, Poland, Romania, Russia, Slovakia, South Africa, Spain, Sweden, Switzerland, Turkey, Ukraine, UK, US, Uruguay
Basel Convention on the Control of Transboundary Movements of Hazardous Wastes and Their Disposal *note*—abbreviated as Hazardous Wastes *opened for signature*—22 March 1989 *entered into force*—5 May 1992 *objective*—to reduce transboundary movements of wastes subject to the Convention to a minimum consistent with the environmentally sound and efficient management of such wastes; to minimize the amount and toxicity of wastes generated and ensure their environmentally sound management as closely as possible to the source of generation; and to assist LDCs in environmentally sound management of the hazardous and other wastes they generate	*parties*—(123) Antigua and Barbuda, Argentina, Australia, Austria, The Bahamas, Bahrain, Bangladesh, Barbados, Belgium, Belize, Benin, Bolivia, Botswana, Brazil, Bulgaria, Burundi, Canada, Chile, China, Colombia, Comoros, Democratic Republic of the Congo, Costa Rica, Cote d'Ivoire, Croatia, Cuba, Cyprus, Czech Republic, Denmark, Dominica, Ecuador, Egypt, El Salvador, Estonia, EU, Finland, France, The Gambia, Germany, Greece, Guatemala, Guinea, Honduras, Hungary, Iceland, India, Indonesia, Iran, Ireland, Israel, Italy, Japan, Jordan, South Korea, Kuwait, Kyrgyzstan, Latvia, Lebanon, Liechtenstein, Luxembourg, The Former Yugoslav Republic of Macedonia, Malawi, Malaysia, Maldives, Mauritania, Mauritius, Mexico, Federated States of Micronesia, Moldova, Monaco, Mongolia, Morocco, Mozambique, Namibia, Nepal, Netherlands, NZ, Nicaragua, Niger, Nigeria, Norway, Oman, Pakistan, Panama, Papua New Guinea, Paraguay, Peru, Philippines, Poland, Portugal, Qatar, Romania, Russia, Saint Kitts and Nevis, Saint Lucia, Saint Vincent and the Grenadines, Saudi Arabia, Senegal, Seychelles, Singapore, Slovakia, Slovenia, South Africa, Spain, Sri Lanka, Sweden, Switzerland, Syria, Tanzania, Thailand, Trinidad and Tobago, Tunisia, Turkey, Turkmenistan, Uganda, UAE, UK, Uruguay, Uzbekistan, Venezuela, Vietnam, Yemen, Zambia *countries that have signed, but not yet ratified*—(3) Afghanistan, Haiti, US
Biodiversity	see Convention on Biological Diversity

Appendix D: Selected International Environmental Agreements (continued)

Convention on Biological Diversity

note—abbreviated as Biodiversity
opened for signature—5 June 1992
entered into force—29 December 1993
objective—to develop national strategies for the conservation and sustainable use of biological diversity

parties—(175) Albania, Algeria, Angola, Antigua and Barbuda, Argentina, Armenia, Australia, Austria, The Bahamas, Bahrain, Bangladesh, Barbados, Belarus, Belgium, Belize, Benin, Bhutan, Bolivia, Botswana, Brazil, Bulgaria, Burkina Faso, Burma, Burundi, Cambodia, Cameroon, Canada, Cape Verde, Central African Republic, Chad, Chile, China, Colombia, Comoros, Democratic Republic of the Congo, Republic of the Congo, Cook Islands, Costa Rica, Cote d'Ivoire, Croatia, Cuba, Cyprus, Czech Republic, Denmark, Djibouti, Dominica, Dominican Republic, Ecuador, Egypt, El Salvador, Equatorial Guinea, Eritrea, Estonia, Ethiopia, EU, Fiji, Finland, France, Gabon, The Gambia, Georgia, Germany, Ghana, Greece, Grenada, Guatemala, Guinea, Guinea-Bissau, Guyana, Haiti, Honduras, Hungary, Iceland, India, Indonesia, Iran, Ireland, Israel, Italy, Jamaica, Japan, Jordan, Kazakhstan, Kenya, Kiribati, North Korea, South Korea, Kyrgyzstan, Laos, Latvia, Lebanon, Lesotho, Liechtenstein, Lithuania, Luxembourg, The Former Yugoslav Republic of Macedonia, Madagascar, Malawi, Malaysia, Maldives, Mali, Marshall Islands, Mauritania, Mauritius, Mexico, Federated States of Micronesia, Moldova, Monaco, Mongolia, Morocco, Mozambique, Namibia, Nauru, Nepal, Netherlands, NZ, Nicaragua, Niger, Nigeria, Niue, Norway, Oman, Pakistan, Palau, Panama, Papua New Guinea, Paraguay, Peru, Philippines, Poland, Portugal, Qatar, Romania, Russia, Rwanda, Saint Kitts and Nevis, Saint Lucia, Saint Vincent and the Grenadines, Samoa, San Marino, Senegal, Seychelles, Sierra Leone, Singapore, Slovakia, Slovenia, Solomon Islands, South Africa, Spain, Sri Lanka, Sudan, Suriname, Swaziland, Sweden, Switzerland, Syria, Tajikistan, Tanzania, Togo, Tonga, Trinidad and Tobago, Tunisia, Turkey, Turkmenistan, Uganda, Ukraine, UK, Uruguay, Uzbekistan, Vanuatu, Venezuela, Vietnam, Yemen, Zambia, Zimbabwe

countries that have signed, but not yet ratified—(12) Afghanistan, Azerbaijan, Kuwait, Liberia, Libya, Malta, Sao Tome and Principe, Thailand, Tuvalu, UAE, US, former Yugoslavia

---

Climate Change

see United Nations Framework Convention on Climate Change

Climate Change-Kyoto Protocol

see Kyoto Protocol to the United Nations Framework Convention on Climate Change

---

Convention on Fishing and Conservation of Living Resources of the High Seas

note—abbreviated as Marine Life Conservation
opened for signature—29 April 1958
entered into force—20 March 1966
objective—to solve through international cooperation the problems involved in the conservation of living resources of the high seas, considering that because of the development of modern technology some of these resources are in danger of being overexploited

parties—(37) Australia, Belgium, Bosnia and Herzegovina, Burkina Faso, Cambodia, Colombia, Denmark, Dominican Republic, Fiji, Finland, France, Haiti, Jamaica, Kenya, Lesotho, Madagascar, Malawi, Malaysia, Mauritius, Mexico, Netherlands, Nigeria, Portugal, Senegal, Sierra Leone, Solomon Islands, South Africa, Spain, Switzerland, Thailand, Tonga, Trinidad and Tobago, Uganda, UK, US, Venezuela, former Yugoslavia

countries that have signed, but not yet ratified—(21) Afghanistan, Argentina, Bolivia, Canada, Costa Rica, Cuba, Ghana, Iceland, Indonesia, Iran, Ireland, Israel, Lebanon, Liberia, Nepal, NZ, Pakistan, Panama, Sri Lanka, Tunisia, Uruguay

---

Convention on Long-Range Transboundary Air Pollution

note—abbreviated as Air Pollution
opened for signature—13 November 1979
entered into force—16 March 1983
objective—to protect the human environment against air pollution and to gradually reduce and prevent air pollution, including long-range transboundary air pollution

parties—(44) Armenia, Austria, Belarus, Belgium, Bosnia and Herzegovina, Bulgaria, Canada, Croatia, Cyprus, Czech Republic, Denmark, EU, Finland, France, Georgia, Germany, Greece, Hungary, Iceland, Ireland, Italy, Latvia, Liechtenstein, Lithuania, Luxembourg, The Former Yugoslav Republic of Macedonia, Malta, Moldova, Netherlands, Norway, Poland, Portugal, Romania, Russia, Slovakia, Slovenia, Spain, Sweden, Switzerland, Turkey, Ukraine, UK, US, former Yugoslavia

countries that have signed, but not yet ratified—(2) Holy See, San Marino

---

Convention on the International Trade in Endangered Species of Wild Flora and Fauna (CITES)

note—abbreviated as Endangered Species
opened for signature—3 March 1973
entered into force—1 July 1975
objective—to protect certain endangered species from overexploitation by means of a system of import/export permits

parties—(137) Afghanistan, Algeria, Antigua and Barbuda, Argentina, Australia, Austria, The Bahamas, Bangladesh, Barbados, Belgium, Belize, Benin, Bolivia, Botswana, Brazil, Brunei, Bulgaria, Burkina Faso, Burundi, Cambodia, Cameroon, Canada, Central African Republic, Chad, Chile, China, Colombia, Comoros, Democratic Republic of the Congo, Republic of the Congo, Costa Rica, Cote d'Ivoire, Cuba, Cyprus, Czech Republic, Denmark, Djibouti, Dominican Republic, Ecuador, Egypt, Equatorial Guinea, Eritrea, Estonia, Ethiopia, Fiji, Finland, France, Gabon, The Gambia, Germany, Ghana, Greece, Guatemala, Guinea, Guinea-Bissau, Guyana, Honduras, Hungary, India, Indonesia, Iran, Israel, Italy, Japan, Jordan, Kenya, Kiribati, South Korea, Latvia, Liberia, Liechtenstein, Luxembourg, Madagascar, Malawi, Malaysia, Mali, Malta, Mauritius, Mexico, Monaco, Mongolia, Morocco, Mozambique, Namibia, Nepal, Netherlands, NZ, Nicaragua, Niger, Nigeria, Norway, Pakistan, Panama, Papua New Guinea, Paraguay, Peru, Philippines, Poland, Portugal, Romania, Russia, Rwanda, Saint Kitts and Nevis, Saint Lucia, Saint Vincent and the Grenadines, Saudi Arabia, Senegal, Seychelles, Sierra Leone, Singapore, Slovakia, Somalia, South Africa, Spain, Sri Lanka, Sudan, Suriname, Swaziland, Sweden, Switzerland, Tanzania, Thailand, Togo, Trinidad and Tobago, Tunisia, Tuvalu, Uganda, UAE, UK, US, Uruguay, Uzbekistan, Vanuatu, Venezuela, Vietnam, Zambia, Zimbabwe

countries that have signed, but not yet ratified—(3) Ireland, Kuwait, Lesotho

Appendix D: Selected International Environmental Agreements (continued)

Convention on the Prevention of Marine Pollution by Dumping Wastes and Other Matter (London Convention) *note*—abbreviated as Marine Dumping *opened for signature*—29 December 1972 *entered into force*—30 August 1975 *objective*—to control pollution of the sea by dumping and to encourage regional agreements supplementary to the Convention	*parties*—(75) Afghanistan, Antigua and Barbuda, Argentina, Australia, Barbados, Belarus, Belgium, Belize, Bosnia and Herzegovina, Brazil, Canada, Cape Verde, Chile, China, Democratic Republic of the Congo, Costa Rica, Cote d'Ivoire, Cuba, Cyprus, Denmark, Dominican Republic, Egypt, Finland, France, Gabon, Germany, Greece, Guatemala, Haiti, Honduras, Hungary, Iceland, Iran, Ireland, Italy, Jamaica, Japan, Jordan, Kenya, Kiribati, Libya, Luxembourg, Malta, Mexico, Monaco, Morocco, Nauru, Netherlands, NZ, Nigeria, Norway, Oman, Panama, Papua New Guinea, Philippines, Poland, Portugal, Russia, Saint Lucia, Seychelles, Slovenia, Solomon Islands, South Africa, Spain, Suriname, Sweden, Switzerland, Tonga, Tunisia, Tuvalu, Ukraine, UAE, UK, US, former Yugoslavia
Convention on the Prohibition of Military or Any Other Hostile Use of Environmental Modification Techniques *note*—abbreviated as Environmental Modification opened for signature—10 December 1976 entered into force—5 October 1978 objective—to prohibit the military or other hostile use of environmental modification techniques in order to further world peace and trust among nations	*parties*—(64) Afghanistan, Algeria, Antigua and Barbuda, Argentina, Australia, Austria, Bangladesh, Belarus, Belgium, Benin, Brazil, Bulgaria, Canada, Cape Verde, Chile, Costa Rica, Cuba, Cyprus, Czech Republic, Denmark, Dominica, Egypt, Finland, Germany, Ghana, Greece, Guatemala, Hungary, India, Ireland, Italy, Japan, North Korea, South Korea, Kuwait, Laos, Malawi, Mauritius, Mongolia, Netherlands, NZ, Niger, Norway, Pakistan, Papua New Guinea, Poland, Romania, Russia, Saint Lucia, Sao Tome and Principe, Slovakia, Solomon Islands, Spain, Sri Lanka, Sweden, Switzerland, Tunisia, Ukraine, UK, US, Uruguay, Uzbekistan, Vietnam, Yemen *countries that have signed, but not yet ratified*—(17) Bolivia, Democratic Republic of the Congo, Ethiopia, Holy See, Iceland, Iran, Iraq, Lebanon, Liberia, Luxembourg, Morocco, Nicaragua, Portugal, Sierra Leone, Syria, Turkey, Uganda
Convention on Wetlands of International Importance Especially as Waterfowl Habitat (Ramsar) *note*—abbreviated as Wetlands *opened for signature*—2 February 1971 *entered into force*—21 December 1975 *objective*—to stem the progressive encroachment on and loss of wetlands now and in the future, recognizing the fundamental ecological functions of wetlands and their economic, cultural, scientific, and recreational value	*parties*—(101) Albania, Algeria, Argentina, Armenia, Australia, Austria, The Bahamas, Bahrain, Bangladesh, Belgium, Brazil, Bulgaria, Burkina Faso, Canada, Chad, Chile, China, Democratic Republic of the Congo, Costa Rica, Cote d'Ivoire, Croatia, Czech Republic, Denmark, Ecuador, Egypt, Estonia, Finland, France, Gabon, The Gambia, Georgia, Germany, Greece, Guatemala, Guinea, Guinea-Bissau, Honduras, Hungary, Iceland, India, Indonesia, Iran, Ireland, Israel, Italy, Jamaica, Japan, Jordan, Kenya, South Korea, Latvia, Liechtenstein, Lithuania, Malawi, Mali, Malta, Mauritania, Mexico, Monaco, Mongolia, Morocco, Namibia, Netherlands, NZ, Nicaragua, Niger, Norway, Pakistan, Panama, Papua New Guinea, Paraguay, Peru, Philippines, Poland, Portugal, Romania, Russia, Senegal, Slovakia, Slovenia, South Africa, Spain, Sri Lanka, Suriname, Sweden, Switzerland, Togo, Trinidad and Tobago, Tunisia, Turkey, UK, US, Uruguay, Venezuela, Vietnam, former Yugoslavia, Zambia
Desertification	see United Nations Convention to Combat Desertification in those Countries Experiencing Serious Drought and/or Desertification, Particularly in Africa
Endangered Species	see Convention on the International Trade in Endangered Species of Wild Flora and Fauna (CITES)
Environmental Modification	see Convention on the Prohibition of Military or Any Other Hostile Use of Environmental Modification Techniques
Hazardous Wastes	see Basel Convention on the Control of Transboundary Movements of Hazardous Wastes and Their Disposal
International Convention for the Regulation of Whaling *note*—abbreviated as Whaling *opened for signature*—2 December 1946 *entered into force*—10 November 1948 *objective*—to protect all species of whales from overhunting; to establish a system of international regulation for the whale fisheries to ensure proper conservation and development of whale stocks; and to safeguard for future generations the great natural resources represented by whale stocks	*parties*—(51) Antigua and Barbuda, Argentina, Australia, Austria, Belize, Brazil, Canada, Chile, China, Costa Rica, Denmark, Dominica, Ecuador, Egypt, Finland, France, Germany, Grenada, Iceland, India, Ireland, Italy, Jamaica, Japan, Kenya, South Korea, Mauritius, Mexico, Monaco, Netherlands, NZ, Norway, Oman, Panama, Peru, Philippines, Russia, Saint Kitts and Nevis, Saint Lucia, Saint Vincent and the Grenadines, Senegal, Seychelles, Solomon Islands, South Africa, Spain, Sweden, Switzerland, UK, US, Uruguay, Venezuela

Appendix D: Selected International Environmental Agreements (continued)

International Tropical Timber Agreement, 1983 *note*—abbreviated as Tropical Timber 83 *opened for signature*—18 November 1983 *entered into force*—1 April 1985; this agreement expired when the International Tropical Timber Agreement, 1994, went into force *objective*—to provide an effective framework for cooperation between tropical timber producers and consumers and to encourage the development of national policies aimed at sustainable utilization and conservation of tropical forests and their genetic resources	*parties*—(54) Australia, Austria, Belgium, Bolivia, Brazil, Burma, Cameroon, Canada, China, Colombia, Democratic Republic of the Congo, Republic of the Congo, Cote d'Ivoire, Denmark, Ecuador, Egypt, EU, Fiji, Finland, France, Gabon, Germany, Ghana, Greece, Guyana, Honduras, India, Indonesia, Ireland, Italy, Japan, South Korea, Liberia, Luxembourg, Malaysia, Nepal, Netherlands, NZ, Norway, Panama, Papua New Guinea, Peru, Philippines, Portugal, Russia, Spain, Sweden, Switzerland, Thailand, Togo, Trinidad and Tobago, UK, US, Venezuela
International Tropical Timber Agreement, 1994 *note*—abbreviated as Tropical Timber 94 opened for signature—26 January 1994 *entered into force*—1 January 1997 *objective*—to ensure that by the year 2000 exports of tropical timber originate from sustainably managed sources; to establish a fund to assist tropical timber producers in obtaining the resources necessary to reach this objective	*parties*—(54) Australia, Austria, Belgium, Bolivia, Brazil, Burma, Cambodia, Cameroon, Canada, Central African Republic, China, Colombia, Democratic Republic of the Congo, Republic of the Congo, Cote d'Ivoire, Denmark, Ecuador, Egypt, EU, Fiji, Finland, France, Gabon, Germany, Ghana, Greece, Guyana, Honduras, India, Indonesia, Italy, Japan, South Korea, Liberia, Luxembourg, Malaysia, Nepal, Netherlands, NZ, Norway, Panama, Papua New Guinea, Peru, Philippines, Spain, Suriname, Sweden, Switzerland, Thailand, Togo, Trinidad and Tobago, UK, US, Venezuela *countries that have signed, but not yet ratified*—(2) Ireland, Portugal
Kyoto Protocol to the United Nations Framework Convention on Climate Change *note*—abbreviated as Climate Change-Kyoto Protocol *opened for signature*—16 March 1998, but not yet in force *objective*—to further reduce greenhouse gas emissions by enhancing the national programs of developed countries aimed at this goal and by establishing percentage reduction targets for the developed countries	*parties*—(7) Antigua and Barbuda, El Salvador, Fiji, Maldives, Panama, Trinidad and Tobago, Tuvalu *countries that have signed, but not yet ratified*—(72) Argentina, Australia, Austria, Belgium, Bolivia, Brazil, Bulgaria, Canada, Chile, China, Cook Islands, Costa Rica, Croatia, Czech Republic, Denmark, Ecuador, Estonia, EU, Finland, France, Germany, Greece, Guatemala, Honduras, Indonesia, Ireland, Israel, Italy, Japan, South Korea, Latvia, Liechtenstein, Lithuania, Luxembourg, Mali, Malta, Marshall Islands, Mexico, Federated States of Micronesia, Monaco, Netherlands, New Zealand, Nicaragua, Niger, Niue, Norway, Papua New Guinea, Paraguay, Peru, Philippines, Poland, Portugal, Romania, Russia, Saint Lucia, Saint Vincent and the Grenadines, Samoa, Seychelles, Slovakia, Slovenia, Solomon Islands, Spain, Sweden, Switzerland, Thailand, Turkmenistan, UK, US, Uruguay, Uzbekistan, Vietnam, Zambia
Law of the Sea	see United Nations Convention on the Law of the Sea (LOS)
Marine Dumping	see Convention on the Prevention of Marine Pollution by Dumping Wastes and Other Matter (London Convention)
Marine Life Conservation	see Convention on Fishing and Conservation of Living Resources of the High Seas
Montreal Protocol on Substances That Deplete the Ozone Layer *note*—abbreviated as Ozone Layer Protection *opened for signature*—16 September 1987 *entered into force*—1 January 1989 *objective*—to protect the ozone layer by controlling emissions of substances that deplete it	*parties*—(168) Algeria, Antigua and Barbuda, Argentina, Australia, Austria, Azerbaijan, The Bahamas, Bahrain, Bangladesh, Barbados, Belarus, Belgium, Belize, Benin, Bolivia, Bosnia and Herzegovina, Botswana, Brazil, Brunei, Bulgaria, Burkina Faso, Burma, Burundi, Cameroon, Canada, Central African Republic, Chad, Chile, China, Colombia, Comoros, Democratic Republic of the Congo, Republic of the Congo, Costa Rica, Cote d'Ivoire, Croatia, Cuba, Cyprus, Czech Republic, Denmark, Dominica, Dominican Republic, Ecuador, Egypt, El Salvador, Estonia, Ethiopia, EU, Fiji, Finland, France, Gabon, The Gambia, Georgia, Germany, Ghana, Greece, Grenada, Guatemala, Guinea, Guyana, Honduras, Hungary, Iceland, India, Indonesia, Iran, Ireland, Israel, Italy, Jamaica, Japan, Jordan, Kazakhstan, Kenya, Kiribati, North Korea, South Korea, Kuwait, Laos, Latvia, Lebanon, Lesotho, Liberia, Libya, Liechtenstein, Lithuania, Luxembourg, The Former Yugoslav Republic of Macedonia, Madagascar, Malawi, Malaysia, Maldives, Mali, Malta, Marshall Islands, Mauritania, Mauritius, Mexico, Federated States of Micronesia, Moldova, Monaco, Mongolia, Morocco, Mozambique, Namibia, Nepal, Netherlands, NZ, Nicaragua, Niger, Nigeria, Norway, Pakistan, Panama, Papua New Guinea, Paraguay, Peru, Philippines, Poland, Portugal (Portugal has also extended the protocol to Macau), Qatar, Romania, Russia, Saint Kitts and Nevis, Saint Lucia, Saint Vincent and the Grenadines, Samoa, Saudi Arabia, Senegal, Seychelles, Singapore, Slovakia, Slovenia, Solomon Islands, South Africa, Spain, Sri Lanka, Sudan, Suriname, Swaziland, Sweden, Switzerland, Syria, Tajikistan, Tanzania, Thailand, Togo, Tonga, Trinidad and Tobago, Tunisia, Turkey, Turkmenistan, Tuvalu, Uganda, Ukraine, UAE, UK, US, Uruguay, Uzbekistan, Vanuatu, Venezuela, Vietnam, Yemen, former Yugoslavia, Zambia, Zimbabwe
Nuclear Test Ban	see Treaty Banning Nuclear Weapons Tests in the Atmosphere, in Outer Space, and Under Water
Ozone Layer Protection	see Montreal Protocol on Substances That Deplete the Ozone Layer

Protocol of 1978 Relating to the International Convention for the Prevention of Pollution From Ships, 1973 (MARPOL)

note—abbreviated as Ship Pollution
opened for signature—17 February 1978
entered into force—2 October 1983
objective—to preserve the marine environment through the complete elimination of pollution by oil and other harmful substances and the minimization of accidental discharge of such substances

parties—(100) Algeria, Antigua and Barbuda, Argentina, Australia, Austria, The Bahamas, Barbados, Belgium, Belize, Brazil, Brunei, Bulgaria, Burma, Cambodia, Canada, Chile, China, Colombia, Cote d'Ivoire, Croatia, Cuba, Cyprus, Czech Republic, Denmark, Djibouti, Ecuador, Egypt, Equatorial Guinea, Estonia, Finland, France, Gabon, The Gambia, Georgia, Germany, Ghana, Greece, Guatemala, Hungary, Iceland, India, Indonesia, Ireland, Israel, Italy, Jamaica, Japan, Kazakhstan, Kenya, North Korea, South Korea, Latvia, Lebanon, Liberia, Lithuania, Luxembourg, Malaysia, Malta, Marshall Islands, Mauritania, Mauritius, Mexico, Monaco, Morocco, Netherlands, Norway, Oman, Pakistan, Panama, Papua New Guinea, Peru, Poland, Portugal, Romania, Russia, Saint Vincent and the Grenadines, Senegal, Seychelles, Singapore, Slovakia, Slovenia, South Africa, Spain, Suriname, Sweden, Switzerland, Syria, Togo, Tonga, Tunisia, Turkey, Tuvalu, Ukraine, UK, US, Uruguay, Vanuatu, Venezuela, Vietnam, former Yugoslavia

---

Protocol on Environmental Protection to the Antarctic Treaty

note—abbreviated as Antarctic-Environmental Protocol
opened for signature—4 October 1991
entered into force—14 January 1998
objective—to enhance the protection of the Antarctic environment and dependent and associated ecosystems

parties—(28) Argentina, Australia, Belgium, Brazil, Bulgaria, Chile, China, Ecuador, Finland, France, Germany, Greece, India, Italy, Japan, South Korea, Netherlands, NZ, Norway, Peru, Poland, Russia, South Africa, Spain, Sweden, UK, US, Uruguay
countries that have signed, but not yet ratified—(15) Austria, Canada, Colombia, Cuba, Czech Republic, Denmark, Guatemala, Hungary, North Korea, Papua New Guinea, Romania, Slovakia, Switzerland, Turkey, Ukraine

---

Protocol to the 1979 Convention on Long-Range Transboundary Air Pollution Concerning the Control of Emissions of Nitrogen Oxides or Their Transboundary Fluxes

note—abbreviated as Air Pollution-Nitrogen Oxides
opened for signature—31 October 1988
entered into force—14 February 1991
objective—to provide for the control or reduction of nitrogen oxides and their transboundary fluxes

parties—(26) Austria, Belarus, Bulgaria, Canada, Czech Republic, Denmark, EU, Finland, France, Germany, Greece, Hungary, Ireland, Italy, Liechtenstein, Luxembourg, Netherlands, Norway, Russia, Slovakia, Spain, Sweden, Switzerland, Ukraine, UK, US
countries that have signed, but not yet ratified—(2) Belgium, Poland

---

Protocol to the 1979 Convention on Long-Range Transboundary Air Pollution Concerning the Control of Emissions of Volatile Organic Compounds or Their Transboundary Fluxes

note—abbreviated as Air Pollution-Volatile Organic Compounds
opened for signature—18 November 1991
entered into force—29 September 1997
objective—to provide for the control and reduction of emissions of volatile organic compounds in order to reduce their transboundary fluxes so as to protect human health and the environment from adverse effects

parties—(17) Austria, Bulgaria, Czech Republic, Denmark, Finland, France, Germany, Hungary, Italy, Liechtenstein, Luxembourg, Netherlands, Norway, Spain, Sweden, Switzerland, UK
countries that have signed, but not yet ratified—(7) Belgium, Canada, EU, Greece, Portugal, Ukraine, US

Protocol to the 1979 Convention on Long-Range Transboundary Air Pollution on Further Reduction of Sulphur Emissions

note—abbreviated as Air Pollution-Sulphur 94
opened for signature—14 June 1994
entered into force—5 August 1998
objective—to provide for a further reduction in sulfur emissions or transboundary fluxes

parties—(21) Austria, Canada, Czech Republic, Denmark, EU, Finland, France, Germany, Greece, Ireland, Italy, Liechtenstein, Luxembourg, Netherlands, Norway, Slovakia, Slovenia, Spain, Sweden, Switzerland, UK
countries that have signed, but not yet ratified—(7) Belgium, Bulgaria, Croatia, Hungary, Poland, Russia, Ukraine

Appendix D: Selected International Environmental Agreements (continued)

Protocol to the 1979 Convention on Long-Range Transboundary Air Pollution on Persistent Organic Pollutants *note*—abbreviated as Air Pollution-Persistent Organic Pollutants *opened for signature*—24 June 1998, but not yet in force *objective*—to provide for the control and reduction of emissions of persistent organic pollutants in order to reduce their transboundary fluxes so as to protect human health and the environment from adverse effects	*partie*—(1) Canada *countries that have signed, but not yet ratified*—(35) Armenia, Austria, Belgium, Bulgaria, Croatia, Cyprus, Czech Republic, Denmark, EU, Finland, France, Germany, Greece, Hungary, Iceland, Ireland, Italy, Latvia, Liechtenstein, Lithuania, Luxembourg, Moldova, Netherlands, Norway, Poland, Portugal, Romania, Slovakia, Slovenia, Spain, Sweden, Switzerland, Ukraine, UK, US
Protocol to the 1979 Convention on Long-Range Transboundary Air Pollution on the Reduction of Sulphur Emissions or Their Transboundary Fluxes by at Least 30% *note*—abbreviated as Air Pollution-Sulphur 85 *opened for signature*—8 July 1985 *entered into force*—2 September 1987 *objective*—to provide for a 30% reduction in sulfur emissions or transboundary fluxes by 1993	*parties*—(21) Austria, Belarus, Belgium, Bulgaria, Canada, Czech Republic, Denmark, Finland, France, Germany, Hungary, Italy, Liechtenstein, Luxembourg, Netherlands, Norway, Russia, Slovakia, Sweden, Switzerland, Ukraine
Ship Pollution	see Protocol of 1978 Relating to the International Convention for the Prevention of Pollution From Ships, 1973 (MARPOL)
Treaty Banning Nuclear Weapon Tests in the Atmosphere, in Outer Space, and Under Water *note*—abbreviated as Nuclear Test Ban *opened for signature*—5 August 1963 *entered into force*—10 October 1963 *objective*—to obtain an agreement on general and complete disarmament under strict international control in accordance with the objectives of the United Nations; to put an end to the armaments race and eliminate incentives for the production and testing of all kinds of weapons, including nuclear weapons	*parties*—(122) Afghanistan, Antigua and Barbuda, Argentina, Armenia, Australia, Austria, The Bahamas, Bangladesh, Belarus, Belgium, Benin, Bhutan, Bolivia, Bosnia and Herzegovina, Botswana, Brazil, Bulgaria, Burma, Canada, Cape Verde, Central African Republic, Chad, Chile, Colombia, Democratic Republic of the Congo, Costa Rica, Cote d'Ivoire, Croatia, Cyprus, Czech Republic, Denmark, Dominican Republic, Ecuador, Egypt, El Salvador, Fiji, Finland, Gabon, The Gambia, Germany, Ghana, Greece, Guatemala, Honduras, Hungary, Iceland, India, Indonesia, Iran, Iraq, Ireland, Israel, Italy, Jamaica, Japan, Jordan, Kenya, South Korea, Kuwait, Laos, Lebanon, Liberia, Libya, Luxembourg, Madagascar, Malawi, Malaysia, Malta, Mauritania, Mauritius, Mexico, Mongolia, Morocco, Nepal, Netherlands, NZ, Nicaragua, Niger, Nigeria, Norway, Pakistan, Panama, Papua New Guinea, Peru, Philippines, Poland, Romania, Russia, Rwanda, Samoa, San Marino, Senegal, Seychelles, Sierra Leone, Singapore, Slovakia, Slovenia, South Africa, Spain, Sri Lanka, Sudan, Suriname, Swaziland, Sweden, Switzerland, Syria, Tanzania, Thailand, Togo, Tonga, Trinidad and Tobago, Tunisia, Turkey, Uganda, Ukraine, UK, US, Uruguay, Venezuela, Yemen, former Yugoslavia, Zambia *countries that have signed, but not yet ratified*—(12) Algeria, Burkina Faso, Burundi, Cameroon, China, Ethiopia, Haiti, Mali, Paraguay, Portugal, Somalia, Vietnam
Tropical Timber 83	see International Tropical Timber Agreement, 1983
Tropical Timber 94	see International Tropical Timber Agreement, 1994

Appendix D: Selected International Environmental Agreements (continued)

United Nations Convention on the Law of the Sea (LOS)

note—abbreviated as Law of the Sea
opened for signature—10 December 1982
entered into force—16 November 1994
objective—to set up a comprehensive new legal regime for the sea and oceans; to include rules concerning environmental standards as well as enforcement provisions dealing with pollution of the marine environment

parties—(130) Algeria, Angola, Antigua and Barbuda, Argentina, Australia, Austria, The Bahamas, Bahrain, Barbados, Belgium, Belize, Benin, Bolivia, Bosnia and Herzegovina, Botswana, Brazil, Brunei, Bulgaria, Burma, Cameroon, Cape Verde, Chile, China, Comoros, Democratic Republic of the Congo, Cook Islands, Costa Rica, Cote d'Ivoire, Croatia, Cuba, Cyprus, Czech Republic, Djibouti, Dominica, Egypt, Equatorial Guinea, EU, Fiji, Finland, France, Gabon, The Gambia, Georgia, Germany, Ghana, Greece, Grenada, Guatemala, Guinea, Guinea-Bissau, Guyana, Haiti, Honduras, Iceland, India, Indonesia, Iraq, Ireland, Italy, Jamaica, Japan, Jordan, Kenya, South Korea, Kuwait, Laos, Lebanon, The Former Yugoslav Republic of Macedonia, Malaysia, Mali, Malta, Marshall Islands, Mauritania, Mauritius, Mexico, Federated States of Micronesia, Monaco, Mongolia, Mozambique, Namibia, Nauru, Nepal, Netherlands, NZ, Nigeria, Norway, Oman, Pakistan, Palau, Panama, Papua New Guinea, Paraguay, Philippines, Poland, Portugal, Romania, Russia, Saint Kitts and Nevis, Saint Lucia, Saint Vincent and the Grenadines, Samoa, Sao Tome and Principe, Saudi Arabia, Senegal, Seychelles, Sierra Leone, Singapore, Slovakia, Slovenia, Solomon Islands, Somalia, South Africa, Spain, Sri Lanka, Sudan, Suriname, Sweden, Tanzania, Togo, Tonga, Trinidad and Tobago, Tunisia, Uganda, UK, Uruguay, Vietnam, Yemen, former Yugoslavia, Zambia, Zimbabwe

countries that have signed, but not yet ratified—(40) Afghanistan, Bangladesh, Belarus, Bhutan, Burkina Faso, Burundi, Cambodia, Canada, Central African Republic, Chad, Colombia, Republic of the Congo, Denmark, Dominican Republic, El Salvador, Ethiopia, Hungary, Iran, North Korea, Lesotho, Liberia, Libya, Liechtenstein, Luxembourg, Madagascar, Malawi, Maldives, Morocco, Nicaragua, Niger, Niue, Qatar, Rwanda, Swaziland, Switzerland, Thailand, Tuvalu, Ukraine, UAE, Vanuatu

---

United Nations Convention to Combat Desertification in Those Countries Experiencing Serious Drought and/or Desertification, Particularly in Africa

note—abbreviated as Desertification
opened for signature—14 October 1994
entered into force—26 December 1996
objective—to combat desertification and mitigate the effects of drought through national action programs that incorporate long-term strategies supported by international cooperation and partnership arrangements

parties—(148) Afghanistan, Algeria, Angola, Antigua and Barbuda, Argentina, Armenia, Austria, Azerbaijan, Bahrain, Bangladesh, Barbados, Belgium, Belize, Benin, Bolivia, Botswana, Brazil, Burkina Faso, Burma, Burundi, Cambodia, Cameroon, Canada, Cape Verde, Central African Republic, Chad, Chile, China, Comoros, Democratic Republic of the Congo, Cook Islands, Costa Rica, Cote d'Ivoire, Cuba, Denmark, Djibouti, Dominica, Dominican Republic, Ecuador, Egypt, El Salvador, Equatorial Guinea, Eritrea, Ethiopia, EU, Fiji, Finland, France, Gabon, The Gambia, Germany, Ghana, Greece, Grenada, Guatemala, Guinea, Guinea-Bissau, Guyana, Haiti, Honduras, Iceland, India, Indonesia, Iran, Ireland, Israel, Italy, Jamaica, Japan, Jordan, Kazakhstan, Kenya, Kiribati, Kuwait, Kyrgyzstan, Laos, Lebanon, Lesotho, Liberia, Libya, Luxembourg, Madagascar, Malawi, Malaysia, Mali, Malta, Marshall Islands, Mauritania, Mauritius, Mexico, Federated States of Micronesia, Moldova, Monaco, Mongolia, Morocco, Mozambique, Namibia, Nauru, Nepal, Netherlands, Nicaragua, Niger, Nigeria, Niue, Norway, Oman, Pakistan, Panama, Paraguay, Peru, Portugal, Romania, Rwanda, Saint Kitts and Nevis, Saint Lucia, Saint Vincent and the Grenadines, Samoa, Sao Tome and Principe, Saudi Arabia, Senegal, Seychelles, Sierra Leone, South Africa, Spain, Sri Lanka, Sudan, Swaziland, Sweden, Switzerland, Syria, Tajikistan, Tanzania, Togo, Tonga, Tunisia, Turkey, Turkmenistan, Tuvalu, Uganda, United Arab Emirates, UK, Uruguay, Uzbekistan, Venezuela, Vietnam, Yemen, Zambia, Zimbabwe

countries that have signed, but not yet ratified—(9) Australia, Colombia, Republic of the Congo, Croatia, Georgia, South Korea, Philippines, US, Vanuatu

---

United Nations Framework Convention on Climate Change

note—abbreviated as Climate Change
opened for signature—9 May 1992
entered into force—21 March 1994
objective—to achieve stabilization of greenhouse gas concentrations in the atmosphere at a low enough level to prevent dangerous anthropogenic interference with the climate system

parties—(177) Albania, Algeria, Antigua and Barbuda, Argentina, Armenia, Australia, Austria, Azerbaijan, The Bahamas, Bahrain, Bangladesh, Barbados, Belgium, Belize, Benin, Bhutan, Bolivia, Botswana, Brazil, Bulgaria, Burkina Faso, Burma, Burundi, Cambodia, Cameroon, Canada, Cape Verde, Central African Republic, Chad, Chile, China, Colombia, Comoros, Democratic Republic of the Congo, Republic of the Congo, Cook Islands, Costa Rica, Cote d'Ivoire, Croatia, Cuba, Cyprus, Czech Republic, Denmark, Djibouti, Dominica, Dominican Republic, Ecuador, Egypt, El Salvador, Eritrea, Estonia, Ethiopia, EU, Fiji, Finland, France, Gabon, The Gambia, Georgia, Germany, Ghana, Greece, Grenada, Guatemala, Guinea, Guinea-Bissau, Guyana, Haiti, Honduras, Hungary, Iceland, India, Indonesia, Iran, Ireland, Israel, Italy, Jamaica, Japan, Jordan, Kazakhstan, Kenya, Kiribati, North Korea, South Korea, Kuwait, Laos, Latvia, Lebanon, Lesotho, Liechtenstein, Lithuania, Luxembourg, The Former Yugoslav Republic of Macedonia, Malawi, Malaysia, Maldives, Mali, Malta, Marshall Islands, Mauritania, Mauritius, Mexico, Federated States of Micronesia, Moldova, Monaco, Mongolia, Morocco, Mozambique, Namibia, Nauru, Nepal, Netherlands, NZ, Nicaragua, Niger, Nigeria, Niue, Norway, Oman, Pakistan, Panama, Papua New Guinea, Paraguay, Peru, Philippines, Poland, Portugal, Qatar, Romania, Russia, Rwanda, Saint Kitts and Nevis, Saint Lucia, Saint Vincent and the Grenadines, Samoa, San Marino, Saudi Arabia, Senegal, Seychelles, Sierra Leone, Singapore, Slovakia, Slovenia, Solomon Islands, South Africa, Spain, Sri Lanka, Sudan, Suriname, Swaziland, Sweden, Switzerland, Syria, Tajikistan, Tanzania, Thailand, Togo, Tonga, Trinidad and Tobago, Tunisia, Turkmenistan, Tuvalu, Uganda, Ukraine, UAE, UK, US, Uruguay, Uzbekistan, Vanuatu, Venezuela, Vietnam, Yemen, former Yugoslavia, Zambia, Zimbabwe

countries that have signed, but not yet ratified—(7) Afghanistan, Angola, Belarus, Liberia, Libya, Madagascar, Sao Tome and Principe

---

Wetlands	see Convention on Wetlands of International Importance Especially As Waterfowl Habitat (Ramsar)
Whaling	see International Convention for the Regulation of Whaling

Appendix E:

Weights and Measures

Mathematical Notation

Mathematical Power	Name
10^{18} or 1,000,000,000,000,000,000	one quintillion
10^{15} or 1,000,000,000,000,000	one quadrillion
10^{12} or 1,000,000,000,000	one trillion
10^{9} or 1,000,000,000	one billion
10^{6} or 1,000,000	one million
10^{3} or 1,000	one thousand
10^{2} or 100	one hundred
10^{1} or 10	ten
10^{0} or 1	one
10^{-1} or 0.1	one-tenth
10^{-2} or 0.01	one-hundredth
10^{-3} or 0.001	one-thousandth
10^{-6} or 0.000 001	one-millionth
10^{-9} or 0.000 000 001	one-billionth
10^{-12} or 0.000 000 000 001	one-trillionth
10^{-15} or 0.000 000 000 000 001	one-quadrillionth
10^{-18} or 0.000 000 000 000 000 001	one-quintillionth

Metric Interrelationships

Prefix	Symbol	Length, weight, or capacity	Area	Volume
exa	E	10^{18}	10^{36}	10^{54}
peta	P	10^{15}	10^{30}	10^{45}
tera	T	10^{12}	10^{24}	10^{36}
giga	G	10^{9}	10^{18}	10^{27}
mega	M	10^{6}	10^{12}	10^{18}
hectokilo	hk	10^{5}	10^{10}	10^{15}
myria	ma	10^{4}	10^{8}	10^{12}
kilo	k	10^{3}	10^{6}	10^{9}
hecto	h	10^{2}	10^{4}	10^{6}
basic unit	—	1 meter, 1 gram, 1 liter	1 meter^2	1 meter^3
deci	d	10^{-1}	10^{-2}	10^{-3}
centi	c	10^{-2}	10^{-4}	10^{-6}
milli	m	10^{-3}	10^{-6}	10^{-9}
decimilli	dm	10^{-4}	10^{-8}	10^{-12}
centimilli	cm	10^{-5}	10^{-10}	10^{-15}
micro	u	10^{-6}	10^{-12}	10^{-18}
nano	n	10^{-9}	10^{-18}	10^{-27}
pico	p	10^{-12}	10^{-24}	10^{-36}
femto	f	10^{-15}	10^{-30}	10^{-45}
atto	a	10^{-18}	10^{-36}	10^{-54}

Appendix E: Weights and Measures (continued)

Conversion Factors	To Convert From	To	Multiply by
	acres	ares	40.468 564 224
	acres	hectares	0.404 685 642 24
	acres	square feet	43,560
	acres	square kilometers	0.004 046 856 422 4
	acres	square meters	4,046.856 422 4
	acres	square miles (statute)	0.001 562 50
	acres	square yards	4,840
	ares	square meters	100
	ares	square yards	119.599
	barrels, US beer	gallons	31
	barrels, US beer	liters	117.347 77
	barrels, US petroleum	gallons (British)	34.97
	barrels, US petroleum	gallons (US)	42
	barrels, US petroleum	liters	158.987 29
	barrels, US proof spirits	gallons	40
	barrels, US proof spirits	liters	151.416 47
	bushels (US)	bushels (British)	0.968 9
	bushels (US)	cubic feet	1.244 456
	bushels (US)	cubic inches	2,150.42
	bushels (US)	cubic meters	0.035 239 07
	bushels (US)	cubic yards	0.046 090 96
	bushels (US)	dekaliters	3.523 907
	bushels (US)	dry pints	64
	bushels (US)	dry quarts	32
	bushels (US)	liters	35.239 070 17
	bushels (US)	pecks	4
	cables	fathoms	120
	cables	meters	219.456
	cables	yards	240
	carat	milligrams	200
	centimeters	feet	0.032 808 40
	centimeters	inches	0.393 700 8
	centimeters	meters	0.01
	centimeters	yards	0.010 936 13
	centimeters, cubic	cubic inches	0.061 023 744
	centimeters, square	square feet	0.001 076 39
	centimeters, square	square inches	0.155 000 31
	centimeters, square	square meters	0.000 1
	centimeters, square	square yards	0.000 119 599

Appendix E: Weights and Measures (continued)

To Convert From	To	Multiply by
chains, square surveyor's	ares	4.046 86
chains, square surveyor's	square feet	4,356
chains, surveyor's	feet	66
chains, surveyor's	meters	20.116 8
chains, surveyor's	rods	4
cords of wood	cubic feet	128
cords of wood	cubic meters	3.624 556
cords of wood	cubic yards	4.740 7
cups	liquid ounces (US)	8
cups	liters	0.236 588 2
degrees Celsius	degrees Fahrenheit	multiply by 1.8 and add 32
degrees Fahrenheit	degrees Celsius	subtract 32 and divide by 1.8
dekaliters	bushels	0.283 775 9
dekaliters	cubic feet	0.353 146 7
dekaliters	cubic inches	610.237 4
dekaliters	dry pints	18.161 66
dekaliters	dry quarts	9.080 829 8
dekaliters	liters	10
dekaliters	pecks	1.135 104
drams, avoirdupois	avoirdupois ounces	0.062 55
drams, avoirdupois	grains	27.344
drams, avoirdupois	grams	1.771 845 2
drams, troy	grains	60
drams, troy	grams	3.887 934 6
drams, troy	scruples	3
drams, troy	troy ounces	0.125
drams, liquid (US)	cubic inches	0.226
drams, liquid (US)	liquid drams (British)	1.041
drams, liquid (US)	liquid ounces	0.125
drams, liquid (US)	milliliters	3.696 69
drams, liquid (US)	minims	60
fathoms	feet	6
fathoms	meters	1.828 8
feet	centimeters	30.48
feet	inches	12
feet	kilometers	0.000 304 8
feet	meters	0.304 8
feet	statute miles	0.000 189 39
feet	yards	0.333 333 3

Appendix E: Weights and Measures (continued)

Conversion Factors	To Convert From	To	Multiply by
	feet, cubic	bushels	0.803 563 95
	feet, cubic	cubic decimeters	28.316 847
	feet, cubic	cubic inches	1,728
	feet, cubic	cubic meters	0.028 316 846 592
	feet, cubic	cubic yards	0.037 037 04
	feet, cubic	dry pints	51.428 09
	feet, cubic	dry quarts	25.714 05
	feet, cubic	gallons	7.480 519
	feet, cubic	gills	239.376 6
	feet, cubic	liquid ounces	957.506 5
	feet, cubic	liquid pints	59.844 16
	feet, cubic	liquid quarts	29.922 08
	feet, cubic	liters	28.316 846 592
	feet, cubic	pecks	3.214 256
	feet, square	acres	0.000 022 956 8
	feet, square	square centimeters	929.030 4
	feet, square	square decimeters	9.290 304
	feet, square	square inches	144
	feet, square	square meters	0.092 903 04
	feet, square	square yards	0.111 111 1
	furlongs	feet	660
	furlongs	inches	7,920
	furlongs	meters	201.168
	furlongs	statute miles	0.125
	furlongs	yards	220
	gallons, liquid (US)	cubic feet	0.133 680 6
	gallons, liquid (US)	cubic inches	231
	gallons, liquid (US)	cubic meters	0.003 785 411 784
	gallons, liquid (US)	cubic yards	0.004 951 13
	gallons, liquid (US)	gills (US)	32
	gallons, liquid (US)	liquid gallons (British)	0.832 67
	gallons, liquid (US)	liquid ounces	128
	gallons, liquid (US)	liquid pints	8
	gallons, liquid (US)	liquid quarts	4
	gallons, liquid (US)	liters	3.785 411 784
	gallons, liquid (US)	milliliters	3,785.411 784
	gallons, liquid (US)	minims	61,440
	gills (US)	centiliters	11.829 4
	gills (US)	cubic feet	0.004 177 517
	gills (US)	cubic inches	7.218 75

Conversion Factors	To Convert From	To	Multiply by
	gills (US)	gallons	0.031 25
	gills (US)	gills (British)	0.832 67
	gills (US)	liquid ounces	4
	gills (US)	liquid pints	0.25
	gills (US)	liquid quarts	0.125
	gills (US)	liters	0.118 294 118 25
	gills (US)	milliliters	118.294 118 25
	gills (US)	minims	1,920
	grains	avoirdupois drams	0.036 571 43
	grains	avoirdupois ounces	0.002 285 71
	grains	avoirdupois pounds	0.000 142 86
	grains	grams	0.064 798 91
	grains	kilograms	0.000 064 798 91
	grains	milligrams	64.798 910
	grains	pennyweights	0.042
	grains	scruples	0.05
	grains	troy drams	0.016 6
	grains	troy ounces	0.002 083 33
	grains	troy pounds	0.000 173 61
	grams	avoirdupois drams	0.564 383 39
	grams	avoirdupois ounces	0.035 273 961
	grams	avoirdupois pounds	0.002 204 622 6
	grams	grains	15.432 361
	grams	kilograms	0.001
	grams	milligrams	1,000
	grams	troy ounces	0.032 150 746 6
	grams	troy pounds	0.002 679 23
	hands (height of horse)	centimeters	10.16
	hands (height of horse)	inches	4
	hectares	acres	2.471 053 8
	hectares	square feet	107,639.1
	hectares	square kilometers	0.01
	hectares	square meters	10,000
	hectares	square miles	0.003 861 02
	hectares	square yards	11,959.90
	hundredweights, long	avoirdupois pounds	112
	hundredweights, long	kilograms	50.802 345
	hundredweights, long	long tons	0.05
	hundredweights, long	metric tons	0.050 802 345
	hundredweights, long	short tons	0.056

Appendix E: Weights and Measures (continued)

Conversion Factors	To Convert From	To	Multiply by
	hundredweights, short	avoirdupois pounds	100
	hundredweights, short	kilograms	45.359 237
	hundredweights, short	long tons	0.044 642 86
	hundredweights, short	metric tons	0.045 359 237
	hundredweights, short	short tons	0.05
	inches	centimeters	2.54
	inches	feet	0.083 333 33
	inches	meters	0.025 4
	inches	millimeters	25.4
	inches	yards	0.027 777 78
	inches, cubic	bushels	0.000 465 025
	inches, cubic	cubic centimeters	16.387 064
	inches, cubic	cubic feet	0.000 578 703 7
	inches, cubic	cubic meters	0.000 016 387 064
	inches, cubic	cubic yards	0.000 021 433 47
	inches, cubic	dry pints	0.029 761 6
	inches, cubic	dry quarts	0.014 880 8
	inches, cubic	gallons	0.004 329 0
	inches, cubic	gills	0.138 528 1
	inches, cubic	liquid ounces	0.554 112 6
	inches, cubic	liquid pints	0.034 632 03
	inches, cubic	liquid quarts	0.017 316 02
	inches, cubic	liters	0.016 387 064
	inches, cubic	milliliters	16.387 064
	inches, cubic	minims (US)	265.974 0
	inches, cubic	pecks	0.001 860 10
	inches, square	square centimeters	6.451 600
	inches, square	square feet	0.006 944 44
	inches, square	square meters	0.000 645 16
	inches, square	square yards	0.000 771 605
	kilograms	avoirdupois drams	564.383 4
	kilograms	avoirdupois ounces	35.273 962
	kilograms	avoirdupois pounds	2.204 622 622
	kilograms	grains	15,432.36
	kilograms	grams	1,000
	kilograms	long tons	0.000 984 2
	kilograms	metric tons	0.001
	kilograms	short hundredweights	0.022 046 23
	kilograms	short tons	0.001 102 31
	kilograms	troy ounces	32.150 75

Conversion Factors	To Convert From	To	Multiply by
	kilograms	troy pounds	2.679 229
	kilometers	meters	1,000
	kilometers	statute miles	0.621 371 192
	kilometers, square	acres	247.105 38
	kilometers, square	hectares	100
	kilometers, square	square meters	1,000,000
	kilometers, square	statute miles	0.386 102 16
	knots (nautical mi/hr)	kilometers/hour	1.852
	knots (nautical mi/hr)	statute miles/hour	1.151
	leagues, nautical	kilometers	5.556
	leagues, nautical	nautical miles	3
	leagues, statute	kilometers	4.828 032
	leagues, statute	statute miles	3
	links, square surveyor's	square centimeters	404.686
	links, square surveyor's	square inches	62.726 4
	links, surveyor's	centimeters	20.116 8
	links, surveyor's	chains	0.01
	links, surveyor's	inches	7.92
	liters	bushels	0.028 377 59
	liters	cubic feet	0.035 314 67
	liters	cubic inches	61.023 74
	liters	cubic meters	0.001
	liters	cubic yards	0.001 307 95
	liters	dekaliters	0.1
	liters	dry pints	1.816 166
	liters	dry quarts	0.908 082 98
	liters	gallons	0.264 172 052
	liters	gills (US)	8.453 506
	liters	liquid ounces	33.814 02
	liters	liquid pints	2.113 376
	liters	liquid quarts	1.056 688 2
	liters	milliliters	1,000
	liters	pecks	0.113 510 4
	meters	centimeters	100
	meters	feet	3.280 839 895
	meters	inches	39.370 079
	meters	kilometers	0.001
	meters	millimeters	1,000
	meters	statute miles	0.000 621 371
	meters	yards	1.093 613 298

Appendix E: Weights and Measures (continued)

Conversion Factors	To Convert From	To	Multiply by
	meters, cubic	bushels	28.377 59
	meters, cubic	cubic feet	35.314 666 7
	meters, cubic	cubic inches	61,023.744
	meters, cubic	cubic yards	1.307 950 619
	meters, cubic	gallons	264.172 05
	meters, cubic	liters	1,000
	meters, cubic	pecks	113.510 4
	meters, square	acres	0.000 247 105 38
	meters, square	hectares	0.000 1
	meters, square	square centimeters	10,000
	meters, square	square feet	10.763 910 4
	meters, square	square inches	1,550.003 1
	meters, square	square yards	1.195 990 046
	microns	meters	0.000 001
	microns	inches	0.000 039 4
	mils	inches	0.001
	mils	millimeters	0.025 4
	miles, nautical	kilometers	1.852 0
	miles, nautical	statute miles	1.150 779 4
	miles, statute	centimeters	160,934.4
	miles, statute	feet	5,280
	miles, statute	furlongs	8
	miles, statute	inches	63,360
	miles, statute	kilometers	1.609 344
	miles, statute	meters	1,609.344
	miles, statute	rods	320
	miles, statute	yards	1,760
	miles, square nautical	square kilometers	3.429 904
	miles, square nautical	square statute miles	1.325
	miles, square statute	acres	640
	miles, square statute	hectares	258.998 811 033 6
	miles, square statute	sections	1
	miles, square statute	square kilometers	2.589 988 110 336
	miles, square statute	square nautical miles	0.755 miles
	miles, square statute	square rods	102,400
	milligrams	grains	0.015 432 358 35
	milliliters	cubic inches	0.061 023 744
	milliliters	gallons	0.000 264 17
	milliliters	gills (US)	0.008 453 5
	milliliters	liquid ounces	0.033 814 02

Conversion Factors	To Convert From	To	Multiply by
	milliliters	liquid pints	0.002 113 4
	milliliters	liquid quarts	0.001 056 7
	milliliters	liters	0.001
	milliliters	minims	16.230 73
	millimeters	inches	0.039 370 078 7
	minims (US)	cubic inches	0.003 759 77
	minims (US)	gills (US)	0.000 520 83
	minims (US)	liquid ounces	0.002 083 33
	minims (US)	milliliters	0.061 611 52
	minims (US)	minims (British)	1.041
	ounces, avoirdupois	avoirdupois drams	16
	ounces, avoirdupois	avoirdupois pounds	0.062 5
	ounces, avoirdupois	grains	437.5
	ounces, avoirdupois	grams	28.349 523 125
	ounces, avoirdupois	kilograms	0.028 349 523 125
	ounces, avoirdupois	troy ounces	0.911 458 3
	ounces, avoirdupois	troy pounds	0.075 954 86
	ounces, liquid (US)	cubic feet	0.001 044 38
	ounces, liquid (US)	centiliters	2.957 35
	ounces, liquid (US)	cubic inches	1.804 687 5
	ounces, liquid (US)	gallons	0.007 812 5
	ounces, liquid (US)	gills (US)	0.25
	ounces, liquid (US)	liquid drams	8
	ounces, liquid (US)	liquid ounces (British)	1.041
	ounces, liquid (US)	liquid pints	0.062 5
	ounces, liquid (US)	liquid quarts	0.031 25
	ounces, liquid (US)	liters	0.029 573 53
	ounces, liquid (US)	milliliters	29.573 529 6
	ounces, liquid (US)	minims	480
	ounces, troy	avoirdupois drams	17.554 29
	ounces, troy	avoirdupois ounces	1.097 143
	ounces, troy	avoirdupois pounds	0.068 571 43
	ounces, troy	grains	480
	ounces, troy	grams	31.103 476 8
	ounces, troy	pennyweights	20
	ounces, troy	troy drams	8
	ounces, troy	troy pounds	0.083 333 3
	paces (US)	centimeters	76.2
	paces (US)	inches	30
	pecks (US)	bushels	0.25

Appendix E: Weights and Measures (continued)

Conversion Factors		
To Convert From	**To**	**Multiply by**
pecks (US)	cubic feet	0.311 114
pecks (US)	cubic inches	537.605
pecks (US)	cubic meters	0.008 809 77
pecks (US)	cubic yards	0.011 522 74
pecks (US)	dekaliters	0.880 976 75
pecks (US)	dry pints	16
pecks (US)	dry quarts	8
pecks (US)	liters	8.809 767 5
pecks (US)	pecks (British)	0.968 9
pennyweights	grains	24
pennyweights	grams	1.555 173 84
pennyweights	troy ounces	0.05
pints, dry (US)	bushels	0.015 625
pints, dry (US)	cubic feet	0.019 444 63
pints, dry (US)	cubic inches	33.600 312 5
pints, dry (US)	dekaliters	0.055 061 05
pints, dry (US)	dry pints (British)	0.968 9
pints, dry (US)	dry quarts	0.5
pints, dry (US)	liters	0.550 610 47
pints, liquid (US)	cubic feet	0.016 710 07
pints, liquid (US)	cubic inches	28.875
pints, liquid (US)	deciliters	4.731 76
pints, liquid (US)	gallons	0.125
pints, liquid (US)	gills (US)	4
pints, liquid (US)	liquid ounces	16
pints, liquid (US)	liquid pints (British)	0.832 67
pints, liquid (US)	liquid quarts	0.5
pints, liquid (US)	liters	0.473 176 473
pints, liquid (US)	milliliters	473.176 473
pints, liquid (US)	minims	7,680
points (typographical)	inches	0.013 837
points (typographical)	millimeters	0.351 459 8
pounds, avoirdupois	avoirdupois drams	256
pounds, avoirdupois	avoirdupois ounces	16
pounds, avoirdupois	grains	7,000
pounds, avoirdupois	grams	453.592 37
pounds, avoirdupois	kilograms	0.453 592 37
pounds, avoirdupois	long tons	0.000 446 428 6

Conversion Factors	To Convert From	To	Multiply by
	pounds, avoirdupois	metric tons	0.000 453 592 37
	pounds, avoirdupois	quintals	0.004 535 92
	pounds, avoirdupois	short tons	0.000 5
	pounds, avoirdupois	troy ounces	14.583 33
	pounds, avoirdupois	troy pounds	1.215 278
	pounds, troy	avoirdupois drams	210.651 4
	pounds, troy	avoirdupois ounces	13.165 71
	pounds, troy	avoirdupois pounds	0.822 857 1
	pounds, troy	grains	5,760
	pounds, troy	grams	373.241 721 6
	pounds, troy	kilograms	0.373 241 721 6
	pounds, troy	pennyweights	240
	pounds, troy	troy ounces	12
	quarts, dry (US)	bushels	0.031 25
	quarts, dry (US)	cubic feet	0.038 889 25
	quarts, dry (US)	cubic inches	67.200 625
	quarts, dry (US)	dekaliters	0.110 122 1
	quarts, dry (US)	dry pints	2
	quarts, dry (US)	dry quarts (British)	0.968 9
	quarts, dry (US)	liters	1.101 221
	quarts, dry (US)	pecks	0.125
	quarts, dry (US)	pints, dry (US)	2
	quarts, liquid (US)	cubic feet	0.033 420 14
	quarts, liquid (US)	cubic inches	57.75
	quarts, liquid (US)	deciliters	9.463 53
	quarts, liquid (US)	gallons	0.25
	quarts, liquid (US)	gills (US)	8
	quarts, liquid (US)	liquid ounces	32
	quarts, liquid (US)	liquid pints (US)	2
	quarts, liquid (US)	liquid quarts (British)	0.832 67
	quarts, liquid (US)	liters	0.946 352 946
	quarts, liquid (US)	milliliters	946.352 946
	quarts, liquid (US)	minims	15,360
	quintals	avoirdupois pounds	220.462 26
	quintals	kilograms	100
	quintals	metric tons	0.1
	rods	feet	16.5
	rods	meters	5.029 2
	rods	yards	5.5

Appendix E: Weights and Measures (continued)

Conversion Factors

To Convert From	To	Multiply by
rods, square	acres	0.006 25
rods, square	square meters	25.292 85
rods, square	square yards	30.25
scruples	grains	20
scruples	grams	1.295 978 2
scruples	troy drams	0.333
sections (US)	square kilometers	2.589 988 1
sections (US)	square statute miles	1
spans	centimeters	22.86
spans	inches	9
steres	cubic meters	1
steres	cubic yards	1.307 95
tablespoons	milliliters	14.786 76
tablespoons	teaspoons	3
teaspoons	milliliters	4.928 922
teaspoons	tablespoons	0.333 333
ton-miles, long	metric ton-kilometers	1.635 169
ton-miles, short	metric ton-kilometers	1.459 972
tons, gross register	cubic feet of permanently enclosed space	100
tons, gross register	cubic meters of permanently enclosed space	2.831 684 7
tons, long (deadweight)	avoirdupois ounces	35,840
tons, long (deadweight)	avoirdupois pounds	2,240
tons, long (deadweight)	kilograms	1,016.046 909 8
tons, long (deadweight)	long hundredweights	20
tons, long (deadweight)	metric tons	1.016 046 908 8
tons, long (deadweight)	short hundredweights	22.4
tons, long (deadweight)	short tons	1.12
tons, metric	avoirdupois pounds	2,204.623
tons, metric	kilograms	1,000
tons, metric	long hundredweights	19.684 130 3
tons, metric	long tons	0.984 206 5
tons, metric	quintals	10
tons, metric	short hundredweights	22.046 23
tons, metric	short tons	1.102 311 3
tons, metric	troy ounces	32,150.75
tons, net register	cubic feet of permanently enclosed space for cargo and passengers	100
tons, net register	cubic meters of permanently enclosed space for cargo and passengers	2.831 684 7
tons, shipping	cubic feet of permanently enclosed cargo space	42

Appendix E: Weights and Measures (continued)

Conversion Factors	To Convert From	To	Multiply by
	tons, shipping	cubic meters of permanently enclosed cargo space	1.189 307 574
	tons, short	avoirdupois pounds	2,000
	tons, short	kilograms	907.184 74
	tons, short	long hundredweights	17.857 14
	tons, short	long tons	0.892 857 1
	tons, short	metric tons	0.907 184 74
	tons, short	short hundredweights	20
	townships (US)	sections	36
	townships (US)	square kilometers	93.239 572
	townships (US)	square statute miles	36
	miles, square statute	acres	640
	miles, square statute	hectares	258.998 811 033 6
	miles, square statute	square feet	27,878,400
	miles, square statute	square meters	2,589,988.110 336
	miles, square statute	square yards	3,097,600
	yards	centimeters	91.44
	yards	feet	3
	yards	inches	36
	yards	meters	0.914 4
	yards	miles	0.000 568 18
	yards, cubic	bushels	21.696 227
	yards, cubic	cubic feet	27
	yards, cubic	cubic inches	46,656
	yards, cubic	cubic meters	0.764 554 857 984
	yards, cubic	gallons	201.974 0
	yards, cubic	liters	764.554 857 984
	yards, cubic	pecks	86.784 91
	yards, square	acres	0.000 206 611 6
	yards, square	hectares	0.000 083 612 736
	yards, square	square centimeters	8,361.273 6
	yards, square	square feet	9
	yards, square	square inches	1,296
	yards, square	square meters	0.836 127 36
	yards, square	square miles	0.000 000 322 830 6

Note: At this time, only three countries—Burma, Liberia, and the US—have not adopted the International System of Units (SI, or metric system) as their official system of weights and measures. Although use of the metric system has been sanctioned by law in the US since 1866, it has been slow in displacing the American adaptation of the British Imperial System known as the US Customary System. The US is the only industrialized nation that does not mainly use the metric system in its commercial and standards activities, but there is increasing acceptance in science, medicine, government, and many sectors of industry.

Appendix F:

Cross-Reference List of Country Data Codes

FIPS 10-4:	*Countries, Dependencies, Areas of Special Sovereignty, and Their Principal Administrative Divisions (FIPS PUB 10-4)* is maintained by the Office of the Geographer and Global Issues (Department of State) and published by the National Institute of Standards and Technology (Department of Commerce). These two-character alphabetic codes are included in the text of the *Factbook* in the **Data code** entry under the Government category. FIPS 10-4 codes are intended for general use throughout the US Government, especially in activities associated with the mission of the Department of State and national defense programs.
ISO 3166:	*Codes for the Representation of Names of Countries (ISO 3166)* is prepared by the International Organization for Standardization. ISO 3166 includes two- and three-character alphabetic codes and three-digit numeric codes that may be needed for activities involving exchange of data with international organizations that have adopted that standard. Except for the numeric codes, ISO 3166 codes have been adopted in the US as FIPS 104-1: *American National Standard Codes for the Representation of Names of Countries, Dependencies, and Areas of Special Sovereignty for Information Interchange.*
Internet:	This is a provisional compilation that generally agrees with the ISO 3166 two-character alphabetic codes.

Entity	FIPS 10-4	ISO 3166			Internet	Comment
Afghanistan	AF	AF	AFG	004	AF	
Albania	AL	AL	ALB	008	AL	
Algeria	AG	DZ	DZA	012	DZ	
American Samoa	AQ	AS	ASM	016	AS	
Andorra	AN	AD	AND	020	AD	
Angola	AO	AO	AGO	024	AO	
Anguilla	AV	AI	AIA	660	AI	
Antarctica	AY	AQ	ATA	010	AQ	ISO defines as the territory south of 60 degrees south latitude
Antigua and Barbuda	AC	AG	ATG	028	AG	
Argentina	AR	AR	ARG	032	AR	
Armenia	AM	AM	ARM	051	AM	
Aruba	AA	AW	ABW	533	AW	
Ashmore and Cartier Islands	AT	—	—	—	—	ISO includes with Australia
Australia	AS	AU	AUS	036	AU	ISO includes Ashmore and Cartier Islands, Coral Sea Islands
Austria	AU	AT	AUT	040	AT	
Azerbaijan	AJ	AZ	AZE	031	AZ	
The Bahamas	BF	BS	BHS	044	BS	
Bahrain	BA	BH	BHR	048	BH	
Baker Island	FQ	—	—	—	—	ISO includes with the US Minor Outlying Islands
Bangladesh	BG	BD	BGD	050	BD	
Barbados	BB	BB	BRB	052	BB	
Bassas da India	BS	—	—	—	—	ISO includes with the Miscellaneous (French) Indian Ocean Islands
Belarus	BO	BY	BLR	112	BY	
Belgium	BE	BE	BEL	056	BE	

Appendix F: Cross-Reference List of Country Data Codes (continued)

Entity	FIPS 10-4	ISO 3166			Internet	Comment
Belize	BH	BZ	BLZ	084	BZ	
Benin	BN	BJ	BEN	204	BJ	
Bermuda	BD	BM	BMU	060	BM	
Bhutan	BT	BT	BTN	064	BT	
Bolivia	BL	BO	BOL	068	BO	
Bosnia and Herzegovina	BK	BA	BIH	070	BA	
Botswana	BC	BW	BWA	072	BW	
Bouvet Island	BV	BV	BVT	074	BV	
Brazil	BR	BR	BRA	076	BR	
British Indian Ocean Territory	IO	IO	IOT	086	IO	
British Virgin Islands	VI	VG	VGB	092	VG	
Brunei	BX	BN	BRN	096	BN	
Bulgaria	BU	BG	BGR	100	BG	
Burkina Faso	UV	BF	BFA	854	BF	
Burma	BM	MM	MMR	104	MM	ISO uses the name Myanmar
Burundi	BY	BI	BDI	108	BI	
Cambodia	CB	KH	KHM	116	KH	
Cameroon	CM	CM	CMR	120	CM	
Canada	CA	CA	CAN	124	CA	
Cape Verde	CV	CV	CPV	132	CV	
Cayman Islands	CJ	KY	CYM	136	KY	
Central African Republic	CT	CF	CAF	140	CF	
Chad	CD	TD	TCD	148	TD	
Chile	CI	CL	CHL	152	CL	
China	CH	CN	CHN	156	CN	see also Taiwan
Christmas Island	KT	CX	CXR	162	CX	
Clipperton Island	IP	—	—	—	—	ISO includes with French Polynesia
Cocos (Keeling) Islands	CK	CC	CCK	166	CC	
Colombia	CO	CO	COL	170	CO	
Comoros	CN	KM	COM	174	KM	
Congo, Democratic Republic of the	CG	ZR	ZAR	180	ZR	formerly Zaire
Congo, Republic of the	CF	CG	COG	178	CG	
Cook Islands	CW	CK	COK	184	CK	
Coral Sea Islands	CR	—	—	—	—	ISO includes with Australia
Costa Rica	CS	CR	CRI	188	CR	
Cote d'Ivoire	IV	CI	CIV	384	CI	
Croatia	HR	HR	HRV	191	HR	
Cuba	CU	CU	CUB	192	CU	
Cyprus	CY	CY	CYP	196	CY	
Czech Republic	EZ	CZ	CZE	203	CZ	
Denmark	DA	DK	DNK	208	DK	
Djibouti	DJ	DJ	DJI	262	DJ	

Appendix F: Cross-Reference List of Country Data Codes (continued)

Entity	FIPS 10-4	ISO 3166			Internet	Comment
Dominica	DO	DM	DMA	212	DM	
Dominican Republic	DR	DO	DOM	214	DO	
East Timor	—	TP	TMP	626	TP	FIPS includes with Indonesia
Ecuador	EC	EC	ECU	218	EC	
Egypt	EG	EG	EGY	818	EG	
El Salvador	ES	SV	SLV	222	SV	
Equatorial Guinea	EK	GQ	GNQ	226	GQ	
Eritrea	ER	ER	ERI	232	ER	
Estonia	EN	EE	EST	233	EE	
Ethiopia	ET	ET	ETH	231	ET	
Europa Island	EU	—	—	—	—	ISO includes with the Miscellaneous (French) Indian Ocean Islands
Falkland Islands (Islas Malvinas)	FA	FK	FLK	238	FK	
Faroe Islands	FO	FO	FRO	234	FO	
Fiji	FJ	FJ	FJI	242	FJ	
Finland	FI	FI	FIN	246	FI	
France	FR	FR	FRA	250	FR	
France, Metropolitan	—	FX	FXX	249	FX	ISO limits to the European part of France, excluding French Guiana, French Polynesia, French Southern and Antarctic Lands, Guadeloupe, Martinique, Mayotte, New Caledonia, Reunion, Saint Pierre and Miquelon, Wallis and Futuna
French Guiana	FG	GF	GUF	254	GF	
French Polynesia	FP	PF	PYF	258	PF	ISO includes Clipperton Island
French Southern and Antarctic Lands	FS	TF	ATF	260	—	FIPS 10-4 does not include the French-claimed portion of Antarctica (Terre Adelie)
Gabon	GB	GA	GAB	266	GA	
The Gambia	GA	GM	GMB	270	GM	
Gaza Strip	GZ	—	—	—	—	
Georgia	GG	GE	GEO	268	GE	
Germany	GM	DE	DEU	276	DE	
Ghana	GH	GH	GHA	288	GH	
Gibraltar	GI	GI	GIB	292	GI	
Glorioso Islands	GO	—	—	—	—	ISO includes with the Miscellaneous (French) Indian Ocean Islands
Greece	GR	GR	GRC	300	GR	
Greenland	GL	GL	GRL	304	GL	
Grenada	GJ	GD	GRD	308	GD	
Guadeloupe	GP	GP	GLP	312	GP	
Guam	GQ	GU	GUM	316	GU	
Guatemala	GT	GT	GTM	320	GT	
Guernsey	GK	—	—	—	—	ISO includes with the United Kingdom
Guinea	GV	GN	GIN	324	GN	
Guinea-Bissau	PU	GW	GNB	624	GW	

Appendix F: Cross-Reference List of Country Data Codes (continued)

Entity	FIPS 10-4	ISO 3166			Internet	Comment
Guyana	GY	GY	GUY	328	GY	
Haiti	HA	HT	HTI	332	HT	
Heard Island and McDonald Islands	HM	HM	HMD	334	HM	
Holy See (Vatican City)	VT	VA	VAT	336	VA	
Honduras	HO	HN	HND	340	HN	
Hong Kong	HK	HK	HKG	344	HK	
Howland Island	HQ	—	—	—	—	ISO includes with the US Minor Outlying Islands
Hungary	HU	HU	HUN	348	HU	
Iceland	IC	IS	ISL	352	IS	
India	IN	IN	IND	356	IN	
Indonesia	ID	ID	IDN	360	ID	
Iran	IR	IR	IRN	364	IR	
Iraq	IZ	IQ	IRQ	368	IQ	
Ireland	EI	IE	IRL	372	IE	
Israel	IS	IL	ISR	376	IL	
Italy	IT	IT	ITA	380	IT	
Jamaica	JM	JM	JAM	388	JM	
Jan Mayen	JN	—	—	—	—	ISO includes with Svalbard
Japan	JA	JP	JPN	392	JP	
Jarvis Island	DQ	—	—	—	—	ISO includes with the US Minor Outlying Islands
Jersey	JE	—	—	—	—	ISO includes with the United Kingdom
Johnston Atoll	JQ	—	—	—	—	ISO includes with the US Minor Outlying Islands
Jordan	JO	JO	JOR	400	JO	
Juan de Nova Island	JU	—	—	—	—	ISO includes with the Miscellaneous (French) Indian Ocean Islands
Kazakhstan	KZ	KZ	KAZ	398	KZ	
Kenya	KE	KE	KEN	404	KE	
Kingman Reef	KQ	—	—	—	—	ISO includes with the US Minor Outlying Islands
Kiribati	KR	KI	KIR	296	KI	
Korea, North	KN	KP	PRK	408	KP	
Korea, South	KS	KR	KOR	410	KR	
Kuwait	KU	KW	KWT	414	KW	
Kyrgyzstan	KG	KG	KGZ	417	KG	
Laos	LA	LA	LAO	418	LA	
Latvia	LG	LV	LVA	428	LV	
Lebanon	LE	LB	LBN	422	LB	
Lesotho	LT	LS	LSO	426	LS	
Liberia	LI	LR	LBR	430	LR	
Libya	LY	LY	LBY	434	LY	
Liechtenstein	LS	LI	LIE	438	LI	

Appendix F: Cross-Reference List of Country Data Codes (continued)

Entity	FIPS 10-4	ISO 3166			Internet	Comment
Lithuania	LH	LT	LTU	440	LT	
Luxembourg	LU	LU	LUX	442	LU	
Macau	MC	MO	MAC	446	MO	
Macedonia, The Former Yugoslav Republic of	MK	MK	MKD	807	MK	
Madagascar	MA	MG	MDG	450	MG	
Malawi	MI	MW	MWI	454	MW	
Malaysia	MY	MY	MYS	458	MY	
Maldives	MV	MV	MDV	462	MV	
Mali	ML	ML	MLI	466	ML	
Malta	MT	MT	MLT	470	MT	
Man, Isle of	IM	—	—	—	—	ISO includes with the United Kingdom
Marshall Islands	RM	MH	MHL	584	MH	
Martinique	MB	MQ	MTQ	474	MQ	
Mauritania	MR	MR	MRT	478	MR	
Mauritius	MP	MU	MUS	480	MU	
Mayotte	MF	YT	MYT	175	YT	
Mexico	MX	MX	MEX	484	MX	
Micronesia, Federated States of	FM	FM	FSM	583	FM	
Midway Islands	MQ	—	—	—	—	ISO includes with the US Minor Outlying Islands
Miscellaneous (French)	—	—	—	—	—	ISO includes Bassas Indian Ocean da India, Europa Islands Island, Glorioso Islands, Juan de Nova Island, Tromelin Island
Moldova	MD	MD	MDA	498	MD	
Monaco	MN	MC	MCO	492	MC	
Mongolia	MG	MN	MNG	496	MN	
Montenegro*	MW	—	—	—	—	see footnote at end of table
Montserrat	MH	MS	MSR	500	MS	
Morocco	MO	MA	MAR	504	MA	
Mozambique	MZ	MZ	MOZ	508	MZ	
Myanmar	—	—	—	—	—	see Burma
Namibia	WA	NA	NAM	516	NA	
Nauru	NR	NR	NRU	520	NR	
Navassa Island	BQ	—	—	—	—	
Nepal	NP	NP	NPL	524	NP	
Netherlands	NL	NL	NLD	528	NL	
Netherlands Antilles	NT	AN	ANT	530	AN	
New Caledonia	NC	NC	NCL	540	NC	
New Zealand	NZ	NZ	NZL	554	NZ	
Nicaragua	NU	NI	NIC	558	NI	
Niger	NG	NE	NER	562	NE	
Nigeria	NI	NG	NGA	566	NG	

Entity	FIPS 10-4	ISO 3166			Internet	Comment
Niue	NE	NU	NIU	570	NU	
Norfolk Island	NF	NF	NFK	574	NF	
Northern Mariana Islands	CQ	MP	MNP	580	MP	
Norway	NO	NO	NOR	578	NO	
Oman	MU	OM	OMN	512	OM	
Pakistan	PK	PK	PAK	586	PK	
Palau	PS	PW	PLW	585	PW	
Palmyra Atoll	LQ	—	—	—	—	ISO includes with the US Minor Outlying Islands
Panama	PM	PA	PAN	591	PA	
Papua New Guinea	PP	PG	PNG	598	PG	
Paracel Islands	PF	—	—	—	—	
Paraguay	PA	PY	PRY	600	PY	
Peru	PE	PE	PER	604	PE	
Philippines	RP	PH	PHL	608	PH	
Pitcairn Islands	PC	PN	PCN	612	PN	
Poland	PL	PL	POL	616	PL	
Portugal	PO	PT	PRT	620	PT	
Puerto Rico	RQ	PR	PRI	630	PR	
Qatar	QA	QA	QAT	634	QA	
Reunion	RE	RE	REU	638	RE	
Romania	RO	RO	ROM	642	RO	
Russia	RS	RU	RUS	643	RU	
Rwanda	RW	RW	RWA	646	RW	
Saint Helena	SH	SH	SHN	654	SH	
Saint Kitts and Nevis	SC	KN	KNA	659	KN	
Saint Lucia	ST	LC	LCA	662	LC	
Saint Pierre and Miquelon	SB	PM	SPM	666	PM	
Saint Vincent and the Grenadines	VC	VC	VCT	670	VC	
Samoa	WS	WS	WSM	882	WS	
San Marino	SM	SM	SMR	674	SM	
Sao Tome and Principe	TP	ST	STP	678	ST	
Saudi Arabia	SA	SA	SAU	682	SA	
Senegal	SG	SN	SEN	686	SN	
Serbia*	SR	—	—	—	—	see footnote at end of table
Serbia and Montenegro*	—	—	—	—	—	see footnote at end of table
Seychelles	SE	SC	SYC	690	SC	
Sierra Leone	SL	SL	SLE	694	SL	
Singapore	SN	SG	SGP	702	SG	
Slovakia	LO	SK	SVK	703	SK	
Slovenia	SI	SI	SVN	705	SI	
Solomon Islands	BP	SB	SLB	090	SB	

Appendix F: Cross-Reference List of Country Data Codes (continued)

Entity	FIPS 10-4	ISO 3166			Internet	Comment
Somalia	SO	SO	SOM	706	SO	
South Africa	SF	ZA	ZAF	710	ZA	
South Georgia and the South Sandwich Islands	SX	GS	SGS	239	GS	
Spain	SP	ES	ESP	724	ES	
Spratly Islands	PG	—	—	—	—	
Sri Lanka	CE	LK	LKA	144	LK	
Sudan	SU	SD	SDN	736	SD	
Suriname	NS	SR	SUR	740	SR	
Svalbard	SV	SJ	SJM	744	SJ	ISO includes Jan Mayen
Swaziland	WZ	SZ	SWZ	748	SZ	
Sweden	SW	SE	SWE	752	SE	
Switzerland	SZ	CH	CHE	756	CH	
Syria	SY	SY	SYR	760	SY	
Taiwan	TW	TW	TWN	158	TW	
Tajikistan	TI	TJ	TJK	762	TJ	
Tanzania	TZ	TZ	TZA	834	TZ	
Thailand	TH	TH	THA	764	TH	
Togo	TO	TG	TGO	768	TG	
Tokelau	TL	TK	TKL	772	TK	
Tonga	TN	TO	TON	776	TO	
Trinidad and Tobago	TD	TT	TTO	780	TT	
Tromelin Island	TE	—	—	—	—	ISO includes with the Miscellaneous (French) Indian Ocean Islands
Tunisia	TS	TN	TUN	788	TN	
Turkey	TU	TR	TUR	792	TR	
Turkmenistan	TX	TM	TKM	795	TM	
Turks and Caicos Islands	TK	TC	TCA	796	TC	
Tuvalu	TV	TV	TUV	798	TV	
Uganda	UG	UG	UGA	800	UG	
Ukraine	UP	UA	UKR	804	UA	
United Arab Emirates	TC	AE	ARE	784	AE	
United Kingdom	UK	GB	GBR	826	UK/GB	ISO includes Guernsey, Isle of Man, Jersey
United States	US	US	USA	840	US	
United States Minor Outlying Islands	—	UM	UMI	581	UM	ISO includes Baker Island, Howland Island, Jarvis Island, Johnston Atoll, Kingman Reef, Midway Islands, Palmyra Atoll, Wake Island
Uruguay	UY	UY	URY	858	UY	
Uzbekistan	UZ	UZ	UZB	860	UZ	
Vanuatu	NH	VU	VUT	548	VU	
Venezuela	VE	VE	VEN	862	UE	
Vietnam	VM	VN	VNM	704	VN	
Virgin Islands	VQ	VI	VIR	850	VI	

Appendix F: Cross-Reference List of Country Data Codes (continued)

Entity	FIPS 10-4	ISO 3166			Internet	Comment
Virgin Islands (UK)	—	—	—	—	—	see British Virgin Islands
Virgin Islands (US)	—	—	—	—	—	see Virgin Islands
Wake Atoll	WQ	—	—	—	—	ISO includes with the US Minor Outlying Islands
Wallis and Futuna	WF	WF	WLF	876	WF	
West Bank	WE	—	—	—	—	
Western Sahara	WI	EH	ESH	732	EH	
Western Samoa	—	—	—	—	—	see Samoa
World	—	—	—	—	—	the *Factbook* uses the W data code from DIAM 65-18 *Geopolitical Data Elements and Related Features*, Data Standard No. 3, December 1994, published by the Defense Intelligence Agency
Yemen	YM	YE	YEM	887	YE	
Yugoslavia*	—	YU	YUG	891	YU	see footnote at end of table
Zaire	—	—	—	—	—	see Democratic Republic of the Congo
Zambia	ZA	ZM	ZWB	894	ZM	
Zimbabwe	ZI	ZW	ZWE	716	ZW	

*Serbia and Montenegro have asserted the formation of a joint independent state, but this entity has not been formally recognized as a state by the US; the US view is that the Socialist Federal Republic of Yugoslavia (SFRY) has dissolved and that none of the successor republics represents its continuation.

Appendix G:

Cross-Reference List of Hydrographic Data Codes

IHO 23-4th:	*Limits of Oceans and Seas*, Special Publication 23, Draft 4th Edition 1986, published by the International Hydrographic Bureau of the International Hydrographic Organization
IHO 23-3rd:	*Limits of Oceans and Seas*, Special Publication 23, 3rd Edition 1953, published by the International Hydrographic Organization
ACIC M 49-1:	*Chart of Limits of Seas and Oceans*, revised January 1958, published by the Aeronautical Chart and Information Center (ACIC), United States Air Force; note—ACIC is now part of the National Imagery and Mapping Agency (NIMA)
DIAM 65-18:	*Geopolitical Data Elements and Related Features*, Data Standard No. 4, Defense Intelligence Agency Manual 65-18, December 1994, published by the Defense Intelligence Agency

The US Government has not yet adopted a standard for hydrographic codes similar to the Federal Information Processing Standards (FIPS) 10-4 country codes. The names and limits of the following oceans and seas are not always directly comparable because of differences in the customers, needs, and requirements of the individual organizations. Even the number of principal water bodies varies from organization to organization. *Factbook* users, for example, find the Atlantic Ocean and Pacific Ocean entries useful, but none of the following standards include those oceans in their entirety. Nor is there any provision for combining codes or overcodes to aggregate water bodies.

Principal Oceans and Seas of the World With Hydrographic Codes by Institution

	IHO 23-4th	IHO 23-3rd*	ACIC M 49-1	DIAM 65-18
Arctic Ocean	9	17	A	5A
Atlantic Ocean	—	—	—	—
North Atlantic Ocean	1	23	B	1A
South Atlantic Ocean	4	32	C	2A
Baltic Sea	2	1	B26	7B
Indian Ocean	5	45	F	6A
Mediterranean Sea	3.1	28	B11	—
Eastern Mediterranean	3.1.2	28 B	—	8E
Western Mediterranean	3.1.1	28 A	—	8W
Pacific Ocean	—	—	—	—
North Pacific Ocean	7	57	D	3A
South Pacific Ocean	8	61	E	4A
South China and Eastern Archipelagic Seas	6	49, 48	D18 plus others	3U plus others

Oceans and Seas of the World With Hydrographic Codes by Institution

	IHO 23-4th	IHO 23-3rd*	ACIC M 49-1	DIAM 65-18
ARCTIC OCEAN	9	17	A	5A
East Siberian Sea	9.1	11	A6	5S
Laptev Sea	9.2	10	A5	5P
Kara Sea	9.3	9	A4	5K
Barents Sea	9.4	7	A2	5B
White Sea	9.5	8	A3	5W

Appendix G: Cross-Reference List of Hydrographic Data Codes (continued)

	IHO 23-4th	IHO 23-23rd*	ACIC M 49-1	DIAM 65-18
North Greenland Sea	9.6	—	—	—
Norwegian Sea	9.7	6	B30	5N
Iceland Sea	9.8	—	—	—
Davis Strait	9.9	15	B2	1V
Hudson Strait	9.10	16 A	A15	1U
Hudson Bay	9.11	16	A10	1H
Baffin Bay	9.12	14 A	A12	1P
Lincoln Sea	9.13	17 A	A13	5L
Northwest Passages (Northwest Passage, Northwestern Passages)	9.14	14	A9	5T
Beaufort Sea	9.15	13	A8	5U
Chukchi Sea	9.16	12	A7	5C
James Bay	—	—	A11	—
Kane Basin	—	—	A14	—
ATLANTIC OCEAN (see North Atlantic Ocean and South Atlantic Ocean)	—	—	—	—
BALTIC SEA	2	1	B26	7B
Gulf of Bothnia	2.1	1 (a)	B29	7T
Gulf of Finland	2.2	1 (b)	B28	7F
Gulf of Riga	2.3	1 (c)	B27	7H
The Sound	2.4	2	—	—
The Great Belt	2.5	2	—	—
The Little Belt	2.6	2	—	—
Kattegat	2.7	2	B25	7K
INDIAN OCEAN	5	45	F	6A
Mozambique Channel	5.1	45 A	F1	6Z
Gulf of Suez	5.2	35	F5	6W
Gulf of Aqaba	5.3	36	—	6Q
Red Sea	5.4	37	F4	6E
Gulf of Aden	5.5	38	F3	6D
Persian Gulf (Gulf of Iran)	5.6	41	F7	6P
Gulf of Oman	5.7	40	F6	6M
Arabian Sea	5.8	39	F2	6R
Laccadive Sea (Lakshadweep Sea)	5.9	42	F9	6L
Gulf of Mannar	5.10	—	F8	—
Palk Strait and Palk Bay	5.11	—	—	—
Bay of Bengal	5.12	43	F10	6B
Andaman Sea (Burma Sea)	5.13	44	F11	6N
Strait of Malacca (Malacca Strait)	5.14	46 (a)	F12	6C
Great Australian Bight	5.15	62	F21	6G
Suez Canal	—	—	—	6U
MEDITERRANEAN REGION	3	—	—	—
Mediterranean Sea	3.1	28	B11	—
Mediterranean Sea, Western Basin	3.1.1	28 A	—	8W
Strait of Gibraltar	3.1.1.1	28 (a)	B7	8S

Appendix G: Cross-Reference List of Hydrographic Data Codes (continued)

	IHO 23-4th	IHO 23-23rd*	ACIC M 49-1	DIAM 65-18
Alboran Sea	3.1.1.2	28 (b)	—	8Y
Balearic Sea (Balear Sea, Iberian Sea)	3.1.1.3	28 (c)	B9	8J
Ligurian Sea (Ligure Sea)	3.1.1.4	28 (d)	B10	8L
Tyrrhenian Sea (Tirreno Sea)	3.1.1.5	28 (e)	B12	8T
Mediterranean Sea, Eastern Basin	3.1.2	28 B	—	8E
Adriatic Sea	3.1.2.1	28 (g)	B14	8D
Strait of Sicily (Strait of Sicilia)	3.1.2.2	—	—	—
Ionian Sea	3.1.2.3	28 (f)	B13	8N
Aegean Sea	3.1.2.4	28 (h)	B15	8G
Sea of Marmara	3.2	29	B16	8M
Black Sea	3.3	30	B17	8B
Sea of Azov	3.4	31	B18	8Z
Gulf of Lion (Gulf of Lions)	—	—	B8	8X
Aral Sea	—	—	—	8R
Bosporus	—	—	—	8P
Caspian Sea	—	—	—	8C
Dardanelles	—	—	—	8U
NORTH ATLANTIC OCEAN	1	23	B	1A
Skagerrak	1.1	3	B24	1S
North Sea	1.2	4	B23	1N
Inner Seas off the West Coast of Scotland	1.3	18	—	1K
Irish Sea and Saint Georges Channel	1.4	19	B22	1R, 1Q
Bristol Channel	1.5	20	B21	1C
Celtic Sea	1.6	21 A	—	—
English Channel	1.7	21	B20	1E
Bay of Biscay	1.8	22	B19	1B
Canarias Sea	1.9	—	—	—
Gulf of Guinea	1.10	34	C4	1G
Caribbean Sea	1.11	27	B6	1X
Gulf of Mexico	1.12	26	B5	1M
Bay of Fundy	1.13	25	B4	1F
Gulf of Saint Lawrence	1.14	24	B3	1T
Labrador Sea	1.15	15 A	—	1L
Greenland Sea	1.16	5	A1	5G
Denmark Strait	—	—	B1	1D
Lake Erie	—	—	—	9E
Lake Huron	—	—	—	9H
Lake Michigan	—	—	—	9M
Lake Ontario	—	—	—	9N
Lake Superior	—	—	—	9S
Panama Canal	—	—	—	1J
Saint Lawrence Seaway	—	—	—	9L
NORTH PACIFIC OCEAN	7	57	D	3A
Philippine Sea	7.1	56	D26	3P
Taiwan Strait (Formosa Strait)	7.2	—	D17	3F
East China Sea (Tung Hai)	7.3	50	D13	3E

Appendix G: Cross-Reference List of Hydrographic Data Codes (continued)

	IHO 23-4th	IHO 23-23rd*	ACIC M 49-1	DIAM 65-18
Yellow Sea (Huang Hai, Hwang Hai)	7.4	51	D14	3Y
Bo Hai (Bo Sea, Gulf of Chihli)	7.5	—	D16	3X
Liaodong Wan (Liaodong Gulf)	7.6	—	—	—
Inland Sea of Japan (Seto Naikai)	7.7	53	—	3N
Sea of Japan (Japan Sea)	7.8	52	D11	3J
Gulf of Tartary	7.9	—	D10	—
Sea of Okhotsk	7.10	54	D8	3Q
Bering Sea	7.11	55	D6	5D
Anadyrskiy Zaliv (Anadyrskiy Gulf)	7.12	—	—	5Y
Gulf of Alaska	7.13	58	D4	5F
Coastal Waters of Southeast Alaska and British Columbia	7.14	59	D3	5E
Gulf of California	7.15	60	D2	3L
Gulf of Panama	7.16	—	D1	—
Amurskiy Liman	—	—	D27	—
Bering Strait	—	—	D7	5R
Bristol Bay	—	—	D5	—
Korea Bay	—	—	D15	3R
Korea Strait	—	—	D12	—
Sakhalinskiy Zaliv	—	—	D28	3B
Zaliv Shelikhova (Zaliv Shelekhova)	—	—	D9	3K
Luzon Strait	—	—	—	3I
Tatar Strait	—	—	—	3D
PACIFIC OCEAN (see North Pacific Ocean and South Pacific Ocean)	—	—	—	—
SOUTH ATLANTIC OCEAN	4	32	C	2A
Rio de la Plata	4.1	33	C1	2R
Drake Passage	—	—	C5	2D
Golfo San Matias	—	—	C2	2M
Golfo San Jorge	—	—	C3	2J
Scotia Sea	—	—	C6	2S
Weddell Sea	—	—	C7	2W
SOUTH CHINA AND EASTERN ARCHIPELAGIC SEAS	6	49 and 48	D18 plus others	3U plus others
South China Sea (Nan Hai)	6.1	49	D18	3U
Gulf of Tonkin	6.2	—	D19	3G
Gulf of Thailand (Gulf of Siam)	6.3	47	D20	3T
Natuna Sea	6.4	—	—	—
Singapore Strait	6.5	46 (b)	—	3Z
Sunda Strait	6.6	—	—	—
Java Sea (Jawa Sea)	6.7	48 (n)	F13	4J
Makassar Strait (Makasar Strait)	6.8	48 (m)	E1	4M
Bali Sea	6.9	48 (l)	F14	4L
Flores Sea	6.10	48 (j)	F16	4F
Sumba Strait	6.11	—	—	—

Appendix G: Cross-Reference List of Hydrographic Data Codes (continued)

	IHO 23-4th	IHO 23-23rd*	ACIC M 49-1	DIAM 65-18
Savu Sea (Sawu Sea)	6.12	48 (o)	F15	6S
Timor Sea	6.13	48 (i)	F19	6T
Joseph Bonaparte Gulf	6.14	—	F20	—
Gulf of Carpentaria	6.15	—	E4	4P
Arafura Sea	6.16	48 (h)	E3	4U
Aru Sea	6.17	—	—	—
Banda Sea	6.18	48 (g)	E2	4B
Teluk Bone (Gulf of Bone, Gulf of Boni)	6.19	48 (k)	F17	4E
Ceram Sea (Seram Sea)	6.20	48 (f)	D25	4Q
Gulf of Berau	6.21	—	—	—
Halmahera Sea	6.22	48 (e)	D24	3H
Molucca Sea (Molukka Sea, Maluku Sea)	6.23	48 (c)	D23	3M
Teluk Tomini (Gulf of Tomini)	6.24	48 (d)	F18	3V
Sulawesi Sea	6.25	—	—	—
Mindanao Sea	6.26	—	—	—
Sulu Sea	6.27	48 (a)	D21	3S
Celebes Sea	—	48 (b)	D22	3C
SOUTH PACIFIC OCEAN	8	61	E	4A
Bismarck Sea	8.1	66	E6	4K
Solomon Sea	8.2	65	E7	4S
Torres Strait	8.3	—	E5	—
Coastal Waters of Great Barrier Reefs	8.4	—	—	—
Coral Sea	8.5	64	E9	4C
Tasman Sea	8.6	63	E10	4T
Bass Strait	8.7	62 A	F22	6F
Amundsen Sea	—	—	E12	4D
Bellingshausen Sea	—	—	E13	4G
Cook Strait	—	—	E8	—
Ross Sea	—	—	E11	4R

* The letters after the numbers are subdivisions, not footnotes.

Appendix H:

Cross-Reference List of Geographic Names

This list indicates where various geographic names—including the location of all United States Foreign Service Posts, alternate names, former names, and political or geographical portions of larger entities—can be found in *The World Factbook*. Spellings are normally those approved by the US Board on Geographic Names (BGN). Additional information is included in brackets.

	Name	Entry in *The World Factbook*	Latitude (deg min)	Longitude (deg min)
A	Abidjan [US Embassy]	Cote d'Ivoire	5 19 N	4 02 W
	Abkhazia [region]	Georgia	43 00 N	41 00 E
	Abu Dhabi [US Embassy]	United Arab Emirates	24 28 N	54 22 E
	Abu Musa [island]	Iran	25 52 N	55 03 E
	Abuja [US Embassy Branch Office]	Nigeria	9 12 N	7 11 E
	Abyssinia	Ethiopia	8 00 N	38 00 E
	Acapulco	Mexico	16 51 N	99 55 W
	Accra [US Embassy]	Ghana	5 33 N	0 13 W
	Adamstown	Pitcairn Islands	25 04 S	130 05 W
	Adana [US Consulate]	Turkey	37 01 N	35 18 E
	Addis Ababa [US Embassy]	Ethiopia	9 02 N	38 42 E
	Adelie Land (Terre Adelie) [claimed by France]	Antarctica	66 30 S	139 00 E
	Aden	Yemen	12 46 N	45 01 E
	Aden, Gulf of	Indian Ocean	12 30 N	48 00 E
	Admiralty Island	United States (Alaska)	57 44 N	134 20 W
	Admiralty Islands	Papua New Guinea	2 10 S	147 00 E
	Adriatic Sea	Atlantic Ocean	42 30 N	16 00 E
	Aegean Islands	Greece	38 00 N	25 00 E
	Aegean Sea	Atlantic Ocean	38 30 N	25 00 E
	Afars and Issas, French Territory of the (FTAI)	Djibouti	11 30 N	43 00 E
	Agalega Islands	Mauritius	10 25 S	56 40 E
	Agana (see Hagatna)	Guam	13 28 N	144 45 E
	Ajaccio	France (Corsica)	41 55 N	8 44 E
	Akmola (see Astana)	Kazakhstan	51 10 N	71 30 E
	Aland Islands	Finland	60 15 N	20 00 E
	Alaska	United States	65 00 N	153 00 W
	Alaska, Gulf of	Pacific Ocean	58 00 N	145 00 W
	Aldabra Islands (Groupe d'Aldabra)	Seychelles	9 25 S	46 22 E
	Alderney [island]	Guernsey	49 43 N	2 12 W
	Aleutian Islands	United States (Alaska)	52 00 N	176 00 W
	Alexander Archipelago	United States (Alaska)	57 00 N	134 00 W
	Alexander Island	Antarctica	71 00 S	70 00 W
	Alexandria	Egypt	31 12 N	29 54 E
	Algiers [US Embassy]	Algeria	36 47 N	2 03 E
	Alhucemas, Penon de	Spain	35 13 N	3 53 W
	Alma-Ata (see Almaty)	Kazakhstan	43 15 N	76 57 E
	Almaty [US Embassy]	Kazakhstan	43 15 N	76 57 E
	Alofi	Niue	19 01 S	169 55 E
	Alphonse Island	Seychelles	7 01 S	52 45 E
	Amami Strait	Pacific Ocean	28 40 N	129 30 E
	Amindivi Islands	India	11 30 N	72 30 E

Name	Entry in *The World Factbook*	Latitude (deg min)	Longitude (deg min)
Amirante Isles (Les Amirantes)	Seychelles	6 00 S	53 10 E
Amman [US Embassy]	Jordan	31 57 N	35 56 E
Amsterdam [US Consulate General]	Netherlands	52 22 N	4 54 E
Amsterdam Island (Ile Amsterdam)	French Southern and Antarctic Lands	37 52 S	77 32 E
Amundsen Sea	Pacific Ocean	72 30 S	112 00 W
Amur River	China, Russia	52 56 N	141 10 E
Anatolia [region]	Turkey	39 00 N	35 00 E
Andaman Islands	India	12 00 N	92 45 E
Andaman Sea	Indian Ocean	10 00 N	95 00 E
Andorra la Vella	Andorra	42 30 N	1 30 E
Andros [island]	Greece	37 45 N	24 42 E
Andros Island	The Bahamas	24 26 N	77 57 W
Anegada Passage	Atlantic Ocean	18 30 N	63 40 W
Angkor Wat [ruins]	Cambodia	13 26 N	103 50 E
Anglo-Egyptian Sudan	Sudan	15 00 N	30 00 E
Anjouan [island]	Comoros	12 15 S	44 25 E
Ankara [US Embassy]	Turkey	39 56 N	32 52 E
Annobon [island]	Equatorial Guinea	1 25 S	5 36 E
Antananarivo [US Embassy]	Madagascar	18 52 S	47 30 E
Antigua [island]	Antigua and Barbuda	14 34 N	90 44 W
Antipodes Islands	New Zealand	49 41 S	178 43 E
Antwerp [European Logistical Support Office]	Belgium	51 13 N	4 25 E
Aozou Strip	Chad	22 00 N	18 00 E
Apia [US Embassy]	Samoa	13 50 S	171 44 N
Aqaba, Gulf of	IIndian Ocean	29 00 N	34 30 E
Aqmola (see Astana)	Kazakhstan	51 10 N	71 30 E
Arab, Shatt al [river]	Iran, Iraq	29 57 N	48 34 E
Arabian Sea	Indian Ocean	15 00 N	65 00 E
Arafura Sea	Pacific Ocean	9 00 S	133 00 E
Aral Sea	Kazakhstan, Uzbekistan	45 00 N	60 00 E
Argun River	China, Russia	53 20 N	121 28 E
Ascension Island	Saint Helena	7 57 S	14 22 W
Ashgabat [US Embassy]	Turkmenistan	37 57 N	58 23 E
Ashkhabad (see Ashgabat)	Turkmenistan	37 57 N	58 23 E
Asmara [US Embassy]	Eritrea	15 20 N	38 53 E
Asmera (see Asmara)	Eritrea	15 20 N	38 53 E
Assumption Island	Seychelles	9 46 S	46 34 E
Astana (Akmola)	Kazakhstan	51 10 N	71 30 E
Asuncion [US Embassy]	Paraguay	25 16 S	57 40 W
Asuncion Island	Northern Mariana Islands	19 40 N	145 24 E
Atacama [region]	Chile	24 30 S	69 15 W
Athens [US Embassy]	Greece	37 59 N	23 44 E
Attu Island	United States	52 55 N	172 57 E
Auckland [US Consulate General]	New Zealand	36 52 S	174 46 E
Auckland Islands	New Zealand	51 00 S	166 30 E
Australes, Iles (Iles Tubuai)	French Polynesia	23 20 S	151 00 W
Avarua	Cook Islands	21 12 S	159 46 W
Axel Heiberg Island	Canada	79 30 N	90 00 W
Azad Kashmir	Pakistan	34 30 N	74 00 E

Name	Entry in *The World Factbook*	Latitude (deg min)	Longitude (deg min)
Azores [islands]	Portugal	38 30 N	28 00 W
Azov, Sea of	Atlantic Ocean	49 00 N	36 00 E
Bab el Mandeb [strait]	Indian Ocean	12 40 N	43 20 E
Babuyan Channel	Pacific Ocean	18 44 N	121 40 E
Babuyan Islands	Philippines	19 10 N	121 40 E
Baffin Bay	Arctic Ocean	73 00 N	66 00 W
Baffin Island	Canada	68 00 N	70 00 W
Baghdad [US Embassy temporarily suspended; US Interests Section located in Poland's embassy in Baghdad]	Iraq	33 21 N	44 25 E
Baki (see Baku)	Azerbaijan	40 23 N	49 51 E
Baku [US Embassy]	Azerbaijan	40 23 N	49 51 E
Baky (see Baku)	Azerbaijan	40 23 N	49 51 E
Balabac Strait	Pacific Ocean	7 35 N	117 00 E
Balearic Islands	Spain	39 30 N	3 00 E
Balearic Sea (Iberian Sea)	Atlantic Ocean	40 30 N	2 00 E
Bali [island]	Indonesia	8 20 S	115 00 E
Bali Sea	Indian Ocean	7 45 S	115 30 E
Balintang Channel	Pacific Ocean	19 49 N	121 40 E
Balintang Islands	Philippines	19 55 N	122 10 E
Balkan Peninsula	Albania, Bosnia and Herzegovina, Bulgaria, Croatia, Greece, Romania, Serbia and Montenegro, Slovenia, The Former Yugoslav Republic of Macedonia, Turkey (European part)	42 00 N	23 00 E
Balleny Islands	Antarctica	67 00 S	163 00 E
Balochistan [region]	Pakistan	28 00 N	63 00 E
Baltic Sea	Atlantic Ocean	57 00 N	19 00 E
Bamako [US Embassy]	Mali	12 39 N	8 00 W
Banaba (Ocean Island)	Kiribati	0 52 S	169 35 E
Bandar Seri Begawan [US Embassy]	Brunei	4 52 S	114 55 E
Banda Sea	Pacific Ocean	5 00 S	128 00 E
Bangkok [US Embassy]	Thailand	13 45 N	100 31 E
Bangui [US Embassy]	Central African Republic	4 22 N	18 35 E
Banjul [US Embassy]	The Gambia	13 28 N	16 39 W
Banks Island	Australia	10 12 S	142 16 E
Banks Island	Canada	75 15 N	121 30 W
Banks Islands (Iles Banks)	Vanuatu	14 00 S	167 30 E
Barbuda [island]	Antigua and Barbuda	17 38 N	61 48 W
Barcelona [US Consulate General]	Spain	41 23 N	2 11 E
Barents Sea	Arctic Ocean	74 00 N	36 00 E
Barranquilla	Colombia	10 59 N	74 48 W
Bashi Channel	Pacific Ocean	22 00 N	121 00 E
Basilan Strait	Pacific Ocean	6 49 N	122 05 E
Basque Provinces	Spain	43 00 N	2 30 W
Bass Strait	Pacific Ocean	39 20 S	145 30 E
Basse-Terre	Guadeloupe	16 00 N	61 44 W
Basseterre	Saint Kitts and Nevis	17 18 N	62 43 W
Bastia	France (Corsica)	42 42 N	9 27 E
Basutoland	Lesotho	29 30 S	28 30 E
Batan Islands	Philippines	20 30 N	121 50 E

Name	Entry in *The World Factbook*	Latitude (deg min)	Longitude (deg min)
Bavaria (Bayern)	Germany	48 30 N	11 30 E
Beagle Channel	Atlantic Ocean	54 53 S	68 10 W
Bear Island (see Bjornoya)	Svalbard	74 26 N	19 5 E
Beaufort Sea	Arctic Ocean	73 00 N	140 00 W
Bechuanaland	Botswana	22 00 S	24 00 E
Beijing [US Embassy]	China	39 56 N	116 24 E
Beirut [US Embassy]	Lebanon	33 53 N	35 30 E
Belau (Palau Islands)	Palau	7 30 N	134 30 E
Belem [US Consular Agency]	Brazil	1 27 S	48 29 W
Belep Islands (Iles Belep)	New Caledonia	19 45 S	163 40 E
Belfast [US Consulate General]	United Kingdom	54 35 N	5 55 W
Belgian Congo	Democratic Republic of the Congo	0 00 N	25 00 E
Belgrade	Serbia and Montenegro	44 50 N	20 30 E
Belize City [US Embassy]	Belize	17 30 N	88 12 W
Belle Isle, Strait of	Atlantic Ocean	51 35 N	56 30 W
Bellingshausen Sea	Pacific Ocean	71 00 S	85 00 W
Belmopan	Belize	17 15 N	88 46 W
Belorussia	Belarus	53 00 N	28 00 E
Bengal, Bay of	Indian Ocean	15 00 N	90 00 E
Bering Sea	Pacific Ocean	60 00 N	175 00 W
Bering Island	Russia	55 00 N	166 30 E
Bering Strait	Pacific Ocean	65 30 N	169 00 W
Berkner Island	Antarctica	79 30 S	49 30 W
Berlin [US Branch Office]	Germany	52 31 N	13 24 E
Berlin, East	Germany	52 30 N	13 33 E
Berlin, West	Germany	52 30 N	12 20 E
Bern [US Embassy]	Switzerland	46 57 N	7 26 E
Bessarabia [region]	Romania, Moldova, Ukraine	47 00 N	28 30 E
Bhopal	India	23 16 N	77 24 E
Biafra [region]	Nigeria	5 30 N	7 30 E
Big Diomede Island	Russia	65 46 N	169 06 W
Bijagos, Arquipelago dos	Guinea-Bissau	11 25 N	16 20 W
Bikini Atoll	Marshall Islands	11 35 N	165 23 E
Bilbao	Spain	43 15 N	2 58 W
Bioko [island]	Equatorial Guinea	3 30 N	8 42 E
Biscay, Bay of	Atlantic Ocean	44 00 N	4 00 W
Bishkek [US Embassy]	Kyrgyzstan	42 54 N	74 36 E
Bishop Rock	United Kingdom	49 52 N	6 27 W
Bismarck Archipelago	Papua New Guinea	5 00 S	150 00 E
Bismarck Sea	Pacific Ocean	4 00 S	148 00 E
Bissau [US Embassy]	Guinea-Bissau	11 51 N	15 35 W
Bjornoya (Bear Island)	Svalbard	74 26 N	19 5 E
Black Forest	Germany	48 00 N	8 15 E
Black Rock	South Georgia and the South Sandwich Islands	53 39 S	41 48 W
Black Sea	Atlantic Ocean	43 00 N	35 00 E
Bloemfontein	South Africa	29 12 S	26 07 E
Boa Vista [island]	Cape Verde	16 05 N	22 50 W
Bogota [US Embassy]	Colombia	4 36 N	74 05 W

Appendix H: Cross-Reference List of Geographic Names (continued)

Name	Entry in *The World Factbook*	Latitude (deg min)	Longitude (deg min)
Bohemia [region]	Czech Republic	50 00 N	14 30 E
Bombay (see Mumbai)	India	18 58 N	72 50 E
Bonaire [island]	Netherlands Antilles	12 10 N	68 15 W
Bonifacio, Strait of	Atlantic Ocean	41 01 N	14 00 E
Bonin Islands	Japan	27 00 N	140 10 E
Bonn [US Embassy]	Germany	50 44 N	7 05 E
Bophuthatswana	South Africa	26 30 S	25 30 E
Bora-Bora [island]	French Polynesia	16 30 S	151 45 W
Bordeaux	France	44 50 N	0 34 W
Borneo [island]	Brunei, Indonesia, Malaysia	0 30 N	114 00 E
Bornholm [island]	Denmark	55 10 N	15 00 E
Bosnia	Bosnia and Herzegovina	44 00 N	18 00 E
Bosporus [strait]	Atlantic Ocean	41 00 N	29 00 E
Bothnia, Gulf of	Atlantic Ocean	63 00 N	20 00 E
Bougainville [island]	Papua New Guinea	6 00 S	155 00 E
Bougainville Strait	Pacific Ocean	6 40 S	156 10 E
Bounty Islands	New Zealand	47 43 S	174 00 E
Brasilia [US Embassy]	Brazil	15 47 S	47 55 W
Bratislava [US Embassy]	Slovakia	48 09 N	17 07 E
Brazzaville [US Embassy]	Republic of the Congo	4 16 S	15 17 E
Bridgetown [US Embassy]	Barbados	13 06 N	59 37 W
Brisbane	Australia	27 28 S	153 02 E
Britain (see Great Britain)	United Kingdom	54 00 N	2 00 W
British East Africa	Kenya, Tanzania, Uganda	1 00 N	38 00 E
British Guiana	Guyana	5 00 N	59 00 W
British Honduras	Belize	17 15 N	88 45 W
British Solomon Islands	Solomon Islands	8 00 S	159 00 E
British Somaliland	Somalia	10 00 N	49 00 E
Brussels [US Embassy, US Mission to European Union (USEU), US Mission to the North Atlantic Treaty Organization (USNATO)]	Belgium	50 50 N	4 20 E
Bubiyan [island]	Kuwait	29 47 N	48 10 E
Bucharest [US Embassy]	Romania	44 26 N	26 06 E
Budapest [US Embassy]	Hungary	47 30 N	19 05 E
Buenos Aires [US Embassy]	Argentina	34 36 S	58 27 W
Bujumbura [US Embassy]	Burundi	3 23 S	29 22 E
Burnt Pine	Norfolk Island	29 02 S	167 56 E
Byelorussia	Belarus	53 00 N	28 00 E
Cabinda [province]	Angola	5 33 S	12 12 E
Cabot Strait	Atlantic Ocean	47 20 N	59 30 W
Caicos Islands	Turks and Caicos Islands	21 56 N	71 58 W
Cairo [US Embassy]	Egypt	30 03 N	31 15 E
Calcutta [US Consulate General]	India	22 32 N	88 22 E
Calgary [US Consulate General]	Canada	51 03 N	114 05 W
California, Gulf of	Pacific Ocean	28 00 N	112 00 W
Campbell Island	New Zealand	52 33 S	169 09 E
Canal Zone	Panama	9 00 N	79 45 W
Canary Islands	Spain	28 00 N	15 30 W
Canberra [US Embassy]	Australia	35 17 S	149 08 E

Name	Entry in *The World Factbook*	Latitude (deg min)	Longitude (deg min)
Canton (Guangzhou)	China	23 06 N	113 16 E
Canton Island (Kanton Island)	Kiribati	2 49 S	171 40 W
Cape Town [US Consulate General]	South Africa	33 55 S	18 22 E
Caracas [US Embassy]	Venezuela	10 30 N	66 56 W
Cargados Carajos Shoals	Mauritius	16 25 S	59 38 E
Caroline Islands	Federated States of Micronesia, Palau	7 30 N	148 00 E
Caribbean Sea	Atlantic Ocean	15 00 N	73 00 W
Carpentaria, Gulf of	Pacific Ocean	14 00 S	139 00 E
Casablanca [US Consulate General]	Morocco	33 39 N	7 35 W
Castries	Saint Lucia	14 01 N	61 00 W
Catalonia [region]	Spain	42 00 N	2 00 E
Cato Island	Australia	23 15 S	155 32 E
Caucasus [region]	Russia	42 00 N	45 00 E
Cayenne	French Guiana	4 56 N	52 20 W
Cebu [US Consular Agency]	Philippines	10 18 N	123 54 E
Celebes [island]	Indonesia	2 00 S	121 00 E
Celebes Sea	Pacific Ocean	3 00 N	122 00 E
Celtic Sea	Atlantic Ocean	51 00 N	6 30 W
Central African Empire	Central African Republic	7 00 N	21 00 E
Ceuta	Spain	35 53 N	5 19 W
Ceylon	Sri Lanka	7 00 N	81 00 E
Chafarinas, Islas	Spain	35 12 N	2 26 W
Chagos Archipelago (Oil Islands)	British Indian Ocean Territory	6 00 S	71 30 E
Channel Islands	Guernsey, Jersey	49 20 N	2 20 W
Charlotte Amalie	Virgin Islands	18 21 N	64 56 W
Chatham Islands	New Zealand	44 00 S	176 30 W
Chechnya (Chechnia)	Russia	43 15 N	45 40 E
Cheju-do [island]	Korea, South	33 20 N	126 30 E
Cheju Strait	Pacific Ocean	34 00 N	126 30 E
Chengdu [US Consulate General]	China	39 39 N	104 04 E
Chennai (Madras) [US Consulate General]	India	13 04 N	80 16 E
Chesterfield Islands (Iles Chesterfield)	New Caledonia	19 52 S	158 15 E
Chiang Mai [US Consulate General]	Thailand	18 47 N	98 59 E
Chihli, Gulf of (see Bo Hai)	Pacific Ocean	38 30 N	120 00 E
China, People's Republic of	China	35 00 N	105 00 E
China, Republic of	Taiwan	23 30 N	105 00 E
Chisinau [US Embassy]	Moldova	47 00 N	28 50 E
Choiseul [island]	Solomon Islands	7 05 S	121 00 E
Christmas Island [Indian Ocean]	Australia	10 25 S	105 39 E
Christmas Island (Kiritimati) [Pacific Ocean]	Kiribati	1 52 N	157 20 W
Chukchi Sea	Arctic Ocean	69 00 N	171 00 W
Ciskei	South Africa	33 00 S	27 00 E
Ciudad Juarez [US Consulate General]	Mexico	31 44 N	106 29 W
Cluj-Napoca [US Branch Office]	Romania	46 47 N	23 36 E
Cochin China [region]	Vietnam	11 00 N	107 00 E
Coco, Isla del	Costa Rica	5 32 N	87 04 W
Cocos Islands	Cocos (Keeling) Islands	12 30 S	96 50 E
Colombo [US Embassy]	Sri Lanka	6 56 N	79 51 E

Name	Entry in *The World Factbook*	Latitude (deg min)	Longitude (deg min)
Colon, Archipielago de (Galapagos Islands)	Ecuador	0 00 N	90 30 W
Commander Islands (Komandorskiye Ostrova)	Russia	55 00 N	167 00 E
Conakry [US Embassy]	Guinea	9 31 N	13 43 W
Congo (Leopoldville)	Democratic Republic of the Congo	15 00 S	30 00 E
Con Son [Islands]	Vietnam	8 43 N	106 36 E
Cook Strait	Pacific Ocean	41 15 S	174 30 E
Copenhagen [US Embassy]	Denmark	55 40 N	12 35 E
Coral Sea	Pacific Ocean	15 00 S	150 00 E
Corfu [island]	Greece	39 40 N	19 45 E
Corinth	Greece	37 56 N	22 56 E
Corisco [island]	Equatorial Guinea	0 55 N	9 19 E
Corn Islands (Islas del Maiz)	Nicaragua	12 15 N	83 00 W
Corocoro Island	Guyana, Venezuela	3 38 N	66 50 W
Corsica (Corse) [island]	France	42 00 N	9 00 E
Cosmoledo Group (Atoll de Cosmoledo)	Seychelles	9 43 S	47 35 E
Cotonou [US Embassy]	Benin	6 21 N	2 26 E
Courantyne River	Guyana, Suriname	5 57 N	57 06 W
Crete [island]	Greece	35 15 N	24 45 E
Crimea [region]	Ukraine	45 00 N	34 00 E
Crimean Peninsula	Ukraine	45 00 N	34 00 E
Crooked Island Passage	Atlantic Ocean	22 55 N	74 35 W
Crozet Islands (Iles Crozet)	French Southern and Antarctic Lands	46 30 S	51 00 E
Curacao [US Consulate General]	Netherlands Antilles	12 11 N	69 00 W
Cyclades [islands]	Greece	37 00 N	25 10 E
Czechoslovakia	Czech Republic, Slovakia	49 00 N	18 00 E
D			
Dahomey	Benin	9 30 N	2 15 E
Daito Islands	Japan	43 00 N	17 00 E
Dakar [US Embassy]	Senegal	14 40 N	17 26 W
Dalmatia [region]	Croatia	43 00 N	17 00 E
Daman (Damao)	India	20 10 N	73 00 E
Damascus [US Embassy]	Syria	33 30 N	36 18 E
Danger Islands (see Pukapuka Atoll)	Cook Islands	10 53 S	165 49 E
Danish Straits	Atlantic Ocean	58 00 N	11 00 E
Danish West Indies	Virgin Islands	18 20 N	64 50 W
Danzig (Gdansk)	Poland	54 23 N	18 40 E
Dao Bach Long Vi [island]	Vietnam	20 08 N	107 44 E
Dardanelles [strait]	Atlantic Ocean	40 15 N	26 25 E
Dar es Salaam [US Embassy]	Tanzania	6 48 S	39 17 E
Davis Strait	Atlantic Ocean	67 00 N	57 00 W
Dead Sea	Israel, Jordan, West Bank	32 30 N	35 30 E
Deception Island	Antarctica	62 56 S	60 34 W
Denmark Strait	Atlantic Ocean	67 00 N	24 00 W
D'Entrecasteaux Islands	Papua New Guinea	9 30 S	150 40 E
Desolation Islands (Isles Kerguelen)	French Southern and Antarctic Lands	49 30 S	69 30 E
Devils Island (Ile du Diable)	French Guiana	5 17 N	52 35 W
Devon Island	Canada	76 00 N	87 00 W
Dhahran [US Consulate General]	Saudi Arabia	26 18 N	50 08 E
Dhaka [US Embassy]	Bangladesh	23 43 N	90 25 E

Name	Entry in *The World Factbook*	Latitude (deg min)	Longitude (deg min)
Dhofar [region]	Oman	17 00 N	54 10 E
Diego Garcia [island]	British Indian Ocean Territory	7 20 S	72 25 E
Diego Ramirez [islands]	Chile	56 30 S	68 43 W
Diomede Islands	Russia [Big Diomede], United States [Little Diomede]	65 47 N	169 00 W
Diu	India	20 42 N	70 59 E
Djibouti [US Embassy]	Djibouti	11 30 N	43 15 E
Dnieper [river] (Dnyapro, Dnepr, Dnipro)	Belarus, Russia, Ukraine	46 30 N	32 18 E
Dniester [river] (Nistru, Dnister)	Moldova, Ukraine	46 18 N	30 17 E
Dodecanese [islands]	Greece	36 00 N	27 05 E
Dodoma	Tanzania	6 11 S	35 45 E
Doha [US Embassy]	Qatar	25 17 N	51 32 E
Donets Basin	Russia, Ukraine	48 15 N	38 30 E
Douala	Cameroon	4 03 N	9 42 E
Douglas	Man, Isle of	54 09 N	4 28 W
Dover, Strait of	Atlantic Ocean	51 00 N	1 30 E
Drake Passage	Atlantic Ocean	60 00 S	60 00 W
Dubai [US Consulate General]	United Arab Emirates	25 18 N	55 18 E
Dubayy (see Dubai)	United Arab Emirates	25 18 N	55 18 E
Dublin [US Embassy]	Ireland	53 20 N	6 15 W
Durban [US Consulate General]	South Africa	29 55 S	30 56 E
Dushanbe [US Embassy]	Tajikistan	38 35 N	68 48 E
Dutch Antilles	Netherlands Antilles	52 05 N	4 18 E
Dutch East Indies	Indonesia	5 00 S	120 00 E
Dutch Guiana	Suriname	4 00 N	56 00 W
Dutch West Indies	Netherlands Antilles	52 05 N	4 18 E
Dzungarian Gate	China, Kazakhstan	45 25 N	82 25 E
East China Sea	Pacific Ocean	30 00 N	126 00 E
East Frisian Islands	Germany	53 44 N	7 25 E
East Germany (German Democratic Republic)	Germany	52 00 N	13 00 E
East Korea Strait (Eastern Channel or Tsushima Strait)	Pacific Ocean	34 00 N	129 00 E
East Pakistan	Bangladesh	24 00 N	90 00 E
East Siberian Sea	Arctic Ocean	74 00 N	166 00 E
East Timor (Portuguese Timor)	Indonesia	9 00 S	126 00 E
Easter Island (Isla de Pascua)	Chile	27 07 S	109 22 W
Eastern Channel (East Korea Strait or Tsushima Strait)	Pacific Ocean	34 00 N	129 00 E
Eastern Samoa	American Samoa	14 20 S	170 00 W
Edinburgh [US Consulate General]	United Kingdom	55 57 N	3 13 W
Eire	Ireland	53 00 N	8 00 W
Elba [island]	Italy	42 46 N	10 17 E
Ellef Ringnes Island	Canada	78 00 N	103 00 W
Ellesmere Island	Canada	81 00 N	80 00 W
Ellice Islands	Tuvalu	8 00 S	178 00 E
Elobey, Islas de	Equatorial Guinea	0 59 N	9 33 E
Enderbury Island	Kiribati	3 08 S	171 5 W
Enewetak Atoll (Eniwetok Atoll)	Marshall Islands	11 30 N	162 15 E
England [region]	United Kingdom	52 30 N	1 30 W
English Channel	Atlantic Ocean	50 20 N	1 00 W
Eniwetok Atoll (see Enewetak Atoll)	Marshall Islands	11 30 N	162 15 E

E

Name	Entry in *The World Factbook*	Latitude (deg min)	Longitude (deg min)
Eolie, Isole	Italy	38 30 N	15 00 E
Epirus, Northern	Albania, Greece	40 00 N	20 30 E
Espana	Spain	40 00 N	4 00 W
Essequibo [region] [claimed by Venezuela]	Guyana	6 59 N	58 23 W
Etorofu (Iturup) [island]	Russia [de facto]	44 55 N	147 40 E
Farquhar Group (Atoll de Farquhar)	Seychelles	10 10 S	51 10 E
Fernando de Noronha	Brazil	3 51 S	32 25 W
Fernando Po [island] (see Bioko)	Equatorial Guinea	3 30 N	8 42 E
Finland, Gulf of	Atlantic Ocean	60 00 N	27 00 E
Florence [US Consulate General]	Italy	43 46 N	11 15 E
Florida, Straits of	Atlantic Ocean	25 00 N	79 45 W
former Soviet Union (FSU)	Armenia, Azerbaijan, Belarus, Estonia, Georgia, Kazakhstan, Kyrgyzstan, Latvia, Lithuania, Moldova, Russia, Tajikistan, Turkmenistan, Ukraine, Uzbekistan		
Formosa [island]	Taiwan	23 30 N	121 00 E
Formosa Strait (see Taiwan Strait)	Pacific Ocean	24 00 N	119 00 E
Fortaleza [US Consular Agency]	Brazil	3 43 S	38 30 W
Fort-de-France	Martinique	14 36 N	61 05 W
Frankfurt am Main [US Consulate General]	Germany	50 07 N	8 40 E
Franz Josef Land [islands]	Russia	81 00 N	55 00 E
Freetown [US Embassy]	Sierra Leone	8 30 N	13 15 W
French Cameroon	Cameroon	6 00 N	12 00 E
French Guinea	Guinea	11 00 N	10 00 E
French Indochina	Cambodia, Laos, Vietnam	15 00 N	107 00 E
French Morocco	Morocco	32 00 N	5 00 W
French Somaliland	Djibouti	11 30 N	43 00 W
French Sudan	Mali	17 00 N	4 00 W
French Territory of the Afars and Issas (FTAI)	Djibouti	11 30 N	43 00 W
French Togo	Togo	8 00 N	1 10 E
French West Indies	Guadeloupe, Martinique	16 30 N	62 00 W
Friendly Islands	Tonga	20 00 S	175 00 W
Frisian Islands	Denmark, Germany, Netherlands	53 35 N	6 40 E
Frunze (see Bishkek)	Kyrgyzstan	42 54 N	74 36 E
Fukuoka [US Consulate]	Japan	33 35 N	130 24 E
Funafuti	Tuvalu	8 30 S	179 12 E
Fundy, Bay of	Atlantic Ocean	45 00 N	66 00 W
Futuna Islands (Hoorn Islands/Iles de Horne)	Wallis and Futuna	14 19 S	178 05 W
Gaborone [US Embassy]	Botswana	24 45 S	25 55 E
Galapagos Islands (Archipielago de Colon)	Ecuador	0 00 N	90 30 W
Galilee [region]	Israel	32 54 N	35 20 E
Galleons Passage	Atlantic Ocean	11 00 N	60 55 W
Gambier Islands (Iles Gambier)	French Polynesia	23 09 S	134 58 W
Gaspar Strait	Pacific Ocean	3 00 S	107 00 E
Geneva [US Consular Agency, US Mission to European Office of the UN and Other International Organizations]	Switzerland	46 12 N	6 10 E
Genoa	Italy	44 25 N	8 57 E
George Town	Malaysia	5 26 N	100 16 E
George Town	The Bahamas	23 30 N	75 46 W

Appendix H: Cross-Reference List of Geographic Names (continued)

Name	Entry in *The World Factbook*	Latitude (deg min)	Longitude (deg min)
George Town	Cayman Islands	19 20 N	81 23 W
Georgetown	The Gambia	13 30 N	14 47 W
Georgetown [US Embassy]	Guyana	6 48 N	58 10 W
German Democratic Republic (East Germany)	Germany	52 00 N	13 00 E
German Southwest Africa	Namibia	22 00 S	17 00 E
Germany, Federal Republic of	Germany	51 00 N	9 00 E
Gibraltar	Gibraltar	36 11 N	5 22 W
Gibraltar, Strait of	Atlantic Ocean	35 57 N	5 36 W
Gidi Pass	Egypt	30 13 N	33 09 E
Gilbert Islands	Kiribati	1 25 N	173 00 E
Goa [state]	India	14 20 N	74 00 E
Godthab (Nuuk)	Greenland	64 11 N	51 44 W
Gold Coast	Ghana	8 00 N	2 00 W
Golan Heights [region]	Syria	33 00 N	35 45 E
Good Hope, Cape of	South Africa	34 24 S	18 30 E
Goteborg	Sweden	57 43 N	11 58 E
Gotland [island]	Sweden	57 30 N	18 33 E
Gough Island	Saint Helena	40 10 S	9 45 W
Grand Banks	Atlantic Ocean	47 06 N	55 48 W
Grand Cayman [island]	Cayman Islands	19 20 N	81 20 W
Grand Turk	Turks and Caicos Islands	21 28 N	71 08 W
Great Australian Bight	Indian Ocean	35 00 S	130 00 E
Great Belt (Store Baelt)	Atlantic Ocean	55 30 N	11 00 E
Great Bitter Lake	Egypt	30 20 N	32 23 E
Great Britain	United Kingdom	54 00 N	2 00 W
Great Channel	Indian Ocean	6 25 N	94 20 E
Greater Sunda Islands	Brunei, Indonesia, Malaysia	2 00 S	110 00 E
Green Islands	Papua New Guinea	4 30 S	154 10 E
Greenland Sea	Arctic Ocean	79 00 N	5 00 W
Grenadines, Northern	Saint Vincent and the Grenadines	13 15 N	61 12 W
Grenadines, Southern	Grenada	12 07 N	61 40 W
Grytviken	South Georgia and the South Sandwich Islands	54 15 S	36 45 W
Guadalajara [US Consulate General]	Mexico	20 40 N	103 20 W
Guadalcanal [island]	Solomon Islands	9 32 S	160 12 E
Guadalupe, Isla de	Mexico	29 11 N	118 17 W
Guangzhou [US Consulate General]	China	23 06 N	113 16 E
Guantanamo Bay [US Naval Base]	Cuba	20 00 N	75 08 W
Guatemala [US Embassy]	Guatemala	14 38 N	90 31 W
Guinea, Gulf of	Atlantic Ocean	3 00 N	2 30 E
Guayaquil [US Consulate General]	Ecuador	2 13 S	79 54 W
Ha'apai Group	Tonga	19 42 S	174 29 W
Habomai Islands	Russia [de facto]	43 30 N	146 10 E
Hadhramaut [region]	Yemen	15 00 N	50 00 E
Hagatna (Agana)	Guam	13 28 N	144 45 E
Hague, The [US Embassy]	Netherlands	52 05 N	4 18 E
Haifa	Israel	32 50 N	35 00 E
Haiphong	Vietnam	20 52 N	106 41 E
Hainan Dao [island]	China	19 00 N	109 30 E

H

Name	Entry in *The World Factbook*	Latitude (deg min)	Longitude (deg min)
Halifax [US Consulate General]	Canada	44 39 N	63 36 W
Halmahera [island]	Indonesia	1 00 N	128 00 E
Hamburg [US Consulate General]	Germany	53 33 N	9 59 E
Hamilton [US Consulate General]	Bermuda	32 17 N	64 46 W
Hanoi [US Embassy]	Vietnam	21 02 N	105 51 E
Harare [US Embassy]	Zimbabwe	17 50 S	31 03 E
Hatay [province]	Turkey	36 30 N	36 15 E
Havana [US post not maintained; representation by US Interests Section (USINT) of the Swiss Embassy]	Cuba	23 08 N	82 22 W
Hawaii	United States	20 00 N	157 45 W
Heard Island	Heard Island and McDonald Islands	53 06 S	73 30 E
Hejaz [region]	Saudi Arabia	24 30 N	38 30 E
Helsinki [US Embassy]	Finland	60 10 N	24 58 E
Hermosillo [US Consulate]	Mexico	29 04 N	110 58 W
Herzegovina	Bosnia and Herzegovina	44 00 N	18 00 E
Hispaniola [island]	Dominican Republic, Haiti	18 45 N	71 00 W
Ho Chi Minh City	Vietnam	10 45 N	106 40 E
Hokkaido [island]	Japan	44 00 N	143 00 E
Holland	Netherlands	52 30 N	5 45 E
Hong Kong [US Consulate General]	Hong Kong	22 15 N	114 10 E
Honiara	Solomon Islands	9 26 S	159 57 E
Honshu [island]	Japan	36 00 N	138 00 E
Hormuz, Strait of	Indian Ocean	26 34 N	56 15 E
Horn, Cape (Cabo de Hornos)	Chile	55 59 S	67 16 W
Horne, Iles de	Wallis and Futuna	14 19 S	178 05 W
Horn of Africa	Djibouti, Eritrea, Ethiopia, Somalia	8 00 N	48 00 E
Hudson Bay	Arctic Ocean	60 00 N	86 00 W
Hudson Strait	Arctic Ocean	62 00 N	71 00 W
Hunter Island	New Caledonia, Vanuatu	22 24 S	172 06 E
Iberian Peninsula	Portugal, Spain	40 00 N	5 00 W
Inaccessible Island	Saint Helena	37 17 S	12 40 W
Indochina	Cambodia, Laos, Vietnam	15 00 N	107 00 E
Inland Sea	Japan	34 20 N	133 30 E
Inner Mongolia (Nei Mongol)	China	42 00 N	113 00 E
Ionian Islands	Greece	38 30 N	20 30 E
Ionian Sea	Atlantic Ocean	38 30 N	18 00 E
Irian Jaya [province]	Indonesia	5 00 S	138 00 E
Irish Sea	Atlantic Ocean	53 30 N	5 20 W
Iron Gate	Romania, Serbia and Montenegro	44 41 N	22 31 E
Islamabad [US Embassy]	Pakistan	33 42 N	73 10 E
Islas Malvinas	Falkland Islands (Islas Malvinas)	51 45 S	59 00 W
Istanbul [US Consulate General]	Turkey	41 01 N	28 58 E
Istrian Peninsula	Croatia, Slovenia	45 00 N	14 00 E
Italian East Africa	Eritrea, Ethiopia, Somalia	8 00 N	38 00 E
Italian Somaliland	Somalia	10 00 N	49 00 E
Iturup (see Etorofu)	Russia [de facto]	44 55 N	147 40 E
Ivory Coast	Cote d'Ivoire	8 00 N	5 00 W
Iwo Jima [island]	Japan	24 47 N	141 20 E

Appendix H: Cross-Reference List of Geographic Names (continued)

Name	Entry in *The World Factbook*	Latitude (deg min)	Longitude (deg min)
J Jakarta [US Embassy]	Indonesia	6 10 S	106 48 E
Jamestown	Saint Helena	15 56 S	5 44 W
Jammu	India	32 42 N	74 52 E
Jammu and Kashmir [region]	India, Pakistan	34 00 N	76 00 E
Japan, Sea of	Pacific Ocean	40 00 N	135 00 E
Jars, Plain of	Laos	19 27 N	103 10 E
Java [island]	Indonesia	7 30 S	110 00 E
Java Sea	Pacific Ocean	5 00 S	110 00 E
Jeddah (see Jiddah)	Saudi Arabia	21 30 N	39 12 E
Jerusalem [US Consulate General]	Israel, West Bank	31 47 N	35 14 E
Jiddah [US Consulate General]	Saudi Arabia	21 30 N	39 12 E
Johannesburg [US Consulate General]	South Africa	26 15 S	28 00 E
Juan de Fuca, Strait of	Pacific Ocean	48 18 N	124 00 W
Juan Fernandez, Isla de	Chile	33 00 S	80 00 W
Jubal, Strait of	Indian Ocean	27 40 N	33 55 E
Judaea [region]	Israel, West Bank	31 35 N	35 00 E
Jutland [region]	Denmark	56 00 N	9 15 E
Juventud, Isla de la (Isle of Youth)	Cuba	21 40 N	82 50 W
K Kabul [US Embassy now closed]	Afghanistan	34 31 N	69 12 E
Kaduna	Nigeria	10 33 N	7 27 E
Kailas Range	China, India	30 00 N	82 00 E
Kalimantan [region]	Indonesia	0 00 N	115 00 E
Kamaran [island]	Yemen	15 21 N	42 34 E
Kamchatka Peninsula (Poluostrov Kamchatka)	Russia	56 00 N	160 00 E
Kampala [US Embassy]	Uganda	0 19 N	32 25 E
Kampuchea	Cambodia	13 00 N	105 00 E
Kanton Island	Kiribati	2 49 S	171 40 W
Karachi [US Consulate General]	Pakistan	24 52 N	67 03 E
Kara Sea	Arctic Ocean	76 00 N	80 00 E
Karakoram Pass	China, India	35 30 N	77 50 E
Karelian Isthmus	Russia	60 25 N	30 00 E
Karimata Strait	Pacific Ocean	2 05 S	108 40 E
Kashmir [region]	India, Pakistan	34 00 N	76 00 E
Katanga [region]	Democratic Republic of the Congo	10 00 S	26 00 E
Kathmandu [US Embassy]	Nepal	27 43 N	85 19 E
Kattegat [strait]	Atlantic Ocean	57 00 N	11 00 E
Kauai Channel	Pacific Ocean	21 45 N	158 50 W
Keeling Islands	Cocos (Keeling) Islands	12 30 S	96 50 E
Kerguelen, Iles	French Southern and Antarctic Lands	49 30 S	69 30 E
Kermadec Islands	New Zealand	29 50 S	178 15 W
Kerulen River	China, Mongolia	48 48 N	117 00 E
Khabarovsk	Russia	48 27 N	135 06 E
Khanka, Lake	China, Russia	45 00 N	132 24 E
Khartoum [US Embassy]	Sudan	15 36 N	32 32 E
Khmer Republic	Cambodia	13 00 N	105 00 E
Khuriya Muriya Islands (Kuria Muria Islands)	Oman	17 30 N	56 00 E
Khyber Pass	Afghanistan, Pakistan	34 05 N	71 10 E
Kiel Canal (Nord-Ostsee Kanal)	Atlantic Ocean	53 53 N	9 08 E

Appendix H: Cross-Reference List of Geographic Names (continued)

Name	Entry in *The World Factbook*	Latitude (deg min)	Longitude (deg min)
Kiev [US Embassy]	Ukraine	50 26 N	30 31 E
Kigali [US Embassy]	Rwanda	1 57 S	30 04 E
Kingston [US Embassy]	Jamaica	18 00 N	76 48 W
Kingston	Norfolk Island	29 03 S	167 58 E
Kingstown	Saint Vincent and the Grenadines	13 09 N	61 14 W
Kinshasa [US Embassy]	Democratic Republic of the Congo	4 18 S	15 18 E
Kirghiziya	Kyrgyzstan	41 00 N	75 00 E
Kiritimati (Christmas Island)	Kiribati	1 52 N	157 20 W
Kishinev (see Chisinau)	Moldova	47 00 N	28 50 E
Kithira Strait	Atlantic Ocean	36 00 N	23 00 E
Kobe	Japan	34 41 N	135 10 E
Kodiak Island	United States	57 49 N	152 23 W
Kola Peninsula (Kol'skiy Poluostrov)	Russia	67 20 N	37 00 E
Kolonia [US Embassy]	Federated States of Micronesia	6 58 N	158 13 E
Korea Bay	Pacific Ocean	39 00 N	124 00 E
Korea, Democratic People's Republic of	North Korea	40 00 N	127 00 E
Korea, Republic of	South Korea	37 00 N	127 30 E
Korea Strait	Pacific Ocean	34 00 N	129 00 E
Koror [US Embassy]	Palau	7 20 N	134 29 E
Kosovo [region]	Serbia and Montenegro	42 30 N	21 00 E
Kowloon	Hong Kong	22 18 N	114 10 E
Kra, Isthmus of	Burma, Thailand	10 20 N	99 00 E
Krakatoa [volcano]	Indonesia	6 07 S	105 24 E
Krakow [US Consulate General]	Poland	50 03 N	19 58 E
Kuala Lumpur [US Embassy]	Malaysia	3 10 N	101 42 E
Kunashiri (Kunashir) [island]	Russia [de facto]	44 20 N	146 00 E
Kunlun Mountains	China	36 00 N	84 00 E
Kuril Islands	Russia [de facto]	46 10 N	152 00 E
Kuwait [US Embassy]	Kuwait	29 20 N	47 59 E
Kuznetsk Basin	Russia	54 00 N	86 00 E
Kwajalein Atoll	Marshall Islands	9 05 N	167 20 E
Kyushu [island]	Japan	33 00 N	131 00 E
Kyyiv (see Kiev)	Ukraine	50 26 N	30 31 E
L Labrador	Canada	54 00 N	62 00 W
Laccadive Islands	India	10 00 N	73 00 E
Laccadive Sea	Indian Ocean	7 00 N	76 00 E
Lagos [US Embassy]	Nigeria	6 27 N	3 24 E
Lahore [US Consulate General]	Pakistan	31 35 N	74 18 E
Lakshadweep (Laccadive Islands)	India	10 00 N	73 00 E
La Paz [US Embassy]	Bolivia	16 30 S	68 09 W
La Perouse Strait	Pacific Ocean	45 45 N	142 00 E
Laptev Sea	Arctic Ocean	76 00 N	126 00 E
Las Palmas	Spain	28 06 N	15 24 W
Lau Group	Fiji	18 20 S	178 30 E
Lefkosa (see Nicosia)	Cyprus	35 10 N	33 22 E
Leipzig [US Consulate General]	Germany	51 19 N	12 20 E
Lemnos [island]	Greece	39 54 N	25 21 E
Leningrad (see Saint Petersburg)	Russia	59 55 N	30 15 E

Appendix H: Cross-Reference List of Geographic Names (continued)

Name	Entry in *The World Factbook*	Latitude (deg min)	Longitude (deg min)
Lesser Sunda Islands	Indonesia	9 00 S	120 00 E
Lesvos [island]	Greece	39 15 N	26 15 E
Leyte [island]	Philippines	10 50 N	124 50 E
Liancourt Rocks [claimed by Japan]	South Korea	37 15 N	131 50 E
Libreville [US Embassy]	Gabon	0 23 N	9 27 E
Ligurian Sea	Atlantic Ocean	43 30 N	9 00 E
Lilongwe [US Embassy]	Malawi	13 59 S	33 44 E
Lima [US Embassy]	Peru	12 03 S	77 03 W
Lincoln Sea	Arctic Ocean	83 00 N	56 00 W
Line Islands	Jarvis Island, Kingman Reef, Kiribati, Palmyra Atoll	0 05 N	157 00 W
Lisbon [US Embassy]	Portugal	38 43 N	9 08 W
Ljubljana [US Embassy]	Slovenia	46 03 N	14 31 E
Lobamba	Swaziland	26 27 S	31 12 E
Lombok Strait	Indian Ocean	8 30 S	115 50 E
Lome [US Embassy]	Togo	6 08 N	1 13 E
London [US Embassy]	United Kingdom	51 30 N	0 10 W
Longyearbyen	Svalbard	78 13 N	15 33 E
Lord Howe Island	Australia	31 30 S	159 00 E
Louisiade Archipelago	Papua New Guinea	11 00 S	153 00 E
Loyalty Islands (Iles Loyaute)	New Caledonia	21 00 S	167 00 E
Luanda [US Embassy]	Angola	8 48 S	13 14 E
Lubumbashi	Democratic Republic of the Congo	11 40 S	27 28 E
Lusaka [US Embassy]	Zambia	15 25 S	28 17 E
Luxembourg [US Embassy]	Luxembourg	49 45 N	6 10 E
Luzon [island]	Philippines	16 00 N	121 00 E
Luzon Strait	Pacific Ocean	20 30 N	121 00 E
Lyakhov Islands	Russia	73 45 N	138 00 E
M Macao	Macau	22 10 N	113 33 E
Macedonia	The Former Yugoslav Republic of Macedonia	41 50 N	22 00 E
Macquarie Island	Australia	30 07 S	147 24 E
Maddalena, Isola	Italy	41 13 N	09 24 E
Madeira Islands	Portugal	32 40 N	16 45 W
Madras (see Chennai)	India	13 04 N	80 16 E
Madrid [US Embassy]	Spain	40 24 N	3 41 W
Magellan, Strait of	Atlantic Ocean	54 00 S	71 00 W
Maghreb	Algeria, Libya, Mauritania, Morocco, Tunisia	30 00 N	5 00 E
Mahe Island	Seychelles	4 41 S	55 30 E
Maiz, Islas del (Corn Islands)	Nicaragua	12 15 N	83 00 W
Majorca Island (Isla de Mallorca)	Spain	39 30 N	3 00 E
Majuro [US Embassy]	Marshall Islands	7 05 N	171 08 E
Makassar Strait	Pacific Ocean	2 00 S	117 30 E
Malabo	Equatorial Guinea	3 45 N	8 47 E
Malacca, Strait of	Indian Ocean	2 30 N	101 20 E
Malagasy Republic	Madagascar	20 00 S	47 00 E
Male	Maldives	4 10 N	73 31 E
Mallorca (Majorca)	Spain	39 30 N	3 00 E
Malpelo, Isla de	Colombia	4 00 N	90 30 W
Malta Channel	Atlantic Ocean	56 44 N	26 53 E

Appendix H: Cross-Reference List of Geographic Names (continued)

Name	Entry in *The World Factbook*	Latitude (deg min)	Longitude (deg min)
Malvinas, Islas	Falkland Islands (Islas Malvinas)	51 45 S	59 00 W
Mamoutzou	Mayotte	12 47 S	45 14 E
Managua [US Embassy]	Nicaragua	12 09 N	86 17 W
Manama [US Embassy]	Bahrain	26 13 N	50 35 E
Manaus [US Consular Agency]	Brazil	3 08 S	60 01 W
Manchukuo	China	44 00 N	124 00 E
Manchuria	China	44 00 N	124 00 E
Manila [US Embassy]	Philippines	14 35 N	121 00 E
Manipa Strait	Pacific Ocean	3 20 S	127 23 E
Mannar, Gulf of	Indian Ocean	8 30 N	79 00 E
Manua Islands	American Samoa	14 13 S	169 35 W
Maputo [US Embassy]	Mozambique	25 58 S	32 35 E
Marcus Island (Minami-tori-shima)	Japan	24 16 N	154 00 E
Mariana Islands	Guam, Northern Mariana Islands	16 00 N	145 30 E
Marion Island	South Africa	46 51 S	37 52 E
Marmara, Sea of	Atlantic Ocean	40 40 N	28 15 E
Marquesas Islands (Iles Marquises)	French Polynesia	9 00 S	139 30 W
Marseille [US Consulate General]	France	43 18 N	5 24 E
Martin Vaz, Ilhas	Brazil	20 30 S	28 51 W
Mas a Tierra (Robinson Crusoe Island)	Chile	33 38 S	78 52 W
Mascarene Islands	Mauritius, Reunion	21 00 S	57 00 E
Maseru [US Embassy]	Lesotho	29 28 S	27 30 E
Matamoros [US Consulate]	Mexico	25 53 N	97 30 W
Mata-Utu	Wallis and Futuna	13 57 S	1 71 56 W
Matsu [island]	Taiwan	26 13 N	119 56 E
Matthew Island	New Caledonia, Vanuatu	22 20 S	171 20 E
Mazatlan	Mexico	23 13 N	106 25 W
Mbabane [US Embassy]	Swaziland	26 18 S	31 06 E
McDonald Islands	Heard Island and McDonald Islands	53 06 S	73 30 E
Mecca	Saudi Arabia	21 27 N	39 49 E
Medan [US Consulate General]	Indonesia	3 35 N	98 40 E
Mediterranean Sea	Atlantic Ocean	36 00 N	15 00 E
Melbourne [US Consulate General]	Australia	37 49 S	144 58 E
Melilla	Spain	35 19 N	2 58 W
Merida [US Consulate]	Mexico	20 58 N	89 37 W
Mesopotamia	Iraq	33 00 N	44 00 E
Messina, Strait of	Atlantic Ocean	38 15 N	15 35 E
Mexico [US Embassy]	Mexico	19 24 N	99 09 W
Mexico, Gulf of	Atlantic Ocean	25 00 N	90 00 W
Milan [US Consulate General]	Italy	45 28 N	9 12 E
Minami-tori-shima (Marcus Island)	Japan	24 16 N	154 00 E
Mindanao [island]	Philippines	8 00 N	125 00 E
Mindoro [island]	Philippines	12 50 N	121 05 E
Mindoro Strait	Pacific Ocean	12 20 N	120 40 E
Minicoy Island	India	8 17 N	73 02 E
Minsk [US Embassy]	Belarus	53 54 N	27 34 E
Minorca Island (Isla de Menorca)	Spain	40 00 N	4 00 E
Mitla Pass	Egypt	30 02 N	32 54 E

Name	Entry in *The World Factbook*	Latitude (deg min)	Longitude (deg min)
Mogadishu	Somalia	2 04 N	45 22 E
Moldavia [region]	Moldova, Romania	47 00 N	29 00 E
Moluccas (Spice Islands)	Indonesia	2 00 S	28 00 E
Mombasa	Kenya	4 03 S	39 40 E
Mona Passage	Atlantic Ocean	18 30 N	67 45 W
Monaco	Monaco	43 44 N	7 25 E
Monrovia [US Embassy]	Liberia	6 18 N	10 47 W
Montenegro	Serbia and Montenegro	42 30 N	19 00 E
Monterrey	Mexico	25 40 N	100 19 W
Montevideo [US Embassy]	Uruguay	34 53 S	56 11 W
Montreal [US Consulate General, US Mission to the International Civil Aviation Organization (ICAO)]	Canada	45 31 N	73 34 W
Moravia [region]	Czech Republic	49 30 N	17 00 E
Moravian Gate	Czech Republic	49 35 N	17 50 E
Moroni	Comoros	11 41 S	43 16 E
Mortlock Islands (Nomoi Islands)	Federated States of Micronesia	5 30 N	153 40 E
Moscow [US Embassy]	Russia	55 45 N	37 35 E
Mount Pinatubo	Philippines	15 08 N	120 21 E
Mozambique Channel	Indian Ocean	19 00 S	41 00 E
Mumbai [US Consulate General]	India	18 58 N	72 50 E
Munich [US Consulate General]	Germany	48 09 N	11 35 E
Musandam Peninsula	Oman, United Arab Emirates	26 18 N	56 24 E
Muscat [US Embassy]	Oman	23 37 N	58 35 E
Muscat and Oman	Oman	21 00 N	57 00 E
Myanma, Myanmar	Burma	22 00 N	98 00 E
Nagorno-Karabakh [region]	Azerbaijan	40 00 N	46 40 E
Nagoya [US Consulate]	Japan	35 10 N	136 55 E
Naha [US Consulate General]	Japan	26 13 N	127 40 E
Nairobi [US Embassy]	Kenya	1 17 S	36 49 E
Nampo-shoto [islands]	Japan	30 00 N	140 00 E
Naples [US Consulate General]	Italy	40 50 N	14 15 E
Nassau [US Embassy]	The Bahamas	25 05 N	77 21 W
Natuna Besar Islands	Indonesia	3 30 N	102 30 E
Naxcivan [region]	Azerbaijan	39 20 N	45 20 E
N'Djamena [US Embassy]	Chad	12 07 N	15 03 E
Negev [region]	Israel	30 30 N	34 55 E
Negros [island]	Philippines	10 00 N	123 00 E
Netherlands East Indies	Indonesia	5 00 S	120 00 E
Netherlands Guiana	Suriname	4 00 N	56 00 W
Nevis [island]	Saint Kitts and Nevis	17 09 N	62 35 W
New Britain [island]	Papua New Guinea	6 00 S	150 00 E
New Delhi [US Embassy]	India	28 36 N	77 12 E
New Guinea	Indonesia, Papua New Guinea	5 00 S	140 00 E
New Hebrides	Vanuatu	16 00 S	167 00 E
New Siberian Islands	Russia	75 00 N	142 00 E
New Territories	Hong Kong	22 24 N	114 10 E
New York, New York [US Mission to the United Nations (USUN)]	United States	40 43 N	74 01 W
Newfoundland [island]	Canada	52 00 N	56 00 W

N

Appendix H: Cross-Reference List of Geographic Names (continued)

Name	Entry in *The World Factbook*	Latitude (deg min)	Longitude (deg min)
Niamey [US Embassy]	Niger	13 31 N	2 07 E
Nicobar Islands	India	8 00 N	93 30 E
Nicosia [US Embassy]	Cyprus	35 10 N	33 22 E
Nightingale Islands	Saint Helena	37 25 S	12 30 W
Nomoi Islands (Mortlock Islands)	Federated States of Micronesia	5 30 N	153 40 E
North Atlantic Ocean	Atlantic Ocean	30 00 N	45 00 W
North Channel	Atlantic Ocean	55 10 N	5 40 W
North Frisian Islands	Denmark, Germany	54 50 N	8 12 E
North Island	New Zealand	39 00 S	176 00 E
North Korea	North Korea	40 00 N	127 00 E
North Pacific Ocean	Pacific Ocean	30 00 N	165 00 E
North Sea	Atlantic Ocean	56 00 N	4 00 E
North Vietnam	Vietnam	23 00 N	106 00 E
North Yemen (Yemen Arab Republic)	Yemen	15 00 N	44 00 E
Northeast Providence Channel	Atlantic Ocean	25 40 N	77 09 W
Northern Epirus	Albania, Greece	40 00 N	20 30 E
Northern Grenadines	Saint Vincent and the Grenadines	12 45 N	61 15 W
Northern Ireland	United Kingdom	54 40 N	6 45 W
Northern Rhodesia	Zambia	15 00 S	30 00 E
Northwest Passages	Arctic Ocean	74 40 N	100 00 W
Norwegian Sea	Atlantic Ocean	66 00 N	6 00 E
Nouakchott [US Embassy]	Mauritania	18 06 N	15 57 W
Noumea	New Caledonia	22 16 S	166 27 E
Novaya Zemlya [islands]	Russia	74 00 N	57 00 E
Nubia	Sudan	20 30 N	33 00 E
Nuku'alofa	Tonga	21 08 S	175 12 W
Nuevo Laredo [US Consulate]	Mexico	27 30 N	99 31 W
Nuuk (Godthab)	Greenland	64 11 N	51 44 W
Nyasaland	Malawi	13 30 S	34 00 E
O	Oahu	United States	21 30 N	158 00 W
Ocean Island (Banaba)	Kiribati	0 52 S	169 35 E
Ocean Island (Kure Island)	United States	28 25 N	178 20 W
Ogaden [region]	Ethiopia, Somalia	7 00 N	46 00 E
Oil Islands (Chagos Archipelago)	British Indian Ocean Territory	6 00 S	71 30 E
Okhotsk, Sea of	Pacific Ocean	53 00 N	150 00 E
Okinawa [island group]	Japan	26 30 N	128 00 E
Oman, Gulf of	Indian Ocean	24 30 N	58 30 E
Ombai Strait	Pacific Ocean	8 30 S	125 00 E
Oran	Algeria	35 43 N	0 43 W
Oranjestad	Aruba	12 33 N	70 06 W
Oresund (The Sound)	Atlantic Ocean	55 50 N	12 40 E
Orkney Islands	United Kingdom	59 00 N	3 00 W
Osaka-Kobe [US Consulate General]	Japan	34 40 N	135 30 E
Oslo [US Embassy]	Norway	59 55 N	10 45 E
Osumi Strait (Van Diemen Strait)	Pacific Ocean	31 00 N	131 00 E
Otranto, Strait of	Atlantic Ocean	40 00 N	19 00 E
Ottawa [US Embassy]	Canada	45 20 N	73 58 W
Ouagadougou [US Embassy]	Burkina Faso	12 22 N	1 31 W
Outer Mongolia	Mongolia	46 00 N	105 00 E

Appendix H: Cross-Reference List of Geographic Names (continued)

Name	Entry in *The World Factbook*	Latitude (deg min)	Longitude (deg min)
P			
Pacific Islands, Trust Territory of the	Marshall Islands, Federated States of Micronesia, Northern Mariana Islands, Palau	10 00 N	155 00 E
Pagan [island]	Northern Mariana Islands	18 8 N	145 47 E
Pago Pago	American Samoa	14 16 S	170 42 W
Palawan [island]	Philippines	9 30 N	118 30 E
Palermo	Italy	38 07 N	13 21 E
Palestine	Israel, West Bank	32 00 N	35 15 E
Palikir	Federated States of Micronesia	6 55 N	158 08 E
Palk Strait	Indian Ocean	10 00 N	79 45 E
Pamirs [mountains]	China, Tajikistan	38 00 N	73 00 E
Pampas [region]	Argentina	35 00 N	63 00 W
Panama [US Embassy]	Panama	8 58 N	79 32 W
Panama Canal	Panama	9 00 N	79 45 W
Panama, Gulf of	Pacific Ocean	8 00 N	79 30 W
Panay [island]	Philippines	11 15 N	122 30 E
Pantelleria, Isola di	Italy	36 47 N	12 00 E
Papeete	French Polynesia	17 32 S	149 34 W
Paramaribo [US Embassy]	Suriname	5 50 N	55 10 W
Parece Vela [island]	Japan	20 20 N	136 00 E
Paris [US Embassy, US Mission to the Organization for Economic Cooperation and Development (OECD), US Observer Mission to the UN Educational, Scientific, and Cultural Organization (UNESCO)]	France	48 52 N	2 20 E
Pascua, Isla de (Easter Island)	Chile	27 07 S	109 22 W
Passion, Ile de la	Clipperton Island	10 17 N	109 13 W
Pashtunistan [region]	Afghanistan, Pakistan	32 00 N	69 00 E
Peking (see Beijing)	China	39 56 N	116 24 E
Pelagian Islands (Isole Pelagie)	Italy	35 40 N	12 40 E
Peleliu (Beliliou) [island]	Palau	7 01 N	134 15 E
Pemba Island	Tanzania	7 31 S	39 25 E
Penang Island	Malaysia	5 23 N	100 15 E
Pentland Firth	Atlantic Ocean	58 44 N	3 13 W
Perim [island]	Yemen	12 39 N	43 25 E
Perouse Strait, La	Pacific Ocean	44 45 N	142 00 E
Persia	Iran	32 00 N	53 00 E
Persian Gulf	Indian Ocean	27 00 N	51 00 E
Perth [US Consulate General]	Australia	31 56 S	115 50 E
Pescadores [islands]	Taiwan	23 30 N	119 30 E
Peshawar [US Consulate]	Pakistan	34 01 N	71 33 E
Peter I Island	Antarctica	68 48 S	90 35 W
Philip Island	Norfolk Island	29 08 S	167 57 E
Philippine Sea	Pacific Ocean	20 00 N	134 00 E
Phnom Penh [US Embassy]	Cambodia	11 33 N	104 55 E
Phoenix Islands	Kiribati	3 30 S	172 00 W
Pines, Isle of (Isla de la Juventud)	Cuba	21 40 N	82 50 W
Pleasant Island	Nauru	0 32 S	166 55 E
Plymouth	Montserrat	16 44 N	62 14 W
Ponape (Pohnpei) [island]	Federated States of Micronesia	6 55 N	158 15 E
Ponta Delgada [US Consulate]	Portugal	37 44 N	25 40 W

Appendix H: Cross-Reference List of Geographic Names (continued)

Name	Entry in *The World Factbook*	Latitude (deg min)	Longitude (deg min)
Port-au-Prince [US Embassy]	Haiti	18 32 N	72 20 W
Port Louis [US Embassy]	Mauritius	20 10 S	57 30 E
Port Moresby [US Embassy]	Papua New Guinea	9 30 S	147 10 E
Porto Alegre [US Consulate]	Brazil	30 04 S	51 11 W
Port-of-Spain [US Embassy]	Trinidad and Tobago	10 39 N	61 31 W
Porto-Novo	Benin	6 29 N	2 37 E
Portuguese East Africa	Mozambique	18 15 S	35 00 E
Portuguese Guinea	Guinea-Bissau	12 00 N	15 00 W
Portuguese Timor (East Timor)	Indonesia	9 00 S	126 00 E
Port-Vila	Vanuatu	17 44 S	168 19 E
Poznan	Poland	52 25 N	16 55 E
Prague [US Embassy]	Czech Republic	40 55 N	21 00 E
Praia [US Embassy]	Cape Verde	14 55 N	23 31 W
Pretoria [US Embassy]	South Africa	25 45 S	28 10 E
Prevlaka peninsula	Croatia	42 24 N	18 31 E
Pribilof Islands	United States	57 00 N	170 00 W
Prince Edward Island	Canada	46 20 N	63 20 W
Prince Edward Islands	South Africa	46 35 S	38 00 E
Prince Patrick Island	Canada	76 30 N	119 00 W
Principe [island]	Sao Tome and Principe	1 38 N	7 25 E
Prussia [region]	Germany, Poland, Russia	53 00 N	14 00 E
Pukapuka Atoll	Cook Islands	10 53 S	165 49 W
Pusan [US Consulate]	South Korea	35 06 N	129 03 E
P'yongyang	North Korea	39 01 N	125 45 E
Q Quebec [US Consulate General]	Canada	52 00 N	72 00 W
Queen Charlotte Islands	Canada	53 00 N	132 00 W
Queen Elizabeth Islands	Canada	78 00 N	95 00 W
Queen Maud Land [claimed by Norway]	Antarctica	73 30 S	12 00 E
Quemoy [island]	Taiwan	24 27 N	118 23 E
Quito [US Embassy]	Ecuador	0 13 S	78 30 W
R Rabat [US Embassy]	Morocco	34 02 N	6 51 W
Ralik Chain	Marshall Islands	8 00 N	167 00 E
Rangoon [US Embassy]	Burma	16 47 N	96 10 E
Ratak Chain	Marshall Islands	9 00 N	171 00 E
Recife [US Consulate]	Brazil	8 03 S	34 54 W
Redonda [island]	Antigua and Barbuda	16 55 N	62 19 W
Red Sea	Indian Ocean	20 00 N	38 00 E
Revillagigedo Island	United States	55 35 N	131 06 W
Revillagigedo Islands	Mexico	19 00 N	112 45 W
Reykjavik [US Embassy]	Iceland	19 00 N	111 30 W
Rhodes [island]	Greece	36 10 N	28 00 E
Rhodesia	Zimbabwe	20 00 S	30 00 E
Rhodesia, Northern	Zambia	15 00 S	30 00 E
Rhodesia, Southern	Zimbabwe	20 00 S	30 00 E
Riga [US Embassy]	Latvia	56 57 N	24 06 E
Rio de Janeiro [US Consulate General]	Brazil	22 54 S	43 14 W
Rio de Oro	Western Sahara	23 45 N	15 45 W
Rio Muni	Equatorial Guinea	1 30 N	10 00 E

Appendix H: Cross-Reference List of Geographic Names (continued)

Name	Entry in The World Factbook	Latitude (deg min)	Longitude (deg min)
Riyadh [US Embassy]	Saudi Arabia	24 38 N	46 43 E
Road Town	British Virgin Islands	18 27 N	64 37 W
Robinson Crusoe Island (Mas a Tierra)	Chile	33 38 S	78 52 W
Rocas, Atol das	Brazil	3 51 S	33 49 W
Rockall [island]	United Kingdom	57 35 N	13 48 W
Rodrigues [island]	Mauritius	19 42 S	63 25 E
Rome [US Embassy, US Mission to the UN Agencies for Food and Agriculture (FODAG)]	Italy	41 54 N	12 29 E
Roncador Cay	Colombia	13 32 N	80 03 W
Roosevelt Island	Antarctica	79 30 S	162 00 W
Roseau	Dominica	15 18 N	61 24 W
Ross Dependency [claimed by New Zealand]	Antarctica	80 00 S	180 00 E
Ross Island	Antarctica	81 30 S	175 00 W
Ross Sea	Antarctica	76 00 S	175 00 W
Rota [island]	Northern Mariana Islands	14 10 N	145 12 E
Rotuma [island]	Fiji	12 30 S	177 30 E
Ryukyu Islands	Japan	26 30 N	128 00 E
Saba [island]	Netherlands Antilles	17 38 N	63 10 W
Sabah [state]	Malaysia	5 20 N	117 10 E
Sable Island	Canada	43 55 N	59 50 W
Safety Islands (Iles du Salut)	French Guiana	5 20 N	52 37 W
Sahel	Burkina Faso, Cape Verde, Chad, The Gambia, Guinea-Bissau, Mali, Mauritania, Niger, Senegal	15 00 N	8 00 W
Saigon (see Ho Chi Minh City)	Vietnam	10 45 N	106 40 E
Saint Brandon (Cargados Carajos Shoals) [island]	Mauritius	16 25 S	59 38 E
Saint Christopher [island]	Saint Kitts and Nevis	17 20 N	62 45 W
Saint Christopher and Nevis	Saint Kitts and Nevis	17 20 N	62 45 W
Saint-Denis	Reunion	20 52 S	55 28 E
Saint George's [US Embassy]	Grenada	12 03 N	61 45 W
Saint George's Channel	Atlantic Ocean	52 00 N	6 00 W
Saint Helier	Jersey	49 12 N	2 37 W
Saint John's	Antigua and Barbuda	17 06 N	61 51 W
Saint Lawrence, Gulf of	Atlantic Ocean	48 00 N	62 00 W
Saint Lawrence Island	United States	49 30 N	67 00 W
Saint Lawrence Seaway	Atlantic Ocean	49 15 N	67 00 W
Saint Martin [island]	Guadeloupe	18 04 N	63 04 W
Saint Martin (Sint Maarten)	Netherlands Antilles	18 04 N	63 04 W
Saint Paul Island	Canada	47 12 N	60 09 W
Saint Paul Island	United States	57 11 N	170 16 W
Saint Paul Island (Ile Saint-Paul)	French Southern and Antarctic Lands	38 43 S	77 29 E
Saint Peter and Saint Paul Rocks (Penedos de Sao Pedro e Sao Paulo)	Brazil	0 23 N	29 23 W
Saint Peter Port	Guernsey	49 27 N	2 32 W
Saint Petersburg [US Consulate General]	Russia	59 55 N	30 15 E
Saint-Pierre	Saint Pierre and Miquelon	46 46 N	56 11 W
Saint Thomas [island]	Virgin Islands	18 21 N	64 55 W
Saint Vincent Passage	Atlantic Ocean	13 30 N	61 00 W
Saipan [island]	Northern Mariana Islands	15 12 N	145 45 E
Sakishima Islands	Japan	24 30 N	124 00 E

S

Appendix H: Cross-Reference List of Geographic Names (continued)

Name	Entry in *The World Factbook*	Latitude (deg min)	Longitude (deg min)
Sakhalin Island (Ostrov Sakhalin)	Russia	51 00 N	143 00 E
Sala y Gomez, Isla	Chile	26 28 S	105 00 W
Salisbury (see Harare)	Zimbabwe	17 50 S	105 00 W
Salvador de Bahia [US Consular Agency]	Brazil	12 59 S	38 31 W
Salzburg	Austria	47 48 N	13 02 E
Samar [island]	Philippines	12 00 N	125 00 E
Samaria [region]	West Bank	32 15 N	35 10 E
Samoa Islands	American Samoa, Samoa	14 00 S	171 00 W
Samos [island]	Greece	37 48 N	26 44 E
Sanaa [US Embassy]	Yemen	15 21 N	44 12 E
San Ambrosio, Isla	Chile	26 21 S	79 52 W
San Andres y Providencia, Archipielago	Colombia	13 00 N	81 30 W
San Bernardino Strait	Pacific Ocean	12 32 N	124 10 E
San Felix, Isla	Chile	26 17 S	80 05 W
San Jose [US Embassy]	Costa Rica	9 56 N	84 05 W
San Juan	Puerto Rico	18 28 N	66 07 W
San Marino	San Marino	43 56 N	12 25 E
San Salvador [US Embassy]	El Salvador	13 42 N	89 12 W
Santa Cruz	Bolivia	17 48 S	63 10 W
Santa Cruz Islands	Solomon Islands	11 00 S	166 15 E
Santiago [US Embassy]	Chile	33 27 S	70 40 W
Santo Antao [island]	Cape Verde	17 05 N	25 10 W
Santo Domingo [US Embassy]	Dominican Republic	18 28 N	69 54 W
Sao Paulo [US Consulate General]	Brazil	23 32 S	46 37 W
Sao Pedro e Sao Paulo, Penedos de [rocks]	Brazil	0 23 N	29 23 W
Sao Tiago [island]	Cape Verde	15 05 N	23 40 W
Sao Tome [island]	Sao Tome and Principe	0 12 N	6 39 E
Sapporo [US Consulate General]	Japan	43 03 N	141 21 E
Sapudi Strait	Pacific Ocean	7 05 S	114 10 E
Sarajevo [US Embassy]	Bosnia and Herzegovina	43 52 N	18 25 E
Sarawak [state]	Malaysia	2 30 N	113 30 E
Sardinia [island]	Italy	40 00 N	9 00 E
Sargasso Sea	Atlantic Ocean	30 00 N	55 00 W
Sark [island]	Guernsey	49 26 N	2 21 W
Saxony [region]	Germany	51 00 N	13 00 E
Schleswig-Holstein [region]	Germany	54 31 N	9 33 E
Scopus, Mount	Israel, West Bank	31 48 N	35 14 E
Scotia Sea	Atlantic Ocean	56 00 S	40 00 W
Scotland [region]	United Kingdom	57 00 N	4 00 W
Scott Island	Antarctica	67 24 S	179 55 W
Senyavin Islands	Federated States of Micronesia	6 55 N	158 00 E
Seoul [US Embassy]	South Korea	37 34 N	127 00 E
Serbia	Serbia and Montenegro	43 00 N	21 00 E
Serrana Bank	Colombia	14 25 N	80 16 W
Serranilla Bank	Colombia	15 51 N	79 46 W
Settlement, The	Christmas Island	18 44 N	64 19 W
Severnaya Zemlya (Northland) [island group]	Russia	79 30 N	98 00 E
Shaba [region]	Democratic Republic of the Congo	8 00 S	27 00 E

Appendix H: Cross-Reference List of Geographic Names (continued)

Name	Entry in *The World Factbook*	Latitude (deg min)	Longitude (deg min)
Shag Island	Heard Island and McDonald Islands	53 00 S	72 30 E
Shag Rocks	South Georgia and the South Sandwich Islands	53 33 S	42 02 W
Shanghai [US Consulate General]	China	31 14 N	121 28 E
Shenyang [US Consulate General]	China	41 48 N	123 27 E
Shetland Islands	United Kingdom	60 30 N	1 30 W
Shikoku [island]	Japan	33 45 N	133 30 E
Shikotan [island]	Russia [de facto]	43 47 N	146 45 E
Siam	Thailand	15 00 N	100 00 E
Siberia [region]	Russia	60 00 N	100 00 E
Sibutu Passage	Pacific Ocean	4 50 N	119 35 E
Sicily [island]	Italy	37 30 N	14 00 E
Sicily, Strait of	Atlantic Ocean	37 20 N	11 20 E
Sidra, Gulf of	Atlantic Ocean	31 30 N	18 00 E
Sikkim [state]	India	27 50 N	88 30 E
Sinai Peninsula	Egypt	29 30 N	34 00 E
Singapore [US Embassy]	Singapore	1 17 N	103 51 E
Singapore Strait	Pacific Ocean	1 15 N	104 00 E
Sinkiang (Xinjiang)	China	42 00 N	86 00 E
Sint Eustatius [island]	Netherlands Antilles	17 29 N	62 58 W
Sint Maarten [island]	Netherlands Antilles	18 04 N	63 04 W
Skagerrak [strait]	Atlantic Ocean	57 45 N	9 00 E
Skopje [US Embassy]	The Former Yugoslav Republic of Macedonia	41 59 N	21 26 E
Society Islands (Iles de la Societe)	French Polynesia	17 00 S	150 00 W
Socotra [island]	Yemen	12 30 N	54 00 E
Sofia [US Embassy]	Bulgaria	42 41 N	23 19 E
Solomon Islands, northern	Papua New Guinea	6 00 S	155 00 E
Solomon Islands, southern	Solomon Islands	8 00 S	159 00 E
Solomon Sea	Pacific Ocean	8 00 S	153 00 E
Songkhla	Thailand	7 12 N	100 36 E
Sound, The (Oresund)	Atlantic Ocean	55 50 N	12 40 E
South Atlantic Ocean	Atlantic Ocean	30 00 S	15 00 W
South China Sea	Pacific Ocean	10 00 N	113 00 E
South Georgia [island]	South Georgia and the South Sandwich Islands	54 15 S	36 45 W
South Island	New Zealand	43 00 S	171 00 E
South Korea	South Korea	37 00 N	127 30 E
South Orkney Islands	Antarctica	61 00 S	45 00 W
South Ossetia [region]	Georgia	42 20 N	44 00 E
South Pacific Ocean	Pacific Ocean	30 00 S	130 00 W
South Sandwich Islands	South Georgia and the South Sandwich Islands	57 45 S	26 30 W
South Shetland Islands	Antarctica	62 00 S	59 00 W
South Tyrol [region]	Italy	46 30 N	10 30 E
South Vietnam	Vietnam	12 00 N	108 00 E
South Yemen (People's Democratic Republic of Yemen)	Yemen	14 00 N	48 00 E
South-West Africa	Namibia	22 00 S	17 00 E
Southern Grenadines	Grenada	12 20 N	61 30 W
Southern Rhodesia	Zimbabwe	20 00 S	30 00 E

Appendix H: Cross-Reference List of Geographic Names (continued)

	Name	Entry in *The World Factbook*	Latitude (deg min)	Longitude (deg min)
	Soviet Union	Armenia, Azerbaijan, Belarus, Estonia, Georgia, Kazakhstan, Kyrgyzstan, Latvia, Lithuania, Moldova, Russia, Tajikistan, Turkmenistan, Ukraine, Uzbekistan		
	Spanish Guinea	Equatorial Guinea	2 00 N	10 00 E
	Spanish Morocco	Morocco	32 00 N	7 00 W
	Spanish North Africa	Spain (Ceuta, Islas Chafarinas, Melilla, Penon de Alhucemas, Penon de Velez de la Gomera)	35 15 N	4 00 W
	Spanish Sahara	Western Sahara	24 30 N	13 00 W
	Spice Islands (Moluccas)	Indonesia	2 00 S	28 00 E
	Spitsbergen [island]	Svalbard	78 00 N	20 00 E
	Stanley	Falkland Islands (Islas Malvinas)	51 42 S	57 41 W
	Stockholm [US Embassy]	Sweden	59 20 N	18 03 E
	Strasbourg [US Consulate General]	France	48 35 N	7 45 E
	Stuttgart	Germany	48 46 N	9 11 E
	Sucre	Bolivia	19 02 S	65 17 W
	Suez Canal	Egypt	29 55 N	32 33 E
	Suez, Gulf of	Indian Ocean	28 10 N	33 27 E
	Sulu Archipelago	Philippines	6 00 N	121 00 E
	Sulu Sea	Pacific Ocean	8 00 N	120 00 E
	Sumatra [island]	Indonesia	0 00 N	102 00 E
	Sumba [island]	Indonesia	10 00 S	120 00 E
	Sunda Islands (Soenda Isles)	Indonesia, Malaysia	2 00 S	110 00 E
	Sunda Strait	Indian Ocean	6 00 S	105 45 E
	Surabaya [US Consulate General]	Indonesia	7 15 S	112 45 E
	Surigao Strait	Pacific Ocean	10 15 N	125 23 E
	Surinam	Suriname	4 00 N	56 00 W
	Suva [US Embassy]	Fiji	18 08 S	178 25 E
	Sverdlovsk (see Yekaterinburg)	Russia	56 50 N	60 39 E
	Swains Island	American Samoa	11 3 S	171 15 W
	Swan Islands	Honduras	17 25 S	83 56 W
	Sydney [US Consulate General]	Australia	33 52 S	151 13 E
T	Tahiti [island]	French Polynesia	17 37 S	149 27 W
	Taipei	Taiwan	25 03 N	121 30 E
	Taiwan Strait	Pacific Ocean	24 00 N	119 00 E
	Tallinn [US Embassy]	Estonia	59 25 N	24 45 E
	Tanganyika	Tanzania	6 00 S	35 00 E
	Tangier	Morocco	35 48 N	5 45 W
	Tarawa [island]	Kiribati	1 25 N	173 00 E
	Tatar Strait	Pacific Ocean	50 00 N	141 00 E
	Tashkent [US Embassy]	Uzbekistan	41 20 N	69 18 E
	Tasmania [island]	Australia	43 00 S	147 00 E
	Tasman Sea	Pacific Ocean	4 30 S	168 00 E
	Taymyr Peninsula (Poluostrov Taymyr)	Russia	76 00 N	104 00 E
	T'bilisi [US Embassy]	Georgia	41 43 N	44 49 E
	Tegucigalpa [US Embassy]	Honduras	14 06 N	87 13 W
	Tehran [US post not maintained; representation by Swiss Embassy]	Iran	35 40 N	51 26 E
	Tel Aviv [US Embassy]	Israel	32 05 N	34 48 E

Appendix H: Cross-Reference List of Geographic Names (continued)

Name	Entry in *The World Factbook*	Latitude (deg min)	Longitude (deg min)
Terre Adelie (Adelie Land) [claimed by France]	Antarctica	66 30 S	139 00 E
Thailand, Gulf of	Pacific Ocean	10 00 N	101 00 E
Thessaloniki [US Consulate General]	Greece	40 38 N	22 56 E
Thimphu	Bhutan	27 28 N	89 39 E
Thuringia [region]	Germany	51 00 N	11 00 E
Thurston Island	Antarctica	72 20 S	99 00 W
Tiberias, Lake	Israel	32 48 N	35 35 E
Tibet (Xizang)	China	32 00 N	90 00 E
Tibilisi (see T'bilisi)	Georgia	41 43 N	44 49 E
Tien Shan [mountains]	China, Kyrgyzstan	42 00 N	80 00 E
Tierra del Fuego	Argentina, Chile	54 00 S	69 00 W
Tijuana [US Consulate General]	Mexico	32 32 N	117 01 W
Timor [island]	Indonesia	9 00 S	125 00 E
Timor Sea	Pacific Ocean	11 00 S	128 00 E
Tinian [island]	Northern Mariana Islands	15 00 N	145 38 E
Tiran, Strait of	Indian Ocean	28 00 N	34 27 E
Tirana [US Embassy]	Albania	41 20 N	19 50 E
Tirane (see Tirana)	Albania	41 20 N	19 50 E
Tirol [region]	Austria, Italy	47 00 N	11 00 E
Tobago [island]	Trinidad and Tobago	11 15 N	60 40 W
Tokyo [US Embassy]	Japan	35 42 N	139 46 E
Tonkin, Gulf of	Pacific Ocean	20 00 N	108 00 E
Toronto [US Consulate General]	Canada	43 39 N	79 23 W
Torres Strait	Pacific Ocean	10 25 S	142 10 E
Torshavn	Faroe Islands	62 01 N	6 46 W
Toshkent (see Tashkent)	Uzbekistan	41 20 N	69 18 E
Transjordan	Jordan	31 00 N	36 00 E
Transkei	South Africa	32 15 S	28 15 E
Transylvania [region]	Romania	46 30 N	24 00 E
Trindade, Ilha de	Brazil	20 31 S	29 20 W
Tripoli	Lebanon	34 26 N	35 51 E
Tripoli [US post not maintained; representation by Belgian Embassy]	Libya	32 54 N	13 11 E
Tristan da Cunha Group	Saint Helena	37 04 S	12 19 W
Trobriand Islands	Papua New Guinea	8 38 S	151 04 E
Trucial Coast	United Arab Emirates	24 00 N	54 00 E
Trucial Oman	United Arab Emirates	24 00 N	54 00 E
Trucial States	United Arab Emirates	24 00 N	54 00 E
Islands	Federated States of Micronesia	7 25 N	151 47 E
Tsugaru Strait	Pacific Ocean	41 35 N	141 00 E
Tuamotu Islands (Iles Tuamotu)	French Polynesia	19 00 S	142 00 W
Tubuai Islands (Iles Tubuai)	French Polynesia	23 00 S	150 00 W
Tunb al Kubra [island]	Iran	26 14 N	55 19 E
Tunb as Sughra [island]	Iran	26 14 N	55 09 E
Tunis [US Embassy]	Tunisia	36 48 N	10 11 E
Turin	Italy	45 04 N	7 40 E
Turkish Straits	Atlantic Ocean	40 40 N	28 00 E
Turkmeniya	Turkmenistan	40 00 N	60 00 E
Turks Island Passage	Atlantic Ocean	21 40 N	71 00 W

Name	Entry in *The World Factbook*	Latitude (deg min)	Longitude (deg min)
Tuscany [region]	Italy	43 25 N	11 00 E
Tutuila [island]	American Samoa	14 18 S	170 42 W
Tyrol, South [region]	Italy	46 30 N	10 30 E
Tyrrhenian Sea	Atlantic Ocean	40 00 N	12 00 E
Udorn (Udon Thani) [US Consulate]	Thailand	17 26 N	102 46 E
Ulaanbaatar [US Embassy]	Mongolia	47 55 N	106 53 E
Ullung-do [island]	South Korea	37 29 N	130 52 E
Unimak Pass [strait]	Pacific Ocean	54 20 N	164 50 W
Union of Soviet Socialist Republics (USSR)	Armenia, Azerbaijan, Belarus, Estonia, Georgia, Kazakhstan, Kyrgyzstan, Latvia, Lithuania, Moldova, Russia, Tajikistan, Turkmenistan, Ukraine, Uzbekistan		
United Arab Republic (UAR)	Egypt, Syria		
Upper Volta	Burkina Faso	13 00 N	2 00 W
Ural Mountains	Kazakhstan, Russia	60 00 N	60 00 E
Ussuri River	China, Russia	48 28 N	135 02 E
Vaduz	Liechtenstein	47 09 N	9 31 E
Vakhan (Wakhan Corridor)	Afghanistan	37 00 N	73 00 E
Valletta [US Embassy]	Malta	35 54 N	14 31 E
Valley, The	Anguilla	18 13 N	63 04 W
Vancouver [US Consulate General]	Canada	49 16 N	123 07 W
Vancouver Island	Canada	49 45 N	126 00 W
Van Diemen Strait (Osumi Strait)	Pacific Ocean	31 00 N	131 00 E
Vatican City [US Embassy]	Holy See	41 54 N	12 27 E
Velez de la Gomera,Penon de	Spain	35 11 N	4 18 W
Venda	South Africa	23 00 S	31 00 E
Verde Island Passage	Pacific Ocean	13 34 N	120 51 E
Victoria	Hong Kong	22 17 N	114 09 E
Victoria	Seychelles	4 38 S	55 27 E
Vienna [US Embassy, US Mission to International Organizations in Vienna (UNVIE)]	Austria	48 12 N	16 22 E
Vientiane [US Embassy]	Laos	17 58 N	102 36 E
Vilnius [US Embassy]	Lithuania	54 41 N	25 19 E
Viti Levu [island]	Fiji	18 00 S	178 00 E
Vladivostok [US Consulate General]	Russia	43 10 N	131 56 E
Volcano Islands	Japan	25 00 N	141 00 E
Vostok Island	Kiribati	10 06 S	152 23 W
Vrangelya, Ostrov (Wrangel Island)	Russia	71 14 N	179 36 W
Wake Island	Wake Atoll	19 17 N	166 36 E
Wakhan Corridor (see Vakhan)	Afghanistan	37 00 N	73 00 E
Wales [region]	United Kingdom	52 30 N	3 30 W
Wallis Islands	Wallis and Futuna	13 17 S	176 10 W
Walvis Bay	Namibia	22 59 S	14 31 E
Warsaw [US Embassy]	Poland	52 15 N	21 00 E
Washington, DC [US Mission to the Organization of American States (OAS)]	United States	38 53 N	77 02 W
Weddell Sea	Atlantic Ocean	72 00 S	45 00 W
Wellington [US Embassy]	New Zealand	41 28 S	174 51 E
West Frisian Islands	Netherlands	53 26 N	5 30 E
West Germany (Federal Republic of Germany)	Germany	53 22 N	5 20 E

Appendix H: Cross-Reference List of Geographic Names (continued)

Name	Entry in *The World Factbook*	Latitude (deg min)	Longitude (deg min)
West Island	Cocos (Keeling) Islands	12 10 S	96 55 E
West Korea Strait (Western Channel)	Pacific Ocean	34 40 N	129 00 E
West Pakistan	Pakistan	30 00 N	70 00 E
West Siberian Plain	Russia	60 00 N	75 00 E
Western Channel (West Korea Strait)	Pacific Ocean	34 40 N	129 00 E
Western Samoa	Samoa	13 35 S	172 20 W
Wetar Strait	Pacific Ocean	8 20 S	126 30 E
White Sea	Arctic Ocean	65 30 N	38 00 E
Willemstad	Netherlands Antilles	12 06 N	68 56 W
Windhoek [US Embassy]	Namibia	22 34 S	17 06 E
Windward Passage	Atlantic Ocean	20 00 N	73 50 W
Wrangel Island (Ostrov Vrangelya)	Russia	71 14 N	179 36 W
Yalu River	China, North Korea	39 55 N	124 20 E
Yamoussoukro	Cote d'Ivoire	6 49 N	5 17 W
Yangon (see Rangoon)	Burma	16 47 N	96 10 E
Yaounde [US Embassy]	Cameroon	3 52 N	11 31 E
Yap Islands	Federated States of Micronesia	9 30 N	138 00 E
Yaren	Nauru	0 32 S	166 55 E
Yekaterinburg (Sverdlovsk) [US Consulate General]	Russia	56 50 N	60 39 E
Yellow Sea	Pacific Ocean	36 00 N	123 00 E
Yemen (Aden) [People's Democratic Republic of Yemen]	Yemen	14 00 N	46 00 E
Yemen Arab Republic	Yemen	15 00 N	44 00 E
Yemen, North [Yemen Arab Republic]	Yemen	15 00 N	44 00 E
Yemen (Sanaa) [Yemen ArabRepublic]	Yemen	15 00 N	44 00 E
Yemen, People's Democratic Republic of	Yemen	14 00 N	46 00 E
Yemen, South [People's Democratic Republic of Yemen]	Yemen	14 00 N	46 00 E
Yerevan [US Embassy]	Armenia	40 11 N	44 30 E
Youth, Isle of (Isla de la Juventud)	Cuba	21 40 N	82 50 W
Yucatan Peninsula	Mexico	19 30 N	89 00 W
Yucatan Channel	Atlantic Ocean	21 45 N	85 45 W
Yugoslavia	Bosnia and Herzegovina, Croatia, The Former Yugoslav Republic of Macedonia, Serbia and Montenegro, Slovenia		
Zagreb [US Embassy]	Croatia	45 48 N	15 58 E
Zaire	Democratic Republic of the Congo	15 00 S	30 00 E
Zanzibar [island]	Tanzania	6 10 S	39 11 E
Zion, Mount	Israel, Jordan	31 46 N	35 14 E
Zurich	Switzerland	47 23 N	8 32 E